A
PRONOUNCING
DICTIONARY

OF

AMERICAN ENGLISH

BY

JOHN SAMUEL KENYON, Ph.D.
Professor of the English Language in Hiram College;
Consulting Editor and Author of the Guide to Pronunciation,
Webster's New International Dictionary, Second Edition

AND

THOMAS ALBERT KNOTT, Ph.D.
Professor of English in the University of Michigan;
Editor of the Middle English Dictionary; General Editor,
Webster's New International Dictionary, Second Edition

G. & C. MERRIAM COMPANY, PUBLISHERS
SPRINGFIELD, MASS., U.S.A.

MADE IN THE U.S.A.
GEORGE BANTA PUBLISHING COMPANY, ELECTROTYPERS, PRINTERS, AND BINDERS
THE COLLEGIATE PRESS, MENASHA, WIS., U.S.A.

To
MYRA POW KENYON
AND
MYRA POWERS KNOTT

This publication was in large part made possible by funds granted by Carnegie Corporation of New York. That Corporation is not, however, the author, owner, publisher, or proprietor of this publication, and is not to be understood as approving by virtue of its grant any of the statements made or views expressed herein.

PREFACE

More than ten years ago several scholars especially interested in American English suggested to one of the present editors the making of a phonetic pronouncing dictionary of the speech of the United States that might serve, both in the United States and elsewhere, the purposes served for Southern British English by Professor Daniel Jones's *English Pronouncing Dictionary*. About six years ago the editors became associated in this work.

Although as a pioneer in the field great credit must go to Professor Jones, who has placed all later lexicographers under inescapable obligation to him, our task is much different from his. He records the pronunciation of a limited and nearly homogeneous class of people in England in a type of speech identical with that of the editor himself. Our problem has been to record without prejudice or preference several different types of speech used by large bodies of educated and cultivated Americans in widely separated areas and with markedly different backgrounds of tradition and culture. Here let it be emphasized once for all that we have no prejudice whatever either for or against any of these varieties of American speech.

As the book is completed, we are keenly aware that only a beginning has been made, subject to later supplementation by other students of the field. On the whole, Southern speech has in the past received least attention. If we have failed to do it the full justice that was our intention, our failure must be laid in part to conflicting testimony, but mainly to the fact that this field has still largely to be investigated.

It was originally intended to include Canadian speech as one of the main regional divisions. A number of questionnaires were sent to Canada, and some correspondents took pains to send us excellent material (see acknowledgments below). The material was not, however, extensive enough to warrant full record of Canadian pronunciation, so that we have had to content ourselves with occasional references thereto. See mention of some Canadian variants (§118).

The scope of this work is limited. It is not intended as a source book for the study of American dialects. That work is being done by the *Linguistic Atlas of the United States and Canada*. It is our aim to record only what is rather vaguely called standard speech (see further, Introduction, §§1–2, 57–58, 76, 90). It is not our purpose even to try to exhaust that field. Almost certainly we have omitted many "good" pronunciations. Many of these are provided for in the Introduction by the lists of variants not fully recorded in the vocabulary (§§90 ff.). Recent studies and records of American speech have made it clear that there exists far greater variety than was formerly supposed in the speech of Americans of unquestioned cultivation and importance. Considering the actual facts of contemporary American pronunciation, the editors feel that on the whole they have been conservative in the variety recorded.

The vocabulary is intended to include the great body of common words in use in America. Besides, it includes a great many somewhat unusual words, inserted for a variety of reasons. Especial attention has been given to American proper names, though an exhaustive treatment of these is far beyond the scope of this work. The editors have had in mind the needs of college and university students, and have therefore included many names of history and literature likely to be encountered by them, as well as a large number of notes on various aspects of the English language. While foreign names are, strictly, outside the scope of a dictionary of American English, it is impossible to avoid including many often heard and used by Americans. The field of British place and personal names, tempting to one interested in pronunciation, has been little entered. A few of general interest must be included, and a considerable number of names of places in England whose pronunciation was verified locally by one of the editors have been inserted. Many of these names are of historical and traditional interest to Americans, and a great number have been transferred to America.

As in all trustworthy dictionaries, the editors have endeavored to base the pronunciations on actual cultivated usage. No other standard has, in point of fact, ever finally settled pronunciation. This book can be taken as a safe guide to pronunciation only insofar as we have succeeded in doing this. According to this standard, no words are, as often said, "almost universally mispronounced," for that is self-contradictory. For an editor the temptation is often strong to prefer what he thinks "ought to be" the right pronunciation; but it has to be resisted. For example, on etymological grounds the word *dahlia* "ought to be" 'dɑljə; by traditional Anglicizing habits of English it should be 'deljə (as it is in England and often in Canada); as a fact, in America it is prevailingly 'dæljə. In this case the variants are current enough to allow free choice; but in many cases the theoretically "right" pronunciation of a word is not even current.

In a work of this sort it is unavoidable to adopt certain devices to save space. These are explained in the Introduction (§§59 ff.). If the reader is now and then annoyed by these, he is asked to reflect that this makes possible the inclusion of far more material than would otherwise be possible, and on the whole makes this material easier for the reader to find.

A question naturally arises as to the relation of this work to the other dictionaries published by G. & C. Merriam Company. This book is published on a different basis from their other publications. For this book they act only as publishers and distributors, without editorial supervision. The Merriam Company is in no way responsible for any statements made in this book. That responsibility rests solely on the two authors.

The purpose of this dictionary is quite new in America. First, it deals solely with pronunciation. Even the entries are determined to a considerable extent by that purpose; for example, certain proper names of persons or places are selected, not for their intrinsic importance, but for some interest or problem in their pronunciation.

But the chief difference between this and the other Merriam dictionaries is that this is a dictionary of colloquial English, of the everyday unconscious speech of cultivated people—of those in every community who carry on the affairs and set the social and educational standards of those communities. *Webster's New International Dictionary, Second Edition* (Introduction, p. xii) thus defines its purpose in regard to pronunciation:

"In this edition, the style adopted for representation is that of formal platform speech—and this must be clearly remembered by consultants of the pronunciations here given. The omission of less precise pronunciations of familiar words does not, of course, indicate either that those pronunciations do not exist or that the editors of the dictionary refuse to recognize them. They do exist, and very naturally so when the occasion suits. . . . The recording of all such colloquial pronunciations of every separate word is not, however, possible in such a Dictionary as the *New International.* . . . The pronunciations contained in this Dictionary are not theoretical. They represent actual speech—the speech of cultivated users of English, speaking formally with a view to being completely understood by their hearers."

On the other hand, the pronunciation which the present editors intend to represent in this book is what has been called "easy English," "the speech of well-bred ease"—not slovenly or careless speech, nor, on the other hand, formal platform speech. Of course the great majority of English words are pronounced alike in colloquial and in formal speech, and much the largest part of the vocabulary will be found to have the same pronunciations in both books, and a large part of the differences will be the differences between colloquial and formal pronunciation. (For fuller discussion of the term *colloquial*, see Introduction, §§1–2.)

The *New International* does not attempt to represent the pronunciation of words as they occur in connected speech. The editors state, "It would be impossible, even were it desirable, to attempt to record the pronunciation of 'running speech,' that is, of words as elements in connected spoken discourse. . . . " The present book does not attempt to do this completely, could not, in fact, but in many instances does show modified pronunciations brought about by the phonetic effect of words on one another. Still more often the pronunciation of words as here indicated has been influenced, not so much by preceding or following sounds, as by rhythm, tempo, intonation, sense stress, etc. This will account for a goodly number of differences between the two books.

Another difference of aim lies in the scope of the two works. The *New*

International avowedly includes the pronunciation "of all parts of the English-speaking world" (p. xii), and puts little emphasis on regional differences within America. This book only occasionally and incidentally represents British or other non-American pronunciation of English, and represents as fully as practicable the main regional differences in America.

In some cases there are differences of accentuation that do not represent real inconsistencies. In the Guide to Pronunciation in the *New International* (p. xxxvi, col. 1) it is pointed out that a great many English words have no fixed accentuation, and that the accent shown in the vocabulary is merely one possible accentuation among others that may be equally correct. In this book, in some instances, the accentuation may depend on the colloquial character of the pronunciation. In some cases, too, differences of accentuation are due merely to a difference of practical policy. For instance, the *New International*, like many dictionaries, usually places no accent mark on a final third syllable though it may have secondary stress; thus the word *calabash* has only the first syllable marked, whereas in this book the mark of secondary accent is regularly placed on such words ('kælə,bæʃ). This represents no difference of accentuation in the two books. but merely a difference of practice, both methods being quite defensible.

The editors believe that this book is a natural complement to *Webster's New International Dictionary, Second Edition*. The *New International* fully recognizes the validity and importance of colloquial English speech. In its Guide to Pronunciation, §8, it states: "The most important of these different styles [of spoken English] is what may be called the cultivated colloquial, which has aptly been termed the style of well-bred ease. This is the most used of the standard styles, it is acceptable to every class of society, whether used by them or not. . . . " The *New International* provides for colloquial pronunciation by means of certain flexible symbols. Thus the Webster symbol *ă* ('italic short *a*') "is used to suggest a variable sound . . . tending . . . , especially in familiar speech, to the neutral vowel [ə]" (Guide, §91). The symbol *ĕ* ('italic short *e*') serves a similar purpose: "In the great majority of everyday words, unaccented *e* before *n* or *l*, and in many words in other unaccented position, as in *quiĕt, propriĕty*, is obscured to the neutral vowel [ə] in colloquial speech" (Guide, §127). Thus our book gives chief emphasis to colloquial speech, while the *New International*, though fully recognizing it, treats it only as one among many features of the English language.

The *New International* has also given a table of the International Phonetic Alphabet for English with full illustration of its use: see especially Guide, pp. xxii–xxv, and thereafter throughout the Guide. The G. & C. Merriam Co. would therefore seem to be in a logical position to publish a dictionary of colloquial American speech in the symbols of the International Phonetic Alphabet. In the upshot, we believe that the actual differences in pronunciation between the Merriam-Webster dictionaries and this one are comparatively few.

The eager and extensive co-operation which the editors have received in the prosecution of this work has gone far beyond our expectation, and has placed us under great obligation to all who have shown interest and given help. First of all we wish to express our thanks to the Carnegie Corporation for a grant-in-aid through the University of Wisconsin to one of the editors, and to that University for inviting him to spend the year 1940–41 in residence to prosecute the work; to the Carnegie Corporation, on recommendation of the American Council of Learned Societies, for extending the grant-in-aid to supply this editor with an instructor at Hiram College in 1941–42 to enable him to give more time to the dictionary; to Dr. Margaret Waterman for competently fulfilling this appointment; and to Hiram College for granting him leave of absence in 1940–41.

We are under very particular obligations to Professor Miles L. Hanley, of the University of Wisconsin, for his hearty encouragement of the dictionary from its beginning, for placing at our disposal his great collection of rimes and spellings at the University of Wisconsin, and for many valuable suggestions; and to Mrs. Louise Hanley for much help in the utilization of the above-mentioned collections, and for many items of expert editorial advice.

We have profited greatly from the material thus far published by the *Linguistic Atlas of the United States and Canada*, and in addition we wish to thank the Directors for placing at our disposal a considerable amount of unpublished material from the collections covering parts of the Central West and of the South.

We thankfully acknowledge our great indebtedness, in common with all students of the English language, to the great *Oxford English Dictionary*.

Intimately associated as the editors have been with *Webster's New International Dictionary, Second Edition*, it is inevitable that we should be influenced by its standards and indebted to its materials in many ways. We gladly acknowledge the deepest obligations to it.

We are indebted to many individuals who have supplied us with details of information in their respective fields; among them, Professors Myles Dillon (Celtic), William Ellery Leonard (English), J. Homer Herriott (Spanish), Joseph L. Russo (Italian), Alexander A. Vasiliev (Russian), R-M. S. Heffner (German and Phonetics), Einar Haugen (Scandinavian), Casimir Zdanowicz (French), Dr. Karl G. Bottke (French and Italian), Mr. Charles E. Condray (Southern speech),—all at the University of Wisconsin; to Mr. Edward Artin, G. & C. Merriam Co., Springfield, Mass. (Eastern speech), Professor J. D. M. Ford, Harvard University (Italian), Professor Bernard Bloch, Brown University (Eastern speech), Dr. George L. Trager, Yale University (Linguistics), Dr. Ruth E. Mulhauser, Hiram

College (Romance Languages), Professor R. H. Stetson, Oberlin College (Syllabics).

To scholars and other competent observers in various parts of the United States and Canada we are under special obligation for material which they have collected on the speech of their regions, with valuable comment and in many instances with phonograph records: to Professors Katherine Wheatley, University of Texas; William A. Read, Louisiana State University; George P. Wilson, Woman's College, University of North Carolina; C. K. Thomas, Cornell University; C. M. Wise, Louisiana State University; Lee S. Hultzén, University of California at Los Angeles; W. Norwood Brigance, Wabash College; Mr. John Kepke, New York City; Mr. L. Sprague de Camp, New York City; Dr. Raven I. McDavid, Jr., South Carolina; Dr. Martin Joos, University of Toronto, Can.

We also wish to thank a number of scholars and teachers who responded to our request for advice on the editing (published in *American Speech*, XI, Oct. 1936, pp. 227–31), replying either in the columns of that journal or by private correspondence. Their suggestions were all carefully considered, and many of them were adopted.

To Mr. Donald A. Bird, Mr. Philip M. Davies, and Mrs. Wayne Caygill of the University of Wisconsin we are indebted for valuable assistance in preparing the manuscript.

In addition to those mentioned above, the editors also have to express lasting obligations to many more scholars, teachers, and others, who made transcriptions of their own and others' speech, and often supplied supplementary notes; in several instances also they sent phonograph records. To those whose names follow and a few that we had no means of identifying we extend our sincere thanks. Titles are omitted; and since it could not be significant without detailed explanation, address and locality are omitted. Suffice it to say that the informants were well distributed over the United States. Those from Canada are so marked.

Virgil A. Anderson, Phyllis B. Arlt, A. M. Barnes, L. L. Barrett, A. C. Baugh, J. F. Bender, C. L. Bennet (Can.), E. B. Birney (Can.), Morton W. Bloomfield (Can.), Hilda Brannon, Alexander Brede, Jr., Christine Broome, William F. Bryan, Donald C. Bryant, C. H. Carruthers (Can.), Philip H. Churchman, Roy B. Clark, T. F. Cummings, Edwin B. Davis, J. de Angulo, L. R. Dingus, Sarah Dodson, Julia Duncan, Norman E. Eliason, Bert Emsley, E. E. Ericson, Paul H. Flint, Frances A. Foster, Elizabeth F. Gardner, James Geddes, Jr., Erma M. Gill, W. Cabell Greet, Louis A. Guerriero, Harold F. Harding, Harry W. Hastings, Grace E. Ingledue, Annie S. Irvine, Cary F. Jacob, Joseph Jones, W. Powell Jones, Claude E. Kantner, Clifford Anne King, C. A. Knudson, C. A. Lloyd, C. M. Lotspeich, William F. Luebke, Klonda Lynn, T. O. Mabbott, John C. McCloskey, Cassa L. McDonald, James B. McMillan, Kemp Malone, Edward W. Mammen, Albert H. Marckwardt, E. K. Maxfield, R. J. Menner,

Alice W. Mills, George Neely, T. Earl Pardoe, Gordon E. Peterson, Holland Peterson (Can.), Louise Pound, E. G. Proudman, Robert L. Ramsay, W. Charles Redding, Loren D. Reid, Stuart Robertson, J. C. Ruppenthal, I. Willis Russell, C. Richard Sanders, Edwin F. Shewmake, Loretta Skelly, Gordon W. Smith, Paul L. Stayner, J. M. Steadman, Jr., W. J. Stevens (Can.), Everett F. Strong, Morris Swadesh, C. H. Thomas, Argus Tresidder, E. H. Tuttle, W. Freeman Twaddell, Charles H. Voelker, Chad Walsh, Lois P. Ware, Raymond Weeks, Walter H. Wilke, Rudolph Willard, A. M. Withers, Robert Withington.

The typesetting and electrotyping of this book were done by the George Banta Publishing Company, of Menasha, Wisconsin. To all members of its staff who were concerned in any way with its making, the editors express their grateful appreciation.

The editors feel that the making of the dictionary has been a co-operative enterprise, and if it has value, this is in large measure due to expert help from many voluntary contributors; for its defects the editors hold themselves solely responsible.

Vachel Lindsay Room, Hiram College   John S. Kenyon
      September, 1943   Thomas A. Knott

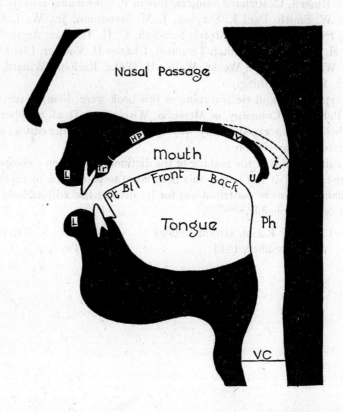

CONVENTIONALIZED DIAGRAM OF THE SPEECH ORGANS

(Reprinted by permission from Kenyon's *American Pronunciation*, 8th ed.)

LL=Lips. Pt=Tongue Point. Bl=Tongue Blade. Tr=Teethridge. HP=Hard Palate. V=Velum (soft palate): black: lowered, or open; dotted: raised, or closed. U=Uvula. Ph=Pharynx. VC=Vocal Cords.

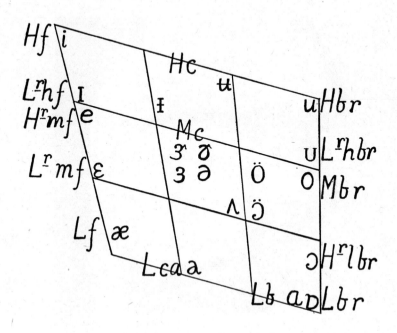

CHART OF THE TONGUE POSITIONS OF THE VOWELS

(Reproduced, with slight changes, from Kenyon's *American Pronunciation,* 8th edition, by permission.)

The left of the figure represents the front of the mouth

Hf = High-front	Hc = High-central	Hbr = High-back round
Lʳhf = Lower high-front		Lʳhbr = Lower high-back round
Hʳmf = Higher mid-front	Mc = Mid-central	Mbr = Mid-back round
Lʳmf = Lower mid-front		Hʳlbr = Higher low-back round
Lf = Low-front	Lca = Low-central advanced	Lbr = Low-back round
		Lb = Low-back

INTRODUCTION

THE STYLE OF SPEECH REPRESENTED

§1. It is the purpose of this dictionary to show the pronunciation of cultivated colloquial English in the United States. The meaning of the word *colloquial* is sometimes misunderstood. A common misunderstanding is that in dictionaries the label *Colloq.* attached to a word or pronunciation brands it as inferior, and therefore to be avoided.

Webster's New International Dictionary, Second Edition, thus defines *colloquial:* "Pertaining to, or used in, conversation, esp. common and familiar conversation; conversational; hence, unstudied; informal; as, *colloquial* phrases or pronunciations; specif., of a word or a sense or use of a word or expression, acceptable and appropriate in ordinary conversational context, as in intimate speech among cultivated people, in familiar letters, in informal speeches or writings, but not in formal written discourse (*flabbergast; go slow; harum-scarum*). Colloquial speech may be as correct as formal speech. 'Every educated person speaks his mother tongue in at least two ways, and the difference between the dignified and the *colloquial* style is considerable.' —*G. L. Kittredge.*" It should be noted that the illustrative words do not refer to pronunciation but to diction, though the definition includes pronunciation.

The definition in the *Oxford Dictionary* is concise and also adequate. Though it does not mention pronunciation, "etc." may safely be taken to include it: "Of words, phrases, etc.: Belonging to common speech; characteristic of or proper to ordinary conversation, as distinguished from formal or elevated language. (The usual sense.)"

Definitions of *colloquial* that only concern choice of words and give as examples only oaths or slang are perhaps in part responsible for some of the popular misunderstanding of the term.

A less frequent, but still not uncommon error is the confusion of *colloquial* with *local,* the assumption that a *colloquialism* is a *localism,* and so to be avoided.

Another not uncommon confusion is to regard *colloquial* English as the opposite of *standard* English (*standard* being confused with *formal* or *literary*). There is standard colloquial English and standard formal or literary English, as there is nonstandard colloquial and nonstandard formal English. As regards pronunciation, one kind of nonstandard formal English is the artificial type in which vowels that are normally unaccented are pronounced with their accented sounds, in which articles (*a, an, the*), prepositions (*to, from, of*), and other normally unstressed particles are pronounced with their emphatic forms instead, in which the tempo and intonation are not those of traditional living speech, in which abnormal accentuation and loudness are practiced, together with similar distortions that detract from unostentatious sincerity.

The accepted meaning of *colloquial* is to be found in the work of such linguistic scholars as Professor Henry Cecil Wyld, of Oxford, whose *History of Modern Colloquial English* deals with the unstudied speech and familiar correspondence of the cultivated classes, and reminds us of the importance both to literature and to general culture of this central core of the English language. Says Professor Wyld, "The style of literary prose is alive and expressive, chiefly insofar as it is rooted in that of colloquial utterance.... The style of Literature is rooted in the life and conversation of the age."[1] Similarly, the American scholar and poet William Ellery

[1] *History of Modern Colloquial English,* London 1925, pp. 157, 188.

Leonard: "In general every good colloquialism is possible in good prose (or verse), for quite rightly good prose (or verse) is becoming more and more a skillful adaptation of the vigorous, compact, racy idiom of the best spoken speech."[2]

§2. Colloquial pronunciation is here treated as the conversational and familiar utterance of cultivated speakers when speaking in the normal contacts of life and concerned with what they are saying, not how they are saying it. There are, of course, different styles of colloquial, from that of the everyday contacts of family life to the somewhat less familiar contacts of social and business or professional life. The variant pronunciations of the same word frequently shown will often reflect the different styles of the colloquial. In all cases of words that are not formal per se, unstudied everyday speech is the basis. It is of course true that the majority of words in general use are the same for colloquial as for formal language, and are pronounced alike in both styles.

The editors are aware that the attempt to represent in fairly accurate symbols the everyday speech of the cultivated is likely now and then to cause surprise and to tempt criticism. The average observer has not been trained to observe speech on the wing, and is too apt to be influenced by unconscious habitual association with spelling forms. No experience is commoner with trained observers than to hear certain pronunciations in the very statements in which the critic is denying them.

It must also be remembered that not all words are of a colloquial nature. Words not in colloquial use have, properly speaking, no colloquial pronunciation. Thus the word *exorcise* does not often occur in conversation. Its pronunciation is therefore what it would be in formal context, with the -*or*- fully sounded. If it should become a popular word, it would sound just like *exercise*. So the word *adhibit*, not being colloquial, receives the full sound of the first vowel as in *add*, while in the more popular word *advise* the first vowel is normally obscured.

THE PHONETIC ALPHABET

§3. Pronunciation in this dictionary is indicated by the alphabet of the International Phonetic Association (IPA). These symbols and the pronunciations represented by them invariably appear in **boldface type**. More than half of these are the ordinary letters of the English alphabet or familiar variations of them.

Each symbol stands for only one speech sound, and each speech sound has only one symbol to represent it. In accord with the practice of many British and American users of this alphabet the accented sounds **ʌ, ɜ, ɝ** are considered to be separate speech sounds from the unaccented sounds **ə** and **ɚ**. Diphthongs are regarded as single sounds and their symbols (**aɪ, aʊ, ɔɪ,** etc.) as single symbols. The same is true of **tʃ, dʒ**.

In using the phonetic alphabet the reader must be careful to give only the one designated sound to those letters which in ordinary spelling represent more than one sound. Thus the symbol **g** has only the sound in *get* **gɛt**, never that in *gem* **dʒɛm; s** has only the sound in *gas* **gæs,** never that in *wise* **waɪz** or that in *vision* **ˈvɪʒən**. The dotted i has only the sound in *machine* **məˈʃin,** never that in *shin* **ʃɪn;** ordinary **e** always has the sound in *gate* **gɛt,** never that in *met* **mɛt**. Below is the list of symbols with key words. The notes after the table give fuller information and additional symbols. The accent mark (ˈ) always precedes the syllable accented.

[2] *American Speech*, VIII, 3, Oct. 1933, p. 57.

VOWELS

Symbol	Spelling	Spoken Form	Symbol	Spelling	Spoken Form
i	bee	**bi**	ʊ	full	**fʊl**
ɪ	pity	**ˈpɪtɪ**	u	tooth	**tuθ**
e	rate	**ret**	ɝ	further	**ˈfɝðɚ** *accented syllable*
ɛ	yet	**jɛt**			*only, r's sounded*
æ	sang	**sæŋ**	ɜ	further	**ˈfɜðɚ** *accented syllable*
a	bath	**baθ** *as heard in the East,*			*only, r's silent*
		between æ (sang)	ɚ	further	**ˈfɝðɚ** *unaccented syllable*
		and ɑ (ah)			*only, r's sounded*
ɑ	ah	**ɑ**	ə	further	**ˈfɜðə** *unaccented syllable*
	far	**fɑr**			*only, r's silent*
ɒ	watch	**wɒtʃ** *between* ɑ (ah) *and*		custom	**ˈkʌstəm** *unaccented syl-*
		ɔ (jaw)		above	**əˈbʌv** *lable*
ɔ	jaw	**dʒɔ**			
	gorge	**gɔrdʒ**	ʌ	custom	**ˈkʌstəm** *accented sylla-*
o	go	**go**		above	**əˈbʌv** *ble*

DIPHTHONGS

aɪ	while	**hwaɪl**	ju	using	**ˈjuzɪŋ**
aʊ	how	**haʊ**		fuse	**fjuz**
ɔɪ	toy	**tɔɪ**	ɪu	fuse	**fɪuz**

CONSONANTS

Symbol	Spelling	Spoken Form	Symbol	Spelling	Spoken Form
p	pity	**ˈpɪtɪ**	dʒ	jaw	**dʒɔ**
b	bee	**bi**		edge	**ɛdʒ**
t	tooth	**tuθ**	m	custom	**ˈkʌstəm**
d	dish	**dɪʃ**	m̩	keep 'em	**ˈkipm̩**
k	custom	**ˈkʌstəm**	n	vision	**ˈvɪʒən**
g	go	**go**	n̩	Eden	**ˈidn̩**
f	full	**fʊl**	ŋ	sang	**sæŋ**
v	vision	**ˈvɪʒən**		angry	**ˈæŋ·grɪ**
θ	tooth	**tuθ**	l	full	**fʊl**
ð	further	**ˈfɝðɚ**	l̩	cradle	**ˈkredl̩**
s	sang	**sæŋ**	w	watch	**wɒtʃ**
z	using	**ˈjuzɪŋ**	hw	while	**hwaɪl**
ʃ	dish	**dɪʃ**	j	yet	**jɛt**
ʒ	vision	**ˈvɪʒən**	r	rate	**ret**
h	how	**haʊ**		very	**ˈvɛrɪ**
tʃ	watch	**wɒtʃ**		far	**fɑr**
	chest	**tʃɛst**		gorge	**gɔrdʒ**

ACCENT MARKS

§4. The mark ' above the line and before a syllable indicates that that syllable has the principal accent, as in *action* **'ækʃən.** The corresponding mark ‚ below the line and before a syllable indicates that that syllable has an accentuation somewhat weaker than the main one, as in *acrobat* **'ækrə‚bæt,** *Aberdeen* ‚æbə'din, *shoemaker* **'ʃu‚mekə.** For discussion of accent, see §§48–54.

LENGTH MARK

§5. The colon (:) after a vowel or a consonant symbol indicates that its sound is prolonged. Thus the form **sæːnd** beside **sæt** means that the **æ** sound in *sand* is longer than in *sat;* and the form **dʒɔɪs:** means that in one pronunciation of the plural *joists* (with omitted **t**) the **s** is longer than it is in *rejoice* **rɪ'dʒɔɪs.** In the vocabulary the length sign is used only occasionally or in certain classes of words. See fuller discussion of length at §55.

NOTES ON THE SYMBOLS

§6. **1.** The symbol **ɪ** is used for accented or unaccented syllables. Though the accented and unaccented vowels in *pity* **'pɪtɪ,** *sitting* **'sɪtɪŋ,** *visit* **'vɪzɪt,** etc., are sometimes different in quality, the differences are here ignored, since they vary with different speakers and with the different sounds that precede or follow. This accords with common practice in transcription.

When final, the unaccented vowel in *pity* **'pɪtɪ** and similar words varies with different speakers in America from a sound like the **ɪ** in *bit* **bɪt,** or like the first **ɪ** in **'pɪtɪ,** to a sound that approaches the **i** in *bee* **bi.** See the ending *-y* in the vocabulary.

§7. **e.** The vowel in *rate* **ret** and other words with "long *a*" is very often (but by no means always) a diphthong (gliding from one vowel to another in the same syllable) **eɪ, ɛɪ, ee,** or the like. On linguistic principles the one symbol **e** properly stands for all varieties of the sound (whether diphthong or not). The variants never distinguish words otherwise alike.

§8. **ɛ.** The symbol **ɛ** is used not only for words like *yet* **jɛt,** *send* **sɛnd,** but also for one type of pronunciation of the vowel sound in *there* **ðɛr,** *swear* **swɛr,** *air* **ɛr,** as pronounced by many. When thus followed by **r,** the **ɛ** sound is usually a little more like the **æ** in *sang* **sæŋ** than is the **ɛ** in *yet* **jɛt,** *send* **sɛnd.** Many speakers pronounce **æ** in such words in both America and England. Both pronunciations are given in the vocabulary (*there* **ðɛr, ðær**).

§9. **æ.** This ligature is a unit symbol (not two letters) standing for a single simple vowel sound. It was the letter used in Anglo-Saxon times for the same sound in Old English as in present English *sat* (OE *sæt*). Originally combined from the Latin letters *a* and *e* (since its sound lay between the two Latin sounds), its present value in the IPA alphabet is the same as in its oldest use in English.

§10. **a.** This vowel sound, not in general use in America as a whole, is about midway between the vowel of *sang* **sæŋ** and the vowel of *ah* **ɑ,** *father* **'fɑðə.** It is often heard in New England and New York City in such words as *ask* **ask,** *chaff* **tʃaf,** *bath* **baθ** (which are also there pronounced **æsk, tʃæf, bæθ** or **ɑsk, tʃɑf, bɑθ**). It commonly begins the diphthongs in *while* and *how.* The vowel **a** is an important sound in French, Spanish, and other foreign languages, and is common in cultivated Northern British, Scottish, Anglo-Irish, and Canadian. The symbol **a** must always be carefully distinguished from **ɑ.** For the use of **a** in Eastern American, see §§102 f.

§11. ɑ. This is the "broad *a*" sound in *ah* ɑ, *far* fɑr, *father* ˈfɑðɚ in most of America. It is also used by the majority of Americans in "short *o*" words such as *top* tɑp, *got* gɑt, *fodder* ˈfɑdɚ, in which some speakers pronounce ɒ.

§12. ɒ. The symbol ɒ represents a vowel not in universal American use. It is the historical "short *o*" now generally used in England in words like *top* tɒp, *got* gɒt, *fodder* ˈfɒdə, by many Easterners and Southerners, and in certain kinds of words by many speakers in all parts of the country. It is a sound about midway between ɑ in *ah* and ɔ in *wall*. It may be approximated by trying to sound ɑ in *ah* while (without moving the tongue) rounding the lips for ɔ in *wall*. As with ɑ, so with ɒ, there is no key word that will convey to all Americans its exact sound. The key word *watch*, here used, frequently is spoken with ɒ in all parts of America, but it is also often pronounced wɑtʃ, with ɑ as in *ah*, and wɔtʃ, with ɔ as in *wall*.

§13. o. Like e, the symbol o represents either a simple vowel or a diphthong (oʊ, öʊ, ɔʊ, etc.). For the same reason stated at e (§7 above) the symbol o is used for both the simple vowel and the diphthong. For ö see *-ow* in the vocabulary.

§14. ʊ, u. The small capital ʊ (*full* fʊl) and the lower-case u (*tooth* tuθ) are to be carefully distinguished from each other.

§15. ɝ. The symbol ɝ represents the accented form of the so-called "*r*-colored" vowel used in the first syllable of *further* ˈfɝðɚ by those who do not "drop their *r*'s." In current spelling it is spelt with a vowel letter followed by the letter *r* (*word, fur, term, firm, earn*). But in sound this vowel ɝ is not followed by r; it is a vowel made while the tongue is at the same time holding the position for r. Such vowels are common in many types of English. The consonantal r sound that formerly followed the vowel (hence the present spelling) long ago merged with the preceding vowel and disappeared as a separate sound, though its effect is still heard in the *r*-coloring of the vowel. The simple proof of the nature of the present sound is that the vowel cannot be pronounced separately from the r without producing a quite different sound, whereas this can easily be done with, say, the ɑ and r of *farm*.

§16. ɜ. The symbol ɜ represents the corresponding vowel in the word *further* of those who "drop their *r*'s," the tongue for this vowel ɜ being in the same general central position in the mouth as for ɝ, but without the simultaneous adjustment of the tongue for the *r*-coloring (usually the elevation of the tip). For those accustomed to pronounce ɝ a fairly good ɜ can be made by trying to pronounce ɝ in *bird* with the point of the tongue placed against the backs of the lower teeth, and with the jaw a trifle more closed than for the vowel ʌ in *sun*. This ɜ is often followed by r, as in *furry* ˈfɜ·rɪ, from *fur* fɜ. While the majority of Americans pronounce *fur* fɝ, and *furry* ˈfɝ·ɪ, most British and many eastern and southern Americans pronounce *fur* fɜ, and *furry* ˈfɜ·rɪ. But in words like *hurry*, which is not derived from a simple form *hur* as *furry* is from *fur*, three American pronunciations are common,—ˈhɜ·ɪ, ˈhɜ·rɪ, ˈhʌ·rɪ, the last being least frequent and tending to become ˈhɜ·rɪ or ˈhɝ·rɪ.

§17. ɚ. The symbol ɚ is the unaccented *r*-colored vowel, like ɝ inseparable from its *r* quality, as pronounced by those who do not "drop their *r*'s." The two symbols ɝ and ɚ are formed from the IPA symbols ɜ and ə (as used, e.g., in the word *Herbert* ˈhɜbət in Ida C. Ward's *Phonetics of English*, Cambridge, Engd. 1939, p. 108), by attaching the hook of retroflexion (*r*-coloring) used by the IPA on the consonants s, z, t, d, etc. (*Le Maître Phonétique*, Jan.–Mar. 1942, inside front cover). This makes easy the comparison of such words as *Herbert* as pronounced by those who "drop their *r*'s" ('hɜbət) and by those who sound them ('hɝbɚt), showing at a glance the phonetic relation between such words in the two types of speech (*further* 'fɝðɚ—'fɝðə, *perverse* pə'vɝs—pɚ'vɝs, *bird* bɜd—bɝd, *over* 'ovɚ—'ovə), all four sounds ɜ, ɝ, ə, ɚ being vowels, none of them here followed by **r**.

§18. **ə**. The symbol **ə** represents the "neutral vowel," or "schwa" ʃwɑ, heard in the unaccented syllable of *custom* 'kʌstəm, or, as just shown above, in that of *further* from those who "drop their *r*'s" ('fɝðə). With many such speakers the ə of 'fɝðə is not exactly like the ə of 'kʌstəm, but is commonly regarded as the same speech sound.

§19. **ʌ**. This represents the accented vowel of *custom* 'kʌstəm, *above* ə'bʌv, *undone* ʌn'dʌn. In ʌn'dʌn the first syllable is not quite without accent, but has sufficient accent (though not marked) to make it audibly more prominent than the *un-* of *unless* (spoken colloquially) ən'lɛs. Compare *unlace* ʌn'les with *unless* ən'lɛs, or *undone* ʌn'dʌn with *and done* in the phrase *over and done with* 'ovɚ ən'dʌn wɪð, or *untilled* with *until* in *This land was untilled until now* ʌn'tɪld ən'tɪl nɑu. The prefix *un-* is commonly pronounced ʌn- with more or less subordinate accent. See *un-* in the vocabulary.

§20. **ɑɪ, ɑu**. For regional varieties of these diphthongs see *Variants* §§105–108.

§21. **ju**. This is a rising diphthong—the last part being stressed more than the first. It begins with the glide consonant **j** (as in *yet* jɛt) and ends with the vowel **u** (as in *tooth* tuθ). **ju** would not be separately listed as a vowel symbol, being a consonant plus vowel, except for comparison with the diphthong **ɪu** (see below), with which it often alternates, for **ju** is of the same nature as other combinations of consonantal **j** plus a vowel (as in *ye* ji, *yea* je, *yaw* jɔ, *yet* jɛt, etc.) or of consonantal **w** plus a vowel (*we* wi, *way* we, *woe* wo, etc.).

§22. **ɪu**. This is either a falling diphthong (first element stressed, as in the diphthongs **ɑɪ, ɑu, ɔɪ**), or a level-stress diphthong, both elements being about equally prominent. If the last element becomes more prominent, then **ɪu** becomes **ju**, as it did historically in such words as *use* juz. The form **ɪu** is heard from many speakers in such words as *fuse* fɪuz, where others pronounce **ju** (fjuz). For the occurrence of **ɪu** in America, see *Variants* §109.

ɪu is a modified form of **ɪu**, occurring chiefly as an alternative to **u** or **ju** that has been reduced from **u** or **ju** by lack of stress (*superb* su'pɝb, sɪu'pɝb, sju'pɝb) or before **r** (*curious* 'kjurɪəs, 'kɪurɪəs). The phonetic surroundings lead without effort to the modified **ɪu** and **ju**.

§23. **ŋ**. It should be noted that this sound is a simple, single sound, which cannot be divided. It is made by contact of the tongue back with the velum, as the simple sound **n** is made by contact of the tongue point with the upper teethridge. The usual spelling with two letters (*ng*) has sometimes led to an impression that **ŋ** is a combination sound. It is also spelt with *n* only (*angry* 'æŋ·grɪ, *ink* ɪŋk). When speakers "drop their *g*'s" (as in *runnin'* for *running*), they drop no sound, but they replace the tongue-back nasal **ŋ** ('rʌnɪŋ) with the tongue-point nasal **n** ('rʌnɪn).

§24. **m̩, n̩, l̩**. These are called syllabic consonants because they form syllables without any vowel whatever, either alone (*stop 'em* 'stɑp·m̩, *button* 'bʌt·n̩, *saddle* 'sæd·l̩) or with other consonants (*opened* 'op·m̩d, *buttoned* 'bʌt·n̩d, *saddled* 'sæd·l̩d). These and such forms as *keep 'em* 'kipm̩, *Eden* 'idn̩, *cradle* 'kredl̩ have no vowel in the unaccented syllable because, for m̩, the lips continue closed throughout pm̩, and, for n̩ and l̩, the tongue point remains in contact with the teethridge throughout tn̩ and dl̩. Between some other consonants, as sn̩ (*lessen* 'lɛsn̩); zn̩ (*reason* 'rizn̩), pl̩ (*apple* 'æpl̩) the transition to the second consonant is so quick, or the opening of the speech organs is so slight, that no vowel intervenes.

All of the foregoing forms can also be uttered with the schwa vowel ə plus a nonsyllabic consonant ('kipəm, 'idən, 'bʌtən, 'kredəl, 'lɛsən, 'rizən, 'æpəl), but in some of these and many others the pronunciation with ə is either not accepted in good use, or is a mark of formal, noncolloquial pronunciation. On this point see further, *Variants* §114.

The remaining nasal consonant ŋ can also be syllabic, as in the colloquial *I can go* ˌaɪkŋ'go. Here the tongue back remains in contact with the velum throughout the k and the ŋ. The syllabic marker is sometimes placed over the symbol ŋ, but is here not deemed necessary, since syllabic ŋ is not frequent, and ŋ is never syllabic in the same position in which it is nonsyllabic. It is always syllabic after a consonant (ˌaɪkŋ'go, 'bægŋ'bægɪdʒ, 'mekŋ) and never syllabic after a vowel (sɪŋ, 'bægɪŋ, 'mekɪŋ).

As 'æpl̩ and 'æpəl show the alternation between a syllabic consonant (l̩) and schwa plus the same consonant (əl), so syllabic consonants may alternate with nonsyllabic consonants, but here sometimes with a difference of meaning: *help 'em eat* 'hɛlpm̩ 'it (3 syllables)—*helpmeet* 'hɛlpˌmit (2 syls.); *ordinance* 'ɔrdn̩əns (3 syls.)—*ordnance* 'ɔrdnəns (2 syls.); *double it* 'dʌbl̩ ɪt (3 syls.)—*doublet* 'dʌblɪt (2 syls.). Such alternation is often shown in the vocabulary in connection with the ending -*ing;* thus *blazoning* is pronounced either 'blez·n̩·ɪŋ or 'blez·nɪŋ; *handling* is either 'hæn·dlɪŋ or 'hæn·dl̩·ɪŋ. The one deemed most usual in colloquial speech is given first; but often there is little choice, the form depending on style of speech.

§25. **hw.** Linguists are disagreed whether **hw** should be regarded as a single speech sound or as two—h followed by w. When regarded as a single phoneme it is often transcribed with inverted w (ʍ). Here the symbol hw is used for the sound spelt *wh* in words like *while* **hwaɪl.** For variation in pronunciation of words spelt with *wh* see *Variants* §113.

§26. **r.** In this book the symbol **r** is used for the consonant, as in *rate* ret, *cradle* 'kredl̩, where it is parallel in phonetic structure to **w** in *wait* wet, *twain* twen, and to **j** in *Yale* jel, *cue* kju, that is, a glide consonant or semivowel before a vowel in the same syllable. In addition, the symbol **r** is here used for the sound in *very* 'vɛrɪ, *far* fɑr, *gorge* gɔrdʒ, which some regard as a nonsyllabic vowel forming a diphthong with the preceding vowel. This is sometimes expressed by the vowel symbol ɚ ('vɛɚɪ, fɑɚ, gɔɚdʒ), which is defensible on laboratory evidence. But the ends of simplicity seem better served to confine the use of ɚ to representing the *syllabic* vowel, so that whenever ɚ occurs in this book it always represents a syllable, either alone, as in *better* 'bɛt·ɚ, or with a consonant, as in *perceive* pɚ'siv. Thus the word *flower*, which is pronounced either with two syllables or with one, can be transcribed with two ('flaʊɚ) or with one (flaʊr). In the speech of those who "drop their *r*'s" the two-syllable pronunciation is shown by separating the syllables with a centered period ('flaʊ·ə) and the one-syllable pronunciation without it (flaʊə). Here the accent mark also implies more than one syllable, but would not help to distinguish three-syllable *cornflower* ES 'kɔənˌflaʊ·ə from two-syllable *corn flour* 'kɔənˌflaʊə, or three-syllable *flower cup* 'flaʊ·əˌkʌp from two-syllable *flour cup* 'flaʊəˌkʌp. In current speech (and often in poetry) all such words as *flower, flour, higher, hire* have either two syllables or one. In this dictionary, as a rule, the number of syllables indicated follows the conventional spelling form.

The symbol **r** is also used between ə and a vowel in such a position as in *flattery* 'flætərɪ, which might (less conveniently) be regarded as *flatter* ꞌflætɚ plus -*y*-ɪ, or by those who "drop their *r*'s" as ꞌflætə plus -rɪ. The slight difference in sound between ꞌflætɚ·ɪ and ꞌflætə·rɪ depends on where the last syllable begins, and is here disregarded.

In a few cases ɚ is used to represent the speech of those who "drop their *r*'s," as in *overact* ₒovɚꞌækt, where all speakers would normally sound the *r* before a vowel.

Besides the usual American sounds of **r,** the symbol **r** indicates certain different sounds in some varieties of English and in foreign languages; as (1) the tongue-point trill (vibration against the upper teethridge) in Scottish, Anglo-Irish, Italian, Spanish, and sometimes German and French; (2) the uvular trill (vibration of the uvula against the back of the tongue) found in French and German; and (3) the uvular fricative, or "scrape," found in French and German. These varieties of **r** have special IPA symbols not needed in this book, where they are all represented by **r.**

ADDITIONAL PHONETIC SYMBOLS

In addition to the symbols given above, a number of symbols are used to express less common English sounds and the sounds of foreign languages recorded in the dictionary. The descriptions of the foreign sounds are only approximate, and are intended for those not familiar with the foreign sounds. The symbols not here described, when used to express foreign pronunciations, have approximately the same sounds as in English words.

§27. **x.** This stands for the consonant in German *ich* ɪx, *ach* ɑx, Scottish *loch* lɒx, Spanish *junto* ꞌxunto, an "open" **k** sound made by forcing voiceless breath through a loose contact of the back of the tongue with the soft palate (velum) at the same point where a firm contact would stop the breath and make the **k** sound. A separate symbol (ç) is sometimes used to express the more forward variety of the sound heard in *ich*. But, as Bloomfield has shown, one symbol is sufficient for both varieties.

§28. **g.** This is the fricative *g* sound (we here use the older and better IPA symbol), pronounced like **x** except with voiced breath (vocal cords vibrating), and related to the English stop **g** just as **x** is related to stop **k.**

§29. **ɬ.** The so-called Welsh fricative *l*, expressed in current Welsh spelling by *ll*, is a kind of *l* sound made by forcible expulsion of voiceless breath at one side of the tongue near the back teeth, the tongue being in contact near the teethridge in front and at the other side. In Anglicized pronunciation of Welsh names **ɬ** is sometimes replaced by English **fl** (*Fluellen* for *Llewelyn*, *Floyd* for *Lloyd*) or by English **θl** (θlænꞌbɛrɪs for *Llanberis*).

§30. **ḷ.** This is ordinary English **l** except that it is voiceless. Its chief use is in the French pronunciation of such words as *debacle* deꞌbɑːkḷ, where the **ḷ** is final after a voiceless consonant. It is almost inaudible to an English ear, and is sometimes actually lost in French conversation. (Voiceless **m** (ṃ) occurs in a word or two; cf *umph*.)

§31. **ṛ.** Voiceless **r** is used in some French words when final after a voiceless consonant (*Joffre* ʒɔ̈fṛ). Like **ḷ,** it is sometimes lost in French speech.

§32. **ʎ.** This is the palatal lateral, or palatal *l* (not the same as palatalized *l*, occasionally represented by **lj** in the vocabulary). It may be approximated by keeping the tongue pressed against the backs of the lower teeth while trying to sound **l.** In the vocabulary **ʎ** is used chiefly in Spanish and Italian words.

§33. **ɲ.** This is palatal *n* (different from palatalized *n*, expressed in the vocabulary, when needed, by **nj**). Like **ʎ,** it can be approximated by keeping the tongue pressed against the backs of the lower teeth while trying to sound **n.** In the vocabulary **ɲ** is used chiefly in French, Spanish, and Italian words.

§34. **ʍ.** Inverted **w,** see **hw.**

§35. **ʔ.** The glottal stop. Not a distinctive speech sound in English (it never distinguishes words otherwise alike). It often occurs before a vowel in English in clear, emphatic utterance. It is formed by closing the glottis as in holding the breath with open mouth. The glottal stop followed by its explosive release is heard in coughing.

§36. **β.** This is the voiced bilabial fricative. It sounds, and is made, somewhat like **v,** but in **β** the upper lip replaces the upper teeth, the voiced breath passing out with friction between the slightly separated lips, instead of (as in v) between the lower lip and the upper teeth. In the vocabulary **β** occurs chiefly in Spanish words (*Habana* a'**βana**).

§37. **Φ.** This, the "candle-blowing" sound, is the voiceless counterpart of **β,** and bears the same relation to **f** that **β** does to **v.** For an example, see *whew* in the vocabulary.

§38. **ɥ.** This sound is used only in French words. It is nearly equivalent to **j** pronounced with rounded lips, being the glide, or semivowel, corresponding to the front rounded vowel **y** (§42 below). It is made by a quick glide (with rounded lips) from the position for **y** to a following vowel, just as the glide semivowel **j** is made by a quick glide (with unrounded lips) from the position of **i** to a following vowel, or as the glide **w** is made by a quick glide from the position for **u** to a following vowel. An example of **ɥ** is seen in French *nuance* **nɥɑ̃:s.**

§39. **ɨ.** This represents a vowel sound about midway between (front) **i** and (back) **u.** It is common in Welsh (*Llandudno* **ɬan'didno**).

§40. **ɪ.** This represents a vowel made with the tongue retracted somewhat from the lower high-front position for ordinary **ɪ** (*bid*). It is regularly heard as the first element of the common American diphthong **ɪu,** in this book written **ɪu** (*fuse* **fɪuz**). The sound **ɪ** is also common in the endings *-ed* (*stated*), *-es* (*glasses*) if they are not pronounced either **-ɪd, -ɪz,** or **-əd, -əz.** See the ending *-ed* in the vocabulary. This symbol is not often used in the vocabulary.

§41. **ʊ.** This is commonly heard as the final element of the American diphthong **ɪu** (*fuse* **fɪuz**). It represents a vowel resembling **u** but with the tongue advanced from the position for **u.** Like **ɪ,** the symbol **ʊ** is not regularly used in the vocabulary, the diphthong **ɪu** being regularly written **ɪu,** and the advanced **ʊ** not being distinguished from **u.** The advanced sound denoted by **ʊ** is also heard by itself in the speech of many who do not use **ɪu,** but who distinguish, for example, *brewed* **brʊd** from *brood* **brud.** See *Variants* **ju, ɪu, u,** §109.

§42. **y.** This is the high-front rounded vowel of German *hübsch* **hypʃ,** *kühn* **ky:n,** or of French *lune* **lyn,** *dur* **dy:r.** It may be approximated by trying to pronounce **ɪ** (*bid*) or **i** (*bee*) with lips rounded as for **u** (*too*).

§43. **ø.** This is the mid-front rounded vowel of German *schön* **ʃø:n** or French *peu* **pø.** It may be approximated by trying to sound **e** (*rate*) with lips rounded as for **o** (*go*).

§44. **œ.** This is the low-front or lower mid-front rounded vowel of German *können* **'kœnən** or French *heure* **œ:r,** and may be approximated by trying to pronounce **ε** or **æ** of *there* **ðεr, ðær** with lips rounded as for **ɔ** (*wall*).

§45. **ǫ** This is the symbol for an *o* sound intermediate between **o** (*go*) and **ɔ** (*wall*). Cf. §98.

§46. ɔ̌. This is a kind of ɔ sound with the tongue pushed farther forward than in *wall*. It may be approximated by sounding ʌ (*sun*) with lips rounded as for ɔ (*wall*). It is nearly the sound of French "short *o*" in *cotte* kɔ̌t, this symbol being regularly used in the vocabulary to denote this French vowel. The symbol ɔ̌ is also used to denote the so-called "New England short *o*," shown in the vocabulary for certain words that usually have the vowel o (*go*), but which, according to Grandgent, are also pronounced with ɔ̌ by many cultivated speakers in New England.

§47. The French nasalized vowels æ̃, ɑ̃, õ, œ̃ are, respectively, the vowel sounds æ, ɑ, o, œ pronounced with the nasal passage open to the throat, the velum being lowered as when breathing through nose and mouth together. In works on French phonetics, for reasons incident to practical transcription, æ̃ is usually written ɛ̃, and õ written ɔ̃, but they are described as æ̃ and õ sounds, and are here so represented.

STRESS, ACCENT, SENSE STRESS

§48. *Stress* is the general term for prominence of a sound or syllable, whether that prominence is produced by force of utterance, by pitch, by duration of sound, or (as usually) by some combination of these elements. *Accent* is the specific term for the prominence of one syllable over others in a plurisyllable (word of more than one syllable), as *practice* ˈpræktɪs, *remain* rɪˈmen, *element* ˈɛləmənt. Monosyllables therefore have no accent in this sense.

§49. *Sense stress*, or *sentence stress*, is the prominence of certain words among others in a group that makes sense—phrase, clause, or sentence; as *The ˈfarmer disˈposed of his ˈholdings*. Here the marked words have more sense stress than the unmarked *the, of, his*. The same marks can show sense stress of monosyllables (*The ˈman has ˈgone to his ˈhouse*). The sense stress of plurisyllables always falls on their accented syllables.

In the vocabulary every word of more than one syllable has a primary accent mark in the pronunciation (*clothing* ˈkloðɪŋ, *amiss* əˈmɪs, *variant* ˈvɛrɪənt, *preceding* prɪˈsidɪŋ, *inflected* ɪnˈflɛktɪd). Some words have two, when two syllables are nearly or quite equal (*redheaded* ˈrɛdˈhɛdɪd).

§50. Syllables more prominent than one or more others in a word, but less prominent than the strongest one in the word, have some degree of subordinate accent, which may or may not be indicated by the secondary accent mark (ˌ), as *hesitate* ˈhɛzəˌtet, *hesitation* ˌhɛzəˈteʃən. Since subordinate accent varies from nearly the weakest to nearly the strongest in words where it can occur, and varies moreover with innumerable styles of speech, no dictionary can accurately mark all instances. Hence the use of secondary accent marks here is largely conventional. Secondary accent is usually marked in words with a clear rhythmical alternation of accents (*satisfy* ˈsætɪsˌfaɪ, *satisfaction* ˌsætɪsˈfækʃən), or when it is adjacent to the chief accent in compound words whose parts are also well known as separate words (*horseplay* ˈhɔrsˌple), and wherever needed to make the whole accentuation clearer (*Winchester* ˈwɪnˌtʃɛstə; cf also *Gambia* and *Gambier* in the vocabulary). Cf §19.

§51. In the vocabulary certain monosyllables that have varying sense stress are marked with primary and secondary accents beside forms without accent, to show how they would be stressed in connected speech. Thus *his* in its stressed forms is marked ˈhɪz, ˌhɪz, as they might occur in *This is his* ˌðɪs ɪz ˈhɪz or *His friend was gone* ˌhɪz ˈfrɛnd wəz ˈgɔn, by the side of its unstressed form, as in *I met his father* aɪ ˈmɛt ɪz ˈfɑðɚ.

§52. In words where a syllabic l or n is followed by an accented syllable beginning with a vowel (*ventilation* ˌvɛntl̩ˈeʃən, *ventilate* ˈvɛntl̩ˌet, *ordination* ˌɔrdn̩ˈeʃən, *ordinary* ˈɔrdn̩ˌɛrɪ), the accent mark is placed after the l or n̩, for if placed before (ˌvɛntˈl̩eʃən, ˌɔrdˈn̩eʃən), this would imply that l or n̩ is accented, which is impossible in English. Stetson's laboratory findings indicate that part of the l or n̩ may be carried over to the following syllable, but without being so markedly doubled or lengthened as it would be in *a little late* ˈlɪtl̩ˈlet or *a sudden need* ˈsʌdn̩ˈnid. Hence the accentuation must be shown as ˌvɛntl̩ˈeʃən, ˌɔrdn̩ˈeʃən, but with the understanding that the syllable division may be within the l or n̩, which is, nevertheless, not so long as ll or n̩n. The problem may be evaded in such words by ignoring the l or n̩ and transcribing ˌvɛntɪˈleʃən, ˌvɛntəˈleʃən, ˌɔrdɪˈneʃən, ˌɔrdəˈneʃən, but to assume that such pronunciations are more usual in cultivated colloquial speech is merely to shut our eyes to the facts. (Syllabic m or ŋ seldom if ever occurs in such situations.)

§53. Shifting accent is often seen in such compound adjectives as *high-strung* ˈhaɪˈstrʌŋ, thus marked with the normal accentuation of the word when spoken alone or when used predicatively as in *He's rather high-strung*. When this is immediately followed by a strong stress (*high-strung nerves*), the second accent is reduced (ˈhigh-ˌstrung ˈnerves). For fuller discussion, see *Webster's New International*, pp. xxxv f., §66. The rhythmic factor involved sometimes brings about permanent changes of accent. Certain adjectives (as *cold-blooded*) occurring often in the attributive position (ˈcold-ˌblooded ˈman) may become generalized with the accent of the attributive use, so that some speakers always say ˈcold-ˌblooded (ˈcold-ˌblooded ˈman, He's ˈcold-ˌblooded), where others would say ˈcold-ˌblooded ˈman, but He's ˈcold-ˈblooded. For the method of showing this in the vocabulary see §54(2). Other words than compound adjectives are subject to the same shift when followed by a strong accent, as *Shaw*ˈnee but ˈShawˌnee ˈtribes. Many examples of these shifts are given in the vocabulary.

Another type of shift in accent is brought about by emphasis. When such adverbs as ˈabsoˌlutely, ˈnecesˌsarily, ˈordiˌnarily are made emphatic, they are likely to be accented ˌabsoˈlutely, ˌnecesˈsarily, ˌordiˈnarily. Most adverbs of this type show this tendency in American English, and in some cases this accentuation has become generalized; i.e., many speakers say ˌordiˈnarily, ˌnecesˈsarily under all circumstances, even when these are not emphatic. The shifted accentuation is usually shown in the vocabulary thus: "*esp. if emphatic* ˌnecesˈsarily," which means that this accentuation may occur at any time, and is especially apt to occur under emphasis.

Shifting or variable secondary accent often occurs in such words as aˌcadeˈmician, ˌanastigˈmatic, ˌimpeccaˈbility, ˌimpenetraˈbility, ˌincompreˈhensible, ˌincorpoˈreity, inˌferiˈority, where in longer words the secondary accent precedes the primary. Here, in actual speech, such alternative accentuations as aˌcadeˈmician or ˌacadeˈmician, ˌimpenetraˈbility or imˌpenetraˈbility, inˌferiˈority or ˌinferiˈority are very common, and do not represent more and less desirable pronunciations, but chiefly show the effect of varying sense stress, emphasis, speech rhythm, semantic distinctions, and other constantly varying factors of connected speech, so that in many such instances the question which accentuation is preferable is irrelevant. See also §57.

§54. In the vocabulary, accent marks are sometimes used on words in ordinary spelling (lightface roman type) when it is desired to show only the accentuation, after a pronunciation already given. This occurs chiefly in two ways:—

(1) As at the entry *heartsore*, where, after the pronunciation and accent in phonetic symbols, there is added "*acct* + 'heart'sore," which means, "Besides the accentuation just given, the following different accentuation is also current."

(2) As at the entry *cloven-footed*, a form in ordinary spelling with accent marks is added in parentheses to show a different accentuation from that already given, especially a shifted accentuation (§53). Thus the basic accentuation is shown in the pronunciation 'klovən'futɪd, but in the attributive construction the accent on -'futɪd is reduced before a following stressed syllable, and this is shown by the phrase in parentheses ('cloven-ˌfooted 'ox). Less usually the same device is used to illustrate or confirm the accentuation just given. Thus after the entry and pronunciation *week-end*, adj, 'wik'ɛnd, the first example in parentheses by its speech rhythm confirms the accentuation just given ('week-'end ˌparty), and the second example illustrates the shift in accent due to a different speech rhythm ('week-ˌend 'trip). The reader can usually confirm the instances of level-stress accentuation by putting the entry word into a phrase with predicate construction, as *The ox is* 'cloven-'footed.

Since it is impossible in the vocabulary to give such examples of variant accentuation at every entry where it would be appropriate, it is to be understood from the occasional examples given that it can occur in all similar cases.

In all cases where accent marks are used with lightface roman type, only accentuation, and no other feature of pronunciation, is referred to.

LENGTH OF VOWELS

§55. As a rule the length of English vowels is not indicated in the vocabulary. In few cases in American English as a whole is time length, or duration, of vowels significant—that is, used to distinguish from each other words otherwise alike. Instances are found here and there, some speakers distinguishing *halve* **hæ:v** from *have* **hæv** by a longer **æ**, or *vary* **vɛ:rɪ** from *very* **vɛrɪ** by a longer **ɛ**.

In the E and S, however, some speakers distinguish certain classes of words by vowel length; e.g., *cart* **kɑ:t** from *cot* **kɑt** by a longer **ɑ**, and this is therefore a convenient way of marking words in which **r** has been dropped after **ɑ** or **a** with a resultant lengthening of the vowel sound, as *farm* **fɑrm**; ES **fɑ:m**, E + **fa:m**. The length sign is sometimes omitted in longer words of this kind when **ɑ** or **a** is noticeably shorter, as in *impartiality* ˌɪmpɑr'fælətɪ; ES ˌɪmpɑ'fælətɪ.

Since the other vowels before a silent *r* in ES are followed by **ə** (**iə, ɪə, ɛə, æə, ɔə, oə, ʊə, uə**), there the length mark is not needed; as *fear* **fɪr**; ES **fɪə(r**, and the length colon is therefore only used with **ɑ** and **a**. On the use of **ɔə** in such words see *Variants* §96.

When the length sign is used, it invariably indicates time length, or duration, not vowel quality, or tamber, and therefore has nothing to do with such distinctions as between so-called "short *i*" (**ɪ**) and "long *i*" (**aɪ**), or between "short *u*" (**ʌ**) and "long *u*" (**ju** or **ɪu**), or between "short *a*" (**æ**) and "long *a*" (**e**), etc.

In cases like *Aachen* 'ɑkən, 'ɑxən (*Ger* 'ɑ:xən), in which the vowel **ɑ** is marked long in the foreign pronunciation (where length is significant) but left unmarked in the English, this does not necessarily mean that the English vowel is shorter than the foreign one, but merely that its length is of no importance, and hence is not indicated.

SINGLE AND DOUBLE CONSONANTS

§56. In reading the pronunciations the consultant should give particular attention to single and double consonants. In ordinary spelling, doubled letters in English words commonly represent only single sounds (*happy* 'hæpɪ, *manner* 'mænɚ, *goodness* 'gʊdnɪs). Only in compounds (*coattail*) or when suffixes are added (*thinness*) are the sounds really doubled ('kot‚tel, 'θɪnnɪs), and not always then (*laterally* 'lætərəlɪ). Strict heed must be paid to the rule—one symbol, one sound; two symbols, two sounds. See §3, 2d paragraph.

In some foreign pronunciations added to compare with the English (esp. Italian) this must be watched; thus in English, *Monticello* has but one l sound (‚mantə'sɛlo), but in Italian it has two (‚monti'tʃɛl‧lo). In Italian when tʃ, dʒ, ts, dz are doubled, tʃ becomes ttʃ (*Puccini* Eng pu-'tʃinɪ, but It put'tʃi:ni), dʒ becomes ddʒ (*Maggiore* Eng mə'dʒorɪ, but It mad'dʒo:re), ts becomes tts (*Tetrazzini* Eng ‚tɛtrə'zinɪ, but It ‚tetrat'tsi:ni), dz becomes ddz (*mezzo* Eng 'mɛdzo, but It 'mɛddzo).

THE ORDER OF VARIANT PRONUNCIATIONS

§57. For words that are in general colloquial use it is intended to give first what is believed to be the most usual colloquial pronunciation. But it must be emphasized that not too much importance should be given to the order. For it is our purpose to give (unless otherwise indicated) only pronunciations that are in general cultivated use—to give none that need be avoided as incorrect or substandard. In a very large number of instances the different pronunciations of a word are of approximately equal frequency and validity, and yet they can be printed only in successive order. In numerous cases it is impossible to maintain on any solid grounds that one pronunciation given is "better" than another, as, for example, that one pronunciation of *swamp* is better than the others given; that kɛr for *care* is either better or worse than kær; that 'kaŋkwɛst is better or worse than 'kankwɛst, bɒg than lag or lɒg, 'lɛvɚ than 'livɚ, and so on. Often, too, the variants given represent only differences of colloquial style, depending on occasion, speed, degree of informality, etc., and having no bearing on the question of correctness.

§58. Where statistics indicate relative frequency, this has been recorded; but fuller collections might change the order. Statistics at present available are often based on the assumption that all words of a given phonetic or historical class (as the "*ask*" words) will be pronounced consistently. But that is not always true. A proof of this is found in the records of the *Linguistic Atlas of New England*, which show that some words that might be expected to have the vowel sound a or ɑ (where British prevailingly has ɑ) are seldom heard with a or ɑ (as *answer*), while others of the same group often or prevailingly have a or ɑ (as *calf, half, aunt*).

DIRECTIONS FOR USE

READING THE ENTRIES AND PRONUNCIATIONS

§59. Each entry, or article, in the vocabulary begins with a head word in lightface roman type, followed without punctuation by the pronunciation in **boldface**.[3] The simplest form of entry is

bequest bɪˈkwɛst

with no derivatives and no variant pronunciations. If the word with the same spelling and pronunciation is also found as a proper name (whether or not it is the same word), it is usually thus indicated:—

clarion, C- ˈklærɪən

which means that *clarion* and *Clarion* are pronounced alike. The proper name may be entered first:—

Cologne, c- kəˈlon

which means that *Cologne* and *cologne* are pronounced alike.

If the entry has a current variant spelling, that is entered in its alphabetical order, unless it would be very near, or has a bearing on the pronunciation, in which case it is given at the same entry. Words alternatively spelt *-tre* are, however, always found with those in *-ter* (*center*).

In the large group of words like *travel(l)ed*, the optional second *l* is disregarded.

WORDS LISTED UNDER HEAD WORDS

§60. If a word is not found in alphabetical order, it is to be looked for under some obviously related head word. Thus many adverbs will be found with the corresponding adjectives; as,

holy ˈholɪ |holily ˈholəlɪ, -lɪlɪ

This method permits the inclusion of far more words than would otherwise be possible.

§61. If a word has variant pronunciations not dependent on locality, they are separated by commas:—

every ˈɛvrɪ, ˈɛvərɪ

defect dɪˈfɛkt, ˈdifɛkt

§62. Commonly, to show such variants only the part that varies is repeated. In representing such fragments of spelling or pronunciation the hyphen shows which part of the word is intended. Thus *de-* is the first part, *-min-* a middle part, and *-ant* a final part. For example,

logwood ˈlɒgˌwʊd, ˈlɑg-, ˈlɒg-

By adding the omitted part (here shown in parentheses) to each fragment we get ˈlɑg(ˌwʊd), ˈlɒg(ˌwʊd) as the 2d and 3d variants.

midday ˈmɪdˌde, -ˈde

By adding the omitted part, with its accent, to the fragment, we get (ˈmɪd)ˈde for the 2d variant.

Lofthouse ˈlɔftəs, ˈlɒft-, -ˌhaʊs

---

[3] In the vocabulary all spelling forms (except catchwords) are printed in light roman type, all pronunciations in **boldface**, and explanatory matter in *italic* (except the regional labels E, S, N, etc.). In the solid print of the Introduction, italic has to be used for spelling forms (as in general usage); but there also, when spelling forms with their pronunciations are set off by themselves, these follow the typography of the vocabulary.

Adding the omitted part to each fragment, we get ˈlɒft(əs), (ˈlɔft)ˌhaʊs, (ˈlɒft)ˌhaʊs as the 2d, 3d, and 4th variants.

Naomi ˈneəˌmaɪ, neˈomaɪ, -mɪ, -mə

Adding the omitted parts in turn to the two fragments, we get (ˈneə)mɪ, (ˈneə)mə, (neˈo)mɪ, (neˈo)mə, six variants in all.

Nazareth ˈnæzərəθ, -rɪθ, ˈnæzr-

Adding the omitted parts, we get, besides the first full pronunciation, (ˈnæzə)rɪθ, ˈnæzr(əθ), ˈnæzr(ɪθ).

ONE ENTRY INCLUDING DIFFERENT WORDS

§63. When more than one spelling appears at the same entry with the same pronunciation, these spellings are not necessarily of the same word or part of speech, especially in proper names. Likewise a single entry may represent two or more words spelt and sounded alike. Thus the word *angle* includes all the words—nouns, verbs, etc., with their different meanings but all with the same pronunciation. When derivative or inflectional endings are added, they are to be fitted only to the appropriate meanings or parts of speech, but this does not affect the pronunciation, and usually need not concern the reader. Thus under *angle* the form *angled* can be the adjective formed from the noun (*wide-angled*) or the past or past participle of the verb (*it angled off*), and the form *angling* can be the adjective (*an angling path*), the participle (*he is angling with flies*), or the noun (*the angling was good*). At the entry *instance* the ending *-es* may be that of the plural of the noun or the 3 sg of the verb. At *intelligence* the entry may be noun or verb, the ending *-es* the plural or 3 sg, the ending *-ed* may be that of the past participle or of the "apparent participle," the adjective formed from the noun. The entry *slew* may be a noun, a verb in the present tense, or the past of the verb *slay*.

LABELS FOR PARTS OF SPEECH

§64. Only when it concerns the pronunciation are these labels added, or in a few cases where there might be doubt whether the various uses of the word had the same pronunciation.

DEFINITIONS

§65. Instead of labels for parts of speech, frequently definitions are appended. These are never full, and are used only to identify the word. Definitions are in quotation marks. Explanatory identification that does not define is without quotation marks.

GEOGRAPHICAL AND LINGUISTIC LABELS

§66. Geographical labels are often appended to place names to indicate the location, or to personal names to indicate residence or nationality. The linguistic abbreviations *Fr*, *Sp*, *Ger*, etc., refer to the pronunciation; thus

Lodi *US* ˈloʊdaɪ; *Italy* ˈlodi (*It* ˈlɔːdi)

means that the various Lodi's in the US are pronounced ˈloʊdaɪ; that Lodi in Italy is pronounced in American English ˈlodi; and that the Italian pronunciation is ˈlɔːdi.

When the linguistic labels *It*, *Fr*, etc., precede the first pronunciation, this means that only the foreign pronunciation is given; as,

voyageur *Fr* vwajaˈʒœːr

THE VERTICAL BAR AND THE ADDITION OF INFLECTIONAL AND DERIVATIVE ENDINGS

§67. The following examples show the uses of the vertical bar:—

press prɛs |presses ˈprɛsɪz |pressed prɛst

Here the bar, in its simplest use, is followed in each case by a new spelling form in roman type, with corresponding pronunciation in boldface.

finish ˈfɪnɪʃ |-es -ɪz |-ed -t

Here, after the first bar, follows a spelling fragment (-es) with its corresponding pronunciation fragment (-ɪz). The simple rule for combining is, Add the spelling fragment (-es) to the first spelling form (finish-es) and the pronunciation fragment (-ɪz) to the first pronunciation form (ˈfɪnɪʃ-ɪz); and so after the next bar (finish-ed ˈfɪnɪʃ-t). Add to the head forms before the first bar, *and add* roman *to* roman, **boldface** *to* **boldface**.

It is important to add each fragment (spelling to spelling, and pronunciation to pronunciation) to the forms before the first bar. The sole exception to this is the adverb ending *-bly* **-blɪ** when the first entry does not end in *-ble* **-bļ**. In that case *-bly* **-blɪ** are fitted to the immediately preceding forms in *-ble* **-bļ**. See *-bly* in the vocabulary.

Hyphenated words are never thus divided after a bar, but are separately entered as head words, to avoid confusing the compounding hyphen with that which separates the fragments.

§68. When the first word in a vocabulary entry is a monosyllable, no accent mark is used (with the exception noted in §51), as *set* sɛt. But when one or more syllables are added after the bar (|) thus, *set* sɛt |-back -ˌbæk |-ting -ɪŋ, then primary accent must be assumed on the plurisyllables, and the entries must be read thus: *set* sɛt |*setback* ˈsɛtˌbæk |*setting* ˈsɛtɪŋ.

§69. There is no significance in the fact that sometimes full forms of the derivatives are given, as in the first example, and sometimes fragments, as in the second. The editors have not sought mere mechanical uniformity, owing to considerations of time, of space, and of other disturbing factors. They have sought only to make each article clear in itself. The occasional full forms may help to make the abbreviated ones clearer.

§70. It should be noted that a pronunciation fragment need not correspond letter for letter with its spelling fragment:—

inflate ɪnˈflet |-d -ɪd

Here, adding spelling *-d* to spelling *inflate* gives *inflated,* and adding pronunciation **-ɪd** to pronunciation ɪnˈflet gives ɪnˈfletɪd. See next example also.

Often, for greater clearness, more than a minimum fragment of pronunciation is given:—

flatten ˈflætṇ |-ed -d |-ing ˈflætṇɪŋ, -tnɪŋ

This is to show that *flattening* is pronounced either ˈflæt·ṇ·ɪŋ (3 syls.) or ˈflæt·nɪŋ (2 syls.). Likewise the frequent adverb ending *-ically* is thus shown:—

symmetric sɪˈmɛtrɪk |-al -ļ |-ally -ļɪ, -ɪklɪ

Here the last two pronunciations are sɪˈmɛtrɪk·ļ·ɪ, sɪˈmɛtrɪk·lɪ, the last being made a little clearer by -ɪklɪ than by -lɪ alone, though -lɪ would be strictly correct.

Some added letters may be silent, as in *bar* bɑr |-red -d, where *-re-* are silent; or letters silent in the first entry may represent sounds in the addition, as *rogue* rog |-ry -ərɪ, where the silent *e* of *rogue* represents ə in *roguery* ˈrogərɪ.

§71. Observe cases like

abut ə'bʌt |-ted -ɪd

where addition of -*ted* doubles the letter *t* (abutted) but not the sound t (ə'bʌtɪd); or like

total 'totļ |-ed -d |-ly -ɪ

where addition of -*ly* doubles the letter *l* (totally) but not the sound l ('totļɪ).

Thus when the final letter of the spelling entry is the same as the first letter of the spelling fragment (total |-ly), it is to be doubled (i.e., the fragment is added regularly). So, too, when the first pronunciation ends with the same sound that begins the pronunciation fragment, this sound also is to be doubled; as,

foreign 'fɔrɪn, 'fɑr-, 'fɒr-, -ən |-ness -nɪs

This is to be expanded into 'fɔrɪnnɪs, 'fɑrɪnnɪs, 'fɒrɪnnɪs, 'fɔrənnɪs, 'fɑrənnɪs, 'fɒrənnɪs, in all cases with double **n.** Whenever space allows, such doubled sounds are shown by doubled symbols; as,

thin θɪn |thinned θɪnd |-ness 'θɪnnɪs

The few exceptions to this rule for doubling are such as to give no trouble. The most usual one consists of words ending in -*th;* as,

truth truθ |-'s -θs |-ths -ðz, -θs

in which the expanded forms are obviously not **truθθs** and **truθðz** or **truθθs,** but **truθs** and **truðz** or **truθs,** since the combinations θθs and θðz do not occur in English.

CUTTING BACK

§72. There are, however, a great many words in which the fragments cannot be added directly to the head words:—

suspicion sə'spɪʃən |-cious -ʃəs

Here, in order to make the proper junction of the spelling fragment, we must take in some letter near the end of the head word to begin the fragment. This we call "cutting back." Thus we cut off the spelling -*cion* and replace it with -*cious* (suspi-cious); and likewise cut off from the head pronunciation the corresponding sounds -ʃən, and replace them with -ʃəs (sə'spɪ-ʃəs).

Cutting back and direct addition are often used in the same word:—

prude prud |-dish -ɪʃ

Since -*ish* cannot be added to *prude,* we take in the *d* and add -*dish* (pru-dish); then, since to add the pronunciation -dɪʃ to prud would wrongly give 'pruddɪʃ, we simply add -ɪʃ directly to prud ('prudɪʃ). Similarly, in

negative 'nɛgətɪv |-d -d |-vism -ˌɪzəm

where -*d* and -**d** are added directly, -*vism* has to be cut back (negati-vism), and -ˌɪzəm (not -ˌvɪzəm) is directly added to 'nɛgətɪv ('nɛgətɪvˌɪzəm).

A "cutback" must always take in more than the final letter of the entry form, for otherwise it would be taken as a direct addition with doubling of the final letter or sound (see the exception above at *truth,* at the end of §71).

§73. In adding suffixes certain familiar changes are made, as of -*y* to -*i;* as,

quarry 'kwɔrɪ |-ied -d, *i.e.,* quarried 'kwɔrɪd

or of *f* to *v;* as in

housewife 'haʊsˌwaɪf |-ves -vz, *i.e.,* housewives 'haʊsˌwaɪvz

where -*ves* and -**vz** are not directly added, but replace -*fe* and **f.**

LISTING OF VERB FORMS

§74. When the past tense and the past participle of strong ("irregular") verbs are given, the past regularly follows the first bar, and the past participle the second bar, usually without labels:—

drive draɪv |droᵥe drov |driven ˈdrɪvən

sing sɪŋ |sang sæŋ or sung sʌŋ |sung sʌŋ

When such verbs end in sibilants, the 3 sg pres precedes the past and pptc:—

choose tʃuz |-s -ɪz |chose tʃoz |chosen ˈtʃozn̩

If the past and pptc are alike, they are given but once:—

shine ʃaɪn |shone ʃon

stand stænd |stood stʊd

fight faɪt |fought fɔt

§75. The bar, not followed by a spelling form, is sometimes used at the end of an article to separate an added item from the immediately preceding one, and to imply its application to the whole article:—

road rod |-ed -ɪd; | NEngd +rɔ̃d

THE MAIN REGIONAL DIVISIONS

§76. For indicating American regional pronunciations the well-known division into three regions is followed, the East (E), the South (S), and, for want of a better term, the North (N). Geographically the East includes New York City (NYC) and environs, and New England east of the Connecticut River. The South includes Virginia, North Carolina, South Carolina, Tennessee, Florida, Georgia, Alabama, Mississippi, Arkansas, Louisiana, Texas, and parts of Maryland, West Virginia, Kentucky, and Oklahoma. The North includes the rest of the US.

In the use of the terms E, S, N, certain modifications must be kept in mind. The speech of the S differs markedly in the more northerly parts from that in the more southerly ones, and (partly coinciding with this) in the more inland regions from that in the coastal ones. Certain features labeled S are therefore not equally applicable to all of the S.

Owing to movements of population, and probably also to the schools, innumerable individuals and often considerable groups in the S speak a type virtually identical with that of the N. The same is true in the E, especially NYC. In NEngd also, and in the southeastern coastal regions, are certain "speech islands" having a similar type, perhaps preserved, by isolation, from a time when it was more general. Allowance must also be made for mixed types of speech in all the border areas between the main regions. The irregular use of the *r* sound is especially noticeable in the border areas.

It is not the function of this dictionary to deal with these more irregular and exceptional features,—to make a dialect map of the country. That work is being done by the *L.A.* Our concern is only with the main types of cultivated American English—something of a fiction, if you will, as all "standard" speech is.

It should be noted that the pronunciations assigned to particular regions are regarded only as the ones prevailing there. It is unsafe to deny the existence of any pronunciation in any region. Thus, when it is indicated that in the S the word *glory* is pronounced ˈglorɪ, while in the E and N it is either ˈglorɪ or ˈglɔrɪ, it is not meant that ˈglorɪ does not exist in the S, but that according to the evidence we have, ˈglɔrɪ is not sufficiently frequent in the S to be recorded as a characteristic S pronunciation. The same may be said of the ɛ sound in such words as *air, there*, etc. Evidence does not show that the vowel ɛ in such words is widespread in the S. The same principle is to be applied to all regional pronunciations.

§77. Linguistically the most generally observed characteristic of the three regions is the treatment of the r sound, the E and the S being in the main alike in this respect in contrast with the N. The S is separated from the E by a number of features, such as the character of the aʊ and aɪ diphthongs, the prevalence of "flat *a*" (æ) in certain groups of words, the "long *e*" sound before r, the tendency to diphthongize many vowels, and many features of intonation and tempo—none of them equally distributed over the S—features that enable the ordinary observer to distinguish a Southerner from an Easterner, but not all of them conveniently or profitably recorded in a work with the scope and purpose of this.

INDICATION OF REGIONAL PRONUNCIATIONS

§78. In the vocabulary, the Eastern (E) and Southern (S) pronunciations are separated from the Northern (N) by semicolons. The pronunciations in entries that contain no regional labels (E, ES, S, N, EN, etc.) are valid for all the US, as *delicious* dɪˈlɪʃəs. When an entry contains a regional label, the unlabeled pronunciations are valid everywhere in the US except in the regions designated; thus

glory ˈglorɪ, ˈglɔrɪ; S ˈglorɪ

means that the first two pronunciations are both valid everywhere except in the S; there only ˈglorɪ prevails; or, stated otherwise, ˈglorɪ and ˈglɔrɪ are characteristic of the E and the N; only ˈglorɪ is so of the S.

perform pɚˈfɔrm; ES pəˈfɔəm

This means that in the US except the E and the S the pronunciation is pɚˈfɔrm; in the E and the S it is pəˈfɔəm.

aircraft ˈɛrˌkræft, ˈær-; E ˈɛə-, ˈæə-, -ˌkraft, -ˌkrɑft; S ˈæəˌkræft

Combining regularly, for the N, besides ˈɛrˌkræft, we get ˈærˌkræft; for the E, ˈɛəˌkræft, ˈæəˌkræft, ˈɛəˌkraft, ˈæəˌkraft, ˈɛəˌkrɑft, ˈæəˌkrɑft; for the S, ˈæəˌkræft.

Very often two regions (usually E and S) have one or more variants in common. They are then usually separated only by commas:—

scarce skɛrs, skærs; E skɛəs, ES skæəs

This means that in the N *scarce* is pronounced skɛrs or skærs; in the E it is pronounced skɛəs, and in both E and S it is pronounced skæəs; or, stated otherwise, in the E it is pronounced skɛəs or skæəs, while in the S only skæəs prevails. See also *board, ear, premonitory* (§80).

ACCENT AS A FACTOR IN COMBINING THE FORMS

§79. Only the forms that agree in accent are to be combined:—

Carew kəˈru, -ˈrɪu, ˈkɛru, ˈke-, -rɪu, -rɪ

For the first accentuation, besides kəˈru we have (kə)ˈrɪu; for the second accentuation, besides ˈkɛru and ˈke(ru) we have (ˈkɛ)rɪu, (ˈke)rɪu, (ˈkɛ)rɪ, (ˈke)rɪ.

empyreal ɛmˈpɪrɪəl, ˌɛmpəˈrɪəl, -paɪ-

Here the first form cannot be combined with -paɪ- because this is not accented, as is the corresponding -'pɪ-. Hence only the second form can combine with -paɪ-, thus: (ˌɛm)paɪ('riəl), the unaccented -paɪ- replacing the unaccented -pə-.

bifurcate v 'baɪfəˌket, baɪ'fɝket; ES 'baɪfə-, -'fɝket, -'fɝket

Here the Eastern and Southern fragment 'baɪfə- can combine only with the omitted part found in 'baɪfəˌket, with the same accent, thus: 'baɪfə(ˌket). The last two fragments must be combined with the omitted part of baɪ'fɝket, having the same accent, thus: (baɪ)'fɝket, (baɪ)'fɝket. (For regional pronunciations see §§76-78.)

discourse n 'dɪskors, dɪ'skors, -ɔrs; ES -oəs, E + -ɔəs

Here the fragment -ɔrs, which does not include the accent mark, will fit both of the first two forms without disturbing their accents, thus: ('dɪsk)ɔrs, (dɪ'sk)ɔrs; and likewise the Eastern and Southern fragments: ES ('dɪsk)oəs, (dɪ'sk)oəs, Eastern also ('dɪsk)ɔəs, (dɪ'sk)ɔəs.

THE PLUS SIGN (+)

§80. The sign (+) is invariably to be read "also." It means that in addition to pronunciations already given, other designated pronunciations are to be heard from cultivated speakers. This sign does not imply that these additional pronunciations have inferior standing, or necessarily are less frequent, though we have not placed it before pronunciations known to be markedly in the majority. The following examples indicate the use of the plus sign:—

hot hɑt; ES + hɒt

This means that the word spelt <i>hot</i> is, in all regions of the US, pronounced **hɑt**; but that there are also many cultivated speakers in the East and the South who usually pronounce it **hɒt**.

fast fæst; E + fast, fɑst

This means that the word <i>fast</i> in all parts of the US is pronounced **fæst**; but that there are also many cultivated speakers in the East who usually pronounce it **fast** or **fɑst**.

board bord, bɔrd; ES boəd, E + bɔəd

This means that <i>board</i> is pronounced **bord** or **bɔrd** in the North, but in the East and the South it is pronounced **boəd**, and in the East, in addition to **boəd**, it is also pronounced **bɔəd**.

ear ɪr; ES ɪə(r, S + ɛə(r

This means that <i>ear</i> is pronounced **ɪr** in the North, but in the East and the South it is pronounced **ɪə(r**, and in the South, in addition to **ɪə(r**, it is also pronounced **ɛə(r**.

premonitory prɪ'mɑnəˌtorɪ, -ˌtɔrɪ; S -ˌtorɪ, ES + -'mɒn-

Where, as here, the pronunciation after + is a fragment, it is to be taken as a pronunciation additional to that of the corresponding parts of the preceding forms. In this example, Eastern has, besides the pronunciations prɪ'mɑnəˌtorɪ and -ˌtɔrɪ, which it shares with the North, also prɪ'mɒnəˌtorɪ and -ˌtɔrɪ; while Southern has, besides prɪ'mɑnəˌtorɪ (but not -ˌtɔrɪ), also prɪ'mɒnəˌtorɪ.

It is believed that any other uses of the sign +, if it is merely read "also," will be clear to the reader as they occur. It should be noted that a pronunciation with + prefixed is never the sole pronunciation of the word.

JOINING REGIONAL FRAGMENTS TO FIRST FORMS

§81. In fitting fragments to forms before the first bar, the regional fragments are to be fitted to the corresponding regional forms before the first bar; as,

woodwork 'wʊdˌwɝk; ES 'wʊdˌwɜk, -ˌwɜk; |-er -ɚ; ES -ə(r

Expanding the fragments after the bar, we get

woodworker ˈwʊdˌwɜ·kə·; ES ˈwʊdˌwɜkə(r, ˈwʊdˌwɜ·kə(r

in which the unlabeled N fragment -ə· is fitted to the first unlabeled (N) pronunciation, and the ES fragment -ə(r is fitted to the first two ES pronunciations.

For the meaning of (r see §82.

LINKING r—THE MEANING OF -ɜ(r, -ɑː(r, -ə(r

§82. When pronunciations are thus indicated,—*fur* fɜ(r, *far* fɑː(r, *bitter* ˈbɪtə(r, *here* hɪə(r, *there* ðɛə(r, ðæə(r, *war* wɔə(r, *more* mɔə(r, *poor* pʊə(r,—this means that (in the E and S) r is not sounded and these words are pronounced fɜ, fɑː, ˈbɪtə, hɪə, ðɛə, ðæə, wɔə, mɔə, pʊə unless a vowel sound follows, either in the same word (by addition of an ending, as *furry* ˈfɜrɪ, *bitterest* ˈbɪtərɪst) or in a word that follows without pause (*the fur is wet* ðə fɜr ɪz wɛt, *far away* fɑr əˈwe, *bitter end* ˈbɪtər ɛnd). The effect of pause on linking r is seen in the following utterance of a distinguished American: *over, and over, and over again* ˈovə, ən ˈovə, ənd ˈovər əˈgɛn.

When -ə(r follows a vowel in the same syllable, as in *here* hɪə(r, *there* ðæə(r, *more* mɔə(r, and a vowel sound is added, then r either replaces ə (*herein* hɪrˈɪn, *here it is* hɪr ɪt ɪz, *therein* ðærˈɪn, *there it goes* ðær ɪt goz, *moreover* mɔrˈovə, *more ice* mɔr aɪs, *poorest* ˈpʊrɪst, *poor and needy* pʊr ən ˈnidɪ), or, less usually, the r is added to ə (hɪərˈɪn, hɪər ɪt ɪz, mɔərˈovə, ˈpʊərɪst, etc.). This alternative is to be understood in all similar cases.

In such words as *adjure* əˈdʒʊr, əˈdʒɪʊr; ES -ə(r, the -ə(r is to be understood as replacing the final r of the N pronunciation.

Some speakers, especially in the S, fail to pronounce linking r before an initial vowel of the following word (*more ice* mɔə aɪs, *when the war ends* hwɛn ðə wɔə ɛndz). Omission of r before a vowel within a word (ˈvɛ·ɪ for ˈvɛrɪ) is regarded as substandard.

§83. In vocabulary entries, when pronunciation fragments are added, the use of (r must be observed. The rule is simple: If the added fragment begins with a vowel sound, the r is sounded in the E and S; if it begins with a consonant sound, the r is not heard in the E and S:—

labor ˈlebə·; ES ˈlebə(r; |-ed -d |-ing -brɪŋ, -bərɪŋ

Here ES ˈlebə(r means ˈlebər or ˈlebə according as a vowel sound immediately follows or not. When -*ed* -d is added, being a consonant sound (*e* silent), we are to understand ES ˈlebəd beside N ˈlebə·d; but when -*ing* -ɪŋ is added, with its vowel sound, then the r is sounded and the ES and the N pronunciations are alike ˈlebrɪŋ or ˈlebərɪŋ.

§84. For the pronunciation of the N in words like *labor* ˈlebə·, when a vowel sound is added (*laboring* ˈlebərɪŋ), then -ər replaces -ə·, since there is no significant difference between ˈlebə·ɪŋ and ˈlebə·rɪŋ. When, as often, *laboring* is contracted, then vowel ə· becomes consonant r (ˈlebrɪŋ). Likewise in the entry *farrier* ˈfærɪə·; ES ˈfærɪ·ə(r; |-*y* -ɪ, the pronunciation of the derivative *farriery* becomes ˈfærɪərɪ, which is also right for the E and S, because a vowel follows -ə(r and therefore r is retained.

INTRUSIVE r

§85. Though not recorded in the vocabulary, intrusive r is appropriately described here. Following the regular habits of his speech a cultivated Easterner or Southerner might normally pronounce *straighter and straighter* ˈstretər ən ˈstretə, sounding final r before the vowel and dropping it at the end. Following the same habits, he might pronounce *strata on strata* ˈstretər ɒn 'stretə, likewise sounding r before the vowel and not at the end. Both procedures are unconscious and phonetically natural.

When the final r is spelt (*straighter*) and pronounced before a vowel it is called Linking r; when it is not spelt but is pronounced before a vowel, it is called Intrusive r. The frequency of intrusive r among cultivated Easterners, Southerners, and British is no longer a matter of doubt except to the uninformed. It is perhaps less frequent in the S than in the E. Words ending in the sound -ə (*Victoria, sofa, idea*) are more apt to show it than are those ending in other vowels. Its use is perhaps less consistent than that of linking r. The same educated Southerner said ðɪs 'mætə ɪz 'dɪfrənt who said ə 'grɛtə ðən 'dʒɒnər ɪz hɪə.

WORD ELEMENTS OMITTED FROM THE VOCABULARY

§86. To save space and relieve the reader from the distraction of needless information, words having certain suffixes with regular pronunciation are often omitted from the vocabulary; as those with -*dom* (*heathendom*), -*hood* (*motherhood*), -*ish* (*darkish*), -*ment* (*announcement*). See §89.

§87. The -(*e*)*s* plural of regular nouns, the third person singular present indicative of verbs, and the possessive case ending of nouns are regularly omitted from the vocabulary, except for words ending in a sibilant sound (s, z, ʃ, ʒ, tʃ, dʒ), where they are regularly given. If the plural and the possessive sound alike, only one is given. If they differ, both are given (see *house*). The possessive plural of regular nouns, formed by adding the apostrophe (') but no sound, is omitted.

Certain nouns ending in a s or z sound closely preceded by a s or z sound vary in current usage in forming the possessive. Unfortunately some printing shops follow their own rules in this, and do not always agree with others or with general usage. Current literary usage in this is set forth in *Webster's New International Dictionary, Second Edition*, at the word *possessive*, and the present work follows this, with a very few exceptions where usage is divided.

The following rules, fully illustrated, will enable the reader to form the regular plural of nouns, the possessive case, and the third singular of verbs, in all cases where these are not recorded in the vocabulary.

§88. Pronunciation of the Plural and Possessive Singular of Nouns and the Third Singular Present of Verbs

Rule I. Add the sound s when the stem of the noun or verb ends in any of the voiceless consonant sounds p, t, k, f, θ. Examples follow:

1. Plural of nouns.
   cap-s kæp-s, *gate-s* get-s, *oak-s* ok-s, *cliff-s* klɪf-s, *growth-s* groθ-s. Words like *leaf* lif—*leaves* livz, *oath* oθ—*oaths* oðz will be found in the vocabulary.

2. Possessives in -'*s* follow the same rule.
   Philip's 'fɪləp-s, *Kate's* ket-s, *Isaac's* 'aɪzək-s, *Joseph's* 'dʒozəf-s, *Edith's* 'idɪθ-s.

3. Third singular present indicatives follow the same rule.
   keep-s kip-s, *get-s* get-s, *look-s* luk-s, *chafe-s* tʃef-s, *froth-s* froθ-s.

Rule II. Add the sound z when the stem of the noun or verb ends in any of the voiced consonant sounds b, d, g, v, ð, m, n, ŋ, l, or in any vowel sound (all vowel sounds are voiced):

1. Plural of nouns.

   robe-s **rob-z,** *bed-s* **bɛd-z,** *rogue-s* **rog-z,** *stove-s* **stov-z,** *lathe-s* **leð-z,** *rim-s* **rɪm-z,** *bone-s* **bon-z,** *thing-s* **θɪŋ-z,** *ball-s* **bɔl-z;** (vowels) *sea-s* **si-z,** *citi-es* **ˈsɪtɪ-z,** *day-s* **de-z,** *ma-s* **mɑ-z,** *law-s* **lɔ-z,** *hoe-s* **ho-z,** *value-s* **ˈvæljʊ-z,** *shoe-s* **ʃu-z,** *fur-s* **fɝ-z, fɜ-z,** *bar-s* **bɑr-z** (§26), **bɑː-z,** *paper-s* **ˈpepɚ-z,** *sofa-s* **ˈsofə-z,** *tie-s* **taɪ-z,** *cow-s* **kaʊ-z,** *toy-s* **tɔɪ-z,** *cue-s* **kju-z, kɪu-z.**

2. Possessives in -*'s* follow the same rule.

   Rob's **rɑb-z,** *Adelaide's* **ˈædl̩ˌed-z,** *Meg's* **mɛg-z,** *Olive's* **ˈɑlɪv-z,** *Blythe's* **blaɪð-z,** *Tom's* **tɑm-z,** *John's* **dʒɑn-z,** *Harding's* **ˈhɑrdɪŋ-z,** *Will's* **wɪl-z;** (vowels) *Lee's* **li-z,** *Betty's* **ˈbɛtɪ-z,** *Ray's* **re-z,** *ma's* **mɑ-z,** *Esau's* **ˈisɔ-z,** *Joe's* **dʒo-z,** *Andrew's* **ˈændru-z,** *Burr's* **bɝ-z, bɜ-z,** *Wilbur's* **ˈwɪlbɚ-z,** *Sarah's* **ˈsɛrə-z,** *Nye's* **naɪ-z,** *Howe's* **haʊ-z,** *Roy's* **rɔɪ-z,** *Hugh's* **hju-z, hɪu-z.**

.3. Third singular present indicatives follow the same rule.

   rub-s **rʌb-z,** *hide-s* **haɪd-z,** *lag-s* **læg-z,** *save-s* **sev-z,** *breathe-s* **brið-z,** *come-s* **kʌm-z,** *run-s* **rʌn-z,** *sing-s* **sɪŋ-z,** *feel-s* **fil-z;** (vowels) *see-s* **si-z,** *piti-es* **ˈpɪtɪ-z,** *stay-s* **ste-z,** *thaw-s* **θɔ-z,** *go-es* **go-z,** *woo-es* **wu-z,** *stir-s* **stɝ-z, stɜ-z,** *scatter-s* **ˈskætɚ-z,** *subpoena-s* **səˈpinə-z,** *tri-es* **traɪ-z,** *allow-s* **əˈlaʊ-z,** *employ-s* **ɪmˈplɔɪ-z,** *hew-s* **hju-z, hɪu-z.**

   (Rules I & II also apply to the pronunciation of -*'s*, the unstressed form of *is, has*.)

Rule III. Plurals, possessives in -*'s*, and third singulars of words ending in the remaining sounds, —the sibilants **s, ʃ, tʃ, z, ʒ, dʒ,**—are regularly given in the vocabulary. These add the syllable **-ɪz** or **-əz** (for variation in the vowel, see -*ed* in the vocabulary): *face-s* **ˈfes-ɪz,** *Nash's* **ˈnæʃ-ɪz,** *catch-es* **ˈkætʃ-ɪz,** *nose-s* **ˈnoz-ɪz,** *rouge-s* **ˈruʒ-ɪz,** *George's* **ˈdʒɔrdʒ-ɪz.**

PREFIXES AND SUFFIXES TREATED IN THE VOCABULARY

§89. Following is a list of word elements, chiefly initial or final, many of which have variant pronunciations. These elements are treated in the vocabulary in alphabetical order.

Where they are not found attached to head words in the vocabulary (as *prideful*, cf *pride*), the reader can add them with their pronunciations. If they are found in the vocabulary with their head words, variant pronunciations not listed at the full word can be found by consulting the separate element in the vocabulary, as, e.g., at *goodness* (see -*ness*) or at *mate* (see -*ed*).

-able	-edly	-hood
-age	-edness	i-, -i-
-ally *see* -ically	em- *see* en-	-ia
-ana	en-	-ial *see* -ia
-ate	-er	-ian *see* -ia
-ative	-es	-ible *see* -able
be-	-ese	-ically
-bly	-ess	-ie *see* -y
-d *see* -ed	-est	-iel *see* -ia
de-	-et	-ien *see* -ia
-dom	ex-	il- *see* in-
e-	-ey *see* -y	im- *see* in-
-ed	-ful	in-

-ing	-ment	-ship
-io, -ion, -ious *see* -ia	-ness	-sia
-ish	-or	-sion
-ism	-ous	-some
-ity	-ow	sub-
-ius *see* -ia	pre-	-tia
-ive	pro-	-tion
-less	re-	un-
-like	-ry	up-
-ly	-s *see* -es	wh-
-man	se-	-y

VARIANTS

§90. Certain classes of variant pronunciations found in cultivated American speech are described here in order to avoid excessive complication of the vocabulary entries. These variants are only those in wide use by cultivated speakers, and do not include those confined to local dialect or substandard speech.

MEDIAL UNACCENTED -*i*-

§91. Medial unaccented short *i* ɪ not followed by a vowel may become -ə- in nearly all words (*editor* ˈɛdɪtɚ, ˈɛdətɚ). When final ɪ becomes medial by the addition of a suffix, this change from ɪ to ə must often be assumed, as in *fragmentary* ˈfrægmənˌtɛrɪ |-*ly* -lɪ = ˈfrægmənˌtɛrɪlɪ or -ˌtɛrəlɪ. See also *i*-, -*i*- in the vocabulary.

UNACCENTED ɪ BEFORE ANOTHER VOWEL

§92. When the vowel sound ɪ (variously spelt) is immediately followed by another vowel sound (*radiate, oceanic, Ephraim, periodic, radio, medium, immediate*), the ɪ sound tends toward i, and thus might properly be shown as in ˈrediˌet, ˌoʃiˈænɪk, ˈifriəm, ˌpɪriˈɑdɪk, ˈrediˌo, ˈmidiəm, ɪˈmidɪɪt. But this would greatly complicate the vocabulary, especially when derivatives vary from the head word, as in *study* ˈstʌdɪ |-*ing* ˈstʌdiɪŋ, and even so would not fully show the extent of the variation of the ɪ. This variation is therefore not shown in the vocabulary. In reading a transcription like ɪˈmidɪɪt the variation will be made automatically.

THE ɔ SOUND (*WAR, HORSE, ALL*)

§93. In most of America ɔ appears to be rather unstable. In most positions except before r final or r plus a consonant (*war, horse*), ɔ varies with many speakers to ɒ or ɑ. A similar variation is reported from Canada. In words in which the sound occurs before l plus a consonant (*walnut, Waldo, salt*), which in Brit have either ɔ or ɒ, the variants ɑ and ɒ are very common in America.

In New England ɒ is an extremely common substitute for ɔ, many speakers having only one phoneme (usually of ɒ quality) in such words as *cot* and *caught* or *collar* and *caller*. In spite of these widespread variants, our collections appear to justify the somewhat regular recording of the standard historical ɔ sound in the appropriate words.

ε FOR æ IN *CARRY, CHARITY*

§94. In words like *carry* ˈkærɪ, *marry* ˈmærɪ, *charity* ˈtʃærətɪ, *comparison* kəmˈpærəsn̩, having historical "short *a*" (æ) before **r** plus a vowel, a widespread pronunciation with ε (ˈkɛrɪ, ˈmɛrɪ, ˈtʃɛrətɪ, kəmˈpɛrəsn̩) is heard in the North and Canada, especially from the younger generations. Many of these speakers pronounce *marry, merry,* and *Mary* all alike —ˈmɛrɪ. This variant appears to be rare in the South, and for New England the *L.A.* shows only a very small percentage with ε.

DREARY, WEARY, POOR

§95. In words like *dreary, weary,* formerly having the vowel sound i before the **r,** while the general tendency is to lower the i to ɪ, some speakers use the higher i, and many use an intermediate vowel somewhat nearer to i than is the ɪ of *bit.* When the **r** is final or followed by a consonant (*year, beard*), the i sound is less apt to occur. Likewise ʊr (*poor*) varies to **ur.**

EASTERN AND SOUTHERN ɔə(r

§96. In words like *form* fɔrm; ES fɔəm, both pronunciations fɔəm and fɔːm are used in the East and the South. In the vocabulary only ɔə is given. This is done, however, with the implication that in such words the vowel varies between ɔə and ɔː, so that for speakers who do not usually pronounce ɔə in such words the symbol ɔə must be taken also to suggest ɔː. In longer words ɔə is more likely to be reduced to ɔ, especially if unaccented. This reduction is shown in such a word as *formality* fɔrˈmælətɪ; ES fɔˈmælətɪ. No sharp line can be drawn. The same speaker may say fɔəm in one breath and fɔːm or fɔm in the next, according to style of speech.

EASTERN AND SOUTHERN ɑə(r

§97. In words like *farm* fɑrm; ES fɑːm, or *far* fɑr; ES fɑː(r, an ə glide is less commonly heard after the ɑ (fɑəm, fɑə(r) than after ɔ in words like *form* (fɔəm). With some speakers in the East and South, however, this is consciously present, so that there is a definite distinction between *father* ˈfɑðə(r and *farther* ˈfɑəðə(r, even when the words are of equal length. As with ɔə(r, the pronunciation ɑə(r is commoner in the shorter words than in longer ones. Thus a speaker may say lɑədʒ for *large,* but ˈlɑːdʒə(r for *larger.* This glide ə after ɑ being much less frequent than after ɔ, it is not shown in the vocabulary.

WORDS LIKE *BOARD*

§98. Besides the two types **bord** and **bɔrd,** regularly shown in the vocabulary, a pronunciation of *board* is heard from some speakers, especially in the North, with a vowel sound about midway between o and ɔ (phonetic symbol ǫ, a lowered o or a raised ɔ). Such speakers also pronounce the same vowel ǫ in words like *horse, form* (pronounced by others hɔrs, fɔrm), so that in their speech *hoarse* is like *horse, boarder* is like *border,* etc. Thus these speakers pronounce all such words uniformly with ǫ, while other speakers that do not distinguish *hoarse* from *horse,* etc., pronounce them uniformly with ɔ.[4]

---

[4] See Kenyon, *American Pronunciation,* 10th ed. §§366–372.

EASTERN AND SOUTHERN VOWEL IN *BIRD*

§99. In words like *bird, further* the first pronunciation for Eastern and Southern is bɜd, ˈfɜðə(r. In both the E and the S, however, a very large number of speakers pronounce ɝ instead of ɜ, saying bɝd, ˈfɜ˞ðə(r (not ˈfɜ˞ðə nor ˈfɜ˞ðə˞), with *r*-coloring in the accented vowel. It is to be noted that this pronunciation is heard from those who otherwise "drop their *r*'s," and it is confined to the stressed vowel. In this type of pronunciation the ə in *further* remains ə as with those who say ˈfɜðə. Thus such speakers would pronounce *The further part is better* ðə ˈfɜ˞ðə pɑːt ɪz ˈbɛtə.

This fact has long been known for Southern speech, but it has also recently been demonstrated for New England by the workers on the *L.A.*, and the same combination of ɝ with otherwise "*r*-less" pronunciation is heard in New York City. These facts have been fully verified by the present editors. Hence, in the vocabulary such words as *furthermore* are regularly represented for ES as ˈfɜ˞ðə,moə(r, ˈfɜ˞ðə,moə(r.

ɜɪ FOR THE VOWEL IN *BIRD*

§100. With many speakers in various parts of the South, and in New York City, a former r sound after ɜ, except when final (*fur*) or followed only by an inflectional ending (*furs*), is changed into something like ɪ, so that a word like *bird* is pronounced bɜɪd.[5]

Whether the NYC ɜɪ in *bird* (popularly but wrongly represented as *boid*) is historically connected with the Southern sound is unknown. But the NYC sound, commonly regarded as local dialect, is used by many educated speakers there, who recognize the sound in their own speech; and in the South it is also used by people of unquestioned cultivation.

EASTERN VARIATION BETWEEN ɑ AND a

§101. In the East, especially New England, the sound ɑ when spelt with *a* (*father, bar, calm*) varies with many speakers toward the sound **a.** A similar sound, but less prevalent, has been reported from near Williamsburg, Va. Since this variant is highly characteristic of New England, it is usually recorded, either in the vocabulary or in a page heading over the appropriate words. But it is not invariably recorded with less common words, and is then to be assumed as a possible variant.

EASTERN VARIATION BETWEEN æ, a, AND ɑ
IN WORDS LIKE *ASK*

§102. In the class of words spelt with *a* that is followed by a voiceless fricative s, f, or θ (*ask, chaff, bath*) or by a nasal plus a consonant (*example, demand*), in which British usually has ɑ, Eastern pronunciation (less commonly Eastern Virginian, see next section) varies between æ, a, and ɑ. The findings of the *L.A.* and the present editors' collections clearly indicate that, with a few exceptions (cf *half, calf, laugh, aunt*), the sound æ in these words in New England and New York City is at least as frequent as **a,** and usually more frequent than ɑ. In the vocabulary this variation is regularly shown by use of the plus sign, meaning "also," as at the word *fast* fæst; E + **fast, fɑst.** For other uses of the plus sign see §80.

---

[5] See Kemp Malone, *Studies for William A. Read*, University, La., 1940, p. 137. The same fact has also been observed by others.

WORDS LIKE *ASK* IN EASTERN VIRGINIA

§103. The words referred to in the preceding section (*ask, last, craft, path, chance,* etc.), in the vicinity of Richmond and Williamsburg, Va., are often pronounced with ɑ, less frequently with a. This pronunciation appears to be somewhat less common now than formerly. The historical and cultural importance of this region precludes regarding this merely as a localism. Yet to list this pronunciation of those words as a regular variant for Southern pronunciation as a whole would give a disproportionate impression, as well as complicate the vocabulary entries. It is therefore to be understood at those entries of such words containing the item "E + -a-, -ɑ-" that in eastern Virginia such words are also sometimes pronounced with ɑ, less often with a.

ɒ FOR ɑ IN *FATHER*

§104. In parts of the South the ɑ sound as in *father* 'fɑðə(r is retracted or raised in the direction of ɔ (*all*) without wholly reaching ɔ, but resembling the intermediate ɒ (§12). The same variant is becoming common in New York City. As a result, we sometimes find the roles of *a* and *o* apparently reversed, *a* being pronounced ɒ and *o* being pronounced ɑ. Thus a native of NYC pronounced *margin* 'mɒːdʒɪn and *Arthur* 'ɒːθə, while in the same breath he pronounced *Conning Tower* 'kɑnɪŋˌtaʊə.

VARIANTS OF THE DIPHTHONG aʊ

§105. For the vowel sound in *out, ground,* one symbol aʊ is used in the vocabulary. This is an inclusive symbol, here serving for all varieties of this diphthong in cultivated American speech. Outside of the South the principal varieties are aʊ and ɑʊ. In aʊ the first element often varies slightly toward ɜ. aʊ and ɑʊ are so nearly alike that most hearers do not notice the difference. These two show no important geographical distribution, and often vary from speaker to speaker. A common variant, very general, is ɑ for aʊ before r (*our* aʊr, ɑr).

§106. In the South are several varieties. These never distinguish words otherwise alike, but there are geographical and sometimes social distinctions. The most striking of these are found in Virginia and bordering North Carolina. In Virginia, mainly east of the Blue Ridge, a diphthong approximately ɜʊ (often written əʊ but with stressed first element) is used before voiceless consonants (*out* ɜʊt, *house* hɜʊs), while æʊ is used before voiced sounds and finally (*ground* græʊnd, *houses* 'hæʊzɪz, *cow* kæʊ). ɜʊ varies somewhat, especially to ʌʊ or oʊ. æʊ varies to aʊ or ɑʊ. Besides, the influence of analogy often breaks down the distinction before voiceless and voiced sounds, giving, e.g., *house* hɜʊs—*houses* 'hɜʊzɪz, or hæʊs—'hæʊzɪz.

In the western and southwestern parts of Virginia the tendency is to use æʊ in all positions, with variation to aʊ or ɑʊ.[6]

Perhaps owing in part to the influence of eastern Virginia, similar varieties are occasionally found in other parts of the South, but appear not to prevail there. The commonest varieties for the South as a whole are æʊ and aʊ, with intermediate shades. The form æʊ often becomes æə (*down* dæʊn, dæən).

[6] E. F. Shewmake, "Laws of Pronunciation in Eastern Virginia," *Mod. Lang. Notes*, xi, 8 (Dec. 1925), pp. 489–492. See also *American Speech*, xviii, 1 (Feb. 1943), pp. 33–38.
Guy S. Lowman, "The Treatment of aʊ in Virginia," *Proc. of the Second International Congress of Phonetic Sciences*, Cambridge, 1936, pp. 122–125.
Argus Tresidder, "Notes on Virginia Speech," *American Speech*, xvi, 2 (April 1941), pp. 112–116.
Unpublished material in the *L.A.* was also consulted.

In parts of Canada (Ontario, Nova Scotia, and probably elsewhere) a distinction is found similar to that of eastern Virginia, the singular of *house* being **hɜʊs** or **hoʊs** and the plural **ˈhaʊzɪz** or **ˈhɑʊzɪz**.

VARIANTS OF THE DIPHTHONG aɪ

§107. As with **aʊ,** so only one symbol **aɪ** is used in the vocabulary for the "long *i*" sound (*white* **hwaɪt,** *rise* **raɪz**). Outside of the South the principal varieties are **aɪ** (with **a** often varying slightly toward ɜ) and **ɑɪ.** The comments on the relation of **aʊ** to **ɑʊ** apply to that of **aɪ** to **ɑɪ.**

§108. In the South the varieties partly behave like those of **aʊ.** In Virginia east of the Blue Ridge many speakers use a sound approximately **ʌɪ** (varying toward ɜɪ) before voiceless consonants (*white* **hwʌɪt,** *wife* **wʌɪf**) but **aɪ** before voiced consonants and finally (*rise* **raɪz,** *wives* **waɪvz,** *high* **haɪ**). In some other parts of the South (as in the Carolinas) a similar distinction is found.

Another distinction, found, e.g., in Virginia and the Carolinas and probably elsewhere, is the use of **aɪ** or **ʌɪ** before voiceless consonants (*wife* **waɪf, wʌɪf**), but simple **a** or **a:** before voiced and finally (*wives* **wavz, wa:vz,** *why* **hwa, hwa:,** *mighty tired* **ˈmʌɪtɪ ta:d**). The simple **a,** less frequently **ɑ,** for **aɪ** is fairly common in many parts of the South (Virginia, North Carolina, South Carolina, Texas, etc.). As with **aʊ,** analogy (as *wife—wives*) tends to break down the distinction **wʌɪf—waɪvz** or **waɪf—wavz,** yielding such pairs as **waɪf—waɪvz** or **waf—wavz.**[7] For the South as a whole **aɪ** may safely be taken as the prevailing sound.

As with **aʊ,** so with **aɪ** a distinction similar to that in Virginia between *wife* **wʌɪf** and *wives* **waɪvz** is also found in Ontario and eastern Canada, probably reflecting a situation found in several Scottish dialects.

VARIATION BETWEEN ju, ɪu, AND u

§109. In words containing "long *u*" there is variation between the sounds **ju, ɪu,** and **u** too complicated to be fully described here.[8] Some misunderstanding has existed as to the prevalence of the diphthong **ɪu** in cultivated American English. Apparently many suppose that words like *duty, new* have but two pronunciations—either **djutɪ** or **dutɪ, nju** or **nu;** or that words like *accuse* have but one—**əˈkjuz.** Grandgent, however, long ago demonstrated the frequency of **ɪu** in America[9] in collections that showed **ɪu** in 35 to 60 per cent of the speakers tested, according to the class of words used. Other American observers have confirmed his findings. Grandgent also accurately described the diphthong as **ɪ** with tongue drawn back somewhat (symbol **ɪ**) followed by **u** with tongue pushed forward (symbol **ʉ**), and either having more stress on **ɪ** than on **ʉ** or having about equal stress on both elements, and with the **ʉ** usually longer than the **ɪ.**

The same speaker often varies between **ɪu** and **ju,** for **ɪu** easily shades into **ju** as the **ɪ** receives less stress and thus becomes more like consonantal **j.** It was thus that modern **ju** developed from Early Modern **ɪu** in all words that now have **ju,** and many Americans have retained the older **ɪu** (except initially) along with other features of Early Modern English.

---

7 See Shewmake and Tresidder, as cited above, footnote 6.
8 See Kenyon, *American Pronunciation,* 8th ed., §§341–350.
9 *Mod. Lang. Notes,* VI, 8 (1891), pp. 466–467.

In one variant of this diphthong the first element has the tongue drawn back as far as to the position for an advanced **u** (**ʉ**), so that the diphthong merges into a monophthongal **ʉ**. Both **ɪu** and this **ʉ** are used by many Americans to distinguish words from similar words that have **u**; as *brewed* **brɪud, brʉd**, distinct from *brood* **brud**, or *lute* **lɪut, lʉt**, distinct from *loot* **lut**.

Present knowledge of the distribution and prevalence of *ju*, **ɪu**, and **u** in the words concerned does not always permit of an accurate order of frequency in the vocabulary. Such order as has been verified is there shown. For example, it appears certain that words like *assume* are prevailingly pronounced with **u**. But in the main all that is attempted is to give the three (or two) current sounds (*duty* **ˈdjutɪ, ˈdɪutɪ, ˈdutɪ;** *blue* **blu, blɪu;** *accuse* **əˈkjuz, əˈkɪuz**) without insistence on order of frequency, all the pronunciations being in cultivated American use.

In the vocabulary the symbol **ɪu** is always to be taken to mean **ʉ**. See §§40, 41.

UNACCENTED *U* IN WORDS LIKE *CALCULATE,*
CONGRATULATE, EDUCATE,
NATURE, VERDURE

§110. In familiar speech unaccented *u* as in *calculate* is most commonly -jə- (**ˈkælkjəˌlet**) unless another vowel follows (*evacuate* **ɪˈvækjuˌet**). It often varies between -jə- and -ju- according to style of speech.

In colloquial pronunciation of words like *congratulate, educate,* unaccented *-tu-* and *-du-* most commonly are -tʃə- (**kənˈgrætʃəˌlet, -ˈgrætʃu-**) and -dʒə- (**ˈɛdʒəˌket, ˈɛdʒu-**), unless a vowel follows (*eventuate* **ɪˈvɛntʃuˌet,** *graduate* **ˈgrædʒuˌet**). In dissyllables the unaccented ending *-ture* is usually -tʃɚ, ES -tʃə(r, in common words (*nature* **ˈnetʃɚ;** ES **ˈnetʃə(r**), and *-dure* is usually -dʒɚ, ES -dʒə(r (*verdure* **ˈvɝˈdʒɚ, -dʒur;** ES **-dʒə(r, -dʒʊə(r**). See *Webster's New International Dictionary, Second Edition,* Guide to Pronunciation, §249, seventh paragraph. In words of three or more syllables not accented on the penult the unaccented ending *-ture* is commonly -tʃɚ or -tʃur according to style or to familiarity of the word (*miniature* **ˈmɪnɪtʃɚ, ˈmɪnɪətʃɚ, ˈmɪnɪəˌtʃur**). If *-ture* has a light accent then it is -ˌtʃur (*literature* **ˈlɪtərəˌtʃur**). Initial unaccented "long *u*" is ju- or ju- according to style (*unite* **juˈnaɪt, juˈnaɪt**).

SOUTHERN ɪ FOR ɛ BEFORE NASAL SOUNDS

§111. In parts of the South the sound of **ɛ** before **m, n,** or **ŋ** (*stem, men, length*) is replaced by, or tends in the direction of, **ɪ** (**stɪm, mɪn, lɪŋkθ**). This pronunciation is not equally distributed over the South and apparently is not equally acceptable in all types of Southern speech. Its omission from the vocabulary is not intended to imply disapproval of it.

VARIATION BETWEEN n AND ŋ BEFORE k OR g

§112. When the letter *n* ends the syllable before a **k** or a **g** sound, it usually represents the sound **ŋ** if the next syllable is final and wholly unaccented, as in *congress* **ˈkɑŋgrəs,** *Concord* **ˈkɑŋkɚd** (compare the pronunciation **ˈkɑnkɔrd,** where the final syllable has an unmarked subordinate accent). In other situations there is much wavering between **n** and **ŋ** that has no bearing on acceptability and is therefore often not shown in the vocabulary.

For the substitution of **n** for **ŋ** in *-ing* words, see *-ing* in the vocabulary.

THE SOUNDS OF *WH*

§113. In words spelt with *wh* (*whale* hwel, *when* hwɛn, *wheel* hwil, etc.) many speakers omit the **h** element and pronounce plain **w**, thus making homophones of *whale*, *wail* wel; *when*, *wen* wɛn; *wheel*, *weal* wil; etc. This is clearly not the prevailing pronunciation for America as a whole, but it appears to be somewhat on the increase, perhaps owing to the influence of Southern British speech. In the vocabulary only **hw** is given for such words. See also *wh-* in the vocabulary.

SYLLABIC ḷ, ṇ, ṃ, VARYING WITH əl, ən, əm

§114. In a great many words there is frequent variation between a syllabic consonant and ə plus a nonsyllabic consonant. In the vocabulary, as a rule, only the one deemed to be colloquially most usual is given. Examples of such variation are: *apple* ˈæpḷ, ˈæpəl; *happen* ˈhæpən, ˈhæpṇ, ˈhæpṃ (when -pṃ results from assimilation of -pṇ, -pəm never occurs); *trouble* ˈtrʌbḷ, ˈtrʌbəl; *buckle* ˈbʌkḷ, ˈbʌkəl; *struggle* ˈstrʌgḷ, ˈstrʌgəl; *castle* ˈkæsḷ, ˈkæsəl; *drizzle* ˈdrɪzḷ, ˈdrɪzəl; *prism* ˈprɪzəm, ˈprɪzṃ (see *-ism* in the vocabulary); *mason* ˈmesṇ, ˈmesən; *prison* ˈprɪzṇ, ˈprɪzən; *bacon* ˈbekən, ˈbekṇ, ˈbekŋ (see §24, 3d par.); *wagon* ˈwægən, ˈwægṇ, ˈwægŋ; *monopoly* məˈnɑpḷɪ, məˈnɑpəlɪ; *obelisk* ˈɑbḷˌɪsk, ˈɑbəˌlɪsk (for the accent see §52); *assassinate* əˈsæsṇˌetˌ əˈsæsəˌnet.

But in many words, while it is phonetically possible to pronounce either form, one of the forms is decidedly prevalent and the other either rare or un-English. Thus *cotton* ˈkɑtṇ, *hidden* ˈhɪdṇ, *little* ˈlɪtḷ, *cradle* ˈkredḷ, and such words as *didn't* ˈdɪdṇt, *oughtn't* ˈɔtṇt, *couldn't* ˈkʊdṇt, *wouldn't* ˈwʊdṇt in standard speech are not pronounced ˈkɑtən, ˈhɪdən, ˈlɪtəl, ˈkredəl, ˈdɪdənt, ˈɔtənt, ˈkʊdənt, ˈwʊdənt. An alternative pronunciation with -əl, -ən, -əm is much less usual when the syllabic consonant is final and follows a consonant made with the same position of the tongue point or of the lips (-tṇ, -dṇ, -tḷ, -dḷ, -nḷ). Syllabic ṃ is less frequent and is heard chiefly after the homorganic **p** (*open* ˈopṃ, *keep 'em* ˈkipṃ) or **b** (*album* ˈælbṃ, *rob 'em* ˈrɑbṃ).

m is not syllabic after **t** (*bottom* ˈbɑtəm) or **d** (*Adam* ˈædəm), though the ə may be very quick. Nasals are not syllabic after nasals (*common* ˈkɑmən, *venom* ˈvɛnəm, *cannon* ˈkænən, *minimum* ˈmɪnəməm) or after **l** (*stolen* ˈstolən or stoln with nonsyllabic **n**, *column* ˈkɑləm). **n** is not usually syllabic after **nd** (*London* ˈlʌndən), but is often so after **nt** (*mountain* ˈmaʊntṇ). Consonants are not syllabic after vowels.

In medial position alternation is frequent even after homorganic consonants (*fatally* ˈfetḷɪ, ˈfetəlɪ; *Adelaide* ˈædḷˌed, ˈædəˌled; *scrutiny* ˈskrutṇɪ, ˈskrutənɪ; *ordinal* ˈɔrdṇəl, ˈɔrdənəl).

In some cases the difference distinguishes words otherwise alike. Thus in Eastern and Southern, ˈsætṇ means "satin," while ˈsætən means "Saturn"; ˈbɪtṇ means "bitten," while ˈbɪtən means "bittern"; ˈpætṇ means "paten" or "patten," while ˈpætən means "pattern"; ˈfɔəmḷɪ means "formally," while ˈfɔəməlɪ means "formerly."

ADDITION OR OMISSION OF CONSONANTS

§115. Certain consonant sounds are inserted or omitted very generally in American English which are not regularly shown as variants in the vocabulary. Thus a **t** sound is often inserted between **n** and the **s** sound (*sense* sɛns, sɛnts, like *cents* sɛnts), between **n** and ʃ (*mansion* ˈmænʃən, ˈmænt·ʃən, *intention* ɪnˈtɛnʃən, ɪnˈtɛnt·ʃən, cf *luncheon* ˈlʌntʃən), between **n** and θ (*ninth* **naɪnθ, naɪntθ,** *tenth* **tɛnθ, tɛntθ**), between l and θ (*health* **hɛlθ, hɛltθ**), between l and s (*false* **fɔls, fɔlts,** like *faults*), between l and ʃ (*Welsh* **wɛlʃ, wɛltʃ,** cf *Welch*); and a p sound between **m** and **f** (*comfort* **ˈkʌmfɚt, ˈkʌmpfɚt,** *camphor* **ˈkæmfɚ, ˈkæmpfɚ,** cf *campfire*).

Omissions: **d** is often omitted between **n** and **z** (*lends* **lɛndz, lɛnz,** like *lens*) or between l and **z** (*fields* **fildz, filz,** like *feels*). The first element of **tʃ** is often omitted after **n** (*bench* **bɛntʃ, bɛnʃ,** *luncheon* **ˈlʌntʃən, ˈlʌnʃən**) or after l (*filch* **filtʃ, filʃ,** cf *Walsh, Welsh*), and the first element of **dʒ** is often omitted after **n** (*revenge* **rɪˈvɛndʒ, rɪˈvɛnʒ**), less frequently after l (*bulge* **bʌldʒ, bʌlʒ**).

LENGTHENED s REPLACING sts

§116. When the ending s is added to words in -st (*nests, beasts, rests*) the **t** sound is very often omitted, and the two s sounds combine into one long s (symbol **s:**). Thus *nests, beasts, rests* are often pronounced **nɛs:, bis:, rɛs:**.

PROPER NAMES

§117. For personal and place names the variant pronunciations given in the vocabulary often refer to different persons or places. Whenever the information was available, the variants have been referred to particular persons or places, but to do so in all cases is beyond the scope of this work.

CANADIAN VARIANTS

§118. In its most noticeable feature—the treatment of the *r* sound—most Canadian speech resembles the speech of the North in the US. The Midwesterner who visits Ontario or southern Quebec feels at home in the matter of speech. Direct British influence is, however, noticeable in details of both pronunciation and vocabulary. The pronunciations **ˈaɪðɚ** and **ˈnaɪðɚ** are rather more frequent than in the East in the US. For *rather* and *can't* **ˈrɑðɚ** and **kɑnt** are often heard. For *dictionary* (and similar words) **ˈdɪkʃənrɪ** is heard beside **ˈdɪkʃənˌɛrɪ**. For *laboratory* **ləˈbɔrətrɪ** is heard beside **ˈlæbrəˌtorɪ**. For *terrible* **ˈtɛrɪbl̩** is heard beside **ˈtɛrəbl̩**. **səˈdʒɛst** for *suggest*, and **ˈfrædʒaɪl** for *fragile*, are frequent. Scottish influence is apparent in Canada, especially in the use of the intermediate **a** for **æ** in "flat *a*" words (*hat, man,* etc.), in Nova Scotia and Alberta, and probably elsewhere. For the **aʊ** diphthong, **oʊ** (§106) and **u** are heard, probably also reflecting Scottish influence.

JUNCTIONAL, OR SANDHI, FORMS

§119. Pronunciations resulting from the effect of an initial sound of a following word (*did you* **ˈdɪdʒu,** *goes shopping* **goʒ ˈʃɑpɪŋ,** *sand pile* **ˈsænˌpaɪl**), or of a final sound of a preceding word (*bag and baggage* **ˈbægṇˈbægɪdʒ,** *good enough* **ˌgʊdṇˈʌf**), are only occasionally recorded in the vocabulary.

SPELLING PRONUNCIATION

§120. The term Spelling Pronunciation is used to designate a pronunciation which replaces that handed on by word of mouth in the spoken language and conforms in some respect more closely to the spelling, which is in some degree unphonetic—fails to correspond with the established pronunciation. Such pronunciations originate, as the *Oxford Dictionary* puts it, by taking a "shot" at the word from the spelling. Every such pronunciation is at first an error (departs from established usage); but innumerable pronunciations of this origin have come to be so general that they are now in unquestioned good standing. For examples see *Bentham, Waltham, Horsham;* and for fuller treatment see Kenyon, *American Pronunciation,* 8th ed., §§142–150.

DISSIMILATION

§121. A phonetic tendency known as Dissimilation is seen in English words in which an *r* sound in one syllable is lost if there is another *r* sound in the word. Thus in those regions where *r* is usually sounded in all positions the commonest colloquial pronunciation of *surprise* is sə'praɪz. Here the presence of the second **r** has led to the loss of the first (that is, in this case, the change of ɝ to ə by loss of its *r*-coloring). This tendency was pointed out for American English by Hempl (*Dialect Notes,* I, vi, 1893). Sometimes instead of being lost the **r** is changed to **l**, as it was in *Salisbury* (formerly *Sarisberie,* cf *Sarum*), or in *Salop* 'Shropshire,' from *Sloppesberie,* earlier *Shrobbesberie* 'Shrewsbury.'

Another example of *r* loss is 'gʌvənɚ, the prevailing pronunciation of *governor* in the North. That this is due to the other *r* sound and not to slovenly pronunciation is shown by the fact that the same speakers who say 'gʌvənɚ do not omit the *r* sound in *governess, govern, governing, governance, government,* which have no second **r.**

R-dissimilation does not often occur in regions where **r** is pronounced only before a vowel, though it might occur there in such a word as *preparatory* if pronounced pə'pærəˌtorɪ, and it may have operated in some words before a second **r** was dropped by the regular loss of **r** in the '*r*-less' regions. The loss of the first *r* in ES *governor* 'gʌvənə(r is not due to *r*-dissimilation, for similar loss is regular in ES *governess* 'gʌvənɪs, *govern* 'gʌvən, which have no other *r;* and *surprise* in ES is sə'praɪz for the same reason that *survive* in ES is sə'vaɪv.

Other examples of dissimilation are: *Bourchier* (cf *Boucher*), *Canterbury, catercornered, caterpillar, elderberry, February, Marylebone, northerner, southerner, Northrup, Otterburn, paraphernalia, particular* (the schoolmastered pronunciation par'tɪkjələ is perhaps a reaction against this), *Pendergast, reservoir, reverbatory, St. Bernard, thermometer, Waterbury.*

The pronunciations sə'praɪz and 'gʌvənɚ are "correct" forms, not because they are phonetically normal, but solely because they are in wide use by cultivated speakers. The same dissimilation is also seen in some pronunciations not so prevalent as to be generally acceptable; as *Arthur, corner, interpret, perform, performance, proportion, secretary, Shrewsbury, Swarthmore.*

ANGLICIZING

§122. A pronouncing dictionary of English must deal with the pronunciation of foreign words that have become more or less a part of the English language. With wholly foreign words it has, strictly speaking, nothing to do. However, a few foreign words or phrases and some foreign names have been entered which are somewhat in use in America but which have as yet no settled English pronunciation. These are given with their foreign pronunciation only, and are so labeled.

For the much larger body of foreign words that have become more or less Anglicized in use, meaning, and pronunciation, the editors follow the same guide as for fully English words—

they try to ascertain and report cultivated usage. But it is just this area of the language in which usage is most unsettled and uncertain, and where dictionary editors must bring to bear certain linguistic principles to supplement the uncertain evidence of usage. Some of these principles and considerations are:—

(1) The English language has shown great vigor and stability in assimilation of foreign material—in making it native. Until comparatively recent times foreign words fully adopted into English use have been adjusted to English laws of sound and accent. In Great Britain especially this is still usual. By radio one often hears foreign words pronounced in the English way by the best-educated leaders of that country; as, for example, the pronunciation ˈnæzɪ for *Nazi*. Whether or not this ever becomes a settled pronunciation, it shows the tendency; and many similar cases could be cited, which are in keeping with English tradition, and are by no means blunders.[10]

(2) The question often arises, Why not pronounce foreign words, especially names, with their foreign sounds? The answer, too little understood, is simple: except for the fractional percentage who speak the foreign language like a native, it is impossible, as the history of sound changes in past borrowings clearly shows. Very few English sounds are exactly like the foreign ones or those spelt with corresponding letters. This is deceptive to those not expert in foreign language. Examples abound. Many apparently suppose, for example, that they are pronouncing *Monticello* as Italian when they call it ˌmɑntɪˈtʃɛlo. In fact, they are giving approximately the Italian sound to three out of the ten sounds (m, tʃ, ɛ), and omitting one. An attempt, sometimes heard, to pronounce *envelope* in the French way by saying ˈɑnvəˌlop results in giving approximately the French sound to the **v** and the **p**. The **l** and all the vowels are quite different, and the **n** is not in the French word. The pronunciation of the fully Americanized name *Valparaiso* as ˌvɑlpəˈraɪzo is not a very successful attempt at the Spanish ˌbalparaˈiso. The American gəˈrɑʒ has two consonants of the French gɑˈrɑːʒ (g, ʒ, the r's being different) and one of its vowels—in the wrong syllable. The underlying fact is, that the speaker not fully conversant with a foreign language in attempting to imitate the foreign pronunciation substitutes his own nearest sounds for the foreign sounds, with a result unacceptable to the native speaker of the foreign language.

Often, too, the attempt to use foreign pronunciations misses the mark. Thus the word *valet* is not from Modern French but from Old French, and has been English (with a **t** sound) for some 400 years. Neither of the hybrid pronunciations væˈle or ˈvæle comes very near to the French vaˈlɛ. The case of *Calais* is similar. For several centuries an English name (for 200 years an English town), it was, and is, pronounced ˈkælɪs in the English way (like *palace* ˈpælɪs from OF *palais*), as in Shakespeare (spelt *Callis, Callice*) and later English poets (riming with *malice, Alice*). The present frequently heard kæˈle, ˈkælɪ are as far from Modern French kɑˈlɛ or kɑˈlɛ as væˈle or ˈvælɪ is from French vaˈlɛ.

The attempt to show knowledge of a foreign language by similar rough or even ludicrous attempts at the foreign pronunciation often shows ignorance instead. Such inaccurate hybrid pronunciations are, however, often taken up by many otherwise well-informed speakers, and so get established in good use, in the same way that hundreds of other linguistic errors and blunders have attained to good standing (witness Dr. Johnson's recommendation of *ache* for

[10] See Brander Matthews's defense of this tradition in *Society for Pure English Tract No. V.*

ake); and a dictionary based on usage must recognize them. Consequently many hybrid pronunciations of foreign derivatives are here given, for, however inaccurate, usage has established them.

(3) Wherever there is room for doubt as to actual usage, however, our policy has been to lean toward the long-established English tradition of full Anglicizing. Certain foreign sounds will, if the words become general, inevitably shift to native English sounds—as French **a** is sure to become either English **æ** or **ɑ**. In most cases the actual foreign pronunciation is added in parentheses, so that the user of the dictionary can adopt the foreign pronunciation if he chooses. And for those who prefer to follow the English tradition the appended foreign pronunciation may serve to show the inaccuracy of some of the attempted imitations.

PRONUNCIATION OF LATIN WORDS

§123. Latin words not usually being American colloquial English, as a rule only the orthodox English Latin pronunciation is given. The so-called Roman pronunciation is very inconsistent in actual practice. Some form of it is sometimes added if it has become widely current in actual use (cf *cum laude*).

MISCELLANEOUS SUGGESTIONS

§124.   1. The Key to pronunciation found at the bottom of every pair of open pages in the vocabulary contains the common English sounds. Each illustrative word in boldface type shows the sound of both vowel and consonant symbols. For fuller information about the phonetic alphabet and its use in this book, see Introduction, §§3–47.

    2. The basis of pronunciation in this dictionary is Cultivated Colloquial English—conversational style, not formal public address or public reading. For discussion of colloquial English, see Introduction, §§1–2.

    3. A Colloquialism is not a Localism or Slang. See Introduction, §§1–2, with the definition of *Colloquial* there quoted from *Webster's New International Dictionary, Second Edition.*

    4. For acceptable pronunciations not regularly listed in the vocabulary, see Introduction, *Variants*, §§90–119.

    5. Certain classes of words have Shifting or Variable Accent. For information on this and on accent and stress in general, see Introduction, §§48–54.

    6. For treatment of Regional Variations, see Introduction, §§76–85.

    7. For the pronunciation of Foreign Words, see §122 on Anglicizing.

    8. Too much importance should not be attached to the Order in which the variant pronunciations are given in the vocabulary. Several factors govern this order. See Introduction, §§57–58.

    9. It is idle to insist on the "correct" pronunciation of words not yet established in general oral use. The correct pronunciation will be whatever usage finally settles on, regardless of whether it agrees with etymology, spelling, or analogy.

  10. "The pronunciation is the actual living form or forms of a word, that is, *the word*

itself, of which the current spelling is only a symbolization—generally, indeed, only the traditionally-preserved symbolization of an earlier form."—*Oxford English Dictionary*.

11. "While we are entitled to display a certain fastidious precision in our saying of words that only the educated use, we deserve not praise but censure if we decline to accept the popular pronunciation of popular words."—H. W. Fowler, *Dictionary of Modern English Usage*.

12. "I do not believe in the feasibility of imposing one particular form of pronunciation on the English-speaking world."—Daniel Jones, *An English Pronouncing Dictionary*, 4th ed.

ABBREVIATIONS

Abbreviated names of English counties are listed in the vocabulary

+	also	*Can*	Canada, -dian
abbr.	abbreviation, -ated	*cf*	compare
acct	accent, -uation	*ch.*	church
acc. to	according to	*Chauc.*	Chaucer
adj	adjective	*chem.*	chemistry
adv	adverb	*Chin*	China, -nese
Afr	Africa, -can	*co.*	county
Ala	Alabama	*Col*	Colorado
Alas	Alaska	*colloq.*	colloquial, -ly
Am	American	*conj*	conjunction
Amer	America	*Conn*	Connecticut
Am Sp	American Spanish (with PI)	*cons., conss.*	consonant, -nants
anat.	anatomy	*Cornw*	Cornwall
Anglic.	Anglicize, -d	*Cumb*	Cumberland
apos.	apostle	*Czech*	Czechish
Arab	Arabic, Arabian	*Dan*	Danish
arch.	archaic	*dat*	dative
Arg	Argentine, -na	*Del*	Delaware
Ark	Arkansas	*Dev*	Devonshire
art.	article	*dial.*	dialect, -al, -ally
attrib.	attributive	*Du*	Dutch
Austral	Australia	E	Eastern, East
aux	auxiliary	*Egyp*	Egypt, -ptian
BBC	British Broadcasting	*emph.*	emphatic, -phasis
	Corporation	EN	Eastern and Northern
bef.	before	*Eng*	English
Belg	Belgium, Belgian	*Engd*	England
Bib.	Bible	*erron.*	erroneous, -ly
Bol	Bolivia	ES	Eastern and Southern
bor.	borough	*esp.*	especially
bot.	botany, botanist	*etym.*	etymology
Braz	Brazil	*fem.*	feminine, female
Brit	British	*Finl*	Finland
C	Canada, -dian	*Fla*	Florida
c (before		*Flem*	Flemish
numerals)	*circa*, about	*Fr*	French
c, cc (after		*freq.*	frequent, -ly
numerals)	century, -ries	*Ga*	Georgia
CA	Central America, -can	*gen*	genitive
Cal	California	*geog.*	geography, -phic, -ically
Camb	Cambridge	*geol.*	geology

(1)

geom.	geometry, -trical	*Mod E*	Modern English
Ger	German	*M. of Ven.*	*Merchant of Venice*
Gk	Greek	*mt., mts.*	mountain, -s
gram.	grammar, -matical	*mus.*	music
Heb	Hebrew	*myth.*	mythology, -logical
Hind	Hindi	*N*	Northern, North
hist.	historical, -ly	*n*	noun
Hung	Hungarian	*naut.*	nautical
Ia	Iowa	*NB*	New Brunswick, Can.
Ice	Iceland, -ic	*NC*	North Carolina
Id	Idaho	*NEngd*	New England
Ill	Illinois	*Neth*	Netherlands
Ind	Indiana	*NH*	New Hampshire
inf	infinitive	*Nicar*	Nicaragua
infreq.	infrequent, -ly	*NJ*	New Jersey
intj	interjection	*NMex*	New Mexico
Ir	Irish	*Norw*	Norwegian
Irel	Ireland	*NY*	New York
isl.	island	*NYC*	New York City
It	Italian	*NZ*	New Zealand
IW	Isle of Wight	*O*	Ohio
Jap	Japanese	*occas.*	occasional, -ly
Kan	Kansas	*OE*	Old English
Ky	Kentucky	*OED*	*Oxford English Dictionary*
L	Latin		*=Oxford Dictionary*
L.A.	*Linguistic Atlas of the US*	*OF*	Old French
	and Canada	*o. f.*	old-fashioned
La	Louisiana	*Okla*	Oklahoma
LI	Long Island	*Oreg*	Oregon
loc.	local, -ly	*Oxf*	Oxford, -shire
Lond	London	*Pa*	Pennsylvania
Mass	Massachusetts	*Pal*	Palestine
math.	mathematics	*perh.*	perhaps
Md	Maryland	*Pers*	Persia, -n
ME	Middle English	*pers*	person (grammar)
Me	Maine	*pers.*	personal
meas.	measure	*Pg*	Portuguese
Mich	Michigan	*Phil*	Philippine
mil.	military	*phil.*	philosopher
Minn	Minnesota	*PI*	Philippine Islands
Miss	Mississippi	*pl*	plural
Mo	Missouri	*poet.*	poetic, -al, poetry
mod.	modern	*Pol*	Polish

Port	Portugal	*surg.*	surgery
poss	possessive	*Sus*	Sussex
pptc	past participle	*Sw*	Swedish
prep	preposition	*Swtz*	Switzerland
pres	present	*syl.*	syllable
pro	pronoun	*Tasm*	Tasmania
prob.	probably	*Tenn*	Tennessee
pron.	pronunciation, pronounce, pronounced	*Tex*	Texas
		trans	transitive
ptc	participle, -cipial	*unstr.*	unstressed
rel	relative pronoun	*Uru*	Uruguay
relig.	religion, -ious	*US*	United States
RI	Rhode Island	*v*	verb
riv.	river	*Va*	Virginia
Rom	Roman	*var.*	variant
Rus	Russian	*vil.*	village
S	Southern, South	*vocab.*	vocabulary
SAmer, SA	South America, -can	*volc.*	volcano
SC	South Carolina	*vow.*	vowel, -s
Sc	Scottish, Scotch	*Vt*	Vermont
Scand	Scandinavian	W	Western, West
schol.	scholar	*w.*	with
Scotl	Scotland	*W²*	*Webster's New International Dictionary, Second Edition*
sculp.	sculptor		
SD	South Dakota		
sg	singular	*Wash*	Washington (state)
Shak.	Shakespeare	*WI*	West Indies
Som	Somersetshire	*Wis*	Wisconsin
Sp	Spanish	*WPacif*	West Pacific
sp.	spelling, spelt	*WVa*	West Virginia
sp. pr., sp. pron.	spelling pronunciation	*Yks*	Yorkshire

In the vocabulary, entries and other spelling forms (except catchwords) are in light roman type, pronunciations and all sounds are in **boldface,** and explanatory matter is in *italic* (except the regional labels E, S, N, W).

Occasionally, earlier spellings of an entry word, with dates of their occurrence in records, are shown as evidence of pronunciation or of other significant facts in the history of the word. Cf. the entries Bicester, kiln.

ADDENDA

A PRONOUNCING DICTIONARY OF AMERICAN ENGLISH

An asterisk (*) *marks words already recorded in the main vocabulary.*
The plus sign (+) *is to be read "also."*

adieux *2d pl of* adieu* ə'djuz, ə'dɪuz, ə'duz
  (*Fr* a'djə)
Aguilar *Col* 'ægwɪˌlɑr; ES -ˌlɑ:(r, E+-ˌlɑ:(r
Ahsahka *Id* ə'sɑkə
Alamosa *Col* ˌælə'mosə, *loc.*+-'musə, -sɪ
Algonquian*, -quin*+-nk-
Amish 'ɑmɪʃ, 'æmɪʃ
Athol* *NY* 'eθəl |A- Springs 'eθəl, 'æθəl
Attu *Alas isl.* 'ætu
bateaux *pl of* bateau* bæ'toz (*Fr* ba'to)
Baugh bɔ—*from* Bach, *cf* Reidenbach, Utah*
Benld *Ill loc.* bə'nɛl, *older* bɛn'ɛldi *from* Ben
  L. Dorsey—*cf* Gnadenhutten*, Ypres*,
  Yreka*, Yvonne*, *in which also the name of
  a letter replaces its usual sound.*
Biloxi *Miss* bə'lɑksɪ, -'lʌk-; ES+-'lɒk-
Blackstone* *cf variant spelling* Blaxton
Blanchester *O* 'blænˌtʃɛstɚ, -tʃɪs-; ES -tə(r
Bogalusa *La* ˌbogə'lusə
Bogoslof Isl. *Alas* 'bogəsˌlɑf, -ˌlɒf, -ˌlɔf
Bois Blanc Isl. *Mich* 'babˌlo'aɪlənd; ES+
  'bɒb-; (*Fr* bwa'blɑ̃)
Boise* *Id*+'bɔɪzɪ
Bollinger *Mo* 'bɑlɪndʒɚ; ES -dʒə(r, 'bɒl-
Bonar*, *Horatius* 'bɑnɚ; ES 'bɑnə(r, 'bɒn-
Bon Homme *SD* bɑn'hɑm; ES+bɒn'hɒm
Borger *Tex* 'bɔrgɚ; ES 'bɔəgə(r
Boscawen* *NH loc.* 'bɑskwaɪn, 'bɒs-
Boston*+'bɔstən, 'bɒstən (*§114*)
Botolph* *loc.*+bə'tɒl ˌstrit
Bouckville *NY* 'baʊkvɪl
Bouquet *NY* bo'kɛt, bə'kɛt
Broadalbin *NY* brɔd'ɔlbɪn, -'ælbɪn
Broome* *NY co. now more often* brum
Bruneau *Id* 'bruno
Buchman 'bʊkmən, 'bʌk- (*Ger* 'bu:xmən)
Buchmanism*, -ite*+'bʊkmən-
Burleigh *ND* 'bɝlɪ; ES 'bɜlɪ, 'bɜlɪ

Busti *NY* 'bʌstaɪ
Cache *Utah* kæʃ |-'s -ɪz
Cadiz* *spell Sp city* Cádiz; *pron.*+kə'dɪz
Cahaba *Ala riv.* kə'hɑbə, kə'hɒbə
Cahoon *surname* kə'hun—*see* Calhoon *below*
Calhoon = Calhoun*—*cf* Colquhoun*
Canaseraga *NY* ˌkænəsə'rɑgə
Canastota *NY* ˌkænə'stotə
Caneadea *NY* ˌkænə'diə ('Caneaˌdea 'Road)
Canisteo *NY* ˌkænə'stio
Canyon de Chelly *Ariz* 'kænjəndə'ʃe
Cape Girardeau *Mo* 'kepdʒə'rɑrdo, -də; ES
  -'rɑːdo, E+-'rɑːdo
Capulin *NMex mt.* kə'pjulɪn, kə'pɪulɪn
Celoron* *NY*+'sɛləˌron, 'sɛlərən
Cerf *surname* sɝf; ES sɜf, sɜf
charm *var. sp. of* chirm* *'din of birds'*
Chateaugay *NY* 'ʃætəˌge, 'ʃætəgɪ
Chehalis *Wash* tʃɪ'helɪs |-'s -ɪz
Cheney *Am vils., surname* 'tʃinɪ
Cheningo *NY* ʃə'nɪŋgo
Chesuncook *Me* tʃɪ'sʌnkʊk
Chichester* *NY* 'tʃaɪˌtʃɛstɚ; ES -tə(r
chile con carne, -li 'tʃɪlɪkən'kɑrnɪ, -kən'k-;
  ES -'kɑːnɪ, -kɒn'k-, E+-'kɑːnɪ
Chittenango *NY* ˌtʃɪtṇ'æŋgo, tʃɪt'næŋgo
Churchill*+-ˌhɪl—*cf* Northampton*
Cleburne *Ala*, *Ark*, *Tex* 'klibɚn; ES 'klibən
climatic klaɪ'mætɪk |-al -l̩ |-ally -l̩ɪ, -ɪklɪ
Cochise *Ariz* ko'tʃis |-'s -ɪz
Coconino *Ariz* ˌkokə'nino
Coeur D'Alene *Id* ˌkɔrdḷ'en; ES ˌkɔəd-
cognizable*+kɑg'naɪzəbḷ, kɒg-
Columbiana *O* kəˌlʌmbɪ'ænə
Combahee *SC* ˌkambə'hi; ES+ˌkɒm-; ('Comba,hee 'River)
Conewango *NY* ˌkɑnə'waŋgo, -'wɒŋ-; ES+
  ˌkɒn-

Key: *See in full §§3–47.* bee bi |pity 'pɪtɪ (§6) |rate ret |yet jɛt |sang sæŋ |angry 'æŋ·grɪ
|bath bæθ; E baθ (§10) |ah ɑ |far fɑr |watch watʃ, wɒtʃ (§12) |jaw dʒɔ |gorge gɔrdʒ |go go
|full fʊl |tooth tuθ |further 'fɝðɚ; ES 'fɜðə |custom 'kʌstəm |while hwaɪl |how haʊ |toy tɔɪ
|using 'juzɪŋ |fuse fjuz, fɪuz |dish dɪʃ |vision 'vɪʒən |Eden 'idṇ |cradle 'kredḷ |keep 'em 'kipm̩

(liii)

Corinth* *NY*, *Vt*, *loc.*+kə'rɪnθ, krɪnθ

Costilla *Col* kɑs'tiə, kɒs-, -'tijə (*Am Sp* kɒs'tija)

coxcombic* *at* ES *read:*+kɒks'kɒmɪk

Coxsackie *NY* kʊk'sɑkɪ, kɑk-, -'sækɪ; ES+kɒk-

cross bun 'krɔs'bʌn, 'krɒs- ('hot ˌcross 'bun)

Crummel, -mmles 'krʌml|(z)—*from* Cromwell

Cunard* *accent*+*as in* 'Cuˌnard 'Line

Cuprum *Id* 'kjuprəm, 'kɪu-, 'ku-

Dahlia* *NY vil.* 'delɪə, 'deljə; *see p. vi*

Darien* *Ga* 'derɪən

Depauville *NY* dɪ'povɪl, dɪ'pɒvɪl

De Ruyter *NY* dɪ'raɪtɚ; ES dɪ'raɪtə(r

Desha *Ark* də'ʃe

dilettantes *pl* ˌdɪlə'tæntɪz |-ti -'tænti

diphosgene*+-'fɑzdʒin; ES+-'fɒz-

Domremy-la-Pucelle*+Domrémy- dŏre'mi-

Dorcheat *La riv.* 'dɔrtʃit; ES 'dɔətʃit

Dravosburg *Pa* drə'vosbɝg; ES -bɜg, -bɚg

Dumas* *Ark* 'dumæs, 'dju-, 'dɪu-

Dunsany* *Brit*+dʌn'sænɪ

Duplin *NC* 'djuplɪn, 'dɪu-, 'du-

Duryea *Pa* dʊr'je, 'dʊrje; ES dʊə'je, 'dʊəje

Ecorse *Mich* 'ikɔrs; ES 'ikɔəs |-'s -ɪz

Edgecombe *NC*, -comb *Me*, *Wash* 'ɛdʒkəm

Edina *Minn* ɪ'daɪnə, i'daɪnə

Elberta ɛl'bɝtə; ES ɛl'bɝtə, ɛl'bɝtə

elegiast ɪ'lidʒɪˌæst, ə'lidʒɪˌæst

Eoanthropus* *put* ˌio'ænθrəpəs *first*

Ephrata *Pa* 'ɛfrətə, *Wash* ɪ'fretə

Ephratah *Bible* 'ɛfrətə, *NY* ɪ'fretə

Esarey, *Logan* 'ɛzərɪ

Etowah *Ala*, *Tenn* 'ɛtəˌwɑ, -ˌwɒ, -wə

Eulalie *Poe's poem* ˌjulə'li (*Fr* øla'li)

existentialism ˌɛgzɪs'tɛnʃəlˌɪzəm, ˌɛksɪs-

Falconer* *NY*+'fælkənɚ; ES 'fælkənə(r

Faust* *NY village* fɔst

Fayette fe'ɛt, fe'jet ('Fayˌette 'City)

Fernandina *Fla* ˌfɝnən'dinə; ES ˌfɝn-, ˌfɝn-

Finisterre* *add:* (*Sp* ˌfinis'tɛrɛ)

Folsom *Cal*, *NMex* 'folsəm, *surname* -o-, -ɑ-

Forsyth* *NY loc.* 'fɔrsaɪθ; ES 'fɔəsaɪθ

Franconia *NH* fræŋ'konɪə

Fremont* *NY loc.* 'fremənt, -mɒnt

frow '*froe*' fro |frow '*woman*' frau

Galway* *NY loc.* 'gælwe

Gansevoort* *NY* 'gænzvɚt, -vʊrt; ES -vət, -vʊət

Ghent* *NY*, *Minn* g-, *Ky* dʒ-, *WVa* dʒ-, g-

Godeffroy *NY* 'gɑdfrɪ, 'gɒd-, *cf* Godfrey*

Gogebic *Mich* go'gibɪk

Gouverneur* *NY*+ˌgʌvə'nʊr, ˌguvə-, *§121*, *loc.*+-'nɝ; ES -'nʊə(r, -'nɝ(r, -'nɝ

Gouverneur Morris ˌgʌvə'nɪr, ˌgʌvə-, *§121*; ES ˌgʌvə'nɪə(r; ('Gouverˌneur 'Morris)

Gravenstein *apple* 'grævənˌstaɪn, -ˌstin

greengage 'grin'gedʒ ('greenˌgage 'plum)

Grosvenor 'grovnɚ, *NY bay loc.* 'grʌvnɚ; ES -nə(r, 'grʌvnə(r

haberdasher* *sometimes* 'hæbəˌdæʃɚ (*§121*)

Hahn *surname* hɑn, hɒn—*cf* Baugh, Utah*

Hallowell 'hæləˌwɛl, -wəl, *Me loc.* 'hɒl-

Hampstead*+'hæmstɛd, 'hæmstɪd

Hapsburg* *see also* Habsburg*

Haralson *Ga* 'hærəlsn̩

Healdsburg *Cal* 'hildzbɝg, -lz-; ES -ɝ-, -ɝ-

Healdton *Okla* 'hildtən, 'hiltən

Hempstead *NY* 'hɛmpstɛd, 'hɛmst-, -stɪd

Henlopen *Del cape* hɛn'lopən

Henrico *Va* hɛn'raɪko

Hermosa *Cal* hɚ'mosə, hɝ-; ES hə-, hɜ-, hɝ-

Hialeah *Fla* ˌhaɪə'liə

Hindman *Ky* 'haɪnmən, 'haɪndmən

Holbrook *Ariz*, *Mass* 'holbrʊk

Honeoye *NY* 'hʌnɪˌɔɪ

Hoosic*+'huzɪk

Houma *La* 'humə

Huerfano *Col* 'wɛrfəˌno, 'wɝ-; ES 'wɛə-, 'wɝ-, 'wɝ-; *loc.*+'ɔrfəˌno

Hyndman *Id mt.* 'haɪnmən, 'haɪndmən

Indianola *Ia*, *Miss* ˌɪndɪə'nolə

Ingraham*+'ɪŋgrəm, 'ɪŋgrəm

Ischua *NY* 'ɪʃʊə, *loc.*+'ɪʃəˌwe—*cf* Nashua*

Ishpeming *Mich* 'ɪʃpɪˌmɪŋ

Itawamba *Miss* ˌɪtə'wɑmbə, -'wɒmbə

Iuka *Miss* aɪ'jukə

Jacquard* *acct*+*as in* 'Jacˌquard 'loom

Java* *NY* 'dʒevə

Juliana*+dʒul'jænə, dʒɪul-

Kalevala*+'kɑlɪˌvɑlə

Kalispell *Mont* ˌkæljə'spɛl, 'kæljəˌspɛl

Kegonsa *Wis lake* kɪ'gɑnsə; ES+-'gɒnsə

Kinderhook *NY* 'kɪndɚˌhʊk; ES 'kɪndəˌhʊk

Kineo *Me mt.* 'kɪnɪˌo

Kissimmee *Fla* kɪ'sɪmɪ

Koshkonong *Wis* 'kɑʃkəˌnɑŋ; ES+'kɒʃkəˌnɒŋ

Kossuth* *Ia* kə'suθ, kɑ-, kɒ-

Key: See in full §§3–47. bee **bi** |pity 'pɪtɪ (§6) |rate **ret** |yet jɛt |sang sæŋ |angry 'æŋ·grɪ |bath bæθ; E baθ (§10) |ah ɑ |far fɑr |watch wɑtʃ, wɒtʃ (§12) |jaw dʒɔ |gorge gɔrdʒ |go go

Kotzebue *Alas* ˈkɑtsəˌbju, -ˌbɪu; ES+ˈkɒt-

La Crosse *Wis* ləˈkrɔs, -ˈkrɒs |-ˈs -ɪz

La Garita *Cal* ˌlɑgəˈritə

La Habra *Cal* ləˈhɑbrə

Lampasas *Tex* læmˈpæsəs |-sas' -səs

Lassellsville *NY* ˈlæs|zˌvɪl—*cf* Lascelles*

Latah *Id* ˈletə, leˈtɔ—*cf* Utah*

Lavaca *Tex* ləˈvækə

Ledyard*+ˈlɛdʒɚd; ES ˈlɛdʒəd

Leelanau *Mich* ˈliləˌnɔ

Lenox *var. sp. of* Lennox* ˈlɛnəks |-ˈs -ɪz

leukemia, -kae- luˈkimɪə, lɪu- |-mic -mɪk

Ligonier* *acct*+, *esp. attrib.*, ˈLigoˌnier

literatus *sg of* literati* ˌlɪtəˈretəs

Livengood *Alas vil.*, *surname* ˈlaɪvənˌgʊd

Lonaconing *Md* ˌlonəˈkonɪŋ

Loogootee *Ind* ləˈgotɪ

Loup *Nebr* lup

Lycoming* *Pa co. loc.*+-ˈkom-, -ˈkʌm-; *NY vil.* laɪˈkomɪŋ

McDermott məkˈdɝmət; ES -ˈdɜmət, -ˈdɝ-

McDiarmid məkˈdɝmɪd; ES -ˈdɜmɪd, -ˈdɝ-

Mahopac *NY* ˈmeoˌpæk, ˈmeəˌpæk

Mannering *surname* ˈmænərɪŋ = Manwaring*, Mainwaring*, Maynwaring*

Matteawan *NY*+, *esp. attrib.*, ˈMatteaˌwan

Mazomanie *Wis* ˌmezəˈmenɪ, ˌmezo-

Mebane *NC* ˈmæbɪn

Montgomery*+məntˈgʌmrɪ, -ˈgʌmərɪ

Montour* *accent*+*as in* ˈMonˌtour ˈFalls

Morenci *Mich* məˈrɛnsɪ

Morris, Gouverneur, *see* Gouverneur Morris

Munising *Mich* ˈmjunəsɪŋ, ˈmɪunəsɪŋ

Muscatatuck *Ind riv.* mʌsˈkætəˌtʌk

Mycenae* *NY loc.* məˈsinə—*cf* məˈzurə

Nauvoo* *accent*+*as in* ˈNauˌvoo ˈstreets

Navarino *NY* ˌnævəˈraɪno

Neligh *Nebr* ˈnilɪ

Neodesha *Kan* ˌniədəˈʃe

Nescopeck *Pa* ˈnɛskəˌpɛk

Neshoba *Miss* nɪˈʃobə

Nevada* *O loc.* nəˈvedə, nɪ-

Newbern* *Tenn*+-bɝn; ES -bɜn, -bɝn

Newfane *NY, Vt* ˈnjuˌfen, ˈnɪu-, ˈnu-; *Vt loc.* +ˌNewˈfane, *also spelt* New Fane

Nisei ˈnise, niˈse

Nootka*+ˈnʊtkə, ˈnutkə, ˈnutkɔ—*cf* Utah*

Nueces *Tex* njuˈesɪs, nɪu-, nu-

Nunda *Ill, NY, loc.* nʌnˈde

Obion *Tenn* oˈbaɪən

Oceana* *WVa* ˌosɪˈænə

Ocheltree *Kan* ˈok|ˌtri, ˈok|trɪ

Ochiltree *Tex* ˈak|ˌtri, ˈak|trɪ; ES+ˈɒk-; *Scotl* ˈok|ˌtri, -trɪ (*Sc* ˈoxɪl-, ˈox|-)

Okanagan *Can* ˌokəˈnagən

Okanogan *Wash* ˌokəˈnagən, -ˈnɒgən

Okemah *Okla* oˈkimə, oˈkima

Oktibbeha *Miss* ɑkˈtɪbɪˌhɔ; ES+ɒk-

Olathe *Kan* oˈleθɪ, əˈleθɪ, -θə

Olean *NY* ˈolɪˌæn, ˌolɪˈæn

Olneyville *RI* ˈonɪˌvɪl—*cf* Olney*

Olustee *Ala, Fla, Okla* oˈlʌstɪ, əˈlʌstɪ

Onawa *Ia* ˈɑnəwə; ES+ˈɒnəwə

Onaway *Mich* ˈɑnəˌwe; ES+ˈɒnəˌwe

Onondaga* *NY loc.*+ˌɑnəˈdɔgə

Onoville *NY* ˈɑnəˌvɪl; ES+ˈɒnəˌvɪl

Opelika *Ala* ˌopəˈlaɪkə, ˌopɪˈlaɪkə

Oregonian ˌɔrəˈgonɪən, ˌɑr-, ˌɒr-

Oriskany *NY* əˈrɪskənɪ, oˈrɪskənɪ

Orleans* *US*, *accent*+*as in* ˈOrˌleans ˈCo.

Osakis *Minn* oˈsekɪs |-ˈs -ɪz

Oskaloosa *Ia* ˌɑskəˈlusə; ES+ˌɒskəˈlusə

Ossining *NY*+ˈɑsn̩ɪŋ; ES+ˈɒsn̩ɪŋ

Otsego *NY* ɑtˈsigo; ES+ɒtˈsigo

Ottumwa *Ia* əˈtʌmwə, ɑˈtʌmwə; ES+ɒˈtʌmwə

Outagamie *Wis* ˌautəˈgæmɪ

Ovid* *Mich, NY*, *occas. pers. name* ˈovɪd

Owyhee *Id* əˈwaɪhi, oˈwaɪhi

Palestine* *Tex loc.* ˈpæləsˌtin

Palomar *Cal* ˌpæləˈmɑr; ES -ˈmɑː(r, E+-ˈmɑː(r; *accent*+*as in* ˈPaloˌmar ˈMountain

Passaconaway *NH* ˌpæsəˈkɑnəˌwe; ES+-ˈkɒn-

Pehlevi 'Pahlavi' ˈpeləˌvi |Pehlvi ˈpelvi

Pend Oreille *Id, Wash* ˌpɑndəˈre, ˌpɛn-

phosgene*+ˈfazdʒin; ES+ˈfɒzdʒin

Picabo *Id loc.* ˈpɪkəˌbu, *elsewhere*+ˈpikəˌbu

pileated ˈpaɪlɪˌetɪd, ˈpɪlɪˌetɪd

Piqua* *O*+ˈpɪkwe—*cf* Pickaway*

Pithecanthropus* *put second pron. first*

Poestenkill *NY* ˈpusn̩ˌkɪl, ˈpostn̩ˌkɪl

princess* *Brit*+prɪnˈsɛs, *but* ˈprɪnsɪs *when attrib.*, *as in* ˈPrincess ˈMary

Pulaski* *US*+pəˈlæskɪ, pju-, pɪu-

Pushmataha *Okla* ˌpuʃməˈtɔhə, -ˈtɑhɑ

Puyallup *Wash* pjuˈæləp, pɪuˈæləp

Rahway *NJ* ˈrɔwe

Ramapo *NY vil.*, *NY, NJ riv.* ˈræməˌpo

|full fʊl |tooth tuθ |further ˈfɝðɚ; ES ˈfɜðə |custom ˈkʌstəm |while hwaɪl |how haʊ |toy tɔɪ |using ˈjuzɪŋ |fuse fjuz, fɪuz |dish dɪʃ |vision ˈvɪʒən |Eden ˈidn̩ |cradle ˈkredl̩ |keep 'em ˈkipm̩

Rangeley *Me* 'rendʒlɪ

Rantoul *Ill* ræn'tul ('Ran,toul 'schools)

Raton* *Col* rə'tun, ræ-; *NMex* rə'ton, rɑ-

Reidenbach *surname* 'raɪdn̩,bɔ—*cf* Baugh

Rensselaer* *NY*+,rensḷ'ɪr; ES -'ɪə(r; *accent* +*as in* 'Rensse,laer 'boy

Robson* *surname*+'robsn̩

Sabinal *Tex* ,sæbə'næl ('Sabi,nal 'bank)

Sacandaga *NY* ,sækən'dɔgə

Sagadahoc* *Me*, *put acct* ,Sagada'hoc *first*

Salida *Col* sə'laɪdə (*Sp* sa'liðа)

Salina *Kan* sə'laɪnə

Salinas *Cal* sə'linəs |-'s -ɪz

Saluda *NC, SC, Va, Ind* sə'ludə

San Bernardino* *Cal*+-,bɝnə'dino, §121

Santanoni *NY* ,sæntə'nonɪ ('Santa,noni 'Mt.)

Sapulpa *Okla* sə'pʌlpə

sarsaparilla*+,sæspə'rɪlə, ,sæsəpə-

Saugerties *NY* 'sɔgɚtɪz, -,tiz; ES 'sɔgə-

Sauquoit *NY* sə'kwɔɪt

Schaefer, -ffer 'ʃefɚ; ES 'ʃefə(r

Schaghticoke *NY* 'skætɪ,kʊk, 'ʃætɪ-, -,kok

Schenevus *NY* skə'nivəs |-'s -ɪz

Schrader 'ʃredɚ; ES 'ʃredə(r

Schroeder 'ʃredɚ, 'ʃrodɚ; ES -də(r; (*Ger* 'ʃrøːdər)

Schuylkill* *SE Pa loc.*+'skʊkḷ

sermonic sɝ'mɑnɪk; ES sɝ-, sɝ-, -'mɒnɪk

Shafer 'ʃefɚ; ES 'ʃefə(r

Shaffer 'ʃefɚ, 'ʃæfɚ; ES -fə(r

shafts '*thills*' ʃævz, ʃæfts; E+ʃɑ-, ʃɑ-; *see* §124.11

Shelbina *Mo* ʃɛl'baɪnə

shindig* *accent*+'ʃɪn,dɪg

slaver '*slave dealer*' 'slevɚ; ES 'slevə(r

slaver '*drool*' 'slævɚ; ES 'slævə(r; |-ed -d |-ing 'slævərɪŋ, 'slævrɪŋ

soot* *cf* boot **but**, foot fʊt, flood flʌd

submersible səb'mɝsəbḷ; ES -'mɜs-, -'mɝs-

Suckow *surname* 'suko

Suffolk*+'sʌfək

Sylacauga *Ala* ,sɪlə'kɔgə

Tahoe *Cal* 'tɑho, 'teho

Talcott, Tallcott 'tɔlkət, 'tælkət

Talladega *Ala* ,tælə'digə

Tallulah *La* tə'lulə

Taughannock Falls *NY* tə'gænək, tə'gænək

Tazewell *Ill, Va* 'tæzwɛl, 'tezwɛl, -wəl

Tehuacana *Tex* tɪ'wakənə, -'wɒk-

Tidioute *Pa* 'tɪdɪ,ut, ,tɪdɪ'ut

Tionesta *Pa* ,taɪə'nɛstə

Totowa *NJ* 'totəwə

Tucumcari *NMex* 'tukəm,kɛrɪ, -,kærɪ; S -æ-

Tuolumne *Cal* 'twaləmnɪ, 'twɒləmnɪ

Tuscola *Mich, Ill* tʌs'kolə

Tyrone* *Pa*, *acct*+*as in* 'taɪ,ron 'strits

Uhrichsville *O* 'jʊrɪks,vɪl

Umatilla *Oreg* ,jumə'tɪlə

Unadilla *NY* ,junə'dɪlə, *loc.*+,ʌnə'dɪlə; *acct*+ *as in* 'Una,dilla 'Forks

Upshire *Engd* 'ʌpʃɪr, -ʃɚ; ES -ʃɪə(r, -ʃə(r

Upshur *surname*, *WVa co.* 'ʌpʃɚ; ES 'ʌpʃə(r

Uvalde *Tex* ju'vældɪ

Valois 'vælwɑ, -wɒ (*Fr* va'lwa), *NY* və'lɔɪs

Vandalia *Am places* væn'deljə

Venango *Pa, Nebr* və'næŋgo

Venezuela*+,vɛnzu'ilə, ,vɛnəzu'ilə

Vergennes *Vt, Ill* vɚ'dʒɛnz; ES və-; |-'s -ɪz

vernacular*+və'nækjəlɚ (§121)

Vevay *Swtz Co. Ind* 'vivɪ, *older* vi've (§6)

Vevey *Switzerland* və've (*Fr* və'vɛ)

Vienna* *some Am places*+vaɪ'ɛnə

Vigo *Ind* 'vaɪgo, 'vigo

Vinita *Okla* və'nitə

Waban *Mass* 'wɒbən

Wabasha *Minn* 'wɑbə,ʃɔ, 'wɒbə-, 'wɔbə-

Wadena *Minn* wɑ'dinə, wɒ'dinə̩

Waha *Id* 'wɔhɔ—*cf* Omaha*, Utah*, Baugh

Walthall *Miss* 'wɒlθɔl—*cf* Waltham*

Wamego *Kan* wə'migo, wɒ-, wɑ-

Wappingers *NY* 'wɑpɪndʒɚz, 'wɒp-; ES -dʒəz

Wasatch 'wɒsætʃ, wɔ'sætʃ ('Wɑ,satch 'Mts.)

Washingtonian ,wɑʃɪŋ'tonɪən, ,wɔʃ-, ,wɒʃ-

Washtenaw *Mich* 'wɑʃtə,nɔ, 'wɒʃ-, 'wɔʃ-

Watauga *NC, Tenn* wɑ'tɔgə, wɒ'tɔgə, wə-

Watervliet *NY* 'wɔtɚ,vlit, 'wɑ-, 'wɒ-, -vḷ,it; ES -tə-; *acct*+,Water'vliet

Watseka *Ill* wɑt'sikə, wɒt'sikə

Waubesa *Wis lake* wɔ'bisə

Waunakee *Wis* ,wɒnə'ki ('Wauna,kee 'mail)

Waupaca *Wis* wɔ'pækə

Waupun *Wis* wɔ'pʌn ('Wau,pun 'schools)

Wauseon *O* 'wɔsɪ,ɑn, -,ɒn, ,wɔsɪ'ɑn, -'ɒn

Weehawken *NJ* wi'hɔkən

Weiser *Id* 'wizɚ; ES 'wizə(r

Wetumka *Okla* wɪ'tʌmkə |-mpka *Ala* wɪ-'tʌmpkə

Wigtownshire* *put* 'wɪgtən,ʃɪr *first*

Winder *Ga* 'waɪndɚ; ES 'waɪndə(r

Winnetka *Ill* wɪ'nɛtkə

Wolcott* *NY loc.* 'wɒlkət

woollen *variant spelling of* woolen*

Zeigler *Ill* 'zɪglɚ; ES 'zɪglə(r

Ziebach *SD* 'zi'bɑk, -'bɑ, -'bɔ—*cf* Baugh

A

PRONOUNCING DICTIONARY

OF

AMERICAN ENGLISH

A, a *letter* e |*pl* A's, As, *poss* A's ez
a *indef. art.* ə, *emph. or hesitating* e—*The use of e, the stressed form of a, in places where the unstressed ə belongs, often gives an artificial effect to public address.*
a, a- *unstressed form of* on ə (a begging, a-foot, afire)
Aachen 'akən, 'axən (*Ger* 'aːxən)
Aaron 'ɛrən, 'ærən, 'erən; S 'ærən, 'erən
abacá ˌabə'ka
aback ə'bæk
abacus 'æbəkəs |-es -ɪz |-ci -ˌsaɪ
abaft ə'bæft; E+ə'baft, ə'baft
abalone, A- ˌæbə'lonɪ
Abana 'æbənə
abandon *n* ə'bændən (*Fr* abũ'dõ)
abandon *v* ə'bændən |-ed -d
abase ə'bes |-s -ɪz |-d -t |-dly -ɪdlɪ
abash ə'bæʃ |-es -ɪz |-ed -t |-edly -ɪdlɪ
abatable ə'betəbḷ
abate ə'bet |abated ə'betɪd
abatis 'æbətɪs, ə'bætɪs |-es -ɪz |-ed -t
abattoir ˌæbə'twar, -'twɔr; ES -'twaː(r, -'twɔə(r; (*Fr* aba'twaːr)
abbacy 'æbəsɪ
Abbana 'æbənə
abbé 'æbe, æ'be (*Fr* a'be)
abbess 'æbɪs, 'æbɛs |abbesses 'æbɪsɪz
Abbeville *US* 'æbɪˌvɪl; S+-vḷ; *France* ab'vil
abbey 'æbɪ |Abbeyville, Abby- 'æbɪˌvɪl
abbot 'æbət
Abbotsford 'æbətsfɚd; ES 'æbətsfəd
abbreviate ə'brivɪˌet |-ated -ˌetɪd

abbreviation əˌbrivɪ'eʃən
ABC· 'e'bi'si |ABC's, ABCs 'e'bi'siz ('AˌBˌC 'book)
abdicate 'æbdəˌket |-cated -ˌketɪd
abdication ˌæbdə'keʃən
Abdiel 'æbdɪəl, -dɪɛl, -dj-
abdomen 'æbdəmən, æb'domən, əb-
abdominal æb'damənḷ, əb-; ES+-'dɒm-; |-ly -ɪ
abduce æb'djus, -'dɪus, -'dus |-s -ɪz |-d -t
abduct æb'dʌkt, əb- |-ed -ɪd |-ction -kʃən
abeam ə'bim
abecedarian ˌebɪsɪ'dɛrɪən, -'der-
À Becket, -ett ə'bɛkɪt
abed ə'bɛd
Abednego ə'bɛdnɪˌgo
Abel 'ebḷ
Abelard 'æbḷˌard; ES 'æbḷˌaːd; (*Fr* abe'laːr)
Aberdeen ˌæbɚ'din; ES ˌæbə'din; ('Aberˌdeen 'Angus) |-shire -ʃɪr, -ʃɚ; ES -ʃɪə(r, -ʃə(r
Abergavenny *Eng town* ˌæbɚgə'vɛnɪ, *family* ˌæbɚ'gɛnɪ, *Shak.* Aburgany ˌæbɚ'gɛnɪ; ES ˌæbə-
aberrance æb'ɛrəns |-ancy -ənsɪ |-ant -ənt
aberration ˌæbə'reʃən
Aberystwyth ˌæbɚ'ɪstwɪθ
abet ə'bɛt |-ted -ɪd |-ter, -tor -ɚ; ES -ə(r
abeyance ə'beəns |-ant -ənt
abhor əb'hɔr, æb-; ES -'hɔə(r; |-red -d
abhorrence əb'hɔrəns, æb-, -'har-, -'hɒr- |-ent -ənt
Abhorson əb'hɔrsn̩; ES -'hɔəsn̩
abidance ə'baɪdn̩s

Key: *See in full §§3–47.* bee bi |pity 'pɪtɪ (§6) |rate ret |yet jɛt |sang sæŋ |angry 'æŋ·grɪ |bath bæθ; E baθ (§10) |ah ɑ |far fɑr |watch wɑtʃ, wɒtʃ (§12) |jaw dʒɔ |gorge gɔrdʒ |go go |full fʊl |tooth tuθ |further 'fɝðɚ; ES 'fɝðə |custom 'kʌstəm |while hwaɪl |how haʊ |toy tɔɪ |using 'juzɪŋ |fuse fjuz, fɪuz |dish dɪʃ |vision 'vɪʒən |Eden 'idn̩ |cradle 'kredḷ |keep 'em 'kipm̩

abide əˈbaɪd |*past* abode əˈbod *or* abided
  əˈbaɪdɪd |*pptc* abode əˈbod *or* abided
  əˈbaɪdɪd, *rarely* abidden əˈbɪdn̩
Abigail ˈæbəˌgel, ˈæbəgl̩
Abijah əˈbaɪdʒə
Abilene *US* ˈæbəˌlin, *Syria* ˌæbəˈlinɪ
ability əˈbɪlətɪ
Abimelech əˈbɪməˌlɛk
Abinadab əˈbɪnəˌdæb
Abingdon ˈæbɪŋdən |-gton -tən
ab initio ˈæbɪˈnɪʃɪˌo
abject æbˈdʒɛkt, ˈæbdʒɛkt (ˈabˌject ˈlook)
abjection æbˈdʒɛkʃən
abjuration ˌæbdʒʊˈreʃən
abjure əbˈdʒʊr, æb-, -ˈdʒɪur; ES -ˈdʒʊə(r,
  -ˈdʒɪuə(r; |-d -d
ablation æbˈleʃən
ablative ˈæblətɪv, ˈæblɪtɪv
ablaut ˈablaʊt, ˈæblaʊt (*Ger* ˈɑplaʊt)
ablaze əˈblez
able ˈebl̩ |-ler ˈeblɚ; ES -lə(r; |-lest ˈeblɪst
-able *unstressed ending* -əbl̩—*often omitted
  from the vocab. when the pron. can be found
  by adding* -əbl̩ *to the head pron. The corresponding adverb ending is* -ably -əblɪ. *For
  the addition of* -bly -blɪ *when the head word
  does not end in* -able, *see the suffix* -bly.
able-bodied ˈebl̩ˈbadɪd; ES+-ˈbɒd-; (ˈable-
  ˌbodied ˈman)
ablution æbˈluʃən, əb-, -ˈlɪuʃən
ably ˈeblɪ
abnegate ˈæbnɪˌget |-gated -ˌgetɪd
abnegation ˌæbnɪˈgeʃən
Abner ˈæbnɚ; ES ˈæbnə(r
abnormal æbˈnɔrml̩, əb-; ES -ˈnɔəml̩; |-ly -ɪ
abnormality ˌæbnɔrˈmælətɪ; ES -nɔˈmælətɪ
abnormity æbˈnɔrmətɪ; ES -ˈnɔəmətɪ
aboard əˈbord, əˈbɔrd; ES əˈboəd, E+əˈbɔəd
abode əˈbod
abolish əˈbalɪʃ; ES+əˈbɒl-; |-es -ɪz |-ed -t
abolition ˌæbəˈlɪʃən |-ism -ˌɪzəm |-ist -ɪst
abominable əˈbɑmnəbl̩, -mən-; ES+əˈbɒm-;
  |-bly -blɪ
abominate əˈbɑməˌnet; ES+əˈbɒm-; |-d -ɪd
aboriginal ˌæbəˈrɪdʒənl̩ |-ly -ɪ |-ne -ˌni
abort əˈbɔrt; ES əˈbɔət; |-ed -ɪd
aborticide əˈbɔrtəˌsaɪd; ES əˈbɔətə-
abortifacient əˌbɔrtəˈfeʃənt; ES əˌbɔətə-
abortion əˈbɔrʃən; ES əˈbɔəʃən

Abou ben Adhem ˈæbubɛnˈædəm, ˈɑbubɛn-
  ˈɑdɛm
abound əˈbaʊnd |-ed -ɪd
about əˈbaʊt
about-face *n* əˈbaʊtˌfes |-s -ɪz
about-face *v* əˌbaʊtˈfes |-s -ɪz |-d -t
about-ship *v* əˌbaʊtˈʃɪp |-ped -t
above əˈbʌv
aboveboard əˈbʌvˌbord, -ˌbɔrd; ES -ˌboəd,
  E+-ˌbɔəd
aboveground əˈbʌvˌgraʊnd
abrade əˈbred, æbˈred |-d -ɪd
Abraham ˈebrəˌhæm, ˈebrɪ-, -həm
Abram ˈebrəm
abrasion əˈbreʒən, æbˈr- |-sive -sɪv, -zɪv
abreaction ˌæbrɪˈækʃən
abreast əˈbrɛst
abridge əˈbrɪdʒ |-s -ɪz |-d -d |-dly -ɪdlɪ
abroad əˈbrɔd
abrogable ˈæbrəgəbl̩
abrogate ˈæbrəˌget, -ro- |-gated -ˌgetɪd
abrogation ˌæbrəˈgeʃən, -ro-
abrupt əˈbrʌpt, æbˈrʌpt
Absalom ˈæbsələm
abscess ˈæbˌsɛs, -sɪs |-es -ɪz |-ed -t
abscissa æbˈsɪsə |-s -z |-sae -si
abscission æbˈsɪʒən, æbˈsɪʃən
abscond æbˈskand, əb-; ES+-ˈskɒnd; |-ed
  -ɪd
absence ˈæbsn̩s |absences ˈæbsn̩sɪz |-sent
  -sn̩t
absent *v* æbˈsɛnt, əb- |-ed -ɪd
absentee ˌæbsn̩ˈti (ˈabsenˌtee ˈlandˌlord)
absent-minded ˈæbsn̩tˈmaɪndɪd
absinthe, -th ˈæbsɪnθ, æbˈsɪnθ
absolute ˈæbsəˌlut, -ˌlɪut, -sl̩ˌjut |-ly -lɪ,
  emph.+ˌabsoˈlutely, ˈabsoˈlutely
absolution ˌæbsəˈluʃən, -ˈlɪuʃən, -sl̩ˈjuʃən
absolutism ˈæbsəlutˌɪzəm, -lɪut-, -sl̩jut-
absolutist ˈæbsəˌlutɪst, -ˌlɪut-, -sl̩ˌjutɪst
absolve æbˈsalv, əb-, -ˈsɒlv, -ˈz- |-d -d
absorb əbˈsɔrb, æb-, -ˈz-; ES -ɔəb; |-ed -d
  |-edly -ɪdlɪ
absorbefacient əbˌsɔrbəˈfeʃənt, æb-, -ˌz-; ES
  -ɔəb-
absorbent əbˈsɔrbənt, æb-, -ˈz-; ES -ɔəb-
absorption əbˈsɔrpʃən, æb-; ES -ˈsɔəp-;
  |-tive -tɪv
abstain əbˈsten, æb- |-ed -d

Key: *See in full §§3–47.* bee **bi** |pity ˈpɪtɪ (§6) |rate **ret** |yet jɛt |sang sæŋ |angry ˈæŋ·grɪ
|bath bæθ; E baθ (§10) |ah ɑ |far fɑr |watch wɑtʃ, wɒtʃ (§12) |jaw dʒɔ |gorge gɔrdʒ |go go

abstemious æb'stimɪəs, əb-, -mjəs
abstention æb'stɛnʃən, əb-
absterge æb'stɝdʒ, əb-; ES -'stɜdʒ, -'stɝdʒ;
|-s -ɪz |-d -d |-gent -ənt
abstersion æb'stɝʃən; ES -'stɜʃ-, -'stɝʃ-
abstinence 'æbstənəns |-s -ɪz
abstract adj æb'strækt ('ab,stract 'thought)
abstract n 'æbstrækt
abstract v æb'strækt, əb-; 'abridge,' 'trace
title' 'æbstrækt |-ed -ɪd
abstractedly æb'stræktɪdlɪ
abstraction æb'strækʃən, əb- |-tive -tɪv
abstriction æb'strɪkʃən
abstruse æb'strus, əb-, -'strɪus
absurd əb'sɝd, æb-, -'z-; ES -ɜd, -ɝd; |-ity
-ətɪ
Abukir ˌæbu'kɪr, ˌɑ-, ə'bukɚ; ES -'kɪə(r,
-kə(r
abulia ə'bjulɪə, ə'bɪul-, ˌæbju'lɪə
abundance ə'bʌndəns |abundant ə'bʌndənt
Abury 'ebərɪ = Avebury
abuse n ə'bjus, ə'bɪus |-s -ɪz
abuse v ə'bjuz, ə'bɪuz |-s -ɪz |-d -d
abusive ə'bjusɪv, ə'bɪusɪv
abut ə'bʌt |-ted -ɪd |-ment -mənt |-tal -ļ
Abydos ə'baɪdɑs, -dəs; ES+-dɒs; |-'s -ɪz
abysm ə'bɪzəm |abysmal ə'bɪzmļ |-ally
-zmļɪ
abyss ə'bɪs |-es -ɪz |-al -ļ
Abyssinia ˌæbə'sɪnɪə, -'sɪnjə |-n -n
acacia ə'keʃə
academe ˌækə'dim
academic ˌækə'dɛmɪk |-al -ļ |-ally -ļɪ, -ɪklɪ
academician ə,kædə'mɪʃən, ˌækədə-
academicism ˌækə'dɛmə,sɪzəm
academy ə'kædəmɪ
Acadia ə'kedɪə, -djə |-n -n—see also Cajun
acanthus ə'kænθəs |-es -ɪz |-thi -θaɪ
a cappella 'ɑ kə'pɛlə (It ˌakkɑp'pɛllɑ)
acariasis ˌækə'raɪəsɪs
acarid 'ækərɪd
acatalectic e,kætļ'ɛktɪk, ə-, æ-, ˌekæt]-,
ˌækæt]-
acaudal e'kɔdļ, ə-, æ-
Accad 'ækæd = Akkad
Accadia ə'kedɪə, ə'kɑ-, -djə |-dian -dɪən,
-djən
accede æk'sid, ək- |-ceded -'sidɪd
accelerable æk'sɛlərəb], ək-

accelerando æk,sɛlə'rændo, ək- (It at,tʃele-
'rɑndo)
accelerant æk'sɛlərənt, ək-
accelerate æk'sɛlə,ret, ək- |-rated -,retɪd
acceleration æk,sɛlə'reʃən, ək-, ˌæksɛlə-
accelerative æk'sɛlə,retɪv, ək- |-tor -tɚ; ES
-tə(r
accent n 'æksɛnt, less freq. 'æksņt
accent v 'æksɛnt, æk'sɛnt, ək- |-ed -ɪd
accentual æk'sɛntʃʊəl, ək- |-ly -ɪ
accentuate æk'sɛntʃʊ,et, ək- |-ated -,etɪd
accentuation æk,sɛntʃʊ'eʃən, ək-, ˌæksɛntʃʊ-
accept ək'sɛpt, ɪk-, æk- |-ed -ɪd |-able -əb]
|-bly -blɪ
acceptability ək,sɛptə'bɪlətɪ, ɪk-, æk-,
ˌæksɛptə-
acceptance ək'sɛptəns, ɪk-, æk- |-s -ɪz
acceptation ˌæksɛp'teʃən
access 'æksɛs |-es -ɪz
accessary æk'sɛsərɪ, ək- |-ries -rɪz
accessibility æk,sɛsə'bɪlətɪ, ək-, ˌæksɛsə-
accessible æk'sɛsəb], ək- |-bly -blɪ
accession æk'sɛʃən, ək- |-ed -d
accessorial ˌæksə'sorɪəl, -'sɔr-; S -'sor-
accessory æk'sɛsərɪ, ək-
accidence 'æksədəns |-dent -dənt
accidental ˌæksə'dɛntļ |-ly -ɪ
acclaim ə'klem |acclaimed ə'klemd
acclamation ˌæklə'meʃən
acclimate ə'klaɪmɪt, 'æklə,met |-d -ɪd
acclimation ˌæklə'meʃən
acclimatization ə,klaɪmətə'zeʃən, -aɪ'z-
acclimatize ə'klaɪmə,taɪz |-s -ɪz |-d -d
acclivity ə'klɪvətɪ
accolade ˌækə'led, -'lɑd |-d -ɪd
Accomac 'ækə,mæk
accommodate ə'kɑmə,det; ES+-'kɒm-; |-d
-ɪd
accommodation ə,kɑmə'deʃən; ES+-,kɒm-
accompaniment ə'kʌmpənɪmənt, ə'kʌmpnɪ-
accompanist ə'kʌmpənɪst, ə'kʌmpnɪst
accompany ə'kʌmpənɪ |-nyist -nɪɪst
accomplice ə'kɑmplɪs; ES+-'kɒm-; |-s -ɪz
accomplish ə'kɑmplɪʃ; ES+-'kɒm-; |-es -ɪz
|-ed -t
accord ə'kɔrd; ES ə'kɔəd; |-ed -ɪd
accordance ə'kɔrdņs; ES ə'kɔəd-; |-dant
-dņt
accordion ə'kɔrdɪən; ES ə'kɔədɪən

|full fʊl |tooth tuθ |further 'fɝðɚ; ES 'fɝðə |custom 'kʌstəm |while hwaɪl |how haʊ |toy tɔɪ
|using 'juzɪŋ |fuse fjuz, fɪuz |dish dɪʃ |vision 'vɪʒən |Eden 'idņ |cradle 'kredļ |keep 'em 'kipm̩

accost əˈkɔst, əˈkɒst |-ed -ɪd

accouchement əˈkuʃmɑ̃, -mənt (*Fr* akuʃˈmɑ̃)

accoucheur ˌækuˈʃɝ; ES ˌækuˈʃɜ(r, -ˈʃɝ; (*Fr* akuˈʃœːr)

accoucheuse ˌækuˈʃɜz |-s -ɪz (*Fr* akuˈʃøːz)

account əˈkaʊnt |accounted əˈkaʊntɪd

accountability əˌkaʊntəˈbɪlətɪ

accountable əˈkaʊntəbl̩ |-bly -blɪ

accountancy əˈkaʊntənsɪ |-tant -tənt

accouter, -tre əˈkutɚ; ES əˈkutə(r; |-(e)d -d

accredit əˈkrɛdɪt |-ed -ɪd

accrete əˈkrit, æˈkrit |-d -ɪd

accretion əˈkriʃən, æˈkriʃən

accrual əˈkruəl, əˈkrɪuəl, æ-

accrue əˈkru, əˈkrɪu, æ- |-d -d

accumbency əˈkʌmbənsɪ |-bent -bənt

accumulate əˈkjumjəˌlet, əˈkɪum- |-d -ɪd |-tive -ɪv |-tor -ɚ; ES -ə(r

accumulation əˌkjumjəˈleʃən, əˌkɪum-

accuracy ˈækjərəsɪ

accurate ˈækjərɪt

accursed əˈkɝsɪd, -st; ES əˈkɜs-, əˈkɝs-; |-sedly -sɪdlɪ

accurst əˈkɝst; ES əˈkɜst, əˈkɝst

accusal əˈkjuzl̩, əˈkɪuzl̩

accusation ˌækjəˈzeʃən, ˌækjʊ-

accusative əˈkjuzətɪv, əˈkɪuz-

accusatorial əˌkjuzəˈtorɪəl, əˌkɪuz-, -ˈtɔr-; S -ˈtor-

accusatory əˈkjuzəˌtorɪ, əˈkɪuz-, -ˌtɔrɪ; S -ˌtorɪ

accuse əˈkjuz, əˈkɪuz |-s -ɪz |-d -d

accustom əˈkʌstəm |-ed -d

ace es |aces ˈesɪz

acentric eˈsɛntrɪk, ə-, æ-

acephalous eˈsɛfələs, ə-, æ-

acerbate *v* ˈæsɚˌbet; ES ˈæsə-; |-d -ɪd

acerbate *adj* əˈsɝbɪt; ES əˈsɜb-, əˈsɝb-

acerbity əˈsɝbətɪ; ES əˈsɜb-, əˈsɝb-

acetamide ˌæsəˈtæmaɪd, əˈsɛtəˌmaɪd, -mɪd |-mid -mɪd

acetanilide ˌæsəˈtænl̩ˌaɪd, -l̩ɪd |-lid -l̩ɪd

acetate ˈæsəˌtet |-tated -ˌtetɪd

acetic əˈsitɪk, əˈsɛtɪk

acetify əˈsɛtəˌfaɪ |-fied -ˌfaɪd

acetone ˈæsəˌton

acetyl ˈæsəˌtɪl |-ene əˈsɛtl̩ˌin

Achaea əˈkiə |Achaia əˈkeə, əˈkaɪə |-n -n

Achates əˈketiz |-tes' -tiz

ache ek |ached ekt—*Before 1700 the verb was spelt* ake, *and the noun was pronounced* etʃ, *pl* ˈetʃɪz.

Achean əˈkiən

Acheron ˈækəˌrɑn, -rən; ES+-ˌrɒn

achieve əˈtʃiv |-d -d |-ment -mənt

Achilles əˈkɪliz |-es' -iz

Achitophel əˈkɪtəˌfɛl

achromatic ˌækrəˈmætɪk, -ro- (ˈachroˌmatic ˈlens)

achromic eˈkromɪk, ə-, æ-

acid ˈæsɪd |acidic əˈsɪdɪk, æˈsɪdɪk

acidify əˈsɪdəˌfaɪ, æ- |-fied -ˌfaɪd

acidimeter ˌæsɪˈdɪmətɚ; ES -tə(r

acidity əˈsɪdətɪ, æ-

acidosis ˌæsɪˈdosɪs

acidulate əˈsɪdʒəˌlet, æ- |-d -ɪd |-lous -ləs

aciform ˈæsɪˌfɔrm; ES -ˌfɔəm

acknowledge əkˈnɑlɪdʒ, æk-, ɪk-, -ədʒ; ES+ -ˈnɒl-; |-d -d

aclinic eˈklɪnɪk, ə-, æ-

acme ˈækmɪ, ˈækmi

acne ˈæknɪ, ˈækni

acolyte ˈækəˌlaɪt

Acoma ˈɑkəˌmɑ, -mə

acorn ˈekɚn, ˈekɔrn; ES ˈekən, ˈekɔən;—*The second pron. arises from false etymology.*

acotyledon ˌekɑtl̩ˈidn̩, əˌkɑt-, æˌkɑt-; ES+ -ɒt-; |-ous -ˈidn̩əs, -ˈɛdn̩əs

acoustic əˈkustɪk, əˈkaʊstɪk |-al -l̩ |-ally -l̩ɪ, -ɪklɪ

acoustician ˌækusˈtɪʃən, -kaʊs-, əˌkus-, əˌkaʊs-

acquaint əˈkwent |-ed -ɪd

acquaintance əˈkwentəns |-s -ɪz

acquiesce ˌækwɪˈɛs |-s -ɪz |-d -t |-nce -n̩s |-nt -n̩t

acquire əˈkwaɪr; ES əˈkwaɪə(r; |-d -d |-rable -əbl̩

acquisition ˌækwəˈzɪʃən

acquit əˈkwɪt |-ted -ɪd |-tal -l̩ |-tance -n̩s

acre ˈekɚ; ES ˈekə(r

acreage ˈekərɪdʒ, ˈekrɪdʒ |-s -ɪz

acre-foot ˈekɚˈfʊt; ES ˈekə-; |-feet -ˈfit

acre-inch ˈekɚˈɪntʃ |-es -ɪz

acrid ˈækrɪd |-ine -ˌin, -ɪn |-in -ɪn

acridity æˈkrɪdətɪ, ə-

acrimonious ˌækrəˈmonɪəs, -njəs

acrimony ˈækrəˌmonɪ

Key: See in full §§3–47. bee bi |pity ˈpɪtɪ (§6) |rate ret |yet jɛt |sang sæŋ |angry ˈæŋ·grɪ |bath bæθ; E baθ (§10) |ah ɑ |far fɑr |watch wɑtʃ, wɒtʃ (§12) |jaw dʒɔ |gorge gɔrdʒ |go go

acrobat ˈækrəˌbæt
acrobatic ˌækrəˈbætɪk |-al -l̩ |-ally -l̩ɪ, -ɪklɪ
acrogen ˈækrədʒən, -dʒɪn
acromegalic ˌækromɪˈgælɪk |-megaly -ˈmɛgəlɪ
acrophobia ˌækrəˈfobɪə
acropolis əˈkrɑpəlɪs; ES+-ˈkrɒp-; |-lises
    -lɪsɪz |Gk pl -leis -ˌles
across əˈkrɔs, əˈkrɒs
acrostic əˈkrɔstɪk, əˈkrɒs-
act ækt |acted ˈæktɪd
Actaeon ækˈtiən
actinic ækˈtɪnɪk |-ally -l̩ɪ, -ɪklɪ
actinism ˈæktɪnˌɪzəm
actinium ækˈtɪnɪəm
action ˈækʃən |-able -əbl̩, -ʃnəbl̩ |-bly -blɪ
Actium ˈæktɪəm, ˈækʃɪəm
activate ˈæktəˌvet |-vated -ˌvetɪd
activation ˌæktəˈveʃən
active ˈæktɪv |-vism -ˌɪzəm |-vist -ɪst
activity ækˈtɪvətɪ
actor ˈæktɚ; ES ˈæktə(r
actress ˈæktrɪs |-es -ɪz
actual ˈæktʃʊəl, -tʃʊl
actuality ˌæktʃʊˈælətɪ
actually ˈæktʃʊəlɪ, -tʃʊlɪ, -tʃəlɪ
actuarial ˌæktʃʊˈɛrɪəl, -ˈer-
actuary ˈæktʃʊˌɛrɪ
actuate ˈæktʃʊˌet |-ated -ˌetɪd
acuity əˈkjuətɪ, əˈkɪuətɪ
acumen əˈkjumɪn, əˈkɪu-, -mən
acute əˈkjut, əˈkɪut
acyclic eˈsaɪklɪk, eˈsɪk-
A.D. ˈeˈdi, ˈænoˈdɑməˌnaɪ; ES+-ˈdɒm-
ad æd
Ada(h) ˈedə
adage ˈædɪdʒ |-s -ɪz
adagio əˈdɑdʒo, əˈdɑdʒɪˌo (It ɑˈdɑːdʒo)
Adair əˈdɛr, əˈdær; E əˈdeə(r, ES əˈdæə(r
Adaline ˈædl̩ˌaɪn, -ˌin
Adam ˈædəm |Adams ˈædəmz |Adams's
    ˈædəmzɪz
adamant ˈædəˌmænt
adamantine ˌædəˈmæntɪn, -tin, -taɪn
Adamic, Louis ˈluɪˈædəmɪk, ˈluɪs-, ˈlɪuɪ(s)-
adapt əˈdæpt |-ed -ɪd
adaptability əˌdæptəˈbɪlətɪ
adaptable əˈdæptəbl̩
adaptation ˌædəpˈteʃən, ˌædæp-
adaptive əˈdæptɪv

add æd |added ˈædɪd
Addams ˈædəmz |Addams's ˈædəmzɪz
addend ˈædɛnd, əˈdɛnd
addendum əˈdɛndəm, æ- |-da -də
adder ˈædɚ; ES ˈædə(r
addible ˈædəbl̩
addict n ˈædɪkt
addict v əˈdɪkt |-ed -ɪd |-ction -kʃən
Addis Ababa ˈædɪsˈɑbəbə, ˈɑdɪs-
Addison ˈædəsn̩
additament əˈdɪtəmənt
addition əˈdɪʃən, æ- |-al -l̩ |-ally -l̩ɪ
additive ˈædətɪv
addle ˈædl̩ |-d -d |-ling ˈædl̩ɪŋ, ˈædlɪŋ
addlebrain ˈædl̩ˌbren
addlebrained ˈædl̩ˈbrend (ˈaddleˌbrained ˈboy)
addleheaded ˈædl̩ˈhɛdɪd
addlepated ˈædl̩ˈpetɪd
address n əˈdrɛs, ˈædrɛs |-es -ɪz
address v əˈdrɛs |-es -ɪz |-ed -t
addressee ədrɛsˈi, ˌædrɛsˈi
adduce əˈdjus, əˈdɪus, əˈdus |-s -ɪz |-d -t
adducible, -ceable əˈdjusəbl̩, əˈdɪus-, əˈdus-
adduct əˈdʌkt |-ed -ɪd
adduction əˈdʌkʃən |-tive -tɪv |-tor -tɚ; ES
    -tə(r
Adel eˈdɛl
Adela ˈædlə
Adelaide ˈædl̩ˌed
Adelbert ˈædl̩bɚt, əˈdɛlbɚt, college əˈdɛlbɚt;
    ES -bət
Adelina ˌædl̩ˈaɪnə, -ˈinə
Adeline ˈædl̩ˌaɪn, -ˌin
Adelphi əˈdɛlfɪ, -faɪ
Aden ˈedn̩, ˈɑdn̩
adenoid ˈædn̩ˌɔɪd |-ism -ˌɪzəm
adenoidal ˌædn̩ˈɔɪdl̩
adept n ˈædɛpt, əˈdɛpt
adept adj əˈdɛpt
adequacy ˈædəkwəsɪ |-quate -kwɪt
adhere ədˈhɪr, æd-; ES -ˈhɪə(r, S+-ˈhɛə(r;
    |-nce -əns |-nt -ənt
adhesion ədˈhiʒən, æd- |-sive -sɪv
adhibit ædˈhɪbɪt |-ed -ɪd
ad hoc ˈædˈhɑk; ES+-ˈhɒk
ad hominem ˈædˈhɑməˌnɛm; ES+-ˈhɒm-
adieu əˈdju, əˈdɪu, əˈdu
ad infinitum ˌædˌɪnfəˈnaɪtəm
ad interim ˈædˈɪntərɪm

|full fʊl |tooth tuθ |further ˈfɝðɚ; ES ˈfɝðə |custom ˈkʌstəm |while hwaɪl |how haʊ |toy tɔɪ
|using ˈjuzɪŋ |fuse fjuz, fɪuz |dish dɪʃ |vision ˈvɪʒən |Eden ˈidn̩ |cradle ˈkredl̩ |keep 'em ˈkipm̩

adipose ˈædəˌpos
adiposity ˌædəˈpɑsətɪ; ES+-ˈpɒs-
Adirondack ˌædəˈrɑndæk; ES+-ˈrɒn-
adit ˈædɪt
adjacency əˈdʒesn̩sɪ |-cent -sn̩t
adjectival ˌædʒɪkˈtaɪvl̩, ˈædʒɪktɪvl̩ |-ly -ɪ
adjective ˈædʒɪktɪv |-ly -lɪ
adjoin əˈdʒɔɪn |-ed -d |-edly -ɪdlɪ, əˈdʒɔɪndlɪ
adjourn əˈdʒɝn; ES əˈdʒɜn, əˈdʒɝn; |-ed -d
adjudge əˈdʒʌdʒ |-s -ɪz |-d -d
adjudicate əˈdʒudɪˌket, əˈdʒɪu- |-d -ɪd
adjudication əˌdʒudɪˈkeʃən, əˌdʒɪu-
adjunct ˈædʒʌŋkt
adjuration ˌædʒʊˈreʃən
adjure əˈdʒʊr, əˈdʒɪur; ES -ə(r; |-d -d
adjust əˈdʒʌst |-ed -ɪd |-able -əbl̩ |-bly
  -blɪ
adjutancy ˈædʒətənsɪ |-tant -tənt
Adler ˈɑdlɚ, ˈæd-; ES -lə(r
ad-lib v ædˈlɪb |-bed -d
ad libitum ˈædˈlɪbɪtəm
administer ədˈmɪnəstɚ, æd-; ES -tə(r; |-ed
  -d |-ing -tərɪŋ, -trɪŋ
administrable ədˈmɪnəstrəbl̩, æd-
administrate ədˈmɪnəˌstret, æd- |-d -ɪd |-tive
  -ɪv
administration ədˌmɪnəˈstreʃən, æd-, ˌæd-
  mɪnə-
administrator ədˈmɪnəˌstretɚ, æd-; ES -tə(r
administratress ədˌmɪnəˈstretrɪs, ˌædmɪnə-
  |-es -ɪz
administratrix ədˌmɪnəˈstretrɪks, ˌædmɪnə-
  |-es -ɪz |-trices -trɪˌsiz
admirable ˈædmərəbl̩ |-bly -blɪ
admiral ˈædmərəl |-ty -tɪ
admiration ˌædməˈreʃən
admire ədˈmaɪr; ES -ˈmaɪə(r; |-d -d |-dly
  -ɪdlɪ, -dlɪ
admissibility ədˌmɪsəˈbɪlətɪ, æd-
admissible ədˈmɪsəbl̩, æd- |-bly -blɪ
admission ədˈmɪʃən, æd-
admit ədˈmɪt, æd- |-ted -ɪd |-tance -n̩s
admix ædˈmɪks, əd- |-es -ɪz |-ed -t
admixture ædˈmɪkstfɚ, əd-; ES -tʃə(r
admonish ədˈmɑnɪʃ, æd-; ES+-ˈmɒn-; |-es
  -ɪz |-ed -t
admonition ˌædməˈnɪʃən
admonitory ədˈmɑnəˌtorɪ, æd-, -ˌtɔrɪ; S
  -ˌtorɪ, ES+-ˈmɒn-

ad nauseam ˈædˈnɔʃɪˌæm, often -ˈnɔz-,
  -ˈnɑs-
ado əˈdu
adobe əˈdobɪ
adolescence ˌædl̩ˈɛsn̩s |-cy -ɪ |-cent -sn̩t
Adolf, -lph ˈædalf, ˈædɒlf, ˈed-
Adolphus əˈdɑlfəs, əˈdɒl- |-ˈs -ɪz
Adonais ˌædəˈne·ɪs |-ˈs -ɪz
Adonijah ˌædəˈnaɪdʒə
Adonis əˈdonɪs |-ˈs -ɪz
adopt əˈdɑpt; ES+əˈdɒpt; |-ed -ɪd
adoptability əˌdɑptəˈbɪlətɪ; ES+əˌdɒp-
adoptable əˈdɑptəbl̩; ES+əˈdɒp-
adoption əˈdɑpʃən; ES+əˈdɒp-; |-tive -tɪv
adorable əˈdorəbl̩, əˈdɔr-; S əˈdor-; |-bly
  -blɪ
adoration ˌædəˈreʃən
adore əˈdor, əˈdɔr; ES əˈdoə(r, E+əˈdɔə(r;
  |-d -d
adorn əˈdɔrn; ES əˈdɔən; |-ed -d
adown əˈdaun
adrenal ædˈrinl̩ |-in ædˈrɛnl̩ɪn
Adrian ˈedrɪən |Adriana ˌedrɪˈænə, -ˈenə
Adrianople ˌedrɪənˈopl̩
Adriatic ˌedrɪˈætɪk
adrift əˈdrɪft
adroit əˈdrɔɪt
adsorb ædˈsɔrb; ES -ˈsɔəb; |-ed -d
adsorption ædˈsɔrpʃən; ES -ˈsɔəpʃən
adulate ˈædʒəˌlet |-d -ɪd |-tion ˌædʒəˈleʃən
adulatory ˈædʒələˌtorɪ, -ˌtɔrɪ; S -ˌtorɪ
Adullam əˈdʌləm |-ite -ˌaɪt
adult əˈdʌlt, ˈædʌlt (ˈaˌdult ˈschool)
adulterant əˈdʌltərənt, -trənt
adulterate adj əˈdʌltərɪt, -ˌret
adulterate v əˈdʌltəˌret |-d -ɪd
adulteration əˌdʌltəˈreʃən
adulterer əˈdʌltərɚ; ES -tərə(r; |-tery -tərɪ,
  -trɪ
adulteress əˈdʌltərɪs, -trɪs |-es -ɪz
adulterine əˈdʌltərɪn, -ˌraɪn
adulterous əˈdʌltərəs, -trəs
adumbrate ædˈʌmbret, ˈædəmˌbret |-d -ɪd
adumbration ˌædəmˈbreʃən, ˌædʌm-
adust əˈdʌst
ad valorem ˌædvəˈlorəm, -ˈlɔrəm, -ɛm; S
  -ˈlor-
advance ədˈvæns; E+-ˈvɑns, -ˈvɒns; |-s -ɪz
  |-d -t

Key: *See in full §§3–47.* bee **bi** |pity ˈpɪtɪ (§6) |rate ret |yet jɛt |sang sæŋ |angry ˈæŋ·grɪ
|bath bæθ; E baθ (§10) |ah ɑ |far fɑr |watch wɑtʃ, wɒtʃ (§12) |jaw dʒɔ |gorge gɔrdʒ |go go

advantage əd'væntɪdʒ; E+-'van-, -'vɑn-;
|-s -ɪz |-d -d
advantageous ˌædvən'tedʒəs, -væn-
advent, A- 'ædvɛnt |-ism -ˌɪzəm |-ist -ɪst
adventitious ˌædvɛn'tɪʃəs, ˌædvən-
adventive æd'vɛntɪv
adventure əd'vɛntʃɚ; ES -tʃə(r; |-d -d |-ring
-'vɛntʃərɪŋ, -'vɛntʃrɪŋ |-rous -tʃərəs, -tʃrəs
adventurer əd'vɛntʃərɚ; ES -tʃərə(r
adventuresome əd'vɛntʃɚsəm; ES -'vɛn-
tʃəsəm
adventuress əd'vɛntʃərɪs, -tʃrɪs |-es -ɪz
adverb 'ædvɝb; ES 'ædvɜb, -vɝb
adverbial əd'vɝbɪəl, æd-, -bjəl; ES -'vɜb-,
-'vɝb-; |-ly -ɪ
adversary 'ædvɚˌsɛrɪ; ES 'ædvə-
adversative əd'vɝsətɪv, æd-; ES -'vɜs-,
-'vɝs-
adverse əd'vɝs, æd-, 'ædvɝs; ES -ɜs, -ɝs;
('winds ad'verse, 'adˌverse 'winds)
adversity əd'vɝsətɪ; ES -'vɜs-, -'vɝs-
advert əd'vɝt, æd-; ES -'vɜt, -'vɝt; |-ed -ɪd
advertence əd'vɝtns, æd-; ES -'vɜt-, -'vɝt-;
|-cy -ɪ |-tent -tnt
advertise, -ize 'ædvɚˌtaɪz, ˌædvɚ'taɪz; ES
-və-; |-s -ɪz |-d -d
advertisement, -tize- ˌædvɚ'taɪzmənt, əd-
'vɝtɪz-, -tɪs-; ES ˌædvə-, -'vɝt-, -'vɝt-
advertising, -tiz- n 'ædvɚˌtaɪzɪŋ; ES 'ædvə-
advice əd'vaɪs |-s -ɪz
advisability ədˌvaɪzə'bɪlətɪ
advisable əd'vaɪzəbḷ |-bly -blɪ
advise əd'vaɪz |-s -ɪz |-d -d |-dly -ɪdlɪ
advisement əd'vaɪzmənt
adviser, -sor əd'vaɪzɚ; ES -'vaɪzə(r; |-sory
-zərɪ
advocacy 'ædvəkəsɪ
advocate n 'ædvəkɪt -ˌket
advocate v 'ædvəˌket |-d -ɪd
advowson əd'vauzn̩
adz, adze ædz |-(e)s -ɪz |-(e)d -d
adzuki æd'zukɪ
Aeacus 'iəkəs |-'s -ɪz
Aëdes e'idiz |-des' -diz
aedile 'idaɪl
Aegean i'dʒiən |-geon -'dʒiən
Aegeus myth. 'idʒjus, -dʒus |-'s -ɪz
Aegina i'dʒaɪnə
aegis 'idʒɪs |-es -ɪz

Aegisthus i'dʒɪsθəs |-'s -ɪz
Aegospotami, -mos ˌigəs'pɑtəˌmaɪ, -məs; ES
+-'pɒt-
Ælfred 'ælfrɪd, 'ælfrəd, 'ælfɚd; ES -frɪd,
-frəd, -fəd
Ælfric 'ælfrɪk
Aemilia i'mɪlɪə |-lius -lɪəs |-lius's -lɪəsɪz
Aeneas ɪ'niəs, i- |-'s -ɪz
Aeneid ɪ'niɪd, i-, -əd
Aeolia i'olɪə |-n -n
Aeolis 'iəlɪs |-'s -ɪz |-t -t |-m -ˌlɪzəm
Aeolus 'iələs, Vt mt. loc. i'oləs |-'s -ɪz
aeon 'iən, 'iɑn; ES+'iɒn
aerate 'eəˌret |-d -ɪd |-tion ˌeə'reʃən
aerial 'airy' e'ɪrɪəl, 'ɛrɪəl, 'ærɪəl; S e'ɪr-,
'ær-; radio 'ɛrɪəl, 'erɪəl |-ly -ɪ
aerie 'ɛrɪ, 'ærɪ, 'ɪrɪ; S 'ærɪ, 'ɪrɪ
aeriform e'ɪrəˌfɔrm, 'ɛrə-, 'ærə-; ES e'ɪrə-
ˌfɔəm, 'ærə-, E+'ɛrə-
aerify e'ɪrəˌfaɪ, 'ɛrə-, 'ærə-; S e'ɪrə-, 'ærə-;
|-fied -ˌfaɪd
aerobic ˌeə'robɪk, ɛ'robɪk |-ally -ḷɪ
aerodrome 'ɛrəˌdrom, 'ærə-; S 'ærə-
aerodynamics ˌɛrodaɪ'næmɪks, ˌæro-, ˌeəro-;
S ˌæro-, ˌeəro-
aerology ˌeə'rɑlədʒɪ; ES+-'rɒl-
aeromechanic ˌɛromɪ'kænɪk, ˌæro-, ˌeəro-; S
ˌæro-, ˌeəro-
aerometer ˌeə'rɑmətɚ; ES -'rɑmətə(r, -'rɒm-
aeronaut 'ɛrəˌnɔt, 'ærə-; S 'ærə-
aeronautic ˌɛrə'nɔtɪk, ˌærə-; S ˌærə-
aeroplane 'ɛrəˌplen, 'ærə-; S 'ærə-
aerostat 'ɛrəˌstæt, 'ærə-; S 'ærə-
aerostatic ˌɛrə'stætɪk, ˌærə-; S ˌærə-
aerostation ˌɛro'steʃən, ˌæro-; S ˌæro-
aery 'airy' 'ɛrɪ, 'ærɪ; S 'ærɪ
aery 'nest' 'ɛrɪ, 'ærɪ, 'ɪrɪ; S 'ærɪ, 'ɪrɪ
Aeschines 'ɛskəˌniz |-'s -ɪz
Aeschylus 'ɛskələs |-'s -ɪz
Aesculapius ˌɛskjə'lepɪəs |-'s -ɪz |-pian
-pɪən
Aesop 'isəp, 'isɑp; ES+'isɒp
aesthesia ɛs'θiʒə, -ʒɪə |-thesis -'θisɪs
aesthete 'ɛsθit
aesthetic ɛs'θɛtɪk |-al -ḷ |-ally -ḷɪ, -ɪklɪ
aestheticism ɛs'θɛtəˌsɪzəm |-thetics -'θɛtɪks
aestival 'ɛstəvḷ, ɛs'taɪvḷ
aestivate 'ɛstəˌvet |-d -ɪd |-tion ˌɛstə'veʃən
aes triplex, A- T- 'iz'traɪplɛks

|full fʊl |tooth tuθ |further 'fɝðɚ; ES 'fɝðə |custom 'kʌstəm |while hwaɪl |how hau |toy tɔɪ
|using 'juzɪŋ |fuse fjuz, fɪuz |dish dɪʃ |vision 'vɪʒən |Eden 'idn̩ |cradle 'kredḷ |keep 'em 'kipm̩

aestuary ˈɛstʃʊˌɛrɪ
aetheling ˈæθəlɪŋ, ˈæðəlɪŋ (OE ˈæð-)
Æthelstan ˈæθəlˌstæn, ˈæðəl-, -stən (OE ˈæð-)
Aethiop ˈiθɪˌɑp; ES+-ˌɒp
Aethiopia ˌiθɪˈopɪə |-n -n
Aethiopic ˌiθɪˈɑpɪk, -ˈopɪk; ES+-ˈɒpɪk
aetiology ˌitɪˈɑlədʒɪ; ES+-ˈɒl-
Aetna ˈɛtnə
afar əˈfɑr; ES əˈfɑː(r, E+əˈfɑː(r
affability ˌæfəˈbɪlətɪ
affable ˈæfəbl̩ |-bly -blɪ
affair əˈfɛr, əˈfær; E əˈfɛə(r, ES əˈfæə(r
affect əˈfɛkt |-ed -ɪd
affectation ˌæfɪkˈteʃən, ˌæfɛk-
affection əˈfɛkʃən |-ed -d |-ate -ɪt
affective əˈfɛktɪv, æˈf-
afferent ˈæfərənt
affiance əˈfaɪəns |-s -ɪz |-d -t |-ant -ənt
affidavit ˌæfəˈdevɪt
affiliate n, adj əˈfɪlɪɪt, -ˌet
affiliate v əˈfɪlɪˌet |-d -ɪd
affiliation əˌfɪlɪˈeʃən
affinity əˈfɪnətɪ
affirm əˈfɝm; ES əˈfɝm, əˈfɝm; |-ed -d
affirmable əˈfɝməbl̩; ES əˈfɝm-, əˈfɝm-; |-bly -blɪ
affirmation ˌæfəˈmeʃən; ES ˌæfə-
affirmative əˈfɝmətɪv; ES əˈfɝm-, əˈfɝm-
affirmatory əˈfɝməˌtorɪ, -ˌtɔrɪ; ES əˈfɝmə-ˌtorɪ, əˈfɝm-, E+-ˌtɔrɪ
affix n ˈæfɪks |-es -ɪz
affix v əˈfɪks |-es -ɪz |-ed -t
afflatus əˈfletəs
afflict əˈflɪkt |-ed -ɪd
affliction əˈflɪkʃən |-tive -tɪv
affluence ˈæfluəns, -flɪu- |-ent -ənt
afflux ˈæflʌks |-es -ɪz
afford əˈford, əˈfɔrd; ES əˈfoəd, E+əˈfɔəd; |-ed -ɪd
afforest əˈfɔrɪst, əˈfɑr-, əˈfɒr- |-ed -ɪd
affranchise əˈfræntʃaɪz |-s -ɪz |-d -d
affranchisement əˈfræntʃɪzmənt
affray əˈfre |-ed -d
affricate n ˈæfrɪkɪt
affricate v ˈæfrɪˌket |-d -ɪd
affricative əˈfrɪkətɪv
affright əˈfraɪt |-ed -ɪd
affront əˈfrʌnt |-ed -ɪd

affy əˈfaɪ |affied əˈfaɪd
afghan, A- ˈæfgən, -gæn
Afghanistan æfˈgænəˌstæn, ˌæfgænəˈstæn
afield əˈfild
afire əˈfaɪr; ES əˈfaɪə(r
aflame əˈflem
afloat əˈflot
aflutter əˈflʌtɚ; ES əˈflʌtə(r
afoot əˈfut
afore əˈfor, əˈfɔr; ES əˈfoə(r, E+əˈfɔə(r
afore-mentioned əˈforˈmɛnʃənd, əˈfɔr-; ES see afore; (aˈfore-ˌmentioned ˈact)
aforesaid əˈforˌsɛd, əˈfɔr-; ES see afore
aforethought əˈforˌθɔt, əˈfɔr-; ES see afore
aforetime əˈforˌtaɪm, əˈfɔr-; ES see afore
a fortiori ˈeˌforʃɪˈoraɪ, -ˌfɔrʃɪˈɔr-; ES -ˌfoəʃɪˈoraɪ, E+-ˌfɔəʃɪˈɔraɪ
afoul əˈfaul
afraid əˈfred; S+əˈfrɛd
afreet ˈæfrit
afresh əˈfrɛʃ
Afric ˈæfrɪk |-a -ə |-an -ən
Afrikaans ˌæfrɪˈkɑnz, -ˈkɑns
Afrikander ˌæfrɪˈkændɚ; ES -də(r
Afro-American ˈæfroəˈmɛrəkən
aft æft; E+aft, ɑft
after ˈæftɚ; ES ˈæftə(r, E+ˈaf-, ˈɑf-
afterbirth ˈæftɚˌbɝθ; ES ˈæftəˌbɝθ, ˈæftəˌbɝθ, E+ˈaf-, ˈɑf-
afterbrain ˈæftɚˌbren; ES see after
afterdamp ˈæftɚˌdæmp; ES see after
afterdeck ˈæftɚˌdɛk; ES see after
after-dinner adj ˈæftɚˈdɪnɚ; ES ˈæftəˈdɪnə(r, E+ˈaf-, ˈɑf-; (ˈafter-ˌdinner ˈmints)
aftereffect ˈæftərəˌfɛkt; E+ˈaf-, ˈɑf-
afterglow ˈæftɚˌglo; ES see after
afterimage ˈæftɚˌɪmɪdʒ; E+ˈaf-, ˈɑf-; |-s -ɪz
afterlife ˈæftɚˌlaɪf; ES see after
aftermath ˈæftɚˌmæθ; ES see after; |-ths -θs
aftermost ˈæftɚˌmost, -məst; ES see after
afternoon ˌæftɚˈnun; ES see after; (ˈafterˌnoon ˈtea)
aftertaste ˈæftɚˌtest; ES see after
afterthought ˈæftɚˌθɔt; ES see after
afterward ˈæftɚwɚd; ES ˈæftəwəd, E+ˈaf-, ˈɑf-; |-s -z— A dissimilated pron. ˈæftəwɚd is often heard (§121).
Agag ˈegæg

Key: See in full §§3–47. bee **bi** |pity ˈpɪtɪ (§6) |rate **ret** |yet **jɛt** |sang **sæŋ** |angry ˈæŋ·grɪ |bath **bæθ**; E **baθ** (§10) |ah **ɑ** |far **fɑr** |watch **wɑtʃ, wɒtʃ** (§12) |jaw **dʒɔ** |gorge **gɔrdʒ** |go **go**

again ə'gɛn, *less freq. or poet.* ə'gen

against ə'gɛnst, *less freq. or poet.* ə'genst

Agamemnon ˌægə'mɛmnən, -nan; ES+-nɒn

agape ə'gep, ə'gæp

agar 'egɑr, 'egɚ, 'agɑr; ES -gɑ:(r, -gə(r

agar-agar 'egɑr'egɑr; ES 'egɑr'egɑ:(r

agaric 'ægərɪk, ə'gærɪk

Agassiz 'ægəsɪ |Agassiz's 'ægəsɪz

agate *n* 'ægɪt, 'ægət

agate *adv* ə'get

Agatha 'ægəθə

agave, A- ə'gevɪ

Agawam 'ægəˌwɔm, -ˌwɑm, -ˌwɒm

agaze ə'gez

age edʒ |ages 'edʒɪz |*past & pptc* aged edʒd

-age *unstressed ending* -ɪdʒ, -ədʒ. *In the vocab. when only* -ɪdʒ *is given, it is to be understood that many speakers pronounce* -ədʒ.

aged *'old'* 'edʒɪd, *'of the age of'* edʒd

agelong 'edʒ'lɔŋ, -'lɒŋ; S+-'lɑŋ; ('ageˌlong 'drift)

agency 'edʒənsɪ |agent 'edʒənt

agenda *pl* ə'dʒɛndə |*sg* agendum ə'dʒɛndəm

ageratum ˌædʒə'retəm

Ageratum ə'dʒɛrətəm, ˌædʒə'retəm

agglomerate *adj, n* ə'glɑmərɪt, -ˌret; ES+ -'glɒm-

agglomerate *v* ə'glɑməˌret; ES+-'glɒm-; |-d -ɪd

agglomeration əˌglɑmə'reʃən; ES+-ˌglɒm-

agglutinate *adj* ə'glutn̩ɪt, -'glɪu-, -ˌet

agglutinate *v* ə'glutn̩ˌet, -'glɪu- |-d -ɪd |-tive -tɪv

agglutination əˌglutn̩'eʃən, -ˌglɪu-

aggrandize 'ægrənˌdaɪz, ə'græn- |-s -ɪz |-d -d

aggrandizement ə'grændɪzmənt

aggravate 'ægrəˌvet |-d -ɪd |-tion ˌægrə'veʃən

aggregate *n, adj* 'ægrɪgɪt, -ˌget

aggregate *v* 'ægrɪˌget |-d -ɪd |-tive -ɪv

aggregation ˌægrɪ'geʃən

aggregatory 'ægrɪgəˌtorɪ, -ˌtɔrɪ; S -ˌtorɪ

aggress ə'grɛs |-es -ɪz |-ed -t

aggression ə'grɛʃən |-sive -sɪv

aggressor ə'grɛsɚ; ES ə'grɛsə(r

aggrieve ə'griv |-d -d |-dly -ɪdlɪ

aghast ə'gæst; E+ə'gast, ə'gɑst

agile 'ædʒəl, 'ædʒɪl |-ly -dʒɪllɪ, -dʒɪlɪ

agility ə'dʒɪlətɪ

Agincourt 'ædʒɪnˌkort, -ˌkɔrt; ES -ˌkoət, E+ -ˌkɔət

agio 'ædʒo, 'ædʒɪˌo (*It* 'ɑ:dʒo)

agiotage 'ædʒətɪdʒ, 'ædʒɪə-

agitate 'ædʒəˌtet |-d -ɪd |-tor -ɚ; ES -ə(r

agitation ˌædʒə'teʃən

Aglaia ə'gleə

aglet 'æglɪt

agley ə'glaɪ=agly *'asquint'*

aglow ə'glo

agly ə'glaɪ=agley—*in Burns rimed with joy, then pronounced* dʒaɪ

agnat 'ægnæt |agnate 'ægnet

Agnes 'ægnɪs, -nəs |-'s -ɪz

Agnew 'ægnju, -nɪu, -nu

agnostic æg'nɑstɪk; ES+-'nɒs-; |-ism -təˌsɪzəm

Agnus Dei 'ægnəs'diaɪ

ago ə'go

agog ə'gɑg, ə'gɒg

agonize 'ægəˌnaɪz |-s -ɪz |-d -d

agony 'ægənɪ |-ied -d

agora 'ægərə |-s -z |-rae -ˌri

agoraphobia ˌægərə'fobɪə

agouti ə'gutɪ

agrarian ə'grɛrɪən, ə'grer- |-ism -ˌɪzəm

agree ə'gri |-d -d |-able -əbl̩ |-bly -blɪ

agreeability əˌgriə'bɪlətɪ

Agricola ə'grɪkələ

agricultural ˌægrɪ'kʌltʃərəl |-ly -ɪ |-ist -ɪst

agriculture 'ægrɪˌkʌltʃɚ; ES -tʃə(r

agriculturist ˌægrɪ'kʌltʃərɪst

agrimony 'ægrəˌmonɪ

Agrippa ə'grɪpə

agrology ə'grɑlədʒɪ; ES+-'grɒl-

agronomic ˌægrə'nɑmɪk; ES+-'nɒm-; |-al -l̩

agronomy ə'grɑnəmɪ; ES+-'grɒn-; |-mist -mɪst

aground ə'graʊnd

ague 'egju |-d -d |aguing 'egjuɪŋ

Aguecheek 'egjuˌtʃik

aguinaldo, A- ˌagi'naldo (*Sp* ˌagi'naldo)

ah ɑ

aha ə'hɑ, ɑ'hɑ, 'ɑ'hɑ

Ahab 'ehæb

Ahasuerus əˌhæzju'ɪrəs, əˌhæʒʊ- |-'s -ɪz

Ahaz 'ehæz |-'s -ɪz

ahead ə'hɛd

ahem ə'hɛm, ˀm̩ˀm̩ˀm̩ˀm̩ *&c.*

|full fʊl |tooth tuθ |further 'fɝðɚ; ES 'fɝðə |custom 'kʌstəm |while hwaɪl |how haʊ |toy tɔɪ |using 'juzɪŋ |fuse fjuz, fɪuz |dish dɪʃ |vision 'vɪʒən |Eden 'idn̩ |cradle 'kredl̩ |keep 'em 'kipm̩

Aherne əˈhɝn; ES əˈhɜn, əˈhɝn
Ahithophel, Ahito- əˈhɪtəˌfɛl
Ahmed ˈɑmɪd, ˈɑmɛd
ahorse əˈhɔrs; ES əˈhɔəs
ahorseback əˈhɔrsˌbæk; ES əˈhɔəs-
Ahoskie əˈhɑskɪ; ES+əˈhɒs-
ahoy əˈhɔɪ
ahungered əˈhʌŋgəd; ES -gəd
Ai ˈeaɪ
aid ed |aided ˈedɪd
Aïda ɑˈidə
aide ed
aide-de-camp ˈeddəˈkæmp, ˈeddəˈkã (Fr
ɛddəˈkã)
aides-de-camp ˈedzdəˈkæmp, ˈedzdəˈkã (Fr
ɛddəˈkã)
aiglet ˈeglɪt
aigrette ˈegrɛt, eˈgrɛt
Aiken ˈekɪn, -ən
ail el |ailed eld |-ment -mənt
ailanthus, A- eˈlænθəs |-es -ɪz
Aileen ˈelin, ˈaɪ-, eˈlin, aɪ-
aileron ˈeləˌrɑn; ES+-ˌrɒn
Ailsa ˈelsə, Sc ˈɛlsə
aim em |aimed emd
ain't ent
Ainu ˈaɪnu
air ɛr, ær; E ɛə(r, ES æə(r
air-cool ˈɛrˌkul, ˈær-; ES see air; |-ed -d
air-cooled adj ˈɛrˈkuld, ˈær-; ES see air;
(ˈair-ˌcooled ˈmotor)
aircraft ˈɛrˌkræft, ˈær-; E ˈɛə-, ˈæə-, -ˌkraft,
-ˌkraft; S ˈæəˌkræft
airdrome ˈɛrˌdrom, ˈær-; ES see air
air-dry ˈɛrˌdraɪ, ˈær-; ES see air; |-ied -d
Airedale ˈɛrˌdel, ˈær-; ES see air
airfield ˈɛrˌfild, ˈær-; ES see air
airfoil ˈɛrˌfɔɪl, ˈær-; ES see air
airily ˈɛrəlɪ, ˈær-, -ɪlɪ; S ˈær-
airplane ˈɛrˌplen, ˈær-; ES see air
airport ˈɛrˌport, ˈær-, -ˌpɔrt; E ˈɛəˌpoət,
ˈæə-, -ˌpɔət; S ˈæəˌpoət
airproof ˈɛrˈpruf, ˈær-; ES see air
airship ˈɛrˌʃɪp, ˈær-; ES see air
airsick ˈɛrˌsɪk, ˈær-; ES see air
airt ɛrt, ært, ert; E ɛət, ES æət, eət
airtight ˈɛrˈtaɪt, ˈær-; ES see air
airway ˈɛrˌwe, ˈær-; ES see air
airy ˈɛrɪ, ˈærɪ; S ˈærɪ

aisle aɪl |aisled aɪld |-less ˈaɪllɪs
Aisne en (Fr. ɛ:n)
aitch etʃ |aitches ˈetʃɪz |-bone -ˌbon
Aix eks |-'s -ɪz (Fr ɛks)
Aix-la-Chapelle ˈekslɑʃæˈpɛl (Fr ɛkslaʃaˈpɛl)
ajar əˈdʒɑr; ES əˈdʒɑ:(r, E+əˈdʒa:(r
Ajax ˈedʒæks |-'s -ɪz
Akbar ˈækbɑr; ES -bɑ:(r, E+-ba:(r
ake 'to ache' ek |-d -t
À Kempis əˈkɛmpɪs |-'s -ɪz
Akenside ˈekɪnˌsaɪd, ˈekən-
akimbo əˈkɪmbo
akin əˈkɪn
Akkad ˈækæd
Akkadian əˈkedɪən, əˈkɑd-
Akron ˈækrən |-ite -ˌaɪt
à la ˈɑlə, ˈɑlɑ (Fr ala)
Alabama ˌæləˈbæmə |-n -n |-mian -mɪən
alabamine ˌæləˈbæmin, -ɪn
alabaster ˈæləˌbæstə; ES -tə(r, E+-ˌbas-,
-ˌbas-
à la carte ˌɑləˈkɑrt; ES -ˈkɑ:t, E+-ˈka:t;
(Fr alaˈkart)
alack əˈlæk
alacrity əˈlækrətɪ
Aladdin əˈlædɪn, əˈlædn̩
Alamannic ˌæləˈmænɪk
alameda ˌæləˈmedə
Alameda ˌæləˈmidə, -ˈmedə (Sp ˌalaˈmeðə)
alamo ˈæləˌmo, ˈɑl- (Sp ˈalaˌmo)
Alamo ˈæləˌmo
alamode ˌɑləˈmod, ˌæglə- (Fr alaˈmöd)
Åland ˈɑlənd, ˈɔ-
Alarbus əˈlɑrbəs; ES əˈlɑ:b-; |-'s -ɪz
Alaric ˈælərɪk
alarm əˈlɑrm; ES əˈlɑ:m, E+əˈla:m
alarum əˈlærəm, əˈlɛrəm; S əˈlærəm
alary ˈelərɪ, ˈæl-
alas əˈlæs; E+əˈlas, əˈlɑs
Alaska əˈlæskə |-n -n
Alastor əˈlæstə, -tɔr; ES -tə(r, -tɔə(r
alate ˈelet |alated ˈeletɪd
alb ælb
Alban ˈɔlbən
alban chem. ˈælbən
Albania ælˈbenɪə, -njə |-n -n
Albans ˈɔlbənz |-'s -ɪz
Albany ˈɔlbənɪ
albatross ˈælbəˌtrɔs, -ˌtrɒs |-es -ɪz

Key: See in full §§3–47. bee **bi** |pity ˈpɪtɪ (§6) |rate ret |yet jɛt |sang sæŋ |angry ˈæŋ·grɪ |bath bæθ; E baθ (§10) |ah ɑ |far fɑr |watch wɑtʃ, wɒtʃ (§12) |jaw dʒɔ |gorge gɔrdʒ |go go

albeit ɔlˈbiːt

Albemarle ˈælbəˌmɑrl; ES -ˌmɑːl, E+ -ˌmɑːl

Albert ˈælbət; ES ˈælbət

Alberta ælˈbɝtə; ES -ˈbɜtə, -ˈbɝtə

Albigenses ˌælbɪˈdʒɛnsiz

albinism ˈælbəˌnɪzəm

albino ælˈbaɪno |-binoism -ˌɪzəm

Albion ˈælbɪən, -bjən

Albright ˈɔlbraɪt

Albro ˈɔlbro, cf Aldborough

album ˈælbəm, -bm̩

albumen ælˈbjumən, -ˈbɪum-

albumin ælˈbjumɪn, -ˈbɪum- |-ate -ɪt, -ˌet

albuminoid ælˈbjumɪˌnɔɪd, -ˈbɪum- |-nose -ˌnos |-nous -nəs

Albuquerque ˈælbəˌkɝkɪ, ˌælbəˈkɝkɪ, -bjʊ-; ES -ɝ-, -ɝ-

alburnum ælˈbɝnəm; ES -ˈbɜn-, -ˈbɝn-

Alcaeus ælˈsiəs |-ʼs -ɪz

Alcaic ælˈkeɪk

alcaide ælˈked (Sp alˈkaiðe)

alcalde ælˈkældɪ (Sp alˈkalde)

Alcatraz ˈælkəˌtræz, ˌælkəˈtræz (Am Sp ˌalkaˈtras)

alcazar, A- ælˈkæzə; ES -zə(r; (Sp alˈkaθar)

Alcestis ælˈsɛstɪs |-ʼs -ɪz

alchemist ˈælkəmɪst |-my -mɪ

Alcibiades ˌælsəˈbaɪəˌdiz |-ʼs -ɪz

Alcides ælˈsaɪdiz |-des' -diz

Alcinoüs ælˈsɪnʊəs |-ʼs -ɪz

Alcmene ælkˈminɪ

Alcoa ælˈkoə

alcohol ˈælkəˌhɔl, -ˌhɒl, -ˌhɑl |-ism -ˌɪzəm

alcoholic ˌælkəˈhɔlɪk, -ˈhɒl-, -ˈhɑl- |-ally -ḷɪ, -ɪklɪ

alcoholicity ˌælkəhɔlˈɪsətɪ, -hɒl-, -hɑl-

Alcoran ˌælkoˈrɑn, -ˈræn

Alcott ˈɔlkət

alcove ˈælkov

Alcuin ˈælkwɪn

Alcyone ælˈsaɪəˌni

Alda ˈɑldə

Aldan Pa ˈɔldən, Russia ɑlˈdɑn

Aldborough ˈɔldˌbɝo, ˈɔlˌb-, -ə; ES -ˌbɜr-, -ˌbʌr-, -ˌbɝ-; Brit ˈɔldbərə, ˈɔlb-, -brə

Aldebaran ælˈdɛbərən

aldehyde ˈældəˌhaɪd

Alden ˈɔldɪn, -dən

alder ˈɔldə; ES ˈɔldə(r

alderman ˈɔldəmən; ES ˈɔldə-; |-men -mən

aldermanic ˌɔldəˈmænɪk; ES ˌɔldə-

Alderney ˈɔldənɪ; ES ˈɔldənɪ

Aldershot ˈɔldəˌʃɑt; ES ˈɔldəˌʃɑt, -ˌʃɒt

Aldine ˈɔldaɪn, ˈɔldin

Aldington ˈɔldɪŋtən

Aldrich ˈɔldrɪtʃ |-ʼs -ɪz

ale el

aleatory ˈeliəˌtorɪ, -ˌtɔrɪ; S -ˌtorɪ

alee əˈli

alehouse ˈelˌhaʊs |-ses -zɪz

Alemannic ˌæləˈmænɪk

alembic əˈlɛmbɪk

Alençon əˈlɛnsən, -sɑn, -sɒn (Fr alɑ̃ˈsõ)

Aleppo əˈlɛpo

alert əˈlɝt; ES əˈlɜt, əˈlɝt; |-ed -ɪd

Alethea ˌæləˈθiə, əˈliθɪə

Aleut ˈælɪˌut

Aleutian əˈluʃən, əˈlɪu-

alewife ˈelˌwaɪf |-wives -ˌwaɪvz

Aleyn ˈælɪn, -ən

Alexander ˌælɪgˈzændə, ˌɛlɪg-; ES -ˈzændə(r; |-dra -drə |-dria -drɪə |-drian -drɪən |-drine -drɪn

Alexas əˈlɛksəs |-xasʼ -ksəs

alexin əˈlɛksɪn

Alexis əˈlɛksɪs |-xisʼ -ksɪs

alfalfa, A- ælˈfælfə

Alfonso ælˈfɑnzo, -so; ES+-ˈfɒn-

Alford ˈɔlfəd; ES ˈɔlfəd

Alfred ˈælfrɪd, -frəd, -fəd; ES -frɪd, -frəd, -fəd

Alfreda ælˈfridə (ˈAlˌfreda ˈBurroughs)

Alfredian ælˈfridɪən

alfresco ælˈfrɛsko

Alfric ˈælfrɪk

alga ˈælgə |algae ˈældʒi

algebra ˈældʒəbrə

algebraic ˌældʒəˈbreɪk |-al -ḷ |-ally -ḷɪ, -ɪklɪ

algebraist ˈældʒəˌbreɪst

Algeciras ˌældʒɪˈsɪrəs |-ʼs -ɪz (Sp ˌalxeˈθiras)

Alger ˈældʒə; ES ˈældʒə(r

Algeria ælˈdʒɪrɪə |-n -n

Algerine ˌældʒəˈrin

Algernon ˈældʒənən; ES ˈældʒə-

algid ˈældʒɪd

Algiers ælˈdʒɪrz; ES -ˈdʒɪəz, S+-ˈdʒɛəz; |-ʼs -ɪz

Algol ˈælgɑl, -gɒl
Algoma ælˈgomə
Algona ælˈgonə
Algonkian ælˈgɑŋkɪən, -ˈgɒŋ-
Algonquian ælˈgɑŋkɪən, -kwɪən, -ˈgɒŋ-
Algonquin ælˈgɑŋkɪn, -kwɪn, -ˈgɒŋ-
algorism ˈælgəˌrɪzəm |algorithm ˈælgəˌrɪðəm
Alhambra ælˈhæmbrə
alias ˈelɪəs |-es -ɪz
Ali Baba ˈælɪˈbæbə, ˈɑlɪˈbɑbə
alibi ˈæləˌbaɪ |-ed -d
Alice ˈælɪs |-ˈs -ɪz
Alicia əˈlɪʃɪə
alien ˈeljən, ˈelɪən
Aliena Shak. ˌelɪˈinə
alienability ˌeljənəˈbɪlətɪ, ˌelɪən-
alienable ˈeljənəbl̩, ˈelɪən-
alienate ˈeljənˌet, ˈelɪən- |-d -ɪd
alienation ˌeljənˈeʃən, ˌelɪən-
alienism ˈeljənˌɪzəm, ˈelɪən- |-ist -ɪst
alight adv əˈlaɪt
alight v əˈlaɪt |-ed -ɪd or alit əˈlɪt
align əˈlaɪn |-ed -d
alike əˈlaɪk
aliment n ˈæləmənt
aliment v ˈæləˌmɛnt |-ed -ɪd
alimental ˌæləˈmɛntl̩ |-ly -ɪ
alimentary ˌæləˈmɛntərɪ, -ˈmɛntrɪ
alimentation ˌæləmɛnˈteʃən
alimony ˈæləˌmonɪ
aline əˈlaɪn |-d -d
Aline əˈlin
aliquant ˈæləkwənt |-quot -kwət
Aliquippa ˌæləˈkwɪpə
Alison ˈæləsn̩
alit past & pptc of alight əˈlɪt
alive əˈlaɪv
alizarin əˈlɪzərɪn |-rine -rɪn -ˌrin
alkahest ˈælkəˌhɛst
alkalescence ˌælkəˈlɛsn̩s |-cy -ɪ |-nt -n̩t
alkali ˈælkəˌlaɪ
alkalify ˈælkələˌfaɪ, ælˈkælə- |-fied -ˌfaɪd
alkaline ˈælkəˌlaɪn, -lɪn
alkalinity ˌælkəˈlɪnətɪ
alkalize ˈælkəˌlaɪz |-s -ɪz |-d -d
alkaloid ˈælkəˌlɔɪd |-al ˌælkəˈlɔɪdl̩
Alkoran ˌælkoˈrɑn, -ˈræn
all ɔl
Allah ˈælə, ˈɑlə

all-American ˈɔləˈmɛrəkən
Allan ˈælən
Allardice ˈælɚˌdaɪs; ES ˈælə-; |-ˈs -ɪz
all-around ˈɔləˈraʊnd (ˈall-aˌround ˈskill)
allay əˈle |-ed -d
Allegan ˈæləgən
Allegany Md, NY ˈæləˌgenɪ
allegation ˌæləˈgeʃən
allege əˈlɛdʒ |-s -ɪz |-d -d |-dly -ɪdlɪ
Alleghany NC, Va ˈæləˌgenɪ
Allegheny Pa city, riv., college ˈæləˌgenɪ
allegiance əˈlidʒəns |-s -ɪz
allegoric ˌæləˈgɔrɪk, -ˈgɑr-, -ˈgɒr- |-al -l̩
    |-ally -lɪ, -ɪklɪ
allegorist ˈæləˌgɔrɪst, -ˌgɑr-, ˈæləgərɪst; S
    -ˌgor-, -gɑr-
allegoristic ˌæləgəˈrɪstɪk
allegorize ˈæləgəˌraɪz |-s -ɪz |-d -d
allegory ˈæləˌgorɪ, -ˌgɔrɪ; S -ˌgorɪ
allegretto ˌæləˈgrɛto (It ˌalleˈgretto)
allegro əˈlegro, əˈlɛgro (It alˈle:gro)
Alleine ˈælɪn, -ən
allelomorph əˈliləˌmɔrf, -ˈlɛl-; ES -ˌmɔəf
alleluia ˌæləˈlujə, -ˈlhujə
allemande ˌæləˈmænd (Fr alˈmɑ̃:d)
Allen ˈælɪn, -ən
Allenby ˈælɪnbɪ, -ən-
Allentown ˈælɪnˌtaʊn, -ən-
allergic əˈlɝdʒɪk; ES -ˈlɜdʒ-, -ˈlɝdʒ-
allergy ˈælɚdʒɪ; ES ˈælədʒɪ
Allerton ˈælɚtən; ES ˈælətən
alleviate əˈlivɪˌet |-d -ɪd -tion əˌlivɪˈeʃən
alley ˈælɪ |-ed -d
Alleyn ˈælɪn, -ən
Allhallows ˌɔlˈhæloz, -ləz
alliance, A- əˈlaɪəns |-s -ɪz |-d -t
allied əˈlaɪd (ˈalˌlied ˈarmies)
Allies ˈælaɪz, əˈlaɪz
alligator ˈæləˌgetɚ; ES -ˌgetə(r
Allingham ˈælɪŋəm
Allison ˈæləsn̩
alliterate əˈlɪtəˌret |-d -ɪd |-tive -ɪv
alliteration əˌlɪtəˈreʃən, ˌælɪtə-
allocable ˈæləkəbl̩
allocate ˈæləˌket, ˈælo- |-d -ɪd
allocation ˌæləˈkeʃən, ˌælo-
allocution ˌæləˈkjuʃən, ˌælo-, -ˈkɪu-
allomorph ˈæləˌmɔrf; ES -ˌmɔəf
allomorphic ˌæləˈmɔrfɪk; ES -ˈmɔəf-

Key: See in full §§3–47. bee bi |pity ˈpɪtɪ (§6) |rate ret |yet jɛt |sang sæŋ |angry ˈæŋ·grɪ |bath bæθ; E baθ (§10) |ah ɑ |far fɑr |watch wɑtʃ, wɒtʃ (§12) |jaw dʒɔ |gorge gɔrdʒ |go go

allopath ˈæləˌpæθ |-ths -θs
allopathic ˌæləˈpæθɪk
allopathist əˈlɑpəθɪst; ES+-ˈlɒp-; |-thy -θɪ
allot əˈlɑt; ES+əˈlɒt; |-ted -ɪd
allotrope ˈæləˌtrop
allotropic ˌæləˈtrɑpɪk; ES+-ˈtrɒp-; |-al -l̩
|-ally -l̩ɪ, -ɪklɪ
allotropy əˈlɑtrəpɪ; ES+əˈlɒt-
allover n ˈɔlˌovɚ; ES -ˌovə(r
allover adj ˈɔlˈovɚ; ES -ˈovə(r; (ən ˈɔlˈovɚ
wən)
allow əˈlaʊ |-ed -d |-edly -ɪdlɪ
allowable əˈlaʊəbl̩ |-bly -blɪ
allowance əˈlaʊəns |-s -ɪz
Alloway ˈæləˌwe
alloy n ˈælɔɪ, əˈlɔɪ
alloy v əˈlɔɪ |-ed -d
all-round ˈɔlˈraʊnd (ˈall-ˌround ˈhelp)
allspice ˈɔlˌspaɪs |-s -ɪz
Allston ˈɔlstən
allude əˈlud, əˈlɪud |-d -ɪd
allure əˈlʊr, əˈlɪʊr; ES əˈlʊə(r, əˈlɪʊə(r;
|-d -d
allusion əˈluʒən, əˈlɪuʒən, æ-
allusive əˈlusɪv, əˈlɪusɪv
alluvial əˈluvɪəl, əˈlɪuv-, -vjəl
alluvion əˈluvɪən, əˈlɪuv- |-vium -vɪəm |-via
-vɪə
ally n ˈælaɪ, əˈlaɪ
ally v əˈlaɪ |allied əˈlaɪd
almagest ˈælməˌdʒɛst
Alma US ˈælmə, Russia ˈɑlmə
Alma Mater ˈælməˈmetɚ, ˈɑlməˈmɑtɚ; ES
-tə(r;—The hybrid ˈælməˈmɑtɚ is frequently heard.
almanac ˈɔlməˌnæk, ˈɔlmənɪk
Alma-Tadema ˈælməˈtædɪmə
almighty, A- ɔlˈmaɪtɪ (ˈalˌmighty ˈtruth)
Almon ˈælmən
almond ˈɑmənd, ˈæmənd—ˈæmənd, now less
freq., is preserved by some old families. In
NEngd ˈælmənd is freq.
almoner ˈælmənɚ, ˈɑmənɚ; ES -nə(r
almonry ˈælmənrɪ, ˈɑmənrɪ
almost ɔlˈmost, ˈɔlˌmost (ˈdone, alˈmost;
ˈalˌmost ˈdone)
alms ɑmz |-giving -ˌgɪvɪŋ |-house -ˌhaʊs
almuce ˈælmjus, -mɪus |-s -ɪz
Aln æln, loc.+el, ˈalən, jɛl

Alne ɔn
Alnmouth ˈælnˌmaʊθ, -məθ, loc.+ˈelməθ,
ˈjɛlməθ
Alnwick ˈænɪk, loc. ˈanɪk
aloe ˈælo |-s -z
aloft əˈlɔft, əˈlɒft
aloha əˈloə, ɑˈlohɑ
alone əˈlon
along əˈlɔŋ, əˈlɒŋ; S+əˈlaŋ
alongshore əˈlɔŋˌʃor, əˈlɒŋ-, -ˌʃɔr; E -ˌʃoə(r,
-ˌʃɔə(r; S -ˌʃoə(r, əˈlaŋ-
alongside əˈlɔŋˈsaɪd, əˈlɒŋ-; S+əˈlaŋ-;
(aˈlongˈside it, aˈlongˌside a ˈbarge)
Alonso, -zo əˈlɑnzo; ES+əˈlɒn-
aloof əˈluf
aloud əˈlaʊd
alow əˈlo
Aloysius ˌæloˈɪsɪəs, -ˈɪʃəs |-'s -ɪz
alp ælp
alpaca ælˈpækə
Alpena ælˈpinə
alpenhorn ˈælpɪnˌhɔrn, -pən-; ES -ˌhɔən
alpenstock ˈælpɪnˌstɑk, -pən-; ES+-ˌstɒk
alpha, A- ˈælfə
alphabet ˈælfəˌbɛt
alphabetic ˌælfəˈbɛtɪk |-al -l̩ |-ally -l̩ɪ, -ɪklɪ
alphabetize ˈælfəbəˌtaɪz |-s -ɪz |-d -d
Alphaeus, -phe- Bib. ælˈfiəs, ˈælf- |-'s -ɪz
Alpheus mod. name ˈælfɪəs, myth. ælˈfiəs
Alphonse ælˈfɑnz, -ˈfɒnz, -ˈfɔnz |-'s -ɪz (Fr
alˈfõːs)
Alphonso ælˈfɑnzo, -so; ES+-ˈfɒn-
Alpine ˈælpaɪn, -pɪn
Alps ælps
already ɔlˈrɛdɪ
alright ɔlˈraɪt
Alsace ælˈses, ˈælsæs |-'s -ɪz (Fr alˈzas)
Alsace-Lorraine ˈælˌsesloˈren, -lɒ-, ˌælˌsæs-
Alsatia ælˈseʃɪə, -ʃə |-tian -ʃən
alsike ˈælsaɪk, ˈɔl-
also ˈɔlso
Altai ælˈtaɪ, ælˈteˌaɪ |Altaic ælˈteˌɪk
Altair ælˈtɑˌɪr; ES -ɪə(r
Altamaha ˌɔltəməˈhɔ
altar ˈɔltɚ; ES ˈɔltə(r; |-ed -d
altarpiece ˈɔltɚˌpis; ES ˈɔltə-; |-s -ɪz
altazimuth ælˈtæzəməθ
alter ˈɔltɚ; ES ˈɔltə(r; |-ed -d |-ing ˈɔltərɪŋ,
ˈɔltrɪŋ

|full fʊl |tooth tuθ |further ˈfɝðɚ; ES ˈfəðə |custom ˈkʌstəm |while hwaɪl |how haʊ |toy tɔɪ
|using ˈjuzɪŋ |fuse fjuz, fɪuz |dish dɪʃ |vision ˈvɪʒən |Eden ˈidn̩ |cradle ˈkredl̩ |keep 'em ˈkipm̩

alterant ˈɔltərənt
alteration ˌɔltəˈreʃən |-rative ˈɔltəˌretɪv
altercate ˈɔltəˌket, ˈæl-; ES -tə-
altercation ˌɔltəˈkeʃən, ˌæl-; ES -tə-
alter ego ˈæltəˈigo, -ˈɛgo
alternant ɔlˈtɜ˞nənt, æl-; ES -ˈtɜn-, -ˈtɜ˞n-
alternate n, adj ˈɔltə˞nɪt, ˈæl-; ES -tə-; |-ly -lɪ,
 acct+alˈternate(ly)
alternate v ˈɔltə˞ˌnet, ˈæl-; ES -tə-; |-d -ɪd
alternation ˌɔltə˞ˈneʃən, ˌæl-; ES -tə-
alternative ɔlˈtɜ˞nətɪv, æl-; ES -ˈtɜn-, -ˈtɜ˞n-
alternator ˈɔltə˞ˌnetə˞, ˈæl-; ES -təˌnetə(r
Altgeld ˈɔltgɛld (Ger ˈɑltgɛlt)
Althaea ælˈθiə
althea, A- ælˈθiə
althorn ˈæltˌhɔrn; ES -ˌhɔən
although, altho ɔlˈðo
altimeter ælˈtɪmətə˞, ˈæltəˌmitə˞; ES -tə(r
altissimo ælˈtɪsəˌmo (It alˈtissiˌmo)
altitude ˈæltəˌtjud, -ˌtɪud, -ˌtud
altitudinal ˌæltəˈtjudn̩l, -ˈtɪud-, -ˈtud-
Altman ˈɔltmən
alto ˈælto
alto-cumulus ˌæltoˈkjumjələs, -ˈkɪum- |-es
 -ɪz |-li -ˌlaɪ
altogether ˌɔltəˈgɛðə˞; ES -ˈgɛðə(r
Alton ˈɔltn̩
Altoona ælˈtunə
alto-relievo ˈælto·rɪˈlivo (It -rilievo ˈɑlto·ri-
 ˈljɛ:vo)
alto-stratus ˈæltoˈstretəs |-es -ɪz |-ti -taɪ
altruism ˈæltrʊˌɪzəm |-ist -ɪst
altruistic ˌæltrʊˈɪstɪk |-ally -ļɪ, -ɪklɪ
Altus ˈæltəs |-’s -ɪz
aludel ˈæljuˌdɛl
alum ˈæləm |-ed -d
alumina əˈlumɪnə, əˈlɪu-
aluminium ˌæljəˈmɪnɪəm
aluminum əˈlumɪnəm, əˈlɪu- |-nous -nəs
alumna əˈlʌmnə |alumnae əˈlʌmni
alumnus əˈlʌmnəs |-’s -ɪz |-ni -naɪ
Alva ˈælvə
alveolar ælˈvɪələ˞; ES -ˈvɪələ(r
alveolus ælˈvɪələs |-li -ˌlaɪ
alway ˈɔlwe
always ˈɔlwɪz, ˈɔlwez, ˈɔlwəz; S ˈɔlwez, -wɪz
alyssum, A- əˈlɪsəm
am stressed ˈæm, ˌæm; unstr. əm, m
A.M., a.m. ˈeˈɛm

Amabel ˈæməˌbɛl
Amadis ˈæmədɪs |-’s -ɪz
Amador ˈæməˌdor, -ˌdɔr; ES -ˌdoə(r, E+
 -ˌdɔə(r; (Sp ˌamaˈðɔr)
amain əˈmen
Amalek ˈæməˌlɛk |-ite ˈæmələˌkaɪt
amalgam əˈmælgəm
amalgamate adj əˈmælgəmɪt, -ˌmet
amalgamate v əˈmælgəˌmet |-d -ɪd
amalgamation əˌmælgəˈmeʃən
Amanda əˈmændə
amanita, A- ˌæməˈnaɪtə, -ˈnitə
amanuensis əˌmænjuˈɛnsɪs |-sis’ -sɪs |pl -nses
 -ˈɛnsiz
amaranth ˈæməˌrænθ |-ths -θs
amaranthine ˌæməˈrænθɪn
Amarillo ˌæməˈrɪlo
amaryllis, A- ˌæməˈrɪlɪs |-lises -lɪsɪz
Amasa ˈæməsə
amass əˈmæs |-es -ɪz |-ed -t
amateur n ˈæməˌtʃur, -ˌtɪur, -ˌtur, -tʃə˞,
 -tə˞, ˌæməˈtɜ˞; ES ˈæməˌtʃuə(r, -ˌtɪuə(r,
 -ˌtuə(r, -tʃə(r, -tə(r, ˌæməˈtɜ(r, -ˈtɜ˞; (Fr
 amaˈtœ:r)—see note below
amateur adj ˈæməˌtʃur, -ˌtɪur, -ˌtur, -tʃə˞,
 -tə˞; ES ˈæməˌtʃuə(r, -ˌtɪuə(r, -ˌtuə(r,
 -tʃə(r, -tə(r; (Fr amaˈtœ:r)—Other prons.
 were reported. The 1st, most freq., accords
 best with the habits of English. The 2d, 3d,
 4th, & 5th are normal variations of the 1st.
amateurish ˌæməˈtɜrɪʃ, -ˈtjurɪʃ, -ˈtɪur-, -ˈtur-;
 ES+-ˈtɜrɪʃ
amative ˈæmətɪv
amatory ˈæməˌtorɪ, -ˌtɔrɪ; S -ˌtorɪ
amaze əˈmez |-s -ɪz |-d -d |-dly -ɪdlɪ
Amaziah ˌæməˈzaɪə
Amazon, a- ˈæməˌzɑn, -zn̩; ES+-ˌzɒn
Amazonian, a- ˌæməˈzonɪən
ambage ˈæmbɪdʒ |-s -ɪz or as L ambages
 æmˈbedʒiz
ambassador æmˈbæsədə˞, əm-; ES -də(r
ambassadorial æmˌbæsəˈdorɪəl, əm-, -ˈdɔr-;
 S -ˈdor-
ambassadress æmˈbæsədrɪs, əm- |-es -ɪz
amber ˈæmbə˞; ES ˈæmbə(r; |-ed -d
ambergris ˈæmbə˞gris, -grɪs; ES ˈæmbə-
ambidexter ˌæmbəˈdɛkstə˞; ES -ˈdɛkstə(r;
 |-trous -trəs
ambidexterity ˌæmbədɛksˈtɛrətɪ

Key: See in full §§3–47. bee bi |pity ˈpɪtɪ (§6) |rate ret |yet jɛt |sang sæŋ |angry ˈæŋ·grɪ
|bath bæθ; E baθ (§10) |ah ɑ |far fɑr |watch wɑtʃ, wɒtʃ (§12) |jaw dʒɔ |gorge gɔrdʒ |go go

ambient ˈæmbɪənt	Amesbury ˈemz͵bɛrɪ, -bərɪ
ambiguity ͵æmbɪˈgjuətɪ, -ˈgɪuətɪ	amethyst ˈæməθɪst
ambiguous æmˈbɪgjʊəs	Amfortas Ger amˈfɔrtas
ambition æmˈbɪʃən |-tious -ʃəs	Amherst ˈæmɚst; ES ˈæməst
ambivalence æmˈbɪvələns |-cy -ɪ |-ent -ənt	amiability ͵emɪəˈbɪlətɪ
amble ˈæmbļ |-d -d |-ling ˈæmblɪŋ, ˈæmbļɪŋ	amiable ˈemɪəbļ |-bly -blɪ
ambler, A- ˈæmblɚ; ES ˈæmblə(r	amic ˈæmɪk
Ambleside ˈæmbļ͵saɪd	amicability ͵æmɪkəˈbɪlətɪ
Ambridge ˈæmbrɪdʒ |-ʼs -ɪz	amicable ˈæmɪkəbļ |-bly -blɪ
Ambrose ˈæmbroz |-ʼs -ɪz	amice ˈæmɪs |-s -ɪz
ambrosia æmˈbroʒɪə, -ʒə |-l -l |-lly -lɪ |-n -n	amid prep əˈmɪd
Ambrosian æmˈbroʒɪən, -ʒən	amide chem. ˈæmaɪd, ˈæmɪd |-mid -mɪd
ambrotype ˈæmbrə͵taɪp, -bro-	amidine ˈæmɪ͵din, -dɪn |-din -dɪn
ambry ˈæmbrɪ	amido əˈmido, ˈæmɪ͵do
ambsace ˈemz͵es, ˈæmz- |-s -ɪz	amidships əˈmɪdʃɪps
ambulance ˈæmbjələns |-s -ɪz |-d -t |-nt -nt	amidst əˈmɪdst
ambulate ˈæmbjə͵let |-d -ɪd	Amiens Shak. ˈæmɪənz, Dublin street ˈemjənz,
ambulation ͵æmbjəˈleʃən	Fr city ˈæmɪənz |-ʼs -ɪz (Fr aˈmjæ̃)
ambulatory ˈæmbjələ͵torɪ, -͵tɔrɪ; S -͵torɪ	amine əˈmin |amin ˈæmɪn
ambuscade ͵æmbəsˈked |-d -ɪd	amino əˈmino
ambush ˈæmbʊʃ |-es -ɪz |-ed -t	amir əˈmɪr; ES əˈmɪə(r
ameba əˈmibə |-s -z |-bae -bi |-n -n	amiss əˈmɪs
amebean ͵æmɪˈbiən	Amite əˈmit
amebic əˈmibɪk |ameboid əˈmibɔɪd	amitosis ͵æməˈtosɪs
ameer əˈmɪr; ES əˈmɪə(r	amity ˈæmətɪ |Amityville ˈæmətɪ͵vɪl
Amelia əˈmiljə	ammeter ˈæm͵mitɚ, ˈæ͵mitɚ; ES -͵mitə(r
ameliorate əˈmiljə͵ret |-d -ɪd	ammine ˈæmin
amelioration ə͵miljəˈreʃən	ammino ˈæmɪ͵no
amen ˈeˈmɛn; worship ˈeˈmɛn, ˈɑ-; singing	Ammon ˈæmən
ˈɑˈmɛn	ammonia əˈmonjə, -nɪə |-niac əˈmonɪ͵æk
Amen Egyp god ˈɑmən	ammoniacal ͵æməˈnaɪəkļ
amenable əˈminəbļ, əˈmɛn- |-bly -blɪ	ammoniate əˈmonɪ͵et |-d -ɪd
Amen Corner ˈe͵mɛnˈkɔrnɚ; ES -ˈkɔənə(r	ammonite ˈæmə͵naɪt
amend əˈmɛnd |-ed -ɪd |-s əˈmɛndz, əˈmɛnz	Ammonite ˈæmən͵aɪt
amenity əˈmɛnətɪ	ammonium əˈmonɪəm
ament ʻcatkinʼ ˈæmənt, ˈemənt	ammunition ͵æmjəˈnɪʃən
ament ʻmoronʼ ˈemənt	amnesia æmˈniʒɪə, -ʒə
amentia eˈmɛnʃɪə, əˈmɛnʃɪə	amnesty ˈæm͵nɛstɪ, ˈæmnəstɪ
amerce əˈmɝs; ES əˈmɜs, əˈmɝs; |-s -ɪz |-d -t	amoeba əˈmibə |-s -z |-bae -bi |-n -n
America əˈmɛrəkə, əˈmɛrɪkə |-n -n |-nism	amoebaean ͵æmɪˈbiən
-n͵ɪzəm	amoebic əˈmibɪk |amoeboid əˈmibɔɪd
Americana ə͵mɛrəˈkenə, -ˈkænə, -ˈkɑnə	amok əˈmʌk, əˈmɑk, əˈmɒk
Americanize əˈmɛrəkən͵aɪz |-s -ɪz |-d -d	among əˈmʌŋ |-st -st, -kst
Americus əˈmɛrɪkəs |-ʼs -ɪz	amoral eˈmɔrəl, eˈmɑrəl, eˈmɒrəl
Americus Vespucius əˈmɛrɪkəs vɛsˈpjuʃəs,	Amorite ˈæmə͵raɪt
-ˈpɪu-	amorous ˈæmərəs
Amerigo Vespucci əˈmɛrɪ͵go vɛsˈputʃɪ (It	amorphism əˈmɔrfɪzəm; ES əˈmɔəf-
͵ameˈri:go vesˈputtʃi)	amorphous əˈmɔrfəs; ES əˈmɔəfəs
Amerind ˈæmə͵rɪnd |-ian ͵æməˈrɪndɪən	amort əˈmɔrt; ES əˈmɔət

|full fʊl |tooth tuθ |further ˈfɝðɚ; ES ˈfɝðə |custom ˈkʌstəm |while hwaɪl |how haʊ |toy tɔɪ
|using ˈjuzɪŋ |fuse fjuz, fɪuz |dish dɪʃ |vision ˈvɪʒən |Eden ˈidn̩ |cradle ˈkredļ |keep ʼem ˈkipm̩

amortization ˌæmɚtəˈzeʃən, əˌmɔrt-, -aɪˈz-;
ES ˌæmə-, əˌmɔət-
amortize ˈæmɚˌtaɪz, əˈmɔrtaɪz; ES ˈæmə-,
əˈmɔə-; |-s -ɪz |-d -d
Amory ˈemərɪ
Amos ˈeməs |-'s -ɪz
Amoskeag ˌæməsˈkɛg
amount əˈmaʊnt |-ed -ɪd
amour əˈmʊr, æ-; ES˙-ˈmʊə(r
amour-propre Fr amurˈprɔpr̩
Amoy əˈmɔɪ
amperage æmˈpɪrɪdʒ, ˈæmˌpɪrɪdʒ |-s -ɪz
Ampère æmˈpɪr, ˈæmpɛr; ES -ˈpɪə(r, -pɛə(r;
(Fr ãˈpɛːr)
ampere ˈæmpɪr, æmˈpɪr; ES -pɪə(r, -ˈpɪə(r
ampersand ˈæmpɚsˌænd, ˌæmpɚsˈænd; ES
-pəs-
amphetamine æmˈfɛtəˌmin, -mɪn
amphibian æmˈfɪbɪən |-bious -bɪəs
amphibrach ˈæmfɪˌbræk
amphictyon æmˈfɪktɪən |-y -ɪ
amphictyonic æmˌfɪktɪˈɑnɪk; ES+-ˈɒn-
Amphion æmˈfaɪən
amphitheater, -tre ˈæmfəˌθɪətɚ, -ˌθɪə-; ES
-tə(r
amphora ˈæmfərə |-s -z |-rae -ˌri
ample ˈæmpl̩ |-r -plɚ; ES -plə(r; |-st -plɪst
amplification ˌæmpləfəˈkeʃən
amplifier ˈæmpləˌfaɪɚ; ES -ˌfaɪ·ə(r
amplify ˈæmpləˌfaɪ |-fied -ˌfaɪd
amplitude ˈæmpləˌtjud, -ˌtɪud, -ˌtud
amply ˈæmplɪ
ampulla æmˈpʌlə, -ˈpʊlə |-s -z |-lae -li
amputate ˈæmpjəˌtet, ˈæmpjʊ- |-d -ɪd
amputation ˌæmpjəˈteʃən, -pjʊ-
Amritsar ʌmˈrɪtsɚ; ES -ˈrɪtsə(r
Amsterdam US ˈæmstɚˌdæm, Neth+ˌæmstɚ-
ˈdæm; ES -stɚ-; (Du ˌamstərˈdam)
Amstutz ˈæmstʌts |-es -ɪz (Ger ˈamʃtʊts)
amuck əˈmʌk
amulet ˈæmjəlɪt
Amundsen ˈamənsn̩, ˈamʊndsn̩
Amur ɑˈmʊr; ES ɑˈmʊə(r
amuse əˈmjuz, əˈmɪuz |-s -ɪz |-d -d |-dly
-ɪdlɪ
amusive əˈmjuzɪv, əˈmɪuzɪv
Amy ˈemɪ
amygdalin əˈmɪgdəlɪn |-line -lɪn, -ˌlaɪn
amyl ˈæmɪl |-ase -ɪˌles |-ene -ɪˌlin

amylolysis ˌæmɪˈlɑləsɪs; ES+-ˈlɒl-
amylose ˈæmɪˌlos |amylum ˈæmɪləm
Amyot ˈemɪət (Fr aˈmjo)
Amzi ˈæmzaɪ
an unstressed ən, n̩; rarely stressed ˈæn, ˌæn
ana ˈenə, ˈɑnə
-ana -ˈenə, -ˈænə, -ˈɑnə
Anabaptist ˌænəˈbæptɪst
anabasis, A- əˈnæbəsɪs |-bases -bəˌsiz
anabolism əˈnæbḷˌɪzəm
anachronism əˈnækrəˌnɪzəm
anachronistic əˌnækrəˈnɪstɪk |-al -ḷ |-ally
-ḷɪ, -ɪklɪ
anachronous əˈnækrənəs
anaclinal ˌænəˈklaɪnḷ
anaclitic ˌænəˈklɪtɪk
anacoluthia ˌænəkəˈluθɪə, -ˈlɪuθ-
anacoluthic ˌænəkəˈluθɪk, -ˈlɪuθ- |-ally -ḷɪ,
-ɪklɪ
anacoluthon ˌænəkəˈluθɑn, -ˈlɪuθ-, -ɒn, -ən
anaconda, A- ˌænəˈkɑndə; ES+-ˈkɒn-
Anacortes ˌænəˈkɔrtɪz, -tɛz, -təs; ES -ˈkɔə-;
|-'s -ɪz
Anacostia ˌænəˈkɑstɪə, -ˈkɒs-, -ˈkɔs-
Anacreon əˈnækrɪən, -ˌɑn; ES+-ˌɒn
Anacreontic əˌnækrɪˈɑntɪk; ES+-ˈɒntɪk
anacrusis ˌænəˈkrusɪs, -ˈkrɪu- |-cruses -siz
Anadarko ˌænəˈdɑrko; ES -ˈdɑːko, E+
-ˈdɑːko
anadem ˈænəˌdɛm
anadromous əˈnædrəməs
anaemia əˈnimɪə |-mic -mɪk
anaerobe ænˈeəˌrob
anaerobic ænˌeəˈrobɪk, ˌænɛˈrobɪk
anaesthesia ˌænəsˈθiʒə, -ʒɪə
anaesthetic ˌænəsˈθɛtɪk |-ally -ḷɪ, -ɪklɪ
anaesthetist əˈnɛsθətɪst
anaesthetize əˈnɛsθəˌtaɪz |-s -ɪz |-d -d
anaglyph ˈænəˌglɪf
anagoge ˌænəˈgodʒɪ |-gogy ˈænəˌgodʒɪ
anagogic ˌænəˈgadʒɪk; ES+-ˈgɒdʒ-; |-al -ḷ
|-ally -ḷɪ, -ɪklɪ
anagram ˈænəˌgræm
anagrammatic ˌænəgrəˈmætɪk |-al -ḷ |-ally
-ḷɪ, -ɪklɪ
Anaheim ˈænəˌhaɪm
Anak ˈenæk |-s -s |-im ˈænəˌkɪm |-ims
ˈænəˌkɪmz
anal ˈenḷ |-ly -ɪ

Key: See in full §§3–47. bee bi |pity ˈpɪtɪ (§6) |rate ret |yet jɛt |sang sæŋ |angry ˈæŋ·grɪ
|bath bæθ; E baθ (§10) |ah ɑ |far fɑr |watch watʃ, wɒtʃ (§12) |jaw dʒɔ |gorge gɔrdʒ |go go

analects 'ænəˌlɛkts |analecta ˌænə'lɛktə
analgesia ˌænæl'dʒɪzɪə, -sɪə |-sic -zɪk, -sɪk
analogic ˌæn|'adʒɪk; ES+-'ɒdʒ-; |-al -|
|-ally -|ɪ, -ɪklɪ
analogist ə'nælədʒɪst
analogize ə'næləˌdʒaɪz |-s -ɪz |-d -d
analogous ə'næləgəs
analogue 'æn|ˌɔg, -ˌɑg, -ˌɒg
analogy ə'nælədʒɪ
analphabetic ˌænælfə'bɛtɪk |-al -| |-ally -|ɪ,
-ɪklɪ
analysable 'æn|ˌaɪzəb|
analyse 'æn|ˌaɪz |-s -ɪz |-d -d
analysis ə'næləsɪs |-yses -əˌsiz
analyst 'æn|ɪst
analytic ˌæn|'ɪtɪk |-al -| |-ally -|ɪ, -ɪklɪ
analytics ˌæn|'ɪtɪks
analyzable 'æn|ˌaɪzəb|
analyze 'æn|ˌaɪz |-s -ɪz |-d -d
Anam ə'næm
Ananias ˌænə'naɪəs |-'s -ɪz
anapaest, -pest 'ænəˌpɛst
anapaestic, -pes- ˌænə'pɛstɪk |-al -| |-ally -|ɪ,
-ɪklɪ
anaphora ə'næfərə |-l -l
anaphoric ˌænə'fɔrɪk, -'far-, -'fɒr- |-al -|
anaphylaxis ˌænəfə'læksɪs
anaplasty 'ænəˌplæstɪ |-tic ˌænə'plæstɪk
anarch 'ænark; ES 'æna:k, E+-a:k
anarchic æn'arkɪk; ES -'a:k-, E+-'a:k-; |-al
-| |-ally -|ɪ, -ɪklɪ
anarchism 'ænəˌkɪzəm; ES 'ænə-
anarchist 'ænəkɪst; ES 'ænəkɪst; |-chy -kɪ
anarchistic ˌænə'kɪstɪk; ES ˌænə-
anastigmatic ˌænəstɪg'mætɪk, ˌænæstɪg-,
ænˌæs-
anastomosis ˌænəstə'mosɪs, əˌnæstə- |-moses
-'mosiz
anastrophe ə'næstrəfɪ
anathema ə'næθəmə
anathematize ə'næθəməˌtaɪz |-s -ɪz |-d -d
Anatolia ˌænə'tolɪə |-n -n
anatomic ˌænə'tamɪk; ES+-'tɒm-; |-al -|
|-ally -|ɪ, -ɪklɪ
anatomist ə'nætəmɪst |-my -mɪ
anatomize ə'nætəˌmaɪz |-s -ɪz |-d -d
Anaxagoras ˌænæks'ægərəs |-'s -ɪz
ancestor 'ænsɛstə; ES -sɛstə(r
ancestral æn'sɛstrəl |-ly -ɪ |-try 'ænsɛstrɪ

ancestress 'ænsɛstrɪs |-es -ɪz
Anchises æn'kaɪsiz, æŋ- |-ses' -siz
anchor 'æŋkə; ES 'æŋkə(r; |-ed -d |-ing
'æŋkərɪŋ, 'æŋkrɪŋ
anchorage 'æŋkərɪdʒ, -krɪdʒ |-s -ɪz
anchoress 'æŋkərɪs, -krɪs |-es -ɪz
anchoret 'æŋkərɪt, -ɛt
anchorite 'æŋkəˌraɪt
anchovy 'ænˌtʃovɪ, 'æntʃəvɪ, æn'tʃovɪ
anchusa æn'tʃuzə, -'tʃiuzə (L æŋ'kjuzə,
-'kɪu-)
ancien régime Fr ɑ̃sjɛ̃·re'ʒim
ancient 'ɛnʃənt
ancillary 'ænsəˌlɛrɪ, Brit æn'sɪlərɪ
ancress 'æŋkrɪs |-es -ɪz=anchoress
and usually unstressed: before vowels ənd, ɛnd,
ṇd ('sno ənd 'aɪs, 'hɛd ṇd 'arm); before
consonants and often before vowels ən ('mæn
ən 'bist), ɛn, ṇ ('rad ṇ 'gʌn, 'fes ṇ 'aɪz),
n ('bʌtə n 'ɛgz); after p or b often m̩ ('kʌp m̩
'sɔsə, 'rʌb m̩ 'palɪʃ); after k or g often ŋ
('dʒæk ŋ 'dʒɪl, 'bæg ŋ 'bægɪdʒ); stressed
or in pause: before vowels 'ænd, ˌænd, or
before consonants 'æn, ˌæn. The forms with
-d occur in ordinary speech before vowels
('fri ənd 'izɪ) or l, r, w, hw, j ('ɜˑlɪ ənd 'let),
but those without -d are also common there
('stap ən 'it), and are regular before other
consonants ('go ən 'si, 'traɪ ən 'du ɪt).
Andalusia ˌændə'luʒə, -'lɪu-, -ʃə |-n -n
Andaman 'ændəmən
andante æn'dæntɪ, an'dantɪ (It an'dante)
Andean æn'diən, 'ændɪən
Andersen 'ændəˌsṇ; ES 'ændəsṇ; |-son -sṇ
Andes 'ændiz |-des' -diz
andiron 'ændˌaɪən, -ˌaɪrn; ES -ˌaɪ·ən, -ˌaɪən
Andorra æn'dɔrə, -'darə, -'dɒrə
Andover 'ændovə; ES -dovə(r; Mass loc.+
'ændəvə(r
Andrade æn'dradɪ
André 'ændrɪ, 'andre
Andrea del Sarto ɑn'drɪədɛl'sarto; ES
-'sa:to; (It an'drɛːadel'sarto)
Andreas 'ændrɪəs |-'s -ɪz
Andrew 'ændru, 'ændrɪu |-s -z |-s's -zɪz
Androcles 'ændrəˌkliz |-'s -ɪz
Androclus 'ændrəkləs |-'s -ɪz
androgen 'ændrədʒən, -dʒɪn |-ic ˌændrə-
'dʒɛnɪk

|full fʊl |tooth tuθ |further 'fɜˑðə; ES 'fɜːðə |custom 'kʌstəm |while hwaɪl |how haʊ |toy tɔɪ
|using 'juzɪŋ |fuse fjuz, fɪuz |dish dɪʃ |vision 'vɪʒən |Eden 'idṇ |cradle 'kredḷ |keep 'em 'kipm̩

androgynous æn'drɑdʒənəs; ES+-'drɒdʒ-
Andromache æn'drɑməki; ES+-'drɒm-
Andromeda æn'drɑmɪdə; ES+-'drɒm-
Andronicus ˌændrə'naɪkəs, *Shak.* æn'drɑnɪ-
  kəs; ES+-'drɒn-; |-'s -ɪz
Andros 'ændrɑs, -drəs; ES+-drɒs; |-'s -ɪz
Androscoggin ˌændrə'skɑgɪn, -'skʊg-
anear ə'nɪr; ES ə'nɪə(r, S+ə'njɛə(r, ə'njɪə(r,
  ə'nɛə(r
anecdotal ˌænɪk'dotḷ ('anecˌdotal 'speech)
anecdote 'ænɪkˌdot |-d -ɪd |-tage -ɪdʒ
anecdotic ˌænɪk'dɑtɪk; ES+-'dɒt-; |-al -ḷ
  |-ally -ḷɪ, -ɪklɪ
anele ə'nil |-d -d
anelectric ˌænɪ'lɛktrɪk
anemia ə'nimɪə |-mic -mɪk
anemometer ˌænə'mɑmətɚ; ES -'mɑmətə(r,
  -'mɒm-
anemometric ˌænəmə'mɛtrɪk |-al -ḷ |-ally -ḷɪ,
  -ɪklɪ
anemone, A- ə'nɛməˌni
anent ə'nɛnt
aneroid 'ænəˌrɔɪd
anesthesia ˌænəs'θiʒə, -ʒɪə
anesthetic ˌænəs'θɛtɪk |-ally -ḷɪ, -ɪklɪ
anesthetist ə'nɛsθətɪst
anesthetize ə'nɛsθəˌtaɪz |-s -ɪz |-d -d
aneurysm, -rism 'ænjəˌrɪzəm
anew ə'nju, ə'nɪu, ə'nu
anfractuous æn'fræktʃʊəs
angary 'æŋgərɪ
angel, A- 'endʒəl
Angela 'ændʒələ
angelic æn'dʒɛlɪk |-al -ḷ |-ally -ḷɪ, -ɪklɪ
Angelica æn'dʒɛlɪkə
Angelina ˌændʒə'linə, -'laɪnə
Angell 'endʒəl
Angelo 'ændʒəˌlo
Angelus 'ændʒələs |-es -ɪz
anger 'æŋgɚ; ES 'æŋgə(r; |-ed -d |-ing
  'æŋgərɪŋ, 'æŋgrɪŋ
angerly 'æŋgɚlɪ; ES 'æŋgəlɪ
Angers 'ændʒɚz, 'æŋgɚz; ES -əz; |-'s -ɪz
  (*Fr* ɑ̃'ʒe)
Angevin 'ændʒəvɪn
Angiers *Shak.* 'ændʒɪrz; ES 'ændʒɪəz; |-'s
  -ɪz
angina æn'dʒaɪnə, *in medicine often* 'ændʒɪnə
angina pectoris æn'dʒaɪnə'pɛktərɪs

angiosperm 'ændʒɪoˌspɝm; ES -ˌspɜm,
  -ˌspɝm
angle 'æŋgḷ |-d -d |-ling 'æŋglɪŋ, 'æŋgḷɪŋ
angler 'æŋglɚ; ES 'æŋglə(r
Angles 'æŋgḷz
Anglesey, -sea 'æŋgḷsɪ
angleworm 'æŋgḷˌwɝm; ES -ˌwɜm, -ˌwɝm
Anglia 'æŋglɪə
Anglican 'æŋglɪkən
Anglicism 'æŋgləˌsɪzəm |-cist -sɪst
Anglicize 'æŋgləˌsaɪz |-s -ɪz |-d -d
Anglify 'æŋgləˌfaɪ |-fied -ˌfaɪd
Anglin 'æŋglɪn
Anglist 'æŋglɪst |-ics æŋ'glɪstɪks
Anglo-American 'æŋgloə'mɛrəkən
Anglo-Catholic 'æŋglo'kæθəlɪk, -'kæθlɪk
Anglo-Catholicism 'æŋglokə'θɑləˌsɪzəm; ES
  +-'θɒl-
Anglo-Egyptian 'æŋglo·ɪ'dʒɪpʃən
Anglo-French 'æŋglo'frɛntʃ
Anglo-Indian 'æŋglo'ɪndɪən, -djən
Anglo-Irish 'æŋglo'aɪrɪʃ
Anglo-Japanese 'æŋgloˌdʒæpə'niz
Anglomania ˌæŋglə'menɪə, -glo- |-niac -nɪˌæk
Anglo-Norman 'æŋglo'nɔrmən; ES -'nɔəmən
Anglophile 'æŋgləˌfaɪl, -glo-
Anglophobe 'æŋgləˌfob, -glo-
Anglophobia ˌæŋglə'fobɪə, -glo-
Anglo-Saxon 'æŋglo'sæksṇ |-dom -dəm |-ism
  -ˌɪzəm
Angola æŋ'golə, æn-
Angora æŋ'gorə, æn-, -'gɔrə, 'æŋgərə; S
  -'gorə, -gɔrə
angostura ˌæŋgəs'tjʊrə, -'tɪʊrə, -'tʊrə
angry 'æŋgrɪ |-grily -grəlɪ, -grɪlɪ
angstrom 'æŋstrəm
anguish 'æŋgwɪʃ |-es -ɪz |-ed -t
angular 'æŋgjələ; ES 'æŋgjələ(r
angularity ˌæŋgjə'lærətɪ
angulate *adj* 'æŋgjəlɪt, -ˌlet
angulate *v* 'æŋgjəˌlet |-d -ɪd
Angus 'æŋgəs |-'s -ɪz
angustura ˌæŋgəs'tjʊrə, -'tɪʊrə, -'tʊrə
anhungered ən'hʌŋgɚd; ES -'hʌŋgəd
anhydride æn'haɪdraɪd, -drɪd |-drid -drɪd
anhydrous æn'haɪdrəs
anil 'ænɪl
anile 'ænaɪl, 'enaɪl
aniline 'ænḷˌin, -ɪn |-in -ɪn

Key: *See in full §§3–47.* bee bi |pity 'pɪtɪ (§6) |rate ret |yet jɛt |sang sæŋ |angry 'æŋ·grɪ
|bath bæθ; E baθ (§10) |ah ɑ |far fɑr |watch wɑtʃ, wɒtʃ (§12) |jaw dʒɔ |gorge gɔrdʒ |go go

anility ə'nɪlətɪ
animadversion ˌænəmæd'vɝʒən, -'vɝʃ-; ES
  -'vɝ-, -'vɝ-
animadvert ˌænəmæd'vɝt; ES -'vɝt, -'vɝt;
  |-ed -ɪd
animal 'ænəml̩ |-ly -ɪ
animalcula pl ˌænə'mælkjələ
animalculae pl ˌænə'mælkjəˌli
animalcule ˌænə'mælkjul, -krʊl
animalculism ˌænə'mælkjəˌlɪzəm
animalculum ˌænə'mælkjələm |-la -lə |-lae
  -ˌli
animalism 'ænəml̩ˌɪzəm
animality ˌænə'mælətɪ
animate adj 'ænəmɪt
animate v 'ænəˌmet |-d -ɪd |-tion ˌænə'meʃən
animism 'ænəˌmɪzəm |animistic ˌænə'mɪstɪk
animosity ˌænə'masətɪ; ES+-'mɒs-
animus 'ænəməs
anion 'ænˌaɪən
anise 'ænɪs
aniseed, anisseed 'ænɪˌsid, 'ænɪsˌsid
anisometric ˌænaɪsə'mɛtrɪk, ænˌaɪsə-
anisotropic ˌænaɪsə'trɑpɪk, ænˌaɪsə-; ES+
  -'trɒp-; |-al -l̩ |-ally -l̩ɪ, -ɪklɪ
Anita ə'nitə
Anjou 'ændʒu (Fr ɑ̃'ʒu)
Ankara 'æŋkərə, 'ɑŋkərə
ankh æŋk
ankle 'æŋkl̩ |ankled 'æŋkl̩d
anklebone 'æŋkl̩ˌbon, -'bon
anklet 'æŋklɪt
ankus 'æŋkəs, 'ʌŋkəʃ |-es -ɪz
ankylose 'æŋkəˌlos |-s -ɪz |-d -t
ankylosis ˌæŋkə'losɪs
anlace 'ænlɪs, -ləs |-s -ɪz
Ann æn
anna, A- 'ænə
Annabel, -lle 'ænəˌbɛl
Annabella ˌænə'bɛlə
annals 'ænl̩z |annalist 'ænl̩ɪst
Annam ə'næm
Annamese ˌænə'miz
Annapolis ə'næpl̩ɪs, -plɪs, -əs |-'s -ɪz
Ann Arbor æn'arbɚ; ES -'ɑ:bə(r, E+
  -'ɑ:bə(r
annates 'ænɪts, 'ænets |annat 'ænæt
Anne æn
anneal ə'nil |-ed -d

Anne Arundel 'æn·ə'rʌndl̩
annelid 'ænl̩ɪd
annex n 'ænɛks |-es -ɪz |-ation ˌænɛks'eʃən
annex v ə'nɛks |-es -ɪz |-ed -t
Annie 'ænɪ
annihilate ə'naɪəˌlet |-d -ɪd |-lable -ləbl̩
annihilation əˌnaɪə'leʃən
anniversary ˌænə'vɝsərɪ, -srɪ; ES -'vɝs-,
  -'vɝs-
anno Domini 'æno'dɑməˌnaɪ; ES+-'dɒm-
annotate 'ænoˌtet |-d -ɪd |-tion ˌæno'teʃən
annotator 'ænoˌtetɚ; ES -ˌtetə(r
announce ə'naʊns |-s -ɪz |-d -t
annoy ə'nɔɪ |-ed -d |-ance -əns |-ances
  -ənsɪz
annual 'ænjʊəl, 'ænjʊl |-ly -ɪ
annuitant ə'nuətənt, ə'nɪu-, ə'nju- |-ity -ətɪ
annul ə'nʌl |-led -d
annular 'ænjələ; ES -lə(r
annulet 'ænjəlɪt
annulus 'ænjələs |-es -ɪz |-li -ˌlaɪ
annum 'ænəm
annunciate ə'nʌnʃɪˌet, -sɪ- |-d -ɪd
annunciation, A- əˌnʌnsɪ'eʃən, -ʃɪ-
annunciator ə'nʌnʃɪˌetɚ, -sɪ-; ES -ˌetə(r
Annunzio, d' də'nunzɪˌo (It dɑn'nuntsjo)
anociassociation əˌnosɪəˌsosɪ'eʃən, -ˌsoʃɪ-
anociation əˌnosɪ'eʃən, əˌnoʃɪ-
anode 'ænod |-dic æn'ɑdɪk; ES+-'rdɪk
anodize 'ænoˌdaɪz |-s -ɪz |-d -d
anodyne 'ænəˌdaɪn, 'æno-
anoint ə'nɔɪnt |-ed -ɪd
Anoka ə'nokə
anolyte 'ænəˌlaɪt
anomalism ə'nɑml̩ˌɪzəm; ES+-'nɒm-
anomalistic əˌnɑml̩'ɪstɪk; ES+-ˌnɒm-; |-al -l̩
  |-ally -l̩ɪ, -ɪklɪ
anomaly ə'nɑməlɪ; ES+-'nɒm-; |-lous -ləs
anon ə'nɑn, ə'nɒn
anonym, -e 'ænəˌnɪm |-nymity ˌænə'nɪmətɪ
anonymous ə'nɑnəməs; ES+ə'nɒn-
anopheles ə'nɑfəˌliz; ES+-'nɒf-
another ə'nʌðɚ; ES ə'nʌðə(r
Anschluss Ger 'anʃlus
Anselm 'ænsɛlm
anserine 'gooselike' 'ænsəˌraɪn, -rɪn
anserine chem. 'ænsəˌrin, -rɪn
Anson 'ænsn̩
Ansonia æn'sonɪə

|full fʊl |tooth tuθ |further 'fɝðɚ; ES 'fɝðə |custom 'kʌstəm |while hwaɪl |how haʊ |toy tɔɪ
|using 'juzɪŋ |fuse fjuz, fɪuz |dish dɪʃ |vision 'vɪʒən |Eden 'idn̩ |cradle 'kredl̩ |keep 'em 'kipm̩

Anstruther 'ænstrʌðɚ; ES -ðə(r
answer 'ænsɚ; ES 'ænsə(r, E+'an-, 'ɑn-;
|-ed -d |-ing -sərɪŋ, -srɪŋ
answerable 'ænsərəbḷ, -srə- |-bly -blɪ; E see
  answer
ant ænt
antacid ænt'æsɪd
Antaeus æn'tiəs |-'s -ɪz
antagonism æn'tægə‚nɪzəm |-nist -nɪst
antagonistic æn‚tægə'nɪstɪk, ‚æntægə- |-al -ḷ
  |-ally -ḷɪ, -ɪklɪ
antagonize æn'tægə‚naɪz |-s -ɪz |-d -d
antalkali ænt'ælkə‚laɪ
antarctic ænt'ɑrktɪk, now rare -'ɑrtɪk; ES
  -'ɑ:-, E+-'ɑ:-; ('ant‚arctic 'circle)
Antarctica ænt'ɑrktɪkə; ES -'ɑ:k-, E+-'ɑ:k-
Antares æn'tɛrɪz, -'tær-; S -'tær-; |-es' -ɪz
ante 'æntɪ
anteater 'ænt‚itɚ; ES -‚itə(r
ante bellum 'æntɪ'bɛləm
antecede ‚æntə'sid |-d -ɪd
antecedence ‚æntə'sidṇs |-cy -ɪ |-dent -dṇt
antecessor ‚æntə'sɛsɚ; ES -'sɛsə(r
antechamber 'æntɪ‚tʃembɚ; ES -‚tʃembə(r
antedate 'æntɪ‚det, ‚æntɪ'det |-d -ɪd
antediluvian ‚æntɪdɪ'luvɪən, -'lɪuv-
antelope 'æntḷ‚op
ante meridiem 'æntɪmə'rɪdɪ‚ɛm, -'rɪdɪəm
antenna ən'tɛnə |-s -z |-nae -ni
Antenor æn'tinɚ, -nɔr; ES -nə(r, -nɔə(r
antepenult ‚æntɪ'pinʌlt, -pɪ'nʌlt
antepenultimate ‚æntɪpɪ'nʌltəmɪt
anterior æn'tɪrɪɚ; ES -'tɪrɪ‚ə(r
anteriority ‚æntɪrɪ'ɔrətɪ, -'ɑr-, -'ɒr-
anteroom 'æntɪ‚rum, -‚rʊm
anthelion ænt'hilɪən, æn'θilɪən |-s -z |-lia
  -lɪə—The 2d is not a spelling pron. Gk
  has θ.
anthelmintic ‚ænθɛl'mɪntɪk
anthem 'ænθəm—a sp. pron. (OE antefn, ME
  antem, 16c anthem with Latinized sp.
  of t)
anther 'ænθɚ; ES 'ænθə(r
anthill 'ænt‚hɪl
anthologize æn'θɑlə‚dʒaɪz; ES+-'ɒl-; |-s
  -ɪz |-d -d
anthology æn'θɑlədʒɪ; ES+-'ɒl-
Anthony 'ænθənɪ, 'æntənɪ, 'æntṇɪ
anthozoan ‚ænθə'zoən

anthracene 'ænθrə‚sin
anthracite 'ænθrə‚saɪt
anthracnose æn'θræknos
anthrax 'ænθræks |-es -ɪz
anthropocentric ‚ænθrəpo'sɛntrɪk
anthropogenesis ‚ænθrəpo'dʒɛnəsɪs
anthropogenetic ‚ænθrə‚podʒə'nɛtɪk
anthropography ‚ænθrə'pɑgrəfɪ, -'pɒg-
anthropoid 'ænθrə‚pɔɪd
anthropological ‚ænθrəpə'lɑdʒɪkḷ; ES+
  -'lɒdʒ-; |-ly -ɪ, -ɪklɪ
anthropology ‚ænθrə'pɑlədʒɪ; ES+-'pɒl-;
  |-gist -dʒɪst
anthropometric ‚ænθrəpo'mɛtrɪk |-al -ḷ |-ally
  -ḷɪ, -ɪklɪ
anthropometry ‚ænθrə'pɑmətrɪ; ES+-'pɒm-
anthropomorphic ‚ænθrəpo'mɔrfɪk; ES
  -'mɔəf-; |-al -ḷ |-ally -ḷɪ, -ɪklɪ |-phism
  -fɪzəm
anthropomorphosis ‚ænθrəpo'mɔrfəsɪs; ES
  -'mɔəf-
anthropomorphous ‚ænθrəpo'mɔrfəs; ES
  -'mɔəfəs
anthroponomy ‚ænθrə'pɑnəmɪ; ES+-'pɒn-
anthropophagi ‚ænθrə'pɑfə‚dʒaɪ; ES+-'pɒf-;
  |-gite -‚dʒaɪt |-gous -gəs
anti n 'æntaɪ, 'æntɪ |-s -z
antiadministration ‚æntɪəd‚mɪnə'streʃən
antiaircraft ‚æntɪ'ɛr‚kræft, -'ær-; E -'ɛə-,
  -'æə-, -‚kraft, -‚kræft; S -'æə‚kræft
antibiosis ‚æntɪbaɪ'osɪs |-otic -'ɑtɪk; ES+
  -'ɒtɪk
antibody 'æntɪ‚bɑdɪ; ES+-‚bɒdɪ
antic 'æntɪk |-ked -t
anticatalyst ‚æntɪ'kætḷɪst
anticathode ‚æntɪ'kæθod
antichlor 'æntɪ‚klor, -‚klɔr; ES -‚kloə(r, E+
  -‚klɔə(r
antichrist 'æntɪ‚kraɪst
anticipant æn'tɪsəpənt
anticipate æn'tɪsə‚pet |-d -ɪd |-tive -ɪv
anticipation æn‚tɪsə'peʃən, ‚æntɪsə-
anticipatory æn'tɪsəpə‚torɪ, -‚tɔrɪ; S -‚torɪ
anticlastic ‚æntɪ'klæstɪk
anticlerical ‚æntɪ'klɛrɪkḷ
anticlimax ‚æntɪ'klaɪmæks |-es -ɪz |-ed -t
anticline 'æntɪ‚klaɪn |-clinal ‚æntɪ'klaɪnḷ
Anticosti ‚æntə'kɑstɪ, -'kɑs-, -'kɒs-
anticyclone ‚æntɪ'saɪklon

anticyclonic ˌæntɪsaɪˈklɑnɪk; ES+-ˈklɒn-;
|-ally -ḷɪ, -ɪklɪ
antidotal ˈæntɪˌdotḷ, ˌæntɪˈdotḷ |-ly -ˈdotḷɪ
antidote ˈæntɪˌdot |-d -ɪd
Antietam ænˈtitəm
antifat ˌæntɪˈfæt (ˈantiˌfat ˈtreatment)
Antifederalist ˌæntɪˈfɛdərəlɪst, -ˈfɛdrəl-
antifreeze ˌæntɪˈfriz |-s -ɪz
antigen ˈæntədʒən -dʒɪn
Antigone ænˈtɪɡəˌni
Antigonus ænˈtɪɡənəs |-'s -ɪz
Antigua ænˈtiɡə, ænˈtiɡwə
anti-imperialism ˌæntɪ·ɪmˈpɪrɪəlˌɪzəm |-ist- ɪst
anti-imperialistic ˌæntɪ·ɪmˌpɪrɪəlˈɪstɪk
antiknock ˌæntɪˈnɑk; ES+-ˈnɒk
antilabor ˌæntɪˈlebɚ; ES -ˈlebə(r
Antilles ænˈtɪliz
antilogarithm ˌæntɪˈlɔɡəˌrɪðəm, -ˈlaɡ-, -ˈlɒɡ-
antilynching ˌæntɪˈlɪntʃɪŋ
antimacassar ˌæntɪməˈkæsɚ; ES -ˈkæsə(r
antimask, -sque ˈæntɪˌmæsk; E+-ˌmask,
-ˌmɑsk
antimonsoon ˌæntɪmɑnˈsun; ES+-mɒn-
antimony ˈæntəˌmonɪ
antimonyl ˈæntɪməˌnɪl
antinomian, A- ˌæntɪˈnomɪən
antinomy ænˈtɪnəmɪ
Antioch ˈæntɪˌɑk; ES+-ˌɒk
Antiochus ænˈtaɪəkəs |-'s -ɪz
antipathetic ænˌtɪpəˈθɛtɪk ˌæntɪpə- |-al -ḷ
|-ally -ḷɪ, -ɪklɪ
antipathy ænˈtɪpəθɪ
antiperiodic ˌæntɪˌpɪrɪˈɑdɪk; ES+-ˈɒd-
antiphlogistic ˌæntɪfloˈdʒɪstɪk
Antipholus ænˈtɪfələs |-'s -ɪz
antiphon ˈæntəˌfɑn, -fən; ES+-ˌfɒn
antiphonal ænˈtɪfənḷ |-ly -ɪ |-phony -fənɪ
antiphonary ænˈtɪfəˌnɛrɪ
antipodal ænˈtɪpədḷ
antipode ˈæntɪˌpod |pl antipodes ænˈtɪpəˌdiz
antipodean ænˌtɪpəˈdiən, ˌæntɪpə-
antipope ˈæntɪˌpop
antiputrid ˌæntɪˈpjutrɪd, -ˈpɪu-
antiquarian ˌæntɪˈkwɛrɪən, -ˈkwer-
antiquary ˈæntɪˌkwɛrɪ
antiquate ˈæntəˌkwet |-d -ɪd
antique ænˈtik (ˈanˌtique ˈtable)
antiquity ænˈtɪkwətɪ
antirrhinum, A- ˌæntɪˈraɪnəm

antirust ˌæntɪˈrʌst
antisaloon ˌæntɪsəˈlun
antiscorbutic ˌæntɪskɔrˈbjutɪk, -ˈbɪu-; ES
-skɔə-
anti-Semitic ˌæntɪsəˈmɪtɪk |-ally -ḷɪ, -ɪklɪ
anti-Semitism ˌæntɪˈsɛməˌtɪzəm
antisepsis ˌæntəˈsɛpsɪs
antiseptic ˌæntəˈsɛptɪk |-ally -ḷɪ, -ɪklɪ
antisepticize ˌæntəˈsɛptəˌsaɪz |-s -ɪz |-d -d
antiserum ˌæntɪˈsɪrəm
antislavery ˌæntəˈslevrɪ, -ˈslevərɪ
antisocial ˌæntɪˈsoʃəl
antistrophe ænˈtɪstrəfɪ, -ˌfi
antistrophic ˌæntɪˈstrɑfɪk, -ˈstrof-; ES+
-ˈstrɒf-; |-ally -ḷɪ, -ɪklɪ
antitank ˌæntɪˈtæŋk (ˈantiˌtank ˈgun)
antithesis ænˈtɪθəsɪs |-theses -θəˌsiz
antithetic ˌæntɪˈθɛtɪk |-al -ḷ |-ally -ḷɪ, -ɪklɪ
antitoxic ˌæntɪˈtɑksɪk; ES+-ˈtɒk-; |-xin
-ksɪn
antitrades ˈæntɪˌtredz
antitrust ˌæntɪˈtrʌst
antitype ˈæntəˌtaɪp
antitypic ˌæntəˈtɪpɪk |-al -ḷ |-ally -ḷɪ, -ɪklɪ
Antium ˈæntɪəm, -ʃɪəm
antivivisection ˌæntɪˌvɪvəˈsɛkʃən |-ist -ɪst
antiwar ˌæntɪˈwɔr; ES -ˈwɔə(r
antler ˈæntlɚ; ES ˈæntlə(r; |-ed -d
Antoinette ˌæntwaˈnɛt (Fr ɑ̃twaˈnɛt)
Antonia ænˈtonɪə
Antoninus ˌæntəˈnaɪnəs |-'s -ɪz
Antonio ænˈtonɪˌo, -njo
Antonius ænˈtonɪəs |-'s -ɪz
antonomasia ˌæntənoˈmeʒə, -ʒɪə
Antony ˈæntənɪ, ˈæntn̩ɪ
antonym ˈæntəˌnɪm
antonymous ænˈtɑnəməs; ES+-ˈtɒn-
antre ˈæntɚ; ES ˈæntə(r
Antrim ˈæntrɪm
antrum ˈæntrəm
Antwerp ˈæntwɝp; ES -wɜp, -wɝp
anus ˈenəs |-es -ɪz |-ni -naɪ
anvil ˈænvɪl |-ed -d
anxiety æŋˈzaɪətɪ, æŋɡˈz-
anxious ˈæŋkʃəs, ˈæŋʃəs
any ˈɛnɪ, unstressed occas. ənɪ, ŋɪ (ˈɡatn̩ɪ
ˈbet?)
anybody ˈɛnɪˌbɑdɪ, -ˌbʌdɪ, -bədɪ; ES+
-ˌbɒdɪ

|full fʊl |tooth tuθ |further ˈfɝðɚ; ES ˈfɜðə |custom ˈkʌstəm |while hwaɪl |how haʊ |toy tɔɪ
|using ˈjuzɪŋ |fuse fjuz, fɪuz |dish dɪʃ |vision ˈvɪʒən |Eden ˈidn̩ |cradle ˈkredḷ |keep 'em ˈkipm̩

Those words below in which the **ɑ** *sound is spelt* o *are often pronounced with* **ɒ** *in E and S*

anyhow **ˈɛnɪˌhaʊ**
anyone **ˈɛnɪˌwʌn, -wən** (**ˌɛnɪwənˈɛls**)
anything **ˈɛnɪˌθɪŋ**
anyway **ˈɛnɪˌwe** |-s **-z**
anywhere **ˈɛnɪˌhwɛr, -ˌhwær**; E **-ˌhweə(r**, ES **-ˌhwæə(r**
anywhere else **ˈɛnɪˌhwɛrˈɛls, -ˌhwær-, -hwɚˈɛls**
anywise **ˈɛnɪˌwaɪz**
Anzac **ˈænzæk**
A one, A 1 **ˈeˈwʌn**
Aonian **eˈonɪən**
aorist **ˈeərɪst**
aoristic **ˌeəˈrɪstɪk** |-ally **-l̩ɪ, -ɪklɪ**
aorta **eˈɔrtə**; ES **eˈɔətə**
apace **əˈpes**
apache *'gangster'* **əˈpɑʃ, əˈpæʃ** |-s **-ɪz** (*Fr* **aˈpaʃ**)
Apache *Indian* **əˈpætʃɪ**
Apalachee, -chi **ˌæpəˈlætʃɪ, -tʃi**
Apalachicola **ˌæpəˌlætʃɪˈkolə**
apanage **ˈæpənɪdʒ** |-s **-ɪz** |-d **-d**
apart **əˈpɑrt**; ES **əˈpɑ:t**, E+**əˈpa:t**
apartment **əˈpɑrtmənt**; ES **əˈpɑ:t-**, E+ **əˈpa:t-**
apartmental **əpɑrtˈmɛntl̩**; ES **əpɑ:t-**, E+ **əpa:t-**
apathetic **ˌæpəˈθɛtɪk** |-al **-l̩** |-ally **-l̩ɪ, -ɪklɪ**
apathy **ˈæpəθɪ**
ape **ep** |aped **ept**
apeak **əˈpik**
Apemantus **ˌæpɪˈmæntəs** |-'s **-ɪz**
Apennines **ˈæpəˌnaɪnz**
aperient **əˈpɪrɪənt**
aperiodic **ˌepɪrɪˈɑdɪk**; ES+**-ˈɒd-**; |-ally **-l̩ɪ, -ɪklɪ**
aperitif *Fr* **aperiˈtif**
aperitive **əˈpɛrətɪv**
aperture **ˈæpɚtʃɚ**; ES **ˈæpətʃə(r**; |-d **-d**
apery **ˈepərɪ**
apetalous **eˈpɛtl̩əs**
apex **ˈepɛks** |-es **-ɪz** |apices **ˈæpɪˌsiz, ˈe-** |-ed **-t**
aphaeresis **əˈfɛrəsɪs, æ-**
aphasia **əˈfeʒə, -ʒɪə**
aphelion **æˈfilɪən, ə-** |-s **-z** |-lia **-lɪə**
apheresis **əˈfɛrəsɪs, æ-**
aphesis **ˈæfəsɪs**
aphid **ˈefɪd, ˈæfɪd**
aphis, A- **ˈefɪs, ˈæfɪs** |-es **-ɪz** |aphides **ˈæfɪˌdiz**
aphorism **ˈæfəˌrɪzəm** |-ist **-rɪst**
aphoristic **ˌæfəˈrɪstɪk** |-al **-l̩** |-ally **-l̩ɪ, -ɪklɪ**
aphorize **ˈæfəˌraɪz** |-s **-ɪz** |-d **-d**
aphrodisiac **ˌæfrəˈdɪzɪˌæk**
Aphrodite **ˌæfrəˈdaɪtɪ**
A P I **ˈeˌpiˈaɪ, asɔ̃sjɑˈsjɔ̃ fɔneˈtik ɛ̃tɛrnasjɔ̃ˈnal**, *cf* I P A
apian **ˈepɪən**
apiarian **ˌepɪˈɛrɪən, -ˈer-**
apiarist **ˈepɪərɪst**
apiary **ˈepɪˌɛrɪ**
apical **ˈæpɪkl̩, ˈe-** |-ly **-ɪ**
apices **ˈæpɪˌsiz, ˈe-**
apicultural **ˌepɪˈkʌltʃərəl**
apiculture **ˈepɪˌkʌltʃɚ**; ES **-tʃə(r**
apiece **əˈpis**
Apis **ˈepɪs**
apish **ˈepɪʃ**
aplenty **əˈplɛntɪ**
aplomb **əˈplɑm, əˈplɔm** (*Fr* **aˈplɔ̃**)
apocalypse, A- **əˈpɑkəˌlɪps** |-s **-ɪz**
apocalyptic **əˌpɑkəˈlɪptɪk** |-al **-l̩** |-ally **-l̩ɪ, -ɪklɪ**
apocopate *adj* **əˈpɑkəpɪt, -ˌpet**
apocopate *v* **əˈpɑkəˌpet** |-d **-ɪd**
apocopation **əˌpɑkəˈpeʃən**
apocope **əˈpɑkəpɪ, -ˌpi**
apocrypha, A- **əˈpɑkrəfə** |-l **-l** |-lly **-lɪ**
apodeictic, -deik- **ˌæpəˈdaɪktɪk** |-al **-l̩** |-ally **-l̩ɪ, -ɪklɪ**
apodictic **ˌæpəˈdɪktɪk** |-al **-l̩** |-ally **-l̩ɪ, -ɪklɪ**
apodosis **əˈpɑdəsɪs** |-doses **-dəˌsiz**
apogee **ˈæpəˌdʒi**
Apollinaris **əˌpɑləˈnɛrɪs, -ˈnærɪs, -ˈnerɪs**
Apollo **əˈpɑlo**
Apollodorus **əˌpɑləˈdorəs, -ˈdɔr-**; S **-ˈdor-**; |-'s **-ɪz**
Apollonius **ˌæpəˈlonɪəs** |-'s **-ɪz**
Apollos **əˈpɑləs** |-'s **-ɪz**
Apollyon **əˈpɑljən**
apologetic **əˌpɑləˈdʒɛtɪk** |-al **-l̩** |-ally **-l̩ɪ, -ɪklɪ**
apologia **ˌæpəˈlodʒɪə**
apologist **əˈpɑlədʒɪst** |-gy **-dʒɪ**
apologize **əˈpɑləˌdʒaɪz** |-s **-ɪz** |-d **-d**
apologue **ˈæpəˌlɔg, -ˌlɑg, -ˌlɒg**
apophthegm **ˈæpəˌθɛm**

Key: *See in full §§3–47.* bee **bi** |pity **ˈpɪtɪ** (§6) |rate **ret** |yet **jɛt** |sang **sæŋ** |angry **ˈæŋ·grɪ** |bath **bæθ**; E **baθ** (§10) |ah **ɑ** |far **fɑr** |watch **wɑtʃ, wɒtʃ** (§12) |jaw **dʒɔ** |gorge **gɔrdʒ** |go **go**

Those words below in which the ɑ sound is spelt o are often pronounced with ɒ in E and S

apophthegmatic ˌæpəθɛɡˈmætɪk |-al -l̩ |-ally -l̩ɪ, -ɪklɪ
apoplectic ˌæpəˈplɛktɪk |-al -l̩ |-ally -l̩ɪ, -ɪklɪ
apoplexed ˈæpəˌplɛkst |apoplexy ˈæpəˌplɛksɪ
aport əˈport, əˈpɔrt; ES əˈpoət, E+əˈpɔət
aposiopesis ˌæpəˌsaɪəˈpisɪs
apostasy əˈpɑstəsɪ
apostate əˈpɑstet, -tɪt
apostatize əˈpɑstəˌtaɪz |-s -ɪz |-d -d
a posteriori ˈepɑsˌtɪrɪˈoraɪ, -ˈɔr-; S -ˈor-
apostle əˈpɑsl̩
apostolate əˈpɑstl̩ɪt, -ˌet
apostolic ˌæpəsˈtɑlɪk |-al -l̩ |-ally -l̩ɪ, -ɪklɪ
apostrophe əˈpɑstrəfɪ
apostrophize əˈpɑstrəˌfaɪz |-s -ɪz |-d -d
apothecary əˈpɑθəˌkɛrɪ
apothegm ˈæpəˌθɛm
apothegmatic ˌæpəθɛɡˈmætɪk |-al -l̩ |-ally -l̩ɪ, -ɪklɪ
apotheosis əˌpɑθɪˈosɪs, ˌæpəˈθiəsɪs
Appalachia ˌæpəˈlætʃɪə
Appalachian ˌæpəˈlætʃɪən, -ˈletʃ-, -tʃən
Appalachians ˌæpəˈlætʃənz, -ˈletʃ-, -ɪənz
appall, -al əˈpɔl |-ed, -led -d
appanage ˈæpənɪdʒ |-s -ɪz |-d -d
Appanoose ˌæpəˈnus |-'s -ɪz
apparatus ˌæpəˈretəs, -ˈrætəs |pl -tuses -təsɪz
|L pl -ratus -ˈretəs
apparel əˈpærəl |-ed -d
apparent əˈpærənt, əˈpɛr-; S əˈpær-
apparition ˌæpəˈrɪʃən
apparitor əˈpærətɚ; ES -tə(r
appeal əˈpil |-ed -d |-able -əbl̩
appealability əˌpiləˈbɪlətɪ
appear əˈpɪr; ES əˈpɪə(r, S+əˈpɛə(r, əˈpjɛə(r;
|-ed -d
appearance əˈpɪrəns; S+əˈpɛr-, əˈpjɛr-;
|-s -ɪz
appeasable əˈpizəbl̩ |-bly -blɪ
appease əˈpiz |-s -ɪz |-d -d
appellant əˈpɛlənt
appellate əˈpɛlɪt |-tive -ɪv, -lətɪv
appellation ˌæpəˈleʃən
appellee ˌæpəˈli
appellor əˈpɛlɔr, ˌæpəˈlɔr; ES -ɔə(r
append əˈpɛnd |-ed -ɪd |-age -ɪdʒ |-ages
-ɪdʒɪz
appendant əˈpɛndənt

appendectomy ˌæpənˈdɛktəmɪ
appendices əˈpɛndəˌsiz
appendicitis əˌpɛndəˈsaɪtɪs
appendix əˈpɛndɪks |-es -ɪz |-dices -dəˌsiz
apperceive ˌæpɚˈsiv; ES ˌæpə-; |-d -d
apperception ˌæpɚˈsɛpʃən; ES ˌæpə-; |-tive
-tɪv
appertain ˌæpɚˈten; ES ˌæpə-; |-ed -d
appetence ˈæpətəns |-cy -ɪ |-tent -tənt
appetite ˈæpəˌtaɪt |-titive -ˌtaɪtɪv
appetize ˈæpəˌtaɪz |-s -ɪz |-d -d
appetizer ˈæpəˌtaɪzɚ; ES -ˌtaɪzə(r
Appian ˈæpɪən
applaud əˈplɔd |-ed -ɪd |-able -əbl̩ |-bly -blɪ
applause əˈplɔz |-s -ɪz
apple ˈæpl̩ |-d -d |-ling ˈæpl̩ɪŋ, ˈæplɪŋ
applejack ˈæpl̩ˌdʒæk
apple pie ˈæpl̩ˈpaɪ (ˈapple-ˌpie ˈorder)
applesauce ˈæpl̩ˌsɔs
Appleton ˈæpl̩tən
appliable əˈplaɪəbl̩ |-bly -blɪ
appliance əˈplaɪəns |-s -ɪz |-ant -ənt
applicability ˌæplɪkəˈbɪlətɪ
applicable ˈæplɪkəbl̩, əˈplɪk- |-bly -blɪ
applicant ˈæpləkənt
application ˌæpləˈkeʃən
applicative ˈæpləˌketɪv |-tor -tɚ; ES -tə(r
applicatory ˈæpləkəˌtorɪ, -ˌtɔrɪ; S -ˌtorɪ
applied əˈplaɪd |appliedly əˈplaɪ-ɪdlɪ
appliqué ˌæplɪˈke (Fr apliˈke)
apply əˈplaɪ |applied əˈplaɪd
appoint əˈpɔɪnt |-ed -ɪd |-ive -ɪv
appointee əpɔɪnˈti, ˌæpɔɪnˈti, əˈpɔɪntɪ
appointor əˈpɔɪntɚ, əpɔɪnˈtɔr; ES -tə(r,
-ˈtɔə(r
Appomattox ˌæpəˈmætəks |-'s -ɪz |-toc -tək
apportion əˈporʃən, əˈpɔr-; ES əˈpoəʃən, E+
əˈpɔə-; |-ed -d |-ing -ʃənɪŋ, -ʃnɪŋ
appose əˈpoz, æ- |-s -ɪz |-d -d |-sable -əbl̩
apposite ˈæpəzɪt
apposition ˌæpəˈzɪʃən
appositive əˈpɑzətɪv
appraise əˈprez |-s -ɪz |-d -d |-sal -l̩
appreciable əˈpriʃɪəbl̩, -ʃəbl̩ |-bly -blɪ
appreciate əˈpriʃɪˌet |-d -ɪd
appreciation əˌpriʃɪˈeʃən |-tive əˈpriʃɪˌetɪv
appreciatory əˈpriʃɪəˌtorɪ, -ˌtɔrɪ; S -ˌtorɪ
apprehend ˌæprɪˈhɛnd |-ed -ɪd

Words below in which a before r (farm) is sounded ɑ are often pronounced in E with a (fa:m)

apprehensible ˌæprɪˈhɛnsəbḷ |-bly -blɪ
apprehension ˌæprɪˈhɛnʃən |-sive -sɪv
apprentice əˈprɛntɪs |-s -ɪz |-d -t |-ship -ˌʃɪp
appressed əˈprɛst, æ-
apprise, -ze *'advise'* əˈpraɪz |-s -ɪz |-d -d
apprize, -se *'appraise'* əˈpraɪz |-s -ɪz |-d -d
approach əˈprotʃ |-es -ɪz |-ed -t
approachability əˌprotʃəˈbɪlətɪ
approachable əˈprotʃəbḷ
approbate ˈæprəˌbet |-d -ɪd |-tion ˌæprəˈbeʃən
approbatory əˈprobəˌtorɪ, -ˌtɔrɪ; S -ˌtorɪ
appropriable əˈproprɪəbḷ
appropriate *adj* əˈproprɪɪt
appropriate *v* əˈproprɪˌet |-d -ɪd |-tive -ɪv
appropriation əˌproprɪˈeʃən
approve əˈpruv |-d -d |-dly -ɪdlɪ |-val -ḷ
approximate *adj* əˈprɑksəmɪt; ES+əˈprɒks-
approximate *v* əˈprɑksəˌmet; ES+əˈprɒks-; |-d -ɪd
approximation əˌprɑksəˈmeʃən; ES+ əˌprɒks-
appurtenance əˈpɝtṇəns; ES əˈpɜt-, əˈpɝt-; |-s -ɪz |-ant -ənt
apricot ˈeprɪˌkɑt, ˈæp-; ES+-ˌkɒt
April ˈeprəl, ˈeprɪl
a priori ˈepraɪˈoraɪ, -ˈɔr-; S -ˈoraɪ
apriority ˌepraɪˈɔrətɪ, -ˈɑr-, -ˈɒr-
apron ˈeprən, ˈepɚn; ES ˈeprən, ˈepən; |-ed -d—*The older pron.* ˈepən, ˈepən *is by no means rare, and appears from the L.A. to be very common in NEngd.*
apropos ˌæprəˈpo
apse æps |apses ˈæpsɪz
apsis ˈæpsɪs |apsides ˈæpsɪˌdiz
apt æpt
apterous ˈæptərəs
apteryx ˈæptəˌrɪks |-es -ɪz
aptitude ˈæptəˌtjud, -ˌtɪud, -ˌtud
Apuleius ˌæpjuˈliəs |-'s -ɪz
Apulia əˈpjulɪə, əˈpɪulɪə
aqua ˈækwə, ˈe- |-s -z |aquae -wi
aqua fortis ˈækwəˈfɔrtɪs, ˈe-; ES -ˈfɔətɪs
aqualon ˈækwəˌlɑn; ES+-ˌlɒn
aquamarine ˌækwəməˈrin
aquaplane ˈækwəˌplen
aqua regia ˈækwəˈridʒɪə, ˈe-
aquarium əˈkwɛrɪəm, əˈkwer- |-s -z |-ria -rɪə

Aquarius əˈkwɛrɪəs, əˈkwer- |-'s -ɪz
aquatic əˈkwætɪk, əˈkwat-, əˈkwɒt-
aquatint ˈækwəˌtɪnt
aqua vitae ˈækwəˈvaɪtɪ
aqueduct ˈækwɪˌdʌkt
aqueous ˈekwɪəs, ˈæk-
Aquidneck əˈkwɪdnɛk
Aquila ˈækwɪlə |-lae -ˌli—*Bible*+əˈkwɪlə, *perh. by association with* Priscilla (*Rom.* 16:3).
aquiline ˈækwəˌlaɪn, -lɪn
Aquinas əˈkwaɪnəs |-'s -ɪz
Aquitaine ˌækwɪˈten |-tania -ɪə
ar ɑr; ES ɑ:(r
Arab ˈærəb, *now less freq.* ˈeræb
Arabella ˌærəˈbɛlə
arabesque ˌærəˈbɛsk
Arabia əˈrebɪə, -bjə |-n -n
Arabic, a- ˈærəbɪk
arabis, A- ˈærəbɪs |-es -ɪz
arable ˈærəbḷ
Araby ˈærəbɪ
Arachne əˈrækni
arachnid əˈræknɪd |-noid -nɔɪd
Aragon ˈærəˌgɑn, -gən; ES+-ˌgɒn; (*Sp* ˌɑrɑˈgɔn)
Aral ˈɛrəl, ˈærəl, ˈerəl; S ˈærəl, ˈerəl
Aram ˈerəm, ˈɛrəm, ˈærəm; S ˈerəm, ˈærəm
Aramaean, -mean ˌærəˈmiən |-maic -ˈme·ɪk
Aransas əˈrænsəs |-sas' -səs
Arapaho, -hoe əˈræpəˌho
Ararat ˈærəˌræt
arbalest, -list ˈɑrbəlɪst; ES ˈɑ:b-
arbiter ˈɑrbɪtɚ; ES ˈɑ:bɪtə(r
arbitrable ˈɑrbətrəbḷ; ES ˈɑ:b-
arbitrage *'arbitration'* ˈɑrbətrɪdʒ; ES ˈɑ:b-; |-s -ɪz
arbitrage *commerce* ˈɑrbətrɪdʒ, ˌɑrbəˈtraʒ; ES ˈɑ:b-, ˌɑ:b-; |-s -ɪz |-d -d
arbitral ˈɑrbətrəl; ES ˈɑ:b-
arbitrament ɑrˈbɪtrəmənt; ES ɑˈbɪt-
arbitrarily ˈɑrbəˌtrɛrəlɪ; ES ˈɑ:b-; *esp. if emph.* ˌɑrbɪˈtrarɪly
arbitrary ˈɑrbəˌtrɛrɪ; ES ˈɑ:b-
arbitrate ˈɑrbəˌtret; ES ˈɑ:b-; |-d -ɪd
arbitration ˌɑrbəˈtreʃən; ES ˌɑ:b-
arbitrator ˈɑrbəˌtretɚ; ES ˈɑ:bəˌtretə(r
arbitress ˈɑrbətrɪs; ES ˈɑ:b-; |-es -ɪz
Arblay, d' ˈdɑrble; ES ˈdɑ:ble

Key: *See in full §§3–47.* bee bi |pity ˈpɪtɪ (§6) |rate ret |yet jɛt |sang sæŋ |angry ˈæŋ·grɪ |bath bæθ; E baθ (§10) |ah ɑ |far fɑr |watch watʃ, wɒtʃ (§12) |jaw dʒɔ |gorge gɔrdʒ |go go

Words below in which a *before* r (farm) *is sounded* ɑ *are often pronounced in* E *with* a (faːm)

arbor, A- ˈɑrbɚ; ES ˈɑːbə(r; |-ed -d
arboraceous ͵ɑrbəˈreʃəs; ES ͵ɑːbə-
arboreal ɑrˈborɪəl, -ˈbɔr-; ES ɑˈborɪəl, E+
-ˈbɔrɪəl
arborescent ͵ɑrbəˈrɛsn̩t; ES ͵ɑːbə-; |-nce
-sn̩s
arboretum ͵ɑrbəˈritəm; ES ͵ɑːbə-
arboriculture ˈɑrbərɪ͵kʌltʃɚ; ES ˈɑːbərɪ-
͵kʌltʃə(r
arborvitae, arbor vitae ˈɑrbɚˈvaɪtɪ; ES
ˈɑːbə-
Arbuckle ˈɑrbʌkl̩; ES ˈɑːb-
Arbuthnot ɑrˈbʌθnət, ˈɑrbəθ͵nɑt; ES ɑː-,
ˈɑː-, -͵nɒt
arbutus ɑrˈbjutəs, -ˈbɪu-; ES ɑː-; |-es -ɪz
arc ɑrk; ES ɑːk; |arced, arcked ɑrkt; ES ɑːkt
Arc, Jeanne d' *Fr* ʒɑːnˈdark
arcade ɑrˈked; ES ɑːˈked; |-d -ɪd
Arcadia ɑrˈkedɪə; ES ɑˈked-; |-n -n
Arcady ˈɑrkədɪ; ES ˈɑːk-
arcanum ɑrˈkenəm; ES ɑːˈken-; |-na -nə
arced ɑrkt; ES ɑːkt
arch ɑrtʃ; ES ɑːtʃ; |-es -ɪz |-ed -t
Archaean ɑrˈkiən; ES ɑːˈkiən
archaeological ͵ɑrkɪəˈlɑdʒɪkl̩;ES ͵ɑːkɪəˈlɑdʒ-,
-ˈlɒdʒ-; |-ly -ɪ, -ɪklɪ
archaeology ͵ɑrkɪˈalədʒɪ; ES ͵ɑːkɪˈal-, -ˈɒl-;
|-gist -dʒɪst
archaeopteryx, A- ͵ɑrkɪˈaptərɪks; ES
͵ɑːkɪˈap-, -ˈɒp-; |-es -ɪz
Archaeornis ͵ɑrkɪˈɔrnɪs; ES ͵ɑːkɪˈɔənɪs
archaic ɑrˈke·ɪk; ES ɑː-; |-al -l̩ |-ally -l̩ɪ,
-ɪklɪ
archaism ˈɑrkɪ͵ɪzəm, ˈɑrke-; ES ˈɑːk-
archaistic ͵ɑrkɪˈɪstɪk, ͵ɑrke-; ES ͵ɑːk-
archaize ˈɑrkɪ͵aɪz, ˈɑrke-; ES ˈɑːk-; |-s -ɪz
|-d -d
archangel, A- ˈɑrkˈendʒəl, -͵endʒəl; ES ˈɑːk-
archangelic ͵ɑrkænˈdʒɛlɪk; ES ͵ɑːk-; |-al -l̩
archbishop ˈɑrtʃˈbɪʃəp; ES ˈɑːtʃ-; (ˈArch-
͵bishop ˈLaud)
archbishopric ͵ɑrtʃˈbɪʃəprɪk; ES ͵ɑːtʃ-
Archbald ˈɑrtʃbɔld; ES ˈɑːtʃ-; |-bold -bold
archdeacon ˈɑrtʃˈdikən, -͵dikən; ES ˈɑːtʃ-
archdiocese ˈɑrtʃˈdaɪə͵sis, -sɪs; ES ˈɑːtʃ-;
|-s -ɪz
archducal ͵ɑrtʃˈdjukl̩, -ˈdɪu-, -ˈdu-; ES
͵ɑːtʃ-

archduchess ˈɑrtʃˈdʌtʃɪs, -͵dʌtʃɪs; ES ˈɑːtʃ-;
|-es -ɪz
archduchy ˈɑrtʃˈdʌtʃɪ; ES ˈɑːtʃ-
archduke ˈɑrtʃˈdjuk, -ˈdɪuk, -ˈduk, -͵d-; ES
ˈɑːtʃ-
Archean ɑrˈkiən; ES ɑːˈkiən
arched ɑrtʃt; ES ɑːtʃt
archenemy ˈɑrtʃˈɛnəmɪ, -͵ɛnəmɪ; ES ˈɑːtʃ-
archeological ͵ɑrkɪəˈlɑdʒɪkl̩; ES ͵ɑːkɪəˈlɑdʒ-,
-ˈlɒdʒ-; |-ly -ɪ, -ɪklɪ
archeology ͵ɑrkɪˈalədʒɪ; ES ͵ɑːkɪˈal-, -ˈɒl-;
|-gist -dʒɪst
Archeozoic ͵ɑrkɪəˈzo·ɪk; ES ͵ɑːkɪə-
archer, A- ˈɑrtʃɚ; ES ˈɑːtʃə(r; |-y -ɪ
archetype ˈɑrkə͵taɪp; ES ˈɑːkə-
archfiend ˈɑrtʃˈfind, -͵find; ES ˈɑːtʃ-
Archibald ˈɑrtʃə͵bɔld; ES ˈɑːtʃ-
Archidamus ͵ɑrkɪˈdeməs; ES ͵ɑːkɪ-; |-'s -ɪz
archidiaconal ͵ɑrkɪdaɪˈækənl̩; ES ͵ɑːkɪ-
archiepiscopacy ͵ɑrkɪəˈpɪskəpəsɪ; ES ͵ɑːkɪ-;
|-pal -pl̩
Archimedean ͵ɑrkɪˈmidɪən, -mɪˈdiən; ES
͵ɑːkɪ-
Archimedes ͵ɑrkəˈmidiz; ES ͵ɑːk-; |-des'
-diz
archipelagic ͵ɑrkɪpəˈlædʒɪk; ES ͵ɑːkɪ-
archipelago ͵ɑrkəˈpɛlə͵go; ES ͵ɑːkə-
architect ˈɑrkə͵tɛkt; ES ˈɑːkə-
architectonic ͵ɑrkɪtɛkˈtɑnɪk;ES ͵ɑːkɪtɛkˈtɑn-,
-ˈtɒn-; |-al -l̩ |-ally -l̩ɪ, -ɪklɪ
architectural ͵ɑrkəˈtɛktʃərəl; ES ͵ɑːkə-;
|-ly -ɪ
architecture ˈɑrkə͵tɛktʃɚ; ES ˈɑːkə͵tɛktʃə(r
architrave ˈɑrkə͵trev; ES ˈɑːkə-; |-d -d
archival ɑrˈkaɪvl̩; ES ɑːˈkaɪvl̩
archive ˈɑrkaɪv; ES ˈɑːk-; |-s -z |-d -d
archivist ˈɑrkəvɪst; ES ˈɑːk-
archivolt ˈɑrkə͵volt; ES ˈɑːkə-
archon ˈɑrkan, -kən; ES ˈɑːkan, -kɒn, -kən
archpriest ˈɑrtʃˈprist; ES ˈɑːtʃ-; |-hood -hʊd
|-ship -ʃɪp
archway ˈɑrtʃ͵we; ES ˈɑːtʃ-
arcing ˈɑrkɪŋ; ES ˈɑːkɪŋ
Arcite ˈɑrsaɪt, ɑrˈsaɪt; ES ˈɑːs-, ɑːˈs-
arcked ɑrkt; ES ɑːkt; |-cking -kɪŋ
Arcola ɑrˈkolə; ES ɑːˈk-
arctic ˈɑrktɪk, *now rare* ˈɑrtɪk; ES ˈɑː-;
|-s -s

Words below in which a *before* r (farm) *is sounded* ɑ *are often pronounced in* E *with* a (fa:m)

Arcturus ɑrk'tjʊrəs, -'tɪʊr-, -'tʊr-; ES ɑ:k-;
|-'s -ɪz
arcuate 'ɑrkjʊɪt, -ˌet; ES 'ɑ:k-; |-d -ˌetɪd
Arden 'ɑrdṇ; ES 'ɑ:dṇ
ardent 'ɑrdṇt; ES 'ɑ:d-; |-ncy -ṇsɪ
Ardmore 'ɑrdmor, -mɔr; ES 'ɑ:dmoə(r,
E+-mɔə(r
ardor 'ɑrdɚ; ES 'ɑ:də(r
arduous 'ɑrdʒʊəs; ES 'ɑ:dʒ-
are *measure* ɛr, ær, ɑr; E ɛə(r, ES æə(r, ɑ:(r
are *v stressed* 'ɑr, ˌɑr; ES 'ɑ:(r, ˌɑ:(r; *unstr.*
ɚ; ES ə(r; |'re -r; ES -ə(r; *see* we're,
you're, they're
area 'ɛrɪə, 'erɪə |-way -ˌwe
arena ə'rinə
aren't ɑrnt; ES ɑ:nt
Areopagite ˌærɪ'ɑpəˌdʒaɪt, -ˌgaɪt; ES+-'ɒp-
Areopagitic ˌærɪˌɑpə'dʒɪtɪk; ES+-ˌɒp-;
|-a -ə
Areopagus ˌærɪ'ɑpəgəs; ES+-'ɒp-; |-'s -ɪz
Ares 'eriz, 'ɛriz, 'æriz; S 'eriz, 'æriz; |-res'
-riz
Arethusa ˌærɪ'θjuzə, -'θɪu-, -'θu-
argal *'argol'* 'ɑrgḷ; ES 'ɑ:gḷ
argal *'ergo'* 'ɑrgḷ; ES 'ɑ:gḷ—*In Shak.'s day*
argal *was pron.* 'ærgḷ *and* ergo 'ærgɔ.
argali 'ɑrgəlɪ; ES 'ɑ:gəlɪ
argent 'ɑrdʒənt; ES 'ɑ:dʒənt
argental ɑr'dʒɛntḷ; ES ɑ:'dʒɛntḷ; |-teous
-tɪəs |-tic -tɪk
argentiferous ˌɑrdʒən'tɪfərəs; ES ˌɑ:dʒən-
Argentina ˌɑrdʒən'tinə; ES ˌɑ:dʒən-
Argentine 'ɑrdʒənˌtin, -ˌtaɪn; ES 'ɑ:dʒ-
argentine 'ɑrdʒəntɪn, -ˌtaɪn; ES 'ɑ:dʒ-
Argentinian ˌɑrdʒən'tɪnɪən; ES ˌɑ:dʒ-
argentite 'ɑrdʒənˌtaɪt; ES 'ɑ:dʒ-
argentous ɑr'dʒɛntəs; ES ɑ:'dʒɛn-
argil 'ɑrdʒɪl; ES 'ɑ:dʒɪl
Argive 'ɑrdʒaɪv; ES 'ɑ:dʒaɪv
Argo 'ɑrgo; ES 'ɑ:go
argol 'ɑrgḷ; ES 'ɑ:gḷ
argon 'ɑrgɑn; ES 'ɑ:gɑn, -gɒn
Argonaut 'ɑrgəˌnɔt; ES 'ɑ:gə-
Argonautic ˌɑrgə'nɔtɪk; ES ˌɑ:gə-
Argonne 'ɑrgɑn; ES 'ɑ:gɑn, -gɒn (*Fr* ar'gɔ̃n)
Argos 'ɑrgɑs, -gəs; ES 'ɑ:gɑs, -gɒs, -gəs;
|-'s -ɪz
argosy 'ɑrgəsɪ; ES 'ɑ:gəsɪ

argot 'ɑrgo, 'ɑrgət; ES 'ɑ:g-
argue 'ɑrgju; ES 'ɑ:g-; |-d -d
argument 'ɑrgjəmənt; ES 'ɑ:g-
argumental ˌɑrgjə'mɛntḷ; ES ˌɑ:g-
argumentation ˌɑrgjəmɛn'teʃən; ES ˌɑ:g-
argumentative ˌɑrgjə'mɛntətɪv; ES ˌɑ:g-
Argus 'ɑrgəs; ES 'ɑ:g-; |-'s -ɪz
Argus-eyed 'ɑrgəsˌaɪd; ES 'ɑ:g-
Argyll, -gyle ɑr'gaɪl; ES ɑ:'g-; |-shire -ʃɪr,
-ʃɚ; ES -ʃɪə(r, -ʃə(r
Argyrol 'ɑrdʒəˌrɔl, -ˌrɑl; ES 'ɑ:dʒ-, -ˌrɒl
aria 'ɑrɪə, 'ɛrɪə, 'ærɪə; S 'ɑrɪə, 'ærɪə
Ariadne ˌærɪ'ædnɪ
Arian 'ɛrɪən, 'ærɪən, 'erɪən; S 'ærɪən, 'er-
arid 'ærɪd |-ity ə'rɪdətɪ, æ-
Ariel 'ɛrɪəl, 'erɪəl, 'ærɪəl; S 'erɪəl, 'ær-
Aries 'ɛriz, 'eriz, 'æriz, -rɪˌiz; S 'er-, 'ær-;
|-es' -iz |*gen* Arietis ə'raɪətɪs
aright ə'raɪt
Ariosto ˌærɪ'ɑsto, -'ɒs-, -'os- (*It* ˌari'ɔsto)
arise ə'raɪz |-s -ɪz |arose ə'roz |arisen ə'rɪzṇ
Aristides ˌærə'staɪdiz |-des' -diz
aristocracy ˌærə'stɑkrəsɪ; ES+-'stɒk-
aristocrat ə'rɪstəˌkræt, 'ærɪstə-
aristocratic əˌrɪstə'krætɪk, ˌærɪstə- |-al -ḷ
|-ally -ḷɪ, -ɪklɪ
Aristophanes ˌærə'stɑfəˌniz; ES+-'stɒf-
Aristotelian ˌærɪstə'tilɪən, əˌrɪstə-, -ljən
Aristotle 'ærəˌstɑtḷ; ES+-ˌstɒtḷ
arithmetic *n* ə'rɪθməˌtɪk
arithmetic *adj* ˌærɪθ'mɛtɪk |-al -ḷ |-ally -ḷɪ,
-ɪklɪ
arithmetician əˌrɪθmə'tɪʃən, ˌærɪθmə-
Arius 'ɛrɪəs, 'ær-, 'er-, ə'raɪəs; S 'ær-, 'er-,
ə'raɪəs; |-'s -ɪz
Arizona ˌærə'zonə |-nan -nən |-nian -nɪən
ark ɑrk; ES ɑ:k; |-ed -t
Arkansan ɑr'kænzən; ES ɑ:'kæn-
Arkansas *state* 'ɑrkənˌsɔ, *o. f.* ɑr'kænzəs; *riv.*
'ɑrkənˌsɔ, *loc.*+ɑr'kænzəs, -z; *city in Ark*
'ɑrkənˌsɔ, *loc.*+ɑr'kænzəs, -z; *city in Kan*
'ɑrkənˌsɔ, *loc.* ɑr'kænzəs, -z; ES 'ɑ:kənˌsɔ,
ɑ:'kænzəs, S+'ɑ:kɪnˌsɔ; |*poss* 'Arkan,sas's
-ˌsɔz |Ar'kansas' -zəs
Arkansawyer 'ɑrkənˌsɔjɚ; ES 'ɑ:kənˌsɔjə(r
Arkwright 'ɑrkˌraɪt; ES 'ɑ:k-
Arlen 'ɑrlɪn, -ən; ES 'ɑ:l-
Arlington 'ɑrlɪŋtən; ES 'ɑ:l-

Words below in which a *before* r (farm) *is sounded* ɑ *are often pronounced in* E *with* a (faːm)

Arliss 'ɑrlɪs; ES 'ɑːl-; |-'s -ɪz
arm ɑrm; ES ɑːm; |-ed -d
armada, A- ɑr'mɑdə, -'medə; ES ɑː'm-
armadillo ˌɑrmə'dɪlo; ES ˌɑːmə-
Armageddon ˌɑrmə'gɛdn̩; ES ˌɑːmə-
armament 'ɑrməmənt; ES 'ɑːmə-
armature 'ɑrmətʃɚ, -ˌtʃʊr; ES 'ɑːmətʃə(r,
  -ˌtʃʊə(r
armchair 'ɑrmˌtʃɛr, -ˌtʃær; E 'ɑːmˌtʃɛə(r,
  ES -ˌtʃæə(r; *acct*+'arm'chair
Armenia ɑr'minɪə; ES ɑ'min-; |-n -n
armful 'ɑrmˌfʊl; ES 'ɑːm-; |-s -z
armhole 'ɑrmˌhol; ES 'ɑːm-
Arminian ɑr'mɪnɪən; ES ɑ'mɪn-
Arminius ɑr'mɪnɪəs; ES ɑ'mɪn-; |-'s -ɪz
armipotent ɑr'mɪpətənt; ES ɑ'mɪp-; |-ence
  -əns
armistice 'ɑrməstɪs; ES 'ɑːm-; |-s -ɪz
Armitage 'ɑrmətɪdʒ; ES 'ɑːm-; |-'s -ɪz
armlet 'ɑrmlɪt; ES 'ɑːm-
armor 'ɑrmɚ; ES 'ɑːmə(r; |-ed -d
armor-bearer 'ɑrmɚˌbɛrɚ, -ˌbærɚ; E 'ɑːmə-
  ˌbɛrə(r, ES -ˌbærə(r
armor-clad 'ɑrmɚˌklæd; ES 'ɑːmə-
armorer 'ɑrmərɚ; ES 'ɑːmərə(r
armorial ɑr'morɪəl, -'mɔr-; ES ɑ'morɪəl,
  E+-'mɔr-
Armoric ɑr'mɔrɪk, -'mɑr-, -'mɒr-; ES ɑː'm-;
  |-a -ə |-an -ən
armory 'ɑrmərɪ; ES 'ɑːmərɪ
armpit 'ɑrmˌpɪt; ES 'ɑːm-
arms ɑrmz; ES ɑːmz
Armstrong 'ɑrmstrɔŋ, -strɒŋ; ES 'ɑːm-
army 'ɑrmɪ; ES 'ɑːmɪ; |-mied -mɪd
arnica 'ɑrnɪkə; ES 'ɑːn-
Arno 'ɑrno; ES 'ɑːno
Arnold 'ɑrnl̩d; ES 'ɑːnl̩d
aroint ə'rɔɪnt
aroma ə'romə
Aroostook ə'rustʊk, *loc.*+-tɪk
arose ə'roz
around ə'raʊnd
arouse ə'raʊz |-s -ɪz |-d -d |-sal -l̩
ARP, A.R.P. 'eˌɑr'pi; ES 'eˌɑː'pi
arpeggio ɑr'pɛdʒɪˌo, -dʒo; ES ɑ'p-
arquebus 'ɑrkwɪbəs; ES 'ɑːk-; |-es -ɪz
arquebusier ˌɑrkwɪbəs'ɪr; ES ˌɑː-kwɪbəs'ɪə(r
arrack 'ærək

Arragon 'ærəˌgɑn, -gən; ES+-ˌgɒn; (*Sp*
  ˌarɑ'gɒn)
arraign ə'ren |-ed -d
arrange ə'rendʒ |-s -ɪz |-d -d
arrant 'ærənt
arras, A- 'ærəs |-es -ɪz (*Fr* a'rɑːs)
array ə're |-ed -d
arrear ə'rɪr; ES ə'rɪə(r, S+ə'rɛə(r; |-s -z
arrearage ə'rɪrɪdʒ |-s -ɪz
arrest ə'rɛst |-ed -ɪd
Arrighi ə'rigi, ɑ- (*It* ɑr'riːgi)
arris 'ærɪs |-es -ɪz
arrive ə'raɪv |-d -d |-val -l̩
arrogance 'ærəgəns |-cy -ɪ |-gant -gənt
arrogate 'ærəˌget, 'æro- |-d -ɪd
arrow 'æro, 'ærə |-ed -d |-ing 'ærəwɪŋ
arrowhead 'æroˌhɛd, 'ærə-
arrowroot 'æroˌrut, 'ærə-, -ˌrʊt
arrowy 'ærəwɪ
arroyo ə'rɔɪo
arsenal 'ɑrsn̩əl, 'ɑrsnəl; ES 'ɑːsn̩əl, 'ɑːsnəl
arsenate *n* 'ɑrsn̩ˌet, -ɪt; ES 'ɑːsn̩-
arsenate *v* 'ɑrsn̩ˌet; ES 'ɑːsn̩-; |-d -ɪd
arsenic *n, v* 'ɑrsn̩ɪk, 'ɑrsnɪk; ES 'ɑːs-;
  |-ked -t
arsenic *adj* ɑr'sɛnɪk; ES ɑː'sɛnɪk; |-al -l̩
arsenide 'ɑrsn̩ˌaɪd, -ɪd; ES 'ɑːsn̩-
arsenious ɑr'sinɪəs; ES ɑ'sin-
arsenite 'ɑrsn̩ˌaɪt; ES 'ɑːsn̩-
arsine ɑr'sin; ES ɑ'sin
arsis 'ɑrsɪs; ES 'ɑːsɪs; |arses -siz
arson 'ɑrsn̩; ES 'ɑːsn̩
arsphenamine ˌɑrsfɛnə'min, -'æmɪn; ES ˌɑːs-
art *n* ɑrt; ES ɑːt; |-y -ɪ
art *v* 2 *pers: stressed* 'ɑrt, ˌɑrt; ES 'ɑːt, ˌɑːt;
  unstr. ɑrt, ɚt; ES ɑt, ət
Artaxerxes ˌɑrtə'zɝksiz; ES ˌɑːtə'zɝk-, ˌɑːtə-
  'zɝk-; |xes' -ksiz
artefact 'ɑrtɪˌfækt; ES 'ɑːtɪ-
Artemidorus ˌɑrtəmɪ'dorəs, -'dɔr-; ES
  ˌɑːtəmɪ'dor-, E+-'dɔr-; |-'s -ɪz
Artemis 'ɑrtəmɪs; ES 'ɑːt-; |-'s -ɪz
Artemus 'ɑrtəməs; ES 'ɑːt-; |-'s -ɪz
arterial ɑr'tɪrɪəl; ES ɑ'tɪr-
arteriosclerosis ɑr'tɪrɪˌosklɪ'rosɪs; ES ɑ'tɪr-
artery 'ɑrtərɪ; ES 'ɑːtərɪ
artesian ɑr'tiʒən; ES ɑː't-; ('ɑrˌtesian 'well)
Artesius ɑr'tiʒəs; ES ɑː't-; |-'s -ɪz

|full fʊl |tooth tuθ |further 'fɝðɚ; ES 'fɝðə |custom 'kʌstəm |while hwaɪl |how haʊ |toy tɔɪ
|using 'juzɪŋ |fuse fjuz, fɪuz |dish dɪʃ |vision 'vɪʒən |Eden 'idn̩ |cradle 'kredl̩ |keep 'em 'kipm̩

Words below in which a *before* r (farm) *is sounded* ɑ *are often pronounced in* E *with* a (fa:m)

Arteveld 'ɑrtə͵vɛlt; ES 'ɑ:tə-
artful 'ɑrtfəl; ES 'ɑ:t-; |-ly -ɪ
Arthabaska ͵ɑrθə'bæskə; ES ͵ɑ:θə-
arthritic ɑr'θrɪtɪk; ES ɑ:'θrɪtɪk; |-al -ļ
arthritis ɑr'θraɪtɪs; ES ɑ:'θr-; |-tes -tiz
arthropod 'ɑrθrə͵pɑd; ES 'ɑ:θrə͵pɑd, -͵pɒd
Arthur 'ɑrθɚ; ES 'ɑ:θə(r;—*In the occas. pron.*
'ɑθɚ *the first* r *is lost by dissimilation*
(§121).
Arthurian ɑr'θjʊrɪən, -'θɪʊr-, -'θʊr-; ES ɑ'θ-
artichoke 'ɑrtɪ͵tʃok; ES 'ɑ:tɪ-
article 'ɑrtɪkļ; ES 'ɑ:tɪ-; |-d -d |-ling -klɪŋ,
-kļɪŋ
articular ɑr'tɪkjələ; ES ɑ'tɪkjələ(r
articulate *adj* ɑr'tɪkjəlɪt; ES ɑ'tɪk-
articulate *v* ɑr'tɪkjə͵let; ES ɑ'tɪk-; |-d -ɪd
articulation ɑr͵tɪkjə'leʃən, ͵ɑrtɪkjə-; ES
ɑ͵tɪk-, ͵ɑ:tɪk-
Artie 'ɑrtɪ; ES 'ɑ:tɪ
artifact 'ɑrtɪ͵fækt; ES 'ɑ:tɪ-
artifice 'ɑrtəfɪs; ES 'ɑ:tə-; |-s -ɪz
artificer ɑr'tɪfəsɚ; ES ɑ'tɪfəsə(r
artificial ͵ɑrtə'fɪʃəl; ES ͵ɑ:tə-; |-ly -ɪ
artificiality ͵ɑrtə͵fɪʃɪ'ælətɪ, -fɪ'ʃælətɪ; ES
͵ɑ:tə-
artillery ɑr'tɪlərɪ; ES ɑ'tɪl-; |-rist -rɪst
artisan 'ɑrtəzn̩; ES 'ɑ:təzn̩; |-ship -͵ʃɪp
artist 'ɑrtɪst; ES 'ɑ:tɪst; |-ry -rɪ
artiste ɑr'tist; ES ɑ:'tist; (*Fr* ɑr'tist)
artistic ɑr'tɪstɪk; ES ɑ:'tɪs-; |-al -ļ |-ally -ļɪ,
-ɪklɪ
artless 'ɑrtlɪs; ES 'ɑ:tlɪs
Artois ɑr'twɑ, -'twɒ; ES ɑ:'t-; (*Fr* ɑr'twa)
arty 'ɑrtɪ; ES 'ɑ:tɪ
Arundel *Engd, Can* 'ærəndļ, *Sus loc.* 'ɑrndļ
(Arndle *1788*); *Md* ə'rʌndļ (*see* Anne
Arundel)
Arveragus ɑr'vɛrəgəs; ES ɑ'vɛr-; |-'s -ɪz
Arviragus ɑr'vɪrəgəs; ES ɑ'vɪr-; |-'s -ɪz
Aryan 'ɛrɪən, 'ær-, 'ɑr-, -rjən; S 'ær-, 'er-,
'ɑr-
arytenoid ͵ærɪ'tinɔɪd, ə'rɪtn̩͵ɔɪd
as *Rom weight* æs |asses 'æsɪz
as *adv, etc: unstressed* əz, z, s; *rarely stressed*
'æz, ͵æz
Asa 'esə
asafetida, -foet- ͵æsə'fɛtɪdə, æs'fɛtɪdə
Asaph 'æsəf, 'esəf, 'esæf

asbestos, -us æs'bɛstəs, æz-
Asbury 'æz͵bɛrɪ, -bərɪ
Ascalon *sword & Pal vil.* 'æskə͵lɑn, -͵lɒn,
-lən
Ascanius ə'skenɪəs, æ- |-'s -ɪz
ascend ə'sɛnd |-ed -ɪd
ascendance, -ence ə'sɛndəns |-cy -ɪ |-nt -nt
ascension, A- ə'sɛnʃən
ascent ə'sɛnt
ascertain ͵æsɚ'ten; ES ͵æsə-; |-ed -d
ascetic ə'sɛtɪk |-al -ļ |-ally -ļɪ, -ɪklɪ
asceticism ə'sɛtə͵sɪzəm
Asch, Sholem 'ʃoləm'æʃ (*Yiddish* 'ʃolɛm'aʃ)
Ascham, a- 'æskəm
Asclepias æs'klipɪəs |-pius -pɪəs |-'s -ɪz
ascot, A- 'æskət
ascribe ə'skraɪb |-d -d
Ascue 'æskju, -kɪu
Ascutney ə'skʌtnɪ, *loc. often* 'skʌtnɪ
asepsis ə'sɛpsɪs, e-, æ-
aseptic ə'sɛptɪk, e-, æ- |-ally -ļɪ, -ɪklɪ
asexual e'sɛkʃʊəl, ə-, æ- |-ly -ɪ
Asgard 'æsgɑrd, 'æz-; ES -gɑ:d
ash, A- æʃ |-es -ɪz |-ed -t
ashamed ə'ʃemd |-medly -mɪdlɪ
Ashanti ə'ʃæntɪ
Ashburn 'æʃbɚn; ES 'æʃbən
Ashburnham *Mass* 'æʃbɚn͵hæm; ES -bən-;
Engd 'æʃ͵bɚnəm; ES -͵bɜn-, -͵bɚn-
Ashburton 'æʃbɚtn̩; ES 'æʃbətn̩
Ashby-de-la-Zouch 'æʃbɪ͵dɛlə'zuʃ, -dələ- |-'s
-ɪz
Ashdod 'æʃdɑd; ES+-dɒd
Ashdown 'æʃ͵daʊn
ashes 'æʃɪz |ashen 'æʃən
Asheville 'æʃvɪl; S+-vļ
Ashkelon 'æʃkə͵lɑn, -͵lɒn, -lən
ashlar, -ler 'æʃlɚ; ES 'æʃlə(r
Ashmole 'æʃmol |-an æʃ'molɪən
Ashokan ə'ʃokən
ashore ə'ʃor, ə'ʃɔr; ES ə'ʃoə(r, E+ə'ʃɔə(r
Ashtabula ͵æʃtə'bjulə, -'bɪulə
Ashtoreth 'æʃtərɪθ, -͵rɛθ |*pl* -taroth -͵rɑθ,
-͵rɒθ
Ashuelot 'æʃwɪ͵lɑt; ES+-͵lɒt; *loc.*+͵æʃʊ'ilət,
͵æʃə'wɪlət, æʃ'wɪlət
Asia 'eʒə, 'eʃə |-n -n —'eʒə *prevails in US,*
'eʃə *in Engd.*

Key: *See in full* §§3–47. bee bi |pity 'pɪtɪ (§6) |rate ret |yet jɛt |sang sæŋ |angry 'æŋ·grɪ
|bath bæθ; E baθ (§10) |ah ɑ |far fɑr |watch wɑtʃ, wɒtʃ (§12) |jaw dʒɔ |gorge gɔrdʒ |go go

Asiatic ˌeʒɪˈætɪk, ˌeʃ- |-al -] |-ally -]ɪ, -ɪklɪ
aside əˈsaɪd
asinine ˈæsn̩ˌaɪn |-ninity ˌæsəˈnɪnətɪ
ask '*newt*' æsk
ask *v* æsk; E ask, æsk, ɑsk; |-ed -skt, -st
askance əˈskæns |askant əˈskænt
Askelon *sword* ˈæskəˌlɑn, -ˌlɒn, -lən
askew əˈskju, əˈskɪu
Askew ˈæskju, -kɪu
aslant əˈslænt; E+əˈslant, əˈslɑnt
asleep əˈslip
aslope əˈslop
Asmodeus ˌæzmoˈdiəs, ˌæs- |-ˈs -ɪz
asp æsp
asparagus əˈspærəgəs
Aspasia æsˈpeʒɪə, -ʃɪə
aspect ˈæspɛkt—*in Shak.* æˈspɛkt
aspen ˈæspɪn, -pən
asperges, A- əˈspɝdʒɪz; ES əˈspɝ-, əˈspɝ-
aspergillum, A- ˌæspɚˈdʒɪləm; ES ˌæspə-; |-s
　-z |-la -lə
asperity æsˈpɛrətɪ, əˈspɛr-
asperse əˈspɝs; ES əˈspɜs, əˈspɝs; |-s -ɪz
　|-d -t
aspersion əˈspɝʒən, -ʃən; ES əˈspɝ-, əˈspɝ-
aspersorium ˌæspɚˈsorɪəm, -ˈsɔr-; ES ˌæspə-
　ˈsor-, E+ˈsɔr-; |-s -z |-ria -rɪə
asphalt ˈæsfɔlt, -fælt |-ed -ɪd
asphaltic æsˈfɔltɪk, -ˈfæltɪk
asphaltum æsˈfæltəm
asphodel ˈæsfəˌdɛl
asphyxia æsˈfɪksɪə |-iate -ɪˌet |-iated -ɪˌetɪd
asphyxiation æsˌfɪksɪˈeʃən ˌæsfɪksɪ-
aspic ˈæspɪk
aspidistra, A- ˌæspɪˈdɪstrə
Aspinwall ˈæspɪnˌwɔl
aspirant əˈspaɪrənt, ˈæspərənt
aspirate *n, adj* ˈæspərɪt, ˈæsprɪt
aspirate *v* ˈæspəˌret |-d -ɪd |-tion ˌæspəˈreʃən
aspirator ˈæspəˌretɚ; ES -ˌretə(r
aspiratory əˈspaɪrəˌtorɪ, -ˌtɔrɪ; S -ˌtorɪ
aspire əˈspaɪr; ES əˈspaɪə(r; |-d -d
aspirin ˈæspərɪn, -prɪn
asquint əˈskwɪnt
Asquith ˈæskwɪθ
ass '*donkey*' æs, '*blockhead*' æs, ɑs |-es -ɪz
assafetida, -foet- ˌæsəˈfɛtɪdə, æsˈfɛt-
assagai ˈæsəˌgaɪ
assai əˈsɑ·i

assail əˈsel |-ed -d |-ant -ənt
Assam æˈsæm, ˈæsæm
assassin əˈsæsɪn |-ate -sn̩ˌet |-ated -sn̩ˌetɪd
assassination əˌsæsn̩ˈeʃən
assault əˈsɔlt |-ed -ɪd
assay *n* əˈse, ˈæse
assay *v* əˈse |-ed -d
assegai ˈæsəˌgaɪ
assemblage əˈsɛmblɪdʒ |-s -ɪz
assemble əˈsɛmbl̩ |-d -d |-ling əˈsɛmblɪŋ,
　-bl̩ɪŋ
assembly əˈsɛmblɪ |-man -mən, -ˌmæn |-men
　-mən, -ˌmɛn
assent əˈsɛnt |-ed -ɪd
assentation ˌæsɛnˈteʃən
assenter, -or əˈsɛntɚ; ES əˈsɛntə(r
Asser ˈæsɚ; ES ˈæsə(r
assert əˈsɝt; ES əˈsɜt, əˈsɝt; |-ed -ɪd
assertion əˈsɝʃən; ES əˈsɜʃ-, əˈsɝʃ-; |-tive
　-tɪv |-tory -tɔrɪ
assess əˈsɛs |-es -ɪz |-ed -t |-or -ɚ; ES -ə(r
assessorial ˌæsəˈsorɪəl, -ˈsɔr-; S -ˈsor-
asset ˈæsɛt |-s -s
asseverate əˈsɛvəˌret |-d -ɪd
asseveration əˌsɛvəˈreʃən
assibilate əˈsɪbl̩ˌet |-d -ɪd
assibilation əˌsɪbl̩ˈeʃən
assiduity ˌæsəˈdjuətɪ, -ˈdɪu-, -ˈdu-
assiduous əˈsɪdʒuəs
assign əˈsaɪn |-ed -d
assignability əˌsaɪnəˈbɪlətɪ
assignable əˈsaɪnəbl̩ |-bly -blɪ
assignat ˈæsɪgˌnæt (*Fr* asiˈɲa)
assignation ˌæsɪgˈneʃən
assignee əsaɪˈni, ˌæsəˈni, ˌæsaɪ-
assigner əˈsaɪnɚ; ES -nə(r
assignor əsaɪˈnɔr, ˌæsəˈnɔr; ES -ˈnɔə(r
assimilability əˌsɪml̩əˈbɪlətɪ
assimilable əˈsɪml̩əbl̩
assimilate *n* əˈsɪml̩ɪt, -ˌet
assimilate *v* əˈsɪml̩ˌet |-d -ɪd |-tive -ɪv
assimilation əˌsɪml̩ˈeʃən
assimilatory əˈsɪml̩əˌtorɪ, -ˌtɔrɪ; S -ˌtorɪ
Assiniboia əˌsɪnəˈbɔɪə
Assiniboine əˈsɪnəˌbɔɪn
Assisi əˈsɪzɪ (*It* ɑsˈsiːzi)
assist əˈsɪst |-ed -ɪd |-ance -əns |-ant -ənt
assize əˈsaɪz |-s -ɪz |-d -d
associable əˈsoʃɪəbl̩, -ʃəbl̩

|full fʊl |tooth tuθ |further ˈfɝðɚ; ES ˈfɝðə |custom ˈkʌstəm |while hwaɪl |how haʊ |toy tɔɪ
|using ˈjuzɪŋ |fuse fjuz, fɪuz |dish dɪʃ |vision ˈvɪʒən |Eden ˈidn̩ |cradle ˈkredl̩ |keep 'em ˈkipm̩

associate *n, adj* ə'soʃɪɪt, -ˌet
associate *v* ə'soʃɪˌet |-d -ɪd |-tive -ɪv
association əˌsosɪ'eʃən, əˌsoʃɪ——*It is doubt-ful which of these prons. prevails.*
assoil ə'sɔɪl |-ed -d
assonance 'æsənəns |-s -ɪz |-d -t |-nant -nənt
assort ə'sɔrt; ES ə'sɔət; |-ed -ɪd
assuage ə'swedʒ |-s -ɪz |-d -d
assuasive ə'swesɪv
assume ə'sum, ə'sɪum, ə'sjum |-d -d
assumpsit ə'sʌmpsɪt
assumption, A- ə'sʌmpʃən |-tive -tɪv
assurance ə'ʃurəns |-s -ɪz
assure ə'ʃur; ES ə'ʃuə(r; |-d -d |-dly -ɪdlɪ
assurgency ə'sɝdʒənsɪ; ES ə'sɜdʒ-, ə'sɝdʒ-; |-ent -ənt
Assyria ə'sɪrɪə |-n -n
Assyriology əˌsɪrɪ'ɑlədʒɪ; ES+-'ɒl-; |-gist -dʒɪst
Astarte æs'tɑrtɪ; ES -'tɑ:tɪ, E+-'tɑ:tɪ
astatic e'stætɪk, ə-, æ- |-ally -ļɪ, -ɪklɪ
Astell 'æstļ
aster, A- 'æstɚ; ES 'æstə(r
asterisk 'æstəˌrɪsk
asterism 'æstəˌrɪzəm
astern ə'stɝn; ES ə'stɜn, ə'stɝn
asteroid 'æstəˌrɔɪd |-al ˌæstə'rɔɪdļ
asthenia æs'θɪnɪə, ˌæsθə'naɪə
asthma 'æzmə, 'æsmə
asthmatic æz'mætɪk, æs- |-al -ļ |-ally -ļɪ, -ɪklɪ
astigmatic ˌæstɪg'mætɪk |-al -ļ |-ally -ļɪ, -ɪklɪ
astigmatism ə'stɪgməˌtɪzəm
astir ə'stɝ; ES ə'stɜ(r, ə'stɝ
astonish ə'stɑnɪʃ; ES+-'stɒn-; |-es -ɪz |-ed -t
astony ə'stɑnɪ; ES+-'stɒn-; |-nied -nɪd
Astor 'æstɚ; ES 'æstə(r
Astoria æs'torɪə, -'tɔrɪə; S -'torɪə
astound ə'staund |-ed -ɪd
astrachan, A- 'æstrəkən
astraddle ə'strædļ
astragal 'æstrəgļ
astrakhan 'æstrəkən
Astrakhan ˌæstrə'kæn
astral 'æstrəl |-ly -ɪ
astray ə'stre

astride ə'straɪd
astringe ə'strɪndʒ |-s -ɪz |-d -d
astringency ə'strɪndʒənsɪ |-gent -dʒənt
astrolabe 'æstrəˌleb
astrologer ə'strɑlədʒɚ; ES ə'strɑlədʒə(r, -'strɒl-; |-gy -dʒɪ |-gist -dʒɪst
astrologic ˌæstrə'lɑdʒɪk; ES+-'lɒdʒ-; |-al -ļ |-ally -ļɪ, -ɪklɪ
astronomer ə'strɑnəmɚ; ES ə'strɑnəmə(r, -'strɒn-; |-my -mɪ
astronomic ˌæstrə'nɑmɪk; ES+-'nɒm-; |-al -ļ |-ally -ļɪ, -ɪklɪ
Astrophel 'æstrəˌfɛl
astrophotographic 'æstrəˌfotə'græfɪk
astrophotography ˌæstrəfo'tɑgrəfɪ, -'tɒg-
astrophysical ˌæstro'fɪzɪkļ |-icist -ɪsɪst
astrophysics ˌæstro'fɪzɪks
astrosphere 'æstrəˌsfɪr; ES-ˌsfɪə(r, S+-ˌsfɛə(r
astrut ə'strʌt
astute ə'stjut, -'strut, -'stut
Astyanax ə'staɪəˌnæks |-'s -ɪz
Asuncion *Am Sp* asun'sjon
asunder ə'sʌndɚ; ES ə'sʌndə(r
asylum ə'saɪləm |-s -z |-la -lə
asymmetric ˌesɪ'mɛtrɪk, ˌæ- |-al -ļ |-ally -ļɪ, -ɪklɪ
asymmetry e'sɪmɪtrɪ, æ-
asymptote 'æsɪmˌtot, 'æsɪmp-
asymptotic ˌæsɪm'tɑtɪk, -sɪmp-; ES+-'tɒt-; |-al -ļ |-ally -ļɪ, -ɪklɪ
asynchronous e'sɪŋkrənəs, æ-, -'sɪn-
asyndeton ə'sɪndətən, -ˌtɑn; ES+-ˌtɒn
at *stressed* 'æt, ˌæt; *unstr.* ət, ɪt
Atalanta ˌætļ'æntə
at all *'to any degree'* ə'tɔl, ət'ɔl——*In* ət'ɔl *the* t *is not aspirated and is usually voiced. This is also the pron. when* at all *is an ordinary prepositional phrase, as in* It stops at some stations, but not at all. *Cf* It stops at no small stations at all (ə'tɔl).
atamasco ˌætə'mæsko
atar 'ætɚ; ES 'ætə(r
Atascosa ˌætə'skosə
atavic ə'tævɪk |atavism 'ætəˌvɪzəm
atavistic ˌætə'vɪstɪk |-ally -ļɪ, -ɪklɪ
ataxia ə'tæksɪə |ataxy ə'tæksɪ
Atchafalaya əˌtʃæfə'laɪə, ˌtʃæfə-, æˌtʃæfə-
Atchison 'ætʃɪsn̩
Ate, ate *myth.* 'etɪ, 'etɪ

Key: *See in full §§3–47.* bee bi |pity 'pɪtɪ (§6) |rate ret |yet jɛt |sang sæŋ |angry 'æŋ·grɪ |bath bæθ; E baθ (§10) |ah ɑ |far fɑr |watch wɑtʃ, wɒtʃ (§12) |jaw dʒɔ |gorge gɔrdʒ |go go

ate *past of* eat **et**—*The past tense* ɛt, *occas.*
in cultivated S, is spelt ate *in Engd, but*
properly belongs to the old past spelling
form eat (*cf* threat, sweat), *as does also the*
old past pron. it (*cf* meat, seat). *See* eat.

-ate *unstressed ending* -ɪt, -ət—*In the vocab.*
when only the pron. -ɪt *is given, it is to be*
understood that many speakers pronounce
-ət, *as in* gamut **ˈgæmət**. *When more or less*
stressed (with or without accent mark), -ate
is pronounced -et, *as in* permeate **ˈpɝmɪˌet**,
mandate **ˈmændet**, oblate **ˈɑblet**.

atelier **ˈætlˌje** (*Fr* atəˈlje)

Athabasca, -ka ˌæθəˈbæskə |-n -n

athanasia ˌæθəˈneʒɪə

Athanasian ˌæθəˈneʒən

Athanasius ˌæθəˈneʃɪəs, -ʃəs |-ˈs -ɪz

athanasy əˈθænəsɪ

Athapascan ˌæθəˈpæskən

atheism **ˈeθɪˌɪzəm** |atheist **ˈeθɪɪst**

atheistic ˌeθɪˈɪstɪk |-al -ḷ |-ally -ḷɪ, -ɪklɪ

atheling **ˈæθəlɪŋ**, **ˈæðəlɪŋ** (*OE* ˈæð-)

Athelstan **ˈæθəlˌstæn**, **ˈæðəl-**, -stən (*OE* ˈæð-)

Athena əˈθinə |Athene əˈθini

athenaeum, A-, -neum ˌæθəˈniəm

Athenian əˈθinɪən

Athens **ˈæθɪnz**, -ənz |-ˈs -ɪz |*N Y+* ˈeθ-

Atherton **ˈæθərtən**; ES **ˈæθətən**

athirst əˈθɝst; ES əˈθɜst, əˈθɝst

athlete **ˈæθlit**

athletic æθˈlɛtɪk |-s -s |-ally -ḷɪ, -ɪklɪ

Athlone æθˈlon

Athol *Mass* **ˈæθɑl**, -ɒl, -əl

Atholl, -ole *Scotl* **ˈæθəl**

at home, at-home ətˈhom—*The pron.* əˈtom,
freq. in Engd, is rare in US.

Athos **ˈæθɑs**, ˈe-, -ɒs

athwart əˈθwɔrt; ES əˈθwɔət; |-ship -ʃɪp

atilt əˈtɪlt

atingle əˈtɪŋgḷ

-ative *ending* -ˌetɪv, -ətɪv, *as in* cumulative,
operative, *etc. When the main accent is on*
the second syllable before -ative, *there is*
usually a secondary accent on the -a- *of*
-ative (inˈiˑtiˌaˑtive ɪˈnɪʃˑɪˌeˑtɪv); *but in*
familiar words some speakers often pro-
nounce -ative *without accent* (-ətɪv), *as*
ɪˈnɪʃɪətɪv. *When only* -ˌetɪv *is given,* -ətɪv
is to be understood as a possible variant.

Atkins **ˈætkɪnz** |-ˈs -ɪz |-kinson **ˈætkɪnsn̩**

Atlanta ətˈlæntə, æt-

atlantean, A- ˌætlænˈtiən

atlantes *pl of* atlas ətˈlæntiz, æt-

Atlantic ətˈlæntɪk

Atlantis ətˈlæntɪs |-ˈs -ɪz

atlas, A- **ˈætləs** |-es -ɪz |atlantes ətˈlæntiz,
æt-

atman, A- **ˈɑtmən**

Atmore **ˈætmor**, -mɔr; ES -moə(r, E+
-mɔə(r

atmosphere **ˈætməsˌfɪr**; ES -ˌfɪə(r, S+
-ˌfɛə(r

atmospheric ˌætməsˈfɛrɪk |-al -ḷ |-ally -ḷɪ,
-ɪklɪ

atoll **ˈætɑl**, -ɒl, əˈtɑl, -ˈtɒl

atom **ˈætəm** |-ism -ˌɪzəm |-y -ɪ

atomic əˈtɑmɪk, æ-; ES+-ˈtɒm-; |-al -ḷ |-ally
-ḷɪ, -ɪklɪ

atomicity ˌætəˈmɪsətɪ

atomization ˌætəməˈzeʃən, -aɪˈz-

atomize **ˈætəmˌaɪz** |-s -ɪz |-d -d

atonal eˈtonḷ, æ- |-ly -ɪ |-ity ˌetoˈnælətɪ

atone əˈton |-d -d

atonic əˈtɑnɪk, e-, æ-; ES+-ˈtɒn-

atonicity ˌætəˈnɪsətɪ, ˌe-, -toˈn-

atony **ˈætənɪ**

atop əˈtɑp; ES+əˈtɒp

atrabilious ˌætrəˈbɪljəs

Atreus **ˈetrus**, -trɪus, **ˈetrɪˑəs** |-ˈs -ɪz

atrip əˈtrɪp

atrium **ˈetrɪəm** |-s -z |-ria -rɪə

atrocious əˈtroʃəs

atrocity əˈtrɑsətɪ; ES+-ˈtrɒs-

atrophy **ˈætrəfɪ** |-phied -fɪd

atropine **ˈætrəˌpin**, -pɪn |-pin -pɪn

Atropos **ˈætrəˌpɑs**; ES+-ˌpɒs; |-ˈs -ɪz

attach əˈtætʃ |-es -ɪz |-ed -t

attaché ˌætəˈʃe, əˈtæʃe (*Fr* ataˈʃe)

attack əˈtæk |-ed -t

attain əˈten |-ed -d

attainable əˈtenəbḷ |-bility əˌtenəˈbɪlətɪ

attainder əˈtendɚ; ES əˈtendə(r

attaint əˈtent |-ed -ɪd

attainture əˈtentʃɚ; ES əˈtentʃə(r

Attala *Miss* **ˈætlə** |Attalla *Ala* əˈtælə

attar **ˈætɚ**; ES **ˈætə(r**

attemper əˈtɛmpɚ; ES -pə(r; |-ed -d |-ing
əˈtɛmpərɪŋ, əˈtɛmprɪŋ

|full fʊl |tooth tuθ |further **ˈfɝðɚ**; ES **ˈfɝðə** |custom **ˈkʌstəm** |while hwaɪl |how haʊ |toy tɔɪ
|using **ˈjuzɪŋ** |fuse fjuz, fɪuz |dish dɪʃ |vision **ˈvɪʒən** |Eden **ˈidn̩** |cradle **ˈkredḷ** |keep 'em **ˈkipm̩**

attempt ə'tɛmpt |-ed -ɪd
attend ə'tɛnd |-ed -ɪd |-ance -əns |-ant -ənt
attent ə'tɛnt
attention ə'tɛnʃən |-tive -tɪv
attenuate adj ə'tɛnjʊɪt
attenuate v ə'tɛnjʊ‚et |-d -ɪd
attenuation ə‚tɛnjʊ'eʃən
Atterbury 'ætə‚bɛrɪ, -bərɪ; ES 'ætə-
attest ə'tɛst |-ed -ɪd |-ation ‚ætɛs'teʃən
attic 'ætɪk
Attic 'ætɪk |-a -ə |-ism 'ætɪ‚sɪzəm
Attila 'ætlə
attire ə'taɪr; ES ə'taɪə(r; |-d -d
attitude 'ætə‚tjud, -‚tɪud, -‚tud
attitudinize ‚ætə'tjudn̩‚aɪz, -'tɪud-, -'tud- |-s -ɪz |-d -d
Atlee 'ætlɪ, 'ætli
Attleboro 'ætl̩‚bɝo, -ə; ES -‚bɝ-, -‚bʌr-, -‚bɝ-
attorn ə'tɝn; ES ə'tɝn, ə'tɝn; |-ed -d
attorney ə'tɝnɪ; ES ə'tɝnɪ, ə'tɝnɪ
attract ə'trækt |-ed -ɪd
attractability ə‚træktə'bɪlətɪ
attraction ə'trækʃən |-tive -tɪv
attribute n 'ætrə‚bjut, -‚bɪut
attribute v ə'trɪbjʊt |-d -bjətɪd |-tive -bjətɪv
attribution ‚ætrə'bjuʃən, -'bɪu-
attrite adj ə'traɪt |-d -ɪd
attrition ə'trɪʃən, æ-
attune ə'tjun, ə'tɪun, ə'tun |-d -d
atwain ə'twen
Atwater 'æt‚wɔtə, -‚wɑtə, -‚wɒtə; ES -tə(r
atypic e'tɪpɪk, æ- |-al -l̩ |-ally -l̩ɪ, -ɪklɪ
au Fr o
Aubrey, -bry 'ɔbrɪ
auburn, A- 'ɔbɝn; ES 'ɔbən
Auckland 'ɔklənd
auction 'ɔkʃən |-ed -d
auctioneer ‚ɔkʃən'ɪr; ES -'ɪə(r, S+-'ɛə(r
audacious ɔ'deʃəs |-dacity ɔ'dæsətɪ
audibility ‚ɔdə'bɪlətɪ
audible 'ɔdəbl̩ |-bly -blɪ
audience 'ɔdɪəns, -djəns |-s -ɪz |-ent -dɪənt
audile 'ɔdɪl
audio 'ɔdɪ‚o |audiogram 'ɔdɪə‚græm
audiometer ‚ɔdɪ'amətə; ES -'amətə(r, -'ɒm-
audiphone, A- 'ɔdə‚fon
audit 'ɔdɪt |-ed -ɪd |-or -ə; ES -ə(r

audition ɔ'dɪʃən |-ed -d |-ing -ʃənɪŋ, -ʃnɪŋ
auditorium ‚ɔdə'torɪəm, -'tɔr-; S -'tor-
auditory 'ɔdə‚torɪ, -‚tɔrɪ; S -‚torɪ
Audley 'ɔdlɪ
Audrey 'ɔdrɪ
Audubon 'ɔdə‚ban; ES+-‚bɒn
Auer 'aʊə; ES 'aʊ·ə(r
au fait o'fe (Fr o'fɛ)
Aufidius ɔ'fɪdɪəs |-'s -ɪz
auf Wiedersehen Ger aʊf'vi:dər‚ze:ən
Augeas ɔ'dʒiəs |-'s -ɪz |-gean -'dʒiən
augend 'ɔdʒɛnd
auger 'ɔgə; ES 'ɔgə(r
aught ɔt
Auglaize ɔ'glez |-'s -ɪz
augment n 'ɔgmɛnt
augment v ɔg'mɛnt |-ed -ɪd |-ative -ətɪv
augmenter ɔg'mɛntə; ES -'mɛntə(r
au gratin o'gratn, o'grætn, -tɪn (Fr ogra'tæ̃)
Augsburg 'ɔgzbɝg; ES -bɝg, -bɝg; (Ger 'aʊksbʊrk)
augur 'ɔgə; ES 'ɔgə(r; |-ed -d |-ing -gərɪŋ, -grɪŋ
augury 'ɔgjərɪ
august ɔ'gʌst ('au‚gust 'office)
August 'ɔgəst
Augusta ɔ'gʌstə, ə'gʌs- |-tan -tən
Augustine saint 'ɔgəs‚tin, ə'gʌstɪn, ɔ-; isl. Alas 'ɔgəstɪn
Augustinian ‚ɔgəs'tɪnɪən
Augustus ɔ'gʌstəs, ə'gʌs- |-'s -ɪz
au jus Fr o'ʒy
auk ɔk |-let -lɪt
auld ɔld
Aulis 'ɔlɪs |-'s -ɪz
Ault ɔlt
Aumerle ɔ'mɝl; ES ɔ'mɝl, ɔ'mɝl
au naturel Fr onaty'rɛl
aunt ænt; E ant, ɑnt, ænt—Sporadic instances of ant, ɑnt occur in the N and S.
aura 'ɔrə |-s -z |-rae -ri
aural 'ɔrəl |-ly -ɪ
Aurangzeb 'ɔrʌŋ'zɛb
aureate adj 'ɔrɪɪt, -‚et
aureate v 'ɔrɪ‚et |-d -ɪd
Aurelia ɔ'rilɪə, -ljə |-n -n
Aurelius ɔ'rilɪəs |-'s -ɪz
aureole 'ɔrɪ‚ol |-d -d
au revoir ‚orə'vɔr; ES -'vɔə(r; (Fr orə'vwa:r)

auric 'ɔrɪk	authenticate ɔ'θɛntɪˌket |-d -ɪd
auricle 'ɔrɪkļ	authentication ɔˌθɛntɪ'keʃən, ˌɔθɛntɪ-
auricular ɔ'rɪkjələ˞; ES -lə(r	authenticity ˌɔθən'tɪsətɪ, -θɛn-
auriculate adj ɔ'rɪkjəlɪt |-lated -ˌletɪd	author 'ɔθə˞; ES 'ɔθə(r; |-ess -ɪs |-esses -ɪsɪz
auriferous ɔ'rɪfərəs	authoritarian əˌθɔrə'tɛrɪən, əˌθɑr-, əˌθɒr-,
Auriga ɔ'raɪgə |gen Aurigae ɔ'raɪdʒi	-'ter- |-ism -ˌɪzəm
Aurignacian ˌɔrɪg'neʃən	authoritative ə'θɔrəˌtetɪv, ə'θɑr-, ə'θɒr-
aurist 'ɔrɪst	authority ə'θɔrətɪ, ə'θɑr-, ə'θɒr-
aurochs 'ɔraks; ES+-ɒks	authorization ˌɔθərə'zeʃən, -aɪ'z-
aurora, A- ɔ'rorə, ə-, -'rɔrə; S -'rorə; |-s -z	authorize 'ɔθəˌraɪz |-s -ɪz |-d -d
|-rae -ri	autism 'ɔtɪzəm |-ist -ɪst |-tistic ɔ'tɪstɪk
aurora australis ɔ'rorə ɔs'trelɪs, ə-, -'rɔrə; S	auto 'ɔto
-'rorə	autobiographic ˌɔtəˌbaɪə'græfɪk |-al -ļ |-ally
aurora borealis ɔ'rorə ˌborɪ'ælɪs, ə-, -'rɔrə	-ļɪ, -ɪklɪ
ˌbɔrɪ-, -'elɪs; S -'rorə ˌborɪ-	autobiography ˌɔtəbaɪ'agrəfɪ, -bɪ-, -'ɒg-
auroral ɔ'rorəl, ə-, -'rɔrəl; S -'rorəl; |-ly -ɪ	autochthon ɔ'takθən; ES+-'tɒk-; |-s -z
aurorean ɔ'rorɪən, ə-, -'rɔr-; S -'ror-	|-es -ˌɪz
Aurorian ɔ'rorɪən, -'rɔr-; S -'ror-	autochthonous ɔ'takθənəs; ES+-'tɒk-
aurum 'ɔrəm |aurous 'ɔrəs	autoclave 'ɔtəˌklev |-d -d
Aurungzeb, -ebe 'ɔrʌŋˌzɛb, -'zib	autocracy ɔ'takrəsɪ; ES+-'tɒk-
Ausable, Au Sable ɔ'sebļ ('Auˌsable 'Chasm)	autocrat 'ɔtəˌkræt
auscultate 'ɔskəlˌtet |-d -ɪd	autocratic ˌɔtə'krætɪk |-al -ļ |-ally -ļɪ, -ɪklɪ
auscultation ˌɔskəl'teʃən	auto-da-fé ˌɔtodə'fe |pl autos- ˌɔtoz-
Auslander 'ɔsˌlændə˞, 'aʊs-; ES -ˌlændə(r	autogenous ɔ'tadʒənəs; ES+-'tɒdʒ-
Ausonia ɔ'sonɪə |-n -n	autogiro, A- ˌɔto'dʒaɪro
auspex 'ɔspɛks |pl auspices 'ɔspɪˌsiz	autograph 'ɔtəˌgræf; E+-ˌgraf, -ˌgraf
auspice 'ɔspɪs |-s -ɪz	autographic ˌɔtə'græfɪk |-al -ļ |-ally -ļɪ,
auspicial ɔ'spɪʃəl |-cious -ʃəs	-ɪklɪ
Austen 'ɔstɪn, -tən	autography ɔ'tagrəfɪ, -'tɒg-
Auster 'ɔstə˞; ES 'ɔstə(r	autogyro, A- ˌɔto'dʒaɪro
austere ɔ'stɪr; ES ɔ'stɪə(r, S+ɔ'stɛə(r	autohypnosis ˌɔtohɪp'nosɪs
austerity ɔ'stɛrətɪ	autoinfection ˌɔto·ɪn'fɛkʃən
Austerlitz 'ɔstə˞ˌlɪts; ES 'ɔstə-; |-'s -ɪz (Ger	autointoxication ˌɔto·ɪnˌtaksə'keʃən; ES+
'aʊstər-)	-ˌtɒk-
Austin 'ɔstɪn, -tən	Autolycus ɔ'taləkəs; ES+-'tɒl-; |-'s -ɪz
austral 'ɔstrəl	automat 'ɔtəˌmæt
Australasia ˌɔstrəl'eʒə, -ʃə |-n -n	automata ɔ'tamətə; ES+-'tɒm-
Australia ɔ'streljə |-n -n	automatic ˌɔtə'mætɪk |-al -ļ |-ally -ļɪ, -ɪklɪ
Austrasia ɔ'streʒə, -ʃə |-n -n	automatism ɔ'taməˌtɪzəm; ES+-'tɒm-
Austria 'ɔstrɪə |-n -n	automaton ɔ'taməˌtan, -tən; ES+ɔ'tɒmə-
Austria-Hungary 'ɔstrɪə'hʌŋgərɪ	ˌtɒn, -tən; |-s -z |-ta -tə
Austro-Hungarian 'ɔstrohʌŋ'gɛrɪən, -'ger-	automobile adj ˌɔtə'mobɪl
Austronesian ˌɔstro'niʒən, -ʃən	automobile n 'ɔtəməˌbil, ˌɔtə'mobil, ˌɔtəmə-
autarch 'ɔtark; ES -ta:k, E+-ta:k; |-y -ɪ	'bil
autarchic ɔ'tarkɪk; ES ɔ'ta:k-, E+ɔ'ta:k-;	automotive ˌɔtə'motɪv
|-al -ļ	autonomic ˌɔtə'namɪk; ES+-'nɒm-; |-al -ļ
autarky 'ɔtarkɪ; ES -ta:kɪ, E+-ta:kɪ; |-kist	|-ally -ļɪ, -ɪklɪ
-kɪst	autonomist ɔ'tanəmɪst; ES+-'tɒn-; |-mous
authentic ɔ'θɛntɪk |-al -ļ |-ally -ļɪ -icly -ɪklɪ	-məs |-my -mɪ

autopsy 'ɔtɑpsɪ, 'ɔtəpsɪ; ES+-tɒp-
autos-da-fé *pl* ˌɔtozdə'fe
autosuggestion ˌɔtəsəg'dʒɛstʃən, -sə'dʒɛs-
autumn 'ɔtəm |-al ə'tʌmn̩ |-ally ə'tʌmn̩ɪ
Auvergne o'vɜˑn; ES o'vɜn, o'vɜˑn; (*Fr* o'vɛrn̩, ɔ̃-)
aux *Fr* o
auxiliary ɔg'zɪljərɪ, -'zɪlərɪ, -'zɪlɪˌɛrɪ
avail ə'vel |-ed -d
availability əˌvelə'bɪlətɪ
available ə'veləb̩ |-bly -blɪ
avalanche 'ævl̩ˌæntʃ; E+-ˌantʃ, -ˌɑntʃ; |-s -ɪz |-d -t
Avalon, -llon 'ævl̩ˌɑn, -ˌɒn (*Fr* ava'lɔ̃)
avarice 'ævərɪs, 'ævrɪs |-cious ˌævə'rɪʃəs
avast ə'væst; E+ə'vast, ə'vɑst
avatar ˌævə'tɑr; ES -'tɑː(r, E+-'tɑː(r
avaunt ə'vɔnt, ə'vɒnt, ə'vɑnt
ave, A- 'evɪ, 'ave
Avebury, Abury 'ebərɪ, 'evˌbɛrɪ, -bərɪ
Ave Maria 'avɪmə'riə
Ave Maria Lane *Lond* 'evɪməˌraɪə'len
Ave Mary 'evɪ'mɛrɪ, -'mɛːrɪ, -'merɪ, -'mærɪ
avenge ə'vɛndʒ |-s -ɪz |-d -d
avens 'ævɪnz, -ɒnz |-es -ɪz
Aventine 'ævənˌtaɪn, -tɪn
aventurine, -in ə'vɛntʃərɪn
avenue 'ævəˌnu, -ˌnɪu, -ˌnju
aver '*assert*' ə'vɜˑ; ES ə'vɜ(r, ə'vɜˑ; |-red -d
aver '*horse*' 'evɚ; ES 'evə(r
average 'ævrɪdʒ, 'ævərɪdʒ |-s -ɪz |-d -d
Avernus ə'vɜˑnəs; ES ə'vɜ-, ə'vɜˑ-; |-'s -ɪz
averse ə'vɜˑs; ES ə'vɜs, ə'vɜˑs
aversion ə'vɜˑʒən, -ʃən; ES ə'vɜ-, ə'vɜˑ-
avert ə'vɜˑt; ES ə'vɜt, ə'vɜˑt; |-ed -ɪd
Avery 'evərɪ, 'evrɪ
Aves *pl of* Avis 'eviz
Avesta ə'vɛstə
avian 'evɪən
aviary 'evɪˌɛrɪ
aviate 'evɪˌet, 'æv- |-d -ɪd |-tor -ɚ; ES -ə(r
aviation ˌevɪ'eʃən, ˌævɪ-
aviculture 'evɪˌkʌltʃɚ; ES -ˌkʌltʃə(r
avid 'ævɪd |avidity ə'vɪdətɪ
Avignon ə'vinjɔ̃, ə'vɪnjən (*Fr* avi'n̩ɔ̃)
Avoca ə'vokə
avocado ˌavə'kado, ˌævə-
avocation ˌævə'keʃən, ˌævo-
avocet 'ævəˌsɛt

avoid ə'vɔɪd |-ed -ɪd |-ance -n̩s
avoirdupois ˌævədə'pɔɪz; ES ˌævə-
Avon 'evən, 'ævən, *Warwickshire* 'evən, *Scotl* 'evən, ɑn
Avon Lake, Avon Park 'evan, -ɒn
avoset 'ævəˌsɛt
avouch ə'vautʃ |-es -ɪz |-ed -t
avow ə'vau |-ed -d |-al -əl |-edly -ɪdlɪ
avuncular ə'vʌŋkjəlɚ; ES -jələ(r; |-late -lɪt
await ə'wet |-ed -ɪd
awake ə'wek |*past* awoke ə'wok *or* awaked ə'wekt |*pptc* awaked ə'wekt *or* awoke ə'wok
awaken ə'wekən |-ed -d |-ing -kənɪŋ, -knɪŋ
award ə'wɔrd; ES ə'wɔəd; |-ed -ɪd
aware ə'wɛr, ə'wær; E ə'wɛə(r, ES ə'wæə(r
awash ə'waʃ, ə'wɔʃ, ə'wɒʃ
away ə'we
awe ɔ |-d -d
aweary ə'wɪrɪ, ə'wirɪ; S+ə'wɜrɪ
awedness 'ɔdnɪs
aweful 'ɔful |-ly -ɪ
aweigh ə'we
aweless 'ɔlɪs |awelessness 'ɔlɪsnɪs
awesome 'ɔsəm
awful '*impressive*' 'ɔful |-ly -ɪ
awful '*great*,' '*ugly*' 'ɔfl̩ |-ly 'ɔfl̩ɪ, 'ɔflɪ
awheel ə'hwil
awhile ə'hwaɪl
awkward 'ɔkwɚd; ES 'ɔkwəd
awl ɔl
awless 'ɔlɪs |awlessness 'ɔlɪsnɪs
awlless 'ɔllɪs
awn ɔn |-ed -d
awning 'ɔnɪŋ
awoke ə'wok |awoken *arch.* ə'wokən
awork ə'wɜˑk; ES ə'wɜk, ə'wɜˑk
awry ə'raɪ
ax, axe æks |axes 'æksɪz |axed ækst
axes *pl of* axis 'æksiz
axial 'æksɪəl |-ly -ɪ
axil 'æksɪl |axile 'æksɪl, -aɪl
axilla æk'sɪlə |-s -z |-lae -li
axillary 'æksəˌlɛrɪ
axiom 'æksɪəm
axiomatic ˌæksɪə'mætɪk |-al -l̩ |-ally -l̩ɪ, -ɪklɪ
axis 'æksɪs |axes 'æksiz
axle 'æksl̩ |-d -d

Key: *See in full §§3–47.* bee bi |pity 'pɪtɪ (§6) |rate ret |yet jɛt |sang sæŋ |angry 'æŋ·grɪ |bath bæθ; E baθ (§10) |ah ɑ |far fɑr |watch watʃ, wɒtʃ (§12) |jaw dʒɔ |gorge gɔrdʒ |go go

axletree ˈæksˌtri, -trɪ
Axminster ˈæksˌmɪnstɚ; ES -ˌmɪnstə(r
axolotl ˈæksəˌlɑtl̩; ES+-ˌlɒtl̩
ay intj ‘alas!’ e
ay, aye ‘always’ e—ay is the better spelling
ayah ˈɑjə
Aydelotte ˈedl̩ˌɑt; ES+-ˌɒt
Ayden ˈedn̩
aye, ay ‘yes’ aɪ—aye is the better spelling
Ayer ɛr, ær; E ɛə(r, ES æə(r
Aylesbury ˈelzˌbɛrɪ, -bərɪ
Aylmer ˈelmɚ; ES ˈelmə(r
Ayr ɛr, ær; E ɛə(r, ES æə(r
Ayres ɛrz, ærz; E ɛəz, ES æəz; |-’s -ɪz
Ayrshire ˈɛrʃɪr, ˈær-, -ʃɚ; E ˈɛəʃɪə(r, -ʃə(r,
  ES ˈæə-
Ayscough, -cue ˈæskju, ˈes-, -kɪu
Ayton, Aytoun ˈetn̩
Azalea əˈzelɪə |azalea əˈzeljə

Azazel əˈzezəl, ˈæzəˌzɛl
Azerbaijan ˌɑzɚbaɪˈdʒɑn, ˌæzɚ-; ES -zə-
azimuth ˈæzəməθ |-al ˌæzəˈmʌθəl
azine ˈæzin, -ɪn |-in -ɪn
Azof ˈɑzɑf, -zɒf
azoic əˈzo·ɪk
azole ˈæzol, əˈzol
Azores əˈzorz, ˈezorz, -ɔrz; ES -ooz, E+
  -ɔəz
azorite ˈæzəˌraɪt
azote ˈæzot, əˈzot
azoth ˈæzɑθ, -ɒθ
Azov ˈɑzɑf, -zɒf, ˈezɑv, ˈezɒv
Azrael ˈæzrɪəl
Aztec ˈæztɛk |-an -ən
azure ˈæʒɚ, ˈeʒɚ; ES -ʒə(r; |-d -d
azurine ˈæʒərɪn, -ˌaɪn
azurite ˈæʒəˌraɪt
Azusa əˈzusə

B

B, b letter bi |pl B’s, Bs, poss B’s biz
baa bæ:, ba:, bɑ: |3 sg baaes, pl n baas -z
  |-ed -d |-ing -ɪŋ
Baal ˈbeəl, bel
babbitt, B- ˈbæbɪt |-ed -ɪd
babble ˈbæbl̩ |-d -d |-ling ˈbæbl̩ɪŋ, -blɪŋ
babe beb
Babel ˈbebl̩, ˈbæbl̩
Bab el Mandeb ˈbæbˌɛlˈmændɛb, ˈbabˌɛl-
  ˈman-
baboo, babu ˈbabu
baboon bæˈbun, bəˈbun
baby ˈbebɪ |-bied -bɪd
Babylon ˈbæbl̩ən
Babylonia ˌbæbl̩ˈonɪə, -njə |-n -n
baccalaureate ˌbækəˈlɔrɪɪt
baccarat, -ra ˌbækəˈra, ˈbækəˌra (Fr bakaˈra)
Bacchae ˈbæki
bacchanal ˈbækənl̩, -ˌnæl
Bacchanalia, b- ˌbækəˈnelɪə, -ljə |-n -n
bacchant ˈbækənt |-s -s |-es bəˈkæntiz, bæ-
bacchante bəˈkæntɪ, -ˈkænt, bæ-, ˈbækənt
Bacchic, b- ˈbækɪk |-al -l̩
Bacchus ˈbækəs |-’s -ɪz
Bach bɑk, bɑx (Ger bɑx)

Bacheller ˈbætʃəlɚ, ˈbætʃlɚ; ES -lə(r
bachelor ˈbætʃəlɚ, ˈbætʃlɚ; ES -lə(r
Bachman ˈbækmən, ˈbak- (Ger ˈbɑxmɑn)
bacillary ˈbæsˌl̩ɛrɪ, ˈbæsɪˌl-
bacillus bəˈsɪləs |-li -laɪ
back bæk |-ed -t |-ache -ˌek
backbite ˈbækˌbaɪt |-bit -ˌbɪt |-bitten -ˌbɪtn̩
backbone ˈbækˈbon, -ˌbon |-d -d
backfire n ˈbækˌfaɪr; ES -ˌfaɪə(r
backfire v ˈbækˌfaɪr, -ˈfaɪr; ES -aɪə(r; |-d -d
backgammon ˈbækˌgæmən, ˌbækˈgæmən
background ˈbækˌgraʊnd
backhand ˈbækˈhænd, -ˌhænd |-ed -ɪd
  (ˈbackˌhand(ed) ˈstroke)
backlash ˈbækˌlæʃ |-es -ɪz |-ed -t
backlog ˈbækˌlɒg, -ˌlag, -ˌlɔg
backset ˈbækˌsɛt
backslide ˈbækˌslaɪd, ˈbækˈslaɪd |-slid -ˌslɪd,
  -ˈslɪd |-slidden -ˌslɪdn̩, -ˈslɪdn̩
backspace ˈbækˌspes |-s -ɪz |-d -t
backspin ˈbækˌspɪn
backstage adv ˈbækˈstedʒ, adj ˈbækˌstedʒ
backstay ˈbækˌste |-ed -d
backstroke ˈbækˌstrok
backswept ˈbækˌswɛpt

|full fʊl |tooth tuθ |further ˈfɝðɚ; ES ˈfɝðə |custom ˈkʌstəm |while hwaɪl |how haʊ |toy tɔɪ
|using ˈjuzɪŋ |fuse fjuz, fɪuz |dish dɪʃ |vision ˈvɪʒən |Eden ˈidn̩ |cradle ˈkredl̩ |keep ’em ˈkipm̩

backward 'bækwəd; ES -wəd; |-s -z

backwash 'bæk₁wɑʃ, -₁wɔʃ, -₁wɒʃ |-es -ɪz |-ed -t

backwater 'bæk₁wɔtɚ, -₁wɑtɚ, -₁wɒtɚ; ES -tə(r

backwoods 'bæk'wʊdz, 'bæk₁wʊdz |-man, -men -mən

bacon, B- 'bekən, 'bekŋ

Baconian be'konɪən, bə-, -njən

bacteria bæk'tɪrɪə |-l -l |sg -ium -m

bactericide bæk'tɪrə₁saɪd

bacterin 'bæktərɪn

bacteriological 'bæk₁tɪrɪə'lɑdʒɪkḷ, bæk₁tɪrɪə-; ES+-'lɒdʒ-

bacteriologist 'bæk₁tɪrɪ'ɑlədʒɪst, bæk₁tɪrɪ-; ES+-'ɒl-; |-gy -dʒɪ

bacteriolysis 'bæk₁tɪrɪ'ɑləsɪs, bæk₁tɪrɪ-; ES+-'ɒl-

bacteriophage bæk'tɪrɪə₁fedʒ |-s -ɪz

Bactria 'bæktrɪə |-n -n

bad bæd

bade past of bid bæd

Baden US 'bedn̩, Germany 'bɑdn̩ (Ger 'bɑːdən)

Baden-Powell 'bedn̩'poəl

badge bædʒ |-s -ɪz |-d -d

badger, B- 'bædʒɚ; ES 'bædʒə(r; |-ed -d |-ing 'bædʒərɪŋ, 'bædʒrɪŋ

Badgworthy 'bædʒərɪ = Bagworthy

badinage 'bædn̩ɪdʒ, ₁bædɪ'nɑʒ (Fr badi'na:ʒ)

badminton, B- 'bædmɪntən

Badon 'bedn̩

Baeda 'bidə, cf Bede

Baedeker 'bedɪkɚ, -də-; ES -kə(r; (Ger 'bɛːdəkər)

baff bæf |-ed -t (Sc baf)

Baffin 'bæfɪn

baffle 'bæfḷ |-d -d |-ling -'bæfḷɪŋ, -flɪŋ

baffy 'bæfɪ (Sc 'bafɪ)

bag bæg |-ged -d |-man, -men -mən

bagasse bə'gæs (Fr ba'gas)

bagatelle ₁bægə'tɛl

Bagdad 'bægdæd, bag'dɑd ('Bag₁dɑd 'rail-₁way)

Bagehot 'bædʒət

bagful 'bæg₁fʊl |-s -z

baggage 'bægɪdʒ |-s -ɪz

Bagot 'bægət

bagpipe 'bæg₁paɪp

Bagworthy Lorna Doone 'bædʒərɪ

bah bɑ, ba, bæ |-ed -d

Bahai bə'hɑ·i |-haism -'hɑ·ɪzəm

Bahama bə'hemə, loc. and Brit bə'hɑmə |-s -z

Bahia bə'hiə (Pg ba'ia)

Baikal baɪ'kɑl

bail bel |-ed -d |-ee 'bel'i

bailey, B- 'belɪ |-liff -lɪf

bailiwick 'belə₁wɪk

Baillie 'belɪ

bailsman 'belzmən |-men -mən

Bainbridge 'benbrɪdʒ |-'s -ɪz

Baird bɛrd, bærd; E bɛəd, ES bæəd

bairn bɛrn, bærn, bern; E bɛən, ES bæən, beən

bait bet |baited 'betɪd

baize bez |baizes 'bezɪz |-d -d

bake bek |baked bekt

bakehouse 'bek₁haʊs |-houses -₁haʊzɪz

Bakelite, b- 'bekə₁laɪt, 'beklaɪt

baker, B- 'bekɚ; ES 'bekə(r; |-kery -kərɪ, -krɪ

baking-powder 'bekɪŋ₁paʊdɚ, 'bekŋ-; ES -də(r

baksheesh, -shish 'bækʃɪʃ

Baku ba'ku

Balaam 'beləm

Balaclava, -klava ₁bælə'klɑvə

balalaika ₁bælə'laɪkə

balance 'bæləns |-s -ɪz |-d -t

Balanga bə₁laŋgə (Sp ba'laŋga)

balata 'bælətə

Balboa bæl'boə

balboa coin bal'boə

balbriggan, B- bæl'brɪgən

balcony 'bælkənɪ |balconied 'bælkənɪd

bald bɔld

baldachin 'bældəkɪn, 'bɔl-

Balder, -dr 'bɔldɚ; ES 'bɔldə(r

balderdash 'bɔldɚ₁dæʃ; ES 'bɔldə-

baldhead 'bɔld₁hɛd

bald-headed 'bɔld'hɛdɪd ('bald -₁headed 'man)

baldpate 'bɔld₁pet |-pated -'petɪd

baldric 'bɔldrɪk, 'bɒdrɪk |-ked -t

Baldwin 'bɔldwɪn, -dɪn

bale, B- bel |baled beld

Bâle bɑl

Balearic ₁bælɪ'ærɪk, bə'lɪrɪk

baleen bə'lin
balefire 'bel,faɪr; ES 'bel,faɪə(r
baleful 'belfəl |-ly -ɪ
baler 'belɚ; ES 'belə(r
Balfour 'bælfʊr; ES 'bælfʊə(r
Baliol 'beljəl, 'belɪəl
balk bɔk |balked bɔkt |balky 'bɔkɪ
Balkan 'bɔlkən
Balkanize 'bɔlkən,aɪz |-s -ɪz |-d -d
ball bɔl |balled bɔld
ballad 'bæləd |balladry 'bælədrɪ
ballade bə'lad, bæ'lad (Fr ba'lad)
ball-and-socket 'bɔlən'sakɪt; ES+-'sɒk-
Ballantrae ,bælən'tre, 'bæləntrɪ
Ballard 'bælɚd; ES 'bæləd
ballast 'bæləst |ballasted 'bæləstɪd
ballerina ,bælə'rinə |-s -z (It ,balle'ri:na)
ballet 'bæle, 'bælɪ, bæ'le (Fr ba'lɛ)
Ballinger 'bælɪndʒɚ; ES -dʒə(r
Balliol 'beljəl, 'belɪəl
ballistic bæ'lɪstɪk, bə- |-s -s
ballonet ,bælə'nɛt
balloon bə'lun, bļ'un |-ed -d
ballot 'bælət |balloted 'bælətɪd
Ballou bə'lu, bæ'lu
ballproof 'bɔl'pruf ('ball,proof 'armor)
ballroom 'bɔl,rum, -,rʊm
ballyhoo 'bælɪ,hu, ,bælɪ'hu |-ed -d
Ballymena ,bælɪ'minə
balm bam |balmed bamd |balmy 'bamɪ; |E+ -a-
Balmoral bæl'mɔrəl, -'marəl, -'mɒrəl
balneal 'bælnɪəl
balneology ,bælnɪ'alədʒɪ; ES+-'ɒl-
baloney bə'lonɪ, bļ'onɪ
balsa 'bɔlsə, 'balsə
balsam 'bɔlsəm |-ed -d
balsamic bɔl'sæmɪk, bæl'sæmɪk |-al -ļ |-ally -ļɪ, -ɪklɪ
baltered 'bɔltɚd; ES -təd; cf blood-boltered
Balthazar bæl'θæzɚ; ES -'θæzə(r; Shak. ,bælθə'zar, -tə'zar; ES -'za:(r
Baltic 'bɔltɪk
Baltimore 'bɔltə,mor, -,mɔr; ES -,moə(r, E+-,mɔə(r; loc. 'bɔltəmɚ, -mə(r
Baluchistan bə,lutʃɪ'stæn, -'stan, bə'lutʃɪ,stæn, -,stan, -ukɪ-
baluster 'bæləstɚ; ES -tə(r; |-ed -d
balustrade ,bælə'stred |-straded -'stredɪd

Balzac 'bælzæk (Fr. bal'zak)
bambino bæm'bino, bam- |-ni -ni (It bam'bi:no)
bamboo bæm'bu ('bam,boo 'pole)
bamboozle bæm'buzļ |-ed -d |-ling -zlɪŋ, -zļɪŋ
ban bæn |banned bænd
banal 'benļ, bə'næl, -'nal, 'bænļ (Fr ba'nal)
banality bə'nælətɪ, be-, bæ-
banana bə'nænə
Banbury 'bæn,bɛrɪ, 'bæm-, -bərɪ, -brɪ
Bancroft 'bænkrɔft, 'bæŋ-, -krɒft
band bænd |banded 'bændɪd
bandage 'bændɪdʒ |-s -ɪz |-d -d
bandanna bæn'dænə
bandbox 'bænd,baks, 'bæn-; ES+-,bɒks; |-es -ɪz
bandeau bæn'do, 'bændo
Bandelier ,bændļ'ɪr; ES -'ɪə(r, S+-'ɛə(r
Bandello bæn'dɛlo (It ban'dɛllo)
banderole 'bændə,rol
bandicoot 'bændɪ,kut
bandit 'bændɪt |-ry -rɪ |-ditti bæn'dɪtɪ
bandmaster 'bænd,mæstɚ, 'bæn-; ES -,mæstə(r, E+-,mas-, -,mɑs-
bandog 'bæn,dɔg, -,dɒg
bandoleer ,bændə'lɪr; ES -'lɪə(r, S+-'lɛə(r
bandore bæn'dor, 'bændor, -ɔr; ES -oə(r, E+-ɔə(r
bandsman 'bændzmən, 'bænz- |-men -mən
bandstand 'bænd,stænd, 'bæn-
bandy 'bændɪ |bandied 'bændɪd
bandy-legged 'bændɪ'lɛgɪd, -'lɛgd, 'bændɪ-,lɛgɪd, -,lɛgd
bane ben |-d -d |-ful -fəl |-fully -fəlɪ
Banff bæmf |-shire -ʃɪr, -ʃɚ; ES -ʃɪə(r, -ʃə(r
bang bæŋ |banged bæŋd
bang 'bhang' bæŋ
Bangkok 'bæŋkak, bæŋ'kak; ES+-ɒk
bangle 'bæŋgļ |-d -d |bangling 'bæŋglɪŋ, -glɪŋ
Bangor Me 'bæŋgɔr, -gɚ, Wales, Irel 'bæŋgɚ; ES -gɔə(r, -gə(r
banish 'bænɪʃ |-es -ɪz |-ed -t
banister 'bænɪstɚ; ES -tə(r; |-ed -d
banjo 'bændʒo |-ed -d
banjorine ,bændʒə'rin
bank bæŋk |banked bæŋkt

|full fʊl |tooth tuθ |further 'fɝðɚ; ES 'fɝðə |custom 'kʌstəm |while hwaɪl |how haʊ |toy tɔɪ |using 'juzɪŋ |fuse fjuz, fɪuz |dish dɪʃ |vision 'vɪʒən |Eden 'idn̩ |cradle 'kredl̩ |keep 'em 'kipm̩

Words below in which a *before* r (farm) *is sounded* ɑ *are often pronounced in* E *with* a (fɑːm)

bankrupt 'bæŋkrʌpt, -rəpt |-ed -ɪd |-ptcy -ptsɪ, -psɪ

Bankside 'bæŋk,saɪd

banner 'bænɚ; ES 'bænə(r

banneret *knight* 'bænərɪt, -,rɛt

banneret, -ette *banner* ,bænə'rɛt

bannock 'bænək

Bannockburn 'bænək,bɝn, ,bænək'bɝn; ES -ɝn, -ɝn

banns, bans bænz

banquet 'bæŋkwɪt, 'bæn- |-ed -ɪd

banquette bæŋ'kɛt

Banquo 'bæŋkwo, 'bæn-, -ko

banshee, -shie 'bænʃi, bæn'ʃi

Banta 'bæntə, *publisher* 'bɑntə

Bantam, b- 'bæntəm

banter 'bæntɚ; ES 'bæntə(r; |-ed -d |-ing -tərɪŋ, -trɪŋ

Banting 'bæntɪŋ

bantingize 'bæntɪŋ,aɪz |-s -ɪz |-d -d

Bantu 'bæn'tu, 'bɑn- ('Ban,tu 'language)

banyan 'bænjən, 'bænjæn

banzai 'bɑn'zɑ·i, 'bɑn'zɑɪ

baobab 'beo,bæb, 'bao,bæb

baptism 'bæptɪzəm

baptismal bæp'tɪzml̩ |-ly -ɪ

Baptist 'bæptɪst

Baptista Minola bæp'tɪstə'mɪnələ

baptistery 'bæptɪstrɪ, -tərɪ |baptistry -trɪ

baptize bæp'taɪz |-s -ɪz |-d -d

bar bɑr; ES bɑː(r; |-red -d

Barabas *Marlowe* 'bærəbəs |-'s -ɪz

Barabbas *Bible* bə'ræbəs, *in Shak.* 'bærəbəs |-'s -ɪz

Baraboo 'bɛrə,bu, 'bær-; S 'bær-

Baraca bə'ræka

Barak 'bɛrək, 'bærək, 'beræk

barb bɑrb; ES bɑːb; |-ed -d, -ɪd

Barbados, -oes bɑr'bedoz, 'bɑrbə,doz; ES bɑː-, 'bɑːb-

Barbara 'bɑrbərə, -brə; ES 'bɑːb-

barbarian bɑr'bɛrɪən, -'bær-, -'ber-, -jən; ES bɑ-

barbaric bɑr'bærɪk; ES bɑː-; |-ally -l̩ɪ, -ɪklɪ

barbarism 'bɑrbə,rɪzəm; ES 'bɑːbə,rɪzəm

barbarity bɑr'bærətɪ; ES bɑ-

barbarous 'bɑrbərəs, -brəs; ES 'bɑːb-

Barbary 'bɑrbərɪ; ES 'bɑːbərɪ

barbecue 'bɑrbɪ,kju, -,kɪu; ES 'bɑː-; |-d -d

barbel 'bɑrbl̩; ES 'bɑːbl̩

barber, B- 'bɑrbɚ; ES 'bɑːbə(r; |-ed -d |-ing -bərɪŋ, -brɪŋ

barberry 'bɑr,bɛrɪ, -bərɪ; ES 'bɑː-

Barberton 'bɑrbətən; ES 'bɑːbətən

barbette bɑr'bɛt; ES bɑː'bɛt

barbican, B- 'bɑrbɪkən; ES 'bɑː-

Barbour 'bɑrbɚ; ES 'bɑːbə(r

Barca 'bɑrkə; ES 'bɑː-; |*pl Eng* -cas -kəz, *Sp* -cas -kas, *It* -che -ke

barcarole, -rolle 'bɑrkə,rol; ES 'bɑːkə,rol

Barcelona ,bɑrsl̩'onə; ES ,bɑː-; (*Sp* ,bɑrθe-'lona)

Barclay 'bɑrklɪ, -le; ES 'bɑːk-

bard bɑrd; ES bɑːd; |-ic -ɪk

Bardolph 'bɑrdɑlf, -dɒlf; ES 'bɑːɹ

bare bɛr, bær; E bɛə(r, ES bæə(r; |-d -d

bareback 'bɛr,bæk, 'bær-; E 'bɛə-, ES 'bæə-

barefaced 'bɛr'fest, 'bær-; E 'bɛə-, ES 'bæə-; |-cedly -sɪdlɪ, -stlɪ ('bare,faced 'lie)

barefoot 'bɛr,fut, 'bær-; E 'bɛə-, ES 'bæə-; |-ed -ɪd

barehead 'bɛr,hɛd, 'bær-; E 'bɛə-, ES 'bæə-

bareheaded 'bɛr'hɛdɪd, 'bær-; E 'bɛə-, ES 'bæə-

baresark 'bɛr,sɑrk, 'bær-; E 'bɛə,sɑːk, ES 'bæə-

bargain 'bɑrgɪn; ES 'bɑːgɪn; |-ed -d

barge bɑrdʒ; ES bɑːdʒ; |-s -ɪz |-d -d

bargeman 'bɑrdʒmən; ES 'bɑːdʒ-; |-men -mən

Barham, *Richard* 'bærəm

baric 'bærɪk

Baring-Gould 'bɛrɪŋ'guld, 'bærɪŋ-; S 'bær-

barite 'bɛraɪt, 'bæraɪt, 'beraɪt; S 'bær-, 'ber-

baritone 'bærə,ton

barium 'bɛrɪəm, 'bær-, 'ber-; S 'bær-, 'ber-

bark bɑrk; ES bɑːk; |-ed -t

barkeeper 'bɑr,kipɚ; ES 'bɑː,kipə(r

barkentine 'bɑrkən,tin; ES 'bɑːk-

Barker, b- 'bɑrkɚ; ES 'bɑːkə(r

barley 'bɑrlɪ; ES 'bɑːlɪ; |-corn -,kɔrn; ES -,kɔən

barm bɑrm; ES bɑːm

barmaid 'bɑr,med; ES 'bɑː,med

Barmecide 'bɑrmə,saɪd; ES 'bɑːm-

Words below in which a *before* r (farm) *is sounded* ɑ *are often pronounced in* E *with* a (fɑ:m)
Words below that have æ *before* r (carry ˈkærɪ) *are often pronounced in* N *with* ɛ (ˈkɛrɪ, §94)

bar mizvah, mitz- ˈbɑrˈmɪtsvə; ES ˈbɑː-
barn bɑrn; ES bɑːn; |-ed -d
Barnabas ˈbɑrnəbəs; ES ˈbɑːnə-; |-ˈs -ɪz
Barnaby ˈbɑrnəbɪ; ES ˈbɑːnəbɪ
barnacle ˈbɑrnəkḷ, ˈbɑrnɪ-; ES ˈbɑːn-; |-d -d
Barnard ˈbɑrnɚd; ES ˈbɑːnəd
Barnardine ˈbɑrnɚˌdin; ES ˈbɑːnə-
barn door ˈbɑrnˈdor, -ˈdɔr; ES ˈbɑːnˈdoə(r,
  E+-ˈdɔə(r; (ˈbarn-ˌdoor ˈfowl)
Barnegat ˌbɑrnɪˈgæt; ES ˌbɑːnɪ-; (ˈBarneˌgat
  ˈBay)
Barnet(t) ˈbɑrnɪt; ES ˈbɑːnɪt; acct+Barˈnett
Barnstable Mass ˈbɑrnstəbḷ; ES ˈbɑːn-
Barnstaple Dev ˈbɑrnstəpḷ; ES ˈbɑːn-; loc.
  -stəbḷ (spelt -ple 1086, -ble 1421)
barnstorm ˈbɑrnˌstɔrm; ES ˈbɑːnˌstɔəm;
  |-ed -d
Barnum ˈbɑrnəm; ES ˈbɑːnəm
barnyard ˈbɑrnˌjɑrd; ES ˈbɑːnˌjɑːd
barogram ˈbærəˌgræm
barograph ˈbærəˌgræf; E+-ˌgraf, -ˌgrɑf
barographic ˌbærəˈgræfɪk
barometer bəˈrɑmətɚ; ES bəˈrɑmətə(r, -ˈrɒm-
barometric ˌbærəˈmɛtrɪk |-al -ḷ |-ally -ḷɪ, -ɪklɪ
baron, B- ˈbærən |-age -ɪdʒ |-ages -ɪdʒɪz
baroness ˈbærənɪs |-es -ɪz
baronet ˈbærənɪt, -ˌnɛt |-ed -ɪd |-age -ɪdʒ
  |-ages -ɪdʒɪz |-cy -sɪ
barong bəˈrɔŋ, bɑˈrɔŋ, -ˈrɒŋ
barony ˈbærənɪ |-nial bəˈronɪəl
baroque bəˈrok (Fr baˈrɔ̃k)
baroscope ˈbærəˌskop
barouche bəˈruʃ, bæ- |-s -ɪz
barque bɑrk; ES bɑːk
barrack ˈbærək |-ed -t
barracuda ˌbærəˈkudə
barrage 'act of barring,' 'bar' ˈbɑrɪdʒ |-s -ɪz
barrage mil. bəˈrɑʒ |-s -ɪz |-d -d
barrator ˈbærətɚ; ES ˈbærətə(r; |-try -trɪ
Barré, Isaac ˈbærɪ, hence next
Barre Mass, Vt ˈbærɪ
barrel ˈbærəl, ˈbærl, ˈbærɪl |-ed -d
barren ˈbærən |-ness ˈbærənnɪs
barret, Barrett ˈbærɪt
barette bəˈrɛt
barricade n ˌbærəˈked, ˈbærəˌked
barricade v ˌbærəˈked |-d -ɪd

Barrie ˈbærɪ
barrier ˈbærɪɚ; ES ˈbærɪ·ə(r
Barrington ˈbærɪŋtən
barrister ˈbærɪstɚ; ES ˈbærɪstə(r
barroom ˈbɑrˌrum, -ˌrʊm; ES ˈbɑːˌr-
barrow, B- ˈbæro, -rə
Barry ˈbærɪ
Barrymore ˈbærəˌmor, -ˌmɔr; ES -ˌmoə(r, E+
  -ˌmɔə(r
Bartas, du djubɑrˈtɑs, drʊ-, du-; ES -bɑːˈtɑs;
  (Fr dybɑrˈtɑ:s) |-ˈs -ɪz
bartender ˈbɑrˌtɛndɚ; ES ˈbɑːˌtɛndə(r
barter ˈbɑrtɚ; ES ˈbɑːtə(r; |-ed -d |-ing
  -tərɪŋ, -trɪŋ
Bartholomew bɑrˈθɑləˌmju, -ˌmɪu; ES
  bɑˈθɑl-, -ˈθɒl-
Bartimeus ˌbɑrtəˈmiəs; ES ˌbɑːtə-; |-ˈs -ɪz
bartizan ˈbɑrtəzṇ, ˌbɑrtəˈzæn; ES ˈbɑːtə-,
  ˌbɑːtə-
Bartlett ˈbɑrtlɪt, -lət; ES ˈbɑːt-
Baruch Bible ˈbɛrək, ˈbærək, ˈberək, -rʊk;
  S ˈbær-, ˈber-
Baruch Bernard bəˈruk
barytone ˈbærəˌton
basal ˈbesḷ |-ly -ɪ
basalt bəˈsɔlt, ˈbæsɔlt
basaltic bəˈsɔltɪk, bæ-
bascule ˈbæskjul, ˈbæskɪul
base bes |bases ˈbesɪz |based best
baseball ˈbesˈbɔl, ˈbesˌbɔl
baseboard ˈbesˌbord, -ˌbɔrd; ES -ˌboəd, E+
  -ˌbɔəd
baseborn ˈbesˈbɔrn; ES -ˈbɔən; (ˈbaseˌborn
  ˈserf)
Basel ˈbɑzḷ—see Basle
basement ˈbesmənt
bases pl of base ˈbesɪz
bases pl of basis ˈbesɪz
bash bæʃ |bashes ˈbæʃɪz |bashed bæʃt
Bashan ˈbeʃæn, ˈbeʃən
bashaw bəˈʃɔ
bashful ˈbæʃfəl |bashfully ˈbæʃfəlɪ
bashi-bazouk ˈbæʃɪbəˈzuk
basic ˈbesɪk |-ally -ḷɪ, -ɪklɪ
basicity beˈsɪsətɪ
basil, B- ˈbæzḷ, -zɪl
basilica bəˈsɪlɪkə, bəˈzɪlɪkə

---

basilisk 'bæsə‚lɪsk 'bæzə‚lɪsk
basin 'besn̩ |basined 'besn̩d
basinet 'bæsənɪt
Basingstoke 'bezɪŋ‚stok
basis 'besɪs |bases 'besiz
bask bæsk; E+bask, bɑsk; |-ed -t
basket 'bæskɪt; E+'baskɪt, 'bɑskɪt
basketball 'bæskɪt‚bɔl; E+'bas-, 'bɑs-
basketful 'bæskɪt‚fʊl; E+'bas-, 'bɑs-; |-s -z
basketry 'bæskɪtrɪ; E+'bas-, 'bɑs-
Basle bɑl
Basque bæsk
Basra 'bʌsrə
bas-relief ‚bɑ·rɪ'lif, ‚bæs-, 'bɑ·rɪ‚lif, 'bæs-
bass *fish* bæs |basses 'bæsɪz
bass *music* bes |basses 'besɪz
Bassanio bə'sɑnɪ‚o, bə'sɑnjo—*trisyllabic in Shak.*
basset, B- 'bæsɪt
Bassianus ‚bæsɪ'enəs |-'s -ɪz
bassinet ‚bæsə'nɛt, 'bæsə‚nɛt
basso 'bæso
bassoon bæ'sun, bə'sun, -'zun
basso-relievo 'bæso·rɪ'livo (*It* -rilievo 'basso-ri'ljɛ:vo)
basswood 'bæs‚wʊd
bast bæst
bastard 'bæstəd; ES 'bæstəd
baste best |basted 'bestɪd |basting 'bestɪŋ
bastille bæs'til (*Fr* bas'ti:j)
bastinado ‚bæstə'nedo
bastion 'bæstʃən, 'bæstɪən
Basutoland bə'suto‚lænd
bat bæt |batted 'bætɪd
Bataan bə'tɑn, bɑ-, bæ-
Batavia bə'tevɪə, -'tevjə
batch bætʃ |batches 'bætʃɪz |batched bætʃt
bate bet |bated 'betɪd
bateau bæ'to
bath, B- bæθ; E+baθ, bɑθ; |-ths -ðz |-th's -θs
bathe beð |bathed beðd |bathing 'beðɪŋ
bathetic bə'θɛtɪk
bathhouse 'bæθ‚haʊs; E+'baθ-, 'bɑθ-
bathos 'beθɑs; ES+-θɒs
bathroom 'bæθ‚rum, -‚rʊm; E+'baθ-, 'bɑθ-
Bathsheba bæθ'ʃibə, 'bæθʃɪbə
Bathurst 'bæθəst; ES 'bæθəst
batik 'bɑtik, bæ'tik, bə-, 'bætɪk
batiste bæ'tist, bə- (*Fr* ba'tist)

baton bæ'tɑn, 'bætn̩, bæ'tɔ̃; ES+-'tɒn; (*Fr* ba'tɔ̃)
Baton Rouge 'bætn̩'ruʒ |-'s -ɪz
batrachian bə'trekɪən
batsman 'bætsmən |-men 'bætsmən
batswing 'bæts‚wɪŋ
battalion bə'tæljən, bæ'tæljən
batten 'bætn̩ |-ed -d |-ing 'bætn̩ɪŋ, 'bætnɪŋ
batter 'bætɚ; ES 'bætə(r; |-ed -d
battery 'bætərɪ, 'bætrɪ
battle 'bætl̩ |-d -d |-ling 'bætl̩ɪŋ, 'bætlɪŋ
Battle Creek 'bætl̩'krɪk, -'krik
battledore 'bætl̩‚dor, -‚dɔr; ES -‚doə(r, E+-‚dɔə(r
battlement *n* 'bætl̩mənt
battlement *v* 'bætl̩‚mɛnt |-mented -‚mɛntɪd
battleplane 'bætl̩‚plen
battleship 'bætl̩‚ʃɪp
battue bæ'tu, bæ'tɪu, bæ'tju (*Fr* ba'ty)
batty 'bætɪ
bauble 'bɔbl̩
Baucis 'bɔsɪs |Baucis' 'bɔsɪs
baudekin 'bɔdəkɪn
Bausch and Lomb 'bɔʃən'lɑm, -'lɒm-, -'lɔm
bauxite 'bɔksaɪt, 'bozaɪt
Bavaria bə'vɛrɪə, bə'verɪə |-n -n
bawcock 'bɔ‚kɑk; ES+'bɔ‚kɒk
bawd bɔd |bawdry 'bɔdrɪ |bawdy 'bɔdɪ
bawl bɔl |bawled bɔld
bay be |bayed bed
bayard, B- 'beəd, *Am statesmen* 'baɪəd; ES -əd
Bayeux be'ju (*Fr* ba'jø)
bayonet 'beənɪt |bayoneted 'beənɪtɪd, -‚nɛtɪd
Bayonne *US* be'on, be'jon; *France*, *Fr* ba'jɔ̃n
bayou 'baɪu, 'baɪju
Bayreuth baɪ'rɔɪt, 'baɪrɔɪt (*Ger* baɪ'rɔyt)
bazaar bə'zɑr; ES bə'zɑ:(r, E+-'zɑ:(r
B.C. 'bi'si
bdellium 'dɛlɪəm
be *v stressed* 'bi, ‚bi; *unstr.* bɪ
be- *unstressed prefix* bɪ-, bə-—*Usually only one pron. is given in the vocab. Where* bə- *is given, usually* bɪ- *would represent a somewhat more careful style; where* bɪ- *is given,* bə- *may often be substituted bef. conss., esp. in a more familiar style. When followed by* l, bl̩- *is a common variant* (believe bl̩'iv).

The **bɪ-** *type with many speakers has the usual tendency toward* **bi-**.

beach bitʃ |-es -ɪz |-ed -t

beachcomber 'bitʃˌkomɚ; ES -ˌkomə(r

beacon 'bikən |-ed -d |-ing 'bikənɪŋ, -knɪŋ

Beaconsfield *in Bucks* 'bɛkənzˌfild

Beaconsfield *Lord* 'bikənzˌfild

bead bid |beaded 'bidɪd

beadle 'bidḷ |-dom -dəm |-ry -rɪ

beadroll 'bidˌrol

beadsman 'bidzmən |-men -mən

beadwork 'bidˌwɝk; ES -ˌwɜk, -ˌwɝk

beagle, B- 'bigḷ

beak bik |-ed -t

beaked *adj* bikt, 'bikɪd

beaker 'bikɚ; ES 'bikə(r

beam bim |-ed -d

beam-ends 'bim'ɛndz, -ˌɛndz, -nz

bean bin |-ed -d

beano 'bino

beanstalk 'binˌstɔk

bear *n* bɛr, bær; E bɛə(r, ES bæə(r

bear *v* bɛr, bær; E bɛə(r, ES bæə(r; |bore bor, bɔr; ES boə(r, E+bɔə(r; |borne born, bɔrn; ES boən, E+bɔən

beard bɪrd; ES bɪəd, S+bɛəd; |-ed -ɪd

Beard bɪrd, bɝd, bærd; ES bɪəd, bɛəd, bæəd

bearer 'bɛrɚ, 'bærɚ; E 'bɛrə(r, ES 'bærə(r

bearskin 'bɛrˌskɪn, 'bær-; E 'bɛə-, ES 'bæə-

beast bist |beasted 'bistɪd |-ly -lɪ

beat bit |*past* beat bit |*pptc* beaten 'bitn̩ *or* beat bit

beatific ˌbiə'tɪfɪk |-al -ḷ |-ally -ḷɪ, -ɪklɪ

beatification bɪˌætəfə'keʃən

beatify bɪ'ætəˌfaɪ |-fied -ˌfaɪd

beatitude bɪ'ætəˌtjud, -ˌtɪud, -ˌtud

Beatrice *fem. name* 'biətrɪs, *in Dante* 'biətrɪs (*It* ˌbea'tri:tʃe) |-'s -ɪz

Beatrix 'biətrɪks |-'s -ɪz

Beattie, -tty 'bitɪ, 'betɪ

beau bo |-s, -x -z |-ed -d

Beaucaire bo'kɛr, -'kær; E -'kɛə(r, ES -'kæə(r; (*Fr* bo'kɛ:r)

Beauchamp *Eng name* 'bitʃəm (*Fr* bo'ʃɑ̃)

Beauclerc, -rk 'boˌklɛr, -ˌklær, -ˌklɑrk; E -ˌklɛə(r, ES -ˌklæə(r, -ˌklɑ:k

Beaufort 'bofɚt, *SC* 'bjufɚt, 'bɪu-, *NC* 'bo-; ES -fət

beau geste *Fr* bo'ʒɛst

beau ideal 'boaɪ'diəl, -'dil, -'dɪəl

Beaulieu *Engd* 'bjulɪ, 'bɪulɪ

Beaumarchais ˌbomar'ʃe; ES -ma:'ʃe; (*Fr* bomar'ʃɛ)

beau monde bo'mɑnd, -'mɒnd (*Fr* bo'mõ:d)

Beaumont 'bomɑnt, -mɒnt

Beauregard 'borəˌgard; ES -ˌgɑ:d, E+-ˌgɑ:d

beauteous 'bjutɪəs, 'bɪu-

beautiful 'bjutəfəl, 'bɪu- |-ly -fəlɪ, -flɪ

beautify 'bjutəˌfaɪ, 'bɪu- |-fied -ˌfaɪd

beauty 'bjutɪ, 'bɪutɪ

Beauvais bo've (*Fr* bo'vɛ)

beaux boz

beaux-arts *Fr* bo'za:r

Beaven 'bɛvən

beaver, B- 'bivɚ; ES 'bivə(r

becalm bɪ'kɑm; E+-'kam; |-ed -d

became bɪ'kem

because bɪ'kɔz, bə-, -'kɒz, -'kʌz

bechance bɪ'tʃæns; E+-'tʃans, -'tʃɑns; |-s -ɪz |-d -t

becharm bɪ'tʃɑrm; ES -'tʃɑ:m, E+-'tʃa:m; |-ed -d

Bechuana ˌbɛtʃu'ɑnə, ˌbɛkju- |-land -ˌlænd

beck bɛk |-ed -t

becket, B- 'bɛkɪt

beckon 'bɛkən |-ed -d |-ing 'bɛkənɪŋ, -knɪŋ

becloud bɪ'klaud |-ed -ɪd

become bɪ'kʌm |became bɪ'kem |become bɪ'kʌm

Becquerel bɛk'rɛl ('Becqueˌrel 'rays)

bed bɛd |bedded 'bɛdɪd

bedabble bɪ'dæbḷ |-d -d |-ling -'dæblɪŋ, -bḷɪŋ

bedaub bɪ'dɔb |-ed -d

bedazzle bɪ'dæzḷ |-d -d |-ling -'dæzlɪŋ, -zḷɪŋ

bedbug 'bɛdˌbʌg

bedchamber 'bɛdˌtʃembɚ; ES -ˌtʃembə(r

bedclothes 'bɛdˌkloz, -ˌkloðz

bedcover 'bɛdˌkʌvɚ; ES -ˌkʌvə(r

bedding 'bɛdɪŋ

Beddoes 'bɛdoz |-'s -ɪz

Bede bid, *Latinized* Baeda 'bidə

bedeck bɪ'dɛk |-ed -t

Bedel, -ll 'bidḷ, bə'dɛl

bedesman 'bidzmən |-men -mən

bedevil bɪ'dɛvḷ |-ed -d |-ing -'dɛvlɪŋ, -vḷɪŋ

bedew bɪ'dju, -'dɪu, -'du |-ed -d

|full fʊl |tooth tuθ |further 'fɝðɚ; ES 'fɝðə |custom 'kʌstəm |while hwaɪl |how haʊ |toy tɔɪ
|using 'juzɪŋ |fuse fjuz, fɪuz |dish dɪʃ |vision 'vɪʒən |Eden 'idn̩ |cradle 'kredḷ |keep 'em 'kipm̩

bedfellow 'bɛdˌfɛlo, -ə
Bedford 'bɛdfəd; ES 'bɛdfəd; |-shire -ˌʃɪr,
-ʃɚ; ES -ˌʃɪə(r, -ʃə(r
bedight bɪ'daɪt
bedim bɪ'dɪm |-med -d
Bedivere 'bɛdəˌvɪr; ES -ˌvɪə(r
bedizen bɪ'dɪzn̩, -'daɪzn̩ |-ed -d |-ing -zn̩ɪŋ,
-znɪŋ—bɪ'daɪzn̩ *is chiefly Brit.*
bedlam, B- 'bɛdləm |-ite -ˌaɪt
Bedloe 'bɛdlo
bedmate 'bɛdˌmet
Bedouin 'bɛduɪn
bedpan 'bɛdˌpæn
bedplate 'bɛdˌplet
bedraggle bɪ'dræɡl̩ |-d -d |-ling -'dræɡlɪŋ,
-ɡl̩ɪŋ
bedrid 'bɛdˌrɪd |bedridden 'bɛdˌrɪdn̩
bedrock 'bɛd'rɑk, -ˌrɑk; ES+-ɒk
bedroll 'bɛdˌrol
bedroom 'bɛdˌrum, -ˌrʊm, -rəm
bedroom door 'bɛdˌrum'dor, 'bɛdrəm-, -'dɔr;
ES -'doə(r, E+-'dɔə(r
Beds *short for* Bedfordshire bɛdz
bedside 'bɛdˌsaɪd
bedsore 'bɛdˌsor, -ˌsɔr; ES -ˌsoə(r, E+
-ˌsɔə(r
bedspread 'bɛdˌsprɛd
bedspring 'bɛdˌsprɪŋ
bedstaff 'bɛdˌstæf; E+-ˌstaf, -ˌstaf; |-staves
-ˌstevz
bedstead 'bɛdˌstɛd, -stɪd
bedstraw 'bɛdˌstrɔ
bedtime 'bɛdˌtaɪm
bedward 'bɛdwəd; ES 'bɛdwəd
bee bi
beech 'bitʃ |-es -ɪz |-en -ən
beechnut 'bitʃnət, -ˌnʌt
beef *n* bif |-'s -s |beeves bivz *or* beefs bifs
beef *v* bif |beefs bifs |beefed bift
beefeater 'bifˌitɚ; ES -ˌitə(r
beefsteak 'bifˌstek
beehive 'biˌhaɪv
beeline 'bi'laɪn ('bee line 'flight)
Beelzebub bɪ'ɛlzɪˌbʌb
been bɪn, bɛn—bin *occurs chiefly as a Briticism, esp. in Canada.* bɛn *is most apt to
occur when unstressed.*
beer, B- bɪr; ES bɪə(r, S+bɛə(r
Beersheba bɪr'ʃibə, 'bɪrʃɪbə; ES bɪə-, 'bɪə-

beeswax 'bizˌwæks |-es -ɪz |-ed -t
beeswing 'bizˌwɪŋ |-ed -d
beet bit
Beethoven 'betovən, 'bet·hovən; *Lond square*
'bit·hovən (*Ger* 'be:t·ho:vən)
beetle 'bitl̩ |-d -d |-ling 'bitlɪŋ, 'bitl̩ɪŋ
beetle-browed 'bitl̩'braud ('beetle-ˌbrowed
'face)
beetlehead 'bitl̩ˌhɛd |-ed 'bitl̩'hɛdɪd
beetroot 'bitˌrut, -ˌrʊt
beeves bivz
befall bɪ'fɔl |-fell -'fɛl |-fallen -'fɔlən, -ln
befit bɪ'fɪt |-ted -ɪd
befog bɪ'fɑg, -'fɔg, -'fɒg |-ged -d
befool bɪ'ful |-ed -d
before bɪ'for, bə-, -'fɔr; ES -'foə(r, E+
-'fɔə(r; |-hand -ˌhænd -time -ˌtaɪm
befoul bɪ'faul |-ed -d
befriend bɪ'frɛnd |-ed -ɪd
befuddle bɪ'fʌdl̩ |-d -d |-ling -'fʌdlɪŋ, -dl̩ɪŋ
beg bɛg |begged bɛgd
begad bɪ'gæd
began bɪ'gæn
begat bɪ'gæt
beget bɪ'gɛt |-got -'gat, *arch.* -gat -'gæt
|-gotten -'gatn̩ *or* -got -'gat; |ES +-'gɒt(n̩)
beggar 'bɛgɚ; ES 'bɛgə(r; |-ed -d |-ing
-gərɪŋ, -grɪŋ |-ly -lɪ |-y -ɪ
begin bɪ'gɪn |-gan -'gæn |-gun -'gʌn |-ning
-ɪŋ
begird bɪ'gɝd |*past* -girt -'gɝt *or* -girded
-'gɝdɪd |*pptc* -girt -'gɝt; | ES -ɜ-, -ɜ-
begohm 'bɛgˌom
begone bɪ'gɔn, -'gɒn, *much less freq.* -'gɑn
begonia, B- bɪ'gonjə, -nɪə
begot bɪ'gat; ES+-'gɒt; |-ten -n̩
begrime bɪ'graɪm |-d -d
begrudge bɪ'grʌdʒ |-s -ɪz |-d -d
beguile bɪ'gaɪl |-d -d
begum *n* 'bigəm
begum *v* bɪ'gʌm |-med -d
begun bɪ'gʌn
behalf bɪ'hæf; E -'haf, -'hæf, -'haf
behave bɪ'hev |-d -d
behavior bɪ'hevjɚ; ES -'hevjə(r; |-ism -ˌɪzəm
behavioristic bɪˌhevjə'rɪstɪk |-ally -ļɪ, -ɪklɪ
behead bɪ'hɛd |-ed -ɪd
beheld bɪ'hɛld
behemoth bɪ'himəθ, 'biəməθ

---

behest bɪˈhɛst
behind bɪˈhaɪnd |-hand bɪˈhaɪndˌhænd
behold bɪˈhold |-held -ˈhɛld |arch. pptc
　-holden -ˈholdən
behoof bɪˈhuf |-s -s
behoove bɪˈhuv |-d -d
behove bɪˈhov |-d -d
Behring ˈbɪrɪŋ, ˈbɛrɪŋ, ˈberɪŋ
beige beʒ |-s -ɪz (Fr bɛːʒ)
being ˈbiɪŋ
Beirut ˈberut, beˈrut
bejewel bɪˈdʒuəl, -ˈdʒɪuəl |-ed -d
bel bɛl
Bel god bɛl, abbr. name bɛl
Bela, Belah ˈbilə
belabor bɪˈlebɚ; ES -ˈlebə(r; |-ed -d |-ing
　-ˈlebərɪŋ, -ˈlebrɪŋ
Belarius bəˈlɛrɪəs, -ˈlær-, -ˈler- |-ˈs -ɪz
belate bɪˈlet |-d -ɪd
belaud bɪˈlɔd |-ed -ɪd
belay bɪˈle |-ed -d
belch, B- bɛltʃ |-es -ɪz |-ed -t
beldam ˈbɛldəm |-dame -dəm, -dem
beleaguer bɪˈligɚ; ES -ˈligə(r; |-ed -d |-ing
　-ˈligərɪŋ, -ˈligrɪŋ
Belfast US ˈbɛlfæst, Irel ˈbɛlfæst, bɛlˈfæst;
　E+-ast, -ɑst
belfry ˈbɛlfrɪ |-fried -frɪd
Belgian ˈbɛldʒɪən, -dʒən |-gium -dʒɪəm,
　-dʒəm
Belgic ˈbɛldʒɪk
Belgrade bɛlˈgred, ˈbɛlgred
Belgravia bɛlˈgrevɪə
Belial ˈbilɪəl, -ljəl
belie bɪˈlaɪ |-d -d
belief bəˈlif, bļˈif, bɪˈlif
believe bəˈliv, bļˈiv, bɪˈliv |-d -d
belike bɪˈlaɪk
Belinda bəˈlɪndə
Belisarius ˌbɛləˈsɛrɪəs, -ˈser- |-ˈs -ɪz
Belisha beacon bəˈliʃəˈbikən
belittle bɪˈlɪtļ |-d -d |-ling -ˈlɪtļɪŋ, -tlɪŋ
belive bɪˈlaɪv
Belize bɛˈliz
Belknap ˈbɛlnæp, bɛlˈnæp
bell, B- bɛl |belled bɛld
belladonna ˌbɛləˈdɑnə; ES+-ˈdɒnə
Bellaire bəˈlɛr, bɛ-, -ˈlær; E -ˈlɛə(r, ES
　-ˈlæə(r

Bellamy ˈbɛləmɪ
bellboy ˈbɛlˌbɔɪ
belle, B- bɛl
Bellefontaine O bɛlˈfauntṇ, -ɑn-, -ɒn-, -tɪn
Bellerophon bəˈlɛrəfən, -ˌfɑn, -ˌfɒn
Bellerus bəˈlɪrəs, -ˈlirəs |-ˈs -ɪz
belles-lettres bɛlˈlɛtrə, -tɚ; ES -trə, -tə(r;
　(Fr bɛlˈlɛtr̩)
belletrist bɛlˈlɛtrɪst |-ic ˌbɛllɛˈtrɪstɪk
bellicose ˈbɛləˌkos
bellicosity ˌbɛləˈkɑsətɪ; ES+-ˈkɒs-
belligerence bəˈlɪdʒərəns |-cy -ɪ |-ent -ənt
Bellingham US ˈbɛlɪŋˌhæm, Engd ˈbɛlɪndʒəm
Bellini beˈlinɪ (It belˈliːni)
bellmouthed ˈbɛlˌmavðd, -θt
Belloc bɛˈlɑk; ES+-ˈlɒk
Bellona bəˈlonə, bɛ-
bellow ˈbɛlo, ˈbɛlə |-ed -d |-ing ˈbɛləwɪŋ
bellows ˈbɛloz, -əz, -əs |double pl bellowses
　ˈbɛləsɪz
Bellows Falls ˈbɛlozˈfɔlz, ˈbɛləz- |-ˈs -ɪz
bellwether ˈbɛlˌwɛðɚ; ES -ˌwɛðə(r
belly ˈbɛlɪ |bellied ˈbɛlɪd
Belmont ˈbɛlmɑnt, -mɒnt
Beloit bəˈlɔɪt
belong bəˈlɔŋ, -ˈlɒŋ; S+-ˈlɑŋ; |-ed -d
belove bɪˈlʌv |-d -d
beloved adj bɪˈlʌvɪd, -ˈlʌvd
below bəˈlo
Belshazzar bɛlˈʃæzɚ; ES -ˈʃæzə(r
belt bɛlt |belted ˈbɛltɪd
Beluchistan bəˌlutʃɪˈstæn, -ˈstan, bəˈlutʃɪ-
　ˌstæn, -ˌstan, -ukɪ-
belvedere, B- ˌbɛlvəˈdɪr; ES -ˈdɪə(r
belying ptc of belie bɪˈlaɪɪŋ
bemaul bɪˈmɔl |-ed -d
bemazed bɪˈmezd
bemean bɪˈmin |-ed -d
bemire bɪˈmaɪr; ES -ˈmaɪə(r; |-d -d
Bemis ˈbimɪs |-ˈs -ɪz
bemoan bɪˈmon |-ed -d
bemock bɪˈmɑk, -ˈmɒk, -ˈmɔk |-ed -t
bemuddle bɪˈmʌdļ |-d -d |-ling -ˈmʌdļɪŋ,
　-dlɪŋ
bemuse bɪˈmjuz, -ˈmɪuz |-s -ɪz |-d -d |-dly
　-ɪdlɪ
Ben bɛn
bename bɪˈnem |-d -d |pptc -d -d or -nempt
　-ˈnɛmpt or -nempted -ˈnɛmptɪd

|full fʊl |tooth tuθ |further ˈfɝðɚ; ES ˈfɝðə |custom ˈkʌstəm |while hwaɪl |how haʊ |toy tɔɪ
|using ˈjuzɪŋ |fuse fjuz, fɪuz |dish dɪʃ |vision ˈvɪʒən |Eden ˈidṇ |cradle ˈkredļ |keep 'em ˈkipm̩

Benares bə'nɑrɪz |-'s -ɪz
Ben Avon *Pa* bɛn'ævən, *Scotl* -'evən, bɛn'ɑn
bench bɛntʃ |-es -ɪz |-ed -t
bend bɛnd |bent bɛnt, *arch.* bended 'bɛndɪd
beneath bɪ'niθ, -'nið
benedicite, B- ˌbɛnə'dɪsətɪ, *Chauc.* ˌbɛndɪs'te
Benedick 'bɛnəˌdɪk
benedict, B- 'bɛnəˌdɪkt
benedictine *liquor* ˌbɛnə'dɪktin
Benedictine *monk* ˌbɛnə'dɪktɪn, -tin
benediction ˌbɛnə'dɪkʃən
Benedictus ˌbɛnɪ'dɪktəs |-es -ɪz
benefaction ˌbɛnə'fækʃən
benefactor 'bɛnəˌfæktɚ, ˌbɛnə'fæktɚ; ES
-tə(r
benefactress 'bɛnəˌfæktrɪs, ˌbɛnə'fæktrɪs |-es
-ɪz
benefic bə'nɛfɪk
benefice 'bɛnəfɪs |-s -ɪz, -ˌfɪsɪz |-d -t
beneficence bə'nɛfəsn̩s |-cent -sn̩t
beneficial ˌbɛnə'fɪʃəl |-ly -ɪ
beneficiary ˌbɛnə'fɪʃərɪ, -'fɪʃɪˌɛrɪ
benefit 'bɛnəfɪt |-ted -ɪd, -ˌfɪtɪd
Beneš 'bɛnɛʃ |-'s -ɪz
Benet 'bɛnɪt
Benét bɛ'ne
benevolence bə'nɛvələns, -vləns |-s -ɪz |-lent
-lənt
Benewah 'bɛnəˌwɑ, -ˌwɒ
Bengal bɛn'gɔl, bɛŋ- ('Benˌgal 'tiger)
Bengalese ˌbɛŋgə'liz, ˌbɛŋ-
Bengali bɛn'gɔlɪ, bɛŋ-
Bengasi, -ghazi bɛn'gɑzɪ, bɛŋ-
Benicia bə'nɪʃə
benighted bɪ'naɪtɪd
benign bɪ'naɪn
benignancy bɪ'nɪgnənsɪ |-nant -nənt |-gnity
-nətɪ
benison 'bɛnəzn̩, -sn̩
Benjamin 'bɛndʒəmən
Ben Lomond bɛn'lomənd
Ben More bɛn'mor, -'mɔr; ES -'moə(r, E+
-'mɔə(r
Bennett 'bɛnɪt
Ben Nevis bɛn'nɛvɪs, -'nivɪs |-'s -ɪz
Bennington 'bɛnɪŋtən
Benoni bə'nonaɪ, bɛ-
Benson 'bɛnsn̩
bent bɛnt

Bentham 'bɛnθəm, 'bɛntəm—'bɛnθəm *is a
sp. pron.*
benthos 'bɛnθɑs; ES+-θɒs
Benton 'bɛntən
benumb bɪ'nʌm |-ed -d |-edness -'nʌmdnɪs,
-ɪdnɪs
Ben Venue ˌbɛnvə'nu, -'nɪu, -'nju
Benvolio bɛn'volɪˌo, -ljo
Ben Vorlich, Voir- bɛn'vɔrlɪk; ES -'vɔə-; (*Sc*
-'vɔrlɪx)
benzaldehyde bɛn'zældəˌhaɪd
benzene, -zine 'bɛnzin, bɛn'zin
benzoate bɛn'zo·ɪt, -et
benzoic bɛn'zo·ɪk
benzoin 'bɛnzo·ɪn, bɛn'zo-
benzol 'bɛnzol, -zɑl, -zɒl |-zole -zol
Beowulf 'beəˌwʊlf
bepaint bɪ'pent |-ed -ɪd
bequeath bɪ'kwið |-ed -d |-al -əl
bequest bɪ'kwɛst
berate bɪ'ret |-rated -'retɪd
Berber 'bɝbɚ; ES 'bɝbə(r, 'bɝbə(r
Berbera 'bɝbərə; ES 'bɝ-, 'bɝ-
berceuse *Fr* bɛr'sø:z
Berea bə'riə |-n -n
bereave bə'riv |-d -d *or* -reft -'rɛft
Berengaria ˌbɛrɪŋ'gɛrɪə, -'ger-
Berenice ˌbɛrə'naɪsɪ
Beresford 'bɛrɪzfɚd, -rɪs-; ES -fəd
beret bə're, 'bɛrɪt (*Fr* be're)
bergamot 'bɝgəˌmɑt; ES 'bɝ-, 'bɝ-, -ˌmɒt
Bergen *NJ* 'bɝgən, *NY* 'bɝdʒɪn, *Norw,
Neth* 'bɝgən, 'bɛrgən; ES 'bɝ-, 'bɝ-, 'bɛə-
Bergerac 'bɝdʒəˌræk; ES 'bɝ-, 'bɝ-; (*Fr*
bɛrʒə'rak)
Bergson 'bɝgsn̩, 'bɛrg-; ES 'bɝg-, 'bɝg-,
'bɛəg-; (*Fr* bɛrg'sõn, bɛrk-) |-ism -ˌɪzəm
berhyme, -rime bɪ'raɪm |-d -d
beribboned bɪ'rɪbənd
beriberi 'bɛrɪ'bɛrɪ
Bering 'bɪrɪŋ, 'bɛr- 'ber-
beringed bɪ'rɪŋd
Berkeley *US* 'bɝklɪ, *Engd* 'bɑrklɪ; ES 'bɝk-,
'bɝk-, 'bɑːk-, E+'bɑːk-
Berkhamsted, -mpstead 'bɝkəmˌstɛd, *loc.+
'bɑrk-; ES 'bɝk-, 'bɝk-, 'bɑːk-;—*The
Brit pron. is* 'bɝkəmstɪd, *loc.+'bɑːk-; the
corresponding Am is as given above.*
Berkley 'bɝklɪ; ES 'bɝklɪ, 'bɝk-

Key: *See in full §§3–47.* bee bi |pity 'pɪtɪ (§6) |rate ret |yet jɛt |sang sæŋ |angry 'æŋ·grɪ
|bath bæθ; E baθ (§10) |ah ɑ |far fɑr |watch wɑtʃ, wɒtʃ (§12) |jaw dʒɔ |gorge gɔrdʒ |go go

Berks *in Engd short for* Berkshire 'bɑrks;
ES 'bɑ:ks; *Pa* bɝks; ES bɜks, bɝks
Berkshire *US* 'bɝkʃɪr, -ʃɚ, *Engd* 'bɑrkʃɪr,
-ʃɚ; ES 'bɜkʃɪə(r, 'bɝkʃɪə(r, 'bɑ:k-, -ʃə(r
berlin bɝ'lɪn, bɚ'lɪn, 'bɝlɪn; ES bɜ'lɪn, bɝ-,
bə-, 'bɜlɪn, 'bɝ-
Berlin *US* 'bɝlɪn; ES 'bɜlɪn, 'bɝ-; *Germany*
bɝ'lɪn, bɚ'lɪn; ES bɜ'lɪn, bɝ-, bə-; (*Ger*
bɛr'li:n) ('Ber‚lin 'wool)
Berlioz 'bɛrlɪ‚oz; ES 'bɛəlɪ‚oz; (*Fr* bɛr'ljɔ̃:z,
-'ljo:z)
berm, -e bɝm; ES bɜm, bɝm
Bermuda bɚ'mjudə, -'mɪudə; ES bə-; |-dian
-dɪən
Bern, -e *US* bɝn, *Swtz* bɝn, bɛrn; ES bɜn,
bɝn, bɛən; (*Fr, Ger* bɛrn)
Bernard 'bɝnəd, 'bɝnɑrd, bɚ'nɑrd; ES
'bɜnəd, 'bɝnəd, -nɑ:d, bə'nɑ:d, E+-a:d;
(*Fr* bɛr'nɑ:r)
Bernardo bɚ'nɑrdo; ES bə'nɑ:do, E+-'nɑ:-
Berners 'bɝnɚz; ES 'bɜnəz, 'bɝnəz
Bernhardt 'bɝnhɑrt; ES 'bɜnhɑ:t, 'bɝnhɑ:t;
(*Fr* bɛr'nɑ:r)
Bernice 'bɝnɪs, bɚ'nɪs; ES 'bɜnɪs, 'bɝ-,
bə'nɪs; |-'s -ɪz
Bernicia bɚ'nɪʃɪə; ES bə'nɪʃ-
bernicle 'bɑrnɪkl̩; ES 'bɑ:n-; =barnacle
Berowne bɪ'run
berretta bə'rɛtə
berrigan 'bɛrɪgən
berry 'bɛrɪ |berried 'bɛrɪd
berserk 'bɝsɝk; ES 'bɜsɜk, 'bɝsɝk; |-er -ɚ;
ES -ə(r
berth bɝθ; ES bɜθ, bɝθ; |-ths -ðs
Bertha, b- 'bɝθə; ES 'bɜθə, 'bɝθə
Bertillon *system* 'bɝtl̩‚ɑn, -‚ɒn; ES 'bɜt-,
'bɝt-; (*Fr* bɛrti'jɔ̃)
Bertram 'bɝtrəm; ES 'bɜtrəm, 'bɝt-
Bertrand 'bɝtrənd; ES 'bɜt-, 'bɝt-; (*Fr*
bɛr'trɑ̃)
bertrandite 'bɝtrənd‚aɪt; ES 'bɜt-, 'bɝt-
beruffled bɪ'rʌfl̩d
Berwick *US* 'bɝwɪk; ES 'bɜwɪk, 'bɝ-; *Scotl*
'bɛrɪk
Berwickshire 'bɛrɪk‚ʃɪr, -ʃɚ; ES -‚ʃɪə(r, -ʃə(r
Berwyn 'bɝwɪn; ES 'bɜwɪn, 'bɝ-
beryl 'bɛrəl, -ɪl
beryllium bə'rɪlɪəm
Besant, *Annie* 'bɛzn̩t, *Sir Walter* bə'zænt

besant 'bɛzn̩t, bə'zænt
beseech bɪ'sitʃ |-es -ɪz |-sought -'sɔt
beseem bɪ'sim |-ed -d
beseen bɪ'sin
beset bɪ'sɛt
beshrew bɪ'ʃru, -'ʃrɪu, *arch.* bɪ'ʃro |-ed-d
beside bɪ'saɪd |-s -z
besiege bɪ'sidʒ |-s -ɪz |-d -d
besmear bɪ'smɪr; ES -'smɪə(r, S+-'smɛə(r;
|-ed -d
besmirch bɪ'smɝtʃ; ES -'smɜtʃ, -'smɝtʃ; |-es
-ɪz |-ed -t
besom 'bizəm |-ed -d
besot bɪ'sɑt; ES+-'sɒt; |-ted -ɪd
besought bɪ'sɔt
bespake bɪ'spek
bespangle bɪ'spæŋgl̩ |-ed -d |-ling -glɪŋ,
-gl̩ɪŋ
bespatter bɪ'spætɚ; ES -'spætə(r; |-ed -d
bespeak bɪ'spik |-spoke -'spok |-spoken
-'spokən
bespouse bɪ'spaʊz; |-s -ɪz |-d -d
bespread bɪ'sprɛd
besprent bɪ'sprɛnt
besprinkle bɪ'sprɪŋkl̩ |-d -d |-ling -klɪŋ,
-kl̩ɪŋ
Bess bɛs |Bess's 'bɛsɪz |-ie -ɪ
Bessarabia ‚bɛsə'rebɪə |-n -n
Bessemer 'bɛsəmɚ; ES 'bɛsəmə(r
best bɛst |bested 'bɛstɪd
best-dressed 'bɛst'drɛst ('best-‚dressed 'man)
bestead, -sted *adj* bɪ'stɛd
bestead *v* bɪ'stɛd |*past* -steaded -'stɛdɪd
|*pptc* -stead -'stɛd
bestial 'bɛstʃəl, -trəl |-ly -ɪ
bestiality ‚bɛstʃɪ'ælətɪ, ‚bɛstɪ-
bestiary 'bɛstɪ‚ɛrɪ
bestir bɪ'stɝ; ES -'stɜ(r, -'stɝ; |-red -d
best-known 'bɛst'non
best-liked 'bɛst'laɪkt ('best-‚liked 'play)
bestow bɪ'sto |-ed -d |-al -əl
bestraddle bɪ'strædl̩ |-d -d |-ling -dlɪŋ, -dl̩ɪŋ
bestrew bɪ'stru, -'strɪu |-ed -d |-ed -d *or*
-n -n
bestride bɪ'straɪd |-strode -'strod |-stridden
-'strɪdn̩
bestrow bɪ'stro |-ed -d |-ed -d *or* -n -n
bet bɛt |*past & pptc* bet bɛt *or* betted 'bɛtɪd
beta *Gk letter* 'betə, 'bitə

|full fʊl |tooth tuθ |further 'fɝðɚ; ES 'fɝðə |custom 'kʌstəm |while hwaɪl |how haʊ |toy tɔɪ
|using 'juzɪŋ |fuse fjuz, fɪuz |dish dɪʃ |vision 'vɪʒən |Eden 'idn̩ |cradle 'kredl̩ |keep 'em 'kipm̩

Beta, b- *'beet'* 'bitə
betaine 'bitɪ‚in
betake bɪ'tek |-took -'tʊk |-taken -'tekən
betel 'bitḷ
Betelgeuse, -geux 'bitḷ‚dʒuz, 'bɛtḷ‚dʒɜz |-'s -ɪz
bête noire 'bet'nwɑr; ES -'nwɑ:(r; (*Fr*
　bɛ:t'nwa:r)
Bethany 'bɛθənɪ
bethel, B- 'bɛθəl
Bethesda bə'θɛzdə
bethink bɪ'θɪŋk |-thought -'θɔt
Bethlehem 'bɛθlɪəm, 'bɛθlɪ‚hɛm
Bethnal 'bɛθnəl
bethought bɪ'θɔt
Bethphage 'bɛθfədʒɪ, -‚dʒi
Bethsaida bɛθ'seədə
Bethune *surnames, US places* bə'θjun, -'θɪun,
　-'θun, 'bitṇ
Béthune bə'θjun, -'θɪun, -'θun (*Fr* be'tyn)
betide bɪ'taɪd |-d -ɪd *or arch.* -tid -'tɪd
betimes bɪ'taɪmz
betoken bɪ'tokən |-ed -d |-ing -'tokənɪŋ,
　-knɪŋ
betook bɪ'tʊk
betray bɪ'tre |-ed -d |-al -əl
betroth bɪ'trɔθ, -'trɒθ, -'troð |-ed -θt, -ðd
　|-al -əl
Betsy 'bɛtsɪ
better 'bɛtɚ; ES 'bɛtə(r; |-ed -d
bettor 'bɛtɚ; ES 'bɛtə(r
Bettws-y-Coed 'bɛtəzɪ'ko·ɪd, -sɪ-
Betty 'bɛtɪ
between bə'twin
betwixt bə'twɪkst
Beulah 'bjulə, 'bɪulə
Bevan 'bɛvən
bevel 'bɛvḷ |-ed -d |-ing 'bɛvlɪŋ, 'bɛvḷɪŋ
Beven 'bɛvən
beverage 'bɛvrɪdʒ, 'bɛvərɪdʒ |-s -ɪz
Beveridge 'bɛvrɪdʒ, 'bɛvərɪdʒ |-'s -ɪz
Beverley, -ly 'bɛvɚlɪ; ES 'bɛvəlɪ
Bevier bɪ'vɪr; ES -'vɪə(r
Bevis 'bivɪs, 'bɛvɪs |-'s- ɪz
bevy 'bɛvɪ
bewail bɪ'wel |-ed -d
beware bɪ'wɛr, -'wær; E -'wɛə(r, ES -'wæə(r;
　|-d -d
beweep bɪ'wip |-wept -'wɛpt
Bewick 'bjuɪk, 'bɪuɪk

bewilder bɪ'wɪldɚ; ES -'wɪldə(r; |-ed -d |-ing
　-'wɪldrɪŋ, -'wɪldərɪŋ
bewitch bɪ'wɪtʃ |-es -ɪz |-ed -t
bewray bɪ're |-ed -d
Bexar *Tex, loc.* bær, bæə(r (*Sp* 'bɛxar)
bey be
beyond bɪ'jand, bɪ'ɑnd, -'jɒnd, -'ɒnd
Beyrouth 'berut, be'rut
Beza 'bizə
bezant, bezz- 'bɛzṇt, bə'zænt
bezel, -il 'bɛzḷ |-ed -d
bezique bə'zik
bezonian bə'zonɪən
bhang bæŋ
Bianca bɪ'æŋkə (*It* 'bjaŋka)
biannual baɪ'ænjuəl |-ly -ɪ
Biarritz 'bɪə‚rɪts (*Fr* bja'rits)
bias 'baɪəs |-es -ɪz |-ed -t
bib bɪb |bibbed bɪbd
bibber 'bɪbɚ; ES 'bɪbə(r
bibcock 'bɪb‚kak; ES+-‚kɒk
bibelot 'bɪblo (*Fr* bi'blo)
Bible 'baɪbḷ
Biblical 'bɪblɪkḷ |-ly -ɪ, -ɪklɪ
Biblicism 'bɪblɪ‚sɪzəm |-cist -sɪst
bibliographer ‚bɪblɪ'agrəfɚ, -'ɒg-; ES -fə(r;
　|-phy -fɪ
bibliographic ‚bɪblɪə'græfɪk |-al -ḷ |-ally -ḷɪ,
　-ɪklɪ
bibliolater ‚bɪblɪ'alətɚ; ES -'alətə(r, -'ɒl-;
　|-try -trɪ
bibliomania ‚bɪblɪə'menɪə, -njə |-iac -ɪ‚æk
bibliophil 'bɪblɪə‚fɪl |-phile -‚faɪl
bibulosity ‚bɪbjə'lasətɪ; ES+-'lɒs-
bibulous 'bɪbjələs
bicameral baɪ'kæmərəl
bicarbonate baɪ'karbənɪt, -‚net; ES -'ka:b-,
　E+-'ka:b-
bicaudal baɪ'kɔdḷ |-date -det
bice baɪs
bicentenary baɪ'sɛntə‚nɛrɪ, ‚baɪsɛn'tɛnərɪ;
　Brit -'tin-, -'tɛn-
bicentennial ‚baɪsɛn'tɛnɪəl |-ly -ɪ
biceps 'baɪsɛps |-es -ɪz
Bicester 'bɪstɚ; ES 'bɪstə(r; (Bister *1634*)
bichlorid baɪ'klorɪd, -'klɔr-; S -'klor-; |-ide
　-aɪd, -ɪd
bichromate *n* baɪ'kromɪt, -met
bichromate *v* baɪ'kromet |-d -ɪd

bicker 'bɪkɚ; ES 'bɪkə(r;|-ed -d |-ing 'bɪkərɪŋ,
 'bɪkrɪŋ
Bickerstaff 'bɪkɚˌstæf; ES 'bɪkə-, E+-ˌstaf,
 -ˌstaf
Bicknell 'bɪknəl
bicolor 'baɪˌkʌlɚ; ES -ˌkʌlə(r; |-ed -d
biconcave baɪ'kankev, -'kaŋ-, ˌbaɪkan'kev;
 ES+-ɒ-
biconvex baɪ'kanvɛks, ˌbaɪkan'vɛks; ES+
 -ɒn-
bicron 'baɪkran, 'bɪk-; ES+-krɒn
bicuspid baɪ'kʌspɪd |-ate -ˌet
bicycle 'baɪˌsɪkl̩, 'baɪsɪkl̩ |-d -d |-ling -klɪŋ,
 -kl̩ɪŋ
bicyclic 'of bicycles' baɪ'sɪklɪk, 'baɪsɪk-
bicyclic 'two-cycled' baɪ'saɪklɪk, -'sɪk-
bicyclist 'b. rider' 'baɪˌsɪklɪst, -sɪklɪst
bid 'ask' bɪd |past bade, bad bæd or. bid bɪd
 |pptc bidden 'bɪdn̩ or bid bɪd
bid 'offer' bɪd |past & pptc bid bɪd
biddable 'bɪdəbl̩ |-bly -blɪ
Biddeford Me 'bɪdəfɚd; ES 'bɪdəfəd
biddy 'bɪdɪ
bide baɪd |past bode bod or bided 'baɪdɪd
 |pptc bided 'baɪdɪd
Bideford Engd 'bɪdəfɚd; ES 'bɪdəfəd
bidentate baɪ'dɛntet
Biela 'bilə
biennial baɪ'ɛnɪəl |-ly -ɪ
bier bɪr; ES bɪə(r, S+bɛə(r
biff bɪf |biffed bɪft
bifid 'baɪfɪd
biflex 'baɪflɛks
bifocal adj baɪ'fokl̩ ('biˌfocal 'lenses)
bifocal n 'baɪfokl̩, baɪ'fokl̩ |-s -z
bifurcate adj 'baɪfɚˌket, baɪ'fɝkɪt; ES 'baɪfə-,
 -'fɝkɪt, -'fɝkɪt
bifurcate v 'baɪfɚˌket, baɪ'fɝket; ES 'baɪfə-,
 -'fɝket, -'fɝket; |-d -ɪd
bifurcation ˌbaɪfɚ'keʃən; ES ˌbaɪfə-
big bɪg
bigamist 'bɪgəmɪst |-mous -məs |-my -mɪ
Bigelow 'bɪgəˌlo, 'bɪglo
bighead 'bɪgˌhɛd |-ed 'bɪg'hɛdɪd
bighorn 'bɪgˌhɔrn; ES -ˌhɔən
Big Horn riv. 'bɪg'hɔrn; ES -'hɔən; (The
 'Big 'Horn, 'Big ˌHorn 'River)
bight baɪt |bighted 'baɪtɪd
Biglow 'bɪglo

bigot, B- 'bɪgət |-ed -ɪd |-ry -rɪ
bigwig 'bɪgˌwɪg |-ged -d |-gery -ərɪ, -rɪ
bijou 'biʒu, bɪ'ʒu
bike baɪk
bilabial baɪ'lebɪəl
bilabiate baɪ'lebɪˌet, -bɪɪt
Bilaspur bɪ'læspʊr, -'las-; ES -pʊə(r
bilateral baɪ'lætərəl |-ly -ɪ
Bilbao bɪl'bao
bilberry 'bɪlˌbɛrɪ, -bərɪ
bilbo 'bɪlbo
Bildad 'bɪldæd
bile baɪl
bilge bɪldʒ |-s -ɪz |-d -d
biliary 'bɪlɪˌɛrɪ
bilinear baɪ'lɪnɪɚ; ES -'lɪnɪ·ə(r
bilingual baɪ'lɪŋgwəl |-ism -ˌɪzəm |-ly -ɪ
bilious 'bɪljəs
biliteral baɪ'lɪtərəl |-ism -ˌɪzəm
bilk bɪlk |bilked bɪlkt
bill bɪl |billed bɪld |-able -əbl̩
billboard 'bɪlˌbord, -ˌbɔrd; ES -ˌboəd, E+
 -ˌbɔəd
Billerica Mass bɪ'lrɪkə
Billericay Engd ˌbɪlə'rɪkɪ
billet 'bɪlɪt |-ed -ɪd
billet-doux 'bɪlɪ'du |pl -doux -'duz (Fr
 bijɛ'du)
billfold 'bɪlˌfold
billhead 'bɪlˌhɛd
billiard 'bɪljɚd; ES 'bɪljəd; |-s -z
billingsgate, B- 'bɪlɪŋzˌget, -gɪt
billion 'bɪljən |-aire ˌbɪljən'ɛr, -'ær; E -'ɛə(r,
 ES -'æə(r; |-th -θ |-ths -θs
billow 'bɪlo, 'bɪlə |-ed -d |-ing 'bɪləwɪŋ |-y
 'bɪləwɪ
billposter 'bɪlˌpostɚ; ES -ˌpostə(r
billsticker 'bɪlˌstɪkɚ; ES -ˌstɪkə(r
billy, B- 'bɪlɪ
bilobate baɪ'lobet |-d -ɪd
bimanual baɪ'mænjʊəl |-ly -ɪ
bimensal baɪ'mɛnsl̩
bimester baɪ'mɛstɚ; ES -'mɛstə(r
bimetallic ˌbaɪmə'tælɪk
bimetallism baɪ'mɛtl̩ˌɪzəm |-ist -ɪst
bimonthly baɪ'mʌnθlɪ
bin bɪn |binned bɪnd
binary 'baɪnərɪ |-nate -net
binaural bɪn'ɔrəl

|full fʊl |tooth tuθ |further 'fɝðɚ; ES 'fɝðə |custom 'kʌstəm |while hwaɪl |how haʊ |toy tɔɪ
|using 'juzɪŋ |fuse fjuz, fɪuz |dish dɪʃ |vision 'vɪʒən |Eden 'idn̩ |cradle 'kredl̩ |keep 'em 'kipm̩

bind baɪnd |bound baʊnd |*arch pptc* bounden
  ˈbaʊndən
binder ˈbaɪndɚ; ES ˈbaɪndə(r; |-y -dərɪ,
  -drɪ
bine baɪn
Binet bɪˈne, bi- (*Fr* biˈnɛ)
Bingen ˈbɪŋən
Bingham ˈbɪŋəm |-ton -tən
Bingley ˈbɪŋlɪ
bingo ˈbɪŋgo
binnacle, binocle ˈbɪnəkl̩
binocular baɪˈnɑkjəlɚ, bɪ-; ES -ˈnɑkjələ(r,
  -ˈnɒk-
binomial baɪˈnomɪəl |-ly -ɪ
Binyon ˈbɪnjən
biochemic ˌbaɪoˈkɛmɪk |-al -l̩ |-ally -l̩ɪ, -ɪklɪ
biochemistry ˌbaɪoˈkɛmɪstrɪ
biogenesis ˌbaɪoˈdʒɛnəsɪs
biogenetic ˌbaɪodʒəˈnɛtɪk |-al -l̩ |-ally -l̩ɪ,
  -ɪklɪ
biogeography ˌbaɪodʒɪˈɑgrəfɪ, -ˈɒg-
biographer baɪˈɑgrəfɚ, bɪ-, -ˈɒg-; ES -fə(r
biographic ˌbaɪəˈgræfɪk |-al -l̩ |-ally -l̩ɪ,
  -ɪklɪ
biography baɪˈɑgrəfɪ, bɪ-, -ˈɒg-
biologic ˌbaɪəˈlɑdʒɪk; ES+-ˈlɒdʒ-; |-al -l̩
  |-ally -l̩ɪ, -ɪklɪ
biology baɪˈɑlədʒɪ; ES+-ˈɒl-; |-gist -dʒɪst
biometric ˌbaɪəˈmɛtrɪk |-al -l̩ |-ally -l̩ɪ, -ɪklɪ
biometry baɪˈɑmətrɪ; ES+-ˈɒm-
Bion ˈbaɪɑn
Biondello ˌbiənˈdɛlo
biophysics ˌbaɪoˈfɪzɪks |-cal -kl̩
biotic baɪˈɑtɪk; ES+-ˈɒt-; |-al -l̩
biotite ˈbaɪəˌtaɪt
biparous ˈbɪpərəs
bipartisan baɪˈpɑrtəzn̩; ES -ˈpɑ:t-, E+-ˈpa:t-;
  |-ship -ˌʃɪp
bipartite baɪˈpɑrtaɪt; ES -ˈpɑ:t-, E+-ˈpa:t-
biped ˈbaɪpɛd |-al -l̩, ˈbɪpədl̩
bipetalous baɪˈpɛtl̩əs
bipinnate baɪˈpɪnet
biplane ˈbaɪˌplen
bipolar baɪˈpolɚ; ES -ˈpolə(r
bipolarity ˌbaɪpoˈlærətɪ
biquadratic ˌbaɪkwɑdˈrætɪk, -kwɒd-
birch bɝtʃ; ES bɝtʃ, bɜtʃ; |-es -ɪz |ed -t |-en
  -ən
bird bɝd; ES bɜd, bɝd; |-ed -ɪd |-ie -ɪ

birdbath ˈbɝdˌbæθ; ES ˈbɜd-, ˈbɝd-, E+
  -ˌbaθ, -ˌbɑθ; |-ths -ðz
birdhouse ˈbɝdˌhaʊs; ES ˈbɜd-, ˈbɝd-; |-ses
  -zɪz
birdlime ˈbɝdˌlaɪm; ES ˈbɜd-, ˈbɝd-
birdseed ˈbɝdˌsid; ES ˈbɜd-, ˈbɝd-
bird's-eye ˈbɝdzˌaɪ; ES ˈbɜdz-, ˈbɝdz-
biretta bəˈrɛtə
Birkenhead ˈbɝkənˌhɛd; ES ˈbɜk-, ˈbɝk-;
  loc. ˌBirkenˈhead
birl bɝl; ES bɜl, bɝl; |-ed -d
Birmingham *US* ˈbɝmɪŋˌhæm, -ŋəm, *Engd*
  ˈbɝmɪŋəm; ES ˈbɜm-, ˈbɝm-
Biron ˈbaɪrən, *in Shak.* bɪˈrun *spelt* Berowne
birr bɝ; ES bɜ(r, bɝ; |-ed -d
Birrell ˈbɪrəl
birth bɝθ; ES bɜθ, bɝθ; |-ths -θs |-day -ˌde
birthmark ˈbɝθˌmɑrk; ES ˈbɜθˌmɑ:k, ˈbɝθ-
  ˌmɑ:k, E+-ˌma:k
birthplace ˈbɝθˌples; ES ˈbɜθ-, ˈbɝθ-; |-s -ɪz
birthright ˈbɝθˌraɪt; ES ˈbɜθ-, ˈbɝθ-
bis bɪs
Biscay ˈbɪskɪ, -ke
biscuit ˈbɪskɪt
bisect *n* ˈbaɪsɛkt
bisect *v* baɪˈsɛkt |-ed -ɪd |-ction -kʃən
bishop, B- ˈbɪʃəp |-ric -rɪk
Bismarck ˈbɪzmɑrk; ES -mɑ:k, E+-ma:k;
  (*Ger* ˈbɪs-)
bismuth ˈbɪzməθ |-al -əl
bismuthic bɪzˈmjuθɪk, -ˈmɪu-, -ˈmʌθɪk
bison ˈbaɪsn̩, -zn̩
Bispham ˈbɪspəm
bisque bɪsk
bister, -tre ˈbɪstɚ; ES ˈbɪstə(r
bisulphate baɪˈsʌlfet
bisulphid baɪˈsʌlfɪd |-ide -aɪd, -ɪd
bisulphite baɪˈsʌlfaɪt
bisymmetric ˌbaɪsɪˈmɛtrɪk |-al -l̩ |-ally -l̩ɪ,
  -ɪklɪ
bisymmetry baɪˈsɪmɪtrɪ
bit bɪt |bitted ˈbɪtɪd
bitch bɪtʃ |bitches ˈbɪtʃɪz |-ed -t
bite baɪt |bit bɪt |bitten ˈbɪtn̩
bitstock ˈbɪtˌstɑk, -ˌstɒk
bitt bɪt |bitted ˈbɪtɪd
bitten ˈbɪtn̩
bitter ˈbɪtɚ; ES ˈbɪtə(r; |-s -z
bittern ˈbɪtɚn; ES ˈbɪtən

Key: *See in full §§3–47.* bee bi |pity ˈpɪtɪ (§6) |rate ret |yet jɛt |sang sæŋ |angry ˈæŋ·grɪ
|bath bæθ; E baθ (§10) |ah ɑ |far fɑr |watch wɑtʃ, wɒtʃ (§12) |jaw dʒɔ |gorge gɔrdʒ |go go

bitternut 'bɪtənət, -ˌnʌt; ES 'bɪtə-
bitterroot 'bɪtəˌrut, -ˌrʊt; ES 'bɪtə-
bittersweet 'bɪtəˌswit, -'swit; ES 'bɪtə-
bitumen bɪ'tjumən, -'tɪu-, -'tu-, 'bɪtʃumən
bituminous bɪ'tjumənəs, baɪ-, -'tɪu-, -'tu-
bivalence baɪ'veləns, 'bɪvələns |-cy -ɪ |-nt
 -nt
bivalve 'baɪˌvælv |-d -d
bivouac 'bɪvʊˌæk, 'bɪvwæk |-ked -t
biweekly baɪ'wiklɪ
biyearly baɪ'jɪrlɪ; ES -'jɪəlɪ, S+-'jɛəlɪ
bizarre bɪ'zɑr; ES -'zɑːr, E+-'zɑːr
Bizet bɪ'ze (Fr bi'zɛ)
Björnson 'bjɝnsn̩; ES 'bjɜn-, 'bjɝn-; (Norw
 'bjø:rnsɔn)
blab blæb |blabbed blæbd
black blæk |blacked blækt
blackamoor 'blækəˌmʊr; ES -ˌmʊə(r
black-and-blue 'blækən'blu, 'blækŋ'blu,
 -'blɪu
blackball 'blækˌbɔl |-ed -d
black-berried 'blæk'bɛrɪd ('black-ˌberried
 'elder)
blackberry 'blækˌbɛrɪ, -bərɪ |-ried -d
blackbird 'blækˌbɝd; ES -ˌbɜd, -ˌbɝd
blackboard 'blækˌbord, -ˌbɔrd; ES -ˌboəd,
 E+-ˌbɔəd
Blackburn 'blækbən; ES 'blækbən
blackcap 'blækˌkæp
blackcock 'blækˌkɑk; ES+-ˌkɒk
blackdamp 'blækˌdæmp
blacken 'blækən |-ed -d |-ing 'blækənɪŋ,
 -knɪŋ
black-eyed 'blæk'aɪd ('black-ˌeyed 'Susan)
Blackfeet 'blækˌfit
blackfellow 'blækˌfɛlo, -ˌfɛlə
blackfish 'blækˌfɪʃ
Blackfoot 'blækˌfʊt |-feet -ˌfit
Blackfriars 'blækˌfraɪəz, -'fraɪəz; ES -ˌfraɪ·əz,
 -'fraɪ·əz
blackguard 'blægəd, 'blægɑrd; ES 'blægəd,
 -gɑːd, E+-gɑːd; |-ed -ɪd |-ry -rɪ
blackhead 'blækˌhɛd
Blackheath 'blækˌhiθ, -'hiθ
blackjack 'blækˌdʒæk |-ed -t
Black Jack 'blæk'dʒæk
blackleg 'blækˌlɛg
blacklist 'blækˌlɪst |-ed -ɪd
blackmail 'blækˌmel |-ed -d

Blackmore 'blækmor, -mɔr; ES -moə(r, E+
 -mɔə(r
blacksmith 'blæksmɪθ |-ths -θs |-ing -ˌsmɪθɪŋ
Blackstone 'blækˌston, -stən
black-throated 'blæk'θrotɪd ('black-ˌthroated
 'warbler)
Blackwells 'blækˌwɛlz, -wəlz
bladder 'blædə; ES 'blædə(r; |-ed -d |-ing
 'blædərɪŋ, -drɪŋ
blade bled |bladed 'bledɪd
blah blɑ
blain blen |blained blend
Blaine blen
Blake blek
blamable 'bleməbl̩ |-bly -blɪ
blame blem |-ed -d |able -əbl̩ |-bly -blɪ
blameful 'blemfəl |-ly -ɪ
blameless 'blemlɪs
blameworthy 'blemˌwɝðɪ; ES -ˌwɜðɪ, -ˌwɝðɪ
Blanc, Mont mɑnt'blæŋk, mʊnt- (Fr mõ'blɑ̃)
blanch blæntʃ; E+blantʃ, blɑntʃ; |-es -ɪz
 |-ed -t
Blanch(e) blæntʃ; E+blantʃ, blɑntʃ; |-'s
 -ɪz
blancmange blə'mɑnʒ, -mɑndʒ
Blanco 'blæŋko
bland blænd
blandish 'blændɪʃ |-es -ɪz |-ed -t
blank blæŋk |blanked blæŋkt
blankbook 'blæŋkˌbʊk, -'bʊk
blanket 'blæŋkɪt |-ed -ɪd
blare blɛr, blær; E blɛə(r, ES blæə(r; |-d -d
blarney, B- 'blɑrnɪ; ES 'blɑːnɪ, E+'blɑːnɪ
blasé blɑ'ze, 'blaze (Fr blɑ'ze)
blaspheme blæs'fim |-d -d
blasphemous 'blæsfɪməs |-my -mɪ, older
 blæs'fim-
blast blæst; E+blast, blɑst; |-ed -ɪd
blastoderm 'blæstəˌdɝm; ES -ˌdɜm, -ˌdɝm
blastula 'blæstʃulə
blat blæt |blatted 'blætɪd
blatancy 'bletnsɪ |blatant 'bletn̩t
blather 'blæðə; ES 'blæðə(r; |-ed -d |-ing
 'blæðrɪŋ, 'blæðərɪŋ
blatherskite 'blæðəˌskaɪt; ES 'blæðə-
blaze blez |blazes 'blezɪz |blazed blezd
blazon 'blezn̩ |-ed -d |-ing 'blezn̩ɪŋ, -znɪŋ
blazonry 'bleznrɪ
bleach blitʃ |bleaches 'blitʃɪz |-ed -t

|full fʊl |tooth tuθ |further 'fɝðə; ES 'fɝðə |custom 'kʌstəm |while hwaɪl |how haʊ |toy tɔɪ
|using 'juzɪŋ |fuse fjuz, fɪuz |dish dɪʃ |vision 'vɪʒən |Eden 'idn̩ |cradle 'kredl̩ |keep 'em 'kipm̩

bleachers 'blitʃɚz; ES 'blitʃəz
bleachery 'blitʃərɪ
bleak blik
blear blɪr; ES blɪə(r, S+blɛə(r; |-ed -d
blearedness 'blɪrɪdnɪs; S+'blɛr-
bleat blit |bleated 'blitɪd
bleb blɛb |-bed -d
bleed blid |bled blɛd
blemish 'blɛmɪʃ |-es -ɪz |-ed -t
blench blɛntʃ |blenches 'blɛntʃɪz |-ed -t
blend blɛnd |blended 'blɛndɪd or blent blɛnt
blende blɛnd
Blenheim 'blɛnəm (Ger Blindheim 'blɪnt-haɪm)
Blennerhassett ˌblɛnɚ'hæsɪt; ES ˌblɛnə-
blenny 'blɛnɪ
blent blɛnt
bless blɛs |blesses 'blɛsɪz |blessed, blest blɛst
blessed adj 'blɛsɪd |-ly -lɪ |-ness -nɪs
blessing 'blɛsɪŋ
blest blɛst
blether 'blɛðɚ; ES 'blɛðə(r
blew blu, blɪu
blight blaɪt |blighted 'blaɪtɪd
blighty, B- 'blaɪtɪ
blimp blɪmp
blind blaɪnd |blinded 'blaɪndɪd
blindfold 'blaɪndˌfold, 'blaɪn- |-ed -ɪd
blindman's buff 'blaɪndˌmænz'bʌf, 'blaɪn-
blindness 'blaɪndnɪs, 'blaɪnnɪs
blindworm 'blaɪndˌwɝm; ES -ˌwɜm, -ˌwɝm
blink blɪŋk |blinked blɪŋkt
bliss blɪs |blisses 'blɪsɪz |-ful -fəl |-fully -fəlɪ
blister 'blɪstɚ; ES 'blɪstə(r; |-ed -d |-ing 'blɪstərɪŋ, 'blɪstrɪŋ
blithe blaɪð |-some -səm
Blithedale 'blaɪðˌdel
blitz blɪts |-es -ɪz |-ed -t
Blitzkrieg 'blɪtsˌkrig (Ger -ˌkri:k)
blizzard 'blɪzɚd; ES 'blɪzəd
bloat blot |bloated 'blotɪd
blob blab; ES+blɒb; |-bed -d
bloc blak; ES+blɒk
Bloch blak; ES+blɒk
block blak; ES+blɒk; |-ed -t
blockade bla'ked; ES+blɒ-; |-d -ɪd
blockhead 'blakˌhɛd; ES+'blɒk-

blockhouse 'blakˌhaʊs; ES+'blɒk-; |-ses -zɪz
Bloemfontein 'blumfənˌten, -fan-, -fɒn-
blond, -e bland, blɒnd
Blondel trouvère blan'dɛl, blɒn-; Brit name 'blʌndl̩
blood blʌd |blooded 'blʌdɪd |-ily -ɪ, -ɪlɪ
blood-boltered 'blʌdˌboltɚd, -ˌboltəd; ES -təd; cf baltered
bloodcurdling 'blʌdˌkɝdlɪŋ; ES -ˌkɜd-, -ˌkɝd-
bloodguilty 'blʌdˌgɪltɪ
bloodhound 'blʌdˌhaʊnd |-ed -ɪd
bloodletting 'blʌdˌlɛtɪŋ
blood-red 'blʌd'rɛd ('blood-ˌred 'wine)
bloodroot 'blʌdˌrut, -ˌrʊt
bloodshed 'blʌdˌʃɛd
bloodshot 'blʌdˌʃat; ES+-ˌʃɒt
bloodstain 'blʌdˌsten |-ed -d
bloodsucker 'blʌdˌsʌkɚ; ES -ˌsʌkə(r
bloodthirsty 'blʌdˌθɝstɪ; ES -ˌθɜstɪ, -ˌθɝstɪ
bloom blum |bloomed blumd |-age -ɪdʒ
bloomers 'blumɚz; ES 'bluməz
bloomery 'blumərɪ
Bloomfield 'blumˌfild
Bloomington 'blumɪŋtən
Bloomsbury 'blumzˌbɛrɪ, -bərɪ
blossom, B- 'blasəm; ES+'blɒsəm; |-ed -d
blot blat; ES+blɒt; |-ted -ɪd
blotch blatʃ; ES+blɒtʃ; |-es -ɪz |-ed -t
blotter 'blatɚ; ES 'blatə(r, 'blɒt-
blotto 'blato; ES+'blɒto
Blount blaʊnt, blʌnt
blouse blaʊs, blaʊz |-s -ɪz |-d -t, -d
blow of wind blo |blew blu, blɪu |blown blon or slang blowed blod
blow 'blossom' blo |blew blu, blɪu |blown blon
blowfly 'bloˌflaɪ
blowgun 'bloˌgʌn
blowhole 'bloˌhol
blown blon
blowoff 'bloˌɔf, -ˌɒf
blowout 'bloˌaʊt
blowpipe 'bloˌpaɪp
blowtorch 'bloˌtɔrtʃ; ES -ˌtɔətʃ; |-es -ɪz
blowup 'bloˌʌp
blowzed blaʊzd |blowzy 'blaʊzɪ
blubber 'blʌbɚ; ES 'blʌbə(r; |-ed -d |-ing 'blʌbrɪŋ, 'blʌbərɪŋ |-y -brɪ, -bərɪ

Key: See in full §§3–47. bee bi |pity 'pɪtɪ (§6) |rate ret |yet jɛt |sang sæŋ |angry 'æŋ·grɪ |bath bæθ; E baθ (§10) |ah ɑ |far fɑr |watch watʃ, wɒtʃ (§12) |jaw dʒɔ |gorge gɔrdʒ |go go

blucher 'blutʃɚ, 'blukɚ; ES -ə(r
Blücher 'blutʃɚ, 'blukɚ; ES -ə(r; (*Ger*
'blyxər)
bludgeon 'blʌdʒən |-ed -d
blue blu, blɪu |-d -d
Bluebeard 'blu‚bɪrd, 'blɪu-; ES -‚bɪəd, S+
-‚bɛəd
bluebell 'blu‚bɛl, 'blɪu-
blueberry 'blu‚bɛrɪ, 'blɪu-, -bərɪ
bluebird 'blu‚bɝd, 'blɪu-; ES -‚bɜd, -‚bɝd
blue-black 'blu'blæk, 'blɪu- ('blue-‚black
'dye)
blue-blooded 'blu'blʌdɪd, 'blɪu-
bluebonnet 'blu‚banɪt, 'blɪu-; ES+-‚bɒnɪt
bluebottle 'blu‚batl̩, 'blɪu-; ES+-‚bɒtl̩
bluecoat 'blu‚kot, 'blɪu-
blue-eyed 'blu'aɪd, 'blɪu- ('blue-‚eyed 'boy)
bluefish 'blu‚fɪʃ, 'blɪu- |-'s -ɪz
bluegill 'blu‚gɪl, 'blɪu-
bluegrass 'blu‚græs, 'blɪu-; E+-‚gras, -‚gras
blueing 'bluɪŋ, 'blɪuɪŋ |-ish -ɪʃ
bluejacket 'blu‚dʒækɪt, 'blɪu-
blue-jay 'blu‚dʒe, 'blɪu-
blue-pencil 'blu'pɛnsl̩, 'blɪu- |-ed -d
blueprint 'blu‚prɪnt, 'blɪu- |-ed -ɪd
Blue Ridge 'blu'rɪdʒ, 'blɪu- ('Blue ‚Ridge
'Mts.)
blues bluz, blɪuz
blue-sky law 'blu'skaɪ‚lɔ, 'blɪu-
bluestocking 'blu‚stakɪŋ, 'blɪu-; ES+-‚stɒk-
bluet 'bluɪt, 'blɪuɪt
bluff blʌf |bluffed blʌft
bluing 'bluɪŋ, 'blɪuɪŋ |-ish -ɪʃ
blunder 'blʌndɚ; ES -də(r; |-ed -d |-ing
'blʌndrɪŋ, 'blʌndərɪŋ
blunderbuss 'blʌndɚ‚bʌs; ES 'blʌndə-; |-es
-ɪz
blunge blʌndʒ |blunges 'blʌndʒɪz |-d -d
blunt, B- blʌnt |blunted 'blʌntɪd
blur blɝ; ES blɝ(r, blɝ; |-red -d
blurb blɝb; ES blɝb, blɝb; |-ed -d
blurry 'blɝɪ; ES 'blɝrɪ, 'blɝɪ
blurt blɝt; ES blɝt, blɝt; |-ed -ɪd
blush blʌʃ |blushes 'blʌʃɪz |blushed blʌʃt
bluster 'blʌstɚ; ES 'blʌstə(r; |-ed -d |-ing
'blʌstərɪŋ, 'blustrɪŋ |-y -tərɪ, -trɪ
-bly -blɪ, *ending of advs corresponding to adjs
in* -able -əbl̩. *In the vocab. this is regularly
added to such adjs in* -able *as have corre-*

*sponding advs, to show the change from
syllabic* l *in* -əbl̩ *to nonsyllabic* l *in* -əblɪ
(dependable dɪ'pɛndəbl̩ |-bly (dɪ'pɛndə)-
blɪ).

When |-bly -blɪ *immediately follows*
|-able -əbl̩, *if the head word does not end in*
-able (pardon 'pardn̩ |-ed -d |-able -əbl̩
|bly -blɪ), *in this case exceptionally the
ending* -blɪ *is to be referred, not as usual to
the head word, but to the immediately preceding form, and pronounced* -əblɪ, *thus
(cf* pardon *in the vocab.):* pardon 'pardn̩
|-ed -d |-able ('par)dnəbl̩, ('par)dn̩əbl̩ |-bly
('pardnə)blɪ, ('pardn̩ə)blɪ. *In such cases,
also, the form in* -bly -(ə)blɪ *includes any
variant prons. of the form in* -able, *as in this
example. The same statements apply to words
in* -ible -əbl̩ *with added* |-bly -blɪ.

Blyth blaɪð, blaɪ |Blythe blaɪð
B'nai B'rith bə'ne·bə'riθ, -'brɪθ
boa 'boə
Boadicea ‚boədɪ'siə
Boanerges ‚boə'nɝdʒiz; ES -'nɜ-, -'nɝ-;
|-ges' -dʒiz
boar bor, bɔr; ES boə(r, E+bɔə(r
board bord, bɔrd; ES boəd, E+bɔəd; |-ed
-ɪd
boarder 'bordɚ, 'bɔr-; ES 'boədə(r, E+
'bɔə-
boardinghouse 'bordɪŋ‚haʊs, 'bɔrd-; ES
'boəd-, E+'bɔəd-; |-ses -zɪz
boardwalk 'bord‚wɔk, 'bɔrd-; ES 'boəd-, E+
'bɔəd-
boarhound 'bor‚haʊnd, 'bɔr-; ES 'boə-, E+
'bɔə-
Boas, *Franz* 'boas, *Frederick S.* 'boæz |-'s -ɪz
boast bost |boasted 'bostɪd
boat bot |boated 'botɪd; |*NEngd*+bɵt (*§46*)
boatful 'bot‚fʊl |-s -z
boatman, -men 'botmən
boatswain, bosun 'bosn̩, *occas.* 'bot‚swen
Boaz *Bible* 'boæz |-'s -ɪz
bob bab; ES+bɒb; |-bed -d
bobbin 'babɪn; ES+'bɒbɪn; |-ed -d
bobbinet ‚babə'nɛt; ES+‚bɒb-
bobby 'babɪ; ES+'bɒbɪ
bobcat 'bab‚kæt; ES+'bɒb-
bobolink 'babl̩‚ɪŋk; ES+'bɒb-
bobsled 'bab‚slɛd; ES+'bɒb-; |-ded -ɪd

|full fʊl |tooth tuθ |further 'fɝðɚ; ES 'fɝðə |custom 'kʌstəm |while hwaɪl |how haʊ |toy tɔɪ
|using 'juzɪŋ |fuse fjuz, fɪuz |dish dɪʃ |vision 'vɪʒən |Eden 'idn̩ |cradle 'kredl̩ |keep 'em 'kipm̩

Those words below in which the ɑ sound is spelt o are often pronounced with ɒ in E and S

bobsleigh 'bab₁sle |-ed -d
bobstay 'bab₁ste
bobtail 'bab₁tel
bobtailed 'bab'teld ('bob₁tailed 'ox)
bobwhite 'bab'hwaɪt
Boccaccio bo'katʃɪ₁o (*It* bok'kattʃo)
Boche, b- baʃ, bɔʃ, boʃ |-s -ɪz
bock bak
bode *past of bide* bod
bode *v* bod |boded 'bodɪd
bodice 'badɪs |-s -ɪz
bodied 'badɪd
bodiless 'badɪlɪs, 'bad|ɪs
bodily 'bad|ɪ, -dɪlɪ
bodkin 'badkɪn
Bodleian bad'liən, 'badliən
Bodley 'badlɪ
Bodmin 'badmɪn
body 'badɪ |-died -d |-guard ₁-gard; ES
   -₁gɑːd, E+-₁gɑːd
Boeotia bɪ'oʃɪə, -ʃə |-tian -ʃən, -ʃɪən
Boer bor, bɔr, bʊr; ES boə(r, bʊə(r, E+
   bɔə(r
Boethius bo'iθɪəs *or* |Boetius bo'iʃɪəs |-'s -ɪz
Boeuf Bayou 'bɛf'baɪu, -'baɪju
bog bag, bɔg, bɒg |-ged -d
bogey 'bogɪ
boggle 'bag|, 'bɒg| |-d -d |-ling -glɪŋ, -g|ɪŋ
bogie 'bogɪ
Bogota *US* bə'gotə, *SAmer* ₁bogə'ta, -'tɔ
   (*Sp* ₁bogo'ta)
bogtrotter 'bag₁tratɚ; 'bɔg-, 'bɒg-; ES
   -₁tratə(r
bogus 'bogəs |-es -ɪz
bogy 'bogɪ
bohea bo'hi
Bohemia bo'himɪə, -mjə |-n -n |-nism -n₁ɪzəm
Bohn bon
Bohr bor, bɔr; ES boə(r, E+bɔə(r
boil bɔɪl |boiled bɔɪld
Boise 'bɔɪsɪ
boisterous 'bɔɪstərəs, -trəs
Bok bak
Bokhara bo'karə
bola 'bolə |bolas 'boləs |-ses -sɪz
bold bold
boldface 'bold₁fes
bold-faced 'bold'fest ('bold-₁faced 'lie)

bold-facedly 'bold'fesɪdlɪ, -'festlɪ
bole bol |boled bold
bolero bo'lɛro, -'lero
Boleyn 'bʊlɪn=Bullen (*in Shak.* Anne
   Bullen)
bolide 'bolaɪd, -lɪd
Bolingbroke 'balɪŋ₁brʊk, 'bʊl-, 'bol- —*All
   except* 'bʊlɪŋ₁brʊk *are spelling pronunciations. The original was* Bul- *and the last
   part is the word* brook.
bolivar 'baləvɚ; ES 'baləvə(r
Bolivar *US* 'baləvɚ; ES 'baləvə(r
Bolivar *SAmer* bo'livar; ES -vɑː(r; (*Sp*
   bo'liβar)
Bolivia, b- bə'lɪvɪə |-n -n (*Sp* bo'liβja)
boll bol |bolled bold
bollard 'balɚd; ES 'baləd
bollworm 'bol₁wɝm; ES -₁wɜm, -₁wɝm
bolly 'bolɪ
bolo 'bolo |-ed -d
Bologna *city* bə'lonjə (*It* bo'loɲɲa)
Bologna *sausage* bə'lonə, -'lonjə, -'lonɪ
bolometer bo'lamətɚ; ES -'lamətə(r
boloney bə'lonɪ, b|'onɪ
Bolshevik, b- 'balʃə₁vɪk, 'bol- |-vism -₁vɪzəm
   |-vist -vɪst
bolster 'bolstɚ; ES 'bolstə(r; |-ed -d
bolt bolt |bolted 'boltɪd; |*NEngd*+bɔ̈lt
   (§46)
bolthead 'bolt₁hɛd
Bolton 'boltn̩
boltrope 'bolt₁rop
bolus 'boləs |-es -ɪz
bomb bam; *less freq.* bʌm |-ed -d
bombard *n* 'bambard; ES 'bambɑːd, E+
   -bɑːd
bombard *v* bam'bard; ES bam'bɑːd, E+
   -'bɑːd; |-ed -ɪd
bombardier ₁bambɚ'dɪr; ES ₁bambə'dɪə(r,
   S+-'dɛə(r
bombasine ₁bambə'zin, 'bambə₁zin
bombast 'bambæst
bombastic bam'bæstɪk |-al -| |-ally -|ɪ, -ɪklɪ
Bombay bam'be ('Bom₁bay 'duck)
bombazine ₁bambə'zin, 'bambə₁zin
bomber 'bamɚ; ES 'bamə(r
bombproof 'bam'pruf ('bomb₁proof 'shelter)
bombshell 'bam₁ʃɛl, 'bʌm₁ʃɛl

Key: *See in full §§3–47.* bee bi |pity 'pɪtɪ (§6) |rate ret |yet jet |sang sæŋ |angry 'æŋ·grɪ
|bath bæθ; E bɑθ (§10) |ah ɑ |far far |watch watʃ, wɒtʃ (§12) |jaw dʒɔ |gorge gɔrdʒ |go go

Those words below in which the ɑ *sound is spelt* o *are often pronounced with* ɒ *in E and S*

Bon **bon**

Bona 'bonə

bona fide 'bonə'faɪdɪ

bonanza bo'nænzə

Bonaparte 'bonə‚pɑrt; ES -‚pɑ:t, E+-‚pɑ:t; |-tist -ɪst

Bonar 'bonɚ; ES 'bonə(r

bonbon 'bɑn‚bɑn (*Fr* bõ'bõ)

bond **band** |bonded 'bɑndɪd |-age -ɪdʒ

bondholder 'bɑnd‚holdɚ; ES -‚holdə(r

bondmaid 'bɑnd‚med |-man -mən |-men -mən

bondsman, -men 'bɑndzmən, 'bɑnz-

bondwoman 'bɑnd‚wumən, -‚wum- |-men -‚wɪmɪn, -ən

bone **bon** |-d -d |-r -ɚ; ES -ə(r; |*NEngd*+ bön (*§46*)

bone-dry 'bon'draɪ ('bone-‚dry 'wood)

boneset 'bon‚sɛt |-ter -ɚ; ES -ə(r

bonfire 'bɑn‚faɪr; ES -‚faɪə(r; |-d -d

Bonheur bə'nɝ, bɔ-; ES -'nɝ(r, -'nɝ; (*Fr* bö'nœ:r)

bonhomie, -mmie ‚bɑnə'mi, 'bɑnə‚mi (*Fr* bönö'mi)

Boniface 'bɑnə‚fes |-'s -ɪz

bonito bə'nito

bon mot *Fr* bõ'mo |*Eng pl* bons mots bõ'moz, *Fr* -'mo

Bonn **ban**

bonne *Fr* bön

bonnet 'bɑnɪt |-ed -ɪd

bonny 'bɑnɪ

bonspiel 'bɑnspil, -spəl

bon ton *Fr* bõ'tõ

bonus 'bonəs |-es-ɪz |-ed -t

bon vivant *Fr* bõvi'vã

bon voyage *Fr* bõvwa'ja:ʒ

bony 'bonɪ; *N Engd*+'bönɪ (*§46*)

boo **bu** |booed bud

boob **bub** |boobery 'bubərɪ |booby 'bubɪ

boodle 'budl̩ |-d -d |-ling 'budlɪŋ, 'budl̩ŋ

boohoo *n* 'bu‚hu

boohoo *intj, v* ‚bu'hu |-ed -d

book **buk** |booked bukt |-ish -ɪʃ

bookbinder 'buk‚baɪndɚ; ES -‚baɪndə(r; |-y -dərɪ, -drɪ

bookcase 'buk‚kes |-s -ɪz

bookkeeper 'buk‚kipɚ; ES -‚kipə(r

booklore 'buk‚lor, -‚lɔr; ES -‚loə(r, E+ -‚lɔə(r

bookmaker 'buk‚mekɚ; ES -‚mekə(r

Bookman 'bukmən

bookman 'bukmən, -‚mæn |-men -mən, -‚mɛn

bookmark 'buk‚mɑrk; ES -‚mɑ:k, E+ -‚mɑ:k

bookplate 'buk‚plet

bookrack 'buk‚ræk

bookseller 'buk‚sɛlɚ; ES -‚sɛlə(r

bookstall 'buk‚stɔl

bookworm 'buk‚wɝm; ES -‚wɝm, -‚wɝ·m

boom **bum** |boomed bumd

boomerang 'bumə‚ræŋ, 'bum‚ræŋ

boon **bun** |booned bund

boondoggle 'bun‚dɑgl̩, -‚dɒgl̩ |-d -d |-ling -glɪŋ, -gl̩ŋ

Boone **bun**

Boonesboro 'bunz‚bɝo, -ə; ES -‚bɝ-, -‚bʌr-, -‚bɝ-

boor **bur**; ES buə(r; |-ish -ɪʃ

boost **bust** |boosted 'bustɪd

boot **but** |booted 'butɪd |-black -‚blæk

bootee bu'ti

Boötes bo'otiz |*gen* -tis -tɪs

booth buθ, buð |-ths -ðs |-'s -θs, -ðz

Booth buθ, buð |-th's -θs, -ðz

Boothbay 'buθ‚be

bootjack 'but‚dʒæk

bootleg 'but‚lɛg |-ged -d |-ger -ɚ; ES -ə(r

bootstrap 'but‚stræp

booty 'butɪ

booze **buz** |boozes 'buzɪz |boozed buzd |-zy -ɪ

bopeep, B- bo'pip

Borachio bo'rɑtʃɪ‚o, -kɪ‚o

boracic bo'ræsɪk

borage 'bɝɪdʒ, 'bɔrɪdʒ, 'bɑrɪdʒ, 'bɒrɪdʒ; ES+'bɝ-, 'bʌr-

Borah 'borə, 'bɔrə; S 'borə

borate *n* 'boret, 'bɔr-, -rɪt; S 'bor-

borate *v* 'boret, 'bɔr-; S 'boret; |-d -ɪd

borax 'boræks, 'bɔr-; S 'boræks

Bordeaux bɔr'do; ES bɔə'do

Borden 'bɔrdn̩; ES 'bɔədn̩; |-town -‚taun

border 'bɔrdɚ; ES 'bɔədə(r; |-ed -d |-ing -dərɪŋ, -drɪŋ, |-land -‚lænd

bore bor, bɔr; ES boə(r, E+bɔə(r; |-d -d

|full ful |tooth tuθ |further 'fɝðɚ; ES 'fɝðə |custom 'kʌstəm |while hwaɪl |how hau |toy tɔɪ |using 'juzɪŋ |fuse fjuz, fɪuz |dish dɪʃ |vision 'vɪʒən |Eden 'idn̩ |cradle 'kredl̩ |keep 'em 'kipm̩

Those words below in which the ɑ sound is spelt o are often pronounced with ɒ in E and S

boreal ˈbɔrɪəl, ˈbɔr-; S ˈbɔrɪəl

borealis ˌbɔrɪˈælɪs, ˌbɔrɪ-, -ˈelɪs; S ˌbɔrɪ-

Boreas ˈbɔrɪəs, ˈbɔr-; S ˈbɔr-; |-ʼs -ɪz

boredom ˈbɔrdəm, ˈbɔr-; ES ˈbɔə-, E+ˈbɔə-

borer ˈbɔrɚ, ˈbɔrɚ; ES ˈbɔrə(r, E+ˈbɔrə(r

boresome ˈbɔrsəm, ˈbɔr-; ES ˈbɔəsəm, E+ˈbɔə-

Borghese bɔrˈgezɪ; ES bɔə-; (*It* borˈge:se)

Borgia ˈbɔrdʒə, -dʒɪə; ES ˈbɔə-

Borglum, Gutzon ˈgʌtsn̩ˈbɔrgləm; ES -ˈbɔəg-

boric ˈbɔrɪk, ˈbɔr-; S ˈbɔrɪk

Boris ˈbɔrɪs, ˈbɔr-; S ˈbɔrɪs; |-ʼs -ɪz

born bɔrn; ES bɔən

borne born, bɔrn; ES bɔən, E+bɔən

Borneo ˈbɔrnɪˌo, ˈbɔr-; ES ˈbɔən-, ˈbɔən-

Borodino ˌbɔrəˈdino, ˌbɑr-, ˌbɒr-

boron ˈbɔrɑn, ˈbɔr-; S ˈbɔrɑn

borough ˈbɝo, ˈbɝə; ES ˈbɜr-, ˈbʌr-, ˈbɝ-

borrow, B- ˈbɔro, -ə, ˈbɑr-, ˈbɒr-; |-ed -d |-ing -rəwɪŋ

bort bɔrt; ES bɔət

borzoi ˈbɔrzɔɪ; ES ˈbɔə-

boscage ˈbɑskɪdʒ |-s -ɪz

Boscawen *NH* ˈbɑskəwən, ˈbɑskwɪn, *Brit name* basˈko·ən, -ˈkɔ·ən

Boscobel ˈbɑskəˌbɛl

bosh bɑʃ |boshes ˈbɑʃɪz |boshed bɑʃt

bosk bɑsk |-age -ɪdʒ |-ages -ɪdʒɪz |-y -ɪ

boʼsʼn ˈbosn̩ = boatswain

Bosnia ˈbɑznɪə |-n -n

bosom ˈbuzəm, ˈbuzəm |-ed -d

Bosphorus ˈbɑsfərəs |-porus -pərəs |-ʼs -ɪz

boss *n* ʻknobʼ, ʻchiefʼ bɔs, bɒs |-es -ɪz |-ed -t

boss *v* ʻembossʼ, ʻorderʼ bɔs, bɒs |-es -ɪz |-ed -t

boss ʻcowʼ bɑs, bɒs

bossy ʻofficiousʼ ˈbɔsɪ, ˈbɒsɪ

bossy ʻcowʼ ˈbɑsɪ, ˈbɒsɪ

Boston, b- ˈbɔstn̩, ˈbɒstn̩—ɔ *prevails in N Engd*

Bostonian bɔsˈtonɪən, bɒs-

bosun ˈbosn̩ = boatswain

Boswell ˈbɑzwɛl, ˈbɒz-, -wəl |-ian bɑzˈwɛlɪən

Bosworth ˈbɑzwɚθ, ˈbɒz-, ˈbɔz-; ES -wɚθ

bot ʻbottʼ bɑt

bot ʻboteʼ bot

botanic boˈtænɪk |-al -l̩ |-ally -l̩ɪ, -ɪklɪ

botanist ˈbɑtn̩ɪst |botany ˈbɑtn̩ɪ

botanize ˈbɑtn̩ˌaɪz |-s -ɪz |-d -d

botch bɑtʃ |-es -ɪz |-ed -t |-edly -ɪdlɪ

bote bot

Botetourt ˈbɑtəˌtɝt; ES -ˌtɜt, -ˌtɝt

botfly ˈbɑtˌflaɪ

both boθ; *N Engd*+bɔθ (§46)

bother ˈbɑðɚ; ES ˈbɑðə(r; |-ed -d |-ing ˈbɑðərɪŋ, ˈbɑðrɪŋ |-some -səm |-ation ˌbɑðəˈreʃən

Bothnia ˈbɑθnɪə

Bothwell ˈbɑθwɛl, ˈbɑð-, -wəl

Botolph ˈbɑtəlf, *Boston street loc.* bəˈtɒlf

bott bɑt

Botticelli ˌbɑtɪˈtʃɛlɪ (*It* ˌbottiˈtʃɛlli)

bottle ˈbɑtl̩ |-d -d |-ling ˈbɑtl̩ɪŋ, ˈbɑtlɪŋ

bottom, B- ˈbɑtəm |-ed -d |-less -lɪs

Bottome bəˈtom = Bottom, bottom

bottomry ˈbɑtəmrɪ |-ried -d

botulism ˈbɑtʃəˌlɪzəm

Botulph ˈbɑtəlf

Botzaris boˈtsɑrɪs |-ʼs -ɪz

Boucher ˈbautʃɚ; ES ˈbautʃə(r

Boucicault ˈbusɪˌkɔlt (*Fr* busiˈko)

bouclé buˈkle

boudoir buˈdwɑr, -ˈdwɔr; ES -ˈdwɑ:(r, -ˈdwɔə(r

bough bau |boughed baud

bought bɔt |boughten ˈbɔtn̩

Boughton *various persons* ˈbotn̩, ˈbɑtn̩, ˈbautn̩

bouillabaisse ˌbuljəˈbes (*Fr* bujaˈbɛs)

bouillon ˈbuljɑn, -jɒn, bulˈjɑn, -ˈjɒn (*Fr* buˈjõ)

boulder, B- ˈboldɚ; ES ˈboldə(r; |-ed -d

boulevard ˈbuləˌvɑrd, ˈbul-; ES -ˌvɑ:d, E+-ˌvɑ:d; (*Fr* bulˈvaːr)

Boulle, Boule bul

Boulogne buˈlon, bə-, -ˈlɔɪn (*Fr* buˈlɔ̃ɲ)

Boult bolt

boun *arch.* baun, *Sc* bun |-(e)d -d

bounce bauns |bounces ˈbaunsɪz |bounced baunst

bound *past & pptc of* bind baund

bound *n, adj, v* baund |-ed -ɪd |-ary -ərɪ, -rɪ

bounden ˈbaundən

bounteous ˈbauntɪəs

bountiful ˈbauntəfəl |-ly -ɪ, -flɪ

bounty ˈbauntɪ |bountied ˈbauntɪd

bouquet *flowers* boˈke, buˈke (*Fr* buˈkɛ)

bouquet ʻaromaʼ buˈke (*Fr* buˈkɛ)

Bourbon ˈbʊrbən; ES ˈbʊəb-; |-ism -ˌɪzəm
|*Ky co. loc.* ˈbɝbən; ES ˈbɝb-, ˈbɝb-
bourbon *whiskey* ˈbʊrbən, ˈbɝb-; ES ˈbʊəb-,
ˈbɝb-, ˈbɝb-
Bourchier *Eng name* ˈbaʊtʃɚ (*cf §121*); ES
ˈbaʊtʃə(r; *Lord Berners* ˈbʊrtʃɪɚ; ES
ˈbʊətʃɪ·ə(r
bourdon ˈbʊrdn̩, ˈbɔrdn̩, ˈbɔrdn̩; ES ˈbʊədn̩,
ˈbɔədn̩, E+ˈbɔədn̩
bourg bʊrg; ES bʊəg; (*Fr* buːr)
bourgeois ˈmiddle-class' bʊrˈʒwɑ, ˈbʊrʒwɑ;
ES bʊə-, ˈbʊə-; (*Fr* burˈʒwa)
bourgeois *type* bɚˈdʒɔɪs, bɝ-; ES bə-, bɝ-, bɝ-
bourgeoise, *pl* -ses bʊrˈʒwɑz; ES bʊə-; (*Fr*
burˈʒwaːz)
bourgeoisie, ˌbʊrʒwɑˈzi; ES ˌbʊə-; (*Fr*
burʒwaˈzi)
bourgeon ˈbɝdʒən; ES ˈbɝdʒ-, ˈbɝdʒ-; |-ed -d
bourn, -e 'limit,' 'brook' bɔrn, bɔrn, bʊrn;
ES bɔən, bʊən, E+bɔən
Bournemouth ˈbɔrnməθ, ˈbɔrn-, ˈbʊrn-; ES
ˈbɔən-, ˈbʊən-, E+ˈbɔən-
bourse bʊrs; ES bʊəs; |-s -ɪz
bouse *naut.* baʊs, baʊz |-s -ɪz |-d -t, -d
bouse, -ze 'drink' buz, baʊz |-s -ɪz |-d -d |-sy,
-zy -ɪ
boustrophedon ˌbustrəˈfidn̩ |-ic buˌstrəfə-
ˈdɑnɪk; ES+-ˌstrɒfəˈdɒnɪk
bout baʊt
boutonniere ˌbutn̩ˈjɛr; ES -ˈjɛə(r; (*Fr*
butöˈnjɛːr)
Bovary ˌbovəˈri (*Fr* bovaˈri) |-rism, -rysm
ˈbovəˌrɪzəm
bovine ˈbovaɪn
bow *n, v* 'prow,' 'nod' baʊ |bowed baʊd
bow *n, v* 'weapon,' 'curve,' 'violin bow' bo
|bowed bod
Bowdich, Bowditch ˈbaʊdɪtʃ |-'s -ɪz
Bowdler ˈbaʊdlɚ; ES ˈbaʊdlə(r
Bowdlerize ˈbaʊdləˌraɪz |-s -ɪz |-d -d
Bowdoin ˈbodn̩
bowel ˈbaʊəl, baʊl |-s -z |-ed -d
bower 'arbor,' *cards* ˈbaʊɚ, baʊr; ES ˈbaʊ·ə(r,
baʊə(r; |-ed -d |-ing ˈbaʊərɪŋ, ˈbaʊrɪŋ |-y -ɪ
bower 'fiddler' ˈboɚ; ES ˈbo·ə(r
bowie ˈbo·ɪ, ˈbu·ɪ
bowknot ˈboˌnat, ˈboˈnat; ES+-ˌnɒt, -ˈnɒt
bowl bol |-s -z |bowled bold
bowlder ˈboldɚ; ES ˈboldə(r

bowleg ˈboˌlɛg
bow-legged ˈboˈlɛgɪd, -ˈlɛgd (ˈbow-ˌlegged
ˈdog)
Bowles bolz |-'s -ɪz
bowline *naut.* ˈbolɪn, -ˌlaɪn
bowling green, B- G- ˈbolɪŋˈgrin
bowman, B- 'archer' ˈbomən |-men -mən
bowman 'front oarsman' baʊmən |-men -mən
Bowmanville ˈbomənˌvɪl
bown(e) baʊn, *Sc* bun |-(e)d -d
Bowness boˈnɛs |-'s -ɪz
bowse 'drink' buz, baʊz |-s -ɪz |-d -d |-sy -zɪ
bowshot ˈboˌʃat; ES+-ˌʃɒt
bowsprit ˈbaʊˌsprɪt, ˈbo-
bowstring ˈboˌstrɪŋ |-ed -d *or* -strung -ˌstrʌŋ
bowyer ˈbojɚ; ES ˈbojə(r
bowze 'drink' buz, baʊz |-s -ɪz |-d -d |-zy -zɪ
box baks; ES+bɒks; |-es -ɪz |-ed -t
boxer, B- ˈbaksɚ; ES ˈbaksə(r, ˈbɒks-
boxful ˈbaksˌful; ES+ˈbɒks-; |-s -z
boxwood ˈbaksˌwʊd; ES+ˈbɒks-
boy bɔɪ |-hood -hʊd
boycott ˈbɔɪˌkat, -ˌkɒt; |-ed -ɪd
Boyesen ˈbɔɪəsn̩
Boyet bɔɪˈɛt (*Fr* bwaˈjɛ)
Boyle bɔɪl
Boyne bɔɪn
boys-and-girls ˈbɔɪzn̩ˈgɝlz; ES -ˈgɝlz, -ˈgɝlz
Boz baz, bɒz—*pron.* boz *by Dickens for* 'Mose'
Bozzaris boˈzærɪs |-'s -ɪz
Brabant brəˈbænt, ˈbrabənt (*Fr* braˈbã),
Shak. ˈBrabant
Brabantio brəˈbænʃo, -ˈbanʃo, -ʃɪˌo
brabble ˈbræbl̩ |-d -d |-ling ˈbræblɪŋ, -blɪŋ
brace bres |braces ˈbresɪz |braced brest
bracelet ˈbreslɪt |-ed -ɪd
brach brætʃ |-es -ɪz
brachial ˈbrekɪəl, ˈbræk-
brachiopod ˈbrækɪəˌpad, ˈbrek-; ES+-ˌpɒd
brachycephalic ˌbrækɪsəˈfælɪk |-lism -ˈsɛfə-
ˌlɪzəm
bracing ˈbresɪŋ
bracken ˈbrækən |-ed -d
Brackenbury ˈbrækənˌbɛrɪ, -bərɪ
Brackenridge ˈbrækənrɪdʒ |-'s -ɪz
bracket ˈbrækɪt |-ed -ɪd
brackish ˈbrækɪʃ
bract brækt |-ed -ɪd |-eal -ɪəl
brad bræd |bradded ˈbrædɪd |-awl -ˌɔl

|full fʊl |tooth tuθ |further ˈfɝðɚ; ES ˈfɝðə |custom ˈkʌstəm |while hwaɪl |how haʊ |toy tɔɪ
|using ˈjuzɪŋ |fuse fjuz, fɪuz |dish dɪʃ |vision ˈvɪʒən |Eden ˈidn̩ |cradle ˈkredl̩ |keep 'em ˈkipm̩

Braddock 'brædək
Bradford 'brædfəd; ES 'brædfəd
Bradshaw 'brædʃɔ
Bradwardine 'brædwədɪn, -ˌaɪn; ES -wəd-
brae bre
brag bræg |bragged brægd
Bragg bræg
braggadocio ˌbrægə'doʃɪˌo
braggart 'brægət; ES 'brægət
Brahe bra (*Dan* 'bra·ɛ)
Brahma *Hindu god* 'bramə, *fowl* 'bramə,
'bremə
Brahman 'bramən |-s -z |-ism -ˌɪzəm
Brahmanic bra'mænɪk |-al -l̩
Brahmaputra ˌbramə'putrə
Brahmin 'bramɪn |-ism -ˌɪzəm
Brahminic bra'mɪnɪk |-al -l̩
Brahms bramz (*Ger* bra:ms) |-'s -ɪz
braid bred |braided 'bredɪd
brail brel |brailed breld
Braille brel |brailled breld (*Fr* bra:j)
brain bren |brained brend
brainpan 'brenˌpæn
brainsick 'brenˌsɪk
Braintree 'brentrɪ, -ˌtri, *in Engd loc.*+'bran-
braise brez |braises 'brezɪz |braised brezd
Braithwaite 'breθwet, *in Engd loc.*+'breθɪt—
cf. Breathitt
brake *arch. past of* break brek
brake *n, v* brek |braked brekt |-age -ɪdʒ
brakeman, -men 'brekmən
brakesman, -men 'breksmən
bramble 'bræmbl̩ |-d -d |-ling -blɪŋ |bly -blɪ
bran, B- bræn
brancard 'bræŋkəd; ES 'bræŋkəd
branch bræntʃ; E+brantʃ, brantʃ; |-es -ɪz
|-ed -t
brand brænd |branded 'brændɪd
Brandeis 'brændaɪs |-'s -ɪz
Brandenburg 'brændənˌbɝg; ES -ˌbɜg, -ˌbɝg;
(*Ger* 'brandənˌburk)
brandied 'brændɪd
brandish 'brændɪʃ |-es -ɪz |-ed -t
brand-new 'bræn'nju, 'brænd-, -'nɪu, -'nu
Brandon 'brændən
brandtail 'brænˌtel
brandy 'brændɪ |brandied 'brændɪd
Brandywine 'brændɪˌwaɪn
Brangwaine 'bræŋwen

bran-new 'bræn'nju, -'nɪu, -'nu
brant brænt
brantail 'brænˌtel
brash bræʃ
brasier 'breʒɚ; ES 'breʒə(r
brass bræs; E+bras, bras; |-es -ɪz |-ed -t
brassard 'bræsard; ES 'bræsa:d, E+-a:d
brassart 'bræsət; ES 'bræsət
brassie, -y, -ey 'bræsɪ; E+'brasɪ, 'brasɪ
brassière brə'zɪr, ˌbræsɪ'ɛr; ES -'zɪə(r, -'ɛə(r
brass-smith 'bræsˌsmɪθ; E+'bras-, 'bras-;
|-ths -θs
brassware 'bræsˌwɛr, -ˌwær; E -ˌwɛə(r,
-ˌwæə(r, 'bras-, 'bras-; S 'bræsˌwæə(r
brasswork 'bræsˌwɝk; ES -ˌwɜk, -ˌwɝk, E+
'bras-, 'bras-
brassy 'bræsɪ; E+'brasɪ, 'brasɪ
brat bræt |-ling -lɪŋ |-tish -ɪʃ
Brathwaite 'breθwet
Bratislava 'bratɪˌslavə, ˌbratɪ'slavə
brattice 'brætɪs |-s -ɪz |-d -t
Brattleboro 'brætl̩ˌbɝo, -ˌbɝə; ES -ˌbɜr-,
-ˌbʌr-, -ˌbɝ-
Brauwer 'brauə; ES 'brauˈə(r
bravado brə'vado, -'vedo |-ed -d
brave brev |braved brevd |-ry -ərɪ, -rɪ
bravo '*well done!*' 'bravo
bravo '*villain*' 'bravo, 'brevo
bravura brə'vjurə, -'vɪurə (*It* bra'vu:ra)
braw *Sc* brɔ, bra
brawl brɔl |brawled brɔld
brawn brɔn |brawned brɔnd |-edness -ɪdnɪs
bray bre |brayed bred
braze brez |brazes 'brezɪz |brazed brezd
brazen 'brezn̩ |-ed -d |-ing 'brezn̩ɪŋ, -znɪŋ
brazenfaced 'brezn̩'fest |-ly -'fesɪdlɪ ('brazen-
ˌfaced 'lie)
brazenness 'brezn̩nɪs
brazier '*brassworker*' 'breʒɚ, 'brezɪɚ; ES
'breʒə(r, -zɪ·ə(r
brazier *for hot coals* 'breʒɚ; ES 'breʒə(r
Brazil, b- brə'zɪl, bə'zɪl |-ian -jən
brazilin 'bræzl̩ɪn
Brazos, -zos' 'brazos, 'brezas, -zɒs
Brea 'brɪə
breach britʃ |breaches 'britʃɪz |-ed -t
bread brɛd |breaded 'brɛdɪd
Breadalbane brɛd'ɔlbən
bread-and-butter 'brɛdn̩'bʌtɚ; ES -'bʌtə(r

Key: *See in full §§3–47.* bee bi |pity 'pɪtɪ (§6) |rate ret |yet jɛt |sang sæŋ |angry 'æŋ·grɪ
|bath bæθ; E baθ (§10) |ah a |far far |watch watʃ, wɒtʃ (§12) |jaw dʒɔ |gorge gɔrdʒ |go go

breadfruit 'brɛdˌfrut, -ˌfrɪut
breadstuff 'brɛdˌstʌf
breadth brɛdθ, brɛtθ |-ths -θs
breadwinner 'brɛdˌwɪnɚ; ES -ˌwɪnə(r
break brek |past broke brok or arch. brake
 brek |pptc broken 'brokən or arch. or slang
 broke brok; |N Engd+brŏk(ən)
breakable 'brekəbļ |-bly -blɪ
breakage 'brekɪdʒ |-s -ɪz
breakbone 'brekˌbon
breakdown 'brekˌdaʊn
breakfast 'brɛkfəst |-ed -ɪd
breakneck 'brekˌnɛk
Breakspeare 'brekˌspɪr; ES -ˌspɪə(r, S+
 -ˌspɛə(r
breakup 'brekˌʌp
breakwater 'brekˌwɔtɚ, -ˌwɑtɚ, -ˌwɒtɚ; ES
 -tə(r
bream brim |breamed brimd
breast brɛst |breasted 'brɛstɪd |-band -ˌbænd
breastbone 'brɛstˌbon, -ˌbon
Breasted 'brɛstɪd
breastpin 'brɛstˌpɪn, 'brɛs-
breastplate 'brɛstˌplet, 'brɛs-
breastsummer 'brɛstˌsʌmɚ, 'brɛsəmɚ; ES
 -ˌsʌmə(r, -səmə(r
breastwork 'brɛstˌwɝk; ES -ˌwɜk, -ˌwɝk
breath brɛθ |-ths -θs |-less -lɪs |-y -ɪ
breathe brið |breathed brið̵d
breathed adj 'having (such) b.,' 'voiceless'
 brɛθt
Breathitt 'brɛθɪt, cf Braithwaite
breccia 'brɛtʃɪə, 'brɛʃɪə (It 'brɛttʃa)
Breckenridge, Breckinridge 'brɛkənrɪdʒ |-'s
 -ɪz
Brecknock 'brɛknək, -nɑk, -nɒk |-shire -ˌʃɪr,
 -ʃɚ; ES -ˌʃɪə(r, -ʃə(r
Brecon 'brɛkən
bred past & pptc of breed brɛd
brede n arch. brid
breech britʃ, brɪtʃ |-es -ɪz |-ed -t
breechblock 'britʃˌblɑk, 'brɪtʃ-; ES+-ˌblɒk
breechcloth 'britʃˌklɔθ, 'brɪtʃ-, -ˌklɒθ |-ths
 -ð̵z, -θs
breeches garment 'brɪtʃɪz
breeching 'brɪtʃɪŋ, 'brɪtʃɪŋ—Those familiar
 with harness call it 'brɪtʃɪŋ.
breechloader 'britʃˌlodɚ, 'brɪtʃ-; ES -ˌlodə(r
breech-pin 'britʃˌpɪn, 'brɪtʃ-

breed brid |bred brɛd
breeks briks
Breese 'briz |-'s -ɪz
breeze briz |breezes 'brizɪz |breezed brizd
Bremen US 'brimən, Germany 'bremən,
 'brɛmən (Ger 'bre:mən)
Bremerton 'brɛmɚtən; ES 'brɛmətən
Brenner 'brɛnɚ; ES 'brɛnə(r
Brereton 'brɪrtn̩; ES 'brɪətn̩, S+'brɛə-
Br'er Rabbit brɚ'ræbɪt; ES brə'ræbɪt
Breslau 'brɛslɔ (Ger 'breslaʊ)
Brest brɛst
Brest Litovsk 'brɛstlɪ'tɔfsk, -'tɒfsk
brethren, B- 'brɛð̵rɪn, -rən
Breton 'brɛtn̩ (Fr brə'tõ)
breve briv
brevet brə'vɛt, 'brɛvɪt |-ed -ɪd |-cy -'vɛtsɪ
breviary 'brivɪˌɛrɪ, 'brɛvɪ-
brevier brə'vɪr; ES -'vɪə(r, S+-'vɛə(r
brevity 'brɛvətɪ
brew bru, brɪu |-ed -d |-ery -ərɪ, -rɪ
brewer, B- 'bruɚ, 'brɪuɚ; ES -ə(r
Brewster 'brustɚ, 'brɪu-; ES -stə(r
Brian 'braɪən
Briand 'brɪɑnd (Fr bri'ɑ̃)
briar 'braɪɚ; ES 'braɪ·ə(r
Briarean braɪ'ɛrɪən, -'er- |-reus -rɪəs |-reus's
 -rɪəsɪz
briarroot 'braɪɚˌrut, -ˌrʊt; ES 'braɪ·ə-
bribe braɪb |bribed braɪbd |-ry -ərɪ, -rɪ
bric-a-brac 'brɪkəˌbræk]-kery -ərɪ, -rɪ
brick brɪk |bricked brɪkt
brickbat 'brɪkˌbæt |-ted -ɪd
brickkiln 'brɪkˌkɪl, -ˌkɪln—cf kiln
bricklayer 'brɪkˌleɚ; ES -ˌle·ə(r
brickle 'brɪkļ
brick-red 'brɪk'rɛd ('brick-ˌred 'paint)
brickwork 'brɪkˌwɝk; ES -ˌwɜk, -ˌwɝk
brickyard 'brɪkˌjɑrd; ES -ˌjɑːd, E+-ˌjɑːd
bridal 'braɪdļ |-ly -ɪ
bride braɪd |brided 'braɪdɪd
bride-ale, brideale 'braɪdˌel
bridechamber 'braɪdˌtʃembɚ; ES -ˌtʃembə(r
bridegroom 'braɪdˌgrum, -ˌgrʊm
bridesmaid 'braɪdzˌmed
bridesman 'braɪdzmən, -ˌmæn |-men -mən
bridewell, B- 'braɪdwɛl, -wəl
bridge brɪdʒ |bridges 'brɪdʒɪz |-d -d
bridgehead 'brɪdʒˌhɛd

Those words below in which the ɑ sound is spelt o are often pronounced with ɒ in E and S

Bridgeport 'brɪdʒˌport, -ˌpɔrt; ES -ˌpoət, E+ -'poət

Bridges 'brɪdʒɪz |Bridges' 'brɪdʒɪz

bridget, B- 'brɪdʒɪt

Bridgewater, -dgw- 'brɪdʒˌwɔtɚ, -ˌwatɚ, -ˌwɒtɚ; ES -tə(r;—*formerly* -Walter

bridgework 'brɪdʒˌwɝk; ES -ˌwɜk, -ˌwɝk

Bridgman 'brɪdʒmən

bridle 'braɪdḷ |-d -d |-ling 'braɪdlɪŋ, -dḷɪŋ

bridleless 'braɪdḷlɪs

Brie bri

brief brif |briefed brift

brier 'braɪɚ; ES 'braɪˌə(r; |-ed -d

brierroot 'braɪɚˌrut, -ˌrʊt; ES 'braɪˌə-

brieve briv

brig brɪg

brigade brɪ'ged |-gaded -'gedɪd

brigadier ˌbrɪgə'dɪr; ES -'dɪə(r, S+-'dɛə(r

brigand 'brɪgənd |-ed -ɪd |-age -ɪdʒ

brigandine 'brɪgənˌdin, -ˌdaɪn

brigantine 'brɪgənˌtin, -ˌtaɪn

Brigham 'brɪgəm

bright, B- braɪt

brighten 'braɪtṇ |-ed -d |-ing 'braɪtṇɪŋ, -tnɪŋ

brighteyes, B- 'braɪtˌaɪz

Brighton 'braɪtṇ

Bright's disease 'braɪtsdɪˌziz

brill brɪl

brilliance 'brɪljəns |-cy -ɪ |-iant -jənt

brilliantine *n* 'brɪljənˌtin, *v* ˌbrɪljən'tin |-d -d

brim brɪm |brimmed brɪmd

brimful, -ll 'brɪm'fʊl ('hearts 'brim'fʊl, 'brɪmˌfʊl 'eye)

brimmer 'brɪmɚ; ES 'brɪmə(r; |-ed -d

brimstone 'brɪmˌston

brinded 'brɪndɪd

Brindisi 'brɪndəzɪ (*It* 'brindizi)

brindle 'brɪndḷ |brindled 'brɪndḷd

brine braɪn |brined braɪnd

bring brɪŋ |brought brɔt

bringing-up 'brɪŋɪŋ'ʌp

brink brɪŋk

briny 'braɪnɪ

brio 'brio

brioche 'brioʃ, 'briaʃ, -nʃ (*Fr* bri'ɔʃ)

briquette, -quet brɪ'kɛt |-(e)d -ɪd

Brisbane 'brɪzben, -bən

Briseis braɪ'siɪs |-'s -ɪz

brisk brɪsk |brisked brɪskt |-en -ən |-ened -ənd

brisket 'brɪskɪt

bristle 'brɪsḷ |-d -d |-ling 'brɪslɪŋ, -sḷɪŋ

bristly 'brɪsḷɪ, 'brɪslɪ

Bristol 'brɪstḷ (Bristow *in 1142*)

Bristow *US* 'brɪsto

Britain 'brɪtṇ, 'brɪtən |-tish -tɪʃ

Britannia brɪ'tænɪə, -njə |-ic -ɪk |-ica -ɪkə

Briticism 'brɪtəˌsɪzəm

Briton 'brɪtṇ, 'brɪtən

Brittain 'brɪtṇ, 'brɪtən

Brittany 'brɪtṇɪ

brittle 'brɪtḷ |brittlely 'brɪtḷɪ, 'brɪtḷɪ |-r -tḷɚ, -tḷɚ; ES -ə(r; |-st -tḷɪst, -tḷɪst

Britton 'brɪtṇ, 'brɪtən

Brno 'bɝno; ES 'bɜno, 'bɝno

broach brotʃ |broaches 'brotʃɪz |-ed -t

broad brɔd |-ax, -axe -ˌæks |-axes -ˌæksɪz

broadbill 'brɔdˌbɪl

broadbrim, B- 'brɔdˌbrɪm

broad-brimmed 'brɔd'brɪmd ('broad-ˌbrimmed 'hat)

broadcast 'brɔdˌkæst; E+-ˌkast, -ˌkɑst; |*past & pptc* -cast, *radio*+-casted -ɪd

broadcloth 'brɔdˌklɔθ, -ˌklɒθ |-ths -θs

broaden 'brɔdṇ |-ed -d |-ing 'brɔdṇɪŋ, -dnɪŋ

broad-gauge 'brɔdˌgedʒ |-s -ɪz

broad-gauged 'brɔd'gedʒd ('broad-ˌgauged 'mind)

broadleaf, B- 'brɔdˌlif

broad-minded 'brɔd'maɪndɪd

Broad Ripple 'brɔdˌrɪpḷ

broadside *n, v* 'brɔdˌsaɪd |-d -ɪd

broadside *adv* 'brɔd'saɪd, -ˌsaɪd

broadsword 'brɔdˌsord, -ˌsɔrd; ES -ˌsoəd, E+ -ˌsɔəd

Broadview 'brɔdˌvju, -ˌvɪu, -'v-

Broadway 'brɔdˌwe

Brobdignag *erron. for next*

Brobdingnag 'brɑbdɪŋˌnæg |-ian ˌbrɑbdɪŋ-'nægɪən

brocade bro'ked |-caded -'kedɪd

brocatel, -lle ˌbrɑkə'tɛl

broccoli 'brɑkəlɪ, 'brɑklɪ (*It* 'brɔkkoli)

brochure bro'ʃjʊr, -'ʃɪʊr, -'ʃʊr; ES -ʊə(r; (*Fr* brɔ'ʃy:r)

brock brɑk

Those words below in which the ɑ *sound is spelt* o *are often pronounced with* ɒ *in E and S*

Brockport 'brak͜ˌport, -ˌpɔrt; ES -ˌpoət, E+ -ˌpɔət

Brockton 'braktən

brocoli 'brakəlɪ, 'braklɪ

Brodhead 'bradˌhɛd, 'brɔd-

brogan 'brogən

brogue brog |brogued brogd

broider 'brɔɪdɚ; ES -də(r; |-ed -d |-ing 'brɔɪdərɪŋ, 'brɔɪdrɪŋ

broil brɔɪl |broiled brɔɪld

brokage 'brokɪdʒ

broke brok; *N Engd*+brōk (*§46*)

broken 'brokən; *N Engd*+'brōkən (*§46*); |-ness -kənnɪs

broken-down 'brokən'daʊn

brokenhearted 'brokən'hartɪd; ES -'ha:tɪd, E+-'ha:tɪd

broken-winded 'brokən'wɪndɪd

broker 'brokɚ; ES 'brokə(r

brokerage 'brokərɪdʒ, 'brokrɪdʒ

bromal 'bromæl

bromate 'bromet |-mated -metɪd

Brom Bones 'bram'bonz |-'s -ɪz

Bromfield 'bramˌfild

bromic 'bromɪk

bromide 'bromaɪd, -mɪd |bromid 'bromɪd

bromine 'bromin, -mɪn |bromin 'bromɪn

Bromley 'brʌmlɪ, 'bram-

Bromwich 'brʌmɪdʒ, 'bram-, -wɪtʃ |-'s -ɪz

bronchi *pl* 'braŋkaɪ

bronchia *pl* 'braŋkɪə

bronchial 'braŋkɪəl |-ly -ɪ

bronchitis bran'kaɪtɪs, braŋ- |-chitic -'kɪtɪk

broncho *see* bronco

bronchoscope 'braŋkəˌskop

bronchus 'braŋkəs |bronchi 'braŋkaɪ

bronco 'braŋko |-buster -ˌbʌstɚ; ES -tə(r

Bronson 'brʌnsn̩, 'bransn̩

Brontë 'brantɪ

Brontosaurus, b- ˌbrantə'sɔrəs |-'s -ɪz

Bronx braŋks |-'s -ɪz |-ville -vɪl

bronze branz |bronzes 'branzɪz |-d -d

brooch brotʃ, brutʃ |-es -ɪz |-ed -t

brood brud |brooded 'brudɪd

brook brʊk |brooked brʊkt |-let -lɪt

Brooke brʊk

Brookline 'brʊklaɪn |-lyn -lɪn

broom brum, brʊm |-ed -d

broomcorn 'brumˌkɔrn, 'brʊm-; ES -ˌkɔən -ˌpɔət

Broome *NY county* brum

broomrape 'brumˌrep, 'brʊm-

broomstick 'brumˌstɪk, 'brʊm-

broth brɔθ, brɒθ |-ths -θs

brothel 'brɔθəl, 'brɒθəl, -ðəl

brother 'brʌðɚ; ES -ðə(r; |-ed -d |-ing 'brʌðərɪŋ, 'brʌðrɪŋ

brotherhood 'brʌðɚˌhʊd; ES 'brʌðə-

brother-in-law 'brʌðərɪnˌlɔ, 'brʌðən̩ˌlɔ; ES 'brʌðərɪnˌlɔ, 'brʌðən̩ˌlɔ

brotherly 'brʌðɚlɪ; ES 'brʌðəlɪ

brothers-in-law 'brʌðɚzɪnˌlɔ, 'brʌðɚzn̩ˌlɔ; ES 'brʌðəzɪnˌlɔ, 'brʌðəzn̩ˌlɔ

brougham 'bruəm, brum, 'broəm

Brougham brum, 'bruəm

brought brɔt

Broun, *Heywood* 'brun

brow braʊ |browed braʊd

Broward 'braʊɚd; ES 'braʊ·əd

browbeat 'braʊˌbit |*past* -beat -ˌbit |*pptc* -beaten -ˌbitn̩

Brower braʊɚ; ES 'braʊ·ə(r

brown braʊn |-ed -d |-ness 'braʊnnɪs

Brown(e) braʊn

Brownell 'braʊnɛl, braʊ'nɛl

brown-eyed 'braʊn'aɪd ('brown-ˌeyed 'Susan)

Brownian 'braʊnɪən

brownie 'braʊnɪ

Browning 'braʊnɪŋ

brownstone 'braʊnˌston

Brownsville 'braʊnzvɪl; S+-vl̩

browntail 'braʊnˌtel

brown-tailed 'braʊn'teld ('brown-ˌtailed 'moth)

browse braʊz |browses 'braʊzɪz |-d -d

Bruce brus, brɪus |-'s -ɪz

bruckle 'brʌkl̩

Bruges 'brudʒɪz, bruʒ (*Fr* bry:ʒ) |Bruges' 'brudʒɪz |Bruges's 'bruʒɪz

Brugmann 'brʊgmən (*Ger* 'brʊgman)

bruin 'bruɪn, 'brɪuɪn

bruise bruz, brɪuz |-s -ɪz |-d -d

bruit brut, brɪut |-ed -ɪd

brumal 'bruml̩, 'brɪuml̩

brume brum, brɪum

brummagem, B- 'brʌmədʒəm

Brummell 'brʌml̩

|full fʊl |tooth tuθ |further 'fɝðɚ; ES 'fɝðə |custom 'kʌstəm |while hwaɪl |how haʊ |toy tɔɪ |using 'juzɪŋ |fuse fjuz, fɪuz |dish dɪʃ |vision 'vɪʒən |Eden 'idn̩ |cradle 'kredl̩ |keep 'em 'kipm̩

Brunanburh 'brunən‚bɝg; ES -‚bɜg, -‚bɝg;
  (OE 'brunɑn‚burx)
Brundisium brʌn'dɪzɪəm
Brunelleschi ‚brun|'ɛskɪ (It ‚brunel'lɛski)
brunet, -tte bru'nɛt, brɪu-
Brunhild 'brunhɪld (Ger 'bru:nhɪlt)
Brunhilde brun'hɪldə (Ger bru:n'hɪldə)
Bruno 'bruno, 'brɪuno
Brunswick 'brʌnzwɪk, -zɪk
brunt brʌnt |brunted 'brʌntɪd
brush, B- brʌʃ |brushes 'brʌʃɪz |-ed -t
brushbush 'brʌʃ‚buʃ |-es -ɪz
brushland 'brʌʃ‚lænd
brushwood 'brʌʃ‚wud
brusque brʌsk, brusk (Fr brysk)
Brussells 'brʌs|z |-ls' -|z
Brussells sprouts 'brʌs|'sprauts, 'brʌs|z's-
Brut brut, brɪut
brutal 'brut|, 'brɪut| |-ly -ɪ
brutality bru'tælətɪ, brɪu-
brutalization ‚brut|ə'zeʃən, ‚brɪut|-, -aɪ'z-
brutalize 'brut|‚aɪz, 'brɪut|- |-s -ɪz |-d -d
brute brut, brɪut |-tify -ə‚faɪ |-tified -ə‚faɪd
brutish 'brutɪʃ, 'brɪutɪʃ
Brutus 'brutəs, 'brɪutəs |-'s -ɪz
Bruyere bru'jɛr; ES -'jɛə(r; (Fr bry'jɛ:r)
Bryan 'braɪən |-ism -‚ɪzəm
Bryant 'braɪənt
Bryce braɪs |-'s -ɪz
Brynhild 'brɪnhɪld (Scand 'bryn-)
Brynmawr, -maur Wales brɪn'mɔr; ES
  -'mɔə(r; (S. Welsh brin'maur)
Bryn Mawr Pa brɪn'mɔr, loc. -'mɑr; ES
  -'mɔə(r, -'mɑ:(r
bryology braɪ'ɑlədʒɪ; ES+-'ɒl-
bryony 'braɪənɪ
bryophyte 'braɪə‚faɪt
Brython 'brɪθən |Brythonic brɪ'θɑnɪk; ES+
  -'θɒn-
bubble 'bʌb| |-d -d |-ling 'bʌblɪŋ, 'bʌb|ɪŋ
bubble and squeak 'bʌb|ən'skwik
bubbler 'bʌblɚ, 'bʌb|ɚ; ES -ə(r; |-bly -blɪ,
  -b|ɪ
bubo 'bjubo, 'brɪubo
bubonalgia ‚bjubən'ældʒɪə, ‚brɪu-
bubonic bju'bɑnɪk, brɪu-; ES+-'bɒnɪk
buccal 'bʌk| |-ly -ɪ
buccaneer ‚bʌkə'nɪr; ES -'nɪə(r, S+-'nɛə(r;
  |-ed -d

Bucephalus bju'sɛfələs, brɪu- |-'s -ɪz
Buchan 'bʌkən (Sc 'bʌxən)
Buchanan bju'kænən, brɪu-, bə-
Bucharest ‚bjukə'rɛst, ‚brɪu-, ‚bu- —acct +
  'Bucha‚rest
Buchmanism 'bʌkmən‚ɪzəm |-ite -‚aɪt
Buchtel 'bʊkt| (Ger 'bʊxtəl)
buck, B- bʌk |bucked bʌkt
buckaroo 'bʌkə‚ru, ‚bʌkə'ru
buckayro bʌk'ero
buckboard 'bʌk‚bord, -‚bɔrd; ES -‚boəd, E+
  -‚bɔəd
bucket 'bʌkɪt |-ed -ɪd |-ful -‚ful |-fuls -‚fulz
buckeye 'bʌk‚aɪ |-d -d
Buckhannon bʌk'hænən
Buckingham US 'bʌkɪŋ‚hæm, Engd 'bʌkɪŋəm
Buckinghamshire 'bʌkɪŋəm‚ʃɪr, -ʃɚ; ES
  -‚ʃɪə(r, -ʃə(r
buckle, B- 'bʌk| |-d -d |-ling 'bʌklɪŋ, -k|ɪŋ
buckler from buckle 'bʌklɚ, 'bʌk|ɚ; ES -ə(r
buckler 'shield' 'bʌklɚ; ES 'bʌklə(r
Bucknell Pa coll. 'bʌknɛl, bʌk'nɛl; Eng places
  'bʌknəl
bucko 'bʌko
buckra 'bʌkrə
buckram 'bʌkrəm |-ed -d
Bucks Pa & short for Buckinghamshire bʌks
bucksaw 'bʌk‚sɔ
buckshot 'bʌk‚ʃɑt; ES+-‚ʃɒt
buckskin 'bʌk‚skɪn |-ned -d
buckthorn 'bʌk‚θɔrn; ES -‚θɔən
bucktooth 'bʌk‚tuθ |-teeth -‚tiθ
buckwheat 'bʌk‚hwit
bucolic, B- bju'kɑlɪk, brɪu-; ES+-'kɒl-
Bucovina ‚bukə'vinə
Bucyrus bju'saɪrəs, brɪu- |-'s -ɪz
bud bʌd |budded 'bʌdɪd
Budapest ‚bjudə'pɛst, ‚brɪudə-, ‚budə-
Buddha 'budə |-ddhism -dɪzəm |-ddhist -dɪst
Buddhistic bud'ɪstɪk |-al -|
buddy 'bʌdɪ
budge bʌdʒ |budges 'bʌdʒɪz |budged bʌdʒd
budget 'bʌdʒɪt |-ed -ɪd |-ary 'bʌdʒɪ‚tɛrɪ
Budle 'bjud|, 'brɪud|
Buell 'bjuəl, 'brɪuəl
Buena Vista US 'bjunə'vɪstə, 'brɪu-; CA
  'bwena'vista (Sp 'bwena'βista)
Buenos Aires 'bonəs'ɛrɪz, -'ærɪz, -'erɪz,
  'bwenəs'aɪrɪz (Sp 'bwenɔs'aires)—In the

Key: See in full §§3–47. bee bi |pity 'pɪtɪ (§6) |rate ret |yet jɛt |sang sæŋ |angry 'æŋ·grɪ
|bath bæθ; E baθ (§10) |ah ɑ |far fɑr |watch wɑtʃ, wɒtʃ (§12) |jaw dʒɔ |gorge gɔrdʒ |go go

19th c. a common Anglicized form in both Engd & America was 'bonəs'ɛrz, -'ærz; E -'ɛəz, ES -'æəz—see §122.

buff bʌf |buffed bʌft
buffalo, B- 'bʌfḷ,o |-ed -d
buffer 'bʌfɚ; ES 'bʌfə(r; |-ed -d
buffet 'stroke,' 'strike' 'bʌfɪt |-ed -ɪd
buffet 'sideboard' bʌ'fe, bə-, bʊ-, Brit 'bʌfɪt
buffet 'restaurant' bʊ'fe, 'bʊfe (Fr by'fɛ)
bufflehead 'bʌfḷ,hɛd
buffo 'bufo (It 'buffo)
Buffon 'bʌfən (Fr by'fõ)
buffoon bʌ'fun |-ed -d |-ery -ərɪ, -rɪ
Bufo 'bjufo, 'bɪu-
Buford 'bjufɚd, 'bɪu-; ES -fəd
Bug riv. bug, bʌg
bug bʌg |bugged bʌgd
bugaboo 'bʌgə,bu
bugbane 'bʌg,ben
bugbear 'bʌg,bɛr, -,bær; E -,bɛə(r, ES -,bæə(r
buggy 'bʌgɪ |-gies -z
bugle 'bjugḷ, 'bɪu- |-d -d |-ling -glɪŋ, -gl̩ŋ
bugloss 'bjuglɑs, 'bɪu-, -glɒs, -glɔs |-es -ɪz
Buhl US bjul, bɪul, bul
Buhl Fr cabinetmaker bul
buhl bul |-work -,wɝk; ES -,wɝk, -,wɝ·k
buhrstone 'bɝ,ston; ES 'bɝ-, 'bɝ-
Buick 'bjuɪk, 'bɪuɪk
build bɪld |built bɪlt or arch. builded -ɪd
built-in 'bɪlt'ɪn ('built-,in 'cupboard)
Bukarest, Bukha- ,bjukə'rɛst, ,bɪu-, ,bu- — acct+'Buka,rest
Bukhara bu'karə
Bukovina ,bukə'vinə
bulb bʌlb |bulbed bʌlbd
bulbose 'bʌlbos |bulbous 'bʌlbəs
bulbul 'bulbul
Bulfinch 'bul,fɪntʃ |-'s -ɪz
Bulgar 'bʌlgɚ, 'bul-, -gɑr; ES -gə(r, -gɑ:(r
Bulgaria bʌl'gɛrɪə, bul-, -'ger- |-n -n
bulge bʌldʒ; S+buldʒ; |-s -ɪz |-d -d
bulk bʌlk, esp. S bulk |-ed -t |-y -ɪ
bulkhead 'bʌlk,hɛd, esp. S 'bulk-
bull, B- bul |bulled buld
bulla 'bulə, 'bʌlə |-lae -i
bullace 'bulɪs, -əs |-s -ɪz
Bullcalf 'bul,kæf; E -,kaf, -,kɑf, -,kæf
bulldog 'bul,dɔg, -,dɒg

bulldoze 'bul,doz |-s -ɪz |-d -d
Bullen 'bulɪn=Boleyn
bullet 'bulɪt |-ed -ɪd
bullethead 'bulɪt,hɛd
bulletheaded 'bulɪt'hɛdɪd ('bullet,headed 'boy)
bulletin 'bulətṇ, -tɪn
bulletproof v 'bulɪt,pruf |-ed -t
bulletproof adj 'bulɪt'pruf ('bullet,proof 'hat)
bullfight 'bul,faɪt
bullfinch, B- 'bul,fɪntʃ |-es -ɪz
bullfrog 'bul,frag, -,frɔg, -,frɒg; S -,frɔg, -,frag, -,frɒg
bullhead 'bul,hɛd
bullheaded 'bul'hɛdɪd ('bull,headed 'obstinacy)
bullion 'buljən
Bullitt 'bulɪt
Bulloch 'bulək
bullock, B- 'bulək
Bullokar 'bulə,kar; ES -,kɑ:(r
Bull Run 'bul'rʌn
bull's-eye 'bulz,aɪ
bully 'bulɪ |bullied 'bulɪd
bulrush 'bul,rʌʃ |-es -ɪz
bulwark 'bulwɚk; ES -wək; |-ed -t
Bulwer 'bulwɚ; ES 'bulwə(r
Bulwer-Lytton 'bulwɚ'lɪtṇ; ES 'bulwə-
bum bʌm |bummed bʌmd
bumblebee 'bʌmbḷ,bi
bumblepuppy 'bʌmbḷ,pʌpɪ
bumboat 'bʌm,bot
bump bʌmp |bumped bʌmpt |-er -ɚ; ES -ə(r
bumpkin 'bʌmpkɪn
bumptious 'bʌmpʃəs
bun bʌn
bunch bʌntʃ |bunches 'bʌntʃɪz |-ed -t
bunco 'bʌŋko |-ed -d
buncombe, B- 'bʌŋkəm
bund bʌnd |bunded 'bʌndɪd
Bund bund (Ger bunt)
bundle 'bʌndḷ |-d -d |-ling 'bʌndlɪŋ, -dl̩ŋ
bung bʌŋ |bunged bʌŋd
bungalow 'bʌŋgə,lo
Bungay 'bʌŋgɪ
bunghole 'bʌŋ,hol
bungle 'bʌŋgḷ |-d -d |-ling 'bʌŋglɪŋ, -gl̩ŋ
bunion 'bʌnjən, -jɪn
bunk bʌŋk |bunked bʌŋkt

bunko 'bʌŋko |-ed -d
bunkum 'bʌŋkəm
bunny 'bʌnɪ
Bunsen 'bʌnsṇ (Ger 'bunzən)
bunt bʌnt |bunted 'bʌntɪd |bunting 'bʌntɪŋ
buntline 'bʌntlɪn, -laɪn
Bunyan 'bʌnjən, -jɪn
Buonaparte 'bonə‚pɑrt; ES -‚pɑːt, E+-‚pɑːt;
   (Fr bu͡ɔna'part, bwɔ̃n-)
buoy bɔɪ, 'buˑɪ |-ed -d
buoyancy 'bɔɪənsɪ, 'bujən- |-ant -ənt
buprestid bju'prɛstɪd, bɪu-
bur bɝ; ES bɜ(r, bɝ; |-red -d
Burbage 'bɝbɪdʒ; ES 'bɜ-, 'bɝ-; |-'s -ɪz
Burbank, b- 'bɝbæŋk; ES 'bɜ-, 'bɝ-; |-ed -t
burberry 'bɝ‚bɛrɪ, -bərɪ; ES 'bɜ-, 'bɝ-
burble 'bɝbḷ; ES 'bɜbḷ, 'bɝbḷ; |-d -d |-ling
   -blɪŋ, -bḷɪŋ
burbot 'bɝbət; ES 'bɜbət, 'bɝbət
burden 'bɝdṇ; ES 'bɜdṇ, 'bɝdṇ; |-ed -d
   |-ing -dṇɪŋ, -dnɪŋ |-some -səm
Burdett(e) bə'dɛt; ES bə-
Burdett-Couts 'bɝdɛt'kuts, bə'dɛt-; ES 'bɜ-,
   'bɝ-, bə- |-'s -ɪz
burdock 'bɝ‚dɑk; ES 'bɜ-, 'bɝ-, -‚dɒk
bureau 'bjuro, -rə, 'bɪu-
bureaucracy bju'rakrəsɪ, bɪu-; ES+-'rɒk-
bureaucrat 'bjurə‚kræt, 'bɪu-
burette, -ret bju'rɛt, bɪu-
burg bɝg; ES bɜg, bɝg; |-age -ɪdʒ
burgeon 'bɝdʒən; ES 'bɜdʒ-, 'bɝdʒ-; |-ed -d
Bürger Ger 'byrgər
burgess, B- 'bɝdʒɪs; ES 'bɜdʒ-, 'bɝdʒ-;
   |-es -ɪz
Burgettstown 'bɝdʒɪts‚taun; ES 'bɜdʒ-,
   'bɝdʒ-
burgh bɝg; ES bɜg, bɝg; (Sc 'bʌro, -ə)
Burgh, de dɪ'bɝg; ES dɪ'bɜg, dɪ'bɝg
burgher, B- 'bɝgɚ; ES 'bɜgə(r, 'bɝgə(r
Burghley, -leigh 'bɝlɪ; ES 'bɜlɪ, 'bɝlɪ
burglar 'bɝglɚ; ES 'bɜglə(r, 'bɝglə(r; |-y -ɪ
burglarize 'bɝglə‚raɪz; ES 'bɜg-, 'bɝg-; |-s
   -ɪz |-d -d
burgle 'bɝgḷ; ES 'bɜgḷ, 'bɝgḷ; |-d -d |-ling
   -glɪŋ, -gḷɪŋ
burgomaster 'bɝgə‚mæstɚ; ES 'bɝgə‚mæstə(r,
   'bɝgə-, E+-‚mas-, -‚mɑs-
burgonet 'bɝgə‚nɛt; ES 'bɜg-, 'bɝg-
burgoo, -gout 'bɝgu, bɝ'gu; ES -ɜ-, -ɝ-

Burgoyne bɚ'gɔɪn; ES bə'gɔɪn
burgrave 'bɝgrev; ES 'bɜ-, 'bɝ-
Burgundian bɚ'gʌndɪən; ES bə'gʌn-
Burgundy 'bɝgəndɪ; ES 'bɜgən-, 'bɝgən-
burial 'bɛrɪəl
burin 'bjurɪn, 'bɪu-
burke, B- bɝk; ES bɜk, bɝk; |-d -t
burl bɝl; ES bɜl, bɝl; |-ed -d
burlap 'bɝlæp; ES 'bɜ-, 'bɝ-; |-ped -t
Burleson 'bɝlɪsṇ; ES 'bɜl-, 'bɝl-
burlesque bɚ'lɛsk, bɝ'lɛsk; ES bə'lɛsk, bɜ-
   bɝ-; |-d -t ('bur‚lesque 'play)
Burley, b- 'bɝlɪ; ES 'bɜlɪ, 'bɝlɪ
Burlingame 'bɝlɪŋ‚gem, -ɪŋəm; ES 'bɜl-,
   'bɝl-; The 1st is a sp. pron. Same word as
   Burlingham.
Burlingham 'bɝlɪŋ‚hæm, -ɪŋəm; ES 'bɜ-,
   'bɝ-
Burlington 'bɝlɪŋtən; ES 'bɜlɪŋ-, 'bɝlɪŋ-
burly 'bɝlɪ; ES 'bɜlɪ, 'bɝlɪ
Burma 'bɝmə; ES 'bɜmə, 'bɝmə; |-n -n
Burmese bɝ'miz; ES bɜ'miz, bɝ'miz
burn bɝn; ES bɜn, bɝn; |-ed -d or -t -t
Burne-Jones 'bɝn'dʒonz; ES 'bɜn-, 'bɝn-;
   |-'s -ɪz
Burnell 'bɝnḷ; ES 'bɜnḷ, 'bɝnḷ
burner 'bɝnɚ; ES 'bɜnə(r, 'bɝnə(r
burnet B- 'bɝnɪt; ES 'bɜnɪt, 'bɝnɪt
Burnett bɚ'nɛt, 'bɝnɪt; ES bɜ-, bɝ-, 'bɜ-,
   'bɝ-
Burney 'bɝnɪ; ES 'bɜnɪ, 'bɝnɪ
Burnham 'bɝnəm; ES 'bɜnəm, 'bɝnəm
burnish 'bɝnɪʃ; ES 'bɜ-, 'bɝ-; |-es -ɪz |-ed -t
burnoose, -nous bɚ'nus, 'bɝnus; ES bə-,
   'bɜ-, 'bɝ-; |-(e)s -ɪz |-(e)d -t
Burns bɝnz; ES bɜnz, bɝnz; |-'s- ɪz |-ian -ɪən
burnside, B- 'bɝn‚saɪd; ES 'bɜn-, 'bɝn-;
   |-s -z
burnt bɝnt; ES bɜnt, bɝnt
Burntisland 'bɝnt'aɪlənd; ES 'bɜnt-, 'bɝnt-;
   Sc+'brʌnt-
burr, B- bɝ; ES bɜ(r, bɝ; |-ed -d
Burrillville 'bɝəl‚vɪl, 'bɝl-; ES 'bɜr-, 'bʌr-,
   'bɝ-, 'bɜl-, 'bɝl-
Burritt 'bɝɪt; ES 'bɜrɪt, 'bʌrɪt, 'bɝɪt
burro 'bɝo, 'buro, -ə; ES 'bɜr-, 'bʌr-, 'bɝ-,
   'bur-
Burroughs 'bɝoz, -əz; ES 'bɜr-, 'bʌr-, 'bɝ-,
   |-'s -ɪz

burrow 'bɝ·o, -ə; ES 'bɜr-, 'bʌr-, 'bɝ-; |-ed -d
burrowing 'bɝəwɪŋ; ES 'bɜrəwɪŋ, 'bʌr-, 'bɝ-
Burrows 'bɝ·oz, -əz; ES 'bɜr-, 'bʌr-, 'bɝ-;
|-'s -ɪz
burrstone 'bɝ·ˌston; ES 'bɜ-, 'bɝ-
bursa 'bɝsə; ES 'bɜsə, 'bɝsə; |-s -z |-sae -si
bursar 'bɝsɚ; ES 'bɜsə(r, 'bɝsə(r; |-y -ɪ
burse bɝs; ES bɜs, bɝs; |-s -ɪz
burst bɝst; ES bɜst, bɝst
burstone 'bɝ·ˌston; ES 'bɜ-, 'bɝ-
burthen 'bɝˈðən; ES 'bɜˈðən, 'bɝˈðən; |-ed -d
Burton 'bɝtn̩; ES 'bɜtn̩, 'bɝtn̩
bury 'bɛrɪ |buried 'bɛrɪd
Bury places 'bɛrɪ, surname 'bɛrɪ, 'bjʊrɪ, 'bɪu-
burying ground 'bɛrɪɪŋˌgraʊnd
bus bʌs |busses, buses 'bʌsɪz
busby, B- 'bʌzbɪ
Busch bʊʃ |-'s -ɪz
bush bʊʃ |bushes 'bʊʃɪz |bushed bʊʃt
bushel 'bʊʃəl |-ed -d |-ing 'bʊʃəlɪŋ, 'bʊʃlɪŋ
bushing 'bʊʃɪŋ
bushman, B-, -men 'bʊʃmən
Bushnell 'bʊʃnəl
bushranger 'bʊʃˌrendʒɚ; ES -ˌrendʒə(r
bushwhack 'bʊʃˌhwæk |-ed -t |-er -ɚ; ES -ə(r
bushy, B- 'bʊʃɪ
busily 'bɪzḷɪ, -zɪlɪ
business 'occupation' 'bɪznɪs |-es -ɪz
business, busy- 'activity' 'bɪzɪnɪs
businesslike 'bɪznɪsˌlaɪk
businessman 'bɪznɪsˌmæn |-men -ˌmɛn
Busiris bju'saɪrɪs, bɪu- |-'s -ɪz
busk bʌsk |busked bʌskt
buskin 'bʌskɪn |-ed -d
busman, -men 'bʌsmən
Busra, -rah 'bʌsrə = Basra
buss bʌs |busses 'bʌsɪz |bussed bʌst
bust n, v bʌst |busted 'bʌstɪd
bustard 'bʌstɚd; ES 'bʌstəd
busticate 'bʌstəˌket |-d -ɪd
bustle 'bʌsḷ |-d -d |-ling 'bʌslɪŋ, 'bʌsḷɪŋ
busy 'bɪzɪ |busied 'bɪzɪd
busybody 'bɪzɪˌbɑdɪ; ES+ -ˌbɒdɪ
busyness 'bɪzɪnɪs
but unstressed bət, stressed or hesit. 'bʌt, ˌbʌt
but-and-ben 'bʌtn̩'bɛn
butane 'bjuten, 'bɪu-, bju'ten, bɪu-
butcher 'bʊtʃɚ; ES 'bʊtʃə(r; |-ed -d |-ing
'bʊtʃərɪŋ, 'bʊtʃrɪŋ |-y -ɪ, -tʃrɪ

butcherbird 'bʊtʃɚˌbɝd; ES 'bʊtʃəˌbɜd,
'bʊtʃəˌbɝd
butcher-knife 'bʊtʃɚˌnaɪf; ES 'bʊtʃə-; |-ives
-aɪvz
Bute bjut, bɪut
butler, B- 'bʌtlɚ; ES 'bʌtlə(r; |-y -ɪ
butt, B- bʌt |butted 'bʌtɪd
butte, B- bjut, bɪut
butter 'bʌtɚ; ES 'bʌtə(r; |-ed -d
butter-and-eggs 'bʌtɚn'ɛgz, 'bʌtərənd'ɛgz;
ES 'bʌtən-, 'bʌtərənd-
buttercup 'bʌtɚˌkʌp; ES 'bʌtə-
butterfat 'bʌtɚˌfæt; ES 'bʌtə-
butterfingers 'bʌtɚˌfɪŋgɚz; ES 'bʌtəˌfɪŋgəz
butterfly 'bʌtɚˌflaɪ; ES 'bʌtə-; |-flies -ˌflaɪz
|-flied -ˌflaɪd
Butterick 'bʌtərɪk, 'bʌtrɪk
butterine 'bʌtəˌrin, -rɪn
butterman 'bʌtɚˌmæn, -mən; ES 'bʌtə-;
|-men -ˌmɛn, -mən
Buttermere 'bʌtɚˌmɪr; ES 'bʌtəˌmɪə(r, S+
-ˌmɛə(r
buttermilk 'bʌtɚˌmɪlk; ES 'bʌtə-
butternut 'bʌtɚnət, -ˌnʌt; ES 'bʌtə-
butterscotch 'bʌtɚ'skɑtʃ; ES 'bʌtə'skɑtʃ,
-'skɒtʃ; |-es -ɪz ('butterˌscotch 'flavor)
Butterwick 'bʌtərɪk, 'bʌtɚwɪk; ES 'bʌtərɪk,
'bʌtəwɪk
Butterworth 'bʌtɚwɚθ, -ˌwɝθ; ES 'bʌtəwəθ,
-ˌwɝθ, 'bʌtəˌwɝθ
buttery 'like butter' 'bʌtɚɪ
buttery 'pantry' 'bʌtrɪ, 'bʌtərɪ
buttle 'bʌtḷ |-d -d |-ling 'bʌtḷɪŋ, 'bʌtlɪŋ
buttock 'bʌtək |buttocked 'bʌtəkt
button, B- 'bʌtn̩ |-ed -d |-ing 'bʌtn̩ɪŋ, -tnɪŋ
buttonhole 'bʌtn̩ˌhol |-d -d
buttonhook 'bʌtn̩ˌhʊk
buttonwood 'bʌtn̩ˌwʊd
buttress 'bʌtrɪs |-es -ɪz |-ed -t
Butts bʌts |-'s -ɪz
butts and bounds 'bʌtsn̩'baʊndz, -nz
buttstock 'bʌtˌstɑk, -ˌstɒk
butyl 'bjutɪl, 'bɪu-
butylene 'bjutḷˌin, 'bɪu-
butyric bju'tɪrɪk, bɪu- |-ally -ḷɪ, -ɪklɪ
butyrin 'bjutərɪn, 'bɪu-
buxom 'bʌksəm
Buxton 'bʌkstən
buy baɪ |bought bɔt

buzz bʌz |buzzes 'bʌzɪz |buzzed bʌzd
buzzard 'bʌzəd; ES 'bʌzəd
Buzzard's Bay 'bʌzədz'be; ES 'bʌzədz-
by stressed 'baɪ, ˌbaɪ; unstr. baɪ, bə
by-and-by 'baɪən'baɪ, 'baɪm'baɪ
bye baɪ
bye-bye n 'baɪˌbaɪ
bye-bye intj 'baɪ'baɪ, 'baɪˌbaɪ
byelaw 'baɪˌlɔ
by-form 'baɪˌfɔrm; ES -ˌfɔəm
bygone 'baɪˌgɔn, -ˌgɒn, much less freq. -ˌgɑn
bylaw 'baɪˌlɔ
byname 'baɪˌnem |-d -d
Bynner 'bɪnɚ; ES 'bɪnə(r
by-pass 'baɪˌpæs; E+-ˌpas, -ˌpɑs; |-es -ɪz
|-ed -t
bypast 'baɪˌpæst; E+-ˌpast, -ˌpɑst
bypath 'baɪˌpæθ; E+-ˌpaθ, -ˌpɑθ; |-ths -ðz
byplay 'baɪˌple
by-product 'baɪˌprɑdəkt, -dʌkt; ES+-ˌprɒd-
Byrd bɝd; ES bɜd, bɝd

byre baɪr; ES baɪə(r
Byrne bɝn; ES bɜn, bɝn
byrnie 'bɝnɪ; ES 'bɜnɪ, 'bɝnɪ
byroad 'baɪˌrod
Byrom 'baɪrəm
Byron 'baɪrən |-esque ˌbaɪrən'ɛsk
Byronian baɪ'ronɪən
Byronic baɪ'rɑnɪk; ES+-'rɒn-; |-ally -ḷɪ,
-ɪklɪ
Byronism 'baɪrənˌɪzəm
byssal 'bɪsḷ
Bysshe bɪʃ |-'s -ɪz
byssus 'bɪsəs |byssuses 'bɪsəsɪz |-ssi -saɪ
bystander 'baɪˌstændɚ; ES -ˌstændə(r
bystreet 'baɪˌstrit
byway 'baɪˌwe
byword 'baɪˌwɝd; ES -ˌwɜd, -ˌwɝd
Byzantian bɪ'zænʃən, -'zæntɪən
Byzantine bɪ'zæntɪn, 'bɪzṇˌtaɪn, -ˌtin
Byzantinism bɪ'zæntɪnˌɪzəm
Byzantium bɪ'zænʃɪəm, -'zæntɪəm

C

C, c letter si |pl C's, Cs, poss C's siz
cab kæb
cabal kə'bæl |caballed kə'bæld
cabala, cabbala 'kæbələ
cabalistic ˌkæbə'lɪstɪk
cabaret 'kæbəˌrɛt, 'café' ˌkæbə're (Fr kaba're)
cabbage 'kæbɪdʒ |-s -ɪz |-d -d (Shak. cabidge)
Cabell 'kæbḷ
cabin 'kæbɪn |cabined 'kæbɪnd
cabinet 'kæbənɪt |-maker -ˌmekɚ; ES -ə(r
cabinetwork 'kæbənɪtˌwɝk; ES -ˌwɜk, -ˌwɝk
cable 'kebḷ |-d -d |-ling 'kebḷɪŋ, 'keblɪŋ
cablegram 'kebḷˌgræm
cabman 'kæbmən |cabmen 'kæbmən, -ˌmɛn
cabob kə'bɑb; ES+kə'bɒb
caboose kə'bus |cabooses kə'busɪz
Cabot 'kæbət
cabriolet ˌkæbrɪə'le, ˌkæbrɪə'lɛt (Fr kabriö'le)
cacao kə'keo, kə'kɑo
cache kæʃ |caches 'kæʃɪz |cached kæʃt
cachet kæ'ʃe, 'kæʃe (Fr ka'ʃɛ)
cachexia kə'kɛksɪə |cachexy kə'kɛksɪ
cachinate 'kækəˌnet |-nated -ˌnetɪd

cachination ˌkækə'neʃən
cachou kə'ʃu, kæ'ʃu (Fr ka'ʃu)
cacique kə'sik
cackle 'kækḷ |-d -d |-ling 'kæklɪŋ, -kḷɪŋ
cacodemon ˌkækə'dimən
cacoethes ˌkæko'iθiz, -θis
cacogenics ˌkækə'dʒɛnɪks
cacophonic ˌkækə'fɑnɪk; ES+-'fɒnɪk
cacophonous kæ'kɑfənəs, kə-; ES+-'kɒf-
cacophony kæ'kɑfənɪ, kə-; ES+-'kɒf-
cactus 'kæktəs |-es -ɪz |cacti 'kæktaɪ
cad kæd
cadaver kə'dævɚ, kə'devɚ; ES -və(r
cadaverous kə'dævərəs, kə'dævrəs
caddie 'kædɪ
caddis, -ice 'kædɪs |-(e)s -ɪz |-(e)d -t
caddy 'kædɪ
Cade ked
cadence 'kedṇs |-s -ɪz |-cy -ɪ |-dent -dṇt
cadenza kə'dɛnzə (It kɑ'dɛntsɑ)
cadet kə'dɛt
cadge kædʒ |cadges 'kædʒɪz |cadged kædʒd
Cadillac 'kædḷˌæk

Key: See in full §§3–47. bee bi |pity 'pɪtɪ (§6) |rate ret |yet jɛt |sang sæŋ |angry 'æŋ·grɪ
|bath bæθ; E baθ (§10) |ah ɑ |far fɑr |watch wɑtʃ, wɒtʃ (§12) |jaw dʒɔ |gorge gɔrdʒ |go go

Cadiz *Spain* ˈkedɪz, *Pl* ˈkɑdis, *O* ˈkædɪz,
ˈkedɪz |-ʾs -ɪzɪz, -isɪz (*Sp* ˈkaðiθ)
Cadman ˈkædmən
cadmium ˈkædmɪəm
Cadmus ˈkædməs |Cadmus's ˈkædməsɪz
Cadnam ˈkædnəm—*cf* Puttenham
Cadogan kəˈdʌɡən
cadre ˈkɑdɚ; ES ˈkɑdə(r; *mil.*+ ˈkædrɪ
caduceus kəˈdjusɪəs, -ˈdɪu-, -ˈdu- |-cei -sɪˌaɪ
Cadwal ˈkædwɑl, -wɒl, -wɔl
Cadwallader kædˈwɑlədɚ, -ˈwɒl-, -ˈwɔl-; ES
-də(r
caecum ˈsikəm |caeca ˈsikə
Caedmon ˈkædmən |-ian kædˈmonɪən |-ic
kædˈmɑnɪk; ES+-ˈmɒnɪk
Caen ˈkeən, ˈkɑn (*Fr* kã)
Caesar ˈsizɚ; ES ˈsizə(r
Caesarea ˌsɛsəˈriə, ˌsɛz- |-rean -ˈriən
Caesarean, -ian *surg.* sɪˈzɛrɪən, -ˈzær-, -ˈzer-
caesium ˈsizɪəm
caesura sɪˈʒʊrə, sɪˈzjʊrə, -ˈzɪʊrə |-l -l
café kəˈfe, kæˈfe
café-au-lait kəˈfe·oˈle, ˌkæfɪoˈle (*Fr* kafeoˈlɛ)
cafeteria ˌkæfəˈtɪrɪə, -təˈriə
caffeine, -in ˈkæfiɪn, -ˌin, ˈkæfin
cage kedʒ |cages ˈkedʒɪz |caged kedʒd
cahoot kəˈhut |-s -s
Caiaphas ˈkeəfəs, ˈkaɪ- |Caiaphas's -fəsɪz
Cain ken
cairn kɛrn, kærn; E keən, ES kæən
Cairo *Egypt* ˈkaɪro, *US* ˈkero, ˈkɛro
caisson ˈkesn̩
Caithness ˈkeθnɛs, keθˈnɛs |-ʾs -ɪz
caitiff ˈketɪf |caitiffs ˈketɪfs
Caius ˈkeəs, *Cambridge college* kiz
cajole kəˈdʒol |cajoled kəˈdʒold |-ry -ərɪ
Cajun, -jan, -jen ˈkedʒən—*see* Acadian
cake kek |caked kekt |caky ˈkekɪ
calabash ˈkæləˌbæʃ |calabashes ˈkæləˌbæʃɪz
calaboose ˈkæləˌbus, ˌkæləˈbus |-s -ɪz
Calabria kəˈlebrɪə |-brian -brɪən
Calais *US* ˈkælɪs; *France* ˈkælɪs, ˈkæle (*mod.
Fr* kɑˈlɛ)—*in Shaks.* ˈCallis, ˈCallice. "*A
town which once sent members to the English
Parliament has a right to an English name.*"
—*John Sargeaunt. See* §122.
calamitous kəˈlæmətəs |calamity kəˈlæmətɪ
calash kəˈlæʃ |calashes kəˈlæʃɪz |-ed -t
Calaveras ˌkæləˈvɛrəs, -ˈverəs |-ʾs -ɪz

calcareous kælˈkɛrɪəs, -ˈkær-, -ˈker-
Calchas ˈkælkəs |Calchas's ˈkælkəsɪz
calcify ˈkælsəˌfaɪ |calcified ˈkælsəˌfaɪd
calcimine ˈkælsəˌmaɪn, -mɪn |-d -d
calcine ˈkælsaɪn, -sɪn |-d -d
calcite ˈkælsaɪt |calcitic kælˈsɪtɪk
calcium ˈkælsɪəm
calculable ˈkælkjələbl̩ |-bly -blɪ
calculate ˈkælkjəˌlet |-lated -ˌletɪd
calculation ˌkælkjəˈleʃən
calculator ˈkælkjəˌletɚ; ES -ˌletə(r
calculus ˈkælkjələs |-es -ɪz |-li -ˌlaɪ
Calcutta kælˈkʌtə
Calderon ˈkɔldərən (*Sp* ˌkaldeˈrɔn)
caldron ˈkɔldrən |-ed -d
Caldwell ˈkɔldwɛl, ˈkɔldwəl, *Yks loc.* ˈkɔdwɛl
Caleb ˈkeləb, ˈkelɪb
Caledonia ˌkæləˈdonɪə, -ˈdonjə |-n -n
calendar ˈkæləndɚ, ˈkælɪn-; ES -də(r; |-ed -d
calender ˈkæləndɚ, ˈkælɪn-; ES -də(r; |-ed -d
calends ˈkæləndz, ˈkælɪndz, -nz
calendula kəˈlɛndʒələ, -dʒʊlə
calenture ˈkælənˌtʃʊɚ, -tʃɚ; ES -ˌtʃʊə(r,
-tʃə(r
Calexico kəˈlɛksɪˌko
calf kæf; E kɑf, kɒf, kæf; |-ʾs -s, -vz |-lves -vz
calf's-foot ˈkævzˌfut; E ˈkɑvz-, ˈkɒvz-, ˈkævz-;
—ˈkævz- *is not the plural, but the older
possessive singular.*
calfskin ˈkæfˌskɪn; E ˈkɑf-, ˈkɒf-, ˈkæf-
Calgary ˈkælgərɪ
Calhoun kəˈhun, kælˈhun
Caliban ˈkæləˌbæn
caliber, -bre ˈkæləbɚ; ES ˈkæləbə(r; |-(e)d -d
calibrate ˈkæləˌbret |-brated -ˌbretɪd
calibration ˌkæləˈbreʃən
calico ˈkæləˌko
Calicut ˈkæləˌkʌt, ˈkæləkət
California ˌkæləˈfɔrnjə, *esp. NEngd* -nɪə; ES
-ˈfɔən-
Caligula kəˈlɪgjʊlə
caliper ˈkæləpɚ; ES ˈkæləpə(r; |-ed -d
caliph ˈkelɪf, ˈkælɪf |-ate ˈkæləˌfet, -fɪt
calisthenics ˌkæləsˈθɛnɪks
calix ˈkelɪks |calices ˈkælɪˌsiz
calk kɔk |calked kɔkt
call kɔl |called kɔld |-er -ɚ; ES -ə(r
calla ˈkælə
Callahan ˈkæləˌhæn

Callao *Peru* ka'jao, *US* 'kælɪ‚o (*Am Sp*
  ka'jao)
Callaway 'kælə‚we
Calles 'kajɛs (*Am Sp* 'kajes)
calligrapher kə'lɪgrəfɚ; ES -fə(r; |-phy -fɪ
calligraphic ‚kælə'græfɪk
calling 'kɔlɪŋ
Calliope kə'laɪə‚pi, -pɪ |Kallyope 'kælɪ‚op
calliper 'kæləpɚ; ES 'kæləpə(r; |-ed -d
callisthenics ‚kæləs'θɛnɪks
Callisto kə'lɪsto
callosity kə'lɑsətɪ, kæ-; ES+-'lɒs-
callous 'kæləs |-es -ɪz |-ed -t
callow 'kælo, 'kælə |-er 'kæləwɚ; ES -wə(r;
  |-est 'kæləwɪst
callus 'kæləs |-es -ɪz |-li -laɪ |-ed -t
calm kɑm; E kɑm, kam; |-ed -d
calomel 'kæləm‚l, 'kælə‚mɛl
caloric kə'lɔrɪk, kə'lɑrɪk, -'lɒr-
calorie, -y 'kælərɪ |-rific ‚kælə'rɪfɪk
calorimeter ‚kælə'rɪmətɚ; ES -tə(r
Calphurnia kæl'fɝnɪə, -njə; ES -'fɜn-, -'fɝn-
Calpurnia kæl'pɜnɪə, -njə; ES -'pɜn-, -'pɝn-
calumet, C- 'kæljʊ‚mɛt, -mɪt, -mət, ‚kæljʊ-
  'mɛt
calumniate kə'lʌmnɪ‚et |-d -ɪd
calumniation kə‚lʌmnɪ'eʃən
calumniatory kə'lʌmnɪə‚torɪ, -‚tɔrɪ; S -‚torɪ
calumny 'kæləmnɪ
Calvary 'kælvərɪ
calve kæv; E kav, kɑv, kæv; |-d -d
calves-foot 'kævz‚fʊt; E 'kavz-, 'kɑvz-,
  'kævz-
Calvin 'kælvɪn |-ism -‚ɪzəm |-ist -ɪst
Calvinistic ‚kælvə'nɪstɪk |-al -‚l |-ally -‚ɪ, -ɪklɪ
calx kælks |calxes 'kælksɪz |calces 'kælsiz
Calydon 'kælə‚dɑn; ES+-‚dɒn
Calydonian ‚kælə'donɪən, -'donjən
Calypso kə'lɪpso
calyx 'kelɪks, 'kæl- |-es -ɪz |calyces 'kælə‚siz
cam kæm |cammed kæmd
camaraderie ‚kɑmə'rɑdərɪ, -‚ri (*Fr* kamara-
  'dri)
camarilla ‚kæmə'rɪlə (*Sp* kama'riʎa)
camber 'kæmbɚ; ES 'kæmbə(r; |-ed -d
cambium 'kæmbɪəm, 'kæmbjəm
Cambodia kæm'bodɪə, kæm'bodjə
Cambria 'kæmbrɪə |Cambrian 'kæmbrɪən
cambric 'kembrɪk

Cambridge 'kembrɪdʒ |-'s -ɪz |-shire -‚ʃɪr, -ʃɚ;
  ES -‚ʃɪə(r, -ʃə(r
Cambs *short for* Cambridgeshire kæmz,
  kæmbz
Cambyses kæm'baɪsiz |-ses' -siz
Camden 'kæmdən
came *past of* come kem
camel 'kæm‚l
camellia kə'mɛlɪə, -'milɪə, -ljə
camelopard kə'mɛlə‚pɑrd; ES -‚pɑ:d, E+
  -‚pɑ:d
Camelot 'kæmə‚lat; ES+-‚lɒt
Camembert 'kæməm‚bɛr, -‚bær; E -‚bɛə(r,
  ES -‚bæə(r; (*Fr* kamã'bɛ:r)
cameo 'kæmɪ‚o, 'kæmjo |-ed -d
camera 'kæmərə |-s -z |-rae -‚ri
Cameron 'kæmərən, 'kæmrən
Cameroon ‚kæmə'run |-roons -'runz
Camilla kə'mɪlə
Camille kə'mil (*Fr* ka'mi:j)
Camillo kə'mɪlo
camisole 'kæmə‚sol
Camoëns 'kæmo‚ɛnz |Camoëns's 'kæmo‚ɛnzɪz
camomile 'kæmə‚maɪl
camouflage 'kæmə‚flaʒ, 'kæmʊ- |-s -ɪz |-d -d
  (*Fr* kamu'fla:ʒ)
camp kæmp |camped kæmpt
Campagna kam'panjə, kæm- (*It* kam'paɲɲa)
campaign kæm'pen |campaigned kæm'pend
Campania kæm'penɪə
campanile ‚kæmpə'nilɪ |-s -z |-li -li
Campaspe kæm'pæspɪ
Campbell 'kæm‚l, 'kæmb‚l |-ite -‚aɪt
Campeius kæm'pɪəs |-'s -ɪz
campfire 'kæmp‚faɪr; ES -‚faɪə(r
camphene 'kæmfin, kæm'fin
camphor 'kæmfɚ, 'kæmpfɚ; ES -fə(r
campstool 'kæmp‚stul
Campton 'kæmptən
campus 'kæmpəs |campuses 'kæmpəsɪz
can *n, v* kæn |canned kænd
can *aux. v stressed* 'kæn, ‚kæn; *unstr.* kən, kn̩,
  kŋ̩ (‚aɪkŋ̩'go)
Cana 'kenə
Canaan 'kenən |Canaanite 'kenən‚aɪt
Canada 'kænədə |-dian kə'nedɪən
canaille kə'nel (*Fr* ka'nɑ:j)
Canajoharie ‚kænədʒo'hærɪ
canal kə'næl |-nalled, -naled -'næld

---

canalization kə‚næləˈzeʃən, ‚kænˌə-, -aɪˈz-
canalize kəˈnælaɪz, ˈkænˌaɪz |-s -ɪz |-d -d
Canal Zone kəˈnælˌzon
Canandaigua ‚kænənˈdegwə
canape ˈkænəpɪ (Fr kanaˈpe)
canard kəˈnard; ES kəˈnɑːd; (Fr kaˈnaːr)
canary, C- kəˈnɛrɪ, kəˈnerɪ
Canberra ˈkænbərə
cancel ˈkænsl̩ |-ed -d |-ing -sl̩ɪŋ, -slɪŋ
cancellation ‚kænsl̩ˈeʃən
cancellous ˈkænsələs
cancer, C- ˈkænsɚ; ES ˈkænsə(r; |Cancri ˈkæŋkraɪ
cancerous ˈkænsərəs, ˈkænsrəs
candelabrum ‚kændl̩ˈebrəm |-s -z |-bra -brə
candent ˈkændənt
candescent kænˈdɛsn̩t |-scence -sn̩s
candid ˈkændɪd, ˈkændəd
Candida ˈkændɪdə
candidate ˈkændəˌdet, -dɪt |-dacy -dəsɪ
Candide kɑnˈdid, kæn- (Fr kɑ̃ˈdid)
Candish ˈkændɪʃ |-ˈs -ɪz=Cavendish
candle kændl̩ |-d -d |-ling ˈkændlɪŋ, -dl̩ɪŋ
candlelight ˈkændl̩ˌlaɪt, ˈkændl̩ˌaɪt
Candlemas ˈkændl̩məs |-es -ɪz
candlestick ˈkændl̩ˌstɪk
candor ˈkændɚ; ES ˈkændə(r
candy ˈkændɪ |candied ˈkændɪd
candytuft ˈkændɪˌtʌft
cane ken |caned kend
canescent kəˈnɛsn̩t |canescence kəˈnɛsn̩s
Canidius kəˈnɪdɪəs |-ˈs -ɪz
canine ˈkenaɪn, kəˈnaɪn
canister ˈkænɪstɚ; ES ˈkænɪstə(r
canker ˈkæŋkɚ; ES ˈkæŋkə(r; |-ed -d |-ing ˈkæŋkərɪŋ, -krɪŋ
cankerous ˈkæŋkərəs, ˈkæŋkrəs
cankerworm ˈkæŋkɚˌwɝm; ES ˈkæŋkəˌwɝm, -kəˌwɜm
canna ˈkænə
Cannae ˈkæni (mod. It Canne ˈkanne)
cannel ˈkænl̩
canner ˈkænɚ; ES ˈkænə(r; |-y ˈkænərɪ
Cannes kæn, kænz (Fr kan) |-ˈs kænz, ˈkænzɪz
cannibal ˈkænəbl̩ |cannibalism ˈkænəbl̩ˌɪzəm
cannikin ˈkænəkɪn
canning, C- ˈkænɪŋ
cannon, C- ˈkænən |-ed -d |-ry -rɪ
cannonade ‚kænənˈed |-d -ɪd

cannoneer ‚kænənˈɪr; ES ‚kænənˈɪə(r, S+ -ˈɛə(r
cannot formal colloq. ˈkænət, kæˈnat, kəˈnat ˈkænət. The usual familiar form is can't.
Emph. kəˈnat, kæˈnat, ˈkænˈnat; ES+-ɒt
canny ˈkænɪ
canoe kəˈnu
canon ˈkænən |-ed -d
cañon ˈkænjən |-ed -d
Canon City ˈkænjənˈsɪtɪ
canoness ˈkænənɪs |-es -ɪz
canonic kəˈnanɪk; ES+-ˈnɒn-; |-al -l̩ |-ally -l̩ɪ, -ɪklɪ
canonicity ‚kænənˈɪsətɪ
canonization ‚kænənəˈzeʃən, -aɪˈz-
canonize ˈkænənˌaɪz |-s -ɪz |-d -d
Canonsburg ˈkænənzˌbɝg; ES -ˌbɜg, -ˌbɝg
Canopic kəˈnopɪk
Canopus kəˈnopəs |-ˈs -ɪz |Canopi kəˈnopaɪ
canopy ˈkænəpɪ |canopied ˈkænəpɪd
Canossa kəˈnasə, kəˈnɒsə, kəˈnɔsə (It kaˈnɔssa)
canst stressed ˈkænst, ‚kænst; unstr. kənst
cant kænt |canted ˈkæntɪd
can't kænt; E kant, kant, kænt
Cantabrigian ‚kæntəˈbrɪdʒɪən
cantaloupe, -lope ˈkæntl̩ˌop, mainly Brit -ˌup
cantankerous kænˈtæŋkərəs, -krəs
cantata kænˈtatə, kən-, -ˈtætə
canteen kænˈtin
canter ˈkæntɚ; ES ˈkæntə(r; |-ed -d |-ing ˈkæntərɪŋ, ˈkæntrɪŋ
Canterbury ˈkæntɚˌberɪ, ˈkæntə-; ES ˈkæntə-;—In the second pron. ɚ is lost by dissimilation (§121).
canticle ˈkæntɪkl̩
cantilever ˈkæntl̩ˌɛvɚ, ˈkæntl̩ˌivɚ; ES -və(r
cantle ˈkæntl̩ |-d -d
canto ˈkænto
canton n ˈkæntən, -tan, kænˈtan; ES+-ɒn
canton v 'divide' ˈkæntən, kænˈtan; ES+-ɒn; 'quarter troops' kænˈtan, -ˈton, -ˈtun; ES+ -ˈtɒn; |-ed -d
Canton China kænˈtan; ES+-ˈtɒn; US ˈkæntən, ˈkæntn̩
Cantonese ‚kæntənˈiz
cantonment kænˈtanmənt, -ˈtun-, -ˈton-; ES+-ˈtɒn-
cantor ˈkæntɔr, -tɚ; ES ˈkæntɔə(r, -tə(r

|full fʊl |tooth tuθ |further ˈfɝðɚ; ES ˈfɝðə |custom ˈkʌstəm |while hwaɪl |how haʊ |toy tɔɪ |using ˈjuzɪŋ |fuse fjuz, fɪuz |dish dɪʃ |vision ˈvɪʒən |Eden ˈidn̩ |cradle ˈkredl̩ |keep 'em ˈkipm̩

Words below in which a *before* r (farm) *is sounded* ɑ *are often pronounced in* E *with* a (fa:m)
Words below that have æ *before* r (carry 'kærɪ) *are often pronounced in* N *with* ɛ ('kɛrɪ, §94)

Canuck kə'nʌk
Canute kə'nut, kə'nɪut, kə'njut
canvas 'kænvəs |canvases 'kænvəsɪz |-ed -t
canvasback 'kænvəs,bæk
canvass 'kænvəs |-es -ɪz |-ed -t
canyon, C- 'kænjən |canyoned 'kænjənd
caoutchouc 'kutʃuk, kau'tʃuk
cap kæp |capped kæpt
capability ,kepə'bɪlətɪ
capable 'kepəbļ |capably 'kepəblɪ
capacious kə'peʃəs
capacitance kə'pæsətəns
capacitate kə'pæsə,tet |-tated -,tetɪd |-ity -ətɪ
cap and gown 'kæpən'gaun, 'kæpm̩'gaun
cap-a-pie ,kæpə'pi
caparison kə'pærəsn̩ |-ed -d
cape kep
cape *writ* 'kepi
Cape Breton 'kep'brɪtn̩, -'brɛtn̩, *loc.* kə'brɪtn̩
Capel, -ll 'kæpļ, 'kepļ
Capella kə'pɛlə
Capen 'kepən
Cape of Good Hope 'kepəv'gud,hop, -'hop
caper 'kepɚ; ES 'kepə(r; |-ed -d
capercaillie ,kæpɚ'keljɪ; ES ,kæpə-; |-cailzie
  -'keljɪ, -'kelzɪ
Capernaum kə'pɜ·nɪəm; ES -'pɜn-, -'pɝn-
Capet 'kepɪt, 'kæpɪt (*Fr* ka'pɛ)
Capetian̩ kə'piʃən
Cape Town, Capetown 'kep'taun, -,taun
Caphis 'kefɪs |-'s -ɪz
capias 'kepɪəs |-es -ɪz
capillary 'kæpļ,ɛrɪ; *Brit* kə'pɪlərɪ; |-arity
  ,kæpļ'ærətɪ
capital 'kæpətļ |-ly -ɪ |-ism -,ɪzəm |-ist -ɪst
capitalization ,kæpətļə'zeʃən, -aɪ'z-
capitalize 'kæpətļ,aɪz |-s -ɪz |-d -d
capitate 'kæpə,tet |-d -ɪd |-tion ,kæpə'teʃən
Capitol, c- 'kæpətļ |-ine -,aɪn
capitular kə'pɪtʃələ·; ES -lə(r; |-lary -,lɛrɪ
capitulate kə'pɪtʃə,let |-lated -,letɪd
capitulation kə,pɪtʃə'leʃən
capon 'kepan, 'kepən; ES+-pɒn
capote kə'pot
Cappadocia ,kæpə'doʃɪə, -ʃə |-n -n
capper, C- 'kæpɚ; ES 'kæpə(r
Capri 'kɑpri

capriccio kə'pritʃɪ,o (*It* ka'prittʃo)
capriccioso kə,pritʃɪ'oso (*It* kaprit'tʃo:so)
caprice kə'pris |caprjces kə'prisɪz
capricious kə'prɪʃəs, *often* -'priʃ-, *cf* caprice
Capricorn 'kæprɪ,kɔrn; ES 'kæprɪ,kɔən
Capron 'kepən; ES 'kepən; *cf* apron
capsize kæp'saɪz |-s -ɪz |-d -d
capstan 'kæpstən
capsular 'kæpsələ·, -sjulə·; ES -lə(r
capsule 'kæpsļ, 'kæpsjul |-d -d
captain 'kæptɪn, 'kæptən, 'kæptn̩ |-cy -sɪ
caption 'kæpʃən |-ed -d |-tious -ʃəs
captivate 'kæptə,vet |captivated 'kæptə,vetɪd
captive 'kæptɪv |-d -d |-vity kæp'tɪvətɪ
captor 'kæptɚ; ES 'kæptə(r
capture 'kæptʃɚ; ES 'kæptʃə(r; |-d -d
Capua 'kæpjuə (*It* 'kapwa)
Capuchin 'kæpju,tʃɪn, -,ʃɪn
Capucius kə'pjuʃəs, -'pɪu- |-'s -ɪz
Capulet 'kæpjə,lɛt, 'kæpjəlɪt
capybara ,kæpɪ'barə
car kɑr; ES kɑ:(r; |-red -d
carabao ,kɑrə'bɑo
carabineer, -nier ,kærəbə'nɪr; ES -'nɪə(r, S+
  -'nɛə(r
Caracas kə'rɑkəs |-'s -ɪz (*Sp* ka'rakas)
carack 'kærək
caracole 'kærə,kol |-col -,kɑl, -,kɒl
Caractacus kə'ræktəkəs |-'s -ɪz
Caradoc 'kærə,dɑk, kə'rædək; ES+-,dɒk;=
  Cradock; *geol.* kə'rædək
carafe kə'ræf; E+-'rɑf, -'rɑf
caramel 'kærəmļ |-ed -d—*In many places*
  'kɑrmļ *is often heard.*
caramelize 'kærəmļ,aɪz |-s -ɪz |-d -d
carapace 'kærə,pes |-s -ɪz |-d -t
carat 'kærət
caravan 'kærə,væn |-ed -d
caravanserai ,kærə'vænsə,raɪ, -,re |-sary -rɪ
caravel, -elle 'kærə,vɛl
caraway 'kærə,we
carbazole 'kɑrbə,zol; ES 'kɑ:-; |-zol -,zɑl,
  -,zɒl
carbide 'kɑrbaɪd, -bɪd; ES 'kɑ:b-
carbine 'kɑrbaɪn; ES 'kɑ:baɪn
carbineer ,kɑrbə'nɪr; ES ,kɑ:bə'nɪə(r, S+
  -'nɛə(r

Key: *See in full §§3–47.*   bee bi |pity 'pɪtɪ (§6) |rate ret |yet jɛt |sang sæŋ |angry 'æŋ·grɪ
|bath bæθ; E baθ (§10) |ah ɑ |far fɑr |watch watʃ, wɒtʃ (§12) |jaw dʒɔ |gorge gɔrdʒ |go go

Words below in which a *before* r (farm) *is sounded* ɑ *are often pronounced in* E *with* a (fɑːm)
Words below that have æ *before* r (carry ˈkæɪɪ) *are often pronounced in* N *with* ɛ (ˈkɛɪɪ, §94)

carbinol ˈkɑrbəˌnol; ES ˈkɑːbə-
carbohydrate ˌkɑrboˈhaɪdret; ES ˌkɑːbo-
carbolated ˈkɑrbəˌletɪd; ES ˈkɑːbə-
carbolic kɑrˈbɑlɪk; ES kɑːˈbɑlɪk, -ˈbɒlɪk
carbolize ˈkɑrbəˌlaɪz; ES ˈkɑːbə-; |-s -ɪz
|-d -d
carbon, C- ˈkɑrbən, -bən; ES ˈkɑːbən, -bɒn,
-bən
carbonaceous ˌkɑrbəˈneʃəs; ES ˌkɑːbə-
carbonate n ˈkɑrbənɪt, -ˌnet; ES ˈkɑːbə-
carbonate v ˈkɑrbəˌnet; ES ˈkɑːbə-; |-d -ɪd
Carbondale ˈkɑrbənˌdel; ES ˈkɑːbən-
carbonic kɑrˈbɑnɪk; ES kɑːˈbɑnɪk, -ˈbɒnɪk
carboniferous ˌkɑrbəˈnɪfərəs; ES ˌkɑːbə-
carbonize ˈkɑrbənˌaɪz; ES ˈkɑːbən-; |-s -ɪz
|-d -d
carbonyl ˈkɑrbəˌnɪl; ES ˈkɑːbə-
carborundum, C- ˌkɑrbəˈrʌndəm; ES ˌkɑːbə-
carboxyl kɑrˈbɑksɪl; ES kɑːˈbɑksɪl, -ˈbɒksɪl
carboy ˈkɑrbɔɪ; ES ˈkɑːbɔɪ; |-ed -d
carbuncle ˈkɑrbʌŋkl̩; ES ˈkɑːbʌŋkl̩; |-d -d
carburate ˈkɑrbəˌret, -bjə-; ES ˈkɑːb-; |-d -ɪd
carburation ˌkɑrbəˈreʃən, -bjə-; ES ˌkɑːb-
carburetor ˈkɑrbəˌretɚ, -bjə-; ES ˈkɑːb-, -təɚ
carburet ˈkɑrbəˌret, -bjə-; ES ˈkɑːb-; |-ed -ɪd
carburetion ˌkɑrbəˈrɛʃən, -bjə-; ES ˌkɑːb-
carburetor, -ttor ˈkɑrbəˌretɚ, -bjəˌretɚ; ES
ˈkɑːb-, -təɚ
carburize ˈkɑrbəˌraɪz, -bjə-; ES ˈkɑːb-;
|-s -ɪz |-d -d
carcajou ˈkɑrkəˌdʒu, -ˌʒu; ES ˈkɑːkə-
carcass, -case ˈkɑrkəs; ES ˈkɑːkəs; |-es -ɪz
|-ed -t
Carchemish ˈkɑrkəˌmɪʃ; ES ˈkɑːk-
carcinogen kɑrˈsɪnədʒən, -dʒɪn, ˈkɑrsənə-;
ES kɑ-, ˈkɑːs-
carcinoma ˌkɑrsəˈnomə; ES ˌkɑːsə-; |-s -z
|-ta -tə
card kɑrd; ES kɑːd; |-ed -ɪd
cardamom, -mum ˈkɑrdəməm; ES ˈkɑːdə-;
|-mon -mən
cardboard ˈkɑrdˌbord, -ˌbɔrd; ES ˈkɑːdˌboəd,
E+-ˌbɔəd
cardcase ˈkɑrdˌkes; ES ˈkɑːd-; |-s -ɪz
Cárdenas ˈkɑrdɪˌnɑs; ES ˈkɑːd-; (*Sp* ˈkɑrðe-
ˌnɑs)
cardiac ˈkɑrdɪˌæk; ES ˈkɑːdɪ-

cardiacal kɑrˈdaɪəkl̩; ES kɑˈdaɪəkl̩
Cardiff ˈkɑrdɪf; ES ˈkɑːdɪf
Cardigan, c- ˈkɑrdɪgən; ES ˈkɑːdɪ-; |-shire
-ˌʃɪr, -ʃɚ; ES -ˌʃɪə(r, -ʃə(r
cardinal, C- ˈkɑrdn̩əl, -dnəl; ES ˈkɑːd-; |-ly -ɪ
cardiograph ˈkɑrdɪəˌgræf; ES ˈkɑːdɪə-, E+
-ˌgrɑf, -ˌgrɑf
carditis kɑrˈdaɪtɪs; ES kɑːˈdaɪtɪs
Cardozo kɑrˈdozo; ES kɑːˈdozo
care kɛr, kær; E kɛə(r, ES kæə(r; |-d -d
careen kəˈrin |careened kəˈrind
career kəˈrɪr; ES kəˈrɪə(r, S+-ˈrɛə(r; |-ed -d
carefree ˈkɛrˌfri, ˈkær-; E ˈkɛə-, ES ˈkæə-
careful ˈkɛrfəl, ˈkær-; E ˈkɛə-, ES ˈkæə-;
|-ly -ɪ
careless ˈkɛrlɪs, ˈkær-; E ˈkɛə-, ES ˈkæə-
caress kəˈrɛs |caresses kəˈrɛsɪz |-ed -t
caret ˈkærət, ˈkerət
caretaker ˈkɛrˌtekɚ, ˈkær-; E ˈkɛəˌtekə(r, ES
ˈkæə-
Carew kəˈru, -ˈrɪu, ˈkɛru, ˈke-, -rɪu, -rɪ
careworn ˈkɛrˌworn, ˈkær-, -ˌwɔrn; E
ˈkɛəˌwoən, ˈkæə-, -ˌwɔən; S ˈkæəˌwoən
Carey ˈkɛrɪ, ˈkeːrɪ, ˈkerɪ, ˈkærɪ; S ˈkerɪ,
ˈkærɪ;—*Some speakers distinguish* Carey
from Kerry *by a longer* ɛ.
carf kɑrf; ES kɑːf
carfare ˈkɑrˌfɛr, -ˌfær; E ˈkɑːˌfɛə(r, ES -ˌfæə(r
cargo ˈkɑrgo; ES ˈkɑːgo
Carhart ˈkɑrˌhɑrt; ES ˈkɑːˌhɑːt
Carib ˈkærɪb |-al -l̩ |-an -ən
Caribbean ˌkærəˈbiən, kəˈrɪbɪən
Caribbee, -ibee ˈkærəˌbi |-s -z
Caribian '*Cariban*' kəˈrɪbɪən—*see* Carib
caribou, C- ˈkærəˌbu
caricature ˈkærɪkətʃɚ, -ˌtʃʊr; ES -tʃəʊ(r,
-ˌtʃʊə(r; |-d -d |-rist -ɪst
caries ˈkɛriz, ˈke-, -rɪˌiz
carillon ˈkærəˌlɑn, -ˌlɒn, -lən, kəˈrɪljən |-ed -d
(*Fr* kariˈjõ)
Carinthia kəˈrɪnθɪə |-n -n
cariole ˈkærɪˌol, -ˌɔl
cark kɑrk; ES kɑːk; |-ed -t
carl, -e, C- kɑrl; ES kɑːl
Carleton ˈkɑrltən; ES ˈkɑːl-
Carlile kɑrˈlaɪl, lɚ-; ES kɑːˈlaɪl, kə-
carlin, -e ˈkɑrlɪn; ES ˈkɑːlɪn

|full fʊl |tooth tuθ |further ˈfɝðɚ; ES ˈfɜðə |custom ˈkʌstəm |while hwaɪl |how haʊ |toy tɔɪ
|using ˈjuzɪŋ |fuse fjuz, fɪuz |dish dɪʃ |vision ˈvɪʒən |Eden ˈidn̩ |cradle ˈkredl̩ |keep 'em ˈkipm̩

Words below in which a *before* r (farm) *is sounded* ɑ *are often pronounced in E with* a (faːm)
Words below that have æ *before* r (carry ˈkærɪ) *are often pronounced in N with* ɛ (ˈkɛrɪ, §94)

car-line ˈkarˌlaɪn; ES ˈkɑ:-
carling *naut.* ˈkarlɪŋ; ES ˈkɑ:lɪŋ
Carlisle karˈlaɪl, kə-; ES kɑ:ˈlaɪl, kə-
Carlotta karˈlɑtə; ES kɑ:ˈlɑtə, -ˈlɒtə
Carlovingian ˌkɑrləˈvɪndʒɪən; ES ˌkɑ:lə-
Carlsbad ˈkarlzbæd; ES ˈkɑ:lzbæd
Carlsruhe ˈkarlzruə; ES ˈkɑ:lzruə
Carlton ˈkarltən; ES ˈkɑ:ltən
Carlyle karˈlaɪl, kə-; ES kɑ:ˈlaɪl, kə-
carmagnole ˌkarmənˈjol; ES ˌkɑ:-; (*Fr* karma-ˈɲɔl)
Carman ˈkarmən; ES ˈkɑ:mən
Carmarthen kəˈmarðən; ES kəˈmɑ:ðən; |-shire -ˌʃɪr, -ʃɚ; ES -ˌʃɪə(r, -ʃə(r
Carmel ˈkarml̩; ES ˈkɑ:ml̩; *Cal* Carˈmel
Carmen ˈkarmən; ES ˈkɑ:mən
Carmi ˈkarmaɪ; ES ˈkɑ:maɪ
Carmichael ˈkarmaɪkl̩; ES ˈkɑ:maɪkl̩
carminative karˈmɪnətɪv; ES kɑˈmɪnətɪv
carmine ˈkarmɪn, -maɪn; ES ˈkɑ:m-; |-d -d
carnage ˈkarnɪdʒ; ES ˈkɑ:n-; |-s -ɪz |-d -d
carnal ˈkarnl̩; ES ˈkɑ:nl̩; |-ly -ɪ
Carnarvon kɚˈnarvən; ES kəˈnɑ:vən; |-shire -ˌʃɪr, -ʃɚ; ES -ˌʃɪə(r, -ʃə(r
Carnatic karˈnætɪk; ES kɑ:ˈnætɪk
carnation karˈneʃən; ES kɑ:ˈneʃən; |-ed -d
Carnegie karˈnegɪ, kɚ-; ES kɑ:ˈnegɪ, kə-; (ˈCarˌnegie ˈHall)
carnelian karˈniljən; ES kɑ:ˈniljən
Carniola ˌkarnɪˈolə; ES ˌkɑ:nɪ-; |-n -n (*It* karˈnjɔ:lɑ)
carnival ˈkarnəvl̩; ES ˈkɑ:nəvl̩
Carnivora karˈnɪvərə; ES kɑˈnɪvərə
carnivore ˈkarnəˌvor, -ˌvɔr; ES ˈkɑ:nəˌvoə(r, E+-ˌvɔə(r
carnivorous karˈnɪvərəs; ES kɑˈnɪvərəs
Carnot *Am name* ˈkarnət, -nat; ES ˈkɑ:nət, -nat, -nɒt, *Fr name* karˈno; ES kɑ:ˈno
carob ˈkærəb
caroche kəˈrotʃ, -ˈrɒʃ |-s -ɪz |-d -t
carol, C- ˈkærəl, kærl |-ed -d
Carolina ˌkærəˈlaɪnə—*see* N. & S. Carolina
Caroline ˈkærəˌlaɪn, -lɪn
Carolingian ˌkærəˈlɪndʒɪən
Carolinian ˌkærəˈlɪnɪən
carom ˈkærəm |caromed ˈkærəmd
carotid kəˈratɪd; ES+-ˈrɒtɪd

carouse kəˈrauz |-s -ɪz |-d -d |-sal -l̩
carousel ˌkærəˈzɛl, ˌkæru-
carp karp; ES kɑ:p; |-ed -t
carpal ˈkarpl̩; ES ˈkɑ:pl̩
Carpathian karˈpeθɪən, -θjən; ES kɑˈpeθ-
carpe diem ˈkarpɪˈdaɪɛm; ES ˈkɑ:pɪ-
carpel ˈkarpl̩; ES ˈkɑ:pl̩; |-lary -ˌɛrɪ
Carpentaria ˌkarpənˈtɛrɪə, -ˈter-; ES ˌkɑ:p-
carpenter, C- ˈkarpəntɚ, ˈkarpm̩tɚ; ES ˈkɑ:p-, -tə(r; |-ed -d |-ing -tərɪŋ, -trɪŋ |-try -trɪ
carpet ˈkarpɪt; ES ˈkɑ:pɪt; |-ed -ɪd
carpetbag ˈkarpɪtˌbæg; ES ˈkɑ:pɪt-; |-ged -d |-ger -ɚ; ES -ə(r
carpus ˈkarpəs; ES ˈkɑ:pəs; |-es -ɪz |-pi -paɪ
Carr kar; ES kɑ:(r
carrack ˈkærək
Carrara kəˈrarə (*It* karˈrɑ:ra)
carraway ˈkærəˌwe
Carrel kəˈrɛl
carrettina ˌkærəˈtinə (*It* ˌkarretˈti:na)
carriage *'vehicle'* ˈkærɪdʒ |-s -ɪz; *'freight charge'* ˈkærɪdʒ
carrier ˈkærɪɚ; ES ˈkærɪ·ə(r
Carrington ˈkærɪŋtən
carriole ˈkærɪˌol, -ˌəl
carrion ˈkærɪən
Carrizo kəˈrizo (*Am Sp* kaˈrriso)
Carroll ˈkærəl |-ton -tən
carronade ˌkærəˈned
carrot ˈkærət |-ed -ɪd
carrousel ˌkærəˈzɛl, ˌkæru-
Carruthers kəˈrʌðɚz; ES -ˈrʌðəz; |-ˈs -ɪz
carry ˈkærɪ |carried ˈkærɪd
carryall ˈkærɪˌɔl = cariole, carriole
Carshalton kɚˈʃɔltn̩; ES kə-
Carson ˈkarsn̩; ES ˈkɑ:sn̩
Carstairs, -stares ˈkarstɛrz, -stærz; E ˈkɑ:stɛəz, ES -stæəz
cart kart; ES kɑ:t; |-ed -ɪd |-age -ɪdʒ |-ful -ˌful
Cartagena ˌkartəˈdʒinə; ES ˌkɑ:tə-
carte kart; ES kɑ:t
carte blanche ˈkartˈblanʃ; ES ˈkɑ:t-; |*pl* cartes ˈkarts-; ES ˈkɑ:ts-; (*Fr* kartˈblã:ʃ)
cartel ˈkartl̩, karˈtɛl; ES ˈkɑ:-, kɑ:-
carter, C- ˈkartɚ; ES ˈkɑ:tə(r
Carteret ˈkartərɪt; ES ˈkɑ:tə-

Key: *See in full* §§3-47. bee bi |pity ˈpɪtɪ (§6) |rate ret |yet jɛt |sang sæŋ |angry ˈæŋ·grɪ |bath bæθ; E baθ (§10) |ah ɑ |far fɑr |watch watʃ, wɒtʃ (§12) |jaw dʒɔ |gorge gɔrdʒ |go go

Words below in which a *before* r (farm) *is sounded* ɑ *are often pronounced in* E *with* a (fɑ:m)

Cartesian kɑrˈtiʒən; ES kɑːˈtiʒən
Carthage ˈkɑrθɪdʒ; ES ˈkɑːθɪdʒ; |-'s -ɪz
Carthaginian ˌkɑrθəˈdʒɪnɪən; ES ˌkɑːθə-
Carthusian kɑrˈθjuʒən, -ˈθɪu-; ES kɑːⁱ
Cartier ˌkɑrtɪˈe, kɑrˈtje; ES ˌkɑː-, kɑː-;
   (*Fr* karˈtje)
cartilage ˈkɑrtḷɪdʒ; ES ˈkɑːt-; |-s -ɪz
cartilaginous ˌkɑrtḷˈædʒənəs; ES ˌkɑːt-
cartle ˈkɑrtḷ; ES ˈkɑːtḷ
cartogram ˈkɑrtəˌgræm; ES ˈkɑːtə-
cartograph ˈkɑrtəˌgræf; ES ˈkɑːtə-, E+
   -ˌgraf, -ˌgrɑf
cartographer kɑrˈtɑgrəfɚ, -ˈtɒg-; ES kɑ-,
   -fə(r; |-phy -fɪ
cartographic ˌkɑrtəˈgræfɪk; ES ˌkɑːtə-; |-al
   -ḷ |-ally -ḷɪ, -ɪklɪ
carton, C- ˈkɑrtn̩, -tan; ES ˈkɑːt-, -tɒn
cartoon kɑrˈtun; ES kɑːˈtun; |-ed -d |-ist -ɪst
cartouche, -ch kɑrˈtuʃ; ES kɑːˈtuʃ; |-s -ɪz
cartridge ˈkɑrtrɪdʒ; ES ˈkɑːtrɪdʒ; |-s -ɪz
cart-track ˈkɑrtˌtræk; ES ˈkɑːt-
cartulary ˈkɑrtʃʊˌlɛrɪ; ES ˈkɑːtʃʊˌlɛrɪ
cartwright, C- ˈkɑrtˌraɪt; ES ˈkɑːt-
Caruso kəˈruso (*It* kaˈruːzo)
Caruthers kəˈrʌðɚz; ES kəˈrʌðəz; |-'s -ɪz
carve kɑrv; ES kɑːv; |-d -d |*arch. pptc* -n -ən
carvel ˈkɑrvḷ
carven ˈkɑrvən; ES ˈkɑːvən
Cary ˈkɛrɪ, ˈkɛːrɪ, ˈkerɪ, ˈkærɪ; S ˈkerɪ, ˈkærɪ;
   see note at Carey
caryatid ˌkærɪˈætɪd |-s -z |-es -ˌiz
casaba kəˈsɑbə
Casabianca ˌkæsəbɪˈæŋkə (*It* ˌkasaˈbjaŋka)
Casablanca ˌkasəˈblaŋkə, ˌkæsəˈblæŋkə
Casanova ˌkæzəˈnovə (*It* ˌkasaˈnɔːva)
Casaubon kəˈsɔbən (*Fr* kazoˈbõ)
Casca ˈkæskə
cascade, C- kæsˈked |-caded -ˈkedɪd
cascara kæsˈkɛrə, -ˈkerə (*Sp* ˈkaskara)
cascarilla ˌkæskəˈrɪlə
cascaron ˌkæskəˈron (*Am Sp* ˌkaskaˈron)
Casco ˈkæsko
case, C- kes |cases ˈkesɪz |cased kest
casease ˈkesɪˌes
caseate ˈkesɪˌet |-d -ɪd
casefy ˈkesəˌfaɪ |-fied -ˌfaɪd
caseharden ˈkesˌhardn̩, -ˈhardn̩; ES -ˌhɑːdn̩,
   -ˈhɑːdn̩; |-ed -d |-ing -dn̩ɪŋ, -dnɪŋ

casein ˈkesɪɪn
case-knife ˈkesˌnaɪf, -ˈnaɪf |-ives -aɪvz
casemate ˈkesˌmet |-mated -ˌmetɪd
casement, C- ˈkesmənt |-ed -ɪd
caseose ˈkesɪˌos |caseous ˈkesɪəs
casern, -e kəˈzɝn; ES -ˈzɜn, -ˈzɝn
Casey ˈkesɪ, *Ill* ˈkezɪ
caseworm ˈkesˌwɝm; ES -ˌwɜm, -ˌwɝm
cash kæʃ |cashes ˈkæʃɪz |cashed kæʃt
casha ˈkæʃə
cash-and-carry ˈkæʃənˈkærɪ
cashaw kəˈʃɔ
cashbook ˈkæʃˌbʊk
cashboy ˈkæʃˌbɔɪ
cashew kəˈʃu, -ˈʃɪu, ˈkæʃ-
cashier *n*, *v* kæˈʃɪr; ES -ˈʃɪə(r, S+-ˈʃɛə(r;
   |-ed -d (ˈcashˌier ˈJones)
cashmere *cloth* ˈkæʃmɪr; ES -mɪə(r
Cashmere *India* kæʃˈmɪr; ES -ˈmɪə(r
cashoo kəˈʃu = catechu
casimere, -mire ˈkæsəˌmɪr, ˈkæzə-; ES -ˌmɪə(r
Casimir ˈkæsəˌmɪr; ES -ˌmɪə(r
casing ˈkesɪŋ
casino, C- kəˈsino |-s -z |-ni -ni
cask kæsk; E+kask, kɑsk; |-ed -t
casket ˈkæskɪt; E ˈkæs-, *much less freq.*
   ˈkas-, ˈkɑs-; |-ed -ɪd
Caslon ˈkæzlən
Caspar, -per ˈkæspɚ; ES ˈkæspə(r
Caspian ˈkæspɪən
casque ˈkæsk |casqued ˈkæskt |-quet ˈkæskɪt
Cass kæs |Cass's ˈkæsɪz
cassaba kəˈsɑbə
Cassandra kəˈsændrə
cassation kæˈseʃən
cassava kəˈsɑvə
Cassel, -ll ˈkæsḷ
casserole ˈkæsəˌrol |-d -d
Cassia ˈkæʃɪə |cassia ˈkæʃə
Cassiepeia ˌkæsɪəˈpiə
Cassil ˈkæsḷ
cassimere ˈkæsəˌmɪr; ES -ˌmɪə(r
cassino kəˈsino
Cassio ˈkæʃɪˌo, ˈkæʃjo
Cassiopeia, -pea ˌkæsɪəˈpiə |-n -n
Cassius ˈkæʃəs, ˈkæʃɪəs |-'s -ɪz
cassock ˈkæsək |-ed -t
cassowary ˈkæsəˌwɛrɪ

|full fʊl |tooth tuθ |further ˈfɝðɚ; ES ˈfɜðə |custom ˈkʌstəm |while hwaɪl |how haʊ |toy tɔɪ
|using ˈjuzɪŋ |fuse fjuz, fɪuz |dish dɪʃ |vision ˈvɪʒən |Eden ˈidn̩ |cradle ˈkredḷ |keep 'em ˈkipm̩

cast kæst; ES+kast, kɑst
Castalia kæs'teliə |-n -n
castanet ˌkæstə'nɛt
castaway 'kæstəˌwe; E+'kast-, 'kɑst-
caste kæst; E+kast, kɑst
castellan 'kæstələn
castellate 'kæstəˌlet |-d -ɪd
caster 'kæstɚ; ES 'kæstə(r, E+'kas-, 'kɑs-
Casterbridge 'kæstɚˌbrɪdʒ; ES 'kæstə-; |-'s
    -ɪz
castigate 'kæstəˌget |-d -ɪd
castigation ˌkæstə'geʃən
Castile kæs'til ('Casˌtile 'soap), NY kæs'taɪl
Castilian kæs'tɪljən, -lɪən
cast-iron adj 'kæst'aɪɚn; ES 'kæst'aɪ·ən, E+
    'kast-, 'kɑst-; ('cast-ˌiron 'pipe)
castle, C- 'kæsḷ; E+'kasḷ, 'kɑsḷ; |-d -d
    |-ling 'kæslɪŋ, 'kæsḷɪŋ
Castlereagh 'kæsḷˌre; E+'kasḷ-, 'kɑsḷ-;
    acct+ˌCastle'reagh
castoff n 'kæstˌɔf, -ˌɒf; E+'kast-, 'kɑst-
castor, C- 'kæstɚ; ES 'kæstə(r, E+'kas-, 'kɑs-
castrate 'kæstret |-d -ɪd
casual 'kæʒuəl, 'kæʒʊl |-ly -ɪ |-ty -tɪ
casuist 'kæʒuɪst |-ry -rɪ
casuistic ˌkæʒʊ'ɪstɪk |-al -ḷ |-ally -ḷɪ, -ɪklɪ
casus belli 'kesəs'bɛlaɪ
Caswell 'kæzwəl, -wɛl
cat kæt |catted 'kætɪd
catabolism kə'tæbḷˌɪzəm
catachresis ˌkætə'krisɪs |-chreses -'krisiz
catachrestic ˌkætə'krɛstɪk |-al -ḷ |-ally -ḷɪ,
    -ɪklɪ
cataclinal ˌkætə'klaɪnḷ
cataclysm 'kætəˌklɪzəm |-al ˌkætə'klɪzmḷ
cataclysmic ˌkætə'klɪzmɪk |-ally -ḷɪ, -ɪklɪ
catacomb 'kætəˌkom
catacumbal ˌkætə'kʌmbḷ
catafalque 'kætəˌfælk
Catahoula ˌkætə'hulə
Catalan 'kætḷən, 'kætḷˌæn
catalase 'kætḷˌes
catalectic ˌkætḷ'ɛktɪk
catalepsis ˌkætḷ'ɛpsɪs |-leptic -'ɛptɪk
catalepsy 'kætḷˌɛpsɪ
Catalina, c- ˌkætḷ'inə
catalogue, -log 'kætḷˌɔg, -ˌɑg, -ˌɒg |-d, -ged -d
Catalonia ˌkætḷ'onɪə |-n -n
catalpa, C- kə'tælpə, occas. kə'tɔlpə

catalysis kə'tæləsɪs |-yses -əˌsiz
catalyst 'kætḷɪst |-lytic ˌkætḷ'ɪtɪk
catalyze 'kætḷˌaɪz |-s -ɪz |-d -d
catamaran ˌkætəmə'ræn
catamount 'kætəˌmaʊnt
Catania kə'tenɪə, -njə (It kɑ'tɑːnjɑ)
catapult 'kætəˌpʌlt |-ed -ɪd
cataract 'kætəˌrækt |-ed -ɪd
catarrh kə'tɑr; ES kə'tɑː(r, E+-'tɑː(r; |-ed -d
    |-al -əl |-ally -əlɪ
Catasauqua ˌkætə'sɔkwə
catastasis kə'tæstəsɪs |-tases -təˌsiz
catastrophe kə'tæstrəfɪ
catastrophic ˌkætə'strɑfɪk; ES+-'strɒf-; |-al
    -ḷ |-ally -ḷɪ, -ɪklɪ
Catawba, c- kə'tɔbə
Catawissa ˌkætə'wɪsə
catbird 'kætˌbɝd; ES -ˌbɜd, -ˌbɝd
catboat 'kætˌbot
catcall 'kætˌkɔl |-ed -d
catch kætʃ, not infreq. kɛtʃ |-es -ɪz |caught kɔt
catchall 'kætʃˌɔl
catcher 'kætʃɚ, 'kɛtʃɚ; ES -tʃə(r
catchpenny 'kætʃˌpɛnɪ
catchpole, -poll 'kætʃˌpol |-d, -ed -d
catchup 'kætʃəp, 'kɛtʃəp
catchword 'kætʃˌwɝd; ES -ˌwɜd, -ˌwɝd
cate ket |cates kets
catechesis ˌkætə'kisɪs |-cheses -'kisiz
catechetical ˌkætə'kɛtɪkḷ |-ly -ɪ
catechism 'kætəˌkɪzəm |-chist -kɪst
catechistic ˌkætə'kɪstɪk |-al -ḷ |-ally -ḷɪ, -ɪklɪ
catechize 'kætəˌkaɪz |-s -ɪz |-d -d
catechu 'kætəˌtʃu
catechumen ˌkætə'kjumən, -'kɪu- |-al -ḷ |-ate
    -ˌet |-ism -ˌɪzəm
categorical ˌkætə'gɔrɪkḷ, -'gar-, -'gɒr- |-ly -ɪ
category 'kætəˌgorɪ, -ˌgɔrɪ; S -ˌgorɪ
catena kə'tinə |-s -z |-nae -ni |-ry -rɪ
catenate 'kætṇˌet |-d -ɪd
cater 'ketɚ; ES 'ketə(r; |-ed -d |-ing 'ketərɪŋ,
    'ketrɪŋ
catercornered 'kætəˌkɔrnɚd, 'kætɚ-; ES
    'kætəˌkɔənəd—In 'kætəˌkɔrnɚd the first ɚ
    was lost by dissimilation (§121).
cater-cousin 'ketɚˌkʌzṇ; ES 'ketə-
caterer 'ketərɚ; ES 'ketərə(r
Caterina ˌkætə'rinə (It ˌkate'riːnɑ)
caterpillar 'kætəˌpɪlɚ, 'kætɚ-; ES 'kætə-

ˌpɪlə(r; |-ed -d—*In* ˈkætəˌpɪlɚ *the first ɚ was lost by dissimilation (§121).*
caterwaul ˈkætɚˌwɔl; ES ˈkætə-; |-ed -d
Catesby ˈketsbɪ
catfall ˈkætˌfɔl
catfish ˈkætˌfɪʃ |-'s -ɪz
catgut ˈkætˌgʌt (ˈkætgət ˈstrɪŋ)
Catharine ˈkæθrɪn, ˈkæθərɪn
catharsis kəˈθɑrsɪs; ES -ˈθɑːs:s, E+-ˈθɑːs:-
cathartic kəˈθɑrtɪk; ES -ˈθɑːt:-, E+-ˈθɑːt:-; |-al -ļ |-ally -ļɪ, -ɪklɪ
Cathay kəˈθe, kæˈθe
Cathcart ˈkæθkɚt, -kɑrt; ES -kət, -kɑːt, E+ -kaːt
cathead ˈkætˌhɛd |-ed -ɪd
cathedra kəˈθidrə, ˈkæθɪdrə
cathedral kəˈθidrəl
Cather ˈkæðɚ; ES ˈkæðə(r
Catherine ˈkæθrɪn, ˈkæθərɪn
Catherwood ˈkæðɚˌwud; ES ˈkæðə-
catheter ˈkæθətɚ; ES ˈkæθətə(r
Cathleen ˈkæθlin
cathode ˈkæθod
cathodic kəˈθɑdɪk; ES+-ˈθɒd-; |-al -ļ |-ally -ļɪ, -ɪklɪ
cat-hole ˈkætˌhol
catholic, C- ˈkæθəlɪk, ˈkæθlɪk
catholicism, C- kəˈθɑləˌsɪzəm; ES+-ˈθɒl-
catholicity ˌkæθəˈlɪsətɪ
catholicize kəˈθɑləˌsaɪz; ES+-ˈθɒl-; |-s -ɪz |-d -d
catholicon kəˈθɑləkən; ES+-ˈθɒl-
Catiline ˈkætļˌaɪn
cation ˈkætˌaɪən
catkin ˈkætkɪn
Catlettsburg ˈkætlɪtsˌbɝg; ES -ˌbɝg, -ˌbɝg
catmint ˈkætˌmɪnt
catnip ˈkætnɪp, -nəp
Cato ˈketo
cat-o'-nine-tails ˌkætəˈnaɪnˌtelz, ˌkætṇˈaɪn-
Catoosa kəˈtusə
catoptric kəˈtɑptrɪk; ES+-ˈtɒp-; |-s -s |-al -ļ |-ally -ļɪ, -ɪklɪ
cat-rigged ˈkætˌrɪgd
Catron kəˈtran; ES+-ˈtrɒn
cat's-cradle ˈkætsˌkredļ
cat's-ear ˈkætsˌɪr; ES -ˌɪə(r, S+-ˌɛə(r
cat's-eye ˈkætsˌaɪ
Catskill ˈkætsˌkɪl

cat's-paw ˈkætsˌpɔ
catsup ˈkætsəp, ˈkɛtʃəp
cattail ˈkætˌtel
Cattaraugus ˌkætəˈrɔgəs |-'s -ɪz
Cattegat ˈkætɪˌgæt, ˌkætɪˈgæt
Cattell kəˈtɛl, kæ-
cattish ˈkætɪʃ |catty ˈkætɪ
cattle ˈkætļ |-less ˈkætļɪs
Catullus kəˈtʌləs |-'s -ɪz
Catulus ˈkætʃələs |-'s -ɪz
catwalk ˈkætˌwɔk
Caucasia kɔˈkeʒə, -ˈkeʃə
Caucasian kɔˈkeʒən, -ˈkeʃən, -ˈkæʒən, -ˈkæʃən
Caucasus ˈkɔkəsəs |-sus' -səs
caucus ˈkɔkəs |-es -ɪz |-ed -t
caudal ˈkɔdļ |-ly -ɪ
caudate ˈkɔdet |-d -ɪd
caudicle ˈkɔdɪkļ
Caudine ˈkɔdaɪn
caudle ˈkɔdļ |-d -d |-ling ˈkɔdlɪŋ, -dļɪŋ
Caudle ˈkɔdļ, *cf* Caldwell
caught kɔt
caul kɔl
cauldron ˈkɔldrən |-ed -d
cauliflower ˈkɔləˌflauɚ; ES -ˌflau·ə(r
caulk kɔk |caulked kɔkt
causal ˈkɔzļ |-ly -ɪ |-ity kɔˈzælətɪ
causation kɔˈzeʃən |causative ˈkɔzətɪv
cause kɔz |causes ˈkɔzɪz |caused kɔzd
causerie ˌkozəˈri (*Fr* koz'ri)
causeway ˈkɔzˌwe |-wayed -ˌwed
causey ˈkɔzɪ |-ed -d
caustic ˈkɔstɪk |-ly -lɪ |-al -ļ |-ally -ļɪ
cautel ˈkɔtļ
cauterization ˌkɔtərəˈzeʃən, -aɪˈz-
cauterize ˈkɔtəˌraɪz |-s -ɪz |-d -d |-tery -rɪ
caution ˈkɔʃən |-ed -d |-ing ˈkɔʃənɪŋ, -ʃnɪŋ
cautionary ˈkɔʃənˌɛrɪ
cautious ˈkɔʃəs
cavalcade ˌkævļˈked |-caded -ˈkedɪd
cavalier, C- ˌkævəˈlɪr; ES -ˈlɪə(r, S+-ˈlɛə(r
cavalry ˈkævļrɪ |-man, -men -mən
cavatina ˌkævəˈtinə (*It* ˌkavəˈtiːna)
cave, C- kev |caved kevd
caveat ˈkevɪˌæt
caveat emptor ˈkevɪˌætˈɛmptɔr; ES -tɔə(r
cave-in ˈkevˌɪn
Cavell, *Edith* ˈkævļ

|full fʊl |tooth tuθ |further ˈfɝðɚ; ES ˈfɝðə |custom ˈkʌstəm |while hwaɪl |how hau |toy tɔɪ |using ˈjuzɪŋ |fuse fjuz, fɪuz |dish dɪʃ |vision ˈvɪʒən |Eden ˈidṇ |cradle ˈkredļ |keep 'em ˈkipm̩

Cavendish, c-, Candish ˈkævəndɪʃ, *loc.*+
 ˈkændɪʃ |-ˈs -ɪz
cavern ˈkævən; ES ˈkævən; |-ed -d |-ous -əs
caviar, -are ˌkævɪˈɑr, ˈkævɪˌɑr; ES -ˈɑ:(r,
 -ˌɑ:(r;—*in Hamlet* caviary, *probably pron.*
 ˌkævɪˈærɪ
cavie ˈkevɪ
cavil ˈkævl̩, -vɪl |-ed -d |-ing ˈkævl̩ɪŋ, -vlɪŋ
Cavite kəˈvite, ka-
cavity ˈkævətɪ |cavitied ˈkævətɪd
cavort kəˈvɔrt; ES -ˈvɔət; |-ed -ɪd
Cavour kəˈvur; ES -ˈvuə(r; (*It* kaˈvu:r)
cavy ˈkevɪ
caw kɔ |cawed kɔd
Cawdor ˈkɔdə; ES ˈkɔdə(r
Cawnpore, -pur kɔnˈpor, -ˈpɔr, -ˈpur; ES
 -ˈpoə(r, -ˈpuə(r, E+-ˈpɔə(r
Caxton ˈkækstən
cay ke, ki, *in West Indies usually* ki
cayenne, C- kaɪˈɛn, keˈɛn (ˈcayˌenne ˈpepper)
cayman ˈkemən |caymans ˈkemənz
Cayman \isls. kaɪˈmɑn
Cayuga keˈugə, -ˈjugə, kɪˈugə, ˈkjugə
Cayuse, c- kaɪˈjus, -ˈjɪus
Cazenovia ˌkæzəˈnovɪə
cease sis |ceases ˈsisɪz |ceased sist
Cebu seˈbu
Cecil *Md co.* ˈsisl̩, -sɪl, *pers. name* ˈsisl̩,ˈsɛsl̩,
 -sɪl
Cecilia sɪˈsɪljə, -ˈsɪlɪə, -ˈsiljə
Cecily ˈsɛsl̩ɪ, ˈsɪsl̩ɪ
Cecropia sɪˈkropɪə
cedar ˈsidə; ES ˈsidə(r; |-ed -d
cede sid |ceded ˈsidɪd
cedilla sɪˈdɪlə
Cedric ˈsɛdrɪk, ˈsidrɪk
cee si
ceil sil |ceiled sild |ceiling ˈsilɪŋ
celandine ˈsɛlənˌdaɪn
Celebes ˈsɛləˌbiz, səˈlibiz
celebrant ˈsɛləbrənt
celebrate ˈsɛləˌbret |-brated -ˌbretɪd
celebration ˌsɛləˈbreʃən
celebrity səˈlɛbrətɪ
celerity səˈlɛrətɪ
celery ˈsɛlərɪ
celesta səˈlɛstə
celeste, C- səˈlɛst
celestial, C- səˈlɛstʃəl |-ly -ɪ

Celia ˈsiljə, *in Shak.* ˈsilɪə
celiac ˈsilɪˌæk
celibate ˈsɛləbɪt, -ˌbet |-bacy -bəsɪ
Celina səˈlaɪnə
cell sɛl |celled sɛld
cellar ˈsɛlə; ES ˈsɛlə(r; |-ed -d
cellarage ˈsɛlərɪdʒ |-s -ɪz
cellarer ˈsɛlərə; ES ˈsɛlərə(r
Cellini tʃɛˈlini (*It* tʃelˈli:ni)
cellist, ˈcellist ˈtʃɛlɪst
cello, ˈcello ˈtʃɛlo |-s -z |-li -i
cellophane, C- ˈsɛləˌfen |-d -d
cellular ˈsɛljələ; ES ˈsɛljələ(r
cellulate ˈsɛljəˌlet |-d -ɪd
cellule ˈsɛljul
celluloid, C- ˈsɛljəˌlɔɪd, ˈsɛlə-
cellulose ˈsɛljəˌlos |-s -ɪz |-d -t |-lous -ləs
Celoron ˈsɛləˌrɑn, -ˌrɒn
Celotex, c- ˈsɛləˌtɛks
Celsius ˈsɛlsɪəs |-ˈs -ɪz
celt sɛlt
Celt sɛlt |-ist -ɪst
Celtic ˈsɛltɪk |-ally -l̩ɪ, -ɪklɪ
Celticism ˈsɛltəˌsɪzəm |-cist -sɪst
cement səˈmɛnt |-ed -ɪd
cementation ˌsimənˈteʃən, ˌsɛmən-
cemetery ˈsɛməˌtɛrɪ, ˈsɛmɪtrɪ
Cenci ˈtʃɛntʃɪ (*It* ˈtʃɛntʃi)
Cenis səˈni
cenobite ˈsɛnəˌbaɪt, ˈsin-
cenotaph ˈsɛnəˌtæf
Cenozoic ˌsinəˈzoˌɪk, ˌsɛnə-
cense sɛns |censes ˈsɛnsɪz |censed sɛnst
censer ˈsɛnsə; ES ˈsɛnsə(r
censor ˈsɛnsə; ES ˈsɛnsə(r; |-ed -d
censorial sɛnˈsorɪəl, -ˈsɔr-; S -ˈsor-
censorious sɛnˈsorɪəs, -ˈsɔr-; S -ˈsor-
censorship ˈsɛnsəˌʃɪp; ES ˈsɛnsə-
censurability ˌsɛnʃərəˈbɪlətɪ
censurable ˈsɛnʃərəbl̩ |-bly -blɪ
censure ˈsɛnʃə; ES ˈsɛnʃə(r; |-d -d |-ring
 ˈsɛnʃərɪŋ, ˈsɛnʃrɪŋ
census ˈsɛnsəs |-es -ɪz |-ed -t |-sus' -səs
cent sɛnt |cental ˈsɛntl̩
centaur ˈsɛntɔr; ES ˈsɛntɔə(r
Centaurus, c- sɛnˈtɔrəs |*gen & pl* -ri -raɪ
 |-ˈs -ɪz
centavo sɛnˈtavo
centenarian ˌsɛntəˈnɛrɪən, -ˈner- |-ism -ˌɪzəm

Key: *See in full §§3–47.* bee **bi** |pity ˈpɪtɪ (§6) |rate ret |yet jɛt |sang sæŋ |angry ˈæŋ·grɪ
|bath bæθ; E baθ (§10) |ah ɑ |far fɑr |watch watʃ, wɒtʃ (§12) |jaw dʒɔ |gorge gɔrdʒ |go go

centenary ˈsɛntəˌnɛrɪ, sɛnˈtɛnərɪ, *mainly Brit*
   sɛnˈtinərɪ
centennial sɛnˈtɛnɪəl, -njəl |-ly -ɪ
center, -tre ˈsɛntɚ; ES ˈsɛntə(r; |-(e)d -d
   |-(r)ing ˈsɛntərɪŋ, ˈsɛntrɪŋ
centerboard, -tre- ˈsɛntɚˌbord, -ˌbɔrd; ES
   ˈsɛntəˌboəd, E+-ˌbɔəd
center-fire, -tre- ˈsɛntɚˈfaɪr; ES ˈsɛntəˈfaɪə(r;
   (ˈcenter-ˌfire ˈshell)
centerpiece, -tre- ˈsɛntɚˌpis; ES ˈsɛntə-;
   |-s -ɪz
centesimal sɛnˈtɛsəml̩ |-ly -ɪ
centesimo sɛnˈtɛsəˌmo
centiar ˈsɛntɪˌar; ES -ˌɑː(r
centiare ˈsɛntɪˌɛr, -ˌær; E -ˌɛə(r, ES -ˌæə(r
centigrade ˈsɛntəˌgred
centigram, -mme ˈsɛntəˌgræm
centiliter, -tre ˈsɛntl̩ˌitɚ; ES -tə(r
centillion sɛnˈtɪljən
centime ˈsantim, sɑnˈtim (*Fr* sɑ̃ˈtim)
centimeter, -tre ˈsɛntəˌmitɚ; ES -ˌmitə(r;
   (*Fr* sɑ̃tiˈmɛtr̩)
centimeter-gram-second, -tre- ˈsɛntəˌmitɚ-
   ˈgræmˈsɛkənd; ES -ˌmitə-
centimo ˈsɛntəˌmo
centipede ˈsɛntəˌpid
centistere ˈsɛntəˌstɪr; ES -ˌstɪə(r
Centlivre sɛntˈlɪvɚ, -ˈlivɚ; ES
   -ˈlɪvə(r, -ˈliv-
centner ˈsɛntnɚ; ES ˈsɛntnə(r; (*Ger* ˈtsɛntnər)
cento ˈsɛnto
central ˈsɛntrəl |-ly -ɪ |-ism -ˌɪzəm |-ist -ɪst
Centralia sɛnˈtrelɪə, -ljə
centrality sɛnˈtrælətɪ
centralization ˌsɛntrələˈzeʃən, -aɪˈz-
centralize ˈsɛntrəlˌaɪz |-s -ɪz |-d -d
centric ˈsɛntrɪk |-al -l̩ |ally -l̩ɪ, -ɪklɪ
centrifugal sɛnˈtrɪfjʊgl̩ |-ly -ɪ
centrifuge ˈsɛntrəˌfjudʒ, -ˌfiudʒ |-s -ɪz
centripetal sɛnˈtrɪpətl̩ |-ly -ɪ
centrist, C- ˈsɛntrɪst
centrosphere ˈsɛntrəˌsfɪr; ES -ˌsfɪə(r, S+
   -ˌsfɛə(r
centuple ˈsɛntʊpl̩, -tjʊ-, sɛnˈtupl̩, -ˈtɪu-,
   -ˈtju- |-d -d |-ling -plɪŋ, -pl̩ɪŋ
centurial sɛnˈtjʊrɪəl, -ˈtɪʊrɪəl, -ˈtʊr-
centurion sɛnˈtjʊrɪən, -ˈtɪʊrɪən, -ˈtʊr-
century ˈsɛntʃərɪ |-ried -d
cephalic səˈfælɪk, sɛ-

Cephalonia ˌsɛfəˈlonɪə, -njə |-n -n
cephalopod ˈsɛfələˌpɑd; ES+-ˌpɒd
Cephalopoda ˌsɛfəˈlɑpədə; ES+-ˈlɒp-
cephalothorax ˌsɛfələˈθoræks, -ˈθɔr-; S -ˈθor-;
   |-es -ɪz
cephalous ˈsɛfələs
Cephalus ˈsɛfələs |-ʼs -ɪz
Cephas ˈsifəs |-ʼs -ɪz
Cepheus ˈsifjus, ˈsifɪəs |-ʼs -ɪz
ceramic səˈræmɪk |-s -s
cerate ˈsɪret
Cerberus ˈsɝbərəs; ES ˈsɜb-, ˈsɝb-; |-ʼs -ɪz
cere sɪr; ES sɪə(r, S+sɛə(r; |-d -d
cereal ˈsɪrɪəl
cerebellar ˌsɛrəˈbɛlɚ; ES -ˈbɛlə(r
cerebellum ˌsɛrəˈbɛləm |-s -z |-la -lə
cerebral ˈsɛrəbrəl |-ly -ɪ
cerebrate ˈsɛrəˌbret |-brated -ˌbretɪd
cerebration ˌsɛrəˈbreʃən
cerebrospinal ˌsɛrəbroˈspaɪnl̩
cerebrum ˈsɛrəbrəm |-s -z |-bra -brə
cerecloth ˈsɪrˌklɔθ, -ˌklɒθ; ES ˈsɪə-; |-ths -ðz,
   -θs
cerement ˈsɪrmənt; ES ˈsɪəmənt
ceremonial ˌsɛrəˈmonɪəl, -njəl |-ly -ɪ
ceremonious ˌsɛrəˈmonɪəs, -njəs
ceremony ˈsɛrəˌmonɪ
Ceres ˈsɪriz, ˈsiriz |-resʼ -rɪz
Cereus, c- ˈsɪrɪəs, ˈsi- |-es -ɪz
cerif, -iph ˈsɛrɪf=serif
Cerigo ˈtʃɛrɪˌgo (*It* ˈtʃɛːrɪˌgo)
Cerimon ˈsɛrɪˌman, -ˌmɒn
cerise səˈriz, -ˈris |-s -ɪz
cerium ˈsɪrɪəm
Cerro Gordo ˈsɛroˈgɔrdo; ES -ˈgɔədo
certain ˈsɝtn̩, -ɪn, -ən; ES ˈsɜt-, ˈsɝt-; |-ty -tɪ
certes ˈsɝtiz; ES ˈsɜt-, ˈsɝt-
certifiable ˈsɝtəˌfaɪəbl̩; ES ˈsɜtə-, ˈsɝtə-;
   |-bly -blɪ
certificate *n* sɚˈtɪfəkɪt; ES səˈtɪf-
certificate *v* sɚˈtɪfəˌket; ES sə-; |-d -ɪd
certification ‘*certifying*’ ˌsɝtəfəˈkeʃən; ES
   ˌsɜtə-, ˌsɝtə-
certification ‘*certificating*’ sɚˌtɪfəˈkeʃən; ES
   sə-
certify ˈsɝtəˌfaɪ; ES ˈsɜtə-, ˈsɝtə-; |-fied -ˌfaɪd
certiorari ˌsɝʃɪəˈrɛrɪ, -ˈrɛrɪ; ES ˌsɜʃɪ-, ˌsɝʃɪ-
certitude ˈsɝtəˌtjud, -ˌtɪud; -ˌtud; ES ˈsɜt-,
   ˈsɝt-

|full fʊl |tooth tuθ |further ˈfɝðɚ; ES ˈfɝðə |custom ˈkʌstəm |while hwaɪl |how haʊ |toy tɔɪ
|using ˈjuzɪŋ |fuse fjuz, fɪuz |dish dɪʃ |vision ˈvɪʒən |Eden ˈidn̩ |cradle ˈkredl̩ |keep ʼem ˈkipm̩

cerulean sə'rulɪən, -'rɪulɪən, -ljən
cerumen sə'rumən, -'rɪumən
ceruse 'sɪrus, sə'rus
Cervantes sɚ'væntiz; ES sə-; |-tes' -tiz (Sp
θɛr'βantes)
cervical 'sɝvɪk|; ES 'sɝv-, 'sɝv-
cervix 'sɝvɪks; ES 'sɝv-, 'sɝv-; |-es -ɪz
|cervices sɚ'vaɪsɪz; ES sə-
César 'sezɑr; ES 'sezɑː(r, E+-zaː(r; (Fr
se'zaːr)
Cesarea ˌsɛsə'rɪə, ˌsɛz- |-rean -'rɪən
Cesarean, c-, -ian surg. sɪ'zɛrɪən, -'zær-, -'zer-
cesium 'sizɪəm
cessation sɛ'seʃən
cession 'sɛʃən
cesspit 'sɛsˌpɪt
cesspool 'sɛsˌpul
cestode 'sɛstod
cestus, C- 'sɛstəs |-es -ɪz
cesura sɪ'ʒurə, sɪ'zjurə, -'zɪurə |-l -l
Cetacea sɪ'teʃə |cetacean sɪ'teʃən
Cetus 'sitəs |gen Ceti 'sitaɪ
cevitamic ˌsivaɪ'tæmɪk
Ceylon sɪ'lɑn; ES+-'lɒn; |-ese ˌsilə'niz
Ceyx 'siɪks |-'s -ɪz
Cézanne sɪ'zæn (Fr se'zan)
cf. 'compare' 'si'ɛf, kən'fɝ; ES -'fɝ(r, -'fɝ
chabouk, -buk 'tʃɑbʊk
Chaco 'tʃɑko
Chad tʃæd, tʃɑd
Chadds Ford 'tʃædz'fɔrd, -'fɔrd; ES -'fɔəd,
E+-'fɔəd
Chadron 'ʃædrən
Chaeronea ˌkɛrə'niə
chafe tʃef |chafed tʃeft
Chafee 'tʃefɪ, 'tʃæfɪ
chafer 'tʃefɚ; ES 'tʃefə(r; |-y -ɪ
chaff tʃæf; E+tʃaf, tʃɑf; |-ed -t
Chaffee 'tʃæfɪ, 'tʃefɪ
chaffer 'tʃæfɚ; ES 'tʃæfə(r; |-ed -d |-ing
'tʃæfərɪŋ, 'tʃæfrɪŋ
Chaffey 'tʃæfɪ, 'tʃefɪ
chaffinch 'tʃæˌfɪntʃ, 'tʃæfˌfɪntʃ |-es -ɪz
Chagres 'tʃɑgrɛs
chagrin ʃə'grɪn |-ed -d
Chagrin Falls ʃə'grɪn'fɔlz, loc.+'ʃugrɪn-,
'ʃægrɪn-
chain tʃen |chained tʃend
chain-stitch 'tʃenˌstɪtʃ |-es -ɪz |-ed -t

chainwork 'tʃenˌwɝk; ES -ˌwɝk, -ˌwɝk
chair tʃɛr, tʃær; E tʃɛə(r, ES tʃæə(r; |-ed -d
chairman 'tʃɛrmən, 'tʃær-; E 'tʃɛə-, ES
'tʃæə-; |-men -mən |-ship -ˌʃɪp
chaise ʃez |chaises 'ʃezɪz |chaised ʃezd
chaise longue 'ʃez'lɔŋg, -'lɒŋg (Fr ʃɛːz'lõg)
Chalcedon 'kælsɪdən, -ˌdɑn, -ˌdɒn
chalcedony kæl'sɛdṇɪ, 'kælsəˌdonɪ
chalcid 'kælsɪd
chalcography kæl'kɑgrəfɪ, -'kɒg-
chalcographic ˌkælkə'græfɪk |-al -ḷ
chalcopyrite ˌkælkə'paɪraɪt, -'pɪr-
Chaldaic kæl'deˑɪk |-al -ḷ
Chaldea kæl'diə |-n -n |-dee kæl'di, 'kældi
chaldron 'tʃɔldrən
chalet ʃæ'le, 'ʃælɪ (Fr ʃɑ'lɛ)
Chalfont Bucks 'tʃælfənt, loc. 'tʃɑfənt
chalice 'tʃælɪs |-s -ɪz |-d -t
chalk tʃɔk |chalked tʃɔkt
challenge 'tʃælɪndʒ, -əndʒ |-s -ɪz |-d -d
challis, -llie 'ʃælɪ
Chalmers 'tʃælmɚz, 'tʃɑm-, 'tʃɒm-; ES -əz;
|-'s -ɪz
cham dial. 'I am' tʃæm
cham 'khan' kæm
chamade ʃə'mɑd
chamber 'tʃembɚ; ES -bə(r; |-ed -d |-ing
'tʃembərɪŋ, 'tʃembrɪŋ
chamberer 'tʃembərɚ; ES 'tʃembərə(r
chamberlain 'tʃembɚlɪn; ES 'tʃembə-
Chamberlain, -lin 'tʃembɚlɪn; ES 'tʃembə-
chambermaid 'tʃembɚˌmed; ES 'tʃembə-
chambray 'ʃæmbre
chameleon kə'milɪən, -ljən
chamfer 'tʃæmfɚ; ES 'tʃæmfə(r; |-ed -d |-ing
'tʃæmfərɪŋ, 'tʃæmfrɪŋ
chamois, -mmy 'ʃæmɪ
chamomile 'kæməˌmaɪl
Chamonix, -mouny 'ʃæmənɪ (Fr ʃamu'ni)
champ tʃæmp |champed tʃæmpt
champac, -pak 'tʃæmpæk, 'tʃʌmpʌk
champagne ʃæm'pen |-d -d
Champagne ʃæm'pen (Fr ʃɑ̃'paɲ)
champaign ʃæm'pen, 'tʃæmpen
Champaign Ill ʃæm'pen
champerty 'tʃæmpɚtɪ; ES 'tʃæmpətɪ
champion, C- 'tʃæmpɪən |-ed -d |-ship -ˌʃɪp
Champlain ʃæm'plen
Champlin 'tʃæmplɪn

Words below in which a *before* r (farm) *is sounded* ɑ *are often pronounced in* E *with* a (faːm)

Champs Élysées *Fr* ʃɑ̃zeliˈze

chance tʃæns; E+tʃɑns, tʃɑns; |-s -ɪz |-d -t

chancel ˈtʃæns‖; E+ˈtʃɑn-, ˈtʃɑn-

chancellery ˈtʃænsələrɪ, -slərɪ; E+ˈtʃɑn-, ˈtʃɑn-

chancellor, C- ˈtʃænsələ, -slə; ES -lə(r, E+ ˈtʃɑn-, ˈtʃɑn-; |-ship -ˌʃɪp

Chancellorsville ˈtʃænsələzˌvɪl, -slə z-; ES -ləz-, E+ˈtʃɑn-, ˈtʃɑn-

chancery ˈtʃænsərɪ; E+ˈtʃɑn-, ˈtʃɑn-

chancre ˈʃæŋkə; ES ˈʃæŋkə(r

chancy, -cey ˈtʃænsɪ; E+ˈtʃɑn-, ˈtʃɑn-

chandelier ˌʃænd‖ˈɪr; ES -ˈɪə(r, S+-ˈɛə(r

chandler, C- ˈtʃændlə; ES -dlə(r, E+ˈtʃɑn-, ˈtʃɑn-

Chandos ˈtʃændɑs, ˈʃæn-; ES+-dɒs; |-'s -ɪz

Chandragupta ˌtʃʌndrəˈguptə

Changchun ˈtʃɑŋˈtʃʊn

change tʃendʒ |changes ˈtʃendʒɪz |-d -d

changeability ˌtʃendʒəˈbɪlətɪ

changeable ˈtʃendʒəb‖ |-bly -blɪ

changeling ˈtʃendʒlɪŋ

Chang Kai-shek ˈtʃɑŋˈkaɪˈʃɛk, ˈtʃæŋ-

channel ˈtʃæn‖ |channeled ˈtʃæn‖d

Channing ˈtʃænɪŋ

chanson ˈʃænsən, -san, -sɒn (*Fr* ʃɑ̃ˈsõ)

chant tʃænt; E+tʃɑnt, tʃɑnt; |-ed -ɪd

chantey, -ty ˈʃæntɪ, ˈtʃæn-; E+-an-, -ɑn-

chanticleer ˈtʃæntɪˌklɪr; ES -ˌklɪə(r, S+-ˌklɛə(r

Chantilly *Va, France* ʃænˈtɪlɪ (*Fr* ʃɑ̃tiˈji)

chantress ˈtʃæntrɪs; E+ˈtʃɑnt-, ˈtʃɑnt-; |-es -ɪz

chantry, C- ˈtʃæntrɪ; E+ˈtʃɑnt-, ˈtʃɑnt-

Chanute tʃəˈnut, ʃəˈnut

chaos ˈkeas; ES+ˈkeɒs; |-es -ɪz

chaotic keˈɑtɪk; ES+-ˈɒtɪk; |-al -‖ |-ally -‖ɪ, -ɪklɪ

chap *'fellow'*, *'crack'* tʃæp |chapped tʃæpt

chap *'jaw'* tʃæp—*cf* chop *'jaw'*

chaparajos ˌtʃɑpəˈrɑhos |-rejos -ˈrehos

chaparral ˌtʃæpəˈræl

chaparreras, -pareras ˌtʃɑpəˈreras

chapbook ˈtʃæpˌbʊk

chape tʃep

chapeau ʃæˈpo |-x, -s -z (*Fr* ʃaˈpo)

chapel, C- ˈtʃæp‖ |-ed -d |-ing ˈtʃæp‖ɪŋ, -plɪŋ

chaperajos ˌtʃʃæpəˈrɑhos

chaperon, -one ˈʃæpəˌron |-ed -d |-age -ɪdʒ

chapfallen ˈtʃæpˌfɔlən, -ˌfɔln—*cf* chopfallen

chaplain ˈtʃæplɪn |-cy -sɪ |-ship -ˌʃɪp

chaplet ˈtʃæplɪt |-ed -ɪd

Chaplin ˈtʃæplɪn

Chapman, c- ˈtʃæpmən |-men -mən

Chappell, -pple ˈtʃæp‖

chappie, -ppy ˈtʃæpɪ

chaptalize ˈʃæpt‖ˌaɪz |-s -ɪz |-d -d

chapter ˈtʃæptə; ES -tə(r; |-ed -d |-ing ˈtʃæptərɪŋ, -trɪŋ

Chapultepec tʃəˈpʌltəˌpɛk (*Sp* tʃaˌpulteˈpɛk)

char tʃɑr; ES tʃɑ:(r; |-red -d

charabanc ˈʃærəˌbæŋk, -ˌbæŋ (*Fr* ʃaraˈbɑ̃)

character ˈkærɪktə, -ək-; ES -tə(r; |-ed -d |-ing -tərɪŋ, -trɪŋ

characteristic ˌkærɪktəˈrɪstɪk, ˌkærək- |-al -‖ |-ally -‖ɪ, -ɪklɪ

characterization ˌkærɪktrəˈzeʃən, -ək-, -tərə-, -aɪˈz-

characterize ˈkærɪktəˌraɪz, ˈkærək- |-s -ɪz |-d -d

charactery ˈkærɪktərɪ, -ək-, -trɪ

charade ʃəˈred

charcoal ˈtʃɑrˌkol; ES ˈtʃɑ:ˌkol; |-ed -d

chard tʃɑrd; ES tʃɑ:d

Chardon ˈʃɑrdn̩; ES ˈʃɑ:dn̩

chare tʃɛr, tʃær; E tʃɛə(r, ES tʃæə(r; |-d -d

charge tʃɑrdʒ; ES tʃɑ:dʒ; |-s -ɪz |-d -d |-able -əb‖ |-bly -blɪ

chargé d'affaires ʃɑrˈʒedæˈfɛr, -ˈfær; E ʃɑːˈʒedæˈfɛə(r, ES -ˈfæə(r; |*pl* chargés -ˈʒez- (*Fr* ʃarʒedaˈfɛːr)

charily ˈtʃɛrəlɪ, ˈtʃær-, ˈtʃer-, -ɪlɪ; S ˈtʃær-, ˈtʃer-

chariness ˈtʃɛrɪnɪs, ˈtʃær-, ˈtʃer-; S ˈtʃær-, ˈtʃer-

Charing Cross ˈtʃærɪŋˈkrɔs, ˈtʃɛr-, -ˈkrɒs; S ˈtʃærɪŋ-; (ˈCharing ˌCross ˈRoad)

chariot ˈtʃærɪət |-ed -ɪd

charioteer ˌtʃærɪəˈtɪr; ES -ˈɪə(r, S+-ˈɛə(r

charitable ˈtʃærətəb‖ |-bly -blɪ

Chariton ˈʃɛrətn̩, ˈʃær-; S ˈʃær-

charity ˈtʃærətɪ

charivari ʃəˌrɪvəˈri, ˌʃɪvəˈri, ˌʃɑrɪˈvɑri—*In* ˌʃɪvəˈri *the first* r *is lost by dissimilation* (*§121). Cf* shivaree

charkha, -ka ˈtʃʌrkə; ES ˈtʃʌːkə

|full fʊl |tooth tuθ |further ˈfɝðə; ES ˈfɝ̃ðə |custom ˈkʌstəm |while hwaɪl |how haʊ |toy tɔɪ
|using ˈjuzɪŋ |fuse fjuz, fɪuz |dish dɪʃ |vision ˈvɪʒən |Eden ˈidn̩ |cradle ˈkred‖ |keep 'em ˈkipm̩

Words below in which a *before* r (farm) *is sounded* ɑ *are often pronounced in* E *with* a (fa:m)

charlatan 'ʃɑrlətn̩; ES 'ʃɑ:lə-; |-ism -ˌɪzəm |-ry -rɪ

charlatanic ˌʃɑrlə'tænɪk; ES ˌʃɑ:lə-; |-al -l̩ |-ally -l̩ɪ, -ɪklɪ

Charlecote 'tʃɑrlkət, -kot; ES 'tʃɑ:l-

Charlemagne 'ʃɑrləˌmen; ES 'ʃɑ:lə-; (Fr ʃarlə'maɲ)

Charleroi Pa ˌʃɑrlə'rɔɪ, 'ʃɑrləˌrɔɪ; ES ˌʃɑ:l-, 'ʃɑ:l-; |Belg -roi, -roy Fr ʃarlə'rwa

Charles tʃɑrlz; ES tʃɑ:lz; |-'s -ɪz |-ton -tən |-town -ˌtaʊn

Charley, -ie 'tʃɑrlɪ; ES 'tʃɑ:lɪ

charlock 'tʃɑrlək; ES 'tʃɑ:lək

Charlotte fem. name 'ʃɑrlət, US places 'ʃɑrlət, ʃɚ'lɑt; ES 'ʃɑ:l-, ʃə-, -'lɒt

Charlottenburg ʃɑr'lɑtn̩ˌbɝg; ES ʃɑ'lɑtn̩ˌbɝg, -'lɒt-, -ˌbɜg (Ger ʃar'lɒtənˌburk)

charlotte russe 'ʃɑrlət'rus, -'ruʃ; ES 'ʃɑ:lət-

Charlottesville 'ʃɑrlətsˌvɪl; ES 'ʃɑ:l-, S+-vl̩

Charlton 'tʃɑrltən; ES 'tʃɑ:l-

charm tʃɑrm; ES tʃɑ:m; |-ed -d |-edly -ɪdlɪ

charmeuse ʃɑr'mɝz; ES ʃɑ:-; (Fr ʃar'mø:z)

Charmian 'tʃɑrmɪən, 'kɑrm-; ES 'tʃɑ:m-, 'kɑ:m-

charnel 'tʃɑrnl̩; ES 'tʃɑ:nl̩

Charon 'kɛrən, 'kærən, 'kerən; S 'kærən, 'kerən

charpoy, -pai 'tʃɑr'pɔɪ, -'paɪ; ES 'tʃɑ:-

chart tʃɑrt; ES tʃɑ:t; |-ed -ɪd

charter 'tʃɑrtɚ; ES 'tʃɑ:tə(r; |-ed -d |-ing -tərɪŋ, -trɪŋ

Charterhouse, c- 'tʃɑrtɚˌhaʊs; ES 'tʃɑ:tə-

chartograph 'kɑrtəˌgræf; ES 'kɑ:tə-, E+ -ˌgrɑf, -ˌgrɒf

chartographer kɑr'tɑgrəfɚ, -'tɒg-; ES kɑ-, -fə(r; |-phy -fɪ

chartographic ˌkɑrtə'græfɪk; ES ˌkɑ:tə-

Chartres 'ʃɑrtrə, ʃɑrt; ES 'ʃɑ:t-, ʃɑ:t; (Fr ʃartr̩)

chartreuse, C- ʃɑr'trɝz; ES ʃɑ:-; (Fr ʃar'trø:z)

chartulary 'kɑrtʃʊˌlɛrɪ; ES 'kɑ:tʃʊˌlɛrɪ

charwoman 'tʃɑrˌwʊmən, -ˌwu-; ES 'tʃɑ:-; |-men -ˌwɪmɪn, -ən

chary 'tʃɛrɪ, 'tʃɛ:rɪ, 'tʃærɪ, 'tʃɛrɪ; S 'tʃærɪ, 'tʃɛrɪ—Some speakers distinguish chary from cherry by a longer ɛ.

Charybdis kə'rɪbdɪs |-'s -ɪz |-dian -dɪən

chase, C- tʃes |chases 'tʃesɪz |chased tʃest

chasm 'kæzəm, much less freq. 'kæzm̩ |-ed -d

chasmal 'kæzml̩ |chasmic 'kæzmɪk

chassé ʃæ'se |-d -d—cf sashay

chasseur ʃæ'sɝ; ES -'sɜ(r, -'sɜ-; (Fr ʃa'sœ:r)

chassis 'ʃæsɪ, 'ʃæsɪs |pl chassis 'ʃæsɪz

chaste tʃest

chasten 'tʃesn̩ |-ed -d |-ing 'tʃesn̩ɪŋ, -snɪŋ

chastise tʃæs'taɪz |-s -ɪz |-d -d

chastisement 'tʃæstɪzmənt, tʃæs'taɪzmənt

chastity 'tʃæstətɪ

chasuble 'tʃæzjʊbl̩, 'tʃæs-

chat tʃæt |chatted 'tʃætɪd

château ʃæ'to |pl -teaux -'toz (Fr ʃɑ'to)

Chateaubriand ʃæ'tobrɪənd, -ˌɑnd (Fr ʃɑtobri'ɑ̃)

Château-Thierry ʃæ'totiə'ri (Fr ʃɑtotje'ri)

chatelain 'ʃætl̩ˌen (Fr ʃɑ'tlɛ̃)

chatelaine 'ʃætl̩ˌen (Fr ʃɑ'tlɛn)

Chatham 'tʃætəm, US places+'tʃæt·hæm, -æm

Chatillon Shak. ʃæ'tɪljən (Fr ʃɑti'jõ)

Chattahoochee ˌtʃætə'hutʃɪ

Chattanooga ˌtʃætn̩'ugə, ˌtʃætə'nugə

chattel 'tʃætl̩ |-ed -d

chatterbox 'tʃætɚˌbɑks; ES 'tʃætəˌbɑks, -ˌbɒks; |-es -ɪz

Chatterton 'tʃætɚtən; ES 'tʃætətən

Chattooga tʃə'tugə

Chaucer 'tʃɔsɚ; ES 'tʃɔsə(r; |-ism -ˌɪzəm

Chaucerian tʃɔ'sɪrɪən

chauffer 'stove' 'tʃɔfɚ; ES 'tʃɔfə(r

chauffeur 'ʃofɚ, ʃo'fɝ; ES 'ʃofə(r, ʃo'fɜ(r, -'fɜ-; |-ed -d

chaulmoogra, -mugra tʃɔl'mugrə

Chauncey 'tʃɔnsɪ, 'tʃɒnsɪ, 'tʃɑnsɪ, 'tʃænsɪ

chaunt tʃɔnt, tʃɒnt, tʃɑnt |-ed -ɪd

Chautauqua, c- ʃə'tɔkwə |-n -n

chauvinism 'ʃovɪnˌɪzəm |-ist -ɪst

chauvinistic ˌʃovɪ'nɪstɪk |-al -l̩ |-ally -l̩ɪ, -ɪklɪ

chaw tʃɔ |chawed tʃɔd

Chazy 'ʃezɪ, ʃe'zi ('Chazy's 'Landing)

cheap tʃip |-ed -t

cheapen 'tʃipən |-ed -d |-ing 'tʃipənɪŋ, -pnɪŋ

Cheapside 'tʃipˌsaɪd, -'saɪd

cheat, C- tʃit |cheated 'tʃitɪd

Cheatham 'tʃitəm—cf Cheetham, Chetham

Cheboygan ʃɪ'bɔɪgən

check tʃɛk |checked tʃɛkt |-book -ˌbʊk

---

checker 'tʃɛkɚ; ES 'tʃɛkə(r; |-ed -d |-ing
'tʃɛkərɪŋ, 'tʃɛkrɪŋ
checkerboard 'tʃɛkɚˌbord, -ˌbɔrd; ES 'tʃɛkə-
ˌboəd, E+-ˌbɔəd; |-ed -ɪd
checkmate 'tʃɛkˌmet |-mated -ˌmetɪd
checkoff 'tʃɛkˌɔf, -ˌɒf
checkrein 'tʃɛkˌren
checkroom 'tʃɛkˌrum, -ˌrʊm
checkrow 'tʃɛkˌro |-ed -d
checkstrap 'tʃɛkˌstræp
Cheddar 'tʃɛdɚ; ES 'tʃɛdə(r
cheek tʃik |cheeked tʃikt
cheekbone 'tʃikˌbon, -'bon
Cheeke tʃik
cheekily 'tʃikḷɪ, -ɪlɪ
cheep tʃip |cheeped tʃipt
cheer tʃɪr; ES tʃɪə(r, S+tʃɛə(r; |-ed -d
cheerful 'tʃɪrfəl; ES 'tʃɪə-, S+'tʃɛə-; |-ly -ɪ
cheerily 'tʃɪrəlɪ, -ɪlɪ
cheerio 'tʃɪrɪˌo
cheerly 'tʃɪrlɪ; ES 'tʃɪəlɪ, S+'tʃɛəlɪ
cheese tʃiz |cheeses 'tʃizɪz |cheesed tʃizd
cheesecake 'tʃizˌkek
cheesecloth 'tʃizˌklɔθ, -ˌklɒθ |-ths -ðz, -θs
cheesemonger 'tʃizˌmʌŋgɚ; ES -ˌmʌŋgə(r
cheeseparing 'tʃizˌpɛrɪŋ, -ˌpærɪŋ; S -ˌpærɪŋ
cheetah 'tʃitə
Cheetham 'tʃitəm—cf Cheatham
chef ʃɛf
chef-d'oeuvre ʃe'dœvrə (Fr ʃɛ'dœ:vr)
Chefoo 'tʃi'fu
Cheke tʃik
Chekov 'tʃɛkɔf, -kɒf
chela 'claw' 'kilə |chelae 'kili
chela 'disciple' 'tʃelɑ
chela measure 'kelɑ
Chelan ʃə'læn
Chelmsford Mass 'tʃɛmzfɚd, 'tʃɛlmz-, Engd
'tʃɛlms-, 'tʃɛms-; ES -fəd
Chelonia kə'lonɪə |chelonian kə'lonɪən
Chelsea 'tʃɛlsɪ
Cheltenham 'tʃɛltnəm, 'tʃɛltṇəm
chemic 'kɛmɪk |-al -ḷ |-ally -ḷɪ, -ɪklɪ
chemise ʃə'miz |-s -ɪz |-sette ˌʃɛmɪ'zɛt
chemist 'kɛmɪst |-ry -rɪ
Chemnitz 'kɛmnɪts |-'s -ɪz
Chemosh 'kimɑʃ, -mɒʃ |-'s -ɪz
chemotherapy ˌkɛmo'θɛrəpɪ
Chemung ʃɪ'mʌŋ

chemurgic kɛm'ɝdʒɪk; ES -'ɜdʒ-, -'ɝdʒ-;
|-al -ḷ
chemurgy 'kɛmɝdʒɪ; ES -ɜdʒɪ, -ɝdʒɪ
Chenango ʃɪ'næŋgo
chenille ʃə'nil
Cheops 'kiɑps; ES+'kiɒps |-'s -ɪz
Chepstow 'tʃɛpsto
cheque tʃɛk |-r -ɚ; ES -ə(r; |-red -ɚd; ES -əd;
|-ring 'tʃɛkərɪŋ, 'tʃɛkrɪŋ
chequerboard 'tʃɛkɚˌbord, -ˌbɔrd; ES 'tʃɛkə-
ˌboəd, E+-ˌbɔəd; |-ed -ɪd
Cheraw 'tʃirɔ, tʃɪ'rɔ
Cherbourg 'ʃɛrburg; ES 'ʃɛəbʊəg; (Fr
ʃɛr'bu:r)
cherish 'tʃɛrɪʃ |-es -ɪz |-ed -t
Cherith 'kɪrɪθ, 'tʃɪrɪθ
Cherokee 'tʃɛrəˌki, ˌtʃɛrə'ki
cheroot ʃə'rut
cherry 'tʃɛrɪ |cherried 'tʃɛrɪd
Chersonese, c- 'kɝsəˌniz; ES 'kɜsə-, 'kɝsə-
chert tʃɝt; ES tʃɜt, tʃɝt
cherub 'tʃɛrəb |-s -z |-im -ɪm, 'tʃɛrjʊbɪm
|-in -ɪn, -jʊbɪn
cherubic tʃə'rubɪk, -'rɪubɪk |-al -ḷ |-ally -ḷɪ,
-ɪklɪ
chervonets tʃɛr'vɒnɪts |pl chervontsi tʃɛr-
'vɒntsi
Cherwell 'tʃɑrwəl, -wɛl; ES 'tʃɑ:-
Chesaning 'tʃɛsṇɪŋ
Chesapeake tʃɛs'pik, ˌtʃɛsə'pik ('Chesaˌpeake
'Bay)
Chesham 'tʃɛʃəm, less freq. 'tʃɛsəm—'tʃɛʃəm
is a sp. pron. Cf Bentham
Cheshire 'tʃɛʃɪr, 'tʃɛʃɚ; ES 'tʃɛʃɪə(r, -ʃə(r
chess tʃɛs |chesses 'tʃɛsɪz
chessboard 'tʃɛsˌbord, -ˌbɔrd; ES -ˌboəd, E+
-ˌbɔəd
chessman 'tʃɛsˌmæn, -mən |-men -ˌmɛn, -mən
chest tʃɛst |chested 'tʃɛstɪd
Chester, c- 'tʃɛstɚ; ES 'tʃɛstə(r
Chesterfield 'tʃɛstɚˌfild; ES 'tʃɛstə-
Chesterton 'tʃɛstɚtən; ES 'tʃɛstətən, -tṇ
Chester White 'tʃɛstɚ'hwaɪt; ES 'tʃɛstə-
chestnut 'tʃɛsnət, -ˌnʌt
chestnut-roan 'tʃɛsnət'ron ('chestnutˌroan
'mare)
chetah 'tʃitə
Chetham 'tʃɛtəm—cf Cheatham
cheval-de-frise ʃə'vældə'friz |pl -vaux- -'vo-

cheval-glass ʃəˈvælˌglæs; E+-ˌglas, -ˌglas;
|-es -ɪz

chevalier ˌʃevəˈlɪr; ES -ˈlɪə(r, S+-ˈlɛə(r

Cheviot *Hills, sheep* ˈtʃevɪət, ˈtʃiv-; *O vil.*
ˈʃɪvɪət, ˈʃev-; |Ch-, ch- *cloth* ˈʃevɪət,
ˈtʃevɪət

Chevrolet ˌʃevrəˈle

chevron ˈʃevrən |-ed -d

chevy, C- ˈtʃevɪ |chevied ˈtʃevɪd

chew, C- tʃu, tʃɪu |-ed -d

chewink tʃɪˈwɪŋk

Cheyenne ʃaɪˈen

Cheyne ˈtʃenɪ, ˈtʃen

chi *Gk letter* kaɪ

Chian ˈkaɪən

Chiang Kai-shek tʃɪˈaŋˈkaɪˈʃɛk, ˈtʃʃaŋ-

Chianti, c- kɪˈæntɪ (*It* ˈkjanti)

chiaroscuro kɪˌarəˈskjuro, -ˈskɪuro (*It* ˌkja:-
roˈsku:ro)

chibouk, -que tʃɪˈbuk, -ˈbʊk

chic ʃik, ʃɪk

Chicago ʃəˈkago, -ˈkɒgo, -ˈkɔgo, ʃɪ-, -ə |-ed -d
|-goan -gəwən

chicane ʃɪˈken |-caned -ˈkend |-canery
-ˈkenərɪ

Chichen Itzá tʃiˈtʃɛnitˈsa

Chichester ˈtʃɪtʃɪstɚ; ES ˈtʃɪtʃɪstə(r

chick tʃɪk

chickadee ˈtʃɪkəˌdi, ˌtʃɪkəˈdi

Chickahominy ˌtʃɪkəˈhamənɪ; ES+-ˈhɒm-

Chickamauga ˌtʃɪkəˈmɔgə (ˈChickaˌmauga
ˈCreek)

chickaree ˈtʃɪkəˌri

Chickasaw ˈtʃɪkaˌsɔ

Chickasawhay ˌtʃɪkəˈsɔwe |-wha -wə

Chickasha ˈtʃɪkəˌʃe

chicken ˈtʃɪkɪn, -ən

chickenhearted ˈtʃɪkɪnˈhartɪd, -ən-; ES
-ˈha:tɪd, E+-ˈha:tɪd; (ˈchickenˌhearted
ˈhero)

chicken-pox ˈtʃɪkɪnˌpaks, -ən-; ES+-ˌpɒks

Chickering ˈtʃɪkərɪŋ, ˈtʃɪkrɪŋ

chickweed ˈtʃɪkˌwid

chicle ˈtʃɪkl̩, ˈtʃikl̩ (*Sp* ˈtʃikle)

Chico ˈtʃiko

Chicopee ˈtʃɪkəˌpi, -pɪ

chicory ˈtʃɪkərɪ, ˈtʃɪkrɪ

chicot ˈtʃiko (*Fr* ʃiˈko)

Chicot ˈʃiko

chide tʃaɪd |*past* chid tʃɪd *or* chided ˈtʃaɪdɪd
|*pptc* chid tʃɪd *or* chidden ˈtʃɪdn̩ *or* chided
ˈtʃaɪdɪd

Chidley ˈtʃɪdlɪ

chief tʃif |-tain -tɪn |-taincy -tɪnsɪ

chield tʃild |chiel tʃil

chiffon ʃɪˈfan, -ˈfɒn, ˈʃɪfən

chiffonier ˌʃɪfəˈnɪr; ES -ˈnɪə(r, S+-ˈnɛə(r,
-ˈnjɛə(r

chigger ˈtʃɪgɚ; ES ˈtʃɪgə(r

chignon ˈʃinjan, -jɒn (*Fr* ʃiˈɲõ)

chigoe ˈtʃɪgo

Chihuahua tʃɪˈwawa, -ˈwɒwɒ

chilblain ˈtʃɪlˌblen |-ed -d |-s -z

child, C-(e) tʃaɪld |-ed -ɪd |*pl see* children

childbearing ˈtʃaɪldˌbɛrɪŋ, -ˌbærɪŋ; S -ˌbær-

childbirth ˈtʃaɪldˌbɝθ; ES -ˌbɝθ, -ˌbɝθ |-ths
-θs

Childermas ˈtʃɪldɚməs; ES ˈtʃɪldə-

childhood ˈtʃaɪldˌhʊd

childlike ˈtʃaɪldˌlaɪk

children ˈtʃɪldrən, -drɪn, -dɚn; ES -drən,
-drɪn, -dən

Childress ˈtʃaɪldrɪs |-'s -ɪz

Chile ˈtʃɪlɪ |-an -ən |-lian -lɪən (*Sp* ˈtʃile)

Chili *US* ˈtʃɪlɪ, *NY* ˈtʃaɪlaɪ

chili, -le ˈtʃɪlɪ

Chilkat ˈtʃɪlkæt

Chilkoot ˈtʃɪlkut

chill tʃɪl |chilled tʃɪld

chilli ˈtʃɪlɪ

Chillicothe ˌtʃɪləˈkaθɪ; ES+-ˈkɒθɪ; (ˈChilli-
ˌcothe ˈRoad)

Chillingworth ˈtʃɪlɪŋwɚθ, -ˌwɝθ; ES -wəθ,
-ˌwɝθ, -ˌwɝθ

Chillon ʃəˈlan, -ˈlɒn, ˈʃɪlən (*Fr* ʃiˈjõ)

chilly ˈtʃɪlɪ

Chiltern ˈtʃɪltɚn; ES ˈtʃɪltən

chimaera kəˈmɪrə, kaɪ-

chimb tʃaɪm

Chimborazo ˌtʃɪmbəˈrezo, -ˈrazo (*Am Sp*
ˌtʃimboˈraso) |+ ʃ-

chime tʃaɪm |chimed tʃaɪmd

chimera kəˈmɪrə, kaɪˈmɪrə

chimerical kəˈmɪrɪkl̩, kaɪ- |-ly -ɪ, -ɪklɪ

chimney ˈtʃɪmnɪ |chimneyed ˈtʃɪmnɪd

chimpanzee ˌtʃɪmpænˈzi, tʃɪmˈpænzɪ, ˌʃ-, ʃ-

chin tʃɪn |chinned tʃɪnd

China, c- ˈtʃaɪnə |-man, -men -mən

Key: See in full §§3–47. bee bi |pity ˈpɪtɪ (§6) |rate ret |yet jɛt |sang sæŋ |angry ˈæŋ·grɪ
|bath bæθ; E baθ (§10) |ah ɑ |far far |watch watʃ, wɒtʃ (§12) |jaw dʒɔ |gorge gɔrdʒ |go go

Those words below in which the ɑ *sound is spelt* o *are often pronounced with* ɒ *in E and S*

chinaware 'tʃaɪnə‚wɛr, -‚wær; E -‚wɛə(r, ES
-‚wæə(r
chincapin 'tʃɪŋkəpɪn
chinch 'tʃɪntʃ |-es -ɪz
chinchilla, C- tʃɪn'tʃɪlə
chincough 'tʃɪn‚kɔf, -‚kɒf
chine tʃaɪn |chined tʃaɪnd
Chinee tʃaɪ'ni
Chinese tʃaɪ'niz |-'s -ɪz ('Chi‚nese 'cabbage)
chink tʃɪŋk |chinked tʃɪŋkt
chinkapin 'tʃɪŋkəpɪn
Chino-Japanese 'tʃaɪno‚dʒæpə'niz
Chinook, c- tʃɪ'nuk, -'nʊk
chinquapin 'tʃɪŋkəpɪn
chinse, chintze *naut.* tʃɪnts |-d -t
chintz tʃɪnts |chintzes 'tʃɪntsɪz
Chios 'kaɪɑs, -ɒs
chip tʃɪp |chipped tʃɪpt
Chipewayan ‚tʃɪpə'weən
Chipewyan ‚tʃɪpə'waɪən
chipmunk 'tʃɪpmʌŋk
Chippawa 'tʃɪpə‚wɑ, -‚wɒ, -‚we, -wə
Chippendale 'tʃɪpən‚del
Chippenham 'tʃɪpənəm
chipper 'tʃɪpɚ; ES 'tʃɪpə(r; |-ed -d |-ing
'tʃɪpərɪŋ, 'tʃɪprɪŋ
Chippewa 'tʃɪpə‚wɑ, -‚wɒ, -‚we, -wə |-way
-‚we
chippy 'tʃɪpɪ
chirk tʃɝk; ES tʃɜk, tʃɝk; |-ed -t
chirm, charm tʃɝm, tʃɑrm; ES tʃɜm, tʃɝm,
tʃɑ:m
chirograph 'kaɪrə‚græf; E+-‚graf, -‚grɑf
chirographer kaɪ'rɑgrəfɚ, -'rɒg-; ES -fə(r;
|-phy -fɪ
chirographic ‚kaɪrə'græfɪk |-al -l̩
Chiron 'kaɪrɑn, -rɒn, -rən
chiropody kaɪ'rɑpədɪ |-dist -dɪst
chiropracter 'kaɪrə‚præktɚ; ES -‚præktə(r
chiropractic ‚kaɪrə'præktɪk
chirp tʃɝp; ES tʃɜp, tʃɝp; |-ed -t
chirr tʃɝ; ES tʃɜ(r, tʃɝ; |-ed -d
chirrup 'tʃɪrəp, 'tʃɝəp; ES+'tʃɜr-, 'tʃʌr-
chirurgeon kaɪ'rɝdʒən; ES -'rɜdʒ-, -'rɝdʒ-
chirurgery kaɪ'rɝdʒərɪ; ES -'rɜdʒ-, -'rɝdʒ-
chirurgic kaɪ'rɝdʒɪk; ES -'rɜdʒ-, -'rɝdʒ-
Chisago ‚tʃɪsə'go
chisel 'tʃɪzl̩ |-ed -d |-ing 'tʃɪzlɪŋ, -zl̩ɪŋ

Chisholm 'tʃɪzəm |Chisolm 'tʃɪzəm
Chiswick 'tʃɪzɪk
chit tʃɪt |chitted 'tʃɪtɪd
chitchat 'tʃɪt‚tʃæt |-ty -ɪ
chiton 'kaɪtn̩, -tɑn, -tɒn
Chittenden 'tʃɪtn̩dən
chitter 'tʃɪtɚ; ES 'tʃɪtə(r; |-ed -d
chitterling 'tʃɪtɚlɪŋ; ES 'tʃɪtə-
chivalric 'ʃɪv‚lrɪk, ʃɪ'vælrɪk |-rous 'ʃɪv‚rəs
chivalry 'ʃɪv‚lrɪ—*The historical pron.* 'tʃɪv‚lrɪ *is
now rare.*
chive tʃaɪv
Chivers 'tʃɪvɚz; ES 'tʃɪvəz
chlamys 'klemɪs, 'klæm- |-es -ɪz |-mydes
'klæmɪ‚diz
Chloë 'klo·ɪ
chloral 'klorəl, 'klɔr-; S 'klorəl
chlorate 'klorɪt, 'klɔr-, -ret; S 'klor-
chloric 'klorɪk, 'klɔr-; S 'klorɪk
chlorid 'klorɪd, 'klɔr-; S 'klorɪd; |-ride -raɪd,
-rɪd
chlorin 'klorɪn, 'klɔr-; S 'klorɪn; |-rine -rin,
-rɪn
chlorinate 'klorɪ‚net, 'klɔr-; S 'klor-; |-d -ɪd
chlorite 'kloraɪt, 'klɔr-; S 'kloraɪt
chloroform 'klorə‚fɔrm, 'klɔrə-; ES 'klorə-
‚fɔəm, E+'klɔrə-
chlorophyll, -yl 'klorə‚fɪl, 'klɔrə-; S 'klorə-
chloroplast 'klorə‚plæst, 'klɔrə-; S 'klorə-
chlorous 'klorəs, 'klɔr-; S 'klorəs
Choate tʃot
choate *adj* 'koet
chock tʃɑk |chocked tʃɑkt
chockablock 'tʃɑkə'blɑk
chock-full 'tʃɑk'ful
chocolate 'tʃɔklɪt, -kəlɪt, 'tʃɑk-, 'tʃɒk-; S
'tʃɑk-, 'tʃɒk-, 'tʃɔk-
Chocorua tʃə'kɔrəwə, ʃə-, -'kɑr, -'kɒr
Choctaw 'tʃɑktɔ
choice tʃɔɪs |choices 'tʃɔɪsɪz
choir kwaɪr; ES kwaɪə(r; |-ed -d
choirboy 'kwaɪr‚bɔɪ; ES 'kwaɪə-
choke tʃok |choked tʃokt; |*N Engd*+tʃõk (§46)
chokebore 'tʃok‚bor, -‚bɔr; ES -‚boə(r, E+
-‚bɔə(r; |-d -d
chokecherry 'tʃok‚tʃɛrɪ
chokedamp 'tʃok‚dæmp
choke-full 'tʃok'ful

Those words below in which the ɑ *sound is spelt* o *are often pronounced with* ɒ *in E and S*

chold *dial.* '*I would*' tʃʊd
choler 'kalə; ES 'kalə(r
cholera 'kalərə
choleric 'kalərık
cholesterol kə'lɛstə‚rol
Cholmley, -meley, -mondeley, Chomley 'tʃʌmlı
choose tʃuz |-s -ız |chose tʃoz |chosen 'tʃozn̩
chop '*jaw*' tʃɑp |-s -s = chap
chop *v* tʃɑp |chopped tʃɑpt
chopfallen 'tʃɑp‚fɔlən, -‚fɔln
Chopin 'ʃopæn, ʃo'pæn (*Fr* ʃo'pæ̃)
chopin, -e *measure* 'tʃɑpın
chopine, -in '*patten*' 'tʃɑpın, tʃo'pin
choppy 'tʃɑpı
chopstick 'tʃɑp‚stık
chop suey, sooy 'tʃɑp'suı, -'sıuı
choral *adj* 'korəl, 'kɔrəl; S 'korəl |-ly -ı
choral, -e *n* ko'ral, kɔ-, 'korəl, 'kɔr-; S ko'ral, 'korəl
Chorazin ko'rezın
chord kɔrd; ES kɔəd; |-ed -ıd
chore tʃor, tʃɔr; ES tʃoə(r, E+tʃɔə(r; |-d -d
chorea ko'riə, kɔ-; S ko'riə; |-l -l |-reic -'riık
choreography ‚korı'ɑgrəfı, ‚kɔ-, -'ng-; S ‚ko-
choric 'korık, 'kɔr-, 'kɑr-, 'kɒr-
chorister 'kɔrıstə, 'kɑr-, 'kɒr-; ES -tə(r
chorography ko'rɑgrəfı, kɔ-, -'rng-; S ko-
choroid 'korɔıd, 'kɔr-; S 'kor-
chortle 'tʃɔrtl̩; ES 'tʃɔətl̩; |-d -d |-ling -tl̩ıŋ, -tlıŋ
chorus 'korəs, 'kɔrəs; S 'korəs; |-es -ız |-ed -t
chose *past of* choose tʃoz
chose '*property*' ʃoz |choses 'ʃozız
chosen *pptc of* choose 'tʃozn̩
Chosen '*Korea*' 'tʃo'sɛn
chough tʃʌf
chouse tʃaʊs |-s -ız
chow tʃaʊ
chowchow 'tʃaʊ‚tʃaʊ
chowder 'tʃaʊdə; ES 'tʃaʊdə(r; |-ed -d |-ing 'tʃaʊdərıŋ, -drıŋ
chow mein 'tʃaʊ'men
Chrestien, -ét-, de Troyes *Fr* kretjæ̃də'trwa
chrestomathy krɛs'tɑməθı
chrism 'krızəm |-ed -d
chrismal 'krızml̩ |chrismale krız'meli
chrisom 'krızəm

crisscross 'krıs‚krɔs, -‚krɒs |-es -ız
Christ *Jesus* kraıst, *given name* krıst, krıs
Christabel 'krıstə‚bɛl
Christchurch 'kraıst‚tʃɜtʃ; ES -‚tʃɜtʃ, -‚tʃɝtʃ
christcross 'krıs‚krɔs, -‚krɒs |-es -ız
christen 'krısn̩ |-ed -d |-ing 'krısn̩ıŋ, -snıŋ
Christendom 'krısn̩dəm
Christian 'krıstʃən
Christiana ‚krıstı'ænə
Christiania ‚krıstı'anıə, krıs'tjanıə
Christianity ‚krıstʃı'ænətı, krıs'tʃænətı
Christianize 'krıstʃən‚aız |-s -ız |-d -d
Christie 'krıstı
Christina krıs'tinə |-tine -'tin ('Chrıs‚tina 'Day)
Christlike 'kraıst‚laık |Christly 'kraıstlı
Christmas 'krısməs |-es -ız |-ed -t
Christmastide 'krısməs‚taıd
Christopher 'krıstəfə; ES 'krıstəfə(r
Christy 'krıstı
chroma 'kromə
chromate 'kromet |-d -ıd
chromatic kro'mætık |-al -l̩ |-ally -l̩ı, -ıklı
chromatin 'kromətın
chrome krom |chromed kromd |chromic 'kromık
chromium 'kromıəm
chromo 'kromo
chromolithograph ‚kromo'lıθə‚græf; E+ -‚graf, -‚graf
chromosome 'kromə‚som
chromosphere 'kromə‚sfır; ES -‚sfıə(r, S+ -‚sfɛə(r
chronic 'krɑnık |-al -l̩ |-ally -l̩ı, -ıklı
chronicle 'krɑnık‚l̩ |-d -d |-ling -kl̩ıŋ, -klıŋ
chronicler 'krɑnıklə; ES -klə(r
Chronicles 'krɑnık‚l̩z
chronograph 'krɑnə‚græf; E+-‚graf, -‚graf
chronographic ‚krɑnə'græfık |-al -l̩ |-ally -l̩ı, -ıklı
chronologer krə'nɑlədʒə; ES -dʒə(r; |-gy -dʒı |-gist -dʒıst
chronologic ‚krɑnə'lɑdʒık |-al -l̩ |-ally -l̩ı, -ıklı
chronometer krə'nɑmətə; ES -'nɑmətə(r; |-try -trı
chronometric ‚krɑnə'mɛtrık |-al -l̩ |-ally -l̩ı, -ıklı

chronoscope ˈkrɑnəˌskop; ES+ˈkrɒn-	cicatrize ˈsɪkəˌtraɪz |-s -ɪz |-d -d
chronoscopic ˌkrɑnəˈskɑpɪk |-ally -lɪ, -ɪklɪ	cicely ˈsɪslɪ |-lies -lɪz
chronoscopy kroˈnɑskəpɪ; ES+-ˈnɒs-	Cicely ˈsɪslɪ
chrysalid ˈkrɪslɪd	Cicero ˈsɪsəˌro |-nian ˌsɪsəˈronɪən
chrysalis ˈkrɪslɪs |-es -ɪz |-lides krɪˈsæləˌdiz	cicerone ˌsɪsəˈronɪ, ˌtʃɪtʃəˈronɪ (It ˌtʃitʃeˈro:ne)
chrysanthemum krɪsˈænθəməm	
Chryseis kraɪˈsiɪs |-'s -ɪz	Cid sɪd (Sp θɪð)
Chrysler ˈkraɪslɚ; ES ˈkraɪslə(r	cider ˈsaɪdɚ; ES ˈsaɪdə(r
chrysoberyl ˈkrɪsəˌbɛrəl, -ɪl	cider-mill ˈsaɪdɚˌmɪl; ES ˈsaɪdə-
chrysolite ˈkrɪslˌaɪt	cider-press ˈsaɪdɚˌprɛs; ES ˈsaɪdə-; |-es -ɪz
chrysoprase ˈkrɪsəˌprez	cigar sɪˈgɑr; ES sɪˈgɑ:(r, E+-ˈgɑ:(r
Chrysostom ˈkrɪsəstəm, krɪsˈɑstəm, -ˈɒs-	cigarette, -ret ˌsɪgəˈrɛt, ˈsɪgəˌrɛt
chthonian ˈθonɪən |-onic ˈθɑnɪk; ES+ˈθɒn-	cilia pl ˈsɪlɪə |sg cilium ˈsɪlɪəm
chub tʃʌb |chubbed ˈtʃʌbɪd	ciliary ˈsɪlɪˌɛrɪ
chubby ˈtʃʌbɪ |chubbily ˈtʃʌbl̩ɪ, -ɪlɪ	ciliate ˈsɪlɪɪt, ˈsɪlɪˌet |-ated -ˌetɪd
chuck tʃʌk |chucked tʃʌkt	Cilicia səˈlɪʃə, -ʃɪə |-n -n
chuck-full ˈtʃʌkˈful	cilium ˈsɪlɪəm
chuckle ˈtʃʌkl̩ |-d -d |-ling ˈtʃʌklɪŋ, -kl̩ɪŋ	Cimabue ˌtʃɪməˈbuɪ (It ˌtʃimaˈbu:e)
chucklehead ˈtʃʌkl̩ˌhɛd	Cimarron ˈsɪməˌrɑn, ˌsɪməˈrɑn (Am Sp ˌsimaˈrrɒn)
chud dial. 'I would' tʃʊd	
chuff tʃʌf |chuffed tʃʌft	Cimber ˈsɪmbɚ; ES ˈsɪmbə(r
chug tʃʌg |chugged tʃʌgd	cimex ˈsaɪmɛks |cimices ˈsɪməˌsiz
chukker, -kar ˈtʃʌkɚ; ES ˈtʃʌkə(r	Cimmerian səˈmɪrɪən
Chulmleigh ˈtʃʌmlɪ	cinch sɪntʃ |cinches ˈsɪntʃɪz |cinched sɪntʃt
chum tʃʌm |chummed tʃʌmd |-my -ɪ	cinchona, C- sɪnˈkonə
chump tʃʌmp |chumped tʃʌmpt	Cincinnati ˌsɪnsəˈnætɪ, -ˈnætə; E+-ˈnɑt-;— -tɪ & -tə seem about equally frequent loc. and generally.
Chungking ˈtʃʊŋˈkɪŋ	
chunk tʃʌŋk |chunked tʃʌŋkt	Cincinnatus ˌsɪnsəˈnetəs |-'s -ɪz
church, C- tʃɝtʃ; ES tʃɜtʃ, tʃɝtʃ; |-es -ɪz |-ed-t	cincture ˈsɪŋktʃɚ; ES ˈsɪŋktʃə(r; |-d -d
Churchill ˈtʃɝtʃɪl, -əl; ES ˈtʃɜtʃ-, ˈtʃɝtʃ-	cinder ˈsɪndɚ; ES ˈsɪndə(r; |-ed -d |-ing ˈsɪndrɪŋ, ˈsɪndərɪŋ
churchman, C-, -men ˈtʃɝtʃmən; ES see church	
churchwarden ˈtʃɝtʃˈwɔrdn̩, -ˌwɔrdn̩; ES ˈtʃɝtʃˈwɔədn̩, ˈtʃɝtʃˈwɔədn̩, -ˌwɔədn̩	Cinderella ˌsɪndəˈrɛlə
	cinema ˈsɪnəmə
churchyard ˈtʃɝtʃˌjɑrd; ES ˈtʃɝtʃˌjɑ:d, ˈtʃɝtʃ-ˌjɑ:d, E+-ˌjɑ:d	cinematograph ˌsɪnəˈmætəˌgræf; E+-ˌgraf, -ˌgrɑf
churl tʃɝl; ES tʃɜl, tʃɝl; |-ed -d |-ish -ɪʃ	cinematography ˌsɪnəməˈtɑgrəfɪ, -ˈtɒg-
churn tʃɝn; ES tʃɜn, tʃɝn; |-ed -d	cineraria, C- ˌsɪnəˈrɛrɪə, -ˈrer-
churr tʃɝ; ES tʃɜ(r, tʃɝ; |-ed -d	cinerarium ˌsɪnəˈrɛrɪəm, -ˈrer- |pl -ria -rɪə
chute ʃut |chuted ˈʃutɪd	cinerary ˈsɪnəˌrɛrɪ
chutney, -nee ˈtʃʌtnɪ	Cingalese ˌsɪŋgəˈliz
Chuzzlewit ˈtʃʌzl̩ˌwɪt	Cinna ˈsɪnə
chyle kaɪl |chylous ˈkaɪləs	cinnabar ˈsɪnəˌbɑr; ES -ˌbɑ:(r, E+-ˌbɑ:(r
chyme kaɪm |chymous ˈkaɪməs	cinnamon ˈsɪnəmən |-ed -d
Cibber ˈsɪbɚ; ES ˈsɪbə(r	cinque sɪŋk
ciborium sɪˈborɪəm, -ˈbɔr-; S -ˈbor-; |-s -z |-ia -ɪə	cinquefoil ˈsɪŋkˌfɔɪl
cicada sɪˈkedə, -ˈkɑdə	Cinque Ports ˈsɪŋkˈports, -ˈpɔrts; ES -ˈpoəts, E+-ˈpɔəts
cicatrix ˈsɪkətrɪks |-es -ɪz |-trices ˌsɪkəˈtraɪsiz	C I O ˈsiˌaɪˈo

cion *'scion'* 'saɪən
Cipango sɪ'pæŋgo
cipher 'saɪfə; ES 'saɪfə(r; |-ed -d |-ing
'saɪfrɪŋ, 'saɪfərɪŋ
cipolin 'sɪpəlɪn
circa 's3ˑkə; ES 's3kə, 's3ˑkə
Circassia sə˞'kæʃɪə, -ʃə; ES sə-; |-n -n
Circe 's3ˑsɪ, -si; ES 's3s-, 's3ˑs-
circinate 's3ˑsn̩ˌet; ES 's3s-, 's3ˑs-
circle 's3ˑk|; ES 's3k|, 's3ˑk|; |-d -d |-ling
-klɪŋ, -k|ɪŋ
circlet 's3ˑklɪt; ES 's3k-, 's3ˑk-
circuit 's3ˑkɪt; ES 's3kɪt, 's3ˑkɪt; |-ed -ɪd
circuitous sə˞'kjuɪtəs, -'kɪu-; ES sə-; |-ty -tɪ
circular 's3ˑkjələ˞; ES 's3kjələ(r, 's3ˑkjələ(r
circularity ˌs3ˑkjə'lærətɪ; ES ˌs3k-, ˌs3ˑk-
circularize 's3ˑkjələˌraɪz; ES 's3k-, 's3ˑk-;
|-s -ɪz |-d -d
circulate 's3ˑkjəˌlet; ES 's3k-, 's3ˑk-; |-d -ɪd
circulation ˌs3ˑkjə'leʃən; ES ˌs3k-, ˌs3ˑk-
circulatory 's3ˑkjələˌtorɪ, -ˌtɔrɪ; ES 's3kjələ-
ˌtorɪ, 's3ˑk-, E+-ˌtɔrɪ
circumambient ˌs3ˑkəm'æmbɪənt; ES ˌs3k-,
ˌs3ˑk-
circumambulate ˌs3ˑkəm'æmbjəˌlet; ES ˌs3k-,
ˌs3ˑk-; |-d -ɪd
circumaviate ˌs3ˑkəm'evɪˌet; ES ˌs3k-, ˌs3ˑk-;
|-d -ɪd
circumcise 's3ˑkəmˌsaɪz; ES 's3k-, 's3ˑk-;
|-s -ɪz |-d -d
circumcision ˌs3ˑkəm'sɪʒən; ES ˌs3k-, ˌs3ˑk-
circumference sə˞'kʌmfərəns, sə'kʌm-; ES
sə-; |-s -ɪz—*In the 2d pron. ə˞ has become ə
by r-dissimilation (§121).*
circumferential sə˞ˌkʌmfə'rɛnʃəl; ES sə-;
|-ly -ɪ
circumflex 's3ˑkəmˌflɛks; ES 's3k-, 's3ˑk-;
|-es -ɪz |-ed -t
circumfluent sə˞'kʌmfluənt; ES sə-
circumfuse ˌs3ˑkəm'fjuz, -'fɪuz; ES ˌs3k-,
ˌs3ˑk-; |-s -ɪz |-d -d
circumjacence ˌs3ˑkəm'dʒesn̩s; ES ˌs3k-,
ˌs3ˑk-; |-cy -ɪ |-cent -sn̩t
circumlocution ˌs3ˑkəmlo'kjuʃən, -'kɪu-; ES
ˌs3k-, ˌs3ˑk-
circumlocutory ˌs3ˑkəm'lɑkjəˌtorɪ, -ˌtɔrɪ; ES
ˌs3k-, ˌs3ˑk-, -'lɒk-, E+-ˌtɔrɪ
circumnavigable ˌs3ˑkəm'nævəgəb|; ES ˌs3k-,
ˌs3ˑk-

circumnavigate ˌs3ˑkəm'nævəˌget; ES ˌs3k-,
ˌs3ˑk-; |-d -ɪd |-tor -ə˞; ES -ə(r
circumnavigation ˌs3ˑkəmˌnævə'geʃən; ES
ˌs3k-, ˌs3ˑk-
circumpolar ˌs3ˑkəm'polə˞; ES ˌs3kəm'polə(r,
ˌs3ˑkəm'polə(r
circumscribe ˌs3ˑkəm'skraɪb; ES ˌs3k-, ˌs3ˑk-;
|-d -d ('circumˌscribed 'halo)
circumscription ˌs3ˑkəm'skrɪpʃən; ES ˌs3k-,
ˌs3ˑk-
circumspect 's3ˑkəmˌspɛkt; ES 's3k-, 's3ˑk-
circumspection ˌs3ˑkəm'spɛkʃən; ES ˌs3k-,
ˌs3ˑk-; |-tive -tɪv
circumstance 's3ˑkəmˌstæns; ES 's3k-, 's3ˑk-;
|-s -ɪz |-d -t
circumstantial ˌs3ˑkəm'stænʃəl; ES ˌs3k-,
ˌs3ˑk-; |-ly -ɪ
circumstantiality ˌs3ˑkəmˌstænʃɪ'ælətɪ; ES
ˌs3k-, ˌs3ˑk-
circumstantiate ˌs3ˑkəm'stænʃɪˌet; ES ˌs3k-,
ˌs3ˑk-; |-d -ɪd
circumvallation ˌs3ˑkəmvæ'leʃən; ES ˌs3k-,
ˌs3ˑk-
circumvent ˌs3ˑkəm'vɛnt; ES ˌs3k-, ˌs3ˑk-;
|-ed -ɪd |-vention -'vɛnʃən
circus, C- 's3ˑkəs; ES 's3k-, 's3ˑk-; |-es -ɪz
Cirencester 'saɪrənˌsɛstə˞, 'sɪsɪtə˞, 'sɪzɪtə˞; ES
-tə(r—*All these prons. (including the -ə˞) are
used in Cirencester and vicinity. The BBC (in
1936) recommended* 'sɪsɪtər, 'saɪərənˌsɛstər.
cirque s3ˑk; ES s3k, s3ˑk
cirrhosis sɪ'rosɪs
cirro-cumulus ˌsɪro'kjumjələs, -'kɪum- |-li
-ˌlaɪ
cirrose 'sɪros
cirro-stratus ˌsɪro'stretəs |-ti -taɪ
cirrus 'sɪrəs |cirri 'sɪraɪ |cirrous 'sɪrəs
cisalpine, C- sɪs'ælpaɪn, -pɪn
cisco, C- 'sɪsko
cismontane, C- sɪs'mɑnten; ES+-'mɒn-
cispadane 'sɪspəˌden, sɪs'peden
cist sɪst, kɪst=kist
Cistercian sɪs't3ˑʃən; ES -'t3ʃ-, -'t3ˑʃ-
cistern 'sɪstə˞n; ES 'sɪstən
citable 'saɪtəb|
citadel, C- 'sɪtəd|, -ˌdɛl
citation saɪ'teʃən
cite saɪt |cited 'saɪtɪd |citeable 'saɪtəb|
cithara 'sɪθərə

Key: *See in full §§3–47.* bee bi |pity 'pɪtɪ (§6) |rate ret |yet jɛt |sang sæŋ |angry 'æŋˑgrɪ
|bath bæθ; E baθ (§10) |ah ɑ |far fɑr |watch wɑtʃ, wɒtʃ (§12) |jaw dʒɔ |gorge gɔrdʒ |go go

cither 'sɪθɚ; ES 'sɪθə(r; |-n -n
citied 'sɪtɪd
citify 'sɪtɪˌfaɪ |-fied -ˌfaɪd
citizen 'sɪtəzn̩, -sn̩ |-ry -rɪ |-ship -ˌʃɪp
citrate 'sɪtret, -rɪt |-d -ɪd |-riç -rɪk
citriculture 'sɪtrɪˌkʌltʃɚ; ES -ˌkʌltʃə(r
citrine 'sɪtrɪn
Citroën 'sɪtroˌɛn
citron 'sɪtrən |-ade ˌsɪtrən'ed
citronella ˌsɪtrən'ɛlə
citrus, C- 'sɪtrəs |citrous 'sɪtrəs
Città del Vaticano It tʃit'ta·delˌvati'ka:no
cittern 'sɪtɚn; ES 'sɪtən
city 'sɪtɪ |citied 'sɪtɪd
city-state 'sɪtɪ'stet
Ciudad Trujillo Am Sp sju'ðaðtru'hijo
civet 'sɪvɪt |-ed -ɪd
civic 'sɪvɪk |-s -s |-ally -ˌlɪ, -ɪklɪ
civil 'sɪvl̩, less freq. 'sɪvɪl |-ly -ɪ
civilian sə'vɪljən |civility sə'vɪlətɪ
civilizable 'sɪvl̩ˌaɪzəbl̩
civilization ˌsɪvl̩ə'zeʃən, -aɪ'z-
civilize 'sɪvl̩ˌaɪz |-s -ɪz |-d -d
clabber 'klæbɚ; ES -bə(r; |-ed -d |-ing
   'klæbərɪŋ, 'klæbrɪŋ
clack klæk |clacked klækt
Clackamas 'klækəməs |-'s -ɪz
Clackmannan klæk'mænən |-shire -ˌʃɪr, -ʃɚ;
   ES -ˌʃɪə(r, -ʃə(r
clad klæd
Claiborne 'klebɚn; ES 'klebən
Claibornian kle'bornɪən, -'bɔrn-; ES -'boən-,
   E+-'bɔən-
claim klem |claimed klemd |-ant -ənt
Clair(e) klɛr, klær; E klɛə(r, ES klæə(r
clairvoyance klɛr'vɔɪəns, klær-; E klɛə-, ES
   klæə-; |-ant -ənt
Clallam 'klæləm
clam klæm |clammed klæmd
clamant 'klemənt
clambake 'klæmˌbek
clamber 'klæmbɚ; ES -bə(r; |-ed -d |-ing
   'klæmbərɪŋ, 'klæmbrɪŋ
clammy 'klæmɪ |-mily -mˌlɪ, -mɪlɪ
clamor 'klæmɚ; ES 'klæmə(r; |-ed -d |-ing
   'klæmrɪŋ, 'klæmərɪŋ
clamorous 'klæmərəs, 'klæmrəs
clamp klæmp |clamped klæmpt
clamshell 'klæmˌʃɛl

clan klæn |clanned klænd |-nish -ɪʃ
clandestine klæn'dɛstɪn
clang klæŋ |clanged klæŋd
clangor 'klæŋgɚ, 'klæŋɚ; ES -ə(r; |-ed -d
   |-ous -əs
clank klæŋk |clanked klæŋkt
clansman 'klænzmən |-men -mən
clap klæp |clapped klæpt
clapboard 'klæbɚd, 'klæbord, 'klæpˌbord,
   -ɔrd; ES 'klæbəd, 'klæboəd, 'klæpˌboəd,
   E+-ɔəd; |-ed -ɪd
clapper 'klæpɚ; ES 'klæpə(r; |-ed -d |-ing
   'klæpərɪŋ, 'klæprɪŋ
clapperclaw 'klæpɚˌklɔ; ES 'klæpə-; |-ed -d
claptrap 'klæpˌtræp
claque klæk
Clara 'klɛrə, 'klærə; S 'klærə
clarabella, C- ˌklærə'bɛlə
Clare klɛr, klær; E klɛə(r, ES klæə(r
Claremont 'klɛrmɑnt, 'klær-; E 'klɛə-, ES
   'klæə-, -mɒnt
Claremore 'klɛrmor, 'klær-, -mɔr; E
   'klɛəmoə(r, 'klæə-, -mɔə(r; S 'klæəmoə(r
Clarence 'klærəns |-'s -ɪz
Clarendon, c- 'klærəndən
claret 'klærət, -ɪt
Claribel 'klærəˌbɛl
Clarice 'klærɪs |-'s -ɪz
clarification ˌklærəfə'keʃən
clarify 'klærəˌfaɪ |-fied -ˌfaɪd
Clarinda klə'rɪndə
clarinet ˌklærə'nɛt ('clariˌnet 'solo)
clarion, C- 'klærɪən
clarionet ˌklærɪə'nɛt
Clarissa klə'rɪsə
clarity 'klærətɪ
Clark, -e klɑrk; ES klɑ:k, E+klɑ:k
Clarksburg 'klɑrksbɚg; ES 'klɑ:ksbɜg,
   'klɑ:ksbɚg, E+'klɑ:ks-
clary 'klɛrɪ, 'klærɪ; S 'klærɪ
clash klæʃ |clashes 'klæʃɪz |clashed klæʃt
clasp klæsp; E+klɑsp, klɒsp; |-ed -t
class klæs; E+klɑs, klɒs; |-es -ɪz |-ed -t
classic 'klæsɪk |-al -l̩ |-ally -lɪ, -ɪklɪ
classicalism 'klæsɪkl̩ˌɪzəm |-ist -ɪst
classicality ˌklæsɪ'kælətɪ
classicism 'klæsəˌsɪzəm |-cist -sɪst
classifiable 'klæsəˌfaɪəbl̩
classification ˌklæsəfə'keʃən

|full fʊl |tooth tuθ |further 'fɝðɚ; ES 'fɝðə |custom 'kʌstəm |while hwaɪl |how haʊ |toy tɔɪ
|using 'juzɪŋ |fuse fjuz, fɪuz |dish dɪʃ |vision 'vɪʒən |Eden 'idn̩ |cradle 'kredl̩ |keep 'em 'kipm̩

classify 'klæsə̩faɪ |-fied -̩faɪd
classman 'klæsmən; E+'klas-, 'klɑs-; |-men
-mən
classmate 'klæs̩met; E+'klas-, 'klɑs-
classroom 'klæs̩rum, -̩rʊm; E+'klas-, 'klɑs-
clatter 'klætə̩; ES 'klætə(r; |-ed -d
Claude Lorrain 'klɔdlo'ren, -lɔ-, -lɒ- (Fr
klodlɔ̃'ræ)
Claudia 'klɔdɪə |-n -n |-ius -s |-ius's -sɪz
Claudio 'klɔdɪ̩o, 'klɔdjo
clause klɔz |clauses 'klɔzɪz |-d -d |-sal -l̩
claustral 'klɔstrəl
claustrophobia ̩klɔstrə'fobɪə
clavate 'klevet |-d -ɪd
clave arch. past of cleave klev
Claverhouse 'klævərəs, 'klævə̩z, 'klævə-
̩haʊs; ES 'klævərəs, 'klævəz, 'klævə̩haʊs;
|-'s -ɪz, Brit+'klev-
clavichord 'klævə̩kɔrd; ES -̩kɔəd
clavicle 'klævəkl̩
clavier 'keyboard' 'klævɪə, klə'vɪr, 'instrument' klə'vɪr; ES 'klævɪ-ə(r, klə'vɪə(r
claw klɔ |clawed klɔd
clay, C- kle |clayed kled
Clayhanger 'kle̩hæŋə; ES -̩hæŋə(r
claymore 'klemor, -mɔr; ES -moə(r, E+
-mɔə(r
Clayton 'kletn̩
clean klin |cleaned klind |-ness 'klinnɪs
clean-cut 'klin'kʌt ('clean-̩cut 'edges)
cleanly adj 'klɛnlɪ
cleanly adv 'klinlɪ
cleanse klɛnz |cleanses 'klɛnzɪz |-d -d
cleanup n 'klin̩ʌp
clear klɪr; ES klɪə(r, S+klɛə(r; |-ed -d
clearance 'klɪrəns; S+'klɛr-; |-s -ɪz
clear-cut 'klɪr'kʌt; ES 'klɪə'kʌt, S+'klɛə-
clear-eyed 'klɪr'aɪd; S+'klɛr-; ('clear-̩eyed
'ox)
Clearfield 'klɪr̩fild; ES 'klɪə-, S+'klɛə-
clearheaded 'klɪr'hɛdɪd; ES 'klɪə-, S+'klɛə-
clearing 'klɪrɪŋ; S+'klɛrɪŋ; |-house -̩haʊs
clear-sighted 'klɪr'saɪtɪd; ES 'klɪə-, S+'klɛə-
clearstarch 'klɪr̩startʃ; E 'klɪə̩sta:tʃ, -̩sta:tʃ;
S 'klɪə̩sta:tʃ, 'klɛə-; |-es -ɪz |-ed -t
clearstory 'klɪr̩storɪ, -̩stɔrɪ; E 'klɪə-; S
'klɪə̩storɪ, 'klɛə-
Clearwater 'klɪr̩wɔtə, -̩watə, -̩wɒtə; ES
'klɪə̩wɔtə(r, -̩wat-, -̩wɒt-, S+'klɛə-

cleat klit |cleated 'klitɪd
cleavable 'klivəbl̩
cleavage 'klivɪdʒ |-s -ɪz
cleave 'cling' kliv |past & pptc cleaved klivd
|arch. past clave klev or clove klov
cleave 'split' kliv |past cleft klɛft or cleaved
klivd or clove klov; arch. clave klev |pptc
cleft klɛft or cleaved klivd or cloven
'klovən; arch. clove klov
Cleaveland, Moses 'klivlənd
cleek klik |-ed -t
clef klɛf
cleft klɛft
cleistogamus klaɪs'tagəməs, -'tɒg-
clematis, C- 'klɛmətɪs |-es -ɪz
Clemenceau ̩klɛmən'so (Fr klemã'so)
Clemens 'klɛmənz |-'s -ɪz
clement, C- 'klɛmənt |clemency 'klɛmənsɪ
Clementina ̩klɛmən'tinə
Clementine fem. name 'klɛmən̩tin, -̩taɪn
Clementine 'of Clement' 'klɛməntɪn, -̩taɪn
clench klɛntʃ |clenches 'klɛntʃɪz |-ed -t
Cleomenes kli'amə̩niz; ES+-'ɒm-; |-'s -ɪz
Cleon 'klian, -ɒn
Cleopatra ̩klɪə'petrə, -'patrə, -'pætrə
clepsydra 'klɛpsɪdrə |-s -z |-drae -̩dri
cleptomania ̩klɛptə'menɪə |-iac -ɪ̩æk
clerestory 'klɪr̩storɪ, -̩stɔrɪ; E 'klɪə-; S
'klɪə̩storɪ, 'klɛə-
clergy 'klɜdʒɪ; ES 'klɜdʒɪ, 'klɜˑdʒɪ; |-man
-mən |-men -mən
cleric 'klɛrɪk |-al -l̩ |-ally -l̩ɪ, -ɪklɪ
clerk klɜk; ES klɜk, klɜˑk; Brit. klɑːk, klɑrk;
|-ed -t |-ly -lɪ
Clerkenwell 'klɜkən̩wɛl; ES 'klɜk-, 'klɜˑk-;
loc. 'klɑːkənwəl
Clermont 'klɛrmant; ES 'klɛəmant, -mɒnt
Clevedon 'klivdən
Cleveland 'klivlənd
clever 'klɛvə; ES 'klɛvə(r; |-er 'klɛvərə,
'klɛvrə; ES -rə(r; |-est -ɪst, -vrɪst
Cleves klivz |-'s -ɪz
clevis 'klɛvɪs |-es -ɪz
clew klu, klɪu |-ed -d
cliché kli'ʃe
click klɪk |clicked klɪkt
clickety-clack 'klɪkətɪ'klæk |-click -'klɪk
client 'klaɪənt |-ed -ɪd |-age -ɪdʒ
clientele ̩klaɪən'tɛl

cliff klıf |cliffed klıft
Clifford 'klıfəd; ES 'klıfəd
Clifton 'klıftən |-ia klıf'tonıə
climacteric klaı'mæktərık, ˌklaımæk'tɛrık
climacterical ˌklaımæk'tɛrıkļ |-ly -ı
climactic klaı'mæktık |-al -ļ |-ally -ļı, -ıklı
climate 'klaımıt |-d -ıd |-tal -ıtļ, -ətļ
climatology ˌklaımə'talədʒı; ES+-'tɒl-
climature 'klaımə,tʃʊr; ES -ˌtʃʊə(r
climax 'klaımæks |-es -ız |-ed -t
climb klaım |climbed klaımd |-er -ɚ; ES -ə(r
clime klaım
clinch, C- klıntʃ |-es -ız |-ed -t
Clinedinst 'klaındınst
cling klıŋ |clung klʌŋ |-stone -ˌston
clinic 'klınık |-al -ļ |-ally -ļı, -ıklı
clinician klı'nıʃən
clink klıŋk |clinked klıŋkt |-er -ɚ; ES -ə(r
clinker-built 'klıŋkɚˌbılt; ES 'klıŋkə-
clinkety-clink 'klıŋkətı'klıŋk
clinometer klaı'namətɚ, klı-; ES -'namətə(r,
   -'nɒm-
clinometric ˌklaınə'mɛtrık |-al -ļ
Clinton 'klıntən
Clio 'klaıo
clip klıp |clipped klıpt |-per -ɚ; ES -ə(r
clique klik, klık
Clitheroe 'klıðəˌro
clitoris 'klaıtərıs, 'klıtərıs |-es -ız
Clitus 'klaıtəs |-'s -ız
Clive klaıv
Cliveden 'klıvdən
cloaca klo'ekə |-s -z |-acae -'esi
cloak klok |cloaked klokt; |NEngd+klōk
cloakroom 'klokˌrum, -ˌrʊm
cloche kloʃ |cloches 'kloʃız (Fr klɔ̄ʃ)
clock klak; ES+klɒk; |-ed -t
clockwise 'klakˌwaız; ES+'klɒk-
clockwork 'klakˌwɝk; ES 'klakˌwɜk, -ˌwɝk,
   'klɒk-
clod klad; ES+klɒd; |-ded -ıd
clodhopper 'kladˌhapɚ; ES 'kladˌhapə(r,
   'klɒdˌhɒpə(r
clodpate 'kladˌpet; ES+'klɒd-; |-d -ıd
clodpoll, -pole 'kladˌpol; ES+'klɒd-
clog klag, klɒg, klɔg |-ged -d
cloisonné ˌklɔızə'ne (Fr klwazɔ̄'ne)
cloister 'klɔıstɚ; ES -stə(r; |-ed -d |-ing
   'klɔıstərıŋ, 'klɔıstrıŋ |-tral -trəl

clootie 'klutı, Sc 'klytı
Cloquet klo'ke
close adj klos; NEngd+klōs (§46)
close n 'end' kloz |-s -ız
close n 'enclosed place' klos |-s -ız
close v kloz |closes 'klozız |closed klozd
closefisted 'klos'fıstıd ('closeˌfisted 'miser)
close-fitting 'klos'fıtıŋ
close-grained 'klos'grend
close-hauled 'klos'hɔld
close-lipped 'klos'lıpt ('close-ˌlipped 'smile)
close-mouthed 'klos'mavðd, -'mavθt
closet 'klazıt, 'klɒzıt |-ed -ıd
close-up 'klosˌʌp
closure 'kloʒɚ; ES 'kloʒə(r; |-d -d
clot klat; ES+klɒt; |-ted -ıd
Cloten 'klotn̩
cloth klɔθ, klɒθ |-ths 'pieces of cloth' -ðz,
   'kinds of cloth' -θs |-'s -θs
clothe v kloð |clothes kloðz |clothed kloðd—
   Note that the 3 sg pres is not kloz, *the usual
   pron. of the noun* clothes, *which occurs far
   oftener.*
clothes n kloz, kloðz—kloz *has been the cultivated colloq. pron. for 200 yrs. Dr. Johnson
   says "always clo's," Sheridan (1780) &
   Walker (1791) give only* kloz. *Oxf. Dict.
   calls it "vulgar or careless." Fowler (Mod.
   Eng. Usage) denies this and says* kloz *is the
   usual pron. [in Engd]. Webster has cor-
   rectly labeled* kloz *'Colloq.' for some 70 yrs.
   The L. A. shows an overwhelming majority
   for* kloz. *The verb* clothes kloðz *keeps its* ð
   from* clothe kloð & clothed kloðd. *The
   noun has no sg* kloð.
clothesbasket 'klozˌbæskıt, 'kloðz-; E+
   -ˌbas-, -ˌbɑs-
clothesbrush 'klozˌbrʌʃ, 'kloðz- |-es -ız
clotheshorse 'klozˌhɔrs, 'kloðz-; ES -ˌhɔəs;
   |-s -ız
clothesline 'klozˌlaın, 'kloðz-
clothespin 'klozˌpın, 'kloðz-
clothespress 'klozˌprɛs, 'kloðz- |-es -ız
clothes-wringer 'klozˌrıŋɚ, 'kloðz-; ES -ˌrıŋə(r
clothier 'kloðjɚ, -ðıɚ; ES 'kloðjə(r, -ı·ə(r
clothing 'kloðıŋ
Clotho 'kloθo
cloths 'pieces of cloth' klɔðz, klɒðz; 'kinds of
   cloth' klɔθs, klɒθs

|full fʊl |tooth tuθ |further 'fɝðɚ; ES 'fɜðə |custom 'kʌstəm |while hwaıl |how hav |toy tɔı
|using 'juzıŋ |fuse fjuz, fıuz |dish dıʃ |vision 'vıʒən |Eden 'idn̩ |cradle 'kredļ |keep 'em 'kipm̩

Those words below in which the ɑ sound is spelt o are often pronounced with ɒ in E and S

cloture 'klotʃɚ, -tʃʊr; ES 'klotʃə(r, -tʃʊə(r; |-d -d

cloud klaʊd |clouded 'klaʊdɪd

cloudburst 'klaʊd‚bɝst; ES -‚bɜst, -‚bɝst

cloud-capped 'klaʊd‚kæpt

cloudland 'klaʊd‚lænd

cloudlet 'klaʊdlɪt

clough klʌf, klaʊ

Clough klʌf, *Irel* klɒx

clout klaʊt |clouted 'klaʊtɪd

clove *'spice'* klov |cloved klovd

clove *past of* cleave klov

Clovelly klo'vɛlɪ

cloven 'klovən

cloven-footed 'klovən'fʊtɪd ('cloven-‚footed 'ox)

cloven-hoofed 'klovən'hʊft, -'hʊft

clover 'klovɚ; ES 'klovə(r; |-ed -d

clover-leaf *adj* 'klovɚ‚lif; ES 'klovə-

Clovis 'klovɪs |-'s -ɪz

clown klaʊn |-ed -d |-age -ɪdʒ |-ery -ərɪ

cloy klɔɪ |-ed -d |-edness -ɪdnɪs

club klʌb |clubbed klʌbd

clubbable, clubable 'klʌbəbl̩

clubfoot 'klʌb'fʊt, -‚fʊt

clubfooted 'klʌb'fʊtɪd ('club‚footed 'sophisms)

clubland 'klʌb‚lænd

clubman 'klʌbmən, -‚mæn |-men -mən, -‚mɛn

clubwoman 'klʌb‚wʊmən, -‚wum- |-men -‚wɪmɪn, -ən

cluck klʌk |clucked klʌkt

clue klu, klɪu |-d -d

clumber 'klʌmbɚ; ES 'klʌmbə(r

clump klʌmp |clumped klʌmpt

clumsy 'klʌmzɪ |-sily -zəlɪ, -zɪlɪ

clung klʌŋ

Cluniac 'klunɪ‚æk, 'klɪunɪ-

Cluny 'klunɪ, 'klɪunɪ (*Fr* kly'ni)

cluster 'klʌstɚ; ES -tə(r; |-ed -d |-ing 'klʌstrɪŋ, 'klʌstərɪŋ

clutch klʌtʃ |clutches 'klʌtʃɪz |-ed -t

clutter 'klʌtɚ; ES 'klʌtə(r; |-ed -d

Clutton-Brock 'klʌtn̩'brɑk

Clyde klaɪd |-bank -‚bæŋk |-sdale -z‚del

Clymer 'klaɪmɚ; ES 'klaɪmə(r

Clytemnestra, -taem- ‚klaɪtəm'nɛstrə

Cnidus 'naɪdəs |-'s -ɪz

Cnossus 'nɑsəs |-sus' -səs

Cnut kə'nut, -'nɪut, -'njut = Canute

coach kotʃ |coaches 'kotʃɪz |coached kotʃt

coach-and-four 'kotʃən'for, -'fɔr; ES -'foə(r, E+-'fɔə(r

Coachella ‚koə'tʃɛlə

coachman 'kotʃmən |-men -mən

coact ko'ækt |-ed -ɪd |-ction -kʃən |-ive -ɪv

coadjutor ko'ædʒətɚ, ‚koə'dʒutɚ; ES -tə(r

coagulate ko'ægjə‚let |-d -ɪd |-lant -lənt

coagulation ko‚ægjə'leʃən, ‚koægjə-

Coahoma ‚koə'homə

Coahuila ‚koə'wilə

coal kol |coaled kold

coalesce ‚koə'lɛs |-s -ɪz |-d -t

coalescence ‚koə'lɛsn̩s |-cy -ɪ |-cent -sn̩t

Coalinga ‚koə'lɪŋgə

coalition ‚koə'lɪʃən ('coa‚lition 'party)

coalless 'kollɪs

coaming 'komɪŋ

coarse kors, kɔrs; ES koəs, E+kɔəs

coarse-grained 'kors'grend, 'kɔrs-; ES 'koəs-, E+'kɔəs-

coarsen 'korsn̩, 'kɔrsn̩; ES 'koəsn̩, E+'kɔəsn̩; |-ed -d |-ing -sn̩ɪŋ, -snɪŋ

coast kost |coasted 'kostɪd |-al -l̩ |-ally -l̩ɪ

coastward 'kostwɚd; ES 'kostwəd

coastways 'kost‚wez |-wise -‚waɪz

coat kot |coated 'kotɪd; |*NEngd*+kɔt (*§46*)

coati ko'ɑtɪ

coattail 'kot‚tel |-ed -d

coauthor ko'ɔθɚ; ES -'ɔθə(r; |-ship -‚ʃɪp

coax koks |coaxes 'koksɪz |coaxed kokst; |*NEngd*+kɔks (*§46*)

coaxal ko'æksl̩ |-xial -ksɪəl |-xially -ksɪəl̩ɪ

cob kab |-bed -d

cobalt, C- 'kobɔlt

Cobbett 'kabɪt

cobble 'kabl̩ |-d -d |-ling 'kablɪŋ, -bl̩ɪŋ

cobbler 'kablɚ; ES 'kablə(r; |-y -ɪ

cobblestone 'kabl̩‚ston

Cobden 'kabdən

Cóbh kov

Cobham 'kabəm, 'kabm̩

Coblenz 'koblɛnts |-'s -ɪz

Cobleskill 'kobl̩z‚kɪl, 'kobl̩‚skɪl

Cobourg *Can* 'kobɝg; ES 'kobɜg, -bɝg

cobra 'kobrə

Key: See in full §§3–47. bee bi |pity 'pɪtɪ (§6) |rate ret |yet jɛt |sang sæŋ |angry 'æŋ·grɪ |bath bæθ; E bɑθ (§10) |ah ɑ |far fɑr |watch watʃ, wɒtʃ (§12) |jaw dʒɔ |gorge gɔrdʒ |go go

Those words below in which the ɑ *sound is spelt* o *are often pronounced with* ɒ *in E and S*

Coburg *Germany* 'kobɝg; ES -bɜg, -bɝg; (*Ger*
  K- 'ko:bʊrk)
Coburn 'kobɝn; ES 'kobən; *cf* Cockburn
cobweb 'kab‚wɛb |-webbery -‚wɛbərı, -brı
coca 'kokə
cocaine, -ain ko'ken, 'koken |-ism -'kenızəm
coccus 'kakəs |cocci 'kaksaı
coccygeal kak'sıdʒıəl
coccyx 'kaksıks |-es -ız |coccyges kak'saıdʒiz
Cochin, c- 'kotʃın, 'katʃın
Cochin China 'kotʃın'tʃaınə, 'katʃ-
cochineal ‚katʃə'nil ('cochi‚neal 'dye)
cochlea 'kaklıə |cochleae 'kaklı‚i
cochlear 'kaklıɝ; ES 'kaklı·ə(r
Cochran, -e 'kakrən
cock kak |cocked kakt
cockade kak'ed |-aded -'edıd
cock-a-doodle ‚kakə'dudl̩ |-d -d
cock-a-doodle-doo 'kakə‚dudl̩'du
cock-a-hoop ‚kakə'hup, -'hʊp
Cockaigne ka'ken
cockalorum ‚kakə'lorəm, -'lɔrəm; S -'lorəm
cock-and-bull story 'kakən'bʊl‚storı, 'kakŋ-,
  -‚stɔrı; S -‚storı
cockatoo ‚kakə'tu ('cocka‚too 'orchis)
cockatrice 'kakətrıs |-s -ız
cockboat 'kak‚bot
Cockburn 'kobɝn; ES 'kobən; *cf* Coburn
cockchafer 'kak‚tʃefɝ; ES -‚tʃefə(r
cockcrow 'kak‚kro
cocker 'kakɝ; ES 'kakə(r; |-ed -d |-ing
  'kakərıŋ, 'kakrıŋ
cockerel 'kakərəl, 'kakrəl
Cockermouth 'kakɝməθ, -‚mauθ; ES 'kakə-
cockeye 'kak‚aı |-d -d
cockfight 'kak‚faıt
cockhorse 'kak'hɔrs; ES -'hɔəs; |-s -ız (a
  'cock‚horse 'air)
cockle 'kakl̩ |-d -d |-ling 'kaklıŋ, 'kakl̩ıŋ
cocklebur 'kakl̩‚bɝ; ES -‚bɜ(r, -‚bɝ
cockleshell 'kakl̩‚ʃɛl
cockloft 'kak‚lɔft, -‚lɒft
cockney, C- 'kaknı |-ism -‚ızəm
cockpit 'kak‚pıt
cockroach 'kak‚rotʃ |-es -ız
cockscomb 'kaks‚kom |-ed -d |-ry -rı
cockshot 'kak‚ʃat
cockshut 'kak‚ʃʌt

cocksure 'kak'ʃʊr; ES -'ʃʊə(r; ('cock‚sure
  'plan)
cockswain 'kaksn̩, 'kak‚swen
cocktail 'kak‚tel |-ed -d
coco 'koko
cocoa 'koko, 'kokə
coconut, cocoa- 'kokənət, 'kokə‚nʌt
cocoon kə'kun, ku'kun
Cocos 'kokas
cocotte ko'kat, kə- (*Fr* kɔ'kɔt)
cocytus, C- ko'saıtəs |-'s -ız
cod, C- kad |codded 'kadıd
C.O.D. 'si‚o'di
coda 'kodə
Coddington 'kadıŋtən
coddle 'kadl̩ |-d -d |-ling 'kadlıŋ, 'kadl̩ıŋ
code kod |coded 'kodıd
codefendant ‚kodı'fɛndənt
codeine 'kodı‚in, 'kodin |-dein -dıın
codex 'kodɛks |-es -ız |codices 'kodə‚siz,
  'kad- —*The* o *in* codices *is by analogy with*
  the singular. The long o *of Latin becomes*
  short in English, as in orator, prominent,
  solitude, nominal, *etc.*
codfish 'kad‚fıʃ |-'s -ız
codger 'kadʒɝ; ES 'kadʒə(r
codices 'kodə‚siz, 'kad- —*see* codex
codicil 'kadəsl̩, -‚sıl
codify 'kadə‚faı, 'kod- |-fied -‚faıd
codling 'kadlıŋ
codpiece 'kad‚pis |-pieces -‚pisız
Cody 'kodı
coed, co-ed 'ko'ɛd, 'ko‚ɛd ('co‚ed 'college)
coeducation ‚koɛdʒə'keʃən |-al -l̩ |-ally -lı
coefficient ‚koə'fıʃənt, ‚ko·ı-
coeliac 'silı‚æk
coempt ko'ɛmpt |-ed -ıd |-ption -pʃən
coenobite 'sɛnə‚baıt, 'sin-
coequal ko'ikwəl |-ed -d |-ly -ı
coequality ‚ko·i'kwalətı, 'kwɒl-
coerce ko'ɝs; ES -'ɜs, -'ɝs; |-s -ız |-d -t
coercion ko'ɝʃən; ES -'ɜʃən, -'ɝʃən |-cive
  -sıv
coeternal ‚ko·i'tɝnl̩; ES -'tɜnl̩, -'tɝnl̩; |-ly -ı
Coeur de Lion ‚kɝdə'lian, -'lian; ES ‚kɜ-,
  ‚kɝ-; (*Fr* kœrdə'ljõ)
coeval ko'ivl̩ |-ly -ı |-ity ‚ko·ı'vælətı
coexecutor ‚ko·ıg'zɛkjətɝ; ES -'zɛkjətə(r

Those words below in which the ɑ sound is spelt o are often pronounced with ɒ in E and S

coexist ˌkoˑɪgˈzɪst |-ed -ɪd |-ence -əns |-ent
-ənt

coextend ˌkoˑɪkˈstɛnd |-ed -ɪd |-tensive -nsɪv

coffee, C- ˈkɔfɪ, ˈkɒfɪ, *much less freq.* ˈkɑfɪ
|-house -ˌhaʊs |-pot -ˌpɑt—*In* coffee ɔ
clearly prevails in all regions of US.

coffer ˈkɔfɚ, ˈkɒfɚ; ES -fə(r; |-dam -ˌdæm

Coffeyville ˈkɔfɪˌvɪl, ˈkɒfɪ-; S+-vl̩

coffin, C- ˈkɔfɪn, ˈkɒfɪn |-ed -d

Coffman ˈkɔfmən, ˈkɒf-, ˈkɑf-

cog kɑg, kɒg, *less freq.* kɔg |-ged -d

cogence ˈkodʒəns |-cy -ɪ |-gent -dʒənt

cogitable ˈkɑdʒɪtəbl̩

cogitate ˈkɑdʒəˌtet |-d -ɪd |-tive -ɪv

cogitation ˌkɑdʒəˈteʃən

cognac ˈkonjæk, ˈkɑn- (*Fr* kõˈɲak)

cognate ˈkɑgnet

cognition kɑgˈnɪʃən |cognitive ˈkɑgnətɪv

cognizable ˈkɑgnəzəbl̩ |-bly -blɪ

cognizance ˈkɑgnəzəns, ˈkɑn- |-s -ɪz |-nt -nt

cognomen kɑgˈnomən |-s -z |-nomina
-ˈnɑmənə

cogwheel ˈkɑgˌhwil, ˈkɒg-, *less freq.* ˈkɔg-

cohabit koˈhæbɪt |-ed -ɪd

cohabitation ˌkohæbəˈteʃən

Cohasset koˈhæsɪt

coheir koˈɛr, -ˈær; E -ˈɛə(r, ES -ˈæə(r; |-ess -ɪs
|-esses -ɪsɪz

cohere koˈhɪr; ES koˈhɪə(r, S+-ˈhɛə(r

coherence koˈhɪrəns; S+-ˈhɛr-; |-ent -ənt

coherer koˈhɪrɚ; ES -ˈhɪrə(r, S+-ˈhɛrə(r

cohesion koˈhiʒən |-hesive -ˈhisɪv

Cohoes koˈhoz |-ʼs -ɪz

cohort ˈkohɔrt; ES ˈkohɔət

cohortative koˈhɔrtətɪv; ES -ˈhɔət-

coif kɔɪf |coifed kɔɪft

coiffeur kwɑˈfɝ ; ES -ˈfɝ(r, -ˈfɝ; (*Fr* kwa-
ˈfœːr)

coiffure kwɑˈfjʊr, -ˈfɪʊr; ES -ˈfjʊə(r, -ˈfɪʊə(r;
(*Fr* kwaˈfyːr)

coign, -e kɔɪn

coil kɔɪl |coiled kɔɪld

coin kɔɪn |-ed -d |-age -ɪdʒ |-ages -ɪdʒɪz

coincide ˌkoˑɪnˈsaɪd |-cided -ˈsaɪdɪd

coincidence koˈɪnsədəns |-s -ɪz |-cy -ɪ |-nt -nt

coincidental koˌɪnsəˈdɛntl̩, ˌkoˑɪn- |-ly -ɪ

coincidently koˈɪnsədəntlɪ

coinsurance ˌkoˑɪnˈʃʊrəns |-s -ɪz

coinsure ˌkoˑɪnˈʃʊr; ES -ˈʃʊə(r; |-d -d

coir kɔɪr; ES kɔɪə(r

coistrel, -il ˈkɔɪstrəl

coition koˈɪʃən

coitus ˈkoˑɪtəs

coke kok |coked kokt

Coke kʊk, kok

colander ˈkʌləndɚ, ˈkɑl-; ES -də(r

Colbert *Am name* ˈkɑlbɚt, ˈkɔl-, ˈkol-; ES
-bət; *Fr name* kõlˈbɛːr

Colby ˈkolbɪ

Colchester ˈkɑlˌtʃɛstɚ; ˈkoltʃɪstɚ; ES -tə(r

colchicum, C- ˈkɑltʃɪkəm

Colchis ˈkɑlkɪs |-ʼs -ɪz

cold kold |colded ˈkoldɪd

cold-blooded ˈkoldˈblʌdɪd, -ˌblʌdɪd (ˈcold-
ˌblooded ˈmalice)

cold-hearted ˈkoldˈhɑrtɪd; ES -ˈhɑːtɪd, E+
-ˈhɑːtɪd

cold-shoulder *v* ˈkoldˈʃoldɚ; ES -ˈʃoldə(r;
|-ed -d |-ing -ˈʃoldərɪŋ, -ˈʃoldrɪŋ

coldslaw ˈkolˌslɔ, ˈkold-

Coldstream ˈkoldˌstrim

cole kol

Coleman ˈkolmən

coleopterous ˌkolɪˈɑptərəs, ˌkɑlɪ-

Coleridge ˈkolrɪdʒ, *not infreq.* ˈkolərɪdʒ |-ʼs -ɪz

coleslaw ˈkolˌslɔ

Colet ˈkɑlɪt

coleus, C- ˈkolɪəs |-es -ɪz

Coleville ˈkolvɪl

colewort ˈkolˌwɝt; ES -ˌwɝt, -ˌwɝt

Colfax ˈkolfæks |-ʼs -ɪz

colic ˈkɑlɪk |colicky ˈkɑlɪkɪ

Colin ˈkɑlɪn

Coliseum ˌkɑləˈsiəm

colitis koˈlaɪtɪs

collaborate kəˈlæbəˌret |-d -ɪd |-tor -ɚ; ES
-ə(r; |-tive -ɪv

collaboration kəˌlæbəˈreʃən

collage kəˈlɑʒ, ko- |-gist -ɪst (*Fr* kõˈlaːʒ)

collapse kəˈlæps |-s -ɪz |-d -t |-sible -əbl̩

collapsibility kəˌlæpsəˈbɪlətɪ

collar ˈkɑlɚ; ES ˈkɑlə(r; |-ed -d

collarbone ˈkɑlɚˈbon, -ˌbon; ES ˈkɑlə-

collaret, -tte ˌkɑləˈrɛt

collate kɑˈlet, kə-, ˈkɑlet |-d -ɪd

collateral kəˈlætərəl |-ly -ɪ

Those words below in which the ɑ *sound is spelt* o *are often pronounced with* ɒ *in E and S*

collation kɑ'leʃən, kə-
colleague n 'kɑlig
colleague v kə'lig, kɑ- |-leagued -'ligd
collect n 'kɑlɛkt
collect v kə'lɛkt |-ed -ɪd
collectanea ˌkɑlɛk'tenɪə
collectibility, -ability kəˌlɛktə'bɪlətɪ
collectible, -able kə'lɛktəbl̩
collection kə'lɛkʃən
collective kə'lɛktɪv |-ism -ˌɪzəm |-ist -ɪst
collectivistic kəˌlɛktə'vɪstɪk |-ally -l̩ɪ, -ɪklɪ
collector kə'lɛktɚ; ES -'lɛktə(r; |-ship -ˌʃɪp
colleen 'kɑlin, kə'lin
college 'kɑlɪdʒ |-s -ɪz
college-bred 'kɑlɪdʒ'brɛd ('college-ˌbred 'man)
collegian kə'lidʒən, -dʒɪən |-giate -dʒɪɪt, -dʒɪt
collet 'kɑlɪt |-ed -ɪd
Colleton 'kɑlətn̩
collide kə'laɪd |-lided -'laɪdɪd
collie 'kɑlɪ
collied 'kɑlɪd
collier 'kɑljɚ; ES 'kɑljə(r; |-y -ɪ
collimate 'kɑləˌmet |-d -ɪd |-tion ˌkɑlə'meʃən
Collingwood 'kɑlɪŋˌwʊd
Collins 'kɑlɪnz |-'s -ɪz
Collinwood 'kɑlɪnˌwʊd
collision kə'lɪʒən |-al -l̩
collocate 'kɑloˌket |-d -ɪd |-tion ˌkɑlo'keʃən
collodion kə'lodɪən
colloid 'kɑlɔɪd |-al kə'lɔɪdl̩
collop 'kɑləp |colloped 'kɑləpt
colloquial kə'lokwɪəl |-ly -ɪ |-ism -ˌɪzəm
colloquiality kəˌlokwɪ'ælətɪ
colloquy 'kɑləkwɪ
collude kə'lud, -'lɪud |-d -ɪd
collusion kə'luʒən, -'lɪuʒən |-sive -sɪv
Colman 'kolmən
Cologne, c- kə'lon (Ger Köln, C- kœln)
Colombia kə'lʌmbɪə (Sp ko'lɔmbja) |-n -n
Colombo kə'lʌmbo, kə'lɑmbo
Colón ko'lɑn, -'lon (Am Sp ko'lon)
colon 'kolən
colon coin ko'lon |-s -z |-es -es
colonel 'kɝnl̩; ES 'kɜnl̩, 'kɝnl̩; |-ed -d |-cy -sɪ
colonial kə'lonɪəl |-ism -ˌɪzəm
colonist 'kɑlənɪst
colonization ˌkɑlənə'zeʃən, -aɪ'z- |-ist -ɪst
colonize 'kɑləˌnaɪz |-s -ɪz |-d -d

colonnade ˌkɑlə'ned |-naded -'nedɪd
colony 'kɑlənɪ
colophon 'kɑləˌfɑn, -fən
color 'kʌlɚ; ES 'kʌlə(r; |-ed -d
colorable 'kʌlərəbl̩ |-bly -blɪ
Colorado ˌkɑlə'rædo, -'rɑdo |-dan -dən—*Observers disagree as to whether* ˌkɑlə'rædo *or* -'rɑdo *prevails in the state. There is little doubt that in the US as a whole* ˌkɑlə'rædo *prevails.*
coloration ˌkʌlə'reʃən
coloratura ˌkʌlərə'tjʊrə, ˌkɑl-, -'tɪʊrə, -'tʊrə
colorature 'kʌlərəˌtʃʊr, 'kɑl-; ES -ˌtʃʊə(r
color-bearer 'kʌlɚˌbɛrɚ, -ˌbærɚ; E 'kʌlə-ˌbɛrə(r, ES -ˌbærə(r
color-blind 'kʌlɚˌblaɪnd; ES 'kʌlə-
colorful 'kʌlɚfəl; ES 'kʌlə-; |-ly -ɪ
colorimeter ˌkʌlə'rɪmətɚ; ES -'rɪmətə(r
colossal kə'lɑsl̩ |-ly -ɪ
Colosseum ˌkɑlə'sɪəm
Colossian kə'lɑʃən |-s -z
colossus kə'lɑsəs |-es -ɪz |-ssi -saɪ |-sus' -səs
colporteur, -ter 'kɑlˌportɚ, -ˌportɚ; ES -ˌpoətə(r, E+-ˌpɔətə(r; (Fr kɔlpör'tœːr)
Colquhoun kə'hun
colt, C- kolt |colted 'koltɪd; |NEngd+kɔlt (§46)
colter 'koltɚ; ES 'koltə(r; |-ed -d
Colton 'koltn̩
Colum 'kɑləm
Columb 'kɑləm
Columba kə'lʌmbə
Columbia kə'lʌmbɪə, -bjə |-n -n
columbine, C- 'kɑləmˌbaɪn
columbium kə'lʌmbɪəm
Columbus kə'lʌmbəs |-'s -ɪz
column 'kɑləm, humorous 'kɑljəm |-ed -d
columnar kə'lʌmnɚ; ES -'lʌmnə(r
columniation 'columning' kəˌlʌmnɪ'eʃən
columnist 'kɑləmɪst, 'kɑləmnɪst
Colusa kə'lusə, kə'lɪusə
Colvin 'kolvɪn, 'kɑl-
coma 'stupor' 'komə |-s -z
coma 'comet's head' 'komə |-ae -i
Comanche ko'mæntʃɪ |-chean -tʃɪən
comatose 'koməˌtos, 'komə-
comb kom |combed komd; |NEngd+kɔm (§46)

Those words below in which the ɑ *sound is spelt* o *are often pronounced with* ɒ *in E and S*

comb *'valley'* kum

combat *n* ˈkɑmbæt, ˈkʌm-

combat *v* ˈkɑmbæt, ˈkʌm-, kəmˈbæt |-ted -ɪd

combatant ˈkɑmbətənt, ˈkʌm-

combative kəmˈbætɪv, ˈkɑmbətɪv, ˈkʌm-

combe kum

comber ˈkomɚ; ES ˈkomə(r

combination ˌkɑmbəˈneʃən

combinative ˈkɑmbəˌnetɪv, kəmˈbaɪnətɪv

combine *n* ˈkɑmbaɪn, kəmˈbaɪn

combine *v* kəmˈbaɪn |-bined -ˈbaɪnd |-dly -ɪdlɪ

combings ˈkomɪŋz

combust kəmˈbʌst |-ed -ɪd

combustibility kəmˌbʌstəˈbɪlətɪ

combustible kəmˈbʌstəbļ |-bly -blɪ

combustion kəmˈbʌstʃən

come *n malting* kom, kum

come *v* kʌm |came kem |come kʌm—*in un-stressed position often* kəm (kəmˈɪn!)

come-and-go ˈkʌmənˈgo

comedian kəˈmidɪən

comédienne kəˌmidɪˈɛn (*Fr* kömeˈdjɛn)

comedy ˈkɑmədɪ

comely ˈkʌmlɪ

comestible kəˈmɛstəbļ

comet ˈkɑmɪt

comfit ˈkʌmfɪt, ˈkɑm-

comfort ˈkʌmfɚt; ES -fət; |-ed -ɪd

comfortable ˈkʌmfɚtəbļ; ES ˈkʌmfətəbļ

comforter ˈkʌmfɚtɚ, ˈkʌmfɚtɚ; ES -fətə(r;— ˈkʌmfətɚ *shows r-dissimilation* (*§121*).

comfry ˈkʌmfrɪ

comic ˈkɑmɪk |-al -ļ |-ally -ļɪ, -ɪklɪ

Cominius kəˈmɪnɪəs, -njəs |-'s -ɪz

Comintern ˌkɑmɪnˈtɝn, ˈkɑmɪnˌtɝn; ES -ɜn, -ɝn

comitatus ˌkɑmɪˈtetəs

comity ˈkɑmətɪ

comma ˈkɑmə |-ed -d

command kəˈmænd; ES+-ˈmɑnd, -ˈmɑnd; |-ed -ɪd

commandant ˌkɑmənˈdænt, -ˈdɑnt

commandeer ˌkɑmənˈdɪr; ES -ˈdɪə(r, S+ -ˈdɛə(r; |-ed -d

commander ˌkəˈmændɚ; ES -də(r, E+ -ˈmɑnd-, -ˈmɑnd-

commander in chief kəˈmændɚɪnˈtʃif; E+ -ˈmɑnd-, -ˈmɑnd-

commandment kəˈmændmənt, -ˈmænmənt; E+-an-, -ɑn-

commemorate kəˈmɛməˌret |-rated -ˌretɪd

commemoration kəˌmɛməˈreʃən

commence kəˈmɛns |-s -ɪz |-d -t |-ment -mənt

commend kəˈmɛnd |-ed -ɪd

commendable kəˈmɛndəbļ |-bly -blɪ

commendation ˌkɑmənˈdeʃən, ˌkɑmɛn-

commendatory kəˈmɛndəˌtorɪ, -ˌtɔrɪ; S -ˌtɔrɪ

commensurability kəˌmɛnʃərəˈbɪlətɪ, -ˌmɛn-sərə-

commensurable kəˈmɛnʃərəbļ, -ˈmɛnsərə- |-bly -blɪ

commensurate *adj* kəˈmɛnʃərɪt, -ˈmɛnsə-

commensurate *v* kəˈmɛnʃəˌret, -ˈmɛnsə- |-d -ɪd

commensuration kəˌmɛnʃəˈreʃən, -ˌmɛnsə-

comment *n* ˈkɑmɛnt

comment *v* ˈkɑmɛnt, *less freq.* kəˈmɛnt |-ed -ɪd

commentary ˈkɑmənˌtɛrɪ

commentator ˈkɑmənˌtetɚ; ES -ˌtetə(r

commerce *n* ˈkɑmɚs, -mɝs; ES ˈkɑməs, -mɜs, -mɝs

commerce *v* kəˈmɝs; ES -ˈmɜs, -ˈmɝs; |-s -ɪz |-d -t

commercial kəˈmɝʃəl; ES -ˈmɜʃ-, -ˈmɝʃ-; |-ly -ɪ |-ism -ˌɪzəm

commercialization kəˌmɝʃələˈzeʃən, -aɪˈz-; ES -ˌmɜʃ-, -ˌmɝʃ-

commercialize kəˈmɝʃəlˌaɪz; ES -ˈmɜʃ-, -ˈmɝʃ-; |-s -ɪz |-d -d

comminate ˈkɑməˌnet |-nated -ˌnetɪd

commination ˌkɑməˈneʃən

commingle kəˈmɪŋgļ |-d -d

comminute ˈkɑməˌnjut, -ˌnɪut, -ˌnut |-d -ɪd

comminution ˌkɑməˈnjuʃən, -ˈnɪu-, -ˈnu-

commiserable kəˈmɪzərəbļ

commiserate kəˈmɪzəˌret |-rated -ˌretɪd

commiseration kəˌmɪzəˈreʃən

commiserative kəˈmɪzəˌretɪv

commissar ˌkɑməˈsɑr; ES -ˈsɑ:(r, E+-ˈsɑ:(r

commissariat ˌkɑməˈsɛrɪət, -ˈsær-, -ˈser-

commissary ˈkɑməˌsɛrɪ

commission kəˈmɪʃən |-ed -d

commissionaire kəˌmɪʃənˈɛr, -ˈær; E -ˈɛə(r, ES -ˈæə(r

commissioner kəˈmɪʃənɚ, -ˈmɪʃnɚ; ES -nə(r

commit kəˈmɪt |-ted -ɪd |-tal -ļ

Key: *See in full §§3–47.*   bee **bi** |pity ˈpɪtɪ (§6) |rate **ret** |yet jɛt |sang sæŋ |angry ˈæŋ·grɪ |bath bæθ; E bɑθ (§10) |ah ɑ |far fɑr |watch wɑtʃ, wɒtʃ (§12) |jaw dʒɔ |gorge gɔrdʒ |go go

Those words below in which the ɑ *sound is spelt* o *are often pronounced with* ɒ *in E and S*

committee kə'mɪtɪ |-d -d |-man -mən, -ˌmæn |-men -mən, -ˌmɛn

commix kə'mɪks, ka- |-es -ɪz |-ed -t

commixture kə'mɪkstʃɚ, ka-; ES -'mɪkstʃə(r

commode kə'mod

commodious kə'modɪəs

commodity kə'madətɪ

commodore 'kaməˌdor, -ˌdɔr; ES -ˌdoə(r, E+ -ˌdɔə(r

common 'kamən |-ed -d |-ness 'kamənnɪs

commonage 'kamənɪdʒ |-s -ɪz

commonality ˌkamən'ælətɪ

commonalty 'kamənəltɪ

commonplace 'kamənˌples |-s -ɪz

common-sense *adj* 'kamən'sɛns ('common-'sense ˌway)

commonweal 'kamənˌwil

commonwealth 'kamənˌwɛlθ, 'kamən'wɛlθ

commotion kə'moʃən

communal 'kamjʊnḷ, kə'mjunḷ, -'mɪu- |-ism -ˌɪzəm |-ist -ɪst |-ly -ɪ

commune *n* 'kamjun, -mɪun

commune *v* kə'mjun, -'mɪun |-d -d

communicability kəˌmjunɪkə'bɪlətɪ, -ˌmɪun-

communicable kə'mjunɪkəbḷ, -'mɪun- |-bly -blɪ

communicant kə'mjunɪkənt, -'mɪun-

communicate kə'mjunəˌket, -'mɪun- |-d -ɪd

communication kəˌmjunə'keʃən, -ˌmɪun-

communicative kə'mjunəˌketɪv, -'mɪun-

communion kə'mjunjən, -'mɪun-

communiqué kəˌmjunə'ke, -ˌmɪun-

communism 'kamjuˌnɪzəm |-ist -nɪst

communistic ˌkamjʊ'nɪstɪk |-al -ḷ |-ally -ḷɪ, -ɪklɪ

community kə'mjunətɪ, -'mɪun-

communize 'kamjuˌnaɪz |-s -ɪz |-d -d

commutable kə'mjutəbḷ, -'mɪut-

commutate 'kamjuˌtet |-d -ɪd |-ter -ɚ; ES -ə(r

commutation ˌkamju'teʃən

commute kə'mjut, -'mɪut |-d -ɪd |-r -ɚ; ES -ə(r

Como 'komo

compact *adj* kəm'pækt ('com,pact 'mass)

compact *n* 'kampækt

compact *v* kəm'pækt |-ed -ɪd

companion kəm'pænjən |-ed -d |-ship -ˌʃɪp

companionable kəm'pænjənəbḷ |bly -blɪ

companionate *adj* kəm'pænjənɪt

companionway kəm'pænjənˌwe

company 'kʌmpənɪ, 'kʌmpnɪ |-nied -nɪd

comparability ˌkampərə'bɪlətɪ

comparable 'kampərəbḷ, -prəbḷ |-bly -blɪ

comparative kəm'pærətɪv

compare kəm'pɛr, -'pær; E -'pɛə(r, ES -'pæə(r

Comparetti ˌkampə'rɛtɪ (*It* ˌkompa'retti)

comparison kəm'pærəsṇ

compartment kəm'partmənt; ES -'pɑ:t-, E+ -'pɑ:t-

compass 'kʌmpəs |-es -ɪz |-ed -t

compassion kəm'pæʃən |-ed -d |-ate -ɪt

compatibility kəmˌpætə'bɪlətɪ

compatible kəm'pætəbḷ |-bly -blɪ

compatriot kəm'petrɪət, *less freq.* -'pæt-

compeer kəm'pɪr, 'kampɪr; ES -ɪə(r, S+-ɛə(r

compel kəm'pɛl |-led -d

compellable kəm'pɛləbḷ |-bly -blɪ

compend 'kampɛnd |-ious kəm'pɛndɪəs

compendium kəm'pɛndɪəm |-s -z |-dia -dɪə

compensable kəm'pɛnsəbḷ

compensate 'kampənˌset, -pɛn-, kəm'pɛnset |-d -ɪd

compensation ˌkampən'seʃən, -pɛn-

compensative 'kampənˌsetɪv, kəm'pɛnsətɪv

compensatory kəm'pɛnsəˌtorɪ, -ˌtɔrɪ; S -ˌtorɪ

compete kəm'pit |-peted -'pitɪd

competence 'kampətəns |-s -ɪz |-cy -ɪ |-nt -nt

competition ˌkampə'tɪʃən

competitive kəm'pɛtətɪv |-tor -tɚ; ES -tə(r

compilation ˌkampḷ'eʃən, -pɪ'leʃən

compile kəm'paɪl |-piled -'paɪld

complacence kəm'plesṇs |-cy -ɪ |-cent -sṇt

complain kəm'plen |-ed -d |-ant -ənt |-t -t -t

complaisance kəm'plezṇs, 'kamplɪˌzæns |-sant -zṇt, -ˌzænt

complement *n* 'kampləmənt

complement *v* 'kampləˌmɛnt |-ed -ɪd

complemental ˌkamplə'mɛntḷ |-ly -ɪ

complementary ˌkamplə'mɛntərɪ, -'mɛntrɪ

complete kəm'plit |-d -ɪd |-tion -'pliʃən

complex *n* 'kamplɛks |-es -ɪz

complex *adj* kəm'plɛks, 'kamplɛks ('com,plex 'act)

complex *v* kəm'plɛks |-es -ɪz |-ed -t

complexion, -plection kəm'plɛkʃən |-ed -d

|full fʊl |tooth tuθ |further 'fɝðɚ; ES 'fɝðə |custom 'kʌstəm |while hwaɪl |how haʊ |toy tɔɪ |using 'juzɪŋ |fuse fjuz, fɪuz |dish dɪʃ |vision 'vɪʒən |Eden 'idṇ |cradle 'kredḷ |keep 'em 'kipm̩

Those words below in which the ɑ sound is spelt o are often pronounced with ɒ in E and S

complexity kəmˈplɛksətɪ
compliance kəmˈplaɪəns |-cy -ɪ |-ant -ənt
complicate *adj* ˈkɑmpləkɪt
complicate *v* ˈkɑmpləˌket |-cated -ˌketɪd
complication ˌkɑmpləˈkeʃən
complice ˈkɑmplɪs |-s -ɪz
complicity kəmˈplɪsətɪ
compliment *n* ˈkɑmpləmənt
compliment ˈkɑmpləˌmɛnt |-ed -ɪd
complimentary ˌkɑmpləˈmɛntərɪ, -ˈmɛntrɪ
complin ˈkɑmplɪn |-pline -plɪn, -plaɪn
comply kəmˈplaɪ |-plied -ˈplaɪd
component kəmˈponənt |-ed -ɪd
comport kəmˈport, -ˈpɔrt; ES -ˈpoət, E+
 -ˈpɔət; |-ed -ɪd
compose kəmˈpoz |-s -ɪz |-d -d |-dly -ɪdlɪ
composite kəmˈpazɪt |-d -ɪd |-tor -ɚ; ES -ə(r
compos mentis ˈkɑmpəsˈmɛntɪs
compost ˈkɑmpost |-ed -ɪd, -pəstɪd
composure kəmˈpoʒɚ; ES -ˈpoʒə(r
compote ˈkɑmpot |-poted -potɪd
compound *n* ˈkɑmpaʊnd
compound *adj* kɑmˈpaʊnd (ˈcomˌpound
 ˈword)
compound *v* kɑmˈpaʊnd, kəm- |-ed -ɪd
comprehend ˌkɑmprɪˈhɛnd |-ed -ɪd |-ible -əbḷ
comprehensibility ˌkɑmprɪˌhɛnsəˈbɪlətɪ
comprehensible ˌkɑmprɪˈhɛnsəbḷ |-bly -blɪ
comprehension ˌkɑmprɪˈhɛnʃən |-sive -sɪv
compress *n* ˈkɑmprɛs |-es -ɪz
compress *v* kəmˈprɛs |-es -ɪz |-ed -t |-edly
 -ɪdlɪ, -ˈprɛstlɪ
compressibility kəmˌprɛsəˈbɪlətɪ
compressible kəmˈprɛsəbḷ |-bly -blɪ
compression kəmˈprɛʃən |-sive -ˈprɛsɪv |-sor
 -ˈprɛsɚ; ES -ə(r
comprise, -ze kəmˈpraɪz |-s -ɪz |-d -d
compromise ˈkɑmprəˌmaɪz |-s -ɪz |-d -d
comptometer, C- kɑmpˈtɑmətɚ; ES -ˈtɑmətə(r
Compton ˈkɑmptən, ˈkʌmptən
comptroller kənˈtrolɚ; ES -lə(r; |-ship -ˌʃɪp
compulsion kəmˈpʌlʃən |-sive -sɪv |-sory -sərɪ
compunction kəmˈpʌŋkʃən |-tious -ʃəs
compurgation ˌkɑmpɝˈgeʃən, -pɚ-; ES -pɝ-,
 -pɝ-, -pə-
computability kəmˌpjutəˈbɪlətɪ, -ˌpɪut-
computable kəmˈpjutəbḷ, -ˈpɪut-, ˈkɑmpjʊtə-
 |-bly -blɪ

computation ˌkɑmpjəˈteʃən, -pjʊ-
compute kəmˈpjut, -ˈpɪut |-d -ɪd
comrade ˈkɑmræd, ˈkʌm-, -rɪd
Comstock ˈkʌmstɑk, -stɒk, -stɔk
Comte kɔnt (*Fr* kõt)
Comus ˈkoməs |-ʼs -ɪz
con ʻ*against*ʼ kɑn
con ʻ*study*ʼ kɑn |conned kɑnd
con amore ˌkɑnəˈmorɪ, -ˈmɔrɪ; S -ˈmorɪ; (*It*
 ˌkonaˈmoːre)
Conan ˈkɑnən, ˈkonən
Conant ˈkonənt
conation koˈneʃən |-al -ḷ |-tive ˈkɑnətɪv
concatenate kɑnˈkætṇˌet, kən- |-d -ɪd
concatenation ˌkɑnkætṇˈeʃən, kənˌkætṇ-
concave *n* ˈkɑnkev, ˈkɑŋ-
concave *adj* kɑnˈkev, kən- (ˈconˌcave ˈsurface)
concave *v* kɑnˈkev, kən- |-d -d |-cavity
 -ˈkævətɪ
concavo-concave kɑnˈkevokɑnˈkev
concavo-convex kɑnˈkevokɑnˈvɛks
conceal kənˈsil |-ed -d |-edly -ɪdlɪ
concede kənˈsid |-ceded -ˈsidɪd
conceit kənˈsit |-ed -ɪd
conceivability kənˌsivəˈbɪlətɪ
conceivable kənˈsivəbḷ |-bly -blɪ
conceive kənˈsiv |-ceived -ˈsivd
concentrate ˈkɑnsṇˌtret, -sɛn- |-d -ɪd
concentration ˌkɑnsṇˈtreʃən, -sɛn-
concentric kənˈsɛntrɪk |-al -ḷ |-ally -ḷɪ, -ɪklɪ
Concepción kənˌsɛpsɪˈon (*Am Sp* kɒn-
 sɛpˈsjon)
concept ˈkɑnsɛpt |-ption, C- kənˈsɛpʃən
conceptual kənˈsɛptʃʊəl, -tʃʊl |-ly -ɪ
concern kənˈsɝn; ES -ˈsɜn, -ˈsɝn; |-ed -d
 |-edly -ɪdlɪ
concert *n* ˈkɑnsɚt, -sət; ES -sɜt, -sɝt, -sət
concert *v* kənˈsɝt; ES -ˈsɜt, -ˈsɝt; |-ed -ɪd
concertina ˌkɑnsɚˈtinə; ES ˌkɑnsə-
concertmaster ˈkɑnsɚtˌmæstɚ; ES ˈkɑnsət-
 ˌmæstə(r, E+-ˌmas-, -ˌmas-
concertmeister ˈkɑnsətˌmaɪstɚ; ES ˈkɑnsət-
 ˌmaɪstə(r; (*Ger* Konzert- kɒnˈtsɛrtˌmaɪstər)
concerto kənˈtʃɛrto; ES -ˈtʃɛəto; (*It* kɒn-
 ˈtʃɛrto)
concession kənˈsɛʃən
concessionaire kənˌsɛʃənˈɛr, -ˈær; E -ˈɛə(r,
 ES -ˈæə(r

Key: *See in full §§3–47.* bee bi |pity ˈpɪtɪ (§6) |rate ret |yet jɛt |sang sæŋ |angry ˈæŋ·grɪ
|bath bæθ; E bɑθ (§10) |ah ɑ |far fɑr |watch wɑtʃ, wɒtʃ (§12) |jaw dʒɔ |gorge gɔrdʒ |go go

Those words below in which the ɑ *sound is spelt* o *are often pronounced with* ɒ *in E and S*

concessionary kənˈsɛʃənˌɛrɪ

concessive kənˈsɛsɪv

conch kɑŋk, kɒŋk |-ed -t

Concho ˈkɑntʃo |Conchos ˈkɑntʃos |-s's -sɪz

conchology kɑŋˈkɑlədʒɪ, kɒŋ- |-gist -dʒɪst

concierge ˌkɑnsɪˈɛrʒ; ES -ˈɛəʒ; (*Fr* kõˈsjɛrʒ)

conciliable kənˈsɪlɪəbḷ

conciliate kənˈsɪlɪˌet |-ated -ˌetɪd

conciliation kənˌsɪlɪˈeʃən

conciliatory kənˈsɪlɪəˌtorɪ, -ˌtɔrɪ; S -ˌtorɪ

concise kənˈsaɪs |-cision kənˈsɪʒən

conclave ˈkɑnklev, ˈkɑŋ-

conclude kənˈklud, -ˈklɪud |-d -ɪd

conclusion kənˈkluʒən, -ˈklɪuʒən |-sive -sɪv

concoct kɑnˈkɑkt, kən- |-ed -ɪd |-ction -kʃən

concomitance kɑnˈkɑmətəns, kən- |-cy -ɪ |-ant -ənt

concord ˈkɑnkɔrd, -ˈkɑŋ-; ES -kɔəd

Concord *Mass, NH* ˈkɑŋkɚd; ES ˈkɑŋkəd; *elsewhere in US, towns & grape* ˈkɑnkɔrd; ES ˈkɑnkɔəd

concordance kɑnˈkɔrdn̩s, kən-; ES -ˈkɔəd-; |-s -ɪz |-d -t |-dant -dn̩t

concordat kɑnˈkɔrdæt; ES -ˈkɔədæt

Concordia kɑnˈkɔrdɪə; ES -ˈkɔədɪə

concourse ˈkɑnkors, ˈkɑŋ-, -kɔrs; ES -koəs, E+-kɔəs; |-s -ɪz

concrete *adj* kɑnˈkrit, ˈkɑnkrit, *much less freq.* kɑŋ-, ˈkɑŋ- (ˈconˌcrete ˈact)

concrete *n* ˈkɑnkrit, kɑnˈkrit, *much less freq.* ˈkɑŋ-, kɑŋ-

concrete *v* '*congeal*' kɑnˈkrit; '*cement*' ˈkɑnkrit, kɑnˈkrit |-d -ɪd—*see n*

concretion kɑnˈkriʃən—*see n*

concubinage kɑnˈkjubənɪdʒ, -ˈkɪub-

concubine ˈkɑŋkjuˌbaɪn, ˈkɑn-

concupiscence kɑnˈkjupəsn̩s, -ˈkɪu- |-cent -sn̩t

concur kənˈkɝ; ES -ˈkɜ(r, -ˈkɝ; |-red -d

concurrence kənˈkɝəns; ES -ˈkɜr-, -ˈkʌr-, -ˈkɝ-; |-cy -ɪ |-ent -ənt

concussion kənˈkʌʃən |-sive -sɪv

condemn kənˈdɛm |-ed -d |-ing -ɪŋ

condemnable '*subject to condemnation*' kənˈdɛməbḷ, '*fit to be condemned*' kənˈdɛmnəbḷ |-bly -blɪ

condemnation ˌkɑndɛmˈneʃən, -dəm-

condemnatory kənˈdɛmnəˌtorɪ, -ˌtɔrɪ; S -ˌtorɪ

condensability kənˌdɛnsəˈbɪlətɪ

condensable kənˈdɛnsəbḷ

condensate kənˈdɛnset

condensation ˌkɑndɛnˈseʃən

condense kənˈdɛns |-s -ɪz |-d -t |-dly -ɪdlɪ

condescend ˌkɑndɪˈsɛnd |-ed -ɪd

condescendence ˌkɑndɪˈsɛndəns |-dent -dənt

condescension ˌkɑndɪˈsɛnʃən

condign kənˈdaɪn (ˈconˌdign ˈcensure)

condiment ˈkɑndəmənt

condition kənˈdɪʃən |-ed -d |-ing -ˌʃənɪŋ, -ˈʃnɪŋ

conditional kənˈdɪʃənḷ, -ʃnəl |-ly -ɪ

condole kənˈdol |-d -d

condolence kənˈdoləns, ˈkɑndələns |-s -ɪz

condominium ˌkɑndəˈmɪnɪəm

condone kənˈdon |-d -d |-nation ˌkɑndoˈneʃən

condor ˈkɑndɚ; ES ˈkɑndə(r

condottiere *It* ˌkɑndotˈtjɛːre

conduce kənˈdjus, -ˈdɪus |-s -ɪz |-d -t |-cive -ɪv

conduct *n* ˈkɑndʌkt

conduct *v* kənˈdʌkt |-ed -ɪd

conductance kənˈdʌktəns |-s -ɪz

conductibility kənˌdʌktəˈbɪlətɪ

conductible kənˈdʌktəbḷ

conduction kənˈdʌkʃən |-tive -tɪv

conductivity ˌkɑndʌkˈtɪvətɪ

conductor kənˈdʌktɚ; ES -ˈdʌktə(r

conduit ˈkɑndɪt, ˈkɑndʊɪt

cone kon |coned kond

Conejos kəˈneəs, -ˈnehəs, -ˈnehos |-'s -ɪz (*Am Sp* koˈnehos)

Conemaugh ˈkɑnəˌmɔ

conenose ˈkonˌnoz |-s -ɪz

Conestoga ˌkɑnəˈstogə

coney ˈkonɪ, ˈkʌnɪ—*see* cony

Coney ˈkonɪ

confab ˈkɑnfæb

confabulate kənˈfæbjəˌlet |-lated -ˌletɪd

confabulation kənˌfæbjəˈleʃən

confect *n* ˈkɑnfɛkt

confect *v* kənˈfɛkt |-ed -ɪd |-ction -kʃən

confectionary kənˈfɛkʃənˌɛrɪ

confectioner kənˈfɛkʃənɚ, -kʃnɚ; ES -nə(r

confectionery kənˈfɛkʃənˌɛrɪ

confederacy, C- kənˈfɛdərəsɪ, -ˈfɛdrəsɪ

confederate, C- *n, adj* kənˈfɛdərɪt, -ˈfɛdrɪt

confederate *v* kənˈfɛdəˌret |-d -ɪd |-tive -ɪv

confederation kənˌfɛdəˈreʃən

|full fʊl |tooth tuθ |further ˈfɝðɚ; ES ˈfɝðə |custom ˈkʌstəm |while hwaɪl |how haʊ |toy tɔɪ |using ˈjuzɪŋ |fuse fjuz, fɪuz |dish dɪʃ |vision ˈvɪʒən |Eden ˈidn̩ |cradle ˈkredḷ |keep 'em ˈkɪpm̩

Those words below in which the ɑ sound is spelt o are often pronounced with ɒ in E and S

confer kən'fɝ; ES -'fɜ(r, -'fɝ; |-red -d
conferee ˌkɑnfə'ri
conference 'kɑnfərəns |-s -ɪz
confess kən'fɛs |-es -ɪz |-ed -t |-edly -ɪdlɪ
Confessio Amantis kən'fɛʃɪˌo ə'mæntɪs
confession kən'fɛʃən |-al -| |-ary -ˌɛrɪ
confessor kən'fɛsɚ; ES -'fɛsə(r
confetti kən'fɛtɪ (*It* kon'fɛtti)
confidant, -nte ˌkɑnfə'dænt, 'kɑnfəˌdænt
confide kən'faɪd |-fided -'faɪdɪd
confidence 'kɑnfədəns |-s -ɪz |-dent -dənt
confidential ˌkɑnfə'dɛnʃəl |-ly -ɪ
configuration kənˌfɪgjə'reʃən |-al -| |-ally -|ɪ
confine *n* 'kɑnfaɪn
confine *v* kən'faɪn |-d -d |-dly -ɪdlɪ
confirm kən'fɝm; ES -'fɜm, -'fɝm; |-ed -d
  |-edly -ɪdlɪ |-atory -əˌtorɪ, -əˌtɔrɪ; S -əˌtorɪ
confirmation ˌkɑnfɚ'meʃən; ES ˌkɑnfə-
confirmative kən'fɝmətɪv; ES -'fɜm-, -'fɝm-
confiscate 'kɑnfɪsˌket, kən'fɪsket |-d -ɪd
confiscation ˌkɑnfɪs'keʃən
confiscatory kən'fɪskəˌtorɪ, -ˌtɔrɪ; S -ˌtorɪ
confiture 'kɑnfɪˌtʃur; ES -ˌtʃuə(r
conflagrate 'kɑnfləˌgret |-grated -ˌgretɪd
conflagration ˌkɑnflə'greʃən
conflate kən'flet |-d -ɪd |-tion -'fleʃən
conflict *n* 'kɑnflɪkt
conflict *v* kən'flɪkt |-ed -ɪd |-ction -kʃən
confluence 'kɑnfluəns, -flɪu- |-s -ɪz |-ent -ənt
conflux 'kɑnflʌks |-es -ɪz
conform kən'fɔrm; ES -'fɔəm; |-ed -d
conformable kən'fɔrməb|; ES -'fɔəm-; |-bly
  -blɪ
conformance kən'fɔrməns; ES -'fɔəm-; |-s -ɪz
conformation ˌkɑnfɔr'meʃən; ES -fɔə-
conformist kən'fɔrmɪst; ES -'fɔəm-
conformity kən'fɔrmətɪ; ES -'fɔəm-
confound kɑn'faʊnd, kən-; '*damn*' 'kɑn'faʊnd
  |-ed -ɪd
confrere 'kɑnfrɛr; ES -frɛə(r
confront kən'frʌnt |-ed -ɪd
Confucian kən'fjuʃən, -'fɪu- |-ism -ˌɪzəm
Confucius kən'fjuʃəs, -'fɪu- |-'s -ɪz
confuse kən'fjuz, -'fɪuz |-s -ɪz |-d -d |-dly
  -ɪdlɪ, -dlɪ
confusion kən'fjuʒən, -'fɪuʒən
confutation ˌkɑnfjʊ'teʃən, -fɪu-
confutative kən'fjutətɪv, -'fɪu-

confute kən'fjut, -'frut |-d -ɪd
Congaree ˌkɑŋgə'ri
congé 'kɑnʒe (*Fr* kõ'ʒe)
congeal kən'dʒil |-ed -d
congee 'kɑndʒi
congener 'kɑndʒɪnɚ; ES -nə(r
congenial kən'dʒinjəl |-ly -ɪ
congeniality kənˌdʒinɪ'ælətɪ, -ˌdʒinjɪ'ælətɪ,
  -ˌdʒin'jælətɪ
congenital kən'dʒɛnət| |-ly -ɪ
conger, C- 'kɑŋgɚ; ES 'kɑŋgə(r
congeries kɑn'dʒɪriz, -'dʒɪrɪˌiz
congest kən'dʒɛst |-ed -ɪd |-ive -ɪv |-stion
  -stʃən
conglobate kɑn'globet, 'kɑŋgloˌbet
conglomerate *n*, *adj* kən'glɑmərɪt; -'glɑmrɪt
conglomerate *v* kən'glɑməˌret |-rated -ˌretɪd
conglomeration kənˌglɑmə'reʃən
Congo 'kɑŋgo
congratulate kən'grætʃəˌlet |-lated -ˌletɪd
congratulation kənˌgrætʃə'leʃən
congratulatory kən'grætʃələˌtorɪ, -ˌtɔrɪ; S
  -ˌtorɪ
congregate 'kɑŋgrɪˌget |-gated -ˌgetɪd
congregation ˌkɑŋgrɪ'geʃən |-al -|, -ʃnəl |-ally
  -|ɪ, -ʃnəlɪ
Congregational ˌkɑŋgrɪ'geʃən|, -ʃnəl |-ism
  -ˌɪzəm |-ist -ɪst
congress 'kɑŋgrəs, -ɪs |-es ɪz |-ed -t
congressional kən'grɛʃən|, -ʃnəl |-ly -ɪ
congressman 'kɑŋgrəsmən |-men -mən
congresswoman 'kɑŋgrəsˌwʊmən, -ˌwu- |-men
  -ˌwɪmɪn, -ən
Congreve 'kɑngriv, 'kɑŋ-
congruence 'kɑŋgruəns, 'kɑnˌgruəns, -ˌgrɪu-
  |-s -ɪz |-cy -ɪ |-ent -ənt
congruity kən'gruətɪ, -'grɪu-
congruous 'kɑŋgruəs
conic 'kɑnɪk |-al -| |-ally -|ɪ, -ɪklɪ
conifer 'konəfɚ, 'kɑn-; ES -fə(r
coniferous ko'nɪfərəs
Coningsby 'kʌnɪŋzbɪ
Coniston 'kɑnɪstən
conjectural kən'dʒɛktʃərəl |-ly -ɪ
conjecture kən'dʒɛktʃɚ; ES -tʃə(r; |-d -d
  |-ring -'dʒɛktʃərɪŋ, -'dʒɛktʃrɪŋ
conjoin kən'dʒɔɪn |-ed -d |-edly -ɪdlɪ |-t -t
conjugal 'kɑndʒʊg| |-ly -ɪ

Those words below in which the ɑ sound is spelt o are often pronounced with ɒ in E and S

conjugality ˌkɑndʒʊˈgælətɪ
conjugate n, adj ˈkɑndʒʊgɪt, -ˌget
conjugate v ˈkɑndʒəˌget |-gated -ˌgetɪd
conjugation ˌkɑndʒəˈgeʃən
conjunct kənˈdʒʌŋkt (ˈconˌjunct ˈverb)
conjunction kənˈdʒʌŋkʃən |-tive -tɪv
conjunctiva ˌkɑndʒʌŋkˈtaɪvə
conjunctivitis kənˌdʒʌŋktəˈvaɪtɪs
conjuncture kənˈdʒʌŋktʃɚ; ES -tʃə(r; |-ral -əl
conjuration ˌkɑndʒʊˈreʃən
conjure *'juggle'* ˈkʌndʒɚ, ˈkɑn-; ES -dʒə(r;
 |-d -d
conjure *'implore'* kənˈdʒʊr, -ˈdʒɪʊr; ES -ə(r;
 |-d -d
conjurer, -or *'juggler'* ˈkʌndʒərɚ, ˈkɑn-; ES
 -rə(r
conjurer, -or *'petitioner'* kənˈdʒʊrɚ, -ˈdʒɪʊ-;
 ES -rə(r
conjuror *'coswearer'* kʌnˈdʒʊrɚ, -ˈdʒɪʊ-; ES
 -rə(r
Conkling ˈkɑŋklɪŋ
Connacht ˈkɑnɔxt, -nət
Connaught ˈkɑnɔt
Conneaut ˈkɑnɪˌɔt
connect kəˈnɛkt |-ed -ɪd |-ible, -able -əbḷ
Connecticut kəˈnɛtɪkət—*The Brit pron.*
 kəˈnɛktɪkət, *based on the current erroneous*
 spelling, has no Am currency.
connection, -nexion kəˈnɛkʃən |-ctive -ktɪv
Connelly ˈkɑnḷɪ
conning ˈkɑnɪŋ
conniption kəˈnɪpʃən
connivance kəˈnaɪvəns |-s -ɪz |-cy -ɪ |-ant -ənt
connive kəˈnaɪv |-nived -ˈnaɪvd |-vent -ənt
connoisseur ˌkɑnəˈsɝ; ES -ˈsɜ(r, -ˈsɝ; (*Fr*
 connaisseur kɔnɛˈsœːr)
connotation ˌkɑnəˈteʃən
connotative ˈkɑnəˌtetɪv, kəˈnotətɪv
connote kəˈnot |-noted -ˈnotɪd
connubial kəˈnubɪəl, -ˈnɪub-, -ˈnjub- |-ly -ɪ
conoid ˈkonɔɪd
conquer ˈkɑŋkɚ, ˈkɒŋkɚ, ˈkɔŋkɚ; ES -kə(r;
 |-ed -d |-ing -kərɪŋ, -krɪŋ |-or -ɚ; ES -ə(r
conquest ˈkɑŋkwɛst, ˈkɒŋ-
conquistador kɑnˈkwɪstəˌdɔr; ES -ˌdɔə(r
Conrad, -e ˈkɑnræd
Conroe ˈkɑnro
consanguine kɑnˈsæŋgwɪn

consanguineous ˌkɑnsæŋˈgwɪnɪəs |-nity -nətɪ
conscience ˈkɑnʃəns |-s -ɪz
conscientious ˌkɑnʃɪˈɛnʃəs, ˌkɑnsɪ-
conscionable ˈkɑnʃənəbḷ |-bly -blɪ
conscious ˈkɑnʃəs
conscribe kənˈskraɪb |-scribed -ˈskraɪbd
conscript n, adj ˈkɑnskrɪpt
conscript v kənˈskrɪpt |-ed -ɪd |-ption -pʃən
consecrate ˈkɑnsɪˌkret |-crated -ˌkretɪd
consecration ˌkɑnsɪˈkreʃən
consecutive kənˈsɛkjətɪv
consensus kənˈsɛnsəs |-suses -səsɪz
consent kənˈsɛnt |-ed -ɪd |-ient -ˈsɛnʃənt
consequence ˈkɑnsəˌkwɛns |-s -ɪz |-quent
 -ˌkwɛnt
consequential ˌkɑnsəˈkwɛnʃəl |-ly -ɪ
consequentiality ˌkɑnsəˌkwɛnʃɪˈælətɪ
conservable kənˈsɝvəbḷ; ES -ˈsɜv-, -ˈsɝv-
conservancy kənˈsɝvənsɪ; ES -ˈsɜv-, -ˈsɝv-
conservation ˌkɑnsɚˈveʃən; ES ˌkɑnsə-
conservatism kənˈsɝvəˌtɪzəm; ES -ˈsɜv-,
 -ˈsɝv-
conservative kənˈsɝvətɪv; ES -ˈsɜv-, -ˈsɝv-
conservatoire kənˌsɝvəˈtwar; ES -ˌsɜvə-
 ˈtwaː(r, -ˌsɝvəˈtwaː(r; (*Fr* kɔ̃sɛrvaˈtwaːr)
conservator *'preserver'* ˈkɑnsɚˌvetɚ, kən-
 ˈsɝvətɚ, *bank officer* kənˈsɝvətɚ; ES
 ˈkɑnsəˌveta(r, kənˈsɜvətə(r, kənˈsɝvətə(r
conservatory kənˈsɝvəˌtorɪ, -ˌtɔrɪ; ES kən-
 ˈsɜvəˌtorɪ, -ˈsɝv-, E+-ˌtɔrɪ
conserve n ˈkɑnsɝv, kənˈsɝv; ES -ɜv, -ɝv
conserve v kənˈsɝv; ES -ˈsɜv, -ˈsɝv; |-d -d
Conshohocken ˌkɑnʃəˈhɑkən
consider kənˈsɪdɚ; ES -ˈsɪdə(r; |-ed -d |-ing
 -ˈsɪdərɪŋ, -ˈsɪdrɪŋ
considerable kənˈsɪdərəbḷ, -ˈsɪdrəbḷ |-bly -blɪ
considerate kənˈsɪdərɪt, -ˈsɪdrɪt
consideration kənˌsɪdəˈreʃən
consign kənˈsaɪn |-ed -d
consignee ˌkɑnsaɪˈni, -sɪˈni
consigner kənˈsaɪnɚ; ES -ˈsaɪnə(r
consignment kənˈsaɪnmənt
consignor kənˈsaɪnɚ; ES -ˈsaɪnə(r; (ˌcon-
 signˈee & ˌconsignˈor)
consist kənˈsɪst |-ed -ɪd
consistence kənˈsɪstəns |-cy -ɪ |-ent -ənt
consistory kənˈsɪstərɪ, -ˈsɪstrɪ
consociate n, adj kənˈsoʃɪɪt, -ʃɪˌet

|full fʊl |tooth tuθ |further ˈfɝðɚ; ES ˈfɜðə |custom ˈkʌstəm |while hwaɪl |how haʊ |toy tɔɪ
|using ˈjuzɪŋ |fuse fjuz, fɪuz |dish dɪʃ |vision ˈvɪʒən |Eden ˈidn̩ |cradle ˈkredḷ |keep 'em ˈkipm̩

Those words below in which the ɑ sound is spelt o are often pronounced with ɒ in E and S

consociate v kən'soʃɪˌet |-ated -ˌetɪd
consociation kənˌsosɪ'eʃən, -ˌsoʃɪ-
consol 'kɑnsɑl, kən'sɑl |-s -z
consolable kən'soləbḷ |-bly -blɪ
consolation ˌkɑnsə'leʃən
consolatory kən'sɑləˌtorɪ, -ˌtɔrɪ; S -ˌtorɪ
console n 'kɑnsol
console v kən'sol |-soled -'sold
consolidate kən'sɑləˌdet |-dated -ˌdetɪd
consolidation kənˌsɑlə'deʃən
consommé ˌkɑnsə'me
consonance 'kɑnsənəns |-cy -ɪ |-ant -ənt
consonantal ˌkɑnsə'næntḷ |-ly -ɪ
consonantly 'kɑnsənəntlɪ
consort n 'kɑnsɔrt; ES -sɔət
consort v kən'sɔrt; ES -'sɔət; |-ed -ɪd
consortium kən'sɔrʃɪəm; ES -'sɔəʃ-; |-ia -ɪə
conspectus kən'spɛktəs |-es -ɪz
conspicuous kən'spɪkjʊəs
conspirator kən'spɪrətɚ; ES -tə(r; |-acy -əsɪ
conspiratorial kənˌspɪrə'torɪəl, -'tɔr-; S -'tor-;
   |-ly -ɪ
conspire kən'spaɪr; ES -'spaɪə(r; |-d -d
conspirer kən'spaɪrɚ; ES -'spaɪrə(r
constable 'kɑnstəbḷ, 'kʌn- —*The sp. pron. is
   now more freq. than the traditional one; see
   next.*
Constable 'kʌnstəbḷ
constabulary kən'stæbjəˌlɛrɪ
Constance 'kɑnstəns |-'s -ɪz
constancy 'kɑnstənsɪ |-tant -tənt
Constantine 'kɑnstənˌtaɪn, -ˌtin
Constantinople ˌkɑnstæntə'nopḷ, -stæntn̩'opḷ
constellation ˌkɑnstə'leʃən
consternate 'kɑnstɚˌnet; ES 'kɑnstə-; |-d -ɪd
consternation ˌkɑnstɚ'neʃən; ES ˌkɑnstə-
constipate 'kɑnstəˌpet |-pated -ˌpetɪd
constipation ˌkɑnstə'peʃən
constituency kən'stɪtʃʊənsɪ |-ent -ənt
constitute 'kɑnstəˌtjut, -ˌtrut, -ˌtut |-d -ɪd
constitution ˌkɑnstə'tjuʃən, -'tru-, -'tu- |-al -ḷ
   |-ally -ḷɪ
constitutionality ˌkɑnstəˌtjuʃən'ælətɪ, -ˌtru-,
   -ˌtu-
constitutive 'kɑnstəˌtjutɪv, -ˌtru-, -ˌtu-
constrain kən'stren |-ed -d |-edly -ɪdlɪ |-t -t
constrict kən'strɪkt |-ed -ɪd |-or -ɚ; ES -ə(r
constriction kən'strɪkʃən |-tive -tɪv

construable kən'struəbḷ, -'strɪu-
construct adj kən'strʌkt ('conˌstruct 'state)
construct n 'kɑnstrʌkt
construct v kən'strʌkt |-ed -ɪd
construction kən'strʌktʃən |-al -ḷ |-ally -ḷɪ
   |-tive -tɪv
construe kən'stru, -'strɪu |-d -d—*in Shak.*
   conster 'kɑnstɚ
consubstantial ˌkɑnsəb'stænʃəl |-ly -ɪ
consubstantiality ˌkɑnsəbˌstænʃɪ'ælətɪ
consubstantiate ˌkɑnsəb'stænʃɪˌet |-ed -ɪd
consubstantiation ˌkɑnsəbˌstænʃɪ'eʃən
consuetude 'kɑnswɪˌtjud, -ˌtrud, -ˌtud
consuetudinary ˌkɑnswɪ'tjudn̩ˌɛrɪ, -'trud-,
   -'tud-
consul 'kɑnsḷ |-ship -ˌʃɪp
consular 'kɑnsḷɚ, 'kɑnsjələ; ES -ə(r
consulate 'kɑnsḷɪt, 'kɑnsjəlɪt
consult n 'kɑnsʌlt, kən'sʌlt
consult v kən'sʌlt |-ed -ɪd |-ant -n̩t
consultation ˌkɑnsḷ'teʃən
consultative kən'sʌltətɪv
consultatory kən'sʌltəˌtorɪ, -ˌtɔrɪ; S -ˌtorɪ
consultory kən'sʌltərɪ
consumable kən'suməbḷ, -'sɪum-, -'sjum-
consume kən'sum, -'sɪum, '-sjum |-d -d
   |-dly -ɪdlɪ
consumer kən'sumɚ, -'sɪumɚ, -'sjumɚ; ES
   -ə(r
consummate adj kən'sʌmɪt
consummate v 'kɑnsəˌmet |-mated -ˌmetɪd
consummation ˌkɑnsə'meʃən
consumption kən'sʌmpʃən |-tive -tɪv
contact 'kɑntækt |-ed -ɪd
contagion kən'tedʒən |-gious -dʒəs
contain kən'ten |-ed -d
contaminate kən'tæməˌnet |-nated -ˌnetɪd
contamination kənˌtæmə'neʃən
contemn kən'tɛm |-ed -d |-edly -nɪdlɪ
contemnible kən'tɛmnəbḷ |-bly -blɪ
contemner kən'tɛmɚ; ES -'tɛmə(r
contemnor kən'tɛmnɚ; ES -'tɛmnə(r
contemplable kən'tɛmpləbḷ
contemplate 'kɑntəmˌplet, kən'templet |-d -ɪd
contemplation ˌkɑntəm'pleʃən
contemplative 'kɑntəmˌpletɪv, kən'tɛmplətɪv
contemporaneity kənˌtɛmpərə'niətɪ
contemporaneous kənˌtɛmpə'renɪəs

Those words below in which the ɑ *sound is spelt* o *are often pronounced with* ɒ *in E and S*

contemporary kən'tɛmpə,rɛrɪ
contempt kən'tɛmpt
contemptible kən'tɛmptəbļ |-bly -blɪ
contemptuous kən'tɛmptʃʊəs
contend kən'tɛnd |-ed -ɪd
content *n* '*satisfaction*' kən'tɛnt, '*what is con-tained*' 'kɑntɛnt, kən'tɛnt
content *adj, v* kən'tɛnt |-ed -ɪd
contention kən'tɛnʃən |-al -ļ |-tious -ʃəs
conterminous kən'tɝmənəs; ES -'tɝm-, -'tɝm-
contest *n* 'kɑntɛst
contest *v* kən'tɛst |-ed -ɪd |-ant -ənt
context 'kɑntɛkst
contextual kən'tɛkstʃʊəl, kɑn- |-ly -ɪ
contexture kən'tɛkstʃɚ, kɑn-; ES -'tɛkstʃə(r
contiguity ,kɑntɪ'gjuətɪ, -'gɪu-
contiguous kən'tɪgjʊəs
continence 'kɑntənəns |-cy -ɪ |-nent -nənt
continental ,kɑntə'nɛntļ |-ly -ɪ
contingence kən'tɪndʒəns |-cy -ɪ |-gent -dʒənt
continual kən'tɪnjʊəl |-ly -ɪ
continuance kən'tɪnjʊəns |-s -ɪz |-ant -ənt
continuation kən,tɪnjʊ'eʃən
continue kən'tɪnjʊ |-d -d |-dly -jʊdlɪ
continuity ,kɑntə'nuətɪ, -'nɪu-, -'nju-
continuous kən'tɪnjʊəs |-nuum -njʊəm |-nua -njʊə
contort kən'tɔrt; ES -'tɔət; |-ed -ɪd
contortion kən'tɔrʃən; ES -'tɔəʃən
contour 'kɑntʊr; ES -tʊə(r; |-ed -d
contra 'kɑntrə
contraband 'kɑntrə,bænd |-age -ɪdʒ |-ist -ɪst
contrabandism 'kɑntrəbænd,ɪzəm
contrabass 'kɑntrə,bes |-es -ɪz
contraception ,kɑntrə'sɛpʃən |-tive -tɪv
contraclockwise ,kɑntrə'klɑk,waɪz
contract *n* 'kɑntrækt
contract *v* '*shrink*' kən'trækt, '*make a con-tract*'+ 'kɑntrækt |-ed -ɪd
contractible kən'træktəbļ |-bly -blɪ
contractile kən'træktļ, -tɪl
contractility ,kɑntræk'tɪlətɪ
contraction kən'trækʃən |-tive -tɪv
contractor 'kɑntræktɚ, kən'træktɚ; ES -tə(r
contractual kən'træktʃʊəl |-ly -ɪ
contradict ,kɑntrə'dɪkt |-ed -ɪd
contradiction ,kɑntrə'dɪkʃən |-tory -tərɪ, -trɪ

contradistinction ,kɑntrədɪ'stɪŋkʃən |-tive -tɪv
contraindication ,kɑntrə,ɪndə'keʃən
contralto kən'trælto
contraposition ,kɑntrəpə'zɪʃən
contraption kən'træpʃən
contrapuntal ,kɑntrə'pʌntļ |-ly -ɪ
contrariety ,kɑntrə'raɪətɪ
contrarily 'kɑntrɛrəlɪ, *esp. if emph.* kən-'trɛrəlɪ, -'trer-
contrarious kən'trɛrɪəs, -'trer-
contrariwise 'kɑntrɛrɪ,waɪz
contrary '*opposite*' 'kɑntrɛrɪ; '*perverse*' 'kɑntrɛrɪ, kən'trɛrɪ, -'trɛrɪ
contrast *n* 'kɑntræst
contrast *v* kən'træst |-ed -ɪd
contravene ,kɑntrə'vin |-vened -'vind
contravention ,kɑntrə'vɛnʃən
contredanse *Fr* kõtrə'dã:s
contretemps *Fr* kõtrə'tã
contribute kən'trɪbjʊt |-d -bjətɪd
contribution ,kɑntrə'bjuʃən, -'brɪuʃən
contributor kən'trɪbjətɚ; ES -tə(r
contributory kən'trɪbjə,tɔrɪ, -,tɔrɪ; S -,tɔrɪ
contrite 'kɑntraɪt, kən'traɪt ('kɑn,trite 'heart, 'hearts con'trite)
contrition kən'trɪʃən
contrivance kən'traɪvəns |-s -ɪz |-cy -ɪ
contrive kən'traɪv |-d -d
control kən'trol |-trolled -'trold
controllable kən'troləbļ |-bly -blɪ
controller kən'trolɚ; ES -'trolə(r; |-ship -,ʃɪp
controversial ,kɑntrə'vɝʃəl, -sɪəl; ES -'vɝ-, -'vɝ-; |-ly -ɪ
controversy 'kɑntrə,vɝsɪ; ES -,vɝsɪ, -,vɝsɪ
controvert 'kɑntrə,vɝt, ,kɑntrə'vɝt; ES -ɝt, -ɝt; |-ed -ɪd
controvertible ,kɑntrə'vɝtəbļ; ES -'vɝt-, -'vɝt-; *acct*+ 'contro,vertible |-bly -blɪ
contumacious ,kɑntjʊ'meʃəs, ,kɑntʊ-
contumacy 'kɑntjʊməsɪ, 'kɑntʊ-
contumelious ,kɑntjʊ'milɪəs, ,kɑntʊ-
contumely 'kɑntjʊməlɪ, 'kɑntʊ-, -,mɪlɪ, kən'tjuməlɪ, -'tɪu-, -'tu- —*Only a book-word. Formerly* 'kɑntjʊ,milɪ, *as in Chap-man and probably Shak. Hood has* kən-'tjumɪlɪ (*rime gloomily*).
contuse kən'tjuz, -'tɪuz, -'tuz |-s -ɪz |-d -d

|full fʊl |tooth tuθ |further 'fɝðɚ; ES 'fɝðə |custom 'kʌstəm |while hwaɪl |how haʊ |toy tɔɪ
|using 'juzɪŋ |fuse fjuz, fɪuz |dish dɪʃ |vision 'vɪʒən |Eden 'idn̩ |cradle 'kredl̩ |keep 'em 'kipm̩

Those words below in which the ɑ *sound is spelt* o *are often pronounced with* ɒ *in E and S*

contusion kən'tjuʒən, -'tɪuʒ-, -'tuʒ-
conundrum kə'nʌndrəm
convalesce ˌkɑnvə'lɛs |-s -ɪz |-d -t
convalescence ˌkɑnvə'lɛsn̩s |-cy -ɪ |-scent -sn̩t
convection kən'vɛkʃən |-al -l̩
convenance 'kɑnvəˌnɑns |-s -ɪz (*Fr* kõv'nã:s)
convene kən'vin |-vened -'vind
convenience kən'vinjəns |-s -ɪz |-ient -jənt
convent 'kɑnvɛnt
conventical kən'vɛntɪkl̩ |-ly -ɪ
conventicle kən'vɛntɪkl̩ |-d -d
convention kən'vɛnʃən |-al -l̩, -ʃnəl |-ally -l̩ɪ, -ʃnəlɪ
conventionalism kən'vɛnʃənl̩ˌɪzəm, -ʃnəl- |-ist -ɪst
conventionality kənˌvɛnʃən'ælətɪ
conventionalize kən'vɛnʃənl̩ˌaɪz, -ʃnəl- |-s -ɪz |-d -d
conventual kən'vɛntʃʊəl |-ly -ɪ
converge kən'vɝdʒ; ES -'vɜdʒ, -'vɝdʒ; |-s -ɪz |-d -d
convergence kən'vɝdʒəns; ES -'vɜdʒ-, -'vɝdʒ-; |-cy -ɪ |-gent -dʒənt
conversance 'kɑnvɚsn̩s, kən'vɝsn̩s; ES -vəs-, -'vɜs-, -'vɝs-; |-cy -ɪ |-sant -sn̩t
conversation ˌkɑnvɚ'seʃən; ES ˌkɑnvə-; |-al -l̩ |-ally -l̩ɪ
conversationalist ˌkɑnvɚ'seʃənl̩ɪst, -ʃnəl-; ES ˌkɑnvə-
converse *n* 'kɑnvɝs; ES -vɜs, -vɝs; |-s -ɪz
converse *adj* kən'vɝs; ES -'vɜs, -'vɝs; ('conˌverse 'wind)
converse *v* kən'vɝs; ES -'vɜs, -'vɝs; |-s -ɪz |-d -t
conversion kən'vɝʃən, -ʒən; ES -'vɜ-, -'vɝ-
convert *n* 'kɑnvɝt; ES -vɜt, -vɝt
convert *v* kən'vɝt; ES -'vɜt, -'vɝt; |-ed -ɪd
convertibility kənˌvɝtə'bɪlətɪ; ES -ˌvɜt-, -ˌvɝt-
convertible kən'vɝtəbl̩; ES -'vɜt-, -'vɝt-; |-bly -blɪ
convex *adj* kɑn'vɛks, kən- ('conˌvex 'surface)
convex *n, v* 'kɑnvɛks |-es -ɪz |-ed -t, *v+* kən'vɛks
convexity kən'vɛksətɪ
convey kən've |-ed -d |-ance -əns |-ances -ənsɪz
convict *n* 'kɑnvɪkt

convict *v* kən'vɪkt |-ed -ɪd |-ction -kʃən
convince kən'vɪns |-s -ɪz |-d -t |-dly -ɪdlɪ
convivial kən'vɪvɪəl |-ly -ɪ
conviviality kənˌvɪvɪ'ælətɪ
convocation ˌkɑnvə'keʃən |-al -l̩ |-ally -l̩ɪ
convoke kən'vok |-voked -'vokt
convolute 'kɑnvəˌlut, -ˌlɪut |-d -ɪd
convolution ˌkɑnvə'luʃən, -'lɪuʃən, -vl̩'juʃən
convolvulus, C- kən'vɑlvjələs |-es -ɪz |-li -ˌlaɪ
convoy *n* 'kɑnvɔɪ
convoy *v* kən'vɔɪ |-ed -d
convulse kən'vʌls |-s -ɪz |-d -t |-dly -ɪdlɪ
convulsion kən'vʌlʃən |-sive -sɪv
Conway 'kɑnwe
Conwell 'kɑnwɛl
cony 'konɪ, 'kʌnɪ—*When the word was popular, it was pron.* 'kʌnɪ; *since it became a book-word, sp. pron. has prevailed.*
conycatcher 'konɪˌkætʃɚ, 'kʌnɪ-; ES -ˌkætʃə(r
coo ku |cooed kud
cook kʊk |cooked kʊkt |-ery -ərɪ, -rɪ |-y, -ie -ɪ
cool kul |cooled kuld
Cooley 'kulɪ
cool-headed 'kul'hɛdɪd ('cool-ˌheaded 'move)
Coolidge 'kulɪdʒ |-'s -ɪz
coolie, -ly 'kulɪ
coolly 'kulɪ, 'kullɪ
coomb, coombe, coom '*valley*' kum
coon kun |cooned kund
co-op ko'ɑp, 'koˌɑp
coop kup, kʊp; S kʊp, kup; |-ed -t
cooper, C- 'kupɚ, 'kupɚ; E -pə(r; S 'kupə(r, 'kup-; |-ed -d |-ing -pərɪŋ, -prɪŋ
co-operate *adj* ko'ɑpərɪt, -'ɑprɪt
co-operate *v* ko'ɑpəˌret |-rated -ˌretɪd
co-operation koˌɑpə'reʃən, ˌkoɑpə-
co-operative ko'ɑpəˌretɪv, -'ɑprətɪv
Cooperstown 'kupɚzˌtaʊn, 'kup-; E -pəz-; S 'kupəz-, 'kup-
co-opt ko'ɑpt |-opted -'ɑptɪd
co-ordinate, *n, adj* ko'ɔrdn̩t, -ˌet; ES -'ɔəd-
co-ordinate *v* ko'ɔrdn̩ˌet; ES -'ɔəd-; |-d -ɪd
co-ordination koˌɔrdn̩'eʃən; ES -ˌɔədn̩'eʃən
co-ordinative ko'ɔrdn̩ˌetɪv; ES -'ɔədn̩ˌetɪv
Coos *NH* ko'ɑs, 'koɑs; *Oreg* kus
coot kut |cooted 'kutɪd
cop kɑp |copped kɑpt
copal 'kopl̩, 'kopæl

Those words below in which the ɑ *sound is spelt* o *are often pronounced with* ɒ *in E and S*

coparcenary koˈpɑrsn̩ˌɛrɪ; ES -ˈpɑːs-, E+
  -ˈpɑːs-
coparcener koˈpɑrsn̩ɚ; ES -ˈpɑːsn̩ə(r, E+
  -ˈpɑːs-
copartner koˈpɑrtnɚ; ES -ˈpɑːtnə(r, E+
  -ˈpɑːt-
cope kop |coped kopt
copeck, -pec ˈkopɛk
Copeland ˈkoplənd
Copenhagen ˌkopənˈhegən (*Dan* ˌkøpn̩ˈhɑʊn)
Copernicus koˈpɜˑnɪkəs; ES -ˈpɜn-, -ˈpɜˑn-;
  |-'s -ɪz |-can -kən
copestone ˈkopˌston
Cophetua koˈfɛtʃʊə
Copiah kəˈpaɪə, ko-
copier ˈkopɪɚ; ES ˈkopɪ·ə(r
coping ˈkopɪŋ
copious ˈkopɪəs
Coplay ˈkoplɪ |Copley ˈkoplɪ
copper ˈkopɚ; ES ˈkopə(r; |-ed -d |-ing
  ˈkopərɪŋ, ˈkoprɪŋ
copperas ˈkopərəs, ˈkoprəs
Copperfield ˈkopɚˌfild; ES ˈkopə-
copperhead, C- ˈkopɚˌhɛd; ES ˈkopə-
copperplate 'engraving' ˈkopɚˌplet; ES ˈkopə-
copperplate 'engrave' ˈkopɚˌplet; ES ˈkopə-;
  |-d -ɪd
copper-plate 'plate with copper' ˈkopɚˈplet; ES
  ˈkopə-; |-d -ɪd (ˈcopper-ˌplated ˈmedal)
coppersmith ˈkopɚˌsmɪθ; ES ˈkopə-; |-ths -θs
coppice ˈkopɪs |-s -ɪz |-d -t
copra ˈkoprə
copse kops |copses ˈkopsɪz |copsed kopst
Copt kopt |Coptic ˈkoptɪk
copula ˈkopjələ
copulate *adj* ˈkopjəlɪt
copulate *v* ˈkopjəˌlet |-lated -ˌletɪd
copulation ˌkopjəˈleʃən |-tive ˈkopjəˌletɪv
copy ˈkopɪ |copied ˈkopɪd |-pyist -ɪst
copybook ˈkopɪˌbʊk
copyhold ˈkopɪˌhold
copyright ˈkopɪˌraɪt |-ed -ɪd
coquet koˈkɛt |-quetted -ˈkɛtɪd
coquetry ˈkokɪtrɪ, koˈkɛtrɪ
coquette koˈkɛt |-quetted -ˈkɛtɪd
Coquille koˈkil
Cora ˈkorə, ˈkɔrə; S ˈkorə
coracle ˈkorəkl̩, ˈkɑr-, ˈkɒr-

coral ˈkorəl, ˈkɑr-, ˈkɒr-, ˈkor- |-ed -d
Coran koˈrɑn, -ˈræn
Coraopolis ˌkorɪˈɑplɪs, -plɪs, ˌkorəˈʔɑp-,
  ˌkɔr-; S ˌkor-
corbel ˈkɔrbl̩; ES ˈkɔəbl̩; |-ed -d
corbie ˈkɔrbɪ; ES ˈkɔəbɪ
Corcoran ˈkɔrkərən; ES ˈkɔəkərən
cord kɔrd; ES kɔəd; |-ed -ɪd |-age -ɪdʒ
Cordelia kɔrˈdiljə; ES kɔəˈdiljə
Cordell kɔrˈdɛl; ES kɔəˈdɛl (ˈCorˌdell ˈHull)
cordial ˈkɔrdʒəl; ES ˈkɔədʒ-; *Brit* -dɪəl |-ly -ɪ
cordiality kɔrˈdʒælətɪ; ES kɔ-; *Brit* -dɪˈæl-
cordillera, C- kɔrˈdɪlərə, ˌkɔrdɪlˈjɛrə; ES kɔ-,
  ˌkɔə-; (*Am Sp* ˌkɔrðiˈjera)
cordite ˈkɔrdaɪt
Córdoba ˈkɔrdovə; ES ˈkɔə-; (*Sp* ˈkɔrðoβa)
cordoba ˈkɔrdəbə; ES ˈkɔə-
cordon ˈkɔrdn̩; ES ˈkɔədn̩; |-ed -d
Cordova ˈkɔrdəvə; ES ˈkɔə-; |-n -n— *some*
  US places Corˈdova
corduroy ˌkɔrdəˈrɔɪ; ES ˌkɔədə-; (ˈcorduˌroy
  ˈroad)
cordwain ˈkɔrdwen; ES ˈkɔəd-; |-er -ɚ; ES
  -ə(r
cordwood ˈkɔrdˌwʊd; ES ˈkɔəd-
core kor, kɔr; ES koə(r, E+kɔə(r; |-d -d
Corea koˈriə |-n -n
corelation ˌko·rɪˈleʃən
coreligionist ˌko·rɪˈlɪdʒənɪst
corella kəˈrɛlə
Corelli kəˈrɛlɪ
coreopsis ˌkorɪˈɑpsɪs, ˌkɔrɪ-; S ˌkorɪ-
corespondent ˌko·rɪˈspandənt
Corfu ˈkɔrfju, -fɪu, kɔrˈfu; ES ˈkɔə-, kɔə-
Corgi ˈkɔrgɪ; ES ˈkɔəgɪ
coriander ˌkorɪˈændɚ, ˌkɔrɪ-; ES ˌkorɪˈændə(r,
  E+ˌkɔrɪ-
Corin ˈkorɪn, ˈkɑr-, ˈkɒr-
Corinna kəˈrɪnə
Corinth ˈkorɪnθ, ˈkɑr-, ˈkɒr- |-ian kəˈrɪnθɪən
Coriolanus ˌkorɪəˈlenəs, ˌkɑr-, ˌkɒr- |-'s -ɪz
Corioles kəˈraɪəˌliz, -lɪz |-'s -ɪz |-li -ˌlaɪ
cork, C- kɔrk; ES kɔək; |-ed -t
corival koˈraɪvl̩, kə-
corkscrew ˈkɔrkˌskru, -ˌskrɪu; ES ˈkɔək-
Corliss ˈkɔrlɪs; ES ˈkɔəlɪs; |-'s -ɪz
corm kɔrm; ES kɔəm
cormorant ˈkɔrmərənt; ES ˈkɔəm-

|full fʊl |tooth tuθ |further ˈfɝðɚ; ES ˈfɜðə |custom ˈkʌstəm |while hwaɪl |how haʊ |toy tɔɪ
|using ˈjuzɪŋ |fuse fjuz, fɪuz |dish dɪʃ |vision ˈvɪʒən |Eden ˈidn̩ |cradle ˈkredl̩ |keep 'em ˈkipm̩

corn **kɔrn**; ES **kɔɔn**; |-ed -**d** |-cake -ˌ**kek** |-cob -ˌ**kɑb**; ES+-ˌ**kɒb**

cornea ˈ**kɔrnɪə**; ES ˈ**kɔɔnɪə**

Corneille kɔrˈ**ne**; ES kɔɔˈ**ne** (*Fr* kɔrˈ**nɛ:j**)

cornel ˈ**kɔrnl̩**, -**nɛl**; ES ˈ**kɔɔn**-

Cornelia kɔrˈ**niljə**, kə-; ES kɔɔˈ**niljə**, kə-

cornelian '*carnelian*' kɔrˈ**niljən**, kə-; ES kɔɔ-, kə-

Cornelius kɔrˈ**niljəs**, kə-; ES kɔɔ-, kə-; |-'s -**ɪz**

Cornell kɔrˈ**nɛl**; ES kɔɔˈ**nɛl**; (ˈ**Cor**ˌnell ˈ**cap**)

corneous ˈ**kɔrnɪəs**; ES ˈ**kɔɔnɪəs**

corner ˈ**kɔrnɚ**; ES ˈ**kɔɔnə(r**; |-ed -**d**—*A dissimilated pron.* ˈ**kɔnɚ** *is sometimes heard* (*§121*).

cornerstone ˈ**kɔrnɚˌston**; ES ˈ**kɔɔnə**-

cornerways ˈ**kɔrnɚˌwez**; ES ˈ**kɔɔnə**-; |-wise -ˌ**waɪz**

cornet ˈ**kɔrnɪt**, kɔrˈ**nɛt**, *musical instr.* kɔrˈ**nɛt**; ES ˈ**kɔɔ**-, kɔɔ-

cornettist, -netist kɔrˈ**nɛtɪst**; ES kɔɔ-

corn-flour ˈ**kɔrnˌflaʊr**; ES ˈ**kɔɔnˌflaʊə(r**

cornflower ˈ**kɔrnˌflaʊɚ**; ES ˈ**kɔɔnˌflaʊ·ə(r**

cornice ˈ**kɔrnɪs**; ES ˈ**kɔɔnɪs**; |-s -**ɪz** |-d -**t**

Cornish ˈ**kɔrnɪʃ**; ES ˈ**kɔɔnɪʃ**; |-man, -men -**mən**

cornstarch ˈ**kɔrnˌstartʃ**, -ˈ**startʃ**; ES ˈ**kɔɔn**-ˌ**stɑ:tʃ**, -ˈ**stɑ:tʃ**, E+-**ɑ:tʃ**

cornucopia ˌ**kɔrnəˈkopɪə**; ES ˌ**kɔɔnə**-; |-n -**n**

Cornwall ˈ**kɔrnwɔl**, -**wəl**; ES ˈ**kɔɔn**-

Cornwallis kɔrnˈ**wɔlɪs**, -ˈ**wɒl**-, -ˈ**wal**-; ES kɔɔn-; |-'s -**ɪz**

corody ˈ**kɔrədɪ**, ˈ**kɑr**-, ˈ**kɒr**-

corolla kəˈ**rɑlə**; ES+-ˈ**rɒlə**

corollary ˈ**kɔrəˌlɛrɪ**, ˈ**kɑr**-, ˈ**kɒr**-, *Brit* kəˈ**rɒlərɪ**

corona, C- kəˈ**ronə** |-s -**z** |-nae -**ni**

coronach ˈ**kɔrənɑx**, ˈ**kɑr**-, ˈ**kɒr**-

coronal *n* ˈ**kɔrənl̩**, ˈ**kɑr**-, ˈ**kɒr**-

coronal *adj* kəˈ**ronl̩**, ˈ**kɔrənl̩**, ˈ**kɑr**-, ˈ**kɒr**- |-ly -**ɪ**

coronary ˈ**kɔrəˌnɛrɪ**, ˈ**kɑr**-, ˈ**kɒr**-

coronation ˌ**kɔrəˈneʃən**, ˌ**kɑr**-, ˌ**kɒr**-

coroner ˈ**kɔrənɚ**, ˈ**kɑr**-, ˈ**kɒr**-; ES -**nə(r**

coronet ˈ**kɔrənɪt**, ˈ**kɑr**-, ˈ**kɒr**- |-ed -**ɪd**, -ˌ**nɛtɪd**

Corot kəˈ**ro**

corporal ˈ**kɔrpərəl**, ˈ**kɔrprəl**; ES ˈ**kɔɔp**-; |-ly -**ɪ**

corporality ˌ**kɔrpəˈrælətɪ**; ES ˌ**kɔɔp**-

corporate *adj* ˈ**kɔrpərɪt**, ˈ**kɔrprɪt**; ES ˈ**kɔɔp**-

corporate *v* ˈ**kɔrpəˌret**; ES ˈ**kɔɔp**-; |-d -**ɪd**

corporation ˌ**kɔrpəˈreʃən**; ES ˌ**kɔɔp**-

corporeal kɔrˈ**porɪəl**, -ˈ**pɔr**-; ES kəˈ**porɪəl**, E+-ˈ**pɔrɪəl**; |-ly -**ɪ**

corporeity ˌ**kɔrpəˈrɪətɪ**; ES ˌ**kɔɔp**-

corposant ˈ**kɔrpəˌzænt**; ES ˈ**kɔɔp**-

corps kor, kɔr; ES koə(r, E+kɔə(r; [*pl* -ps -**z**

corpse kɔrps; ES kɔɔps; |-s -**ɪz**

corpulence ˈ**kɔrpjələns**; ES ˈ**kɔɔp**-; |-cy -**ɪ** |-nt -**nt**

corpus ˈ**kɔrpəs**; ES ˈ**kɔɔp**-; |-es -**ɪz** |-pora -**pərə**

Corpus Christi ˈ**kɔrpəsˈkrɪstɪ**; ES ˈ**kɔɔp**-; *Church* +-**taɪ**

corpuscular kɔrˈ**pʌskjəlɚ**; ES kəˈ**pʌskjələ(r**

corpuscle ˈ**kɔrpəsl̩**, ˈ**kɔrpʌsl̩**; ES ˈ**kɔɔp**-

corpus delicti ˈ**kɔrpəsdɪˈlɪktaɪ**; ES ˈ**kɔɔp**-

corral kəˈ**ræl** |-led -**d**

correct kəˈ**rɛkt** |-ed -**ɪd**

correction kəˈ**rɛkʃən** |-tive -**tɪv**

correctitude kəˈ**rɛktəˌtjud**, -ˌ**tɪud**, -ˌ**tud**

corrector kəˈ**rɛktɚ**; ES -ˈ**rɛktə(r**

Corregidor kəˈ**rɛgəˌdɔr**; ES -ˌ**dɔə(r**; (*Am Sp* kəˌ**rrɛhiˈðɔr**)

correlate ˈ**kɔrəˌlet**, ˈ**kɑr**-, ˈ**kɒr**- |-d -**ɪd**

correlation ˌ**kɔrəˈleʃən**, ˌ**kɑr**-, ˌ**kɒr**-

correlative kəˈ**rɛlətɪv** |-vity kəˌ**rɛləˈtɪvətɪ**

correspond ˌ**kɔrəˈspand**, ˌ**kɑr**-, ˌ**kɒr**-; ES+-ˈ**spɒnd**; |-ed -**ɪd** |-ence -**əns** |-ent -**ənt**

corridor ˈ**kɔrədɚ**, ˈ**kɑr**-, ˈ**kɒr**-, *geog.*+-ˌ**dɔr**; ES -**də(r**, -ˌ**dɔə(r**; |-ed -**d**

corrie ˈ**kɔrɪ**, ˈ**kɑrɪ**, ˈ**kɒrɪ**

Corrigan ˈ**kɔrəgən**, ˈ**kɑr**-, ˈ**kɒr**-

corrigendum ˌ**kɔrɪˈdʒɛndəm**, ˌ**kɑr**-, ˌ**kɒr**- |-da -**də**

corrigibility ˌ**kɔrədʒəˈbɪlətɪ**, ˌ**kɑr**-, ˌ**kɒr**-

corrigible ˈ**kɔrədʒəbl̩**, ˈ**kɑr**-, ˈ**kɒr**- |-bly -**blɪ**

corrival kəˈ**raɪvl̩**

corrobboree, -ri *n* kəˈ**rabərɪ**; ES+-ˈ**rɒb**-

corroborant kəˈ**rabərənt**; ES+-ˈ**rɒb**-

corroborate *adj* kəˈ**rabərɪt**; ES+-ˈ**rɒb**-

corroborate *v* kəˈ**rabəˌret**; ES+-ˈ**rɒb**-; |-d -**ɪd** |-tive -**tɪv**

corroboration kəˌ**rabəˈreʃən**; ES+-ˌ**rɒb**-

corroboratory kəˈ**rabərəˌtorɪ**, -ˌ**tɔrɪ**; S -ˌ**torɪ**

corroboree, -ri *n* kəˈ**rabərɪ**; ES+-ˈ**rɒb**-

corroboree *v* kəˈ**rabəˌri** |-d -**d**

corrode kəˈ**rod** |-roded -ˈ**rodɪd**

corrosion kəˈ**roʒən** |-sive -**sɪv**

corrugate *adj* ˈ**kɔrəgɪt**, ˈ**kɔrjə**-, ˈ**kɑr**-, ˈ**kɒr**-, -ˌ**get**

Those words below in which the ɑ sound is spelt o are often pronounced with ɒ in E and S

corrugate *v* ˈkɔrəˌget, ˈkɔrjə-, ˈkɑr-, ˈkɒr-
|-d -ɪd

corrugation ˌkɔrəˈgeʃən, ˌkɔrjə-, ˌkɑr-, ˌkɒr-

corrupt kəˈrʌpt |-ed -ɪd |-ption -pʃən

·corruptibility kəˌrʌptəˈbɪlətɪ

corruptible kəˈrʌptəbļ |-bly -blɪ

Corry ˈkɔrɪ, ˈkɑrɪ, ˈkɒrɪ

corsage kɔrˈsɑʒ; ES kɔəˈsɑʒ; |-s -ɪz

corsair ˈkɔrsɛr, -sær; E ˈkɔəsɛə(r, ES -sæə(r

corse kɔrs; ES kɔəs; |-s -ɪz

corselet *'armor'* ˈkɔrslɪt; ES ˈkɔəs-; *'under-garment'* ˌkɔrsļˈɛt; ES ˌkɔəs-

corset ˈkɔrsɪt; ES ˈkɔəsɪt; |-ed -ɪd

Corsica ˈkɔrsɪkə; ES ˈkɔəsɪkə; |-n -n

Corsicana ˌkɔrsɪˈkænə; ES ˌkɔəs-

corslet ˈkɔrslɪt; ES ˈkɔəslɪt

Corson ˈkɔrsņ; ES ˈkɔəsņ

cortege kɔrˈteʒ, -ˈtɛʒ; ES kɔə-; (*Fr* kɔrˈtɛːʒ)

Cortes *Sp & Pg legisl.* ˈkɔrtɪz; ES ˈkɔət-; (*Sp* ˈkɔrtes, *Pg* ˈkɔrtɛʃ)

Cortes, -ez *Sp soldier* ˈkɔrtɛz; ES ˈkɔətɛz; (*Sp* kɔrˈtes) |-'s -ɪz

cortex ˈkɔrtɛks; ES ˈkɔə-; |-es -ɪz |-tices -tɪˌsiz

cortez kɔrˈtes; ES kɔə-; |-es -ɪz

cortical ˈkɔrtɪkļ; ES ˈkɔə-; |-ly -ɪ

corticate *adj* ˈkɔrtɪkɪt, -ˌket; ES ˈkɔə-; |-cated -ˌketɪd

Cortland ˈkɔrtlənd, ˈkɔrt-; ES ˈkɔət-, E+ ˈkɔət-

corundum kəˈrʌndəm

coruscant kəˈrʌskənt

coruscate ˈkɔrəsˌket, ˈkɑr-, ˈkɒr- |-d -ɪd

coruscation ˌkɔrəsˈkeʃən, ˌkɑr-, ˌkɒr-

Corvallis kɔrˈvælɪs; ES kɔə-; |-'s -ɪz

corvée kɔrˈve; ES kɔəˈve; (*Fr* kɔrˈve)

corvette, -vet kɔrˈvɛt; ES kɔəˈvɛt

Corybant ˈkɔrəˌbænt, ˈkɑr-, ˈkɒr- |-s -s |-es ˌkɔrəˈbæntiz |-ic ˌkɔrəˈbæntɪk

Corydon ˈkɔrədņ, ˈkɑr-, ˈkɒr-, -ˌdɑn, -ˌdɒn

Coryell ˌkɔrɪˈɛl, ˌkɑr-; S ˌkɔr-

corymb ˈkɔrɪmb, ˈkɑr-, ˈkɒr-, -ɪm

coryphaeus ˌkɔrəˈfiəs, ˌkɑr-, ˌkɒr- |-es -ɪz |-phaei -ˈfiaɪ

coryphee ˌkɔrəˈfe, ˌkɑrəˈfe, ˌkɒrəˈfe |-s -z (*Fr* kɔriˈfe)

coryza kəˈraɪzə

cose *'kos'* kos

cose *'coze'* koz |coses ˈkozɪz |cosed kozd

cosecant koˈsikənt, -kænt

cosey *'cozy'* ˈkozɪ

Cosgrave ˈkazgrev, ˈkɒz-

Coshocton kəˈʃaktən

cosie *'cozy'* ˈkozɪ

cosignatory koˈsɪgnəˌtorɪ, -ˌtɔrɪ; S -ˌtorɪ

cosine ˈkosaɪn

Cos lettuce ˈkasˌlɛtɪs, ˈkɒs-, -əs

cosmetic kazˈmɛtɪk |-al -ļ |-ally -ļɪ, -ɪklɪ

cosmic ˈkazmɪk |-al -ļ |-ally -ļɪ, -ɪklɪ

cosmogony kazˈmagənɪ, -ˈmɒng-

cosmographic ˌkazməˈgræfɪk |-al -ļ |-ally -lɪ, -ɪklɪ

cosmography kazˈmagrəfɪ, -ˈmɒng-

cosmology kazˈmalədʒɪ

cosmopolitan ˌkazməˈpalətņ |-ism -ˌɪzəm

cosmopolitanize ˌkazməˈpalətņˌaɪz |-s -ɪz |-d -d

cosmopolite kazˈmapəˌlaɪt

cosmos ˈkazməs, -mas |-es -ɪz

Cossack ˈkasæk, ˈkɒs-, -ək

cosset ˈkasɪt, ˈkɒsɪt |-ed -ɪd

cost kɔst, kɒst

costa ˈkastə |-tae -ti |-tal -tļ |-tally -tļɪ

costard, C- ˈkastəˈd; ES ˈkastəd

Costa Rica ˈkastəˈrikə, ˈkɒs-, -ˈkɔs-, ˈkos- |-n -n

costermonger ˈkastɚˌmʌŋgɚ, ˈkɒs-; ES -təˌmʌŋgə(r

costive ˈkastɪv, ˈkɒs-

costly ˈkɔstlɪ, ˈkɒst-

costmary ˈkastˌmɛrɪ, ˈkɒst-, -ˌmærɪ; S -ˌmærɪ, -ˌmerɪ

costrel ˈkastrəl, ˈkɒs-

costume *n* ˈkastjum, ˈkɒs-, -tɪum, -tum

costume *v* kasˈtjum, kɒs-, -ˈtɪum, -ˈtum |-d -d |-r -ɚ; ES -ə(r

costumier kasˈtjumɪɚ; -ˈtɪum-, -ˈtum-; ES -ɪˌə(r; (*Fr* kɔstyˈmje)

cosy *'cozy'* ˈkozɪ

cot kat |cotted ˈkatɪd—*see* cote

cotangent koˈtændʒənt

cotangential ˌkotænˈdʒɛnʃəl

cote kot—cot & cote *are distinct, but related, words in the oldest English, but have become confused in spelling.*

cotemporaneous koˌtɛmpəˈreniəs, ˈkotɛmpə-

cotemporary koˈtɛmpəˌrɛrɪ

Those words below in which the ɑ sound is spelt o are often pronounced with ɒ in E and S

cotenant ko'tɛnənt |-ancy -ənsɪ
coterie 'kotərɪ
coterminous ko'tɜ˞mənəs; ES -'tɜm-, -'tɜ˞m-
cothurnus ko'θɜ˞nəs; ES -'θɜn-, -'θɜ˞n-; |-ni -naɪ
cotidal ko'taɪdḷ
cotillion, -llon ko'tɪljən
Cotopaxi ˌkotə'pæksɪ (*Am Sp* ˌkoto'pa·hi)
Cotswold 'kɑtswold, -wəld |-s -z
cottage 'kɑtɪdʒ |-s -ɪz |-d -d
cotter, -ar 'kɑtɚ; ES 'kɑtə(r
Cotterell 'kɑtərəl, 'kɑtrəl
cottier 'kɑtɪɚ; ES 'kɑtɪ·ə(r
cotton, C- 'kɑtn̩ |-ed -d
Cottonian kɑ'tonɪən
cottonmouth 'kɑtn̩ˌmaʊθ |-ths -ðz
cottonseed 'kɑtn̩ˌsid
cottontail 'kɑtn̩ˌtel
cottonwood 'kɑtn̩ˌwʊd
Cottrell 'kɑtrəl
cotyledon ˌkɑtḷ'idn̩ |-ous -'idn̩əs, -'ɛdn̩əs
couch kaʊtʃ |couches 'kaʊtʃɪz |couched kaʊtʃt
Couch kaʊtʃ, kutʃ |-'s -ɪz
couchant 'kaʊtʃənt
Coudersport 'kaʊdɚzˌport; ES 'kaʊdəzˌpoət, E+-ˌpɔət
Coué ku'e
Coues kaʊz |-'s -ɪz
cougar 'kugɚ; ES 'kugə(r
cough kɔf, kɒf |-ed -t
Coughlin 'kɔglən, 'kɒg-
could *stressed* 'kʊd, ˌkʊd; *unstr.* kəd
couldest 'kʊdɪst
couldn't 'kʊdn̩t, *before some conss.*+'kʊdn̩ ('kʊdn̩'se)—*The pron.* 'kʊdənt *is substandard.*
couldst *stressed* 'kʊdst, ˌkʊdst; *unstr.* kədst
coulee 'kulɪ (*Fr* coulée ku'le)
coulomb, C- ku'lɑm, -'lɒm
coulter, C- 'koltɚ; ES 'koltə(r; |-ed -d
Coulton 'koltn̩
council 'kaʊnsḷ
Council Bluffs 'kaʊnsḷ'blʌfs
councilman 'kaʊnsḷmən |-men -mən
councilor, -llor 'kaʊnsḷɚ, -slɚ; ES -ə(r
counsel 'kaʊnsḷ |-ed -d |-ing 'kaʊnsḷɪŋ, -slɪŋ
counselor, -llor 'kaʊnsḷɚ, -slɚ; ES -ə(r

count kaʊnt |counted 'kaʊntɪd
countenance 'kaʊntənəns |-s -ɪz |-d -t
counter 'kaʊntɚ; ES 'kaʊntə(r; |-ed -d
counteraccusation ˌkaʊntɚˌækju'zeʃən
counteract ˌkaʊntɚ'ækt |-ed -ɪd
counteraction ˌkaʊntɚ'ækʃən ('action & 'counterˌaction)
counterattack *n* 'kaʊntərəˌtæk
counterattack *v* ˌkaʊntərə'tæk |-ed -t
counterattraction ˌkaʊntərə'trækʃən
counterbalance *n* 'kaʊntɚˌbæləns; ES -tə-; |-s -ɪz
counterbalance *v* ˌkaʊntɚ'bæləns; ES -tə-; |-s -ɪz |-d -t
counterblast 'kaʊntɚˌblæst; ES -tə-, E+-ˌblast, -ˌblɑst
counterchange *v* ˌkaʊntɚ'tʃendʒ; ES -tə-; |-s -ɪz |-d -d
countercharge *n* 'kaʊntɚˌtʃɑrdʒ; ES 'kaʊntɚˌtʃɑ·dʒ, E+-ˌtʃɑ:dʒ; |-s -ɪz
countercharge *v* ˌkaʊntɚ'tʃɑrdʒ; ES ˌkaʊntɚ'tʃɑ·dʒ, E+-'tʃɑ:dʒ; |-s -ɪz |-d -d
countercheck *n* 'kaʊntɚˌtʃɛk; ES 'kaʊntə-
counterclaim *n* 'kaʊntɚˌklem; ES 'kaʊntə-
counterclaim *v* ˌkaʊntɚ'klem; ES ˌkaʊntə-; |-ed -d
counterclockwise ˌkaʊntɚ'klɑkˌwaɪz; ES ˌkaʊntɚ'klɑk-
counterdemonstration ˌkaʊntɚˌdɛmən'streʃən; ES ˌkaʊntə-
counterespionage ˌkaʊntɚ'ɛspɪənɪdʒ, -ə'spaɪənɪdʒ
counterfeit 'kaʊntɚfɪt; ES 'kaʊntə-; |-ed -ˌfɪtɪd
counterfoil 'kaʊntɚˌfɔɪl; ES 'kaʊntə-
counterirritant ˌkaʊntɚ'ɪrətənt
counterjumper 'kaʊntɚˌdʒʌmpɚ; ES 'kaʊntəˌdʒʌmpə(r
countermand *n* 'kaʊntɚˌmænd; ES 'kaʊntə-, E+-ˌmand, -ˌmɑnd
countermand *v* ˌkaʊntɚ'mænd; ES ˌkaʊntə-, E+-'mand, -'mɑnd; |-ed -ɪd ('counterˌmand 'orders)
countermarch *n* 'kaʊntɚˌmɑrtʃ; ES 'kaʊntəˌmɑ:tʃ, E+-ˌmɑ:tʃ; |-es -ɪz
countermarch *v* ˌkaʊntɚ'mɑrtʃ; ES ˌkaʊntə'mɑ:tʃ, E+-'mɑ:tʃ; |-es -ɪz |-ed -t
countermine *n* 'kaʊntɚˌmaɪn; ES 'kaʊntə-

Key: See in full §§3–47. bee bi |pity 'pɪtɪ (§6) |rate ret |yet jɛt |sang sæŋ |angry 'æŋ·grɪ |bath bæθ; E baθ (§10) |ah ɑ |far fɑr |watch wɑtʃ, wɒtʃ (§12) |jaw dʒɔ |gorge gɔrdʒ |go go

countermine *v* ˌkaʊntɚˈmaɪn; ES ˌkaʊntə-;
|-d **-d**
countermove ˈkaʊntɚˌmuv; ES ˈkaʊntə-
counteroffensive ˌkaʊntərəˈfɛnsɪv (ofˈfensive
& ˈcounterofˌfensive)
counterpane ˈkaʊntɚˌpen; ES ˈkaʊntə-;
|-d **-d**
counterpart ˈkaʊntɚˌpart; ES ˈkaʊntəˌpɑːt,
E+-ˌpɑːt
counterplot *n*, *v* ˈkaʊntɚˌplɑt; ES ˈkaʊntə-
ˌplɑt, -ˌplɒt; |-ted **-ɪd**
counterpoint ˈkaʊntɚˌpɔɪnt; ES ˈkaʊntə-
counterpoise *n*, *v* ˈkaʊntɚˌpɔɪz; ES ˈkaʊntə-;
|-s **-ɪz** |-d **-d**
counterproposal ˈkaʊntɚprəˌpozl̩; ES ˈkaʊntə-
counterreformation ˌkaʊntɚˌrɛfəˈmeʃən; ES
ˌkaʊntəˌrɛfəˈmeʃən
counterrevolution ˌkaʊntɚˌrɛvəˈluʃən, -ˈlɪuʃən,
-ˌrɛvl̩ˈjuʃən; ES ˌkaʊntə-; |-ary -ˌɛrɪ
counterscarp ˈkaʊntɚˌskarp; ES ˈkaʊntə-
ˌskɑːp, E+-ˌskɑːp
countershaft ˈkaʊntɚˌʃæft; ES ˈkaʊntə-, E+
-ˌʃaft, -ˌʃaft
countersign *n* ˈkaʊntɚˌsaɪn; ES ˈkaʊntə-
countersign *v* ˈkaʊntɚˌsaɪn, ˌkaʊntɚˈsaɪn; ES
-tə-; |-ed **-d**
countersignature ˌkaʊntɚˈsɪgnətʃɚ; ES
ˌkaʊntəˈsɪgnətʃə(r; (ˈsignature & ˈcounter-
ˌsignature)
countersink *n* ˈkaʊntɚˌsɪŋk; ES ˈkaʊntə-
countersink *v* ˈkaʊntɚˌsɪŋk, ˌkaʊntɚˈsɪŋk; ES
-tə-; |-sunk -ˌsʌŋk, -ˈsʌŋk
counterstatement ˈkaʊntɚˌstetmənt; ES
ˈkaʊntə-
counterstroke ˈkaʊntɚˌstrok; ES ˈkaʊntə-
countersuggestion ˈkaʊntɚsəgˌdʒɛstʃən, -sə-
ˌdʒɛstʃən; ES ˈkaʊntə-
counterthrust ˈkaʊntɚˌθrʌst; ES ˈkaʊntə-
countervail ˌkaʊntɚˈvel; ES ˌkaʊntə-; |-ed **-d**
counterweigh ˌkaʊntɚˈwe; ES ˌkaʊntə-; |-ed
-d
counterweight ˈkaʊntɚˌwet; ES ˈkaʊntə-
counterwork *n* ˈkaʊntɚˌwɝk; ES ˈkaʊntə-
ˌwɝk, -ˌwɝk
counterwork *v* ˌkaʊntɚˈwɝk; ES ˌkaʊntə-
ˈwɝk, -ˈwɝk
countess ˈkaʊntɪs |-es **-ɪz**
countinghouse ˈkaʊntɪŋˌhaʊs |-ses **-zɪz**
country ˈkʌntrɪ |-trified, -tryf- ˈkʌntrɪˌfaɪd

country-bred ˈkʌntrɪˈbrɛd (ˈcountry-ˌbred
ˈman)
country-dance ˈkʌntrɪˈdæns, -ˌdæns; E+
-ans, -ɑns; |-s **-ɪz**
countryfolk ˈkʌntrɪˌfok
countryman ˈkʌntrɪmən |-men -mən
countryseat ˈkʌntrɪˌsit, -ˈsit
countryside ˈkʌntrɪˌsaɪd (ˈwhole ˈcountry-
ˈside)
country-style ˈkʌntrɪˌstaɪl, -ˈstaɪl
country-wide ˈkʌntrɪˈwaɪd
countrywoman ˈkʌntrɪˌwʊmən, ˌwu- |-women
-ˌwɪmɪn, -ən
county ˈkaʊntɪ
coup *'upset'*, *'drink'* kop, kup |-ed **-t**
coup *'stroke'* ku
coup de grâce *Fr* kudəˈgrɑːs
coup de main *Fr* kudəˈmæ̃
coup d'état ˈkudeˈta (*Fr* kudeˈta)
coupé *'carriage'* kuˈpe; *'auto'* kup, *less freq.*
kuˈpe
couple ˈkʌpl̩ |-d **-d** |-ling ˈkʌplɪŋ, ˈkʌpl̩ɪŋ
coupler ˈkʌplɚ; ES ˈkʌplə(r
couplet ˈkʌplɪt
coupling *n* ˈkʌplɪŋ
coupon ˈkupɑn, ˈkju-, ˈkɪu-, -pɒn
courage ˈkɝɪdʒ; ES ˈkɝɪdʒ, ˈkʌr-, ˈkɝ-; |-d **-d**
courageous kəˈredʒəs
courante kuˈrɑnt (*Fr* kuˈrɑ̃)
courier ˈkʊrɪɚ, ˈkɝɪɚ; ES ˈkʊrɪ·ə(r, ˈkɝɪ-,
ˈkʌr-, ˈkɝ-
course kors, kɔrs, *esp. in 'of course'* kʊrs; ES
koəs, kʊəs, E+kɔəs |-s **-ɪz** |-d **-t**
courser ˈkorsɚ, ˈkɔr-; ES ˈkoəsə(r, E+ˈkɔə-
court kort, kɔrt; ES koət, E+kɔət; |-ed **-ɪd**
courteous ˈkɝtɪəs; ES ˈkɝtɪəs, ˈkɝt-
courtesan, -zan ˈkortəzn̩, ˈkɔrt-, ˈkɝt-; ES
ˈkoət-, ˈkɝt-, ˈkɝt-, E+ˈkɔət-
courtesy *'politeness'* ˈkɝtəsɪ; ES ˈkɝtəsɪ, ˈkɝt-
courtesy *'curtsy'* kɝtsɪ; ES ˈkɝtsɪ, ˈkɝt-; |-ied
-d
Courthope ˈkortəp, ˈkɔrt-, -ˌhop; ES ˈkoət-,
E+ˈkɔət-
courthouse ˈkortˌhaʊs, ˈkɔrt-; ES ˈkoət-, E+
ˈkɔət-; |-ses **-zɪz**
courtier ˈkortɪɚ, ˈkɔrt-, -tjɚ; ES ˈkoətɪ·ə(r,
-tjə(r, E+ˈkɔət-
courtly ˈkortlɪ, ˈkɔrt-; ES ˈkoət-, E+ˈkɔət-
court-martial ˈkortˈmarʃəl, ˈkɔrt-; ES ˈkoət-

|full fʊl |tooth tuθ |further ˈfɝðɚ; ES ˈfɝðə |custom ˈkʌstəm |while hwaɪl |how haʊ |toy tɔɪ
|using ˈjuzɪŋ |fuse fjuz, fɪuz |dish dɪʃ |vision ˈvɪʒən |Eden ˈidn̩ |cradle ˈkredl̩ |keep 'em ˈkipm̩

'maːʃəl, E+'kɔət-, -'maːʃəl; |-ed -d |-ing
-ʃəlɪŋ, -ʃlɪŋ

court-plaster 'kɔrt͵plæstɚ, 'kɔrt-; ES 'kɔət-
͵plæstə(r, E+'kɔət-, -͵plas-, -͵plas-

courtroom 'kɔrt͵rum, 'kɔrt-, -͵rʊm; ES
'kɔət-, E+'kɔət-

courtship 'kɔrtʃɪp, 'kɔrt-; ES 'kɔət-, E+
'kɔət-

courtyard 'kɔrt͵jard, 'kɔrt-; ES 'kɔət͵jaːd,
E+'kɔət-, -͵jaːd

cousin 'kʌzn̩ |-ed -d |-ing 'kʌzn̩ɪŋ, 'kʌznɪŋ

cousin-german 'kʌzn̩'dʒɝmən; ES -'dʒɝm-,
-'dʒɝˑm-; |pl cousins- 'kʌzn̩z-

Cousins 'kʌzn̩z |-'s -ɪz

couth kuθ

couturier Fr kuty'rje |fem -rière -'rjɛːr

Couzens 'kʌzn̩z |-'s -ɪz

cove kov |coved kovd

covenant, C- 'kʌvənənt, 'kʌvnənt |-ed -ɪd

covenanter, -or 'kʌvənəntɚ, 'kʌvn-; ES -tə(r

Covenanter 'kʌvə͵næntɚ, ͵kʌvə'næntɚ; ES
-tə(r

Covent 'kʌvənt, 'kav-; ES+'kɒv-

Coventry 'kʌvəntrɪ, 'kav-; ES+'kɒv-; |-ied
-d—Both a(ɒ) and ʌ appear to be historical.

cover 'kʌvɚ; ES 'kʌvə(r; |-ed -d |-ing
'kʌvərɪŋ, 'kʌvrɪŋ

coverage 'kʌvərɪdʒ, 'kʌvrɪdʒ |-s -ɪz

Coverdale 'kʌvɚ͵del; ES 'kʌvə-

covering n 'kʌvrɪŋ

coverlet 'kʌvɚlɪt; ES 'kʌvə-

Coverley 'kʌvɚlɪ; ES 'kʌvə-

coverlid 'kʌvɚ͵lɪd; ES 'kʌvə-

covert 'kʌvɚt; ES 'kʌvət

coverture 'kʌvɚtʃɚ; ES 'kʌvətʃə(r

covet 'kʌvɪt |-ed -ɪd |-ous -əs

covey 'kʌvɪ |-ed -d

covin 'kʌvɪn

Covina ko'vinə

Covington 'kʌvɪŋtən

cow kau |cowed kaud

coward, C- 'kauɚd; ES 'kau-əd; |-ice -ɪs

cowbell 'kau͵bɛl

cowbird 'kau͵bɝd; ES -͵bɝd, -͵bɝd

cowboy 'kau͵bɔɪ

cowcatcher 'kau͵kætʃɚ, -͵kɛtʃɚ; ES -tʃə(r

cower 'kauɚ; ES 'kau·ə(r; |-ed -d |-ing
'kauərɪŋ, 'kaurɪŋ

Cowes kauz |-'s -ɪz

cowherd 'kau͵hɝd; ES -͵hɝd, -͵hɝd

cowhide 'kau͵haɪd |-d -ɪd

cowl, C- kaul |-ed -d

Cowley 'kaulɪ

cowlick 'kau͵lɪk

cowling, C- 'kaulɪŋ

co-worker ko'wɝkɚ; ES -'wɝkə(r, -'wɝkə(r

cowpea 'kau͵pi

Cowpens SC 'kau͵pɛnz, loc.+'kʌpɪnz

Cowper 'kupɚ, 'kaupɚ; ES -pə(r;—the same
word as Cooper, 'kaupɚ being a spelling
pronunciation.

cowpox 'kau͵paks; ES+-͵pɒks

cowpuncher 'kau͵pʌntʃɚ; ES -͵pʌntʃə(r

cowrie, -ry 'kaurɪ

cowskin 'kau͵skɪn

cowslip 'kau͵slɪp—cf oxlip

cox kaks; ES+kɒks; |-es -ɪz

coxcomb 'kaks͵kom; ES+'kɒks-; |-ry -rɪ

coxcombic kaks'kamɪk, -'kom-; ES+-'kɒm-;
|-al -l̩ |-ally -lɪ, -ɪklɪ

coxswain 'kaksn̩, 'kak͵swen; ES+'kɒk-

coy kɔɪ |coyed kɔɪd

coyote kaɪ'ot, kaɪ'otɪ, 'kaɪot

coz kʌz

coze koz |cozes 'kozɪz |cozed kozd

cozen 'kʌzn̩ |-ed -d |-ing 'kʌzn̩ɪŋ, 'kʌznɪŋ

cozenage 'kʌzn̩ɪdʒ, 'kʌznɪdʒ

cozy 'kozɪ

Cozzens 'kʌzn̩z |-'s -ɪz

crab kræb |crabbed kræbd

Crabbe kræb

crabbed adj 'kræbɪd |-ly -lɪ

crabby 'kræbɪ

crack kræk |cracked krækt

crackajack 'krækə͵dʒæk

crackbrain 'kræk͵bren

crackbrained 'kræk'brend ('crack͵brained
'wits)

cracker 'krækɚ; ES 'krækə(r

crackerjack 'krækɚ͵dʒæk; ES 'krækə-

crackle 'krækl̩ |-d -d |-ling 'kræklɪŋ, -kl̩ɪŋ

crackling n 'kræklɪŋ

cracknel 'kræknl̩

cracksman 'kræksmən |-men -mən

crack-up 'kræk͵ʌp

Cracow 'kreko, 'krækau (see Kraków)

Craddock 'krædək

cradle 'kredl̩ |-d -d |-ling 'kredlɪŋ, 'kredl̩ɪŋ

Cradock 'krædək = Caradoc *knight*
craft kræft; ES+kraft, kraft; |-y -ɪ
craftsman 'kræftsmən; E+'krafts-, 'krafts-;
|-men -mən |-manship -mən‚ʃɪp
crag kræg |cragged 'krægɪd |-gy -ɪ
Craigenputtock ‚kregən'pʌtək
Craigie 'kregɪ
crake krek |craked krekt
crakow 'krækaʊ
cram kræm |crammed kræmd
crambo 'kræmbo
cramp kræmp |cramped kræmpt
crampon 'kræmpən
cranage 'krenɪdʒ
Cranage 'krænɪdʒ |-'s -ɪz
cranberry 'kræn‚bɛrɪ, -bərɪ
Crandall 'krændḷ
crane, C- kren |craned krend
Cranford 'krænfəd; ES 'krænfəd
cranial 'krenɪəl |-ly -ɪ
craniological ‚krenɪə'ladʒɪkḷ; ES+-'lɒdʒ-;
|-ly -ɪ
craniology ‚krenɪ'alədʒɪ; ES+-'ɒl-
craniometer ‚krenɪ'amətə; ES -'amətə(r,
-'ɒm-
craniometric ‚krenɪə'mɛtrɪk |-al -ḷ |-ally -ḷɪ,
-ɪklɪ
craniometry ‚krenɪ'amətrɪ; ES+-'ɒm-
cranium 'krenɪəm |-s -z |-nia -nɪə
crank kræŋk |cranked kræŋkt
crankcase 'kræŋk‚kes |-cases -‚kesɪz
crankle 'kræŋkḷ |-d -d |-ling 'kræŋkḷɪŋ, -klɪŋ
crankpin 'kræŋk‚pɪn
crankshaft 'kræŋk‚ʃæft; E+-‚ʃaft,-‚ʃaft
Cranmer 'krænmə; ES 'krænmə(r
crannog 'krænəg
cranny 'krænɪ |crannied 'krænɪd
Cranston 'krænstən
crape krep |craped krept
crappie 'kræpɪ, 'krapɪ
craps kræps
crapulous 'kræpjʊləs
crash kræʃ |-es -ɪz |-ed -t
Crashaw 'kræʃɔ
crasis 'kresɪs |crases 'kresiz
crass kræs
Crassus 'kræsəs |-sus' -səs
cratch, C- krætʃ |cratches 'krætʃɪz
Cratchit 'krætʃɪt

crate kret |crated 'kretɪd
crater 'kretə; ES 'kretə(r; |-ed -d
cravat krə'væt |-vatted -'vætɪd
crave krev |craved krevd
craven 'krevən |-ed -d |-ing 'krevənɪŋ, -vnɪŋ
cravenette, C- ‚krævə'nɛt, ‚krev- |-d -d -ɪd
craving 'krevɪŋ
craw krɔ
crawfish 'krɔ‚fɪʃ |-es -ɪz |-ed -t
Crawford 'krɔfəd; ES 'krɔfəd; |-sville -z‚vɪl
crawl krɔl |crawled krɔld |-y -ɪ
Crawley 'krɔlɪ
crayfish 'kre‚fɪʃ |-'s -ɪz
crayon 'kreən |crayoned 'kreənd
craze krez |crazes 'krezɪz |crazed krezd
crazy 'krezɪ |crazily 'krezḷɪ, -zɪlɪ
creak krik |creaked krikt
cream krim |creamed krimd |-ery -ərɪ,
'krimrɪ
cream-faced 'krim'fest ('cream-‚faced 'loon)
crease kris |creases 'krisɪz |creased krist
creasy 'krisɪ
create krɪ'et |created krɪ'etɪd |-tion -'eʃən
creative krɪ'etɪv |-tor -tə; ES -tə(r
creature 'kritʃə; ES 'kritʃə(r; |-ral -əl
crèche krɛʃ, kreʃ |-s -ɪz (*Fr* krɛːʃ)
Crécy 'krɛsɪ (*Fr* kre'si)
credence 'kridn̥s |-dent -dn̥t
credential krɪ'dɛnʃəl |-ed -d
credibility ‚krɛdə'bɪlətɪ
credible 'krɛdəbḷ |-bly -blɪ
credit 'krɛdɪt |credited 'krɛdɪtɪd
creditability ‚krɛdɪtə'bɪlətɪ
creditable 'krɛdɪtəbḷ |-bly -blɪ
creditor 'krɛdɪtə; ES 'krɛdɪtə(r
credo, C- 'krido, 'kredo
credulity krə'dulətɪ, -'dɪu-, -'dju-
credulous 'krɛdʒələs
Cree kri
creed krid |creeded 'kridɪd
creek krik, krɪk—krɪk *is much less freq. in the*
S, but appears to be the native form in the
N & E. krɪk, *originally a North British dia-*
lect form, is still native in the Appalachians.
According to Horn's, Jordan's, and Luick's
Historical English Grammars, krɪk *repre-*
sents the original word (*ME* crike), *later*
altered to krik *and then spelt* creek. *Crike is*
much the earlier recorded form. At first krɪk

was not a spelling pronunciation, but the spelling creek *doubtless encouraged its spread. Luick thinks that American* krık *represents the normal standard English development.*

Creek krik
creel kril |creeled krild
creep krip |crept krɛpt |-er 'kripɚ; ES -pə(r
creepmouse 'krip,maʊs |-'s -ız |-mice -,maıs
creese kris |creeses 'krisız
Creighton 'kretn̩, 'kraıtn̩
cremate 'krimet |-d -ıd |-tor -ɚ; ES -ə(r
crematory 'krimə,torı, 'krɛm-, -,tɔrı; S -,torı
crème de menthe *Fr* krɛmdə'mãt
Cremona krı'monə
crenate 'krinet |-d -ıd |-tion krı'neʃən
crenel 'krɛnl̩ |creneled 'krɛnl̩d
crenelate, -ll- 'krɛnl̩,et |-d -ıd
crenelation, -ll- ,krɛnl̩'eʃən
Creole, c- 'kriol
Creon 'krian, -ɒn
creosote 'kriə,sot |creosoted 'kriə,sotıd
crepe, crêpe krep |-d -t
crepe de Chine ,krepdə'ʃin
crepitant 'krɛpətənt |-itate -,tet |-tated -,tetıd
crept krɛpt
crepuscle krı'pʌsl̩ |-cular -kjələ; ES -lə(r
crescendo krə'ʃɛndo, -'sɛn- (*It* kre'ʃɛndo)
crescent 'krɛsn̩t |-ed -ıd
cresol 'krisol
cress krɛs |cresses 'krɛsız |cressed krɛst
cresset 'krɛsıt
Cressida *in Shak.* 'krɛsıdə—*see* Criseyde
Cressy 'krɛsı (*Fr* Crécy kre'si)
crest krɛst |crested 'krɛstıd
crestfallen 'krɛst,fɔlən, -,fɔln
Crestline 'krɛstlaın, 'krɛslaın
cretaceous krı'teʃəs
Crete krit |Cretan 'kritn̩
cretin 'kritın |-ism -,ızəm, -tn̩-
cretonne krı'tɒn, -'tɒn, 'kritɒn, -tɒn
crevasse krə'væs |-s -ız |-d -t
crevice 'krɛvıs |-s -ız |-d -t
crew kru, krıu
Crewe kru, krıu
crewel 'kruəl, 'krıuəl
crib krıb |cribbed krıbd
cribbage 'krıbıdʒ |-s -ız |-d -d
cribwork 'krıb,wɜk; ES -,wɜk, -,wɜk
Crichton 'kraıtn̩

crick krık |cricked krıkt
cricket 'krıkıt |-ed -ıd |-er -ɚ; ES -ə(r
cricoid 'kraıkɔıd
cried kraıd
crier 'kraıɚ; ES 'kraı·ə(r
cries kraız
Crile kraıl
crime kraım |crimed kraımd
Crimea kraı'miə, krı- |-n -n
criminal 'krımənl̩, 'krımnl̩ |-ly -ı
criminality ,krımə'nælətı
criminate 'krımə,net |-nated -,netıd
crimination ,krımə'neʃən
criminologic ,krımənə'lɑdʒık, ,krımnə-; ES+
-'lɒdʒ-; |-al -l̩
criminologist ,krımə'nɑlədʒıst, krım'nɑl-;
ES+-'nɒl-; |-gy -dʒı
crimp krımp |crimped krımpt
crimple 'krımpl̩ |-d -d |-ling -'krımplıŋ, -pl̩ıŋ
crimson 'krımzn̩ |crimsoned 'krımznd
cringe krındʒ |cringes 'krındʒız |-d -d
cringle 'krıŋgl̩
crinkle 'krıŋkl̩ |-d -d |-ling 'krıŋklıŋ, -kl̩ıŋ
crinkly 'krıŋklı
crinoid 'kraınɔıd, 'krın-
crinoline 'krınl̩ın, -,ın
cripple 'krıpl̩ |-d -d |-ling 'krıplıŋ, -pl̩ıŋ
Cripple Creek 'krıpl̩'krık, -'krik
Cripplegate 'krıpl̩,get, -gıt
Criseyde *in Chaucer* krı'sedə
crisis 'kraısıs |crises 'kraısiz
crisp krısp |crisped krıspt
crisscross 'krıs,krɔs, -,krɒs |-es -ız |-ed -t
Cristobal krıs'tobl̩ (*Sp* kris'toβal)
criterion kraı'tırıən |-teria -'tırıə
critic 'krıtık |-al -l̩ |-ally -l̩ı, -ıklı
criticaster 'krıtık,æstɚ; ES -,æstə(r
criticism 'krıtə,sızəm
criticize 'krıtə,saız |-s -ız |-d -d
critique krı'tik
Crito 'kraıto
Crittendon 'krıtn̩dən
croak krok |croaked krokt
croaker, C- 'krokɚ; ES 'krokə(r
Croat 'kroæt, -ət
Croatia kro'eʃə, -ʃıə |-n -n
Croce 'krotʃı (*It* 'kro:tʃe)
crochet *n* 'kroʃıt; ES+'krɒtʃıt
crochet *v* kro'ʃe |-cheted -'ʃed |-cheting -'ʃe·ıŋ

crock krak; ES+krɒk; |-ed -t |-ery -ərɪ, -rɪ
Crockett ˈkrakɪt; ES+ˈkrɒkɪt
crocodile ˈkrakəˌdaɪl; ES+ˈkrɒk-
crocodilian ˌkrakəˈdɪlɪən; ES+ˌkrɒk-
crocus, C- ˈkrokəs |-es -ɪz |-ci -saɪ
Croesus ˈkrisəs |-sus' -səs
croft krɔft, krɒft
Croix krɔɪ (Fr krwɑ)
Croix de guerre Fr krwad ˈgɛːr
Croker ˈkrokɚ; ES ˈkrokə(r
crokinole, C- ˈkrokəˌnol
Cro-Magnon kroˈmægnɑn, -nɒn (Fr kromaˈŋõ)
Cromarty ˈkramɚtɪ; ES ˈkramətɪ, ˈkrɒm-
cromlech ˈkramlɛk; ES+ˈkrɒm-
Crompton ˈkramptən; ES+ˈkrɒmp-
Cromwell ˈkramwəl, -wɛl, ˈkrʌm-; ES+ˈkrɒm-
Cromwellian kramˈwɛlɪən, -ljən; ES+krɒm-
crone kron
Cronus ˈkronəs |-'s -ɪz
crony ˈkronɪ |cronied ˈkronɪd
crook krʊk |crooked krʊkt
crookback ˈkrʊkˌbæk |-ed -t
crooked adj ˈkrʊkɪd
Crookes krʊks |-'s -ɪz
crookneck ˈkrʊkˌnɛk |-ed -t
croon krun |crooned krund
crop krap; ES+krɒp; |-ped -t
crop-eared ˈkrapˈɪrd; ES ˈkrapˈɪəd, ˈkrɒp-, S+-ˈɛəd; (ˈcrop-ˌeared ˈcur)
cropper ˈkrapɚ; ES ˈkrapə(r, ˈkrɒp-
croppie ˈkrapɪ; ES+ˈkrɒpɪ
croquet kroˈke |croqueted kroˈked |-ing -ˈke·ɪŋ
croquette kroˈkɛt
croquignole ˈkrokəˌnol, -kɪnˌjol (Fr krŏkiˈɲɔl)
crore kror, krɔr; ES kroə(r, E+krɔə(r
Crosby ˈkrɔzbɪ, ˈkrɒz-, ˈkraz-
crosier, C- ˈkroʒɚ; ES ˈkroʒə(r; |-ed -d
cross krɔs, krɒs |-es -ɪz |-ed -t
crossbar ˈkrɔsˌbar, ˈkrɒs-; ES -ˌbɑ:(r, E+-ˌbɑ:(r; |-red -d
crossbeam ˈkrɔsˌbim, ˈkrɒs-
crossbill ˈkrɔsˌbɪl, ˈkrɒs-
crossbones ˈkrɔsˌbonz, ˈkrɒs-
crossbow ˈkrɔsˌbo, ˈkrɒs- |-man -mən |-men -mən
crossbred ˈkrɔsˈbrɛd, ˈkrɒs- (ˈcrossˌbred ˈdog)

crossbreed n ˈkrɔsˌbrid, ˈkrɒs-
crossbreed v ˈkrɔsˈbrid, ˈkrɒs-, -ˌbrid |-bred -ˈbrɛd, -ˌbrɛd
crosscut ˈkrɔsˌkʌt, ˈkrɒs-
crosse krɔs, krɒs |-s -ɪz
cross-examination ˈkrɔsɪɡˌzæməˈneʃən, ˈkrɒs-
cross-examine ˈkrɔsɪɡˈzæmɪn, ˈkrɒs- |-d -d
cross-eye ˈkrɔsˌaɪ, ˈkrɒs-
cross-eyed ˈkrɔsˈaɪd, ˈkrɒs- (ˈcross-ˌeyed ˈbear)
cross-fertilization ˈkrɔsˌfɝtḷəˈzeʃən, ˈkrɒs-, -aɪˈz-; ES -ˌfɜtḷ-, -ˌfɜtḷ-
cross-fertilize ˈkrɔsˈfɝtḷˌaɪz, ˈkrɒs-; ES -ˈfɜtḷ-, -ˈfɜtḷ-; |-s -ɪz |-d -d
cross-gartered ˈkrɔsˈgartɚd, ˈkrɒs-; ES -ˈgɑ:təd, E+-ˈgɑ:təd
cross-grained ˈkrɔsˈgrend, ˈkrɒs-
crosshatch ˈkrɔsˌhætʃ, ˈkrɒs- |-es -ɪz |-ed -t
cross-legged ˈkrɔsˈlɛgɪd, -ˈlɛgd, ˈkrɒs- (ˈsit ˌcross-ˈlegged, ˈcross-ˌlegged ˈknight)
crossover n ˈkrɔsˌovɚ, ˈkrɒs-; ES -ˌovə(r
crosspatch ˈkrɔsˌpætʃ, ˈkrɒs- |-es -ɪz
crosspiece ˈkrɔsˌpis, ˈkrɒs- |-s -ɪz
cross-pollinate ˈkrɔsˈpaləˌnet, ˈkrɒs-; ES+-ˈpɒl-; |-d -ɪd
cross-pollination ˈkrɔsˌpaləˈneʃən, ˈkrɒs-; ES+-ˌpɒl-
cross-purpose ˈkrɔsˈpɝpəs, ˈkrɒs-; ES -ˈpɜp-, -ˈpɝp-; |-s -ɪz
cross-question ˈkrɔsˈkwɛstʃən, ˈkrɒs- |-ed -d
crossruff ˈkrɔsˌrʌf, ˈkrɒs- |-ed -t
cross-section v ˈkrɔsˈsɛkʃən, ˈkrɒs- |-ed -d
cross-stitch ˈkrɔsˌstɪtʃ, ˈkrɒs- |-es -ɪz |-ed -t
crosstrees ˈkrɔsˌtriz, ˈkrɒs-
crossways ˈkrɔsˌwez, ˈkrɒs- |-wise -ˌwaɪz
crossword ˈkrɔsˌwɝd, ˈkrɒs-; ES -ˌwɜd, -ˌwɝd
crotch kratʃ; ES+krɒtʃ; |-es -ɪz |-ed -t
crotched adj ˈkratʃt, ˈkratʃɪd; ES+ˈkrɒtʃ-
crotchet ˈkratʃɪt; ES+ˈkrɒtʃɪt; |-ed -ɪd
Crothers ˈkrʌðɚz; ES ˈkrʌðəz; |-'s -ɪz
croton, C- ˈkrotn̩
crouch krautʃ |crouches ˈkrautʃɪz |-ed -t
croup krup |-ed -t
crouper 'crupper' ˈkrupɚ, ˈkrʊpɚ; ES -pə(r
croupier ˈkrupɪɚ; ES ˈkrupɪ·ə(r
crouton kruˈtan, -ˈtɒn (Fr kruˈtõ)
crow kro |past crew kru, krɪu or crowed krod |pptc crowed krod
crowbar ˈkroˌbar; ES -ˌbɑ:(r, E+-ˌbɑ:(r

|full fʊl |tooth tuθ |further ˈfɝðɚ; ES ˈfɜðə |custom ˈkʌstəm |while hwaɪl |how haʊ |toy tɔɪ
|using ˈjuzɪŋ |fuse fjuz, fɪuz |dish dɪʃ |vision ˈvɪʒən |Eden ˈidn̩ |cradle ˈkredl̩ |keep 'em ˈkipm̩

crowd kraʊd |crowded 'kraʊdɪd

Crowell 'kroəl

crowfoot 'kro͵fʊt |pl -feet -͵fit, plant -foots -͵fʊts

Crowley 'krolɪ, 'kraʊlɪ

crown kraʊn |crowned kraʊnd

crownpiece 'kraʊn͵pis |-pieces -͵pisɪz

crow's-foot 'kroz͵fʊt |-feet -͵fit

crow's-nest 'kroz͵nɛst

Croydon 'krɔɪdn̩

crozier, C- 'kroʒɚ; ES 'kroʒə(r; |-ed -d

cruces pl of crux 'krusiz, 'krɪusiz

crucial 'kruʃəl, 'krɪuʃəl |-ly -ɪ

cruciate adj 'kruʃɪɪt, 'krɪu-, -ɪ͵et

cruciate v 'kruʃɪ͵et, 'krɪu- |-ated -͵etɪd

crucible 'krusəbl̩, 'krɪu- |-d -d

crucifix 'krusə͵fɪks, 'krɪu- |-es -ɪz

crucifixion ͵krusə'fɪkʃən, ͵krɪu-

cruciform 'krusə͵fɔrm, 'krɪu-; ES -͵fɔəm

crucify 'krusə͵faɪ, 'krɪu- |-fied -͵faɪd

crude krud, krɪud |-dity -ətɪ

cruel 'kruəl, 'krɪuəl |-ly -ɪ |-ty -tɪ

cruet 'kruɪt, 'krɪuɪt

Cruikshank 'krʊkʃæŋk

cruise kruz, krɪuz |-s -ɪz |-d -d

cruiser 'kruzɚ, 'krɪuzɚ; ES -zə(r

cruller 'krʌlɚ; ES 'krʌlə(r

crumb, C- krʌm |crumbed krʌmd

crumble 'krʌmbl̩ |crumbled 'krʌmbl̩d |-bly -blɪ

crump krʌmp |crumped krʌmpt

crumpet 'krʌmpɪt

crumple 'krʌmpl̩ |-d -d |-ling 'krʌmplɪŋ, -pl̩ɪŋ

crumply 'krʌmplɪ

crunch krʌntʃ |crunches 'krʌntʃɪz |-ed -t

crupper 'krʌpɚ, 'krʊpɚ; ES -pə(r

crural 'krʊrəl, 'krɪʊrəl

crusade, C- kru'sed, krɪu- |-d -ɪd

cruse kruz, krɪuz, -s |-s -ɪz

crush krʌʃ |crushes 'krʌʃɪz |crushed krʌʃt

Crusoe 'kruso, 'krɪuso

crust krʌst |crusted 'krʌstɪd

crustacean krʌs'teʃən |-ceous -ʃəs

crutch krʌtʃ |crutches 'krʌtʃɪz |-ed -t

crux krʌks |-es -ɪz |cruces 'krusiz, 'krɪu-

cry kraɪ |cried kraɪd |-baby -͵bebɪ

cryolite 'kraɪə͵laɪt

crypt krɪpt |crypted 'krɪptɪd

cryptic 'krɪptɪk |-al -l̩ |-ally -l̩ɪ, -ɪklɪ

cryptogam 'krɪptə͵gæm |-ic ͵krɪptə'gæmɪk

cryptogamous krɪp'tagəməs, -'tɒg- |-my -mɪ

cryptogram 'krɪptə͵græm

cryptograph 'krɪptə͵græf; E+-͵graf, -͵graf

cryptographer krɪp'tagrəfɚ, -'tɒg-; ES -fə(r; |-phy -fɪ

cryptographic ͵krɪptə'græfɪk |-al -l̩ |-ally -l̩ɪ, -ɪklɪ

crystal, C- 'krɪstl̩ |-ed -d

crystalline 'krɪstl̩ɪn, -͵aɪn, poet.+krɪs'tæl-

crystallization ͵krɪstl̩ə'zeʃən, -aɪ'z-

crystallize 'krɪstl̩͵aɪz |-s -ɪz |-d -d

crystallography ͵krɪstl̩'agrəfɪ, -'ɒg-

crystalloid 'krɪstl̩͵ɔɪd |-al ͵krɪstl̩'ɔɪdl̩

Ctesiphon 'tɛsə͵fan, -͵fɒn

cub kʌb |cubbed kʌbd

Cuba 'kjubə, 'kɪubə |-n -n (Sp 'kuβa)

cubbyhole 'kʌbɪ͵hol

cube kjub, kɪub |-d -d

cubeb 'kjubɛb, 'kɪubɛb

cubic 'kjubɪk, 'kɪu- |-al -l̩ |-ally -l̩ɪ |-icly -ɪklɪ

cubicle 'kjubɪkl̩, 'kɪu-

cubism 'kjubɪzəm, 'kɪub- |-ist -ɪst

cubistic kju'bɪstɪk, kɪu-

cubit 'kjubɪt, 'kɪubɪt |-ed -ɪd

cuboid 'kjubɔɪd, 'kɪubɔɪd

Cuchulainn, -llin ku'kʌlɪn, 'kuxʊlɪn

cucking-stool 'kʌkɪŋ͵stul

cuckold 'kʌkl̩d |-ed -ɪd |-ry -rɪ

cuckoo 'kuku, ku'ku |-ed -d

cuckooflower 'kuku͵flaʊɚ; ES -͵flaʊ-ə(r

cucumber 'kjukʌmbɚ, 'kɪu-; ES -kʌmbə(r

cud kʌd

Cudahy 'kʌdəhɪ

cuddle 'kʌdl̩ |-d -d |-ling 'kʌdlɪŋ, 'kʌdl̩ɪŋ

cuddly 'kʌdlɪ

cuddy, C- 'kʌdɪ

cudgel 'kʌdʒəl |cudgeled 'kʌdʒəld

cue kju, kɪu |cued kjud, kɪud

cuff kʌf |cuffed kʌft

Cufic 'kjufɪk, 'kɪu-

cuirass kwɪ'ræs |-es -ɪz |-ed -t

cuirassier ͵kwɪrə'sɪr; ES -'sɪə(r

cuisine kwɪ'zin

cuisse kwɪs |cuisses 'kwɪsɪz

cul-de-sac 'kʌldə'sæk, 'kʊl- (Fr kyd'sak, kyt-)

Culebra ku'lebrə

culex, C- 'kjulɛks, 'kɪu- |-lices -lɪ͵siz

culinary 'kjulə͵nɛrɪ, 'kɪulə-

---

cull kʌl |culled kʌld
Cullen 'kʌlɪn, -ən
cullender 'kʌləndɚ, 'kʌlɪn-; ES -də(r
cullion 'kʌljən |-ry -rɪ
Culloden kə'lɑdn̩, -'lɒdn̩, -'lodn̩
culm kʌlm |culmed kʌlmd
culminate 'kʌlmə,net |-nated -,netɪd
culmination ,kʌlmə'neʃən
culpability ,kʌlpə'bɪlətɪ
culpable 'kʌlpəbl̩ |-bly -blɪ
Culpeper 'kʌlpɛpɚ; ES 'kʌlpɛpə(r
culprit 'kʌlprɪt
cult kʌlt
cultivability ,kʌltəvə'bɪlətɪ
cultivable 'kʌltəvəbl̩ |-bly -blɪ
cultivate 'kʌltə,vet |-vated -,vetɪd
cultivation ,kʌltə'veʃən
cultivator 'kʌltə,vetɚ; ES -,vetə(r
cultural 'kʌltʃərəl |-ly -ɪ
culture 'kʌltʃɚ; ES 'kʌltʃə(r; |-d -d
culver, C- 'kʌlvɚ; ES 'kʌlvə(r
culverin 'kʌlvərɪn
culvert 'kʌlvɚt; ES 'kʌlvət; |-ed -ɪd
cumber 'kʌmbɚ; ES 'kʌmbə(r; |-ed -d |-ing
'kʌmbrɪŋ, 'kʌmbərɪŋ
Cumberland 'kʌmbɚlənd; ES 'kʌmbə-
cumbersome 'kʌmbɚsəm; ES 'kʌmbə-
cumbrance 'kʌmbrəns |-s -ɪz |-brous -brəs
Cumbria 'kʌmbrɪə |-n -n
cumin, cumm- 'kʌmɪn
cum laude 'kʌm'lɔdɪ, 'kum'laudɪ
Cummings 'kʌmɪŋz |-'s -ɪz
Cummins 'kʌmɪnz |-'s -ɪz
cumquat 'kʌmkwɑt, -kwɒt
cumshaw 'kʌmʃɔ
cumulate adj 'kjumjəlɪt, 'kɪum-, -,let
cumulate v 'kjumjə,let, 'kɪum- |-lated -,letɪd
cumulation ,kjumjə'leʃən, ,kɪumjə-
cumulative 'kjumjə,letɪv, 'kɪumjə-
cumulo-cirrus ,kjumjəlo'sɪrəs, ,kɪum- |-ri -raɪ
cumulo-nimbus ,kjumjəlo'nɪmbəs, ,kɪum-
|-bi -baɪ
cumulo-stratus ,kjumjəlo'stretəs, ,kɪum- |-ti
-taɪ
cumulous 'kjumjələs, 'kɪum-
cumulus 'kjumjələs, 'kɪum- |-es -ɪz |-li -,laɪ
Cunard kju'nɑrd, kɪu-; ES -'nɑ:d, E+-'nɑ:d
cunctator kʌŋk'tetɚ; ES -'tetə(r; |-ship -,ʃɪp
cuneate 'kjunɪt, 'kɪun-, -ɪ,et

cuneiform 'kjunɪə,fɔrm, 'kɪun-, -nɪ,fɔrm,
kju'nɪə-, kɪu-; ES -,fɔəm
cuniform 'kjunɪ,fɔrm, 'kɪunɪ-; ES -,fɔəm
cunner 'kʌnɚ; ES 'kʌnə(r
cunning 'kʌnɪŋ
Cunningham 'kʌnɪŋ,hæm, 'kʌnɪŋəm
cup kʌp |cupped kʌpt
cupalo, -olo 'kjupə,lo, 'kɪu- |-ed -d—'kjupə,lo
represents a 17c variant of cupola still widely
heard in US.
cupbearer 'kʌp,bɛrɚ, -,bærɚ; E -,bɛrə(r, ES
-,bærə(r
cupboard 'kʌbɚd; ES 'kʌbəd; |-ed -ɪd
cupful 'kʌp,ful |-s -z
Cupid, c- 'kjupɪd, 'kɪupɪd
cupidity kju'pɪdətɪ, kɪu-
cupola 'kjupələ, 'kɪu- |-ed -d—see cupalo
cupreous 'kjuprɪəs, 'kɪup- |-rous -rəs |-ric -rɪk
cur kɝ; ES kɝ(r, kɝ
curability ,kjurə'bɪlətɪ, ,kɪurə-
curable 'kjurəbl̩, 'kɪur- |-bly -blɪ
Curaçao, c-, -çoa ,kjurə'so, ,kɪurə-
curacy 'kjurəsɪ, 'kɪurəsɪ
Curan 'kɝən; ES 'kɝən, 'kʌrən, 'kɝən
curassow 'kjurə,so, 'kɪurə-
curate 'kjurɪt, 'kɪurɪt
curative 'kjurətɪv, 'kɪu-
curator kju'retɚ, kɪu'retɚ, law+'kjurətɚ,
'kɪur-; ES -tə(r
curatorial ,kjurə'torɪəl, ,kɪurə-, -'tɔr-; S
-'tor-
curb kɝb; ES kɝb, kɝb; |-ed -d |-stone -,ston
curculio kɝ'kjulɪ,o, -'kɪulɪ-; ES kɝ-, kɝ-
curd kɝd; ES kɝd, kɝd; |-ed -ɪd
curdle 'kɝdl̩; ES 'kɝdl̩, 'kɝdl̩; |-d -d |-ling
-dl̩ɪŋ, -dlɪŋ
cure kjur, kɪur; ES -ə(r; |-d -d
curé kju're, kɪu're (Fr ky're)
cure-all 'kjur,ɔl, 'kɪur,ɔl
curette kju'rɛt, kɪu- |-d -ɪd
curfew 'kɝfju, -fɪu; ES 'kɝ-, 'kɝ-
curia 'kjurɪə, 'kɪurɪə |-iae -ɪ,i
Curie, c- 'kjurɪ, 'kɪu-, kju'ri, kɪu- (Fr ky'ri)
curio, C- 'kjurɪ,o, 'kɪurɪ-
curiosity ,kjurɪ'ɑsətɪ, ,kɪurɪ-; ES+-'ɒs-
curious 'kjurɪəs, 'kɪurɪ-
curl kɝl; ES kɝl, kɝl; |-ed -d
curlew 'kɝlu, -lɪu, 'kɝlju; ES 'kɝ-, 'kɝ-
curlicue 'kɝlɪ,kju, -,kɪu; ES 'kɝlɪ-, 'kɝlɪ-

|full ful |tooth tuθ |further 'fɝðɚ; ES 'fɝðə |custom 'kʌstəm |while hwaɪl |how hau |toy tɔɪ
|using 'juzɪŋ |fuse fjuz, fɪuz |dish dɪʃ |vision 'vɪʒən |Eden 'idn̩ |cradle 'kredl̩ |keep 'em 'kipm̩

curmudgeon kəˈmʌdʒən; ES kə-
currant ˈkɝənt; ES ˈkɝrənt, ˈkʌr-, ˈkɝ-
currency ˈkɝənsɪ; ES ˈkɝrənsɪ, ˈkʌr-, ˈkɝ-
current ˈkɝənt; ES ˈkɝrənt, ˈkʌr-, ˈkɝ-
curricle ˈkɝɪkḷ; ES ˈkɝrɪkḷ, ˈkʌr-, ˈkɝ-;
|-d -d |-ling -klɪŋ, -kḷɪŋ
curricular kəˈrɪkjələ˞; ES -lə(r
curriculum kəˈrɪkjələm |-s -z |-la -lə
currier, C- ˈkɝɪ˞; ES ˈkɝɪ·ə(r, ˈkʌrɪ-, ˈkɝɪ-
Currier and Ives ˈkɝɪ˞nˈaɪvz, ˈkɝɪərəndˈaɪvz;
ES ˈkɝrɪənˈaɪvz, ˈkʌrɪənˈaɪvz, ˈkɝɪənˈaɪvz,
ˈkɝrɪərəndˈaɪvz ˈkʌrɪərəndˈaɪvz, ˈkɝɪərənd-
ˈaɪvz
currish ˈkɝɪʃ; ES ˈkɝrɪʃ, ˈkɝ-
curry ˈkɝɪ; ES ˈkɝrɪ, ˈkʌrɪ, ˈkɝɪ; |-ied -d
|-comb -ˌkom
curse kɝs; ES kɝs, kɝs; |-s -ɪz |-d -t
cursed adj ˈkɝsɪd, kɝst; ES ˈkɝs-, ˈkɝs-,
kɝst, kɝst; |-ly -ɪdlɪ
cursive ˈkɝsɪv; ES ˈkɝs-, ˈkɝs-; |-sory -sərɪ
cursorial kɝˈsorɪəl, -ˈsor-; ES kɝˈsorɪəl, kɝ-,
E+-ˈsor-
Cursor Mundi ˈkɝsorˈmʌndaɪ, ˈkɝsə˞-, -dɪ;
ES ˈkɝsɔə-, -sə-, ˈkɝsɔə-, ˈkɝsə-
curst kɝst; ES kɝst, kɝst
curt kɝt; ES kɝt, kɝt
curtail kɝˈtel, kə-; ES kɝ-, kɝ-, kə-; |-ed -d
(ˈcurˌtail ˈspending)
curtain ˈkɝtṇ, -tɪn, -tən; ES ˈkɝt-, ˈkɝt-;
|-ed -d |-ing -ɪŋ, -tnɪŋ
curtal ˈkɝtḷ; ES ˈkɝtḷ, ˈkɝtḷ
curtesy ˈkɝtəsɪ; ES ˈkɝt-, ˈkɝt-
curtilage ˈkɝtḷɪdʒ; ES ˈkɝt-, ˈkɝt-; |-s -ɪz
Curtis, -ss ˈkɝtɪs; ES ˈkɝt-, ˈkɝt-; |-'s -ɪz
curtsy -sey ˈkɝtsɪ; ES ˈkɝt-, ˈkɝt-; |-ied -d
curule ˈkjurul, ˈkɪur-, -rul
curvature ˈkɝvətʃə˞; -ˌtʃur; ES ˈkɝvətʃə(r,
ˈkɝvətʃə(r, -ˌtʃuə(r
curve kɝv; ES kɝv, kɝv; |-d -d |-dly -ɪdlɪ
curvet n ˈkɝvɪt; ES ˈkɝv-, ˈkɝv-
curvet v ˈkɝvɪt, kəˈvɛt; ES ˈkɝvɪt, ˈkɝv-,
kəˈvɛt; |-(t)ed -ɪd
curvilineal ˌkɝvəˈlɪnɪəl; ES ˌkɝvə-, ˌkɝvə-;
|-ear -ɪ˞; ES -ɪ·ə(r
Curwood ˈkɝˌwud; ES ˈkɝˌwud, ˈkɝ-
Curzon ˈkɝzṇ; ES ˈkɝzṇ, ˈkɝzṇ
Cusco ˈkusko
cusec ˈkjusɛk, ˈkɪusɛk
Cush kʌʃ |-'s -ɪz |-ite -aɪt |-itic kʌʃˈɪtɪk

cushaw kəˈʃɔ
Cushing ˈkuʃɪŋ
Cushman ˈkuʃmən
cushion ˈkuʃən, -ɪn |-ed -d
cusp kʌsp |cusped kʌspt |-id -ɪd |-idal -ɪdḷ
cuspate ˈkʌspɪt, -pet |-d -petɪd
cuspidate ˈkʌspɪˌdet |-dated -ˌdetɪd
cuspidor ˈkʌspəˌdɔr; ES -ˌdɔə(r
cuss kʌs |cusses ˈkʌsɪz |cussed kʌst
cussed adj ˈkʌsɪd |-ly -lɪ
cuss-word ˈkʌsˌwɝd; ES -ˌwɝd, -ˌwɝd
custard ˈkʌstə˞d; ES ˈkʌstəd
Custer ˈkʌstə˞; ES ˈkʌstə(r
Custis ˈkʌstɪs |-'s -ɪz
custodial kʌsˈtodɪəl |-an -ən |-anship -ənˌʃɪp
custody ˈkʌstədɪ
custom ˈkʌstəm |-ed -d
customarily ˈkʌstəmˌɛrəlɪ, esp. if emph.
ˌkʌstəˈmɛrəlɪ
customary ˈkʌstəmˌɛrɪ
customer ˈkʌstəmə˞; ES ˈkʌstəmə(r
customhouse ˈkʌstəmˌhaus |-ses -zɪz
custom-made ˈkʌstəmˈmed (ˈcustom-ˌmade
ˈhat)
cut kʌt
cut-and-fill ˈkʌtṇˈfɪl
cutaneous kjuˈtenɪəs, kɪu-
cutaway ˈkʌtəˌwe
cutback ˈkʌtˌbæk
cute kjut, kɪut
Cuthbert ˈkʌθbə˞t; ES ˈkʌθbət
cuticle ˈkjutɪkḷ, ˈkɪut-
cutlass, -las ˈkʌtləs |-es -ɪz
cut-leaf ˈkʌtˌlif |-leaved -ˌlivd
cutler ˈkʌtlə˞; ES ˈkʌtlə(r; |-ess -ɪs |-y -ɪ
cutlet ˈkʌtlɪt
cutoff ˈkʌtˌɔf, -ˌɒf
cutout ˈkʌtˌaut
cutover ˈkʌtˌovə˞; ES -ˌovə(r
cutpurse ˈkʌtˌpɝs; ES -ˌpɝs, -ˌpɝs; |-s -ɪz
cut-rate ˈkʌtˈret (ˈcut-ˌrate ˈstore)
cutter ˈkʌtə˞; ES ˈkʌtə(r
cutthroat ˈkʌtˌθrot
cutting ˈkʌtɪŋ
cuttle, C- ˈkʌtḷ |-bone -ˌbon |-fish -ˌfɪʃ
cutty ˈkʌtɪ
Cuttyhunk ˈkʌtɪˌhʌŋk
cutworm ˈkʌtˌwɝm; ES -ˌwɝm, -ˌwɝm
Cuvier ˈkjuvɪˌe, ˈkɪu- (Fr kyˈvje)

Key: See in full §§3–47. bee bi |pity ˈpɪtɪ (§6) |rate ret |yet jɛt |sang sæŋ |angry ˈæŋ·grɪ
|bath bæθ; E baθ (§10) |ah ɑ |far fɑr |watch watʃ, wɒtʃ (§12) |jaw dʒɔ |gorge gɔrdʒ |go go

Cuyahoga kaɪˈhɑgə, ˌkaɪə-, kə-, -ˈhɒgə,
-ˈhɔgə, *old-fash.* -ˈhogə
Cuyahoga Falls kəˈhɑgəˈfɔlz, kaɪ-, -ˈhɒgə-,
-ˈhɔgə-, *old-fash.* -ˈhogə-
Cuzco ˈkusko
cyanamide ˌsaɪəˈnæmaɪd, saɪˈænəˌmaɪd, -mɪd
|-mid -mɪd
cyanate ˈsaɪəˌnet
cyanic saɪˈænɪk
cyanide ˈsaɪəˌnaɪd, -nɪd |-nid -nɪd |-d -ɪd
cyanogen saɪˈænədʒən, -dʒɪn
cyanosis ˌsaɪəˈnosɪs
Cybele, c- ˈsɪbl̩ˌi
Cyclades ˈsɪkləˌdiz
cyclamen ˈsɪkləmən, -ˌmɛn
cycle ˈsaɪkl̩ |-d -d |-ling ˈsaɪklɪŋ, ˈsaɪkl̩ɪŋ
cyclic ˈsaɪklɪk, ˈsɪk- |-al -l̩ |-ally -l̩ɪ, -ɪklɪ
cyclist ˈsaɪklɪst, ˈsaɪkl̩ɪst
cycloid ˈsaɪklɔɪd |-al saɪˈklɔɪdl̩ |-ally saɪ-
ˈklɔɪdl̩ɪ
cyclometer saɪˈklɑmətɚ; ES -ˈklɑmətə(r,
-ˈklɒm-
cyclone ˈsaɪklon |-d -d
cyclonic saɪˈklɑnɪk; ES+-ˈklɒn-; |-al -l̩ |-ally
-l̩ɪ, -ɪklɪ
Cyclopean, c- ˌsaɪkləˈpiən
cyclopedia, -paed- ˌsaɪkləˈpidɪə
cyclopedic, -paed- ˌsaɪkləˈpidɪk |-al -l̩ |-ally
-l̩ɪ, -ɪklɪ
Cyclops ˈsaɪklɑps; ES+-klɒps; |-es -ɪz
|-clopes saɪˈklopiz
cyclorama ˌsaɪkləˈræmə, -ˈrɑmə
cygnet ˈsɪgnɪt
Cygnus ˈsɪgnəs |-'s -ɪz |*gen* Cygni ˈsɪgnaɪ
cylinder ˈsɪlmdɚ; ES -də(r; |-ed -d |-ing
ˈsɪlɪndrɪŋ, -dərɪŋ
cylindric sɪˈlɪndrɪk |-al -l̩ |-ally -l̩ɪ, -ɪklɪ
cymbal ˈsɪmbl̩ |-ed -d |-ing ˈsɪmbl̩ɪŋ, -blɪŋ
cymbalist ˈsɪmbl̩ɪst, ˈsɪmblɪst

Cymbeline ˈsɪmbl̩ˌin
cyme saɪm |cymose ˈsaɪmos, saɪˈmos
cymous ˈsaɪməs
Cymric ˈsɪmrɪk, ˈkɪmrɪk |-ry -rɪ
Cynewulf ˈkɪnɪˌwʊlf
cynic ˈsɪnɪk |-al -l̩ |-ally -l̩ɪ, -ɪklɪ
cynicism ˈsɪnəˌsɪzəm |-cist -sɪst
cynocephalic ˌsɪnosɛˈfælɪk, ˌsaɪno-
cynocephalus ˌsɪnoˈsɛfələs, ˌsaɪ- |-lous -ləs
cynosure ˈsaɪnəˌʃʊr, ˈsɪnə-; ES -ˌʃʊə(r
Cynthia ˈsɪnθɪə |Cynthiana ˌsɪnθɪˈænə
cypher ˈsaɪfɚ; ES ˈsaɪfə(r; |-ed -d |-ing
ˈsaɪfrɪŋ, ˈsaɪfərɪŋ
cypress ˈsaɪprəs |-es -ɪz |-ed -t
Cyprian ˈsɪprɪən
cyprinoid ˈsɪprəˌnɔɪd
Cypriot ˈsɪprɪət |-ote -ˌot
cypripedium, C- ˌsɪprəˈpidɪəm |-dia -dɪə
Cyprus, c- ˈsaɪprəs |-'s -ɪz
Cyrano de Bergerac ˈsɪrəˌnodəˈbɚˈdʒəˌræk;
ES -ˈbɜdʒ-, -ˈbɝˈdʒ-; (*Fr* siranodbɛrʒəˈrak)
Cyrenaic ˌsɪrəˈne·ɪk, ˌsaɪrə- |-naica -ˈneəkə
Cyrene *pers. name* saɪˈrin, *Gk city* saɪˈrini
Cyril ˈsɪrəl, -ɪl
Cyrus ˈsaɪrəs |-'s -ɪz
cyst sɪst |-ed -ɪd |-itis sɪsˈtaɪtɪs
Cythera sɪˈθɪrə
Cytherea ˌsɪθəˈriə |-n -n
cytology saɪˈtɑlədʒɪ; ES+-ˈtɒl-; |-gist -st
cytoplasm ˈsaɪtəˌplæzəm |-ic ˌsaɪtəˈplæzmɪk
czar zɑr; ES zɑ:(r, E+zɑ:(r
czarevitch ˈzɑrəˌvɪtʃ; E+ˈzɑrə-; |-'s -ɪz
czarevna zɑˈrɛvnə; E+zɑ-
czarina zɑˈrinə; E+zɑ-
Czech tʃɛk |-ic -ɪk |-ish -ɪʃ
Czechoslovak, Czecho-Sl- ˌtʃɛkəˈslovæk, -vɑk
Czechoslovakia, Czecho-Sl- ˌtʃɛkəsloˈvækɪə,
-ˈvɑk-, -kjə |-n -n
Czernowitz ˈtʃɛrnəˌvɪts |-'s -ɪz

|full fʊl |tooth tuθ |further ˈfɝˈðɚ; ES ˈfɝˈðə |custom ˈkʌstəm |while hwaɪl |how haʊ |toy tɔɪ
|using ˈjuzɪŋ |fuse fjuz, fɪuz |dish dɪʃ |vision ˈvɪʒən |Eden ˈidn̩ |cradle ˈkredl̩ |keep 'em ˈkipm̩

D

D, d *letter* di |*pl* D's, Ds, *poss* D's **diz**
-d *ending see* -ed
'd *abbr. spelling of unstressed* had, would, *as in*
  I'd **aɪd**, he'd **hid**, she'd **ʃid**, it'd **ɪtəd**, we'd
  wid, you'd **jud**, they'd **ðed**, there'd **ðerd**,
  ðeəd, *etc.*
dab **dæb** |dabbed **dæbd**
dabble **'dæbļ** |-d -d |-ling **'dæbļɪŋ, 'dæblɪŋ**
dabster **'dæbstə**; ES **'dæbstə(r**
da capo *It* **da'ka:po**
dace des |daces **'desɪz**
dachshund **'daks,hʊnd, 'dæks,hʌnd** (*Ger*
  'daks,hʊnt
Dacia **'deʃɪə, 'deʃə** |-n -n
dacoit də'kɔɪt |dacoitage də'kɔɪtɪdʒ |-y -ɪ
dactyl, D- **'dæktɪl, -tļ** |Dactyli **'dæktɪ,laɪ**
dactylic dæk'tɪlɪk
dad dæd |daddy **'dædɪ**
dado **'dedo** |dadoed **'dedod**
Daedalus **'dɛdļəs** |Daedalus's **'dɛdļəsɪz**
daemon **'dimən** |-s -z |daemones **'dimən,iz**
daffodil **'dæfə,dɪl** |-dilly -,dɪlɪ
daffy **'dæfɪ**
daffydowndilly **'dæfɪ,daʊn'dɪlɪ**
Dafoe **'defo**
daft dæft; E+daft, daft
dag dæg |dagged dægd
dagger **'dægə**; ES **'dægə(r**
daggle **'dægļ** |-d -d |daggling **'dæglɪŋ, -glɪŋ**
Dago '*Italian*' **'dego**; *Darfur Negro* **'dago**
Dagobert **'dægəbət, 'dægo,bзt**; ES **'dægə-**
  bət, 'dægo,bзt, -,bзt
Dagon **'degan, -gən**; ES+**'degɒn**
Daguerre *Fr* da'gɛːr
daguerreotype də'gɛrə,taɪp, də'gɛrɪə-
Dahl dɑl
Dahlgren **'dælgrɪn, -ən**
dahlia **'dæljə, 'daljə, 'deljə**—*The regular*
  Anglicized form is **'deljə**, *prevalent in Engd*
  and formerly in Amer. **'daljə** *is formed on*
  Sw Dahl, *and* **'dæljə** *is an Am modification*
  of **'daljə.**
Dahomey də'homɪ, da'home
Dail Eireann **'dɔɪl'erən, 'daɪl-, -'ɛrən**
daily, D- **'delɪ**
daimio **'daɪmjo**
Daimler **'demlə, 'daɪmlə**; ES -lə(r

daimon **'daɪman**; ES+**'daɪmɒn**
Daingerfield **'dendʒə,fild**; ES **'dendʒə-**
Dai Nippon **'daɪ nɪ'pan, -'pɒn, 'nɪp'pan, -'pɒn**
  (*Jap* **'njɪppon**)
dainty **'dentɪ** |-tily **'dentļɪ, -tɪlɪ**
dairy **'dɛrɪ, 'dɛːrɪ, 'derɪ** |-man -mən, -,mæn
  |-men -mən, -,mɛn—*Some speakers distin-*
  guish dairy *from* Derry *by a longer* ɛ.
dais **'de·ɪs,** des |daises **'de·ɪsɪz, 'desɪz**—"*The*
  dissyllabic pronunciation of dais *is a 'shot' at*
  the word from the spelling."—*OED.*
daisy **'dezɪ** |daisied **'dezɪd**
dak, dawk dɔk, dak
Dakar da'kar, də-; ES -'ka:(r, E+-'ka:(r
Dakin **'dekɪn**
Dakota də'kotə, dɪ'kotə
Dalai Lama də'laɪ'lamə, 'dalaɪ-
dale del |-man, -men -mən |-sman, -smen
  -zmən
Dalhousie *college* dæl'haʊzɪ, *Quebec* dæl'huzɪ
Dallas **'dæləs,** *Texas loc.*+**'dælɪs** |-'s -ɪz
dalles, D- dælz
dalliance **'dælɪəns, 'dæljəns** |-s -ɪz
dally **'dælɪ** |dallied **'dælɪd**
Dalmatia dæl'meʃɪə, -'meʃə |-n -n
dalmatic, D- dæl'mætɪk
Dalrymple **'dælrɪmpļ,** dæl'rɪmpļ
Dalton **'dɔltn̩**
Daly **'delɪ**
Dalzel, -ll, -ziel *Am name* dæl'zɛl; *Scotl*
  dal'jɛl, -'zɛl, dɪ'ɛl, di'ɛl, də'ɛl
dam dæm |dammed dæmd
damage **'dæmɪdʒ** |-s -ɪz |-d -d
Damariscotta ,dæmərɪ'skatə; ES+-'skɒtə;
  loc. ,dæmə'skɒtɪ
Damascene **'dæmə,sin,** ,dæmə'sin
Damascus də'mæskəs |-'s -ɪz
damask **'dæməsk**
dame dem
Damien **'demɪən, -mjən** (*Fr* da'mjæ̃)
damn dæm |-ed -d |damning **'dæmɪŋ,**
  'dæmnɪŋ
damnable **'dæmnəbļ** |-bly -blɪ |-ation dæm-
  'neʃən
damnatory **'dæmnə,torɪ, -,tɔrɪ**; S **'dæmnə-**
  ,tɔrɪ
damnify **'dæmnə,faɪ** |damnified **'dæmnə,faɪd**

Key: *See in full §§3–47.* bee bi |pity **'pɪtɪ** (§6) |rate ret |yet jɛt |sang sæŋ |angry **'æŋ·grɪ**
|bath bæθ; E baθ (§10) |ah ɑ |far fɑr |watch watʃ, wɒtʃ (§12) |jaw dʒɔ |gorge gɔrdʒ |go go

Words below in which a *before* r (farm) *is sounded* ɑ *are often pronounced in* E *with* a (fɑːm)

Damocles 'dæmə‚kliz |Damocles's 'dæmə-
‚klɪzɪz
Damon 'demən
damosel, -zel 'dæmə‚zɛl |-zell ‚dæmə'zɛl
damosella ‚dæmə'zɛlə
damp dæmp |damped dæmpt
dampen 'dæmpən |-ed -d |-ing -pənɪŋ, -pnɪŋ
damper 'dæmpɚ; ES 'dæmpə(r
Dampier 'dæmpɪr, 'dæmpɪ‧ɚ, -pjɚ; ES -pɪə(r,
-pɪ‧ə(r, -pjə(r
Damrosch 'dæmraʃ; ES+-rɒʃ; |-'s -ɪz
damsel 'dæmzl̩
damson 'dæmzn̩
Dan dæn
Dana 'denə
Danaë 'dænɪ‚i
Danai 'dænɪ‚aɪ
Danbury 'dæn‚bɛrɪ, 'dænbərɪ
dance dæns; E+dans, dɑns; |-s -ɪz |-d -t
dandelion 'dændl̩‚aɪən, 'dændɪ‚laɪən
dander 'dændɚ; ES 'dændə(r
Dandie 'dændɪ
dandify 'dændɪ‚faɪ |-fied -‚faɪd
dandle 'dændl̩ |-d -d |-ling 'dændlɪŋ, 'dændl̩ɪŋ
dandler 'dændlɚ; ES 'dændlə(r
dandruff 'dændrəf
dandy 'dændɪ
Dane den |-geld -‚geld |-lagh, -law -‚lɔ
Danenhower 'dænən‚hauɚ; ES -‚hau‧ə(r
danger 'dendʒɚ; ES 'dendʒə(r; |-ous -əs,
-dʒrəs
Dangerfield 'dendʒɚ‚fild; ES 'dendʒə-
dangle 'dæŋgl̩ |-d -d |-ling 'dæŋglɪŋ, -gl̩ɪŋ
Daniel 'dænjəl, *old-fash.* 'dænl̩ |-s -z
Danielson *Conn* 'dænl̩sn̩, 'dænjəlsn̩
Danish 'denɪʃ
Danite 'dænaɪt
dank dæŋk
d'Annunzio də'nunzɪ‚o (*It* dɑn'nuntsjo)
danseuse dɑn'sɜz, dæn- |-s -ɪz (*Fr* dãsøːz)
Dante 'dæntɪ, 'dɑntɪ (*It* 'dante)
Dantean 'dæntɪən, dæn'tiən, 'dɑn-, dɑn-
Dantesque dæn'tɛsk, dɑn-
Danton 'dæntən, *Fr leader* ʒɜrʒ ʒɑːk dã'tõ
Danube 'dænjub, 'dænjub |-bian dæn'jubɪən
Danvers 'dænvɚz; ES 'dænvəz; |-'s -ɪz
Danzig 'dæntsɪg (*Ger* 'dɑntsɪx)
dap dæp |dapped dæpt

Daphne 'dæfnɪ
Daphnis 'dæfnɪs |Daphnis's 'dæfnɪsɪz
dapper 'dæpɚ; ES 'dæpə(r
dapple 'dæpl̩ |-d -d |-ling 'dæplɪŋ, -pl̩ɪŋ
dapple-gray 'dæpl̩'gre ('dapple-‚gray 'mare)
Darbishire 'dɑrbɪ‚ʃɪr, -ʃɚ; ES 'dɑːbɪ‚ʃɪə(r,
-ʃə(r
Darby 'dɑrbɪ; ES 'dɑːbɪ
Dardanelles ‚dɑrdn̩'ɛlz; ES ‚dɑːdn̩-
Dardanius dɑr'denɪəs; ES dɑ-; |-'s -ɪz
dare dɛr, dær; E dɛə(r, ES dæə(r; |-d -d
or durst dɜst; ES dɜst, dɜst; *pptc* -d -d
daredevil 'dɛr‚dɛvl̩, 'dær-; E 'dɛə-, ES 'dæə-;
|-try -trɪ
daren't dɛrnt, dærnt; E dɛənt, ES dæənt
Dares 'dɛriz, 'dæriz, 'deriz; S 'dæriz, 'deriz;
|-es' -ɪz
Darfur dɑr'fur, 'dɑrfɚ; ES dɑ:'fuə(r, 'dɑ:fə(r
daric 'dærɪk
Darien *Panama* ‚dɛrɪ'ɛn, ‚dær-, 'dɛrɪ‚ɛn,
'dær-, -ən; S ‚dær-, 'dær-; *Conn* -'ɛn
daring 'dɛrɪŋ, 'dærɪŋ; S 'dærɪŋ
Darius də'raɪəs |Darius's də'raɪəsɪz
Darjeeling, -jil- dɑr'dʒilɪŋ; ES dɑ:'dʒ-
dark dɑrk; ES dɑ:k; |darked dɑrkt; ES dɑ:kt
darken 'dɑrkən; ES 'dɑ:k-; |-ed -d |-ing
-kənɪŋ, -knɪŋ
darkey 'dɑrkɪ; ES 'dɑ:kɪ
darkling 'dɑrklɪŋ; ES 'dɑ:klɪŋ
darkroom 'dɑrk‚rum, -‚rum; ES 'dɑ:k-
darksome 'dɑrksəm; ES 'dɑ:ksəm
darky 'dɑrkɪ; ES 'dɑ:kɪ
Darlan 'dɑrlən; ES 'dɑ:l-; (*Fr* dɑr'lã)
darling 'dɑrlɪŋ; ES 'dɑ:lɪŋ
Darmstadt 'dɑrm‚stɑt; ES 'dɑ:m-; (*Ger*
'dɑrm‚ʃtɑt)
darn dɑrn; ES dɑ:n; |-ed -d |-edest -dɪst
Darnal, -ll 'dɑrnl̩; ES 'dɑ:nl̩
Darnay dɑr'ne; ES dɑ:'ne
darnel 'dɑrnl̩; ES 'dɑ:nl̩
Darnel, -ll 'dɑrnl̩, dɑr'nɛl; ES 'dɑ:nl̩, dɑ:'nɛl
Darnley 'dɑrnlɪ; ES 'dɑ:nlɪ
Darrow 'dæro, -ə
Darsie 'dɑrsɪ; ES 'dɑ:sɪ
dart dɑrt; ES dɑ:t; |-ed -ɪd
Dartford 'dɑrtfɚd; ES 'dɑ:tfəd
dartle 'dɑrtl̩; ES 'dɑ:tl̩; |-d -d |-ling -tl̩ɪŋ,
-tlɪŋ

|full fʊl |tooth tuθ |further 'fɝðɚ; ES 'fɜðə |custom 'kʌstəm |while hwaɪl |how hau |toy tɔɪ
|using 'juzɪŋ |fuse fjuz, fruz |dish dɪʃ |vision 'vɪʒən |Eden 'idn̩ |cradle 'kredl̩ |keep 'em 'kipm̩

Words below in which a *before* r (farm) *is sounded* ɑ *are often pronounced in* E *with* a (faːm)

Dartmoor ˈdɑrtˌmʊr, -ˌmor, -ˌmɔr; ES ˈdɑːt-ˌmʊə(r, -ˌmoə(r, E+-ˌmɔə(r

Dartmouth ˈdɑrtməθ; ES ˈdɑːtməθ

Darwin ˈdɑrwɪn; ES ˈdɑːwɪn; |-ism -ˌɪzəm

Darwinian dɑrˈwɪnɪən; ES dɑˈwɪnɪən

Dasent ˈdesn̩t

dash dæʃ |dashes ˈdæʃɪz |-ed -t |-edly -ɪdlɪ

dashboard ˈdæʃˌbord, -ˌbɔrd; ES ˈdæʃˌboəd, E+-ˌbɔəd

dastard ˈdæstəd; ES ˈdæstəd

data ˈdetə, ˈdætə, ˈdɑtə

datary ˈdetərɪ |dataria dəˈtɛrɪə, de-, -ˈter-

date det |dated ˈdetɪd

dative ˈdetɪv

datum ˈdetəm |data ˈdetə, ˈdætə, ˈdɑtə

daub dɔb |daubed dɔbd

Daubeney ˈdɔbənɪ, ˈdɔbnɪ

Daubigny doˈbinjɪ (Fr dobiˈɲi)

Daudet doˈde, ˈdode (Fr doˈdɛ)

daughter ˈdɔtɚ; ES ˈdɔtə(r

daughter-in-law ˈdɔtərɪnˌlɔ, ˈdɔtɚnˌlɔ; ES ˈdɔtərɪnˌlɔ, ˈdɔtənˌlɔ

daughters-in-law ˈdɔtɚzɪnˌlɔ, ˈdɔtɚzn̩ˌlɔ; ES ˈdɔtəzɪnˌlɔ, ˈdɔtəzn̩ˌlɔ

daunt dɔnt, dɒnt, dɑnt |-ed -ɪd |-less -lɪs

dauphin ˈdɔfɪn |-ess -ɪs, -ˌɛs (Fr doˈfæ̃)

davenport, D- ˈdævənˌport, ˈdævm̩ˌport, -ˌpɔrt; ES -ˌpoət, E+-ˌpɔət

Daventry ˈdævəntrɪ, loc. ˈdentrɪ

David ˈdevɪd |-son -sn̩

Davies ˈdevɪz, ˈdevɪs, ˈdevɪz |-'s -ɪz

Daviess ˈdevɪs |-'s -ɪz

da Vinci, Leonardo ˌliəˈnɑrdo dəˈvɪntʃɪ; ES -ˈnɑːdo; (It ˌleoˈnɑrdo dɑˈvintʃi)

Davis ˈdevɪs |Davis's ˈdevɪsɪz |-on -n̩

davit ˈdævɪt

Davy ˈdevɪ

daw dɔ

dawdle ˈdɔdl̩ |-d -d |-ling ˈdɔdlɪŋ, ˈdɔdl̩ŋ

Dawes dɔz |Dawes's ˈdɔzɪz

dawk dɔk, dɑk

dawn dɔn |dawned dɔnd

Dawson ˈdɔsn̩

day, D- de |-book -ˌbʊk |-break -ˌbrek

Dayak ˈdaɪæk

daydream ˈdeˌdrim |-ed -d

dayflower ˈdeˌflauɚ, -ˌflaur; ES -ˌflau·ə(r, -ˌflauə(r

daylight ˈdeˌlaɪt

daylight-saving ˈdeˌlaɪtˈsevɪŋ (ˈdaylight-ˌsaving ˈtime)

dayspring ˈdeˌsprɪŋ

daystar ˈdeˌstɑr; ES ˈdeˌstɑː(r

daytime ˈdeˌtaɪm

Dayton ˈdetn̩ |-ian deˈtonɪən

Daytona deˈtonə

daze dez |dazes ˈdezɪz |dazed dezd |-dly -ɪdlɪ

dazzle ˈdæzl̩ |-d -d |-ling ˈdæzlɪŋ, dæzl̩ŋ

de- *prefix. When wholly unaccented, de- varies between* dɪ- *and* də-. *When only one of these is given in the vocab., it is to be understood that the other is used by many speakers, or often by the same speaker in different styles. The* dɪ- *type with many speakers has the usual tendency toward* dɪ-.

deacon ˈdikən |-ed -d |-ate -ɪt |-ess -ɪs |-esses -ɪsɪz

dead dɛd |deaded ˈdɛdɪd |-ly -lɪ

deaden ˈdɛdn̩ |-ed -d |-ing ˈdɛdn̩ɪŋ, ˈdɛdnɪŋ

deadeye, D- ˈdɛdˌaɪ

deadfall ˈdɛdˌfɔl

deadhead ˈdɛdˌhɛd |-headed -ˌhɛdɪd

deadliness ˈdɛdlɪnɪs

deadlock ˈdɛdˌlɑk; ES+-ˌlɒk; |-ed -t

deadwood, D- ˈdɛdˌwʊd

deaf dɛf, *now much less freq.* dif

deaf-and-dumb ˈdɛfən'dʌm (ˈdeaf-and-ˈdumb ˌschool, ˈdeaf-and-ˌdumb ˈboy)

deafen ˈdɛfən |-ed -d |-ing ˈdɛfənɪŋ, ˈdɛfnɪŋ

deaf-mute ˈdɛfˈmjut, -ˈmɪut, -ˌmjut, -ˌmɪut

deal dil |dealt dɛlt

dean dˈin |deaned dind |-ery -ərɪ, -rɪ |-ship -ʃɪp

Dean(e) din

dear dɪr; ES dɪə(r, S+dɛə(r, djɛə(r

Dearborn ˈdɪrbən, -ˌbɔrn; ES ˈdɪəbən, -ˌbɔən, S+ˈdɛə-, ˈdjɛə-

dearth dɝθ; ES dɜθ, dɝθ; |-ths -θs

deary, -ie ˈdɪrɪ; S+ˈdɛrɪ, ˈdjɛrɪ

death dɛθ |-ths -θs |-ly -lɪ |-like -ˌlaɪk

deathbed ˈdɛθˌbɛd

deathblow ˈdɛθˌblo

death's-head ˈdɛθsˌhɛd

deathwatch ˈdɛθˌwɑtʃ, -ˌwɒtʃ, -ˌwɔtʃ |-es -ɪz

Deauville ˈdovɪl (Fr doˈvil)

debacle deˈbɑkl̩, dɪ-, -ˈbækl̩ (Fr deˈbɑːkl̩)

debar dɪˈbɑr; ES -ˈbɑː(r; |-red -d

Key: See in full §§3–47. bee bi |pity ˈpɪtɪ (§6) |rate ret |yet jɛt |sang sæŋ |angry ˈæŋ·grɪ |bath bæθ; E baθ (§10) |ah ɑ |far fɑr |watch wɑtʃ, wɒtʃ (§12) |jaw dʒɔ |gorge gɔrdʒ |go go

debark dɪˈbɑrk; ES -ˈbɑːk, E+-ˈbɑːk; |-ed -t
debarkation ˌdibɑrˈkeʃən; ES -bɑː-, E+-bɑː-
debase dɪˈbes |-s -ɪz |-d -t |-dness -ɪdnɪs
debatable, -bateable dɪˈbetəbḷ
debate dɪˈbet |-bated -ˈbetɪd
debauch dɪˈbɔtʃ |-es -ɪz |-ed -t |-edly -ɪdlɪ
debauchee ˌdɛbəˈtʃi, -ˈʃi
debauchery dɪˈbɔtʃərɪ, -tʃrɪ
debenture dɪˈbɛntʃɚ; ES -ˈbɛntʃə(r; |-d -d
debilitate dɪˈbɪləˌtet |-tated -ˌtetɪd
debilitation dɪˌbɪləˈteʃən
debility dɪˈbɪlətɪ
debit ˈdɛbɪt |debited ˈdɛbɪtɪd
debonair, -aire ˌdɛbəˈnɛr, -ˈnær; E -ˈnɛə(r,
  ES -ˈnæə(r
Deborah ˈdɛbərə
debouch dɪˈbuʃ |-es -ɪz |-ed -t
debris, dé- dəˈbri, ˈdebri, Brit ˈdɛbri
Debs dɛbz |-ˈs -ɪz
debt dɛt |debtor ˈdɛtɚ; ES ˈdɛtə(r
debunk diˈbʌŋk |-ed -t
De Burgh dɪˈbɝg; ES -ˈbɝg, -ˈbɝg
Debussy dəˈbjusɪ, -ˈbɪu- (Fr dəbyˈsi)
debut dɪˈbju, de-, -ˈbɪu, ˈdebju, -bɪu |-ed -d
  (Fr deˈby)
debutante ˌdɛbjuˈtɑnt ˈdɛbjəˌtænt
decade ˈdɛked, dɛkˈed
decadence dɪˈkedn̩s, ˈdɛkədəns |-cy -ɪ |-dent
  dɪˈkedn̩t, ˈdɛkədənt
decagon ˈdɛkəˌgɑn; ES+-ˌgɒn
decagram, -mme ˈdɛkəˌgræm
decahedral ˌdɛkəˈhidrəl
decahedron ˌdɛkəˈhidrən |-s -z |-dra -drə
decalcify diˈkælsəˌfaɪ |-fied -ˌfaɪd
decalescence ˌdikəˈlɛsn̩s |-scent -sn̩t
decaliter, -tre ˈdɛkəˌlitɚ; ES -ˌlitə(r
Decalogue, -log ˈdɛkəˌlɔg, -ˌlɑg, -ˌlɒg
Decameron dɪˈkæmərən, dɛ-
decameter verse dɪˈkæmətɚ; ES -ˈkæmətə(r
decameter, -tre meas. ˈdɛkəˌmitɚ; ES -tə(r
decamp dɪˈkæmp |-camped -ˈkæmpt
de Camp dɪˈkæmp
decanal ˈdɛkənḷ, dɪˈkenḷ |-ly -ɪ
decane ˈdɛken
decant dɪˈkænt |-ed -ɪd |-er -ɚ; ES -ə(r
decantation ˌdikænˈteʃən
decapitate dɪˈkæpəˌtet |-tated -ˌtetɪd
decapitation dɪˌkæpəˈteʃən, ˌdikæpə-
decapod ˈdɛkəˌpɑd; ES+-ˌpɒd

Decapolis dɪˈkæpəlɪs |-ˈs -ɪz
decarbonate diˈkɑrbənˌet; ES -ˈkɑːb-, E+
  -ˈkɑːb-; |-ated -ˌetɪd
decarbonize diˈkɑrbənˌaɪz; ES -ˈkɑːb-, E+
  -ˈkɑːb-; |-s -ɪz |-d -d
decarburize diˈkɑrbjəˌraɪz, -ˈkɑrbə-; ES
  -ˈkɑːb-, E+-ˈkɑːb-
decasyllable ˈdɛkəˌsɪləbḷ |-bic ˌdɛkəsɪˈlæbɪk
decathlon dɪˈkæθlən; ES+-lɒn
Decatur dɪˈketɚ; ES -ˈketə(r
decay dɪˈke |-cayed -ˈked
Deccan ˈdɛkən
decease dɪˈsis |-s -ɪz |-d -t
decedent dɪˈsidn̩t
deceit dɪˈsit |-ful -fəl |-fully -fəlɪ
deceive dɪˈsiv |-ceived -ˈsivd
decelerate diˈsɛləˌret |-rated -ˌretɪd
deceleration diˌsɛləˈreʃən, ˌdisɛlə-
December dɪˈsɛmbɚ; ES -ˈsɛmbə(r
decemvir dɪˈsɛmvɚ; ES -ˈsɛmvə(r; |-s -z |-i
  -ˌaɪ
decemvirate dɪˈsɛmvərɪt, -ˌret, -vrɪt
decency ˈdisn̩sɪ |decent ˈdisn̩t
decennial dɪˈsɛnɪəl |-ly -ɪ
decenter, -tre diˈsɛntɚ; ES -ˈsɛntə(r; |-(e)d -d
  |-(r)ing -ˈsɛntərɪŋ, -ˈsɛntrɪŋ
decentralization ˌdisɛntrələˈzeʃən, diˌsɛn-,
  -aɪˈz-
decentralize diˈsɛntrəlˌaɪz |-s -ɪz |-d -d
deception dɪˈsɛpʃən |-tive -tɪv
decibel ˈdɛsəˌbɛl
decide dɪˈsaɪd |-cided -ˈsaɪdɪd
deciduous dɪˈsɪdʒʊəs
decigram, -mme ˈdɛsəˌgræm
decile, -il ˈdɛsɪl
deciliter, -tre ˈdɛsəˌlitɚ; ES -ˌlitə(r
decillion dɪˈsɪljən |-th -θ |-ths -θs
decimal ˈdɛsəmḷ |-ly -ɪ
decimate ˈdɛsəˌmet |-d -ɪd |-tion ˌdɛsəˈmeʃən
decimeter, -tre ˈdɛsəˌmitɚ; ES -ˌmitə(r
decipher dɪˈsaɪfɚ; ES -ˈsaɪfə(r; |-ed -d |-ing
  -ˈsaɪfərɪŋ, -ˈsaɪfrɪŋ
decision dɪˈsɪʒən |-al -ḷ
decisive dɪˈsaɪsɪv
decistere ˈdɛsəˌstɪr; ES -ˌstɪə(r
Decius ˈdiʃəs, -ʃəs |-ˈs -ɪz
deck dɛk |decked dɛkt |-house -ˌhaʊs
deckle, -ckel ˈdɛkḷ
deckle-edged ˈdɛkḷˈɛdʒd(ˈdeckle-ˌedgedˈbond)

|full fʊl |tooth tuθ |further ˈfɝðɚ; ES ˈfɝðə |custom ˈkʌstəm |while hwaɪl |how haʊ |toy tɔɪ
|using ˈjuzɪŋ |fuse fjuz, fɪuz |dish dɪʃ |vision ˈvɪʒən |Eden ˈidn̩ |cradle ˈkredḷ |keep ’em ˈkipm̩

declaim dɪˈklem |-claimed -ˈklemd
declamation ˌdɛkləˈmeʃən
declamatory dɪˈklæməˌtorɪ, -ˌtɔrɪ; S -ˌtorɪ
declaration ˌdɛkləˈreʃən
declarative dɪˈklærətɪv
declaratory dɪˈklærəˌtorɪ, -ˌtɔrɪ; S -ˌtorɪ
declare dɪˈklɛr, -ˈklær; E -ˈklɛə(r, ES
 -ˈklæə(r; |-d -d |-dly -ɪdlɪ |-r -ɚ; ES -ə(r
declension dɪˈklɛnʃən |-al -|̩ |-ally -|ɪ
declinable dɪˈklaɪnəb|̩
declination ˌdɛkləˈneʃən |-al -|̩
decline dɪˈklaɪn |-clined -ˈklaɪnd
declivitous dɪˈklɪvətəs |-ty -tɪ
decoct dɪˈkɑkt; ES+-ˈkɒkt; |-ed -ɪd
decoction dɪˈkɑkʃən; ES+-ˈkɒk-; |-tive -tɪv
decode diˈkod |-coded -ˈkodɪd
decollate dɪˈkɑlet; ES+-ˈkɒl-; |-d -ɪd
décolleté ˌdekɑlˈte, -kɑləˈte, -kɒl- (Fr de-
 kɔlˈte)
decolorant diˈkʌlərənt
decolorate diˈkʌləˌret |-rated -ˌretɪd
decoloration ˌdikʌləˈreʃən
decolorize diˈkʌləˌraɪz |-s -ɪz |-d -d
decompose ˌdikəmˈpoz |-s -ɪz |-d -d
decomposition ˌdikɑmpəˈzɪʃən; ES+-kɒm-
decompound ˌdikəmˈpaʊnd |-ed -ɪd
decompress ˌdikəmˈprɛs |-es -ɪz |-ed -t
décor deˈkɔr; ES -ˈkɔə(r; (Fr deˈkɔ:r)
Decorah dɪˈkorə, -ˈkɔrə; S -ˈkorə
decorate ˈdɛkəˌret |-d -ɪd |-tion ˌdɛkəˈreʃən
decorative ˈdɛkəˌretɪv |-tor -tɚ; ES -tə(r
decorous ˈdɛkərəs, dɪˈkorəs; EN+-ˈkɔr-
decorum dɪˈkorəm, -ˈkɔr-; S -ˈkorəm
decoy n dɪˈkɔɪ, ˈdikɔɪ
decoy v dɪˈkɔɪ |-ed -d
decrease n ˈdikris, ˌdiˈkris, dɪ- |-s -ɪz
decrease v dɪˈkris, ˌdi- |-s -ɪz |-d -t (ˈde-
 ˌcreased ˈbuying)
decree dɪˈkri |-creed -ˈkrid
decrement ˈdɛkrəmənt
decrepit dɪˈkrɛpɪt
decrepitude dɪˈkrɛpəˌtjud, -ˌtɪud, -ˌtud
decrescendo ˌdikrəˈʃɛndo, ˌde- (It dekre-
 ˈʃɛndo)
decretal dɪˈkritl̩
decry dɪˈkraɪ |-cried -ˈkraɪd |-crial -ˈkraɪəl
decumbent dɪˈkʌmbənt
decuple ˈdɛkjʊp|̩, dɛkˈjup|̩ |-d -d |-ling -plɪŋ,
 -p|ɪŋ

decurrent dɪˈkɝənt; ES -ˈkɝr-, -ˈkʌr-, -ˈkɝ-
Dedham ˈdɛdəm
dedicate ˈdɛdəˌket |-d -ɪd |-tor -ɚ; ES -ə(r
dedication ˌdɛdəˈkeʃən
dedicatory ˈdɛdəkəˌtorɪ, -ˌtɔrɪ; S -ˌtorɪ
deduce dɪˈdjus, -ˈdɪus, -ˈdus |-s -ɪz |-d -t
deducibility dɪˌdjusəˈbɪlətɪ, -ˌdɪus-, -ˌdus-
deducible dɪˈdjusəb|̩, -ˈdɪus-, -ˈdus- |-bly
 -blɪ
deduct dɪˈdʌkt |-ed -ɪd |-ible -əb|̩
deduction dɪˈdʌkʃən |-tive -tɪv
Dee di
dee ˈdie' di
dee ˈdamn' di |-d -d
dee letter di
deed did |deeded ˈdidɪd
deem dim |deemed dimd
Deems dimz |-'s -ɪz
deemster ˈdimstɚ; ES ˈdimstə(r
deep dip
deepen ˈdipən |-ed -d |-ing ˈdipənɪŋ, ˈdipnɪŋ
deep-mouthed ˈdipˈmaʊðd, -θt (ˈdeep-
 ˌmouthed ˈbay)
deep-rooted ˈdipˈrutɪd, -ˈrutɪd
deep-sea ˈdipˈsi (ˈdeep-ˈsea ˌlife)
deep-seated ˈdipˈsitɪd (ˈdeep-ˌseated ˈfaith)
deer dɪr; ES dɪə(r, S+dɛə(r, djɛə(r; |-hound
 -ˌhaʊnd -skin -ˌskɪn -stalking -ˌstɔkɪŋ
Deerfield ˈdɪrˌfild; ES ˈdɪəˌfild, S+ˈdɛə-,
 ˈdjɛə-
deface dɪˈfes |-s -ɪz |-d -t |-able -əb|̩
de facto dɪˈfækto
defalcate dɪˈfælket, -ˈfɔl- |-d -ɪd |-tor -ɚ; ES
 -ə(r
defalcation ˌdifælˈkeʃən, -fɔl-
defamation ˌdɛfəˈmeʃən, ˌdi-
defamatory dɪˈfæməˌtorɪ, -ˌtɔrɪ; S -ˌtorɪ
defame dɪˈfem |-famed -ˈfemd
default dɪˈfɔlt |-ed -ɪd
defeasibility dɪˌfizəˈbɪlətɪ
defeasible dɪˈfizəb|̩
defeat dɪˈfit |-ed -ɪd |-ism -ɪzəm |-ist -ɪst
defecate ˈdɛfəˌket |-d -ɪd |-tion ˌdɛfəˈkeʃən
defect dɪˈfɛkt, ˈdifɛkt
defection dɪˈfɛkʃən |-tive -tɪv
defend dɪˈfɛnd |-ed -ɪd |-ant -ənt
defense, Brit -ce dɪˈfɛns |-s -ɪz |-sive -ɪv
defensibility dɪˌfɛnsəˈbɪlətɪ
defensible dɪˈfɛnsəb|̩ |-bly -blɪ

Key: See in full §§3–47. bee **bi** |pity ˈpɪtɪ (§6) |rate **ret** |yet **jɛt** |sang **sæŋ** |angry ˈæŋ·grɪ
|bath **bæθ**; E **baθ** (§10) |ah **ɑ** |far **fɑr** |watch **watʃ, wɒtʃ** (§12) |jaw **dʒɔ** |gorge **gɔrdʒ** |go **go**

defer dɪˈfɝ; ES -ˈfɜ(r, -ˈfɝ; |-red -d
deference ˈdɛfərəns
deferential ˌdɛfəˈrɛnʃəl |-ly -ɪ
deferrer dɪˈfɝɚ; ES -ˈfɜrə(r, -ˈfɝə(r
defiance, D- dɪˈfaɪəns |-s -ɪz |-ant -ənt
deficiency dɪˈfɪʃənsɪ |-cient -ʃənt
deficit ˈdɛfəsɪt, Brit + dɪˈfɪsɪt
defier dɪˈfaɪɚ; ES -ˈfaɪ·ə(r
defile 'befoul' dɪˈfaɪl |-filed -ˈfaɪld
defile 'march off' dɪˈfaɪl, ˈdifaɪl |-d -d
defile n dɪˈfaɪl, ˈdifaɪl
definable dɪˈfaɪnəbl̩ |-bly -blɪ
define dɪˈfaɪn |-fined -ˈfaɪnd
definite ˈdɛfənɪt |-tion ˌdɛfəˈnɪʃən
definitive dɪˈfɪnətɪv
deflate dɪˈflet |-d -ɪd |-flation -ˈfleʃən
deflationary dɪˈfleʃənˌɛrɪ
deflect dɪˈflɛkt |-ed -ɪd
deflection, -flexion dɪˈflɛkʃən
deflower dɪˈflaʊɚ; ES -ˈflaʊ·ə(r; |-ed -d
Defoe, De Foe dɪˈfo
deforce dɪˈfors, -ˈfɔrs; ES -ˈfoəs, E+-ˈfɔəs;
 |-s -ɪz |-d -t
deforest dɪˈfɔrɪst, -ˈfɑr-, -ˈfɒr- |-ed -ɪd
deforestation dɪˌfɔrɪsˈteʃən, -ˌfɑr-, -ˌfɒr-, ˌdif-
deform dɪˈfɔrm; ES -ˈfɔəm; |-ed -d |-edly
 -ɪdlɪ
deformation ˌdifɔrˈmeʃən, ˌdɛfɚ-; ES ˌdifɔə-,
 ˌdɛfə-
deformity dɪˈfɔrmətɪ; ES -ˈfɔəmətɪ
defraud dɪˈfrɔd |-ed -ɪd
defray dɪˈfre |-ed -d |-able -əbl̩ |-al -əl
defrock diˈfrɑk; ES+-ˈfrɒk; |-ed -t
defrost diˈfrɔst, -ˈfrɒst |-ed -ɪd
deft dɛft
defunct dɪˈfʌŋkt
defy n dɪˈfaɪ, ˈdifaɪ
defy v dɪˈfaɪ |-fied -ˈfaɪd
degenerate adj dɪˈdʒɛnərɪt, -ˈdʒɛnrɪt |-racy
 -rəsɪ, -nrəsɪ
degenerate v dɪˈdʒɛnəˌret |-d -ɪd |-tive -ɪv
degeneration dɪˌdʒɛnəˈreʃən, ˌdidʒɛnə-
deglutinate dɪˈglutn̩ˌet, -ˈglut- |-d -ɪd
deglutition ˌdiglʊˈtɪʃən, -glu-
degrade dɪˈgred |-d -ɪd |-dation ˌdɛgrəˈdeʃən
degree dɪˈgri |-d -d
De Groot dəˈgrot=Grotius
degum diˈgʌm |-gummed -ˈgʌmd
dehisce dɪˈhɪs |-s -ɪz |-d -t |-nce -n̩s |-nt -n̩t

dehorn diˈhɔrn; ES -ˈhɔən; |-ed -d
dehydrate diˈhaɪdret |-drated -dretɪd
deictic ˈdaɪktɪk |-al -l̩ |-ally -l̩ɪ, -ɪklɪ
deification ˌdiəfəˈkeʃən
deiform ˈdiəˌfɔrm; ES -ˌfɔəm
deify ˈdiəˌfaɪ |-fied -ˌfaɪd
deign den |deigned dend
Dei gratia ˈdiaɪˈgreʃɪə
deil dil
Deiphobus diˈɪfəbəs |-'s -ɪz
Deira ˈdeərə
Deirdre ˈdɪrdrɪ, ˈdɛrdrɪ; ES ˈdɪə-, ˈdɛə-; Ir
 ˈderdre
deism ˈdiɪzəm |-ist -ɪst
deistic diˈɪstɪk |-al -l̩ |-ally -l̩ɪ, -ɪklɪ
deity ˈdiətɪ
deject dɪˈdʒɛkt |-ed -ɪd |-ction -kʃən
déjeuné, -ner n ˈdeʒəˌne (Fr deʒœˈne)
de jure diˈdʒʊrɪ, -ˈdʒɪurɪ
De Kalb dɪˈkælb
Dekker ˈdɛkɚ; ES ˈdɛkə
dekle ˈdɛkl̩
De Koven dɪˈkovən
Delafield ˈdɛləˌfild
Delagoa ˌdɛləˈgoə (ˈDelaˌgoa ˈBay)
delaine, D- dəˈlen
de la Mare, D- ˈdɛləˌmɛr, -ˌmær; E -ˌmɛə(r,
 ES -ˌmæə(r; acct + ˌde la ˈMare
Delamere ˈdɛləˌmɪr; ES -ˌmɪə(r, S+-ˌmɛə(r
De Land dɪˈlænd
Deland dɪˈlænd, Brit name ˈdilənd
Delano ˈdɛləˌno
De la Pole ˌdɛləˈpol
delate dɪˈlet |-lated -ˈletɪd
Delavan ˈdɛləvən
Delaware ˈdɛləˌwɛr, -ˌwær; E -ˌwɛə(r, ES
 -ˌwæə(r
Delawarean ˌdɛləˈwɛrɪən, -ˈwær-; S -ˈwærɪən
De La Warr ˈdɛləˌwɛr -ˌwær; E -ˌwɛə(r, ES
 -ˌwæə(r
delay dɪˈle |-layed -ˈled
dele ˈdilɪ |deled ˈdilɪd
delectable dɪˈlɛktəbl̩ |-bly -blɪ
delectation ˌdilɛkˈteʃən, dɪˌlɛkˈteʃən
delegate n ˈdɛləˌget, ˈdɛləgɪt |-gacy -gəsɪ
delegate v ˈdɛləˌget |-d -ɪd |-tion ˌdɛləˈgeʃən
de Lesseps dəˈlɛsəps (Fr dəlɛˈsɛps) |-'s -ɪz
delete dɪˈlit |-leted -ˈlitɪd |-letion -ˈliʃən
deleterious ˌdɛləˈtɪrɪəs

---

delft, D- dɛlft |-ware -ˌwɛr, -ˌwæer; E
-ˌwɛə(r, ES -ˌwæə(r
Delhi US ˈdɛlhaɪ, India ˈdɛlɪ
Delia ˈdiljə, -lɪə |-n -n
deliberate adj dɪˈlɪbərɪt, -brɪt
deliberate v dɪˈlɪbəˌret |-d -ɪd |-tion dɪˌlɪbə-
ˈreʃən
deliberative dɪˈlɪbəˌretɪv |-tor -tɚ; ES -tə(r
delicate ˈdɛləkət, -kɪt |-cacy -kəsɪ
delicatessen ˌdɛləkəˈtɛsṇ
delicious dɪˈlɪʃəs
delight dɪˈlaɪt |-ed -ɪd |-ful -fəl |-fully -fəlɪ
Delilah dɪˈlaɪlə
delimit dɪˈlɪmɪt |-ed -ɪd
delimitation dɪˌlɪməˈteʃən, ˌdilɪmə-
delineate dɪˈlɪnɪˌet |-d -ɪd |-tion dɪˌlɪnɪˈeʃən
delineative dɪˈlɪnɪˌetɪv |-tor -tɚ; ES -tə(r
delinquency dɪˈlɪŋkwənsɪ |-quent -kwənt
deliquesce ˌdɛləˈkwɛs |-s -ɪz |-d -t
deliquescence ˌdɛləˈkwɛsṇs |-cent -sṇt
delirium dɪˈlɪrɪəm |-s -z |-ria -rɪə |-rious -rɪəs
Delisle, De l'Isle US dɪˈlaɪl, Fr name dəˈlil
Delitzsch ˈdelɪtʃ |-ˈs -ɪz
Delius ˈdilɪəs |-ˈs -ɪz
deliver dɪˈlɪvɚ; ES -ˈlɪvə(r; |-ed -d |-ing
-ˈlɪvərɪŋ, -ˈlɪvrɪŋ |-ance -vərəns, -vrəns
deliverer dɪˈlɪvərɚ, -ˈlɪvrɚ; ES -rə(r; |-very
-vərɪ, -vrɪ
dell, D- dɛl |Della ˈdɛlə
Della Robbia ˌdɛləˈrabɪə, -ˈrɒb- (It ˌdella-
ˈrobbja)
Delmarva dɛlˈmarvə; ES -ˈmɑːvə, E+
-ˈmaːvə
Delmonico dɛlˈmanɪˌko, -ˈmɒn-
Delos ˈdilas, -lɒs |-ˈs -ɪz
delouse diˈlaus, -ˈlauz |-s -ɪz |-d -t, -d
Delphi ˈdɛlfaɪ |-phian -fɪən |-phic -fɪk
delphinium, D- dɛlˈfɪnɪəm |-s -z
Delphos ˈdɛlfəs, -fas, -fɒs |-ˈs -ɪz
Del Rio dɛlˈrio
Delsarte dɛlˈsart; ES -ˈsaːt, E+-ˈsaːt
del Sarto, Andrea ˈandrɪədɛlˈsarto; ES
-ˈsaːto, E+-ˈsaːto; (It anˈdrɛːadelˈsarto)
delta, D- ˈdɛltə |-ic dɛlˈteˑɪk |-toid ˈdɛltɔɪd
delude dɪˈlud, -ˈlɪud |-d -ɪd
deluge ˈdɛljudʒ |-s -ɪz |-d -d
delusion dɪˈluʒən, -ˈlɪuʒən
delusive dɪˈlusɪv, -ˈlɪus- |-sory -sərɪ
de luxe dɪˈluks, -ˈlʌks (Fr dəˈlyks)

delve dɛlv |delved dɛlvd
demagnetization ˌdimægnətəˈzeʃən, diˌmæg-,
-aɪˈz-
demagnetize diˈmægnəˌtaɪz |-s -ɪz |-d -d
demagogic ˌdɛməˈgadʒɪk, -ˈgɒdʒ-, -ˈgag-,
-ˈgɒg- |-al -ḷ |-ally -ḷɪ, -ɪklɪ
demagogism ˈdɛməˌgɔgɪzəm, -ˌgag-, -ˌgɒg-
demagogue, -gog ˈdɛməˌgɔg, -ˌgag, -ˌgɒg
|-guery -ərɪ, -rɪ
demagogy ˈdɛməˌgodʒɪ, -ˌgɔgɪ, -ˌgagɪ, -ˌgɒgɪ
demand dɪˈmænd; E+-ˈmand, -ˈmɑnd; |-ed
-ɪd
demarcate dɪˈmɑrket, ˈdimarˌket; ES -aːk-,
E+-aːk-; |-d -ɪd
demarcation ˌdimɑrˈkeʃən; ES -maːˈk-, E+
-maːˈk-
Demas ˈdiməs |-ˈs -ɪz
dematerialize ˌdiməˈtɪrɪəlˌaɪz |-s -ɪz |-d -d
demean dɪˈmin |-ed -d |-or -ɚ; ES -ə(r
dement dɪˈmɛnt |-ed -ɪd |-ia -ˈmɛnʃɪə, -ʃə
demerit diˈmɛrɪt |-ed -ɪd
demesne dɪˈmen, -ˈmin |-nial -ɪəl
Demeter dɪˈmitɚ; ES -ˈmitə(r
Demetrius dɪˈmitrɪəs |-ˈs -ɪz
demigod ˈdɛməˌgad, -ˌgɒd
demijohn ˈdɛməˌdʒan, -ˌdʒɒn
demilitarize diˈmɪlətəˌraɪz |-s -ɪz |-d -d
demimondaine ˌdɛmɪmanˈden, -mɒn- (Fr
dəmimõˈdɛn)
demimonde ˈdɛmɪˌmand, -ˌmɒnd, ˌdɛmɪˈm-
(Fr dəmiˈmõːd)
Deming ˈdɛmɪŋ
demirep ˈdɛmɪˌrep
demise dɪˈmaɪz |-s -ɪz |-d -d
demisemiquaver ˌdɛmɪˈsɛməˌkwevɚ; ES
-ˌkwevə(r
demission dɪˈmɪʃən |-ary -ˌɛrɪ
demit n dɪˈmɪt, ˈdimɪt
demit v dɪˈmɪt |-ted -ɪd
demitasse ˈdɛməˌtæs, -ˌtas (Fr dəmiˈtaːs)
demitint ˈdɛmɪˌtɪnt
demiurge ˈdɛmɪˌɝdʒ; ES -ˌɝdʒ, -ˌɜˑdʒ; |-s -ɪz
demobilization ˌdimobḷəˈzeʃən, dɪˌmobḷə-,
-aɪˈz-
demobilize diˈmobḷˌaɪz |-s -ɪz |-d -d
democracy dəˈmakrəsɪ; ES+-ˈmɒk-
democrat, D- ˈdɛməˌkræt
democratic ˌdɛməˈkrætɪk |-al -ḷ |-ally -ḷɪ,
-ɪklɪ

---

democratize də'makrə‚taɪz; ES+-'mɒk-; |-s -ɪz |-d -d

Democritus dɪ'makrɪtəs; ES+-'mɒk-; |-'s -ɪz

Demogorgon ‚dimə'gɔrgən, ‚dɛmə-; ES -'gɔəgən

demography dɪ'magrəfɪ, di-, -'mɒg-

demoiselle ‚dɛmwa'zɛl (Fr dəmwa'zɛl)

demolish dɪ'malɪʃ; ES+-'mɒl-; |-es -ɪz |-ed -t

demolition ‚dɛmə'lɪʃən, ‚dimə-

demon 'dimən

demonetization di‚manətə'zeʃən, -‚mʌn-, -aɪ'z-; ES+-‚mɒn-

demonetize di'manə‚taɪz, -'mʌn-; ES+ -'mɒn-; |-s -ɪz |-d -d

demoniac dɪ'monɪ‚æk

demoniacal ‚dimə'naɪəkl̩ |-ly -ɪ, -əklɪ

demonic di'manɪk; ES+-'mɒn-; |-al -l̩

demonism 'dimən‚ɪzəm |-ist -ɪst

demonolater ‚dimən'alətɚ; ES -'alətə(r, -'ɒl-; |-try -trɪ |-logy -lədʒɪ

demonstrability ‚dɛmənstrə'bɪlətɪ, dɪ‚manstrə-; ES+-‚mɒn-

demonstrable 'dɛmənstrəbl̩, dɪ'manstrə-; ES+-'mɒn-; |-bly -blɪ

demonstrant dɪ'manstrənt; ES+-'mɒn-

demonstrate 'dɛmən‚stret |-strated -‚stretɪd

demonstration ‚dɛmən'streʃən

demonstrative dɪ'manstrətɪv; ES+-'mɒn-; in sense 'showy'+'dɛmən‚stretɪv

demonstrator 'dɛmən‚stretɚ; ES -‚stretə(r

demoralization dɪ‚mɔrələ'zeʃən, -‚mar-, -‚mɒr-, -aɪ'z-

demoralize dɪ'mɔrəl‚aɪz, -'mar-, -'mɒr- |-s -ɪz |-d -d

De Morgan dɪ'mɔrgən; ES -'mɔəgən

demos 'dimas, -mɒs |-mi -maɪ

Demosthenes dɪ'masθə‚niz, -'mɒs- |-'s -ɪz

demote dɪ'mot |-moted -'motɪd |-tion -'moʃən

demotics di'matɪks; ES+-'mɒt-

demount di'maʊnt |-able -əbl̩

dempster 'dɛmpstɚ; ES -stə(r

demulcent dɪ'mʌlsn̩t

demur dɪ'mɝ; ES -'mɝ(r, -'mɝ; |-red -d

demure dɪ'mjʊr, -'mɪur; ES -'mjʊə(r, -'mɪuə(r

demurrage dɪ'mɝɪdʒ; ES -'mɝr-, -'mʌr-, -'mɝ-

demurrer 'objector² dɪ'mɝɚ; ES -'mɝrə(r, -'mɝə(r

demurrer 'objection' dɪ'mɝɚ; ES -'mɝrə(r, -'mʌr-, -'mɝə(r

demy dɪ'maɪ

den dɛn |denned dɛnd

denarius dɪ'nɛrɪəs, -'ner- |-s -ɪz |-rii -rɪ‚aɪ

denary 'dɛnərɪ, 'dinərɪ

denationalize di'næʃən‚aɪz, -ʃnəl- |-s -ɪz |-d -d

denaturalization di‚nætʃrələ'zeʃən, -aɪ'z-

denaturalize di'nætʃrəl‚aɪz, -tʃərəl- |-s -ɪz |-d -d

denaturant di'netʃərənt

denature di'netʃɚ; ES -tʃə(r; |-d -d |-ring -'netʃərɪŋ, -'netʃrɪŋ

Denbigh 'dɛnbɪ |-shire -‚ʃɪr, -ʃɚ; ES -‚ʃɪə(r, -ʃə(r

dendrite 'dɛndraɪt

dendroid 'dɛndrɔɪd |-al dɛn'drɔɪdl̩

dendrology dɛn'dralədʒɪ; ES+-'drɒl-

Deneb 'dɛnɛb

dengue 'dɛŋgɪ, 'dɛŋge

Denham 'dɛnəm

denial dɪ'naɪəl, -'naɪl |-able -'naɪəbl̩

denier 'contradicter' dɪ'naɪɚ; ES -'naɪ‚ə(r

denier coin də'nɪr; ES -'nɪə(r; (Fr də'nje)

denigrate 'dɛnə‚gret |-grated -‚gretɪd

denim 'dɛnəm, 'dɛnɪm

Denis 'dɛnɪs |-'s -ɪz (Fr də'ni)

Denise də'niz |-'s -ɪz

Denison 'dɛnəsn̩

denitrate di'naɪtret |-trated -tretɪd

denizen 'dɛnəzn̩ |-ed -d

Denmark 'dɛnmark; ES -ma:k, E+-ma:k

Dennis 'dɛnɪs |-'s -ɪz

Dennison 'dɛnəsn̩

Denny 'dɛnɪ |-s -s |-s's -sɪz

denominate adj dɪ'namənɪt, -‚net; ES+ -'nɒm-

denomination dɪ‚namə'neʃən; ES+-‚nɒm-; |-al -l̩, -ʃnəl |-ally -l̩ɪ, -ʃnəlɪ -alism -l̩‚ɪzəm, -ʃnəl-

denominative dɪ'namə‚netɪv, -nətɪv; ES+ -'nɒm-

denominator dɪ'namə‚netɚ; ES-'namə‚netə(r, -'nɒm-

denotation ‚dino'teʃən

denotative dɪ'notətɪv, esp. in contrast with connotative 'dino‚tetɪv

denote dɪ'not |-noted -'notɪd

---

denouement de'numã (*Fr* denu'mã)
denounce dɪ'naʊns |-s -ɪz |-d -t
de novo di'novo
dense dɛns |density 'dɛnsətɪ
dent dɛnt |dented 'dɛntɪd
dental 'dɛntḷ |-ly -ɪ
dentate 'dɛntet |-tated -tetɪd |-tion dɛn'teʃən
denticulate *adj* dɛn'tɪkjəlɪt, -ˌlet |-d -ɪd
dentifrice 'dɛntəˌfrɪs |-s -ɪz
dentilabial ˌdɛntɪ'lebɪəl
dentin 'dɛntɪn |dentine 'dɛntin, -tɪn
dentist 'dɛntɪst |-ry -rɪ
dentition dɛn'tɪʃən
Denton 'dɛntən
denture 'dɛntʃɚ; ES 'dɛntʃə(r; |-ral -əl
denudation ˌdinju'deʃən, ˌdɛn-, -nɪu-, -nu-
denude dɪ'njud, -'nɪud, -'nud |-d -ɪd
denunciate dɪ'nʌnsɪˌet, -ʃɪ- |-d -ɪd |-tive -ɪv
denunciation dɪˌnʌnsɪ'eʃən, -ʃɪ'eʃən
denunciatory dɪ'nʌnsɪəˌtorɪ, -ʃɪ-, -ˌtɔrɪ; S
    -ˌtorɪ
Denver 'dɛnvɚ; ES 'dɛnvə(r
deny dɪ'naɪ |denied dɪ'naɪd
Denys 'dɛnɪs |-'s -ɪz (*Fr* də'ni)
deodand 'diəˌdænd
deodar 'diəˌdɑr; ES -ˌdɑ:(r, E+-ˌdɑ:(r
deodorant di'odərənt
deodorize di'odəˌraɪz |-s -ɪz |-d -d
Deo gratias 'dio'greʃɪˌæs
Deo volente 'diovo'lɛntɪ
deoxidize di'ɑksəˌdaɪz; ES+-'ɒks-; |-s -ɪz
    |-d -d
depart dɪ'pɑrt; ES -'pɑ:t, E+-'pa:t; |-ed -ɪd
    |-ment -mənt
departmental dɪˌpɑrt'mɛntḷ, ˌdipɑrt-; ES
    -ɑ:t-, E+-a:t-; |-ly -ɪ
departure dɪ'pɑrtʃɚ; ES -'pɑ:tʃə(r, E+-'pa:t-
depend dɪ'pɛnd |-ed -ɪd
dependability dɪˌpɛndə'bɪlətɪ
dependable dɪ'pɛndəbḷ |-bly -blɪ
dependence dɪ'pɛndəns |-cy -ɪ
dependent, -ant dɪ'pɛndənt
Depere dɪ'pɪr; ES -'pɪə(r
Depew dɪ'pju, -'pɪu
depict dɪ'pɪkt |-ed -ɪd
depiction dɪ'pɪkʃən |-ture -tʃɚ; ES -tʃə(r
depilate 'dɛpəˌlet |-lated -ˌletɪd
depilatory dɪ'pɪləˌtorɪ, -ˌtɔrɪ; S -ˌtorɪ
deplete dɪ'plit |-d -ɪd |-tion -'pliʃən

deplorable dɪ'plorəbḷ, -'plɔr-; S -'plor-; |-bly
    -blɪ
deplore dɪ'plor, -'plɔr; ES -'ploə(r, E+
    -'plɔə(r; |-d -d
deploy dɪ'plɔɪ |-ed -d
deplume dɪ'plum, -'plɪum |-d -d
depolarization ˌdipolərə'zeʃən, diˌpol-, -aɪ'z-
depolarize di'poləˌraɪz |-s -ɪz |-d -d
depone dɪ'pon |-d -d |-nt -ənt
depopulate di'pɑpjəˌlet; ES+-'pɒp-; |-d -ɪd
depopulation ˌdipɑpjə'leʃən, diˌpɑp-; ES+
    -ɒp-
deport dɪ'port, -'pɔrt; ES -'poət, E+-'pɔət;
    |-ed -ɪd
deportation ˌdipor'teʃən, -pɔr-; ES -poə-,
    E+-pɔə-
deportee ˌdipor'ti, -pɔr-; ES -poə-, E+-pɔə-
deportment dɪ'portmənt, -'pɔrt-; ES -'poət-,
    E+-'pɔət-
depose dɪ'poz |-s -ɪz |-d -d |-sal -ḷ
deposit, D- dɪ'pazɪt; ES+-'pɒz-; |-ed -ɪd
depositary dɪ'pazəˌtɛrɪ; ES+-'pɒz-
deposition ˌdɛpə'zɪʃən, ˌdi-
depositor dɪ'pazɪtɚ; ES -'pazɪtə(r, -'pɒz-
depository dɪ'pazəˌtorɪ, -ˌtɔrɪ; S -ˌtorɪ,
    ES+-'pɒz-
depot 'dipo, *Brit usually* 'dɛpo
depravation ˌdɛprə'veʃən
deprave dɪ'prev |-d -d |-pravity -'prævətɪ
deprecate 'dɛprəˌket |-d -ɪd |-tive -ɪv
deprecation ˌdɛprə'keʃən
deprecatory 'dɛprəkəˌtorɪ, -ˌtɔrɪ; S -ˌtorɪ
depreciable dɪ'priʃɪəbḷ
depreciate dɪ'priʃɪˌet |-ated -ˌetɪd
depreciation dɪˌpriʃɪ'eʃən
depreciative dɪ'priʃɪˌetɪv |-tor -tɚ; ES -tə(r
depreciatory dɪ'priʃɪəˌtorɪ, -ˌtɔrɪ; S -ˌtorɪ
depredate 'dɛprɪˌdet |-d -ɪd |-tor -ɚ; ES -ə(r
depredation ˌdɛprɪ'deʃən
depress dɪ'prɛs |-es -ɪz |-ed -t |-ant -ṇt
depression dɪ'prɛʃən |-sive -'prɛsɪv
deprival dɪ'praɪvḷ
deprivation ˌdɛprə'veʃən
deprive dɪ'praɪv |-prived -'praɪvd
de profundis ˌdiprə'fʌndɪs
Deptford 'dɛtfɚd; ES 'dɛtfəd
depth dɛpθ |-ths -θs
Depue dɪ'pju, -'pɪu
deputation ˌdɛpjə'teʃən

---

depute dɪ'pjut, -'pɪʊt |-d -ɪd	Descartes de'kart; ES -'ka:t, E+-'ka:t; (Fr
deputize 'dɛpjəˌtaɪz |-s -ɪz |-d -d |-ty -tɪ	de'kart, dɛ-)
De Quincey, -cy dɪ'kwɪnsɪ	descend dɪ'sɛnd |-ed -ɪd |-ible, -able -əbļ
derail di'rel |-railed -'reld	descendant n, adj dɪ'sɛndənt
derange dɪ'rendʒ |-s -ɪz |-d -d	descendent adj dɪ'sɛndənt
Derby Engd 'darbɪ, 'dɝbɪ; Am races 'dɝbɪ,	descent dɪ'sɛnt
less freq. 'darbɪ; Eng races 'darbɪ; US	Deschamps Fr de'ʃã, dɛ-
places 'dɝbɪ; ES 'da:bɪ, 'dɜbɪ, 'dɝbɪ,	Deschutes de'ʃut
E+'da:bɪ; |-shire -ˌʃɪr, -ʃɝ; ES -ˌʃɪə(r, -ʃə(r	describable dɪ'skraɪbəbļ |-bly -blɪ
—The Brit pron. of all these is 'da:bɪ, 'darbɪ,	describe dɪ'skraɪb |-scribed -'skraɪbd
less freq. 'dɜbɪ, 'dɝbɪ.	description dɪ'skrɪpʃən |-tive -tɪv
derby 'dɝbɪ; ES 'dɜbɪ, 'dɝbɪ; Brit 'da:bɪ,	descry dɪ'skraɪ |-scried -'skraɪd
'darbɪ	Desdemona ˌdɛzdə'monə
derelict 'dɛrəˌlɪkt |-ction ˌdɛrə'lɪkʃən	desecrate 'dɛsɪˌkret |-crated -ˌkretɪd
deride dɪ'raɪd |-rided -'raɪdɪd	desecration ˌdɛsɪ'kreʃən
de rigueur Fr dəri'gœːr	desensitization ˌdisɛnsətə'zeʃən, diˌsɛn-,
derision dɪ'rɪʒən |-risible dɪ'rɪzəbļ	-aɪ'z-
derisive dɪ'raɪsɪv |-sory -sərɪ	desensitize di'sɛnsəˌtaɪz |-s -ɪz |-d -d
derivable dɪ'raɪvəbļ |-bly -blɪ	desert 'merit' dɪ'zɝt; ES -'zɜt, -'zɝt
derivation ˌdɛrə'veʃən	desert 'a waste' 'dɛzɝt; ES 'dɛzət
derivative də'rɪvətɪv	desert 'abandon' dɪ'zɝt; ES -'zɜt, -'zɝt; |-ed
derive də'raɪv |-rived -'raɪvd	-ɪd
derma 'dɝmə; ES 'dɜmə, 'dɝmə	desertion dɪ'zɝʃən; ES -'zɜʃ-, -'zɝʃ-
dermatitis ˌdɝmə'taɪtɪs; ES ˌdɜmə-, ˌdɝmə-	deserve dɪ'zɝv; ES -'zɜv, -'zɝv; |-d -d |-dly
dermatological ˌdɝmətə'ladʒɪkļ; ES ˌdɜmə-,	-ɪdlɪ
ˌdɝmə-, -'lɒdʒ-	deshabille ˌdɛzə'bil, cf Fr déshabillé dezabi'je
dermatology ˌdɝmə'talədʒɪ; ES ˌdɜmə-,	& Eng dishabille
ˌdɝmə-, -'tɒl-; |-gist -dʒɪst	desiccant 'dɛsəkənt
dermis 'dɝmɪs; ES 'dɜmɪs, 'dɝmɪs	desiccate 'dɛsəˌket |-d -d |-tive -ɪv
Dermott 'dɝmət; ES 'dɜmət, 'dɝmət	desiderate dɪ'sɪdəˌret |-rated -ˌretɪd
Derna 'dɝnə; ES 'dɜnə	desideratum dɪˌsɪdə'retəm |-rata -'retə
dernier 'dɝnɪɝ; ES 'dɜnɪ·ə(r, 'dɝn-; (Fr	design dɪ'zaɪn |-signed -'zaɪnd |-edly -ɪdlɪ
dɛr'nje)	designate adj 'dɛzɪgnɪt, 'dɛs-, -ˌnet
dernier cri Fr dɛrnje'kri	designate v 'dɛzɪgˌnet, 'dɛs- |-d -d -ɪd
dernier ressort Fr dɛrnjɛrə'sɔːr	designation ˌdɛzɪg'neʃən, ˌdɛs-
derogate 'dɛrəˌget |-gated -ˌgetɪd	designative 'dɛzɪgˌnetɪv, 'dɛs-
derogation ˌdɛrə'geʃən	designee ˌdɛzɪg'ni, ˌdɛs-
derogative dɪ'ragətɪv, -'rɒg-	desirability dɪˌzaɪrə'bɪlətɪ
derogatory dɪ'ragəˌtorɪ, -'rɒg-, -ˌtɔrɪ; S	desirable dɪ'zaɪrəbļ |-bly -blɪ
-ˌtɒrɪ; |-rily -rəlɪ	desire dɪ'zaɪr; ES dɪ'zaɪə(r; |-d -d |-dly -ɪdlɪ
Deronda də'randə; ES+-'rɒn-	|-rous -əs
derrick, D- 'dɛrɪk |-ed -t	desist dɪ'zɪst |-ed -ɪd |-ance -əns |-ive -ɪv
derring-do 'dɛrɪŋ'du	desk dɛsk |desked dɛskt
derringer, D- 'dɛrɪndʒɝ; ES -dʒə(r	Des Moines dɪ'mɔɪn, -'mɔɪnz |-'s -z, -nzɪz
Derry 'dɛrɪ	desolate adj 'dɛsļɪt
dervish 'dɝvɪʃ; ES 'dɜv-, 'dɝv-; |-es -ɪz	desolate v 'dɛsļˌet |-d -ɪd |-tor -ɝ; ES -ə(r
Derwent 'dɝwənt, -wɛnt; ES 'dɜ-, 'dɝ-	De Soto dɪ'soto, -'sotə
descant n 'dɛskænt	despair dɪ'spɛr, -'spær; E -'spɛə(r, ES
descant v dɛs'kænt, dɪ'skænt |-ed -ɪd	-'spæə(r; |-ed -d

despatch dɪˈspætʃ |-es -ɪz |-ed -t = dispatch
desperado ˌdɛspəˈredo
desperate ˈdɛsprɪt, -pərɪt |-tion ˌdɛspəˈreʃən
despicable ˈdɛspɪkɪbḷ, less freq. dɪˈspɪkəbḷ
 |-bly -blɪ
despise dɪˈspaɪz |-s -ɪz |-d -d |-dness -ɪdnɪs
despite dɪˈspaɪt |-d -ɪd |-ful -fəl |-fully -fəlɪ
Des Plaines dɛsˈplenz (Fr deˈplɛn)
despoil dɪˈspɔɪl |-ed -d
despoliation dɪˌspolɪˈeʃən
despond dɪˈspɑnd, -ˈspɒnd |-ed -ɪd |-ence
 -əns |-ency -ənsɪ |-ent -ənt
despot ˈdɛspət, -pɑt; ES+-pɒt
despotic dɪˈspɑtɪk; ES+-ˈspɒt-; |-al -ḷ |-ally
 -ḷɪ |-ly -lɪ
despotism ˈdɛspətˌɪzəm
despumate dɪˈspjumet, -ˈspɪu-, ˈdɛspjʊˌmet
 |-d -ɪd
desquamate ˈdɛskwəˌmet |-mated -ˌmetɪd
dessert dɪˈzɝt; ES -ˈzɜt, -ˈzɝt; |-spoon -ˌspun,
 -ˌspʊn
de Stijl dəˈstil
destination ˌdɛstəˈneʃən
destine ˈdɛstɪn |-d -d |-tiny -tənɪ
destitute ˈdɛstəˌtjut, -ˌtɪut, -ˌtut |-d -ɪd
destitution ˌdɛstəˈtjuʃən, -ˈtɪu-, -ˈtu-
destroy dɪˈstrɔɪ |-ed -d |-er -ɝ; ES -ə(r
destructibility dɪˌstrʌktəˈbɪlətɪ
destructible dɪˈstrʌktəbḷ
destruction dɪˈstrʌkʃən |-tive -tɪv
destructivity ˌdistrʌkˈtɪvətɪ, dɪˌstrʌkˈtɪv-
desuetude ˈdɛswɪˌtjud, -ˌtɪud, -ˌtud
desulphurize diˈsʌlfəˌraɪz, -fjə- |-s -ɪz |-d -d
desultory ˈdɛsḷˌtorɪ, -ˌtɔrɪ; S -ˌtorɪ; |-rily
 -rəlɪ, -rɪlɪ
detach dɪˈtætʃ |-es -ɪz |-ed -t |-edly -ɪdlɪ
detachability dɪˌtætʃəˈbɪlətɪ
detachable dɪˈtætʃəbḷ |-bly -blɪ
detail n ˈditel, dɪˈtel
detail v dɪˈtel |-ed -d |-edly -ɪdlɪ
detain dɪˈten |-ed -d
detect dɪˈtɛkt |-ed -ɪd |-able -əbḷ |-bly -blɪ
detection dɪˈtɛkʃən |-tive -tɪv |-tor -tɝ; ES
 -tə(r
detent dɪˈtɛnt
detention dɪˈtɛnʃən
deter dɪˈtɝ; ES -ˈtɜ(r, -ˈtɝ; |-red -d
deterge dɪˈtɝdʒ; ES -ˈtɜdʒ, -ˈtɝdʒ; |-s -ɪz
 |-d -d |-nce -əns |-ncy -ənsɪ |-nt -ənt

deteriorate dɪˈtɪrɪəˌret |-rated -ˌretɪd
deterioration dɪˌtɪrɪəˈreʃən
determinable dɪˈtɝmɪnəbḷ; ES -ˈtɜm-, -ˈtɝm-;
 |-bly -blɪ
determinant dɪˈtɝmənənt; ES -ˈtɜm-, -ˈtɝm-
determinate adj dɪˈtɝmənɪt; ES -ˈtɜm-,
 -ˈtɝm-; n -nɪt, -ˌnet
determination dɪˌtɝməˈneʃən; ES -ˌtɜm-,
 -ˌtɝm-
determine dɪˈtɝmɪn; ES -ˈtɜm-, -ˈtɝm-; |-d -d
 |-dly -dlɪ, -ɪdlɪ |-nism -ˌɪzəm |-nist -ɪst
deterrent dɪˈtɝrənt, -ˈtɛr-; ES -ˈtɜr-, -ˈtʌr-,
 -ˈtɝ-, -ˈtɛr-
detest dɪˈtɛst |-ed -ɪd |-able -əbḷ |-bly -blɪ
detestation ˌditɛsˈteʃən
dethrone dɪˈθron, di- |-d -d
de Tocqueville dɪˈtɑkvɪl, -ˈtɒk- (Fr dətɔkˈvil)
detonate ˈdɛtənˌet, -ton- |-d -ɪd |-tor -ɝ; ES
 -ə(r
detonation ˌdɛtəˈneʃən, -to-
detour ˈditur, dɪˈtur |-ed -d
detract dɪˈtrækt |-ed -ɪd |-or -ɝ; ES -ə(r
detraction dɪˈtrækʃən |-tory -tərɪ
detrain diˈtren |-trained -ˈtrend
detriment ˈdɛtrəmənt
detrimental ˌdɛtrəˈmɛntḷ |-ly -ɪ
detrition dɪˈtrɪʃən
detritus dɪˈtraɪtəs
Detroit dɪˈtrɔɪt |-er -ɝ; ES -ə(r
de trop Fr dəˈtro
Deucalion djuˈkelɪən, dɪu-, du-, -ljən
deuce djus, dɪus, dus |-s -ɪz |-d -ɪd, -t |-dly
 -ɪdlɪ
Deuel ˈdjuəl, ˈdɪuəl, ˈduəl
deus ex machina ˈdiəsˌɛksˈmækɪnə
deuterium djuˈtɪrɪəm, dɪu-, du-
Deuteronomy ˌdjutəˈrɑnəmɪ, ˌdɪu-, ˌdu-;
 ES+-ˈrɒn-
Deutsches Reich Ger ˈdɔytʃəsˈraɪx
Deutschland Ger ˈdɔytʃˌlant
De Valera ˌdəvəˈlerə, -ˈlɛrə, -ˈlɪrə
devaluate diˈvæljuˌet |-ated -ˌetɪd
devaluation ˌdivæljuˈeʃən
devastate ˈdɛvəsˌtet |-tated -ˌtetɪd
devastation ˌdɛvəsˈteʃən
develop dɪˈvɛləp |-ed -t
De Vere dɪˈvɪr; ES -ˈvɪə(r
Devereux ˈdɛvəˌru, -ˌrɪu
deviate ˈdivɪˌet |-d -ɪd |-tion ˌdivɪˈeʃən

Key: See in full §§3–47. bee bi |pity ˈpɪtɪ (§6) |rate ret |yet jɛt |sang sæŋ |angry ˈæŋ‧grɪ
|bath bæθ; E baθ (§10) |ah ɑ |far fɑr |watch wɑtʃ, wɒtʃ (§12) |jaw dʒɔ |gorge gɔrdʒ |go go

device dɪˈvaɪs |-vices -ˈvaɪsɪz
devil ˈdɛvl̩ |-ed -d |-ing ˈdɛvlɪŋ, ˈdɛvl̩ŋ
devilfish ˈdɛvl̩ˌfɪʃ |-ˈs -ɪz
devilish ˈdɛvl̩ʃ, ˈdɛvl̩ʃ
devil-may-care ˈdɛvl̩mɪˈkɛr, -ˈkær; E -ˈkɛə(r,
ES -ˈkæə(r; (ˈdevil-may-ˌcare ˈwit)
devilment ˈdɛvl̩mənt
devilry ˈdɛvl̩rɪ |deviltry ˈdɛvl̩trɪ
devious ˈdivɪəs, -vjəs
devisable dɪˈvaɪzəbl̩
devise dɪˈvaɪz |-s -ɪz |-d -d |-sal -l̩
devisee dɪˌvaɪzˈi, ˌdɛvɪˈzi (deˌvisˈee & de-
ˌvisˈor)
devisor dɪˈvaɪzɚ, dɪˌvaɪzˈɔr; ES -ə(r, -ˈɔə(r
devitalization diˌvaɪtl̩əˈzeʃən, ˌdivaɪt-, -aɪˈz-
devitalize diˈvaɪtl̩ˌaɪz |-s -ɪz |-d -d
Devizes dɪˈvaɪzɪz |-zes' -zɪz
devoice diˈvɔɪs |-s -ɪz |-d -d -t
devoid dɪˈvɔɪd
devoir dəˈvwɑr, ˈdɛvwɑr; ES -wɑː(r; (Fr
dəˈvwaːr)
devolution ˌdɛvəˈluʃən, -ˈlɪuʃən, -vl̩ˈjuʃən
devolve dɪˈvɑlv, -ˈvɒlv |-d -d
Devon ˈdɛvən |Devonian dəˈvonɪən
Devonport ˈdɛvənˌport, ˈdɛvm̩-, -ˌpɔrt; ES
-ˌpoət, E+-ˌpɔət
Devonshire ˈdɛvənˌʃɪr, -ʃɚ; ES -ˌʃɪə(r, -ʃə(r
devote dɪˈvot |-d -ɪd
devotee ˌdɛvəˈti
devotion dɪˈvoʃən |-al -l̩ |-ally -l̩ɪ
devour dɪˈvaur; ES -ˈvauə(r; |-ed -d |-ing
-ˈvaurɪŋ
devout dɪˈvaut
De Vries dəˈvris |-ˈs -ɪz
dew dju, dɪu, du |-ed -d
Dewar ˈdjuɚ, ˈdɪuɚ, ˈduɚ; ES -ə(r
dewberry ˈdjuˌbɛrɪ, ˈdɪu-, ˈdu-, -bərɪ
dewdrop ˈdjuˌdrɑp, ˈdɪu-, ˈdu-; ES+-ˌdrɒp
Dewey ˈdjuɪ, ˈdɪuɪ, ˈduɪ
Dewitt, De-Witt v dɪˈwɪt |-ed -ɪd
dewlap ˈdjuˌlæp, ˈdɪu-, ˈdu- |-ped -t
dewy ˈdjuɪ, ˈdɪuɪ, ˈduɪ
dexter, D- ˈdɛkstɚ; ES ˈdɛkstə(r
dexterity dɛksˈtɛrətɪ
dexterous ˈdɛkstrəs, -tərəs
dextral ˈdɛkstrəl |-ly -ɪ
dextrin ˈdɛkstrɪn |-trine -trɪn, -trin
dextrose ˈdɛkstros
dextrous ˈdɛkstrəs

dey de
Dhaulagiri ˌdauləˈgɪrɪ
dhole dol
dhoti, dhooti ˈdotɪ
dhow dau
diabase ˈdaɪəˌbes |-sic ˌdaɪəˈbesɪk
diabetes ˌdaɪəˈbitɪs, -tiz
diabetic ˌdaɪəˈbɛtɪk, -ˈbitɪk |-al -l̩
diablerie dɪˈablərɪ (Fr djabləˈri)
diabolic ˌdaɪəˈbɑlɪk; ES+-ˈbɒl-; |-al -l̩ |-ally
-l̩ɪ, -ɪklɪ
diabolism daɪˈæbəˌlɪzəm
diachronic ˌdaɪəˈkrɑnɪk; ES+-ˈkrɒn-
diacid daɪˈæsɪd
diaconate daɪˈækənɪt, -ˌnet |-nal -nl̩
diacritic ˌdaɪəˈkrɪtɪk |-al -l̩ |-ally -l̩ɪ, -ɪklɪ
diadem ˈdaɪəˌdɛm |-demed -ˌdɛmd
diaeresis daɪˈɛrəsɪs |-eses -əˌsiz
diagnose ˌdaɪəgˈnos, -ˈnoz |-s -ɪz |-d -t, -d
diagnosis ˌdaɪəgˈnosɪs |-noses -ˈnosiz
diagnostic ˌdaɪəgˈnɑstɪk; ES+-ˈnɒs-; |-ally
-l̩ɪ, -ɪklɪ
diagnostician ˌdaɪəgnɑsˈtɪʃən; ES+-nɒs-
diagonal daɪˈægənl̩ |-ly -ɪ, -ˈægnəlɪ
diagram ˈdaɪəˌgræm |-(m)ed -d
diagrammatic ˌdaɪəgrəˈmætɪk |-al -l̩ |-ally
-l̩ɪ, -ɪklɪ
dial ˈdaɪəl, daɪl |-ed -d
dialect ˈdaɪəˌlɛkt
dialectal ˌdaɪəˈlɛktl̩ |-ly -ɪ
dialectic ˌdaɪəˈlɛktɪk |-al -l̩ |-ally -l̩ɪ, -ɪklɪ
dialectician ˌdaɪəlɛkˈtɪʃən
dialectology ˌdaɪəlɛkˈtɑlədʒɪ; ES+-ˈtɒl-
dialogist daɪˈælədʒɪst
dialogue, -log ˈdaɪəˌlɔg, -ˌlɑg, -ˌlɒg |-d, -ged -d
dialysis daɪˈæləsɪs |-yses -əˌsiz
dialytic ˌdaɪəˈlɪtɪk |-ally -l̩ɪ, -ɪklɪ
diamagnetic ˌdaɪəmægˈnɛtɪk |-ally -l̩ɪ, -ɪklɪ
diamagnetism ˌdaɪəˈmægnəˌtɪzəm
diameter daɪˈæmətɚ; ES -ˈæmətə(r
diametric ˌdaɪəˈmɛtrɪk |-al -l̩ |-ally -l̩ɪ, -ɪklɪ
diamond ˈdaɪmənd, ˈdaɪə- |-ed -ɪd—ˈdaɪmənd
is common from the 16c (often spelt dimond),
being found in Shak., Milton, Pope, Cowper,
Keats, Tennyson.
Dian ˈdaɪən |Diana daɪˈænə
dianthus, D- daɪˈænθəs |-es -ɪz
diapason ˌdaɪəˈpezn̩, -ˈpesn̩
diaper ˈdaɪəpɚ; ES ˈdaɪəpə(r; |-ed -d

|full fʊl |tooth tuθ |further ˈfɝðɚ; ES ˈfɝðə |custom ˈkʌstəm |while hwaɪl |how hau |toy tɔɪ
|using ˈjuzɪŋ |fuse fjuz, fɪuz |dish dɪʃ |vision ˈvɪʒən |Eden ˈidn̩ |cradle ˈkredl̩ |keep 'em ˈkipm̩

diaphanous daɪˈæfənəs
diaphone ˈdaɪəˌfon
diaphonic ˌdaɪəˈfɑnɪk; ES+-ˈfɒn-; |-al -ḷ
diaphoresis ˌdaɪəfəˈrisɪs
diaphoretic ˌdaɪəfəˈrɛtɪk |-al -ḷ
diaphragm ˈdaɪəˌfræm |-ed -d
diaphragmatic ˌdaɪəfrægˈmætɪk |-ally -ḷɪ,
 -ɪklɪ
diarchy ˈdaɪɑrkɪ; ES -ɑːkɪ, E+-ɑːkɪ
diarist ˈdaɪərɪst
diarrhea, -rrhoea ˌdaɪəˈriə
diary ˈdaɪərɪ
Diaspora daɪˈæspərə
diastase ˈdaɪəˌstes
diastole daɪˈæstəˌli
diastolic ˌdaɪəˈstɑlɪk; ES+-ˈstɒl-
diastrophism daɪˈæstrəˌfɪzəm
diathermic ˌdaɪəˈθɝmɪk; ES -ˈθɝm-, -ˈθɝm-
diathermy ˈdaɪəˌθɝmɪ; ES -ˌθɝmɪ, -ˌθɝmɪ
diatom ˈdaɪətəm, -ˌtɑm; ES+-ˌtɒm
diatomaceous ˌdaɪətəˈmeʃəs
diatonic ˌdaɪəˈtɑnɪk; ES+-ˈtɒn-; |-al -ḷ |-ally
 -ḷɪ, -ɪklɪ
diatribe ˈdaɪəˌtraɪb |-tribed -ˌtraɪbd
Díaz ˈdias |-ʼs -ɪz
dib dɪb |dibbed dɪbd
dibase ˈdaɪˌbes |-sic daɪˈbesɪk
dibble ˈdɪbḷ |-d -d |-ling ˈdɪblɪŋ, ˈdɪbḷɪŋ
dice daɪs |diced daɪst |-ʼs -ɪz
dichlorid daɪˈklorɪd, -ˈklɔr-; S -ˈklor-; |-ride
 -raɪd, -rɪd
dichotomous daɪˈkɑtəməs; ES+-ˈkɒt-; |-my
 -mɪ
dichromatic ˌdaɪkroˈmætɪk |-tism daɪˈkromə-
 ˌtɪzəm
Dick dɪk
dickcissel dɪkˈsɪsḷ, ˈdɪkˌs-
Dickens, d- ˈdɪkɪnz |-ʼs -ɪz |-ian dɪˈkɛnzən
dicker ˈdɪkɚ; ES ˈdɪkə(r; |-ed -d |-ing ˈdɪkər-
 ɪŋ, ˈdɪkrɪŋ
Dickinson, Dicken- ˈdɪkɪnsn̩
dicotyledon ˌdaɪkɑtḷˈidn̩, daɪˌkɑt-; ES+-ɒt-;
 |-ous -ˈidn̩əs, -ˈɛdn̩əs
dictaphone, D- ˈdɪktəˌfon
dictate n ˈdɪktet
dictate v ˈdɪktet, dɪkˈtet |-d -ɪd
dictation dɪkˈteʃən
dictator ˈdɪktetɚ, dɪkˈtetɚ; ES -tə(r; |-ship
 -ˌʃɪp

dictatorial ˌdɪktəˈtorɪəl, -ˈtɔr-; S -ˈtor-;
 |-ly -ɪ
dictic ˈdɪktɪk |-al -ḷ |-ally -ḷɪ, -ɪklɪ
diction ˈdɪkʃən
dictionary ˈdɪkʃənˌɛrɪ, as a Briticism+ˈdɪk-
 ʃənərɪ, -ʃənrɪ, -ʃnərɪ
dictograph, D- ˈdɪktəˌgræf; E+-ˌgraf, -ˌgrɑf
dictum ˈdɪktəm |-s -z |-ta -tə
did dɪd—for forms see do
didactic daɪˈdæktɪk |-al -ḷ |-ally -ḷɪ, -ɪklɪ
diddest ˈdɪdɪst—see do
diddle ˈdɪdḷ |-d -d |-ling ˈdɪdlɪŋ, ˈdɪdḷɪŋ
Diderot ˈdidəˌro (Fr diˈdro)
didest ˈdɪdɪst—see do
didn't ˈdɪdn̩t, before some conss.+ˈdɪdn̩
 (ˌdɪdn̩ˈgo)—The pron. ˈdɪdənt is substandard.
Dido, d- ˈdaɪdo
didst dɪdst—see do
Didymus ˈdɪdəməs |-ʼs -ɪz
die 'cube' daɪ |pl dice daɪs
die 'tool' daɪ |pl dies daɪz
die 'expire' daɪ |died daɪd
die-hard ˈdaɪˌhɑrd; ES -ˌhɑːd, E+-ˌhɑːd
dielectric ˌdaɪəˈlɛktrɪk |-al -ḷ |-ally -ḷɪ, -ɪklɪ
Dieman, van væn ˈdimən
Dieppe dɪˈɛp (Fr djɛp)
dieresis daɪˈerəsɪs |-eses -əˌsiz
dies 'expires,' 'colors,' 'tools' daɪz
dies 'day' ˈdaɪɪz
Dies, Martin daɪz |-ʼs -ɪz
Diesel ˈdizḷ, ˈdisḷ
Dies Irae ˈdaɪɪzˈaɪri
diet ˈdaɪət |-ed -ɪd |-ary ˈdaɪəˌtɛrɪ
dietetic ˌdaɪəˈtɛtɪk |-al -ḷ |-ally -ḷɪ, -ɪklɪ
dietician ˌdaɪəˈtɪʃən |-titian -ˈtɪʃən
differ ˈdɪfɚ; ES -fə(r; |-ed -d |-ing ˈdɪfrɪŋ,
 ˈdɪfərɪŋ
difference ˈdɪfrəns, ˈdɪfəns, ˈdɪfərəns; ES
 -frəns, -fər-, -fəns; |-s -ɪz |-nt -nt
differentia ˌdɪfəˈrɛnʃɪə |-tiae -ʃɪˌi
differential ˌdɪfəˈrɛnʃəl |-ly -ɪ
differentiate ˌdɪfəˈrɛnʃɪˌet |-ated -ˌetɪd
differentiation ˌdɪfəˌrɛnʃɪˈeʃən
difficile ˌdɪfəˈsil, formerly dɪˈfɪsḷ
difficult ˈdɪfəˌkʌlt, ˈdɪfəkəlt, -kḷt
difficulty ˈdɪfəˌkʌltɪ, -kəltɪ, -kḷtɪ
diffidence ˈdɪfədəns |-dent -dənt
diffract dɪˈfrækt |-ed -ɪd |-ction -kʃən

---

diffuse, *adj* dɪˈfjus, -ˈfɪus
diffuse *v* dɪˈfjuz, -ˈfɪuz |-s -ɪz |-d -d |-dly -ɪdlɪ
diffusibility dɪˌfjuzəˈbɪlətɪ, -ˌfɪuz–
diffusible dɪˈfjuzəbļ, -ˈfɪuz- |-bly -blɪ
diffusion dɪˈfjuʒən, -ˈfɪu- |-sive -sɪv
dig dɪg |*past & pptc* dug dʌg, *or arch.* digged
  dɪgd
digamma daɪˈgæmə
digest *n* ˈdaɪdʒɛst
digest *v* dəˈdʒɛst, daɪˈdʒɛst |-ed -ɪd
digestibility dəˌdʒɛstəˈbɪlətɪ, daɪ-
digestible dəˈdʒɛstəbļ, daɪ- |-bly -blɪ
digestion dəˈdʒɛstʃən, daɪ- |-gestive -ˈdʒɛstɪv
digger ˈdɪgɚ; ES ˈdɪgə(r; |digging ˈdɪgɪŋ
Diggory ˈdɪgərɪ
dight daɪt |*past & pptc* dight daɪt, *or* dighted
  ˈdaɪtɪd
Dighton ˈdaɪtņ
digit ˈdɪdʒɪt |-al -ļ |-ally -ļɪ
digitalin ˌdɪdʒəˈtelɪn
digitalis ˌdɪdʒəˈtelɪs, -ˈtælɪs
digitate *adj* ˈdɪdʒəˌtet |-d -ɪd
digitigrade ˈdɪdʒɪtəˌgred |-ism -gredˌɪzəm
dignify ˈdɪgnəˌfaɪ |-fied -ˌfaɪd
dignitary ˈdɪgnəˌtɛrɪ
dignity ˈdɪgnətɪ
digraph ˈdaɪgræf; E+-graf, -graf
digress dəˈgrɛs, daɪ- |-es -ɪz |-ed -t
digression dəˈgrɛʃən, daɪ- |-sive -ˈgrɛsɪv
dihedral daɪˈhidrəl |-dron -drən
Dijk, van vænˈdaɪk
Dijon ˈdiʒɑn, -ʒɒn, diˈʒ- (*Fr* diˈʒõ)
dike daɪk |-d -t
dilantin daɪˈlæntɪn
dilapidate dəˈlæpəˌdet |-dated -ˌdetɪd
dilapidation dəˌlæpəˈdeʃən
dilatation ˌdɪləˈteʃən, ˌdaɪlə-
dilate daɪˈlet, dɪ- |-d -ɪd |-lation -ˈleʃən
dilatory ˈdɪləˌtorɪ, -ˌtɔrɪ; S -ˌtɔrɪ; |-rily -rəlɪ,
  -rɪlɪ
dilemma dəˈlɛmə, daɪ-
dilettante ˌdɪləˈtæntɪ |-ism -tɪˌɪzəm |-tism
  -ˈtæntɪzəm
diligence ˈdɪlədʒəns |-s -ɪz |-gent -dʒənt
dill dɪl
Dillon ˈdɪlən
dillydally ˈdɪlɪˌdælɪ |-ied -d
diluent ˈdɪljʊənt
dilute dɪˈlut, daɪ-, -ˈlɪut |-d -ɪd |-tion -ʃən

diluvial dɪˈluvɪəl, -ˈlɪu- |-an -ən -ne
dim dɪm |dimmed dɪmd
dime daɪm
dimension dəˈmɛnʃən |-ed -d |-al -ļ |-ally -ļɪ
dimeter ˈdɪmətɚ; ES ˈdɪmətə(r
diminish dəˈmɪnɪʃ |-es -ɪz |-ed -t
diminuendo dəˌmɪnjʊˈɛndo
diminution ˌdɪməˈnjuʃən, -ˈnɪu-, -ˈnu-
diminutive dəˈmɪnjətɪv
dimissory ˈdɪməˌsorɪ, dəˈmɪsərɪ; EN+-ˌsorɪ
dimity ˈdɪmətɪ
Dimmesdale ˈdɪmzdel
Dimond ˈdaɪmənd
dimorphism daɪˈmɔrfɪzəm; ES -ˈmɔəf-
dimple ˈdɪmpļ |-d -d |-ling ˈdɪmplɪŋ, -pļɪŋ
din dɪn |dinned dɪnd
Dinah ˈdaɪnə
dinar dɪˈnɑr; ES -ˈnɑː(r
dine daɪn |dined daɪnd
ding dɪŋ |dinged dɪŋd
dingdong ˈdɪŋˌdɒŋ, -ˌdɒŋ; S+-ˌdɑŋ; |-ed -d
dinghy, -gey, -gy ˈdɪŋgɪ
dingle ˈdɪŋgļ |-d -d |-ling ˈdɪŋglɪŋ, -gļɪŋ
dingo ˈdɪŋgo
dingy '*dinghy*' ˈdɪŋgɪ
dingy '*dusky*' ˈdɪndʒɪ
dinkey, -ky ˈdɪŋkɪ
Dinmont, d- ˈdɪnmənt, -mɑnt; ES+-mɒnt
dinner ˈdɪnɚ; ES ˈdɪnə(r
dinnerware ˈdɪnɚˌwɛr, -ˌwær; E ˈdɪnəˌwɛə(r,
  ES -ˌwæə(r
dinosaur ˈdaɪnəˌsɔr; ES -ˌsɔə(r
Dinosauria ˌdaɪnəˈsɔrɪə |d-n ˌdaɪnəˈsɔrɪən
dinosaurus ˌdaɪnəˈsɔrəs |-rai -raɪ
dinothere ˈdaɪnəˌθɪr; ES -ˌθɪə(r
Dinotherium ˌdaɪnəˈθɪrɪəm
dint dɪnt |dinted ˈdɪntɪd
Dinwiddie dɪnˈwɪdɪ, ˈdɪnwɪdɪ
diocesan daɪˈɑsəsņ, ˈdaɪəˌsɪsņ; ES+-ˈɒs-
diocese ˈdaɪəˌsɪs |-s -ɪz
Diocles ˈdaɪəˌkliz |-'s -ɪz
Diocletian ˌdaɪəˈkliʃən
Diodorus ˌdaɪəˈdorəs, -ˈdɔr-; S -ˈdɔr-; |-'s -ɪz
Diogenes daɪˈɑdʒəˌniz; ES+-ˈɒdʒ-; |-'s -ɪz
Diomed ˈdaɪəˌmɛd |-mede -ˌmid
Diomedes ˌdaɪəˈmidiz |-des' -diz
Dion ˈdaɪən
Dionysia ˌdaɪəˈnɪʃɪə, -sɪə |-iac -ˈnɪsɪˌæk
Dionysian ˌdaɪəˈnɪʃən, -ˈnɪsɪən

|full fʊl |tooth tuθ |further ˈfɝðɚ; ES ˈfɝðə |custom ˈkʌstəm |while hwaɪl |how haʊ |toy tɔɪ
|using ˈjuzɪŋ |fuse fjuz, fɪuz |dish dɪʃ |vision ˈvɪʒən |Eden ˈidņ |cradle ˈkredļ |keep 'em ˈkipm̩

Dionysius ˌdaɪəˈnɪʃɪəs, -ˈnɪsɪəs |-ˈs -ɪz
Dionysus ˌdaɪəˈnaɪsəs |-sus' -səs
Dionyza ˌdaɪəˈnaɪzə
diopter daɪˈaptɚ; ES -ˈaptə(r, -ˈɒp-
dioptric daɪˈaptrɪk; ES+-ˈɒp-; |-s -s
diorama ˌdaɪəˈræmə, -ˈramə
diorite ˈdaɪəˌraɪt
Dioscuri ˌdaɪəˈskjʊraɪ, -ˈskɪʊ- |-rian -rɪən
dioxide daɪˈaksaɪd, -ɪd; ES+-ˈɒks-; |-id -ɪd
dip dɪp |dipped dɪpt
diphase ˈdaɪˌfez |-phasic daɪˈfezɪk
diphosgene daɪˈfasdʒɪn; ES+-ˈfɒs-
diphtheria dɪfˈθɪrɪə, dɪp-; S+-ˈθɛr-; |-l -l
diphtheretic ˌdɪfθəˈrɛtɪk, ˌdɪp- |-ally -ʃɪ, -ɪklɪ
diphthong ˈdɪfθɔŋ, ˈdɪp-, -θɒŋ |-ed -d
diphthongal dɪfˈθɔŋgḷ, dɪp-, -ˈθɒŋḷ, -ˈθɒŋ-
|-ly -ɪ
diphthongization ˌdɪfθɔŋəˈzeʃən, ˌdɪp-,
-θɒŋgə-, -θɒŋ-, -aɪˈz-
diphthongize ˈdɪfθɔŋˌaɪz, ˈdɪp-, -θɒŋˌgaɪz,
-θɒŋ- |-s -ɪz |-d -d
diplococcus ˌdɪpləˈkakəs; ES+-ˈkɒk-; |-ci
-ksaɪ
diploma dɪˈplomə |-s -z |-ed -d |-cy -sɪ
diplomat ˈdɪpləˌmæt |-ist dɪˈplomətɪst
diplomatic ˌdɪpləˈmætɪk |-al -ḷ |-ally -ʃɪ, -ɪklɪ
dipody ˈdɪpədɪ
dipolar daɪˈpolɚ; ES -ˈpolə(r; |-pole ˈdaɪˌpol
dipper ˈdɪpɚ; ES ˈdɪpə(r
dipsomania ˌdɪpsəˈmenɪə |-maniac -ˈmenɪˌæk
dipterous ˈdɪptərəs
dire daɪr; ES daɪə(r
direct dəˈrɛkt, daɪ- |-ed -ɪd |-ive -ɪv
direction dəˈrɛkʃən, daɪ- |-al -ḷ |-ally -ʃɪ
director dəˈrɛktɚ, daɪ-; ES -tə(r; |-ate -ɪt
|-ship -ˌʃɪp
directorial dəˌrɛkˈtorɪəl, ˌdaɪrɛk-, -ˈtɔr-; S
-ˈtor-; |-ly -ɪ
directory dəˈrɛktərɪ, -ˈrɛktrɪ
directress dəˈrɛktrɪs, daɪ- |-es -ɪz
directrix dəˈrɛktrɪks, daɪ- |-es -ɪz |for any that
desire it -trices ˌdaɪrɛkˈtraɪsiz
direful ˈdaɪrfəl; ES ˈdaɪəfəl; |-ly -ɪ
dirge dɝdʒ; ES dɜdʒ, dɝdʒ; |-s -ɪz |-d -d
dirigibility ˌdɪrədʒəˈbɪlətɪ
dirigible ˈdɪrədʒəbḷ, Brit + dɪˈrɪdʒəbḷ
dirk, D- dɝk; ES dɜk, dɝk; |-ed -t
dirt dɝt; ES dɜt, dɝt; |-ed -ɪd |-y -ɪ |-ied -ɪd
|-ily -ʃɪ, -ɪlɪ

Dis dɪs |-ˈs -ɪz
disability ˌdɪsəˈbɪlətɪ
disable dɪsˈebḷ, dɪz- |-d -d
disabuse ˌdɪsəˈbjuz, -ˈbɪuz |-s -ɪz |-d -d
disaccord ˌdɪsəˈkɔrd; ES -ˈkɔəd; |-ed -ɪd
disaccustom ˌdɪsəˈkʌstəm |-ed -d
disadvantage ˌdɪsədˈvæntɪdʒ; E+-ˈvan-,
-ˈvɑn-; |-s -ɪz |-d -d
disadvantageous dɪsˌædvənˈtedʒəs, ˌdɪsæd-
vən-
disaffect ˌdɪsəˈfɛkt |-ed -ɪd |-ction -kʃən
disagree ˌdɪsəˈgri |-d -d |-able -əbḷ |-bly -blɪ
disallow ˌdɪsəˈlaʊ |-ed -d |-ance -əns
disannul ˌdɪsəˈnʌl |-led -d
disappear ˌdɪsəˈpɪr; ES -ˈpɪə(r, S+-ˈpɛə(r,
-ˈpjɛə(r; |-ed -d |-ance -əns |-ances -ənsɪz
disappoint ˌdɪsəˈpɔɪnt |-ed -ɪd |-ment -mənt
disapprobation ˌdɪsæprəˈbeʃən, dɪsˌæprə-
disapprove ˌdɪsəˈpruv |-d -d |-val -vḷ
disarm dɪsˈɑrm, dɪz-; ES -ˈɑːm, E+-ˈɑːm; |-ed
-d |-ament -əmənt
disarrange ˌdɪsəˈrendʒ |-s -ɪz |-d -d
disarray ˌdɪsəˈre |-ed -d
disaster dɪzˈæstɚ; ES -ˈæstə(r, E+-ˈas-,
-ˈɑs-; |-trous -trəs
disavow ˌdɪsəˈvaʊ |-ed -d |-edly -ɪdlɪ |-al -əl
disband dɪsˈbænd |-ed -ɪd
disbar dɪsˈbɑr; ES -ˈbɑː(r, E+-ˈbɑː(r; |-red -d
disbark dɪsˈbɑrk; ES -ˈbɑːk, E+-ˈbɑːk; |-ed -t
disbelieve ˌdɪsbəˈliv |-d -d |-lief -ˈlif
disburden dɪsˈbɝdn̩; ES -ˈbɜdn̩, -ˈbɝdn̩;
|-ed -d
disburse dɪsˈbɝs; ES -ˈbɜs, -ˈbɝs; |-s -ɪz
|-d -t
disc dɪsk
discard n ˈdɪskɑrd; ES -kɑːd, E+-kɑːd
discard v dɪsˈkɑrd; ES -ˈkɑːd, E+-ˈkɑːd; |-ed
-ɪd
discern dɪˈzɝn, -ˈsɝn; ES -ɜn, -ɝn; |-ed -d
|-ible -əbḷ |-bly -blɪ
discharge dɪsˈtʃɑrdʒ; ES -ˈtʃɑːdʒ, E+
-ˈtʃɑːdʒ; |-s -ɪz |-d -d
disciple, D- dɪˈsaɪpḷ |-d -d |-ship -ˌʃɪp
disciplinable ˈdɪsəˌplɪnəbḷ
disciplinarian ˌdɪsəplɪnˈɛrɪən, -ˈer-
disciplinary ˈdɪsəplɪnˌɛrɪ
discipline n ˈdɪsəplɪn
discipline v ˈdɪsəˌplɪn |-d -d
disclaim dɪsˈklem |-ed -d

Key: *See in full §§3–47.* bee bi |pity ˈpɪtɪ (§6) |rate ret |yet jɛt |sang sæŋ |angry ˈæŋ·grɪ
|bath bæθ; E baθ (§10) |ah ɑ |far fɑr |watch watʃ, wɒtʃ (§12) |jaw dʒɔ |gorge gɔrdʒ |go go

disclose dɪs'kloz |-s -ɪz |-d -d |-sure -ʒɚ; ES -ʒə(r

discolor dɪs'kʌlɚ; ES -'kʌlə(r; |-ed -d

discoloration ˌdɪskʌlə'reʃən, dɪsˌkʌlə-

discombobulate ˌdɪskəm'bɑbḷˌet; ES+-'bɒb-; |-d -ɪd

discomfit dɪs'kʌmfɪt |-ed -ɪd |-ure -fɪtʃɚ; ES -fɪtʃə(r

discomfort dɪs'kʌmfɚt; ES -'kʌmfət; |-ed -ɪd

discommode ˌdɪskə'mod |-d -ɪd

discompose ˌdɪskəm'poz |-s -ɪz |-d -d |-dly -ɪdlɪ |-sure -'poʒɚ; ES -'poʒə(r

disconcert ˌdɪskən'sɝt; ES -'sɜt, -'sɝt; |-ed -ɪd

disconnect ˌdɪskə'nɛkt |-ed -ɪd

disconnection, -nexion ˌdɪskə'nɛkʃən

disconsolate dɪs'kɑnsḷɪt; ES+-'kɒn-

disconsolation ˌdɪskɑnsə'leʃən, dɪsˌkɑnsə-; ES+-ɒn-

discontent ˌdɪskən'tɛnt |-ed -ɪd

discontinuance ˌdɪskən'tɪnjuəns |-s -ɪz

discontinuation ˌdɪskənˌtɪnju'eʃən

discontinue ˌdɪskən'tɪnju |-d -d |-uous -juəs

discontinuity ˌdɪskəntə'nuətɪ, -'nɪu-, -'nju-; ES+-kɒn-

discord n 'dɪskɔrd; ES -kɔəd

discord v dɪs'kɔrd; ES -'kɔəd; |-ed -ɪd

discordance dɪs'kɔrdn̩s; ES -'kɔəd-; |-s -ɪz |-dant -dn̩t

discount n 'dɪskaʊnt

discount v 'dɪskaʊnt, dɪs'kaʊnt |-ed -ɪd

discountenance dɪs'kaʊntənəns |-s -ɪz |-d -t

discourage dɪs'kɝɪdʒ; ES -'kɜr-, -'kʌr-, -'kɝ-; |-s -ɪz |-d -d

discourse n 'dɪskors, dɪ'skors, -ɔrs; ES -oəs, E+-ɔəs; |-s -ɪz

discourse v dɪ'skors, -'skɔrs; ES -'skoəs, E+-'skɔəs; |-s -ɪz |-d -t

discourteous dɪs'kɝtɪəs; ES -'kɜt-, -'kɝt-; |-esy -əsɪ

discover dɪ'skʌvɚ; ES -'skʌvə(r; |-ed -d |-ing -'skʌvərɪŋ, -'skʌvrɪŋ |-y -'skʌvrɪ, -vərɪ

discredit dɪs'krɛdɪt |-ed -ɪd

discreditable dɪs'krɛdɪtəbḷ |-bly -blɪ

discreet dɪ'skrit

discrepance dɪ'skrɛpəns |-cy -ɪ |-ant -ənt

discrete dɪ'skrit

discretion dɪ'skrɛʃən |-al -ḷ |-ally -ḷɪ

discretionary dɪ'skrɛʃənˌɛrɪ

discriminate adj dɪ'skrɪmənɪt

discriminate v dɪ'skrɪməˌnet |-d -ɪd |-tive -ɪv

discrimination dɪˌskrɪmə'neʃən

discriminatory dɪ'skrɪmənəˌtorɪ, -ˌtɔrɪ; S -ˌtorɪ

discrown dɪs'kraʊn |-ed -d

discursive dɪ'skɝsɪv; ES -'skɜs-, -'skɝs-; |-sory -sərɪ

discus 'dɪskəs |-es -ɪz |disci 'dɪsaɪ

discuss dɪ'skʌs |-es -ɪz |-ed -t |-ion -'skʌʃən

disdain dɪs'den, dɪz- |-ed -d

disdainful dɪs'denfəl, dɪz- |-ly -ɪ

disease dɪ'ziz |-s -ɪz |-d -d |-dly -ɪdlɪ

disembark ˌdɪsɪm'bɑrk; ES -'bɑːk, E+-'bɑːk; |-ed -t

disembarkation ˌdɪsɛmbɑr'keʃən, dɪsˌɛm-; ES -bɑː-, E+-bɑː-

disembarrass ˌdɪsɪm'bærəs, -ɪs |-es -ɪz |-ed -t

disembody ˌdɪsɪm'bɑdɪ; ES+-'bɒdɪ; |-ied -d

disembowel ˌdɪsɪm'baʊəl, -'baʊl |-ed -d

disenchant ˌdɪsɪn'tʃænt; E+-'tʃɑnt, -'tʃɑnt; |-ed -ɪd

disencumber ˌdɪsɪn'kʌmbɚ; ES -'kʌmbə(r; |-ed -d |-ing -'kʌmbərɪŋ, -'kʌmbrɪŋ

disenfranchise ˌdɪsɪn'fræntʃaɪz |-s -ɪz |-d -d

disenfranchisement ˌdɪsɪn'fræntʃɪzmənt

disengage ˌdɪsɪn'gedʒ |-s -ɪz |-d -d |-dness -ɪdnɪs, -dnɪs

disentangle ˌdɪsɪn'tæŋgḷ |-d -d |-ling -'tæŋglɪŋ, -'tæŋgḷɪŋ

disestablish ˌdɪsə'stæblɪʃ |-es -ɪz |-ed -t

disesteem ˌdɪsə'stim |-ed -d

disfavor dɪs'fevɚ; ES -'fevə(r; |-ed -d |-ing -'fevərɪŋ, -'fevrɪŋ

disfiguration ˌdɪsfɪgjə'reʃən, dɪsˌfɪgjə-

disfigure dɪs'fɪgjɚ; ES -'fɪgjə(r; |-d -d

disfranchise dɪs'fræntʃaɪz |-s -ɪz |-d -d

disfranchisement dɪs'fræntʃɪzmənt

disgorge dɪs'gɔrdʒ; ES -'gɔədʒ; |-s -ɪz |-d -d

disgrace dɪs'gres |-s -ɪz |-d -t

disgraceful dɪs'gresfəl |-ly -ɪ

disgruntle dɪs'grʌntḷ |-d -d

disguise dɪs'gaɪz |-s -ɪz |-d -d |-dly -ɪdlɪ

disgust dɪs'gʌst, dɪz- |-ed -ɪd

dish dɪʃ |dishes 'dɪʃɪz |dished dɪʃt

dishabille ˌdɪsə'bil, cf deshabille

disharmonious ˌdɪs·hɑr'monɪəs; ES -hɑ-, E -ha-

|full fʊl |tooth tuθ |further 'fɝðɚ; ES 'fɝðə |custom 'kʌstəm |while hwaɪl |how haʊ |toy tɔɪ |using 'juzɪŋ |fuse fjuz, fɪuz |dish dɪʃ |vision 'vɪʒən |Eden 'idn̩ |cradle 'kredḷ |keep 'em 'kipm̩

disharmony dɪsˈharmənɪ; ES -ˈhɑːm-, E+ -ˈhɑːm-

dishcloth ˈdɪʃˌklɔθ, -ˌklɒθ |-ths -ðz, -θs

dishearten dɪsˈhɑrtn̩; ES -ˈhɑːtn̩, E+-ˈhɑːtn̩; |-ed -d |-ing -tnɪŋ, -tn̩ɪŋ

disherison dɪsˈhɛrəzn̩ |-ed -d

dishevel dɪˈʃɛvl̩ |-ed -d |-ing -ˈʃɛvl̩ɪŋ, -vlɪŋ

dishful ˈdɪʃˌful |-s -z

dishonest dɪsˈanɪst, dɪz-; ES+-ˈɒn-; |-y -ɪ

dishonor dɪsˈanɚ, dɪz-; ES -ˈɑnə(r, -ˈɒn-; |-able -əbl̩ |-bly -blɪ

disillusion ˌdɪsɪˈluʒən, -ˈlɪu- |-ed -d

disinclination ˌdɪsɪnkləˈneʃən, dɪsˌɪnklə-

disincline ˌdɪsɪnˈklaɪn |-clined -ˈklaɪnd

disinfect ˌdɪsɪnˈfɛkt, ˌdɪsn̩- |-ed -ɪd |-ant -ənt |-ction -kʃən

disingenuous ˌdɪsɪnˈdʒɛnjuəs, ˌdɪsn̩-

disinherit ˌdɪsɪnˈhɛrɪt, ˌdɪsn̩- |-ed -ɪd

disintegrable dɪsˈɪntəgrəbl̩

disintegrate dɪsˈɪntəˌgret |-grated -ˌgretɪd

disintegration ˌdɪsɪntəˈgreʃən, dɪsˌɪntə-

disinter ˌdɪsɪnˈtɚ; ES -ˈtɜ(r, -ˈtɜ; |-red -d

disinterested dɪsˈɪntərəstɪd, -ˈɪntrɪstɪd, -ˈɪntəˌrɛstɪd—see interesting

disjoin dɪsˈdʒɔɪn |-ed -d |-t -t |-ted -tɪd

disjunct dɪsˈdʒʌŋkt |-ction -kʃən |-ive -ɪv

disk dɪsk |-ed -t

dislike dɪsˈlaɪk |-liked -ˈlaɪkt

dislocate ˈdɪsloˌket, dɪsˈloket |-d -ɪd

dislocation ˌdɪsloˈkeʃən

dislodge dɪsˈladʒ; ES+-ˈlɒdʒ; |-s -ɪz |-d -d

disloyal dɪsˈlɔɪəl, -ˈlɔjəl |-ly -ɪ |-ty -tɪ

dismal ˈdɪzml̩ |-ly -ɪ

dismantle dɪsˈmæntl̩ |-d -d |-ling -tl̩ɪŋ, -tlɪŋ

dismast dɪsˈmæst; E+-ˈmast, -ˈmɑst; |-ed -ɪd

dismay dɪsˈme, dɪz- |-ed -d |-edness -dnɪs, -ɪdnɪs

dismember dɪsˈmɛmbɚ; ES -ˈmɛmbə(r; |-ed -d |-ing -ˈmɛmbrɪŋ, -ˈmɛmbərɪŋ

dismiss dɪsˈmɪs |-ed -d |-al -l̩

dismount dɪsˈmaunt |-ed -ɪd

disobedience ˌdɪsəˈbidɪəns |-ent -ənt

disobey ˌdɪsəˈbe |-ed -d

disoblige ˌdɪsəˈblaɪdʒ |-s -ɪz |-d -d

disorder dɪsˈɔrdɚ, dɪz-; ES -ˈɔədə(r; |-ed -d |-ing -dərɪŋ, -drɪŋ

disorganic ˌdɪsɔrˈgænɪk; ES -ɔəˈgæn-

disorganization dɪsˌɔrgənəˈzeʃən, ˌdɪsɔr-; ES -ˌɔəgənə-, -ˌɔəg-, -aɪˈz-

disorganize dɪsˈɔrgəˌnaɪz; ES -ˈɔəgə-; |-s -ɪz |-d -d

disown dɪsˈon, dɪz- |-ed -d

disparage dɪˈspærɪdʒ |-es -ɪz |-d -d

disparate ˈdɪspərɪt |disparity dɪsˈpærətɪ

dispart dɪsˈpart; ES -ˈpɑːt, E+-ˈpaːt; |-ed -ɪd

dispassion dɪsˈpæʃən |-ed -d |-ate -ɪt

dispatch dɪˈspætʃ |-es -ɪz |-ed -t

dispel dɪˈspɛl |-led -d

dispensable dɪˈspɛnsəbl̩

dispensary dɪˈspɛnsərɪ

dispensation ˌdɪspənˈseʃən, -pɛn-

dispensatory dɪˈspɛnsəˌtorɪ, -ˌtɔrɪ; S -ˌtorɪ

dispense dɪˈspɛns |-s -ɪz |-d -t

disperse dɪˈspɝs; ES -ˈspɜs, -ˈspɝs; |-s -ɪz |-d -t |-sal -l̩

dispersion dɪˈspɝʃən, -ˈspɝʒ-; ES -ˈspɝ-, -ˈspɝ-; |-sive -sɪv

dispirit dɪˈspɪrɪt |-ed -ɪd

displace dɪsˈples |-s -ɪz |-d -t

display dɪˈsple |-ed -d

displease dɪsˈpliz |-s -ɪz |-d -d

displeasure dɪsˈplɛʒɚ; ES -ˈplɛʒə(r; |-d -d

disport dɪˈsport, -ˈspɔrt; ES -ˈspoət, E+ -ˈspɔət; |-ed -ɪd

disposable dɪˈspozəbl̩ |-sal -zl̩

dispose dɪˈspoz |-s -ɪz |-d -d

disposition ˌdɪspəˈzɪʃən

dispossess ˌdɪspəˈzɛs |-es -ɪz |-ed -t

disposure dɪˈspoʒɚ; ES -ˈspoʒə(r

dispraise dɪsˈprez |-s -ɪz |- d -d

disprize dɪsˈpraɪz |-s -ɪz |- d -d

disproof dɪsˈpruf (ˈproof and ˈdisˌproof)

disproportion ˌdɪsprəˈporʃən, -ˈpɔr-; ES -ˈpoə-, E+-ˈpɔə-; |-al -l̩ |-ally -l̩ɪ |-ate -ɪt

disprove dɪsˈpruv |-proved -ˈpruvd |-val -l̩

disputable dɪˈspjutəbl̩, -ˈsprut-, ˈdɪspjutəbl̩ |-bly -blɪ—The accentuation of disˈputable like disˈpute has inevitably won its way into good use.

disputant ˈdɪspjutənt, dɪˈspjutn̩t, -ˈsprut-

disputation ˌdɪspjuˈteʃən |-tious -ʃəs

disputative dɪˈspjutətɪv, -ˈsprut-

dispute dɪˈspjut, -ˈsprut |-d -ɪd

disqualification ˌdɪskwaləfəˈkeʃən, dɪsˌkw-, -wɒl-

disqualify dɪsˈkwaləˌfaɪ, -ˈkwɒl- |-fied -ˌfaɪd

disquiet dɪsˈkwaɪət |-ed -ɪd

disquietude dɪsˈkwaɪəˌtjud, -ˌtɪud, -ˌtud

Key: See in full §§3–47. bee bi |pity ˈpɪtɪ (§6) |rate ret |yet jɛt |sang sæŋ |angry ˈæŋ·grɪ |bath bæθ; E baθ (§10) |ah ɑ |far fɑr |watch watʃ, wɒtʃ (§12) |jaw dʒɔ |gorge gɔrdʒ |go go

disquisition ˌdɪskwəˈzɪʃən
Disraeli dɪzˈrɛlɪ
disrate dɪsˈret |-rated -ˈretɪd
disregard ˌdɪsrɪˈgɑrd; ES -ˈgɑːd, E+-ˈgɑːd;
  |-ed -ɪd
disrelish dɪsˈrɛlɪʃ |-es -ɪz |-ed -t
disrepair ˌdɪsrɪˈpɛr, -ˈpær; E -ˈpɛə(r, ES
  -ˈpæə(r
disreputability dɪsˌrɛpjətəˈbɪlətɪ, ˌdɪsrɛp-
disreputable dɪsˈrɛpjətəbl̩ |-bly -blɪ
disrepute ˌdɪsrɪˈpjut, -ˈpɪut
disrespect ˌdɪsrɪˈspɛkt |-ed -ɪd
disrespectful ˌdɪsrɪˈspɛktfəl |-ly -ɪ
disrobe dɪsˈrob |-robed -ˈrobd
disrupt dɪsˈrʌpt |-ed -ɪd |-ption -pʃən |-ive -ɪv
dissatisfaction ˌdɪssætɪsˈfækʃən, ˌdɪsæt- |-tory
  -tərɪ
dissatisfy dɪsˈsætɪsˌfaɪ, dɪˈsæt- |-fied -ˌfaɪd
dissect dɪˈsɛkt |-ed -ɪd |-ction -kʃən
disseize dɪsˈsiz |-s -ɪz |-d -d
dissemblance dɪˈsɛmbləns
dissemble dɪˈsɛmbl̩ |-d -d |-ling -blɪŋ, -bl̩ɪŋ
disseminate dɪˈsɛməˌnet |-nated -ˌnetɪd
dissemination dɪˌsɛməˈneʃən
dissention dɪˈsɛnʃən
dissent dɪˈsɛnt |-ed -ɪd |-er -ɚ; ES -ə(r
dissentience dɪˈsɛnʃəns |-cy -ɪ |-ent -ənt
dissert dɪˈsɜt; ES -ˈsɜt, -ˈsɜt; |-ed -ɪd
dissertation ˌdɪsɚˈteʃən; ES ˌdɪsə-
disservice dɪsˈsɜvɪs; ES -ˈsɜv-, -ˈsɜv-; |-s -ɪz
  |-d -t
dissever dɪˈsɛvɚ; ES -ˈsɛvə(r; |-ed -d |-ing
  -ˈsɛvərɪŋ, -ˈsɛvrɪŋ
dissidence ˈdɪsədəns |-dent -dənt
dissimilar dɪˈsɪmələ, dɪsˈs-; ES -ˈsɪmələ(r
dissimilarity dɪˌsɪməˈlærətɪ, dɪsˌs-, ˌdɪssɪm-
dissimilate dɪˈsɪməˌlet, dɪsˈs- |-d -ɪd
dissimilation dɪˌsɪməˈleʃən, dɪsˌs-, ˌdɪssɪm-
dissimilitude ˌdɪssɪˈmɪləˌtjud, -ˌtɪud, -ˌtud
dissimulate dɪˈsɪmjəˌlet |-lated -ˌletɪd
dissimulation dɪˌsɪmjəˈleʃən
dissipate ˈdɪsəˌpet |-d -ɪd |-tion ˌdɪsəˈpeʃən
dissociate dɪˈsoʃɪˌet |-ated -ˌetɪd
dissociation dɪˌsosɪˈeʃən, -ˌsoʃɪ-
dissociative dɪˈsoʃɪˌetɪv
dissolubility dɪˌsɑljəˈbɪlətɪ; ES+-ˌsɒl-
dissoluble dɪˈsɑljəbl̩; ES+-ˈsɒl-;—*The accentuation* disˈsoluble *has displaced* ˈdissoluble
  by analogy of ˈsoluble *and* disˈsolve.

dissolute ˈdɪsəˌlut, -ˌlɪut, ˈdɪslˌjut
dissolution ˌdɪsəˈluʃən, -ˈlɪu-, -sl̩ˈjuʃən
dissolve dɪˈzɑlv, -ˈzɒlv |-d -d |-nt -ənt
dissonance ˈdɪsənəns |-s -ɪz |-cy -ɪ |-ant -ənt
dissuade dɪˈswed |-d -ɪd
dissuasion dɪˈsweʒən |-sive -ˈswesɪv
dissyllabic ˌdɪssɪˈlæbɪk, ˌdɪsɪ-
dissyllable dɪˈsɪləbl̩, ˈdɪsˌsɪləbl̩
distaff ˈdɪstæf; E+ˈdɪstɑf, ˈdɪstɑf
distain dɪˈsten |-ed -d
distal ˈdɪstl̩ |-ly -ɪ
distance ˈdɪstəns |-s -ɪz |-d -t |-tant -tənt
distaste dɪsˈtest |-tasted -ˈtestɪd
distasteful dɪsˈtestfəl |-ly -ɪ
distemper dɪsˈtɛmpɚ; ES -pə(r; |-ed -d
  |-pərɪŋ, -prɪŋ
distend dɪˈstɛnd |-ed -ɪd
distensible dɪˈstɛnsəbl̩
distention, -sion dɪˈstɛnʃən
distich ˈdɪstɪk
distill, -til dɪˈstɪl |-(l)ed -d
distillate ˈdɪstl̩ˌɪt, -ˌet
distillation ˌdɪstl̩ˈeʃən, -stɪl-
distiller dɪˈstɪlɚ; ES -ˈstɪlə(r; |-y -ɪ
distinct dɪˈstɪŋkt |-ction -kʃən |-ctive -ktɪv
distingué ˌdistæŋˈge, dɪˈstæŋge (*Fr* distæˈge)
distinguish dɪˈstɪŋgwɪʃ |-es -ɪz |-ed -t
distinguishable dɪˈstɪŋgwɪʃəbl̩ |-bly -blɪ
distort dɪsˈtɔrt; ES -ˈtɔət; |-ed -ɪd
distortion dɪsˈtɔrʃən; ES -ˈtɔəʃən
distract dɪˈstrækt |-ed -ɪd
distraction dɪˈstrækʃən |-tive -tɪv
distrain dɪˈstren |-ed -d |-t -t
distrait dɪˈstre |-e -t (*Fr* disˈtrɛ(t))
distraught dɪˈstrɔt
distress dɪˈstrɛs |-es -ɪz |-ed -t |-edly -ɪdlɪ
distressful dɪˈstrɛsfəl |-ly -ɪ
distributable dɪˈstrɪbjətəbl̩
distribute dɪˈstrɪbjut |-d -bjətɪd |-tive -bjətɪv
distribution ˌdɪstrəˈbjuʃən, -ˈbɪuʃən
distributor dɪˈstrɪbjətɚ; ES -tə(r
district ˈdɪstrɪkt |-ed -ɪd
distrust dɪsˈtrʌst |-ed -ɪd
distrustful dɪsˈtrʌstfəl |-ly -ɪ
disturb dɪˈstɜb; ES -ˈstɜb, -ˈstɜb; |-ed -d
  |-ance -əns |-ances -ənsɪz
disulphate, -fate daɪˈsʌlfet
disulphide, -fide daɪˈsʌlfaɪd, -fɪd |-phid, -fid
  -fɪd

Those words below in which the ɑ *sound is spelt* o *are often pronounced with* ɒ *in E and S*

disunion dɪs'junjən

disunite ˌdɪsju'naɪt |-nited -'naɪtɪd

disuse *n* dɪs'jus |-s -ɪz

disuse *v* dɪs'juz |-s -ɪz |-d -d

disyllable dɪ'sɪləbḷ |disyllabic ˌdɪsɪ'læbɪk

ditch dɪtʃ |ditches 'dɪtʃɪz |ditched dɪtʃt

dither 'dɪðɚ; ES -ə(r; |-ed -d |-ing -ðərɪŋ, -ðrɪŋ

dithyramb 'dɪθəˌræm, -ˌræmb

dithyrambic ˌdɪθə'ræmbɪk |-ally -ḷɪ, -ɪklɪ

ditto 'dɪto |-ed -d

ditty 'dɪtɪ |-ied -d

diuretic ˌdaɪju'rɛtɪk |-al -ḷ |-ally -ḷɪ, -ɪklɪ

diurnal daɪ'ɝnḷ; ES -'ɝnḷ, -'ɝnḷ; |-ly -ɪ

diva 'divə

divagate 'daɪvəˌget |-d -ɪd |-tion ˌdaɪvə'geʃən

divalent daɪ'velənt, 'dɪvələnt

divan 'daɪvæn, dɪ'væn

divaricate də'værəˌket, daɪ- |-d -ɪd

divarication dəˌværə'keʃən, daɪ-

dive daɪv |*past* dove dov *or* dived daɪvd |*pptc* dived daɪvd

diver 'daɪvɚ; ES 'daɪvə(r

diverge də'vɝdʒ, daɪ-; ES -'vɝdʒ, -'vɝdʒ; |-s -ɪz |-d -d |-nce -əns |-ncy -ənsɪ |-nt -ənt

divers 'swimmers,' 'various' 'daɪvɚz; ES 'daɪvəz

diverse də'vɝs, daɪ-; ES -'vɝs, -'vɝs; ('dɪˌverse 'forces)

diversification dəˌvɝsəfə'keʃən, daɪ-; ES -ˌvɝs-, -ˌvɝs-

diversify də'vɝsəˌfaɪ, daɪ-; ES -'vɝs-, -'vɝs-; |-fied -ˌfaɪd

diversion də'vɝʒən, daɪ-, -ʃən; ES -'vɝ-, -'vɝ-

diversity də'vɝsətɪ, daɪ-; ES -'vɝs-, -'vɝs-

divert də'vɝt, daɪ-; ES -'vɝt, -'vɝt; |-ed -ɪd

divertisement də'vɝtɪzmənt; ES -'vɝt-, -'vɝt-

divertissement *Fr* divɛrtis'mã

Dives 'daɪviz |-ves' -viz

divest də'vɛst, daɪ- |-ed -ɪd

divide də'vaɪd |-vided -'vaɪdɪd

dividend 'dɪvəˌdɛnd

divination ˌdɪvə'neʃən

divine də'vaɪn |-vineness -'vaɪnnɪs

divinity də'vɪnətɪ

divisibility dəˌvɪzə'bɪlətɪ

divisible də'vɪzəbḷ |-bly -blɪ

division də'vɪʒən |-al -ḷ |-ally -ḷɪ

divisive də'vaɪsɪv

divisor də'vaɪzɚ; ES -'vaɪzə(r; |-ry -ɪ

divorce də'vors, -'vɔrs; ES -'voəs, E+-'vɔəs; |-s -ɪz |-d -t

divorcé, -cée dəˌvor'se, -ˌvɔr-; ES -ˌvoə-, E+-ˌvɔə-; |-cee -'si (*Fr* divör'se)

divot 'dɪvət

divulge də'vʌldʒ |-s -ɪz |-d -d |-nce -əns

Dixie 'dɪksɪ

Dixon 'dɪksṇ

dizen 'dɪzṇ, 'daɪzṇ |-ed -d |-ing -zṇɪŋ, -znɪŋ

dizzy 'dɪzɪ |dizzied 'dɪzɪd

Dnepropetrovsk ˌdnjɛpropjɛ'trɔfsk

Dnieper 'nipɚ; ES 'nipə(r

Dniester 'nistɚ; ES 'nistə(r

do *music, Jap geography* do

do *v stressed forms:*—|do 'du, ˌdu |*2 sg arch.* dost 'dʌst, ˌdʌst *or* doest 'duɪst, ˌduɪst |*3 sg* does 'dʌz, ˌdʌz *or arch.* doth 'dʌθ, ˌdʌθ *or* doeth 'duɪθ, ˌduɪθ |*past 2 sg arch.* didst 'dɪdst, ˌdɪdst *or* diddest, didest 'dɪdɪst, ˌdɪdɪst |*past 1 & 3 sg, 1–3 pl* did 'dɪd, ˌdɪd |*pptc* done dʌn, ˌdʌn; *unstressed forms (auxiliaries):*—|do *bef. vowels* du (ˌso du 'aɪ); *bef. conss.* də (ˌso də 'ðe) |dost dəst ('hwaɪ dəst ðaʊ ˌpaɪn wɪð'ɪn?) |doth dəθ (dəθ 'æsk ə 'drɪŋk dɪ'vaɪn) |does dəz (ˌhaʊ dəz ɪt 'lʊk?), dz (ˌhaʊdzɪt 'sim?), ts (ˌhwʌttsɪt 'mætɚ?) |did dɪd (ˌhwɛn dɪd ɪt 'kʌm?), dəd (ˌhaʊ dəd 'hi ˌno?), d (ˌhaʊdɪt 'go? ˌhaʊd ðe 'laɪk ɪt?)

doable 'duəbḷ

dob dɑb, dɒb |-bed -d

Dobbin, d- 'dɑbɪn

Dobell do'bɛl

Dobruja, -dja 'dobrudʒə

Dobson, d- 'dɑbsṇ

docent 'dosṇt (*Ger* dozent do'tsɛnt)

docibility ˌdɑsə'bɪlətɪ

docile 'dɑsḷ, 'dɑsɪl |-ly -ɪ

docility do'sɪlətɪ, dɑ'sɪl-

dock dɑk |docked dɑkt |-age -ɪdʒ

docket 'dɑkɪt |-ed -ɪd

dockyard 'dɑkˌjɑrd; ES -ˌjɑːd, E+-ˌjɑːd

doctor 'dɑktɚ; ES -tə(r; |-ed -d |-ing 'dɑktərɪŋ, 'dɑktrɪŋ

doctoral 'dɑktərəl |-ly -ɪ |-rate -tərɪt, -trɪt

Key: *See in full §§3–47.* bee bi |pity 'pɪtɪ (§6) |rate ret |yet jɛt |sang sæŋ |angry 'æŋ·grɪ |bath bæθ; E baθ (§10) |ah ɑ |far fɑr |watch wɑtʃ, wɒtʃ (§12) |jaw dʒɔ |gorge gɔrdʒ |go go

Those words below in which the ɑ sound is spelt o *are often pronounced with* ɒ *in E and S*

doctrinaire ˌdɑktrɪˈnɛr, -ˈnær; ES -ˈnɛə(r, ES
 -ˈnæə(r
doctrine ˈdɑktrɪn |-al -| |-ally -|ɪ
document *n* ˈdɑkjəmənt |-al ˌdɑkjəˈmɛnt|
document *v* ˈdɑkjəˌmɛnt |-ed -ɪd
documentary ˌdɑkjəˈmɛntərɪ, -trɪ |-rily -rəlɪ
documentation ˌdɑkjəmɛnˈteʃən
dodder ˈdɑdɚ; ES ˈdɑdə(r; |-ed -d |-ing
 ˈdɑdərɪŋ, ˈdɑdrɪŋ
dodecagon doˈdɛkəˌgɑn, -gən
dodecahedron ˌdodɛkəˈhidrən |-s -z |-dra -drə
Dodecanese ˌdodɛkəˈnis, doˌdɛk- |-nesus
 -ˈnisəs
dodge, D- dɑdʒ |-s -ɪz |-d -d|-r -ɚ; ES -ə(r
Dodgson ˈdɑdʒsən
dodo ˈdodo
Dodona doˈdonə
doe, D- do
does dʌz—*for forms see* do
doesn't ˈdʌznt, *before some conss.*+ˈdʌzn̩
 (ˌdʌzn̩ˈkɛr)—ˈdʌzənt *is substandard*
doest ˈduɪst—*for forms see* do
doeth ˈduɪθ—*for forms see* do
doff dɑf, dɒf, dɔf |-ed -t
dog dɔg, dɒg, *much less freq.* dɑg |-ged -d
Dogberry, d- ˈdɔgˌbɛrɪ, ˈdɒg-, -bərɪ
dogcart ˈdɔgˌkɑrt, ˈdɒg-; ES -ˌkɑːt, E+-ˌkɑːt
doge dodʒ |-ʼs -ɪz
dog-ear ˈdɔgˌɪr ˈdɒg-; ES -ˌɪə(r, S+-ˌɛə(r;
 |ed -d
dogged *adj* ˈdɔgɪd, ˈdɒg-
dogger ˈdɔgɚ, ˈdɒgɚ; ES -ə(r
doggerel ˈdɔgərəl, ˈdɒg-, ˈdɑg-, -grəl
dogie ˈdogɪ
dogma ˈdɔgmə, ˈdɒg-, ˈdɑg- |-tism -ˌtɪzəm
 |-tist -tɪst
dogmatic dɔgˈmætɪk, dɒg-, dɑg- |-al -| |-ally
 -|ɪ, -ɪklɪ
dogmatize ˈdɔgməˌtaɪz, ˈdɒg-, ˈdɑg- |-s -ɪz
 |-d -d
dog-tired ˈdɔgˈtaɪrd, ˈdɒg-; ES -ˈtaɪəd
dogtooth ˈdɔgˌtuθ, ˈdɒg- |-teeth -ˌtiθ |-ed
 -θt, -ðd
dogtrot ˈdɔgˌtrɑt, ˈdɒg-
dogwatch ˈdɔgˌwɑtʃ, ˈdɒg-, -ˌwɒtʃ, -ˌwɔtʃ
 |-es -ɪz
dogwood ˈdɔgˌwʊd, ˈdɒg-
dogy ˈdogɪ

doily ˈdɔɪlɪ
doings ˈduɪŋz, *humorous* ˈduɪnz
doit dɔɪt
Dolabella ˌdɑləˈbɛlə
dolce far niente ˈdoltʃɪˌfɑr·nɪˈɛntɪ; ES -fɑː-
 (*It* ˈdoltʃeˌfɑrˈnjɛnte)
doldrum ˈdɑldrəm |-s -z
dole dol |doled dold |-ful -fəl |-fully -fəlɪ
dolerite ˈdɑləˌraɪt
Dolgelly dɑlˈgɛθlɪ, -ˈgɛlɪ (*Welsh* dɔlˈgɛɬi)
Dolgeville ˈdɑldʒvɪl
dolichocephalic ˈdɑlɪˌkosəˈfælɪk
doll dɑl, dɒl, dɔl |-ed -d
dollar ˈdɑlɚ; ES ˈdɑlə(r
Dollard ˈdɑlɚd; ES ˈdɑləd
dolly, D- ˈdɑlɪ, ˈdɒlɪ, ˈdɔlɪ
dolman ˈdɑlmən |-s -z
dolmen ˈdɑlmɛn |-s -z
dolomite ˈdɑləˌmaɪt
Dolomites ˈdɑləˌmaɪts
dolor ˈdolɚ; ES ˈdolə(r; |-ous ˈdolərəs, ˈdɒl-
Dolores dəˈlorɪs, -ɪz, -ˈlɔr-; S -ˈlor-; |-ʼs -ɪz
dolphin ˈdɑlfɪn
dolt dolt; *N Engd*+dölt (*§46*)
-dom *unstressed ending* -dəm—*Many words in*
 -dom *are omitted from the vocab.*
domain doˈmen |-ial -ɪəl
Dombey ˈdɑmbɪ
dome dom |domed domd |domal ˈdom|
domesday, D- ˈdumzˌde=doomsday
domestic dəˈmɛstɪk |-al -| |-ally -|ɪ, -ɪklɪ
domesticate dəˈmɛstəˌket |-cated -ˌketɪd
domestication dəˌmɛstəˈkeʃən
domesticity ˌdomɛsˈtɪsətɪ, dəˌmɛsˈtɪsətɪ
domicile ˈdɑməs|, -sɪl |-d -d
domiciliary ˌdɑməˈsɪlɪˌɛrɪ
dominance ˈdɑmənəns |-cy -ɪ |-nant -nənt
dominate ˈdɑməˌnet |-d -ɪd |-tion ˌdɑmə-
 ˈneʃən
domineer ˌdɑməˈnɪr; ES -ˈnɪə(r, S+-ˈnɛə(r,
 -ˈnjɛə(r; |-ed -d
Domingo dəˈmɪŋgo
Dominic ˈdɑmənɪk
Dominica dəˈmɪnɪkə, ˌdɑməˈnikə |-n -n
dominical dəˈmɪnɪk|
dominie ˈdɑmənɪ, ʻ*pastor*ʼ+ˈdomənɪ
dominion dəˈmɪnjən
domino ˈdɑməˌno

|full fʊl |tooth tuθ |further ˈfɝðɚ; ES ˈfɝðə |custom ˈkʌstəm |while hwaɪl |how haʊ |toy tɔɪ
|using ˈjuzɪŋ |fuse fjuz, fɪuz |dish dɪʃ |vision ˈvɪʒən |Eden ˈidn̩ |cradle ˈkredl̩ |keep ʼem ˈkipm̩

Those words below in which the ɑ sound is spelt o are often pronounced with ɒ in E and S

Domitian də'mɪʃən, -ʃɪən |-tius -ʃəs, -ʃɪəs |-tius's -əsɪz

Domremy-la-Pucelle *Fr* dõrəmilapy'sɛl

don, D- dɑn |donned dɑnd

Don Adriano de Armado ˌdɑn·ɑdrɪ'ɑnoˌdear-'mɑdo; ES -ɑ:'mɑdo

Donalbain 'dɑnlˌben

Donald 'dɑnld |-son 'dɑnlsn̩, 'dɑnldsən

donate 'donet |-nated -netɪd |-tion do'neʃən

Donatello ˌdɑnə'tɛlo (*It* ˌdonɑ'tɛllo)

Donati do'nɑtɪ

donative 'dɑnətɪv, 'don-

Donatus do'netəs |-'s -ɪz

Doncaster 'dɑŋkæstə, 'dɑn-; ES -kæstə(r

done dʌn

done for 'dʌnˌfɔr; ES -ˌfɔə(r

done up 'dʌn'ʌp

done with 'dʌnˌwɪð, -ˌwɪθ

donee do'ni

Donegal 'dɑnɪˌgɔl, ˌdɑnɪ'gɔl

Donelson 'dɑnlsn̩

Don Giovanni ˌdɑn·dʒɪə'vɑnɪ, -dʒo- (*It* ˌdondʒo'vɑnni)

Dongola 'dɑŋgələ

Donizetti ˌdɑnə'zɛtɪ, (*It* ˌdoni'dzetti)

donjon 'dʌndʒən, 'dɑn-

Don Juan dɑn'dʒuən, -'dʒɪuən (*Sp* dɔn-'xwɑn)

donkey 'dɑŋkɪ, 'dɒŋkɪ, 'dɔŋkɪ, 'dʌŋkɪ

Donley 'dɑnlɪ

donna, D- 'dɑnə (*It* 'dɔnnɑ)

Donne dʌn

Donnelly 'dɑnlˌɪ, 'dɑnlɪ

Donnithorne 'dɑnəˌθɔrn; ES -ˌθɔən

Donnybrook 'dɑnɪˌbrʊk

Donohue 'dɑnəˌhju, -ˌhɪu, -ˌhu, 'dʌn-

donor 'donə; ES 'donə(r; (do'ni ən do'nɔr)

Donora do'norə, -'nɔrə; S -'norə

do-nothing 'duˌnʌθɪŋ

Don Pedro dɑn'pidro

Don Quixote ˌdɑnkɪ'hotɪ, dɑn'kwɪksət (*Sp* -ki'xote)

don't dont, *bef. some conss. often* don (don'tek ɪt), *bef.* n *often* don, do (don'no, do'no), *bef.* p, b, m *often* domp (dompprɪ'tɛnd ˌtu, dompbə'liv ɪt, domp'maɪnd ɪt), *bef.* k, g *often* doŋ, doŋk (doŋ'kær, doŋk'kær, doŋ'go, doŋk'go); |*NEngd*+dõnt (*§46*)

doodlebug 'dudlˌbʌg

doom dum |doomed dumd

doomsday, D- 'dumzˌde

Doon(e) dun

door, D- dor, dɔr; ES doə(r, E+dɔə(r; |-ed -d

doorjamb 'dorˌdʒæm, 'dɔr-; ES 'doə-, E+'dɔə-

doorman 'dorˌmæn, -mən |-men -ˌmɛn, -mən

doornail 'dorˌnel, 'dɔr-, -'nel; ES 'doə-, E+'dɔə-

dooryard 'dorˌjard, 'dɔr-; ES 'doəˌjɑːd, E+'dɔə-, -ˌjaːd

dope dop |doped dopt

dor, -rr dɔr; ES dɔə(r

Dora 'dorə, 'dɔrə; S 'dorə

Dorcas 'dɔrkəs; ES 'dɔəkəs; |-'s -ɪz

Dorchester 'dɔrˌtʃɛstə, 'dɔrtʃɪstə; ES 'dɔə-, -tə(r

Dordogne dɔr'dɔnjə (*Fr* dɔr'dɔ̃ɲ)

Dordrecht 'dɔrdrɛkt, -drɛxt

Doré do're, dɔ-; S do're; (*Fr* dɔ're)

Dorian 'dorɪən, 'dɔr-; S 'dorɪən

Doric 'dorɪk, 'dɑr-, 'dɒr-

Doricles 'dorəˌkliz, 'dɑr-, 'dɒr- |-'s -ɪz

Dorigen 'dorəgɪn, -gən, 'dɑr-, 'dɒr-

Doris 'dorɪs, 'dɑr-, 'dɒr- |-'s -ɪz

Dorking 'dɔrkɪŋ; ES 'dɔəkɪŋ

dormancy 'dɔrmənsɪ; ES 'dɔəm-; |-mant -mənt

dormer 'dɔrmə; ES 'dɔəmə(r; |-ed -d

dormitory 'dɔrməˌtorɪ, -ˌtɔrɪ; ES 'dɔəməˌtorɪ, E+-ˌtɔrɪ

dormouse 'dɔrˌmaʊs; ES 'dɔə-; |-'s -ɪz |-mice -ˌmaɪs |-mice's -ˌmaɪsɪz

dormy, -mie 'dɔrmɪ; ES 'dɔəmɪ

Dorothea ˌdorə'θiə, ˌdɑr-, ˌdɒr-

Dorothy 'dorəθɪ, 'dɑr-, 'dɒr-

Dorrit 'dorɪt, 'dɑr-, 'dɒr-

dorsal 'dɔrsl; ES 'dɔəsl; |-ly -ɪ

Dorset 'dɔrsɪt; ES 'dɔəsɪt; |-shire -ˌʃɪr, -ʃə; ES -ˌʃɪə(r, -ʃə(r

Dortmund 'dɔrtmənd; ES 'dɔət-; (*Ger* 'dɔrtmʊnt)

dory- D- 'dorɪ, 'dɔrɪ; S 'dorɪ

dos-à-dos *Fr* dozɑ'do

dosage 'dosɪdʒ |-s -ɪz

dose dos |doses 'dosɪz |dosed dost; |*NEngd*+dõs (*§46*)

Key: *See in full §§3–47.* bee bi |pity 'pɪtɪ (§6) |rate ret |yet jɛt |sang sæŋ |angry 'æŋ·grɪ |bath bæθ; E bɑθ (§10) |ah ɑ |far fɑr |watch wɑtʃ, wɒtʃ (§12) |jaw dʒɔ |gorge gɔrdʒ |go go

Dos Passos dɑs'pæsos; ES+dɒs-; |-sos' -sos

dossier 'dɑsɪ,e, 'dɑsɪɚ; ES 'dɑsɪ,e, 'dɑsɪ·ə(r, 'dɒs-; (Fr do'sje)

dost dʌst—see do

Dostoevski ˌdɑstɔ'jɛfskɪ, ˌdɒs-

dot 'dowry' dɑt; ES+dɒt; (Fr döt)

dot 'point' dɑt; ES+dɒt; |-ted -ɪd

dotard 'dotɚd; ES 'dotəd

dote dot |doted 'dotɪd |dotage 'dotɪdʒ

doth dʌθ—see do

Dothan 'doθən, 'doθæn

Dotheboys Hall 'duðə,bɔɪz'hɔl

dotterel 'dɑtərəl; ES+'dɒt-

Douai, -ay du'e ('Douˌai 'Bible)

double 'dʌbḷ |-d -d |-ling 'dʌblɪŋ, 'dʌbḷɪŋ

double-barreled 'dʌbḷ'bærəld

double-breasted 'dʌbḷ'brɛstɪd

double-cross 'dʌbḷ'krɔs, -'krɒs |-es -ɪz |-ed -t

double-edged 'dʌbḷ'ɛdʒd, -'ɛdʒɪd

double-entendre 'dublɑn'tɑndrə (Fr dublɑ̃-'tɑ̃:dr)

double-faced 'dʌbḷ'fest |-facedly -'fesɪdlɪ

double-leaded 'dʌbḷ'lɛdɪd

double-lived 'dʌbḷ'laɪvd ('double-ˌlived 'bards)

double-quick 'dʌbḷ'kwɪk ('double-ˌquick 'time)

doublet 'dʌblɪt |-ed -ɪd

doubletree 'dʌbḷˌtri, -trɪ

double-U letter 'dʌb·lju, 'dʌbḷju, 'dʌbju

doubloon dʌ'blun

doubly 'dʌblɪ

doubt daʊt |-ed -ɪd |-ful -fəl |-fully -fəlɪ

Douce daʊs, dus |-'s -ɪz

douceur du'sɝ; ES -'sɜ(r, -'sɝ; (Fr du'sœːr)

douche duʃ |douches 'duʃɪz |douched duʃt

Dougal, -ll 'dugḷ

dough do |doughed dod |-y -ɪ |-boy -ˌbɔɪ

Dougherty 'doɚtɪ, 'dɔɚtɪ, 'dɑhɚtɪ; ES 'doə-, 'dɔə-, 'dɑhə-

doughfaced 'doˌfest

doughnut 'donət, -ˌnʌt

doughty 'daʊtɪ

Douglas, -ss 'dʌgləs |-'s -ɪz

dour dur, dʊr, daʊr; ES dʊə(r, dʊə(r, daʊə(r

Dousabel 'dusəˌbɛl

douse daʊs |douses 'daʊsɪz |doused daʊst

dove 'pigeon' dʌv

dove 'dived' dov

Dove Eng name dʌv, Ger name 'dovə

dovecot 'dʌvˌkɑt; ES+-ˌkɒt;—see cot

dovecote 'dʌvˌkot—see cot, cote

Dovedale 'dʌvˌdel

Dover 'dovɚ; ES 'dovə(r

dovetail 'dʌvˌtel |-tailed -ˌteld

Dow daʊ

dowager 'daʊədʒɚ; ES 'daʊədʒə(r

Dowagiac də'wɒdʒæk

Dowden 'daʊdn̩

dowdy 'daʊdɪ

dowel 'daʊəl |-ed -d

dower 'daʊɚ; ES 'daʊ·ə(r; |-ed -d |-ing 'daʊərɪŋ, 'daʊrɪŋ

down daʊn |downed daʊnd

down-and-out 'daʊnən'aʊt, 'daʊnənd'aʊt

downcast 'daʊnˌkæst; E+-ˌkast, -ˌkɑst

downfall 'daʊnˌfɔl |-en -ən, -ˌfɔln

downgrade adj, adv 'daʊn'gred, cf upgrade

downhearted 'daʊn'hɑrtɪd; ES -'hɑːt-, E+ -'hɑːt-

downhill n 'daʊnˌhɪl, daʊn'hɪl

Downing 'daʊnɪŋ

downpour 'daʊnˌpor, -ˌpɔr, -ˌpʊr; ES -ˌpoə(r, -ˌpʊə(r, E+-ˌpɔə(r

downright adj 'daʊnˌraɪt

downright adv 'daʊnˌraɪt, daʊn'raɪt

downside 'daʊn'saɪd, 'daʊnˌsaɪd

downstage adj, adv, v 'daʊn'stedʒ |-s -ɪz |-d -d

downstairs n daʊn'stɛrz, -'stærz; E -'stɛəz, ES -'stæəz; acct+'downˌstairs, adj, adv 'down'stairs

downstream adj, adv 'daʊn'strim; v daʊn-'strim |-ed -d

downtown n daʊn'taʊn, 'daʊnˌtaʊn

downtown adj, adv 'daʊn'taʊn ('upˌtown & 'downˌtown)

downtrodden 'daʊn'trɑdn̩; ES+-'trɒdn̩

downward 'daʊnwɚd; ES 'daʊnwəd |-s -z

dowry 'daʊrɪ

dowsabel 'daʊsəˌbɛl

doxology dɑks'ɑlədʒɪ; ES+dɒks'ɒl-

doyen 'dɔɪən (Fr dwa'jæ̃)

Doyle dɔɪl

Doylestown 'dɔɪlzˌtaʊn

doze doz |dozes 'dozɪz |dozed dozd

dozen 'stun' 'dɒzn̩ |-ed -d

dozen 'twelve' 'dʌzn̩ |-ed -d

dozy 'dozɪ

drab dræb |drabbed dræbd

|full fʊl |tooth tuθ |further 'fɝðɚ; ES 'fɜðə |custom 'kʌstəm |while hwaɪl |how haʊ |toy tɔɪ |using 'juzɪŋ |fuse fjuz, fɪuz |dish dɪʃ |vision 'vɪʒən |Eden 'idn̩ |cradle 'kredḷ |keep 'em 'kipm̩

drabble 'dræb| |-d -d |-ling 'dræblıŋ, -b|ıŋ
drachm dræm
drachma 'drækmə |-s -z |-mae -mi
Draco 'dreko |gen Draconis dre'konıs
Draconian dre'konıən
Dracula 'drækjʊlə
Dracut 'drekət
draff dræf
draft dræft; E+draft, draft; |-ed -ıd
draftsman 'dræftsmən; E+'draft-, 'draft-;
 |-men -mən
drag dræg |dragged drægd
draggle 'dræg| |-d -d |-ling 'dræglıŋ, -g|ıŋ
draggly 'dræglı
dragnet 'dræg͵nɛt
dragoman 'drægəmən |-mans -mənz |-men
 -mən
dragon 'drægən |-et -ıt |-fly -͵flaı
dragonnade ͵drægə'ned
dragoon drə'gun |-ed -d |-age -ıdʒ
dragrope 'dræg͵rop
drain dren |drained drend |-age -ıdʒ
drake, D- drek
dram dræm
drama 'drɑmə, 'dræmə, 'dramə, rarely
 'dremə
dramatic drə'mætık |-al -| |-ally -|ı, -ıklı
dramatis personae 'dræmətıspə'soni; ES
 -pə-
dramatization ͵dræmətə'zefən, -aı'z-
dramatize 'dræmə͵taız |-s -ız |-d -d
dramaturgic ͵dræmə'tɝdʒık; ES -'tɝdʒ-,
 -'tɝdʒ-
dramaturgy 'dræmə͵tɝdʒı; ES -͵tɝdʒı, -͵tɝdʒı
dramshop 'dræm͵fap; ES+-͵fɒp
drank dræŋk
drape drep |-d -t |-r -ɚ; ES -ə(r; |-ry -ɚı, -rı
drastic 'dræstık |-ally -|ı, -ıklı
drat dræt |dratted 'drætıd
draught dræft; E+draft, draft; |-ed -ıd
draughtsman 'dræftsmən; E+'draft-, 'draft-;
 |-men -mən
Drava 'drɑvə
Dravida 'drɑvıdə |-vidian drə'vıdıən
draw drɔ |drew dru, drıu |drawn drɔn
drawbar 'drɔ͵bar; ES -͵ba:(r, E+-͵ba:(r
drawboard 'drɔ͵bord, -͵bord; ES -͵boəd,
 E+-͵bɔəd
drawbridge 'drɔ͵brıdʒ |-s -ız

drawee drɔ'i
drawer 'one who draws' 'drɔɚ; ES 'drɔ·ə(r
drawer of a dresser drɔr; ES drɔə(r; |-s -z
drawing-room 'drɔ·ıŋ͵rum, -͵rʊm
drawknife 'drɔ͵naıf |-knives -͵naıvz
drawl drɔl |drawled drɔld
drawn drɔn
drawshave 'drɔ͵fev
dray dre |-ed -d |-age -ıdʒ |-man, -men -mən
Drayton 'dretn̩
dread drɛd |-ed -ıd |-ful -fəl |-fully -fəlı
dreadnought, -naught, D- 'drɛd͵nɔt
dream drim |dreamed drimd or dreamt
 drɛmpt
dreamland 'drim͵lænd, -lənd
drear drır; ES drıə(r, S+drɛə(r
dreary 'drırı, 'drırı; S+'drɛrı
dredge drɛdʒ |-s -ız |-d -d
dregs drɛgz
Dreiser 'draısɚ, -zɚ; ES 'draısə(r, -zə(r
drench drɛntf |-es -ız |-ed -t
Dresden 'drɛzdən
dress drɛs |-es -ız |-ed or drest 'drɛst
dressmaker 'drɛs͵mekɚ; ES -͵mekə(r
dress suit 'drɛs'sut, -'sıut, -'sjut ('dress-'suit
 ͵case, 'dress-͵suit ͵case)
drew, D- dru, drıu
Dreyfus 'drefəs, 'draı- |-'s -ız (Fr drɛ'fys)
dribble 'drıb| |-d -d |-ling 'drıblıŋ, -b|ıŋ
dribbler 'drıblɚ; ES 'drıblə(r
driblet, dribb- 'drıblıt
dried draıd
drier 'draıɚ; ES 'draı·ə(r
dries draız
drift drıft |drifted 'drıftıd |-wood -͵wʊd
drill drıl |drilled drıld
drily 'draılı
drink drıŋk |drank dræŋk |drunk drʌŋk
drinkable 'drıŋkəb| |-bly -blı
Drinkwater 'drıŋk͵wɔtɚ, -͵watɚ, -͵wɒtɚ; ES
 -tə(r
drip drıp |dripped drıpt
drippings 'drıpıŋz
drivable, driveable 'draıvəb|
drive draıv |drove drov |driven 'drıvən
drivel 'drıv| |-ed -d |-ing 'drıv|ıŋ, -vlıŋ
driveling adj 'drıvlıŋ
driveway 'draıv͵we
drizzle 'drız| |-d -d |-ling 'drızlıŋ, -z|ıŋ

Key: See in full §§3–47. bee bi |pity 'pıtı (§6) |rate ret |yet jɛt |sang sæŋ |angry 'æŋ·grı
|bath bæθ; E baθ (§10) |ah ɑ |far far |watch watf, wɒtf (§12) |jaw dʒɔ |gorge gɔrdʒ |go go

drizzly ˈdrɪzlɪ
Drogheda ˈdrɔədə, ˈdrɔ·ɪdə
drogher, droger ˈdrogɚ; ES ˈdrogə(r
droll drol |-ed -d |ery -ərɪ |-y ˈdrollɪ, -olɪ
dromedary ˈdrɑməˌdɛrɪ, ˈdrʌm-; ES+-ˈdrɒm-
Dromio ˈdromjo, ˈdromɪˌo
drone dron |droned drond |-age -ɪdʒ
Drood drud
drool drul |drooled druld
droop drup |drooped drupt
drop drɑp; ES+drɒp; |-ped, -t -t
drop-forge ˈdrɑpˈfɔrdʒ, -ˈfordʒ; ES -ˈfoədʒ,
 -ˈfɔədʒ; |-s -ɪz |-d -d—see forge
droplet ˈdrɑplɪt; ES+ˈdrɒp-
droplight ˈdrɑpˌlaɪt; ES+ˈdrɒp-
dropper ˈdrɑpɚ; ES ˈdrɑpə(r, ˈdrɒp-
dropsical ˈdrɑpsɪk|; ES+ˈdrɒp-; |-ly -ɪ
dropsy ˈdrɑpsɪ; ES+ˈdrɒp-; |-ied -d
dropt drɑpt; ES+drɒpt
droshky ˈdrɑʃkɪ; ES+ˈdrɒʃ-
Drosophila, d- dro·ˈsɑfələ; ES+-ˈsɒf-; |-lae
 -ˌli
dross drɔs, drɒs |-es -ɪz |-ed -t
drought draʊt
drouth draʊθ |-ths -θs—Drouth *is not an
error for* drought, *but a normal historical
variant in wide American use.*
drove drov |droved drovd
drover ˈdrovɚ; ES ˈdrovə(r
drown draʊn |drowned draʊnd
drowse draʊz |-s -ɪz |-d -d
drowsy ˈdraʊzɪ |-sily ˈdraʊzˌlɪ, -zɪlɪ
drub drʌb |drubbed drʌbd |-bing -ɪŋ
drudge drʌdʒ |-s -ɪz |-d -d |-ry -ərɪ, -rɪ
drug drʌg |drugged drʌgd |-gist -ɪst
drugget ˈdrʌgɪt
drugstore ˈdrʌgˌstor, -ˌstɔr; ES -ˌstoə(r,
 E+-ˌstɔə(r
druid, D- ˈdruɪd, ˈdrɪuɪd
druidic druˈɪdɪk, drɪu- |-al -|
drum drʌm |drummed drʌmd |-mer -ɚ; ES
 -ə(r
drumfire ˈdrʌmˌfaɪr; ES -ˌfaɪə(r
drumhead ˈdrʌmˌhɛd
drumlin ˈdrʌmlɪn
Drummond ˈdrʌmənd
drumstick ˈdrʌmˌstɪk
drunk drʌŋk |-en -ən |-ard -ɚd; ES -əd
drunkenness ˈdrʌŋkənnɪs

drupaceous druˈpeʃəs, drɪu-
drupe drup, drɪup |-let -lɪt
Drury Lane ˈdrʊrɪˈlen, ˈdrɪʊrɪ-
Drusilla druˈsɪlə, drɪu-
dry draɪ |dried draɪd
dryad ˈdraɪəd, -æd
Dryasdust ˈdraɪəzˌdʌst
Dryburgh ˈdraɪˌbɝo, -ə; ES -ˌbɝr-, -ˌbʌr-,
 -ˌbɜr-; *Brit* ˈdraɪbərə
dry-clean ˈdraɪˈklin, -ˌklin |-ed -d
Dryden ˈdraɪdn̩
dryer ˈdraɪɚ; ES ˈdraɪ·ə(r
dryly ˈdraɪlɪ
dry-nurse ˈdraɪˌnɝs; ES -ˌnɜs, -ˌnɝs; |-s -ɪz
 |-d -t
drysalter ˈdraɪˌsɔltɚ; ES -ˌsɔltə(r; |-y -ɪ
dry-shod ˈdraɪˈʃɑd; ES -ˈʃɒd
'dst *'wouldst'* dst
dual ˈdjuəl, ˈdɪuəl, ˈduəl |-ism -ˌɪzəm
dualistic ˌdjuəlˈɪstɪk, ˌdɪu-, ˌdu- |-ally -|ɪ,
 -ɪklɪ
duality djuˈælətɪ, dɪu-, du-
dub dʌb |dubbed dʌbd
Du Barry djuˈbærɪ, dɪu- du- (*Fr* dybaˈri)
Du Bartas djubarˈtas, dɪu-, du-; ES -baːˈtas;
 (*Fr* dybarˈtɑːs) |-'s -ɪz
dubiety djuˈbaɪətɪ, dɪu-, du-
dubious ˈdjubɪəs, ˈdɪu-, ˈdu-
dubitable ˈdjubɪtəb|, ˈdɪu-, ˈdu- |-bly -blɪ
dubitate ˈdjubəˌtet, ˈdɪu-, ˈdu- |-d -ɪd |-tive
 -ɪv
dubitation ˌdjubəˈteʃən, ˌdɪu- ˌdu-
Dublin ˈdʌblɪn
Dubois, Du Bois dəˈbɔɪs, du-, ˈdubɔɪs |-'s -ɪz
Dubuque dəˈbjuk, du-, -ˈbɪuk
ducal ˈdjuk|, ˈdɪu-, ˈdu- |-ly -ɪ
Du Cange djuˈkændʒ, dɪu-, du- |-'s -ɪz (*Fr*
 dyˈkɑ̃ːʒ)
ducat ˈdʌkət
duce *It* ˈduːtʃe
Duchesne *in Utah* duˈʃen, dɪu-; *Fr name*
 dyˈʃɛːn
duchess ˈdʌtʃɪs |-'s -ɪz
duchy ˈdʌtʃɪ
duck dʌk |ducked dʌkt |-ling ˈdʌklɪŋ
duct dʌkt |-ed -ɪd
ductile ˈdʌkt|, -tɪl |-ly -ɪ
ductility dʌkˈtɪlətɪ
dud dʌd

Duddon 'dʌdn̩
dude dʒud, dɪud, dud
dudgeon 'dʌdʒən
Dudley 'dʌdlɪ
due dju, dɪu, du
duel 'dju̯əl, 'dɪu-, 'du- |-ed -d |-ist -ɪst
duello dju'ɛlo, dɪu-, du- (*It* du'ɛllo)
duenna dju'ɛnə, dɪu-, du-
duet dju'ɛt, dɪu-, du- |-ted -ɪd
duff dʌf |duffed dʌft |-el -l̩ | |-er -ɚ; ES -ə(r
dug dʌg
Dugdale 'dʌgdel
dugong 'dugaŋ, -gɒŋ, -gɔŋ
dugout 'dʌg͵aʊt
dugway 'dʌg͵we
duke dʒuk, dɪuk, duk |-dom -dəm |-ry -ərɪ
dulcet 'dʌlsɪt
dulcimer 'dʌlsəmɚ; ES 'dʌlsəmə(r
Dulcinea dʌl'sɪnɪə, ͵dʌlsə'nɪə (*Sp* ͵dulθi'nea)
dulia dju'laɪə, dɪu-, du-
dull dʌl |dulled dʌld |-ard -ɚd; ES -əd
dully 'dʌllɪ, 'dʌlɪ
Duluth də'luθ, du-, -'lɪuθ
Dulwich 'dʌlɪdʒ, -ɪtʃ |-'s -ɪz
duly 'djulɪ, 'dɪulɪ, 'dulɪ
Dumain dju'men, dɪu-, du-
Dumas dju'mɑ, dɪu-, du-, *acct*+'Dumas (*Fr* dy'ma)
Du Maurier dju'mɔrɪ͵e, dɪu-, du- (*Fr* dymɔ'rje)
dumb dʌm |-ed -d |-bell -͵bel
Dumbarton dʌm'bɑrtn̩; ES -'bɑ:tn̩, E+ -'bɑ:tn̩; |-shire -͵ʃɪr, -ʃɚ; ES -͵ʃɪə(r, -ʃə(r
dumdum 'dʌmdʌm
dumfound, dumbf- dʌm'faʊnd |-ed -ɪd
Dumfries dʌm'fris |-shire -ʃɪr, -ʃɚ; ES -ʃɪə(r, -ʃə(r
dummy 'dʌmɪ |-ied -d
dump dʌmp |dumped dʌmpt |-ling -lɪŋ
dun dʌn |dunned dʌnd
Dunbar *US* 'dʌnbɑr; ES -bɑ:(r, E+-bɑ:(r; *Scotl* Dun'bar
Duncan 'dʌŋkən
Duncannon dʌn'kænən
dunce dʌns |dunces 'dʌnsɪz
Dunciad 'dʌnsɪ͵æd
Dundas dʌn'dæs |-'s -ɪz
Dundee dʌn'di ('Dun͵dee 'road)
dunderhead 'dʌndɚ͵hɛd; ES 'dʌndə-

dunderpate 'dʌndɚ͵pet; ES 'dʌndə-
Dundreary, d- dʌn'drɪrɪ
dune dʒun, dɪun, dun
Dun Edin, Dunedin dʌn'idn̩, -dɪn
Dunfermline dʌn'fɝmlɪn, dʌm-; ES -'fɝm-, -'fɜm-; *loc*.+-'fɛrm-, -'farm-
dung dʌŋ |-ed -d
dungaree, -ri ͵dʌŋgə'ri
dungeon 'dʌndʒən |-ed -d
dung-fork 'dʌŋ͵fɔrk; ES -͵fɔək
dunghill 'dʌŋ͵hɪl
Dunkard 'dʌŋkɚd; ES 'dʌŋkəd
Dunker 'dʌŋkɚ; ES 'dʌŋkə(r
Dunkirk *US* 'dʌnkɝk; ES -kɜk, -kɝk, *France* 'Dunkirk, Dun'kirk
Dunmore dʌn'mor, -'mɔr; ES -'moə(r, E+-'mɔə(r
Dunmow 'dʌnmo
dunnage 'dʌnɪdʒ |-s -ɪz |-d -d
Duns dʌnz, dʌns |-'s -ɪz
Dunsany dʌn'senɪ
Dunsinane 'dʌnsə͵nen, ͵dʌnsə'nen
Dunsmuir 'dʌnzmjʊr, -mɪur
Duns Scotus 'dʌnz'skotəs, *earlier* 'dʌns- |-'s -ɪz
Dunstan 'dʌnstən
Dunster 'dʌnstɚ; ES 'dʌnstə(r
duo *It* 'du:o
duo- 'djuo, 'dɪuo, 'duo, -ə
duodecimal ͵djuə'dɛsəml̩, ͵dɪuə-, ͵duə- |-ly -ɪ |-mo -͵mo
duodenal ͵djuə'dinl̩, ͵dɪuə-, ͵duə- |-num -nəm |-na -nə
duologue 'djuə͵lɔg, 'dɪuə-, 'duə-, -͵lag, -͵lɒg
dupe djup, dɪup, dup |-d -t |-ry -ərɪ, -rɪ
duple 'djupl̩, 'dɪupl̩, 'dupl̩
duplex 'djuplɛks, 'dɪu-, 'du- |-es -ɪz |-ed -t
duplicate, *n, adj* 'djupləkɪt, 'dɪu-, 'du-, -͵ket
duplicate *v* 'djuplə͵ket, 'dɪu-, 'du- |-d -ɪd |-tor -ɚ; ES -ə(r
duplication ͵djuplə'keʃən, ͵dɪu-, ͵du-
duplicity dju'plɪsətɪ, dɪu-, du-
Dupont 'djupant, 'dɪu-, 'du-; ES+-pɒnt; *acct*+Du'pont ('Du͵pont 'product)
Duquesne dju'ken, dɪu-, du-
Du Quoin dju'kɔɪn, dɪu-, du-
durability ͵djʊrə'bɪlətɪ, ͵dɪur-, ͵dur-
durable 'djʊrəbl̩, 'dɪur-, 'dur- |-bly -blɪ

Key: *See in full §§3–47.* bee bi |pity 'pɪtɪ (§6) |rate ret |yet jɛt |sang sæŋ |angry 'æŋ·grɪ |bath bæθ; E baθ (§10) |ah ɑ |far fɑr |watch watʃ, wɒtʃ (§12) |jaw dʒɔ |gorge gɔrdʒ |go go

duralumin, D- djʊˈræljəˌmɪn, dɪʊ-, dʊ-

durance ˈdjʊrəns, ˈdɪʊr-, ˈdʊr-

Durand djʊˈrænd, dɪʊ-, dʊ-

Durango djʊˈræŋgo, dɪʊ-, dʊ-

Durant djʊˈrænt, dɪʊ-, dʊ-

duration djʊˈreʃən, dɪʊ-, dʊ-

durative ˈdjʊrətɪv, ˈdɪʊr-, ˈdʊr-

Durazzo dʊˈrɑtso

Durban ˈdɝbən, dɚˈbæn; ES ˈdɜb-, ˈdɝb-, də-

durbar ˈdɝbɑr; ES ˈdɜbɑ:(r, ˈdɝbɑ:(r, E+-bɑ:(r

D'Urberville ˈdɝbəˌvɪl; ES ˈdɜbə-, ˈdɝbə-

Durbeyfield ˈdɝbɪˌfild; ES ˈdɜbɪ-, ˈdɝbɪ-

dure djʊr, dɪʊr, dʊr; ES -ə(r; |-d -d

duress ˈdjʊrɪs, ˈdɪʊr-, ˈdʊr-, acct+duˈress

D'Urfey, Durfey ˈdɝfɪ; ES ˈdɜfɪ, ˈdɝfɪ

Durham ˈdɝəm; ES ˈdɜrəm, ˈdʌr-, ˈdɝ-

during ˈdʊrɪŋ, ˈdɪʊrɪŋ, ˈdjʊrɪŋ

durn dɝn; ES dɜn, dɝn; |-ed -d |-edest -dɪst

Duroc ˈdjʊrɑk, ˈdɪʊr-, ˈdʊr-; ES+-ɒk

durst dɝst; ES dɜst, dɝst |-stn't -snt—before some conss.+-sn (ˌdɝsnˈgo)

durum ˈdjʊrəm, ˈdɪʊr-, ˈdʊr-

Duse ˈduzɪ (It ˈdu:ze)

dusk dʌsk |dusked dʌskt

Düsseldorf ˈdɪsḷˌdɔrf, ˈdʌsḷ-; ES -ˌdɔəf; (Ger ˈdysəlˌdɔrf)

dust dʌst |dusted ˈdʌstɪd

dustman ˈdʌstmən |-men -mən

dustpan ˈdʌstˌpæn, ˈdʌsˌpæn

dustproof ˈdʌstˈpruf (ˈdustˌproof ˈbearings)

Dutch dʌtʃ |dutches ˈdʌtʃɪz |dutched dʌtʃt

Dutchman ˈdʌtʃmən |-men -mən

Dutchman's-breeches ˈdʌtʃmənzˈbrɪtʃɪz

duteous ˈdjutɪəs, ˈdɪu-, ˈdu-

dutiable ˈdjutɪəbḷ, ˈdɪu-, ˈdu-

dutiful ˈdjutɪfəl, ˈdɪu-, ˈdu- |-ly -ɪ

duty ˈdjutɪ, ˈdɪu-, ˈdu-

duty-free ˈdjutɪˈfri, ˈdɪu-, ˈdu-

duumvir djuˈʌmvɚ, dɪu-, du-; ES -ˈʌmvə(r; |-ate -ɪt

Duxbury ˈdʌksˌbɛrɪ, -bərɪ

Duyckinck ˈdaɪkɪŋk

Dvina dviˈnɑ

Dvořák ˈdvɔrʒɑk, dəˈvɔrʒɑk, ˈvɔrʒæk, ˈvɔrˌʃæk; ES -ɔə-

dwarf dwɔrf; ES dwɔəf; |-ed -t |-ish -ɪʃ

dwarvish ˈdwɔrvɪʃ; ES ˈdwɔəvɪʃ

dwell dwɛl |dwelt dwɛlt, arch. dwelled dwɛld

dwelling ˈdwɛlɪŋ

dwindle ˈdwɪndḷ |-d -d |-ling ˈdwɪndḷɪŋ, -dlɪŋ

Dwight dwaɪt

Dyak ˈdaɪæk

dyarchy ˈdaɪɑrkɪ; ES -ɑːkɪ, E+-ɑːkɪ

Dyce daɪs |-'s -ɪz

Dyck, van vænˈdaɪk

dye daɪ |dyed daɪd |-ing -ɪŋ |-r -ɚ; ES -ə(r

dyed-in-the-wool ˈdaɪdnðəˈwʊl, ˈdaɪdɪnðə-

dyeing from dye ˈdaɪɪŋ

dyestuff ˈdaɪˌstʌf

dying from die ˈdaɪɪŋ

Dyke, van vænˈdaɪk

dyke daɪk |dyked daɪkt

Dykema ˈdaɪkəmə

Dykstra ˈdaɪkstrə

Dymond ˈdaɪmənd

dynameter daɪˈnæmətɚ; ES -ˈnæmətə(r

dynamic daɪˈnæmɪk |-al -ḷ |-ally -ḷɪ, -ɪklɪ

dynamism ˈdaɪnəˌmɪzəm |-mist -mɪst

dynamite ˈdaɪnəˌmaɪt |-mited -ˌmaɪtɪd

dynamo ˈdaɪnəˌmo

dynamometer ˌdaɪnəˈmɑmətɚ; ES -ˈmɑmətə(r, -ˈmɒm-

dynast ˈdaɪnæst, ˈdaɪnəst

dynastic daɪˈnæstɪk |-al -ḷ |-ally -ḷɪ, -ɪklɪ

dynasty ˈdaɪnəstɪ, ˈdaɪnæstɪ—ˈdɪnəstɪ is mainly Brit.

dyne daɪn

Dysart ˈdaɪzɚt, -zɑrt; ES ˈdaɪzət, -zɑ:t

dysentery ˈdɪsṇˌtɛrɪ

dysgenic dɪsˈdʒɛnɪk

Dyson ˈdaɪsṇ

dyspepsia dɪˈspɛpʃə, -ʃɪə

dyspeptic dɪˈspɛptɪk |-al -ḷ |-ally -ḷɪ, -ɪklɪ

dysphasia dɪsˈfeʒə, -ʒɪə

dyspnea, -noea dɪspˈniə

dysprosium dɪsˈprosɪəm, -ˈproʃɪəm

|full fʊl |tooth tuθ |further ˈfɝðɚ; ES ˈfɝðə |custom ˈkʌstəm |while hwaɪl |how haʊ |toy tɔɪ
|using ˈjuzɪŋ |fuse fjuz, fɪuz |dish dɪʃ |vision ˈvɪʒən |Eden ˈidṇ |cradle ˈkredḷ |keep 'em ˈkipm̩

E

E, e *letter* i |*pl* E's, Es, *poss* E's **iz**
e- *word initial. When unstressed, this varies as*
i-, ɪ-, ɛ-, *or* **ə-** *according to style of speech or*
commonness of the word. **ə-** *is esp. freq. be-*
fore **l** (elect ɪ'lɛkt, ə'lɛkt). *When only one*
or two prons. are given in the vocab., it is to
be understood that one or more of the others
are used by many speakers.
each itʃ |each's 'itʃɪz
Eads **idz** |Eads's 'idzɪz
eager 'igɚ; ES 'igə(r
eagle 'igḷ |eaglet 'iglɪt
eagre 'igɚ, 'egɚ; ES 'igə(r, 'egə(r
Eakins 'ekɪnz |-'s -ɪz
Eames **emz, imz** |Eames's 'emzɪz, 'imzɪz
Eamon de Valera 'ɪəmən dəvə'lerə, -'lɛrə,
-'lɪrə
ean **in** |eaned **ind** |eanling 'inlɪŋ
ear **ɪr**; ES ɪə(r, S+ɛə(r; |-ed -**d**
earache 'ɪrˌek; S+'ɛrˌek
eardrop 'ɪrˌdrɑp; ES 'ɪəˌdrɑp, 'ɪəˌdrɒp,
S+'ɛə-
eardrum 'ɪrˌdrʌm; ES 'ɪəˌdrʌm, S+'ɛə-
earl **ɝl**; ES ɜl, ɝl; |-dom -**dəm**
early 'ɝlɪ; ES 'ɜlɪ, 'ɝlɪ
earmark 'ɪrˌmɑrk; E 'ɪəˌmɑːk, -ˌmɑːk; S
'ɪəˌmɑːk, 'ɛə-
earn **ɝn**; ES ɜn, ɝn; |-ed -**d**
earnest 'ɝnɪst, -əst; ES 'ɜn-, 'ɝn-
earnings 'ɝnɪŋz; ES 'ɜnɪŋz, 'ɝn-
earphone 'ɪrˌfon; ES 'ɪəˌfon, S+'ɛə-
earring 'ɪrˌrɪŋ; ES 'ɪəˌrɪŋ, S+'ɛəˌrɪŋ
Earsdon 'ɪrzdən; ES 'ɪəz-; *loc.*+'jɔzn̩
earshot 'ɪrˌʃɑt; ES 'ɪəˌʃɑt, 'ɪəˌʃɒt, S+'ɛə-
earth **ɝθ**; ES ɜθ, ɝθ; |-th's -**θs**
earthborn 'ɝθˌbɔrn; ES 'ɜθˌbɔən, 'ɝθˌbɔən
earthbound 'ɝθˌbaʊnd; ES 'ɜθ-, 'ɝθ-
earthen 'ɝθən; ES 'ɜθən, 'ɝθən
earthenware 'ɝθənˌwɛr, -ˌwær; E 'ɜθən-
ˌwɛə(r, 'ɝθ-, ES -ˌwæə(r
earthling 'ɝθlɪŋ; ES 'ɜθlɪŋ, 'ɝθlɪŋ
earthly 'ɝθlɪ; ES 'ɜθlɪ, 'ɝθlɪ
earthquake 'ɝθˌkwek; ES 'ɜθ-, 'ɝθ-
earthshine 'ɝθˌʃaɪn; ES 'ɜθ-, 'ɝθ-
earthward 'ɝθwɚd; ES 'ɜθwəd, 'ɝθwəd
earthwork 'ɝθˌwɝk; ES 'ɜθˌwɜk, 'ɝθˌwɝk
earthworm 'ɝθˌwɝm; ES 'ɜθˌwɜm, 'ɝθˌwɝm

earwig 'ɪrˌwɪg; ES 'ɪəˌwɪg, S+'ɛə-; |-wigged
-ˌwɪgd
Easdale 'izˌdel
ease **iz** |-s -**ɪz** |-d -**d** |-ful -**fəl** |-fully -**fəlɪ**
easel 'izḷ
easement 'izmənt
easily 'izḷɪ, 'izɪlɪ
Easley 'izlɪ
east, E- **ist**
Eastbourne 'istˌborn, -ˌbɔrn, -bən; ES 'ist-
ˌboən, -bən, E+-ˌbɔən
Eastcheap 'istˌtʃip, 'isˌtʃip
Easter 'istɚ; ES 'istə(r
easterly 'istɚlɪ; ES 'istəlɪ
eastern 'istɚn; ES 'istən; |-er -ɚ; ES -ə(r;
|-most -ˌmost, -məst—'istənɚ *is sometimes*
heard by r-dissimilation (§121).
Eastertide 'istɚˌtaɪd; ES 'istəˌtaɪd
East Greenwich *RI* 'ist'grinwɪtʃ, *loc.*+
-'grɪnɪdʒ, -ɪtʃ
Eastham 'istəm, *Mass loc.*+'istæm
East Ham 'ist'hæm
Eastman 'istmən
Easton 'istən
eastward 'istwɚd; ES 'istwəd
easy 'izɪ |-going -'goɪŋ ('easyˌgoing 'man)
eat **it** |ate **et** |eaten 'itn̩ |eat *dial. past* ɛt, **it**—
ɛt *is occas. in cultivated S, see* ate.
eatable 'itəbḷ
Eaton 'itn̩ |Eatonton 'itn̩tən |-town 'itn̩ˌtaʊn
Eau Claire ˌo'klɛr, ˌo'klær; E ˌo'klɛə(r, ES
ˌo'klæə(r
Eau de Cologne ˌodəkə'lon
eaves **ivz**
eavesdrop 'ivzˌdrɑp; ES+-ˌdrɒp; |-ped -**t**
ebb **ɛb** |ebbed **ɛbd** |ebb-tide 'ɛb'taɪd, -ˌtaɪd
Ebenezer ˌɛbə'nizɚ; ES ˌɛbə'nizə(r
Ebensburg 'ɛbənzˌbɝg; ES -ˌbɜg, -ˌbɝg
ebon 'ɛbən |ebony 'ɛbənɪ
ebriate *adj* 'ibrɪt |ebriated 'ibrɪˌetɪd
ebriety i'braɪətɪ
Ebro 'ibro, 'ebro
ebullience ɪ'bʌljəns, ɪ'bʌlɪəns |-cy -ɪ |-nt -nt
ebullition ˌɛbə'lɪʃən
écarté ˌekɑr'te; ES ˌekɑ'te; (*Fr* ekar'te)
ecce homo 'ɛksɪ'homo, 'ɛkɛ-
eccentric ɪk'sɛntrɪk, ɛk- |-al -ḷ |-ally -ḷɪ, -ɪklɪ

Key: *See in full §§3–47.* bee **bi** |pity 'pɪtɪ (§6) |rate **ret** |yet **jɛt** |sang **sæŋ** |angry 'æŋ·grɪ
|bath **bæθ**; E baθ (§10) |ah **ɑ** |far **fɑr** |watch **wɑtʃ, wɒtʃ** (§12) |jaw **dʒɔ** |gorge **gɔrdʒ** |go **go**

eccentricity ˌɛksən'trɪsətɪ, ˌɛksɛn-

Ecclefechan ˌɛkl̩'fɛkən, -'fɛxən

Eccles 'ɛkl̩z |-'s -ɪz

Ecclesiastes ɪˌklizɪ'æstiz |-tes' -tiz

ecclesiastic ɪˌklizɪ'æstɪk |-al -l̩ |-ally -l̩ɪ, -ɪklɪ

ecclesiasticism ɪˌklizɪ'æstəˌsɪzəm

Ecclesiasticus ɪˌklizɪ'æstɪkəs |-'s -ɪz

echelon 'ɛʃəˌlɑn, -ˌlɒn (Fr ɛʃ'lõ)

echinoderm ɛ'kaɪnəˌdɝm, 'ɛkɪnə-; ES -ˌdɜm, -ˌdɝm

echinus ɛ'kaɪnəs |echini ɛ'kaɪnaɪ

echo 'ɛko |echoed 'ɛkod |-ing 'ɛkəwɪŋ

echoic ɛ'ko·ɪk

éclair e'klɛr, e'klær, ɪ-; E -'klɛə(r, ES -'klæə(r

éclat ɪ'klɑ, e'klɑ (Fr e'kla)

eclectic ɪk'lɛktɪk, ɛk- |-ticism -ˌsɪzəm

eclipse ɪ'klɪps |eclipses ɪ'klɪpsɪz |-d -t

ecliptic ɪ'klɪptɪk, i-

eclogue 'ɛklɔg, -lɑg, -lɒg

ecology i'kalədʒɪ; ES+-'kɒl-

economic ˌikə'nɑmɪk, ˌɛk-; ES+-'nɒm-; |-s -s |-al -l̩ |-ally -l̩ɪ, -ɪklɪ

economist ɪ'kɑnəmɪst, i-; ES+-'kɒn-

economize ɪ'kɑnəˌmaɪz, i-; ES+-'kɒn-; |-s -ɪz |-d -d |-my -mɪ

ecru 'ɛkru, 'ɛkru, e'kru (Fr e'kry)

ecstasy 'ɛkstəsɪ

ecstatic ɪk'stætɪk, ɛk- |-ally -l̩ɪ, -ɪklɪ

ectoderm 'ɛktəˌdɝm; ES -ˌdɜm, -ˌdɝm

ectoplasm 'ɛktəˌplæzəm

Ecuador 'ɛkwəˌdɔr; ES 'ɛkwəˌdɔə(r

Ecuadorian ˌɛkwə'dorɪən, -'dɔr-; S -'dɔrɪən

ecumenic ˌɛkju'mɛnɪk |-al -l̩ |-ally -l̩ɪ, -ɪklɪ

eczema 'ɛksəmə, 'ɛgzəmə, -ɪmə, ɪg'zimə

-ed, -d ending of the past and pptc, and of certain adjectives. Pronounced -t after voiceless consonant sounds except t (walk-ed wɔk-t, price-d praɪs-t, reach-ed ritʃ-t); pronounced -d after vowel and voiced consonants sounds except d (paw-ed pɔ-d, free-d fri-d, dragg-ed dræg-d, prize-d praɪz-d, horn-ed hɔrn-d, age-d edʒ-d); pronounced -ɪd or -əd after t & d (state-d 'stet-ɪd, -əd, fatt-ed 'fæt-ɪd, -əd, wood-ed 'wʊd-ɪd, -əd, raid-ed 'red-ɪd, -əd, padd-ed 'pæd-ɪd, -əd); in a few adjectives pronounced -ɪd, -əd also after other consonants than t & d (age-d 'edʒ-ɪd, -əd, crabb-ed 'kræb-ɪd, -əd, bless-ed 'blɛs-ɪd,

-əd, two-legg-ed 'tu'lɛg-ɪd, -əd). *With different speakers the unstressed vowel of* -ed *(when sounded at all) varies from a sound like that in* bit **bɪt** *to one like the last vowel in* method **'mɛθəd**. *Very often it is a sound made with the tongue higher than the central position (that for* ə*), and back of that for* ɪ *(phonetic symbol* ɪ*). In the vocabulary, as a rule, only the pronunciation* -ɪd *is given, it being understood that many speakers instead pronounce* -ɪd, *or (fewer in the E & S)* -əd *as in* method **'mɛθəd**. *The difference between* -əd & -ɪd *or* -əz & -ɪz *is sometimes phonemic—used to distinguish words otherwise alike, as* quotaed *(Jefferson)* **'kwotəd**, quoted **'kwotɪd**, *or* Louisa's **lu'izəz**, Louise's **lu'izɪz**, *and often in ES:* Caesars **'sizəz**, seizes **'sizɪz** *or* mattered **'mætəd**, matted **'mætɪd**.

Edam 'idəm, 'idæm (Du e'dɑm)

Edda 'ɛdə

eddy, E- 'ɛdɪ |eddied 'ɛdɪd

Eddystone light 'ɛdɪstən, Pa bor. 'ɛdɪˌston

edelweiss 'edl̩ˌvaɪs |-es -ɪz

edema i'dimə |-mata -mətə |-tous -təs

Eden 'idn̩ |-ton 'idn̩tən

Edgar 'ɛdgɚ; ES 'ɛdgə(r

edge ɛdʒ |edges 'ɛdʒɪz |edged ɛdʒd

Edgerton 'ɛdʒɚtən; ES 'ɛdʒətən

edgeways 'ɛdʒˌwez |edgewise 'ɛdʒˌwaɪz

Edgeworth 'ɛdʒwɚθ; ES 'ɛdʒwəθ

edible 'ɛdəbl̩ |edibility ˌɛdə'bɪlətɪ

edict 'idɪkt

edification ˌɛdəfə'keʃən

edifice 'ɛdəfɪs |edifices 'ɛdəfɪsɪz |-d -t

edify 'ɛdəˌfaɪ |edified 'ɛdəˌfaɪd

edile 'idaɪl

Edinburg US 'ɛdn̩ˌbɝg, 'ɛdɪn-; ES -ˌbɜg, -ˌbɝg

Edinburgh Scotl 'ɛdn̩ˌbɝo, 'ɛdɪn-, -ə; ES -ˌbɜr-, -ˌbʌr-, -ˌbɝ-; (Brit. pron. 'ɛdɪnbrə, 'ɛdn̩-, -bərə, -ˌbʌrə)

Edison 'ɛdəsn̩

edit 'ɛdɪt |edited 'ɛdɪtɪd

Edith 'idɪθ

edition ɪ'dɪʃən, i'dɪʃən

editor 'ɛdɪtɚ; ES 'ɛdɪtə(r; |-ship -ˌʃɪp

editorial ˌɛdə'torɪəl, -'tɔr-; S -'tɔr-; |-ly -ɪ

-edly ending of advs formed on -ed words, as

designedly dɪˈzaɪnɪdlɪ—*Advs in* -edly *are
only given in the vocabulary when the pron.
cannot be inferred from the form in* -ed, *as
disguised* dɪsˈgaɪzd *but disguisedly* dɪs-
ˈgaɪzɪdlɪ. *But disgustedly* dɪsˈgʌstɪdlɪ *is
not entered, since the pron. can be found by
adding* -lɪ *directly to* dɪsˈgʌstɪd. *For the
vowels in* -edly *see* -ed & -ly *in the vocab.
The pron. of* -edness *as* -ɪdnɪs *or* -dnɪs
usually follows that of -edly.

Edmondson, -nson ˈɛdmənsn̩

Edmonton ˈɛdməntən

Edmund ˈɛdmənd, *before some conss.*+ˈɛdmən
(ˈɛdməndˈsmɪθ, ˈɛdmənˈsmɪθ)

Edmundston ˈɛdmənstən

Edna ˈɛdnə

-edness *ending, see* -edly

Edom ˈidəm |Edomite ˈidəmˌaɪt

educability ˌɛdʒəkəˈbɪlətɪ, ˌɛdʒʊ-

educable ˈɛdʒəkəbl̩, ˈɛdʒʊ-

educate ˈɛdʒəˌket, ˈɛdʒʊ- |-d -ɪd

educator ˈɛdʒəˌketə, ˈɛdʒʊ-; ES -ˌketə(r

education ˌɛdʒəˈkeʃən, ˌɛdʒʊ-

educational ˌɛdʒəˈkeʃənl̩, ˌɛdʒʊ-, -ʃnəl |-ist
-ɪst |-ly -ɪ

educative ˈɛdʒəˌketɪv, ˈɛdʒʊ-

educe ɪˈdjus, ɪˈdɪus, ɪˈdus, i- |-s -ɪz |-d -t

eductive ɪˈdʌktɪv, i- |-tion -kʃən

Edward ˈɛdwəd; ES ˈɛdwəd; |-s -z |-s's -zɪz

Edwardian, -dean ɛdˈwɔrdɪən; ES ɛdˈwɔədɪən

Edwin ˈɛdwɪn |Edwina ɛdˈwinə, -ˈwɪnə

eel il

eelgrass ˈilˌgræs; E+-ˌgras, -ˌgrɑs

eelpout ˈilˌpaʊt

e'en in

e'er ɛɚ; ES ɛə(r

eerie, -ry ˈɪrɪ, ˈirɪ

ef ɛf

efface ɪˈfes, ɛ- |-faces -ˈfesɪz |-faced -ˈfest

effect əˈfɛkt, ɪˈfɛkt, ɛ- |-fected -ˈfɛktɪd

effective əˈfɛktɪv, ɪ-

effector əˈfɛktə, ɪ-; ES -ˈfɛktə(r

effectual əˈfɛktʃʊəl, -tʃʊl, ɪ- |-ly -ɪ

effectuality əˌfɛktʃʊˈælətɪ, ɪ-

effectuate əˈfɛktʃʊˌet, ɪ- |-ated -ˌetɪd

effeminacy əˈfɛmənəsɪ, ɪ- |-nate -nɪt

efferent ˈɛfərənt

effervesce ˌɛfəˈvɛs; ES ˌɛfəˈvɛs; |-s -ɪz |-d -t
|-cence -n̩s |-cent -n̩t

effete ɛˈfit, ɪ-

efficacious ˌɛfəˈkeʃəs

efficacy ˈɛfəkəsɪ

efficiency əˈfɪʃənsɪ, ɪ-, |-ent -ənt

Effie ˈɛfɪ

effigy ˈɛfədʒɪ

Effingham *US* ˈɛfɪŋˌhæm; *Engd* -ɪŋəm

effloresce ˌɛfloˈrɛs, -flɔ-; S -flo-; |-s -ɪz |-d -t
|-cence -n̩s |-cency -n̩sɪ

effluence ˈɛflʊəns, ˈɛflɪʊəns |-s -ɪz

effluvium ɛˈfluvɪəm, ɪ-, -ˈflɪu- |-via -vɪə

efflux ˈɛflʌks |effluxes ˈɛflʌksɪz

effort ˈɛfət; ES ˈɛfət

effrontery əˈfrʌntərɪ, ɪ-

effulge ɛˈfʌldʒ, ɪ- |-s -ɪz |-d -d |-nce -əns
|-ncy -ənsɪ |-nt -ənt

effuse *adj* ɛˈfjus, ɪ-, -ˈfɪus |-sive -ɪv

effuse *v* ɛˈfjuz, ɪ-, -ˈfɪuz |-s -ɪz |-d -d

effusion əˈfjuʒən, ɪ-, ɛ-, -ˈfɪuʒən

eft ɛft |eftsoon ɛftˈsun |-soons -ˈsunz

e.g. ˈiˈdʒi, ɪgˈzɛmplaɪˈgreʃɪə, fərɪgˈzæmpl̩

egad ɪˈgæd, iˈgæd

egalitarian ɪˌgæləˈtɛrɪən, i-, -ˈter-

Egbert ˈɛgbət; ES ˈɛgbət

Egerton ˈɛdʒətən; ES ˈɛdʒətən

egest iˈdʒɛst |-ed -ɪd

Egeus *myth.* ˈidʒjus, -dʒus, *Shak.* iˈdʒiəs
|-ˈs -ɪz

egg ɛg |egged ɛgd

Eggleston ˈɛgl̩ztən, ˈɛgl̩stən

eggnog ˈɛgˌnɑg, ˈɛgˌnɔg, -ˈnɒg, -ˌnɒg

eggplant ˈɛgˌplænt; E+-ˌplant, -ˌplɑnt

eggshell ˈɛgˌʃɛl

egis ˈidʒɪs |egises ˈidʒɪsɪz

Eglamore ˈɛgləˌmor, -ˌmɔr; ES -ˌmoə(r,
E+-ˌmɔə(r; |-mour -ˌmur; ES -ˌmʊə(r

eglantine ˈɛglənˌtaɪn, -ˌtin

ego ˈigo, ˈɛgo |-ism -ˌɪzəm |-ist -ɪst

egocentric ˌigoˈsɛntrɪk, ˌɛgo-

egotism ˈigəˌtɪzəm, ˈɛg- |-tist -tɪst

egotistic ˌigəˈtɪstɪk, ˌɛg- |-al -l̩ |-ally -l̩ɪ, -ɪklɪ

egregious ɪˈgridʒəs, ɪˈgridʒɪəs

egress *n* ˈigrɛs |egresses ˈigrɛsɪz

egress *v* ɪˈgrɛs, i- |-es -ɪz |-ed -t

egret ˈigrɪt, -grɛt, ˈɛ-

Egypt ˈidʒəpt, ˈidʒɪpt |-ptian ɪˈdʒɪpʃən, i-

Egyptology ˌidʒɪpˈtɑlədʒɪ; ES+-ˈtɒl-

eh e, ɛ *and various other inquiring sounds*

eider ˈaɪdɚ; ES ˈaɪdə(r

Key: See in full §§3–47. bee bi |pity ˈpɪtɪ (§6) |rate ret |yet jɛt |sang sæŋ |angry ˈæŋ·grɪ
|bath bæθ; E baθ (§10) |ah ɑ |far fɑr |watch wɑtʃ, wɒtʃ (§12) |jaw dʒɔ |gorge gɔrdʒ |go go

Eiffel ˈaɪfḷ
eight et |eighth etθ |eighty ˈetɪ |-ieth -ɪɪθ
|-ieths -ɪɪθs
eighteen eˈtin, ˈeˈtin (ˈeighˌteen ˈyears)
eightfold adj, adv ˈetˈfold (ˈeightˌfold ˈloss)
eightpenny ˈetˌpɛnɪ, -pənɪ
eikon, E- ˈaɪkɑn; ES+ˈaɪkɒn
Eileen aɪˈlin (ˈEiˌleen ˈJohnson)
Einstein ˈaɪnstaɪn |-ian aɪnˈstaɪnɪən
Eire ˈɛrə, ˈɛrə |Eireann ˈɛrən, ˈɛrən
eisteddfod eˈstɛðvad, ɛ-, -vɒd
either ˈiðɚ, much less freq. ˈaɪðɚ; ES -ðə(r
ejaculate ɪˈdʒækjəˌlet, iˈdʒækju- |-d -ɪd
ejaculation ɪˌdʒækjəˈleʃən, iˌdʒækju-
ejaculatory ɪˈdʒækjələˌtorɪ, iˈdʒækju-, -ˌtɔrɪ;
S -ˌtorɪ
eject n ˈidʒɛkt
eject v ɪˈdʒɛkt, i- |-jected -ˈdʒɛktɪd
ejecta iˈdʒɛktə
ejection ɪˈdʒɛkʃən, i- |-tment -ˈdʒɛktmənt
eke adv ik
eke v ik |eked ikt
el ɛl
elaborate adj ɪˈlæbərɪt, ə-, -ˈlæbrɪt
elaborate v ɪˈlæbəˌret, ə- |-rated -ˌretɪd
elaboration ɪˌlæbəˈreʃən, ə-
Elaine ɪˈlen, əˈlen
Elam ˈiləm |-ite -ˌaɪt |-itic ˌiləˈmɪtɪk
élan Fr eˈlɑ̃
eland ˈilənd
elapse ɪˈlæps, ə- |-s -ɪz |-d -t
elastic ɪˈlæstɪk, ə- |-ally -ḷɪ, -ɪklɪ
elasticity ɪˌlæsˈtɪsətɪ, ə-, ˌilæsˈtɪsətɪ
elate ɪˈlet, i- |-lated -ˈletɪd
elation ɪˈleʃən, i-
Elba ˈɛlbə
Elbe ɛlb (Ger ˈɛlbə)
Elbert ˈɛlbɚt; ES ˈɛlbət
elbow ˈɛlˌbo |elbowed ˈɛlˌbod
elbowroom ˈɛlboˌrum, -ˌrʊm
eld ɛld
elder ˈɛldɚ; ES ˈɛldə(r
elderberry ˈɛldɚˌbɛrɪ, ˈɛldə-, -bərɪ, -brɪ; ES
ˈɛldə-; The second pron. results from
r-dissimilation (§121).
elderly ˈɛldɚlɪ; ES ˈɛldəlɪ
eldest ˈɛldɪst
Eldora ɛlˈdorə, -ˈdɔrə; S -ˈdorə
El Dorado myth. ˌɛldəˈrado, Ark city -ˈredo

Eldorado Calif ˌɛldəˈrado; Ill, Kas, Mo
ˌɛldəˈredo
eldritch, E- ˈɛldrɪtʃ |Eldritch's ˈɛldrɪtʃɪz
Eleanor ˈɛlənɚ, ˈɛlɪnɚ; ES -nə(r
Eleanora ˌɛləˈnorə, ˌɛlɪə-, -ˈnɔrə; S -ˈnorə
Eleazar, -er ˌɛlɪˈezɚ; ES ˌɛlɪˈezə(r
elecampane ˌɛləkəmˈpen, ˌɛlɪ-
elect ɪˈlɛkt, əˈlɛkt |-lected -ˈlɛktɪd
election ɪˈlɛkʃən, əˈlɛkʃən
electioneer ɪˌlɛkʃənˈɪr, ə-; ES -ˈɪə(r, S+-ˈɛə(r;
|-ed -d
elective ɪˈlɛktɪv, əˈlɛktɪv
elector ɪˈlɛktɚ, ə-; ES -ˈlɛktə(r
electoral ɪˈlɛktərəl, ə- |-ly -ɪ |-rate -rɪt, -trɪt
Electra ɪˈlɛktrə
electress ɪˈlɛktrɪs, ə- |-es -ɪz
electric ɪˈlɛktrɪk, ə- |-al -ḷ |-ally -ḷɪ, -ɪklɪ
electrician ɪˌlɛkˈtrɪʃən, ə-, ˌilɛkˈtrɪʃən
electricity ɪˌlɛkˈtrɪsətɪ, ə-, ˌilɛkˈtrɪsətɪ
electrification ɪˌlɛktrəfəˈkeʃən, ə-
electrify ɪˈlɛktrəˌfaɪ, ə- |-fied -ˌfaɪd
electro ɪˈlɛktro, ə-
electroanalysis ɪˌlɛktroəˈnæləsɪs, ə-
electrochemical ɪˌlɛktroˈkɛmɪkḷ, ə- |-ly -ɪ
electrochemist ɪˌlɛktroˈkɛmɪst, ə- |-ry -rɪ
electrocute ɪˈlɛktrəˌkjut, ə-, -ˌkɪut |-d -ɪd
electrocution ɪˌlɛktrəˈkjuʃən, ə-, -ˈkɪuʃən
electrode ɪˈlɛktrod, ə-
electrodeposit ɪˌlɛktrodɪˈpazɪt, ə-; ES+
-ˈpɒzɪt
electrodynamics ɪˌlɛktrodaɪˈnæmɪks, ə-
electroencephalograph ɪˌlɛktro·ɛnˈsɛfələˌgræf,
ə-; E+-ˌgraf, -ˌgrɑf
electrograph ɪˈlɛktroˌgræf, ə-; E+-af, -ɑf
electrokinetics ɪˌlɛktrokɪˈnɛtɪks, ə-, -kaɪ-
electrolysis ɪˌlɛkˈtraləsɪs, ə-; ES+-ˈtrɒl-
electrolyte ɪˈlɛktrəˌlaɪt, ə-
electrolytic ɪˌlɛktrəˈlɪtɪk, ə-
electrolyze ɪˈlɛktrəˌlaɪz, ə- |-s -ɪz |-d -d
electromagnet ɪˌlɛktroˈmægnɪt, ə-
electromagnetic ɪˌlɛktromægˈnɛtɪk, ə- |-s -s
electromagnetism ɪˌlɛktroˈmægnəˌtɪzəm, ə-
electrometallurgy ɪˌlɛktroˈmɛtḷˌɚdʒɪ, ə-, -mɛ-
ˈtælɚdʒɪ; ES -ˌɜdʒɪ, -ˌɜˈdʒɪ, -ˈtælədʒɪ
electrometer ɪˌlɛkˈtramətɚ, ə-, ˌilɛk-; ES
-ˈtramətə(r, -ˈtrɒmətə(r
electromotive ɪˌlɛktrəˈmotɪv, ə-
electromotor ɪˌlɛktrəˈmotɚ, ə-; ES -ˈmotə(r
electron ɪˈlɛktrɑn, ə-; ES+-trɒn

electroplate ɪˈlɛktrəˌplet, ə- |-d -ɪd
electroscope ɪˈlɛktrəˌskop, ə-
electroscopic ɪˌlɛktrəˈskɑpɪk, ə-; ES+-ˈskɒp-
electrostatic ɪˌlɛktrəˈstætɪk, ə- |-al -l̩ |-ally
  -l̩ɪ, -ɪklɪ
electrotherapeutic ɪˌlɛktroˌθɛrəˈpjutɪk, ə-,
  -ˈpɪu- |-al -l̩
electrotherapy ɪˌlɛktroˈθɛrəpɪ, ə-
electrotype ɪˈlɛktrəˌtaɪp, ə- |-d -t
electrum ɪˈlɛktrəm, ə-
electuary ɪˈlɛktʃuˌɛrɪ, ə-
eleemosynary ˌɛləˈmɑsn̩ˌɛrɪ, ˌɛlɪə-; ES+
  -ˈmɒs-
elegance ˈɛləgəns |-cy -ɪ |-gant -gənt
elegiac ɪˈlidʒɪˌæk, ə-, ˌɛləˈdʒaɪæk, -ək
elegiacal ˌɛləˈdʒaɪəkl̩
elegize ˈɛləˌdʒaɪz |-s -ɪz |-d -d
elegy ˈɛlədʒɪ |-gist -dʒɪst
element ˈɛləmənt
elemental ˌɛləˈmɛntl̩ |-ly -ɪ |-tary -tərɪ, -trɪ
Elena ˈɛlənə
Eleonora ˌɛləˈnorə, ˌɛlɪə-, -ˈnɔrə; S -ˈnorə
elephant ˈɛləfənt |-a ˌɛləˈfæntə
elephantiasis ˌɛləfənˈtaɪəsɪs, -fæn-
elephantine ˌɛləˈfæntin, -taɪn, -tɪn
Eleusinian ˌɛljuˈsɪnɪən
Eleusis ɛˈlusɪs, ə-, -ˈlɪusɪs |-sis' -sɪs
elevate ˈɛləˌvet |-d -ɪd |-tor -ɚ; ES -ə(r
elevation ˌɛləˈveʃən
eleven ɪˈlɛvən, ɪˈlɛvm̩, ə- |-th -ənθ |-ths -ənθs
elf ɛlf |-'s -s |elves ɛlvz |-in -ɪn
elfish ˈɛlfɪʃ, ˈɛlvɪʃ
elflock ˈɛlfˌlɑk; ES+-ˌlɒk
Elfrida ɛlˈfridə
Elgar ˈɛlgɚ; ES ˈɛlgə(r
Elgin US ˈɛldʒɪn; C, Scotl, Lord, marble
  ˈɛlgɪn
Elginshire ˈɛlgɪnˌʃɪr, -ʃɚ; ES -ˌʃɪə(r, -ʃə(r
El Greco ɛlˈgreko, -ˈgrɛko
Eli ˈilaɪ
Elia ˈilɪə
Elias ɪˈlaɪəs |-'s -ɪz
elicit ɪˈlɪsɪt |-ed -ɪd
elide ɪˈlaɪd |-lided -ˈlaɪdɪd
eligibility ˌɛlɪdʒəˈbɪlətɪ
eligible ˈɛlɪdʒəbl̩ |-bly -blɪ
Elihu Bible ɪˈlaɪhju, -hɪu; Am name ˈɛləˌhju,
  -ˌhɪu
Elijah ɪˈlaɪdʒə, ə-

Elimelech ɪˈlɪməˌlɛk, ə-
eliminate ɪˈlɪməˌnet, ə- |-nated -ˌnetɪd
elimination ɪˌlɪməˈneʃən, ə-
Elinor ˈɛlɪnɚ; ES ˈɛlɪnə(r
Eliot ˈɛlɪət, ˈɛljət
Eliphalet ɪˈlɪfəlɪt, ə-
Eliphaz ˈɛləˌfæz |-'s -ɪz
Elis ˈilɪs |-'s -ɪz
Elisabeth ɪˈlɪzəbəθ, ə-—see Elizabeth
Elisha ɪˈlaɪʃə, ə-
elision ɪˈlɪʒən
elite ɪˈlit, eˈlit
elixir ɪˈlɪksɚ; ES ɪˈlɪksə(r
Eliza ɪˈlaɪzə
Elizabeth ɪˈlɪzəbəθ, ə- |-ton -tən |-town
  -ˌtaʊn—spelt with z in the 1611 Bible
Elizabethan ɪˌlɪzəˈbiθən, ə-, -ˈbɛθən, ɪˈlɪzə-
  ˌbɛθən
elk ɛlk
Elkanah ˈɛlkənə, ɛlˈkenə
Elkhart ˈɛlkˌhart; ES -ˌhɑːt, E+-ˌhɑːt
ell ɛl—The n sound was lost from ell (OE eln
  measure) in the same way as from kiln, mill,
  Milne.
Ella ˈɛlə
Ellen ˈɛlɪn, -ən
Ellesmere ˈɛlzmɪr; ES -mɪə(r
Ellice Islands ˈɛlɪsˈaɪləndz, -lənz
Elliott ˈɛlɪət, ˈɛljət
ellipse ɪˈlɪps, ə- |-s -ɪz
ellipsis ɪˈlɪpsɪs, ə- |-pses -psiz
ellipsoid ɪˈlɪpsɔɪd, ə-
ellipsoidal ɪˌlɪpˈsɔɪdl̩, ə-, ˌɛlɪpˈsɔɪdl̩
elliptic ɪˈlɪptɪk, ə- |-al -l̩ |-ally -l̩ɪ, -ɪklɪ
ellipticity ɪˌlɪpˈtɪsətɪ, ə-, ˌɛlɪpˈtɪsətɪ
Ellis ˈɛlɪs |-'s -ɪz
Ellsworth ˈɛlzwɚθ; ES ˈɛlzwəθ
elm ɛlm
Elmer ˈɛlmɚ; ES ˈɛlmə(r
Elmira ɛlˈmaɪrə
Elmo ˈɛlmo
El Modena ˌɛlmoˈdinə
Elmore ˈɛlmor, -mɔr; ES -moə(r, E+-mɔə(r
elocution ˌɛləˈkjuʃən, -ˈkɪu- |-ary -ˌɛrɪ
Elohim ɛˈlohɪm, -him |-hist -hɪst |-hism
  -hɪzəm
Elohistic ˌɛloˈhɪstɪk
eloign, eloin ɪˈlɔɪn |-ed -d
Eloise 'Heloise' ˌeloˈiz, Eng name ˌɛləˈwiz

elongate ɪˈlɔŋget, ɪˈlɒŋ-; S+ɪˈlaŋ-; |-gated
-getɪd

elongation ɪˌlɔŋˈgeʃən, ɪˌlɒŋ-, ˌilɔŋ-, ˌilɒŋ-;
S+-aŋ-

elope ɪˈlop, ə- |-d -t

eloquence ˈɛləkwəns |-quent -kwənt

El Paso ɛlˈpæso

Elphinstone ˈɛlfɪnstən

Elsa ˈɛlsə (Ger ˈɛlzɑ:)

El Salvador ɛlˈsælvəˌdɔr; ES -ˌdɔɔ(r; (Sp
-ˌsalβaˈðɔr)

Elsass Ger ˈɛlzɑs

else ɛls |else's ˈɛlsɪz

El Segundo ˌɛlsəˈgʌndo, -ˈgʊn-

elsewhere ˈɛlsˌhwɛr, -ˌhwær; E -ˌhwɛə(r, ES
-ˌhwæə(r

Elsie ˈɛlsɪ

Elsinore ˈɛlsəˌnor, -ˌnɔr; ES -ˌnoə(r, E+
-ˌnɔə(r; acct+ˌElsiˈnore

Elsmere ˈɛlzmɪr; ES -mɪə(r

Elspeth ˈɛlspəθ

Elsworthy ˈɛlzwɝˈðɪ; ES -wɜˈðɪ, -wɝˈðɪ

Eltham Kent ˈɛltəm, ˈɛlθəm—ˈɛlθəm is a sp.
pron.

elucidate ɪˈlusəˌdet, ɪˈlɪus- |-d -ɪd

elucidation ɪˌlusəˈdeʃən, ɪˌlɪus-

elude ɪˈlud, ɪˈlɪud |-d -ɪd

elusive ɪˈlusɪv, ɪˈlɪusɪv |-sory -sərɪ

elves ɛlvz

Elvira ɛlˈvaɪrə

elvish ˈɛlvɪʃ

Ely ˈilɪ, pers. name+ˈilaɪ, cf Eli

Elyot ˈɛlɪət, ˈɛljət

Elyria ɪˈlɪrɪə, ə-

Elysia ɪˈlɪʒɪə, ɪˈlɪzɪə

Elysian ɪˈlɪʒən, ɪˈlɪʒɪən

Elysium ɪˈlɪʒɪəm, ɪˈlɪzɪəm

elzevir, E- ˈɛlzəvɚ, -ˌvɪr; ES -və(r, -ˌvɪə(r

em ɛm

'em unstressed only əm, after p or b+m (keep
'em ˈkipm̩, mob 'em ˈmɑbm̩)—When unstressed, hem, the native Eng word for 'them,'
lost its h sound just as do he, her, his, him
when unstressed. Hem and hit lost the letter
h also. The mistaken belief that 'em is an
abbreviation of them has led some to avoid it,
but it is in excellent colloquial use.

em- unstressed prefix ɪm-, ɛm——see en-

emaciate ɪˈmeʃɪˌet |-ated -ˌetɪd

emaciation ɪˌmeʃɪˈeʃən, ɪˌmesɪ-

emanate ˈɛməˌnet |-d -ɪd |-tion ˌɛməˈneʃən

emancipate ɪˈmænsəˌpet |-pated -ˌpetɪd

emancipation ɪˌmænsəˈpeʃən

Emanuel ɪˈmænjʊəl, -ˌɛl

emasculate ɪˈmæskjəˌlet |-lated -ˌletɪd

emasculation ɪˌmæskjəˈleʃən

embalm ɪmˈbɑm |-ed -d

embank ɪmˈbæŋk |-ed -t

embar ɛmˈbɑr; ES -ˈbɑ:(r, E+-ˈbɑ:(r; |-red -d

embarcation ˌɛmbɑrˈkeʃən; ES -bɑ:-, E+
-bɑ:-

embargo ɪmˈbɑrgo; ES -ˈbɑ:-, E+-ˈbɑ:-;
|-ed -d

embark ɪmˈbɑrk; ES -ˈbɑ:k, E+-ˈbɑ:k; |-ed -t

embarkation ˌɛmbɑrˈkeʃən; ES -bɑ:-, E+
-bɑ:-

embarrass ɪmˈbærəs, -ɪs |-es -ɪz |-ed -t

embassador ɪmˈbæsədɚ; ES -ˈbæsədə(r

embassage ˈɛmbəsɪdʒ |-s -ɪz |-bassy -bəsɪ

embattle ɛmˈbætl̩ |-d -d |-ling -ˈbætl̩ɪŋ, -tlɪŋ

embay ɛmˈbe |-ed -d

embed ɪmˈbɛd |-ded -ɪd

embellish ɪmˈbɛlɪʃ |-es -ɪz |-ed -t

ember ˈɛmbɚ; ES ˈɛmbə(r

embezzle ɪmˈbɛzl̩ |-ed -d |-ling -ˈbɛzlɪŋ, -zl̩ɪŋ

embitter ɪmˈbɪtɚ; ES -ˈbɪtə(r; |-ed -d

emblaze ɛmˈblez |-s -ɪz |-d -d

emblazon ɛmˈblezn̩ |-ed -d |-ing -zn̩ɪŋ, -znɪŋ

emblem ˈɛmbləm |-ed -d

emblematic ˌɛmbləˈmætɪk |-al -l̩ |-ally -l̩ɪ,
-ɪklɪ

embodiment ɪmˈbadɪmənt; ES+-ˈbɒdɪ-

embody ɪmˈbadɪ; ES+-ˈbɒdɪ; |-ied -d

embolden ɪmˈboldn̩ |-ed -d |-ing -dn̩ɪŋ, -dnɪŋ

embolic ɛmˈbalɪk; ES+-ˈbɒl-

embolism ˈɛmbəˌlɪzəm |-lus -ləs |-li -ˌlaɪ

embonpoint Fr ãbõˈpwæ̃

embosom ɛmˈbuzəm, -ˈbuzəm |-ed -d

emboss ɪmˈbɔs, -ˈbɒs |-es -ɪz |-ed -t

embouchure ˌãmbuˈʃur; ES -ˈʃuə(r; (Fr
ãbuˈʃy:r)

embow ɛmˈbo |-ed -d

embowel ɛmˈbaʊəl, -ˈbaʊl |-ed -d

embower ɛmˈbaʊɚ; ES -ˈbaʊ·ə(r; |-ed -d |-ing
-ˈbaʊərɪŋ, -ˈbaʊrɪŋ

embrace ɪmˈbres |-s -ɪz |-d -t

embraceor ɛmˈbresɚ; ES -ˈbresə(r; |-cery -ɪ

embracer ɪmˈbresɚ; ES -ˈbresə(r

embranchment ɛmˈbræntʃmənt; E+-ˈbrantʃ-, -ˈbrantʃ-

embrasure ɛmˈbreʒɚ; ES -ˈbreʒə(r; |-d -d

embrocate ˈɛmbroˌket |-cated -ˌketɪd

embrocation ˌɛmbroˈkeʃən

embroider ɪmˈbrɔɪdɚ; ES -ˈbrɔɪdə(r; |-ed -d |-ing -dərɪŋ, -drɪŋ |-y -dərɪ, -drɪ

embroil ɛmˈbrɔɪl |-ed -d

embrown ɛmˈbraʊn |-ed -d

embrue ɛmˈbru, -ˈbrɪu |-d -d

embryo ˈɛmbrɪˌo

embryologic ˌɛmbrɪəˈlɑdʒɪk; ES+-ˈlɒdʒ-; |-al -ḷ |-ally -ḷɪ, -ɪklɪ

embryologist ˌɛmbrɪˈɑlədʒɪst; ES+-ˈɒl-; |-gy -dʒɪ

embryonic ˌɛmbrɪˈɑnɪk; ES+-ˈɒn-; |-ally -ḷɪ, -ɪklɪ

Emden ˈɛmdən

emeer əˈmɪr; ES əˈmɪə(r; |-ate -ɪt

Emeline ˈɛməˌlaɪn, -ˌlin

emend ɪˈmɛnd |-ed -ɪd

emendate ˈimənˌdet |-dated -ˌdetɪd

emendation ˌimɛnˈdeʃən, -mən-, ˌɛmən-ˈdeʃən

emendator ˈimənˌdetɚ, ˈɛmən-; ES -ˌdetə(r

emendatory ɪˈmɛndəˌtorɪ, -ˌtɔrɪ; S -ˌtɔrɪ

emerald ˈɛmərəld, ˈɛmrəld

emerge ɪˈmɝdʒ; ES ɪˈmɜdʒ, ɪˈmɝˈdʒ; |-s -ɪz |-d -d

emergence ɪˈmɝdʒəns; ES ɪˈmɜdʒ-, ɪˈmɝˈdʒ-; |-cy -ɪ |-gent -dʒənt

emeritus ɪˈmɛrətəs |-ti -ˌtaɪ

emersed iˈmɝst; ES iˈmɜst, iˈmɝˈst

emersion iˈmɝʃən, -ʒən; ES -ˈmɜ-, -ˈmɝˈ-

Emerson ˈɛmɚsn̩; ES ˈɛməsn̩

emery ˈɛmərɪ, ˈɛmrɪ |-ied -d

emetic ɪˈmɛtɪk |-al -ḷ |-ally -ḷɪ, -ɪklɪ

emigrant ˈɛməgrənt, -ˌgrænt

emigrate ˈɛməˌgret |-d -ɪd |-tion ˌɛməˈgreʃən

émigré ˈɛməˌgre (Fr emiˈgre)

Emil ˈiml̩

Emilia ɪˈmɪlɪə, ɪˈmɪljə

Emily ˈɛml̩ɪ

eminence ˈɛmənəns |-cy -ɪ |-nent -nənt

emir əˈmɪr; ES əˈmɪə(r; |-ate -ɪt

emissary ˈɛməˌsɛrɪ

emission ɪˈmɪʃən

emit ɪˈmɪt |emitted ɪˈmɪtɪd

Emma ˈɛmə

Emmanuel ɪˈmænjʊəl

Emmaus ɛˈmeəs, ˈɛmɪəs |-ˈs -ɪz

Emmeline ˈɛməˌlaɪn, -ˌlin

emmet, E- ˈɛmɪt

Emmetsburg, Emmits- ˈɛmɪtsˌbɝg; ES -ˌbɝg, -ˌbɝˈg

emollient ɪˈmaljənt, -lɪənt; ES+-ˈmɒl-

emolument ɪˈmaljəmənt; ES+-ˈmɒl-

Emory ˈɛmərɪ

emotion ɪˈmoʃən |-al -ḷ, -ʃnəl |-ally -ḷɪ, -ʃnəlɪ

emotionalism ɪˈmoʃənḷˌɪzəm, -ˈmoʃnəlˌɪzəm

emotionality ɪˌmoʃənˈælətɪ

emotionalization ɪˌmoʃənḷəˈzeʃən, -ʃnələ-, -aɪˈz-

emotionalize ɪˈmoʃənḷˌaɪz, -ʃnəl- |-s -ɪz |-d -d

emotive ɪˈmotɪv

empale ɪmˈpel |-d -d

empanel ɪmˈpænḷ |-ed -d

empathic ɛmˈpæθɪk |-ally -ḷɪ, -ɪklɪ

empathy ˈɛmpəθɪ

Empedocles ɛmˈpɛdəˌkliz |-ˈs -ɪz

emperor ˈɛmpərɚ; ES ˈɛmpərə(r

empery ˈɛmpərɪ

emphasis ˈɛmfəsɪs |-phases -fəˌsiz

emphasize ˈɛmfəˌsaɪz |-s -ɪz |-d -d

emphatic ɪmˈfætɪk |-al -ḷ |-ally -ḷɪ, -ɪklɪ

empire ˈɛmpaɪr; ES ˈɛmpaɪə(r

empiric ɛmˈpɪrɪk |-al -ḷ |-ally -ḷɪ, -ɪklɪ

empiricism ɛmˈpɪrəˌsɪzəm |-cist -sɪst

emplacement ɪmˈplesmənt

employ ɪmˈplɔɪ |-ed -d |-ment -mənt

employee, -ye, -yé ɪmˈplɔɪ·i, ˌɛmplɔɪˈi

employer ɪmˈplɔɪɚ, -ˈplɔjɚ; ES -ˈplɔɪ·ə(r, -ˈplɔjə(r

empoison ɛmˈpɔɪzn̩ |-ed -d |-ing -znɪŋ, -znɪŋ

Emporia ɛmˈporɪə, -ˈpɔr-; S -ˈpɔrɪə

emporium ɛmˈporɪəm, -ˈpɔr-; S -ˈpɔrɪəm; |-s -z |-ia -ɪə

empower ɪmˈpaʊɚ; ES -ˈpaʊ·ə(r; |-ed -d |-ing -ˈpaʊrɪŋ, -ˈpaʊərɪŋ

empress ˈɛmprɪs |-es -ɪz

emprise, -ze ɛmˈpraɪz |-s -ɪz

emption ˈɛmpʃən |-al -ḷ

empty ˈɛmptɪ |-ied -d

empurple ɛmˈpɝpḷ; ES -ˈpɝpḷ, -ˈpɝˈpḷ; |-d -d |-ling -plɪŋ, -pl̩ɪŋ

empyema ˌɛmpɪˈimə, -paɪ- |-mata -ˈimətə, -ˈɛmətə

empyreal ɛmˈpɪrɪəl, ˌɛmpəˈriəl, -paɪ-

Key: *See in full §§3–47.* bee bi |pity ˈpɪtɪ (§6) |rate ret |yet jɛt |sang sæŋ |angry ˈæŋ·grɪ |bath bæθ; E baθ (§10) |ah ɑ |far fɑr |watch wɑtʃ, wɒtʃ (§12) |jaw dʒɔ |gorge gɔrdʒ |go go

empyrean ˌɛmpəˈriən, -paɪ-

emu ˈimju, ˈimɪu

emulate adj ˈɛmjəlɪt

emulate v ˈɛmjəˌlet |-lated -ˌletɪd |-tive -ɪv

emulation ˌɛmjəˈleʃən

emulator ˈɛmjəˌletɚ; ES -ˌletə(r

emulous ˈɛmjələs

emulsification ɪˌmʌlsəfəˈkeʃən

emulsify ɪˈmʌlsəˌfaɪ |-fied -ˌfaɪd

emulsion ɪˈmʌlʃən

en ɛn

en- *prefix* ɪn-, ɛn-—*When wholly unstressed in familiar words, pronounced* ɪn-, *sometimes* ən-. *Since words vary in familiarity, and since styles and personal habits vary, many such words are pronounced with either* ɪn- *or* ɛn-. *Observe that many such words are spelt with either* en- *or* in-, *as endorse, indorse. These facts will explain seeming inconsistencies in the pron. of such words in the vocabulary. The same statements apply to the variant em-. In these prefixes,* ɪm-, ɪn- *are heard in more familiar words; cf* ɪmˈbɛzl̩ *with* ɛmˈblezn̩, *or* ɪˈnæml̩ *with* ɛnˈklæsp.

enable ɪnˈebl̩ |-d -d |-ling -ˈeblɪŋ, -ˈebl̩ŋ

enact ɪnˈækt |-ed -ɪd |-ive -ɪv |-ory -ərɪ

enamel ɪˈnæml̩ |-ed -d |-ing -ml̩ŋ, -mlɪŋ

enamor ɪnˈæmɚ; ES -ˈæmə(r; |-ed -d

en bloc ɛnˈblɑk; ES+-ˈblɒk; (*Fr* ɑ̃ˈblɔ̈k)

encage ɛnˈkedʒ |-s -ɪz |-d -d

encamp ɪnˈkæmp |-ed -t |-ment -mənt

encase ɪnˈkes |-s -ɪz |-d -t

encaustic ɛnˈkɔstɪk |-ally -l̩ɪ, -ɪklɪ

enceinte ɛnˈsent (*Fr* ɑ̃ˈsæ̃t)

Enceladus ɛnˈsɛlədəs |-ʼs -ɪz

encephalic ˌɛnsəˈfælɪk

encephalitis ˌɛnsɛfəˈlaɪtɪs, ɛnˌsɛfə-

encephalon ɛnˈsɛfəˌlɑn, -ˌlɒn |-la -lə

enchain ɛnˈtʃen |-chained -ˈtʃend

enchant ɪnˈtʃænt; E+-ˈtʃant, -ˈtʃɑnt; |-ed -ɪd |-ress -rɪs |-resses -rɪsɪz

enchase ɛnˈtʃes |-s -ɪz |-d -t

encircle ɪnˈsɝkl̩; ES -ˈsɜkl̩, -ˈsɝkl̩; |-d -d |-ling -klɪŋ, -kl̩ŋ

Encke ˈɛŋkə

enclasp ɛnˈklæsp; E+-ˈklasp, -ˈklɑsp; |-ed -t

enclave n ˈɛnklev (*Fr* ɑ̃ˈklɑːv)

enclave v ɛnˈklev |-claved -ˈklevd

enclitic ɛnˈklɪtɪk |-al -l̩ |-ally -l̩ɪ, -ɪklɪ

enclose ɪnˈkloz |-s -ɪz |-d -d

enclosure ɪnˈkloʒɚ; ES -ˈkloʒə(r

encomiast ɛnˈkomɪˌæst

encomiastic ɛnˌkomɪˈæstɪk |-al -l̩ |-ally -l̩ɪ, -ɪklɪ

encomium ɛnˈkomɪəm |-s -z |-comia -mɪə

encompass ɪnˈkʌmpəs |-es -ɪz |-ed -t

encore n, v ˈɑŋkor, ˈɑn-, -kɔr; ES -koə(r, E+-kɔə(r; |-d -d—v+enˈcore

encounter ɪnˈkauntɚ; ES -ˈkauntə(r; |-ed -d |-ing -tərɪŋ, -trɪŋ

encourage ɪnˈkɝɪdʒ; ES -ˈkɜr-, -ˈkʌr-, -ˈkɝ-; |-s -ɪz |-d -d

encrimson ɛnˈkrɪmzn̩ |-ed -d

encroach ɪnˈkrotʃ |-es -ɪz |-ed -t

encrust ɪnˈkrʌst |-ed -ɪd

encumber ɪnˈkʌmbɚ; ES -ˈkʌmbə(r; |-ed -d |-ing -bərɪŋ, -brɪŋ

encumbrance ɪnˈkʌmbrəns |-s -ɪz

encyclical ɛnˈsɪklɪkl̩, -ˈsaɪk-

encyclopedia, -paed- ɪnˌsaɪkləˈpidɪə

encyclopedic, -paed- ɪnˌsaɪkləˈpidɪk |-al -l̩ |-ally -l̩ɪ, -ɪklɪ

encyclopedism, -paed- ɪnˌsaɪkləˈpidɪzəm |-ist -ɪst

encyst ɛnˈsɪst |-ed -ɪd

end ɛnd |ended ˈɛndɪd

endanger ɪnˈdendʒɚ; ES -ˈdendʒə(r; |-ed -d |-ing -dʒərɪŋ, -dʒrɪŋ

endear ɪnˈdɪr; ES -ˈdɪə(r, S+-ˈdeə(r, -ˈdjeə(r; |-ed -d

endeavor ɪnˈdɛvɚ; ES -ˈdɛvə(r; |-ed -d |-ing -ˈdɛvərɪŋ, -ˈdɛvrɪŋ

endemic ɛnˈdɛmɪk |-al -l̩ |-ally -l̩ɪ, -ɪklɪ

Enderby ˈɛndɚbɪ; ES ˈɛndəbɪ

endermic ɛnˈdɝmɪk; ES -ˈdɜm-, -ˈdɝm-; |-al -l̩ |-ally -l̩ɪ, -ɪklɪ

Endicott ˈɛndɪˌkɑt, -kət; ES+-ˌkɒt

endive ˈɛndaɪv, ˈɑndiv (*Fr* ɑ̃ˈdiːv)

endlong ˈɛndˌlɔŋ, -ˌlɒŋ; S+-ˌlɑŋ

endmost ˈɛndˌmost, ˈɛnˌmost

endocarditis ˌɛndokɑrˈdaɪtɪs; ES -kɑː-, E+-kɑ:-

endocardium ˌɛndoˈkɑrdɪəm; ES -ˈkɑːd-, E+-ˈkɑːd-

endocarp ˈɛndoˌkɑrp; ES -ˌkɑːp, E+-ˌkɑːp

endocrin ˈɛndoˌkrɪn

endocrine ˈɛndoˌkraɪn |-nal ˌɛndoˈkraɪnl̩

endocrinology ˌɛndokraɪˈnɑlədʒɪ; ES+-ˈnɒl-

|full fʊl |tooth tuθ |further ˈfɝðɚ; ES ˈfɜðə |custom ˈkʌstəm |while hwaɪl |how hau |toy tɔɪ
|using ˈjuzɪŋ |fuse fjuz, fɪuz |dish dɪʃ |vision ˈvɪʒən |Eden ˈidn̩ |cradle ˈkredl̩ |keep ʼem ˈkipm̩

endoderm ˈɛndoˌdɜˑm; ES -ˌdɜm, -ˌdɜˑm
endogamy ɛnˈdɑgəmɪ, -ˈdɒg-
endogenous ɛnˈdɑdʒənəs; ES+-ˈdɒdʒ-
endolymph ˈɛndoˌlɪmf, -ˌlɪmpf
endoparasite ˌɛndoˈpærəˌsaɪt
endoplasm ˈɛndoˌplæzəm
Endor ˈɛndɚ, -dɔr; ES ˈɛndə(r, -dɔə(r
endorse ɪnˈdɔrs; ES -ˈdɔəs; |-s -ɪz |-d -t
endorsee ɪnˌdɔrˈsi, ˌɛndɔrˈsi; ES -ˌdɔə-, -dɔə-
endoscope ˈɛndəˌskop
endothelium ˌɛndoˈθiliəm |-lia -lɪə
endothermic ˌɛndoˈθɜˑmɪk; ES -ˈθɜm-, -ˈθɜˑm-
endow ɪnˈdaʊ |endowed ɪnˈdaʊd
endue ɪnˈdju, -ˈdɪu, -ˈdu |-d -d
endurance ɪnˈdjʊrəns, -ˈdɪʊr-, -ˈdʊr-
endure ɪnˈdjʊr, -ˈdɪʊr, -ˈdʊr; ES -ə(r
endways ˈɛndˌwez |-wise -ˌwaɪz
Endymion ɛnˈdɪmɪən
Eneas ɪˈniəs |-'s -ɪz
Eneid ɪˈniɪd, -əd
enema ˈɛnəmə
enemy ˈɛnəmɪ
energetic ˌɛnɚˈdʒɛtɪk; ES ˌɛnə-; |-al -ļ |-ally
-ļɪ, -ɪklɪ
energize ˈɛnɚˌdʒaɪz; ES ˈɛnə-; |-s -ɪz |-d -d
energy ˈɛnɚdʒɪ; ES ˈɛnədʒɪ
enervate adj ɪˈnɜˑvɪt; ES ɪˈnɜv-, ɪˈnɜˑv-
enervate v ˈɛnɚˌvet; ES ˈɛnə-; |-d -ɪd
enervation ˌɛnɚˈveʃən; ES ˌɛnə-
enfeeble ɪnˈfibļ |-d -d |-ling -blɪŋ, -bļɪŋ
enfeoff ɛnˈfɛf |-ed -t
Enfield ˈɛnfild
enfilade ˌɛnfəˈled |-laded -ˈledɪd
enfold ɪnˈfold |-ed -ɪd
enforce ɪnˈfors, -ˈfɔrs; ES -ˈfoəs, E+-ˈfɔəs;
|-s -ɪz |-d -t |-dly -ɪdlɪ
enfranchise ɛnˈfræntʃaɪz |-s -ɪz |-d -d
enfranchisement ɛnˈfræntʃɪzmənt
engage ɪnˈgedʒ |-s -ɪz |-d -d |-dly -ɪdlɪ
engarland ɛnˈgɑrlənd; ES -ˈgɑːl-, E+-ˈgɑːl-;
|-ed -ɪd
Engedi ɛnˈgɪdaɪ
Engels Ger ˈɛŋəls
engender ɪnˈdʒɛndɚ; ES -ˈdʒɛndə(r; |-ed -d
|-ing -ˈdʒɛndrɪŋ, -ˈdʒɛndərɪŋ
engine ˈɛndʒən |-d -d |-ry -rɪ
engineer ˌɛndʒəˈnɪr; ES -ˈnɪə(r, S+-ˈnɛə(r,
-ˈnjɛə(r; |-ed -d
engird ɛnˈgɜˑd; ES -ˈgɜd, -ˈgɜˑd; |-ed -ɪd

England ˈɪŋglənd |-er -ɚ; ES -ə(r; freq.
ˈɪŋlənd, which many regard as careless
Englefield ˈɛŋgļˌfild
Englewood ˈɛŋgļˌwʊd
English ˈɪŋglɪʃ |-ed -t |-man -mən |-men -mən
|-ry -rɪ |-woman -ˌwʊmən, -ˌwʊ- |-women
-ˌwɪmɪn, -ən—freq. ˈɪŋlɪʃ; see England
engorge ɛnˈgɔrdʒ; ES -ˈgɔədʒ; |-s -ɪz |-d -d
engraft ɛnˈgræft; E+-ˈgraft, -ˈgrɑft; |-ed -ɪd
engrain ɪnˈgren |-ed -d |-edly -ɪdlɪ
engrave ɪnˈgrev |-graved -ˈgrevd
engross ɪnˈgros |-es -ɪz |-ed -t |-edly -ɪdlɪ
engulf ɪnˈgʌlf |-ed -t
enhance ɪnˈhæns; E+-ˈhans, -ˈhɑns; |-s -ɪz
|-d -t
enharmonic ˌɛnhɑrˈmɑnɪk; ES -hɑːˈmɑnɪk,
-ˈmɒn-, E+-hɑː-; |-al -ļ |-ally -ļɪ, -ɪklɪ
Enid ˈinɪd
enigma ɪˈnɪgmə
enigmatic ˌɛnɪgˈmætɪk, ˌi- |-al -ļ |-ally -ļɪ,
-ɪklɪ
enjambment, -bement ɪnˈdʒæmmənt (Fr
ãʒãbˈmã)
enjoin ɪnˈdʒɔɪn |-ed -d
enjoy ɪnˈdʒɔɪ |-ed -d
enkindle ɛnˈkɪndļ |-d -d |-ling -dlɪŋ, -dļɪŋ
enlace ɪnˈles |-s -ɪz |-d -t
enlarge ɪnˈlɑrdʒ; ES -ˈlɑːdʒ, E+-ˈlɑːdʒ; |-s
-ɪz |-d -d |-dly -ɪdlɪ, -dlɪ
enlighten ɪnˈlaɪtṇ |-ed -d |-ing -tṇɪŋ, -tnɪŋ
enlist ɪnˈlɪst |-ed -ɪd
enliven ɪnˈlaɪvən |-ed -d |-ing -vənɪŋ, -vnɪŋ
en masse ɛnˈmæs (Fr ãˈmas)
enmesh ɛnˈmɛʃ |-es -ɪz |-ed -t
enmity ˈɛnmətɪ
ennoble ɪˈnobļ, ɛnˈnobļ |-d -d |-ling -ˈnoblɪŋ,
-ˈnobļɪŋ
ennui ˈɑnwi (Fr ãˈnɥi)
Enobarb ˈinəˌbɑrb, ˈɛnə-; ES -ˌbɑːb, E+
-ˌbɑːb
Enobarbus ˌinəˈbɑrbəs, ˌɛnə-; ES -ˈbɑːb-,
E+-ˈbɑːb-; |-'s -ɪz
Enoch ˈinək
enorm ɪˈnɔrm; ES ɪˈnɔəm
enormous ɪˈnɔrməs; ES ɪˈnɔəməs; |-mity
-mətɪ
Enos ˈinəs |-'s -ɪz
enough əˈnʌf, ɪˈnʌf—after t, d, s, z, often ṇˈʌf
(gʊdṇˈʌf, ðætsṇˈʌf)

enounce i'nauns |-s -ız |-d -t
enow ı'nau
enplane ɛn'plen |-planed -'plend
enquire ın'kwaır; ES -'kwaıə(r; |-d -d |-ry -ı
enrage ın'redʒ |-s -ız |-d -d |-dly -ıdlı, -dlı
enrapture ın'ræptʃɚ; ES -'ræptʃə(r; |-d -d
enravish ɛn'rævıʃ |-es -ız |-ed -t
enregister ɛn'redʒıstɚ; ES -tə(r; |-ed -d |-ing
  -trıŋ, -tərıŋ
enrich ın'rıtʃ |-es -ız |-ed -t
enrobe ɛn'rob |-robed -'robd
enroll, -ol ın'rol |-(l)ed -d
enroot ɛn'rut, -'rut |-ed -ıd
Enroughty ɛn'rautı—'dɑ:bı *is not a pronun-*
  ciation of Enroughty, *but a substitution for*
  it.
en route an'rut (*Fr* ɑ̃'rut)
ensample ɛn'sæmpḷ; E+-'sampḷ, -'sɑmpḷ
ensanguine ɛn'sæŋgwın |-d -d
ensconce ɛn'skɑns; ES+-'skɒns; |-s -ız |-d -t
ensemble an'sambḷ (*Fr* ɑ̃'sɑ̃:bl)
enshade ɛn'ʃed |-shaded -'ʃedıd
enshrine ın'ʃraın |-d -d
enshroud ɛn'ʃraud |-ed -ıd
ensign *n* 'ɛnsaın, *mil.*+'ɛnsn̩
ensign *v* ɛn'saın |-ed -d
ensilage 'ɛnsḷıdʒ
ensile ɛn'saıl, 'ɛnsaıl |-d -d
enslave ın'slev |-slaved -'slevd
ensnare ɛn'snɛr, -'snær; E -'snɛə(r, ES
  -'snæə(r; |-d -d
ensphere ɛn'sfır; ES -'sfıə(r, S+-'sfɛə(r
ensue ɛn'su, -'sıu, -'sju |-d -d
en suite an'swit (*Fr* ɑ̃'sɥit)
ensure ın'ʃur; ES -'ʃuə(r; |-d -d
enswathe ɛn'sweð |-swathed -'sweðd
entablature ɛn'tæblətʃɚ; ES -tʃə(r
entablement ɛn'tebḷmənt
entail ın'tel |-ed -d
entangle ın'tæŋgḷ |-d -d |-ling -glıŋ, -gḷıŋ
entelechy ɛn'tɛləkı
entente an'tant (*Fr* ɑ̃'tɑ̃:t)
enter 'ɛntɚ; ES -tə(r; |-ed -d |-ing -tərıŋ,
  -trıŋ
enteric ɛn'tɛrık |-ritis ˌɛntə'raıtıs
enteron 'ɛntəˌrɑn; ES+-ˌrɒn
enterprise 'ɛntɚˌpraız, 'ɛntə-; ES 'ɛntə-; |-s
  -ız |-d -d—*In the second pron.* ɚ *becomes* ə
  by dissimilation (*§121*).

entertain ˌɛntɚ'ten; ES ˌɛntə-; |-ed -d
enthrall, -al ın'θrɔl |-(l)ed -d
enthrone ın'θron |-d -d
enthronize ɛn'θronaız |-s -ız |-d -d
enthuse ın'θjuz, -'θıuz, -'θuz |-s -ız |-d -d
enthusiasm ın'θjuzıˌæzəm, -'θıuz-, -'θuz-
  |-ast -ˌæst
enthusiastic ınˌθjuzı'æstık, -ˌθıuz-, -ˌθuz- |-al
  -ḷ |-ally -ḷı, -ıklı
enthymeme 'ɛnθəˌmim
entice ın'taıs |-s -ız |-d -t
entire ın'taır; ES -'taıə(r; |-ty -tı ('ɛnˌtire
  'length)
entitle ın'taıtḷ |-d -d |-ling -tḷıŋ, -tlıŋ
entity 'ɛntətı
entoil ɛn'tɔıl |-ed -d
entomb ın'tum |-ed -d |-ment -'tummənt
entomologic ˌɛntəmə'lɑdʒık; ES+-'lɒdʒ-;
  |-al -ḷ |-ally -ḷı, -ıklı
entomologist ˌɛntə'mɑlədʒıst; ES+-'mɒl-;
  |-gy -dʒı
entourage ˌantu'rɑʒ (*Fr* ɑ̃tu'ra:ʒ)
entr'acte an'trækt (*Fr* ɑ̃'trakt)
entrails 'ɛntrəlz
entrain ın'tren |-ed -d
entrance *n* 'ɛntrəns |-s -ız |-trant -trənt
entrance *v* ın'træns; E+-'trans, -'trɑns; |-s
  -ız |-d -t |-dly -ıdlı
entrap ın'træp |-trapped -'træpt
entreasure ɛn'trɛʒɚ; ES -'trɛʒə(r; |-d -d
entreat ın'trit |-ed -ıd |-y -ı
entree 'antre (*Fr* ɑ̃'tre)
entremets 'antrəˌme |*pl* -mets -ˌmez (*Fr*
  ɑ̃trə'mɛ)
entrench ın'trɛntʃ |-es -ız |-ed -t
entre nous *Fr* ɑ̃trə'nu
entrepôt 'antrəˌpo (*Fr* ɑ̃trə'po)
entrepreneur ˌantrəprə'nɝ; ES -'nɜ(r, -'nɝ;
  (*Fr* ɑ̃trəprə'nœ:r)
entropy 'ɛntrəpı
entrust ın'trʌst |-ed -ıd
entry 'ɛntrı
entwine ın'twaın |-d -d
entwist ɛn'twıst |-ed -ıd
enucleate *adj* ı'njuklııt, ı'nıu-, ı'nu-, -ˌet
enucleate *v* ı'njuklıˌet, ı'nıu-, ı'nu- |-d -ıd
enucleation ıˌnjuklı'eʃən, ıˌnıu-, ıˌnu-
enumerate ı'njuməˌret, ı'nıu-, ı'nu- |-d -ıd
enumeration ıˌnjumə'reʃən, ıˌnıu-, ıˌnu-

|full fʊl |tooth tuθ |further 'fɝðɚ; ES 'fɜðə |custom 'kʌstəm |while hwaıl |how hau |toy tɔı
|using 'juzıŋ |fuse fjuz, fıuz |dish dıʃ |vision 'vıʒən |Eden 'idn̩ |cradle 'kredḷ |keep 'em 'kipm̩

enunciate ɪ'nʌnsɪˌet, -ʃɪ- |-d -ɪd
enunciation ɪˌnʌnsɪ'eʃən, ɪˌnʌnʃɪ-
enure ɪn'jʊr; ES ɪn'jʊə(r; |-d -d
envelop n, v ɪn'vɛləp |-ed -t
envelope n 'ɛnvəˌlop, 'an-, ɪn'vɛləp (Fr
  ã'vlɔ̃p)—'anvəˌlop is pseudo-French.
envelopment ɪn'vɛləpmənt
envenom ɛn'vɛnəm |-ed -d
enviable 'ɛnvɪəbl̩ |-bly -blɪ |-vious -vɪəs
environ v ɪn'vaɪrən |-ed -d
environs n ɪn'vaɪrənz, 'ɛnvərənz
envisage ɛn'vɪzɪdʒ |-s -ɪz |-d -d
envision ɛn'vɪʒən |-ed -d
envoy 'postscript' 'ɛnvɔɪ (Fr ã'vwa)
envoy 'messenger' 'ɛnvɔɪ
envy 'ɛnvɪ |-ied -d
enwrap ɛn'ræp |-wrapped -'ræpt
enwreathe ɛn'rið |-d -d
enzym 'ɛnzɪm |-zyme - zaɪm, -zɪm
Eoanthropus ˌioæn'θropəs |-'s -ɪz
Eocene 'iəˌsin
Eohippus ˌio'hɪpəs |-'s -ɪz
Eolia i'oliə |-n -n
Eolis 'iəlɪs |-'s -ɪz |-t -t |-m -ˌlɪzəm
eolith 'iəˌlɪθ |-ths -θs |-ic ˌiə'lɪθɪk
Eolus 'iələs, Vt mt. loc. i'oləs |-'s -ɪz
eon 'iən, 'ian; ES+'iɒn
Eos 'ias; ES+-ɒs; |-'s -ɪz
eosin 'iəˌsɪn
Eothen i'oθɛn
Epaminondas ɛˌpæmə'nandəs; ES+-'nɒn-
eparch 'epark; ES 'epɑːk, E+-aːk
epaulet, -tte 'ɛpəˌlet, 'ɛpəlɪt
epencephalon ˌɛpɛn'sɛfəˌlan, -ˌlɒn
ephah 'ifə
ephedrine, -in ɛ'fɛdrɪn, chem.+'ɛfəˌdrin
ephemera, E- ə'fɛmərə |-s -z |-rae -ˌri
ephemeral ə'fɛmərəl |-ly -ɪ |-rid -rɪd
Ephesian ɪ'fiʒən
Ephesus 'ɛfəsəs, -zəs |-us' -əs
ephod 'ɛfəd, 'i-, -fad; ES+-fɒd
Ephraim 'ifrɪəm |-ite -ˌaɪt
epic 'ɛpɪk |-al -l̩ |-ally -l̩ɪ |-ly -lɪ
epicene 'ɛpəˌsin
epicenter, -tre 'ɛpɪˌsɛntə; ES -ˌsɛntə(r
Epictetus ˌɛpɪk'titəs |-'s -ɪz
epicure 'ɛpɪˌkjur, -ˌkɪur; ES -ə(r
Epicurean ˌɛpɪkju'riən, -kɪu'riən |-ism -ˌɪzəm
epicurism 'ɛpɪkjuˌrɪzəm, -kɪu-

Epicurus ˌɛpɪ'kjurəs, -'kɪurəs |-'s -ɪz
epicycle 'ɛpəˌsaɪkl̩
epicyclic ˌɛpə'saɪklɪk, -'sɪk- |-al -l̩
epidemic ˌɛpə'dɛmɪk |-al -l̩ |-ally -l̩ɪ, -ɪklɪ
epidermic ˌɛpə'dɜmɪk; ES -'dɜm-, -'dɝm-;
  |-al -l̩ |-ally -l̩ɪ, -ɪklɪ
epidermis ˌɛpə'dɜmɪs; ES -'dɜm-, -'dɝm-; ▸
  |-mal -ml̩
epigene 'ɛpəˌdʒin |-genesis ˌɛpə'dʒɛnəsɪs
epiglottal ˌɛpə'glatl̩; ES+-'glɒtl̩
epiglottis ˌɛpə'glatɪs; ES+-'glɒt-; |-es -ɪz
epigram 'ɛpəˌgræm
epigrammatic ˌɛpəgrə'mætɪk |-al -l̩ |-ally -l̩ɪ,
  -ɪklɪ
epigraph 'ɛpəˌgræf; E+-ˌgraf, -ˌgraf
epigraphy ɛ'pɪgrəfɪ
epilepsy 'ɛpəˌlɛpsɪ
epileptic ˌɛpə'lɛptɪk |-al -l̩ |-ally -l̩ɪ, -ɪklɪ
epilogue, -log 'ɛpəˌlɔg, -ˌlɑg, -ˌlɒg |-d, -ged -d
Epimenides ˌɛpə'mɛnəˌdiz |-'s -ɪz
Épinal 'ɛpɪnl̩ (Fr epi'nal)
Epiphany ɪ'pɪfənɪ
epiphyte 'ɛpɪˌfaɪt |-tic ˌɛpɪ'fɪtɪk
Epipsychidion ˌɛpɪsaɪ'kɪdɪən, -sɪ'kɪdɪən
Epirus ɛ'paɪrəs |-'s -ɪz
episcopacy ɪ'pɪskəpəsɪ
episcopal, E- ɪ'pɪskəpl̩ |-ly -ɪ
episcopalian, E- ɪˌpɪskə'peljən, -lɪən
episcopate ɪ'pɪskəpɪt, -ˌpet
episode 'ɛpəˌsod, -ˌzod
episodic ˌɛpə'sadɪk, -'zad-; ES+-ɒd-; |-al -l̩
  |-ally -l̩ɪ, -ɪklɪ
epistemology ɪˌpɪstə'malədʒɪ; ES+-'mɒl-
epistle ɪ'pɪsl̩
epistolary ɪ'pɪstəˌlɛrɪ
epistyle 'ɛpɪˌstaɪl
epitaph 'ɛpəˌtæf; ES+-ˌtaf, -ˌtaf; |-ed -t
epithalamium ˌɛpɪθə'lemɪəm |-s -z |-lamia
  -mɪə
epithelium ˌɛpə'θilɪəm |-s -z |-lia -lɪə
epithet 'ɛpəˌθɛt |-theted -ˌθɛtɪd
epithetic ˌɛpə'θɛtɪk |-al -l̩ |-ally -l̩ɪ, -ɪklɪ
epitome ɪ'pɪtəmɪ
epitomize ɪ'pɪtəˌmaɪz |-s -ɪz |-d -d
epoch 'ɛpək |-al -l̩ |-ally -l̩ɪ—'ipɒk is mainly
  Brit.
epode 'ɛpod
eponym 'ɛpəˌnɪm |-ous ɛ'panəməs; ES+
  -'pɒn-

epos ˈɛpɑs; ES+-ɒs; |-es -ɪz
Epping ˈɛpɪŋ
epsilon ˈɛpsələn, -ˌlɑn, -ˌlɒn, Brit ɛpˈsaɪlən
Epsom ˈɛpsəm
Epworth ˈɛpwɚ·θ; ES ˈɛpwəθ
equable ˈɛkwəbḷ, ˈik- |-bly -blɪ
equal ˈikwəl |-ed -d |-ly -ɪ
equalitarian ɪˌkwɑləˈtɛrɪən, -ˌkwɒl-, -ˈter-
equality ɪˈkwɑlətɪ, ɪˈkwɒl-
equalization ˌikwələˈzeʃən, -aɪˈz-
equalize ˈikwəlˌaɪz |-s -ɪz |-d -d
equanimity ˌikwəˈnɪmətɪ
equate ɪˈkwet |equated ɪˈkwetɪd
equation ɪˈkweʒən, -ʃən |-al -ḷ |-ally -ḷɪ
equator ɪˈkwetɚ; ES ɪˈkwetə(r
equatorial ˌikwəˈtorɪəl, ˌɛk-, -ˈtɔr-; S -ˈtor-;
   |-ly -ɪ
equerry ˈɛkwərɪ
equestrian ɪˈkwɛstrɪən |-ienne ɪˌkwɛstrɪˈɛn
equiangular ˌikwɪˈæŋgjəlɚ; ES -ˈæŋgjələ(r
equidistance ˌikwəˈdɪstəns |-tant -tənt
equilateral ˌikwəˈlætərəl |-ly -ɪ
equilibrant ɪˈkwɪləbrənt
equilibrate ˌikwəˈlaɪbret, ɪˈkwɪləˌbret |-d -ɪd
equilibrist ɪˈkwɪləbrɪst
equilibrium ˌikwəˈlɪbrɪəm |-s -z |-ria -rɪə
equine ˈikwaɪn
equinoctial ˌikwəˈnɑkʃəl; ES+-ˈnɒk-; |-ly -ɪ
equinox ˈikwəˌnɑks; ES+-ˌnɒks; |-es -ɪz
equip ɪˈkwɪp |equipped ɪˈkwɪpt
equipage ˈɛkwəpɪdʒ |-s -ɪz
equipoise ˈɛkwəˌpɔɪz, ˈi- |-s -ɪz |-d -d
equiponderance ˌikwɪˈpɑndərəns; ES+-ˈpɒn-
equiponderate ˌikwɪˈpɑndəˌret; ES+-ˈpɒn-;
   |-d -ɪd
equipotential ˌikwɪpoˈtɛnʃəl
equisetum ˌɛkwəˈsitəm |-s -z |-ta -tə
equitable ˈɛkwɪtəbḷ |-bly -blɪ
equitation ˌɛkwɪˈteʃən
equity ˈɛkwətɪ
equivalence ɪˈkwɪvələns |-cy -ɪ |-lent -lənt
equivocal ɪˈkwɪvəkḷ |-ly -ɪ, -əklɪ
equivocate ɪˈkwɪvəˌket |-cated -ˌketɪd
equivocation ɪˌkwɪvəˈkeʃən
equivoque, -oke ˈɛkwɪˌvok
er intj of hesitation ə, ɜ:, ʌ, ʌ: of various
   lengths. This spelling originated with writers
   who did not sound the r. It is a blunder in
   reading to pronounce it ɚ or ɝ.

-er ending of agent nouns (maker) and the
   comparative degree (slower) -ɚ; ES -ə(r. In
   the vocab. usually omitted when its sound can
   be added directly to that of the head word, as
   make mek, maker ˈmek-ɚ; ES ˈmek-ə(r;
   slow slo, slower ˈslo-ɚ; ES ˈslo-ə(r. When
   -ɚ follows -r-, as in blusterer ˈblʌs·tə·rɚ,
   ˈblʌs·trɚ, or syllabic ḷ or ṇ, as in handler
   ˈhænd·ḷ·ɚ, ˈhænd·lɚ, or fastener ˈfæs·ṇ·ɚ,
   ˈfæs·nɚ, there are usually the same alterna-
   tives as in the addition of -ing in similar
   cases. See also -est.

era ˈɪrə, ˈirə
eradiate iˈrediˌet |-ated -ˌetɪd
eradicable ɪˈrædɪkəbḷ
eradicate ɪˈrædɪˌket |-d -ɪd |-tor -ɚ; ES -ə(r
eradication ɪˌrædɪˈkeʃən
erase ɪˈres |-s -ɪz |-d -t |-r -ɚ; ES -ə(r
Erasmus ɪˈræzməs |-'s -ɪz
Erastus ɪˈræstəs |-'s -ɪz
erasure ɪˈreʒɚ, ɪˈreʃɚ; ES -ə(r
Erath iˈræθ
erbium ˈɝ·bɪəm; ES ˈɝb-, ˈɝ·b-
ere ɛr, ær; ES ɛə(r, æə(r
Erebus ˈɛrəbəs |-'s -ɪz
Erechtheum ˌɛrɪkˈθiəm
Erechtheus ɪˈrɛkθjus, -θɪus |-'s -ɪz
erect ɪˈrɛkt |-ed -ɪd |-ile -ḷ, -ɪl
erectility ɪˌrɛkˈtɪlətɪ, ˌirɛkˈtɪlətɪ
erection ɪˈrɛkʃən
erelong ɛrˈlɒŋ, ær-, -ˈlɔŋ; ES ɛə-, æə-,
   S+-ˈlɑŋ
eremite ˈɛrəˌmaɪt
erenow ɛrˈnaʊ, ær-; ES ɛə-, æə-
Eretria ɪˈritrɪə, ɪˈrɛt- |-n -n
erewhile ɛrˈhwaɪl, ær-; ES ɛə-, æə-
Erewhon ˈɛrəhwən
erg ɝg; ES ɜg, ɝg
ergo ˈɝ·go; ES ˈɝgo, ˈɝ·go; see argal
ergon ˈɝ·gɑn; ES ˈɝgɑn, ˈɝ-, -gɒn
ergosterol ɚˈgɑstəˌrol; ES əˈgɑs-, əˈgɒs-
ergot ˈɝ·gət; ES ˈɝgət, ˈɝ·gət
Eric ˈɛrɪk |-son, -riccson ˈɛrɪksṇ
Erie ˈɪrɪ; S+ˈirɪ
Erin ˈɛrɪn, ˈɪrɪn
Erinys ɪˈrɪnɪs, ɪˈraɪnɪs |-'s -ɪz |pl Erinyes
   ɪˈrɪnɪˌiz
Eris ˈɪrɪs, ˈirɪs, ˈɛrɪs |-'s -ɪz
Eritrea ˌɛrɪˈtriə |-n -n (It eriˈtrɛ:ɑ)

|full fʊl |tooth tuθ |further ˈfɝ·ðɚ; ES ˈfɝ·ðə |custom ˈkʌstəm |while hwaɪl |how haʊ |toy tɔɪ
|using ˈjuzɪŋ |fuse fjuz, fɪuz |dish dɪʃ |vision ˈvɪʒən |Eden ˈidṇ |cradle ˈkredḷ |keep 'em ˈkipm̩

erlking ˈɝlˌkɪŋ; ES ˈɝl-, ˈɜl-—*The pronuncia-*
tion ˈɛrlˌkɪŋ *is a mixture of Ger and Eng.*
The Ger is Erlkönig ˈɛrlˌkønɪx.
Erma ˈɝmə; ES ˈɝmə, ˈɜmə
Ermengarde ˈɝmənˌgard; ES ˈɝmənˌgɑːd,
ˈɜm-
ermine ˈɝmɪn; ES ˈɝmɪn, ˈɜm-; |-d -d
Erminia ɝˈmɪnɪə; ES ɝˈmɪnɪə, ɜ-
erne, ern ɝn; ES ɜn, ɝn
Ernest ˈɝnɪst; ES ˈɝnɪst, ˈɜ-
Ernestine *fem. name* ˈɝnɪsˌtin; ES ˈɝ-, ˈɜ-
Ernestine *adj* ˈɝnɪstɪn; ES ˈɝ-, ˈɜ-
erode ɪˈrod |-d -ɪd
Eroica ɪˈroˑɪkə
Eros ˈɪrɑs, ˈi-, ˈɛ-, -rɒs |-ˈs -ɪz
erosion ɪˈroʒən
erotic ɪˈrɑtɪk; ES+-ˈrɒt-; |-al -l̩ |-ally -l̩ɪ,
-ɪklɪ
eroticism ɪˈrɑtəˌsɪzəm; ES+-ˈrɒt-
Erpingham ˈɝpɪŋˌhæm, ˈɝpɪŋəm; ES ˈɝp-,
ˈɜp-; *in Shak.* ˈErpingˌham
err ɝ; ES ɜ(r, ɝ; |-ed -d
errand ˈɛrənd
errant ˈɛrənt |-ry -rɪ
errata ɪˈretə, ɛ-, -ˈrɑtə
erratic əˈrætɪk |-al -l̩ |-ally -l̩ɪ, -ɪklɪ
erratum ɪˈretəm, ɛ-, -ˈrɑt- |-ta -tə
erring ˈɝrɪŋ; ES ˈɝrɪŋ, ˈɜrɪŋ; *less freq.* ˈɛrɪŋ
erroneous əˈronɪəs, ɛ-
error ˈɛrɚ; ES ˈɛrə(r
ersatz *Ger* ɛrˈzɑts
Erse ɝs; ES ɜs, ɝs
Erskine ˈɝskɪn; ES ˈɜs-, ˈɝs-
erst ɝst; ES ɜst, ɝst; |-while -ˌhwaɪl
eruct ɪˈrʌkt |-ed -ɪd |-ate -et |-ated -etɪd
eructation ɪˌrʌkˈteʃən, ˌirʌk-
erudite ˈɛruˌdaɪt, ˈɛrju-
erudition ˌɛruˈdɪʃən, ˌɛrju-
erupt ɪˈrʌpt |-ed -ɪd |-ption -pʃən
Ervine ˈɝvɪn; ES ˈɝvɪn, ˈɜ-
Erwin ˈɝwɪn; ES ˈɝwɪn, ˈɜ-
erysipelas ˌɛrəˈsɪpləs, ˌɪrə-
erythrocyte ɪˈrɪθroˌsaɪt, ɛ-
-es, -s *ending for pl & poss of nouns, & for 3*
sg pres of verbs. Pron. *-s after voiceless*
consonant sounds except s, ʃ, tʃ (cap-s
kæp-s, Kate's ket-s, chafe-s tʃef-s); *pron.*
z *after vowel & voiced consonant sounds ex-*
cept z, ʒ, dʒ (ball-s bɔl-z, Joe's dʒo-z,

save-s sev-z); *pron.* -ɪz *or* -əz *after the*
voiceless and voiced sibilants s, ʃ, tʃ, z, ʒ, dʒ
(face-s ˈfes-ɪz, Nash's ˈnæʃ-ɪz, catch-es
ˈkætʃ-ɪz, nose-s ˈnoz-ɪz, rouge-s ˈruʒ-ɪz,
George's ˈdʒɔrdʒ-ɪz). *For the variation in*
unstressed vowel between -ɪz *&* -əz, *see fuller*
statement of the same variation at -ed *in the*
vocab., and for full illustration of the ending
-es, -s *see §88.*
Esau ˈisɔ
escadrille ˌɛskəˈdrɪl (*Fr* ɛskaˈdriːj)
escalade ˌɛskəˈled |-laded -ˈledɪd
escalator, E- ˈɛskəˌletɚ; ES -ˌletə(r
escalop, -ll- ɛˈskɑləp, ɛˈskæləp; ES+-ˈskɒl-;
|-ed -t
Escalus ˈɛskələs |-'s -ɪz
Escanes ˈɛskəˌniz |-'s -ɪz
escapade ˈɛskəˌped, ˌɛskəˈped
escape əˈskep, ɪ-, ɛ- |-d -t |-pism -ɪzəm |-pist
-ɪst
escarp ɛˈskɑrp; ES ɛˈskɑːp, E+ɛˈska:p;
|-ed -t
eschatological ˌɛskætəˈlɑdʒɪkl̩; ES+-ˈlɒdʒ-
eschatologist ˌɛskəˈtɑlədʒɪst; ES+-ˈtɒl-; |-gy
-dʒɪ
escheat ɛsˈtʃit |-ed -ɪd |-age -ɪdʒ
eschew ɛsˈtʃu, -ˈtʃɪu |-ed -d |-al -əl
Escorial ɛsˈkorɪəl, -ˈkɔr-; S -ˈkor-; (*Sp*
eskoriˈal)
escort *n* ˈɛskɔrt; ES ˈɛskɔət
escort *v* ɪˈskɔrt; ES ɪˈskɔət; |-ed -ɪd
escritoire ˌɛskrɪˈtwɑr, -ˈtwɔr; ES -ˈtwɑ:(r,
-ˈtwɔə(r; (*Fr* écritoire ekriˈtwaːr)
escrow ˈɛskro, ɛˈskro
esculent ˈɛskjələnt
escutcheon ɪˈskʌtʃən |-ed -d
Esdraelon ˌɛzdrəˈilən, ˌɛs-
Esdras ˈɛzdrəs |-'s -ɪz
-ese *word ending* (Chinese, Burmese) -ˈiz, -ˌiz,
-iz; *in America much less often* -s
esker, -kar ˈɛskɚ; ES ˈɛskə(r
Eskimo ˈɛskəˌmo |-mauan, -moan ˌɛskəˈmoən
Esmeralda ˌɛzməˈrældə
Esmond ˈɛzmənd
esophagus iˈsɑfəgəs; ES+-ˈsɒf-; |-es -ɪz |-gi
-ˌdʒaɪ
Esopus iˈsopəs |-'s -ɪz
esoteric ˌɛsəˈtɛrɪk |-al -l̩ |-ally -l̩ɪ, -ɪklɪ
espalier ɛˈspæljɚ; ES -jə(r; |-ed -d

especial ə'spɛʃəl |-ly -ɪ, -ʃlɪ
esperance 'ɛspərəns |-s -ɪz
Esperanto ˌɛspə'rɑnto, -'rænto
espial ɪ'spaɪəl
espionage 'ɛspɪənɪdʒ, ə'spaɪənɪdʒ (Fr espion-
nage ɛspjŏ'na:ʒ)
esplanade ˌɛsplə'ned
espouse ɪ'spaʊz |-s -ɪz |-d -d |-sal -ḷ
esprit ɛ'spri
esprit de corps ɛ'spridə'kor, -'kɔr; ES -'koə(r,
E+-'kɔə(r; (Fr ɛsprid'kŏ:r)
espy ə'spaɪ |-ied -d
Espy 'ɛspɪ
Esquimau 'ɛskəˌmo |-maux -ˌmo, -ˌmoz
|-mauan ˌɛskə'moən
esquire ə'skwaɪr; ES ə'skwaɪə(r; |-d -d
ess ɛs |esses 'ɛsɪz
-ess fem. ending -ɪs, -əs; if lightly accented,
esp. in verse, sometimes -ɛs. In the vocab.
if only -ɪs is given, it is to be understood that
-əs and -ɛs are also possible. Often omitted
when the pron. can be found by adding -ɪs,
-əs, -ɛs to the head pronunciation.
essay 'composition' 'ɛsɪ, 'ɛse; 'trial' ɛ'se,
'ɛse
essay 'try' ə'se, ɛ'se |-ed -d
esse 'ɛsɪ
Essen 'ɛsṇ
essence 'ɛsṇs |-s -ɪz
Essene 'ɛsin, ɛ'sin
essential ə'sɛnʃəl |-ly -ɪ |-ity əˌsɛnʃɪ'ælətɪ
Essex 'ɛsɪks |-'s -ɪz
-est unstressed superlative & archaic 2 sg pres
ending -ɪst or -əst; if lightly stressed, esp.
in verse, sometimes -ɛst. In the vocab. if
only -ɪst is given, it is to be understood that
many speakers (fewer in the E & S) also
pronounce -əst as in August 'ɔgəst. For the
vowel see also -ed.
establish ə'stæblɪʃ |-es -ɪz |-ed -t
estaminet Fr ɛstami'nɛ
estate ə'stet |-d -ɪd
esteem ə'stim |-ed -d
Estella ɛ'stɛlə |Estelle ɛ'stɛl
ester 'ɛstɚ; ES 'ɛstə(r
Estes 'ɛstɪz |-tes' -tɪz
Esther 'ɛstɚ; ES 'ɛstə(r
esthesia ɛs'θiʒə, -ʒɪə |-thesis -'θisɪs
esthete 'ɛsθit

esthetic ɛs'θɛtɪk |-al -ḷ |-ally -ḷɪ, -ɪklɪ
estheticism ɛs'θɛtəˌsɪzəm |-thetics -'θɛtɪks
Esthonia ɛs'tonɪə, -'θon- |-n -n=Estonia
estimable 'ɛstəməbḷ |-bly -blɪ
estimate n 'ɛstəmɪt, -ˌmet
estimate v 'ɛstəˌmet |-d -ɪd |-tion ˌɛstə'meʃən
estival 'ɛstəvḷ, ɛs'taɪvḷ
estivate 'ɛstəˌvet |-d -ɪd |-tion ˌɛstə'veʃən
Estmere 'ɛstmɪr; ES -mɪə(r, S+-mɛə(r
Estonia ɛs'tonɪə |-n -n
estop ɛ'stɑp; ES+ɛ'stɒp; |-ped -t |-pel -ḷ
estovers ɛ'stovɚz; ES -vəz
estrange ə'strendʒ |-s -ɪz |-d -d |-dness -ɪdnɪs,
-dnɪs
estray ɪ'stre
estreat ɪ'strit |-ed -ɪd
estrous 'ɛstrəs, 'ɪs-
estrum 'ɛstrəm, 'ɪs- |-trus -trəs |-truses
-trəsɪz
estuary 'ɛstʃʊˌɛrɪ |-arial ˌɛstʃu'ɛrɪəl
esurient ɪ'sjʊrɪənt, ɪ'sɪʊr-, ɪ'sʊr-
et 'and' ɛt
-et unstressed word terminal, as in pocket,
tablet, comet, carpet, rivet, etc. -ɪt, -ət.
In the vocab. when only -ɪt is given, it is to
be understood that many speakers (fewer in
the E & S) also pron. -ət as in pilot 'paɪlət.
eta Gk letter 'etə, 'itə
etaoin 'ɛtɪˌɔɪn—cf shrdlu
et cetera ɛt'sɛtərə, -'sɛtrə |-s -z
etch ɛtʃ |etches 'ɛtʃɪz |etched ɛtʃt
eternal ɪ'tɝnḷ; ES ɪ'tɜnḷ, ɪ'tɝnḷ; |-ly -ɪ
eternalize ɪ'tɝnḷˌaɪz; ES ɪ'tɜn-, ɪ'tɝn-; |-s -ɪz
|-d -d
eterne ɪ'tɝn; ES ɪ'tɜn, ɪ'tɝn |-nity -ətɪ
eternization ɪˌtɝnə'zeʃən, -aɪ'z-; ES ɪˌtɜn-,
ɪˌtɝn-
eternize ɪ'tɝnaɪz; ES ɪ'tɜn-, ɪ'tɝn-; |-s -ɪz
|-d -d
Ethan 'iθən
ethane 'ɛθen
Ethel 'ɛθəl
Ethelbald 'ɛθəlˌbɔld
Ethelbert 'ɛθəlbɚt; ES -bət
Ethelberta ˌɛθəl'bɝtə; ES -'bɜtə, -'bɝtə
Ethelred 'ɛθəlˌrɛd |Ethelwulf 'ɛθəlˌwʊlf
ether 'iθɚ; ES 'iθə(r
ethereal ɪ'θɪrɪəl |-ly -ɪ
ethereality ɪˌθɪrɪ'ælətɪ

Etherege ˈɛθərɪdʒ |-ʼs -ɪz
etherization ˌiθərəˈzeʃən, -aɪˈz-
etherize ˈiθəˌraɪz |-s -ɪz |-d -d
ethic ˈɛθɪk |-al -ḷ |-ally -ḷɪ, -ɪklɪ
Ethiop ˈiθɪˌɑp; ES+-ˌɒp
Ethiopia ˌiθɪˈopɪə |-n -n
Ethiopic ˌiθɪˈɑpɪk, -ˈopɪk; ES+-ˈɒp-
ethmoid ˈɛθmɔɪd
ethnic ˈɛθnɪk |-al -ḷ |-ally -ḷɪ, -ɪklɪ
ethnographic ˌɛθnəˈgræfɪk |-al -ḷ |-ally -ḷɪ, -ɪklɪ
ethnography ɛθˈnɑgrəfɪ, -ˈnɒg-
ethnologic ˌɛθnəˈlɑdʒɪk; ES+-ˈlɒdʒ-; |-al -ḷ |-ally -ḷɪ, -ɪklɪ
ethnology ɛθˈnɑlədʒɪ; ES+-ˈnɒl-
ethos ˈiθɑs; ES+-θɒs
ethyl, E- ˈɛθəl, -ɪl
ethylate ˈɛθəˌlet |-lated -ˌletɪd
ethylene ˈɛθəˌlin
ethylic ɪˈθɪlɪk
etiology ˌitɪˈɑlədʒɪ; ES+-ˈɒl-
etiquette ˈɛtɪˌkɛt
Etna, e- ˈɛtnə
Eton ˈitn̩ |-tonian iˈtonɪən
Etruria ɪˈtrʊrɪə |-n -n
Etruscan ɪˈtrʌskən
Ettrick ˈɛtrɪk
étude eˈtjud, eˈtɪud, eˈtud (Fr eˈtyd)
etymologic ˌɛtəməˈlɑdʒɪk; ES+-ˈlɒdʒ-; |-al -ḷ |-ally -ḷɪ, -ɪklɪ
etymologist ˌɛtəˈmɑlədʒɪst; ES+-ˈmɒl-; |-gy -dʒɪ
etymologize ˌɛtəˈmɑləˌdʒaɪz; ES+-ˈmɒl-; |-s -ɪz |-d -d
etymon ˈɛtəˌmɑn, -ˌmɒn |-s -z |-ma -mə
Euboea juˈbiə |-n -n |-boic -ˈboˌɪk
eucalypt ˈjukəˌlɪpt |-ic ˌjukəˈlɪptɪk
eucalyptus, E- ˌjukəˈlɪptəs |-es -ɪz |-ti -taɪ
Eucharist ˈjukərɪst
Eucharistic ˌjukəˈrɪstɪk |-al -ḷ |-ally -ḷɪ, -ɪklɪ
euchre ˈjukɚ; ES ˈjukə(r; |-d -d |-ring -kərɪŋ, -krɪŋ
Euclid ˈjuklɪd |-ean juˈklɪdɪən
eudaemon, -dem- juˈdimən |-monia ˌjudɪˈmonɪə
eudiometer ˌjudɪˈɑmətɚ; ES -ˈɑmətə(r, -ˈɒm-
eudiometric ˌjudɪəˈmɛtrɪk |-al -ḷ |-ally -ḷɪ, -ɪklɪ
Eudora juˈdorə, -ˈdɔrə; S -ˈdorə

Euganean ˌjugəˈniən, juˈgenɪən
Eugene juˈdʒin |-nia -ɪə |-nius -ɪəs |-nius's -ɪəsɪz
eugenic juˈdʒɛnɪk |-al -ḷ |-ally -ḷɪ, -ɪklɪ
Eugénie Fr øʒeˈni
eugenism ˈjudʒəˌnɪzəm |-nist -nɪst
Eulalia juˈlelɪə, -ljə
eulogia juˈlodʒɪə |-giae -dʒɪˌi
eulogist ˈjulədʒɪst |-gy -dʒɪ
eulogistic ˌjuləˈdʒɪstɪk |-al -ḷ |-ally -ḷɪ, -ɪklɪ
eulogize ˈjuləˌdʒaɪz |-s -ɪz |-d -d
Eumenides juˈmɛnəˌdiz
Eunice ˈjunɪs |-ʼs -ɪz
eunuch ˈjunək
eupepsia juˈpɛpʃə, -ʃɪə |-ptic -tɪk
Euphemia juˈfimɪə
euphemism ˈjufəˌmɪzəm |-mist -mɪst
euphemistic ˌjufəˈmɪstɪk |-al -ḷ |-ally -ḷɪ, -ɪklɪ
euphonic juˈfɑnɪk; ES+-ˈfɒn-; |-al -ḷ |-ally -ḷɪ, -ɪklɪ
euphony ˈjufənɪ |-phonious juˈfonɪəs
Euphorbia, e- juˈfɔrbɪə; ES -ˈfɔəb-
Euphrates juˈfretiz, in Shak. ˈjufrəˌtiz |-tesʼ -tiz
Euphronius juˈfronɪəs |-ʼs -ɪz
Euphrosyne juˈfrɑsəˌni, -ˈfrɒs-
Euphues ˈjufjuˌiz |-ʼs -ɪz
euphuism ˈjufjuˌɪzəm |-ist -ɪst
euphuistic ˌjufjuˈɪstɪk |-al -ḷ |-ally -ḷɪ, -ɪklɪ
Eurasia juˈreʒə, -ˈreʃə |-n -n
Eureka, e- juˈrikə
eurhythmic juˈrɪðmɪk |-al -ḷ |-my -mɪ
Euripedes juˈrɪpəˌdiz |-ʼs -ɪz
Euroclydon juˈrɑklɪˌdan; ES+-ˈrɒklɪˌdɒn
Europa juˈropə
Europe ˈjʊrəp |-an ˌjurəˈpiən
europium juˈropɪəm
Eurus ˈjʊrəs |-ʼs -ɪz
Eurydice juˈrɪdəˌsi
eurythmic juˈrɪðmɪk |-al -ḷ |-my -mɪ
Eusebius juˈsibɪəs |-ʼs -ɪz
Eustace ˈjustɪs, -təs |-ʼs -ɪz
Eustachian juˈstekɪən, -ʃɪən, -ʃən
Eustis ˈjustɪs |-ʼs -ɪz
Euston ˈjustən
Eutaw ˈjutɔ
eutectic juˈtɛktɪk
Euterpe juˈtɝpɪ; ES -ˈtɜpɪ, -ˈtɝpɪ

Key: See in full §§3–47. bee **bi** |pity ˈpɪtɪ (§6) |rate ret |yet jɛt |sang sæŋ |angry ˈæŋ·grɪ |bath bæθ; E baθ (§10) |ah ɑ |far fɑr |watch wɑtʃ, wɒtʃ (§12) |jaw dʒɔ |gorge gɔrdʒ |go go

euthanasia ˌjuθə'neʒə, -ʒɪə
euthenics ju'θɛnɪks |-ist 'juθənɪst
euxenite 'juksə͵naɪt
Euxine 'juksɪn, -aɪn
Eva 'ivə, 'ɛvə
evacuant ɪ'vækjʊənt
evacuate ɪ'vækju͵et |-d -ɪd |-tion ɪ͵vækju-
'eʃən
evacuee ɪ'vækju͵i, ɪ͵vækju'i, -'e (Fr eva'kɥe)
evadable, -ible ɪ'vedəb̦
evade ɪ'ved |evaded ɪ'vedɪd
evaluate ɪ'vælju͵et |-d -ɪd |-tion ɪ͵vælju'eʃən
Evan 'ɛvən
Evander ɪ'vændɚ; ES ɪ'vændə(r
evanesce ͵ɛvə'nɛs |-s -ɪz |-d -t
evanescence ͵ɛvə'nɛsn̩s |-cy -ɪ |-ent -n̩t
evangel ɪ'vændʒəl
evangelic ͵ivæn'dʒɛlɪk, ͵ɛvən- |-al -l̩ |-ally
-l̩ɪ, -ɪklɪ
Evangeline ɪ'vændʒə͵lin, -lɪn, -͵laɪn
evangelism ɪ'vændʒə͵lɪzəm |-list -lɪst
evangelistic ɪ͵vændʒə'lɪstɪk |-ally -l̩ɪ, -ɪklɪ
evangelize ɪ'vændʒə͵laɪz |-s -ɪz |-d -d
evanish ɪ'vænɪʃ |-es -ɪz |-ed -t
Evans 'ɛvənz |-'s -ɪz |-ville -͵vɪl
Evanston 'ɛvən·stən, 'ɛvənz·tən
evaporability ɪ͵væpərə'bɪlətɪ
evaporable ɪ'væpərəb̦, -prəb̦
evaporate ɪ'væpə͵ret |-rated -͵retɪd
evaporation ɪ͵væpə'reʃən
Evarts 'ɛvɚts; ES 'ɛvəts; |-'s -ɪz
evasion ɪ'veʒən |-sive -sɪv
eve iv
Eve iv
Eveleth 'ɛvəlɪθ
Evelina ͵ɛvə'laɪnə, -'linə
Eveline 'ɛvə͵laɪn, -lɪn, 'ɛvlɪn
Evelyn 'ɛvəlɪn, 'ɛvlɪn, 'ivlɪn
even 'ivən |-fall -͵fɔl
evener 'ivnɚ, 'ivənɚ; ES -nə(r
evenhanded 'ivən'hændɪd ('even͵handed 'justice)
evening 'ivnɪŋ
evenness 'ivənnɪs
evensong 'ivən͵sɔŋ, -͵sɒŋ; S+-͵sɑŋ
event ɪ'vɛnt
eventide 'ivən͵taɪd
eventual ɪ'vɛntʃʊəl |-ly -ɪ, ɪ'vɛntʃʊlɪ
eventuality ɪ͵vɛntʃʊ'ælətɪ

eventuate ɪ'vɛntʃʊ͵et |-ated -͵etɪd
ever 'ɛvɚ; ES 'ɛvə(r
Everest 'ɛvrɪst, 'ɛvərɪst
Everett, -itt 'ɛvrɪt, 'ɛvərɪt
everglade, E- 'ɛvɚ͵gled; ES 'ɛvə͵gled
evergreen 'ɛvɚ͵grin; ES 'ɛvə͵grin
everlasting ͵ɛvɚ'læstɪŋ; ES ͵ɛvə-, E+-'last-,
-'lɑst-; ('ever͵lasting 'whip͵cord)
evermore ͵ɛvɚ'mor, -'mɔr; ES -'moə(r,
E+-'mɔə(r
eversion ɪ'vɝʃən, -ʒən; ES ɪ'vɜ-, ɪ'vɜ-
evert ɪ'vɝt; ES ɪ'vɜt, ɪ'vɜt; |-ed -ɪd
every 'ɛvrɪ, 'ɛvərɪ
everybody 'ɛvrɪ͵bɑdɪ, -͵bʌdɪ, -bədɪ; ES+
-͵bɒdɪ
everyday 'ɛvrɪ'de ('every͵day 'clothes)
Everyman 'ɛvrɪ͵mæn
everyone 'ɛvrɪ͵wʌn, -wən
everything 'ɛvrɪ͵θɪŋ
everywhere 'ɛvrɪ͵hwɛr, -͵hwær; E -͵hwɛə(r,
ES -͵hwæə(r
Evesham 'ivʃəm, 'ivzəm, loc.+'iʃəm, 'isəm
evict ɪ'vɪkt |-ed -ɪd |-ction ɪ'vɪkʃən
evidence 'ɛvədəns |-s -ɪz |-d -t |-dent -dənt
evidential ͵ɛvə'dɛnʃəl |-ly -ɪ
evidently 'ɛvədəntlɪ, -dɛntlɪ, sometimes if
emphatic ͵ɛvə'dɛntlɪ
evil 'iv̦, formal, esp. in church,+'ivɪl |-ly -ɪ,
'ivlɪ
evince ɪ'vɪns |-s -ɪz |-d -t
eviscerate ɪ'vɪsə͵ret |-rated -͵retɪd
evisceration ɪ͵vɪsə'reʃən
evocable 'ɛvəkəb̦ |-cation ͵ɛvo'keʃən
evocative ɪ'vɑkətɪv, ɪ'vok-; ES+-'vɒk-
evoke ɪ'vok |evoked ɪ'vokt
evolute n, adj, v 'ɛvə͵lut, -͵lɪut |-d -ɪd
evolution ͵ɛvə'luʃən, -'lɪu-, ͵ɛvl̩'juʃən |-ary
-͵ɛrɪ
evolve ɪ'vɑlv, ɪ'vɒlv |-d -d
Ewart 'juɚt; ES 'ju·ət
ewe ju, jo—The historical variant jo is still
common among sheep breeders both in England and America.
Ewen 'juɪn, -ən
ewer 'juɚ; ES 'ju·ə(r
Ewers 'juɚz, jurz; ES 'ju·əz, juəz; |-'s -ɪz
Ewing 'juɪŋ
ex ɛks |exes 'ɛksɪz
ex- prefix. When quite unaccented, the vowel

|full fʊl |tooth tuθ |further 'fɝðɚ; ES 'fɝðə |custom 'kʌstəm |while hwaɪl |how haʊ |toy tɔɪ
|using 'juzɪŋ |fuse fjuz, fɪuz |dish dɪʃ |vision 'vɪʒən |Eden 'idn̩ |cradle 'kred̦ |keep 'em 'kipm̩

is usually ɪ in current speech, less freq. ə or ɛ, of the two ə being more likely in rapid speech & ɛ in careful. In the vocab. when only ɪ is given, it is to be understood that ə or ɛ may also occur.

exacerbate ɪg'zæsə‚bet, ɪk'sæs-; ES -æsə-; |-d -ɪd

exacerbation ɪg‚zæsə'beʃən, ɪk‚sæs-; ES -æsə-

exact ɪg'zækt |-ed -ɪd |-ction -kʃən

exactitude ɪg'zæktə‚tjud, -‚tɪud, -‚tud

exactly ɪg'zæktlɪ, ɪg'zæklɪ

exaggerate ɪg'zædʒə‚ret |-d -ɪd |-tive -ɪv

exaggeration ɪg‚zædʒə'reʃən

exalt ɪg'zɔlt |-ed -ɪd |-ation ‚ɛgzɔl'teʃən

exam ɪg'zæm |-ination ɪg‚zæmə'neʃən

examine ɪg'zæmɪn |-d -d |-nee ɪg‚zæmə'ni

example ɪg'zæmpļ; E+-'zam-, -'zɑm-; |-d -d |-ling -plɪŋ, -pļɪŋ

exanimate *adj* ɪg'zænəmɪt, -‚met

exanimate *v* ɪg'zænə‚met |-mated -‚metɪd

exarch 'ɛksɑrk; ES 'ɛksɑ:k, E+-a:k

exasperate ɪg'zæspə‚ret |-reted -‚retɪd

exasperation ɪg‚zæspə'reʃən

Excalibur ɛks'kæləbə‧; ES -bə(r

ex cathedra ‚ɛkskə'θidrə, ɛks'kæθɪdrə

excavate 'ɛkskə‚vet |-d -ɪd |-tor -ə‧; ES -ə(r

excavation ‚ɛkskə'veʃən

exceed ɪk'sid |-ed -ɪd

excel ɪk'sɛl |-celled -'sɛld

excellence 'ɛksļəns |-cy -ɪ |-ent -ənt

excelsior ɪk'sɛlsɪə‧; ES -'sɛlsɪ·ə(r

except ɪk'sɛpt |-ed -ɪd |-ption -'sɛpʃən

exceptionable ɪk'sɛpʃənəbļ, -ʃnəbļ |-bly -blɪ

exceptional ɪk'sɛpʃənļ, -ʃnəl |-ly -ɪ

excerpt *n* 'ɛksɝpt; ES -sɝpt, -sɝpt

excerpt *v* ɪk'sɝpt; ES -'sɝpt, -'sɝpt; |-ed -ɪd |-ption -pʃən

excess ɪk'sɛs |-es -ɪz |-ed -t ('ɛk‚sɛs 'ret)

exchange ɪks'tʃendʒ |-s -ɪz |-d -d

exchangeability ɪks‚tʃendʒə'bɪlətɪ

exchangeable ɪks'tʃendʒəbļ |-bly -blɪ

exchequer ɪks'tʃɛkə‧, 'ɛkstʃɛkə‧; ES -kə(r

excise *n* ɪk'saɪz ('ex‚cise 'duty)

excise *v* ɪk'saɪz |-s -ɪz |-d -d

excision ɪk'sɪʒən

excitability ɪk‚saɪtə'bɪlətɪ

excitable ɪk'saɪtəbļ

excitation ‚ɛksaɪ'teʃən

excitatory ɪk'saɪtə‚torɪ, -‚torɪ; S -‚torɪ

excite ɪk'saɪt |-cited -'saɪtɪd

exclaim ɪk'sklem |-ed -d

exclamation ‚ɛksklə'meʃən

exclamatory ɪk'sklæmə‚torɪ, -‚torɪ; S -‚torɪ

exclave 'ɛksklev

exclude ɪk'sklud, -'sklɪud |-d -ɪd

exclusion ɪk'skluʒən, -'sklɪu- |-sive -sɪv

excogitate ɛks'kɑdʒə‚tet; ES+-'kɒdʒ-; |-d -ɪd

excogitation ɛks‚kɑdʒə'teʃən; ES+-‚kɒdʒ-

excommunicable ‚ɛkskə'mjunɪkəbļ, -'mɪun-

excommunicate ‚ɛkskə'mjunə‚ket, -'mɪun- |-d -ɪd

excommunication ‚ɛkskə‚mjunə'keʃən, -‚mɪun-

excoriate ɪk'skorɪ‚et, -'skɔr-; S -'skor-; |-d -ɪd

excoriation ɪk‚skorɪ'eʃən, ‚ɛkskorɪ-, -kɔr-; S -kor-

excrement 'ɛkskrɪmənt

excremental ‚ɛkskrɪ'mɛntļ |-tary -tərɪ

excrescence ɪk'skrɛsņs |-cy -ɪ |-scent -sņt

excreta ɛk'skritə |-tal -tļ

excrete ɪk'skrit |-d -ɪd |-tion -'skriʃən

excretory 'ɛkskrɪ‚torɪ, -‚torɪ; S -‚torɪ

excruciate ɪk'skruʃɪ‚et, -'skrɪu- |-d -ɪd

excruciation ɪk‚skruʃɪ'eʃən, -‚skrɪu-, -sɪ-

exculpate 'ɛkskʌl‚pet, ɪk'skʌlpet |-d -ɪd

exculpation ‚ɛkskʌl'peʃən

exculpatory ɪk'skʌlpə‚torɪ, -‚torɪ; S -‚torɪ

excursion ɪk'skɝʒən, -ʃən; ES -'skɝ-, -'skɝ-; |-sive -sɪv

excursus ɛk'skɝsəs; ES -'skɝs-, -'skɝs-; |-es -ɪz

excusability ɪk‚skjuzə'bɪlətɪ, -‚skɪuz-

excusable ɪk'skjuzəbļ, -'skɪuz- |-bly -blɪ

excusatory ɪk'skjuzə‚torɪ, -'skɪuz-, -‚torɪ; S -‚torɪ

excuse *n* ɪk'skjus, -'skɪus |-s -ɪz

excuse *v* ɪk'skjuz, -'skɪuz |-s -ɪz |-d -d

Exe ɛks |-'s -ɪz

execrable 'ɛksɪkrəbļ |-bly -blɪ

execrate 'ɛksɪ‚kret |-crated -‚kretɪd

execration ‚ɛksɪ'kreʃən

execratory 'ɛksɪkrə‚torɪ, -‚torɪ, -‚kretərɪ; S -‚torɪ, -‚kretərɪ

executable 'ɛksɪ‚kjutəbļ, -‚kɪut-, ɪg'zɛkjutəbļ

executant ɪg'zɛkjutənt

execute 'ɛksɪ‚kjut, -‚kɪut |-d -ɪd

execution ‚ɛksɪ'kjuʃən, -'kɪu-

Key: *See in full §§3–47.* bee **bi** |pity **'pɪtɪ** (§6) |rate **ret** |yet **jɛt** |sang **sæŋ** |angry **'æŋ·grɪ** |bath **bæθ**; E **baθ** (§10) |ah **ɑ** |far **fɑr** |watch **wɑtʃ, wɒtʃ** (§12) |jaw **dʒɔ** |gorge **gɔrdʒ** |go **go**

executive ɪɡˈzɛkjʊtɪv
executor *'performer'* ˈɛksɪˌkjutɚ, -ˌkɪu-, *law* ɪɡˈzɛkjətɚ; ES -tə(r
executory ɪɡˈzɛkjəˌtorɪ, -ˌtɔrɪ; S -ˌtorɪ
executrix ɪɡˈzɛkjətrɪks |-es -ɪz |*L pl* -trices ɪɡˌzɛkjəˈtraɪsiz
exegesis ˌɛksəˈdʒɪsɪs |-geses -ˈdʒisiz
exegetic ˌɛksəˈdʒɛtɪk |-al -l̩ |-ally -l̩ɪ, -ɪklɪ
exemplar ɪɡˈzɛmplɚ; ES -ˈzɛmplə(r; |-y -ɪ
exemplification ɪɡˌzɛmpləfəˈkeʃən
exemplify ɪɡˈzɛmpləˌfaɪ |-fied -ˌfaɪd
exempli gratia ɪɡˈzɛmplaɪˈɡreʃɪə
exempt ɪɡˈzɛmpt |-ed -ɪd |-ption -pʃən
exequatur ˌɛksɪˈkwetɚ; ES -ˈkwetə(r
exequy ˈɛksɪkwɪ |-quies -kwɪz
exercise ˈɛksɚˌsaɪz; ES ˈɛksɚ-; |-s -ɪz |-d -d
exercitation ɪɡˌzɜˈsɪˈteʃən; ES -ˌzɜ-, -ˌzɜˈ-
exert ɪɡˈzɜt; ES -ˈzɜt, -ˈzɜt; |-ed -ɪd
exertion ɪɡˈzɜʃən; ES -ˈzɜʃ-, -ˈzɜʃ-
Exeter ˈɛksɪtɚ; ES ˈɛksɪtə(r
exeunt ˈɛksɪənt, ˈɛksɪˌʌnt
exhalant ɛksˈhelənt, ɪɡˈzelənt
exhalation ˌɛksəˈleʃən, ˌɛɡzə-
exhale ɛksˈhel, ɪɡˈzel |-d -d
exhaust ɪɡˈzɔst |-ed -ɪd |-ion -stʃən |-ive -ɪv
exhibit ɪɡˈzɪbɪt |-ed -ɪd
exhibition ˌɛksəˈbɪʃən |-ism -ˌɪzəm |-ist -ɪst
exhibitive ɪɡˈzɪbɪtɪv
exhibitory ɪɡˈzɪbəˌtorɪ, -ˌtɔrɪ; S -ˌtorɪ
exhilarate ɪɡˈzɪləˌret |-d -ɪd |-rant -rənt
exhilaration ɪɡˌzɪləˈreʃən
exhort ɪɡˈzɔrt; ES -ˈzɔət; |-ed -ɪd
exhortation ˌɛɡzɚˈteʃən, ˌɛksɚ-, -ɔrˈteʃən; ES ˌɛɡzɚ-, ˌɛksɚ-, -ɔəˈteʃən
exhume ɪɡˈzjum, ɪkˈsjum, -ɪum, -um |-d -d
exigence ˈɛksədʒəns |-cy -ɪ |-gent -dʒənt
exiguity ˌɛksəˈɡjuətɪ, -ˈɡɪu-
exiguous ɪɡˈzɪɡjʊəs, ɪkˈsɪɡ-
exile *n* ˈɛɡzaɪl, ˈɛksaɪl
exile *v* ˈɛɡzaɪl, ˈɛksaɪl, ɪɡˈzaɪl |-d -d
exist ɪɡˈzɪst |-ed -ɪd |-ence -əns |-ent -ənt
exit ˈɛɡzɪt, ˈɛksɪt |-ed -ɪd
ex libris ɛksˈlaɪbrɪs
Exmoor ˈɛksˌmʊr; ES -ˌmʊə(r
Exmouth ˈɛksˌmaʊθ, ˈɛksməθ
exodontia ˌɛksəˈdɑnʃə, -ʃɪə; ES+-ˈdɒn-
exodus, E- ˈɛksədəs |-es -ɪz
ex officio ˌɛksəˈfɪʃɪˌo

exonerate ɪɡˈzɑnəˌret; ES+-ˈzɒn-; |-d -ɪd
exorable ˈɛksərəbl̩
exorbitance ɪɡˈzɔrbətəns; ES -ˈzɔəb-; |-nt -nt
exorcise, -ze ˈɛksɔrˌsaɪz; ES ˈɛksɔə-; |-s -ɪz |-d -d |-cism -ˌsɪzəm
exordium ɪɡˈzɔrdɪəm, ɪkˈs-; ES -ɔəd-; |-s -z |-ia -ɪə
exoskeleton ˌɛksoˈskɛlətn̩ |-tal -tl̩
exoteric ˌɛksəˈtɛrɪk |-al -l̩ |-ally -l̩ɪ, -ɪklɪ
exotic ɪɡˈzɑtɪk; ES+-ˈzɒt-; |-ally -l̩ɪ, -ɪklɪ
expand ɪkˈspænd |-ed -ɪd
expanse ɪkˈspæns |-s -ɪz |-sion -ʃən |-sive -ɪv
expansibility ɪkˌspænsəˈbɪlətɪ
expansible ɪkˈspænsəbl̩ |-bly -blɪ
expansile ɪkˈspænsl̩, -sɪl
ex parte ɛksˈpɑrtɪ; ES -ˈpɑːtɪ, E+-ˈpaːtɪ
expatiate ɪkˈspeʃɪˌet |-d -ɪd
expatiation ɪkˌspeʃɪˈeʃən
expatriate *adj* ɛksˈpetrɪɪt, -ˌet
expatriate *v* ɛksˈpetrɪˌet |-d -ɪd
expatriation ɛksˌpetrɪˈeʃən, ˌɛkspetrɪ-
expect ɪkˈspɛkt |-ed -ɪd
expectance ɪkˈspɛktəns |-cy -ɪ |-ant -ənt
expectation ˌɛkspɛkˈteʃən
expectorant ɪkˈspɛktərənt
expectorate ɪkˈspɛktəˌret |-rated -ˌretɪd
expectoration ɪkˌspɛktəˈreʃən
expedience ɪkˈspidɪəns |-cy -ɪ |-ent -ənt
expedite ˈɛkspɪˌdaɪt |-dited -ˌdaɪtɪd
expedition ˌɛkspɪˈdɪʃən |-ary -ˌɛrɪ |-tious -ʃəs
expel ɪkˈspɛl |-led -d |-lant, -lent -ənt
expend ɪkˈspɛnd |-ed -ɪd
expenditure ɪkˈspɛndɪtʃɚ, -ˌtʃʊr; ES -tʃə(r, -ˌtʃʊə(r
expense ɪkˈspɛns |-s -ɪz |-sive -ɪv
experience ɪkˈspɪrɪəns; S+-ˈspɛr-; |-s -ɪz |-d -t
experiential ɪkˌspɪrɪˈɛnʃəl; S+-ˌspɛr-; |-ly -ɪ
experiment ɪkˈspɛrəmənt
experimental ɪkˌspɛrəˈmɛntl̩, ˌɛkspɛrə- |-ly -ɪ |-ism -ˌɪzəm |-ist -ɪst
experimentation ɪkˌspɛrəmɛnˈteʃən, -mən-
expert *n* ˈɛkspɜt; ES -spɜt, -spɜt
expert *adj* ɪkˈspɜt, ˈɛkspɜt; ES -pɜt, -pɜt (ˈexˌpert ˈworkman)
expert *v* ɪkˈspɜt; ES -ˈspɜt, -ˈspɜt; |-ed -ɪd
expiable ˈɛkspɪəbl̩
expiate ˈɛkspɪˌet |-d -ɪd |-tion ˌɛkspɪˈeʃən
expiatory ˈɛkspɪəˌtorɪ, -ˌtɔrɪ; S -ˌtorɪ

|full fʊl |tooth tuθ |further ˈfɜˈðɚ; ES ˈfɜðə |custom ˈkʌstəm |while hwaɪl |how haʊ |toy tɔɪ |using ˈjuzɪŋ |fuse fjuz, fɪuz |dish dɪʃ |vision ˈvɪʒən |Eden ˈidn̩ |cradle ˈkredl̩ |keep 'em ˈkipm̩

expiration ˌɛkspəˈreʃən
expiratory ɪkˈspaɪrəˌtorɪ, -ˌtɔrɪ; S -ˌtorɪ
expire ɪkˈspaɪr; ES -ˈspaɪə(r; |-d -d
expiry ɪkˈspaɪrɪ, ˈɛkspərɪ
explain ɪkˈsplen |-ed -d
explanation ˌɛkspləˈneʃən
explanatory ɪkˈsplænəˌtorɪ, -ˌtɔrɪ; S -ˌtorɪ
expletive ˈɛksplɪtɪv
explicable ˈɛksplɪkəbl̩, less freq. ɪkˈsplɪkəbl̩—
cf inexplicable
explicate ˈɛksplɪˌket |-d -ɪd |-tive -ɪv
explication ˌɛksplɪˈkeʃən
explicatory ˈɛksplɪkəˌtorɪ, -ˌtɔrɪ; S -ˌtorɪ;
Brit ˈɛksplɪˌketərɪ, ɪksˈplɪkətərɪ, -trɪ
explicit 'here ends' ˈɛksplɪsɪt
explicit 'precise' ɪkˈsplɪsɪt
explode ɪkˈsplod |-d -ɪd
exploit n ˈɛksplɔɪt, ɪkˈsplɔɪt
exploit v ɪkˈsplɔɪt |-ed -ɪd
exploitation ˌɛksplɔɪˈteʃən
exploration ˌɛkspləˈreʃən, -splo-
exploratory ɪkˈsplorəˌtorɪ, -ˈsplɔrəˌtɔrɪ; S
ɪkˈsplorəˌtorɪ
explore ɪkˈsplor, -ˈsplɔr; ES ɪkˈsploə(r, E+
-ˈsplɔə(r; |-d -d
explosion ɪkˈsploʒən |-sive -sɪv
exponent ɪkˈsponənt
exponential ˌɛkspoˈnɛnʃəl |-ly -ɪ
export n ˈɛksport, -pɔrt; ES -poət, E+-pɔət
export v ɪksˈport, -ˈpɔrt; ES ɪksˈpoət, E+
-ˈpɔət; |-ed -ɪd—acct+ˈexport, esp. in con-
trast to import v.
exportation ˌɛksporˈteʃən, -pɔr-; ES -poə-,
E+-pɔə-
expose ɪkˈspoz |-s -ɪz |-d -d |-dness -ɪdnɪs,
-dnɪs
exposé ˌɛkspoˈze
exposition ˌɛkspəˈzɪʃən
expositor ɪkˈspazɪtɚ; ES ɪkˈspazɪtə(r, -ˈspɒz-;
|-tory -ˌtorɪ, -ˌtɔrɪ; S -ˌtorɪ
ex post facto ˈɛksˌpostˈfækto
expostulate ɪkˈspastʃəˌlet; ES+-ˈspɒs-; |-d
-ɪd
expostulation ɪkˌspastʃəˈleʃən; ES+-ˌspɒs-
expostulatory ɪkˈspastʃələˌtorɪ, -ˌtɔrɪ; S
-ˌtorɪ, ES+-ˈspɒs-
exposure ɪkˈspoʒɚ; ES -ˈspoʒə(r
expound ɪkˈspaund |-ed -ɪd
ex-president ˈɛksˈprɛzədənt, -ˈprɛzdənt

express ɪkˈsprɛs |-es -ɪz |-ed -t |-ive -ɪv
expressible ɪkˈsprɛsəbl̩ |-bly -blɪ
expression ɪkˈsprɛʃən |-ism -ˌɪzəm |-ist -ɪst
expressionistic ɪkˌsprɛʃənˈɪstɪk
expressman ɪkˈsprɛsmən |-men -mən
expropriate ɛksˈproprɪˌet |-d -ɪd
expropriation ɛksˌproprɪˈeʃən, ˌɛkspropri-
expulsion ɪkˈspʌlʃən |-sive -sɪv
expunction ɪkˈspʌŋkʃən
expunge ɪkˈspʌndʒ |-s -ɪz |-d -d
expurgate adj ˈɛkspɚˌgɪt, -ˌget; ES -pə-
expurgate v ˈɛkspɚˌget, ɪkˈspɚˈget; ES
ˈɛkspə-, -ˈspɜ-, -ˈspɜ-; |-d -ɪd
expurgation ˌɛkspɚˈgeʃən; ES ˌɛkspə-
expurgatory ɪkˈspɚgəˌtorɪ, -ˌtɔrɪ; ES ɪk-
ˈspɜgəˌtorɪ, -ˈspɜ-, E+-ˌtɔrɪ
exquisite ˈɛkskwɪzɪt, less freq. ɪkˈskwɪzɪt
exscind ɛkˈsɪnd |-ed -ɪd
exsect ɛkˈsɛkt |-ed -ɪd
exsert ɛkˈsɜt; ES -ˈsɜt, -ˈsɜt; |-ed -ɪd
ex-service ˈɛksˈsɜvɪs; ES -ˈsɜv-, -ˈsɜv-
exsiccate ˈɛksɪˌket |-d -ɪd
exsufflicate adj ɛksˈsʌflɪˌket, -kɪt
extant ɪkˈstænt, ˈɛkstənt
extemporal ɪkˈstɛmpərəl |-ly -ɪ
extemporaneity ɪkˌstɛmpərəˈniətɪ
extemporaneous ɪkˌstɛmpəˈreniəs
extemporary ɪkˈstɛmpəˌrɛrɪ |-rarily -rəlɪ, esp.
if emph. ɪkˌstɛmpəˈrɛrəlɪ
extempore ɪkˈstɛmpərɪ, -ˌrɪ
extemporize ɪkˈstɛmpəˌraɪz |-s -ɪz |-d -d
extend ɪkˈstɛnd |-ed -ɪd
extensibility ɪkˌstɛnsəˈbɪlətɪ
extensible ɪkˈstɛnsəbl̩
extensile ɪkˈstɛnsl̩, -sɪl
extensimeter ˌɛkstɛnˈsɪmətɚ; ES -ˈsɪmətə(r
extension ɪkˈstɛnʃən |-sive -sɪv
extensometer ˌɛkstɛnˈsɑmətɚ; ES -ˈsɑmətə(r,
-ˈsɒm-
extensor ɪkˈstɛnsɚ, as L -sɔr; ES -sə(r,
-sɔə(r
extent ɪkˈstɛnt
extenuate ɪkˈstɛnjuˌet |-d -ɪd |-tive -ɪv
extenuation ɪkˌstɛnjuˈeʃən
extenuatory ɪkˈstɛnjuəˌtorɪ, -ˌtɔrɪ-; S -ˌtorɪ
exterior ɪkˈstɪrɪɚ; ES -ˈstɪrɪ·ə(r
exteriorize ɪkˈstɪrɪəˌraɪz |-s -ɪz |-d -d
exterminable ɪkˈstɜmɪnəbl̩; ES -ˈstɜm-,
-ˈstɜm-

Key: See in full §§3–47. bee bi |pity ˈpɪtɪ (§6) |rate ret |yet jɛt |sang sæŋ |angry ˈæŋ·grɪ
|bath bæθ; E baθ (§10) |ah ɑ |far fɑr |watch wɑtʃ, wɒtʃ (§12) |jaw dʒɔ |gorge gɔrdʒ |go go

exterminate ɪk'stɝməˌnet; ES -'stɝm-,
-'stɝ·m-; |-d -ɪd |-tor -ɚ; ES -ə(r
extermination ɪkˌstɝmə'neʃən; ES -ˌstɝm-,
-ˌstɝ·m-
external ɪk'stɝn̩|; ES -'stɜn̩, -'stɝ·n̩|; |-ly -ɪ
externality ˌɛkstɚ'nælətɪ; ES ˌɛkstɚ-
exterritorial ˌɛkstɛrə'torɪəl, -'tɔr-; S -'tor-;
|-ly -ɪ
exterritoriality ɛksˌtɛrəˌtorɪ'ælətɪ, ˌɛkstɛrə-,
-ˌtɔr-; S -ˌtor-
extinct ɪk'stɪŋkt |-ction -'stɪŋkʃən
extinguish ɪk'stɪŋgwɪʃ |-es -ɪz |-ed -t
extirpate 'ɛkstɚˌpet, ɪk'stɝpet; ES -stə-,
-'stɜ-, -'stɝ·-; |-d -ɪd
extirpation ˌɛkstɚ'peʃən; ES ˌɛkstə-
extol, -ll ɪk'stɑl, -'stɒl, -'stol |-(l)ed -d
Exton 'ɛkstən
extort ɪk'stɔrt; ES -'stɔət; |-ed -ɪd
extortion ɪk'stɔrʃən; ES -'stɔəʃən; |-ary -ˌɛrɪ
|-ate -ɪt
extra 'ɛkstrə—'ɛkstrɪ *is often heard from educated speakers, esp. before a vowel* (extra
allowance).
extract *n* 'ɛkstrækt
extract *v* ɪk'strækt |-ed -ɪd |-ction -kʃən
extractable, -ible ɪk'stræktəb|
extracurricular ˌɛkstrəkə'rɪkjələ; ES -lə(r
extraditable 'ɛkstrəˌdaɪtəb|
extradite 'ɛkstrəˌdaɪt |-dited -ˌdaɪtɪd
extradition ˌɛkstrə'dɪʃən
extrados ɛk'stredɑs; ES+-dɒs; |-es -ɪz
extrajudicial ˌɛkstrədʒu'dɪʃəl, -dʒɪu- |-ly -ɪ
extralegal ˌɛkstrə'lig| |-ly -ɪ
extramarital ˌɛkstrə'mærət| |-ly -ɪ
extramundane ˌɛkstrə'mʌnden
extramural ˌɛkstrə'mjʊrəl, -'mɪu- |-ly -ɪ
extraneous ɪk'strenɪəs
extraofficial ˌɛkstrɪə'fɪʃəl, ˌɛkstrə·ə'fɪʃəl
extraordinarily ɪk'strɔrdn̩ˌɛrəlɪ, *esp. if emph.*
ɪkˌstrɔrdn̩'ɛrəlɪ; ES -ɔədn̩-
extraordinary ɪk'strɔrdn̩ˌɛrɪ, *envoy* ˌɛkstrə-
'ɔrdn̩ˌɛrɪ, -trɪ-; ES -ɔədn̩-
extraterritorial ˌɛkstrəˌtɛrə'torɪəl, -'tɔr-; S
-'tor-; |-ly -ɪ
extraterritoriality ˌɛkstrəˌtɛrəˌtorɪ'ælətɪ, -ˌtɔr-;
S -ˌtor-
extravagance ɪk'strævəgəns |-cy -ɪ |-ant -ənt
extravaganza ɪkˌstrævə'gænzə
extravert *n* 'ɛkstrəˌvɝt; ES -ˌvɝt, -ˌvɝt

extravert *v* ˌɛkstrə'vɝt; ES -'vɝt, -'vɝt; |-ed
-ɪd
extreme ɪk'strim (the 'exˌtreme 'verge)
extremism ɪk'strimɪzəm |-ist -ɪst
extremity ɪk'strɛmətɪ
extricable 'ɛkstrɪkəb| |-bly -blɪ
extricate 'ɛkstrɪˌket |-cated -ˌketɪd
extrication ˌɛkstrɪ'keʃən
extrinsic ɛk'strɪnsɪk |-al -| |-ally -|ɪ, -ɪklɪ
extrorse ɛk'strɔrs; ES -'strɔəs
extroversion ˌɛkstro'vɝʃən, -'vɝʒ-; ES -'vɝ-,
-'vɝ-
extrovert *n* 'ɛkstroˌvɝt; ES -ˌvɝt, -ˌvɝt
extrovert *v* ˌɛkstro'vɝt; ES -'vɝt, -'vɝt; |-ed
-ɪd
extrude ɪk'strud, -'strɪud |-d -ɪd
extrusion ɪk'struʒən, -'strɪu- |-sive -sɪv
exuberance ɪg'zjubərəns, -'zɪu-, -'zu- |-cy -ɪ
|-ant -ənt
exude ɪg'zjud, -'zɪud, -'zud, ɪk'sjud, -'sɪud,
-'sud |-d -ɪd |exudation ˌɛksju'deʃən
exult ɪg'zʌlt |-ed -ɪd |-ant -n̩t
exultation ˌɛgzʌl'teʃən, ˌɛksʌl-
-ey *ending see* -y
eyas 'aɪəs |-es -ɪz
Eyck, van væn'aɪk
eye aɪ |eyed aɪd |-ful -ˌfʊl |-fuls -ˌfʊlz
eyeglass 'aɪˌglæs; E+-ˌglas, -ˌglɑs; |-es -ɪz
eyehole 'aɪˌhol
eyelash 'aɪˌlæʃ |-es -ɪz
eyeless 'aɪlɪs
eyelet 'aɪlɪt |-ed -ɪd |-lid 'aɪˌlɪd
eye-minded 'aɪ'maɪndɪd ('eye-ˌminded 'man)
eye-opener 'aɪˌopənɚ, -ˌopnɚ; ES -nə(r
eyeservant 'aɪˌsɝvənt; ES -ˌsɝv-, -ˌsɝv-
eyeservice 'aɪˌsɝvɪs; ES -ˌsɝv-, -ˌsɝv-
eyeshot 'aɪˌʃɑt; ES+-ˌʃɒt
eyesight 'aɪˌsaɪt
eyesore 'aɪˌsor, -ˌsɔr; ES -ˌsoə(r, E+-ˌsɔə(r
eyestrain 'aɪˌstren
eyetooth 'aɪ'tuθ, -ˌtuθ |-teeth -'tiθ, -ˌtiθ
eyewash 'aɪˌwɑʃ, -ˌwɔʃ, -ˌwɒʃ |-es -ɪz
eyewater 'aɪˌwɔtɚ, -ˌwɑtɚ, -ˌwɒtɚ; ES -tə(r
eyewitness 'aɪ'wɪtnɪs, -ˌwɪt- |-es -ɪz |-ed -t
eyne *'eyes'* aɪn
eyre, E- ɛr, ær; E ɛə(r, ES æə(r
eyrie, -ry 'ɛrɪ, 'ærɪ, 'ɪrɪ; S 'ærɪ, 'ɪrɪ
Ezekiel ɪ'zikɪəl, -kjəl
Ezra 'ɛzrə

F

F, f *letter* ɛf |*pl* F's, Fs, *poss* F's ɛfs
fa *music* fɑ
Faber *Eng name* ˈfebɚ, *Ger name* ˈfɑbɚ; ES
-bə(r
Fabian ˈfebɪən |-ism -ˌɪzəm |-ist -ɪst
Fabius ˈfebɪəs |-'s -ɪz
fable ˈfebḷ |-d -d |-ling ˈfeblɪŋ, -bḷɪŋ
Fabre ˈfɑbɚ, ˈfɑbrə; ES -bə(r, -brə; (*Fr* fabr)
fabric ˈfæbrɪk |-ation ˌfæbrɪˈkeʃən
fabricate ˈfæbrɪˌket |-d -ɪd |-tor -ɚ; ES -ə(r
Fabrikoid ˈfæbrɪˌkɔɪd
fabulous ˈfæbjələs
Fabyan ˈfebɪən
façade fəˈsɑd, fæˈsɑd |-d -ɪd (*Fr* faˈsad)
face fes |faces ˈfesɪz |faced fest
facet ˈfæsɪt |-ed -ɪd
facetiae fəˈsiʃɪˌi
facetious fəˈsiʃəs
facial ˈfeʃəl |-ly -ɪ
facile ˈfæsḷ, -sɪl
facilely ˈfæsḷɪ, -sḷlɪ, -sɪlɪ, -sɪllɪ
facilitate fəˈsɪləˌtet |-tated -ˌtetɪd
facilitation fəˌsɪləˈteʃən
facility fəˈsɪlətɪ
facing ˈfesɪŋ
facsimile fækˈsɪməlɪ, -ˈsɪməˌli |-s -z
fact fækt |facts fækts, fæks
faction ˈfækʃən |-tious -ʃəs
factitious fækˈtɪʃəs
factitive ˈfæktətɪv
factor ˈfæktɚ; ES ˈfæktə(r; |-ed -d |-ing
ˈfæktərɪŋ, ˈfæktrɪŋ
factorial fækˈtorɪəl, -ˈtɔrɪəl; S -ˈtorɪəl
factory ˈfæktrɪ, ˈfæktərɪ
factotum fækˈtotəm
factual ˈfæktʃʊəl |-ly -ɪ
facultative ˈfækḷˌtetɪv
faculty ˈfækḷtɪ
fad fæd |faddish ˈfædɪʃ |faddist ˈfædɪst
fade fed |faded ˈfedɪd
faeces ˈfisɪz
faerie, -ry, F- ˈfeərɪ, ˈfɛrɪ, ˈfeːrɪ, ˈfærɪ; S
ˈfeərɪ, ˈfærɪ, ˈfɛrɪ—*Some speakers distinguish* faerie & fairy *from* ferry *by a longer*
ɛ.
Faeroes ˈferoz, ˈfæroz, ˈferoz; S ˈfæroz, ˈferoz
Fafnir ˈfɑvnɪr, ˈfɑf-, -nɚ; ES -nɪə(r, -nə(r

fag fæg |fagged fægd
Fagin ˈfegɪn
fagot, fagg- ˈfægət |-ed -ɪd
Fahrenheit ˈfærənˌhaɪt, ˈfɑrən-
faience faɪˈɑns, feˈɑns (*Fr* faˈjɑ̃:s)
fail fel |failed feld |-ure -jɚ; ES -jə(r
fain fen
faineant ˈfenɪənt, -njənt (*Fr* feneˈɑ̃)
faint fent |fainted ˈfentɪd
fainthearted ˈfentˈhɑrtɪd; ES -ˈhɑːtɪd, E+
-ˈhaːt-; (ˈfaintˌhearted ˈhero)
fair fɛr, fær; E fɛə(r, ES fæə(r; |-ed -d |-er -ɚ;
ES -ə(r
Fairfax ˈfɛrˌfæks, ˈfær-; E ˈfɛə-, ES ˈfæə-;
|-fax's -ˌfæksɪz
Fair Haven, Fairhaven ˈfɛrˈhevən, ˈfær-; E
ˈfɛə-, ES ˈfæə-
fair-lead ˈfɛrˌlid, ˈfær-; E ˈfɛə-, ES ˈfæə-
fair-minded ˈfɛrˈmaɪndɪd, ˈfær-; E ˈfɛə-, ES
ˈfæə-
Fairport ˈfɛrˌport, ˈfær-, -ˌpɔrt; E ˈfɛəˌpoət,
ˈfæə-, -ˌpɔət; S ˈfæəˌpoət
fair-spoken ˈfɛrˈspokən, ˈfær-; E ˈfɛə-, ES
ˈfæə-; (ˈfair-ˌspoken ˈman)
Fairview ˈfɛrˌvju, ˈfær-, -ˌvɪu; E ˈfɛə-, ES
ˈfæə-
fairway ˈfɛrˌwe, ˈfær-; E ˈfɛə-, ES ˈfæə-
Fairweather ˈfɛrˌwɛðɚ, ˈfær-; E ˈfɛəˌwɛðə(r,
ES ˈfæə-
fairy ˈfɛrɪ, ˈfeːrɪ, ˈfærɪ; S ˈfærɪ, ˈfɛrɪ; |-land
-ˌlænd—*see note at* faerie
fait accompli *Fr* fɛtakõˈpli
faith feθ |-ths -θs |-ful -fəl |-fully -fəlɪ
Faiyum faɪˈjum
fake fek |faked fekt |faker ˈfekɚ; ES ˈfekə(r
fakir fəˈkɪr, ˈfekɚ; ES fəˈkɪə(r, ˈfekə(r
Falangist fəˈlændʒɪst
falchion ˈfɔltʃən, ˈfɔlʃən
falcon ˈfɔlkən, *esp. among falconers* ˈfɔkən
Falconbridge ˈfɔkənˌbrɪdʒ, ˈfɔlkən- |-'s -ɪz
Falconer ˈfɔknɚ, ˈfɔlkənɚ; ES -nə(r
falderal ˈfældəˌræl—*see* folderol
Falernian fəˈlɝnɪən, fæ-; ES -ˈlɜn-, -ˈlɝn-
Falkirk ˈfɔlkɝk, ˈfɔk-; ES -kɜk, -kɝk
Falkland ˈfɔklənd, ˈfɔlklənd
Falkner ˈfɔknɚ; ES ˈfɔknə(r
fall fɔl |fell fɛl |fallen ˈfɔlən, fɔln

Words below that have æ *before* r (carry ˈkærɪ) *are often pronounced in* N *with* ɛ (ˈkɛrɪ, *§94*)
Words below in which a *before* r (farm) *is sounded* ɑ *are often pronounced in* E *with* a (faːm)

fallacy ˈfæləsɪ |-lacious fəˈleʃəs
fallibility ˌfæləˈbɪlətɪ
fallible ˈfæləbḷ |fallibly ˈfæləblɪ
Falloden ˈfælədn̩
Fallon ˈfælən
Fallopian fəˈlopɪən, fæ-
fallow ˈfælo, ˈfælə |-ed -d |-ing ˈfæləwɪŋ
Falmouth ˈfælməθ
false fɔls |falsed fɔlst
falsehearted ˈfɔlsˈhɑrtɪd; ES ˈfɔlsˈhɑːtɪd;
   (ˈfalseˌhearted ˈknave)
falsehood ˈfɔls·hʊd
falsetto fɔlˈsɛto, -ˈsɛtə
falsification ˌfɔlsəfəˈkeʃən
falsify ˈfɔlsəˌfaɪ |falsified ˈfɔlsəˌfaɪd
falsity ˈfɔlsətɪ
Falstaff ˈfɔlstæf; E+-staf, -staf
Falstaffian fɔlˈstæfɪən; E+-ˈstaf-, -ˈstɑf-
falter ˈfɔltɚ; ES ˈfɔltə(r; |-ed -d |-ing ˈfɔltərɪŋ
   ˈfɔltrɪŋ
fame fem |famed femd |famous ˈfeməs
familiar fəˈmɪljɚ; ES fəˈmɪljə(r
familiarity fəˌmɪlɪˈærətɪ, fəˌmɪljɪˈærətɪ, fə-
   ˌmɪlˈjærətɪ
familiarize fəˈmɪljəˌraɪz |-s -ɪz |-d -d
family ˈfæmlɪ, ˈfæməlɪ
famine ˈfæmɪn
famish ˈfæmɪʃ |famishes ˈfæmɪʃɪz |-ed -t
fan fæn |fanned fænd
fanatic fəˈnætɪk |-al -ḷ |-ally -ḷɪ, -ɪklɪ
fanaticism fəˈnætəˌsɪzəm
fanciful ˈfænsɪfəl |-ly -ɪ
fancy ˈfænsɪ |fancied ˈfænsɪd
fancy-free ˈfænsɪˈfri (ˈfancy-ˌfree ˈmaiden)
fandango fænˈdæŋgo
fane fen
Faneuil ˈfænḷ, ˈfænjəl, -juəl, *older* ˈfʌnḷ
fanfare ˈfænˌfɛr, -ˌfær; E -ˌfɛə(r, ES -ˌfæə(r
fanfaron ˈfænfəˌrɑn; ES+-ˌrɒn
fanfaronade ˌfænfərəˈned, -færə-
fang fæŋ |fanged fæŋd
fangle ˈfæŋgḷ |fangled ˈfæŋgḷd
fanlight ˈfænˌlaɪt |-ed -ɪd
fanner ˈfænɚ; ES ˈfænə(r
fantail ˈfænˌtel |fantailed ˈfænˌteld
fan-tan ˈfænˌtæn
fantasia fænˈteʒɪə, -ʒə, -zɪə (*It* ˌfantaˈziːa)

fantasm ˈfæntæzəm
fantastic fænˈtæstɪk |-al -ḷ |-ally -ḷɪ, -ɪklɪ
fantasy ˈfæntəsɪ, ˈfæntəzɪ |-ied -d
far fɑr; ES fɑː(r
farad ˈfærəd, ˈfæræd
Faraday, f- ˈfærədɪ, ˈfærəˌde
faradic fəˈrædɪk, fæˈrædɪk
faraway *adj, n* ˈfɑrəˈwe (ˈfaraˌway ˈlook)
farce fɑrs; ES fɑːs; |-s -ɪz |-d -t
farcical ˈfɑrsɪkḷ; ES ˈfɑːsɪkḷ; |-ly -ɪ, -ɪklɪ
fardle ˈfɑrdḷ; ES ˈfɑːdḷ
fare fɛr, fær; E fɛə(r, ES fæə(r; |-ed -d
farewell *intj* ˈfɛrˈwɛl, ˈfær-; ES *see* fare
farewell *n* ˌfɛrˈwɛl, ˌfær-; ES *see* fare; (ˈfare-
   ˌwell ˈspeech)
farfetched ˈfɑrˈfɛtʃt; ES ˈfɑː-; (ˈfarˌfetched
   ˈpun)
far-flung ˈfɑrˈflʌŋ; ES ˈfɑːˈflʌŋ
far-forth ˈfɑrˌforθ, -ˌfɔrθ; ES ˈfɑːˌfoəθ, E+
   -ˌfɔəθ; *acct varies*
Fargo ˈfɑrgo; ES ˈfɑːgo
Faribault ˈfɛrəˌbo, ˈfærəˌbo; S ˈfærəˌbo
farina fəˈrinə, -ˈraɪnə |-naceous ˌfærəˈneʃəs
farinose ˈfærəˌnos
farm fɑrm; ES fɑːm; |-ed -d |-er -ɚ; ES -ə(r
farmer-general ˈfɑrmɚˈdʒɛnərəl, -ˈdʒɛnrəl;
   ES ˈfɑːmə-
farmhouse ˈfɑrmˌhaʊs; ES ˈfɑːmˌhaʊs; |-ses
   -zɪz
farmstead ˈfɑrmˌstɛd; ES ˈfɑːmˌstɛd
farmyard ˈfɑrmˌjɑrd; ES ˈfɑːmˌjɑːd
Farne Islands ˈfɑrnˈaɪləndz, -ənz; ES ˈfɑːn-
Farnham ˈfɑrnəm; ES ˈfɑːn-
faro ˈfɛro, ˈfæro; S ˈfæro
Faroe ˈfɛro, ˈfæro, ˈfero
Faroese ˌfɛroˈiz, ˌfær-, ˌfer-
far-off *n, adj* ˈfɑrˈɔf, -ˈɒf (ˈfar-ˌoff ˈlook)
Farquhar ˈfɑrkwɚ, -kwɑr, -kɚ; ES ˈfɑːkwə(r,
   -kwɑː(r, -kə(r
farrago fəˈrego, fəˈrago
Farragut ˈfærəgət, ˈfærəˌgʌt
Farrand ˈfærənd
Farrar ˈfærɚ; ES ˈfærə(r; *Geraldine* fəˈrɑr;
   ES fəˈrɑː(r
far-reaching ˈfɑrˈritʃɪŋ; ES ˈfɑːˈritʃɪŋ
Farrell ˈfærəl
Farrer ˈfærɚ; ES ˈfærə(r

Words below that have æ before r .(carry **'kærɪ**) *are often pronounced in N with* ɛ (**'kɛrɪ**, *§94*)
Words below in which a *before* r (farm) *is sounded* ɑ *are often pronounced in E with* a (**fa:m**)

farrier **'færɪɚ**; ES **'færɪ·ə(r**; |-y -ɪ
farrow **'færo, -ə** |-ed -d |-ing **'færəwɪŋ**
farse **fɑrs**; ES **fɑ:s**; |-s -ɪz |-d -t
farseeing **'fɑr'siɪŋ**; ES **'fɑ:'siɪŋ**
farsighted **'fɑr'saɪtɪd**; ES **'fɑ:'saɪtɪd**
farther **'fɑrðɚ**; ES **'fɑ:ðə(r**; |-most -ˌmost,
  -məst
farthest **'fɑrðɪst**; ES **'fɑ:ðɪst**
farthing **'fɑrðɪŋ**; ES **'fɑ:ðɪŋ**
farthingale **'fɑrðɪŋˌgel**; ES **'fɑ:ðɪŋˌgel**
fasces **'fæsiz** L *pl of* fascis **'fæsɪs**
fasciate **'fæʃɪˌet** |fasciated **'fæʃɪˌetɪd**
fascicle **'fæsɪkl̩** |fasicled **'fæsɪkl̩d**
fascinate **'fæsn̩ˌet** |-d -ɪd |-tor -ɚ; ES -ə(r
fascination ˌfæsn̩'eʃən
fascine fæ'sin, fə'sin |-d -d
fascis **'fæsɪs** |*pl* fasces **'fæsiz**
Fascism **'fæʃˌɪzəm** |-ist -ɪst
Fascisti fə'ʃɪsti, fæ'ʃɪsti (*It* fa'ʃisti)
Fascistic fə'ʃɪstɪk |-ally -ļɪ, -ɪklɪ
fashion **'fæʃən** |-ed -d |-ing **'fæʃənɪŋ, 'fæʃnɪŋ**
fashionable **'fæʃnəbl̩, 'fæʃənəbl̩** |-bly -blɪ
Fashoda fə'ʃodə
fast fæst; E+fast, fɑst; |-ed -ɪd
fasten **'fæsn̩**; E+**'fɑsn̩, 'fɑsn̩**; |-ed -d |-ing
  -snɪŋ, -sn̩ɪŋ
fastidious fæs'tɪdɪəs, -djəs
fastness **'fæstnɪs** |-es -ɪz; E *see* fast
Fastolf, -e **'fæstɑlf, -tɒlf**
fat fæt |fatted **'fætɪd**
fatal **'fetl̩** |-ly -ɪ |-ism -ˌɪzəm |-ist -ɪst
fatalistic ˌfetl̩'ɪstɪk |-ally -ļɪ, -ɪklɪ
fatality fe'tælətɪ, fə'tælətɪ, fɪ'tælətɪ
Fata.Morgana **'fɑtəmɔr'gɑnə**; ES -mɔɚ'gɑnə
father **'fɑðɚ**; ES -ðə(r, E+**'fɑð-**; |-hood -ˌhud
father-in-law **'fɑðɚrɪnˌlɔ, 'fɑðənˌlɔ**; ES **'fɑ-
  ðərɪnˌlɔ, 'fɑðənˌlɔ**, E+**'fɑð-**
fatherland **'fɑðɚˌlænd**; ES **'fɑðə-**, E+**'fɑðə-**
fathers-in-law **'fɑðɚzɪnˌlɔ, 'fɑðɚzn̩ˌlɔ**; ES
  'fɑðəzɪnˌlɔ, 'fɑðəzn̩ˌlɔ, E+**'fɑð-**
fathom **'fæðəm** |fathomed **'fæðəmd**
fatigable **'fætɪgəbl̩**
fatigate **'fætɪˌget** |fatigated **'fætɪˌgetɪd**
fatigue fə'tig |fatigued fə'tigd
Fatima **'fætɪmə, 'fɑtɪmə**
fatling **'fætlɪŋ**
fatten **'fætn̩** |-ed -d |-ing **'fætn̩ɪŋ, 'fætnɪŋ**

fattish **'fætɪʃ** |fatty **'fætɪ**
fatuitous fə'tjuətəs, -'tɪu-, -'tu- |-ity -ətɪ
fatuous **'fætʃuəs**
fat-witted **'fæt'wɪtɪd** (**'fat-ˌwitted 'Falstaff**)
fauces **'fɔsiz**
faucet **'fɔsɪt**, *occas.* **'fæsɪt, 'fɑsɪt**
Faucit **'fɔsɪt**
faugh fɔ, pf, *and various puffs of breath*
Faulconbridge **'fɔkənˌbrɪdʒ, 'fɔlkən-** |-'s -ɪz
Faulkner **'fɔknə**; ES **'fɔknə(r**
fault fɔlt |faulted **'fɔltɪd** |faulty **'fɔltɪ**
faultfinding **'fɔltˌfaɪndɪŋ**
faun fɔn |fauna **'fɔnə**
Fauntleroy **'fɔntləˌrɔɪ, 'fɒnt-, 'fɑnt-**
Fauquier fɔ'kɪr; ES -'kɪə(r, S+-'kɛə(r
Faust faust |Faustian **'faustɪən, 'fɔs-**
Faustus **'fɔstəs** |Faustus's **'fɔstəsɪz**
faux pas **'fo'pɑ** |*pl* -'pɑz (*Fr pl* -'pɑ)
Faversham **'fævɚʃəm**; ES **'fævə-**
favor **'fevɚ**; ES **'fevə(r**; |-ed -d |-ing **'fevrɪŋ,
  'fevərɪŋ** |-able **'fevrəbl̩, 'fevərəbl̩** |-bly -blɪ
favorite **'fevrɪt, 'fevərɪt** |-tism -ˌɪzəm
Fawcett **'fɔsɪt**
Fawkes fɔks |Fawkes's |'fɔksɪz
fawn fɔn |fawned fɔnd
fay fe
Fayal faɪ'ɑl
Fayum faɪ'jum
faze fez |fazes **'fezɪz** |fazed fezd—*less prop-
  erly spelt* feaze
feal '*turf*' fil
fealty **'fiəltɪ, 'filtɪ**
fear fɪr; ES fɪə(r, S+fɛə(r, fjɪə(r, fjɛə(r; |-ful
  -fəl |-fully -fəlɪ, -flɪ
fearnought **'fɪrˌnɔt**; ES **'fɪə-**, S+**'fɛə-, 'fjɪə-,
  'fjɛə-**
fearsome **'fɪrsəm**; ES **'fɪəsəm**, S+**'fɛə-, 'fjɪə-,
  'fjɛə-**
feasance **'fizn̩s**
feasibility ˌfizə'bɪlətɪ
feasible **'fizəbl̩** |-bly -blɪ
feast fist |feasted **'fistɪd**
feat fit
feather **'fɛðɚ**; ES **'fɛðə(r**; |-ed -d |-ing
  'fɛðərɪŋ, 'fɛðrɪŋ
featherbrain **'fɛðɚˌbren**; ES **'fɛðə-**; |-ed -d
featherhead **'fɛðɚˌhɛd**; ES **'fɛðə-**; |-ed -ɪd

Key: *See in full §§3–47.* bee **bi** |pity **'pɪtɪ** (§6) |rate **ret** |yet **jɛt** |sang **sæŋ** |angry **'æŋ·grɪ**
|bath **bæθ**; E **bɑθ** (§10) |ah **ɑ** |far **fɑr** |watch **wɑtʃ, wɒtʃ** (§12) |jaw **dʒɔ** |gorge **gɔrdʒ** |go **go**

featherstitch ˈfɛðɚˌstɪtʃ; ES ˈfɛðə-; |-es -ɪz
|-ed -t

featherweight ˈfɛðɚˌwet; ES ˈfɛðə-

feathery ˈfɛðɚɪ, ˈfɛðɪ

feature ˈfitʃɚ; ES ˈfitʃə(r; |-d -d

feaze 'feeze' fiz |-s -ɪz |-d -d, cf faze

febrifuge ˈfɛbrɪˌfjudʒ, -ˌfɪudʒ |-s -ɪz

febrile ˈfibrəl, ˈfɛb-

February ˈfɛbruˌɛrɪ, ˈfɛbjuˌɛrɪ, -ərɪ—Loss of
r in ˈfɛbjuˌɛrɪ is due to dissimilation and the
influence of ˈdʒænjuˌɛrɪ (§121).

feces ˈfisiz

feckless ˈfɛklɪs

feculence ˈfɛkjuləns |-lent -lənt

fecund ˈfikənd, ˈfɛk-, -ʌnd

fecundate ˈfikənˌdet, ˈfɛk- |-d -ɪd

fecundity fɪˈkʌndətɪ

fed fɛd

federacy ˈfɛdərəsɪ

federal, F- ˈfɛdərəl, ˈfɛdrəl |-ly -ɪ |-ist -ɪst

federalize ˈfɛdərəlˌaɪz, ˈfɛdrəl- |-s -ɪz |-d -d

federate n, adj ˈfɛdərɪt, ˈfɛdrɪt

federate, v ˈfɛdəˌret |-d -ɪd

federation ˌfɛdəˈreʃən

fedora, F- fɪˈdorə, -ˈdɔrə; S -ˈdorə

fee fi |past & pptc feed fid

feeble ˈfibl̩ |-bly -blɪ |-bler -blɚ; ES -blə(r;
|-blest -blɪst

feeble-minded ˈfibl̩ˈmaɪndɪd (ˈfeeble-ˌminded
ˈman)

feed past & pptc of fee fid

feed v fid |fed fɛd

feedback ˈfidˌbæk

feel fil |felt fɛlt

feere 'mate' arch. fɪr; ES fɪə(r, S+fɛə(r

fee-simple ˈfiˈsɪmpl̩

feet fit

feeze fiz |feezes ˈfiziz |-d -d

feign fen |feigned fend |-edly -ɪdlɪ

feint fent |feinted ˈfentɪd

feldspar ˈfɛldˌspɑr, ˈfɛl-; ES -ˌspɑː(r, E+
-ˌspɑː(r

Felicia fəˈlɪʃɪə, -ʃə

felicitate fəˈlɪsəˌtet |-tated -ˌtetɪd

felicitation fəˌlɪsəˈteʃən

felicity fəˈlɪsətɪ |-tous -təs

feline ˈfilaɪn

Felix ˈfilɪks |-ʼs -ɪz

fell past of fall fɛl

fell n, v, adj fɛl |felled fɛld

fellah ˈfɛlə |Arab pl -ahin, -aheen ˌfɛləˈhin

fellmonger ˈfɛlˌmʌŋgɚ; ES -gə(r

felloe 'wheel rim' ˈfɛlo, -ə—Felloe, mainly
Brit, comes from the OE pl felga; cf felly.

fellow ˈfɛlo, ˈfɛlə |-ed -d |-ship -ˌʃɪp

felly 'wheel rim' ˈfɛlɪ—Felly, Am and Brit,
comes from the OE dative sg felge; cf felloe.

felly adv 'cruelly' ˈfɛllɪ, ˈfɛlɪ

felon ˈfɛlən |-y -ɪ |-lonious fəˈlonɪəs, fɛ-

felsite ˈfɛlsaɪt

felspar ˈfɛlˌspɑr; ES -ˌspɑː(r, E+-ˌspɑː(r

felt past & pptc of feel fɛlt

felt n, v fɛlt |felted ˈfɛltɪd

felucca fəˈlʌkə, fɛ-

female ˈfimel

feme fɛm

feme covert ˈfɛmˈkʌvɚt; ES -ˈkʌvət

feme sole ˈfɛmˈsol

feminacy ˈfɛmənəsɪ |-neity ˌfɛməˈniətɪ

feminie ˈfɛmənɪ

feminine ˈfɛmənɪn |feminineness ˈfɛmənɪnnɪs

femininity ˌfɛməˈnɪnətɪ

feminism ˈfɛməˌnɪzəm |-nist -nɪst

femme de chambre Fr famdəˈʃɑ̃ːbr

femoral ˈfɛmərəl

femur ˈfimɚ; ES -mə(r; |-s -z |-mora ˈfɛmərə

fen fɛn

fence fɛns |-s -ɪz |-d -t

fencible ˈfɛnsəbl̩

fend fɛnd |fended ˈfɛndɪd |-er -ɚ; ES -ə(r

Fénelon ˈfɛnl̩ˌan, -ˌɒn (Fr fenˈlõ)

Fenian ˈfinɪən, -njən |-ism -ˌɪzəm

fennel ˈfɛnl̩

Fennimore Wis, Feni- Cooper ˈfɛnəˌmor,
-ˌmɔr; ES -ˌmoə(r, E+-ˌmɔə(r

fenny ˈfɛnɪ

Fenton ˈfɛntən

fenugreek ˈfɛnjuˌgrik

feod fjud, fɪud |-al -l̩ |-ary -ərɪ

feodality fjuˈdælətɪ, fɪu-

feoff fɛf, fif |-ed -t

feoffee fɛfˈi, fifˈi

feoffor ˈfɛfɚ, ˈfifɚ; ES -ə(r; (fɛfˈi ən fɛfˈɔr)

feracious fəˈreʃəs, fɛ-

feral ˈfɪrəl

Ferber ˈfɝbɚ; ES ˈfɝbə(r, ˈfɝbə(r

fer-de-lance Fr fɛrdəˈlɑ̃ːs

Ferdinand ˈfɝdn̩ˌænd; ES ˈfɝd-, ˈfɝd-

|full fʊl |tooth tuθ |further ˈfɝðɚ; ES ˈfɝðə |custom ˈkʌstəm |while hwaɪl |how haʊ |toy tɔɪ
|using ˈjuzɪŋ |fuse fjuz, fɪuz |dish dɪʃ |vision ˈvɪʒən |Eden ˈidn̩ |cradle ˈkredl̩ |keep ʼem ˈkipm̩

fere *'mate'* arch. **fɪr**; ES **fɪə(r, S+fɛə(r**
feretory **'fɛrəˌtorɪ, -ˌtɔrɪ; S -ˌtorɪ**
Ferguson, -sson **'fɝgəsn̩; ES 'fɝg-, 'fɝg-**
Feringi **fəˈrɪŋgɪ**
ferly **'fɝlɪ, 'fɛrlɪ; ES 'fɝlɪ, 'fɛəlɪ, 'fɝlɪ**
ferment *n* **'fɝmɛnt; ES 'fɝ-, 'fɝ-**
ferment *v* **fəˈmɛnt; ES fə-; |-ed -ɪd |-able -əbl̩**
fermentation **ˌfɝmənˈteʃən, -mɛn-; ES ˌfɝ-, ˌfɝ-**
fern **fɝn; ES fɝn, fɝn; |-ery -ərɪ, -rɪ**
ferocious **fəˈroʃəs, fɪ-, emph.+ˈfiˈroʃəs**
ferocity **fəˈrɑsətɪ, fɪ-; ES+-ˈrɒs-**
Ferrara **fəˈrɑrə, fɛ- (It fer'rɑːrɑ)**
ferrate **'fɛret |-d -ɪd**
ferret **'fɛrɪt |-ed -ɪd**
ferriage **'fɛrɪɪdʒ |-s -ɪz**
ferric **'fɛrɪk**
ferrite **'fɛraɪt**
ferroconcrete **ˌfɛroˈkɑnkrit, -kɑnˈkrit; ES+ -ɒn-**
ferromagnetic **ˌfɛromægˈnɛtɪk**
ferrous **'fɛrəs**
ferruginous **fɛˈrudʒənəs, fə-**
ferrule *'ring'* **'fɛrəl |-d -d**
ferry **'fɛrɪ |-ied -d |-boat -ˌbot**
fertile **'fɝtl̩; ES 'fɝtl̩, 'fɝtl̩; |-tilely -tl̩ɪ, -tl̩ɪ**
fertility **fɝˈtɪlətɪ; ES fɝ-, fɝ-**
fertilization **ˌfɝtl̩əˈzeʃən, -aɪˈz-; ES ˌfɝt-, ˌfɝt-**
fertilize **'fɝtl̩ˌaɪz; ES 'fɝt-, 'fɝt-; |-s -ɪz |-d -d**
ferule *'ruler'* **'fɛrəl, 'fɛrul |-d -d**
fervency **'fɝvənsɪ; ES 'fɝv-, 'fɝv-; |-ent -ənt**
fervid **'fɝvɪd; ES 'fɝvɪd, 'fɝv-**
fervor **'fɝvɚ; ES 'fɝvə(r, 'fɝvə(r**
fescue **'fɛskju, 'fɛskɪu**
Fessenden **'fɛsn̩dən**
festal **'fɛstl̩ |-ly -ɪ**
Feste **'fɛstɪ**
fester **'fɛstɚ; ES -tə(r; |-ed -d |-ing 'fɛstərɪŋ, 'fɛstrɪŋ**
festival **'fɛstəvl̩**
festive **'fɛstɪv |-vity fɛsˈtɪvətɪ**
festoon **fɛsˈtun |-ed -d |-ery -ərɪ**
fetal **'fitl̩ |-ism -ˌɪzəm**
fetation **fiˈteʃən**
fetch **fɛtʃ |fetches 'fɛtʃɪz |fetched fɛtʃt**
fete, fête **fet |-d -ɪd (Fr fɛːt)**
feterita **ˌfɛtəˈritə**
feticide **'fitəˌsaɪd |-dal ˌfitəˈsaɪdl̩**

fetid **'fɛtɪd, 'fitɪd**
fetish, -ich **'fitɪʃ, 'fɛtɪʃ |-ed -t**
fetlock **'fɛtˌlɑk; ES+-ˌlɒk; |-ed -t**
fetter **'fɛtɚ; ES 'fɛtə(r; |-ed -d**
fettle **'fɛtl̩ |-d -d |-ling 'fɛtl̩ɪŋ, 'fɛtlɪŋ**
fetus **'fitəs |-es -ɪz**
Fetzer **'fɛtsɚ; ES 'fɛtsə(r**
feu **fju, fɪu |-ed -d**
feud **fjud, frud |-ist -ɪst**
feudal **'fjudl̩, 'frudl̩ |-ism -ˌɪzəm |-ist -ɪst |-ly -ɪ**
feudalize **'fjudl̩ˌaɪz, 'frud- |-s -ɪz |-d -d**
feudatory **'fjudəˌtorɪ, 'frud-, -ˌtɔrɪ; S -ˌtorɪ**
fever **'fivɚ; ES 'fivə(r; |-ed -d |-ing 'fivərɪŋ, 'fivrɪŋ |-ous -vərəs, -vrəs**
feverfew **'fivɚˌfju, -ˌfɪu; ES 'fivə-**
Feversham **'fɛvɚʃəm; ES 'fɛvə-**
few, F- **fju, fru**
Fewkes **fjuks, fruks |-'s -ɪz**
fey **fe**
fez, F- **fɛz |fezzes 'fɛzɪz |fezzed fɛzd**
fiacre **fɪˈɑkɚ; ES -ˈɑkə(r; (Fr fjakr̩)**
fiancé **ˌfiənˈse, fiˌɑnˈse, fiˈɑnse (Fr fjɑ̃ˈse)**
fiancée *pron. like* fiancé
Fianna Fail **'fiənəˈfɔɪl, -ˈfaɪl**
fiasco **fɪˈæsko**
fiat **'faɪət, 'faɪæt |-ed -ɪd**
fib **fɪb |fibbed fɪbd**
fiber, -bre **'faɪbɚ; ES 'faɪbə(r; |-ed, -d -d**
fibril **'faɪbrəl, -brɪl |-led -d**
fibrin **'faɪbrɪn |-ation ˌfaɪbrɪˈneʃən**
fibrinogen **faɪˈbrɪnədʒən, -ˌdʒɛn**
fibroid **'faɪbrɔɪd |fibrous 'faɪbrəs**
fibster **'fɪbstɚ; ES 'fɪbstə(r**
fibula **'fɪbjələ |-s -z |-lae -ˌli**
Fichte **'fɪxtə |-tean -tɪən |-teanism -tɪənˌɪzəm**
fichu **'fɪʃu, -ʃɪu, -ʃju (Fr fiˈʃy)**
fickle **'fɪkl̩**
fico **'fiko**
fictile **'fɪktl̩, -tɪl**
fiction **'fɪkʃən |-al -l̩ |-ally -l̩ɪ**
fictitious **fɪkˈtɪʃəs |fictive 'fɪktɪv**
fid **fɪd |fidded 'fɪdɪd**
fiddle **'fɪdl̩ |-d -d |-ling 'fɪdlɪŋ, 'fɪdl̩ɪŋ**
fiddle-dee-dee **ˌfɪdl̩ˈdiˈdi, ˌfɪdl̩dɪˈdi**
fiddle-faddle **'fɪdl̩ˌfædl̩ |-d -d |-ling -dl̩ɪŋ, -dlɪŋ**
fiddlehead **'fɪdl̩ˌhɛd**
fiddler **'fɪdlɚ, 'fɪdl̩ɚ; ES -ə(r**

fiddlestick 'fɪdl̩ˌstɪk
Fidele fɪ'dili
Fidelia fɪ'diljə, -lɪə
Fidelio fɪ'delɪo, -ljo
fidelity faɪ'dɛlətɪ, fə-
fidget 'fɪdʒɪt |-ed -ɪd
fiducial fɪ'duʃəl, -'dɪu-, -'dju- |-ly -ɪ
fiduciary fɪ'duʃɪˌɛrɪ, -'dɪu-, -'dju-, -ʃərɪ
fie faɪ |fie-fie adj, v 'faɪˌfaɪ |-d -d
fief fif
field, F- fild |-ed -ɪd
fieldfare 'fildˌfɛr, -ˌfær; E -ˌfɛə(r, ES -ˌfæə(r
Fielding 'fildɪŋ
fieldpiece 'fildˌpis |-s -ɪz
fiend find |fiends findz, finz
fierce fɪrs; ES fɪəs, S+fɛəs, fjɛəs
fiery 'faɪrɪ, 'faɪərɪ
Fiesole fi'ezəlɪ (It 'fjɛːzole)
fiesta fɪ'ɛstə (Sp 'fjesta)
fife, F- faɪf |-d -t |-shire -ʃɪr, -ʃɚ; ES -ʃɪə(r, -ʃə(r
fifteen fɪf'tin, 'fɪf'tin ('fif ˌteen 'men)
fifteenth fɪf'tinθ, 'fɪf- |-ths -θs
fifth fɪfθ |-ths -θs
fifty 'fɪftɪ |-tieth -tɪɪθ |-fold -'fold ('fifty ˌfold 'loss)
fig fɪg
Figaro 'fɪgəˌro (Fr figa'ro)
fight faɪt |fought fɔt
figment 'fɪgmənt |figmental fɪg'mɛntl̩
figurate adj 'fɪgjərɪt
figurate v 'fɪgjəˌret |-d -ɪd
figuration ˌfɪgjə'reʃən
figurative 'fɪgjərətɪv, 'fɪgərətɪv, 'fɪgrətɪv
figure 'fɪgjɚ, 'fɪgɚ; ES -ə(r; |-d -d |-ring -gjərɪŋ, -gərɪŋ, -grɪŋ—In America 'fɪgɚ, -ə(r is less freq.
figurehead 'fɪgjɚˌhɛd, 'fɪgɚ-; ES 'fɪgjə-, -gə-
figurine ˌfɪgjə'rin
Fiji 'fidʒi |Figian fi'dʒɪən, 'fidʒɪən
filament n 'fɪləmənt |filimented 'fɪləməntɪd
filament v 'fɪləˌmɛnt |-ed -ɪd
filar 'faɪlɚ; ES -lə(r
filbert 'fɪlbɚt; ES 'fɪlbət
filch fɪltʃ |-es -ɪz |-ed -t
file faɪl |filed faɪld
filet 'fillet' 'fɪlɪt |fileted 'fɪlɪtɪd
filet de sole Eng 'fɪlɪəv'sol, Fr filɛ d'sɔl
filet mignon fi'le min'jɔ̃ (Fr filɛ mi'ɲɔ̃)

filial 'fɪlɪəl, -ljəl |-ly -ɪ
filiate 'fɪlɪˌet |-d -ɪd |-tion ˌfɪlɪ'eʃən
filibuster 'fɪləˌbʌstɚ; ES -ˌbʌstə(r; |-ed -d |-ing -ˌbʌstərɪŋ, -trɪŋ
filibusterer ˌfɪlə'bʌstərɚ; ES -rə(r; |-terism -təˌrɪzəm |-terous -tərəs, -trəs
filiform 'fɪləˌfɔrm, 'faɪlə-; ES -ˌfɔəm
filigree 'fɪləˌgri |-d -d
filing 'faɪlɪŋ
Filipino ˌfɪlə'pino |fem -pina -'pinə, -ɑ
fill fɪl |filled fɪld
fillet 'fɪlɪt |filleted 'fɪlɪtɪd
fillip 'fɪləp |filliped 'fɪləpt
Fillmore 'fɪlmor, -mɔr; ES -moə(r, E+ -mɔə(r
filly 'fɪlɪ
film fɪlm |filmed fɪlmd
filose 'faɪlos
filter 'fɪltɚ; ES -tə(r; |-ed -d |-ing 'fɪltərɪŋ, 'fɪltrɪŋ
filterable 'fɪltərəbl̩, 'fɪltrəbl̩
filth fɪlθ |-ths -θs |-y -ɪ |filthily 'fɪlθəlɪ
filtrable 'fɪltrəbl̩
filtrate n 'fɪltret, 'fɪltrɪt
filtrate v 'fɪltret |-d -ɪd |-tion fɪl'treʃən
fin fɪn |finned fɪnd
finable 'faɪnəbl̩
finagle fə'negl̩ |-nagler -'neglɚ; ES -lə(r
final 'faɪnl̩ |-ism -ˌɪzəm |-ist -ɪst |-ly -ɪ
finale fɪ'nɑlɪ (It fi'nɑːle)
finality faɪ'nælətɪ
finance fə'næns, 'faɪnæns |-s -ɪz |-d -t
financial fə'nænʃəl, faɪ'nænʃəl |-ly -ɪ
financier ˌfɪnən'sɪr, ˌfaɪnən-; ES -'sɪə(r; |-ed -d
finback 'fɪnˌbæk
finch fɪntʃ |finches 'fɪntʃɪz |finched fɪntʃt
Finchley 'fɪntʃlɪ
find faɪnd |found faʊnd
fin de siècle Fr fæ̃də'sjɛkl̩
Findlay 'fɪnlɪ, less freq. 'fɪndlɪ
fine faɪn |fined faɪnd |fineness 'faɪnnɪs
fineable 'faɪnəbl̩
finery 'faɪnərɪ
finespun 'faɪn'spʌn ('fine ˌspun 'theory)
finesse fə'nɛs |-s -ɪz |-d -t
Fingal 'fɪŋgl̩
finger 'fɪŋgɚ; ES 'fɪŋgə(r; |-ed -d |-ing 'fɪŋgərɪŋ, 'fɪŋgrɪŋ

|full fʊl |tooth tuθ |further 'fɝðɚ; ES 'fɝðə |custom 'kʌstəm |while hwaɪl |how haʊ |toy tɔɪ |using 'juzɪŋ |fuse fjuz, fɪuz |dish dɪʃ |vision 'vɪʒən |Eden 'idn̩ |cradle 'kredl̩ |keep 'em 'kipm̩

fingerer ˈfɪŋgərɚ; ES -rə(r
fingerling ˈfɪŋgɚlɪŋ; ES ˈfɪŋgə-
fingernail ˈfɪŋgɚˌnel, ˌfɪŋgɚˈnel; ES -gə-
fingerprint ˈfɪŋgɚˌprɪnt; ES ˈfɪŋgə-; |-ed -ɪd
finial ˈfɪnɪəl, ˈfaɪnɪəl
finical ˈfɪnɪk|̩ |-ly -ɪ, -ɪklɪ
finicking ˈfɪnɪkɪŋ |-cky -kɪ
finikin ˈfɪnɪkɪn
finis ˈfaɪnɪs |finises ˈfaɪnɪsɪz |+ˈfɪnɪs
finish ˈfɪnɪʃ |-es -ɪz |-ed -t
Finistère Fr finisˈtɛːr
Finisterre ˌfɪnɪsˈtɛr; ES -ˈtɛə(r
finite ˈfaɪnaɪt
finitude ˈfɪnəˌtjud, ˈfaɪnə-, -ˌtrud, -ˌtud
Finland ˈfɪnlənd
finland 'home of fish' ˈfɪnˌlænd
Finlay ˈfɪnlɪ |Finley ˈfɪnlɪ
Finn fɪn |-ish -ɪʃ
finnan haddie ˈfɪnənˈhædɪ
finny ˈfɪnɪ
fiord fjord, fjɔrd; ES fjoəd, E+fjɔəd
fipple ˈfɪp|̩
fir fɝ; ES fɝ(r, fɝ; |-ry -ɪ
fire faɪr; ES faɪə(r; |-d -d |-ring ˈfaɪrɪŋ
firearm ˈfaɪrˌarm; ES -ˌɑːm, E+-ˌɑːm
fireball ˈfaɪrˌbɔl; ES ˈfaɪə-
firebird ˈfaɪrˌbɝd; ES ˈfaɪəˌbɝd, ˈfaɪəˌbɝd
firebox ˈfaɪrˌbaks; ES ˈfaɪəˌbaks, -ˌbɒks; |-es -ɪz
firebrand ˈfaɪrˌbrænd; ES ˈfaɪə-; |-ed -ɪd
firebreak ˈfaɪrˌbrek; ES ˈfaɪə-
firebrick ˈfaɪrˌbrɪk; ES ˈfaɪə-
firebug ˈfaɪrˌbʌg; ES ˈfaɪə-
firecracker ˈfaɪrˌkrækɚ; ES ˈfaɪəˌkrækə(r
firedamp ˈfaɪrˌdæmp; ES ˈfaɪə-
firedog ˈfaɪrˌdɔg, -ˌdɒg; ES ˈfaɪə-
firedrake ˈfaɪrˌdrek; ES ˈfaɪə-
fire-eater ˈfaɪrˌitɚ; ES ˈfaɪrˌitə(r
firefang ˈfaɪrˌfæŋ; ES ˈfaɪə-; |-ed -d
firefly ˈfaɪrˌflaɪ; ES ˈfaɪə-
fireguard ˈfaɪrˌgard; ES ˈfaɪəˌgaːd, E+-ˌgaːd
firelock ˈfaɪrˌlak; ES ˈfaɪəˌlak, -ˌlɒk
fireman ˈfaɪrmən; ES ˈfaɪəmən; |-men -mən
fireplace ˈfaɪrˌples; ES ˈfaɪə-; |-s -ɪz
fireproof adj ˈfaɪrˈpruf; ES ˈfaɪə-; (ˈfireˌproof ˈvault)
fireproof v ˈfaɪrˌpruf; ES ˈfaɪə-; |-ed -t
fireside ˈfaɪrˌsaɪd; ES ˈfaɪə-
firetrap ˈfaɪrˌtræp; ES ˈfaɪə-

firewarden ˈfaɪrˌwɔrdn̩; ES ˈfaɪəˌwɔədn̩
firewater ˈfaɪrˌwɔtɚ, -ˌwatɚ, -ˌwɒtɚ; ES ˈfaɪə-, -tə(r
firewood ˈfaɪrˌwʊd; ES ˈfaɪə-
firework ˈfaɪrˌwɝk; ES ˈfaɪəˌwɝk, -ˌwɝk; |-s -s
firkin ˈfɝkɪn; ES ˈfɝkɪn, ˈfɝ-; |-ed -d
firm fɝm; ES fɝm, fɝm; |-ed -d
firmament ˈfɝməmənt; ES ˈfɝm-, ˈfɝm-
firman ˈfɝmən, fɚˈman; ES ˈfɝm-, ˈfɝm-, fə-
Firman pers. name ˈfɝmən; ES ˈfɝm-, ˈfɝm-
first fɝst; ES fɝst, fɝst
first-born ˈfɝstˈbɔrn; ES ˈfɝstˈbɔən, ˈfɝstˈbɔən
first-class ˈfɝstˈklæs; ES ˈfɝst-, ˈfɝst-, E+-ˈklas, -ˈklas; (ˈfirst-ˌclass ˈfare)
firsthand ˈfɝstˈhænd; ES ˈfɝst-, ˈfɝst-
firstling ˈfɝstlɪŋ; ES ˈfɝst-, ˈfɝst-
firstly ˈfɝstlɪ; ES ˈfɝstlɪ, ˈfɝstlɪ
first-rate ˈfɝstˈret, ˈfɝstˈret; ES ˈfɝ-, ˈfɝ-
firth fɝθ; ES fɝθ, fɝθ; |-ths -θs
fisc fɪsk
fiscal ˈfɪsk|̩ |-ly -ɪ
fish fɪʃ |fishes ˈfɪʃɪz |fished fɪʃt
fisher, F- ˈfɪʃɚ; ES ˈfɪʃə(r; |-man, -men -mən
fishery ˈfɪʃərɪ
fishhook ˈfɪʃˌhʊk, ˈfɪʃˌʊk
fishmonger ˈfɪʃˌmʌŋgɚ; ES -ˌmʌŋgə(r
fishwife ˈfɪʃˌwaɪf |-'s -s, -vz |-wives -ˌwaɪvz
fishy ˈfɪʃɪ
fisk, F- fɪsk
fissile ˈfɪs|̩, ˈfɪsɪl
fission ˈfɪʃən |-ed -d
fissure ˈfɪʃɚ; ES ˈfɪʃə(r; |-d -d
fist fɪst |fisted ˈfɪstɪd |-ic -ɪk |-ical -ɪk|̩
fisticuff ˈfɪstɪˌkʌf |-ed -t
fistula ˈfɪstʃʊlə |-s -z |-lae -ˌli
fit fɪt |fitted ˈfɪtɪd
Fitch fɪtʃ |Fitch's ˈfɪtʃɪz
fitchew ˈfɪtʃu, ˈfɪtʃɪu
fitful ˈfɪtfəl |-ly -ɪ
fitting ˈfɪtɪŋ
Fitzgerald fɪtsˈdʒɛrəld
FitzGerald Eng poet fɪtsˈdʒɛrəld
Fitzhugh fɪtsˈhju, -ˈhɪu (ˈFitzˌhugh ˈLee)
Fitzsimmons fɪtˈsɪmənz, fɪtsˈs- |-'s -ɪz
Fitzwalter ˈfɪtsˌwɔltɚ; ES -ˌwɔltə(r
Fitzwater ˈfɪtsˌwɔtɚ, -ˌwatɚ, -ˌwɒtɚ; ES -tə(r; formerly Fitzwalter

---

Key: See in full §§3–47. bee bi |pity ˈpɪtɪ (§6) |rate ret |yet jɛt |sang sæŋ |angry ˈæŋ·grɪ |bath bæθ; E baθ (§10) |ah ɑ |far fɑr |watch watʃ, wɒtʃ (§12) |jaw dʒɔ |gorge gɔrdʒ |go go

Fiume *It* ˈfjuːme

five faɪv |-r ˈfaɪvɚ; ES -və(r

fivefold *adj, adv* ˈfaɪvˈfold (ˈfaɪvˌfold ˈloss)

fivepence ˈfaɪvpəns, *now less freq.* ˈfɪpəns

fivepenny ˈfaɪvˌpɛnɪ, -pənɪ

fix fɪks |fixes ˈfɪksɪz |fixed, fixt fɪkst |-edly -ɪdlɪ

fixate ˈfɪkset |-d -ɪd |-tion fɪksˈeʃən

fixative ˈfɪksətɪv

fixity ˈfɪksətɪ

fixt fɪkst

fixture ˈfɪkstʃɚ; ES ˈfɪkstʃə(r

fizgig ˈfɪzˌgɪg

fizz fɪz |-es -ɪz |-ed -d |-y -ɪ

fizzle ˈfɪzl̩ |-d -d |-ling ˈfɪzlɪŋ, ˈfɪzl̩ɪŋ

fjord fjord, fjɔrd; ES fjoəd, E+fjɔəd

flabbergast ˈflæbɚˌgæst; ES ˈflæbə-; |-ed -ɪd

flabby ˈflæbɪ

flabellum fləˈbɛləm |-bella -ˈbɛlə

flaccid ˈflæksɪd |-ity flækˈsɪdətɪ

flag flæg |flagged flægd

flagellant ˈflædʒələnt, fləˈdʒɛlənt

flagellate ˈflædʒəˌlet |-d -ɪd

flageolet ˌflædʒəˈlɛt

flaggy ˈflægɪ

flagitious fləˈdʒɪʃəs

flagman ˈflægmən |-men -mən

flagon ˈflægən

flagrancy ˈflegrənsɪ |flagrant ˈflegrənt

flagship ˈflægˌʃɪp

Flagstad ˈflægstæd

flagstaff, F- ˈflægˌstæf; E+-ˌstaf, -ˌstaf; |-s -s—*The pl* flagstaves -ˌstevz *is rare in America.*

flagstone ˈflægˌston

Flaherty ˈflæɚtɪ; ES ˈflæ·ətɪ

flail flel |flailed fleld

flair flɛr, flær; E flɛə(r, ES flæə(r; |-ed -d

flake flek |flaked flekt |flaky ˈflekɪ

flam flæm |flammed flæmd

flambeau ˈflæmbo |-beaux *or* -beaus -boz

flamboyance flæmˈbɔɪəns |-cy -ɪ |-ant -ənt

flame flem |flamed flemd

flame-color ˈflemˌkʌlɚ; ES -ˌkʌlə(r; |-ed -d

flamingo fləˈmɪŋgo, flæ-

Flaminius fləˈmɪnɪəs, -njəs |-'s -ɪz

flan *pastry* flæn (*Fr* flɑ̃)

Flanders ˈflændɚz; ES ˈflændəz; |-'s -ɪz

flange flændʒ |-s -ɪz |-d -d

flank flæŋk |flanked flæŋkt

flannel ˈflænl̩ |-ed -d

flannelette, -let ˌflænl̩ˈɛt

flap flæp |flapped flæpt

flapdoodle ˈflæpˌdudl̩

flapjack ˈflæpˌdʒæk

flapper ˈflæpɚ; ES ˈflæpə(r; |-ed -d

flare flɛr, flær; E flɛə(r, ES flæə(r; |-d -d

flare-up ˈflɛrˌʌp, ˈflærˌʌp; S ˈflærˌʌp

flash flæʃ |flashes ˈflæʃɪz |flashed flæʃt

flashboard ˈflæʃˌbord, -ˌbɔrd; ES -ˌboəd, E+-ˌbɔəd

flashlight ˈflæʃˌlaɪt |-ed -ɪd

flask flæsk; E+flask, flɑsk

flat flæt |flatted ˈflætɪd

flatboat ˈflætˌbot

flatcar ˈflætˌkɑr; ES -ˌkɑː(r, E+-ˌkɑː(r

flatfish ˈflætˌfɪʃ |-es -ɪz

flat-footed ˈflætˈfʊtɪd (ˈflat-ˌfooted ˈway)

flathead, F- ˈflætˌhɛd

flatiron ˈflætˌaɪɚn, -ˌaɪrn; ES -ˌaɪ·ən, -ˌaɪən

flatten ˈflætn̩ |-ed -d |-ing ˈflætnɪŋ, -tnɪŋ

flatter ˈflætɚ; ES -tə(r; |-ed -d |-ing ˈflætərɪŋ, ˈflætrɪŋ

flattery ˈflætərɪ, ˈflætrɪ

flatulence ˈflætʃələns |-cy -ɪ |-lent -lənt

flatus ˈfletəs |-es -ɪz

flatways ˈflætˌwez |flatwise ˈflætˌwaɪz

flaunt flɔnt, flɒnt, flɑnt |-ed -ɪd

flauntily ˈflɔntl̩ɪ, ˈflɒnt-, ˈflɑnt-

flautist ˈflɔtɪst

Flavius ˈflevɪəs, -vjəs |-'s -ɪz

flavor ˈflevɚ; ES -və(r; |-ing ˈflevrɪŋ, -vərɪŋ

flaw flɔ |flawed flɔd |-less -lɪs |-y ˈflɔ·ɪ

flax flæks |flaxes ˈflæksɪz |-ed -t |-en -n̩

flaxseed ˈflæksˌsid, ˈflækˌsid

flay fle |flayed fled

flea fli |-bane -ˌben |-bite -ˌbaɪt

flea-bitten ˈfliˌbɪtn̩

Fleance ˈfliəns |-'s -ɪz

Fleay fle

fleck flɛk |flecked flɛkt

Flecknoe ˈflɛkno

flection ˈflɛkʃən |-al -l̩

fled *past & pptc of* flee fled

fledge flɛdʒ |-s -ɪz |-d -d |-dgling, -dgeling -lɪŋ

flee fli |fled fled

fleece flis |fleeces ˈflisɪz |fleeced flist

|full fʊl |tooth tuθ |further ˈfɝðɚ; ES ˈfɝðə |custom ˈkʌstəm |while hwaɪl |how haʊ |toy tɔɪ |using ˈjuzɪŋ |fuse fjuz, fɪuz |dish dɪʃ |vision ˈvɪʒən |Eden ˈidn̩ |cradle ˈkredl̩ |keep 'em ˈkipm̩

fleer *'gibe'* flır; ES flıə(r, S+flɛə(r; |-ed -d
fleer *'one who flees'* 'fliʒ; ES 'fli·ə(r
fleet flit |fleeted 'flitıd
Fleming 'flɛmıŋ |Flemish 'flɛmıʃ
flense, flence flɛns |-s -ız |-d -t
flesh flɛʃ |fleshes 'flɛʃız |fleshed flɛʃt
fleshly 'flɛʃlı |fleshy 'flɛʃı
fleshpot 'flɛʃˌpat; ES+-ˌpɒt
fletch flɛtʃ |-es -ız |-ed -t
fletcher 'flɛtʃʒ; ES 'flɛtʃə(r
Fletcherism 'flɛtʃəˌrızəm |-rite -ˌraıt
Fletcherize 'flɛtʃəˌraız |-s -ız |-d -d
fleur-de-lis ˌflʒdə'li, -'lis; ES ˌflɜ-, ˌflʒ-; |*pl*
  -lis -'liz *or* -lises -'lisız
flew *'dog's lip'* flu, flıu |-s -z |-ed -d
flew *past of* fly flu, flıu
flex flɛks |flexes 'flɛksız |flexed flɛkst
flexibility ˌflɛksə'bılətı
flexible 'flɛksəbl̩ |-bly -blı
flexion 'flɛkʃən |-al -l̩
Flexner 'flɛksnʒ; ES 'flɛksnə(r
flexor 'flɛksʒ; ES 'flɛksə(r
flexure 'flɛkʃʒ; ES 'flɛkʃə(r; |-xuous -kʃuəs
flibbertigibbet, F- 'flıbʒtıˌdʒıbıt; ES 'flıbə-
flick flık |flicked flıkt
flicker 'flıkʒ; ES 'flıkə(r; |-ed -d |-ing
  'flıkərıŋ, 'flıkrıŋ
flier 'flaıʒ; ES 'flaı·ə(r
flies flaız
flight flaıt |-y -ı
flimflam 'flımˌflæm |-med -d
flimsy 'flımzı
flinch flıntʃ |flinches 'flıntʃız |-ed -t
flinder 'flındʒ; ES 'flındə(r
fling flıŋ |flung flʌŋ
flint, F- flınt |flinted 'flıntıd
flintlock 'flıntˌlak; ES+-ˌlɒk
Flintshire 'flıntʃır, -ʃʒ; ES -ʃıə(r, -ʃə(r
flip flıp |flipped flıpt
flippancy 'flıpənsı |-ant -ənt
flirt flʒt; ES flɜt, flʒt; |-ed -ıd
flirtatious flʒ'teʃəs; ES flɜ-, flʒ-
flit flıt |flitted 'flıtıd
flitch flıtʃ |flitches 'flıtʃız |-ed -t
flite flaıt |-d -ıd |-ting 'flaıtıŋ
flitter 'flıtʒ; ES 'flıtə(r; |-ed -d
flivver 'flıvʒ; ES 'flıvə(r; |-ed -d |-ing
  'flıvərıŋ, 'flıvrıŋ
float flot |floated 'flotıd |-age -ıdʒ

floatation flo'teʃən
floc flak; ES+flɒk
floccose 'flakos, fla'kos; ES+-ɒk-
flocculence 'flakjələns; ES+'flɒk-; |-nt -nt
flock flak; ES+flɒk; |-ed -t
Flodden 'fladn̩; ES+'flɒdn̩
floe flo
flog flag, flɒg, flɔg |-ged -d
flood flʌd |flooded 'flʌdıd |-gate -ˌget
floodlight 'flʌdˌlaıt |-ed -ıd
floor flor, flɔr; ES floə(r, E+flɔə(r
floorcloth 'florˌklɔθ, 'flɔr-, -ˌklɒθ; ES 'floə-,
  E+'flɔə-; |-ths -ðz, -θs
flooring 'florıŋ, 'flɔrıŋ; S 'florıŋ
floorwalker 'florˌwɔkʒ, 'flɔr-; ES 'floəˌwɔkə(r,
  E+'flɔə-
flop flap; ES+flɒp; |-ped -t |-py -ı
Flora 'florə, 'flɔrə; S 'florə
floral 'florəl, 'flɔrəl; S 'florəl
Florala flo'rælə, fla-, flɒ-
Florence 'florəns, 'flar-, 'flɒr- |-'s -ız |-entine
  -ənˌtin
flores 'florız, 'flɔrız; S 'florız
florescence flo'rɛsn̩s, flɔ-; S flo-; |-nt -n̩t
Floresville 'florısˌvıl, 'flɔ-; S 'flo-, S+-vl̩
floriculture 'florıˌkʌltʃʒ, 'flɔ-; ES 'florı-
  ˌkʌltʃə(r, E+'flɔ-
florid 'florıd, 'flarıd, 'flɒrıd
Florida 'florədə, 'flar-, 'flɒr- |-n -n
Floridian flo'rıdıən, flɔ-, fla-, flɒ-
Florimel 'florəˌmɛl, 'flar-, 'flɒr-
florin 'florın, 'flar-, 'flɒr-, 'florın
florist 'florıst, 'flɔr-, 'flar-, 'flɒr-
Florizel 'florəˌzɛl, 'flar-, 'flɒr-
floss flɔs, flɒs |-es -ız |-ed -t
flota 'flotə
flotage 'flotıdʒ |-s -ız
flotation flo'teʃən
flotilla flo'tılə
flotsam 'flatsəm; ES+'flɒtsəm; *less freq.*
  'flotsəm (*19c* floatsome)
flounce flauns |flounces 'flaunsız |-d -t
flounder 'flaundʒ; ES -də(r; |-ed -d |-ing
  'flaundərıŋ, 'flaundrıŋ
flour flaur; ES flavə(r; |-ed -d
flourish 'flʒıʃ; ES 'flɜrıʃ, 'flʌrıʃ, 'flʒıʃ; |-es
  -ız |-ed -t
flout flaut |flouted 'flautıd
flow flo |flowed flod

Key: *See in full §§3–47.* bee bi |pity 'pıtı (§6) |rate ret |yet jɛt |sang sæŋ |angry 'æŋ·grı
|bath bæθ; E baθ (§10) |ah ɑ |far far |watch watʃ, wɒtʃ (§12) |jaw dʒɔ |gorge gɔrdʒ |go go

flower 'flauɚ, flaur; ES 'flau·ə(r, flauə(r;
  |-ed **-d**
flower-de-luce 'flaurdı'lus, -'lıus; ES 'flauə-;
  |-s **-ız**
floweret 'flaurıt
flowerpot 'flaur₁pɑt; ES 'flauə₁pɑt, -₁pɒt
flowery 'flaurı, 'flauərı
flown flon
flu flu, flıu
fluctuate 'flʌktʃu₁et |-ated -₁etıd |-ant -ənt
fluctuation ₁flʌktʃu'eʃən
flue flu, flıu
Fluellen flu'ɛlın, -ən
fluent 'fluənt, 'flıuənt |-ency -ənsı
fluff flʌf |fluffed flʌft
Flügel 'fligḷ (Ger 'fly:gəl)
fluid 'fluıd, 'flıuıd
fluidity flu'ıdətı, flıu-
fluke fluk, flıuk |-d **-t** |-ky **-ı**
flume, F- flum, flıum
flummery 'flʌmərı
flummox 'flʌməks |-es **-ız** |-ed **-t**
flung flʌŋ
flunk flʌŋk |flunked flʌŋkt
fluor 'fluɚ, 'flıuɚ; ES -ə(r
fluoresce ₁fluə'rɛs, ₁flıu- |-s **-ız** |-d **-t** |-nce **-ns**
  |-nt **-n̩t**
fluoric flu'ɔrık, flıu-, -'arık, -'ɒrık
fluorine 'fluə₁rin, 'flıu-, -rın |-rin **-rın**
fluorite 'fluə₁rart 'flıu-
fluoroscope 'flurə₁skop, 'flıu-
flurry 'flɝı; ES 'flɜrı, 'flʌrı, 'flɝı
flush flʌʃ |flushes 'flʌʃız |flushed flʌʃt
fluster 'flʌstɚ; ES 'flʌstə(r; |-ed **-d** |-ing
  'flʌstərıŋ, 'flʌstrıŋ
flustrate 'flʌstret |-terate -tə₁ret, -tret |-d **-ıd**
flute flut, flıut |-d **-ıd**
flutter 'flʌtɚ; ES 'flʌtə(r; |-ed **-d**
fluty 'flutı, 'flıutı
Fluvanna flu'vænə, flıu-
fluvial 'fluvıəl, 'flıu-
flux flʌks |fluxes 'flʌksız |fluxed flʌkst
fluxion 'flʌkʃən
fly flaı |flew flu, flıu |flown flon
flyaway 'flaıə₁we
flycatcher 'flaı₁kætʃɚ; ES -₁kætʃə(r
flyer 'flaıɚ; ES 'flaı·ə(r
flyleaf 'flaı₁lif |-leaves -₁livz
flyproof 'flaı'pruf ('fly₁proof 'ointment)

flyspeck 'flaı₁spɛk |-ed **-t**
flyte flart |-d **-ıd** |-ting **-ıŋ**
flytrap 'flaı₁træp
flyweight 'flaı₁wet
flywheel 'flaı₁hwil
foal fol |foaled fold
foam fom |foamed fomd
f.o.b. 'ɛf₁o'bi
fob fɑb; ES+fɒb; |-bed **-d**
focal 'fokḷ |-ly **-ı**
focalize 'fokḷ₁aız |-s **-ız** |-d **-d**
Foch foʃ, fɔk (Fr fɔʃ, Ger fɔk)
focus 'fokəs |-es **-ız** |-ed **-t** |foci 'fosaı
fodder 'fɑdɚ; ES 'fɑdə(r, 'fɒd-; |-ed **-d** |-ing
  -dərıŋ, -drıŋ
foe fo
foehn fen (Ger fø:n)
foeman 'fomən |-men **-mən**
foetal 'fitḷ |-ism -₁ızəm
foetation fi'teʃən
foeticide 'fitə₁saıd |-dal ₁fitə'saıdḷ
foetus 'fitəs |-es **-ız**
fog fɑg, fɔg, fɒg |-ged **-d** |-gy **-ı**
foghorn 'fɑg₁hɔrn, 'fɔg-, 'fɒg-; ES -₁hɔən
fogy 'fogı
foible 'fɔıbḷ
foie gras Fr fwa'grɑ
foil fɔıl |foiled fɔıld
foison 'fɔızn̩
foist fɔıst |foisted 'fɔıstıd
fold fold |folded 'foldıd
folderol 'fɑldə₁rɑl; ES+'fɒldə₁rɒl
Folger 'foldʒɚ; ES 'foldʒə(r
foliage 'folııdʒ |-s **-ız** |-d **-d**
foliate adj 'folııt, -₁et
foliate v 'folı₁et |-ated -₁etıd
folio 'folı₁o, -ljo |-ed **-d**
folium 'folıəm |-s **-z** |-lia **-ə**
folk fok |-s **-s**; N Engd+fɔ̃ks (§46)
Folkestone 'fok₁ston, Brit 'fokstən
folklore 'fok₁lor, -₁lɔr; ES -₁loə(r, E+-₁lɔə(r
folkmoot 'fok₁mut |folkmote, -mot 'fok₁mot
folkway 'fok₁we
Follansbee 'fɑlənzbı; ES+'fɒl-
follicle 'fɑlıkḷ; ES+'fɒl-
follow 'fɑlo, -ə; ES+'fɒl-; |-ed **-d** |-ing -ləwıŋ
follow-up 'fɑlo₁ʌp, 'fɑlə₁wʌp; ES+'fɒl-
folly 'fɑlı; ES+'fɒlı
foment n 'fomɛnt

|full ful |tooth tuθ |further 'fɝðɚ; ES 'fɜðə |custom 'kʌstəm |while hwaıl |how hau |toy tɔı
|using 'juzıŋ |fuse fjuz, fıuz |dish dıʃ |vision 'vıʒən |Eden 'idn̩ |cradle 'kredḷ |keep 'em 'kipm̩

foment *v* fo'mɛnt |-ed **-ıd** ('foment 'trouble)

fomentation ˌfomən'teʃən, -mɛn-

fond fand, fɒnd

fondant 'fandənt, 'fɒn-

Fond du Lac 'fandʒəˌlæk, -dʒʊ-, 'fandə-, 'fɒn-

fondle 'fandl̩, 'fɒn- |-d -d |-ling -dlıŋ, -dl̩ıŋ

fondler 'fandlɚ, 'fɒn-; ES -lə(r

fondue 'fandu, fan'du, -ɒn- (*Fr* fõ'dy)

font fant; ES+fɒnt

Fontaine, La læfan'ten, -fɒn- (*Fr* lafõ'tɛn)

Fontainebleau 'fantınˌblo, ˌfantın'blo, -ɒn- (*Fr* fõtɛn'blo)

fontanel, -lle ˌfantə'nɛl; ES+ˌfɒn-

Foochow 'fu'tʃaʊ (*Chin* -'dʒo)

food fud |foodstuff 'fudˌstʌf

fool ful |fooled fuld |-ery -ərı

foolhardy 'fulˌhardı; ES -ˌhɑːdı, E+-ˌhɑːdı

foolish 'fulıʃ

foolproof 'ful'pruf ('foolˌproof 'gadget)

foolscap 'fulzˌkæp, *paper often* 'fulˌskæp

foot fʊt |footed 'fʊtıd |-age -ıdʒ |-ing -ıŋ

football 'fʊtˌbɔl

footboard 'fʊtˌbord, -ˌbɔrd; ES -ˌboəd, E+ -ˌbɔəd

footboy 'fʊtˌbɔı

footbridge 'fʊtˌbrıdʒ |-s -ız

foot-candle 'fʊt'kændl̩

footfall 'fʊtˌfɔl

footgear 'fʊtˌgır; ES -ˌgıə(r, S+-ˌgɛə(r

foothill 'fʊtˌhıl

foothold 'fʊtˌhold

footle 'fʊtl̩ |-d -d |-ling 'fʊtlıŋ, 'fʊtl̩ıŋ

footlights 'fʊtˌlaıts

footling *adv, adj* 'fʊtlıŋ

foot-loose 'fʊtˌlus

footman 'fʊtmən |-men -mən

footmark 'fʊtˌmark; ES -ˌmɑːk, E+-ˌmɑːk

footnote 'fʊtˌnot |-d -ıd

footpad 'fʊtˌpæd

footpath 'fʊtˌpæθ; E+-ˌpɑθ, -ˌpɑθ; |-ths -ðz

foot-pound 'fʊt'paʊnd

footprint 'fʊtˌprınt |-ed -ıd

footrest 'fʊtˌrɛst

footrope 'fʊtˌrop

footsore 'fʊtˌsor, -ˌsɔr; ES -ˌsoə(r, E+-ˌsɔə(r

footstep 'fʊtˌstɛp

footstock 'fʊtˌstak; ES+-ˌstɒk

footstool 'fʊtˌstul

foot-ton 'fʊt'tʌn

footway 'fʊtˌwe

footwear 'fʊtˌwɛr, -ˌwær; E -ˌwɛə(r, ES -ˌwæə(r

footwork 'fʊtˌwɝk; ES -ˌwɜk, -ˌwɝk

footworn 'fʊtˌworn, -ˌwɔrn; ES -ˌwoən, E+-ˌwɔən

foozle 'fuzl̩ |-d -d |-ling 'fuzl̩ıŋ, 'fuzlıŋ

fop fap; ES+fɒp; |-pery -ərı, -rı

for *stressed* 'fɔr, ˌfɔr; ES 'fɔə(r, ˌfɔə(r; *unstr.* fɚ; ES fə(r

forage 'fɔrıdʒ, 'far-, 'fɒr- |-s -ız |-d -d

Foraker 'fɔrəkɚ, 'far-, 'fɒr-; ES -kə(r

foramen fo'remən |-s -z |foramina fo'ræmənə

forasmuch ˌfɔrəz'mʌtʃ

foray 'fɔre, 'fɑre, 'fɒre |-ed -d

forbade fɚ'bæd; ES fə'bæd

forbear *'ancestor'* 'fɔrˌbɛr, -ˌbær; E 'fɔəˌbɛə(r, ES -ˌbæə(r

forbear *v* fɔr'bɛr, fɚ-, -'bær; E fɔə'bɛə(r, fə-, ES -'bæə(r; |-bore -'bor, -'bɔr; ES -'boə(r, E+-'bɔə(r; |-borne -'born, -'bɔrn; ES -'boən, E+-'bɔən; ('bear and 'forˌbear)

forbearance fɔr'bɛrəns, fɚ-, -'bærəns; E fɔə-, fə-; S fɔə'bærəns, fə-

Forbes-Robertson 'fɔrbz'rabɚtsn̩; ES 'fɔəbz-'rabətsn̩, -'rɒb-

forbid fɚ'bıd; ES fə'bıd; |-bad, -bade -'bæd |-bidden -'bıdn̩ |-dance -ns

forbore fɔr'bor, fɚ-, -'bɔr; ES fɔə'boə(r, fə-, E+-'bɔə(r; |-rne -n

forby, -bye fɔr'baı; ES fɔə'baı

force fors, fɔrs; ES foəs, E+fɔəs; |-s -ız |-d -t |-dly -ıdlı

forceable *'coerceable'* 'forsəbl̩, 'fɔrs-; ES 'foəs-, E+'fɔəs-

forceful 'forsfəl, 'fɔrs-; ES 'foəs-, E+'fɔəs-; |-ly -ı

forcemeat 'forsˌmit, 'fɔrs-; ES 'foəs-, E+ 'fɔəs-

forceps 'fɔrsəps; ES 'fɔəsəps

forcible *'violent'* 'forsəbl̩, 'fɔrs-; ES 'foəs-, E+'fɔəs-; |-bly -blı

ford, F- ford, fɔrd; ES foəd, E+fɔəd; |-ed -ıd

Fordham 'fordəm, 'fɔr-; ES 'foədəm, E+ 'fɔə-

fordo fɔr'du; ES fɔə-; |-does -'dʌz |-did -'dıd |-done -'dʌn

Key: *See in full* §§3–47. bee bi |pity 'pıtı (§6) |rate ret |yet jɛt |sang sæŋ |angry 'æŋ·grı |bath bæθ; E baθ (§10) |ah ɑ |far fɑr |watch watʃ, wɒtʃ (§12) |jaw dʒɔ |gorge gɔrdʒ |go go

Fordyce 'fɔrdaɪs; ES 'fɔə-; |-'s -ɪz, *Scotl*
For'dyce
fore for, fɔr; ES foə(r, E+fɔə(r
fore-and-aft 'forən'æft, 'fɔr-, -ənd-; E+-'aft,
 -'aft; S 'forən(d)'æft
forearm *n* 'for‚ɑrm, 'fɔr-; ES 'for‚ɑːm,
 E+'fɔr-, -‚ɑːm
forearm *v* for'ɑrm, fɔr-; ES for'ɑːm, E+fɔr-,
 -'ɑːm; |-ed -d
forebear *'ancestor'* 'for‚bɛr, 'fɔr-, -‚bær; E
 'foə‚bɛə(r, 'fɔə-, -‚bæə(r; S 'foə‚bæə(r
forebode for'bod, fɔr-; ES foə-, E+fɔə-; |-d
 -ɪd |-ding -ɪŋ
forebrain 'for‚bren, 'fɔr-; ES 'foə-, E+'fɔə-
forecast *n* 'for‚kæst, 'fɔr-; ES 'foə-, E+'fɔə-,
 -‚kast, -‚kɑst
forecast *v* for'kæst, fɔr-; ES foə-, E+fɔə-,
 -'kast, -'kɑst; |*past* -cast, -casted -ɪd
 |*acct*+'fore‚cast(ed)
forecastle *naut.* 'foks|, *as sp. pron.* 'for‚kæs|,
 'fɔr-; ES 'foə-, E+'fɔə-, -‚kas|, -‚kɑs|
foreclose for'kloz, fɔr-; ES foə-, E+fɔə-; |-s
 -ɪz |-d -d |-sure -ʒɚ; ES -ʒə(r
foredo for'du, fɔr-; ES foə-, E+fɔə-; |-does
 -'dʌz |-did -'dɪd |-done -'dʌn
foredoom *n* 'for‚dum, 'fɔr-; ES 'foə-, E+'fɔə-
foredoom *v* for'dum, fɔr-; ES foə-, E+fɔə-;
 |-ed -d
forefather 'for‚fɑðɚ, 'fɔr-; ES 'foə‚fɑðə(r,
 E+'fɔə-, -‚fɑðə(r
forefend for'fɛnd, fɔr-; ES foə-, E+fɔə-;
 |-ed -ɪd
forefinger 'for‚fɪŋgɚ, 'fɔr-; ES 'foə‚fɪŋgə(r,
 E+'fɔə-
forefoot 'for‚fʊt, 'fɔr-; ES 'foə-, E+'fɔə-;
 |-feet -‚fit—*acct*+'fore'f-
foregather for'gæðɚ, fɔr-; ES foə'gæðə(r,
 E+fɔə-; |-ed -d |-ing -'gæðərɪŋ, -'gæðrɪŋ
forego for'go, fɔr-; ES foə-, E+fɔə-; |-went
 -'wɛnt |-gone -'gɔn, -'gɒn, *less freq.* -'gan
foregoing for'go‚ɪŋ, fɔr-; ES foə-, E+fɔə-;
 ('fore‚going 'day)
foregone for'gɔn, fɔr-, -'gɒn; ES foə-, E+fɔə-;
 ('fore‚gone con'clusion)
foreground 'for‚graʊnd, 'fɔr-; ES 'foə-, E+
 'fɔə-
forehand 'for‚hænd, 'fɔr-; ES 'foə-, E+'fɔə-
forehanded 'for'hændɪd, 'fɔr-; ES 'foə-,
 E+'fɔə-

forehead 'fɔrɪd, 'fɑr-, 'fɒr-, -əd, 'fɔr‚hɛd
foreign 'fɔrɪn, 'fɑr-, 'fɒr-, -ən |-ness -nɪs
forejudge for'dʒʌdʒ, fɔr-; ES foə-, E+fɔə-;
 |-s -ɪz |-d -d
foreknow for'no, fɔr-; ES foə-, E+fɔə-;
 |-knew -'nju, -'nɪu, -'nu |-known -'non
foreknowledge 'for‚nɑlɪdʒ, 'fɔr-; ES 'foə‚nɑl-,
 -‚nɒl-, E+'fɔə-; *acct*+fore'knowledge
forelady 'for‚ledɪ, 'fɔr-; ES 'foə-, E+'fɔə-
foreland 'forlənd, 'fɔr-; ES 'foə-, E+'fɔə-
foreleg 'for‚lɛg, 'fɔr-; ES 'foə-, E+'fɔə-;
 acct+'fore'leg
forelimb 'for‚lɪm, 'fɔr-; ES 'foə-, E+'fɔə-;
 acct+'fore'limb
forelock 'for‚lɑk, 'fɔr-; ES 'foə‚lɑk, -‚lɒk,
 E+'fɔə-
foreman 'formən, 'fɔr-; ES 'foə-, E+'fɔə-;
 |-men -mən
foremast 'for‚mæst, 'fɔr-; ES 'foə‚mæst,
 E+'fɔə-, -‚mast, -‚mɑst
foremost 'for‚most, 'fɔr-, -məst; ES 'foə-,
 E+'fɔə-
forename 'for‚nem, 'fɔr-; ES 'foə-, E+'fɔə-;
 |-d -d
forenoon for'nun, fɔr-; ES foə-, E+fɔə-;
 ('fore‚noon 'task)
forensic fə'rɛnsɪk, fo- |-al -| |-ally -|ɪ, -ɪklɪ
foreordain ‚forɔr'den, ‚fɔr-; ES ‚forɔə'den,
 E+‚fɔr-; |-ed -d
foreordinate *v* for'ɔrdn‚et, fɔr-; ES for'ɔədn-,
 E+fɔr-; |-d -ɪd
foreordination ‚forɔrdn'eʃən, ‚fɔr-; ES ‚for-
 ɔdn-, E+‚fɔr-
Forepaugh 'for‚pɔ, 'fɔr-; ES 'foə-, E+'fɔə-
forepaw, F- 'for‚pɔ, 'fɔr-; ES 'foə-, E+'fɔə-
forequarter 'for‚kwɔrtɚ, 'fɔr-; ES 'foə-,
 ‚kwɔətə(r, E+'fɔə-
forerun for'rʌn, fɔr-; ES foə'rʌn, E+fɔə-;
 |-ran -'ræn |*pptc* -run -'rʌn |-ner -ɚ; ES
 -ə(r; *acct*+'fore‚runner
foresaid 'for‚sɛd, 'fɔr-; ES 'foə-, E+'fɔə-
foresail 'for‚sel, 'fɔr-; ES 'foə-, E+'fɔə-
foresee for'si, fɔr-; ES foə-, E+fɔə-; |-saw
 -'sɔ |-seen -'sin
foreshadow *n* 'for‚ʃædo, 'fɔr-, -ə; ES 'foə-,
 E+'fɔə-
foreshadow *v* for'ʃædo, fɔr-, -ə; ES foə-,
 E+fɔə-; |-ed -d |-ing -'ʃædəwɪŋ
foreshank 'for‚ʃæŋk, 'fɔr-; ES 'foə-, E+'fɔə-

|full fʊl |tooth tuθ |further 'fɝðɚ; ES 'fɝðə |custom 'kʌstəm |while hwaɪl |how haʊ |toy tɔɪ
|using 'juzɪŋ |fuse fjuz, fɪuz |dish dɪʃ |vision 'vɪʒən |Eden 'idn̩ |cradle 'kredl̩ |keep 'em 'kipm̩

foresheet 'for‚ʃit, 'fɔr-; ES 'foə-, E+'fɔə-

foreshore 'for‚ʃor, 'fɔr‚ʃɔr; ES 'foə‚ʃoə(r, E+'fɔə‚ʃɔə(r

foreshorten for'ʃɔrtn̩, fɔr-; ES foə'ʃɔətn̩, E+ fɔə-; |-ed -d |-ing -tn̩ɪŋ, -tnɪŋ

foreside 'for‚saɪd, 'fɔr-; ES 'foə-, E+'fɔə-; acct+'fore'side

foresight 'for‚saɪt, 'fɔr-; ES 'foə-, E+'fɔə-

foresighted 'for'saɪtɪd, 'fɔr-; ES 'foə-, E+ 'fɔə-; ('fore‚sighted 'act)

foreskin 'for‚skɪn, 'fɔr-; ES 'foə-, E+'fɔə-

forespeak for'spik, fɔr-; ES foə-, E+fɔə-; |-spoke -'spok |-spoken -'spokən

forest 'fɔrɪst, 'far-, 'fɒr-, -əst |-ed -ɪd |-ry -rɪ

forestall for'stɔl, fɔr-; ES foə-, E+fɔə-; |-ed -d

forestation ‚fɔrɪs'teʃən, ‚far-, ‚fɒr-

foretaste n 'for‚test, 'fɔr-; ES 'foə-, E+'fɔə-

foretaste v for'test, fɔr-; ES foə-, E+fɔə-; |-d -ɪd

foretell for'tɛl, fɔr-; ES foə-, E+fɔə-; |-told -'told

forethink for'θɪŋk, fɔr-; ES foə-, E+fɔə-; |-thought -'θɔt

forethought n 'for‚θɔt, 'fɔr-; ES 'foə-, E+'fɔə-

foretime 'for‚taɪm, 'fɔr-; ES 'foə-, E+'fɔə-

foretimed 'timed before' for'taɪmd, fɔr-; ES foə-, E+fɔə-

foretoken n 'for‚tokən, 'fɔr-; ES 'foə-, E+'fɔə-

foretoken v for'tokən, fɔr-; ES foə-, E+fɔə-; |-ed -d |-ing -'tokənɪŋ, -'toknɪŋ

foretop 'for‚tap, 'fɔr-; ES 'foə‚tap, -‚tɒp, E+'fɔə-

fore-topmast for'tap‚mæst, fɔr-; ES foə'tap‚mæst, -'tɒp-, E+fɔə-, -‚mast, -‚mast

fore-topsail for'tap‚sel, naut. -sl̩, fɔr-; ES foə'tap-, -'tɒp-, E+fɔə-

forever fə'ɛvɚ; ES -'ɛvə(r

forevermore fə‚ɛvɚ'mor, -'mɔr; ES fə‚ɛvə-'moə(r, E+-'mɔə(r

forewarn for'wɔrn, fɔr-; ES foə'wɔən, E+fɔə-; |-ed -d

forewent past of forego for'wɛnt, fɔr-; ES foə-, E+fɔə-

forewoman 'for‚wumən, 'fɔr-, -‚wum-; ES 'foə-, E+'fɔə-; |-women -‚wɪmɪn, -mən— see woman

foreword 'for‚wɝd, 'fɔr-; ES 'foə‚wɝd, 'foə-‚wɝd, E+'fɔə-

foreyard 'for‚jard, 'fɔr-; ES 'foə‚ja:d, E+ 'fɔə-, -‚ja:d

Forfar 'fɔrfɚ; loc. 'fɒrfər; ES 'fɔəfə(r; |-shire -‚ʃɪr, -ʃɚ; ES -‚ʃɪə(r, -ʃə(r

forfeit 'fɔrfɪt; ES 'fɔəfɪt; |-ed -ɪd

forfeiture 'fɔrfɪtʃɚ; ES 'fɔəfɪtʃə(r

forfend fɔr'fɛnd; ES foə'fɛnd; |-ed -ɪd

forgather fɔr'gæðɚ; ES fɔə'gæðə(r; |-ed -d |-ing -'gæðərɪŋ, -'gæðrɪŋ

forgave fə'gev; ES fə'gev

forge fɔrdʒ, fordʒ; ES foədʒ, fɔədʒ; |-s -ɪz |-d -d—The pron. with ɔ by many who say ford, forθ, etc., results from ME double forms 'fɒrdʒə & 'fɔ:rdʒə.

forger 'fɔrdʒɚ, 'fordʒɚ; ES 'foədʒə(r, 'fɔə-; |-y -ɪ—see forge

forget fə'gɛt; ES fə-; |past -got -'gat |pptc -gotten, -got -'gatn̩, -'gat; |ES+-'gɒt(n̩

forgetful fə'gɛtfəl; ES fə-; |-ly -ɪ

forgetive 'fɔrdʒətɪv, 'for-; ES 'foədʒ-, 'fɔədʒ- —see forge

forget-me-not fə'gɛtmɪ‚nat; ES fə'gɛtmɪ‚nat, -‚nɒt

forgettable fə'gɛtəbl̩; ES fə-

forgive fə'gɪv; ES fə-; |-gave -'gev |-given -'gɪvən |-ness -nɪs

forgo fɔr'go; ES foə'go; |-went -'wɛnt |-gone -'gɒn, -'gɒn, less freq. -'gan

forgot fɚ'gat; ES fə'gat, -'gɒt; |-ten -n̩

forjudge fɔr'dʒʌdʒ; ES fɔə-; |-s -ɪz |-d -d

fork fɔrk; ES fɔək; |-ed -t

forked adj fɔrkt, 'fɔrkɪd; ES fɔək-

forlorn fɚ'lɔrn; ES fə'lɔən; |-ness -nɪs

form fɔrm; ES fɔəm; |-ed -d |-al -l̩ |-ally -lɪ— The pron. form for the sense 'rank,' 'bench,' once current in Engd, comes from a ME variant furme, fourme 'fu:rmə. Cf course.

formaldehyde fɔr'mældə‚haɪd; ES fɔ'mæl-

formalin, F- 'fɔrməlɪn; ES 'fɔəm-

formalism 'fɔrml̩‚ɪzəm; ES 'fɔəm-; |-ist -ɪst

formality fɔr'mælətɪ; ES fɔ-

formalize 'fɔrml̩‚aɪz; ES 'fɔəm-; |-s -ɪz |-d -d

formant 'fɔrmənt; ES 'fɔəm-

format 'fɔrmæt (Fr fɔr'ma)

formation fɔr'meʃən; ES fɔə-

formative 'fɔrmətɪv; ES 'fɔəm-

forme fɔrm; ES fɔəm

former 'fɔrmɚ; ES 'fɔəmə(r; |-ly -lɪ— 'fɔrmlɪ, by r-dissimilation, is often heard,

---

leading to easier confusion with formally
(*§121*).

formic 'fɔrmɪk; ES 'fɔəm-; |-ary -ˌɛrɪ
formicate *adj* 'fɔrmɪkɪt; ES 'fɔəm-
formicate *v* 'fɔrmɪˌket; ES 'fɔəm-; |-d -ɪd
formidable 'fɔrmɪdəb|; ES 'fɔəm-; |-bly -blɪ
—*Brit*+fə'mɪd-
Formosa fɔr'mosə; ES fɔə-
formula 'fɔrmjələ; ES 'fɔəm-; |-s -z |-lae -ˌli
|-lary -ˌlɛrɪ
formulate 'fɔrmjəˌlet; ES 'fɔəm-; |-d -ɪd
formulation ˌfɔrmjə'leʃən; ES ˌfɔəm-
fornicate 'fɔrnɪˌket; ES 'fɔən-; |-d -ɪd
fornication ˌfɔrnɪ'keʃən; ES ˌfɔən-
Forres 'fɔrɪs, 'farɪs, 'fɒrɪs, -ɪz |-'s -ɪsɪz, -ɪzɪz
Forrest 'fɔrɪst, 'farɪst, 'fɒrɪst
forsake fɚ'sek; ES fə-; |-sook -'sʊk |-saken
-'sekən
forsooth fɚ'suθ; ES fə'suθ
forspend fɔr'spɛnd; ES fɔə-; |-spent -'spɛnt
forswear fɔr'swɛr, -'swær; E fɔə'swɛə(r, ES
fɔə'swæə(r; |-swore -'swor, -'swɔr; ES
-'swoə(r, E+-'swɔə(r; |-sworn -'sworn,
-'swɔrn; ES -'swoən, E+-'swɔən
Forsyte 'fɔrsaɪt; ES 'fɔəsaɪt
Forsyth fɚ'saɪθ; ES fə'saɪθ
forsythia, F- fɚ'sɪθɪə, fɔr-, -'saɪθ-, -θjə; ES
fə-, fɔ-; *The 1st pron. follows English Latin
tradition, as in* Lydia (*L* Lȳdia); *the 2d,
the analogy of* Forsyth.
fort fort, fɔrt; ES foət, E+fɔət
forte '*strong point*' fort, fɔrt; ES foət, E+fɔət
forte *music* 'fɔrtɪ, -te; ES 'fɔət-
Fortescue 'fɔrtɪsˌkju, -ˌkɪu; ES 'fɔət-
forth, F- forθ, fɔrθ; ES foəθ, E+fɔəθ
forthcoming 'forθ'kʌmɪŋ, 'fɔrθ-; ES 'foəθ-,
E+'fɔəθ-
forthright *adj, adv* forθ'raɪt, fɔrθ-; ES foəθ-,
E+fɔəθ-; ('forthˌright 'mind)
forthwith forθ'wɪθ, fɔrθ-, -'wɪð; ES foəθ-,
E+fɔəθ-
fortification ˌfɔrtəfə'keʃən; ES ˌfɔətə-
fortify 'fɔrtəˌfaɪ; ES 'fɔətə-; |-fied -ˌfaɪd
Fortinbras 'fɔrtn̩ˌbræs, 'fɔrtɪn-; ES 'fɔət-
fortissimo fɔr'tɪsəˌmo; ES fɔ'tɪs-; (*It* fɔr-
'tissiˌmo)
fortitude 'fɔrtəˌtjud, -ˌtɪud, -ˌtud; ES 'fɔət-
fortnight 'fɔrtnaɪt, 'fort-, -nɪt, -nət; ES
'fɔət-, 'foət-; |-ly -lɪ—*All the pronuncia-*

tions of fortnight *here given are regular
phonetic or analogical developments.*

fortress 'fɔrtrɪs, -trəs; ES 'fɔət-; |-es -ɪz
|-ed -t
fortuitous fɔr'tjuətəs, -'tru-, -'tu-; ES fɔ-;
|-tism -ˌtɪzəm |-ty -tɪ
Fortuna fɔr'tjunə, -'tru-, -'tu-; ES fɔə-
fortune 'fɔrtʃən; ES 'fɔə-; |-nate -ɪt
fortuneteller 'fɔrtʃənˌtɛlɚ; ES 'fɔətʃənˌtɛlə(r
forty 'fɔrtɪ; ES 'fɔətɪ; |-tieth -tɪɪθ |-fold -'fold
forty-niner ˌfɔrtɪ'naɪnɚ; ES ˌfɔətɪ'naɪnə(r
forum 'forəm, 'fɔrəm; S 'forəm; |-s -z |-ra -rə
forward 'fɔrwɚd; ES 'fɔəwəd; |-s -z—*Some
good speakers still use the historical pron.*
'fɔrɚd; ES 'fɔrəd.
forwent *past of* forgo fɔr'wɛnt; ES fɔə-
forwhy fɔr'hwaɪ; ES fɔə'hwaɪ
fosse fɔs, fɒs |-s -ɪz |-d -t
fossil 'fɑs|, 'fɒs|; |-ize -ˌaɪz |-izes -ˌaɪzɪz |-ized
-ˌaɪzd
foster, F- 'fɔstɚ, 'fɑs-, 'fɒs-; ES -tə(r; |-ed -d
|-ing -tərɪŋ, -trɪŋ
Fostoria fɑs'torɪə, fɒs-, -'tɔr-; S -'tor-
Fotheringay 'fɑðərɪŋˌge, -ðrɪŋ-; ES+'fɒð-
fought fɔt
foul faʊl |-ed -d |-ly 'faʊllɪ, 'faʊlɪ
foulard fu'lard, fə'lard; ES -'la:d, E+-'la:d
foul-breathed 'faʊl'brɛθt
foulmouthed 'faʊl'maʊðd, -θt |-thedly -ðɪdlɪ
foulness 'faʊlnɪs |-es -ɪz
Foulness ˌfaʊl'nɛs |-'s -ɪz
found *past & pptc of* find faʊnd
found *v* faʊnd |founded 'faʊndɪd
foundation faʊn'deʃən |-al -| |-ally -ɪ
founder *n* 'faʊndɚ; ES -də(r; |-dress -drɪs
founder *v* 'faʊndɚ; ES -də(r; |-ed -d |-ing
'faʊndərɪŋ, -drɪŋ
foundery 'faʊndərɪ, 'faʊndrɪ |-dry -drɪ
fount faʊnt
fountain 'faʊntn̩, -tɪn, -tən
four for, fɔr; ES foə(r, E+fɔə(r
Fourdrinier fur'drɪnɪɚ; ES fuə'drɪnɪ·ə(r
four-flush 'for'flʌʃ, 'fɔr-; ES 'foə-, E+'fɔə-;
|-es -ɪz |-ed -t |-er -ɚ; ES -ə(r
fourfold *adj, adv* 'for'fold, 'fɔr-; ES 'foə-,
E+'fɔə-
four-footed 'for'fʊtɪd, 'fɔr-; ES 'foə-, E+'fɔə-
Fourier ˌfurɪ'e, 'furɪɚ; ES ˌfurɪ'e, 'furɪ·ə(r;
(*Fr* fu'rje)

Fourierism ˈfʊrɪəˌɪzəm |-ist -ɪst

four-in-hand ˈfɔrɪnˌhænd, ˈfɔr-; S ˈfor-

four-legged ˈforˈlɛgɪd, ˈfɔr-, -ˈlɛgd; ES ˈfɔə-, E+ˈfɔə-

four-masted ˈforˈmæstɪd, ˈfɔr-; ES ˈfɔə-, E+ˈfɔə-, -ˈmast-, -ˈmɑst-

four-o'clock ˈforəˌklak, ˈfɔrə-; ES ˈforəˌklak, -ˌklɒk, E+ˈfɔrə-

fourpence ˈforpəns, ˈfɔr-; ES ˈfɔə-, E+ˈfɔə-; |-penny -ˌpɛnɪ, -pənɪ

four-poster ˈforˈpostɚ, ˈfɔr-; ES ˈfɔəˈpostə(r, E+ˈfɔə-

fourscore ˈforˈskor, ˈfɔrˈskɔr; ES ˈfɔəˈskoə(r, E+ˈfɔəˈskɔə(r; (ˈfourˌscore and ˈten)

foursome ˈforsəm, ˈfɔr-; ES ˈfɔə-, E+ˈfɔə-

foursquare ˈforˈskwɛr, ˈfɔr-, -ˈskwær; E ˈfɔəˈskwɛə(r, ˈfɔə-, -ˈskwæə(r; S ˈfɔəˈskwæə(r; (ˈfourˌsquare ˈroom)

fourteen forˈtin, fɔr-; ES fɔə-, E+fɔə-; (ˌhe's ˈfourˈteen, ˈfourˌteen ˈmen)

fourteenth forˈtinθ, fɔr-; ES fɔə-, E+fɔə-; |-ths -θs—acct+ˈfourˈteenth

fourth forθ, fɔrθ; ES fɔəθ, E+fɔəθ; |-ths -θs

four-wheel adj, n ˈforˌhwil, ˈfɔr-; ES ˈfɔə-, E+ˈfɔə-

four-wheeled ˈforˈhwild, ˈfɔr-; ES ˈfɔə-, E+ˈfɔə-; (ˈfour-ˌwheeled ˈtruck)

fouter, -tre ˈfutɚ; ES ˈfutə(r

fowl faʊl |fowled faʊld |fowling ˈfaʊlɪŋ

fox faks; ES+fɒks; |-es -ɪz |-ed -t |-glove -ˌglʌv |-hound -ˌhaʊnd |-tail -ˌtel

foy v fɔɪ |-ed -d

foyer 'pilot' ˈfɔɪɚ; ES ˈfɔɪ·ə(r

foyer 'lobby' ˈfɔɪɚ, ˈfɔɪ·e; ES ˈfɔɪ·ə(r, ˈfɔɪ·e; (Fr fwaˈje)

fra, F- frɑ

fracas ˈfrekəs |-es -ɪz; Brit ˈfræka, pl -kaz

fraction ˈfrækʃən |-ed -d |-al -ļ |-ally -ļɪ

fractionate ˈfrækʃənˌet |-d -ɪd

fractious ˈfrækʃəs

fracture ˈfræktʃɚ; ES -tʃə(r; |-d -d

frae stressed ˈfre, ˌfre; unstr. fre, frɪ

fragile ˈfrædʒəl, -dʒɪl |-gilely -dʒəlɪ, -dʒɪlɪ, -əlɪ, -ɪllɪ

fragility fræˈdʒɪlətɪ, frə-

fragment ˈfrægmənt

fragmental frægˈmɛntļ |-ly -ɪ

fragmentary ˈfrægmənˌtɛrɪ |-ly -lɪ, esp. if emph. ˌfrægmənˈtɛrəlɪ

fragrance ˈfregrəns |-cy -ɪ |-ant -ənt

frail frel |-ly ˈfrellɪ, ˈfrelɪ |-ty -tɪ

fraise frez |-s -ɪz |-d -d

frame frem |-d -d

frame-up ˈfremˌʌp

framework ˈfremˌwɝk; ES -ˌwɜk, -ˌwɝ·k

Framingham Mass ˈfremɪŋˌhæm, Engd -mɪŋəm

franc fræŋk

France fræns; E+frans, frɑns; |-'s -ɪz

Frances ˈfrænsɪs E+ˈfran-, ˈfrɑn-; |-ces' -sɪs

Francesca franˈtʃɛska (It franˈtʃeska)

franchise ˈfræntʃaɪz |-s -ɪz |-d -d

franchisement ˈfræntʃɪzmənt

Francis ˈfrænsɪs; E+ˈfran-, ˈfrɑn-; |-cis' -sɪs

Francisca frænˈsɪskə |-can -kən |-co -ko

Franck fraŋk (Fr frɑ̃:k, Ger fraŋk)

Francke, Kuno ˈkunoˈfraŋkə

Franco-American ˈfræŋkoəˈmɛrəkən

Franco-British ˈfræŋkoˈbrɪtɪʃ

Franco-German ˈfræŋkoˈdʒɝmən; ES -ˈdʒɝm-, -ˈdʒɝ·m-

Francophile ˈfræŋkəˌfaɪl

Francophobe ˈfræŋkəˌfob |-bia ˌfræŋkəˈfobɪə

Franco-Prussian ˈfræŋkoˈprʌʃən

frangible ˈfrændʒəbļ |-bility ˌfrændʒəˈbɪlətɪ

frangipane ˈfrændʒəˌpen

frangipani ˌfrændʒɪˈpænɪ, -ˈpanɪ

frank, F- fræŋk |-ed -t

Frankenstein ˈfræŋkənˌstaɪn, -kɪn-

Frankfort ˈfræŋkfɚt; ES ˈfræŋkfət

Frankfurt ˈfræŋkfɚt; ES ˈfræŋkfət; (Ger ˈfraŋkfurt)

frankfurter, F- ˈfræŋkfɚtɚ; ES ˈfræŋkfətə(r

frankincense ˈfræŋkɪnˌsɛns

franklin, F- ˈfræŋklɪn |-ite -ˌaɪt

frankpledge ˈfræŋkˌplɛdʒ |-s -ɪz

frantic ˈfræntɪk |-ly -lɪ |-ally -ļɪ

frappé fræˈpe |-ed -d (Fr fraˈpe)

Fraser ˈfrezɚ, ˈfrezɚ; ES -ə(r; (Sc ˈfre:ʒər)

frater ˈfretɚ; ES ˈfretə(r

fraternal frəˈtɝnļ, fre-; ES -ˈtɜnļ, -ˈtɝnļ; |-ly -ɪ

fraternity frəˈtɝnətɪ; ES -ˈtɜn-, -ˈtɝn-

fraternize ˈfrætɚˌnaɪz, ˈfret-; ES -tə-; |-s -ɪz |-d -d

fratricide ˈfrætrəˌsaɪd, ˈfretrə-

fratricidal ˌfrætrəˈsaɪdļ, ˌfretrə-

fraud frɔd |-ful -fəl |-fully -fəlɪ

Key: See in full §§3–47. bee bi |pity ˈpɪtɪ (§6) |rate ret |yet jɛt |sang sæŋ |angry ˈæŋ·grɪ |bath bæθ; E baθ (§10) |ah ɑ |far fɑr |watch watʃ, wɒtʃ (§12) |jaw dʒɔ |gorge gɔrdʒ |go go

fraudulence ˈfrɔdʒələns |-cy -ɪ |-lent -lənt
fraught frɔt
Fraunhofer ˈfraʊnˌhofɚ; ES -ˌhofə(r
fray fre |-ed -d
Frazer ˈfrezɚ, ˈfreʒɚ; ES -ə(r; (Sc ˈfreːʒər)
Frazier ˈfreʒɚ; ES ˈfreʒə(r; cf Fraser, Frazer
frazzle ˈfræzl̩ |-d -d |-ling ˈfræzlɪŋ, -zl̩ɪŋ
freak frik
freckle ˈfrɛkl̩ |-d -d |-ling ˈfrɛklɪŋ, -kl̩ɪŋ
Frederic, -ick ˈfrɛdərɪk, ˈfrɛdrɪk
Frederica ˌfrɛdəˈrikə
Fredericksburg ˈfrɛdrɪksˌbɝg; ES -ˌbɜg,
-ˌbɝg
Fredonia NY, Kan friˈdonɪə; Colombia fre-
ˈdonjə (Am Sp freˈðonja)
free fri |freer ˈfriɚ; ES ˈfri·ə(r
freeboard ˈfriˌbord, -ˌbɔrd; ES -ˌboəd, E+
-ˌbɔəd
freebooter ˈfriˌbutɚ; ES -ˌbutə(r
freeborn ˈfriˌbɔrn; ES -ˌbɔən
Freeborn ˈfribɚn; ES ˈfribən
freedman, F- ˈfridmən |-men -mən
freedom, F- ˈfridəm
freedwoman ˈfridˌwʊmən, -ˌwu- |-men
-ˈwɪmɪn, -ən—see woman
free-for-all ˈfrifɚˈɔl (ˈfree-for-ˌall ˈfight)
freehand ˈfriˌhænd
freehanded ˈfriˈhændɪd
freehold ˈfriˌhold
freeman, F- ˈfrimən |-men -mən
Freemason ˈfriˌmesn̩, ˌfriˈmesn̩ |-ry -rɪ
freer, F- ˈfriɚ; ES ˈfri·ə(r
free-soil, F- ˈfriˈsɔɪl (ˈFree-ˌsoil ˈparty)
free-spoken ˈfriˈspokən
freestone, F- ˈfriˌston
freethinker ˈfriˈθɪŋkɚ; ES -ˈθɪŋkə(r
freeze, F- friz |-s -ɪz |froze froz |frozen ˈfrozn̩
Freiburg ˈfraɪbɝg; ES -bɜg, -bɝg; (Ger
ˈfraɪbʊrk)
freight fret |freighted ˈfretɪd
Frémont John C. ˈfrimɑnt, -mɒnt, frɪˈm-
Fremont O ˈfrimɑnt, -mɒnt
French frɛntʃ |-'s -ɪz |-man, -men -mən
|-woman -ˌwʊmən |-women -ˌwɪmɪn, -ən—
see woman
Frenchify ˈfrɛntʃəˌfaɪ |-fied -ˌfaɪd
Freneau frɪˈno, frɛ-
frenetic frəˈnɛtɪk, frɪ- |-al -l̩ |-ally -l̩ɪ
frenzy ˈfrɛnzɪ |-ied -d

frequence ˈfrikwəns |-s -ɪz |-cy -ɪ |-nt -nt
frequent v frɪˈkwɛnt |-ed -ɪd
Frere frɪr; ES frɪə(r, S+frɛə(r
fresco ˈfrɛsko |-ed -d
fresh frɛʃ |-es -ɪz |-ed -t
freshen ˈfrɛʃən |-ed -d |-ing ˈfrɛʃənɪŋ, -ʃnɪŋ
freshet ˈfrɛʃɪt
freshman ˈfrɛʃmən |-men -mən
Fresno ˈfrɛzno
fret frɛt |-ted -ɪd |-ful -fəl |-fully -fəlɪ
fretsome ˈfrɛtsəm
fretwork ˈfrɛtˌwɝk; ES -ˌwɜk, -ˌwɝk
Freud frɔɪd (Ger frɔyt) |Freudian ˈfrɔɪdɪən
Frey fre, Swiss statesm. fraɪ
Freya ˈfreə |Freyja ˈfrejə
friable ˈfraɪəbl̩
friar, F- ˈfraɪɚ, fraɪr; ES ˈfraɪ·ə(r, fraɪə(r
friary ˈfraɪərɪ
fribble ˈfrɪbl̩ |-d -d |-ling ˈfrɪblɪŋ, -bl̩ɪŋ
fricassee ˌfrɪkəˈsi |-d -d
fricative ˈfrɪkətɪv
friction ˈfrɪkʃən |-ed -d
Friday ˈfraɪdɪ—spelt Fridy in 1642
fried past & pptc of fry fraɪd
friedcake ˈfraɪdˌkek
friend frɛnd |-ly -lɪ |-ship -ʃɪp, ˈfrɛnʃɪp
frier ˈfryer' ˈfraɪɚ; ES ˈfraɪ·ə(r
Fries Sw bot., Ger philos. fris; Am schol. friz
|-'s -ɪz
fries from fry fraɪz
Friesian ˈfriʒən |-sic -zɪk |-sish -zɪʃ
Friesland ˈfrizlənd, -ˌlænd
frieze friz |-s -ɪz |-d -d
frigate ˈfrɪgɪt
Frigg frɪg |Frigga ˈfrɪgɑ
fright fraɪt |-ed -ɪd
frighten ˈfraɪtn̩ |-ed -d |-ing ˈfraɪtn̩ɪŋ, -tnɪŋ
frightful ˈfraɪtfəl |-ly -ɪ
frigid ˈfrɪdʒɪd |-ity frɪˈdʒɪdətɪ
frijol, -e ˈfrihol, -ˈhol
frill frɪl |-ed -d
fringe frɪndʒ |-s -ɪz |-d -d
frippery ˈfrɪpərɪ
Frisian ˈfrɪʒən, ˈfrɪʒɪən
frisk frɪsk |-ed -t
frit frɪt
frith frɪθ |-ths -θs
fritillary ˈfrɪtl̩ˌɛrɪ
fritter ˈfrɪtɚ; ES ˈfrɪtə(r; |-ed -d

frivol ˈfrɪvl̩ |-ed -d |-ing ˈfrɪvl̩ɪŋ, -vl̩ɪŋ

frivolity frɪˈvɑlətɪ; ES+-ˈvɒl-

frivolous ˈfrɪvələs, ˈfrɪvləs

friz, -zz frɪz |frizzes ˈfrɪzɪz |frizzed frɪzd

frizzle ˈfrɪzl̩ |-d -d |-ling ˈfrɪzl̩ɪŋ, -zlɪŋ

fro fro

Fröbel ˈfrebl̩ (Ger ˈfrøːbəl)

Frobisher ˈfrobɪʃɚ; ES ˈfrobɪʃə(r

frock frɑk; ES+frɒk; |-ed -t

froe fro

Froebel ˈfrebl̩ (Ger ˈfrøːbəl)

frog frɑg, frɔg, frɒg; S frɔg, frɑg, frɒg; |-eye -ˌaɪ

Frohman ˈfromən

Froissart ˈfrɔɪsɑrt; ES -saːt, E+-saːt; (Fr frwɑˈsaːr)

frolic ˈfrɑlɪk; ES+ˈfrɒlɪk; |-some -səm

from stressed ˈfrɑm, ˌfrɑm, ˈfrɒm, ˌfrɒm, ˈfrʌm, ˌfrʌm; unstr. frəm

Frome Eng rivs. & places frum—A sp. pron. from is also heard in Engd.

frond frɑnd, frɒnd

Fronde Fr frõːd

front frʌnt |fronted ˈfrʌntɪd |-age -ɪdʒ |-ages -ɪdʒɪz |-al -l̩ |-ally -l̩ɪ

Frontenac ˈfrɑntəˌnæk, ˈfrɒn-, in C+Fr frõtəˈnak

frontier frʌnˈtɪr, frɑn-, frɒn-, ˈfrʌntɪr, ˈfrɑn-, ˈfrɒn-; ES -ˈtɪə(r, -tɪə(r, S+-ˈtɛə(r, -tɛə(r; |-sman -zmən |-smen -zmən

frontispiece ˈfrʌntɪsˌpis, ˈfrɑn-; ES+ˈfrɒn-; |-s -ɪz

frontlet ˈfrʌntlɪt

frore arch. fror, frɔr; ES froə(r, E+frɔə(r

frost frɔst, frɒst |-ed -ɪd |-ing -ɪŋ

frostbite ˈfrɔstˌbaɪt, ˈfrɒst- |-bit -ˌbɪt |-bitten -ˌbɪtn̩

frostflower ˈfrɔstˌflauɚ, ˈfrɒst-, -ˌflaʊr; ES -ˌflauˑə(r, -ˌflauə(r

frostwork ˈfrɔstˌwɝk, ˈfrɒst-; ES -ˌwɜk, -ˌwɝˑk

froth frɔθ, frɒθ |-ths -θs |-ed -t

Froude frud

frou-frou ˈfrufru

frounce frauns |-s -ɪz |-d -t

frouzy ˈfrauzɪ

froward ˈfroɚd, ˈfrowɚd; ES -əd, -wəd

frown fraun |-ed -d

frowsty ˈfraustɪ

frowzy ˈfrauzɪ

froze froz |frozen ˈfrozn̩

fructification ˌfrʌktəfəˈkeʃən

fructify ˈfrʌktəˌfaɪ |-fied -ˌfaɪd |-tose -tos

fructuous ˈfrʌktʃuəs

frugal ˈfrugl̩, ˈfrɪugl̩ |-ity fruˈgælətɪ, frɪu-

fruit frut, frɪut |-ed -ɪd |-ful -fəl |-fully -fəlɪ

fruitcake ˈfrutˌkek, ˈfrɪut-

fruiterer ˈfrutərɚ, ˈfrɪut-; ES -tərə(r

fruition fruˈɪʃən, frɪu-

frumenty ˈfruməntɪ, ˈfrɪu-

frump frʌmp |-ed -t

frustrate ˈfrʌstret |-d -ɪd |-tion frʌsˈtreʃən

frustrum erron. for frustum ˈfrʌstrəm |-s -z |-tra -trə

frustum ˈfrʌstəm |-s -z |-ta -tə

fry fraɪ |fried fraɪd |fryer ˈfraɪɚ; ES -ə(r

Fryeburg ˈfraɪbɝg; ES -bɜg, -bɝg

fuchsia, F- ˈfjuʃə, ˈfɪu-, -ʃɪə, generic ˈfuksɪə

fuchsin ˈfuksɪn |-sine -sɪn, -sin

fuddle ˈfʌdl̩ |-d -d |-ling ˈfʌdl̩ɪŋ, ˈfʌdlɪŋ

fudge fʌdʒ |fudges ˈfʌdʒɪz |fudged fʌdʒd

Fuegian fjuˈidʒɪən, fɪu-, ˈfwedʒ-

Fuehrer ˈfɪrɚ, ˈfju-; ES -rə(r; (Ger ˈfyːrər)

fuel ˈfjuəl, ˈfɪuəl |-ed -d

fugacious fjuˈgeʃəs, fɪu-

fugitive ˈfjudʒətɪv, ˈfɪu-

fugleman ˈfjuglˌmən, ˈfɪu- |-men -mən

fugue fjug, frɪug |-d -d

Führer ˈfɪrɚ, ˈfju-; ES -rə(r; (Ger ˈfyːrər)

Fuji ˈfudʒi |Fujiyama ˌfudʒɪˈjamə

-ful unstressed ending forming adjectives (play-ful), pron. -fəl, -f̩, less freq. -fʊl. Only the pron. -fəl is given in the vocabulary, it being understood that -f̩ is a common variant, and -fʊl a less freq. one, being heard chiefly in formal style or consciously careful speech. Many adjectives in -ful are omitted from the vocabulary.

-ful half-stressed ending of compound nouns (cupful ˈkʌpˌfʊl).

-ful, -full stressed second element of compound adjectives (brimful, -ll ˈbrɪmˈfʊl, -ˌfʊl, half-full ˈhæfˈfʊl, -ˌfʊl).

fulcrum ˈfʌlkrəm |-s -z |-ra -rə

fulfill, -fil fʊlˈfɪl |-(l)ed -d

fulgent ˈfʌldʒənt |-gid -dʒɪd

fulgor ˈfʌlgɚ; ES -gə(r; |-ous -əs

full fʊl |fulled fʊld |fully ˈfʊlɪ

fullback 'fʊlˌbæk
fuller 'fʊlɚ; ES 'fʊlə(r; |-ed -d
fulmar 'fʊlmɚ; ES 'fʊlmə(r
fulminate 'fʌlməˌnet |-d -ɪd |-nant -nənt
fulmination ˌfʌlmə'neʃən |-nous 'fʌlmənəs
fulsome 'fʊlsəm, 'fʌl-
Fulton 'fʊltn̩
Fulvia 'fʌlvɪə, -vjə
fulvous 'fʌlvəs
fumarole 'fjuməˌrol, 'fɪu-
fumatory 'fjuməˌtorɪ, 'fɪu-, -ˌtɔrɪ; S -ˌtorɪ
fumble 'fʌmbl̩ |-d -d |-ling 'fʌmblɪŋ, -bl̩ɪŋ
fume fjum, frum |-d -d
fumet 'fjumɪt, 'fɪu- |fumette fju'mɛt, frɪu-
fumigate 'fjuməˌget, 'fɪu- |-d -ɪd
fumiter 'fjumətɚ, 'fɪu-; ES -tə(r
fumitory 'fjuməˌtorɪ, 'fɪu-, -ˌtɔrɪ; S -ˌtorɪ
fumy 'fjumɪ, 'fɪumɪ
fun fʌn |funned fʌnd
function 'fʌŋkʃən |-ed -d |-al -l̩ |-ally -lɪ
functionary 'fʌŋkʃənˌɛrɪ
fund fʌnd |funded 'fʌndɪd
fundament 'fʌndəmənt
fundamental ˌfʌndə'mɛntl̩ |-ly -ɪ |-ism -ˌɪzəm
   |-ist -ɪst
fundus 'fʌndəs |-es -ɪz
Fundy 'fʌndɪ
funeral 'fjunərəl, 'fɪu-
funereal fju'nɪrɪəl, frɪu- |-ly -ɪ
funest fju'nɛst, frɪu-
fungi 'fʌndʒaɪ
fungicide 'fʌndʒəˌsaɪd
fungoid 'fʌŋgɔɪd |-al fʌŋ'gɔɪdl̩
fungous adj 'fʌŋgəs
fungus n 'fʌŋgəs |-es -ɪz |fungi 'fʌndʒaɪ
funicle 'fjunɪkl̩, 'fɪu-
funicular fju'nɪkjələ, frɪu-; ES -lə(r
funk fʌŋk |funked fʌŋkt
funnel 'fʌnl̩ |-ed -d
funny 'fʌnɪ
fur fɝ; ES fɝ(r, fɝ; |-red -d
furbelow 'fɝbl̩ˌo; ES 'fɝ-, 'fɝ-; |-ed -d
furbish 'fɝbɪʃ; ES 'fɝ-, 'fɝ-; |-es -ɪz |-ed -t
furcate adj 'fɝket, -kɪt; ES 'fɝ-, 'fɝ-
furcate v 'fɝket; ES 'fɝ-, 'fɝ-; |-d -ɪd
furfur 'fɝfɚ; ES 'fɝfə(r, 'fɝfə(r; |-es -ˌiz |-al
   -ˌæl
furibund 'fjurɪˌbʌnd, 'frɪu-
furious 'fjurɪəs, 'frɪu-

furl fɝl; ES fɝl, fɝl; |-ed -d
furlong 'fɝlɔŋ, -lɒŋ; ES 'fɝ-, 'fɝ-, S+-laŋ
furlough 'fɝlo; ES 'fɝlo, 'fɝlo
furmenty 'fɝməntɪ; ES 'fɝ-, 'fɝ-
furmity 'fɝmətɪ; ES 'fɝ-, 'fɝ-
furnace 'fɝnɪs, -əs; ES 'fɝ-, 'fɝ-; |-s -ɪz
Furnas 'fɝnɪs, -əs; ES 'fɝ-, 'fɝ-; |-'s -ɪz
Furness, -niss 'fɝnɪs, -əs; ES 'fɝ-, 'fɝ-; |-'s
   -ɪz
furnish 'fɝnɪʃ; ES 'fɝ-, 'fɝ-; |-es -ɪz |-ed -t
furniture 'fɝnɪtʃɚ; ES 'fɝnɪtʃə(r, 'fɝnɪtʃə(r
Furnival, -all 'fɝnəvl̩; ES 'fɝn-, 'fɝn-
furor 'fjuror, 'frɪu-; ES -rɔə(r
furrier 'fɝɪɚ; ES 'fɝɪ·ə(r, 'fʌr-, 'fɝɪ·ə(r
furring 'fɝɪŋ; ES 'fɝɪŋ, 'fɝɪŋ
furrow 'fɝo, -ə; ES 'fɝr-, 'fʌr-, 'fɝ-; |-ed -d
furrowing 'fɝəwɪŋ; ES 'fɝəwɪŋ, 'fʌr-, 'fɝ-
furry 'fɝɪ; ES 'fɝɪ, 'fɝɪ
further 'fɝðɚ; ES 'fɝðə(r, 'fɝðə(r; |-ed -d
   |-ing -ðərɪŋ, -ðrɪŋ |-ance -əns, -ðrəns
furthermore 'fɝðɚˌmor, 'fɝðə-, -ˌmɔr; ES
   'fɝðəˌmoə(r, 'fɝðəˌmoə(r, E+-ˌmɔə(r;—In
   the 2d pron. ɚ has become ə by dissimilation
   (§121).
furthermost 'fɝðɚˌmost; ES 'fɝðə-, 'fɝðə-
furthest 'fɝðɪst; ES 'fɝ-, 'fɝ-
furtive 'fɝtɪv; ES 'fɝ-, 'fɝ-
fury 'fjurɪ, 'frɪurɪ
furze fɝz; ES fɝz, fɝz; |-s -ɪz |-d -d
fusain 'fjuzen, 'frɪu-, fju'zen, frɪu- (Fr fy'zæ̃)
fuscous 'fʌskəs
fuse fjuz, frɪuz |-s -ɪz |-d -d
fusee gun fju'zi, frɪu-
fusée mus. Fr fy'ze
fusel 'fjuzl̩, 'frɪu-, -sl̩
fuselage 'fjuzl̩ɪdʒ, 'frɪu-, -ˌɑʒ; |-s -ɪz (Fr
   fyz'la:ʒ)
fusibility ˌfjuzə'bɪlətɪ, ˌfrɪu-
fusible 'fjuzəbl̩, 'frɪu- |-bly -blɪ
fusiform 'fjuzəˌfɔrm, 'frɪu-; ES -ˌfɔəm
fusil 'fjuzl̩, 'frɪu-, -zɪl
fusilier, -eer ˌfjuzl̩'ɪr, ˌfrɪu-; ES -'ɪə(r, S+
   -'ɛə(r
fusillade ˌfjuzl̩'ed, ˌfrɪu- |-d -ɪd
fusion 'fjuʒən, 'frɪu-
fuss fʌs |fusses 'fʌsɪz |fussed fʌst
fustian 'fʌstʃən
fustic 'fʌstɪk
fustigate 'fʌstəˌget |-d -ɪd |-tor -ɚ; ES -ə(r

---

fusty 'fʌstɪ |-tily -t̩ɪ, -tɪlɪ
futhorc, -rk 'fuθɔrk; ES 'fuθɔək
futile 'fjut̩l̩, 'fɪu-, -tɪl |-ly -ɪ
futilitarian ˌfjutɪlə'tɛrɪən, ˌfɪu-, -'ter-, -rjən,
  acct+fuˌtili'tarian
futility fju'tɪlətɪ, fɪu-
Futrall 'fjutrəl, 'fɪu-
Futrell 'fjutrəl, 'fɪu-
Futrelle fju'trɛl, fɪu-

futtock 'fʌtək
future 'fjutʃɚ, 'fɪu-; ES -tʃə(r; |-rism -ˌɪzəm
  |-ist -ɪst
futuristic ˌfjutʃə'rɪstɪk, ˌfɪu-
futurity fju'tʊrətɪ, fɪu-, -'tɪur-, -'tjʊr- |-ric
  -rɪk
fuze fjuz, fɪuz |-s -ɪz |-d -d
fuzee fju'zi, fɪu-
fuzz fʌz |fuzzes 'fʌzɪz |fuzzed fʌzd |-y -ɪ

G

G, g letter dʒi |pl G's, Gs, poss G's dʒiz
gab gæb |gabbed gæbd
gabardine, -ber- 'gæbɚˌdin, ˌgæbɚ'din; ES
  -bə-
gabble 'gæbl̩ |-d -d |-ling 'gæbl̩ɪŋ, 'gæblɪŋ
gabby 'gæbɪ
gable 'gebl̩ |-d -d |-ling 'gebl̩ɪŋ, 'geblɪŋ
Gabriel 'gebrɪəl
gad, G- gæd |gadded 'gædɪd
gadabout 'gædəˌbaʊt
Gadarine ˌgædə'rin, 'gædəˌrin
Gades 'gediz |-es' -iz
gadfly 'gædˌflaɪ
gadget 'gædʒɪt
gadolinium ˌgædə'lɪnɪəm, -'lɪnjəm
Gadsden 'gædzdən
Gadshill 'gædzˌhɪl
gadzooks 'gæd'zuks, 'gæd'zʊks
Gaea 'dʒiə
Gaekwar 'dʒikwɑr; ES 'dʒikwɑː(r
Gael gel |Gaelic 'gelɪk |Gaelicist 'geləsɪst
gaff gæf |gaffed gæft
gaffer 'gæfɚ; ES 'gæfə(r
gaff-topsail 'gæf'tɑpsl̩, -ˌsel; ES+-'tɒp-
gag gæg |gagged gægd
gage gedʒ |gages 'gedʒɪz |gaged gedʒd
Gaia 'geə, 'gaɪə
gaiety 'geətɪ |gaily 'gelɪ
gaillardia ge'lardɪə, gɪ-; ES -'lɑːdɪə, E+
  -'lɑːd-
gain gen |-ed -d |-ful -fəl |-fully -fəlɪ
Gainesville 'genzvɪl; S+-vl̩
gainly 'genlɪ
gainsay gen'se |-says -'sez, -'sɛz |-said -'sed,
  -'sɛd, acct+'gainˌsay, -ˌsaid

Gainsborough 'genzˌbɾo, -ə; ES -ˌbɚ-,
  -ˌbʌr-, -ˌbɝ-; Brit -bərə, -brə
Gairdner 'gardnɚ, 'gerd-, 'gærd-; ES
  'gɑːdnə(r, 'gæəd-, E+'gaːd-, 'gɛəd-
gait get |gaited 'getɪd
gaiter 'getɚ; ES 'getə(r
Gaius 'geəs, 'gaɪəs |-'s -ɪz
gala 'gelə
galactic gə'læktɪk
galactose gə'læktos
Galahad 'gæləˌhæd
Galapagos gə'lapəˌgos (Sp ga'lapagɔs)
Galashiels ˌgælə'ʃilz
Galatea ˌgælə'tiə
Galatia gə'leʃə, gə'leʃɪə |-tians -ʃənz, -ʃɪənz
Galax, g- 'gelæks |-'s -ɪz |-ias gə'læksɪəs
galaxy 'gæləksɪ |-xian gə'læksɪən
Galba 'gælbə
gale gel |galed geld
Galen 'gelən, 'gelɪn
galena, G- gə'linə
Galesburg 'gelzbɝg; ES -bɜg, -bɝg
Galicia gə'lɪʃɪə, -'lɪʃə |-cian -ʃɪən, -ʃən
Galilee 'gæləˌli |Galilean ˌgælə'liən
Galileo ˌgælə'lio (It ˌgali'lɛːo)
galingale 'gælɪnˌgel, 'gælɪŋˌgel
Galion 'gælɪən
gall gɔl |galled gɔld
Gall gɔl, gɑl, gæl
gallant adj 'brave' 'gælənt
gallant adj 'amorous' gə'lænt, 'gælənt
gallant n 'gælənt, gə'lænt |-ry 'gæləntrɪ
gallant v gə'lænt |gallanted gə'læntɪd
Gallatin 'gælətɪn
galleass 'gælɪˌæs, 'gælɪəs |-es -ɪz

Key: See in full §§3–47. bee bi |pity 'pɪtɪ (§6) |rate ret |yet jɛt |sang sæŋ |angry 'æŋ·grɪ
|bath bæθ; E baθ (§10) |ah ɑ |far fɑr |watch watʃ, wɒtʃ (§12) |jaw dʒɔ |gorge gɔrdʒ |go go

galleon **'gælɪən, 'gæljən**
gallery **'gælərɪ, -lrɪ** |-ied **-d**
galley **'gælɪ**
gallfly **'gɔl͵flaɪ**
Gallia **'gælɪə**
galliard **'gæljəd; ES 'gæljəd**
galliardise **'gæljəd͵iz; ES 'gæljəd͵iz**
gallic, G- **'gælɪk**
Gallicism **'gælə͵sɪzəm**
Galli-Curci **'galɪ'kurtʃɪ, 'gælɪ'kɝtʃɪ; ES -'kuə-, -'kɝ-, -'kɝ-;** (*It* **'galli'kurtʃi**)
gallimaufry **͵gælə'mɔfrɪ**
gallinaceous **͵gælə'neʃəs**
gallinule **'gælə͵njul, -͵nɪul, -͵nul**
Gallipoli **gə'lɪpəlɪ, gə'lɪpə͵li**
Gallipolis *O* **͵gælɪpə'lis** |-lis's **-'lisɪz**
gallipot **'gælə͵pat; ES+-͵pɒt**
Gallitzin *Pa* **gə'lɪtsɪn**
gallium **'gælɪəm**
gallivant **'gælə͵vænt, ͵gælə'vænt** |-ed **-ɪd**
gall-less **'gɔllɪs**
gallnut **'gɔl͵nʌt**
galloglass **'gælo͵glæs** |-glasses **-͵glæsɪz**
gallon **'gælən**
gallop **'gæləp** |galloped **'gæləpt**
Galloway **'gælə͵we**
gallowglass **'gælo͵glæs** |-glasses **-͵glæsɪz**
gallows **'gæloz, -əz** |gallowses *rare* **'gælozɪz, -ləzɪz** |*dial.* gallus **'gæləs** |galluses **'gæləsɪz**
gallstone **'gɔl͵ston**
Gallup **'gæləp**
Gallus **'gæləs** |-li **-laɪ** |-'s **-ɪz**
galop **'gæləp** |galoped **'gæləpt**
galore **gə'lor, -'lɔr; ES -'loə(r, E+-'lɔə(r**
galosh **gə'laʃ; ES+-'lɒʃ;** |-es **-ɪz**
Galsworthy **'gɔlz͵wɝðɪ, 'gælz-; ES -͵wɝ'ðɪ, -͵wɝ'ðɪ;** *Dev* **'gælzərɪ**
galumph **gə'lʌmf** |galumphed **gə'lʌmft**
Galvani **gæl'vanɪ** (*It* **gal'va:ni**)
galvanic **gæl'vænɪk** |galvanism **'gælvə͵nɪzəm**
galvanize **'gælvə͵naɪz** |-s **-ɪz** |-d **-d**
galvanometer **͵gælvə'namətɚ; ES -'namət(r, -'nɒm-;** |-metry **-mətrɪ**
galvanoscope **gæl'vænə͵skop, 'gælvənə͵skop**
Galveston **'gælvɪstn̩, 'gælvəstn̩**
Galway **'gɔlwe**
gam **gæm** |gammed **gæmd**
Gamaliel **gə'melɪəl, gə'meljəl**
Gambetta **gæm'bɛtə**

Gambia **'gæmbɪ·ə**
Gambier *O* **'gæm͵bɪr; ES -͵bɪə(r;** *loc.*+**gæm-'bɪr**
gambier **'gæm͵bɪr; ES -͵bɪə(r**
gambit **'gæmbɪt**
gamble **'gæmbl̩** |-d **-d** |-ling **'gæmblɪŋ, 'gæmbl̩ɪŋ**
gambrel **'gæmbrəl** |gambreled **'gæmbrəld**
Gambrinus **gæm'braɪnəs** |-'s **-ɪz**
game gem |-d **-d** |-some **-səm**
gamecock **'gem͵kak; ES+-͵kɒk**
gamester **'gemstɚ; ES 'gemstə(r**
gamete **'gæmit, gə'mit, gæ'mit**
gamin **'gæmɪn** (*Fr* **ga'mæ̃**)
gamma **'gæmə**
gammer **'gæmɚ; ES 'gæmə(r**
gammon **'gæmən**
Gamp **gæmp**
gamut **'gæmət**
gamy **'gemɪ**
gan **gæn**
Gananoque **͵gænə'nok,** *loc.*+**-'nakwɪ** (*Fr* **gana'nɔ̃k**)
gander **'gændɚ; ES 'gændə(r**
Gandhi **'gandɪ, 'gandi, 'gændi, 'gændɪ**
ganef **'ganəf**
gang **gæŋ** |ganged **gæŋd** |ganging **'gæŋɪŋ**
gange **gændʒ** |-s **-ɪz** |-d **-d**
Ganges **'gændʒiz** |Ganges' **gændʒiz**
gangling **'gæŋglɪŋ** |-gly **-glɪ**
ganglion **'gæŋglɪən** |ganglia **'gæŋglɪə**
gangplank **'gæŋ͵plæŋk**
gangrene **'gæŋgrin, 'gæn-, gæŋ'grin, gæn-** |-d **-d**
gangster **'gæŋstɚ; ES 'gæŋstə(r**
gangue **gæŋ**
gangway **'gæŋ͵we**
gannet, G- **'gænɪt**
ganof **'ganəf**
ganoid **'gænɔɪd** |ganoidal **gə'nɔɪdl̩**
Gans **gænz** |-'s **-ɪz** (*Ger* **gans**)
Gansevoort **'gænsvurt; ES -vuət**
gantlet **'gæntlɪt**—*see* gauntlet
gantline **'gænt͵laɪn**
gantry **'gæntrɪ**
Ganymede **'gænə͵mid**
gaol **dʒel** |gaoled **dʒeld,** *formerly* gel, geld—
"*Some..again are boring their very Noses with hot Irons, in rage that they cannot come*

|full ful |tooth tuθ |further **'fɝðɚ; ES 'fɝðə** |custom **'kʌstəm** |while hwaɪl |how haʊ |toy tɔɪ
|using **'juzɪŋ** |fuse fjuz, fɪuz |dish dɪʃ |vision **'vɪʒən** |Eden **'idn̩** |cradle **'kredl̩** |keep 'em **'kipm̩**

Words below in which a *before* r (farm) *is sounded* ɑ *are often pronounced in* E *with* a (faːm)
Words below that have æ *before* r (carry ˈkærɪ) *are often pronounced in* N *with* ɛ (ˈkɛrɪ, §94)

to a Resolution, whether they shall say.. | Garrick ˈgærɪk
Jayl or Gaol."—R. L'Estrange (OED). | garrison ˈgærəsn̩ |-ed -d
gaolbird ˈdʒelˌbɜ˞d; ES -ˌbɜd, -ˌbɜ˞d | garrote, -tte gəˈrot, gəˈrɑt; ES+-ˈrɒt; |-d -ɪd
gap gæp |gapped gæpt | garrulity gəˈrulətɪ, gəˈrɪulətɪ
gape gep, gæp |gaped gept, gæpt—see gaup | garrulous ˈgærələs, ˈgærjələs
gapingstock ˈgepɪŋˌstɑk, ˈgæp-; ES+-ˌstɒk | Garry ˈgærɪ
gar gɑr; ES gɑːr | garter ˈgɑrtɚ; ES ˈgɑːtə(r; |-ed -d
garage gəˈrɑʒ, gəˈrɑdʒ, ˈgærɑʒ |-s -ɪz |-d -d | garth gɑrθ; ES gɑːθ; |-ths -θs
  (Fr gaˈraːʒ)—The fully Anglicized ˈgærɪdʒ | Gary ˈgerɪ, ˈgɛːrɪ, ˈgærɪ, ˈgerɪ; S ˈgerɪ, ˈgærɪ—
  (cf carriage ˈkærɪdʒ) is not general in | Some speakers distinguish Gary from Gerry
  American cultivated use. | by a longer ɛ.
Garand ˈgærənd |
garb gɑrb; ES gɑːb; |-ed -d | gas n gæs |gases ˈgæsɪz |gassy ˈgæsɪ
garbage ˈgɑrbɪdʒ; ES ˈgɑːbɪdʒ | gas v gæs |gasses ˈgæsɪz |gassed gæst
garble ˈgɑrbl̩; ES ˈgɑːbl̩; |-d -d |-ling -bl̩ɪŋ, | Gascoigne gæsˈkɔɪn, ˈgæskɔɪn, ˈgæskɪn
  -blɪŋ | Gascon ˈgæskən |Gascony ˈgæskənɪ
garboard ˈgɑrˌbord, -ˌbɔrd; ES ˈgɑːˌboəd, | gasconade ˌgæskənˈed |-aded -ˈedɪd
  E+-ˌbɔəd | gaseous ˈgæsɪəs, ˈgæsjəs, ˈgæz-
Garcia ˈgɑrʃɪə, -ʃə, -sɪə, Col gɑrˈsiə; ES -ɑː-; | gash gæʃ |gashes ˈgæʃɪz |gashed gæʃt
  (Am Sp gɑrˈsia) | gasiform ˈgæsəˌfɔrm; ES -ˌfɔəm
garden ˈgɑrdn̩, ˈgɑrdɪn; ES ˈgɑːdn̩, -dɪn | gasify ˈgæsəˌfaɪ |-fied -ˌfaɪd
gardener, G- ˈgɑrdnɚ, ˈgɑrdn̩ɚ; ES ˈgɑːd- | Gaskell ˈgæskl̩
gardenia gɑrˈdɪnɪə, -njə; ES gɑˈdin- | gasket ˈgæskɪt |gasketed ˈgæskɪtɪd
Gardiner ˈgɑrdnɚ, ˈgɑrdnɚ, ˈgɑrdɪnɚ; ES | gaslight ˈgæsˌlaɪt |-lighted -ˌlaɪtɪd
  ˈgɑːdnə(r, -dnə(r, -dɪnə(r | gasoline, -lene ˈgæsl̩ˌin, ˌgæsl̩ˈin, ˈgæz-,
Gardner ˈgɑrdnɚ; ES ˈgɑːdnə(r | ˌgæz-
Gareth ˈgærɪθ, ˈgærəθ | gasometer gæsˈɑmətɚ; ES -ˈɑmətə(r, -ˈɒmə-
Garfield ˈgɑrfild; ES ˈgɑːfild | tə(r
Gargantua gɑrˈgæntʃʊə; ES gɑˈgæntʃʊə; | gasp gæsp; E+gɑsp, gɑsp; |-ed -t
  |-n -n | Gaspé gæsˈpe (Fr gasˈpe) (ˈGasˌpé ˈtourist)
gargle ˈgɑrgl̩; ES ˈgɑːgl̩; |-d -d |-ling -glɪŋ, | gaspergou ˌgæspɚˈgu, ˈgæspɚˌgu; ES -pə-
  -glɪŋ | gastight ˈgæsˈtaɪt (ˈgasˌtight ˈjoint)
gargoyle ˈgɑrgɔɪl; ES ˈgɑːgɔɪl; |-d -d | Gaston US ˈgæstən; Fr name gæsˈtɔn, -ˈtɑn,
Gargrave ˈgɑrgrev; ES ˈgɑːgrev | -ˈtɒn (Fr gasˈtɔ̃)
Garibaldi ˌgærəˈbɔldɪ (It ˌgariˈbaldi) | gastric ˈgæstrɪk |gastritis gæsˈtraɪtɪs
garish ˈgerɪʃ, ˈgærɪʃ; S ˈgærɪʃ | gastroenteritis ˈgæstroˌɛntəˈraɪtɪs
garland, G- ˈgɑrlənd; ES ˈgɑːlənd; |-ed -ɪd | gastronomic ˌgæstrəˈnɑmɪk; ES+-ˈnɒmɪk;
garlic ˈgɑrlɪk; ES ˈgɑːlɪk | |-al -l̩ |-ally -lɪ, -ɪklɪ
garment ˈgɑrmənt; ES ˈgɑːmənt; |-ed -ɪd | gastronomy gæsˈtrɑnəmɪ; ES+-ˈtrɒnəmɪ
garner ˈgɑrnɚ; ES ˈgɑːnə(r; |-ed -d | gastropod ˈgæstrəˌpɑd; ES+-ˌpɒd
garnet ˈgɑrnɪt; ES ˈgɑːnɪt; |-ed -ɪd | gastroscope ˈgæstrəˌskop
garnish ˈgɑrnɪʃ; ES ˈgɑːnɪʃ; |-es -ɪz |-ed -t | gat gæt
garnishee ˌgɑrnɪˈʃi; ES ˌgɑː-; |-d -d | gate get |gated ˈgetɪd |-way -ˌwe
garniture ˈgɑrnɪtʃɚ; ES ˈgɑːnɪtʃə(r | gate-leg ˈgetˌlɛg |gate-legged ˈgetˌlɛgd
Garrard ˈgærəd; ES ˈgærəd | Gath gæθ
garret ˈgærɪt | gather ˈgæðɚ; ES ˈgæðə(r; |-ed -d |-ing
Garrett ˈgærɪt |-sville -sˌvɪl | ˈgæðrɪŋ, ˈgæðərɪŋ
| Gatling ˈgætlɪŋ

Key: See in full §§3–47. bee bi |pity ˈpɪtɪ (§6) |rate ret |yet jɛt |sang sæŋ |angry ˈæŋ·grɪ
|bath bæθ; E baθ (§10) |ah ɑ |far fɑr |watch wɑtʃ, wɒtʃ (§12) |jaw dʒɔ |gorge gɔrdʒ |go go

Gatun gɑ'tun
gauche goʃ
gaucherie ˌgoʃə'ri, 'goʃəˌri (*Fr* goʃ'ri)
Gaucho 'gautʃo
gaud gɔd |gaudy 'gɔdɪ |-ed -ɪd
gauffer 'gɔfɚ, 'gɒfɚ, 'gafɚ; ES -fə(r; |-ed -d
|-ing -fərɪŋ, -frɪŋ
gauge gedʒ |gauges 'gedʒɪz |gauged gedʒd
Gaul gɔl
gaunt, G- gɔnt, gɒnt, gant
gauntlet 'gɔntlɪt, 'gɒnt-, 'gant—*cf* gantlet
gaup gɔp |gauped gɔpt—*see* gape
gauss gaʊs |gausses 'gaʊsɪz
Gauss *Christian, Karl* gaʊs; *Clarence* gɔs
|-'s -ɪz
Gautama 'gɔtəmə
gauze gɔz |gauzes 'gɔzɪz |gauzy 'gɔzɪ
gave gev
gavel 'gævl̩ |-ed -d |-ing 'gævl̩ɪŋ, 'gævlɪŋ
gavelkind 'gævl̩ˌkaɪnd
Gawain 'gawɪn, 'gɔwɪn
gawk gɔk |gawky 'gɔkɪ
gay ge |gayety 'geətɪ
Gaza *Palestine* 'gezə, *Mozambique* 'gazə
gaze gez |gazes 'gezɪz |gazed gezd
gazelle gə'zɛl
gazette gə'zɛt |gazetted gə'zɛtɪd
gazetteer ˌgæzə'tɪr; ES -'tɪə(r, S+-'tɛə(r
Gdynia gə'dɪnjə, -nɪə (*Pol* 'gdiɲa)
gear gɪr; ES gɪə(r, S+gɛə(r; |-ed -d |-shift
-ˌʃɪft
Geauga dʒɪ'ɔgə
gecko 'gɛko
Geddes 'gɛdɪz, -ɪs |-'s -ɪz
gee dʒi |geed dʒid
geese gis |geese's 'gisɪz
geest gist
geezer 'gizɚ; ES 'gizə(r
Geffrey 'dʒɛfrɪ
Gehenna gɪ'hɛnə
Gehrkens 'gɝkɪnz, 'gɛr-; ES 'gɜ-, 'gɝ-,
'gɛə-; |-'s -ɪz
Geierstein 'gaɪɚˌstaɪn; ES 'gaɪə-
Geikie 'gikɪ
geisha 'geʃə
gel *chem.* dʒɛl |gelled dʒɛld
gelatin, -e 'dʒɛlətn̩ |-(e)d -d
gelatinate dʒə'lætn̩ˌet |-d -ɪd |-nous -əs
gelation dʒɛl'eʃən, dʒə'l-

geld *n* gɛld
geld *v* gɛld |gelded 'gɛldɪd *or* gelt gɛlt
Gelderland 'gɛldɚlənd; ES 'gɛldə-
gelding 'gɛldɪŋ
gelid 'dʒɛlɪd |-ity dʒə'lɪdətɪ, dʒɛ-
gelt *past & pptc of* geld gɛlt
gem dʒɛm |gemmed dʒɛmd
geminate *n, adj* 'dʒɛmənɪt
geminate *v* 'dʒɛməˌnet |-d -ɪd
gemination ˌdʒɛmə'neʃən
Gemini 'dʒɛməˌnaɪ, *as intj* 'dʒɪmənɪ
gemot, -e gə'mot
gemsbok 'gɛmzbak; ES+-bɒk
gendarme 'ʒandarm; ES -da:m, E+-da:m;
|-ry -ərɪ, -rɪ (*Fr* ʒã'darm)
gender 'dʒɛndɚ; ES -də(r; |-ed -d |-ing -dərɪŋ,
-drɪŋ
gene dʒin
genealogical ˌdʒɛnɪə'ladʒɪkl̩, ˌdʒini-; ES+
-'lɒdʒ-; |-ly -ɪ
genealogy ˌdʒini'ælədʒɪ, ˌdʒɛni-, -'alədʒɪ;
ES+-'ɒl-; |-gist -st; *The* a *or* ɒ *sound is
found in all parts of the US and in Canada.
The* -ology *words have influenced it.*
genera *pl of* genus 'dʒɛnərə
general 'dʒɛnərəl, 'dʒɛnrəl |-cy -sɪ
generalissimo ˌdʒɛnərəl'ɪsəˌmo, ˌdʒɛnrəl-
generality ˌdʒɛnə'rælətɪ
generalization ˌdʒɛnərələ'zeʃən, 'dʒɛnrəl-,
-aɪ'z-
generalize 'dʒɛnərəlˌaɪz, 'dʒɛnrəl- |-s -ɪz
|-d -d
generally 'dʒɛnərəlɪ, 'dʒɛnrəlɪ
generalty 'dʒɛnərəltɪ, 'dʒɛnrəltɪ
generate 'dʒɛnəˌret |-d -ɪd |-tor -ɚ; ES -ə(r
generation ˌdʒɛnə'reʃən
generic dʒə'nɛrɪk |-al -l̩ |-ally -l̩ɪ, -ɪklɪ
generosity ˌdʒɛnə'rasətɪ; ES+-'rɒs-
generous 'dʒɛnərəs, 'dʒɛnrəs
Genesee ˌdʒɛnə'si ('Geneˌsee 'River)
Geneseo ˌdʒɛnə'sio
genesis, G- 'dʒɛnəsɪs |*pl* geneses 'dʒɛnəˌsiz
Genest, Genêt dʒə'nɛt, ʒə'ne (*Fr* ʒə'nɛ)
genet, -tte 'dʒɛnɪt, dʒə'nɛt
genetic dʒə'nɛtɪk |-al -l̩ |-ally -l̩ɪ, -ɪklɪ |-s -s
geneticism dʒə'nɛtəˌsɪzəm |-cist -sɪst
Geneva dʒə'nivə |-van -vən
Genevese ˌdʒɛnə'viz
Genevieve 'dʒɛnəˌviv, ˌdʒɛnə'viv

|full fʊl |tooth tuθ |further 'fɝðɚ; ES 'fɜðə |custom 'kʌstəm |while hwaɪl |how haʊ |toy tɔɪ
|using 'juzɪŋ |fuse fjuz, fɪuz |dish dɪʃ |vision 'vɪʒən |Eden 'idn̩ |cradle 'kredl̩ |keep 'em 'kipm̩

Genevieve, -viève *saint* 'dʒɛnəˌviv (*Fr*
ʒənˈvjɛːv)
Genghis Khan 'dʒɛn·gɪzˈkan, 'dʒɛŋgɪz-
genial '*cheerful*' 'dʒinjəl |-ly -ɪ
genial '*generative*' 'dʒiniəl
genial '*of the chin*' dʒɪˈnaɪəl
geniality ˌdʒiniˈælətɪ, -nˈjæl-, -njɪˈælətɪ
genic 'dʒɛnɪk
geniculate *adj* dʒəˈnɪkjəlɪt
genie 'dʒinɪ
genii 'dʒiniˌaɪ
genital 'dʒɛnətl̩
genitival ˌdʒɛnəˈtaɪvl̩ |-ly -ɪ
genitive 'dʒɛnətɪv
genito-urinary ˌdʒɛnətoˈjʊrəˌnɛrɪ
geniture 'dʒɛnɪtʃɚ; ES -tʃə(r
genius 'dʒinjəs, '*spirit*'+-nɪəs |-'s -ɪz |*pl*
geniuses 'dʒinjəsɪz, '*spirits*' genii 'dʒiniˌaɪ
Gennesaret gəˈnɛsərɪt, dʒə-
Genoa *Italy* 'dʒɛnəwə, dʒəˈnoə (*It* Genova
'dʒɛːnova); *US* dʒəˈnoə
Genoese ˌdʒɛnəˈwiz
genotype 'dʒɛnoˌtaɪp
genotypic ˌdʒɛnoˈtɪpɪk |-al -l̩ |-ally -l̩ɪ, -ɪklɪ
genre 'ʒɑnrə (*Fr* ʒɑ̃ːr)
genro 'gɛnˈro
gens dʒɛnz |*pl* gentes 'dʒɛntiz
Genseric 'dʒɛnsərɪk, 'gɛn-
gent dʒɛnt
genteel dʒɛnˈtil |-ly -'tɪllɪ, -'tɪlɪ
gentes *pl of* gens 'dʒɛntiz
gentian 'dʒɛnʃən, -ʃɪən
gentile, G- 'dʒɛntaɪl
gentilesse 'dʒɛntl̩ˌɛs, *ME* 'dʒɛntɪˌlɛssə
gentility dʒɛnˈtɪlətɪ
gentle 'dʒɛntl̩ |-d -d |-ling -tlɪŋ, -tl̩ɪŋ |-r -tlɚ;
ES -tlə(r; |-st -tlɪst, -tl̩ɪst
gentlefolk 'dʒɛntl̩ˌfok |-s -s
gentleman 'dʒɛntl̩mən |-men -mən |-ly -lɪ
gentlewoman 'dʒɛntl̩ˌwʊmən, -ˌwu- |-men
-ˌwɪmɪn, -ən—*see* woman
gently 'dʒɛntlɪ
gentrice 'dʒɛntrɪs
gentry 'dʒɛntrɪ
genuflect 'dʒɛnjuˌflɛkt |-ed -ɪd
genuflection, -flexion ˌdʒɛnjuˌflɛkʃən
genuflexuous ˌdʒɛnjuˈflɛkʃʊəs
genuine 'dʒɛnjʊɪn |-ineness 'dʒɛnjʊɪnnɪs
Genung dʒɪˈnʌŋ

genus 'dʒinəs |*pl* genera 'dʒɛnərə |*less freq.*
-es -ɪz
geocentric ˌdʒio'sɛntrɪk |-al -l̩ |-ally -l̩ɪ, -ɪklɪ
geochemistry ˌdʒioˈkɛmɪstrɪ
geode 'dʒiod
geodesic ˌdʒiəˈdɛsɪk, -'dis- |-al -l̩
geodesist dʒiˈadəsɪst; ES+-'ɒd-
geodesy dʒiˈadəsɪ; ES+-'ɒd-
geodetic ˌdʒiəˈdɛtɪk |-al -l̩ |-ally -l̩ɪ, -ɪklɪ
Geoffrey 'dʒɛfrɪ
geographer dʒiˈagrəfɚ, -'ɒg-; ES -fə(r
geographic ˌdʒiəˈgræfɪk |-al -l̩ |-ally -l̩ɪ, -ɪklɪ
geography dʒiˈagrəfɪ, -'ɒg-
geoid 'dʒiɔɪd |-al dʒiˈɔɪdl̩
geologic ˌdʒiəˈladʒɪk; ES+-'lɒdʒ-; |-al -l̩
|-ally -l̩ɪ, -ɪklɪ
geologist dʒiˈalədʒɪst; ES+-'ɒl-
geologize dʒiˈaləˌdʒaɪz; ES+-'ɒl-; |-s -ɪz
|-d -d
geology dʒiˈalədʒɪ; ES+-'ɒl-
geomancer 'dʒiəˌmænsɚ; ES -sə(r; |-cy -sɪ
geometer dʒiˈamətɚ; ES -'amətə(r, -'ɒm-
geometric ˌdʒiəˈmɛtrɪk |-al -l̩ |-ally -l̩ɪ, -ɪklɪ
geometrician ˌdʒiəməˈtrɪʃən, dʒiˌamə-; ES+
-ˌɒm-
geometrize dʒiˈaməˌtraɪz; ES+-'ɒm-; |-s -ɪz
|-d -d
geometry dʒiˈamətrɪ; ES+-'ɒm-
geomorphic ˌdʒiəˈmɔrfɪk; ES -'mɔə-
geophysics ˌdʒioˈfɪzɪks
geopolitics ˌdʒioˈpalətɪks; ES+-'pɒl-
geoponic ˌdʒiəˈpanɪk; ES+-'pɒnɪk; |-al -l̩
George dʒɔrdʒ; ES dʒɔədʒ; |-'s -ɪz
Georgette dʒɔrˈdʒɛt; ES dʒɔə-
Georgia 'dʒɔrdʒə, -dʒɪə; ES 'dʒɔədʒ-; |-n -n
Georgiana dʒɔrˈdʒænə, -dʒɪˈænə; ES dʒɔə-
georgic, G- 'dʒɔrdʒɪk; ES 'dʒɔə-; |-al -l̩
geostatic ˌdʒiəˈstætɪk |-s -s
geosyncline ˌdʒioˈsɪnklaɪn |-nal -sɪnˈklaɪnl̩
geotectonic ˌdʒiotɛkˈtanɪk; ES+-'tɒn-
geotropic ˌdʒiəˈtrapɪk; ES+-'trɒpɪk
geotropism dʒiˈatrəˌpɪzəm; ES+-'ɒt-
gerah 'girə, 'gɪrə
Geraint dʒəˈrent
Gerald 'dʒɛrəld |-ine -ˌin, -ɪn
geranium dʒəˈreniəm, -njəm
Gerard dʒəˈrard; ES -'rɑːd, E+-'rɑːd; *Brit*+
'dʒɛrɑːd, -rəd
gerent 'dʒɪrənt

gerfalcon ˈdʒɝˌfɔlkən, -ˌfɔkən; ES ˈdʒɜ-,
  ˈdʒɝ-
Gergesenes ˈgɝgəˌsinz; ES ˈgɝ-, ˈgɝ-
Gerhard ˈgɝhɑrd; ES ˈgɝhɑːd, ˈgɝ-, E+-hɑːd
Gerizim gəˈraɪzɪm, ˈgɛrəzɪm
germ dʒɝm; ES dʒɝm, dʒɝm
german ˈdʒɝmən; ES ˈdʒɝm-, ˈdʒɝm-
German ˈdʒɝmən; ES ˈdʒɝm-, ˈdʒɝm-; |-ism
  -ˌɪzəm |-y -ɪ
germander dʒɝˈmændɚ; ES dʒɝˈmændə(r
germane dʒɝˈmen, dʒɝ-; ES dʒɝ-, dʒɝ-,
  dʒə-; |-maneness -ˈmennɪs
Germanic dʒɝˈmænɪk, dʒɝ-; ES dʒɝ-, dʒɝ-,
  dʒə-
germanium dʒɝˈmenɪəm, -njəm; ES dʒɝ-,
  dʒɝ-
Germantown ˈdʒɝmənˌtaʊn; ES ˈdʒɝm-,
  ˈdʒɝm-
germen ˈdʒɝmɪn, -ən; ES ˈdʒɝm-, ˈdʒɝm-;
  |-s -z |-mina -mɪnə
germicide ˈdʒɝməˌsaɪd; ES ˈdʒɝm-, ˈdʒɝm-
germinal ˈdʒɝmən!; ES ˈdʒɝm-, ˈdʒɝm-;
  |-ly -ɪ
germinant ˈdʒɝmənənt; ES ˈdʒɝm-, ˈdʒɝm-
germinate ˈdʒɝməˌnet; ES ˈdʒɝm-, ˈdʒɝm-;
  |-d -ɪd |-tive -ɪv
germination ˌdʒɝməˈneʃən; ES ˌdʒɝm-,
  ˌdʒɝm-
Gerontius dʒəˈrɑntɪəs; ES+-ˈrɒn-; |-'s -ɪz
Gerrard ˈdʒɛrɚd; ES ˈdʒɛrəd
Gerrold ˈdʒɛrəld
Gerry ˈdʒɛrɪ
gerrymander ˈgɛrɪˌmændɚ, ˈdʒɛrɪ-; ES -də(r
Gertrude ˈgɝtrud; ES ˈgɝt-, ˈgɝt-
gerund ˈdʒɛrənd, -ʌnd |-ive dʒəˈrʌndɪv
Geryon ˈdʒɪrɪən, ˈgɛrɪən |-es dʒɪˈraɪəˌniz, gə-
gest, -e dʒɛst
Gestapo gəˈstapo (Ger gəˈʃtɑpo)
gestate ˈdʒɛstet |-d -ɪd |-tion dʒɛsˈteʃən
gesticulate dʒɛsˈtɪkjəˌlet |-d -ɪd
gesticulation ˌdʒɛstɪkjəˈleʃən, dʒɛsˌtɪk-
gesticulatory dʒɛsˈtɪkjələˌtorɪ, -ˌtɔrɪ; S -ˌtorɪ
gestion ˈdʒɛstʃən
gesture ˈdʒɛstʃɚ; ES -tʃə(r; |-d -d
get gɛt |past got gɑt, arch. gat gæt |pptc got
  gɑt or gotten ˈgɑtn̩; ES+gɒt(n̩) — in unstressed position often gɪt (wɪ ˌkænt gɪtˈɪn)
get-at-able gɛtˈætəb!, gɪtˈætəb!
getaway ˈgɛtəˌwe

Gethsemane gɛθˈsɛmənɪ
Gettysburg ˈgɛtɪzˌbɝg; ES -ˌbɝg, -ˌbɝg
getup ˈgɛtˌʌp
gewgaw ˈgjugɔ, ˈgɪu- |-ed -d |-ry -ɪɪ
geyser 'spring' ˈgaɪzɚ, ˈgaɪsɚ, water-heater
  Brit ˈgizɚ; ES -ə(r
ghast arch. gæst |-ful -fəl |-fully -fəlɪ
ghastly ˈgæstlɪ; E+ˈgast-, ˈgast-
ghat, ghaut gɔt
ghazi, G- ˈgɑzi
ghee gi
Ghent Belg gɛnt, O dʒɛnt
gherkin ˈgɝkɪn; ES ˈgɝk-, ˈgɝk-
ghetto ˈgɛto
Ghibelline ˈgɪb!ɪn, -ˌin
Ghoorka ˈgʊrkə; ES ˈgʊəkə
ghost gost |-ed -ɪd |-ly -lɪ
ghoul gul |-ish -ɪʃ
Ghurka ˈgʊrkə; ES ˈgʊəkə
ghyl 'ravine' gɪl
giant ˈdʒaɪənt |-ess -ɪs |-esses -ɪsɪz
giaour dʒaʊr; ES dʒaʊə(r
gib, G- gɪb
gibber v 'jabber' ˈdʒɪbɚ, ˈgɪbɚ; ES -bə(r; |-ed
  -d |-ing -bərɪŋ, -brɪŋ |-ish -bərɪʃ, -brɪʃ
gibber n 'hump' ˈgɪbɚ; ES ˈgɪbə(r
gibbet ˈdʒɪbɪt |-ed -ɪd
gibbon, G- ˈgɪbən
gibbosity gɪˈbɑsətɪ; ES+-ˈbɒs-; |-bous ˈgɪbəs
gib-cat 'Gilbert cat' ˈgɪbˌkæt
gibe dʒaɪb |gibed dʒaɪbd
Gibeon ˈgɪbɪən |-ites -ˌaɪts
giblet ˈdʒɪblɪt
Gibralter dʒɪbˈrɔltɚ; ES -tə(r
Gibson ˈgɪbsn̩
giddy ˈgɪdɪ
Gideon ˈgɪdɪən |-s -z |-ite -ˌaɪt
Gielgud ˈgilgʊd
gier-eagle ˈdʒɪrˌig!
gift gɪft |gifted ˈgɪftɪd
gig gɪg |gigged gɪgd
gigantean ˌdʒaɪgænˈtɪən |-tesque -ˈtɛsk
gigantic dʒaɪˈgæntɪk |-ally -!ɪ, -ɪklɪ (ˈgi-
  ˌgantic ˈhound)
gigantism ˈdʒaɪgænˌtɪzəm, dʒaɪˈgæntɪzəm
gigantomachy ˌdʒaɪgænˈtɑməkɪ; ES+-ˈtɒm-
giggle ˈgɪg! |-d -d |-ling ˈgɪglɪŋ, ˈgɪg!ɪŋ
giglet ˈgɪglɪt
gigolo ˈdʒɪgəˌlo (Fr ʒigŏˈlo)

|full fʊl |tooth tuθ |further ˈfɝðɚ; ES ˈfɝðə |custom ˈkʌstəm |while hwaɪl |how haʊ |toy tɔɪ
|using ˈjuzɪŋ |fuse fjuz, fɪuz |dish dɪʃ |vision ˈvɪʒən |Eden ˈidn̩ |cradle ˈkred! |keep 'em ˈkipm̩

gigue ʒig
Gila ˈhilə
gilbert, G- ˈgɪlbɚt; ES -bət
Gilbert and Ellice Islands ˈgɪlbɚtn̩ˈɛlɪs-
　ˈaɪləndz, -lənz; ES -bət-
Gilbertian gɪlˈbɚtɪən; ES -ˈbɜt-, -ˈbɚt-
Gilboa gɪlˈboə
Gilchrist ˈgɪlkrɪst
gild gɪld |gilded ˈgɪldɪd or gilt gɪlt
Gilead ˈgɪlɪəd |-ites -ˌaɪts
Giles dʒaɪlz |-ʼs -ɪz
Gilfillan gɪlˈfɪlən
gill ‘quarter pint’ dʒɪl
Gill Jack & Gill dʒɪl
gill ‘ravine’ gɪl
gill of a fish gɪl |gilled gɪld
Gillespie gɪˈlɛspɪ
Gillett, -e dʒəˈlɛt, ˈdʒɪlɪt
Gillian ˈdʒɪlɪən, -ljən
gillie, -y ‘servant,’ ‘serve’ ˈgɪlɪ |-d -d
Gilliss ˈgɪlɪs |-ʼs -ɪz
gill-less ˈgɪllɪs
gillyflower ˈdʒɪlɪˌflauɚ, -ˌflaur; ES -ˌflau·ə(r,
　-ˌflauə(r
gilt past & pptc of gild gɪlt
gilt-edged ˈgɪltˈɛdʒd (ˈgilt-ˌedged ˈbook)
gimbals ˈdʒɪmbl̩z, ˈgɪm-
gimcrack ˈdʒɪmˌkræk
gimlet ˈgɪmlɪt |-ed -ɪd
gimmal ˈgɪml̩, ˈdʒɪml̩ |-ed -d
gimmick ˈgɪmɪk
gimp ‘trimming’ gɪmp |-ed -t
gin ‘begin’ gɪn |past gan gæn |pptc gun gʌn
gin liquor dʒɪn
gin machine dʒɪn |ginned dʒɪnd
Ginevra dʒɪˈnɛvrə
ginger ˈdʒɪndʒɚ; ES -dʒə(r; |-ly -lɪ |-bread
　-ˌbrɛd |-snap -ˌsnæp
gingham ˈgɪŋəm |-ed -d
gingival dʒɪnˈdʒaɪvl̩, ˈdʒɪndʒəvl̩
gingko, ginko ˈgɪŋko, ˈdʒɪŋko
gink gɪŋk
Ginn gɪn
ginseng, -sing ˈdʒɪnsɛŋ, -sɪŋ
Giotto ˈdʒato, ˈdʒɒto (It ˈdʒɔtto)
gip dʒɪp |-ped -t
gip ‘cut fish’ gɪp |-ped -t
gipon dʒɪˈpan, ˈdʒɪpan; ES+-ɒn
gipsy ˈdʒɪpsɪ

giraffe dʒəˈræf; E+-ˈraf, -ˈrɑf
girandole ˈdʒɪrənˌdol
Girard dʒəˈrard; ES -ˈraːd, E+-ˈraːd
gird ‘encircle’ gɚd |past & pptc girt gɚt or
　girded ˈgɚdɪd; |ES -ɜ-, -ɚ-
gird ‘sill,’ ‘sneer’ gɚd; ES gɜd, gɚd; |-ed -ɪd
girdle ˈgɚdl̩; ES ˈgɜdl̩, ˈgɚdl̩; |-d -d |-ling
　-dl̩ɪŋ, -dlɪŋ |-ler -dlɚ, -dl̩ɚ; ES -dlə(r,
　-dl̩ə(r
girl gɚl, much less freq. gɛrl; ES gɜl, gɚl, gɛəl;
　|-hood -hʊd
Girondist dʒəˈrandɪst; ES+-ˈrɒn-
girt gɚt; ES gɜt, gɚt; |-ed -ɪd
girth gɚθ; ES gɜθ, gɚθ; |-ths -θs |-ed -t
gisarme gɪˈzarm; ES -ˈzaːm, E+-ˈzaːm
Gissing ˈgɪsɪŋ
gist dʒɪst
gittern ˈgɪtɚn; ES ˈgɪtən
give gɪv |gave gev |given ˈgɪvən
give-and-take ˈgɪvənˈtek
giveaway ˈgɪvəˌwe
given ˈgɪvən
Giza ˈgizə |Gizeh ˈgizɛ
gizzard ˈgɪzɚd; ES ˈgɪzəd
glabrous ˈglebrəs
glacé glæˈse (Fr glaˈse)
glacial ˈgleʃəl, -ʃɪəl |-ly -ɪ
glaciate ˈgleʃɪˌet |-d -ɪd
glacier ˈgleʃɚ; ES ˈgleʃə(r; Brit usually
　ˈglæsɪə, ˈglæsjə
glacis ˈglesɪs, ˈglæsɪs (Fr glaˈsi) |-es -ɪz
glad glæd |gladded ˈglædɪd
gladden, G- ˈglædn̩ |-ed -d |-ing ˈglædn̩ɪŋ,
　-dnɪŋ
glade gled
gladiator ˈglædɪˌetɚ; ES -ˌetə(r
gladiatorial ˌglædɪəˈtorɪəl, -ˈtɔr-; S -ˈtor-
gladiola ˌglædɪˈolə, gləˈdaɪələ |pl -s -z
gladiolus plant ˌglædɪˈoləs |pl -es -ɪz |-li -laɪ
Gladiolus the genus gləˈdaɪələs |pl -li -ˌlaɪ
gladsome ˈglædsəm
Gladstone ˈglædˌston, -stən—W. E. Glad-
　stone pronounced his name ˈgladˌston
　(Wyld).
Gladys ˈglædɪs |-ʼs -ɪz
glair glɛr, glær; E glɛə(r, ES glæə(r; |-ed -d
　|-eous -ɪəs |-y -ɪ
glaive glev |glaived glevd
Glamis Scotl glamz, in Shak. ˈglamɪs |-ʼs -ɪz

Key: See in full §§3–47. bee **bi** |pity ˈpɪtɪ (§6) |rate **ret** |yet **jɛt** |sang **sæŋ** |angry ˈæŋ·grɪ
|bath **bæθ**; E baθ (§10) |ah **ɑ** |far **fɑr** |watch **watʃ**, **wɒtʃ** (§12) |jaw **dʒɔ** |gorge **gɔrdʒ** |go **go**

Glamorganshire glə'mɔrgən‚ʃır, -ʃɚ; ES -'mɔəgən‚ʃıə(r, -ʃə(r
glamorous 'glæmərəs, 'glæmrəs
glamour, -mor 'glæmɚ; ES 'glæmə(r
glance glæns; E+glans, glɑns; |-s -ız |-d -t
gland glænd
glanders 'glændɚz; ES 'glændəz
glandular 'glændʒələ; ES 'glændʒələ(r; |-lous -ləs
glandule 'glændʒul
glans glænz |pl glandes 'glændiz
Glansdale 'glænz‚del, -dḷ
glare glɛr, glær; E glɛə(r, ES glæə(r; |-d -d
Glarus Swtz 'glɑrəs (Fr Glaris glɑ'ris), Wis 'glærəs |-'s -ız
Glasgow 'glæsgo, 'glæz-, 'glæsko, Brit+'glaglass glæs; E+glɑs, glɑs; |-es -ız |-ed -t
glassful 'glæs‚ful; E+'glɑs-, 'glɑs-; |-s -z
glasshouse 'glæs‚havs; E+'glɑs-, 'glɑs-; |-houses -‚havzız
glassmaker 'glæs‚mekɚ; ES -‚mekə(r, E+ 'glɑs-, 'glɑs-
glassman 'glæsmən; E+'glɑs-, 'glɑs-; |-men -mən
glassware 'glæs‚wɛr, -‚wær; E -‚wɛə(r, -‚wæə(r, 'glɑs-, 'glɑs-; S 'glæs‚wæə(r
glasswork 'glæs‚wɝk; ES -‚wɜk, -‚wɝk, E+'glɑs-, 'glɑs-
Glastonbury 'glæstən‚bɛrı, 'glæsṇ-, -bərı
Glaswegian glæs'widʒən, -dʒıən
Glauber 'glaubɚ; ES 'glaubə(r
glaucoma glɔ'komə
glaucous, G- 'glɔkəs
glaze glez |glazes 'glezız |glazed glezd
glazier 'gleʒɚ; ES 'gleʒə(r
gleam glim |-ed -d
glean glin |-ed -d
glebe glib
glee gli |-ful -fəl |-fully -fəlı |-man -mən |-men -mən
glee v 'squint' gli |gleed glid—see agley
gleet glit |gleeted 'glitıd
glen glɛn
Glencairn glɛn'kɛrn, -'kærn; E -'kɛən, ES -'kæən
Glencoe US 'glɛnko, Scotl glɛn'ko
Glendower 'glɛndauɚ, glɛn'dauɚ; ES -ə(r
Glengarry glɛn'gærı
gley v 'squint' glaı |gleyed glaıd—see agley

glib glıb |glibbed glıbd
glide glaıd |glided 'glaıdıd |-r -ɚ; ES -ə(r
glim glım
glimmer 'glımɚ; ES -ə(r; |-ed -d |-ing 'glımərıŋ, 'glımrıŋ
glimpse glımps |-s -ız |-d -t
glint glınt |glinted 'glıntıd
glissade glı'sad, -'sed |-d -ıd
glissando glı'sando |pl -di -di (pseudo-It)
glisten 'glısṇ |-ed -d |-ing 'glısṇıŋ, -snıŋ
glister 'glıstɚ; ES -tə(r; |-ed -d |-ing 'glıstərıŋ, 'glıstrıŋ
glitter 'glıtɚ; ES -tə(r; |-ed -d
gloam glom |-ed -d |-ing -ıŋ
gloat glot |gloated 'glotıd
global 'globḷ |-ly -ı
globate 'globet |-d -ıd
globe glob |globed globd
globeflower 'glob‚flauɚ, -‚flaur; ES -‚flau·ə(r, -‚flauə(r
globoid 'globɔıd
globose 'globos, glo'bos |-bous 'globəs
globular 'glɑbjələ; ES 'glɑbjələ(r, 'glɒb-
globule 'glɑbjul; ES+'glɒb-
globulin 'glɑbjəlın; ES+'glɒb-
Glocester 'glɑstɚ, 'glɒs-; ES -tə(r
glockenspiel 'glakən‚spil; ES+'glɒk-; (Ger 'glɔkən‚ʃpi:l)
glomerate adj 'glɑmərıt, -mrıt; ES+'glɒm-
glomerate v 'glɑmə‚ret; ES+'glɒm-; |-d -ıd
glomeration ‚glɑmə'reʃən; ES+‚glɒm-
gloom glum |gloomed glumd |-y -ı
Gloria 'glorıə, 'glɔr-; S 'glorıə; |G- Patri -'patrı, -'petraı
Gloriana ‚glorı'ænə, ‚glɔr-, -'enə; S ‚glor-
glorification ‚glorəfə'keʃən, ‚glɔr-; S ‚glor-
glorify 'glorə‚faı, 'glɔr-; S 'glor-; |-fied -‚faıd |-fier -‚faıɚ; ES -‚faı·ə(r
glorious 'glorıəs, 'glɔr-; S 'glor-
glory 'glorı, 'glɔrı; S 'glorı; |-ried -rıd
Glos. abbr. for Gloucestershire glas, glɒs, glɔs
gloss glɔs, glɒs |-es -ız |-ed -t
glossary 'glasərı, 'glɒs-, 'glɔs-
Gloster Ga, La, Minn, Miss 'glastɚ, 'glɒs-; ES -tə(r
glottal 'glatḷ; ES+'glɒtḷ
glottalize 'glatḷ‚aız; ES+'glɒt-; |-s -ız |-d -d
glottis 'glatıs; ES+'glɒt-; |-es -ız
Gloucester 'glastɚ, 'glɒs-, 'glɔs-; ES -tə(r; in

Engd loc. 'glɔs- |-shire -ˌʃɪr, -ʃɚ; ES -ˌʃɪə(r,
-ʃə(r
Glouster *O* 'glaustɚ; ES 'glaustə(r
glove glʌv |gloved glʌvd
Gloversville 'glʌvɚzˌvɪl; ES -vəz-
glow glo |glowed glod
glower 'glauɚ; ES 'glau·ə(r; |-ed -d |-ing
'glaurɪŋ, 'glauərɪŋ
glowfly 'gloˌflaɪ
glowworm 'gloˌwɝm; ES -ˌwɜm, -ˌwɝm
gloxinia, G- glɑk'sɪnɪə, -njə; ES+glɒk-
gloze gloz |glozes 'glozɪz |glozed glozd
glucinum, -nium glu'saɪnəm, -'sɪnɪəm, glɪu-
Gluck glʊk
glucose 'glukos, 'glɪu- |-coside -kəˌsaɪd
glue glu, glɪu |-d -d
Glueck glʊk
glum glʌm
glume glum, glɪum
glut glʌt |glutted 'glʌtɪd
gluten 'glutn̩, 'glɪutn̩ |-ous -əs
glutinus 'glutɪnəs, 'glɪu-
glutton 'glʌtn̩ |-ous -əs |-y -ɪ
glyceric glɪ'sɛrɪk, 'glɪsərɪk
glycerin 'glɪsrɪn, -sərɪn |-ine -rɪn, -səˌrin
glycerol 'glɪsəˌrol, -ˌral, -ˌrɒl
glyceryl 'glɪsəˌrɪl
glycine 'glaɪsin, glaɪ'sin
glycogen 'glaɪkədʒən, -dʒɪn
glycol glaɪkol, -kɑl, -kɒl
glycoprotein ˌglaɪkə'protiɪn
glyph glɪf
glyptic 'glɪptɪk |-al -l̩
G-man 'dʒiˌmæn |-men -ˌmɛn
Gnadenhutten *O, loc.* dʒɪ'nednˌhʌtn̩ (*Ger*
-hütten 'gnɑːdənˌhytən)
gnarl nɑrl; ES nɑːl, E+nɑːl; |-ed -d
gnash næʃ |gnashes 'næʃɪz |gnashed næʃt
gnat næt
gnaw nɔ |gnawed nɔd |-er 'nɔɚ; ES 'nɔ·ə(r
gneiss naɪs
gnome nom
gnomic 'nomɪk |-al -l̩ |-ally -l̩ɪ, -ɪklɪ
gnomon 'nomɑn, 'nomɒn
Gnossus 'nɑsəs; ES+'nɒs-; |-sus' -səs
gnostic 'nɑstɪk; ES+'nɒs-; |-al -l̩ |-ally -l̩ɪ,
-ɪklɪ |-ism -təˌsɪzəm
gnu nu, nɪu, nju
go go |went wɛnt |gone gɔn, gɒn, *much less*

freq. gan — *in unstressed position often* gʊ
(ˌlɛts gʊ'ɪn), *or* gə (ˌlɛts gə'daʊn)
goad god |goaded 'godɪd
go-ahead *adj* 'goə'hɛd ('go-a'head ˌchap,
'go-aˌhead 'spirit)
go-ahead *n* 'goəˌhɛd
goal gol |-ed -d, *children's game*+gul
goalkeeper 'golˌkipɚ; ES -ˌkipə(r
goalless 'gollɪs
goat got
goatee go'ti
goatherd 'gotˌhɝd; ES -ˌhɜd, -ˌhɝd
goatsbeard 'gotsˌbɪrd; ES -ˌbɪəd, S+-ˌbɛəd
goatsucker 'gotˌsʌkɚ; ES -ˌsʌkə(r
gob, G- gɑb; ES+gɒb
gobbet 'gɑbɪt; ES+'gɒbɪt
gobble 'gɑbl̩; ES+'gɒbl̩; |-d -d |-ling -blɪŋ,
bl̩ɪŋ
gobbler 'gɑblɚ; ES 'gɑblə(r, 'gɒb-
Gobbo 'gɑbo; ES+'gɒbo
Gobelin 'gɑbəlɪn, 'gob-; ES+'gɒb-; (*Fr*
gɔ'blæ̃)
go-between 'gobəˌtwin
Gobi 'gobɪ, 'gobi
goblet 'gɑblɪt; ES+'gɒb-
goblin 'gɑblɪn; ES+'gɒb-; *In 'Little Orphant
Annie' Riley pronounced it* 'gɑbəˌlɪn.
goby 'gobɪ
go-by 'goˌbaɪ
gocart 'goˌkɑrt; ES -ˌkɑːt, E+-ˌkɑːt
god gɑd, gɒd
God gɑd, gɒd, *less freq.* gɔd
Godalming 'gɑdl̩mɪŋ, 'gɒd-
godchild 'gɑdˌtʃaɪld, 'gɒd-
goddaughter 'gɑdˌdɔtɚ, 'gɒd-; ES -tə(r
goddess 'gɑdɪs, 'gɒd- |-es -ɪz
godfather 'gɑdˌfɑðɚ, 'gɒd-; ES -ˌfɑðə(r,
E+-ˌfɑðə(r
god-fearing 'gɑdˌfɪrɪŋ, 'gɒd-; S+-ˌfɛrɪŋ,
-ˌfjɪrɪŋ, -ˌfjɛrɪŋ
god-forsaken 'gɑdfɚ'sekən, 'gɒd-; ES -fə-;
('god-forˌsaken 'place)
Godfrey 'gɑdfrɪ, 'gɒd-
godhead 'gɑdhɛd, 'gɒd- |-hood -hʊd
Godiva go'daɪvə
godlike 'gɑdˌlaɪk, 'gɒd-
godly 'gɑdlɪ, 'gɒdlɪ
godmother 'gɑdˌmʌðɚ, 'gɒd-; ES -ˌmʌðə(r
godown '*a drink*' 'goˌdaʊn

Key: *See in full §§3-47.* bee bi |pity 'pɪtɪ (§6) |rate ret |yet jɛt |sang sæŋ |angry 'æŋ·grɪ
|bath bæθ; E baθ (§10) |ah ɑ |far fɑr |watch wɑtʃ, wɒtʃ (§12) |jaw dʒɔ |gorge gɔrdʒ |go go

godown *'warehouse'* go'daʊn

godparent 'gad͵pɛrənt, 'gɒd-, -͵pær-, -͵per-

godsend 'gad͵sɛnd, 'gɒd-

godson 'gad͵sʌn, 'gɒd-

Godspeed 'gad͵spid, 'gɒd-, -'spid

Godward 'gadwəd, 'gɒd-; ES -wəd

Goebbels *Ger* 'gœbəls

goer 'goɚ; ES 'go·ə(r

Goethals 'goθəlz |-'s -ɪz

Goethe 'getɪ, 'gɜtə (*Ger* 'gøːtə)

Goffe gɔf, gɒf

goffer 'gafɚ, 'gɒfɚ, 'gɔfɚ; ES -fə(r; |-ed -d
|-ing -fərɪŋ, -frɪŋ

Gog gag, gɒg, gɔg

go-getter 'go'gɛtɚ; ES -'gɛtə(r

goggle 'gagl̩, 'gɒgl̩ |-d -d |-ling -glɪŋ, -gl̩ɪŋ

goggles 'gagl̩z, 'gɒg-

Gogmagog 'gagmə͵gag, 'gɒgmə͵gɒg

Gogol 'gogal, 'gogɒl

Goidelic gɔɪ'dɛlɪk

goiter, -tre 'gɔɪtɚ; ES 'gɔɪtə(r; |-(e)d -d

Golconda gal'kandə; ES+gɒl'kɒndə

gold gold, *formerly* guld

goldbeater 'gold͵bitɚ; ES -͵bitə(r

golden 'goldn̩

goldenrod 'goldn̩͵rad; ES+-͵rɒd

goldfinch 'gold͵fɪntʃ |-es -ɪz

goldfish 'gold͵fɪʃ |-es -ɪz |-'s -ɪz

goldilocks, G- 'goldɪ͵laks; ES+-͵lɒks; |-'s -ɪz

gold-plate *v* 'gold'plet |-plated -'pletɪd

goldsmith, G- 'gold͵smɪθ |-ths -θs

Goldwin, Gouldin 'goldwɪn, 'goldɪn

golf galf, gɒlf, gɔlf, *much less freq.* gaf, gɒf
|-ed -t

Golgotha 'galgəθə, 'gɒl-

goliard 'goljəd; ES 'goljəd

Goliath gə'laɪəθ

Gollancz 'galənts, -ænts; ES+'gɒl-; |-'s -ɪz

golliwog 'galɪ͵wag, -͵wɒg; ES+'gɒl-

golosh gə'laʃ; ES+-'lɒʃ; |-es -ɪz

Gomorrah, -rrha gə'mɔrə, -'mar-, -'mɒr-

gonad 'ganæd, 'gɒn-

gondola 'gandələ, 'gɒn- |-ed -d

gondolier ͵gandə'lɪr, ͵gɒn-; ES -'lɪə(r, S+
-'lɛə(r

gone gɔn, gɒn, *much less freq.* gan

goneness 'gɔnnɪs, 'gɒn-, *much less freq.* 'gan-

Goneril 'ganərəl, 'gɒn-, -rɪl

gonfalon 'ganfələn, 'gɒn-

gonfalonier ͵ganfələ'nɪr, ͵gɒn-; ES -'nɪə(r,
S+-'nɛə(r

gonfanon 'ganfənən, 'gɒn-

gong gɔŋ, gɒŋ, gaŋ |-ed -d

gonococcus ͵ganə'kakəs |*pl* -cocci -'kaksaɪ;
|ES+͵gɒnə'kɒk-

gonof 'ganəf, 'gɒn-

gonorrhea ͵ganə'riə, ͵gɒn-

Gonzaga gən'zagə (*It* gon'dzaːga)

Gonzalo gən'zalo

goober 'gubɚ, 'gubɚ; ES -bə(r

good gʊd |goodly 'gʊdlɪ

good-by, -bye gʊd'baɪ

good deal *'good bargain'* 'gʊd'dil, *'much'*
gʊ'dil

goodhearted 'gʊd'hartɪd; ES -'haːtɪd, E+
-'haːtɪd

good-humored 'gʊd'jumɚd, -'hjumɚd; ES
-məd

goodman 'gʊdmən |-men -mən

good-natured 'gʊd'netʃɚd; ES -'netʃəd;
('good-͵natured 'dog)

goodness 'gʊdnɪs |-es -ɪz

goods gʊdz

good-tempered 'gʊd'tɛmpɚd; ES -'tɛmpəd

goodwife 'gʊd͵waɪf — *see* wife

Goodwin 'gʊdwɪn

goody 'gʊdɪ

Goodyear 'gʊdʒɪr, 'gʊdjɪr; ES -ɪə(r, S+
-ɛə(r

goof guf |-y -ɪ

googly 'guglɪ

goon gun

Goop gup

goose gus |-'s -ɪz |geese gis |geese's 'gisɪz

gooseberry 'gus͵bɛrɪ, 'guz-, -bərɪ, *rarely*
'guz-

gooseherd 'gus͵hɝd; ES -͵hɜd, -͵hɝd; *formerly* 'gazəd, 'gɒz-

gooseneck 'gus͵nɛk |-ed -t

gopher 'gofɚ; ES -fə(r; |-ed -d |-ing 'gofərɪŋ,
'gofrɪŋ

Gordian 'gɔrdɪən, -djən; ES 'gɔəd-

gore gor, gɔr; ES goə(r, E+gɔə(r; |-d -d

gorge gɔrdʒ; ES gɔədʒ; |-s -ɪz |-d -d |-ous -əs

gorget 'gɔrdʒɪt; ES 'gɔədʒɪt; |-ed -ɪd

Gorgon 'gɔrgən; ES 'gɔəgən

Gorgonian gɔr'gonɪən, -njən; ES gɔ-

Gorgonzola ͵gɔrgən'zolə; ES ͵gɔəgən-

Gorham ˈgɔrəm, *NH* ˈgorəm, ˈgɔrəm
gorilla gəˈrɪlə
Gorky, -ki ˈgɔrkɪ; ES ˈgɔəkɪ
gormand ˈgɔrmənd; ES ˈgɔəmənd
gormandize ˈgɔrmənˌdaɪz; ES ˈgɔəm-; |-s -ɪz
|-d -d
gorse gɔrs; ES gɔəs; |-s -ɪz
gory ˈgorɪ, ˈgɔrɪ; S ˈgorɪ
goshawk ˈgasˌhɔk, ˈgɒs-
Goshen ˈgoʃən
gosling ˈgazlɪŋ, ˈgɒz-
gospel ˈgaspļ, ˈgɒs- |-ed -d
gossamer ˈgasəmɚ; ES ˈgasəmə(r, ˈgɒs-
Gosse gɔs, gɒs, gas
gossip ˈgasəp; ES+ˈgɒs-; |-ed -t
gossoon gaˈsun; ES+gɒ-
got gat; ES+gɒt
Gotama ˈgɒtəmə, ˈgɒt-
Göteborg ˈjetəˌbɔrg *or* Gothenburg ˈgatņ̩-
ˌbɝg; ES ˈjetəˌbɔəg, ˈgatņ̩ˌbɝg, -ˌbɝg, ˈgɒt-;
(*Sw* ˌjøtəˈbɔrj)
Goth gaθ, gɒθ, gɔθ |-ths -θs
Gotham 'New York' ˈgaθəm, ˈgɒθəm, ˈgoθəm,
in Notts ˈgatəm, ˈgɒtəm, *loc.* ˈgotəm
Gothard ˈgatɚd; ES ˈgatəd, ˈgɒt-; (*Fr*
gɔˈtaːr)
Gothic ˈgaθɪk, ˈgɒθɪk |-ism -θəˌsɪzəm
Gotland ˈgatlənd, ˈgɒt-
gotten ˈgatņ; ES+ˈgɒtņ
Götterdämmerung *Ger* ˈgœtərˌdɛməˌrʊŋ
Gotthard ˈgatɚd; ES ˈgatəd, ˈgɒt-; (*Fr*
gɔˈtaːr)
Gottland ˈgatlənd, ˈgɒt-
gouge gaʊdʒ |gouges ˈgaʊdʒɪz |gouged gaʊdʒd
—*Brit*+gudʒ
Gough gɔf, gɒf, gaf
goulash ˈgulæʃ, -laʃ |-es -ɪz
Gouldin = Goldwin ˈgoldɪn
Gouldsboro ˈguldzˌbɝo, -ə; ES -ˌbɝ-, -ˌbʌr-,
-ˌbɝ-; *Me loc.* ˈgulzbrə
Gounod ˈguno (*Fr* guˈno)
gourd gord, gɔrd, gʊrd; E goəd, gɔəd, gʊəd;
S goəd
gourmand ˈgʊrmənd; ES ˈgʊəmənd; (*Fr*
gurˈmã)
gourmet ˈgʊrme; ES ˈgʊəme; (*Fr* gurˈmɛ)
gout gaʊt
Gouverneur *NY* ˌgʌvɚˈnʊr; ES ˌgʌvəˈnʊə(r
govern ˈgʌvɚn; ES ˈgʌvən; |-ed -d

governance ˈgʌvɚnəns; ES ˈgʌvənəns; |-s -ɪz
governess ˈgʌvɚnɪs; ES ˈgʌvənɪs; |-es -ɪz
government ˈgʌvɚmənt, ˈgʌvɚnmənt; ES
ˈgʌvəmənt, ˈgʌvənmənt, ˈgʌvm̩ənt; *No
competent observer can doubt the prevalence
of* ˈgʌvɚmənt, ˈgʌvəmənt *among the leading
statesmen of US and England, even in formal
public address.*
governor ˈgʌvənɚ, ˈgʌvnɚ, ˈgʌvɚnɚ; ES
ˈgʌvənə(r, ˈgʌvnə(r;—ə *for* ɚ *in* ˈgʌvənɚ
shows dissimilation (§121).
gowan ˈgaʊən
Gowanda gəˈwandə, go-, -ˈwɒndə
Gower *ME poet* ˈgoɚ, ˈgaʊɚ, *Lond street*
ˈgaʊɚ; ES ˈgo·ə(r, ˈgaʊ·ə(r
gown gaʊn |-ed -d
grab græb |grabbed græbd
grabble ˈgræbļ |-d -d |-ling ˈgræblɪŋ, -bḷɪŋ
Gracchus ˈgrækəs |-'s -ɪz |*pl* -chi ˈgrækaɪ
grace, G- gres |-'s -ɪz |-s -ɪz |-d -t
gracile ˈgræsḷ, -ɪl
gracious ˈgreʃəs
grackle ˈgrækḷ
gradate ˈgredet |-d -ɪd
gradation greˈdeʃən |-ed -d |-al -ḷ |-ally -ḷɪ
grade gred |graded ˈgredɪd
Gradgrind, g- ˈgrædˌgraɪnd |-ian -ɪən |-ism
-ˌɪzəm
gradient ˈgredɪənt, -djənt
gradual ˈgrædʒʊəl, -dʒʊl |-ly -ɪ, -dʒəlɪ
graduate *n, adj* ˈgrædʒʊɪt, -ˌet
graduate *v* ˈgrædʒʊˌet |-d -ɪd
graduation ˌgrædʒʊˈeʃən
Gradus, g- ˈgredəs |-es -ɪz
graft græft; E+graft, grɑft; |-ed -ɪd
graham, G- ˈgreəm
grail grel
grain gren |-ed -d
grainery, -ary ˈgrenərɪ, ˈgrenrɪ—*cf* granary.
Both grainery, -ary *and* granary *date from
the 16c. In US* ˈgrenərɪ, ˈgrenrɪ *appears to
prevail.*
gram græm
gramarye, -ry ˈgræmərɪ
gramercy grəˈmɝsɪ; ES -ˈmɝsɪ, -ˈmɝsɪ;
(ˈGramercy ˈPark)
grammar ˈgræmɚ; ES ˈgræmə(r
grammarian grəˈmɛrɪən, -ˈmær-, -ˈmer-
grammatical grəˈmætɪkḷ |-ly -ɪ, -ɪklɪ

Key: *See in full* §§3–47. bee bi |pity ˈpɪtɪ (§6) |rate ret |yet jɛt |sang sæŋ |angry ˈæŋ·grɪ
|bath bæθ; E baθ (§10) |ah ɑ |far fɑr |watch watʃ, wɒtʃ (§12) |jaw dʒɔ |gorge gɔrdʒ |go go

gramme **græm**
gramophone, G- **ˈgræməˌfon**
Grampian **ˈgræmpɪən, -pjən** |-s **-z**
grampus **ˈgræmpəs** |-es **-ɪz**
Granada **grəˈnɑdə** (*Sp* **grɑˈnɑðɑ**)
granary **ˈgrænərɪ**—*cf* grainery. Granary
  ˈgrænərɪ *comes from Latin* grānārium;
  grainery, -ary *from English* grain.
Granby **ˈgrænbɪ**; *in Mass loc.* **ˈgræmbɪ**
Gran Chaco **ˈgrɑnˈtʃɑko**
grand **grænd**, *before some conss.*+**græn** (*cf*
  ˈgrændˈlek *with* **ˈgrænˈvju**)
grandad **ˈgrænˌdæd** |-dy **-ɪ**
grandam **ˈgrændəm**
grandame **ˈgrændem, -dəm**
grandaunt **ˈgrændˈænt**, *much less freq.* **-ˈɑnt**;
  E **-ˈant, -ˈɑnt, -ˈænt**
grandchild **ˈgrænˌtʃaɪld, ˈgrænd-** |-ren **-ˌtʃɪl-**
  drən
Grand Coulee **ˈgrændˈkulɪ, -ˈkuli**
granddad **ˈgrænˌdæd** |-dy **-ɪ**
granddaughter **ˈgrænˌdɔtɚ, ˈgrænd-**; ES
  -ˌdɔtə(r
grandee **grænˈdi**
grandeur **ˈgrændʒɚ, -dʒʊr**; ES **ˈgrændʒɚ(r,**
  -dʒʊə(r
grandfather **ˈgrænˌfɑðɚ, ˈgrænd-**; ES **-ˌfɑðə(r,**
  E+**-ˌfɑðə(r**; |-ly **-lɪ**
Grandgent **ˈgrændʒənt**
grandiloquence **grænˈdɪləkwəns** |-ent **-ənt**
grandiose **ˈgrændɪˌos**
grandiosity **ˌgrændɪˈɑsətɪ**; ES+**-ˈɒsətɪ**
Grandison **ˈgrændəsn̩**
grandma **ˈgrænma, ˈgræmmɑ, ˈgræma,**
  ˈgræmə, ˈgrændma
grandmamma **ˈgrænˌmamə, ˈgrænd-, -məˌma**
grandmother **ˈgrænˌmʌðɚ, ˈgrænd-**; ES
  -ˌmʌðə(r; |-ly **-lɪ**
grandnephew **ˈgrænˈnɛfju, ˈgrænd-**, *much less*
  freq. **-ˈnɛvju**
grandniece **ˈgrænˈnis, ˈgrænd-** |-s **-ɪz**
grandpa **ˈgrænpa, ˈgræmpa, ˈgræmpə, ˈgrænd-**
  pa
grandpapa **ˈgrænˌpapə, -pəˈpa, ˈgrænd-**
grandparent **ˈgrænˌpɛrənt, ˈgrænd-, -ˌpær-,**
  -ˌper-; S **-ˌpær-, -ˌper-**
Grand Pré **ˈgrænˈpre, ˈgrænd-** (*Fr* **grɑ̃ˈpre**)
Grandpré *Shak.* **ˈgrænpre, ˈgrændp-**; *Fr vil.*
  grɑ̃ˈpre

grandsire **ˈgrænˌsaɪr, ˈgrænd-**; ES **-ˌsaɪə(r**
grandson **ˈgrænˌsʌn, ˈgrænd-**
grandstand **ˈgrænˌstænd, ˈgrænd-**
Grand Teton **ˈgrænˈtitn̩, ˈgrænd-, -tɑn, -tɒn**
granduncle **ˈgrændˈʌŋkl̩**
grange, G- **grendʒ** |-s **-ɪz**
Granicus **grəˈnaɪkəs** |-ˈs **-ɪz**
granite **ˈgrænɪt** |-tic **grəˈnɪtɪk, græ-**
granny **ˈgrænɪ**
grant **grænt**; E+**grant, grɑnt**; |-ed **-ɪd**
Grant **grænt**
grantee **grænˈti**; E+**gran-, grɑn-**
grantor **ˈgræntɚ, grænˈtɔr**; ES **-tə(r, -ˈtɔə(r,**
  E+**gran-, grɑn-**
granular **ˈgrænjəlɚ**; ES **ˈgrænjələ(r**
granulate *adj* **ˈgrænjəlɪt**
granulate *v* **ˈgrænjəˌlet** |-d **-ɪd**
granulation **ˌgrænjəˈleʃən**
granule **ˈgrænjʊl**
Granville **ˈgrænvɪl**
grape **grep**
grapefruit **ˈgrepˌfrut, -ˌfrɪut**
grapeshot **ˈgrepˌʃɑt**; ES+**-ˌʃɒt**
grapevine **ˈgrepˌvaɪn** |-d **-d**
graph **græf**; E+**graf, grɑf**; |-ed **-t**
graphic **ˈgræfɪk** |-ly **-lɪ** |-ally **-ļɪ**
graphite **ˈgræfaɪt** |-d **-ɪd**
graphophone, G- **ˈgræfəˌfon**
grapnel **ˈgræpnəl** |-ed **-d**
grapple **ˈgræpl̩** |-d **-d** |-ling **ˈgræplɪŋ, -pļɪŋ**
Grasmere **ˈgræsmɪr**; ES **-mɪə(r, E+ˈgras-,**
  ˈgrɑs-
grasp **græsp**; E+**grasp, grɑsp**; |-ed **-t**
grass **græs**; E+**gras, grɑs**; |-es **-ɪz** |-ed **-t**
Grasse, de **dəˈgras**
grasshopper **ˈgræsˌhapɚ**; ES **-ˌhapə(r, -ˌhɒpə(r,**
  E+**ˈgras-, ˈgrɑs-**
Grassmann **ˈgrasman**
grate **gret** |grated **ˈgretɪd**
grateful '*thankful*' **ˈgretfəl** |-ly **-ɪ**
grateful '*filled grate*' **ˈgretˌful** |-s **-z**
Gratiano **ˌgræʃɪˈano, ˌgraʃ-**, *Brit* **ˌgreʃ-**
gratification **ˌgrætəfəˈkeʃən**
gratify **ˈgrætəˌfaɪ** |-fied **-faɪd**
gratin **ˈgrætæ̃** (*Fr* **graˈtæ̃**)
grating **ˈgretɪŋ**
Gratiot **ˈgræʃɪət, ˈgre-**
gratis **ˈgretɪs**
gratitude **ˈgrætəˌtjud, -ˌtɪud, -ˌtud**

Grattan 'grætn̩

gratuitous grə'tjuətəs, -'tɪu-, -'tu- |-ty -tɪ

gratulate 'grætʃə‚let, -tʃʊ-

gravamen grə'vemɛn |-s -z |-mina -'væmɪnə

grave grev |*past* graved grevd |*pptc* graven
'grevən *or* graved grevd

gravel 'grævl̩ |-ed -d |-ing 'grævl̩ɪŋ, -vlɪŋ

gravel-blind 'grævl̩‚blaɪnd

graven 'grevən

gravestone 'grev‚ston

graveyard 'grev‚jɑrd; ES -‚jɑːd, E+-‚jɑːd

gravid 'grævɪd |-ity grə'vɪdətɪ

gravitate 'grævə‚tet |-d -ɪd

gravitation ‚grævə'teʃən

gravity 'grævətɪ

gravure 'grevjər, -jʊr; ES 'grevjə(r, -jʊə(r
-gravure -grə'vjʊr; ES -'vjʊə(r

gravy 'grevɪ

gray, G- gre

graybeard 'gre‚bɪrd; ES -‚bɪəd, S+-‚bɛəd

grayling 'grelɪŋ

graze grez |grazes 'grezɪz |grazed grezd

grazier 'greʒɚ; ES 'greʒə(r

grease *n* gris |greases 'grisɪz

grease *v* gris, griz; S griz; |-s -ɪz |-d -grist,
grizd — 'grizɪ *and* tə griz *are phonetically*
normal; 'grisɪ *and* tə gris *imitate the noun*
grease (gris).

greasewood 'gris‚wʊd

greasy 'grisɪ, 'grizɪ; S 'grizɪ — *Some distin-*
guish 'grisɪ *'covered with grease' from* 'grizɪ
'slimy'.

great gret; S *occas.* grɛt, *a historical form, cf*
threat θrɛt; *The pronunciation* grɛt *paral-*
lels that of bread, deaf, sweat, thread, tread,
etc.

great-aunt 'gret'ænt, *much less freq.* -'ɑnt; E
-'ɑnt, -'ɑnt, -'ænt

Great Britain 'gret'brɪtn̩, -tən

greatcoat 'gret‚kot |-ed -ɪd

great deal *'important bargain'* 'gret'dil,
'large amount' 'gre'dil, 'gret'dil

greaten 'gretn̩ |-ed -d |-ing 'gretn̩ɪŋ, -tnɪŋ

Greatheart 'gret‚hɑrt; ES -‚hɑːt, E+-‚hɑːt

greathearted 'gret'hɑrtɪd; ES -'hɑːtɪd, E+
-'hɑːtɪd

great-uncle 'gret'ʌŋkl̩

greave griv |greaved grivd

grebe grib

Grecian 'griʃən

gree gri

Greece gris |-'s -ɪz

greed grid |-y -ɪ |-ily 'gridl̩ɪ, -dɪlɪ

Greek grik

Greeley 'grilɪ

green grin |greened grind |-ness 'grinnɪs

Greenaway 'grinə‚we

greenback 'grin‚bæk

green-backed 'grin'bækt ('green-‚backed 'bird)

greenbrier, G- 'grin‚braɪɚ; ES -‚braɪ‚ə(r

greenery 'grinərɪ, 'grinrɪ

green-eyed 'grin'aɪd ('green-‚eyed 'Becky)

greengrocer 'grin‚grosɚ; ES -‚grosə(r; |-y -ɪ,
-srɪ

greenhorn 'grin‚hɔrn; ES -‚hɔən

greenhouse 'grin‚haʊs |-s -‚haʊzɪz

Greenland 'grinlənd

greensward 'grin‚swɔrd; ES -‚swɔəd; |-ed -ɪd

Greenville 'grinvɪl; S+-vl̩

Greenwich *Engd* 'grɪnɪdʒ, 'grɛn-, -ɪtʃ; *US*
places usually 'grinwɪtʃ. *How far* 'grɪnɪtʃ,
'grɛn- *are traditional and prevalent for some*
Eastern places, or recent imitations of Brit
is doubtful. 'grɛnɪtʃ *appears to prevail for*
Greenwich Village, NY.

greenwood, G- 'grin‚wʊd

greet grit |greeted 'gritɪd

Greet, William Cabell 'wɪljəm'kæbl̩'grit

gregarious grɪ'gɛrɪəs, -'gær-, -'ger-

Gregorian grɛ'gorɪən, -'gɔr-; S -'gorɪən

Gregory 'grɛgərɪ

gremial 'grimɪəl

Gremio 'grimɪ‚o, 'grimjo

Grenada *Miss* grɪ'nɑdə, *Brit colony* grɪ'nedə

grenade grɪ'ned

grenadier ‚grɛnə'dɪr; ES -'dɪə(r, S+-'dɛə(r

grenadine ‚grɛnə'din, 'grɛnə‚din

Grendel 'grɛndl̩

Gresham 'grɛʃəm, 'grɛsəm — 'grɛʃəm *is a*
sp. pron.

Gretchen 'grɛtʃɪn

Gretel 'gretl̩ — *see* Hänsel and Gretel

Gretna 'grɛtnə

Gretna Green 'grɛtnə'grin

Greville 'grɛvl̩, -ɪl

grew *past of* grow gru, grɪu

grewsome 'grusəm, 'grɪu-

grey, G- gre

Key: See in full §§3-47. bee bi |pity 'pɪtɪ (§6) |rate ret |yet jɛt |sang sæŋ |angry 'æŋ·grɪ
|bath bæθ; E baθ (§10) |ah ɑ |far fɑr |watch wɑtʃ, wɒtʃ (§12) |jaw dʒɔ |gorge gɔrdʒ |go go

greyhound 'gre͵haʊnd
grid grɪd |gridded 'grɪdɪd
griddle 'grɪdl̩ |-d -d |-ling 'grɪdlɪŋ, -dl̩ɪŋ
griddlecake 'grɪdl̩͵kek
gride graɪd |grided 'graɪdɪd
gridiron 'grɪd͵aɪəˑn, -͵aɪrn; ES -͵aɪˑən, -͵aɪən
grief grif
Grieg grig
Grierson 'grɪrsn̩; ES 'grɪəsn̩
grievance 'grivəns |-s -ɪz
grieve griv |-d -d |-dly -ɪdly |-vous -əs
griff grɪf
griffin 'grɪfɪn |griffon 'grɪfən
Griffith 'grɪfɪθ
grifter 'grɪftɚ; ES 'grɪftə(r
grig grɪg |grigged grɪgd
grill, -e grɪl |grilled grɪld
grim grɪm
grimace grɪ'mes |-s -ɪz |-d -t
grimalkin grɪ'mælkɪn, -'mɔlkɪn, -'mɔkɪn
grime, G- graɪm |grimed graɪmd |grimy
    'graɪmɪ
Grimm grɪm
grin grɪn |grinned grɪnd
grind graɪnd |ground graʊnd
grindstone 'graɪn͵ston, 'graɪnd-
gringo 'grɪŋgo
Grinnell grɪ'nɛl
grip grɪp |gripped grɪpt
gripe graɪp |griped graɪpt
grippe grɪp
gripsack 'grɪp͵sæk
Griqualand 'grikwə͵lænd, 'grɪkwə-
Griselda grɪ'zɛldə
grisly 'ghastly' 'grɪzlɪ
grisly 'gristly' 'grɪslɪ, 'grɪsl̩ɪ
grist grɪst
gristle 'grɪsl̩ |-tly 'grɪslɪ, 'grɪsl̩ɪ
gristmill 'grɪst͵mɪl
Griswold 'grɪzwəld
grit grɪt |gritted 'grɪtɪd |gritty 'grɪtɪ
grith grɪθ |-ths -θs
grits grɪts |-tten 'grɪtn̩
grizzle 'grɪzl̩ |-d -d |-ling 'grɪzl̩ɪŋ, -zlɪŋ
grizzly 'grɪzlɪ
groan gron |groaned grond
groat grot
grocer 'grosɚ; ES 'grosə(r; |-y -ɪ, -srɪ
Groesbeck 'grosbɛk

grog grɑg, grɒg, grɔg |-ged -d |-gery -ərɪ
    |-gy -ɪ
grogram 'grɑgrəm, 'grɒg-, 'grɔg-
groin grɔɪn |groined grɔɪnd
grommet 'grɑmɪt; ES+'grɒmɪt
Groningen 'groninɡən
groom grum, grʊm |-ed -d
groomsman 'grumzmən, 'grʊmz- |-men -mən
groove gruv |grooved gruvd
grope grop |groped gropt
grosbeak 'gros͵bik
grosgrain 'gro͵gren |-ed -d
gross gros |-es -ɪz|-ed -t
grot coin grot |pl grote 'grotə or groten 'grotən
grot 'grotto' grɑt; ES+grɒt
grotesque gro'tɛsk |-rie -ərɪ, -skrɪ
Grotius 'groʃɪəs |or De Groot də'grot |Gro-
    tius's -ɪz
Groton US places variously pron. 'grɑtn̩,
    'grɒtn̩, 'grɔtn̩, 'grɒtn̩ — in NEngd & NY
    usually 'grɑtn̩, 'grɒtn̩
grotto 'grɑto; ES+'grɒto
grouch graʊtʃ |-es -ɪz |-ed -t
ground graʊnd |-ed -ɪd |-ling -lɪŋ
ground-hog 'graʊnd͵hɑg, -͵hɔg, -͵hɒg; S
    -͵hɔg, -͵hɑg, -͵hɒg
groundnut 'graʊnd͵nʌt, 'graʊn͵nʌt
groundsel 'graʊnsl̩, 'graʊndsl̩
groundwork 'graʊnd͵wɝk; ES -͵wɜk, -͵wɝk
group grup |grouped grupt
grouse bird graʊs |3 sg -s -ɪz |-d -t
grousy 'having grouse' 'graʊzɪ, -sɪ
grout graʊt |grouted 'graʊtɪd
grove grov |groved grovd
grovel 'grɑvl̩, 'grʌvl̩; ES+'grɒvl̩; |-ed -d |-ling
    -vl̩ɪŋ, -vlɪŋ — ʌ shows the original vowel,
    ɑ being a sp. pron.
Grover 'grovɚ; ES 'grovə(r
grow gro |grew gru, grɪu |grown gron
growl graʊl |growled graʊld
grown gron
grown-up n 'gron͵ʌp
grown-up adj 'gron'ʌp ('grown-͵up 'boys)
growth groθ |-ths -θs
grub grʌb |grubbed grʌbd
grubstake 'grʌb͵stek |-staked -͵stekt
grudge grʌdʒ |grudges 'grʌdʒɪz |grudged
    grʌdʒd
gruel 'gruəl, 'grɪuəl |-ed -d

|full fʊl |tooth tuθ |further 'fɝðɚ; ES 'fɜðə |custom 'kʌstəm |while hwaɪl |how haʊ |toy tɔɪ
|using 'juzɪŋ |fuse fjuz, fɪuz |dish dɪʃ |vision 'vɪʒən |Eden 'idn̩ |cradle 'kredl̩ |keep 'em 'kipm̩

gruesome 'grusəm, 'grɪu-
gruff grʌf
grumble 'grʌmbl̩ |-d -d |-ling 'grʌmblɪŋ,
  -bl̩ɪŋ
Grumio 'grumɪˌo, 'grumjo
grumpy 'grʌmpɪ
Grundy 'grʌndɪ |-ism -ˌɪzəm |-dyist -ɪst
grunt grʌnt |grunted 'grʌntɪd
Gruyère gru'jɛr, grɪ'jɛr; ES -'jɛə(r; (Fr
  gry'jɛːr)
gryphon 'grɪfən
Guadalquivir ˌgwadl̩'kwɪvɚ, ˌgwɒd-; ES
  -və(r; (Sp ˌgwaðalki'ßir)
Guadalupe Tex 'gɒdl̩ˌup, ˌgɒdl̩'up, ˌgwadl̩'up,
  ˌgwɒd- (Sp ˌgwaða'lupe)
Guadalupe Hidalgo Mex ˌgwadl̩'up·hɪ'dælgo,
  ˌgwɒd- (Sp ˌgwaða'lupe·i'ðalgo)
Guadeloupe WI ˌgɒdl̩'up, ˌgwad-, ˌgwɒd-
Guam gwam, gwɒm
guanine 'gwanin, 'gwɒn-
guano 'gwano, 'gwɒno
guarantee ˌgærən'ti |-d -d
guarantor 'gærəntɚ, -tɔr, in contrast -'tɔr; ES
  -tə(r, -tɔə(r, -'tɔə(r
guaranty 'gærəntɪ |-tied -tɪd
guard gard; ES gaːd, E+gaːd; |-ed -ɪd
guardhouse 'gardˌhaʊs |-houses -ˌhaʊzɪz; ES
  see guard
guardian 'gardɪən; ES see guard
guardroom 'gardˌrum, -ˌrʊm; ES see guard
guardsman 'gardzmən |-men -mən; ES see
  guard
Guatemala ˌgwatə'malə, ˌgwɒt-, older ˌgɒtə-
  'mɒlə |-n -n
guava 'gwavə, 'gwɒvə
Guayaquil ˌgwaɪə'kil (Sp ˌgwaja'kil)
gubernatorial ˌgjubɚnə'torɪəl, ˌgɪu-, -'tɔr-;
  ES -bənə-, S -'tor-
gudgeon 'gʌdʒən |-ed -d
Gudrun 'gʊdrun
guelder-rose 'gɛldɚˌroz; ES 'gɛldə-
Guelph gwɛlf
guerdon 'gɝdn̩; ES 'gɜdn̩, 'gɝdn̩ |-ed -d
  |-ing -dn̩ɪŋ, -dnɪŋ
Guernsey, g- 'gɝnzɪ; ES 'gɜnzɪ, 'gɝnzɪ
guerrilla, gueri- gə'rɪlə
guess gɛs |guesses 'gɛsɪz |guessed gɛst
guesswork 'gɛsˌwɝk; ES -ˌwɜk, -ˌwɝk
guest gɛst |guested 'gɛstɪd

guffaw gʌ'fɔ, gə'fɔ |-ed -d
Guiana gɪ'ænə, gɪ'anə (Sp 'gjana)
guidance 'gaɪdn̩s |-s -ɪz
guide gaɪd |guided 'gaɪdɪd
Guiderius gwɪ'dɪrɪəs, -rjəs |-'s -ɪz
guidon 'gaɪdn̩
guild gɪld
Guildenstern 'gɪldn̩ˌstɝn; ES -ˌstɜn, -ˌstɝn
guilder 'gɪldɚ; ES 'gɪldə(r
Guildford 'gɪlfɚd; ES 'gɪlfəd
guildhall, G- 'gɪld'hɔl—cf Am 'town 'hall
guile gaɪl |-ful -fəl |-fully -fəlɪ |-less 'gaɪllɪs
Guilford 'gɪlfɚd; ES 'gɪlfəd
guillemot 'gɪləˌmat; ES+-ˌmɒt
guillotine n 'gɪləˌtin
guillotine v ˌgɪlə'tin, 'gɪləˌtin |-d -d
guilt gɪlt |-y -ɪ |-ily 'gɪltəlɪ, -tlɪ
guimpe 'chemisette' gæmp, gɪmp (Fr gæ̃ːp)
Guinea, g- 'gɪnɪ
Guinevere, -ver 'gwɪnəˌvɪr, -vɚ; ES -ˌvɪə(r,
  -və(r
Guiney 'gaɪnɪ
guise gaɪz |guises 'gaɪzɪz |guised gaɪzd
guitar gɪ'tar; ES -'taː(r, E+-'taː(r
Guiterman 'gɪtɚmən; ES 'gɪtə-
gulch gʌltʃ |gulches 'gʌltʃɪz |gulched gʌltʃt
gulden 'gʊldən
gules gjulz, gɪulz
gulf gʌlf |gulfed gʌlft
gulfweed 'gʌlfˌwid
gull gʌl |gulled gʌld
Gullah 'gʌlə
gullet 'gʌlɪt |-ed -ɪd
gullibility ˌgʌlə'bɪlətɪ
gullible 'gʌləbl̩ |-bly -blɪ
Gulliver 'gʌləvɚ; ES 'gʌləvə(r
gully 'gʌlɪ |gullied 'gʌlɪd
gulp gʌlp |gulped gʌlpt
gum gʌm |gummed gʌmd
gum arabic ˌgʌm'ærəbɪk, now rare ˌgʌmə-
  'rebɪk
gumbo 'gʌmbo
gumdrop 'gʌmˌdrap; ES+-ˌdrɒp
gumption 'gʌmpʃən |-tious -ʃəs
gums 'alveoli' gʌmz, much less freq. gumz,
  gʊmz
gumshoe 'gʌmˌʃu, 'gʌmˌʃɪu
gumwood 'gʌmˌwʊd
gun gʌn |gunned gʌnd

Key: See in full §§3–47. bee **bi** |pity **'pɪtɪ** (§6) |rate **ret** |yet **jɛt** |sang **sæŋ** |angry **'æŋ·grɪ**
|bath **bæθ**; E **baθ** (§10) |ah **ɑ** |far **fɑr** |watch **watʃ**, **wɒtʃ** (§12) |jaw **dʒɔ** |gorge **gɔrdʒ** |go **go**

gunboat 'gʌn‚bot
guncotton 'gʌn‚katn̩; ES+-‚kɒtn̩
gunfire 'gʌn‚faɪr; ES -‚faɪə(r
gunman 'gʌn‚mæn, -mən |-men -‚mɛn, -mən
Gunnar 'gʊnɑr, Am pers. name 'gʌnɚ; ES
   -ɑː(r, -ə(r
gunnel 'gʌnl̩
gunner 'gʌnɚ; ES 'gʌnə(r; |-y -ɪ
gunny 'gʌnɪ
gunpowder, G- 'gʌn‚paʊdɚ; ES -‚paʊdə(r
gunrunning 'gʌn‚rʌnɪŋ
gunshot 'gʌn‚ʃat; ES+-‚ʃɒt
gunwale 'gʌnl̩
gurge gɝdʒ; ES gɜdʒ, gɝdʒ; |-s -ɪz |-d -d
gurgitation ‚gɝdʒə'teʃən; ES ‚gɜdʒ-, ‚gɝdʒ-
gurgle 'gɝgl̩; ES 'gɜgl̩, 'gɝgl̩; |-d -d |-ling
   -glɪŋ, -glɪŋ
Gurkha 'gʊrkə; ES 'gʊəkə
gurnard 'gɝnɚd; ES 'gɜnəd, 'gɝnəd
Gurney, -nee 'gɝnɪ; ES 'gɜnɪ, 'gɝnɪ
gush gʌʃ |gushes 'gʌʃɪz |gushed gʌʃt
gusset 'gʌsɪt |gusseted 'gʌsɪtɪd
gust gʌst |gusty 'gʌstɪ
gustation gʌs'teʃən
gustatory 'gʌstə‚torɪ, -‚tɔrɪ; S -‚torɪ
Gustavus gʌs'tevəs |-'s -ɪz
gusto 'gʌsto
gut gʌt |gutted 'gʌtɪd
Gutenberg 'gutn̩‚bɝg; ES -‚bɜg, -‚bɝg; (Ger
   'gu:tən‚bɛrk)
Guthrie 'gʌθrɪ
Guthrun 'gʊðrun
gutta 'gʌtə
gutta-percha 'gʌtə'pɝtʃə; ES -'pɜtʃə, -'pɝtʃə
Guttenberg US 'gʌtn̩‚bɝg; ES -‚bɜg, -‚bɝg
gutter 'gʌtɚ; ES 'gʌtə(r; |-ed -d
guttersnipe 'gʌtɚ‚snaɪp; ES 'gʌtɚ-

guttural 'gʌtərəl |-ly -ɪ
guy gaɪ |guyed gaɪd
Guyandot 'gaɪən‚dat; ES+-‚dɒt
guzzle 'gʌzl̩ |-d -d |-ling 'gʌzlɪŋ, 'gʌzlɪŋ
Gwendolen, -ine, -yn 'gwɛndl̩ɪn
Gwinnett gwɪ'nɛt
gybe dʒaɪb |-d -d
gymnasium dʒɪm'nezɪəm, -zjəm |-s -z |-sia
   -zɪə
gymnast 'dʒɪmnæst
gymnastic dʒɪm'næstɪk |-al -l̩ |-ally -l̩ɪ, -ɪklɪ
gynae- see gyne-
gynarchy 'dʒaɪnɑrkɪ; ES -ɑːkɪ, E+-ɑːkɪ
gynecologic ‚dʒaɪnɪkə'ladʒɪk, ‚gaɪn-; ES+
   -'lɒdʒ-; |-al -l̩
gynecologist ‚dʒaɪnɪ'kalədʒɪst, ‚gaɪnɪ-; ES+
   -'kɒl-
gynecology ‚dʒaɪnɪ'kalədʒɪ, ‚gaɪnɪ-; ES+
   -'kɒl-;—One form is as 'correct' as the
   other. The first is more Englished.
gyp dʒɪp |gypped dʒɪpt
gypsum 'dʒɪpsəm
gypsy 'dʒɪpsɪ
gyral 'dʒaɪrəl |-ly -ɪ
gyrate 'dʒaɪret |-d -ɪd |-tion dʒaɪ'reʃən
gyrator dʒaɪ'retɚ, 'dʒaɪretɚ; ES -tə(r
gyratory 'dʒaɪrə‚torɪ, -‚tɔrɪ; S -‚torɪ
gyre dʒaɪr; ES dʒaɪə(r; |-d -d
gyrfalcon 'dʒɝ‚fɔlkən, -‚fɔkən; ES 'dʒɜ-,
   'dʒɝ-
gyro 'dʒaɪro
gyrocompass 'dʒaɪro‚kʌmpəs |-es -ɪz
gyroscope 'dʒaɪrə‚skop
gyroscopic ‚dʒaɪrə'skapɪk; ES+-'skɒp-; |-ally
   -l̩ɪ, -ɪklɪ
gyrostatic ‚dʒaɪrə'stætɪk |-ally -l̩ɪ, -ɪklɪ
gyve dʒaɪv |gyved dʒaɪvd

H

H, h letter etʃ |pl H's, Hs, poss H's 'etʃɪz
ha intj, n ha |pl has, ha's haz
ha v ha |haes haz |haed had |haing 'ha·ɪŋ
Haarlem 'harləm; ES 'ha:ləm, E+'ha:ləm
Habakkuk hə'bækək, 'hæbə‚kʌk
Habana 'Havana' Sp a'βana
habeas corpus 'hebɪəs'kɔrpəs; ES -'kɔəpəs

haberdasher 'hæbɚ‚dæʃɚ; ES 'hæbə‚dæʃə(r;
   |-y -ɪ, -ʃrɪ
habergeon 'hæbɚdʒən; ES 'hæbədʒən
habiliment hə'bɪləmənt
habilitate hə'bɪlə‚tet |-tated -‚tetɪd
habit 'hæbɪt |-ed -ɪd |-able -əbl̩ |-bly -blɪ
habitant 'hæbətənt

|full fʊl |tooth tuθ |further 'fɝðɚ; ES 'fɝðə |custom 'kʌstəm |while hwaɪl |how haʊ |toy tɔɪ
|using 'juzɪŋ |fuse fjuz, fɪuz |dish dɪʃ |vision 'vɪʒən |Eden 'idn̩ |cradle 'kredl̩ |keep 'em 'kipm̩

habitat 'hæbə,tæt |-tation ,hæbə'teʃən

habitual hə'bɪtʃʊəl, -tʃʊl |-ly -ɪ

habituate hə'bɪtʃʊ,et |-ated -,etɪd

habitude 'hæbə,tjud, -,tɪud, -,tud

habitué hə'bɪtʃʊ,e, hə,bɪtʃʊ'e (Fr abi'tɥe)

Habsburg 'hæpsbɝg; ES -bɜg, -bɝg; (Ger 'ha:psbʊrk)—see Hapsburg

hacienda ,hɑsɪ'ɛndə (Sp a'sjenda)

hack hæk |hacked hækt

hackamore 'hækə,mor, -,mɔr; ES -,moə(r, E+-,mɔə(r

hackberry 'hæk,bɛrɪ, -bərɪ

hackbut 'hækbʌt—see hagbut

hackle 'hækḷ |-d -d |-ling 'hæklɪŋ, 'hækḷɪŋ

hackman 'hækmən, -,mæn |hackmen 'hæk- mən, -,mɛn

hackney 'hæknɪ |hackneyed 'hæknɪd

had stressed 'hæd, ,hæd; unstr. həd, hɛd, əd, ɛd, ɪd |'d d

Haddington 'hædɪŋtən

haddock 'hædək

Hades 'hediz |Hades' 'hediz

hadj hædʒ |hadjes 'hædʒɪz |hadji 'hædʒi

hadn't 'hædn̩t, before some conss.+'hædn̩ ('hædn̩ 'sɪnɪm)

Hadrian 'hedrɪən

hadst stressed 'hædst, ,hædst; unstr. hədst, ədst, dst

haem- see hem-

haemo- see hemo-

Haensel 'hɛnsḷ=Hänsel

haft hæft |hafted 'hæftɪd

hag hæg

Hagar 'hegɚ, 'hegɑr; ES 'hegə(r, 'hegɑ:(r

hagbut 'hægbʌt

Hagen 'hɑgən

Hagerstown 'hegɚz,taʊn; ES 'hegɚz-

haggada hə'gɑdə, -da |pl haggadoth hə'gɑdoθ

Haggai 'hægɪ,aɪ, 'hægaɪ

haggard, H- 'hægɚd; ES 'hægəd

haggis 'hægɪs |-es -ɪz

haggle 'hægḷ |-d -d |-ling 'hæglɪŋ, 'hægḷɪŋ

hagiography ,hægɪ'ɑgrəfɪ, ,hedʒɪ-, -'ɒg-

hagiolatry ,hægɪ'ɑlətrɪ, ,hedʒɪ-; ES+-'ɒl-

hagiology ,hægɪ'ɑlədʒɪ, ,hedʒɪ-; ES+-'ɒl-

Hague heg

Hahnemann 'hɑnəmən (Ger 'ha:nə,man)

Haidarabad 'haɪdərə,bæd, ,haɪdərə'bɑd

haikwan 'haɪ'kwɑn

hail hel |hailed held |hailstone 'hel,ston

Haile Selassie 'haɪlɪsə'lɑsɪ, -sə'læsɪ

hailstorm 'hel,stɔrm; ES 'hel,stɔəm

hair hɛr, hær; E hɛə(r, ES hæə(r; |-ed -d |-y -ɪ

hairbreadth 'hɛr,brɛdθ, 'hær-; ES see hair

hairbrush 'hɛr,brʌʃ, 'hær-; ES see hair

haircloth 'hɛr,klɔθ, 'hær-, -,klɒθ; ES see hair; pl see cloth

haircut 'hɛr,kʌt, 'hær-; ES see hair

hair-do 'hɛr,du, 'hær-; ES see hair

hairdresser 'hɛr,drɛsɚ, 'hær-; ES -ə(r, see hair

hairline 'hɛr,laɪn, 'hær-; ES see hair

hair's-breadth 'hɛrz'brɛdθ, 'hærz-, -,brɛdθ; E 'hɛəz-, ES 'hæəz-

hairsplitter 'hɛr,splɪtɚ, 'hær-; ES -,splɪtə(r, see hair

hairspring 'hɛr,sprɪŋ, 'hær-; ES see hair

Haiti 'hetɪ |Haitian 'hetɪən

hake hek

Hakluyt 'hæklut, 'hæklaɪt, 'hæklɪt

halation he'leʃən, hæ'leʃən

halberd 'hælbɚd; ES 'hælbəd; |-rt -t—formerly 'hɔlb-, 'hɒb-, spelt haubert, holberd

halcyon 'hælsɪən

Haldane 'hɔlden

hale hel |haled held

half hæf; E haf, hæf, hɑf; |-'s -s |-lves -vz

half-and-half 'hæfn̩'hæf; E see half

halfback 'hæf,bæk; E see half

half-baked 'hæf'bekt; E see half; ('half-,baked 'scheme)

half-blooded 'hæf'blʌdɪd; E see half; ('half-,blooded 'Indian)

half-breed 'hæf,brid; E see half

half-caste 'hæf,kæst; E+'haf,kast, 'hɑf,kast

half-full 'hæf'fʊl; E see half

halfhearted 'hæf'hɑrtɪd; ES -'hɑ:tɪd, E+ -'ha:tɪd—see half; ('half,hearted 'effort)

half-hour 'hæf'aʊr; ES -'aʊə(r, E see half

half-length 'hæf'lɛŋkθ, -'lɛŋθ; E see half

half-mast 'hæf'mæst; E+'haf'mast, 'hɑf- 'mast

half-moon 'hæf'mun; E see half

halfpenny Brit 'hepnɪ, 'hepənɪ |pl halfpence 'hepəns, halfpennies 'hepnɪz, 'hepənɪz

half-timbered 'hæf'tɪmbɚd; ES -'tɪmbəd, see half

half-tone 'hæf,ton; E see half

Key: See in full §§3–47. bee bi |pity 'pɪtɪ (§6) |rate ret |yet jɛt |sang sæŋ |angry 'æŋ·grɪ |bath bæθ; E baθ (§10) |ah ɑ |far fɑr |watch wɑtʃ, wɒtʃ (§12) |jaw dʒɔ |gorge gɔrdʒ |go go

half-truth ˈhæfˌtruθ; E *see* half
halfway ˈhæfˈwe; E *see* half; (ˈhalfˌway ˈup)
half-witted ˈhæfˈwɪtɪd; E *see* half
Haliburton ˈhæləˌbɝtn̩; ES -ˌbɝtn̩, -ˌbɝtn̩
halibut ˈhæləbət, ˈhaləbət; ES+ˈhɒl-
Halicarnassus ˌhælɪkɑrˈnæsəs; ES -kɑːˈn-; |-sus' -səs
halide ˈhælaɪd, ˈhelaɪd
halidom ˈhælɪdəm |halidome ˈhælɪˌdom
Halifax ˈhæləˌfæks |Halifax's ˈhæləˌfæksɪz
Haligonian ˌhæləˈɡonɪən, ˌhælɪ-
halitosis ˌhæləˈtosɪs
Haliver ˈhæləvɚ, ˈhæˌlɪvɚ; ES -və(r
hall, H- hɔl
Hallam ˈhæləm
Halle *Am name* ˈhælɪ; *Ger city* ˈhalə
Halleck ˈhælɪk, ˈhælək
hallelujah, -iah ˌhæləˈlujə, -ˈlɪujə
Halley ˈhælɪ
Halliburton ˈhæləˌbɝtn̩; ES -ˌbɝtn̩, -ˌbɝtn̩
Halliday ˈhæləˌde
Halliwell ˈhæləˌwɛl, ˈhæləwəl
hallmark ˈhɔlˌmark; ES ˈhɔlˌmaːk, E+ -ˌmaːk; |-ed -t
hallo, -loa həˈlo
halloo həˈlu |hallooed həˈlud
hallow ˈhælo, -ə |-ed -d, *worship* ˈhæləwɪd |-ing ˈhæləwɪŋ
Halloween ˌhæloˈin, ˌhaloˈin (ˈHallowˌeen ˈjoke)
Hallowmas ˈhæloˌmæs, -məs |-es -ɪz
hallucinate həˈlusn̩ˌet, -ˈlɪu- |-d -ɪd
hallucination həˌlusn̩ˈeʃən, -ˌlɪu-
hallucinatory həˈlusn̩əˌtorɪ, -ˈlɪu-, -ˌtɔrɪ; S -ˌtorɪ
hallway ˈhɔlˌwe
halo ˈhelo |haloed ˈhelod
halogen ˈhælədʒən, -dʒɪn
haloid ˈhælɔɪd, ˈhelɔɪd
Halpin, -ine ˈhælpɪn
Hals, Frans ˈfransˈhals, ˈfrænsˈhæls |-'s -ɪz
Halstead ˈhɔlstɛd, ˈhɔlstɪd, ˈhæl-
halt hɔlt |halted ˈhɔltɪd
halter ˈhɔltɚ; ES ˈhɔltə(r
halve hæv; E hav, hæv, hav |-d -d
halyard ˈhæljɚd; ES ˈhæljəd
ham, H- hæm
hamadryad ˌhæməˈdraɪəd, -ˈdraɪæd
Haman ˈhemən

Hamburg ˈhæmbɝɡ; ES ˈhæmbɝɡ, -bɝɡ; (*Ger* ˈhamburk)
hamburger ˈhæmbɝɡɚ; ES ˈhæmbɝɡə(r, -bɝɡə(r
hame hem
Hamilcar həˈmɪlkɑr, ˈhæml-; ES -kɑː(r, E+-kɑː(r
Hamilton ˈhæmḷtən |Hamiltonian ˌhæml-ˈtonɪən
Hamite ˈhæmaɪt |-tic hæmˈɪtɪk, həˈmɪtɪk
hamlet, H- ˈhæmlɪt
hammer ˈhæmɚ; ES ˈhæmə(r; |-ed -d |-ing ˈhæmərɪŋ, ˈhæmrɪŋ
hammerhead ˈhæmɚˌhɛd; ES ˈhæməˌhɛd; |-ed -ɪd
hammock ˈhæmək
Hammurabi ˌhaməˈrabɪ, ˌhamuˈrabɪ
Hampden ˈhæmpdən, ˈhæmdən
hamper ˈhæmpɚ; ES ˈhæmpə(r; |-ed -d |-ing ˈhæmpərɪŋ, ˈhæmprɪŋ
Hampshire ˈhæmpʃɪr, ˈhæmpʃɚ; ES -ʃɪə(r, -ʃə(r
Hampstead ˈhæmpstɛd, ˈhæmpstɪd
Hampton ˈhæmptən
hamstring ˈhæmˌstrɪŋ |-strung -ˌstrʌŋ *or* -stringed -ˌstrɪŋd
Hamsun, Knut ˈknutˈhæmsən, -ˈhamsʊn
Hamtramck *Mich* hæmˈtræmɪk
Han han
hanaper ˈhænəpɚ; ES ˈhænəpə(r
Hancock ˈhænkɑk; ES+ˈhænkɒk
hand hænd |handed ˈhændɪd
handbag ˈhændˌbæɡ, ˈhænˌbæɡ
handball ˈhændˌbɔl, ˈhænˌbɔl
handbarrow ˈhændˌbæro, ˈhænˌbæro, -ə
handbill ˈhændˌbɪl, ˈhænˌbɪl
handbook ˈhændˌbʊk, ˈhænˌbʊk
handbreadth ˈhændˌbrɛdθ, ˈhænˌbrɛdθ |-ths -θs
handcar ˈhændˌkar, ˈhæn-; ES -ˌkɑː(r, E+ -ˌkɑː(r
handcart ˈhændˌkart, ˈhæn-; ES -ˌkaːt, E+-ˌkaːt
Handcock ˈhænkɑk; ES+-kɒk
handcuff ˈhændˌkʌf, ˈhænˌkʌf |-cuffed -ˌkʌft
Handel ˈhændl̩ (*Ger* Händel ˈhɛndəl)
Handelian hænˈdilɪən, -ˈdiljən
handfast ˈhændˌfæst, ˈhæn-; E+-ˌfast, -ˌfast
handful ˈhændˌfʊl, ˈhænˌfʊl |-s -z

Words below in which a *before* r (farm) *is sounded* ɑ *are often pronounced in E with* a (faːm)

handgrip ˈhændˌɡrɪp, ˈhænˌɡrɪp

handicap ˈhændɪˌkæp |handicapped ˈhændɪ-ˌkæpt

handicraft ˈhændɪˌkræft; E+-ˌkraft, -ˌkrɑft

handicraftsman ˈhændɪˌkræftsmən; E+ -ˌkrafts-, -ˌkrɑfts-; |-men -mən

handiwork ˈhændɪˌwɜˑk; ES -ˌwɜk, -ˌwɝk

handkerchief ˈhæŋkɚtʃɪf, -ˌtʃif; ES -kə-; |-s -tʃɪvz, -tʃɪfs, -ˌtʃivz, -ˌtʃifs

hand-knit ˈhændˈnɪt, ˈhænˈnɪt |-ted -ɪd

handle ˈhændl̩ |-d -d |-ling ˈhændlɪŋ, -dl̩ɪŋ

handleless ˈhændl̩lɪs

handmade ˈhændˈmed, ˈhæn- (ˈhandˌmade ˈshoe)

handmaid ˈhændˌmed, ˈhæn- |-en -ˌmedn̩

hand-me-down ˈhænmɪˌdaʊn

handout ˈhændˌaʊt

handrail ˈhændˌrel

handsaw ˈhændˌsɔ, ˈhæn-

handsel ˈhænsl̩ |-ed -d

handset ˈhændˈsɛt, ˈhæn- (ˈhandˌset ˈtype)

handsome ˈhænsəm

handspike ˈhænˌspaɪk, ˈhænd-

handspring ˈhænˌsprɪŋ, ˈhænd-

hand-to-mouth ˈhændtəˈmaʊθ, ˈhænːtə-

handwork ˈhændˌwɜˑk; ES -ˌwɜk, -ˌwɝk

handwriting ˈhændˌraɪtɪŋ

handy ˈhændɪ

hang hæŋ |hung hʌŋ *or* hanged hæŋd |-ing ˈhæŋɪŋ

hangar ˈhæŋɚ, ˈhæŋɡar; ES ˈhæŋə(r, ˈhæŋ-ɡɑː(r

Hangchow ˈhæŋˈtʃaʊ (*Chin* ˈxaŋˈdʒo)

hangdog ˈhæŋˌdɔɡ, ˈhæŋˌdɒɡ

hanger ˈhæŋɚ; ES ˈhæŋə(r

hanger-on ˈhæŋɚˈɑn, -ˈɒn, -ˈɔn

hangers-on ˈhæŋɚzˈɑn, -ˈɒn, -ˈɔn; ES ˈhæŋəz-

hangman ˈhæŋmən |hangmen ˈhæŋmən

hangnail ˈhæŋˌnel

hank hæŋk |hanked hæŋkt

hanker ˈhæŋkɚ; ES ˈhæŋkə(r; |-ed -d |-ing ˈhæŋkərɪŋ, ˈhæŋkrɪŋ

Hankow ˈhænˈkaʊ, ˈhæŋˈkaʊ (*Chinese* ˈxanˈko)

hanky-panky ˈhæŋkɪˈpæŋkɪ

Hanley ˈhænlɪ

Hannah ˈhænə

Hannibal ˈhænəbl̩

Hanover ˈhænovɚ; ES ˈhænovə(r; (*Ger* Hannover haˈnoːvər, *loc.* haˈnoːfər)

Hanoverian ˌhænoˈvɪrɪən

Hans hæns, -z (*Ger* hans)

Hansard ˈhænsɚd, ˈhænsard; ES ˈhænsəd, -saːd

hanse hæns |hanses ˈhænsɪz

Hanseatic ˌhænsɪˈætɪk, ˌhænzɪˈætɪk

hansel ˈhænsl̩ |hanseled ˈhænsl̩d

Hänsel and Gretel ˈhɛnsl̩ənˈɡretl̩

hansom ˈhænsəm

Hants *short for* Hampshire hænts

hap hæp |happed hæpt |haply ˈhæplɪ

haphazard ˌhæpˈhæzɚd; ES -ˈhæzəd

haploid ˈhæplɔɪd |-loidic hæpˈlɔɪdɪk

haplosis hæpˈlosɪs

happen ˈhæpən, -pm̩ |-ed -d |-ing -pənɪŋ, -pnɪŋ

happy ˈhæpɪ |-pily -pl̩ɪ, -pɪlɪ

happy-go-lucky ˈhæpɪˌɡoˈlʌkɪ

Hapsburg ˈhæpsbɝɡ; ES -bɜɡ, -bɝɡ; (*Ger* ˈhaːpsbʊrk)

hara-kiri ˈhɑrəˈkɪrɪ, ˈhærə-

harangue həˈræŋ |-d -d |-guing -ˈræŋɪŋ

harass ˈhærəs, həˈræs; S+ˈhærɪs; |-es -ɪz |-ed -t—*The pronunciation* həˈræs *instead of the older* ˈhærəs *appears to be on the increase.*

Harbin ˈhɑrˈbɪn; ES ˈhɑːˈbɪn

harbinger ˈhɑrbɪndʒɚ; ES ˈhɑːbɪndʒə(r; |-ed -d

harbor ˈhɑrbɚ; ES ˈhɑːbə(r; |-ed -d |-ing -bərɪŋ, -brɪŋ |-age -bərɪdʒ, -brɪdʒ

Harcourt ˈhɑrkort, -kɔrt, -kɚt; ES -koət, -kət, E+-kɔət

hard hard; ES hɑːd

hard-bitted ˈhardˈbɪtɪd; ES ˈhɑːd-; (ˈhardˌbitted ˈhorse)

hard-bitten ˈhardˈbɪtn̩; ES ˈhɑːd-

hard-boiled ˈhardˈbɔɪld; ES ˈhɑːd-

harden ˈhardn̩; ES ˈhɑːdn̩; |-ed -d |-ing -dn̩ɪŋ, -dnɪŋ

hard-featured ˈhardˈfitʃɚd; ES ˈhɑːdˈfitʃəd

hard-fisted ˈhardˈfɪstɪd; ES ˈhɑːd-

hardhack ˈhardˌhæk; ES ˈhɑːdˌhæk

hardhanded ˈhardˈhændɪd; ES ˈhɑːd-

hardhead ˈhardˌhɛd; ES ˈhɑːd-

hardheaded ˈhardˈhɛdɪd; ES ˈhɑːd-

Words below in which a *before* r (farm) *is sounded* ɑ *are often pronounced in E with* a (fɑ:m)
Words below that have æ *before* r (carry ˈkæɪ) *are often pronounced in N with* ɛ (ˈkɛɪ, §94)

hardhearted ˈhɑrdˈhɑrtɪd; ES ˈhɑːdˈhɑːtɪd
hardihood ˈhɑrdɪˌhʊd; ES ˈhɑːdɪ-
hardly ˈhɑrdlɪ; ES ˈhɑːdlɪ
hardmouthed ˈhɑrdˈmaʊðd, -θt; ES ˈhɑːd-;
 (ˈhardˌmouthed ˈhorse)
hardpan ˈhɑrdˌpæn; ES ˈhɑːd-
hard-shell ˈhɑrdˌʃɛl; ES ˈhɑːd-; |-ed -d
hardship ˈhɑrdʃɪp; ES ˈhɑːd-
hardtack ˈhɑrdˌtæk; ES ˈhɑːd-
hardware ˈhɑrdˌwɛr, -ˌwær; E ˈhɑːdˌwɛə(r,
 ES -ˌwæə(r
hardwood ˈhɑrdˌwʊd; ES ˈhɑːd-
hardy, H- ˈhɑrdɪ; ES ˈhɑːdɪ; |-dily -dļɪ, -dɪlɪ
hare hɛr, hær; E hɛə(r, ES hæə(r; |-d -d
harebell ˈhɛrˌbɛl, ˈhær-; ES *see* hare
harebrained ˈhɛrˈbrend, ˈhær-; ES *see* hare
harelip ˈhɛrˈlɪp, ˈhær-, -ˌlɪp; ES *see* hare
harelipped ˈhɛrˈlɪpt, ˈhær-; ES *see* hare;
 (ˈhareˌlipped ˈboy)
harem ˈhɛrəm, ˈhær-, ˈher-; S ˈhærəm, ˈher-
Harfleur ˈhɑrflɝ; ES ˈhɑːflɝ(r, ˈhɑːflɝ; (*Fr*
 arˈflœːr)—*in Shak* Harflew ˈhɑrflu, -flɪu;
 ES ˈhɑːf-
haricot ˈhærɪˌko |-coed -ˌkod
hark hɑrk; ES hɑːk; |-ed -t
harken ˈhɑrkən; ES ˈhɑːk-; |-ed -d |-ing
 -kənɪŋ, -knɪŋ
Harleian ˈhɑrlɪən, hɑrˈliən; ES ˈhɑːl-, hɑːˈl-
Harlem ˈhɑrləm; ES ˈhɑːləm
harlequin, H- ˈhɑrləkwɪn, -kɪn; ES ˈhɑːl-
harlequinade ˌhɑrləkwɪnˈed, -kɪn-; ES ˌhɑːl-
Harley ˈhɑrlɪ; ES ˈhɑːlɪ
harlot ˈhɑrlət; ES ˈhɑːlət; |-ry -rɪ
harm hɑrm; ES hɑːm; |-ed -d |-ful -fəl |-fully
 -fəlɪ
harmonic hɑrˈmɑnɪk; ES hɑːˈmɑnɪk, -ˈmɒn-;
 |-a -ə |-ally -ļɪ, -ɪklɪ
harmonious hɑrˈmonɪəs; ES hɑːˈmon-; |-nium
 -nɪəm
harmonize ˈhɑrməˌnaɪz; ES ˈhɑːm-; |-s -ɪz
 |-d -d
harmony ˈhɑrmənɪ; ES ˈhɑːm-; |-nied -nɪd
harness ˈhɑrnɪs; ES ˈhɑːnɪs; |-es -ɪz |-ed -t
Harold ˈhærəld
harp hɑrp; ES hɑːp; |-ed -t
harpoon hɑrˈpun; ES hɑːˈpun; |-ed -d
harpsichord ˈhɑrpsɪˌkɔrd; ES ˈhɑːpsɪˌkɔəd

Harpy ˈhɑrpɪ; ES ˈhɑːpɪ
harquebus ˈhɑrkwɪbəs; ES ˈhɑːkwɪbəs; |-es
 -ɪz
harquebusier ˌhɑrkwɪbəsˈɪr; ES ˌhɑːkwɪbəs-
 ˈɪə(r, S+-ˈɛə(r
harridan ˈhærədən
harrier ˈhærɪɚ; ES ˈhærɪ·ə(r
Harriet ˈhærɪət, ˈhærɪt
Harrison ˈhærəsņ
Harrisburg ˈhærɪsˌbɝg; ES -ˌbɝg, -ˌbɝg
harrow, H- ˈhæro, -ə |-ed -d |-ing ˈhærəwɪŋ
harry, H- ˈhærɪ |harried ˈhærɪd
harsh hɑrʃ; ES hɑːʃ
hart hɑrt; ES hɑːt
Harte hɑrt; ES hɑːt
hartebeest ˈhɑrtəˌbist; ES ˈhɑːtəˌbist
Hartford ˈhɑrtfɚd; ES ˈhɑːtfəd
hartshorn ˈhɑrtsˌhɔrn; ES ˈhɑːtsˌhɔən
Harum ˈhɛrəm, ˈhærəm; S ˈhærəm
harum-scarum ˌhɛrəmˈskɛrəm, ˌhærəm-
 ˈskærəm; S ˌhærəmˈskærəm; (ˈharum-
 ˌscarum ˈmanners)
Harun-al-Raschid ˌhærunælˈræʃɪd, hɑˈrun-
 ˌɑrrəˈʃid
haruspex həˈrʌspɛks, ˈhærəs- |-pexes -ˌpɛksɪz
 |haruspices həˈrʌspɪˌsiz
Harvard ˈhɑrvɚd; ES ˈhɑːvəd
harvest ˈhɑrvɪst, -vəst; ES ˈhɑːvɪst; |-ed -ɪd
Harvey ˈhɑrvɪ; ES ˈhɑːvɪ
Harwich *Engd* ˈhærɪdʒ, ˈhærɪtʃ; *Mass* ˈhɑr-
 wɪtʃ; ES ˈhɑːwɪtʃ; |-ʼs -ɪz
Harz hɑrts; ES hɑːts
has *stressed* ˈhæz, ˌhæz; *unstr.* həz, əz |ʼs z, s
has-been ˈhæzˌbɪn
Hasbrouck ˈhæzbrʊk
Hasdrubal ˈhæzdrubļ, ˈhæzdrʊˌbæl
hash hæʃ |hashes ˈhæʃɪz |hashed hæʃt
hashish, -eesh ˈhæʃɪʃ
hasnʼt ˈhæznt, *bef. some conss.*+ˈhæzņ (ˈhæzņ
 ˈgɑn)
hasp hæsp; E+hɑsp, hɑsp; |-ed -t
hassock ˈhæsək |-ed -t
hast *stressed* ˈhæst, ˌhæst; *unstr.* həst, əst, st
haste hest |hasted ˈhestɪd
hasten ˈhesņ |-ed -d |-ing ˈhesņɪŋ, ˈhesnɪŋ
Hastings ˈhestɪŋz |-ʼs -ɪz
hasty ˈhestɪ |hastily ˈhestļɪ, -tɪlɪ

|full fʊl |tooth tuθ |further ˈfɝðɚ; ES ˈfɝðə |custom ˈkʌstəm |while hwaɪl |how haʊ |toy tɔɪ
|using ˈjuzɪŋ |fuse fjuz, fɪuz |dish dɪʃ |vision ˈvɪʒən |Eden ˈidņ |cradle ˈkredļ |keep ʼem ˈkipm̩

hat **hæt** |hatted **'hætɪd**

hatband **'hæt,bænd**

hatbox **'hæt,bɑks**; ES+-,bɒks; |-es -z

hatch **hætʃ** |hatches **'hætʃɪz** |hatched **hætʃt**

hatchel **'hætʃəl** |hatcheled **'hætʃəld**

hatchery **'hætʃərɪ**, **'hætʃrɪ**

hatchet **'hætʃɪt** |-ed -ɪd

hatchway **'hætʃ,we**

hate **het** |hated **'hetɪd** |hateful **'hetfəl** |-fully -fəlɪ

hath *stressed* **'hæθ**, ,hæθ; *unstr.* həθ, əθ

Hathaway **'hæθə,we**

Hathorn(e) **'hɔθɔrn**; ES **'hɔθɔən;**—*The BBC recommends* **'hæθɔrn** *for the British name.*

hatred **'hetrɪd**

hatter **'hætɚ**; ES **'hætə(r**

Hatteras **'hætərəs** |Hatteras's **'hætərəsɪz**

hauberk **'hɔbɝk**; ES **'hɔbɜk**, **'hɔbɝk**

Haugen **'hauɡən**

haughty **'hɔtɪ** |-tily -t|ɪ, -tɪlɪ

haul **hɔl** |hauled **hɔld** |haulage **'hɔlɪdʒ**

haunch **hɔntʃ**, **hɒntʃ**, **hɑntʃ** |-es -ɪz |-ed -t

haunt **hɔnt**, **hɒnt**, **hɑnt** |-ed -ɪd

Hauptmann **'hauptmən**, **'haupm-** (*Ger* **'hauptman**)

hautboy **'hobɔɪ**, **'obɔɪ** (*Fr* o'bwɑ)

hauteur **ho'tɝ**, **o'tɝ**; ES -'tɜ(r -'tɝ; (*Fr* o'tœːr)

Havana **hə'vænə** (*Sp* Habana a'βana)

have *stressed* **'hæv**, ,hæv; *unstr.* həv, əv |'ve v |have to *bef. conss.* **'hæftə**, *bef. vow.* **'hæftʊ**, **'hæftə**—*In* "I could of done it," *of is merely a misspelling for* have. *Their pronunciation is identical. The pron.* **'hæftə**, **'hæftʊ** *is universal in unaffected familiar speech in US and England.*

Havelock, -lok, h- **'hævlɑk**; ES+-lɒk

haven **'hevən** |havened **'hevənd**

haven't **'hævṇt**, *bef. some conss.*+**'hævṇ** (**'hævṇ 'sɪnɪm**)

Haverford **'hævɚfɚd**; ES **'hævəfəd**

Haverhill **'hevɚɪl**, **'hevrɪl**, -rəl

haversack **'hævɚ,sæk**; ES **'hævə,sæk**

Haverstraw **'hævɚ,strɔ**; ES **'hævə,strɔ**

havior **'hevjɚ**; ES **'hevjə(r**

havoc **'hævək**

Havre *US* **'hævɚ**; ES **'hævə(r**

Havre *France* **'hɑvɚ**, **'hɑvrə**; ES **'hɑvə(r**, **'hɑvrə**; (*Fr* lə'ɑːvr)

Havre de Grace **'hævɚdə'græs**, -'gres; ES **'hævə-**

haw **hɔ** |hawed **hɔd**

Hawaii **hə'waɪjə**, **hə'wajə**, **hə'wɒjə**, **hə-'waɪ·i**, **hə'wɑ·i**

Hawarden *US* **'hewɑrdṇ**; ES -wɑːdṇ; *Wales* **'hɔ·ɚdṇ**, **'hɑrdṇ**; ES **'hɔ·ədṇ**, **'hɑːdṇ**

hawk **hɔk** |hawked **hɔkt**

hawk-eyed **'hɔk,aɪd**

Hawkins **'hɔkɪnz** |Hawkins's **'hɔkɪnzɪz**

hawse **hɔz** |hawses **'hɔzɪz**

hawsehole **'hɔz,hol**, **'hɔs-**

hawser **'hɔzɚ**; ES **'hɔzə(r**

hawthorn, Hawthorn(e) **'hɔ,θɔrn**; ES -,θɔən

hay **he** |hayed **hed** |haying **'he·ɪŋ**

Hayakawa **,haɪə'kɑwə**

haycock **'he,kɑk**; ES+**'he,kɒk**

Hayden **'hedṇ**

Haydn **'haɪdṇ**, **'hedṇ**

Haydon **'hedṇ**

Hayes **hez** |Hayes's **'hezɪz**

hayfork **'he,fɔrk**; ES **'he,fɔək**

hayloft **'he,lɔft**, **'he,lɒft**

haymarket **'he,mɑrkɪt**; ES **'he,mɑːkɪt**

haymow **'he,mau**

hayrack **'he,ræk** |-rick -,rɪk

hayseed **'he,sid** |-stack -,stæk

Hayti **'hetɪ**, *US places*+**'hetaɪ**

Hayward **'hewɚd**; ES **'hewəd**

hayward **'he,wɚd**, -wɚd; ES **'he,wɔəd**, -wəd

hazard **'hæzɚd**; ES **'hæzəd**; |-ed -ɪd |-ous -əs

haze **hez** |hazes **'hezɪz** |hazed **hezd**

hazel, H- **'hezḷ** |-nut -nət, -,nʌt

Hazledean **'hezḷ,din**

Hazleton **'hezḷtən**

Hazlitt **'hæzlɪt**

hazy **'hezɪ** |-zily -z|ɪ, -zɪlɪ

he *stressed* **'hi**, ,hi; *unstr.* i, ɪ, hɪ

head **hɛd** |headed **'hɛdɪd**

headache **'hɛd,ek**

headband **'hɛd,bænd**

headboard **'hɛd,bord**, -,bɔrd; ES -,boəd, E+-,bɔəd

headcheese **'hɛd,tʃiz** |-s -ɪz

headdress **'hɛd,drɛs** |-es -ɪz

headfirst **'hɛd'fɝst**; ES -'fɜst, -'fɝst

headforemost **'hɛd'for,most**, -'fɔr-, -məst; ES -'foə-, E+-'fɔə-

headgear **'hɛd,ɡɪr**; ES -,ɡɪə(r, S+-,ɡɛə(r

Key: *See in full §§3–47.* bee **bi** |pity **'pɪtɪ** (§6) |rate **ret** |yet **jɛt** |sang **sæŋ** |angry **'æŋ·ɡrɪ** |bath **bæθ**; E **bɑθ** (§10) |ah **ɑ** |far **fɑr** |watch **wɑtʃ**, **wɒtʃ** (§12) |jaw **dʒɔ** |gorge **ɡɔrdʒ** |go **ɡo**

Words below in which ea *before* r (heart) *is sounded* ɑ *are often pronounced in* E *with* a (hɑ:t)

heading ˈhɛdɪŋ

headland *unplowed land* ˈhɛdˌlænd, ‘*promontory*’ ˈhɛdlənd

headlight ˈhɛdˌlaɪt

headline ˈhɛdˌlaɪn |-d -d

headlock ˈhɛdˌlɑk; ES+-ˌlɒk

headlong ˈhɛdˈlɔŋ, -ˌlɔŋ, -ɒŋ; S+-ɑŋ

headman ˈhɛdmən |-men -mən

headmaster ˈhɛdˈmæstɚ; ES -təˌr, E+-ˈmɑs-, -ˈmɑs-

head-on ˈhɛdˈɑn, -ˈɒn, -ˈɔn (ˈhead-ˌon ˈcrash)

headphone ˈhɛdˌfon

headpiece ˈhɛdˌpis |-s -ɪz

headquarters ˈhɛdˈkwɔrtɚz, -ˌkw-; ES -ˈkwɔətəz, -ˌkw-

headrest ˈhɛdˌrɛst

headsman ˈhɛdzmən |-men -mən

headspring ˈhɛdˌsprɪŋ

headstock ˈhɛdˌstɑk; ES+-ˌstɒk

headstone ˈhɛdˌston

headstrong ˈhɛdˌstrɔŋ, -ˌstrɒŋ; S+-ˌstrɑŋ

headwater ˈhɛdˌwɔtɚ, -ˌwɑtɚ, -ˌwɒtɚ; ES -təˌr

headway ˈhɛdˌwe

headwork ˈhɛdˌwɝk; ES -ˌwɜk, -ˌwɝk

heal hil |healed hild

health hɛlθ |-ths -θs |-ful -fəl |-fully -fəlɪ

healthy ˈhɛlθɪ |-thily -θəlɪ, -θɪlɪ

heap hip |heaped hipt

hear hɪr; ES hɪə(r, S+hjɛə(r, hjɪə(r, hɛə(r; |heard hɝd; ES hɜd, hɝd

hearken ˈhɑrkən; ES ˈhɑ:kən; |-ed -d |-ing -kənɪŋ, -knɪŋ

hearsay ˈhɪrˌse; ES ˈhɪə-, S+ˈhjɛə-, ˈhjɪə-, ˈhɛə-

hearse hɝs; ES hɜs, hɝs; |-d -t

heart hɑrt; ES hɑ:t

heartache ˈhɑrtˌek; ES ˈhɑ:t-

heartbreak ˈhɑrtˌbrek; ES ˈhɑ:t-

heartbroken ˈhɑrtˌbrokən, -ˈbrokən; ES ˈhɑ:t-

heartburn ˈhɑrtˌbɝn; ES ˈhɑ:tˌbɜn, ˈhɑ:tˌbɝn; |-ed -d

hearten ˈhɑrtn̩; ES ˈhɑ:tn̩; |-ed -d |-ing -tn̩ɪŋ, -tnɪŋ

heartfelt ˈhɑrtˌfɛlt, -ˈfɛlt; ES ˈhɑ:t-

hearth hɑrθ; ES hɑ:θ; |-ths -θs—*Poetic* hɝθ, hɜθ *is still occas. heard.*

hearthstone ˈhɑrθˌston; ES ˈhɑ:θ-;—*see* hearth

heartily ˈhɑrtl̩ɪ, -ɪlɪ; ES ˈhɑ:t-

heartsease ˈhɑrtsˌiz; ES ˈhɑ:ts-

heartsick ˈhɑrtˌsɪk, -ˈsɪk; ES ˈhɑ:t-

heartsore ˈhɑrtˌsor, -ˌsɔr; ES -ˌsoə(r, E+-ˌsɔə(r; *acct*+ˈheartˈsore

heartstring ˈhɑrtˌstrɪŋ; ES ˈhɑ:t-

heart-to-heart ˈhɑrttəˈhɑrt; ES ˈhɑ:ttəˈhɑ:t

heart-whole ˈhɑrtˈhol; ES ˈhɑ:t-; (ˈheartˌwhole ˈmaid)

heartwood ˈhɑrtˌwʊd; ES ˈhɑ:t-

heat hit |heated ˈhitɪd

heath hiθ |-ths -θs

heathen ˈhiðən |-ism -ˌɪzəm |-ness -ˌðənnɪs

heathenesse *arch.* ˈhiðənˌɛs

heather ˈhɛðɚ; ES ˈhɛðə(r; |-ed -d

heatstroke ˈhitˌstrok

heaume hom

heave hiv |heaved hivd *or* hove hov

heaven ˈhɛvən, ˈhɛvm̩ |-ward -wɚd; ES -wəd

Heavener ˈhivnɚ; ES ˈhivnə(r

heavily ˈhɛvl̩ɪ, -ɪlɪ

Heaviside ˈhɛvɪˌsaɪd

heavy ‘*weighty*’ ˈhɛvɪ

heavy ‘*broken-winded*’ ˈhivɪ

heavy-hearted ˈhɛvɪˈhɑrtɪd; ES -ˈhɑ:tɪd

heavyweight ˈhɛvɪˌwet

hebdomad ˈhɛbdəˌmæd

hebdomadal hɛbˈdɑmədl̩; ES+-ˈdɒm-; |-ly -ɪ

Hebe ˈhibɪ

Hebraic hiˈbre·ɪk |-al -l̩ |-ally -l̩ɪ

Hebraism ˈhibrɪˌɪzəm |-ist -ɪst

Hebraistic ˌhibrɪˈɪstɪk |-al -l̩ |-ally -l̩ɪ, -ɪklɪ

Hebrew ˈhibru, ˈhibrɪu

Hebrides ˈhɛbrəˌdiz

Hebron ˈhibrən

Hecate ˈhɛkətɪ, *in Shak.* ˈhɛkɪt

hecatomb ˈhɛkəˌtom, -ˌtum

Hecht hɛkt

heckle ˈhɛkl̩ |-d -d |-ling ˈhɛklɪŋ, ˈhɛkl̩ɪŋ

hectare ˈhɛkter, -tær; E -tɛə(r, ES -tæə(r

hectic ˈhɛktɪk |-ly -lɪ |-al -l̩ |-ally -l̩ɪ

hectograph ˈhɛktəˌgræf; E+-ˌgrɑf, -ˌgrɑf

Hector ˈhɛktɚ; ES ˈhɛktə(r

hector ˈhɛktɚ; ES ˈhɛktə(r; |-ed -d |-ing ˈhɛktərɪŋ, ˈhɛktrɪŋ

Hecuba ˈhɛkjʊbə

he'd abbr. spelling of he had, he would, stressed
'hid, ˌhid; unstr. id, ɪd, hɪd

heddle 'hɛdļ |-d -d |-ling -dļɪŋ, -dlɪŋ

hedge hɛdʒ |hedges 'hɛdʒɪz |hedged hɛdʒd

hedgehog 'hɛdʒˌhɑg, -ˌhɔg, -ˌhɒg; S -ˌhɔg,
-ˌhɑg, -ˌhɒg

hedgerow 'hɛdʒˌro

Hedjaz hɛ'dʒaz

hedonic hi'danɪk; ES+-'dɒn-; |-al -ļ |-ally -ļɪ

hedonism 'hidņˌɪzəm |-ist -ɪst

Hedwig 'hɛdwɪg

heed hid |heeded 'hidɪd |-ful -fəl |-fully -fəlɪ

heedless 'hidlɪs

heehaw 'hiˌhɔ, 'iˌhɔ̃ (nasal i) |-ed -d

heel hil |heeled hild |-less 'hillɪs

heelpiece 'hilˌpis |-s -ɪz |-d -t

heeltap 'hilˌtæp |-tapped -ˌtæpt

Heep, Uriah juˈraɪəˈhip

heft hɛft |hefted 'hɛftɪd |-y -ɪ

Hegel 'hegļ

Hegelian he'gelɪən, hi'dʒilɪən

hegemony hi'dʒɛmənɪ, 'hɛdʒəˌmonɪ

hegira, H- hi'dʒaɪrə, 'hɛdʒərə

Heidelberg 'haɪdļˌbɝg; ES -ˌbɝg, -ˌbɝˈg; (Ger
'haɪdəlˌbɛrk)

heifer 'hɛfɚ; ES 'hɛfə(r

Heifetz 'haɪfɪts |-'s -ɪz

heigh intj he, haɪ

heigh-ho intj, n, v 'he'ho, 'haɪ'ho |-ed -d

height haɪt—cf highth

heighten 'haɪtņ |-ed -d |-ing 'haɪtņɪŋ, -tnɪŋ

Heine 'haɪnə

Heinie, -ne nickname 'haɪnɪ

heinous 'henəs

Heinz haɪnts, haɪnz |-'s -ɪz

heir ɛr, ær; E ɛə(r, ES æə(r; |-ess -ɪs |-esses
-ɪsɪz

heirloom 'ɛr'lum, 'ær-, -ˌlum; E 'ɛə-, ES 'æə-

Hejaz hɛ'dʒaz

hejira, H- hi'dʒaɪrə, 'hɛdʒərə

Hekate 'hɛkətɪ, in Shak. 'hɛkɪt

held hɛld

Helen 'hɛlɪn, -ən

Helena 'hɛlɪnə, hɛ'linə; cf Saint H. & Lena

Helgoland 'hɛlgoˌlænd (Ger -ˌlɑnt)

heliacal hɪ'laɪəkļ |-ly -ɪ, -əklɪ

helical 'hɛlɪkļ |-ly -ɪ

Helicanus ˌhɛlɪ'kenəs |-'s -ɪz

helicline 'hɛlɪˌklaɪn

helicoid 'hɛlɪˌkɔɪd

helicoidal ˌhɛlɪ'kɔɪdļ |-ly -ɪ

Helicon, h- 'hɛlɪˌkan, -kən; ES+-ˌkɒn

helicopter 'hɛlɪˌkaptɚ, 'hi-; ES -tə(r, -ˌkɒp-

Heligoland 'hɛlɪgoˌlænd

heliocentric ˌhilɪo'sɛntrɪk |-al -ļ |-ally -ļɪ,
-ɪklɪ

Heliogabalus ˌhilɪə'gæbələs |-'s -ɪz

heliograph 'hilɪəˌgræf; E+-ˌgraf, -ˌgrɑf

heliometer ˌhilɪ'amətɚ; ES -'amətə(r, -'ɒm-

Heliopolis ˌhilɪ'apəlɪs; ES+-'ɒp-; |-'s -ɪz

Helios 'hilɪˌas; ES+-ˌɒs

helioscope 'hilɪəˌskop, 'hiljə-

heliotherapy ˌhilɪo'θɛrəpɪ

heliotrope 'hiljəˌtrop, 'hilɪə-

helium 'hilɪəm

helix 'hilɪks |-es -ɪz |helices 'hɛlɪˌsiz

hell hɛl

he'll abbr. spelling of he will, stressed 'hil, ˌhil;
unstr. il, ɪl, hɪl

hellbender 'hɛlˌbɛndɚ; ES -ˌbɛndə(r

hellbroth 'hɛlˌbrɔθ, -ˌbrɒθ |-ths -θs

hellcat 'hɛlˌkæt

hell-diver 'hɛlˌdaɪvɚ; ES -ˌdaɪvə(r

hellebore 'hɛləˌbor, -ˌbɔr; ES -ˌboə(r, E+
-ˌbɔə(r

Hellen 'hɛlɪn, -ən, -ɛn

Hellene 'hɛlin |Hellenes 'hɛlinz

Hellenic hɛ'lɛnɪk, -'lin- |-ally -ļɪ, -ɪklɪ

Hellenism 'hɛlɪnˌɪzəm, -lən- |-ist -ɪst

Hellenistic ˌhɛlɪn'ɪstɪk, -lən- |-al -ļ |-ally -ļɪ,
-ɪklɪ

Hellenize 'hɛlɪnˌaɪz, -lən- |-s -ɪz |-d -d

Hellespont 'hɛləˌspant, -ˌspɒnt

hell-fire, H- 'hɛl'faɪr, -ˌfaɪr; ES -aɪə(r

hellgrammite 'hɛlgrəˌmaɪt

hellhound 'hɛlˌhaʊnd

hellion 'hɛljən

hellkite 'hɛlˌkaɪt

hello hɛ'lo, hə'lo, 'hɛlo, 'hʌlo, emph. 'hɛl'lo,
'hʌl'lo

helm hɛlm |helmed hɛlmd

helmet 'hɛlmɪt |helmeted 'hɛlmɪtɪd

Helmholtz 'hɛlmˌholts |-'s -ɪz

helmsman 'hɛlmzmən |-men -mən

Heloise Eng name ˌhɛlo'iz |-'s -ɪz

Héloise wife of Abélard ˌelo'iz |-'s -ɪz (Fr
elɔ'iːz

Helot, h- 'hɛlət, 'hilət |-ism -ˌɪzəm |-ry -rɪ

Key: See in full §§3–47. bee bi |pity 'pɪtɪ (§6) |rate ret |yet jɛt |sang sæŋ |angry 'æŋ·grɪ
|bath bæθ; E baθ (§10) |ah ɑ |far fɑr |watch watʃ, wɒtʃ (§12) |jaw dʒɔ |gorge gɔrdʒ |go go

help hɛlp |helped hɛlpt |holp *arch. past &*
pptc holp |holpen *arch. pptc* 'holpən
helpful 'hɛlpfəl |-ly -ɪ
helpmate 'hɛlp,met |helpmeet 'hɛlp,mit
Helsingfors 'hɛlsɪŋ,fɔrz, -,fɔrs; ES -,fɔəz,
-,fɔəs
Helsinki 'hɛlsɪŋkɪ
helter-skelter 'hɛltɚ'skɛltɚ; ES 'hɛltə'skɛl-
tə(r
helve hɛlv |helved hɛlvd
Helvetia hɛl'viʃə, -ʃɪə |-n -n
Helvetii hɛl'viʃɪ,aɪ
hem hɛm |hemmed hɛmd
Hemans 'hɛmənz, 'himənz |-'s -ɪz
hematic, hae- hi'mætɪk
hematite, haem- 'hɛmə,taɪt
hemicycle 'hɛmə,saɪk]
hemicyclic ,hɛmə'saɪklɪk, -'sɪk-
hemidemisemiquaver,hɛmɪ,dɛmɪ'sɛmə,kwevɚ;
ES -,kwevə(r
hemin, hae- 'himɪn
Hemingway 'hɛmɪŋ,we
hemiplegy 'hɛmɪ,plidʒɪ |-gia ,hɛmɪ'plidʒɪə
hemisphere 'hɛməs,fɪr; ES -,fɪə(r, S+-,fɛə(r
hemispheric ,hɛmə'sfɛrɪk |-al -] |-ally -]ɪ
hemispheroid ,hɛmə'sfɪrɔɪd
hemistich 'hɛmə,stɪk
hemlock 'hɛmlɑk; ES+-lɒk
hemoglobin, haem- ,himə'globɪn, ,hɛmə-
hemophilia, haem- ,himə'fɪlɪə, ,hɛmə-
hemorrhage, haem- 'hɛmərɪdʒ, 'hɛmrɪdʒ |-s
-ɪz
hemorrhoid, haem- 'hɛmə,rɔɪd, 'hɛm,rɔɪd
hemp hɛmp |hempen 'hɛmpən |-seed -,sid
Hempl, *George, Am scholar* 'hɛmp]
hemstitch 'hɛm,stɪtʃ |-es -ɪz |-ed -t
hen hɛn |henbane 'hɛn,ben
hence hɛns
henceforth ,hɛns'forθ, -'fɔrθ; ES -'foəθ,
E+-'fɔəθ
henceforward ,hɛns'fɔrwəd; ES -'fɔəwəd
henchman 'hɛntʃmən |-men -mən
hencoop 'hɛn,kup, -,kʊp—*see* coop
hendiadys hɛn'daɪədɪs
henequen, -quin 'hɛnəkɪn
Hengist 'hɛŋgɪst, 'hɛndʒɪst
Henley 'hɛnlɪ
henna 'hɛnə |hennaed 'hɛnəd
Hennepin 'hɛnəpɪn (*Fr* ɛn'pɛ̃)

hennery 'hɛnərɪ
henpeck 'hɛn,pɛk |-pecked -,pɛkt
Henrietta ,hɛnrɪ'ɛtə
henry, H- 'hɛnrɪ
hepatic hɪ'pætɪk |-a -ə |-al -]
Hephaestus hi'fɛstəs |-'s -ɪz
Hephzibah 'hɛfzɪbə
Hepplewhite 'hɛp],hwaɪt
heptagon 'hɛptə,gɑn; ES+-,gɒn
heptagonal hɛp'tægən]
heptameter hɛp'tæmətɚ; ES -'tæmətə(r
heptarchy, H- 'hɛptɑrkɪ; ES -tɑːkɪ, E+-tɑːkɪ
Heptateuch 'hɛptə,tjuk, -,tɪuk, -,tuk
Hepzibah Pyncheon 'hɛpzɪbə'pɪntʃən
her *stressed* 'hɝ, ,hɝ; ES 'hɜ(r, ,hɜ(r, 'hɝ, ,hɝ;
unstr. ɚ, hɚ; ES ə(r, hə(r
Hera 'hirə, 'hɪrə
Heracles 'hɛrə,kliz |-'s -ɪz
Heraclitus ,hɛrə'klaɪtəs |-'s -ɪz
Herakles 'hɛrə,kliz |-'s -ɪz
herald 'hɛrəld, hɛrld |-ed -ɪd |-ry -rɪ
heraldic hɛ'rældɪk |-al -] |-ally -]ɪ, -ɪklɪ
herb ɝb, hɝb; ES ɜb, hɜb, ɝb, hɝb
herbaceous hɝ'beʃəs; ES hɜ-, hɝ-
herbage 'ɝbɪdʒ, 'hɝb-; ES 'ɜb-, 'hɜb-, 'ɝb-,
'hɝb-
herbal 'hɝb], 'ɝb]; ES 'hɜb], 'ɜb], 'hɝb], 'ɝb];
|-ism -,ɪzəm |-ist -ɪst
herbarium hɝ'bɛrɪəm, -'bær-, -'ber-; ES hɜ-,
hɝ-; |-s -z |-ia -ɪə
Herbert 'hɝbɚt; ES 'hɜbət, 'hɝbət
herbiferous hɝ'bɪfərəs; ES hɜ-, hɝ-
herbivorous hɝ'bɪvərəs; ES hɜ-, hɝ-
Herculaneum ,hɝkjə'lenɪəm; ES ,hɜ-, ,hɝ-
herculean, H- hɝ'kjulɪən, -'kɪul-, ,hɝkjə'liən;
ES -ɜ-, -ɝ-
Hercules 'hɝkjə,liz; ES 'hɜ-, 'hɝ-; |-'s -ɪz
herd hɝd; ES hɜd, hɝd; |-ed -ɪd
Herder *Ger poet* 'hɛrdɚ; ES 'hɛədə(r
herdsman 'hɝdzmən; ES 'hɜdz-, 'hɝdz-;
|-men -mən
here hɪr; ES hɪə(r, S+hjɛə(r, hjɪə(r, jɛə(r,
hɛə(r
Here 'hiri=Hera
hereabout ,hɪrə'baʊt, 'hɪrə,baʊt; S+*see* here
hereafter hɪr'æftɚ; ES hɪr'æftə(r, E+-'af-,
-'ɑf-, S+*see* here
hereat hɪr'æt; S+*see* here
hereby hɪr'baɪ; ES hɪə'baɪ, S+*see* here

|full fʊl |tooth tuθ |further 'fɝðɚ; ES 'fɝðə |custom 'kʌstəm |while hwaɪl |how haʊ |toy tɔɪ
|using 'juzɪŋ |fuse fjuz, fɪuz |dish dɪʃ |vision 'vɪʒən |Eden 'idn̩ |cradle 'kred] |keep 'em 'kipm̩

hereditable həˈrɛdətəbļ |-bly -blɪ
hereditament ˌhɛrəˈdɪtəmənt
hereditary həˈrɛdəˌtɛrɪ |-dity -dətɪ
herefor hɪrˈfɔr; ES hɪəˈfɔə(r, S+*see* here
Hereford ˈhɛrəfəd, *by Am stockmen usually*
ˈhɝfəd; ES ˈhɛrəfəd, ˈhɑf-, ˈhɝfəd; |-shire
-ˌʃɪr, -ʃɚ; ES -ˌʃɪə(r, -ʃə(r
herefrom hɪrˈfram, -ˈfrɒm; ES hɪə-, S+*see*
here
herein hɪrˈɪn; S+*see* here
hereinafter ˌhɪrɪnˈæftɚ; ES -ˈæftə(r, E+-ˈaf-,
-ˈɑf-, S+*see* here
hereinbefore ˌhɪrɪnbɪˈfor, -ˈfɔr; ES -ˈfoə(r,
E+-ˈfɔə(r, S+*see* here
hereinto hɪrˈɪntu, -tʊ; S+*see* here—*acct*+
ˌhereinˈto
hereof hɪrˈav, -ˈɑf, -ˈɒ-; S+*see* here
hereon hɪrˈan, -ˈɒn, -ˈɔn; S+*see* here
heresy ˈhɛrəsɪ |heretic ˈhɛrətɪk
heretical həˈrɛtɪkḷ |-ly -ɪ, -ɪklɪ
hereto hɪrˈtu; ES hɪəˈtu, S+*see* here
heretofore ˌhɪrtəˈfor, -ˈfɔr; ES ˌhɪətəˈfoə(r,
E+-ˈfɔə(r, S+*see* here
hereunder hɪrˈʌndɚ; ES -ˈʌndə(r, S+*see* here
hereunto hɪrˈʌntu, -tʊ; S+*see* here—*acct*+
ˌhereunˈto
hereupon ˌhɪrəˈpan, -ˈpɒn, -ˈpɔn; S+*see* here
Hereward ˈhɛrəwɚd; ES ˈhɛrəwəd
herewith hɪrˈwɪθ, -ˈwɪð; ES hɪə-, S+*see* here;
cf wherewith
Herford ˈhɝfəd; ES ˈhɝfəd, ˈhɝfəd
Hergesheimer ˈhɝgəsˌhaɪmɚ; ES ˈhɝgəs-
ˌhaɪmə(r, ˈhɝgəsˌhaɪmə(r
Herington ˈhɛrɪŋtən
heriot, H- ˈhɛrɪət
heritable ˈhɛrətəbḷ |-bly -blɪ
heritage ˈhɛrətɪdʒ |-tance -təns |-s -ɪz
heritor ˈhɛrətɚ; ES ˈhɛrətə(r
Herkimer ˈhɝkəmɚ; ES ˈhɝkəmə(r, ˈhɝkə-
mə(r
herl hɝl; ES hɝl, hɝl
Herman ˈhɝmən; ES ˈhɝm-, ˈhɝm-
hermaphrodite hɝˈmæfrəˌdaɪt; ES hɝ-, hɝ-
hermaphroditic hɝˌmæfrəˈdɪtɪk; ES hɝ-, hɝ-;
|-al -ļ |-ally -ļɪ, -ɪklɪ
hermeneutic ˌhɝmənˈjutɪk, -məˈnɪutɪk, -ˈnu-;
ES ˌhɝ-, ˌhɝ-; |-al -ļ |-ally -ļɪ, -ɪklɪ
Hermes ˈhɝmiz; ES ˈhɝmiz, ˈhɝmiz; |-mes'
-miz

hermetic hɝˈmɛtɪk; ES hɝ-, hɝ-; |-al -ļ
|-ally -ļɪ, -ɪklɪ
Hermia ˈhɝmɪə, -mjə; ES ˈhɝm-, ˈhɝm-
Hermione hɝˈmaɪənɪ; ES hɝ-, hɝ
hermit ˈhɝmɪt; ES ˈhɝm-, ˈhɝm-; |-age -ɪdʒ
|-ages -ɪdʒɪz
Hermon ˈhɝmən; ES ˈhɝm-, ˈhɝm-
hernia ˈhɝnɪə, -njə; ES ˈhɝn-, ˈhɝn-; |-s -z
|-niae -nɪˌi
hero, H- ˈhɪro, ˈhiro
Herod ˈhɛrəd |-rodian hɛˈrodɪən
Herodias həˈrodɪəs, hɛ- |-'s -ɪz
Herodotus həˈradətəs; ES+-ˈrɒd-; |-'s -ɪz
heroic hɪˈro·ɪk, hə-, hɛ- |-al -ļ |-ally -ļɪ |-icly
-ɪklɪ
heroin, H- *drug* ˈhɛro·ɪn
heroine '*heroic woman*' ˈhɛro·ɪn
heroism ˈhɛroˌɪzəm
heron ˈhɛrən |-ry -rɪ
heronsew, -sewe *arch.* ˈhɛrənˌsju, -ˌsɪu, -ˌsu
|-shaw -ˌʃɔ
herpes ˈhɝpiz; ES ˈhɝ-, ˈhɝ-
herpetology ˌhɝpəˈtalədʒɪ; ES ˌhɝp-, ˌhɝp-,
-ˈtɒl-
Herr *Ger title* hɛr; ES hɛə(r
Herrick ˈhɛrɪk
herring ˈhɛrɪŋ |-bone -ˌbon
Herriot *Am pers. name* ˈhɛrɪət, *Fr statesman*
ɛrˈjo
hers hɝz; ES hɝz, hɝz
Herschel ˈhɝʃəl; ES ˈhɝʃ-, ˈhɝʃ-
herself həˈsɛlf,+*if not initial or after a pause*
ɚˈself; ES hə-, ə-
Hertford *US* ˈhɝtfəd; ES ˈhɝtfəd, ˈhɝtfəd;
Engd ˈharfəd, ˈhartfəd; ES ˈhɑːfəd,
ˈhɑːtfəd, E+ˈhɑː-; |-shire -ˌʃɪr, -ʃɚ; ES
-ˌʃɪə(r, -ʃə(r
Herts *short for* Hertfordshire harts, hɝts; ES
hɑːts, hɝts, hɝts, E+hɑːts
Hertz hɛrts, hɝts; ES hɛəts, hɝts, hɝts; |-'s
-ɪz |-ian -ɪən
he's *abbr. spelling of* he has, he is, *stressed* ˈhiz,
ˌhiz; *unstr.* iz, ɪz, hiz, hɪz
Hesiod ˈhisɪəd, ˈhɛs-
Hesione hɪˈsaɪənɪ, hɛ-
hesitance ˈhɛzətəns |-cy -ɪ |-tant -tənt
hesitate ˈhɛzəˌtet |-d -ɪd |-tion ˌhɛzəˈteʃən
Hesper ˈhɛspɚ; ES ˈhɛspə(r
Hesperia hɛsˈpɪrɪə |-n -n -n

Key: *See in full §§3–47.* bee bi |pity ˈpɪtɪ (§6) |rate ret |yet jɛt |sang sæŋ |angry ˈæŋ·grɪ
|bath bæθ; E baθ (§10) |ah ɑ |far fɑr |watch watʃ, wɒtʃ (§12) |jaw dʒɔ |gorge gɔrdʒ |go go

Hesperides hɛsˈpɛrəˌdiz
Hesperus ˈhɛspərəs |-'s -ɪz
Hesse *Ger region* hɛs, ˈhɛsɪ (*Ger* Hessen
ˈhɛsən)—*The Ger word* Hesse ˈhɛsə *means
'resident of Hesse'* (*Ger* Hessen).
Hessian ˈhɛʃən
hest hɛst
Hester ˈhɛstɚ; ES ˈhɛstə(r
Hestia ˈhɛstɪə
hetaera hɪˈtɪrə |hetaira hɪˈtaɪrə
Hetch Hetchy Valley ˈhɛtʃˈhɛtʃɪˈvælɪ
heterodox ˈhɛtərəˌdɑks, ˈhɛtrə-; ES+ˌdɒks;
|-y -ɪ
heterodyne ˈhɛtərəˌdaɪn
heterogeneity ˌhɛtərədʒəˈniətɪ, ˌhɛtəro-
heterogeneous ˌhɛtərəˈdʒɪnɪəs, -njəs
heteronym ˈhɛtərəˌnɪm
heterosyllabic ˌhɛtəˌro·sɪˈlæbɪk
hetman ˈhɛtmən |*pl* hetmans ˈhɛtmənz
hew hju, hɪu |*past* -ed -d |*pptc* -ed -d *or* -n -n
hex hɛks |hexes ˈhɛksɪz |hexed hɛkst
hexachord ˈhɛksəˌkɔrd; ES -ˌkɔəd
hexa·emeron ˌhɛksəˈɛməˌrɑn, ES+-ˌrɒn
hexagon ˈhɛksəˌgɑn, -gən; ES+-ˌgɒn
hexagonal hɛksˈægənḷ |-ly -ɪ
hexagram ˈhɛksəˌgræm
hexahedral ˌhɛksəˈhidrəl
hexahedron ˌhɛksəˈhidrən |-s -z |-dra -drə
hexahemeron ˌhɛksəˈhɛməˌrɑn; ES+-ˌrɒn
hexameter hɛksˈæmətɚ; ES -ˈæmətə(r; |-ed -d
hexane ˈhɛksen
hexangular hɛksˈæŋgjəlɚ; ES -ˈæŋgjələ(r
hexapla ˈhɛksəplə
hexapod ˈhɛksəˌpɑd; ES+-ˌpɒd
hexarchy ˈhɛksɑrkɪ; ES ˈhɛksɑ:kɪ, E+-a:kɪ
Hexateuch ˈhɛksəˌtjuk, -ˌtɪuk, -ˌtuk
hey he |heyday ˈheˌde
Heyne ˈhaɪnə
Heywood ˈhewʊd
Hezekiah ˌhɛzəˈkaɪə
hiatus haɪˈetəs |-es -ɪz
Hiawatha ˌhaɪəˈwɑθə, -ˈwɒθə
hibernal haɪˈbɝnḷ; ES -ˈbɝnḷ, -ˈbɝnḷ
hibernate ˈhaɪbɚˌnet; ES -bəˌnet; |-d -ɪd
hibernation ˌhaɪbɚˈneʃən; ES ˌhaɪbə-
Hibernia haɪˈbɝnɪə; ES -ˈbɝn-, -ˈbɝn-; |-n -n
|-nicism -nəˌsɪzəm
hibiscus, H- haɪˈbɪskəs, hɪ- |-es -ɪz
hiccough *erroneous sp. for* hiccup

hiccup ˈhɪkʌp, ˈhɪkəp |-ed -t
hickory, H- ˈhɪkrɪ, ˈhɪkərɪ
hickory-nut ˈhɪkrɪnət, ˈhɪkərɪ-, -ˌnʌt, *dial.*
ˈhɪkɚnət
hid hɪd
hidalgo, H- hɪˈdælgo (*Sp* iˈðalgo)
hide 'conceal' haɪd |hid hɪd |hidden ˈhɪdṇ,
hid hɪd
hide 'skin' haɪd |hided ˈhaɪdɪd
hide-and-seek ˈhaɪdṇˈsik
hidebound ˈhaɪdˌbaʊnd
hideous ˈhɪdɪəs
hie haɪ |hied haɪd
Hiems, h- ˈhaɪəmz |-'s -ɪz
hierarch ˈhaɪəˌrɑrk; ES -ˌrɑ:k, E+-ˌrɑ:k;
|-y -ɪ
hieratic ˌhaɪəˈrætɪk |-al -ḷ |-ally -ḷɪ, -ɪklɪ
hieroglyph ˈhaɪərəˌglɪf, ˈhaɪrə-
hieroglyphic ˌhaɪərəˈglɪfɪk, ˌhaɪrə- |-al -ḷ
|-ally -ḷɪ, -ɪklɪ
Hieronymus ˌhaɪəˈrɑnəməs, -ˈrɒn-
higgle ˈhɪgḷ |-d -d |-ling ˈhɪglɪŋ, ˈhɪglɪŋ
higgledy-piggledy ˈhɪgḷdɪˈpɪgḷdɪ
high haɪ |-er ˈhaɪɚ; ES ˈhaɪ·ə(r; |-est -ɪst
Higham ˈhaɪəm
highball ˈhaɪˌbɔl
highbinder ˈhaɪˌbaɪndɚ; ES -ˌbaɪndə(r
highborn ˈhaɪˈbɔrn; ES -ˈbɔən; (ˈhighˌborn
ˈlass)
highboy ˈhaɪˌbɔɪ
highbred ˈhaɪˈbred
high-brow ˈhaɪˌbraʊ
highfalutin, -ting, -ten ˌhaɪfəˈlutṇ, -ˈlɪutṇ
highflier ˈhaɪˌflaɪɚ; ES -ˌflaɪ·ə(r
high-flown ˈhaɪˈflon (ˈhigh-ˌflown ˈspeech)
Highgate *US* ˈhaɪˌget, *Engd* ˈhaɪgɪt
highhanded ˈhaɪˈhændɪd
highjacker ˈhaɪˌdʒækɚ; ES -ˌdʒækə(r
highland, H- ˈhaɪlənd |-er -ɚ; ES -ə(r
highlight *v* ˈhaɪˌlaɪt |-ed -ɪd
highminded ˈhaɪˈmaɪndɪd
high-pitched ˈhaɪˈpɪtʃt (ˈhigh-ˌpitched ˈnote)
high-pressure ˈhaɪˈprɛʃɚ; ES -ˈprɛʃə(r
highroad ˈhaɪˌrod, -ˈrod
high-spirited ˈhaɪˈspɪrɪtɪd
high-strung ˈhaɪˈstrʌŋ (ˈhigh-ˌstrung ˈnerves)
hight *arch.* *v* 'call,' 'called' haɪt
hight *var. sp. of* height haɪt
high-test ˈhaɪˈtɛst

|full fʊl |tooth tuθ |further ˈfɝðɚ; ES ˈfɝðə |custom ˈkʌstəm |while hwaɪl |how haʊ |toy tɔɪ
|using ˈjuzɪŋ |fuse fjuz, fɪuz |dish dɪʃ |vision ˈvɪʒən |Eden ˈidṇ |cradle ˈkredḷ |keep 'em ˈkipm̩

highth *doublet of* height haɪtθ, *Brit*+haɪθ—
Highth *is not an error for* height, *but a phonetically normal historical variant, found
e.g. in Milton.*

high-toned ˈhaɪˈtond

highty-tighty ˈhaɪtɪˈtaɪtɪ

highway ˈhaɪˌwe

highwayman *'robber'* ˈhaɪˌwemən, haɪˈwe-

highwayman *'road overseer'* ˈhaɪweˌmæn
|-men -ˌmɛn

hike haɪk |hiked haɪkt

Hilaire hɪˈlɛr, -ˈlær; E -ˈlɛə(r, ES -ˈlæə(r

hilarious həˈlɛrɪəs, hɪ-, haɪ-, -ˈlær-, -ˈler-

hilarity həˈlærətɪ, hɪ-, haɪ-

Hilda ˈhɪldə

Hildebrand ˈhɪldəˌbrænd (*Ger* ˈhɪldəˌbrant)

Hildegarde ˈhɪldəˌgard; ES -ˌgaːd, E+-ˌgaːd

hilding ˈhɪldɪŋ

hill hɪl |hilled hɪld

hillbilly ˈhɪlˌbɪlɪ

Hillis ˈhɪlɪs |-'s -ɪz

hill-less ˈhɪllɪs

hillock ˈhɪlək |hillocked ˈhɪləkt

hillside ˈhɪlˌsaɪd

hilt hɪlt |hilted ˈhɪltɪd

hilum ˈhaɪləm |-s -z |-la -lə

him *stressed* ˈhɪm, ˌhɪm; *unstr.* ɪm, hɪm

Himalaya hɪˈmaljə, -ˈmaləjə, ˌhɪməˈleə |-n -n
|-s -z—*In Engd the traditional Anglicized
pron. still prevails (Jones says* hɪˈmaləjə *is
rare), as it once did in America, but the pron.
more like the native one has recently become
frequent here.*

himself hɪmˈsɛlf,+*if not initial or after a
pause* ɪmˈsɛlf

hind haɪnd

hindbrain ˈhaɪndˌbren, ˈhaɪn-

hinder *'back'* ˈhaɪndɚ; ES ˈhaɪndə(r

hinder *'obstruct'* ˈhɪndɚ; ES ˈhɪndə(r; |-ed -d
|-ing ˈhɪndrɪŋ, ˈhɪndərɪŋ

hindermost ˈhaɪndɚˌmost; ES ˈhaɪndə-

Hindi ˈhɪndi, ˈhɪnˈdi

hindmost ˈhaɪndˌmost, ˈhaɪn-

Hindoo ˈhɪndu, ˈhɪnˈdu |-ism ˈhɪndʊˌɪzəm
|-stani ˌhɪndʊˈstænɪ, -ˈstanɪ

Hindostan ˌhɪndʊˈstæn, -ˈstan |-i -ɪ

hindquarter ˈhaɪndˈkwɔrtɚ, ˈhaɪn-; ES
-ˈkwɔətə(r

hindrance ˈhɪndrəns |-s -ɪz

hindside ˈhaɪndˌsaɪd, ˈhaɪn-

hind-side-foremost ˈhaɪndˌsaɪdˈforˌmost,ˈhaɪn-,
-ˈfɔr-; ES -ˈfoə-, E+-ˈfɔə-

hindsight ˈhaɪndˌsaɪt, ˈhaɪn-

Hindu ˈhɪndu, ˈhɪnˈdu (ˈHinˌdu ˈraces)

Hinduism ˈhɪndʊˌɪzəm

Hindu Kush ˈhɪndʊˈkuʃ, -du-

Hindustan ˌhɪndʊˈstæn, -ˈstɑn |-i -ɪ

hinge hɪndʒ |hinges ˈhɪndʒɪz |hinged hɪndʒd

Hingham ˈhɪŋəm

hinny ˈhɪnɪ

Hinsdale ˈhɪnzdel

hint hɪnt |hinted ˈhɪntɪd

hinterland ˈhɪntɚˌlænd; ES ˈhɪntə-; (*Ger*
-ˌlant)

hip hɪp |hipped hɪpt |-bone -ˈbon, -ˌbon

hippocampus ˌhɪpəˈkæmpəs |-es -ɪz |-pi -paɪ

hippocras ˈhɪpəˌkræs

Hippocrates hɪˈpɑkrəˌtiz; ES+-ˈpɒk-; |-'s -ɪz

Hippocratic ˌhɪpəˈkrætɪk

Hippocrene ˈhɪpəˌkrin, ˌhɪpəˈkrini

hippodrome ˈhɪpəˌdrom

hippogriff, -gryff ˈhɪpəˌgrɪf

Hippolyta hɪˈpɑlɪtə; ES+-ˈpɒl-; |-tus -təs
|-tus's -təsɪz

hippopotamus ˌhɪpəˈpɑtəməs; ES+-ˈpɒt-;
|-es -ɪz |-mi -ˌmaɪ

Hiram ˈhaɪrəm

hircine ˈhɝsaɪn, -sɪn; ES ˈhɜ-, ˈhɝ-

hire haɪr; ES haɪə(r; |-d -d |-ling -lɪŋ

Hirohito ˌhɪroˈhito

Hirsch hɝʃ; ES hɜʃ, hɝʃ; |-'s -ɪz

hirsute ˈhɝsut, -sɪut, -sjut; ES ˈhɜ-, ˈhɝ-

his *stressed* ˈhɪz, ˌhɪz; *unstr.* ɪz, hɪz—*When
entirely unstressed, his has no* h, *just like* he,
her, him, 'em, it.

Hispania hɪsˈpenɪə, -njə |-nic hɪsˈpænɪk

Hispaniola ˌhɪspənˈjolə

hispid ˈhɪspɪd |hispidity hɪsˈpɪdətɪ

hiss hɪs |hisses ˈhɪsɪz |hissed hɪst

hist hɪst |histed ˈhɪstɪd

histology hɪsˈtɑlədʒɪ; ES+-ˈtɒl-

historian hɪsˈtorɪən, -ˈtɔr-; S -ˈtor-

historic hɪsˈtɔrɪk, -ˈtɑrɪk, -ˈtɒrɪk |-al -l̩ |-ally
-lɪ, -ɪklɪ

historicity ˌhɪstəˈrɪsətɪ

historiographer ˌhɪstorɪˈɑgrəfɚ, hɪsˌtorɪ-, -ɔrɪ,
-ˈɒg-; S -orɪ-, ES -fə(r

history ˈhɪstrɪ, ˈhɪstərɪ |-ried -rɪd

Key: *See in full §§3-47.* bee bi |pity ˈpɪtɪ (§6) |rate ret |yet jɛt |sang sæŋ |angry ˈæŋˌgrɪ
|bath bæθ; E baθ (§10) |ah ɑ |far fɑr |watch wɑtʃ, wɒtʃ (§12) |jaw dʒɔ |gorge gɔrdʒ |go go

histrionic ˌhɪstrɪˈɑnɪk; ES+-ˈɒn-; |-al -ļ
|-ally -ļɪ, -ɪklɪ
hit hɪt
hit-and-miss ˈhɪtņˈmɪs
hit-and-run ˈhɪtņˈrʌn (ˈhit-and-ˌrun ˈdriver)
hitch hɪtʃ |hitches ˈhɪtʃɪz |hitched hɪtʃt
hitchhike ˈhɪtʃˌhaɪk |-hiked -ˌhaɪkt
hithe, H- haɪð
hither ˈhɪðɚ; ES ˈhɪðə(r; |-most -ˌmost
hitherto ˌhɪðɚˈtu; ES ˌhɪðə-; (ˈhitherˌto
ˈcame)
hitherward ˈhɪðɚwɚd; ES ˈhɪðəwəd; |-s -z
Hitler ˈhɪtlɚ; ES ˈhɪtlə(r; |-ism -ˌɪzəm |-ite
-ˌaɪt
Hitlerian hɪtˈlɪrɪən
hit-or-miss ˈhɪtɚˈmɪs; ES ˈhɪtəˈmɪs
hit-skip ˈhɪtˈskɪp |-ped -t (ˈhit-ˌskip ˈdriver)
Hittite ˈhɪtaɪt
hive haɪv |hived haɪvd
h'm, hm hm—*the* h *nasal, with closed lips*
ho ho
hoar, H- hor, hɔr; ES hoə(r, E+hɔə(r
hoard hord, hɔrd; ES hoəd, E+hɔəd; |-ed -ɪd
hoarfrost ˈhorˌfrɔst, ˈhɔr-, -ˌfrɒst; ES ˈhoə-,
E+ˈhɔə-
hoarhound ˈhorˌhaʊnd, ˈhɔr-; ES ˈhoə-,
E+ˈhɔə-
hoarse hors, hɔrs; ES hoəs, E+hɔəs
hoary ˈhorɪ, ˈhɔrɪ; S ˈhorɪ
hoaryheaded ˈhorɪˈhɛdɪd, ˈhɔrɪ-; S ˈhorɪ-;
(ˈhoaryˌheaded ˈjoke)
hoax hoks |hoaxes ˈhoksɪz |hoaxed hokst;
|*N Engd*+hŏks (*§46*)
hob hɑb; ES+hɒb; |-bed -d
hob-and-nob ˈhɑbənˈnɑb; ES+ˈhɒbənˈnɒb
Hobart *Tasm* ˈhobɚt, -bɑrt, *US pers. name*
ˈhobɚt; ES -bət, -bɑːt
Hobbes hɑbz; ES+hɒbz; |-'s -ɪz
hobble ˈhɑbļ; ES+ˈhɒbļ; |-d -d |-ling -blɪŋ,
-bļɪŋ
hobbledehoy ˈhɑbļdɪˌhɔɪ; ES+ˈhɒb-
hobby ˈhɑbɪ; ES+ˈhɒbɪ; |-horse -ˌhɔrs; ES
-ˌhɔəs
hobgoblin ˈhɑbˌgɑblɪn; ES+ˈhɒbˌgɒblɪn
hobman-blind ˈhɑbmənˈblaɪnd; ES+ˈhɒb-;
see hodman-blind
hobnail ˈhɑbˌnel; ES+ˈhɒb-; |-ed -d
hobnob ˈhɑbˌnɑb; ES+ˈhɒbˌnɒb; |-bed -d
hobo ˈhobo

Hoboken ˈhobokən
Hobson ˈhɑbsņ; ES+ˈhɒbsņ
hock hɑk; ES+hɒk; |-ed -t
hockey ˈhɑkɪ; ES+ˈhɒkɪ
hocus ˈhokəs |hocuses ˈhokəsɪz |hocused
ˈhokəst
hocus-pocus ˈhokəsˈpokəs |-ed -t
hod hɑd; ES+hɒd
Hodgenville ˈhɑdʒənˌvɪl; ES+ˈhɒdʒ-, S+-vļ
hodgepodge ˈhɑdʒˌpɑdʒ; ES+ˈhɒdʒˌpɒdʒ;
|-s -ɪz |-d -d
hodman-blind ˈhɑdmənˈblaɪnd; ES+ˈhɒd-;
see hoodman-blind
hoe ho |hoed hod |-cake -ˌkek
hog hɑg, hɔg, hɒg; S hɔg, hɑg, hɒg; |-ged -d
Hogarth ˈhogɑrθ; ES -gɑ:θ, E+-gɑ:θ
Hogarthian hoˈgɑrθɪən; ES -ˈgɑ:θ-, E+
-ˈgɑ:θ-
hogback ˈhɑgˌbæk, ˈhɔg-, ˈhɒg- |-ed -t—*cf* hog
hogmanay ˌhɑgməˈne, ˌhɒg-
hognose ˈhɑgˌnoz, ˈhɔg-, ˈhɒg- |-d -d—*cf* hog
hognut ˈhɑgˌnʌt, ˈhɔg-, ˈhɒg-, -nət—*cf* hog
hogshead ˈhɑgzˌhɛd, ˈhɔgz-, ˈhɒgz-, -zɪd—*cf*
hog
hogwash ˈhɑgˌwɑʃ, ˈhɔg-, ˈhɒg-, -ˌwɔʃ, -ˌwɒʃ
—*cf* hog
Hohenlinden ˈhoənˌlɪndən
Hohenstaufen *Ger* ˌhoːənˈʃtaʊfən
Hohenzollern ˈhoənˌzɑlɚn; ES -ˌzɑlən, -ˌzɒl-:
(*Ger* ˌhoːənˈtsɔlərn)
hoicks hɔɪks
hoiden ˈhɔɪdņ |-ed -d |-ing -dņɪŋ, -dnɪŋ
hoi polloi ˈhɔɪpəˈlɔɪ
hoise *arch.* hɔɪz |hoised hɔɪzd *or* hoist hɔɪst
hoist *v pres* hɔɪst |-ed -ɪd
hokeypokey ˈhokɪˈpokɪ
Hokkaido hɑˈkaɪdo, hɒ-
hokum ˈhokəm
Holbein ˈholbaɪn, ˈhɑl-, ˈhɒl-
Holborn *Lond* ˈhobɚn, ˈhol-; ES -bən; *Scotl*
holˈborn, -ˈbɔrn; ES -ˈboən, E+-ˈbɔən
hold hold |held hɛld |*arch. pptc* holden ˈholdən
holdall ˈholdˌɔl
holdback ˈholdˌbæk
Holden ˈholdən, -dɪn
holder ˈholdɚ; ES ˈholdə(r
holdfast ˈholdˌfæst; E+-ˌfast, -ˌfɑst
holdup ˈholdˌʌp
hole hol |holed hold

|full fʊl |tooth tuθ |further ˈfɝðɚ; ES ˈfɝðə |custom ˈkʌstəm |while hwaɪl |how haʊ |toy tɔɪ
|using ˈjuzɪŋ |fuse fjuz, fɪuz |dish dɪʃ |vision ˈvɪʒən |Eden ˈidņ |cradle ˈkredļ |keep 'em ˈkipm̩

holiday 'halə,de; ES+'hɒl-
holiness, H- 'holɪnɪs |-'s -ɪz
Holinshed 'halɪnz,hɛd, 'halɪn,ʃɛd; ES+
'hɒl-; -,ʃɛd *is a sp. pron.; the second part=*
'head.'
holla 'halə, hə'la—*see* hollo
Holland 'halənd; ES+'hɒl-
hollandaise ,halən'dez; ES+,hɒl-; ('hollan-
,daise 'sauce)
hollo 'halo, hə'lo—*This word&* holla*are hardly*
in current use. The living word is holler
'halɚ; ES 'halə(r, 'hɒl-, *shunned by many.*
hollow 'halo, 'halə; ES+'hɒl-; |-ed -d |-ing
-ləwɪŋ |-er -ləwɚ; ES -wə(r; |-est -ləwɪst
holly 'halɪ; ES+'hɒlɪ
hollyhock 'halɪ,hak, -,hɔk; ES+'hɒlɪ,hɒk;
The pronunciation 'halɪ,hɔk *is evidenced*
from all parts of US and from Canada.
Hollywood 'halɪ,wʊd; ES+'hɒlɪ-
holm hom
Holmes homz; *NEngd*+hŏmz (*§46*) |-'s -ɪz
holmia 'holmɪə |holmium 'holmɪəm |-mic
-mɪk
holocaust 'halə,kɔst; ES+'hɒl-
Holofernes, -pher- ,halə'fɝniz; ES ,halə-
'fɝniz, ,hɒl-, -'fɝniz; |-nes' -niz
holograph 'halə,græf; ES+'hɒl-, E+-,graf,
-,graf
holophote 'halə,fot; ES+'hɒl-
holp *arch. past & pptc of* help holp
holpen *arch. pptc of* help 'holpən
Holstein 'holstaɪn, *with US farmers usually*
'holstin (*Ger* 'hɔlʃtaɪn)
Holstein-Friesian 'holstaɪn'friʒən, -stin-
holster 'holstɚ; ES -stə(r; |-ed -d |-ing 'hol-
stərɪŋ, 'holstrɪŋ
holt, H- holt; *NEngd*+hŏlt (*§46*)
holy 'holɪ |holily 'holəlɪ, -lɪlɪ
holyday 'holɪ,de
Holyhead *Wales* 'halɪ,hɛd, -'hɛd; ES+'hɒlɪ-
Holyoke 'holɪ,ok, *Mass city & college* 'holjok
Holyrood *Scotl* 'halɪ,rud; ES+'hɒlɪ-
holystone 'holɪ,ston |-d -d
holytide 'holɪ,taɪd
Holywell 'halɪ,wɛl, -wəl; ES+'hɒlɪ-
homage 'hamɪdʒ, 'am-; ES+'hɒm-, 'ɒm-;
|-s -ɪz |-d -d
hombre *Sp* '*man*' 'ɔmbre |*pl* -bres -bres
hombre '*omber*' 'ambɚ; ES 'ambə(r, 'ɒm-

home hom |homed homd; |*NEngd*+hŏm
(*§46*)
homebred 'hom'brɛd ('home,bred 'mink)
homeland 'hom,lænd
homelike 'hom,laɪk
homely 'homlɪ; *NEngd*+'hŏmlɪ (*§46*)
homemade 'hom'med
homemaker 'hom,mekɚ; ES -,mekə(r
homeopath 'homɪə,pæθ |-ths -θs
homeopathic ,homɪə'pæθɪk |-ally -ļɪ, -ɪklɪ
homeopathist ,homɪ'apəθɪst; ES+-'ɒp-; |-thy
-θɪ
homer 'homɚ; ES 'homə(r
Homer 'homɚ; ES 'homə(r
Homeric ho'mɛrɪk |-al -ļ |-ally -ļɪ, -ɪklɪ
homesick 'hom,sɪk
homespun 'hom,spʌn
homestead, H- 'hom,stɛd, 'homstɪd
homestretch 'hom'strɛtʃ |-es -ɪz
homeward 'homwɚd; ES 'homwəd
homework 'hom,wɝk; ES -,wɜk, -,wɝk
homey 'homɪ
homicidal ,hamə'saɪdļ; ES+-,hɒm-; |-ly -ɪ
homicide 'hamə,saɪd; ES+'hɒm-
homiletic ,hamə'lɛtɪk; ES+,hɒm-; |-al -ļ
|-ally -ļɪ, -ɪklɪ
homily 'hamļɪ; ES+'hɒm-
hominy 'hamənɪ; ES+'hɒm-
homo, H- 'homo |*pl* homines 'hamə,niz;
ES+'hɒm-
homogamic ,homə'gæmɪk, ,ham-; ES+,hɒm-
homogamy ho'magəmɪ, -'mɒg-
homogeneity ,homədʒə'niətɪ, ,ham-; ES+
,hɒm-
homogeneous ,homə'dʒinɪəs, ,ham-; ES+
,hɒm-
homogenesis ,homə'dʒɛnəsɪs, ,ham-; ES+
,hɒm-
homogenize ho'madʒə,naɪz; ES+ -'mɒdʒ-
homologous ho'maləgəs; ES+-'mɒl-
homologue 'homə,lɔg, -,lag, -,lɒg; ES+'hɒm-
homology ho'malədʒɪ; ES+-'mɒl-
homonym 'hamə,nɪm; ES+'hɒm-
homonymous ho'manəməs; ES+-'mɒn-;
|-my -mɪ
homophone 'hamə,fon; ES+'hɒm-
homophonic ,hamə'fanɪk; ES+,homə'fɒnɪk
homophonous ho'mafənəs; ES+-'mɒf-; |-ny
-nɪ

homorganic ˌhomərˈgænɪk, ˌham-; ES ˌhomɔəˈgænɪk, ˌham-, ˌhɒm-
Homo sapiens ˈhomoˈsepɪˌɛnz
homunculus hoˈmʌŋkjələs |-li -ˌlaɪ
Honan ˈhoˈnæn, -ˈnɑn (Chin ˈxʌˈnɑn)
Honduran hɑnˈdʊrən, -ˈdɪʊr-, -ˈdjʊr-; ES+ hɒn-; |-ras -rəs |-ras's -rəsɪz
hone hon |honed hond
honest ˈɑnɪst; ES+ˈɒn-; |-y -ɪ
honey ˈhʌnɪ |honeyed ˈhʌnɪd |-bee -ˌbi
honeycomb ˈhʌnɪˌkom |-ed -d
honeydew ˈhʌnɪˌdju, -ˌdɪu, -ˌdu
honeymoon ˈhʌnɪˌmun |-ed -d
honeysuckle ˈhʌnɪˌsʌkl̩ |-d -d
honey-tongued ˈhʌnɪˈtʌŋd (ˈhoney-ˌtongued ˈAnn)
Hong Kong ˈhɑŋˈkɑŋ, ˈhɒnˈkɒŋ
Honiton ˈhɑnɪtn̩, loc. ˈhʌnɪtn̩; ES+ˈhɒn-
honk ˈhɑŋk, ˈhaŋk, ˈhɒŋk |-ed -t
Honolulu ˌhɑnəˈlulə, -lu; ES+ˌhɒn-; native ˈhoˈnoˈluˈlu (even stress)
honor ˈɑnɚ; ES ˈɑnə(r, ˈɒnə(r; |-ed -d |-ing -nərɪŋ, -nrɪŋ |-able -əbl̩, -nrəbl̩ |-bly -blɪ
honorarium ˌɑnəˈrɛrɪəm, -ˈrær-, -ˈrer-; ES+ˌɒn-; |-s -z |-ria -rɪə
honorary ˈɑnəˌrɛrɪ; ES+ˈɒn-
honorific ˌɑnəˈrɪfɪk; ES+ˌɒn-; |-al -l̩ |-ally -lɪ, -ɪklɪ
Honshu ˈhɑnʃu, ˈhɒn-
hooch hutʃ
hood, H- hʊd |hooded ˈhʊdɪd
-hood ending, pron. -hʊd, -ˌhʊd according to number of syllables; as ˈmænhʊd, ˈlaɪklɪˌhʊd. The pron. of all such words omitted from the vocab. can be found by adding -hʊd or -ˌhʊd directly to the main word.
hoodlum ˈhʊdləm
hoodman ˈhʊdmən |-men -mən
hoodman-blind ˈhʊdmənˈblaɪnd
hoodoo ˈhudu |hoodooed ˈhudud
hoodwink ˈhʊdˌwɪŋk |-ed -t
hooey ˈhuɪ
hoof hʊf, huf |-s -s |rarely hooves -vz |-ed -t— The pronunciation hʊf clearly prevails in the N, E, and S, and probably in Canada.
Hooghly, -gly ˈhuglɪ
hook hʊk |hooked hʊkt
hookah, -ka ˈhʊkə
hooked adj ˈhʊkɪd, hʊkt |-ness ˈhʊkɪdnɪs

Hooker ˈhʊkɚ; ES ˈhʊkə(r
hookup ˈhʊkˌʌp
hookworm ˈhʊkˌwɝm; ES -ˌwɜm, -ˌwɝm
hooky ˈhʊkɪ
hooligan ˈhulɪgən |-ism -ˌɪzəm
hoop hup, hup |-ed -t
hooping-cough ˈhupɪŋˌkɔf, ˈhupɪŋ-, -ˌkɒf
hoopoe ˈhupu
hooray huˈre, hu-
Hoosac ˈhusək, -sæk
hoosegow, hoosg- ˈhusgaʊ
Hoosic, -sick ˈhusɪk
Hoosier ˈhuʒɚ; ES ˈhuʒə(r
hoot hut |hooted ˈhutɪd
Hoover ˈhuvɚ; ES ˈhuvə(r
hooves pl of hoof hʊvz, huvz
hop hɑp; ES+hɒp; |-ped -t
Hopatcong hoˈpætkɑŋ, hə-, -kɒŋ
hope, H- hop |hoped hopt; [N Engd+hɔ̈p (§46)
Hopeh, -pei ˈhoˈpe
hoplite ˈhɑplaɪt; ES+ˈhɒp-
hop-o'-my-thumb ˈhɑpəmaɪˈθʌm; ES+ˈhɒp-
hopper ˈhɑpɚ; ES ˈhɑpə(r, ˈhɒp-
hopscotch ˈhɑpˌskɑtʃ; ES+ˈhɒpˌskɒtʃ; |-ed -t
Horace ˈhɑrɪs, ˈhar-, ˈhɒr-, -əs |-'s -ɪz
Horatian həˈreʃən, ho-, -ʃɪən
Horatio həˈreʃo, ho-, -ʃɪo
Horatius həˈreʃəs, ho-, -ʃɪəs |-'s -ɪz
horde hord, hɔrd; ES hoəd, E+hɔəd; |-d -ɪd
Horeb ˈhorəb, ˈhɔr-, -ɛb; S ˈhor-
Hore-Belisha ˈhorbəˈliʃə, ˈhɔr-; ES ˈhoə-, E+-ˈhɔə-
horehound ˈhorˌhaʊnd, ˈhɔr-; ES ˈhoə-, E+ˈhɔə-
horizon həˈraɪzn̩ |-ed -d |-ing -ˈraɪznɪŋ, -znɪŋ
horizontal ˌhɔrəˈzantl̩, ˌhar-, ˌhɒr-; ES+-ˈzɒn-; |-ly -ɪ
hormone ˈhɔrmon; ES ˈhɔəmon
Hormuz ˈhɔrmʌz; ES ˈhɔəmʌz; |-'s -ɪz
horn, H- hɔrn; ES hɔən; |-ed -d
hornblende ˈhɔrnˌblɛnd; ES ˈhɔən-
hornbook ˈhɔrnˌbʊk; ES ˈhɔən-
Hornell hɔrˈnɛl; ES hɔəˈnɛl
Horner ˈhɔrnɚ; ES ˈhɔənə(r
hornet ˈhɔrnɪt; ES ˈhɔənɪt
Hornie ˈhɔrnɪ; ES ˈhɔənɪ
horn-mad ˈhɔrnˈmæd; ES ˈhɔən-
hornpipe ˈhɔrnˌpaɪp; ES ˈhɔən-

|full fʊl |tooth tuθ |further ˈfɝðɚ; ES ˈfɜðə |custom ˈkʌstəm |while hwaɪl |how haʊ |toy tɔɪ |using ˈjuzɪŋ |fuse fjuz, fɪuz |dish dɪʃ |vision ˈvɪʒən |Eden ˈidn̩ |cradle ˈkredl̩ |keep 'em ˈkipm̩

horologe ˈhɒrəˌlodʒ, ˈhɑr-, ˈhɒr-, -ˌlɑdʒ;
ES+-ˌlɒdʒ; |-s -ɪz
horologer hoˈrɑlədʒɚ, hɔ-; ES -ˈrɑlədʒə(r,
-ˈrɒl-; |-gist -dʒɪst |-gy -dʒɪ
horoscope ˈhɒrəˌskop, ˈhɑrə-, ˈhɒrə-
horoscopy hoˈrɑskəpɪ, hɔ-; ES+-ˈrɒs-
horrendous hɔˈrɛndəs, ˈhɑ-, hɒ-
horrent ˈhɒrənt, ˈhɑr-, ˈhɒr-
horrible ˈhɒrəbl̩, ˈhɑr-, ˈhɒr- |-bly -blɪ
horrid ˈhɒrɪd, ˈhɑr-, ˈhɒr-
horrific hɔˈrɪfɪk, hɑ-, hɒ-
horrification ˌhɒrəfəˈkeʃən, ˌhɑr-, ˌhɒr-
horrify ˈhɒrəˌfaɪ, ˈhɑr-, ˈhɒr- |-fied -ˌfaɪd
Horrocks ˈhɒrəks, ˈhɑr-, ˈhɒr- |-'s -ɪz
horror ˈhɒrɚ, ˈhɑr-, ˈhɒr-; ES -rə(r
Horsa ˈhɔrsə; ES ˈhɔəsə
hors de combat ˌɔrdəˈkɑmbɑ; ES ˌɔədə-,
-ˈkɒm-; (Fr ɔ̃rdəkõˈbɑ)
hors d'oeuvre ɔrˈdœvrə, -ˈdʌv; ES ɔə-; (Fr
ɔ̃rˈdœːvr)
horse hɔrs; ES hɔəs; |-s -ɪz |-d -t
horse-and-buggy adj ˈhɔrsn̩ˈbʌgɪ; ES ˈhɔəs-
horseback ˈhɔrsˌbæk; ES ˈhɔəs-
horsecar ˈhɔrsˌkɑr; ES ˈhɔəsˌkɑː(r, E+-ˌkɑː(r
horsecloth ˈhɔrsˌklɒθ, -ˌklɒθ |-ths -θs, -ðz—see
cloth
horseflesh ˈhɔrsˌflɛʃ; ES ˈhɔəs-
horsefly ˈhɔrsˌflaɪ; ES ˈhɔəs-
horsehair ˈhɔrsˌhɛr, -ˌhær; E ˈhɔəsˌhɛə(r, ES
ˈhɔəsˌhæə(r
horsehide ˈhɔrsˌhaɪd; ES ˈhɔəs-
horsejockey ˈhɔrsˌdʒɑkɪ; ES ˈhɔəs-, -ˌdʒɒkɪ
horselaugh ˈhɔrsˌlæf; ES ˈhɔəs-, E+-ˌlaf,
-ˌlɑf; |-ed -t
horseleech ˈhɔrsˌlitʃ; ES ˈhɔəs-; |-es -ɪz
horseman rider, manager ˈhɔrsmən; ES
ˈhɔəs-; |-men -mən
horseman racing sport, expert ˈhɔrsˌmæn; ES
ˈhɔəs-; |-men -ˌmɛn
horseplay ˈhɔrsˌple; ES ˈhɔəs-
horsepower ˈhɔrsˌpaʊɚ; ES ˈhɔəsˌpaʊ·ə(r
horse-radish ˈhɔrsˌrædɪʃ; ES ˈhɔəs-; |-es -ɪz
horseshoe ˈhɔrʃˌʃu, ˈhɔrsˌʃu, -ˌʃɪu; ES ˈhɔəʃ-,
ˈhɔəs-; |-d -d
horsetail ˈhɔrsˌtel; ES ˈhɔəs-
horsewhip ˈhɔrsˌhwɪp; ES ˈhɔəs-; |-ped -t
horsewoman ˈhɔrsˌwʊmən, -ˌwum-; ES
ˈhɔəs-; |-women -ˌwɪmɪn—see woman
Horsham ˈhɔrʃəm; ES ˈhɔəʃəm; sp. pron.

Horst Wessel ˈhɔrstˈvɛsl̩; ES ˈhɔəst-
horsy ˈhɔrsɪ; ES ˈhɔəsɪ
hortative ˈhɔrtətɪv; ES ˈhɔətə-
hortatory ˈhɔrtəˌtorɪ, -ˌtɔrɪ; ES ˈhɔətəˌtorɪ,
E+-ˌtɔrɪ
Hortense hɔrˈtɛns; ES hɔə-; |-'s -ɪz (Fr
ɔ̃rˈtɑ̃ːs)
Hortensia hɔrˈtɛnsɪə, -ˌʃɪə; ES hɔ- |-ius -s
|-ius's -sɪz
Hortensio hɔrˈtɛnsɪˌo, -ˈtɛnʃjo; ES hɔ-
horticulture ˈhɔrtɪˌkʌltʃɚ; ES ˈhɔətɪˌkʌltʃə(r
hosanna, H- hoˈzænə
hose hoz |hoses ˈhozɪz |hosed hozd
Hosea prophet hoˈziə, pers. name hoˈziə, ˈhozɪə
(ˈHoˌsea ˈBiglow)
hosier ˈhoʒɚ; ES ˈhoʒə(r; |-y -ɪ, -ʒrɪ
Hosmer ˈhazmɚ; ES ˈhazmə(r, ˈhɒz-
hospice ˈhɑspɪs, ˈhɒs- |-s -ɪz
hospitable ˈhɑspɪtəbl̩, ˈhɒs-, much less freq.
hasˈpɪtəbl̩, hɒs- |-bly -blɪ
hospital ˈhɑspɪtl̩, ˈhasˌpɪtl̩, ˈhɒs-
hospitality ˌhɑspɪˈtælətɪ, ˌhɒs-
hospitalization ˌhɑspɪtl̩əˈzeʃən, ˌhɒs-, -aɪˈz-
hospitalize ˈhɑspɪtl̩ˌaɪz, ˈhɒs- |-s -ɪz |-d -d
host host |hosted ˈhostɪd
hostage ˈhastɪdʒ; ES+ˈhɒs-; |-s -ɪz |-d -d
hostel ˈhastl̩; ES+ˈhɒs-; |-ry -rɪ
hosteler ˈhastlɚ; ES ˈhastlə(r, ˈhɒs-
hostess ˈhostɪs |hostesses ˈhostɪsɪz
hostile ˈhastl̩, -tɪl; ES+ˈhɒs-
hostility hasˈtɪlətɪ; ES+hɒs-
hostler ˈhaslɚ, ˈaslɚ; ES ˈhaslə(r, ˈaslə(r
ˈhɒs-, ˈɒs-
hot hɑt; ES+hɒt
hotbed ˈhatˌbed; ES+ˈhɒt-
hot-blooded ˈhatˈblʌdɪd; ES+ˈhɒt-
hotbox ˈhatˌbaks; ES+ˈhɒtˌbɒks; |-es -ɪz
hot-breathed ˈhatˈbrɛθt; ES+ˈhɒt-
hotchpot ˈhatʃˌpat; ES+ˈhɒtʃˌpɒt
hotchpotch ˈhatʃˌpatʃ; ES+ˈhɒtʃˌpɒtʃ; |-es
-ɪz |-ed -t
hotel hoˈtɛl (ˈHoˌtel ˈCleveland)
hotfoot ˈhatˌfʊt; ES+ˈhɒt-; |-ed -ɪd
hothead ˈhatˌhɛd; ES+ˈhɒt-
hotheaded ˈhatˈhɛdɪd; ES+ˈhɒt-
hothouse ˈhatˌhaʊs; ES+ˈhɒt-; |-ses -zɪz
hotspur, H- ˈhatˌspɚ; ES ˈhatˌspɜ(r, -ˌspɝ,
ˈhɒt-
Hottentot ˈhatn̩ˌtat; ES+ˈhɒtn̩ˌtɒt

Houdini hu'dını
hough hɑk; ES+hɒk; |-ed -t (Sc hɒx)
Hough hʌf, hɔf, hɑf, hɒf
Houghton 'hotn̩, 'hɑutn̩, 'hɔtn̩
Houlton 'holtn̩
hound haund |hounded 'haundıd
Hounslow 'haunzlo
hour aur; ES auə(r
hourglass 'aur͵glæs; ES 'auə-, E+-͵glɑs,
 -͵glɑs; |-es -ız
houri 'hurı, 'haurı
Housatonic ͵husə'tɑnık; ES+-'tɒn-; loc.+
 ͵huzə-
house n haus |house's 'hausız |houses 'hauzız
house v hauz |houses 'hauzız |housed hauzd
houseboat 'haus͵bot |-ed -ıd
housebreaking 'haus͵brekıŋ
housebroken 'haus͵brokən
housecarl 'haus͵kɑrl; ES -͵kɑːl, E+-͵kɑːl
housefly 'haus͵flaı
houseful 'haus͵ful |fuls -͵fulz
household 'haus͵hold, -͵old
housekeeper 'haus͵kipɚ; ES -͵kipə(r
housel 'hauzl̩ |houseled 'hauzl̩d
houseless 'hauslıs
housemaid 'haus͵med
house-raising 'haus͵rezıŋ
housetop 'haus͵tɑp; ES+-͵tɒp
housewarming 'haus͵wɔrmıŋ; ES -͵wɔəmıŋ
housewife 'woman' 'haus͵waıf |-ves -vz
housewife 'sewing-kit' 'hʌzıf, 'haus͵waıf |-fes
 -fs |-ves -vz
housewife v 'haus͵waıf |-s -s |-d -t
housewifery 'haus͵waıfrı, -fərı, 'hʌzıfrı
housework 'haus͵wɝk; ES -͵wɜk, -͵wɝ·k
housing 'hauzıŋ
Housman 'hausmən
Houston Tex soldier & city 'hjustən, 'hıus-;
 Eng botanist 'hustən, NYC street, Ga co.
 'haustən, Scotl 'hustən
Houyhnhnm hu'ınəm, 'hwınəm, 'hwın-
 ˀmˀmˀm---
hove n & past of heave hov
hovel 'hʌvl̩, much less freq. 'hɑvl̩; ES+'hɒvl̩;
 |-ed -d |-ing -vl̩ıŋ, -vlıŋ
hover 'hʌvɚ, much less freq. 'hɑvɚ; ES -və(r,
 'hɒv-; |-ed -d |-ing -vərıŋ, -vrıŋ
how hau
How(e) hau

Howard 'hauɚd; ES 'hau·əd
howbeit hau'biıt
howdah 'haudə
how-do-you-do 'haudəjə'du, 'haudəju'du,
 'haudəjı'du, 'haudjə'du, 'haudju'du, 'haudı'du, 'haud'du
how-dy-do 'haudı'du
howe'er hau'ɛr; ES hau'ɛə(r
Howells 'haualz |-'s -ız
however hau'ɛvɚ; ES hau'ɛvə(r
howitzer 'hauıtsɚ; ES 'hauıtsə(r
howl haul |howled hauld |-er -ɚ; ES -ə(r
howlet 'haulıt
howsoever ͵hauso'ɛvɚ; ES -'ɛvə(r
hoy hɔı |hoyed hɔıd
hoyden 'hɔıdn̩ |-ed -d |-ing -dn̩ıŋ, -dnıŋ
hub hʌb |hubbed hʌbd
Hubbell 'hʌbl̩
hubbub 'hʌbʌb
Hubert 'hjubɚt, 'hıu-; ES -bət
huckaback 'hʌkə͵bæk
huckle 'hʌkl̩ |-back -͵bæk |-backed -͵bækt
huckleberry, H- 'hʌkl̩͵bɛrı, -bərı
hucklebone 'hʌkl̩͵bon
huckster 'hʌkstɚ; ES 'hʌkstə(r
hucksterer 'hʌkstərɚ; ES 'hʌkstərə(r
huddle 'hʌdl̩ |-d -d |-ling 'hʌdlıŋ, 'hʌdl̩ıŋ
Hudibras 'hjudı͵bræs, 'hıu- |-'s -ız
Hudibrastic ͵hjudı'bræstık, ͵hıu-
Hudson 'hʌdsn̩
hue hju, hıu |hued hjud, hıud
Huebner 'hjubnɚ, 'hıub-, 'hib-; ES -nə(r;
 (Ger 'hyːbnər)
Huerta 'wɛrtə (Sp 'werta)
huff hʌf |huffed hʌft
hug hʌg |hugged hʌgd
huge hjudʒ, hıudʒ, judʒ
huggermugger 'hʌgɚ͵mʌgɚ; ES 'hʌgə͵mʌgə(r
Hugh hju, hıu
Hughes hjuz, hıuz |-'s -ız
Hugli 'huglı
Hugo 'hjugo, 'hıugo
Huguenot 'hjugə͵nɑt, 'hıu-; ES+-͵nɒt
huh hʌ (nasal ʌ) & various other grunts
Huidekoper 'haıdı͵kopɚ; ES -͵kopə(r
hula or hula-hula 'hulə, 'hulə'hulə
hulk hʌlk |hulked hʌlkt
hull hʌl |hulled hʌld
hullabaloo 'hʌləbə͵lu, 'hʌləbə'lu

|full ful |tooth tuθ |further 'fɝðɚ; ES 'fɜðə |custom 'kʌstəm |while hwaıl |how hau |toy tɔı
|using 'juzıŋ |fuse fjuz, fıuz |dish dıʃ |vision 'vıʒən |Eden 'idn̩ |cradle 'kredl̩ |keep 'em 'kipm̩

hullo hə'lo |hulloed hə'lod

Hulme hjum, hɪum, hʌlm

Hultzén hʊl'tsen

hum hʌm |hummed hʌmd

human 'hjumən, 'hɪumən, 'jumən |-ness -mənnɪs

humane hju'men, hɪu'men, ju'men |-ness -'mennɪs

humanism 'hjumən‚ɪzəm, 'hɪu- |-ist -ɪst

humanitarian hju‚mænə'tɛrɪən, hɪu-, -'ter-, ‚hjumænə-, ‚hɪu-

humanity hju'mænətɪ, hɪu-

Humber 'hʌmbɚ; ES 'hʌmbə(r

Humbert 'hʌmbɚt; ES 'hʌmbət

humble 'hʌmbl̩, 'ʌmbl̩ |-d -d—The historical 'ʌmbl̩ is well preserved in the S.

humblebee 'hʌmbl̩‚bi

humbler 'hʌmblɚ, 'ʌm-; ES -blə(r; |-blest -blɪst |-bly -blɪ

Humboldt 'hʌmbolt (Ger 'hʊmbɔlt)

humbug 'hʌm‚bʌg |humbugged 'hʌm‚bʌgd

humdrum 'hʌm‚drʌm |humdrummed 'hʌm-‚drʌmd

Hume hjum, hɪum

humerus 'hjumərəs, 'hɪu- |-es -ɪz |-ri -‚raɪ

humid 'hjumɪd, 'hɪumɪd

humidify hju'mɪdə‚faɪ, hɪu- |-fied -‚faɪd

humidity hju'mɪdətɪ, hɪu-

humidor 'hjumɪ‚dɔr, 'hɪu-; ES -‚dɔə(r

humiliate hju'mɪlɪ‚et, hɪu- |-ated -‚etɪd

humiliation hju‚mɪlɪ'eʃən, hɪu-, ‚hjumɪlɪ-, ‚hɪu-

humiliatory hju'mɪlɪə‚torɪ, hɪu-, -‚tɔrɪ; S -‚torɪ

humility hju'mɪlətɪ, hɪu-

hummer 'hʌmɚ; ES 'hʌmə(r

hummingbird 'hʌmɪŋ‚bɝd; ES -‚bɜd, -‚bɝd

hummock 'hʌmək |hummocked 'hʌməkt

humor 'hjumɚ, 'hɪu-, 'ju-; ES -mə(r; |-ed -d |-ing -mərɪŋ, -mrɪŋ—The pron. 'jumɚ, 'jumə(r is most likely to occur in 'sense of humor,' 'mood,' and in the verb.

humoresque ‚hjumə'rɛsk, ‚hɪu-

humorist 'hjumərɪst, 'hɪu-, 'ju-

humoristic ‚hjumə'rɪstɪk, ‚hɪu-, ‚ju- |-al -l̩

humorous 'hjumərəs, 'hɪu-, 'ju-

hump hʌmp |humped hʌmpt

humpback 'hʌmp‚bæk |-backed -‚bækt

Humperdinck 'hʊmpɚ‚dɪŋk; ES 'hʊmpə-

humph hm̥m̥m̥ & various other grunts & nasal puffs

Humphrey, -ry 'hʌmfrɪ, 'ʌm-, -pfrɪ |-s -z |-s' -z

humus 'hjuməs, 'hɪu-

Hun hʌn

hunch hʌntʃ |hunches 'hʌntʃɪz |hunched hʌntʃt

hunchback 'hʌntʃ‚bæk |-backed -‚bækt

hundred 'hʌndrəd, -drɪd, -dəd; ES -drəd, -drɪd, -dəd; |-th -θ |-fold -'fold, -‚fold |-weight -'wet, -‚wet —'hʌndəd, -dəd has been current from the 14c to Tennyson and King George V.

hung hʌŋ

Hungary 'hʌŋgərɪ |-rian hʌŋ'gɛrɪən, -'ger-

hunger 'hʌŋgɚ; ES 'hʌŋgə(r; |-ed -d |-ing 'hʌŋgərɪŋ, 'hʌŋgrɪŋ |-gry -grɪ

hunh hʌ (nasal ʌ) & other similar sounds

hunk hʌŋk

hunky 'hʌŋkɪ

hunky-dory ‚hʌŋkɪ'dorɪ, -'dɔrɪ; S -'dorɪ

Hunnish 'hʌnɪʃ

hunt hʌnt |hunted 'hʌntɪd

hunter, H- 'hʌntɚ; ES 'hʌntə(r

Hunterian hʌn'tɪrɪən

Huntingdon 'hʌntɪŋdən |-shire -‚ʃɪr, -ʃɚ; ES -‚ʃɪə(r, -ʃə(r

Huntington 'hʌntɪŋtən

Hunts short for Huntingdonshire hʌnts

huntsman 'hʌntsmən |-men -mən

hurdle 'hɝdl̩; ES 'hɜdl̩, 'hɝdl̩; |-d -d |-ling -dlɪŋ, -dl̩ɪŋ

hurdy-gurdy 'hɝdɪ‚gɝdɪ; ES 'hɜdɪ‚gɜdɪ, 'hɝdɪ‚gɝdɪ

hurl hɝl; ES hɜl, hɝl; |-ed -d

hurly-burly 'hɝlɪ‚bɝlɪ; ES 'hɜlɪ‚bɜlɪ, 'hɝlɪ‚bɝlɪ

Huron 'hjʊrən, 'hɪu-

hurrah hə'rɔ, hə'rɑ, hʊ-

hurray hə're, hʊ-

hurricane 'hɝɪ‚ken; ES 'hɜrɪ-, 'hʌrɪ-, 'hɝɪ-

hurry 'hɝɪ; ES 'hɜrɪ, 'hʌrɪ, 'hɝɪ; |-ried -d

hurry-scurry, -sk- 'hɝɪ'skɝɪ; ES 'hɜrɪ'skɜrɪ, 'hʌrɪ'skʌrɪ, 'hɝɪ'skɝɪ |-ried -d

hurt hɝt; ES hɜt, hɝt; |-ful -fəl |-fully -fəlɪ

hurtle 'hɝtl̩; ES 'hɜtl̩, 'hɝtl̩; |-d -d |-ling -tlɪŋ, -tl̩ɪŋ

husband 'hʌzbənd |husbanded 'hʌzbəndɪd

Key: See in full §§3–47. bee bi |pity 'pɪtɪ (§6) |rate ret |yet jɛt |sang sæŋ |angry 'æŋ‚grɪ |bath bæθ; E baθ (§10) |ah ɑ |far fɑr |watch wɑtʃ, wɒtʃ (§12) |jaw dʒɔ |gorge gɔrdʒ |go go

husbandman ˈhʌzbəndmən, -bənmən |-men
-mən

husbandry ˈhʌzbəndrɪ

hush hʌʃ |hushed hʌʃt |-edly -ɪdlɪ

hushaby ˈhʌʃəˌbaɪ

Hushai ˈhjuʃɪˌaɪ, ˈhɪu-, -ʃaɪ

husk hʌsk |husked hʌskt

husky ˈhʌskɪ |Husky ˈhʌskɪ

Huss hʌs |Huss's ˈhʌsɪz |-ite -aɪt

hussar huˈzɑr; ES huˈzɑːr, E+-ˈzaː(r

hussy ˈhʌsɪ, ˈhʌzɪ

hustings ˈhʌstɪŋz

hustle ˈhʌsl̩ |-d -d |-ling ˈhʌslɪŋ, ˈhʌsl̩ɪŋ

huswife ˈhʌzɪf

hut hʌt |hutted ˈhʌtɪd

hutch hʌtʃ |hutches ˈhʌtʃɪz |hutched hʌtʃt

Hutten, von fənˈhʊtn̩

Huxley ˈhʌkslɪ

Huygens ˈhaɪgənz

huzza həˈzɑ, huˈzɑ

Hwang-ho ˈhwæŋˈho, ˈhwɑŋ-

hyacinth, H- ˈhaɪəˌsɪnθ |-ths -θs

Hyads ˈhaɪədz |Hyades ˈhaɪəˌdiz

hyaena haɪˈinə

hyaline ˈhaɪəlɪn

hyalogen haɪˈælədʒən, -dʒɪn

Hyannis haɪˈænɪs |-'s -ɪz

Hybla ˈhaɪblə

hybrid ˈhaɪbrɪd |-ity haɪˈbrɪdətɪ

hybridization ˌhaɪbrɪdəˈzeʃən, -aɪˈz-

hybridize ˈhaɪbrɪdˌaɪz |-s -ɪz |-d -d

Hydaspes haɪˈdæspiz |-pes' -piz

Hyderabad, Hydra- ˈhaɪdərəˌbæd, ˌhaɪdərə-
ˈbɑd, ˈhaɪdrə-, ˌhaɪdrə-

Hydra ˈhaɪdrə |-s -z |-drae -dri

hydracid haɪˈdræsɪd

hydrangea, H- haɪˈdrendʒə, -ˈdrændʒɪə, -dʒə

hydrant ˈhaɪdrənt

hydrate n ˈhaɪdret, -drɪt

hydrate v ˈhaɪdret |hydrated ˈhaɪdretɪd

hydraulic haɪˈdrɔlɪk |-al -l̩ |-ally -l̩ɪ, -ɪklɪ

hydride ˈhaɪdraɪd, -drɪd |drid -drɪd

hydrocarbon ˌhaɪdroˈkɑrbən, -ban; ES ˈkɑːb-,
-bɒn, E+ˈkɑːb-

hydrocephaly ˌhaɪdroˈsefəlɪ |-lic -səˈfælɪk

hydrochloric ˌhaɪdrəˈklorɪk, -ˈklɔr-; S -ˈklor-

hydrochloride ˌhaɪdrəˈkloraɪd, -ˈklɔr-, -ɪd; S
-ˈklor-; |-rid -ɪd

hydrocyanic ˌhaɪdrosaɪˈænɪk

hydrodynamics ˌhaɪdrodaɪˈnæmɪks

hydroelectric ˌhaɪdro·ɪˈlɛktrɪk

hydrogen ˈhaɪdrədʒən, -dʒɪn |-ate -ˌet |-ated
-ˌetɪd

hydrogenize ˈhaɪdrədʒənˌaɪz |-s -ɪz |-d -d

hydrogenous haɪˈdrædʒənəs; ES+-ˈdrɒdʒ-

hydrographer haɪˈdrɑgrəfɚ, -ˈdrɒg-; ES
-fə(r; |-phy -fɪ

hydroid ˈhaɪdrɔɪd

hydrolysis haɪˈdrɑləsɪs; ES+-ˈdrɒl-; |-yses
-ˌsiz

hydromechanics ˌhaɪdromɪˈkænɪks

hydromel ˈhaɪdrəˌmɛl

hydrometer haɪˈdrɑmətɚ; ES -ˈdrɑmətə(r,
-ˈdrɒm-

hydropathic ˌhaɪdrəˈpæθɪk |-al -l̩

hydropathy haɪˈdrɑpəθɪ; ES+-ˈdrɒp-

hydrophobia ˌhaɪdrəˈfobɪə

hydroplane ˈhaɪdrəˌplen

hydroponics ˌhaɪdrəˈpɑnɪks; ES+-ˈpɒn-

hydroponist haɪˈdrɑpənɪst; ES+-ˈdrɒp-

hydropsy ˈhaɪdrɑpsɪ; ES+-drɒp-

hydroquinone ˌhaɪdrokwɪˈnon

hydrosphere ˈhaɪdrəˌsfɪr; ES -ˌsfɪə(r, S+
-ˈsfɛə(r

hydrostatic ˌhaɪdrəˈstætɪk |-s -s |-al -l̩ |-ally
-l̩ɪ, -ɪklɪ

hydrosulphide, -fide, ˌhaɪdroˈsʌlfaɪd, -fɪd
|-phid, -fɪd -fɪd

hydrosulphite ˌhaɪdroˈsʌlfaɪt

hydrotherapeutics ˌhaɪdroˌθɛrəˈpjutɪks, -ˈpɪu-

hydrous ˈhaɪdrəs

hydroxide haɪˈdrɑksaɪd, -ɪd; ES+-ˈdrɒks-;
|-id -ɪd

hydroxyl haɪˈdrɑksɪl; ES+-ˈdrɒk-

hydrozoan, H- ˌhaɪdrəˈzoən

hyena haɪˈinə

Hygeia haɪˈdʒiə

hygiene ˈhaɪdʒin, ˈhaɪdʒɪˌin

hygienic ˌhaɪdʒɪˈɛnɪk |-s -s |-al -l̩ |-ally -l̩ɪ,
-ɪklɪ

hygienist ˈhaɪdʒɪənɪst

hygrometer haɪˈgrɑmətɚ; ES -ˈgrɑmətə(r,
-ˈgrɒm-

hygrometric ˌhaɪgrəˈmɛtrɪk |-al -l̩ |-ally -l̩ɪ,
-ɪklɪ

hygroscope ˈhaɪgrəˌskop

hying ptc of hie ˈhaɪɪŋ

Hyksos ˈhɪksos, -sɑs; ES+-sɒs

|full fʊl |tooth tuθ |further ˈfɝðɚ; ES ˈfɝðə |custom ˈkʌstəm |while hwaɪl |how haʊ |toy tɔɪ
|using ˈjuzɪŋ |fuse fjuz, fɪuz |dish dɪʃ |vision ˈvɪʒən |Eden ˈidn̩ |cradle ˈkredl̩ |keep 'em ˈkipm̩

Hymen, h- ˈhaɪmən
hymeneal ˌhaɪməˈniəl |-ly -ɪ |-nean -ˈniən
hymenopterous ˌhaɪməˈnɑptərəs, -trəs; ES+
  -ˈnɒp-
Hymettus haɪˈmɛtəs |-ˈs -ɪz
hymn hɪm |hymned hɪmd |hymning ˈhɪmɪŋ
hymnal ˈhɪmnəl |-nist -nɪst |-nody -nədɪ
hymnbook ˈhɪmˌbʊk
hymnology hɪmˈnɑlədʒɪ; ES+ˈnɒl-
hyoid ˈhaɪɔɪd
Hypatia haɪˈpeʃɪə, -ʃə
hyperacid ˌhaɪpəˈæsɪd
hyperacidity ˌhaɪpərəˈsɪdətɪ, -æˈsɪdətɪ
hyperbola haɪˈpɝbələ; ES -ˈpɜ-, -ˈpɝ-; |-s -z
hyperbole haɪˈpɝbəˌli, -lɪ; ES -ˈpɜ-, -ˈpɝ-;
  |-s -z
hyperbolic ˌhaɪpəˈbɑlɪk; ES ˌhaɪpəˈbɑlɪk,
  -ˈbɒl-; |-ally -ļɪ |-icly -ɪklɪ
hyperbolize haɪˈpɝbəˌlaɪz; ES -ˈpɜ-, -ˈpɝ-;
  |-s -ɪz |-d -d
hyperborean, H- ˌhaɪpəˈboriən, -ˈbɔr-; ES
  ˌhaɪpəˈbor-, E+-ˈbɔr-
hypercivilized ˌhaɪpəˈsɪvļˌaɪzd; ES ˌhaɪpə-
hypercritic ˌhaɪpəˈkrɪtɪk; ES ˌhaɪpə-; |-al -ļ
  |-ally -ļɪ, -ɪklɪ |-ticism -təˌsɪzəm
hyperfunction ˌhaɪpəˈfʌŋkʃən; ES ˌhaɪpə-
Hyperion haɪˈpɪrɪən
hyperopia ˌhaɪpəˈopɪə
hypersensitive ˌhaɪpəˈsɛnsətɪv; ES ˌhaɪpə-;
  |-vity -ˌsɛnsəˈtɪvətɪ
hyperthyroidism ˌhaɪpəˈθaɪrɔɪdˌɪzəm; ES
  ˌhaɪpə-
hypertrophy haɪˈpɝtrəfɪ; ES -ˈpɜ-, -ˈpɝ-;
  |-phied -fɪd
hyphen ˈhaɪfən |-ed -d |-ate -ˌet |-ated -ˌetɪd
hyphenize ˈhaɪfənˌaɪz |-s -ɪz |-d -d
hypnosis hɪpˈnosɪs |-noses -ˈnosiz

hypnotic hɪpˈnɑtɪk; ES+-ˈnɒt-; |-ally -ļɪ,
  -ɪklɪ
hypnotism ˈhɪpnəˌtɪzəm |-tist -tɪst
hypnotize ˈhɪpnəˌtaɪz |-s -ɪz |-d -d
hypo ˈhaɪpo
hypochondria ˌhaɪpəˈkɑndrɪə, ˌhɪp-; ES+
  -ˈkɒn-; |-driac -drɪˌæk
hypocrisy hɪˈpɑkrəsɪ; ES+-ˈpɒk-
hypocrite ˈhɪpəˌkrɪt
hypocritical ˌhɪpəˈkrɪtɪkļ |-ly -ɪ, -ɪklɪ
hypodermic ˌhaɪpəˈdɝmɪk; ES -ˈdɜm-,
  -ˈdɝm-; |-ally -ļɪ, -ɪklɪ
hypogene ˈhɪpəˌdʒin, ˈhaɪpə-
hypophosphate ˌhaɪpəˈfɑsfet; ES+-ˈfɒs-;
  |-phite -faɪt
hypophosphorous ˌhaɪpəˈfɑsfərəs; ES+-ˈfɒs-
hyposulphite ˌhaɪpəˈsʌlfaɪt
hyposulphurous ˌhaɪpəˈsʌlfərəs, -sʌlˈfju-,
  -ˈfru-
hypotenuse, -poth- haɪˈpɑtņˌus, -ˌɪus, -ˌjus,
  -z; ES+-ˈpɒt-; |-s -ɪz
hypothecate haɪˈpɑθəˌket; ES+-ˈpɒθ-; |-d -ɪd
hypothecation haɪˌpɑθəˈkeʃən; ES+-ˌpɒθ-
hypothesis haɪˈpɑθəsɪs; ES+-ˈpɒθ-; |-ses
  -ˌsiz
hypothesize haɪˈpɑθəˌsaɪz; ES+-ˈpɒθ-; |-s -ɪz
  |-d -d
hypothetic ˌhaɪpəˈθɛtɪk |-al -ļ |-ally -ļɪ, -ɪklɪ
hyrax, H- ˈhaɪræks |-es -ɪz |-races -rəˌsiz
Hyrcania hɝˈkenɪə; ES hɝ-, hɝ-; |-n -n
hyson ˈhaɪsņ
hyssop ˈhɪsəp
hysteresis ˌhɪstəˈrisɪs
hysteretic ˌhɪstəˈrɛtɪk |-ally -ļɪ, -ɪklɪ
hysteria hɪsˈtɪrɪə, less freq. hɪsˈtɛrɪə
hysteric hɪsˈtɛrɪk |-s -s |-al -ļ |-ally -ļɪ, -ɪklɪ
hythe, H- haɪð

I

I, i *letter* aɪ |*pl* I's, Is, *poss* I's aɪz
I *pro stressed* ˈaɪ, ˌaɪ; *unstr.* aɪ, ɔɪ, *familiar* ə
i-, -i- ɪ, ə—*The nonfinal unaccented vowel
spelt* i *and originally pron.* ɪ *shows a tendency
in innumerable words of normal conversation
to be obscured in the direction of the sound* ə,
as in possible ˈpɑsəbļ, divide dəˈvaɪd. *As a*

rule only one pronunciation (ə *or* ɪ) *is shown
in the vocab. The alternative pron. with* ɪ *is
permissible if it does not sound artificial* (*as
it would in* possible), *or with* ə *if it does not
sound slovenly* (*as it would in* sluggish).
*But such judgments depend somewhat on
habit, and as regional practice varies con-*

siderably, only an enlightened judgment and observation can decide.

-ia *ending* (mania), -ia- *plus consonant* (trivial, ruffian), -ie- *plus cons.* (alien), -io (Bassanio), -io- *plus cons.* (scorpion), -ious (tedious), -ius (radius). *These and similar combinations of unstressed* i *plus vowel regularly have double prons.* ɪə & jə. *In the vocab. usually the one believed to be most common in ordinary speech is given, with the understanding that the other pron. is also more or less common.*

Iachimo ˈjɑkɪˌmo; *so Shak.; mod.*+aɪˈækəˌmo

Iago ɪˈɑgo

-ial *see* -ia

iamb ˈaɪæmb |-ic aɪˈæmbɪk

iambus aɪˈæmbəs |-es -ɪz |-bi aɪˈæmbaɪ

-ian *see* -ia

iarovize ˈjɑrəˌvaɪz |-s -ɪz |-d -d

Iberia aɪˈbɪrɪə |-ian -ɪən

ibex, I- ˈaɪbɛks |-es -ɪz |ibices ˈɪbɪˌsiz, ˈaɪibidem *abbr.* ibid. ɪˈbaɪdɛm, ˈɪbɪd, ˈaɪbɪd

ibis ˈaɪbɪs |-es -ɪz

-ible *see* -able

Ibsen ˈɪbsn̩

-ically *ending of advs to words in* -ic (comic) *or in* -ical (radical), *pron.* -ɪk·|·ɪ (ˈrædɪk·|·ɪ) *or* -ɪk·lɪ (ˈrædɪk·lɪ). *The pron. with* -ɪk·lɪ *is very common colloquially, and in a good many words is recognized by the spelling, which usually lags behind pronunciation; as in* authentically, -thenticly, cubically, -icly, heroically, -icly, rustically, -icly, specifically, -icly, symbolically, -icly, tyrannically, -icly, *etc.*

Icarian ɪˈkɛrɪən, ɪˈker-

Icarus ˈɪkərəs, ˈaɪ- |-ˈs -ɪz

ice aɪs |ices ˈaɪsɪz |iced aɪst

iceberg ˈaɪsˌbɝg; ES -ˌbɝg, -ˌbɝg

iceboat ˈaɪsˌbot

icebound ˈaɪsˌbaʊnd

icebox ˈaɪsˌbɑks; ES+-ˌbɒks; |-es -ɪz

ice cream ˈaɪsˈkrim

ice-cream ˈaɪsˈkrim (ˈice-ˈcream ˌcone, ˈiceˌcream ˈsoda)

icehouse ˈaɪsˌhaʊs |-ses -zɪz

Iceland ˈaɪslənd |-ic aɪsˈlændɪk

iceman ˈaɪsˌmæn, -mən |-men -ˌmɛn, -mən

Ichabod ˈɪkəˌbɑd, -ˌbɒd

ichneumon ɪkˈnjumən, -ˈnɪu-, -ˈnu-

ichor ˈaɪkɔr, -kɚ; ES ˈaɪkɔə(r, ˈaɪkə(r

ichthyologic ˌɪkθɪəˈlɑdʒɪk; ES+-ˈlɒdʒ-; |-al -|ˌ|-ally -|ɪ, -ɪklɪ

ichthyologist ˌɪkθɪˈɑlədʒɪst; ES+-ˈɒl-; |-gy -dʒɪ

ichthyosaur ˈɪkθɪəˌsɔr; ES -ˌsɔə(r

ichthyosaurus, I- ˌɪkθɪəˈsɔrəs |-es -ɪz |-ri -raɪ

icicle ˈaɪˌsɪk|, ˈaɪsɪk| |-d -d

icily ˈaɪs|ɪ, ˈaɪsɪlɪ

icing ˈaɪsɪŋ

Ickes ˈɪkɪs, -əs, -ɪz |-ˈs -ɪz

icon ˈaɪkɑn, -kɒn |-s -z |-es ˈaɪkəˌniz

iconoclasm aɪˈkɑnəˌklæzəm; ES+-ˈkɒn-; |-clast -ˌklæst

iconoclastic aɪˌkɑnəˈklæstɪk, ˌaɪkɑnə-; ES+-ɒn-; |-ally -|ɪ, -ɪklɪ

iconography ˌaɪkənˈɑgrəfɪ, -ˈɒg-

icosahedron ˌaɪkosəˈhidrən |-dra -drə

ictus ˈɪktəs |-es -ɪz

icy ˈaɪsɪ

I'd *abbr. spelling of* I had, I would, *stressed* ˈaɪd, ˌaɪd; *unstr.* aɪd, əɪd, *occas.* əd

Idaho ˈaɪdəˌho, ˈaɪdɪˌho |-an -ən

idea aɪˈdiə, aɪˈdɪə, *occas. by sentence rhythm* ˈaɪdɪə

ideal aɪˈdiəl, aɪˈdil, aɪˈdɪəl |-ism -ˌɪzəm |-ist -ɪst

idealistic ˌaɪdiəlˈɪstɪk, -dɪəl-, aɪˌd- |-al -|ˌ|-ally -|ɪ, -ɪklɪ

ideality ˌaɪdɪˈælətɪ

idealization aɪˌdiələˈzeʃən, -ˌdɪəl-, -aɪˈz-

idealize aɪˈdiəlˌaɪz, aɪˈdɪəl- |-s -ɪz |-d -d

ideate *n* aɪˈdiɪt, -et

ideate *v* aɪˈdiet, -ˈdɪet |-d -ɪd

ideation ˌaɪdɪˈeʃən

ideatum ˌaɪdɪˈetəm |-ta -tə

idem ˈaɪdɛm

idempotent aɪˈdɛmpətənt

Iden ˈaɪdn̩

identic aɪˈdɛntɪk |-al -| |-ally -|ɪ, -ɪklɪ

identification aɪˌdɛntəfəˈkeʃən

identify aɪˈdɛntəˌfaɪ |-fied -ˌfaɪd

identity aɪˈdɛntətɪ

ideogram ˈɪdɪəˌgræm, ˈaɪdɪə-

ideograph ˈɪdɪəˌgræf, ˈaɪdɪə-; E+-ˌgraf, -ˌgraf

ideographic ˌɪdɪəˈgræfɪk, ˌaɪdɪə-

ideography ˌɪdɪˈɑgrəfɪ, ˌaɪdɪ-, -ˈɒg-

|full fʊl |tooth tuθ |further ˈfɝðɚ; ES ˈfɝðə |custom ˈkʌstəm |while hwaɪl |how haʊ |toy tɔɪ |using ˈjuzɪŋ |fuse fjuz, fɪuz |dish dɪʃ |vision ˈvɪʒən |Eden ˈidn̩ |cradle ˈkredl̩ |keep 'em ˈkipm̩

ideology ˌaɪdɪˈɑlədʒɪ, ˌɪd-; ES+-ˈɒl-
ides aɪdz
id est *'that is'* ˌɪdˈɛst
idiocy ˈɪdɪəsɪ
idiom ˈɪdɪəm
idiomatic ˌɪdɪəˈmætɪk |-al -| |-ally -|ɪ, -ɪklɪ
idiosyncrasy ˌɪdɪəˈsɪnkrəsɪ, -ˈsɪŋ-
idiosyncratic ˌɪdɪosɪnˈkrætɪk |-al -| |-ally -|ɪ, -ɪklɪ
idiot ˈɪdɪət |-ism -ˌɪzəm
idiotic ˌɪdɪˈɑtɪk; ES+-ˈɒtɪk; |-al -| |-ally -|ɪ, -ɪklɪ
idle ˈaɪdl̩ |-d -d |-ling ˈaɪdlɪŋ, -d|ɪŋ |-r -dlɚ; ES -dlə(r; |-st -dlɪst
idly ˈaɪdlɪ
idol ˈaɪdl̩ |-ed -d |-ing ˈaɪdl̩ɪŋ
idolater aɪˈdɑlətɚ; ES aɪˈdɑlətə(r, -ˈdɒl-; |-tress -trɪs |-try -trɪ
idolization ˌaɪdl̩əˈzeʃən, -aɪˈz-
idolize ˈaɪdl̩ˌaɪz |-s -ɪz |-d -d
Idomeneus aɪˈdɑmənˌjus, -məˌnɪus, -məˌnus; ES+-ˈdɒm-; |-ʼs -ɪz
Idumaea, -mea ˌɪdjuˈmiə, ˌaɪd-, -dʊ- |-n -n
Idun ˈidʊn=Ithunn
idyl, -ll ˈaɪdl̩
idyllic aɪˈdɪlɪk |-al -| |-ally -|ɪ, -ɪklɪ
-ie *ending see* -y
-iel *ending see* -ia
-ien *ending see* -ia
if ɪf, f
igloo ˈɪglu
Ignatius Loyola ɪgˈneʃəs lɔɪˈolə, lɔˈjolə
igneous ˈɪgnɪəs
ignescent ɪgˈnɛsn̩t
ignis fatuus ˈɪgnɪsˈfætʃuəs |ignes fatui ˈɪgnizˈfætʃuˌaɪ
ignite ɪgˈnaɪt |-d -ɪd |-nition ɪgˈnɪʃən
ignoble ɪgˈnobl̩ |-bly -blɪ
ignominious ˌɪgnəˈmɪnɪəs
ignominy ˈɪgnəˌmɪnɪ
ignoramus ˌɪgnəˈreməs |-es -ɪz
ignorance ˈɪgnərəns |-rant -rənt
ignore ɪgˈnor, -ˈnɔr; ES ɪgˈnoə(r, E+-ˈnɔə(r; |-d -d
Igorot ˌɪgəˈrot, ˌi- (*Sp* ˌigoˈrrɔte)
Igraine ɪˈgren
iguana ɪˈgwɑnə
il- *'not' see* in- *prefix*
Il Duce ɪlˈdutʃɪ (*It* ilˈduːtʃe)

ileum ˈɪlɪəm |ileac, iliac ˈɪlɪˌæk
ilex, I- ˈaɪlɛks |-es -ɪz
Ilfracombe ˈɪlfrəˌkum, ˌɪlfrəˈkum
iliac ˈɪlɪˌæk=ileac
Iliac *'of Ilium'* ˈɪlɪˌæk
Iliad ˈɪlɪəd
Ilion ˈɪlɪən |Ilium ˈɪlɪəm
ilium ˈɪlɪəm
ilk ɪlk
ill ɪl
I'll *abbr. spelling of* I will aɪl—*not a contraction of* I shall (= ˈaɪʃl̩) *but often substituted for it*
ill-advised ˈɪlədˈvaɪzd |-sedly -zɪdlɪ
illation ɪˈleʃən |illative ˈɪlətɪv
ill-boding ˈɪlˈbodɪŋ
ill-bred ˈɪlˈbrɛd
illegal ɪˈligl̩, ɪlˈligl̩ |-ly -ɪ
illegality ˌɪliˈgælətɪ
illegibility ˌɪlɛdʒəˈbɪlətɪ, ˌɪllɛdʒ-, ɪˌlɛdʒ-
illegible ɪˈlɛdʒəbl̩, ɪlˈlɛdʒ- |-bly -blɪ
illegitimacy ˌɪlɪˈdʒɪtəməsɪ, ˌɪllɪ- |-mate -mɪt
ill-fated ˈɪlˈfetɪd (ˈill-ˌfated ˈproject)
ill-favored ˈɪlˈfevɚd; ES ˈfevəd
ill-gotten ˈɪlˈgɑtn̩; ES+-ˈgɒtn̩
ill-humor ˈɪlˈjumɚ, -ˈhjumɚ, -ˈhɪu-; ES -mə(r; |-ed -d
illiberal ɪˈlɪbərəl, ɪˈlɪbrəl, ɪlˈl- |-ly -ɪ
illiberality ˌɪlɪbəˈrælətɪ, ˌɪllɪb-
illicit ɪˈlɪsɪt, ɪlˈlɪs-
illimitable ɪˈlɪmɪtəbl̩, ɪlˈlɪm- |-bly -blɪ
illinium ɪˈlɪnɪəm
Illinoian ˌɪləˈnɔɪən
Illinois ˌɪləˈnɔɪ, -ˈnɔɪz |-nois's -ˈnɔɪz, -ˈnɔɪzɪz
—ˌɪləˈnɔɪz, *not infrequent generally, is esp. common in the S.*
Illinoisan ˌɪləˈnɔɪən, -ˈnɔɪzən
illiteracy ɪˈlɪtərəsɪ, ɪlˈlɪt- |-rate -rɪt, -trɪt
ill-looking ˈɪlˈlʊkɪŋ
ill-mannered ˈɪlˈmænɚd; ES -ˈmænəd
ill-natured ˈɪlˈnetʃɚd; ES -ˈnetʃəd
illness ˈɪlnɪs |-es -ɪz
illogical ɪˈlɑdʒɪkl̩, ɪlˈl-; ES+-ˈlɒdʒ-; |-ly -ɪ, -ɪklɪ
ill-omened ˈɪlˈomɪnd, -mənd
ill-starred ˈɪlˈstɑrd; ES -ˈstɑːd, E+-ˈstɑːd
ill-tempered ˈɪlˈtɛmpɚd; ES -ˈtɛmpəd
ill-timed ˈɪlˈtaɪmd (ˈill-ˌtimed ˈstart)
ill-treat ɪlˈtrit |-ed -ɪd
illume ɪˈlum, ɪˈlɪum |-d -d

Key: *See in full* §§3–47. bee bi |pity ˈpɪtɪ (§6) |rate ret |yet jɛt |sang sæŋ |angry ˈæŋ·grɪ |bath bæθ; E baθ (§10) |ah ɑ |far fɑr |watch watʃ, wɒtʃ (§12) |jaw dʒɔ |gorge gɔrdʒ |go go

illuminant ɪˈlumənənt, ɪˈlɪum-
illuminate ɪˈluməˌnet, ɪˈlɪum- |-d -ɪd
illuminati, I- ɪˌluməˈnetaɪ, ɪˌlumɪˈnɑti, ɪˌlɪum-
illumination ɪˌluməˈneʃən, ɪˌlɪum-
illuminative ɪˈluməˌnetɪv, ɪˈlɪum-
illuminator ɪˈluməˌnetɚ, ɪˈlɪum-; ES -tə(r
illumine ɪˈlumɪn, ɪˈlɪumɪn |-d -d
ill-usage ˈɪlˈjusɪdʒ, -ˈjuz- |-s -ɪz
ill-use n ˈɪlˈjus |-s -ɪz
ill-use v ɪlˈjuz |-s -ɪz |-d -d
illusion ɪˈluʒən, ɪˈlɪuʒən |-ed -d
illusive ɪˈlusɪv, ɪˈlɪusɪv |-sory -sərɪ
illustrate ˈɪləstret, ɪˈlʌstret |-d -ɪd
illustration ˌɪləsˈtreʃən, ɪˌlʌsˈtreʃən
illustrative ɪˈlʌstrətɪv, ˈɪləsˌtretɪv, ɪˈlʌsˌtretɪv
illustrator ˈɪləsˌtretɚ, ɪˈlʌsˌtretɚ; ES -tə(r
illustrious ɪˈlʌstrɪəs
illy substandard for adv ill ˈɪlɪ
Illyria ɪˈlɪrɪə |-n -n
Ilokano ˌiloˈkɑno
Il Penseroso ˌɪlpɛnsəˈroso (It ilˌpenseˈroːso)
I'm abbr. spelling of I am, stressed ˈaɪm, ˌaɪm;
  unstr. aɪm, occas. əm
im- 'not' see in- prefix
image ˈɪmɪdʒ |-s -ɪz |-d -d
imagery ˈɪmɪdʒrɪ, -dʒərɪ
imaginable ɪˈmædʒɪnəbl̩, ɪˈmædʒnəbl̩ |-bly
  -blɪ
imaginary ɪˈmædʒəˌnɛrɪ
imagination ɪˌmædʒəˈneʃən |-tive ɪˈmædʒə-
  ˌnetɪv
imagine ɪˈmædʒɪn |-d -d
imagist ˈɪmədʒɪst |-gism -ˌdʒɪzəm
imago ɪˈmego |pl -s -z |imagines ɪˈmædʒɪˌniz
imam ɪˈmɑm |imaum ɪˈmɑm, ɪˈmɔm
imbalm ɪmˈbɑm; E+-ˈbɑm; |-ed -d
imbark ɪmˈbɑrk; ES -ˈbɑːk, E+-ˈbɑːk; |-ed -t
imbecile ˈɪmbəsl̩, -ˌsɪl |-lity ˌɪmbəˈsɪlətɪ
imbed ɪmˈbɛd |-bedded -ˈbɛdɪd
imbibe ɪmˈbaɪb |-bibed -ˈbaɪbd
imbitter ɪmˈbɪtɚ; ES -ˈbɪtə(r; |-ed -d
imbody ɪmˈbɑdɪ; ES+-ˈbɒdɪ; |-died -dɪd
imbolden ɪmˈboldn̩ |-ed -d |-ing -ˈboldn̩ɪŋ,
  -ˈboldnɪŋ
imbosom ɪmˈbuzəm, -ˈbʊzəm |-ed -d
imbower ɪmˈbaʊɚ; ES -ˈbaʊ·ə(r
imbricate adj ˈɪmbrɪkɪt, -ˌket
imbricate v ˈɪmbrɪˌket |- d -ɪd
imbrication ˌɪmbrɪˈkeʃən

imbroglio ɪmˈbroljo (It imˈbrɔʎʎo)
imbrue ɪmˈbru, -ˈbrɪu |-d -d
imbrute ɪmˈbrut, -ˈbrɪut |-d -ɪd
imbue ɪmˈbju, -ˈbɪu |-d -d
imid ˈɪmɪd |imide ˈɪmaɪd, ˈɪmɪd
imidogen ɪˈmɪdədʒən, ɪˈmɪdə-, -dʒɪn
imine ɪˈmin
imitable ˈɪmɪtəbl̩
imitate ˈɪməˌtet |-tated -ˌtetɪd |-tive -ɪv
imitation ˌɪməˈteʃən
imitator ˈɪməˌtetɚ; ES -ˌtetə(r
immaculate ɪˈmækjəlɪt
immane ɪˈmen
immanence ˈɪmənəns |-nent -nənt
Immanuel ɪˈmænjuəl
immaterial ˌɪməˈtɪrɪəl |-ly -ɪ |-ism -ˌɪzəm
immateriality ˌɪməˌtɪrɪˈælətɪ
immature ˌɪməˈtʊr, -ˈtɪʊr, -ˈtjur; ES -ə(r;
  |-rity -ətɪ
immeasurable ɪˈmɛʒrəbl̩, ɪmˈm-, -ˈmɛʒərə-
  |-bly -blɪ
immediacy ɪˈmidɪəsɪ
immediate ɪˈmidɪt, esp. C ɪˈmidjət
immemorial ˌɪməˈmorɪəl, ˌɪmmə-, -ˈmɔr-; S
  -ˈmor-; |-ly -ɪ
immense ɪˈmɛns |-sity -ətɪ
immerse ɪˈmɝs; ES ɪˈmɜs, ɪˈmɝˑs; |-s -ɪz |-d -t
immersion ɪˈmɝʃən; ES ɪˈmɜʃ-, ɪˈmɝˑʃ-
immigrant ˈɪməgrənt, -ˌgrænt
immigrate ˈɪməˌgret |-d -ɪd |-tion ˌɪməˈgreʃən
imminence ˈɪmənəns |-nent -nənt
immiscible ɪˈmɪsəbl̩ |-bly -blɪ
immix ɪmˈmɪks |-es -ɪz |-ed -t
immixture ɪmˈmɪkstʃɚ; ES -ˈmɪkstʃə(r
immobile ɪˈmobl̩, ɪmˈm-, -bɪl, -bɪl
immobility ˌɪmoˈbɪlətɪ, ˌɪmmo-
immobilization ɪˌmobl̩əˈzeʃən, ɪmˌmo-, ˌɪmob-,
  ˌɪmmob-, -aɪˈz-
immobilize ɪˈmobl̩ˌaɪz, ɪmˈmo- |-s -ɪz |-d -d
immoderate ɪˈmɑdərɪt, ɪmˈmɑd-, -drɪt; ES+
  -ˈmɒd-
immodest ɪˈmɑdɪst, ɪmˈmɑd-; ES+-ˈmɒd-;
  |-y -ɪ
immolate ˈɪməˌlet |-d -ɪd |-tion ˌɪməˈleʃən
immolator ˈɪməˌletɚ; ES -ˌletə(r
immoral ɪˈmɔrəl, ɪmˈm-, -ˈmɑr-, -ˈmɒr- |-ly -ɪ
immorality ˌɪməˈrælətɪ, -mɔ-, -mɑ-, -mɒ-,
  -mo-

---

immortal ɪˈmɔrtl̩; ES ɪˈmɔɜtl̩
immortality ˌɪmɔrˈtælɪtɪ; ES ˌɪmɔˈtælɪtɪ
immortalize ɪˈmɔrtl̩ˌaɪz; ES ɪˈmɔɜtl̩-; |-s -ɪz
|-d -d
immortelle ˌɪmɔrˈtɛl; ES ˌɪmɔɜˈtɛl
immovability ɪˌmuvəˈbɪlətɪ, ɪmˌmuv-, ˌɪmuv-,
ˌɪmmuvə-
immovable ɪˈmuvəbl̩, ɪmˈmuv- |-bly -blɪ
immune ɪˈmjun, ɪˈmɪun |-nity -ətɪ
immunization ˌɪmjʊnəˈzeʃən, -aɪˈz-
immunize ˈɪmjəˌnaɪz, -jʊ- |-s -ɪz |-d -d
immunology ˌɪmjəˈnalədʒɪ, -jʊ-; ES+-ˈnɒl-
immure ɪˈmjʊr, ɪˈmɪur; ES -ə(r; |-d -d
immutability ɪˌmjutəˈbɪlətɪ, -ˌmɪut-, ˌɪmjut-,
ˌɪmɪut-, ˌɪmm-
immutable ɪˈmjutəbl̩, ɪˈmɪut- |-bly -blɪ
Imogen ˈɪmədʒɪn, -ən |-gene -ˌdʒin
imp ɪmp |imped ɪmpt
impact n ˈɪmpækt
impact v ɪmˈpækt |-pacted -ˈpæktɪd
impair ɪmˈpɛr, -ˈpær; E -ˈpɛə(r, ES -ˈpææ(r;
|-ed -d
impale ɪmˈpel |-d -d
impalpability ˌɪmpælpəˈbɪlətɪ, ɪmˌpæl-
impalpable ɪmˈpælpəbl̩ |-bly -blɪ
impanel ɪmˈpænl̩ |-ed -d
imparadise ɪmˈpærəˌdaɪs |-s -ɪz |-d -t
impark ɪmˈpark; ES ɪmˈpɑːk, E+-ˈpɑːk;
|-ed -t
impart ɪmˈpart; ES -ˈpɑːt, E+-ˈpɑːt; |-ed -ɪd
impartation ˌɪmparˈteʃən; ES -pɑː-, E+-pɑː-
impartial ɪmˈparʃəl; ES -ˈpɑːʃəl, E+-ˈpɑːʃəl;
|-ly -ɪ
impartiality ˌɪmparˈʃælətɪ, -ʃɪˈæl-; ES -pɑ-,
E+-pɑ-
impassability ˌɪmpæsəˈbɪlətɪ, ɪmˌpæs-; E+
-pas-, -ˌpas-, -pɑs-, -ˌpɑs-
impassable ɪmˈpæsəbl̩; E+-ˈpas-, -ˈpɑs-;
|-bly -blɪ
impasse ɪmˈpæs, ˈɪmpæs; E+-a-, -ɑ- |-s -ɪz
(Fr æ̃ˈpɑːs)
impassible ɪmˈpæsəbl̩ |-bly -blɪ
impassionate adj ɪmˈpæʃənɪt
impassionate v ɪmˈpæʃənˌet |-d -ɪd
impassioned ɪmˈpæʃənd
impassive ɪmˈpæsɪv |-sivity ˌɪmpæˈsɪvətɪ
impaste ɪmˈpest |-d -ɪd
impatience ɪmˈpeʃəns |-tient -ʃənt
impavid ɪmˈpævɪd

impeach ɪmˈpitʃ |-es -ɪz |-ed -t
impeachability ˌɪmpitʃəˈbɪlətɪ, ɪmˌpitʃə-
impeachable ɪmˈpitʃəbl̩
impearl ɪmˈpɝl; ES ɪmˈpɜl, -ˈpɝl; |-ed -d
impeccability ˌɪmpɛkəˈbɪlətɪ, ɪmˌpɛk-
impeccable ɪmˈpɛkəbl̩ |-bly -blɪ
impecuniosity ˌɪmpɪˌkjunɪˈasətɪ, -ˌkɪunɪ-;
ES+-ˈɒs-
impecunious ˌɪmpɪˈkjunɪəs, -ˈkɪun-
impede ɪmˈpid |-d -ɪd |-dance -ˈpidn̩s
impediment ɪmˈpɛdəmənt
impedimenta ˌɪmpɛdəˈmɛntə, ɪmˌpɛd-
impedimentary ɪmˌpɛdəˈmɛntərɪ, -trɪ
impel ɪmˈpɛl |-pelled -ˈpɛld
impend ɪmˈpɛnd |-ed -ɪd
impenetrability ˌɪmpɛnətrəˈbɪlətɪ, ɪmˌpɛn-
impenetrable ɪmˈpɛnətrəbl̩ |-bly -blɪ
impenitence ɪmˈpɛnətəns |-tent -tənt
imperative ɪmˈpɛrətɪv
imperator ˌɪmpəˈretɚ; ES -ˈretə(r
imperatorial ɪmˌpɛrəˈtorɪəl, ɪmˌpɛrə-, -ˈtɔr-;
S -ˈtor-
imperceptibility ˌɪmpɚˌsɛptəˈbɪlətɪ; ES ˌɪmpə-
imperceptible ˌɪmpɚˈsɛptəbl̩; ES ˌɪmpə-;
|-bly -blɪ
imperceptive ˌɪmpɚˈsɛptɪv; ES ˌɪmpə-
imperfect ɪmˈpɝfɪkt; ES -ˈpɜf-, -ˈpɝf-
imperfection ˌɪmpɚˈfɛkʃən; ES ˌɪmpə-
imperforate adj, n ɪmˈpɝfərɪt; ES -ˈpɜf-,
-ˈpɝf-
imperforated ɪmˈpɝfəˌretɪd; ES -ˈpɜf-, -ˈpɝf-
imperial ɪmˈpɪrɪəl |-ly -ɪ
imperialism ɪmˈpɪrɪəlˌɪzəm |-ist -ɪst
imperialistic ɪmˌpɪrɪəlˈɪstɪk |-ally -ļɪ, -ɪklɪ
imperil ɪmˈpɛrəl, -ɪl |-ed -d
imperious ɪmˈpɪrɪəs
imperishability ˌɪmpɛrɪʃəˈbɪlətɪ, ɪmˌpɛr-
imperishable ɪmˈpɛrɪʃəbl̩, |-bly -blɪ
imperium ɪmˈpɪrɪəm |-ria -rɪə
impermanent ɪmˈpɝmənənt; ES -ˈpɜm-,
-ˈpɝm-
impermeability ˌɪmpɝmɪəˈbɪlətɪ, ɪmˌpɝm-;
ES -ɜ-, -ɝ-
impermeable ɪmˈpɝmɪəbl̩; ES -ˈpɜm-, -ˈpɝm-;
|-bly -blɪ
impersonal ɪmˈpɝsn̩l̩, -ˈpɝsnəl; ES -ˈpɜs-,
-ˈpɝs-; |-ly -ɪ
impersonality ˌɪmpɝsn̩ˈælətɪ, ɪmˌpɝs-; ES
-ɜ-, -ɝ-

Key: See in full §§3–47. bee bi |pity ˈpɪtɪ (§6) |rate ret |yet jɛt |sang sæŋ |angry ˈæŋ·grɪ |bath bæθ; E baθ (§10) |ah ɑ |far fɑr |watch watʃ, wɒtʃ (§12) |jaw dʒɔ |gorge gɔrdʒ |go go

impersonate ɪmˈpɝsṇˌet; ES -ˈpɜs-, -ˈpɝs-; |-d -ɪd

impersonation ˌɪmpɝsṇˈeʃən, ɪmˌpɝs-; ES -ɜ-, -ɝ-

impertinence ɪmˈpɝtṇəns; ES -ˈpɜt-, -ˈpɝt-; |-s -ɪz |-tinent -tṇənt

imperturbability ˌɪmpɚˌtɝbəˈbɪlətɪ; ES -pə-ˌtɜb-, -pəˌtɝb-

imperturbable ˌɪmpɚˈtɝbəbļ; ES -pəˈtɜb-, -pəˈtɝb-; |-bly -blɪ

imperturbation ˌɪmpɝtɚˈbeʃən; ES -pɜtə-, -pɝtə-

impervious ɪmˈpɝvɪəs; ES -ˈpɜv-, -ˈpɝv-

impetigo ˌɪmpɪˈtaɪgo

impetuosity ˌɪmpɛtʃʊˈɑsətɪ, ɪmˌpɛt-; ES+ -ˈɒs-

impetuous ɪmˈpɛtʃʊəs

impetus ˈɪmpətəs |-es -ɪz

Impey ˈɪmpɪ |-an -ən

impiety ɪmˈpaɪətɪ |impious ˈɪmpɪəs

impinge ɪmˈpɪndʒ |-s -ɪz |-d -d

impish ˈɪmpɪʃ

implacability ˌɪmplekəˈbɪlətɪ, ɪmˌplek-, -læk-

implacable ɪmˈplekəbļ, -ˈplæk- |-bly -blɪ

implant ɪmˈplænt; E+-ˈplant, -ˈplant; |-ed -ɪd

implausible ɪmˈplɔzəbļ |-bly -blɪ

implead ɪmˈplid |-ed -ɪd

implement n ˈɪmpləmənt

implement v ˈɪmpləˌmɛnt |-ed -ɪd

implemental ˌɪmpləˈmɛntļ

implementation ˌɪmpləmɛnˈteʃən

implicate adj ˈɪmplɪkɪt

implicate v ˈɪmplɪˌket |-d -ɪd

implication ˌɪmplɪˈkeʃən |-tive ˈɪmplɪˌketɪv

implicit ɪmˈplɪsɪt

implore ɪmˈplor, -ˈplɔr; ES -ˈploə(r, E+ -ˈplɔə(r; |-d -d

imply ɪmˈplaɪ |-plied -ˈplaɪd |-pliedly -ˈplaɪ-ɪdlɪ

impolite ˌɪmpəˈlaɪt

impolitic ɪmˈpɑləˌtɪk; ES+-ˈpɒl-

imponderability ˌɪmpɑndərəˈbɪlətɪ, ɪmˌpɑn-; ES+ -ɒn-

imponderable ɪmˈpɑndərəbļ; ES+-ˈpɒn-; |-bly -blɪ

import n ˈɪmport, -pɔrt; ES -poət, E+-ˈpɔət

import v ɪmˈport, -ˈpɔrt; ES -ˈpoət, E+-ˈpɔət; |-ed -ɪd—acct+ˈimport, esp. in contrast to export, v.

importance ɪmˈpɔrtṇs; ES -ˈpɔətṇs; |-tant -tṇt

importation ˌɪmporˈteʃən, -pər-; ES -poə-, E+-pɔə-

importunate adj ɪmˈpɔrtʃənɪt; ES -ˈpɔə-

importunate v ɪmˈpɔrtʃəˌnet; ES -ˈpɔə-; |-d -ɪd

importune adj, v ˌɪmpɚˈtjun, -ˈtɪun, -ˈtun, ɪmˈpɔrtʃən; ES ˌɪmpə-, ɪmˈpɔətʃ-; |-d -d

importunity ˌɪmpɚˈtjunətɪ, -ˈtɪun-, -ˈtun-; ES ˌɪmpə-

impose ɪmˈpoz |-s -ɪz |-d -d |-sing -ɪŋ

imposition ˌɪmpəˈzɪʃən

impossibility ˌɪmpɑsəˈbɪlətɪ, ɪmˌpɑs-; ES+ -ɒs-

impossible ɪmˈpɑsəbļ; ES+-ˈpɒs-; |-bly -blɪ

impost ˈɪmpost |-ed -ɪd

impostor ɪmˈpɑstɚ; ES -ˈpɑstə(r, -ˈpɒs-

impostume ɪmˈpɑstʃum; ES+-ˈpɒs-

imposture ɪmˈpɑstʃɚ; ES -ˈpɑstʃə(r, -ˈpɒs-

impotence ˈɪmpətəns |-tent -tənt

impound ɪmˈpaʊnd |-ed -ɪd |-age -ɪdʒ

impoverish ɪmˈpavərɪʃ, -vrɪʃ; ES+-ˈpɒv-; |-es -ɪz |-ed -t

impracticability ˌɪmpræktɪkəˈbɪlətɪ, ɪmˌpræk-

impracticable ɪmˈpræktɪkəbļ |-bly -blɪ

impractical ɪmˈpræktɪkļ

impracticality ˌɪmpræktɪˈkælətɪ, ɪmˌpræk-

imprecate ˈɪmprɪˌket |- d -ɪd

imprecation ˌɪmprɪˈkeʃən

imprecatory ˈɪmprɪkəˌtorɪ, -ˌtɔrɪ; S -ˌtorɪ

impregnability ˌɪmprɛgnəˈbɪlətɪ, ɪmˌprɛg-

impregnable ɪmˈprɛgnəbļ |-bly -blɪ

impregnate adj ɪmˈprɛgnɪt

impregnate v ɪmˈprɛgnet |-d -ɪd

impregnation ˌɪmprɛgˈneʃən

impresario ˌɪmprɪˈsɑrɪˌo

imprescriptible ˌɪmprɪˈskrɪptəbļ |-bly -blɪ

impress n ˈɪmprɛs |-es -ɪz

impress v ɪmˈprɛs |-es -ɪz |-ed -t |-edly -ɪdlɪ

impressibility ˌɪmprɛsəˈbɪlətɪ, ɪmˌprɛs-

impressible ɪmˈprɛsəbļ |-bly -blɪ

impression ɪmˈprɛʃən |-al -ļ |-ally -ļɪ

impressionability ɪmˌprɛʃənəˈbɪlətɪ, -ʃnə-

impressionable ɪmˈprɛʃənəbļ, -ʃnə- |-bly -blɪ

impressionism ɪmˈprɛʃənˌɪzəm |-ist -ɪst

impressionistic ɪmˌprɛʃənˈɪstɪk |-ally -ļɪ, -ɪklɪ

impressive ɪmˈprɛsɪv

|full fʊl |tooth tuθ |further ˈfɝðɚ; ES ˈfɜðə |custom ˈkʌstəm |while hwaɪl |how haʊ |toy tɔɪ |using ˈjuzɪŋ |fuse fjuz, fɪuz |dish dɪʃ |vision ˈvɪʒən |Eden ˈidṇ |cradle ˈkredļ |keep 'em ˈkipm̩

imprest *adj, n* 'ımprɛst
imprest *v* ım'prɛst |-prested -'prɛstıd
imprimatur ˌımprı'metɚ; ES -'metə(r
imprimis ım'praımıs
imprint *n* 'ımprınt
imprint *v* ım'prınt |-ed -ıd
imprison ım'prızn̩ |-ed -d |-ing -'prızn̩ıŋ,
-znıŋ
improbability ˌımprɑbə'bılətı, ım‚pr-; ES+
-rɒb-
improbable ım'prɑbəb!; ES+-'prɒb-; |-bly
-blı
improbity ım'probətı, -'prɑbətı; ES+-'prɒb-
impromptu ım'prɑmptu, -tıu, -tju; ES+
-'prɒmp-
improper ım'prɑpɚ; ES -'prɑpə(r, -'prɒp-
impropriety ˌımprə'praıətı, ˌımpə'praıətı—*In*
ˌımpə'praıətı r *is lost by dissimilation*
(*§121*).
improvability ım‚pruvə'bılətı
improvable ım'pruvəb! |-bly -blı
improve ım'pruv |-d -d
improvidence ım'prɑvədəns; ES+-'prɒv-;
|-nt -nt
improvisation ˌımprəvaı'zeʃən, -prɑvə'ze-;
ES+-prɒv-
improvise 'ımprə‚vaız, ˌımprə'vaız |-s -ız |-d
-d |-visedly -'vaızıdlı
imprudence ım'prudn̩s, -'prıud- |-dent -dn̩t
impudence 'ımpjədəns, -pju- |-dent -dənt
impugn ım'pjun, -'prun |-ed -d |-er -ɚ; ES
-ə(r; |-able -əb! |-bly -blı
impugnable '*unconquerable*' ım'pʌgnəb!
impuissance ım'pjuɪsn̩s, -'pıu- |-sant -sn̩t
impulse *n* 'ımpʌls |-s -ız
impulse *v* ım'pʌls |-s -ız |-d -t
impulsion ım'pʌlʃən |-sive -sıv
impunity ım'pjunətı, -'prun-
impure ım'pjur, -'pıur; ES -ə(r; |-rity -ətı
imputability ım‚pjutə'bılətı, -‚prut-, ˌımp-
imputable ım'pjutəb!, -'prut- |-bly -blı
imputation ˌımpju'teʃən
impute ım'pjut, -'prut |-d -ıd
in *adj, adv* ın
in *prep stressed* 'ın, ˌın; *unstr.* ın, n̩ (cut in two
'kʌtn̩'tu), *occas. nonsyllabic* n *before the
article* a ə (I'm in a hurry ˌaımnə'hɝı,
He'll go in a minute hil'gonə'mınıt)
in- *prefix. In words like* inactive, *where* in-

means '*not,*' *and the second part clearly has
its separate meaning, the* in- *just before the
main accent has a slight stress that could be
marked thus:* ˌın'æktıv, *or under emphasis
even* 'ın'æktıv. *But if the second part does
not show a clear meaning, being fused with
the* in- *into a simple word, as* insipid ın-
'sıpıd, *then the* in- *is quite stressless. Since
with different speakers and styles of speech
there are all grades between no stress and full
stress, it is not feasible to mark this accent,
though it often exists in speech. The same
statements apply to the variants* il- *and* im-.
inability ˌınə'bılətı
in absentia ˌınəb'sɛnʃıə
inaccessibility ˌınək‚sɛsə'bılətı, ˌınæk-
inaccessible ˌınək'sɛsəb!, ˌınæk- |-bly -blı
inaccuracy ın'ækjərəsı |-rate -rıt
inaction ın'ækʃən |-active -'æktıv
inactivity ˌınæk'tıvətı
inadequacy ın'ædəkwəsı |-quate -kwıt
inadmissibility ˌınəd‚mısə'bılətı
inadmissible ˌınəd'mısəb! |-bly -blı
inadvertence ˌınəd'vɝtn̩s; ES -'vɝt-, -'vɝt-;
|-cy -ı |-ent -tn̩t
inadvisability ˌınəd‚vaızə'bılətı
inadvisable ˌınəd'vaızəb! |-bly -blı
inalienability ın‚eljənə'bılətı, ın‚eljən-, -lıən-
inalienable ın'eljənəb!, -'elıən- |-bly -blı
inalterable ın'ɔltərəb! |-bly -blı
inamorata ın‚æmə'ratə, ˌınæm-
inane ın'en
inanimate ın'ænəmıt
inanity ın'ænətı |inanition ˌınə'nıʃən
inappeasable ˌınə'pizəb!
inapplicability ˌınæplıkə'bılətı, ın‚æp-
inapplicable ın'æplıkəb! |-bly -blı
inapposite ın'æpəzıt
inappreciable ˌınə'priʃɪəb! |-bly -blı
inappreciative ˌınə'priʃɪ‚etıv
inapproachability ˌınə‚protʃə'bılətı
inapproachable ˌınə'protʃəb! |-bly -blı
inappropriate ˌınə'proprıt
inapt ın'æpt
inaptitude ın'æptə‚tjud, -‚trud, -‚tud
inarm ın'arm; ES -'a:m, E+-'a:m; |-ed -d
inarticulate ˌınar'tıkjəlıt; ES -ɑ-, E+-ɑ-
inartistic ˌınar'tıstık; ES -ɑ:'tıs-, E+-ɑ:'tıs-;
|-al -! |-ally -l̩ı, -ıklı

Key: *See in full §§3–47.* bee bi |pity 'pıtı (§6) |rate ret |yet jɛt |sang sæŋ |angry 'æŋ·grı
|bath bæθ; E baθ (§10) |ah ɑ |far fɑr |watch wɑtʃ, wɒtʃ (§12) |jaw dʒɔ |gorge gɔrdʒ |go go

inasmuch ˌɪnəzˈmʌtʃ
inattention ˌɪnəˈtɛnʃən |-tive -tɪv
inaudibility ˌɪnɔdəˈbɪlətɪ, ɪnˌɔd-
inaudible ɪnˈɔdəbl̩ |-bly -blɪ
inaugural ɪnˈɔgjərəl, ɪnˈɔgərəl
inaugurate ɪnˈɔgjəˌret, -ˈɔgə- |-d -ɪd
inauguration ɪnˌɔgjəˈreʃən, -ˌɔgə-
inauspicious ˌɪnɔˈspɪʃəs
inboard ˈɪnˌbord, -ˌbɔrd; ES -ˌboəd, E+
   -ˌbɔəd
inborn ɪnˈbɔrn; ES -ˈbɔən; (ˈɪnˌborn ˈgrace)
inbound ˈɪnˈbaʊnd (ˈɪnˌbound ˈship)
inbreathe ɪnˈbrið |-d -d
inbred adj ɪnˈbrɛd (ˈɪnˌbred ˈtact)
inbreed ɪnˈbrid |-bred -ˈbrɛd
Inca ˈɪŋkə
incalculability ˌɪnkælkjələˈbɪlətɪ, ɪnˌkæl-
incalculable ɪnˈkælkjələbl̩ |-bly -blɪ
incandesce ˌɪnkənˈdɛs, -kæn- |-s -ɪz |-d -t
incandescence ˌɪnkənˈdɛsn̩s |-cy -ɪ |-nt -n̩t
incantation ˌɪnkænˈteʃən
incapability ˌɪnkepəˈbɪlətɪ, ɪnˌkep-
incapable ɪnˈkepəbl̩ |-bly -blɪ
incapacitate ˌɪnkəˈpæsəˌtet |-d -ɪd |-ity -tɪ
incarcerate ɪnˈkɑrsəˌret; ES -ˈkɑːs-, E+
   -ˈkɑːs-; |-d -ɪd
incarceration ɪnˌkɑrsəˈreʃən; ES -ˌkɑːs-,
   E+-ˌkɑːs-; ˌɪnk-
incarnadine ɪnˈkɑrnəˌdaɪn, -dɪn; ES -ˈkɑː-,
   E+-ˈkɑː-; |-d -d
incarnate adj ɪnˈkɑrnɪt, -net; ES -ˈkɑː-,
   E+-ˈkɑː-
incarnate v ɪnˈkɑrnet; ES -ˈkɑː-, E+-ˈkɑː-;
   |-d -ɪd
incarnation, I- ˌɪnkɑrˈneʃən; ES -kɑː-,
   E+-kɑː-
incase ɪnˈkes |-cases -ˈkesɪz |-cased -ˈkest
incaution ɪnˈkɔʃən |-tious -ʃəs
incendiary ɪnˈsɛndɪˌɛrɪ |-arism -əˌrɪzəm
incense n ˈɪnsɛns |adj - d -t
incense v ɪnˈsɛns |-s -ɪz |-d -t
incentive ɪnˈsɛntɪv
incept ɪnˈsɛpt |-ed -ɪd
inception ɪnˈsɛpʃən |-tive -tɪv
inceration ˌɪnsəˈreʃən
incertitude ɪnˈsɝtəˌtjud, -ˌtɪud, -ˌtud; ES
   -ˈsɝt-, -ˈsɝt-
incessancy ɪnˈsɛsn̩sɪ |-sant -sn̩t
incest ˈɪnsɛst |-uous ɪnˈsɛstʃʊəs

inch ɪntʃ |inches ˈɪntʃɪz |inched ɪntʃt
Inchbald ˈɪntʃbɔld
inchoate adj ɪnˈko·ɪt
inchoate v ˈɪnkoˌet |-d -ɪd
inchworm ˈɪntʃˌwɝm; ES -ˌwɝm, -ˌwɝm
incidence ˈɪnsədəns |-dent -dənt
incidental ˌɪnsəˈdɛntl̩ |-ly -ɪ
incinerate ɪnˈsɪnəˌret |-d -ɪd |-tor -ɚ; ES -ə(r
incipience ɪnˈsɪpɪəns |-cy -ɪ |-ent -ənt
incipit 'here begins' ˈɪnsɪpɪt
incise ɪnˈsaɪz |-s -ɪz |-d -d
incision ɪnˈsɪʒən
incisive ɪnˈsaɪsɪv, -zɪv
incisor ɪnˈsaɪzɚ; ES -ˈsaɪzə(r
incite ɪnˈsaɪt |-d -ɪd |-tation ˌɪnsaɪˈteʃən
incivility ˌɪnsəˈvɪlətɪ
inclemency ɪnˈklɛmənsɪ |-clement -ˈklɛmənt
inclinable ɪnˈklaɪnəbl̩
inclination ˌɪnkləˈneʃən
incline n ˈɪnklaɪn, ɪnˈklaɪn
incline v ɪnˈklaɪn |-d -d
inclinometer ˌɪnklɪˈnɑmətɚ; ES -ˈnɑmətə(r,
   -ˈnɒm-
inclose ɪnˈkloz |-s -ɪz |-d -d
inclosure ɪnˈkloʒɚ; ES -ʒə(r
include ɪnˈklud, -ˈklɪud |-d -ɪd
inclusion ɪnˈkluʒən, -ˈklɪu-
inclusive ɪnˈklusɪv, -ˈklɪu-, -zɪv
incog ɪnˈkɑg, -ˈkɒg
incognito ɪnˈkɑgnɪˌto, -ˈkɒg-
incoherence ˌɪnkoˈhɪrəns |-cy -ɪ |-ent -ənt
incombustibility ˌɪnkəmˌbʌstəˈbɪlətɪ
incombustible ˌɪnkəmˈbʌstəbl̩ |-bly -blɪ
income ˈɪnˌkʌm, ˈɪŋˌkʌm
incoming ˈɪnˌkʌmɪŋ
incommensurability ˌɪnkəˌmɛnʃərəˈbɪlətɪ,
   -sərə-
incommensurable ˌɪnkəˈmɛnʃərəbl̩, -sərə-
   |-bly -blɪ
incommensurate ˌɪnkəˈmɛnʃərɪt, -sərɪt
incommode ˌɪnkəˈmod |-d -ɪd |-dious -ɪəs
incommodity ˌɪnkəˈmɑdətɪ; ES+-ˈmɒd-
incommunicability ˌɪnkəˌmjunɪkəˈbɪlətɪ,
   -ˌmɪun-
incommunicable ˌɪnkəˈmjunɪkəbl̩, -ˈmɪun-
   |-bly -blɪ
incommunicado ˌɪnkəˌmjunɪˈkado, -ˌmɪun-
incommunicative ˌɪnkəˈmjunəˌketɪv, -ˈmɪun-
incompact ˌɪnkəmˈpækt

Those words below in which the ɑ *sound is spelt* o *are often pronounced with* ɒ *in E and S*

incomparability ˌɪnkɑmpərəˈbɪlətɪ, -prə-, ɪnˌkɑm-

incomparable ɪnˈkɑmpərəbļ, -prə- |-bly -blɪ

incompatibility ˌɪnkəmˌpætəˈbɪlətɪ

incompatible ˌɪnkəmˈpætəbļ |-bly -blɪ

incompetence ɪnˈkɑmpətəns |-cy -ɪ |-tent tənt

incomplete ˌɪnkəmˈplit |-pletion -ˈpliʃən

incompliance ˌɪnkəmˈplaɪəns |-cy -ɪ |-nt -nt

incomprehensibility ˌɪnkɑmprɪˌhɛnsəˈbɪlətɪ, ɪnˌkɑm-

incomprehensible ˌɪnkɑmprɪˈhɛnsəbļ, ɪnˌkɑm- |-bly -blɪ |-sive -sɪv

incompressible ˌɪnkəmˈprɛsəbļ |-bly -blɪ

incomputable ˌɪnkəmˈpjutəbļ, -ˈpɪut-

inconceivability ˌɪnkənˌsivəˈbɪlətɪ

inconceivable ˌɪnkənˈsivəbļ |-bly -blɪ

inconclusive ˌɪnkənˈklusɪv, -ˈklɪu-

inconformity ˌɪnkənˈfɔrmətɪ; ES -ˈfɔəmətɪ

incongruence ɪnˈkɑŋgrʊəns |-ent -ənt

incongruity ˌɪnkɑŋˈgruətɪ, -kəŋ-, -nˈgru-, -ˈgrɪu-

incongruous ɪnˈkɑŋgrʊəs

inconsecutive ˌɪnkənˈsɛkjətɪv

inconsequence ɪnˈkɑnsəˌkwɛns |-quent -ˌkwɛnt

inconsequential ˌɪnkɑnsəˈkwɛnʃəl |-ly -ɪ

inconsequentiality ˌɪnkɑnsəˌkwɛnʃɪˈælətɪ, ɪnˌkɑn-

inconsiderable ˌɪnkənˈsɪdərəbļ, -ˈsɪdrə- |-bly -blɪ

inconsiderate ˌɪnkənˈsɪdərɪt, -ˈsɪdrɪt

inconsideration ˌɪnkənˌsɪdəˈreʃən

inconsistence ˌɪnkənˈsɪstəns |-cy -ɪ |-nt -nt

inconsolability ˌɪnkənˌsoləˈbɪlətɪ

inconsolable ˌɪnkənˈsoləbļ |-bly -blɪ

inconsonance ɪnˈkɑnsənəns |-nant -nənt

inconspicuous ˌɪnkənˈspɪkjʊəs

inconstancy ɪnˈkɑnstənsɪ |-tant -tənt

incontestable ˌɪnkənˈtɛstəbļ |-bly -blɪ

incontinence ɪnˈkɑntənəns |-cy -ɪ |-nt -nt

incontrollable ˌɪnkənˈtroləbļ |-bly -blɪ

incontrovertability ˌɪnkɑntrəˌvɝtəˈbɪlətɪ, ɪnˌkɑn-; ES -ˌvɝt-, -ˌvɝˑt-

incontrovertible ˌɪnkɑntrəˈvɝtəbļ, ɪnˌkɑn-; ES -ˈvɝt-, -ˈvɝˑt-; *acct*+inˈcontroˌvertible |-bly -blɪ

inconvenience ˌɪnkənˈvinjəns |-s -ɪz |-d -t |-nt -nt

inconvertibility ˌɪnkənˌvɝtəˈbɪlətɪ; ES -ˌvɝt-, -ˌvɝˑt-

inconvertible ˌɪnkənˈvɝtəbļ; ES -ˈvɝt-, -ˈvɝˑt-; |-bly -blɪ

inconvincibility ˌɪnkənˌvɪnsəˈbɪlətɪ

inconvincible ˌɪnkənˈvɪnsəbļ |-bly -blɪ

in-co-ordinate ˌɪnkoˈɔrdṇɪt; ES -ˈɔədṇɪt; |-nated -dṇˌetɪd

in-co-ordination ˌɪnkoˌɔrdṇˈeʃən; ES -ˌɔədṇ-ˈeʃən

incorporable ɪnˈkɔrpərəbļ; ES -ˈkɔəp-

incorporate *adj* ɪnˈkɔrpərɪt, -prɪt; ES -ˈkɔəp-

incorporate *v* ɪnˈkɔrpəˌret; ES -ˈkɔəp-; |-d -ɪd |-rative -ˌretɪv

incorporation ɪnˌkɔrpəˈreʃən; ES -ˌkɔəp-; ˌɪnk-

incorporeal ˌɪnkɔrˈporɪəl, -ˈpɔr-; ES ˌɪnkɔ-ˈporɪəl, E+-ˈpɔrɪəl

incorporeity ɪnˌkɔrpəˈriətɪ; ES -kɔp-; ɪnˌk-

incorrect ˌɪnkəˈrɛkt (ˈincorˌrect ˈanswer)

incorrigibility ˌɪnkɔrɪdʒəˈbɪlətɪ, ɪnˌkɔr-, -ɑr-, -ɒr-

incorrigible ɪnˈkɔrɪdʒəbļ, -ˈkɑr-, -ˈkɒr- |-bly -blɪ

incorrupt ˌɪnkəˈrʌpt |-ed -ɪd

incorruptibility ˌɪnkəˌrʌptəˈbɪlətɪ

incorruptible ˌɪnkəˈrʌptəbļ |-bly -blɪ

incorruption ˌɪnkəˈrʌpʃən

increase *n* ˈɪnkris, ˈɪŋk- |-s -ɪz

increase *v* ɪnˈkris |-s -ɪz |-d -t |-dly -ɪdlɪ

increasingly ɪnˈkrisɪŋlɪ

incredibility ˌɪnkrɛdəˈbɪlətɪ, ɪnˌkrɛdə-

incredible ɪnˈkrɛdəbļ |-bly -blɪ

incredulity ˌɪnkrəˈdulətɪ, -ˈdɪul-, -ˈdjul-

incredulous ɪnˈkrɛdʒələs

increment ˈɪnkrəmənt, ˈɪŋk- |-al ˌɪnkrəˈmɛntļ

incriminate ɪnˈkrɪməˌnet |-d -ɪd

incrimination ɪnˌkrɪməˈneʃən, ˌɪnkrɪmə-

incriminator ɪnˈkrɪməˌnetɚ; ES -ˌnetə(r

incriminatory ɪnˈkrɪmənəˌtorɪ, -ˌtɔrɪ; S -ˌtorɪ

incrust ɪnˈkrʌst |-ed -ɪd

incrustation ˌɪnkrʌsˈteʃən

incubate ˈɪnkjəˌbet, ˈɪŋk- |-d -ɪd

incubation ˌɪnkjəˈbeʃən, ˌɪŋk-

incubator ˈɪnkjəˌbetɚ, ˈɪŋk-; ES -tə(r

incubus ˈɪnkjəbəs, ˈɪŋk- |-es -ɪz |-bi -ˌbaɪ

inculcate ɪnˈkʌlket, ˈɪnkʌlˌket |-d -ɪd

inculcation ˌɪnkʌlˈkeʃən

Key: *See in full §§3–47.* bee **bi** |pity ˈpɪtɪ (§6) |rate **ret** |yet **jɛt** |sang **sæŋ** |angry ˈæŋ�·grɪ |bath **bæθ**; E **bɑθ** (§10) |ah **ɑ** |far **fɑr** |watch **wɑtʃ, wɒtʃ** (§12) |jaw **dʒɔ** |gorge **gɔrdʒ** |go **go**

inculpate ɪnˈkʌlpet, ˈɪnkʌlˌpet |-d -ɪd
inculpation ˌɪnkʌlˈpeʃən
inculpatory ɪnˈkʌlpəˌtorɪ, -ˌtɔrɪ; S -ˌtorɪ
incult ɪnˈkʌlt (ˈinˌcult ˈbeard)
incumbency ɪnˈkʌmbənsɪ |-bent -bənt
incumber ɪnˈkʌmbɚ; ES -ˈkʌmbə(r; |-ed -d
  |-ing -ˈkʌmbrɪŋ, -bərɪŋ
incumbrance ɪnˈkʌmbrəns |-s -ɪz
incunabula ˌɪnkjuˈnæbjələ |sg -lum -ləm
incur ɪnˈkɝ; ES -ˈkɜ(r, -ˈkɝ; |-red -d
incurability ˌɪnkjʊrəˈbɪlətɪ, -kɪʊr-, ɪnˌk-
incurable ɪnˈkjʊrəbl̩, -ˈkɪʊr- |-bly -blɪ
incuriosity ˌɪnkjʊrɪˈɑsətɪ, -kɪʊr-; ES+-ˈɒs-
incurious ɪnˈkjʊrɪəs, -ˈkɪʊr-
incurrence ɪnˈkɝəns; ES -ˈkɜrəns, -ˈkʌrəns,
  -ˈkɝəns; |-s -ɪz
incursion ɪnˈkɝʒən, -ˈkɝʃ-; ES -ˈkɜ-, -ˈkɝ-
incursive ɪnˈkɝsɪv; ES -ˈkɜs-, -ˈkɝs-
incurvate adj ɪnˈkɝvɪt, -vet; ES -ˈkɜv-, -ˈkɝv-
incurvate ɪnˈkɝvet; ES -ˈkɜv-, -ˈkɝv-; |-d -ɪd
incurvation ˌɪnkɝˈveʃən; ES -kɜˈv-, -kɝˈv-
incurve n ˈɪnˌkɝv; ES -ˌkɜv, -ˌkɝv
incurve v ɪnˈkɝv; ES -ˈkɜv, -ˈkɝv; |-d -d
incus ˈɪŋkəs |-es -ɪz |-cudes ɪnˈkjudiz, -ˈkɪu-
Ind ˈIndiaˈ ɪnd, aɪnd—The historical pron. is
  aɪnd, as in Chauc. and Shak.
indamin ˈɪndəmɪn |-mine -ˌmin, -mɪn
indebt ɪnˈdɛt |-ed -ɪd -edness -ɪdnɪs
indecency ɪnˈdisn̩sɪ |-cent -sn̩t
indecipherability ˌɪndɪˌsaɪfrəˈbɪlətɪ, -fərə-
indecipherable ˌɪndɪˈsaɪfrəbl̩, -fərə- |-bly -blɪ
indecision ˌɪndɪˈsɪʒən |-cisive -ˈsaɪsɪv
indeclinable ˌɪndɪˈklaɪnəbl̩ |-bly -blɪ
indecorous ɪnˈdɛkərəs, ˌɪndɪˈkorəs; EN+
  -ˈkɔr-
indecorum ˌɪndɪˈkorəm, -ˈkɔr-; S -ˈkorəm
indeed ɪnˈdid, n̩ˈdid, emph.+ˈɪnˈdid (ˈjɛsn̩-
  ˈdid)
indefatigability ˌɪndɪˌfætɪgəˈbɪlətɪ
indefatigable ˌɪndɪˈfætɪgəbl̩ |-bly -blɪ
indefeasible ˌɪndɪˈfizəbl̩ |-bly -blɪ
indefensible ˌɪndɪˈfɛnsəbl̩ |-bly -blɪ
indefinable ˌɪndɪˈfaɪnəbl̩ |-bly -blɪ
indefinite ɪnˈdɛfənɪt
indehiscence ˌɪndiˈhɪsn̩s |-scent -sn̩t
indelibility ˌɪndɛləˈbɪlətɪ, ɪnˌdɛl-
indelible ɪnˈdɛləbl̩ |-bly -blɪ
indelicate ɪnˈdɛləkət, -kɪt |-cacy -kəsɪ
indemnification ɪnˌdɛmnəfəˈkeʃən

indemnify ɪnˈdɛmnəˌfaɪ |-fied -ˌfaɪd |-ity -tɪ
indemonstrable ɪnˈdɛmənstrəbl̩, ˌɪndɪˈmən-
  strəbl̩; ES+-ˈmɒn-; |-bly -blɪ
indene ˈɪndin
indent n ɪnˈdɛnt, ˈɪndɛnt
indent v ɪnˈdɛnt |-ed -ɪd |-ation ˌɪndɛnˈteʃən
indention ɪnˈdɛnʃən
indenture ɪnˈdɛntʃɚ; ES -ˈdɛntʃə(r; |-d -d
independence ˌɪndɪˈpɛndəns |-cy -ɪ |-nt -nt
indescribable ˌɪndɪˈskraɪbəbl̩ |-bly -blɪ
indestructibility ˌɪndɪˌstrʌktəˈbɪlətɪ
indestructible ˌɪndɪˈstrʌktəbl̩ |-bly -blɪ
indeterminable ˌɪndɪˈtɝmɪnəbl̩; ES -ˈtɝm-,
  -ˈtɝm-; |-bly -blɪ
indeterminate ˌɪndɪˈtɝmənɪt; ES -ˈtɝm-,
  -ˈtɝm-
indetermination ˌɪndɪˌtɝməˈneʃən; ES -ˌtɝm-,
  -ˌtɝm-
indeterminism ˌɪndɪˈtɝmənˌɪzəm; ES -ˈtɝm-,
  -ˈtɝm-; |-ist -ɪst
index ˈɪndɛks |-es -ɪz |indices ˈɪndəˌsiz |-ed -t
India ˈɪndɪə, ˈɪndjə |-n -n |-man -mən |-men
  -mən
Indiana ˌɪndɪˈænə—BBC ɪndɪˈɑːnə is not Am.
Indianapolis ˌɪndɪənˈæplɪs, -ˈæplɪs, -əs |-ˈs -ɪz
Indianian ˌɪndɪˈænɪən, -njən
Indic ˈɪndɪk
indic ˈɪndɪk |indican ˈɪndɪkən
indicant ˈɪndɪkənt
indicate ˈɪndəˌket |-d -ɪd |-tion ˌɪndəˈkeʃən
indicative ɪnˈdɪkətɪv, -ˈdɪkɪtɪv
indicator ˈɪndəˌketɚ; ES -ˌketə(r
indices pl of index ˈɪndəˌsiz
indict ɪnˈdaɪt |-ed -ɪd |-er, -or -ɚ; ES -ə(r
indictable ɪnˈdaɪtəbl̩ |-bly -blɪ
indictee ˌɪndaɪtˈi
indiction ɪnˈdɪkʃən
indictment ɪnˈdaɪtmənt
Indies ˈɪndɪz, ˈɪndiz
indifference ɪnˈdɪfrəns, -ˈdɪfərəns |-nt -nt
indigence ˈɪndədʒəns |-gent -dʒənt
indigene ˈɪndəˌdʒin
indigenous ɪnˈdɪdʒənəs
indigestibility ˌɪndəˌdʒɛstəˈbɪlətɪ
indigestible ˌɪndəˈdʒɛstəbl̩ |-bly -blɪ
indigestion ˌɪndəˈdʒɛstʃən
indign ɪnˈdaɪn
indignant ɪnˈdɪgnənt |-gnation ˌɪndɪgˈneʃən
indignity ɪnˈdɪgnətɪ

|full fʊl |tooth tuθ |further ˈfɝðɚ; ES ˈfɝðə |custom ˈkʌstəm |while hwaɪl |how haʊ |toy tɔɪ
|using ˈjuzɪŋ |fuse fjuz, fɪuz |dish dɪʃ |vision ˈvɪʒən |Eden ˈidn̩ |cradle ˈkredl̩ |keep ʼem ˈkipm̩

indigo 'ɪndɪˌgo |-digoid -dɪˌgɔɪd
indigotin ɪn'dɪgətɪn, ˌɪndɪ'gotɪn
Indio 'ɪndɪˌo
indirect ˌɪndə'rɛkt |-rection -'rɛkʃən
indiscernible ˌɪndɪ'zɝnəbļ, -'sɝn-; ES -ɜn-,
    -ɝn-; |-bly -blɪ
indiscreet ˌɪndɪ'skrit |-scretion -'skrɛʃən
indiscriminate ˌɪndɪ'skrɪmənɪt
indiscrimination ˌɪndɪˌskrɪmə'neʃən
indispensability ˌɪndɪˌspɛnsə'bɪlətɪ
indispensable ˌɪndɪ'spɛnsəbļ |-bly -blɪ
indispose ˌɪndɪ'spoz |-s -ɪz |-d -d
indisposition ˌɪndɪspə'zɪʃən
indisputability ˌɪndɪˌspjutə'bɪlətɪ, -ˌsprut-,
    ɪnˌdɪspjutə'bɪlətɪ
indisputable ˌɪndɪ'spjutəbļ, -'sprut-, ɪn'dɪs-
    pjutəbļ |-bly -blɪ—Usage appears to be
    sensibly following the analogy of dispute.
indissolubility ˌɪndɪˌsaljə'bɪlətɪ, ɪnˌdɪsļju-
    'bɪlətɪ; ES+-ˌsɒl-
indissoluble ˌɪndɪ'saljəbļ, ɪn'dɪsļjubļ; ES+
    -'sɒl-; |-bly -blɪ
indistinct ˌɪndɪ'stɪŋkt
indistinguishability ˌɪndɪˌstɪŋgwɪʃə'bɪlətɪ
indistinguishable ˌɪndɪ'stɪŋgwɪʃəbļ |-bly -blɪ
indite ɪn'daɪt |-d -ɪd
indium 'ɪndɪəm
individual ˌɪndə'vɪdʒʊəl, -dʒʊl |-ly -ɪ |-ism
    -ˌɪzəm |-ist -ɪst
individualistic ˌɪndəˌvɪdʒʊəl'ɪstɪk, -dʒʊl-
    |-ally -ļɪ, -ɪklɪ
individuality ˌɪndəˌvɪdʒʊ'ælətɪ
individualization ˌɪndəˌvɪdʒʊələ'zeʃən, -dʒʊl-,
    -aɪ'z-
individualize ˌɪndə'vɪdʒʊəlˌaɪz, -dʒʊl- |-s -ɪz
    |-d -d
indivisibility ˌɪndəˌvɪzə'bɪlətɪ
indivisible ˌɪndə'vɪzəbļ |-bly -blɪ
Indo-Aryan 'ɪndo'ɛrɪən, -'ær-, -'ɑr-, -rjən;
    S -'ær-, -'er-, -'ɑr-
Indo-British 'ɪndo'brɪtɪʃ
Indo-Chinese 'ɪndotʃaɪ'niz
indocile ɪn'dɑsļ, -sɪl; ES+-'dɒs-
indocility ˌɪndo'sɪlətɪ
indoctrinate ɪn'dɑktrɪnˌet; ES+-'dɒk-; |-d
    -ɪd
indoctrination ɪnˌdɑktrɪ'neʃən, ˌɪndak-; ES+
    -ɒ-
Indo-European ˌɪndəˌjʊrə'piən, ˌɪndo-

Indo-Germanic ˌɪndodʒɝ'mænɪk, -dʒɝ-; ES
    -dʒə-, -dʒɜ-, -dʒɝ-
indol 'ɪndol, -dɑl, -dɒl |-dole -dol
indolence 'ɪndələns |-lent -lənt
indomitable ɪn'dɑmətəbļ; ES+-'dɒm-; |-bly
    -blɪ
Indonesian ˌɪndo'niʃən, -ʒən
indoor 'ɪnˌdor, -ˌdɔr; ES -ˌdoə(r, E+-ˌdɔə(r
indoors n ɪn'dorz, -'dɔrz; ES -'doəz, E+
    -'dɔəz
indoors adj 'ɪnˌdorz, -ˌdɔrz; ES -ˌdoəz,
    E+-ˌdɔəz
indoors adv 'ɪn'dorz, -'dɔrz; ES -'doəz,
    E+-'dɔəz
indophenol ˌɪndo'finol, -nɑl, -nɒl
indorse ɪn'dɔrs; ES -'dɔəs; |-s -ɪz |-d -t
indoxyl ɪn'dɑksɪl; ES+-'dɒk-
Indra 'ɪndrə
indraft, -draught 'ɪnˌdræft; E+-ˌdraft, -ˌdrɑft
indrawn 'ɪn'drɔn ('ɪnˌdrawn 'breath)
indubitable ɪn'djubɪtəbļ, -'dru-, -'du- |-bly
    -blɪ
induce ɪn'djus, -'drus, -'dus |-s -ɪz |-d -t
    |-cible -əbļ |-dly -ɪdlɪ
induct ɪn'dʌkt |-ed -ɪd |-ance -əns
inductile ɪn'dʌktļ, -tɪl
inductility ˌɪndʌk'tɪlətɪ
induction ɪn'dʌkʃən |-tive -tɪv
inductivity ˌɪndʌk'tɪvətɪ
inductor ɪn'dʌktɚ; ES -'dʌktə(r
indue ɪn'dju, -'dɪu, -'du |-d -d
indulge ɪn'dʌldʒ |-s -ɪz |-d -d
indulgence ɪn'dʌldʒəns |-s -ɪz |-d -t |-nt -nt
indulin 'ɪndjulɪn |-line -ˌlin, -lɪn
indurate adj 'ɪndjʊrɪt, -dʊrɪt
indurate v 'ɪndjʊˌret, -dʊˌret |-d -ɪd
induration ˌɪndjʊ'reʃən, -dʊ-
Indus 'ɪndəs |-'s -ɪz
industrial ɪn'dʌstrɪəl |-ly -ɪ |-ism -ˌɪzəm |-ist
    -ɪst
industrialization ɪnˌdʌstrɪələ'zeʃən, -aɪ'z-
industrialize ɪn'dʌstrɪəlˌaɪz |-s -ɪz |-d -d
industrious ɪn'dʌstrɪəs
industry 'ɪndəstrɪ, 'ɪnˌdʌstrɪ
indwell ɪn'dwɛl |-dwelt -'dwɛlt
indweller 'ɪnˌdwɛlɚ; ES -ˌdwɛlə(r
indwelling n 'ɪnˌdwɛlɪŋ
inearth ɪn'ɝθ; ES -'ɜθ, -'ɝθ; |-ed -t
inebriacy ɪn'ibrɪəsɪ |-briant -brɪənt

inebriate *adj* ɪn'ibrɪɪt
inebriate *n* ɪn'ibrɪɪt, -ɪˌet
inebriate *v* ɪn'ibrɪˌet |-d -ɪd
inebriation ɪnˌibrɪ'eʃən
inebriety ˌɪnɪ'braɪətɪ
inedibility ˌɪnɛdə'bɪlətɪ, ɪnˌɛdə-
inedible ɪn'ɛdəbḷ
inedited ɪn'ɛdɪtɪd
ineducability ˌɪnɛdʒəkə'bɪlətɪ, -dʒʊ-
ineducable ɪn'ɛdʒəkəbḷ, -dʒʊ-
ineffability ˌɪnɛfə'bɪlətɪ, ɪnˌɛfə-
ineffable ɪn'ɛfəbḷ |-bly -blɪ
ineffaceable ˌɪnə'fesəbḷ |-bly -blɪ
ineffective ˌɪnə'fɛktɪv
ineffectual ˌɪnə'fɛktʃʊəl, -tʃʊl |-ly -ɪ
ineffectuality ˌɪnəˌfɛktʃʊ'ælətɪ
inefficacious ˌɪnɛfə'keʃəs |-cacy ɪn'ɛfəkəsɪ
inefficience ˌɪnə'fɪʃəns |-cy -ɪ |-nt -nt
inelastic ˌɪnɪ'læstɪk
inelasticity ˌɪnɪlæs'tɪsətɪ
inelegance ɪn'ɛləgəns |-s -ɪz |-cy -ɪ |-nt -nt
ineligibility ˌɪnɛlɪdʒə'bɪlətɪ, ɪnˌɛlɪdʒə-
ineligible ɪn'ɛlɪdʒəbḷ |-bly -blɪ
ineluctable ˌɪnɪ'lʌktəbḷ |-bly -blɪ
inept ɪn'ɛpt
ineptitude ɪn'ɛptəˌtjud, -ˌtrud, -ˌtud
inequality ˌɪnɪ'kwɑlətɪ, -'kwɒl-
inequitable ɪn'ɛkwɪtəbḷ |-bly -blɪ |-ty -tɪ
ineradicable ˌɪnɪ'rædɪkəbḷ |-bly -blɪ
inerrancy ɪn'ɛrənsɪ |-rant -rənt
inert ɪn'ɝt; ES ɪn'ɜt, -'ɝt
inertia ɪn'ɝʃə; ES -'ɜʃə, -'ɝʃə
inescapable ˌɪnə'skepəbḷ |-bly -blɪ
in esse ɪn'ɛsɪ
inessential ˌɪnə'sɛnʃəl
inestimable ɪn'ɛstəməbḷ |-bly -blɪ
inevitability ˌɪnɛvətə'bɪlətɪ, ɪnˌɛv-
inevitable ɪn'ɛvətəbḷ |-bly -blɪ
inexact ˌɪnɪg'zækt
inexactitude ˌɪnɪg'zæktəˌtjud, -ˌtrud, -ˌtud
inexcusable ˌɪnɪk'skjuzəbḷ, -'skɪuz- |-bly -blɪ
inexhaustibility ˌɪnɪgˌzɔstə'bɪlətɪ
inexhaustible ˌɪnɪg'zɔstəbḷ |-bly -blɪ
inexorable ɪn'ɛksərəbḷ |-bly -blɪ
inexpedience ˌɪnɪk'spidɪəns |-cy -ɪ |-nt -nt
inexpensive ˌɪnɪk'spɛnsɪv
inexperience ˌɪnɪk'spɪrɪəns |-d -t
inexpert ˌɪnɪk'spɝt; ES -'spɜt, -'spɝt; ('inexˌpert 'help)

inexpiable ɪn'ɛkspɪəbḷ |-bly -blɪ
inexplainable ˌɪnɪk'splenəbḷ
inexplicability ɪnˌɛksplɪkə'bɪlətɪ, ˌɪnɛks-
inexplicable ɪn'ɛksplɪkəbḷ |-bly -blɪ—*Brit
   occasional* ˌɪnɪk'splɪkəbḷ *seems to be gaining
   ground here.*
inexpressible ˌɪnɪk'sprɛsəbḷ |-bly -blɪ
inexpressive ˌɪnɪk'sprɛsɪv
inexpugnable ˌɪnɪk'spʌgnəbḷ |-bly -blɪ
in extenso ˌɪnɪk'stɛnso
inextinguishable ˌɪnɪk'stɪŋgwɪʃəbḷ |-bly -blɪ
in extremis ˌɪnɪk'strimɪs
inextricable ɪn'ɛkstrɪkəbḷ |-bly -blɪ
infallibility ˌɪnfælə'bɪlətɪ, ɪnˌfælə-
infallible ɪn'fæləbḷ |-bly -blɪ
infamous 'ɪnfəməs |infamy 'ɪnfəmɪ
infancy 'ɪnfənsɪ |-fant -fənt
infanta ɪn'fæntə |infante ɪn'fænte
infanticide ɪn'fæntəˌsaɪd
infantile 'ɪnfənˌtaɪl, -təl, -tɪl
infantine 'ɪnfənˌtaɪn, -tɪn
infantry 'ɪnfəntrɪ |-man -mən |-men -mən
infatuate ɪn'fætʃʊˌet |-d -ɪd
infatuation ɪnˌfætʃʊ'eʃən
infeasible ɪn'fizəbḷ
infect ɪn'fɛkt |-ed -ɪd
infection ɪn'fɛkʃən |-tious -ʃəs |-tive -tɪv
infelicitous ˌɪnfə'lɪsətəs |-ty -tɪ
infelt 'ɪnˌfɛlt
infer ɪn'fɝ; ES -'fɜ(r, -'fɝ; |-red -d
inferable ɪn'fɝəbḷ, 'ɪnfərəbḷ; ES+-'fɝəbḷ
inference 'ɪnfərəns |-s -ɪz
inferential ˌɪnfə'rɛnʃəl |-ly -ɪ
inferior ɪn'fɪrɪɚ; ES -'fɪrɪ·ə(r
inferiority ɪnˌfɪrɪ'ɔrətɪ, -'ɑr-, -'ɒr-, ˌɪnfɪr-
infernal ɪn'fɝnḷ; ES -'fɜnḷ, -'fɝnḷ; |-ly -ɪ
inferno, I- ɪn'fɝno; ES -'fɜno, -'fɝno
inferrible ɪn'fɝəbḷ; ES+-'fɝəbḷ
infertile ɪn'fɝtḷ, -tɪl; ES -'fɜ-, -'fɝ-; |-ly -ɪ
infertility ˌɪnfɝ'tɪlətɪ; ES ˌɪnfə-
infest ɪn'fɛst |-ed -ɪd |-ation ˌɪnfɛs'teʃən
infidel 'ɪnfədḷ |-delity ˌɪnfə'dɛlətɪ
infield 'ɪnˌfild
infiltrate ɪn'fɪltret |-d -ɪd
infiltration ˌɪnfɪl'treʃən
infinite, I- 'ɪnfənɪt, *worship occas.* -ˌnaɪt
infinitesimal ˌɪnfɪnə'tɛsəmḷ |-ly -ɪ
infinitival ˌɪnfɪnə'taɪvḷ, ɪnˌfɪnə- |-ly -ɪ
infinitive ɪn'fɪnətɪv

|full fʊl |tooth tuθ |further 'fɝðɚ; ES 'fɝðə |custom 'kʌstəm |while hwaɪl |how haʊ |toy tɔɪ
|using 'juzɪŋ |fuse fjuz, fɪuz |dish dɪʃ |vision 'vɪʒən |Eden 'idn̩ |cradle 'kredḷ |keep 'em 'kipm̩

infinitude ɪnˈfɪnəˌtjud, -ˌtɪud, -ˌtud
infinity ɪnˈfɪnətɪ
infirm ɪnˈfɜ˞m; ES -ˈfɜm, -ˈfɜ˞m; |-ary -ərɪ, -rɪ
|-ity -ətɪ
infix n ˈɪnˌfɪks |-es -ɪz
infix v ɪnˈfɪks |-es -ɪz |-ed -t
inflame ɪnˈflem |-d -d |-dly -ɪdlɪ
inflammability ɪnˌflæməˈbɪlətɪ, ˌɪnflæmə-
inflammable ɪnˈflæməbl̩ |-bly -blɪ
inflammation ˌɪnfləˈmeʃən
inflammatory ɪnˈflæməˌtorɪ, -ˌtɔrɪ; S -ˌtorɪ
inflate ɪnˈflet |-d -ɪd
inflation ɪnˈfleʃən |-ary -ˌɛrɪ |-ism -ˌɪzəm |-ist
-ɪst
inflect ɪnˈflɛkt |-ed -ɪd
inflection ɪnˈflɛkʃən |-al -l̩ |-ally -l̩ɪ
inflexibility ɪnˌflɛksəˈbɪlətɪ, ˌɪnflɛksə-
inflexible ɪnˈflɛksəbl̩ |-bly -blɪ
inflexion ɪnˈflɛkʃən
inflict ɪnˈflɪkt |-ed -ɪd |-ction -kʃən
inflorescence ˌɪnfloˈrɛsn̩s, -flə-; S -flo-; |-s -ɪz
|-cent -sn̩t
inflow n ˈɪnˌflo
influence ˈɪnfluəns, -flɪuəns |-s -ɪz |-d -t
influential ˌɪnfluˈɛnʃəl, -flɪu- |-ly -ɪ
influenza ˌɪnfluˈɛnzə, -flɪu-
influx ˈɪnˌflʌks |-es -ɪz
infold ɪnˈfold |-ed -ɪd
inform ɪnˈfɔrm; ES -ˈfɔəm; |-ed -d |-edly -ɪdlɪ
informal ɪnˈfɔrml̩; ES -ˈfɔəml̩; |-ly -ɪ
informality ˌɪnfɔrˈmælətɪ; ES -fɔˈmælətɪ
informant ɪnˈfɔrmənt; ES -ˈfɔəmənt
information ˌɪnfɚˈmeʃən; ES ˌɪnfə-
informative ɪnˈfɔrmətɪv; ES -ˈfɔəmətɪv
infra ˈɪnfrə
infract ɪnˈfrækt |-ed -ɪd
infra dig short for infra dignitatem ˈɪnfrə-
ˈdɪg(nɪˈtetɛm)
infrangible ɪnˈfrændʒəbl̩ |-bly -blɪ
infrared ˌɪnfrəˈred
infrequence ɪnˈfrikwəns |-cy -ɪ |-nt -nt
infringe ɪnˈfrɪndʒ |-s -ɪz |-d -d
infundibulum ˌɪnfʌnˈdɪbjələm |-la -lə
infuriate adj ɪnˈfjʊrɪɪt, -ˈfɪur-
infuriate v ɪnˈfjʊrɪˌet, -ˈfɪur- |-d -ɪd
infuse ɪnˈfjuz, -ˈfɪuz |-s -ɪz |-d -d |-dly -ɪdlɪ
infusible ɪnˈfjuzəbl̩, -ˈfɪuz-
infusion ɪnˈfjuʒən, -ˈfɪuʒən
infusive ɪnˈfjusɪv, -ˈfɪus-

infusoria, I- ˌɪnfjuˈsorɪə, -fɪu-, -ˈsɔrɪə; S
-ˈsorɪə; |-l -l |-n -n
-ing ending of pres ptc & verbal n, pronounced
-ɪŋ, -ŋ, -ɪn, -ən, n̩. Syllabic -ŋ frequently
replaces -ɪŋ after a k or g sound, as making
ˈmekɪŋ, ˈmekŋ, or dragging ˈdrægɪŋ,
ˈdrægŋ. The pronunciation with -ɪn, -ən
(running ˈrʌnɪn, ˈrʌnən) or with -ŋ (getting
ˈgɛtŋ) is occasionally heard in the informal
speech of the cultivated in all parts of the
US & C. It is more frequent in the S, where
it is not infrequently heard also on formal
occasions. In this vocabulary only -ɪŋ is
given, and this is usually omitted if the pronunciation can be inferred by adding the
sounds -ɪŋ directly to the head pronunciation.
Ingaevones ˌɪndʒɪˈvoniz
ingather ɪnˈgæðɚ; ES -ˈgæðə(r; |-ed -d |-ing
-ˈgæðrɪŋ, -ˈgæðərɪŋ
ingathering n ˈɪnˌgæðrɪŋ, -ˌgæðərɪŋ
Inge Dean of St. Paul's ɪŋ
Ingelow ˈɪndʒəˌlo
ingeminate ɪnˈdʒɛməˌnet |-d -ɪd
ingenerate adj ɪnˈdʒɛnərɪt
ingenerate v ɪnˈdʒɛnəˌret |-d -ɪd
ingenious ɪnˈdʒinjəs
ingénue Fr æʒeˈny
ingenuity ˌɪndʒəˈnuətɪ, -ˈnɪu-, -ˈnju-
ingenuous ɪnˈdʒɛnjuəs
Ingersoll ˈɪŋgɚˌsɔl, -ˌsɑl, -ˌsɒl, -ˌsɔl; ES ˈɪŋgə-
ingest ɪnˈdʒɛst |-ed -ɪd |-gestion -ˈdʒɛstʃən
Ingham ˈɪŋəm
ingle ˈɪŋgl̩ |-nook -ˌnʊk
inglobe ɪnˈglob |-d -d
inglorious ɪnˈglorɪəs, -ˈglɔr-; S -ˈglor-
ingoing ˈɪnˌgoɪŋ
Ingold ˈɪngold, ˈɪŋgold
Ingoldsby ˈɪŋgl̩zbɪ, ˈɪŋgəldzbɪ
ingot ˈɪŋgət |-ed -ɪd
Ingraham ˈɪŋgrɪəm, ˈɪŋgrəhəm
ingrain n ˈɪnˌgren
ingrain adj, v ɪnˈgren |-ed -d (ˈɪnˌgrain ˈrug)
ingrained adj ɪnˈgrend |-nedly -nɪdlɪ, -ndlɪ
Ingram ˈɪŋgrəm
ingrate n ˈɪngret
ingratiate ɪnˈgreʃɪˌet |-d -ɪd
ingratiatory ɪnˈgreʃɪəˌtorɪ, -ˌtɔrɪ; S -ˌtorɪ
ingratitude ɪnˈgrætəˌtjud, -ˌtɪud, -ˌtud

Key: See in full §§3–47. bee bi |pity ˈpɪtɪ (§6) |rate ret |yet jɛt |sang sæŋ |angry ˈæŋ·grɪ
|bath bæθ; E baθ (§10) |ah ɑ |far fɑr |watch watʃ, wɒtʃ (§12) |jaw dʒɔ |gorge gɔrdʒ |go go

ingredient ɪn'ɡridɪənt
ingress n 'ɪnɡrɛs |-es -ɪz
ingress v ɪn'ɡrɛs |-es -ɪz |-ed -t
ingression ɪn'ɡrɛʃən |-sive -'ɡrɛsɪv
ingrow 'ɪnˌɡro |-grew -ˌɡru, -ˌɡrɪu |-grown -ˌɡron
ingrown adj 'ɪn'ɡron ('ɪnˌɡrown 'habit)
ingrowth 'ɪnˌɡroθ |-ths -θs
inguinal 'ɪŋɡwɪn‖
ingulf ɪn'ɡʌlf |-ed -t
ingurgitate ɪn'ɡɝˌdʒɜ‖tet; ES -'ɡɜdʒ-, -'ɡɝˌdʒ-; |d -ɪd
inhabit ɪn'hæbɪt |-ed -ɪd
inhabitability 'habitability' ɪnˌhæbɪtə'bɪlətɪ
inhabitability 'nonhabitability' ˌɪnhæbɪtə-'bɪlətɪ
inhabitable 'habitable' ɪn'hæbɪtəb‖
inhabitable 'not habitable' 'ɪn'hæbɪtəb‖
inhabitancy ɪn'hæbətənsɪ |-tant -tənt
inhabitation ɪnˌhæbə'teʃən
inhalant ɪn'helənt
inhale ɪn'hel |-d -d |-lation ˌɪnhə'leʃən
inharmonic ˌɪnhɑr'mɑnɪk; ES -hɑː'mɑnɪk, -'mɒn-, E+-hɑː-
inharmonious ˌɪnhɑr'monɪəs; ES -hɑː'mon-, E+-hɑ-
inhere ɪn'hɪr; ES -'hɪə(r, S+-'hɛə(r; |-d -d
inherence ɪn'hɪrəns |-cy -ɪ |-nt -nt
inheritable ɪn'hɛrətəb‖ |-bly -blɪ
inheritance ɪn'hɛrətəns |-s -ɪz
inheritor ɪn'hɛrətɚ; ES -'hɛrətə(r; |-tress -trɪs |-tress's -trɪsɪz
inheritrix ɪn'hɛrətrɪks |-es -ɪz
inhibit ɪn'hɪbɪt |-ed -ɪd
inhibition ˌɪnɪ'bɪʃən, ˌɪnhɪ-
inhibitive ɪn'hɪbɪtɪv
inhibitory ɪn'hɪbəˌtorɪ, -ˌtɔrɪ; S -ˌtorɪ
inhospitable ɪn'hɑspɪtəb‖; ES+-'hɒs-; much less freq. ˌɪnhos'pitable |-bly -blɪ
inhospitality ˌɪnhɑspə'tælətɪ; ES+-hɒs-
inhuman ɪn'hjumən, -'hɪumən, -'jumən
inhumane ˌɪnhju'men, -hɪu'men, -ju'men
inhumanity ˌɪnhju'mænətɪ, -hɪu-, -ju'mæn-
inhumation ˌɪnhju'meʃən, -hɪu- |-tionist -ɪst
inhume ɪn'hjum, -'hɪum |-d -d
Inigo 'ɪnɪˌɡo
inimical ɪn'ɪmɪk‖ |-ly -ɪ, -ɪklɪ
inimitability ˌɪnɪmɪtə'bɪlətɪ
inimitable ɪn'ɪmətəb‖ |-bly -blɪ

inion 'ɪnɪən
iniquitous ɪ'nɪkwətəs |-ty -tɪ
initial ɪ'nɪʃəl |-ly -ɪ
initiate n, adj ɪ'nɪʃɪɪt, -ˌet
initiate v ɪ'nɪʃɪˌet |-d -ɪd
initiation ɪˌnɪʃɪ'eʃən
initiative ɪ'nɪʃɪˌetɪv, ɪ'nɪʃɪətɪv
initiatory ɪ'nɪʃɪəˌtorɪ, -ˌtɔrɪ; S -ˌtorɪ
inject ɪn'dʒɛkt |-ed -ɪd |-ction -kʃən
injector ɪn'dʒɛktɚ; ES -'dʒɛktə(r
injudicious ˌɪndʒu'dɪʃəs, -dʒɪu-
injunction ɪn'dʒʌŋkʃən |tive -tɪv
injure 'ɪndʒɚ; ES -dʒə(r; |-d -d |-ry -ɪ
injurious ɪn'dʒurɪəs, -'dʒɪu-
injustice ɪn'dʒʌstɪs |-s -ɪz
ink ɪŋk |-ed -t |-horn -ˌhɔrn; ES -ˌhɔən
inkling 'ɪŋklɪŋ
inkstand 'ɪŋkˌstænd
inkwell 'ɪŋkˌwɛl
inland adj 'ɪnlənd
inland n, adv 'ɪnˌlænd, 'ɪnlənd
inlander 'ɪnləndɚ; ES -də(r
inlaw n 'ɪnˌlɔ, v ɪn'lɔ |-ed ɪn'lɔd
inlay n 'ɪnˌle, v ɪn'le |-laid ɪn'led
inlet n 'ɪnˌlɛt, v ɪn'lɛt
inly 'ɪnlɪ
inmate 'ɪnmet
in medias res ɪn 'mɪdɪˌæs 'riz
in memoriam ˌɪnmə'morɪˌæm, -'mɔrɪ-, -ˌɑn. S -'morɪ-
inmost 'ɪnˌmost, -məst
inn ɪn |inned ɪnd
innate ɪ'net, ɪn'net ('ɪnˌnate 'poise)
inner 'ɪnɚ; ES 'ɪnə(r; |-most -ˌmost, -məst
innervate ɪ'nɝvet, 'ɪnɚˌvet; ES ɪ'nɝv-, ɪ'nɝv-, 'ɪnə-; |-d -ɪd
innervation ˌɪnɚ'veʃən; ES ˌɪnə-
innerve ɪ'nɝv, ɪn'nɝv; ES -'nɝv, -'nɝv; |-d -d
Innes, Inness 'ɪnɪs |-'s -ɪz
innholder 'ɪnˌholdɚ; ES -ˌholdə(r
inning 'ɪnɪŋ
innkeeper 'ɪnˌkipɚ; ES -ˌkipə(r
innocence 'ɪnəsn̩s |-cy -ɪ |-cent -sn̩t
innocuous ɪ'nɑkjuəs; ES+-'nɒk-
innominate adj ɪ'nɑmənɪt, ɪn'n-; ES+-'nɒm-
innovate 'ɪnəˌvet |-d -ɪd |-tion ˌɪnə'veʃən
innoxious ɪ'nɑkʃəs, ɪn'n-; ES+-'nɒk-
Innsbruck 'ɪnzbruk (Ger 'ɪnsbruk)

|full ful |tooth tuθ |further 'fɝðɚ; ES 'fɝðə |custom 'kʌstəm |while hwaɪl |how haʊ |toy tɔɪ
|using 'juzɪŋ |fuse fjuz, fɪuz |dish dɪʃ |vision 'vɪʒən |Eden 'idn̩ |cradle 'kred‖ |keep 'em 'kipm̩

innuendo ˌɪnjuˈɛndo
innumerable ɪˈnjumərəb|, ɪnˈn-, -ˈnɪum-, -ˈnum- |-bly -blɪ
innumerous ɪnˈnjumərəs, -ˈnɪum-, -ˈnum-
innutrition ˌɪnjuˈtrɪʃən, ˌɪnnju-, -nɪu-, -nu- |-tious -ʃəs
inobservance ˌɪnəbˈzɝvəns; ES -ˈzɝv-, -ˈzɝˑv-; |-nt -nt
inoculable ɪnˈakjələb|; ES+-ˈɒk-
inoculate ɪnˈakjəˌlet; ES+-ˈɒk-; |-d -ɪd
inoculation ɪnˌɑkjəˈleʃən; ES+-ˌɒk-
inodorous ɪnˈodərəs
inoffensive ˌɪnəˈfɛnsɪv
inofficious ˌɪnəˈfɪʃəs
inoperable ɪnˈɑpərəb|; ES+-ˈɒp-
inoperative ɪnˈɑpəˌretɪv, -ˈɑpərətɪv, -ˈɑprətɪv; ES+-ˈɒp-
inopportune ˌɪnɑpəˈtjun, ɪnˌɑp-, -ˈtɪun, -ˈtun; ES+-ɒp-, -ˌɒp-
inordinate ɪnˈɔrdn̩ɪt; ES -ˈɔədn̩ɪt
inorganic ˌɪnɔrˈgænɪk; ES -ɔəˈgæn-; |-al -| |-ally -|ɪ, -ɪklɪ
inosculate ɪnˈɑskjəˌlet; ES+-ˈɒs-; |-d -ɪd
inositol ɪˈnosɪˌtol
inpatient ˈɪnˌpeʃənt
inphase adj ˈɪnˌfez
inpour n ˈɪnˌpor, -ˌpɔr, -ˌpʊr; ES -ˌpoə(r, -ˌpʊə(r, E+-ˌpɔə(r
inpour v ɪnˈpor, -ˈpɔr-, -ˈpʊr; ES -ˈpoə(r, -ˈpʊə(r, E+-ˈpɔə(r; |-ed -d
input ˈɪnˌpʊt
inquest ˈɪnkwɛst
inquiet ɪnˈkwaɪət
inquietude ɪnˈkwaɪəˌtjud, -ˌtɪud, -ˌtud
inquire ɪnˈkwaɪr; ES -ˈkwaɪə(r; |-d -d
inquiry ɪnˈkwaɪrɪ, ˈɪnkwərɪ
inquisition ˌɪnkwəˈzɪʃən
inquisitive ɪnˈkwɪzətɪv |-tor -tɚ; ES -tə(r
inquisitorial ɪnˌkwɪzəˈtorɪəl, ˌɪnkwɪzə-, -ˈtɔr-; S -ˈtor-
in re ɪnˈri
inroad ˈɪnˌrod
inrush n ˈɪnˌrʌʃ |-es -ɪz
inrush v ɪnˈrʌʃ |-es -ɪz |-ed -t
insalivate ɪnˈsæləˌvet |-d -ɪd
insalubrious ˌɪnsəˈlubrɪəs, -ˈlɪub- |-brity -brətɪ
insane ɪnˈsen (ˈɪnˌsane ˈroot)
insanitary ɪnˈsænəˌtɛrɪ

insanity ɪnˈsænətɪ
insatiability ɪnˌseʃɪəˈbɪlətɪ, -ˌseʃə-, ˌɪnseʃ-
insatiable ɪnˈseʃɪəb|, -ˈseʃə- |-bly -blɪ
insatiate ɪnˈseʃɪɪt |-ated -ˌetɪd
inscribe ɪnˈskraɪb |-d -d
inscription ɪnˈskrɪpʃən
inscroll ɪnˈskrol |-ed -d
inscrutability ɪnˌskrutəˈbɪlətɪ, -ˌskrɪut-, ˌɪn-skr-
inscrutable ɪnˈskrutəb|, -ˈskrɪut- |-bly -blɪ
insculp ɪnˈskʌlp |-ed -t |-ture -tʃɚ; ES -tʃə(r
insect ˈɪnsɛkt
insectarium ˌɪnsɛkˈtɛrɪəm, -ˈter-
insectary ˈɪnsɛkˌtɛrɪ
insecticide ɪnˈsɛktəˌsaɪd |-dal -ˌsɛktəˈsaɪd|
insectival ˌɪnsɛkˈtaɪv|, ɪnˈsɛktəv|
insectivore ɪnˈsɛktəˌvor, -ˌvɔr; ES -ˌvoə(r, E+-ˌvɔə(r
insectivorous ˌɪnsɛkˈtɪvərəs, -ˈtɪvrəs
insecure ˌɪnsɪˈkjur, -ˈkɪur; ES -ə(r
insecurity ˌɪnsɪˈkjurətɪ, -ˈkɪurətɪ
inseminate ɪnˈsɛməˌnet |-d -ɪd
insemination ɪnˌsɛməˈneʃən, ˌɪnsɛmə-
insensate ɪnˈsɛnset, -sɪt
insensibility ˌɪnsɛnsəˈbɪlətɪ, ɪnˌsɛnsə-
insensible ɪnˈsɛnsəb| |-bly -blɪ
insensitive ɪnˈsɛnsətɪv
insensitivity ˌɪnsɛnsəˈtɪvətɪ, ɪnˌsɛnsə-
insentient ɪnˈsɛnʃɪənt, -ʃənt
inseparability ˌɪnsɛpərəˈbɪlətɪ, ɪnˌsɛpərə-, -prə-
inseparable ɪnˈsɛpərəb|, -prə- |-bly -blɪ
insert n ˈɪnsɝt; ES -sɝt, -sɝt
insert v ɪnˈsɝt; ES -ˈsɝt, -ˈsɝt; |-ed -ɪd
insertion ɪnˈsɝʃən; ES -ˈsɝʃən, -ˈsɝʃən
inset n ˈɪnˌsɛt, v ɪnˈsɛt
insheathe ɪnˈʃið |-d -d
inshore adj ˈɪnˌʃor, -ˌʃɔr; ES -ˌʃoə(r, E+ -ˌʃɔə(r; adv ˈɪnˈshore
inside n, adj ˈɪnˈsaɪd (ˈɪnˌside ˈdoor)
inside adv ˈɪnˈsaɪd (ˈɪnˌside & ˈoutˌside)
inside prep ɪnˈsaɪd
insider ɪnˈsaɪdɚ; ES -ˈsaɪdə(r
insidious ɪnˈsɪdɪəs
insight ˈɪnˌsaɪt
insignia ɪnˈsɪgnɪə
insignificance ˌɪnsɪgˈnɪfəkəns |-cant -kənt
insincere ˌɪnsɪnˈsɪr; ES -ˈsɪə(r, S+-ˈsɛə(r
insincerity ˌɪnsɪnˈsɛrətɪ

Key: See in full §§3–47. bee bi |pity ˈpɪtɪ (§6) |rate ret |yet jɛt |sang sæŋ |angry ˈæŋˑgrɪ |bath bæθ; E baθ (§10) |ah ɑ |far fɑr |watch wɑtʃ, wɒtʃ (§12) |jaw dʒɔ |gorge gɔrdʒ |go go

insinuate ɪnˈsɪnjʊˌet |-d -ɪd
insinuation ɪnˌsɪnjʊˈeʃən
insipid ɪnˈsɪpɪd |-ity ˌɪnsɪˈpɪdətɪ
insipience ɪnˈsɪpɪəns |-ent -ənt
insist ɪnˈsɪst |-ed -ɪd
insistence ɪnˈsɪstəns |-cy -ɪ |-ent -ənt
in situ ɪnˈsaɪtju, -tɪu-, -tu
insnare ɪnˈsnɛr, -ˈsnær; E -ˈsnɛə(r, ES
   -ˈsnæə(r; |-d -d
insobriety ˌɪnsəˈbraɪətɪ, ˌɪnso-
insociability ˌɪnsoʃəˈbɪlətɪ, ɪnˌsoʃə-
insociable ɪnˈsoʃəbl̩ |-bly -blɪ
insolate ˈɪnsoˌlet |-d -ɪd
insolation ˌɪnsoˈleʃən
insole ˈɪnˌsol |-d -d
insolence ˈɪnsələns |-s -ɪz |-cy -ɪ |-nt -nt
insolubility ˌɪnsɑljəˈbɪlətɪ; ES+-sɒl-
insoluble ɪnˈsɑljəbl̩; ES+-ˈsɒl-; |-bly -blɪ
insolvable ɪnˈsɑlvəbl̩, -ˈsɒlv- |-bly -blɪ
insolvency ɪnˈsɑlvənsɪ, -ˈsɒlv- |-vent -vənt
insomnia ɪnˈsɑmnɪə; ES+-ˈsɒm-
insomuch ˌɪnsoˈmʌtʃ, -so-
insouciance ɪnˈsusɪəns (Fr æsuˈsjɑ̃:s)
insouciant ɪnˈsusɪənt (Fr æsuˈsjɑ̃)
inspan ɪnˈspæn |-ned -d
inspect ɪnˈspɛkt |-ed -ɪd |-ction -kʃən
inspector ɪnˈspɛktɚ; ES -ˈspɛktə(r; |-ate -ɪt
insphere ɪnˈsfɪr; ES -ˈsfɪə(r, S+-ˈsfɛə(r
inspirable ɪnˈspaɪrəbl̩
inspiration ˌɪnspəˈreʃən |-al -l̩ |-ally -l̩ɪ
inspiratory ɪnˈspaɪrəˌtorɪ, -ˌtɔrɪ; S -ˌtorɪ
inspire ɪnˈspaɪr; ES -ˈspaɪə(r; |-d -d |-dly
   -ɪdlɪ
inspirit ɪnˈspɪrɪt |-ed -ɪd
inspissate ɪnˈspɪset |-d -ɪd
instability ˌɪnstəˈbɪlətɪ
install ɪnˈstɔl |-ed -d
installation ˌɪnstəˈleʃən
installment, -stalm- ɪnˈstɔlmənt
instance ˈɪnstəns |-s -ɪz |-d -t |-stant -stənt
instantaneous ˌɪnstənˈtenɪəs
instanter ɪnˈstæntɚ; ES -ˈstæntə(r
instar n ˈɪnstɑr; ES -stɑ:(r, E+-stɑ:(r
instar v ɪnˈstɑr; ES -ˈstɑ:(r, E+-ˈstɑ:(r;
   |-red -d
instate ɪnˈstet |-d -ɪd
in statu quo ɪnˈstetjuˈkwo, -ˈstætʃu-
instaurate ɪnˈstɔret |-d -ɪd
instauration ˌɪnstəˈreʃən

instead ɪnˈstɛd—*The historical doublet* ɪnˈstɪd
   is frequently heard.
instep ˈɪnˌstɛp
instigate ˈɪnstəˌget |-d -ɪd |-tor -ɚ; ES -ə(r
instigation ˌɪnstəˈgeʃən
instill, -il ɪnˈstɪl |-ed, -led -d
instillation ˌɪnstɪˈleʃən
instinct n ˈɪnstɪŋkt
instinct adj ɪnˈstɪŋkt |-ive -ɪv
institute ˈɪnstəˌtjut, -ˌtɪut-, -ˌtut |-d -ɪd
institution ˌɪnstəˈtjuʃən, -ˈtɪu-, -ˈtu- |-ary
   -ˌɛrɪ
institutionalize ˌɪnstəˈtjuʃənl̩ˌaɪz, -ʃnəl- |-s
   -ɪz |-d -d
institutive ˈɪnstəˌtjutɪv, -ˌtɪu-, -ˌtu-
instruct ɪnˈstrʌkt |-ed -ɪd |-ction -kʃən |-ive
   -ɪv |-or -ɚ; ES -ə(r
instrument ˈɪnstrəmənt
instrumental ˌɪnstrəˈmɛntl̩ |-ist -ɪst |-ly -ɪ
instrumentality ˌɪnstrəmɛnˈtælətɪ
instrumentation ˌɪnstrəmɛnˈteʃən
insubordinate ˌɪnsəˈbɔrdn̩ɪt; -dn̩ɪt; ES -ˈbɔəd-
insubordination ˌɪnsəˌbɔrdn̩ˈeʃən; ES -ˌbɔəd-
insubstantial ˌɪnsəbˈstænʃəl
insubstantiality ˌɪnsəbˌstænʃɪˈælətɪ
insufferable ɪnˈsʌfrəbl̩, -fərə- |-bly -blɪ
insufficience ˌɪnsəˈfɪʃəns |-cy -ɪ |-ent -ənt
insufflate ɪnˈsʌflet, ˈɪnsəˌflet |-d -ɪd
insufflation ˌɪnsəˈfleʃən
insular ˈɪnsələ, ˈɪnsjʊ-; ES -lə(r
insularity ˌɪnsəˈlærətɪ, ˌɪnsjʊ-
insulate ˈɪnsəˌlet, ˈɪnsjʊ- |-tor -ɚ; ES -ə(r
insulation ˌɪnsəˈleʃən, -sjʊ-
insulin ˈɪnsəlɪn, -sjʊ-
insulize ˈɪnsəˌlaɪz, -sjʊ- |-s -ɪz |-d -d
insult n ˈɪnsʌlt, v ɪnˈsʌlt |-ed ɪnˈsʌltɪd
insuperability ɪnˌsupərəˈbɪlətɪ, -ˌsɪu-, -ˌsju-,
   ˌɪns-
insuperable ɪnˈsupərəbl̩, -ˈsɪu-, -ˈsju- |-bly
   -blɪ
insupportable ˌɪnsəˈportəbl̩, -ˈpɔrt-; ES
   -ˈpoət-, E+-ˈpɔət-; |-bly -blɪ
insuppressible ˌɪnsəˈprɛsəbl̩ |-bly -blɪ
insurable ɪnˈʃʊrəbl̩ |-ability ɪnˌʃʊrəˈbɪlətɪ
insurance ɪnˈʃʊrəns |-s -ɪz
insure ɪnˈʃʊr; ES -ˈʃʊə(r; |-d -d
insurer ɪnˈʃʊrɚ; ES -rə(r
insurgence ɪnˈsɝdʒəns; ES -ˈsɜdʒ-, -ˈsɝdʒ-;
   |-cy -ɪ |-ent -ənt

|full fʊl |tooth tuθ |further ˈfɝðɚ; ES ˈfɝðə |custom ˈkʌstəm |while hwaɪl |how haʊ |toy tɔɪ
|using ˈjuzɪŋ |fuse fjuz, fɪuz |dish dɪʃ |vision ˈvɪʒən |Eden ˈidn̩ |cradle ˈkredl̩ |keep 'em ˈkipm̩

insurmountable ˌɪnsɚˈmaʊntəbḷ; ES -sə-;
|-bly -blɪ
insurrection ˌɪnsəˈrɛkʃən |-ary -ˌɛrɪ
insusceptibility ˌɪnsəˌsɛptəˈbɪlətɪ
insusceptible ˌɪnsəˈsɛptəbḷ |-bly -blɪ
inswathe ɪnˈsweð |-d -d
inswept ˈɪnˌswɛpt
intact ɪnˈtækt
intaglio ɪnˈtæljo, -ˈtaljo (It inˈtaʎʎo)
intake ˈɪnˌtek
intangible ɪnˈtændʒəbḷ |-bly -blɪ
integer ˈɪntədʒɚ; ES -dʒə(r
integral ˈɪntəgrəl |-ly -ɪ |-grable -grəbḷ
integrality ˌɪntəˈgrælətɪ
integrant ˈɪntəgrənt |-grand -ˌgrænd
integrate ˈɪntəˌgret |-grated -ˌgretɪd
integration ˌɪntəˈgreʃən
integrator ˈɪntəˌgretɚ; ES -ˌgretə(r
integrity ɪnˈtɛgrətɪ
integument n ɪnˈtɛgjəmənt
integument v ɪnˈtɛgjəˌmɛnt |-ed -ɪd
intellect ˈɪntḷˌɛkt
intellection ˌɪntḷˈɛkʃən |-tive -tɪv
intellectual ˌɪntḷˈɛktʃʊəl, -tʃʊl |-ly -ɪ |-ism
-ˌɪzəm |-ist -ɪst
intellectuality ˌɪntḷˌɛktʃʊˈælətɪ
intellectualize ˌɪntḷˈɛktʃʊəlˌaɪz, -tʃʊl- |-s -ɪz
|-d -d
intelligence ɪnˈtɛlədʒəns |-s -ɪz |-d -t
intelligent ɪnˈtɛlədʒənt
intelligential ɪnˌtɛləˈdʒɛnʃəl
intelligentsia ɪnˌtɛləˈdʒɛntsɪə, -ˈgɛntsɪə
intelligibility ɪnˌtɛlɪdʒəˈbɪlətɪ
intelligible ɪnˈtɛlɪdʒəbḷ |-bly -blɪ
intemperance ɪnˈtɛmpərəns, -prəns
intemperate ɪnˈtɛmpərɪt, -prɪt
intend ɪnˈtɛnd |-ed -ɪd |-ance -əns |-ant -ənt
intense ɪnˈtɛns |-sity -ətɪ |-sive -ɪv
intensification ɪnˌtɛnsəfəˈkeʃən
intensify ɪnˈtɛnsəˌfaɪ |-fied -ˌfaɪd
intension ɪnˈtɛnʃən
intent ɪnˈtɛnt
intention ɪnˈtɛnʃən |-al -ḷ, -ʃnəl |-ally -ḷɪ,
-ʃnəlɪ
inter ɪnˈtɝ; ES -ˈtɝ(r, -ˈtɝ; |-red -d
inter- prefix ˈɪntɚ-; ES ˈɪntə(r-
interact ˌɪntɚˈækt |-ed -ɪd |-ion -kʃən |-ive -ɪv
interblend ˌɪntɚˈblɛnd; ES ˌɪntə-; |-ed -ɪd
interbreed ˌɪntɚˈbrid; ES ˌɪntə-; |-bred -ˈbrɛd

intercalary ɪnˈtɝkəˌlɛrɪ; ES -ˈtɝk-, -ˈtɝk-
intercalate ɪnˈtɝkəˌlet; ES -ˈtɝk-, -ˈtɝk-; |-d
-ɪd |-tive -ɪv
intercalation ɪnˌtɝkəˈleʃən; ES -ˌtɝk-, -ˌtɝk-
intercede ˌɪntɚˈsid; ES ˌɪntə-; |-d -ɪd
intercellular ˌɪntɚˈsɛljəlɚ; ES ˌɪntəˈsɛljələ(r
intercept n ˈɪntɚˌsɛpt; ES ˈɪntə-
intercept v ˌɪntɚˈsɛpt; ES ˌɪntə-; |-ed -ɪd
|-ption -pʃən
intercession ˌɪntɚˈsɛʃən; ES ˌɪntə-
intercessory ˌɪntɚˈsɛsərɪ; ES ˌɪntə-
interchange n ˈɪntɚˌtʃendʒ; ES ˈɪntə-; |-s -ɪz
interchange v ˌɪntɚˈtʃendʒ; ES ˌɪntə-; |-s -ɪz
|-d -d
interchangeability ˌɪntɚˌtʃendʒəˈbɪlətɪ; ES
ˌɪntə-
interchangeable ˌɪntɚˈtʃendʒəbḷ; ES ˌɪntə-;
|-bly -blɪ
interclass ˈɪntɚˈklæs; ES ˈɪntə-, E+-ˈklɑs,
-ˈklas; (ˈɪntɚˌclass ˈgame)
intercollegiate ˌɪntɚkəˈlidʒɪɪt, -dʒɪt; ES ˌɪntə-
intercolonial ˌɪntɚkəˈlonɪəl; ES ˌɪntə-; |-ly -ɪ
intercommunicate ˌɪntɚkəˈmjunəˌket, -ˈmɪun-;
ES ˌɪntə-; |-d -ɪd
intercommunication ˌɪntɚkəˌmjunəˈkeʃən,
-ˌmɪun-; ES ˌɪntə-
intercommunion ˌɪntɚkəˈmjunjən, -ˈmɪun-;
ES ˌɪntə-
interconnect ˌɪntɚkəˈnɛkt; ES ˌɪntə-; |-ed -ɪd
interconnection ˌɪntɚkəˈnɛkʃən; ES ˌɪntə-
intercostal ˌɪntɚˈkɑstḷ, -ˈkɒs-, -ˈkɔs-; ES
ˌɪntə-; |-ly -ɪ
intercourse ˈɪntɚˌkors, -ˌkɔrs; ES ˈɪntəˌkoəs,
E+-ˌkɔəs
intercurrent ˌɪntɚˈkɝənt; ES ˌɪntəˈkɝr-,
-ˈkʌr-, -ˈkɝ-
interdenominational ˌɪntɚdɪˌnɑməˈneʃənḷ,
-ʃnəl; ES ˌɪntɚdɪˌnɑmə-, -ˌnɒmə-
interdental ˌɪntɚˈdɛntḷ; ES ˌɪntə-; |-ly -ɪ
interdepartmental ˌɪntɚdɪˌpɑrtˈmɛntḷ, -ˌdi-
pɑrt-; ES ˌɪntɚdɪˌpɑːt-, -ˌdipɑːt-, E+-ˌpɑːt-,
-pɑːt:; |-ly -ɪ
interdependence ˌɪntɚdɪˈpɛndəns; ES ˌɪntə-;
|-ent -ənt
interdict n ˈɪntɚˌdɪkt; ES ˈɪntə-
interdict v ˌɪntɚˈdɪkt; ES ˌɪntə-; |-ed -ɪd
interdiction ˌɪntɚˈdɪkʃən; ES ˌɪntə-
interest n ˈɪntərɪst, ˈɪntrɪst
interest v ˈɪntərɪst, ˈɪntrɪst, ˈɪntəˌrɛst

interested 'ɪntərɪstɪd, -rəs-, 'ɪntrɪstɪd, -trəs-,
'ɪntəˌrɛstɪd
interesting 'ɪntərɪstɪŋ, -rəs-, 'ɪntrɪstɪŋ, -trəs-,
'ɪntəˌrɛstɪŋ—*The former pron.* ˌɪntə'rɛstɪd,
-ɪŋ, *is now somewhat old-fashioned* (*though
still heard both in America and England*),
but 'ɪntəˌrɛstɪd, -ɪŋ *are still in excellent use,
esp. in England.*
interfere ˌɪntə'fɪr; ES ˌɪntə'fɪə(r, S+-'fɛə(r;
|-d -d |-nce -əns |-nces -ənsɪz
interferometer ˌɪntəfɪ'rɑmətə; ES ˌɪntəfɪ-
'rɑmətə(r, -'rɒm-
interfuse ˌɪntə'fjuz, -'fɪuz; ES ˌɪntə-; |-s -ɪz
|-d -d |-sion -ʒən
interglacial ˌɪntə'gleʃəl; ES ˌɪntə-
intergrade *n* 'ɪntəˌgred; ES 'ɪntə-
intergrade *v* ˌɪntə'gred; ES ˌɪntə-; |-d -ɪd
interim 'ɪntərɪm
interior ɪn'tɪrɪə; ES -'tɪrɪ·ə(r
interiority ɪnˌtɪrɪ'ɔrətɪ, -'ɑr-, -'ɒr-
interject ˌɪntə'dʒəkt; ES ˌɪntə-; |-ed -ɪd
interjection ˌɪntə'dʒɛkʃən; ES ˌɪntə-; |-al -|
|-ally -|ɪ |-tory -tərɪ
interknit ˌɪntə'nɪt; ES ˌɪntə-; |*past & pptc*
-knit -'nɪt *or* -knitted -'nɪtɪd
interlace ˌɪntə'les; ES ˌɪntə-; |-s -ɪz |-d -t
Interlaken 'ɪntəˌlɑkən; ES 'ɪntə-
interlard ˌɪntə'lɑːd; ES ˌɪntə'lɑːd, E+-'lɑːd;
|-ed -ɪd
interlay *n* 'ɪntəˌle; ES 'ɪntə-
interlay *v* ˌɪntə'le; ES ˌɪntə-; |-laid -'led
interleaf *n* 'ɪntəˌlif; ES 'ɪntə-; |-leaves -vz
interleaf *v* ˌɪntə'lif; ES ˌɪntə-; |-s -s |-ed -t
interleave *v* ˌɪntə'liv; ES ˌɪntə-; |-s -z |d -d
interline *n* 'ɪntəˌlaɪn; ES 'ɪntə-
interline *v* ˌɪntə'laɪn; ES ˌɪntə-; |d -d
interlineal ˌɪntə'lɪnɪəl; ES ˌɪntə-; |-ly -ɪ
interlinear ˌɪntə'lɪnɪə; ES ˌɪntə'lɪnɪ·ə(r
interlineate ˌɪntə'lɪnɪˌet; ES ˌɪntə-; |-d -ɪd
interlineation ˌɪntəˌlɪnɪ'eʃən; ES ˌɪntə-
interlink *n* 'ɪntəˌlɪŋk; ES 'ɪntə-
interlink *v* ˌɪntə'lɪŋk; ES ˌɪntə-; |-ed -t
interlocate ˌɪntə'loket; ES ˌɪntə-; |-d -ɪd
interlock *n* 'ɪntəˌlɑk; ES 'ɪntəˌlɑk, -ˌlɒk
interlock *v* ˌɪntə'lɑk; ES ˌɪntə'lɑk, -'lɒk;
|-ed -t
interlocution ˌɪntələ'kjuʃən, -'kɪu-; ES ˌɪntə-
interlocutor ˌɪntə'lɑkjətə; ES ˌɪntə'lɑkjətə(r,
-'lɒk-; |-tory -ˌtorɪ, -ˌtɔrɪ; S -ˌtorɪ

interlope ˌɪntə'lop; ES ˌɪntə-; |-d -t |-r -ə;
ES -ə(r; *acct*+'interˌloper
interlude 'ɪntəˌlud, -ˌlɪud; ES 'ɪntə-
interlunar ˌɪntə'lunə, -'lɪunə; ES ˌɪntə-
'lunə(r, -'lɪu-
intermarriage ˌɪntə'mærɪdʒ; ES ˌɪntə-; |-s
-ɪz
intermarry ˌɪntə'mærɪ; ES ˌɪntə-; |-ied -d
intermeddle ˌɪntə'mɛd|; ES ˌɪntə-; |-d -d
|-ling -'mɛdlɪŋ, -'mɛd|ɪŋ
intermediacy ˌɪntə'midɪəsɪ; ES ˌɪntə-
intermediary ˌɪntə'midɪˌɛrɪ; ES ˌɪntə-
intermediate *adj* ˌɪntə'midɪɪt; ES ˌɪntə-
intermediate *v* ˌɪntə'midɪˌet; ES ˌɪntə-; |-d -ɪd
interment ɪn'tɜmənt; ES -'tɜ-, -'tɜ-
intermezzo ˌɪntə'mɛtso, -'mɛdzo; ES ˌɪntə-;
(*It* ˌinter'mɛddzo)
interminable ɪn'tɜmɪnəb|; ES -'tɜm-, -'tɜm-;
|-bly -blɪ
intermingle ˌɪntə'mɪŋg|; ES ˌɪntə-; |-d -d
|-ling -'mɪŋglɪŋ, -g|ɪŋ
intermission ˌɪntə'mɪʃən; ES ˌɪntə-
intermit ˌɪntə'mɪt; ES ˌɪntə-; |-ted -ɪd |-tent
-ṇt
intermix ˌɪntə'mɪks; ES ˌɪntə-; |-es -ɪz |-ed
-t |-ture -tʃə; ES -tʃə(r
intern, -e *adj* ɪn'tɜn; ES -'tɜn, -'tɜn
intern, -e *n* 'ɪntɜn; ES -tɜn, -tɜn
intern *v* '*segregate*' ɪn'tɜn; ES -'tɜn, -'tɜn;
|-ed -d
intern *v* '*act as intern*' 'ɪntɜn; ES -tɜn, -tɜn;
|-ed -d
internal ɪn'tɜn|; ES -'tɜn|, -'tɜn|; |-ly -ɪ
internal-combustion ɪn'tɜn|kəm'bʌstʃən; ES
-'tɜn|-, -'tɜn|-; |*acct*+'internal-
internality ˌɪntə'nælətɪ; ES ˌɪntə-
international, I- ˌɪntə'næʃən|, -ʃnəl; ES
ˌɪntə-; |-ly -ɪ |-ism -ˌɪzəm |-ist -ɪst
internationalization ˌɪntəˌnæʃənələ'zeʃən,
-ʃnələ-, -aɪ'z-; ES ˌɪntə-
internationalize ˌɪntə'næʃən|ˌaɪz, -ʃnəl-; ES
ˌɪntə-; |-s -ɪz |-d -d
internecine ˌɪntə'nisɪn, -saɪn; ES ˌɪntə-
internment ɪn'tɜnmənt; ES -'tɜn-, -'tɜn-
internship, -terne- 'ɪntɜnˌʃɪp, ɪn'tɜnʃɪp; ES
-ɜn-, -ɜn-
internuncio ˌɪntə'nʌnʃɪˌo; ES ˌɪntə-
interoceanic ˌɪntəˌoʃɪ'ænɪk; ES ˌɪntə-
interpellant ˌɪntə'pɛlənt; ES ˌɪntə-

---

interpellate ˌɪntɚˈpɛlet, ɪnˈtɝpɪˌlet; ES ˌɪntə-,
-ˈtɝ-, -ˈtɝ-; |-d -ɪd
interpellation ˌɪntɚpɛˈleʃən, ɪnˌtɝpɪˈleʃən; ES
ˌɪntə-, -ˌtɝ-, -ˌtɝ-
interpellator ˌɪntɚpɛˈletɚ, ɪnˈtɝpɪˌletɚ; ES
ˌɪntəpɛˈletə(r, ɪnˈtɝpɪˌletə(r, -ˈtɝpɪˌletə(r
interpenetrate ˌɪntɚˈpɛnəˌtret; ES ˌɪntə-;
|-d -ɪd
interpenetration ˌɪntɚˌpɛnəˈtreʃən; ES ˌɪntə-
interplanetary ˌɪntɚˈplænəˌtɛrɪ; ES ˌɪntə-
interplay n ˈɪntɚˌple; ES ˌɪntə-
interplay v ˌɪntɚˈple; ES ˌɪntə-; |-ed -d
interplead ˌɪntɚˈplid; ES ˌɪntə-; |-ed -ɪd or
-plead, -pled -ˈplɛd
interpolate ɪnˈtɝpəˌlet; ES -ˈtɝ-, -ˈtɝ-; |-d -ɪd
|-tor -ɚ; ES -ə(r
interpolation ɪnˌtɝpəˈleʃən; ES -ˌtɝ-, -ˌtɝ-
interposal ˌɪntɚˈpoz|; ES ˌɪntə-
interpose ˌɪntɚˈpoz; ES ˌɪntə-; |-s -ɪz |-d -d
interposition ˌɪntɚpəˈzɪʃən; ES ˌɪntə-
interpret ɪnˈtɝprɪt; ES -ˈtɝp-, -ˈtɝp-; |-ed -ɪd
—*The occasional pron.* ɪnˈtɝpɪt *is due to
dissimilation (§121).*
interpretability ɪnˌtɝprɪtəˈbɪlətɪ; ES -ˌtɝp-,
-ˌtɝp-
interpretation ɪnˌtɝprɪˈteʃən; ES -ˌtɝp-,
-ˌtɝp-
interpretative ɪnˈtɝprɪˌtetɪv; ES -ˈtɝp-, -ˈtɝp-
interpretive ɪnˈtɝprɪtɪv; ES -ˈtɝp-, -ˈtɝp-
interracial ˌɪntɚˈreʃəl, -ʃɪəl; ES ˌɪntə-
interregnum ˌɪntɚˈrɛgnəm; ES ˌɪntə-; |-s -z
|-na -nə
interrelate ˌɪntɚrɪˈlet; ES ˌɪntə-; |-d -ɪd |-tion
-ˈleʃən
interrenal ˌɪntɚˈrin|; ES ˌɪntə-
interrex ˈɪntɚˌrɛks; ES ˈɪntə-; |-reges ˌɪntə-
ˈridʒiz; ES ˌɪntə-
interrogate ɪnˈtɛrəˌget |-d -ɪd |-tor -ɚ; ES
-ə(r
interrogation ɪnˌtɛrəˈgeʃən |-al -|
interrogative ˌɪntəˈragətɪv, -ˈrɒg- |-tory -ˌtorɪ,
-ˌtɔrɪ; S -ˌtɔrɪ
interrupt ˌɪntəˈrʌpt |-ed -ɪd |-ption -pʃən
interscholastic ˌɪntɚskəˈlæstɪk, -sko-; ES
ˌɪntə-
intersect ˌɪntɚˈsɛkt; ES ˌɪntə-; |-ed -ɪd
|-ction -kʃən
interspace n ˈɪntɚˌspes; ES ˈɪntə-; |-s -ɪz
interspace v ˌɪntɚˈspes; ES ˌɪntə-; |-s -ɪz |-d -t

interspatial ˌɪntɚˈspeʃəl; ES ˌɪntə-; |-ly -ɪ
intersperse ˌɪntɚˈspɝs; ES ˌɪntəˈspɝs, -ˈspɝs;
|-s -ɪz |-d -t |-dly -ɪdlɪ |-sion -ʃən, -ʒən
interstate ˌɪntɚˈstet; ES ˌɪntə-; (ˈɪnterˌstate
ˈact)
interstellar ˌɪntɚˈstɛlɚ; ES ˌɪntəˈstɛlə(r
interstice ɪnˈtɝstɪs; ES -ˈtɝs-, -ˈtɝs-; |-s -ɪz
|-d -t
interstitial ˌɪntɚˈstɪʃəl; ES ˌɪntə-; |-ly -ɪ
intertribal ˌɪntɚˈtraɪb|; ES ˌɪntə-
intertwine n ˈɪntɚˌtwaɪn; ES ˈɪntə-
intertwine v ˌɪntɚˈtwaɪn; ES ˌɪntə-; |-d -d
intertwist n ˈɪntɚˌtwɪst; ES ˈɪntə-
intertwist v ˌɪntɚˈtwɪst; ES ˌɪntə-; |-ed -ɪd
interurban ˌɪntɚˈɝbən; ES ˌɪntəˈɝbən, -ˈɝb-
interval ˈɪntɚv|; ES ˈɪntə-; |-ed -d
intervale ˈɪntɚˌvel, *attrib.*+-v|, -vɪl; ES ˈɪntə-
intervene ˌɪntɚˈvin; ES ˌɪntə-; |-d -d
intervenience ˌɪntɚˈvinjəns; ES ˌɪntə-; |-cy -ɪ
|-ient -jənt
intervention ˌɪntɚˈvɛnʃən; ES ˌɪntə-; |-al -|
|-ism -ˌɪzəm |-ist -ɪst
interview ˈɪntɚˌvju, -ˌvɪu; ES ˈɪntə-; |-ed -d
intervocal ˌɪntɚˈvok|; ES ˌɪntə-; |-ly -ɪ
intervocalic ˌɪntɚvoˈkælɪk; ES ˌɪntə-; |-ally
-|ɪ, -ɪklɪ
interweave ˌɪntɚˈwiv; ES ˌɪntə-; |-wove -ˈwov
|-woven -ˈwovən or -wove -ˈwov
intestate ɪnˈtɛstet, -tɪt |-tacy -təsɪ
intestine ɪnˈtɛstɪn |-nal -| |-nally -|ɪ (*BBC*
ˌɪntɛsˈtaɪn|)
inthrall, -al ɪnˈθrɔl |-(l)ed -d
inthrone ɪnˈθron |-d -d
intimate *adj* ˈɪntəmɪt |-macy -məsɪ
intimate v ˈɪntəˌmet |-d -ɪd |-tion ˌɪntəˈmeʃən
intimidate ɪnˈtɪməˌdet |-d -ɪd
intimidation ɪnˌtɪməˈdeʃən
intitle ɪnˈtaɪt| |-d -d |-ling -t|ɪŋ, -tlɪŋ
intitule ɪnˈtɪtjul |-d -d
into *before vowel* ˈɪntu, ˈɪntə; *before cons.* ˈɪntə;
before pause ˈɪntu; *in poetry often* ɪnˈtu
intolerability ɪnˌtɑlərəˈbɪlətɪ; ES+-ˌtɒl-
intolerable ɪnˈtɑlərəb|; ES+-ˈtɒl-; |-bly -blɪ
intolerance ɪnˈtɑlərəns; ES+-ˈtɒl-; |-ant -ənt
intomb ɪnˈtum |-ed -d |-ment ɪnˈtummənt
intonate ˈɪntoˌnet |-nated -ˌnetɪd
intone ɪnˈton |-d -d |-nation ˌɪntoˈneʃən
intorsion ɪnˈtɔrʃən; ES -ˈtɔəʃən
intort ɪnˈtɔrt; ES -ˈtɔət; |-ed -ɪd

Key: *See in full §§3–47.* bee bi |pity ˈpɪtɪ (§6) |rate ret |yet jɛt |sang sæŋ |angry ˈæŋ·grɪ
|bath bæθ; E baθ (§10) |ah ɑ |far fɑr |watch wɑtʃ, wɒtʃ (§12) |jaw dʒɔ |gorge gɔrdʒ |go go

in toto ɪn'toto
intoxicant ɪn'tɑksəkənt; ES+-'tɒks-
intoxicate ɪn'tɑksə‚ket; ES+-'tɒks-; |-tive
  -ɪv
intoxication ɪn‚tɑksə'keʃən; ES+-‚tɒks-
intra 'ɪntrə
intracellular ‚ɪntrə'sɛljələ‚; ES -lə(r
intracollegiate ‚ɪntrəkə'lidʒɪɪt, -dʒɪt
intractability ‚ɪntræktə'bɪlətɪ, ɪn‚træktə-
intractable ɪn'træktəb!, |-bly -blɪ
intractile ɪn'trækt!, -tɪl
intrados ɪn'tredɑs; ES+-dɒs; |-es -ɪz
intramolecular ‚ɪntrəmə'lɛkjələ‚; ES -lə(r
intramural ‚ɪntrə'mjʊrəl, -'mɪʊrəl
intramuscular ‚ɪntrə'mʌskjələ‚; ES -lə(r
intransigence ɪn'trænsədʒəns |-cy -ɪ |-ent -ənt
intransitive ɪn'trænsətɪv
intrant 'ɪntrənt
intrastate ‚ɪntrə'stet ('intra‚state 'trade)
intravenous ‚ɪntrə'vinəs
intreat ɪn'trit |-ed -ɪd
intrench ɪn'trɛntʃ |-es -ɪz |-ed -t
intrepid ɪn'trɛpɪd |-pidity ‚ɪntrə'pɪdətɪ
intricate 'ɪntrəkɪt |-cacy -kəsɪ
intrigue n ɪn'trig, 'ɪntrig
intrigue v ɪn'trig |-d -d
intrinsic ɪn'trɪnsɪk |-al -! |-ally -!ɪ, -ɪklɪ
intrinsicate ɪn'trɪnsɪkɪt, -‚ket
introduce ‚ɪntrə'djus, -'dɪus, -'dus |-s -ɪz |-d -t
introduction ‚ɪntrə'dʌkʃən |-tive -tɪv |-tory
  -tərɪ, -trɪ
introit ɪn'tro·ɪt
introjection ‚ɪntrə'dʒɛkʃən
intromission ‚ɪntrə'mɪʃən
intromit ‚ɪntrə'mɪt |-ted -ɪd |-tent -ṇt
introrse ɪn'trɔrs; ES -'trɔəs
introspect ‚ɪntrə'spɛkt |-ed -ɪd
introspection ‚ɪntrə'spɛkʃən |-tive -tɪv
introversion ‚ɪntrə'vɝʃən, -ʒən; ES -'vɝ-,
  -'vɝ-; |-sive -sɪv
introvert n 'ɪntrə‚vɝt; ES -‚vɝt, -‚vɝt
introvert v ‚ɪntrə'vɝt; ES -'vɝt, -'vɝt; |-ed -ɪd
  |-ive -ɪv
intrude ɪn'trud, -'trɪud |-d -ɪd
intrusion ɪn'truʒən, -'trɪuʒən |-sive -sɪv
intrust ɪn'trʌst |-ed -ɪd
intuit 'ɪntjʊɪt, -tɪu-, -tu-, ɪn'tjuɪt, -'trɪu-,
  -'tu- |-ed -ɪd
intuition ‚ɪntu'ɪʃən, -tɪu-, -tju-

intuitive ɪn'tjuɪtɪv, -'trɪu-, -'tu-
intumescence ‚ɪntju'mɛsṇs, -trɪu-, -tu- |-nt -ṇt
inturn 'ɪn‚tɝn; ES -‚tɝn, -‚tɝn; |-ed -d
intussuscept ‚ɪntəssə'sɛpt |-ed -ɪd |-ion -pʃən
intwine ɪn'twaɪn |-d -d
inulin 'ɪnjəlɪn
inunction ɪn'ʌŋkʃən
inundate 'ɪnən‚det, -ʌn-, ɪn'ʌndet |-d -ɪd
inundation ‚ɪnən'deʃən, ‚ɪnʌn-
inure ɪn'jʊr; ES -'jʊə(r; |-d -d
inurn ɪn'ɝn; ES -'ɝn, -'ɝn; |-ed -d
inutile ɪn'jut!, -tɪl |-ly -ɪ
inutility ‚ɪnju'tɪlətɪ
in vacuo ɪn'vækju‚o
invade ɪn'ved |-vaded -'vedɪd
invalid 'not valid' ɪn'vælɪd
invalid n, adj 'sick' 'ɪnvəlɪd |-ism -‚ɪzəm
invalid v 'ɪnvə‚lɪd |-lided -‚lɪdɪd
invalidate ɪn'vælə‚det |-dated -‚detɪd
invalidation ɪn‚vælə'deʃən, ‚ɪnvælə-
invalidity ‚ɪnvə'lɪdətɪ
invaluable ɪn'væljəb!, -'væljʊəb! |-bly -blɪ
invariability ‚ɪnvɛrɪə'bɪlətɪ, -ver-, -vær-,
  ɪn‚v-
invariable ɪn'vɛrɪəb!, -'ver-, -'vær- |-bly -blɪ
invasion ɪn'veʒən |-sive -sɪv
invective ɪn'vɛktɪv
inveigh ɪn've |-ed -d
inveigle ɪn'vig!, -'veg! |-d -d |-ling -g!ɪŋ,
  -g!ɪŋ
invent ɪn'vɛnt |-ed -ɪd |-ive -ɪv |-ntion -nʃən
inventory 'ɪnvən‚torɪ, -‚tɔrɪ; S -‚torɪ
Inverness ‚ɪnvɚ'nɛs; ES -və-; ('Inver‚ness
  'cape) |-ness-shire -'nɛsʃɪr,- 'nɛʃʃ-, -ʃɚ; ES
  -ʃɪə(r, -ʃə(r
inverse n, adj ɪn'vɝs; ES -'vɝs, -'vɝs; ('in-
  ‚verse 'ratio)
inverse v ɪn'vɝs; ES -'vɝs, -'vɝs; |-s -ɪz |-d -t
  |-dly -ɪdlɪ, -tlɪ
inversion ɪn'vɝʃən, -ʒən; ES -'vɝ-, -'vɝ-
invert n, adj 'ɪnvɝt; ES -vɝt, -vɝt
invert v ɪn'vɝt; ES -'vɝt, -'vɝt; |-ed -ɪd
invertebrate n, adj ɪn'vɝtəbrɪt, -‚bret; ES
  -'vɝt-, -'vɝt-; |-d -‚bretɪd
invest ɪn'vɛst |-ed -ɪd
investigable ɪn'vɛstɪgəb! |-gatable -‚getəb!
investigate ɪn'vɛstə‚get |-d -ɪd |-tor -ɚ; ES
  -ə(r
investigation ɪn‚vɛstə'geʃən

investiture ɪnˈvɛstətʃɚ; ES -tʃə(r
investment ɪnˈvɛstmənt |-stor -tɚ; ES -tə(r
inveteracy ɪnˈvɛtərəsɪ |-rate -rɪt
Invictus ɪnˈvɪktəs
invidious ɪnˈvɪdɪəs
invigorate ɪnˈvɪgəˌret |-rated -ˌretɪd
invigoration ɪnˌvɪgəˈreʃən
invincibility ɪnˌvɪnsəˈbɪlətɪ, ˌɪnvɪnsə-
invincible ɪnˈvɪnsəbl̩ |-bly -blɪ
inviolability ɪnˌvaɪələˈbɪlətɪ, ˌɪnvaɪələ-
inviolable ɪnˈvaɪələbl̩ |-bly -blɪ
inviolate ɪnˈvaɪəlɪt, -ˌlet
invisibility ˌɪnvɪzəˈbɪlətɪ, ɪnˌvɪzə-
invisible ɪnˈvɪzəbl̩ |-bly -blɪ
invitation ˌɪnvəˈteʃən
invite n ˈɪnvaɪt
invite v ɪnˈvaɪt |-vited -ˈvaɪtɪd
invocate ˈɪnvəˌket |-d -ɪd |-tion ˌɪnvəˈkeʃən
invoice ˈɪnvɔɪs |-s -ɪz |-d -t
invoke ɪnˈvok |-voked -ˈvokt
involucre ˈɪnvəˌlukɚ, -ˌlɪukɚ; ES -kə(r; |-d -d
involuntary ɪnˈvɑlənˌtɛrɪ; ES -ˈvɒl-; |-rily
-rəlɪ, esp. if emph. ˌɪnvəlunˈtarɪlɪ
involute ˈɪnvəˌlut, -ˌlɪut |-d -ɪd
involution ˌɪnvəˈluʃən, -ˈlɪuʃən, -v]ˈjuʃən
involve ɪnˈvɑlv, -ˈvɒlv |-d -d |-dly -ɪdlɪ
invulnerability ˌɪnvʌlnərəˈbɪlətɪ, ɪnˌvʌl-, -nrə-
invulnerable ɪnˈvʌlnərəbl̩, -nrə- |-bly -blɪ
inwall n ˈɪnˌwɔl, v ɪnˈwɔl |-ed ɪnˈwɔld
inward ˈɪnwɚd; ES ˈɪnwəd; |-s -z
inweave ɪnˈwiv |-wove -ˈwov |-woven -ˈwovən
or -wove -ˈwov
inwind ɪnˈwaɪnd |-wound -ˈwaʊnd
inwork ɪnˈwɝk; ES -ˈwɜk, -ˈwɝk; |-ed -t or
-wrought -ˈrɔt
inwound ɪnˈwaʊnd
inwove ɪnˈwov |-woven -ˈwovən (ˈɪnˌwoven
ˈhue)
inwrap ɪnˈræp |-ped -t
inwreathe ɪnˈrið |-d -d
inwrought ɪnˈrɔt (ˈɪnˌwrought ˈcolors)
Io ˈaɪo
-io ending see -ia
iodate ˈaɪəˌdet |-dated -ˌdetɪd
iodide ˈaɪəˌdaɪd, -dɪd |iodid ˈaɪədɪd
iodin ˈaɪədɪn
iodine ˈaɪəˌdaɪn, -dɪn, chem. usually -ˌdin
iodize ˈaɪəˌdaɪz |-s -ɪz |-d -d
iodoform aɪˈodəˌfɔrm, -ˈad-; ES -ˌfɔəm, -ˈɒd-

Iola aɪˈolə
Iolanthe ˌaɪəˈlænθɪ
-ion ending see -ia
ion ˈaɪən, ˈaɪɑn, -ɒn
Ion ˈaɪən, -ɒn
Iona aɪˈonə
Ione heroine aɪˈonɪ
Ione village, geol. formation aɪˈon
Ionia aɪˈonɪə, -njə |-n -n
ionic, I- aɪˈɑnɪk, -ˈɒn-
ionium aɪˈonɪəm
ionization ˌaɪənəˈzeʃən, -aɪˈz-
ionize ˈaɪənˌaɪz |-s -ɪz |-d -d
Iosco aɪˈasko; ES+-ˈɒs-
iota aɪˈotə |-cism -ˌsɪzəm
iotize ˈaɪəˌtaɪz |-s -ɪz |-d -d
I O U ˈaɪˌoˈju
-ious ending see -ia
Iowa ˈaɪəwə, loc.+ˈaɪəˌwe
I P A ˈaɪˌpiˈe, ˌɪntɚˈnæʃən] foˈnɛtɪk əˌsosɪ-
ˌeʃən, əˌsoʃɪ-; ES ˌɪntə-; cf A P I
ipecac ˈɪpɪˌkæk |-uanha -juˈænə
Iphigenia ˌɪfədʒɪˈnaɪə, mod. name -ˈdʒinjə
ipse dixit ˈɪpsɪˈdɪksɪt
ipso facto ˈɪpsoˈfækto
Ipswich ˈɪpswɪtʃ |-ˈs -ɪz
Iquique iˈkike
iracund ˈaɪrəˌkʌnd
irade iˈradɪ
Iran aɪˈræn, iˈran |-ian aɪˈrenɪən
Iraq iˈrak |-i -ɪ
Iras ˈaɪrəs |-ˈs -ɪz
irascibility aɪˌræsəˈbɪlətɪ, ɪˌræsə-
irascible aɪˈræsəbl̩, ɪˈræsə- |-bly -blɪ
irate ˈaɪret, aɪˈret (ˈirate ˈforeman)
ire aɪr; ES aɪə(r; |-ful -fəl |-fully -fəlɪ
Iredell ˈaɪrdɛl; ES ˈaɪə-
Ireland ˈaɪrlənd; ES ˈaɪələnd
Irenaeus ˌaɪrəˈniəs |-ˈs -ɪz
Irene aɪˈrin, myth. aɪˈrini
irenic aɪˈrɛnɪk, -rinɪk |-al -l̩ |-ally -l̩ɪ, -ɪklɪ
iridaceous ˌaɪrɪˈdeʃəs, ˌɪrɪ-
iridesce ˌɪrəˈdɛs |-s -ɪz |-d -t
iridescence ˌɪrəˈdɛsn̩s |-cy -ɪ |-ent -sn̩t
iridium aɪˈrɪdɪəm, ɪ-
Irion ˈɪrɪən, -ɑn, -ɒn
iris, I- ˈaɪrɪs |-es -ɪz |-ed -t
Irish ˈaɪrɪʃ |-man -mən |-men -mən |-woman
-ˌwumən, -ˌwu- |-women -ˌwɪmɪn, -ən

---

iritis aɪ'raɪtɪs |-tic -'rɪtɪk

irk ɜ˞k; ES ɜk, ɜ˞k; |-ed -t |-some -səm

Irkutsk ɪr'kʊtsk; ES ɪə-

Irma 'ɜ˞mə; ES 'ɜmə, 'ɜ˞mə

iron, I- 'aɪə˞n; ES 'aɪ·ən |-ed -d

ironclad 'aɪə˞n'klæd; ES 'aɪ·ən-; ('iron‚clad 'shoe)

iron-gray, -grey 'aɪə˞n'gre; ES 'aɪ·ən-; ('iron‚gray 'hair)

ironic aɪ'rɑnɪk; ES+-'rɒn-; |-al -l̩ |-ally -l̩ɪ, -ɪklɪ

ironmonger 'aɪə˞n‚mʌŋgə˞; ES 'aɪ·ən‚mʌŋgə(r; |-y -gərɪ, -grɪ

ironside, I- 'aɪə˞n‚saɪd; ES 'aɪ·ən-; |-s -z

ironsmith 'aɪə˞n‚smɪθ; ES 'aɪ·ən-; |-ths -θs

ironstone 'aɪə˞n‚ston; ES 'aɪ·ən-

ironware 'aɪə˞n‚wɛr, -‚wær; E 'aɪ·ən‚wɛə(r, ES -‚wæə(r

ironwork 'aɪə˞n‚wɜ˞k; ES 'aɪ·ən‚wɜk, 'aɪ·ən-‚wɜ˞k

irony 'like iron' 'aɪə˞nɪ; ES 'aɪ·ənɪ

irony kind of humor 'aɪrənɪ

Iroquoian ‚ɪrə'kwɔɪən

Iroquois 'ɪrə‚kwɔɪ, -‚kwɔɪz |-'s -‚kwɔɪz, -‚kwɔɪzɪz

irradiance ɪ'redɪəns |-cy -ɪ |-ant -ənt

irradiate ɪ'redɪ‚et |-ated -‚etɪd |-tive -ɪv

irradiation ‚ɪredɪ'eʃən, ɪ‚redɪ-

irrational ɪ'ræʃənl̩, ɪr'ræʃ-; ES ɪ'r-, ɪə'r-; |-ly -ɪ

irrationality ɪ‚ræʃə'nælətɪ, ‚ɪrræʃə-; ES ɪ‚ræʃə-, ‚ɪəræʃə-

Irrawaddy ‚ɪrə'wɑdɪ, -'wɒdɪ

irreclaimability ‚ɪrɪ‚klemə'bɪlətɪ, ‚ɪrrɪ-; ES ‚ɪrɪ-, ‚ɪərɪ-

irreclaimable ‚ɪrɪ'klem[bl̩, ‚ɪrrɪ-; ES ‚ɪrɪ-, ‚ɪərɪ-; |-bly -blɪ

irreconcilability ɪ‚rɛkən‚saɪlə'bɪlətɪ, ɪr‚rɛk-; ES ɪ‚rɛk-, ɪə‚rɛk-

irreconcilable ɪ'rɛkən‚saɪləbl̩, ɪr'rɛk-; ES ɪ'rɛk-, ɪə'rɛk-; emph.+‚irrecon'cilable |-bly -blɪ

irrecoverable ‚ɪrɪ'kʌvərəbl̩, ‚ɪrrɪ-, -vrə-; ES ‚ɪrɪ-, ‚ɪərɪ-; |-bly -blɪ

irredeemable ‚ɪrɪ'dimɘbl̩, ‚ɪrrɪ-; ES ‚ɪrɪ-, ‚ɪərɪ-; |-bly -blɪ

Irredentist ‚ɪrɪ'dɛntɪst

irreducible ‚ɪrɪ'djusəbl̩, ‚ɪrrɪ-, -'dɪus-, -'dus-; ES ‚ɪrɪ-, ‚ɪərɪ-; |-bly -blɪ

irrefragability ɪ‚rɛfrəgə'bɪlətɪ, ɪr‚rɛf-; ES ɪ‚rɛf-, ‚ɪə‚rɛf-

irrefragable ɪ'rɛfrəgəbl̩, ɪr'rɛf-; ES ɪ'rɛf-, ɪə'rɛf-; |-bly -blɪ

irrefutability ɪ‚rɛfjutə'bɪlətɪ, ɪr‚rɛf-, ‚ɪrɪ-‚fjutə-, ‚ɪrrɪ-, -‚fɪutə-; ES ɪ‚rɛf-, ɪə‚rɛf-, ‚ɪrɪ‚f-, ‚ɪərɪ‚f-

irrefutable ɪ'rɛfjutəbl̩, ɪr'rɛf-, ‚ɪrɪ'fjutəbl̩, ‚ɪrrɪ-, -'fɪutə-; ES ɪ'rɛf-, ɪə'rɛf-, ‚ɪrɪ'f-, ‚ɪərɪ'f-

irregular ɪ'rɛgjələ˞, ɪr'rɛg-; ES ɪ'rɛgjələ(r, ɪə'rɛg-

irregularity ‚ɪregjə'lærətɪ, ‚ɪrreg-, ɪ‚reg-, ɪr‚reg-; ES ‚ɪreg-, ‚ɪəreg-, ɪ‚reg-, ɪə‚reg-; |-lation -jə'leʃən

irrelative ɪ'rɛlətɪv, ɪr'rɛl-; ES ɪ'rɛl-, ɪə'rɛl-

irrelevance ɪ'rɛlɘvəns, ɪr'rɛl-; ES ɪ'rɛl-, ɪə'rɛl-; |-cy -ɪ |-ant -ənt

irreligion ‚ɪrɪ'lɪdʒən, ‚ɪrrɪ-; ES ‚ɪrɪ-, ‚ɪərɪ-; |-gious -dʒəs

irremediable ‚ɪrɪ'midɪəbl̩, ‚ɪrrɪ-; ES ‚ɪrɪ-, ‚ɪərɪ-; |-bly -blɪ

irremovability ‚ɪrɪ‚muvə'bɪlətɪ, ‚ɪrrɪ-; ES ‚ɪrɪ-, ‚ɪərɪ-

irremovable ‚ɪrɪ'muvəbl̩, ‚ɪrrɪ-; ES ‚ɪrɪ-, ‚ɪərɪ-; |-bly -blɪ

irreparability ‚ɪrɛpərə'bɪlətɪ, ‚ɪrrɛp-, ɪ‚rɛp-, ɪr‚rɛp-; ES ‚ɪrɛp-, ‚ɪərɛp-, ɪ‚rɛp-, ɪə‚rɛp-

irreparable ɪ'rɛpərəbl̩, ɪr'rɛp-; ES ɪ'rɛp-, ɪə'rɛp-; |-bly -blɪ

irrepealable ‚ɪrɪ'piləbl̩, ‚ɪrrɪ-; ES ‚ɪrɪ-, ‚ɪərɪ-; |-bly -blɪ

irreplaceable ‚ɪrɪ'plesəbl̩, ‚ɪrrɪ-; ES ‚ɪrɪ-, ‚ɪərɪ-; |-bly -blɪ

irrepressibility ‚ɪrɪ‚prɛsə'bɪlətɪ, ‚ɪrrɪ-; ES ‚ɪrɪ-, ‚ɪərɪ-

irrepressible ‚ɪrɪ'prɛsəbl̩, ‚ɪrrɪ-; ES ‚ɪrɪ-, ‚ɪərɪ-; |-bly -blɪ

irreproachable ‚ɪrɪ'protʃəbl̩, ‚ɪrrɪ-; ES ‚ɪrɪ-, ‚ɪərɪ-; |-bly -blɪ

irresistibility ‚ɪrɪ‚zɪstə'bɪlətɪ, ‚ɪrrɪ-; ES ‚ɪrɪ-, ‚ɪərɪ-

irresistible ‚ɪrɪ'zɪstəbl̩, ‚ɪrrɪ-; ES ‚ɪrɪ-, ‚ɪərɪ-; |-bly -blɪ

irresolute ɪ'rɛzə‚lut, ɪr'rɛz-, -‚lɪut, -'rɛz‚l̩jut; ES ɪ'rɛz-, ɪə'rɛz-

irresolution ‚ɪrɛzə'luʃən, ‚ɪrrɛz-, ɪ‚rɛz-, ɪr‚rɛz-, -'lɪu-, -z‚l̩'juʃən; ES ‚ɪrɛz-, ‚ɪərɛz-, ɪ‚rɛz-, ɪə‚rɛz-

|full fʊl |tooth tuθ |further 'fɝðɚ; ES 'fɜðə |custom 'kʌstəm |while hwaɪl |how haʊ |toy tɔɪ |using 'juzɪŋ |fuse fjuz, fɪuz |dish dɪʃ |vision 'vɪʒən |Eden 'idn̩ |cradle 'kredl̩ |keep 'em 'kipm̩

Those words below in which the ɑ sound is spelt o are often pronounced with ɒ in E and S

irresolvable ˌɪrɪˈzɑlvəbḷ, ˌɪrrɪ-, -ˈzɒlv-; ES ˌɪrɪ-, ˌɪərɪ-

irrespective ˌɪrɪˈspɛktɪv, ˌɪrrɪ-; ES ˌɪrɪ-, ˌɪərɪ-

irresponsibility ˌɪrɪˌspɑnsəˈbɪlətɪ, ˌɪrrɪ-; ES ˌɪrɪ-, ˌɪərɪ-

irresponsible ˌɪrɪˈspɑnsəbḷ, ˌɪrrɪ-; ES ˌɪrɪ-, ˌɪərɪ-; |-bly -blɪ

irresponsive ˌɪrɪˈspɑnsɪv, ˌɪrrɪ-; ES ˌɪrɪ-, ˌɪərɪ-

irretraceable ˌɪrɪˈtresəbḷ, ˌɪrrɪ-; ES ˌɪrɪ-, ˌɪərɪ-; |-bly -blɪ

irretrievability ˌɪrɪˌtrivəˈbɪlətɪ, ˌɪrrɪ-; ES ˌɪrɪ-, ˌɪərɪ-

irretrievable ˌɪrɪˈtrivəbḷ, ˌɪrrɪ-; ES ˌɪrɪ-, ˌɪərɪ-; |-bly -blɪ

irreverence ɪˈrɛvərəns, ɪrˈrɛv-; ES ɪˈrɛv-, ɪəˈrɛv-; |-ent -ənt

irreversibility ˌɪrɪˌvɝsəˈbɪlətɪ, ˌɪrrɪ-; ES ˌɪrɪˌvɝs-, -ˌvɝˑs-, ˌɪərɪ-

irreversible ˌɪrɪˈvɝsəbḷ, ˌɪrrɪ-; ES ˌɪrɪˈvɝs-, -ˈvɝˑs-, ˌɪərɪ-; |-bly -blɪ

irrevocability ɪˌrɛvəkəˈbɪlətɪ, ɪrˌrɛv-; ES ɪˌrɛv-, ɪəˌrɛv-

irrevocable ɪˈrɛvəkəbḷ, ɪrˈrɛv-; ES ɪˈrɛv-, ɪəˈrɛv-; |-bly -blɪ—*Cultivated speakers often pron.* ˌɪrɪˈvokəbḷ, *by confusion of* revocable *with* revokable.

irrigable ˈɪrɪgəbḷ |-bly -blɪ

irrigate ˈɪrəˌget |-d -ɪd |-tion ˌɪrəˈgeʃən

irritability ˌɪrətəˈbɪlətɪ

irritable ˈɪrətəbḷ |-bly -blɪ

irritant ˈɪrətənt

irritate ˈɪrəˌtet |-tated -ˌtetɪd |-tive -ɪv

irritation ˌɪrəˈteʃən

irruption ɪˈrʌpʃən |-tive -tɪv

Irvine ˈɝvɪn; ES ˈɝvɪn, ˈɝˑvɪn

Irving ˈɝvɪŋ; ES ˈɝvɪŋ, ˈɝˑvɪŋ |-ton -tən

Irwin ˈɝwɪn; ES ˈɝwɪn, ˈɝˑwɪn

is *stressed* ˈɪz, ˌɪz; *unstr. & sometimes spelt* 's: *after voiced sounds except sibilants* z; *after voiceless sounds except sibilants* s; *after the sibilants* (s, z, ʃ, ʒ, tʃ, dʒ) ɪz—*see* 's *& §88.*

Isaac ˈaɪzək |-s -s |-s's -sɪz

Isabel ˈɪzəˌbɛl, -bḷ |-la ˌɪzəˈbɛlə

Isadora ˌɪzəˈdorə, -ˈdɔrə; S -ˈdorə

isagoge ˈaɪsəˈgodʒɪ

isagogic ˌaɪsəˈgadʒɪk |-al -ḷ |-ally -ḷɪ, -ɪklɪ

Isaiah aɪˈzeə, aɪˈzaɪə

isatin ˈaɪsətɪn

Iscariot ɪsˈkærɪət

ischium ˈɪskɪəm |-ia -ɪə

Iseult ɪˈsult

Isfahan ˌɪsfəˈhɑn, -ˈhæn

-ish *adj ending* -ɪʃ—*often omitted when the pron. can be found by adding* -ɪʃ *to the head pronunciation*

Ishbosheth ɪʃˈbɒʃɪθ

Ishmael ˈɪʃmɪəl |-ite -ˌaɪt

Ishtar ˈɪʃtɑr; ES -tɑːr, E+-tɑːr

Isiac ˈaɪsɪˌæk

Isidore ˈɪzəˌdor, -ˌdɔr; S -ˌdor

Isidorian ˌɪzəˈdorɪən, -ˈdɔr-; S -ˈdor-

isinglass ˈaɪzɪŋˌglæs; E+-ˌglɑs, -ˌglɑs

Isis ˈaɪsɪs |Isis' ˈaɪsɪs

Islam ˈɪsləm, ɪsˈlɑm |-ic ɪsˈlæmɪk, -ˈlɑmɪk

Islamite ˈɪsləmˌaɪt |-tic ˌɪsləˈmɪtɪk

island ˈaɪlənd

isle aɪl |-d -d |-less ˈaɪllɪs

Isle Royale ˈaɪlˈrɔɪəl, -ˈrɔjəl

islet ˈaɪlɪt

Isleton ˈaɪltən

Isleworth ˈaɪzḷwəθ; ES -wəθ

Islington ˈɪzlɪŋtən

Islip *Oxf, LI* ˈaɪslɪp, *Northants*+ˈaɪz-

ism *n* ˈɪzəm

-ism *ending* -ɪzəm, -ɪzm̩—*The pron.* -ɪzm̩ *is less frequent, though the vowel in* -ɪzəm *is often very brief. In the vocab. only* -ɪzəm *is given, it being understood that* -ɪzm̩ *is also a possible pron. If the syllable before has the main accent, as in* ˈtruism, -ɪz- *has slightly more stress than* -əm, *though usually the accent mark is not used. If* -ism *follows an unaccented syllable, it has a secondary accent* (ˈlɪtərəlˌɪzəm, ˈfɛməˌnɪzəm, ˈfetḷˌɪzəm).

Ismail *Rus city, Egyp viceroy* ˌɪsmɑˈil

isn't ˈɪzn̩t, *before some conss.*+ˈɪzn̩ (There isn't time ˈðɚˌɪzn̩ˈtaɪm)

isobar ˈaɪsəˌbɑr; ES -ˌbɑːr, E+-ˌbɑːr

isobaric ˌaɪsəˈbærɪk

Isobel ˈɪzəbḷ, -ˌbɛl

isochromatic ˌaɪsəkroˈmætɪk

isochronal aɪˈsɑkrənḷ |-ly -ɪ |-nous -nəs

isochronize aɪˈsɑkrəˌnaɪz |-s -ɪz |-d -d

isoclinal ˌaɪsəˈklaɪnḷ |-clinic -ˈklɪnɪk

Key: *See in full §§3–47.* bee bi |pity ˈpɪtɪ (§6) |rate ret |yet jɛt |sang sæŋ |angry ˈæŋ·grɪ |bath bæθ; E baθ (§10) |ah ɑ |far fɑr |watch wɑtʃ, wɒtʃ (§12) |jaw dʒɔ |gorge gɔrdʒ |go go

Those words below in which the ɑ *sound is spelt* o *are often pronounced with* ɒ *in E and S*

isocline ˈaɪsəˌklaɪn
isocracy aɪˈsɑkrəsɪ
Isocrates aɪˈsɑkrəˌtiz |-ˈs -ɪz
isodynamic ˌaɪsədaɪˈnæmɪk |-al -ḷ
isoelectric ˌaɪsoˈɪˈlɛktrɪk |-ally -ḷɪ, -ɪklɪ
isogenous aɪˈsɑdʒənəs
isogeotherm ˌaɪsəˈdʒiəˌθɝˑm; ES -ˌθɝm, -ˌθɝˑm
isogonal aɪˈsɑgənḷ |-ly -ɪ |-gonic ˌaɪsəˈgɑnɪk
isolable ˈaɪsələbḷ, ˈɪs-
isolate ˈaɪsḷˌet, ˈɪs- |-ated -ˌetɪd |-tive - ɪv
isolation ˌaɪsḷˈeʃən, ˌɪs-
Isolda ɪˈsoldə, ɪˈzol-
Isolde ɪˈsold, ɪˈsoldə, ɪˈzol- (Ger iːˈzɔldə)
isomagnetic ˌaɪsəmægˈnɛtɪk
isomer ˈaɪsəmɚ; ES -mə(r
isomere ˈaɪsəˌmɪr; ES -ˌmɪə(r
isomeric ˌaɪsəˈmɛrɪk |-al -ḷ |-ally -ḷɪ, -ɪklɪ
isomerism aɪˈsɑməˌrɪzəm |-rous -rəs
isometric ˌaɪsəˈmɛtrɪk |-al -ḷ |-ally -ḷɪ, -ɪklɪ
isometry aɪˈsɑmətrɪ
isomorph ˈaɪsəˌmɔrf; ES -ˌmɔɔf
isomorphic ˌaɪsəˈmɔrfɪk; ES -ˈmɔɔfɪk; |-phism
   -fɪzəm |-phous -fəs
isopiestic ˌaɪsəpaɪˈɛstɪk |-ally -ḷɪ, -ɪklɪ
isopleth ˈaɪsəˌplɛθ |-ths -θs
isopod ˈaɪsəˌpɑd
isoprene ˈaɪsəˌprin
isosceles aɪˈsɑsḷˌiz
isoseismal ˌaɪsəˈsaɪzmḷ, -ˈsaɪs-
isoseismic ˌaɪsəˈsaɪzmɪk, -ˈsaɪs- |-al -ḷ
isostasy aɪˈsɑstəsɪ
isostatic ˌaɪsəˈstætɪk |-al -ḷ |-ally -ḷɪ, -ɪklɪ
isothere ˈaɪsəˌθɪr; ES -ˌθɪə(r
isotherm ˈaɪsəˌθɝˑm; ES -ˌθɝm, -ˌθɝˑm
isothermal ˌaɪsəˈθɝˑmḷ; ES -ˈθɝmḷ, -ˈθɝˑmḷ
isotonic ˌaɪsəˈtɑnɪk |-ity ˌaɪsətoˈnɪsətɪ
isotope ˈaɪsəˌtop |-pic ˌaɪsəˈtɑpɪk
isotrope ˈaɪsəˌtrop |-pic ˌaɪsəˈtrɑpɪk
isotropy aɪˈsɑtrəpɪ
Ispahan ˌɪspəˈhɑn, -ˈhæn
Israel ˈɪzrɪəl |-ite -ˌaɪt |-itish -ˌaɪtɪʃ
Issachar ˈɪsəkɚ; ES -kə(r
issuable ˈɪʃʊəbḷ, ˈɪʃjʊ- |-bly -blɪ
issuance ˈɪʃʊəns, ˈɪʃjʊ- |-s -ɪz |-ant -ənt
issue ˈɪʃʊ, ˈɪʃjʊ |-d -d—ˈɪʃju is mainly Brit.
Issus ˈɪsəs |Issus' ˈɪsəs
Istanbul ˌɪstanˈbul, ˌɪstɑm-
isthmus ˈɪsməs |-es -ɪz |-mian -mɪən

Istria ˈɪstrɪə |-n -n
it stressed ˈɪt, ˌɪt; unstr. ɪt or (spelt 't) t- —
   see 'tis, 't'll, 'twas, 'twere, 'twill, 'twould
Italian ɪˈtæljən, ə-, now less freq. aɪˈtæljən
Italianate adj ɪˈtæljənˌet, -ɪt
Italianate v ɪˈtæljənˌet |-ated -ˌetɪd
Italianize ɪˈtæljənˌaɪz |-s -ɪz |-d -d
italic, I- ɪˈtælɪk |-ally -ḷɪ, -ɪklɪ
italicize ɪˈtæləˌsaɪz |-s -ɪz |-d -d
Italy ˈɪtḷɪ
Itasca aɪˈtæskə
itch ɪtʃ |itches ˈɪtʃɪz |itched ɪtʃt
Itchen ˈɪtʃɪn, -ən
it'd 'it would' ˈɪtəd
item L adv ˈaɪtɛm
item n, v ˈaɪtəm |-ed -d
itemize ˈaɪtəmˌaɪz |-s -ɪz |-d -d
iterate ˈɪtəˌret |-d -ɪd |-tive -ɪv
iteration ˌɪtəˈreʃən
Ithaca ˈɪθəkə, ˈɪθɪkə
Ithamar ˈɪθəˌmar; ES -ˌmɑːr, E+-ˌmaːr
Ithunn, -un ˈɪðʊn=Idun
Ithuriel ɪˈθjʊrɪəl, ɪˈθɪʊrɪəl
itineracy aɪˈtɪnərəsɪ, ɪ- |-ancy -ənsɪ |-ant -ənt
itinerary aɪˈtɪnəˌrɛrɪ, ɪ-
itinerate aɪˈtɪnəˌret, ɪ- |-rated -ˌretɪd
it'll 'it will' ˈɪtḷ
its poss ɪts |it's 'it is,' 'it has' ɪts
itself ɪtˈsɛlf
-ity word ending (fatality, familiarity, au-
   thority) -ətɪ, -ɪtɪ. It seems clear that -ətɪ is
   the prevailing pron. in colloq. speech, -ɪtɪ is
   probably somewhat more common in the
   E & S than in the N.
-ius ending see -ia
Ivan ˈaɪvən
Ivanhoe ˈaɪvənˌho
I've 'I have' aɪv
-ive unstressed ending -ɪv—often omitted from
   the vocab. when its pron. may be added directly to that of the head word
Ives aɪvz |-'s -ɪz
ivory, I- ˈaɪvrɪ, ˈaɪvərɪ
ivy ˈaɪvɪ |-ied -d
iwis, y- ɪˈwɪs |erron. I wis aɪˈwɪs
Ixion ɪksˈaɪən
izard, I- ˈɪzɚd; ES ˈɪzəd
izzard ˈɪzɚd; ES ˈɪzəd

|full fʊl |tooth tuθ |further ˈfɝˑðɚ; ES ˈfɝˑðə |custom ˈkʌstəm |while hwaɪl |how haʊ |toy tɔɪ
|using ˈjuzɪŋ |fuse fjuz, fɪuz |dish dɪʃ |vision ˈvɪʒən |Eden ˈidn̩ |cradle ˈkredḷ |keep 'em ˈkipm̩

J

J, j *letter* dʒe |*pl* J's, Js, *poss* J's dʒez
jab dʒæb |jabbed dʒæbd
jabber 'dʒæbɚ; ES -bə(r; |-ed -d |-ing
   'dʒæbrɪŋ, 'dʒæbərɪŋ
Jabberwock 'dʒæbɚˌwak, -ˌwɒk; ES 'dʒæbə-
Jabesh-gilead 'dʒebɛʃ'gɪlɪəd
Jabez 'dʒebɪz |-'s -ɪz
jabot ʒæ'bo (*Fr* ʒa'bo)
jacinth 'dʒesɪnθ |-ths -θs
Jack, j- dʒæk |jacked dʒækt
jack-a-dandy ˌdʒækə'dændɪ
jackal 'dʒækɔl
jackanapes 'dʒækəˌneps |-napeses -ˌnepsɪz
jackass 'dʒækˌæs |-es -ɪz |-ed -t
jackdaw 'dʒækˌdɔ
jacket 'dʒækɪt |-ed -ɪd
jack-in-a-box 'dʒækɪnəˌbaks; ES+-ˌbɒks;
   |-es -ɪz
jack-in-the-box 'dʒækɪnðəˌbaks; ES+-ˌbɒks;
   |-es -ɪz
jack-in-the-pulpit 'dʒækɪnðə'pʊlpɪt
jackknife 'dʒækˌnaɪf |-knives -ˌnaɪvz
Jack-of-all-trades, j- ˌdʒækəv'ɔlˌtredz
jack-o'-lantern 'dʒækəˌlæntɚn, 'dʒækˌl-; ES
   -tən
jack-rabbit 'dʒækˌræbɪt
jackscrew 'dʒækˌskru, -ˌskrɪu
Jackson 'dʒæksn̩ |-ville -ˌvɪl; S+-vl̩
Jacksonian dʒæk'sonɪən
jackstay 'dʒækˌste
jackstraw 'dʒækˌstrɔ
jack-tar 'dʒæk'tɑr; ES -'tɑ:(r, E+-'tɑ:(r
Jacob 'dʒekəb, 'dʒekəp
Jacobean ˌdʒækə'bɪən ('Jacoˌbean 'style)
Jacobi *Am* dʒɚ'kobɪ, *various Germans* jɚ-
   'kobɪ (*Ger* jɑ'ko:bi:)
Jacobian dʒə'kobɪən, dʒe-
Jacobin 'dʒækəbɪn
Jacobinic ˌdʒækə'bɪnɪk |-al -l̩ |-ally -l̩ɪ, -ɪklɪ
Jacobite 'dʒækəˌbaɪt
Jacobitic ˌdʒækə'bɪtɪk |-al -l̩ |-ally -l̩ɪ, -ɪklɪ
jacobus dʒə'kobəs |-es -ɪz
jacoby 'dʒækəbɪ
Jacoby, *Harold* dʒə'kobɪ, *Johann* jɚ-
Jacquard, j- dʒə'kɑrd; ES -'kɑ:d, E+-'kɑ:d;
   (*Fr* ʒa'ka:r)
Jacqueline 'dʒækwəlɪn, -ˌlin

Jacquerie *Fr* ʒak'ri
jactation dʒæk'teʃən |-titation -tɪ'teʃən
jade dʒed |jaded 'dʒedɪd
jaeger, jäg- *bird* 'jegɚ, 'dʒe-, *rifleman* 'jegɚ;
   ES -gə(r; (*Ger* 'jɛːgər)
Jael 'dʒeəl
Jaffa 'dʒæfə
Jaffrey 'dʒæfrɪ
jag dʒæg |jagged dʒægd
jagged *adj* 'dʒægɪd
jagged-toothed 'dʒægɪd'tuθt, -ðd
jaguar 'dʒægwɑr, 'dʒægjʊˌɑr; ES -wɑ:(r, -ˌɑ:(r
Jahveh 'javɛ |-vism -vɪzəm |-vist -vɪst
   |-vistic jɑ'vɪstɪk
Jahweh 'jawɛ |-wism -wɪzəm |-wist -wɪst
   |-wistic jɑ'wɪstɪk
jail dʒel |jailed dʒeld |-er -ɚ; ES -ə(r; *cf* gaol
jailbird 'dʒelˌbɚd; ES -ˌbɝd, -ˌbɝd
Jain dʒaɪn |-a -ə |-ism -ɪzəm |-ist -ɪst
Jaipur dʒaɪ'pʊr; ES -'pʊə(r; *acct+*'Jaipur
Jairus dʒe'aɪrəs, 'dʒeərəs |-'s -ɪz
jalap 'dʒæləp
Jalna 'dʒɑlnə
jalopy dʒə'lɑpɪ; ES+-'lɒpɪ
jalousie ˌʒælʊ'zi (*Fr* ʒalu'zi)
jam dʒæm |jammed dʒæmd
Jam dʒɑm
Jamaica dʒə'mekə |-n -n
jamb, -e dʒæm
jambeau 'dʒæmbo |-x -z
jamboree ˌdʒæmbə'ri
James dʒemz |-ian -ɪən |-'s -ɪz
Jameson 'dʒemsn̩
Jamestown 'dʒemzˌtaʊn
Jamestown weed 'dʒɪmsn̩ˌwid
Jamieson 'dʒeməsn̩
Jamy 'dʒemɪ
Jan dʒæn
Jane dʒen
Janeiro dʒə'nɪro, -'nero (*Pg* ʒa'nɛirʊ)
Janesville 'dʒenzvɪl
Janet *fem. name* 'dʒænɪt, dʒə'nɛt; *Fr writer*
   ʒə'ne (*Fr* ʒa'nɛ)
jangle 'dʒæŋgl̩ |-d -d |-ling 'dʒæŋglɪŋ, -gl̩ɪŋ
Janice 'dʒænɪs |-'s -ɪz
Janicula dʒə'nɪkjələ
Janiculum dʒə'nɪkjələm

janitor 'dʒænətɚ; ES -tə(r; |-ed -d |-ing
  'dʒænətərɪŋ, -trɪŋ
Janizary 'dʒænəˌzɛrɪ
Jansen 'dʒænsn̩ |-ism -ˌɪzəm |-ist -ɪst
January 'dʒænjuˌɛrɪ, 'dʒænjʊərɪ
Janus 'dʒenəs |-'s -ɪz
Jap dʒæp
Japan, j- dʒə'pæn, dʒæ- |-ned -d
Japanese ˌdʒæpə'niz ('Japaˌnese 'beetle)
jape dʒep |japed dʒept
Japhet 'dʒefɪt
Japheth 'dʒefɪθ, -fɪt
Japhetic dʒə'fɛtɪk, dʒe-
Jaqueline 'dʒækwəlɪn, -ˌlin
Jaquenetta ˌdʒækwə'nɛtə, ˌdʒækə-
Jaques surname dʒæks, dʒeks; in Shak.
  'dʒekwɪz, -kwɪz |-'s -ɪz
jar dʒɑr; ES dʒɑ:(r, E+dʒa:(r; |-red -d
jardiniere ˌdʒɑrdn̩'ɪr; E ˌdʒɑ:dn̩'ɪə(r, ˌdʒa:d-;
  S ˌdʒɑ:dn̩'ɪə(r, -'ɛə(r; (Fr ʒardi'njɛːr)
Jared 'dʒerɪd
jarful 'dʒɑrˌful; ES 'dʒɑ:-, E+'dʒa:-; |-s -z
jargon 'dʒɑrgən, -gɑn, -gɒn |-ed -d
jarl jɑrl; ES jɑ:l, E+ja:l; |-ess -ɪs
jarless 'without jar' 'dʒɑrlɪs; ES 'dʒɑ:-,
  E+'dʒa:-
jarovize 'jɑrəˌvaɪz |-s -ɪz |-d -d
Jarrow 'dʒæro, -ə
Jarvis 'dʒɑrvɪs; ES 'dʒɑ:-, E+'dʒa:-; |-'s -ɪz
jasmine, -min 'dʒæsmɪn, 'dʒæz-
Jason 'dʒesn̩
jasper, J- 'dʒæspɚ; ES 'dʒæspə(r; |-ed -d
Jassy 'jɑsɪ, 'dʒæsɪ
Jastrow 'dʒæstro
jaundice 'dʒɔndɪs, 'dʒɒn-, 'dʒɑn- |-s -ɪz |-d -t
jaunt dʒɔnt, dʒɒnt, dʒɑnt |-ed -ɪd |-y -ɪ
Java 'dʒɑvə |-n -n
Javan Bible 'dʒevən, 'dʒevæn
Javanese ˌdʒævə'niz ('Javaˌnese 'people)
javelin 'dʒævlɪn |-ed -d
jaw dʒɔ |jawed dʒɔd
jawbone 'dʒɔ'bon, -ˌbon
jawbreaker 'dʒɔˌbrekɚ; ES -ˌbrekə(r
jay, J- dʒe
jayhawk 'dʒeˌhɔk |-ed -t |-er -ɚ; ES -ə(r
jaywalk 'dʒeˌwɔk |-ed -t |-er -ɚ; ES -ə(r
jazz dʒæz |jazzes 'dʒæzɪz |-ed -d |-ily -ˌɪ, -ɪlɪ
Jeaffreson 'dʒɛfɚsn̩; ES 'dʒɛfəsn̩
jealous 'dʒɛləs |y -ɪ

Jeames dʒimz |-'s -ɪz
Jean Eng name dʒin, Fr name ʒɑ̃
jean cloth dʒin, dʒen
Jeanne Eng name dʒin, Fr name ʒɑːn
Jeanne d'Arc Fr ʒɑːn'dark
Jeannette dʒə'nɛt
Jeans dʒinz |-'s -ɪz
Jebusite 'dʒɛbjuˌzaɪt |-sitic ˌdʒɛbju'zɪtɪk
Jedburgh 'dʒɛdˌbɝo, -ə; ES -ˌbɜr, -ˌbʌr-,
  -ˌbɝ-; Brit 'dʒɛdbərə
Jedediah ˌdʒɛdɪ'daɪə
jeer dʒɪr; ES dʒɪə(r, S+dʒɛə(r; |-ed -d
Jefferies 'dʒɛfrɪz |-ries' -rɪz
Jefferson 'dʒɛfɚsn̩; ES 'dʒɛfəsn̩
Jeffersonian ˌdʒɛfɚ'sonɪən; ES ˌdʒɛfə-
Jeffrey, -fferey 'dʒɛfrɪ
Jeffreys 'dʒɛfrɪz |-reys' -rɪz
Jeffries 'dʒɛfrɪz |-ries' -rɪz
jehad dʒɪ'hɑd
Jehoiakim dʒɪ'hɔɪəˌkɪm
Jehoram dʒɪ'horəm, -'hɔr-; S -'horəm
Jehoshaphat dʒɪ'hɑʃəˌfæt, -'hɑs-; ES+-'hɒ-
Jehovah dʒɪ'hovə
Jehu 'dʒihju, -hɪu
jejune dʒɪ'dʒun, -'dʒɪun ('jeˌjune 'diet)
jejunum dʒɪ'dʒunəm, -'dʒɪunəm
Jekyll 'dʒikl̩, 'dʒɛkl̩
jelly 'dʒɛlɪ |-ied -d |-fish -ˌfɪʃ
Jemima dʒə'maɪmə
jemmy, J- 'dʒɛmɪ
Jena 'jenə
Jenghiz Khan, -is 'dʒɛn·gɪz'kɑn, 'dʒɛŋgɪz-
Jenkins 'dʒɛŋkɪnz |-'s -ɪz
Jenner 'dʒɛnɚ; ES 'dʒɛnə(r
jennet 'dʒɛnɪt
Jenny, j- 'dʒɛnɪ
jeopard 'dʒɛpɚd; ES 'dʒɛpəd; |-ed -ɪd |-y -ɪ
jeopardize 'dʒɛpɚdˌaɪz; ES 'dʒɛpəd-; |-s -ɪz
  |-d -d
Jephtha 'dʒɛfθə, 'dʒɛpθə
Jerauld dʒə'rɔld
jerboa dʒɚ'boə; ES dʒə'boə
jeremiad ˌdʒɛrə'maɪəd, -æd
Jeremiah ˌdʒɛrə'maɪə
Jeremy 'dʒɛrəmɪ
Jericho 'dʒɛrəˌko
Jeritza 'jɛrɪtsə
jerk dʒɝk; ES dʒɝk, dʒɝk; |-ed -t
jerkin 'dʒɝkɪn; ES 'dʒɝk-, 'dʒɝk-; |-ed -d

Those words below in which the ɑ *sound is spelt* o *are often pronounced with* ɒ *in E and S*

Jeroboam, j- ˌdʒɛrə'boəm

Jerome dʒə'rom, 'dʒɛrəm

Jerrold 'dʒɛrəld

Jerry, j- 'dʒɛrɪ

jerry-build 'dʒɛrɪˌbɪld |-built -ˌbɪlt

Jersey, j- 'dʒɝ˞zɪ; ES 'dʒɝzɪ, 'dʒɝ˞zɪ; |-ed -d

Jerusalem dʒə'rusələm, -'rɪu-

Jervaulx *Yks* 'dʒɑrvɪs, 'dʒɝ˞vo; ES 'dʒɑ:vɪs, 'dʒɝvo, 'dʒɝ˞vo, E+'dʒɑ:vɪs; |-'s -ɪsɪz, -voz

Jervis 'dʒɝ˞vɪs, 'dʒɑrvɪs; ES 'dʒɝvɪs, 'dʒɝ˞v-, 'dʒɑ:v-, E+'dʒɑ:v-; |-'s -ɪz

Jervois *Austral* 'dʒɝ˞vɪs; ES 'dʒɝv-, 'dʒɝ˞v-

Jeshurun 'dʒɛʃjurən, 'dʒɛʃu-

Jespersen 'jɛspɚsn̩; ES 'jɛspəsn̩

jess dʒɛs |jesses 'dʒɛsɪz |jessed dʒɛst

jessamine, J- 'dʒɛsəmɪn

Jesse 'dʒɛsɪ |Jessie 'dʒɛsɪ |-sica 'dʒɛsɪkə

Jessopp, Jessup 'dʒɛsəp

jest dʒɛst |jested 'dʒɛstɪd

Jesu 'dʒizju, 'dʒis-, -ɪu, -u

Jesuit 'dʒɛʒʊɪt, 'dʒɛzju- |-ry -rɪ

Jesuitic, j- ˌdʒɛʒʊ'ɪtɪk, ˌdʒɛzju- |-al -l̩ |-ally -l̩ɪ, -ɪklɪ

Jesup 'dʒɛsəp

Jesus 'dʒizəs |-sus' -zəs

jet dʒɛt |jetted 'dʒɛtɪd

jet-black 'dʒɛt'blæk ('jet-ˌblack 'eyes)

Jethro 'dʒɛθro

jetsam 'dʒɛtsəm

jettison 'dʒɛtəsn̩, -zn̩ |-ed -d

jetty 'dʒɛtɪ |jettied 'dʒɛtɪd

jeu d'esprit *Fr* ʒødɛs'pri

Jevons 'dʒɛvənz |-'s -ɪz

Jew dʒu, dʒɪu |-ess -ɪs |-ry -rɪ

jewel, J- 'dʒuəl, 'dʒɪuəl |-ry -rɪ

Jewett 'dʒuɪt, 'dʒɪuɪt

jew's-harp 'dʒuzˌharp, 'dʒus-, 'dʒɪu-; ES -ˌhɑ:p, E+-ˌhɑ:p; 'dʒusˌharp *preserves a regular old form, dissociated from* Jew's.

Jezebel 'dʒɛzəbl̩

Jezreel 'dʒɛzrɪəl, dʒɛz'ril |-ite 'dʒɛzrɪəlˌaɪt

jib dʒɪb |jibbed dʒɪbd

jibber 'dʒɪbɚ; ES -ə(r; |-ed -d |-ing -bərɪŋ, -brɪŋ

jibboom 'dʒɪb'bum

jibe dʒaɪb |jibed dʒaɪbd

jiffy 'dʒɪfɪ

jig dʒɪg |jigged dʒɪgd

jigger 'dʒɪgɚ; ES -ə(r; |-ed -d |-ing -ɪŋ, -grɪŋ

jiggle 'dʒɪgl̩ |-d -d |-ling 'dʒɪglɪŋ, -gl̩ɪŋ

jigsaw 'dʒɪgˌsɔ |-ed -d

jihad dʒɪ'had

Jill dʒɪl

jilt dʒɪlt |jilted 'dʒɪltɪd

Jim dʒɪm

jimjams 'dʒɪmˌdʒæmz

jimmy, J- 'dʒɪmɪ |-ied -d

Jimson weed 'dʒɪmsn̩ˌwid

Jinghis Khan 'dʒɪn·gɪz'kan, 'dʒɪŋgɪz-

jingle 'dʒɪŋgl̩ |-d -d |-ling 'dʒɪŋglɪŋ, -gl̩ɪŋ

jingo 'dʒɪŋgo |-ed -d |-ism -ˌɪzəm

jink dʒɪŋk |jinked dʒɪŋkt

jinn *pl* dʒɪn

jinnee, -nni dʒɪ'ni |*pl* jinn dʒɪn

jinniyeh dʒɪ'nijɛ |*pl* jinn dʒɪn

jinricksha, -rikisha dʒɪn'rɪkʃə, -ʃə

jinx dʒɪŋks |jinxes 'dʒɪŋksɪz |jinxed dʒɪŋkst

jitney 'dʒɪtnɪ

jitters 'dʒɪtɚz; ES 'dʒɪtəz; |-ery -ərɪ

jiujitsu, jiujutsu dʒu'dʒɪtsu, dʒɪu-

Joab 'dʒoæb

Joachim, -akim *Bible* 'dʒoəˌkɪm, *violinist* 'joəˌkɪm (*Ger* jo'ɑxɪm)

Joan dʒon, 'dʒoən, dʒo'æn—dʒo'æn *is a spelling pron., not used by those familiar with the traditional pron.*

Joanna dʒo'ænə

Joan of Arc 'dʒonəv'ɑrk, dʒo'æn-; ES -'ɑ:k, E+-'ɑ:k;—*see* Joan

Joaquin hwa'kin (*Am Sp* hwa-)

job dʒab |-bed -d |-ber -ɚ; ES -ə(r

Job dʒob

Jobson 'dʒabsn̩, 'dʒob-

Jocasta dʒo'kæstə

Jocelin, -ine, -lyn 'dʒaslɪn, 'dʒasəlɪn

Jock dʒak

jockey 'dʒakɪ |-ed -d

jocko 'dʒako

jocose dʒo'kos |-sity -'kasətɪ

jocular 'dʒakjəlɚ; ES -lə(r; |-ity ˌdʒakjə-'lærətɪ

jocund 'dʒakənd, -ʌnd |-ity dʒo'kʌndətɪ

jodel 'jodl̩ |-ed -d |-ing 'jodlɪŋ, 'jodl̩ɪŋ

Jodhpur dʒod'pur; ES -'puə(r; *acct+*'Jodhpur

jodhpurs 'dʒadpɚz, 'dʒod-; ES -pəz

Joe dʒo

Key: *See in full* §§3–47. bee bi |pity 'pɪtɪ (§6) |rate ret |yet jɛt |sang sæŋ |angry 'æŋ·grɪ |bath bæθ; E baθ (§10) |ah ɑ |far fɑr |watch watʃ, wɒtʃ (§12) |jaw dʒɔ |gorge gɔrdʒ |go go

Those words below in which the ɑ sound is spelt o are often pronounced with ɒ in E and S

Joel 'dʒoəl
Joffre *Fr* ʒɔ́fṛ
jog dʒɑg |jogged dʒɑgd
joggle 'dʒɑgḷ |-d -d |-ling 'dʒɑglɪŋ, -gḷɪŋ
Johanna dʒo'hænə
Johannes, j- dʒo'hæniz |-es' -iz
Johannesburg dʒo'hænɪsˌbɝg, jo-; ES -ˌbɜg,
    -ˌbɝg
John dʒɑn, dʒɒn |-ian 'dʒoniən
johnnycake 'dʒɑnɪˌkek
Johnny-jump-up 'dʒɑnɪ'dʒʌmpˌʌp
Johnson 'dʒɑnsṇ |-ese ˌdʒɑnsṇ'iz
Johnsonian dʒɑn'soniən
Johnston 'dʒɑnstən
Johnstown 'dʒɑnzˌtaʊn
joie-de-vivre *Fr* ʒwadə'vivṛ
join dʒɔɪn |-ed -d
joinder 'dʒɔɪndɚ; ES 'dʒɔɪndə(r
joiner 'dʒɔɪnɚ; ES 'dʒɔɪnə(r; |-ed -d |-y -ɪ
joint dʒɔɪnt |-ed -ɪd |-ress -rɪs |-resses -rɪsɪz
joint-stock 'dʒɔɪnt'stɑk ('joint-ˌstock 'bank)
jointure 'dʒɔɪntʃɚ; ES 'dʒɔɪntʃə(r; |-d -d
joist dʒɔɪst, dʒɔɪs |-joists dʒɔɪsts, dʒɔɪs:
joke dʒok |joked dʒokt
Joliet *Ill* 'dʒolɪˌɛt, -ət, ˌdʒolɪ'ɛt, -ɑl-
Jolliet, Joli- *explorer* 'dʒolɪˌɛt, -ət, ˌdʒolɪ'ɛt,
    -ɑl- (*Fr* ʒɔ́'ljɛ)
jollification ˌdʒɑləfə'keʃən
jollify 'dʒɑləˌfaɪ |-fied -ˌfaɪd
jolly 'dʒɑlɪ |jollity 'dʒɑlətɪ
jolt dʒolt |jolted 'dʒoltɪd
Jon dʒɑn
Jonah 'dʒonə
Jonas 'dʒonəs |-'s -ɪz
Jonathan 'dʒɑnəθən
Jones dʒonz |-'s -ɪz
jonglery 'dʒʌŋglərɪ
jongleur 'dʒʌŋglɚ; ES 'dʒʌŋglə(r; (*Fr* ʒɔ̃-
    'glœ:r)
jonquil 'dʒɑŋkwɪl, 'dʒɑn-
Jonson 'dʒɑnsṇ |-ian dʒɑn'soniən
Joplin 'dʒɑplɪn
Joppa 'dʒɑpə
Jordan 'dʒɔrdṇ; ES 'dʒɔədṇ
jorum 'dʒorəm, 'dʒɔr-; S 'dʒorəm
Joseph 'dʒozəf |-phine 'dʒozəˌfin
Josepha dʒo'sifə |-phus -fəs |-phus's -fəsɪz
josh dʒɑʃ |joshes 'dʒɑʃɪz |joshed dʒɑʃt

Joshua 'dʒɑʃuə, *o.f.* 'dʒɑʃəˌwe
Josiah dʒo'saɪə
joss dʒɑs, dʒɒs |-es -ɪz
jostle 'dʒɑsḷ |-d -d |-ling 'dʒɑslɪŋ, -sḷɪŋ
jot dʒɑt |jotted 'dʒɑtɪd
Jotunn, -un 'jɔtʊn, 'jɒt- |-heim -ˌhem
Joule dʒaʊl, dʒul, dʒol |joule dʒaʊl, dʒul
jounce dʒaʊns |jounces 'dʒaʊnsɪz |-d -t
Jourdain *Shak.* dʒʊr'den; ES dʒʊə-; *Fr name*
    ʒur'dæ̃
journal 'dʒɝnḷ; ES 'dʒɜnḷ, 'dʒɝnḷ; |-ed -d
    |-ism -ˌɪzəm |-ist -ɪst
journalese ˌdʒɝnḷ'iz, -'is; ES ˌdʒɜnḷ-, ˌdʒɝnḷ-
journalistic ˌdʒɝnḷ'ɪstɪk; ES ˌdʒɜnḷ-, ˌdʒɝnḷ-;
    |-ally -ḷɪ, -ɪklɪ
journalize 'dʒɝnḷˌaɪz; ES 'dʒɜnḷ-, 'dʒɝnḷ-;
    |-s -ɪz |-d -d
journey 'dʒɝnɪ; ES 'dʒɜnɪ, 'dʒɝnɪ; |-ed -d
    |-man -mən |-men -mən
joust dʒʌst, dʒaʊst |-ed -ɪd
Jove dʒov |Jovian 'dʒoviən
jovial 'dʒovjəl, -vɪəl |-ity ˌdʒovɪ'ælətɪ
Jovinian dʒo'vɪnɪən
Jowett 'dʒaʊɪt
jowl dʒaʊl, dʒol |-ed -d
joy dʒɔɪ |-ed -d |-ful -fəl |-fully -fəlɪ |-ous -əs
Joyce dʒɔɪs |-'s -ɪz
Juab 'dʒuæb, 'dʒɪuæb
Juan 'dʒuən, 'dʒɪuən (*Sp* xwan)
Juanita wɔ'nitə, wɒ-, wɑ- (*Sp* xwa'nita)
Juarez, Juárez 'hwɑres (*Am Sp* 'hwares)
Jubal 'dʒubḷ, 'dʒɪubḷ
jubilance 'dʒubḷəns, 'dʒɪu- |-cy -ɪ |-ant -ənt
jubilate 'dʒubḷˌet, 'dʒɪu- |-d -ɪd
Jubilate ˌdʒubə'leti, ˌdʒɪu-
jubilation ˌdʒubḷ'eʃən, ˌdʒɪu-
jubilee 'dʒubḷˌi, 'dʒɪu-
Judaea dʒu'diə, dʒɪu- |-n -n
Judah 'dʒudə, 'dʒɪudə
Judaic dʒu'de·ɪk, dʒɪu- |-al -ḷ |-ally -ḷɪ, -ɪklɪ
Judaism 'dʒudɪˌɪzəm, 'dʒɪu-
judaize 'dʒudɪˌaɪz, 'dʒɪu- |-s -ɪz |-d -d
Judas 'dʒudəs, 'dʒɪu- |-'s -ɪz
Judd dʒʌd
Jude dʒud, dʒɪud
Judea dʒu'diə, dʒɪu- |-n -n
judge dʒʌdʒ |judges 'dʒʌdʒɪz |-d -d
judgement 'dʒʌdʒmənt

|full fʊl |tooth tuθ |further 'fɝðɚ; ES 'fɜðə |custom 'kʌstəm |while hwaɪl |how haʊ |toy tɔɪ
|using 'juzɪŋ |fuse fjuz, fɪuz |dish dɪʃ |vision 'vɪʒən |Eden 'idṇ |cradle 'kredḷ |keep 'em 'kipm̩

Judges 'dʒʌdʒɪz
judgeship 'dʒʌdʒʃɪp
judgmatic dʒʌdʒ'mætɪk |-al -ļ |-ally -ļɪ, -ɪklɪ
judgment 'dʒʌdʒmənt
judicable 'dʒudɪkəbļ, 'dʒɪu-
judicatory 'dʒudɪkə‚torɪ, 'dʒɪu-, -‚tɔrɪ; S -‚torɪ
judicature 'dʒudɪkətʃɚ, 'dʒɪu-; ES -tʃə(r
judiciable dʒu'dɪʃɪəbļ, dʒɪu-
judicial dʒu'dɪʃəl, dʒɪu- |-ly -ɪ
judiciary dʒu'dɪʃɪ‚ɛrɪ, dʒɪu-, -'dɪʃərɪ
judicious dʒu'dɪʃəs, dʒɪu-
Judith 'dʒudɪθ, 'dʒɪu-
Judson 'dʒʌdsn̩
Judy 'dʒudɪ, 'dʒɪudɪ
jug dʒʌg |jugged dʒʌgd
Juggernaut, j- 'dʒʌgɚ‚nɔt; ES 'dʒʌgə-; |-ed -ɪd
juggle 'dʒʌgļ |-d -d |-ling 'dʒʌglɪŋ, -gļɪŋ
jugglery 'dʒʌglərɪ
Jugoslav n 'jugo‚slav, -‚slæv
Jugoslav adj 'jugo'slav, -'slæv ('Jugo‚slav 'state)
Jugoslavia 'jugo'slavɪə, -vjə |-n -n
Jugoslavic ‚jugo'slavɪk, -'slæv-
jugular 'dʒʌgjələ, less freq. 'dʒug-; ES -lə(r
Jugurtha dʒu'gɝθə; ES -'gɜθə, -'gɝθə
juice dʒus, dʒɪus |-s -ɪz |-d -d |-cy -ɪ
jujitsu dʒu'dʒɪtsu, dʒɪu-
juju 'dʒudʒu |-ism -‚ɪzəm |-ist -ɪst
jujube 'dʒudʒub, 'dʒɪudʒɪub (Fr ʒy'ʒyb)
jujutsu dʒu'dʒɪtsu, dʒɪu-
Jukes dʒuks, dʒɪuks |-'s -ɪz
julep 'dʒulɪp, 'dʒɪu-, -ləp
Julia 'dʒuljə, 'dʒɪul- |-n -n
Juliana ‚dʒulɪ'ænə, ‚dʒɪul-, -jɪ'ænə
Julien 'dʒuljən, 'dʒɪuljən
julienne ‚dʒulɪ'ɛn, ‚dʒɪul-
Juliet 'dʒuljət, 'dʒɪul-, -lɪət—*The frequent modern pron.* ‚dʒulɪ'ɛt *has no basis in Shakespeare's verse. Of some 47 occurrences, 43 show only two syllables and initial accent; in the 4 cases of three syllables (all highly emotional) there is no evidence that the last syllable had more than secondary accent.*
Julius 'dʒuljəs, 'dʒɪul- |-'s -ɪz
July dʒu'laɪ, dʒɪu- ('Ju‚ly 'first)
jumble 'dʒʌmbļ |-d -d |-ling 'dʒʌmblɪŋ, -bļɪŋ
Jumbo, j- 'dʒʌmbo

jump dʒʌmp |jumped dʒʌmpt
junco, J- 'dʒʌŋko
junction 'dʒʌŋkʃən |-ed -d
juncture 'dʒʌŋktʃɚ; ES 'dʒʌŋktʃə(r
June dʒun, dʒɪun
Juneau 'dʒuno, 'dʒɪu-
Jungfrau 'juŋ‚frau
jungle 'dʒʌŋgļ |-d -d
Juniata ‚dʒunɪ'ætə, ‚dʒɪu-
junior 'dʒunjɚ, 'dʒɪun-; ES -jə(r
juniority dʒun'jɔrətɪ, dʒɪun-, -'jɑr-, -'jɒr-
juniper 'dʒunəpɚ, 'dʒɪun-; ES -pə(r
Junius 'djunjəs, 'dʒɪun-, -nɪəs |-'s -ɪz
junk dʒʌŋk |junked dʒʌŋkt
Junker, j- 'juŋkɚ; ES 'juŋkə(r
junket 'dʒʌŋkɪt |-ed -ɪd
Juno 'dʒuno, 'dʒɪuno
junta 'dʒʌntə |junto 'dʒʌnto
Jupiter 'dʒupətɚ, 'dʒɪu-; ES -tə(r
Jura 'dʒurə, 'dʒɪurə (Fr ʒy'ra)
jural 'dʒurəl, 'dʒɪur- |-ly -ɪ
jurant 'dʒurənt, 'dʒɪur-
jurassic dʒu'ræsɪk, dʒɪu-
jurat 'dʒuræt, 'dʒɪur-
juridical dʒu'rɪdɪkļ, dʒɪu- |-ly -ɪ, -ɪklɪ
jurisconsult ‚dʒurɪskən'sʌlt, ‚dʒɪur-, -'kan‑sʌlt; ES+-'kɒn-
jurisdiction ‚dʒurɪs'dɪkʃən, ‚dʒɪur- |-al -ļ |-ally -ļɪ
jurisprudence ‚dʒurɪs'prudn̩s, ‚dʒɪurɪs'prɪud-|-dent -dn̩t
jurist 'dʒurɪst, 'dʒɪur-
juristic dʒu'rɪstɪk, dʒɪu- |-al -ļ |-ally -ļɪ, -ɪklɪ
juror 'dʒurɚ, 'dʒɪurɚ; ES -rə(r
jury 'dʒurɪ, 'dʒɪurɪ |-man -mən |-men -mən
jury-rigged 'dʒurɪ‚rɪgd, 'dʒɪurɪ-
Jusserand Fr ʒy'srã
just dʒʌst, *lightly stressed adv often* dʒəst, dʒɛst
justice 'dʒʌstɪs |-s -ɪz |-d -t |-ship -‚ʃɪp
justiciable dʒʌs'tɪʃɪəbļ
justiciar dʒʌs'tɪʃɪɚ; ES -'tɪʃɪ‑ə(r
justiciary dʒʌs'tɪʃɪ‚ɛrɪ
justifiability ‚dʒʌstə‚faɪə'bɪlətɪ
justifiable 'dʒʌstə‚faɪəbļ |-bly -blɪ
justification ‚dʒʌstəfə'keʃən
justificatory dʒʌs'tɪfəkə‚torɪ, 'dʒʌstəfə‚ke‑tərɪ; EN+-‚tɔrɪ

Key: *See in full §§3–47.* bee **bi** |pity 'pɪtɪ (§6) |rate **ret** |yet jɛt |sang sæŋ |angry 'æŋ·grɪ |bath bæθ; E baθ (§10) |ah ɑ |far fɑr |watch watʃ, wɒtʃ (§12) |jaw dʒɔ |gorge gɔrdʒ |go **go**

justify ˈdʒʌstəˌfaɪ |-fied -ˌfaɪd
Justin ˈdʒʌstɪn |-ian dʒʌsˈtɪnɪən
Justus ˈdʒʌstəs |-'s -ɪz
jut dʒʌt |jutted ˈdʒʌtɪd
jute, J- dʒut, dʒɪut
Jutland ˈdʒʌtlənd

Juvenal ˈdʒuvənḷ, ˈdʒɪuv-
juvenescence ˌdʒuvəˈnɛsn̩s, ˌdʒɪu- |-ent -n̩t
juvenile ˈdʒuvənḷ, ˈdʒɪu-, -nɪl, -ˌnaɪl
juvenility ˌdʒuvəˈnɪlətɪ, ˌdʒɪu-
juxtapose ˌdʒʌkstəˈpoz |-s -ɪz |-d -d
juxtaposition ˌdʒʌkstəpəˈzɪʃən |-al -ḷ

K

K, k *letter* ke |*pl* K's, Ks, *poss* K's kez
Kaaterskill ˈkɔtɚzˌkɪl, ˈkat-; ES -təz-
Kabul ˈkɑbʊl
Kadesh-Barnea ˈkedɛʃˈbɑrnɪə; ES -ˈbɑ:n-,
  E+-ˈba:n-
Kaffir, Kafir ˈkæfɚ; ES ˈkæfə(r
Kahoka kəˈhokə
kaiser, K- ˈkaɪzɚ; ES ˈkaɪzə(r
Kalamazoo ˌkæləməˈzu
kale kel
kaleidoscope kəˈlaɪdəˌskop
kaleidoscopic kəˌlaɪdəˈskɑpɪk; ES+-ˈskɒp-;
  |-al -ḷ |-ally -ḷɪ, -ɪklɪ
kalends ˈkælɪndz, -əndz, -nz
Kalevala ˌkɑlɪˈvɑlə
Kalkaska kælˈkæskə
Kallyope '*calliope*' ˈkælɪˌop
Kalmuck, k-, -muk ˈkælmʌk
kalsomine ˈkælsəˌmaɪn |-d -d
Kama ˈkɑmə
Kamchatka kæmˈtʃætkə
Kamerun ˌkæməˈrun (*Ger* ˌkɑməˈru:n)
Kanaka kəˈnækə, ˈkænəkə
Kanawha kəˈnɔwə
Kanchanjanga ˌkʌntʃənˈdʒɑŋɡə
Kandahar ˌkændəˈhɑr, ˌkʌndə-; ES -ˈhɑ:(r
Kandy ˈkændɪ, ˈkan-
Kane ken
kangaroo ˌkæŋɡəˈru |-ed -d
Kankakee ˌkæŋkəˈki
Kansas ˈkænzəs, *rarely* -səs; S+-zɪs; |-an -ən
  |-sas' -əs, -ɪs
Kant kænt (*Ger* kɑnt) |-ian -ɪən |-ism -ɪzəm
  |-ianism -ɪənˌɪzəm
kaoliang ˌkɑolɪˈæŋ
kaolin, -ine ˈkeəlɪn
kapok ˈkepɑk, ˈkæpək; ES+-pɒk
kappa ˈkæpə

Karakoram ˌkɑrəˈkorəm, ˌkærə-; EN+
  -ˈkɔrəm
Karelia kəˈrilɪə
Karl kɑrl; ES kɑ:l, E+kɑ:l
Karlsbad ˈkɑrlzbæd; ES ˈkɑ:lz-, E+ˈkɑ:lz-;
  (*Ger* ˈkɑrlsbɑt)
Karlsruhe ˈkɑrlzruə; ES ˈkɑ:lz-, E+ˈkɑ:lz-;
  (*Ger* ˈkɑrlsru:ə, -ˈru:ə)
karma ˈkɑrmə, ˈkɝmə; ES ˈkɑ:mə, ˈkɜmə,
  ˈkɝmə; (*Hind* ˈkʌrmə)
Karnak ˈkɑrnæk; ES ˈkɑ:-, E+ˈkɑ:-
Karroo, Karoo, k- kəˈru, kæˈru
Kashmir *India* kæʃˈmɪr; ES -ˈmɪə(r; |-ian
  -ɪən
Kaskaskia kæsˈkæskɪə
Katahdin kəˈtɑdɪn, -dn̩
Kate, k- ket
Katharina ˌkæθəˈrinə
Katharine ˈkæθrɪn, ˈkæθərɪn
katharsis kəˈθɑrsɪs; ES -ˈθɑ:s-, E+-ˈθɑ:s-
Katherine ˈkæθrɪn, ˈkæθərɪn
Kathleen ˈkæθlin
kathode ˈkæθod
Kathrine ˈkæθrɪn, ˈkæθərɪn
Katrine ˈkætrɪn, ˈkætrin, *Sc* ˈkat-
Kattegat ˈkætɪˌgæt, ˌkætɪˈgæt
katydid ˈketɪˌdɪd |-dided -ˌdɪdɪd
Kauai ˈkɑ·uˈɑ·i
Kauffman ˈkɔfmən |Kaufman ˈkɔfmən (*Ger*
  ˈkaʊfmən)
Kaukauna kəˈkɔnə
Kavanagh ˈkævəˌnɔ, -nə
Kavanaugh ˈkævəˌnɔ, -nə
kay ke
Kay ke
kayak ˈkaɪæk
Kaye ke |Kaye-Smith ˈkeˈsmɪθ
Kazan kəˈzan

|full fʊl |tooth tuθ |further ˈfɝðɚ; ES ˈfɜðə |custom ˈkʌstəm |while hwaɪl |how haʊ |toy tɔɪ
|using ˈjuzɪŋ |fuse fjuz, fɪuz |dish dɪʃ |vision ˈvɪʒən |Eden ˈidn̩ |cradle ˈkredḷ |keep 'em ˈkipm̩

Kean, -e kin

Kearny, -ey ˈkɑrnɪ; ES ˈkɑːnɪ, E+ˈkɑːnɪ

Kearsarge ˈkɪrsɑrdʒ; ES ˈkɪəsɑːdʒ, E+ -sɑːdʒ; |-'s -ɪz

Keats kits |-'s -ɪz

Keble ˈkibl̩

Kedar ˈkidɚ; ES ˈkidə(r

kedge kɛdʒ |kedges ˈkɛdʒɪz |kedged kɛdʒd

kedgeree ˈkɛdʒəˌri, ˌkɛdʒəˈri

Kedron ˈkidrən

keel kil |keeled kild |-less ˈkillɪs

keelhaul ˈkilˌhɔl |-ed -d

keelson ˈkɛlsn̩, ˈkil-

keen kin |-ness ˈkinnɪs

Keene kin

keep kip |kept kɛpt |-sake ˈkipˌsek

Keewatin kiˈwɑtɪn, -ˈwɒt-

keg kɛg L.A. shows that keg & less freq. kæg are used by cultured informants.

Keighly Yks ˈkiθlɪ

Keightley ˈkitlɪ

Keijo ˈkeˈdʒo

Keith kiθ

Kellar, -er ˈkɛlɚ; ES ˈkɛlə(r

Kelley, -ly, k- ˈkɛlɪ |kellied ˈkɛlɪd

Kellogg ˈkɛləg, -ɑg, -ɒg

Kelmscot ˈkɛmskət (Kelm- *1274*, Kemscott *1695*), ˈkɛlm-

kelp kɛlp

kelpie, -py ˈkɛlpɪ

Kelsey ˈkɛlsɪ

Kelso ˈkɛlso

kelson ˈkɛlsn̩

Kelt kɛlt |-ist -ɪst

kelter ˈkɛltɚ; ES ˈkɛltə(r

Keltic ˈkɛltɪk |-ally -l̩ɪ, -ɪklɪ

Kelticism ˈkɛltəˌsɪzəm |-cist -sɪst

Kelvin ˈkɛlvɪn

Kemal kəˈmɑl, ˈkemɑl

kemb kɛm |kembed kɛmd or kempt kɛmpt

Kemble ˈkɛmbl̩

Kemmerer ˈkɛmərɚ; ES ˈkɛmərə(r

kemp, K- kɛmp

Kempis ˈkɛmpɪs |-'s -ɪz

ken kɛn |kenned kɛnd

Kendal, -ll ˈkɛndl̩ |-ville -ˌvɪl

Kenedy ˈkɛnədɪ

Kenelm ˈkɛnəlm, -ɛlm

Kenilworth ˈkɛnl̩ˌwɝθ; ES -ˌwɜθ, -ˌwɝθ

Kenmore US ˈkɛnmor, -mɔr; ES -moə(r, E+ -mɔə(r; Scotl Kenˈmore

Kennan ˈkɛnən

Kennebec ˌkɛnəˈbɛk (ˈKenneˌbec ˈRiver)

Kennebunk ˌkɛnəˈbʌŋk

Kennebunkport ˌkɛnəbʌŋkˈport -ˈpɔrt; ES -ˈpoət, E+-ˈpɔət

Kennedy ˈkɛnədɪ

kennel ˈkɛnl̩ |-ed -d |-ly ˈkɛnl̩ɪ

Kennerly ˈkɛnɚlɪ; ES ˈkɛnəlɪ

Kennesaw ˈkɛnəˌsɔ

Kenneth ˈkɛnɪθ

Kennett Square ˈkɛnɪtˈskwɛr, -ˈskwær; E -ˈskwɛə(r, ES -ˈskwæə(r

keno ˈkino

Kenora kəˈnorə, -ˈnɔrə; S -ˈnorə

Kenosha kəˈnoʃə

Kenova kəˈnovə

Kensington ˈkɛnzɪŋtən

Kent kɛnt |-ish -ɪʃ

Kenton ˈkɛntən

Kentucky kənˈtʌkɪ, loc.+kɛnˈtʌkɪ |-kian -ən

Kenya ˈkɛnjə, loc.+ˈkinjə

Kenyon ˈkɛnjən

Keokuk ˈkiəˌkʌk

kepi ˈkɛpɪ

Kepler ˈkɛplɚ; ES ˈkɛplə(r

kept kɛpt, before some conss.+kɛp (ˈkɛpˈtɔkɪŋ)

Ker, -rr kɝ, kɑr; ES kɜ(r, kɝ, kɑː(r, E+kɑː(r

keratin ˈkɛrətɪn

kerb kɝb; ES kɜb, kɝb; |-stone -ˌston

kerchief ˈkɝtʃɪf; ES ˈkɜ-, ˈkɝ-; |-s -s |-ed -t

kerf kɝf, kɑrf; ES kɜf, kɝf, kɑːf, E+kɑːf

kermes ˈkɝmiz; ES ˈkɜm-, ˈkɝm-

kermis, -mess ˈkɝmɪs; ES ˈkɜm-, ˈkɝm-; |-es -ɪz

kern kɝn; ES kɜn, kɝn; |-ed -d

Kernahan, -no- ˈkɝnəˌhæn, ˈkɑr-; ES ˈkɜ-, ˈkɝ-, ˈkɑː-, E+ˈkɑː-

kernel ˈkɝnl̩; ES ˈkɜnl̩, ˈkɝnl̩; |-ed -d

kernelless ˈkɝnl̩lɪs; ES ˈkɜn-, ˈkɝn-

kerosene ˈkɛrəˌsin, ˌkɛrəˈsin |-d -d

Kerr kɝ, kɑr; ES kɜ(r, kɝ, kɑː(r, E+kɑː(r

Kerry ˈkɛrɪ

kersey, K- ˈkɝzɪ; ES ˈkɜzɪ, ˈkɝzɪ

Kershaw kɝˈʃɔ; ES kɜ-, kɝ-

Kesteven Lincs ˈkɛstivən, loc.+kɛsˈtivən

kestrel ˈkɛstrəl

Keswick ˈkɛzɪk

Key: See in full §§3–47. bee bi |pity ˈpɪtɪ (§6) |rate ret |yet jɛt |sang sæŋ |angry ˈæŋ·grɪ |bath bæθ; E bɑθ (§10) |ah ɑ |far fɑr |watch wɑtʃ, wɒtʃ (§12) |jaw dʒɔ |gorge gɔrdʒ |go go

ketch, K- kɛtʃ |-es -ɪz
ketchup ˈkɛtʃəp
ketene ˈkitin
ketone ˈkiton
kettle, K- ˈkɛtl̩ |-drum -ˌdrʌm—ˈkɪtl̩, *a his-*
torical variant, is still not infrequently heard.
Keturah kɪˈtjurə, -ˈtɪurə
Keuka kɪˈjukə, ˈkjukə
Kew kju, kɪu
Kewanee kəˈwani, -ˈwɒni
Kewaunee kəˈwɔni
Keweenaw ˈkiwɪˌnɔ
key, K- ki |-ed -d |-board -ˌbord, -ˌbɔrd; ES
    -ˌboəd, E+-ˌbɔəd
Keyes kiz, kaɪz |-'s -ɪz
keyhole ˈkiˌhol
keyman ˈkiˌmæn, -ˈmæn |-men -ˌmɛn, -ˈmɛn
Keynes kenz |-'s -ɪz
keynote ˈkiˌnot, -ˈnot
Keyport ˈkiˌport, -ˌpɔrt; ES -ˌpoət, E+-ˌpɔət
Keyser ˈkaɪzɚ; ES ˈkaɪzə(r
keystone, K- ˈkiˌston |-d -d
Key West ˈkiˈwɛst
Kezia, -h kəˈzaɪə
khaddar ˈkʌdɚ; ES ˈkʌdə(r
khaki ˈkakɪ, ˈkækɪ |-ed -d
khan, K- kɑn, kæn
Kharkov ˈkarkɔf, -kɒf; ES ˈka:-, E+ˈka:-
Khartoum, -tum karˈtum; ES ka:-, E+ka:-
Khayyám kaɪˈam, -ˈæm, -ˈjam, -ˈjæm
khedive, K- kəˈdiv |-vial -ɪəl, -jəl |-viate -ɪɪt
Khmer kmɛr; ES kmɛə(r
Khyber ˈkaɪbɚ; ES ˈkaɪbə(r
Kiangsu ˈkjæŋˈsu (*Chin* ˈdʒjaŋˈsu)
Kiaochow ˈkjauˈtʃau (*Chin* ˈdʒjauˈdʒo)
kibe kaɪb |kibed kaɪbd
kibitzer ˈkɪbɪtsɚ, kəˈbɪt-; ES -sə(r
kibosh ˈkaɪbɑʃ, kɪˈbɑʃ; ES+-ɒʃ
kick kɪk |-ed -t |-back -ˌbæk |-off -ˌɔf, -ˌɒf
kickshaw ˈkɪkʃɔ
kickup ˈkɪkˌʌp
kid kɪd |kidded ˈkɪdɪd |-dy -ɪ
Kidd kɪd
kidnap ˈkɪdnæp |-(p)ed -t
kidney ˈkɪdnɪ
Kidron ˈkɪdrən
kidskin ˈkɪdˌskɪn
Kiel kil
Kiev kiˈɛv, -ˈɛf, ˈkiɛv, -ɛf

Kilauea ˌkilauˈeə
Kildare kɪlˈdɛr, -ˈdær; E -ˈdɛə(r, ES -ˈdæə(r
kilderkin ˈkɪldɚkɪn; ES ˈkɪldə-
kilerg ˈkɪlˌɝg; ES -ˌɜg, -ˌɝg
Kilkenny kɪlˈkɛnɪ (ˈKilˌkenny ˈcats)
kill kɪl |killed kɪld |-able -əbl̩
Killarney kɪˈlarnɪ; ES -ˈla:nɪ, E+-ˈla:nɪ
killdeer ˈkɪlˌdɪr;ES -ˌdɪə(r, S+-ˌdɛə(r, -ˌdjɛə(r
Killiecrankie ˌkɪlɪˈkræŋkɪ
Killigrew ˈkɪləˌgru, -ˌgrɪu
killjoy ˈkɪlˌdʒɔɪ
Kilmarnock kɪlˈmarnək; ES -ˈma:n-, E+
    -ˈma:n-
Kilmer ˈkɪlmɚ; ES ˈkɪlmə(r
kiln kɪl, kɪln—*spelt* kill *since 1470* (*so in the*
    1611 Bible)—*The* n *sound was lost from*
    kiln *in the same way as it was from* ell, mill,
    Milne.
kiln-dry ˈkɪlˌdraɪ |-dried -ˌdraɪd
kilo ˈkɪlo, ˈki-
kilocalorie ˈkɪləˌkælərɪ
kilocycle ˈkɪləˌsaɪkl̩
kilogram, -mme ˈkɪləˌgræm
kiloliter, -tre ˈkɪləˌlitɚ; ES -ˌlitə(r
kilometer, -tre ˈkɪləˌmitɚ, *much less freq.*
    kɪˈlamətɚ; ES -tə(r, -ˈlɒm-
kilowatt ˈkɪləˌwat, -ˌwɒt
kilowatt-hour ˈkɪləˌwatˈaur, -ˌwɒt-; ES
    -ˈauə(r
Kilpatrick kɪlˈpætrɪk
kilt kɪlt |kilted ˈkɪltɪd
kilter ˈkɪltɚ; ES ˈkɪltə(r
Kim kɪm |-ball -bl̩ |-berley -bɚlɪ; ES -bəlɪ
Kimbolton *O* kɪmˈboltn̩, *NC* ˈkɪmbl̩tən,
    Hunts kɪmˈboltn̩, *formerly* ˈkɪml̩tən (*Shak.*
    Kymmalton)
kimono kəˈmonə, -no
kin kɪn
kinaesthesia ˌkɪnɪsˈθiʒə, -zɪə |-thetic -ˈθɛtɪk
Kincaid kɪnˈked, kɪŋˈked
Kincardine kɪnˈkardɪn, kɪŋ-; ES -ˈka:d-,
    E+-ˈka:d-
Kinchinjunga ˌkɪntʃɪnˈdʒʌŋgə
kind kaɪnd
kindergarten ˈkɪndɚˌgartn̩; ES ˈkɪndəˌga:tn̩;
    E+-ˌga:tn̩; |-tner, -tener -tnɚ; ES -tnə(r
kindhearted ˈkaɪndˈhartɪd; ES -ˈha:t-, E+
    -ˈha:t-; (ˈkindˌhearted ˈman)
kindle ˈkɪndl̩ |-d -d |-ling -dlɪŋ, -dl̩ɪŋ

|full fʊl |tooth tuθ |further ˈfɝðɚ; ES ˈfɜðə; |custom ˈkʌstəm |while hwaɪl |how hau |toy tɔɪ
|using ˈjuzɪŋ |fuse fjuz, fɪuz |dish dɪʃ |vision ˈvɪʒən |Eden ˈidn̩ |cradle ˈkredl̩ |keep 'em ˈkipm̩

kindling *n* 'kındlıŋ
kindness 'kaındnıs, 'kaınnıs |-es -ız
kindred 'kındrıd, -əd
kine kaın |-pox -₁paks; ES+-₁pɒks
kinema 'kınəmə
kinematic ₁kınə'mætık |-al -ļ |-ally -ļı, -ıklı
kinematograph ₁kınə'mætə₁græf; E+-₁graf,
     -₁graf
kinesthesia ₁kınıs'θiʒə, -zıə |-thetic -'θɛtık
kinetic kı'nɛtık, kaı- |-al -ļ |-ally -ļı, -ıklı
kinfolk 'kın₁fok
king, K- kıŋ
kingbird 'kıŋ₁bɜˑd; ES -₁bɜd, -₁bɜˑd
kingbolt 'kıŋ₁bolt
kingcraft 'kıŋ₁kræft; E+-₁kraft, -₁kraft
kingdom 'kıŋdəm
Kingdon 'kıŋdən
kingfisher 'kıŋ₁fıʃɚ; ES -₁fıʃə(r
kinglet 'kıŋlıt
kingpin 'kıŋ₁pın
Kingsbury 'kıŋz₁bɛrı, -bərı
kingship 'kıŋʃıp
Kingsley 'kıŋzlı
Kingston, -e 'kıŋ·stən, 'kıŋz·tən, 'kıŋks-
Kingstown 'kıŋz₁taʊn
kink kıŋk |kinked kıŋkt |kinky 'kıŋkı
Kinkaid kın'ked, kıŋ'ked
kinkajou 'kıŋkə₁dʒu
kinnikinnick, -kinic ₁kınıkə'nık
Kinross kın'rɔs, -'rɒs |-ross-shire -'rɔsʃır,
     -'rɒʃʃ-, -'rɒ-, -ʃɚ; ES -ʃıə(r, -ʃə(r
Kinsey 'kınsı, -zı
kinsfolk 'kınz₁fok
kinship 'kınʃıp
kinsman, K- 'kınzmən |-men -mən
kinswoman 'kınz₁wʊmən, -₁wu- |-women
     -₁wımın, -ən
kiosk kı'ask, 'kaıask; ES+-'ɒsk, -ɒsk
Kioto 'kjoto
Kiowa *US* places 'kaıəwə
Kiowa, -way *Indian* 'kaıə₁we, -wə
Kipling 'kıplıŋ
kipper 'kıpɚ; ES 'kıpə(r; |-ed -d
Kirby 'kɜˑbı; ES 'kɜbı, 'kɜˑbı
Kirghiz kır'giz; ES kıɚ-; |-'s -ız
kirk, K- kɜˑk; ES kɜk, kɜˑk
Kirkby 'kɜˑkbı, 'kɜˑbı; ES 'kɜ-, 'kɜˑ-
Kirkcaldy kɜˑ'kɔldı, -'kɔdı, -'kadı; ES kɜ-,
     kɜˑ-

Kirkcudbright kɜˑ'kubrı; ES kɜ-, kɜˑ-; |-shire
     -₁ʃır, -ʃɚ; ES -₁ʃıə(r, -ʃə(r
Kirkland 'kɜˑklənd; ES 'kɜk-, 'kɜˑk-
kirmess 'kɜˑmıs; ES 'kɜm-, 'kɜˑm-; |-es -ız
Kirtland 'kɜˑtlənd; ES 'kɜt-, 'kɜˑt-
kirtle 'kɜˑtļ; ES 'kɜtļ, 'kɜˑtļ; |-d -d
kismet 'kızmɛt, 'kıs-
kiss kıs |kisses 'kısız |kissed kıst
kist kıst
kit, K- kıt |-ty -ı
kitcat 'kıt₁kæt
kitchen, K- 'kıtʃın, -ən
Kitchener, k- 'kıtʃınɚ, -ənɚ, -tʃnɚ; ES -nə(r
kitchenette ₁kıtʃın'ɛt, -ən-
kitchenware 'kıtʃın₁wɛr, -ən-, -₁wær; E
     -₁wɛə(r, ES -₁wæə(r
Kitchin 'kıtʃın
kite kaıt |kited 'kaıtıd
kith kıθ
Kittanning kı'tænıŋ
Kittatinny ₁kıtə'tını
kitten 'kıtņ—*The pron.* 'kıtən *is substandard.*
Kittery 'kıtərı
Kittitas 'kıtı₁tæs |-'s -ız
kittiwake 'kıtı₁wek
kittle 'kıtļ
Kittredge 'kıtrıdʒ |-'s -ız
kitty, K- 'kıtı
Kitty Hawk 'kıtı'hɔk |Kittyhawk 'kıtı₁hɔk
kiva 'kivə
Kiwanian kə'wanıən, -'wɒn- |-wanis -nıs
kiwi 'kiwı
Klaeber 'klɛbɚ; ES 'klɛbə(r
Klamath 'klæməθ
KleinSmid, von fən'klaın₁smıd
kleptomania ₁klɛptə'menıə |-niac -'menı₁æk
klieg klig
Klingsor 'klıŋzor, -zɔr; ES -zoə(r, E+-zɔə(r
Klondike 'klandaık; ES+'klɒn-
Klopstock 'klapstak; ES+'klɒpstɒk; (*Ger*
     'klɒpʃtɔk)
Kluge *Ger scholar* 'klugə; *Eng name* kludʒ,
     klıudʒ
knack næk |knacked nækt
knag næg |knagged 'nægıd |-gy -ı
knap næp |knapped næpt |-sack -₁sæk
knar nar; ES na:(r, E+na:(r; |-red -d -ry -ı
knave nev |-d -d |-ry -ərı, -rı |-ship -ʃıp
knead nid |kneaded 'nidıd

---

knee **ni** |kneed **nid** |-cap -ˌ**kæp**
knee-deep **ˈniˈdip** (ˈknee-ˌdeep ˈclover)
knee-high **ˈniˈhaɪ**
kneel **nil** |knelt **nɛlt** *or* kneeled **nild**
kneepad **ˈniˌpæd** |-pan -ˌ**pæn**
knell **nɛl** |knelled **nɛld**
Kneller **ˈnɛlɚ**; ES **ˈnɛlə(r**
knelt **nɛlt**
knew **nju, nɪu, nu**
knicker **ˈnɪkɚ**; ES **ˈnɪkə(r**; |-ed -**d**
Knickerbocker, k- **ˈnɪkɚˌbakɚ**; ES **ˈnɪkɚ-**
ˌ**bakə(r, -ˌbɒk-**; |-ed -**d**
knickknack **ˈnɪkˌnæk** |-ery -ɚɪ, -rɪ
knife *n* **naɪf** |knife's **naɪfs** (*in Shak.* knives
naɪvz) |*pl* knives **naɪvz**—*The pronunciation*
naɪvz *for* knife's *is the older possessive singu-*
lar.
knife *v* **naɪf** |knifes **naɪfs** |knifed **naɪft**
knifeful **ˈnaɪfˌful** |-s -**z**
knight **naɪt** |knighted **ˈnaɪtɪd** |-age -ɪdʒ
knight-errant **ˈnaɪtˈɛrənt** |-ry -rɪ
knighthood **ˈnaɪt·hʊd**
knit **nɪt** |knit **nɪt** *or* knitted **ˈnɪtɪd**
knives **naɪvz** |knive's **naɪvz**—*see* knife *n*
knob **nab**; ES+**nɒb**; |-bed -**d, -ɪd** |-by -**ɪ**
knobble **ˈnabl̩**; ES+**ˈnɒbl̩**; |-d -**d** |-ling -**blɪŋ,**
-**bl̩ɪŋ** |-bly -**bl̩ɪ, -blɪ**
Knoblock **ˈnablak**; ES+**ˈnɒblɒk**
knock **nak**; ES+**nɒk**; |-ed -**t** |-about -əˌ**baʊt**
knockdown **ˈnakˌdaʊn**; ES+**ˈnɒk-**
knock-knee **ˈnakˌni**; ES+**ˈnɒk-**; |-d -**ˈnid**
knockout **ˈnakˌaʊt**; ES+**ˈnɒk-**
knoll **nol** |-ed -**d** |-y -**ɪ**
knop **nap**; ES+**nɒp**; |-ped -**t** |-py -**ɪ**
Knossus **ˈnasəs**; ES+**ˈnɒs-**; |-sus' -səs
knot **nat**; ES+**nɒt**; |-ted -**ɪd** |-ty -**ɪ**
knothole **ˈnatˌhol**; ES+**ˈnɒt-**
Knott **nat**; ES+**nɒt**
knout **naʊt** |knouted **ˈnaʊtɪd**
know **no** |knew **nju, nɪu, nu** |known **non**
knowledge **ˈnalɪdʒ**; ES+**ˈnɒl-**; |-s -ɪz |-d -**d**
|-able -əbl̩ |-bly -**blɪ**
Knowles **nolz** |-'s -ɪz
know-nothing, K-N- **ˈnoˌnʌθɪŋ**
Knox **naks**; ES+**nɒks**; |-'s -ɪz |-ville -vɪl;
S+-**vl̩**
knuckle **ˈnʌkl̩** |-d -**d** |-ling -**klɪŋ, -kl̩ɪŋ**
knucklebone **ˈnʌkl̩ˌbon**
Knudsen **ˈnudsn̩, ˈnrudsn̩, ˈnjudsn̩**

knur, -rr **nɝ**; ES **nɝ(r, nɝ**; |-(r)ed -**d**
knurl **nɝl**; ES **nɝl, nɝl**; |-ed -**d**
Knut **kəˈnut, -ˈnrut, -ˈnjut**=Canute
knut '*nut*' *humorous* **kəˈnʌt**
Knutsford **ˈnʌtsfɚd**; ES **ˈnʌtsfəd**
Kobe **ˈkobɪ**
Koblenz **ˈkoblɛnts** |-'s -ɪz
kobold **ˈkobald, -bɒld, -bold** (*Ger* **ˈkoːbɔlt**)
Kobuk **koˈbʊk**
Koch *Ger* **kɔx**; '*Assamese*' **kotʃ** |-es**ˈkotʃɪz**
Kodak **ˈkodæk** |kodaked **ˈkodækt**
Kodiak **ˈkodɪˌæk**
Koekeritz **ˈkɛkərɪts** |-'s -ɪz
Koheleth **koˈhɛlɪθ**
Koh-i-noor, Kohinoor, -nur ˌ**koˈɪˈnʊr**; ES
-**ˈnʊə(r**
kohl, K- **kol** |Kohlan **ˈkolən**
Kohler **ˈkolɚ**; ES **ˈkolə(r**
kohlrabi **ˈkolˌrabɪ, ˈkolˈrabɪ**
koine **ˈkɔɪnɪ, -ni**
Kokomo **ˈkokəˌmo**
kola **ˈkolə**
Komintern ˌ**kamɪnˈtɝn, ˈkamɪnˌtɝn**; ES -ɝn,
-ɝn, -ɒm-
Kongo **ˈkaŋgo**; ES+**ˈkɒŋ-**
Königsberg **ˈkenɪgzˌbɝg**; ES -ˌ**bɝg, -ˌbɝg**;
(*Ger* **ˈkøːnɪksˌbɛrk**)
koodoo **ˈkudu**
Kootenay, -nai **ˈkutn̩ˌe**
kopeck, -pek **ˈkopɛk**
kopje **ˈkapɪ**; ES+**ˈkɒpɪ**
kor **kor, kɔr**; ES **koə(r, E+kɔə(r**
Koran **koˈran, -ˈræn**
Korea *India* **ˈkorɪˌa, ˈkɔr-**; S **ˈkor-**
Korea *Japan* **koˈriə, kɔ-**; S **ko-**; |-n -**n**
Korzybski **kərˈzɪbskɪ**; ES **kɔə-**
Kosciusko ˌ**kasɪˈʌsko**; ES+ˌ**kɒs-**; *mt.* -zɪ-
kosher **ˈkoʃɚ**; ES **ˈkoʃə(r**
Kossuth **kaˈsuθ, kɒ-** (*Hung* **ˈkɒʃut**)
kotow **koˈtaʊ** |-ed -**d**
koumis, -ss, -yss **ˈkumɪs**
Koussevitzky ˌ**kusəˈvɪtskɪ**
kowtow **kaʊˈtaʊ, ko-** |-ed -**d**
Koyukuk **kəˈjukʊk, ko-**
kraal **kral** |kraaled **krald**
kraft **kræft**; E+**kraft, krɑft**
Kraft, -fft **kraft, kræft**
Krag **krag, kræg**
Krakatao ˌ**krakəˈtao**

Kraków ˈkreko, ˈkrækaʊ (*Pol* ˈkrakʊf)

Krapotkin *city* krəˈpɑtkɪn, -ˈpɒt-

kraut kraʊt

Kreisler ˈkraɪslə; ES ˈkraɪslə(r

kremlin, K- ˈkrɛmlɪn

Kresge ˈkrɛsɡɪ, ˈkrɛskɪ

kreutzer, K-, kreuz- ˈkrɔɪtsə; ES ˈkrɔɪtsə(r

Kreymborg ˈkrɛmbɔrɡ; ES -bɔəɡ

kriegspiel ˈkriɡˌspil

Kriemhild ˈkrimhɪld (*Ger* ˈkriːmhɪlt)

Krimhild ˈkrɪmhɪld

kris kris |krises ˈkrisɪz

Krishna ˈkrɪʃnə |-ism -ˌɪzəm |-ist -ɪst

Kriss Kringle ˈkrɪsˈkrɪŋɡḷ

krona ˈkronə (*Sw* ˈkruːnə) |*pl* -nor -nɔr

krone ˈkronə |*Ger pl* kronen ˈkronən

krone ˈkronɛ |*Dan pl* kroner ˈkronɛr

Kropotkin *anarchist* krəˈpɑtkɪn, -ˈpɒt-

Kruger ˈkruɡə; ES ˈkruɡə(r

Krupp krʌp, krʊp (*Ger* krʊp)

Krutch krutʃ |-'s -ɪz

krypton ˈkrɪptɑn, -tɒn

Kshatriya ˈkʃætrijə

Kubelik ˈkubəlɪk

Kublai Khan *Chin ruler* ˈkublaɪˈkan

Kubla Kahn *poem* ˈkubləˈkan

kudos ˈkjudɑs, -dɒs, ˈkɪu- |-ed -t

kudu ˈkudu

Kufic ˈkjufɪk, ˈkɪu-

Ku-Klux, Kuklux ˈkjuˌklʌks, ˈkɪu- |-es -ɪz |-ed -t

kulak kuˈlɑk |-ism -ɪzəm

kultur ˈkʊltʊr; ES -tʊə(r; (*Ger* kʊlˈtuːr)

kumiss ˈkumɪs

kümmel ˈkɪmḷ (*Ger* ˈkyməl)

kumquat ˈkʌmkwɑt, -kwɒt

Kundry ˈkʊndrɪ

Kuomintang ˈkwomɪnˈtæŋ, ˈɡwo-, -ˈtɑŋ

Kurath, Hans ˈhænsˈkjuræθ, -ˈkɪu-, ˈhans-ˈkurɑt

Kurd kɝd, kurd; ES kɜd, kɝd, kuəd

Kurdistan ˌkɝdɪˈstæn, ˌkur-, -ˈstɑn; ES ˌkɜd-, ˌkɝd-, ˌkuəd-

Kure ˈkure

Kuril ˈkurɪl |-ian kuˈrɪlɪən, -ljən

Kurland ˈkurlənd; ES ˈkuə-

Kutztown ˈkutsˌtaʊn

Kwangsi ˈkwæŋˈsi, ˈɡwaŋ-

Kwangtung *China* ˈkwæŋˈtʌŋ, ˈɡwaŋˈdʊŋ

Kwantung *Manchuria* ˈkwænˈtʌŋ, ˈɡwanˈdʊŋ

Kweichow ˈkweˈtʃaʊ, ˈɡweˈdʒo

Kyd kɪd

Kyoto, Kio- ˈkjoto

Kyrie eleison ˈkɪrɪˌi əˈleəsṇ

Kythera ˈkɪθərə

L

L, l *letter* ɛl |*pl* L's, Ls, *poss* L's ɛlz

la *intj* lɔ, lɑ; *music* lɑ; *Fr article* la

laager 'camp' ˈlɑɡə; ES ˈlɑɡə(r; |-ed -d

Laban ˈlebən

label ˈlebḷ |-ed -d |-ing ˈleblɪŋ, ˈlebḷɪŋ

labellum ləˈbɛləm |-la -ˈbɛlə

labial ˈlebɪəl |-ly -ɪ

labialize ˈlebɪəlˌaɪz |-s -ɪz |-d -d

labiate *adj* ˈlebɪˌet, -bɪt

labile ˈlebḷ, -bɪl

labium ˈlebɪəm |-bia -bɪə

labor ˈlebə; ES -bə(r; |-ed -d |-ing -brɪŋ, -bərɪŋ

laboratory ˈlæbrəˌtorɪ, ˈlæbərə-, -brɪ-, -ˌtɔrɪ; S -ˌtorɪ

laborer ˈlebərə; ES ˈlebərə(r

laborious ləˈborɪəs, -ˈbɔr-; S -ˈbor-

laborite, L- ˈlebəˌraɪt

labor-saving ˈlebəˌsevɪŋ; ES ˈlebə-

Labrador ˈlæbrəˌdɔr; ES -ˌdɔə(r

laburnum ləˈbɝnəm; ES -ˈbɜn-, -ˈbɝn-

labyrinth ˈlæbəˌrɪnθ |-ths -θs

labyrinthian ˌlæbəˈrɪnθɪən

labyrinthine ˌlæbəˈrɪnθɪn, -θɪn

lac læk

lace les |laces ˈlesɪz |laced lest

Lacedaemon ˌlæsəˈdimən

Lacedaemonian ˌlæsədɪˈmonɪən, -njən

lacerate ˈlæsəˌret |-d -ɪd |-tion ˌlæsəˈreʃən

laches ˈlætʃɪz

Lachesis ˈlækəsɪs |-sis' -sɪs

lachrymal ˈlækrəmḷ

Key: *See in full §§3–47.* bee **bi** |pity ˈpɪtɪ (§6) |rate ret |yet jɛt |sang sæŋ |angry ˈæŋ·ɡrɪ |bath bæθ; E baθ (§10) |ah ɑ |far fɑr |watch wɑtʃ, wɒtʃ (§12) |jaw dʒɔ |gorge ɡɔrdʒ |go go

lachrymatory ˈlækrəməˌtɔrɪ, -ˌtɔrɪ; S -ˌtɔrɪ
lachrymose ˈlækrəˌmos
laciniate ləˈsɪnɪˌet, -ɪt |-ated -ˌetɪd
lack læk |lacked lækt
lackadaisical ˌlækəˈdezɪkl̩ |-ly -ɪ, -ɪklɪ
lackaday ˈlækəˌde
Lackawanna ˌlækəˈwɑnə, -ˈwɒnə
lackey ˈlækɪ |-ed -d
lackluster, -tre ˈlækˌlʌstɚ; ES -tə(r
Laconia ləˈkonɪə |-n -n
laconic, L- ləˈkɑnɪk; ES+-ˈkɒn-; |-ally -ļɪ, -ɪklɪ
lacquer ˈlækɚ; ES -ə(r; |-ed -d |-ing ˈlækərɪŋ, ˈlækrɪŋ
lacrosse, L- ləˈkrɔs, -ˈkrɒs |-ʼs -ɪz
lactate ˈlæktet |-d -ɪd |-tation lækˈteʃən
lacteal ˈlæktɪəl |lactic ˈlæktɪk
lactometer lækˈtɑmətɚ; ES -ˈtɑmətə(r, -ˈtɒm-
lactone ˈlækton |-tose -tos
lacuna ləˈkjunə, -ˈkɪu- |-s -z |-nae -ni
lacustrine ləˈkʌstrɪn
lacy ˈlesɪ
lad læd |laddie ˈlædɪ
ladder ˈlædɚ; ES -də(r; |-ed -d |-ing -dərɪŋ, -drɪŋ
lade led |past -d -ɪd |pptc -d -ɪd or laden ˈledn̩
laden v ˈledn̩ |-ed -d |-ing ˈledn̩ɪŋ, ˈlednɪŋ
ladle ˈledḷ |-d -d |-ling ˈledḷɪŋ, ˈledlɪŋ
Ladoga Finl ˈladogə, US places ləˈdogə
ladrone ləˈdron, Sc ˈlædrən
lady ˈledɪ |ladies, ladies', lady's ˈledɪz
ladybird ˈledɪˌbɝd; ES -ˌbɝd, -ˌbɝd
ladybug ˈledɪˌbʌg
ladyfinger ˈledɪˌfɪŋgɚ; ES -gə(r
lady-killer ˈledɪˌkɪlɚ; ES -lə(r
ladylike ˈledɪˌlaɪk
ladylove ˈledɪˌlʌv
ladyship ˈledɪˌʃɪp
lady-slipper ˈledɪˌslɪpɚ; ES -pə(r
lady's-slipper ˈledɪzˌslɪpɚ; ES -pə(r
Laertes lɪˈɝtiz, le-; ES -ˈɝtiz, -ˈɝtiz; |-tesʼ -tiz
La Farge ləˈfarʒ, commonly Anglic. ləˈfardʒ; ES -ˈfɑː-, E+-ˈfɑː-; |-ʼs -ɪz
Lafayette Fr general ˌlafɪˈɛt (Fr lafaˈjɛt), US places pron. variously ˌlæfɪˈ(j)ɛt, ˌlefɪˈ(j)ɛt, ləˈfe(j)ɪt
Lafeu, Shak. Lafew ləˈfju, -ˈfɪu
La Follette ləˈfɑlɪt; ES+-ˈfɒl-
La Fontaine ləfɑnˈten, -fɒn- (Fr lafõˈtɛn)

lag læg |lagged lægd
lager 'camp' ˈlagɚ; ES -gə(r; |-ed -d
lager beer ˈlagɚ, ˈlɔgɚ; ES -gə(r
Lagerlöf Sw ˈlɑːgərˌløːv
laggard ˈlægɚd; ES ˈlægəd
lagniappe, -gnap- lænˈjæp, ˈlænjæp
lagoon ləˈgun
La Guardia ləˈgwardɪə, -ˈgar-; ES -aːd-, E+-aːd-; (It laˈgwardja)
Lahore ləˈhor, -ˈhɔr; ES -ˈhoə(r, E+-ˈhɔə(r
laic ˈleˌɪk |-al -ļ |-ally -ļɪ, -ɪklɪ
laid past & pptc of lay led
lain pptc of lie len
lair lɛr, lær; E lɛə(r, ES læɚ(r; |-ed -d
laird lɛrd, lærd, Sc lerd; E lɛəd, ES læəd
laissez faire, laisser ˌleseˈfɛr, -ˈfær; E -ˈfɛə(r, ES -ˈfæə(r; (Fr lɛseˈfɛːr)
laity ˈleˌɪtɪ, ˈleˌɪtɪ
La Junta ləˈhʌntə (Am Sp laˈhunta)
lake lek
Lalla Rookh ˈlaləˈruk, Brit ˈlæləˈruk
L'Allegro laˈlegro (It lalˈleːgro)
lam læm |-med -d
lama ˈlɑmə
Lamar ləˈmɑr; ES ləˈmɑː(r, E+-ˈmɑː(r
Lamarck ləˈmɑrk; ES -ˈmɑːk, E+-ˈmɑːk; |-ian -ɪən (Fr laˈmark)
lamasery ˈlɑməˌsɛrɪ
lamb læm |lambed læmd |lambing ˈlæmɪŋ
lambaste læmˈbest |-d -ɪd
lambda ˈlæmdə
lambency ˈlæmbənsɪ |-bent -bənt
Lambeth ˈlæmbɪθ, -bəθ, -bɛθ
lambkin ˈlæmkɪn
lamblike ˈlæmˌlaɪk
lambrekin ˈlæmbɚˌkɪn, ˈlæmbrə-; ES ˈlæmbə-, -brə-
lambskin ˈlæmˌskɪn
lame lem |lamed lemd
Lamech ˈlemək, -mɛk
lamella ləˈmɛlə |-s -z |-lae -ˈmɛli
lament ləˈmɛnt |-ed -ɪd
lamentable ˈlæməntəbḷ |-bly -blɪ
lamentation ˌlæmənˈteʃən
La Mesa ləˈmesə |Lamesa ləˈmisə
Lamia poem ˈlemɪə; Gk town ləˈmiə, ˈlemɪə
lamina ˈlæmənə |-s -z |-nae -ˌni |-nar -nɚ; ES -nə(r
laminate adj ˈlæmənɪt, -ˌnet

|full fʊl |tooth tuθ |further ˈfɝðɚ; ES ˈfɝðə |custom ˈkʌstəm |while hwaɪl |how haʊ |toy tɔɪ |using ˈjuzɪŋ |fuse fjuz, fɪuz |dish dɪʃ |vision ˈvɪʒən |Eden ˈidn̩ |cradle ˈkredḷ |keep 'em ˈkipm̩

laminate *v* 'læmə‚net |-d -ɪd |-tion ‚læmə-
  'neʃən
Lammas 'læməs |-tide -‚taɪd
Lammermoor 'læmɚ‚mʊr; ES 'læmə‚mʊə(r;
  (*Sc* ‚lamər'muːr)
Lammermuir 'læmɚ‚mjʊr, -‚mɪʊr; ES 'læmə-
  ‚mjʊə(r, -‚mɪʊə(r; (*Sc* ‚lamər'mjuːr)
Lamont lə'mant; ES+-'mɒnt
lamp læmp |lamped læmpt
lampad 'læmpæd
lampblack 'læmp‚blæk |-ed -t
lamplight 'læmp‚laɪt |-er -ɚ; ES -ə(r
Lampman 'læmpmən
lampoon læm'pun |-ed -d
lamppost 'læmp‚post
Lamprecht 'læmprɛkt (*Ger* 'lamprɛxt)
lamprey 'læmprɪ
Lanark 'lænɚk; ES 'lænək; |-shire -‚ʃɪr, -ʃɚ;
  ES -‚ʃɪə(r, -ʃə(r
Lancashire 'læŋkə‚ʃɪr, -ʃɚ; ES -‚ʃɪə(r, -ʃə(r
Lancaster *Engd* 'læŋkəstɚ; ES -tə(r; *US*
  places variously 'læŋkəstɚ, 'læŋ‚kæstɚ,
  'læn‚kæstɚ; ES -tə(r
Lancastrian læŋ'kæstrɪən
lance læns; E+lans, lɑns; |-s -ɪz |-d -t
Lancelot 'lænsələt, 'lan-, -‚lat; ES+-‚lɒt
lanceolate 'lænsɪəlɪt, -‚let
Lancs *short for* Lancashire læŋks
land lænd |landed 'lændɪd
landau 'lændɔ
landfall 'lænd‚fɔl, 'læn-
land-grant 'lænd‚grænt, 'læn-; E+-‚grant,
  -‚grant
landgrave 'lænd‚grev, 'læn-
landgravine 'lændgrə‚vin, 'læn-
landholder 'lænd‚holdɚ; ES -‚holdə(r
landlady 'lænd‚ledɪ, 'læn-
landless 'lændlɪs
landlocked 'lænd‚lakt; ES+-‚lɒkt
landlord 'lænd‚lɔrd, 'læn-; ES -‚lɔəd
landlubber 'lænd‚lʌbɚ; ES -‚lʌbə(r
landmark 'lænd‚mark, 'læn-; ES -‚maːk,
  E+-‚maːk
land-office 'lænd‚ɔfɪs, -‚ɒfɪs, -‚afɪs |-s -ɪz
Landor 'lændɚ, -dɔr; ES -də(r, -dɔə(r
landowner 'lænd‚onɚ; ES -‚onə(r
land-poor 'lænd‚pur, 'læn-; ES -'pʊə(r,
  -'pʊə(r, -'pɔə(r
landscape 'lænskep, 'lænd- |-d -t

Landseer 'lændsɪr, 'læn-; ES -sɪə(r
Land's End 'lændz'ɛnd, 'lænz-
landskip *arch.* '*landscape*' 'lændskɪp
landslide 'lænd‚slaɪd, 'læn-
landslip 'lænd‚slɪp, 'læn-
landsman 'lændzmən, 'lænz- |-men -mən
landward 'lændwɚd; ES 'lændwəd; |-s -z
lane len
Lanett lə'nɛt
Lanfranc 'lænfræŋk
Langlade 'læŋled (*Fr* lɑ̃'glad)
Langland 'læŋlənd
Langley 'læŋlɪ
Langmuir 'læŋmjʊr, -mɪʊr; ES -ə(r
langsyne 'læŋ'saɪn, *in the song often* -'zaɪn
Langtree, -try 'læŋtrɪ
language 'læŋgwɪdʒ |-s -ɪz |-d -d
langue d'oc, L- *Fr* lɑ̃g'dɔk
langue d'oil *Fr* lɑ̃g'dɔil, -'dɔːj
languid 'læŋgwɪd
languish 'læŋgwɪʃ |-es -ɪz |-ed -t
languor 'læŋgɚ; ES 'læŋgə(r; |-ous -əs, -grəs
laniard 'lænjɚd; ES 'lænjəd
Lanier lə'nɪr; ES -'nɪə(r
lank læŋk |-ily 'læŋklɪ, -ɪlɪ
lanolin 'lænəlɪn |-line -lɪn, -‚lin
Lansdowne 'lænzdaʊn
Lansing 'lænsɪŋ
lantern 'læntɚn; ES 'læntən
lanthanum 'lænθənəm
lanthorn *arch. sp. of* lantern 'læntɚn; ES -tən
lanyard 'lænjɚd; ES 'lænjəd
Laocoön le'akə‚wan, -‚wɒn, -ko‚an, -‚ɒn;
  ES+-'ɒk-
Laodamia ‚leodə'maɪə
Laodicea ‚leədə'siə, ‚leo-, le‚adə'siə; ES+
  -‚ɒd-; |-n -n
Laomedon le'amə‚dan, -'ɒmə‚dɒn, -dən
lap læp |lapped læpt
La Paz lə'pas (*Am Sp* la'pas)
lapboard 'læp‚bord, -‚bɔrd; ES -‚boəd,
  E+-‚bɔəd
lapel lə'pɛl |lapelled lə'pɛld
lapful 'læp‚fʊl |-s -z
lapidary 'læpə‚dɛrɪ
lapin 'læpɪn (*Fr* la'pæ̃)
lapis lazuli 'læpɪs'læzjə‚laɪ, -jʊ-
Lapithe 'læpɪ‚θi
Laplace lə'plæs, læ- |-'s -ɪz (*Fr* la'plas)

Key: See in full §§3–47. bee bi |pity 'pɪtɪ (§6) |rate ret |yet jɛt |sang sæŋ |angry 'æŋ·grɪ
|bath bæθ; E baθ (§10) |ah ɑ |far far |watch watʃ, wɒtʃ (§12) |jaw dʒɔ |gorge gɔrdʒ |go go

Words below in which a *before* r (farm) *is sounded* ɑ *are often pronounced in* E *with* a (fɑːm)
Words below that have æ *before* r (carry ˈkærɪ) *are often pronounced in* N *with* ɛ (ˈkɛrɪ, §94)

La Place ləˈples |-'s -ɪz
Lapland ˈlæpˌlænd
Laplander ˈlæpˌlændɚ, -ləndɚ; ES -də(r
La Plata ləˈplɑtə (Sp laˈplata)
Lapp læp
lappet ˈlæpɪt |-ed -ɪd
lapse læps |lapses ˈlæpsɪz |lapsed læpst
lapsus linguae ˈlæpsəsˈlɪŋgwi
Laputa ləˈpjutə, -ˈpɪu- |-tan -tn̩
lapwing ˈlæpˌwɪŋ
lar lɑr; ES lɑː(r; |Latin pl lares ˈleriz |Eng pl
　lars -z
Laramie ˈlærəmɪ
larboard ˈlɑrbɚd, -ˌbord, -ˌbɔrd; ES ˈlɑːbəd,
　-ˌboəd, E+-ˌbɔəd
larcener ˈlɑrsn̩ɚ; ES ˈlɑːsn̩ə(r; |-cenous -sn̩əs
　|-ceny -sn̩ɪ
larch lɑrtʃ; ES lɑːtʃ; |-es -ɪz
lard lɑrd; ES lɑːd; |-ed -ɪd
larder ˈlɑrdɚ; ES ˈlɑːdə(r
Lardner ˈlɑrdnɚ; ES ˈlɑːdnə(r
Laredo ləˈredo, lɑ-, -ˈri-
lares L pl of lar ˈleriz
large lɑrdʒ; ES lɑːdʒ
large-hearted ˈlɑrdʒˈhɑrtɪd; ES ˈlɑːdʒˈhɑːtɪd
large-scale ˈlɑrdʒˈskel; ES ˈlɑːdʒ-; (ˈlarge-
　ˌscale ˈbuying)
largess, -sse ˈlɑrdʒɪs; ES ˈlɑːdʒɪs; |-es, -s -ɪz
larghetto lɑrˈgɛto; ES lɑː-; (It lɑrˈgetto)
largo ˈlɑrgo; ES ˈlɑːgo
lariat n ˈlærɪət
lariat v ˈlærɪˌæt |-ed -ɪd
lark lɑrk; ES lɑːk; |-ed -t
larkspur ˈlɑrkˌspɝ; ES ˈlɑːkˌsp3(r, -ˌspɝ
Larned ˈlɑrnɪd; ES ˈlɑːnɪd
larrikin ˈlærəˌkɪn
larrup ˈlærəp |larruped ˈlærəpt
Lars Porsena ˈlɑrzˈpɔrsɪnə; ES ˈlɑːzˈpɔəsɪnə
larum ˈlærəm, ˈlɛrəm; S ˈlærəm
larva ˈlɑrvə; ES ˈlɑːvə; |-vae -vi |-val -vl̩
laryngal ləˈrɪŋgl̩
laryngeal ləˈrɪndʒɪəl |-gitis ˌlærɪnˈdʒaɪtɪs
laryngology ˌlærɪŋˈgɑlədʒɪ; ES+-ˈgɒl-
laryngoscope ləˈrɪŋgəˌskop
larynx ˈlærɪŋks |-es -ɪz |larynges ləˈrɪndʒiz
La Salle ləˈsæl (Fr laˈsal)
lascar, L- ˈlæskɚ; ES ˈlæskə(r

Las Casas lɑsˈkɑsəs (Sp lasˈkasas)
Lascelles ˈlæslz̩, ləˈsɛlz |-'s -ɪz (Lassells 1574)
lascivious ləˈsɪvɪəs, læ-
Las Cruces lɑsˈkrusɪs (Am Sp lasˈkruses)
lash læʃ |lashes ˈlæʃɪz |lashed læʃt
lass læs |lasses ˈlæsɪz |lassie ˈlæsɪ
lassitude ˈlæsəˌtjud, -ˌtɪud, -ˌtud
lasso ˈlæso, older læ'su |-ed -d
last n, adj, v læst; E+last, lɑst; |-ed -ɪd—bef.
　conss. often læs (ˈlæsˈnaɪt)
Las Vegas lɑsˈvegəs |-'s -ɪz
latch lætʃ |latches ˈlætʃɪz |latched lætʃt
latchet ˈlætʃɪt
latchkey ˈlætʃˌki
latchstring ˈlætʃˌstrɪŋ, -ˌʃtrɪŋ
late let
lateen læˈtin
latency ˈletn̩sɪ |-tent -tn̩t
lateral ˈlætərəl |-ly -ɪ
Lateran ˈlætərən
latex ˈletɛks |-es -ɪz |latices ˈlætəˌsiz
lath n læθ; E+laθ, lɑθ; |-ths -ðz, -θs
lath v læθ; E+laθ, lɑθ; |-ths -θs |-ed -t
Lathbury ˈlæθˌbɛrɪ, -bərɪ
lathe leð |-thes -ðz
lather 'one who laths' ˈlæθɚ; ES ˈlæθə(r,
　E+ˈlaθ-, ˈlɑθ-
lather 'lathe-worker' ˈleðɚ; ES ˈleðə(r
lather 'foam' ˈlæðɚ; ES ˈlæðə(r; |-ed -d |-ing
　ˈlæðərɪŋ, ˈlæðrɪŋ
Lathrop ˈleθrəp
lathwork ˈlæθˌwɝk; ES -ˌwɜk, -ˌwɝk, E+
　ˈlaθ-, ˈlɑθ-
lathy 'like a lath' ˈlæθɪ; E+ˈlaθɪ, ˈlɑθɪ
Latimer ˈlætəmɚ; ES ˈlætəmə(r
Latin ˈlætn̩, ˈlætɪn |-ed -d |-ism -ˌɪzəm |-ist
　-ɪst
Latinity læˈtɪnətɪ
Latinize ˈlætn̩ˌaɪz, -tɪnˌaɪz |-s -ɪz |-d -d
latish ˈletɪʃ
latitude ˈlætəˌtjud, -ˌtɪud, -ˌtud
latitudinarian ˌlætəˌtjudn̩ˈɛrɪən, -ˌtɪud-,
　-ˌtud-, -ˈer-
Latium ˈleʃɪəm
Latona ləˈtonə, le-
latrine ləˈtrin
Latrobe ləˈtrob

|full fʊl |tooth tuθ |further ˈfɝðɚ; ES ˈfɜðə |custom ˈkʌstəm |while hwaɪl |how haʊ |toy tɔɪ
|using ˈjuzɪŋ |fuse fjuz, fɪuz |dish dɪʃ |vision ˈvɪʒən |Eden ˈidn̩ |cradle ˈkredl̩ |keep 'em ˈkipm̩

latron 'letrən

latten 'lætn̩

latter 'lætɚ; ES 'lætə(r; |-ly -lɪ

lattice 'lætɪs |-s -ɪz |-d -t

latticework 'lætɪsˌwɝk; ES -ˌwɜk, -ˌwɝk

Latvia 'lætvɪə |-n -n

laud, L- lɔd |lauded 'lɔdɪd

laudability ˌlɔdə'bɪlətɪ

laudable 'lɔdəbl̩ |-bly -blɪ

laudanum 'lɔdn̩əm, 'lɔdnəm

laudation lɔ'deʃən

laudatory 'lɔdəˌtorɪ, -ˌtɔrɪ; S -ˌtorɪ

Lauder 'lɔdɚ; ES 'lɔdə(r; |-derdale -ˌdel

laugh læf; E laf, læf, laf; |-ed -t

laughable 'læfəbl̩ |-bly -blɪ; E see laugh

laughingstock 'læfɪŋˌstak; ES+-ˌstɒk, E see laugh

Laughlin 'læflɪn, 'laf-, 'lak-, 'lax-; ES+'lɒ-, E+'la-

laughter 'læftɚ; ES -tə(r, E see laugh

Launce lɔns, lɒns, lans |-'s -ɪz

Launcelot 'lɔnsələt, 'lɒn-, 'lan-, -ˌlat; ES+-ˌlɒt

Launceston Tasm 'lɔnˌsɛstən, 'lan-; Cornw 'lɔnstən, loc. 'lan-, 'lɒn-, -sn̩

launch lɔntʃ, lɒntʃ, lantʃ |-es -ɪz |-ed -t

launder 'lɔndɚ, 'lɒn-, 'lan-; ES -də(r; |-ed -d |-ing -drɪŋ, -dərɪŋ

laundress 'lɔndrɪs, 'lɒn-, 'lan- |-es -ɪz

laundry 'lɔndrɪ, 'lɒn-, 'lan-; N Engd+'lan-; |-dried -drɪd

Laura 'lɔrə

laureate n 'lɔrɪɪt |-ship -ˌʃɪp

laureate v 'lɔrɪˌet |-d -ɪd

laurel 'lɔrəl, 'lar-, 'lɒr- |-ed -d

Laurence 'lɔrəns, 'lar-, 'lɒr- |-'s -ɪz

Laurens 'lɔrəns, 'lar-, 'lɒr-, -ənz |-'s -ɪz

Laurentian lɔ'rɛnʃɪən, -ʃən, la-, lɒ-

Laurie 'lɔrɪ, 'lɒr-

Laurier 'lɔrɪɚ, 'lar-, 'lɒr-; ES -ɪ·ə(r; C statesman 'lɔrɪˌe, 'lar-, 'lɒr-

Lausanne lo'zæn (Fr lo'zan)

lava 'lavə, 'lævə

lavabo, L- lə'vebo

Lavache lə'vætʃ |-'s -ɪz, in Shak. Lavatch

lavaliere, -ier ˌlævə'lɪr; ES -'lɪə(r; (Fr lavaˈljeːr)

lavatory 'lævəˌtorɪ, -ˌtɔrɪ; S -ˌtorɪ

lave lev |laved levd

lavender 'lævəndɚ; ES -də(r

Lavengro lə'vɛŋgro, læ-

laver 'levɚ; ES 'levə(r

Lavinia lə'vɪnɪə, -njə

lavish 'lævɪʃ |-es -ɪz |-ed -t

law lɔ |lawed lɔd |-ful -fəl |-fully -fəlɪ

law-abiding 'lɔəˌbaɪdɪŋ

lawbreaker 'lɔˌbrekɚ; ES -ˌbrekə(r

lawgiver 'lɔˌgɪvɚ; ES -ˌgɪvə(r

lawmaker 'lɔˌmekɚ; ES -ˌmekə(r

lawmaking 'lɔˌmekɪŋ

lawn lɔn |lawned lɔnd

Lawrence, -ance 'lɔrəns, 'lar-, 'lɒr- |-'s -ɪz

lawsuit 'lɔˌsut, -ˌsɪut, -ˌsjut

lawyer 'lɔjɚ; ES 'lɔjə(r

lax læks |laxes 'læksɪz

laxative 'læksətɪv |laxity 'læksətɪ

lay past of lie le

lay v le |laid led

lay n, adj le

Layamon 'leəmən, 'lajəmən

layer 'leɚ, lɛr; ES 'le·ə(r, lɛə(r; |-ed -d

layette le'ɛt

layman, L- 'lemən |laymen -mən

layoff 'leˌɔf, -ˌɒf

layout 'leˌaʊt

layover 'leˌovɚ; ES -ˌovə(r

lazar 'lezɚ; ES -zə(r;—The a in lazar was lengthened after the word was shortened from Lazarus.

lazaret, -tte ˌlæzə'rɛt |-retto -'rɛto

Lazarus 'læzərəs, -zrəs |-'s -ɪz

laze lez |lazes 'lezɪz |lazed lezd

lazy 'lezɪ |-bones -ˌbonz

lazzarone ˌlæzə'rone |pl -ni -ni (It ˌladdzaˈroːne)

lea, L- li

leach, L- litʃ |leaches 'litʃɪz |leached litʃt

Leacock 'liˌkak, 'le-; ES+-ˌkɒk

lead n, v lid |led lɛd

lead metal lɛd |leaded 'lɛdɪd

Lead lid

leaden v, adj 'lɛdn̩ |-ed -d |-ing 'lɛdnɪŋ, 'lɛdn̩ɪŋ

leader 'guide' 'lidɚ; ES 'lidə(r

leader 'lead-worker' 'lɛdɚ; ES 'lɛdə(r

leadoff 'lidˌɔf, -ˌɒf

lead-pencil 'lɛdˌpɛnsl̩, -ˌpɛnsl̩

leadsman 'lɛdzmən |-men -mən

Leadville 'lɛdvɪl

leaf *n* lif |leaf's lifs |leaves livz

leaf *v* lif |leafs lifs |-ed -t—*cf* leave *v*

leafage 'lifɪdʒ |-s -ɪz

leaflet 'liflɪt

leafy 'lifɪ—*cf* leavy

league lig |leagued ligd

leaguer 'ligɚ; ES -gə(r; |-ed -d .|-ing -gərɪŋ, -grɪŋ

Leah 'liə

Leahy *Am diplomat* 'le·ɪ, 'lehɪ

leak lik |leaked likt |leaky 'likɪ |-age -ɪdʒ

leal lil

Leamington 'lɛmɪŋtən, *cf* Lemington

lean lin |leaned lind *or* leant lɛnt

Leander lɪ'ændɚ; ES -'ændə(r

leanness 'linnɪs

leant *past &* *pptc of* lean lɛnt

lean-to 'lin,tu

leap lip |leaped lipt, lɛpt *or* leapt lɛpt, lipt

leapfrog 'lip,frɑg, -,frɔg, -,frɒg; S -,frɔg, -,frɑg, -,frɒg; |-ged -d

leapt *past &* *pptc of* leap lɛpt, lipt

Lear lɪr; ES lɪə(r, S+lɛə(r

learn lɝn; ES lɝn, lɜn; |-ed -d, -t *or* -t -t

learned *past &* *pptc* lɝnd, lɝnt; ES lɜn-, lɝn-; *adj* -ned -nɪd

learnt *past &* *pptc of* learn lɝnt; ES lɜnt, lɝnt

lease 'rent' lis |-s -ɪz |-d -t

lease 'tell a lie' 'liz |-s -ɪz |-d -d

leasehold 'lis,hold

leash liʃ |leashes 'liʃɪz |leashed liʃt

leasing 'falsehood' 'lizɪŋ

least list

leastways 'list,wez |leastwise 'list,waɪz

leather 'lɛðɚ; ES 'lɛðə(r; |-n -n |-y -ɪ, -ðrɪ

leatherette, L- ,lɛðə'rɛt |-roid 'lɛðə,rɔɪd

leave *n* liv, *dial. &* *Brit army*+lif

leave 'to leaf' liv |leaved livd

leave 'depart' liv |left lɛft

leaved *adj* livd

leaven 'lɛvən |-ed -d |-ing 'lɛvənɪŋ, -vnɪŋ

Leavenworth 'lɛvənwɚθ, -,wɝθ; ES -wəθ, -,wɝθ, -,wɜθ

leaves *pl of* leaf *&* leave *n, 3 sg of* leave *v* livz

leave-taking 'liv,tekɪŋ

Leavit, -tt 'lɛvɪt

leavy 'livɪ

leaze 'tell a lie' liz |-s -ɪz |-d -d

leazing 'falsehood' 'lizɪŋ

Lebanon 'lɛbənən

Le Beau lə'bo, *in Shakespeare's day* lə'bɪu

Lebrun *Fr* lə'brœ̃

lecher, L- 'lɛtʃɚ; ES 'lɛtʃə(r; |-ous -əs, -tʃrəs |-y -ɪ, -tʃrɪ

lecithin 'lɛsəθɪn

Lecky 'lɛkɪ

Le Conte lɪ'kɑnt; ES+-'kɒnt

lectern 'lɛktɚn; ES 'lɛktən

lection 'lɛkʃən |-ary -,ɛrɪ

lector 'lɛktɚ; ES 'lɛktə(r

lecture 'lɛktʃɚ; ES -tʃə(r; |-d -d |-ring 'lɛk-tʃərɪŋ, 'lɛktʃrɪŋ

lectureship 'lɛktʃɚ,ʃɪp; ES 'lɛktʃə-

led *past &* *pptc of* lead lɛd

Leda 'lidə

ledger 'lɛdʒɚ; ES -dʒə(r; |-ed -d |-ing 'lɛdʒərɪŋ, 'lɛdʒrɪŋ

Ledyard 'lɛdjɚd; ES 'lɛdjəd

lee, L- li

leeboard 'li,bord, -,bɔrd; ES -,bɔəd, E+-,bɔəd

leech 'litʃ |leeches 'litʃɪz |leeched litʃt

Leeds lidz |Leeds's 'lidzɪz

leek, L- lik

leer lɪr; ES lɪə(r, S+lɛə(r; |-ed -d

lees liz

leese 'lose' (*1611 Bible*) liz

leet lit

leeward 'liwɚd, *naut.* 'luɚd, 'lɪuɚd; ES 'liwəd, 'lu·əd, 'lɪu·əd

Leeward Islands 'liwɚd'aɪləndz, -lənz; ES 'liwəd-

leeway 'li,we

leeze 'lose' liz=leese

Lefevre lə'fivɚ; ES -'fivə(r

left lɛft

left-hand 'lɛft'hænd ('left-,hand 'turn)

left-handed 'lɛft'hændɪd

leg lɛg |legged *v* lɛgd

legacy 'lɛgəsɪ

legal 'ligl |-ly -ɪ |-ism -,ɪzəm |-ist -ɪst

legalistic ,ligl'ɪstɪk |-ally -|ɪ, -ɪklɪ

legality lɪ'gælətɪ

legalization ,liglə'zeʃən, -aɪ'z-

legalize 'ligl,aɪz |-s -ɪz |-d -d

legate 'lɛgɪt

legatee ,lɛgə'ti

legatine 'lɛgətɪn, -ˌtaɪn
legation lɪ'geʃən
legato lɪ'gɑto (*It* le'gɑːto)
legend 'lɛdʒənd |-ary -ˌɛrɪ
Leger 'lɛdʒɚ; ES 'lɛdʒə(r
legerdemain ˌlɛdʒɚdɪ'men; ES ˌlɛdʒə-
legged *past of* leg *v* lɛgd, *adj* 'lɛgɪd, lɛgd
leggings 'lɛgɪŋz |leggins 'lɛgɪnz
leghorn 'lɛgɚn, 'lɛgˌhɔrn; ES 'lɛgən, -ˌhɔən
Leghorn *Italy* 'lɛgˌhɔrn; ES -ˌhɔən; *fowl*
 'lɛgɚn, -ˌhɔrn; ES 'lɛgən, -ˌhɔən
legibility ˌlɛdʒə'bɪlətɪ
legible 'lɛdʒəbḷ |-bly -blɪ
legion 'lidʒən |-ary -ˌɛrɪ
legionnaire ˌlidʒən'ɛr, -'ær; E -'ɛə(r, ES
 -'æə(r
legislate 'lɛdʒɪsˌlet |-d -ɪd |-lative -ˌletɪv
legislation ˌlɛdʒɪs'leʃən
legislator 'lɛdʒɪsˌletɚ; ES -ˌletə(r
legislature 'lɛdʒɪsˌletʃɚ; ES -ˌletʃə(r
legist 'lidʒɪst
legitimate *adj* lɪ'dʒɪtəmɪt |-macy -məsɪ
legitimate *v* lɪ'dʒɪtəˌmet |-d -ɪd
legitimist lɪ'dʒɪtəmɪst |-matist -'dʒɪtəmətɪst
legitimize lɪ'dʒɪtəˌmaɪz |-s -ɪz |-d -d
leg-of-mutton *adj* 'lɛgə'mʌtṇ, 'lɛgəv-
Legree lɪ'gri
legume 'lɛgjum, lɪ'gjum, -'gɪum
legumen lɪ'gjumən, lɛ-, -'gɪu- |-s -z |-mina
 -mɪnə
legumin lɪ'gjumɪn, lɛ-, -'gɪumɪn |-ous -əs
Le Havre *France* lə'hɑvɚ, -'hɑvrə; ES
 -'hɑvə(r, -'hɑvrə; (*Fr* lə'ɑːvr)
Lehigh 'lihaɪ
Lehman 'limən, 'lemən
lehua lɪ'hua
lei le, 'le·ɪ
Leibnitz 'laɪbnɪts |-'s -ɪz (*Ger* Leibniz
 'laɪpnɪts)
Leica 'laɪkə
Leicester 'lɛstɚ; ES 'lɛstə(r; |-shire -ˌʃɪr, -ʃɚ;
 ES -ˌʃɪə(r, -ʃə(r
Leiden 'laɪdṇ
Leif Ericson 'lif'ɛrɪksṇ
Leigh *pers. name* li; *places* li, laɪ
Leila 'lilə
Leinster 'lɛnstɚ; ES 'lɛnstə(r
Leipsic 'laɪpsɪk, O 'lɪpsɪk
Leipzig 'laɪpsɪg, -sɪk (*Ger* 'laɪptsɪx)

leisure 'liʒɚ, *now less freq.* 'lɛʒɚ; ES -ʒə(r;
 |-d -d
Leitch litʃ |-'s -ɪz
Leith liθ
leitmotiv, -tif 'laɪtmoˌtif
Leland 'lilənd
Lelia 'lilɪə, -ljə
leman 'lɛmən
Leman *lake* 'limən
Lemington 'lɛmɪŋtən, *cf* Leamington
lemma 'lɛmə |-s -z |-mata -tə
lemming 'lɛmɪŋ
lemon 'lɛmən |-ade ˌlɛmən'ed
Lemuel 'lɛmjuəl
lemur 'limɚ; ES 'limə(r
Lena 'linə
Lenawee 'lɛnəwɪ, -ˌwi
lend lɛnd |lent lɛnt
L'Enfant 'lɑnfant (*Fr* lɑ̃'fɑ̃)
length lɛŋkθ, lɛŋθ |-ths -θs |-thy -ɪ
lengthen 'lɛŋkθən, 'lɛŋθən |-ed -d |-ing
 -θənɪŋ, -θnɪŋ
lengthways 'lɛŋkθˌwez, 'lɛŋθ- |-wise -ˌwaɪz
lenience 'linɪəns, -njəns |-cy -ɪ |-ent -ənt
Lenin 'lɛnɪn |-grad -ˌgræd, -ˌgrɑd
lenitive 'lɛnətɪv |-ty 'lɛnətɪ
Lennox 'lɛnəks |-'s -ɪz
Lenoir *US places* lə'nor, -'nɔr; ES -'noə(r,
 E+-'nɔə(r
Lenoir, Étienne *Fr* e'tjɛn lə'nwɑːr
Lenore lə'nor, -'nɔr; ES -'noə(r, E+-'nɔə(r
lens lɛnz |lenses 'lɛnzɪz |lensed lɛnzd
lent lɛnt
Lent lɛnt |Lenten 'lɛntən
lenticular lɛn'tɪkjələ; ES -lə(r
lentigo lɛn'taɪgo |lentigines lɛn'tɪdʒəˌniz
lentil 'lɛntḷ, -tɪl
lento *It* 'lɛnto
l'envoi, -voy 'lɛnvɔɪ, lɛn'vɔɪ (*Fr* lɑ̃'vwa)
Leo 'lio
Leominster *Mass* 'lɛmɪnstɚ, *Engd* 'lɛmstɚ,
 'lɛmɪn-; ES -stə(r
Leon *US places* 'liən, *PI* le'on
Leonard 'lɛnɚd; ES 'lɛnəd
Leonardo ˌliə'nardo; ES -'nɑːdo
Leonardo da Vinci ˌliə'nardo də'vɪntʃɪ; ES
 -'nɑːdo; (*It* ˌleo'nardo da'vintʃi)
Leonato ˌliə'nato
Leonatus ˌliə'netəs |-'s -ɪz

Key: See in full §§3–47. bee bi |pity 'pɪtɪ (§6) |rate ret |yet jɛt |sang sæŋ |angry 'æŋ·grɪ
|bath bæθ; E baθ (§10) |ah ɑ |far fɑr |watch wɑtʃ, wɒtʃ (§12) |jaw dʒɔ |gorge gɔrdʒ |go go

Leonid 'liənɪd
Leonidas lɪ'anədəs; ES+-'ɒn-; |-'s -ɪz
leonine, L- 'liə͵naɪn
Leonora ͵liə'norə, -'nɔrə; S -'norə
Leontes lɪ'ɑntiz, -'ɒntiz
leopard 'lɛpəd; ES 'lɛpəd; |-ess -ɪs
Leopold 'liə͵pold, older 'lɛp|d
Lepanto lɪ'pænto
leper 'lɛpə; ES 'lɛpə(r; |-ed -d
lepidopterous ͵lɛpə'dɑptərəs, -trəs; ES+
-'dɒp-
Lepidus 'lɛpɪdəs |-'s -ɪz
leprechaun 'lɛprə͵kɔn
leprosy 'lɛprəsɪ |leprous 'lɛprəs
Lesbian 'lɛzbɪən
Lesbos 'lɛzbɒs, -bɑs; ES+-bɒs
lese majesty 'liz'mædʒɪstɪ
lesion 'liʒən
Leslie 'lɛslɪ
less lɛs |lesser 'lɛsə; ES 'lɛsə(r
-less *unstressed suffix* -lɪs, -ləs. *The pronunciation* -lɛs *is not normal to conversational
style, but occurs occasionally in deliberate
reading style, especially in rime. In the
vocab. only the pron.* -lɪs *is given, but it is
to be understood that many speakers (fewer
in the E and S) also pronounce* -ləs *as in
stylus* 'staɪləs. *In the vocabulary the ending*
-less *is usually not given. When* -less *is
added to words ending in* -l *or* -|, *two* l
sounds are pronounced, as in soulless 'sollɪs,
bridleless 'braɪd|lɪs. Cf* -ness.
lessee lɛs'i
lessen 'lɛsn̩ |-ed -d |-ing 'lɛsn̩ɪŋ, 'lɛsnɪŋ
Lesseps 'lɛsəps |-'s -ɪz (*Fr* lɛ'sɛps)
Lessing 'lɛsɪŋ
lesson 'lɛsn̩ |-ed -d |-ing 'lɛsn̩ɪŋ, 'lɛsnɪŋ
lessor 'lɛsɔr; ES 'lɛsɔə(r; (lɛs'see & lɛs'sor)
lest lɛst
Lester 'lɛstə; ES 'lɛstə(r
L'Estrange lɛ'strendʒ |-'s -ɪz
Le Sueur lə'sur; ES -'suə(r; (*Fr* Lesueur
lə'sɥœ:r)
let lɛt |-down 'lɛt͵daʊn
Letcher 'lɛtʃə; ES 'lɛtʃə(r
lethal 'liθəl |-ly -ɪ
lethargic lɪ'θɑrdʒɪk, lɛ-; ES -'θɑ:dʒ-; |-al -|
|-ally -|ɪ, -ɪklɪ
lethargy 'lɛθədʒɪ; ES 'lɛθədʒɪ

Lethe 'liθɪ, 'liθi |-d -d |-thied -θɪd
Lethean li'θiən
Letitia lɪ'tɪʃɪə, -ʃə
Leto 'lito
let's lɛts, lɛs
let's see lɛts'si, lɛt'si (*originally* let see)
Lett lɛt
letter 'lɛtə; ES 'lɛtə(r; |-ed -d
letterhead 'lɛtə͵hɛd; ES 'lɛtə-
letter-perfect 'lɛtə'pɜfɪkt; ES 'lɛtə'pɜf-,
-'pɜf-
letterpress 'lɛtə͵prɛs; ES 'lɛtə-
Lettice 'lɛtɪs |-'s -ɪz
Lettish 'lɛtɪʃ
lettuce 'lɛtɪs, -əs |-s -ɪz
letup 'lɛt͵ʌp
leucocyte 'lukə͵saɪt, 'lɪukə-
leucorrhea, -rhoea ͵lukə'riə, ͵lɪukə-
leud lud, lɪud |-s -z |-es -ɪz
Leutner 'lɔɪtnə; ES 'lɔɪtnə(r
Levant lə'vænt
Levantine lə'væntɪn, 'lɛvən͵taɪn
levator lə'vetə; ES -'vetə(r; |-tores ͵lɛvə-
'toriz
levee 'bank' 'lɛvɪ |-d -d, 'reception'+lə'vi
level 'lɛv|, older & still occas. 'lɛvɪl |-ly -ɪ
|-ed -d |-ing 'lɛvlɪŋ, -v|ɪŋ
levelheaded 'lɛv|'hɛdɪd ('level͵headed 'move)
lever 'lɛvə, 'livə; E -və(r; S 'livə(r, 'lɛvə(r;
|-ed -d |-ing -vərɪŋ, -vrɪŋ |-age -ɪdʒ, -vrɪdʒ
Levi 'livaɪ
leviable 'lɛvɪəb|
leviathan, L- lə'vaɪəθən
levigate 'lɛvə͵get |-d -ɪd
levin 'lɛvɪn
Levis 'livɪs (*Fr* lɛ'vi)
levitate 'lɛvə͵tet |-d -ɪd |-tion ͵lɛvə'teʃən
Levite 'livaɪt
Levitic lə'vɪtɪk |-al -| |-ally -|ɪ |-us -əs
levity 'lɛvətɪ
levulose 'lɛvjə͵los
levy 'lɛvɪ |levied 'lɛvɪd
lewd lud, lɪud
Lewes, -is 'luɪs, 'lɪuɪs |-'s -ɪz
lewisite 'luɪs͵aɪt, 'lɪuɪs-
Lewisohn 'luɪ͵zon, 'lɪuɪ-, -͵son
Lewiston 'luɪstən, 'lɪuɪs-
lex lɛks |leges 'lidʒiz
lexical 'lɛksɪk|

|full fʊl |tooth tuθ |further 'fɜðə; ES 'fɜðə |custom 'kʌstəm |while hwaɪl |how haʊ |toy tɔɪ
|using 'juzɪŋ |fuse fjuz, fɪuz |dish dɪʃ |vision 'vɪʒən |Eden 'idn̩ |cradle 'kred| |keep 'em 'kipm̩

lexicographer ˌlɛksəˈkɑɡrəfɚ, -ˈkɒɡ-; ES -fə(r; |-phy -fɪ

lexicon ˈlɛksɪkən

Lexington ˈlɛksɪŋtən

Leyden ˈlaɪdn̩

Lhasa ˈlɑsə

liable ˈlaɪəbl̩ |liability ˌlaɪəˈbɪlətɪ

liaison ˌlieˈzɔ̃ (Fr ljɛˈzõ)

liar ˈlaɪɚ; ES ˈlaɪ·ə(r

libation laɪˈbeʃən

Libby ˈlɪbɪ

libel ˈlaɪbl̩ |-ed -d |-ing ˈlaɪbl̩ɪŋ, ˈlaɪblɪŋ

libelant, -llant ˈlaɪbl̩ənt

libelee, -llee ˌlaɪbl̩ˈi

libelous, -llous ˈlaɪbl̩əs

liberal ˈlɪbərəl, ˈlɪbrəl |-ly -ɪ |-ism -ˌɪzəm

liberality ˌlɪbəˈrælətɪ

liberalize ˈlɪbərəlˌaɪz, -brəl- |-s -ɪz |-d -d

liberate ˈlɪbəˌret

liberation ˌlɪbəˈreʃən

liberator ˈlɪbəˌretɚ; ES -ˌretə(r

Liberia laɪˈbɪrɪə |-n -n

libertarian ˌlɪbɚˈtɛrɪən, -ˈter-; ES ˌlɪbə-

liberticide lɪˈbɝtəˌsaɪd; ES -ˈbɝt-, -ˈbɝt-

libertinage ˈlɪbɚtɪnɪdʒ; ES ˈlɪbə-

libertine ˈlɪbɚˌtin; ES ˈlɪbəˌtin; |-nism -tin-ˌɪzəm, -tɪnˌɪzəm

liberty ˈlɪbɚtɪ; ES ˈlɪbətɪ

libidinous lɪˈbɪdnəs

libido lɪˈbaɪdo

Libra ˈlaɪbrə |-brae -bri

librarian laɪˈbrɛrɪən, -ˈbrer- |-ship -ˌʃɪp

library ˈlaɪˌbrɛrɪ, -brɪ, -brərɪ—In the occas. prons. ˈlaɪˌbɛrɪ, ˈlaɪbərɪ r is lost by dissimilation (§121), and ˈlaɪbrɪ is due to contraction.

librate ˈlaɪbret |-d -ɪd |-tion laɪˈbreʃən

librettist lɪˈbrɛtɪst

libretto lɪˈbrɛto |-s -z |-ti -ti

Libya ˈlɪbɪə |-n -n

lice laɪs |lice's ˈlaɪsɪz

license, -nce ˈlaɪsn̩s |-s -ɪz |-d -t

licensee, -cee ˌlaɪsn̩ˈsi

licensor ˈlaɪsn̩sɚ; ES -sə(r; (ˌlaɪsn̩ˈsi ən ˌlaɪsn̩ˈsɔr)

licentiate n, adj laɪˈsɛnʃɪt, -ˌet

licentious laɪˈsɛnʃəs

Lichas ˈlaɪkəs |-'s -ɪz

lichen ˈlaɪkɪn, -kən |-ed -d |-ous -əs

Lichfield Engd ˈlɪtʃfild

lich-gate ˈlɪtʃˌget

licit ˈlɪsɪt

lick lɪk |licked lɪkt

lickerish adj ˈlɪkərɪʃ

Licking ˈlɪkɪŋ

lickspittle ˈlɪkˌspɪtl̩ |-d -d |-ling -ˌspɪtl̩ɪŋ, -ˌspɪtlɪŋ

licorice ˈlɪkərɪs, ˈlɪkərɪʃ, -krɪ-

lictor ˈlɪktɚ; ES ˈlɪktə(r

lid lɪd |lidded ˈlɪdɪd

Liddell ˈlɪdl̩

Liddesdale ˈlɪdzˌdel

Lidice ˈlidɪtsɪ, -tse (Czech liˈdji·tsɛ)

lie n laɪ

lie ‘falsify’ laɪ |lied laɪd |lying ˈlaɪɪŋ

lie ‘recline’ laɪ |lay le |lain len |lying -ɪŋ

Liebig ˈlibɪg (Ger ˈli:bɪx)

Liechtenstein ˈlɪktənˌstaɪn (Ger ˈlɪxtənˌʃtaɪn)

lied past of lie laɪd

lied ‘song’ lid |pl lieder ˈlidɚ; ES ˈlidə(r; (Ger li:t, ˈli:dər)

lief lif |liefer ˈlivɚ, ˈlifɚ; ES -ə(r; |liefest ˈlivɪst, ˈlifɪst—see lieve

liege lidʒ |-s -ɪz

Liége lɪˈeʒ, -ˈɛʒ (Fr ljɛ:ʒ)

lien lin, ˈliən

lieu lu, lɪu

lieutenancy luˈtɛnənsɪ, lɪu-

lieutenant luˈtɛnənt, lɪu-; Brit army lɛf-, Brit navy lu- (Jones)

lieve liv |liever ˈlivɚ; ES -və(r; |-est -ɪst

life laɪf |life's laɪfs (in Shak. lives laɪvz) |pl lives laɪvz—The pronunciation laɪvz for life's is the older possessive singular.

lifeblood ˈlaɪfˌblʌd, emph.+-ˈblʌd

lifeboat ˈlaɪfˌbot

lifeguard ˈlaɪfˌgard; ES -ˌga:d, E+-ˌga:d

lifelike ˈlaɪfˌlaɪk

lifelong ˈlaɪfˈlɒŋ, -ˈlɔŋ; S+-ˈlɑŋ; (ˈlaɪfˌlɒŋ ˈfriend)

lifesaver ˈlaɪfˌsevɚ; ES -ˌsevə(r

life-size ˈlaɪfˈsaɪz |-d -d

lifetime ˈlaɪfˌtaɪm

lifework ˈlaɪfˈwɝk, -ˈwɝk; ES -ɝk, -ɝk

lift lɪft |-ed -ɪd or arch. lift lɪft

ligament ˈlɪgəmənt |-al ˌlɪgəˈmɛntl̩

Ligarius lɪˈgɛrɪəs, -ˈger- |-s -ɪz

ligate ˈlaɪget |-d -ɪd |-tion laɪˈgeʃən

---

ligature 'lɪgəˌtʃʊr, -tʃɚ; ES -ˌtʃʊə(r, -tʃə(r; |-d -d

ligeance 'laɪdʒəns, 'lidʒ- |-s -ɪz

light laɪt |lighted 'laɪtɪd *or* lit lɪt

lighten 'laɪtn̩ |-ed -d |-ing 'laɪtn̩ɪŋ, -tnɪŋ

lighter 'laɪtɚ; ES 'laɪtə(r; |-ed -d

lighterage 'laɪtərɪdʒ |-s -ɪz

light-fingered 'laɪt'fɪŋgɚd; ES -'fɪŋgəd

Lightfoot 'laɪtˌfʊt

light-footed 'laɪt'fʊtɪd

lighthead 'laɪtˌhɛd

lightheaded 'laɪt'hɛdɪd ('light‚headed 'youth)

lighthearted 'laɪt'hɑrtɪd; ES -'hɑːtɪd, E+ -'hɑːt-

lighthouse 'laɪtˌhaʊs |-ses -zɪz

lightning 'laɪtnɪŋ |lightninged 'laɪtnɪŋd

light-o'-love 'laɪtə'lʌv

lightship 'laɪtˌʃɪp

lightsome 'laɪtsəm

light-struck 'laɪtˌstrʌk

lightweight 'laɪt'wet ('light‚weight 'coin)

lightwood 'laɪtˌwʊd, *loc. S* 'laɪtəd

light-year 'laɪt'jɪr, -ˌjɪr; ES -ɪə(r; *cf* year

ligneous 'lɪgnɪəs

lignify 'lɪgnəˌfaɪ |-fied -ˌfaɪd

lignin 'lɪgnɪn

lignite 'lɪgnaɪt

lignose 'lɪgnos |-nous -nəs

lignum vitae 'lɪgnəm'vaɪtɪ, -ti

Ligonier ˌlɪgə'nɪr; ES -'nɪə(r

ligule 'lɪgjul

ligure 'lɪgjʊr; ES 'lɪgjʊə(r

Liguria lɪ'gjʊrɪə, -'gɪʊrɪə |-n -n

Li Hung Chang 'li'hʊŋ'ɪʃæŋ, -'hʌŋ-, -'tʃaŋ

likable, likeable 'laɪkəbl̩

like laɪk |liked laɪkt

-like *suffix* -ˌlaɪk—*Words in* -like *are usually omitted from the vocab., since the pron. can always be found by adding* -ˌlaɪk *to the sound of the head word* (manlike 'mænˌlaɪk). *When the head word ends in a* l *sound, two* l *sounds are heard* (taillike 'telˌlaɪk, eaglelike 'igl̩-ˌlaɪk, bell-like 'bɛlˌlaɪk).

likelihood 'laɪklɪˌhʊd

likely 'laɪklɪ

liken 'laɪkən |-ed -d |-ing 'laɪkənɪŋ, -knɪŋ

likeness 'laɪknɪs |-es -ɪz

likewise 'laɪkˌwaɪz

likin 'li'kin

liking 'laɪkɪŋ

lilac 'laɪlək, *older* 'laɪlæk

Lilian 'lɪlɪən, -ljən

lilied 'lɪlɪd

Lilith 'lɪlɪθ

Lille lil

lillibullero ˌlɪlɪbə'liro

Lilliput 'lɪləˌpʌt, -pət

Lilliputian ˌlɪlə'pjuʃən, -'pɪu-

Lilly 'lɪlɪ

lilt lɪlt |lilted 'lɪltɪd

lily 'lɪlɪ |lilied 'lɪlɪd

lily-livered 'lɪlɪ'lɪvɚd; ES -'lɪvəd

Lima *US* 'laɪmə, *Peru* 'limə, *bean* 'laɪmə

limb lɪm |limbed lɪmd

limbeck, -bec 'lɪmbɛk

limber *'tree trimmer'* 'lɪmɚ; ES 'lɪmə(r

limber *'flex,' 'flexible'* 'lɪmbɚ; ES 'lɪmbə(r; |-ed -d |-ing 'lɪmbərɪŋ, 'lɪmbrɪŋ

limbo 'lɪmbo

Limburg, -bourg *Belg* 'lɪmbɚg; ES 'lɪmbɜg, -bɝg; (*Fr* læ̃'buːr)

Limburger 'lɪmbɚgɚ; ES 'lɪmbɜgə(r, -bɝgə(r

lime laɪm |limed laɪmd

Limehouse *Lond* 'laɪmˌhaʊs, *loc.* 'lɪməs (Les Lymostes *1367*, Lymost *1496*, Lymehurst *1535*, Lymehouse *1547*—*a triumph of literate ignorance*)

limekiln 'laɪmˌkɪl, -ˌkɪln—*see* kiln

limelight 'laɪmˌlaɪt

limen 'laɪmɛn

limerick, L- 'lɪmərɪk, 'lɪmrɪk

limestone 'laɪmˌston

limewater 'laɪmˌwɔtɚ, -ˌwɑtɚ, -ˌwɒtɚ; ES -tə(r

limit 'lɪmɪt |limited 'lɪmɪtɪd

limn lɪm |limned lɪmd |-ing 'lɪmɪŋ, 'lɪmnɪŋ

limner 'lɪmɚ, 'lɪmnɚ; ES -ə(r

Limoges lɪ'moʒ |-'s -ɪz

limonene 'lɪməˌnin

limonite 'laɪməˌnaɪt

limousine 'lɪməˌzin, ˌlɪmə'zin

limp lɪmp |limped lɪmpt

limpet 'lɪmpɪt

limpid 'lɪmpɪd |-pidity lɪm'pɪdətɪ

limy 'laɪmɪ

linage 'laɪnɪdʒ |-s -ɪz

linchpin 'lɪntʃˌpɪn |-pinned -ˌpɪnd

Lincoln 'lɪŋkən

Lincolnian lıŋˈkonıən
Lincolniana ˌlıŋkənıˈenə, -ko-, -ˈænə, -ˈɑnə
Lincolnshire ˈlıŋkənˌʃır, -ʃɚ; ES -ˌʃıə(r, -ʃə(r
Lincs *short for* Lincolnshire lıŋks
Lind lınd
Lindbergh ˈlınbɝg, ˈlınd-; ES -bɝg, -bɝg
linden, L- ˈlındən
Lindisfarne ˈlındısˌfɑrn; ES -ˌfɑ:n, E+-ˌfa:n
Lindley ˈlındlı, ˈlınlı
Lindsay ˈlınzı, ˈlındzı |Vachel ˈvetʃəl
Lindsey ˈlınzı, ˈlındzı
line laın |lined laınd
lineage *'alignment'* ˈlaınıdʒ |-s -ız
lineage *'family'* ˈlınrıdʒ |-s -ız |-d -d
lineal ˈlınıəl |-ly -ı |-neament ˈlınıəmənt
linear ˈlınıɚ; ES ˈlını·ə(r
lineate *adj* ˈlınııt, -ˌet |-ated -ˌetıd
lineman ˈlaınmən |-men -mən
linen ˈlının, -ən
liner ˈlaınɚ; ES ˈlaınə(r
linesman ˈlaınzmən |-men -mən
line-up ˈlaınˌʌp
ling lıŋ
linger ˈlıŋgɚ; ES ˈlıŋgə(r; |-ed -d |-ing
  ˈlıŋgərıŋ, ˈlıŋgrıŋ
lingerie ˈlænʒəˌri (*Fr* læʒˈri)
lingo ˈlıŋgo
lingua franca ˈlıŋgwəˈfræŋkə
lingual ˈlıŋgwəl
linguaphone, L- ˈlıŋgwəˌfon
linguiform ˈlıŋgwıˌfɔrm; ES -ˌfɔəm
linguist ˈlıŋgwıst
linguistic lıŋˈgwıstık |-s -s |-al -ļ |-ally -ļı,
  -ıklı
liniment ˈlınəmənt
lining ˈlaınıŋ
link lıŋk |links lıŋks |linked lıŋkt
linkage ˈlıŋkıdʒ |-s -ız
linkboy ˈlıŋkˌbɔı
linked ˈlıŋkt, *poet.* ˈlıŋkıd
Linklater ˈlıŋkˌletɚ; ES -ˌletə(r
linkwork ˈlıŋkˌwɝk; ES -ˌwɝk, -ˌwɝk
Linley ˈlınlı—*see* Lindley
Linlithgow lınˈlıθgo
Linnaeus lıˈniəs |-'s -ız |-aean, -ean -ˈnıən
linnet ˈlınıt
linoleum lıˈnolıəm, -ljəm
Linotype ˈlaınəˌtaıp |-d -t
linseed ˈlınˌsid

linsey-woolsey ˈlınzıˈwʊlzı
linstock ˈlınˌstɑk; ES+-ˌstɒk
lint lınt
lintel ˈlıntļ |-ed -d
linter ˈlıntɚ; ES ˈlıntə(r
Lin Yutang ˈlınjuˈtæŋ
lion, L- ˈlaıən |-ess -ıs |-ess's -ısız
Lionel ˈlaıənļ, ˈlaıəˌnɛl
lionheart ˈlaıənˌhɑrt; ES -ˌhɑ:t, E+-ˌha:t
lion-hearted ˈlaıənˈhɑrtıd; ES -ˈhɑ:t-, E+
  -ˈha:t-
lionize ˈlaıənˌaız |-s -ız |-d -d
lip lıp |lipped lıpt
lipase ˈlaıpes
lipide ˈlaıpaıd, ˈlıpıd |-pid -pıd
Lippi ˈlıpı (*It* ˈlippi)
Lippmann ˈlıpmən
lipstick ˈlıpˌstık |-sticked -ˌstıkt
liquefaction ˌlıkwıˈfækʃən
liquefy ˈlıkwəˌfaı |-fied -ˌfaıd
liquescence lıˈkwɛsn̩s |-cy -ı |-scent -sn̩t
liqueur lıˈkɝ; ES -ˈkɝ(r, -ˈkɝ; *Brit* lıˈkjʊə(r;
  (*Fr* liˈkœ:r)
liquid ˈlıkwıd
liquidambar, -ber, L- ˈlıkwıdˌæmbɚ; ES
  -ˌæmbə(r
liquidate ˈlıkwıˌdet |-d -ıd
liquidation ˌlıkwıˈdeʃən
liquidator ˈlıkwıˌdetɚ; ES -ˌdetə(r
liquidity lıˈkwıdətı
liquor ˈlıkɚ; ES ˈlıkə(r; |-ed -d
liquorice ˈlıkɚıs, -krıs, -rıʃ
liquorish *'lickerish'* ˈlıkɚıʃ
liquorish *'licorice'* ˈlıkɚıʃ, -krıʃ
lira ˈlırə |-s -z |lire ˈlıre (*It* ˈliːrɑ, -re)
liripipe ˈlırıˌpaıp |-poop -ˌpup
Lisa *Eng name* ˈlaızə, ˈlisə, *It name* ˈlizɑ
Lisbon ˈlızbən
lisle, L- laıl (*Fr* lil)
lisp lısp |lisped lıspt
lissome, -som ˈlısəm
list lıst |-ed -ıd
list *'please'* lıst |*past* listed ˈlıstıd *or arch.* list
  lıst |*pptc* listed ˈlıstıd
listel ˈlıstļ
listen ˈlısn̩ |-ed -d |-ing ˈlısn̩ıŋ, ˈlısnıŋ
listener ˈlısnɚ, ˈlısnə; ES -nə(r
lister, L- ˈlıstɚ; ES ˈlıstə(r
Listerine, l- ˈlıstəˌrin

Key: See in full §§3–47.   bee bi |pity ˈpıtı (§6) |rate ret |yet jɛt |sang sæŋ |angry ˈæŋ·grı
|bath bæθ; E baθ (§10) |ah ɑ |far fɑr |watch watʃ, wɒtʃ (§12) |jaw dʒɔ |gorge gɔrdʒ |go go

listless 'lɪstl̩ɪs
Liszt lɪst
lit lɪt
litany, L- 'lɪtn̩ɪ
Litchfield US 'lɪtʃfild
liter, -tre 'litɚ; ES 'litə(r
literacy 'lɪtərəsɪ
literal 'lɪtərəl |-ly -ɪ |-ism -ˌɪzəm |-ist -ɪst
literary 'lɪtəˌrɛrɪ
literate 'lɪtərɪt
literati ˌlɪtə'retaɪ, ˌlɪtə'ratɪ
literatim ˌlɪtə'retɪm
literature 'lɪtərəˌtʃʊr, -tʃɚ, 'lɪtrə-, -ˌtjʊr; ES -ˌtʃʊə(r, -tʃə(r, -ˌtjʊə(r
litharge 'lɪθɑrdʒ; ES -ɑ:dʒ, E+-θɑ:dʒ
lithe laɪð |-some -səm
lither 'more lithe' 'laɪðɚ; ES 'laɪðə(r
lither 'bad,' 'agile' 'lɪðɚ; ES 'lɪðə(r
lithia 'lɪθɪə, -θjə |-ium -ɪəm |-ic -ɪk
lithograph 'lɪθəˌgræf; E+-ˌgraf, -ˌgraf; |-ed -t
lithographer lɪ'θɑgrəfɚ, -'θɒg-; ES -fə(r; |-phy -fɪ
lithographic ˌlɪθə'græfɪk |-al -] |-ally -ḷ, -ɪklɪ
lithosphere 'lɪθəˌsfɪr; ES -ˌsfɪə(r, S+-ˌsfɛə(r
Lithuania ˌlɪθju'enɪə, ˌlɪθʊ'enɪə |-n -n
litigable 'lɪtɪgəb] |-gant 'lɪtəgənt
litigate 'lɪtəˌget |-d -ɪd |-tion ˌlɪtə'geʃən
litigious lɪ'tɪdʒɪəs
litmus 'lɪtməs
litotes 'laɪtəˌtiz, 'laɪto-
litro 'litro
Littell 'lɪtl̩, lɪ'tɛl
litten 'lɪtn̩
litter 'lɪtɚ; ES 'lɪtə(r; |-ed -d
littérateur ˌlɪtərə'tɝ; ES -'tɜ(r, -'tɝ; (Fr litera'tœːr)
little 'lɪtl̩ |-r 'lɪtl̩ɚ, 'lɪtlɚ; ES -ə(r; |-st 'lɪtl̩ɪst, 'lɪtl̩ɪst
Littlejohn 'lɪtl̩ˌdʒɑn, -ˌdʒɒn
littleneck 'lɪtl̩ˌnɛk
Littleton 'lɪtl̩tən
littoral 'lɪtərəl
liturgical lɪ'tɝdʒɪk]; ES -'tɜdʒ-, -'tɝdʒ-; |-ly -ɪ, -ɪklɪ |-gics -dʒɪks
liturgism 'lɪtɚˌdʒɪzəm; ES 'lɪtə-; |-gist -dʒɪst
liturgy 'lɪtɚdʒɪ; ES 'lɪtədʒɪ
Litvinov lɪt'vinɔf, -ɒf
livable, liveable 'lɪvəb]
live adj laɪv

live 'lief' Shak. lɪv
live v lɪv |lived lɪvd
lived 'having life' laɪvd—cf long-lived
livelihood 'laɪvlɪˌhud
livelong n, adj 'lɪvˌlɔŋ, -ˌlɒŋ; S+-ˌlɑŋ
lively 'laɪvlɪ
liven 'laɪvən |-ed -d |-ing 'laɪvənɪŋ, -vnɪŋ
liver 'lɪvɚ; ES -və(r; |-ed -d |-ing -vərɪŋ, -vrɪŋ
liver Liverpool arms 'laɪvɚ; ES 'laɪvə(r
liveried 'lɪvərɪd, 'lɪvrɪd
liverish 'lɪvərɪʃ, 'lɪvrɪʃ
Livermore 'lɪvɚˌmor, -ˌmɔr; ES 'lɪvəˌmoə(r, E+-ˌmɔə(r
Liverpool 'lɪvɚˌpul; ES 'lɪvəˌpul
Liverpudlian ˌlɪvɚ'pʌdlɪən; ES ˌlɪvə-
liverwort 'lɪvɚˌwɝt; ES 'lɪvəˌwɜt, 'lɪvəˌwɝt
liverwurst 'lɪvɚˌwɝst, -ˌwurst; ES 'lɪvə-ˌwɜst, 'lɪvəˌwɝst, -ˌwuəst
livery 'lɪvərɪ, -vrɪ |-ied -d |-man -mən |-men -mən
lives pl of life laɪvz |live's laɪvz—see life
lives 3 sg of live v lɪvz
lives 'lief' dial. lɪvz
livestock 'laɪvˌstɑk; ES+-ˌstɒk
Livia 'lɪvɪə
livid 'lɪvɪd |-vidity lɪ'vɪdətɪ
living 'lɪvɪŋ |-s -z
Livingston, -e 'lɪvɪŋstən
Livonia lɪ'vonɪə, -njə
Livy 'lɪvɪ
lizard, L- 'lɪzɚd; ES 'lɪzəd
-'ll abbr. spelling of unstressed will in I'll aɪl, you'll jul, he'll hil, she'll ʃil, we'll wil, they'll ðel, it'll 'ɪt]; after nouns rarely abbreviated in spelling but often in pronunciation, as father will go 'fɑðɚ əl̩go, George will go 'dʒɔrdʒ əl̩go, that will do 'ðæt]'du, Lucy will go 'lusɪ əl̩go, Joe will go 'dʒol̩go. See will
llama 'lɑmə
Llanarmon læ'nɑrmən, θlæ-; ES -'nɑːm-; (Welsh ɬa'narmon)
Llanberis læn'bɛrɪs, θlæn- (Welsh ɬan'beris)
Llandudno læn'dʌdno, θlæn- (Welsh ɬan-'didno)
Llanelly læ'nɛlɪ, θlæ'nɛθlɪ (S. Welsh ɬa'neɬi)
Llangollen læn'gɑlɪn, θlæn'gaθl-, -'gɒ-, -ən (Welsh ɬan'goɬen)

Those words below in which the ɑ sound is spelt o are often pronounced with ɒ in E and S

llano, L- ˈlano, ˈlæno

Llano Estacado ˈlano͵estəˈkado, ˈleno͵estə-
 ˈkedo

Llewellyn, -elyn luˈɛlɪn, lɪu- (*Welsh* ɬ͡ɵ-
 ˈwelɪn)

Lloyd lɔɪd

Lloyd George ˈlɔɪdˈdʒɔrdʒ; ES -ˈdʒɔədʒ; |-ʼs
 -ɪz

Llywelyn luˈɛlɪn, lɪu- (*Welsh* ɬ͡ɵˈwelin)

lo lo

loach lotʃ |loaches ˈlotʃɪz

load lod |loaded ˈlodɪd

loadstar ˈlod͵star; ES -͵stɑ:(r, E+-͵stɑ:(r

loadstone ˈlod͵ston

loaf *n* lof |loafʼs lofs |loaves lovz

loaf *v* lof |loafs lofs |loafed loft

loam lom |loamed lomd

loan lon |loaned lond

loan *Phil measure* loˈɑn |loanes loˈɑnes

loath loθ

loathe loð |loathed loðd

loathful ˈloðfəl |-ly -ɪ

loathly *adj* ˈloðlɪ

loathly *adv* ˈloθlɪ, ˈloðlɪ (*older form*)

loathsome ˈloðsəm

lob, L- lab |lobbed labd

lobar ˈlobɚ; ES ˈlobə(r

lobby ˈlabɪ |lobbied ˈlabɪd |lobbyist ˈlabɪɪst

lobe lob |lobed lobd

lobelia, L- loˈbiljə

loblolly ˈlablalɪ

lobo ˈlobo

Lobos ˈlobos |-ʼs -ɪz

lobster ˈlabstɚ; ES ˈlabstə(r

local ˈlokḷ |-ed -d |-ly -ɪ

locale, -al loˈkæl, -ˈkɑl (*Fr* lɔˈkal)

localism ˈlokḷ͵ɪzəm |-istic ͵lokḷˈɪstɪk

locality loˈkælətɪ

localization ͵lokḷəˈzeʃən, -aɪˈz-

localize ˈlokḷ͵aɪz |-s -ɪz |-d -d

Locarno loˈkarno; ES -ˈkɑ:no, E+-ˈkɑ:no

locate ˈloket, loˈket |-d -ɪd

location loˈkeʃən |-al -ḷ

locative ˈlakətɪv, ˈlakɪtɪv

loch, L- lak, lax (*Sc* lɒx, lox)

Lochaber laˈkæbɚ, lɒ-, -ˈxæb-, -abɚ; ES
 -bə(r

Lochiel laˈkil, lɒ-, -ˈxil

Lochinvar ͵lakɪnˈvar, ͵lɒ-, -xɪn-; ES -ˈva:(r,
 E+-ˈva:(r

loci *pl of* locus ˈlosaɪ

lock lak |locked lakt |-age -ɪdʒ |-et -ɪt

Locke lak

Lockerbie ˈlakɚbɪ; ES ˈlakəbɪ

Lockhart ˈlakhart, -kət; ES -ha:t, -kət,
 E+-ha:t

lockjaw ˈlak͵dʒɔ

lockout ˈlak͵aut

Lockport ˈlak͵port, -͵pɔrt; ES -͵poət, E+
 -͵pɔət

Locksley ˈlakslɪ

locksmith ˈlak͵smɪθ |-ths -θs

lockup ˈlak͵ʌp

Lockyer ˈlakjɚ; ES ˈlakjə(r

loco ˈloko |locoed ˈlokod

locomotion ͵lokəˈmɔʃən |-motive -ˈmotɪv

locomotor ͵lokəˈmotɚ; ES -ˈmotə(r

Locrine loˈkraɪn, -ˈkrin

Locris ˈlokrɪs |-ʼs -ɪz

loculus ˈlakjələs |-es -ɪz |-li -͵laɪ

locum tenens ˈlokəmˈtininz, -ənz

locus ˈlokəs |loci ˈlosaɪ

locust ˈlokəst

locution loˈkjuʃən, -ˈkɪu-

locutory ˈlakjə͵torɪ, -͵tɔrɪ; S -͵torɪ

lode lod |-star -͵star; ES -͵sta:(r, E+-͵sta:(r;
 |-stone -͵ston

lodge ladʒ |lodges ˈladʒɪz |lodged ladʒd

Lodge ladʒ |-ʼs -ɪz

lodgment, -dge- ˈladʒmənt

Lodi *US* ˈlodaɪ; *Italy* ˈlodi (*It* ˈlɔ:di)

Lodore loˈdor, -ˈdɔr; ES -ˈdoə(r, E+-ˈdɔə(r

Lodovico ͵lodəˈviko

Lodowic, -ick ˈlodəwɪk, ˈlad-

Loeb leb, lɛb, lob (*Ger* løːp)

loess ˈlo·ɪs (*Ger* löss lœs)

loft lɔft, lɒft

Lofthouse ˈlɔftəs, ˈlɒft-, -͵haus |-ʼs -ɪz

Loftus ˈlɔftəs, ˈlɒf- |-ʼs -ɪz

lofty ˈlɔftɪ, ˈlɒf- |-tily -tḷɪ, -tɪlɪ

log lɔg, lag, lɒg |-ged -d

Logan ˈlogən |-sport -z͵port, -z͵pɔrt; ES
 -z͵poət, E+-z͵pɔət

logarithm ˈlɔgə͵rɪðəm, ˈlag-, ˈlɒg-, -θəm

logarithmic ͵lɔgəˈrɪðmɪk, ͵lag-, ͵lɒg-, -θmɪk
 |-al -ḷ |-ally -ḷɪ, -ɪklɪ

Key: See in full §§3–47. bee bi |pity ˈpɪtɪ (§6) |rate ret |yet jɛt |sang sæŋ |angry ˈæŋ·grɪ
|bath bæθ; E baθ (§10) |ah ɑ |far fɑr |watch watʃ, wɒtʃ (§12) |jaw dʒɔ |gorge gɔrdʒ |go go

Those words below in which the ɑ sound is spelt o are often pronounced with ɒ in E and S

logbook ˈlɔɡˌbʊk, ˈlɑɡ-, ˈlɒɡ-
loge loʒ (*Fr* lɔ̃:ʒ)
loggerhead ˈlɔɡɚˌhɛd, ˈlɑɡ-, ˈlɒɡ-; ES -ɡə-; |-ed -ɪd
loggia ˈlɑdʒɪə, -dʒə, ˈlɒdʒ-, ˈlɔdʒ- |-s -z (*It* ˈlɔddʒɑ |*pl* loggie ˈlɔddʒe)
logic ˈlɑdʒɪk |-al -əl̩ |-ally -ļɪ, -ɪklɪ
logicality ˌlɑdʒɪˈkælətɪ
logician loˈdʒɪʃən
logos, L- ˈlɑɡɑs, ˈlɒɡ-
logroll ˈlɔɡˌrol, ˈlɑɡ-, ˈlɒɡ- |-ed -d
logwood ˈlɔɡˌwʊd, ˈlɑɡ-, ˈlɒɡ-
logy ˈloɡɪ
Lohengrin ˈloənˌɡrɪn, -ˌɡrin
loin lɔɪn |loined lɔɪnd
Loire lwɑr; ES lwɑ:(r, E+lwɑ:(r; (*Fr* lwa:r)
Lois ˈlo·ɪs |-'s -ɪz
loiter ˈlɔɪtɚ; ES -tə(r; |-ed -d |-ing -tərɪŋ, -trɪŋ
Loki ˈloki (*Ice* ˈlɔkɪ)
Lola ˈlolə
loll lɑl |lolled lɑld
Lollard ˈlɑlɚd; ES ˈlɑləd; |-ry -rɪ |-y -ɪ
lollipop ˈlɑlɪˌpɑp
Lomax ˈlomæks |-'s -ɪz
Lombard ˈlɑmbɚd, ˈlʌm-, -bɑrd; ES -bəd, -bɑ:d, E+-bɑ:d
Lombardic lɑmˈbɑrdɪk, lʌm-; ES -ˈbɑ:d-, E+-ˈbɑ:d-
Lombardy ˈlɑmbɚdɪ, ˈlʌm-; ES -bədɪ
Lomond ˈlomənd
London ˈlʌndən
Londonderry ˈlʌndənˌdɛrɪ, *Irel* ˌlʌndənˈdɛrɪ
Londres, l- *cigar* ˈlɑndrɛs (*Fr* lɔ̃ˈdrɛ:s)
lone lon |lonely ˈlonlɪ |-some -səm; *N Engd*+ lɔ̃n(-) (*§46*)
long lɔŋ, lɒŋ; S+lɑŋ; |-er -ɡɚ; ES -ɡə(r; |-est -ɡɪst
long-and-short ˈlɔŋənˈʃɔrt, ˈlɒŋ-; ES -ˈʃɔət, S+ˈlɑŋ-
Longaville ˈlɔŋɡəˌvɪl, ˈlɒŋɡə-; S+ˈlɑŋ-
longboat ˈlɔŋˌbot, ˈlɒŋ-; S+ˈlɑŋ-
longbow ˈlɔŋˌbo, ˈlɒŋ-; S+ˈlɑŋ-
long-distance ˈlɔŋˈdɪstəns, ˈlɒŋ-; S+ˈlɑŋ-; (ˈlong-ˌdistance ˈcall)
longeron ˈlɑndʒərən (*Fr* lɔ̃ʒeˈrɔ̃)
longevity lɑnˈdʒɛvətɪ
Longfellow ˈlɔŋˌfɛlo, ˈlɒŋ-; S+ˈlɑŋ-

longhand ˈlɔŋˌhænd, ˈlɒŋ-; S+ˈlɑŋ-
longhorn ˈlɔŋˌhɔrn, ˈlɒŋ-; ES -ˌhɔən, S+ˈlɑŋ-
Longinus lɑnˈdʒaɪnəs |-'s -ɪz
longish ˈlɔŋɪʃ, ˈlɒŋ-; S+ˈlɑŋ-
longitude ˈlɑndʒəˌtjud, -ˌtɪud, -ˌtud
longitudinal ˌlɑndʒəˈtjudn̩l, -ˈtɪud-, -ˈtud-, -dənəl |-ly -ɪ
long-legged ˈlɔŋˈlɛɡɪd, ˈlɒŋ-, -ˈlɛɡd; S+ˈlɑŋ-
long-lived ˈlɔŋˈlaɪvd, ˈlɒŋ-, *by false etym.*+ -ˈlɪvd; S+ˈlɑŋ-
longshoreman ˈlɔŋˌʃormən, ˈlɒŋ-, -ˌʃɔr-; E -ˌʃoə-, -ˌʃɔə-; S -ˌʃoə-,+ˈlɑŋ-; |-men -mən
Longstreet ˈlɔŋˌstrit, ˈlɒŋ-; S+ˈlɑŋ-
longsuffering ˈlɔŋˈsʌfrɪŋ, ˈlɒŋ-, -fərɪŋ; S+ˈlɑŋ-
Longsword ˈlɔŋˌsord, ˈlɒŋ-, -ˌsɔrd; E -ˌsoəd, -ˌsɔəd; S -ˌsoəd, +ˈlɑŋ-
longways ˈlɔŋˌwez, ˈlɒŋ-; S+ˈlɑŋ-; |-wise -ˌwaɪz
long-winded ˈlɔŋˈwɪndɪd, ˈlɒŋ-; S+ˈlɑŋ-
loo lu |looed lud
looby ˈlubɪ
look lʊk |looked lʊkt
looker-on ˌlʊkɚˈɑn, -ˈɒn, -ˈɔn |lookers- ˌlʊkɚz-; ES ˌlʊkəz-
lookout, L- ˈlʊkˌaʊt
loom lum |loomed lumd
loon lun |loonery ˈlunərɪ
Loon, van væn ˈlon
loony, -ey ˈlunɪ
loop lup |looped lupt |-hole -ˌhol
loose lus |looses ˈlusɪz |loosed lust
loosen ˈlusn̩ |-ed -d |-ing ˈlusn̩ɪŋ, -snɪŋ
loosestrife ˈlusˌstraɪf
loot lut |looted ˈlutɪd
lop lɑp |lopped lɑpt
lope lop |loped lopt
López ˈlopɛz (*Am Sp* ˈlopes)
lop-sided ˈlɑpˈsaɪdɪd (ˈlop-ˌsided ˈmind)
loquacious loˈkweʃəs |-quacity -ˈkwæsətɪ
Lora ˈlorə, ˈlɔrə; S ˈlorə
Lorain, -e loˈren
lord, L- lɔrd; ES lɔəd; |-ed -ɪd |-ling -lɪŋ |-ship -ʃɪp
lord-and-lady ˈlɔrdn̩ˈledɪ; ES ˈlɔəd-
lore lor, lɔr; ES loə(r, E+lɔə(r
Lorelei ˈlorəˌlaɪ, ˈlɒr- (*Ger* ˈlo:rəˌlaɪ)
Lorenzo loˈrɛnzo, lə-

|full fʊl |tooth tuθ |further ˈfɝðɚ; ES ˈfɝðə |custom ˈkʌstəm |while hwaɪl |how haʊ |toy tɔɪ
|using ˈjuzɪŋ |fuse fjuz, fɪuz |dish dɪʃ |vision ˈvɪʒən |Eden ˈidn̩ |cradle ˈkredḷ |keep 'em ˈkipm̩

Those words below in which the ɑ sound is spelt o are often pronounced with ɒ in E and S

lorgnette lɔrn'jɛt; ES lɔɔn-; (*Fr* lȯr'nɛt)

lorimer, L- 'lɔrəmə, 'lar-, 'lɒr-; ES -mə(r

lorn lɔrn; ES lɔɔn

Lorna 'lɔrnə; ES 'lɔɔnə

Lorrain lo'ren (*Fr* lȯ'rǣ)

Lorraine lo'ren (*Fr* lȯ'rɛn)

Lorris, Guillaume de *Fr* gijomdəlȯ'ris

lorry 'lɔrɪ, 'larɪ, 'lɒrɪ |-ied -d

lory 'lorɪ, 'lɔrɪ; S 'lorɪ

losable, loseable 'luzəbl̩

Los Angeles *Cal* lɔs'æŋgələs, lɒs-, -'ændʒələs, -lɪs, -ndʒə͵liz |-'s -ɪz—*Other pronunciations exist. A resident phonetician writes, "The only one I've never heard is* los'aŋheles."

Los Angeles *Chile, Am Sp* los'aŋheles

Los Angelean lɔs͵æŋgə'liən, lɒs-, -ndʒə'liən

lose luz |loses 'luzɪz |lost lɔst, lɒst

Los Gatos lɔs'gatos, *loc.* -'gætəs |-'s -ɪz

loss lɔs, lɒs |-es -ɪz

lost lɔst, lɒst

lot lɑt |lotted 'lɑtɪd

Lot *Eng name* lɑt; *Fr riv.* lo, *loc.* lȯt

loth loθ |-ful 'loðfəl |-fully 'loðfəlɪ

Lothaire, -thair lo'θɛr, -'θær; E -'θɛə(r, ES -'θæə(r; (*Fr* lȯ'tɛːr)

Lothario lo'θɛrɪ͵o, -'θær-, -'θer-

Lothian 'loðɪən

lothly *adj* 'loðlɪ, *adv* 'loθ-, 'loð-

lothsome 'loðsəm

lotion 'loʃən

lotos 'lotəs |-es -ɪz

Lotos-Eaters 'lotəs͵itəz; ES -͵itəz

Lotta 'lɑtə, 'lɑtɪ

lottery 'lɑtərɪ

Lottie 'lɑtɪ

lotto 'lɑto

lotus, L- 'lotəs |-es -ɪz |-eater -͵itə; ES -ə(r

Lou lu, lɪu

loud laʊd

louden 'laʊdn̩ |-ed -d |-ing 'laʊdn̩ɪŋ, -dnɪŋ

loudmouthed 'laʊd'maʊðd, -θt

Loudon 'laʊdn̩ -ville -͵vɪl |-doun -dn̩

loud-speaker 'laʊd'spikə; ES -'spikə(r

lough lɑx, lɒx

Loughborough 'lʌf͵bʒo, -ə; ES -͵bʒr-, -͵bʌr-, -͵bʒ-

Loughrig 'lʌfrɪg

Louis *Fr name* 'lʊɪ (*Fr* lwi)

Louis *Eng name* 'lʊɪs, 'lɪuɪs, 'lʊɪ, 'lɪuɪ |-'s

  -ɪz, -z

Louisa lu'izə |-'s lu'izəz

Louisburg 'lʊɪs͵bʒg, 'lɪuɪs-; ES -͵bʒg, -͵bʒg

louis d'or ͵lʊɪ'dɔr, ͵lɪuɪ-; ES -'dɔə(r

Louise lu'iz, |Louise's lu'izɪz

Louisiana ͵luɪzɪ'ænə, lu͵izɪ'ænə |-nian -nɪən

  —*Competent observers also report* lu͵izɪ'ænə, ͵luizɪ'ænə, ͵luɪzɪ'ænə, lə͵wizɪ'ænə, *and the accentuations* 'Louisi͵ana, Lou'isi͵ana.

Louisville 'lʊɪs͵vɪl, 'lɪuɪs-; *Ky* 'lʊɪ͵vɪl, 'lɪuɪ-, *less freq.* -ɪs͵vɪl; S+'lʊɪvl̩, 'lʊəvl̩

lounge laʊndʒ |-s -ɪz |-d -d

Lounsbury 'laʊnz͵bɛrɪ, -bərɪ

loup-garou *Fr* luga'ru |*pl* loups- lu-

lour laʊr; ES laʊə(r; |-ed -d |-y -ɪ |-ing 'laʊrɪŋ

Lourdes lʊrd; ES lʊəd; (*Fr* lurd)

louse *n* laʊs |-'s -ɪz |lice laɪs |lice's |laɪsɪz

louse, *v* laʊz |-s -ɪz |-d -d |lousy 'laʊzɪ

lout laʊt |-ed -ɪd

Louth *Irel* laʊð, *Lincs* laʊθ

Louvain lu'ven (*Fr* lu'vǣ)

louver 'luvə; ES 'luvə(r; |-ed -d

L'Ouverture, Toussaint *Fr* tusǣluvɛr'tyːr

Louvre 'luvrə, 'luvə, luv; ES 'luvrə, 'luvə(ɪ

  luv; (*Fr* luːvr)

lovability, loveab- ͵lʌvə'bɪlətɪ

lovable, loveable 'lʌvəbl̩ |-bly -blɪ

lovat, L- 'lʌvət

love lʌv |loved lʌvd

love-in-idleness 'lʌvɪn'aɪdl̩nɪs |-es -ɪz

Lovel, -ll 'lʌvl̩

Lovelace 'lʌvles, 'lʌvlɪs |-'s -ɪz

lovelock 'lʌv͵lɑk

lovelorn 'lʌv͵lɔrn; ES -͵lɔən

lovesick 'lʌv͵sɪk

Lovett 'lʌvɪt

loving-kindness 'lʌvɪŋ'kaɪndnɪs, -'kaɪnnɪs

low lo |lowed lod

Low, -e lo

lowborn 'lo'bɔrn; ES -'bɔən; ('low͵born 'lass)

lowboy 'lo͵bɔɪ

lowbred 'lo'brɛd ('low͵bred 'horse)

low-brow 'lo͵braʊ

low-browed 'lo'braʊd ('low͵browed 'taste)

low-down *n* 'lo͵daʊn

low-down *adj* 'lo'daʊn ('low-͵down 'trick)

Lowell 'loəl, 'lo·ıl
lower *'frown'* 'laʊɚ; ES 'laʊ·ə(r; |-ed -d |-ing
  'laʊrıŋ, 'laʊərıŋ
lower *adj 'less high'* 'loɚ; ES 'lo·ə(r
lower *'let down'* 'loɚ; ES 'lo·ə(r; |-ed -d |-ing
  'loərıŋ, 'lorıŋ
lowermost 'loɚˌmost; ES 'lo·əˌmost
lowery 'laʊrı, 'laʊərı
Lowes loz |Lowes's 'lozız
Lowestoft 'lostɔft, -tɒft, *loc.* + 'lostəf
lowland 'loˌlænd, -lənd, *adj* -lənd
lowlander 'loləndɚ; ES 'loləndə(r
low-lifed 'lo'laıvd ('low-'lifed ˌfellow)
lowlihead 'lolıˌhɛd
low-lived 'lo'laıvd ('low-ˌlived 'face)
lowly 'lolı
Lowman 'lomən
Lowndes laʊndz, laʊnz |-'s -ız
low-pressure 'lo'prɛʃɚ; ES -'prɛʃə(r
lowrie, L- *'fox'* 'laʊrı
lowrie *'lory'* 'lorı, 'lɔrı; S 'lorı
low-test 'lo'tɛst ('low-ˌtest 'gas)
Lowth laʊθ
Lowville 'laʊvɪl
loyal 'lɔıəl, 'lɔjəl |-ly -ı |-ty -tı |-ism -ˌızəm
  |-ist -ıst
Loyd lɔıd
Loyola lɔı'olə, lɔ'jolə
Loyolite 'lɔıoˌlaıt, 'lɔjəˌlaıt |-lism -ˌlızəm
lozenge 'lazındʒ; ES + 'lɒz-; |-s -ız |-d -d
lubber 'lʌbɚ; ES 'lʌbə(r; |-ed -d |-ly -lı
Lubbock 'lʌbək
Lubec 'lubɛk, 'lıubɛk
Lübeck 'lubɛk, 'lıu- (*Ger* 'ly:bɛk)
Lubeck 'lubɛk, 'lıu- |-bish -bıʃ |-bs -bz
lubric 'lubrık, 'lıu- |-al -ļ
lubricant 'lubrıkənt, 'lıu-
lubricate 'lubrıˌket, 'lıu- |-d -ıd |-tor -ɚ; ES
  -ə(r
lubrication ˌlubrı'keʃən, ˌlıu-
lubricious lu'brıʃəs, lıu- |-city -'brısətı
lubricous 'lubrıkəs, 'lıu-
Lucan 'lukən, 'lıu-
Lucas 'lukəs, 'lıu- |-'s -ız
Lucasta lu'kæstə, lıu-
luce, L- lus, lıus |-s -ız |-'s -ız
lucence 'lusņs, 'lıu- |-cy -ı |-cent -sņt
Lucentio lu'sɛnʃıˌo, lıu-, -ʃjo
lucerne, -rn lu'sɝn, lıu-; ES -'sɜn, -'sɝn

Lucerne lu'sɝn, lıu-; ES -'sɜn, -'sɝn; (*Ger*
  Luzern lu'tsɛrn)
Lucetta lu'sɛtə, lıu-
Lucia 'luʃə, 'lıu-, -ʃıə |-n -n
Lucia di Lammermoor lu'tʃıədı'læməˌmʊr;
  ES -'læməˌmʊə(r; (*It* lu'tʃi:adiˌlammer-
  'mu:r)
Luciana ˌluʃı'ænə, ˌlıu-, -'ɑnə |-nus -nəs
lucid 'lusıd, 'lıusıd |-ity lu'sıdətı, lıu-
Lucifer, l- 'lusəfɚ, 'lıu-; ES -fə(r
Lucile, -lle lu'sil, lıu-
Lucilius lu'sılıəs, lıu-, -ljəs |-'s -ız
Lucina lu'saınə, lıu-
Lucinda lu'sındə, lıu-
Lucio 'luʃıˌo, 'lıu-, -ʃjo
lucite 'lusaıt, 'lıu-
Lucius 'luʃəs, 'lıu-, -ʃıəs |-'s -ız
luck lʌk |-y -ı |-ily 'lʌkļı, 'lʌkılı
Lucknow 'lʌknaʊ
lucrative 'lukrətıv, 'lıu-
lucre 'lukɚ, 'lıu-; ES -kə(r
Lucrece lu'kris, lıu- |-'s -ız
Lucretia lu'kriʃə, lıu-, -ʃıə
Lucretius lu'kriʃəs, lıu-, -ʃıəs |-'s -ız
lucubrate 'lukjuˌbret, 'lıu-, -kʊ- |-brated
  -ˌbretıd
lucubration ˌlukju'breʃən, ˌlıu-, -kʊ-
Lucullus lu'kʌləs, lıu- |-'s -ız |-lan -lən |-lian
  -lıən
Lucy 'lusı, 'lıusı
Lud lʌd |Luddite 'lʌdaıt
Ludendorf 'ludņˌdɔrf; ES -ˌdɔɔf
Ludgate 'lʌdˌget, 'lʌdgıt
ludicrous 'ludıkrəs, 'lıu-
Ludington 'lʌdıŋtən
Ludlow 'lʌdlo |-lovian lʌd'lovıən
Ludovic 'ludəvık |-wick -wık
Ludwig 'lʌdwıg, -wık (*Ger* 'lu:tvıx, 'lu:d-)
Luella lu'ɛlə, lıu-
lues 'luiz, 'lıu-
luff lʌf |luffed lʌft
lug lʌg |lugged lʌgd |luggage 'lʌgıdʒ
lugger 'lʌgɚ; ES 'lʌgə(r
lugsail 'lʌgˌsel, 'lʌgsļ
lugubrious lu'gjubrıəs, lıu'gıu-, lu'gub-
Luke luk, lıuk |-kan, -can -kən
lukewarm 'luk'wɔrm, 'lıuk-; ES -'wɔəm
  ('lukeˌwarm 'zeal)
lull, L- lʌl |-ed -d |-aby -əˌbaı

|full fʊl |tooth tuθ |further 'fɝðɚ; ES 'fɝðə |custom 'kʌstəm |while hwaıl |how haʊ |toy tɔı
|using 'juzıŋ |fuse fjuz, fıuz |dish dıʃ |vision 'vıʒən |Eden 'idņ |cradle 'kredļ |keep 'em 'kipm̩

lumbago lʌmˈbego
lumbar ˈlʌmbɚ; ES ˈlʌmbə(r
lumber ˈlʌmbɚ; ES -bə(r; |-ed -d |-ing
 ˈlʌmbrɪŋ, -bərɪŋ
lumberjack ˈlʌmbɚˌdʒæk; ES ˈlʌmbə-
lumber-room ˈlʌmbɚˌrum, -ˌrʊm; ES ˈlʌmbə-
lumen ˈlumɪn, ˈlɪu-, -mən |-s -z |-mina -mɪnə
luminary ˈluməˌnɛrɪ, ˈlɪu-
lumine ˈlumɪn, ˈlɪu- |-d -d
luminesce ˌluməˈnɛs, ˌlɪu- |-s -ɪz |-d -t
luminescence ˌluməˈnɛsn̩s, ˌlɪu- |-scent -sn̩t
luminosity ˌluməˈnɑsətɪ, ˌlɪu-; ES+-ˈnɒs-
luminous ˈlumənəs, ˈlɪu-
Lumley, -ly ˈlʌmlɪ
Lummis ˈlʌmɪs |-'s -ɪz
lummox ˈlʌməks |-es -ɪz
lump lʌmp |lumped lʌmpt
Lumpkin ˈlʌmpkɪn
Luna, l- ˈlunə, ˈlɪunə
lunacy ˈlunəsɪ, ˈlɪu-
lunar ˈlunɚ, ˈlɪunɚ; ES -nə(r; |-y -ɪ
lunate ˈlunet, ˈlɪu-, -nɪt |-tion luˈneʃən, lɪu-
lunatic ˈlunəˌtɪk, ˈlɪu-
lunatical luˈnætɪkl̩, lɪu- |-ly -ɪ, -ɪklɪ
lunch lʌntʃ |lunches ˈlʌntʃɪz |lunched lʌntʃt
luncheon ˈlʌntʃən |-ed -d
lunchroom ˈlʌntʃˌrum, -ˌrʊm
lune lun, lɪun
Lunenburg ˈlunənˌbɝg; ES -ˌbɝg, -ˌbɝg
lunette luˈnɛt, lɪu-
lung lʌŋ |lunged lʌŋd
lunge lʌndʒ |lunges ˈlʌndʒɪz |lunged lʌndʒd
lunger from lung ˈlʌŋɚ; ES ˈlʌŋə(r
Lunger surname ˈlʌŋɚ; ES ˈlʌŋə(r
lunger from lunge ˈlʌndʒɚ; ES ˈlʌndʒə(r
lunkhead ˈlʌŋkˌhɛd
lunn, L- lʌn
luny ˈlunɪ, ˈlɪunɪ
Lupercal ˈlupɚˌkl̩, ˈlɪu-, -ˌkæl
Lupercalia ˌlupɚˈkelɪə, ˌlɪu-, -ˈkeljə
lupine 'wolfish' ˈlupaɪn, ˈlɪu-
lupine, -in plant ˈlupɪn, ˈlɪu-
lupus, L- ˈlupəs, ˈlɪu- |-pi -paɪ
Luquiens luˈkæn, lɪu- (Fr lyˈkjæ̃)
Luray luˈre, lɪu- (ˈLuˌray ˈCaverns)
lurch lɝtʃ; ES lɝtʃ, lɝtʃ; |-es -ɪz |-ed -t
lurdan, -e ˈlɝdn̩; ES ˈlɝdn̩, ˈlɝdn̩
lure lʊr, lɪʊr |-d -d
lure 'trumpet' ˈlʊrə |pl luren ˈlʊrən

lurid ˈlʊrɪd, ˈlɪʊ-
lurk lɝk; ES lɝk, lɝk; |-ed -t
Lurlei ˈlʊrlaɪ; ES ˈlʊə-; (Ger ˈlʊrlaɪ)
luscious ˈlʌʃəs
lush lʌʃ
Lusiad ˈlusɪˌæd, ˈlɪu- |-s -z
Lusitania ˌlusəˈtenɪə, ˌlɪu-
lust lʌst |lusted ˈlʌstɪd |-ful -fəl |-fully -fəlɪ
luster, -tre ˈlʌstɚ; ES -tə(r; |-(e)d -d |lust(e)-
 ring ˈlʌstərɪŋ, ˈlʌstrɪŋ
lusterer ˈlʌstərɚ; ES ˈlʌstərə(r
lusterware, lustre- ˈlʌstɚˌwɛr, -ˌwær; E
 ˈlʌstɚˌwɛə(r, ES -ˌwæə(r
lustihead ˈlʌstɪˌhɛd |lustihood ˈlʌstɪˌhʊd
lustral ˈlʌstrəl
lustrate ˈlʌstret |-d -ɪd |-tion lʌsˈtreʃən
lustrous ˈlʌstrəs
lustrum ˈlʌstrəm |-s -z |-tra -trə
lutanist ˈlutn̩ɪst, ˈlɪut-
lute lut, lɪut |-d -ɪd
lutecium luˈtiʃɪəm, lɪu-
Luther ˈluθɚ, ˈlɪu-; ES -θə(r; |-an -ən, -θrən
Lutterworth ˈlʌtɚwɚθ; ES ˈlʌtəwɚθ
Luttrell ˈlʌtrəl
Lutz luts, lʌts |-'s -ɪz
lux lʌks |-es -ɪz |L pl luces ˈlusiz, ˈlɪu-
luxe lʊks, lʌks (Fr lyks)
Luxembourg ˈlʌksəmˌbɝg; ES -ˌbɝg, -ˌbɝg;
 (Fr lyksɑ̃ˈbu:r)
Luxemburg ˈlʌksəmˌbɝg; ES -ˌbɝg, -ˌbɝg;
 (Ger ˈlʊksəmˌbʊrk)
Luxor ˈlʌksɔr; ES ˈlʌksɔə(r
luxuriance lʌgˈʒʊrɪəns, lʌkˈʃʊr- |-cy -ɪ |-ant
 -ənt—see luxurious
luxuriate lʌgˈʒʊrɪˌet, lʌkˈʃʊr- |-d -ɪd—see
 luxurious
luxurious lʌgˈʒʊrɪəs, lʌkˈʃʊr-——The pron.
 with -gʒ- is phonetically normal; that with
 -kʃ- is due to the analogy of ˈlʌkʃərɪ, q.v.
luxury ˈlʌkʃərɪ, much less freq. ˈlʌgʒ-——The
 pron. with -kʃ- is phonetically normal (owing
 to accent); that with -gʒ- is due to analogy of
 lʌgˈʒʊrɪəs.
Luzerne Pa luˈzɝn, lɪu-; ES -ˈzɝn, -ˈzɝn
Luzon luˈzɑn, -ˈzɒn
-ly ending of adjs (timely) & advs (boldly) -lɪ,
 -li—Very many words in -ly (esp. advs) are
 omitted from the vocab. when the pron. can
 be found by adding the sounds -lɪ directly to

the corresponding head pron., as slow **slo,** slowly **'slo-lɪ.** *But if some question of pronunciation is involved, the* -ly *form is entered, as in* real **'rɪəl** |-ly **-ɪ** *or* full **fʊl** |-ly **-ɪ,** *where only a single* l *is sounded, or in* sole **sol** |-ly **'solɪ,** *where both are sounded, or in* wholly **'holɪ, 'hɒlɪ,** *which varies. For variation between* ɪ *&* i *see* -y *in the vocab.*

Lyall **'laɪəl**
lycanthropy **laɪ'kænθrəpɪ**
lyceum **laɪ'sɪəm, 'laɪsɪəm** |L- **laɪ'sɪəm**
Lychorida **laɪ'kɔrɪdə, -'kɑr-, -'kɒr-**
Lycia **'lɪʃɪə** |Lycian **'lɪʃɪən**
Lycidas **'lɪsədəs** |-'s -ɪz
Lycoming **laɪ'kʌmɪŋ;** ES+-'kɒm-
Lycurgus **laɪ'kɝgəs;** ES -'kɜg-, -'kɝg-; |-'s -ɪz
lyddite **'lɪdaɪt**
Lydekker **laɪ'dɛkɚ, lɪ-;** ES -dɛkə(r
Lydenberg **'laɪdṇ,bɝg;** ES -,bɜg, -,bɝg
Lydgate **'lɪdget, -gɪt**
Lydia **'lɪdɪə** |-n -n
lye *'alkali'* **laɪ** |lyed **laɪd** |lying **'laɪɪŋ**
Lyell **'laɪəl**
lying *'deceiving,' 'reclining,' 'treating with lye'* **'laɪɪŋ**
Lykens **'laɪkɪnz, -kənz** |-'s -ɪz
Lyly **'lɪlɪ**
Lyme Regis **'laɪm'ridʒɪs** |-'s -ɪz
lymph **lɪmf, lɪmpf** |-atic **lɪm'fætɪk**
lymphocyte **'lɪmfə,saɪt** |-tic **,lɪmfə'sɪtɪk**
lymphoid **'lɪmfɔɪd**
Lympne **lɪm**
lyncean **lɪn'sɪən**
lynch, L- **lɪntʃ** |lynches **'lɪntʃɪz** |-ed -t

Lynchburg **'lɪntʃbɝg;** ES -bɜg, -bɝg
Lyndhurst **'lɪndhɝst;** ES -hɜst, -hɝst
Lyndsay **'lɪnzɪ, 'lɪndzɪ**
Lynmouth **'lɪnməθ**
Lynn **lɪn**
lynx **lɪŋks** |lynxes **'lɪŋksɪz**
lynx-eyed **'lɪŋks'aɪd** ('lynx-,eyed 'scout)
Lyon *Eng name* **'laɪən;** *Fr city see* Lyons
lyonnaise **,laɪə'nez** (*Fr* ljɔ̃'nɛːz)
Lyonness, -sse **,laɪə'nɛs** |-'s -ɪz
Lyons *Eng name* **'laɪənz,** *Fr city* **'laɪənz** |-'s -ɪz (*Fr* Lyon ljɔ̃)
Lyra, l- **'laɪrə** |gen Lyrae **'laɪri**
lyrate **'laɪret, -rɪt**
lyre **laɪr;** ES laɪə(r; |-d -d
lyrebird **'laɪr,bɝd;** ES **'laɪə,bɜd, 'laɪə,bɝd**
lyric **'lɪrɪk** |-al -ḷ |-ally -ḷɪ, -ɪklɪ
lyricism **'lɪrə,sɪzəm** |-cist -sɪst
lyricize **'lɪrə,saɪz** |-s -ɪz |-d -d
lyrist *lyre-player* **'laɪrɪst, 'lɪr-**
lyrist *lyric poet* **'lɪrɪst**
Lysander **laɪ'sændɚ;** ES -'sændə(r
lyse **laɪs** |lyses **'laɪsɪz** |lysed **laɪst**
Lysias **'lɪsɪəs** |-'s -ɪz
Lysimachus **laɪ'sɪməkəs** |-'s -ɪz
lysimeter **laɪ'sɪmətɚ;** ES -tə(r
lysin **'laɪsɪn** |-sine **'laɪsin, -sɪn**
Lysippus **laɪ'sɪpəs** |-'s -ɪz
lysis **'laɪsɪs**
lysol **'laɪsal, -sɒl, -sɔl**
Lyte **laɪt**
Lytell **'laɪtḷ, 'lɪtḷ, lɪ'tɛl**
Lytle **'laɪtḷ, 'lɪtḷ**
Lyttleton **'lɪtḷtən**
Lytton **'lɪtṇ**

M

M, m *letter* ɛm |*pl* M's, Ms, *poss* M's ɛmz
'm *unstressed form of* am *after* I, m
ma'am **mæm, mɑm, -ṃ, -m**
Mab **mæb**
Mabel **'mebḷ**
Mabinogion **,mæbə'nogɪən**
Mac-, Mc-, M'- *pron.* **mə-, mɪ-, mək-, mɪk-**
—*alphabetically* M' *&* Mc *are placed with* Mac

macabre **mə'kɑbrə, mə'kɑbɚ;** ES -'kɑbrə, -'kɑbə(r
macadam, **mə'kædəm** |-ize -,aɪz |-izes -,aɪzɪz |-ized -,aɪzd
MacAdam **mək'ædəm, mæk'ædəm** |-s -z |-s's -zɪz
macadamization **mə,kædəmə'zeʃən, -maɪ-'zeʃən**
McAdoo **'mækə,du**

McAllister, Macalister mə'kæləstəɔ; ES -tə(r
macaroni ˌmækə'roni
macaronic ˌmækə'rɑnɪk; ES+-'rɒnɪk
macaroon ˌmækə'run ('macaˌroon 'tart)
MacArthur mək'ɑrθəɔ; ES mək'ɑ:θə(r, E+
-'a:θ-
Macassar mə'kæsəɔ; ES mə'kæsə(r
Macaulay mə'kɔlɪ
Macbeth mæk'bɛθ, mək'bɛθ
Maccabees 'mækəˌbiz |-bean ˌmækə'biən
Maccabeus ˌmækə'biəs |Maccabeus's -'biəsɪz
M'Carthy mə'kɑrθɪ; ES mə'kɑ:θɪ, E+-'ka:θɪ
McClellan mə'klɛlən
Macclesfield 'mækļzˌfild
McColl mə'kɔl
McCormack mə'kɔrmək; ES mə'kɔəmək
McCormick mə'kɔrmɪk; ES mə'kɔəmɪk
MacCracken mə'krækən
McCrae mə'kre
McCrea mə'kre
McCulloch, -ough mə'kʌləx, -'kʌlək, -lə, -lɪ
McDougal, -ll mək'dugļ, mæk-
MacDowell composer mək'dauəl
McDowell Am general mək'dauəl
Macduff mæk'dʌf, mək'dʌf
mace mes |maces 'mesɪz |maced mest
Macedon 'mæsəˌdɑn; ES+'mæsəˌdɒn
Macedonia ˌmæsə'donɪə, -'donjə |-n -n
macerate 'mæsəˌret |macerated 'mæsəˌretɪd
McFarland mək'farlənd, -lən; ES -'fa:l-,
E+-'fa:l-
MacFarlane mək'farlɪn, -lən; ES -'fa:l-,
E+-'fa:l-
MacFlecknoe mək'flɛkno, mæk-
McGehee mə'gihi
McGill university mə'gɪl, mɪ'gɪl
Macgillicuddy mə'gɪləˌkʌdɪ, 'mægļˌk-, 'mæ-
gļɪˌk-
MacGillivray mə'gɪləvrɪ, mə'gɪləvɔrɪ
Machen Arthur 'mækən
McHenry mək'hɛnrɪ, mə'kɛnrɪ
machete ma'tʃete, mə'ʃɛt, mə'ʃɛtɪ (Sp ma-
'tʃete)
Machias mə'tʃaɪəs |-'s -ɪz
Machiavelli ˌmækɪə'vɛlɪ, -kjə- (It ˌmakja-
'vɛlli)
Machiavellian ˌmækɪə'vɛlɪən, -kjə-, -ljən
machinate 'mækəˌnet |-d -ɪd |-tion ˌmækə-
'neʃən

machine mə'ʃin |-d -d |-ry -ərɪ, -rɪ |-ist -ɪst
McIlrath 'mækļˌræθ, 'mækļˌrɑθ
McIntosh 'mækɪnˌtɑʃ; ES+-ˌtɒʃ; |-'s -ɪz
MacIvor, Flora mək'aɪvəɔ, -'ivəɔ; ES -və(r
mackerel 'mækərəl, 'mækrəl
Mackinac co., isl., and strait 'mækəˌnɔ
Mackinaw 'mækəˌnɔ
McKinley mə'kɪnlɪ
mackintosh 'mækɪnˌtɑʃ; ES+-ˌtɒʃ; |-es -ɪz
McLaughlin mə'klɑklɪn, -'gl-, -ɑx-, -ɑf-;
ES+-ɒ-
McLean mə'klen, mək'len
MacLeish mək'liʃ |MacLeish's mək'liʃɪz
McLeod mə'klaud
McLoughlin mə'klɑklɪn; ES+-ɒk-
MacManus mək'mænəs, -'mɑnəs, -'menəs
|-'s -ɪz
McMechan, -en mək'mɛkən
MacMillan mæk'mɪlən, mək'mɪlən
MacMonnies mək'mʌnɪz |-Monnies' -'mʌnɪz
Macomb mə'kom, Mich mə'kum, -'kom
Macon 'mekən, 'mekɑn, 'mekɒn
MacReady mə'kredɪ, mə'kridɪ
Macrobius mə'krobɪəs |-crobius's -'krobɪəsɪz
macrocosm 'mækrəˌkɑzəm; ES+-ˌkɒzəm
macron 'mekrən, 'mekrɑn, 'mekrɒn, 'mæk-
McShea mək'ʃe
MacTavish mək'tævɪʃ, mæk'tævɪʃ
maculate adj 'mækjəlɪt, 'mækjʊlɪt
maculate v 'mækjəˌlet, 'mækjʊˌlet |-d -ɪd
maculation ˌmækjə'leʃən, ˌmækjʊ'leʃən
MacVeagh mək've
mad mæd |madded 'mædɪd
Madagascar ˌmædə'gæskəɔ; ES -kə(r; |-can
-kən
madam 'mædəm
madame 'mædəm (Fr ma'dam, pl mesdames
me'dam)
madcap 'mædˌkæp
madden, M- 'mædn̩ |-ed -d |-ing 'mædnɪŋ,
'mædn̩ɪŋ
madder 'mædəɔ; ES 'mædə(r
made med
Madeira mə'dɪrə
Madeleine 'mædļˌen
Madeline 'mædļˌaɪn, 'mædļɪn
mademoiselle ˌmædəmə'zɛl (Fr madmwa'zɛl,
mam'zɛl)
made-up 'med'ʌp ('made-ˌup 'story)

Madge mædʒ |Madge's 'mædʒɪz—*cf* Margery
and see §121

madhouse 'mæd͜ˌhaʊs |-houses -ˌhaʊzɪz

Madison 'mædəsn̩

madman 'mædˌmæn, 'mædmən |-men -mən

Madonna mə'dɑnə; ES+mə'dɒnə

madras mə'dræs, 'mædrəs, mə'drɑs

Madras mə'dræs, mə'drɑs |-'s -ɪz

Madrid *US* 'mædrɪd, *Spain* mə'drɪd (*Sp*
ma'ðrɪð, ma'ðri)

madrigal 'mædrɪgl̩

Madura *Brit India* 'mædʒʊrə, -djʊ-; *Du E.
Indies* ma'durɑ

maduro mə'dʊro (*Sp* ma'ðuro)

Mae me

Maeander mɪ'ændɚ; ES mɪ'ændə(r

Maecenas mɪ'sinəs, mi- |Maecenases -'sinəsɪz

maelstrom, M- 'melstrəm

maenad 'minæd |-s -z |maenades 'mɛnəˌdiz

maestro 'maɪstro (*It* ma'ɛstro)

Maeterlinck 'metɚˌlɪŋk, 'metɚ-; ES 'metə-,
'mɛtɚ-; (*Du* 'matərˌlɪŋk, *Fr* matɛr'lɛ̃)

magazine *'storehouse'* ˌmægə'zin, *'periodical'*
ˌmægə'zin, 'mægəˌzin

Magdalen *Bible* 'mægdəlɪn, -lən, *Oxf college*
'mɔdlɪn

Magdalene *Bible* 'mægdəˌlin, ˌmægdə'lini,
Camb college 'mɔdlɪn

Magdeburg 'mægdəˌbɝg; ES 'mægdəˌbɜg,
-ˌbɝg; (*Ger* 'makdəˌbʊrk)

Magellan mə'dʒɛlən |Magellanic ˌmædʒə-
'lænɪk

magenta, M- mə'dʒɛntə

Maggiore mə'dʒɔrɪ, mə'dʒɔrɪ; S mə'dʒɔrɪ;
(*It* mad'dʒo:re)

maggot 'mægət |maggoty 'mægətɪ

Maggy 'mægɪ—*cf* Margaret *and see §121*

Magi 'medʒaɪ

magic 'mædʒɪk |-al -l̩ |-ally -l̩ɪ, -ɪklɪ

magician mə'dʒɪʃən

Maginot 'mæʒəˌno, 'maʒ- (*Fr* maʒi'no)

magisterial ˌmædʒɪs'tɪrɪəl |-ly -ɪ

magistery 'mædʒɪsˌtɛrɪ

magistral 'mædʒɪstrəl |-ly -ɪ |-stracy -strəsɪ

magistrate 'mædʒɪsˌtret, 'mædʒɪstrɪt

magma 'mægmə |magmas 'mægməz |mag-
mata 'mægmətə

Magna Charta, Carta 'mægnə'kɑrtə; ES
-'kɑ:tə, E+-'kɑ:tə

magnanimous mæg'nænəməs |-mity ˌmægnə-
'nɪmətɪ

magnate 'mægnet

magnesia mæg'niʃə, -ʒə |-sium -ʃɪəm, -ʒɪəm

magnesite 'mægnɪˌsaɪt

magnet 'mægnɪt

magnetic mæg'nɛtɪk |-al -l̩ |-ally -l̩ɪ, -ɪklɪ

magnetism 'mægnəˌtɪzəm

magnetite 'mægnəˌtaɪt

magnetize 'mægnəˌtaɪz |-tizes -ˌtaɪzɪz |-d -d

magneto mæg'nito

magnetogenerator mægˌnito'dʒɛnəˌretɚ; ES
-tɚ(r

magnetometer ˌmægnə'tɑmətɚ; ES -tə(r,
-'tɒm-

magnetoscope mæg'nitəˌskop, mæg'nɛtə-

magnific mæg'nɪfɪk |-al -l̩ |-ally -l̩ɪ, -ɪklɪ

Magnificat mæg'nɪfɪˌkæt

magnification ˌmægnəfə'keʃən

magnificence mæg'nɪfəsn̩s |-cent -sn̩t

magnifico mæg'nɪfəˌko

magnify 'mægnəˌfaɪ |-fied -ˌfaɪd

magniloquence mæg'nɪləkwəns |-quent
-kwənt

magnitude 'mægnəˌtjud, -ˌtɪud, -ˌtud

magnolia mæg'nolɪə, -'noljə

magnum 'mægnəm

Magog 'megɑg, 'megɒg

Magoun mə'gun

magpie 'mægˌpaɪ

maguey 'mægwe (*Sp* ma'ge·i)

Magus 'megəs |Magi 'medʒaɪ

Magyar 'mægjɑr; ES 'mægjɑ:(r, E+-gjɑ:(r;
(*Hung* 'mɒdjɒr)

Mahan mə'hæn, 'me·ən

Mahanoy ˌmɑhə'nɔɪ

maharaja, -h ˌmɑhə'rɑdʒə (*Hind* mə'hɑ-
'rɑdʒə)

maharani, -nee ˌmɑhə'rɑni (*Hind* mə'hɑ'rɑni)

mahatma mə'hætmə, mə'hɑtmə

Mahdi 'mɑdi

mah-jongg, -ng mɑ'dʒɔŋ, -'dʒɒŋ, -'dʒɑŋ

mahogany mə'hɑgənɪ, mə'hɒgənɪ

Mahometan mə'hɑmətən, -'hɒm-

Mahommed mə'hɑmɪd, mə'hɒmɪd |-an -ən

Mahon *Am name* 'mean, mə'hun, -'hɒn

Mahoning mə'honɪŋ

Mahound mə'haʊnd, mə'hund

mahout mə'haʊt

maid **med** |maiden **'medn̩**

maidenhair **'medn̩ˌhɛr, -ˌhær**; E **-ˌhɛə(r**, ES **-ˌhæə(r**

maidenhead **'medn̩ˌhɛd** |maidenhood **'medn̩ˌhʊd**

maidservant **'medˌsɝvənt; -ˌsɜvənt, -ˌsɝvənt**

Maidstone *Engd* **'medstən, 'medˌston**

mail **mel** |mailed **meld** |mailable **'meləbl̩**

mailbag **'melˌbæg**

mailbox **'melˌbɑks**; ES+**'melˌbɒks**; |-es **-ɪz**

mailman **'melˌmæn** |mailmen **'melˌmɛn, 'melmən**

maim **mem** |maimed **memd** |-edly **-ɪdlɪ**

main **men**

Maine **men**

mainland **'menˌlænd, 'menlənd**

mainmast **'menˌmæst, -məst**; E+**-ˌmast, -ˌmast**

mainsail **'menˌsel**, *naut.* **'mensl̩**

mainsheet **'menˌʃit**

mainspring **'menˌsprɪŋ**

mainstay **'menˌste** |mainstayed **'menˌsted**

maintain **men'ten, mən'ten** |-tained **-'tend**

maintenance **'mentənəns, -tɪn-** |-s **-ɪz**

Mainwaring **'mænərɪŋ, 'menwɔrɪŋ, -wɑr-, -wɒr-**

maître d'hôtel *Fr* **mɛtrədɔ̃'tɛl, mɛtdɔ̃'tɛl**

maize **mez** |maizes **'mezɪz**

majestic **mə'dʒɛstɪk** |-al **-l̩** |-ally **-l̩ɪ, -ɪklɪ**

majesty **'mædʒɪstɪ, 'mædʒəstɪ**

majolica **mə'dʒɑlɪkə, mə'jɑl-**; ES+**-ɒl-**

major **'medʒɝ**; ES **'medʒə(r**; |-ed **-d**

Majorca **mə'dʒɔrkə**; ES **mə'dʒɔəkə**

major-domo **'medʒɚ'domo**; ES **'medʒə'domo**

majority **mə'dʒɔrətɪ, -'dʒɑr-, -'dʒɒr-**

majuscule **mə'dʒʌskjul, -kɪul**

make **mek** |made **med**

makebate **'mekˌbet**

make-believe **'mekbəˌliv**

makeshift **'mekˌʃɪft**

make-up **'mekˌʌp**

makeweight **'mekˌwet**

Malabar **'mæləˌbɑr, ˌmælə'bɑr**; ES **-ɑː(r, E+-ɑː(r; ('Malaˌbar 'Coast)**

Malacca **mə'lækə**

Malachi **'mæləˌkaɪ**

malachite **'mæləˌkaɪt**

maladaptation **ˌmælədæp'teʃən, ˌmælædəp-'teʃən**

maladjusted **ˌmælə'dʒʌstɪd** |-justment **-'dʒʌstmənt**

maladminister **ˌmæləd'mɪnəstɚ**; ES **-'mɪnəstə(r**

maladministration **ˌmælədˌmɪnə'streʃən**

maladroit **ˌmælə'drɔɪt** (**'malaˌdroit 'move**)

malady **'mælədɪ**

Malaga **'mæləgə**

malaise **mæ'lez** (*Fr* **ma'lɛːz**)

malapert **'mæləˌpɝt**; ES **-ˌpɝt, -ˌpɝt**

Malaprop **'mæləˌprɑp**; ES+**-ˌprɒp**

malapropism **'mæləprɑpˌɪzəm**; ES+**-prɒp-**

malapropos **ˌmælæprə'po**

malaria **mə'lɛrɪə, mə'lerɪə, mə'lærɪə** |-l **-l**

malassimilation **'mæləˌsɪmə'leʃən**

Malay **mə'le, 'mele** |-an **mə'leən**

Malaysian **mə'leʃən, mə'leʒən**

Malchus **'mælkəs** |Malchus's **'mælkəsɪz**

Malcolm **'mælkəm**, *formerly* **'mɔkəm**

malcontent **'mælkənˌtɛnt** |-ed **ˌmælkən'tɛntɪd**

mal de mer *Fr* **maldə'mɛːr**

Malden **'mɔldən, 'mɔldɪn** |Maldon **'mɔldən**

male **mel**

maledict **'mæləˌdɪkt** |-ed **-ɪd** |-ion **ˌmælə-'dɪkʃən**

maledictory **ˌmælə'dɪktərɪ, -trɪ**

malefaction **ˌmælə'fækʃən** |-tor **-tɚ**; ES **-tə(r**

malefic **mə'lɛfɪk** |-al **-l̩** |-ally **-l̩ɪ, -ɪklɪ**

maleficence **mə'lɛfəsṇs** |-cent **-sṇt**

malevolence **mə'lɛvələns** |-lent **-lənt**

malfeasance **ˌmæl'fizṇs** |-feasances **-'fizṇsɪz**

malformation **ˌmælfɔr'meʃən**; ES **-fɔə'meʃən**

malformed **mæl'fɔrmd**; ES **-'fɔəmd**

malic **'mælɪk, 'melɪk**

malice **'mælɪs** |-licious **mə'lɪʃəs**

malign **mə'laɪn**

malignance **mə'lɪgnəns** |-cy **-ɪ** |-nant **-nənt**

malignity **mə'lɪgnətɪ**

malines, -line **mə'lin** (*Fr* **ma'lin**)

malinger **mə'lɪŋgɚ**; ES **-gə(r**; |-ed **-d** |-ing **-gərɪŋ, -grɪŋ**

malingerer **mə'lɪŋgərɚ**; ES **-'lɪŋgərə(r**

malison **'mæləzṇ, -sṇ**

malkin **'mɔkɪn** |Malkin **'mælkɪn, 'mɔkɪn**

mall '*maul*' **mɔl** |-ed **-d**

Mall **mæl, mɔl**—*see* Pall Mall

mallard **'mæləd**; ES **'mæləd**

malleable **'mælɪəbl̩** |-bility **ˌmælɪə'bɪlətɪ**

mallet, M- **'mælɪt**

mallow ˈmælo, -ə
Malmesbury ˈmɑmzˌbɛrɪ, ˈmɑmzbərɪ
malmsey, M- ˈmɑmzɪ
malnutrition ˌmælnjuˈtrɪʃən, -nɪu-, -nu-
malodor mælˈodɚ; ES mælˈodə(r; |-ous
   -ˈodərəs
Malone məˈlon
malonic məˈlɑnɪk, məˈlonɪk; ES+-ˈlɒnɪk
Malory ˈmælərɪ
malpractice mælˈpræktɪs |-tices -tɪsɪz
malt mɔlt |malted ˈmɔltɪd
Malta ˈmɔltə
Maltese mɔlˈtiz |-s -ɪz (ˈMalˌtese ˈcat)
Malthus ˈmælθəs |Malthus's ˈmælθəsɪz
Malthusian mælˈθjuzɪən, -ˈθɪuz-, -ˈθuz-, -jən
maltose ˈmɔltos
maltreat mælˈtrit |-ed -ɪd |-ment -mənt
Malvern US ˈmælvɚn, mælˈvɝn, Engd, Aus-
   tralia ˈmɔlvɝn, ˈmɔlvɚn; ES -ən, -ɜn, -ɝn
malversation ˌmælvɚˈseʃən; ES ˌmælvə-
   ˈseʃən
Malvolio mælˈvolɪˌo, mælˈvoljo
mama ˈmɑmə, now rare məˈmɑ
Mamaroneck məˈmærəˌnɛk
mamba ˈmɑmbə
Mameluke, m- ˈmæməˌluk, ˈmæməˌlɪuk
Mamilius məˈmɪlɪəs, -ˈmɪljəs |-'s -ɪz
mamma 'mother' ˈmɑmə, now rare məˈmɑ
mamma 'milk gland' ˈmæmə |mammae
   ˈmæmi
mammal ˈmæml |mammalia mæˈmelɪə, -ljə
mammalogy mæˈmælədʒɪ |-gist -dʒɪst
mammary ˈmæmərɪ |mammilary ˈmæməˌlɛrɪ
mammon, M- ˈmæmən
mammoth ˈmæməθ |-ths -θs
mammy ˈmæmɪ
man, M- mæn |men mɛn |manned mænd
-man, -men second element of compound nouns
   (policeman). In most popular words pronounced in sg & pl -mən. In deliberate
   speech or sometimes with special meaning,
   the sg & pl -mən often becomes sg -ˌmæn,
   pl -ˌmɛn (horsemen 'cavalry' ˈhɔrsmən;
   'racing sports' ˈhɔrsˌmɛn). In the vocab.
   usually only the popular and colloquial forms
   are given.
manacle ˈmænəkl̩, -ɪkl̩ |-d -d |-ling -kl̩ɪŋ,
   -klɪŋ
manage ˈmænɪdʒ |-s -ɪz |-d -d |-ment -mənt

manageability ˌmænɪdʒəˈbɪlətɪ
manageable ˈmænɪdʒəbl̩ |-bly -blɪ
manageress ˈmænɪdʒɚɪs, -dʒɪrɪs |-esses -ɪsɪz
managerial ˌmænəˈdʒɪrɪəl |-ly -ɪ
mañana mɑˈnjɑnɑ (Sp maˈɲana)
Manasquan ˈmænəˌskwɑn, -ˌskwɒn
Manassas məˈnæsəs |-nassas' -ˈnæsəs
Manasseh məˈnæsə, -sɪ
man-at-arms ˈmænətˈɑrmz; ES -ˈɑːmz, E+
   -ˈɑːmz
manatee, M- ˌmænəˈti
Manchester ˈmænˌtʃɛstɚ, ˈmæntʃɪstɚ; ES
   -tə(r
Manchu mænˈtʃu (ˈManˌchu ˈlanguage)
Manchukuo ˌmæntʃuˈkwo, ˌmæntʃukuˈo,
   mænˈtʃuko
Manchukuoan ˌmæntʃuˈkwoən, -kuˈoən,
   mænˈtʃukəwən
Manchuria mænˈtʃʊrɪə
manciple ˈmænsəpl̩
Mandalay ˈmændəˌle, ˌmændəˈle
mandamus mænˈdeməs |-damuses -ˈdeməsɪz
   |-ed -t
mandarin n ˈmændərɪn, v ˌmændəˈrin |-d -d
mandatary ˈmændəˌtɛrɪ
mandate n ˈmændet, -dɪt, v -det |-d -ɪd
mandator mænˈdetɚ; ES mænˈdetə(r
mandatory ˈmændəˌtorɪ, -ˌtɔrɪ; S -ˌtorɪ
Mandeville ˈmændəˌvɪl
mandible ˈmændəbl̩
mandolin ˈmændl̩ˌɪn, ˌmændl̩ˈɪn
mandragora mænˈdrægərə
mandrake ˈmændrɪk, ˈmændrek
mandrel, -il ˈmændrəl, ˈmændrɪl
mandrill ˈmændrɪl
mane men |maned mend
man-eater ˈmænˌitɚ; ES ˈmænˌitə(r
manege mæˈnɛʒ, mæˈneʒ |-s -ɪz (Fr maˈnɛːʒ)
manes ˈmeniz
Manet məˈne (Fr maˈnɛ)
maneuver məˈnuvɚ; ES -ˈnuvə(r; |-ed -d |-ing
   -ˈnuvərɪŋ, -ˈnuvrɪŋ
maneuverability məˌnuvərəˈbɪlətɪ
Manfred ˈmænfrɪd, ˈmænfrɛd
manful ˈmænfəl |-ly -ɪ
manganese ˈmæŋɡəˌnis, ˈmæn-, ˌmæŋɡəˈnis,
   ˌmæn-, -ˌniz, -ˈniz
manganic mænˈɡænɪk, mæŋˈɡænɪk
manganite ˈmæŋɡəˌnaɪt, ˈmæŋɡəˌnaɪt

|full fʊl |tooth tuθ |further ˈfɝðɚ; ES ˈfɝðə |custom ˈkʌstəm |while hwaɪl |how haʊ |toy tɔɪ
|using ˈjuzɪŋ |fuse fjuz, fɪuz |dish dɪʃ |vision ˈvɪʒən |Eden ˈidn̩ |cradle ˈkredl̩ |keep 'em ˈkipm̩

mange **mendʒ** |manged **mendʒd** |mangy
  'mendʒɪ
mangel-wurzel **'mæŋgļ'wɝz|**, -**'wɝts|**; ES
  -**'wɝ-**, -**'wɝ-**; *acct+*-₁wurzel
manger **'mendʒɚ**; ES **'mendʒə(r**
mangle **'mæŋgļ** |-d -d |-ling **'mæŋglɪŋ, -g|ɪŋ**
mango **'mæŋgo**
mangonel **'mæŋgə₁nɛl**
mangosteen **'mæŋgə₁stin**
mangrove **'mæŋgrov, 'mæn-**
manhandle **'mæn₁hændļ, ₁mæn'hændļ** |-d -d
  |-ling -dlɪŋ, -d|ɪŋ
Manhattan **mæn'hætn̩** ('Man₁hattan 'Borough)
Manheim *US* **'mænhaɪm**
manhole **'mæn₁hol**
manhood **'mænhʊd**
man-hour **'mæn'aʊr**; ES **'mæn'aʊə(r**
mania **'menɪə** |-niac **'menɪ₁æk**
maniacal **mə'naɪək|** |-ly -ɪ
manic **'menɪk, 'mænɪk**
Manichean **₁mænə'kiən**
manicure **'mænɪ₁kjʊr, -₁kɪʊr**; ES **-₁kjʊə(r,
  -₁kɪʊ-**
manifest **'mænə₁fɛst** |-fested -₁fɛstɪd
manifestation **₁mænəfɛs'teʃən, -fəs'tɛʃən**
manifesto **₁mænə'fɛsto**
manifold **'mænə₁fold** |-folded -₁foldɪd
manikin **'mænəkɪn**
Manila, -lla, m- **mə'nɪlə**
manioc **'mænɪ₁ak, 'menɪ₁ak**; ES+-₁ɒk
maniple **'mænəpļ** |manipled **'mænəp|d**
manipulate **mə'nɪpjə₁let** |-lated -₁letɪd |-lator
  -₁letɚ; ES -₁letə(r
manipulation **mə₁nɪpjə'leʃən**
Manistee **₁mænə'sti**
Manistique **₁mænə'stik**
manito **'mænə₁to** |manitou, -tu **'mænə₁tu**
Manitoba **₁mænə'tobə, ₁mænəto'bɑ** |-ban
  -'tobən
Manitou **'mænə₁tu**
Manitoulin **₁mænə'tulɪn**
Manitowoc **₁mænətə'wak, -'wɒk**
Mankato **mæn'keto**
mankind **mæn'kaɪnd** ('man₁kind & 'woman-
  ₁kind)
Manley **'mænlɪ**
manlike **'mæn₁laɪk**
Manlius **'mænlɪəs** |-'s -ɪz

manly, M- **'mænlɪ**
Mann, Horace **'hɔrɪs'mæn, 'harɪs, 'hɒrɪs, -əs**
Mann, Thomas **'tɑməs'mæn, 'man**; ES+
  'tɒməs; (*Ger* **'to:mas'man**)
manna **'mænə**
mannequin **'mænəkɪn**
manner **'mænɚ**; ES **'mænə(r; |-s -z |-ed -d
mannerism **'mænə₁rɪzəm**
Mannheim **'mænhaɪm** (*Ger* **'manhaɪm**)
mannish **'mænɪʃ**
mannitol **'mænə₁tol, 'mænə₁tɑl, -₁tɒl
Manoah **mə'noə**
manoeuvre **mə'nuvɚ**; ES -**'nuvə(r; |- d -d
  |-ring -'nuvərɪŋ, -'nuvrɪŋ
man-of-war **'mænəv'wɔr, 'mænə'wɔr**; ES
  -**'wɔə(r
manometer **mə'namətɚ**; ES -**'namətə(r,
  -'nɒm-
manor **'mænɚ**; ES **'mænə(r
manorial **mə'norɪəl, mæ-, -'nɔr-**; S -**'nor-
mansard **'mænsard**; ES **'mænsɑ:d, E+-sɑ:d
manse **mæns** |manses **'mænsɪz
manservant **'mæn₁sɝvənt** |menservants **'mɛn-
  ₁sɝvənts**; |ES -₁sɝv-, -₁sɝv-
Mansfield **'mænz₁fild, 'mæns₁fild
mansion **'mænʃən** |mansioned **'mænʃənd** |-ry
  -rɪ
manslaughter **'mæn₁slɔtɚ**; ES -tə(r
manslayer **'mæn₁sleɚ**; ES **'mæn₁sle·ə(r
mansuetude **'mænswɪ₁tjud, -₁tɪud, -₁tud
manteau **'mænto** (*Fr* mɑ̃'to)
Manteca **mæn'tikə
mantel **'mæntļ** |manteled **'mæntļd
Mantell **mæn'tɛl, 'mæntɛl
mantelpiece **'mæntļ₁pis** |-pieces -₁pisɪz
Manti **'mæntaɪ
mantic **'mæntɪk
mantilla **mæn'tɪlə
mantis **'mæntɪs** |-es -ɪz |mantes **'mæntiz
mantissa **mæn'tɪsə
mantle **'mæntļ** |-d -d |-ling **'mæntļɪŋ, -tlɪŋ
mantrap **'mæn₁træp
mantua **'mæntʃʊə, 'mæntʊə
Mantua **'mæntʃʊə, 'mæntʊə, *O* 'mæntə₁we
manual **'mænjʊəl** |-ly -ɪ
Manuel **'mænjʊəl, 'mænjʊ₁ɛl
manufactory **₁mænjə'fæktərɪ, -'fæktrɪ
manufacture **₁mænjə'fæktʃɚ, ₁mænə'fæktʃɚ**;
  ES -tʃə(r; |-d -d |-ring -tʃərɪŋ, -tʃrɪŋ

Words below in which a *before* r (farm) *is sounded* ɑ *are often pronounced in* E *with* a (fɑ:m)
Words below that have æ *before* r (carry 'kærɪ) *are often pronounced in* N *with* ɛ ('kɛrɪ, §94)

manumission ˌmænjə'mɪʃən, ˌmænjʊ-
manumit ˌmænjə'mɪt, ˌmænjʊ- |-ted -ɪd
manure mə'njʊr, mə'nɪʊr, mə'nʊr; ES -ə(r;
|-d -d
manuscript 'mænjəˌskrɪpt
manward 'mænwəd; ES 'mænwəd; |-s -z
Manwaring 'mænərɪŋ, 'mænwɔrɪŋ, -wɑr-,
-wɒr-
manwise 'mænˌwaɪz
Manx mæŋks
Manxman 'mæŋksmən, -ˌmæn |-men -mən,
-ˌmɛn
many 'mɛnɪ |many's 'mɛnɪz |occas. unstressed
mənɪ (how many men 'haʊmənɪ'mɛn)
manysided 'mɛnɪ'saɪdɪd ('manyˌsided 'man)
Maori 'maʊrɪ, 'marɪ
map mæp |mapped mæpt
maple, M- 'mepl̩ |mapled 'mepl̩d
Mapleton 'mepl̩tən, 'mæpl̩-
Mappleton 'mæpl̩tən
Maquoketa mə'kokɪtə
mar mɑr; ES mɑ:(r; |-red -d
Maracaibo ˌmærə'kaɪbo, ˌmɑrə-
maraschino, M- ˌmærə'skino
marathon, M- 'mærəˌθɑn, -ˌθɒn, -θən
maraud mə'rɔd |marauded mə'rɔdɪd
Marazion ˌmærə'zaɪən
marble 'mɑrbl̩; ES 'mɑ:bl̩; |-d -d |-ling -blɪŋ,
-bl̩ɪŋ
Marblehead 'mɑrbl̩ˌhɛd, 'mɑrbl̩'hɛd; ES
'mɑ:bl̩-
Marburg 'mɑrbɝg; ES 'mɑ:bɝg, 'mɑ:bɝg;
(Ger 'mɑrbʊrk)
Marcade 'mɑrkəˌdi; ES 'mɑ:k-
marcasite 'mɑrkəˌsaɪt; ES 'mɑ:kəˌsaɪt
marcel mɑr'sɛl; ES mɑ:'sɛl; ('marˌcel 'wave)
Marceline ˌmɑrsl̩'in; ES ˌmɑ:s-
Marcella mɑr'sɛlə; ES mɑ:'sɛlə
Marcellus mɑr'sɛləs; ES mɑ:-; |-'s -ɪz
march, M- mɑrtʃ; ES mɑ:tʃ; |-es -ɪz |-ed -t
marchesa mɑr'kezə; ES mɑ:'kezə; (It
mɑr'ke:za)
marchese mɑr'keze; ES mɑ:'keze; (It mɑr-
'ke:ze)
marchioness 'mɑrʃənɪs, ˌmɑrʃə'nɛs; ES
'mɑ:ʃənɪs, ˌmɑ:ʃə'nɛs; |-es -ɪz
marchpane 'mɑrtʃˌpen; ES 'mɑ:tʃˌpen

Marcius 'mɑrʃɪəs, -ʃəs; ES 'mɑ:ʃ-; |-'s -ɪz
Marco 'mɑrko; ES 'mɑ:ko
Marconi mɑr'konɪ; ES mɑ:'konɪ
marconigram mɑr'konɪˌgræm; ES mɑ'konɪ-
ˌgræm
Marcus 'mɑrkəs; ES 'mɑ:kəs; |-'s -ɪz
Mardian 'mɑrdɪən, -djən; ES 'mɑ:d-
Mardi gras 'mɑrdɪ'grɑ, -'grɔ; ES 'mɑ:dɪ-
mare mɛr, mær; E mɛə(r, ES mæə(r
Marengo, m- mə'rɛŋgo
mares-nest 'mɛrzˌnɛst, 'mærz-; E 'mɛəz-, ES
'mæəz-
mare's-tail 'mɛrzˌtel, 'mærz-; E 'mɛəz-, ES
'mæəz-
Margaret 'mɑrgrɪt, 'mɑrgərɪt; ES 'mɑ:g-
margaric mɑr'gærɪk, -'gɑrɪk; ES mɑ:'g-
margarine 'mɑrdʒəˌrin, -rɪn, much less freq.
'mɑrgə-; ES 'mɑ:dʒ-, 'mɑ:g-; acct+
ˌmarga'rine
Margarita ˌmɑrgə'ritə; ES ˌmɑ:gə'ritə
Margate Engd 'mɑrgɪt, NJ 'mɑrget, -gɪt; ES
'mɑ:g-
marge mɑrdʒ; ES mɑ:dʒ; |-s -ɪz |-d -d
margent 'mɑrdʒənt; ES 'mɑ:dʒənt
Margery 'mɑrdʒərɪ, -dʒrɪ; ES 'mɑ:dʒ-
margin 'mɑrdʒɪn; ES 'mɑ:dʒɪn; |-ed -d
marginal 'mɑrdʒɪnl̩; ES 'mɑ:dʒ-; |-ly -ɪ
marginalia ˌmɑrdʒə'nelɪə, -ljə; ES ˌmɑ:dʒ-
Margot Eng name (from Margaret) 'mɑrgət,
Fr name 'mɑrgo; ES 'mɑ:g-
margrave 'mɑrgrev; ES 'mɑ:grev
margravine 'mɑrgrəˌvin; ES 'mɑ:grəˌvin
marguerite, M- ˌmɑrgə'rit; ES ˌmɑ:gə'rit
Maria mə'raɪə, mə'riə
Marian 'mɛrɪən, 'mærɪən, 'mɛrɪən
Mariana ˌmɛrɪ'ænə, ˌmær-, ˌmer-, Sp schol.
ˌmɑrɪ'ɑnə (Sp ˌmari'ana)
Marianne ˌmɛrɪ'æn, ˌmɛrɪ'æn
Maria Theresa mə'raɪətə'rizə, -tə'rɛsə (It
mə'ri:ɑte'rɛ:za)
Marie mə'ri, 'mɑrɪ, 'mærɪ
Marietta ˌmɛrɪ'ɛtə, ˌmɛrɪ-
marigold 'mærəˌgold
marijuana ˌmɑrɪ'hwɑnə (Sp ˌmari'xwana)
marimba mə'rɪmbə
Marina mə'rinə, -'raɪnə
marine mə'rin

Words below in which a *before* r (farm) *is sounded* ɑ *are often pronounced in E with* a (fɑ:m)
Words below that have æ *before* r (carry ˈkærɪ) *are often pronounced in N with* ɛ (ˈkɛrɪ, §94)

mariner ˈmærənɚ; ES ˈmærənə(r
Mariolatry ˌmɛrɪˈɑlətrɪ, ˌmɛrɪ-; ES+-ˈɒl-
Marion ˈmɛrɪən, ˈmæ-, ˈme-, *NC* ˈme-, *SC* ˈmæ-
marionette ˌmærɪəˈnɛt
Mariposa ˌmærəˈposə, -ˈpozə
marish *'marsh'* ˈmærɪʃ |marishes ˈmærɪʃɪz
marish *'like a mare'* ˈmɛrɪʃ, ˈmærɪʃ; S ˈmær-
Marissa məˈrɪsə
marital ˈmærətl̩ |-ly -ɪ; (*Brit* məˈraɪtl̩)
maritime ˈmærəˌtaɪm
Marius ˈmɛrɪəs, ˈmærɪəs, ˈmerɪəs |-ʼs -ɪz
marjoram ˈmɑrdʒərəm; ES ˈmɑːdʒərəm
Marjoribanks ˈmɑrtʃˌbæŋks, ˈmɑrʃ-; ES ˈmɑːtʃ-, ˈmɑːʃ-
Marjorie, -ry ˈmɑrdʒərɪ, -dʒrɪ; ES ˈmɑːdʒ-
mark, M- mɑrk; ES mɑːk; |-ed -t |-edly -ɪdlɪ
Mark Antony ˈmɑrkˈæntənɪ; ES ˈmɑːk-
market ˈmɑrkɪt; ES ˈmɑːkɪt; |-ed -ɪd |-able -əbl̩ |-bly -blɪ
marketability ˌmɑrkɪtəˈbɪlətɪ; ES ˌmɑːk-
Markham ˈmɑrkəm; ES ˈmɑːkəm
marksman ˈmɑrksmən; ES ˈmɑːks-; |-men -mən
marl mɑrl; ES mɑːl; |-ed -d
Marlborough, -ro *US* ˈmɑrlˌbɝo, -ə; ES ˈmɑːl-, ˌbɝ-, -ˌbʌr-, -ˌbɝ-; *Mass*+ˈmɒlbrə; *Engd* ˈmɔlbərə, -brə
Marlin ˈmɑrlɪn; ES ˈmɑːlɪn
marline ˈmɑrlɪn; ES ˈmɑːlɪn; |-spike -ˌspaɪk
Marlow, -lowe ˈmɑrlo; ES ˈmɑːlo
Marmaduke ˈmɑrməˌdjuk, -ˌdɪuk, -ˌduk; ES ˈmɑːmə-
marmalade ˈmɑrml̩ˌed, ˌmɑrml̩ˈed; ES ˈmɑː-mə-, ˌmɑːmə-
Marmara ˈmɑrmərə; ES ˈmɑːmərə
Marmion ˈmɑrmɪən, ˈmɑrmjən; ES ˈmɑːm-
Marmora ˈmɑrmərə, mɑrˈmorə, -ˈmɔrə; ES ˈmɑːmərə, mɑːˈmorə, E+mɑːˈmɔrə
marmoreal mɑrˈmorɪəl, -ˈmɔr-; ES mɑ-ˈmorɪəl, E+-ˈmɔr-
marmoset ˈmɑrməˌzɛt; ES ˈmɑːməˌzɛt
marmot ˈmɑrmət; ES ˈmɑːmət
Marne mɑrn; ES mɑːn; (*Fr* marn)
maroon məˈrun |marooned məˈrund
marplot ˈmɑrˌplɑt; ES ˈmɑːˌplɑt, -ˌplɒt
Marprelate ˈmɑrˌprɛlɪt; ES ˈmɑːˌprɛlɪt

Marquand mɑrˈkwɑnd, -ˈkwɒnd; ES mɑ:-; (ˈMarˌquand ˈHall)
marque mɑrk; ES mɑːk
marquee mɑrˈki; ES mɑːˈki
Marquesas mɑrˈkesəs, mɑrˈkesæs; ES mɑː-ˈkes-
marquetry ˈmɑrkətrɪ; ES ˈmɑːkətrɪ
Marquette mɑrˈkɛt; ES mɑːˈkɛt
marquis, -ess ˈmɑrkwɪs; ES ˈmɑːkwɪs; |-ʼs -ɪz (*Fr* mɑrˈki)
marquisette ˌmɑrkɪˈzɛt, -kwɪˈzɛt; ES ˌmɑːk-
marriage ˈmærɪdʒ |-s -ɪz |-able -əbl̩
marriageability ˌmærɪdʒəˈbɪlətɪ
marrow ˈmæro, ˈmærə |-ed -d |-ing ˈmærəwɪŋ
marrowbone ˈmæroˌbon, ˈmærə-
marrowfat ˈmærəˌfæt, ˈmæro-
marrowy ˈmærəwɪ
marry ˈmærɪ |married ˈmærɪd
Marryat ˈmærɪət, ˈmærɪˌæt
Mars mɑrz; ES mɑːz; |-ʼs -ɪz
Marseillaise ˌmɑrsl̩ˈez; ES ˌmɑːsl̩ˈez; (*Fr* mɑrsɛˈjɛːz)
Marseilles, m- mɑrˈselz; ES mɑːˈselz; |-ʼs -ɪz (*Fr* Marseille mɑrˈsɛːj)
marsh, M- mɑrʃ; ES mɑːʃ; |-es -ɪz |-y -ɪ
marshal, M- ˈmɑrʃəl; ES ˈmɑːʃəl; |-ed -d
Marshalsea ˈmɑrʃl̩ˌsi; ES ˈmɑːʃl̩ˌsi
marshmallow ˈmɑrʃˌmælo, -ˌmælə; ES ˈmɑːʃ-
marsupial mɑrˈsupɪəl, -ˈsɪu-, -ˈsju-; ES mɑ-
mart, M- mɑrt; ES mɑːt
Martel mɑrˈtɛl; ES mɑːˈtɛl
marten ˈmɑrtɪn, ˈmɑrtn̩; ES ˈmɑːt-
Martha ˈmɑrθə; ES ˈmɑːθə
martial, M- ˈmɑrʃəl; ES ˈmɑːʃəl; |-ly -ɪ
Martian ˈmɑrʃɪən, ˈmɑrʃjən; ES ˈmɑːʃ-
martin, M- ˈmɑrtɪn, ˈmɑrtn̩; ES ˈmɑːt-
Martineau ˌmɑrtɪˈno, ˌmɑrtn̩ˈo; ES ˌmɑːt-
martinet ˌmɑrtn̩ˈɛt, ˈmɑrtn̩ˌɛt; ES ˌmɑːt-, ˈmɑːt-
Martinez mɑrˈtinɪz; ES mɑː-; |-nezʼ -nɪz
martingale ˈmɑrtn̩ˌgel; ES ˈmɑːtn̩ˌgel
Martinique ˌmɑrtn̩ˈik; ES ˌmɑːtn̩ˈik
Martinmas ˈmɑrtɪnməs; ES ˈmɑːtɪnməs; |-es -ɪz
martlet ˈmɑrtlɪt; ES ˈmɑːtlɪt
martyr ˈmɑrtɚ; ES ˈmɑːtə(r; |-ed -d |-dom -dəm

Key: See in full §§3–47. bee bi |pity ˈpɪtɪ (§6) |rate ret |yet jɛt |sang sæŋ |angry ˈæŋ·grɪ |bath bæθ; E bɑθ (§10) |ah ɑ |far fɑr |watch wɑtʃ, wɒtʃ (§12) |jaw dʒɔ |gorge gɔrdʒ |go go

Words below in which a *before* r (farm) *is sounded* ɑ *are often pronounced in* E *with* a (fɑːm)

martyrological ˌmɑrtərəˈlɑdʒɪkl̩; ES ˌmɑːtə-, -ˈlɒdʒ-

martyrologist ˌmɑrtəˈrɑlədʒɪst; ES ˌmɑːtə-, -ˈrɒl-; |-gy -dʒɪ

Marullus məˈrʌləs |-ʼs -ɪz

marvel ˈmɑrvl̩; ES ˈmɑːvl̩; |-ed -d |-ing -vl̩ɪŋ, -vl̩ɪŋ |-ous -vl̩əs, -vləs

Marvel, -ll ˈmɑrvl̩; ES ˈmɑːvl̩

Marx mɑrks; ES mɑːks; |-ian -ɪən, -jən |-ʼs -ɪz

Mary ˈmɛrɪ, ˈmɛːrɪ, ˈmerɪ, ˈmærɪ—*Some speakers distinguish* Mary *from* merry *by a longer* ɛ (§55).

Maryland ˈmɛrələnd, ˈmɛrɪlənd

Marylebone *Lond road* ˈmærələbən, -ˌbon, ˈmærəbən—*see* St. Mary-le-Bone. ˈmærəbən *came from the original* Maryburn *by r-dissimilation* (§121).

Masaryk ˈmɑsəˌrik

Mascagni masˈkɑnjɪ, mæs- (*It* masˈkɑɲɲi)

mascara mæsˈkærə, masˈkɑrə (*It* masˈkɑːrɑ)

mascot ˈmæskət, -kɑt; ES+-kɒt

masculine ˈmæskjəlɪn |-linity ˌmæskjəˈlɪnətɪ

Masefield ˈmesˌfild, ˈmez-

mash mæʃ |mashes ˈmæʃɪz |mashed mæʃt

mashie, -y ˈmæʃɪ |mashies ˈmæʃɪz

mask mæsk; E+mask, mɑsk |-ed -t

masochism ˈmæzəˌkɪzəm

mason, M- ˈmesn̩ |masonry ˈmesn̩rɪ

masonic məˈsɑnɪk; ES+məˈsɒnɪk

Masora, -h məˈsorə, məˈsɔrə; S məˈsorə

masque mæsk; E+mask, mɑsk

masquerade ˌmæskəˈred |-raded -ˈredɪd

mass mæs |masses ˈmæsɪz |massed mæst

Mass mæs |Masses ˈmæsɪz

Massac ˈmæsək, -æk

Massachusetts ˌmæsəˈtʃusɪts, -ˈtʃuz-, -əts *L.A. of N Engd shows that about 28 per cent of the cultured informants pronounce* z.

massacre ˈmæsəkə; ES -kə(r; |-d -d |-ring -krɪŋ, -kərɪŋ

massage məˈsɑʒ |-sages -ˈsɑʒɪz |-saged -ˈsɑʒd

Massasoit ˈmæsəˌsɔɪt

Massena məˈsinə

Massenet ˌmæsəˈne (*Fr* masˈnɛ)

masseur mæˈsɝ; ES mæˈsɝ(r, -ˈsɝ; (*Fr* maˈsœːr)

masseuse mæˈsɜz |-s -ɪz |-ʼs -ɪz (*Fr* maˈsøːz)

massicot ˈmæsɪˌkɑt; ES+-ˌkɒt

massif ˈmæsɪf (*Fr* maˈsif)

Massillon ˈmæslən, ˈmæsələn

Massinger ˈmæsn̩dʒə; ES -dʒə(r

massive ˈmæsɪv |massey ˈmæsɪ

Masson ˈmæsn̩

mast *'pole,' 'nuts'* mæst; E+mast, mɑst; |-ed -ɪd

master ˈmæstə; ES -tə(r, E+ˈmɑs-, ˈmɑs-; |-ed -d |-ing -tərɪŋ, -trɪŋ |-ful -fəl |-fully -fəlɪ |-ly -lɪ |-y -tərɪ, -trɪ

master-at-arms ˈmæstərətˈɑrmz; ES -ˈɑːmz, E+ˈmɑs-, ˈmɑs- |-ʼs -ɪz

masterpiece ˈmæstəˌpis; ES ˈmæstə-, E+ˈmɑs-, ˈmɑs-; |-s -ɪz

masterwork ˈmæstəˌwɝk; ES ˈmæstəˌwɝk, ˈmæstəˌwɝk, E+ˈmɑs-, ˈmɑs-

masthead ˈmæstˌhɛd; E+ˈmɑst-, ˈmɑst-

mastic ˈmæstɪk

masticate ˈmæstəˌket |-d -ɪd |-tion ˌmæstəˈkeʃən

masticatory ˈmæstəkəˌtorɪ, -ˌtɔrɪ; S -ˌtorɪ

mastiff ˈmæstɪf; E+ˈmɑstɪf, ˈmɑstɪf

mastitis mæsˈtaɪtɪs

mastodon ˈmæstəˌdɑn; ES+ˈmæstəˌdɒn

mastoid ˈmæstɔɪd |mastoiditis ˌmæstɔɪdˈaɪtɪs

masturbation ˌmæstəˈbeʃən; ES ˌmæstəˈbeʃən

masurium məˈsjurɪəm, məˈsɪurɪəm, məˈsurɪəm

mat mæt |matted ˈmætɪd |matting ˈmætɪŋ

Matabele ˌmætəˈbilɪ |-leland -ˌlænd

matador ˈmætəˌdɔr; ES ˈmætəˌdɔə(r; (*Sp* ˌmataˈðɔr)

Matamoras ˌmætəˈmorəs, -ˈmɔr-; S -ˈmor-; |-ʼs -ɪz

Matanzas məˈtænzəs |-zasʼ -zəs (*Am Sp* maˈtansas)

Matawan ˌmætəˈwan, -ˈwɒn

match mætʃ |matches ˈmætʃɪz |matched mætʃt

matchlock ˈmætʃˌlɑk; ES+ˈmætʃˌlɒk

matchmaker ˈmætʃˌmekə; ES ˈmætʃˌmekə(r

matchwood ˈmætʃˌwud

mate met |mated ˈmetɪd

maté, -te ˈmate, ˈmæte

mater *'mother'* ˈmetə, ˈmɑtə; ES -tə(r

|full fʊl |tooth tuθ |further ˈfɝðə; ES ˈfɝðə |custom ˈkʌstəm |while hwaɪl |how haʊ |toy tɔɪ |using ˈjuzɪŋ |fuse fjuz, fɪuz |dish dɪʃ |vision ˈvɪʒən |Eden ˈidn̩ |cradle ˈkredl̩ |keep ʼem ˈkipm̩

materfamilias ˌmetɚfəˈmɪlɪˌæs; ES ˌmetə-
material məˈtɪrɪəl |-ism -ˌɪzəm |-ist -ɪst |-ly -ɪ
materiality məˌtɪrɪˈælətɪ
materialize məˈtɪrɪəlˌaɪz |-s -ɪz |-d -d
materia medica məˈtɪrɪəˈmɛdɪkə
matériel məˌtɪrɪˈɛl (Fr mateˈrjɛl)
maternal məˈtɝnḷ; ES məˈtɜnḷ, -ˈtɝnḷ; |-ly -ɪ
maternity məˈtɝnətɪ; ES -ˈtɜnətɪ, -ˈtɝn-
mathematic ˌmæθəˈmætɪk |-s -s |-al -ḷ |-ally
-ḷɪ, -ɪklɪ
mathematician ˌmæθəməˈtɪʃən
Mather ˈmæðɚ; ES ˈmæðə(r
Mathew ˈmæθju
Mathias məˈθaɪəs |Mathias's məˈθaɪəsɪz
Mathilda, -tilda məˈtɪldə
matin ˈmætɪn
matinee ˌmætn̩ˈe (ˈmatiˌnee ˈseat)
matrass, -ttrass chem. ˈmætrəs |-es -ɪz
matriarch ˈmetrɪˌɑrk; ES -ˌɑːk; |-ate -ɪt |-y -ɪ
matrices pl of matrix ˈmetrɪˌsiz, ˈmæt-
matricide ˈmetrəˌsaɪd, ˈmætrəˌsaɪd
matriculate məˈtrɪkjəˌlet |-d -ɪd
matriculation məˌtrɪkjəˈleʃən
matrimonial ˌmætrəˈmonɪəl, -ˈmonjəl |-ly -ɪ
matrimony ˈmætrəˌmonɪ
matrix ˈmetrɪks, ˈmætrɪks |-es -ɪz |matrices
ˈmetrɪˌsiz, ˈmætrɪˌsiz
matron ˈmetrən
matronymic ˌmætrəˈnɪmɪk
Mattaponi ˌmætəpəˈnaɪ
matte mæt |matted ˈmætɪd
Matteawan ˌmætəˈwɑn, ˌmætəˈwɒn
matter ˈmætɚ; ES ˈmætə(r; |-ed -d
matterate ˈmætəˌret |-d -ɪd |-tion ˌmætə-
ˈreʃən
Matterhorn ˈmætɚˌhɔrn; ES ˈmætəˌhɔən
matter-of-course ˈmætərəvˈkors, -ˈkɔrs; ES
-ˈkoəs, E+-ˈkɔəs
matter-of-fact ˈmætərəvˈfækt, ˈmætərəˈfækt
(ˈmatter-of-ˌfact ˈstyle)
Matthew ˈmæθju |-s -z |-s's -zɪz
Matthias məˈθaɪəs |Matthias's məˈθaɪəsɪz
mattock ˈmætək |-ed -t
Mattoon mæˈtun, mə-
mattress ˈmætrɪs, ˈmætrəs |-es -ɪz |-ed -t
maturate ˈmætʃuˌret, ˈmætjuˌret |-d -ɪd
maturation ˌmætʃuˈreʃən, ˌmætjuˈreʃən
mature məˈtjur, -ˈtɪur, -ˈtur |-d -d |-rity -ətɪ
matutinal məˈtjutɪnḷ, məˈtɪu-, məˈtu-

matzoth ˈmætsōθ, ˈmatsoθ
Mauch Chunk ˈmɔkˈtʃʌŋk
Maud, -e mɔd
maudlin ˈmɔdlɪn
mauger, -gre ˈmɔgɚ; ES ˈmɔgə(r
Maugham mɔm
maul mɔl |-ed -d
Maulmein maʊlˈmen, mɔl-, mol-
maulstick ˈmɔlˌstɪk
Maumee mɔˈmi (ˈMauˌmee ˈRiver)
maumet ˈmɔmɪt |maumetry ˈmɔmɪtrɪ
Mauna Kea ˈmaʊnəˈkeə, ˈmɔnəˈkiə
Mauna Loa ˈmaʊnəˈloə, ˈmɔnəˈloə
maunder ˈmɔndɚ; ES -də(r; |-ed -d |-ing
ˈmɔndərɪŋ, ˈmɔndrɪŋ
Maundy Thursday ˈmɔndɪˈθɝzdɪ; ES -ˈθɜz-,
-ˈθɝz-
Maupassant, de dəˈmopəˌsɑnt (Fr dəmopa-
ˈsã)
Mauretania, -ri- ˌmɔrəˈtenɪə, ˌmar-, ˌmɒr-,
-njə
Maurice ˈmɔrɪs, ˈmarɪs, ˈmɒrɪs |-'s -ɪz
Maurois Fr ˈmorwa, moˈrwa
mausoleum, M- ˌmɔsəˈliəm |-s -z |-lea -ˈlɪə
mauve mov
maverick, M- ˈmævrɪk, ˈmævərɪk
mavis, M- ˈmevɪs |-es -ɪz
mavourneen, -nin, M- məˈvurnin, -ˈvor-,
-ˈvɔr-; ES -ˈvuə-, -ˈvoə-, E+-ˈvɔə-
maw mɔ
Mawer ˈmɔɚ; ES ˈmɔ·ə(r
mawkin ˈmɔkɪn = malkin
mawkish ˈmɔkɪʃ
maxilla mæksˈɪlə |-lae -li
maxillary ˈmæksəˌlɛrɪ, mæksˈɪlərɪ
maxim, M- ˈmæksɪm
Maximilian ˌmæksəˈmɪlɪən, -ˈmɪljən
maximite ˈmæksəˌmaɪt
maximize ˈmæksəˌmaɪz |-s -ɪz |-d -d
maximum ˈmæksəməm |-s -z |-ma -mə
maxwell, M- ˈmækswɛl, ˈmækswəl
may stressed ˈme, ˌme; unstr. mɪ, mə
May me
Maya ˈmajə |Mayan ˈmajən
maybe ˈmebɪ, ˈmebi, ˈmɛbɪ—ˈmɛbɪ, occasionally heard, is phonetically normal, being
parallel to ˈbrɛkfəst for breakfast.
mayest ˈme·ɪst
Mayfair ˈmeˌfɛr, -ˌfær; E -ˌfɛə(r, ES -ˌfæə(r

Mayflower, m- 'me͟ı‚flaʋɚ, -‚flaʋr; ES 'me-
‚flaʋ·ə(r, -‚flaʋə(r

mayhap 'me͟ı‚hæp, me'hæp |-s -s

mayhem 'mehɛm, 'meəm

Mayhew 'mehju, 'mehɪu

mayn't mɛnt

Maynwaring 'mænərɪŋ, 'menwɔrɪŋ, -wɑr-,
-wɒr-

Mayo surname 'meo, Am Indian 'mɑjo

mayonnaise ‚meə'nez ('mayon‚naise 'dress-
ing)

mayor, M- 'meɚ, mɛr; ES 'me·ə(r, mɛə(r;
|-alty -əltɪ

Maypole, m- 'me͟ı‚pol

maypop 'mepɑp; ES+'mepɒp

mayst mest

Maytide 'me͟ı‚taɪd

mazard 'mæzɚd; ES 'mæzəd

Mazatlán ‚mɑzə'tlɑn (Am Sp ‚masa'tlan)

mazda, M- 'mæzdə

Mazdaism, Mazde- 'mæzdə‚ɪzəm

maze mez |mazes 'mezɪz |mazed mezd |-dly
-ɪdlɪ

mazer 'mezɚ; ES 'mezə(r

mazurka mə'zɝkə, -'zʋrkə; ES -'zɝkə,
-'zɝkə, -'zʋəkə

mazzard 'mæzɚd; ES 'mæzəd

Mazzini mæt'sinɪ, mɑt'sinɪ (It mɑt'tsi:ni,
mɑd'dz-)

Mc- alphabetized under Mac-
me stressed 'mi, ‚mi; unstr. mɪ

mead mid |Mead, -e mid

meadow 'mɛdo, 'mɛdə |-ed -d |-ing 'mɛdəwɪŋ

Meadville 'midvɪl; S+-vl̩

meager, -gre 'migɚ; ES 'migə(r; |-(e)d -d

Meagher mɑr; ES mɑ:(r, E+mɑ:(r

meal mil |-ed -d |-less 'millɪs

mealie, -y 'corn' 'milɪ |-lies -z

mealtime 'mil‚taɪm

mealy adj 'milɪ

mealymouthed 'milɪ'maʋðd, -θt |-thedly
-ðɪdlɪ, -ðdlɪ, -θtlɪ

mean min |meant mɛnt |-ness 'minnɪs

meander, M- mɪ'ændɚ; ES -'ændə(r; |-ed -d
|-ing -'ændrɪŋ, -'ændərɪŋ

meant mɛnt

meantime 'min‚taɪm |meanwhile 'min‚hwaɪl

measles 'mizl̩z |measly 'mizlɪ

measurability ‚mɛʒərə'bɪlətɪ

measurable 'mɛʒrəbl̩, 'mɛʒərəbl̩ |-bly -blɪ

measure 'mɛʒɚ; ES 'mɛʒə(r; |-d -d |-ring
'mɛʒrɪŋ, 'mɛʒərɪŋ

meat mit |meated 'mitɪd

Meath Ir co. miθ

meatman 'mit‚mæn |-men -‚mɛn

meatus mɪ'etəs |-es -ɪz |L pl -tus -təs

Mecca 'mɛkə

mechanic mə'kænɪk |-al -l̩ |-ally -l̩ɪ, -ɪklɪ

mechanician ‚mɛkə'nɪʃən

mechanism 'mɛkə‚nɪzəm |-nist -nɪst

mechanistic ‚mɛkə'nɪstɪk |-ally -l̩ɪ, -ɪklɪ

mechanization ‚mɛkənə'zeʃən, -aɪ'z-

mechanize 'mɛkə‚naɪz |-s -ɪz |-d -d

Mechlin 'mɛklɪn

Mecklenburg US, Germany 'mɛklɪn‚bɝg,
-lən-; ES -‚bɝg, -‚bɝg; (Ger 'me:klən‚bʋrk,
'mɛk-)

medal 'mɛdl̩ |-ed -d |-ist -ɪst

medallic mə'dælɪk, mɪ- |-ally -l̩ɪ, -ɪklɪ

medallion mə'dæljən, mɪ- |-ist -ɪst

meddle 'mɛdl̩ |-d -d |-ling 'mɛdlɪŋ, 'mɛdl̩ɪŋ

meddlesome 'mɛdl̩səm

Mede mid

Medea mi'diə

Medford 'mɛdfɚd; ES 'mɛdfəd

media, M- 'midɪə |pl mediae 'midɪ‚i

media pl of medium 'midɪə

mediacy 'midɪəsɪ

mediaeval ‚midɪ'ivl̩, ‚mɛd- |-ly -ɪ |-ism -‚ɪzəm
|-ist -ɪst

medial 'midɪəl |-ly -ɪ

median, M- 'midɪən

mediate adj 'midɪɪt

mediate v 'midɪ‚et |-d -ɪd |-tion ‚midɪ'eʃən

mediatize 'midɪə‚taɪz |-s -ɪz |-d -d

mediator 'midɪ‚etɚ; ES -‚etə(r

mediatory 'midɪə‚torɪ, -‚tɔrɪ; S -‚torɪ

medic 'mɛdɪk |Medic 'midɪk

medical 'mɛdɪkl̩ |-ly -ɪ, -ɪklɪ |-cable -kəbl̩

medicament n mə'dɪkəmənt, 'mɛdɪkə-

medicament v mə'dɪkə‚mɛnt |-ed -ɪd

medicamental ‚mɛdɪkə'mɛntl̩ |-ly -ɪ

medicate 'mɛdɪ‚ket |-d -ɪd |-tion ‚mɛdɪ'keʃən

Medicean ‚mɛdə'siən

Medici 'mɛdə‚tʃi (It 'mɛ:di‚tʃi)

medicinable mə'dɪsn̩əbl̩, in Shak. 'mɛdsɪnəbl̩

medicinal mə'dɪsn̩l̩ |-ly -ɪ

medicine 'mɛdəsn̩ |-cined -snd

medico 'mɛdɪˌko
medicodental ˌmɛdɪko'dɛntl̩
medicolegal ˌmɛdɪko'ligl̩ |-ly -ɪ
medieval ˌmidɪ'ivl̩, ˌmɛd- |-ly -ɪ |-ism -ˌɪzəm
|-ist -ɪst
Medina *NY, O, Spenser's F.Q.* mə'daɪnə, mɪ-;
Tex co., Arab city, Belg painter, IW river
mə'dinə, me-, mɪ-; *Sp & SAm persons &*
places me'ðina
mediocre 'midɪˌokɚ, ˌmidɪ'okɚ; ES -kə(r
mediocrity ˌmidɪ'akrətɪ; ES+-'ɒk-
meditate 'mɛdəˌtet |-d -ɪd |-tive -ɪv
meditation ˌmɛdə'teʃən
Mediterranean, m- ˌmɛdətə'renɪən |-neous
-nɪəs
medium 'midɪəm |-s -z |-dia -dɪə
medlar 'mɛdlɚ; ES 'mɛdlə(r
medley 'mɛdlɪ |-ed, -lied -d
Medoc, Mé- 'médak, mɪ'dak; ES+-ɒk; (*Fr*
me'dɔk)
medulla mɪ'dʌlə |-s -z |-lae -li
medullary 'mɛdl̩ˌɛrɪ, mɪ'dʌlərɪ
Medusa mə'djusə, -'dɪu-, -'du-, -zə
Medway 'mɛdˌwe
meed mid
meek, M- mik
meerschaum 'mɪrʃəm, -ʃɔm; ES 'mɪə-
meet mit |met mɛt
meetinghouse 'mitɪŋˌhaʊs |-houses -ˌhaʊzɪz
Meg mɛg
megacephalic ˌmɛgəsə'fælɪk |-lous -'sɛfələs
megafarad ˌmɛgə'færəd, -'færæd
megalith 'mɛgəˌlɪθ |-ths -θs |-ic ˌmɛgə'lɪθɪk
megalomania ˌmɛgələ'menɪə |-iac -ɪˌæk
megalophonous ˌmɛgə'lɑfənəs; ES+-'lɒf-
megameter *instrument* mɛ'gæmətɚ; ES
-'gæmətə(r
megameter *'million meters'* 'mɛgəˌmitɚ; ES
-tə(r
megaphone 'mɛgəˌfon |-d -d |-ist -ɪst
Megara 'mɛgərə |-rian mɛ'gɛrɪən, -'gær-,
-'ger-
megatherium ˌmɛgə'θɪrɪəm
Megiddo mə'gɪdo
megohm 'mɛgˌom
megrim 'migrɪm
Mehetabel mə'hɛtəbl̩ |Mehitable mə'hɪtəbl̩
Meier 'maɪɚ; ES 'maɪ·ə(r
Meighen 'miən

Meigs mɛgz |-'s -ɪz
Meikle 'mikl̩
Meiklejohn 'mɪkl̩ˌdʒɑn, -ˌdʒɒn, 'mikl̩-
mein men
meiosis maɪ'osɪs
Meistersinger 'maɪstɚˌsɪŋɚ; ES 'maɪstə-
ˌsɪŋə(r
melancholia ˌmɛlən'kolɪə |-lic -'kɑlɪk; ES+
-'kɒlɪk
melancholy 'mɛlənˌkɑlɪ; ES+-ˌkɒlɪ
Melanchthon mə'læŋkθən |-ian ˌmɛlæŋk-
'θonɪən
Melanesia ˌmɛlə'niʃə, -ʃɪə, -'niʒ- |-n -n
mélange me'lɑ̃ʒ |-s -ɪz |-d -d (*Fr* me'lɑ̃:ʒ)
melanic mə'lænɪk |-niferous ˌmɛlə'nɪfərəs
melanin 'mɛlənɪn |melanism 'mɛləˌnɪzəm
melanotic ˌmɛlə'nɑtɪk; ES+-'nɒt-
Melba 'mɛlbə
Melbourne 'mɛlbɚn; ES 'mɛlbən
Melcher 'mɛltʃɚ; ES 'mɛltʃə(r
Melchers 'mɛltʃɚz; ES 'mɛltʃəz; |-'s -ɪz
Melchizedek mɛl'kɪzədɪk, -ˌdɛk
meld mɛld |melded 'mɛldɪd
Meleager ˌmɛlɪ'edʒɚ; ES -'edʒə(r
melee *'fray'* me'le, 'mele, 'mɛle (*Fr* me'le)
melee *'diamond'* 'mɛli
Melibeus, -boeus ˌmɛlə'biəs |-'s -ɪz
Melicent 'mɛləsn̩t
melinite 'mɛlɪˌnaɪt
meliorate 'miljəˌret |-d -ɪd |-tive -ɪv
melioration ˌmiljə'reʃən
Melissa mə'lɪsə
Mellen 'mɛlɪn, -ən
mellifluence mə'lɪflʊəns |-nt -nt |-uous -ʊəs
Mellon 'mɛlən
mellow 'mɛlo, -ə |-ed -d |-ing 'mɛləwɪŋ |-er
'mɛləwɚ; ES -wə(r; |-est 'mɛləwɪst
melodic mə'lɑdɪk; ES+-'lɒd-; |-al -l̩ |-ally
-l̩ɪ, -ɪklɪ
melodion mə'lodɪən |-dious -dɪəs
melodist 'mɛlədɪst
melodrama 'mɛləˌdrɑmə, -ˌdræmə
melodramatic ˌmɛlədrə'mætɪk |-al -l̩ |-ally
-l̩ɪ, -ɪklɪ
melody 'mɛlədɪ |-ied -d
melon 'mɛlən
Melos, m- 'milas, -lɒs
Melpomene mɛl'pamənɪ, -ˌni; ES+-'pɒm-
Melrose 'mɛlroz |-'s -ɪz

---

melt mɛlt |-ed -ɪd |*arch. pptc* molten ˈmoltn̩

melton, M- ˈmɛltn̩

Melton Mowbray ˈmɛltn̩ˈmobrɪ

Melun məˈlʌn (*Fr* məˈlœ̃)

Melville ˈmɛlvɪl; S+ˈmɛlvl̩

member ˈmɛmbɚ; ES ˈmɛmbə(r; |-ed -d |-ship -ˌʃɪp

membrane ˈmɛmbren |-d -d

membranous ˈmɛmbrənəs, mɛmˈbrenəs (ˈmemˌbranous ˈcroup) |-neous mɛmˈbrenɪəs

memento mɪˈmɛnto

memento mori mɪˈmɛntoˈmoraɪ, -ˈmɔ-; S -ˈmo-

Memnon ˈmɛmnɑn, -nɒn

memoir ˈmɛmwɑr, -wɔr; ES -wɑ:(r, -wɔə(r

memorabilia, M- ˌmɛmərəˈbɪlɪə

memorable ˈmɛmərəbl̩, ˈmɛmrə- |-bly -blɪ

memorandum ˌmɛməˈrændəm |-s -z |-da -də

memorial məˈmorɪəl, -ˈmɔr-; S -ˈmor-; |-ly -ɪ

memorialize məˈmorɪəlˌaɪz, -ˈmɔr-; S -ˈmor-; |-s -ɪz |-d -d

memorization ˌmɛmərəˈzeʃən, -aɪˈz-

memorize ˈmɛməˌraɪz |-s -ɪz |-d -d

memory ˈmɛmərɪ, -mrɪ |-ied -d

Memphis ˈmɛmfɪs |-ˈs -ɪz

Memphremagog ˌmɛmfrɪˈmegɑg, -gɒg

mem-sahib ˈmɛmˌsɑ·ɪb, -ˌsahɪb

men mɛn |men's mɛnz

menace ˈmɛnɪs, -əs |-s -ɪz |-d -t

menad ˈminæd |menades ˈmɛnəˌdiz

ménage, me- məˈnɑʒ, me- |-s -ɪz (*Fr* meˈna:ʒ)

menagerie məˈnædʒɔrɪ, -ˈnæʒ- (*Fr* menaʒˈri)

Menander mɪˈnændɚ; ES -ˈnændə(r

Menands məˈnændz, -ˈnænz |-ˈs -ɪz

Menard məˈnɑrd; ES -ˈnɑ:d, E+-ˈnɑ:d

Menas ˈminəs |-ˈs -ɪz

Menasha məˈnæʃə

Mencken ˈmɛŋkɪn, -ən

mend mɛnd |mended ˈmɛndɪd

mendacious mɛnˈdeʃəs |-dacity -ˈdæsətɪ

Mendel ˈmɛndl̩ |-ian mɛnˈdilɪən

Mendelssohn ˈmɛndl̩sn̩, -ˌson

Mendelyeev ˌmɛndəˈleɛf, ˌmɛndjɛˈljeɛf

mendicancy ˈmɛndɪkənsɪ |-cant -kənt

mendicity mɛnˈdɪsətɪ

Mendota mɛnˈdotə

Mendoza mɛnˈdozə (*Am Sp* menˈðosa)

Menecrates məˈnɛkrəˌtiz |-ˈs -ɪz

Menelaus ˌmɛnəˈleəs |-ˈs -ɪz

mene, mene, tekel, upharsin ˈminɪˈminɪˈtikǁjuˈfɑrsɪn, -ˈtɛkǁ-; ES -ˈfɑ:s-, E+-ˈfɑ:s-

menfolk ˈmɛnˌfok |-s -s

menhaden mɛnˈhedn̩

menhir ˈmɛnhɪr; ES -hɪə(r

menial ˈminɪəl, -njəl |-ly -ɪ |-ism -ˌɪzəm

Menifee ˈmɛnəˌfi

meninges məˈnɪndʒiz |-ningeal -ˈnɪndʒɪəl

meningitis ˌmɛnɪnˈdʒaɪtɪs |*L pl* -gitides -ˈdʒɪtɪˌdiz

meninx ˈminɪŋks |meninges məˈnɪndʒiz

Mennonite ˈmɛnənˌaɪt

Menominee, -nie məˈnɑməˌni; ES+-ˈnɒm-

menopause ˈmɛnəˌpɔz |-s -ɪz

menservants ˈmɛnˌsɝvənts; ES -ˌsɝv-, -ˌsɝv-

menses ˈmɛnsiz |mensal ˈmɛnsl̩

menstruate ˈmɛnstruˌet |-d -ɪd |-al -struəl

menstruation ˌmɛnstruˈeʃən

mensuration ˌmɛnʃəˈreʃən, -səˈreʃən, -sju-

-ment *unstressed ending of nouns* -mənt, *older & less freq.* -mɪnt. *The pronunciation* -mɛnt *for unstressed* -ment (*as in* judgment) *is artificial. Words in* -ment *are usually omitted from the vocab. if the pron. can be found by adding* -mənt *to the head pron. Verbs in* -ment (*with secondary accent*) *are usually given, as also a few nouns like* ˈaugment, ˈcomment, ˈferment, ˈtorment, *in which* -ment *has an* (*unmarked*) *subordinate accent.*

mental ˈmɛntl̩ |-ly -ɪ |-ity mɛnˈtælətɪ

Menteith mɛnˈtiθ

menthol ˈmɛnθol, -ɵɑl, -ɵɒl, -ɵɔl

mentholated ˈmɛnθəˌletɪd

mention ˈmɛnʃən |-ed -d |-ing -ʃənɪŋ, -ʃnɪŋ

mentor, M- ˈmɛntɚ; ES ˈmɛntə(r

menu ˈmɛnju, ˈmenju, ˈmɛnu, ˈmenu (*Fr* məˈny)

Menuhin ˈmɛnjuɪn

Menzies ˈmɛnzɪz (*Sc* ˈmɪŋɪz, *orig.* ˈmiɲɪz)

Mephibosheth mɪˈfɪbəˌʃɛθ

Mephistophelean ˌmɛfɪstəˈfilɪən, ˌmɛfəˌstɑfəˈliən, -ˌstɒf-

Mephistopheles ˌmɛfəˈstɑfəˌliz, -ˈstɒf- |-ˈs -ɪz

Mephistophelian ˌmɛfɪstəˈfilɪən

mephitic mɛˈfɪtɪk |-al -l̩ |-tis -ˈfaɪtɪs

Meramec ˈmɛrəˌmɛk

mercantile ˈmɝkəntɪl, -ˌtaɪl; ES mɝ-, ˈmɝ-; |-ly -lɪ |+-ˌtil

---

mercaptan mə'kæptæn; ES mə-
Mercator mɜ'ketɚ; ES mɜ'ketə(r, mɜ'ketə(r
Merced mə'sɛd; ES mə-
Mercedes mɜ'sidiz; ES mɜ-, mɜ-; |-des' -diz
mercenary 'mɜsn̩ˌɛrɪ; ES 'mɜs-, 'mɜs-
mercer, M- 'mɜsɚ; ES 'mɜsə(r, 'mɜsə(r
mercerize 'mɜsəˌraɪz; ES 'mɜs-, 'mɜs-; |-s
  -ɪz |-d -d
merchandise n 'mɜtʃənˌdaɪz, -ˌdaɪs; ES
  'mɜtʃ-, 'mɜtʃ-
merchandise v 'mɜtʃənˌdaɪz; ES 'mɜtʃ-,
  'mɜtʃ-; |-s -ɪz |-d -d
merchant 'mɜtʃənt; ES 'mɜtʃ-, 'mɜtʃ-; |-man
  -mən |-men -mən
Mercia 'mɜʃɪə, -ʃə |-cian -ʃən, -ʃən, -sɪən
Mercier 'mɜsɪɚ; ES 'mɜsɪ·ə(r, 'mɜsɪ·ə(r; (Fr
  mɛr'sje)
merciful 'mɜsɪfəl; ES 'mɜs-, 'mɜs-; |-ly -ɪ
mercurate 'mɜkjəˌret; ES 'mɜk-, 'mɜk-; |-d
  -ɪd
mercurial mɜ'kjʊrɪəl, -'kɪʊ-; ES mɜ-, mɜ-;
  |-ly -ɪ
mercuric mɜ'kjʊrɪk, -'kɪʊ-; ES mɜ-, mɜ-
mercurous mɜ'kjʊrəs, 'mɜkjə-, -'kɪʊ-; ES
  -ɜ-, -ɜ-
Mercury 'mɜkjərɪ, 'mɜkərɪ, -krɪ; ES 'mɜk-,
  'mɜk-
Mercutio mɜ'kjuʃɪˌo, -'kɪʊ-, -ʃjo; ES mɜ-,
  mɜ-
mercy, M- 'mɜsɪ; ES 'mɜsɪ, 'mɜsɪ
mere mɪr; ES mɪə(r, S+ mɛə(r
Meredith 'mɛrədɪθ
Meres mɪrz; ES mɪəz; |-'s -ɪz
meretricious ˌmɛrə'trɪʃəs
merganser mə'gænsɚ; ES mə'gænsə(r
merge mɜdʒ; ES mɜdʒ, mɜdʒ; |-s -ɪz |-d -d
merger 'mɜdʒɚ; ES 'mɜdʒə(r, 'mɜdʒə(r
mergence 'mɜdʒəns; ES 'mɜdʒ-, 'mɜdʒ-
Mergenthaler 'mɜgənˌθalɚ; ES 'mɜgən-
  ˌθalə(r, 'mɜg-; (Ger 'mɛrgənˌta:lər)
Meriden 'mɛrədn̩, -dɪn
meridian, M- mə'rɪdɪən |-al -l̩ |-ally -ʝɪ
meringue mə'ræŋ |-d -d (Fr mə'rɛ̃:g)
Merino, m- mə'rino
Merionethshire ˌmɛrɪ'anɪθˌʃɪr, -ʃɚ; ES -'anɪθ-
  ˌʃɪə(r, -'ɒn-, -ʃə(r
merit 'mɛrɪt |-ed -ɪd
meritorious ˌmɛrə'torɪəs, -'tɔr-; S -'tor-
Merivale 'mɛrəˌvel

merl, -e mɜl; ES mɜl, mɜl
merlin, M- 'mɜlɪn; ES 'mɜl-, 'mɜl-
merlon 'mɜlən; ES 'mɜl-, 'mɜl-
mermaid 'mɜˌmed; ES 'mɜ-, 'mɜ-
merman 'mɜˌmæn; ES 'mɜ-, 'mɜ-; |-men
  -ˌmɛn
Merope 'mɛrəpɪ, -ˌpi
Merovingian ˌmɛrə'vɪndʒɪən, -dʒən
Merriam 'mɛrɪəm
Merrick 'mɛrɪk
Merrilies 'mɛrəˌliz |-'s -ɪz
Merrill 'mɛrəl
Merrimack, -mac 'mɛrəˌmæk
merriment 'mɛrɪmənt
merry 'mɛrɪ |-rily 'mɛrəlɪ, -rɪlɪ
merry-andrew 'mɛrɪ'ændru, -drɪu
merry-go-round 'mɛrɪgəˌraʊnd, -go-
Mersey 'mɜzɪ; ES 'mɜzɪ, 'mɜzɪ
Merton 'mɜtn̩; ES 'mɜtn̩, 'mɜtn̩
mesa, M- 'mesə (Am Sp 'mɛsa)
Mesaba mə'sabə |-bi -bɪ
mésalliance me'zælɪəns |-s -ɪz (Fr meza'ljɑ̃:s)
Mesa Verde ˌmesə'vɜd; ES -'vɜd, -'vɜd;
  (Am Sp ˌmesa'βɛrðe)
mescal mɛs'kæl |-ism -ɪzəm
mesdames me'dam (Fr me'dam)
meseems mi'simz
mesencephalon ˌmɛsɛn'sɛfəˌlan, -ˌlɒn
mesentery 'mɛsn̩ˌtɛrɪ |-ric ˌmɛsn̩'tɛrɪk
mesh mɛʃ |meshes 'mɛʃɪz |meshed mɛʃt
Meshach 'miʃæk
Meshek 'miʃɛk
Mesmer 'mɛsmɚ, 'mɛz-; ES -mə(r; (Ger
  'mɛsmər, Fr mɛz'mɛ:r)
mesmeric mɛs'mɛrɪk, mɛz- |-al -l̩ |-ally -l̩ɪ,
  -ɪklɪ—see mesmerism
mesmerism 'mɛsməˌrɪzəm, 'mɛz- (Ger
  ˌmɛsmə'rɪsmʊs, Fr mɛzme'rɪsm̩)
mesmerize 'mɛsməˌraɪz, 'mɛz- |-s -ɪz |-d -d
mesne min
Meso-Gothic, Mesog- ˌmiso'gaθɪk, -'gɒθɪk
Mesopotamia ˌmɛsəpə'temɪə |-n -n
mesothorium ˌmɛsə'θorɪəm, ˌmɛz-, -'θɔr-; S
  -'θor-
Mesozoic ˌmɛsə'zo·ɪk
mesquite 'mɛskit, mɛs'kit
mess mɛs |messes 'mɛsɪz |messed mɛst
message 'mɛsɪdʒ |-s -ɪz |-d -d
Messala mɛ'selə |-lian -lɪən

Messeigneurs, m- ˌmɛsen'jɝz; ES -'jɜz, -'jɝz; (Fr mesɛ'ɲœːr)

messenger 'mɛsn̩dʒɚ; ES 'mɛsn̩dʒə(r

Messiah mə'saɪə |Messias mə'saɪəs |-s's -sɪz

messianic, M- ˌmɛsɪ'ænɪk |-al -l̩ |-ally -lɪ, -ɪklɪ

Messieurs, m- 'mɛsɚz; ES 'mɛsəz (Fr me'sjø)

Messina mə'sinə, mɛ-

messmate 'mɛsˌmet

Messrs. 'mɛsɚz; ES 'mɛsəz (Fr me'sjø)

messuage 'mɛswɪdʒ |-s -ɪz

mestizo mɛs'tizo

met mɛt

meta 'mitə |-s -z |-tae -ti

metabolic ˌmɛtə'balɪk; ES+-'bɒl-; |-al -l̩

metabolism mə'tæbl̩ˌɪzəm, mɛ-

metabolize mə'tæbl̩ˌaɪz, mɛ- |-s -ɪz |-d -d

metacarpal ˌmɛtə'karpl̩; ES -'kɑːpl̩

metacarpus ˌmɛtə'karpəs; ES -'kɑːpəs; |-es -ɪz |-pi -paɪ

metacenter, -tre 'mɛtəˌsɛntɚ; ES -ˌsɛntə(r

metacentral ˌmɛtə'sɛntrəl |-tric -trɪk

metagalaxy ˌmɛtə'gæləksɪ |-lactic -gə'læktɪk

metage 'mitɪdʒ |-s -ɪz

metal 'mɛtl̩ |-ed -d

metallic mə'tælɪk |-al -l̩ |-ally -lɪ, -ɪklɪ

metalliferous ˌmɛtl̩'ɪfərəs

metallurgic ˌmɛtl̩'ɝdʒɪk; ES -'ɝdʒ-, -'ɝdʒ-; |-al -l̩ |-ally -lɪ, -ɪklɪ

metallurgy 'mɛtl̩ˌɝdʒɪ, mɛ'tælɚdʒɪ; ES -ˌɝdʒɪ, -ˌɝdʒɪ, -'tælədʒɪ

metamorphic ˌmɛtə'mɔrfɪk; ES -'mɔəfɪk

metamorphize ˌmɛtə'mɔrfaɪz; ES -'mɔə-; |-s -ɪz |-d -d

metamorphose ˌmɛtə'mɔrfoz, -fos; ES -'mɔə-; |-s -ɪz |-d -d, -t

metamorphosis ˌmɛtə'mɔrfəsɪs; ES -'mɔə-; |-ses -ˌsiz

metaphor 'mɛtəfɚ; ES 'mɛtəfə(r

metaphoric ˌmɛtə'fɔrɪk, -'far-, -'fɒr- |-al -l̩ |-ally -lɪ, -ɪklɪ

metaphysic ˌmɛtə'fɪzɪk |-al -l̩ |-ally -lɪ, -ɪklɪ

metaphysician ˌmɛtəfə'zɪʃən

metapsychosis ˌmɛtəsaɪ'kosɪs, less sensibly mɪˌtæpsɪ'kosɪs

metastasis mə'tæstəsɪs |-ses -ˌsiz

metatarsal ˌmɛtə'tarsl̩; ES -'tɑːsl̩; |-sus -səs |-si -saɪ

metathesis mə'tæθəsɪs |-ses -ˌsiz

Metazoa ˌmɛtə'zoə

Metcalf, -e 'mɛtkæf; E+-kaf, -kɑf

Metchnikoff 'mɛtʃnɪˌkɔf, -ˌkɒf, -ˌkɑf

mete mit |meted 'mitɪd

Metellus mɪ'tɛləs |-'s -ɪz

metempsychosis ˌmɛtəmsaɪ'kosɪs, məˌtɛmp-sɪ'kosɪs |-ses -siz

meteor 'mitɪɚ; ES 'mitɪ·ə(r; |-ite -ˌaɪt

meteoric ˌmitɪ'ɔrɪk, -'ar-, -'ɒr- |-al -l̩ |-ally -lɪ, -ɪklɪ

meteorologic ˌmitɪərə'ladʒɪk, -ˌɔrə-, -ˌarə-, -ˌɒrə-; ES+-'lɒdʒɪk; |-al -l̩ |-ally -lɪ, -ɪklɪ

meteorologist ˌmitɪə'ralədʒɪst; ES+-'rɒl-; |-gy -dʒɪ

meter, -tre 'mitɚ; ES 'mitə(r; |-(e)d -d

methane 'mɛθen |-nol 'mɛθəˌnol

metheglin mə'θɛglɪn

methinks mɪ'θɪŋks |methought mɪ'θɔt

method 'mɛθəd

methodic mə'θadɪk; ES+-'θɒd-; |-al -l̩ |-ally -lɪ, -ɪklɪ

Methodism 'mɛθədˌɪzəm |-ist -ɪst

methodology ˌmɛθəd'alədʒɪ; ES+-'ɒl-

methought mɪ'θɔt

Methow 'mɛt·haʊ, mɛt'haʊ ('Metˌhow 'River)

Methuen Mass mɪ'θjuɪn, -'θɪu-, -ən; surname 'mɛθjuɪn, -ən

Methuselah mə'θjuzlə, -'θɪuz-, -zlə

methyl 'mɛθəl, -ɪl

methylamene ˌmɛθələ'min

methylate 'mɛθəˌlet |-lated -ˌletɪd

methylene 'mɛθəˌlin

meticulous mə'tɪkjələs

métier Fr me'tje

métis, métisse Fr me'tiːs

metonymy mə'tanəmɪ; ES -'tɒn-

metope 'mɛtəˌpi

metric 'mɛtrɪk |-al -l̩ |-ally -lɪ, -ɪklɪ

metrician mɛ'trɪʃən, mə-

metrics 'mɛtrɪks |-trist -trɪst

metrology mɪ'tralədʒɪ; ES+-'trɒl-

metronome 'mɛtrəˌnom

metronomic ˌmɛtrə'namɪk; ES+-'nɒm-; |-al -l̩ |-ally -lɪ, -ɪklɪ

metronymic ˌmitrə'nɪmɪk

metropolis mə'traplɪs, -plɪs; ES+-'trɒp-; |-es -ɪz

metropolitan ˌmɛtrə'palətn̩; ES+-'pɒl-

|full fʊl |tooth tuθ |further 'fɝðɚ; ES 'fɝðə |custom 'kʌstəm |while hwaɪl |how haʊ |toy tɔɪ |using 'juzɪŋ |fuse fjuz, fɪuz |dish dɪʃ |vision 'vɪʒən |Eden 'idn̩ |cradle 'kredl̩ |keep 'em 'kipm̩

Metternich 'mɛtəˌnɪk; ES 'mɛtənɪk
mettle 'mɛtɫ |-d -d |-some -səm
Metuchen məˈtʌtʃɪn, -ən
Metz mɛts |-'s -ɪz
Meung Fr mœ̃
Meuse mjuz, mɪuz |-'s -ɪz (Fr mø:z)
mew mju, mɪu |-ed -d
mewl mjul, mɪul |-ed -d
Mexia Tex məˈhiə, loc.+-ˈheə
Mexicali ˌmɛksɪˈkɑlɪ, -ˈkælɪ
Mexico 'mɛksɪˌko |-can -kən
Meyer 'maɪə; ES 'maɪ·ə(r; |-s -z
Meyerbeer 'maɪəˌbɪr; ES 'maɪ·əˌbɪə(r; (Ger
'maɪərˌbeːr)
Meynell 'mɛnɫ, 'mɛnɫ
Meyrick 'mɛrɪk, 'me-
mezzanine 'mɛzəˌnin, -nɪn
mezzo 'mɛtso, 'mɛzo, 'mɛdzo (It 'mɛddzo)
mezzo-soprano 'mɛtsosəˈpræno, 'mɛzo-,
'mɛdzo-, -ˈprano
mezzotint 'mɛtsəˌtɪnt, 'mɛzə-, 'mɛdzə- |-ed
-ɪd
mho mo
mi mi
Miami maɪˈæmə, -ˈæmɪ
miaow, -ou mɪˈau, mjau |-ed -d
miasma maɪˈæzmə, mɪ- |-s -z |-mata -mətə
|-l -mɫ
miasmatic ˌmaɪəzˈmætɪk |-al -ɫ |-ally -ɫɪ,
-ɪklɪ
miaul mɪˈaul, mjaul |-ed -d
mib mɪb
mica 'maɪkə |-caceous, -cacious maɪˈkeʃəs
Micah 'maɪkə |Micaiah maɪˈkeə
Micawber məˈkɔbə; ES -ˈkɔbə(r
mice maɪs |mice's 'maɪsɪz
Michael 'maɪkɫ
Michaelmas 'mɪkɫməs |-es -ɪz
Michaud, -chault, -chaut mɪˈʃo (Fr miˈʃo)
Michelangelo ˌmaɪkɫˈændʒəˌlo, ˌmɪkɫ- (It
ˌmiːkelˈandʒeˌlo)
Michelson 'maɪkɫsn̩
Michigan 'mɪʃəgən |-der ˌmɪʃəˈgændə; ES
-də(r; Brit 'mɪtʃɪgən is not current in
America.
Michiganite 'mɪʃəgənˌaɪt
mickle, M- 'mɪkɫ
Micmac 'mɪkmæk
microampere ˌmaɪkroˈæmpɪr; ES -ˈæmpɪə(r

microanalysis ˌmaɪkroəˈnæləsɪs |-ses -ˌsiz
microbe 'maɪkrob
microbiology ˌmaɪkrobaɪˈɑlədʒɪ; ES+-ˈɒl-
microcephalic ˌmaɪkrosəˈfælɪk |-lous -ˈsɛfələs
microchemistry ˌmaɪkroˈkɛmɪstrɪ
microcosm 'maɪkrəˌkɑzəm; ES+-ˌkɒz-
microfarad ˌmaɪkroˈfærəd, -ˈfæræd
microfilm 'maɪkrəˌfɪlm |-ed -d
microgram 'maɪkroˌgræm
micrography maɪˈkrɑgrəfɪ, -ˈkrɒg-
micrometer tool maɪˈkrɑmətə; ES -ˈkrɑmə-
tə(r, -ˈkrɒm-
micrometer 'millionth of a meter' 'maɪkro-
ˌmitə; ES -ˌmitə(r
micrometry maɪˈkrɑmətrɪ; ES+-ˈkrɒm-
micron 'maɪkrɑn; ES+-krɒn; |-s -z |-cra -krə
Micronesia ˌmaɪkrəˈniʒə, -ʃə |-n -n
microorganism ˌmaɪkroˈɔrgənˌɪzəm; ES -ˈɔə-
gən-
microphone 'maɪkrəˌfon |-d -d
microphysics ˌmaɪkroˈfɪzɪks
microscope 'maɪkrəˌskop |-d -t
microscopic ˌmaɪkrəˈskɑpɪk; ES+-ˈskɒp-;
|-al -ɫ |-ally -ɫɪ, -ɪklɪ
microscopy maɪˈkrɑskəpɪ, 'maɪkrəˌskopɪ; ES
+-ˈkrɒs-; |-pist -pɪst
microtomy maɪˈkrɑtəmɪ; ES+ˈkrɒt-
microvolt 'maɪkrəˌvolt
microwatt 'maɪkrəˌwat -ˌwɒt
micturate 'mɪktʃəˌret |-rated -ˌretɪd
micturition ˌmɪktʃəˈrɪʃən
mid mɪd |-most -ˌmost |'mid mɪd
Midas 'maɪdəs |-'s -ɪz
midbrain 'mɪdˌbren
midday 'mɪdˌde, -ˈde
midden 'mɪdn̩
middle 'mɪdɫ |-d -d |-ling 'mɪdɫɪŋ, 'mɪdlɪŋ
middle-aged 'mɪdɫˈedʒd ('middle-ˌaged 'man)
Middleboro 'mɪdɫˌbɝo, -ə; ES -ˌbɜr-, -ˌbʌr-,
-ˌbɝ-
Middlebury 'mɪdɫˌbɛrɪ, -bərɪ
middleman 'mɪdɫˌmæn |-men -ˌmɛn
Middlemarch 'mɪdɫˌmartʃ; ES -ˌma:tʃ, E+
-ˌma:tʃ
middler 'mɪdlə; ES 'mɪdlə(r
Middlesex 'mɪdɫˌsɛks |-'s -ɪz
Middleton 'mɪdɫtən |-town -ˌtaun
middleweight 'mɪdɫˌwet
middling adj, adv, n 'mɪdlɪŋ

Key: See in full §§3–47. bee bi |pity 'pɪtɪ (§6) |rate ret |yet jɛt |sang sæŋ |angry 'æŋ·grɪ
|bath bæθ; E baθ (§10) |ah ɑ |far fɑr |watch watʃ, wɒtʃ (§12) |jaw dʒɔ |gorge gɔrdʒ |go go

Midgard 'mɪd¡gard; ES -¡gɑ:d, E+-¡gɑ:d
midge mɪdʒ |midges 'mɪdʒɪz
midget 'mɪdʒɪt
Midi Fr mi'di
Midian 'mɪdɪən |-ite -¡aɪt
midiron 'mɪd¡aɪɚn, -¡aɪrn; ES -¡aɪ·ən, -¡aɪən
midland, M- 'mɪdlənd
Midlothian mɪd'loðɪən
midmost 'mɪd¡most
midnight 'mɪd¡naɪt
midnoon 'mɪd'nun ('mid¡noon 'heat)
midrash, M- 'mɪdræʃ |-es -ɪz |Heb pl -im
   mɪd'rɑʃim |-oth -'rɑʃoθ
midrib 'mɪd¡rɪb |-bed -d
midriff 'mɪdrɪf
midship 'mɪd¡ʃɪp |-man -mən |-men -mən
midst mɪdst, mɪtst
midsummer, M- 'mɪd'sʌmɚ; ES -'sʌmə(r
midway, M- n 'mɪd¡we
midway adv, adj 'mɪd'we ('mid¡way 'out,
   'mid¡way 'air)
midweek 'mɪd'wik ('mid¡week 'meeting)
Midwest 'mɪd'wɛst ('Mid¡west 'custom)
Midwestern mɪd'wɛstɚn; ES -tən; |-er -ɚ;
   ES -ə(r
midwife 'mɪd¡waɪf |-wives -¡waɪvz |-wife's
   -waɪfs |-ry -ərɪ, -rɪ
midwinter 'mɪd'wɪntɚ; ES -'wɪntə(r
midyear 'mɪd¡jɪr; ES -¡jɪə(r, S+-¡jɛə(r
mien min
miff mɪf |miffed mɪft
might maɪt |-y -ɪ |-ily 'maɪtlɪ, -ɪlɪ
mightest 'maɪtɪst
might-have-been n 'maɪtəv¡bɪn, 'maɪtə¡bɪn
mightn't 'maɪtn̩t, before some conss.+'maɪtn̩
   (mightn't go 'maɪtn̩'go)
mignon 'minion' 'mɪnjən
mignon 'small' 'mɪnjɑn, -jɒn (Fr mi'n̩õ
Mignon Ala 'mɪnjən; in Goethe Fr mi'n̩õ
mignonette ¡mɪnjən'ɛt
mignonne 'mɪnjən (Fr mi'n̩ɒn)
migraine 'maɪgren, mɪ'gren
migrant 'maɪgrənt
migrate 'maɪgret |-d -ɪd |-tion maɪ'greʃən
migratory 'maɪgrə¡torɪ, -¡tɔrɪ; S -¡torɪ
mikado, M- mə'kɑdo
mike, M- maɪk
mil mɪl
mil Scand measure mil

milady mɪ'ledɪ—not current in America
Milan US 'maɪlən; Italy mɪ'læn, 'mɪlən (It
   Milano mi'lɑ:no)
Milanese ¡mɪlən'iz
Milburn 'mɪlbɚn; ES 'mɪlbən
milch mɪltʃ
mild maɪld |-en -n̩ |-ened -n̩d |-ening -dn̩ɪŋ,
   -dnɪŋ
mildew 'mɪl¡dju, -¡dɪu, -¡du |-ed -d
Mildred 'mɪldrɪd
mile maɪl |-age -ɪdʒ |-ages -ɪdʒɪz
milepost 'maɪl¡post
Miles maɪlz |Miles's 'maɪlzɪz
Milesian mə'liʒən, -ʃən
milestone 'maɪl¡ston
Miletus maɪ'litəs |-'s -ɪz
milfoil 'mɪl¡fɔɪl
Milford 'mɪlfɚd; ES 'mɪlfəd
miliary 'mɪlɪ¡ɛrɪ, 'mɪljərɪ
Milicent 'mɪləsn̩t
milieu Fr mi'ljø
militant 'mɪlətənt |-tancy -tənsɪ
militarism 'mɪlətə¡rɪzəm |-rist -rɪst
militaristic ¡mɪlətə'rɪstɪk |-ally -ḷɪ, -ɪklɪ
militarization ¡mɪlətərə'zeʃən, -trə-, -aɪ'z-
militarize 'mɪlətə¡raɪz |-s -ɪz |-d -d
military 'mɪlə¡tɛrɪ |-tate -¡tet |-tated -¡tetɪd
militia mə'lɪʃə |-man -mən |-men -mən
milk mɪlk |milked mɪlkt |-maid -¡med
milkman retailer 'mɪlk¡mæn |-men -¡mɛn
milkman producer 'mɪlkmən |-men -mən,
   -¡mɛn
milksop 'mɪlk¡sɑp; ES+-¡sɒp
milkweed 'mɪlk¡wid
mill, M- mɪl |-ed -d—The n sound was lost
   from mill (OE myln 'gristmill') in the same
   way as from ell, kiln, Milne.
Millais mɪ'le |-lais's -'lez |pl Millais mɪ'lez
Millard 'mɪlɚd; ES 'mɪləd
Millay mɪ'le
Millbourne 'mɪlbən; ES 'mɪlbən
Millburn 'mɪlbɚn; ES 'mɪlbən
Millbury 'mɪl¡bɛrɪ, -bərɪ
milldam 'mɪl¡dæm
Milledgeville 'mɪlɪdʒ¡vɪl; S+-vḷ
millenarian ¡mɪlə'nɛrɪən, -'ner- |-anism
   -¡ɪzəm
millenary 'mɪlə¡nɛrɪ
millennial mə'lɛnɪəl |-ly -ɪ |-alism -¡ɪzəm

|full fʊl |tooth tuθ |further 'fɝðɚ; ES 'fɝðə |custom 'kʌstəm |while hwaɪl |how haʊ |toy tɔɪ
|using 'juzɪŋ |fuse fjuz, fɪuz |dish dɪʃ |vision 'vɪʒən |Eden 'idn̩ |cradle 'kredḷ |keep 'em 'kipm̩

millennium mə'lɛnɪəm |-s -z |-nia -nɪə

millepede 'mɪlə͵pid

miller, M- 'mɪlɚ; ES 'mɪlə(r; |-ite -͵aɪt

millet *'grass'* 'mɪlɪt; *relig. group*+mɪ'lɛt

Millet *Am painter* 'mɪlɪt, *Fr sculp., painter* mɪ'le (*Fr* mi'lɛ, mi'jɛ)

milliampere ͵mɪlɪ'æmpɪr; ES -pɪə(r

milliard 'mɪljɚd, -jard; ES -jəd, -jɑːd

Millicent 'mɪləsn̩t

Milligan 'mɪləgən

milligram 'mɪlə͵græm

Millikan 'mɪləkən

milliliter, -tre 'mɪlə͵litɚ; ES -͵litə(r

millimeter, -tre 'mɪlə͵mitɚ; ES -͵mitə(r

millimicron ͵mɪlə'maɪkran; ES+-krɒn

milliner 'mɪlənɚ; ES 'mɪlənə(r; |-y -͵nɛrɪ, -nərɪ

million 'mɪljən |-th -θ |-ths -θs

millionaire ͵mɪljən'ɛr, -'ær; E -'ɛə(r, ES -'æə(r

millipede 'mɪlə͵pid

millpond 'mɪl͵pand, -͵pɒnd, -͵pɔnd

millrace 'mɪl͵res |-s -ɪz

millstone 'mɪl͵ston

millstream 'mɪl͵strim

millwright 'mɪl͵raɪt

Miln, -e mɪl, mɪln—*When the* n *sound is heard, it is a spelling pronunciation; see* mill.

Milner 'mɪlnɚ; ES 'mɪlnə(r

Milnes mɪlz, mɪlnz |-'s -ɪz

Milo *US name and places* 'maɪlo; *'Melos'* 'milo

milord mɪ'lɔrd; ES -'lɔəd;—*not current in America*

milreis *coin* 'mɪl͵res |*pl same*

milt, M- mɪlt |-ed -ɪd

Miltiades mɪl'taɪə͵diz |-'s -ɪz

Milton 'mɪltn̩ |-tonian mɪl'tonɪən

Miltonic mɪl'tɑnɪk; ES+-'tɒn-; |-ally -l̩ɪ

Milwaukee mɪl'wɔkɪ ('Mɪl͵waukee 'Road)

mime maɪm |mimed maɪmd

mimeograph, M- 'mɪmɪə͵græf; E+-͵graf, -͵graf; |-ed -t

mimeographic ͵mɪmɪə'græfɪk |-ally -l̩ɪ, -ɪklɪ

mimetic mɪ'mɛtɪk, maɪ- |-al -l̩ |-ally -l̩ɪ, -ɪklɪ

mimic 'mɪmɪk |-ked -t |-ally -l̩ɪ |-ry -rɪ

mimosa, M- mɪ'mosə, -zə

mina 'maɪnə |-s -z |-nae -ni

Mina 'maɪnə

minaret ͵mɪnə'rɛt, 'mɪnə͵rɛt |-ed -ɪd

minatorial ͵mɪnə'torɪəl, -'tɔr-; S -'tor-; |-ly -ɪ

minatory 'mɪnə͵torɪ, -͵tɔrɪ; S -͵torɪ

mince mɪns |minces 'mɪnsɪz |-d -t |-meat -͵mit

mind maɪnd |minded 'maɪndɪd |-ful -fəl |-fully -fəlɪ

mine *n, v* maɪn |mined maɪnd |*pro* maɪn

Mineola ͵mɪnɪ'olə

miner, M- 'maɪnɚ; ES 'maɪnə(r

mineral, M- 'mɪnərəl, 'mɪnrəl

mineralogic ͵mɪnərə'lɑdʒɪk; ES+-'lɒdʒ-; |-al -l̩ |-ally -l̩ɪ, -ɪklɪ

mineralogist ͵mɪnɚ'ælədʒɪst, -'al-; ES+-'ɒl-; |-gy -dʒɪ

Minerva mə'nɝvə; ES -'nɜvə, -'nɝvə

Ming mɪŋ

mingle 'mɪŋgl̩ |-d -d |-ling 'mɪŋglɪŋ, -gl̩ɪŋ

Mingo 'mɪŋgo

miniature 'mɪnɪtʃɚ, 'mɪnɪə-; ES -tʃə(r; |-d -d

Minie ball 'mɪnɪ͵bɔl (*Fr* mi'nje)

minify 'mɪnə͵faɪ |-fied -͵faɪd

minikin 'mɪnɪkɪn

minim 'mɪnɪm

minimal 'mɪnɪml̩ |-ly -ɪ

minimize 'mɪnə͵maɪz |-s -ɪz |-d -d

minimum 'mɪnəməm |-s -z |-ma -mə

minion, M- 'mɪnjən

minish 'mɪnɪʃ |-es -ɪz |-ed -t

minister 'mɪnɪstɚ; ES -tə(r; |-ed -d |-ing 'mɪnɪstərɪŋ, 'mɪnɪstrɪŋ

ministerial ͵mɪnəs'tɪrɪəl |-ly -ɪ

ministrant 'mɪnɪstrənt |-stry -strɪ

ministration ͵mɪnə'streʃən

miniver, M- 'mɪnəvɚ; ES 'mɪnəvə(r

mink mɪŋk

Minneapolis ͵mɪnɪ'æpl̩ɪs, -'æplɪs, -əs |-'s -ɪz

Minnehaha ͵mɪnɪ'hɑhɑ

minnesinger, M- 'mɪnɪ͵sɪŋɚ; ES -͵sɪŋə(r

Minnesota ͵mɪnɪ'sotə |-tan -tn̩

Minnewit 'mɪnjʊɪt, 'mɪnəwɪt=Minuit

Minnie 'mɪnɪ

minnow 'mɪno, -ə |minny 'mɪnɪ

minny-bass 'mɪnɪ͵bæs |-'s -ɪz

Minoan mɪ'noən

Minola 'mɪnələ

minor, M- 'maɪnɚ; ES 'maɪnə(r

Minorca mə'nɔrkə; ES -'nɔəkə; |-n -n

Minorite, m- 'maɪnəˌraɪt
minority mə'nɔrətɪ, maɪ-, -'nɑr-, -'nɒr-
Minos 'maɪnɑs, -nɒs; ES+-nɒs; |-'s -ɪz
Minot 'maɪnət
Minotaur 'mɪnəˌtɔr; ES -ˌtɔə(r
minster 'mɪnstɚ; ES 'mɪnstə(r
minstrel 'mɪnstrəl |-ed -d |-sy -sɪ
mint mɪnt |minted 'mɪntɪd |-age -ɪdʒ
minuend 'mɪnjuˌɛnd
minuet ˌmɪnju'ɛt |-ed -ɪd
Minuit 'mɪnjuɪt, 'mɪnəwɪt=Minnewit
minus 'maɪnəs |-es -ɪz
minuscule mɪ'nʌskjul, -kɪul
minute n, v 'mɪnɪt |-d -ɪd
minute 'small' mə'njut, maɪ-, -'nɪut, -'nut
minuteman 'mɪnɪtˌmæn |-men -ˌmɛn
minutia mɪ'njuʃɪə, -'nɪu-, -'nu- |-tiae -ʃɪˌi
minx mɪŋks |minxes 'mɪŋksɪz
Miocene 'maɪəˌsin |-cenic ˌmaɪə'sɛnɪk
Miquelon ˌmɪkə'lɑn, -'lɒn (Fr mi'klõ)
Mirabeau 'mɪrəˌbo (Fr mira'bo)
miracle 'mɪrəkl̩, 'mɪrɪ- |-d -d |-ling -klɪŋ,
   -kl̩ɪŋ
miraculous mə'rækjələs
Miraflores ˌmɪrə'flores |-'s -ɪz
mirage mə'rɑʒ |-s -ɪz |-d -d
Miranda mə'rændə
mire maɪr; ES maɪə(r; |-d -d
Miriam 'mɪrɪəm, 'mɛrɪəm—cf Syracuse
mirk mɝk; ES mɜk, mɝk; |-some -səm |-y -ɪ
mirror 'mɪrɚ; ES 'mɪrə(r; |-ed -d
mirth mɝθ; ES mɜθ, mɝθ; |-ful -fəl |-fully
   -fəlɪ
miry 'maɪrɪ
Mirza 'mɝzə; ES 'mɜzə, 'mɝzə; (Pers
   'mirzɑ)
misadventure ˌmɪsəd'vɛntʃɚ; ES -tʃə(r; |-d -d
misalliance ˌmɪsə'laɪəns |-s -ɪz
misanthrope 'mɪsənˌθrop, 'mɪz-
misanthropic ˌmɪsən'θrɑpɪk; ES+-'θrɒp-; |-al
   -l̩ |-ally -l̩ɪ, -ɪklɪ
misanthropism mɪs'ænθrəˌpɪzəm |-pist -pɪst
misanthropy mɪs'ænθrəpɪ
misapplication ˌmɪsæplə'keʃən
misapply ˌmɪsə'plaɪ |-ied -d
misapprehend ˌmɪsæprɪ'hɛnd |-ed -ɪd
misapprehension ˌmɪsæprɪ'hɛnʃən
misappropriate adj ˌmɪsə'proprɪɪt
misappropriate v ˌmɪsə'proprɪˌet |-d -ɪd

misappropriation ˌmɪsəˌproprɪ'eʃən
misbecoming ˌmɪsbɪ'kʌmɪŋ
misbegotten ˌmɪsbɪ'gɑtn̩; ES+-'gɒtn̩
misbehave ˌmɪsbɪ'hev |-d -d |-vior -jɚ; ES
   -jə(r
misbelieve ˌmɪsbə'liv, -bl̩'iv |-d -d |-r -ɚ; ES
   -ə(r
miscalculate mɪs'kælkjəˌlet |-d -ɪd
miscalculation ˌmɪskælkjə'leʃən
miscall mɪs'kɔl |-ed -d
miscarriage mɪs'kærɪdʒ |-s -ɪz; in sense 'fail-
   ure'+-'kærɪdʒ
miscarry mɪs'kærɪ |-ied -d
miscegenation ˌmɪsɪdʒə'neʃən
miscellaneous ˌmɪsl̩'enɪəs, -njəs
miscellany 'mɪsl̩ˌɛnɪ
mischance mɪs'tʃæns; E+-'tʃɑns, -'tʃɑns; |-s
   -ɪz |-d -t
mischief 'mɪstʃɪf |-chievous -tʃɪvəs
miscolor mɪs'kʌlɚ; ES -'kʌlə(r; |-ed -d
misconceive ˌmɪskən'siv |-d -d
misconception ˌmɪskən'sɛpʃən
misconduct n mɪs'kɑndʌkt; ES+-'kɒn-
misconduct v ˌmɪskən'dʌkt |-ed -ɪd
misconster 'misconstrue' Shak. mɪs'kɑnstɚ;
   ES -'kɑnstə(r, -'kɒn- |-ed -d
misconstruct ˌmɪskən'strʌkt |-ed -ɪd
misconstruction ˌmɪskən'strʌkʃən
misconstrue ˌmɪskən'stru, -'strɪu, mɪs'kɑn-
   stru, -strɪu, ES+-'kɒn-; |-d -d
miscount mɪs'kaʊnt |-ed -ɪd
miscreance 'mɪskrɪəns |-cy -ɪ |-ant -ənt
miscreate ˌmɪskrɪ'et |-d -ɪd |-tion -'eʃən
miscue mɪs'kju, -'kɪu |-d -d
misdate mɪs'det |-dated -'detɪd
misdeal mɪs'dil |-dealt -'dɛlt
misdeed mɪs'did
misdemean ˌmɪsdɪ'min |-ed -d |-ant -ənt
misdemeanor ˌmɪsdɪ'minɚ; ES -'minə(r
misdirect ˌmɪsdə'rɛkt |-ed -ɪd |-ction -kʃən
misdo mɪs'du |-did -'dɪd |-done -'dʌn
misdoubt mɪs'daʊt |-ed -ɪd
mise miz, maɪz |-s -ɪz
misease mɪs'iz |-d -d
miser, M- 'maɪzɚ; ES 'maɪzə(r; |-ly -lɪ
miserable 'mɪzrəbl̩, -zərə- |-bly -blɪ
Miserere ˌmɪzə'rɛrɪ, -'rɪrɪ
misericord, -e ˌmɪzərɪ'kɔrd, mɪ'zɛrɪˌkɔrd; ES
   -ɔəd

|full fʊl |tooth tuθ |further 'fɝðɚ; ES 'fɝðə |custom 'kʌstəm |while hwaɪl |how haʊ |toy tɔɪ
|using 'juzɪŋ |fuse fjuz, fɪuz |dish dɪʃ |vision 'vɪʒən |Eden 'idn̩ |cradle 'kredl̩ |keep 'em 'kipm̩

misery 'mɪzrɪ, 'mɪzərɪ

misestimate mɪs'ɛstəˌmet |-mated -ˌmetɪd

misestimation ˌmɪsɛstə'meʃən, mɪsˌɛstə-

misfeasance mɪs'fizn̩s |-s -ɪz

misfire mɪs'faɪr; ES -'faɪə(r; |-d -d

misfit mɪs'fɪt |-ted -ɪd ('mɪsˌfɪt 'suit)

misfortune mɪs'fɔrtʃən; ES -'fɔətʃ-; |-d -d

misgive mɪs'gɪv |-gave -'gev |-given -'gɪvən

misgiving mɪs'gɪvɪŋ

misgovern mɪs'gʌvən; ES -'gʌvən; |-ed -d

misguide mɪs'gaɪd |-d -ɪd |-dance -n̩s

mishandle mɪs'hænd̩l |-d -d |-ling -dlɪŋ, -d̩lɪŋ

mishap 'mɪsˌhæp, mɪs'hæp

Mishawaka ˌmɪʃə'wɔkə

Mishnah, -na 'mɪʃnə |Heb pl -nayoth ˌmɪʃna-
'joθ

misinform ˌmɪsɪn'fɔrm, ˌmɪsn̩-; ES -'fɔəm;
|-ed -d

misinformation ˌmɪsɪnfə'meʃən; ES -fə'me-

misinterpret ˌmɪsɪn'tɝprɪt, ˌmɪsn̩-; ES -'tɝp-,
-'tɝp-; |-ed -ɪd

misinterpretation ˌmɪsɪnˌtɝprɪ'teʃən, ˌmɪsn̩-;
ES -ˌtɝp-, -ˌtɝp-

misjudge mɪs'dʒʌdʒ |-s -ɪz |-d -d

mislabel mɪs'leb̩l |-ed -d |-ing -blɪŋ, -b̩lɪŋ

mislay mɪs'le |-laid -'led

mislead mɪs'lid |-led -'lɛd

mismanage mɪs'mænɪdʒ |-s -ɪz |-d -d

mismatch mɪs'mætʃ |-es -ɪz |-ed -t

mismate mɪs'met |-mated -'metɪd

misname mɪs'nem |-named -'nemd

misnomer mɪs'nomə; ES -'nomə(r; |-ed -d
|-ing -'nomərɪŋ, -'nomrɪŋ

misogamist mɪ'sagəmɪst; ES+-'sɒg-; |-my
-mɪ

misogynist mɪ'sadʒənɪst; ES+-'sɒdʒ-; |-ny
-nɪ

misplace mɪs'ples |-s -ɪz |-d -t

misplay mɪs'ple |-ed -d

misprint n mɪs'prɪnt, 'mɪsˌprɪnt

misprint v mɪs'prɪnt |-ed -ɪd

misprision mɪs'prɪʒən

misprize mɪs'praɪz |-s -ɪz |-d -d

mispronounce ˌmɪsprə'naʊns, -pə- |-s -ɪz
|-d -t

mispronunciation ˌmɪsprəˌnʌnsɪ'eʃən, -pə-,
-ʃɪ-

misquotation ˌmɪskwo'teʃən

misquote mɪs'kwot |-d -ɪd

misread mɪs'rid |-read -'rɛd

misreport ˌmɪsrɪ'port, -'pɔrt; ES -'poət,
E+-'pɔət; |-ed -ɪd

misrepresent ˌmɪsrɛprɪ'zɛnt |-ed -ɪd

misrepresentation ˌmɪsrɛprɪzɛn'teʃən

misrule mɪs'rul, -'rɪul |-d -d ('rule or 'mis-
ˌrule)

miss, M- mɪs |misses 'mɪsɪz |missed mɪst

missal 'mɪs̩l

Missaukee mɪ'sɔkɪ

missay mɪs'se |-said -'sɛd

misseem mɪs'sim |-ed -d

misshape mɪs'ʃep, mɪʃ'ʃep |-d -t |-n -ən

missile 'mɪs̩l, -ɪl

mission 'mɪʃən |-ed -d |-ary -ˌɛrɪ

Missisquoi mɪ'sɪskwɔɪ

Mississippi ˌmɪsə'sɪpɪ, ˌmɪs:'sɪpɪ ('Missis-
ˌsippi 'River) |-an -ən

missive 'mɪsɪv

Missoula mɪ'zulə

Missouri mə'zʊrɪ, -'zʊrə |-rian -rɪən

misspeak mɪs'spik |-spoke -'spok |-spoken
-'spokən

misspell mɪs'spɛl |-ed -d or -spelt -'spɛlt

misspend mɪs'spɛnd |-spent -'spɛnt

misstate mɪs'stet |-d -ɪd

misstep mɪs'stɛp |-ped -t

mist mɪst |misted 'mɪstɪd

mistakable mə'stekəb̩l |-bly -blɪ

mistake mə'stek |-took mɪs'tʊk |-n mə-
'stekən—mistook is less familiar than
mistake & was (were) mistaken; hence the
difference in syllable division.

mistaught mɪs'tɔt

misteach mɪs'titʃ |-es -ɪz |-taught -'tɔt

mistell mɪs'tɛl |-told -'told

Mister, m- 'mɪstə; ES 'mɪstə(r; |-ed -d

misthink mɪs'θɪŋk |-thought -'θɔt

mistime mɪs'taɪm |-d -d

mistletoe 'mɪs̩lˌto

mistook mɪs'tʊk—see mistake

mistral wind 'mɪstrəl, mɪs'tral (Fr mis'tral)

Mistral poet, Fr mis'tral

mistranslate ˌmɪstræns'let, -trænz- |-d -ɪd

mistreat mɪs'trit |-ed -ɪd

mistress 'mɪstrɪs |-es -ɪz |-'s -ɪz

mistrial mɪs'traɪəl

mistrust mɪs'trʌst |-ed -ɪd; dial. in sense
'expect,' 'think' mɪ'strʌst

Key: See in full §§3–47. bee bi |pity 'pɪtɪ (§6) |rate ret |yet jɛt |sang sæŋ |angry 'æŋ·grɪ
|bath bæθ; E baθ (§10) |ah ɑ |far fɑr |watch watʃ, wɒtʃ (§12) |jaw dʒɔ |gorge gɔrdʒ |go go

Those words below in which the ɑ sound is spelt o are often pronounced with ɒ in E and S

misunderstand ˌmɪsʌndəˈstænd; ES -ʌndə-;
|-stood -ˈstʊd
misusage mɪsˈjusɪdʒ, -zɪdʒ
misuse *n* mɪsˈjus |-uses -ˈjusɪz
misuse *v* mɪsˈjuz |-uses -ˈjuzɪz |-used -ˈjuzd
misword mɪsˈwɝd; ES -ˈwɜd, -ˈwɜˑd; |-ed -ɪd
miswrite mɪsˈraɪt |-wrote -ˈrot |-written -ˈrɪtn̩
Mitchell ˈmɪtʃəl
mite maɪt
miter, -tre ˈmaɪtɚ; ES ˈmaɪtə(r; |-(e)d -d
Mithras ˈmɪθræs |-'s -ɪz
Mithridates ˌmɪθrəˈdetiz |-tes' -tiz
mitigable ˈmɪtəgəbl̩
mitigate ˈmɪtəˌget |-d -ɪd |-tion ˌmɪtəˈgeʃən
mitosis mɪˈtosɪs |-toses -ˈtosiz
mitrailleur ˌmitreˈjɝ; ES -ˈjɜ(r, -ˈjɝ; (*Fr*
mitraˈjœːr)
mitrailleuse ˌmitreˈjɜz |-s -ɪz (*Fr* mitraˈjøːz)
mitral ˈmaɪtrəl
mitt mɪt |-en ˈmɪtn̩ |-ened ˈmɪtn̩d
mittimus ˈmɪtəməs |-es -ɪz |-ed -t
mitzvah, mits- ˈmɪtsva |*Heb pl* -voth -voθ
mix, M- mɪks |-es -ɪz |-ed -t |-edly -ɪdlɪ, -tlɪ
mixture ˈmɪkstʃɚ ES ˈmɪkstʃə(r
Mizpah, -peh ˈmɪzpə
mizzen ˈmɪzn̩ |-mast -məst, -ˌmæst; E+
-ˌmast, -ˌmast
mizzle ˈmɪzl̩ |-d -d |-ling ˈmɪzl̩ɪŋ, -zlɪŋ
mnemonic niˈmɑnɪk |-al -ˈmɑnɪkl̩ |-ally -l̩ɪ,
-ɪklɪ
Mnemosyne niˈmɑsn̩ˌi, -ˈmɑz-, -ˈmɒ-
Moab ˈmoæb |-ite ˈmoəbˌaɪt
moan mon |moaned mond |-ful -fəl |-fully
-fəlɪ
moat mot |moated ˈmotɪd
mob mɑb |-bed -d
mobble '*muffle*' ˈmɑbl̩ |-d -d
Moberly ˈmobɚlɪ; ES ˈmobəlɪ
Mobile moˈbil (ˈMoˌbile ˈBay)
mobile ˈmobl̩, ˈmobil, -bɪl |-bility moˈbɪlətɪ
mobilization ˌmoblə'zeʃən, -aɪ'z-
mobilize ˈmoblˌaɪz |-s -ɪz |-d -d
moble '*muffle*' ˈmɑbl̩ |-d -d
moble '*movable*' ˈmobl̩
Mobridge ˈmobrɪdʒ |-'s -ɪz
Moby Dick ˈmobɪˈdɪk
moccasin ˈmɑkəsn̩, -zn̩ |-ed -d
Mocha ˈmokə

mock mɑk, mɒk, mɔk |-ed -t |-ery -ərɪ—mɔk
is widespread in the N and C, and not in-
frequent in the E and S.
mock-heroic ˈmɑkhɪˈroˑɪk, ˈmɒk-, ˈmɔk- |-al
-l̩ |-ally -l̩ɪ, -ɪklɪ
mockingbird ˈmɑkɪŋˌbɝd, ˈmɒk-, ˈmɔk-; ES
-ˌbɝd, -ˌbɝˑd
modal ˈmodl̩ |-ly -ɪ |-ity moˈdælətɪ
mode mod
model ˈmɑdl̩ |-ed -d |-ing ˈmɑdl̩ɪŋ, ˈmɑdlɪŋ
moderate *n, adj* ˈmɑdərɪt, ˈmɑdrɪt
moderate *v* ˈmɑdəˌret |-d -ɪd |-tor -ɚ; ES -ə(r
moderation ˌmɑdəˈreʃən
modern ˈmɑdɚn; ES ˈmɑdən, *esp. attrib.*
ˈmɑdn̩
modernism ˈmɑdɚnˌɪzəm; ES ˈmɑdən-, -dn̩-
modernity maˈdɝnətɪ, mo-; ES -ˈdɜn-, -ˈdɝn-
modernization ˌmɑdɚnəˈzeʃən, -aɪˈz-; ES
ˌmɑdən-, -dn̩-
modernize ˈmɑdɚnˌaɪz; ES ˈmɑdən-, -dn̩-; |-s
-ɪz |-d -d
modernness ˈmɑdɚnnɪs; ES ˈmɑdənnɪs,
ˈmɑdn̩nɪs
modest ˈmɑdɪst |modesty ˈmɑdəstɪ
Modesto moˈdɛsto
modicum ˈmɑdɪkəm |-s -z
modifiable ˈmɑdəˌfaɪəbl̩ |-bly -blɪ
modification ˌmɑdəfəˈkeʃən
modify ˈmɑdəˌfaɪ |-fied -ˌfaɪd
modish ˈmodɪʃ
modiste moˈdist (*Fr* mɔˈdist)
Modjeska məˈdʒɛskə
Modoc ˈmodak
Modred ˈmodrɪd
modulate ˈmɑdʒəˌlet |-d -ɪd |-tor -ɚ; ES -ə(r
modulation ˌmɑdʒəˈleʃən
module ˈmɑdʒul, -dʒɪul
modulus ˈmɑdʒələs |-es -ɪz |-li -ˌlaɪ
modus operandi ˈmodəsˌɑpəˈrændaɪ
modus vivendi ˈmodəsvɪˈvɛndaɪ
Moeso-Gothic, Moesog- ˌmisoˈgɑθɪk, -ˈgɒθɪk
Moffat, -et, -tt ˈmɑfɪt, -ət
Mogador ˌmɑgəˈdor, -ˈdɔr; ES -ˈdoə(r,
E+-ˈdɔə(r; *Ohio* ˈMogaˌdore
Mogul ˈmogʌl, moˈgʌl (ˈGreat Moˈgul)
mohair ˈmoˌhɛr, -ˌhær; E -ˌhɛə(r, ES -ˌhæə(r
Mohammed moˈhæmɪd |-an -ˈhæmədən
Mohave, -jave moˈhavɪ (*Am Sp* moˈhaβe)

Those words below in which the ɑ *sound is spelt* o *are often pronounced with* ɒ *in E and S*

Mohawk ˈmohɔk

Mohican moˈhikən

Mohock ˈmohɑk, -hɔk

Mohonk moˈhaŋk, -ˈhɒŋk

moidore ˈmɔɪdor, -dɔr; ES -doə(r, E+-dɔə(r

moiety ˈmɔɪətɪ, ˈmɔjətɪ

moil mɔɪl |moiled mɔɪld

Moira ˈmɔɪrə

moire mwɑr, mwɔr, mor, mɔr; ES mwɑ:(r, mwɔə(r, moə(r, E+mɔə(r

moist mɔɪst

moisten ˈmɔɪsn̩ |-ed -d |-ing ˈmɔɪsn̩ɪŋ, -snɪŋ

moisture ˈmɔɪstʃɚ; ES ˈmɔɪstʃə(r

Mojave moˈhavɪ (*Am Sp* moˈhaβe)

molar ˈmolɚ; ES ˈmolə(r

molasses məˈlæsɪz

mold mold |-ed -ɪd |-y -ɪ

Moldavia malˈdevɪə, -vjə |-n -n

moldboard ˈmoldˌbord, ˈmol-, -ˌbɔrd, *dial.* ˈmʌl-; ES -ˌboəd, E+-ˌbɔəd

molder ˈmoldɚ; ES ˈmoldə(r; |-ed -d |-ing ˈmoldrɪŋ, ˈmoldərɪŋ

moldwarp ˈmoldˌwɔrp; ES -ˌwɔəp

mole mol |moled mold

Mole ˈmole

molecular məˈlɛkjələ˞; ES -ˈlɛkjələ(r

molecule ˈmaləˌkjul, -ˌkɪul

molehill ˈmolˌhɪl |moleskin -ˌskɪn

molest məˈlɛst |-ed -ɪd

molestation ˌmoləsˈteʃən, ˌmal-

Moliére ˌmolɪˈɛr, -lˈjɛr; ES -ɛə(r; (*Fr* mɔ̈-ˈljɛ:r)

Moline moˈlin

Moll mal, mɒl, mɔl |-y -ɪ

mollification ˌmaləfəˈkeʃən

mollify ˈmaləˌfaɪ |-fied -ˌfaɪd

mollusk, -sc ˈmaləsk |-ed -t |-scan məˈlʌskən

mollycoddle ˈmalɪˌkadl̩ |-d -d |-ling -ˌkadlɪŋ, -ˌkadl̩ɪŋ

Moloch ˈmolak

Moloney, -ny məˈlonɪ

molt molt |molted ˈmoltɪd; |*N Engd*+mɔ̈lt (*§46*)

molten ˈmoltn̩

Moltke ˈmoltkə (*Ger* ˈmɔltkə)

Molucca məˈlʌkə |-n -n |-s -z

moly ˈmolɪ

molybdenum məˈlɪbdənəm, ˌmalɪbˈdinəm

molybdic məˈlɪbdɪk |-dite -daɪt

Molyneux ˈmʌlɪˌnuks, -ˌnju, -ˌnɪu, -ˌnu |-x's -ˌnuksɪz, -ˌnjuz, -ˌnɪuz, -ˌnuz

Mombasa mamˈbæsə, -ˈbɑsə

Momence moˈmɛns |-'s -ɪz

moment ˈmomənt |-mentary -mənˌtɛrɪ

momentaneous ˌmomənˈtenɪəs

momentarily ˈmomənˌtɛrəlɪ, *esp. if emph.* ˌmomənˈtɛrəlɪ

momentous moˈmɛntəs |-tum -təm |-tums -təmz |-ta -tə

Mommsen ˈmamsn̩, -zn̩ (*Ger* ˈmɔmzən)

Momus ˈmoməs |-'s -ɪz

Monaca ˈmanəkə

monachal ˈmanəkl̩ |-chism -ˌkɪzəm

monacid manˈæsɪd

Monaco ˈmanəˌko

monad ˈmanæd, ˈmonæd

Monadnoc *poem* məˈnædnak |*mt.* -nock -nak

Monaghan ˈmanəgən, ˈmanəhən, -xən

Mona Lisa ˈmonəˈlizə, ˈmanə- (*It* ˈmonə-ˈli:za)

monandric məˈnændrɪk |-drous -drəs |-dry -drɪ

monarch ˈmanɚk; ES ˈmanək; |-ed -t

monarchal məˈnɑrkl̩; ES -ˈnɑ:kl̩, E+-ˈnɑ:kl̩; |-ly -ɪ |-chial -kɪəl

monarchic məˈnɑrkɪk; ES -ˈnɑ:k-, E+ -ˈnɑ:k-; |-al -l̩ |-ally -l̩ɪ, -ɪklɪ

monarchy ˈmanɚkɪ; ES ˈmanəkɪ; |-chism -ˌkɪzəm |-chist -kɪst

monastery ˈmanəsˌtɛrɪ |-rial ˌmanəˈstɪrɪəl

monastic məˈnæstɪk |-al -l̩ |-ally -l̩ɪ, -ɪklɪ

monasticism məˈnæstəˌsɪzəm

Monboddo manˈbado

Monckton ˈmʌŋktən

Monday ˈmʌndɪ—*spelt* Mundy *in 1647, cf* Friday

Monel, m- moˈnɛl

Monet moˈne (*Fr* mɔ̈ˈnɛ)

monetary ˈmʌnəˌtɛrɪ, ˈmanə-

monetize ˈmʌnəˌtaɪz, ˈmanə- |-s -ɪz |-d -d

money ˈmʌnɪ |-s, -nies -z |-ed, -nied -d

moneybag ˈmʌnɪˌbæg

monger ˈmʌŋgɚ; ES ˈmʌŋgə(r; |-ing -grɪŋ, -gərɪŋ

Mongol ˈmaŋgəl, -gal, -gol

Mongolia maŋˈgolɪə, man-, -ljə |-n -n

Key: *See in full §§3–47.* bee bi |pity ˈpɪtɪ (§6) |rate ret |yet jɛt |sang sæŋ |angry ˈæŋ·grɪ |bath bæθ; E baθ (§10) |ah ɑ |far fɑr |watch watʃ, wɒtʃ (§12) |jaw dʒɔ |gorge gɔrdʒ |go go

Those words below in which the ɑ *sound is spelt* o *are often pronounced with* ɒ *in E and S*

mongoose, -goos 'maŋgus, 'mʌŋ-, 'man-
|-(e)s -ɪz
mongrel 'mʌŋgrəl, 'maŋ-, 'man-, -grɪl
'mongst mʌŋst, mʌŋkst
Monhegan man'higən
Monica, m- 'manɪkə
monied 'mʌnɪd |monies 'mʌnɪz
moniker, -icker 'manɪkɚ; ES 'manɪkə(r
monish 'manɪʃ |-es -ɪz |-ed -t
monism 'manɪzəm, 'mon- |-ist -ɪst
monistic mo'nɪstɪk |-al -l̩ |-ally -l̩ɪ, -ɪklɪ
monition mo'nɪʃən
monitor 'manətɚ; ES 'manətə(r; |-ed -d |-ing
-tərɪŋ, -trɪŋ
monitory 'manə͵torɪ, -͵tɔrɪ; S -͵torɪ
monk mʌŋk |-craft -͵kræft; E+-͵kraft,
-͵kraft
monkey 'mʌŋkɪ |-ed -d |-shine -͵ʃaɪn
Monkwearmouth 'mʌŋk'wɪrməθ; ES -'wɪə-
məθ
Monmouth 'manməθ |-shire -͵ʃɪr, -ʃɚ; ES
-͵ʃɪə(r, -ʃə(r
Monna Lisa 'manə'lizə (*It* 'mɔnɑ'li:zɑ)
monniker 'manɪkɚ; ES 'manɪkə(r
monoacid ͵mano'æsɪd
monobasic ͵manə'besɪk
Monocacy mə'nakəsɪ
monocarpous ͵manə'karpəs; ES -'kɑ:pəs,
E+-'kɑ:p-
monochord 'manə͵kɔrd; ES -͵kɔəd
monochrome 'manə͵krom
monocle 'manəkl̩ |-d -d
monoclinal ͵manə'klaɪnl̩ |-ly -ɪ |-nous -nəs
monocline 'manə͵klaɪn
monoclinic ͵manə'klɪnɪk
monocotyledon ͵manə͵katl̩'idn̩ |-ous -'idn̩əs,
-'ɛdn̩əs
monocracy mo'nakrəsɪ
monody 'manədɪ
monogamist mə'nagəmɪst |-mous -məs |-my
-mɪ
monogram 'manə͵græm |-med -d
monograph 'manə͵græf; E+-͵graf, -͵graf;
|-ed -t
monolith 'manl̩͵ɪθ |-ths -θs |-ic ͵manl̩'ɪθɪk
monologue, -log 'manl̩͵ɔg, -͵ɑg, -͵ɒg |-d,
-ged -d
monomania ͵manə'menɪə, -njə |-iac -ɪ͵æk

monometallic ͵manəmə'tælɪk
monometallism ͵manə'mɛtl̩͵ɪzəm |-ist -ɪst
monomial mo'nomɪəl
Monona mə'nonə
Monongahela mə͵naŋgə'hilə, -͵nan-
Monongalia ͵monən'gelɪə
monophthong 'manəf͵θɔŋ, 'manə͵θ-, -͵θɒŋ
monophthongal ͵manəf'θɔŋgl̩, -ə'θ-, -ɒŋ-, -ɒl̩
monophthongize 'manəf͵θɔŋ͵aɪz, 'manə͵θ-,
-͵θɒŋ͵gaɪz, -ɒŋ- |-s -ɪz |-d -d
monoplane 'manə͵plen
monopolism mə'napl̩͵ɪzəm |-ist -ɪst
monopolization mə͵napl̩ə'zeʃən, -aɪ'z-
monopolize mə'napl̩͵aɪz |-s -ɪz |-d -d
monopoly mə'napl̩ɪ, -'naplɪ
monorail 'manə͵rel
monorailroad 'manə͵relrod |-railway -͵relwe
monosyllabic ͵manəsɪ'læbɪk |-al -l̩ |-ally -l̩ɪ,
-ɪklɪ
monosyllabism ͵manə'sɪlə͵bɪzəm
monosyllable 'manə͵sɪləbl̩
monotheism 'manəθi͵ɪzəm |-ist -͵θiɪst
monotheistic ͵manəθi'ɪstɪk |-al -l̩ |-ally -l̩ɪ,
-ɪklɪ
monotone 'manə͵ton
monotonous mə'natn̩əs |-tony -tn̩ɪ
monotype 'manə͵taɪp
Monroe mən'ro |-rovia -'rovɪə
Monseigneur, m- ͵mansen'jɝ; ES -'jɜ(r, -'jɚ;
(*Fr* mõsɛ'ɲœːr)
Monsieur, m- mə'sjɝ; ES -'sjɜ(r; (*Fr* mə'sjø)
Monsignor, m- man'sinjɚ; ES -jə(r; (*It*
monsiɲ'ɲo:re)
Monson 'mʌnsn̩
monsoon man'sun |-al -l̩
monster 'manstɚ; ES 'manstə(r; |-ed -d
monstrance 'manstrəns |-s -ɪz
monstrous 'manstrəs |-strosity man'strasətɪ
Montagu, -e 'mantə͵gju, -͵gɪu
Montaigne man'ten
Montana man'tænə |-n -n
Montano man'tæno
Montauk man'tɔk ('Mon͵tauk 'Point)
Mont Blanc mant'blæŋk, mɒnt- (*Fr* mõ'blã)
Montcalm mant'kam
Montclair mant'klɛr, -'klær; E -'klɛə(r, ES
-'klæə(r
Montebello ͵mantə'bɛlo

|full fʊl |tooth tuθ |further 'fɝðɚ; ES 'fɜðə |custom 'kʌstəm |while hwaɪl |how haʊ |toy tɔɪ
|using 'juzɪŋ |fuse fjuz, fɪuz |dish dɪʃ |vision 'vɪʒən |Eden 'idn̩ |cradle 'kredl̩ |keep 'em 'kipm̩

Those words below in which the ɑ sound is spelt o are often pronounced with ɒ in E and S

Monte Carlo ˌmɑntɪˈkɑrlo; ES -ˈkɑ:-, E+ -ˈkɑ:-

Monte Cristo, Montecristo ˌmɑntɪˈkrɪsto

Montenegro ˌmɑntəˈnigro |-grin -ˈnigrɪn

Monterey, -rrey ˌmɑntəˈre (*Am Sp* ˌmontɛ- ˈrrɛi)

Montesquieu ˌmɑntəˈskju, -ˈskɪu (*Fr* mõtɛs- ˈkjø)

Montessori ˌmɑntəˈsorɪ, -ˈsɔrɪ; S -ˈsorɪ (*It* ˌmontes'so:ri)

Montevideo *US* ˌmɑntəˈvɪdɪˌo; *Uru*+ˌman- təvɪˈdeo (*Am Sp* ˌmonteβiˈðeo)

Montezuma ˌmɑntəˈzumə

Montferrat ˌmɑntfəˈræt (*It* ˌmonferˈrɑ:to, *Fr* mõfɛˈra)

Montgomery mɑntˈgʌmrɪ, -ˈgʌmərɪ |-shire -ˌʃɪr, -ʃɚ; ES -ˌʃɪə(r, -ʃə(r

month mʌnθ |months mʌnθs, mʌnts

Monticello ˌmɑntəˈsɛlo, -ə (*It* ˌmontiˈtʃɛllo)

Montmorency *US, Can, France* ˌmɑntmə- ˈrɛnsɪ (*Fr* mõmõrãˈsi)

Montour mɑnˈtʊr; ES -ˈtʊə(r

Montpelier mɑntˈpiljɚ; ES -ˈpiljə(r

Montpellier *France* mɑntˈpɛlɪˌe (*Fr* mõpəˈlje, -pɛ-)

Montreal ˌmɑntrɪˈɔl, ˌmʌnt-

Montrose mɑntˈroz |-'s -ɪz

Mont-Saint-Michel *Fr* mõsæmiˈʃɛl

Montserrat ˌmɑntsəˈræt (*Sp* ˌmɔntsɛˈrrat)

monument *n* ˈmɑnjəmənt

monument *v* ˈmɑnjəˌmɛnt |-mented -ˌmɛntɪd

monumental ˌmɑnjəˈmɛntḷ |-ly -ɪ

moo mu |mooed mud

mooch mutʃ |mooches ˈmutʃɪz |mooched mutʃt

mood mud |moody, M- ˈmudɪ

moolly, mooly ˈmulɪ, ˈmulɪ

moon, M- mun |mooned mund |-beam -ˌbim

mooncalf ˈmunˌkæf; E -ˌkaf, -ˌkɑf, -ˌkæf; |-lves -vz

mooneye ˈmunˌaɪ |moon-eyed ˈmunˌaɪd

moonlight ˈmunˌlaɪt |-ed -ɪd *or* -lit -ˌlɪt

moonrise ˈmunˌraɪz |-s -ɪz

moonset ˈmunˌsɛt

moonshine ˈmunˌʃaɪn |-shined -ˌʃaɪnd

moonstone ˈmunˌston

moon-struck ˈmunˌstrʌk

moor, M- mʊr; ES mʊə(r; |-ed -d |-age -ɪdʒ

Moore mor, mɔr, mʊr; ES moə(r, mʊə(r, E+mɔə(r

Moorehead ˈmʊrˌhɛd, ˈmor-, ˈmɔr-; ES ˈmʊə-, ˈmoə-, E+ˈmɔə-

Moorgate ˈmʊrˌget, ˈmor-, ˈmɔr-; ES ˈmʊə-, ˈmoə-, E+ˈmɔə-; *loc.* -git

Moorhead ˈmorˌhɛd, ˈmɔr-, ˈmʊr-; ES ˈmoə-, ˈmʊə-, E+ˈmɔə-

Moorish ˈmʊrɪʃ

moose mus |moose's ˈmusɪz

Moosehead ˈmusˌhɛd

Moosilauke ˈmusḷˌɔk, ˌmusḷˈɔkɪ

moot mut |mooted ˈmutɪd

mop mɑp |-ped -t

mope mop |moped mopt

moppet ˈmɑpɪt

Mopsa ˈmɑpsə

moraine moˈren |-nal -ḷ |-nic -ɪk

moral ˈmɔrəl, ˈmɑr-, ˈmɒr- |-ly -ɪ |-ist -ɪst

morale məˈræl, mo-, mɔ-, -ˈral (*Fr* mõˈral)

morality mɔˈrælətɪ, ma-, mɒ-, mɑ-, mo-

moralize ˈmɔrəlˌaɪz, ˈmar-, ˈmɒr- |-s -ɪz |-d -d

moralless ˈmɔrəllɪs, ˈmar-, ˈmɒr-

Moran moˈræn, mɔ-, mə-, ˈmorən, ˈmɔr-; S mo-, mə-, ˈmor-

morass moˈræs, mɔ-, mə-; S mo-, mə-; |-es -ɪz

moratorium ˌmɔrəˈtorɪəm, ˌmar-, ˌmɒr-, -ˈtɔr-; S -ˈtorɪəm

Moravia moˈrevɪə, mə- |-n -n

Moray *Scotl* ˈmɝɪ (*Sc* ˈmʌre); ES ˈmɝɪ, ˈmʌrɪ, ˈmɝɪ; *Am fem. name often* ˈmorɪ, ˈmɔrɪ

moray ˈmore, moˈre, ˈmo-, mɔ-; S ˈmo-, mo-

morbid ˈmɔrbɪd; ES ˈmɔəbɪd

morbidity mɔrˈbɪdətɪ; ES mɔˈbɪdətɪ

mordacious mɔrˈdeʃəs; ES mɔə-

mordancy ˈmɔrdn̩sɪ; ES ˈmɔədn̩sɪ; |-dant -dn̩t

Mordecai ˌmɔrdɪˈkeaɪ, ˈmɔrdɪˌkaɪ; ES -əədɪ-

mordent ˈmɔrdn̩t; ES ˈmɔədn̩t

more, M- mor, mɔr; ES moə(r, E+mɔə(r

morel, M- məˈrɛl, mɔ-, mɑ-, mɒ-

Moreland ˈmorlənd, ˈmɔr-; ES ˈmoə-, E+ ˈmɔə-

Moreno məˈrino

more or less ˈmorəˈlɛs, ˈmorəˈlɛs, ˈmɔr-; ES ˈmorəˈlɛs, E+ˈmɔrə-——*In the 2d pron.* ɚ *becomes* ə *by dissimilation* (§121).

moreover mor'ovɚ, mɔr-; ES mor'ovə(r,
  E+mɔr-
mores 'moriz, 'mɔr-; S 'mor-
Morgan 'mɔrgən; ES 'mɔəgən
morganatic ‚mɔrgə'nætɪk; ES ‚mɔəg-; |-al -|
  |-ally -|ɪ, -ɪklɪ
Morganton 'mɔrgəntən; ES 'mɔəg-; |-town
  -‚taʊn
Morgenthau 'mɔrgən‚θɔ; ES 'mɔəg-; (Ger
  'mɔrgən‚taʊ)
morgue mɔrg; ES mɔəg
Moriah mə'raɪə, mo-
Moriarty ‚mɔrɪ'artɪ, ‚mar-, ‚mɒr-; ES -'a:tɪ
moribund 'mɔrə‚bʌnd, 'mar-, 'mɒr-, -bənd
moribundity ‚mɔrə'bʌndətɪ, ‚mar-, ‚mɒr-
Morisco, m- mə'rɪsko
Morison 'mɔrəsn̩, 'mar-, 'mɒr-
Morland 'mɔrlənd; ES 'mɔələnd
Morley 'mɔrlɪ; ES 'mɔəlɪ
Mormon 'mɔrmən; ES 'mɔəmən; |-ism -‚ɪzəm
morn mɔrn; ES mɔən; |-ing -ɪŋ
Morocco, m- mə'rako; ES+-'rɒko; |-can -kən
moron 'moran, 'mɔr-; S 'mor-, ES+-ɒn
moronic mo'ranɪk, mə-; S mo-, ES+-'rɒn-
morose mo'ros, mə-
morpheme 'mɔrfim; ES 'mɔə-; |-mic mɔr-
  'fimɪk; ES mɔə-
Morpheus 'mɔrfɪəs, -fjus; ES 'mɔəf-; |-'s -ɪz
morphine 'mɔrfin; ES 'mɔəfin
morphology mɔr'falədʒɪ; ES mɔ'fal-, -'fɒl-
Morris, m- 'mɔrɪs, 'mar-, 'mɒr- |-'s -ɪz
Morrison 'mɔrəsn̩, 'mar-, 'mɒr-
Morristown 'mɔrɪs‚taʊn, 'mar-, 'mɒr-
morrow, M- 'mɔro, 'mar-, 'mɒr-, -ə
Morse mɔrs; ES mɔəs; |-'s -ɪz
morsel 'mɔrsl̩; ES 'mɔəsl̩; |-ed -d
mort mɔrt; ES mɔət
mortal 'mɔrtl̩; ES 'mɔətl̩; |-ly -ɪ
mortality mɔr'tælətɪ; ES mɔ-
mortar 'mɔrtɚ; ES 'mɔətə(r; |-ed -d
mortarboard 'mɔrtɚ‚bord, -‚bɔrd; ES 'mɔətə-
  ‚boəd, E+-‚bɔəd
Morte d'Arthur, Mort Darthur 'mɔrt'darθɚ;
  ES 'mɔət'da:θə(r; (Fr mörtdar'ty:r)
mortgage 'mɔrgɪdʒ; ES 'mɔə-; |-s -ɪz |-d -d
mortgagee ‚mɔrgɪ'dʒi; ES ‚mɔə-
mortgagor, -er 'mɔrgɪdʒɚ; ES 'mɔəgɪdʒə(r;
  (‚mortga'gee & ‚mortga'gor -'dʒɔr)
mortice 'mɔrtɪs; ES 'mɔə-; |-s -ɪz |-d -t

mortification ‚mɔrtəfə'keʃən; ES ‚mɔətə-
mortify 'mɔrtə‚faɪ; ES 'mɔətə-; |-fied -‚faɪd
Mortimer 'mɔrtəmɚ; ES 'mɔətəmə(r
mortise 'mɔrtɪs; ES 'mɔə-; |-s -ɪz |-d -t
mortmain 'mɔrtmen; ES 'mɔət-; |-ed -d
Morton 'mɔrtn̩, 'mɔrtn̩; ES 'moətn̩, E+
  'mɔətn̩
mortuary 'mɔrtʃʊ‚ɛrɪ; ES 'mɔətʃʊ-
Mosaic, m- mo'ze·ɪk |-al -|̩ |-ally -|ɪ, -ɪklɪ
Mosby 'mozbɪ
Moschus 'maskəs, 'mɒs-; |-'s -ɪz
Moscow Id 'masko, 'mɒs-; Russia -kaʊ, -ko
Moseley 'mozlɪ
Moselle mo'zɛl
Moses 'mozɪz, -əz, -əs, -ɪs—'mozəz & 'mozəs
  are less freq. in the S.
Moslem 'mazləm, 'mas-; ES+'mɒ-
mosque mask, mɒsk, mɔsk
mosquito mə'skito, -ə
moss, M- mɔs, mɒs |-es -ɪz |-ed -t |-back -‚bæk
most most; N Engd+möst (§46)
mot Fr mo
mote arch. v mot |past moste most, mod. must
mote n mot |moted 'motɪd
motet mo'tɛt
moth mɔθ, mɒθ |-ths -ðz, -θs |-th's -θs
mother 'mʌðɚ; ES 'mʌðə(r; |-ed -d |-ing
  'mʌðrɪŋ, 'mʌðərɪŋ
mother-in-law 'mʌðərɪn‚lɔ, 'mʌðɚn‚lɔ; ES
  'mʌðərɪn‚lɔ, 'mʌðən‚lɔ
motherland 'mʌðɚ‚lænd; ES 'mʌðə-
mothers-in-law 'mʌðɚzɪn‚lɔ, 'mʌðɚzn̩‚lɔ; ES
  'mʌðəzɪn‚lɔ, 'mʌðəzn̩‚lɔ
moths mɔðz, mɒðz, -θs
mothy 'mɔθɪ, 'mɒθɪ
motif mo'tif
motile 'motl̩, 'motɪl
motion 'moʃən |-ed -d
motivate 'motə‚vet |-d -ɪd |-tion ‚motə'veʃən
motive 'motɪv |-d -d
mot juste Fr mo'ʒyst
motley, M- 'matlɪ; ES+'mɒt-
motor 'motɚ; ES 'motə(r; |-ed -d |-y -ɪ
motorboat 'motɚ‚bot; ES 'motə-
motorbus 'motɚ‚bʌs; ES 'motə-; |-(s)es -ɪz
motorcar 'motɚ‚kar; ES 'motə‚ka:(r, E+
  -‚ka:(r
motorcycle 'motɚ‚saɪkl̩; ES 'motə-; |-d -d
  |-ling -‚saɪklɪŋ, -‚saɪkl̩ɪŋ

|full fʊl |tooth tuθ |further 'fɝðɚ; ES 'fɝðə |custom 'kʌstəm |while hwaɪl |how haʊ |toy tɔɪ
|using 'juzɪŋ |fuse fjuz, fɪuz |dish dɪʃ |vision 'vɪʒən |Eden 'idn̩ |cradle 'kredl̩ |keep 'em 'kipm̩

motorman ˈmotɚmən; ES ˈmotəmən; |-men -mən

Motteux maˈtju, mɒ-, -ˈtɪu, -ˈtu (Fr möˈtø)

mottle ˈmatḷ; ES+ˈmɒtḷ; |-d -d |-ling -tḷɪŋ, -tḷɪŋ

motto ˈmato, -ə; ES+ˈmɒt-; |-ed -d

mouch ˈmutʃ |mouches ˈmutʃɪz |mouched mutʃt

moue Fr mu

Moukden mukˈdɛn, ˈmukdən

mould mold |-ed -ɪd |-y -ɪ

mouldboard ˈmoldˌbord, ˈmol-, -ˌbɔrd, dial. ˈmʌl-; ES -ˌboəd, E+-ˌbɔəd

moulder ˈmoldɚ; ES ˈmoldə(r; |-ed -d |-ing ˈmoldrɪŋ, ˈmoldərɪŋ

mouldwarp ˈmoldˌwɔrp; ES -ˌwɔəp

Moulmein maulˈmen, mɔl-, mol-

moult molt |moulted ˈmoltɪd; |N Engd+mölt (§46)

Moulton ˈmoltṇ

Moultrie US places ˈmoltrɪ, Fort & general ˈmutrɪ, ˈmultrɪ (formerly spelt Moutrie)

mound, M- maund |mounded ˈmaundɪd

Mounseer 'Monsieur' arch. & humorous maunˈsɪr; ES -ˈsɪə(r

mount, M- maunt |mounted ˈmauntɪd

mountain ˈmauntṇ, -tɪn, -tən |-ous -əs

mountaineer ˌmauntṇˈɪr, -tɪn-, -tən-; ES -ˈɪə(r, S+-ˈɛə(r

mountainside ˈmauntṇˌsaɪd, -tɪn-, -tən-

Mount Desert ˌmauntdɪˈzɝt, -ˈdɛzɚt; ES -ˈzɝt, -ˈzɝt, -zət; (ˈMount ˌDesert ˈIsland)

mountebank ˈmauntəˌbæŋk

Mountjoy ˈmauntdʒɔɪ

mourn morn, mɔrn; ES moən, E+mɔən; |-ed -d

mouse n maus |-'s -ɪz |mice maɪs |mice's -ɪz

mouse v mauz |mouses ˈmauzɪz |moused mauzd

mousehole ˈmausˌhol |Mousehole Cornw ˈmauzḷ

mouser ˈmauzɚ; ES ˈmauzə(r; |-y ˈmausərɪ, -srɪ

mousse mus |mousses ˈmusɪz

moustache ˈmʌstæʃ, məˈstæʃ |-s -ɪz |-d -t

mousy ˈmausɪ, ˈmauzɪ

mouth n mauθ |-th's -θs |-ths -ðz

mouth v mauð |mouthed mauðd |-y ˈmauðɪ, -θɪ

mouthful ˈmauθˌful |-fuls -ˌfulz

mouthpiece ˈmauθˌpis |-s -ɪz

movability, movea- ˌmuvəˈbɪlətɪ

movable, movea- ˈmuvəbḷ |-bly -blɪ

move muv |moved muvd |movie ˈmuvɪ

mow 'haymow' mau |mowed maud

mow 'reap' mo |mowed mod |mowed mod or mown mon

mow 'grimace' mau, mo |-ed -d

Mowbray ˈmobrɪ

mower 'mowing machine' ˈmoɚ; ES ˈmo·ə(r

Mower ˈmauɚ; ES ˈmau·ə(r

Mowgli ˈmauglɪ

mown mon

Mozambique ˌmozəmˈbik

Mozart ˈmozart; ES -zaːt; (Ger ˈmoːtsart)

Mr. ˈmɪstɚ; ES ˈmɪstə(r

Mrs. ˈmɪsɪz, -əz, ˈmɪsɪs, -əs; S ˈmɪzɪz, mɪz: —Some speakers say ˈmɪsɪs before voiceless sounds, and ˈmɪsɪz before voiced (ˈmɪsɪs ˈpræt, ˈmɪsɪz ˈbraun).

mu Gk letter mju, mɪu, mu; Chin meas. mu

much mʌtʃ

mucid ˈmjusɪd, ˈmɪusɪd

mucilage ˈmjusḷɪdʒ, ˈmɪu-, -slɪdʒ

mucilaginous ˌmjusḷˈædʒənəs, ˌmɪusḷ-

muck mʌk |mucked mʌkt

muckle ˈmʌkḷ

muckrake ˈmʌkˌrek |-raked -ˌrekt

mucous ˈmjukəs, ˈmɪu- |mucus ˈmjukəs, ˈmɪu-

mud mʌd |mudded ˈmʌdɪd |-dy -ɪ |-died -ɪd

muddle ˈmʌdḷ |-d -d |-ling ˈmʌdlɪŋ, -dḷɪŋ

muddleheaded ˈmʌdḷˈhɛdɪd (ˈmuddleˌheaded ˈJoe)

mudguard ˈmʌdˌgard; ES -ˌgaːd, E+-ˌgaːd

mudsill ˈmʌdˌsɪl

muezzin mjuˈɛzɪn, mɪu-

muff mʌf |muffed mʌft

muffin ˈmʌfɪn

muffle ˈmʌfḷ |-d -d |-ling ˈmʌflɪŋ, ˈmʌfḷɪŋ

muffler ˈmʌflɚ; ES ˈmʌflə(r

mufti ˈmʌftɪ

mug mʌg |mugged mʌgd |-gy -ɪ |-wump -ˌwʌmp

Muhammad muˈhæməd |-an -ən

Muhlenberg ˈmjulənˌbɝg, ˈmɪu-; ES -ˌbɜg, -ˌbɝg

Muir mjur, mɪur |-head -ˌhɛd

Key: See in full §§3–47. bee bi |pity ˈpɪtɪ (§6) |rate ret |yet jɛt |sang sæŋ |angry ˈæŋ·grɪ |bath bæθ; E baθ (§10) |ah ɑ |far far |watch watʃ, wɒtʃ (§12) |jaw dʒɔ |gorge gɔrdʒ |go go

Mukden mʊk'dɛn, 'mʊkdən
mulatto mə'læto, mjʊ-, mɪʊ-, -ə
mulberry, M- 'mʌlˌbɛrɪ, -bərɪ
Mulcaster 'mʌlkæstɚ; ES -kæstə(r
mulch mʌltʃ |mulches 'mʌltʃɪz |mulched
  mʌltʃt
mulct mʌlkt |mulcted 'mʌlktɪd
mule mjul, mɪul |-lish -ɪʃ
muleteer ˌmjulə'tɪr; ES -'tɪə(r, S+-'tɛə(r
muley 'mjulɪ, 'mɪu-, 'mʊlɪ, 'mulɪ
mull mʌl |mulled mʌld
mullah, M-, -la 'mʌlə, 'mʊlə
mullein, -len 'mʌlɪn, -ən
Mullens, -ins 'mʌlɪnz, -ənz |-'s -ɪz
Muller 'mʌlɚ; ES 'mʌlə(r
Müller, Max 'mæks'mɪlɚ; ES -'mɪlə(r; (Ger
  'maks'mylər)
mullet 'mʌlɪt
mulley 'mʊlɪ, 'mulɪ
mulligatawny ˌmʌlɪgə'tɔnɪ
mulligrubs 'mʌlɪˌgrʌbz
mullion 'mʌljən |-ed -d
Mulock 'mjulək, 'mɪu-, -lak; ES+-lɒk
multicellular ˌmʌltɪ'sɛljəlɚ; ES -'sɛljələ(r
multifarious ˌmʌltə'fɛrɪəs, -'fær-, -'fer-
multifold 'mʌltəˌfold
multiform 'mʌltəˌfɔrm; ES -ˌfɔəm
multigraph, M- 'mʌltəˌgræf; E+-ˌgraf, -ˌgrɑf
multilateral ˌmʌltɪ'lætərəl |-ly -ɪ
multilingual ˌmʌltɪ'lɪŋgwəl
multimillionaire ˌmʌltəˌmɪljən'ɛr, -'ær; E
  -'ɛə(r, ES -'æə(r
multinuclear ˌmʌltɪ'njuklɪɚ, -'nɪu-, -'nu-; ES
  -lɪ·ə(r
multiparous mʌl'tɪpərəs
multiped 'mʌltəˌpɛd |-pede -ˌpid
multiphase 'mʌltəˌfez
multiple 'mʌltəpḷ |-plex -ˌplɛks
multiplicand ˌmʌltəplɪ'kænd
multiplicate 'mʌltəplɪˌket
multiplication ˌmʌltəplə'keʃən, ˌmʌltəpə- —
  In the 2d pron. the 2d l is lost by l-dissimila-
  tion (§121).
multiplicity ˌmʌltə'plɪsətɪ
multiplier 'mʌltəˌplaɪɚ; ES -ˌplaɪ·ə(r
multiply v 'mʌltəˌplaɪ |-plied -ˌplaɪd
multiply adv 'mʌltəplɪ, -pḷɪ
multipolar ˌmʌltə'polɚ; ES -'polə(r
multitude 'mʌltəˌtjud, -ˌtɪud-, -ˌtud

multitudinous ˌmʌltə'tjudn̩əs, -'tɪud-, -'tud-
multivalence ˌmʌltə'veləns, mʌl'tɪvə- |-cy -ɪ
  |-lent -lənt
Multnomah mʌlt'nomə
mum, mumm mʌm |mummed mʌmd
mumble 'mʌmbḷ |-d -d |-ling 'mʌmblɪŋ, -bḷɪŋ
Mumbo Jumbo 'mʌmbo'dʒʌmbo
mummer 'mʌmɚ; ES 'mʌmə(r; |-y -ɪ
mummify 'mʌmɪˌfaɪ |-fied -ˌfaɪd
mummy 'mʌmɪ |mummied 'mʌmɪd
mumps mʌmps
munch mʌntʃ |munches 'mʌntʃɪz |munched
  mʌntʃt
Munchausen mʌn'tʃɔzn̩ ('Munˌchausen 'tales)
Muncie 'mʌnsɪ |Muncy 'mʌnsɪ
mundane 'mʌnden
Munday 'mʌndɪ
Munhall 'mʌnhɔl
Munich 'mjunɪk, 'mɪu- (Ger München
  'mynxən)
municipal mju'nɪsəpḷ, mɪu- |-ly -pḷɪ, -plɪ
municipality ˌmjunɪsə'pælətɪ, ˌmɪu-, mju-
  ˌnɪsə-, mɪu-
munificence mju'nɪfəsn̩s, mɪu- |-cy -ɪ |-nt
  -sn̩t
muniment 'mjunəmənt, 'mɪu-
munition mju'nɪʃən, mɪu- |-ed -d
Munro, -roe mən'ro
Munsey 'mʌnsɪ, -zɪ
Munson 'mʌnsn̩
Munster 'mʌnstɚ; ES 'mʌnstə(r
Münster 'mɪnstɚ; ES 'mɪnstə(r; (Ger
  'mynstər)
Münsterberg 'mɪnstɚˌbɝg; ES 'mɪnstəˌbɜg,
  'mɪnstəˌbɝg; (Ger 'mynstərˌbɛrk)
mural 'mjurəl, 'mɪurəl |-ly -ɪ
Murat Am name mju'ræt, mɪu-, Fr general
  mju'ræt, mɪu-, my'ra (Fr my'ra)
murder 'mɝdɚ; ES 'mɝdə(r, 'mɜdə(r; |-ed -d
  |-ing -dərɪŋ, -drɪŋ
murderer 'mɝdərɚ; ES 'mɜdərə(r, 'mɝdərə(r
murderous 'mɝdərəs, -drəs; ES 'mɜd-, 'mɝd-
murex, M- 'mjurɛks, 'mɪu- |-es -ɪz |-rices
  -rəˌsiz
Murfreesboro 'mɝfrɪzˌbɝo, -ə; ES 'mɝfrɪz-
  ˌbɜr-, 'mɝf-, -ˌbʌr-, -ˌbɜ-
muriate 'mjurɪˌet, 'mɪu-, -ɪt |-d -ˌetɪd
muriatic ˌmjurɪ'ætɪk, ˌmɪu- ('muriˌatic 'acid)
Muriel 'mjurɪəl, 'mɪu-

|full fʊl |tooth tuθ |further 'fɝðɚ; ES 'fɝðə |custom 'kʌstəm |while hwaɪl |how haʊ |toy tɔɪ
|using 'juzɪŋ |fuse fjuz, fɪuz |dish dɪʃ |vision 'vɪʒən |Eden 'idn̩ |cradle 'kredḷ |keep 'em 'kipm̩

Murillo mju'rɪlo, mɪʊ- (*Sp* mu'riʌo)

murk mɝk; ES mɜk, mɝk; |-some -səm |-y -ɪ

murmur 'mɝmɚ; ES 'mɜmə(r, 'mɝmə(r; |-ed
-d |-ing -mrɪŋ, -mərɪŋ

Murphy 'mɝfɪ; ES 'mɜfɪ, 'mɝfɪ

Murphysboro 'mɝfɪz͵bɝo, -ə; ES 'mɜfɪz-
͵bɜr-, 'mɝf-, -͵bʌr-, -͵bɝ-

murrain 'mɝɪn; ES 'mɜrɪn, 'mʌrɪn, 'mɝrɪn;
|-ed -d

Murray 'mɝɪ; ES 'mɜrɪ, 'mʌrɪ, 'mɝɪ

murrey 'mɝɪ; ES 'mɜrɪ, 'mʌrɪ, 'mɝɪ

murther 'mɝðɚ; ES 'mɜðə(r, 'mɝðə(r; |-ed -d
|-ing -ðərɪŋ, -ðrɪŋ

muscadine 'mʌskədɪn, -͵daɪn

muscat 'mʌskət, -kæt

muscatel ͵mʌskə'tɛl ('musca͵tel 'wine)

Muscatine ͵mʌskə'tin

muscle, M- 'mʌsl̩ |-d -d |-ling 'mʌslɪŋ, -sl̩ɪŋ

Muscoda ͵mʌskə'de

Muscogee mʌs'kogɪ

Muscovy 'mʌskəvɪ |-vite -͵vaɪt

muscular 'mʌskjəlɚ; ES 'mʌskjələ(r

muscularity ͵mʌskjə'lærətɪ

musculature 'mʌskjələtʃɚ; ES -tʃə(r

muse, M- mjuz, mɪuz |-s -ɪz |-d -d

museum mju'zɪəm, mɪʊ-, -'zɪəm, 'mjuzɪəm,
'mɪʊ-

mush mʌʃ |-es -ɪz |-ed -t

mushroom 'mʌʃrum, -rʊm, *less freq.* -run

music 'mjuzɪk, 'mɪʊ- |-al -l̩ |-ally -l̩ɪ, -ɪklɪ

musicale ͵mjuzɪ'kæl, ͵mɪʊ- (*Fr* myzi'kal)

musician mju'zɪʃən, mɪʊ-

musicologist ͵mjuzɪ'kalədʒɪst, ͵mɪʊ-; ES+
-'kɒl-; |-gy -dʒɪ

musk mʌsk |musked mʌskt

muskallonge 'mʌskə͵landʒ, -͵lɒndʒ |-s -ɪz

Muskegon mʌs'kigən

muskellunge, -kall- 'mʌskə͵lʌndʒ |-s -ɪz

musket 'mʌskɪt |-ry -rɪ

musketeer ͵mʌskə'tɪr; ES -'tɪə(r, S+-'teə(r

Muskingum mʌs'kɪŋgəm, *recently*+mʌs'kɪŋ-
əm

muskmelon 'mʌsk͵mɛlən

Muskogee mʌs'kogɪ

muskrat 'mʌsk͵ræt, 'mʌs͵kræt

muslin 'mʌzlɪn

musquash 'mʌskwɒʃ, -kwɒʃ |-es -ɪz

muss mʌs |musses 'mʌsɪz |mussed mʌst

mussel 'mʌsl̩ |-ed -d

Musset mə'se (*Fr* my'sɛ)

Mussolini ͵musl̩'inɪ, ͵mʊs- (*It* ͵musso'li:ni)

Mussulman 'mʌsl̩mən |-s -z *or* -men -mən

must *stressed* 'mʌst, ͵mʌst; *unstr.* məst, *before*
conss.+məs (͵wi məs 'go)

mustache 'mʌstæʃ, mə'stæʃ |-s -ɪz |-d -t

mustachio mə'stɑʃo |-ed -d

Mustafa Kemal, -pha 'mʌstəfəkə'mal, -'kemal

mustang 'mʌstæŋ

mustard 'mʌstɚd; ES 'mʌstəd

muster 'mʌstɚ; ES 'mʌstə(r; |-ed -d |-ing
'mʌstərɪŋ, 'mustrɪŋ

mustn't 'mʌsn̩t, *before some conss.*+'mʌsn̩
('mʌsn̩ 'du ɪt)

mutability ͵mjutə'bɪlətɪ, ͵mɪutə-

mutable 'mjutəbl̩, 'mɪut- |-bly -blɪ

mutate 'mjutet, 'mɪʊ- |-tated - tetɪd

mutation mju'teʃən, mɪu-

mutatis mutandis mju'tetɪs mju'tændɪs,
mɪu'tetɪs mɪu-

mute mjut, mɪut |-d -ɪd

mutilate 'mjutl̩͵et, 'mɪʊ- |-d -ɪd

mutilation ͵mjutl̩'eʃən, ͵mɪʊ-

mutineer ͵mjutn̩'ɪr, ͵mɪʊt-; ES -'ɪə(r, S+
-'ɛə(r, -'jɛə(r; |-ed -d

mutinous 'mjutn̩əs, 'mɪʊt- |-ny -n̩ɪ

Mutius 'mjuʃəs, 'mɪʊ-, -ʃɪəs |-'s -ɪz

mutt mʌt

mutter 'mʌtɚ; ES 'mʌtə(r; |-ed -d |-ing
'mʌtərɪŋ, 'mʌtrɪŋ

mutton, M- 'mʌtn̩—*The pron.* 'mʌtən *is not*
in general use.

mutual 'mjutʃʊəl, 'mɪʊ- |-ly -ɪ

mutuality ͵mjutʃʊ'ælətɪ, ͵mɪʊ-

muzhik, -zjik mu'ʒik, 'muʒik

muzzle 'mʌzl̩ |-d -d |-ling 'mʌzlɪŋ, 'mʌzl̩ɪŋ

my *stressed* 'maɪ, ͵maɪ; *unstr. before vowels*
məɪ, *before conss.* mə, *Brit stage sometimes*
mɪ

Mycenae maɪ'sini |-naean ͵maɪsɪ'niən

mycologist maɪ'kalədʒɪst; ES+-'kɒl-; |-gy
-dʒɪ

Myer 'maɪɚ; ES 'maɪ·ə(r; |-s -z |-s's -zɪz

Mynheer, m- maɪn'hɛr, -'hɪr; ES -'hɛə(r,
-'hɪə(r; (*Du* mijnheer mə'ne:r)

myocardiograph ͵maɪo'kardɪə͵græf; ES -'kɑ:-
dɪə-, E+-͵grɑf, -͵graf, -'ka:d-

myope 'maɪop |myopia maɪ'opɪə

---

myopic **maɪˈɑpɪk**; ES+-ˈɒp-; |-al -ḷ |-ally -ḷɪ, -ɪklɪ
myosis **maɪˈosɪs**
myosotis **ˌmaɪəˈsotɪs** |-es **-ɪz**
Myra **ˈmaɪrə**
myriad **ˈmɪrɪəd**
myriapod **ˈmɪrɪəˌpɑd**; ES+-ˌpɒd
Myrick **ˈmaɪrɪk, ˈmɛrɪk**
Myrmidon, m- **ˈmɝˑməˌdɑn, -dən**; ES **ˈmɝmə-, ˈmɝˑmə-, -ˌdɒn**
Myron **ˈmaɪrən**
myrrh **mɝ**; ES **mɝ(r, mɝ**; |-ed **-d** |-ic **-ɪk, ˈmɪrɪk**
Myrrha **ˈmɪrə**
Myrtle, m- **ˈmɝˑtḷ**; ES **ˈmɝtḷ, ˈmɝˑtḷ**
myself **məˈsɛlf, maɪˈsɛlf**
Mysia **ˈmɪʃɪə** |-n **-n**
Mysore **maɪˈsor, -ˈsɔr**; ES **-ˈsoə(r, E+-ˈsɔə(r**

mysterious **mɪsˈtɪrɪəs, mɪˈstɪrɪəs**
mystery *'trade'* **ˈmɪstərɪ**
mystery *'secret'* **ˈmɪstrɪ, ˈmɪstərɪ**
mystic, M- **ˈmɪstɪk** |-al -ḷ |-ally -ḷɪ, -ɪklɪ
mysticism **ˈmɪstəˌsɪzəm**
mystification **ˌmɪstəfəˈkeʃən**
mystify **ˈmɪstəˌfaɪ** |-fied -ˌfaɪd
myth **mɪθ** |-ths **-θs**
mythic **ˈmɪθɪk** |-al -ḷ |-ally -ḷɪ, -ɪklɪ
mythological **ˌmɪθəˈlɑdʒɪkḷ**; ES+-ˈlɒdʒ-; |-ly -ɪ, -ɪklɪ
mythologist **mɪˈθɑlədʒɪst**; ES+-ˈθɒl-; |-gy -dʒɪ
mythologize **mɪˈθɑləˌdʒaɪz**; ES+-ˈθɒl-; |-s -ɪz |-d -d
Mytilene **ˌmɪtḷˈinɪ**
myxedema, -oedema **ˌmɪksɪˈdimə**
myxoid **ˈmɪksɔɪd**

N

N, n *letter* **ɛn** |*pl* N's, Ns, *poss* N's **ɛnz**
Naaman **ˈneəmən, ˈnemən**
Naamathite **ˈneəməˌθaɪt**
nab **næb** |nabbed **næbd**
Nabal **ˈnebḷ**
nabob **ˈnebɑb**; ES+ˈnebɒb
Naboth **ˈnebɑθ**; ES+ˈnebɒθ
nacelle **nəˈsɛl**
Nacogdoches **ˌnækəˈdotʃɪz** |-es' -tʃɪz
nacre **ˈnekɚ**; ES **ˈnekə(r**
nadir **ˈnedɚ**; ES **ˈnedə(r**
nag **næg** |nagged **nægd**
Nagasaki **ˌnægəˈsakɪ, ˌnɑgəˈsɑkɪ**
Nahant **nəˈhænt**; E+nəˈhɑnt, nəˈhɑnt
Nahuatl **ˈnɑwɑtḷ** |Nahuatlan **ˈnɑwɑtlən**
Nahum **ˈneəm, ˈnehʌm**
naiad **ˈneæd, ˈnaɪæd, -əd** |-s **-z** |-es **-əˌdiz**
naïf **nɑˈif** |naïfs **nɑˈifs**=naïve
nail **nel** |nailed **neld**
Nain **ˈne·ɪn, nen**
nainsook **ˈnensʊk, ˈnænsʊk**
Nairn **nɛrn, nærn, nern**; ES **næən, neən,** E+neən; |-shire -ʃɪr, -ʃɚ; ES -ʃɪə(r, -ʃə(r
Naismith **ˈnesmɪθ**
naïve **nɑˈiv** |naïveté **nɑˌivˈte, nɑˈivte**
naked **ˈnekɪd,** *old fash.* **ˈnɛkɪd**

namable, nameable **ˈneməbḷ** |-bly **-blɪ**
namby-pamby **ˈnæmbɪˈpæmbɪ** (ˈnamby-ˌpamby ˈair)
name **nem** |named **nemd** |namely **ˈnemlɪ**
Nameoki **ˌnæmɪˈokɪ**
namesake **ˈnemˌsek**
Namur **ˈnemʊr**; ES **ˈnemʊə(r**; (*Fr* nɑˈmyːr)
Nanchang **ˈnænˈtʃæŋ** (*Chin* ˈnanˈtʃaŋ)
Nancy *pers. name* **ˈnænsɪ**; *France* **ˈnænsɪ** (*Fr* nɑ̃ˈsi)
nankeen, -kin **nænˈkin**
Nanking **nænˈkɪŋ** |Nankin **nænˈkɪn**
Nannette **nænˈɛt**
Nannie **ˈnænɪ** |nanny-goat **ˈnænɪˌgot**
Nansemond **ˈnænsɪmənd**
Nansen **ˈnænsṇ** (*Norw* ˈnɑnsən)
Nantasket **nænˈtæskɪt**
Nantes **nænts** |-'s -ɪz (*Fr* nɑ̃ːt)
Nanticoke **ˈnæntɪˌkok**
Nanti-Glo **ˈnæntɪˈglo**
Nantucket **nænˈtʌkɪt** (ˈNanˌtucket ˈcoast)
Naomi **ˈneəˌmaɪ, neˈomaɪ, -mɪ, -mə**
nap **næp** |napped **næpt**
Napa **ˈnæpə**
Napanee **ˈnæpəˌni**
nape **nep, næp**

|full fʊl |tooth tuθ |further ˈfɝðɚ; ES ˈfɝðə |custom ˈkʌstəm |while hwaɪl |how haʊ |toy tɔɪ
|using ˈjuzɪŋ |fuse fjuz, fɪuz |dish dɪʃ |vision ˈvɪʒən |Eden ˈidṇ |cradle ˈkredḷ |keep 'em ˈkipm̩

Naperville ˈnepəˌvɪl; ES ˈnepə-
napery ˈnepərɪ, ˈneprɪ
Naphtali ˈnæftəˌlaɪ
naphtha ˈnæpθə, ˈnæfθə
naphthalene ˈnæfθəˌlin, ˈnæp-
naphthene ˈnæfθin, ˈnæp-
naphthol ˈnæfθɒl, ˈnæp-, -θɔl, -θɒl, -θɑl
Napier ˈnepɪəˌ, ˈnepjəˌ, nəˈpɪr; ES ˈnepɪˌə(r,
ˈnepjə(r, nəˈpɪə(r
Napierville ˈnepɪəˌvɪl, -pjəˌ-; ES ˈnepɪˌə-,
-pjə-
napkin ˈnæpkɪn |napkined ˈnæpkɪnd
Naples ˈnepl̩z |-ˈs -ɪz
napoleon, N- nəˈpoljən, nəˈpoliən
Napoleonic nəˌpolɪˈɑnɪk; ES+-ˈɒnɪk
Nappanee ˈnæpəˌni, ˌnæpəˈni
Narbonne narˈban; ES nɑːˈban, -ˈbɒn; (Fr
narˈbɔ̃n)
narceine, -in ˈnarsɪˌin, -ɪn; ES ˈnɑːs-
narcism ˈnarˌsɪzəm; ES ˈnɑːˌsɪzəm
narcissism narˈsɪsˌɪzəm; ES nɑˈsɪsˌɪzəm
Narcissus narˈsɪsəs; ES nɑːˈs-; |-sus' -səs
narcosis narˈkosɪs; ES nɑːˈkosɪs
narcotic narˈkatɪk; ES nɑːˈkatɪk, -ˈkɒtɪk
narcoticism narˈkatəˌsɪzəm; ES nɑˈkat-,
-ˈkɒt-
narcotism ˈnarkəˌtɪzəm; ES ˈnɑːk-
nard nard; ES nɑːd
narghile, -gile ˈnargəlɪ, -ˌle; ES ˈnɑːg-
Nares nɛrz, nærz; E nɛəz, ES næəz; |-ˈs -ɪz
naris ˈnerɪs |pl nares ˈneriz
Narragansett ˌnærəˈgænsɪt
narrate næˈret, ˈnæret |-d -ɪd
narration næˈreʃən |narrative ˈnærətɪv
narrow ˈnæro, ˈnærə |-ed -d |-ing ˈnærəwɪŋ
|-er ˈnærəwəˌ; ES -wə(r; |-est ˈnærəwɪst
narrow-gauge ˈnæroˈgedʒ, ˈnærə-
narrowish ˈnærəwɪʃ
narrow-minded ˈnæroˈmaɪndɪd, ˈnærə- (ˈnar-
row-ˌminded ˈhate)
narthex ˈnarθɛks; ES ˈnɑːθ-; |-es -ɪz
Narvaez Sp narˈβa·eθ
Narvik ˈnarvɪk; ES ˈnɑːvɪk
narwhal, -e, -wal ˈnarhwəl, -wəl; ES ˈnɑː-
nasal ˈnezl̩ |-ly -ɪ
nasalization ˌnezlˈ̩əˈzeʃən, -aɪˈz-
nasalize ˈnezl̩ˌaɪz |-s -ɪz |-d -d
Nasby ˈnæzbɪ
nascency ˈnæsn̩sɪ |nascent ˈnæsn̩t

Naseby ˈnezbɪ
Nash(e) næʃ |-ˈs ˈnæʃɪz
Nashua ˈnæʃʊə, loc.+ˈnæʃəˌwe
Nashville ˈnæʃvɪl; S+ˈnæʃvl̩
Nasmyth ˈnesmɪθ
Nassau US ˈnæsɔ, Germany ˈnɑsaʊ
Nast næst
nasturtium næˈstɝʃəm, nə-; ES -ˈstɝʃ-,
-ˈstɝʃ-
nasty ˈnæstɪ; E+ˈnɑstɪ, ˈnɑstɪ
natal ˈnetl̩
Natal S Afr nəˈtæl, Braz nəˈtɑl
Natalie ˈnætl̩ɪ, ˈnetl̩ɪ (Fr nataˈli)
natant ˈnetn̩t |natation neˈteʃən
natatorial ˌnetəˈtorɪəl, -ˈtɔr-; S -ˈtor-
natatorium ˌnetəˈtorɪəm, -ˈtɔr-; S -ˈtor-; |-s -z
|-ria -rɪə
natatory ˈnetəˌtorɪ, -ˌtɔrɪ; S -ˌtorɪ
Natches ˈnætʃɪz |Natches' ˈnætʃɪz
Natchitoches ˈnækɪˌtaʃ |-ˈs -ɪz
Nathan ˈneθən |-iel nəˈθænjəl
natheless, -thless arch. ˈneθlɪs, ˈnæθlɪs
Natick ˈnetɪk
nation ˈneʃən |-hood -ˌhʊd
national ˈnæʃənl̩, ˈnæʃnəl |-ism -ˌɪzəm |-ist
-ɪst |-ly -ɪ
nationalistic ˌnæʃənl̩ˈɪstɪk, -ʃnəl- |-al -l̩ |-ally
-l̩ɪ, -ɪklɪ
nationality ˌnæʃənˈælətɪ
nationalize ˈnæʃənl̩ˌaɪz, -ʃnəl- |-s -ɪz |-d -d
native ˈnetɪv
nativity neˈtɪvətɪ, nə-
Natrona nəˈtronə
natty ˈnætɪ
natural ˈnætʃərəl, ˈnætʃrəl |-ly -ɪ
naturalism ˈnætʃərəlˌɪzəm, ˈnætʃrəl- |-ist -ɪst
naturalize ˈnætʃərəlˌaɪz, ˈnætʃrəl- |-s -ɪz |-d -d
nature ˈnetʃəˌ; ES ˈnetʃə(r
Naugatuck ˈnɔgəˌtʌk
naught nɔt |naughty ˈnɔtɪ
nausea ˈnɔʒə, ˈnɔzɪə, ˈnɔsɪə, ˈnɔʃɪə, ˈnɔʃə,
ˈnɔʒɪə
nauseate ˈnɔʒɪˌet, ˈnɔzɪ-, ˈnɔsɪ-, ˈnɔʃɪ-
nauseous ˈnɔʒəs, ˈnɔzɪəs, ˈnɔsɪəs, ˈnɔʃəs
Nausicaä nɔˈsɪkɪə
nautch nɔtʃ |nautches ˈnɔtʃɪz
nautical ˈnɔtɪkl̩ |-ly -ɪ
nautilus ˈnɔtləs |nautiluses ˈnɔtləsɪz
Nauvoo nɔˈvu

Key: See in full §§3–47. bee bi |pity ˈpɪtɪ (§6) |rate ret |yet jɛt |sang sæŋ |angry ˈæŋ·grɪ
|bath bæθ; E baθ (§10) |ah ɑ |far fɑr |watch watʃ, wɒtʃ (§12) |jaw dʒɔ |gorge gɔrdʒ |go go

Navaho, -jo ˈnævəˌho

naval ˈnevl̩ |-ly -ɪ

Navarino ˌnævəˈrino (*It* ˌnavaˈriːno)

Navarre nəˈvɑr; ES nəˈvɑː(r, E+-ˈvɑː(r

nave nev

navel ˈnevl̩

Navesink ˈnævəˌsɪŋk, ˈnevə-, ˈnɛvə-

navigability ˌnævəgəˈbɪlətɪ

navigable ˈnævəgəbl̩ |-bly -blɪ

navigate ˈnævəˌget |-d -ɪd |-tor -tɚ; ES -tə(r

navigation ˌnævəˈgeʃən

navvy ˈnævɪ

navy ˈnevɪ

nawab nəˈwɑb, nəˈwɔb

nay ne

Nazarene ˌnæzəˈrin (ˈNazaˌrene ˈGospel)

Nazareth ˈnæzərəθ, -rɪθ, ˈnæzr-

Nazarite ˈnæzəˌraɪt

Nazi ˈnɑtsɪ, ˈnætsɪ |-ism -ˌɪzəm (*Ger* ˈnɑːtsiː)

Nazimova nɑˈzimoˌvɑ

Neanderthal nɪˈændɚˌtɑl; ES -ˈændə-; (*Ger* neˈandərˌtɑːl)

neap nip |neaped nipt

Neapolitan ˌniəˈpɑlətn̩; ES+-ˈpɒl-

near nɪr; ES nɪə(r, S+njɛə(r, njɪə(r, nɛə(r

near-by ˈnɪrˈbaɪ; ES ˈnɪə-, S+ˈnjɛə-, ˈnjɪə-, ˈnɛə-; (ˈnear-ˌby ˈtown)

nearsighted ˈnɪrˈsaɪtɪd; ES ˈnɪə-, S+ˈnjɛə-, ˈnjɪə-, ˈnɛə-

neat nit |neated ˈnitɪd

ˈneath niθ, nĭð

neatherd ˈnitˌhɜd; ES -ˌhɜd, -ˌhɜ̆d

neat's-foot ˈnitsˌfʊt

neb nɛb |nebbed nɛbd

Nebo ˈnibo

Nebraska nəˈbræskə |-n -n

Nebuchadnezzar ˌnɛbjəkədˈnɛzɚ, ˌnɛbə-; ES -ˈnɛzə(r; |-drezzar -ˈrɛzɚ; ES -ˈrɛzə(r

nebula ˈnɛbjələ |-s -z -lae -ˌli -lous -ləs

nebulosity ˌnɛbjəˈlɑsətɪ; ES+-ˈlɒs-

necessarily ˈnɛsəˌsɛrəlɪ, *esp. if emph.* ˌnɛsəˈsɛrəlɪ

necessary ˈnɛsəˌsɛrɪ

necessitate nəˈsɛsəˌtet |-d -ɪd |-tous -təs |-ty -tɪ

neck nɛk |necked nɛkt

neckerchief ˈnɛkɚtʃɪf; ES ˈnɛkətʃɪf

necklace ˈnɛklɪs |-s -ɪz |-d -t

necktie ˈnɛkˌtaɪ

necrology nɛˈkrɑlədʒɪ; ES+-ˈkrɒl-

necromancer ˈnɛkrəˌmænsɚ; ES -sə(r; |-cy -sɪ

necropolis nɛˈkrɑpəlɪs; ES+-ˈkrɒp-; |-es -ɪz

necropsy ˈnɛkrɑpsɪ; ES+-krɒp-

necrosis nɛˈkrosɪs |-croses -ˈkrosiz

nectar ˈnɛktɚ; ES ˈnɛktə(r; |-ed -d |-ous -əs

nectarine ˈnɛktəˌrin, ˌnɛktəˈrin

nee ne

need nid |-ed -ɪd |-ful -fəl |-fully -fəlɪ

needle ˈnidl̩ |-d -d |-ful -ˌfʊl |-fuls -ˌfʊlz

needle-point ˈnidl̩ˌpɔɪnt |-ed -ɪd

needlewoman ˈnidl̩ˌwʊmən, -ˌwu- |-men -ˌwɪmɪn, -ən

needlework ˈnidl̩ˌwɜk; ES -ˌwɜk, -ˌwɜ̆k

needn't ˈnidn̩t, *before some conns.*+ˈnidn̩ (ˈnidn̩ ˈbɑ̆ðɚ)—*The pron.* ˈnidənt *is not in general use.*

Neenah ˈninə

ne'er nɛr; ES nɛə(r

ne'er-do-weel ˈnɛrduˌwil; ES ˈnɛəduˌwil

ne'er-do-well ˈnɛrduˌwɛl; ES ˈnɛəduˌwɛl

nefarious nɪˈfɛrɪəs, -ˈfær-, -ˈfer-

negate ˈniget, nɪˈget |-d -ɪd |-tion nɪˈgeʃən

negative ˈnɛgətɪv |-d -d |-vism -ˌɪzəm

Negaunee nɪˈgɔnɪ

neglect nɪˈglɛkt |-ed -ɪd |-ful -fəl |-fully -fəlɪ

negligee ˌnɛglɪˈʒe (*Fr* negliˈʒe) (ˈnegliˌgee ˈwear)

negligence ˈnɛglədʒəns |-cy -ɪ |-gent -dʒənt

negligible ˈnɛglədʒəbl̩ |-bly -blɪ

negotiability nɪˌgoʃɪəˈbɪlətɪ, -ˌgoʃə-

negotiable nɪˈgoʃɪəbl̩, -ˈgoʃə-

negotiate nɪˈgoʃɪˌet |-d -ɪd |-tor -ɚ; ES -ə(r

negotiation nɪˌgoʃɪˈeʃən

negress ˈnigrɪs |-es -ɪz

negro, N- ˈnigro, *esp.* S ˈnɪgro, ˈnɪgrə

Negroid ˈnigrɔɪd

Negros *PI* ˈnegros |-'s -ɪz

Negus, n- ˈnigəs |-'s -ɪz

Nehemiah ˌniəˈmaɪə

neigh ne |neighed ned

neighbor ˈnebɚ; ES ˈnebə(r; |-ed -d |-ing ˈnebrɪŋ, ˈnebərɪŋ |-hood -ˌhʊd

Neilson ˈnilsn̩

neither ˈniðɚ, *much less freq.* ˈnaɪðɚ; ES -ðə(r

Nell nɛl |Nellie ˈnɛlɪ |Nelly ˈnɛlɪ

Nelson ˈnɛlsn̩ |-ville -ˌvɪl; S+-vl̩

nematode ˈnɛməˌtod

Nemean nɪˈmiən, ˈnimɪən

|full fʊl |tooth tuθ |further ˈfɝðɚ; ES ˈfɝ̆ðə |custom ˈkʌstəm |while hwaɪl |how haʊ |toy tɔɪ |using ˈjuzɪŋ |fuse fjuz, fɪuz |dish dɪʃ |vision ˈvɪʒən |Eden ˈidn̩ |cradle ˈkredl̩ |keep 'em ˈkipm̩

Nemesis, n- 'nɛməsɪs |-eses -ə͵siz
Neocene 'niə͵sin
neoimpressionism ͵nio·ɪm'prɛʃən͵ɪzəm |-ist
-ɪst
neolith 'niə͵lɪθ |-ths -θs |-ic ͵niə'lɪθɪk
neologism ni'alə͵dʒɪzəm; ES+-'ɒl-; |-ist -ɪst
neologistic ni͵alə'dʒɪstɪk; ES+-͵ɒl-; |-al -ḷ
neology ni'alədʒɪ; ES+-'ɒl-
neon 'nian, 'niɒn
neophyte 'niə͵faɪt
Neoplatonism ͵nio'pletn͵ɪzəm
Neozoic ͵niə'zo·ɪk
Nepal, -paul nɪ'pɔl
nepenthe nɪ'pɛnθɪ
nephew 'nɛfju, -jʊ, -ɪu, *much less freq.* 'nɛv-
nephritic nɛ'frɪtɪk |-al -ḷ |-tis -'fraɪtɪs
ne plus ultra 'niplʌs'ʌltrə
nepotism 'nɛpə͵tɪzəm
Neptune 'nɛptʃun, -tʃʊun, -tjun
Nereid, n- 'nɪrɪɪd
Nerissa nə'rɪsə, nɛ-
Nero 'niro, 'nɪro
nerve nɝv; ES nɜv, nɝ·v; |-d -d |-vous -əs
ness nɛs |nesses 'nɛsɪs
-ness *unstressed ending* -nɪs, -nəs. *The pron.*
-nɛs is not normal to conversation but is
occasional in reading style or rime. When
only -nɪs *is given in the vocab., it is to be*
understood that many speakers (fewer in the
E & S) also pron. -nəs, *riming* slyness *with*
sinus. *When* -ness *is added to words ending*
in -n *or* -ņ, *two* n *sounds are pronounced*
(thinness 'θɪnnɪs, fineness 'faɪnnɪs, sudden-
ness 'sʌdņņɪs); *cf* -less.
nest nɛst |nested 'nɛstɪd
nestle 'nɛsḷ |-d -d |-ling 'nɛslɪŋ, 'nɛsḷɪŋ
nestling n 'nɛstlɪŋ, 'nɛslɪŋ
Nestor 'nɛstɚ; ES 'nɛstə(r
Nestorian nɛs'torɪən, -'tɔr-; S -'tor-
net nɛt |netted 'nɛtɪd
nether 'nɛðɚ; ES 'nɛðə(r
Netherlander 'nɛðɚ͵lændɚ, -ləndɚ; ES
'nɛðə͵lændə(r, -ləndə(r
Netherlands 'nɛðɚləndz, -nz; ES 'nɛðə-
nethermost 'nɛðɚ͵most, -məst; ES 'nɛðə-
Nettie 'nɛtɪ
netting 'nɛtɪŋ
nettle 'nɛtḷ |-d -d |-ling 'nɛtḷɪŋ, 'nɛtlɪŋ
network 'nɛt͵wɝk; ES -͵wɜk, -͵wɝ·k

Neufchâtel ͵njuʃə'tɛl, ͵nɪu-, ͵nu- (*Fr* nœʃa-
'tɛl) ('Neufchâ͵tel 'cheese)
neural 'njurəl, 'nɪurəl, 'nʊrəl
neuralgia nju'ræld͡ʒə, nɪu-, nu-
neurasthenia ͵njurəs'θinɪə, ͵nɪu-, ͵nu-
neurasthenic ͵njurəs'θɛnɪk, ͵nɪu-, ͵nu- |-al -ḷ
|-ally -ḷɪ, -ɪklɪ
neuritis nju'raɪtɪs, nɪu-, nu-
neurologist nju'rɑlədʒɪst, nɪu-, nu-; ES+
-'rɒl-; |-gy -dʒɪ
neuron 'njurɑn, 'nɪu-, 'nu-, -rɒn |-rone -ron
neuropathic ͵njurə'pæθɪk, ͵nɪu-, ͵nu- |-al -ḷ
|-ally -ḷɪ, -ɪklɪ
neuropathist nju'rɑpəθɪst, nɪu-, nu-; ES+
-'rɒp-; |-thy -θɪ
neuropsychosis ͵njurosaɪ'kosɪs, ͵nɪu-, ͵nu-
neurosis nju'rosɪs, nɪu-, nu- |-roses -'rosiz
neurotic nju'rɑtɪk, nɪu-, nu-; ES+-'rɒt-;
|-ally -ḷɪ, -ɪklɪ
Neustria 'njustrɪə, 'nɪu-, 'nu- |-n -n
neuter 'njutɚ, 'nɪu-, 'nu-; ES -tə(r
neutral 'njutrəl, 'nɪu-, 'nu- |-ly -ɪ
neutrality nju'trælətɪ, nɪu-, nu-
neutralization ͵njutrələ'zeʃən, ͵nɪu-, ͵nu-,
-aɪ'z-
neutralize 'njutrəl͵aɪz, 'nɪu-, 'nu- |-s -ɪz |-d -d
neutron 'njutrɑn, 'nɪu-, 'nu-, -trɒn
Nevada *state* nə'vædə, nɪ-, -'vadə |-n -n; *Ia,*
Mo cities, Ark co. loc. -'vedə
never 'nɛvɚ; ES 'nɛvə(r
nevermore ͵nɛvɚ'mor, -'mɔr; ES ͵nɛvə'moə(r,
E+-'mɔə(r
nevertheless ͵nɛvɚðə'lɛs; ES ͵nɛvə-
Neville 'nɛvḷ, -vɪl
Nevin 'nɛvɪn
Nevis 'nɛvɪs, 'nivɪs |-'s -ɪz
new nju, nɪu, nu
Newark 'njuɚk, 'nɪu-, 'nu-; ES -ək; *Del*+
-ark; ES -ɑ:k
New Bern 'njubɚn, 'nɪu-, 'nu-; ES -bən
Newbern 'njubɚn, 'nɪu-, 'nu-; ES -bən
Newberry, -bery 'nju͵bɛrɪ, 'nɪu-, 'nu-, -bərɪ
newborn 'nju'bɔrn, 'nɪu-, 'nu-; ES -'bɔən;
('new͵born 'lamb)
Newburgh 'njubɝg, 'nɪu-, 'nu-; ES -bɜg,
-bɝ·g
Newbury 'nju͵bɛrɪ, 'nɪu-, 'nu-, -bərɪ |-port
-͵port, -͵pɔrt, -brɪ-; ES -͵poət, E+-͵pɔət
('Newbury & ͵Newbury'port)

Key: *See in full §§3–47.* bee **bi** |pity **'pɪtɪ** (§6) |rate **ret** |yet **jɛt** |sang **sæŋ** |angry **'æŋ·grɪ**
|bath **bæθ**; E **baθ** (§10) |ah **ɑ** |far **far** |watch **wɑtʃ, wɒtʃ** (§12) |jaw **dʒɔ** |gorge **gɔrdʒ** |go **go**

Newcastle 'nju͜ɪkæsḷ, 'nɪu-, 'nu-; E+-ˌkasḷ,
-ˌkasḷ; *Engd loc.* nju'kasḷ

Newcomb, -mbe, -me 'njukəm, 'nɪu-, 'nu-

newcome 'nju͜ɪkʌm, 'nɪu-, 'nu-

newcomer 'nju͜ɪkʌmɚ, 'nɪu-, 'nu-; ES -mə(r;
acct+new'comer

Newcomerstown 'njukʌmɚzˌtaʊn, 'nɪu-, 'nu-;
ES -kʌməz-

Newdigate 'njudɪgɪt, 'nɪu-, 'nu-, -ˌget

newel, Newell 'njuəl, 'nɪuəl, 'nuəl

New England nju'ɪŋglənd, nɪu-, nu-

newfangled ˌnju'fæŋgḷd, ˌnɪu-, ˌnu- ('new-
ˌfangled 'whims)

Newfoundland *isl.* ˌnjufənd'lænd, ˌnɪu-, ˌnu-,
'njufəndlənd, 'nɪu-, 'nu-; *dog* nju'faʊnd-
lənd, nɪu-, nu-

Newfoundlander nju'faʊndləndɚ, nɪu-, nu-;
ES -də(r

Newgate 'njugɪt, -get

New Hampshire nju'hæmpʃɚ, nɪu-, nu-, -ʃɪr;
ES -ʃə(r, -ʃɪə(r

New Haven nju'hevən, nɪu-, nu-, *loc.*+
-'hevm̩

New Jersey nju'dʒɝʒɪ, nɪu-, nu-; ES -'dʒɝ̃ʒɪ,
-'dʒɝʒɪ

new-laid 'nju'led, 'nɪu-, 'nu- ('new-ˌlaid 'egg)

Newman 'njumən, 'nɪu-, 'nu-

Newmarket 'nju͜ɪmɑrkɪt, 'nɪu-, 'nu-; ES
-ˌmɑ:kɪt, E+-ˌma:kɪt

New Mexico nju'mɛksəˌko, nɪu-, nu-

Newnan 'njunən, 'nɪu-, 'nu-

New Orleans nju'ɔrlɪənz, nɪu-, nu-; ES
-'ɔəlɪənz;—*The older pron.* ˌnjuɚ'linz *is
not uncommon, and is regular in* New
Orleans molasses. *Cf* Orleans.

Newport 'nju͜ɪport, 'nɪu-, 'nu-, -ˌpɔrt; ES
-ˌpoət, E+-ˌpɔət

news njuz, nɪuz, nuz |-boy -ˌbɔɪ

New Salem nju'seləm, nɪu-, nu-; *Mass loc.*
'New ˌSalem (*cf* Salem, *Mass*)

newspaper 'njuzˌpepɚ, 'njus-, 'nɪu-, 'nu-; ES
-ˌpepə(r; |-man -ˌmæn |-men -ˌmɛn

newsprint 'njuzˌprɪnt, 'nɪuz-, 'nuz-

newsreel 'njuzˌril, 'nɪuz-, 'nuz-

newssheet 'njuzˌʃit, 'njuʒ-, 'nɪu-, 'nu-

newsstand 'njuzˌstænd, 'nɪuz-, 'nuz-

newt njut, nɪut, nut

Newton 'njutn̩, 'nɪu-, 'nu- |-town -ˌtaʊn

Newtonian nju'tonɪən, nɪu-, nu-

New Year's 'nju͜ɪjɪrz, 'nɪu-, 'nu-; ES -ˌjɪəz,
S+-ˌjɛəz; |Day -ˌde |Eve -'iv

New York nju'jɔrk, nɪu-, nu-, nʊ-; ES -'jɔək;
('New ˌYork 'City)

New Zealand nju'zilənd, nɪu-, nu-

next nɛkst, *before some conss.*+nɛks ('nɛks
'de, 'nɛks 'flor)

nexus 'nɛksəs |-es -ɪz

Ney ne

Nez Perce 'nɛz'pɝs; ES -'pɜs, -'pɝ̃s; |-s -ɪz
(*Fr* nepɛr'se |-cés -'se)

Niagara naɪ'ægrə, -gərə ('Niˌagara 'Falls)

nib nɪb |nibbed nɪbd

nibble 'nɪbḷ |-d -d |-ling 'nɪblɪŋ, 'nɪbḷɪŋ

Nibelung 'nibḷˌʊŋ |-enlied -ənˌlid (*Ger* -ˌlit)

niblick, -ic 'nɪblɪk |-cked -t

Nicaea naɪ'siə |-n -n

Nicanor nɪ'kenɚ, naɪ-; ES -'kenə(r

Nicaragua ˌnɪkə'rɑgwə, -'rɔgwə |-n -n

nice naɪs |-ty 'naɪsətɪ

Nice nis |-'s -ɪz

Nicene naɪ'sin ('Niˌcene 'Creed)

niche nɪtʃ |niches 'nɪtʃɪz |niched nɪtʃt

Nicholas 'nɪkḷəs, 'nɪkḷəs |-'s -ɪz

Nichols 'nɪkḷz |-'s -ɪz -lson 'nɪkḷsn̩

nick, N- nɪk |nicked nɪkt

nickel 'nɪkḷ |-ed -d |-ing 'nɪkḷɪŋ, 'nɪkḷɪŋ

nickelodeon ˌnɪkḷ'odɪən

nickel-plate *v* 'nɪkḷ'plet |-d -ɪd ('Nickel-
ˌplate 'Railˌroad)

Nickleby 'nɪkḷbɪ

nicknack 'nɪkˌnæk

nickname 'nɪkˌnem |-named -ˌnemd

Nicodemus ˌnɪkə'diməs |-'s -ɪz

Nicolas 'nɪkḷəs, 'nɪkləs |-'s -ɪz

Nicolay 'nɪkḷˌe

nicotine 'nɪkəˌtin, -tɪn |-tin -tɪn

niece nis |nieces 'nisɪz

Niemen 'nimən (*Pol* 'njɛmən)

Niemeyer 'nimaɪɚ; ES -maɪ·ə(r

Niemöller *Ger* 'nimœlər

Nietzsche 'nitʃə

nifty 'nɪftɪ

Nigel 'naɪdʒəl

Niger 'naɪdʒɚ, 'naɪgɚ; ES -dʒə(r, -gə(r

Nigeria naɪ'dʒɪrɪə |-n -n

niggard 'nɪgɚd; ES 'nɪgəd; |-ly -lɪ

nigger 'nɪgɚ; ES 'nɪgə(r; |-ed -d |-ing 'nɪgɚɪŋ,
'nɪgrɪŋ

|full fʊl |tooth tuθ |further 'fɝðɚ; ES 'fɝ̃ðə |custom 'kʌstəm |while hwaɪl |how haʊ |toy tɔɪ
|using 'juzɪŋ |fuse fjuz, fɪuz |dish dɪʃ |vision 'vɪʒən |Eden 'idn̩ |cradle 'kredḷ |keep 'em 'kipm̩

Those words below in which the ɑ sound is spelt o are often pronounced with ɒ in E and S

niggle 'nɪgl̩ |-d -d |-ling 'nɪglɪŋ, 'nɪgl̩ɪŋ
niggler 'nɪglɚ; ES 'nɪglə(r
niggling *n* 'nɪglɪŋ
nigh naɪ |nighed naɪd
night naɪt |-ed -ɪd |-cap -ˌkæp |-capped -ˌkæpt
nightdress 'naɪtˌdrɛs |-es -ɪz
nightfall 'naɪtˌfɔl
nightgown 'naɪtˌgaʊn |-ed -d
nighthawk 'naɪtˌhɔk
nightingale, N- 'naɪtn̩ˌgel, 'naɪtɪn-, 'naɪtɪŋ-
nightjar 'naɪtˌdʒɑr; ES -ˌdʒɑ:(r, E+-ˌdʒɑ:(r
nightlong 'naɪtˌlɔŋ, -ˌlɒŋ; S+-ˌlɑŋ
nightmare 'naɪtˌmɛr, -ˌmær; E -ˌmɛə(r, ES
   -ˌmæə(r; |-d -d
nightshade 'naɪtˌʃed
nightshirt 'naɪtˌʃɝt; ES -ˌʃɝt, -ˌʃɝt; |-ed -ɪd
nighttime 'naɪtˌtaɪm
nightwalker 'naɪtˌwɔkɚ; ES -ˌwɔkə(r
nightward 'naɪtwɚd; ES 'naɪtwəd
night-watch 'naɪtˌwɑtʃ, -ˌwɒtʃ, -ˌwɔtʃ |-es -ɪz
night-watchman 'naɪtˈwɑtʃmən, -ˈwɒtʃ-,
   -ˈwɔtʃ- |-men -mən ('night-ˌwatchman
   'Jones)
nihil 'naɪhɪl
nihilism 'naɪəlˌɪzəm |-ist -ɪst
Nike 'naɪki
nil nɪl
Nile naɪl |Niles naɪlz |Niles's 'naɪlzɪz
Nilotic naɪ'lɑtɪk
Nilus 'naɪləs |-'s -ɪz
nimble 'nɪmbl̩ |-d -d |-ling 'nɪmblɪŋ, 'nɪmbl̩ɪŋ
nimbus 'nɪmbəs |-es -ɪz |-bi -baɪ |-ed -t
Nîmes nim
Nimrod 'nɪmrɑd
Nina *fem. name* 'naɪnə; *goddess* 'ninə
nincompoop 'nɪnkəmˌpup, ˌnɪnkəm'pup, -ɪŋ-
   kəm-
nine naɪn
ninefold *adj, adv* 'naɪn'fold ('nineˌfold 'gain)
ninepence 'naɪnpəns |-s -ɪz
ninepenny 'naɪnˌpɛnɪ, -pənɪ
ninepins 'naɪnˌpɪnz
nineteen naɪn'tin, 'naɪn'tin ('nineˌteen 'years)
ninety 'naɪntɪ |-tieth 'naɪntɪɪθ |-tieths -ɪθs
   |-fold -'fold
Nineveh 'nɪnəvə |-vite -ˌvaɪt
ninny 'nɪnɪ
ninth naɪnθ |-ths -θs

Ninus 'naɪnəs |-'s -ɪz
Niobe 'naɪəbɪ, -ˌbi
niobium naɪ'obɪəm
Niobrara ˌnaɪə'brɛrə, -'bræɪə, -'brerə
nip nɪp |nipped nɪpt
nip-and-tuck 'nɪpən'tʌk, 'nɪpm̩'tʌk
Nipissing 'nɪpəˌsɪŋ
nipper 'nɪpɚ; ES 'nɪpə(r; |-ed -d
nipple 'nɪpl̩ |-d -d |-ling 'nɪplɪŋ, 'nɪpl̩ɪŋ
Nippon nɪ'pɑn, -'pɒn, 'nɪpɑn, -pɒn
Nipponese ˌnɪpən'iz
nirvana, N- nɝ'vænə, nɪr-, -'vɑnə; ES nɝ-,
   nɝ-, nɪə-
nisi 'naɪsaɪ |nisi prius -'praɪəs
Nismes nim
nit nɪt
niter, -tre 'naɪtɚ; ES 'naɪtə(r; |-(e)d -d
niton 'naɪtɑn, -tɒn
nitrate *n* 'naɪtret, -trɪt
nitrate *v* 'naɪtret |-d -ɪd |-tion naɪ'treʃən
nitric 'naɪtrɪk |-trid -trɪd |-tride -traɪd, -trɪd
nitrify 'naɪtrəˌfaɪ |-fied -ˌfaɪd
nitrite 'naɪtraɪt
nitrobacteria ˌnaɪtrobæk'tɪrɪə
nitrocellulose ˌnaɪtro'sɛljəˌlos
nitrogen 'naɪtrədʒən, -dʒɪn |-ate -ˌet |-ated
   -ˌetɪd
nitrogenous naɪ'trɑdʒənəs
nitroglycerin ˌnaɪtrə'glɪsrɪn, -sərɪn |-ine -rɪn,
   -səˌrin
nitrous 'naɪtrəs
nitwit 'nɪtˌwɪt
nix nɪks |nixes 'nɪksɪz |-ie -ɪ
Nizam naɪ'zæm, nɪ-, -'zɑm
no no |noes noz |noed nod
Noah 'noə
nob nɑb |nobbed nɑbd |nobby 'nɑbɪ
Nobel no'bɛl ('Noˌbel 'prize)
nobility no'bɪlətɪ
noble 'nobl̩ |-r 'noblɚ; ES -blə(r; |-st 'noblɪst
Nobleboro 'noblˌbɝo, -ə; ES -ˌbɝr-, -ˌbʌr-,
   -ˌbɝ-
nobleman 'nobl̩mən |-men -mən
noble-minded 'nobl̩'maɪndɪd ('noble-ˌminded
   'man)
noblesse no'blɛs
noblesse oblige no'blɛso'bliʒ (*Fr* nŏblɛsŏ-
   'bli:ʒ)

Key: See in full §§3–47. bee bi |pity 'pɪtɪ (§6) |rate ret |yet jɛt |sang sæŋ |angry 'æŋ·grɪ
|bath bæθ; E baθ (§10) |ah ɑ |far fɑr |watch wɑtʃ, wɒtʃ (§12) |jaw dʒɔ |gorge gɔrdʒ |go go

Those words below in which the ɑ *sound is spelt* o *are often pronounced with* ɒ *in E and S*

noblewoman 'nobḷ‚wʊmən, -‚wu- |-men
-‚wɪmɪn, -ən
nobly 'noblɪ
nobody 'no‚bɑdɪ, 'no‚bʌdɪ, 'nobədɪ
nociassociation ‚nosɪə‚sosɪ'eʃən, -‚soʃɪ-
nock nɑk |nocked nɑkt
noctambulation ‚nɑktæmbjə'leʃən, nɑk‚tæm-
noctambulism nɑk'tæmbjə‚lɪzəm |-list -lɪst
nocturnal nɑk't3·nḷ; ES -'t3n-, -'t3·n- |-ly -ɪ
nocturne 'nɑkt3·n, nɑk't3·n; ES -3n, -3·n
nocuous 'nɑkjʊəs
nod nɑd |nodded 'nɑdɪd
nodal 'nodḷ |-dality no'dælətɪ
noddle 'nɑdḷ |-d -d |-ling 'nɑdḷɪŋ, 'nɑdlɪŋ
node nod |noded 'nodɪd
nodular 'nɑdʒələ·; ES 'nɑdʒələ(r
nodule 'nɑdʒul
Noel *pers. name* 'noəl; *'Christmas'* no'ɛl
nog, nogg nɑg |nogged nɑgd
noggin 'nɑgɪn
nohow 'no‚haʊ
noil nɔɪl |-age -ɪdʒ
noise nɔɪz |noises 'nɔɪzɪz |noised nɔɪzd
noisome 'nɔɪsəm
Nokomis no'komɪs |-'s -ɪz
Noll nɑl
nolle prosequi 'nɑlɪ'prɑsɪ‚kwaɪ
nolo contendere 'nolokən'tɛndə‚ri
nol-pros ‚nɑl'prɑs |-ses -ɪz |-sed -t
nomad 'nomæd, 'nɑmæd |-ism -‚ɪzəm
nomadic no'mædɪk |-al -ḷ |-ally -ḷɪ, -ɪklɪ
nombles 'nʌmbḷz = numbles
nom de plume 'nɑmdə‚plum, -‚plɪum (*Fr*
nõdə'plym)
Nome nom
nomenclature 'nomən‚kletʃə·; ES -‚kletʃə(r—
no'mɛnklətʃə(r *is chiefly Brit.*
nominal 'nɑmənḷ |-ly -ɪ
nominate *adj* 'nɑmənɪt
nominate *v* 'nɑmə‚net |-d -ɪd |-tion ‚nɑmə-
'neʃən
nominative 'nɑmə‚netɪv, *gram.* + 'nɑmənətɪv,
-mnə-
nominee ‚nɑmə'ni
nomology no'mɑlədʒɪ |-gist -dʒɪst
nonacceptance ‚nɑnək'sɛptəns, -ɪk-
nonage 'nɑnɪdʒ, 'nonɪdʒ
nonagenarian ‚nɑnədʒə'nɛrɪən, ‚nonə-, -'ner-

nonaggression ‚nɑnə'grɛʃən
nonalcoholic ‚nɑnælkə'hɑlɪk, -'hɒl-, -'hɑl-
nonappearance ‚nɑnə'pɪrəns; S+-'pɛr-,
-'pjɛr-; |-s -ɪz
nonassessable ‚nɑnə'sɛsəbḷ
nonattendance ‚nɑnə'tɛndəns |-s -ɪz
nonbeliever ‚nɑnbə'livə·; -bḷ'ivə·; ES -və(r
nonbelligerent ‚nɑnbə'lɪdʒərənt
nonce nɑns
nonchalance 'nɑnʃələns, ‚nɑnʃə'lɑns (*Fr*
nõʃa'lɑ̃:s) |-nt -nt (*Fr* -'lɑ̃)
noncollapsible ‚nɑnkə'læpsəbḷ
noncom nɑn'kɑm
nomcombatant nɑn'kɑmbətənt, -'kʌm-
noncombustible ‚nɑnkəm'bʌstəbḷ
noncommissioned ‚nɑnkə'mɪʃənd
noncommittal ‚nɑnkə'mɪtḷ |-ly -ɪ
noncompliance ‚nɑnkəm'plaɪəns |-s -ɪz
non compos mentis 'nɑn‚kɑmpəs'mɛntɪs
nonconditioned ‚nɑnkən'dɪʃənd
nonconductive ‚nɑnkən'dʌktɪv |-tor -tə·; ES
-tə(r
nonconformance ‚nɑnkən'fɔrməns; ES -'fɔəm-
nonconformist ‚nɑnkən'fɔrmɪst; ES -'fɔəm-
noncontemporary ‚nɑnkən'tɛmpə‚rɛrɪ
noncontraband nɑn'kɑntrə‚bænd
non-co-operation ‚nɑnko‚apə'reʃən
non-co-operative ‚nɑnko'apə‚retɪv
noncorroding ‚nɑnkə'rodɪŋ |-rosive -'rosɪv
nondelivery ‚nɑndɪ'lɪvərɪ, -'lɪvrɪ
nondescript 'nɑndɪ‚skrɪpt
nondivisible ‚nɑndə'vɪzəbḷ
nondramatic ‚nɑndrə'mætɪk
none *'ninth hour'* non |nones nonz
none *'not any'* nʌn
nonentity nɑn'ɛntətɪ
nonessential ‚nɑnə'sɛnʃəl
nonesuch 'nʌn‚sʌtʃ |-es -ɪz
nonexistence ‚nɑnɪg'zɪstəns |-tent -tənt
nonexplosive ‚nɑnɪk'splosɪv
nonfactual nɑn'fæktʃʊəl
nonfeasance nɑn'fizṇs
nonfiction nɑn'fɪkʃən
nonflammable nɑn'flæməbḷ
nonfulfillment ‚nɑnfʊl'fɪlmənt
nonhuman nɑn'hjumən, -'hɪu-
nonillion no'nɪljən
nonimmune ‚nɑnɪ'mjun, -'mɪun

|full fʊl |tooth tuθ |further 'f3·ðə·; ES 'f3ðə |custom 'kʌstəm |while hwaɪl |how haʊ |toy tɔɪ
|using 'juzɪŋ |fuse fjuz, fɪuz |dish dɪʃ |vision 'vɪʒən |Eden 'idṇ |cradle 'kredḷ |keep 'em 'kipm̩

Those words below in which the ɑ *sound is spelt* o *are often pronounced with* ɒ *in E and S*

nonindustrial ˌnɑnɪn'dʌstrɪəl

noninflammable ˌnɑnɪn'flæməbļ

noninjurious ˌnɑnɪn'dʒʊrɪəs

nonintercourse nɑn'ɪntɚˌkors, -ˌkɔrs; ES -'ɪntəˌkoəs, E+-ˌkɔəs

noninterference ˌnɑnɪntɚ'fɪrəns; ES -ɪntə-, S+-'fɛr-

nonintervention ˌnɑnɪntɚ'vɛnʃən; ES -ɪntə-

nonintoxicant ˌnɑnɪn'taksəkənt |-cating -ˌketɪŋ

nonjoinder nɑn'dʒɔɪndɚ; ES -'dʒɔɪndə(r

nonjuror nɑn'dʒʊrɚ, -'dʒɪʊrɚ; ES -rə(r

nonmember nɑn'mɛmbɚ; ES -'mɛmbə(r

nonmetal nɑn'mɛtļ |-talic ˌnɑnmə'tælɪk

nonmoral nɑn'mɔrəl, -'mɑr-, -'mɒr-

nonnegotiable ˌnɑnnɪ'goʃɪəbļ, -'goʃə-

nonobservance ˌnɑnəb'zɝvəns; ES -'zɝv-, -'zɝ·v-; |-ant -ənt

nonofficial ˌnɑnə'fɪʃəl |-ly -ɪ

nonpareil ˌnɑnpə'rɛl ('nonpaˌreil 'type)

nonparticipant ˌnɑnpɚ'tɪsəpənt; ES -pɚ'tɪs-

nonparticipation ˌnɑnpɚˌtɪsə'peʃən; ES -pə-

nonpartisan, -zan nɑn'pɑrtəzņ; ES -'pɑːt-, E+-'pɑːt-

nonpaying nɑn'pe·ɪŋ |-payment -'pemənt

nonperformance ˌnɑnpɚ'fɔrməns; ES -pə-'fɔəm-

nonperiodical ˌnɑnpɪrɪ'ɑdɪkļ

nonpermanent nɑn'pɝmənənt; ES -'pɝm-, -'pɝm-

nonperpendicular ˌnɑnpɝpən'dɪkjələ,-pɚpm̩-; ES -pɚpən'dɪkjələ(r, -pɚpm̩-, -pɚ-

nonphysical nɑn'fɪzɪkļ

nonplus nɑn'plʌs, 'nɑnplʌs |-es -ɪz |-ed -t

nonpoetic ˌnɑnpo'ɛtɪk

nonpoisonous nɑn'pɔɪznəs, -znəs

nonpolitical ˌnɑnpə'lɪtɪkļ

nonproducer ˌnɑnprə'djusɚ, -'dɪu-, -'du-; ES -sə(r

nonproductive ˌnɑnprə'dʌktɪv

nonprofessional ˌnɑnprə'fɛʃənļ, -ʃnəl

nonprofit nɑn'prɑfɪt

non-Protestant nɑn'prɑtəstənt

nonreality ˌnɑnrɪ'ælətɪ

nonrecoverable ˌnɑnrɪ'kʌvrəbļ, -'kʌvərəbļ

nonrefillable ˌnɑnrɪ'fɪləbļ

nonreligious ˌnɑnrɪ'lɪdʒəs

nonresidence nɑn'rɛzədəns |-dent -dənt

nonresidential ˌnɑnrɛzə'dɛnʃəl

nonresistance ˌnɑnrɪ'zɪstəns |-tant -tənt

nonrestricted ˌnɑnrɪ'strɪktɪd

nonreturnable ˌnɑnrɪ'tɝnəbļ; ES -'tɝn-, -'tɝn-

nonrigid nɑn'rɪdʒɪd

nonrustable nɑn'rʌstəbļ

nonsectarian ˌnɑnsɛk'tɛrɪən, -'terɪən

nonsense 'nɑnsɛns

nonsensical nɑn'sɛnsɪkļ |-ally -ļɪ, -ɪklɪ

non sequitur nɑn'sɛkwɪtɚ; ES -'sɛkwɪtə(r

nonsharing nɑn'ʃɛrɪŋ, -'ʃær-; S -'ʃær-

nonskid 'nɑn'skɪd ('nonˌskid 'tread)

nonsmoker nɑn'smokɚ; ES -'smokə(r

nonstainable nɑn'stenəbļ

nonstarter nɑn'stɑrtɚ; ES -'stɑːtə(r, E+-'stɑːt-

nonstop 'nɑn'stɑp ('nonˌstop 'flight)

nonstriker nɑn'straɪkɚ; ES -'straɪkə(r

nonsuit nɑn'sut, -'sɪut, -'sjut, 'nɑnˌs- |-ed -ɪd

nonsupport ˌnɑnsə'port, -'pɔrt; ES -'poət, E+-'pɔət

nonsustaining ˌnɑnsə'stenɪŋ

nonsyllabic ˌnɑnsɪ'læbɪk

nontaxable nɑn'tæksəbļ

nontheatrical ˌnɑnθɪ'ætrɪkļ

nonthinking nɑn'θɪŋkɪŋ

nonunion nɑn'junjən ('nonˌunion 'shop)

nonvoter nɑn'votɚ; ES -'votə(r

noodle 'nudļ |-d -d |-ling 'nudlɪŋ, 'nudļɪŋ

nook nʊk |nooked nʊkt |-ery -ərɪ, -rɪ

noon nun |nooned nund |-day -ˌde |-tide -ˌtaɪd |-time -ˌtaɪm

no-one 'noˌwʌn, 'nowən

noose nus |nooses 'nusɪz |noosed nust

Nootka 'nutkə

no-par 'no'pɑr; ES -'pɑː(r, E+-'pɑː(r; ('noˌpar 'stock)

nor *usual form* nɚ; ES nə(r; *stressed* 'nɔr, ˌnɔr; ES 'nɔə(r, ˌnɔə(r

Nora, -h 'norə, 'nɔrə; S 'nɔrə

Nordic 'nɔrdɪk; ES 'nɔədɪk; |-icism -dəˌsɪzəm

Nordica 'nɔrdɪkə; ES 'nɔədɪkə

Norfolk 'nɔrfək; ES 'nɔəfək; *Mass loc.* 'nɔrfək, 'nɔəfək

norm nɔrm; ES nɔəm

Norma 'nɔrmə; ES 'nɔəmə

normal, N- 'nɔrmļ; ES 'nɔəmļ; |-ly -ɪ |-cy -sɪ

Key: *See in full* §§3–47. bee **bi** |pity 'pɪtɪ (§6) |rate ret |yet jɛt |sang sæŋ |angry 'æŋ·grɪ |bath bæθ; E bɑθ (§10) |ah ɑ |far fɑr |watch wɑtʃ, wɒtʃ (§12) |jaw dʒɔ |gorge gɔrdʒ |go go

normality nɔrˈmælətɪ; ES nɔˈmælətɪ

normalization ˌnɔrmlə'zeʃən, -aɪˈz-; ES ˌnɔɔm-

normalize 'nɔrmlˌaɪz; ES 'nɔɔm-; |-s -ɪz |-d -d

Norman 'nɔrmən; ES 'nɔɔmən; |-dy -dɪ

Norn nɔrn; ES nɔɔn

Norridgewock 'nɔrɪdʒˌwɑk, 'nɑr-, 'nɒr-, -ˌwɒk

Norris 'nɔrɪs, 'nɑr-, 'nɒr- |-'s -ɪz

Norse nɔrs; ES nɔɔs; |-man -mən |-men -mən

north, N- nɔrθ; ES nɔɔθ; |-ed -t

Northallerton nɔrθˈælətən; ES nɔθˈælətən

Northampton nɔrθˈhæmptən, nɔrˈθæm-; ES nɔɔ-; |-shire -ˌʃɪr, -ʃɚ; ES -ˌʃɪə(r, -ʃə(r

Northanger 'nɔrθəndʒɚ, nɔrˈθæŋgɚ; ES -ɔɔ-, -ə(r

Northants *short for* Northamptonshire nɔrθ-'hænts, nɔrˈθænts; ES nɔɔ-

North Carolina ˌnɔrθkærə'laɪnə, -kɚˈlaɪnə, -kə'laɪnə; ES ˌnɔɔθkærə-, -kə-; *loc.*+ -'la:nə, -kææ'la:nə—*In* ˌnɔrθkə'laɪnə kɚ *becomes* kə *by dissimilation (§121).*

Northcliffe 'nɔrθklɪf; ES 'nɔɔθ-; |-cote -kət, -kot

North Dakota ˌnɔrθdə'kotə, -dɪ-; ES ˌnɔɔθ-

northeast, N- ˌnɔrθ'ist; ES ˌnɔɔθ-; ('north-ˌeast 'wind)—*naut.*+nɔr'ist |-er -ɚ; ES -ə(r; |-ern -ɚn; ES -ən

northeastward ˌnɔrθ'istwɚd; ES ˌnɔɔθ'istwəd; |-s -z

norther 'nɔrðɚ; ES 'nɔɔðə(r; |-n -n |-ly -lɪ |-most -ˌmost

northerner, N- 'nɔrðɚnɚ, 'nɔrðənɚ; ES 'nɔɔðənə(r;—*In* 'nɔrðənɚ ə *results from* ɚ *by dissimilation (§121); this is less freq. in* northern 'nɔrðən.

northernmost 'nɔrðɚnˌmost, -məst; ES 'nɔɔðən-

Northfield 'nɔrθˌfild; ES 'nɔɔθ-

northing 'nɔrθɪŋ, -ðɪŋ; ES 'nɔɔ-

northland, N- 'nɔrθlənd, -ˌlænd

Northman 'nɔrθmən; ES 'nɔɔθ-; |-men -mən

Northop *see* Northrup

Northport 'nɔrθˌport, -ˌpɔrt; ES 'nɔɔθˌpoət, E+-ˌpɔət

Northrup, -rop 'nɔrθrəp, -θəp; ES 'nɔɔθ-; *The pron.* 'nɔrθəp *is due to r-dissimilation (§121).*

Northumberland nɔrθ'ʌmbələnd; ES nɔθ-'ʌmbələnd

Northumbria nɔrθ'ʌmbrɪə; ES nɔθ'ʌm-; |-n -n

Northup *see* Northrup

northward 'nɔrθwɚd; ES 'nɔɔθwəd; |-s -z

northwest, N- ˌnɔrθ'wɛst; ES ˌnɔɔθ-; *naut.*+ nɔr'w-; ES nɔɔ'w-; |-er -ɚ; ES -ə(r |-ern -ɚn; ES -ən

Norton 'nɔrtn̩; ES 'nɔɔtn̩

Norumbega ˌnɔrəm'bigə, ˌnɑr-, ˌnɒr-

Norwalk 'nɔrwɔk; ES 'nɔɔwɔk

Norway 'nɔrwe; ES 'nɔɔwe

Norwegian nɔr'widʒən; ES nɔɔ-

Norwich *US* 'nɔrwɪtʃ; ES 'nɔɔ-; *Engd* 'nɔrɪdʒ, 'nɑr-, 'nɒr- |-'s -ɪz

nose noz |noses 'nozɪz |nosed nozd |-sy -ɪ

noseband 'nozˌbænd |-ed -ɪd

nosebleed 'nozˌblid

nose-dive 'nozˌdaɪv |-dived -ˌdaɪvd

nosegay 'nozˌge

nosepiece 'nozˌpis |-s -ɪz

nosology no'sɑlədʒɪ; ES+-'sɒl-; |-gist -dʒɪst

nostalgia nɑ'stældʒɪə, nɒ-, -dʒə |-gic -dʒɪk

nostril 'nɑstrəl, 'nɒs-, 'nɔs-, -trɪl

nostrum 'nɑstrəm, 'nɒs-, 'nɔs-

not *stressed* 'nɑt, ˌnɑt; ES+-ɒt; *unstressed, rarely* -nət *in* cannot |-n't *enclitic* -nt, -n̩t, -t, -n̩—*see* aren't, doesn't, can't, *etc.*

nota bene 'notə'binɪ

notability ˌnotə'bɪlətɪ

notable 'notəbl̩ |-bly -blɪ

notarial no'tɛrɪəl, -'tær-, -'ter- |-ly -ɪ

notary 'notərɪ |-ied -d

notation no'teʃən

notch nɑtʃ; ES+nɒtʃ; |-es -ɪz |-ed -t

note not |noted 'notɪd |-book -ˌbʊk; |*N Engd*+ nɔt (§46)

noteworthy 'notˌwɝˌðɪ; ES -ˌwɝðɪ, -ˌwɝdɪ

nothing 'nʌθɪŋ

notice 'notɪs |-s -ɪz |-d -t

noticeable 'notɪsəbl̩ |-bly -blɪ

notification ˌnotəfə'keʃən

notify 'notəˌfaɪ |-fied -ˌfaɪd

notion 'noʃən |-ed -d |-al -l̩ |-ally -lɪ

notochord 'notəˌkɔrd; ES -ˌkɔəd

notoriety ˌnotə'raɪətɪ

notorious no'torɪəs, -'tɔr-; S -'tor-

Notre Dame *US* ˌnotɚ'dem; ES ˌnotə'dem; *Paris* ˌnotrə'dam (*Fr* nɔtrə'dam)

Nottaway 'nɑtəˌwe; ES+-'nɒt-

|full fʊl |tooth tuθ |further 'fɝðɚ; ES 'fɝðə |custom 'kʌstəm |while hwaɪl |how haʊ |toy tɔɪ
|using 'juzɪŋ |fuse fjuz, fɪuz |dish dɪʃ |vision 'vɪʒən |Eden 'idn̩ |cradle 'kredl̩ |keep 'em 'kipm̩

Nottingham *US* 'nɑtɪŋˌhæm, *Engd* 'nɑtɪŋəm; ES+'nɒt-; |-shire -ˌʃɪr, -ʃɚ; ES -ˌʃɪə(r, -ʃə(r

Notts *short for* Nottinghamshire nɑts; ES+ nɒts

notwithstanding ˌnɑtwɪθ'stændɪŋ, -wɪð-; ES+ˌnɒt-

nougat 'nugət, 'nugɑ

nought nɔt

noun naʊn |-al -ḷ |-ally -ḷɪ

nourish 'nɝɪʃ; ES 'nɜɪʃ, 'nʌr-, 'nɜ˞-; |-es -ɪz |-ed -t

nous nus, naʊs

nouveau riche *Fr* nuvo'riʃ

nova 'novə |novas 'novəz |novae 'novi

Nova Scotia 'novə'skoʃə |-n -n

Nova Zembla 'novə'zɛmblə

novel 'navḷ |novelly 'navḷɪ, 'navlɪ; ES+'nɒv-; |-ist -ɪst

novelette ˌnavḷ'ɛt; ES+ˌnɒv-

novelize 'navḷˌaɪz; ES+'nɒv-; |-s -ɪz |-d -d

novelty 'navḷtɪ; ES+'nɒv-

November no'vɛmbɚ; ES no'vɛmbə(r

novena no'vinə |-s -z |-nae -ni

Novgorod 'nɑvgəˌrad; ES+'nɒvgəˌrɒd

Novial 'novɪəl, ˌnovɪ'ɑl

novice 'navɪs; ES+'nɒv-; |-s -ɪz

novitiate, novici- no'vɪʃɪɪt, -ˌet

Novocain, -e 'novəˌken

now naʊ |-adays 'naʊəˌdez, 'naʊˌdez

noway 'noˌwe |-ways -ˌwez

nowhere 'noˌhwɛr, -ˌhwær; E -ˌhwɛə(r, ES -ˌhwæə(r

nowhither 'noˌhwɪðɚ; ES -ˌhwɪðə(r

nowise 'noˌwaɪz

noxious 'nakʃəs; ES+'nɒk-

Noyes nɔɪz |-'s -ɪz

nozzle 'nazḷ; ES+'nɒzḷ; |-d -d |-ling -zlɪŋ, -zḷɪŋ

-n't *abbrev. spelling of unstressed* not *after auxiliaries* -nt, -ṇt, -ṇ, -t, *as in* don't, doesn't, can't; *see these and similar combinations in the vocab.*

nth ɛnθ

n-tuple 'ɛntʊpḷ, -tjʊpḷ, ɛn'tupḷ, -'tɪu-, -'tju- |-d -d |-ling -plɪŋ, -pḷɪŋ

nu *Gk letter* nu, nju, nɪu

nuance nju'ɑns, nɪu-, nu-, 'njuɑns, 'nɪu-, 'nu- |-s -ɪz |-d -t (*Fr* nɥã:s)

nub nʌb |nubbed nʌbd |nubbin 'nʌbɪn

nubble 'nʌbḷ |-d -d |-bly -blɪ

Nubia 'njubɪə, 'nɪu-, 'nu- |-n -n

nubile 'njubḷ, 'nɪu-, 'nu-, -bɪl

nuclear 'njuklɪɚ, 'nɪu-, 'nu-; ES -klɪ·ə(r

nucleate *adj* 'njuklɪɪt, 'nɪu-, 'nu-, -ˌet

nucleate *v* 'njuklɪˌet, 'nɪu-, 'nu- |-d -ɪd

nuclei 'njuklɪˌaɪ, 'nɪu-, 'nu-

nucleic nju'kliɪk, nɪu-, nu-

nuclein 'njuklɪɪn, 'nɪu-, 'nu-

nucleolar nju'kliələ, nɪu-, nu-; ES -lə(r

nucleolate *adj* nju'kliəlɪt, nɪu-, nu-, -ˌlet |-d -ˌletɪd

nucleolus nju'kliələs, nɪu-, nu- |-es -ɪz |-li -ˌlaɪ

nucleus 'njuklɪəs, 'nɪu-, 'nu- |-es -ɪz |-lei -lɪˌaɪ

nude njud, nɪud, nud |-d -ɪd |-ism -ɪzəm |-ist -ɪst

nudge nʌdʒ |nudges 'nʌdʒɪz |nudged nʌdʒd

nudity 'njudətɪ, 'nɪu-, 'nu-

nugatory 'njugəˌtorɪ, 'nɪu-, 'nu-, -ˌtɔrɪ; S -ˌtorɪ

nugget 'nʌgɪt

nuisance 'njusṇs, 'nɪu-, 'nu- |-s -ɪz

null nʌl |nulled nʌld

null and void 'nʌlən'vɔɪd

nullification ˌnʌləfə'keʃən

nullify 'nʌləˌfaɪ |-fied -ˌfaɪd

nullity 'nʌlətɪ

numb nʌm |numbed nʌmd

number '*more numb*' 'nʌmɚ; ES 'nʌmə(r

number '*count*' 'nʌmbɚ; ES 'nʌmbə(r; |-ed -d |-ing 'nʌmbrɪŋ, 'nʌmbərɪŋ

numbest 'nʌmɪst

numbles 'nʌmbḷz

numbly 'nʌmlɪ

numbskull 'nʌmˌskʌl |-ed -d |-edness -ɪdnɪs |-ery -ərɪ |-ism -skʌlˌɪzəm

numerable 'njumərəbḷ, 'nɪu-, 'nu-, -mrə- |-bly -blɪ

numeral 'njumrəl, 'nɪu-, 'nu-, -mərəl |-ly -ɪ

numerate *adj* 'njumərɪt, 'nɪu-, 'nu-, -ˌret

numerate *v* 'njuməˌret, 'nɪu-, 'nu- |-d -ɪd |-tor -ɚ; ES -ə(r

numeration ˌnjumə'reʃən, ˌnɪu-, ˌnu-

numerical nju'mɛrɪkḷ, nɪu-, nu- |-ly -ɪ, -ɪklɪ

numerology ˌnjumə'ralədʒɪ, ˌnɪu-, ˌnu-; ES+-'ɒl-

Those words below in which the ɑ *sound is spelt* o *are often pronounced with* ɒ *in E and S*

numerous ˈnjumrəs, ˈnɪu-, ˈnu-, -mərəs

Numidia njuˈmɪdɪə, nɪu-, nu- |-n -n

numismatic ˌnjumɪzˈmætɪk, ˌnɪu-, ˌnu-, -mɪs-
|-al -ļ |-ally -ļɪ, -ɪklɪ

numskull ˈnʌmˌskʌl |-ed -d |-edness -ɪdnɪs
|-ery -ərɪ |-ism -skʌlˌɪzəm

nun nʌn |nunned nʌnd

Nun *Bible* nʌn

Nunc Dimittis ˈnʌŋkdɪˈmɪtɪs |-es -ɪz

nuncheon ˈnʌntʃən

nuncio ˈnʌnʃɪˌo

nuncle ˈnʌŋkļ

nuncupative ˈnʌnkjʊˌpetɪv, nʌnˈkjupətɪv,
-ˈkɪu-

Nuneaton nʌnˈitn̩

nunnery ˈnʌnərɪ

nuptial ˈnʌpʃəl, ˈnʌptʃəl |-s -z |-ed -d

Nuremberg ˈnjʊrəmˌbɝg, ˈnɪu-, ˈnu-; ES
-ˌbɜg, -ˌbɝg; (*Ger* Nürnberg ˈnyrnbɛrk)

nurse nɝs; ES nɜs, nɝs; |-s -ɪz |-d -t

nursegirl ˈnɝsˌgɝl; ES ˈnɜsˌgɜl, ˈnɝsˌgɝl

nursemaid ˈnɝsˌmed; ES ˈnɜs-, ˈnɝs-

nursery ˈnɝsrɪ, ˈnɝsərɪ; ES ˈnɜs-, ˈnɝs-;
|-ied -d |-maid -ˌmed

nurseryman ˈnɝsrɪmən, ˈnɝsərɪ-; ES ˈnɜs-,
ˈnɝs-; |-men -mən

nursling, nursel- ˈnɝslɪŋ; ES ˈnɜs-, ˈnɝs-

nurture ˈnɝtʃɚ; ES ˈnɜtʃə(r, ˈnɝtʃə(r; |-d -d

nut nʌt |nutted ˈnʌtɪd

nutant ˈnjutn̩t, ˈnɪu-, ˈnu-

nutation njuˈteʃən, nɪu-, nu-

nutcracker ˈnʌtˌkrækɚ; ES -ˌkrækə(r

Nuthall, Nuttall ˈnʌtɔl, *Engd* ˈnʌtļ

nuthatch ˈnʌtˌhætʃ |-es -ɪz

Nutley ˈnʌtlɪ

nutmeg ˈnʌtmɛg |-ged -d |-gy -ɪ

nutrient ˈnjutrɪənt, ˈnɪu-, ˈnu-

nutriment ˈnjutrəmənt, ˈnɪu-, ˈnu-

nutrition njuˈtrɪʃən, nɪu-, nu- |-tious -ʃəs

nutritive ˈnjutrɪtɪv, ˈnɪu-, ˈnu-

nutshell ˈnʌtˌʃɛl |-ed -d

Nuttall ˈnʌtɔl, *Engd* ˈnʌtļ

nutty ˈnʌtɪ

nux vomica ˈnʌksˈvɑmɪkə

nuzzle ˈnʌzļ |-d -d |-ling ˈnʌzlɪŋ, ˈnʌzļɪŋ

Nyack ˈnaɪæk

Nyanza naɪˈænzə, nɪ-

Nyasa naɪˈæsə, nɪ- |-land -ˌlænd

Nye naɪ

nylon ˈnaɪlɑn, -ɒn

Nym nɪm

nymph nɪmf, nɪmpf |-al -ļ |-ic -ɪk |-ical -ɪkļ

O

O, o *letter* o |*pl* O's, Os, *poss* O's oz

O *intj* o

o' *prep unstressed form of* on ə (o' nights
əˈnaɪts) *or of* of (o'clock əˈklɑk)

oaf of |-'s -s |oafs ofs *or* oaves ovz

Oahu oˈɑhu

oak ok |oaken ˈokən

Oakes oks |-'s -ɪz

Oakland ˈoklənd

oakum ˈokəm

oar or, ɔr; ES oə(r, E+ɔə(r; |-ed -d |-lock
-ˌlɑk

oarsman ˈorzmən, ˈɔrz-; ES ˈoəz-, E+ˈɔəz-;
|-men -mən

oasis oˈesɪs, ˈoəsɪs |oases -siz

oast ost |-house -ˌhaʊs |-houses -ˌhaʊzɪz

oat ot |oaten ˈotn̩ |-cake -ˌkek |-meal -ˌmil

oath oθ |oath's oθs |oaths oðz

Oaxaca wɑˈhɑkɑ (*Am Sp* waˈhaka)

Obadiah ˌobəˈdaɪə

Oban ˈobən

obbligato ˌɑblɪˈgato

obduracy ˈɑbdjərəsɪ, -djʊ-

obdurate ˈɑbdjərɪt, -djʊ-, -də-

obeah, O- ˈobɪə |obeahed ˈobɪəd

Obed ˈobɪd, ˈobɛd

obedience əˈbidɪəns |-cy -ɪ |-ent -ənt

obeisance oˈbesn̩s, -ˈbɪsn̩s |-sant -sn̩t

obelisk ˈɑbļˌɪsk

obelus ˈɑbļəs |-es -ɪz |-li ˈɑbļˌaɪ

Oberammergau ˌobɚˈæməˌgaʊ, -ˈɑmə-; ES
-məˌgaʊ

Oberon ˈobəˌrɑn, ˈobərən

obese oˈbis |-sity oˈbisətɪ, oˈbɛs-

|full fʊl |tooth tuθ |further ˈfɝðɚ; ES ˈfɝðə |custom ˈkʌstəm |while hwaɪl |how haʊ |toy tɔɪ
|using ˈjuzɪŋ |fuse fjuz, fɪuz |dish dɪʃ |vision ˈvɪʒən |Eden ˈidn̩ |cradle ˈkredļ |keep 'em ˈkipm̩

Those words below in which the α sound is spelt o are often pronounced with ɒ in E and S

obey ə'be, o'be |-ed -d

obfuscate ab'fʌsket, əb-, 'abfəs,ket |-d -ɪd

obfuscation ,abfʌs'keʃən, ,abfəs-

obiter dictum 'abɪtə'dɪktəm, 'ob-; ES -tə-

obituary ə'bɪtʃu,ɛrɪ, o-

object n 'abdʒɪkt

object v əb'dʒɛkt |-jected -'dʒɛktɪd

objectify əb'dʒɛktə,faɪ |-fied -,faɪd

objection əb'dʒɛkʃən |-able -əb|, -ʃnəb| |-bly -blɪ

objective əb'dʒɛktɪv ('sub,jective & 'ob-,jective)

objectivity ,abdʒɛk'tɪvətɪ

objector əb'dʒɛktə; ES -'dʒɛktə(r

objurgate 'abdʒɚ,get, əb'dʒɝget; ES 'abdʒə-, əb'dʒɝg-, -'dʒɝg-; |-d -ɪd

oblate n, adj 'ablet, əb'let

oblate v əb'let |-lated -'letɪd

oblation əb'leʃən, ab-

oblatory 'ablə,torɪ, -,tɔrɪ; S -,torɪ

obligate 'ablə,get |-d -ɪd |-tion ,ablə'geʃən

obligato ,ablɪ'gato

obligatory ə'blɪgə,torɪ, 'ablɪgə-, -,tɔrɪ; S -,torɪ

oblige ə'blaɪdʒ |-s -ɪz |-d -d |-dly -ɪdlɪ

obligee ,ablɪ'dʒi (,obli'gee & ,obli'gor)

obligor 'ablɪ,gɔr; ES -,gɔə(r; *see above*

oblique ə'blik |obliqued ə'blikt—ə'blaɪk *is o.f. or military.*

obliquity ə'blɪkwətɪ

obliterate ə'blɪtə,ret |-rated -,retɪd

obliteration ə,blɪtə'reʃən

oblivion ə'blɪvɪən |-ous -əs

oblong 'ablɔŋ, -lɒŋ; S+-laŋ

obloquy 'abləkwɪ

obnoxious əb'nakʃəs, ab-

oboe 'obo, 'obɔɪ

obol 'ab|

obolus 'abləs |-es -ɪz |-li 'ab|,aɪ

Obrdlik *Czech scholar* 'bɚd,lik; ES 'ɔbəd-

obscene əb'sin, ab- ('ob,scene 'mind)

obsceneness əb'sinnɪs

obscenity əb'sɛnətɪ, -'sinətɪ

obscurant əb'skjurənt, -'skɪur- |-ism -,ɪzəm

obscuration ,abskju'reʃən, -skɪu-

obscure əb'skjur, -'skɪur; ES -'skjuə(r, -'skɪuə(r; |-d -d |-dly -ɪdlɪ

obscurity əb'skjurətɪ, -'skɪurətɪ

obsequious əb'sikwɪəs

obsequy 'absɪkwɪ

observable əb'zɝvəb|; ES -'zɔv-, -'zɜˑv-; |-bly -blɪ

observance ɛb'zɝvəns; ES -'zɔv-, -'zɜˑv-; |-s -ɪz |-ant -ənt |-vation ,abzɚ'veʃən; ES -zə-

observatory əb'zɝvə,torɪ, -,tɔrɪ; ES əb'zɝvə-,torɪ, -'zɜˑv-, E+-,tɔrɪ

observe əb'zɝv; ES -'zɔv, -'zɜˑv; |-d -d |-dly -ɪdlɪ

obsess əb'sɛs |-es -ɪz |-ed -t |-ion -'sɛʃən

obsidian əb'sɪdɪən

obsolescence ,absə'lɛsn̩s |-scent -sn̩t

obsolete 'absə,lit

obstacle 'abstək|, 'abstɪk|

obstetric əb'stɛtrɪk |-al -| |-ally -|ɪ, -ɪklɪ

obstetrician ,abstɛ'trɪʃən

obstinacy 'abstənəsɪ |-nate -nɪt

obstreperous əb'strɛpərəs, ab-

obstruct əb'strʌkt |-ed -ɪd |-ion -'strʌkʃən

obtain əb'ten |-ed -d |-able -əb|

obtrude əb'trud, -'trɪud |-d -ɪd

obtrusion əb'truʒən, -'trɪuʒən |-sive -sɪv

obtuse əb'tus, -'tɪus, -'tjus

obverse n 'abvɝs; ES 'abvɜs, -vɜˑs

obverse adj əb'vɝs, 'abvɝs; ES -3s, -3ˑs

obvert əb'vɝt; ES əb'vɜt, -'vɜˑt; |-ed -ɪd

obviate 'abvɪ,et |-d -ɪd |-tion ,abvɪ'eʃən

obvious 'abvɪəs

ocarina ,akə'rinə

Occam 'akəm

occasion ə'keʒən |-ed -d

occasional ə'keʒən|, -'keʒnəl |-ly -ɪ

occident 'aksədənt

occidental ,aksə'dɛnt| |-ly -ɪ |-ism -,ɪzəm

occidentalize ,aksə'dɛnt|,aɪz |-s -ɪz |-d -d

occipital ak'sɪpət| |-ly -ɪ

occiput 'aksɪ,pʌt, 'aksəpət |-pita ak'sɪpɪtə

occlude ə'klud, -'klɪud |-d -ɪd |-clusion -ʒən

occult ə'kʌlt |-ed -ɪd ('oc,cult 'science)

occultation ,akʌl'teʃən, -kəl-

occupancy 'akjəpənsɪ |-pant -pənt

occupation ,akjə'peʃən

occupy 'akjə,paɪ |-pied -,paɪd

occur ə'kɝ; ES ə'kɜ(r, ə'kɜˑ; |-red -d

occurrence ə'kɝəns; ES ə'kɜr-, ə'kʌr-, ə'kɜˑ-

ocean 'oʃən |-ic ,oʃɪ'ænɪk |Oceanica -'ænɪkə

Oceana o'siənə, ,oʃɪ'enə, *Mich* ,oʃɪ'ænə

Key: *See in full §§3–47.* bee bi |pity 'pɪtɪ (§6) |rate ret |yet jɛt |sang sæŋ |angry 'æŋ·grɪ |bath bæθ; E baθ (§10) |ah ɑ |far fɑr |watch watʃ, wɒtʃ (§12) |jaw dʒɔ |gorge gɔrdʒ |go go

Those words below in which the ɑ *sound is spelt* o *are often pronounced with* ɒ *in E and S*

Oceania ˌoʃɪˈænɪə, -ˈɑn-, -ˈen-
Oceanid oˈsɪənɪd |Oceano ˌoʃɪˈæno
oceanography ˌoʃɪənˈɑgrəfɪ, ˌoʃən-, -ˈɒg-
Oceanus oˈsɪənəs |-ˈs -ɪz
ocelot ˈosəˌlat, ˈɑsə-, -lət
ocher, ochre ˈokɚ; ES ˈokə(r; |-(e)d -d |-ing
　ˈokərɪŋ, ˈokrɪŋ
ochroid ˈokrɔɪd
Ockham ˈɑkəm
o'clock əˈklɑk
Ocmulgee okˈmʌlgɪ—*traditional & loc. pron.*
octachord ˈɑktəˌkɔrd; ES -ˌkɔəd
octad ˈɑktæd
octagon ˈɑktəˌgɑn, -gən
octagonal ɑkˈtægənl̩ |-ly -ɪ
octahedral ˌɑktəˈhidrəl
octameter ɑkˈtæmətɚ; ES -ˈtæmətə(r
octane ˈɑkten
octangle ˈɑktæŋgl̩ |-gular ɑkˈtæŋgjələ; ES
　-ə(r
octaroon ˌɑktəˈrun
octave ˈɑktev, ˈɑktɪv
Octavia ɑkˈtevɪə |-vius -s |-vius's -sɪz
octavo ɑkˈtevo
octennial ɑkˈtɛnɪəl |-ly -ɪ
octet, -tte ɑkˈtɛt (ˈocˌtet & ˈsesˌtet)
October ɑkˈtobɚ; ES -ˈtobə(r
octodecimo ˌɑktoˈdɛsəˌmo
octogenarian ˌɑktədʒəˈnɛrɪən, -ˈner-
octogenary ɑkˈtɑdʒəˌnɛrɪ
octopus ˈɑktəpəs |-es -ɪz |-pi -ˌpaɪ
octoroon ˌɑktəˈrun
octosyllable ˈɑktəˌsɪləbl̩ |-bic ˌɑktəsɪˈlæbɪk
octroi ˈɑktrɔɪ (*Fr* ɔkˈtrwɑ)
octuple *n, adj, v* ˈɑktʊpl̩, -tjʊpl̩, ɑkˈtupl̩,
　-ˈtɪu-, -ˈtju- |-d -d |-ling -plɪŋ, -pl̩ɪŋ
.ocular ˈɑkjələ; ES ˈɑkjələ(r; |-list -lɪst
Od, 'Od, Odd *intj* ɑd, ɒd |-ˈs -z
odalisque, -sk ˈodl̩ɪsk
odd ɑd, ɒd |-s -z |-ity -ətɪ |-ment -mənt
Oddfellow, Odd Fellow ˈɑdˌfɛlo, ˈɒd-, -ə
ode od
Oder ˈodɚ; ES ˈodə(r
Odessa oˈdɛsə
Odin ˈodɪn
odious ˈodɪəs |odium ˈodɪəm
Odoacer ˌodoˈesɚ; ES -ˈesə(r
odometer oˈdɑmətɚ; ES oˈdɑmətə(r

odontology ˌodɑnˈtɑlədʒɪ, ˌɑd-
odor ˈodɚ; ES ˈodə(r; |-ous -əs
odoriferous ˌodəˈrɪfərəs, -frəs
'Od's bodikins, odsb- ˈɑdzˈbɑdɪkɪnz
Odysseus oˈdɪsjus, oˈdɪsɪəs |-eus' -jus, -ɪəs
Odyssey ˈɑdəsɪ
oecumenic ˌɛkjuˈmɛnɪk |-al -l̩ |-ally -l̩ɪ, -ɪklɪ
oedema iˈdimə |*pl* -mata -mətə |-tous -təs
Oedipus ˈɛdəpəs |-ˈs -ɪz
Oeneus ˈinjus |-ˈs -ɪz
Oenone iˈnonɪ
o'er or, ɔr; ES oə(r, E+ɔə(r
oersted ˈɝstɛd; ES ˈɜstɛd, ˈɝs-
oesophagus iˈsɑfəgəs |-es -ɪz |-gi -ˌdʒaɪ
oestrous ˈɛstrəs, ˈis-
oestrum ˈɛstrəm, ˈis-
oestrus ˈɛstrəs, ˈis- |-es -ɪz
of *stressed* ˈɑv, ˌɑv, ˈɒv, ˌɒv, ˈʌv, ˌʌv; *unstr.*
　əv, *before conss.*+ə (ðə ˈlɑd ə ˈkɔl), *or after*
　vowels + v (ðɪ aɪˈdɪə v ˌðæt)
off ɔf, ɒf
offal ˈɔfl̩, ˈɒfl̩, ˈɑfl̩
off and on ˈɔfənˈɑn, ˈɒf-, -ˈɒn, -ˈɔn
offcast ˈɔfˈkæst, ˈɒf-; E+-ˈkast, -ˈkɑst; (ˈoff-
　ˌcast ˈclothes)
off-color ˈɔfˈkʌlɚ, ˈɒf-; ES -ˈkʌlə(r; (ˈoff-
　ˌcolor ˈstory)
Offenbach ˈɔfənˌbɑk, ˈɒf-, -ɑf- (*Ger* ˈɔfənˌbɑx)
offend əˈfɛnd |offended əˈfɛndɪd
offense, -ce əˈfɛns |-s -ɪz (ˈɔˌfɛnsn̩ˈdiˌfɛns)
offensive əˈfɛnsɪv
offer ˈɔfɚ, ˈɒfɚ, ˈɑfɚ; ES -fə(r; |-ed -d |-ing
　-fərɪŋ, -frɪŋ
offertory ˈɔfɚˌtorɪ, ˈɒf-, ˈɑf-, -ˌtɔrɪ; ES
　-fəˌtorɪ, E+-ˌtɔrɪ
offhand ˈɔfˈhænd, ˈɒf-; E+- (ˈoffˌhand ˈway)
office ˈɔfɪs, ˈɒfɪs, ˈɑfɪs |-s -ɪz |-d -t
officeholder ˈɔfɪsˌholdɚ, ˈɒf-, ˈɑf-; ES -ə(r
officer ˈɔfəsɚ, ˈɒf-, ˈɑf-; ES -fəsə(r
official əˈfɪʃəl |-ly -ɪ |-dom -dəm
officiant əˈfɪʃɪənt
officiary əˈfɪʃɪˌɛrɪ
officiate əˈfɪʃɪˌet |-ated -ˌetɪd
officinal əˈfɪsɪnl̩
officious əˈfɪʃəs
offing ˈɔfɪŋ, ˈɒfɪŋ
offish ˈɔfɪʃ, ˈɒfɪʃ
offprint ˈɔfˌprɪnt, ˈɒf- |-ed -ɪd

|full fʊl |tooth tuθ |further ˈfɝðɚ; ES ˈfɜðə |custom ˈkʌstəm |while hwaɪl |how haʊ |toy tɔɪ
|using ˈjuzɪŋ |fuse fjuz, fɪuz |dish dɪʃ |vision ˈvɪʒən |Eden ˈidn̩ |cradle ˈkredl̩ |keep 'em ˈkipm̩

offscouring 'ɔf,skaʊrɪŋ, 'ɒf-
offset *n* 'ɔf,sɛt, 'ɒf-
offset *v* ɔf'sɛt, ɒf- |-setting -'sɛtɪŋ
offshoot 'ɔf,ʃut, 'ɒf-
offshore 'ɔf'ʃor, 'ɒf-, -'ʃɔr; ES -'ʃoə(r, E+
 -'ʃɔə(r
offspring 'ɔf,sprɪŋ, 'ɒf-
oft ɔft, ɒft |-times -,taɪmz
often 'ɔfən, 'ɒftən, 'ɒf- |-times -,taɪmz
oftener 'ɔfənɚ, 'ɒf-, -fnɚ, -tənɚ, -tnɚ; ES
 -nə(r; |-nest -nɪst
Og ɑg, ɒg, ɔg
Ogden 'ɑgdən, 'ɒgdən, 'ɔgdən
ogee o'dʒi, 'odʒi |-d -d
Ogilby 'ogḷbɪ |Ogilvy, -ie 'ogḷvɪ
ogive 'odʒaɪv, o'dʒaɪv |-d -d
ogle 'ogḷ |ogled 'ogḷd |-ling 'oglɪŋ, 'ogḷɪŋ
Ogleby 'ogḷbɪ |Oglethorpe -,θɔrp; ES -,θɔəp
Ogpu 'ɑgpu, 'ɒgpu, 'ɔgpu
ogre 'ogɚ; ES 'ogə(r; |-ish, -grish -gərɪʃ, -grɪʃ
oh o |oh's, ohs oz |ohed od |ohing 'o·ɪŋ
O'Hara o'hærə, o'hɑrə
Ohio o'haɪo |Ohioan o'haɪəwən—*see* -ow
ohm, O- om |-age -ɪdʒ |-ages -ɪdʒɪz
oho *intj* o'ho
oil ɔɪl |oiled ɔɪld |oily 'ɔɪlɪ |-less 'ɔɪllɪs
oilcloth 'ɔɪl,klɒθ, -,klɒθ |-ths -ðz, -θs—*see*
 cloth
oilproof 'ɔɪl'pruf |-ed -t ('oil,proof 'paint)
oilskin 'ɔɪl,skɪn
oilstone 'ɔɪl,ston
ointment 'ɔɪntmənt
Oireachtas 'ɛrəxtəs |-'s -ɪz
Ojibway, -wa o'dʒɪbwe
O.K., OK 'o'ke |-'s -'kez |-'d -'ked|-'ing
 -'ke·ɪŋ
okapi o'kɑpɪ
Okeechobee ,okɪ'tʃobɪ, -bi
Oklahoma ,oklə'homə |-n -n
okra 'okrə
Olaf 'oləf, 'olaf
old old |olden 'oldn̩ |oldened 'oldn̩d
Oldcastle 'old,kæsḷ; E+-,kɑsḷ, -,kɑsḷ
old-fashioned 'old'fæʃənd, 'ol'f- ('old-,fash-
 ioned 'girl)
old-fogyish, -gey- 'old'fogɪʃ, 'ol'f-
Oldham 'oldəm
old-maidish 'old'medɪʃ, 'ol'm- ('old-,maidish
 'air)

oldster 'oldstɚ, 'ols-; ES -stə(r
oldwife 'old,waɪf |-'s -,waɪfs |-wives -,waɪvz
old-womanish 'old'wʊmənɪʃ, -'wʊm-
old-world 'old'wɝld; ES -'wɝld, -'wɝld
oleaginous ,olɪ'ædʒənəs
oleander ,olɪ'ændɚ; ES -də(r; ('ole,ander
 'leaf)
oleaster ,olɪ'æstɚ; ES -'æstə(r
oleate 'olɪ,et, 'olɪt
olefin 'oləfɪn |-fine -fɪn, -,fin
oleic o'liɪk, 'olɪk |olein 'olɪɪn |oleo 'olɪ,o
oleomargarine, -in ,olɪə'mɑrdʒə,rin, -rɪn,
 much less freq. -'mɑrg-; ES -'mɑ:-, E+
 -'ma:-
oleoresin ,olɪo'rɛzn̩, -'rɛzɪn
olfactory al'fæktərɪ, -'fæktrɪ; ES+ɒl-
Olga 'ɑlgə, 'ɒlgə
olibanum o'lɪbənəm
oligarch 'ɑlɪ,gɑrk; ES 'ɑlɪ,gɑ:k, 'ɒlɪ-; |-y -ɪ
oligarchic ,ɑlɪ'gɑrkɪk; ES -'gɑ:k-, ,ɒl-
Oligocene 'ɑlɪgo,sin; ES+'ɒl-
olio 'olɪ,o
olivary 'ɑlə,vɛrɪ; ES+'ɒl-
olive, O- 'ɑlɪv; ES+'ɒlɪv
Oliver 'ɑləvɚ; ES 'ɑləvə(r, 'ɒl-
Olivet 'ɑlə,vɛt, 'ɑləvɪt; ES+'ɒl-
Olivia o'lɪvɪə, o'lɪvjə
olla *L word* 'ɑlə; ES+'ɒlə; |ollae -li
olla 'ɑlə; ES+'ɒlə; |*pl* ollas -ləz (*Sp* 'oʎa,
 'oʎas)
olla-podrida 'ɑləpə'dridə; ES+'ɒl-; (*Sp*
 'oʎapo'ðriða)
Olmsted 'ɑmstɛd, 'ɒm-, 'ʌm-, -stɪd
Olney *US* 'ɑlnɪ, 'ɒlnɪ, *Engd* 'olnɪ, *loc.* 'onɪ
ology 'ɑlədʒɪ; ES+'ɒl-
Olympia o'lɪmpɪə, -pjə |-n -n |-piad -pɪ,æd
Olympic o'lɪmpɪk |-pus -pəs |-pus's -pəsɪz
Omaha 'omə,hɔ, 'omə,hɑ
Omar 'omɚ, 'omɑr; ES 'omə(r, 'omɑ:(r
omber, -bre 'ɑmbɚ; ES 'ɑmbə(r, 'ɒm-
omega, O- o'mɛgə, o'migə, 'omɪgə
omelet, -tte 'ɑmlɪt, 'ɑməlɪt; ES+'ɒm-
omen 'omɪn, 'omən
omer, O- 'omɚ; ES 'omə(r
omicron 'ɑmɪ,krɑn, 'o-; ES+'ɒmɪ,krɒn
ominous 'ɑmənəs; ES+'ɒm-
omissible o'mɪsəbḷ |-bly -blɪ
omission o'mɪʃən ('o,mission and 'com-
 ,mission)

Key: *See in full §§3–47.* bee bi |pity 'pɪtɪ (§6) |rate ret |yet jɛt |sang sæŋ |angry 'æŋ·grɪ
|bath bæθ; E baθ (§10) |ah ɑ |far fɑr |watch wɑtʃ, wɒtʃ (§12) |jaw dʒɔ |gorge gɔrdʒ |go go

omissive o'mɪsɪv

omit o'mɪt, ə'mɪt |omitted -'mɪtɪd

omnibus 'ɑmnə,bʌs, 'ɑmnəbəs; ES+'ɒm-; |-es -ɪz

omnifarious ,ɑmnə'fɛrɪəs, -'fær-, -'fer-; ES+,ɒm-

omnific ɑm'nɪfɪk; ES+ɒm-

omnipotence ɑm'nɪpətəns; ES+ɒm-; |-ent -ənt

omnipresence ,ɑmnɪ'prɛzn̦s; ES+,ɒm-; |-nt -n̦t

omniscience ɑm'nɪʃəns; ES+ɒm-; |-ent -ənt

omnium gatherum 'ɑmnɪəm'gæðərəm; ES+'ɒm-

omnivorous ɑm'nɪvərəs, -'nɪvrəs; ES+ɒm-

on ɑn, ɒn, ɔn—ɒn is commonest in S and W.

onager 'ɑnədʒɚ; ES 'ɑnədʒə(r, 'ɒn-; |pl -s -z |-gri -,ɡraɪ

onanism 'onən,ɪzəm |-ist -ɪst

once wʌns

oncoming 'ɑn,kʌmɪŋ, 'ɒn-, 'ɔn-

ondometer ɑn'dɑmətɚ; ES ɑn'dɑmətə(r, ɒn'dɒm-

one stressed 'wʌn, ,wʌn; unstr. wən |-s -z

one-horse 'wʌn'hɔrs; ES 'wʌn'hɔəs; ('one-,horse 'shay)

Oneida o'naɪdə, Ky o'nidə

O'Neill o'nil

one-legged 'wʌn'lɛɡɪd, -ɡd ('one-,legged 'man)

oneness 'wʌnnɪs

Oneonta NY ,onɪ'ɑntə; ES+-'ɒntə

onerous 'ɑnərəs; ES+'ɒn-

oneself wʌn'sɛlf, wʌnz'sɛlf, wən-

one-sided 'wʌn'saɪdɪd ('one-,sided 'view)

one-step 'wʌn,stɛp |one-stepped 'wʌn,stɛpt

one-way 'wʌn'we ('one-,way 'traffic)

onion 'ʌnjən, 'ʌnjɪn

Onions 'ʌnjənz |-'s -ɪz

onionskin 'ʌnjən,skɪn, 'ʌnjɪn-

onlooker 'ɑn,lʊkɚ, 'ɒn-, 'ɔn-; ES -,lʊkə(r

only 'onlɪ; NEngd+'ɔnlɪ (§46)

onomatapoeia ,ɑnə,mætə'pɪə, o,nɑmətə-; ES+,ɒn-, o,nɒm-; |-poeic -'piɪk

onomatapoetic ,ɑnə,mætəpo'ɛtɪk; ES+,ɒn-

Onondaga ,ɑnən'dɔɡə, -'dɑɡə; ES+,ɒn-

onrush 'ɑn,rʌʃ, 'ɒn-, 'ɔn- |-es -ɪz

onset 'ɑn,sɛt, 'ɒn-, 'ɔn-

onslaught 'ɑn,slɔt, 'ɒn-, 'ɔn-

Ontarian ɑn'tɛrɪən, -'ter-; ES+ɒn- |-io -ɪ,o

onto bef. pause 'ɑntu, 'ɒn-, 'ɔn-; bef. conss. -tə; bef. vow. -tʊ, -tə

ontogeny ɑn'tɑdʒənɪ; ES+ɒn'tɒdʒ-; |-ist -ɪst

ontology ɑn'tɑlədʒɪ; ES+ɒn'tɒl-

onus 'onəs |onuses 'onəsɪz

onward 'ɑnwɚd, 'ɒn-, 'ɔn-; ES -wəd; |-s -z

onyx 'ɑnɪks, 'onɪks; ES+'ɒn-; |-es -ɪz

oögenesis ,oə'dʒɛnəsɪs

oölite 'oə,laɪt |oölitic ,oə'lɪtɪk

oölogy o'ɑlədʒɪ; ES+-'ɒl-; |-gist -dʒɪst

oolong, O- 'ulɔŋ, 'ulɒŋ, 'ulɑŋ

oomiak 'umɪ,æk

oösperm 'oə,spɝm; ES 'oə,spɜm, -,spɝm

oösphere 'oə,sfɪr; ES 'oə,sfɪə(r, S+-,sfɛə(r

oöspore 'oə,spor, -,spɔr; ES 'oə,spoə(r, E+-,spɔə(r

ooze uz |oozes 'uzɪz |oozed uzd |oozy 'uzɪ

opacity o'pæsətɪ

opal 'opl̦ |opaline n 'opl̦,in

opalescence ,opl̦'ɛsn̦s |opalescent ,opl̦'ɛsn̦t

opaline adj 'opl̦ɪn, 'opl̦,aɪn

opaque o'pek, ə'pek

ope op |oped opt

open 'opən, 'opm̦ |-ed -d |-ing 'opənɪŋ, 'opn̦ɪŋ; NEngd+'ɔp- (§46)

open-air 'opən'ɛr, -'ær; E -'ɛə(r, ES -'æə(r

open-eyed 'opən'aɪd |-eyedly -'aɪdlɪ, -'aɪdlɪ

openhanded 'opən'hændɪd ('open,handed 'giver)

openhearted 'opən'hɑrtɪd; ES -'hɑːtɪd, E+'hɑːtɪd

open-hearth 'opən'hɑrθ; ES -'hɑːθ, E+-'hɑːθ

open-minded 'opən'maɪndɪd ('open-,minded 'man)

openmouthed 'opən'maʊðd, -θt

openness 'opənnɪs

openwork 'opən,wɝk; ES 'opən,wɜk, -,wɝk

opera 'ɑpərə, 'ɑprə; ES+'ɒp-

operable 'ɑpərəbl̦, 'ɑprə-; ES+'ɒp-; |-bly -blɪ

opéra bouffe 'ɑpərə'buf, 'ɑprə-; ES+'ɒp-; (Fr ɔpera'buf)

opéra comique Fr ɔpera-kɔ'mik

operate 'ɑpə,ret; ES+'ɒp-; |-d -ɪd

operatic ,ɑpə'rætɪk; ES+,ɒp-; |-ally -l̦ɪ, -ɪklɪ

operation ,ɑpə'reʃən; ES+,ɒp-

operative 'ɑpə,retɪv, 'ɑpərətɪv, 'ɑprətɪv; ES+'ɒp-

|full fʊl |tooth tuθ |further 'fɝðɚ; ES 'fɜðə |custom 'kʌstəm |while hwaɪl |how haʊ |toy tɔɪ
|using 'juzɪŋ |fuse fjuz, fruz |dish dɪʃ |vision 'vɪʒən |Eden 'idn̦ |cradle 'kredl̦ |keep 'em 'kipm̦

operator 'ɑpəˌretəˈ; ES 'ɑpəˌretə(r, 'ɒp-
opere citato, op. cit. 'ɑpəˌri·sai'teto, 'ɑp'sit;
ES+'ɒp-
operetta ˌɑpə'retə; ES+ˌɒp-; |-s -z |-te -ti
Ophelia ə'filjə, o'filjə
ophidian o'fidiən
Ophir 'ofəˈ; ES 'ofə(r
ophthalmia af'θælmiə, -mjə; ES+ɒf-; |-mic
-mik
ophthalmitis ˌafθæl'maitis; ES+ˌɒf-
ophthalmology ˌafθæl'mɑlədʒi; ES+ˌɒfθæl-
'mɒl-
ophthalmoscope af'θælməˌskop; ES+ɒf-
opiate 'opiˌet, 'opiit
opine o'pain |opined o'paind
opinion ə'pinjən |opinioned ə'pinjənd
opinionated ə'pinjənˌetid |-ative -ˌetiv
opium 'opiəm, 'opjəm
Oporto o'porto, o'pɔrto; ES o'poəto, E+
o'pɔəto
opossum 'pɑsəm, ə'pɑsəm; ES+'pɒs-, ə'pɒs-
Oppenheim 'ɑpənˌhaim; ES+'ɒp-
opponent ə'ponənt
opportune ˌɑpəˈ'tjun, -'tiun, -'tun; ES+ˌɒp-;
|-nist -ist |-nity -əti |-neness -nis
opposable ə'pozəbl̩ |-bly -bli
oppose ə'poz |-s -iz |-d -d
opposite 'ɑpəzit; ES+'ɒp-
opposition ˌɑpə'ziʃən; ES+ˌɒp-
oppress ə'prɛs |-es -iz |-ed -t
oppression ə'prɛʃən |oppressive ə'prɛsiv
oppressor ə'prɛsəˈ; ES ə'prɛsə(r
opprobrious ə'probriəs |-brium -briəm
oppugn ə'pjun, ə'piun |-ed -d
oppugnant ə'pʌgnənt
opsonic ɑp'sɑnik; ES+ɒp'sɒnik
opsonin 'ɑpsənin; ES+'ɒp-
opt ɑpt; ES+ɒpt; |-ed -id
optative 'ɑptətiv; ES+'ɒp-
optic 'ɑptik; ES+'ɒp-; |-s -s |-al -l̩ |-ally -l̩i,
-ikli
optician ɑp'tiʃən; ES+ɒp-
optime 'ɑptəˌmi; ES+'ɒp-
optimism 'ɑptəˌmizəm; ES+'ɒp-; |-mist
-mist
optimistic ˌɑptə'mistik; ES+ˌɒp-; |-al -l̩
|-ally -l̩i, -ikli
optimum 'ɑptəməm; ES+'ɒp-
option 'ɑpʃən; ES+'ɒp-; |-d -d |-al -l̩ |-ally -l̩i

optometer ɑp'tɑmətəˈ; ES ɑp'tɑmətə(r, ɒp-
'tɒm-; |-trist -trist)-try -tri
opulence 'ɑpjələns; ES+'ɒp-; |-cy -i |-nt -nt
opus 'opəs |-es -iz |opera 'ɑpərə; ES+'ɒp-
opuscule o'pʌskjul, -kiul
or conj, usual form əˈ; ES ə(r; stressed 'ɔr,
ˌɔr; ES 'ɔə(r, ˌɔə(r
or 'ere' ɔr; ES ɔə(r
-or ending -əˈ; ES -ə(r; usually not pron. -ɔr,
-ɔə(r unless contrast is expressed or implied,
as 'vɛndɔr—vɛn'di
oracle 'ɔrəkl̩, 'ɑrɪkl̩, 'ɑr-, 'ɒr- |-d -d
oracular ɔ'rækjələˈ, a'r-, ɒ'r, o'r-; ES -lə(r
oral 'orəl, 'ɔrəl; S 'orəl; |-ly -i
orange 'ɔrindʒ, 'ɑr-, 'ɒr-, -əndʒ |-s -iz |-ade
-'ed
orangeman 'ɔrindʒmən, 'ɑ-, 'ɒ-, -ən- |-men
-mən
orangery 'ɔrindʒri, 'ɑ-, 'ɒ-, -əndʒ-
orangutan, -outang o'ræŋuˌtæn, -ˌtæŋ (Malay
'oraŋ'utaŋ)
orate 'oret, 'ɔret, o'ret, ɔ-; S 'o-, o-
oration o'reʃən, ɔ'reʃən; S o'reʃən
orator 'ɔrətəˈ, 'arətəˈ, 'ɒrətəˈ; ES -tə(r
oratorical ˌɔrə'tɔrikl̩, ˌarə'tar-, ˌɒrə'tɒr- |-ly
-i, -ikli
oratorio ˌɔrə'torio, ˌar-, ˌɒr-, -'tɔr-; S -'tor-
oratory 'ɔrəˌtori, 'ar-, 'ɒr-, -ˌtɔri; S -ˌtori
orb ɔrb; ES ɔəb; |-ed -d, adj poetic -id
orbicular ɔr'bikjələˈ; ES ɔ'bikjələ(r
orbit 'ɔrbit; ES 'ɔəbit; |-bital -bitl̩
orby 'ɔrbi; ES 'ɔəbi
orc ɔrk; ES ɔək
Orcadian ɔr'kediən; ES ɔ'kediən
orcein 'ɔrsiin; ES 'ɔəsiin
orchard 'ɔrtʃəˈd; ES 'ɔətʃəd
orchestra 'ɔrkistrə; ES 'ɔəkistrə
orchestral ɔr'kɛstrəl; ES ɔə'kɛstrəl |-ly -i
orchestrate 'ɔrkisˌtret; ES 'ɔək-; |-d -id
orchestration ˌɔrkis'treʃən; ES ˌɔəkis-
orchestrion ɔr'kɛstriən; ES ɔ'kɛstriən
orchid 'ɔrkid; ES 'ɔəkid
orchis 'ɔrkis; ES 'ɔəkis; |-es -iz
orcinol 'ɔrsiˌnol, -ˌnal, -ˌnɒl; ES 'ɔə-
ordain ɔr'den; ES ɔə'den; |-ed -d
ordeal ɔr'dil, -'diəl, 'ɔrd-; ES ɔə'd-, 'ɔəd-
order 'ɔrdəˈ; ES 'ɔədə(r; |-ed -d |-ing -dəriŋ,
-driŋ
ordinal 'ɔrdn̩əl; ES 'ɔədn̩əl; |-ly -i

---

ordinance 'ɔrdn̩əns, 'ɔrdnəns; ES 'ɔəd-; |-s -ɪz

ordinary 'ɔrdn̩ˌɛrɪ, 'ɔrdnɛrɪ; ES 'ɔəd-; |-ily -rəlɪ, esp. if emph. ˌordi'narily

ordinate n, adj 'ɔrdn̩ˌet, 'ɔrdn̩ɪt; ES 'ɔəd-

ordinate v 'ɔrdn̩ˌet; ES 'ɔəd-; |-d -ɪd

ordination ˌɔrdn̩'eʃən; ES ˌɔədn̩'eʃən

ordnance 'ɔrdnəns; ES 'ɔədnəns

ordo 'ɔrdo; ES 'ɔədo; |-dines -dɪˌniz

ordonnance 'ɔrdənəns; ES 'ɔəd-; (Fr ɔ̃rdɔ̃-'nɑ̃:s)

Ordovician ˌɔrdə'vɪʃən; ES ˌɔədə'vɪʃən

ordure 'ɔrdʒɚ, 'ɔrdjʊr; ES 'ɔədʒə(r, -djʊə(r

öre Dan coin sg & pl 'ørə

ore or, ɔr; ES oə(r, E+ɔə(r

oread 'ɔrɪˌæd, 'ɔrɪˌæd; S 'or-

Oregon 'ɔrɪˌgɑn, 'ar-, 'ɒr-, -gən

Orestes o'rɛstiz, ɔ-; S o-; |-tes' -tiz

organ 'ɔrgən; ES 'ɔəgən

organdy 'ɔrgəndɪ; ES 'ɔəgəndɪ

organic ɔr'gænɪk; ES ɔə'gænɪk; |-ally -l̩ɪ, -ɪklɪ

organism 'ɔrgənˌɪzəm; ES 'ɔəgənˌɪzəm; |-ist -ɪst

organization ˌɔrgənə'zeʃən, -aɪ'z-; ES ˌɔəg-

organize 'ɔrgənˌaɪz; ES 'ɔəgən-; |-s -ɪz |-d -d

organon 'ɔrgəˌnɑn; ES 'ɔəgəˌnɑn, -ˌnɒn; |-s -z |-gana -gənə

organum 'ɔrgənəm; ES 'ɔəg-; |-s -z |-gana -gənə

orgasm 'ɔrgæzəm; ES 'ɔəgæzəm

orgiastic ˌɔrdʒɪ'æstɪk; ES ˌɔədʒ-; |-al -l̩

orgy 'ɔrdʒɪ; ES 'ɔədʒɪ

oriel 'orɪəl, 'ɔrɪəl; S 'orɪəl

orient, O- n 'orɪˌɛnt, 'ɔr-, -ənt; S 'or-

orient adj 'orɪənt, 'ɔr-; S 'orɪənt

orient v 'orɪˌɛnt, 'ɔr-; S 'orɪˌɛnt; |-ed -ɪd

oriental ˌorɪ'ɛntl̩, ˌɔr-; S ˌor-; |-ism -ˌɪzəm |-ist -ɪst |-ly -ɪ |-ize -ˌaɪz |-izes -ˌaɪzɪz |-ized -ˌaɪzd

orientate 'orɪɛnˌtet, ˌorɪ'ɛntet, 'ɔr-, ˌɔr-; S 'or-, ˌor-; |-d -ɪd

orientation ˌorɪɛn'teʃən, ˌɔr-; S ˌor-

orifice 'ɔrəfɪs, 'ar-, 'ɒr-

oriflamme, -amb 'ɔrəˌflæm, 'ar-, 'ɒr-

Origen 'ɔrɪdʒɪn, 'ɔrɪˌdʒɛn, 'ar-, 'ɒr-

origin 'ɔrədʒɪn, 'ar-, 'ɒr-

original ə'rɪdʒənl̩ |-ly -ɪ

originality əˌrɪdʒə'nælətɪ

originate ə'rɪdʒəˌnet |-d -ɪd |-tive -ɪv

orinasal ˌorɪ'nezl̩, ˌɔr-; S ˌor-; |-ly -ɪ

Orinoco ˌorə'noko, ˌɔr-; S ˌor-

oriole 'orɪˌol, 'ɔr-; S 'or-

Orion o'raɪən |-'s -z |gen ˌɔrɪ'onɪs, ˌɑr-, ˌɒr-

orison 'ɔrɪzn̩, 'ar-, 'ɒr-

Orizaba ˌɔrɪ'savə, ˌɔr-; S ˌor-; (Am Sp ˌori'saβa)

Orkney 'ɔrknɪ; ES 'ɔəknɪ

Orlando ɔr'lændo; ES ɔə'lændo

Orleans La, France 'ɔrlɪənz; ES 'ɔəlɪənz; most US places ɔr'linz; ES ɔə'l-; (Fr ɔ̃rle'ɑ̃), cf New Orleans

orlop 'ɔrlɑp; ES 'ɔəlɑp, -lɒp

Ormazd, -muzd 'ɔrməzd; ES 'ɔəməzd

ormolu 'ɔrməˌlu; ES 'ɔəməˌlu

Ormuz 'ɔrmʌz; ES 'ɔəmʌz; |-'s -ɪz

ornament n 'ɔrnəmənt, v 'ɔrnəˌmɛnt; ES 'ɔən-; |-ed -ɪd

ornamental ˌɔrnə'mɛntl̩; ES ˌɔən-; |-ly -ɪ

ornamentation ˌɔrnəmɛn'teʃən, -mən-; ES ˌɔənə-

ornate ɔr'net; ES ɔə'net

ornery 'ɔrnərɪ; ES 'ɔənərɪ

ornithology ˌɔrnə'θalədʒɪ; ES ˌɔənə-, -'θɒl-

orogeny ə'radʒənɪ; ES+ə'rɒdʒ-

orography ə'ragrəfɪ, ə'rɒg-

oroide 'oroˌaɪd, 'ɔr-; S 'or-

orology o'ralədʒɪ, ɔ-; S o-, ES+-'rɒl-

Orono 'orəˌno, 'ɔr-; S 'or-

Orosius ə'rosɪəs, -sjəs |-us' -əs

orotund 'orəˌtʌnd, 'ɔr-, 'ar-, 'ɒr-

orphan 'ɔrfən; ES 'ɔəfən; |-ed -d |-age -ɪdʒ

Orpheus 'ɔrfɪəs, 'ɔrfjus; ES 'ɔəf-; |-'s -ɪz

Orphic 'ɔrfɪk; ES 'ɔəfɪk

orphrey 'ɔrfrɪ; ES 'ɔəfrɪ; |-ed -d

orpiment 'ɔrpɪmənt; ES 'ɔəp-

orpine, -pin 'ɔrpɪn; ES 'ɔəpɪn

Orpington 'ɔrpɪŋtən; ES 'ɔəp-

orrery 'ɔrərɪ, 'ar-, 'ɒr-

orris 'ɔrɪs, 'arɪs, 'ɒrɪs

Orsino ɔr'sino; ES ɔə'sino

orthodontia ˌɔrθə'danʃə, -ʃɪə; ES ˌɔəθə-, -'dɒn-

orthodox 'ɔrθəˌdaks; ES 'ɔəθə-, -ˌdɒks; |-y -ɪ

orthoepy ɔr'θo·ɪpɪ, 'ɔrθo·ɪˌpɪ; ES ɔ'θo-, 'ɔəθo-

orthographic ˌɔrθə'græfɪk; ES ˌɔəθə-; |-al -l̩ |-ally -l̩ɪ, -ɪklɪ

orthography ɔr'θagrəfɪ, -'θɒg-; ES ɔˌθ-

orthopedic, -paed- ˌɔrθəˈpidɪk; ES ˌɔəθə-;
|-s -s
orthophonic ˌɔrθəˈfɑnɪk; ES ˌɔəθəˈfɑn-, -ˈfɒn-
orthophosphoric ˌɔrθɑfɑsˈfɔrɪk, -ˈfar-, -ˈfɒr-;
ES ˌɔəθɑfɑs-, -fɒs-
orthopsychiatry ˌɔrθəsaɪˈkaɪətrɪ; ES ˌɔəθə-
orthopter ɔrˈθɑptɚ; ES ɔəˈθɑptə(r, -ˈθɒp-
oryx, O- ˈɔrɪks, ˈɔr-, ˈar-, ˈɒr- |-es -ɪz
os 'bone' as; ES+ɒs; |pl ossa -ə
os 'mouth' as; ES+ɒs; |pl ora ˈorə, ˈɔrə; S
ˈɔrə
Osage oˈsedʒ, ˈosedʒ |-s -ɪz (ˈOˌsage ˈorange)
Osaka oˈsɑkə (Jap ˈo:sɑkɑ)
Osawatomie ˌosəˈwɑtəmɪ, ˌɑsə-, ˌɒs-, -ˈwɒt-,
loc. ˌosə-
Osborn, -e ˈɔzbɚn, ˈɒz-, ˈaz-; ES -bən
Oscan ˈɑskən, ˈɒskən, ˈɔskən
Oscar ˈɔskɚ, ˈɒskɚ, ˈaskɚ; ES -kə(r
Osceola ˌɑsɪˈolə; ES+ˌɒs-
oscillate ˈɑsˌɪet; ES+ˈɒs-; |-d -ɪd
oscillation ˌɑsɪˈeʃən; ES+ˌɒs-
oscillator ˈɑsˌɪetɚ; ES ˈɑsˌɪetə(r, ˈɒs-
oscillograph əˈsɪləˌgræf; E+-ˌgraf, -ˌgrɑf
oscular ˈɑskjəlɚ; ES ˈɑskjələ(r, ˈɒs-
osculate ˈɑskjəˌlet; ES+ˈɒs-; |-d -ɪd
osculation ˌɑskjəˈleʃən; ES+ˌɒs-
Osgood ˈɑzgʊd, ˈɒz-, ˈɔz-
O'Shaughnessy oˈʃɑnəsɪ
O'Shea oˈʃe, oˈʃi
Oshkosh ˈɑʃkɑʃ; ES+ˈɒʃkɒʃ
osier ˈoʒɚ; ES ˈoʒə(r; |-ed -d
Osiris oˈsaɪrɪs |Osiris's oˈsaɪrɪsɪz
Osler ˈoslɚ, ˈozlɚ, ˈas-, ˈɒs-; ES -lə(r
Oslo ˈazlo, ˈaslo, ˈɒ- (Norw ˈoslo, ˈʊslʊ)
Osman ˈazmɑn, ˈas-, ˈɒ-, -mən
Osmanli azˈmænlɪ, ɑs-, ɒ-
osmic ˈazmɪk; ES+ˈɒz-; |-mious -mɪəs
|-mium -mɪəm
osmose ˈazmos, ˈas-; ES+ˈɒ-
osmosis azˈmosɪs, ɑs-; ES+ɒ-
osmotic azˈmɑtɪk, ɑs-; ES+ɒzˈmɒtɪk, ɒs-
osmund, O- ˈazmənd; ES+ˈɒz-
osprey ˈasprɪ, ˈɒsprɪ, ˈɔsprɪ
Osric ˈazrɪk, ˈɒz-
Ossa ˈasə; ES+ˈɒsə
ossein ˈasiɪn; ES+ˈɒs-
osseous ˈasɪəs, -jəs; ES+ˈɒs-
Ossian ˈaʃən, ˈasɪən; ES+ˈɒ-
Ossianic ˌasɪˈænɪk, ˌaʃɪ-; ES+ˌɒ-

ossification ˌɑsəfəˈkeʃən; ES+ˌɒs-
ossify ˈɑsəˌfaɪ; ES+ˈɒs-; |-fied -ˌfaɪd
Ossining ˈɑsɪˌnɪŋ; ES+ˈɒs-
Ossipee ˈɑsəˌpi, -pɪ; ES+ˈɒs-; loc.+ˈɔspɪ
osteal ˈɑstɪəl; ES+ˈɒs-
Ostend ɑsˈtɛnd; ES+ɒs-
ostensible ɑsˈtɛnsəbḷ; ES+ɒs-; |-bly -blɪ
ostentation ˌɑstənˈteʃən, -tɛn-; ES+ˌɒs-
ostentatious ˌɑstənˈteʃəs, -tɛn-; ES+ˌɒs-
osteology ˌɑstɪˈɑlədʒɪ; ES+ˌɒstɪˈɒlədʒɪ
osteopath ˈɑstɪəˌpæθ; ES+ˈɒs-
osteopathic ˌɑstɪəˈpæθɪk; ES+ˌɒs-; |-ally -ļɪ
osteopathy ˌɑstɪˈɑpəθɪ; ES+ˌɒstɪˈɒpəθɪ
ostiary ˈɑstɪˌɛrɪ; ES+ˈɒs-
ostler ˈɑslɚ; ES ˈɑslə(r, ˈɒs-
ostracism ˈɑstrəˌsɪzəm, ˈɒs-, ˈɔs-
ostracize ˈɑstrəˌsaɪz, ˈɒs-, ˈɔs- |-s -ɪz |-d -d
ostrich ˈɔstrɪtʃ, ˈɒs-, ˈas- |-es -ɪz
Ostrogoth ˈɑstrəˌgɑθ, ˈɒstrəˌgɒθ |-ths -θs
Oswald, -wold ˈazwəld, ˈazwald, ˈɒzwɒld,
ˈɒzwɔld
Oswego asˈwigo; ES+ɒs-
Oswestry ˈazwəstrɪ, ˈɒz-, -wɛs-
Othello oˈθɛlo, əˈθɛlo
other ˈʌðɚ; ES ˈʌðə(r
otherwhile ˈʌðɚˌhwaɪl; ES ˈʌðəˌhwaɪl
otherwise ˈʌðɚˌwaɪz; ES ˈʌðəˌwaɪz
otherworldly ˈʌðɚˈwɝldlɪ; ES ˈʌðəˈwɝldlɪ,
ˈʌðəˈwɝldlɪ
Othin ˈoðɪn
Othman ˈɑθmən, ˈɒθ-, -mən
otiose ˈoʃɪˌos, ˈotɪˌos
otology oˈtɑlədʒɪ; ES+-ˈtɒl-; |-gist -dʒɪst
Otranto oˈtrænto, ɑ-, ɒ- (It ˈɔ:trɑnto)
ottava rima əˈtɑvəˈrimə (It otˈtɑ:vɑˈri:mɑ)
Ottawa ˈɑtəwə, ˈɑtəˌwɑ, -ˌwɒ; ES+ˈɒt-
otter ˈɑtɚ; ES ˈɑtə(r, ˈɒtə(r
Otterburn ˈɑtɚˌbɝn, ˈɑtəbɚn; ES ˈɑtəˌbɝn,
ˈɒtə-, -təˌbɝn, -bən; The pron. ˈɑtəbɚn is
due to r-dissimilation (§121).
Otto ˈɑto; ES+ˈɒto
Ottoman ˈɑtəmən, ˈato-; ES+ˈɒt-
Ouachita ˈwɑʃɪˌtɔ, ˈwɒʃ-, ˈwɔʃ-
ouananiche ˌwɑnəˈniʃ, ˌwɒ- (Fr wanaˈniʃ)
oubliette ˌublɪˈɛt
ouch aʊtʃ |ouches ˈaʊtʃɪz |ouched aʊtʃt
ought ɔt |ought to ˈɔttʊ, ˈɔttə, ˈɔtʊ, ˈɔtə, ˈɔttu
oughtn't ˈɔtṇt, bef. some conss.+ˈɔtṇ (ˈɔtṇ-
ˈdʒɑn təˈgo?)

Key: See in full §§3–47.   bee **bi** |pity ˈpɪtɪ (§6) |rate ret |yet jɛt |sang sæŋ |angry ˈæŋˌgrɪ
|bath bæθ; E baθ (§10) |ah ɑ |far fɑr |watch wɑtʃ, wɒtʃ (§12) |jaw dʒɔ |gorge gɔrdʒ |go go

Ouida ˈwidə
Ouija ˈwidʒə
ounce aʊns |ounces ˈaʊnsɪz
Oundle ˈaʊndl̩
our aʊr, ɑr; ES aʊə(r, ɑ:(r; |-s -z
ourself aʊrˈsɛlf, ɑr-; ES aʊə-, ɑ:-; |-lves -vz
Oursler ˈaʊrzlɚ, ˈaʊz-, ˈɑz-, ˈɒz-; ES -lə(r;
  see §121
-ous *adj ending, always unstressed* -əs
Ouse uz
ousel ˈuzl̩
ousia uˈsiə
oust aʊst |ousted ˈaʊstɪd
out aʊt
out-and-out ˈaʊtn̩ˈaʊt (ˈout-and-ˌout ˈthief)
outargue aʊtˈɑrgjʊ; ES -ˈɑːgjʊ, E+-ˈɑːg-;
  |-d -d
outbalance aʊtˈbæləns |-s -ɪz |-d -t
outbid aʊtˈbɪd |*past & pptc* -bid -ˈbɪd
outboard ˈaʊtˌbord, -ˌbɔrd; ES -ˌboəd, E+
  -ˌbɔəd
outbound ˈaʊtˈbaʊnd (ˈoutˌbound ˈtrain)
outbrag aʊtˈbræg |-bragged -ˈbrægd
outbranch aʊtˈbræntʃ; E+-ˈbrantʃ, -ˈbrɑntʃ;
  |-es -ɪz |-ed -t
outbrave aʊtˈbrev |outbraved aʊtˈbrevd
outbuilding ˈaʊtˌbɪldɪŋ
outcast *n* ˈaʊtˌkæst; E+-ˌkast, -ˌkɑst; *v*
  outˈcast
outcaste *n* ˈaʊtˌkæst; E+-ˌkast, -ˌkɑst
outcaste *v* aʊtˈkæst; E+-ˈkast, -ˈkɑst; |-d -ɪd
outclass aʊtˈklæs; E+-ˈklas, -ˈklɑs; |-es -ɪz
  |-ed -t
outcome ˈaʊtˌkʌm
outcrop *n* ˈaʊtˌkrɑp; ES+-ˌkrɒp
outcrop *v* aʊtˈkrɑp; ES+-ˈkrɒp; |-ped -t
outcry *n* ˈaʊtˌkraɪ
outcry *v* aʊtˈkraɪ |-cried -ˈkraɪd
outdare aʊtˈdɛr, -ˈdær; E -ˈdɛə(r, ES -ˈdæə(r
outdistance aʊtˈdɪstəns |-s -ɪz |-d -t
outdo aʊtˈdu |-does -ˈdʌz |-did -ˈdɪd |-done
  -ˈdʌn
outdoor ˈaʊtˌdor, -ˌdɔr; ES -ˌdoə(r, E+-ˌdɔə(r
outdoors *n* aʊtˈdorz -ˈdɔrz; ES -ˈdoəz,
  E+-ˈdɔəz
outdoors *adj* ˈaʊtˌdorz, -ˌdɔrz; ES -ˌdoəz,
  E+-ˌdɔəz
outdoors *adv* aʊtˈdorz, -ˈdɔrz; ES -ˈdoəz,
  E+-ˈdɔəz

outer ˈaʊtɚ; ES ˈaʊtə(r; |-most -ˌmost, -məst
outface aʊtˈfes |-faces -ˈfesɪz |-faced -ˈfest
outfall ˈaʊtˌfɔl
outfield *n* ˈaʊtˈfild, ˈaʊtˌfild
outfit ˈaʊtˌfɪt |outfitted ˈaʊtˌfɪtɪd
outflank aʊtˈflæŋk |outflanked aʊtˈflæŋkt
outflow *n* ˈaʊtˌflo
outflow *v* aʊtˈflo |outflowed aʊtˈflod
outfoot aʊtˈfʊt |outfooted aʊtˈfʊtɪd
outgeneral aʊtˈdʒɛnərəl, -ˈdʒɛnrəl |-ed -d
outgo *n* ˈaʊtˌgo
outgo *v* aʊtˈgo |-went -ˈwɛnt |-gone -ˈgɔn,
  -ˈgɒn, *much less freq.* -ˈgɑn
outgoing aʊtˈgoɪŋ (ˈoutˌgoɪŋ ˈtrain)
outgrow aʊtˈgro |-grew -ˈgru, -ˈgrɪu |-grown
  -ˈgron
outgrowth ˈaʊtˌgroθ |-growths -ˌgroθs
outguess aʊtˈgɛs |-guesses -ˈgɛsɪz |-ed -t
out-Herod aʊtˈhɛrəd (ˈout-ˌHerods ˈHerod)
  |-ed -ɪd
outhouse ˈaʊtˌhaʊs |-houses -ˌhaʊzɪz
outing ˈaʊtɪŋ
outland *n* ˈaʊtˌlænd
outland *adj* ˈaʊtˌlænd, -lənd |-er -ɚ; ES -ə(r
outlandish aʊtˈlændɪʃ (ˈoutˌlandish ˈhats)
outlast aʊtˈlæst; E+-ˈlast, -ˈlɑst; |-ed -ɪd
outlaw ˈaʊtˌlɔ |-lawed -ˌlɔd |-lawry -ˌlɔrɪ
outlay *n* ˈaʊtˌle
outlay *v* aʊtˈle |-laid -ˈled
outlet ˈaʊtˌlɛt
outlier ˈaʊtˌlaɪɚ; ES -ˌlaɪ·ə(r
outline ˈaʊtˌlaɪn |-lined -ˌlaɪnd
outlive aʊtˈlɪv |-lived -ˈlɪvd
outlook *n* ˈaʊtˌlʊk
outlook *v* aʊtˈlʊk |-looked -ˈlʊkt
outlying ˈaʊtˌlaɪŋ
outmaneuver, -noeu- ˌaʊtməˈnuvɚ; ES -və(r;
  |-ed -d |-ring -vərɪŋ, -vrɪŋ
outmode aʊtˈmod |-moded -ˈmodɪd
outmost ˈaʊtˌmost, -məst
outnumber aʊtˈnʌmbɚ; ES -ˈnʌmbə(r; |-ed
  -d |-ing -brɪŋ, -bərɪŋ
out-of-date ˈaʊtəvˈdet, ˈaʊtəˈdet
out-of-door ˈaʊtəvˈdor, -ˈdɔr; ES -ˈdoə(r,
  E+-ˈdɔə(r
out-of-the-way ˈaʊtəðəˈwe, ˈaʊtəvðəˈwe (ˈout-
  of-the-ˌway ˈplace)
outpatient ˈaʊtˌpeʃənt
outplay aʊtˈple |-played -ˈpled

|full fʊl |tooth tuθ |further ˈfɝðɚ; ES ˈfɝðə |custom ˈkʌstəm |while hwaɪl |how haʊ |toy tɔɪ
|using ˈjuzɪŋ |fuse fjuz, fɪuz |dish dɪʃ |vision ˈvɪʒən |Eden ˈidn̩ |cradle ˈkredl̩ |keep 'em ˈkipm̩

outpoint aʊt'pɔɪnt |-pointed -'pɔɪntɪd

outpost 'aʊt‚post

outpour n 'aʊt‚por, -‚pɔr; ES -‚poə(r, E+ -‚pɔə(r

outpour v aʊt'por, -'pɔr; ES -'poə(r, E+ -'pɔə(r

output 'aʊt‚pʊt

outrage 'aʊt‚redʒ |-rages -‚redʒɪz |-d -d

outrageous aʊt'redʒəs

outrange aʊt'rendʒ |-ranges -'rendʒɪz |-d -d

outrank aʊt'ræŋk |-ranked -'ræŋkt

outré u'tre ('ou‚tré 'styles)

outreach n 'aʊt‚ritʃ |outreaches 'aʊt‚ritʃɪz

outreach v aʊt'ritʃ |-es -ɪz |-ed -t

outremer, Outre-Mer ‚utrə'mɛr; ES -'mɛə(r

outrider 'aʊt‚raɪdɚ; ES 'aʊt‚raɪdə(r

outrigger 'aʊt‚rɪgɚ; ES 'aʊt‚rɪgə(r

outright adj 'aʊt‚raɪt

outright adv 'aʊt'raɪt ('out‚right 'lazy)

outrival aʊt'raɪvl̩ |-ed -d |-ing -vlɪŋ, -vlɪ̩ŋ

outroot aʊt'rut, -'rʊt |-ed -ɪd

outrun aʊt'rʌn |past -'ræn |p ptc -'rʌn

outrunner aʊt'rʌnɚ, 'aʊt‚rʌnɚ; ES -ə(r

outsell aʊt'sɛl |-sold -'sold

outset n 'aʊt‚sɛt, v aʊt'sɛt

outshine aʊt'ʃaɪn |-shone -'ʃon

outshoot n 'aʊt‚ʃut

outshoot v aʊt'ʃut |-shot -'ʃat; ES+-'ʃɒt

outside n, adj 'aʊt'saɪd ('out‚side 'door)

outside adv 'aʊt'saɪd ('out‚side & 'in‚side)

outside prep aʊt'saɪd

outsider aʊt'saɪdɚ; ES aʊt'saɪdə(r

outsit aʊt'sɪt |outsat aʊt'sæt

outsize n 'aʊt‚saɪz |-sizes -‚saɪzɪz

outsized adj 'aʊt'saɪzd ('out‚sized 'pair)

outskirt 'aʊt‚skɝt; ES -‚skɜt, -‚skɝt

outsmart aʊt'smɑrt; ES -'smɑːt, E+-'smɑːt; |-ed -ɪd

outsoar aʊt'sor, -'sɔr; ES -'soə(r, E+-'sɔə(r; |-ed -d

outspan aʊt'spæn |outspanned aʊt'spænd

outspeak aʊt'spik |-spoke -'spok |-spoken -'spokən

outspent aʊt'spɛnt

outspoken 'aʊt'spokən ('out‚spoken 'leader)

outspokenness aʊt'spokənnɪs

outspread n 'aʊt‚sprɛd

outspread v aʊt'sprɛd

outstand aʊt'stænd |-stood -'stʊd

outstanding adj 'aʊt'stændɪŋ

outstare aʊt'stɛr, -'stær; E -'stɛə(r, ES -'stæə(r; |-d -d

outstation n 'aʊt‚steʃən

outstation v aʊt'steʃən |-ed -d

outstay aʊt'ste |-stayed -'sted

outstretch aʊt'strɛtʃ |-es -ɪz |-ed -t

outstrip aʊt'strɪp |-stripped -'strɪpt

outtalk aʊt'tɔk |-talked -'tɔkt

outtell aʊt'tɛl |-told -'told

outtop aʊt'tɑp; ES+-'tɒp; |-ped -t

outturn n 'aʊt‚tɝn; ES -‚tɜn, -‚tɝn

outvote aʊt'vot |-voted -'votɪd

outward 'aʊtwɚd; ES 'aʊtwəd; |-s -z

outwatch aʊt'watʃ, -'wɒtʃ, -'wɔtʃ |-es -ɪz |-ed -t

outwear aʊt'wɛr, -'wær; E -‚wɛə(r, ES -'wæə(r; |-wore -'wor, -'wɔr; ES -'woə(r, E+-'wɔə(r; |-worn -'worn, -'wɔrn; ES -'woən, E+-'wɔən

outweigh aʊt'we |-weighed -'wed

outwind 'uncoil' aʊt'waɪnd |-wound -'waʊnd

outwind 'exhaust' aʊt'wɪnd |-winded -'wɪndɪd

outwit aʊt'wɪt |-witted -'wɪtɪd

outwork n 'aʊt‚wɝk; ES -‚wɜk, -‚wɝk

outwork v aʊt'wɝk; ES -'wɜk, -'wɝk; |-ed -t or -wrought -'rɔt

outworn adj 'aʊt'worn, -'wɔrn; ES -'woən, E+-'wɔən; ('out‚worn 'joke)

outwrite aʊt'raɪt |-wrote -'rot |-written -'rɪtn̩

ouzel 'uzl̩

ova pl 'ovə |sg ovum 'ovəm

oval 'ovl̩ |-ly -ɪ

ovarian o'vɛrɪən, -'vær-, -'ver-

ovary 'ovərɪ, 'ovrɪ

ovate 'ovet, 'ovɪt

ovation o'veʃən

oven 'ʌvən |-bird -‚bɝd; ES -‚bɜd, -‚bɝd

over 'ovɚ; ES 'ovə(r

over- Compounds in over- vary in accent according to meaning, rhythm, and sense stress. In compound verbs, over='excessively' is apt to have more stress than over='above' (cf 'over'do with ‚over'flow)

overact 'ovɚ'ækt |-acted -'æktɪd

overage 'surplus' 'ovərɪdʒ, 'ovrɪdʒ |-s -ɪz

overage 'too old' 'ovɚ'edʒ |-d -'edʒɪd, -'edʒd

over-all adj 'ovɚ‚ɔl ('over-‚all 'width)

overall adv ‚ovɚ'ɔl

overalls 'ovɚ͵ɔlz, -͵hɔlz; ES 'ovɚ͵ɔlz, 'ovə͵h-

overanxious 'ovɚ'æŋkʃəs -'æŋʃ- |-iety -æŋ-'zaɪətɪ

overawe ͵ovɚ'ɔ |-awed -'ɔd

overbalance ͵ovɚ'bæləns; ES ͵ovə-; |-s -ɪz |-d -t

overbear ͵ovɚ'bɛr, -'bær; E ͵ovɚ'bɛə(r, ES -'bæə(r; |-bore -'bor, -'bɔr; ES -'boə(r, E+-'bɔə(r; |-borne -'born, -'bɔrn; ES -'boən, E+-'bɔən

overbearing ͵ovɚ'bɛrɪŋ, -'bærɪŋ; E ͵ovə-'bɛrɪŋ, ES -'bærɪŋ

overbid n 'ovɚ͵bɪd; ES 'ovə͵bɪd

overbid v ͵ovɚ'bɪd; ES ͵ovə-; |past & pptc -bid -'bɪd

overblow ͵ovɚ'blo; ES ͵ovə-; |-blew -'blu, -'blɪu |-blown -'blon

overboard 'ovɚ͵bord, -͵bɔrd; ES 'ovə͵boəd, E+-͵bɔəd

overbold 'ovɚ'bold; ES 'ovə-; ('over͵bold 'act)

overbuild 'ovɚ'bɪld; ES 'ovə-; |-built -'bɪlt

overburden n 'ovɚ͵bɝdn̩; ES 'ovə͵bɝdn̩, 'ovə͵bɝˑdn̩

overburden v 'ovɚ'bɝdn̩; ES 'ovə'bɝdn̩, 'ovə'bɝˑdn̩; |-ed -d |-ing -dn̩ɪŋ, -dnɪŋ

Overbury 'ovɚ͵bɛrɪ, -bərɪ; ES 'ovə-

overbuy 'ovɚ'baɪ; ES 'ovə-; |-bought -'bɔt

overcall n 'ovɚ͵kɔl; ES 'ovə-

overcall v 'ovɚ'kɔl; ES 'ovə-; |-ed -d

overcapitalize 'ovɚ'kæpət͡l͵aɪz; ES 'ovə-; |-s -ɪz |-d -d

overcareful 'ovɚ'kɛrfəl, -'kær-; E 'ovə-'kɛəfəl, ES -'kæəfəl; |-ly -ɪ

overcast n 'ovɚ͵kæst; ES 'ovə-, E+-͵kast, -͵kast

overcast v ͵ovɚ'kæst; ES ͵ovə-, E+-'kast, -'kast; in sense 'sew' acct+'over͵cast, ptc adj ͵over'cast, 'over͵cast

overcharge n 'ovɚ͵tʃɑrdʒ; ES 'ovə͵tʃɑ:dʒ, E+-͵tʃɑ:dʒ; |-s -ɪz

overcharge v 'ovɚ'tʃɑrdʒ; ES 'ovə'tʃɑ:dʒ, E+-'tʃɑ:dʒ; |-s -ɪz |-d -d

overcloud ͵ovɚ'klaʊd; ES ͵ovə-; |-ed -ɪd

overcoat 'ovɚ͵kot; ES 'ovə-

overcome ͵ovɚ'kʌm; ES ͵ovə-; |past -came -'kem |pptc -come -'kʌm

overconfidence 'ovɚ'kɑnfədəns; ES 'ovə-'kɑn-, -'kɒn-; |-s -ɪz

overdevelop 'ovɚdɪ'vɛləp; ES 'ovə-; |-ed -t

overdo 'ovɚ'du; ES 'ovə-; |-does -'dʌz |-did -'dɪd |-done -'dʌn

overdose n 'ovɚ͵dos; ES 'ovə-; |-s -ɪz

overdose v 'ovɚ'dos; ES 'ovə-; |-s -ɪz |-d -t

overdraft, -draught 'ovɚ͵dræft; ES 'ovə-, E+-͵draft, -͵drɑft

overdraw 'ovɚ'drɔ; ES 'ovə-; |-drew -'dru, -'drɪu |-drawn -'drɔn

overdress 'ovɚ'drɛs; ES 'ovə-; |-es -ɪz |-ed -t

overdue 'ovɚ'dju, -'drɪu, -'du; ES 'ovə-; ('over͵due 'note)

overeat 'ovɚ'it |-ate -'et |-eaten -'itn̩ |-eat dial. past -'ɛt, cf ate

overemphasis 'ovɚ'ɛmfəsɪs |pl -ses -͵siz

overemphasize 'ovɚ'ɛmfə͵saɪz |-s -ɪz |-d -d

overestimate n 'ovɚ'ɛstəmɪt, -͵met

overestimate v 'ovɚ'ɛstə͵met |-d -ɪd

overexcite 'ovɚɪk'saɪt |-d -ɪd

overexert 'ovɚɪg'zɝt; ES -'zɝt, -'zɝt |-ed -ɪd

overexertion 'ovɚɪg'zɝʃən; ES -'zɝʃ-, -'zɝʃ-

overexpose 'ovɚɪk'spoz |-s -ɪz |-d -d |-sure -ʒɚ; ES -ʒə(r

overfeed n, adj 'ovɚ͵fid; ES 'ovə-

overfeed v 'ovɚ'fid; ES 'ovə-; |-fed -'fɛd

overflow n 'ovɚ͵flo; ES 'ovə͵flo

overflow v ͵ovɚ'flo; ES ͵ovə-; |-ed -d

overgarment 'ovɚ͵gɑrmənt; ES 'ovə͵gɑ:mənt, E+-͵gɑ:m-

overgild ͵ovɚ'gɪld; ES ͵ovə-; |-ed -ɪd

overglaze n 'ovɚ͵glez; ES 'ovə-; |-s -ɪz

overglaze v ͵ovɚ'glez; ES ͵ovə-; |-s -ɪz |-d -d

overgrow 'ovɚ'gro; ES 'ovə-; |-grew -'gru, -'grɪu |-grown -'gron

overhand adj, adv 'ovɚ'hænd; ES 'ovə-; |-ed -ɪd ('over͵hand 'play)

overhand n, v 'ovɚ͵hænd; ES 'ovə-; |-ed -ɪd

overhang n 'ovɚ͵hæŋ; ES 'ovə-

overhang v ͵ovɚ'hæŋ; ES ͵ovə-; |-hung -'hʌŋ

overhaul n 'overhauling' 'ovɚ͵hɔl; ES 'ovə-

overhaul v ͵ovɚ'hɔl; ES ͵ovə-; |-ed -d

overhauls 'overalls' 'ovɚ͵hɔlz; ES 'ovə-

overhead n, adj 'ovɚ͵hɛd; ES 'ovə-

overhead adv 'ovɚ'hɛd; ES 'ovə-

overhear ͵ovɚ'hɪr; ES ͵ovə'hɪə(r, S+-'hjɛə(r, -'hjɪə(r, -'hɛə(r; |-heard -'hɝd; ES -'hɜd, -'hɝd

overheat 'ovɚ'hit; ES 'ovə-; |-heated -'hitɪd

overindulge 'ovɚɪn'dʌldʒ |-s -ɪz |-d -d

|full fʊl |tooth tuθ |further 'fɝðɚ; ES 'fɜðə |custom 'kʌstəm |while hwaɪl |how haʊ |toy tɔɪ |using 'juzɪŋ |fuse fjuz, fɪuz |dish dɪʃ |vision 'vɪʒən |Eden 'idn̩ |cradle 'kredl̩ |keep 'em 'kipm̩

overjoy 'ovɚ'dʒɔɪ; ES 'ovə-; |-ed -d
overlaid ˌovɚ'led; ES ˌovə-; ('over ˌlaid 'gold)
overland adj, adv 'ovɚˌlænd; ES 'ovə-
overland v 'ovɚˌlænd, ˌovɚ'lænd; ES -və-;
|-ed -ɪd
overlap n 'ovɚˌlæp; ES 'ovə-
overlap v ˌovɚ'læp; ES ˌovə-; |-ped -t
overlay past of overlie ˌovɚ'le; ES ˌovə-
overlay n 'ovɚˌle; ES 'ovə-
overlay v ˌovɚ'le; ES ˌovə-; |-laid -'led
overleaf adv 'ovɚ'lif; ES 'ovə-; n 'overˌleaf
overleap ˌovɚ'lip; ES ˌovə-; |-leaped -'lipt,
-'lɛpt or -leapt -'lɛpt, -'lipt
overlie ˌovɚ'laɪ; ES ˌovə-; |past -lay -'le |pptc
-lain -'len
overlook n 'ovɚˌlʊk; ES 'ovə-
overlook v ˌovɚ'lʊk; ES ˌovə-; |-ed -t
overlord 'ovɚˌlɔrd; ES 'ovəˌlɔəd
overly 'ovɚlɪ; ES 'ovəlɪ
overman 'foreman' 'ovɚmən; ES 'ovə-; |-men
-mən, 'superman' -ˌmæn |-men -ˌmɛn
overman v 'ovɚ'mæn; ES 'ovə-; |-ned -d
overmaster ˌovɚ'mæstɚ; ES ˌovə'mæstə(r,
E+-'mas-, -'mɑs-
overmatch ˌovɚ'mætʃ; ES ˌovə-; |-es -ɪz
|-ed -t
overmuch adj, adv 'ovɚ'mʌtʃ; ES 'ovə-;
('over ˌmuch 'joy)
overnight adj, adv 'ovɚ'naɪt; ES 'ovə-;
('over ˌnight 'bag)
overnight n 'ovɚˌnaɪt; ES 'ovə-
overpass n 'ovɚˌpæs; ES 'ovə-, E+-ˌpas,
-ˌpɑs; |-es -ɪz
overpass v ˌovɚ'pæs; ES ˌovə'pæs, E+-'pas,
-'pɑs; |-es -ɪz |-ed -t
overpay 'ovɚ'pe; ES 'ovə-; |-paid -'ped
overpersuade 'ovɚpɚ'swed; ES 'ovəpə-; |-d
-ɪd
overplus 'ovɚˌplʌs; ES 'ovə-; |-es -ɪz
overpower ˌovɚ'pauɚ; ES ˌovə'pau·ə(r; |-ed
-d |-ing -'pauərɪŋ, -'paʊrɪŋ
overprint n 'ovɚˌprɪnt; ES 'ovə-
overprint v ˌovɚ'prɪnt; ES ˌovə-; |-ed -ɪd
overprize 'ovɚ'praɪz; ES 'ovə-; |-s -ɪz |-d -d
overproduction 'ovɚprə'dʌkʃən; ES 'ovə-
overproportion 'ovɚprə'porʃən, -'pɔr-; ES
'ovəprə'pɔəʃən, E+-'pɔə-; |-ed -d
overrate 'ovɚ'ret; ES 'ovə'ret; |-rated -'retɪd
Overreach 'ovɚˌritʃ; ES 'ovə-; |-'s -ɪz

overreach ˌovɚ'ritʃ; ES ˌovə-; |-es -ɪz |-ed -t
override ˌovɚ'raɪd; ES ˌovə-; |-rode -'rod
|-ridden -'rɪdn̩
overripe 'ovɚ'raɪp; ES 'ovə-
overrule ˌovɚ'rul, -'rʊl; ES ˌovə-; |-d -d
overrun n 'ovɚˌrʌn; ES 'ovə-
overrun v ˌovɚ'rʌn; ES ˌovə-; |-ran -'ræn
overscrupulous 'ovɚ'skrupjələs, -rɪu-; ES
'ovə-
oversea 'ovɚ'si; ES 'ovə-; |-s -z ('over ˌsea
'voyage)
oversee ˌovɚ'si; ES ˌovə-; |-saw -'sɔ |-seen
-'sin
overseer 'ovɚˌsiɚ, -ˌsɪr, ˌovɚ'sɪr; ES 'ovə-
ˌsi·ə(r, -ˌsɪə(r, ˌovə'sɪə(r
oversell 'ovɚ'sɛl; ES 'ovə-; |-sold -'sold
overset n 'ovɚˌsɛt; ES 'ovə-
overset v ˌovɚ'sɛt; ES ˌovə-
oversew 'ovɚˌso, ˌovɚ'so; ES 'ovə-, ˌovə-;
|past -ed -d |pptc -ed -d or -n -n
overshade ˌovɚ'ʃed; ES ˌovə-; |-d -ɪd
overshadow ˌovɚ'ʃædo, -də; ES ˌovə-; |-ed -d
|-ing -'ʃædəwɪŋ
overshine ˌovɚ'ʃaɪn; ES ˌovə-; |-shone -'ʃon
overshoe 'ovɚˌʃu, -ˌʃɪu; ES 'ovə-
overshoot ˌovɚ'ʃut; ES ˌovə-; |-shot -'ʃat;
ES+-'ʃɒt
oversight 'ovɚˌsaɪt; ES 'ovə-
oversize adj 'ovɚ'saɪz; ES 'ovə-; |-d -d ('over-
ˌsize(d) 'bolt)
oversize n 'ovɚˌsaɪz; ES 'ovə-; |-s -ɪz
oversize v ˌovɚ'saɪz; ES ˌovə-; |-s -ɪz |-d -d
overskirt 'ovɚˌskɚt; ES 'ovəˌskɜt, 'ovəˌskɝt
oversleep 'ovɚ'slip; ES 'ovə-; |-slept -'slɛpt
oversoon 'ovɚ'sun, -'sʊn; ES 'ovə-
oversoul 'ovɚˌsol; ES 'ovə-
overspend 'ovɚ'spɛnd; ES 'ovə-; |-spent
-'spɛnt
overspread ˌovɚ'sprɛd; ES ˌovə-
overstate 'ovɚ'stet; ES 'ovə-; |-d -ɪd
overstay 'ovɚ'ste; ES 'ovə-; |-stayed -'sted
overstep ˌovɚ'stɛp; ES ˌovə-; |-ped -t
overstride ˌovɚ'straɪd; ES ˌovə-; |-strode
-'strod |-stridden -'strɪdn̩
overstrung 'ovɚ'strʌŋ; ES 'ovə-
overstuff 'ovɚ'stʌf; ES 'ovə-; |-ed -t
oversubscribe 'ovɚsəb'skraɪb; ES 'ovə-;
|-d -d
overt o'vɝt; ES o'vɜt, o'vɝt; ('oˌvert 'act)

Key: See in full §§3–47. bee bi |pity 'pɪtɪ (§6) |rate ret |yet jɛt |sang sæŋ |angry 'æŋ·grɪ
|bath bæθ; E baθ (§10) |ah ɑ |far fɑr |watch wɑtʃ, wɒtʃ (§12) |jaw dʒɔ |gorge gɔrdʒ |go go

overtake ˌovɚˈtek; ES ˌovə-; |-took -ˈtʊk |-taken -ˈtekən

overtax ˈovɚˈtæks; ES ˈovə-; |-es -ɪz |-ed -t

over-the-counter ˈovɚðəˈkaʊntɚ; ES ˈovəðə-ˈkaʊntə(r

overthrow n ˈovɚˌθro; ES ˈovə-

overthrow v ˌovɚˈθro; ES ˌovə-; |-threw -ˈθru, -ˈθrɪu |-thrown -ˈθron

overtime n ˈovɚˌtaɪm; ES ˈovə-

overtime v ˌovɚˈtaɪm; ES ˌovə-; |-d -d

overtone ˈovɚˌton; ES ˈovə-

overtop ˌovɚˈtɑp; ES ˌovəˈtɑp, -ˈtɒp; |-ped -t

overtrade ˈovɚˈtred; ES ˈovə-; |-d -ɪd

overtrick ˈovɚˌtrɪk; ES ˈovə-

overtrump ˌovɚˈtrʌmp; ES ˌovə-; |-ed -t

overture ˈovɚtʃɚ, -ˌtʃʊr; ES ˈovətʃə(r, -ˌtʃʊə(r

overturn n ˈovɚˌtɝn; ES ˈovəˌtɜn, ˈovəˌtɝn

overturn v ˌovɚˈtɝn; ES ˌovəˈtɜn, ˌovəˈtɝn; |-ed -d

overvalue ˈovɚˈvælju; ES ˈovə-; |-d -d

overwatch ˈovɚˈwɑtʃ, -ˈwɒtʃ, -ˈwɔtʃ; ES ˈovə-; |-es -ɪz |-ed -t

overwear ˈovɚˈwɛr, -ˈwær; E ˈovəˈwɛə(r, ES -ˈwæə(r; |-wore -ˈwor, -ˈwɔr; ES -ˈwoə(r, E+-ˈwɔə(r; |-worn -ˈworn, -ˈwɔrn; ES -ˈwoən, E+-ˈwɔən

overweary ˈovɚˈwɪrɪ, -ˈwɪrɪ; ES ˈovə-, S+-ˈwɛrɪ; |-ied -d

overween ˈovɚˈwin; ES ˈovə-; |-ed -d |-ing -ɪŋ

overweigh ˈovɚˈwe; ES ˈovə-; |-ed -d

overweight n ˈovɚˌwet; ES ˈovə-

overweight adj ˈovɚˈwet; ES ˈovə-; (ˈover-ˌweight ˈparcel)

overweight v ˈovɚˈwet; ES ˈovə-; |-ed -ɪd

overwhelm ˌovɚˈhwɛlm; ES ˌovə-; |-ed -d

overwind ˈovɚˈwaɪnd; ES ˈovə-; |-wound -ˈwaʊnd

overwork n ‘too hard w.’ ˈovɚˈwɝk; ES ˈovəˈwɜk, ˈovəˈwɝk; ‘extra w.’ ˈoverˌwork

overwork v ˈovɚˈwɝk; ES ˈovəˈwɜk, ˈovə-ˈwɝk; |-ed -t or -wrought -ˈrɔt

overwrought ˈovɚˈrɔt; ES ˈovəˈrɔt; (ˈover-ˌwrought ˈnerves)

Ovid ˈɑvɪd; ES+ˈɒvɪd

Ovidian oˈvɪdɪən

oviduct ˈovɪˌdʌkt

oviparous oˈvɪpərəs

oviposit ˌovɪˈpɑzɪt; ES+-ˈpɒz-; |-ed -ɪd

Ovoca əˈvokə

ovoid ˈovɔɪd

ovule ˈovjul

ovum ˈovəm |pl ova ˈovə

-ow suffix -o, -ö, -ə. The ending -ow is seldom pronounced (except with artificial care) with a full o as in elbow. The commonest prons. are with an advanced ö, nearly like ʊ, and with ə. ö differs from ə chiefly in its lip-rounding. In these words the symbol ö is not used in the vocab., the symbol o being under-stood to include the pron. with fronted ö. When a vowel follows the -ə (as in -ing, -er) a w or r intervenes; as follow ˈfalə, following ˈfaləwɪŋ or ˈfalərɪŋ. An ö sound, nearly ʊ, is also heard in medial syllables of such words as whatsoever.

owe o |-d -d |owing ˈo·ɪŋ

Owego əˈwigo, o-

Owen ˈo·ɪn, -ən

owl aʊl |-et -ɪt

own on |owned ond

ownership ˈonɚˌʃɪp; ES ˈonəˌʃɪp

Owosso əˈwaso, əˈwɒso

ox aks; ES+ɒks; |-’s -ɪz |-en -n̩

oxalate ˈaksəˌlet; ES+ˈɒks-; |-d -ɪd

oxalic aksˈælɪk; ES+ɒks-

oxalis ˈaksəlɪs; ES+ˈɒks-

oxazine ˈaksəˌzin, -zɪn; ES+ˈɒks-

oxbow ˈaksˌbo; ES+ˈɒks-

oxen ˈaksn̩; ES+ˈɒksn̩

oxeye ˈaksˌaɪ; ES+ˈɒks-; |-d -d

Oxford ˈaksfɚd; ES ˈaksfəd, ˈɒks-; |-shire -ˌʃɪr, -ʃɚ; ES -ˌʃɪə(r, -ʃə(r

oxidase ˈaksəˌdes, -ˌdez; ES+ˈɒks-

oxidate ˈaksəˌdet; ES+ˈɒks-; |-d -ɪd

oxide ˈaksaɪd, ˈaksɪd; ES+ˈɒks-

oxidize ˈaksəˌdaɪz; ES+ˈɒks-; |-s -ɪz |-d -d

oxime ˈaksim, ˈaksɪm; ES+ˈɒks-

oxlip ˈaksˌlɪp; ES+ˈɒks-;—The earlier form was ox-slip. The present syl. division may be due to confusion with the word lip; cf cowslip.

Oxonian aksˈonɪən; ES+ɒks-

oxtongue ˈaksˌtʌŋ; ES+ˈɒks-; |-d -d

oxyacetylene ˌaksɪəˈsɛtl̩ˌin; ES+ˌɒks-

oxycalcium ˌaksɪˈkælsɪəm; ES+ˌɒks-

oxygen ˈaksədʒən, ˈaksɪ-, -dʒɪn; ES+ˈɒks-

oxygenate ˈaksədʒənˌet; ES+ˈɒks-; |-d -ɪd

oxygenize 'aksədʒənˌaɪz; ES+'ɒks-; |-s -ɪz
|-d -d
oxyhydrogen ˌaksɪ'haɪdrədʒən, -dʒɪn; ES+
ˌɒks-
oxymoron ˌaksɪ'moran, -'mɔr-; ES ˌaksɪ-
'moran, ˌɒksɪ'mɒrɒn, E+-'mɔr-
oxysalt 'aksɪˌsɔlt; ES+'ɒks-
oxysulphide, -fide ˌaksɪ'sʌlfaɪd, -fɪd; ES+
ˌɒks-; |-phid, -fid -fɪd

oxytocic ˌaksɪ'tosɪk, -'tɑsɪk; ES+ˌɒksɪ'tosɪk,
ˌɒksɪ'tɒsɪk
oxytone 'aksɪˌton; ES+'ɒks-
oyer 'ojɚ, 'ɔɪɚ; ES 'ojə(r, 'ɔɪ·ə(r
oyez, -yes 'ojɛs, 'ojɛz |-es -ɪz
oyster 'ɔɪstɚ; ES 'ɔɪstə(r
Ozark 'ozark; ES 'oza:k, E+'oza:k
ozone 'ozon, o'zon
ozonize 'ozəˌnaɪz |-s -ɪz |-d -d |-nous -nəs

P

P, p *letter* pi |*pl* P's, Ps, *poss* P's piz
pabulum 'pæbjələm
pace pes |paces 'pesɪz |paced pest
pacemaker 'pesˌmekɚ; ES 'pesˌmekə(r
Pachaug pə'tʃɔg, *cf* Patchogue
pachisi pə'tʃizɪ, pa-—*see* parcheesi
pachyderm 'pækəˌdɝm; ES -ˌdɝm, -ˌdɝm
pacifiable 'pæsəˌfaɪəbḷ |-bly -blɪ
pacific, P- pə'sɪfɪk |-ally -ḷɪ, -ɪklɪ
pacification ˌpæsəfə'keʃən
pacificator 'pæsəfəˌketɚ; ES -ˌketə(r
pacificatory pə'sɪfəkəˌtorɪ, -ˌtɔrɪ; S -ˌtorɪ
pacificism pə'sɪfəˌsɪzəm
pacifism 'pæsəˌfɪzəm |-fist -fɪst
pacify 'pæsəˌfaɪ |pacified 'pæsəˌfaɪd
pack pæk |packed pækt |-age -ɪdʒ |-ages
-ɪdʒɪz
Packard 'pækɚd; ES 'pækəd
packet 'pækɪt |packeted 'pækɪtɪd
packhorse 'pækˌhɔrs; ES 'pækˌhɔəs; |-s -ɪz
packsack 'pækˌsæk
packsaddle 'pækˌsædḷ |-d -d
packthread 'pækˌθrɛd
pact pækt
pad pæd |padded 'pædɪd
paddle 'pædḷ |-d -d |-ling 'pædlɪŋ, 'pædlɪŋ
paddock 'pædək |paddocked 'pædəkt
paddy, padi '*rice*' 'pædɪ
Paddy '*Irishman*' 'pædɪ
Padelford pə'dɛlfɚd; ES -fəd
Paderewski ˌpædə'rɛfskɪ, -'rɛv-, -'ruskɪ,
-'rɪuskɪ
padishah 'padɪˌʃa
padlock 'pædˌlak; ES+-ˌlɒk; |-ed -t
padre 'padrɪ (*It* 'pa:dre, *Sp* 'paðre)

Padriac Colum 'padrɪk'kaləm, -'kɒləm
padrone pə'dronɪ |-s -z (*It* pa'dro:ne |*pl* -ni
-ni)
Padua 'pædʒʊə, 'pædjʊə |-n -n (*It* 'pa:dova)
Paducah pə'djukə, -'dɪu-, -'du-
paean 'piən
paediatric ˌpidɪ'ætrɪk, ˌpɛd- |-s -s
paediatrician ˌpidɪə'trɪʃən, ˌpɛd-
pagan 'pegən |paganism 'pegənˌɪzəm
Paganini ˌpægə'ninɪ (*It* ˌpaga'ni:ni)
paganize 'pegənˌaɪz |-s -ɪz |-d -d
page pedʒ |pages 'pedʒɪz |paged pedʒd
Page pedʒ |Page's 'pedʒɪz
pageant 'pædʒənt |-ry -rɪ
Paget 'pædʒɪt
paginate 'pædʒəˌnet |-nated -ˌnetɪd
pagination ˌpædʒə'neʃən
pagoda pə'godə
Pago Pago 'paŋo'paŋo=Pangopango
pah *int, v* pa, pa, pæ, *etc.* |-ed -d
Pahlavi, p- 'palə,vi=Pehlevi
paid *past & pptc of* pay ped
pail pel |-ed -d |-ful -ˌfʊl |-fuls -ˌfʊlz
pain pen |pained pend |-ful -fəl |-fully -fəlɪ
Paine pen
painstaking 'penzˌtekɪŋ
paint pent |painted 'pentɪd
paintbrush 'pentˌbrʌʃ |-es -ɪz
pair pɛr, pær; E pɛə(r, ES pæə(r; |-ed -d
Paisley 'pezlɪ
Paiute paɪ'jut ('Paiˌute 'language)
pajama pə'dʒæmə, pə'dʒamə |-s -z
pal pæl |palled pæld
palace 'pælɪs, -əs |-s -ɪz
paladin 'pælədɪn

Palamon 'pæləmən, -ˌmɑn, -ˌmɒn

palanquin, -keen ˌpælən'kin, -əŋ'k- |-ed -d

palatability ˌpælətə'bɪlətɪ

palatable 'pælətəb| |-bly -blɪ

palatal 'pælət|

palatalization ˌpælət|ə'zeʃən, -aɪ'z-

palatalize 'pælət|ˌaɪz |-s -ɪz |-d -d

palate 'pælɪt

palatial pə'leʃəl |-ly -ɪ

palatinate, P- pə'lætn̩ˌet, -ɪt

palatine, P- 'pæləˌtaɪn, -tɪn

Palatka pə'lætkə

palaver pə'lævɚ; ES pə'lævə(r; |-ed -d |-ing
     pə'lævərɪŋ, pə'lævrɪŋ

pale pel |paled peld

pale-, paleo- 'pelɪ-, 'pelɪo-, Brit usually 'pæl-

paleethnology ˌpelɪɛθ'nɑlədʒɪ; ES+-'nɒl-

paleface 'pelˌfes |-faces -ˌfesɪz

paleobotany ˌpelɪo'bɑtn̩ɪ; ES+-'bɒt-

paleographer ˌpelɪ'ɑgrəfɚ, -'ɒg-; ES -fə(r

paleographic ˌpelɪə'græfɪk |-al -| |-ally -|ɪ

paleography ˌpelɪ'ɑgrəfɪ, -'ɒg- |-phist -fɪst

paleolith 'pelɪəˌlɪθ |-ths -θs

paleolithic ˌpelɪə'lɪθɪk

paleontologic ˌpelɪˌɑntə'lɑdʒɪk; ES+-ˌɒntə-
     'lɒdʒɪk; |-al -| |-ally -|ɪ, -ɪklɪ

paleontology ˌpelɪɑn'tɑlədʒɪ; ES+-ɒn'tɒl-;
     |-gist -dʒɪst

Paleozoic ˌpelɪə'zo·ɪk

paleozoology 'pelɪˌo·zo'ɑlədʒɪ; ES+-'ɒl-

Palermo pə'lɝmo; ES -'lɜmo, -'lɜˑmo; (It
     pɑ'lɛrmo)

Palestine 'pæləsˌtaɪn

Palestinian ˌpæləs'tɪnɪən, -'tɪnjən

paletot 'pæləˌto, 'pælto

palette 'pælɪt

Paley 'pelɪ

palfrey, P- 'pɒlfrɪ

Palgrave 'pɒlgrev, 'pæl-

Pali 'pɑli

palikar 'pælɪˌkɑr; ES 'pælɪˌkɑ:(r

palimpsest 'pælɪmpˌsɛst

palindrome 'pælɪnˌdrom

paling 'pelɪŋ

palingenesis ˌpælɪn'dʒɛnəsɪs |-sist -sɪst

palinode 'pælɪˌnod |-d -ɪd

palisade ˌpælə'sed |-d -ɪd |Palisades -'sedz

pall pɒl |palled pɒld

Palladian pə'ledɪən

palladic pə'lædɪk, pə'ledɪk

palladium, P- pə'ledɪəm |-s -z |-dia -dɪə

palladous pə'ledəs, 'pælədəs

Pallas 'pæləs |Pallas's 'pæləsɪz

pallbearer 'pɒlˌbɛrɚ, -ˌbærɚ; E -ˌbɛrə(r, ES
     -ˌbærə(r

pallet 'pælɪt

palliate 'pælɪˌet |-d -ɪd |-ative -ˌetɪv

palliation ˌpælɪ'eʃən

pallid 'pælɪd

pallium 'pælɪəm |-s -z |pallia 'pælɪə

pall-mall game 'pɛl'mɛl

Pall Mall London street 'pɛl'mɛl, 'pæl'mæl

pallor 'pælɚ; ES 'pælə(r

palm pɑm |palmed pɑmd |-ist -ɪst |-istry
     -ɪstrɪ

palmate 'pælmet, 'pælmɪt |-mated -metɪd

palmer, P- 'pɑmɚ; ES 'pɑmə(r

Palmerston 'pɑmɚstən; ES 'pɑməstən

palmetto pæl'mɛto

palmitate 'pælməˌtet |-mitic pæl'mɪtɪk

palmitin 'pælmətɪn |-tine -tɪn, -ˌtin

palmy 'pɑmɪ

Palmyra, p- pæl'maɪrə

Palo Alto Cal, Pa 'pælo'ælto; Ia, Tex+
     'pɑlo'ɑlto

palpable 'pælpəb| |-bly -blɪ

palpitant 'pælpətənt

palpitate 'pælpəˌtet |-tated -ˌtetɪd

palpitation ˌpælpə'teʃən

palsy 'pɒlzɪ |palsied 'pɒlzɪd

palter 'pɒltɚ; ES 'pɒltə(r; |-ed -d |-ing
     'pɒltərɪŋ, 'pɒltrɪŋ |-try -trɪ

paly 'pelɪ

pam pæm

Pamela 'pæmələ

Pamlico 'pæmlɪˌko

pampas 'pæmpəz, attrib. -pəs

Pampas S Amer plains 'pæmpəz

pamper 'pæmpɚ; ES 'pæmpə(r; |-ed -d |-ing
     'pæmpərɪŋ, 'pæmprɪŋ

pamphlet 'pæmflɪt, 'pæmpflɪt |-ed -ɪd

pamphleteer ˌpæmflɪ'tɪr; ES -'tɪə(r, S+
     -'tɛə(r; |-ed -d

Pamunkey pə'mʌŋkɪ

pan, P- pæn |panned pænd

panacea ˌpænə'siə, -'sɪə

Panama, p- 'pænəˌmɑ, -ˌmɔ, ˌpænə'mɑ, -'mɔ
     (Sp ˌpana'ma)

Words below that have æ before r (carry ˈkærɪ) are often pronounced in N with ɛ (ˈkɛrɪ, §94)

Panamanian ˌpænəˈmenɪən, -ˈmenjən, -ˈman-
Pan-American ˈpænəˈmɛrəkən
Panay pəˈnaɪ (*Sp* paˈnai)
pancake ˈpænˌkek, ˈpæŋ-
panchromatic ˌpænkroˈmætɪk
Pancras ˈpæŋkrəs—*see* St. Pancras
pancreas ˈpænkrɪəs, ˈpæŋ-
pancreatic ˌpænkrɪˈætɪk, ˌpæŋ-
pancreatin ˈpænkrɪətɪn, ˈpæŋ-
panda ˈpændə
Pandar ˈpændɚ; ES ˈpændə(r; *cf* pander
Pandarus ˈpændərəs |Pandarus's ˈpændərəsɪz
pandect, P- ˈpændɛkt
pandemic pænˈdɛmɪk
Pandemonium, p- ˌpændɪˈmonɪəm, -ˈmonjəm
pander, -ar ˈpændɚ; ES ˈpændə(r; |-ed -d
    |-ing ˈpændərɪŋ, ˈpændrɪŋ
Pandora pænˈdorə, -ˈdɔrə; S -ˈdorə
pandowdy pænˈdaʊdɪ
Pandulph ˈpændʌlf
pane pen |paned pend
panegyric ˌpænəˈdʒɪrɪk |-al -l̩ |-ally -l̩ɪ, -ɪklɪ
panegyrize ˈpænədʒəˌraɪz |-s -ɪz |-d -d
panel ˈpænl̩ |-ed -d
panful ˈpænˌfʊl |-s -z
pang pæŋ
pangenesis pænˈdʒɛnəsɪs
Pangopango ˈpaŋoˈpaŋo=Pago Pago
panhandle, P- ˈpænˌhændl̩ |-d -d |-dling
    -dl̩ɪŋ, -dlɪŋ
Panhellenic ˈpænhəˈlɛnɪk, -hɛˈlɛnɪk
panic ˈpænɪk |-icked -t |panicky ˈpænɪkɪ
panicle ˈpænɪk|l̩ |panicled ˈpænɪk|d
Panjab pʌnˈdʒab |-i -ɪ
panjandrum, P- pænˈdʒændrəm
panne pæn
pannier ˈpænjɚ, ˈpænɪɚ; ES ˈpænjə(r, -nɪ·ə(r
pannikin ˈpænəkɪn
panoply ˈpænəplɪ |-plied -plɪd
panorama ˌpænəˈræmə, *less freq.* -ˈramə
panoramic ˌpænəˈræmɪk |-ally -l̩ɪ, -ɪklɪ
pansy ˈpænzɪ
pant pænt |panted ˈpæntɪd
Pantagruel pænˈtægruˌɛl (*Fr* pãtagryˈɛl)
pantalets, -ttes ˌpæntl̩ˈɛts
pantaloon ˌpæntl̩ˈun |-ed -d
pantechnicon pænˈtɛknɪˌkan, -kən; ES+
    -ˌkɒn

pantheism ˈpænθiˌɪzəm |-ist -ɪst
pantheistic ˌpænθiˈɪstɪk |-al -l̩ |-ally -l̩ɪ, -ɪklɪ
pantheon, P- ˈpænθɪən, -ˌan, pænˈθiən;
    ES+-ˌɒn
panther ˈpænθɚ; ES ˈpænθə(r
Panthino pænˈθino
pantofle ˈpæntəfl̩, pænˈtafl̩, -ˈtufl̩; ES+-ˈtɒf-
pantomime ˈpæntəˌmaɪm |-d -d |-mimist -ɪst
pantomimic ˌpæntəˈmɪmɪk
pantry ˈpæntrɪ
pants pænts
Panurge pænˈɝdʒ; ES -ˈɜdʒ, -ˈɝdʒ; |-'s -ɪz
    (*Fr* paˈnyrʒ)
panzer ˈpænzɚ, ˈpʌntsɚ; ES -ə(r; (*Ger* ˈpan-
    tsər)
Paola pɪˈolə, pe-, *Italy* ˈpɑːolɑ
Paoli pɪˈolaɪ, pe- (*It* ˈpɑːoli)
pap pæp |papped pæpt
papa ˈpapə, *now rare* pəˈpa
papacy ˈpepəsɪ
papain pəˈpe·ɪn
papal ˈpepl̩ |papally ˈpepl̩ɪ
papaverine pəˈpævəˌrin, -rɪn, -ˈpev-
papaw ˈpɔpɔ
papaya pəˈpaɪə, pəˈpajə
Papeete ˌpapɪˈete
paper ˈpepɚ; ES ˈpepə(r; |-ed -d |-ing ˈpe-
    pərɪŋ, ˈpeprɪŋ
paperer ˈpepərɚ, ˈpeprɚ; ES ˈpepərə(r,
    ˈpeprə(r
papeterie ˈpæpətrɪ (*Fr* papˈtri)
papier-mâché ˈpepɚməˈʃe, ˌpæpjemæˈʃe; ES
    ˈpepəməˈʃe, ˌpæpjemæˈʃe; (*Fr* papjema-
    ˈʃe)
papist ˈpepɪst
papistic peˈpɪstɪk, pə- |-al -l̩ |-ally -l̩ɪ, -ɪklɪ
papoose pæˈpus |-s -ɪz
paprika, -ca pæˈprikə, pə-
Papua ˈpæpjʊə |Papuan ˈpæpjʊən
papyrus pəˈpaɪrəs |-es -ɪz |papyri pəˈpaɪraɪ
par par; ES pɑː(r, E+pɑː(r; |-red -d
Pará paˈra (ˈPará ˈrubber)
parable ˈpærəbl̩ |-d -d |-ling -bl̩ɪŋ, -blɪŋ
parabola pəˈræbələ |-loid -ˌlɔɪd
parabolic ˌpærəˈbalɪk; ES+-ˈbɒl-; |-ally -l̩ɪ,
    -ɪklɪ
paraboloidal pəˌræbəˈlɔɪdl̩
Paracelsus ˌpærəˈsɛlsəs |-sus' -səs

Key: *See in full §§3–47.* bee bi |pity ˈpɪtɪ (§6) |rate ret |yet jɛt |sang sæŋ |angry ˈæŋ·grɪ
|bath bæθ; E baθ (§10) |ah ɑ |far fɑr |watch watʃ, wɒtʃ (§12) |jaw dʒɔ |gorge gɔrdʒ |go go

Words below in which a *before* r (farm) *is sounded* ɑ *are often pronounced in* E *with* a (fɑːm)
Words below that have æ *before* r (carry 'kærɪ) *are often pronounced in* N *with* ɛ ('kɛrɪ, §94)

parachute 'pærə͵ʃut |-chuted -͵ʃutɪd
paraclete 'pærə͵klit
parade pə'red |paraded pə'redɪd
paradigm 'pærə͵dɪm, -͵daɪm
paradigmatic ͵pærədɪg'mætɪk |-al -| |-ally -|ɪ, -ɪklɪ
paradisaic ͵pærədɪ'se·ɪk |-al -| |-ally -|ɪ, -ɪklɪ
paradise, P- 'pærə͵daɪs |-dises -͵daɪsɪz
paradox 'pærə͵dɑks; ES+-͵dɒks; |-es -ɪz
paradoxical ͵pærə'dɑksɪk|; ES+-'dɒks-; |-ally -|ɪ, -ɪklɪ
paraffin 'pærəfɪn |-fine -fɪn, -͵fin
paragenesis ͵pærə'dʒɛnəsɪs
paragon 'pærə͵gɑn, -gən; ES+-͵gɒn
paragraph 'pærə͵græf |-ed -t; ES+-af, -ɑf
paragraphic ͵pærə'græfɪk |-al -| |-ally -|ɪ, -ɪklɪ
Paraguay 'pærə͵gwe, -͵gwaɪ (*Sp* ͵para'gwai)
Paraguayan ͵pærə'gwean, -'gwaɪən
parakeet 'pærə͵kit
paraldehyde pə'rældə͵haɪd
paralipsis, -lep-, -leip- ͵pærə'lɪpsɪs, -'lɛp-, -'laɪp- |-ses -siz
parallax 'pærə͵læks |-es -ɪz |-ed -t
parallel 'pærə͵lɛl |-ed -d |-ism -lɛl͵ɪzəm
parallelepiped 'pærə͵lɛlə'paɪpɪd, -'pɪpɪd
parallelogram ͵pærə'lɛlə͵græm
paralysis pə'ræləsɪs |-ses -͵siz
paralytic ͵pærə'lɪtɪk
paralyze 'pærə͵laɪz |-lyzes -͵laɪzɪz |-d -d
paramount, P- 'pærə͵maʊnt |-cy -sɪ
paramour 'pærə͵mʊr; ES -͵mʊə(r
Paraná ͵pærə'nɑ, -'nɔ (*Sp* ͵para'na)
parang pɑ'rɑŋ
paranoia ͵pærə'nɔɪə |-noiac -'nɔɪæk
parapet 'pærəpɪt, -͵pɛt |-peted -pɪtɪd, -͵pɛtɪd
paraphernalia ͵pærəfə'nelɪə, -fə-, -ljə; ES -fə-;—*In the first pron.* ɚ *is lost by dissimilation* (§121).
paraphrase 'pærə͵frez |-s -ɪz |-d -d
paraphrastic ͵pærə'fræstɪk |-al -| |-ally -|ɪ, -ɪklɪ
parapsychology ͵pærəsaɪ'kɑlədʒɪ; ES+-'kɒl-
parasang 'pærə͵sæŋ
parasite 'pærə͵saɪt |-sitism -saɪt͵ɪzəm
parasitic ͵pærə'sɪtɪk |-al -| |-ally -|ɪ, -ɪklɪ
parasol 'pærə͵sɔl, -͵sɒl, -͵sɑl

parasynthesis ͵pærə'sɪnθəsɪs
parasynthetic ͵pærəsɪn'θɛtɪk |-al -| |-ally -|ɪ, -ɪklɪ
paratactic ͵pærə'tæktɪk |-al -| |-ally -|ɪ, -ɪklɪ
parataxis ͵pærə'tæksɪs
parathyroid ͵pærə'θaɪrɔɪd |-al -θaɪ'rɔɪd|
paratyphoid ͵pærə'taɪfɔɪd
parboil 'pɑr͵bɔɪl; ES 'pɑː͵bɔɪl; |-ed -d
parbuckle 'pɑr͵bʌk|; ES 'pɑː͵bʌk|; |-d -d |-ling -͵bʌk|ɪŋ, -͵bʌk|ɪŋ
parcel 'pɑrs|; ES 'pɑːs|; |-ed -d |-ing -s|ɪŋ, -s|ɪŋ
parcener 'pɑrsnɚ; ES 'pɑːsnə(r; |-nary -͵ɛrɪ
parch pɑrtʃ; ES pɑːtʃ; |-es -ɪz |-ed -t |-edly -ɪdlɪ
parcheesi, -chesi, -chisi pə'tʃizɪ, pɑː-; N+pɚ-, pɑr-
parchment 'pɑrtʃmənt; ES 'pɑːtʃ-; |-ed -ɪd
pard pɑrd; ES pɑːd
Pardee pɑr'di; ES pɑː'di
pardie *intj* pɑr'di; ES pɑː'di
pardon 'pɑrdn̩; ES 'pɑː'dn̩; |-ed -d |-ing -dn̩ɪŋ, -dnɪŋ |-able -dnəb|, -dnəb| |-bly -blɪ
pare pɛr, pær; E pɛə(r, ES pæə(r; |-d -d
paregoric ͵pærə'gɔrɪk, -'gɑrɪk, -'gɒrɪk
parent 'pɛrənt, 'pærənt, 'perənt |-age -ɪdʒ
parental pə'rɛnt| |parentally pə'rɛnt|ɪ
parenthesis pə'rɛnθəsɪs |-theses -θə͵siz
parenthesize pə'rɛnθə͵saɪz |-s -ɪz |-d -d
parenthetic ͵pærən'θɛtɪk |-al -| |-ally -|ɪ, -ɪklɪ
paresis pə'risɪs, 'pærəsɪs
paretic pə'rɛtɪk, pə'ritɪk
par excellence pɑr'ɛksə͵lɑns (*Fr* parɛksɛ-'lãːs)
parfait pɑr'fe, pɑr'fɛ; ES pɑː-; (*Fr* pɑr'fɛ)
parhelion pɑr'hilɪən, -ljən; ES pɑː-; |-ia -ɪə
pariah pə'raɪə, 'pærɪə, 'pɑr-
Parian 'pɛrɪən, 'pær-, 'per-; S 'pær-, 'per-
parietal pə'raɪət|
pari mutuel 'pærɪ'mjutʃʊəl, -'mɪu- (*Fr* parimy'tɥɛl)
Paris 'pærɪs, *jocularly* pæ'ri |-'s -ɪz (*Fr* pa'ri)
Paris, Gaston gæs'tɔnpæ'ris |-'s -ɪz (*Fr* gas-tõpa'riːs)
parish 'pærɪʃ |parished 'pærɪʃt
parishioner pə'rɪʃənɚ, -'rɪʃnɚ; ES -nə(r

Words below in which a before r (farm) is sounded ɑ are often pronounced in E with a (fa:m)
Words below that have æ before r (carry ˈkæɪɪ) are often pronounced in N with ɛ (ˈkɛɪɪ, §94)

Parisian pəˈrɪʒən, pəˈrɪzɪən
parity ˈpærətɪ
park pɑrk; ES pɑːk; |-ed -t |-way -ˌwe
parka ˈpɑrkə; ES ˈpɑːkə
Parker ˈpɑrkɚ; ES ˈpɑːkə(r
Parkman ˈpɑrkmən; ES ˈpɑːkmən
parlance ˈpɑrləns; ES ˈpɑːləns; |-s -ɪz
parlay ˈpɑrlɪ; ES ˈpɑːlɪ
parle pɑrl; ES pɑːl
parley ˈpɑrlɪ; ES ˈpɑːlɪ; |-ed -d
parliament ˈpɑrləmənt; ES ˈpɑːləmənt
parliamentarian ˌpɑrləmɛnˈtɛrɪən, -ˈter-; ES ˌpɑːl-
parliamentary ˌpɑrləˈmɛntərɪ, -trɪ; ES ˌpɑːl-
parlor, P- ˈpɑrlɚ; ES ˈpɑːlə(r; |-maid -ˌmed
parlous ˈpɑrləs; ES ˈpɑːləs
Parmesan ˌpɑrməˈzæn; ES ˌpɑːm-; (ˈParmeˌsan ˈCheese)
Parnassian pɑrˈnæsɪən, -sjən; ES pɑˈn-
Parnassus pɑrˈnæsəs; ES pɑːˈn-; |-sus' -səs
Parnell pɑrˈnɛl, ˈpɑrnḷ, *Irish leader* ˈpɑrnḷ; ES pɑːˈn-, ˈpɑːn-
parochial pəˈrokɪəl, -kjəl |-ly -ɪ
parody ˈpærədɪ |parodied ˈpærədɪd |-dist -dɪst
parol, -e *'word'* pəˈrol
parole pəˈrol |-d -d |-lable -əbḷ
Parolles pəˈrɑlɪs, -ˈrɒl- |-'s -ɪz
paronomasia ˌpærənoˈmeʒə, -ʒɪə
parotid pəˈrɑtɪd; ES+-ˈrɒtɪd
paroxysm, P- ˈpærəksˌɪzəm
paroxytone pærˈɑksəˌton; ES+-ˈɒks-
parquet pɑrˈke, -ˈkɛt; ES pɑː-; |-ed -ˈked, -ˈkɛtɪd
parquetry ˈpɑrkɪtrɪ; ES ˈpɑːk-
parricidal ˌpærəˈsaɪdḷ |-ly -ɪ
parricide ˈpærəˌsaɪd
Parrish ˈpærɪʃ |-'s -ɪz
parrot ˈpærət |parroted ˈpærətɪd
parry ˈpærɪ |parried ˈpærɪd
parse pɑrs; ES pɑːs; |-d -t (*Brit* pɑːz)
parsec ˈpɑrˌsɛk; ES ˈpɑːˌsɛk
Parsi, -see ˈpɑrsi, pɑrˈsi; ES ˈpɑːsi, pɑːˈsi
Parsifal ˈpɑrsəfḷ, -ˌfal; ES ˈpɑːs-; (*Ger* ˈpɑrziˌfal)—*see* Parzival
parsimonious ˌpɑrsəˈmonɪəs, -njəs; ES ˌpɑːs-
parsimony ˈpɑrsəˌmonɪ; ES ˈpɑːs-

parsley ˈpɑrslɪ; ES ˈpɑːslɪ
parsnip ˈpɑrsnəp, -nɪp; ES ˈpɑːs-
parson ˈpɑrsn̩; ES ˈpɑːsn̩; |-age -ɪdʒ
part pɑrt; ES pɑːt; |-ed -ɪd |-ly -lɪ
partake pəˈtek, pɑr-; ES pəˈtek, pɑː-; |-took -ˈtʊk |-taken -ˈtekən
parterre pɑrˈtɛr; ES pɑː-; |-d -d (*Fr* pɑrˈtɛːr)
parthenogenesis ˌpɑrθənoˈdʒɛnəsɪs; ES ˌpɑː-θ-
Parthenon ˈpɑrθəˌnɑn, -nən; ES ˈpɑː-θ-, -ˌnɒn
Parthenope pɑrˈθɛnəˌpi, -pɪ; ES pɑˈθɛn-
Parthia ˈpɑrθɪə, -θjə; ES ˈpɑː-θ-; |-n -n
partial ˈpɑrʃəl; ES ˈpɑːʃəl; |-ly -ɪ
partiality pɑrˈʃælɪtɪ, ˌpɑrʃɪˈæl-; ES pɑˈʃæl-, ˌpɑːʃɪˈælɪtɪ
partible ˈpɑrtəbḷ; ES ˈpɑːtəbḷ
participant pɚˈtɪsəpənt, pɑr-; ES pə-, pɑ-
participate *adj* pɚˈtɪsəpɪt, pɑr-, -ˌpet; ES pə-, pɑ-
participate *v* pɚˈtɪsəˌpet, pɑr-; ES pə-, pɑ-; |-d -ɪd
participation pɚˌtɪsəˈpeʃən, pɑr-; ES pə-, pɑ-
participial ˌpɑrtəˈsɪpɪəl, -pjəl; ES ˌpɑːtə-; |-ly -ɪ
participle ˈpɑrtəsəpḷ, ˈpɑrtsəpḷ, ˈpɑrtəˌsɪpḷ; ES ˈpɑːt-
particle ˈpɑrtɪkḷ; ES ˈpɑːt-; |-d -d
parti-colored ˈpɑrtɪˌkʌlɚd; ES ˈpɑːtɪˌkʌləd
particular pɚˈtɪkjələ, pə-, pɑr-; ES pəˈtɪkjələ(r, pɑ-;—*In the 2d pron. ɚ is lost by dissimilation (§121).*
particularity pɚˌtɪkjəˈlærətɪ, pə-, pɑr-; ES pə-, pɑ- —*see note above*
particularize pɚˈtɪkjələˌraɪz, pə-, pɑr-; ES pə-, pɑ-; |-s -ɪz |-d -d—*see note above*
Partington ˈpɑrtɪŋtən; ES ˈpɑːtɪŋ-
partisan, -zan ˈpɑrtəzn̩; ES ˈpɑːtəzn̩
partition pɚˈtɪʃən, pɑr-; ES pə-, pɑ-; |-ed -d
partitive ˈpɑrtətɪv; ES ˈpɑːtətɪv
partlet, P- ˈpɑrtlɪt; ES ˈpɑːtlɪt
partly ˈpɑrtlɪ; ES ˈpɑːtlɪ
partner ˈpɑrtnɚ; ES ˈpɑːtnə(r
partook pɚˈtʊk, pɑr-; ES pəˈtʊk, pɑ:-
partridge ˈpɑrtrɪdʒ; ES ˈpɑːtrɪdʒ; |-s -ɪz
parturition ˌpɑrtjʊˈrɪʃən; ES ˌpɑːt-
party ˈpɑrtɪ; ES ˈpɑːtɪ
party-colored ˈpɑrtɪˌkʌlɚd; ES ˈpɑːtɪˌkʌləd
parure pəˈrʊr; ES pəˈrʊə(r; (*Fr* paˈryːr)

Key: *See in full §§3–47.* bee bi |pity ˈpɪtɪ (§6) |rate ret |yet jɛt |sang sæŋ |angry ˈæŋ·grɪ |bath bæθ; E bɑθ (§10) |ah ɑ |far fɑr |watch wɑtʃ, wɒtʃ (§12) |jaw dʒɔ |gorge gɔrdʒ |go go

Words below in which a *before* r (farm) *is sounded* ɑ *are often pronounced in* E *with* a (fɑːm)

parvenu ˈpɑrvəˌnju, -ˌnɪu, -ˌnu; ES ˈpɑːv-; (Fr parvəˈny)

parvoline ˈpɑrvəˌlin, -lɪn; ES ˈpɑːv-

Parzival ˈpɑrtsəvḷ, -ˌval; ES ˈpɑːts-; (Ger ˈpɑrtsiˌval)

pas Fr pɑ

Pascal ˈpæskḷ (Fr pɑsˈkal)

Pasch pæsk |Pascha ˈpæskə |paschal ˈpæskḷ

pasha ˈpæʃə, ˈpɑʃə, pəˈʃɑ

Paso Robles ˈpæsoˈrobḷz, -bləs, ˈpɑsoˈroblɛs

pasquinade ˌpæskwɪˈned |-d -ɪd

pass pæs; E+pas, pɑs; |-es -ɪz |-ed -t |-able -əbḷ |-bly -blɪ

passado pəˈsɑdo

passage ˈpæsɪdʒ |-s -ɪz |-d -d |-way -ˌwe

Passaic pəˈse·ɪk, pæ-

Passamaquoddy ˌpæsəməˈkwɑdɪ, -ˈkwɒdɪ

passbook ˈpæsˌbʊk; E+ˈpas-, ˈpɑs-

passé, fem. passée pæˈse (Fr pɑˈse) (ˈpɑsˌsée ˈbelle)

passementerie pæsˈmɛntrɪ (Fr pɑsmɑ̃ˈtri)

passenger ˈpæsṇdʒɚ; ES ˈpæsṇdʒɚ(r

passe partout n ˌpæspɚˈtu, -pɑr-; ES -pəˈtu, -pɑːˈtu; (Fr pɑspɑrˈtu)

passe-partout v ˌpæspɚˈtu, -pɑr-; ES -pəˈtu, -pɑːˈtu; |-ed -d

passer-by ˈpæsɚˈbaɪ; ES ˈpæsə-, E+ˈpas-, ˈpɑs-

passim ˈpæsɪm

passion, P- ˈpæʃən |-ed -d |-ate -ɪt, -ʃnɪt

passive ˈpæsɪv |-sivity pæˈsɪvətɪ

passkey ˈpæsˌki; E+ˈpas-, ˈpɑs-

passover ˈpæsˌovɚ; ES -ˌovə(r, E+ˈpas-, ˈpɑs-

passport ˈpæsˌport, -ˌpɔrt; ES -ˌpoət, E+ˈpas-, ˈpɑs-, -ˌpɔət

password ˈpæsˌwɝd; ES -ˌwɜd, -ˌwɝd, E+ˈpas-, ˈpɑs-

Passy pæˈsi (Fr pɑˈsi)

past pæst; E+past, pɑst

paste pest |pasted ˈpestɪd

pasteboard ˈpestˌbord, ˈpes-, -ˌbɔrd; ES -ˌboəd, E+-ˌbɔəd

pastel pæsˈtɛl (ˈpasˌtel ˈdrawing)

pastern ˈpæstɚn; ES ˈpæstən

Pasteur pæsˈtɝ; ES -ˈtɜ(r, -ˈtɝ; (Fr pɑsˈtœːr)

pasteurization ˌpæstərəˈzeʃən, ˌpæstʃə-, -aɪˈz-

pasteurize ˈpæstəˌraɪz, ˈpæstʃə- |-s -ɪz |-d -d

pastille pæsˈtil |pastil ˈpæstɪl |-tile -tɪl |-(e)d -d

pastime ˈpæsˌtaɪm; E+ˈpas-, ˈpɑs-

pastor ˈpæstɚ; ES ˈpæstə(r, E+ˈpas-, ˈpɑs-; |-ate -ɪt, -trɪt

pastoral ˈpæstərəl, -trəl; E+ˈpas-, ˈpɑs-; |-ly -ɪ

pastorale ˌpæstəˈrɑlɪ (It ˌpɑstoˈrɑːle)

pastorium pæsˈtorɪəm, -ˈtɔr-; S -ˈtor-

pastry ˈpestrɪ

pasturage ˈpæstʃərɪdʒ

pasture ˈpæstʃɚ; ES ˈpæstʃə(r, E+ˈpas-, ˈpɑs-

pasty 'pie,' chiefly Brit ˈpæstɪ, ˈpɑstɪ

pasty 'like paste' ˈpestɪ

pat pæt |patted ˈpætɪd

pat-a-cake ˈpætɪˌkek, ˈpætə- |-d -t

Patagonia ˌpætəˈgonjə, -ˈgonɪə |-n -n

patch pætʃ |patches ˈpætʃɪz |-ed -t |-able -əbḷ

Patchogue pæˈtʃɔg, pə-, cf Pachaug

patchouli, -ly ˈpætʃʊlɪ, pəˈtʃulɪ

patchwork ˈpætʃˌwɝk; ES -ˌwɜk, -ˌwɝk

pate pet |pated ˈpetɪd

pâté Fr pɑˈte

patella pəˈtɛlə |-s -z |-lae -li

paten ˈpætṇ

patency ˈpetṇsɪ

patent 'obvious' ˈpetṇt, 'letters patent' ˈpætṇt |-ed -ɪd

patentee ˌpætṇˈti

patentor ˈpætṇtɚ, contrasted with patentee ˌpætṇˈtɔr; ES -tə(r, -ˈtɔə(r

pater, P- ˈpetɚ; ES ˈpetə(r

paterfamilias ˈpetɚfəˈmɪlɪˌæs, -əs; ES ˈpetə-; |-es -ɪz

paternal pəˈtɝnḷ; ES pəˈtɜnḷ, -ˈtɝnḷ; |-ism -ˌɪzəm |-ist -ɪst |-ly -ɪ |-ize -ˌaɪz |-izes -ˌaɪzɪz |-ized -ˌaɪzd

paternalistic pəˌtɝnḷˈɪstɪk; ES -ˌtɜnḷ-, -ˌtɝnḷ-

paternity pəˈtɝnətɪ; ES pəˈtɜnətɪ, -ˈtɝn-

paternoster ˈpetɚˈnɑstɚ, ˈpætɚ-; ES ˈpetə-ˈnɑstə(r, ˈpætə-, -ˈnɒstə(r; Lond street ˈpætɚˌnɑstɚˈro; ES ˈpætəˌnɑstə-, -ˌnɒstə-

Paterson ˈpætɚsṇ; ES ˈpætəsṇ

path pæθ; E+pɑθ, pɑθ; |-'s -s |-θs |-ths -ðz |-thed -θt

Pathan pəˈtɑn, pətˈhɑn

pathetic pəˈθɛtɪk |-al -ḷ |-ally -ḷɪ, -ɪklɪ

|full fʊl |tooth tuθ |further ˈfɝðɚ; ES ˈfɝðə |custom ˈkʌstəm |while hwaɪl |how haʊ |toy tɔɪ |using ˈjuzɪŋ |fuse fjuz, fɪuz |dish dɪʃ |vision ˈvɪʒən |Eden ˈidṇ |cradle ˈkredḷ |keep 'em ˈkipm̩

pathfinder 'pæθ₁faɪndəˈ; ES -də(r, E+'paθ-, 'paθ-
pathogenesis ₁pæθə'dʒɛnəsɪs |-netic -dʒə-'nɛtɪk
pathogenic ₁pæθə'dʒɛnɪk
pathologic ₁pæθə'lɑdʒɪk; ES+-'lɒdʒɪk; |-al -ļ |-ally -ļɪ, -ɪklɪ
pathologist pæ'θɑlədʒɪst, pə-; ES+-'θɒl-; |-gy -dʒɪ
pathos 'peθɑs; ES+'peθɒs
pathway 'pæθ₁we; E+'paθ-, 'paθ-; |-ed -d
patience, P- 'peʃəns |-'s -ɪz |patient 'peʃənt
patina 'pan' 'pætɪnə |-nae -₁ni
patina 'film' 'pætṇə |-s -z
patio 'patɪ₁o (Sp 'patjo)
Patmore 'pætmor, -mɔr; ES -moə(r, E+ -mɔə(r
Patmos 'pætməs, 'pætmɑs; ES+-mɒs; |-'s -ɪz
patois 'pætwɑ, -wɒ (Fr pa'twɑ)
patriarch 'petrɪ₁ɑrk; ES -₁ɑːk, E+-₁ɑːk; |-ate -ɪt
patriarchal ₁petrɪ'ɑrkļ; ES -'ɑːkļ, E+-'ɑːkļ; |-ly -ɪ
Patricia pə'trɪʃə, -ʃɪə
patrician pə'trɪʃən
Patrick 'pætrɪk
patrimonial ₁pætrə'monɪəl, -njəl |-ly -ɪ
patrimony 'pætrə₁monɪ
patriot 'petrɪət, 'petrɪ₁ɑt; ES+-₁ɒt
patriotic ₁petrɪ'ɑtɪk; ES+-'ɒtɪk; |-al -ļ |-ally -ļɪ, -ɪklɪ
patristic pə'trɪstɪk
Patroclus pə'trokləs |-'s -ɪz
patrol pə'trol |-led -d |-man, -men -mən
patron 'petrən
patronage 'petrənɪdʒ, 'pæt-
patroness 'petrənɪs, 'pæt- |-es -ɪz
patronize 'petrən₁aɪz |-s -ɪz |-d -d |+'pæt-
patronymic ₁pætrə'nɪmɪk
patroon pə'trun
Pattee pæ'ti
patten 'pætṇ |pattened 'pætṇd
patter 'pætəˈ; ES 'pætə(r; |-ed -d
pattern 'pætəˈn; ES 'pætən
Patti 'pætɪ, 'pæti (It 'patti)
Pattison 'pætəsṇ
patty, P- 'pætɪ |patty-cake 'pætɪ₁kek
paucity 'pɔsətɪ

paul pɒl |-ed -d
Paul pɒl |Paula 'pɒlə |Paulist 'pɒlɪst
Paulina pə'laɪnə, pɒ'laɪnə
Pauline fem. name pɒ'lin; 'of Paul' 'pɒlaɪn
Paulinus pɒ'laɪnəs |-'s -ɪz
paunch pɒntʃ, pɒntʃ, pɑntʃ |-es -ɪz |-ed -t
pauper 'pɔpəˈ; ES 'pɔpə(r; |-age -ɪdʒ |-ism -₁ɪzəm
pauperize 'pɔpə₁raɪz |-s -ɪz |-d -d
pause pɔz |pauses 'pɔzɪz |paused pɔzd
pave pev |past & pptc -d -d |rare pptc -ven -vən
pavement 'pevmənt
Pavey, -vy 'pevɪ, cf Peavey
Pavia bot. 'pevɪə; It city pɑ'viə (It pa'viːɑ)
pavilion pə'vɪljən |pavilioned pə'vɪljənd
pavior 'pevjəˈ; ES 'pevjə(r
paw pɔ |pawed pɔd |pawing 'pɔ·ɪŋ
pawky 'pɔkɪ
pawl pɔl |-ed -d
pawn pɒn |pawned pɒnd |-broker -₁brokəˈ; ES -ə(r
pawnee pɒn'i |-nor 'pɒnəˈ, -n'ɔr; ES -nə(r, -n'ɔə(r
Pawnee pɒ'ni
pawnshop 'pɒn₁ʃɑp; ES+-₁ʃɒp
pawpaw 'pɔpɔ=papaw
Paw Paw 'pɔpɔ
Pawtucket pɒ'tʌkɪt
pax pæks |paxes 'pæksɪz
pay pe |paid, naut. payed ped |-ing 'pe·ɪŋ
payee pe'i
paymaster 'pe₁mæstəˈ; ES -₁mæstə(r, E+ -₁mas-, -₁mɑs-
payment 'pemənt
Payne pen
paynim 'penɪm
pay-roll 'pe₁rol
Paz, La lə'pas (Am Sp la'pas)
pea pi
Peabody 'pi₁bɑdɪ, -bədɪ; ES+-₁bɒdɪ
peace pis |-s -ɪz |-d -t |-ful -fəl |-fully -fəlɪ
peaceable 'pisəbļ |-bly -blɪ
peacemaker 'pis₁mekəˈ; ES -₁mekə(r
peach pitʃ |peaches 'pitʃɪz |peached pitʃt
peachick 'pi₁tʃɪk
peach-tree 'pitʃ₁tri
peacock 'pi₁kɑk; ES+-₁kɒk; |peafowl 'pi₁faʊl
peag, -e pig
pea-green 'pi'grin ('pea-₁green 'dress)

Key: See in full §§3–47. bee bi |pity 'pɪtɪ (§6) |rate ret |yet jɛt |sang sæŋ |angry 'æŋ·grɪ |bath bæθ; E baθ (§10) |ah ɑ |far fɑr |watch wɑtʃ, wɒtʃ (§12) |jaw dʒɔ |gorge gɔrdʒ |go go

peahen 'pi,hɛn
peak pik |peaked pikt
peaked adj 'pikɪd, pikt; N Engd+'pɪkɪd
peal pil |pealed pild
pean 'heraldic pattern,' 'peen' pin
pean 'paean' 'piən
peanut 'pinət, 'pi,nʌt
pear pɛr, pær; E pɛə(r, ES pæə(r
Pearce pɪrs; ES pɪəs, S+pɛəs; |-'s -ɪz
pearl, P- pɝl; ES pɜl, pɝˑl; |-ed -d |-ite -aɪt
pearmain 'pɛrmen, 'pær-; E 'pɛə-, ES 'pæə-
peart 'pert' pɝt, pɪrt; ES pɝt, pɝt, pɪət,
    S+pɛət
Pears pɛrz, pærz; E pɛəz, ES pæəz; |-'s -ɪz
Pearsall 'pɪrsɔl, 'pɪrsḷ; ES 'pɪə-
Pearse pɪrs, pɝs; ES pɪəs, pɝs, pɝˑs; |-'s -ɪz
Pearson 'pɪrsn̩; ES 'pɪəsn̩
Peary 'pɪrɪ
peasant 'pɛznt̩ |-ry -ɪ
pease piz |-cod -,kɑd; ES+-,kɒd
Peaseblossom 'piz,blasəm; ES+-,blɒs-
peat pit |-ery -ərɪ |-wood -,wʊd
peavey, -vy 'pivɪ
Peavey 'pevɪ, 'pivɪ, cf Pavey
pebble 'pɛbḷ |-d -d |-ling -blɪŋ, -bḷɪŋ
pebbly 'pɛblɪ, 'pɛbḷɪ
pecan pɪ'kɑn, pə-, pɪ'kæn, 'pikæn—pɪ'kɑn
    appears to prevail in the S, but pɪ'kæn is not
    uncommon there.
peccable 'pɛkəbḷ |-bility ,pɛkə'bɪlətɪ
peccadillo ,pɛkə'dɪlo
peccant 'pɛkənt |-ancy -ənsɪ
peccary 'pɛkərɪ
peccavi pɪ'kevaɪ, pɛ- |-s -z
peck pɛk |pecked pɛkt
Peckham 'pɛkəm
Pecksniff 'pɛksnɪf |-ian pɛk'snɪfɪən
Pecock 'pi,kɑk; ES+-,kɒk
Pecos 'pekəs, -os |-'s -ɪz
pectin 'pɛktɪn |-al -ḷ |-ase -,es |-ate -,et
pectoral 'pɛktərəl |-ly -ɪ
peculate 'pɛkjə,let |-d -ɪd |-tor -ɚ; ES -ə(r
peculation ,pɛkjə'leʃən
peculiar pɪ'kjuljɚ, -'kɪul-; ES -jə(r
peculiarity pɪ,kjulɪ'ærətɪ, pɪ,kjuljɪ'ærətɪ, pɪ-
    ,kjul'jærətɪ, -,kɪul-
pecuniary pɪ'kjunɪ,ɛrɪ, -'kɪun-
pedagogic ,pɛdə'gɑdʒɪk, -'godʒ-; ES+
    -'gɒdʒ-; |-al -ḷ |-ally -ḷɪ, -ɪklɪ

pedagogue, -gog 'pɛdə,gɑg, -,gɒg, -,gɔg |-d,
    -ged -d |-guism, -ogism -,ɪzəm
pedagogy 'pɛdə,godʒɪ, -,gɑdʒɪ; ES+-,gɒdʒɪ
pedal n, v 'pɛdḷ |-ed -d |-ing 'pɛdḷɪŋ
pedal adj 'pɛdḷ, 'pidḷ
pedaler 'pɛdḷɚ; ES 'pɛdḷə(r; cf peddler
pedant 'pɛdnt̩ |-ry -rɪ
pedantic pɪ'dæntɪk |-al -ḷ |-ally -ḷɪ, -ɪklɪ
peddle 'pɛdḷ |-d -d |-ling 'pɛdḷɪŋ, 'pɛdlɪŋ
peddler 'pɛdlɚ; ES 'pɛdlə(r
pedestal 'pɛdɪstḷ |-ed -d
pedestrian pə'dɛstrɪən |-ism -,ɪzəm
pediatric ,pidɪ'ætrɪk, ,pɛdɪ- |-s -s
pediatrician ,pidɪə'trɪʃən, ,pɛdɪ-
pedicel 'pɛdəsḷ |-ed -d
pedicle 'pɛdɪkḷ
pedigree 'pɛdə,gri |-d -d
pediment 'pɛdəmənt |-al ,pɛdə'mɛntḷ
pedimented 'pɛdə,mɛntɪd, 'pɛdəməntɪd
pedlar 'pɛdlɚ; ES 'pɛdlə(r
pedometer pɪ'damətɚ, pɛd'am-; ES -'damə-
    tə(r, -'am-, -'dɒm-, -'ɒm-
pedro 'pidro
Pedro 'pidro, 'ped- (Sp 'peðro)
peduncle pɪ'dʌŋkḷ |-d -d
pee pi
Peebles 'pibḷz |-'s -ɪz |-shire -,ʃɪr, -ḷʒ,ʃɪr, -ʃɚ,
    -ḷʃɚ; ES -,ʃɪə(r, -ʃə(r
peek pik |peeked pikt
peel, P- pil |peeled pild
peen pin |peened pind
peep pip |peeped pipt |-hole -,hol
peer pɪr; ES pɪə(r, S+pɛə(r; |-ed -d
peerage 'pɪrɪdʒ; S+'pɛr-; |-s -ɪz
peeve piv |peeved pivd |-dly -ɪdlɪ, -dlɪ
peg, P- |pegged pɛgd |peggy, P- 'pɛgɪ
Pegasus 'pɛgəsəs |-sus' -səs
Peggotty 'pɛgətɪ
peignoir pen'war, 'penwar, -ɔr; ES -aː(r,
    -ɔə(r
Peiping 'pe'pɪŋ (Chin 'be'pɪŋ)
Peiraeus paɪ'riəs |-'s -ɪz
Peirce pɪrs; ES pɪəs, S+pɛəs; |-'s -ɪz
pejorative 'pidʒə,retɪv, pɪ'dʒɔrətɪv, -'dʒɑr-,
    -'dʒɒr-
Pekin US 'pikɪn, China 'pi'kɪn |-king 'pi'kɪŋ
Pekingese ,pikɪŋ'iz |-kinese -kɪn'iz |-'s -ɪz
pekoe 'piko, Brit+'pɛko
pelage 'pɛlɪdʒ |-s -ɪz

pelagian, P- pə'ledʒɪən |pelagic pə'lædʒɪk
Pelasgian pə'læzdʒɪən, -gɪən |-gic -dʒɪk
Pelee *isl.* 'pili |Pelée *mt.* pə'le
Peleus 'piljus |-'s -ɪz
pelf pɛlf
Pelham 'pɛləm
pelican 'pɛlɪkən |-ry -rɪ
Pelion 'pilɪən
pelisse pə'lis |-s -ɪz
pellagra pə'legrə, -'læg- |-grous -grəs
pellet 'pɛlɪt |-ed -ɪd
pellicle 'pɛlɪkḷ
pell-mell, pellmell 'pɛl'mɛl |-ed -d
pellucid pə'lusɪd, -'lɪusɪd
Peloponnese ˌpɛləpə'nis |-sos, -sus -əs
Peloponnesian ˌpɛləpə'niʃən, -ʒən
Pelops 'pilɑps; ES+-lɒps; |-'s -ɪz
pelt pɛlt |pelted 'pɛltɪd |-ry -rɪ
pelter 'pɛltɚ; ES 'pɛltə(r; |-ed -d
pelvis 'pɛlvɪs |-es -ɪz |-ves -viz |-vic -vɪk
Pembina 'pɛmbɪnə, -ˌnɔ |Pembine 'pɛmbaɪn
Pemberton 'pɛmbɚtṇ; ES 'pɛmbətṇ
Pembroke *US, C* 'pɛmbrok, *Wales, Irel* -bruk
Pembrokeshire 'pɛmbrukˌʃɪr, -ʃɚ; ES -ˌʃɪə(r,
   -ʃə(r
Pemigewasset ˌpɛmɪdʒə'wɑsɪt, -'wɒsɪt
Pemiscot 'pɛmɪˌskɑt; ES+-ˌskɒt
pemmican 'pɛmɪkən
pen *n* pɛn
pen *v 'write'* pɛn |penned pɛnd
pen *v 'shut'* pɛn |penned pɛnd
penal 'pinḷ |-ly -ɪ
penalize 'pinḷˌaɪz, 'pɛnḷ- |-s -ɪz |-d -d—*The
   pronunciation* 'pɛnḷˌaɪz *is influenced by*
   'pɛnḷtɪ, *which is heard oftener than* 'pinḷ
   (penal).
penalty 'pɛnḷtɪ
penance 'pɛnəns |-s -ɪz |-d -t
pen-and-ink 'pɛnən'ɪŋk, *less freq.* 'pɛnənd'ɪŋk
Pen Argyl pɛn'ɑrdʒɪl; ES -'ɑːdʒɪl
penates, P- pə'netiz
Penbrook 'pɛnˌbruk
pence pɛns, *in combination* -pəns, -pɛns
penchant 'pɛntʃənt (*Fr* pɑ̃'ʃɑ̃)
pencil 'pɛnsḷ |-ed -d
pend pɛnd |-ed -ɪd |-ing -ɪŋ
pendant 'pɛndənt |-ed -ɪd
pendency 'pɛndənsɪ |pendent 'pɛndənt
Pendennis pɛn'dɛnɪs |-'s -ɪz

Pendergast 'pɛndɚˌgæst; ES 'pɛndə-;—*r has
   been lost by dissimilation* (*§121*)—*see*
   Prendergast.
Pendleton 'pɛndḷtən
pendragon, P- pɛn'drægən
pendulous 'pɛndʒələs
pendulum 'pɛndʒələm, 'pɛndḷəm, 'pɛndjələm
Penelope pə'nɛləpɪ |-an pəˌnɛlə'piən
peneplain, -plane 'pinəˌplen, ˌpinə'plen
penetrability ˌpɛnətrə'bɪlətɪ
penetrable 'pɛnətrəbḷ |-bly -blɪ
penetrate 'pɛnəˌtret |-d -ɪd |-tion ˌpɛnə-
   'treʃən
penguin 'pɛngwɪn, 'pɛŋgwɪn |-ery -ˌɛrɪ
penholder 'pɛnˌholdɚ; ES -ˌholdə(r
penicillin ˌpɛnɪ'sɪlɪn (*cf L* ˌpeni'cillus)
peninsula, P- pə'nɪnsələ, -sjulə, -ʃulə |-r -ɚ;
   ES -ə(r
penis 'pinɪs |-es -ɪz |-nes -niz
penitence 'pɛnətəns |-tent -tənt
penitential ˌpɛnə'tɛnʃəl |-ly -ɪ
penitentiary ˌpɛnə'tɛnʃərɪ, -'tɛntʃərɪ
penknife 'pɛnˌnaɪf, 'pɛnaɪf |-knives -aɪvz
penman 'pɛnmən |-men -mən |-ship -ˌʃɪp
Penn pɛn
pen-name 'pɛnˌnem
pennant 'pɛnənt
pennate 'pɛnet |-d -ɪd
Pennell 'pɛnḷ
penniless 'pɛnḷɪs, 'pɛnɪlɪs
Pennine 'pɛnaɪn
pennon 'pɛnən |-ed -d
Pennsylvania ˌpɛnsḷ'venjə, -nɪə, -sɪl- |-n -n
penny 'pɛnɪ |-ies -z |pence pɛns
penny-a-liner ˌpɛnɪə'laɪnɚ; ES -'laɪnə(r
Penn Yan ˌpɛn'jæn
pennyroyal ˌpɛnə'rɔɪəl, -'rɔjəl, -'rɔɪl
pennyweight 'pɛnɪˌwet
penny-wise 'pɛnɪ'waɪz ('penny-ˌwise 'move)
pennyworth 'pɛnɪˌwɝθ; ES -ˌwɜθ, -ˌwɝθ;
   |-ths -θs
Penobscot pə'nɑbskɑt, -skət; ES+-'nɒbskɒt
penology pi'nɑlədʒɪ; ES+-'nɒl-; |-gist -dʒɪst
Penrith 'pɛnrɪθ, pɛn'rɪθ
Penrod 'pɛnrɑd; ES+-rɒd
Pensacola ˌpɛnsə'kolə
Pensauken pɛn'sɔkən
penseroso, P- ˌpɛnsə'roso
pensile 'pɛnsḷ, 'pɛnsɪl

Key: *See in full §§3–47.* bee bi |pity 'pɪtɪ (§6) |rate ret |yet jɛt |sang sæŋ |angry 'æŋ·grɪ
|bath bæθ; E baθ (§10) |ah ɑ |far fɑr |watch wɑtʃ, wɒtʃ (§12) |jaw dʒɔ |gorge gɔrdʒ |go go

pension *'payment'* 'pɛnʃən |-ed -d
pension *'lodging'* 'pɑnsɪˌɑn, -ˌɒn (*Fr* pɑ̃'sjõ)
pensionary 'pɛnʃənˌɛrɪ
pensive 'pɛnsɪv |-d -d
penstock 'pɛnˌstɑk; ES+-ˌstɒk
pent pɛnt
pentagon 'pɛntəˌgɑn; ES+-ˌgɒn
pentagonal pɛn'tægənḷ |-ly -ɪ
pentahedron ˌpɛntə'hidrən |-dral -drəl
pentameter pɛn'tæmətɚ; ES -'tæmətə(r
pentane 'pɛnten
Pentateuch 'pɛntəˌtjuk, -ˌtɪuk, -ˌtuk
pentathlon pɛn'tæθlən, -lɑn, -lɒn
Pentecost 'pɛntɪˌkɔst, -ˌkɒst, -ˌkɑst
Penthesilea ˌpɛnθɛsḷ'iə
penthouse 'pɛntˌhaʊs |-ses -zɪz |-d -ˌhaʊst
pentice 'pɛntɪs |-s -ɪz |-d -t=penthouse
pentose 'pɛntos
pent-up 'pɛnt'ʌp ('pent-ˌup 'wrath)
penult 'pinʌlt, pɪ'nʌlt
penultima pɪ'nʌltəmə |-mate -mɪt
penumbra pɪ'nʌmbrə |-s -z |-brae -bri
penurious pə'nʊrɪəs, -'nɪʊ-, -'njʊ-
penury 'pɛnjərɪ
Penzance pɛn'zæns |-'s -ɪz
peon 'piən |-age -ɪdʒ |-ism -ˌɪzəm
peony 'piənɪ—*The well-known popular* 'paɪnɪ
represents piony, *in literary use* 15–19 *cc*
(*Cowper has* pioney). *Peony dates from the*
16*c.*
people 'pipḷ |-d -d |-ling 'piplɪŋ, 'pipḷɪŋ
peopleless 'pipḷlɪs
Peoria pɪ'orɪə, -'ɔrɪə; S -'orɪə
pep pɛp |-ped -t |-py -ɪ |-pily -ḷɪ, -ɪlɪ
Pepin *lake, Wis co.* 'pɛpɪn; *Franks king* 'pɛpɪn
(*Fr* pe'pæ̃)
pepper 'pɛpɚ; ES 'pɛpə(r; |-ed -d |-ing
'pɛpərɪŋ, 'pɛprɪŋ |-box -ˌbɑks; ES+-ˌbɒks
pepper-and-salt 'pɛpɚn'sɔlt, 'pɛpərən-; ES
'pɛpən-, ˌpɛpərən-
peppercorn 'pɛpɚˌkɔrn; ES 'pɛpəˌkɔən
Pepperell 'pɛpərəl, 'pɛprəl
pepperidge 'pɛpərɪdʒ, 'pɛprɪdʒ |-s -ɪz
peppermint 'pɛpɚˌmɪnt; ES 'pɛpə-, 'pɛpm̩ˌɪnt
Pepperrell 'pɛpərəl, 'pɛprəl
pepperwort 'pɛpɚˌwɝt; ES 'pɛpəˌwɜt, 'pɛpə-
ˌwɝt
pepsin, -e 'pɛpsɪn |-ate -ˌet |-ated -ˌetɪd
peptic 'pɛptɪk |-al -ḷ

peptone 'pɛpton
Pepys *diarist &* Ir *family* pips; *Eng family*
'pɛpɪs |-'s -ɪz
Pequawket pɪ'kwɔkɪt, -'kwɒkɪt
Pequot 'pikwɑt, -kwɒt
per *prep w. object* pɚ; ES pə(r; *without obj.*
pɝ; ES pɝ(r, pɝ
peradventure ˌpɝəd'vɛntʃɚ; ES ˌpɝəd-
'vɛntʃə(r, ˌpɝəd'vɛntʃə(r
perambulate pɚ'æmbjəˌlet |-d -ɪd |-tor -ɚ;
ES -ə(r
perambulation pɚˌæmbjə'leʃən
per annum pɚ'ænəm
percale pɚ'kel; ES pə'kel; (*Fr* pɛr'kal)
per capita pɚ'kæpɪtə; ES pə'kæp-
perceive pɚ'siv; ES pə'siv; |-d -d
per cent, percent pɚ'sɛnt; ES pə-; |-s -s
percentage pɚ'sɛntɪdʒ; ES pə-; |-s -ɪz
percentile pɚ'sɛntaɪl, -tḷ, -tɪl; ES pə-
percept 'pɝsɛpt; ES 'pɝ-, 'pɝ-
perceptible pɚ'sɛptəbḷ; ES pə-; |-bly -blɪ
perception pɚ'sɛpʃən; ES pə-; |-tive -tɪv
perceptual pɚ'sɛptʃʊəl; ES pə-; |-ly -ɪ
Percival, -ce-, -e 'pɝsəvḷ; ES 'pɝs-, 'pɝs-
perch pɝtʃ; ES pɝtʃ, pɝtʃ; |-es -ɪz |-ed -t
perchance pɚ'tʃæns; ES pə-, E+-'tʃɑns,
-'tʃɒns
Percheron 'pɝtʃərən, -ˌɑn; ES 'pɝtʃ-, 'pɝtʃ-,
-ˌɒn
perchlorate pɝ'kloret, -'klɔr-; ES pɝ'klor-,
pɝ-, E+-'klɔr-; |-ric -rɪk |-rid -rɪd |-ride
-raɪd, -rɪd
percipience pɚ'sɪpɪəns; ES pə-; |-ent -ənt
percolate *n* 'pɝkəlɪt, -ˌlet; ES 'pɝk-, 'pɝk-
percolate *v* 'pɝkəˌlet; ES 'pɝk-, 'pɝk-; |-d -ɪd
|-tor -ɚ; ES -ə(r
percuss pɚ'kʌs; ES pə-; |-es -ɪz |-ed -t |-ion
-'kʌʃən
Percy 'pɝsɪ; ES 'pɝsɪ, 'pɝsɪ
perdie pɚ'di; ES pə'di
per diem pɚ'daɪəm, -ɛm; ES pə-
Perdita 'pɝdɪtə; ES 'pɝd-, 'pɝd-
perdition pɚ'dɪʃən; ES pə'dɪʃən
perdu, -due pɚ'dju, -'dɪu, -'du; ES pə-
perdurable pɚ'djʊrəbḷ, -'dɪʊr-, -'dʊr-; ES
pə-; |-bly -blɪ
peregrin 'pɛrəgrɪn |-grine -grɪn, -ˌgrɪn
peregrinate 'pɛrəgrɪˌnet |-nated -ˌnetɪd
peregrination ˌpɛrəgrɪ'neʃən

peremptory pə'rɛmptərɪ, -trɪ, 'pɛrəmp͵torɪ, -͵tɔrɪ; S -͵torɪ; |-rily -rəlɪ, -rɪlɪ

perennial pə'rɛnɪəl |-ly -ɪ

perfect *adj* 'pɝfɪkt; ES 'pɝf-, 'pɝf-

perfect *v* pɚ'fɛkt, *now less freq.* 'pɝfɪkt; ES pə'fɛkt, 'pɝf-, 'pɝf-; |-ed -ɪd

perfection pɚ'fɛkʃən; ES pə'fɛkʃən

perfervid pɝ'fɝ·vɪd; ES pɜ'fɝvɪd, pɝ'fɝ·vɪd

perfidious pɚ'fɪdɪəs; ES pə'fɪdɪəs

perfidy 'pɝfədɪ; ES 'pɜfədɪ, 'pɝfədɪ

perforate *adj* 'pɝfərɪt, -͵ret; ES 'pɜf-, 'pɝf-

perforate *v* 'pɝfə͵ret; ES 'pɜf-, 'pɝf-; |-d -ɪd

perforation ͵pɝfə'reʃən; ES ͵pɜfə-, ͵pɝfə-

perforce pɚ'fors, -'fɔrs; ES pə'foəs, E+-'fɔəs

perform pɚ'fɔrm; ES pə'fɔəm; |-ed -d |-ance -əns—*A dissimilated pron.* pə'fɔrm(əns) *is sometimes heard (§121).*

perfume *n* 'pɝfjum, -fɪum, pɚ'fjum, -'fɪum; ES 'pɜ-, 'pɝ-, pə-

perfume *v* pɚ'fjum, -'fɪum; ES pə-; |-d -d

perfumery pɚ'fjumərɪ, -mrɪ, -'fɪum-; ES pə-; —*A dissimilated pron.* pə'fjumərɪ *is often heard (§121).*

perfunctory pɚ'fʌŋktərɪ; ES pə-; |-rily -rəlɪ, -rɪlɪ

perfuse pɚ'fjuz, -'fɪuz; ES pə-; |-s -ɪz |-d -d

Pergamum 'pɝgəməm; ES 'pɜg-, 'pɝg-; |-amus -məs |-amus's -məsɪz

pergola 'pɝgələ; ES 'pɜg-, 'pɝg-

perhaps pɚ'hæps, pɚ'æps, præps; ES pə-'hæps, pə'ræps, præps

peri 'pɪrɪ, 'pirɪ

pericarditis ͵pɛrɪkɑr'daɪtɪs; ES -kɑ:-

pericardium ͵pɛrɪ'kɑrdɪəm; ES -'kɑ:d-; |-dia -dɪə

Pericles 'pɛrə͵kliz |-'s -ɪz |-ean ͵pɛrə'kliən

perigee 'pɛrə͵dʒi

perihelion ͵pɛrɪ'hilɪən

peril 'pɛrəl |-ed -d |-ous -əs

perimeter pə'rɪmətɚ; ES -'rɪmətə(r

perimetric *geom.* ͵pɛrə'mɛtrɪk |-al -l̩ |-ally -l̩ɪ, -ɪklɪ

perimetric *anat.* ͵pɛrə'mitrɪk |-trium -trɪəm

perineum ͵pɛrə'nɪəm |-nea -'nɪə

period 'pɪrɪəd, 'pir-, -rɪɪd

periodic ͵pɪrɪ'ɑdɪk, ͵pir-; ES+-'ɒd-; |-al -l̩ |-ally -l̩ɪ, -ɪklɪ

periodicity ͵pɪrɪə'dɪsətɪ, ͵pir-

periosteum ͵pɛrɪ'ɑstɪəm; ES+-'ɒs-; |-tea -tɪə

periostitis ͵pɛrɪɑs'taɪtɪs; ES+-ɒs-

peripatetic ͵pɛrəpə'tɛtɪk |-al -l̩ |-ally -l̩ɪ, -ɪklɪ

peripheral pə'rɪfərəl |-ly -ɪ |-ry -rɪ

periphrase 'pɛrə͵frez |-s -ɪz |-d -d

periphrasis pə'rɪfrəsɪs |-rases -rə͵siz

periphrastic ͵pɛrə'fræstɪk |-al -l̩ |-ally -l̩ɪ, -ɪklɪ

peripteral pə'rɪptərəl |-ry -rɪ

perique pə'rik

periscope 'pɛrə͵skop

periscopic ͵pɛrə'skɑpɪk; ES+-'skɒp-; |-al -l̩

perish 'pɛrɪʃ |-es -ɪz |-ed -t

perishability ͵pɛrɪʃə'bɪlətɪ

perishable 'pɛrɪʃəb̩l |-bly -blɪ

peristalsis ͵pɛrə'stælsɪs |-stalses -'stælsiz

peristaltic ͵pɛrə'stæltɪk |-ally -l̩ɪ, -ɪklɪ

peristyle 'pɛrə͵staɪl

peritoneum, -nae- ͵pɛrətə'nɪəm |-nea, -naea -'nɪə |-neal, -naeal -'nɪəl |-neally, -naeally -'nɪəlɪ

peritonitis ͵pɛrətə'naɪtɪs

periwig 'pɛrə͵wɪg |-ged -d

periwinkle 'pɛrə͵wɪŋk̩l |-d -d

Perizzite 'pɛrə͵zaɪt

perjure 'pɝdʒɚ; ES 'pɜdʒə(r, 'pɝdʒə(r; |-d -d |-ring -dʒərɪŋ, -dʒrɪŋ |-ry -ɪ, -dʒrɪ

perjurer 'pɝdʒərɚ; ES 'pɜdʒərə(r, 'pɝdʒərə(r

perk pɝk; ES pɜk, pɝk; |-ed -t

Perkin, p- 'pɝkɪn; ES 'pɜk-, 'pɝk-

Perkins 'pɝkɪnz; ES 'pɜk-, 'pɝk-; |-'s -ɪz

perlite 'pɝlaɪt; ES 'pɜl-, 'pɝl-

permanence 'pɝmənəns; ES 'pɜm-, 'pɝm-; |-cy -ɪ |-nent -nənt

permanganate pɝ'mæŋgə͵net; ES pɜ-, pɝ-

permeability ͵pɝmɪə'bɪlətɪ; ES ͵pɜ-, ͵pɝ-

permeable 'pɝmɪəb̩l; ES 'pɜ-, 'pɝ-; |-bly -blɪ

permeance 'pɝmɪəns; ES 'pɜ-, 'pɝ-; |-ant -ənt

permeate 'pɝmɪ͵et; ES 'pɜ-, 'pɝ-; |-d -ɪd

Permiak 'pɝmɪ͵æk; ES 'pɜ-, 'pɝ-; |-ian -ɪən

permissibility pɚ͵mɪsə'bɪlətɪ; ES pə-

permissible pɚ'mɪsəb̩l; ES pə-; |-bly -blɪ

permission pɚ'mɪʃən; ES pə-; |-sive -'mɪsɪv

permit *n* '*leave*' 'pɝmɪt, pɚ'mɪt; ES 'pɜ-, 'pɝ-, pə-

permit *v* pɚ'mɪt; ES pə-; |-ted -ɪd

permit *n* '*pompano*' pɚ'mɪt; ES pə-

permutation ͵pɝmjə'teʃən; ES ͵pɜ-, ͵pɝ-

permute pɚ'mjut, -'mɪut; ES pə-; |-d -ɪd

Key: *See in full §§3–47.* bee bi |pity 'pɪtɪ (§6) |rate ret |yet jɛt |sang sæŋ |angry 'æŋ·grɪ |bath bæθ; E baθ (§10) |ah ɑ |far fɑr |watch wɑtʃ, wɒtʃ (§12) |jaw dʒɔ |gorge gɔrdʒ |go go

Pernambuco ˌpɜˑnəmˈbjuko, -ˈbɪu-; ES ˌpɜ-, ˌpɜˑ-

pernicious pəˈnɪʃəs; ES pə-

pernickety pəˈnɪkɪtɪ; ES pə-

perorate ˈpɛrəˌret |-d -ɪd |-tion ˌpɛroˈreʃən

peroxid pəˈrɑksɪd; ES+-ˈrɒks-; |-ide -aɪd

perpend n ˈpɜˑpənd; ES ˈpɜ-, ˈpɜˑ-

perpend v pəˈpɛnd; ES pə-; |-ed -ɪd

perpendicular ˌpɜˑpənˈdɪkjələ, ˌpɜˑpm̩-; ES ˌpɜpənˈdɪkjələ(r, ˌpɜpm̩-, ˌpɜˑ-

perpendicularity ˌpɜˑpənˌdɪkjəˈlærətɪ, ˌpɜˑpm̩-; ES ˌpɜ-, ˌpɜˑ-

perpetrate ˈpɜˑpəˌtret; ES ˈpɜ-, ˈpɜˑ-; |-d -ɪd

perpetration ˌpɜˑpəˈtreʃən; ES ˌpɜ-, ˌpɜˑ-

perpetual pəˈpɛtʃʊəl; ES pə-; |-ly -ɪ

perpetuate pəˈpɛtʃʊˌet; ES pə-; |-d -ɪd

perpetuation pəˌpɛtʃʊˈeʃən; ES pə-

perpetuity ˌpɜˑpəˈtjuətɪ, -ˈtɪu-, -ˈtu-; ES ˌpɜ-, ˌpɜˑ-

perplex pəˈplɛks; ES pə-; |-es -ɪz |-ed -t |-edly -ɪdlɪ |-ity -ətɪ

perquisite ˈpɜˑkwəzɪt; ES ˈpɜ-, ˈpɜˑ-

Perrault pɛˈro

Perry, p- ˈpɛrɪ

persalt ˈpɜˑˌsɔlt; ES ˈpɜ-, ˈpɜˑ-

Perse, p- pɜˑs; ES pɜs, pɜˑs; |-s -ɪz

per se ˈpɜˑˈsi; ES ˈpɜ-, ˈpɜˑ-

persecute ˈpɜˑsɪˌkjut, -ˌkɪut; ES ˈpɜ-, ˈpɜˑ-; |-d -ɪd

persecution ˌpɜˑsɪˈkjuʃən, -ˈkɪu-; ES ˌpɜ-, ˌpɜˑ-

Perseid ˈpɜˑsɪɪd; ES ˈpɜ-, ˈpɜˑ-

Persephone pəˈsɛfənɪ; ES pə-

Persepolis pəˈsɛpəlɪs; ES pə-; |-'s -ɪz

Perseus ˈpɜˑsjus, ˈpɜˑsɪəs; ES ˈpɜs-, ˈpɜˑs-; |-seus' -sjus, -ɪəs

perseverance ˌpɜˑsəˈvɪrəns; ES ˌpɜ-, ˌpɜˑ-

persevere ˌpɜˑsəˈvɪr; ES ˌpɜsəˈvɪə(r, ˌpɜˑsə-ˈvɪə(r; |-d -d

Pershing ˈpɜˑʃɪŋ; ES ˈpɜ-, ˈpɜˑ-

Persia ˈpɜˑʒə, ˈpɜˑʃə; ES ˈpɜ-, ˈpɜˑ-; |-n -n

persiflage ˈpɜˑsɪˌflɑʒ; ES ˈpɜ-, ˈpɜˑ-; (Fr pɛrsiˈflɑːʒ)

persimmon pəˈsɪmən; ES pə-

persist pəˈzɪst, -ˈsɪst; ES pə-; |-ed -ɪd

persistence pəˈzɪstəns, -ˈsɪst-; ES pə-; |-nt -nt

persnickety pəˈsnɪkɪtɪ; ES pə-

person, P- ˈpɜˑsn̩; ES ˈpɜ-, ˈpɜˑ-

persona pəˈsonə; ES pə-; |-nae -ni

personable ˈpɜˑsn̩əbl̩, ˈpɜˑsnə-; ES ˈpɜ-, ˈpɜˑ-; |-bly -blɪ

personage ˈpɜˑsn̩ɪdʒ, ˈpɜˑsnɪdʒ; ES ˈpɜ-, ˈpɜˑ-; |-s -ɪz

persona grata pəˈsonəˈgretə, -ˈgrɑtə; ES pə-

personal ˈpɜˑsn̩l̩, ˈpɜˑsnəl; ES ˈpɜ-, ˈpɜˑ-; |-ly -ɪ

personality ˌpɜˑsn̩ˈælətɪ; ES ˌpɜ-, ˌpɜˑ-

personalty ˈpɜˑsn̩l̩tɪ; ES ˈpɜ-, ˈpɜˑ-

persona non grata pəˈsonəˌnanˈgretə, -ˈgrɑtə; ES pə-, -ˌnɒn-

personate ˈpɜˑsn̩ˌet; ES ˈpɜ-, ˈpɜˑ-; |-d -ɪd

personation ˌpɜˑsn̩ˈeʃən; ES ˌpɜ-, ˌpɜˑ-

personification pəˌsanəfəˈkeʃən; ES pə-, ˌsɑnə-, -ˌsɒnə-

personify pəˈsanəˌfaɪ; ES pəˈsɑn-, -ˈsɒn-; |-fied -ˌfaɪd

personnel ˌpɜˑsn̩ˈɛl; ES ˌpɜ-, ˌpɜˑ-

perspective pəˈspɛktɪv; ES pə-; |-d -d

perspicacious ˌpɜˑspɪˈkeʃəs; ES ˌpɜ-, ˌpɜˑ-; |-cacity -ˈkæsətɪ

perspicuity ˌpɜˑspɪˈkjuətɪ, -ˈkɪu-; ES ˌpɜ-, ˌpɜˑ-

perspicuous pəˈspɪkjuəs; ES pə-

perspiration ˌpɜˑspəˈreʃən; ES ˌpɜ-, ˌpɜˑ-

perspiratory pəˈspaɪrəˌtorɪ, -ˌtɔrɪ; ES pə-ˈspaɪrəˌtorɪ, E+-ˌtɔrɪ

perspire pəˈspaɪr; ES pəˈspaɪə(r; |-d -d

persuadable pəˈswedəbl̩; ES pə-; |-bly -blɪ

persuade pəˈswed; ES pə-; |-d -ɪd

persuasible pəˈswesəbl̩; ES pə-; |-bly -blɪ

persuasion pəˈsweʒən; ES pə-; |-sive -sɪv

pert pɜt; ES pɜt, pɜˑt

pertain pəˈten; ES pə-; |-ed -d

Perth pɜˑθ; ES pɜθ, pɜˑθ; |-shire -ʃɪr, -ʃə; ES -ʃɪə(r, -ʃə(r

Perth Amboy ˈpɜˑθˈæmbɔɪ; ES ˈpɜθ-, ˈpɜˑθ-

pertinacious ˌpɜˑtn̩ˈeʃəs; ES ˌpɜt-, ˌpɜˑt-; |-acity -ˈæsətɪ

pertinence ˈpɜˑtn̩əns; ES ˈpɜt-, ˈpɜˑt-; |-cy -ɪ |-ent -ənt

perturb pəˈtɜb; ES pəˈtɜb, pəˈtɜˑb; |-ed -d |-edly -ɪdlɪ

perturbation ˌpɜˑtəˈbeʃən; ES ˌpɜtə-, ˌpɜˑtə-

Peru pəˈru, pəˈrɪu

Perugino ˌpɛruˈdʒino, ˌpɜˑrju- (It ˌperuˈdʒiːno)

peruke pəˈruk, pəˈrɪuk

peruse pəˈruz, -ˈrɪuz; |-s -ɪz -d -d |-sal -l̩

Peruvian pəˈruvɪən, -ˈrɪu-

pervade pəˈved; ES pəˈved; |-d -ɪd

|full fʊl |tooth tuθ |further ˈfɜˑðə; ES ˈfɜˑðə |custom ˈkʌstəm |while hwaɪl |how haʊ |toy tɔɪ |using ˈjuzɪŋ |fuse fjuz, fɪuz |dish dɪʃ |vision ˈvɪʒən |Eden ˈidn̩ |cradle ˈkredl̩ |keep 'em ˈkipm̩

pervasion pɚˈveʒən; ES pə-; |-sive -sɪv

perverse pɚˈvɝs; ES pəˈvɝs, pəˈvɝs; |-sion -ʒən, -ʃən

perversity pɚˈvɝsətɪ; ES pəˈvɝs-, pəˈvɝs-; |-ive -ɪv

pervert *n* ˈpɝvɝt; ES ˈpɝvɝt, ˈpɝvɝt

pervert *v* pɚˈvɝt; ES pəˈvɝt, pəˈvɝt; |-ed -ɪd

pervious ˈpɝvɪəs; ES ˈpɝ-, ˈpɝ-

peseta pəˈsetə, -ˈsetə (*Sp* peˈseta)

pesky ˈpɛskɪ

peso ˈpeso

pessimism ˈpɛsəˌmɪzəm |-mist -mɪst

pessimistic ˌpɛsəˈmɪstɪk |-al -ḷ |-ally -ḷɪ, -ɪklɪ

pest pɛst

Pestalozzi ˌpɛstəˈlɑtsɪ; ES+-ˈlɒtsɪ

pester ˈpɛstɚ; ES ˈpɛstə(r; |-ed -d |-ing ˈpɛstrɪŋ, ˈpɛstərɪŋ

pesthole ˈpɛstˌhol

pesthouse ˈpɛstˌhaʊs |-ses -zɪz

pestiferous pɛsˈtɪfərəs, -frəs

pestilence ˈpɛstḷəns |-s -ɪz |-ent -ənt

pestilential ˌpɛstḷˈɛnʃəl |-ly -ɪ

pestle ˈpɛsḷ, ˈpɛstḷ |-d -d |-ling -ɪŋ, -sḷɪŋ, -stḷɪŋ

pet pɛt |petted ˈpɛtɪd

Pétain *Fr* peˈtɛ̃

petal ˈpɛtḷ |-ed -d |-less ˈpɛtḷɪs

Petaluma ˌpɛtḷˈumə

petard pɪˈtɑrd; ES -ˈtɑːd, E+-ˈtɑːd

petcock ˈpɛtˌkɑk; ES+-ˌkɒk

peter, P- ˈpitɚ; ES ˈpitə(r; |-ed -d

Peterboro, -borough ˈpitɚˌbɝo, -ə; ES ˈpitə-ˌbɝr-, -ˌbʌr-, -ˌbɝ-

Petersburg ˈpitɚzˌbɝg; ES ˈpitəzˌbɝg, -təzˌbɝg

Petersen, -son ˈpitɚsn̩; ES ˈpitəsn̩

Petersham *Mass* ˈpitɚzˌhæm, *Engd, Austral* ˈpitɚʃəm; ES ˈpitə-; *Both* ˈpitɚzˌhæm *and* ˈpitɚʃəm *are spelling pronunciations. The traditional pron. is* ˈpitɚzəm.

petiolate ˈpɛtɪəˌlet |-lated -ˌletɪd

petiole ˈpɛtɪˌol |-d -d

petit ˈpɛtɪ |petite pəˈtit

petition pəˈtɪʃən |-ed -d |-ing -ˈtɪʃənɪŋ, -ʃnɪŋ |-ary -ʃəˌnɛrɪ

Peto ˈpito

Petoskey pəˈtɑskɪ, -ˈtɒs-

Petrarch ˈpitrɑrk; ES -trɑːk, E+-trɑːk; |-ism -ˌɪzəm |-ist -ɪst

Petrarchal pɪˈtrɑrkḷ; ES -ˈtrɑːkḷ, E+-ˈtrɑːkḷ; |-chan -kən |-chian -kɪən |-chianism -kɪənˌɪzəm

petrel ˈpɛtrəl

petrifaction ˌpɛtrəˈfækʃən

petrification ˌpɛtrəfəˈkeʃən

petrify ˈpɛtrəˌfaɪ |-fied -ˌfaɪd

Petrograd ˈpɛtrəˌgræd

petrography piˈtrɑgrəfɪ, -ˈtrɒg-

petrol ˈpɛtrəl |-ed -d

petrolatum ˌpɛtrəˈletəm

petroleum, P- pəˈtrolɪəm

petrologic ˌpɛtrəˈlɑdʒɪk; ES+-ˈlɒdʒ-; |-al -ḷ |-ally -ḷɪ, -ɪklɪ

petrology piˈtrɑlədʒɪ; ES+-ˈtrɒl-; |-gist -dʒɪst

petronel ˈpɛtrənəl

Petronius pɪˈtronɪəs |-ˈs -ɪz

Petroskey pɪˈtrɑskɪ, -ˈtrɒs-

petrous ˈpɛtrəs, ˈpitrəs

Petruchio pəˈtrukɪˌo, -ˈtrɪuk-, -kjo

petticoat ˈpɛtɪˌkot |-ed -ɪd |-ism -kotˌɪzəm

pettifog ˈpɛtɪˌfɑg, -ˌfɒg, -ˌfɔg |-ged -d |-gery -ərɪ, -rɪ

pettish ˈpɛtɪʃ

pettitoes ˈpɛtɪˌtoz

petty ˈpɛtɪ |-ily -ḷɪ, -ɪlɪ

petulance ˈpɛtʃələns |-cy -ɪ |-lant -lənt

petunia pəˈtjunjə, -ˈtɪun-, -ˈtun-, -nɪə

Petworth ˈpɛtwɚθ, ˈpɛtəθ; ES -wəθ, ˈpɛtəθ

pew pju, pɪu |-ed -d

pewee ˈpiwi

pewit ˈpiwɪt, ˈpjuɪt, ˈpɪuɪt

pewter ˈpjutɚ, ˈpɪu-; ES -tə(r

pewterer ˈpjutərɚ, ˈpɪu-; ES -tərə(r

pfennig ˈpfɛnɪg, ˈfɛnɪg |-s -z (*Ger* ˈpfɛnɪx |-e -nɪgə, -nɪjə)

Phaedo ˈfido

Phaedra ˈfidrə |Phaedrus ˈfidrəs |-s's -drəsɪz

Phaëthon ˈfeəθən, ˈfeətn̩

phaeton, P- ˈfeətn̩

phagocyte ˈfægəˌsaɪt

phalange ˈfælændʒ, fəˈlændʒ |-s -ɪz

phalanx, P- ˈfelæŋks |-es -ɪz |-nges fəˈlændʒiz

phallic ˈfælɪk |-al -ḷ |-ism ˈfæləˌsɪzəm

phallus ˈfæləs |-es -ɪz |-li -laɪ

phanerogam ˈfænərəˌgæm |-ic ˌfænərəˈgæmɪk

phantasm ˈfæntæzəm

phantasma fænˈtæzmə |-s -z |-mata -mətə

---

phantasmagoria ˌfæntæzməˈgorɪə, -ˈgɔr-; S -ˈgor-; |-l -l |-lly -lɪ

phantasmic fænˈtæzmɪk |-al -] |-ally -]ɪ, -ɪklɪ

phantasy ˈfæntəsɪ, -zɪ |-ied -d

phantom ˈfæntəm

Pharaoh ˈfɛro, ˈfe-, -rɪ,o

Pharisaic, p- ˌfærəˈse·ɪk |-al -] |-ally -]ɪ, -ɪklɪ

Pharisaism ˈfærəseˌɪzəm |-ist -ˌse·ɪst

Pharisee ˈfærəˌsi |-ism -siˌɪzəm

pharmaceutic ˌfɑrməˈsjutɪk, -ˈsɪu-, -ˈsu-; ❡ES ˌfɑːmə-, E+ˌfɑːmə-; |-al -] |-ally -]ɪ, -ɪklɪ

pharmacist ˈfɑrməsɪst; ES ˈfɑːmə-, E+ˈfɑːmə-

pharmacology ˌfɑrməˈkɑlədʒɪ; ES ˌfɑːmə-ˈkɑl-, -ˈkɒl-, E+ˌfɑːmə-

pharmacopoea ˌfɑrməkəˈpiə; ES ˌfɑːm-, E+ˌfɑːm-

pharmacy ˈfɑrməsɪ; ES ˈfɑːm-, E+ˈfɑːm-

Pharpar, -phar ˈfɑrpɑr, -fɑr; ES ˈfɑːpɑː(r, -fɑː(r, E+-ɑː-

Pharsala ˈfɑrsələ; ES ˈfɑːsə-, E+ˈfɑːsə-

Pharsalia fɑrˈseliə; ES fɑ-, E+fɑ-; |-n -n

pharyngal fəˈrɪŋg]

pharyngeal fəˈrɪndʒɪəl, ˌfærɪnˈdʒiəl

pharynges fəˈrɪndʒiz

pharyngitis ˌfærɪnˈdʒaɪtɪs

pharyngoscope fəˈrɪŋgəˌskop

pharynx ˈfærɪŋks |-es -ɪz -rynges fəˈrɪndʒiz

phase fez |phases ˈfezɪz |phased fezd

phasis ˈfesɪs |phases ˈfesiz

pheasant ˈfɛzn̩t

Phebe, p- ˈfibɪ

Phelps fɛlps |-'s -ɪz

phenacetin, -e fəˈnæsətɪn

phenazin ˈfɛnəzɪn |-zine -ˌzin, -zɪn

Phenicia fəˈnɪʃɪə, -ʃə

Phenician fəˈnɪʃən, fəˈniʃən |-s -z

phenix, ˈfinɪks |-es -ɪz

phenol ˈfinɔl, -nɒl, -nɑl, -nol |-phthælein -ˈθælin

phenomenal fəˈnɑmənl̩; ES+-ˈnɒm-; |-ly -ɪ

phenomenon fəˈnɑməˌnɑn; ES+-ˈnɒməˌnɒn; |-mena -mənə

phew fju, fɪu, pfju &ᶜ various other puffs

phi Gk letter faɪ

phial faɪl, ˈfaɪəl |-ed -d

Phi Beta Kappa ˈfaɪˌbetəˈkæpə, -ˌbitə-

Phidias ˈfɪdɪəs |-'s -ɪz |-an -ən

Philadelphia ˌfɪləˈdɛlfjə, -fɪə |-n -n

philander, P- fəˈlændɚ; ES -ˈlændə(r; |-ed -d |-ing -ˈlændrɪŋ, -ˈlændərɪŋ

philanthropic ˌfɪlənˈθrɑpɪk; ES+-ˈθrɒp-; |-al -] |-ally -]ɪ, -ɪklɪ

philanthropist fəˈlænθrəpɪst |-py -pɪ

Philario fɪˈlɑrɪˌo, -rjo

philatelist fəˈlæt]ɪst |-ly -t]ɪ

Philemon fəˈlimən, faɪ-

philharmonic, P- ˌfɪləˈmɑnɪk, ˌfɪlhɑr-; ES ˌfɪlə-, ˌfɪlhɑ:-, -ˈmɒn-, E+-hɑ:-

Philip ˈfɪləp |Philippa fəˈlɪpə |-pan fəˈlɪpən

Philippi fəˈlɪpaɪ, ˈfɪləˌpaɪ; WVa -ˈlɪpɪ, ˈfɪləpɪ

Philippians fəˈlɪpɪənz |-pic fəˈlɪpɪk

Philippine ˈfɪləˌpin

Philippsburg ˈfɪləpsˌbɝg; ES -ˌbɜg, -ˌbɝg; (Ger ˈfiːlɪpsˌburk)

Philips, -pps ˈfɪləps |-'s -ɪz

Philipsburg ˈfɪləpsˌbɝg; ES -ˌbɜg, -ˌbɝg

Philistia fəˈlɪstɪə

Philistine, p- fəˈlɪstɪn, ˈfɪləsˌtin, ˈfɪləsˌtaɪn

philistinism, P- fəˈlɪstɪnˌɪzəm, ˈfɪləstɪnˌɪzəm

Phillips, -pps ˈfɪləps |-'s -ɪz

Phillipsburg ˈfɪləpsˌbɝg; ES -ˌbɜg, -ˌbɝg

Phillis ˈfɪlɪs |-'s -ɪz

Phillpot ˈfɪlpət

Philo ˈfaɪlo

philogynist fɪˈlɑdʒənɪst; ES+-ˈlɒdʒ-; |-ny -nɪ

philologer fɪˈlɑlədʒɚ; ES -ˈlɑlədʒə(r, -ˈlɒl-; |-gist -dʒɪst |-gy -dʒɪ

philologic ˌfɪləˈlɑdʒɪk; ES+-ˈlɒdʒ-; |-al -] |-ally -]ɪ, -ɪklɪ

philomel, P- ˈfɪləˌmɛl |Philomela ˌfɪləˈmilə

philopena ˌfɪləˈpinə

philosopher fəˈlɑsəfɚ; ES -ˈlɑsəfə(r, -ˈlɒs-; |-phy -fɪ

philosophical ˌfɪləˈsɑfɪk]; ES+-ˈsɒf-; |-ly -ɪ, -ɪklɪ

philosophize fəˈlɑsəˌfaɪz; ES+-ˈlɒs-; |-s -ɪz |-d -d

Philostrate ˈfɪləˌstret

Philostratus fɪˈlɑstrətəs; ES+-ˈlɒs-; |-'s -ɪz

Philotus fɪˈlotəs |-'s -ɪz

Philpot, -pott, -putt ˈfɪlpət

philter, -tre ˈfɪltɚ; ES ˈfɪltə(r; |-(e)d -d |-(r)ing -tərɪŋ, -trɪŋ

Phineas ˈfɪnɪəs |-'s -ɪz

phlebitis flɪˈbaɪtɪs, flɛ-

phlebotomy flɪˈbɑtəmɪ, flɛ-; ES+-ˈbɒt-

Phlegethon ˈflɛgəˌθɑn, -ˌθɒn

|full fʊl |tooth tuθ |further ˈfɝðɚ; ES ˈfɝðə |custom ˈkʌstəm |while hwaɪl |how haʊ |toy tɔɪ |using ˈjuzɪŋ |fuse fjuz, fɪuz |dish dɪʃ |vision ˈvɪʒən |Eden ˈidn̩ |cradle ˈkred] |keep 'em ˈkipm̩

Those words below in which the ɑ *sound is spelt* o *are often pronounced with* ɒ *in E and S*

phlegm flɛm

phlegmatic flɛgˈmætɪk |-al -l̩ |-ally -l̩ɪ |-icly -ɪklɪ

phloem ˈfloɛm

phlogistic floˈdʒɪstɪk |-al -l̩ |-ton -tən

. phlox flɑks |-es -ɪz

phobia ˈfobɪə |-ic -ɪk |-ism -ɪzəm |-ist -ɪst

Phocian ˈfoʃən |Phocis ˈfosɪs |Phocis' -sɪs

Phoebe, p- ˈfibɪ |Phoebus ˈfibəs |-bus's -bəsɪz

Phoenicia fəˈnɪʃɪə, -ʃə

Phoenician fəˈnɪʃən, fəˈniʃən |-s -z

phoenix, P- ˈfinɪks |-es -ɪz

phonation foˈneʃən

phone fon |phoned fond

phoneme ˈfonim

phonemic foˈnimɪk |-ly -lɪ

phonetic foˈnɛtɪk, fə- |-al -l̩ |-ally -l̩ɪ, -ɪklɪ

phonetician ˌfonəˈtɪʃən

phoneticist foˈnɛtəsɪst, fə-

phonetism ˈfonəˌtɪzəm |-tist -tɪst

phonic ˈfɑnɪk, ˈfon-

phonodeik ˈfonəˌdaɪk

phonogram ˈfonəˌgræm

phonograph ˈfonəˌgræf; E+-ˌgraf, -ˌgraf

phonographic ˌfonəˈgræfɪk |-ally -l̩ɪ, -ɪklɪ

phonography foˈnɑgrəfɪ, -ˈnɒg-

phonological ˌfonəˈlɑdʒɪkl̩ |-ly -ɪ, -ɪklɪ

phonologist foˈnɑlədʒɪst |-gy -dʒɪ

phosgene ˈfɑsdʒin

phosphate ˈfɑsfet |-d -ɪd |-tic fɑsˈfætɪk

phosphid ˈfɑsfɪd |-fide -faɪd, -fɪd

phosphin ˈfɑsfɪn |-fine -fin, -fɪn

phosphite ˈfɑsfaɪt

phosphor ˈfɑsfɚ; ES ˈfɑsfə(r

phosphore ˈfɑsfor, -fɔr; ES -foə(r, E+-fɔə(r

phosphoresce ˌfɑsfəˈrɛs |-s -ɪz |-d -t

phosphorescence ˌfɑsfəˈrɛsn̩s |-scent -sn̩t

phosphoric fɑsˈfɔrɪk, -ˈfɑr-, -ˈfɒr-, -ˈfor-

phosphorous ˈfɑsfərəs, fɑsˈforəs, EN+-ˈfɔr-

phosphorus, P- ˈfɑsfərəs |Phosphori ˈfɑsfəˌraɪ

phot fɑt, fot

photic ˈfotɪk |-tism -tɪzəm

photo ˈfoto |-ed -d |-ing ˈfotəwɪŋ

photochemist ˌfotəˈkɛmɪst |-ry -rɪ

photodrama ˌfotəˈdrɑmə, -ˈdræmə

photodynamics ˌfotədaɪˈnæmɪks

photoelectric ˌfoto·ɪˈlɛktrɪk |-al -l̩ |-ally -l̩ɪ, -ɪklɪ

photoengrave ˌfoto·ɪnˈgrev |-d -d

photogenic ˌfotəˈdʒɛnɪk |-ally -l̩ɪ, -ɪklɪ

photograph ˈfotəˌgræf; E+-ˌgraf, -ˌgraf; |-ed -t

photographer fəˈtɑgrəfɚ, fo-, -ˈtɒg-; ES -fə(r; |-phy -fɪ

photographic ˌfotəˈgræfɪk |-al -l̩ |-ally -l̩ɪ, -ɪklɪ

photogravure ˌfotəgrəˈvjʊr, -ˈgrevjɚ; ES -ˈvjʊə(r, -ˈgrevjə(r

photolithograph ˌfotəˈlɪθəˌgræf; E+-ˌgraf, -ˌgraf; |-ed -t

photolithographer ˌfotəlɪˈθɑgrəfɚ, -ˈθɒg-; ES -fə(r

photometer foˈtɑmətɚ; ES -ˈtɑmətə(r; |-try -trɪ

photometric ˌfotəˈmɛtrɪk |-al -l̩ |-ally -l̩ɪ, -ɪklɪ

photon ˈfotɑn

photoplay ˈfotəˌple

photosensitive ˌfotəˈsɛnsətɪv

photospectroscope ˌfotəˈspɛktrəˌskop

photosphere ˈfotəˌsfɪr; ES -ˌsfɪə(r, S+-ˌsfɛə(r

photostat, P- ˈfotəˌstæt |-ed -ɪd

photostatic ˌfotəˈstætɪk |-ally -l̩ɪ, -ɪklɪ

photosynthesis ˌfotəˈsɪnθəsɪs

phototropism foˈtatrəˌpɪzəm

phototype ˈfotəˌtaɪp

phrasal ˈfrezl̩ |-ly -ɪ

phrase frez |phrases ˈfrezɪz |phrased frezd

phraseological ˌfrezɪəˈlɑdʒɪkl̩ |-ly -ɪ, -ɪklɪ

phraseologist ˌfrezɪˈɑlədʒɪst |-gy -dʒɪ

phrenetic frɪˈnɛtɪk |-al -l̩ |-ally -l̩ɪ, -ɪklɪ

phrenologist frɛˈnɑlədʒɪst, frɪ- |-gy -dʒɪ

phrensy ˈfrɛnzɪ |-ied -d

Phrygia ˈfrɪdʒɪə |-n -n

Phrynia ˈfrɪnɪə

phthisic ˈtɪzɪk |-al -l̩—Phthisic *is a 16c pedantic spelling of ME* tisik *that little affected the pronunciation.* Phthisis *is learned Latin.*

phthisis ˈθaɪsɪs

phut *intj* ft, fʌt, fət, *etc.*

Phut fʌt

Phyfe faɪf

phylactery fəˈlæktərɪ, -trɪ

Phyle ˈfaɪli

Phyllis ˈfɪlɪs |-'s -ɪz

phylloxera fɪˈlɑksərə, ˌfɪləkˈsɪrə

Those words below in which the ɑ *sound is spelt* o *are often pronounced with* ɒ *in E and S*

phylon 'faɪlɑn |phylum 'faɪləm |phyla 'faɪlə

physic 'fɪzɪk |-icked -t |-al -| |-ally -|ɪ, -ɪklɪ |-s -s

physician fə'zɪʃən |-ed -d

physicist 'fɪzəsɪst

physiocrat 'fɪzɪəˌkræt |-ic ˌfɪzɪə'krætɪk

physiogenesis ˌfɪzɪo'dʒɛnəsɪs

physiogenetic ˌfɪzɪˌodʒə'nɛtɪk

physiogeny ˌfɪzɪ'adʒənɪ |-genic -o'dʒɛnɪk

physiognomy ˌfɪzɪ'agnəmɪ, -'anəmɪ

physiographer ˌfɪzɪ'agrəfɚ, -'ɒg-; ES -fə(r; |-phy -fɪ

physiographic ˌfɪzɪə'græfɪk |-al -| |-ally -|ɪ, -ɪklɪ

physiologic ˌfɪzɪə'ladʒɪk |-al -| |-ally -|ɪ, -ɪklɪ

physiologist ˌfɪzɪ'alədʒɪst |-gy -dʒɪ

physiotherapist ˌfɪzɪo'θɛrəpɪst |-py -pɪ

physique fɪ'zik |-d -t

phytogenesis ˌfaɪto'dʒɛnəsɪs

phytogenetic ˌfaɪtodʒə'nɛtɪk |-al -| |-ally -|ɪ, -ɪklɪ

phytogenic ˌfaɪto'dʒɛnɪk

phytology faɪ'talədʒɪ |-gist -dʒɪst

pi paɪ

pia mater 'paɪə'metɚ; ES -'metə(r

pianissimo ˌpiə'nɪsəˌmo (*It* pjɑ'nissiˌmo)

pianist pɪ'ænɪst, 'piənɪst

piano *n* pɪ'æno, -ə, *less freq.* pɪ'ano

piano '*soft,*' '*softly*' pɪ'ano (*It* 'pjɑ:no)

pianoforte pɪ'ænəˌfort, -ˌfortɪ, -ˌfɔr-; ES -ˌfoɚ, E+-ˌfɔə-

pianola ˌpiə'nolə

piaster, -tre pɪ'æstɚ; ES -'æstə(r

Piatt 'paɪət

piazza pɪ'æzə (*It* 'pjɑttsɑ)

pibroch 'pibrɑk (*Sc* -brɒx)

pica, P- 'paɪkə

picador 'pɪkəˌdɔr; ES -ˌdɔə(r

Picardy 'pɪkɚdɪ; ES 'pɪkədɪ

picaresque ˌpɪkə'rɛsk

picaroon ˌpɪkə'run

picayune ˌpɪkɪ'jun, ˌpɪkɪ'un, ˌpɪkə'jun

Piccadilly ˌpɪkə'dɪlɪ ('Piccaˌdilly 'Circus)

piccalilli ˌpɪkə'lɪlɪ

piccaninny 'pɪkəˌnɪnɪ

piccolo 'pɪkəˌlo

Piccolomini ˌpɪkə'lomənɪ (*It* ˌpikko'lɔ:mini)

pice paɪs

Pichon pɪ'ʃan, -'ʃɒn

pick pɪk |picked pɪkt |-edly -ɪdlɪ

pickaback 'pɪkəˌbæk

pickaninny 'pɪkəˌnɪnɪ

Pickaway 'pɪkəˌwe

pickax, -e 'pɪkˌæks |-(e)s -ɪz |-(e)d -t

picked *adj* '*pointed*' 'pɪkɪd, pɪkt

Pickens 'pɪkɪnz |-'s -ɪz

pickerel 'pɪkərəl, 'pɪkrəl

Pickering 'pɪkərɪŋ, 'pɪkrɪŋ

picket 'pɪkɪt |-ed -ɪd |Pickett 'pɪkɪt

pickle, P- 'pɪk| |-d -d |-ling 'pɪklɪŋ, -k|ɪŋ

picklock 'pɪkˌlak

pickpocket 'pɪkˌpakɪt |-ed -ɪd

pickthank 'pɪkˌθæŋk

pickup 'pɪkˌʌp

Pickwick 'pɪkwɪk |-ian pɪk'wɪkɪən

picnic, P- 'pɪknɪk |-icked -t

Pico *isl.*, *volc.*, *It count* 'piko; *Vt mt.* 'paɪko

picot 'piko

picric 'pɪkrɪk

picrite 'pɪkraɪt

Pict pɪkt

pictograph 'pɪktəˌgræf; E+-ˌgraf, -ˌgrɑf

pictorial pɪk'torɪəl, -'tɔr-; S -'tor-; |-ly -ɪ

picture 'pɪktʃɚ; ES -tʃə(r; |-d -d |-ring 'pɪktʃərɪŋ, 'pɪktʃrɪŋ

picturesque ˌpɪktʃə'rɛsk

picul 'pɪkʌl

piddle 'pɪd| |-d -d |-ling 'pɪdlɪŋ, 'pɪd|ɪŋ

piddling *adj* 'pɪdlɪŋ

pidgin English, pigeon 'pɪdʒɪn'ɪŋglɪʃ

pie paɪ |pied paɪd; *Sp meas.* pje, *Sp pl* pjes

piè *It meas.* pjɛ, *It pl* 'pjɛ:·i

piebald 'paɪˌbɔld

piece pis |pieces 'pisɪz |-d -t |-meal -ˌmil

pièce de résistance *Fr* pjɛsdərezis'tã:s

piecework 'pisˌwɝk; ES -ˌwɜk, -ˌwɝk

pied paɪd

piedmont, P- 'pidmant

piedmontese, P- ˌpidmɑn'tiz

pieplant 'paɪˌplænt

pier pɪr; ES pɪə(r, S+pɛə(r; |-ed -d

pierce, P- pɪrs; ES pɪəs, S+pɛəs; |-s -ɪz |-d -t

Pierian paɪ'ɪrɪən

Pierpont 'pɪrpant; ES 'pɪəpant

Pierre *SD* pɪr; ES pɪə(r, S+pɛə(r; '*Peter*' pɪ'ɛr, pjɛr; ES -ɛə(r

---

|full fʊl |tooth tuθ |further 'fɝðɚ; ES 'fɜðə |custom 'kʌstəm |while hwaɪl |how haʊ |toy tɔɪ
|using 'juzɪŋ |fuse fjuz, fɪuz |dish dɪʃ |vision 'vɪʒən |Eden 'idn̩ |cradle 'kredl̩ |keep 'em 'kipm̩

Pierrot ˌpiəˈro (*Fr* pjɛˈro)
Piers Plowman ˈpɪrzˈplaʊmən; ES ˈpɪəz-,
S+ˈpɛəz-
Pierson ˈpɪrsn̩; ES ˈpɪəsn̩, S+ˈpɛəsn̩
pietism, P- ˈpaɪəˌtɪzəm |-tist -tɪst |-ty -tɪ
pietistic ˌpaɪəˈtɪstɪk |-al -l̩ |-ally -lɪ, -ɪklɪ
piezoelectricity paɪˌizo·ɪˌlɛkˈtrɪsətɪ
piffle ˈpɪfl̩ |-d -d |-ling ˈpɪflɪŋ, ˈpɪflɪŋ
piffling *adj* ˈpɪflɪŋ
pig pɪg |pigged pɪgd |-pen -ˌpɛn |-skin -ˌskɪn
|-sty -ˌstaɪ |-tail -ˌtel
pigeon ˈpɪdʒən, ˈpɪdʒɪn—*cf* pidgin
pigeonhearted ˈpɪdʒənˈhɑrtɪd, -dʒɪn-; ES
-ˈhɑːt-, E+-ˈhɑːt-
pigeonhole ˈpɪdʒənˌhol, ˈpɪdʒɪn- |-holed -ˌhold
pigeon-livered ˈpɪdʒənˈlɪvɚd, -dʒɪn-; ES
-ˈlɪvəd
pigeon-toed ˈpɪdʒənˌtod, ˈpɪdʒɪn-
piggery ˈpɪgərɪ
piggin ˈpɪgɪn, -ən
piggy ˈpɪgɪ |-back -ˌbæk
pigheaded ˈpɪgˈhɛdɪd (ˈpɪgˌheaded ˈlout)
pigment ˈpɪgmənt |-ed -ɪd |-ary ˈpɪgmənˌtɛrɪ
pigmentation ˌpɪgmənˈteʃən
Pigmy, p- ˈpɪgmɪ |-ied -d
pignut ˈpɪgˌnʌt, ˈpɪgnət
pike, P- paɪk |piked paɪkt
piked *adj* ˈpaɪkɪd, paɪkt
Pikes Peak ˈpaɪksˈpik
pikestaff ˈpaɪkˌstæf; ES+-ˌstaf, -ˌstɑf
pilaster pəˈlæstɚ; ES -ˈlæstə(r; |-ed -d |-ing
-tərɪŋ, -trɪŋ
Pilate ˈpaɪlət
pilchard ˈpɪltʃɚd; ES ˈpɪltʃəd
pile paɪl |piled paɪld
pilfer ˈpɪlfɚ; ES -fə(r; |-ed -d |-ing -fərɪŋ,
-frɪŋ
pilgrim ˈpɪlgrɪm, -əm |-ed -d
pilgrimage ˈpɪlgrəmɪdʒ |-s -ɪz
pill pɪl |pilled pɪld
pillage ˈpɪlɪdʒ |-s -ɪz |-d -d
pillar ˈpɪlɚ; ES ˈpɪlə(r; |-ed -d
pillbox ˈpɪlˌbɑks; ES+-ˌbɒks; |-es -ɪz
pilledness ˈpɪlɪdnɪs, ˈpɪldnɪs
pillion ˈpɪljən |-ed -d
pillory ˈpɪlərɪ |-ied -d
pillow ˈpɪlo, -ə |-ed -d |-ing ˈpɪləwɪŋ
pillowcase ˈpɪloˌkes, ˈpɪlə- |-s -ɪz
pillowy ˈpɪləwɪ

Pillsbury ˈpɪlzˌbɛrɪ, -bərɪ
pilose ˈpaɪlos
pilot ˈpaɪlət |-ed -ɪd
pilothouse ˈpaɪlətˌhaʊs |-houses -ˌhaʊzɪz
Pilsen ˈpɪlzn̩ |-er -znɚ, -snɚ, -n̩ɚ; ES -ə(r
Pilsudski pɪlˈsʊtskɪ, -ˈsʌdskɪ
Piltdown ˈpɪltˌdaʊn
pimento pɪˈmɛnto |pimiento pɪmˈjɛnto
pimola pɪˈmolə
pimp pɪmp |pimped pɪmpt |-ery -ərɪ, -rɪ
pimple ˈpɪmpl̩ |-d -d |-ply -plɪ, -pl̩ɪ
pin pɪn |pinned pɪnd
pinafore, P- ˈpɪnəˌfor, -ˌfɔr; ES -ˌfoə(r,
E+-ˌfɔə(r
pince-nez ˈpænsˌne, ˈpɪns- |*pl* -nez -ˌnez (*Fr*
pæsˈne)
pincers ˈpɪnsɚz; ES ˈpɪnsəz; *cf* pinchers.
ˈpɪnsɚz *is from ME* pynsours *and is rare in*
Am use. The usual word ˈpɪntʃɚz *is from*
pinch, *and is not a mistake for* pincers.
pinch pɪntʃ |pinches ˈpɪntʃɪz |pinched pɪntʃt
pinchbeck ˈpɪntʃbɛk
pinchers ˈpɪntʃɚz; ES ˈpɪntʃəz; *see* pincers
pinch-hit *n* ˈpɪntʃˌhɪt
pinch-hit *v* ˈpɪntʃˈhɪt, -ˌhɪt
Pinchot ˈpɪnʃo, ˈpɪntʃo
Pinckney ˈpɪŋknɪ |-ville -ˌvɪl; S+-vl̩
pincushion ˈpɪnˌkʊʃən, -ɪn
Pindar ˈpɪndɚ; ES ˈpɪndə(r
pindaric, P- pɪnˈdærɪk |-al -l̩ |-ally -lɪ, -ɪklɪ
Pindarus ˈpɪndərəs |-'s -ɪz
pindling ˈpɪndlɪŋ
Pindus ˈpɪndəs |-'s -ɪz
pine, P- paɪn |pined paɪnd |-ny -ɪ |-ville -vɪl;
S+-vl̩
pineal ˈpɪnɪəl |-ism -ˌɪzəm
pineapple ˈpaɪnˌæpl̩
Pinero pəˈnɪro, -ˈniro, -ˈnɛro
pinetum paɪˈnitəm |-s -z |-ta -tə
pinfeather ˈpɪnˌfɛðɚ; ES -ˌfɛðə(r; |-ed -d
pinfold ˈpɪnˌfold |-folded -ˌfoldɪd
ping pɪŋ |pinged pɪŋd
pinge pɪndʒ |pinges ˈpɪndʒɪz |pinged pɪndʒd
ping-pong, P- ˈpɪŋˌpaŋ, -ˌpɒŋ, -ˌpɔŋ |-ed -d
pinhead ˈpɪnˌhɛd |-ed -ɪd
pinhole ˈpɪnˌhol |-holed -ˌhold
pinion ˈpɪnjən |-ed -d
pink pɪŋk |pinked pɪŋkt
Pinkerton ˈpɪŋkɚtn̩; ES ˈpɪŋkətn̩

Key: *See in full* §§3–47. bee bi |pity ˈpɪtɪ (§6) |rate ret |yet jɛt |sang sæŋ |angry ˈæŋ·grɪ
|bath bæθ; E baθ (§10) |ah ɑ |far fɑr |watch wɑtʃ, wɒtʃ (§12) |jaw dʒɔ |gorge gɔrdʒ |go go

Pinkney 'pɪŋknɪ

pinnace 'pɪnɪs, -əs |-s -ɪz

pinnacle 'pɪnək|, -ɪk| |-d -d |-ling -k|ɪŋ, -klɪŋ

pinnate 'pɪnet, 'pɪnɪt

pinochle, -cle 'pi,nʌk|

piñon 'pɪnjən, 'pinjon (*Am Sp* pi'non)

pint paɪnt

pintail 'pɪn,tel |-tailed -,teld

pintle 'pɪnt|

pinto, P- 'pɪnto

pioneer ,paɪə'nɪr; ES ,paɪə'nɪə(r, S+-'nɛə(r; |-ed -d

pious 'paɪəs

pip pɪp |pipped pɪpt

pipage 'paɪpɪdʒ

pipe paɪp |piped paɪpt |-ful -,fʊl

pipestem 'paɪp,stɛm

pipestone, P- 'paɪp,ston

pipette, -pet pɪ'pɛt |-(te)d -ɪd

pipit 'pɪpɪt

Pippa 'pɪpə

pippin 'pɪpɪn

pipsissewa pɪp'sɪsəwə

Piqua 'pɪkwə

piquancy 'pikənsɪ |-quant -kənt

pique '*anger*' pik |piqued pikt

pique *insect* pik, 'pike

piqué pɪ'ke

piquet pɪ'kɛt

piracy 'paɪrəsɪ

Piraeus paɪ'riəs |-'s -ɪz

Pirandello ,pɪrən'dɛlo (*It* ,piran'dɛllo)

pirate 'paɪrət, -rɪt |-d -ɪd

piratic paɪ'rætɪk |-al -| |-ally -|ɪ, -ɪklɪ

Pirithous paɪ'rɪθʊəs, *Shak.*+'paɪrɪ,θus |-'s -ɪz

pirogue pə'rog, pɪ-

pirouette ,pɪru'ɛt |-d -ɪd

Pisa 'pizə (*It* 'pi:sa)

Pisanio pɪ'zanɪ,o, -njo

Piscataqua pɪs'kætəkwə, *loc.*+,kwe |-quis -kwɪs |-quog -,kwɑg, -,kwɒg

piscatology ,pɪskə'talədʒɪ; ES+-'tɒl-

piscatorial ,pɪskə'torɪəl, -'tɔr-; S -'tor-

Pisces 'pɪsiz |*gen* Piscium 'pɪʃɪəm

piscina pɪ'saɪnə |piscinal 'pɪsɪn|

Pisgah 'pɪzgə

pish *n, v* pɪʃ |pishes 'pɪʃɪz |pished pɪʃt

pish *intj* pʃ, pɪʃ

Pisistratus pɪ'sɪstrətəs, paɪ- |-'s -ɪz

pismire 'pɪs,maɪr; ES -,maɪə(r; |-ism -maɪ-,rɪzəm

pistachio pɪs'taʃɪ,o, -'tæʃ-

pistareen ,pɪstə'rin

pistil 'pɪst|, -tɪl |-late -ɪt, -,et

pistol, P- 'pɪst| |-ed -d

pistole pɪs'tol

piston 'pɪstn, -tən

pit pɪt |pitted 'pɪtɪd

pitapat 'pɪtə,pæt, 'pɪtɪ-

Pitcairn 'pɪtkɛrn, -kærn; E -kɛən, ES -kæən

pitch pɪtʃ |pitches 'pɪtʃɪz |pitched pɪtʃt

pitchblende 'pɪtʃ,blɛnd

pitch-dark 'pɪtʃ'dɑrk; ES -'dɑ:k, E+-'dɑ:k

pitcher 'pɪtʃɚ; ES 'pɪtʃə(r; |-ful -,fʊl

pitchfork 'pɪtʃ,fɔrk; ES -,fɔək

piteous 'pɪtɪəs

pitfall 'pɪt,fɔl |-ed -d

pith pɪθ |piths pɪθs |pithed pɪθt

Pithecanthropus ,pɪθɪkæn'θropəs, -'kænθrə-pəs |-'s -ɪz

pitiable 'pɪtɪəb| |-bly -blɪ

pitiful 'pɪtɪfəl |-ly -ɪ

Pitkin 'pɪtkɪn |-s -z |-s's -zɪz

pitman, P- 'pɪtmən |pitmen 'pɪtmən

pittance 'pɪtns |-s -ɪz

pitter-patter 'pɪtɚ,pætɚ; ES 'pɪtə,pætə(r

Pittsboro 'pɪts,bɝo, -ə; ES -,bɜr-, -,bʌr-, -,bɝ-

Pittsburg, -gh 'pɪtsbɝg; ES -bɜg, -bɝg

Pittsylvania ,pɪts|'venjə, -nɪə, -sɪl-

pituitary pɪ'tjuə,tɛrɪ, -'trʊ-, -'tu-

pity 'pɪtɪ |pitied 'pɪtɪd

Pius 'paɪəs |-'s -ɪz

Piute paɪ'jut ('Pi,ute 'language)

pivot 'pɪvət, 'pɪvɪt |-ed -ɪd |-al -| |-ally -|ɪ (pevet *1763*)

pix pɪks |pixes 'pɪksɪz |pixed pɪkst

pixilate 'pɪks|,et |-ed -ɪd

pixy, -ie 'pɪksɪ

Pizarro pɪ'zaro (*Sp* pi'θarrɔ)

placable 'plekəb|, 'plæk- |-bly -blɪ

placard *n* 'plækard; ES -ɑ:d, E+-ɑ:d

placard *v* 'plækard, plæ'kard; ES -ɑ:d, E+-ɑ:d; |-ed -ɪd

placate 'pleket, 'plæk- |-d -ɪd

placatory 'plekə,torɪ, 'plæk-, -,tɔrɪ; S -,torɪ

place ples |places 'plesɪz |placed plest

placebo plə'sibo

---

placenta plə'sɛntə |-s -z |-tae -ti
placer *'disposer'* 'plesɚ; ES 'plesə(r
placer *mining* 'plæsɚ; ES 'plæsə(r
Placer 'plæsɚ; ES 'plæsə(r; |-ville -ˌvɪl
placid, P- 'plæsɪd |-ity plə'sɪdətɪ, plæ-
placket 'plækɪt
plagiarism 'pledʒəˌrɪzəm
plagiarize 'pledʒəˌraɪz |-s -ɪz |-d -d
plague pleg, plɛg |-d -d |-guy -ɪ
plagued *adj* 'plegɪd, 'plɛg-
plaice ples |plaices 'plesɪz
plaid plæd |plaided 'plædɪd
plain plen |plained plend |-ness 'plennɪs
plainsman 'plenzmən |-men -mən
plainsong 'plenˌsɔŋ, -ˌsɒŋ
plain-spoken 'plen'spokən ('plain-ˌspoken
  'man)
plaint plent
plaintiff 'plentɪf |plaintive 'plentɪv
Plaisance plə'zɑns (*Fr* plɛ'zɑ̃:s)
plaister 'plestɚ; ES 'plestə(r
plait plet |-ed -ɪd—*see* plat, pleat. *The words*
  plit, plæt, *and* **plet** *are sometimes spelt*
  plait, *but there is a proper spelling for each.*
plan plæn |planned plænd
planchet 'plæntʃɪt
planchette plæn'ʃɛt (*Fr* plɑ̃'ʃɛt)
Planck plɑŋk
plane plen |planed plend
planet 'plænɪt |-ary 'plænəˌtɛrɪ
planetarium ˌplænə'tɛrɪəm -'tær-, -'ter- |-s
  -z |-ria **-rɪə**
planetesimal ˌplænə'tɛsəmļ
plangency 'plændʒənsɪ |-gent -dʒənt
plank plæŋk |planked plæŋkt
plankton 'plæŋktən
Plano 'pleno
plant plænt; E+plant, plɑnt; |-ed -ɪd
Plantagenet plæn'tædʒənɪt
plantain 'plæntɪn
plantation plæn'teʃən; S+plænt'eʃən
plantigrade 'plæntəˌgred
plaque plæk
plash plæʃ |plashes 'plæʃɪz |plashed plæʃt
plasm 'plæzəm |plasma 'plæzmə
plaster 'plæstɚ; ES 'plæstə(r, E+'plas-,
  'plɑs-; |-ed -d |-ing -trɪŋ, -tərɪŋ
plastic 'plæstɪk |-ally -ļɪ, -ɪklɪ
plasticine, P- 'plæstəˌsin

plasticity plæs'tɪsətɪ
plat plæt |platted 'plætɪd—*see* plait, pleat
Plata 'plɑtə (*Sp* 'plata)
plate plet |plated 'pletɪd |-ful -ˌfʊl
plateau plæ'to
platen 'plætņ
plater 'pletɚ; ES 'pletə(r
platform 'plætˌfɔrm; ES -ˌfɔəm; |-ed -d
platinum 'plætņəm |-tinous -tņəs
platitude 'plætəˌtjud, -ˌtɪud, -ˌtud
platitudinous ˌplætə'tjudņəs, -'tɪud-, -'tud-
Plato 'pleto |-nism 'pletņˌɪzəm |-nist -tņɪst
Platonic ple'tɑnɪk, plə-; ES+-'tɒn-; |-al -ļ
  |-ally -ļɪ, -ɪklɪ
platoon plæ'tun, plə'tun
Platte plæt
platter 'plætɚ; ES 'plætə(r
Plattsburg 'plætsbɝg; ES -bɝg, -bɝg
Plattsmouth 'plætsməθ
platypus 'plætəpəs |-es -ɪz |-pi -ˌpaɪ
plaudit 'plɔdɪt
plausibility ˌplɔzə'bɪlətɪ
plausible 'plɔzəbļ |-bly -blɪ
Plautus 'plɔtəs |-'s -ɪz |-tine -taɪn, -tɪn
play ple |played pled |-boy -ˌbɔɪ |-day -ˌde
  |-fellow 'pleˌfɛlo, -ə |-ground -ˌgraʊnd
playful 'plefəl |-ly -ɪ
playhouse 'pleˌhaʊs |-s -zɪz |-mate 'pleˌmet
plaything 'pleˌθɪŋ |-time 'pleˌtaɪm
playwright 'pleˌraɪt
plaza 'plæzə, 'plɑzə (*Sp* 'plaθa)
plea pli
pleach plitʃ |pleaches 'plitʃɪz |-ed -t
plead plid |pleaded 'plidɪd *or* plead, pled plɛd
pleasance 'plɛzņs |-sant -zņt |-santry -zņtrɪ
please pliz |pleases 'plizɪz |pleased plizd
pleasurable 'plɛʒrəbļ, -ʒərəbļ |-bly -blɪ
pleasure 'plɛʒɚ; ES 'plɛʒə(r; |-d -d
pleat plit |-ed -ɪd—*see* plat, plait
pleb plɛb |plebe plib
plebeian plɪ'biən |-ism -ˌɪzəm
plebiscite 'plɛbəˌsaɪt, 'plɛbəsɪt
plebs plɛbz |plebes 'plibiz
plectrum 'plɛktrəm |-s -z |-tra -trə
pled plɛd
pledge plɛdʒ |pledges 'plɛdʒɪz |pledged plɛdʒd
pledget 'plɛdʒɪt
pledgee plɛdʒ'i
Pleiad 'pliəd, 'plaɪəd |-s -z |-ades -əˌdiz

Key: *See in full §§3–47.* bee **bi** |pity 'pɪtɪ (§6) |rate ret |yet jɛt |sang sæŋ |angry 'æŋ·grɪ
|bath bæθ; E baθ (§10) |ah ɑ |far fɑr |watch watʃ, wɒtʃ (§12) |jaw dʒɔ |gorge gɔrdʒ |go go

pleiosyllabic ˌplaɪəsɪˈlæbɪk
pleiosyllable *'plurisyllable'* ˈplaɪəˌsɪləbḷ
Pleistocene ˈplaɪstəˌsin
plenary ˈplinərɪ, ˈplɛn-
plenipotentiary ˌplɛnəpəˈtɛnʃərɪ, -ʃɪˌɛrɪ
plenitude ˈplɛnəˌtjud, -ˌtɪud, -ˌtud
plenteous ˈplɛntɪəs
plentiful ˈplɛntɪfəl |-ly -ɪ
plenty ˈplɛntɪ
plenum ˈplinəm |-s -z |-na -nə
pleonasm ˈpliəˌnæzəm
pleonastic ˌpliəˈnæstɪk |-al -ḷ |-ally -ḷɪ, -ɪklɪ
plethora ˈplɛθərə
plethoric ˈplɛθərɪk, plɛˈθɔrɪk, -ˈθɑr-, -ˈθɒr-
plethorical plɛˈθɔrɪkḷ, -ˈθɑr-, -ˈθɒr- |-ly -ɪ
pleura ˈplʊrə, ˈplɪʊrə |-l -l |-risy -rəsɪ
plexus ˈplɛksəs |-es -ɪz |*L pl* -xus -ksəs
pliability ˌplaɪəˈbɪlətɪ
pliable ˈplaɪəbḷ |-bly -blɪ
pliancy ˈplaɪənsɪ |pliant ˈplaɪənt
plicate ˈplaɪket |-d -ɪd
plied plaɪd
pliers ˈplaɪɚz; ES ˈplaɪ·əz
plies plaɪz
plight plaɪt |plighted ˈplaɪtɪd
Plinlimmon plɪnˈlɪmən
plinth plɪnθ |-ths -θs
Pliny ˈplɪnɪ |Plinian ˈplɪnɪən
Pliocene ˈplaɪəˌsin
plod plɑd; ES+plɒd; |-ded -ɪd
plop plɑp; ES+plɒp; |-ped -t
plosion ˈploʒən |-sive -sɪv
plot plɑt; ES+plɒt; |-ted -ɪd
plover ˈplʌvɚ; ES ˈplʌvə(r
plow, -ough plaʊ |-ed -d |-share -ˌʃɛr, -ˌʃær;
 E -ˌʃɛə(r, ES -ˌʃæə(r
ploy plɔɪ |ployed plɔɪd
pluck plʌk |plucked plʌkt
plug plʌg |plugged plʌgd
plugugly ˈplʌgˌʌglɪ
plum, P- plʌm
plumage ˈplumɪdʒ, ˈplɪum- |-s -ɪz |-d -d
Plumas ˈpluməs, ˈplɪuməs |-'s -ɪz
plumb plʌm |plumbed plʌmd |-er -ɚ; ES -ə(r
plumbago plʌmˈbego
plume plum, plɪum |-d -d |-d *adj* -d, -ɪd
plumelet ˈplumlɪt, ˈplɪum-
plummet ˈplʌmɪt |-ed -ɪd
plump plʌmp |plumped plʌmpt

Plumptre ˈplʌmptrɪ
plumule ˈplumjul, ˈplɪum-
plumy ˈplumɪ, ˈplɪumɪ
plunder ˈplʌndɚ; ES -də(r; |-ed -d |-ing
 ˈplʌndrɪŋ, ˈplʌndərɪŋ
plunge plʌndʒ |plunges ˈplʌndʒɪz |-d -d
plunk plʌŋk |plunked plʌŋkt
Plunkett ˈplʌŋkɪt
pluperfect pluˈpɝfɪkt, plɪu-; ES -ˈpɝf-, -ˈpɝf-;
 (ˈpluˌperfect ˈtense)
plural ˈplʊrəl, ˈplɪʊ- |-ly -ɪ
plurality plʊˈrælətɪ, plɪʊ-
plurisyllabic ˌplʊrɪsɪˈlæbɪk, ˌplɪʊ-
plurisyllable ˈplʊrəˌsɪləbḷ, ˈplɪʊ-
plus plʌs |plusses ˈplʌsɪz |plussed plʌst
plush plʌʃ |plushes ˈplʌʃɪz |plushed plʌʃt
Plutarch ˈplutɑrk, ˈplɪu-; ES -tɑ:k, E+-tɑ:k
Pluto ˈpluto, ˈplɪu-
plutocracy pluˈtɑkrəsɪ, plɪu-; ES+-ˈtɒk-
plutocrat ˈplutəˌkræt, ˈplɪu-
plutocratic ˌplutəˈkrætɪk, ˌplɪu- |-al -ḷ |-ally
 -ḷɪ, -ɪklɪ
Plutonian pluˈtonɪən, plɪu-
plutonic pluˈtɑnɪk; ES+-ˈtɒn-
Plutus ˈplutəs, ˈplɪu- |-'s -ɪz
pluvial ˈpluvɪəl, ˈplɪu-
pluviometer ˌpluvɪˈɑmətɚ, ˌplɪu-; ES -ˈɑmə-
 tə(r, -ˈɒm-
ply plaɪ |plied plaɪd |-ers -ɚz; ES -əz
Plymouth ˈplɪməθ
Plynlimon plɪnˈlɪmən
P.M., p.m. ˈpiˈɛm
pneumatic njuˈmætɪk, nɪu-, nu- |-ally -ḷɪ,
 -ɪklɪ
pneumococcus ˌnjuməˈkɑkəs, ˌnɪu-, ˌnu-;
 ES+-ˈkɒk-; |-cci -ksaɪ
pneumogastric ˌnjuməˈgæstrɪk, ˌnɪu-, ˌnu-
pneumonia njuˈmonjə, nɪu-, nu-, -nɪə
Po po
poach potʃ |poaches ˈpotʃɪz |poached potʃt
Pocahontas ˌpokəˈhɑntəs, -ˈhɒn- |-'s -ɪz
Pocatello ˌpokəˈtɛlo
pock pɑk; ES+pɒk; |-ed -t
pocket ˈpɑkɪt; ES+ˈpɒk-; |-ed -ɪd |-book
 -ˌbʊk |-knife -ˌnaɪf |-ful -ˌfʊl
pockmark ˈpɑkˌmɑrk; ES ˈpɑkˌmɑ:k, ˈpɒk-,
 E+-ˌmɑ:k
Pocomoke ˈpokəˌmok
Pocono ˈpokəˌno

|full fʊl |tooth tuθ |further ˈfɝðɚ; ES ˈfɝðə |custom ˈkʌstəm |while hwaɪl |how haʊ |toy tɔɪ
|using ˈjuzɪŋ |fuse fjuz, fɪuz |dish dɪʃ |vision ˈvɪʒən |Eden ˈidṇ |cradle ˈkredḷ |keep 'em ˈkipm̩

Those words below in which the ɑ *sound is spelt* o *are often pronounced with* ɒ *in E and S*

pod pad |-ded -ɪd

podgy ˈpadʒɪ

podiatry poˈdaɪətrɪ

podium ˈpodɪəm |-dia -dɪə

Poe po

poem ˈpo·ɪm, -əm

poesy ˈpo·ɪsɪ, -əsɪ, -zɪ

poet ˈpo·ɪt, -ət |-ry -rɪ

poetaster ˈpo·ɪtˌæstə, -ət-; ES -ˌæstə(r

poetic poˈɛtɪk |-al -ļ |-ally -ļɪ, -ɪklɪ

poetize ˈpo·ɪtˌaɪz |-s -ɪz |-d -d

Pogram ˈpogrəm

pogrom ˈpogrəm, ˈpag-, ˈpɒg-, poˈgram, -ˈgrɒm

poh po

poi pɔɪ, ˈpo·ɪ

poignancy ˈpɔɪnənsɪ, -njɒnsɪ |-ant -ənt

poilu ˈpwalu, pɔɪˈlu (*Fr* pwaˈly)

Poincaré *Fr* pwæ̃kaˈre

Poins pɔɪnz |-ʼs -ɪz; *in Shak prob.* pɔɪnts (*spelt* Pointz)

poinsettia, P- pɔɪnˈsɛtɪə

point pɔɪnt |pointed ˈpɔɪntɪd

point-blank ˈpɔɪntˈblæŋk (ˈpoint-ˌblank ˈaim)

Point Pelee ˈpɔɪntˈpili

poise pɔɪz |poises ˈpɔɪzɪz |poised pɔɪzd

poison ˈpɔɪzn̩ |-ed -d |-ing ˈpɔɪznɪŋ, -zn̩ɪŋ

poisonous ˈpɔɪznəs, ˈpɔɪzn̩əs

Poitiers pɔɪˈtɪrz; ES -ˈtɪəz; |-ʼs -ɪz (*Fr* pwaˈtje)

Poitou pɔɪˈtu (*Fr* pwaˈtu)

poke pok |poked pokt |poky, -key ˈpokɪ; |*N Engd* + pʊ̆k (*§46*)

pokeberry ˈpokˌbɛrɪ, -bərɪ; *N Engd* + ˈpʊ̆k- (*§46*)

poker ˈpokɚ; ES -kə(r; |-ing ˈpokərɪŋ, -krɪŋ; *N Engd* + ˈpʊ̆k- (*§46*)

Polack ˈpolæk, -lak

polack, -lak '*balsa*' poˈlak

Poland ˈpolənd |-er -ləndɚ, -læn-; ES -ə(r

polar ˈpolɚ; ES ˈpolə(r; |-ity poˈlærətɪ

Polaris poˈlɛrɪs, -ˈlær-, -ˈler-

polariscope poˈlɛrəˌskop

polarization ˌpolərəˈzeʃən, -aɪˈz-

polarize ˈpoləˌraɪz |-s -ɪz |-d -d

Pole *surname* pol, pul; '*Polander*' pol

pole pol |-d -d |-ax(e) -ˌæks |-axes -ˌæksɪz

polecat ˈpolˌkæt

polemic poˈlɛmɪk |-al -ļ |-ally -ļɪ, -ɪklɪ

polenta poˈlɛntə

polestar ˈpolˌstar; ES -ˌsta:(r, E+-ˌsta:(r

police pəˈlis |-s -ɪz |-d -t |-man, -men -mən

policy ˈpaləsɪ |-cied -sɪd

poliomyelitis ˌpalɪoˌmaɪəˈlaɪtɪs

polish ˈpalɪʃ |-es -ɪz |-ed -t

Polish ˈpolɪʃ

polite pəˈlaɪt

politic ˈpaləˌtɪk |-s -s |-ian ˌpaləˈtɪʃən

political pəˈlɪtɪkļ |-ly -ɪ, -ɪklɪ

politico pəˈlɪtɪˌko

polity ˈpalətɪ

Polixenes pəˈlɪksəˌniz |-ʼs -ɪz

Polk pok; *N Engd* + pʊ̆k (*§46*)

polka ˈpolkə, ˈpokə; *N Engd* + ˈpʊ̆- (*§46*); |-ed -d

polkadot ˈpokəˌdat

Poll, p- '*Polly*' pal

poll *adj* '*polled*' pol

poll '*head*,' '*cut*,' '*vote*' pol |-ed -d

pollack ˈpalək

pollard, P- ˈpaləd; ES ˈpaləd; |-ed -ɪd

pollen ˈpalən |-ed -d

pollinate ˈpaləˌnet |-d -ɪd |-tion ˌpaləˈneʃən

polliwog ˈpalɪˌwag, -ˌwɒg

pollock, P- ˈpalək

pollute pəˈlut, -ˈlɪut |-d -ɪd

pollution pəˈluʃən, -ˈlɪuʃən

Pollux ˈpaləks |-ʼs -ɪz

Polly ˈpalɪ |-anna ˌpalɪˈænə

pollywog ˈpalɪˌwag, -ˌwɒg

polo, P- ˈpolo

polonaise ˌpoləˈnez, ˌpalə- |-s -ɪz |-d -d

polonium pəˈlonɪəm

Polonius pəˈlonɪəs, -njəs |-ʼs -ɪz

poltroon palˈtrun |-ery -ərɪ, -rɪ

polyandrous ˌpalɪˈændrəs |-dry -drɪ, ˈpalɪˌæn-

Polybius pəˈlɪbɪəs |-ʼs -ɪz

Polycarp ˈpalɪˌkarp; ES -ˌka:p, E+-ˌka:p

polychromatic ˌpalɪkroˈmætɪk

polychrome ˈpalɪˌkrom |-d -d

Polycrates pəˈlɪkrəˌtiz |-ʼs -ɪz

Polydore ˈpalɪˌdor, -ˌdɔr; ES -ˌdoə(r, E+-ˌdɔə(r

Polydorus ˌpalɪˈdorəs, -ˈdɔr-; S -ˈdor-; |-ʼs -ɪz

polygamy pəˈlɪgəmɪ |-mous -məs |-mist -mɪst

Key: *See in full §§3–47.* bee bi |pity ˈpɪtɪ (§6) |rate ret |yet jɛt |sang sæŋ |angry ˈæŋ·grɪ |bath bæθ; E baθ (§10) |ah ɑ |far far |watch watʃ, wɒtʃ (§12) |jaw dʒɔ |gorge gɔrdʒ |go go

Those words below in which the ɑ sound is spelt o are often pronounced with ɒ in E and S

polyglot ˈpɑlɪˌglɑt

polygon ˈpɑlɪˌgɑn |-al pəˈlɪgən|

polygyny pəˈlɪdʒənɪ

polyhedron ˌpɑlɪˈhidrən |-dral -drəl

Polyhymnia ˌpɑlɪˈhɪmnɪə

polymer ˈpɑlɪmɚ; ES -mə(r; |-e -ˌmɪr; ES -ˌmɪə(r

polymeric ˌpɑlɪˈmɛrɪk

polymerize ˈpɑlɪməˌraɪz, pəˈlɪmə- |-s -ɪz |-d -d

Polynesia ˌpɑləˈniʃə, -ʒə |-n -n

polynomial ˌpɑlɪˈnomɪəl

polyp ˈpɑlɪp

polyped ˈpɑlɪˌpɛd

polyphase ˈpɑlɪˌfez |-sal ˌpɑlɪˈfezḷ

Polyphemus ˌpɑlɪˈfiməs |-'s -ɪz

polyphonic ˌpɑlɪˈfɑnɪk |-ny pəˈlɪfənɪ

polypus ˈpɑləpəs |-pi -ˌpaɪ |-'s -ɪz

polysyllabic ˌpɑləsɪˈlæbɪk |-al -ḷ |-ally -ḷɪ, -ɪklɪ

polysyllabism ˌpɑləˈsɪləˌbɪzəm

polysyllable ˈpɑləˌsɪləbḷ

polytechnic, P- ˌpɑləˈtɛknɪk |-al -ḷ

polytheism ˈpɑləθiˌɪzəm

polytheistic ˌpɑləθiˈɪstɪk |-al -ḷ |-ally -ḷɪ, -ɪklɪ

Polyxena pəˈlɪksɪnə

pomace ˈpʌmɪs, -əs |-ous poˈmeʃəs

pomade poˈmed, -ˈmɑd

pome pom

pomegranite ˈpʌmˌgrænɪt, ˈpɑm-, pʌmˈgræn-, pɑm-

Pomerania ˌpɑməˈrenɪə |-n -n

Pomerene ˈpɑməˌrin

Pomeroy ˈpɑməˌrɔɪ, ˈpʌmə-, -mrɔɪ

Pomfret ˈpʌmfrɪt, ˈpɑm-

pommel *n* ˈpʌmḷ, ˈpɑmḷ |-ed -d

pommel *v* ˈpʌmḷ |-ed -d |-ing ˈpʌmḷɪŋ, ˈpɑmlɪŋ

pomology poˈmɑlədʒɪ

Pomona pəˈmonə

pomp pɑmp |pomped pɑmpt

pompadour, P- ˈpɑmpəˌdor, -ˌdɔr, -ˌdur; ES -ˌdoə(r, -ˌduə(r, E+-ˌdɔə(r

pompano, P- ˈpɑmpəˌno

Pompei *It province* pɑmˈpe·i (*It* pomˈpɛ:i)

Pompeian pɑmˈpeən, -ˈpiən

Pompeii *anc. city* pɑmˈpe·i, -ˈpe, ˈpɑmpɪˌaɪ

Pompeius pɑmˈpiəs |-'s -ɪz

Pompey ˈpɑmpɪ

pompon ˈpɑmpɑn (*Fr* põˈpõ)

pompous ˈpɑmpəs |pomposity pɑmˈpɑsətɪ

Ponce ˈponse

Ponce de Leon ˈpɑnsdəˈliən (*Sp* ˈpɔnθeˈðeleˈɔn)

poncho ˈpɑntʃo

pond pɑnd, pɒnd, pɔnd

ponder ˈpɑndɚ; ES -də(r; |-ed -d |-ing ˈpɑndrɪŋ, ˈpɑndərɪŋ

ponderable ˈpɑndərəbḷ, ˈpɑndrə- |-rous -rəs

Pondicherry ˌpɑndɪˈtʃɛrɪ (*Fr* Pondichéry põdiʃeˈri)

pone *'corn bread'* pon

pone *L v* ˈponi

pongee pɑnˈdʒi (ˈpɑnˌgee ˈsilk)

poniard ˈpɑnjɚd; ES ˈpɑnjəd; |-ed -ɪd

pons asinorum ˈpɑnzˌæsɪˈnorəm, -ˈnɔr-; S -ˈnor-

Pons, Lily ˈlɪlɪˈpɑnz (*S Fr* liliˈpõ:ns) |-'s -ɪz

Pontchartrain ˈpɑntʃɚˌtren; ES ˈpɑntʃə-

Pontefract ˈpʌmfrɪt, ˈpɑm-, ˈpɑntɪˌfrækt

Pontiac ˈpɑntɪˌæk

pontifex, P- ˈpɑntəˌfɛks |-fices pɑnˈtɪfəˌsiz

pontiff ˈpɑntɪf

pontifical pɑnˈtɪfɪkḷ |-ly -ɪ |-cate -kɪt, -ˌket

pontifices pɑnˈtɪfəˌsiz

Pontius ˈpɑntʃəs, -nʃəs, -ntɪəs |-'s -ɪz

pontoon pɑnˈtun |-ed -d (ˈpɑnˌtoon ˈbridge)

Pontotoc ˌpɑntəˈtɑk

Pontus ˈpɑntəs |-'s -ɪz

pony ˈponɪ |ponied ˈponɪd

poodle ˈpudḷ |-d -d |-ling ˈpudlɪŋ, ˈpudḷɪŋ

pooh pu, pʊ *& various other breath puffs*

Pooh-Bah ˌpuˈbɑ

pooh-pooh ˈpuˈpu, ˈpuˌpu |-ed -d

pool pul |-ed -d |-room ˈpulˌrum, -ˌrʊm

poop pup |pooped pupt

poor pʊr; ES pʊə(r, poə(r, pɔə(r

poor-farm *'poorhouse'* ˈpʊrˌfɑrm; ES ˈpʊə-ˌfɑːm, ˈpoə-, ˈpɔə-, E+-ˌfɑːm

poor farm *'bad farm'* *acct* ˈpoorˈfɑrm

poorhouse ˈpʊrˌhaʊs; ES ˈpʊə-, ˈpoə-, ˈpɔə- |-ses -zɪz

pop pɑp |popped pɑpt |-corn -ˌkɔrn; ES -ˌkɔən

pope, P- pop |-ry -ərɪ, -rɪ |-pish -ɪʃ

popgun ˈpɑpˌgʌn |-gunned -ˌgʌnd

Popilius poˈpɪlɪəs, -ljəs |-'s -ɪz

popinjay ˈpɑpɪnˌdʒe

poplar ˈpɑplɚ; ES ˈpɑplə(r

poplin ˈpɑplɪn |-ette ˌpɑplɪnˈɛt

|full fʊl |tooth tuθ |further ˈfɝðɚ; ES ˈfɜðə |custom ˈkʌstəm |while hwaɪl |how haʊ |toy tɔɪ |using ˈjuzɪŋ |fuse fjuz, fɪuz |dish dɪʃ |vision ˈvɪʒən |Eden ˈidn̩ |cradle ˈkredḷ |keep 'em ˈkɪpm̩

Those words below in which the ɑ sound is spelt o are often pronounced with ɒ in E and S

Popocatepetl ˌpopə'kætəˌpɛt|, poˌpokə'tepət|
—*Whatever the Aztec, the first pron. is well
established. A learned colleague once rimed:*
—*'What is home without a kettle?
Popocat- without a -petl.'*
popover 'papˌovɚ; ES -ˌovə(r
popper 'papɚ; ES 'papə(r
poppet 'papɪt |-ed -ɪd
popple, P- 'pap|
poppy 'papɪ |poppied 'papɪd
poppycock 'papɪˌkak
populace 'papjəlɪs, -ləs |-'s -ɪz
popular 'papjələ˞; ES -lə(r; |-ity ˌpapjə-
'lærətɪ
popularize 'papjələˌraɪz |-s -ɪz |-d -d
populate 'papjəˌlet |-lated -ˌletɪd |-lous -ləs
population ˌpapjə'leʃən
Populist 'papjəlɪst
porcelain 'porslɪn, 'por-, -s|ɪn, -ən, -s|ˌen; ES
-'pɔə-, 'pɔə-
porch portʃ, pɔrtʃ; ES poətʃ, E+pɔətʃ; |-es -ɪz
|-ed -t
porcine 'porsaɪn, -sɪn; ES 'pɔə-
porcupine, P- 'pɔrkjəˌpaɪn; ES 'pɔək-; |-d -d
pore por, pɔr; ES poə(r, E+pɔə(r; |-d -d
porgy 'pɔrgɪ; ES 'pɔəgɪ
pork pork, pɔrk; ES poək, E+pɔək
pornographic ˌpɔrnə'græfɪk; ES ˌpɔənə-
pornography por'nagrəfɪ, -'nɒg-; ES pɔ'n-
porosity po'rasətɪ, pɔ-; S po-
porous 'porəs, 'pɔrəs; S 'porəs
porphyry, P- 'pɔrfərɪ; ES 'pɔə-
porpoise 'pɔrpəs; ES 'pɔəpəs; |-s -ɪz
porridge 'pɔrɪdʒ, 'par-, 'pɒr- |-s -ɪz |-d -d
porringer 'pɔrɪndʒɚ, 'par-, 'pɒr-; ES -dʒə(r
Porsena 'pɔrsɪnə; ES 'pɔə-
port port, pɔrt; ES poət, E+pɔət; |-ed -ɪd
|-able -əb| |-bly -blɪ
portability ˌportə'bɪlətɪ, ˌpɔr-; ES ˌpoətə-,
E+ˌpɔətə-
portage, P- 'portɪdʒ, 'pɔr-; ES 'poə-, E+
'pɔə-; |-s -ɪz |-d -d
portal 'port|, 'pɔrt|; ES 'poət|, E+'pɔə-;
|-ed -d
Port Angeles port'ændʒələs, pɔrt-, -ˌliz; ES
poət, E+pɔt-
Port-au-Prince ˌporto'prɪns, ˌpɔrt-; ES ˌpoət-,
E+ˌpɔət-; (*Fr* pɔ̃rto'præ̃:s)

portcullis port'kʌlɪs, pɔrt-; ES poət-, E+
pɔət-; |-es -ɪz |-ed -t
Porte port, pɔrt; ES poət, E+pɔət
portend por'tɛnd, pɔr-; ES poə-, E+pɔə-;
|-ed -ɪd
portent 'portɛnt, 'pɔr-; ES 'poə-, E+'pɔə-
portentous por'tɛntəs, pɔr-; ES poə-, E+pɔə-
porter, P- 'portɚ, 'pɔr-; ES 'poətə(r, E+
'pɔətə(r; |-ed -d
porterhouse 'portɚˌhaus, 'pɔr-; ES 'poətə-, E+
'pɔətə-; |*pl* -houses '*liquor-house*' -ˌhauzɪz,
'*steak*' -ˌhausɪz
portfolio port'folɪˌo, pɔrt-, -ljo; ES poət-,
E+pɔt-
porthole 'portˌhol, 'pɔrt-; ES 'poət-, E+'pɔət-
Port Huron port'hjurən, pɔrt-, -'hɪu-; ES
poət-, E+pɔət-
Portia 'porʃə, 'pɔr-, -ʃɪə; ES 'poə-, E+'pɔə-
portico 'portɪˌko, 'pɔr-; ES 'poə-, E+'pɔə-;
|-ed -d
portiere ˌportɪ'ɛr, ˌpɔr-; ES ˌpoə-, E+ˌpɔə-;
(*Fr* pɔr'tjɛ:r)
portion 'porʃən, 'pɔr-; ES 'poə-, E+'pɔə-;
|-ed -d |-ing -ʃənɪŋ, -ʃnɪŋ
Port Jervis port'dʒɝvɪs, pɔrt-; ES poət-
'dʒɝvɪs, -'dʒɝv-, E+pɔət-; |-'s -ɪz
Portland 'portlənd, 'pɔrt-; ES 'poət-, E+
'pɔət-
portmanteau port'mænto, pɔrt-; ES poət-,
E+pɔət-
Portobello ˌportə'bɛlo, ˌpɔrtə-; ES ˌpoətə-,
E+ˌpɔətə-
Porto Bello ˌportə'bɛlo, ˌpɔrtə-; ES 'poətə-,
E+ˌpɔətə-; (*Am Sp* ˌpɔrto'βejo)
Porto Rico ˌportə'riko, ˌpɔrtə-; ES ˌpoətə-,
E+ˌpɔətə-; |-can -kən
portrait 'portret, 'pɔr-, -trɪt; ES 'poə-, E+
'pɔə-
portraiture 'portrɪtʃɚ, 'pɔr-; ES 'poətrɪtʃə(r,
E+'pɔə-
portray por'tre, pɔr-; ES poə-, E+pɔə-; |-ed
-d |-al -əl
Port Said port'sed, pɔrt-, -'saɪd, -sɑ'id; ES
poət-, E+pɔət-
Portsmouth 'portsməθ, 'pɔrts-; ES 'poəts-,
E+'pɔəts-
Portugal 'portʃəg|, 'pɔr-; ES 'poə-, E+'pɔə-;
|-guese -ˌgiz

Key: *See in full §§3–47.* bee bi |pity 'pɪtɪ (§6) |rate ret |yet jɛt |sang sæŋ |angry 'æŋ·grɪ
|bath bæθ; E baθ (§10) |ah ɑ |far fɑr |watch watʃ, wɒtʃ (§12) |jaw dʒɔ |gorge gɔrdʒ |go go

Those words below in which the ɑ *sound is spelt* o *are often pronounced with* ɒ *in E and S*

portulaca **ˌportʃəˈlækə, ˌpɔr-;** ES **ˌpoə-,** E+**ˌpɔə-;** |P- **-ˈlekə**
pose **poz** |poses **ˈpozɪz** |posed **pozd**
Poseidon **poˈsaɪdn̩, pə-**
Posey **ˈpozɪ**
poseur **poˈzɝ;** ES **-ˈzɜ(r, -ˈzɝ;** (*Fr* poˈzœ:r)
posit **ˈpɑzɪt** |-ed **-ɪd**
position **pəˈzɪʃən** |-ed **-d** |-al **-l̩,** '*placing*' **po-**
positive **ˈpɑzətɪv, -ztɪv** |-d **-d** |-vism **-ˌɪzəm**
positively **ˈpɑzətɪvlɪ, -ztɪv-,** *emph. occas.* **ˌpɑzəˈtɪvlɪ**
posse **ˈpɑsɪ** |-man **-mən** |-men **-mən**
posse comitatus **ˈpɑsɪˌkɑmɪˈtetəs**
possess **pəˈzɛs** |-es **-ɪz** |-ed **-t** |-edly **-ɪdlɪ**
possession **pəˈzɛʃən** |-ed **-d** |-ive **-sɪv** |-al **-l̩**
possessor **pəˈzɛsɚ;** ES **-ˈzɛsə(r;** |-y **-ɪ**
posset **ˈpɑsɪt** |-ed **-ɪd**
possibility **ˌpɑsəˈbɪlətɪ**
possible **ˈpɑsəbl̩** |-bly **-blɪ**
possum **ˈpɑsəm** |-ed **-d**
post **post** |posted **ˈpostɪd** |-age **-ɪdʒ** |-al **-l̩**
post-chaise *n* **ˈpostˌʃez** |-s **-ɪz**
post-chaise *v* **ˌpostˈʃez** |-s **-ɪz** |-d **-d**
postdate **ˌpostˈdet** |-dated **-ˈdetɪd**
posterior **pɑsˈtɪrɪɚ;** ES **-ˈtɪrɪ·ə(r**
posterity **pɑsˈtɛrətɪ**
postern **ˈpostɚn, ˈpɑs-;** ES **-tən**
postgraduate **postˈgrædʒʊɪt, posˈg-, -ˌet**
posthaste **ˈpostˈhest** (ˈpostˌhaste ˈjourney)
posthumous **ˈpɑstʃʊməs**
Posthumus **postˈhjuməs, -ˈhɪu-** |-'s **-ɪz**
postilion, -ll- **poˈstɪljən, pɑ-** |-ed **-d**
postlude **ˈpostˌlud, -ˌlɪud**
postman **ˈpostmən** |-men **-mən**
postmark **ˈpostˌmɑrk;** ES **-ˌmɑ:k,** E+**-ˌma:k;** |-ed **-t**
postmaster **ˈpostˌmæstɚ, ˈposˌm-;** ES **-ˌmæs-tə(r,** E+**-ˌmas-, -ˌmɑs-**
post meridiem **ˈpostməˈrɪdɪˌɛm, -ˈrɪdɪəm**
postmistress **ˈpostˌmɪstrɪs, ˈposˌm-** |-es **-ɪz**
post-mortem **postˈmɔrtəm;** ES **-ˈmɔətəm;** |-ed **-d**
postnatal **postˈnetl̩**
post-obit **postˈobɪt, -ˈɑb-**
post-office **ˈpostˌɔfɪs, -ˌɒf-, -ˌɑf-** |-s **-ɪz**
postpaid **ˈpostˈped, ˈposˈp-** (ˈpostˌpaid ˈparcel)
postpone **postˈpon, posˈp-** |-poned **-ˈpond**
postprandial **postˈprændɪəl** |-ly **-ɪ**
postscript **ˈpos·skrɪpt, ˈpost-** |-ed **-ɪd**
postulant **ˈpɑstʃələnt**
postulate *n* **ˈpɑstʃəlɪt, -ˌlet**
postulate *v* **ˈpɑstʃəˌlet** |-lated **-ˌletɪd**
postulation **ˌpɑstʃəˈleʃən**
posture **ˈpɑstʃɚ;** ES **-tʃə(r;** |-d **-d**
posy **ˈpozɪ**
pot **pɑt** |potted **ˈpɑtɪd**
potable **ˈpotəbl̩**
potash **ˈpɑtˌæʃ** |-es **-ɪz** |-ed **-t**
potassium **pəˈtæsɪəm**
potation **poˈteʃən**
potato **pəˈteto, -ə**
Potawatomi, -ami **ˌpɑtəˈwɑtəmɪ, -ˈwɒt-**
potbelly **ˈpɑtˌbɛlɪ** |-ied **-d**
potboiler **ˈpɑtˌbɔɪlɚ;** ES **-ˌbɔɪlə(r**
potboy **ˈpɑtˌbɔɪ**
Poteat **poˈtit**
poteen **poˈtin, pə-**
potence **ˈpotn̩s** |-cy **-ɪ** |-tent **-tn̩t**
potentate **ˈpotn̩ˌtet**
potential **pəˈtɛnʃəl** |-ly **-ɪ** |-ity **-ˌtɛnʃɪˈælətɪ**
potentiometer **pəˌtɛnʃɪˈɑmətɚ;** ES **-ˈɑmətə(r**
potheen **poˈtin, pə-**
pother **ˈpɑðɚ;** ES **ˈpɑðə(r;** |-ed **-d**
potherb **ˈpɑtˌɝb, -ˌhɝb;** ES **-ˌɜb, -ˌɝb, -ˌhɜb, -ˌhɝb**
potholder **ˈpɑtˌholdɚ;** ES **-ˌholdə(r**
pothole **ˈpɑtˌhol** |-hook **-ˌhʊk**
pothouse **ˈpɑtˌhaʊs** |-ses **-zɪz**
pothunter **ˈpɑtˌhʌntɚ;** ES **-ˌhʌntə(r**
potion **ˈpoʃən** |-ed **-d**
Potiphar **ˈpɑtəfɚ;** ES **ˈpɑtəfə(r**
potlatch, P- **ˈpɑtˌlætʃ** |-es **-ɪz** |-ed **-t**
potlicker, -likk- **ˈpɑtˌlɪkɚ;** ES **-ˌlɪkə(r**
pot-liquor **ˈpɑtˌlɪkɚ;** ES **-ˌlɪkə(r**
potluck **ˈpɑtˌlʌk, ˈpɑtˈlʌk**
Potomac **pəˈtomək**
Potosi *Bol* **ˌpotoˈsi;** *US* **pəˈtosɪ**
potpie **ˈpɑtˌpaɪ**
potpourri **pɑtˈpʊrɪ** (*Fr* **popuˈri**)
Potsdam **ˈpɑtsˌdæm**
potsherd **ˈpɑtˌʃɝd;** ES **-ˌʃɜd, -ˌʃɝd**
pottage **ˈpɑtɪdʒ**
Pottawattamie, -wato- **ˌpɑtəˈwɑtəmɪ, -ˈwɒt-**
potter **ˈpɑtɚ;** ES **ˈpɑtə(r;** |-ed **-d** |-y **-ɪ**
pottle **ˈpɑtl̩** |-d **-d**
Pottstown **ˈpɑtsˌtaʊn** |-ville **-vɪl;** S+**-vl̩**

pouch **pautʃ** |pouches **'pautʃɪz** |pouched
  pautʃt
pouf **puf**
Poughkeepsie **pə'kɪpsɪ**
poult **polt**
poulterer **'poltɚ**; ES **'poltərə(r**
poultice **'poltɪs** |-s -ɪz |- d -t
Poultney **'poltnɪ**
poultry **'poltrɪ**
pounce **paʊns** |-s -ɪz |-d -t
pound **paʊnd** |pounded **'paʊndɪd** |-cake -ˌkek
pound-foolish **'paʊnd'fʊlɪʃ** ('pound-ˌfoolish
  'act)
Pounds **paʊndz, paʊnz** |-'s -ɪz
pour **por, pɔr, pʊr**; ES **poə(r, pʊə(r, E+pɔə(r**;
  |-ed -d
pourboire **'pʊrˌbwar**; ES **'pʊəˌbwɑ:(r**; (Fr
  pur'bwa:r)
pourparler, -ley **pʊr'parlɪ**; ES **pʊə'pɑ:lɪ**; |-ed
  -d (Fr purpar'le)
pou sto **'pu'sto**
pout **paʊt** |pouted **'paʊtɪd**
poverty **'pavɚtɪ**; ES **'pavətɪ, 'pɒv-**
Pow **paʊ**
powder **'paʊdɚ**; ES **-də(r**; |-ed -d |-ing
  'paʊdrɪŋ, 'paʊdərɪŋ
Powell **'paʊəl** |Baden-P-, F. York P- **'poəl**
power, P- **'paʊɚ**; ES **'paʊ·ə(r**; |-ed -d |-ful
  -fəl |-fully -fəlɪ, -flɪ
Poweshiek **ˌpaʊə'ʃik**
Powhatan **ˌpaʊə'tæn**
Pownal, -ll **'paʊnl**
powwow **'paʊˌwaʊ** |-ed -d
Powys **'po·ɪs** |-'s -ɪz
pox **paks**; ES+**pɒks**
praam **pram**
practicability **ˌpræktɪkə'bɪlətɪ**
practicable **'præktɪkəbl** |-bly -blɪ
practical **'præktɪkl** |-ly -ɪ, 'virtually' -ɪklɪ
practicality **ˌpræktɪ'kælətɪ**
practice, v+-tise **'præktɪs** |-s -ɪz |-d -t
practitioner **præk'tɪʃənɚ, -ʃnɚ**; ES -nə(r
Praed **pred**
praedial **'pridɪəl** |-ity **ˌpridɪ'ælətɪ**
praefect **'prifɛkt**
praetor **'pritɚ**; ES **'pritə(r**
praetorian **prɪ'torɪən, -'tɔr-**; S -'tor-
pragmatic **præg'mætɪk** |-al -l |-ally -l̩ɪ, -ɪklɪ
pragmatism **'prægməˌtɪzəm** |-tist -tɪst

Prague **preg, prag** (Czech **'praha**, Ger **prak**)—
  The hybrid pronunciation **prag** is now accepted beside **preg**.
prairie **'prɛrɪ, 'prerɪ**
Prairie du Chien **ˌprɛrɪdə'ʃin, ˌprerɪ-**
praise **prez** |praises **'prezɪz** |praised **prezd**
praiseworthy **'prezˌwɝðɪ**; ES -ˌwɝðɪ, -ˌwɝðɪ
Prakrit **'prakrɪt**
praline **'pralin**; S+**'prɔ-**
pram **præm**, 'praam' **pram**
prance **præns**; E+**prans, prɒns**; |-s -ɪz |-d -t
prandial **'prændɪəl** |-ly -ɪ
prank **præŋk** |pranked, prankt **præŋkt**
prate **pret** |prated **'pretɪd**
pratique **præ'tik, 'prætɪk** (Fr pra'tik)
Pratt **præt**
prattle **'prætl** |-d -d |-ling **'prætlɪŋ, -tl̩ɪŋ**
prawn **prɔn**
Praxiteles **præks'ɪtl̩ˌiz** |-'s -ɪz
pray **pre** |prayed **pred**
prayer 'petition' **prɛr, prær**; E **prɛə(r**, ES
  præə(r
prayer 'supplicant' **'pre·ɚ**; ES **'pre·ə(r**
prayer-rug **'prɛrˌrʌg, 'prær-**; E **'prɛəˌrʌg**, ES
  'præə-
pre- prefix, stressed **'pri-, ˌpri-, 'prɛ-, ˌprɛ-**;
  unstr. **prɪ-, prə-, pri-**. For the unstr., when
  only **prɪ-** is given in the vocab., it is to be
  understood that many speakers, both British
  and American, use **prə-** as in propose
  prə'poz, or **pri-** as in precede **pri'sid**. The
  pron. **pɚ-** is also not infrequently heard from
  speakers of unquestioned cultivation.
preach **pritʃ** |-es -ɪz |-ed -t |-er -ɚ; ES -ə(r
preachify **'pritʃəˌfaɪ** |-fied -ˌfaɪd
preamble **'priæmbl, prɪ'æmbl** |-d -d |-ling
  -blɪŋ, -bl̩ɪŋ
prearrange **ˌpriə'rendʒ** |-s -ɪz |-d -d
prebend **'prɛbənd** |-ary -ˌɛrɪ |-al prɪ'bɛndl̩
Preble **'prɛbl**
precarious **prɪ'kɛrɪəs, -'kær-, -'ker-**
precaution **prɪ'kɔʃən** |-al -l̩ |-ary -ˌɛrɪ |-tious
  -ʃəs
precede **pri'sid, prɪ-** |-d -ɪd
precedence **prɪ'sidns, 'prɛsədəns** |-s -ɪz |-cy -ɪ
precedent n **'prɛsədənt**
precedent adj **prɪ'sidn̩t**
precedent v **'prɛsəˌdɛnt** |-ed -ɪd
precentor **prɪ'sɛntɚ**; ES -'sɛntə(r

Key: See in full §§3–47. bee **bi** |pity **'pɪtɪ** (§6) |rate **ret** |yet **jɛt** |sang **sæŋ** |angry **'æŋ·grɪ**
|bath **bæθ**; E **baθ** (§10) |ah **ɑ** |far **far** |watch **watʃ, wɒtʃ** (§12) |jaw **dʒɔ** |gorge **gɔrdʒ** |go **go**

precept ˈprisɛpt |-ed -ɪd
preceptive prɪˈsɛptɪv |-tor -tɚ; ES -tə(r
preceptress prɪˈsɛptrɪs |-es -ɪz
preceptual prɪˈsɛptʃʊəl |-ly -ɪ
precession priˈsɛʃən, prɪ- |-al -ļ
precinct ˈprisɪŋkt
preciosity ˌprɛʃɪˈɑsətɪ, ˌprɛsɪ-; ES+-ˈɒs-
precious ˈprɛʃəs
precipice ˈprɛsəpɪs |-s -ɪz |-d -t
precipitance prɪˈsɪpətəns |-cy -ɪ |-tant -tənt
precipitate n, adj prɪˈsɪpəˌtet, -tɪt
precipitate v prɪˈsɪpəˌtet |-tated -ˌtetɪd
precipitation prɪˌsɪpəˈteʃən
precipitous prɪˈsɪpətəs
précis n preˈsi, ˈpresi (Fr preˈsi) |pl précis -z
précis v preˈsi |précises preˈsiz |précised
 preˈsid—acct+ˈprécis
precise prɪˈsaɪs |-s -ɪz |-d -t
precisian prɪˈsɪʒən |-ism -ˌɪzəm |-ist -ɪst
precision prɪˈsɪʒən
preclinical priˈklɪnɪkļ
preclude prɪˈklud, -ˈklɪud |-d -ɪd
preclusion prɪˈkluʒən, -ˈklɪu- |-sive -sɪv
precocious prɪˈkoʃəs
precocity prɪˈkɑsətɪ; ES+-ˈkɒs-
preconceive ˌprikənˈsiv |-d -d
preconception ˌprikənˈsɛpʃən
preconcert n priˈkɑnsɚt, -sɚt; ES -ˈkɑnsɜt,
 -ˈkɒn-, -sɜt, -sət
preconcert v ˌprikənˈsɚt; ES -ˈsɜt, -ˈsɜt; |-ed
 -ɪd
precontract n priˈkɑntrækt; ES+-ˈkɒn-
precontract v ˌprikənˈtrækt, priˈkɑntrækt;
 ES+-ˈkɒn-; |-ed -ɪd
precook priˈkʊk |-ed -t
precool priˈkul |-ed -d
precursor prɪˈkɚsɚ; ES -ˈkɜsə(r, -ˈkɜsə(r
precursory prɪˈkɚsərɪ; ES -ˈkɜs-, -ˈkɜs-
predaceous, -cious prɪˈdeʃəs |-city -ˈdæsətɪ
predate priˈdet |-dated -ˈdetɪd
predatory ˈprɛdəˌtorɪ, -ˌtɔrɪ; S -ˌtorɪ; |-rily
 -rəlɪ, -rɪlɪ, emph+ˌpredaˈtorily
predecessor ˌprɛdɪˈsɛsɚ, ˈprɛdɪˌsɛsɚ; ES -sə(r
predestinarian prɪˌdɛstəˈnɛrɪən, -ˈner- |-ism
 -ˌɪzəm
predestinate adj prɪˈdɛstənɪt
predestinate v prɪˈdɛstəˌnet |-nated -ˌnetɪd
predestination prɪˌdɛstəˈneʃən, ˌprɪdɛstə-
predestine prɪˈdɛstɪn |-d -d

predetermine ˌpridɪˈtɚmɪn; ES -ˈtɜm-, -ˈtɜm-;
 |-d -d
predial ˈpridɪəl |-ity ˌpridɪˈælətɪ
predicable ˈprɛdɪkəbļ |-bly -blɪ
predicament prɪˈdɪkəmənt |-al prɪˌdɪkə-
 ˈmɛntļ
predicate n, adj ˈprɛdɪkɪt, -ət
predicate v ˈprɛdɪˌket |-d -ɪd
predication ˌprɛdɪˈkeʃən |-tive ˈprɛdɪˌketɪv
predict prɪˈdɪkt |-ed -ɪd |-ction -kʃən
predigest ˌpridəˈdʒɛst, -daɪ- |-ed -ɪd
predilection ˌpridļˈɛkʃən, ˌpred-
predispose ˌpridɪsˈpoz |-s -ɪz |-d -d |- dly -ɪdlɪ
predisposition ˌpridɪspəˈzɪʃən
predominance prɪˈdɑmənəns; ES+-ˈdɒm-;
 |-cy -ɪ |-nant -nənt
predominate prɪˈdɑməˌnet; ES+-ˈdɒm-; |-d
 -ɪd
predomination prɪˌdɑməˈneʃən; ES+-ˌdɒm-
pre-eminence prɪˈɛmənəns |-cy -ɪ |-nent -nənt
pre-empt prɪˈɛmpt |-ed -ɪd |-ption -pʃən
preen prin |preened prind
pre-exist ˌprɪgˈzɪst |-ed -ɪd |-ence -əns
preface ˈprɛfɪs, -əs |-s -ɪz |-d -t
prefatorial ˌprɛfəˈtorɪəl, -ˈtɔr-; S -ˈtor-
prefatory ˈprɛfəˌtorɪ, -ˌtɔrɪ; S -ˌtorɪ
prefect ˈprifɛkt
prefecture ˈprifɛktʃɚ; ES -fɛktʃə(r
prefer prɪˈfɚ; ES -ˈfɜ(r, -ˈfɜ; |-red -d
preferability ˌprɛfərəˈbɪlətɪ
preferable ˈprɛfrəbļ, ˈprɛfərə- |-bly -blɪ
preference ˈprɛfrəns, ˈprɛfərəns |-s -ɪz
preferential ˌprɛfəˈrɛnʃəl |-ly -ɪ
preferment prɪˈfɚmənt; ES -ˈfɜ-, -ˈfɜ-
prefiguration ˌprifɪgjəˈreʃən, -fɪgə-, prɪˌfɪg-
prefigure priˈfɪgjɚ, -ˈfɪgɚ; ES -ə(r; |-d -d
prefix n ˈpriˌfɪks |-es -ɪz
prefix v priˈfɪks |-es -ɪz |-ed -t
pregnable ˈprɛgnəbļ
pregnance ˈprɛgnəns |-cy -ɪ |-nant -nənt
preheat priˈhit |-heated -ˈhitɪd
prehensile prɪˈhɛnsļ, -sɪl
prehistoric ˌpriʌsˈtɔrɪk, ˌprihɪs-, -ˈtar-, -ˈtɒr-
 |-al -ļ |-ally -ļɪ, -ɪklɪ
preignition ˌprɪgˈnɪʃən
prejudge priˈdʒʌdʒ |-s -ɪz ˌ-d -d
prejudice ˈprɛdʒədɪs |-s -ɪz |-d -t
prejudicial ˌprɛdʒəˈdɪʃəl |-ly -ɪ
pre-judicial ˌpridʒuˈdɪʃəl, -dʒɪu-

|full fʊl |tooth tuθ |further ˈfɚðɚ; ES ˈfɜðə |custom ˈkʌstəm |while hwaɪl |how haʊ |toy tɔɪ
|using ˈjuzɪŋ |fuse fjuz, fɪuz |dish dɪʃ |vision ˈvɪʒən |Eden ˈidņ |cradle ˈkredļ |keep 'em ˈkipm̩

prelacy ˈprɛləsɪ
prelate ˈprɛlɪt |-tism -ˌɪzəm
preliminary prɪˈlɪməˌnɛrɪ
prelude ˈprɛljud, ˈpri-, ˈprilud, ˈprilɪud |-d -ɪd
premarital priˈmærətl̩
premature ˌpriməˈtjʊr, -ˈtɪʊr, -ˈtʊr, ˈprɪməˌt-, -ˌtʃʊr; ES -ə(r; (ˈpreməˌture ˈdeath)
premedical priˈmɛdɪkl̩
premeditate prɪˈmɛdəˌtet |-tated -ˌtetɪd
premeditation ˌprimɛdəˈteʃən, prɪˌmɛdə-
premier n ˈprimɪɚ, prɪˈmɪr; ES ˈprimɪ·ə(r, prɪˈmɪə(r; Brit+ˈprɛmɪ·ə(r, -mjə(r
premier adj ˈprimɪɚ; ES ˈprimɪ·ə(r; Brit+ˈprɛmɪ·ə(r, -mjə(r
première prɪˈmɪr; ES -ˈmɪə(r; (Fr prəˈmjɛːr)
premise, -iss n ˈprɛmɪs |-s -ɪz
premise v prɪˈmaɪz, ˈprɛmɪs |-s -ɪz |-d -d, -t
premium ˈprimɪəm
premolar priˈmolɚ; ES -ˈmolə(r
premonition ˌpriməˈnɪʃən
premonitory prɪˈmanəˌtorɪ, -ˌtɔrɪ; S -ˌtorɪ, ES+-ˈmɒn-
prenatal priˈnetl̩ |-ly -ɪ
Prendergast ˈprɛndɚˌgæst; ES ˈprɛndə-
prentice, ʼp-, P- ˈprɛntɪs |-s -ɪz |-d -t
preoccupation priˌɑkjəˈpeʃən, ˌpriakjə-; ES+-ˌɒk-, -ɒk-
preoccupy priˈɑkjəˌpaɪ; ES+-ˈɒk-; |-pied -ˌpaɪd
preordain ˌpriɔrˈden; ES -ɔəˈden; |-ed -d
preordination ˌpriɔrdn̩ˈeʃən; ES -ɔdn̩ˈeʃən
prepaid priˈped (ˈpreˌpaid ˈcharges)
preparation ˌprɛpəˈreʃən
preparative prɪˈpærətɪv
preparatory prɪˈpærəˌtorɪ, -ˌtɔrɪ; S -ˌtorɪ
prepare prɪˈpɛr, -ˈpær; E -ˈpɛə(r, ES -ˈpæə(r; |-d -d |-dness -ɪdnɪs, -dnɪs
prepay priˈpe |-paid -ˈped (ˈpreˌpay ˈrent)
prepense prɪˈpɛns |-s -ɪz |-d -t
preponderance prɪˈpandrəns, -dərəns; ES+-ˈpɒn-; |-cy -ɪ |-ant -ənt
preponderate prɪˈpandəˌret; ES+-ˈpɒn-; |-d -ɪd
preposition gram. ˌprɛpəˈzɪʃən |-al -l̩ |-ally -l̩ɪ
preposition ʻposition beforeʼ ˌpripəˈzɪʃən
prepossess ˌpripəˈzɛs |-es -ɪz |-ed -t
prepossessing ˌpripəˈzɛsɪŋ (ˈpreposˌsessing ˈeye)
prepossession ˌpripəˈzɛʃən

preposterous prɪˈpastrəs, -tərəs; ES+-ˈpɒs-
prepotence prɪˈpotn̩s |-cy -ɪ |-tent -tn̩t
preprint priˈprɪnt, ˈpriˌprɪnt
preprofessional ˌpriprəˈfɛʃənl̩, ˌpripə-, -ˈfɛʃnəl —In the 2d pron. r is lost by dissimilation (§121).
prepuce ˈpripjus, -pɪus |-s -ɪz
Pre-Raphaelite, pre-R- prɪˈræfɪəˌlaɪt, -ˈræfjə-, -ˈræfə-
prerequisite priˈrɛkwəzɪt
prerogative prɪˈragətɪv, -ˈrɒg- |-d -d
presage n ˈprɛsɪdʒ |-s -ɪz, in Shak. prɪˈsedʒ
presage v prɪˈsedʒ |-s -ɪz |-d -d |- r -ɚ; ES -ə(r
presbyopia ˌprɛzbɪˈopɪə
presbyter ˈprɛzbɪtɚ; ES -tə(r; |-y -bɪˌtɛrɪ
Presbyterian ˌprɛzbəˈtɪrɪən |-ism -ˌɪzəm
preschool priˈskul (ˈpreˌschool ˈtraining)
prescience ˈprɛʃɪəns, ˈpri- |-ent -ənt
pre-science priˈsaɪəns
prescind prɪˈsɪnd |-ed -ɪd
prescission prɪˈsɪʒən, -ˈsɪʃən
Prescot, -tt ˈprɛskət
prescribe prɪˈskraɪb |-d -d
prescript adj prɪˈskrɪpt (ˈpreˌscript ˈrule)
prescript n ˈpriskrɪpt
prescription prɪˈskrɪpʃən, pɚˈskrɪpʃən
prescriptive prɪˈskrɪptɪv
presence ˈprɛzn̩s |-s -ɪz |-d -t
present n ˈprɛznt; mil. prɪˈzɛnt
present v prɪˈzɛnt |-ed -ɪd
presentable prɪˈzɛntəbl̩ |-bly -blɪ
presentation ˌprɛznˈteʃən, ˌprizɛnˈteʃən
presentative prɪˈzɛntətɪv
present-day ˈprɛzntˈde (ˈpresent-ˌday ˈlaws)
presentiment prɪˈzɛntəmənt
presentment prɪˈzɛntmənt
preservation ˌprɛzɚˈveʃən; ES ˌprɛzə-
preservative prɪˈzɝvətɪv; ES -ˈzɝv-, -ˈzɜv-
preserve prɪˈzɝv; ES -ˈzɝv, -ˈzɜv; |-d -d
preshow priˈʃo |-ed -ˈʃod |-n -ˈʃon or -ed -ˈʃod
preside prɪˈzaɪd |-d -ɪd
presidency ˈprɛzədənsɪ, ˈprɛzdən- |-dent -dənt
presidential ˌprɛzəˈdɛnʃəl |-ly -ɪ
presidio prɪˈsɪdɪˌo (Sp preˈsiðjo)
Presque Isle Me, Pa ˌprɛskˈaɪl, Mich -ˈil
press prɛs |presses ˈprɛsɪz |pressed prɛst
pressmark ˈprɛsˌmark; ES -ˌmɑːk, E+-ˌmɑːk; |-ed -t

pressroom 'prɛs,rum, -,rʊm
pressure 'prɛʃɚ; ES 'prɛʃə(r
presswork 'prɛs,wɝk; ES -,wɜˑk, -,wɝk
Prester John 'prɛstɚ'dʒɑn, -'dʒɒn; ES -tə-
prestidigitation ,prɛstɪ,dɪdʒɪ'teʃən
prestidigitate ,prɛstɪ'dɪdʒɪ,tet |-d -ɪd
prestidigitator ,prɛstɪ'dɪdʒɪ,tetɚ; ES -tə(r
prestige 'prɛstɪdʒ, prɛs'tiʒ (Fr prɛs'tiːʒ)
prestissimo prɛs'tɪsə,mo (It prɛs'tissi,mo)
presto 'prɛsto
Preston 'prɛstən
Prestwich 'prɛstwɪtʃ, loc.+-tɪdʒ |-'s -ɪz
Prestwick 'prɛstwɪk, 'prɛstɪk
presumable prɪ'zuməb|, -'zɪum-, -zjum- |-bly
  -blɪ
presume prɪ'zum, -'zɪum, -'zjum |-d -d |-dly
  -ɪdlɪ
presumption prɪ'zʌmpʃən |-tive -tɪv |-tuous
  -tʃʊəs
presuppose ,prisə'poz |-s -ɪz |-d -d
presupposition ,prisʌpə'zɪʃən
pretence prɪ'tɛns |-s -ɪz
pretend prɪ'tɛnd |-ed -ɪd |-ant -ənt
pretender, P- prɪ'tɛndɚ; ES -'tɛndə(r
pretense prɪ'tɛns |-s -ɪz
pretension prɪ'tɛnʃən |-tentious -'tɛnʃəs
preterit, -ite 'prɛtərɪt |-ive prɪ'tɛrətɪv
pretermission ,pritɚ'mɪʃən; ES ,pritə-
pretermit ,pritɚ'mɪt; ES ,pritə-; |-ted -ɪd
preternatural ,pritɚ'nætʃərəl, -tʃrəl; ES
  ,pritə-; |-ly -ɪ
pretext n 'pritɛkst |adj -ed 'pritɛkstɪd
pretext v prɪ'tɛkst |-ed -ɪd
pretor 'pritɚ; ES 'pritə(r
Pretoria prɪ'torɪə, -'tɔr-; S -'tor-
pretorian prɪ'torɪən, -'tɔr-; S -'tor-
prettify 'prɪtɪ,faɪ |-fied -,faɪd
pretty stressed 'prɪtɪ, unstr. pɚtɪ['gʊd], prɪtɪ-,
  prətɪ-, prʊtɪ-, pʊrtɪ-; ES+pətɪ-, pʊtɪ-; the
  unstressed form pɚtɪ can be heard as the last
  two syllables of property ['prɑ]pɚtɪ. Another common unstr. form is pɪtɪ-, in which
  ɪ represents an ɪ with simultaneous retroflexion of the tongue.
pretzel 'prɛts|
prevail prɪ'vel |-ed -d
prevalence 'prɛvələns |-cy -ɪ |-lent -lənt
prevaricate prɪ'værə,ket |-d -ɪd |-tor -ɚ; ES
  -ə(r

prevarication prɪ,værə'keʃən
prevent prɪ'vɛnt |-ed -ɪd |-able, -ible -əb|
preventability prɪ,vɛntə'bɪlətɪ
preventative prɪ'vɛntətɪv
prevention prɪ'vɛnʃən |-tive -'vɛntɪv
preview n 'pri,vju, -,vɪu
preview v pri'vju, -'vɪu |-ed -d
previous 'privɪəs, 'privjəs
previse prɪ'vaɪz |-s -ɪz |-d -d
prevision prɪ'vɪʒən |-ed -d |-ing -ʒənɪŋ, -ʒnɪŋ
prevocal pri'vok| |-ly -ɪ
prevocational ,privo'keʃən|
prewar pri'wɔr; ES -'wɔə(r; ('pre,war 'price)
prey pre |preyed pred
Priam 'praɪəm
Pribilof 'prɪbə,lɑf, -,lɒf, -,lɔf ('Pribi,lof 'Isls.)
price praɪs |prices 'praɪsɪz |priced praɪst
Prichard 'prɪtʃɚd; ES 'prɪtʃəd
prick prɪk |pricked prɪkt
prickle 'prɪk| |-d -d |-ling 'prɪklɪŋ, -k|ɪŋ
prickly 'prɪklɪ
pride praɪd |prided 'praɪdɪd
pried praɪd
prie-dieu Fr pri'djø
prier from pry 'praɪɚ; ES 'praɪˑə(r
pries praɪz
priest, P- prist |-ed -ɪd
priestcraft 'prist,kræft; E+-,kraft, -,krɑft
priesthood 'prist·hʊd
Priestley 'pristlɪ
prig prɪg |-ged -d |-gery -ərɪ |-gish -ɪʃ
prim prɪm |primmed prɪmd
primacy 'praɪməsɪ
prima donna ,primə'dɑnə; ES+-'dɒnə; (It
  ,primɑ'dɒnnɑ)
prima facie 'praɪmə'feʃɪ,i, -'feʃɪ
primage 'praɪmɪdʒ |-s -ɪz
primal 'praɪm|
primarily 'praɪ,mɛrəlɪ, -lɪ, 'praɪmər-, esp. if
  emph. praɪ'mɛr-, -'mer-
primary 'praɪ,mɛrɪ, -mərɪ
primate 'praɪmɪt, -met
prime praɪm |primed praɪmd
primer 'what primes' 'praɪmɚ; ES -mə(r
primer 'first book,' type 'prɪmɚ; ES 'prɪmə(r
primeval praɪ'miv| |-ly -ɪ |-ism -,ɪzəm
primitive 'prɪmətɪv |-vism -,ɪzəm
primogenitor ,praɪmə'dʒɛnətɚ; ES -tə(r
primogeniture ,praɪmə'dʒɛnətʃɚ; ES -tʃə(r

|full fʊl |tooth tuθ |further 'fɝðɚ; ES 'fɜˑðə |custom 'kʌstəm |while hwaɪl |how haʊ |toy tɔɪ
|using 'juzɪŋ |fuse fjuz, fɪuz |dish dɪʃ |vision 'vɪʒən |Eden 'idn̩ |cradle 'kred| |keep 'em 'kipm̩

Those words below in which the ɑ sound is spelt o are often pronounced with ɒ in E and S

primordial praɪˈmɔrdɪəl; ES -ˈmɔəd-; |-ly -ɪ
primp prɪmp |primped prɪmpt
primrose ˈprɪmˌroz |-s -ɪz |-d -d
primula, P- ˈprɪmjʊlə
primus ˈpraɪməs
prince prɪns |-s -ɪz |-d -t
princess ˈprɪnsɪs |-es -ɪz |-cess' -sɪs
princesse prɪnˈsɛs, ˈprɪnsɪs |-(e)s -ɪz
Princeton ˈprɪnstən
principal ˈprɪnsəp| |-ly -p|ɪ, -plɪ
principality ˌprɪnsəˈpælətɪ
principle ˈprɪnsəp| |-d -d |-ling -plɪŋ, -p|ɪŋ
pringle, P- ˈprɪŋg| |-d -d |-ling -glɪŋ, -g|ɪŋ
prink prɪŋk |prinked prɪŋkt
print prɪnt |printed ˈprɪntɪd |-able -əb|
prior, P- ˈpraɪɚ; ES ˈpraɪ·ə(r; |-y -ɪ
prioress ˈpraɪərɪs |-'s -ɪz
priority praɪˈɔrətɪ, -ˈɑr-, -ˈɒr-
Priscian ˈprɪʃɪən, ˈprɪʃən
Priscilla prɪˈsɪlə
prise praɪz |prises ˈpraɪzɪz |prised praɪzd
prism ˈprɪzəm |-ed ˈprɪzəmd
prismatic prɪzˈmætɪk |-al -| |-ally -|ɪ, -ɪklɪ
prison ˈprɪzn̩ |-ed -d |-ing ˈprɪznɪŋ, -zn̩ɪŋ
prisoner ˈprɪznɚ, ˈprɪzn̩ɚ; ES -ə(r
prissy ˈprɪsɪ |prissily ˈprɪs|ɪ, -sɪlɪ
pristine ˈprɪstin, -tɪn, -taɪn
Pritchard ˈprɪtʃɚd; ES ˈprɪtʃəd; |-chett -tʃɪt
prithee ˈprɪðɪ
privacy ˈpraɪvəsɪ |-vate -vɪt
privateer ˌpraɪvəˈtɪr, -vɪ-; ES ˈtɪə(r, S+ -ˈtɛə(r
privation praɪˈveʃən
privative ˈprɪvətɪv
privet ˈprɪvɪt
privilege ˈprɪvlɪdʒ, ˈprɪv|ɪdʒ |-s -ɪz |-d -d
privity ˈprɪvətɪ
privy *n, adj* ˈprɪvɪ |-vily ˈprɪv|ɪ, -vɪlɪ
prize praɪz |prizes ˈpraɪzɪz |prized praɪzd
pro pro
pro- *unstressed prefix* prə-, pro-. *When wholly unstressed in familiar words, the usual pron. is* prə-. *It varies from this through* prʊ- *to* pro- (*with brief* o) *in less familiar words or more deliberate style. The pron.* pɚ-, pə- *is also often heard from cultivated speakers.*
proa ˈproə
pro-Ally proˈælaɪ, ˌproəˈlaɪ

probability ˌprɑbəˈbɪlətɪ
probable ˈprɑbəb| |-bly -blɪ
probate ˈprobet |-bated -betɪd
probation proˈbeʃən |-al -| |-ary -ˌɛrɪ
probative ˈprobətɪv, ˈprɑb-
probatory ˈprobəˌtorɪ, -ˌtɔrɪ; S -ˌtorɪ
probe prob |probed probd |-able -əb|
probity ˈprobətɪ, ˈprɑb-
problem ˈprɑbləm, -lɪm, -lɛm
problematic ˌprɑbləˈmætɪk |-al -| |-ally -|ɪ, -ɪklɪ
pro bono publico ˈproˈbonoˈpʌblɪˌko
proboscis proˈbɑsɪs |-es -ɪz |*L pl* -scides -ˈbɑsəˌdiz
procedural proˈsidʒərəl
procedure prəˈsidʒɚ; ES -ˈsidʒə(r
proceed prəˈsid |-s -ˈsidz |-ed -ɪd
proceeds *n* ˈprosidz
process ˈprɑsɛs, *mainly Brit* ˈprosɛs |-es -ɪz |-ed -t
process '*march in procession*' proˈsɛs, -ˈsɛʃ |-es -ɪz |-ed -t
procession prəˈsɛʃən, pro- |-al -| |-ally -|ɪ
proclaim proˈklem |-claimed -ˈklemd
proclamation ˌprɑkləˈmeʃən
proclitic proˈklɪtɪk
proclivity proˈklɪvətɪ |-tous -təs
proconsul proˈkɑns| |-ar -s|ɚ, -sjələ; ES -lə(r
proconsulate proˈkɑns|ɪt, -ˈkɑnsjəlɪt
procrastinate proˈkræstəˌnet |-nated -ˌnetɪd
procrastination proˌkræstəˈneʃən
procreant ˈprokrɪənt
procreate ˈprokrɪˌet |-d -ɪd |-tive -tɪv
procreation ˌprokrɪˈeʃən
Procrustes proˈkrʌstiz |-tes' -tiz |-tean -tɪən
Procter, proctor, P- ˈprɑktɚ; ES ˈprɑktə(r
Proctorknott ˈprɑktɚˈnɑt; ES ˈprɑktə-
Proculeius ˌprokjuˈliəs |-'s -ɪz
procumbent proˈkʌmbənt
procurable proˈkjʊrəb|, -ˈkɪʊr-
procuracy ˈprɑkjərəsɪ
procurance proˈkjʊrəns, -ˈkɪʊ-
procurator ˈprɑkjəˌretɚ; ES -ˌretə(r
procure proˈkjʊr, -ˈkɪʊr |-d -d
Procyon ˈprosɪˌɑn, -sɪən
prod prɑd |prodded ˈprɑdɪd
prodigal ˈprɑdɪg| |-ly -ɪ, -ɪglɪ
prodigality ˌprɑdɪˈgælətɪ

Key: *See in full §§3–47.* bee bi |pity ˈpɪtɪ (§6) |rate ret |yet jɛt |sang sæŋ |angry ˈæŋ·grɪ |bath bæθ; E baθ (§10) |ah ɑ |far fɑr |watch wɑtʃ, wɒtʃ (§12) |jaw dʒɔ |gorge gɔrdʒ |go go

Those words below in which the ɑ sound is spelt o are often pronounced with ɒ in E and S

prodigy 'prɑdədʒɪ |-digious prə'dɪdʒəs

produce *n* 'prɑdjus, 'pro-, -dɪus, -dus

produce *v* prə'djus, -'dɪus, -'dus |-s -ɪz |-d -t

producible prə'djusəbḷ, -'dɪus-, -'dus-

product 'prɑdəkt, -dʌkt

production prə'dʌkʃən |-tive -tɪv

productivity ˌprɑdʌk'tɪvətɪ

proem 'proɛm, -ɪm

profanation ˌprɑfə'neʃən

profane prə'fen |-faned -'fend |-nity -'fænətɪ

profaneness prə'fennɪs

profess prə'fɛs |-es -ɪz |-ed -t |-edly -ɪdlɪ

profession prə'fɛʃən |-al -ḷ, -ʃnəl |-ly -ɪ

professor prə'fɛsɚ; ES -'fɛsə(r; |-ate -ɪt

professorial ˌprɑfə'sorɪəl, ˌprɑfə-, -'sɔr-; S -'sor-; |-ly -ɪ

professorship prə'fɛsɚˌʃɪp; ES -'fɛsə-

proffer 'prɑfɚ; ES 'prɑfə(r; |-ed -d |-ing 'prɑfrɪŋ, 'prɑfərɪŋ

proficiency prə'fɪʃənsɪ |-cient -ʃənt

profile 'profaɪl |-filed -faɪld

profit 'prɑfɪt |-ed -ɪd

profitable 'prɑfɪtəbḷ, 'prɑftə- |-bly -blɪ

profiteer ˌprɑfə'tɪr; ES -'tɪə(r, S+-'tɛə(r; |-ed -d

profligacy 'prɑfləgəsɪ |-gate -gɪt, -ˌget

pro forma pro'fɔrmə; ES -'fɔəmə

profound prə'faʊnd |-ness -nɪs, -'faʊnnɪs

profundity prə'fʌndətɪ

profuse prə'fjus, -'fɪus |-sive -ɪv

profusion prə'fjuʒən, -'fɪu-

progenitor pro'dʒɛnətɚ; ES -'dʒɛnətə(r

progeniture pro'dʒɛnətʃɚ; ES -'dʒɛnətʃə(r

progeny 'prɑdʒənɪ

prognathic prɑg'næθɪk

prognathous 'prɑgnəθəs, prɑg'neθəs

prognosis prɑg'nosɪs |-noses -'nosiz

prognostic prɑg'nɑstɪk |-al -ḷ |-ally -ḷɪ, -ɪklɪ

prognosticate prɑg'nɑstɪˌket |-cated -ˌketɪd

prognostication prɑgˌnɑstɪ'keʃən, ˌprɑgnɑstɪ-

program, -mme 'progræm, -grəm |-(me)d -d

progress *n* 'prɑgrɛs, 'pro-, -grɪs |-es -ɪz

progress *v* prə'grɛs |-es -ɪz |-ed -t

progression prə'grɛʃən |-sive -'grɛsɪv

prohibit pro'hɪbɪt |-ed -ɪd |-ive -ɪv

prohibition ˌproə'bɪʃən

project *n* 'prɑdʒɛkt, -dʒɪkt

project *v* prə'dʒɛkt |-ed -ɪd |-ction -kʃən

projectile prə'dʒɛktḷ, -tɪl

projective prə'dʒɛktɪv |-tor -tɚ; ES -tə(r

Prokosch 'prokɑʃ |-'s -ɪz

prolate 'prolet, pro'let

proletarian ˌprolə'tɛrɪən, -'tær-, -'ter- |-iat -ɪət

proliferate pro'lɪfəˌret |-d -ɪd |-rous -rəs

proliferation proˌlɪfə'reʃən

prolific prə'lɪfɪk |-al -ḷ |-ally -ḷɪ |-ly -lɪ

prolix pro'lɪks |-ity -ətɪ ('proˌlix 'style)

prologue, -log 'prolɑg, -lɑg, -lɒg |-d, -ged -d

prolong prə'lɒŋ, -'lɒŋ; S+-'lɑŋ; |-ed -d

prolongate prə'iɒŋget, -'lɒŋ-; S+-'lɑŋ-; |-d -ɪd

prolongation ˌprolɒŋ'geʃən, -lɒŋ-; S+-lɑŋ-

promenade ˌprɑmə'ned, -'nɑd |-d -ɪd

Promethean prə'miθɪən, -θjən

Prometheus prə'miθjəs, -jus, -ɪəs |-'s -ɪz

prominence 'prɑmənəns |-s -ɪz |-cy -ɪ |-nt -nt

promiscuity ˌprɑmɪs'kjuətɪ, ˌpro-, -'kɪu-

promiscuous prə'mɪskjuəs

promise 'prɑmɪs |-s -ɪz |-d -t

promisee ˌprɑmɪs'i

promisor 'prɑmɪsˌɔr; ES -ˌɔə(r; (ˌpromis'ee & ˌpromis'or)

promissory 'prɑməˌsorɪ, -ˌsɔrɪ; S -ˌsorɪ

promontory 'prɑmənˌtorɪ, -ˌtɔrɪ; S -ˌtorɪ

promote prə'mot |-d -ɪd |-tion prə'moʃən

prompt prɑmpt |prompted 'prɑmptɪd

promptitude 'prɑmptəˌtjud, -ˌtɪud, -ˌtud

promulgate prə'mʌlget |-d -ɪd—'prɑməlˌget *is mainly Brit.*

promulgation ˌprɑmʌl'geʃən—ˌprɑməl- *is mainly Brit.*

prone pron |proned prond |proneness 'pronnɪs

prong prɒŋ, prɒŋ; S+praŋ; |-ed -d

pronominal prə'nɑmənḷ, pro- |-ly -ɪ

pronoun 'pronaʊn

pronounce prə'naʊns, pɚ- |-s -ɪz |-d -t |-dly -ɪdlɪ

pronto 'prɑnto (*Sp* 'prɒnto)

pronunciamento prəˌnʌnsɪə'mɛnto, -ˌnʌnʃ-

pronunciation prəˌnʌnsɪ'eʃən, pɚ-, -ˌnʌnʃɪ-

proof pruf |-ed -t—pruf *is often heard, esp. in compounds.*

proofread *v* 'prufˌrid |-read -ˌrɛd

prop prɑp |propped prɑpt

propaganda *sg* ˌprɑpə'gændə |-ed -d

Those words below in which the ɑ *sound is spelt* o *are often pronounced with* ɒ *in E and S*

propagandism ˌprɑpəˈgændɪzəm |-ist -ɪst

propagandum *false sg* ˌprɑpəˈgændəm

propagate ˈprɑpəˌget |-d -ɪd |-tion ˌprɑpəˈgeʃən

pro patria proˈpetrɪə

propel prəˈpɛl |-led -d |-lant, -lent -ənt

propensity prəˈpɛnsətɪ

proper ˈprɑpɚ; ES ˈprɑpə(r

property ˈprɑpɚtɪ; ES ˈprɑpətɪ; |-ied -d

prophecy ˈprɑfəsɪ

prophesy ˈprɑfəˌsaɪ |-sied -ˌsaɪd

prophet ˈprɑfɪt |-ess -ɪs |-esses -ɪsɪz

prophetic prəˈfɛtɪk |-al -ḷ |-ally -ḷɪ, -ɪklɪ

prophylactic ˌprofəˈlæktɪk, ˌprɑfə- |-al -ḷ |-ally -ḷɪ, -ɪklɪ |-laxis -ˈlæksɪs

propinquity proˈpɪŋkwətɪ, -ˈpɪŋ-

propitiate *adj* prəˈpɪʃɪɪt, -ɪˌet

propitiate *v* prəˈpɪʃɪˌet |-ated -ˌetɪd

propitiatory prəˈpɪʃɪəˌtorɪ, -ˌtɔrɪ; S -ˌtorɪ

propitious prəˈpɪʃəs

proponent prəˈponənt

Propontic proˈpɑntɪk

proportion prəˈporʃən, -ˈpɔr-; ES -ˈpoə-, E+-ˈpɔə-; |-ed -d |-able -əbḷ, -ʃnəbḷ |-bly -blɪ |-al -ḷ, -ʃnəl |-ally -ḷɪ, -ʃnəlɪ |-ate -ɪt, -ʃnɪt—*A dissimilated form* pəˈporʃən *is sometimes heard (§121).*

propose prəˈpoz |-s -ɪz |-d -d |-sal -zḷ

proposition ˌprɑpəˈzɪʃən |-al -ḷ |-ally -ḷɪ

propound prəˈpaʊnd |-ed -ɪd

propraetor, -pret- proˈpritɚ; ES -ˈpritə(r

proprietary prəˈpraɪəˌtɛrɪ

proprietor prəˈpraɪətɚ, pəˈpraɪ-; ES -tə(r; |-tress -trɪs—*The 2d pron. is due to r-dis-similation (§121).*

propriety prəˈpraɪətɪ—*A dissimilated pron.* pəˈpraɪətɪ *is probably less freq. than* ˌɪmpəˈpraɪətɪ *and* pəˈpraɪətɚ *(§121).*

propulsion prəˈpʌlʃən |-sive -sɪv

propylaeum ˌprɑpəˈliəm |-laea -ˈliə

pro rata proˈretə

prorate *n* ˈproret, *v* proˈret |-rated -ˈretɪd

prorogue proˈrog |-d -d |-gation ˌprorəˈgeʃən

prosaic proˈze·ɪk |-al -ḷ |-ally -ḷɪ, -ɪklɪ

prosateur ˌprozəˈtɝ; ES -ˈtɝ(r, -ˈtɝ; *(Fr* prozaˈtœːr)

proscenium proˈsinɪəm

proscribe proˈskraɪb |-d -d

proscription proˈskrɪpʃən |-tive -tɪv

prose proz |proses ˈprozɪz |prosed prozd

prosecute ˈprɑsɪˌkjut, -ˌkɪut |-d -ɪd

prosecution ˌprɑsɪˈkjuʃən, -ˈkɪu-

prosecutor ˈprɑsɪˌkjutɚ, -ˌkɪu-; ES -tə(r

proselyte ˈprɑsḷˌaɪt |-d -ɪd |-tism -aɪtˌɪzəm |-tist -ˌaɪtɪst

Proserpina proˈsɝpɪnə; ES -ˈsɝp-, -ˈsɝ·p-; |-ne -ˌni, ˈprɑsɚˌpaɪn; ES -sə-

prosit ˈprosɪt *(Ger* ˈproːzɪt)

proslavery proˈslevrɪ, -vərɪ |-ryism -ˌɪzəm

prosodist ˈprɑsədɪst |-dy -dɪ

prospect ˈprɑspɛkt |-ed -ɪd |-ive prəˈspɛktɪv

prospector ˈprɑspɛktɚ, prəˈspɛk-; ES -tə(r

prospectus prəˈspɛktəs, prɑ- |-es -ɪz

prosper ˈprɑspɚ; ES -pə(r; |-ed -d |-ing ˈprɑspərɪŋ, ˈprɑsprɪŋ |-ous -prəs, -pərəs

prosperity prɑsˈpɛrətɪ

Prospero ˈprɑspəˌro

Prospice ˈprɑspɪˌsi

prostate ˈprɑstet |-tic proˈstætɪk

prostitute ˈprɑstəˌtjut, -ˌtɪut, -ˌtut |-d -ɪd

prostitution ˌprɑstəˈtjuʃən, -ˈtɪu-, -ˈtu-

prostrate ˈprɑstret |-d -ɪd |-tion prɑˈstreʃən

prosy ˈprozɪ

protagonist proˈtægənɪst |-nism -ˌɪzəm

Protagoras proˈtægərəs |-'s -ɪz

protean *adj* ˈprotɪən, proˈtiən

protean *n chem.* ˈprotɪən

protect prəˈtɛkt |-ed -ɪd |-ion -kʃən |-ive -ɪv

protector prəˈtɛktɚ; ES -tə(r; |-ate -ɪt, -trɪt

protégé, -ée ˈprotəˌʒe, ˌprotəˈʒe *(Fr* prŏteˈʒe)

proteid ˈprotiɪd |-ide -ˌaɪd, -ɪd

protein ˈprotiɪn

pro tem proˈtɛm |pro tempore proˈtɛmpəˌri

Proterozoic ˌpratərəˈzo·ɪk

protest *n* ˈprotɛst

protest *v* prəˈtɛst |-ed -ɪd

protestant, P- ˈprɑtɪstənt |-ism -ˌɪzəm

protestation ˌprɑtəsˈteʃən

Proteus ˈprotjus, ˈprotɪəs |-'s -ɪz

prothalamion, P- ˌproθəˈlemɪˌɑn, -ən

Prothero ˈprɑðəˌro

prothonotary proˈθɑnəˌtɛrɪ, ˌproθəˈnotərɪ

protocol ˈprotəˌkɑl, -ˌkɒl

proton ˈprotɑn

protoplasm ˈprotəˌplæzəm |-ic ˌprotəˈplæzmɪk

prototype ˈprotəˌtaɪp

Key: *See in full §§3–47.* bee bi |pity ˈpɪtɪ (§6) |rate ret |yet jɛt |sang sæŋ |angry ˈæŋ·grɪ |bath bæθ; E baθ (§10) |ah ɑ |far fɑr |watch wɑtʃ, wɒtʃ (§12) |jaw dʒɔ |gorge gɔrdʒ |go go

Those words below in which the ɑ sound is spelt o are often pronounced with ɒ in E and S

prototypic ˌprotəˈtɪpɪk |-al -|̣ |-ally -|ɪ, -ɪklɪ

Protozoa, p- ˌprotəˈzoə |-n -n |-zoic -ˈzoˑɪk

protract proˈtrækt |-ed -ɪd |-ile -|̣, -ɪl

protraction proˈtrækʃən |-tor -tɚ; ES -tə(r

protrude proˈtrud, -ˈtrɪud |-d -ɪd

protrusion proˈtruʒən, -ˈtrɪu- |-sive -sɪv

protuberance proˈtjubərəns, -ˈtɪu-, -ˈtu- |-s -ɪz |-ant -ənt

proud praʊd

Proust prust

prove pruv |-d -d |-d -d *or* -n -ən

provenance ˈprɑvənəns

Provençal ˌprɑvənˈsɑl, ˌprɑv- (*Fr* prɔ̃vɑ̃ˈsɑl)

Provence ˈprɑvɛns, proˈvɑns |-ˈs -ɪz (*Fr* prɔ̃ˈvɑ̃:s)

provender ˈprɑvəndɚ; ES ˈprɑvəndə(r; |-ed -d

provenience proˈvinɪəns, -njəns |-ent -ənt

proverb ˈprɑvɝb, -ɚb; ES -ɜb, -ɝb, -əb |-ed -d

proverbial prəˈvɝbɪəl; ES -ˈvɜb-, -ˈvɝb-; |-ly -ɪ

provide prəˈvaɪd |-vided -ˈvaɪdɪd

providence, P- ˈprɑvədəns |-ˈs -ɪz |-nt -nt

providential ˌprɑvəˈdɛnʃəl |-ly -ɪ

province ˈprɑvɪns |-s -ɪz

Provincetown ˈprɑvɪnsˌtaʊn

provincial prəˈvɪnʃəl |-ly -ɪ |-ism -ˌɪzəm

provinciality prəˌvɪnʃɪˈælətɪ

provision prəˈvɪʒən |-ed -d |-al -|̣ |-ally -|ɪ

proviso prəˈvaɪzo |-r prəˈvaɪzɚ; ES -zə(r

provocation ˌprɑvəˈkeʃən |-tive prəˈvɑkətɪv

provoke prəˈvok |-d -t

provost ˈprɑvəst |p- marshal ˈprovoˈmɑrʃəl; ES -ˈmɑ:ʃ-, E+-ˈmɑ:ʃ-

prow praʊ |prowed praʊd

Prowers ˈproɚz; ES ˈproˑəz; |-ˈs -ɪz |-ite -ˌaɪt

prowess ˈpraʊɪs |-ed -t

prowl praʊl |prowled praʊld |-er -ɚ; ES -ə(r

proximal ˈprɑksəm|̣ |-ly -ɪ |-mate *adj* -mɪt

proximate *v* ˈprɑksəˌmet |-d -ɪd

proximity prɑkˈsɪmətɪ

proxy ˈprɑksɪ |proxied ˈprɑksɪd

prude prud, prɪud |-ry -ərɪ |-dish -ɪʃ

prudence, P- ˈprudn̩s, ˈprɪudn̩s |-ˈs -ɪz |-nt -n̩t

prudential, P- pruˈdɛnʃəl, prɪu- |-ly -ɪ

prune prun, prɪun |-d -d

prunella, P- pruˈnɛlə, prɪu-

prunes and prism ˈprunzn̩ˈprɪzəm, ˈprɪunz-

prurience ˈprurɪəns, ˈprɪu- |-cy -ɪ |-ent -ənt

Prussia ˈprʌʃə |-n -n

prussic ˈprʌsɪk

pry, P- praɪ |pried praɪd

Prynne prɪn

Pryor ˈpraɪɚ; ES ˈpraɪˑə(r

prythee ˈprɪðɪ

Przemyśl ˈpʃɛmɪʃ|̣, -s|̣

psalm sɑm |psalmed sɑmd |-ist -ɪst

psalmody ˈsɑmədɪ, ˈsælmədɪ

Psalter, p- ˈsɔltɚ; ES ˈsɔltə(r

psaltery ˈsɔltrɪ, ˈsɔltərɪ

pseudo ˈsjudo, ˈsɪu-, ˈsu- |-nym -dn̩ˌɪm

pseudonymous sjuˈdɑnəməs, sɪu-, su-

pshaw ʃɔ |pshawed ʃɔd

psi saɪ (*Gk* psi)

psoriasis səˈraɪəsɪs

Psyche ˈsaɪkɪ

psychiatric ˌsaɪkɪˈætrɪk |-al -|̣ |-ally -|ɪ, -ɪklɪ

psychiatry saɪˈkaɪətrɪ |-trist -trɪst

psychic ˈsaɪkɪk |-al -|̣ |-ally -|ɪ, -ɪklɪ

psychoanalysis ˌsaɪkoəˈnæləsɪs

psychoanalyst ˌsaɪkoˈænl̩ɪst

psychoanalytic ˌsaɪkoˌænl̩ˈɪtɪk |-al -|̣ |-ally -|ɪ, -ɪklɪ

psychoanalyze ˌsaɪkoˈænl̩ˌaɪz |-s -ɪz |-d -d

psychological ˌsaɪkəˈlɑdʒɪk|̣ |-ly -ɪ, ɪklɪ

psychologism saɪˈkɑləˌdʒɪzəm

psychologize saɪˈkɑləˌdʒaɪz |-s -ɪz |-d -d |-gy -dʒɪ

psychometry saɪˈkɑmətrɪ

psychoneurosis ˌsaɪko·njuˈrosɪs, -nɪu-, -nu- |-roses -ˈrosiz

psychopath ˈsaɪkəˌpæθ |-ths -θs

psychopathic ˌsaɪkəˈpæθɪk

psychopathology ˌsaɪkopəˈθɑlədʒɪ

psychopathy saɪˈkɑpəθɪ

psychosis saɪˈkosɪs |-choses -ˈkosiz

psychotherapy ˌsaɪkoˈθɛrəpɪ

ptarmigan ˈtɑrməgən; ES ˈtɑ:m-, E+ˈtɑ:m-

pteridophyte ˈtɛrədoˌfaɪt

pterodactyl ˌtɛrəˈdæktɪl, -t|̣

Ptolemaic ˌtɑləˈme·ɪk |-al -|̣

Ptolemy ˈtɑləmɪ

ptomaine, -ain ˈtomen, toˈmen

ptosis ˈtosɪs

ptyalin ˈtaɪəlɪn

pub pʌb

puberty ˈpjubɚtɪ, ˈpɪu-; ES -bətɪ

pubescence pjuˈbɛsn̩s, pɪu- |-cy -ɪ |-nt -n̩t

pubic ˈpjubɪk, ˈpɪu-

pubis ˈpjubɪs, ˈpɪu- |-bes -biz

public ˈpʌblɪk

publican ˈpʌblɪkən

publication ˌpʌblɪˈkeʃən

publicist ˈpʌblɪsɪst

publicity pʌbˈlɪsətɪ, pəˈblɪs-

publicize ˈpʌblɪˌsaɪz |-s -ɪz |-d -d

publish ˈpʌblɪʃ |-es -ɪz |-ed -t

Publius ˈpʌblɪəs |-ˈs -ɪz

Puccini puˈtʃinɪ (It putˈtʃiːni)

Puccinia pʌkˈsɪnɪə

puce pjus, pɪus

Pucelle, La læpjuˈsɛl, -pɪu- (Fr lapyˈsɛl)

puck, P- pʌk |-ish -ɪʃ

pucka ˈpʌkə

pucker ˌˈpʌkɚ; ES ˈpʌkə(r; |-ed -d |-ing ˈpʌkrɪŋ, ˈpʌkərɪŋ

pudding ˈpʊdɪŋ, humorous ˈpʊdn̩

puddle ˈpʌdl̩ |-d -d |-ling ˈpʌdlɪŋ, ˈpʌdl̩ɪŋ

puddly ˈpʌdlɪ, ˈpʌdl̩ɪ

pudd'nhead, P- ˈpʊdn̩ˌhɛd

pudency ˈpjudn̩sɪ, ˈpɪu- |-dent -dn̩t

pudendum pjuˈdɛndəm, pɪu- |-da -də

pudgy ˈpʌdʒɪ

Pueblo, p- ˈpwɛblo, loc. pjuˈɛblo, pɪu-

puerile ˈpjuəˌrɪl, ˈpɪu-, -rəl

puerility ˌpjuəˈrɪlətɪ, ˌpɪuə-

puerperal pjuˈɜpərəl, pɪu-; ES -ˈɜp-, -ˈɜ̣p-

Puerto Rico ˌpwɛrtəˈriko |-can -kən

puff, P- pʌf |-ed -t |-ball -ˌbɔl

puffin ˈpʌfɪn

pug pʌg |-gged pʌgd

Puget ˈpjudʒɪt, ˈpɪu-

Pugh(e) pju, pɪu

pugilism ˈpjudʒəˌlɪzəm, ˈpɪu- |-list -lɪst

pugilistic ˌpjudʒəˈlɪstɪk, ˌpɪu- |-al -l̩ |-ally -l̩ɪ, -ɪklɪ

pugnacious pʌgˈneʃəs |-nacity -ˈnæsətɪ

pug-nosed ˈpʌgˈnozd (ˈpug-ˌnosed ˈlassie)

puisne ˈpjunɪ, ˈpɪunɪ

puissance ˈpjuɪsn̩s, ˈpɪu-, pjuˈɪsn̩s, pɪu-, ˈpwɪsn̩s |-sant -sn̩t

puke pjuk, pɪuk |-d -t

pukka ˈpʌkə

Pulaski Count puˈlæskaɪ, -kɪ; US pəˈlæskaɪ

pulchritude ˈpʌlkrɪˌtjud, -ˌtɪud, -ˌtud

pulchritudinous ˌpʌlkrɪˈtjudn̩əs, -ˈtɪud-, -ˈtud-

pule pjul, pɪul |-d -d

Pulitzer ˈpjulɪtsɚ, ˈpɪu-, formerly ˈpʊl-; ES -sə(r

pull pʊl |pulled pʊld

pullet ˈpʊlɪt

pulley ˈpʊlɪ

Pullman ˈpʊlmən |-s -z

pull-over n ˈpʊlˌovɚ; ES -ˌovə(r

pullulate ˈpʌljəˌlet |-d -ɪd |-tion ˌpʌljəˈleʃən

pulmonary ˈpʌlməˌnɛrɪ

Pulmotor, p- ˈpʌlˌmotɚ, ˈpʊl-; ES -ˌmotə(r

pulp pʌlp |pulped pʌlpt

pulpit ˈpʊlpɪt |-ed -ɪd |-er -ɚ; ES -ə(r

pulpiteer ˌpʊlpɪtˈɪr; ES -ˈɪə(r, S+-ˈɛə(r

pulpwood ˈpʌlpˌwʊd

pulque ˈpʊlkɪ, ˈpulke

pulsate ˈpʌlset |-d -ɪd |-tion pʌlˈseʃən

pulsatile ˈpʌlsətl̩, -tɪl

pulse pʌls |pulses ˈpʌlsɪz |pulsed pʌlst

Pulteney ˈpʌltnɪ, ˈpolt-

pulverization ˌpʌlvərəˈzeʃən, -aɪˈz-

pulverize ˈpʌlvəˌraɪz |-s -ɪz |-d -d

puma ˈpjumə, ˈpɪu-

pumice ˈpʌmɪs |-s -ɪz |-d -t

pumice-stone ˈpʌmɪsˌston, ˈpʌmɪˌston

pummel ˈpʌml̩ |-ed -d

pummice ˈpʌmɪs |-s -ɪz

pump pʌmp |pumped pʌmpt

pumpernickel ˈpʌmpɚˌnɪkl̩; ES ˈpʌmpə-

pumpkin ˈpʌmpkɪn, ˈpʌŋkɪn—A L.A. informant said, "We were drilled in school not to say ˈpʌŋkɪn," eloquent testimony to its prevalence. The two prons. are almost equally common. Both are phonetically normal. ˈpʌŋkɪn is historically parallel to ˈpʌmpkɪn, both being normal phonetic developments from earlier ˈpʌmkɪn (pumkin). Cf §124.11.

pumpkin-headed ˈpʌŋkɪnˈhɛdɪd

pun pʌn |punned pʌnd

punch, P- pʌntʃ |-es -ɪz |-ed -t

Punch-and-Judy ˈpʌntʃənˈdʒudɪ, -ˈdʒɪu-

puncheon ˈpʌntʃən

punchinello ˌpʌntʃəˈnɛlo

punctilio pʌŋkˈtɪlɪˌo |-tilious -ˈtɪlɪəs, -ljəs

punctual ˈpʌŋktʃʊəl, -tʃʊl |-ly -ɪ |-ity ˌpʌŋktʃʊˈælətɪ

punctuate ˈpʌŋktʃʊˌet |-d -ɪd

punctuation ˌpʌŋktʃʊˈeʃən

puncture 'pʌŋktʃɚ; ES 'pʌŋktʃə(r; |-d -d |-ring 'pʌŋktʃərɪŋ, 'pʌŋktʃrɪŋ
pundit 'pʌndɪt |-ical pʌn'dɪtɪk|
pung pʌŋ |punged pʌŋd
pungence 'pʌndʒəns |-cy -ɪ |-gent -dʒənt
Punic 'pjunɪk, 'pɪu-
punish 'pʌnɪʃ |-es -ɪz |-ed -t |-able -əb|
punitive 'pjunətɪv, 'pɪu-
Punjab pʌn'dʒab |-i -ɪ
punk pʌŋk
punkah, -ka 'pʌŋkə
punkin 'pʌŋkɪn
punster 'pʌnstɚ; ES 'pʌnstə(r
punt pʌnt |punted 'pʌntɪd
Punxsutawney ˌpʌŋksə'tɔnɪ
puny 'pjunɪ, 'pɪu-
pup pʌp |pupped pʌpt |-py -ɪ
pupa 'pjupə, 'pɪu- |-l -p|
pupil 'pjup|, 'pɪu- |-ed -d |-age -ɪdʒ
Pupin pju'pin, pɪu-
puppet 'pʌpɪt
pur pɝ; ES pɜ(r, pɝ; |-red -d
Purbeck 'pɝbɛk; ES 'pɜ-, 'pɝ-
purblind 'pɝˌblaɪnd; ES 'pɜ-, 'pɝ-
Purcell *composer* 'pɝs|; ES 'pɜ-, 'pɝ-
Purcell *Okla* pɚ'sɛl; ES pə'sɛl; *Can* 'pɝs|; ES 'pɜs|, 'pɝs|
Purchas 'pɝtʃəs; ES 'pɜ-, 'pɝ-; |-'s -ɪz
purchasability ˌpɝtʃəsə'bɪlətɪ; ES ˌpɜ-, ˌpɝ-
purchasable 'pɝtʃəsəb|; ES 'pɜ-, 'pɝ-
purchase 'pɝtʃəs, -ɪs; ES 'pɜ-, 'pɝ-; |-s -ɪz |-d -t
purdah 'pɝdə; ES 'pɜ-, 'pɝ-
Purdue pɚ'dju, -'dɪu, -'du; ES pə-
pure pjʊr, pɪur; ES pjʊə(r, pɪuə(r; |-d -d
purebred 'pjʊr'brɛd, 'pɪur-; ES 'pjʊə-, 'pɪuə-; ('pureˌbred 'horse)
purée pju're, pɪu-, 'pjʊre, 'pɪure (*Fr* py're)
purfle 'pɝf|; ES 'pɜ-, 'pɝ-; |-d -d |-ling -f|ɪŋ, -f|ɪŋ |*n* -f|ɪŋ
purgation pɝ'geʃən; ES pɜ-, pɝ-
purgatory, P- 'pɝgəˌtorɪ, -ˌtɔrɪ; ES 'pɝgə-ˌtorɪ, 'pɝ-, E+-ˌtɔrɪ
purge pɝdʒ; ES pɜdʒ, pɝdʒ; |-s -ɪz |-d -d
purgery 'pɝdʒərɪ; ES 'pɜdʒ-, 'pɝdʒ-
purification ˌpjʊrəfə'keʃən, ˌpɪurə-
purify 'pjʊrəˌfaɪ, 'pɪurə- |-fied -ˌfaɪd
Purim 'pjʊrɪm, 'pɪu-, 'pu- (*Heb* pu'rim)
purism 'pjʊrɪzəm, 'pɪur- |-ist -ɪst

puristic pju'rɪstɪk, pɪu- |-al -| |-ally -|ɪ, -ɪklɪ
Puritan, p- 'pjʊrətn̩, 'pɪurə- |-ism -ˌɪzəm
puritanic ˌpjʊrə'tænɪk, ˌpɪurə- |-al -| |-ally -|ɪ, -ɪklɪ
purity 'pjʊrətɪ, 'pɪurətɪ
purl pɝl; ES pɜl, pɝl; |-ed -d
purlieu 'pɝlu, -lɪu; ES 'pɜ-, 'pɝ-
purloin pɝ'lɔɪn, pə-; ES pɜ-, pɝ-, pə-; |-ed -d
purple 'pɝp|; ES 'pɜp-, 'pɝp-; |-d -d |-ling -p|ɪŋ, -p|ɪŋ |-lish -p|ɪʃ, -p|ʃ
purport *n* 'pɝport, -pɔrt; ES 'pɝpoət, 'pɝpɔət, E+-pɔət
purport *v* pɚ'port, 'pɝport, -ɔrt; ES pə'poət, 'pɝpoət, 'pɝpɔət, E+-ɔət; |-ed -ɪd
purpose 'pɝpəs; ES 'pɜ-, 'pɝ-; |-s -ɪz |-d -t |-dly -tlɪ |-sive -ɪv
purr pɝ; ES pɜ(r, pɝ; |-ed -d
purse pɝs; ES pɜs, pɝs; |-s -ɪz |-d -t
purse-proud 'pɝsˌpraʊd; ES 'pɜs-, 'pɝs-
purser 'pɝsɚ; ES 'pɜsə(r, 'pɝsə(r
purslane 'pɝslɪn, -len; ES 'pɜs-, 'pɝs-
pursuance pɚ'suəns, -'sɪu-, -'sju-; ES pə-; |-s -ɪz |-ant -ənt
pursue pɚ'su, -'sɪu, -'sju; ES pə-; |-d -d |-suit -t
pursuivant 'pɝswɪvənt; ES 'pɜs-, 'pɝs-
pursy 'pɝsɪ; ES 'pɜsɪ, 'pɝsɪ; *substandard* 'pʌsɪ
purulence 'pjʊrələns, 'pɪurə-, -rjələns |-cy -ɪ |-lent -lənt
Purvey 'pɝvɪ; ES 'pɜvɪ, 'pɝvɪ
purvey pɚ've; ES pə've; |-ed -d |-ance -əns
purveyor pɚ'veɚ; ES pə've·ə(r
purview 'pɝvju, -vɪu; ES 'pɜ-, 'pɝ-
pus pʌs |*pl* puses 'pʌsɪz
Pusey 'pjuzɪ, 'pɪu- |-ism -ˌɪzəm
push *n, v* pʊʃ |pushes 'pʊʃɪz |pushed pʊʃt
push *intj* pʊʃ, pʃ *& various other puffs*
pushball 'pʊʃˌbɔl
pushcart 'pʊʃˌkɑrt; ES -ˌkɑːt, E+-ˌkɑːt
Pushkin 'pʊʃkɪn
pusillanimity ˌpjus|ə'nɪmətɪ, ˌpɪu-
pusillanimous ˌpjus|'ænəməs, ˌpɪu-
puss pʊs
pussy '*cat*' 'pʊsɪ
pussy '*like pus*' 'pʌsɪ
pussy '*pursy*' 'pʌsɪ
pussyfoot 'pʊsɪˌfʊt |-ed -ɪd
pustular 'pʌstʃələ; ES -lə(r

|full fʊl |tooth tuθ |further 'fɝðɚ; ES 'fɝðə |custom 'kʌstəm |while hwaɪl |how haʊ |toy tɔɪ
|using 'juzɪŋ |fuse fjuz, fɪuz |dish dɪʃ |vision 'vɪʒən |Eden 'idn̩ |cradle 'kredl̩ |keep 'em 'kipm̩

pustulation ˌpʌstʃə'leʃən
pustule 'pʌstʃʊl |-d -d
put n 'throw,' v 'place' pʊt
put n 'rustic' pʌt
put 'putt' pʌt |putted 'pʌtɪd
Put pʌt
putative 'pjutətɪv, 'pɪu-
Put in Bay ˌpʊtɪn'be
Putman 'pʌtmən
Putnam 'pʌtnəm |-ney 'pʌtnɪ
putrefaction ˌpjutrə'fækʃən, ˌpɪu-
putrefy, -ri- 'pjutrəˌfaɪ, 'pɪu- |-fied -ˌfaɪd
putrescence pju'trɛsn̩s, pɪu- |-cy -ɪ |-nt -sn̩t
putrid 'pjutrɪd, 'pɪu-
Putsch Ger pʊtʃ
putt pʌt |putted 'pʌtɪd
puttee 'pʌtɪ |-d -d
Puttenham 'pʌtn̩əm, 'pʌtnəm—see Putnam
putter 'who putts' 'pʌtɚ; ES 'pʌtə(r
putter 'who puts' 'pʊtɚ; ES 'pʊtə(r
putter v 'pʌtɚ; ES 'pʌtə(r; |-ed -d
putty 'pʌtɪ |puttied 'pʌtɪd
Puvis de Chavannes pju'visdəʃə'væn, pɪu-
  (Fr pyvi:sdəʃa'van, pyvidʃa'van)
puzzle 'pʌzl̩ |-d -d |-ling 'pʌzlɪŋ, 'pʌzl̩ɪŋ
pyemia, -aemia paɪ'imɪə
Pygmalion pɪg'meljən, -lɪən
Pygmy, p- 'pɪgmɪ |-ied -d
pyjama pə'dʒæmə, pə'dʒamə |-s -z
pylon 'paɪlɑn; ES+-lɒn
pyloric pə'lɔrɪk, paɪ-, -'lɑr-, -'lɒr-
pylorus pə'lorəs, paɪ-, -'lɔr-; S -'lor-

Pym pɪm
Pynchon, -cheon 'pɪntʃən
pyorrhea, -rhoea ˌpaɪə'riə, paɪ'riə
pyramid, P- 'pɪrəmɪd |-mided -ˌmɪdɪd
pyramidal pɪ'ræmədl̩ |-ly -ɪ
Pyramus 'pɪrəməs |-'s -ɪz
pyre paɪr; ES paɪə(r
Pyrenees 'pɪrəˌniz |-nean ˌpɪrə'niən
pyrethrum, P- paɪ'rɛθrəm, -'riθ-
pyretic paɪ'rɛtɪk
Pyrex, p- 'paɪrɛks
pyridin 'pɪrədɪn |-dine -ˌdin, -dɪn
pyriform 'pɪrəˌfɔrm; ES -ˌfɔəm
pyrites pə'raɪtiz, paɪ-, 'paɪraɪts
pyrography paɪ'rɑgrəfɪ, -'rɒg-
pyromancy 'paɪrəˌmænsɪ
pyromania ˌpaɪrə'menɪə
pyrotechnic ˌpaɪrə'tɛknɪk |-al -l̩ |-ally -l̩ɪ,
  -ɪklɪ |-s -s
Pyrrha 'pɪrə
pyrrhic, P- 'pɪrɪk
Pyrrhus 'pɪrəs |-'s -ɪz
Pythagoras pɪ'θægərəs |-'s -ɪz
Pythagorean pɪˌθægə'riən
Pythian 'pɪθɪən
Pythias 'pɪθɪəs |-'s -ɪz
Pythius 'pɪθɪəs |-'s -ɪz
Python, p- 'paɪθɑn, -θən; ES+-θɒn
pythoness 'paɪθənɪs |-'s -ɪz
pyx pɪks |pyxes 'pɪksɪz |pyxed pɪkst
pyxidium pɪks'ɪdɪəm |-dia -dɪə
pyxie 'pɪksɪ

Q

Q, q letter kju, kɪu |pl Q's, Qs, poss Q's kjuz,
  kɪuz
Qirghiz kɪr'giz; ES kɪə-; |-'s -ɪz
quack kwæk |-ed -t |quackery 'kwækərɪ, -rɪ
quad kwad, kwɒd |-rat -rət
Quadragesima ˌkwadrə'dʒɛsəmə, ˌkwɒd-
quadragesimal ˌkwadrə'dʒɛsəml̩, ˌkwɒd- |-ly -ɪ
quadrangle 'kwadræŋgl̩, 'kwɒd- |-d -d
quadrant 'kwadrənt, 'kwɒd- |-al kwad'ræntl̩
quadrate adj, n 'kwadrɪt, 'kwɒd-, -ret
quadrate v 'kwadret, 'kwɒd- |-d -ɪd
quadratic kwad'rætɪk, kwɒd-

quadrature 'kwadrətʃɚ, 'kwɒd-, -ˌtʃʊr; ES
  -tʃə(r, -ˌtʃʊə(r
quadrennial kwad'rɛnɪəl, kwɒd-, -njəl |-ly -ɪ
quadrennium kwad'rɛnɪəm, kwɒd-
quadricentennial ˌkwadrɪsɛn'tɛnɪəl, ˌkwɒd-,
  -njəl |-ly -ɪ
quadrilateral ˌkwadrə'lætərəl, -trəl, ˌkwɒd-
  |-ly -ɪ
quadrille kwə'drɪl, kə'drɪl |-d -d
quadripartite ˌkwadrɪ'partaɪt, ˌkwɒd-; ES
  -'pɑːt-, E+-'pɑːt-
quadrisyllabic ˌkwadrəsɪ'læbɪk, ˌkwɒd-

Key: See in full §§3–47. bee bi |pity 'pɪtɪ (§6) |rate ret |yet jɛt |sang sæŋ |angry 'æŋ·grɪ
|bath bæθ; E baθ (§10) |ah ɑ |far fɑr |watch watʃ, wɒtʃ (§12) |jaw dʒɔ |gorge gɔrdʒ |go go

quadrisyllable ˈkwɑdrəˌsɪləbḷ, ˈkwɒd-
quadrivalent ˌkwɑdrəˈvelənt, ˌkwɒd-, kwɑd-ˈrɪvələnt, kwɒd-
quadrivial kwɑdˈrɪvɪəl, kwɒd- |-vium -vɪəm
quadroon kwɑdˈrun, kwɒd-
quadruped ˈkwɑdrəˌpɛd, ˈkwɒd-
quadruple n, adj, v ˈkwɑdrʊpḷ, ˈkwɒd-, kwɑdˈrupḷ, kwɒd-, -ˈrɪu- |-d -d |-ling -plɪŋ, -pḷɪŋ
quadruplets ˈkwɑdrʊˌplɪts, ˈkwɒd-, kwɑdˈruplɪts, kwɒd-, -ˈrɪu-
quadruplicate adj kwɑdˈruplɪkɪt, kwɒd-, -ˈrɪu-, -ˌket
quadruplicate v kwɑdˈruplɪˌket, kwɒd-, -ˈrɪu- |-d -ɪd
quaestor ˈkwɛstɚ; ES ˈkwɛstə(r
quaff kwæf, kwɑf, kwɒf, kwɔf; E+kwaf; |-ed -t
quaggy ˈkwægɪ, ˈkwɑgɪ, ˈkwɒgɪ
quagmire ˈkwægˌmaɪr, ˈkwɑg-, ˈkwɒg-; ES -ˌmaɪə(r
quahog, -haug ˈkwɔhɑg, ˈko-, -hɒg, kwəˈhɔg, -ˈhɒg
quail kwel |quailed kweld
quaint kwent
quait kwet |quaits kwets=quoit—Quaits is not a corruption of quoits, but is probably the earlier spoken form, still used by players.
Quaitso ˈkwetso
quake kwek |quaked kwekt
Quaker ˈkwekɚ; ES ˈkwekə(r; |-ism -ˌɪzəm
qualification ˌkwɑləfəˈkeʃən, ˌkwɒl-
qualify ˈkwɑləˌfaɪ, ˈkwɒl- |-fied -ˌfaɪd
qualitative ˈkwɑləˌtetɪv, ˈkwɒlə-
quality ˈkwɑlətɪ, ˈkwɒl- |-ied -d
qualm kwɑm, kwɒm, kwɔm
Quanah ˈkwɑnə, ˈkwɒnə
quandary ˈkwɑndrɪ, ˈkwɒn-, -dərɪ
quantify ˈkwɑntəˌfaɪ, ˈkwɒn- |-fied -ˌfaɪd
quantitative ˈkwɑntəˌtetɪv, ˈkwɒn-
quantity ˈkwɑntətɪ, ˈkwɒn-
quantum ˈkwɑntəm, ˈkwɒn- |-ta -tə
quarantine ˈkwɔrənˌtin, ˈkwɑr-, ˈkwɒr- |-d -d
Quarles kwɔrlz, kwɑrlz; ES kwɔɔlz, kwɑːlz; |-'s -ɪz
quarrel ˈkwɔrəl, ˈkwɑr-, ˈkwɒr-, -rl |-ed -d
quarry ˈkwɔrɪ, ˈkwɑrɪ, ˈkwɒrɪ |-ied -d
quart kwɔrt; ES kwɔɔt
quartan ˈkwɔrtn̩; ES ˈkwɔɔtn̩

quarter ˈkwɔrtɚ; ES ˈkwɔɔtə(r; |-ed -d—A dissimilated form ˈkwɔtɚ is sometimes heard (§121).
quarterback ˈkwɔrtɚˌbæk; ES ˈkwɔɔtɚ-
quarter-deck ˈkwɔrtɚˌdɛk; ES ˈkwɔɔtɚ-
quartermaster ˈkwɔrtɚˌmæstɚ; ES ˈkwɔɔtɚ-ˌmæstə(r, E+-ˌmas-, -ˌmɑs-
quarterstaff ˈkwɔrtɚˌstæf; ES ˈkwɔɔtɚ-, E+-ˌstaf, -ˌstɑf; |pl -s -s or -staves -ˌstevz, -ˌstævz; E+-ˌstavz, -ˌstɑvz
quartet, -tte kwɔrˈtɛt; ES kwɔɔˈtɛt
quartile ˈkwɔrtaɪl, -tḷ, -tɪl; ES ˈkwɔɔt-
quarto ˈkwɔrto; ES ˈkwɔɔto
quartz kwɔrts; ES kwɔɔts; |-ite -aɪt
quash kwɑʃ, kwɒʃ |-es -ɪz |-ed -t
quasi ˈkwesaɪ, ˈkwezaɪ, ˈkwɑsɪ
Quassia, q- ˈkwɑʃɪə, ˈkwɒʃ-, -ʃə
quaternary kwəˈtɝnərɪ; ES -ˈtɜn-, -ˈtɝn-
quaternion kwəˈtɝnɪən, -njən; ES -ˈtɜn-, -ˈtɝn-
quatorze kæˈtɔrz, kə-; ES -ˈtɔɔz
quatrain ˈkwɑtren, ˈkwɒt-
Quatre Bras Fr katrəˈbra
quatrefoil ˈkætɚˌfɔɪl, ˈkætrə-; ES ˈkætə-, ˈkætrə-; |-ed -d
quaver ˈkwevɚ; ES ˈkwevə(r; |-ed -d |-ing ˈkwevərɪŋ, ˈkwevrɪŋ
quay ki |-ed kid |-age ˈkiɪdʒ
quean kwin
queasy ˈkwizɪ
Quebec kwɪˈbɛk
quebracho keˈbratʃo
queen kwin |queened kwind
Queens kwinz |-'s -ɪz |-land -ˌlænd, -lənd |-town -ˌtaun |-ton -tən
queer kwɪr; ES kwɪə(r, S+kwɛə(r; |-ed -d
quell kwɛl |quelled kwɛld
quench kwɛntʃ |quenches ˈkwɛntʃɪz |-ed -t |-able -əbḷ |-bly -blɪ
quercetin ˈkwɝsɪtɪn; ES ˈkwɜs-, ˈkwɝs-
quercine ˈkwɝsɪn, -aɪn; ES ˈkwɜs-, ˈkwɝs-
Quercus ˈkwɝkəs; ES ˈkwɜkəs, ˈkwɝk-
quern kwɝn; ES kwɜn, kwɝn
querulous ˈkwɛrələs, ˈkwɛrjələs, -rʊləs
query ˈkwɪrɪ |queried ˈkwɪrɪd
Quesnay keˈne (Fr kɛˈnɛ)
quest kwɛst |quested ˈkwɛstɪd
question ˈkwɛstʃən |-ed -d |-able -əbḷ |-bly -blɪ |-ary -ˌɛrɪ

|full fʊl |tooth tuθ |further ˈfɝðɚ; ES ˈfɝðə |custom ˈkʌstəm |while hwaɪl |how hau |toy tɔɪ
|using ˈjuzɪŋ |fuse fjuz, fɪuz |dish dɪʃ |vision ˈvɪʒən |Eden ˈidn̩ |cradle ˈkredḷ |keep 'em ˈkipm̩

questionnaire ˌkwɛstʃən'ɛr, -'ær; E -'ɛə(r,
  ES -'æə(r
questor 'kwɛstɚ; ES 'kwɛstə(r
queue kju, kɪu |queued kjud, kɪud
Quezon 'kezɑn, -zɒn (Am Sp 'keson)
quibble 'kwɪbl̩ |-d -d |-ling 'kwɪblɪŋ, -bl̩ɪŋ
quick kwɪk |-ed -t |-en -ən |-ened -ənd |-ening
  'kwɪkənɪŋ, 'kwɪknɪŋ
quicklime 'kwɪkˌlaɪm
Quickly 'kwɪklɪ
quicksand 'kwɪkˌsænd
quickstep 'kwɪkˌstɛp |-stepped -ˌstɛpt
quick-witted 'kwɪk'wɪtɪd ('quick-ˌwitted 'man)
quid kwɪd
quiddity 'kwɪdətɪ
quidnunc 'kwɪdˌnʌŋk
quiescence kwaɪ'ɛsn̩s |-scent -sn̩t
quiet 'kwaɪət |quieted 'kwaɪətɪd
quietude 'kwaɪəˌtjud, -ˌtɪud, -ˌtud
quietus kwaɪ'itəs |quietuses kwaɪ'itəsɪz
quill kwɪl |quilled kwɪld
quillet 'kwɪlɪt
Quiller-Couch 'kwɪlɚ'kutʃ; ES 'kwɪlə-; |-'s
  -ɪz
quilt kwɪlt |quilted 'kwɪltɪd
quinary 'kwaɪnərɪ
quinazoline kwɪn'æzəˌlin, -lɪn
quince kwɪns |quinces 'kwɪnsɪz
quincunx 'kwɪnkʌŋks, 'kwɪŋ- |-cunxes
  -kʌŋksɪz
Quincy 'kwɪnsɪ; Mass city & family 'kwɪnzɪ
quindecennial ˌkwɪndɪ'sɛnɪəl, -njəl |-ly -ɪ
quinine 'kwaɪnaɪn
quinnat 'kwɪnæt
quinoidine kwɪ'nɔɪdin, -dɪn |-din -dɪn
quinoline 'kwɪnl̩ˌin, -ɪn |-lin -ɪn
quinone kwɪ'non ('quinˌone 'compound)
Quinquagesima ˌkwɪnkwə'dʒɛsəmə, ˌkwɪŋ-
quinquennial kwɪn'kwɛnɪəl, kwɪŋ-, -njəl |-ly
  -ɪ |-nium -nɪəm, -njəm
quinsy 'kwɪnzɪ
quint cards kwɪnt, kɪnt
quintain 'kwɪntɪn
quintal 'kwɪntl̩
quintan 'kwɪntən

quintessence kwɪn'tɛsn̩s |-s -ɪz
quintessential ˌkwɪntə'sɛnʃəl |-ly -ɪ
quintet, -tte kwɪn'tɛt
Quintilian kwɪn'tɪljən, -lɪən
quintillion kwɪn'tɪljən
Quints, q- kwɪnts
quintuple n, adj, v 'kwɪntʊpl̩, -tjʊpl̩, kwɪn-
  'tʊpl̩, -'tɪu-, -'tju- |-d -d |-ling -plɪŋ, -pl̩ɪŋ
quintuplets 'kwɪntəplɪts, -tu-, kwɪn'tuplɪts,
  -'tɪu-, -'tju-, -'tʌp-
quip kwɪp |-ped -t |-ster -stɚ; ES -stə(r
quire kwaɪr; ES kwaɪə(r; |-d -d
Quirinal 'kwɪrənl̩
quirk kwɝk; ES kwɜk, kwɝk; |-ed -t
quirt kwɝt; ES kwɜt, kwɝt; |-ed -ɪd
Quisling 'kwɪzlɪŋ
quit kwɪt |-ted -ɪd or quit kwɪt
quitclaim 'kwɪtˌklem |-claimed -ˌklemd
quite kwaɪt
Quito 'kito
quitrent 'kwɪtˌrɛnt
quittance 'kwɪtn̩s |-s -ɪz
quiver 'kwɪvɚ; ES 'kwɪvə(r; |-ed -d |-ing
  'kwɪvrɪŋ, 'kwɪvərɪŋ
Quixote, Don ˌdɑnkɪ'hotɪ, -'kwɪksət; ES+
  ˌdɒn-; (Sp -ki'xote)
quixotic kwɪks'ɑtɪk; ES+-'ɒt-; |-al -l̩ |-ally
  -l̩ɪ, -ɪklɪ
quiz kwɪz |quizzes 'kwɪzɪz |quizzed kwɪzd
quizzical 'kwɪzɪkl̩ |-ly -ɪ, -ɪklɪ
quohog, -haug 'kwɔhɔg, 'ko-, -hɒg, kwə'hɔg,
  -'hɒg=quahog
quoin kɔɪn, kwɔɪn |-ed -d
quoit kwɔɪt |quoits kwɔɪts, less freq. kɔɪt(s)—
  see quait
quondam 'kwɑndəm, 'kwɒndəm
quorum 'kworəm, 'kwɔrəm; S 'kworəm
quota 'kwotə |quotaed 'kwotəd
quotation kwo'teʃən, less freq ko'teʃən
quote kwot, less freq. kot |-d -ɪd |-table -əbl̩
  |-bly -blɪ
quoth kwoθ |quotha 'kwoθə
quotidian kwo'tɪdɪən, -'tɪdjən
quotient 'kwoʃənt
quo warranto 'kwo wɔ'rænto, wɑ-, wɒ-, wə-

R

R, r *letter* ɑr; ES ɑ:(r; |*pl* R's, Rs, *poss* R's ɑrz; ES ɑ:z, E+a:(r, a:z
rabbet 'ræbɪt |rabbeted 'ræbɪtɪd
rabbi 'ræbaɪ
rabbinical ræ'bɪnɪkḷ, rə- |-ly -ɪ
rabbit 'ræbɪt |rabbited 'ræbɪtɪd
rabble 'ræbḷ
Rabelais ˌræbḷ'e, 'ræbḷˌe (*Fr* ra'blɛ)
Rabelaisian ˌræbḷ'ezɪən, -ʒən
rabid 'ræbɪd
rabies 'rebiz, 'rebɪˌiz, 'ræb-
Rabindranath Tagore rə'bɪndrəˌnɑttə'gor, -'gɔr; ES -'goə(r, E+-'gɔə(r
raccoon ræ'kun
race res |races 'resɪz |raced rest
racecourse 'resˌkors, -ˌkɔrs; ES -ˌkoəs, E+ -ˌkɔəs; |-s -ɪz
raceme re'sim, rə'sim |-d -d
Rachel *name* 'retʃəl, *powder Fr* ra'ʃɛl
rachitis rə'kaɪtɪs |-chitic -'kɪtɪk
Rachmaninov, -off rɑk'mɑnɪˌnɔf, ræk-, -ˌnɒf
racial 'reʃəl, 'reʃɪəl |-ly -ɪ
Racine rə'sin, (*Fr* ra'sin)
rack ræk |racked ækt
racket 'rækɪt |racketed 'rækɪtɪd
racketeer ˌrækɪt'ɪr; ES -'ɪə(r; S+-'ɛə(r |-ed -d
raconteur ˌrækɑn'tɝ; ES -kɑn'tɜ(r, -kɒn-, -'tɝ
racquet 'rækɪt
racy 'resɪ |racily 'resḷɪ, -sɪlɪ
Radcliff(e), -clyffe 'rædklɪf
raddle 'rædḷ |-d -d |-ling 'rædḷɪŋ, 'rædlɪŋ
raddleman 'rædḷmən |-men -mən
radial 'redɪəl |-ly -ɪ
radiance 'redɪəns, 'redjəns |-s -ɪz |-ant -ənt
radiate 'redɪˌet |-d -ɪd |-tion ˌredɪ'eʃən
radiator 'redɪˌetɚ; ES 'redɪˌetə(r
radical 'rædɪkḷ |-ly -ɪ, -ɪklɪ
radio 'redɪˌo |-ed -d |-active ˌredɪo'æktɪv
radioactivity 'redɪˌoæk'tɪvətɪ
radiobroadcast 'redɪo'brɔdˌkæst; E+-ˌkast, -ˌkɑst
radiogram 'redɪəˌgræm
radiograph 'redɪəˌgræf; ES+-ˌgraf, -ˌgrɑf; |-ed -t
radiographer ˌredɪ'ɑgrəfɚ, -'ɒg-; ES -fə(r; |-phy -fɪ

radiolarian ˌredɪo'lɛrɪən, -'le-
radiology ˌredɪ'ɑlədʒɪ; ES+-'ɒl-
radiometer ˌredɪ'ɑmətɚ; ES -'ɑmətə(r, -'ɒm-
radiophone 'redɪəˌfon
radioscope 'redɪəˌskop
radioscopy ˌredɪ'ɑskəpɪ; ES+-'ɒs-
radiotelegram 'redɪo'tɛləˌgræm
radiotelegraphy 'redɪˌotə'lɛgrəfɪ
radiotelephony 'redɪˌotə'lɛfənɪ
radiotherapy 'redɪo'θɛrəpɪ
radiothorium ˌredɪo'θorɪəm, -'θɔr-; S -'θor-
radish 'rædɪʃ |radishes 'rædɪʃɪz
radium 'redɪəm
radiumtherapy 'redɪəm'θɛrəpɪ
radius 'redɪəs |-es -ɪz |radii 'redɪˌaɪ
Radnor 'rædnɚ; ES -nə(r; |-shire -ˌʃɪr, -ʃɚ; ES -ˌʃɪə(r, -ʃə(r
radon 'redɑn; ES+-dɒn
Raeburn 'rebɝn; ES 'rebən
Raemaekers 'rɑmɑkɚz; ES 'rɑmɑkəz; |-'s -ɪz
Rafael 'ræfɪəl, 'refɪəl
raff ræf |raffish 'ræfɪʃ
raffia 'ræfɪə, -fjə
raffle 'ræfḷ |-d -d |-ling 'ræfḷɪŋ, 'ræflɪŋ
raft ræft; E+raft, rɑft; |-ed -ɪd
rafter 'ræftɚ; ES 'ræftə(r, E+'raf-, 'rɑf-
rag ræg |ragged rægd
ragamuffin 'rægəˌmʌfɪn, 'rægˌmʌfɪn
rage redʒ |rages 'redʒɪz |raged redʒd
ragged *adj* 'rægɪd
raglan 'ræglən
ragman 'rægˌmæn, -mən |-men -mən
ragman *document* 'rægmən
ragout ræ'gu |-s -z |-ed -d |-ing -ɪŋ
ragpicker 'rægˌpɪkɚ; ES -ˌpɪkə(r
ragtime 'rægˌtaɪm
ragweed 'rægˌwid
raid red |raided 'redɪd
rail rel |railed reld
railhead 'relˌhɛd
raillery 'relərɪ—rallery 'rælərɪ, *an old variant, is said to be still heard.*
railroad 'relˌrod |railroaded 'relˌrodɪd
railway 'relˌwe
raiment 'remənt |-ed -ɪd
rain ren |rained rend
rainbow 'renˌbo |-bowed -ˌbod

|full fʊl |tooth tuθ |further 'fɝðɚ; ES 'fɝðə |custom 'kʌstəm |while hwaɪl |how haʊ |toy tɔɪ |using 'juzɪŋ |fuse fjuz, fɪuz |dish dɪʃ |vision 'vɪʒən |Eden 'idn̩ |cradle 'kredḷ |keep 'em 'kipm̩

raincoat 'ren₁kot |-ed -ɪd
raindrop 'ren₁drɑp; ES+-₁drɒp
rainfall 'ren₁fɔl
Rainier, *Mount* re'nɪr; ES re'nɪə(r
rainier *'wetter'* 'renɪɚ; ES 'renɪ·ə(r
rainproof *adj* 'ren'pruf ('rain₁proof 'hat)
rainproof *v* 'ren₁pruf |-proofed -₁pruft
rainstorm 'ren₁stɔrm; ES 'ren₁stɔəm
raintight 'ren'taɪt ('rain₁tight 'roof)
rainwater 'ren₁wɔtɚ, -₁wɑtɚ, -₁wɒtɚ; ES -tə(r
rainworm 'ren₁wɝm; ES -₁wɜm, -₁wɝm
raise rez |raises 'rezɪz |raised rezd
raisin 'rezṇ
raison d'être 'rezɔn'dɛt (*Fr* rɛzõ'dɛ:tr̥)
raj rɑdʒ |raja, -jah 'rɑdʒə
Rajput 'rɑdʒput
rake rek |raked rekt
Raleigh 'rɔlɪ
rally 'rælɪ |rallied 'rælɪd
Ralph rælf—ref *is chiefly British*
ram ræm |rammed ræmd
Ramadan ₁ræmə'dɑn
ramble 'ræmbḷ |-d -d |-ling 'ræmblɪŋ, -b̩ɪŋ
ramekin 'ræməkɪn
Rameses 'ræmə₁siz |-'s -ɪz |+rə'misiz
ramie 'ræmɪ
ramification ₁ræməfə'keʃən
ramiform 'ræmə₁fɔrm; ES 'ræmə₁fɔəm
ramify 'ræmə₁faɪ |ramified 'ræmə₁faɪd
ramp ræmp |ramped ræmpt
rampage *n* 'ræmpedʒ |-geous ræm'pedʒəs
rampage *v* ræm'pedʒ |-s -ɪz |-d -d
rampant 'ræmpənt |-pancy -pənsɪ
rampart 'ræmpɑrt, 'ræmpɚt; ES -pɑ:t, -pət,
  E+-pɑ:t
ramrod 'ræm₁rɑd; ES+-₁rɒd
Ramsay, -sey 'ræmzɪ
Ramses 'ræmsiz |-ses' -siz
Ramsgate 'ræmz₁get, *Brit* 'ræmzgɪt
ramshackle 'ræmʃækḷ |-d -d
ramson 'ræmzṇ, -sṇ
ramtil 'ræmtɪl
ran ræn
ranch ræntʃ |ranches 'ræntʃɪz |ranched
  ræntʃt
ranchero ræn'tʃero (*Sp* ran-)
ranchman 'ræntʃmən |-men -mən
rancho 'ræntʃo, 'ran-
rancid 'rænsɪd |rancidity ræn'sɪdətɪ

rancor 'ræŋkɚ; ES 'ræŋkə(r; |-ous -əs, -krəs
Randolph 'rændɑlf, -dɒlf
random 'rændəm
rang ræŋ
range rendʒ |ranges 'rendʒɪz |ranged rendʒd
Rangely 'rendʒlɪ
Rangoon ræŋ'gun
rangy, -gey 'rendʒɪ
Ranier re'nɪr; ES -'nɪə(r
rank ræŋk |ranked ræŋkt
rankle 'ræŋkḷ |-d -d |-ling 'ræŋklɪŋ, -k̩ɪŋ
ransack 'rænsæk |ransacked 'rænsækt
ransom 'rænsəm |ransomed 'rænsəmd
rant rænt |ranted 'ræntɪd
rap ræp |rapped ræpt
rapacious rə'peʃəs |-pacity -'pæsətɪ
rape rep |raped rept
rapeseed 'rep₁sid
Raphael *painter* 'ræfɪəl, *pers. name* 'ræf-,
  'ref-
rapid 'ræpɪd
Rapidan ₁ræpə'dæn
rapid-fire 'ræpɪd'faɪr; ES -'faɪə(r; ('rapid-₁fire
  'gun)
rapidity rə'pɪdətɪ
rapier 'repɪɚ, 'repjɚ; ES 'repɪ·ə(r, -pjə(r
rapine 'ræpɪn
Rappahannock ₁ræpə'hænək
rapparee ₁ræpə'ri
rapport ræ'port, -'pɔrt; ES -'poət, E+-'pɔət;
  (*Fr* ra'pɔ̃:r)
rapprochement *Fr* raprɔʃ'mã
rapscallion ræp'skæljən
rapt ræpt
rapture 'ræptʃɚ; ES 'ræptʃə(r; |-rous -əs
rara avis 'rerə'evɪs |rarae aves 'reri'eviz
rare rɛr, rær; E rɛə(r, ES ræə(r; |rarer -rɚ;
  ES -rə(r
rarebit *erron. for* (Welsh) rabbit 'rɛr₁bɪt,
  'rær-; ES *see* rare; rarebit *is unknown*
  apart from Welsh rarebit.
rarefaction ₁rɛrə'fækʃən, ₁rær-; S ₁rær-;
  |-tive -tɪv
rarefy 'rɛrə₁faɪ, 'rær-; S 'rær-; |-fied -₁faɪd
Raritan 'rærətṇ
rarity 'rɛrətɪ, 'rær-; S 'rær-
rascal 'ræskḷ |rascally 'ræskḷɪ
rascality ræs'kælətɪ
rase rez |rases 'rezɪz |rased rezd

---

rash ræʃ |rashes ˈræʃɪz
rasher ˈræʃɚ; ES ˈræʃə(r
Rask rɑsk
Rasmussen ˈrɑsmʌsn̩
rasp ræsp; E+rasp, rɑsp; |-ed -t
raspberry ˈræz,bɛrɪ, -bərɪ; E+ˈraz-, ˈrɑz-
Rasputin ræsˈpjutɪn, -ˈpɪu-, rɑsˈputin
Rasselas ˈræsə,læs, -ləs |-'s -ɪz
rasure ˈreʒɚ; ES ˈreʒə(r
rat ræt |ratted ˈrætɪd
ratable, ratea- ˈretəbl̩ |-bly -blɪ
ratafia ˌrætəˈfiə
ratan ræˈtæn |-ned -d
rataplan ˌrætəˈplæn |-ned -d
ratch rætʃ |ratches ˈrætʃɪz |ratched rætʃt
ratchet ˈrætʃɪt |racheted ˈrætʃɪtɪd
Ratcliff, -e ˈrætklɪf
rate ret |rated ˈretɪd
Rathbone ˈræθ,bon, -bən
rathe reð
rather ˈræðɚ; ES ˈræðə(r, ˈra̍ð-, ˈrɑð-;—*In
NEngd the* Linguistic Atlas *shows that*
ˈræðə(r, ˈrɛð-, ˈrʌð-, ˈrað- *among cultivated
informants are more frequent than* ˈrɑðə(r,
and that ˈræðə(r *is more frequent than*
ˈrɑðə(r. *In the US as a whole* ˈræðɚ,
ˈræðə(r *overwhelmingly prevails,* ˈrɑð-,
ˈrað-, ˈrɛð-, ˈrʌð- *being only sporadic. The
most regular form, historically, is* ˈræðɚ,
ˈræðə(r, *like* gather, lather, Cather,
Mather, blather, slather, fathom. *The
Brit form is* ˈrɑðə(r.
rathskeller ˈrɑts,kɛlɚ; ES -,kɛlə(r
ratification ˌrætəfəˈkeʃən
ratify ˈrætə,faɪ |ratified ˈrætə,faɪd
ratio ˈreʃo (*as L* ˈreʃɪ,o)
ratiocinate *v* ˌræʃɪˈɑsn̩,et; ES+-ˈɒs-; |-d -d
ratiocinate *adj* ˌræʃɪˈɑsn̩ɪt; ES+-ˈɒs-
ratiocination ˌræʃɪ,ɑsn̩ˈeʃən; ES+-,ɒs-
ration ˈræʃən, ˈreʃən; *mil.* ˈræʃən |-ed -d
|-ing -ʃənɪŋ, -ʃnɪŋ
rational ˈræʃənl̩ |-ly -ɪ |-ism -,ɪzəm |-ist -ɪst
rationale ˌræʃəˈnæl, -ˈnɑlɪ, -ˈnelɪ
rationalistic ˌræʃənl̩ˈɪstɪk |-al -l̩ |-ally -l̩ɪ,
-ɪklɪ
rationality ˌræʃəˈnælətɪ
rationalize ˈræʃənl̩,aɪz, -ʃnəl- |-s -ɪz |-d -d
Ratisbon ˈrætɪz,bɑn, ˈrætɪs-; ES+-,bɒn
ratline, -lin ˈrætlɪn |-lined -lɪnd

Raton ræˈtun (ˈRa,ton ˈPass)
ratoon ræˈtun |-ed -d
ratsbane ˈræts,ben
rattail ˈræt,tel
rattan ræˈtæn |-ned -d
rattle ˈrætl̩ |-d -d |-ling ˈrætl̩ɪŋ, ˈrætlɪŋ
rattlebrain ˈrætl̩,bren |-ed -d
rattlehead ˈrætl̩,hɛd |-headed -ˈhɛdɪd (ˈrattle-
,headed ˈnotion)
rattler ˈrætlɚ, ˈrætl̩ɚ; ES ˈrætlə(r, ˈrætl̩ə(r
rattlesnake ˈrætl̩,snek
rattletrap ˈrætl̩,træp
rattly ˈrætl̩ɪ, ˈrætlɪ
rattrap ˈræt,træp
raucous ˈrɔkəs
ravage ˈrævɪdʒ |-s -ɪz |-d -d
rave rev |raved revd
ravel ˈrævl̩ |-ed -d |-ing ˈrævlɪŋ, ˈrævl̩ɪŋ
raven *bird* ˈrevən
raven *v* ˈrævɪn, -ən |-ed -d
Ravena rəˈvinə
Ravenna rəˈvɛnə, *in Ohio*+rɪˈvænə
ravenous ˈrævənəs
ravin, -ine '*rapine*' ˈrævɪn |-ed -d
ravine '*gorge*' rəˈvin
ravish ˈrævɪʃ |-es -ɪz |-ed -t
raw rɔ
rawboned ˈrɔˈbond (ˈraw,boned ˈhorse)
Rawdon ˈrɔdn̩
rawhide ˈrɔ,haɪd |rawhided ˈrɔ,haɪdɪd
ray, R- re |rayed red
Rayleigh ˈrelɪ
Raymond ˈremənd
Raynham ˈrenəm, *Mass loc.*+ˈrenhæm
rayon ˈrean, -ɒn
raze rez |razes ˈrezɪz |razed rezd
razor ˈrezɚ; ES ˈrezə(r
razorback ˈrezɚ,bæk; ES ˈrezə-; |-ed -t
razz ræz |razzes ˈræzɪz |razzed ræzd
razzle-dazzle *n* ˈræzl̩,dæzl̩
razzle-dazzle *v* ˌræzl̩ˈdæzl̩, ˈræzl̩,dæzl̩ |-d -d
|-ling -zlɪŋ, -zl̩ɪŋ
r-colored ˈɑr,kʌlɚd; ES ˈɑ:,kʌləd, E+ˈa:-
re *music* re, *prep* ri
re- *prefix: stressed* ˈri-, ˌri-, ˈrɛ-, ˌrɛ-; *unstr.*
rɪ-, ri-, rə-; *for the unstr. form when only* rɪ-
*is given in the vocabulary, it is to be under-
stood that many speakers* (*both British and
American*) *also pronounce* ri- (*esp. in more*

careful speech or when a vowel follows), or
rə- *as in* Ramona rə'monə.

're *abbr. sp. of unstressed* are *in* you're, we're,
they're -r; ES -ə(r

Rea re, 'riə, ri
reabsorb ˌriəb'sɔrb, -'zɔrb; ES -ɔəb; |-ed -d
reabsorption ˌriəb'sɔrpʃən; ES -'sɔəpʃən
reach ritʃ |reaches 'ritʃɪz |reached ritʃt
react rɪ'ækt |-ed -ɪd |-ction -kʃən
re-act ˌri'ækt |-ed -ɪd
reactionary rɪ'ækʃənˌɛrɪ
read *n, v* rid |*past* read rɛd |*pptc* read rɛd
Read rid
readability ˌridə'bɪlətɪ
readable 'ridəbḷ |-bly -blɪ
readily 'rɛdḷɪ, -ɪlɪ |-iness -ɪnɪs
Reading 'rɛdɪŋ
readjust ˌriə'dʒʌst |-ed -ɪd |-able -əbḷ
readmit ˌriəd'mɪt |-ted -ɪd |-mission -'mɪʃən
ready 'rɛdɪ
ready-made 'rɛdɪ'med ('ready-ˌmade 'clothes)
reaffirm ˌriə'fɝm; ES -'fɜm, -'fɝm; |-ed -d
reaffirmation ˌriæfɚ'meʃən; ES ˌriæfə-
Reagan 'regən
reagent ri'edʒənt |-gency -dʒənsɪ
real 'riəl, ril, 'rɪəl
real *coin* 'riəl, ril (*Sp* re'al)
Real 'riəl
real estate 'riləˌstet, 'riəl-, 'rɪəl-
realism 'riəlˌɪzəm, 'rɪəl- |-ist -ɪst
realistic ˌriə'lɪstɪk, ˌrɪə- |-ally -ḷɪ, -ɪklɪ
reality rɪ'ælətɪ
realization ˌriələ'zeʃən, ˌrɪəl-, -aɪ'z-
realize 'riəˌlaɪz, 'rɪə- |-s -ɪz |-d -d
really 'riəlɪ, 'rilɪ, 'rɪəlɪ, 'rɪlɪ
realm rɛlm
realtor 'riəltɚ, -tər; ES -tə(r, -tɔə(r
realty 'riəltɪ
ream rim |reamed rimd
reanimate ri'ænəˌmet |-d -ɪd
reanimation ˌriænə'meʃən
reap rip |reaped ript |-er -ɚ; ES -ə(r
reappear ˌriə'pɪr; ES -'pɪə(r, S+-'pɛə(r,
-'pjɛə(r; |-ed -d
reappoint ˌriə'pɔɪnt |-ed -ɪd
rear rɪr; ES rɪə(r, S+rɛə(r; |-ed -d
rearm ri'arm; ES -'ɑ:m, E+'a:m; |-ed -d
rearmament ri'arməmənt; ES -'a:m-, E+
-'a:m-

rearmost 'rɪrˌmost; ES 'rɪə-, S+'rɛə-
rearrange ˌriə'rendʒ |-s -ɪz |-d -d
rearward *'backward'* 'rɪrwɚd; ES 'rɪəwəd,
S+'rɛə-
rearward *'rear guard'* 'rɪrˌwɔrd; ES 'rɪəˌwɔəd,
S+'rɛə-
reason 'rizṇ |-ed -d |-ing 'riznɪŋ, 'rɪznɪŋ
reasonable 'riznəbḷ, 'rɪzṇə- |-bly -blɪ
reassemble ˌriə'sɛmbḷ |-d -d |-ling -'sɛmblɪŋ,
-'sɛmbḷɪŋ
reassert ˌriə'sɝt; ES -'sɜt, -'sɝt; |-ed -ɪd
reassign ˌriə'saɪn |-ed -d
reassure ˌriə'ʃʊr; ES -'ʃʊə(r; |-d -d |-dly -ɪdlɪ
|-rance -əns |-rances -ənsɪz
Reaumur, Ré- 'reəˌmjʊr, -ˌmɪʊr; ES -ə(r;
(*Fr* reo'my:r)
reave riv |reaved rivd *or* reft rɛft
reawaken ˌriə'wekən |-ed -d
rebate *'rabbet'* 'ræbɪt, 'ribet |-d -ɪd
rebate *'discount'* 'ribet, rɪ'bet; |-d -ɪd
rebec, -eck 'ribɛk
Rebecca, -bekah rɪ'bɛkə
rebel *n, adj* 'rɛbḷ
rebel *v* rɪ'bɛl |-led -d |-lion -jən |-lious -jəs
rebirth ri'bɝθ; ES -'bɜθ, -'bɝθ ('birth &
're₁birth)
reborn ri'bɔrn; ES -'bɔən; ('re₁born 'soul)
rebound *n* 'riˌbaʊnd, rɪ'baʊnd
rebound *v 'recoil'* rɪ'baʊnd |-ed -ɪd
rebound *pptc of* rebind ˌri'baʊnd
rebroadcast ri'brɔdˌkæst; E+-ˌkast, -ˌkɑst;
|*past & pptc* -cast, *radio*+-casted -ɪd
rebuff rɪ'bʌf |-ed -t
rebuild ri'bɪld |-built -'bɪlt *or arch.* -builded
-'bɪldɪd
rebuke rɪ'bjuk, -'bɪuk |-d -t
rebus 'ribəs |-es -ɪz |-ed -t
rebut rɪ'bʌt |-ted -ɪd |-tal -ḷ
rebutter *'who rebuts'* rɪ'bʌtɚ; ES -tə(r
re-butter *'butter again'* ˌri'bʌtɚ; ES -tə(r
recalcitrance rɪ'kælsɪtrəns |-cy -ɪ |-nt -nt
recall *n* 'riˌkɔl, rɪ'kɔl
recall *v* rɪ'kɔl |-ed -d
recant rɪ'kænt |-ed -ɪd |-ation ˌrikæn'teʃən
recapitulate ˌrikə'pɪtʃəˌlet |-d -ɪd
recapitulation ˌrikəˌpɪtʃə'leʃən
recapture ri'kæptʃɚ; ES -tʃə(r; |-d -d
recast *n* 'riˌkæst; E+-ˌkast, -ˌkɑst
recast *v* ri'kæst; E+-'kast, -'kɑst

---

recede *'go back'* rɪ'sid |-d -ɪd
re-cede *'cede back'* ˌri'sid |-d -ɪd
receipt rɪ'sit |-ed -ɪd
receivable rɪ'sivəbḷ |-s -z
receive rɪ'siv |-d -d |-r -ɚ; ES -ə(r
receivership rɪ'sivɚˌʃɪp; ES -'sivə-
recency 'risn̩sɪ |recent 'risn̩t
recension rɪ'sɛnʃən
receptacle rɪ'sɛptəkḷ, -tɪkḷ
reception rɪ'sɛpʃən |-tive -tɪv
receptivity rɪˌsɛp'tɪvətɪ, ˌrisɛp'tɪv-
recess *n* rɪ'sɛs, 'risɛs |-es -ɪz
recess *v* rɪ'sɛs |-es -ɪz |-ed -t
recession *'going back'* rɪ'sɛʃən |-sive -sɪv
recession *'ceding back'* ˌri'sɛʃən
recharge ri'tʃɑrdʒ; ES -'tʃɑːdʒ, E+-'tʃɑːdʒ;
  |-s -ɪz |-d -d
rechate rɪ'tʃet=recheat
recheat rɪ'tʃit
recherché rə'ʃɛrʃe; ES -'ʃɛəʃe; (*Fr* rəʃɛr'ʃe)
recidivous rɪ'sɪdəvəs |-vism -ˌvɪzəm
Recife re'sifə
recipe 'rɛsəpɪ, -ˌpi
recipient rɪ'sɪpɪənt
reciprocal rɪ'sɪprəkḷ |-ly -ɪ
reciprocate rɪ'sɪprəˌket |-d -ɪd
reciprocation rɪˌsɪprə'keʃən
reciprocity ˌrɛsə'prɑsətɪ; ES+-'prɒs-
recital rɪ'saɪtḷ |-ist -ɪst
recitation ˌrɛsə'teʃən
recitative *n* ˌrɛsətə'tiv
recitative *adj* 'rɛsəˌtetɪv, rɪ'saɪtətɪv
recite rɪ'saɪt |-d -ɪd
reck rɛk |recked rɛkt |-less -lɪs
reckon 'rɛkən |-ed -d |-ing 'rɛkənɪŋ, -knɪŋ
reclaim rɪ'klem |-ed -d
reclamation ˌrɛklə'meʃən
recline *n* rɪ'klaɪn, 'riklaɪn
recline *v* rɪ'klaɪn |-d -d
recluse *n* 'rɛklus, -lɪus, rɪ'klus, -'klɪus |-s -ɪz
recluse *adj* rɪ'klus, -'klɪus
recognition ˌrɛkəg'nɪʃən
recognizable 'rɛkəgˌnaɪzəbḷ |-bly -blɪ
recognizance rɪ'kɑgnɪzəns, -'kɑnɪ-, -'kɒ- |-s
  -ɪz
recognize 'rɛkəgˌnaɪz, -ɪg- |-s -ɪz |-d -d
re-cognize *'cognize again'* ˌri'kɑgnaɪz, -'kɒg-
  |-s -ɪz |-d -d
recoil rɪ'kɔɪl |-ed -d

re-coil *'coil again'* ˌri'kɔɪl |-ed -d
recollect *'remember'* ˌrɛkə'lɛkt |-ed -ɪd |-ction
  -kʃən
re-collect *'collect again'* ˌrikə'lɛkt |-ed -ɪd
  |-ction -kʃən
recombine ˌrikəm'baɪn |-d -d
recommence ˌrikə'mɛns |-s -ɪz |-d -t
recommend ˌrɛkə'mɛnd |-ed -ɪd
re-commend *'c. again'* ˌrikə'mɛnd |-ed -ɪd
recommendation ˌrɛkəmɛn'deʃən
recommit ˌrikə'mɪt |-ted -ɪd |-tal -ḷ
recompense 'rɛkəmˌpɛns |-s -ɪz |-d -t
reconcilable 'rɛkənˌsaɪləbḷ, *emph.*+ˌrɛkən-
  'saɪl- |-bly -blɪ
reconcile 'rɛkənˌsaɪl |-d -d |-less -ˌsaɪllɪs
reconciliation ˌrɛkənˌsɪlɪ'eʃən
recondite 'rɛkənˌdaɪt, rɪ'kɑndaɪt; ES+-'kɒn-
reconnaissance rɪ'kɑnəsəns; ES+-'kɒn-; |-s
  -ɪz
reconnoissance rɪ'kɑnəsəns; ES+-'kɒn-; |-s
  -ɪz
reconnoiter, -tre ˌrikə'nɔɪtɚ, ˌrɛkə-; ES -tə(r;
  |-(e)d -d |-ing -tərɪŋ, -trɪŋ
reconquer ri'kɑŋkɚ, -'kɒŋ-, -'kɑŋ-; ES -kə(r;
  |-ed -d |-ing -kərɪŋ, -krɪŋ
reconsider ˌrikən'sɪdɚ; ES -də(r; |-ed -d
  |-ing -dərɪŋ, -drɪŋ
reconsideration ˌrikənˌsɪdə'reʃən
reconstitute ri'kɑnstəˌtjut, -ˌtɪut, -ˌtut |-d -ɪd
reconstruct ˌrikən'strʌkt |-ed -ɪd |-ion -kʃən
record *n* 'rɛkɚd; ES 'rɛkəd;—'rɛkɔrd *is*
  mainly Brit.
record *v* rɪ'kɔrd; ES -'kɔəd; |-ed -ɪd
reorder rɪ'kɔrdɚ; ES -'kɔədə(r
recount *n* 'riˌkaʊnt, ri'kaʊnt
recount *v* *'tell'* rɪ'kaʊnt |-ed -ɪd
re-count *'c. again'* ˌri'kaʊnt |-ed -ɪd
recoup rɪ'kup |-ed -t
recourse 'rikors, rɪ'kors, -ɔrs; ES -ɔəs,
  E+-ɔəs
recover *'get back'* rɪ'kʌvɚ; ES -'kʌvə(r; |-ed
  -d |-ing -'kʌvrɪŋ, -'kʌvərɪŋ |-y -'kʌvrɪ,
  -'kʌvərɪ
re-cover *'c. again'* ˌri'kʌvɚ; ES -'kʌvə(r; |-ed
  -d |-ing -vrɪŋ, -vərɪŋ
recreance 'rɛkrɪəns |-cy -ɪ |-ant -ənt
recreate *'refresh'* 'rɛkrɪˌet |-d -ɪd
re-create *'c. anew'* ˌrikrɪ'et |-d -ɪd
recreation *'play'* ˌrɛkrɪ'eʃən |-al -ḷ

|full fʊl |tooth tuθ |further 'fɝðɚ; ES 'fɝðə |custom 'kʌstəm |while hwaɪl |how haʊ |toy tɔɪ
|using 'juzɪŋ |fuse fjuz, fɪuz |dish dɪʃ |vision 'vɪʒən |Eden 'idn̩ |cradle 'kredḷ |keep 'em 'kipm̩

re-creation '*c. anew*' ˌrikrɪ'eʃən
recreative 'rɛkrɪˌetɪv
recriminate rɪ'krɪməˌnet |-d -ɪd
recrimination rɪˌkrɪmə'neʃən
recriminatory rɪ'krɪmənəˌtorɪ, -ˌtɔrɪ; S -ˌtorɪ
recross ri'krɔs, -'krɒs |-es -ɪz |-ed -t
recrudesce ˌrikru'dɛs, -krɪu- |-s -ɪz |-d -t
recrudescence ˌrikru'dɛsn̩s |-cy -ɪ |-nt -sn̩t
recruit rɪ'krut, -'krɪut |-ed -ɪd
rectangle 'rɛktæŋgl̩ |-d -d
rectangular rɛk'tæŋgjələ; ES -lə(r
rectification ˌrɛktəfə'keʃən
rectify 'rɛktəˌfaɪ |-fied -ˌfaɪd
rectilinear ˌrɛktə'lɪnɪɚ; ES -'lɪnɪ·ə(r
rectitude 'rɛktəˌtjud, -ˌtɪud, -ˌtud
recto 'rɛkto
rector 'rɛktɚ; ES -tə(r; |-ate -ɪt |-y -ɪ, -trɪ
rectum 'rɛktəm |-ta -tə |-tal -tl̩
recumbency rɪ'kʌmbənsɪ |-bent -bənt
recuperate rɪ'kjupəˌret, -'kɪu-, -'ku- |-d -ɪd
recuperation rɪˌkjupə'reʃən, -ˌkɪu-, -ˌku-
recur rɪ'kɝ; ES -'kɝ(r, -'kɝ; |-red -d
recurrence rɪ'kɝəns; ES -'kɝr-, -'kʌr-, -'kɝ-;
  |-s -ɪz |-ent -ənt
recurve rɪ'kɝv; ES -'kɝv, -'kɝv; |-d -d
recusancy 'rɛkjuzn̩sɪ, rɪ'kjuz-, -'kɪuz- |-nt -n̩t
red, R- rɛd |redded 'rɛdɪd
redact rɪ'dækt |-ed -ɪd |-ction -kʃən
redan, R- rɪ'dæn
redbird 'rɛdˌbɝd; ES -ˌbɝd, -ˌbɝd
red-blooded 'rɛd'blʌdɪd ('red-ˌblooded 'worm)
redbreast 'rɛdˌbrɛst
redbud 'rɛdˌbʌd
redcap 'rɛdˌkæp
redcoat 'rɛdˌkot
red-coated 'rɛd'kotɪd ('red-ˌcoated 'glory)
Red Cross 'rɛd'krɔs, -'krɒs ('red-ˌcross 'seal)
redden 'rɛdn̩ |-ed -d |-ing 'rɛdn̩ɪŋ, 'rɛdnɪŋ
reddish 'rɛdɪʃ
Redditch 'rɛdɪtʃ |-'s -ɪz
reddle 'rɛdl̩ |-man -mən |-men -mən
rede rid |*arch. past* red rɛd
redeem rɪ'dim |-ed -d |-able -əbl̩ |-bly -blɪ
redemption rɪ'dɛmpʃən |-tive -tɪv |-tory -tərɪ
Redgauntlet 'rɛdˌgɒntlɪt
red-handed 'rɛd'hændɪd ('red-ˌhanded 'Orchis)
redhead 'rɛdˌhɛd
redheaded 'rɛd'hɛdɪd ('red-ˌheaded 'lark)

red-hot *adj* 'rɛd'hɑt; ES+-'hɒt
red-hot *n* 'rɛdˌhɑt; ES+-ˌhɒt
redintegrate rɪ'dɪntəˌgret, rɛd'ɪn- |-d -ɪd
redintegration rɪˌdɪntə'greʃən, rɛdˌɪn-
redirect ˌridə'rɛkt, -daɪ- |-ed -ɪd
rediscount ri'dɪskaʊnt |-ed -ɪd
rediscover ˌridɪ'skʌvɚ; ES -'skʌvə(r; |-ed -d
  |-ing -'skʌvərɪŋ, -'skʌvrɪŋ
redistribute ˌridɪ'strɪbjut |-d -bjətɪd
redistribution ˌridɪstrə'bjuʃən, -'bɪu-
redistrict ri'dɪstrɪkt |-ed -ɪd
Redlands 'rɛdˌlændz, -ləndz, -nz |-'s -ɪz
red-letter 'rɛd'lɛtɚ; ES -tə(r; |-ed -d ('red-
  ˌletter 'journey)
redolence 'rɛdl̩əns |-cy -ɪ |-lent -dl̩ənt
Redondo rɪ'dando; ES+-'dɒn-
redouble ri'dʌbl̩ |-d -d |-ling -'dʌblɪŋ, -bl̩ɪŋ
redoubt rɪ'daʊt |-ed -ɪd |-able -əbl̩ |-bly -blɪ
redound rɪ'daʊnd |-ed -ɪd
redpoll 'rɛdˌpol
redraft *n* 'riˌdræft; E+-ˌdraft, -ˌdrɑft
redraft *v* ri'dræft; E+-'draft, -'drɑft; |-ed -ɪd
redraw ri'drɔ |-drew -'dru, -'drɪu |-drawn
  -'drɔn
redress *n* 'ridrɛs, rɪ'drɛs
redress *v* '*repair*' rɪ'drɛs |-es -ɪz |-ed -t
re-dress '*d. again*' ˌri'drɛs |-es -ɪz |-ed -t
Redriff 'rɛdrɪf=Rotherhithe
Redruth 'rɛdruθ, rɛd'ruθ
redskin 'rɛdˌskɪn
reduce rɪ'djus, -'drus, -'dus |-s -ɪz |-d -t
reducible rɪ'djusəbl̩, -'drus-, -'dus- |-bly -blɪ
reductio ad absurdum rɪ'dʌkʃɪoˌædəb-
  'sɝdəm; ES -'sɝd-, -'sɝd-
reduction rɪ'dʌkʃən |-tive -tɪv
redundance rɪ'dʌndəns |-cy -ɪ |-dant -dənt
reduplicate '*n, adj* rɪ'djupləkɪt, -'dru-, -'du-,
  -ˌket
reduplicate *v* rɪ'djupləˌket, -'dru-, -'du- |-d
  -ɪd
reduplication rɪˌdjuplə'keʃən, -ˌdru-, -ˌdu-
redwood, R- 'rɛdˌwʊd
re-echo ri'ɛko |-ed -d |-ing -'ɛkəwɪŋ
reed, R- rid |reeded 'ridɪd
re-educate ri'ɛdʒəˌket, -'ɛdʒu- |-d -ɪd
reef rif |reefed rift
reek rik |reeked rikt
reel ril |reeled rild
re-elect ˌriə'lɛkt |-ed -ɪd |-ction -kʃən

Key: See in full §§3–47. bee bi |pity 'pɪtɪ (§6) |rate ret |yet jɛt |sang sæŋ |angry 'æŋ·grɪ
|bath bæθ; E baθ (§10) |ah ɑ |far fɑr |watch wɑtʃ, wɒtʃ (§12) |jaw dʒɔ |gorge gɔrdʒ |go go

re-embark ˌriɪm'bɑrk; ES -'bɑːk, E+-'baːk; |-ed -t

re-emphasize ri'ɛmfəˌsaɪz |-s -ɪz |-d -d

re-enact ˌriɪn'ækt |-acted -'æktɪd

re-enforce ˌriɪn'fors, -'fɔrs; ES -'foəs, E+ -'fɔəs; |-s -ɪz |-d -t

re-engrave ˌriɪn'grev |-graved -'grevd

re-enter ri'ɛntɚ; ES -'ɛntə(r; |-ed -d |-ing -'ɛntərɪŋ, -'ɛntrɪŋ |-try -trɪ

re-establish ˌriə'stæblɪʃ |-es -ɪz |-ed -t

reeve n riv

reeve v riv |rove rov or reeved rivd

re-examination ˌriɪgˌzæmə'neʃən

re-examine ˌriɪg'zæmɪn |-d -d

re-export n ri'ɛksˌport, -ˌpɔrt; ES -ˌpoət, E+-ˌpɔət

re-export v ˌriɪks'port, -'pɔrt; ES -'poət, E+-'pɔət; |-ed -ɪd

refashion ri'fæʃən |-ed -d |-ing -ʃənɪŋ, -ʃnɪŋ

refection rɪ'fɛkʃən |-tory -tərɪ

refer rɪ'fɝ; ES -'fɜ(r, -'fɝ; |-red -d

referable 'rɛfrəbl̩, 'rɛfərə-, rɪ'fɝəbl̩; ES 'rɛfrə, -fərə-, -'fɜrə-, -'fɝə-

referee ˌrɛfə'ri |-d -d

reference 'rɛfrəns, 'rɛfərəns |-s -ɪz |-d -t

referendum ˌrɛfə'rɛndəm |-s -z |-da -də

referent 'rɛfrənt, 'rɛfərənt

referential ˌrɛfə'rɛnʃəl |-ly -ɪ

referrible rɪ'fɝəbl̩; ES -'fɜrə-, -'fɝə-

refill n 'riˌfɪl

refill ri'fɪl |-ed -d

refine rɪ'faɪn |-fined -'faɪnd |-ry -ərɪ, -rɪ

refit n ri'fɪt, 'riˌfɪt

refit v ri'fɪt |-ted -ɪd

reflect rɪ'flɛkt |-ed -ɪd |-ion -kʃən |-ive -ɪv

reflector rɪ'flɛktɚ; ES -'flɛktə(r

reflex n, adj 'riflɛks |-es -ɪz

reflex v rɪ'flɛks |-es -ɪz |-ed -t

reflexion rɪ'flɛkʃən |-xive -'flɛksɪv

refloat ri'flot |-ed -ɪd

reforest ri'fɔrɪst, -'fɑr-, -'fɒr-, -əst |-ed -ɪd

reforestation ˌrifɔrɪs'teʃən, -fɑr-, -fɒr-, -əs-

reform rɪ'fɔrm; ES -'fɔəm; |-ed -d

re-form 'f. anew' ˌri'fɔrm; ES -'fɔəm; |-ed -d

reformation ˌrɛfɚ'meʃən; ES ˌrɛfə-

re-formation 'f. anew' ˌrifɔr'meʃən; ES -fɔə-

reformatory rɪ'fɔrməˌtorɪ, -ˌtɔrɪ; ES -'fɔəmə-ˌtorɪ, E+-ˌtɔrɪ

refract rɪ'frækt |-ed -ɪd |-ction -kʃən

refractive rɪ'fræktɪv |-tory -tərɪ

refrain rɪ'fren |-frained -'frend

refrangibility rɪˌfrændʒə'bɪlətɪ

refrangible rɪ'frændʒəbl̩

refresh rɪ'frɛʃ |-es -ɪz |-ed -t

refrigerant rɪ'frɪdʒərənt

refrigerate rɪ'frɪdʒəˌret |-d -ɪd

refrigeration rɪˌfrɪdʒə'reʃən

refrigerator rɪ'frɪdʒəˌretɚ; ES -ˌretə(r

reft rɛft

refuel ri'fjuəl, -'frʊəl |-ed -d

refuge 'rɛfjudʒ |-s -ɪz

refugee ˌrɛfju'dʒi ('refuˌgee 'family)

refulgence rɪ'fʌldʒəns |-cy -ɪ |-ent -ənt

refund n 'riˌfʌnd

refund 'pay back' rɪ'fʌnd |-ed -ɪd

refund 'f. anew' ˌri'fʌnd |-ed -ɪd

refurbish ri'fɝbɪʃ; ES -'fɜ-, -'fɝ-; |-es -ɪz |-ed -t

refusal rɪ'fjuzl̩, -'frʊ-

refuse n, adj 'rɛfjus, -juz

refuse 'deny' rɪ'fjuz, -'frʊz |-s -ɪz |-d -d

re-fuse 'melt again,' 'replace fuse' ˌri'fjuz, -'frʊz |-s -ɪz |-d -d

refutation ˌrɛfju'teʃən

refute rɪ'fjut, -'frʊt |-d -ɪd

regain rɪ'gen |-gained -'gend

regal 'rigl̩ |-ly -ɪ

regale 'feast' rɪ'gel |-galed -'geld

regale 'prerogative' rɪ'geli

regalia rɪ'gelɪə, -ljə

regality ri'gælətɪ

Regan 'rigən

regard rɪ'gard; ES -'gɑːd, E+-'gaːd; |-ed -ɪd

regatta rɪ'gætə

regency 'ridʒənsɪ

regenerate n, adj rɪ'dʒɛnərɪt

regenerate v rɪ'dʒɛnəˌret |-rated -ˌretɪd

regeneration rɪˌdʒɛnə'reʃən, ˌridʒɛnə-

regent 'ridʒənt |-ship -ˌʃɪp

Reggie 'rɛdʒɪ

regicidal ˌrɛdʒə'saɪdl̩ ('regiˌcidal 'prince)

regicide 'rɛdʒəˌsaɪd

regime rɪ'ʒim, re-

regimen 'rɛdʒəˌmɛn, -mən

regiment n 'rɛdʒəmənt

regiment v 'rɛdʒəˌmɛnt |-ed -ɪd

regimental ˌrɛdʒə'mɛntl̩ |-ed -d |-ly -ɪ

regimentary ˌrɛdʒə'mɛntərɪ

|full fʊl |tooth tuθ |further 'fɝðɚ; ES 'fɜðə |custom 'kʌstəm |while hwaɪl |how haʊ |toy tɔɪ
|using 'juzɪŋ |fuse fjuz, frʊz |dish dɪʃ |vision 'vɪʒən |Eden 'idn̩ |cradle 'kredl̩ |keep 'em 'kipm̩

regimentation ˌrɛdʒəmɛnˈteʃən
Regina rɪˈdʒaɪnə |-nal -n|
Reginald ˈrɛdʒɪn|d
region ˈridʒən |-ed -d |-al -| |-ally -|ɪ
regionalism ˈridʒən|ˌɪzəm |-ist -ɪst
Regis ˈridʒɪs |-ˈs -ɪz
register ˈrɛdʒɪstə˞; ES -tə(r; |-ed -d |-ing
ˈrɛdʒɪstrɪŋ, -tərɪŋ
registrable ˈrɛdʒɪstrəb| |-strant -strənt
registrar ˈrɛdʒɪˌstrɑr, ˌrɛdʒɪˈstrɑr; ES -ɑ:(r,
E+-a:(r
registration ˌrɛdʒɪˈstreʃən |-stry ˈrɛdʒɪstrɪ
Regius, r- ˈridʒɪəs
regnal ˈrɛgnəl |-nancy -nənsɪ |-nant -nənt
regrant riˈgrænt; E+-ˈgrant, -ˈgrɑnt; |-ed -ɪd
regrate rɪˈgret |-grated -ˈgretɪd
regress n ˈrigrɛs |-es -ɪz
regress v rɪˈgrɛs |-es -ɪz |-ed -t
regression rɪˈgrɛʃən |-sive -ˈgrɛsɪv
regret rɪˈgrɛt |-ted -ɪd
regrettable rɪˈgrɛtəb| |-bly -blɪ
regular ˈrɛgjələ˞; ES ˈrɛgjələ(r
regularity ˌrɛgjəˈlærətɪ
regularize ˈrɛgjələˌraɪz |-rized -ˌraɪzd
regulate ˈrɛgjəˌlet |-d -ɪd |-tion ˌrɛgjəˈleʃən
regulatory ˈrɛgjələˌtorɪ, -ˌtɔrɪ; S -ˌtorɪ
regurgitate riˈgɝdʒəˌtet; ES -ˈgɝdʒ-, -ˈgɝdʒ-;
|-tated -ˌtetɪd
regurgitation rɪˌgɝdʒəˈteʃən, ˌrigɝdʒə-; ES
-ˌdʒ, -ˌdʒ-
rehabilitate ˌriəˈbɪləˌtet, ˌrihə- |-d -ɪd
rehabilitation ˌriəˌbɪləˈteʃən, ˌrihə-
Rehan ˈriən, ˈreən
rehash n ˈriˌhæʃ |-es -ɪz
rehash v riˈhæʃ |-es -ɪz |-ed -t
rehearsal rɪˈhɝs|; ES -ˈhɝs|, -ˈhɝs|
rehearse rɪˈhɝs; ES -ˈhɝs, -ˈhɝs; |-s -ɪz |-d -t
Rehoboam ˌriəˈboəm, ˌrihə-
Rehoboth US rɪˈhobəθ; Afr people ˈreəˌboθ,
ˈrehə-
Reich raɪk |-stag -sˌtɑg (Ger ˈraɪx, -sˌtɑk)
reichsmark ˈraɪksˌmɑrk; ES -ˌmɑ:k, E+
-ˌmɑ:k; (Ger ˈraɪxsˌmɑrk)
Reid rid
reign ren |reigned rend
Reikjavik ˈrekjəˌvik
Reilly ˈraɪlɪ
reimburse ˌriɪmˈbɝs; ES -ˈbɝs, -ˈbɝs; |-s -ɪz
|-d -t

Reims rimz |-ˈs -ɪz (Fr rɛ̃:s)
rein ren |reined rend
reincarnate ˌriɪnˈkɑrnet; ES -ˈkɑ:-, E+-ˈka:-;
|-d -ɪd
reincarnation ˌriɪnkɑrˈneʃən; ES -kɑ:-, E+
-ka:-
reindeer ˈrenˌdɪr; ES -ˌdɪə(r, S+-ˌdeə(r,
-ˌdjeə(r
reinforce ˌriɪnˈfors, -ˈfɔrs; ES -ˈfoəs, E+
-ˈfɔəs; |-s -ɪz |-d -t (ˈreinˌforced ˈconcrete)
Reinhardt, -hart ˈraɪnhɑrt; ES -hɑ:t
reinstate ˌriɪnˈstet |-d -ɪd
reinsure ˌriɪnˈʃʊr; ES -ˈʃʊə(r; |-d -d |-rance
-əns
reintegrate riˈɪntəˌgret |-d -ɪd
reintegration ˌriɪntəˈgreʃən, riˌɪntə-
reintroduce ˌriɪntrəˈdjus, -ˈdɪus, -ˈdus |-s -ɪz
|-d -t
reinvest ˌriɪnˈvɛst |-ed -ɪd
reinvigorate ˌriɪnˈvɪgəˌret |-d -ɪd
reinvigoration ˌriɪnˌvɪgəˈreʃən
reissue riˈɪʃʊ, -ˈɪʃju |-d -d
reiterate riˈɪtəˌret |-rated -ˌretɪd
reiteration riˌɪtəˈreʃən, ˌriɪtə-
reject n ˈridʒɛkt
reject v rɪˈdʒɛkt |-ed -ɪd |-ction -kʃən
rejoice rɪˈdʒɔɪs |-s -ɪz |-d -t
rejoin ˈreply' rɪˈdʒɔɪn |-ed -d |-der -də˞; ES
-də(r
rejoin ˈj. anew' ˌriˈdʒɔɪn |-ed -d
rejuvenate rɪˈdʒuvəˌnet, -ˈdʒɪu- |-d -ɪd |-tor
-tə˞; ES -tə(r
rejuvenation rɪˌdʒuvəˈneʃən, -ˌdʒɪu- |-nes-
cence -ˈnɛsns |-nescent -ˈnɛsnt
rekindle riˈkɪnd| |-d -d |-ling -dlɪŋ, -d|ɪŋ
relabel riˈleb| |-ed -d |-ing -b|ɪŋ, -blɪŋ
relapse rɪˈlæps |-s -ɪz |-d -t
relate rɪˈlet |-lated -ˈletɪd
relation rɪˈleʃən |-al -| |-ally -|ɪ
relative ˈrɛlətɪv |-tivity ˌrɛləˈtɪvətɪ
relax rɪˈlæks |-es -ɪz |-ed -t |-edly -ɪdlɪ
relaxation ˌrilæksˈeʃən
relay n, adj ˈrile, rɪˈle (ˈrelay ˌrace)
relay v ˈpass on' rɪˈle, ˈrile |-ed -d
relay v ˈl. anew, ˌriˈle |-laid -ˈled
release ˈfree(dom)' rɪˈlis |-s -ɪz |-d -t
re-lease ˈl. anew' ˌriˈlis |-s -ɪz |-d -t
relegate ˈrɛləˌget |-d -ɪd |-tion ˌrɛləˈgeʃən
relent rɪˈlɛnt |-ed -ɪd |-less -lɪs

Key: See in full §§3–47. bee bi |pity ˈpɪtɪ (§6) |rate ret |yet jɛt |sang sæŋ |angry ˈæŋ·grɪ
|bath bæθ; E baθ (§10) |ah ɑ |far fɑr |watch wɑtʃ, wɒtʃ (§12) |jaw dʒɔ |gorge gɔrdʒ |go go

relet ri'lɛt
relevance 'rɛləvəns |-cy -ɪ |-vant -vənt
reliability rɪˌlaɪə'bɪlətɪ
reliable rɪ'laɪəbļ |-bly -blɪ
reliance rɪ'laɪəns |-s -ɪz |-ant -ənt
relict n 'rɛlɪkt
relict adj rɪ'lɪkt |-ed -ɪd
relied rɪ'laɪd
relief rɪ'lif
relieve rɪ'liv |-d -d |-dly -ɪdlɪ
relievo rɪ'livo (It rilievo ri'ljɛːvo)
relight ri'laɪt |-ed -ɪd
religion rɪ'lɪdʒən |-gious -dʒəs
religiosity rɪˌlɪdʒɪ'ɑsətɪ; ES+-'ɒs-
relinquish rɪ'lɪŋkwɪʃ |-es -ɪz |-ed -t
reliquary 'rɛləˌkwɛrɪ
relique 'rɛlɪk, rɪ'lik
relish 'rɛlɪʃ |-es -ɪz |-ed -t
relive ri'lɪv |-d -d
reload ri'lod |-ed -ɪd
relocate ri'loket |-d -ɪd
reluctance rɪ'lʌktəns |-cy -ɪ |-ant -ənt
relume ri'lum, -'lɪum |-d -d
rely rɪ'laɪ |-lied -'laɪd
remain rɪ'men |-ed -d |-der -dɚ; ES -də(r
remake ri'mek |-made -'med
remand rɪ'mænd; E+-'mand, -'mɑnd; |-ed
    -ɪd
remark rɪ'mɑrk; ES -'mɑːk, E+-'maːk; |-ed
    -t |-able -əbļ |-bly -blɪ
re-mark 'm. anew' ˌri'mɑrk; ES see remark
    |-ed -t
remarry ri'mærɪ |-ied -d |-iage -dʒ
Rembrandt 'rɛmbrænt (Du -brant)
remediable rɪ'midɪəbļ |-bly -blɪ
remedial rɪ'midɪəl |-ly -ɪ
remedy 'rɛmədɪ |-ied -d |-diless -lɪs, rɪ-
    'mɛdəlɪs
remember rɪ'mɛmbɚ; ES -bə(r; |-ed -d |-ing
    -'mɛmbrɪŋ, -'mɛmbərɪŋ
remembrance rɪ'mɛmbrəns |-s -ɪz |-r -ɚ; ES
    -ə(r
Reményi 'rɛmɪnjɪ, 'rɛmenjɪ
remind rɪ'maɪnd |-ed -ɪd |-er -ɚ; ES -ə(r
Remington 'rɛmɪŋtən
reminisce ˌrɛmə'nɪs |-s -ɪz |-d -t
reminiscence ˌrɛmə'nɪsņs |-s -ɪz |-nt -sņt
remise rɪ'maɪz; fencing -'miz |-s -ɪz |-d -d
remiss rɪ'mɪs |-es -ɪz |-ed -t |-ible -əbļ

remission rɪ'mɪʃən |-sive -'mɪsɪv
remit rɪ'mɪt |-ted -ɪd |-tal -ļ |-tance -ņs
    |-tent -ņt
remnant, R- 'rɛmnənt
remodel ri'mɑdļ; ES+-'mɒdļ; |-ed -d |-ing
    -dlɪŋ, -dļɪŋ
remold ri'mold |-ed -ɪd
remonstrance rɪ'mɑnstrəns; ES+-'mɒn-; |-s
    -ɪz |-ant -ənt
remonstrate rɪ'mɑnstret; ES+-'mɒn-; |-d -ɪd
    |-tive -strətɪv
remonstration ˌrɪmɑn'streʃən, ˌrɛmən-; ES+
    -mɒn-
remora, R- 'rɛmərə
remorse rɪ'mɔrs; ES -'mɔəs; |-ful -fəl |-fully
    -fəlɪ
remote rɪ'mot |-tion -'moʃən
remould ri'mold |-ed -ɪd
remount ri'maʊnt |-ed -ɪd
remove rɪ'muv |-d -d |-dly -ɪdlɪ |-val -ļ
Remsen 'rɛmsņ, 'rɛmzņ
remunerate rɪ'mjunɚˌret, -'mɪu- |-d -ɪd |-tive
    -ˌretɪv, -rətɪv
remuneration rɪˌmjunɚ'reʃən, -ˌmɪu-
Remus 'riməs |-'s -ɪz
Renaissance ˌrɛnə'zɑns, -'sɑns, rɪ'nesņs |-s
    -ɪz (Fr rənɛ'sãːs)
renal 'rinļ
rename ri'nem |-d -d
Renan rɪ'næn (Fr rə'nã)
renascence, R- rɪ'næsņs |-s -ɪz |-nt -sņt
rencontre rɛn'kɑntɚ; ES -'kɑntə(r, -'kɒn-;
    (Fr rã'kõːtṛ)
rencounter rɛn'kaʊntɚ; ES -tə(r; |-ed -d
    |-ing -'kaʊntrɪŋ, -tərɪŋ
rend rɛnd |rent rɛnt
render 'rɛndɚ; ES -də(r; |-ed -d |-ing
    'rɛndrɪŋ, -dərɪŋ
rendezvous 'rɑndəˌvu, 'rɛn- |pl -vous -ˌvuz
    |-ed -d (Fr rãde'vu)
rendition rɛn'dɪʃən
renegade 'rɛnɪˌged |-d -ɪd
renege rɪ'nɪg, -'nig |-d -d
renew rɪ'nju, -'nɪu, -'nu |-ed -d |-edly -ɪdlɪ
Renfrew 'rɛnfru, -frɪu |-shire -ˌʃɪr, -ʃɚ; ES
    -ˌʃɪə(r, -ʃə(r
Reni 'renɪ (It 're:ni)
reniform 'rɛnəˌfɔrm, 'rinə-; ES -ˌfɔəm
renig rɪ'nɪg |-ged -d

rennet 'rɛnɪt |rennin 'rɛnɪn
Reno US 'rino; Italy 'reno (It 'rɛ:no)
renominate ri'nama,net; ES+-'nɒm-; |-d -ɪd
renomination ,rinamə'neʃən; ES+-nɒm-
renounce rɪ'naʊns |-s -ɪz |-d -t
renovate 'rɛnə,vet |-d -ɪd |-tor -ɚ; ES -ə(r
renovation ,rɛnə'veʃən
Renovo rɪ'novo
renown rɪ'naʊn |-ed -d |-edly -ɪdlɪ
Rensselaer 'rɛnslɚ; ES 'rɛnslə(r
rent rɛnt |rented 'rɛntɪd |rental 'rɛntl̩
renumber ri'nʌmbɚ; ES -bə(r; |-ed -d |ing
  -'nʌmbrɪŋ, -'nʌmbərɪŋ
renunciation rɪ,nʌnsɪ'eʃən, -,nʌnʃɪ-
renunciative rɪ'nʌnʃɪ,etɪv, -sɪ- |-tory -,torɪ,
  -,tɔrɪ; S -,torɪ
Renwick, James 'rɛnwɪk, Cumb+'rɛnɪk
reoccupation ,riakjə'peʃən; ES+-ɒk-
reoccupy ri'akjə,paɪ; ES+-'ɒk-; |-ied -d
reopen ri'opən, -'opm̩ |-ed -d |-ing -'opənɪŋ,
  -'opnɪŋ
reorder ri'ɔrdɚ; ES -'ɔədə(r; |-ed -d |-ing
  -drɪŋ, -dərɪŋ
reorganization ,riɔrgənə'zeʃən, -aɪ'z-; ES
  -əgən-
reorganize ri'ɔrgə,naɪz; ES -'ɔəgə,naɪz; |-s -ɪz
  |-d -d
rep rɛp |repped rɛpt
repack ri'pæk |-packed -'pækt
repaid 'paid back' rɪ'ped, 'paid again' ,ri-
repaint ri'pent |-ed -ɪd
repair rɪ'pɛr, -'pær; E -'pɛə(r, ES -'pæə(r;
  |-ed -d |-man -,mæn, -mən |-men -,mɛn,
  -mən |-able -əbl̩
reparable 'rɛpərəbl̩ |-bly -blɪ
reparation ,rɛpə'reʃən
repartee ,rɛpɚ'ti; ES ,rɛpə-; |-d -d
repass ri'pæs; E+-'pas, -'pɑs; |-es -ɪz |-ed -t
repast rɪ'pæst; E+-'past, -'pɑst; |-ed -ɪd
repatriate ri'petrɪ,et |-d -ɪd
repatriation ,ripetrɪ'eʃən, ri,petrɪ-
repay 'p. back' rɪ'pe |-paid -'ped
repay 'p. anew' ,ri'pe |-paid -'ped
repeal rɪ'pil |-ed -d
repeat rɪ'pit |-ed -ɪd
repel rɪ'pɛl |-led -d
repellant, -ent rɪ'pɛlənt |-ance, -ence -əns
repent rɪ'pɛnt |-ed -ɪd |-ance -əns |-ant -ənt
repeople ri'pipl̩ |-d -d |-ling -plɪŋ, -pl̩ɪŋ

repercussion ,ripɚ'kʌʃən; ES ,ripə-; |-ive
  -'kʌsɪv
repertoire 'rɛpɚ,twɑr, -,twɔr; ES 'rɛpə-
  ,twɑ:(r, -,twɔə(r; (Fr repɛr'twa:r)
repertory 'rɛpɚ,torɪ, -,tɔrɪ; ES 'rɛpə,torɪ,
  E+-,tɔrɪ
repetend 'rɛpə,tɛnd, ,rɛpə'tɛnd
repetition ,rɛpɪ'tɪʃən |-tious -ʃəs
repetitive rɪ'pɛtɪtɪv
rephrase ri'frez |-s -ɪz |-d -d
repine rɪ'paɪn |-pined -'paɪnd
replace 'restore' rɪ'ples |-s -ɪz |-d -t
replace 'p. anew' ,ri'ples |-s -ɪz |-d -t
replant ri'plænt; E+-'plant, -'plɑnt; |-ed -ɪd
replay ri'ple |-ed -d
replenish rɪ'plɛnɪʃ |-es -ɪz |-ed -t
replete rɪ'plit |-tion -'pliʃən
replevin rɪ'plɛvɪn |-ed -d |-vy -vɪ |-vied -vɪd
replica 'rɛplɪkə
replicate n, adj 'rɛplɪkɪt
replicate v 'rɛplɪ,ket |-cated -,ketɪd
reply rɪ'plaɪ |-plied -'plaɪd
report rɪ'port, -'pɔrt; ES -'poət, E+-'pɔət;
  |-ed -ɪd
reportorial ,rɛpɚ'torɪəl, -'tɔr-; ES ,rɛpə'tor-,
  E+-'tɔr-; |-ly -ɪ
repose rɪ'poz |-s -ɪz |-d -d |-dly -ɪdlɪ
repository rɪ'pazə,torɪ, -,tɔrɪ; S -,torɪ, ES+
  -'pɒz-
repossess ,ripə'zɛs |-es -ɪz |-ed -t |-ion -'zɛʃən
repousse Fr rəpu'se
repp rɛp |repped rɛpt
Repplier 'rɛplɪr; ES -lɪə(r
reprehend ,rɛprɪ'hɛnd |-ed -ɪd
reprehensible ,rɛprɪ'hɛnsəbl̩ |-bly -blɪ
reprehension ,rɛprɪ'hɛnʃən |-sive -sɪv
represent ,rɛprɪ'zɛnt |-ed -ɪd |-ative -ətɪv
representation ,rɛprɪzɛn'teʃən
repress rɪ'prɛs |-es -ɪz |-ed -t |-edly -ɪdlɪ
repressible rɪ'prɛsəbl̩ |-bly -blɪ
repression rɪ'prɛʃən |-sive -sɪv
repressure ri'prɛʃɚ; ES -'prɛʃə(r; |-d -d
reprieve rɪ'priv |-d -d
reprimand v 'rɛprə,mænd, ,rɛprə'mænd; E+
  -and, -ɑnd; |-ed -ɪd, n 'rɛprɪ,mand
reprint n 'ri,prɪnt
reprint v ri'prɪnt |-ed -ɪd
reprise rɪ'praɪz |-s -ɪz |-d -d |-sal -l̩
reproach rɪ'protʃ |-es -ɪz |-ed -t

Key: See in full §§3–47. bee bi |pity 'pɪtɪ (§6) |rate ret (§6) |yet jɛt |sang sæŋ |angry 'æŋ·grɪ
|bath bæθ; E baθ (§10) |ah ɑ |far fɑr |watch watʃ, wɒtʃ (§12) |jaw dʒɔ |gorge gɔrdʒ |go go

reproachable rɪˈprotʃəbl̩ |-bly -blɪ
reprobate ˈrɛprəˌbet |-d -ɪd
reprobation ˌrɛprəˈbeʃən
reproduce ˌriprəˈdjus, -ˈdɪus, -ˈdus |-s -ɪz
|-d -t
reproduction ˌriprəˈdʌkʃən |-tive -tɪv
reproof rɪˈpruf
re-proof ˈproof again' ˌriˈpruf |-ed -t
reproval rɪˈpruvl̩
reprove rɪˈpruv |-d -d |-vable -əbl̩ |-bly -blɪ
reptile ˈrɛptl̩, -tɪl |-lism -ˌɪzəm
reptilian rɛpˈtɪlɪən
republic rɪˈpʌblɪk |-an -ən |-anism -ənˌɪzəm
republication ˌripʌblɪˈkeʃən
republish riˈpʌblɪʃ |-es -ɪz |-ed -t
repudiate rɪˈpjudɪˌet, -ˈpɪu- |-d -ɪd
repudiation rɪˌpjudɪˈeʃən, -ˌpɪu-
repugnance rɪˈpʌɡnəns |-cy -ɪ |-nant -nənt
repulse rɪˈpʌls |-s -ɪz |-d -t
repulsion rɪˈpʌlʃən |-sive -sɪv
repurchase riˈpɝˈtʃəs, -ɪs; ES -ˈpɜtʃ-, -ˈpɝˈtʃ-;
|-s -ɪz |-d -t
reputability ˌrɛpjətəˈbɪlətɪ
reputable ˈrɛpjətəbl̩ |-bly -blɪ
reputation ˌrɛpjəˈteʃən
repute rɪˈpjut, -ˈpɪut |-d -ɪd
request rɪˈkwɛst |-ed -ɪd
requiem, R- ˈrikwɪəm, ˈrɛk-
requiescat ˌrɛkwɪˈɛskæt
require rɪˈkwaɪr; ES -ˈkwaɪə(r; |-d -d
requisite ˈrɛkwəzɪt |-tion ˌrɛkwəˈzɪʃən
requite rɪˈkwaɪt |-d -ɪd |-tal -l̩
reread pres riˈrid |past -read -ˈrɛd
re-recover ˌrirɪˈkʌvɚ; ES -ˈkʌvə(r
reredos ˈrɪrdɑs; ES ˈrɪədɑs, -dɒs; |-es -ɪz
re-refine ˌrirɪˈfaɪn |-d -d
re-revise ˌrirɪˈvaɪz |-s -ɪz |-d -d
reroute riˈrut, -ˈraut |-d -ɪd
rerun riˈrʌn |-ran -ˈræn |-run -ˈrʌn
Resaca rɪˈsɑkə
resale riˈsel (ˈriˌsale ˈprice)
resartus, R- rɪˈsɑrtəs; ES -ˈsɑːt-, E+-ˈsɑːt-
rescind rɪˈsɪnd |-ed -ɪd
rescission rɪˈsɪʒən, -ˈsɪʃən
rescript ˈriskrɪpt
rescue ˈrɛskju |-d -d
reseal riˈsil |-ed -d
research n ˈrisɝˈtʃ, rɪˈsɝˈtʃ; ES -ɜtʃ, -ɝˈtʃ;
|-es -ɪz

research v rɪˈsɝˈtʃ, ˈrisɝˈtʃ; ES -ɜtʃ, -ɝˈtʃ; |-es
-ɪz |-ed -t
reseat riˈsit |-ed -ɪd
resell riˈsɛl |-sold -ˈsold
resemblance rɪˈzɛmbləns |-s -ɪz
resemble rɪˈzɛmbl̩ |-d -d |-ling -blɪŋ, -bl̩ɪŋ
resend riˈsɛnd |-sent -ˈsɛnt
resent ˈobject to' rɪˈzɛnt |-ed -ɪd
resent ˈsent again' riˈsɛnt
reservation ˌrɛzɚˈveʃən; ES ˌrɛzə-
reserve rɪˈzɝˈv; ES -ˈzɜv, -ˈzɝˈv; |-d -d |-dly
-ɪdlɪ
re-serve ˈs. anew' ˌriˈsɝˈv; ES -ˈsɜv, -ˈsɝˈv;
|-d -d
reservoir ˈrɛzɚˌvɔr, ˈrɛzə-, -ˌvwɔr, -ˌvwɑr; ES
ˈrɛzəˌvɔə(r, -ˌvwɔə(r, -ˌvwɑ:(r;—ɚ becomes
ə in ˈrɛzəˌvɔr by dissimilation (§121).
reset n ˈrisɛt, riˈsɛt, v riˈsɛt
resettle riˈsɛtl̩ |-d -d |-ling -ˈsɛtl̩ŋ, -tl̩ɪŋ
reshape riˈʃep |-d -t |-d -t or -n -ən
reship riˈʃɪp |-ped -t
reside rɪˈzaɪd |-d -ɪd
residence ˈrɛzədəns |-cy -ɪ |-dent -dənt
residential ˌrɛzəˈdɛnʃəl |-ly -ɪ
residual rɪˈzɪdʒʊəl |-duary -dʒʊˌɛrɪ
residue ˈrɛzəˌdju, -ˌdɪu, -ˌdu
residuum rɪˈzɪdʒʊəm |-dua -dʒʊə
resign ˈgive up' rɪˈzaɪn |-ed -d |-edly -ɪdlɪ
re-sign ˈs. again' ˌriˈsaɪn |-ed -d
resignation ˌrɛzɪɡˈneʃən, ˌrɛs-
resilience rɪˈzɪlɪəns |-cy -ɪ |-ent -ənt
resin ˈrɛzn̩, -zɪn |-ous -əs
resist rɪˈzɪst |-ed -ɪd |-ance -əns |-ant -ənt
resistible rɪˈzɪstəbl̩ |-table -təbl̩ |-bly -blɪ
resold riˈsold
resole riˈsol |-soled -ˈsold
resolute ˈrɛzəˌlut, -ˌlɪut, ˈrɛzl̩ˌjut
resolution ˌrɛzəˈluʃən, -ˈlɪu-, -zl̩ˈjuʃən
resolve rɪˈzalv, -ˈzɒlv |-d -d |-dly -ɪdlɪ
resolvent rɪˈzalvənt, -ˈzɒlv-
resonance ˈrɛznəns |-s -ɪz |-cy -ɪ |-ant -ənt
resort rɪˈzɔrt; ES -ˈzɔət; |-ed -ɪd
re-sort ˈs. anew' ˌriˈsɔrt; ES -ˈsɔət; |-ed -ɪd
resound ˈecho' rɪˈzaund |-ed -ɪd
re-sound ˈs. anew' ˌriˈsaund |-ed -ɪd
resource rɪˈsors, ˈrisors, -ɔrs; ES -oəs, E
-ɔəs; |-s -ɪz
resourceful rɪˈsorsfəl, -ˈsɔrs-; ES -ˈsoəs-,
E+-ˈsɔəs-; |-ly -ɪ

|full fʊl |tooth tuθ |further ˈfɝˈðɚ; ES ˈfɜðə |custom ˈkʌstəm |while hwaɪl |how hau |toy tɔɪ
|using ˈjuzɪŋ |fuse fjuz, fɪuz |dish dɪʃ |vision ˈvɪʒən |Eden ˈidn̩ |cradle ˈkredl̩ |keep ˈem ˈkipm̩

respect rɪ'spɛkt |-ed -ɪd |-able -əb‖ |-bly -blɪ
|-ive -ɪv

respectability rɪˌspɛktə'bɪlətɪ

respell ri'spɛl |-ed -d *or* -spelt -'spɛlt

respiration ˌrɛspə'reʃən

respirator 'rɛspəˌretɚ; ES -ˌretə(r

respiratory rɪ'spaɪrəˌtorɪ, -ˌtɔrɪ; S -ˌtorɪ

respire rɪ'spaɪr; ES -'spaɪə(r; |-d -d

respite 'rɛspɪt |-d -ɪd

resplendence rɪ'splɛndəns |-cy -ɪ |-dent -dənt

respond rɪ'spɑnd; ES+-'spɒnd; |-ed -ɪd |-ent
-ənt

response rɪ'spɑns; ES+-'spɒns; |-s -ɪz

responsibility rɪˌspɑnsə'bɪlətɪ; ES+-ˌspɒns-

responsible rɪ'spɑnsəb‖; ES+-'spɒns-; |-bly
-blɪ

responsive rɪ'spɑnsɪv; ES+-'spɒns-

rest rɛst |-rested 'rɛstɪd

restate ri'stet |-stated -'stetɪd

restaurant 'rɛstərənt, -ˌrɑnt

restaurateur ˌrɛstərə'tɝ; ES -'tɜ(r, -'tɝ; (*Fr*
rɛstöra'tœ:r)

Restigouche ˌrɛstɪ'guʃ |-'s -ɪz

restitution ˌrɛstə'tjuʃən, -'tɪu-, -'tu-

restive 'rɛstɪv

restock ri'stɑk; ES+-'stɒk; |-ed -t

restoration ˌrɛstə'reʃən

restorative rɪ'storətɪv, -'stɔr-; S -'stor-

restore rɪ'stor, -'stɔr; ES -'stoə(r, E+-'stɔə(r;
|-d -d

restrain rɪ'stren |-ed -d |-edly -ɪdlɪ, -dlɪ

restraint rɪ'strent

restrict rɪ'strɪkt |-ed -ɪd

restriction rɪ'strɪkʃən |-tive -tɪv

restring ri'strɪŋ |-strung -'strʌŋ

result rɪ'zʌlt |-ed -ɪd |-ant -'zʌltn̩t

resume rɪ'zum, -'zɪum, -'zjum |-d -d

résumé ˌrɛzu'me, ˌrɛzju'me |-ed -d

resumption rɪ'zʌmpʃən |-tive -tɪv

resurface ri'sɝfɪs, -əs; ES -'sɜf-, -'sɝf-; |-s
-ɪz |-d -t

resurge rɪ'sɝdʒ; ES -'sɜdʒ, -'sɝdʒ; |-s -ɪz |-d
-d |-nce -əns |-ncy -ənsɪ |-nt -ənt

resurrect ˌrɛzə'rɛkt |-ed -ɪd |-ction -kʃən

resurvey *n* ri'sɝve, ˌrisɚ've; ES -'sɜ-, -'sɝ-,
ˌrisə-

resurvey *v* ˌrisɚ've; ES -sə've; |-ed -d

resuscitate rɪ'sʌsəˌtet |-d -ɪd

resuscitation rɪˌsʌsə'teʃən

ret rɛt |retted 'rɛtɪd

retail *n, adj* 'ritel

retail *v* 'ritel, '*repeat*'+rɪ'tel |-ed -d

retain rɪ'ten |-ed -d |-er -ɚ; ES -ə(r

retake *n* 'riˌtek

retake *v* ri'tek |-took -'tʊk |-taken -'tekən

retaliate rɪ'tælɪˌet |-d -ɪd |-tive -ɪv

retaliation rɪˌtælɪ'eʃən

retaliatory rɪ'tælɪəˌtorɪ, -ˌtɔrɪ; S -ˌtorɪ

retard rɪ'tɑrd; ES -'tɑ:d, E+-'tɑ:d; |-ed -ɪd

retardation ˌritar'deʃən; ES -tɑ:-, E+-tɑ:-

retch rɛtʃ |retch 'rɛtʃɪz |retched rɛtʃt

retell ri'tɛl |-told -'told

retention rɪ'tɛnʃən |-tive -tɪv

retentivity ˌriten'tɪvətɪ

retiarius ˌriʃɪ'ɛrɪəs, -'erɪəs |-'s -ɪz |-rii -rɪˌaɪ
|-ary 'riʃɪˌɛrɪ

reticence 'rɛtəsn̩s |-cy -ɪ |-cent -sn̩t

reticulate *adj* rɪ'tɪkjəlɪt, -ˌlet

reticulate *v* rɪ'tɪkjəˌlet |-lated -ˌletɪd

reticulation rɪˌtɪkjə'leʃən

reticule 'rɛtɪˌkjul, -ˌkɪul |-d -d

reticulum rɪ'tɪkjələm |-la -lə

retina 'rɛtn̩ə, -tɪnə |-s -z |-nae -tn̩ˌi, -tɪˌni

retinue 'rɛtn̩ˌju, -ˌɪu, -ˌu, -tɪˌnju, -ˌnɪu, -ˌnu
|-d -d

retire rɪ'taɪr; ES -'taɪə(r; |-d -d

re-tire '*change tires*' ˌri'taɪr; ES -'taɪə(r

retold ri'told

retook ri'tʊk

retort rɪ'tɔrt; ES -'tɔət; |-ed -ɪd

retouch ri'tʌtʃ |-es -ɪz |-ed -t

retrace '*t. back*' rɪ'tres |-s -ɪz |-d -t

re-trace '*t. again*' ˌri'tres |-s -ɪz |-d -t

retract rɪ'trækt |-ed -ɪd |-ile -‖, -ɪl

retractation ˌritræk'teʃən

retraction rɪ'trækʃən |-tive -tɪv

retread *tire* ˌri'trɛd |-ed -ɪd |*n* 'riˌtrɛd

retread, re-t- '*t. anew*' ri'trɛd |-trod -'trɑd
|-trodden -'trɑdn̩ *or* -trod -'trɑd; |ES+
-'trɒd(n̩)

retreat rɪ'trit |-ed -ɪd

retrench rɪ'trɛntʃ |-es -ɪz |-ed -t

retrial ri'traɪəl, -'traɪl

retribution ˌrɛtrə'bjuʃən, -'bɪu-

retributive rɪ'trɪbjətɪv |-tory -ˌtorɪ, -ˌtɔrɪ;
S -ˌtorɪ

retrieve rɪ'triv |-d -d |-al -‖

retroact ˌrɛtro'ækt |-ed -ɪd

retroaction ˌrɛtro'ækʃən |-tive -tɪv
retrocede ˌrɛtro'sid |-d -ɪd |-nce -ṇs |-nt -ṇt
retrocession ˌrɛtro'sɛʃən |-sive -'sɛsɪv
retroflex 'rɛtrəˌflɛks |-es -ɪz |-ed -t
retroflexion, -ction ˌrɛtrə'flɛkʃən
retrograde 'rɛtrəˌgred |-d -ɪd
retrogress v 'rɛtrəˌgrɛs, ˌrɛtrə'grɛs |-es -ɪz
  |-ed -t
retrogression ˌrɛtrə'grɛʃən |-sive -'grɛsɪv
retrospect 'rɛtrəˌspɛkt |-ed -ɪd
retrospection ˌrɛtrə'spɛkʃən |-tive -tɪv
retry ri'traɪ |-tried -'traɪd
return rɪ'tɝn; ES -'tɜn, -'tɝn; |-ed -d
retuse rɪ'tjus, -'tɪus, -'tus
Reuben 'rubɪn, 'rɪu-, -ən
reune ri'jun |-d -d |-nion -jən |-nioned -jənd
reunite ˌriju'naɪt |-d -ɪd
Reuter 'rɔɪtɚ; ES 'rɔɪtə(r; (Ger 'rɔytər)
revalue ri'vælju |-d -d |-uation ˌrivælju'eʃən
revamp ri'væmp |-ed -t
reveal rɪ'vil |-ed -d
reveille 'rɛvḷˌi, -ɪ, ˌrɛvḷ'i (Fr réveillez rɛvɛ'je)
revel 'rɛvḷ |-ed -d |-ing -vlɪŋ, -vḷɪŋ
revelation, R- ˌrɛvḷ'eʃən
reveler 'rɛvlɚ, 'rɛvḷɚ; ES -ə(r; |-lry -vḷrɪ
Revelstoke 'rɛvḷˌstok
revenge rɪ'vɛndʒ |-s -ɪz |-d -d
revenue 'rɛvəˌnju, -ˌnɪu, -ˌnu |-d -d
reverbatory rɪ'vɝbəˌtorɪ, -ˌtɔrɪ; ES -'vɝbə-
  ˌtorɪ, -'vɝb-, E+-ˌtɔrɪ—reduced from reverberatory by r-dissimilation (§121)
reverberate adj rɪ'vɝbərɪt, -ˌret; ES -'vɝb-,
  -'vɝb-
reverberate v rɪ'vɝbəˌret; ES -'vɝb-, -'vɝb-;
  |-d -ɪd
reverberation rɪˌvɝbə'reʃən; ES -ˌvɝb-,
  -ˌvɝb-
reverberatory rɪ'vɝbrəˌtorɪ, -bərə-, -ˌtɔrɪ; ES
  -'vɝbrəˌtorɪ, -'vɝb-, -bərə-, E+-ˌtɔrɪ
revere, R- rɪ'vɪr; ES -'vɪə(r, S+-'vɛə(r; |-d -d
reverence 'rɛvrəns, -vərəns |-s -ɪz |-d -t
reverend 'rɛvrənd, -vərənd, as a title+-rən
reverent 'rɛvrənt, 'rɛvərənt
reverential ˌrɛvə'rɛnʃəl |-ly -ɪ
reverie 'rɛvərɪ, 'rɛvrɪ
reverify ri'vɛrəˌfaɪ |-fied -ˌfaɪd
revers rə'vɪr, -'vɛr; ES -'vɪə(r, -'vɛə(r; (Fr
  rə'veːr)
reversal rɪ'vɝsḷ; ES -'vɝs-, -'vɝs-

reverse rɪ'vɝs; ES -'vɝs, -'vɝs; |-s -ɪz |-d -t
  |-dly -ɪdlɪ, -tlɪ
reversible rɪ'vɝsəbḷ; ES -'vɝs-, -'vɝs-; |-bly
  -blɪ
reversion rɪ'vɝʒən, -'vɝʃ-; ES -'vɝ-, -'vɝ-;
  |-al -ḷ |-ally -ḷɪ |-ary -ˌɛrɪ
revert rɪ'vɝt; ES -'vɝt, -'vɝt; |-ed -ɪd
revery 'rɛvərɪ, 'rɛvrɪ
revet rɪ'vɛt |-ted -ɪd
revictual ri'vɪtḷ |-ed -d
review rɪ'vju, -'vɪu |-ed -d
revile rɪ'vaɪl |-viled -'vaɪld
revise rɪ'vaɪz |-s -ɪz |-d -d
revision rɪ'vɪʒən |-al -ḷ |-ary -ˌɛrɪ
revisit ri'vɪzɪt |-ed -ɪd
revisory rɪ'vaɪzərɪ
revitalize ri'vaɪtḷˌaɪz |-s -ɪz |-d -d
revival rɪ'vaɪvḷ |-ism -ˌɪzəm |-ist -ɪst
revive rɪ'vaɪv |-d -d
revivify ri'vɪvəˌfaɪ |-fied -ˌfaɪd
revocable 'rɛvəkəbḷ |-bly -blɪ, cf irrevocable
revocation ˌrɛvə'keʃən
revokable rɪ'vokəbḷ, cf revocable
revoke rɪ'vok |-d -t
revolt rɪ'volt |-ed -ɪd
revolution, R- ˌrɛvə'luʃən, -'lɪu-, ˌrɛvḷ'juʃən
  |-ary -ˌɛrɪ |-ize -ˌaɪz |-izes -ˌaɪzɪz |-ized
  -ˌaɪzd
revolve rɪ'vɑlv, -'vɒlv |-d -d |-r -ɚ; ES -ə(r
revue rɪ'vju, -'vɪu (Fr rə'vy)
revulsion rɪ'vʌlʃən
reward rɪ'wɔrd; ES -'wɔəd; |-ed -ɪd
rewire ri'waɪr; ES -'waɪə(r; |-d -d
reword ri'wɝd; ES -'wɝd, -'wɝd; |-ed -ɪd
rework ri'wɝk; ES -'wɝk, -'wɝk; |-ed -t
rewrite ri'raɪt |-wrote -'rot |-written -'rɪtṇ
rex, R- rɛks |Rex's 'rɛksɪz |L pl reges 'ridʒiz
Reykjavik 'rekjəˌvik
Reynaldo rɪ'nældo
Reynard 'rɛnɚd, 'rɛnɚd; ES -nəd
Reynolds 'rɛnḷdz, 'rɛnḷz |-'s -ɪz
rhachitis rə'kaɪtɪs |-chitic -'kɪtɪk
Rhadamanthus ˌrædə'mænθəs |-'s -ɪz
Rhaetia 'rɪʃɪə, -ʃə |-n 'rɪʃən
Rhaeto-Romance 'ritoˌro'mæns |-manic
  -'mænɪk
rhapsodic ræp'sɑdɪk; ES+-'sɒd-; |-al -ḷ
  |-ally -ḷɪ, -ɪklɪ
rhapsodist 'ræpsədɪst |-dy -dɪ |-died -dɪd

|full fʊl |tooth tuθ |further 'fɝðɚ; ES 'fɝðə |custom 'kʌstəm |while hwaɪl |how haʊ |toy tɔɪ
|using 'juzɪŋ |fuse fjuz, fɪuz |dish dɪʃ |vision 'vɪʒən |Eden 'idṇ |cradle 'kredḷ |keep 'em 'kipṃ

rhapsodize 'ræpsəˌdaɪz |-s -ɪz |-d -d
Rhea, r- 'riə, *Tenn co.* re
Rheims rimz |-'s -ɪz (*Fr* rǣːs)
Rheingold 'raɪnˌgold
Rhemish 'rimɪʃ
Rhenish 'rɛnɪʃ
rhenium 'riniəm
rheostat 'riəˌstæt |-ic ˌriə'stætɪk
Rhesus, r- 'risəs |-sus' -səs
rhetoric 'rɛtərɪk |-rician ˌrɛtə'rɪʃən
rhetorical rɪ'tɔrɪkḷ, -'tɑr-, -'tɒr- |-ly -ɪ, -ɪklɪ
rheum rum, rɪum |-atism -əˌtɪzəm
rheumatic ru'mætɪk, rɪu- |-al -ḷ |-ally -ḷɪ, -ɪklɪ
rhinal 'raɪnḷ
Rhine raɪn |-land -ˌlænd
Rhinelander 'raɪnləndɚ; ES -də(r
rhinestone 'raɪnˌston
rhinitis raɪ'naɪtɪs
rhino 'raɪno
rhinoceros raɪ'nɑsərəs, -srəs; ES+-'nɒs-; |-'s -ɪz
rhizoid 'raɪzɔɪd |-zome -zom
rho ro
Rhoades rodz |-'s -ɪz
Rhoda 'rodə
Rhode Island rod'aɪlənd, ro'daɪ-
Rhodes rodz |-'s -ɪz |-dian -dɪən
Rhodesia ro'diʒɪə, -ʒə—*see* -sia
rhodium 'rodɪəm
rhododendron ˌrodə'dɛndrən |-s -z |-dra -drə
rhodomontade ˌradəman'ted, -'tad; ES+ˌrɒdəmɒn-; (*Fr* rɔ̃dɔ̃mɔ̃'tad)
rhodora, R- ro'dorə, -'dɔrə; S -'dorə
Rhoecus 'rikəs |-'s -ɪz
rhomb rɑmb, rʌm, rɒ- |-bus -mbəs
Rhone ron
rhotacism 'rotəˌsɪzəm
rhubarb 'rubarb, 'rɪu-; ES -bɑːb, E+-baːb
rhumb rʌm, rʌmb
rhumba 'rʌmbə (*Sp* 'rumba)
rhyme raɪm |rhymed raɪmd |-ster -stɚ; ES -stə(r
Rhyolite 'raɪəˌlaɪt
Rhys ris |Rhys's 'risɪz
rhythm 'rɪðəm, *less freq.* 'rɪðm̩
rhythmic 'rɪðmɪk |-al -ḷ |-ally -ḷɪ, -ɪklɪ
rhythmproof 'rɪðəmˌpruf ('rhythmˌproof 'ear)
Rialto, r- rɪ'ælto (*It* ri'alto)

rib rɪb |ribbed rɪbd
ribald 'rɪbḷd |-ry -rɪ
riband 'rɪbənd, 'rɪbən
ribband '*ribbon*' 'rɪbənd, 'rɪbən
ribband, rib-band *shipbuilding* 'rɪbˌbænd, 'rɪbənd, 'rɪbən
ribbon 'rɪbən |-ed -d
rice, R- raɪs |Rice's 'raɪsɪz
rich rɪtʃ |riches 'rɪtʃɪz |riched rɪtʃt
Richard 'rɪtʃɚd; ES 'rɪtʃəd; |-son -sn̩
Richelieu ˌrɪʃə'lu, -'lɪu (*Fr* riʃə'ljø)
Richland 'rɪtʃlənd
Richmond 'rɪtʃmənd
Richter 'rɪktɚ, 'rɪx-; ES -tə(r; (*Ger* 'rɪxtər)
rick rɪk |ricked rɪkt
Rickard 'rɪkɚd; ES 'rɪkəd; |-s -z
rickets 'rɪkɪts |-ty -tɪ
rickey 'rɪkɪ
ricksha, -shaw 'rɪkʃɔ
ricochet ˌrɪkə'ʃe, -'ʃɛt |-cheted -'ʃed |-chetted -'ʃɛtɪd
rid rɪd |rid rɪd *or* ridded 'rɪdɪd
ridable 'raɪdəbḷ |-bly -blɪ
Ridd rɪd
riddance 'rɪdn̩s |-s -ɪz
Riddell 'rɪdḷ, rɪ'dɛl
ridden 'rɪdn̩—'rɪdən *is seldom heard.*
riddle 'rɪdḷ |-d -d |-ling 'rɪdlɪŋ, 'rɪdḷɪŋ
ride raɪd |rode rod |ridden 'rɪdn̩
rideable 'raɪdəbḷ |-bly -blɪ
Rider, r- 'raɪdɚ; ES 'raɪdə(r
ridge rɪdʒ |ridges 'rɪdʒɪz |ridged rɪdʒd
ridgepole 'rɪdʒˌpol |-d -d
Ridgeway, -dgway 'rɪdʒˌwe
ridicule 'rɪdɪˌkjul, -ˌkɪul |-d -d
ridiculous rɪ'dɪkjələs
Ridley 'rɪdlɪ
Rienzi rɪ'ɛnzɪ |-zo -zo (*It* ri'ɛntsi, -tso)
rifacimento rɪˌfatʃɪ'mɛnto (*It* riˌfatʃi'mento)
rife raɪf
riffle 'rɪfḷ |-d -d |-ling 'rɪflɪŋ, 'rɪfḷɪŋ
riffraff 'rɪfˌræf
rifle 'raɪfḷ |-d -d |-ling 'raɪflɪŋ, 'raɪfḷɪŋ
rifleman 'raɪfḷmən |-men -mən
rift rɪft |rifted 'rɪftɪd
rig rɪg |rigged rɪgd
Riga 'rigə, *NY* 'raɪgə
Rigdon 'rɪgdən
Rigel 'raɪgḷ, 'raɪdʒəl

Key: See in full §§3–47. bee bi |pity 'pɪtɪ (§6) |rate ret |yet jɛt |sang sæŋ |angry 'æŋ·grɪ |bath bæθ; E baθ (§10) |ah ɑ |far fɑr |watch wɑtʃ, wɒtʃ (§12) |jaw dʒɔ |gorge gɔrdʒ |go go

right **raɪt** |righted **'raɪtɪd**
rightabout **'raɪtəˌbaʊt**
right-and-left **'raɪtn̩'lɛft**
right-angled **'raɪt'æŋɡld** ('right-ˌangled 'turn)
righteous **'raɪtʃəs**
rightful **'raɪtfəl** |-ly -ɪ
right-hand **'raɪt'hænd** ('right-ˌhand 'screw,
  'right-'hand ˌone)
right-handed **'raɪt'hændɪd**
right-of-way ˌraɪtəv'we, ˌraɪtə'we
rigid **'rɪdʒɪd** |-ity rɪ'dʒɪdətɪ
rigmarole **'rɪɡməˌrol** |-d -d |-lery -ərɪ, -rɪ
Rigoletto ˌrɪɡə'lɛto (It ˌrigo'lettо)
rigor **'rɪɡɚ**; ES **'rɪɡə(r**; |-ous -əs, -grəs
rigor mortis **'raɪɡɔr'mɔrtɪs, 'rɪɡɚ-**; ES
  'raɪɡɔə'mɔətɪs, 'rɪɡə-
Rig-Veda rɪɡ'vedə, -'vidə
Riis **'ris** |-'s -ɪz
Rijswijk **'raɪswaɪk**
Rikki-Tiki-Tavi ˌrɪkɪˌtɪkɪ'tevɪ, -'tɑvɪ
rile **raɪl** |riled raɪld |-y -ɪ
Riley **'raɪlɪ**
rill **rɪl** |rilled rɪld
rim **rɪm** |rimmed rɪmd
rime **raɪm** |rimed raɪmd |-ster -stɚ; ES -stə(r
Rimmon **'rɪmən**
Rimski-Korsakov **'rɪmskɪ'kɔrsəˌkɔf, -ˌkɒf;**
  ES **-'kɔəsə-**
rimy **'raɪmɪ**
Rinaldo rɪ'nældo
rind **raɪnd, raɪn**
rinderpest **'rɪndɚˌpɛst**; ES **'rɪndə-**
Rinehart **'raɪnhɑrt**; ES **-hɑ:t,** E+-ha:t
ring 'circle,' 'provide with a ring' rɪŋ |ringed
  rɪŋd or rung rʌŋ
ring 'sound' rɪŋ |rang ræŋ |rung rʌŋ
ringbolt **'rɪŋˌbolt**
ringdove **'rɪŋˌdʌv**
ringleader **'rɪŋˌlidɚ, -'lidɚ**; ES -də(r
ringlet **'rɪŋlɪt** |-ed -ɪd
ringside **'rɪŋˌsaɪd**
ringworm **'rɪŋˌwɝm**; ES -ˌwɜm, -ˌwɝm
rink **rɪŋk** |rinked rɪŋkt
rinse **rɪns** |rinses **'rɪnsɪz** |rinsed rɪnst
Rio de Janeiro **'riodədʒə'nɪro, -deʒə'nero**
  (Pg **'riʊðəʒa'neirʊ**)
Rio Grande US ˌriə'ɡrænd, ˌrio-, ˌraɪə-,
  ˌrio'ɡrændɪ; Nicar, Bol ˌrio'ɡrande; Braz
  ˌriʊ'ɡrandə

riot **'raɪət** |-ed -ɪd |-ous -əs
rip rɪp |ripped rɪpt
riparian rɪ'pɛrɪən, raɪ-, -'pær-, -'per-
ripe raɪp |riped raɪpt
ripen **'raɪpən, -pm̩** |-ed -d |-ing 'raɪpnɪŋ,
  -pənɪŋ
Ripley **'rɪplɪ**
Ripman **'rɪpmən**
Ripon **'rɪpən**
riposte, -st rɪ'post |-(e)d -ɪd
ripper **'rɪpɚ**; ES **'rɪpə(r**
ripple **'rɪpl̩** |-d -d |-ling 'rɪplɪŋ, 'rɪpl̩ɪŋ
riprap **'rɪpˌræp** |-ped -t
ripsaw **'rɪpˌsɔ** |-ed -d
Rip van Winkle ˌrɪpvæn'wɪŋkl̩, -vən-
rise **raɪz** |-s -ɪz |rose roz |risen **'rɪzn̩**—raɪs for
  the noun rise once had some currency, but
  evidently never prevailed. Both meaning and
  pronunciation come from the verb.
risibility ˌrɪzə'bɪlətɪ
risible **'rɪzəbl̩** |-bly -blɪ
risk **rɪsk** |risked rɪskt |-y -ɪ
risqué rɪs'ke (Fr ris'ke)
Rita **'ritə**
ritardando ˌritɑr'dændo, -'dɑn-; ES -tɑ:-
rite raɪt
Ritson **'rɪtsn̩**
Rittenhouse **'rɪtn̩ˌhaʊs** |-'s -ɪz
ritual **'rɪtʃʊəl** |-ly -ɪ |-ism -ˌɪzəm |-ist -ɪst
ritualistic ˌrɪtʃʊəl'ɪstɪk |-ally -l̩ɪ, -ɪklɪ
ritualless **'rɪtʃʊəllɪs**
rivage **'rɪvɪdʒ** |-s -ɪz
rival **'raɪvl̩** |-ed -d |-ing 'raɪvlɪŋ, -vl̩ɪŋ
rivaless **'raɪvlɪs** |-es -ɪz
rivalless **'raɪvl̩lɪs**
rivalry **'raɪvl̩rɪ**
rive raɪv |-d -d |-d -d or riven 'rɪvən
river 'who rives' **'raɪvɚ**; ES **'raɪvə(r**
river 'stream' **'rɪvɚ**; ES **'rɪvə(r**; |-side -ˌsaɪd
Rivers **'rɪvɚz**; ES **'rɪvəz**; |-'s -ɪz
Rives **rɪvz** |-'s -ɪz
rivet **'rɪvɪt** |-ed -ɪd
Rivett **'rɪvɪt**
Riviera ˌrɪvɪ'ɛrə (It ri'vjɛ:rɑ)
rivulet **'rɪvjəlɪt**
rix-dollar **'rɪksˌdɑlɚ**; ES **-ˌdɑlə(r, -ˌdɒl-**
roach rotʃ |-es -ɪz |-ed -t
road rod |-ed -ɪd; |N Engd+rɔd (§46)
roadbed **'rodˌbɛd**

|full fʊl |tooth tuθ |further **'fɝðɚ**; ES **'fɜðə** |custom **'kʌstəm** |while hwaɪl |how haʊ |toy tɔɪ
|using **'juzɪŋ** |fuse fjuz, fɪuz |dish dɪʃ |vision **'vɪʒən** |Eden **'idn̩** |cradle **'kredl̩** |keep 'em **'kipm̩**

Those words below in which the ɑ sound is spelt o are often pronounced with ɒ in E and S

roadhouse 'rod₁haʊs |-houses -₁haʊzɪz

roadstead 'rod₁stɛd

roadster 'rodstɚ; ES 'rodstə(r

roadway 'rod₁we

roam rom |roamed romd |-age -ɪdʒ

roan ron

roanoke ₁roə'nok

Roanoke 'roə₁nok, 'ronok

roar ror, rɔr; ES roə(r, E+rɔə(r; |-ed -d

roast rost |roasted 'rostɪd

roast beef 'rost'bif, 'ros'bif

rob, R- rab |-bed -d |-ber -ɚ; ES -ə(r

robbery 'rabrɪ, 'rabərɪ

robe rob |robed robd

Robert 'rabɚt; ES 'rabət

Roberta ro'bɝtə; ES -'bɝtə, -'bɝtə

Robeson *surname* 'robsn̩; *NC* 'rabəsn̩

Robespierre 'robzpjɛr, -pɪr; ES -pjɛə(r, -pɪə(r; (*Fr* rɔ̃bɛs'pjɛːr)

robin, R- 'rabɪn |-son -sn̩

robot 'robət, 'rab-, -bat

Rob Roy 'rab'rɔɪ

Robsart 'rabsart; ES 'rabsɑːt, E+-saːt

Robson 'rabsn̩

robust ro'bʌst |-ious -'bʌstʃəs ('ro₁bust 'boy)

roc rak

Rochambeau ₁roʃæm'bo (*Fr* rɔ̃ʃɑ̃'bo)

Rochdale 'ratʃdel

Rochelle ro'ʃɛl

Rochester 'ra₁tʃɛstɚ, 'ratʃɪstɚ; ES -tə(r

rochet 'ratʃɪt |-ed -ɪd

rock rak |rocked rakt

rockaway, R- 'rakə₁we

rock-bottom 'rak'batəm ('rock-₁bottom 'price)

rock-bound 'rak₁baʊnd, -'baʊnd

Rockefeller 'rakɪ₁fɛlɚ, 'rakə-; ES -₁fɛlə(r

rocket 'rakɪt |-ed -ɪd

Rockingham *Marquis* 'rakɪŋəm; *US* 'rakɪŋ₁hæm

Rockford 'rakfɚd; ES 'rakfəd

rock-garden 'rak₁gardn̩, -dɪn; ES -₁gɑːd-, E+-₁gaːd-

Rock Island 'rak'aɪlənd

rock-ribbed 'rak'rɪbd ('rock-₁ribbed 'hills)

rock salt 'rak'sɔlt

rockweed 'rak₁wid

rococo rə'koko (*Fr* rɔkɔ'ko, roko-)

rod rad |rodded 'radɪd

rode rod

rodent 'rodn̩t

rodeo 'rodɪ₁o, ro'deo (*Sp* ro'ðeo), *cf* roleo

Roderic, -ick 'radərɪk, 'radrɪk

Roderigo ₁radə'rigo

Rodin ro'dæn |-esque ₁rodæn'ɛsk (*Fr* ro'dæ̃)

rodman, R- 'radmən |-men -mən

Rodney 'radnɪ

Rodolph 'rodalf

rodomontade ₁radəman'ted, -'tad (*Fr* rɔdɔmɔ̃'tad)

roe, R- ro |roed rod

roebuck, R- 'ro₁bʌk

Roentgen 'rɛntgən (*Ger* 'rœntgən)

rogation ro'geʃən

rogatory 'ragə₁torɪ, -₁tɔrɪ; S -₁torɪ

Roger 'radʒɚ; ES 'radʒə(r; |-s -z |-s's -zɪz

rogerian, R- ro'dʒɪrɪən

Roget *Eng author* 'roʒe, ro'ʒe

rogue rog |rogued rogd |-ry -ərɪ |-guish -ɪʃ

roil rɔɪl, *'vex'*+ raɪl |-ed -d |-y -ɪ

roister 'rɔɪstɚ; ES 'rɔɪstə(r; |-ed -d |-ing 'rɔɪstrɪŋ, 'rɔɪstərɪŋ

roister-doister, R-D- 'rɔɪstɚ₁dɔɪstɚ; ES 'rɔɪstə₁dɔɪstə(r

Roland 'rolənd

role, rôle rol

roleo 'rolɪ₁o—*cf* rodeo

Rolfe ralf

roll rol |rolled rold

Rolla 'ralə

Rolle rol

rollick 'ralɪk |-ed -t

Rollin 'ralɪn |-s -z |-s's -zɪz

rolling-mill 'rolɪŋ₁mɪl

rolling-pin 'rolɪŋ₁pɪn

Rollo 'ralo, -ə

Rolls-Royce 'rolz'rɔɪs |-s -ɪz

Rölvaag 'rolvag, 'rɔlvɔg (*Norw* 'rœlvɔg)—*the American family prefer* 'rolvag.

roly-poly 'rolɪ₁polɪ ('roly'poly ₁one)

Romaic ro'me·ɪk

Romain ro'men (*Fr* rɔ'mæ̃)

romaine ro'men ('ro₁maine 'lettuce)

Roman 'romən |-ism -₁ɪzəm |-ist -ɪst

Romance ro'mæns ('Ro₁mance 'language)

romance *n* ro'mæns, rə-, 'romæns |-s -ɪz

romance *v* ro'mæns, rə- |-s -ɪz |-d -t

Key: See in full §§3–47.   bee bi |pity 'pɪtɪ (§6) |rate ret |yet jɛt |sang sæŋ |angry 'æŋ·grɪ |bath bæθ; E baθ (§10) |ah ɑ |far fɑr |watch watʃ, wɒtʃ (§12) |jaw dʒɔ |gorge gɔrdʒ |go go

Those words below in which the ɑ *sound is spelt* o *are often pronounced with* ɒ *in E and S*

Romanes roˈmɑnɪz |-es' -ˈmɑnɪz
Romanesque ˌromənˈɛsk (ˈRomanˌesque ˈstyle)
Romanic roˈmænɪk |-ally -ḷɪ, -ɪklɪ
romanize ˈromənˌaɪz |-s -ɪz |-d -d
Romanov ˈromɑˌnɔf, roˈmɑnɔf, -ɒf
Romansh, -sch roˈmænʃ, -ˈmɑnʃ
romantic roˈmæntɪk, rə- |-al -ḷ |-ally -ḷɪ, -ɪklɪ
romanticism roˈmæntəˌsɪzəm |-cist -sɪst
romanticize roˈmæntəˌsaɪz |-s -ɪz |-d -d
Romany, Romm- ˈrɑmənɪ
ɪomaunt, R- roˈmɑnt, -ˈmɔnt, -ˈmɒnt
Rome rom
Romeo ˈromɪˌo, ˈromjo
Romic ˈromɪk
Romney ˈrɑmnɪ, ˈrʌmnɪ—*The historical pron. is* ˈrʌmnɪ.
Romola ˈrɑmələ
romp ramp |romped rampt |-ers -ɚz; ES -əz
Romulus ˈrɑmjələs |-'s -ɪz
Ronald ˈrɑnḷd
Ronan ˈronən, ˈranən, ˈrɒn-
Roncesvalles ˈrɑnsəˌvælz (*Sp* ˌrɔnθesˈβaʎes)
Roncevaux *Fr* rõsˈvo
Ronceverte ˈrɑnsəˌvɝt; ES -ˌvɝt, -ˌvɝt
rondeau ˈrando, ranˈdo (*Fr* rõˈdo)
rondel ˈrandḷ, -dɛl
rondelle ranˈdɛl (*Fr* rõˈdɛl)
rondo ˈrando, ranˈdo
Rondout ˈrandaʊt
Roney ˈronɪ
Ronsard ˈrɑnsard, ranˈsard; ES -ɑːd (*Fr* rõˈsaːr)
Röntgen ˈrɛntgən (*Ger* ˈrœntgən)
ronyon, runnion ˈrʌnjən
rood, R- rud
roof ruf, rʊf |-ed -t—rʊf *is less freq. in the S.*
rooftree ˈrufˌtri, ˈrʊf-
rook rʊk |-ed -t |-ery -ərɪ |-eried -ərɪd
rookie, -y ˈrʊkɪ
room rum, rʊm |-ed -d |-ful -ˌfʊl |-fuls -ˌfʊlz
—rʊm *is frequent in all parts of the US, but apparently less so than* rum.
roommate ˈrumˌmet, ˈrʊm-
roorback, -ch ˈrʊrbæk; ES ˈrʊə-
Roosevelt ˈrozəˌvɛlt, ˈrozvɛlt, ˈrozəvḷt
roost rust |roosted ˈrustɪd
rooster ˈrustɚ, *less freq.* ˈrus-; ES -təˌr

root, R- rut, rʊt |-ed -ɪd—rʊt *is less freq. in the S.*
rootstalk ˈrutˌstɔk, ˈrʊt-
rootstock ˈrutˌstɑk, ˈrʊt-
Rootstown ˈrutsˌtaʊn, ˈruts-, *loc.* ˈrʊts-
rope rop |roped ropt |-walk -ˌwɔk |-py, -pey -ɪ
Roquefort ˈrokfɚt; ES -fət; (*Fr* rɔkˈfɔːr)
Rorke rork, rɔrk; ES roək, E+rɔək; *loc.*+ ˈrorək
rorqual ˈrɔrkwəl; ES ˈrɔək-
Rosa ˈrozə
Rosabel ˈrozəˌbɛl |-la ˌrozəˈbɛlə
rosace ˈrozes |-s -ɪz (*Fr* roˈzas)
rosacean roˈzeʃən |-ceous -ʃəs
Rosalind ˈrazlɪnd, ˈrɑzlɪnd—*in Shak.*+-aɪnd
Rosaline ˈrazḷɪn, -ˌaɪn, ˈrozḷˌin
Rosamond ˈrazəmənd, ˈrozə-
rosary ˈrozərɪ
Roscius ˈraʃɪəs |-'s -ɪz
Roscoe ˈrasko
Roscommon rasˈkamən
rose, R- roz |-s -ɪz |-d -d
roseate ˈrozɪɪt
Rosecrans ˈrozɪˌkrænz |-'s -ɪz
Roselle roˈzɛl
rosemary, R- ˈrozˌmɛrɪ, -ˈmærɪ
Rosencrantz ˈrozṇˌkrænts |-'s -ɪz
Rosenwald ˈrozṇˌwɔld
roseola roˈzɪələ
Roseto roˈzito
Rosetta roˈzɛtə
rosette roˈzɛt |-d -ɪd
Rosh Hashana ˈraʃhəˈʃɑnə, ˈroʃ-
Rosicrucian ˌrozəˈkruʃən, -ˈkrɪu- |-ism -ˌɪzəm
rosily ˈrozḷɪ, -zɪlɪ
rosin ˈrazṇ, ˈrazɪn |-ed -d
Rosinante ˌrazṇˈæntɪ
Ross, -sse rɑs, rɒs |-'s -ɪz
Rossetti roˈsɛtɪ, -ˈzɛtɪ
Rossillion roˈsɪljən, ru-, *in Shak.* Roˈsillion, Rosˈs-
Rossini roˈsinɪ (*It* rosˈsiːni)
Ross-shire ˈrɑsʃɪr, ˈrɒʃʃ-, ˈrɒ-, -ʃɚ; ES -ʃɪə(r, -ʃə(r
Rostand ˈrastænd, ˈrɒs- (*Fr* rõsˈtã)
roster ˈrastɚ; ES ˈrastə(r; |-ed -d |-ing ˈrastərɪŋ, -strɪŋ
rostral ˈrastrəl, ˈrɒs- |-ly -ɪ

|full fʊl |tooth tuθ |further ˈfɝðɚ; ES ˈfɝðə |custom ˈkʌstəm |while hwaɪl |how haʊ |toy tɔɪ
|using ˈjuzɪŋ |fuse fjuz, fɪuz |dish dɪʃ |vision ˈvɪʒən |Eden ˈidṇ |cradle ˈkredḷ |keep 'em ˈkipm̩

Those words below in which the ɑ *sound is spelt* o *are often pronounced with* ɒ *in E and S*

rostrum 'rɑstrəm, 'rɒs- |-s -z |-tra -trə

rosy 'rozɪ |rosied 'rozɪd

rot rɑt |rotted 'rɑtɪd

rota, R- 'rotə |-l -tḷ

rotacism 'rotəˌsɪzəm

Rotarian ro'tɛrɪən, -'tær-, -'ter-

rotary, R- 'rotərɪ

rotate 'rotet |-d -ɪd |-tion ro'teʃən

rote rot |roted 'rotɪd

rother 'rɑðɚ, 'rʌðɚ; ES -ðə(r

Rotherham 'rɑðərəm

Rotherhithe 'rɑðɚˌhaɪð; *loc.*+'rɛdrɪf; ES 'rɑðə-; *spelt* Rediff *1595*

Rothermel 'rɑðɚˌmɛl; ES 'rɑðə-

Rothesay 'rɑθsɪ, -se

Rothley 'roθlɪ

Rothschild 'rɑθtʃaɪld, 'rɑstʃ-, 'rɑθstʃ- (*Ger* 'roːtʃʃɪlt)

Rothwell 'rɑθwɛl, *loc.*+'roəl

rotogravure ˌrotəgrə'vjʊr, -'grevjɚ; ES -'vjʊə(r, -jə(r

rotor 'rotɚ; ES 'rotə(r

rotten 'rɑtṇ |-ness 'rɑtṇnɪs

rotten-egg v ˌrɑtṇ'ɛg |-ed -d

Rotterdam 'rɑtɚˌdæm; ES 'rɑtə-

rotund ro'tʌnd |-ed -ɪd ('roˌtund 'style)

rotunda ro'tʌndə |-dity -tɪ

rouble 'rubḷ

roué ru'e

Rouen ru'ɑn, ru'ɑ̃ (*Fr* rwɑ̃)

rouge ruʒ |-s -ɪz |-d -d

Rougemont 'ruʒmɑnt

rough rʌf |roughed rʌft

rough-and-ready 'rʌfṇ'rɛdɪ

rough-and-tumble 'rʌfṇ'tʌmbḷ

roughcast 'rʌfˌkæst; E+-ˌkast, -ˌkɑst

roughdry adj 'rʌfˌdraɪ

roughdry v ˌrʌf'draɪ |-dried -'draɪd

roughen 'rʌfən |-ed -d |-ing 'rʌfənɪŋ, -fnɪŋ

roughhew ˌrʌf'hju, -'hɪu |-ed -d |-ed -d *or* -n -n

roughhouse n 'rʌfˌhaʊs

roughhouse v 'rʌfˌhaʊs |-s -ˌhaʊsɪz |-d -ˌhaʊst

roughneck 'rʌfˌnɛk

roughrider 'rʌfˌraɪdɚ; ES -ˌraɪdə(r

roughshod 'rʌf'ʃɑd; ES+-'ʃɒd; ('rough,shod 'nag)

roulade ru'lɑd |-d -ɪd

roulette ru'lɛt

Roum rum

Roumania ru'menɪə |-n -n

rouncy 'raʊnsɪ

round raʊnd |-ed -ɪd

roundabout n, adj 'raʊndəˌbaʊt

round about adv, prep 'raʊndə'baʊt ('round aˌbout 'town)

roundel 'raʊndḷ |-ay 'raʊndəˌle, -dḷˌe

roundhead, R- 'raʊndˌhɛd

roundhouse 'raʊndˌhaʊs |-ses -zɪz

roundness 'raʊndnɪs, 'raʊnnɪs

round-shouldered 'raʊnd'ʃoldɚd, 'raʊn-; ES -dəd

roundup 'raʊndˌʌp

roup rup

Rourke rork, rɔrk; ES roək, E+rɔək

rouse n raʊz, raʊs *spelt* rouce *in Shak.*

rouse v raʊz |rouses 'raʊzɪz |roused raʊzd

Rouse raʊs |-'s -ɪz

Rouses Point 'raʊsɪz'pɔɪnt

Rousillon, Rouss- ro'sɪljən, ru- (*Fr* rusi'jõ), *in Shak.* Ro'sillion, Ros's-

Rousseau ru'so |-ism -ɪzəm

roustabout 'raʊstəˌbaʊt |-ed -ɪd

rout raʊt |routed ˌraʊtɪd

route rut, raʊt |-d -ɪd

routine ru'tin |-d -d ('rouˌtine 'work)

Routledge 'rʌtlɪdʒ, 'raʊt- |-'s -ɪz

rove past of reeve rov

rove v rov |roved rovd

row n, v '*brawl*' raʊ |rowed raʊd

row n, v with oars ro |rowed rod

row n, v '*rank*' ro |rowed rod

rowan tree 'roən, 'raʊən

rowan '*tuft of wool*' 'raʊən

Rowan Stephen 'roən, Ky, NC ro'æn

rowboat 'roˌbot

Rowe ro

rowel 'raʊəl |-ed -d

rowen 'raʊən

Rowena ro'inə, rə'winə

rower '*disturber*,' '*napper*' 'raʊɚ, '*oarsman*' 'roɚ; ES -ə(r

Rowland 'rolənd

Rowlesburg 'rolzbɝg; ES -bɝg, -bɝg

Rowley 'raʊlɪ, 'rolɪ

rowlock 'roˌlɑk, 'rʌlək

Roxana raks'ænə; ES+rɒks-
Roxburgh, -ghe 'raksˌbɝo, -ə; ES -ˌbɝr-,
-ˌbʌr-, -ˌbɝ-, 'rɒks-, *Brit* 'rɒksbrə |-shire
-ˌʃɪr, -ʃɝ; ES -ˌʃɪə(r, -ʃə(r
Roxbury 'raksˌbɛrɪ, -bərɪ; ES+'rɒks-
Roy rɔɪ
royal 'rɔɪəl, 'rɔjəl |-ism -ˌɪzəm |-ist -ɪst
Royalton 'rɔɪəltən, 'rɔjəltən
royalty 'rɔɪəltɪ, 'rɔjəltɪ
Royce rɔɪs |-'s -ɪz
rub rʌb |rubbed rʌbd
rub-a-dub 'rʌbəˌdʌb, ˌrʌbə'dʌb
Rubáiyát ˌrubaɪ'jat, 'rubaɪˌjat, ˌrubɪ'jat
rubato ru'bato
rubber 'rʌbɝ; ES -bə(r; |-ed -d |-ing
'rʌbərɪŋ, 'rʌbrɪŋ
rubberize 'rʌbəˌraɪz |-s -ɪz |-d -d
rubberneck 'rʌbɝˌnɛk; ES 'rʌbə-; |-ed -t
rubber-stamp *adj* 'rʌbɝ'stæmp; ES 'rʌbə-;
('rubber-ˌstamp 'vote)
rubber-stamp *v* ˌrʌbɝ'stæmp; ES ˌrʌbə-;
|-ed -t
rubbish 'rʌbɪʃ
rubble 'rʌbļ |-d -d |-ling -bļɪŋ, -blɪŋ
rubbly 'rʌblɪ
Rube, r- rub, rɪub
Rubens 'rubɪnz, 'rɪu-, -ənz |-'s -ɪz
rubescence ru'bɛsn̩s, rɪu- |-scent -sn̩t
Rubicon 'rubɪˌkan, 'rɪu-; ES+-ˌkɒn
rubicund 'rubəˌkʌnd, 'rɪu-
rubicundity ˌrubə'kʌndətɪ, ˌrɪu-
rubidium ru'bɪdɪəm, rɪu-
rubied 'rubɪd, 'rɪu-
Rubinstein 'rubɪnˌstaɪn, 'rɪu-
ruble 'rubļ
rubric 'rubrɪk, 'rɪu- |-ked -t |-al -ļ |-ally -ļɪ,
-ɪklɪ
rubricate *adj* 'rubrɪkɪt, 'rɪu-, -ˌket
rubricate *v* 'rubrɪˌket, 'rɪu- |-d -ɪd
ruby, R- 'rubɪ, 'rɪu- |-ied -d
ruche ruʃ, rɪuʃ |-s -ɪz |-d -t (*Fr* ryʃ)
ruck rʌk |rucked rʌkt
ruction 'rʌkʃən
Rudbeckia rʌd'bɛkɪə
rudder 'rʌdɝ; ES 'rʌdə(r; |-ed -d
Ruddigore, Ruddy- 'rʌdɪˌgor, -ˌgɔr; ES
-ˌgoə(r, E+-ˌgɔə(r
ruddle 'rʌdļ |-d -d |-ling 'rʌdļɪŋ, 'rʌdlɪŋ
ruddleman 'rʌdļmən |-men -mən

ruddy 'rʌdɪ
rude rud, rɪud
rudiment 'rudəmənt, 'rɪudə-
rudimental ˌrudə'mɛntļ, ˌrɪu- |-tary -tərɪ, -trɪ
Rudolf, -lph 'rudalf, 'rɪu-, -dɒlf
Rudyard 'rʌdjɝd, 'rʌdʒɝd; ES -əd
rue ru, rɪu |-d -d |-ful -fəl |-fully -fəlɪ
ruff rʌf |ruffed rʌft
ruffian 'rʌfɪən, -fjən |-ism -ˌɪzəm
ruffle 'rʌfļ |-d -d |-ling 'rʌflɪŋ, 'rʌfļɪŋ
ruffly 'rʌflɪ
rufous 'rufəs, 'rɪu-
Rufus, r- 'rufəs, 'rɪu- |-'s -ɪz
rug rʌg |rugged '*provided with rugs*' rʌgd
Rugbeian rʌg'bian
Rugby 'rʌgbɪ
rugged '*rough*' 'rʌgɪd
Ruhr rur; ES ruə(r; (*Ger* ruːr)
ruin 'ruɪn, 'rɪuɪn |-ed -d |-ous -əs
ruinate 'ruɪnˌet, 'rɪu- |-ated -ˌetɪd
ruination ˌruɪn'eʃən, ˌrɪu-
rule rul, rɪul |-d -d |-rship -ɝˌʃɪp; ES -əˌʃɪp
rum *liquor* rʌm, *dye* rum
Rum Cum
Rumania ru'menɪə |-n -n
rumba 'rʌmbə (*Sp* 'rumba)
rumble 'rʌmbļ |-d -d |-ling 'rʌmblɪŋ, -bļɪŋ
rumen 'rumɪn, 'rɪu-, -mən |-mina -ə
Rumford 'rʌmfɝd; ES 'rʌmfəd
Rumina ru'maɪnə, rɪu-
ruminant 'rumənənt, 'rɪu-
ruminate 'ruməˌnet, 'rɪu- |-d -ɪd |-tive -ɪv
rumination ˌrumə'neʃən, ˌrɪu-
rummage 'rʌmɪdʒ |-s -ɪz |-d -d
rumor 'rumɝ, 'rɪumɝ; ES -mə(r; |-ed -d
rump rʌmp |rumped rʌmpt
rumple 'rʌmpļ |-d -d |-ling 'rʌmplɪŋ, -pļɪŋ
rumpus 'rʌmpəs |-es -ɪz
run rʌn |ran ræn |run rʌn |running 'rʌnɪŋ
runabout 'rʌnəˌbaut
runagate 'rʌnəˌget
runaway 'rʌnəˌwe
runcinate *adj* 'rʌnsɪnɪt, -ˌnet
rundle 'rʌndļ |-d -d
run-down 'rʌn'daun ('run-ˌdown 'health)
rune run, rɪun |-d -d
rung *from* ring rʌŋ
rung *of ladder* rʌŋ |runged rʌŋd
runic 'runɪk, 'rɪu- |-ally -ļɪ, -ɪklɪ

|full fʊl |tooth tuθ |further 'fɝðɝ; ES 'fɝðə |custom 'kʌstəm |while hwaɪl |how hau |toy tɔɪ
'using 'juzɪŋ |fuse fjuz, fɪuz |dish dɪʃ |vision 'vɪʒən |Eden 'idn̩ |cradle 'kredļ |keep 'em 'kipm̩

runnel 'rʌnl̩
Runnemede 'rʌnɪ‚mid
runner 'rʌnɚ; ES 'rʌnə(r; |-ed -d
runnion 'rʌnjən
Runnymede 'rʌnɪ‚mid
runt rʌnt |runted 'rʌntɪd
runway 'rʌn‚we
rupee ru'pi
Rupert 'rupɚt, 'rɪu-; ES -pət
rupture 'rʌptʃɚ; ES -tʃə(r; |-d -d |-ring
   -tʃərɪŋ, -tʃrɪŋ
rural 'rurəl, 'rɪurəl |-ly -ɪ |-ism -‚ɪzəm
Ruritania ‚rurə'tenɪə, ‚rɪu- |-n -n
ruse ruz, rɪuz |-s -ɪz (Fr ry:z)
rush, R- rʌʃ |-es -ɪz |-ed -t |-ville -vɪl
Rushworth 'rʌʃwɚθ; ES 'rʌʃwəθ
rusk rʌsk |rusked rʌskt
Ruskin 'rʌskɪn
Russ rʌs |-'s -ɪz
Russell 'rʌsl̩ |-ville -‚vɪl; S+-vl̩
russet 'rʌsɪt
Russia 'rʌʃə |-n -n
Russo-Japanese 'rʌso‚dʒæpə'niz
rust rʌst |rusted 'rʌstɪd
Rustam, -tem 'rʌstəm
rustic 'rʌstɪk |-al -l̩ |-ally -l̩ɪ |-ly -lɪ
rusticate 'rʌstɪ‚ket |-cated -‚ketɪd
rustication ‚rʌstɪ'keʃən
rusticity rʌs'tɪsətɪ
rustle 'rʌsl̩ |-d -d |-ling 'rʌslɪŋ, 'rʌsl̩ɪŋ

rustler 'rʌslɚ; ES 'rʌslə(r
Rustum 'rʌstəm
rusty 'rʌstɪ
rut rʌt |rutted 'rʌtɪd
rutabaga ‚rutə'begə, -'bɛgə
Rutgers 'rʌtgɚz; ES 'rʌtgəz; |-'s -ɪz
ruth, R- ruθ, rɪuθ
Ruthene ru'θin, rɪu- |-nia -nɪə |-nian -nɪən
ruthenium ru'θinɪəm, rɪu-
Rutherford 'rʌðɚfɚd; ES 'rʌðəfəd; |-ton -tən
Rutherfurd 'rʌðɚfɚd; ES 'rʌðəfəd
ruthful 'ruθfəl, 'rɪuθ- |-ly -ɪ
ruthless 'ruθlɪs, 'rɪuθ-
Ruthven 'ruθvən (Sc 'rʌθvən, 'rɪvən)
Ruthwell 'rʌðwəl, 'rʌθ-, Sc+'rɪvl̩
Rutland 'rʌtlənd |-shire -‚ʃɪr, -ʃɚ; ES -‚ʃɪə(r,
   -ʃə(r
Rutledge 'rʌtlɪdʒ |-'s -ɪz
Ruud rud
-ry unstressed ending -rɪ, -ri. For the sound of
   the vowel, see -y.
Ryan 'raɪən
Rydal Mount 'raɪdl̩'maunt
Ryder 'raɪdɚ; ES 'raɪdə(r
rye, R- raɪ
Ryerson 'raɪɚ‚sn̩; ES 'raɪ·ə-
Rylstone 'rɪlstən, 'rɪlz-
Rymer 'raɪmɚ; ES 'raɪmə(r
ryot 'raɪət
Ryswick 'raɪswɪk, 'rɪz-

S

S, s letter ɛs |pl S's, Ss, poss S's 'ɛsɪz
-s pl, poss, & 3 sg ending, see -es
's abbr. spelling of has, is, us, as in he's hiz,
   she's ʃiz, it's ɪts, there's ðɛrz, ðɛəz, let's
   lɛts, this's a fine day ðɪs: ə faɪn de
-'s possessive ending, see §§87–88.
Saar sɑr; ES sɑ:(r, E+sɑ:r; (Ger zɑ:r, Fr
   sa:r)
Saarbrücken Ger 'zɑ:r‚brykən
Sabaoth 'sæbɪ‚ɑθ, -‚ɒθ, -‚ɔθ
Sabatini ‚sæbə'tini (It ‚saba'ti:ni)
Sabbatarian ‚sæbə'tɛrɪən, -'tær-, -'ter-
Sabbath 'sæbəθ |Sabbaths 'sæbəθs
sabbatical, S- sə'bætɪk |-ly -ɪ, -ɪklɪ

saber, -bre 'sebɚ; ES 'sebə(r; |-ed, -d -d |-ing,
   -bring -brɪŋ, -bərɪŋ
saber-toothed 'sebɚ‚tuθt, -‚tuðd; ES 'sebə-
Sabine people 'sebaɪn, places sə'bin
sable 'sebl̩ |sabled 'sebl̩d
sabot 'sæbo, 'sæbət (Fr sa'bo)
sabotage 'sæbə‚tɑʒ, 'sæbətɪdʒ (Fr sabö'ta:ʒ)
Sabrina sə'braɪnə
sac sæk
Sac sæk, sɔk=Sauk |Sac City Ia sɔk
saccharin 'sækərɪn
saccharine n 'sækərɪn, -‚rin; adj -‚raɪn, -rɪn
saccule 'sækjul
sacerdotal ‚sæsɚ'dotl̩; ES ‚sæsə-; |-ly -ɪ

sachem ˈsetʃəm
sachet sæˈʃe (*Fr* saˈʃɛ)
Sacheverell səˈʃɛvərəl
sack sæk |sacked sækt
sackbut ˈsækˌbʌt
sackcloth ˈsækˌklɔθ, -ˌklɒθ—*see* cloth
sackful ˈsækˌfʊl |-s -z
Saco ˈsɔko
sacque sæk
sacral ˈsekrəl
sacrament ˈsækrəmənt
sacramental ˌsækrəˈmɛntl̩ |-ly -ɪ |-ism ˌɪzəm
    |-ist -ɪst
sacramentarian ˌsækrəmɛnˈtɛrɪən, -ˈter-
Sacramento ˌsækrəˈmɛnto
sacred ˈsekrɪd
sacrifice *n*, *v* ˈsækrəˌfaɪs, -ˌfaɪz |-s -ɪz |-d
    -ˌfaɪst, -ˌfaɪzd—*The pron. with* z *is now less*
    frequent.
sacrificial ˌsækrəˈfɪʃəl |-ly -ɪ
sacrilege ˈsækrəlɪdʒ |-s -ɪz
sacrilegious ˌsækrɪˈlɪdʒəs, -ˈlidʒ- —*British*
    and American ˌsækrɪˈlɪdʒəs *is probably due*
    to the analogy of ˈsækrəlɪdʒ *and the unre-*
    lated rɪˈlɪdʒəs.
sacring ˈsekrɪŋ
sacristan ˈsækrɪstən |sacristy ˈsækrɪstɪ
sacrosanct ˈsækroˌsæŋkt
sacrum ˈsekrəm |-ra -rə
sad sæd
sadden ˈsædn̩ |-ed -d |-ing ˈsædn̩ɪŋ, ˈsædnɪŋ
saddle ˈsædl̩ |-d -d |-ling ˈsædl̩ɪŋ, ˈsædlɪŋ
saddlebag ˈsædl̩ˌbæg |-ged -d
saddlebow ˈsædl̩ˌbo
saddleless ˈsædl̩lɪs
saddler, S- ˈsædlɚ; ES ˈsædlə(r
Sadducee ˈsædʒəˌsi, ˈsædjʊ-
sadiron ˈsædˌaɪɚn; ES -ˌaɪ·ən
sadism ˈsædɪzəm, ˈsed- |-ist -ɪst
sadistic sæˈdɪstɪk, se- |-ally -ļɪ, -ɪklɪ
safari səˈfɑrɪ
safe sef
safeblower ˈsefˌbloɚ; ES -ˌblo·ə(r
safe-conduct ˈsefˈkɑndʌkt; ES+-ˈkɒn-
safeguard ˈsefˌgɑrd; ES -ˌgɑːd, E+-ˌgɑːd;
    |-ed -ɪd
safekeeping ˈsefˈkipɪŋ
safety ˈseftɪ
safety-pin ˈseftɪˌpɪn

safety-valve ˈseftɪˌvælv
safflower ˈsæˌflaʊɚ, -ˌflaʊr; ES -ˌflaʊ·ə(r,
    -ˌflaʊə(r
saffron ˈsæfrən, ˈsæfən; ES -frən, -fən; *cf*
    apron
sag sæg |sagged sægd
saga ˈsɑgə
sagacious səˈgeʃəs, se- |-gacity səˈgæsətɪ
Sagadahoc ˈsægədɪˌhɑk, -ˌhɒk
sagamore, S- ˈsægəˌmor, -ˌmɔr; ES -ˌmoə(r,
    E+-ˌmɔə(r
sage sedʒ |sages ˈsedʒɪz |-d -d |-brush -ˌbrʌʃ
Saghalien ˌsægəˈlin, səˈgɑlɪən=Sakhalin
Saginaw ˈsægəˌnɔ
Sagitta, s- səˈdʒɪtə |*pl & gen sg* -tae -ti
Sagittarius ˌsædʒɪˈtɛrɪəs, -ˈter- |*gen* -rii -rɪˌaɪ
sago ˈsego
Saguache səˈwɑtʃ, -ˈwɒtʃ |-'s -ɪz (*Am Sp*
    saˈwɑtʃe)=Sawatch
saguaro səˈgwɑro, -ˈwɑro
Saguenay ˌsægəˈne
Sahara səˈhɛrə, -ˈherə, -ˈhɑrə
sahib, S- ˈsɑ·ɪb, ˈsɑhɪb
said sɛd, *unstressed* səd (said he səd ˈhi)
Saigon ˌsɑ·iˈgon, saɪˈgon (*Fr* sa·iˈgõ)
sail sel |sailed seld |-boat -ˌbot
sailcloth ˈselˌklɔθ, -ˌklɒθ, *see* cloth
sailer ˈselɚ; ES ˈselə(r
sailless ˈsellɪs
sailor ˈselɚ; ES ˈselə(r
sainfoin ˈsenfɔɪn
saint, S- sent—*Unstressed forms* sɪnt, sənt,
    sn̩t, sɪn, sən, sn̩ *are chiefly British. For*
    additional names in Saint-, St.- *see the sec-*
    ond part of the name.
Saint Agnes's Eve ˈægnɪsɪz (*in Keats* St.
    Agnes' ˈægnɪs)
Saint Albans ˈɔlbənz |-'s -ɪz
Saint Asaph ˈæsəf, ˈesəf, ˈesæf
Saint Augustine *ch. father, missionary* ˈɔgəs-
    ˌtin, əˈgʌstɪn, ɔ-; *Fla city* ˈɔgəsˌtin
Saint Bernard *La, O* ˈbɝnəd; ES ˈbɝnəd,
    ˈbɝnəd; *mt. pass, dog* bəˈnɑrd, bəˈnɑrd;
    ES bəˈnɑːd, E+-ˈnɑːd; (*Fr* bɛrˈnəːr)—*In*
    bəˈnɑrd ɚ *became* ə *by dissimilation* (*§121*).
Saint Cecilia sɪˈsɪljə, -ˈsɪlɪə, -ˈsɪljə
Saint Christopher ˈkrɪstəfɚ; ES ˈkrɪstəfə(r
Saint Clair ˈklɛr, ˈklær; E ˈklɛə(r, ES ˈklæə(r
Saint Columb ˈkɑləm; ES+ˈkɒləm

|full fʊl |tooth tuθ |further ˈfɝðɚ; ES ˈfɝðə |custom ˈkʌstəm |while hwaɪl |how haʊ |toy tɔɪ
|using ˈjuzɪŋ |fuse fjuz, fɪuz |dish dɪʃ |vision ˈvɪʒən |Eden ˈidn̩ |cradle ˈkredl̩ |keep 'em ˈkipm̩

Saint Croix ˈkrɔɪ, *Me, NB loc.*+sɪŋˈ-, sɪntˈ-
Saint Cuthbert ˈkʌθbɚt; ES ˈkʌθbət
Sainte-Anne-de-Beaupré -ˈændəboˈpre
Sainte-Beuve *Fr* sæ̃tˈbœːv
St. Elmo ˈɛlmo
Saint Gall ˈgɔl, ˈgɑl, ˈgæl
Saint-Gaudens -ˈgodn̩z |-ʼs -ɪz
Saint Giles ˈdʒaɪlz |-ʼs -ɪz
Saint Gotthard, Goth- ˈgɑtɚd; ES ˈgɑtəd,
   ˈgɒt-; (*Fr* sæ̃gɔˈtaːr)
Saint Helena *saint* ˈhɛlɪnə, -lə-, *isl. & La, Cal*
   places həˈlinə, ˌsentˈlinə
St. Ives ˈaɪvz, *novel*+ˈivz |-ʼs -ɪz
St. John *surname* ˈsɪndʒən, sentˈdʒɑn,
   -ˈdʒɒn; *apos. & places* sentˈdʒɑn, -ˈdʒɒn;
   in NB loc. sn̩ˈdʒɒn—*Lowell rimed* St. John
   with Mohawk Injun.
Saint Julien ˈdʒuljən, ˈdʒɪuljən
Saint Lawrence ˈlɔrəns, ˈlɑr-, ˈlɒr- |-ʼs -ɪz
St. Leger *surname, race* sentˈlɛdʒɚ, *less freq.*
   ˈsɛlɪndʒɚ; ES -dʒə(r
Saint Louis *US places* ˈluɪs, ˈlɪuɪs |-ʼs -ɪz
St. Mary-le-bone *church, borough* ˈmɛrɪləˈbon
Saint-Mihiel *Fr* sæ̃-miˈjɛl
Saint-Moritz -ˈmorɪts, -ˈmɔr-; S -ˈmor-; |-ʼs
   -ɪz
St. Pancras ˈpæŋkrəs |-ʼs -ɪz
St. Regis ˈridʒɪs |-ʼs -ɪz
St. Ronan ˈronən, ˈrɑnən, ˈrɒn-
Saint-Saëns *Fr* sæ̃ˈsɑ̃
Saint Sophia soˈfaɪə, sə-
Saint Swithin ˈswɪðɪn, ˈswɪθɪn
Saint Valentine ˈvælənˌtaɪn
Saint Vitus ˈvaɪtəs |-ʼs -ɪz, *in* St. Vitus's
   dance+ˈvaɪtəs
saith sɛθ
sake sek
saké *Jap drink* ˈsɑkɪ
Sakhalin ˌsækəˈlin=Saghalien
Saki ˈsɑki, ˈsɔki
sal *chem., geol.* sæl; *tree* sɑl, sɔl
salaam səˈlɑm |salaamed səˈlɑmd
salability, salea- ˌseləˈbɪlətɪ
salable ˈseləbl̩ |-bly -blɪ
salacious səˈleʃəs
salad ˈsæləd
Saladin ˈsælədɪn
Salamanca ˌsæləˈmæŋkə, -ˈmænkə
salamander ˈsæləˌmændɚ; ES -ˌmændə(r

Salamis ˈsæləmɪs |-ʼs -ɪz
sal-ammoniac ˌsæləˈmonɪˌæk, -njæk
Salarino ˌsæləˈrino
salary ˈsælərɪ |salaried ˈsælərɪd
sale sel |-able -əbl̩ |-bly -blɪ
Salem ˈseləm
saleratus ˌsæləˈretəs
Salerio səˈlɛrɪˌo, -ˈlɪrɪˌo, -rjo
Salerno səˈlɜno; ES -ˈlɜno, -ˈlɜno; (*It*
   sɑˈlɛrno)
Salesbury ˈselzˌbɛrɪ, -bərɪ, -brɪ—*distinct from*
   Salisbury
salesclerk ˈselzˌklɝk; ES -ˌklɝk, -ˌklɜk
salesman ˈselzmən |-men -mən
salesroom ˈselzˌrum, -ˌrʊm
saleswoman ˈselzˌwʊmən, -ˌwum- |-women
   -ˌwɪmɪn, -ən
Salian ˈselɪən
Salic ˈsælɪk, ˈselɪk=Salique (*Fr* saˈlik)
salicin ˈsæləsɪn
salicylate ˈsæləsɪˌlet, səˈlɪsəˌlet |-lated -ˌletɪd
salicylic ˌsæləˈsɪlɪk
salience ˈselɪəns |salient ˈselɪənt, -ljənt
salify ˈsæləˌfaɪ |-fied -ˌfaɪd
saline ˈselaɪn |-linity səˈlɪnətɪ
Saline səˈlin |-ville -vɪl
Salique ˈsælɪk, ˈselɪk=Salic (*Fr* saˈlik)
Salisbury ˈsɔlzˌbɛrɪ, -bərɪ, -brɪ—*cf* §121
saliva səˈlaɪvə |-vous -vəs |-ry ˈsæləˌvɛrɪ
salivate ˈsæləˌvet |-d -ɪd |-tion ˌsæləˈveʃən
sallet ˈsælɪt
sallow ˈsælo, -ə |-ed -d |-ing ˈsæləwɪŋ |-er
   ˈsæləwɚ; ES -wə(r; |-est ˈsæləwɪst
Sallust ˈsæləst
sally, S- ˈsælɪ |sallied ˈsælɪd
sally lunn, S- L- ˈsælɪˈlʌn
salmagundi, S- ˌsælməˈgʌndɪ
salmon ˈsæmən
Salmon *surname* ˈsæmən, ˈsam-; *Bible*
   ˈsælmən
Salome səˈlomɪ
salon *Fr* saˈlɔ̃
Salonika, -ca, -ki ˌsæləˈnikə, ˌsɑl-, -ˈnaɪ-, -kɪ,
   səˈlɑnɪkə; ES+-ˈlɒn-
saloon səˈlun
Salop *short for* Shropshire ˈsæləp—*cf* §121
Salopian səˈlopɪən
Salpiglossis, s- ˌsælpɪˈglɑsɪs, -ˈglɒs-
salpinx ˈsælpɪŋks |salpinges sælˈpɪndʒiz

---

salsify ˈsælsəfɪ	Samian ˈsemɪən, ˈsemjən
sal soda ˈsælˈsodə	samite ˈsæmaɪt
salt sɔlt |salted ˈsɔltɪd	Samnite ˈsæmnaɪt
salt-and-pepper ˈsɔltn̩ˈpɛpɚ; ES -ˈpɛpə(r	Samoa səˈmoə |Samoan səˈmoən
saltant ˈsæltənt |saltation sælˈteʃən	Samos ˈsemɑs, -mɒs |-ˈs -ɪz
saltarello ˌsæltəˈrɛlo (It ˌsaltaˈrɛllo)	Samothrace ˈsæməˌθres |-ˈs -ɪz |-cian ˌsæmə-
saltatory ˈsæltəˌtorɪ, -ˌtɔrɪ; S -ˌtorɪ	ˈθreʃən
saltcellar ˈsɔltˌsɛlɚ; ES -ˌsɛlə(r	samovar ˈsæməˌvɑr; ES -ˌvɑː(r, E+-ˌvɑː(r
Salter ˈsɔltɚ; ES ˈsɔltə(r	samp sæmp
Salt Lake City ˈsɔltˌlekˈsɪtɪ	sampan ˈsæmpæn
saltmarsh, S- ˈsɔltˌmɑrʃ; ES -ˌmɑːʃ, E+	samphire ˈsæmfaɪr; ES ˈsæmfaɪə(r
-ˌmɑːʃ; |-es -ɪz	sample ˈsæmpl̩; E+ˈsam-, ˈsɑm-; |-d -d
Salton Sink ˈsɔltn̩ˈsɪŋk	|-ling -plɪŋ, -pl̩ɪŋ
Saltonstall ˈsɔltn̩ˌstɔl	sampler ˈsæmplɚ; ES ˈsæmplə(r, E+ˈsam-,
saltpeter, -tre ˈsɔltˈpitɚ; ES -ˈpitə(r	ˈsɑm-
saltworks ˈsɔltˌwɝks; ES -ˌwɜks, -ˌwɝks	Samson, -pson ˈsæmpsn̩, ˈsæmsn̩
salubrious səˈlubrɪəs, -ˈlɪu- |-brity -brətɪ	Samuel ˈsæmjʊəl, ˈsæmjʊl, ˈsæmjəl
salutary ˈsæljəˌtɛrɪ, -jʊ-	samurai ˈsæmʊˌraɪ
salutation ˌsæljəˈteʃən, -jʊ-	San Antonio ˌsænənˈtonɪo, ˌsænæn-, loc.+
salutatorian səˌlutəˈtorɪən, -ˌlɪu-, -ˈtɔr-; S	ˌsænənˈton
-ˈtor-	sanatorium ˌsænəˈtorɪəm, -ˈtɔr-; S -ˈtor- |-s -z
salutatory səˈlutəˌtorɪ, -ˈlɪu-, -ˌtɔrɪ; S -ˌtorɪ	|-ria -rɪə
salute səˈlut, -ˈlɪut |-d -ɪd	sanatory ˈsænəˌtorɪ, -ˌtɔrɪ; S -ˌtorɪ
Saluzzo səˈlutso (It saˈluttso)	San Bernardino ˈsænˌbɝnəˈdino, -nɑr-; ES
Salvador, El ɛlˈsælvəˌdɔr; ES -ˌdɔə(r; (Sp	-ˌbɜnə-, -ˌbɝnə-, -nɑː-
-ˌsalβaˈðɔr)	Sancho Panza ˈsæŋkoˈpænzə (Sp ˈsantʃo-
Salvadoran, ˌsælvəˈdorən, -ˈdɔr-; S -ˈdor-;	ˈpanθa)
|-dorian -rɪən	sanctification ˌsæŋktəfəˈkeʃən
salvage ˈsælvɪdʒ |-s -ɪz |-d -d |-able -əbl̩	sanctify ˈsæŋktəˌfaɪ |-fied -ˌfaɪd |-fiedly
salvation sælˈveʃən (ˈSalˌvation ˈArmy)	-ˌfaɪdlɪ, -ˌfaɪdlɪ
salve n 'ointment,' v 'anoint' sæv; E+sav,	sanctimonious ˌsæŋktəˈmonɪəs, -ˈmonjəs
sɑv; |-d -d	sanctimony ˈsæŋktəˌmonɪ
salve v 'salvage' sælv |-d -d |-vable -əbl̩	sanction ˈsæŋkʃən |-ed -d
Salve, s- intj ˈsælvɪ	sanctity ˈsæŋktətɪ
salver 'tray' ˈsælvɚ; ES ˈsælvə(r	sanctuary ˈsæŋktʃʊˌɛrɪ
salvia ˈsælvɪə, ˈsælvjə	sanctum ˈsæŋktəm |-s -z |rarely -ta ˈsæŋktə
Salvini sælˈvini (It salˈviːni)	Sanctus ˈsæŋktəs |-es -ɪz
salvo ˈsælvo |-ed -d	sand sænd |sanded ˈsændɪd
sal volatile ˈsælvoˈlætl̩ˌi	Sand, George ˈdʒɔrdʒˈsænd; ES ˈdʒɔədʒ-;
salvor ˈsælvɚ; ES ˈsælvə(r	(Fr ʒɔ̃rʒəˈsɑ̃, -ˈsɑ̃ːd)
Sam sæm	sandal ˈsændl̩ |-ed -d |-ing ˈsændl̩ɪŋ, -dl̩ɪŋ
samara ˈsæmərə	sandalwood ˈsændl̩ˌwʊd
Samaria səˈmɛrɪə, səˈmerɪə |-n -n	sandbag ˈsændˌbæg, ˈsænˌbæg |-bagged
Samaritan səˈmærətn̩, səˈmɛr- |-ism -ˌɪzəm	-ˌbægd
samarium səˈmærɪəm, səˈmɛr-, səˈmer-	sand-blind ˈsændˌblaɪnd, ˈsæn-
Samarkand ˌsæməˈkænd; ES ˌsæməˈkænd	sandbur, -rr ˈsændˌbɝ, ˈsæn-; ES -ˌbɜ(r, -ˌbɝ
sambo, S- ˈsæmbo	Sandburg ˈsændbɝg, ˈsæn-; ES -bɜg, -bɝg
sambuke ˈsæmbjuk, -bɪuk	Sanders ˈsændɚz, ˈsɑn-; ES -dəz; |-ˈs -ɪz
same sem	Sandford, Sanf- ˈsænfɚd; ES ˈsænfəd

|full fʊl \|tooth tuθ \|further ˈfɝðɚ; ES ˈfɝðə \|custom ˈkʌstəm \|while hwaɪl \|how haʊ \|toy tɔɪ
\|using ˈjuzɪŋ \|fuse fjuz, fɪuz \|dish dɪʃ \|vision ˈvɪʒən \|Eden ˈidn̩ \|cradle ˈkredl̩ \|keep 'em ˈkipm̩

Words below in which a *before* r (farm) *is sounded* ɑ *are often pronounced in* E *with* a (faːm)

sandglass 'sænd͜ˌglæs, 'sæn-; E+-ˌglas, -ˌglɑs; |-es -ɪz

sandhi 'sændhi, 'sɑn-, 'sʌn-, -di

Sandhurst 'sændhɝst; ES -hɜst, -hɝst

San Diego ˌsæn·di'ego

sandman 'sændˌmæn |-men -ˌmɛn

sandpaper 'sændˌpepɚ, 'sæn-; ES -ˌpepə(r; |-ed -d |-ing -ˌpeprɪŋ, -ˌpepərɪŋ

sandpiper 'sændˌpaɪpɚ, 'sæn-; ES -ˌpaɪpə(r

Sandringham 'sændrɪŋəm

Sandrocottus ˌsændro'kɑtəs; ES+-'kɒt-; |-'s -ɪz

Sands sændz, sænz |-'s -ɪz

sandstone 'sændˌston, 'sæn-

Sandusky sən'dʌskɪ, sæn-

sandwich, S- 'sændwɪtʃ, 'sæn- |-es -ɪz |-ed -t

Sandys 'sændz, sænz |-'s -ɪz, *in Shak. spelt* Sandys, Sands

sane sen |saneness 'sennɪs

Sanford, Sand- 'sænfɚd; ES 'sænfəd

San Francisco ˌsænfrən'sɪsko

sang sæŋ

sangaree ˌsæŋgə'ri

Sanger 'sæŋɚ, 'sæŋgɚ; ES -ə(r

sang-froid *Fr* sã'frwa

Sangraal sæŋ'grel

sanguine 'sæŋgwɪn |-nary -ˌɛrɪ |-neness -gwɪnnɪs |-neous sæŋ'gwɪnɪəs

Sanhedrin, -im 'sænɪˌdrɪn, -ˌdrɪm

sanitarian ˌsænə'tɛrɪən, -'ter- |-rium -rɪəm

sanitary 'sænəˌtɛrɪ |-tation ˌsænə'teʃən

sanity 'sænətɪ

San Joaquin *Cal* ˌsænwə'kin, *PI* ˌsænhoə'kin

San Jose ˌsænho'ze, -no'ze ('San Joˌse 'scale)

San Juan sæn'hwɑn, -'wɑn, -ɒn

sank sæŋk

San Miguel ˌsænmi'gel

Sannazaro ˌsænə'zaro (*It* ˌsanna'dzaːro)

sans sænz (*Fr* sã)

San Salvador sæn'sælvəˌdɔr; ES -ˌdɔə(r; (*Sp* ˌsalβa'ðɔr)

sans-culotte ˌsænzkju'lɑt, -kə-, -'lɒt |-tism -ɪzəm |-tist -ɪst (*Fr* sãky'lɔt)

Sanskrit, -crit 'sænskrɪt |-ic sæn'skrɪtɪk

sans-serif, sanserif sæn'sɛrɪf, sænz's-

Santa Ana, Anna ˌsæntə'ænə, ˌsæntɪ'ænə

Santa Barbara ˌsæntə'barbərə, -brə; ES -'baːb-

Santa Catalina ˌsæntəˌkæt͜l'inə

Santa Claus 'sæntɪˌklɔz, 'sæntə- |-'s -ɪz

Santa Cruz *US, WI* ˌsæntə'kruz; *PI* ˌsæntə-'krus (*Am Sp* ˌsanta'krus); |-'s -ɪz |*W Pacif* ˌsæntə'kruθ (*Sp* ˌsanta'kruθ)

Santa Cruz de Tenerife ˌsæntə'kruz·dɪˌtenə-'rif (*Sp* ˌsanta'kruθ·ðeˌtene'rife)

Santa Fe *NMex* 'sæntəˌfe, ˌsæntə'fe, *older* -ˌfi, -'fi

Santa Fé *Arg* ˌsantə'fe (*Sp* ˌsanta'fe)

Santayana ˌsæntɪ'ænə, -'anə (*Sp* ˌsanta'jana)

Santee sæn'ti

Santiago ˌsæntɪ'ego, -'ago (*Sp* ˌsanti'ago)

Santo Domingo ˌsæntodə'mɪŋgo (*Sp* ˌsanto-ðo'miŋgo)

São Paulo *Pg* ˌsãu'paulu

Saorstat Eireann 'sɛːrˌstət'erən, -'ɛrən

sap sæp |sapped sæpt |-head -ˌhɛd

sapheaded 'sæp'hɛdɪd ('sapˌheaded 'lout)

sapid 'sæpɪd |-ity sæ'pɪdətɪ, sə-

sapience 'sepɪəns, -pjəns |-ent -ənt

sapiential ˌsepɪ'ɛnʃəl |-ly -ɪ

Sapir sə'pɪr, sa-; ES -'pɪə(r

sapling 'sæplɪŋ

sapodilla ˌsæpə'dɪlə

saponaceous ˌsæpə'neʃəs

saponification səˌpɑnəfə'keʃən; ES+-ˌpɒn-

saponine 'sæpənɪn, -ˌnin |-nin -nɪn

saponite 'sæpəˌnaɪt

Sapphic 'sæfɪk

Sapphira sə'faɪrə

sapphire 'sæfaɪr; ES 'sæfaɪə(r; |-d -d

sapphirine 'sæfərɪn, -ˌrin

Sappho 'sæfo

sappy 'sæpɪ

saprophyte 'sæproˌfaɪt |-tic ˌsæpro'fɪtɪk

sapsucker 'sæpˌsʌkɚ; ES 'sæpˌsʌkə(r

sapwood 'sæpˌwud

Saracen 'særəsn̩

Saragossa ˌsærə'gɑsə, -'gɒsə

Sarah, -ra 'sɛrə, *esp.* S 'serə

Sarajevo 'sarajeˌvo, ˌsarə'jɛvo

Saranac 'særəˌnæk

Sarasota ˌsærə'sotə

Saratoga ˌsærə'togə ('Saraˌtoga 'chips)

sarcasm 'sarkæzəm; ES 'saːkæzəm

sarcastic sar'kæstɪk; ES saː-; |-ally -l̩ɪ, -ɪklɪ

sarcoma sar'komə; ES saː'komə

***

Key: *See in full* §§3–47. bee bi |pity 'pɪtɪ (§6) |rate ret |yet jɛt |sang sæŋ |angry 'æŋ·grɪ |bath bæθ; E baθ (§10) |ah ɑ |far far |watch wɑtʃ, wɒtʃ (§12) |jaw dʒɔ |gorge gɔrdʒ |go go

Words below in which a *before* r (farm) *is sounded* ɑ *are often pronounced in* E *with* a (fɑːm)

sarcophagus sɑrˈkɑfəgəs; ES sɑːˈkɑf-, -ˈkɒf-;
|-es -ɪz |-gi -ˌdʒaɪ

sard, S- sɑrd; ES sɑːd

Sardanapalus ˌsɑrdəˈnæpələs; ES ˌsɑːd-; |-'s
-ɪz

sardine *stone* ˈsɑrdɪn, -daɪn; ES ˈsɑːd-

sardine *fish* sɑrˈdin; ES sɑːˈdin (ˈsar-
ˌdine ˈsalad)

Sardinia sɑrˈdɪnɪə, -njə; ES sɑːˈd-; |-n -n

Sardis ˈsɑrdɪs; ES ˈsɑːdɪs; |-'s -ɪz

sardius ˈsɑrdɪəs; ES ˈsɑːdɪəs; |-es -ɪz

sardonic sɑrˈdɑnɪk; ES sɑːˈdɑnɪk, -ˈdɒnɪk;
|-ally -ḷɪ, -ɪklɪ

sardonyx ˈsɑrdənɪks; ES ˈsɑːd-; |-es -ɪz

sargasso, S- sɑrˈgæso; ES sɑːˈgæso

Sargeant, -gent, -geaunt ˈsɑrdʒənt; ES
ˈsɑːdʒ-

Sargon ˈsɑrgɑn; ES ˈsɑːgɑn, -gɒn

sari ˈsɑri

sark sɑrk; ES sɑːk; |-ed -t

sarong səˈrɔŋ, ˈsɑrɔŋ, -ɒŋ

Saroyan səˈrɔjən

Sarpedon sɑrˈpidṇ, -dɑn; ES sɑːˈpidṇ, -dɑn,
-dɒn

sarsaparilla ˌsɑrspəˈrɪlə, ˌsɑrsə-; ES ˌsɑːs-

sarsenet ˈsɑrsnɪt; ES ˈsɑːsnɪt

Sarto, del dɛlˈsɑrto; ES -ˈsɑːto

sartorial sɑrˈtorɪəl, -rjəl, -ˈtɔr-; ES sɑˈtor-,
E+-ˈtɔr-

Sartor Resartus ˈsɑrtɚrɪˈsɑrtəs; ES ˈsɑːtərɪ-
ˈsɑːtəs

Sarum ˈsɛrəm, ˈsær-, ˈser- —*cf* Salisbury

sash sæʃ |sashes ˈsæʃɪz |sashed sæʃt

sashay sæˈʃe |-ed -d

Saskatchewan sæsˈkætʃəˌwan, səs-, -ˌwɒn,
-ˌwɔn, -wən

Saskatoon ˌsæskəˈtun

sassafras ˈsæsəˌfræs, ˈsæsf-

Sassenach ˈsæsṇˌæk, -əx

Sassoon sæˈsun, səˈsun

sassy ˈsæsɪ

sat sæt

Satan ˈsetṇ

satanic seˈtænɪk, sə- |-al -ḷ |-ally -ḷɪ, -ɪklɪ

satchel ˈsætʃəl |-ed -d

sate *past of* sit set, sæt

sate *'fill'* set |sated ˈsetɪd

sateen sæˈtin

satellite ˈsætḷˌaɪt

satiability ˌseʃɪəˈbɪlətɪ, ˌseʃə-

satiable ˈseʃɪəbḷ, ˈseʃə- |-bly -blɪ

satiate ˈseʃɪˌet |-d -ɪd

satiety səˈtaɪətɪ, sæˈt-

satin ˈsætṇ, ˈsætɪn |-ed -d

satinette, -net ˌsætṇˈɛt, -tɪˈnɛt

satinwood ˈsætṇˌwʊd, ˈsætɪn-

satire ˈsætaɪr; ES ˈsætaɪə(r

satiric səˈtɪrɪk, sæ- |-al -ḷ |-ally -ḷɪ, -ɪklɪ

satirist ˈsætərɪst

satirize ˈsætəˌraɪz |-s -ɪz |-d -d

satisfaction ˌsætɪsˈfækʃən |-tory -trɪ, -tərɪ
|-torily -trəlɪ, -tərəlɪ

satisfy ˈsætɪsˌfaɪ |-fied -ˌfaɪd

satrap ˈsetræp, -trəp |-y ˈsetrəpɪ, ˈsætrəpɪ

saturable ˈsætʃərəbḷ |-bly -blɪ

saturant ˈsætʃərənt

saturate ˈsætʃəˌret |-d -ɪd |-tion ˌsætʃəˈreʃən

Saturday ˈsætɚdɪ; ES ˈsætə-; *see* Monday

Saturn ˈsætɚn; ES ˈsætən

Saturnale ˌsætɚˈneli; ES ˌsætə-; -lia -lɪə, -ljə

Saturnian sæˈtɝnɪən; ES -ˈtɜn-, -ˈtɝn-

saturnine, S- ˈsætɚˌnaɪn; ES ˈsætəˌnaɪn

Saturninus ˌsætɚˈnaɪnəs; ES ˌsætə-; |-'s -ɪz

satyr ˈsætɚ, ˈsetɚ; ES ˈsætə(r, ˈsetə(r

sauce sɔs |sauces ˈsɔsɪz |sauced sɔst

saucebox ˈsɔsˌbɑks; ES+-ˌbɒks; |-es -ɪz

saucepan ˈsɔsˌpæn, -pən

saucer ˈsɔsɚ; ES ˈsɔsə(r; |-ed -d

saucy ˈsɔsɪ

sauerkraut ˈsaʊrˌkraʊt; ES ˈsaʊəˌkraʊt

Sauk Center *Minn*, Sauk City *Wis* sɔk

Saul sɔl

Sault Sainte Marie ˈsuˌsentməˈri

Saunders ˈsɔndɚz, ˈsɒn-, ˈsɑn-, ˈsæn- |-'s -ɪz

saunter ˈsɔntɚ, ˈsɒn-, ˈsɑn-; ES -tə(r; |-ed -d
|-ing -tərɪŋ, -trɪŋ

saurian ˈsɔrɪən

sauropod ˈsɔrəˌpɑd; ES+-ˌpɒd

sausage ˈsɔsɪdʒ, ˈsɒs-, ˈsɑs- |-s -ɪz

Sausalito ˌsɔsəˈlito, -ə

sauté soˈte |-téed -ˈted (ˈsauˌté ˈhash)

sauterne, S- soˈtɝn; ES soˈtɜn, -ˈtɝn

savage ˈsævɪdʒ |-s -ɪz |-ry -rɪ

savanna, -ah, S- səˈvænə

savant səˈvɑnt, ˈsævənt (*Fr* saˈvɑ̃)

save sev |saved sevd

save-all 'sɛv‚ɔl
saver 'sevɚ; ES 'sevə(r
savings-bank 'sevɪŋz‚bæŋk
savior, Saviour 'sevjɚ; ES 'sevjə(r
savoir-faire 'sævwɑr'fɛr, -'fær; E 'sævwɑ:-
'fɛə(r, ES -'fæə(r; (Fr savwar'fɛ:r)
Savonarola ‚sævənə'rolə (It ‚savona'rɔ:la)
savor 'sevɚ; ES 'sevə(r; |-ed -d |-ing -vərɪŋ,
-vrɪŋ
savory 'sevərɪ, 'sevrɪ
Savoy sə'vɔɪ
Savoyard sə'vɔɪɚd, sə'vɔjɚd; ES -əd, -jəd;
(Fr savɔ'ja:r)
savvy, -ey 'sævɪ |-ied, -eyed 'sævɪd
saw sɔ |past sawed sɔd |pptc sawed sɔd or
sawn sɔn |-ing 'sɔ·ɪŋ
saw past of see sɔ
Sawatch sə'watʃ, -'wɒtʃ |-'s -ɪz, cf Saguache
sawbones 'sɔ‚bonz |-'s -ɪz
sawbuck 'sɔ‚bʌk
sawdust 'sɔ‚dʌst |sawdusted 'sɔ‚dʌstɪd
sawfish 'sɔ‚fɪʃ |-fish's -‚fɪʃɪz
sawfly 'sɔ‚flaɪ
sawhorse 'sɔ‚hɔrs; ES -‚hɔəs; |-s -ɪz
sawmill 'sɔ‚mɪl
sawn one pptc of saw sɔn
saw-toothed 'sɔ‚tuθt, -‚tuðd
sawyer, S- 'sɔjɚ; ES 'sɔjə(r
Saxe sæks |-'s -ɪz
saxhorn 'sæks‚hɔrn; ES -‚hɔən
saxifrage 'sæksəfrɪdʒ |-gous sæks'ɪfrəgəs
Saxon 'sæksn̩ |Saxony 'sæksən̩ɪ, 'sæksn̩ɪ
saxophone 'sæksə‚fon |-d -d |-nist -ɪst
say se |says sɛz |saith sɛθ |said sɛd; unstressed
səz (səz 'hi), səd (səd 'hi)
Sayce ses |-'s -ɪz
say-so 'se‚so
'sblood zblʌd
scab skæb |scabbed skæbd
scabbard 'skæbɚd; ES 'skæbəd; |-ed -ɪd
scabbed adj 'skæbɪd, skæbd |-ness -ɪdnɪs
scabies 'skebɪ‚iz, 'skebiz
Scabiosa ‚skebɪ'osə |scabious 'skebɪəs
scabrous 'skebrəs
Scafell 'skɔ'fɛl |S- Pike 'skɔ‚fɛl'paɪk
scaffold 'skæfl̩d, 'skæfold |-ed -ɪd
scaffoldage 'skæfl̩dɪdʒ |-ding -dɪŋ
scalawag, -ll- 'skælə‚wæg |-ery -ərɪ, -rɪ
scald skɔld |scalded 'skɔldɪd

scale skel |scaled skeld
scalene ske'lin ('sca‚lene 'triangle)
Scaliger 'skælɪdʒɚ; ES 'skælɪdʒə(r
scallion 'skæljən
scallop 'skɑləp, 'skæl-; ES+'skɒl-; |-ed -t
Scalopus skə'lopəs
scalp skælp |scalped skælpt
scalpel 'skælpɛl |scalpeled 'skælpɛld
scaly 'skɛlɪ
Scamander, s- skə'mændɚ; ES -'mændə(r;
|-ed -d |-ing -dərɪŋ, -drɪŋ
scamp skæmp |scamped skæmpt
scamper 'skæmpɚ; ES -pə(r; |-ed -d |-ing
-pərɪŋ, -prɪŋ
scan skæn |scanned skænd
scandal 'skændl̩ |-ed -d |-ing -dl̩ɪŋ, -dlɪŋ
scandalize 'skændl̩‚aɪz |-s -ɪz |-d -d
scandalous 'skændl̩əs, -dləs
Scanderbeg 'skændɚ‚bɛg; ES 'skændə-
Scandinavia ‚skændə'nevɪə, -vjə |-n -n
scandium 'skændɪəm
scansion 'skænʃən
scant skænt |scanted 'skæntɪd
scantling 'skæntlɪŋ |-ed -d
scanty 'skæntɪ |-tily -tl̩ɪ, -tɪlɪ
Scapa Flow 'skæpə'flo, 'skɑpə-
'scape, scape skep |-ed -t |-goat -‚got
scapegrace 'skep‚gres |-graces -‚gresɪz
scapula 'skæpjələ |-s -z |-lae -‚li
scar skɑr; ES skɑ:(r, E+skɑ:(r; |-red -d
scarab 'skærəb |-oid -‚ɔɪd
scarabaeus ‚skærə'biəs |-es -ɪz |-baei -'biaɪ
Scaramouch, s- 'skærə‚mautʃ, -‚muʃ |-es -ɪz
Scarboro, -rough 'skar‚bɚo, -ə; ES 'skɑ:‚bɜr-,
-‚bʌr-, -‚bɝ-, E+'skɑ:-
scarce skɛrs, skærs; E skɛəs, ES skæəs;
|-city -ətɪ
scare skɛr, skær; E skɛə(r, ES skæə(r; |-d -d
|-crow -‚kro
scarf skɑrf; ES skɑ:f, E+skɑ:f; |-rves -vz or
-rfs -s |-ed -t |-rved -vd
scarification ‚skærəfə'keʃən
scarify 'skærə‚faɪ |-fied -‚faɪd
scarlatina ‚skɑrlə'tinə; ES ‚skɑ:l-, E+‚skɑ:l-
Scarlatti skɑr'latɪ, -'lætɪ; ES skɑ:l-; (It
skɑr'latti)
scarlet 'skɑrlɪt; ES 'skɑ:lɪt, E+'skɑ:l-
scarp skɑrp; ES skɑ:p, E+skɑ:p; |-ed -t
Scarsdale 'skɑrz‚del; ES 'skɑ:z-, E+'skɑ:z-

Key: See in full §§3–47. bee bi |pity 'pɪtɪ (§6) |rate ret |yet jɛt |sang sæŋ |angry 'æŋ·grɪ
|bath bæθ; E baθ (§10) |ah ɑ |far fɑr |watch watʃ, wɒtʃ (§12) |jaw dʒɔ |gorge gɔrdʒ |go go

scarved **skɑrvd**; ES **skɑːvd**, E+**skɑːvd**
scarves **skɑrvz**; ES **skɑːvz**, E+**skɑːvz**
scary **'skɛrɪ**, **'skeːrɪ**, **'skærɪ**; S **'skærɪ**—*Some
speakers distinguish* scary *from* skerry *by a
longer* ɛ.
scat *card game* **skɑt**
scat *'git!'* **skæt** |-ted -**ɪd**
scathe **skeˈð**|scathed **skeˈðd** |-thing-**ɪŋ** |-less-**lɪs**
scatter **'skætɚ**; ES **'skætə(r**, |-ed -**d**
scatterbrain **'skætɚˌbren** |-s -**z** |-ed -**d**
scaup **skɔp**
scavenge **'skævɪndʒ** |-s -**ɪz** |-d -**d** |-r -**ɚ**; ES
-**ə(r**
scenario sɪ**'nɛrɪˌo**, -**'nær-**, -**'nɑr-** (*It* ʃe**'nɑːrjo)**
|-rist -**rɪst**
scene **sin** |scened **sind** |-ry -**ərɪ**, -**rɪ**
scenic **'sinɪk**, **'sɛn-** |-al -**l̩** |-ally -**l̩ɪ**, -**ɪklɪ**
scenography si**'nɑgrəfɪ**, -**'nɒg-**
scent **sɛnt** |scented **'sɛntɪd**
scepter, -tre **'sɛptɚ**; ES **'sɛptə(r**; |-(e)d -**d**
|-(r)ing **'sɛptərɪŋ**, -**ptrɪŋ**
sceptic **'skɛptɪk** |-al -**l̩** |-ally -**l̩ɪ**, -**ɪklɪ**
scepticism **'skɛptəˌsɪzəm**
Schacht *Ger* **ʃɑxt**
schedule **'skɛdʒʊl** |-d -**d**, *Brit* **'ʃɛdjul**
scheelite **'ʃilaɪt**
Scheherazade ʃəˌhɛrə**'zɑdə**, -ˌhærə-, -ˌhɪrə-
Scheldt **skɛlt**
schematic ski**'mætɪk** |-ally -**l̩ɪ**, -**ɪklɪ**
schematism **'skiməˌtɪzəm**
schematize **'skiməˌtaɪz** |-s -**ɪz** |-d -**d**
scheme **skim** |schemed **skimd**
Schenectady skə**'nɛktədɪ**
scherzando skɛr**'tsɑndo**, -**'tsændo** (*It* sker-
'tsɑndo)
scherzo **'skɛrtso** |-s -**z** |-zi -**tsi** (*It* **'skertso)**
Schiaparelli skɪˌɑpə**'rɛlɪ**, ˌskjɑp- (*It* ˌskjɑpɑ-
'rɛlli)
Schick **ʃɪk** |S- test **'ʃɪkˌtɛst**
Schiller **'ʃɪlɚ**; ES **'ʃɪlə(r**; (*Ger* **'ʃɪlər)**
schism **'sɪzəm** |-atism **'sɪzməˌtɪzəm**
schismatic sɪz**'mætɪk** |-al -**l̩** |-ally -**l̩ɪ**, -**ɪklɪ**
schist **ʃɪst** |-ic -**ɪk** |-ose -**os** |-ous -**əs**
schizocarp **'skɪzəˌkɑrp**; ES -ˌkɑːp, E+-ˌkɑːp
schizophrenia ˌskɪzə**'frinɪə** |-ic -**'frɛnɪk**
Schlegel **'ʃlegl̩** (*Ger* **'ʃleːgəl)**
Schleswig **'ʃlɛswɪg**, **'ʃlɛs-** (*Ger* **'ʃleːsvɪx**, **'ʃlɛs-)**
|S- -Holstein -**'holstaɪn**
Schley *Am admiral, Ga co.* **slaɪ** (*Ger* ʃlaɪ)

Schliemann **'ʃlimən** (*Ger* **'ʃliːmɑn)**
Schmidt ʃmɪt
schnapps ʃnæps, ʃnɑps (*Ger* schnaps ʃnɑps)
schnauzer **'ʃnauzɚ**; ES **'ʃnauzə(r**; (*Ger*
'ʃnautsər)
Schoenbrunn *O* **'ʃenbrən**, -**brʊn** (*Ger* ʃøːn-
'brʊn)
Schofield **'skofild**
Schoharie sko**'hærɪ**
scholar **'skɑlɚ**; ES **'skɑlə(r**, **'skɒl-**; |-ship -ˌʃɪp
scholastic sko**'læstɪk** |-al -**l̩** |-ally -**l̩ɪ** |-ly -**lɪ**
|-ism -təˌsɪzəm
Scholes **skolz** |-'s -**ɪz**
scholiast **'skolɪˌæst** |-ic ˌskolɪ**'æstɪk**
scholium **'skolɪəm** |-lia -lɪə
Schönbrunn **'ʃenbrʊn** (*Ger* ʃøːn**'brʊn)**
school **skul** |-ed -**d** |-book -ˌbʊk |-boy -ˌbɔɪ
schoolfellow **'skulˌfɛlo**, -ə
schoolgirl **'skulˌgɝl**; ES -ˌgɜl, -ˌgɝl
schoolhouse **'skulˌhaʊs** |-ses -zɪz
schoolma'am **'skulˌmɑm**, -ˌmæm
schoolman *'scholastic'* **'skulmən** |-men -mən
schoolman *'schoolteacher'* **'skulˌmæn** |-men
-ˌmɛn
schoolmarm **'skulˌmɑm**, -ˌmɑrm; ES -ˌmɑːm,
E+-ˌmɑːm
schoolmaster **'skulˌmæstɚ**; ES -ˌmæstə(r,
E+-ˌmɑs-, -ˌmɑs-; |-ed -**d** |-ing -tərɪŋ, -trɪŋ
schoolmate **'skulˌmet**
schoolmistress **'skulˌmɪstrɪs** |-es -**ɪz**
schoolroom **'skulˌrum**, -ˌrʊm
schoolteacher **'skulˌtitʃɚ**; ES -ˌtitʃə(r
schoolyard **'skulˌjɑrd**; ES -ˌjɑːd, E+-ˌjɑːd
schooner **'skunɚ**; ES **'skunə(r**
schooner-rigged **'skunɚˌrɪgd**; ES **'skunə-**
Schopenhauer **'ʃopənˌhaʊɚ**; ES -ˌhaʊ·ə(r
schottische, -sch **'ʃɑtɪʃ**; ES+**'ʃɒt-**; |-(e)s -**ɪz**
|-(e)d -**t**
Schroon **skrun**
Schubert **'ʃubɚt**, **'ʃiu-**; ES -bət; (*Ger* **'ʃuːbərt)**
Schulenburg **'ʃulənˌbɝg**; ES -ˌbɜg, -ˌbɝg
Schumann **'ʃumɑn**, **'ʃiu-** |S- -Heink -**'haɪŋk**
Schurman **'ʃʊrmən**; ES **'ʃuəmən**
Schurz ʃʊrts; ES ʃuəts; |-'s -**ɪz**
Schuyler **'skaɪlɚ**; ES **'skaɪlə(r**; |-ville -ˌvɪl
Schuylkill **'skulkɪl**
schwa ʃwɑ (*Ger* ʃvɑː)
Schwab ʃwɑb, ʃwɒb, ʃwɔb
Schwartz swɔrts; ES swɔəts; |-'s -**ɪz**

|full fʊl |tooth tuθ |further **'fɝðɚ**; ES **'fɝðə**; |custom **'kʌstəm** |while hwaɪl |how haʊ |toy tɔɪ
|using **'juzɪŋ** |fuse fjuz, fɪuz |dish dɪʃ |vision **'vɪʒən** |Eden **'idn̩** |cradle **'kredl̩** |keep 'em **'kipm̩**

schweizerkäse 'swaɪtsəˌkezə; ES -tsə-; (*Ger*
ˈʃvaɪtsərˌkɛːzə)
sciagram 'saɪəˌgræm |-graph -ˌgræf; E+
-ˌgraf -ˌgraf
sciagraphy saɪ'ægrəfɪ
sciatic saɪ'ætɪk |-al -ḷ |-ally -ḷɪ, -ɪklɪ
sciatica saɪ'ætɪkə
science 'saɪəns |-s -ɪz |-d -t
scientific ˌsaɪən'tɪfɪk |-al -ḷ |-ally -ḷɪ, -ɪklɪ
scientist, S- 'saɪəntɪst
scientistic ˌsaɪən'tɪstɪk |-ally -ḷɪ, -ɪklɪ
scilicet 'sɪlɪˌset
Scilla '*Scylla*' 'sɪlə (*It* 'ʃilla)
Scilla '*squill*' 'sɪlə
Scilly Isles 'sɪlɪ'aɪlz
scimitar, -ter 'sɪmətɚ; ES 'sɪmətə(r; |-ed -d
scintilla sɪn'tɪlə
scintillate 'sɪntḷˌet |-d -ɪd |-tor -ɚ; ES -ə(r
scintillation ˌsɪntḷ'eʃən
sciolism 'saɪəˌlɪzəm |-list -lɪst
scion 'saɪən
Scioto saɪ'otə, -to
Scipio 'sɪpɪˌo
scire facias 'saɪrɪ'feʃɪˌæs
scirrhus 'sɪrəs, 'skɪr- |-rhous -əs
scission 'sɪʒən, 'sɪʃən
scissor 'sɪzɚ; ES 'sɪzə(r; |-s -z |-ed -d
Scituate 'sɪtʃuˌet, 'sɪtʃəˌwet
sclaff sklæf |sclaffed sklæft
scleriasis sklɪ'raɪəsɪs
sclerometer sklɪ'ramətɚ; ES -'ramətə(r,
-'rɒm-
sclerosis sklɪ'rosɪs |-roses -'rosiz
sclerotic sklɪ'ratɪk; ES+-'rɒt-; |-al -ḷ
sclerous 'sklɪrəs
scoff skɔf, skɒf |-ed -t
scold skold |scolded 'skoldɪd
Scollard 'skaləˑd; ES 'skaləd, 'skɒl-
Scollay 'skʌlɪ, *sp. pron.* 'skalɪ, ES+'skɒlɪ
scollop 'skaləp; ES+'skɒl-; |-ed -t
sconce skans; ES+skɒns; |-s -ɪz |-d -t
scone skon, skɒn
Scone skun, skon
scoop skup |scooped skupt |-ful 'skupˌful
scoot skut |scooted 'skutɪd
scop skap, skop; ES+skɒp
scope skop
scopolamin sko'paləmɪn, -'pɒl-, ˌskopə-
'læmɪn |-ine -in, -ɪn

scorbutic skɔr'bjutɪk, -'bɪu-; ES skɔə-; |-al -ḷ
|-ally -ḷɪ, -ɪklɪ
scorch skɔrtʃ; ES skɔətʃ; |-es -ɪz |-ed -t
score skor, skɔr; ES skoə(r, E+skɔə(r; |-d -d
scoria 'skorɪə, 'skɔr-; S 'skor-; |-riae -rɪˌi
scoriaceous ˌskorɪ'eʃəs, ˌskɔr-; S ˌskor-
scorify 'skorəˌfaɪ, 'skɔr-; S 'skor-; |-fied -ˌfaɪd
scorn skɔrn; ES skɔən; |-ed -d |-ful -fəl
|-fully -fəlɪ
Scorpio 'skɔrpɪˌo; ES 'skɔəpɪˌo
scorpion 'skɔrpɪən; ES 'skɔəpɪən
Scot, s- skat; ES+skɒt
Scotch skatʃ; ES+skɒtʃ; |-man -mən |-men
-mən
scotch skatʃ; ES+skɒtʃ; |-es -ɪz |-ed -t
Scotch-Irish 'skatʃ'aɪrɪʃ; ES+'skɒtʃ-
scoter 'skotɚ; ES 'skotə(r
scot-free 'skat'fri; ES+'skɒt-; ('scot-ˌfree
'trip)
Scotia 'skoʃə, -ʃɪə
Scotland 'skatlənd; ES+'skɒt-
Scots skats; ES+skɒts; |-man -mən |-men
-mən
Scotswoman 'skatsˌwumən, -ˌwu-; ES+
'skɒts-; |-women -ˌwɪmɪn, -ən
Scott skat; ES+skɒt; |-dale -ˌdel
Scotticism 'skatəˌsɪzəm; ES+'skɒtə-
Scottish 'skatɪʃ; ES+'skɒt-
Scottsbluff 'skatsˌblʌf; ES+'skɒts-
Scotts Bluff 'skats'blʌf; ES+'skɒts-
Scotus 'skotəs |-'s -ɪz
scoundrel 'skaundrəl |-ly -ɪ
scour skaur; ES skauə(r; |-ed -d |-ing
'skaurɪŋ
scourge skɝdʒ; ES skɝdʒ, skɜˑdʒ; |-s -ɪz |-d -d
scouse skaus |-s -ɪz
scout skaut |scouted 'skautɪd
scoutmaster 'skautˌmæstɚ; ES -ˌmæstə(r,
E+-ˌmas-, -ˌmɑs-
scow skau |scowed skaud
scowl skaul |scowled skauld
scrabble 'skræbḷ |-d -d |-ling -blɪŋ, -bḷɪŋ
scrag skræg |scragged skrægd
scragged *adj* 'skrægɪd |-gled -ḷd |-gling -lɪŋ
|-gly -lɪ |-gy -ɪ |-gily -ḷɪ, -ɪlɪ
scram skræm |scrammed skræmd
scramble 'skræmbḷ |-d -d |-ling -blɪŋ, -bḷɪŋ
scrannel 'skrænḷ
Scranton 'skræntən

scrap **skræp** |scrapped **skræpt** |-book -ˌbʊk
scrape **skrep** |scraped **skrept**
scraper **ˈskrepɚ**; ES **ˈskrepə(r**
scrapper **ˈskræpɚ**; ES **ˈskræpə(r**
scrapple **ˈskræpl̩**
scrappy **ˈskræpɪ** |-ily -l̩ɪ, -ɪlɪ
scratch **skrætʃ** |scratches **ˈskrætʃɪz** |-ed -t
scratch-awl **ˈskrætʃˌɔl**
scrawl **skrɔl** |scrawled **skrɔld**
scrawny **ˈskrɔnɪ**
screak **skrik** |screaked **skrikt**
scream **skrim** |screamed **skrimd**
scree **skri**
screech **skritʃ** |screeches **ˈskritʃɪz** |-ed -t
screech-owl **ˈskritʃˌaʊl**
screed **skrid** |screeded **ˈskridɪd**
screen **skrin** |screened **skrind**
Screven **ˈskrɪvɪn, -ən**
screw **skru, skrɪu** |-ed -d |-driver -ˌdraɪvɚ; ES
  -ˌdraɪvə(r
Scriabin **skriˈɑbɪn, ˈskriəbɪn**
scribble **ˈskrɪbl̩** |-d -d |-ling **ˈskrɪblɪŋ, -bl̩ɪŋ**
scribbler **ˈskrɪblɚ**; ES **ˈskrɪblə(r**
scribe **skraɪb** |scribed **skraɪbd**
Scribner **ˈskrɪbnɚ**; ES **ˈskrɪbnə(r**
scrim **skrɪm**
scrimmage **ˈskrɪmɪdʒ** |-s -ɪz |-d -d
scrimp **skrɪmp** |scrimped **skrɪmpt**
scrimshaw **ˈskrɪmʃɔ** |-ed -d
scrip **skrɪp** |-page **ˈskrɪpɪdʒ**
script **skrɪpt**
scriptorium **skrɪpˈtorɪəm, -ˈtɔr-**; S -ˈtor-; |-ria
  -rɪə
scriptural, S- **ˈskrɪptʃərəl** |-ly -ɪ |-ism -ˌɪzəm
scripture, S- **ˈskrɪptʃɚ**; ES **ˈskrɪptʃə(r**; |-d -d
Scriven **ˈskrɪvən**
scrivener, S- **ˈskrɪvnɚ, -vənɚ**; ES -nə(r
scrod **skrɑd**; ES+skrɒd
scrofula **ˈskrɔfjələ, ˈskrɒf-, ˈskrɑf-** |-lous -ləs
scroll **skrol** |scrolled **skrold**
scrooch **skrutʃ** |-es -ɪz |-ed -t
Scrooge **skrudʒ** |-'s -ɪz
Scroop **skrup**
scrotum **ˈskrotəm** |-tal -tl̩
scrouge **skrudʒ, skraʊdʒ** |-s -ɪz |-d -d
scrounge **skraʊndʒ** |-s -ɪz |-d -d
scrub **skrʌb** |scrubbed **skrʌbd**
scrubbed *adj* **ˈskrʌbɪd**
scrub-brush **ˈskrʌbˌbrʌʃ** |-es -ɪz

scrubby **ˈskrʌbɪ**
scruff **skrʌf**
scrummage **ˈskrʌmɪdʒ** |-s -ɪz |-d -d
scrumptious **ˈskrʌmpʃəs**
scrunch **skrʌntʃ** |-es -ɪz |-ed -t
scruple **ˈskrupl̩, ˈskrɪu-** |-d -d |-ling -plɪŋ,
  -pl̩ɪŋ, |-pulous -pjələs
scrupulosity **ˌskrupjəˈlɑsətɪ, ˌskrɪu-**; ES+
  -ˈlɒs-
scrutinize **ˈskrutn̩ˌaɪz, ˈskrɪu-** |-s -ɪz |-d -d
  |-ny -ɪ
Scrymgeour, -e, -miger, -migar **ˈskrɪmdʒɚ**;
  ES -dʒə(r
scud **skʌd** |scudded **ˈskʌdɪd** |-der, S- -ɚ; ES
  -ə(r
Scudéry *Fr* skydeˈri
scudo *It* **ˈsku:do** |-di -di
scuff **skʌf** |scuffed **skʌft**
scuffle **ˈskʌfl̩** |-d -d |-ling **ˈskʌflɪŋ, -fl̩ɪŋ**
sculduddery **skʌlˈdʌdərɪ, -drɪ** |-duggery
  -ˈdʌgərɪ, -grɪ
sculk **skʌlk** |sculked **skʌlkt**
scull **skʌl** |sculled **skʌld**
scullduddery, -dugg- *see* sculduddery
scullery **ˈskʌlərɪ**
scullion **ˈskʌljən**
sculp **skʌlp** |-ed -t
sculpin **ˈskʌlpɪn**
sculptor **ˈskʌlptɚ**; ES **ˈskʌlptə(r**
sculptress **ˈskʌlptrɪs** |-es -ɪz
sculptural **ˈskʌlptʃərəl** |-ly -ɪ
sculpture **ˈskʌlptʃɚ**; ES -tʃə(r; |-d -d
sculpturesque **ˌskʌlptʃəˈrɛsk**
scum **skʌm** |scummed **skʌmd** |-my -ɪ
scumble **ˈskʌmbl̩** |-d -d |-ling **ˈskʌmblɪŋ,**
  -bl̩ɪŋ
scup **skʌp** |scupped **skʌpt**
scupper **ˈskʌpɚ**; ES -pə(r; |-ed -d |-ing
  ˈskʌpərɪŋ, ˈskʌprɪŋ
scuppernong **ˈskʌpɚˌnɔŋ, -ˌnɒŋ, -ˌnɑŋ**; ES
  ˈskʌpə-
scurf **skɝf**; ES skɜf, skɝf; |-ed -t |-y -ɪ
scurrile **ˈskɝɪl, -əl**; ES **ˈskɜr-, ˈskʌr-, ˈskɝ-**;
  |-lous -əs
scurrility **skəˈrɪlətɪ, skɝˈɪl-**; ES+skɝˈrɪl-,
  skʌ-
scurry, S- **ˈskɝɪ**; ES **ˈskɜrɪ, ˈskʌrɪ, ˈskɝɪ**
scurvy **ˈskɝvɪ**; ES **ˈskɜvɪ, ˈskɝvɪ**
scut **skʌt** |scutted **ˈskʌtɪd**

|full fʊl |tooth tuθ |further ˈfɝðɚ; ES ˈfɝðə |custom ˈkʌstəm |while hwaɪl |how haʊ |toy tɔɪ
|using ˈjuzɪŋ |fuse fjuz, fɪuz |dish dɪʃ |vision ˈvɪʒən |Eden ˈidn̩ |cradle ˈkredl̩ |keep 'em ˈkipm̩

Scutari ˈskutərɪ, skuˈtɑrɪ
scutate ˈskjutet, ˈskɪu-
scutch skʌtʃ |scutches ˈskʌtʃɪz |-ed -t
scutcheon ˈskʌtʃən |-ed -d
scute skjut, skɪut
scutella skjuˈtɛlə, skɪu- |-lae -i
scutellate ʻplatterlikeʼ ˈskjutḷˌet, ˈskɪu-
scutellate ʻscalyʼ skjuˈtɛlɪt, ˈskjutḷˌet, -kɪu-
scutellum skjuˈtɛləm, skɪu- |-la -ə
scutter ˈskʌtɚ; ES ˈskʌtə(r; |-ed -d
scuttle ˈskʌtḷ |-d -d |-ling ˈskʌtḷɪŋ, -tlɪŋ
Scylla ˈsɪlə
scythe saɪð |scythed saɪðd
Scythia ˈsɪθɪə |-n -n
ʼsdeath zdɛθ
se music se
se- unstressed word initial sɪ-, sə-, si- (sedate
  sɪˈdet, səˈdet, siˈdet); before l often sḷ-
  (select sḷˈɛkt). In the vocab. when only one
  pron. is given (usually sɪ-), it is to be understood that many speakers also pronounce sə-,
  si-, sḷ- (si- esp. in deliberate speech).
sea si |-beach -ˌbitʃ |-beaches -ˌbitʃɪz
Seabeach ˈsiˌbitʃ, loc. ˈsɪbɪdʒ |-ʼs -ɪz
seaboard ˈsiˌbord, -ˌbɔrd; ES -ˌboəd, E+
  -ˌbɔəd
sea-born ˈsiˌbɔrn; ES -ˌbɔən
sea-borne ˈsiˌborn, -ˌbɔrn; ES -ˌboən, E+
  -ˌbɔən
Seabright ˈsiˌbraɪt
seacoast ˈsiˌkost
seafarer ˈsiˌfɛrɚ, -ˌfærɚ; E -ˌfɛrə(r, ES
  -ˌfærə(r
seafaring ˈsiˌfɛrɪŋ, -ˌfær-; S -ˌfær-
Seaford ˈsifɚd; ES ˈsifəd
seafowl ˈsiˌfaʊl
Seager ˈsigɚ; ES ˈsigə(r
seagirt ˈsiˌgɝt; ES -ˌgɜt, -ˌgɝt
seagoing ˈsiˌgo·ɪŋ
seal sil |sealed sild |sealery ˈsilərɪ
sealless ˈsillɪs
Sealyham ˈsilɪˌhæm, ˈsilɪəm
seam sim |seamed simd
seaman ˈsimən |-men -mən |-like -ˌlaɪk |-ly -lɪ
  |-ship -ˌʃɪp
seamark ˈsiˌmɑrk; ES -ˌmɑːk, E+-ˌmɑːk
seamstress ˈsimstrɪs, older ˈsɛm- |-es -ɪz
Seamus ˈʃeməs |-ʼs -ɪz
Seanad Eireann ˈsænadˈerən, -ˈɛrən

séance ˈseɑns, ˈsiɑns |-s -ɪz (Fr seˈɑ̃:s)
seaplane ˈsiˌplen
seaport ˈsiˌport, -ˌpɔrt; ES -ˌpoət, E+-ˌpɔət
sear sɪr; ES sɪə(r, S+sɛə(r; |-ed -d
search sɝtʃ; ES sɜtʃ, sɝtʃ; |-es -ɪz |-ed -t
  |-light -ˌlaɪt
search-warrant ˈsɝtʃˌwɔrənt, -ˌwɑr-, -ˌwɒr-;
  ES ˈsɜtʃ-, ˈsɝtʃ-
Searcy ˈsɝsɪ; ES ˈsɜsɪ, ˈsɝsɪ
Searle sɝl; ES sɜl, sɝl; |-s -z |-sʼs -zɪz
Sears sɪrz; ES sɪəz; |-ʼs -ɪz
seascape ˈsiˌskep
seascout ˈsiˌskaʊt
seashore, S- ˈsiˌʃor, -ˌʃɔr; ES -ˌʃoə(r, E+
  -ˌʃɔə(r
seasick ˈsiˌsɪk
seaside ˈsiˌsaɪd
season ˈsizn̩ |-ed -d |-ing ˈsizn̩ɪŋ, ˈsiznɪŋ
seasonable ˈsiznəbḷ, ˈsizn̩ə- |-bly -blɪ
seasonal ˈsizn̩əl |-ly -ɪ
seat sit |seated ˈsitɪd
Seattle siˈætḷ, ˈsiætḷ (ˈSeˌattle ˈWash.)
seaward ˈsiwɚd; ES ˈsiwəd; |-s -z
seaway ˈsiˌwe
seaweed ˈsiˌwid
seaworthy ˈsiˌwɝðɪ; ES -ˌwɜðɪ, -ˌwɝðɪ
sebaceous sɪˈbeʃəs
Sebago sɪˈbego
Sebastian sɪˈbæstʃən
Sebastopol sɪˈbæstəpḷ, Russia+ˌsɛbəsˈtopḷ
Sebring ˈsibrɪŋ
sebum ˈsibəm, ˈsibm̩
sec sɛk
secant ˈsikənt, ˈsikænt
Secaucus sɪˈkɔkəs |-ʼs -ɪz
secede siˈsid, sɪ- |-d -ɪd
secession siˈsɛʃən, sɪ- |-ism -ˌɪzəm |-ist -ɪst
Sechuana sɛˈtʃwɑnə
Seckel pear ˈsɛkḷ, ˈsɪkḷ
seclude sɪˈklud, -ˈklɪud |-d -ɪd
seclusion sɪˈkluʒən, -ˈklɪuʒən
second n, adj, adv ˈsɛkənd, ˈsɛkənt, before
  some conss.+ˈsɛkən (ˈsɛkənˈget)
second v ˈsɛkənd, -nt |-ed -əndɪd
secondary ˈsɛkənˌdɛrɪ
secondarily ˈsɛkənˌdɛrəlɪ, -ɪlɪ, esp. if emph.
  ˌsɛkənˈdɛr-
second-class ˈsɛkəndˈklæs, ˈsɛkən-, ˈsɛkŋ-;
  E+-ˈklas, -ˈklɑs (ˈsecond-ˌclass ˈfare)

Key: See in full §§3–47. bee bi |pity ˈpɪtɪ (§6) |rate ret |yet jɛt |sang sæŋ |angry ˈæŋ·grɪ
|bath bæθ; E baθ (§10) |ah ɑ |far fɑr |watch watʃ, wɒtʃ (§12) |jaw dʒɔ |gorge gɔrdʒ |go go

second-hand *adj, adv* ˈsɛkəndˈhænd, -ənt-
(ˈsecond-ˌhand ˈbook)
secondhand *n* ˈsɛkəndˌhænd, -ənt-
secondly ˈsɛkəndlɪ
second-rate ˈsɛkəndˈret
secret ˈsikrɪt |secrecy ˈsikrəsɪ
secretarial ˌsɛkrəˈtɛrɪəl, -ˈter-
secretariat ˌsɛkrəˈtɛrɪət, -ˌæt, -ˈter- |-ate -ɪt
secretary ˈsɛkrəˌtɛrɪ, ˈsɛkəˌtɛrɪ—*The first r
is lost from* ˈsɛkəˌtɛrɪ *by dissimilation*
(*§121*).
secrete sɪˈkrit |-d -ɪd |-tion -ˈkriʃən
secretive sɪˈkritɪv |-tory -tərɪ
sect sɛkt |-ary -ərɪ
sectarian sɛkˈtɛrɪən, -ˈter- |-ism -ˌɪzəm
sectile ˈsɛktɪl |-lity sɛkˈtɪlətɪ
section ˈsɛkʃən |-ed -d |-ing -ʃənɪŋ, -ʃnɪŋ
sectional ˈsɛkʃənḷ |-ly -ɪ |-ism -ˌɪzəm
sectionalize ˈsɛkʃənḷˌaɪz |-s -ɪz |-d -d
sector ˈsɛktɚ; ES -tə(r; |-ed -d |-ing ˈsɛktərɪŋ,
ˈsɛktrɪŋ
secular ˈsɛkjəlɚ; ES -lə(r; |-ism -ˌɪzəm
secularity ˌsɛkjəˈlærətɪ
secularization ˌsɛkjələrəˈzeʃən, -aɪˈz-
secularize ˈsɛkjələˌraɪz |-s -ɪz |-d -d
secund ˈsikʌnd
secure sɪˈkjʊr, -ˈkɪur; ES -ˈkjʊə(r, -ˈkɪu-;
|-d -d |-rity -ətɪ
Sedalia sɪˈdelɪə, -ljə
Sedan, s- sɪˈdæn (*Fr* səˈdɑ̃)
sedate sɪˈdet
sedative ˈsɛdətɪv
sedentarily ˈsɛdṇˌtɛrəlɪ, -ɪlɪ, *esp. if emph.*
ˌsedenˈtarily
sedentary ˈsɛdṇˌtɛrɪ
sedge sɛdʒ |sedges ˈsɛdʒɪz |sedged sɛdʒd
Sedgwick ˈsɛdʒwɪk, ˈsɛdʒɪk
sedgy ˈsɛdʒɪ
sediment ˈsɛdəmənt
sedimental ˌsɛdəˈmɛntḷ |-tary -tərɪ
sedimentation ˌsɛdəmənˈteʃən, -mɛn-
sedition sɪˈdɪʃən |-tious -ʃəs
Sedley ˈsɛdlɪ
Sedlitz ˈsɛdlɪts |-’s -ɪz
seduce sɪˈdjus, -ˈdɪus, -ˈdus |-s -ɪz |-d -t
seduction sɪˈdʌkʃən |-tive -tɪv
sedulity sɪˈdjulətɪ, -ˈdɪu-, -ˈdu-
sedulous ˈsɛdʒələs
Sedum, s- ˈsidəm

see si |saw sɔ |seen sin—*unstressed often* sɪ
(sɪˈhɪr!)
seed sid |seeded ˈsidɪd |-ling -lɪŋ
seedtime ˈsidˌtaɪm
seek sik |sought sɔt
Seek-No-Further *apple* ˈsiknəˌfɝðɚ, ˈsɪgnə-;
ES -ˌfɝðə(r, -ˌfɝðə(r;—*The 2d pron., probably now rare, shows the normal phonetic
development of the proper name dissociated
from the meaning of* seek.
Seekonk ˈsikɑŋk, -kɒŋk
Seeley, Seelye ˈsilɪ
seem sim |seemed simd |seemly ˈsimlɪ
seen sin
seep sip |seeped sipt |-age -ɪdʒ
seer *'who sees'* ˈsiɚ; ES ˈsi·ə(r
seer *'prophet'* sɪr; ES sɪə(r, S+sɛə(r; |-ess -ɪs
seersucker ˈsɪrˌsʌkɚ; ES -ˌsʌkə(r, S+ˈsɛə-
seesaw ˈsiˌsɔ |-sawed -ˌsɔd
seethe sið |-d -d *or arch.* sod sɑd; ES+sɒd;
|-d -d *or arch.* sodden ˈsɑdṇ; ES+ˈsɒdṇ
sefari səˈfɑrɪ
segment ˈsɛgmənt |-ed -ɪd |-ary -mənˌtɛrɪ
segmental sɛgˈmɛntḷ |-ly -ɪ
segmentation ˌsɛgmənˈteʃən
segregate *adj* ˈsɛgrɪgɪt, -ˌget
segregate *v* ˈsɛgrɪˌget |-d -ɪd |-tive -ɪv
segregation ˌsɛgrɪˈgeʃən
Seguin sɪˈgin, ˈsigɪn (*Fr* səˈgæ̃)
seiche seʃ (*Fr* sɛʃ)
Seidl ˈsaɪdḷ, ˈzaɪdḷ
Seidlitz ˈsɛdlɪts |-’s -ɪz
seigneur sinˈjɝ; ES -ˈjɝ(r, -ˈjɝ; (*Fr* sɛˈnœːr)
seignior ˈsinjɚ; ES ˈsinjə(r; |-age -ɪdʒ |-y -ɪ
seignorial sinˈjorɪəl, -ˈjɔr-; S -ˈjor-
seine sen |seined send
Seine sen (*Fr* sɛːn)
seise siz |seises ˈsizɪz |seised sizd
seisin ˈsizɪn
seism ˈsaɪzəm, ˈsaɪsəm
seismic ˈsaɪzmɪk, ˈsaɪs- |-al -ḷ |-ally -ḷɪ, -ɪklɪ
seismogram ˈsaɪzməˌgræm, ˈsaɪs-
seismograph ˈsaɪzməˌgræf, ˈsaɪs-; E+-ˌgraf,
-ˌgrɑf
seismographic ˌsaɪzməˈgræfɪk, ˌsaɪs- |-al -ḷ
seismologic ˌsaɪzməˈlɑdʒɪk, ˌsaɪs-; ES+
-ˈlɒdʒ-; |-al -ḷ |-ally -ḷɪ, -ɪklɪ
seismologist saɪzˈmɑlədʒɪst, saɪs-; ES+
-ˈmɒl-; |-gy -dʒɪ

|full fʊl |tooth tuθ |further ˈfɝðɚ; ES ˈfɝðə |custom ˈkʌstəm |while hwaɪl |how haʊ |toy tɔɪ
|using ˈjuzɪŋ |fuse fjuz, fɪuz |dish dɪʃ |vision ˈvɪʒən |Eden ˈidṇ |cradle ˈkredḷ |keep ’em ˈkipm̩

seismometer saɪz'mɑmətɚ, saɪs-; ES -'mɑmə-
tə(r, -'mɒm-
seize siz |seizes 'siziz |seized sizd
seizin 'sizɪn
seizure 'siʒɚ; ES 'siʒə(r
Sejanus sɪ'dʒenəs |-'s -ɪz
selah 'silə
Selden 'sɛldɪn, -dən
seldom 'sɛldəm
select sə'lɛkt |-ed -ɪd |-ive -ɪv |-ion -kʃən
selectivity sə,lɛk'tɪvətɪ
selectman sə'lɛktmən |-men -mən, in N Engd
(1) səlɛkt'mæn, sɪ-, s|-, -k'mæn (2) sə-
'lɛktmæn, sɪ-, s|'ɛkt-, -kmæn, -mən
(3) 'silɛkt,mæn, -k,mæn |pl (1) -'mɛn
(2) -mɛn, -mən (3) -,mɛn (L.A.)
selector sə'lɛktɚ; ES -'lɛktə(r
Selene sə'lini |-na -nə
selenite 'sɛlə,naɪt
Selenite 'moon-dweller' 'sɛlə,naɪt, sə'linaɪt
selenium sə'liniəm
Seleucia sə'luʃɪə, -'lɪu- |-n -n
Seleucid sə'lusɪd, -'lɪu- |-ae -sə,di |-an -ən
Seleucus sə'lukəs, -'lɪu- |-'s -ɪz
self sɛlf |self's sɛlfs |selves sɛlvz
self-abasement ,sɛlfə'besmənt
self-abnegation ,sɛlfæbnɪ'geʃən
self-assertion ,sɛlfə'sɝʃən; ES -'sɝʃ-, -'sɝʃ-
self-assurance ,sɛlfə'ʃurəns |-s -ɪz
self-assured ,sɛlfə'ʃurd; ES -'ʃuəd
self-centered, -tred 'sɛlf'sɛntɚd; ES -təd;
('self-,centered 'hero)
self-command ,sɛlfkə'mænd; ES+-'mand,
-'mɑnd
self-complacence ,sɛlfkəm'plesn̩s |-cy -ɪ |-nt
-n̩t
self-conceit ,sɛlfkən'sit |-ed -ɪd
self-condemned ,sɛlfkən'dɛmd |-nedly -mnɪdlɪ
self-confidence 'sɛlf'kɑnfədəns; ES+-'kɒn-;
|-dent -dənt
self-conscious 'sɛlf'kɑnʃəs; ES+-'kɒn-
self-consistency ,sɛlfkən'sɪstənsɪ |-tent -tənt
self-contained ,sɛlfkən'tend |-nedly -nɪdlɪ
self-control ,sɛlfkən'trol |-led -d
self-declared ,sɛlfdɪ'klɛrd, -'klærd; E -'klɛəd,
ES -'klæəd; |-redly -rɪdlɪ
self-defense, Brit -nce ,sɛlfdɪ'fɛns
self-denial ,sɛlfdɪ'naɪəl, -'naɪl
self-denying ,sɛlfdɪ'naɪɪŋ

self-determination ,sɛlfdɪ,tɝmə'neʃən; ES
-,tɝm-, -,tɝm-
self-esteem ,sɛlfə'stim
self-evident 'sɛlf'ɛvədənt
self-explanatory ,sɛlfɪk'splænə,torɪ, -,tɔrɪ; S
-,torɪ
self-expression ,sɛlfɪk'sprɛʃən
self-governed 'sɛlf'gʌvɚnd; ES -'gʌvənd;
|-ning -nɪŋ
self-government 'sɛlf'gʌvɚmənt, -'gʌvɚn-
mənt; ES -vɚ-, -vən-
self-help 'sɛlf'hɛlp
selfhood 'sɛlfhud
self-importance ,sɛlfɪm'pɔrtn̩s; ES -'pɔət-;
|tant -tn̩t
self-indulgence ,sɛlfɪn'dʌldʒəns |-ent -ənt
self-interest 'sɛlf'ɪntərɪst, -'ɪntrɪst
selfish 'sɛlfɪʃ
self-made 'sɛlf'med ('self-,made 'woman)
self-mastery 'sɛlf'mæstərɪ, -trɪ; E+-'mas-,
-'mɑs-
self-possessed ,sɛlfpə'zɛst |-sedly -sɪdlɪ
self-possession ,sɛlfpə'zɛʃən
self-preservation ,sɛlfprɛzɚ'veʃən; ES -zə-
self-realization ,sɛlfrɪələ'zeʃən, -aɪ'z-
self-regard ,sɛlfrɪ'gɑrd; ES -'gɑːd, E+-'gɑːd
self-reliance ,sɛlfrɪ'laɪəns |-ant -ənt
self-reproach ,sɛlfrɪ'protʃ |-es -ɪz |-ed -t
self-respect ,sɛlfrɪ'spɛkt
self-restraint ,sɛlfrɪ'strent
Selfridge 'sɛlfrɪdʒ |-'s -ɪz
self-righteous 'sɛlf'raɪtʃəs
self-rising 'sɛlf'raɪzɪŋ ('self-,rising 'flour)
self-sacrifice 'sɛlf'sækrə,faɪs, -,faɪz |-s -ɪz
selfsame 'sɛlf'sem ('self,same 'hour)
self-satisfaction ,sɛlfsætɪs'fækʃən
self-satisfied 'sɛlf'sætɪs,faɪd
self-seeker 'sɛlf'sikɚ; ES -'sikə(r
self-service 'sɛlf'sɝvɪs; ES -'sɝv-, -'sɝv-
self-starter 'sɛlf'stɑrtɚ; ES -'stɑːtə(r, E+
-'stɑːt-
self-sufficiency ,sɛlfsə'fɪʃənsɪ |-ent -ənt
self-sustaining ,sɛlfsə'stenɪŋ
self-taught 'sɛlf'tɔt ('self-,taught 'sage)
self-will 'sɛlf'wɪl |-ed -d
Seligman 'sɛlɪgmən
Selim 'silɪm, sə'lim
Selinsgrove 'silɪnz,grov
Seljuk sɛl'dʒuk |-ian -ɪən

Key: *See in full* §§3–47. bee bi |pity 'pɪtɪ (§6) |rate ret |yet jɛt |sang sæŋ |angry 'æŋ·grɪ
|bath bæθ; E bɑθ (§10) |ah ɑ |far fɑr |watch wɑtʃ, wɒtʃ (§12) |jaw dʒɔ |gorge gɔrdʒ |go go

Selkirk ˈsɛlkɝk; ES -kɜk, -kɝk; |-shire -ˌʃɪr, -ʃɚ; ES -ˌʃɪə(r, -ʃə(r

sell sɛl |sold sold |-out n ˈsɛlˌaʊt

Seltzer, s- ˈsɛltsɚ; ES ˈsɛltsə(r

selvage, -vedge ˈsɛlvɪdʒ |-s -ɪz |-d -d

selves sɛlvz

semanteme səˈmæntim

semantic səˈmæntɪk |-ally -ļɪ, -ɪkļɪ |-s -s

semaphore ˈsɛməˌfor, -ˌfɔr; ES -ˌfoə(r, E+ -ˌfɔə(r

semasiological səˌmesɪəˈlɑdʒɪkļ; ES+-ˈlɒdʒ-; |-ly -ɪ, -ɪkļɪ

semasiologist səˌmesɪˈɑlədʒɪst; ES+-ˈɒl-; |-gy -dʒɪ

semblable ˈsɛmbləbļ |-bly -blɪ

semblance ˈsɛmbləns |-s -ɪz |-ant -ənt

Semele ˈsɛməˌli

semen ˈsimən |semina ˈsɛmɪnə

semester səˈmɛstɚ; ES -ˈmɛstə(r

semiannual ˌsɛmɪˈænjʊəl |-ly -ɪ

semibreve ˈsɛməˌbriv

semicentennial ˌsɛməsɛnˈtɛnɪəl |-ly -ɪ

semicircle ˈsɛməˌsɝkļ; ES -ˌsɜkļ, -ˌsɝkļ

semicircular ˌsɛməˈsɝkjələ; ES -ˈsɜkjələ(r, -ˈsɝkjələ(r

semicircumference ˌsɛməsɚˈkʌmfərəns, -frəns; ES -səˈkʌm-; |-s -ɪz

semicolon ˈsɛməˌkolən

semiconscious ˌsɛməˈkɑnʃəs; ES+-ˈkɒn-

semidarkness ˌsɛməˈdɑrknɪs; ES -ˈdɑːk-, E+-ˈdaːk-

semidetached ˌsɛmədɪˈtætʃt

semifinal ˌsɛməˈfaɪnļ (ˈsemiˌfinal ˈround)

semifluid ˌsɛməˈfluɪd, -ˈflɪu-

semimonthly ˌsɛməˈmʌnθlɪ

seminal ˈsɛmənļ |-ly -ɪ

seminar ˈsɛməˌnɑr, ˌsɛməˈnɑr; ES -ɑː(r, E+-aː(r

seminary ˈsɛməˌnɛrɪ

Seminole ˈsɛməˌnol

semiofficial ˌsɛmɪəˈfɪʃəl |-ly -ɪ

semiprofessional ˌsɛməprəˈfɛʃənļ, -ʃnəl |-ly -ɪ

semiquaver ˈsɛməˌkwevɚ; ES -ˌkwevə(r

Semiramis səˈmɪrəmɪs |-ˈs -ɪz

semirigid ˌsɛməˈrɪdʒɪd

semiskilled ˌsɛməˈskɪld

Semite ˈsɛmaɪt, ˈsi-

Semitic səˈmɪtɪk |-ticism -ˈmɪtəˌsɪzəm

Semitism ˈsɛməˌtɪzəm, ˈsimə-

semitone ˈsɛməˌton

semitropical ˌsɛməˈtrɑpɪkļ; ES+-ˈtrɒp-

semivowel ˈsɛməˌvaʊəl, -ˌvaʊl, -ɪl

semiweekly ˌsɛməˈwiklɪ

semiyearly ˌsɛməˈjɪrlɪ; ES -ˈjɪəlɪ, S+-ˈjɛəlɪ

sempiternal ˌsɛmpɪˈtɝnļ; ES -ˈtɜnļ, -ˈtɝnļ; |-ly -ɪ |-nity -nətɪ

Sempronius sɛmˈpronɪəs, -njəs |-ˈs -ɪz

sempstress ˈsɛmpstrɪs |-es -ɪz

sen sɛn

senate ˈsɛnɪt |-tor -ɚ, -nətɚ; ES -tə(r

senatorial ˌsɛnəˈtorɪəl, ˌsɛnɪ-, -ˈtɔr-; S -ˈtor-

send sɛnd |sent sɛnt

sendal ˈsɛndļ

send-off ˈsɛndˌɔf, -ˌɒf

Seneca ˈsɛnɪkə |-n -n

Senegal ˌsɛnɪˈgɔl (Fr seneˈgal)

Senegalese ˌsɛnɪgəˈliz, -gɔˈliz

Senegambia ˌsɛnəˈgæmbɪə |-n -n

senescence səˈnɛsņs |-cy -ɪ |-scent -sņt

seneschal ˈsɛnəʃəl |-ed -d

senile ˈsinaɪl, -nɪl, -nļ |-lity səˈnɪlətɪ, sɪ-

senior ˈsinjɚ; ES ˈsinjə(r

seniority sinˈjɔrətɪ, -ˈjɑr-, -ˈjɒr-

Senlac ˈsɛnlæk

senna ˈsɛnə

Sennacherib səˈnækəˌrɪb

sennight ˈsɛnaɪt, -nɪt

señor sɛnˈjɔr; ES -ˈjɔə(r; (Sp seˈɲor)

señora sɛnˈjorə, -ˈjɔrə; S -ˈjorə; (Sp seˈɲora)

señorita ˌsɛnjəˈritə (Sp seɲoˈrita)

sensation sɛnˈseʃən |-al ļ |-ally -ļɪ

sensationalism sɛnˈseʃənļˌɪzəm, -ʃnəl- |-ist -ɪst

sense sɛns |senses ˈsɛnsɪz |sensed sɛnst

sense stress ˈsɛnsˌstrɛs |-es -ɪz

sensibility ˌsɛnsəˈbɪlətɪ

sensible ˈsɛnsəbļ |-bly -blɪ

sensitive ˈsɛnsətɪv |-tivity ˌsɛnsəˈtɪvətɪ

sensitization ˌsɛnsətəˈzeʃən, -aɪˈz-

sensitize ˈsɛnsəˌtaɪz |-s -ɪz |-d -d

sensorial sɛnˈsorɪəl, -ˈsɔr-; S -ˈsor-

sensory ˈsɛnsorɪ

sensual ˈsɛnʃʊəl |-ly -ɪ |-ism -ˌɪzəm |-ist -ɪst

sensuality ˌsɛnʃʊˈælətɪ

sensualize ˈsɛnʃʊəlˌaɪz |-s -ɪz |-d -d

sent sɛnt

sentence ˈsɛntəns |-s -ɪz |-d -t

sententious sɛnˈtɛnʃəs

|full fʊl |tooth tuθ |further ˈfɝðɚ; ES ˈfɜðə |custom ˈkʌstəm |while hwaɪl |how haʊ |toy tɔɪ |using ˈjuzɪŋ |fuse fjuz, fɪuz |dish dɪʃ |vision ˈvɪʒən |Eden ˈidņ |cradle ˈkredļ |keep 'em ˈkipm̩

sentience ˈsɛnʃəns, -ʃɪəns |-ent -ənt
sentiment ˈsɛntəmənt
sentimental ˌsɛntəˈmɛntḷ |-ly -ɪ |-ism -ˌɪzəm
sentimentality ˌsɛntəmɛnˈtælətɪ, -mən-
sentimentalize ˌsɛntəˈmɛntḷˌaɪz |-s -ɪz |-d -d
sentinel ˈsɛntənḷ |-ed -d
sentry ˈsɛntrɪ
Senour ˈsinjɚ; ES ˈsinjə(r
Senusi, -nousi səˈnusɪ
Seoul soḷ, seˈol
sepal ˈsipḷ |-ed -d
separability ˌsɛpərəˈbɪlətɪ, ˌsɛprə-
separable ˈsɛpərəbḷ, ˈsɛprə- |-bly -blɪ
separate adj, n ˈsɛprɪt, ˈsɛpərɪt
separate v ˈsɛpəˌret, -pret |-d -ɪd
separation ˌsɛpəˈreʃən
separatism ˈsɛpərəˌtɪzəm, ˈsɛprə-
separatist ˈsɛpəˌretɪst
separator ˈsɛpəˌretɚ; ES -ˌretə(r
Sephardi Heb sɪˈfardi; ES -ˈfɑːdi; |pl -dim
   -dɪm
sepia ˈsipɪə
sepoy ˈsipɔɪ
sepsis ˈsɛpsɪs
sept sɛpt
September sɛpˈtɛmbɚ, səp-; ES -ˈtɛmbə(r
septenary ˈsɛptəˌnɛrɪ
septennial sɛpˈtɛnɪəl |-ly -ɪ
septentrional sɛpˈtɛntrɪənḷ |-ly -ɪ
septet, -tte sɛpˈtɛt
septic ˈsɛptɪk |-al -ḷ |-ally -ḷɪ, -ɪklɪ
septicemia, -caem- ˌsɛptəˈsimɪə
septillion sɛpˈtɪljən
septuagenarian ˌsɛptʃʊədʒəˈnɛrɪən, -ˈner-
septuagenary ˌsɛptʃʊˈædʒəˌnɛrɪ, Brit -əˈdʒi-
   nərɪ
septuagesima, S- ˌsɛptʃʊəˈdʒɛsəmə |-mal -mḷ
Septuagint ˈsɛptuəˌdʒɪnt, ˈsɛptʃʊə-
septum ˈsɛptəm |-ta -tə
septuple n, adj, v ˈsɛptʊpḷ, -tjʊpḷ, sɛpˈtupḷ,
   -ˈtɪu-, -ˈtju- |-d -d |-ling -plɪŋ, -pḷɪŋ
sepulcher, -chre ˈsɛpḷkɚ; ES -kə(r; |-(e)d -d
sepulchral səˈpʌlkrəl |-ly -ɪ
sepulture ˈsɛpḷtʃɚ; ES ˈsɛpḷtʃə(r; |-d -d
sequel ˈsikwəl |-a sɪˈkwilə |-ae sɪˈkwili
sequence ˈsikwəns |-cy -ɪ |-ent -ənt
sequential sɪˈkwɛnʃəl |-ly -ɪ
sequester sɪˈkwɛstɚ; ES -tə(r; |-ed -d |-ing
   -ˈkwɛstərɪŋ, -trɪŋ

sequestrate sɪˈkwɛstret |-d -ɪd
sequestration sɪˌkwɛsˈtreʃən, ˌsikwɛs-
sequin ˈsikwɪn
sequitur ˈsɛkwɪtɚ; ES ˈsɛkwɪtə(r
sequoia, S- tree sɪˈkwɔɪə, -ˈkwɔjə
Sequoya pers. name sɪˈkwɔjə, -ˈkwɔɪə
seraglio sɪˈræljo, -ˈral- (It serˈraʎʎo)
Serajevo ˈsɛrəjɛˌvo, ˌsɛrəˈjɛvo
serape sɛˈrɑpɪ (Sp seˈrape)
seraph ˈsɛrəf |-s -s |-im ˈsɛrəˌfɪm
seraphic səˈræfɪk, sɛ- |-al -ḷ |-ally -ḷɪ, -ɪklɪ
Serapis səˈrepɪs |-'s -ɪz
Serb sɝb; ES sɜb, sɝb |-ia -ɪə |-ian -ɪən
Serbo-Croatian ˈsɝboˌkroˈeʃən, -ʃɪən; ES
   ˈsɜb-, ˈsɝb-
sere sɪr; ES sɪə(r, S+sɛə(r
sere Heb grammar ˈsere
Sere Negroid ˈsere
Serena Chile seˈrenə; Am name səˈrinə
serenade ˌsɛrəˈned |-d -ɪd
serendipity ˌsɛrənˈdɪpətɪ
serene səˈrin |-nity səˈrɛnətɪ
sereneness səˈrinnɪs
serf sɝf; ES sɜf, sɝf; |-dom -dəm
serge sɝdʒ; ES sɜdʒ, sɝdʒ; |-s -ɪz
sergeancy, -jean- ˈsardʒənsɪ; ES ˈsaːdʒ-,
   E+ˈsaːdʒ-; |-ant -ənt
Sergeant, -jeant, -gent ˈsardʒənt; ES ˈsaːdʒ-,
   E+ˈsaːdʒ-
serial ˈsɪrɪəl |-ly -ɪ
seriate adj ˈsɪrɪɪt, -ˌet
seriate v ˈsɪrɪˌet |-d -ɪd
seriatim ˌsɪrɪˈetɪm, ˌsɛrɪ-
sericultural ˌsɛrɪˌkʌltʃərəl
sericulture ˈsɛrɪˌkʌltʃɚ; ES -ˌkʌltʃə(r
series ˈsɪrɪz, ˈsiriz, ˈsɪriz, ˈsiriz
serif ˈsɛrɪf
seriocomic ˌsɪrɪoˈkɑmɪk; ES+-ˈkɒm-; |-al -ḷ
   |-ally -ḷɪ, -ɪklɪ
serious ˈsɪrɪəs
serjeancy ˈsardʒənsɪ; ES ˈsaːdʒ-, E+-ˈsaːdʒ-;
   |-ant -ənt
sermon ˈsɝmən; ES ˈsɜm-, ˈsɝm-; |-ed -d
   |-ize -ˌaɪz |-izes -ˌaɪzɪz |-ized -ˌaɪzd
serous ˈsɪrəs
serpentine, S- ˈsɝpənˌtin, -ˌtaɪn; ES ˈsɜp-,
   ˈsɝp-; |-d -d
serrate adj ˈsɛrɪt, -et
serrate v ˈsɛret |-d -ɪd |-tion sɛˈreʃən

serry ˈsɛrɪ |serried ˈsɛrɪd

serum ˈsɪrəm |-s -z |-ra -rə

servant ˈsɝvənt; ES ˈsɝv-, ˈsɝv-

serve sɝv; ES sɝv, sɝv; |-d -d

Servia ˈsɝvɪə; ES ˈsɝv-, ˈsɝv-; |-n -n

service, S- ˈsɝvɪs; ES ˈsɝv-, ˈsɝv-; |-s -ɪz |-d -t

serviceability ˌsɝvɪsəˈbɪlətɪ; ES ˌsɝv-, ˌsɝv-

serviceable ˈsɝvɪsəb|; ES ˈsɝv-, ˈsɝv-; |-bly -blɪ

serviette ˌsɝvɪˈɛt; ES ˌsɝv-, ˌsɝv-

servile ˈsɝv|, -ɪl; ES ˈsɝv-, ˈsɝv-; |-ly -lɪ, -ɪ

servility səˈvɪlətɪ, sɝ-; ES sə-, sɝ-, sɝ-

Servilius səˈvɪlɪəs, sɝ-, -ljəs; ES sə-, sɝ-, sɝ-; |-'s -ɪz

servitor ˈsɝvətɚ; ES ˈsɝvətə(r, ˈsɝvətə(r

servitude ˈsɝvəˌtjud, -ˌtɪud, -ˌtud; ES ˈsɝv-, ˈsɝv-

sesame ˈsɛsəmɪ

sesquicentennial ˌsɛskwɪsɛnˈtɛnɪəl, -njəl

sesquipedalian ˌsɛskwɪpəˈdelɪən, -ljən

sessile ˈsɛs|, -ɪl

session ˈsɛʃən |-ed -d |-al -| |-ally -ʃɪ

sesterce ˈsɛstɝs; ES -tɝs, -tɝs; |-s -ɪz

sestet, -tte sɛsˈtɛt (ˈsesˌtet ˈrimes)

Sestos ˈsɛstəs, -tɑs; ES+-tɒs; |-'s -ɪz

set sɛt |-back -ˌbæk |-ting -ɪŋ

Setebos ˈsɛtəˌbɑs, -bəs; ES+-ˌbɒs; |-'s -ɪz

Seth sɛθ |Seth's sɛθs

Seton ˈsitn̩, ˈsitən

settee sɛˈti

setter ˈsɛtɚ; ES ˈsɛtə(r

settle ˈsɛt| |-d -d |-ling ˈsɛt|ɪŋ, ˈsɛt|ɪŋ

settlings n ˈsɛt|ɪŋz

set-to ˈsɛtˌtu, -ˈtu

setup ˈsɛtˌʌp

Seul Choix loc. ˈsɪʃəˌwe, -wə

Sevastopol sɪˈvæstəp|, Russia+ˌsɛvəsˈtop|

seven ˈsɛvən, ˈsɛvm̩ |-s ˈsɛvənz

sevenfold adj, adv ˈsɛvənˈfold, ˈsɛvm̩- (ˈsevenˌfold ˈloss)

sevenpenny ˈsɛvənˌpɛnɪ, ˈsɛvm̩-

seventeen ˌsɛvənˈtin, ˈsɛvənˈtin (ˈsevenˌteen ˈyears) |-th -θ |-ths -θs

seventh ˈsɛvənθ |-ths -θs

seventh-day ˈsɛvənθˌde (ˈseventh-ˈday ˌman)

seventy ˈsɛvəntɪ |-tieth -tɪɪθ |-tieths -tɪɪθs |-fold -ˈfold

sever ˈsɛvɚ; ES ˈsɛvə(r; |-ed -d |-ing ˈsɛvərɪŋ, ˈsɛvrɪŋ

several ˈsɛvrəl, ˈsɛvərəl |-ly -ɪ |-ty -tɪ

severance ˈsɛvərəns, ˈsɛvrəns |-s -ɪz

Severance ˈsɛvrəns, ˈsɛvərəns |-'s -ɪz

severe səˈvɪr; ES -ˈvɪə(r, S+-ˈvɛə(r

severity səˈvɛrətɪ

Severn ˈsɛvɚn; ES ˈsɛvən

Severus səˈvɪrəs |-'s -ɪz

Sevier səˈvɪr; ES -ˈvɪə(r, S+-ˈvɛə(r

Seville US səˈvɪl; Spain səˈvɪl, ˈsɛvɪl (Sp Sevilla seˈβiʎa)

Sèvres ˈsɛvrə, ˈsɛvɚ, -vəz; ES -vrə, -və(r, -vəz; (Fr sɛːvr)

sew so |sewed sod |sewed sod or sewn son

sewage ˈsjuɪdʒ, ˈsɪu-, ˈsu-

Sewall ˈsjuəl, ˈsɪu-, ˈsu-

Sewanee səˈwɒnɪ, ˈswɒnɪ

Seward ˈsjuɚd, ˈsɪu-, ˈsu-; ES -əd

Sewell ˈsjuəl, ˈsɪu-, ˈsu-

sewer 'who sews' ˈsoɚ; ES ˈso·ə(r

sewer 'servant,' 'drain' ˈsjuɚ, ˈsɪuɚ, ˈsuɚ; ES -ə(r; |-age -ɪdʒ

Sewickley səˈwɪklɪ

sewn son

sex sɛks |sexes ˈsɛksɪz |sexed sɛkst

sexagenarian ˌsɛksədʒəˈnɛrɪən, -ˈner-

sexagenary sɛksˈædʒəˌnɛrɪ

Sexagesima ˌsɛksəˈdʒɛsəmə |-mal -m|

sext sɛkst

sextant ˈsɛkstənt

sextet, -tte sɛksˈtɛt

sextile ˈsɛkst|, -tɪl

sextillion sɛksˈtɪljən

sexton ˈsɛkstən

sextuple n, adj, v ˈsɛkstʊp|, -tjʊp|, sɛksˈtʊp|, -ˈtɪu-, -ˈtju-; |-d -d |-ling -plɪŋ, -p|ɪŋ

sextuplets ˈsɛkstuˌplɪts, -tju-, sɛksˈtuplɪts, -ˈtɪu-, -ˈtju-

Sextus ˈsɛkstəs |-'s -ɪz

sexual ˈsɛkʃuəl |-ly -ɪ |-ality ˌsɛkʃuˈælətɪ

Seymour ˈsimor, -mɔr, -mɚ; ES -moə(r, -mə(r, E+-mɔə(r

Seyton ˈsitn̩

shabby ˈʃæbɪ |shabbily ˈʃæb|ɪ, -ɪlɪ

shack ʃæk |shacked ʃækt

shackle ˈʃæk| |-d -d |-ling ˈʃæklɪŋ, -k|ɪŋ

Shackleton ˈʃæk|tən

shad ʃæd

shadberry ˈʃædˌbɛrɪ, -bərɪ

shadbush ˈʃædˌbʊʃ |-es -ɪz

|full fʊl |tooth tuθ |further ˈfɝðɚ; ES ˈfɝðə |custom ˈkʌstəm |while hwaɪl |how haʊ |toy tɔɪ |using ˈjuzɪŋ |fuse fjuz, fɪuz |dish dɪʃ |vision ˈvɪʒən |Eden ˈidn̩ |cradle ˈkred| |keep 'em ˈkipm̩

shaddock 'ʃædək

shade ʃed |shaded 'ʃedɪd |-dy -ɪ

shadow 'ʃædo, -ə |-ed -d |-ing 'ʃædəwɪŋ

shadowy 'ʃædəwɪ

Shadrach 'ʃedræk

Shadwell 'ʃædwɛl, -wəl

shaft ʃæft; E+ʃaft, ʃaft |-ed -ɪd

Shaftesbury, Shafts- 'ʃæfts,bɛrɪ, -bərɪ; E+ 'ʃafts-, 'ʃafts-

shag ʃæg |shagged ʃægd |shaggy 'ʃægɪ

shagbark 'ʃæg,bark; ES -,ba:k, E+-,ba:k

shagged adj 'ʃægɪd

shagreen ʃə'grin |-ed -d

shah, S- ʃa

Shairp ʃarp, ʃɛrp, ʃærp; ES ʃa:p, ʃæəp, E+ʃɛəp, ʃa:p

shake ʃek |shook ʃʊk |shaken 'ʃekən

shake-down 'ʃek,daʊn

shaker, S- 'ʃekɚ; ES 'ʃekə(r

Shakespeare 'ʃek,spɪr; ES -,spɪə(r, S+-,spɛə(r

Shakespearean, -ian ʃek'spɪrɪən; S+-'spɛr-

Shakespeareana, -iana ,ʃekspɪrɪ'enə, -'ænə, -'anə

shake-up 'ʃek,ʌp

shako 'ʃæko, 'ʃeko

Shakopee 'ʃækəpɪ

Shakspere, -speare 'ʃek,spɪr; ES -,spɪə(r, S+-,spɛə(r

shaky 'ʃekɪ

shale, S- ʃel |-r -ɚ; ES -ə(r

shall stressed 'ʃæl, ,ʃæl; unstr. ʃəl, ʃ|

shalloon ʃə'lun, ʃæ-

shallop 'ʃæləp

shallott ʃə'lat; ES+-'lɒt

shallow, S- 'ʃælo, -ə |-er 'ʃæləwɚ; ES -wə(r; |-est 'ʃæləwɪst |-ed -d |-ing 'ʃæləwɪŋ

Shalmaneser ,ʃælmə'nizɚ; ES -'nizə(r

Shalott ʃə'lat; ES+-'lɒt

shalt stressed 'ʃælt, ,ʃælt; unstr. ʃəlt, ʃ|t

sham ʃæm |shammed ʃæmd

shaman 'ʃamən, 'ʃæm-, 'ʃe-

shamble 'ʃæmb| |-d -d |-ling 'ʃæmblɪŋ, -b|ɪŋ |-s -z

shambling n, adj 'ʃæmblɪŋ

shame ʃem |shamed ʃemd

shamefaced 'ʃem,fest |-ly -lɪ, ʃem'fesɪdlɪ

shamefacedness 'ʃem,festnɪs, ʃem'fesɪdnɪs

shammy 'ʃæmɪ=chamois

Shamokin ʃə'mokɪn

shamoy 'ʃæmɔɪ=chamois

shampoo ʃæm'pu |-pooed -'pud

shamrock, S- 'ʃæmrak; ES+-rɒk

Shandy 'ʃændɪ

Shanghai 'ʃæŋ'haɪ ('Shang,hai 'rooster)

shanghai n 'ʃæŋhaɪ

shanghai v 'ʃæŋhaɪ, ʃæŋ'haɪ |-ed -d

shank ʃæŋk |shanked ʃæŋkt

Shannon 'ʃænən

shan't ʃænt; E+ʃant, ʃant

shantey, -ty 'chantey' 'ʃæntɪ; E+'ʃan-, 'ʃan-

Shantung 'ʃæn'tʌŋ, 'ʃan'dʊŋ

Shantung, s- 'silk' ʃæn'tʌŋ

shanty 'shed' 'ʃæntɪ |-ied -d

shape ʃep |-d -t |-d -t or arch -n 'ʃepən

Shapley 'ʃæplɪ

shard ʃard; ES ʃa:d, E+ʃa:d; |-ed -ɪd

share ʃɛr, ʃær; E ʃɛə(r, ES ʃæə(r; |-d -d |-holder -,holdɚ; ES -də(r

shark ʃark; ES ʃa:k, E+ʃa:k; |-ed -t

Sharon 'ʃɛrən, 'ʃærən; S 'ʃærən, 'ʃerən

sharp, S- ʃarp; ES ʃa:p, E+ʃa:p; |-ed -t

sharpen 'ʃarpən, -pm̩; ES 'ʃa:p-, E+'ʃa:p-; |-ed -d |-ing -pənɪŋ, -pnɪŋ

Sharples 'ʃarp|z; ES 'ʃa:p-, E+'ʃa:p-; |-'s -ɪz

Sharpsburg 'ʃarpsbɝg; ES 'ʃa:psbɝg, 'ʃa:psbɝg, E+'ʃa:ps-

sharpshooter 'ʃarp,ʃutɚ; ES 'ʃa:p,ʃutə(r, E+'ʃa:p-

sharp-sighted 'ʃarp'saɪtɪd; ES see sharp

sharp-witted 'ʃarp'wɪtɪd; ES see sharp ('sharp-,witted 'sneer)

Shasta 'ʃæstə

shatter 'ʃætɚ; ES 'ʃætə(r; |-ed -d

Shaughnessy 'ʃɔnəsɪ

shave ʃev |-d -d |-d -d or -n 'ʃevən

shaveling 'ʃevlɪŋ

Shavian 'ʃevɪən

shaw, S- ʃɔ

Shawanese ,ʃowə'niz ('Shawa,nese 'salad)

Shawangunk 'ʃɔŋgəm, 'ʃɒŋ-, 'ʃaŋ-

Shawano Wis 'ʃono, 'ʃowə,no

Shawinigan ʃə'wɪnəgən

shawl ʃɔl |shawled ʃɔld |-less 'ʃɔllɪs

shawm ʃɔm

Shawnee ʃɔ'ni ('Shaw,nee 'tribes)

shawneewood ʃɔ'ni,wʊd

shay ʃe

Shays ʃez |Shays's 'ʃezɪz |Shays' ʃez

Key: See in full §§3–47. bee **bi** |pity 'pɪtɪ (§6) |rate **ret** |yet **jɛt** |sang **sæŋ** |angry 'æŋ·grɪ |bath **baθ**; E **baθ** (§10) |ah **ɑ** |far **fɑr** |watch **wɑtʃ, wɒtʃ** (§12) |jaw **dʒɔ** |gorge **gɔrdʒ** |go **go**

she *stressed* ˈʃi, ˌʃi; *unstr.* ʃɪ	Shekina ʃɪˈkaɪnə
shea ʃi	Shelburn, -e ˈʃɛlbən; ES ˈʃɛlbən
Shea ʃe	Shelby ˈʃɛlbɪ |-ville -ˌvɪl; S+-vl̩
sheaf *n* ʃif |sheaf's ʃifs |sheaves ʃivz	Shelden, -on ˈʃɛldən, -ɪn—*double pron. perh.*
sheaf *v* ʃif |sheafed ʃift	*due to double etym.* (*OE* -dun, -denu)
shear ʃɪr; ES ʃɪə(r, S+ʃɛə(r; |-ed -d *or arch.*	sheldrake ˈʃɛlˌdrek |-duck -ˌdʌk
shore ʃor, ʃɔr; ES ʃoə(r, E+ʃɔə(r; |-ed -d *or*	shelf *n* ʃɛlf |shelf's ʃɛlfs |shelves ʃɛlvz
shorn ʃorn, ʃɔrn; ES ʃoən, E+ʃɔən	shelf *v* ʃɛlf |shelfed ʃɛlft
sheard ʃard; ES ʃɑːd, E+ʃɑːd	shell ʃɛl |shelled ʃɛld
shearman ˈʃɪrmən; ES ˈʃɪə-, S+ˈʃɛə-; |-men	she'll *'she will'* stressed ˈʃil, ˌʃil; *unstr.* ʃil, ʃɪl
-mən	shellac, -ack ʃəˈlæk
Shearman ˈʃɜmən; ES ˈʃɜm-, ˈʃɝm-	Shelley ˈʃɛlɪ |-an, -eian ˈʃɛlɪən
shearwater ˈʃɪrˌwɔtɚ, -ˌwɑtɚ, -ˌwɒtɚ; ES	shellfire ˈʃɛlˌfaɪr; ES -ˌfaɪə(r
ˈʃɪə-, -tə(r, S+ˈʃɛə-	shellfish ˈʃɛlˌfɪʃ |-'s -ɪz
sheath ʃiθ |sheath's ʃiθs |sheaths ʃiðz	shell-less ˈʃɛllɪs
sheathe ʃið |sheathed ʃiðd	shellproof ˈʃɛlˈpruf (ˈshellˌproof ˈshelter)
sheathing ˈʃiðɪŋ, ˈʃiθɪŋ	shelly ˈʃɛlɪ
sheave ʃiv |sheaved ʃivd	shelter ˈʃɛltɚ; ES -tə(r; |-ed -d |-ing ˈʃɛltərɪŋ,
Sheba ˈʃibə	ˈʃɛltrɪŋ
she-bear ˈʃiˈbɛr, -ˈbær; E -ˈbɛə(r, ES -ˈbæə(r	shelve ʃɛlv |shelves ʃɛlvz |shelved ʃɛlvd
Sheboygan ʃɪˈbɔɪgən	Shem ʃɛm |-ite -aɪt
shed *'shelter'* ʃed |shedded ˈʃɛdɪd	Shenandoah ˌʃɛnənˈdoə
shed *'cast off'* ʃed	Shenango ʃəˈnæŋgo
she'd *abbr. spelling of* she had, she would,	shenanigan ʃəˈnænəˌgæn, -gən
stressed ˈʃid, ˌʃid; *unstr.* ʃid, ʃɪd	shend ʃɛnd |-shent ʃɛnt
she-devil ˈʃiˈdɛvl̩ (ˈshe-ˌdevil ˈmood)	Shenstone ˈʃɛnstən, -ˌston
Shee ʃi	Sheol, s- ˈʃiol
sheen ʃin |-ed -d	Shepard, Shepp-, -pherd ˈʃɛpɚd; ES ˈʃɛpəd
sheep ʃip |-ed -t	shepherd ˈʃɛpɚd; ES ˈʃɛpəd; |-ed -ɪd |-ess -ɪs
sheepcot ˈʃipˌkat; ES+-ˌkɒt; |-cote -ˌkot—*see*	Sheraton ˈʃɛrətn̩
cote	sherbet ˈʃɝbɪt; ES ˈʃɜb-, ˈʃɝb-
sheepfold ˈʃipˌfold	Sherborne, -burn(e) ˈʃɝbən; ES ˈʃɜbən,
sheepherder ˈʃipˌhɝdɚ; ES -ˌhɜdə(r, -ˌhɝdə(r	ˈʃɝbən
sheephook ˈʃipˌhʊk	Sherbrook ˈʃɝbrʊk; ES ˈʃɜ-, ˈʃɝ-
sheepman ˈʃipˌmæn, -mən |-men -ˌmɛn, -mən	sherd ʃard, ʃɝd; ES ʃɑːd, ʃɜd, ʃɝd, E+ʃɑːd
sheepshank ˈʃipˌʃæŋk	Sheridan ˈʃɛrədn̩
sheepshead ˈʃipsˌhɛd	sherif, -reef ʃəˈrif
sheepshearing ˈʃipˌʃɪrɪŋ; S+-ˌʃɛrɪŋ	sheriff ˈʃɛrɪf
sheepshed ˈʃipˌʃɛd	Sherlock ˈʃɝlak; ES ˈʃɜlak, ˈʃɝ-, -ˈlɒk
sheepskin ˈʃipˌskɪn	Sherman ˈʃɝmən; ES ˈʃɜm-, ˈʃɝm-
sheer ʃɪr; ES ʃɪə(r, S+ʃɛə(r; |-ed -d	Sherrill ˈʃɛrəl
sheerness ˈʃɪrnɪs; ES ˈʃɪə-, S -ˈʃɛə-	sherry ˈʃɛrɪ
Sheerness ʃɪrˈnɛs; ES ʃɪə-, S+ʃɛə-; |-'s -ɪz	Sherwood ˈʃɝwʊd; ES ˈʃɜ-, ˈʃɝ-
sheet ʃit |sheeted ˈʃitɪd	she's *'she is,' 'she has,'* stressed ˈʃiz, ˌʃiz;
Sheffield ˈʃɛfild	*unstr.* ʃiz, ʃɪz
she-goat ˈʃiˈgot	Shetland ˈʃɛtlənd
sheik, -kh ʃik, *Brit* ʃek	Shetucket ʃɪˈtʌkɪt
Sheila ˈʃilə	shew ʃo |shewed ʃod |shewn ʃon *or* shewed ʃod
shekel ˈʃɛkl̩	shewbread ˈʃoˌbrɛd

Shewmake 'ʃuˌmek, 'ʃɪu-
she-wolf 'ʃiˈwʊlf |-lves -lvz
Sheyenne ʃaɪˈɛn
Shiah 'ʃiə
Shiawassee ˌʃaɪəˈwɒsɪ
shibboleth 'ʃɪbəlɪθ |-ths -θs
Shickshinny 'ʃɪkˌʃɪnɪ
shied ʃaɪd
Shiel ʃil
shield ʃild |shielded 'ʃildɪd
shier 'ʃaɪɚ; ES 'ʃaɪ·ə(r
shies ʃaɪz
shift ʃɪft |shifted 'ʃɪftɪd
Shih ʃi
Shiite 'ʃiaɪt |-itic ʃiˈɪtɪk
Shikoku ʃiˈkoku
shillelagh, -lah, -ly, shillalah, -la, S-ʃəˈlelə, -lɪ
shilling, S- 'ʃɪlɪŋ
shilly-shally 'ʃɪlɪˌʃælɪ |-ied -d
Shilo, Shiloh 'ʃaɪlo
shily 'ʃaɪlɪ
shim ʃɪm |shimmed ʃɪmd
shimmer 'ʃɪmɚ; ES 'ʃɪmə(r; |-ed -d |-ing
   'ʃɪmərɪŋ, 'ʃɪmrɪŋ
shimmy 'ʃɪmɪ |-ied -d
shin, S- ʃɪn |shinned ʃɪnd
Shinar 'ʃaɪnɑr, -nɚ; ES -nɑː(r, -nə(r
shindig 'ʃɪndɪg |shindy 'ʃɪndɪ
shine ʃaɪn |shone ʃon, Brit ʃɒn, or arch. (except
   in sense 'polish') shined ʃaɪnd
shingle 'ʃɪŋgl̩ |-d -d |-ling 'ʃɪŋglɪŋ, -gl̩ɪŋ
shingly 'ʃɪŋglɪ
shinny 'ʃɪnɪ |-ied -d
shinplaster 'ʃɪnˌplæstɚ; ES -ˌplæstə(r, E+
   -ˌplas-, -ˌplɑs-
Shinto 'ʃɪnto |-ism -ˌɪzəm
shiny 'ʃaɪnɪ
ship ʃɪp |shipped ʃɪpt
-ship abstract noun ending, ˌunstressed -ʃɪp or
   half-stressed -ˌʃɪp. Words in -ship are often
   omitted from the vocab. when their pron. is
   obvious.
shipboard 'ʃɪpˌbord, -ˌbɔrd; ES -ˌboəd,
   E+-ˌbɔəd
shipbuilder 'ʃɪpˌbɪldɚ; ES -ˌbɪldə(r
shipload 'ʃɪpˌlod
shipman 'ʃɪpmən |-men -mən
shipmaster 'ʃɪpˌmæstɚ; ES -ˌmæstə(r, E+
   -ˌmas-, -ˌmɑs-

shipmate 'ʃɪpˌmet
shippable 'ʃɪpəbl̩
Shippen 'ʃɪpən |-sburg -zˌbɝg; ES -zˌbɜg,
   -zˌbɝg
shipshape 'ʃɪpˌʃep
shipwreck 'ʃɪpˌrɛk |-wrecked -ˌrɛkt
shipwright 'ʃɪpˌraɪt
shipyard 'ʃɪpˌjɑrd; ES -ˌjɑːd, E+-ˌjɑːd
Shiras 'ʃaɪrəs |-'s -ɪz
Shiraz ʃɪˈrɑz, 'ʃɪræz |-'s -ɪz
shire ʃaɪr; ES ʃaɪə(r
-shire -ʃɪr, -ʃɚ; ES -ʃɪə(r, -ʃə(r
shirk ʃɝk; ES ʃɜk, ʃɝk; |-ed -t
Shirley 'ʃɝlɪ; ES 'ʃɜ-, 'ʃɝ-
shirr ʃɝ; ES ʃɝ(r, ʃɝ; |-ed -d
shirt ʃɝt; ES ʃɜt, ʃɝt; |-ed -d |-tail -ˌtel
shirtwaist 'ʃɝtˌwest; ES 'ʃɜt-, 'ʃɝt-
shitta 'ʃɪtə
shittim 'ʃɪtɪm |-wood -ˌwʊd
Shiva 'ʃivə, 'ʃɪvə |-ism -ˌɪzəm
shivaree ˌʃɪvəˈri—see charivari |-d -d
shive ʃaɪv |shived ʃaɪvd
shiver 'ʃɪvɚ; ES 'ʃɪvə(r; |-ed -d |ing -vrɪŋ,
   -vərɪŋ
shivery 'ʃɪvrɪ, 'ʃɪvərɪ
shoal ʃol |shoaled ʃold
shoat ʃot
shock ʃak; ES+ʃɒk; |-ed -t
shockheaded 'ʃakˈhɛdɪd; ES+'ʃɒk-; ('shock-
   ˌheaded 'boy)
shod ʃad; ES+ʃɒd
shoddy 'ʃadɪ; ES+'ʃɒdɪ
shoe ʃu, ʃɪu (sp. shew 16–17cc.) |-horn -ˌhɔrn;
   ES -ˌhɔən; |-lace -ˌles |-laces -ˌlesɪz
   |-maker -ˌmekɚ; ES -ˌmekə(r; |-string
   -ˌstrɪŋ
shoer 'ʃuɚ, 'ʃɪuɚ; ES 'ʃu·ə(r, 'ʃɪu-
Shogun 'ʃoˌgʌn, -ˌgun |-ate -ɪt, -gʌnˌet, -gun-
shone ʃon, Brit ʃɒn
shoo ʃu |-ed -d
shook past of shake ʃʊk
shook n, v ʃʊk |shooked ʃʊkt
shoon ʃun
shoot ʃut |shot ʃat; ES+ʃɒt; |arch. pptc
   shotten 'ʃatn̩; ES+'ʃɒtn̩
shop ʃap; ES+ʃɒp; |-ped -t |-girl -ˌgɝl; ES see
   girl
shopkeeper 'ʃapˌkipɚ; ES -ˌkipə(r, 'ʃɒp-
shoplifter 'ʃapˌlɪftɚ; ES -ˌlɪftə(r, 'ʃɒp-

shopwalker 'ʃɑpˌwɔkɚ; ES -ˌwɔkə(r, 'ʃɒp-
shopwindow 'ʃɑp'wɪndo, -ˌwɪn-, -də; ES+
'ʃɒp-
shopwoman 'ʃɑpˌwʊmən, -ˌwu-; ES+'ʃɒp-;
|-men -ˌwɪmɪn, -ən
shopworn 'ʃɑpˌworn, -ˌwɔrn; ES -ˌwoən,
'ʃɒp-, E+-ˌwɔən
shore ʃor, ʃɔr; ES ʃoə(r, E+ʃɔə(r; |-d -d
|-ward -wɚd; ES -wəd
Shorey 'ʃorɪ, 'ʃɔrɪ; S 'ʃorɪ
shorn ʃorn, ʃɔrn; ES ʃoən, E+ʃɔən
short ʃɔrt; ES ʃɔət; |-ed -ɪd |-age -ɪdʒ
short-and-long 'ʃɔrtn̩'lɔŋ, -'lɒŋ; ES 'ʃɔət-,
S+-'lɑŋ
shortbread 'ʃɔrtˌbrɛd; ES 'ʃɔət-
short-breathed 'ʃɔrt'brɛθt; ES 'ʃɔət-
shortcake 'ʃɔrtˌkek; ES 'ʃɔət-
shortchange ˌʃɔrt'tʃendʒ; ES ˌʃɔət-; |-s -ɪz
|-d -d
short-circuit ˌʃɔrt'sɚkɪt; ES ˌʃɔət'sɜk-, ˌʃɔət-
'sɜk-; |-ed -ɪd
shortcoming 'ʃɔrtˌkʌmɪŋ, -'kʌm- |-s -z
short-eared 'ʃɔrt'ɪrd; ES 'ʃɔət'ɪəd, S+-'ɛəd;
('short-ˌeared 'owl)
shorten 'ʃɔrtn̩; ES 'ʃɔətn̩; |-ed -d |-ing -tnɪŋ,
-tn̩ɪŋ
Shorter C. K. 'ʃɔrtɚ; ES 'ʃɔətə(r; Ga college+
'ʃautɚ; ES -tə(r
shorthand 'ʃɔrtˌhænd; ES 'ʃɔət-; |-ed -ɪd
shorthanded 'ʃɔrt'hændɪd; ES 'ʃɔət-; ('short-
ˌhanded 'job)
shorthorn 'ʃɔrtˌhɔrn; ES 'ʃɔətˌhɔən
Shorthouse 'ʃɔrtˌhaʊs; ES 'ʃɔət-; |-'s -ɪz
short-lived 'ʃɔrt'laɪvd; ES 'ʃɔət-; — The pron.
'ʃɔrt'lɪvd is a misapprehension, now accepted in England.
shortsighted 'ʃɔrt'saɪtɪd; ES 'ʃɔət-
short-skirted 'ʃɔrt'skɚtɪd; ES 'ʃɔət'skɜt-,
'ʃɔət'skɜt-; ('short-ˌskirted 'coat)
short-tempered 'ʃɔrt'tɛmpɚd; ES 'ʃɔət-
'tɛmpəd
short-winded 'ʃɔrt'wɪndɪd; ES 'ʃɔət-
Shoshone ʃo'ʃonɪ |-nian -nɪən |-nean -nɪən,
ˌʃoʃə'niən
shot ʃat; ES+ʃɒt; |-ted -ɪd |-gun -ˌgʌn
shote ʃot
shotten 'ʃatn̩; ES+'ʃɒtn̩
Shottery 'ʃatərɪ; ES+'ʃɒt-
should stressed 'ʃʊd, ˌʃʊd; unstr. ʃəd, ʃd, ʃt

shoulder 'ʃoldɚ; ES 'ʃoldə(r; |-ed -d |-ing
-dərɪŋ, -drɪŋ
shouldest 'ʃʊdɪst
shouldn't 'should not' 'ʃʊdn̩t—The pron.
'ʃʊdənt is not in general use.
shouldst stressed 'ʃʊdst, ˌʃʊdst; unstr. ʃədst
shout ʃaʊt |shouted 'ʃaʊtɪd
shove 'shive' ʃov
shove 'push' ʃʌv |shoved ʃʌvd
shovel 'ʃʌvl̩ |-ed -d |-ing 'ʃʌvlɪŋ, 'ʃʌvl̩ɪŋ
shovelboard 'ʃʌvl̩ˌbord, -ˌbɔrd; ES -ˌboəd,
E+-ˌbɔəd
shovelful 'ʃʌvl̩ˌfʊl |-fuls -ˌfʊlz
show ʃo |-ed ʃod |-n ʃon or -ed ʃod
showboat 'ʃoˌbot
showbread 'ʃoˌbrɛd
showcase 'ʃoˌkes |-s -ɪz
showdown 'ʃoˌdaʊn
shower 'who shows' 'ʃoɚ; ES 'ʃo·ə(r
shower 'rain' 'ʃaʊɚ, ʃaʊr; ES 'ʃaʊ·ə(r,
ʃaʊə(r; |-ed -d |-ing 'ʃaʊrɪŋ, 'ʃaʊərɪŋ |-y
'ʃaʊrɪ, 'ʃaʊərɪ
showman 'ʃomən |-men -mən |-ship -ˌʃɪp
shown ʃon
show-off 'ʃoˌɔf, -ˌɒf
showroom 'ʃoˌrum, -ˌrʊm
shrank ʃræŋk
shrapnel 'ʃræpnəl |-ed -d
shrdlu ʃɚd'lu; ES ʃəd'lu; cf etaoin
shred ʃrɛd |shred ʃrɛd or shredded 'ʃrɛdɪd
Shreveport 'ʃrivˌport, -ˌpɔrt; ES -ˌpoət,
E+-ˌpɔət
shrew ʃru, ʃrɪu, arch. ʃro (thus in Shak.)
shrewd ʃrud, ʃrɪud, arch. ʃrod |-ly -lɪ
Shrewsbury 'ʃruzˌbɛrɪ, 'ʃrɪuz-, 'ʃroz-, -bərɪ,
in Mass loc.+'ʃɪuzbərɪ, the first r being lost
by dissimilation (§121)
shriek ʃrik |shrieked ʃrikt
shrievalty 'ʃrivl̩tɪ
shrift ʃrɪft
shrike ʃraɪk |-d -t
shrill ʃrɪl |shrilled ʃrɪld
shrilly adj 'ʃrɪlɪ, adv 'ʃrɪllɪ
shrimp ʃrɪmp |shrimped ʃrɪmpt
shrine ʃraɪn |shrined ʃraɪnd |-nal -l̩
Shriner 'ʃraɪnɚ; ES 'ʃraɪnə(r
shrink ʃrɪŋk |shrank ʃræŋk or shrunk ʃrʌŋk
|shrunk ʃrʌŋk or shrunken 'ʃrʌŋkən |-able
-əbl̩ |-age -ɪdʒ

|full fʊl |tooth tuθ |further 'fɚðɚ; ES 'fɜðə |custom 'kʌstəm |while hwaɪl |how haʊ |toy tɔɪ
|using 'juzɪŋ |fuse fjuz, fɪuz |dish dɪʃ |vision 'vɪʒən |Eden 'idn̩ |cradle 'kredl̩ |keep 'em 'kipm̩

shrive ʃraɪv |shrived ʃraɪvd *or* shrove ʃrov
|shriven 'ʃrɪvən *or* shrived ʃraɪvd
shrivel 'ʃrɪvl̩ |-ed -d |-ing 'ʃrɪvlɪŋ, -vl̩ɪŋ
Shropshire 'ʃrɑpʃɪr, -ʃɚ; ES -ʃɪə(r, -ʃə(r,
'ʃrɒp-
shroud ʃraʊd |shrouded 'ʃraʊdɪd
shrove, S- ʃrov |Shrovetide 'ʃrov͵taɪd
shrub ʃrʌb |shrubbed ʃrʌbd |-bery -ərɪ, -rɪ
shrug ʃrʌg |shrugged ʃrʌgd
shrunk ʃrʌŋk |-en -ən
shuck ʃʌk |shucked ʃʌkt
shudder 'ʃʌdɚ; ES 'ʃʌdə(r; |-ed -d |-ing
'ʃʌdərɪŋ, 'ʃʌdrɪŋ |-y -dərɪ, -drɪ
shuffle 'ʃʌfl̩ |-d -d |-ling 'ʃʌflɪŋ, -fl̩ɪŋ
shuffleboard 'ʃʌfl̩͵bord, -͵bɔrd; ES -͵boəd,
E+-͵bɔəd
Shuhite 'ʃuhaɪt, 'ʃɪu-
shun ʃʌn |shunned ʃʌnd
shunt ʃʌnt |shunted 'ʃʌntɪd
shush ʃʌʃ, ʃ: |-ed -t
shut ʃʌt |-down -͵daʊn |shut-in 'ʃʌt͵ɪn
shutter 'ʃʌtɚ; ES 'ʃʌtə(r; |-ed -d
shuttle 'ʃʌtl̩ |-d -d |-ling 'ʃʌtl̩ɪŋ, 'ʃʌtl̩ɪŋ
shuttlecock 'ʃʌtl̩͵kɑk; ES+-͵kɒk; |-ed -t
shy ʃaɪ |shied ʃaɪd
Shylock 'ʃaɪlɑk; ES+-lɒk
shyly 'ʃaɪlɪ
shyster 'ʃaɪstɚ; ES 'ʃaɪstə(r
si *music* si
-sia *unstressed ending* (magnesia) *variously
pronounced* -ʃə, -ʃɪə, -ʃjə, -ʒə, -ʒɪə, -ʒjə,
-sɪə, -sjə, -zɪə, -zjə. *Besides the pron. given
in the vocab. it is to be understood that one
or more of the other variants are often heard.*
Siam saɪ'æm, 'saɪæm
Siamese ͵saɪə'miz ('Sia͵mese 'pheasant)
Siamese *v* ͵saɪə'miz |-s -ɪz |-d -d
Siasconset ͵saɪə'skɑnsɪt; ES+-'skɒn-; *loc.*
'skɒnsɪt, 'skɒn-
sib sɪb
sibboleth 'sɪbəlɪθ |-ths -θs
Sibelius sɪ'belɪəs, -'bi- |-'s -ɪz
Siberia saɪ'bɪrɪə, sə- |-n -n
sibilance 'sɪbl̩əns |-cy -ɪ |-ant -ənt
sibyl, S- 'sɪbl̩, -ɪl |-line 'sɪbl̩͵in, -ɪn
Sibylla, -illa, s- sɪ'bɪlə
sic sɪk |sicked sɪkt
Sicilia sɪ'sɪlɪə, -ljə |-n -n
Sicily 'sɪsl̩ɪ, -ɪlɪ

Sicinius sɪ'sɪnɪəs, -njəs |-'s -ɪz
sick sɪk |sicked sɪkt |-bed -͵bɛd
sick-abed *adj* 'sɪkə'bɛd, *n* 'sɪkə͵bɛd
sicken 'sɪkən |-ed -d |-ing 'sɪknɪŋ, -kənɪŋ
sickle 'sɪkl̩ |sickled 'sɪkl̩d
Sickles 'sɪkl̩z |-'s -ɪz
sickly 'sɪklɪ
sic transit gloria mundi 'sɪk'trænsɪt'glorɪə-
'mʌndaɪ, -'glɒr-; S -'glor-
Siddons 'sɪdn̩z |-'s -ɪz
siddur 'sɪdʊr; ES -dʊə(r
side saɪd |sided 'saɪdɪd
sideboard 'saɪd͵bord, -͵bɔrd; ES -͵boəd,
E+-͵bɔəd
sideburns 'saɪd͵bɝnz; ES -͵bɜnz, -͵bɝnz
sidecar 'saɪd͵kɑr; ES -͵kɑ:(r, E+-͵kɑ:(r
sidehill 'saɪd'hɪl ('side͵hill 'grove)
sideling 'moving aside' 'saɪdlɪŋ, -dlɪŋ
sideling 'sideways' 'saɪdlɪŋ
sidelong 'saɪd͵lɒŋ, -͵lɒŋ; S+-͵lɑŋ
sideral 'sɪdərəl
sidereal saɪ'dɪrɪəl |-ly -ɪ
sidesaddle 'saɪd͵sædl̩
sideslip 'saɪd͵slɪp |-ped -t
sidesplitting 'saɪd͵splɪtɪŋ
side-step 'saɪd͵stɛp |-ped -t
sideswipe 'saɪd͵swaɪp |- d -t
sidetrack 'saɪd͵træk |-ed -t
sidewalk 'saɪd͵wɔk
sideward 'saɪdwɚd; ES -wəd; |-s -z
sideways 'saɪd͵wez |-wise -͵waɪz
Sidgwick 'sɪdʒwɪk, 'sɪdʒɪk
siding 'saɪdɪŋ
sidle 'saɪdl̩ |-d -d |-ling 'saɪdlɪŋ, 'saɪdlɪŋ
sidling 'moving aside' 'saɪdlɪŋ, 'saɪdlɪŋ
sidling 'sideways' 'saɪdlɪŋ
Sidney 'sɪdnɪ
Sidon 'saɪdn̩ |-donian saɪ'donɪən
siècle *Fr* sjɛkl̩
siege sidʒ |sieges 'sidʒɪz |sieged sidʒd
Siegfried 'sigfrid (*Ger* 'ziːkfriːt)
Siena sɪ'ɛnə (*It* 'sjɛːnɑ)
Sienkiewicz ʃɛn'kjevɪtʃ |-'s -ɪz
sienna sɪ'ɛnə
sierra sɪ'ɛrə, 'sɪrə
Sierra Leone sɪ'ɛrəlɪ'onɪ, 'sɪrəlɪ'on
Sierra Nevada sɪ'ɛrənə'vædə, 'sɪrə-, -'vɑdə
siesta sɪ'ɛstə
sieve sɪv |sieved sɪvd

Sievers ˈzivɚz, ˈsiv-; ES -vəz; |-'s -ɪz (Ger
ˈziːfərs, -vərs)
sift sɪft |sifted ˈsɪftɪd |-age -ɪdʒ
sigh saɪ |sighed saɪd
sight saɪt |sighted ˈsaɪtɪd |-ly -lɪ
sight-seeing ˈsaɪtˌsiɪŋ
sight-seer ˈsaɪtˌsiɚ; ES -ˌsi·ə(r
sigil ˈsɪdʒəl, -ɪl
sigillum sɪˈdʒɪləm |-la -ə
Sigismond, -und ˈsɪdʒɪsmənd, ˈsɪgɪs- (Ger
ˈziːgɪsˌmunt)
sigma ˈsɪgmə |-moid -mɔɪd
sigmoidal sɪgˈmɔɪdl̩ |-ly -ɪ
sign saɪn |signed saɪnd
signal ˈsɪgn̩l |-ed -d |-ly -ɪ
signalize ˈsɪgnəˌlaɪz |-s -ɪz |-d -d
signalman ˈsɪgn̩lˌmæn, -mən |-men -ˌmɛn,
-mən
signatory ˈsɪgnəˌtorɪ, -ˌtɔrɪ; S -ˌtorɪ
signature ˈsɪgnətʃɚ, ˈsɪgnɪ-; ES -tʃə(r; |-d -d
signboard ˈsaɪnˌbord, -ˌbɔrd; ES -ˌboəd, E+
-ˌbɔəd
signet ˈsɪgnɪt |-ed -ɪd
significance sɪgˈnɪfəkəns |-cy -ɪ |-ant -ənt
signification sɪgˌnɪfəˈkeʃən, ˌsɪgnɪfə-
significative sɪgˈnɪfəˌketɪv
signify ˈsɪgnəˌfaɪ |-fied -ˌfaɪd
signor, S- ˈsinjor, -jɔr; ES -joə(r, E+-jɔə(r;
(It siɲˈnor)
signora sinˈjorə (It siɲˈnoːra)
signore sinˈjore (It siɲˈnoːre)
signorina ˌsinjəˈrinə (It ˌsiɲɲoˈriːna)
signory ˈsinjərɪ
signpost ˈsaɪnˌpost
Sigourney ˈsɪgɚnɪ; ES ˈsɪgənɪ
Sigurd ˈsɪgɚd; ES ˈsɪgəd; (Ger ˈziːgurt, Ice
ˈsɪgurður)
Sikes saɪks |-'s -ɪz
Sikh sik
silage ˈsaɪlɪdʒ |-s -ɪz
Silas ˈsaɪləs |-'s -ɪz
silence ˈsaɪləns |-s -ɪz |-d -t |-ent -ənt
Silenus saɪˈlinəs |-'s -ɪz
Silesia saɪˈliʃɪə, sə-, -ʃə |-n -n
silex ˈsaɪlɛks
silica ˈsɪlɪkə
silicate n ˈsɪlɪkɪt, -ˌket
silicate v ˈsɪlɪˌket |-d -ɪd

silicic səˈlɪsɪk
silicon ˈsɪlɪkən
silicosis ˌsɪlɪˈkosɪs |-cotic -ˈkatɪk; ES+-ˈkɒt-
Silius ˈsɪlɪəs |-'s -ɪz
silk sɪlk |silked sɪlkt
silken ˈsɪlkən |-ed -d
silkworm ˈsɪlkˌwɝm; ES -ˌwɜm, -ˌwɝm
sill, S- sɪl |silled sɪld
sillabub, silli- ˈsɪləˌbʌb, ˈsɪlɪ·
silly ˈsɪlɪ |-iness -nɪs
silo ˈsaɪlo |siloed ˈsaɪlod
Siloam saɪˈloəm, sə-, -ˈlom
silt sɪlt |silted ˈsɪltɪd
Silurian səˈlurɪən, -ˈlɪur-, saɪ-
silva ˈsɪlvə |silvan ˈsɪlvən
Silvanus sɪlˈvenəs |-'s -ɪz
silver ˈsɪlvɚ; ES ˈsɪlvə(r; |-ed -d |-ing
ˈsɪlvərɪŋ, ˈsɪlvrɪŋ
silver-plate 'plate with silver' ˈsɪlvɚˈplet; ES
ˈsɪlvə-; |-d -ɪd
silversmith ˈsɪlvɚˌsmɪθ; ES ˈsɪlvə-
silverware ˈsɪlvɚˌwɛr, -ˌwær; E ˈsɪlvəˌwɛə(r,
ES -ˌwæə(r
Silvester sɪlˈvɛstɚ; ES -ˈvɛstə(r
Silvia ˈsɪlvɪə
silvicultural ˌsɪlvɪˈkʌltʃərəl |-ly -ɪ
silviculture ˈsɪlvɪˌkʌltʃɚ; ES -ˌkʌltʃə(r
Silvius ˈsɪlvɪəs |-'s -ɪz
Simcoe ˈsɪmko
Simcox ˈsɪmkaks, ˈsɪmp-; ES+-kɒks; |-'s -ɪz
Simeon ˈsɪmɪən
simian ˈsɪmɪən
similar ˈsɪmələ; ES ˈsɪmələ(r
similarity ˌsɪməˈlærətɪ
simile ˈsɪməˌli, -lɪ
similitude səˈmɪləˌtjud, -ˌtɪud, -ˌtud
Simla ˈsɪmlə
simmer ˈsɪmɚ; ES ˈsɪmə(r; |-ed -d |-ing
ˈsɪmərɪŋ, ˈsɪmrɪŋ
Simms sɪmz |-'s -ɪz
simnel, S- ˈsɪmnəl
Simoïs ˈsɪmo·ɪs, ˈsɪməwɪs
simoleon səˈmolɪən
Simon ˈsaɪmən
simoniac səˈmonɪˌæk
simoniacal ˌsaɪməˈnaɪəkl̩, ˌsɪm- |-ly -ɪ, -ɪklɪ
Simonides saɪˈmanəˌdiz, -ˈmɒn- |-'s -ɪz
Simoniz ˈsaɪmənˌaɪz |-es -ɪz |-ed -d
simon-pure ˈsaɪmənˈpjur, -ˈpɪur; ES -ə(r

|full fʊl |tooth tuθ |further ˈfɝðɚ; ES ˈfɜðə |custom ˈkʌstəm |while hwaɪl |how haʊ |toy tɔɪ
|using ˈjuzɪŋ |fuse fjuz, fɪuz |dish dɪʃ |vision ˈvɪʒən |Eden ˈidn̩ |cradle ˈkredl̩ |keep 'em ˈkipm̩

simony 'saɪmənɪ, 'sɪm-
simoom sɪ'mum, saɪ- |-moon -'mun
simp sɪmp
Simpcox 'sɪmpkɑks; ES+-kɒks; |-'s -ɪz
simper 'sɪmpɚ; ES 'sɪmpə(r; |-ed -d |-ing
'sɪmpərɪŋ, 'sɪmprɪŋ
simple, S- 'sɪmpl̩ |-d -d |-ling 'sɪmplɪŋ, -pl̩ɪŋ
|-r -plɚ; ES -plə(r; |-st -plɪst
simple-minded 'sɪmpl̩'maɪndɪd
simpleton 'sɪmpl̩tən |-tonian ˌsɪmpl̩'tonɪən
simplex 'sɪmplɛks |-es -ɪz |-ed -t
simplicity sɪm'plɪsətɪ
simplification ˌsɪmpləfə'keʃən
simplify 'sɪmpləˌfaɪ |-fied -ˌfaɪd
Simplon 'sɪmplɑn, -plɒn
simply 'sɪmplɪ
Simpson, Simson 'sɪmpsn̩, 'sɪmsn̩
Sims sɪmz |-'s -ɪz
simulacre 'sɪmjəˌlekɚ; ES -ˌlekə(r
simulacrum ˌsɪmjə'lekrəm |-cra -krə
simulate adj 'sɪmjəlɪt, -ˌlet
simulate 'sɪmjəˌlet |-d -ɪd |-tion ˌsɪmjə'leʃən
simultaneity ˌsaɪml̩tə'nɪətɪ, ˌsɪml̩-
simultaneous ˌsaɪml̩'tenɪəs, ˌsɪml̩-, -njəs
sin sɪn |sinned sɪnd |-ful -fəl |-fully -fəlɪ
Sinai 'saɪnaɪ, 'saɪnɪˌaɪ
Sinaitic ˌsaɪnɪ'ɪtɪk |-us -əs
Sinbad 'sɪnbæd
since sɪns
sincere sɪn'sɪr, sn̩-; ES -'sɪə(r, S+-'sɛə(r
sincerity sɪn'sɛrətɪ, sn̩-
Sinclair Brit name 'sɪŋklɛr, 'sɪn-, -klær,
'sɪŋklɚ; E -klɛə(r, ES -klæə(r, 'sɪŋklə(r
Sinclair Am name sɪn'klɛr, -'klær; E -'klɛə(r,
ES -'klæə(r
Sindbad 'sɪnbæd
sine math. saɪn
sine 'without' 'saɪnɪ
sinecure 'saɪnɪˌkjʊr, 'sɪnɪ-, -ˌkɪʊr; ES -ə(r;
|-rist -ɪst
sine die 'saɪnɪ'daɪ·i
sine qua non 'saɪnɪkwe'nɑn, -'nɒn
sinew 'sɪnju, 'sɪnɪu, 'sɪnu
sinewy 'sɪnjəwɪ, 'sɪnəwɪ
sing sɪŋ |sang sæŋ or sung sʌŋ |sung sʌŋ
Singapore 'sɪŋgəˌpor, 'sɪŋə-, -ˌpɔr; ES -ˌpoə(r,
E+-ˌpɔə(r; acct+ˌSinga'pore
singe sɪndʒ |singes 'sɪndʒɪz |singed sɪndʒd
singer 'who sings' 'sɪŋɚ; ES 'sɪŋə(r

singer 'who singes' 'sɪndʒɚ; ES 'sɪndʒə(r
singh, S- sɪŋ
Singhalese ˌsɪŋgə'liz |-'s -ɪz
single 'sɪŋgl̩ |-d -d |-ling 'sɪŋglɪŋ, -gl̩ɪŋ
singlehanded 'sɪŋgl̩'hændɪd
singlehearted 'sɪŋgl̩'hɑrtɪd; ES -'hɑ:t-, E+
-'hɑ:t-
singlestick 'sɪŋgl̩ˌstɪk
singlet 'sɪŋglɪt
Singleton, s- 'sɪŋgl̩tən
singletree 'sɪŋgl̩ˌtri, -trɪ
singly 'sɪŋglɪ
Sing Sing 'sɪŋˌsɪŋ
singsong 'sɪŋˌsɔŋ, -ˌsɒŋ; S+-ˌsɑŋ
singular 'sɪŋgjəlɚ; ES -lə(r
singularity ˌsɪŋgjə'lærətɪ
Sinhalese ˌsɪnhə'liz |-'s -ɪz
sinister 'sɪnɪstɚ; ES 'sɪnɪstə(r; |-tral -trəl
sink sɪŋk |sank sæŋk or sunk sʌŋk |sunk sʌŋk
sinkhole 'sɪŋkˌhol
sinner 'sɪnɚ; ES 'sɪnə(r
Sinn Fein 'ʃɪn'fen |-ism -ɪzəm
Sino-Japanese ˌsaɪnoˌdʒæpə'niz, ˌsɪno-
Sinology saɪ'nɑlədʒɪ, sɪ-; ES+-'nɒl-
Sinon 'saɪnən
sinter 'sɪntɚ; ES 'sɪntə(r; |-ed -d
sinuate adj 'sɪnjuɪt, -ˌet
sinuate v 'sɪnjuˌet |-d -ɪd
sinuosity ˌsɪnju'ɑsətɪ; ES+-'ɒs-
sinuous 'sɪnjuəs
sinus 'saɪnəs |-es -ɪz
Sion 'Zion' 'saɪən
-sion unstressed ending -ʃən, -ʃn̩—The pron.
-ʃn̩ is less common in America than in England.
Sioux su |pl Sioux su, suz |Siouan 'suən
sip sɪp |sipped sɪpt
siphon 'saɪfən, -fɑn, -fɒn |-ed -d |-age -fənɪdʒ
|-al -fənl̩
sir stressed 'sɝ, ˌsɝ; ES 'sɜ(r, 'sɝ, ˌsɜ(r, ˌsɝ;
unstr. sɚ; ES sə(r
sirdar, S- sɚ'dɑr; ES sə'dɑ:(r, E+-'dɑ:(r
sire saɪr; ES saɪə(r; |-d -d
siren 'saɪrən
sirenic saɪ'rɛnɪk |-al -l̩ |-ally -l̩ɪ, -ɪklɪ
Sirius 'sɪrɪəs |-'s -ɪz
sirloin 'sɝlɔɪn; ES 'sɜ-, 'sɝ-
sirocco sə'rako; ES+-'rɒko
sirrah 'sɪrə

sirup ˈsɪrəp, ˈsɜ˞əp; E ˈsɪrəp, ˈsɜrəp, ˈsɜ˞əp;
S ˈsɜrəp, ˈsʌrəp, ˈsɪrəp, ˈsɜ˞əp, ˈserəp—*The
pron.* ˈsɛrəp, *found also occasionally in N
& E, is a normal traditional form. Cf*
Syracuse, Miriam.

sisal ˈsaɪsl̩, ˈsɪsl̩

Sisam ˈsaɪsəm

Sisera ˈsɪsərə

sissify ˈsɪsɪˌfaɪ |-fied -ˌfaɪd |sissy ˈsɪsɪ

Sisson ˈsɪsn̩

sister ˈsɪstɚ; ES -tə(r; |-ed -d |-ing -trɪŋ,
-tərɪŋ

sister-in-law ˈsɪstərɪnˌlɔ, ˈsɪstən̩ˌlɔ; ES ˈsɪstərɪnˌlɔ, ˈsɪstənˌlɔ

sisters-in-law ˈsɪstɚzɪnˌlɔ, ˈsɪstɚzn̩ˌlɔ; ES
ˈsɪstəzɪnˌlɔ, ˈsɪstəzn̩ˌlɔ

Sistine ˈsɪstin, -tɪn

Sisyphus ˈsɪsəfəs |-ˈs -ɪz |-phean ˌsɪsəˈfiən

sit sɪt |sat sæt, *arch.* sate set, sæt |sat sæt

sit-down ˈsɪtˌdaʊn

sit down sɪˈdaʊn, sɪtˈdaʊn—sɪˈdaʊn *is the
usual conversational pronunciation.* Sat
down, *being less frequent, keeps the* t *sound.*

site saɪt |sited ˈsaɪtɪd

sith sɪθ

Sitka ˈsɪtkə

sitology saɪˈtɑlədʒɪ; ES+-ˈtɒl-

sitting ˈsɪtɪŋ

Sittingbourne ˈsɪtɪŋˌborn, -ˌbɔrn; ES -ˌboən,
E+-ˌbɔən

situate *adj* ˈsɪtʃʊɪt, -ˌet

situate *v* ˈsɪtʃuˌet |-d -ɪd

situation ˌsɪtʃuˈeʃən, ˌsɪtʃəˈweʃən

situs ˈsaɪtəs

Sitwell ˈsɪtwəl, -wɛl

Siva ˈsivə, ˈʃivə, -ɪvə |-ism -ˌɪzəm

Siward ˈsjuɚd, ˈsɪu-, ˈsu-; ES -əd

siwash, S- ˈsaɪwɑʃ, -wɔʃ, -wɒʃ |-es -ɪz |-ed -t

six sɪks |sixes ˈsɪksɪz

sixes and sevens ˈsɪksɪzn̩ˈsɛvənz

sixfold *adj, adv* ˈsɪksˈfold (ˈsɪxˌfold ˈloss)

sixpence ˈsɪkspəns |-s -ɪz

sixpenny ˈsɪksˌpɛnɪ, -pənɪ

sixscore ˈsɪksˈskor, ˈsɪkˈsk-, -ˈskɔr; ES
-ˈskoə(r, E+-ˈskɔə(r; (ˈsɪxˌscore ˈyears)

six-shooter ˈsɪksˈʃutɚ, ˈsɪkʃˈʃ-; ES -ˈʃutə(r

sixteen sɪksˈtin, ˈsɪksˈtin (ˈsɪxˌteen ˈmen)

sixteenmo sɪksˈtinmo

sixteenth sɪksˈtinθ, ˈsɪksˈ- |-ths -θs

sixth sɪksθ |sixths sɪksθs, sɪks:

Sixtus ˈsɪkstəs |-ˈs -ɪz

sixty ˈsɪkstɪ |-ieth -ɪθ |-ieths -ɪθs |-fold -ˈfold
(ˈsixtyˌfold ˈgain)

sizable ˈsaɪzəbl̩ |-bly -blɪ

sizar, -er ˈsaɪzɚ; ES ˈsaɪzə(r

size saɪz |sizes ˈsaɪzɪz |sized saɪzd

sizeable ˈsaɪzəbl̩ |-bly -blɪ

sizzle ˈsɪzl̩ |-d -d |-ling ˈsɪzlɪŋ, ˈsɪzl̩ɪŋ

Skager Rack, -er-Rak, -errak ˈskægɚˌræk,
ˌskægɚˈræk; ES -gə-

Skagit ˈskægɪt

Skagway ˈskægwe

skald skɔld, skɑld

Skaneateles ˌskænɪˈætləs, *loc.* ˌskɪnɪˈætləs
|-ˈs -ɪz—*The loc. pron. apparently comes
from an older form* Skeneateles ˌskɪnɪ-.

skat 'scat' skæt |skatted ˈskætɪd

skat *game* skɑt

skate sket |skated ˈsketɪd

Skeat skit

skedaddle skɪˈdædl̩ |-d -d |-ling -dlɪŋ, -dl̩ɪŋ

skee 'ski' ski

skeesicks, -zix ˈskizɪks, -zəks |-ˈs -ɪz

skeet skit

skein sken |skeined skend

skeleton ˈskɛlətn̩ |-ed -d |-tal -tl̩

skeletonize ˈskɛlətn̩ˌaɪz |-s -ɪz |-d -d

skelp skɛlp |skelped skɛlpt

Skelton ˈskɛltn̩

skeptic ˈskɛptɪk |-al -l̩ |-ally -l̩ɪ, -ɪklɪ

skepticism ˈskɛptəˌsɪzəm

skerry ˈskɛrɪ

sketch skɛtʃ |-es -ɪz |-ed -t |-book -ˌbʊk

skew skju, skɪu |-ed -d |-er -ɚ; ES -ə(r

ski ski |skis skiz |skied skid (*Norw, Sw* ʃi)

skiagram ˈskaɪəˌgræm |-graph -ˌgræf; E+
-ˌgraf, -ˌgrɑf

skiagraphy skaɪˈægrəfɪ

skid skɪd |skidded ˈskɪdɪd

Skiddaw ˈskɪdɔ

skier 'who skis' ˈskiɚ; ES ˈski·ə(r

skier 'skyer' ˈskaɪɚ; ES ˈskaɪ·ə(r

skies skaɪz

skiff skɪf |skiffed skɪft

skiing ˈskiɪŋ

skill skɪl |skilled skɪld

skillet ˈskɪlɪt

skillful, skilf- ˈskɪlfəl |-ly -ɪ

skill-less 'skɪllıs
skim skɪm |skimmed skɪmd |-mer -ɚ; ES -ə(r
skim milk 'skɪm'mɪlk
skimp skɪmp |skimped skɪmpt |-y -ı
skin skɪn |skinned skɪnd |-ny -ı
skin-deep 'skɪn'dip ('skin-ˌdeep 'cut)
skinflint 'skɪnˌflɪnt
skinful 'skɪnˌfʊl |-fuls -ˌfʊlz
skinner, S- 'skɪnɚ; ES 'skɪnə(r
skintight 'skɪn'taɪt ('skinˌtight 'boots)
skip skɪp |skipped skɪpt
skipper 'skɪpɚ; ES 'skɪpə(r; |-ed -d |-y -ı
skirl skɝl; ES skɜl, skɝl; |-ed -d
skirmish 'skɝmɪʃ; ES 'skɜm-, 'skɝm-; |-es
    -ız |-ed -t
skirr skɝ; ES skɜ(r, skɝ; |-ed -d
skirt skɝt; ES skɜt, skɝt; |-ed -ıd
skit skɪt |skitted 'skɪtɪd
skitter 'skɪtɚ; ES 'skɪtə(r; |-ed -d
skittish 'skɪtɪʃ
skittle 'skɪtl̩ |-d -d |-s -z
skoal skol |skoaled skold
Skowhegan skau'higən
skua 'skjuə, 'skɪuə
skulduddery skʌl'dʌdɚɪ, -drı |-duggery
    -'dʌgɚɪ, -grı
skulk skʌlk |skulked skʌlkt
skull 'head' skʌl |skulled skʌld
skull 'scull' skʌl |skulled skʌld
skullcap 'skʌlˌkæp, -'kæp
skullduddery, -dugg- see skulduddery
skull-less 'skʌllıs
skunk skʌŋk |skunked skʌŋkt
sky skaɪ |skied or skyed skaɪd |-ey -ı
Skye skaɪ
skyer 'high hit' 'skaɪɚ; ES 'skaɪ-ə(r
skylark 'skaɪˌlɑrk; ES -ˌlɑ:k, E+-ˌlɑ:k; |-ed -t
skylight 'skaɪˌlaɪt |-ed -ıd
skyrocket 'skaɪˌrɑkɪt; ES+-ˌrɒk-; |-ed -ıd
skyscraper 'skaɪˌskrepɚ; ES -ˌskrepə(r
skyward 'skaɪwɚd; ES -wəd
slab slæb |slabbed slæbd
slab-sided 'slæb'saɪdɪd ('slab-ˌsided 'gawk)
slack slæk |slacked slækt
slacken 'slækən |-ed -d |-ing -kənıŋ, -knıŋ
slag slæg |slagged slægd
slain slen
Slaithwaite 'sleθwet, loc.+'sloət
slake slek |slaked slekt

slam slæm |slammed slæmd
slander 'slændɚ; ES 'slændə(r; |-ed -d |-ing
    'slændrıŋ, -dərıŋ |-ous -drəs, -dərəs
slang slæŋ |slanged slæŋd |-y -ı
slant slænt; E+slant, slɑnt; |-ed -ıd
slap slæp |slapped slæpt
slapdash 'slæpˌdæʃ |-es -ız |-ed -t |-ery -ɚı,
    -rı
slapjack 'slæpˌdʒæk
slapstick 'slæpˌstɪk
slash slæʃ |slashes 'slæʃız |slashed slæʃt
slat slæt |slatted 'slætɪd
slate slet |slated 'sletɪd
slate-pencil 'sletˌpɛnsl̩
slather 'slæðɚ, 'sle-; ES -ðə(r; |-ed -d |-ing
    -ðrıŋ, -ðərıŋ
slattern 'slætɚn; ES 'slætən
slaty 'sletı
slaughter, S- 'slɔtɚ; ES -tə(r; |-ed -d |-ing
    'slɔtərıŋ, 'slɔtrıŋ |-ous -əs, -trəs
Slav slɑv, slæv
slave slev |slaved slevd |-ry -rı, -ərı
slaveholder 'slevˌholdɚ; ES -ˌholdə(r
slavey 'slevı
Slavic 'slævɪk, 'slɑv-
Slavonia slə'vonıə |-n -n
Slavonic slə'vɑnık; ES+-'vɒn-; |-ally -ļı,
    -ıklı
slaw slɔ
slay sle |slew slu, slɪu |slain slen
slazy 'sleazy', 'slezı
sleave sliv |sleaved slivd
sleazy 'slezı, 'slizı
sled slɛd |sledded 'slɛdɪd
sledge slɛdʒ |sledges 'slɛdʒız |sledged slɛdʒd
sleek slik |sleeked slikt, cf slick
sleep slip |slept slɛpt |-y -ı
sleepwalker 'slipˌwɔkɚ; ES -ˌwɔkə(r
sleepyhead 'slipıˌhɛd
sleet slit |sleeted 'slitɪd
sleeve sliv |sleeved slivd
sleigh sle |sleighed sled
sleight slaɪt
slender, S- 'slɛndɚ; ES 'slɛndə(r; |-er -drɚ
    -dərɚ; ES -rə(r
slept slɛpt
sleuth sluθ, slɪuθ |-ed -t
slew slu, slɪu |-ed -d
slice slaɪs |slices 'slaɪsız |sliced slaɪst

slick **slɪk** |slicked **slɪkt**
slicker **'slɪkɚ**; ES **'slɪkə(r**
slide **slaɪd** |slid **slɪd** |slid **slɪd** or slidden **'slɪdn̩**
Slidell **slaɪ'dɛl, 'slaɪdḷ**
slier **'slaɪɚ**; ES **'slaɪ·ə(r**
slight **slaɪt** |slighted **'slaɪtɪd**
Sligo **'slaɪgo**
slily **'slaɪlɪ**
slim **slɪm** |slimmed **slɪmd**
slime **slaɪm** |slimed **slaɪmd**
slimish **'slaɪmɪʃ**
slimmish **'slɪmɪʃ**
slimpsy **'slɪmpsɪ**
slimsy **'slɪmzɪ, 'slɪmpsɪ**
slimy **'slaɪmɪ**
sling **slɪŋ** |slung **slʌŋ** or arch. slang **slæŋ** |slung **slʌŋ**
slingshot **'slɪŋˌʃɑt**; ES+-**ˌʃɒt**
slink **slɪŋk** |slunk **slʌŋk** or arch. slank **slæŋk** |slunk **slʌŋk**
slip **slɪp** |slipped **slɪpt** |-per **-ɚ**; ES **-ə(r**
slipknot **'slɪpˌnat**; ES+-**ˌnɒt**
slippery **'slɪprɪ, 'slɪpərɪ** |-rier **'slɪprɪɚ**; ES **-rɪ·ə(r**; |-riest **'slɪprɪɪst**
slippery elm **'slɪprɪ'ɛlm**
slipshod **'slɪpˌʃɑd**; ES+-**ˌʃɒd**
slipslop **'slɪpˌslap**; ES+-**ˌslɒp**; |-ped **-t**
slit **slɪt** |past & pptc slit **slɪt** or rare slitted **'slɪtɪd**
slither **'slɪðɚ**; ES **'slɪðə(r**; |-ed **-d** |-ing **'slɪðrɪŋ, 'slɪðərɪŋ** |-y **-ðrɪ, -ðərɪ**
slithy **'slaɪðɪ**
sliver **'slɪvɚ**; ES **-və(r**; |-ed **-d** |-ing **'slɪvərɪŋ, -vrɪŋ** |-y **-vərɪ, -vrɪ**
slob **slab**; ES+**slɒb**
slobber **'slabɚ**; ES **'slabə(r, 'slɒb-**; |-y **-brɪ, -bərɪ**
slobberer **'slabərɚ**; ES **'slabərə(r, 'slɒb-**
sloe **slo**
slog **slag, slɒg** |-ged **-d**
slogan **'slogən**
sloo 'slough' **slu**
sloop **slup**
slop **slap**; ES+**slɒp**; |-ped **-t** |-py **-ɪ**
slope **slop** |sloped **slopt**
slosh **slaʃ**; ES+**slɒʃ**; |-es **-ɪz** |-ed **-t**
Slosson **'slasn̩, 'slɒsn̩, 'slɔsn̩**
slot **slat**; ES+**slɒt**; |-ted **-ɪd**
sloth **sloθ, slɔθ, slɒθ** |-ful **-fəl** |-fully **-fəlɪ**

slouch **slaʊtʃ** |slouches **'slaʊtʃɪz** |-ed **-t**
slough 'mudhole' **slaʊ**, 'marsh' **slu, slɪu**
slough 'shed skin' **slʌf** |-ed **-t**
Slough Engd **slau**
Slovak **'slovæk, slo'væk**
Slovakia **slo'vakɪə, -'væk-** |-n **-n**
sloven **'slʌvən** |-ed **-d** |-ly **-lɪ**
Slovene **slo'vin, 'slovin**
Slovenia **slo'vinɪə** |-n **-n**
slow **slo** |slowed **slod**
slow-motion **'slo'moʃən** ('slow-ˌmotion 'film)
slowworm **'sloˌwɝm**; ES **-ˌwɜm, -ˌwɝm**
sloyd **slɔɪd**
slub **slʌb** |slubbed **slʌbd**
slubber **'slʌbɚ**; ES **-bə(r**; |-ed **-d** |-ing **'slʌbrɪŋ, 'slʌbərɪŋ** |-y **-brɪ, -bərɪ**
slubberer **'slʌbərɚ**; ES **'slʌbərə(r**
sludge, S- **slʌdʒ** |sludges **'slʌdʒɪz** |-d **-d**
slue **slu, slɪu**
slug **slʌg** |slugged **slʌgd**
slugabed **'slʌgəˌbɛd**
sluggard **'slʌgɚd**; ES **'slʌgəd**; |-gish **'slʌgɪʃ**
sluice **slus, slɪus** |-s **-ɪz** |-d **-t**
slum **slʌm** |slummed **slʌmd**
slumber **'slʌmbɚ**; ES **-bə(r**; |-ed **-d** |-ing **-brɪŋ, -bərɪŋ** |-ous **-brəs, -bərəs**
slumbrous **'slʌmbrəs**
slump **slʌmp** |slumped **slʌmpt**
slung **slʌŋ**
slunk **slʌŋk**
slur **slɝ**; ES **slɜ(r, slɝ**; |-red **-d**
slurp **slɝp**; ES **slɜp, slɝp**; |-ed **-t**
slurry **'slɝɪ**; ES **'slɜrɪ, 'slɝɪ**
slush **slʌʃ** |slushes **'slʌʃɪz** |slushed **slʌʃt**
slut **slʌt** |sluttish **'slʌtɪʃ**
sly **slaɪ** |slyly **'slaɪlɪ**
slyer 'slier' **'slaɪɚ**; ES **'slaɪ·ə(r**
smack **smæk** |smacked **smækt**
Smackover **'smækovɚ**; ES **'smækovə(r**
small **smɔl** |smalled **smɔld**
smallclothes **'smɔlˌkloz, -ˌkloðz**
smallpox **'smɔlˌpaks**; ES+-**ˌpɒks**; |-'s **-ɪz**
smalt **smɔlt**
smaragd **'smæræɡd** |-ine **smə'ræɡdɪn**
smart **smart**; ES **smɑːt**, E+**smɑːt**; |-ed **-ɪd**
smarten **'smartn̩**; ES see smart; |-ed **-d** |-ing **-tnɪŋ, -tn̩ɪŋ**
smash **smæʃ** |smashes **'smæʃɪz** |smashed **smæʃt**

|full **fʊl** |tooth **tuθ** |further **'fɝðɚ**; ES **'fɝðə** |custom **'kʌstəm** |while **hwaɪl** |how **haʊ** |toy **tɔɪ** |using **'juzɪŋ** |fuse **fjuz, fɪuz** |dish **dɪʃ** |vision **'vɪʒən** |Eden **'idn̩** |cradle **'kredḷ** |keep 'em **'kipm̩**

smashup **ˈsmæʃˌʌp**
smatter **ˈsmætɚ**; ES **-tə(r**; |-ed **-d** |-ing **-tərɪŋ, -trɪŋ**
smear **smɪr**; ES **smɪə(r**, S+**smɛə(r**; |-ed **-d**
smearcase **ˈsmɪrˌkes**; ES *see* smear; (*Ger* **ˈʃmi:rˌkɛ:zə**)
smell **smɛl** |smelled **smɛld** *or* smelt **smɛlt**
smellage **ˈsmɛlɪdʒ**
smell-less **ˈsmɛllɪs**
smelt **smɛlt** |-ed **-ɪd** |-ery **-ərɪ**
Smetana **ˈsmɛtn̩ə**
Smethport **ˈsmɛθˌport, -ˌpɔrt**; ES **-ˌpoət**, E+**-ˌpɔət**
Smethwick **ˈsmɛðɪk**
smilax **ˈsmaɪlæks** |-es **-ɪz**
smile **smaɪl** |smiled **smaɪld** |-less **ˈsmaɪllɪs**
Smintheus **ˈsmɪnθjus** |-'s **-ɪz**
smirch **smɝtʃ**; ES **smɜtʃ, smɝtʃ**; |-es **-ɪz** |-ed **-t**
smirk **smɝk**; ES **smɜk, smɝk**; |-ed **-t**
smite **smaɪt** |smote **smot** |smitten **ˈsmɪtn̩** *or* smit **smɪt** *or* smote **smot**
smith, S- **smɪθ** |-ths **-θs** |-ery **-ərɪ, -rɪ**
smither **ˈsmɪðɚ**; ES **-ðə(r**; |-s **-z**
smithereens **ˌsmɪðəˈrinz**
Smithers **ˈsmɪðɚz**; ES **ˈsmɪðəz**; |-'s **-ɪz**
Smithfield **ˈsmɪθfild**
smithier **ˈsmɪðɪɚ, -ðjɚ**; ES **-ə(r**
Smithson **ˈsmɪθsən** |-sonian **smɪθˈsonɪən**
Smithville **ˈsmɪθvɪl**; S+**-vl̩**
smithy **ˈsmɪθɪ, ˈsmɪðɪ—ˈsmɪðɪ** *is the older pronunciation.* **ˈsmɪθɪ** *imitates* smith *as* **ˈgrisɪ** *imitates the noun* grease (**gris**).
smitten **ˈsmɪtn̩**
smock **smɑk**; ES+**smɒk**; |-ed **-t**
smoke **smok** |smoked **smokt** |-ky **-ɪ**; |*NEngd* +**smŏk** (*§46*)
smokestack **ˈsmokˌstæk**
Smokies **ˈsmokɪz**
smolder **ˈsmoldɚ**; ES **-də(r**; |-ed **-d** |-ing **-drɪŋ, -dərɪŋ**
Smolensk **smoˈlɛnsk, smɔ-, -ˈljɛnsk**
Smollett **ˈsmɑlɪt**; ES+**ˈsmɒl-**
smolt **smolt**
smooth **smuð** |smoothed **smuðd**
smoothbore **ˈsmuðˌbor, -ˌbɔr**; ES **-ˌboə(r**, E+**-ˌbɔə(r**
smoothen **ˈsmuðən** |-ed **-d** |-ing **ˈsmuðnɪŋ, -ðənɪŋ**
smooth-spoken **ˈsmuðˈspokən** (ˈsmooth-ˌspoken ˈman)
smote **smot**
smother **ˈsmʌðɚ**; ES **ˈsmʌðə(r**; |-ed **-d** |-ing **ˈsmʌðrɪŋ, -ðərɪŋ**
smoulder **ˈsmoldɚ**; ES **-də(r**; |-ed **-d** |-ing **-drɪŋ, -dərɪŋ**
smudge **smʌdʒ** |smudges **ˈsmʌdʒɪz** |smudged **smʌdʒd**
smug **smʌg** |smugged **smʌgd**
smuggle **ˈsmʌgl̩** |-d **-d** |-ling **ˈsmʌglɪŋ, -gl̩ɪŋ**
smut **smʌt** |smutted **ˈsmʌtɪd** |-ty **-ɪ**
smutch **smʌtʃ** |smutches **ˈsmʌtʃɪz** |-smutched **smʌtʃt**
Smuts **smʌts** |-'s **-ɪz**
Smyrna **ˈsmɝnə**; ES **ˈsmɜnə, ˈsmɝnə**
Smyth **smɪθ, smaɪθ** |Smythe **smaɪð, smaɪθ**
snack **snæk** |snacked **snækt**
snaffle **ˈsnæfl̩** |-d **-d** |-ling **ˈsnæflɪŋ, -fl̩ɪŋ**
snag **snæg** |snagged **snægd**
snaggletooth **ˈsnægl̩ˌtuθ**
snail **snel** |snailed **sneld**
snail-paced **ˈsnelˌpest**
snake, S- **snek** |snaked **snekt** |-ky **-ɪ**
snakeroot **ˈsnekˌrut, -ˌrʊt**
snap **snæp** |snapped **snæpt** |-per **-ɚ**; ES **-ə(r**
snapdragon **ˈsnæpˌdrægən**
snapshot **ˈsnæpˌʃɑt**; ES+**-ˌʃɒt**
snare **snɛr, snær**; E **snɛə(r**, ES **snæə(r**; |-d **-d**
snark **snɑrk**; ES **snɑ:k**, E+**sna:k**
snarl **snɑrl**; ES **snɑ:l**, E+**sna:l**; |-ed **-d**
snatch **snætʃ** |snatches **ˈsnætʃɪz** |-ed **-t**
snath **snæθ** |-ths **-θs** |snathe **sneð**
sneak **snik** |sneaked **snikt**
sneer **snɪr**; ES **snɪə(r**, S+**snɛə(r**; |-ed **-d**
sneeze **sniz** |sneezes **ˈsnizɪz** |sneezed **snizd**
snell, S- **snɛl** |snelled **snɛld**
Snelling **ˈsnɛlɪŋ**
snick **snɪk** |snicked **snɪkt**
snickersnee **ˈsnɪkɚˌsni**; ES **ˈsnɪkə-**; |-d **-d**
sniff **snɪf** |sniffed **snɪft**
sniffle **ˈsnɪfl̩** |-d **-d** |-ling **ˈsnɪflɪŋ, -fl̩ɪŋ**
snigger **ˈsnɪgɚ**; ES **-gə(r**; |-ed **-d** |-ing **ˈsnɪgərɪŋ, ˈsnɪgrɪŋ**
snip **snɪp** |snipped **snɪpt** |py **-ɪ**
snipe **snaɪp** |sniped **snaɪpt**
snippet **ˈsnɪpɪt**
snitch **snɪtʃ** |snitches **ˈsnɪtʃɪz** |-ed **-t**
snivel **ˈsnɪvl̩** |-ed **-d** |-ing **ˈsnɪvlɪŋ, -vl̩ɪŋ**

Key: *See in full §§3–47.* bee **bi** |pity **ˈpɪtɪ** (§6) |rate **ret** |yet **jɛt** |sang **sæŋ** |angry **ˈæŋ·grɪ** |bath **bæθ**; E **baθ** (§10) |ah **ɑ** |far **fɑr** |watch **wɑtʃ, wɒtʃ** (§12) |jaw **dʒɔ** |gorge **gɔrdʒ** |go **go**

Those words below in which the ɑ *sound is spelt* o *are often pronounced with* ɒ *in E and S*

snob snɑb |-bery -ərɪ, -rɪ |-bish -ɪʃ

Snoddy 'snɑdɪ

Snodgrass 'snɑd‚græs; E+-‚grɑs, -‚grɑs; |-'s -ɪz

Snohomish sno'homɪʃ |-'s -ɪz

snood snud |snooded 'snudɪd

snook snuk, snʊk

snoop snup |snooped snupt

snoot snut |snooty 'snutɪ

snooze snuz |snoozes 'snuzɪz |snoozed snuzd

Snoqualmie sno'kwɑlmɪ

snore snor, snɔr; ES snoə(r, E+snɔə(r; |-d -d

snort snɔrt; ES snɔət; |-ed -ɪd

snout snaʊt |snouted 'snaʊtɪd

snow, S- sno |snowed snod |-y -ɪ

snowball 'sno‚bɔl |-ed -d

snowbank 'sno‚bæŋk

snowbird 'sno‚bɝd; ES -‚bɜd, -‚bɝd

snow-blind 'sno‚blaɪnd |-ed -ɪd |-ness -nɪs

snowbound, S- 'sno‚baʊnd

snow-capped 'sno‚kæpt

Snowden, -don 'snodn̩ |-donian sno'donɪən

snowdrift 'sno‚drɪft |-drop -‚drɑp

snowfall 'sno‚fɔl |-flake -‚flek

snowplow 'sno‚plaʊ

snowshoe 'sno‚ʃu |-storm -‚stɔrm; ES -‚stɔəm

snow-white 'sno'hwaɪt ('snow-‚white 'dove)

Snow White 'sno‚hwaɪt

snub snʌb |snubbed snʌbd |-ber -ɚ; ES -ə(r

snub-nose 'snʌb‚noz |-s -ɪz

snub-nosed 'snʌb‚nozd ('snub-‚nosed 'Auk)

snuff snʌf |snuffed snʌft |-y -ɪ

snuffbox 'snʌf‚bɑks |-es -ɪz

snuffers 'snʌfɚz; ES 'snʌfəz

snuffle 'snʌfl̩ |-d -d |-ling 'snʌflɪŋ, -fl̩ɪŋ

snug snʌg |snugged snʌgd |-gery -ərɪ

snuggle 'snʌgl̩ |-d -d |-ling 'snʌglɪŋ, -gl̩ɪŋ

Snyder 'snaɪdɚ; ES 'snaɪdə(r

so *stressed* 'so, ‚so; *unstr.* so, sə, su

soak sok |soaked sokt; |N Engd+sɔk (§46)

soaken *adj* 'sokən

so-and-so 'soən‚so

soap sop |soaped sopt |-stone -‚ston |-suds -‚sʌdz

soapwort 'sop‚wɝt; ES -‚wɜt, -‚wɝt

soar sor, sɔr; ES soə(r, E+sɔə(r; |-ed -d

sob sɑb |sobbed sɑbd

sobeit so'bɪit

sober 'sobɚ; ES 'sobə(r; |-ed -d |-ing 'sobərɪŋ, -brɪŋ

Sobieski ‚sobɪ'ɛskɪ, so'bjɛskɪ

sobriety sə'braɪətɪ, so-

sobriquet 'sobrɪ‚ke (*Fr* söbri'kɛ)

socage, socc- 'sɑkɪdʒ |-s -ɪz

so-called 'so'kɔld ('so-‚called 'learning)

soccer 'sɑkɚ; ES 'sɑkə(r

sociability ‚soʃə'bɪlətɪ

sociable 'soʃəbl̩ |-bly -blɪ

social 'soʃəl |-ly -ɪ |-ism -‚ɪzəm |-ist -ɪst

socialistic ‚soʃə'lɪstɪk |-ally -ḷɪ, -ɪklɪ

socialite 'soʃə‚laɪt

sociality ‚soʃɪ'ælətɪ

socialize 'soʃə‚laɪz |-s -ɪz |-d -d

societal sə'saɪətḷ |-ly -ɪ

society sə'saɪətɪ

sociological ‚soʃɪə'lɑdʒɪkḷ, ‚sosɪ- |-ly -ɪ

sociology ‚soʃɪ'ɑlədʒɪ, ‚sosɪ- |-gist -dʒɪst

sock sɑk |socked sɑkt

sockdolager sɑk'dɑlədʒɚ; ES -'dɑlədʒə(r

socket 'sɑkɪt |-ed -ɪd

Socrates 'sɑkrə‚tiz |-'s -ɪz

Socratic so'krætɪk |-al -ḷ |-ally -ḷɪ, -ɪklɪ

sod sɑd |sodded 'sɑdɪd

soda 'sodə

sodality so'dælətɪ

sodden 'sɑdn̩ |-ness 'sɑdn̩nɪs

sodium 'sodɪəm

Sodom 'sɑdəm |-ist -ɪst |-ite -‚aɪt |-y -ɪ

soever so'ɛvɚ, su'ɛvɚ; ES -'ɛvə(r

sofa 'sofə

Sofia 'sofɪə, so'fiə

Sofronia so'fronɪə

soft sɔft, sɒft

soft-boiled 'sɔft'bɔɪld, 'sɒft-

soften 'sɔfən, 'sɒf- |-ed -d |-ing -fənɪŋ, -fnɪŋ |-er -fənɚ, -fnɚ; ES -ə(r

softhead 'sɔft‚hɛd, 'sɒft-

soft-headed 'sɔft'hɛdɪd, 'sɒft-

softhearted 'sɔft'hɑrtɪd, 'sɒft-; ES -'hɑːt-, E+-'hɑːt-; ('soft‚hearted 'judge)

soft-pedal ‚sɔft'pɛdḷ, ‚sɒft- |-ed -d

soft-shell *n* 'sɔft‚ʃɛl, 'sɒft-

soft-shell *adj* 'sɔft'ʃɛl, 'sɒft- |-ed -d ('soft-‚shell 'crab)

soft-soap 'sɔft'sop, 'sɒft- |-ed -t

soft-spoken 'sɔft'spokən, 'sɒft-

|full fʊl |tooth tuθ |further 'fɝðɚ; ES 'fɝðə |custom 'kʌstəm |while hwaɪl |how haʊ |toy tɔɪ
|using 'juzɪŋ |fuse fjuz, fɪuz |dish dɪʃ |vision 'vɪʒən |Eden 'idn̩ |cradle 'kredl̩ |keep 'em 'kipm̩

Those words below in which the ɑ *sound is spelt* o *are often pronounced with* ɒ *in E and S*

sogdologer sag'dalədʒɚ; ES -'daladʒə(r

soggy 'sagɪ

soho so'ho |sohoed so'hod

Soho so'ho, 'soho ('Soˌho 'Square)

Sohrab 'soræb, 'sorəb, 'sɔr-; S 'sor-

soi-disant *Fr* swadi'zã

soil sɔɪl |soiled sɔɪld |-less 'sɔɪlɪs

soiree swa're (*Fr* swa're)

Soissons *Fr* swa'sõ

sojourn *n* 'sodʒɝn; ES -dʒɜn, -dʒɝn

sojourn *v* so'dʒɝn, 'sodʒɝn; ES -ɜn, -ɝn; |-ed -d

soke sok |soken 'sokən

sokeman 'sokmən |-men -mən

Sokoloff 'sokəˌlɔf, -ˌlɒf, -ləv

Sol sal, sɒl, sɔl

sol *music, coin* sol

sol *chem.* sal, sol

solace 'salɪs, -əs |-s -ɪz |-d -t

Solanio sə'lanɪo, -njo

solar 'solɚ; ES 'solə(r

solarium so'lɛrɪəm, -'ler- |-s -z |-ia -ɪə

solarize 'soləˌraɪz |-s -ɪz |-d -d

sold sold

Soldan, s- 'saldən

solder 'sadɚ; ES 'sadə(r; |-ed -d |-ing 'sadərɪŋ, -drɪŋ

soldier 'soldʒɚ; ES -dʒə(r; |-ed -d |-y -ɪ

sole sol |soled sold |-ly 'sollɪ

solecism 'saləˌsɪzəm

soleless 'sollɪs

solemn 'saləm |-ity sə'lɛmnətɪ

solemnization ˌsaləmnə'zeʃən, -naɪ'z-

solemnize 'saləmˌnaɪz |-s -ɪz |-d -d

solenoid 'soləˌnɔɪd

solenoidal ˌsolə'nɔɪdl̩ |-ly -ɪ

Solent 'solənt

sol-fa sol'fa |-ed -d ('sol-ˌfa 'syllables)

solfeggio sal'fɛdʒo, -dʒɪˌo (*It* sol'feddʒo)

solicit sə'lɪsɪt |-ed -ɪd |-ous -əs

solicitation səˌlɪsə'teʃən

solicitor sə'lɪsətɚ; ES -'lɪsətə(r

solicitude sə'lɪsəˌtjud, -ˌtɪud, -ˌtud

solid 'salɪd |-arity ˌsalə'dærətɪ

solidification sə'lɪdəfə'keʃən

solidify sə'lɪdəˌfaɪ |-fied -ˌfaɪd

solidity sə'lɪdətɪ

solidus 'salɪdəs |-di -ˌdaɪ

soliloquize sə'lɪləˌkwaɪz |-s -ɪz |-d -d

soliloquy sə'lɪləkwɪ |-quist -kwɪst

Solinus sə'laɪnəs |-'s -ɪz

solitaire ˌsalə'tɛr, -'tær; E -'tɛə(r, ES -'tæə(r; *acct*+'soliˌtaire

solitary 'saləˌtɛrɪ |-tude -ˌtjud, -ˌtɪud, -ˌtud

solo, S- 'solo |-ed -d |-ing 'soˌlo-ɪŋ, -ləwɪŋ

soloist 'soˌlo-ɪst, 'soləwɪst

Solomon 'saləmən

Solomon's-seal ˌsaləmənz'sil, -mən'sil

Solon 'solən |-ian so'lonɪən |-ic so'lanɪk

solstice 'salstɪs |-s -ɪz

solstitial sal'stɪʃəl |-ly -ɪ

solubility ˌsaljə'bɪlətɪ

soluble 'saljəbl̩ |-bly -blɪ

solus 'soləs |sola 'solə

solute 'saljut, 'soljut, 'solut, -lɪut

solution sə'luʃən, -'lɪu-

solvability ˌsalvə'bɪlətɪ, ˌsɒlv-

solvable 'salvəbl̩, 'sɒlv-

Solvay 'salve

solve salv, sɒlv |-d -d |-ncy -ənsɪ |-nt -ənt

Solway 'salwe

Solyman 'salɪmən

Somali so'malɪ, sə- |-land -ˌlænd

somatic so'mætɪk |-al -l̩ |-ally -l̩ɪ, -ɪklɪ

somber, -bre 'sambɚ; ES -bə(r; |-(e)d -d |-ing -bərɪŋ, -brɪŋ

sombrero sam'brɛro, -'brɪro, -'brero |-ed -d

some *stressed* 'sʌm, ˌsʌm; *unstr.* səm, sm̩, *before* more sə (sə'mor 'tɪ)

-some *unstressed adj ending* -səm—*often omitted in the vocab.*

somebody 'sʌmˌbadɪ, -ˌbʌdɪ, 'sʌmbədɪ

somehow 'sʌmˌhaʊ

someone 'sʌmˌwʌn, 'sʌmwən

Somers 'sʌmɚz; ES 'sʌməz; |-'s -ɪz

somersault 'sʌmɚˌsɔlt; ES 'sʌmə-; |-ed -ɪd

somerset 'sʌmɚˌsɛt; ES 'sʌmə-; |-ed -ɪd

Somerset 'sʌmɚˌsɛt, -sɪt; ES 'sʌmə-; |-shire -ˌsɛtˌʃɪr, -sɪtˌʃɪr, -sɪtʃɚ; ES -ˌʃɪə(r, -ʃə(r

Somerville, -vile 'sʌmɚˌvɪl; ES 'sʌmə-

something 'sʌmpθɪŋ, 'sʌmθɪŋ

sometime 'sʌmˌtaɪm

sometimes 'sʌmˌtaɪmz, sʌm'taɪmz, səm'taɪmz

someway 'sʌmˌwe

somewhat 'sʌmˌhwɑt, -ˌhwɒt, 'sʌmhwət

Key: *See in full §§3–47.* bee bi |pity 'pɪtɪ (§6) |rate ret |yet jɛt |sang sæŋ |angry 'æŋ·grɪ |bath bæθ; E baθ (§10) |ah ɑ |far fɑr |watch wɑtʃ, wɒtʃ (§12) |jaw dʒɔ |gorge gɔrdʒ |go go

Those words below in which the ɑ sound is spelt o are often pronounced with ɒ in E and S

somewhere ˈsʌmˌhwɛr, -ˌhwær; E -ˌhwɛə(r, ES -ˌhwæə(r

somewhither ˈsʌmˌhwɪðɚ; ES -ˌhwɪðə(r

Somme sʌm, səm (*Fr* sɔ̃m)

somnambulate samˈnæmbjəˌlet |-d -ɪd

somnambulation ˌsamnæmbjəˈleʃən, samˌnæmbjə-

somnambulism samˈnæmbjəˌlɪzəm |-list -lɪst

somniferous samˈnɪfərəs

somnolence ˈsamnələns |-cy -ɪ |-lent -lənt

Somnus, s- ˈsamnəs |-ʼs -ɪz

son sʌn |sonny ˈsʌnɪ

sonance ˈsonəns |-cy -ɪ |-nant -nənt

sonantal soˈnæntl̩ |-tic -tɪk

sonata səˈnatə

sonatina ˌsanəˈtinə, ˌsonə- (*It* ˌsonaˈti:na)

song sɔŋ, sɒŋ; S+saŋ; |-bird -ˌbɝd; ES -ˌbɜd, -ˌbɝd

song-and-dance ˈsɔŋənˈdæns, ˈsɒŋ-; E+ -ˈdans, -ˈdɑns; S ˈsɔŋənˈdæns, ˈsɒŋ-, ˈsaŋ-

songster ˈsɔŋstɚ, ˈsɒŋkstɚ, ˈsɒŋ-; ES -stə(r, S+ˈsaŋ-

songstress ˈsɔŋstrɪs, ˈsɒŋ-; S+ˈsaŋ-; |-es -ɪz

son-in-law ˈsʌnɪnˌlɔ |sons-in-law ˈsʌnzɪnˌlɔ, ˈsʌnzn̩ˌlɔ

sonnet ˈsanɪt |-ed -ɪd

sonneteer ˌsanəˈtɪr; ES -ˈtɪə(r, S+-ˈtɛə(r

sonometer soˈnamətɚ; ES -ˈnamətə(r

Sonora soˈnorə, -ˈnɔrə; S -ˈnorə

sonorant səˈnorənt, -ˈnɔr-; S -ˈnor-

sonority səˈnɔrətɪ, -ˈnar-, -ˈnɒr-

sonorous səˈnorəs, -ˈnɔr-; S -ˈnor-

Soo su

Soochow ˈsuˈtʃau

soon sun, sʊn

Sooner, s- ˈsunɚ, ˈsʊn-; ES -nə(r

soot sʊt, sut, *less freq.* sʌt—sʌt *is better preserved in the S.*

sooth suθ |-ly -lɪ

soothe suð |soothed suðd

soothsay ˈsuθˌse |-er -ɚ; ES -ə(r

sooty ˈsʊtɪ, ˈsutɪ, *less freq.* ˈsʌtɪ

sop sap |sopped sapt

Sophia *saint* soˈfaɪə, sə-; *Am name* səˈfaɪə, ˈsofɪə; *cf* Sophy

sophism ˈsafɪzəm |-ist -ɪst |-ister -ɪstɚ; ES -tə(r

sophistic səˈfɪstɪk |-al -l̩ |-ally -lɪ, -ɪklɪ

sophisticate səˈfɪstɪˌket |-d -ɪd

sophistication səˌfɪstɪˈkeʃən

sophistry ˈsafɪstrɪ

Sophocles ˈsafəˌkliz |-ʼs -ɪz |-clean ˌsafəˈklɪən

sophomore ˈsafm̩ˌor, -ˌɔr; ES -ˌoə(r, E+-ˌɔə(r

sophomoric ˌsafəˈmorɪk, -ˈmɑr-, -ˈmɒr-

Sophronia soˈfronɪə, sə-

Sophy ˈsofɪ

soporiferous ˌsopəˈrɪfərəs, ˌsapə-

soporific ˌsopəˈrɪfɪk, ˌsapə- |-al -l̩ |-ally -lɪ, -ɪklɪ

sopping ˈsapɪŋ

soprano səˈpræno, -ˈprano

Sorbonne sɔrˈban, -ˈbʌn (*Fr* sɔrˈbɔ̃n)

sorcerer ˈsɔrsərɚ; ES ˈsɔəsərə(r; |-cery -sərɪ

sorceress ˈsɔrsərɪs; ES ˈsɔəsə-; |-es -ɪz

Sordello sɔrˈdɛlo; ES sɔə-

sordid ˈsɔrdɪd; ES ˈsɔədɪd

sore sor, sɔr; ES soə(r, E+sɔə(r; |-head -ˌhɛd

soreheaded ˈsorˈhɛdɪd, ˈsɔr-; ES ˈsoə-, E+ˈsɔə-

sorghum ˈsɔrgəm; ES ˈsɔəgəm

sorority səˈrɔrətɪ, -ˈrar-, -ˈrɒr-

sorosis, S- səˈrosɪs

sorption ˈsɔrpʃən; ES ˈsɔəp-

sorrel, S- ˈsɔrəl, ˈsar-, ˈsɒr-

sorrento, S- səˈrɛnto

sorrow ˈsaro, ˈsɒro, ˈsɔro, -ə |-ed -d |-ing -rəwɪŋ

sorry ˈsɔrɪ, ˈsarɪ, ˈsɒrɪ

sort sɔrt; ES sɔət; |-ed -ɪd

sortie ˈsɔrti, -tɪ; ES ˈsɔə-; |-d -d

sortilege ˈsɔrtl̩ɪdʒ; ES ˈsɔət-

S O S *n* ˈɛsˌoˈɛs *pl* -ʼs -ɪz

S O S *v* ˈɛsˌoˈɛs |-ʼes -ɪz |-ʼed -t

soso ˈsoˌso

sot sat |sotted ˈsatɪd |sottish ˈsatɪʃ

Sothern ˈsʌðɚn; ES ˈsʌðən

sotto voce ˈsatoˈvotʃɪ (*It* ˈsottoˈvo:tʃe)

sou su

soubrette suˈbrɛt |-tish -ɪʃ

soubriquet ˈsubrɪˌke

souchong, S- suˈʃɔŋ, -ˈtʃɔŋ, -ɒŋ (ˈsouˌchong ˈtea)

Soudan suˈdæn |-ese ˌsudəˈniz

soufflé suˈfle, ˈsufle |-ed -d

souffle ˈsufl̩

|full fʊl |tooth tuθ |further ˈfɝðɚ; ES ˈfɝðə |custom ˈkʌstəm |while hwaɪl |how hau |toy tɔɪ
|using ˈjuzɪŋ |fuse fjuz, fɪuz |dish dɪʃ |vision ˈvɪʒən |Eden ˈidn̩ |cradle ˈkredl̩ |keep ʼem ˈkipm̩

sough sʌf, saʊ |soughed sʌft, saʊd	southron 'sʌðrən, 'sʌðərən

sough sʌf, saʊ |soughed sʌft, saʊd
sought sɔt
soul sol |souled sold |-less 'sollıs
sound saʊnd |-ed -ıd |-ness -nıs, 'saʊnnıs
soundboard 'saʊnd,bord, 'saʊn-, -,bɔrd; ES -,boəd, E+-,bɔəd
sound-box 'saʊnd,bɑks, 'saʊn-; ES+-,bɒks; |-es -ız
sound-wave 'saʊnd,wev
soup sup |souped supt
soup-and-fish 'supən'fıʃ, 'supm̩'fıʃ
soupçon Fr sup'sõ
sour saʊr; ES saʊə(r; |-ed -d
source sors, sɔrs; ES soəs, E+sɔəs; |-s -ız
sourdough 'saʊr,do; ES 'saʊə,do
Souris 'sʊrıs |-'s -ız
Sousa 'suzə, 'susə
souse saʊs |souses 'saʊsız |soused saʊst
soutane su'tɑn
souter, -ar 'sutɚ; ES 'sutə(r
south, S- n, adj, adv saʊθ
south v saʊð, saʊθ |-ed -ðd, -θt
Southampton saʊθ'hæmptən, saʊ'θæmptən
Southbridge 'saʊθbrıdʒ |-'s -ız
South Carolina ,saʊθkærə'laınə, -kɚ'laınə; ES ,saʊθkærə'laınə, -kə'laınə; loc.+,sæʊθkærə'la:nə, -kæə'la:nə, -kərə'la:nə
South Dakota ,saʊdə'kotə, -dı'kotə
Southdown 'saʊθ,daʊn |S- Downs 'saʊθ'daʊnz
southeast, S- ,saʊθ'ist ('south,east 'wind)
southeaster ,saʊθ'istɚ; ES -'istə(r; |-n -n
southeastward ,saʊθ'istwɚd; ES -wəd; |-s -z
southerly 'sʌðɚlı; ES 'sʌðəlı
southermost 'sʌðɚ,most; ES 'sʌðə-
southern, Southerne 'sʌðɚn; ES 'sʌðən; |-most -,most, -məst
southerner 'sʌðɚnɚ, 'sʌðənɚ; ES 'sʌðənə(r;
—In 'sʌðənɚ ə has been changed from ɚ by dissimilation (§121); this is less freq. in easterner & westerner.
Southey 'saʊðı, 'sʌðı
Southgate 'saʊθ,get, -gıt
southing 'saʊðıŋ
Southington 'sʌðıŋtən
southland 'saʊθlənd, -,lænd
southpaw 'saʊθ,pɔ
Southport 'saʊθ,port, -,pɔrt; ES -,poət, E+-,pɔət

southron 'sʌðrən, 'sʌðərən
southward 'saʊθwɚd; ES -wəd; |-s -z
Southwark 'sʌðɚk, 'saʊθwɚk; ES -ək
Southwell 'saʊθ,wɛl, -wəl; Notts 'sʌðəl
southwest ,saʊθ'wɛst |-er -ɚ; ES -ə(r; |-n -n
—naut.+,saʊ'w- ('south,west 'wind)
Southwick 'saʊθwık, 'sʌðık
Southworth 'saʊθwɚθ; ES 'saʊθwəθ
souvenir ,suvə'nır, 'suvə,nır; ES -ıə(r
Souza 'sozə, 'suzə
sovereign 'sɑvrın, 'sʌv-, 'sɒv-, -rən |-ty -tı
soviet, S- 'sovıɪt, -ət, -vı,ɛt, ,sovı'ɛt
sovietism 'sovıə,tızəm |-tize -,taız
sovran 'sɑvrən, 'sɒv-, 'sʌv-
sow 'hog' saʊ
sow 'seed' so |sowed sod |sown son or sowed sod
Sowerby Lancs, Yks, Cumb 'saʊəbı; ES 'saʊ·əbı
soy sɔı |soybean 'sɔı'bin, -,bin
sozin 'sozın
spa spɑ |Spa spɑ, spɔ
space spes |spaces 'spesız |spaced spest
spacious 'speʃəs
spade sped |spaded 'spedıd |-ful -,fʊl
spadix 'spedıks |-es -ız |-dices spı'daısiz
Spaeth, Sigmund 'sıgmənd speθ
spaghetti spə'gɛtı
spahi, -hee 'spɑhi
Spain spen
spake spek
Spalding 'spɔldıŋ
spall spɔl |spalled spɔld
spalpeen 'spælpin, spæl'pin
span spæn |spanned spænd
spandrell 'spændrəl
spangle 'spæŋgl̩ |-d -d |-ling 'spæŋglıŋ, -g|ıŋ
Spangler 'spæŋglɚ; ES 'spæŋglə(r
Spaniard 'spænjɚd; ES 'spænjəd
spaniel 'spænjəl |-ed -d
Spanish 'spænıʃ
spank spæŋk |spanked spæŋkt
spanner 'spænɚ; ES 'spænə(r
span-new 'spæn'nju, -'nıu, -'nu ('span-,new 'hat)
spar spɑr; ES spɑ:(r, E+spɑ:(r; |-red -d
spare spɛr, spær; E spɛə(r, ES spæə(r; |-d -d
sparerib 'spɛr,rıb, 'spær-; E 'spɛə,rıb, ES 'spæə-

Key: See in full §§3–47. bee bi |pity 'pıtı (§6) |rate ret |yet jɛt |sang sæŋ |angry 'æŋ·grı |bath bæθ; E baθ (§10) |ah ɑ |far fɑr |watch wɑtʃ, wɒtʃ (§12) |jaw dʒɔ |gorge gɔrdʒ |go go

Spargo 'spɑrgo; ES 'spɑːgo, E+'spɑːgo

spark spɑrk; ES spɑːk, E+spɑːk; |-ed -t

sparkle 'spɑrkl̩; ES 'spɑːkl̩, E+'spɑːkl̩; |-d -d
|-ling -klɪŋ, -kl̩ɪŋ |-r -klɚ; ES -klə(r

sparrow 'spæro, -ə |-ish 'spærəwɪʃ |-y -rəwɪ

sparse spɑrs; ES spɑːs, E+spɑːs; |-sity -ətɪ

Sparta 'spɑrtə; ES 'spɑːtə, E+'spɑːtə; |-n -tn̩

Spartacus 'spɑrtəkəs; ES 'spɑːt-, E+'spɑːt-;
|-'s -ɪz

Spartanburg 'spɑrtn̩ˌbɝg; ES 'spɑːtn̩ˌbɝg,
'spɑːtn̩ˌbɝg, E+'spɑːtn̩-

spasm 'spæzəm

spasmodic spæz'mɑdɪk; ES+-'mɒd-; |-al -l̩
|-ally -l̩ɪ, -ɪklɪ

spastic 'spæstɪk |-ally -l̩ɪ, -ɪklɪ

spat past of spit spæt

spat spæt |spatted 'spætɪd

spatchcock 'spætʃˌkak; ES+-ˌkɒk; |-ed -t

spate spet |spated 'spetɪd

spathe speð |spathed speðd

spathic 'spæθɪk

spatial 'speʃəl |-ly -ɪ

spatialize 'speʃəlˌaɪz |-s -ɪz |-d -d

spatter 'spætɚ; ES 'spætə(r; |-ed -d

spatula 'spætʃələ

spatulate adj 'spætʃəlɪt, -ˌlet

spatulate v 'spætʃəˌlet |-d -ɪd

Spaulding 'spɔldɪŋ

spavin 'spævɪn |-ed -d

spawn spɔn |spawned spɔnd

spay spe |spayed sped

speak spik |spoke spok or arch. spake spek
|spoken 'spokən or arch. spoke spok

spear spɪr; ES spɪə(r, S+spɛə(r, spjɛə(r; |-ed
-d |-head -ˌhɛd |-man -mən |-men -mən
|-mint -ˌmɪnt

special 'spɛʃəl |-ly -ɪ |-ism -ˌɪzəm |-ist -ɪst

speciality ˌspɛʃɪ'ælətɪ

specialize 'spɛʃəlˌaɪz |-s -ɪz |-d -d

specialty 'spɛʃəltɪ

specie 'spiʃɪ

species 'spiʃɪz, -ʃiz, L pl 'spiʃɪˌiz

specifiable 'spɛsəˌfaɪəbl̩

specific spɪ'sɪfɪk |-al -l̩ |-ally -l̩ɪ |-ly -lɪ

specification ˌspɛsəfə'keʃən

specify 'spɛsəˌfaɪ |-fied -ˌfaɪd

specimen 'spɛsəmən

speciosity ˌspiʃɪ'ɑsətɪ; ES+-'ɒs-

specious 'spiʃəs

speck spɛk |specked spɛkt

speckle 'spɛkl̩ |-d -d |-ling 'spɛklɪŋ, -kl̩ɪŋ

spectacle 'spɛktəkl̩, -tɪkl̩, -ˌtɪkl̩ |-d -d

spectacular spɛk'tækjələ; ES -'tækjələ(r

spectator 'spɛktetɚ, spɛk'tetɚ; ES -tə(r

specter, -tre 'spɛktɚ; ES -tə(r; |-(e)d -d

spectra 'spɛktrə

spectral 'spɛktrəl |-ly -ɪ

spectrochemistry ˌspɛktro'kɛmɪstrɪ

spectrometer spɛk'trɑmətɚ; ES -'trɑmətə(r,
-'trɒm-

spectrophotometer ˌspɛktrofo'tɑmətɚ; ES
-'tɑmətə(r, -'tɒm-

spectroscope 'spɛktrəˌskop

spectroscopic ˌspɛktrə'skɑpɪk; ES+-'skɒp-;
|-al -l̩ |-ally -l̩ɪ, -ɪklɪ

spectroscopy spɛk'trɑskəpɪ, 'spɛktrəˌskopɪ;
ES+-'trɒs-; |-pist -pɪst

spectrum 'spɛktrəm |-s -z |-tra -trə

specular 'spɛkjələ; ES 'spɛkjələ(r

speculate 'spɛkjəˌlet |-d -ɪd |-tive -ɪv

speculation ˌspɛkjə'leʃən

speculum 'spɛkjələm |-s -z |-la -lə

sped spɛd

speech spitʃ |speeches 'spitʃɪz |-ed -t

speechify 'spitʃəˌfaɪ |-fied -ˌfaɪd

speed, S- spid |speeded 'spidɪd or sped spɛd

speedboat 'spidˌbot

speedily 'spidl̩ɪ, -ɪlɪ

speedometer spi'dɑmətɚ; ES -'dɑmətə(r,
-'dɒm-

speed-up n 'spidˌʌp

speed up v 'spid'ʌp |speeded up 'spidɪd'ʌp

speer spɪr; ES spɪə(r, S+spɛə(r; |-ed -d

Speght, Speight spet

Speiser 'spaɪzɚ; ES 'spaɪzə(r

spell spɛl |spelled spɛld or spelt spɛlt

spellbind 'spɛlˌbaɪnd |-bound -ˌbaʊnd

spelling-bound 'spɛlɪŋˌbaʊnd

spelt spɛlt

spelter 'spɛltɚ; ES 'spɛltə(r; |-ed -d

spence, S- spɛns |Spence's 'spɛnsɪz

spencer, S- 'spɛnsɚ; ES 'spɛnsə(r

Spencerian spɛn'sɪrɪən

spend spɛnd |spent spɛnt

spendthrift 'spɛndˌθrɪft, 'spɛnˌθrɪft

Spens spɛns |-'s -ɪz

Spenser 'spɛnsɚ; ES 'spɛnsə(r

Spenserian spɛn'sɪrɪən

|full fʊl |tooth tuθ |further 'fɝðɚ; ES 'fɝðə |custom 'kʌstəm |while hwaɪl |how haʊ |toy tɔɪ
|using 'juzɪŋ |fuse fjuz, fɪuz |dish dɪʃ |vision 'vɪʒən |Eden 'idn̩ |cradle 'kredl̩ |keep 'em 'kipm̩

spent spɛnt

sperm spɜˑm; ES spɜm, spɜˑm

spermaceti ˌspɜˑməˈsɛtɪ, -ˈsitɪ; ES ˌspɜm-, ˌspɜˑm-

spermatic spɜˈmætɪk; ES spɜ-, spɜˑ-; |-al -ḷ |-ally -ḷɪ, -ɪklɪ

spermatophyte ˈspɜˑmətəˌfaɪt; ES ˈspɜm-, ˈspɜˑm-

spermatozoon ˌspɜˑmətəˈzoɑn, -ɒn, -ən; ES ˌspɜm-, ˌspɜˑm-; |-zoa -ˈzoə

spew spju, spɪu |-ed -d

Spey spe

sphagnum, S- ˈsfægnəm

spheral ˈsfɪrəl; S+ˈsfɛrəl

sphere sfɪr; ES sfɪə(r, S+sfɛə(r; |-d -d

spheric ˈsfɛrɪk |-al -ḷ |-ally -ḷɪ, -ɪklɪ

sphericity sfɪˈrɪsətɪ

sphericle ˈsfɛrɪkḷ

spheroid ˈsfɪrɔɪd; S+ˈsfɛr-

spheroidal sfɪˈrɔɪdḷ; S+sfɛ-; |-ly -ɪ

sphery ˈsfɪrɪ; S+ˈsfɛrɪ

sphincter ˈsfɪŋktɚ; ES ˈsfɪŋktə(r; |-al -əl

sphinx sfɪŋks |-es ˈsfɪŋksɪz |-nges ˈsfɪndʒiz

sphragistic sfrəˈdʒɪstɪk |-s -s

sphygmograph ˈsfɪgməˌgræf; E+-ˌgraf, -ˌgrɑf

spica, S- ˈspaɪkə |-cal -kḷ

spicate ˈspaɪket |-d -ɪd

spice spaɪs |-s ˈspaɪsɪz |-d -t |-ry -ərɪ, -rɪ

spicily ˈspaɪsḷɪ, -ɪlɪ

spick spɪk |spicked spɪkt

spick-and-span ˈspɪkənˈspæn, ˈspɪkṇˈspæn

spicket ˈspɪkɪt

spiculate ˈspɪkjəˌlet |-lated -ˌletɪd

spicule ˈspɪkjul

spicy ˈspaɪsɪ

spider ˈspaɪdɚ; ES ˈspaɪdə(r; |-ed -d

spied from spy spaɪd

spiel spil |spieled spild (Ger ʃpiːl)

spier 'speer,' 'screen' spɪr; ES spɪə(r, S+ spɛə(r; |-ed -d

spier 'who spies' ˈspaɪɚ; ES ˈspaɪˑə(r

spies spaɪz

spiffy ˈspɪfɪ

spigot ˈspɪgət |-ed -ɪd

spike spaɪk |spiked spaɪkt

spikenard ˈspaɪknɚd, -nɑrd; ES -nəd, -nɑːd, E+-naːd

spile spaɪl |spiled spaɪld

spill spɪl |spilled spɪld or spilt spɪlt

spillway ˈspɪlˌwe

spilt spɪlt

spin spɪn |spun spʌn or arch. span spæn |spun spʌn

spinach ˈspɪnɪtʃ, -ɪdʒ |-es -ɪz—ˈspɪnɪtʃ clearly prevails in US, though ˈspɪnɪdʒ is also traditional here. Both go back to OF.

spinal ˈspaɪnḷ |-ly -ɪ

spindle ˈspɪndḷ |-d -d |-ling -dlɪŋ, -dḷɪŋ

spindle-legged ˈspɪndḷˌlegɪd, -ˌlegd

spindlelegs ˈspɪndḷˌlegz

spindling adj ˈspɪndlɪŋ |spindly ˈspɪndlɪ

spindrift ˈspɪnˌdrɪft

spine spaɪn |spined spaɪnd

spinet ˈspɪnɪt

Spingarn ˈspɪŋgɑrn; ES -gɑːn, E+-gaːn

Spink, s- spɪŋk

spinnaker ˈspɪnəkɚ, ˈspɪnɪ-; ES -kə(r

spinney ˈspɪnɪ

spinose ˈspaɪnos |spinous ˈspaɪnəs

Spinoza spɪˈnozə

spinster ˈspɪnstɚ; ES -stə(r; |-hood -ˌhʊd

spinstress ˈspɪnstrɪs |-es -ɪz

spinule ˈspaɪnjul, ˈspɪn-

spiny ˈspaɪnɪ

spiraea, S- spaɪˈriə

spiral ˈspaɪrəl |-ed -d |-ly -ɪ

spire spaɪr; ES spaɪə(r; |-d -d |-ry -ɪ

spirea, S- spaɪˈriə

spirit ˈspɪrɪt |-ed -ɪd |-ous -əs

spiritual ˈspɪrɪtʃʊəl, -tʃʊl, -tʃəl |-ly -ɪ |-ism -ˌɪzəm |-ist -ɪst

spirituality ˌspɪrɪtʃʊˈælətɪ

spiritualize ˈspɪrɪtʃʊəlˌaɪz, -tʃʊl-, -tʃəl- |-s -ɪz |-d -d

spirituel, -elle ˌspɪrɪtʃʊˈɛl (Fr spiriˈtɥel)

spirituous ˈspɪrɪtʃʊəs

spirochete, -chaete ˈspaɪrəˌkit

spirogyra, S- ˌspaɪrəˈdʒaɪrə

spirometer spaɪˈrɑmətɚ; ES -ˈrɑmətə(r, -ˈrɒm-

spirt spɜt; ES spɜt, spɜˑt; |-ed -ɪd

spit 'saliva' spɪt |spit spɪt or spat spæt

spit 'stick' spɪt |spitted ˈspɪtɪd

spital ˈspɪtḷ |Spitalfields ˈspɪtḷˌfildz

spit and image, spit an' image ˈspɪtṇˈɪmɪdʒ (sometimes misapprehended as spittin' image ˈspɪtṇˈɪmɪdʒ)

spitchcock ˈspɪtʃˌkɑk; ES+-ˌkɒk; |-ed -t

spite spaɪt |spited 'spaɪtɪd |-ful -fəl |-fully
-fəlɪ
spitfire 'spɪtˌfaɪr; ES -ˌfaɪə(r; |-d -d
spitful 'spɪtˌfʊl |-s -z
Spithead 'spɪt'hɛd ('Spitˌhead 'route)
Spitsbergen 'spɪtsbɝgən; ES -bɜg-, -bɝg-
spittle 'spɪtl̩
spittoon spɪ'tun
spitz spɪts |spitzes 'spɪtsɪz
Spitzbergen 'spɪtsbɝgən; ES -bɜg-, -bɝg-
Spitzenburg, -berg 'spɪtsn̩ˌbɝg; ES -ˌbɜg,
-ˌbɝg
splash splæʃ |splashes 'splæʃɪz |-ed -t
splatter 'splætɚ; ES 'splætə(r; |-ed -d
splay sple |splayed spled |-foot -ˌfʊt
spleen splin |spleened splind
splendent 'splɛndənt
splendid 'splɛndɪd |-diferous splɛn'dɪfərəs,
-frəs
splendor 'splɛndɚ; ES 'splɛndə(r; |-ed -d
splenetic splɪ'nɛtɪk |-al -l̩ |-ally -l̩ɪ, -ɪklɪ
splenetive 'splɛnətɪv
splenic 'splɛnɪk, 'splin- |-al -l̩
splice splaɪs |splices 'splaɪsɪz |-d -t
splint splɪnt |splinted 'splɪntɪd
splint-bottom 'splɪntˌbɑtəm; ES+-ˌbɒt-;
|-ed -d
splinter 'splɪntɚ; ES -tə(r; |-ed -d |-ing
'splɪntərɪŋ, -trɪŋ |-y -ɪ, -trɪ
split splɪt |split splɪt or splitted 'splɪtɪd
splotch splɒtʃ; ES+splɒtʃ; |-es -ɪz |-ed -t
splurdge splɝdʒ; ES splɜdʒ, splɝdʒ; |-s -ɪz
|-d -d
splutter 'splʌtɚ; ES 'splʌtə(r; |-ed -d
Spofford 'spɑfɚd; ES 'spɑfəd, 'spɒf-
spoil spɔɪl |spoiled spɔɪld or spoilt spɔɪlt
spoilsman 'spɔɪlzmən |-men -mən
Spokane spo'kæn
spoke from speak spok
spoke of a wheel spok |spoked spokt
spokeshave 'spokˌʃev
spokesman 'spoksmən |-men -mən
spoliate 'spolɪˌet |-d -ɪd |-tion ˌspolɪ'eʃən
spondaic spɑn'de·ɪk; ES+spɒn-; |-al -l̩
spondee 'spɑndi; ES+spɒn-
sponge spʌndʒ |-s -ɪz |-d -d |-gy -ɪ
sponsion 'spɑnʃən; ES+'spɒn-
sponson 'spɑnsn̩; ES+'spɒn-
sponsor 'spɑnsɚ; ES 'spɑnsə(r, 'spɒn-; |-ed -d

spontaneity ˌspɑntə'niətɪ; ES+ˌspɒn-
spontaneous spɑn'tenɪəs; ES+spɒn-
spontoon spɑn'tun; ES+spɒn-
spoof spuf |spoofed spuft
spook spuk, spʊk |-ed -t
spool spul |spooled spuld
spoon spun, spʊn |-ed -d—spun is freq. in
compounds like teaspoon.
spoondrift 'spunˌdrɪft
Spooner 'spunɚ; ES 'spunə(r
spoonerism 'spunəˌrɪzəm
spoon-fed 'spunˌfɛd, 'spun-
spoonful 'spunˌfʊl, 'spun- |-fuls -ˌfʊlz
spoor spʊr, spor, spɔr; ES spʊə(r, spoə(r, E+
spɔə(r; |-ed -d
sporadic spo'rædɪk, spɔ-; S spo-; |-al -l̩ |-ally
-lɪ, -ɪklɪ
spore spor, spɔr; ES spoə(r, E+spɔə(r; |-d
-d
sport sport, spɔrt; ES spoət, E+spɔət; |-ed
-ɪd |-sman -smən |-smen -smən
spot spɑt; ES+spɒt; |-ted -ɪd |-light -ˌlaɪt
Spotswood 'spɑtsˌwʊd; ES+'spɒts-
Spotsylvania ˌspɑtsl̩'venjə, -sɪl-; ES+ˌspɒt-
Spottiswood, -e 'spɑtɪsˌwʊd, 'spɑts-; ES+
'spɒt-
Spottswood 'spɑtsˌwʊd; ES+'spɒts-
spousal 'spaʊzl̩ |-ly -ɪ
spouse spaʊz, spaʊs |-s -ɪz |-d -d, -t
spout spaʊt |spouted 'spaʊtɪd
Sprague spreg, sprɛg
sprain spren |sprained sprend
sprang spræŋ
sprat, S- spræt |spratted 'sprætɪd
sprawl sprɔl |sprawled sprɔld
spray spre |sprayed spred
spread sprɛd
spread-eagle 'sprɛdˌigl̩ |-d -d |-ling -ˌiglɪŋ,
-ˌiglɪŋ
spree spri |spreed sprid
sprier 'spraɪɚ; ES 'spraɪ·ə(r; |-est -ɪst
sprig sprɪg |sprigged sprɪgd
sprightly 'spraɪtlɪ
spring sprɪŋ |sprang spræŋ or sprung sprʌŋ
|sprung sprʌŋ
springboard 'sprɪŋˌbord, -ˌbɔrd; ES -ˌboəd,
E+-ˌbɔəd
springbok 'sprɪŋˌbɑk; ES+-ˌbɒk
springe sprɪndʒ |-s -ɪz |-d -d

springer, S- ˈsprɪŋɚ; ES ˈsprɪŋə(r
Springfield ˈsprɪŋˌfild
springhalt ˈsprɪŋˈhɔlt, -ˌhɔlt
springtime ˈsprɪŋˌtaɪm |-tide -ˌtaɪd
springy ˈsprɪŋɪ
sprinkle ˈsprɪŋkl̩ |-d -d |-ling -klɪŋ, -kl̩ɪŋ
sprinkling n, adj ˈsprɪŋklɪŋ
sprint sprɪnt |sprinted ˈsprɪntɪd
sprit sprɪt
sprite spraɪt
sprocket ˈsprɑkɪt; ES+ˈsprɒk-
Sproul spraʊl
sprout spraʊt |sprouted ˈspraʊtɪd
spruce, S- sprus, sprɪus |-s -ɪz |-d -t
sprung sprʌŋ
spry spraɪ
spud spʌd |spudded ˈspʌdɪd
spue spju, spɪu |-d -d
spume spjum, spɪum |-d -d
spun spʌn
spunk spʌŋk |-ie, y -ɪ |-ed -t
spur spɝ; ES spɜ(r, spɝ; |-red -d
spurge spɝdʒ; ES spɜdʒ, spɝdʒ; |-s -ɪz |-d -d
Spurgeon ˈspɝdʒən; ES ˈspɜdʒ-, ˈspɝdʒ-
spurious ˈspjʊrɪəs, ˈspɪʊrɪəs
spurn spɝn; ES spɜn, spɝn; |-ed -d
spurt spɝt; ES spɜt, spɝt; |-ed -ɪd
sputter ˈspʌtɚ; ES ˈspʌtə(r; |-ed -d
sputum ˈspjutəm, ˈspɪutəm |-ta -tə
Spuyten Duyvil ˈspaɪtn̩ˈdaɪvl̩
spy spaɪ |spied spaɪd |-er -ɚ; ES -ə(r
spyglass ˈspaɪˌglæs; E+-ˌglas, -ˌglɑs; |-es -ɪz
squab skwɑb, skwɒb |-bed -d
squabble ˈskwɑbl̩, ˈskwɒbl̩ |-d -d |-ling -blɪŋ, -bl̩ɪŋ
squad skwɑd, skwɒd |-ded -ɪd
squadron ˈskwɑdrən, ˈskwɒd- |-ed -d
squalid ˈskwɑlɪd, ˈskwɒl-
squall skwɔl |squalled skwɔld |-y -ɪ
squalor ˈskwɑlɚ, ˈskwɒlɚ, less freq. ˈskwelɚ; ES -lə(r
Squam, s- skwɑm, skwɒm
squama ˈskwemə |-mae -mi |-mate -met |-mose -mos |-mous -məs
squander ˈskwɑndɚ, ˈskwɒn-; ES -də(r; |-ed -d |-ing -drɪŋ, -dərɪŋ
Squantum, s- ˈskwɑntəm, ˈskwɒn-
square, S- skwɛr, skwær; E skwɛə(r, ES skwæə(r; |-d -d |-head -ˌhɛd

square-rigged ˈskwɛrˈrɪgd, ˈskwær-; E ˈskwɛə-, ES ˈskwæə-
squash skwɑʃ, skwɒʃ |-es -ɪz |-ed -t
squat skwɑt, skwɒt |-ted -ɪd
squaw skwɔ
squawk skwɔk |squawked skwɔkt
squeak skwik |squeaked skwikt
squeal skwil |squealed skwild
squeamish ˈskwimɪʃ
squeegee ˈskwidʒi, skwiˈdʒi |-d -d
Squeers skwɪrz; ES skwɪəz; |-ʼs -ɪz
squeeze skwiz |squeezes ˈskwizɪz |-d -d
squelch skwɛltʃ |squelches ˈskwɛltʃɪz |-ed -t
squib skwɪb |squibbed skwɪbd
squid skwɪd |squidded ˈskwɪdɪd
squill skwɪl
squint skwɪnt |squinted ˈskwɪntɪd
squint-eyed ˈskwɪntˈaɪd (ˈsquint-ˌeyed ˈboy)
squire, S- skwaɪr; ES skwaɪə(r; |-d -d
squirearchy ˈskwaɪˌrɑrkɪ; ES -ˌrɑːkɪ, E+ -ˌrɑːkɪ
Squires skwaɪrz; ES skwaɪəz; |-ʼs -ɪz
squirm skwɝm; ES skwɜm, skwɝm; |-ed -d
squirrel ˈskwɝəl, skwɝl, less freq. ˈskwɪrəl, ˈskwʌrəl; ES ˈskwɜrəl, ˈskwʌrəl, ˈskwɝəl, skwɜl, skwɝl, ˈskwɛrəl, less freq. ˈskwɪrəl
squirt skwɝt; ES skwɜt, skwɝt; |-ed -d
St. ʻSaintʼ stressed ˈsent, ˌsent; unstr. sent, sənt, sɪnt—sənt & sɪnt are rarer in Amer than in Engd, where sn̩t & sn̩ are also common. Words beginning with St.=Saint are listed alphabetically with Saint words.
stab stæb |stabbed stæbd
Stabat Mater ˈstɑbɑtˈmɑtɚ, Eng L ˈstebæt-ˈmetɚ; ES -tə(r
stability stəˈbɪlətɪ, ste-
stabilization ˌstebl̩əˈzeʃən, -aɪˈz-
stabilize ˈsteblˌaɪz |-s -ɪz |-d -d
stable ˈstebl̩ |-d -d |-ling ˈsteblɪŋ, -bl̩ɪŋ
stableman ˈsteblˌmæn, -mən |-men -ˌmɛn, -mən
stablish ˈstæblɪʃ |-es -ɪz |-ed -t
staccato stəˈkɑto (It stakˈkɑːto)
stack stæk |stacked stækt
stacte ˈstæktɪ
Stacy, -cey ˈstesɪ
staddle ˈstædl̩ |-d -d |-ling ˈstædlɪŋ, -dl̩ɪŋ
stadholder ˈstædˌholdɚ; ES -ˌholdə(r; |stadt-ˈstæt-

Words below in which a *before* r (farm) *is sounded* ɑ *are often pronounced in* E *with* a (fɑːm)

stadia ˈstedɪə |-s -z

stadium ˈstedɪəm |-s -z |-dia -dɪə

Staël stɑl, ˈstɑɛl (*Fr* stɑl)

staff stæf; E+staf, stɑf; |-'s -s |-s -s |-ed -t
|staves stevz, stævz; E+stavz, stɑvz

Stafford ˈstæfəd; ES ˈstæfəd; |-shire -ˌʃɪr,
-ʃə; ES -ˌʃɪə(r, -ʃə(r

Staffs *short for* Staffordshire stæfs

staffs *one pl of* staff stæfs; E+stafs, stɑfs·

stag stæg |stagged stægd

stage stedʒ |stages ˈstedʒɪz |staged stedʒd

stagecoach ˈstedʒˌkotʃ |-es -ɪz

stagecraft ˈstedʒˌkræft; E+-ˌkraft, -ˌkrɑft

stager ˈstedʒɚ; ES ˈstedʒə(r

stagey ˈstedʒɪ

stagger ˈstægɚ; ES ˈstægə(r; |-ed -d |-ing
ˈstægərɪŋ, ˈstægrɪŋ

staghound ˈstægˌhaʊnd

staging ˈstedʒɪŋ

Stagira stəˈdʒaɪrə |-rite ˈstædʒəˌraɪt

stagnant ˈstægnənt |-nancy -nənsɪ

stagnate ˈstægnet |-d -ɪd |-tion stægˈneʃən

stagy ˈstedʒɪ

Stahl *Am surname* stɔl (*Ger* ʃtɑːl)

Stahr *Am surname* stɛr, stær; E stɛə(r, ES
stæə(r

staid sted

stain sten |stained stend

stair stɛr, stær; E stɛə(r, ES stæə(r; |-ed -d
|-case -ˌkes |-way -ˌwe

stake stek |staked stekt

stakeholder ˈstekˌholdɚ; ES -ˌholdə(r

stalactite stəˈlæktaɪt |-lagmite -ˈlægmaɪt

stale stel |staled steld

stalemate ˈstelˌmet |-d -ɪd

Stalin ˈstɑlɪn, ˈstɑlin |-grad -ˌgræd, -ˌgrɑd

Stalinsk stɑˈlɪnsk

stalk stɔk |stalked stɔkt |-y -ɪ

Stalky ˈstɔkɪ, ˈstɔlkɪ

stall stɔl |stalled stɔld

stallion ˈstæljən

stalwart ˈstɔlwət; ES ˈstɔlwət

Stambaugh ˈstæmbɔ

Stambul, -boul stɑmˈbul, stæm-

stamen ˈstemən |stamened ˈstemənd

Stamford ˈstæmfəd; ES ˈstæmfəd

stamina ˈstæmənə

staminate *adj* ˈstæmənɪt, -ˌnet

staminate *v* ˈstæməˌnet |-d -ɪd

stammer ˈstæmɚ; ES ˈstæmə(r; |-ed -d |-ing
ˈstæmərɪŋ, ˈstæmrɪŋ

stamp stæmp |stamped stæmpt

stampede stæmˈpid |-peded -ˈpidɪd

stance stæns |stances ˈstænsɪz |-d -t

stanch '*stop*' stæntʃ, stantʃ |-es -ɪz |-ed -t

stanch '*firm*' stantʃ, *less freq.* stæntʃ

stanchion ˈstænʃən, -tʃən |-ed -d

stand stænd |stood stud |-ard -əd; ES -əd

standardization ˌstændədəˈzeʃən, -aɪˈz-; ES
ˌstændəd-

standardize ˈstændədˌaɪz; ES -dəd-; |-s -ɪz
|-d -d

stand-by ˈstændˌbaɪ, ˈstænˌbaɪ

standee stænˈdi

standfast ˈstændˌfæst, ˈstæn-; E+-ˌfast,
-ˌfɑst

Standish ˈstændɪʃ |-'s -ɪz

standoff ˈstændˌɔf, -ˌɒf

standoffish stændˈɔfɪʃ, -ˈɒfɪʃ

standpat ˈstændˌpæt, ˈstæn- |-ter -ə; ES -ə(r

standpipe ˈstændˌpaɪp, ˈstæn-

standpoint ˈstændˌpɔɪnt, ˈstæn-

standstill ˈstændˌstɪl, ˈstæn-

Stanfield ˈstænˌfild |-ford -fəd; ES -fəd

Stanhope ˈstænhop, ˈstænəp

Stanislas ˈstænɪsləs |-'s -ɪz

Stanislaus *Cal* ˌstænɪsˈlau

stank ˈstæŋk

Stanley, -ly ˈstænlɪ

stannary ˈstænərɪ

stannic ˈstænɪk

stannum ˈstænəm |-nous ˈstænəs

Stanton ˈstæntən

Stanwix ˈstænwɪks |-'s -ɪz

stanza ˈstænzə |stanzaed ˈstænzəd

stapes ˈstepiz

staple ˈstepḷ |-d -d |-ling ˈsteplɪŋ, -pḷɪŋ

stapler ˈsteplɚ; ES ˈsteplə(r

Staples ˈstepḷz |-'s -ɪz

star stɑr; ES stɑː(r; |-red -d

starboard ˈstɑrˌbord, -ˌbɔrd; ES ˈstɑːˌboəd,
E+-ˌbɔəd

starch stɑrtʃ; ES stɑːtʃ; |-es -ɪz |-ed -t

stare stɛr, stær; E stɛə(r, ES stæə(r; |-d -d

starfish ˈstɑrˌfɪʃ; ES ˈstɑː-; |-'s -ɪz

stargaze ˈstɑrˌgez; ES ˈstɑː-; |-s -ɪz |-d -d

Words below in which a *before* r (farm) *is sounded* ɑ *are often pronounced in* E *with* a (fa:m)

stark **stɑrk**; ES **stɑːk**; |-ed -**t**

Stark, -ke **stɑrk**; ES **stɑːk**

starlet **ˈstɑrlɪt**; ES **ˈstɑːlɪt**

starlight **ˈstɑrˌlaɪt**; ES **ˈstɑː-**; |-ed -**ɪd**

starling **ˈstɑrlɪŋ**; ES **ˈstɑːlɪŋ**

starlit adj **ˈstɑrˌlɪt**; ES **ˈstɑː-**; |-ten -ˌlɪtn̩

Starr **stɑr**; ES **stɑː(r**

starry **ˈstɑrɪ**

star-spangled **ˈstɑrˌspæŋgļd**; ES **ˈstɑː-**

start **stɑrt**; ES **stɑːt**; |-ed -**ɪd**

startle **ˈstɑrtļ**; ES **ˈstɑːtļ**; |-d -**d** |-ling -tlɪŋ, -tļɪŋ

starvation **stɑrˈveʃən**; ES **stɑː-**

starve **stɑrv**; ES **stɑːv**; |-d -**d** |-dly -ɪdlɪ

starveling **ˈstɑrvlɪŋ**; ES **ˈstɑːvlɪŋ**

stasis **ˈstesɪs** |stases **ˈstesiz**

Stassen **ˈstæsn̩**

state **stet** |stated **ˈstetɪd** |-ly -lɪ |-dly -ɪdlɪ

statecraft **ˈstetˌkræft**; E+-ˌkraft, -ˌkrɑft

Statehouse **ˈstetˌhaʊs** |-ses -zɪz

Staten Island **ˈstætn̩ˈaɪlənd**

stateroom **ˈstetˌrum**, -ˌrʊm

statesman **ˈstetsmən** |-men -mən |-like -ˌlaɪk |-ly -lɪ |-ship -ˌʃɪp

state-wide **ˈstetˈwaɪd** (ˈstate-ˌwide ˈtour)

static **ˈstætɪk** |-al -ļ |-ally -ļɪ, -ɪklɪ

station **ˈsteʃən** |-ed -**d** |-ing **ˈsteʃənɪŋ**, -ʃnɪŋ

stationary **ˈsteʃənˌɛrɪ**

stationer **ˈsteʃənɚ**, **ˈsteʃnɚ**; ES -nə(r

stationery **ˈsteʃənˌɛrɪ**

statist **ˈstetɪst**

statistic **stəˈtɪstɪk** |-s -s |-al -ļ |-ally -ļɪ, -ɪklɪ

statistician **ˌstætəˈstɪʃən**

Statius **ˈsteʃɪəs** |-'s -ɪz

stator **ˈstetɚ**; ES **ˈstetə(r**

statoscope **ˈstætəˌskop**

statuary **ˈstætʃʊˌɛrɪ**

statue **ˈstætʃʊ** |-d -**d**

statuesque **ˌstætʃʊˈɛsk**

statuette **ˌstætʃʊˈɛt**

stature **ˈstætʃɚ**; ES **ˈstætʃə(r**; |-d -**d**

status **ˈstetəs**, **ˈstætəs** |-es -ɪz

status quo **ˈstetəsˈkwo**, **ˈstætəs-**

statute **ˈstætʃʊt** |-d -ɪd

statutory **ˈstætʃʊˌtorɪ**, -ˌtɔrɪ; S -ˌtorɪ

staunch **stɔntʃ**, **stɒntʃ**, **stɑntʃ** |-es -ɪz |-ed -t

Staunton Va **ˈstæntən**; Ind, Ill, Engd **ˈstɔntən**, **ˈstɒntən**, **ˈstɑntən**

Stavanger **stəˈvæŋɚ**, **stɑˈvɑŋɚ**; ES -ə(r

stave 'break' **stev** |staved **stevd** or stove **stov**

stave n **stev**

staves pl of staff, stave **stevz**, **stævz**; E+ **stavz**, **stɑvz**

stay **ste** |stayed **sted** or arch. staid **sted**

stead **stɛd** |steaded **ˈstɛdɪd**

steadfast **ˈstɛdˌfæst**, -fəst; E+-ˌfast, -ˌfɑst

steady **ˈstɛdɪ** |steadied **ˈstɛdɪd**

steak **stek**

steal **stil** |stole **stol** |stolen **ˈstolən** or arch. stoln **stoln**

stealth **ˈstɛlθ** |-y -ɪ |-ily -əlɪ, -ɪlɪ

steam **stim** |-ed -**d** |-boat -ˌbot |-ship -ˌʃɪp

steam engine n **ˈstimˈɛndʒən**

steam-engine adj **ˈstimˌɛndʒən**

steamer-rug **ˈstimɚˌrʌg**; ES **ˈstimɚˌrʌg**

steamtight **ˈstimˈtaɪt** (ˈsteamˌtight ˈjoint)

stearic **stɪˈærɪk**, **ˈstɪrɪk**

stearin **ˈstiərɪn**, **ˈstɪrɪn**

Stearn, -e **stɜn**; ES **stɜn**, **stɝn**; |-s -z |-s's -zɪz

stedfast **ˈstɛdˌfæst**, -fəst; E+-ˌfast, -ˌfɑst

steed **stid**

steel **stil** |steeled **stild** |-less **ˈstillɪs**

Steele **stil**

steelyard **ˈstɪljɚd**, **ˈstilˌjard**; ES **ˈstɪljəd**, **ˈstilˌjaːd**; |-s -z—When steelyards were in common use, the phonetically normal **ˈstɪljɚdz** was usual; **ˈstilˌjardz** is a spelling pronunciation.

steep **stip** |steeped **stipt**

steepen **ˈstipən** |-ed -**d** |-ing **ˈstipnɪŋ**, -pənɪŋ

steeple **ˈstipļ** |-d -**d** |-ling -plɪŋ, -pļɪŋ

steeplechase **ˈstipļˌtʃes** |-s -ɪz |-d -t

steepleless **ˈstipļlɪs**

steer **stɪr**; ES **stɪə(r**, S+**stɛə(r**; |-sman -zmən |smen -zmən

Steevens **ˈstivənz** |-'s -ɪz

Stefansson **ˈstɛfənsn̩**

Steffens **ˈstɛfənz** |-'s -ɪz

Steger **ˈstigɚ**; ES **ˈstigə(r**

stegomya **ˌstɛgəˈmaɪə**

stein **staɪn**

Steinmetz **ˈstaɪnmɛts** |-'s -ɪz

stele 'arrow shaft' **stil**

stele 'pillar' **ˈstili**

stella, S- **ˈstɛlə** |-lar -lɚ; ES -lə(r

stellate **ˈstɛlɪt**, -let

---

stem stɛm |stemmed stɛmd
stem-winder ˈstɛmˈwaɪndɚ, -ˌwaɪndɚ; ES -də(r
stench stɛntʃ |-es -ɪz |-ed -t
stencil ˈstɛnsl̩ |-ed -d |-ing -slɪŋ, -slɪŋ
stenograph ˈstɛnəˌgræf; E+-ˌgraf, -ˌgraf; |-ed -t
stenographer stəˈnɑgrəfɚ, -ˈnɒg-; ES -fə(r; |-phy -fɪ
stenographic ˌstɛnəˈgræfɪk |-al -| |-ally -ḷ, -ɪklɪ
stent stɛnt |stented ˈstɛntɪd
Stentor ˈstɛntɔr; ES -tɔə(r
stentorian stɛnˈtorɪən, -ˈtɔr-; S -ˈtor-
step stɛp |stepped stɛpt
stepbrother ˈstɛpˌbrʌðɚ; ES -ˌbrʌðə(r
stepchild ˈstɛpˌtʃaɪld |-children -ˌtʃɪldrən, -drɪn, -dən; ES -drən, -drɪn, -dən
stepdame ˈstɛpˌdem
stepdaughter ˈstɛpˌdɔtɚ; ES -ˌdɔtə(r
stepfather ˈstɛpˌfɑðɚ; ES -ˌfɑðə(r, E+ -ˌfaðə(r
Stephano *Tempest* ˈstɛfəˌno, *M. of Ven.* stəˈfɑno
Stephen ˈstivən |-s -z |-son -sn̩
Stephenville ˈstivənˌvɪl; S+-vl̩
stepladder ˈstɛpˌlædɚ; ES -ˌlædə(r
stepmother ˈstɛpˌmʌðɚ; ES -ˌmʌðə(r
Stepney ˈstɛpnɪ
stepparent ˈstɛpˌpɛrənt, -ˌpær-, -ˌper-
steppe stɛp
steppingstone ˈstɛpɪŋˌston
stepsister ˈstɛpˌsɪstɚ; ES -ˌsɪstə(r
stepson ˈstɛpˌsʌn
stere stɪr; ES stɪə(r
stereopticon ˌstɛrɪˈɑptɪkən, ˌstɪrɪ-; ES+ -ˈɒp-
stereoscope ˈstɛrɪəˌskop, ˈstɪrɪə-
stereoscopic ˌstɛrɪəˈskɑpɪk, ˌstɪrɪə-; ES+ -ˈskɒp-; |-al -| |-ally -ḷ, -ɪklɪ
stereoscopy ˌstɛrɪˈɑskəpɪ, ˌstɪrɪ-; ES+-ˈɒs-
stereotype ˈstɛrɪəˌtaɪp, ˈstɪrɪə- |-d -t
stereotypy ˈstɛrɪəˌtaɪpɪ, ˈstɪrɪə-
sterile ˈstɛrəl, -ɪl
sterility stəˈrɪlətɪ, stɛ-
sterilization ˌstɛrələˈzeʃən, -aɪˈz-
sterilize ˈstɛrəˌlaɪz |-s -ɪz |-d -d
sterling, S- ˈstɝlɪŋ; ES ˈstɜ-, ˈstɝ-
stern, S- stɝn; ES stɜn, stɝn

Sterne stɝn; ES stɜn, stɝn
sternforemost ˌstɝnˈformost, -ˈfɔr-, -məst; ES ˌstɜnˈfoə-, ˌstɝn-, E+-ˈfɔə-
sternmost ˈstɝnˌmost, -məst; ES ˈstɜn-, ˈstɝn-
sternness ˈstɝnnɪs; ES ˈstɜn-, ˈstɝn-
sternpost ˈstɝnˌpost; ES ˈstɜn-, ˈstɝn-
sternum ˈstɝnəm; ES ˈstɜn-, ˈstɝn-; |-s -z |-na -nə
sterol ˈstɛrol, -ɑl, -ɒl
stertorous ˈstɝtərəs; ES ˈstɜ-, ˈstɝ-
stet stɛt |stetted ˈstɛtɪd
stethoscope ˈstɛθəˌskop
stethoscopic ˌstɛθəˈskɑpɪk; ES+ˈskɒp-; |-al -| |-ally -ḷ, -ɪklɪ
stethoscopy stɛˈθɑskəpɪ; ES+-ˈθɒs-
Stetson ˈstɛtsn̩
Steuben *Baron* ˈstjubɪn, ˈstɪu-, ˈstu- |-ville -ˌvɪl
Steuben *US places* stjuˈbɛn, stɪu-, stu-
stevedore ˈstivəˌdor, -ˌdɔr; ES -ˌdoə(r, E+ -ˌdɔə(r
Stevens ˈstivənz |-'s -ɪz |-on ˈstivənsn̩
stew stju, stɪu, stu |-ed -d
steward, S- ˈstjuwɚd, ˈstɪu-, ˈstu-; ES -əd
Stewart ˈstjuɚt, ˈstɪu-, ˈstu-; ES -ət
stewpan ˈstjuˌpæn, ˈstɪu-, ˈstu-
Steyn staɪn
Steyne stin
stibium ˈstɪbɪəm
stick *of wood* stɪk |sticked stɪkt
stick *'stab'* stɪk |stuck stʌk
stickit ˈstɪkɪt
stickle ˈstɪkl̩ |-d -d |-ling ˈstɪklɪŋ, -kl̩ɪŋ
stickleback ˈstɪkl̩ˌbæk
stickler ˈstɪklɚ; ES ˈstɪklə(r
Stickney ˈstɪknɪ
stickpin ˈstɪkˌpɪn
Stieglitz ˈstiglɪts |-'s -ɪz
sties staɪz
stiff stɪf |stiffed stɪft
stiffen ˈstɪfən |-ed -d |-ing ˈstɪfənɪŋ, -fnɪŋ
stiff-necked ˈstɪfˈnɛkt (ˈstiff-ˌnecked ˈox)
stifle ˈstaɪfl̩ |-d -d |-ling ˈstaɪflɪŋ, -fl̩ɪŋ
stigma ˈstɪgmə |-s -z |-mata -mətə
stigmatic stɪgˈmætɪk |-al -| |-ally -ḷ, -ɪklɪ
stigmatization ˌstɪgmətəˈzeʃən, -aɪˈz-
stigmatize ˈstɪgməˌtaɪz |-s -ɪz |-d -d
Stikine stɪˈkin

|full fʊl |tooth tuθ |further ˈfɝðɚ; ES ˈfɝðə |custom ˈkʌstəm |while hwaɪl |how haʊ |toy tɔɪ |using ˈjuzɪŋ |fuse fjuz, fɪuz |dish dɪʃ |vision ˈvɪʒən |Eden ˈidn̩ |cradle ˈkredl̩ |keep 'em ˈkipm̩

stile staɪl

Stiles staɪlz |-'s -ɪz

stiletto stɪˈlɛto |-ed -d

Stilicho ˈstɪlɪˌko

still stɪl |stilled stɪld

stillbirth ˈstɪlˌbɝ̇θ; ES -ˌbɝ̇θ, -ˌbɝ̇θ; |-ths -θs

stillborn ˈstɪlˈbɔrn; ES -ˈbɔən; (ˈstɪlˌborn ˈhopes)

Stillson ˈstɪlsn̩

stilly adj ˈstɪlɪ

stilly adv ˈstɪllɪ

stilt stɪlt |stilted ˈstɪltɪd

Stilton ˈstɪltn̩

stimie ˈstaɪmɪ |stimied ˈstaɪmɪd

Stimson ˈstɪmsn̩, ˈstɪmpsn̩

stimulance ˈstɪmjələns |-cy -ɪ |-lant -lənt

stimulate ˈstɪmjəˌlet |-d -ɪd |-tive -ɪv

stimulation ˌstɪmjəˈleʃən

stimulus ˈstɪmjələs |-es -ɪz |-li -ˌlaɪ

stimy ˈstaɪmɪ |stimied ˈstaɪmɪd

sting stɪŋ |stung stʌŋ or arch. stang stæŋ |stung stʌŋ

stingaree ˈstɪŋəˌri, ˌstɪŋəˈri

stinge stɪndʒ |-s -ɪz |-d -d |stingeing -ɪŋ

stinger 'who stinges' ˈstɪndʒɝ̇; ES -dʒə(r

stinger 'what stings' ˈstɪŋɝ̇; ES ˈstɪŋə(r

stingy 'miserly' ˈstɪndʒɪ

stingy 'stinging' ˈstɪŋɪ

stink stɪŋk |stunk stʌŋk or stank stæŋk |stunk stʌŋk

stinkpot ˈstɪŋkˌpat; ES+-ˌpɒt

stint stɪnt |stinted ˈstɪntɪd

stipate ˈstaɪpet

stipe staɪp |stiped staɪpt

stipel ˈstaɪpl̩

stipend ˈstaɪpɛnd |-iary staɪˈpɛndɪˌɛrɪ

stipple ˈstɪpl̩ |-d -d |-ling -plɪŋ, -plɪŋ

stipulate adj ˈstɪpjəlɪt, -ˌlet

stipulate v ˈstɪpjəˌlet |-lated -ˌletɪd

stipulation ˌstɪpjəˈleʃən

stipule ˈstɪpjul |-d -d

stir stɝ̇; ES stɝ(r, stɝ̇; |-red -d

Stirling ˈstɝ̇lɪŋ; ES ˈstɝ-, ˈstɝ̇-; |-shire -ˌʃɪr, -ʃɝ̇; ES -ˌʃɪə(r, -ʃə(r

stirps stɝ̇ps; ES stɝps, stɝ̇ps; |-pes -piz

stirrup ˈstɝ̇əp, ˈstɪrəp, ˈstɛrəp; E ˈstɪrəp, ˈstɝ̇əp, ˈstɝ̇əp, ˈstɛrəp; S ˈstɝ̇rəp, ˈstʌrəp, ˈstɪrəp, ˈstɝ̇əp, ˈstɛrəp

stitch stɪtʃ |stitches ˈstɪtʃɪz |-ed -t

stithy ˈstɪðɪ, ˈstɪθɪ

stiver ˈstaɪvɝ̇; ES ˈstaɪvə(r

stoa, S- ˈstoə |-s -z |stoae ˈstoi

stoat stot

stock stak; ES+stɒk; |-ed -t

stockade stakˈed; ES+stɒk-; |-aded -ˈedɪd

Stockbridge ˈstakbrɪdʒ; ES+ˈstɒk-; |-'s -ɪz

stockbroker ˈstakˌbrokɝ̇; ES ˈstakˌbrokə(r, ˈstɒk-

stockholder ˈstakˌholdɝ̇; ES ˈstakˌholdə(r, ˈstɒk-

Stockholm ˈstakˌhom, -ˌholm; ES+ˈstɒk-

stockinet ˌstakɪnˈɛt; ES+ˌstɒk-

stocking ˈstakɪŋ; ES+ˈstɒk-; |-ed -d

stocking-feet ˈstakɪŋˌfit; ES+ˈstɒk-

stockman, ˈstakmən, -ˌmæn; ES+ˈstɒk-; |-men -mən, -ˌmɛn

Stockport ˈstakˌport, -ˌpɔrt; ES ˈstakˌpoət, ˈstɒk-, E+-ˌpɔət

stock-still ˈstakˈstɪl; ES+ˈstɒk-

Stockton ˈstaktən; ES+ˈstɒk-

stockyard ˈstakˌjard; ES ˈstakˌjaːd, ˈstɒk-, E+-ˌjaːd

Stoddard ˈstadɝ̇d; ES ˈstadəd, ˈstɒd-

stodgy ˈstadʒɪ; ES+ˈstɒdʒɪ

stogie, -gy ˈstogɪ

Stoic, s- ˈstoˌɪk |-al -l |-ally -l̩ɪ, -ɪklɪ

Stoicism, s- ˈstoˌɪˌsɪzəm

stoke, S- stok |stoked stokt

Stoke Poges ˈstokˈpodʒɪs, -ɪz |-'s -ɪz |-ges' -dʒɪz

Stokes stoks |-'s -ɪz

Stokowski stoˈkɔfskɪ, -ˈkɔvskɪ, -ˈkɒ-

stole stol |stoled stold

stolen ˈstolən, stoln (nonsyllabic n)

stolid ˈstalɪd; ES+ˈstɒl-

stolidity stəˈlɪdətɪ

stoln stoln (nonsyllabic n)

stolon ˈstolan; ES+-ɒn

stoma ˈstomə |-ta ˈstomətə, ˈstam-; ES+ˈstɒm-

stomach ˈstʌmək |-ed -t |-er -ɝ̇; ES -ə(r

stomach-ache ˈstʌmək¦ek

stomatoscope stoˈmætəˌskop, ˈstamətə-, ˈsto-; ES+ˈstɒm-

stomp stamp, stɒmp, stɔmp

stone, S- ston |-ed -d; |N Engd+stön (§46)

stonecutter ˈstonˌkʌtɝ̇; ES -ˌkʌtə(r

stone-deaf ˈstonˈdɛf (ˈstone-ˌdeaf ˈadder)

Key: See in full §§3–47. bee bi |pity ˈpɪtɪ (§6) |rate ret |yet jɛt |sang sæŋ |angry ˈæŋ·grɪ |bath bæθ; E baθ (§10) |ah ɑ |far far |watch watʃ, wɒtʃ (§12) |jaw dʒɔ |gorge gɔrdʒ |go go

Stoneham ˈstonəm
Stonehenge ˈstonhɛndʒ, -ˈhɛndʒ |-ˈs -ɪz
stonemason ˈstonˌmesn̩, -ˈmesn̩ |-ry -rɪ
stonewall adj ˈstonˌwɔl
Stonewall ˈstonˌwɔl
stonewall v ˌstonˈwɔl |-ed -d
stone wall ˈstonˈwɔl
stonework ˈstonˌwɝk; ES -ˌwɜk, -ˌwɝk
Stonington ˈstonɪŋtən
stonish ˈstanɪʃ; ES+ˈstɒn-; |-es -ɪz |-ed -t
stony ˈstonɪ; N Engd+ˈstönɪ
stood stʊd
stooge studʒ |stooges ˈstudʒɪz
stook stuk, stʊk |-ed -t
stool stul |stooled stuld
stoop stup |stooped stupt
stop stɑp; ES+stɒp; |-ped -t
stopcock ˈstɑpˌkak; ES+ˈstɒpˌkɒk
stope stop |stoped stopt
stopgap ˈstɑpˌgæp; ES+ˈstɒp-
stopover ˈstɑpˌovɚ; ES ˈstɑpˌovə(r, ˈstɒp-
stoppage ˈstɑpɪdʒ; ES+ˈstɒp-; |-s -ɪz
stopple ˈstɑpl̩; ES+ˈstɒpl̩; |-d -d |-ling -plɪŋ,
    -pl̩ɪŋ
storage ˈstorɪdʒ, ˈstɔr-; S ˈstor-; |-s -ɪz
store stor, stɔr; ES stoə(r, E+stɔə(r; |-d -d
storehouse ˈstorˌhaʊs, ˈstɔr-; ES ˈstoə-,
    E+ˈstɔə-; |-ses -zɪz
storekeeper ˈstorˌkipɚ, ˈstɔr-; ES ˈstoəˌkipə(r,
    E+ˈstɔə-
storeroom ˈstorˌrum, ˈstɔr-, -ˌrʊm; ES ˈstoə-,
    E+ˈstɔə-
storey, S- ˈstorɪ, ˈstɔrɪ; S ˈstorɪ; |-ed -d
storied ˈstorɪd, ˈstɔrɪd; S ˈstorɪd
storiette ˌstorɪˈɛt, ˌstɔrɪ-; S ˌstorɪ-
stork stɔrk; ES stɔək
storm, S- stɔrm; ES stɔəm; |-ed -d
Stormonth ˈstɔrmənθ, -mʌnθ; ES ˈstɔəm-
Storrs stɔrz; ES stɔəz; |-ˈs -ɪz
Storthing, -ting ˈstorˌtɪŋ, ˈstɔr-; ES ˈstoə-,
    E+ˈstɔə-
story, S- ˈstorɪ, ˈstɔrɪ; S ˈstorɪ; |-ied -d
storyteller ˈstorɪˌtɛlɚ, ˈstɔrɪ-; ES ˈstorɪ-
    ˌtɛlə(r, E+ˈstɔrɪ-
Stoughton ˈstotn̩
stound staʊnd |stounded ˈstaʊndɪd
stoup stup
Stourbridge ˈstʊrbrɪdʒ, ˈstaʊr-, ˈstɝ-; ES
    ˈstʊə-, ˈstaʊə-, ˈstɜ-, ˈstɝ-; |-ˈs -ɪz

stout, S- staʊt
stouten ˈstaʊtn̩ |-ed -d |-ing -tn̩ɪŋ, -tn̩ɪŋ
stouthearted ˈstaʊtˈhɑrtɪd; ES -ˈhɑːt-, E+
    -ˈhɑːt-; (ˈstoutˌhearted ˈlass)
stove stov |stoved stovd |-pipe -ˌpaɪp
stow sto |stowed stod |-age -ɪdʒ
Stow, -e sto, Scotl staʊ
stowaway ˈstoəˌwe
strabismal strəˈbɪzml̩ |-ly -ɪ
strabismic strəˈbɪzmɪk |-al -l̩
strabismus strəˈbɪzməs
Strabo ˈstrebo
Strachan strɔn
Strachey ˈstretʃɪ
straddle ˈstrædl̩ |-d -d |-ling -dlɪŋ, -dl̩ɪŋ
Stradivarius ˌstrædəˈvɛrɪəs, -ˈver-; |-ˈs -ɪz
strafe stref, straf (Ger ˈʃtraːfə)
Strafford ˈstræfəd; ES ˈstræfəd
straggle ˈstrægl̩ |-d -d |-ling -glɪŋ, -gl̩ɪŋ
straggly ˈstræglɪ
straight stret |straighted ˈstretɪd
straightaway ˈstretəˌwe
straightedge ˈstretˌɛdʒ |-s -ɪz |-d -d
straighten ˈstretn̩ |-ed -d |-ing -tn̩ɪŋ, -tn̩ɪŋ
straightforward ˌstretˈfɔrwəd; ES -ˈfɔəwəd;
    (ˈstraightˌforward ˈstyle)
straight-grained ˈstretˈgrend (ˈstraight-
    ˌgrained ˈoak)
straight-out n ˈstretˌaʊt
straight-out adj ˈstretˈaʊt
straightway ˈstretˌwe
strain stren |strained strend |-edly -ɪdlɪ, -dlɪ
strait stret
straiten ˈstretn̩ |-ed -d |-ing -tn̩ɪŋ, -tn̩ɪŋ
strait-laced ˈstretˈlest (ˈstrait-ˌlaced ˈsect)
strake strek |straked strekt
strand, S- strænd |stranded ˈstrændɪd
strange, S- strendʒ |Strange's ˈstrendʒɪz
stranger ˈstrendʒɚ; ES -dʒə(r; |-ed -d
strangle ˈstræŋgl̩ |-d -d |-ling -glɪŋ, -gl̩ɪŋ
strangulate ˈstræŋgjəˌlet |-lated -ˌletɪd
strangulation ˌstræŋgjəˈleʃən
strap stræp |strapped stræpt
Strasbourg ˈstræsbɝg; ES -bɜg, -bɝg (Fr
    strasˈbuːr, straz-; Ger ˈʃtraːsbʊrk)
Strasburg US ˈstræsbɝg; ES -bɜg, -bɝg;
    O loc.+ˈstrɔzbɝg
strata ˈstretə, ˈstrætə
stratagem ˈstrætədʒəm |-gist -dʒɪst |-gy -dʒɪ

|full fʊl |tooth tuθ |further ˈfɝðɚ; ES ˈfɜðə |custom ˈkʌstəm |while hwaɪl |how haʊ |toy tɔɪ
|using ˈjuzɪŋ |fuse fjuz, fɪuz |dish dɪʃ |vision ˈvɪʒən |Eden ˈidn̩ |cradle ˈkredl̩ |keep 'em ˈkipm̩

strategic strə'tidʒɪk |-al -] |-ally -|ɪ, -ɪklɪ
Stratford 'strætfəd; ES 'strætfəd
Stratford-on-Avon 'strætfədɑn'evən, -ɒn-,
 -ɔn-; ES -fəd-
strath stræθ |-ths -θs
Strathclyde stræθ'klaɪd |-cona -'konə
Strathmore stræθ'mor, -'mɔr; ES -'moə(r,
 E+-'mɔə(r; US & attrib. 'Strath,more
strathspey, S- stræθ'spe, 'stræθ,spe
stratification ,strætəfə'keʃən
stratiform 'strætə,fɔrm; ES -,fɔəm
stratify 'strætə,faɪ |-fied -,faɪd
stratigraphic ,strætə'græfɪk |-al -] |-ally -|ɪ,
 -ɪklɪ
stratigraphy strə'tɪgrəfɪ
Stratton 'strætn̩
Strato 'streto
stratosphere 'strætə,sfɪr, 'stretə-; ES -,sfɪə(r,
 S+-,sfɛə(r
stratospheric ,strætə'sfɛrɪk, ,stretə-
stratum 'stretəm, 'stræt- |-ta -tə |-s -z
stratus 'stretəs |strati 'stretaɪ
straught strɔt
Straus, -ss straus |-'s -ɪz (Ger ʃtraus)
Stravinski strə'vɪnskɪ
straw strɔ |strawed strɔd
strawberry 'strɔ,bɛrɪ, -bərɪ
strawboard 'strɔ,bord, -,bɔrd; ES -,boəd,
 E+-,bɔəd
strawy 'strɔ·ɪ
stray stre |strayed stred
streak strik |streaked strikt
streaked adj 'strikɪd, strikt
stream strim |streamed strimd |-let -lɪt
streamline 'strim,laɪn |-lined -,laɪnd
Streatham 'strɛtəm
Streator 'stritɚ; ES 'stritə(r
street, S- strit |streeted 'stritɪd
Streitberg 'straɪtbɝg; ES -bɝg, -bɝg; (Ger
 'ʃtraɪtbɛrk)
strength strɛŋkθ, strɛŋθ |-ths -θs
strengthen 'strɛŋkθən, 'strɛŋθ- |-ed -d |-ing
 -θənɪŋ, -θnɪŋ
strenuosity ,strɛnjʊ'ɑsətɪ; ES+-'ɒsətɪ
strenuous 'strɛnjʊəs
streptococcus ,strɛptə'kɑkəs; ES+-'kɒk-;
 |-cci -ksaɪ
Stresa 'strɛzə, 'strezə (It 'stre:za)
Stresemann 'strezəmən (Ger 'ʃtre:zə,man)

stress strɛs |stresses 'strɛsɪz |-ed -t
stretch strɛtʃ |stretches 'strɛtʃɪz |-ed -t
Stretford 'strɛtfəd; ES 'strɛtfəd
strew stru, strɪu |-ed -d |-ed -d or -n -n
striate adj 'straɪɪt, -et
striate v 'straɪet |-d -ɪd |-tion straɪ'eʃən
stricken 'strɪkən |-ness 'strɪkənnɪs
Strickland 'strɪklənd
strickle 'strɪk] |-d -d |-ling -klɪŋ, -k]ɪŋ
strickler 'strɪklɚ; ES 'strɪklə(r
strict strɪkt |-ly -ktlɪ, -klɪ
stricture 'strɪktʃɚ; ES 'strɪktʃə(r; |-d -d
stride straɪd |strode strod |stridden 'strɪdn̩
stridence 'straɪdn̩s |-cy -ɪ |-dent -dn̩t
stridulate 'strɪdʒə,let |-lated -,letɪd
stridulation ,strɪdʒə'leʃən
strife straɪf
strike straɪk |struck strʌk |struck strʌk or
 stricken 'strɪkən
strikebreaker 'straɪk,brekɚ; ES -,brekə(r
Strindberg 'strɪndbɝg, 'strɪnb-; ES -bɝg,
 -bɝg
string strɪŋ |strung strʌŋ
stringed adj strɪŋd
stringency 'strɪndʒənsɪ |-gent -dʒənt
stringhalt 'strɪŋ'hɔlt, -,hɔlt
stringhalted 'strɪŋ'hɔltɪd ('string,halted 'nag)
stringpiece 'strɪŋ,pis |-s -ɪz
stringy 'strɪŋɪ
strip strɪp |stripped strɪpt
stripe straɪp |striped straɪpt
striped adj 'straɪpɪd, straɪpt
stripling 'strɪplɪŋ
stripper 'strɪpɚ; ES 'strɪpə(r
stripy 'straɪpɪ
strive straɪv |strove strov or strived straɪvd
 |striven 'strɪvən or strived straɪvd or rarely
 strove strov
stroboscope 'strobə,skop
stroboscopic ,strabə'skapɪk; ES+,strobə-
 'skɒp-; |-al -]
stroboscopy stro'baskəpɪ; ES+-'bɒs-
strode, S- strod
stroke strok |stroked strokt
stroll strol |strolled strold
strong, S- strɔŋ, strɒŋ; S+straŋ; |-er -gɚ; ES
 -gə(r; |-est -gɪst
stronghold 'strɔŋ,hold, 'strɒŋ-; S+'straŋ-
strongish 'strɔŋɪʃ, 'strɒŋ-; S+'straŋ-

Key: See in full §§3-47. bee bi |pity 'pɪtɪ (§6) |rate ret |yet jɛt |sang sæŋ |angry 'æŋ·grɪ
|bath bæθ; E baθ (§10) |ah ɑ |far fɑr |watch wɑtʃ, wɒtʃ (§12) |jaw dʒɔ |gorge gɔrdʒ |go go

Words formed with sub- *often shift their accent for contrast* ('editor & 'sub͵editor)

strong-minded 'strɔŋ'maɪndɪd, 'strɒŋ-; S+ 'strɒŋ-
strontia 'strɒnʃɪə; ES+'strɒn-; |-ium -m
strook strʊk
strop strɒp; ES+strɒp; |-ped -t
strophe 'stroʊfɪ
strophic 'strɒfɪk, 'strof-; ES+'strɒf-; |-al -ḷ |-ally -ḷɪ, -ɪklɪ
Strother 'strʌðɚ; ES 'strʌðə(r, 'strʌð-
Stroud straʊd |-sburg -zbɝg; ES -zbɜg, -zbɝg
strove stroʊv
strow stro |strowed strod |strown stron *or* strowed strod
stroy strɔɪ |stroyed strɔɪd
struck strʌk
structural 'strʌktʃərəl |-ly -ɪ
structure 'strʌktʃɚ; ES 'strʌktʃə(r; |-d -d
struggle 'strʌgḷ |-d -d |-ling -glɪŋ, -gḷɪŋ
struggler 'strʌglɚ; ES 'strʌglə(r
strum strʌm |strummed strʌmd
strumpet 'strʌmpɪt |-ed -ɪd
strung strʌŋ
strut strʌt |strutted 'strʌtɪd
Struthers 'strʌðɚz; ES 'strʌðəz; |-'s -ɪz
Strutt strʌt
strychnin, -e 'strɪknɪn |-nic -nɪk
Stuart 'stjuɚt, 'strʊ-, 'stu-; ES -ət
stub stʌb |stubbed stʌbd
stubbed *adj* 'stʌbɪd, stʌbd
stubble 'stʌbḷ |-d -d |-ling 'stʌblɪŋ, -bḷɪŋ
stubbly 'stʌblɪ, 'stʌbḷɪ
stubborn 'stʌbɚn; ES 'stʌbən; |-ness -nɪs
stubby 'stʌbɪ
stucco 'stʌko |stuccoed 'stʌkod
stuck stʌk
stuck-up 'stʌk'ʌp ('stuck-͵up 'manner)
stud stʌd |studded 'stʌdɪd
Studebaker 'stjudə͵bekɚ, 'strʊ-, 'stu-; ES -ə(r
student 'stjudṇt, 'strʊ-, 'stu-
studied 'stʌdɪd
studio 'stjudɪ͵o, 'strʊ-, 'stu- |-ious -ɪəs
study 'stʌdɪ |studied 'stʌdɪd
stuff stʌf |stuffed stʌft |-y -ɪ
stultification ͵stʌltəfə'keʃən
stultify 'stʌltə͵faɪ |-fied -͵faɪd
stumble 'stʌmbḷ |-d -d |-ling -blɪŋ, -bḷɪŋ
stump stʌmp |stumped stʌmpt

stun stʌn |stunned stʌnd
stung stʌŋ
stunk stʌŋk
stunt stʌnt |stunted 'stʌntɪd
stupe stjup, strup, stup |-d -t
stupefacient ͵stjupə'feʃənt, ͵strɪ-, ͵stu- |-faction -'fækʃən
stupefy 'stjupə͵faɪ, 'strɪ-, 'stu- |-fied -͵faɪd
stupendous stju'pɛndəs, strɪ-, stu-
stupid 'stjupɪd, 'strɪ-, 'stu-
stupidity stju'pɪdətɪ, strɪ-, stu-
stupor 'stjupɚ, 'strɪ-, 'stu-; ES -pə(r
Sturbridge 'stɝbrɪdʒ; ES 'stɝ-, 'stɝ-; |-'s -ɪz
sturdy 'stɝdɪ; ES 'stɝ-, 'stɝ-; |-dily -dḷɪ, -dɪlɪ
sturgeon, S- 'stɝdʒən; ES 'stɝ-, 'stɝ-
Sturgis 'stɝdʒɪs, 'stɝ-, 'stɝ-; |-'s -ɪz
stutter 'stʌtɚ; ES 'stʌtə(r
Stuttgart 'stʌtgɚt, -gɑrt; ES -gət, -gɑːt (*Ger* 'ʃtʊtgart)
Stuyvesant 'staɪvəsṇt
sty staɪ |sties staɪz |stied staɪd
stye staɪ |sties, styes staɪz
Stygian 'stɪdʒɪən
style staɪl |styled staɪld |-list -ɪst
styleless 'staɪllɪs
stylistic staɪ'lɪstɪk |-al -ḷ |-ally -ḷɪ, -ɪklɪ
stylite 'staɪlaɪt |-tism -͵ɪzəm
Stylites staɪ'laɪtiz |-tes' -tiz
stylize 'staɪlaɪz |-s -ɪz |-d -d
stylus 'staɪləs |styluses 'staɪləsɪz
stymie 'staɪmɪ |-d -d
styptic 'stɪptɪk |-al -ḷ
Styria 'stɪrɪə |-n -n
Styx stɪks |-'s -ɪz |-ian -ɪən
suable 'suəbḷ, 'sɪu-, 'sju- |-bly -blɪ
suasion 'sweʒən |suasive 'swesɪv
suave swɑv, swev |-vity 'swævətɪ, 'swɑv-
sub sʌb
sub- *prefix, stressed* 'sʌb-, ͵sʌb-; *unstr.* səb-;
　　—*The accent mark is usually omitted from partly accented* sʌb- *before an accented syllable.*
subacid sʌb'æsɪd ('sub͵acid 'juice)
subalpine sʌb'ælpaɪn, -pɪn
subaltern səb'ɔltɚn, *logic*+'sʌbḷ͵tɝn; ES -'ɔltən, -͵tɜn, -͵tɝn
subalternate səb'ɔltɚnɪt, -'æl-; ES -tə-

Words formed with sub- *often shift their accent for contrast* ('editor & 'sub,editor)

subalternating səb'ɔltɚ,netɪŋ, -'æl-; ES -tə-
subalternation səb,ɔltɚ'neʃən, ,sʌbɔltɚ-, -,æl-, -æl-; ES -tə-
subaqueous sʌb'ekwɪəs, -'æk-
subarctic sʌb'arktɪk, *now rare* -'art-; ES -'ɑ:-, E+-'a:-
subaudible sʌb'ɔdəbl̩
subbase 'sʌb,bes |-s -ɪz
subbass 'sʌb,bes |-es -ɪz
subclass 'sʌb,klæs; E+-,klas, -,klas; |-es -ɪz |-ed -t
subcommittee 'sʌbkə,mɪtɪ
subconscious sʌb'kanʃəs; ES+-'kɒn-
subcontract *n* sʌb'kantrækt; ES+-'kɒn-
subcontract *v* ,sʌbkən'trækt |-ed -ɪd
subcutaneous ,sʌbkju'tenɪəs, -kɪu-
subdeacon sʌb'dikən |-ate -ɪt |-ess -ɪs |-ry -rɪ
subdean sʌb'din |-ery -ərɪ, -'dinrɪ
subdeb sʌb'dɛb
subdebutante sʌb,dɛbju'tant, ,sʌbdɛb-, sʌb-'dɛbjə,tænt
subdivide ,sʌbdə'vaɪd |-d -ɪd (di'vide & 'subdi,vide)
subdivision ,sʌbdə'vɪʒən, 'sʌbdə,vɪʒən
subduct səb'dʌkt |-ed -ɪd |-ction -kʃən
subdue səb'dju, -'dɪu, -'du |-d -d |-dly -dlɪ, -ɪdlɪ
subedit sʌb'ɛdɪt |-ed -ɪd |-or -ɚ; ES -ə(r
subgroup *n* 'sʌb,grup
subgroup *v* sʌb'grup |-ed -t
subhead 'sʌb,hɛd
subjacency sʌb'dʒesn̩sɪ |-cent -sn̩t
subject *n, adj* 'sʌbdʒɪkt
subject *v* səb'dʒɛkt |-ed -ɪd |-ion -kʃən |-ive -ɪv
subjectivity ,sʌbdʒɛk'tɪvətɪ
subjoin səb'dʒɔɪn |-ed -d
sub-jugate *adj* sʌb'dʒugɪt, -'dʒɪu-
subjugate *v* 'sʌbdʒə,get |-gated -,getɪd
subjugation ,sʌbdʒə'geʃən
subjunct *n* 'sʌbdʒʌŋkt
subjunction səb'dʒʌŋkʃən |-tive -tɪv
subkingdom sʌb'kɪŋdəm, 'sʌb,kɪŋdəm
sublease *n* 'sʌb,lis |-s -ɪz
sublease *v* sʌb'lis |-s -ɪz |-d -t
sublet sʌb'lɛt ('let & 'sub,let)
Sublette sə'blɛt
sublimate *n, adj* 'sʌbləmɪt, -,met

sublimate *v* 'sʌblə,met |-mated -,metɪd
sublimation ,sʌblə'meʃən
sublime sə'blaɪm |-d -d
subliminal sʌb'lɪmənl̩, -'laɪm- |-ly -ɪ
sublimity sə'blɪmətɪ
sublunar sʌb'lunɚ, -'lɪu-; ES -nə(r; |-y -ɪ
submarginal sʌb'mardʒɪnl̩; ES -'ma:-; |-ly -ɪ
submarine *adj* ,sʌbmə'rin ('subma,rine 'life)
submarine *n, v* 'sʌbmə,rin |-d -d
submerge səb'mɝdʒ; ES -'mɜdʒ, -'mɝdʒ; |-s -ɪz |-d -d |-gence -dʒəns
submerse səb'mɝs; ES -'mɜs, -'mɝs; |-s -ɪz |-d -t |-sion -ʃən, -ʒən
submission səb'mɪʃən |-sive -'mɪsɪv
submit səb'mɪt |-ted -ɪd |-tal -l̩
subnormal sʌb'nɔrml̩; ES -'nɔəml̩
suborder sʌb'ɔrdɚ, 'sʌb,ɔrdɚ; ES -'ɔədə(r, -,ɔə-
subordinate *n, adj* sə'bɔrdn̩ɪt, -dn̩ɪt; ES -'bɔəd-
subordinate *v* sə'bɔrdn̩,et; ES -'bɔəd-; |-d -ɪd
subordination sə,bɔrdn̩'eʃən; ES -,bɔəd-
suborn sə'bɔrn, sʌ-; ES -'bɔən; |-ed -d
subornation ,sʌbɔr'neʃən; ES ,sʌbɔə-
subplot 'sʌb,plat; ES+-,plɒt
subpoena, -pena sə'pinə, səb'pinə |-ed -d
sub rosa sʌb'rozə
subscribe səb'skraɪb |-d -d
subscript 'sʌbskrɪpt
subscription səb'skrɪpʃən |-tive -tɪv
subsection sʌb'sɛkʃən, 'sʌb,sɛkʃən
subsequence 'sʌbsɪ,kwɛns, -kwəns |-cy -ɪ |-nt -nt
subserve səb'sɝv; ES -'sɜv, -'sɝv; |-d -d
subservience səb'sɝvɪəns; ES -'sɜv-, -'sɝv-; |-cy -ɪ |-ient -ɪənt
subside səb'saɪd |-d -ɪd
subsidence səb'saɪdn̩s, 'sʌbsədəns |-s -ɪz
subsidiary səb'sɪdɪ,ɛrɪ
subsidization ,sʌbsədə'zeʃən, -aɪ'z-
subsidize 'sʌbsə,daɪz |-s -ɪz |-d -d |-dy -dɪ
subsist səb'sɪst |-ed -ɪd
subsistence səb'sɪstəns |-cy -ɪ |-ent -ənt
subsoil 'sʌb,sɔɪl |-ed -d
subsolar sʌb'solɚ; ES -'solə(r
subspecies sʌb'spiʃɪz, 'sʌb,spiʃɪz, -ʃɪz
substance 'sʌbstəns |-s -ɪz
substandard sʌb'stændɚd; ES -dəd

Key: *See in full §§3–47.* bee **bi** |pity **'pɪtɪ** (§6) |rate **ret** |yet **jɛt** |sang **sæŋ** |angry **'æŋ·grɪ** |bath **bæθ**; E **baθ** (§10) |ah **ɑ** |far **far** |watch **watʃ, wɒtʃ** (§12) |jaw **dʒɔ** |gorge **gɔrdʒ** |go **go**

Words formed with sub- *often shift their accent for contrast* ('editor & 'sub‚editor)

substantial səb'stænʃəl |-ly -ɪ

substantiality səb‚stænʃɪ'ælətɪ |-ation -'eʃən

substantival ‚sʌbstən'taɪv| |-ly -ɪ

substantive 'sʌbstəntɪv |-ly 'sʌbstəntɪvlɪ

substitute 'sʌbstə‚tjut, -‚trut, -‚tut |-d -ɪd |-tutive -ɪv

substitution ‚sʌbstə'tjuʃən, -'tru-, -'tu-

substratum sʌb'stretəm, -'stræt-, 'sʌb‚str- |-ta -tə

substructure sʌb'strʌktʃɚ, 'sʌb‚str-; ES -tʃə(r

subsume səb'sum, -'srum, -'sjum |-d -d

subsumption səb'sʌmpʃən

subtangent sʌb'tændʒənt

subtenancy sʌb'tɛnənsɪ |-nant -nənt

subtend səb'tɛnd |-ed -ɪd

subterfuge 'sʌbtɚ‚fjudʒ, -‚frudʒ; ES 'sʌbtə-; |-s -ɪz |-d -d

subterranean ‚sʌbtə'renɪən |-neous -nɪəs

subtile 'sʌt|, 'sʌbtɪl |-ly 'sʌt|ɪ, 'sʌtlɪ, 'sʌbt|ɪ

subtility sʌb'tɪlətɪ

subtilize 'sʌt|‚aɪz, 'sʌbt|- |-s -ɪz |-d -d

subtilty 'sʌt|tɪ, 'sʌbt|tɪ

subtitle 'sʌb‚taɪt| |-d -d |-ling -t|ɪŋ, -tlɪŋ

subtle 'sʌt| |-ty -tɪ |-r -tlɚ, -t|ɚ; ES -ə(r; |-st -tlɪst, -t|ɪst

subtly 'sʌtlɪ, 'sʌt|ɪ

subtonic sʌb'tɑnɪk; ES+-'tɒn-

subtract səb'trækt |-ed -ɪd

subtraction səb'trækʃən |-tive -tɪv

subtrahend 'sʌbtrə‚hɛnd, 'sʌbtrɪ-

subtropical sʌb'trɑpɪk|; ES+-'trɒp-

suburb 'sʌbɝb; ES 'sʌbɜb, -ɝb

suburban sə'bɝbən; ES -'bɜb-, -'bɝb-; |-ite -‚aɪt |-bia -bɪə

subvene səb'vin |-d -d |-ntion -'vɛnʃən

subversion səb'vɝʃən, -ʒən; ES -'vɜ-, -'vɝ-; |-sive -sɪv

subvert səb'vɝt; ES -'vɜt, -'vɝt; |-ed -ɪd

subway 'sʌb‚we

succeed sək'sid |-ed -ɪd

success sək'sɛs |-es -ɪz |-ful -fəl |-fully -fəlɪ

succession sək'sɛʃən |-ive -'sɛsɪv |-sor -'sɛsɚ; ES -ə(r

succinct sək'sɪŋkt

succor 'sʌkɚ; ES 'sʌkə(r; |-ed -d

succory 'sʌkərɪ

succotash 'sʌkə‚tæʃ |-'s -ɪz

succubus 'sʌkjəbəs |-es -ɪz |-bi -‚baɪ

succulence 'sʌkjələns |-cy -ɪ |-lent -lənt

succumb sə'kʌm |-ed -d

such sʌtʃ, *unstressed sometimes* sətʃ

suck sʌk |sucked sʌkt |-er -ɚ; ES -ə(r

suckle 'sʌk| |-d -d |-ling 'sʌk|ɪŋ, -klɪŋ

suckling, S- *n* 'sʌklɪŋ

sucrose 'sukros, 'sɪu-, 'sju-

suction 'sʌkʃən |-al -|

sud sʌd |suds sʌdz |sudded 'sʌdɪd |-sy -zɪ

Sudan su'dæn |-ese ‚sudə'niz

sudary 'sudərɪ, 'sɪu-, 'sju-

sudatorium ‚sudə'torɪəm, ‚sɪu-, ‚sju-, -'tɔr-; S -'tor-

sudatory 'sudə‚torɪ, 'sɪu-, 'sju-, -‚tɔrɪ; S -‚torɪ

Sudbury 'sʌd‚bɛrɪ, -bərɪ

sudden 'sʌdn̩, *less freq.* 'sʌdɪn |-ness 'sʌdn̩nɪs, 'sʌdɪnnɪs

Sudermann 'sudɚmən; ES 'sudə-; (*Ger* 'zu:dər‚man)

Sudeten su'detn̩ (*Ger* zu'de:tən)

Sudetes su'ditiz |-detic -'dɛtɪk

sudorific ‚sudə'rɪfɪk, ‚sɪu-, ‚sju-

suds sʌdz |-es -ɪz |-ed -d

sue su, sɪu, sju |-d -d

suede swed (*Fr* sɥɛd)

suet 'suɪt, 'sɪuɪt, 'sjuɪt

Suetonius swɪ'tonɪəs |-'s -ɪz

Suez 'suɛz, 'sɪu-, 'sju-, su'ɛz, sɪu-, sju- |-'s -ɪz

suffari sə'fɑrɪ

suffer 'sʌfɚ; ES 'sʌfə(r; |-ed -d |-ing 'sʌfrɪŋ, -fərɪŋ

sufferable 'sʌfrəb|, 'sʌfərə- |-bly -blɪ

sufferance 'sʌfrəns, 'sʌfərəns |-s -ɪz

Suffern 'sʌfɚn; ES 'sʌfən

suffice sə'faɪs, -'faɪz |-s -ɪz |-d -'faɪst, -'faɪzd

sufficiency sə'fɪʃənsɪ |-cient -ʃənt

Suffield 'sʌfild

suffix *n* 'sʌfɪks |-es -ɪz

suffix *v* sə'fɪks, 'sʌfɪks |-es -ɪz |-ed -t

suffocate 'sʌfə‚ket |-d -ɪd |-tive -ɪv

suffocation ‚sʌfə'keʃən

Suffolk 'sʌfək

suffragan 'sʌfrəgən |-ganate -‚et

suffrage 'sʌfrɪdʒ |-s -ɪz |-tte ‚sʌfrə'dʒɛt

suffuse sə'fjuz, -'fɪuz |-s -ɪz |-d -d

|full fʊl |tooth tuθ |further 'fɝðɚ; ES 'fɝðə |custom 'kʌstəm |while hwaɪl |how haʊ |toy tɔɪ |using 'juzɪŋ |fuse fjuz, fɪuz |dish dɪʃ |vision 'vɪʒən |Eden 'idn̩ |cradle 'kred| |keep 'em 'kipm̩

suffusion səˈfjuʒən, -ˈfɪuʒ- |-sive -sɪv
Sufi ˈsufɪ |-sm ˈsufɪzəm
sugar ˈʃʊgɚ; ES ˈʃʊgə(r; |-ed -d |-ing ˈʃʊgrɪŋ,
  ˈʃʊgərɪŋ |-plum -ˌplʌm
sugary ˈʃʊgrɪ, ˈʃʊgərɪ
suggest səgˈdʒɛst, less freq. səˈdʒɛst |-ed -ɪd
suggestibility səgˌdʒɛstəˈbɪlətɪ, səˌdʒɛst-
suggestible səgˈdʒɛstəbḷ, səˈdʒɛst- |-bly -blɪ
suggestion səgˈdʒɛstʃən, səˈdʒɛs- |-tive -tɪv
suicidal ˌsuəˈsaɪdḷ, ˌsɪu-, ˌsju- |-ly -ɪ
suicide ˈsuəˌsaɪd, ˈsɪu-, ˈsju- |-d -ɪd
sui generis ˈsjuɪˈdʒɛnərɪs, ˈsɪu-, ˈsu-
suit sut, sɪut, sjut |-ed -ɪd
suitability ˌsutəˈbɪlətɪ, ˌsɪu-, ˌsju-
suitable ˈsutəbḷ, ˈsɪu-, ˈsju- |-bly -blɪ
suitcase ˈsutˌkes, ˈsɪut-, ˈsjut- |-s -ɪz
suite ‘suit’ sut, sɪut, sjut |-d -ɪd
suite ‘staff,’ ‘set’ swit, ‘furniture’+sut, sɪut,
  sjut
suitor ˈsutɚ, ˈsɪu-, ˈsju-; ES -tə(r
sulcal ˈsʌlkḷ |-ize -ˌaɪz |-izes -ˌaɪzɪz |-ized
  -ˌaɪzd
Suleiman ˈsulɪˌmɑn
sulfanilamide ˌsʌlfəˈnɪləˌmaɪd
sulfate ˈsʌlfet |-d -ɪd
sulfathiazole ˌsʌlfəˈθaɪəˌzol |-zol -ˌzol, -ˌzɑl,
  -ˌzɒl, -ˌzɔl
sulfid ˈsʌlfɪd |-fide -faɪd, -fɪd
sulfite ˈsʌlfaɪt
sulfone ˈsʌlfon
sulfur ˈsʌlfɚ; ES ˈsʌlfə(r; |-ed -d |-ing
  ˈsʌlfərɪŋ, ˈsʌlfrɪŋ
sulfurate adj ˈsʌlfərɪt, -frɪt
sulfurate v ˈsʌlfəˌret |-rated -ˌretɪd
sulfureous sʌlˈfjʊrɪəs, -ˈfɪu-
sulfuret n ˈsʌlfjərɪt
sulfuret v ˈsʌlfjəˌret |-ed -ɪd
sulfuric sʌlˈfjʊrɪk, -ˈfɪu- (ˈsulˌfuric ˈacid)
sulfurous ˈsʌlfərəs, -fjərəs, chem.+sʌlˈfjʊrəs,
  -ˈfɪu-
sulfury ˈsʌlfərɪ, ˈsʌlfrɪ
Sulgrave ˈsʌlgrev
Suliman ˈsulɪˌmɑn
sulk sʌlk |-ed -t |-y -ɪ |-ily -ḷɪ, -ɪlɪ
Sulla ˈsʌlə
sullen ˈsʌlɪn, -ən |-ness ˈsʌlɪnnɪs, -lənnɪs
Sullivan ˈsʌləvən |-vant -vənt
sully, S- ˈsʌlɪ |sullied ˈsʌlɪd
sulphanilamide ˌsʌlfəˈnɪləˌmaɪd

sulphate ˈsʌlfet |-d -ɪd
sulphathiazole ˌsʌlfəˈθaɪəˌzol |-zol -ˌzol, -ˌzɑl,
  -ˌzɒl, -ˌzɔl
sulphid ˈsʌlfɪd |-phide -faɪd, -fɪd
sulphite ˈsʌlfaɪt
sulphone ˈsʌlfon
sulphur ˈsʌlfɚ; ES ˈsʌlfə(r; |-ed -d |-ing
  ˈsʌlfərɪŋ, -frɪŋ
sulphurate adj ˈsʌlfərɪt, -frɪt
sulphurate v ˈsʌlfəˌret |-rated -ˌretɪd
sulphureous sʌlˈfjʊrɪəs, -ˈfɪu-
sulphuret n ˈsʌlfjərɪt
sulphuret v ˈsʌlfjəˌrɛt |-ed -ɪd
sulphuric sʌlˈfjʊrɪk, -ˈfɪu- (ˈsulˌphuric ˈacid)
sulphurous ˈsʌlfərəs, -fjərəs, chem.+sʌl-
  ˈfjʊrəs, -ˈfɪu-
sulphury ˈsʌlfərɪ, ˈsʌlfrɪ
sultan, S- ˈsʌltṇ |-a sʌlˈtænə, -ˈtɑnə
sultanate ˈsʌltṇɪt, -ˌet
sultry ˈsʌltrɪ
Sulu ˈsulu
sum sʌm |summed sʌmd
sumac, -ach ˈʃumæk, ˈʃɪu-, ˈsu-, ˈsɪu-, ˈsju-,
  ˈʃumek, ˈʃɪu—The historically natural
  pron. (which still prevails) is ˈʃumæk, ˈʃɪu-
  (cf sugar, sure), ˈsumæk being clearly a
  spelling pron. used only by the literate.
  Perh. from use in tanning, it was early also
  called ˈʃumek, ˈʃɪu- (shoemake 1600), still
  not uncommon. A N Engd informant said,
  “ˈʃumek, used to dye shoes.”
Sumatra suˈmɑtrə, -ˈmetrə |-n -n
Sumer ˈsumɚ, ˈsɪu-, ˈsju-; ES -mə(r
Sumerian suˈmɪrɪən, sɪu-, sju-
summa cum laude ˈsʌməˌkʌmˈlɔdɪ, ˈsumə-
  ˌkumˈlaudɪ
summarily ˈsʌmərəlɪ, emph.+sʌˈmɛrəlɪ
summarization ˌsʌmərəˈzeʃən, -aɪˈz-
summarize ˈsʌməˌraɪz |-s -ɪz |-d -d
summary ˈsʌmərɪ
summation sʌmˈeʃən
summer ˈsʌmɚ; ES ˈsʌmə(r; |-ed -d |-ing
  ˈsʌmərɪŋ, ˈsʌmrɪŋ
Summers ˈsʌmɚz; ES ˈsʌməz; |-’s -ɪz
summersault ˈsʌməˌsɔlt; ES ˈsʌmə-; |-ed -ɪd
summerset ˈsʌməˌsɛt; ES ˈsʌmə-; |-ed -ɪd
summertime ˈsʌməˌtaɪm; ES ˈsʌmə-
Summerville ˈsʌməˌvɪl; ES ˈsʌmə-, S+-vḷ
summit, S- ˈsʌmɪt

---

summon 'sʌmən |-ed -d |-er -ɚ; ES -ə(r

summons 'sʌmənz |-es 'sʌmənzɪz |-ed
'sʌmənzd

summum bonum 'sʌməm'bonəm

Sumner 'sʌmnɚ; ES 'sʌmnə(r

sump sʌmp |sumped sʌmpt

sumpter 'sʌmptɚ; ES 'sʌmptə(r

sumptuary 'sʌmptʃʊˌɛrɪ |-tuous -tʃʊəs

Sumter 'sʌmptɚ, 'sʌmtɚ; ES -tə(r

sun sʌn |sunned sʌnd

Sunapee 'sʌnəpɪ, -ˌpi

sunbonnet 'sʌnˌbɑnɪt; ES+-ˌbɒn-; |-ed -ɪd

sunbow 'sʌnˌbo

sunburn 'sʌnˌbɝn; ES -ˌbɜn, -ˌbɝn; |-ed -d
or -t -t

sunburst 'sʌnˌbɝst; ES -ˌbɜst, -ˌbɝst

Sunbury 'sʌnˌbɛrɪ, -bərɪ

sundae 'sʌndɪ

Sunday 'sʌndɪ |-ed -d—see Monday

sunder 'sʌndɚ; ES -də(r; |-ed -d |-ing -dərɪŋ,
-drɪŋ

sunderance 'sʌndrəns, -dərəns |-s -ɪz

Sunderland 'sʌndɚlənd; ES 'sʌndə-

sundew 'sʌnˌdju, -ˌdɪu, -ˌdu

sundial 'sʌnˌdaɪəl, -ˌdaɪl

sundog 'sʌnˌdɔg, -ˌdɒg, much less freq. -ˌdɑg

sundown 'sʌnˌdaʊn

sundry 'sʌndrɪ |-ies -z

sun-dry 'sʌnˌdraɪ |-ied -d

sunfast 'sʌnˌfæst; E+-ˌfast, -ˌfɑst

sunfish 'sʌnˌfɪʃ |-'s -ɪz

sunflower, S- 'sʌnˌflaʊɚ, -ˌflaʊr; ES -ˌflaʊ-
ə(r, -ˌflaʊə(r

sung sʌŋ

Sung sʊŋ

sunglass 'sʌnˌglæs; E+-ˌglas, -ˌglɑs; |-es -ɪz

sunglow 'sʌnˌglo

sunk sʌŋk |-en -ən

sunlight 'sʌnˌlaɪt |-ed -ɪd |-lit -ˌlɪt

Sunna, -h 'sʊnə |-nite 'sʊnaɪt

sunny 'sʌnɪ

sunproof 'sʌn'pruf ('sun,proof 'dye)

sunrise 'sʌnˌraɪz |-s -ɪz

sunroom 'sʌnˌrum, -ˌrʊm

sunset 'sʌnˌsɛt

sunshade 'sʌnˌʃed

sunshine 'sʌnˌʃaɪn |-d -d |-ny -ɪ

sunspot 'sʌnˌspɑt; ES+-ˌspɒt; |-ted -ɪd

sunstroke 'sʌnˌstrok

sun-struck 'sʌnˌstrʌk

sunup 'sʌnˌʌp

sunward 'sʌnwɚd; ES -wəd; |-s -z

Sun Yat-sen 'sʌn'jæt'sɛn, 'sun'jɑt'sɛn

sup sʌp |supped sʌpt

super 'supɚ, 'sɪu-, 'sju-; ES -pə(r

superable 'supərəbl̩, 'suprə-, 'sɪu-, 'sju- |-bly
-blɪ

superabound ˌsupərə'baʊnd, ˌsɪu-, ˌsju- |-ed
-ɪd

superabundance ˌsupərə'bʌndəns, ˌsɪu-, ˌsju-
|-cy -ɪ |-dant -dənt

superadd ˌsupɚ'æd, ˌsɪu-, ˌsju- |-ed -ɪd

superannuate ˌsupɚ'ænjʊˌet, ˌsɪu-, ˌsju- |-d
-ɪd

superannuation ˌsupɚˌænjʊ'eʃən, ˌsɪu-, ˌsju-

superb sʊ'pɝb, sə-, sɪu-, sju-; ES -'pɝb,
-'pɜb

supercargo ˌsupɚ'kɑrgo, ˌsɪu-, ˌsju-; ES
-pə'kɑ:go, E+-'kɑ:go; acct.+'superˌcargo

supercharge n 'supɚˌtʃɑrdʒ, 'sɪu-, 'sju-; ES
-pəˌtʃɑ:dʒ, E+-ˌtʃɑ:dʒ; |-s -ɪz |-r -ɚ; ES
-ə(r

supercharge v ˌsupɚ'tʃɑrdʒ, ˌsɪu-, ˌsju-; ES
-pə'tʃɑ:dʒ, E+-'tʃɑ:dʒ; |-s -ɪz |-d -d

superciliary ˌsupɚ'sɪlɪˌɛrɪ, ˌsɪu-, ˌsju-; ES
-pə'sɪl-; |-ious -'sɪlɪəs

superdreadnought ˌsupɚ'drɛdˌnɔt, ˌsɪu-, ˌsju-;
ES -pə'drɛd-

superego ˌsupɚ'igo, ˌsɪu-, ˌsju-, -'ɛgo

supereminent ˌsupɚ'ɛmənənt, ˌsɪu-, ˌsju-

supererogate ˌsupɚ'ɛrəˌget, ˌsɪu-, ˌsju- |-d -ɪd
|-tion -ˌɛrə'geʃən

supererogative ˌsupərə'rɑgətɪv, ˌsɪu-, ˌsju-,
-'rɒg- |-tory -ˌtorɪ, -ˌtɔrɪ; S -ˌtorɪ

superficial ˌsupɚ'fɪʃəl, ˌsɪu-, ˌsju-; ES -pə-;
|-ly -ɪ |-ity -ˌfɪʃɪ'ælətɪ

superficies ˌsupɚ'fɪʃɪˌiz, ˌsɪu-, ˌsju-, -'fɪʃiz;
ES -pə-

superfine ˌsupɚ'faɪn, ˌsɪu-, ˌsju-; ES -pə-;
|-ness -'faɪnnɪs ('superˌfine 'taste)

superfluity ˌsupɚ'fluətɪ, ˌsɪupɚ'flɪu-, ˌsjupɚ-
'flu-; ES -pə-

superfluous sʊ'pɝfluəs, sə-; ES -'pɜ-, -'pɝ-

superheat n 'supɚˌhit, 'sɪu-, 'sju-; ES -pə-;

superheat v ˌsupɚ'hit, ˌsɪu-, ˌsju-; ES -pə-;
|-ed -ɪd

superheterodyne ˌsupɚ'hɛtərəˌdaɪn, ˌsɪu-,
ˌsju-; ES -pə-

---

superhuman ˌsupɚˈhjumən, ˌsɪupɚˈhɪu-, ˌsjupɚˈhju-, -ˈjumən; ES -pə-

superimpose ˌsupɚɪmˈpoz, ˌsɪu-, ˌsju- |-s -ɪz |-d -d

superimposition ˌsupɚˌɪmpəˈzɪʃən, ˌsɪu-, ˌsju-

superincumbent ˌsupərɪnˈkʌmbənt, ˌsɪu-, ˌsju-

superinduce ˌsupərɪnˈdjus, -ˈdus, ˌsɪupərɪnˈdɪus, ˌsjupərɪnˈdjus |-s -ɪz |-d -t

superintend ˌsuprɪnˈtɛnd, ˌsɪu-, ˌsju-, -pərɪn- |-ed -ɪd |-ence -əns |-ency -ənsɪ |-ent -ənt

superior, S- səˈpɪrɪɚ, su-; ES -ˈpɪrɪ·ə(r

superioress səˈpɪrɪərɪs, su- |-ˈs -ɪz

superiority səˌpɪrɪˈɔrətɪ, su-, -ˈar-, -ˈɒr-

superlative səˈpɝlətɪv, su-, sɪu-, sju-; ES -ˈpɝ-, -ˈpɝ-

superman ˈsupɚˌmæn, ˈsɪu-, ˈsju-; ES -pə-; |-men -ˌmɛn

supernal suˈpɝnl̩, sɪu-, sju-; ES -ˈpɝ-, -ˈpɝ-; |-ly -ɪ

supernatural ˌsupɚˈnætʃrəl, ˌsɪu-, ˌsju-, -tʃərəl |-ly -ɪ |-ism -ˌɪzəm

supernumerary ˌsupɚˈnjuməˌrɛrɪ, -ˈnu-, ˌsɪupɚˈnɪu-, ˌsjupɚˈnju-; ES -pə-

superphosphate ˌsupɚˈfɑsfet, ˌsɪu-, ˌsju-; ES -pəˈfɑs-, -ˈfɒs-

superpose ˌsupɚˈpoz, ˌsɪu-, ˌsju-; ES -pə-; |-s -ɪz |-d -d

superposition ˌsupɚpəˈzɪʃən, ˌsɪu-, ˌsju-; ES -pəpə-

superpower ˌsupɚˈpaʊɚ, ˌsɪu-, ˌsju-, -ˈpaʊr; ES -pəˈpaʊ·ə(r, -ˈpaʊə(r; |-ed -d

superrealism ˌsupɚˈrɪəlˌɪzəm, ˌsɪu-, ˌsju-; ES -pə-

supersaturate ˌsupɚˈsætʃəˌret, ˌsɪu-, ˌsju-; ES -pə-; |-d -ɪd

superscribe ˌsupɚˈskraɪb, ˌsɪu-, ˌsju-; ES -pə-; |-d -d

superscript ˈsupɚˌskrɪpt, ˈsɪu-, ˈsju-; ES -pə-

superscription ˌsupɚˈskrɪpʃən, ˌsɪu-, ˌsju-; ES -pə-

supersede ˌsupɚˈsid, ˌsɪu-, ˌsju-; ES -pə-; |-d -ɪd |-dure -dʒɚ; ES -dʒə(r

superstate ˈsupɚˌstet, ˈsɪu-, ˈsju-; ES -pə-

superstition ˌsupɚˈstɪʃən, ˌsɪu-, ˌsju-; ES -pə-; |-tious -ʃəs

superstructure ˈsupɚˌstrʌktʃɚ, ˈsɪu-, ˈsju-; ES -pəˌstrʌktʃə(r

supertax ˈsupɚˌtæks, ˈsɪu-, ˈsju-; ES -pə-; |-es -ɪz

supervene ˌsupɚˈvin, ˌsɪu-, ˌsju-; ES -pə-; |-d -d |-vention -ˈvɛnʃən

supervise n ˈsupɚˌvaɪz, ˈsɪu-, ˈsju-; ES -pə-; |-s -ɪz

supervise v ˌsupɚˈvaɪz, ˌsɪu-, ˌsju-; ES -pə-; |-s -ɪz |-d -d |-sion -ˈvɪʒən

supervisor ˌsupɚˈvaɪzɚ, ˌsɪu-, ˌsju-; ES -pəˈvaɪzə(r;—acct. + ˈsuperˌvisor

supine n ˈsupaɪn, ˈsɪu-, ˈsju-

supine adj suˈpaɪn, sɪu-, sju- |-ness -ˈpaɪnnɪs

supper ˈsʌpɚ; ES ˈsʌpə(r; |-ed -d |-ing -pərɪŋ, -prɪŋ

supplant səˈplænt; E+-ˈplant, -ˈplɑnt; |-ed -ɪd

supple ˈsʌpl̩ |-d -d |-ling ˈsʌplɪŋ, -pl̩ɪŋ |-r -plɚ; ES -plə(r; |-st -plɪst

supplely ˈsʌpl̩ɪ, ˈsʌpl̩ɪ

supplement n ˈsʌpləmənt

supplement v ˈsʌpləˌmɛnt |-mented -ˌmɛntɪd

supplementary ˌsʌpləˈmɛntrɪ, -ˈmɛntərɪ

suppliance 'entreaty' ˈsʌplɪəns |-cy -ɪ |-ant -ənt

suppliance 'supply' səˈplaɪəns |-s -ɪz

supplicancy ˈsʌplɪkənsɪ |-cant -kənt

supplicate ˈsʌplɪˌket |-d -ɪd

supplication ˌsʌplɪˈkeʃən

supply v səˈplaɪ |-plied -ˈplaɪd

supply 'supplely' ˈsʌplɪ

support səˈport, -ˈpɔrt; ES -ˈpoət, E+-ˈpɔət; |-ed -ɪd |-able -əbl̩ |-bly -blɪ

suppose səˈpoz |-s -ɪz |-d -d |-dly -ɪdlɪ |N Engd + səˈpōz (§46)

supposition ˌsʌpəˈzɪʃən

supposititious səˌpɑzəˈtɪʃəs; ES+-ˌpɒz-

suppository səˈpɑzəˌtorɪ, -ˌtɔrɪ; ES -ˈpɑzəˌtorɪ, -ˈpɒz-, E+-ˌtɔrɪ

suppress səˈprɛs |-es -ɪz |-ed -t |-edly -ɪdlɪ

suppressible səˈprɛsəbl̩

suppression səˈprɛʃən |-sive -ˈprɛsɪv

suppurate ˈsʌpjəˌret |-rated -ˌretɪd |-tive -ɪv

suppuration ˌsʌpjəˈreʃən

supra ˈsuprə, ˈsɪu-, ˈsju-

supremacy səˈprɛməsɪ, su-, sɪu-, sju-

supreme səˈprim, su-, sɪu-, sju-

Surat ˈsurət, suˈræt, ˈsurʌt

Surbiton ˈsɝbɪtn; ES ˈsɝb-, ˈsɝb-

surcease sɝˈsis; ES sɝ-, sɝ-; |-s -ɪz |-d -t

surcharge n ˈsɝˌtʃɑrdʒ; ES ˈsɝˌtʃɑːdʒ, ˈsɝˌtʃɑːdʒ, E+-ˌtʃɑːdʒ; |-s -ɪz

---

Key: *See in full §§3–47.* bee **bi** |pity **ˈpɪtɪ** (§6) |rate **ret** |yet **jɛt** |sang **sæŋ** |angry **ˈæŋ·grɪ** |bath **bæθ**; E **baθ** (§10) |ah **ɑ** |far **fɑr** |watch **wɑtʃ, wɒtʃ** (§12) |jaw **dʒɔ** |gorge **gɔrdʒ** |go **go**

surcharge *v* sɜ·'tʃɑrdʒ; ES sɜ'tʃɑːdʒ, sɜ-
'tʃɑːdʒ, E+-'tʃɑːdʒ; |-s -ɪz |-d -d ('sur-
,charged 'mind)
surcingle 'sɜ·sɪŋg|; ES 'sɜ-, 'sɜ·-; |-d -d
surcoat 'sɜ·,kot; ES 'sɜ-, 'sɜ·-
surd sɜd; ES sɜd, sɜ·d
sure ʃur; ES ʃuə(r, ʃoə(r, ʃɔə(r; |-ly -lɪ
sure-footed 'ʃur'futɪd; ES 'ʃuə-, 'ʃoə-, 'ʃɔə-;
('sure-,footed 'mule)
surety 'ʃurtɪ, 'ʃurətɪ; ES 'ʃuətɪ, 'ʃoə-, 'ʃɔə-,
'ʃurətɪ
surf sɜf; ES sɜf, sɜ·f; |-ed -t
surface 'sɜ·fɪs, -əs; ES 'sɜf-, 'sɜ·f-; |-s -ɪz
|-d -t
surfboat 'sɜ·f,bot; ES 'sɜf-, 'sɜ·f-
surfeit 'sɜ·fɪt; ES 'sɜf-, 'sɜ·f-; |-ed -ɪd
surge sɜ·dʒ; ES sɜdʒ, sɜ·dʒ; |-s -ɪz |-d -d
surgeon 'sɜ·dʒən; ES 'sɜdʒ-, 'sɜ·dʒ-; |-ed -d
|-ery -ərɪ, -dʒrɪ
surgical 'sɜ·dʒɪk|; ES 'sɜdʒ-, 'sɜ·dʒ-; |-ly -ɪ,
-ɪklɪ
Surinam ,surɪ'nɑm, -'næm
surly 'sɜ·lɪ; ES 'sɜlɪ, 'sɜ·lɪ; |-lily -lɪlɪ
surmise *n* sɚ'maɪz, 'sɜ·maɪz; ES sɚ-, 'sɜ-, 'sɜ·-
surmise *v* sɚ'maɪz; ES sə-; |-s -ɪz |-d -d |-dly
-ɪdlɪ
surmount sɚ'maunt; ES sə'maunt; |-ed -ɪd
surname 'sɜ·,nem; ES 'sɜ-, 'sɜ·-; |-d -d
surpass sɚ'pæs; ES sə-, E+-'pas, -'pɑs; |-es
-ɪz |-ed -t
surplice 'sɜ·plɪs; ES 'sɜ-, 'sɜ·-; |-s -ɪz |-d -t
surplus 'sɜ·plʌs, -pləs; ES 'sɜ-, 'sɜ·-; |-es -ɪz
surprise sə'praɪz, sɚ-; ES sə-; |-s -ɪz |-d -d
|-dly -ɪdlɪ—*In the first pron.* sɚ- *became* sə-
by dissimilation (*§121*).
surrealism sə'rɪəl,ɪzəm |-ist -ɪst
surrealistic sə,rɪəl'ɪstɪk |-ally -|ɪ, -ɪklɪ
surrebut ,sɜ·rɪ'bʌt; ES ,sɜ·rɪ'bʌt, ,sɜ·rɪ-;
|-ted -ɪd |-tal -|
surrejoin ,sɜ·rɪ'dʒɔɪn; ES ,sɜ·rɪ-, ,sɜ·rɪ-;
|-ed -d |-der -dɚ; ES -də(r
surrender sə'rɛndɚ; ES -də(r; |-ed -d |-ing
-'rɛndrɪŋ, -'rɛndərɪŋ
surreptitious ,sɜ·əp'tɪʃəs; ES ,sɜr-, ,sʌr-, ,sɜ·-
surrey, S- 'sɜ·ɪ; ES 'sɜrɪ, 'sʌrɪ, 'sɜ·ɪ
surrogate 'sɜ·ə,get; ES 'sɜrə-, 'sʌrə-, 'sɜ·ə-
surround sə'raund |-ed -ɪd
Surry 'sɜ·ɪ; ES 'sɜrɪ, 'sʌrɪ, 'sɜ·ɪ
surtax 'sɜ·,tæks; ES 'sɜ-, 'sɜ·-; |-es -ɪz |-ed -t

Surtees 'sɜ·tiz; ES 'sɜ-, 'sɜ·-; |-tees' -tiz
surtout sɚ'tut, -'tu; ES sə-; (*Fr* syr'tu)
surveillance sɚ'veləns, -'veljəns; ES sə-; |-s
-ɪz
survey *n* 'sɜ·ve, sɚ've; ES 'sɜ-, 'sɜ·-, sə-
survey *v* sɚ've; ES sə've; |-ed -d
surveyor sɚ'veɚ, sə'veɚ; ES sə've·ə(ɪ;
sə've ɚ *is due to r-dissimilation* (*§121*).
survival sɚ'vaɪv|; ES sə-; |-ism -,ɪzəm |-ist
-ɪst
survive sɚ'vaɪv; ES sə-; |-d -d
Susa 'susə
Susan 'suzn̩, 'sɪuzn̩, 'sjuzn̩
Susanna, -h su'zænə, sɪu-, sju-
susceptibility sə,sɛptə'bɪlətɪ
susceptible sə'sɛptəb| |-bly -blɪ
suspect '*suspected person*' 'sʌspɛkt
suspect '*suspicion*' sə'spɛkt
suspect *v* sə'spɛkt |-ed -ɪd
suspend sə'spɛnd |-ed -ɪd |-nse -ns
suspension sə'spɛnʃən |-sive -sɪv |-sory -sərɪ
suspicion sə'spɪʃən |-cious -ʃəs
suspiration ,sʌspə'reʃən
suspire sə'spaɪr; ES -'spaɪə(r; |-d -d
Susquehanna ,sʌskwɪ'hænə
Sussex 'sʌsɛks, -ɪks |-'s -ɪz
sustain sə'sten |-ed -d |-edly -ɪdlɪ
sustenance 'sʌstənəns |-s -ɪz
sustentation ,sʌstɛn'teʃən
Sutherland 'sʌðɚlənd; ES 'sʌðə-; |-shire
-,ʃɪr, -ʃɚ; ES -,ʃɪə(r, -ʃə(r
Sutherlandia ,sʌðɚ'lændɪə; ES ,sʌðə-
sutler 'sʌtlɚ; ES 'sʌtlə(r; |-age -ɪdʒ |-y -ɪ
sutor 'sutɚ, 'sɪu-, 'sju-; ES -tə(r
sutra 'sutrə
Sutro 'sutro
suttee sʌ'ti, 'sʌti
suttle 'sʌt|
Sutton 'sʌtn̩
suture 'sutʃɚ, 'sɪu-, 'sju-; ES -tʃə(r; |-d -d
Suwannee sə'wɔni, su-, 'swɔni, swɔ'ni
Suzanne su'zæn, sɪu-, sju-
suzerain 'suzərɪn, -,ren, 'sɪu-, 'sju-; |-ty -tɪ
svarabhakti ,svarə'bæktɪ, -'bɑk-
svelte svɛlt (*Fr* svɛlt, zvɛlt)
swab swab, swɒb |-bed -d |-ber -ɚ; ES -ə(r
Swabia 'swebɪə |-n -n
swaddle 'swad|, 'swɒd| |-d -d |-ling -d|ɪŋ,
-dlɪŋ

|full fʊl |tooth tuθ |further 'fɝðɚ; ES 'fɝðə |custom 'kʌstəm |while hwaɪl |how haʊ |toy tɔɪ
|using 'juzɪŋ |fuse fjuz, fɪuz |dish dɪʃ |vision 'vɪʒən |Eden 'idn̩ |cradle 'kred| |keep 'em 'kipm̩

swaddling *adj* 'swɑdlıŋ, 'swɒd-
swag swæg |swagged swægd
swage swedʒ |swages 'swedʒız |swaged
swedʒd
swagger 'swægɚ; ES 'swægǝ(r; |-ed -d |-ing
'swægǝrıŋ, 'swægrıŋ
Swahili swɑ'hilı
swain, S- swen |-ed -d
swale, S- swel |swaled sweld
swallow 'swɑlo, 'swɒlo, -lǝ |-ed -d |-ing -lǝwıŋ
swam swæm
swamp swɑmp, swɔmp, swɒmp; E swɒmp,
swɔmp, swæmp; S swɔmp, swæmp, swɒmp
—*These orders of prevalence are based on
known collections. Fuller statistics might
change them.*
Swampscott 'swɒmpskǝt, 'swɔmp-, 'swæmp-
swan swɑn, swɒn, swɔn |-ned -d
Swanage 'swɑnıdʒ, 'swɒn- |-'s -ız
swang swæŋ
swank swæŋk |swanked swæŋkt
swan's-down 'swɑnz,dɑun, 'swɒnz-, 'swɔnz-
Swansea 'swɑnsı, 'swɒnsı, -zı
Swanwick 'swɑnık, 'swɒn-
Swanzey 'swɑnzı, 'swɒnzı
swap swɑp, swɒp, swɔp |-ped -t
Swaraj, s- swǝ'rɑdʒ |-ism -ızǝm |-ist -ıst
sward swɔrd; ES swɔǝd; |-ed -ıd
sware swɛr, swær; E swɛǝ(r, ES swæǝ(r
swarm swɔrm; ES swɔǝm; |-ed -d
swart swɔrt; ES swɔǝt
swarth swɔrθ; ES swɔǝθ
Swarthmore 'swɔrθmor, -mɔr; ES 'swɔǝθ-
moǝ(r, E+-mɔǝ(r; *loc.*+'swɑθmor—*In*
'swɑθmor *the first* r *is lost by dissimilation*
(§*121*).
Swarthout 'swɔrθɑut; ES 'swɔǝθ-
swarthy 'swɔrðı, -θı; ES 'swɔǝ-
swash swɑʃ, swɒʃ |-es -ız |-ed -t
swashbuckle 'swɑʃ,bʌkḷ, 'swɒʃ- |-d -d |-ling
-,bʌklıŋ, -,bʌkḷıŋ |-r -,bʌklǝ; ES -,bʌklǝ(r
swastika 'swɑstıkǝ, 'swɒs-, 'swæs-
swat swɑt, swɒt |-ted -ıd
swath swɑθ, swɑð, swɔθ, swɒ- |-'s -θs, -ðz
|-ths -θs, -ðz
swathe '*swath*' sweð |-thes -ðz
swathe *v* sweð |swathed sweðd
sway swe |swayed swed
Swaziland 'swɑzı,lænd

swear swɛr, swær; E swɛǝ(r, ES swæǝ(r;
|swore swor, swɔr; ES swoǝ(r, E+swɔǝ(r;
or arch. sware swɛr, swær; E swɛǝ(r, ES
swæǝ(r; |sworn sworn, swɔrn; ES swoǝn,
E+swɔǝn
sweat swɛt |*past & p ptc* sweat swɛt *or* sweated
'swɛtıd
sweatily 'swɛtḷı, -ılı
Swede swid |Sweden 'swidṇ |-dish -ıʃ
Swedenborg 'swidṇ,bɔrg; ES -,bɔǝg
Swedenborgian ,swidṇ'bɔrdʒıǝn; ES -'bɔǝdʒ-
sweep swip |swept swɛpt |-stake -,stek
sweet, S- swit |sweeted 'switıd |-bread -,brɛd
sweet-breathed 'swit'brɛθt
Sweetbriar, S- Briar 'swit,braıɚ; ES -,braı·ǝ(r
sweetbrier, -ar 'swit,braıɚ; ES -,braı·ǝ(r
sweeten 'switṇ |-ed -d |-ing 'switṇıŋ, -tnıŋ
sweetheart 'swit,hɑrt; ES -,hɑːt, E+-,haːt
sweetmeat 'swit,mit
sweet-potato 'switpǝ,teto, -'teto, -tǝ
swell swɛl |swelled swɛld |swelled swɛld *or*
swollen 'swolǝn, swoln
swelp swɛlp
swelter 'swɛltɚ; ES 'swɛltǝ(r; |-ed -d |-ing
'swɛltǝrıŋ, 'swɛltrıŋ |-try -trı
swerve swɝv; ES swɜv, swɝv; |-d -d
Swete swit
Sweyn swen
swift, S- swıft |-en -ǝn |-ened -ǝnd
swift-footed 'swıft'futıd ('swift-,footed 'deer)
swig swıg |swigged swıgd
swill swıl |swilled swıld
swim swım |swam swæm |swum swʌm *or*
arch. swam swæm
Swinburne 'swınbɚn; ES 'swınbǝn
swindle 'swındḷ |-d -d |-ling -dlıŋ, -dḷıŋ
swindler 'swındlɚ; ES 'swındlǝ(r
Swindon 'swındǝn
swine swaın |-herd -,hɝd; ES -,hɜd, -,hɝd
swing swıŋ |swung swʌŋ |-er -ɚ; ES -ǝ(r
swinge swındʒ |-s -ız |-d -d |-r -ɚ; ES -ǝ(r
swingle 'swıŋgḷ |-d -d |-ling -glıŋ, -gḷıŋ
swingletree 'swıŋgḷ,tri, -trı
swinish 'swaınıʃ
swink *arch.* swıŋk |swank swæŋk *or* swonk
swʌŋk *or* swinked swıŋkt |swonk swʌŋk *or*
swonken 'swʌŋkǝn *or* swinked swıŋkt
Swinnerton 'swınɚtǝn; ES 'swınǝ-
Swinton 'swıntǝn

Key: See in full §§*3–47.* bee bi |pity 'pıtı (§6) |rate ret |yet jɛt |sang sæŋ |angry 'æŋ·grı
|bath bæθ; E baθ (§10) |ah ɑ |far fɑr |watch wɑtʃ, wɒtʃ (§12) |jaw dʒɔ |gorge gɔrdʒ |go go

swipe **swaɪp** |swiped **swaɪpt**

swirl **swɜ˞l**; ES **swɜl, swɜ˞l**; |-ed **-d**

swish **swɪʃ** |swishes **ˈswɪʃɪz** |-swished **swɪʃt**

Swiss **swɪs** |-ˈs **-ɪz**

switch **swɪtʃ** |switches **ˈswɪtʃɪz** |-ed **-t** |-board -ˌbord, -ˌbɔrd; ES -ˌbʊəd, E+-ˌbɔəd

switchel **ˈswɪtʃəl**

swith **swɪθ** |swithe **swaɪð**

Swithin **ˈswɪðɪn, -θɪn**

Switzer **ˈswɪtsə˞**; ES **ˈswɪtsə(r**; |-land -lənd

swivel **ˈswɪvl** |-ed **-d** |-ing **ˈswɪvlɪŋ, -vl̩ɪŋ**

swizzle **ˈswɪzl̩** |-d **-d** |-ling **ˈswɪzlɪŋ, -zl̩ɪŋ**

swob **swɑb, swɒb** |-bed **-d**

swollen **ˈswolən, swoln** |swoln **swoln**

swollenness **ˈswolənnɪs**

swoon **swun** |swooned **swund**

swoop **swup** |swooped **swupt**

swop **swɑp, swɒp** |-ped **-t**

sword **sord, sɔrd**; ES **soəd, E+sɔəd**; |-fish -ˌfɪʃ |-play -ˌple |-sman -zmən |-smen -zmən

swore **swor, swɔr**; ES **swoə(r, E+swɔə(r**; |-rn **-n**

swot **swɑt, swɒt** |-ted **-ɪd**

swound *arch.* **swaʊnd, swund, saʊnd** |-ed **-ɪd** 'swounds **zwaʊndz, zaʊndz, -nz**

Swoyersville **ˈswɔɪə˞z̩ˌvɪl**; ES **ˈswɔɪəz-**

swum **swʌm**

swung **swʌŋ**

Sybaris **ˈsɪbərɪs** |-ˈs **-ɪz** |-rite **ˈsɪbəˌraɪt**

Sybaritic **ˌsɪbəˈrɪtɪk** |-al **-l̩** |-ally **-l̩ɪ, -ɪklɪ**

sybil, S- **ˈsɪbl̩, -ɪl** |-line **ˈsɪbl̩ˌin, -ɪn**

sycamore, S- **ˈsɪkəˌmor, -ˌmɔr**; ES -ˌmoə(r, E+-ˌmɔə(r

syce **saɪs** |syces **ˈsaɪsɪz**

sycophancy **ˈsɪkəfənsɪ** |-phant -fənt

sycophantic **ˌsɪkəˈfæntɪk** |-al **-l̩** |-ally **-l̩ɪ, -ɪklɪ**

Sydenham **ˈsɪdn̩əm, ˈsɪdnəm**

Sydney **ˈsɪdnɪ**

Sylla **ˈsɪlə**

syllabi **ˈsɪləˌbaɪ**

syllabic **sɪˈlæbɪk** |-al **-l̩** |-ally **-l̩ɪ, -ɪklɪ**

syllabicate **sɪˈlæbɪˌket** |-d **-ɪd**

syllabication **sɪˌlæbɪˈkeʃən**

syllabification **sɪˌlæbəfəˈkeʃən**

syllabify **sɪˈlæbəˌfaɪ** |-fied **-ˌfaɪd**

syllable **ˈsɪləbl̩** |-d **-d** |-ling **-bl̩ɪŋ, -blɪŋ**

syllabus **ˈsɪləbəs** |-es **-ɪz** |-bi **-ˌbaɪ**

syllogism **ˈsɪləˌdʒɪzəm** |-gist **-dʒɪst**

syllogistic **ˌsɪləˈdʒɪstɪk** |-al **-l̩** |-ally **-l̩ɪ, -ɪklɪ**

sylph **sɪlf** |-ic **-ɪk** |-id **-ɪd**

sylva **ˈsɪlvə** |sylvan **ˈsɪlvən**

Sylvania **sɪlˈvenɪə, -njə**

Sylvester **sɪlˈvɛstə˞**; ES -ˈvɛstə(r

Sylvia **ˈsɪlvɪə** |Sylvian **ˈsɪlvɪən**

symbiosis **ˌsɪmbaɪˈosɪs, ˌsɪmbɪ-**

symbiotic **ˌsɪmbaɪˈɑtɪk, -bɪ-**; ES+-ˈɒt-; |-al -l̩ |-ally -l̩ɪ, -ɪklɪ

symbol **ˈsɪmbl̩** |-ed **-d** |-ing **ˈsɪmbl̩ɪŋ, -blɪŋ**

symbolic **sɪmˈbɑlɪk**; ES+-ˈbɒl-; |-al **-l̩** |-ally -l̩ɪ |-ly -lɪ

symbolism **ˈsɪmbl̩ˌɪzəm** |-ist **-ɪst**

symbolistic **ˌsɪmbl̩ˈɪstɪk** |-al **-l̩** |-ally **-l̩ɪ, -ɪklɪ**

symbolization **ˌsɪmbl̩əˈzeʃən, -aɪˈz-**

symbolize **ˈsɪmbl̩ˌaɪz** |-s **-ɪz** |-d **-d**

symmetric **sɪˈmɛtrɪk** |-al **-l̩** |-ally **-l̩ɪ, -ɪklɪ**

symmetry **ˈsɪmɪtrɪ**

Symonds, -ons **ˈsaɪməndz, ˈsɪm-, -nz** |-ˈs **-ɪz**

sympathetic **ˌsɪmpəˈθɛtɪk** |-al **-l̩** |-ally -l̩ɪ, -ɪklɪ

sympathize **ˈsɪmpəˌθaɪz** |-s **-ɪz** |-d **-d**

sympathy **ˌsɪmpəθɪ**

symphonic **sɪmˈfɑnɪk**; ES+-ˈfɒn-; |-ally -l̩ɪ, -ɪklɪ

symphony **ˈsɪmfənɪ**

symposium **sɪmˈpozɪəm** |-s **-z** |-sia **-zɪə**

symptom **ˈsɪmptəm**

symptomatic **ˌsɪmptəˈmætɪk** |-al **-l̩** |-ally -l̩ɪ, -ɪklɪ

synaesthesia **ˌsɪnəsˈθiʒɪə, -ʒə**

synagogue **ˈsɪnəˌgɔg, -ˌgɑg, -ˌgɒg**

synapse **sɪˈnæps** |-sis **-ɪs** |-ses **-iz**

synchromesh **ˈsɪŋkrəˌmɛʃ, ˈsɪn-** |-es **-ɪz**

synchronal **ˈsɪŋkrən̩l, ˈsɪn-**

synchronic **sɪnˈkrɑnɪk, sɪŋ-**; ES+-ˈkrɒn-; |-al **-l̩** |-ally -l̩ɪ, -ɪklɪ

synchronism **ˈsɪŋkrəˌnɪzəm, ˈsɪn-**

synchronize **ˈsɪŋkrəˌnaɪz, ˈsɪn-** |-s **-ɪz** |-d **-d**

synchronous **ˈsɪŋkrənəs, ˈsɪn-**

synclinal **sɪnˈklaɪnl̩, sɪŋ-, ˈsɪŋklɪnl̩, ˈsɪn-** |-ly **-ɪ**

syncline **ˈsɪŋklaɪn, ˈsɪn-**

syncopate **ˈsɪŋkəˌpet, ˈsɪn-** |-d **-ɪd**

syncopation **ˌsɪŋkəˈpeʃən, ˌsɪn-**

syncope **ˈsɪŋkəpɪ, ˈsɪn-, -ˌpi**

syncretism **ˈsɪŋkrɪˌtɪzəm, ˈsɪn-**

syndic **ˈsɪndɪk** |-al **-l̩** |-alism **-l̩ˌɪzəm**

syndicate *n* 'sındıkıt, -ˌket
syndicate *v* 'sındıˌket |-d -ıd
syne saın, *in the song often* zaın
synecdoche sı'nɛkdəkı
synesthesia ˌsınəs'θiʒıə, -ʒə
Synge sıŋ
ˌsynod sınəd |-al -| |-ally -|ı
synodic sı'nɑdık; ES+-'nɒd-; |-al -| |-ally -|ı, -ıklı
synonym 'sınəˌnım
synonymous sı'nɑnəməs; ES+-'nɒn-; |-my -mı
synopsis sı'nɑpsıs; ES+-'nɒp-; |-pses -psiz
synoptic sı'nɑptık; ES+-'nɒp-; |-al -| |-ally -|ı, -ıklı
syntactical sın'tæktık| |-ly -ı
syntax 'sıntæks |-es -ız
synthesis 'sınθəsıs |-theses -θəˌsiz
synthesize 'sınθəˌsaız |-s -ız |-d -d
synthetic sın'θɛtık |-al -| |-ally -|ı, -ıklı
syphilis 'sıf|ıs |-lous -|əs
syphilitic ˌsıf|'ıtık |-ally -|ı, -ıklı
syphon 'saıfən, -fɑn, -fɒn |-ed -d |-age -fənıdʒ |-al -fən|

Syracusan ˌsırə'kjuzən, -'kıu-, -sən
Syracuse *NY* 'sırəˌkjus, 'sɛr-, -ˌkıus, ˌsırə'k-, ˌsɛr- |-'s -ız—*The traditional, phonetically regular, pron. is clearly* 'sɛr-, ˌsɛr- (*cf.* 'mɛrıəm *for* Miriam), *still in use, but largely superseded by the spelling pronunciation* 'sır-, ˌsır-. *Cf* Terrell. *In Sicily* 'sırəˌkjus, -ˌkıus, *Brit* 'saırəˌkjuz
Syria 'sırıə |Syrian 'sırıən |Syriac 'sırıˌæk
syringa sə'rıŋɡə
syringe 'sırındʒ |-s -ız |-d -d
syrinx, S- 'sırıŋks |-es -ız |-nges sə'rındʒiz
syrup 'sırəp, 'sɝəp; E 'sırəp, 'sɝrəp, 'sɝəp; S 'sɝrəp, 'sʌrəp, 'sırəp, 'sɝəp, 'sɛrəp—*see* sirup
system 'sıstəm, -tım
systematic ˌsıstə'mætık |-al -| |-ally -|ı, -ıklı
systematism 'sıstəməˌtızəm |-tist -tıst
systematize 'sıstəməˌtaız |-s -ız |-d -d
systemic sıs'tɛmık |-ally -|ı, -ıklı
systole 'sıstəˌli, -lı
systolic sıs'tɑlık; ES+-'tɒl-
syzygy 'sızədʒı
Szechwan 'sɛ'tʃwan, 's3tʃwæn

T

T, t *letter* ti |*pl* T's, Ts, *poss* T's tiz
't (1) *abbr. spelling of unstressed* it *in* 'tis, 't'll, 'twas, 'twere, 'twill, 'twould t-
't (2) *abbr. spelling of* not *in* can't -t
tab tæb |tabbed tæbd
tabard, T- 'tæbəd; ES 'tæbəd; |-ed -ıd
tabaret 'tæbərıt
Tabasco tə'bæsko
tabby, T- 'tæbı
tabernacle, T- 'tæbəˌnæk|, -ˌnɛk|; ES 'tæbə-; |-d -d |-ling -k|ıŋ, -k|ıŋ
tabes 'tebiz
tabetic tə'bɛtık, -'bitık
Tabitha 'tæbəθə
tablature 'tæbləˌtʃur, -tʃɚ; ES -ˌtʃuə(r, -tʃə(r
table 'teb| |-d -d |-ling -b|ıŋ, -b|ıŋ
tableau 'tæblo, tæb'lo |-ed -d
tablecloth 'teb|ˌklɔθ, -ˌklɒθ—*see* cloth
table d'hote 'tæb|'dot, 'tab|- (*Fr* tablə'do:t)

tableknife 'teb|ˌnaıf |-knives -ˌnaıvz
tableland 'teb|ˌlænd
tableless 'teb|ıs
tablespoon 'teb|ˌspun, -ˌspun
tablespoonful 'teb|spunˌful, -spun-, ˌteb|-'spunˌful, -'spun-
tablet 'tæblıt |-ed -ıd
tableware 'teb|ˌwɛr, -ˌwær; E -ˌwɛə(r, ES -ˌwæə(r
tabloid, T- 'tæblɔıd
taboo tə'bu, tæ'bu |-ed -d
tabor 'tebɚ; ES 'tebə(r; |-ed -d |-ing -bərıŋ, -brıŋ
taboret ˌtæbə'rɛt, 'tæbərıt
tabret 'tæbrıt
tabu tə'bu, tæ'bu |-ed -d
tabular 'tæbjələ; ES -lə(r
tabulate 'tæbjəˌlet |-d -ıd |-tor -ɚ; ES -ə(r
tache tætʃ |taches 'tætʃız
tachiol 'tækıˌol, -ˌɑl; ES+-ˌɒl

tachometer tə'kɑmətɚ, tæ-; ES -'kɑmətə(r,
  -'kɒm-
tachygraphy tæ'kɪgrəfɪ
tachymeter tə'kɪmətɚ, tæ-; ES -'kɪmətə(r;
  |-try -trɪ
tacit 'tæsɪt
taciturn 'tæsəˌtɜˑn; ES -ˌtɜn, -ˌtɝn
taciturnity ˌtæsə'tɝnətɪ; ES -'tɜn-, -'tɝn-
Tacitus 'tæsətəs |Tacitus's 'tæsətəsɪz
tack tæk |tacked tækt
tackle 'tækḷ |-d -d |-ling -klɪŋ, -kḷɪŋ
Tacna 'tɑknə (Sp 'takna)
Tacoma tə'komə
tact tækt |-ful -fəl |-fully -fəlɪ
tactic 'tæktɪk |-s -s |-al -ḷ |-ally -ḷɪ, -ɪklɪ
tactician tæk'tɪʃən
tactile 'tæktḷ, 'tæktɪl
tactual 'tæktʃʊəl |-ly -ɪ
tad, T- tæd |-pole -ˌpol
tael tel
ta'en arch. pptc of take 'ten
taeniafuge 'tinɪəˌfjudʒ, -ˌfɪudʒ |-s -ɪz
taeniasis ti'naɪəsɪs
taffeta 'tæfɪtə |taffity 'tæfətɪ
taffrail 'tæfˌrel
taffy, T- 'tæfɪ |-fied -fɪd
tag tæg |tagged tægd
Tagalog 'tægəˌlɑg, -ˌlɒg, -ˌlɔg
Tagore tə'gor, tə'gɔr; ES tə'goə(r, E+-'gɔə(r
tagrag 'tægˌræg |-ed -d |-gery -ərɪ, -rɪ
Tagus 'tegəs |Tagus's 'tegəsɪz
Tahiti tɑ'hitɪ, -ti |-tian -tɪən
Tai, t- 'tɑ·i
tail tel |tailed teld
tailboard 'telˌbord, -ˌbɔrd; ES -ˌboəd, E+
  -ˌbɔəd
Tailefer, Taill- surname 'tɑləvɚ, 'tʌl-; ES
  -və(r, 'tɒl-
taille tel
tailless 'tellɪs
taillight 'telˌlaɪt
tailor, T- 'telɚ; ES 'telə(r; |-ed -d |-ing -ɪŋ
tailor-made 'telɚ'med; ES 'telə-; ('tailor-
  ˌmade 'suit)
tailpiece 'telˌpis |-pieces -ˌpisɪz
tailrace 'telˌres |-races -ˌresɪz
tailstock 'telˌstɑk; ES+-ˌstɒk
Taine ten (Fr tɛn)
taint tent |tainted 'tentɪd

Taiwan 'taɪ'wɑn
Taj Mahal 'tɑdʒmə'hɑl, 'tɑʒ-
take tek |took tʊk |taken 'tekən
take care te'kɛr, tek'kɛr, -'kær; E -'kɛə(r, ES
  -'kæə(r
takedown 'tekˌdaʊn
take-off 'tekˌɔf, -ˌɒf
taker 'tekɚ; ES 'tekə(r
Talbot, t- 'tɔlbət
talc tælk |-ose 'tælkos |-um 'tælkəm
tale tel
talebearer 'telˌbɛrɚ, -ˌbærɚ; E -ˌbɛrə(r, ES
  -ˌbærə(r
talecarrier 'telˌkærɪɚ; ES -ˌkærɪ·ə(r
talemonger 'telˌmʌŋgɚ; ES -ˌmʌŋgə(r
talent 'tælənt |-ed -ɪd
taler 'tɑlɚ; ES 'tɑlə(r; (Ger 'tɑ:lər)
tales 'jurymen' 'teliz
talesman 'telzmən, 'teliz- |-men -mən
taleteller 'telˌtelɚ; ES -ˌtelə(r
Taliaferro Ga 'tɑləvɚ, 'tʌl-; ES -və(r, 'tɒl-
Taliesin ˌtælɪ'ɛsɪn
talion 'tælɪən, -ljən
talisman 'tælɪsmən, 'tælɪz- |-mans -mənz
talk tɔk |talked tɔkt |-ative -ətɪv |-ie -ɪ
talking-to 'tɔkɪŋˌtu
tall tɔl
tallage 'tælɪdʒ |-s -ɪz |-d -d
Tallahassee ˌtælə'hæsɪ
Tallahatchie ˌtælə'hætʃɪ
Tallapoosa ˌtælə'pusə
tallboy 'tɔlˌbɔɪ
Talleyrand-Perigord, de 'tælɪˌrænd (Fr də
  tajrã·peri'gɔːr, talrã-)
tallith 'tælɪθ
tallow 'tælo, 'tælə |-ed -d |-ing 'tæləwɪŋ
tallowy 'tæləwɪ
tally 'tælɪ |tallied 'tælɪd
tallyho intj ˌtælɪ'ho
tallyho n, v 'tælɪˌho |-hoed -ˌhod
Talmage 'tælmɪdʒ |Talmage's 'tælmɪdʒɪz
Talmud 'tælmʌd, 'tælməd |-ic tæl'mʌdɪk
talon 'tælən |taloned 'tælənd
talus 'teləs |taluses 'teləsɪz |tali 'telaɪ
tamale tə-ˌmɑlɪ
Tamar 'temɚ; ES 'temə(r
tamarack 'tæməˌræk, 'tæmræk
tamarind 'tæməˌrɪnd
tamarisk 'tæməˌrɪsk

|full fʊl |tooth tuθ |further 'fɝðɚ; ES 'fɝðə |custom 'kʌstəm |while hwaɪl |how haʊ |toy tɔɪ
|using 'juzɪŋ |fuse fjuz, fɪuz |dish dɪʃ |vision 'vɪʒən |Eden 'idṇ |cradle 'kredḷ |keep 'em 'kipm̩

Words below in which a *before* r (farm) *is sounded* ɑ *are often pronounced in* E *with* a (fɑːm)

tamasha tə'maʃə	tansy 'tænzɪ
tamber 'tæmbɚ; ES 'tæmbə(r = timbre	tantalize 'tænt]ˌaɪz |-s -ɪz |-d -d
tambour 'tæmbʊr; ES 'tæmbʊə(r; |-ed -d	tantalum 'tænt]əm
tambourin 'tæmbʊˌrɪn (Fr tãbu'ræ̃)	Tantalus 'tænt]əs |Tantalus's 'tænt]əsɪz
tambourine ˌtæmbə'rin |-d -d	tantamount 'tæntəˌmaʊnt
tame tem |tamed temd |-mable, -meable -əb]	tantara 'tæntərə, tæn'tærə, -'tɑrə
Tamerlane 'tæmɚˌlen; ES 'tæmə-	tantivy, T- tæn'tɪvɪ |-tivied -'tɪvɪd
Tamil 'tæm], 'tæmɪl	tantrum 'tæntrəm
Tammany 'tæmənɪ	Taos NMex taʊs, 'taʊəs, 'taəs (Am Sp taus)
Tamora 'tæmərə, 'tæmrə	|-'s -ɪz
Tam o'Shanter 'tæmə'ʃæntɚ; ES -'ʃæntə(r	Taoism 'taoˌɪzəm, 'taʊɪzəm
tam-o'shanter ˌtæmə'ʃæntɚ; ES -tə(r; |-ed -d	tap tæp |tapped tæpt
tamp tæmp |tamped tæmpt	tapa 'tɑpə
Tampa 'tæmpə	tape tep |taped tept |-line 'tepˌlaɪn
tamper 'tæmpɚ; ES 'tæmpə(r; |-ed -d |-ing	taper 'tepɚ; ES 'tepə(r; |-ed -d |-ing -pərɪŋ,
'tæmpərɪŋ, 'tæmprɪŋ	-prɪŋ
Tampico tæm'piko, 'tæmpɪˌko (Sp tam'piko)	tapestry 'tæpɪstrɪ |-tried -trɪd
tampion 'tæmpɪən, -pjən |-ed -d	tapeworm 'tepˌwɝm; ES -ˌwɜm, -ˌwɝm
tampon 'tæmpan, -pɒn	taphouse 'tæpˌhaʊs |-houses -ˌhaʊzɪz
Tamworth 'tæmwɚθ; ES 'tæmwəθ	tapioca ˌtæpɪ'okə
tan tæn |tanned tænd	tapir 'tepɚ; ES 'tepə(r
tanager 'tænədʒɚ, 'tænɪ-; ES -dʒə(r	tapis tæ'pi, 'tæpi, 'tæpɪs (Fr ta'pi)
Tanagra 'tænəgrə	tappa 'tɑpə
tanbark 'tænˌbark; ES -ˌbɑːk	Tappan 'tæpən
Tancred 'tæŋkrɪd, 'tænkrɪd	tappet 'tæpɪt
tandem 'tændəm	taproom 'tæpˌrum, -ˌrʊm
Taney justice 'tonɪ	taproot 'tæpˌrut, -ˌrʊt |-ed -ɪd
tang tæŋ |tanged tæŋd |tanging 'tæŋɪŋ	tapster 'tæpstɚ; ES 'tæpstə(r
Tanganyika ˌtæŋgən'jikə, ˌtæŋgæn-	tar tar; ES tɑː(r; |-red -d |-ring 'tarɪŋ
tangelo 'tændʒəˌlo	Tara Irel 'tærə, goddess 'tarə
tangent 'tændʒənt |tangency 'tændʒənsɪ	taradiddle 'tærəˌdɪd] |-d -d |-ling -d]ɪŋ, -dlɪŋ
tangential tæn'dʒɛnʃəl |-ly -ɪ	tarantella ˌtærən'tɛlə
Tangerine 'of Tangier' ˌtændʒə'rin	Taranto tə'rænto (It 'taːranto)
tangerine fruit 'tændʒəˌrin, ˌtændʒə'rin	tarantula tə'ræntʃələ |-s -z |-lae -li
tangibility ˌtændʒə'bɪlətɪ	tarboosh tar'buʃ; ES tɑː'buʃ; |-ed -t
tangible 'tændʒəb] |-bly -blɪ	Tarbox 'tarˌbaks; ES 'tɑːˌbaks, -ˌbɒks; |-'s
Tangier tæn'dʒɪr; ES tæn'dʒɪə(r	-ɪz
tangle 'tæŋg] |-d -d |-ling 'tæŋglɪŋ, -g]ɪŋ	tardigrade 'tardɪˌgred; ES 'tɑːdɪ-
Tanglewood 'tæŋg]ˌwʊd	tardy 'tardɪ; ES 'tɑːdɪ; |-dily -d]ɪ, -dɪlɪ
tango 'tæŋgo |-ed -d	tare tɛr, tær; E tɛə(r, ES tæə(r; |-d -d
tank tæŋk |tanked tæŋkt	Tarentum tə'rɛntəm
tankard 'tæŋkɚd; ES 'tæŋkəd	targe tardʒ; ES tɑːdʒ; |-s -ɪz |-d -d
tanker 'tæŋkɚ; ES 'tæŋkə(r	target 'targɪt; ES 'tɑːgɪt; |-ed -ɪd
tannate 'tænet	tariff 'tærɪf |tariffed 'tærɪft
tanner, T- 'tænɚ; ES 'tænə(r; |-y 'tænərɪ	Tarkington 'tarkɪŋtən; ES 'tɑːk-
Tannhäuser 'tænˌhɔɪzɚ, 'tan-; ES -ˌhɔɪzə(r;	tarlatan, -le- 'tarlətn̩; ES 'tɑːl-; |-ed -d
(Ger 'tanˌhɔyzər)	Tarleton 'tarltən; ES 'tɑːl-
tannic 'tænɪk |tannin 'tænɪn	tarn tarn; ES tɑːn; |-side -ˌsaɪd

Key: See in full §§3–47. bee bi \|pity 'pɪtɪ (§6) \|rate ret \|yet jɛt \|sang sæŋ \|angry 'æŋ·grɪ \|bath bæθ; E baθ (§10) \|ah ɑ \|far far \|watch watʃ, wɒtʃ (§12) \|jaw dʒɔ \|gorge gɔrdʒ \|go go

Words below in which a *before* r (farm) *is sounded* ɑ *are often pronounced in E with* a (fɑːm)
Words below that have æ *before* r (carry *ˈ*kærɪ) *are often pronounced in N with* ɛ (ˈkɛrɪ, §94)

tarnish ˈtɑrnɪʃ; ES ˈtɑːn-; |-es -ɪz |-ed -t

taro ˈtɑro

tarpaulin tarˈpɔlɪn; ES tɑːˈpɔlɪn; |-ed -d

Tarpeia tarˈpiə; ES tɑːˈpiə; |-n -n

tarpon ˈtɑrpɑn; ES ˈtɑːpɑn, -pɒn, S+tɑːˈpɒn

Tarquin ˈtɑrkwɪn; ES ˈtɑːkwɪn

tarradiddle ˈtærəˌdɪdl̩ |-d -d |-ling -dl̩ɪŋ, -dlɪŋ

tarragon ˈtærəˌgɑn; ES+-ˌgɒn

Tarrant ˈtærənt

tarriance ˈtærɪəns |-s -ɪz

tarry *'like tar'* ˈtɑrɪ

tarry *'stay'* ˈtærɪ |tarried ˈtærɪd

tarsal ˈtɑrsl̩; ES ˈtɑːsl̩

Tarshish ˈtɑrʃɪʃ; ES ˈtɑːʃɪʃ; |-'s -ɪz

tarsometatarsus ˈtɑrsoˌmɛtəˈtɑrsəs; ES ˈtɑːso-ˌmɛtəˈtɑːsəs; |-si -saɪ

tarsus, T- ˈtɑrsəs; ES ˈtɑːsəs; |tarsi -saɪ |-sus' səs

tart tɑrt; ES tɑːt; |-ed -ɪd

tartan ˈtɑrtn̩; ES ˈtɑːtn̩; |-ed -d

tartar, T- ˈtɑrtɚ; ES ˈtɑːtə(r

Tartarean, -ian tarˈtɛrɪən, -ˈtær-, -ˈter-; ES tɑˈt-

tartare sauce ˈtɑrtɚˌsɔs; ES ˈtɑːtə-

tartaric tarˈtærɪk, -ˈtɑrɪk; ES tɑːˈt-

Tartarus ˈtɑrtərəs; ES ˈtɑːtərəs; |-'s -ɪz

Tartary ˈtɑrtərɪ; ES ˈtɑːtərɪ; =Tatary

tartlet ˈtɑrtlɪt; ES ˈtɑːtlɪt

tartrate ˈtɑrtret; ES ˈtɑːtret; |-d -ɪd

Tartufe, -ffe tarˈtuf; ES tɑːˈtuf; (*Fr* tarˈtyf)

task tæsk; E+task, tɑsk; |-ed -t

taskmaster ˈtæskˌmæstɚ; ES ˈtæskˌmæstə(r, E+ˈtaskˌmastə(r, ˈtɑskˌmɑstə(r

Tasman ˈtæzmən

Tasmania tæzˈmenɪə, -njə |-n -n

tasse tæs |tasses ˈtæsɪz

tassel ˈtæsl̩ |-ed -d |-ing ˈtæsl̩ɪŋ, ˈtæslɪŋ—*cf* tossel

Tasso ˈtæso (*It* ˈtɑsso)

taste test |-d -ɪd |-ful ˈtestfəl |-fully -fəlɪ

tasty ˈtestɪ |tastily ˈtestl̩ɪ, -tɪlɪ

tat tæt |tatted ˈtætɪd

ta-ta ˈtɑˌtɑ *accent varies*

Tatar ˈtɑtɚ; ES ˈtɑtə(r;=Tartar

Tatarian tɑˈtɛrɪən, -ˈtær-, -ˈter-

Tataric tɑˈtærɪk

Tatary ˈtɑtərɪ

tatler, T- ˈtætlɚ; ES ˈtætlə(r

tatterdemalion ˌtætɚdɪˈmeljən, -lɪən; ES ˌtætə-

Tattersall ˈtætɚˌsɔl, -səl; ES ˈtætə-

Tattershall *Lincs* ˈtætɚʃɔl, -səl; ES ˈtætə-; ʃ *by sp. pron.*

tattle ˈtætl̩ |-d -d |-ling ˈtætl̩ɪŋ, ˈtætlɪŋ

tattler ˈtætlɚ, ˈtætlɚ; ES -ə(r

tattoo tæˈtu |tattooed tæˈtud

tau tɔ, taʊ

Tauchnitz ˈtaʊknɪts (*Ger* ˈtaʊxnɪts) |-'s -ɪz

taught *past pptc of* teach tɔt

taunt tɔnt, tɒnt, tɑnt |-ed -ɪd

Taunton *Engd, Mass* ˈtɔntən, ˈtɒn-, *loc.* ˈtɑntən, *Mass+*ˈtɑntn̩

taupe top (*Fr* toːp)

Taurus ˈtɔrəs |Taurus's ˈtɔrəsɪz |*gen* -ri -raɪ

taut tɔt |-en -n̩ |-ened -n̩d |-ening -n̩ɪŋ, -nɪŋ

tautog ˈtɔtɑg, -tɒg, -tɔg

tautological ˌtɔtl̩ˈadʒɪkl̩; ES+-ˈɒdʒ-; |-ly -ɪ, -ɪklɪ

tautology tɔˈtɑlədʒɪ; ES+-ˈtɒl-; |-gism -ˌdʒɪzəm |-gist -dʒɪst |-gous -gəs

tautosyllabic ˌtɔtəsɪˈlæbɪk

tavern ˈtævɚn; ES ˈtævən; |-ed -d

Tavistock ˈtævɪsˌtɑk; ES+-ˌtɒk

taw tɔ |tawed tɔd

Tawas ˈtɔwəs |-'s -ɪz

tawdry ˈtɔdrɪ

tawny ˈtɔnɪ

tax tæks |taxes ˈtæksɪz |taxed tækst

taxability ˌtæksəˈbɪlətɪ

taxable ˈtæksəbl̩ |-bly -blɪ |-ation tæksˈeʃən

tax-exempt ˈtæksɪgˈzɛmpt (ˈtax-exˌempt ˈbond)

taxi *n* ˈtæksɪ |taxis ˈtæksɪz

taxi, -y *v* ˈtæksɪ |taxies ˈtæksɪz |taxied -d

taxicab ˈtæksɪˌkæb |-cabbed -ˌkæbd

taxidermal ˌtæksəˈdɝml̩; ES -ˈdɜml̩, -ˈdɝml̩; |-mic -mɪk

taxidermist ˈtæksəˌdɝmɪst; ES -ˌdɜmɪst, -ˌdɝmɪst; |-my -mɪ

taximeter ˈtæksɪˌmitɚ; ES -ˌmitə(r

taxiplane ˈtæksɪˌplen |-ed -d

taxis ˈtæksɪs

taxonomy tæksˈɑnəmɪ; ES+-ˈɒn-

|full fʊl |tooth tuθ |further ˈfɝðɚ; ES ˈfɜðə; |custom ˈkʌstəm |while hwaɪl |how haʊ |toy tɔɪ |using ˈjuzɪŋ |fuse fjuz, fruz |dish dɪʃ |vision ˈvɪʒən |Eden ˈidn̩ |cradle ˈkredl̩ |keep 'em ˈkipm̩

Tay te
Tayler 'telɚ; ES 'telə(r
Taylor 'telɚ; ES 'telə(r
Tchad tʃæd, tʃɑd
Tchaikovsky, -wsky tʃaɪ'kɔfskɪ, -'kɒf-, -vskɪ, -'kaʊskɪ
tea ti |teaed tid
tea-ball 'ti‚bɔl
teacake 'ti‚kek
teach titʃ |teaches 'titʃɪz |taught tɔt
teachability ‚titʃə'bɪlətɪ
teachable 'titʃəb! |-bly -blɪ
teacher 'titʃɚ; ES 'titʃə(r
teacup 'ti‚kʌp |-ful 'tikʌp‚fʊl |-fuls -‚fʊlz
Teagarden 'ti‚gɑrdn̩, -dɪn; ES -‚gɑ:d-, E+ -‚gɑ:d-
Teague tig
teak tik |-wood -‚wʊd
teakettle 'ti‚kɛtl̩, 'tikɪtl̩
teal til
team tim |teamed timd |-ster -stɚ; ES -stə(r
teammate 'tim‚met
teamwork 'tim‚wɝk; ES -‚wɜk, -‚wɝ·k
teapot 'ti‚pɑt; ES+-‚pɒt
teapotful 'tipɑt‚fʊl; ES+-pɒt-; |-fuls -‚fʊlz
tear 'eyewater' tɪr; ES tɪə(r, S+tɛə(r; |-ed -d
tear 'rip' tɛr, tær; E tɛə(r, ES tæə(r; |tore tor, tɔr; ES toə(r, E+tɔə(r; |torn torn, tɔrn; ES toən, E+tɔən
tearoom 'ti‚rum, -‚rʊm
Tearsheet 'tɛr‚ʃit, 'tær-; E 'tɛə-, ES 'tæə-
Teasdale 'tizdl̩, -‚del—cf Tisdall, Tees
tease tiz |teases 'tizɪz |teased tizd
teasel 'tizl̩ |-ed -d |-ing 'tizl̩ɪŋ, -zlɪŋ
teashop 'ti‚ʃɑp; ES+-‚ʃɒp
teaspoon 'ti‚spun, -‚spʊn, 'tis‚p-
teaspoonful 'tispun‚fʊl, -spʊn- |-fuls -‚fʊlz
teat tit
Teaticket ‚ti'tɪkɪt
teazel, -zle 'tizl̩ |-(e)d -d |-(l)ing -zl̩ɪŋ, -zlɪŋ
Teazle 'tizl̩
technic 'tɛknɪk |-al -l̩ |-ally -l̩ɪ, -ɪklɪ
technicality ‚tɛknɪ'kælətɪ
technician tɛk'nɪʃən
technique tɛk'nik
technocracy tɛk'nɑkrəsɪ; ES+-'nɒk-
technocrat 'tɛknə‚kræt |-ic ‚tɛknə'krætɪk
technologic ‚tɛknə'lɑdʒɪk; ES+-'lɒdʒ-; |-al -l̩ |-ally -l̩ɪ, -ɪklɪ

technology tɛk'nɑlədʒɪ; ES+-'nɒl-
techy 'tɛtʃɪ |-chily -tʃəlɪ, -tʃɪlɪ
tectal 'tɛktl̩
tectum 'tɛktəm |-ta -tə
Tecumseh tɪ'kʌmsɪ, -'kʌmpsɪ
ted tɛd |tedded 'tɛdɪd
Teddy 'tɛdɪ
Te Deum tɪ'diəm, ti-
tedious 'tidɪəs, 'tidʒəs
tedium 'tidɪəm |-s -z
tee ti |teed tid
teem tim |teemed timd
teen tin |-s -z
teen-age 'tin‚edʒ
teenage 'tinɪdʒ
teeny 'tinɪ
teepee 'tepee' 'tipi
Tees tiz |-'s -ɪz |-dale -‚del, -dl̩
teeter 'titɚ; ES 'titə(r; |-ed -d
teeth tiθ |-less -lɪs
teethe tið |teethed tiðd |-thing 'tiðɪŋ
teethridge 'tiθ‚rɪdʒ |-s -ɪz
teetotal ti'totl̩ |-ed -d |-ing -'totl̩ɪŋ, -tlɪŋ
teetotaler, -ller ti'totlɚ, -'totlɚ; ES -ə(r
teetotalism ti'totl̩‚ɪzəm |-ist -ɪst
teetotally ti'totl̩ɪ, emph.+'ti'totl̩ɪ
teetotum ti'totəm |-ed -d
tegument 'tɛgjəmənt |-al ‚tɛgjə'mɛnt]
tegumentary ‚tɛgjə'mɛntərɪ
te-hee ti'hi |-te-heed ti'hid
Teheran ‚tɪə'rɑn, ‚tɛhə'rɑn, tɛ'rɑn
Tehuantepec tə‚wɑntə'pɛk, tə'wɑntə‚pɛk, -ɒntə-
Teign tɪn, tin, ten
Teignmouth 'tɪnməθ
tekel 'tikl̩, 'tɛkl̩—cf mene
Tekoa tɪ'koə
Telamon 'tɛləmən
telautograph tɛl'ɔtə‚græf; E+-‚grɑf, -‚grɑf
telegram 'tɛlə‚græm |-med -d
telegraph 'tɛlə‚græf; E+-‚grɑf, -‚grɑf; |-ed -t
telegrapher tə'lɛgrəfɚ; ES -fə(r; |-phy -fɪ
telegraphic ‚tɛlə'græfɪk |-al -l̩ |-ally -l̩ɪ, -ɪklɪ
Telemachus tə'lɛməkəs |-'s -ɪz
teleological ‚tɛlɪə'lɑdʒɪkl̩, ‚tilɪ-; ES+-'lɒdʒ-; |-ly -ɪ
teleology ‚tɛlɪ'ɑlədʒɪ, ‚tilɪ-; ES+-'ɒl-
telepathic ‚tɛlə'pæθɪk |-ally -l̩ɪ, -ɪklɪ
telepathy tə'lɛpəθɪ

Key: See in full §§3-47. bee bi |pity 'pɪtɪ (§6) |rate ret |yet jɛt |sang sæŋ |angry 'æŋ·grɪ |bath bæθ; E baθ (§10) |ah ɑ |far fɑr |watch wɑtʃ, wɒtʃ (§12) |jaw dʒɔ |gorge gɔrdʒ |go go

telephone 'tɛləˌfon |-d **-d**
telephonic ˌtɛlə'fɑnɪk; ES+-'fɒn-; |-al -|
  |-ally -|ɪ, -ɪklɪ
telephony tə'lɛfənɪ
telephotography ˌtɛləfo'tɑgrəfɪ, -'tɒg-
telescope 'tɛləˌskop |-d **-t**
telescopic ˌtɛlə'skɑpɪk; ES+-'skɒp-; |-al -|
  |-ally -|ɪ, -ɪklɪ
telescopy tə'lɛskəpɪ
teletype, T- 'tɛləˌtaɪp |-d **-t**
teletypewriter ˌtɛlə'taɪpˌraɪtɚ; ES -ˌraɪtə(r
television 'tɛləˌvɪʒən |-visor -ˌvaɪzɚ; ES -zə(r
tell tɛl |told **told**
telltale 'tɛlˌtel
tellurium tɛ'lʊrɪəm, -'lɪʊ-
Temanite 'timənˌaɪt
temblor tɛm'blɔr; ES -'blɔə(r; (*Sp* tem'blɔr)
temerity tə'mɛrətɪ
Temescal ˌtɛmə'skæl
Tempe 'tɛmpɪ
temper 'tɛmpɚ; ES -pə(r; |-ed **-d** |-ing 'tɛm-
  pərɪŋ, -prɪŋ
temperament 'tɛmprəmənt, -pərə-
temperamental ˌtɛmprə'mɛnt|, -pərə- |-ly -ɪ
temperance 'tɛmprəns, -pərəns
temperate 'tɛmprɪt, -pərɪt
temperature 'tɛmprətʃɚ, -pərə-; ES -tʃə(r
tempest 'tɛmpɪst |-ed **-ɪd**
tempestuous tɛm'pɛstʃʊəs
Templar 'tɛmplɚ; ES 'tɛmplə(r
temple, T- 'tɛmp| |-d **-d** |-ton **-tən**
tempo 'tɛmpo |-s **-z** |-pi **-pi**
temporal 'tɛmpərəl, -prəl |-ly -ɪ
temporarily 'tɛmpəˌrɛrəlɪ, *esp. if emph.*
  ˌtɛmpə'rɛrəlɪ
temporary 'tɛmpəˌrɛrɪ
temporize 'tɛmpəˌraɪz |-s **-ɪz** |-d **-d**
tempt tɛmpt |-ed **-ɪd** |-ation tɛmp'teʃən
tempus fugit 'tɛmpəs'fjudʒɪt, -'fɪu-
ten tɛn
tenability ˌtɛnə'bɪlətɪ
tenable 'tɛnəb| |-bly **-blɪ**
tenacious tɪ'neʃəs |-city tɪ'næsətɪ
Tenafly 'tɛnəˌflaɪ
tenancy 'tɛnənsɪ |-ant **-ənt** |-anted **-əntɪd**
tenantry 'tɛnəntrɪ
tench tɛntʃ |tenches 'tɛntʃɪz
tend tɛnd |-ed **-ɪd** |-ance **-əns** |-ency **-ənsɪ**
tendencious, -tious tɛn'dɛnʃəs

tender 'tɛndɚ; ES 'tɛndə(r; |-ed **-d** |-ing
  'tɛndərɪŋ, -drɪŋ
tenderer 'tɛndərɚ, 'tɛndrɚ; ES -dərə(r,
  -drə(r
tenderfoot 'tɛndɚˌfʊt; ES 'tɛndə-
tender-footed 'tɛndɚ'fʊtɪd; ES 'tɛndə-
tenderhearted 'tɛndɚ'hɑrtɪd; ES 'tɛndə-
  'hɑːtɪd, E+-'hɑːtɪd; ('tɛndɚˌhearted 'father)
tenderloin 'tɛndɚˌlɔɪn; ES 'tɛndə-; |-ed **-d;**
tendinous, -donous 'tɛndənəs
tendon 'tɛndən
tendril 'tɛndrɪl, -əl |-ed **-d**
Tenebrae 'tɛnəˌbri
tenebrous 'tɛnəbrəs
Tenedos 'tɛnədəs, -ˌdɑs; ES+-ˌdɒs; |-'s **-ɪz**
tenement 'tɛnəmənt |-ed **-ɪd**
Tenerife, -ffe ˌtɛnə'rɪf, -'rif (*Sp* ˌtene'rife)
tenet 'tɛnɪt, 'tinɪt
tenfold *adj, adv* 'tɛn'fold ('tenˌfold 'loss)
teniafuge 'tinɪəˌfjudʒ, -ˌfɪudʒ |-s **-ɪz**
teniasis tɪ'naɪəsɪs
Teniers 'tɛnjɚz, -ɪɚz; ES 'tɛnjəz, -ɪ·əz; |-'s
  -ɪz (*Flem* tɛ'nirs, *Fr* te'nje)
Tennessean ˌtɛnə'siən
Tennessee ˌtɛnə'si, 'tɛnəˌsi ('Tennesˌsee 'air)
tennis 'tɛnɪs
Tennyson 'tɛnəsn̩
tenon 'tɛnən |-ed **-d**
tenor 'tɛnɚ; ES 'tɛnə(r; |-ed **-d**
tenpenny 'tɛnˌpɛnɪ, -pənɪ
tenpins 'tɛnˌpɪnz
Tensas 'tɛnsɔ
tense tɛns |tenses 'tɛnsɪz |tensed tɛnst
tensile 'tɛnsl̩, -sɪl
tension 'tɛnʃən |-sity 'tɛnsətɪ
tensor 'tɛnsɚ, -sɔr; ES 'tɛnsə(r, -sɔə(r
ten-strike 'tɛnˌstraɪk
tent tɛnt |tented 'tɛntɪd
tentacle 'tɛntək|, -ɪk| |-d **-d**
tentative 'tɛntətɪv
tenterhook 'tɛntɚˌhʊk; ES 'tɛntə-
tenth tɛnθ |-ths **-θs**
tenuity tɛn'juətɪ, tɪ'nɪʊətɪ, tɪ'nʊətɪ
tenuous 'tɛnjʊəs
tenure 'tɛnjɚ; ES 'tɛnjə(r
tepee 'tipi
tepid 'tɛpɪd |-ity tɪ'pɪdətɪ
Terah 'tɪrə, 'tirə

|full fʊl |tooth tuθ |further 'fɝðɚ; ES 'fɝðə |custom 'kʌstəm |while hwaɪl |how haʊ |toy tɔɪ
|using 'juzɪŋ |fuse fjuz, fɪuz |dish dɪʃ |vision 'vɪʒən |Eden 'idn̩ |cradle 'kred| |keep 'em 'kipm̩

teraph 'tɛrəf |-im 'tɛrəˌfɪm

Terbeek 'tɝbɪk, tɚ'bik; ES 'tɝb-, 'tɝb-, tə'b-; (*Du* tər'be:k)

terbium 'tɝbɪəm; ES 'tɝb-, 'tɝb-

tercel 'tɝs|; ES 'tɝs|, 'tɝs|

tercentenary tɝ'sɛntəˌnɛrɪ, ˌtɝsɛn'tɛnərɪ; ES -ɝ-, -ɝ-; *mainly Brit* -sɛn'tinərɪ

terebinth 'tɛrəˌbɪnθ |-ths -θs

Terence 'tɛrəns |-'s -ɪz

Teresa tə'risə, -'rizə, -'rɛsə (*It* te'rɛ:za)

tergiversate 'tɝdʒɪvɚˌset; ES 'tɝdʒɪvə-, 'tɝdʒɪvə-; |-d -ɪd

tergiversation ˌtɝdʒɪvɚ'seʃən; ES ˌtɝdʒɪvə-, ˌtɝdʒɪvə-

Terhune tɝ'hjun, -'hɪun; ES tɝ-, tɝ-

term tɝm; ES tɝm, tɝm; |-ed -d

Termagant, t- 'tɝməgənt; ES 'tɝm-, 'tɝm-; |-gancy -gənsɪ

terminable 'tɝmɪnəb|; ES 'tɝm-, 'tɝm-; |-bly -blɪ

terminal 'tɝmən|; ES 'tɝm-, 'tɝm-; |-ly -ɪ

terminate 'tɝməˌnet; ES 'tɝm-, 'tɝm-; |-d -ɪd

termination ˌtɝmə'neʃən; ES ˌtɝm-, ˌtɝm-

terminer 'tɝmɪnɚ; ES 'tɝmɪnə(r, 'tɝmɪnə(r

terminology ˌtɝmə'nalədʒɪ; ES ˌtɝm-, ˌtɝm-, -'nɒl-

terminus 'tɝmənəs; ES 'tɝm-, 'tɝm-; |-es -ɪz |-ni -ˌnaɪ

termite 'tɝmaɪt; ES 'tɝm-, 'tɝm-

tern tɝn; ES tɝn, tɝn

ternary 'tɝnərɪ; ES 'tɝn-, 'tɝn-

ternate 'tɝnɪt, -net; ES 'tɝn-, 'tɝn-

Terpsichore tɝp'sɪkərɪ, -ˌri; ES tɝp-, tɝp-

terpsichoreal ˌtɝpsɪkə'riəl; ES ˌtɝp-, ˌtɝp-; |-ly -ɪ |-an -ən

terrace 'tɛrɪs, -əs |-s -ɪz |-d -t

terra cotta, -ra-c- 'tɛrə'katə; ES+-'kɒtə

Terra del Fuego 'tɛrəˌdɛlfu'ego, -'fwego

terra firma 'tɛrə'fɝmə; ES -'fɝmə, -'fɝmə

terrain tɛ'ren, 'tɛren

terrane tɛ'ren, 'tɛren

terrapin 'tɛrəpɪn

Terre Haute 'tɛrə'hot, *loc.*+'tɛrɪ'hʌt

Terrell 'tɛrəl, *cf* Tyrrell, Syracuse

terrene tɛ'rin ('tɛrˌrene 'days)

terrestrial tə'rɛstrɪəl |-ly -ɪ

terrible 'tɛrəb| |-bly -blɪ

terrier 'tɛrɪɚ; ES 'tɛrɪ·ə(r; *dial.* 'tærɪɚ, *cf* farrier

terrific tə'rɪfɪk |-al -| |-ally -|ɪ |-icly -ɪklɪ

terrify 'tɛrəˌfaɪ |-fied -ˌfaɪd

territorial, T- ˌtɛrə'torɪəl, -'tɔr-; S -'tor-; |-ly -ɪ

territoriality ˌtɛrəˌtorɪ'ælətɪ, -ˌtɔrɪ-; S -ˌtorɪ-

territory 'tɛrəˌtorɪ, -ˌtɔrɪ; S -ˌtorɪ

terror 'tɛrɚ; ES 'tɛrə(r; |-ed -d |-some -səm

terrorism 'tɛrəˌrɪzəm |-rist -rɪst

terrorize 'tɛrəˌraɪz |-s -ɪz |-d -d

Terry 'tɛrɪ

terse tɝs; ES tɝs, tɝs

tertian 'tɝʃən; ES 'tɝʃən, 'tɝʃən

tertiary, T- 'tɝʃɪˌɛrɪ, -ʃərɪ; ES 'tɝʃ-, 'tɝʃ-

tertium quid 'tɝʃɪəm'kwɪd; ES 'tɝʃ-, 'tɝʃ-

Tertullian tɚ'tʌlɪən, -ljən; ES tə-; |-ism -ˌɪzəm

terza rima 'tɛrtsə'rimə; ES 'tɛətsə-; (*It* 'tɛrtsɑ'ri:mɑ)

Tesla 'tɛslə

tesselate *adj* 'tɛs|ɪt, -ˌet

tesselate *v* 'tɛs|ˌet |-d -ɪd

test tɛst |tested 'tɛstɪd |-acy -əsɪ

testament *n* 'tɛstəmənt

testament *v* 'tɛstəˌmɛnt |-ed -ɪd

testamental ˌtɛstə'mɛntļ |-ly -ɪ |-tary -tərɪ, -trɪ

testate 'tɛstet |-tated -tetɪd

testator 'tɛstetɚ, tɛs'tetɚ; ES -tə(r

testatrix tɛs'tetrɪks |-es -ɪz |-trices -trɪˌsiz

testicle 'tɛstɪkļ

testify 'tɛstəˌfaɪ |-fied -ˌfaɪd

testimonial ˌtɛstə'monɪəl, -njəl |-alist -ɪst

testimony 'tɛstəˌmonɪ

teston 'tɛstn̩

test-tube 'tɛstˌtjub, -ˌtɪub, -ˌtub

testudo tɛs'tjudo, -'tɪu-, -'tu- |-dines -dn̩ˌiz

testy 'tɛstɪ -tily -t|ɪ, -tɪlɪ

tetanus 'tɛtnəs |tetany 'tɛtn̩ɪ

tetchy 'tɛtʃɪ

tête-à-tête 'tetə'tet (*Fr* tɛta'tɛ:t)

tether 'tɛðɚ; ES -ðə(r; |-ed -d |-ðərɪŋ, -ðrɪŋ

Teton 'titn̩, -tan; ES+-tɒn; |-s -z

tetotum ti'totəm |-ed -d

tetrachord 'tɛtrəˌkɔrd; ES -ˌkɔəd

tetraethyl ˌtɛtrə'ɛθəl, -ɪl

tetragon 'tɛtrəˌgan; ES+-ˌgɒn

tetrahedron ˌtɛtrə'hidrən |-dral -drəl

tetralogy tɛ'trælədʒɪ

tetrameter tɛ'træmətɚ; ES -mətə(r

---

tetrarch ˈtitrɑrk, ˈtɛt-; ES -ɑːk, E+-aːk
tetrasyllabic ˌtɛtrəsɪˈlæbɪk
tetrasyllable ˈtɛtrəˌsɪləbļ
Tetrazzini ˌtɛtrəˈzinɪ (It ˌtetrɑtˈtsiːni)
tetter ˈtɛtɚ; ES ˈtɛtə(r, |-ed -d |-ous -əs
Tetzel ˈtɛtsļ
Teucer ˈtjusɚ, ˈtɪu-, ˈtu-; ES -sə(r
Teufelsdröckh, -droeckh ˈtɔɪfļzˌdrɛk
Teuton ˈtjutņ, ˈtɪu-, ˈtu-
Teutonic tjuˈtɑnɪk, tɪu-, tu-; ES+-ˈtɒn-
Teviot ˈtiviət, ˈtɛv-, ˈtɪv-
Tewkesbury, -ksb- ˈtjuksˌbɛrɪ, ˈtɪu-, ˈtu-,
 -bərɪ
Texan ˈtɛksņ, ˈtɛksən
Texarkana ˌtɛkşɑrˈkænə; ES ˌtɛksɑːˈk-
Texas ˈtɛksəs; S+ˈtɛksɪs, -səz, -sɪz; |-as'
 -s, -z
text tɛkst |texted ˈtɛkstɪd |-book -ˌbʊk
textile ˈtɛkstļ, -tɪl, -taɪl
textual ˈtɛkstʃʊəl |-ly -ɪ
textural ˈtɛkstʃərəl |-ly -ɪ
texture ˈtɛkstʃɚ; ES ˈtɛkstʃə(r; |-d -d
Tezel ˈtɛtsļ
Thackeray ˈθækərɪ, ˈθækrɪ |-ayan -ən |-ayite
 -ˌaɪt
Thackerayana ˌθækərɪˈenə, -ˈænə, -ˈɑnə
Thackley ˈθæklɪ
Thaddaeus -deus Bib. θæˈdiəs, ˈθædɪəs
Thaddeus mod. name ˈθædɪəs |-'s -ɪz
Thai ˈtɑˑi
Thailand ˈtaɪlənd
Thais courtesan ˈθeˑɪs, opera tɑˈis |-'s -ɪz
Thaisa θeˈɪsə, ˈθeˑɪsə, -zə
thaler ˈtɑlɚ; ES ˈtɑlə(r; (Ger ˈtaːlər)
Thaler ˈθelɚ; ES ˈθelə(r
Thales ˈθeliz |-les' -liz
Thalia Muse θəˈlaɪə, fem. name ˈθelɪə, -ljə
Thaliard ˈθæljɚd; ES ˈθæljəd
thallium ˈθælɪəm
Thames US θemz, tɛmz, temz; C, Engd, NZ
 tɛmz |-'s -ɪz
than usually unstressed ðən, ðɛn, ðņ, ņ, n;
 stressed ˈðæn, ˌðæn
thanatopsis, T- ˌθænəˈtɑpsɪs; ES+-ˈtɒp-
thane θen |-ess -ɪs |-esses -ɪsɪz
Thanet ˈθænɪt—a sp. pron.; OE Tænett
thank θæŋk |-ed -t
thankful ˈθæŋkfəl |-ly -ɪ |-ness -nɪs
thankless ˈθæŋklɪs |-ness -nɪs

thanksgiving, T- ˌθæŋksˈgɪvɪŋ (ˈThanks-
ˌgiving ˈturkey)
Thanksgiving Day ˌθæŋksˈgɪvɪŋˌde
thankworthy ˈθæŋkˌwɝˈðɪ; ES -ˌwɝðɪ, -ˌwɝˈðɪ
that demonstrative ðæt; conj, relative ðət
thatch θætʃ |thatches ˈθætʃɪz |-ed -t
thaumaturgic ˌθɔməˈtɝˈdʒɪk; ES -ˈtɝdʒ-,
 -ˈtɝˈdʒ-
thaumaturgy ˈθɔməˌtɝˈdʒɪ; ES -ˌtɝdʒɪ, -ˌtɝˈdʒɪ
thaw θɔ |thawed θɔd |-y ˈθɔˑɪ
Thaxter ˈθækstɚ; ES ˈθækstə(r
Thayer θer, θær; E θeə(r, ES θæə(r
the usually unstressed: before conss. ðə; before
 vowels, & often before j- or hi-, hɪ-, he-, hɛ-
 pronounced ðɪ, in the S+ðə; rarely stressed
 ˈðɪ, ˌðɪ
Thea ˈθiə
thearchy ˈθiɑrkɪ; ES -ɑːkɪ, E+-aːkɪ
theater, -tre ˈθiətɚ, ˈθɪə-; ES -tə(r
theatric θɪˈætrɪk |-s -s |-al -ļ |-ally -ļɪ, -ɪklɪ
Thebes θibz |-'s -ɪz |Theban ˈθibən
The Dalles ðəˈdælz
thé dansant, pl thés dansants Fr tedɑ̃ˈsɑ̃
thee ði, unstressed+ðɪ
theft θɛft
thegn θen
thein ˈθiɪn |-ine -in, -ɪn
their ðɛr, ðær, ðer; ES ðɛə(r, ðæə(r, ðeə(r;
 unstressed+ðɚ; ES ðə(r
theirs ðɛrz, ðærz, ðerz; ES ðɛəz, ðæəz, ðeəz
theism ˈθiɪzəm |-ist -ɪst
theistic θiˈɪstɪk |-al -ļ |-ally -ļɪ, -ɪklɪ
them stressed ˈðɛm, ˌðɛm; unstr. ðəm, ðm̩
thematic θiˈmætɪk |-al -ļ |-ally -ļɪ, -ɪklɪ
theme θim |themed θimd
Themistocles θəˈmɪstəˌkliz |-'s -ɪz
themselves ðəmˈsɛlvz
then ðɛn |thenness ˈðɛnnɪs
thence ðɛns, less freq. θɛns—cf thither
thenceforth ˌðɛnsˈforθ, ˌθɛns-, -ˈfɔrθ; ES
 -ˈfoəθ, E+-ˈfɔəθ, acct+ˈthenceˌforth
thenceforward ˌðɛnsˈfɔrwɚd, ˌθɛns-; ES
 -ˈfɔəwəd
Theobald Am name ˈθiəˌbɔld, Shak. editor
 ˈtɪbļd |-'s ˈθiəˌbɔldz, ˈtɪbļdz, ˈtɪbļz
theocracy θiˈɑkrəsɪ; ES+-ˈɒk-; |-rasy -rəsɪ
theocrat ˈθiəˌkræt
theocratic ˌθiəˈkrætɪk |-al -ļ |-ally -ļɪ, -ɪklɪ
Theocritus θiˈɑkrɪtəs; ES+-ˈɒk-; |-'s -ɪz

|full fʊl |tooth tuθ |further ˈfɝˈðɚ; ES ˈfɝðə |custom ˈkʌstəm |while hwaɪl |how haʊ |toy tɔɪ
|using ˈjuzɪŋ |fuse fjuz, fɪuz |dish dɪʃ |vision ˈvɪʒən |Eden ˈidņ |cradle ˈkredļ |keep 'em ˈkipm̩

theodolite θiˈɑdlˌaɪt; ES+-ˈɒd-
Theodora ˌθiəˈdorə, -ˈdɔrə; S -ˈdorə
Theodore ˈθiəˌdor, -ˌdɔr; ES -ˌdoə(r, E+ -ˌdɔə(r
Theodoric θiˈɑdərɪk; ES+-ˈɒd-
Theodosia ˌθiəˈdoʃɪə |-sian -ʃən, -ʃɪən
Theodosius ˌθiəˈdoʃɪəs |-ʼs -ɪz
theologian ˌθiəˈlodʒən, -dʒɪən
theologic ˌθiəˈlɑdʒɪk; ES+-ˈlɒdʒ-; |-al -|
|-ally -|ɪ, -ɪklɪ
theologue, -log ˈθiəˌlɑg, -ˌlɑg, -ˌlɒg
theology θiˈɑlədʒɪ; ES+-ˈɒl-
Theophilus θiˈɑfələs; ES+-ˈɒf-; |-ʼs -ɪz
Theophrastus ˌθiəˈfræstəs |-ʼs -ɪz
theorbo θiˈɔrbo; ES -ˈɔəbo
theorem ˈθiərəm
theoretic ˌθiəˈrɛtɪk |-al -| |-ally -|ɪ, -ɪklɪ
theorism ˈθiəˌrɪzəm |-ist -rɪst
theorize ˈθiəˌraɪz |-s -ɪz |-d -d
theory ˈθiərɪ, ˈθɪərɪ
theosophic ˌθiəˈsɑfɪk; ES+-ˈsɒf-; |-al -| |-ally -|ɪ, -ɪklɪ
theosophy θiˈɑsəfɪ; ES+-ˈɒs-; |-phist -fɪst
therapeutic ˌθɛrəˈpjutɪk, -ˈpɪu- |-al -| |-ally -|ɪ, -ɪklɪ |-s -s
therapy ˈθɛrəpɪ
there *'in that place' (stressed)* ˈðɛr, ˈðær, ˌðɛr, ˌðær; E ˈðɛə(r, ˌðɛə(r, ES ˈðæə(r, ˌðæə(r
there *meaningless expletive (unstressed)* ðɚ; ES ðə(r; *(lightly stressed)* ðɛr, ðær; E ðɛə(r, ES ðæə(r
thereabout ˌðɛrəˈbaʊt, ˌðærə-; S ˌðærə-; |-s -s
thereafter ðɛrˈæftɚ, ðær-; E ðɛrˈæftə(r, ES ðær-, E+-ˈɑftə(r, -ˈɑftə(r
thereat ðɛrˈæt, ðær-; S ðær-
thereby ðɛrˈbaɪ, ðær-; E ðɛəˈbaɪ, ES ðæə-
therefor ðɛrˈfɔr, ðær-; E ðɛəˈfɔə(r, ES ðæə-
therefore ˈðɛrˌfor, ˈðær-, -ˌfɔr; E ˈðɛəˌfoə(r, ˈðæə-, -ˌfɔə(r; S ˈðæəˌfoə(r; *o.f.* ˈðɝ-, ˈðɝ-
therefrom ðɛrˈfrɑm, ðær-, -ˈfrɒm; E ðɛə-, ES ðæə-
therein ðɛrˈɪn, ðær-; S ðærˈɪn
thereinafter ˌðɛrɪnˈæftɚ, ˌðær-; E ˌðɛrɪn-ˈæftə(r, ES ˌðær-, E+-ˈɑftə(r, -ˈɑftə(r
thereinbefore ˌðɛrɪnbɪˈfor, ˌðær-, -ˈfɔr; E -ˈfoə(r, -ˈfɔə(r; S ˌðærɪnbɪˈfoə(r
thereinto ðɛrˈɪntu, ðær-, -tʊ, ˌðɛrɪnˈtu, ˌðær-; S ðærˈɪn-, ˌðærɪnˈtu

thereof ðɛrˈɑv, ðær-, ðɚ-, -ˈɑf, -ˈɒ-; S ðær-, ðɚ-
thereon ðɛrˈɑn, ðær-, -ˈɒn, -ˈɔn; S ðærˈɒn, -ˈɒn, *less freq.* -ˈɑn
there's *stressed* ˈðɛrz, ˈðærz, ˌðɛrz, ˌðærz; E ˈðɛəz, ˌðɛəz, ES ˈðæəz, ˌðæəz; *unstr.* ðɚz; ES ðəz
Theresa təˈrisə, θə-, -ˈrizə, -ˈrɛsə *(It* teˈrɛːza)
therethrough ðɛrˈθru, ðær-; E ðɛə-, ES ðæə-
thereto ðɛrˈtu, ðær-; E ðɛə-, ES ðæə-; (ˈthereˌto ˈadded)
theretofore ˌðɛrtəˈfor, ˌðær-, -ˈfɔr; E ˌðɛətə-ˈfoə(r, ˌðæə-, -ˈfɔə(r; S ˌðæətəˈfoə(r
thereunder ðɛrˈʌndɚ, ðær-; E ðɛrˈʌndə(r, ES ðær-
thereunto ðɛrˈʌntu, ðær-, -tʊ, ˌðɛrʌnˈtu, ˌðær-; S ðærˈʌn-, ˌðærʌnˈtu
thereupon ˌðɛrəˈpɑn, ˌðær-, -ˈpɒn, -ˈpɔn; S ˌðær-
therewith ðɛrˈwɪθ, ðær-, -ˈwɪð; E ðɛə-, ðæə-; *cf* wherewith
therewithal ˌðɛrwɪðˈɔl, ˌðær-; E ˌðɛə-, ES ˌðæə-
therm, -e θɝm; ES θɝm, θɝm; |-al -| |-ally -|ɪ
thermic ˈθɝmɪk; ES ˈθɝm-, ˈθɝm-; |-al -| |-ally -|ɪ, -ɪklɪ
thermion ˈθɝmɪən; ES ˈθɝm-, ˈθɝm-
thermionic ˌθɝmɪˈɑnɪk; ES ˌθɝm-, ˌθɝm-, -ˈɒn-; |-ally -|ɪ, -ɪklɪ
thermit, T- ˈθɝmɪt; ES ˈθɝm-, ˈθɝm-; |-mite -maɪt
thermocouple ˈθɝmoˌkʌpl̩; ES ˈθɝm-, ˈθɝm-
thermodynamic ˌθɝmodaɪˈnæmɪk; ES ˌθɝm-, ˌθɝm-; |-al -| |-ally -|ɪ, -ɪklɪ |-s -s
thermometer θəˈmɑmətɚ, θɚ-; ES θəˈmɑmə-tə(r, -ˈmɒm-—*In* θəˈmɑmətɚ θɚ- *has become* θə- *by dissimilation* (§121).
thermometric ˌθɝməˈmɛtrɪk; ES ˌθɝm-, ˌθɝm-; |-al -| |-ally -|ɪ, -ɪklɪ
Thermopylae θɚˈmɑplˌi; ES θəˈmɑp-, -ˈmɒp-
thermos, T- ˈθɝməs; ES ˈθɝm-, ˈθɝm-
thermostat ˈθɝməˌstæt; ES ˈθɝm-, ˈθɝm-
thermostatic ˌθɝməˈstætɪk; ES ˌθɝm-, ˌθɝm-; |-ally -|ɪ, -ɪklɪ
Thersites θɚˈsaɪtiz; ES θə-; |-tes' -tiz
thesaurus θɪˈsɔrəs |-es -ɪz |-ri -raɪ
these ðiz
Theseus ˈθisjus, ˈθisus, ˈθisɪəs |-eus' -s
thesis ˈθisɪs |theses ˈθisiz

Key: *See in full §§3–47.* bee bi |pity ˈpɪtɪ (§6) |rate ret |yet jɛt |sang sæŋ |angry ˈæŋ·grɪ |bath bæθ; E baθ (§10) |ah ɑ |far fɑr |watch wɑtʃ, wɒtʃ (§12) |jaw dʒɔ |gorge gɔrdʒ |go go

Thespis 'θɛspɪs |-'s -ɪz |-pian -pɪən
Thessalonian ˌθɛsə'lonɪən |-s -z
Thessalonica ˌθɛsələ'naɪkə, -'lɑnɪkə; ES+
  -'lɒn-
Thessalonike ˌθɛsələ'nikɪ
Thessaly 'θɛslɪ |-lian θɛ'selɪən
theta 'θetə, 'θitə
Thetis 'θitɪs |-'s -ɪz
theurgic θi'ɝˈdʒɪk; ES -'ɝˈdʒ-, -'ɝˈdʒ-; |-al -ḷ
  |-ally -ḷɪ, -ɪklɪ
theurgy 'θiɝˈdʒɪ; ES -ɝˈdʒɪ, -ɝˈdʒɪ; |-gist
  -dʒɪst
thew θju, θɪu, θu |-s -z |-ed -d
they ðe; *unstressed sometimes* ðɛ, ðɪ
they'd *'they would,' 'they had'* ðed
they'll *'they will'* ðel—They'll *is an abbreviation of* they will, *not of* they shall ('ðeʃəl),
  though it often replaces 'ðeʃəl.
they're *'they are'* ðer, ðɛr; ES ðeə(r, ðɛə(r
they've *'they have'* ðev; *unstressed sometimes*
  ðɛv, ðɪv, ðəv
thiazole 'θaɪəˌzol |-zol -ˌzol, -ˌzɑl, -ˌzɒl, -ˌzɔl
Thibet tɪ'bɛt, 'tɪbɪt |-an -n̩
Thibodaux ˌtɪbə'do
thick θɪk |thicked θɪkt
thick-and-thin 'θɪkən'θɪn, 'θɪkn̩-, 'θɪkŋ-
thicken 'θɪkən |-ed -d |-ing 'θɪkənɪŋ, -knɪŋ
thicket 'θɪkɪt |-ed -ɪd
thickheaded 'θɪk'hɛdɪd ('thickˌheaded 'fly)
thickset 'θɪk'sɛt
thick-skinned 'θɪk'skɪnd
thick-witted 'θɪk'wɪtɪd
thief θif |thief's θifs |thieves θivz
Thiel til
thieve θiv |thieved θivd |-ry -ərɪ, -rɪ
thigh θaɪ |thighed θaɪd
thill θɪl
thimble 'θɪmbḷ |-d -d |-ling 'θɪmblɪŋ, -bḷɪŋ
thimbleful 'θɪmbḷˌful |-fuls -ˌfulz
thimblerig 'θɪmbḷˌrɪg |-ged -d
thin θɪn |thinned θɪnd |-ness 'θɪnnɪs
thine ðaɪn
thing θɪŋ |-umajig 'θɪŋəməˌdʒɪg
thingumbob 'θɪŋəmˌbɑb, 'θɪŋəˌbɑb; ES+
  -ˌbɒb
think θɪŋk |thought θɔt |-able -əbḷ |-bly -blɪ
thinnish 'θɪnɪʃ
thin-skinned 'θɪn'skɪnd ('thin-ˌskinned 'face)
third θɝˈd; ES θɜd, θɝˈd

third-class 'θɝˈd'klæs; ES 'θɜd-, 'θɝˈd-, E+
  -'klɑs, -'klɑs
Thirlmere 'θɝˈlmɪr; ES 'θɜlmɪə(r, 'θɝˈlmɪə(r
thirst θɝˈst; ES θɜst, θɝˈst; |-ed -ɪd |-y -ɪ
thirteen θɝˈ'tin; ES θɜ-, θɝˈ-; (ˌhe's 'thir'teen,
  'thirˌteen 'men)
thirty 'θɝˈtɪ; ES 'θɜtɪ, 'θɝˈtɪ; |-tieth -tɪɪθ
  |-tieths -tɪɪθs |-fold -'fold
this ðɪs |these ðiz
Thisbe 'θɪzbɪ
thistle 'θɪsḷ |-d -d |-ling 'θɪslɪŋ, -sḷɪŋ
thistledown, T- 'θɪsḷˌdaun
thither 'θɪðɚ, 'ðɪðɚ; ES -ðə(r; |-ward -wɚd;
  ES -wəd; *For* thither, *now chiefly a book
  word,* 'θɪðɚ *is replacing older* 'ðɪðɚ, *but for*
  thence, *more often heard,* ðɛns *is still usual.*
tho' ðo
thole θol |tholed θold
Thomas 'tɑməs; ES+'tɒm-; |-'s -ɪz |-a -ə
  |-in, -ine -ɪn
Thomaston 'tɑməstən; ES+'tɒm-; |-town
  -ˌtaun |-ville -ˌvɪl; S+-vḷ
Thomism 'tomɪzəm, 'θom- |-ist -ɪst
Thompson 'tɑmpsn̩, -msn̩; ES+'tɒm-
Thomson 'tɑmpsn̩, -msn̩; ES+'tɒm-
thong θɑŋ, θɒŋ; S+θaŋ; |-ed -d
Thopas 'topəs |-'s -ɪz
Thor θɔr; ES θɔə(r
thoracic θo'ræsɪk |-al -ḷ
thorax 'θoræks |-es -ɪz |-races -rəˌsiz
Thoreau 'θoro, θə'ro, 'θɝˈo; ES+'θɔro, 'θʌro
thorium 'θorɪəm |-rite 'θoraɪt
thorn θɔrn; ES θɔən; |-ed -d
Thorold 'θorold
thoron 'θorɑn; ES+-ɒn
thorough 'θɝˈo, -ə; ES 'θɜr-, 'θʌr-, 'θɝˈ-;
  |-bred -ˌbrɛd, -'brɛd |-fare -ˌfɛr, -ˌfær; E
  -ˌfɛə(r, ES -ˌfæə(r; |-going -'go·ɪŋ
thorp, -pe, T- θɔrp; ES θɔəp
those ðoz
thou ðau
though ðo
thought θɔt |-ful -fəl |-fully -fəlɪ
thousand 'θauzn̩d, 'θauzn̩ |-th -θ |-ths -θs
  |-fold -'fold
Thrace θres |-'s -ɪz |-cian 'θreʃən
Thrale θrel
thrall θrɔl |thralled θrɔld |-dom -dəm
thrall-less 'θrɔllɪs

---

thrash θræʃ |thrashes 'θræʃɪz |-ed -t—Thrash *is not an error for* thresh, *but a historical variant in literary use since the 16c. It is the usual word in American agriculture.*

Thraso 'θreso

thrasonical θre'sɑnɪk|; ES+-'sɒn-; |-ly -|ɪ, -ɪklɪ

thrave θrev |thraved θrevd

thread θrɛd |threaded 'θrɛdɪd

threadbare 'θrɛd,bɛr, -,bær; E -,bɛə(r, ES -,bæə(r

Threadneedle 'θrɛd,nidḷ

threat θrɛt |threated 'θrɛtɪd

threaten 'θrɛtn̩ |-ed -d |-ing 'θrɛtnɪŋ, -tn̩ɪŋ

three θri

threefold 'θri'fold ('three,fold 'gain)

three-four 'θri'for, -'fɔr; ES -'foə(r, E+-'fɔə(r; ('three-,four 'time)

three-legged 'θri'lɛgɪd, -'lɛgd

threepence 'θrɪpəns, 'θrɛp- |-s -ɪz

threepenny 'θri,pɛnɪ, -pənɪ, 'θrɪpənɪ

three-ply 'θri'plaɪ ('three-,ply 'tire)

threescore 'θri'skor, -'skɔr; ES -'skoə(r, E+-'skɔə(r

threescore-and-ten 'θri,skorən'tɛn, -,skɔr-; S -,skor-

threesome 'θrisəm

threnody 'θrɛnədɪ

thresh θrɛʃ |threshes 'θrɛʃɪz |-ed -t—*see* thrash

threshold 'θrɛʃold, 'θrɛʃhold

threw θru, θrɪu

thrice θraɪs

thrift θrɪft |thrifted 'θrɪftɪd

thrifty 'θrɪftɪ -tily -t|ɪ, -tɪlɪ

thrill θrɪl |thrilled θrɪld

thrips θrɪps |-es -ɪz

thrive θraɪv |throve θrov *or* thrived θraɪvd |thrived θraɪvd *or* thriven 'θrɪvən

throat θrot |throated 'θrotɪd; |N Engd+θrɔt (§46)

throb θrɑb; ES+θrɒb; |-bed -d

Throckmorton 'θrɑkmortn̩, -mɔrtn̩; ES -mɔətn̩, -mɔətn̩, 'θrɒk-

throe θro |throed θrod

thrombosis θrɑm'bosɪs, θrɒm-

throne θron |throned θrond

throng θrɔŋ, θrɒŋ; S+θraŋ; |-ed -d

Throop trup, θrup

throstle 'θrɑsḷ; ES+'θrɒsḷ

throttle 'θrɑtḷ |-d -d |-ling -t|ɪŋ, -tlɪŋ

through θru, θrɪu |-out -'aut

throve θrov

throw θro |threw θru, θrɪu |thrown θron

throwback 'θro,bæk

thrum θrʌm |thrummed θrʌmd

thrush θrʌʃ |thrushes 'θrʌʃɪz

thrust θrʌst |arch. thrusted 'θrʌstɪd

Thucydides θju'sɪdə,diz, θɪu-, θu- |-'s -ɪz

thud θʌd |thudded 'θʌdɪd

thug θʌg |thugged θʌgd

Thule 'θjulɪ, 'θɪu-, 'θu-, -li

thulia 'θjulɪə, 'θɪu-, 'θu- |-ium -ɪəm

thumb θʌm |thumbed θʌmd

thumbnail 'θʌm'nel, -,nel ('thumb,nail 'sketch)

thumbscrew 'θʌm,skru, -,skrɪu |-ed -d

thumbtack 'θʌm,tæk |-ed -t

Thummim 'θʌmɪm

thump θʌmp |thumped θʌmpt

thunder 'θʌndɚ; ES 'θʌndə(r; |-ed -d |-ing 'θʌndrɪŋ, -dərɪŋ |-bolt -,bolt

thundercloud 'θʌndɚ,klaud; ES 'θʌndə-

thunderhead 'θʌndɚ,hɛd; ES 'θʌndə-

thunderous 'θʌndərəs, -drəs

thundershower 'θʌndɚ,ʃauɚ, -,ʃaur; ES 'θʌndə,ʃau-ə(r, -,ʃauə(r

thunderstone 'θʌndɚ,ston; ES 'θʌndə-

thunderstorm 'θʌndɚ,stɔrm; ES 'θʌndə-,stɔəm

thunderstruck 'θʌndɚ,strʌk; ES 'θʌndə-

thurible 'θjurəbḷ, 'θɪur-

Thuringia θju'rɪndʒɪə, θɪu-, θu- |-n -n

Thurio 'θjurɪ,o, 'θɪur-, 'θur-

Thursday 'θɝzdɪ; ES 'θɜz-, 'θɝz- —*see* Monday

Thurston 'θɝstn̩; ES 'θɜs-, 'θɝs-

thus ðʌs |thusly 'ðʌslɪ

thwack θwæk |thwacked θwækt

thwart θwɔrt; ES θwɔət; |-ed -ɪd

Thwing twɪŋ

thy ðaɪ

thyme taɪm |thymed taɪmd

thymol 'θaɪmol, -mɑl, -mɒl

thymus, T- 'θaɪməs |-es -ɪz

thyreoid 'θaɪrɪ,ɔɪd

Thyreus 'θaɪrɪəs |-'s -ɪz

thyroid 'θaɪrɔɪd

Key: *See in full §§3–47.* bee bi |pity 'pɪtɪ (§6) |rate ret |yet jɛt |sang sæŋ |angry 'æŋ·grɪ |bath bæθ; E baθ (§10) |ah ɑ |far fɑr |watch watʃ, wɒtʃ (§12) |jaw dʒɔ |gorge gɔrdʒ |go go

Thyrsis 'θɜˈsɪs; ES 'θɜs-, 'θɜˈs-; |-sis' -sɪs
thyrsus 'θɜˈsəs; ES 'θɜs-, 'θɜˈs-; |-si -saɪ
thyself ðaɪˈsɛlf
ti ti
-tia *ending, variously pronounced* -ʃə, -ʃɪə,
-ʃjə. *Besides the pron. given in the vocab.,
one or more of the variants are often heard.*
tiara taɪˈɛrə, -ˈɛrə, tɪˈɑrə
Tibbalds 'tɪb|dz, -b|z |-'s -ɪz
Tibbals 'tɪb|z |-'s -ɪz
Tiber 'taɪbɚ; ES 'taɪbə(r
Tiberias taɪˈbɪrɪəs |-ius -ɪəs |-'s -ɪz
Tibet tɪˈbɛt, 'tɪbɪt |-an -n̩
tibia 'tɪbɪə |-s -z |-biae -bɪˌi
Tibullus tɪˈbʌləs |-'s -ɪz
tic tɪk
tick tɪk |ticked tɪkt
Tickell 'tɪk|
ticket 'tɪkɪt |-ed -ɪd
tickle 'tɪk| |-d -d |-ling 'tɪklɪŋ, -k|ɪŋ
ticklish 'tɪklɪʃ, 'tɪk|ɪʃ
Ticknor 'tɪknɚ; ES 'tɪknə(r
ticktacktoe ˌtɪktækˈto, ˌtɪttætˈto |-too -ˈtu
ticktock 'tɪkˈtɑk, -ˌtɑk, tɪkˈtɑk; ES+-ɒk;
|-ed -t
Ticonderoga ˌtaɪkɑndəˈrogə, taɪˌkɑn-; ES+
-ɒn-
tidal 'taɪd| |-ly -ɪ
tidbit 'tɪdˌbɪt
tiddledywinks 'tɪd|dɪˌwɪŋks
tiddlywinks 'tɪd|ɪˌwɪŋks, 'tɪdlɪ-
tide taɪd |tided 'taɪdɪd |-dings -ɪŋz
tidewater 'taɪdˌwɔtɚ, -ˌwɑtɚ, -ˌwɒtɚ; ES
-tə(r
tidy 'taɪdɪ |tidied 'taɪdɪd
tie taɪ |tied taɪd
Tieck tik
Tientsin 'tjɛnˈtsɪn, 'tɪn-
tier *'who ties'* 'taɪɚ; ES 'taɪˈə(r
tier *'layer'* tɪr; ES tɪə(r, S+tɛə(r
tierce tɪrs; ES tɪəs; S+tɛəs
Tierra del Fuego tɪˈɛrəˌdɛlfuˈego, 'tjɛrə-,
-'fwego (*Sp* 'tjɛrra·ðɛlˈfwego)
tie-up 'taɪˌʌp
tiff tɪf |tiffed tɪft
Tiffany 'tɪfənɪ
tiffin, T- 'tɪfɪn |tiffined 'tɪfɪnd
Tiflis 'tɪflɪs |-'s -ɪz
tiger 'taɪgɚ; ES 'taɪgə(r; |-ed -d

tigerish 'taɪgərɪʃ, 'taɪgrɪʃ
Tigert 'taɪgɚt; ES 'taɪgət
Tighe taɪ
tight taɪt |-s -s
tighten 'taɪtn̩ |-ed -d |-ing 'taɪtn̩ɪŋ, -tnɪŋ
tightfisted 'taɪtˈfɪstɪd
tightrope 'taɪtˌrop |-roped -ˌropt
tightwad 'taɪtˌwɑd, -ˌwɒd
Tiglath-pileser 'tɪglæθpəˈlizɚ, -paɪ-; ES -zə(r
tiglon 'taɪglɑn, -ɒn, -ən
tigress 'taɪgrɪs |-'s -ɪz
Tigris 'taɪgrɪs |-'s -ɪz
tigrish 'taɪgrɪʃ
tike taɪk
Tilbury, t- 'tɪlˌbɛrɪ, -bərɪ
Tilda 'tɪldə
tilde 'tɪldə, -dɪ
Tilden 'tɪldɪn, -ən
tile taɪl |tiled taɪld
till *v* tɪl |tilled tɪld
till *conj, prep* tɪl, t|; *rarely stressed* 'tɪl, ˌtɪl
tiller 'tɪlɚ; ES 'tɪlə(r; |-ed -d
Tillotson 'tɪlətsn̩
Tilsit 'tɪlzɪt
tilt tɪlt |tilted 'tɪltɪd
tilth tɪlθ
Tilton 'tɪltn̩ |-ville -ˌvɪl
tiltyard 'tɪltˌjɑrd; ES -ˌjɑːd, E+-ˌjɑːd
Timandra tɪˈmændrə
timbal 'tɪmb|
timbale 'tɪmb| (*Fr* tæ̃ˈbal)
timber 'tɪmbɚ; ES 'tɪmbə(r; |-ed -d |-ing
'tɪmbərɪŋ, -brɪŋ
timbre 'tɪmbɚ, 'tæm-; ES -bə(r; (*Fr* tæ̃:mbr)
timbrel 'tɪmbrəl |-ed -d
Timbuctoo *poem* ˌtɪmbʌkˈtu, tɪmˈbʌktu
Timbuktu *town* tɪmˈbʌktu
time taɪm |timed taɪmd |-ly -lɪ
time-honored 'taɪmˈɑnəd; ES -ˈɑnəd, -ˈɒn-;
('taɪm-ˌhonored 'custom)
timekeeper 'taɪmˌkipɚ; ES -ˌkipə(r
timepiece 'taɪmˌpis |-s -ɪz
timeserving 'taɪmˌsɝvɪŋ; ES -ˌsɝv-, -ˌsɝˈv-
timetable 'taɪmˌteb|
timid 'tɪmɪd |-midity tɪˈmɪdətɪ, tə-
Timnite 'tɪmnaɪt
Timon 'taɪmən
timorous 'tɪmərəs, 'tɪmrəs
Timotheus tɪˈmoθɪəs, -θjəs |-'s -ɪz

|full fʊl |tooth tuθ |further 'fɝðɚ; ES 'fɝðə |custom 'kʌstəm |while hwaɪl |how haʊ |toy tɔɪ
|using 'juzɪŋ |fuse fjuz, fɪuz |dish dɪʃ |vision 'vɪʒən |Eden 'idn̩ |cradle 'kred| |keep 'em 'kipm̩

Timothy, t- 'tɪməθɪ
timpanist 'tɪmpənɪst
timpano 'tɪmpəˌno |pl -ni -ˌni (It 'timpaˌno)
Timpanogos ˌtɪmpə'nogəs |-'s -ɪz
tin tɪn |tinned tɪnd
tinct tɪŋkt |tincted 'tɪŋktɪd
tincture 'tɪŋktʃɚ; ES -tʃə(r; |-d -d
Tindal, -dale 'tɪndl̩
tinder 'tɪndɚ; ES 'tɪndə(r; |-ed -d
tinderbox 'tɪndɚˌbɑks; ES 'tɪndəˌbɑks,
  -ˌbɒks; |-es -ɪz
tine taɪn |tined taɪnd
tin-foil 'tɪnˌfɔɪl |-ed -d
ting tɪŋ |-ed -d
tinge tɪndʒ |tinges 'tɪndʒɪz |-d -d
tinged past of ting tɪŋd |of tinge tɪndʒd
tingle 'tɪŋgl̩ |-d -d |-ling 'tɪŋglɪŋ, -glɪŋ
tinhorn adj 'tɪnˌhɔrn; ES -ˌhɔən
tinker, T- 'tɪŋkɚ; ES 'tɪŋkə(r; |-ed -d |-ing
  'tɪŋkərɪŋ, -krɪŋ
tinkle 'tɪŋkl̩ |-d -d |-ling 'tɪŋklɪŋ, -kl̩ɪŋ
tinner 'tɪnɚ; ES 'tɪnə(r; |-y -ɪ
tinnitus tɪ'naɪtəs
tinny 'tɪnɪ
tinsel 'tɪnsl̩ |-ed -d
tinsmith 'tɪnˌsmɪθ |-ths -θs
tint tɪnt |tinted 'tɪntɪd
Tintagel tɪn'tædʒəl
Tintern 'tɪntɚn; ES 'tɪntən
tintinnabular ˌtɪntɪ'næbjələ; ES -lə(r; |-y
  -ˌlɛrɪ |-lous -ləs |-lum -ləm
tintinnabulation ˌtɪntɪˌnæbjə'leʃən
Tintoretto ˌtɪntə'rɛto (It ˌtinto'retto)
tintype 'tɪnˌtaɪp
tinware 'tɪnˌwɛr, -ˌwær; E -ˌwɛə(r, ES
  -ˌwæə(r
tinwork 'tɪnˌwɝk; ES -ˌwɜk, -ˌwɝk
tiny 'taɪnɪ
Tioga taɪ'ogə
-tion unstressed ending -ʃən, -ʃn̩—The pron.
  -ʃn̩ is less common in America than in
  England.
tip tɪp |tipped tɪpt
Tippecanoe ˌtɪpəkə'nu
Tipperary ˌtɪpə'rɛrɪ
tippet 'tɪpɪt |-ed -ɪd
tipple 'tɪpl̩ |-d -d |-ling 'tɪplɪŋ, -pl̩ɪŋ
tippler 'tɪplɚ, 'tɪpl̩ɚ; ES -ə(r
Tippoo Sahib tɪ'pu'saˑɪb, -'sahɪb

tipstaff 'tɪpˌstæf; E+-ˌstaf, -ˌstɑf; |-s -s
  |-staves -ˌstevz
tipster 'tɪpstɚ; ES 'tɪpstə(r
tipsy 'tɪpsɪ
tiptoe 'tɪpˌto |-d -d
Tipton 'tɪptən
tiptop 'tɪp'tɑp; ES+-'tɒp; ('tɪpˌtop 'day)
tirade 'taɪred, tə'red |-d -d
tire taɪr; ES taɪə(r; |-d -d |-some -səm
Tiresias tə'rɛsɪəs, taɪ-, -'rɪs-, -ʃɪəs |-'s -ɪz
tirewoman 'taɪrˌwʊmən; ES 'taɪə-
tiro 'taɪro
Tirol 'tɪrəl, -ɑl, -ɒl, tɪ'rol
Tirolean tɪ'rolɪən, ˌtɪrə'liən
Tirolese ˌtɪrə'liz
Tirzah 'tɝzə; ES 'tɜzə, 'tɝzə
'tis 'it is' 'tɪz, ˌtɪz (ˌjɛs'tɪz, 'jɛsˌtɪz)—when
  without stress, replaced in US by it's its
  (ɪts'kold).
Tisbury 'tɪzˌbɛrɪ, -bərɪ
Tischendorf 'tɪʃənˌdɔrf; ES -ˌdɔəf
Tisdall, -dale 'tɪzdl̩
Tishbite 'tɪʃbaɪt
tissue 'tɪʃu |-d -d
tissue-paper 'tɪʃuˌpepɚ, 'tɪʃə-; ES -pə(r
tit tɪt |titted 'tɪtɪd
Titan, t- 'taɪtn̩
Titania tɪ'tenɪə, taɪ- |-n -n
titanic, T- taɪ'tænɪk |-al -l̩ |-ally -l̩ɪ, -ɪklɪ
titanium taɪ'tenɪəm, tɪ-
titbit 'tɪtˌbɪt, 'tɪdˌbɪt
Titchener 'tɪtʃənɚ, 'tɪtʃnɚ; ES -nə(r
Titcomb 'tɪtkəm
tit for tat 'tɪtfɚ'tæt; ES -fə-
tithe taɪð |tithed taɪðd
Tithonus tɪ'θonəs |-'s -ɪz
Titian, t- 'tɪʃən, -ʃɪən
Titicaca ˌtɪtɪ'kɑkə (Sp ˌtiti'kɑkɑ)
titillate 'tɪtl̩ˌet |-ated -ˌetɪd
titillation ˌtɪtl̩'eʃən
Titinius tɪ'tɪnɪəs, taɪ- |-'s -ɪz
titivate 'tɪtəˌvet |-d -ɪd |-tion ˌtɪtə'veʃən
titlark 'tɪtˌlɑrk; ES -ˌlɑːk, E+-ˌlɑːk
title 'taɪtl̩ |-d -d |-ling 'taɪtl̩ɪŋ, -tl̩ɪŋ
titleless 'taɪtl̩ɪs
Titmarsh 'tɪtmɑrʃ; ES -mɑːʃ, E+-mɑːʃ; |-'s
  -ɪz
titmouse 'tɪtˌmaʊs |-'s -ɪz |-mice -ˌmaɪs
titter 'tɪtɚ; ES 'tɪtə(r; |-ed -d

tittivate ˈtɪtəˌvet |-d -ɪd |-tion ˌtɪtəˈveʃən

tittle ˈtɪtl̩

tittle-tattle ˈtɪtl̩ˌtætl̩ |-d -d

titular ˈtɪtʃələ˞, ˈtɪtjə-; ES -lə(r; |-y -ˌlɛrɪ

Titus ˈtaɪtəs |-'s -ɪz |-ville -ˌvɪl

Tiverton ˈtɪvɚtən; ES ˈtɪvə-

Tivoli, t- ˈtɪvəlɪ (It ˈtiːvoli)

tivy ˈtɪvɪ |tivied ˈtɪvɪd

'tˈll 'it will' tl̩

tmesis ˈtmisɪs, təˈmisɪs |tmeses -siz

TNT ˈtiˌɛnˈti

to stressed ˈtu, ˌtu; unstr: before conss. tə;
before vowels tʊ, tə; after -t often ə (ought to
go ˈɔtəˈgo)

toad tod; N Engd + tɔ̈d (§46)

toadflax ˈtodˌflæks |-es -ɪz

toadstone ˈtodˌston

toadstool ˈtodˌstul

toady ˈtodɪ |toadied ˈtodɪd

to-and-fro ˈtuənˈfro

toast tost |toasted ˈtostɪd

toastmaster ˈtostˌmæstɚ; ES -ˌmæstə(r,
E+-ˌmas-, -ˌmɑs-

tobacco təˈbæko, -ə |-nist təˈbækənɪst

Tobago təˈbego

Tobiah toˈbaɪə, tə- |-bias -ˈbaɪəs |-as's -sɪz

Tobit ˈtobɪt

toboggan təˈbɑgən, -ˈbɒg-

Tobolsk təˈbalsk, -ˈbɒlsk

Tobruk toˈbruk, ˈtoˌbruk (ˈToˌbruk ˈHarbor)

Toby ˈtobɪ

toccata təˈkɑtə (It tokˈkɑːtɑ)

tocome təˈkʌm

Tocqueville ˈtakvɪl; ES+ˈtɒk-; (Fr tɔ̈kˈvil)

tocsin ˈtaksɪn; ES+ˈtɒk-

today, to-day təˈde

Todd tad; ES+tɒd

toddle ˈtadl̩; ES+ˈtɒdl̩; |-d -d |-ling -dlɪŋ,
-dl̩ɪŋ

toddy ˈtadɪ; ES+ˈtɒdɪ; |-ied -d

to-do təˈdu

toe to |toed tod |-nail n ˈtoˈnel, ˈtoˌnel

toenail v ˈtoˌnel |-nailed -ˌneld

toff tɔf, tɒf

toffee, -ffy ˈtɔfɪ, ˈtɒfɪ, ˈtɑfɪ

toft, T- tɔft, tɒft

tog tag, tɒg |-s -z |-ged -d |-gery -ərɪ, -rɪ

toga ˈtogə |-ed -d

together təˈgɛðɚ; ES -ˈgɛðə(r

toggle ˈtagl̩, ˈtɒgl̩ |-d -d |-ling -glɪŋ, -gl̩ɪŋ

Togo ˈtogo |-land -ˌlænd

toil tɔɪl |-ed -d |-some -səm |-less ˈtɔɪllɪs

toilet ˈtɔɪlɪt |-ed -ɪd |-ry -rɪ

toilette tɔɪˈlɛt, twaˈlɛt (Fr twaˈlɛt)

toilworn ˈtɔɪlˌworn, -ˌwɔrn; ES -ˌwoən, E+
-ˌwɔən

Tokay toˈke

token ˈtokən |-ed -d |-ing ˈtokənɪŋ, -knɪŋ

Tokyo, -kio ˈtokɪˌo, -kjo

Toland ˈtolənd

tolbooth, toll- ˈtolˌbuθ, ˈtal-, ˈtɒl-, -ˌbuð

told told

tole tol |toled told

Toledo təˈlido, tlˈido, -də (Sp toˈleðo)

tolerable ˈtalərəbl̩, ˈtalrə-; ES+ˈtɒl-; |-bly
-blɪ

tolerance ˈtalərəns, -lrəns; ES+ˈtɒl-; |-cy -ɪ
|-nt -nt

tolerate ˈtaləˌret; ES+ˈtɒl-; |-d -ɪd

toleration ˌtaləˈreʃən; ES+ˌtɒl-

toll tol |tolled told |-gate -ˌget

Tolland ˈtalənd; ES+ˈtɒlənd

tollgatherer ˈtolˌgæðərə˞; ES -ˌgæðərə(r

Tolstoy ˈtalstɔɪ, ˈtɒl-

Toluca təˈlukə

toluene ˈtaljuˌin; ES+ˈtɒl-

Tom tam, tɒm

tomahawk ˈtaməˌhɔk, ˈtamɪ-; ES+ˈtɒm-;
|-ed -t

tomato təˈmeto, -ə, much less freq. -ˈmat-,
-ˈmat-, -ˈmæt-

tomb tum |tombed tumd |-stone -ˌston

Tombigbee tamˈbɪgbɪ; ES+tɒm-

tomboy ˈtamˌbɔɪ, ˈtɒm-

tomcat ˈtamˌkæt, ˈtɒm-

Tom, Dick, and Harry ˈtamˌdɪkn̩ˈhærɪ,
ˈtɒm-, -ˌdɪkŋ-

tome tom

tomfool ˈtamˈful, ˈtɒm- |-ed -d (ˈtomˌfool
ˈjoke)

tomfoolery ˌtamˈfulərɪ, ˌtɒm-, -ˈfulrɪ

Tomlinson ˈtamlɪnsn̩, ˈtɒm-

Tommy ˈtamɪ, ˈtɒmɪ

tomorrow, to-m- təˈmɔro, -ˈmar-, -ˈmɒr-, -ə

Tompkins, Tomk- ˈtampkɪnz, ˈtɒmp- |-'s -ɪz

tomtit ˈtamˌtɪt, ˈtɒm-

tom-tom ˈtamˌtam; ES+ˈtɒmˌtɒm; |-ed -d

ton tʌn

|full fʊl |tooth tuθ |further ˈfɝðɚ; ES ˈfɝðə |custom ˈkʌstəm |while hwaɪl |how haʊ |toy tɔɪ
|using ˈjuzɪŋ |fuse fjuz, fruz |dish dɪʃ |vision ˈvɪʒən |Eden ˈidn̩ |cradle ˈkredl̩ |keep 'em ˈkipm̩

Those words below in which the **ɑ** *sound is spelt* o *are often pronounced with* ɒ *in E and S*

ton *Fr* tõ

tonal 'tonḷ |-ly -ɪ |-ity to'nælətɪ

Tonawanda ˌtɑnə'wɑndə, -'wɒn-

Tonbridge 'tʌnbrɪdʒ |-'s -ɪz

tone, t'one (*better* 'tone) *'the one'* tʌn—*see* tother

tone *v* ton |toned tond

toneme 'tonim |-mic to'nimɪk

tong tɔŋ, tɒŋ; S+tɑŋ; |-s -z

Tongaland 'tɑŋgəˌlænd, 'tɒŋ-

tongue tʌŋ |tongued tʌŋd |-guey, -guy -ɪ

tongue-tie 'tʌŋˌtaɪ |-tied -ˌtaɪd

tonic 'tɑnɪk |-ally -ḷɪ, -ɪklɪ

tonicity to'nɪsətɪ

tonight, to-night tə'naɪt

tonite 'tonaɪt

tonnage 'tʌnɪdʒ |-s -ɪz |-d -d

tonneau tə'no, tʌ- |-s, -x -z |-ed -d

tonsil 'tɑnsḷ, -sɪl |-lar, -ar -ɚ; ES -ə(r

tonsillectomy ˌtɑnsḷ'ɛktəmɪ

tonsillitis ˌtɑnsḷ'aɪtɪs

tonsillotomy ˌtɑnsḷ'ɑtəmɪ

tonsorial tɑn'soriəl, -'sɔr-; S -'sor-

Tonstall 'tʌnstḷ

tonsure 'tɑnʃɚ; ES 'tɑnʃə(r |-d -d

tontine 'tɑntin, tɑn'tin

tony, T- 'tonɪ

too tu

Tooele tu'ɛlə

took tʊk

Tooke tʊk

tool tul |tooled tuld

Toombs tumz |-'s -ɪz

toot tut |tooted 'tutɪd

tooth *n* tuθ |teeth tiθ |*adj* toothed -θt, -ðd

tooth *v* tuθ, tuð |-ed -θt, -ðd

toothache 'tuθˌek

toothbrush 'tuθˌbrʌʃ |-es -ɪz

toothpick 'tuθˌpɪk

toothsome 'tuθsəm |toothy 'tuθɪ

tootle 'tutḷ |-d -d |-ling 'tutḷɪŋ, -tlɪŋ

top tɑp |topped tɑpt

topaz 'topæz |-es -ɪz

topcoat 'tɑpˌkot |-ed -ɪd

tope top |toped topt |-r 'topɚ; ES 'topə(r

Topeka tə'pikə

topgallant ˌtɑp'gælənt, *naut.* tə'gælənt

top-heavy 'tɑpˌhɛvɪ

Tophet, -th 'tofɪt, -ɛt

topic 'tɑpɪk |-al -ḷ |-ally -ḷɪ, -ɪklɪ

topknot 'tɑpˌnɑt |-ted -ɪd

Toplady 'tɑpˌledɪ

toplofty 'tɑp'lɔftɪ, -'lɒf- ('topˌlofty 'air)

topmast 'tɑpˌmæst, *naut.* -məst; E+-ˌmast, -ˌmɑst

topmost 'tɑpˌmost, -məst

top-notch 'tɑp'nɑtʃ ('top-ˌnotch 'story)

topographer to'pɑgrəfɚ, tə-, -'pɒg-; ES -fə(r; |-phy -fɪ

topographic ˌtɑpə'græfɪk |-al -ḷ |-ally -ḷɪ, -ɪklɪ

topple 'tɑpḷ |-d -d |-ling 'tɑpḷɪŋ, -plɪŋ

topsail 'tɑpˌsel, *naut.* 'tɑpsḷ

Topsham 'tɑpsəm

topside 'tɑp'saɪd ('topˌside 'cut)

topsoil 'tɑpˌsɔɪl |-ed -d

Topsy 'tɑpsɪ

topsy-turvy 'tɑpsɪ'tɝvɪ; ES -'tɜvɪ, -'tɝvɪ; |-ied -d

toque tok

torah, -ra, T- 'torə, 'tɔrə; S 'torə; |-s -z |-roth -roθ

torch tɔrtʃ; ES tɔətʃ; |-es -ɪz |-ed -t

torchon 'tɔrʃɑn; ES 'tɔəʃɑn; (*Fr* tɔr'ʃõ)

tore tor, tɔr; ES toə(r, E+tɔə(r

toreador 'tɔrɪəˌdɔr, 'tɒr-; ES -ˌdɔə(r; (*Sp* ˌtorea'ðɔr)

toric 'tɔrɪk, 'tar-, 'tɒr-

torment *n* 'tɔrmɛnt; ES 'tɔə-

torment *v* tɔr'mɛnt; ES tɔə-; |-ed -ɪd

torn tɔrn, tɒrn; ES tɔən, E+tɒən

tornado tɔr'nedo; ES tɔə-

Toronto tə'rɑnto

torpedo tɔr'pido; ES tɔə-; |-ed -d |-ing -'pidəwɪŋ

torpid 'tɔrpɪd; ES 'tɔəpɪd

torpidity tɔr'pɪdətɪ; ES tə'pɪdətɪ

torpor 'tɔrpɚ; ES 'tɔəpə(r

Torquay tɔr'ki; ES tɔə'ki

torque tɔrk; ES tɔək; |-d -t

Torquemada ˌtɔrkɪ'mɑdə; ES ˌtɔək-; (*Sp* ˌtɔrke'maða)

Torrence, Torrens 'tɔrəns, 'tar-, 'tɒr- |-'s -ɪz

torrent 'tɔrənt, 'tar-, 'tɒr-

torrential tɔ'rɛnʃəl, tɑ-, tɒ- |-ly -ɪ

Torres Strait 'tɔrɪz'stret, 'tar-, 'tɒr-, -ɪs's-

Key: *See in full §§3–47.* bee bi |pity 'pɪtɪ (§6) |rate ret |yet jɛt |sang sæŋ |angry 'æŋ·grɪ |bath bæθ; E bɑθ (§10) |ah ɑ |far fɑr |watch wɑtʃ, wɒtʃ (§12) |jaw dʒɔ |gorge gɔrdʒ |go go

Torrey 'tɔrɪ, 'tɑrɪ, 'tɒrɪ
Torricelli ˌtɔrɪ'tʃɛlɪ, ˌtɒr- (*It* ˌtorri'tʃɛlli)
torrid 'tɔrɪd, 'tɑr-, 'tɒr-
torridity tɔ'rɪdətɪ, tɑ-, tɒ-
Torrington 'tɔrɪŋtən, 'tɑr-, 'tɒr-
torsion 'tɔrʃən; ES 'tɔəʃən; |-al -] |-ally -lɪ
torso 'tɔrso; ES 'tɔəso
tort tɔrt; ES tɔət
tortilla *Am Sp* tɔr'tija
tortious 'tɔrʃəs; ES 'tɔəʃəs
tortoise 'tɔrtəs, -tɪs; ES 'tɔət-; |-s -ɪz
tortoise-shell 'tɔrtəsˌʃɛl, -tɪs-, -ʃˌʃɛl
Tortuga tɔr'tugə; ES tɔə-
tortuosity ˌtɔrtʃu'asətɪ; ES ˌtɔətʃu-, -'ɒs-
tortuous 'tɔrtʃuəs; ES 'tɔətʃuəs
torture 'tɔrtʃɚ; ES 'tɔətʃə(r; |-d -d |-rous -əs
torus 'tɔrəs, 'tɔr-; S 'tor-; |-es -ɪz |-ri -raɪ
Tory 'tɔrɪ, 'tɔrɪ; S 'torɪ
Toscanini ˌtaskə'ninɪ, ˌtɒs-, ˌtʌs- (*It* ˌtoska-'ni:ni)
tosh taʃ; ES+tɒʃ; |-es -ɪz |-ed -t
toss tɔs, tɒs |-es -ɪz |-ed -t |-up -ˌʌp
tossel 'tas], 'tɒsḷ |-ed -d |-ing -sḷɪŋ, -slɪŋ
Tosti 'tɔstɪ, 'tɒs-, 'tas- (*It* 'tɒsti)
tot tat; ES+tɒt; |-ted -ɪd
total 'tot] |-ed -d |-ly -ɪ |-ity to'tælətɪ
totalitarian ˌtotælə'tɛrɪən, toˌtælə-, -'ter-, *less freq.* ˌtotḷə't-
totalization ˌtotḷə'zeʃən, -aɪ'z-
totalizator 'totḷəˌzetɚ; ES -ˌzetə(r
totalize 'totḷˌaɪz |-s -ɪz |-d -d
tote tot |toted 'totɪd
totem 'totəm
tother, t'other (*better* 'tother) 'tʌðɚ; ES -ðə(r
— *In this and in* tone, '*the one,' initial* t *was final* t *of the old definite article* that, *not the initial of modern* the.
Tottel 'tat]; ES+'tɒt]
Totten 'tatṇ; ES+'tɒtṇ
Tottenham 'tatnəm, 'tatṇəm; ES+'tɒt-
totter 'tatɚ; ES 'tatə(r, 'tɒt-
toucan 'tukæn, tu'kan
touch tʌtʃ |touches 'tʌtʃɪz |-ed -t |-down -ˌdaun
touch-and-go 'tʌtʃən'go
touchstone, T- 'tʌtʃˌston, 'tʌtʃˌʃton
tough tʌf |toughed tʌft
toughen 'tʌfṇ |-ed -d |-ing 'tʌfnɪŋ, -fṇɪŋ
Toulon tu'lan, -'lɒn (*Fr* tu'lõ)

Toulouse tu'luz |-'s -ɪz (*Fr* tu'lu:z)
toupee tu'pe, tu'pi (*Fr* toupét tu'pɛ)
tour tur; ES tuə(r; |-ed -d |-ist -ɪst
Touraine tu'ren (*Fr* tu'rɛn)
tour de force ˌturdə'fɔrs, -'fɔrs; ES -'fɔəs, E+'fɔəs; (*Fr* turdə'fɔrs)
tournament 'tɝnəmənt, 'tur-; ES 'tɜn-, 'tɝn-'tuən-
Tourneur 'tɝnɚ; ES 'tɜnə(r, 'tɝnə(r
tourney 'tɝnɪ, 'turnɪ; ES 'tɜnɪ, 'tɝnɪ, 'tuənɪ
tourniquet 'turnɪˌkɛt, -ˌke, 'tɝn-; ES 'tuən-, 'tɜn-, 'tɝn-
Tours tur; ES tuə(r; (*Fr* tu:r)
tousle 'tauz] |-d -d |-ling 'tauzlɪŋ, -zḷɪŋ
Toussaint L'Ouverture *Fr* tusæ̃·luver'ty:r
tout taut |touted 'tautɪd
tow to |towed tod |-age -ɪdʒ
Towanda to'wandə, -'wɒn-
toward *adj* tord, tɔrd; ES toəd, E+tɔəd
toward *prep* tord, tɔrd, tə'word; ES toəd, tə'wɔəd, E+tɔəd; |-s -z
towboat 'toˌbot
Towcester 'tostɚ, *loc.*+'taustɚ; ES -tə(r
towel taul, 'tauəl |-ed -d
tower '*who tows*' 'toɚ; ES 'to·ə(r
tower *building* 'tauɚ, taur; ES 'tau·ə(r, tauə(r; |-ed -d |-ing 'taurɪŋ, 'tauərɪŋ
towhead 'toˌhɛd
towhee 'tauhi, 'tohi
towline 'toˌlaɪn
town taun |-ed -d |-ship -ʃɪp
town hall 'taun'hɔl |townhouse 'taunˌhaus
Townsend, -shend 'taunzṇd
townsfolk 'taunzˌfok
townspeople 'taunzˌpipḷ
towpath 'toˌpæθ; E+-ˌpaθ, -ˌpɑθ; |-ths -ðz
towrope 'toˌrop
toxemia, -aemia taks'imɪə; ES+tɒks-; |-ic -ɪk
toxic 'taksɪk; ES+'tɒks-; |-al -] |-ally -lɪ, -ɪklɪ
toxicity taks'ɪsətɪ; ES+tɒks-
toxicology ˌtaksɪ'kalədʒɪ; ES+ˌtɒksɪ'kɒl-
toxin 'taksɪn; ES+'tɒks-; |-ine -ɪn, -in
toy tɔɪ |toyed tɔɪd
Toynbee 'tɔɪnbɪ
trace tres |traces 'tresɪz |-ed -t |-ry -ərɪ, -rɪ
traceable 'tresəb] |-bly -blɪ
trachea 'trekɪə, trə'kiə |-s -z |-cheae -'ki·i

|full fʊl |tooth tuθ |further 'fɝðɚ; ES 'fɝðə |custom 'kʌstəm |while hwaɪl |how hau |toy tɔɪ
|using 'juzɪŋ |fuse fjuz, fɪuz |dish dɪʃ |vision 'vɪʒən |Eden 'idṇ |cradle 'kredḷ |keep 'em 'kipm̩

trachoma trə'komə, tre-

track træk |tracked trækt |-age -ɪdʒ

tract trækt

tractability ˌtræktə'bɪlətɪ

tractable 'træktəb! |-bly -blɪ

tractarian træk'tɛrɪən, -'ter- |-ism -ˌɪzəm

tractate 'træktet

tractile 'træktl̩, -tɪl

traction 'trækʃən |-tive -tɪv

tractor 'træktɚ; ES 'træktə(r

Tracy 'tresɪ

trade tred |traded 'tredɪd |-sman -zmən |-smen -zmən

trade-mark 'tredˌmɑrk; ES -ˌmɑːk, E+ -ˌmɑːk; |-ed -t

trade-union 'tred'junjən |-ism -ˌɪzəm

tradition trə'dɪʃən |-al -l̩ |-ally -l̩ɪ

traduce trə'djus, -'dɪus, -'dus |-s -ɪz |-d -t

Trafalgar Spain, London trə'fælgɚ; ES -'fælgə(r; (Sp trafal'gar)

traffic 'træfɪk |-ked -t

Trafford 'træfɚd; ES 'træfəd

tragacanth 'trægəˌkænθ |-ths -θs

tragedian trə'dʒidɪən

tragedienne trəˌdʒidɪ'ɛn (Fr traʒe'djɛn)

tragedy 'trædʒədɪ

tragic 'trædʒɪk |-al -l̩ |-ally -l̩ɪ, -ɪklɪ

tragicomedy ˌtrædʒɪ'kɑmədɪ; ES+-'kɒm-

trail, T-, Traill trel |trailed treld

train tren |-ed -d |-band -ˌbænd

trainman 'trenmən |-men -mən, -ˌmɛn

trait tret

traitor 'tretɚ; ES 'tretə(r; |-ess -ɪs, -trɪs |-ous -əs, -trəs

traitress 'tretrɪs |-es -ɪz

Trajan 'tredʒən

traject n 'trædʒɛkt

traject v trə'dʒɛkt |-ed -ɪd |-ction -kʃən

trajectory trə'dʒɛktərɪ, -trɪ

tram træm |trammed træmd

trammel 'træml̩ |-ed -d

tramp træmp |tramped træmpt

trample 'træmpl̩ |-d -d |-ling -plɪŋ, -pl̩ɪŋ

trance træns; E+trans, trans; |-s -ɪz |-d -t

Tranio 'trenɪˌo, 'trɑn-, -njo

tranquil 'træŋkwɪl, 'træŋ- |-ly -ɪ, -kwəlɪ

tranquillity træn'kwɪlətɪ, træŋ-

transact træns'ækt, trænz- |-ed -ɪd |-ion -kʃən

transalpine træns'ælpɪn, trænz-, -paɪn

transatlantic ˌtrænsət'læntɪk, ˌtrænz- |-ally -l̩ɪ, -ɪklɪ

transcend træn'sɛnd |-ed -ɪd

transcendence træn'sɛndəns |-cy -ɪ |-ent -ənt

transcendental ˌtrænsɛn'dɛntl̩ |-ly -ɪ |-ism -ˌɪzəm |-ist -ɪst

transcontinental ˌtrænskɑntə'nɛntl̩; ES+ -kɒn-

transcribe træn'skraɪb |-scribed -'skraɪbd

transcript 'trænˌskrɪpt |-ption træn'skrɪpʃən

transept 'trænsɛpt |-al træn'sɛptl̩

transfer n 'trænsfɝ; ES -fɝ, -fɝ

transfer v træns'fɝ; ES -'fɝ(r, -'fɝ; |-red -d

transferability ˌtrænsfɝə'bɪlətɪ; ES+-fɝə-; acct+trans,fera'bility

transferable træns'fɝəb!; ES+-'fɝə-; |-bly -blɪ

transference træns'fɝəns; ES+-'fɝəns

transfiguration ˌtrænsfɪgjə'reʃən, trænsˌfɪgjə-

transfigure træns'fɪgjɚ; ES -'fɪgjə(r; |-d -d

transfix træns'fɪks |-es -ɪz |-ed -t |-ion -kʃən

transform træns'fɔrm; ES -'fɔəm; |-ed -d

transformation ˌtrænsfɚ'meʃən; ES -fə- 'meʃən

transfuse træns'fjuz, -'fɪuz |-s -ɪz |-d -d

transfusion træns'fjuʒən, -'fɪu-

transgress træns'grɛs, trænz- |-es -ɪz |-ed -t

transgression træns'grɛʃən, trænz-

transience 'trænʃəns |-cy -ɪ |-ent -ənt

transigent 'trænsədʒənt

transit 'trænsɪt, -zɪt

transition træn'zɪʃən, træns'ɪʃən

transitive 'trænsətɪv

transitory 'trænsəˌtorɪ, 'trænzə-, -ˌtɔrɪ; S -ˌtɔrɪ

Trans-Jordan træns'dʒɔrdn̩, trænz-; ES -'dʒɔədn̩

Transjordania ˌtrænsdʒɔr'denɪə, ˌtrænz-, -njə; ES -dʒɔ'den-; |-n -n

translate træns'let, trænz- |-d -ɪd |-tion -'leʃən

transliterate træns'lɪtəˌret, trænz- |-d -ɪd

transliteration ˌtrænslɪtə'reʃən, ˌtrænz-

translucence træns'lusn̩s, trænz-, -'lɪu- |-cy -ɪ |-cent -sn̩t

transmigrate træns'maɪgret, trænz- |-d -ɪd

transmigration ˌtrænsmaɪ'greʃən, ˌtrænz-

transmissible træns'mɪsəb!, trænz-

transmission træns'mɪʃən, trænz-
Trans-Mississippi ˌtrænsmɪsə'sɪpɪ, ˌtrænz-
transmit træns'mɪt, trænz- |-ted -ɪd |-tal -l̩
transmutation ˌtrænsmju'teʃən, ˌtrænz-,
-mɪu-
transmute træns'mjut, trænz-, -'mɪut |-d -ɪd
transoceanic ˌtrænsoʃɪ'ænɪk, ˌtrænz-
transom 'trænsəm |-ed -d
transpacific ˌtrænspə'sɪfɪk
transparence træns'pɛrəns, -'pær-; S -'pær-;
|-cy -ɪ |-rent -rənt
transpire træn'spaɪr; ES -'spaɪə(r; |-d -d
transplant træns'plænt; E+-'plant, -'plɑnt;
|-ed -ɪd
transport n 'trænsport, -pɔrt; ES -poət,
E+-pɔət
transport v træns'port, -'pɔrt; ES -'poət,
E+-'pɔət; |-ed -ɪd
transportation ˌtrænspɚ'teʃən; ES -pə-
transposal træns'pozl̩
transpose træns'poz |-s -ɪz |-d -d ('trans-
ˌposed 'accent)
transposition ˌtrænspə'zɪʃən
transship træns'ʃɪp, trænʃ'ʃɪp |-ped -t
Trans-Siberian ˌtrænssaɪ'bɪrɪən, ˌtrænsaɪ-
transubstantiate ˌtrænsəb'stænʃɪˌet |-d -ɪd
transubstantiation ˌtrænsəbˌstænʃɪ'eʃən
Transvaal træns'vɑl, trænz-
transversal træns'vɝsl̩, trænz-; ES -'vɝsl̩,
-'vɝs]; |-ly -ɪ
transverse træns'vɝs, trænz-; ES -'vɝs,
-'vɝs; ('transˌverse 'section)
Transylvania ˌtrænsl̩'venjə, -nɪə |-n -n
trap træp |trapped træpt
trapeze træ'piz, trə- |-s -ɪz
trapezium trə'pizɪəm |-s -z |-zia -zɪə
trapezoid 'træpəˌzɔɪd |-al ˌtræpə'zɔɪdl̩
Trappist, t- 'træpɪst
traprock 'træpˌrɑk; ES+-ˌrɒk
trapshooting 'træpˌʃutɪŋ
trash træʃ |trashes 'træʃɪz |-ed -t |-y -ɪ
trauma 'trɔmə, 'traʊmə |-s -z |-mata -mətə
traumatic trɔ'mætɪk |-ally -l̩ɪ, -ɪklɪ
traumatism 'trɔməˌtɪzəm
travail 'trævel, -vl̩ |-ed -d
travail 'trave' trə'vel (Fr tra'va:j)
travel 'trævl̩ |-ed -d |-ing 'trævlɪŋ, -vl̩ɪŋ
traveler, -ller 'trævlɚ, 'trævlɚ; ES -ə(r
travelogue, -log 'trævl̩ˌɔg, -ˌɑg, -ˌɒg

Travers 'trævɚz; ES 'trævəz; |-'s -ɪz
traverse 'trævɚs, 'trævɝs; ES -vəs, -vɝs,
-vɝs; |-s -ɪz |-d -t—acct+tra'verse
Traverse 'trævɚs; ES 'trævəs; |-'s -ɪz
travertin 'trævɚtɪn; ES 'trævə-; |-tine -tɪn,
-ˌtin
travesty 'trævɪstɪ, -vəstɪ |-tied -d
Travis 'trævɪs |-'s -ɪz
trawl trɔl |trawled trɔld
tray tre |trayed tred
treacherous 'trɛtʃərəs, 'trɛtʃrəs |-ry -rɪ
treacle 'trikl̩ |-d -d |-ling 'triklɪŋ, -klɪŋ
tread trɛd |trod trɑd; ES+trɒd; |trodden
'trɑdn̩ or trod trɑd; ES+-ɒ-
treaded adj 'trɛdɪd
treadle 'trɛdl̩ |-d -d |-ling 'trɛdlɪŋ, -dl̩ɪŋ
treadmill 'trɛdˌmɪl |-ed -d
treason 'trizn̩ |-ed -d |-ing -zn̩ɪŋ, -znɪŋ
treasonable 'triznəbl̩, 'triznə- |-bly -blɪ
treasonous 'triznəs, 'triznəs
treasure 'trɛʒɚ; ES -ʒə(r; |-d -d |-ring
'trɛʒərɪŋ, -ʒrɪŋ |-ry -ʒərɪ, -ʒrɪ
treasurer 'trɛʒrɚ, -ʒərɚ; ES -rə(r
treasure-trove 'trɛʒɚ'trov; ES 'trɛʒə-
treat, T- trit |treated 'tritɪd
treatise 'tritɪs |-s -ɪz |treaty 'tritɪ
Trebizond 'trɛbɪˌzɑnd; ES+-ˌzɒnd
treble 'trɛbl̩ |-d -d |-bly -blɪ
Trebonius trɪ'bonɪəs, -njəs |-'s -ɪz
tree tri |treed trid
treeman 'triˌmæn |-men -ˌmɛn
treenail, tren- 'triˌnel, 'trɛnl̩, 'trʌnl̩
tree-run 'tri'rʌn ('treeˌrun 'apples)
tree-toad 'triˌtod
trefoil 'trifɔɪl
Treitschke 'traɪtʃkə
trek trɛk |trekked trɛkt
Trelawny trɪ'lɔnɪ
trellis 'trɛlɪs |-es -ɪz |-ed -t
tremble 'trɛmbl̩ |-d -d |-ling -blɪŋ, -bl̩ɪŋ
trembly 'trɛmblɪ
tremendous trɪ'mɛndəs—trɪ'mɛndʒʊəs, -dʒəs
is an old variant frequently heard, spelt
tremenduous in 1632, 1742 (Young's Night
Thoughts), 1796.
tremolo 'trɛml̩ˌo, 'trɛməˌlo |-ed -d
Tremont US places trɪ'mɑnt, in Me loc.
'trɪmɒnt; ES+-'mɒnt; Boston street 'trɛ-
mənt, 'trɛmɑnt, 'trɪmɑnt; ES+-mɒnt

|full fʊl |tooth tuθ |further 'fɝðɚ; ES 'fɝðə |custom 'kʌstəm |while hwaɪl |how haʊ |toy tɔɪ
|using 'juzɪŋ |fuse fjuz, fɪuz |dish dɪʃ |vision 'vɪʒən |Eden 'idn̩ |cradle 'kredl̩ |keep 'em 'kipm̩

tremor 'trɛmɚ, 'trimɚ; ES -mə(r
tremulous 'trɛmjələs
trenail 'tri͵nel, 'trɛn͟l, 'trʌn͟l
trench trɛntʃ |trenches 'trɛntʃɪz |-ed -t
trenchancy 'trɛntʃənsɪ |-chant -tʃənt
trencherman 'trɛntʃɚmən; ES -tʃə-; |-men -mən
trend trɛnd |trended 'trɛndɪd
Trent trɛnt
Trenton 'trɛntən
trepan trɪ'pæn |-panned -'pænd
trephine trɪ'faɪn, -'fin |-d -d
trepid 'trɛpɪd |-ity trə'pɪdətɪ
trepidation ͵trɛpə'deʃən
trespass 'trɛspəs, -͵pæs; E+-͵pas, -͵pɑs; |-es -ɪz |-ed -t
tress trɛs |tresses 'trɛsɪz |tressed trɛst
Tressel 'trɛs͟l
trestle 'trɛs͟l |-d -d |-ling -slɪŋ, -s͟lɪŋ
Trevelyan trɪ'vɛljən, -'vɪl-
Treves trivz |-'s -ɪz (Fr trɛːv, Ger Trier triːr)
Trevisa trə'visə
trews truz, trɪuz |-man -mən |-men -mən
trey tre |trey-ace 'tre'es
triable 'traɪəb͟l
triad 'traɪæd, -əd
trial 'traɪəl, traɪl
triangle 'traɪ͵æŋg͟l |-d -d |-ling -glɪŋ, -g͟lɪŋ
triangular traɪ'æŋgjəlɚ; ES -'æŋgjələ(r
triangularity ͵traɪæŋgjə'lærətɪ, traɪ͵æŋ-
triangulate adj traɪ'æŋgjəlɪt, -͵let
triangulate v traɪ'æŋgjə͵let |-lated -͵letɪd
triangulation ͵traɪæŋgjə'leʃən, traɪ͵æŋ-
Trias 'traɪəs |-sic traɪ'æsɪk
tribal 'traɪb͟l |-ly -ɪ
tribase 'traɪ͵bes |-sic traɪ'besɪk
tribe traɪb |-sman -zmən |-smen -zmən
tribrach 'traɪbræk, 'trɪb-
tribulation ͵trɪbjə'leʃən
tribunal trɪ'bjun͟l, traɪ-, -'bɪun-
tribunate 'trɪbjənɪt, -͵net
tribune 'trɪbjun, newspapers often trɪ'bjun, -'bɪun
tributary 'trɪbjə͵tɛrɪ
tribute 'trɪbjut |-buted -bjutɪd
trice traɪs |trices 'traɪsɪz |triced traɪst
tricentennial ͵traɪsɛn'tɛnɪəl, -njəl
triceps 'traɪsɛps |-es -ɪz |-cipites traɪ'sɪpə͵tiz
trichina trɪ'kaɪnə |-nae -ni |-nous 'trɪkənəs

Trichinopoly, -li ͵trɪtʃɪ'napəlɪ; ES+-'nɒp-
trichinosis ͵trɪkə'nosɪs
trick trɪk |tricked trɪkt |-ery -ərɪ, -rɪ
trickle 'trɪk͟l |-d -d |-ling -klɪŋ, -k͟lɪŋ
trickster 'trɪkstɚ; ES -stə(r; |-cksy -ksɪ |-cky -kɪ
tricolor 'traɪ͵kʌlɚ; ES -͵kʌlə(r; |-ed -d
tricot 'triko (Fr tri'ko)
tricotine ͵trɪkə'tin (Fr trikɔ'tin)
tricuspid traɪ'kʌspɪd
tricycle 'traɪsɪk͟l |-d -d |-ling -klɪŋ, -k͟lɪŋ
trident 'traɪdṇt
tridental traɪ'dɛnt͟l |-tate -tet
tried traɪd
triennial traɪ'ɛnɪəl |-ly -ɪ
trier 'traɪɚ; ES 'traɪ·ə(r
Trier trɪr; ES trɪə(r; (Ger triːr)
tries traɪz
Trieste trɪ'ɛst (It tri'ɛste)
trifle 'traɪf͟l |-d -d |-ling 'traɪflɪŋ, -f͟lɪŋ
trifling adj 'traɪflɪŋ |-fler -flɚ; ES -flə(r
trifoliate traɪ'folɪɪt, -lɪ͵et
triforium traɪ'forɪəm, -'fɔr-; S -'for-; |-s -z |-ria -ɪə
trig trɪg |trigged trɪgd
trigger 'trɪgɚ; ES 'trɪgə(r; |-ed -d
triglyph 'traɪglɪf |-ed -t |-al -͟l
triglyphic traɪ'glɪfɪk |-al -͟l
trigonometric ͵trɪgənə'mɛtrɪk |-al -͟l |-ally -͟lɪ, -ɪklɪ
trigonometry ͵trɪgə'nɑmətrɪ; ES+-'nɒm-
trigraph 'traɪgræf; E+-graf, -grɑf
trihedron traɪ'hidrən |-s -z |-dra -drə
trilateral traɪ'lætərəl |-ly -ɪ
Trilby 'trɪlbɪ
trilinear traɪ'lɪnɪɚ; ES -'lɪnɪ·ə(r
trilingual traɪ'lɪŋgwəl
triliteral traɪ'lɪtərəl |-ly -ɪ
trill trɪl |trilled trɪld
trillion 'trɪljən |-th -θ |-ths -θs
trillium 'trɪlɪəm |-s -z
trilobate traɪ'lobet |-d -ɪd |-bal -b͟l
trilobite 'traɪlə͵baɪt
trilogic trɪ'lɑdʒɪk, traɪ-; ES+-'lɒdʒ-
trilogy 'trɪlədʒɪ
trim trɪm |-med -d |-mer -ɚ; ES -ə(r
trimeter 'trɪmətɚ; ES 'trɪmətə(r
trimetric traɪ'mɛtrɪk |-al -͟l
trimonthly traɪ'mʌnθlɪ

Key: See in full §§3–47. bee bi |pity 'pɪtɪ (§6) |rate ret |yet jɛt |sang sæŋ |angry 'æŋ·grɪ |bath bæθ; E baθ (§10) |ah ɑ |far fɑr |watch watʃ, wɒtʃ (§12) |jaw dʒɔ |gorge gɔrdʒ |go go

Those words below in which the ɑ sound is spelt o are often pronounced with ɒ in E and S

Trinculo 'trɪŋkjə‚lo

trine, T- traɪn |-nal -ḷ

Trinidad 'trɪnə‚dæd |-ian ‚trɪnə'dædɪən

Trinitarian ‚trɪnə'tɛrɪən, -'ter- |-ism -‚ɪzəm

trinitrotoluene traɪ‚naɪtro'taljʊ‚in

trinity, T- 'trɪnətɪ

trinket 'trɪŋkɪt |-ed -ɪd |-ry -rɪ

trinomial traɪ'nomɪəl |-ly -ɪ |-ism -‚ɪzəm

trio *music* 'trio, *'group of three'* 'trio, 'traɪo

Trio 'trio

triolet 'traɪəlɪt

trip trɪp |tripped trɪpt

tripartite traɪ'pɑrtaɪt, 'trɪpɚ‚taɪt; ES -'pɑːt-,
-pə-, E+-'paːt-

tripe traɪp

triphthong 'trɪfθɔŋ, 'trɪp-, -θɒŋ |-ed -d

triphthongal trɪf'θɔŋgḷ, trɪp-, -'θɒŋḷ, -'θɒŋ-
|-ly -ɪ

triplane 'traɪ‚plen

triple 'trɪpḷ |-d -d |-ling -plɪŋ, -pḷɪŋ

triplet 'trɪplɪt |-s -s

triplex 'trɪplɛks, 'traɪ-

triplicate *n, adj* 'trɪpləkɪt, -‚ket

triplicate *v* 'trɪplə‚ket |-cated -‚ketɪd

triplication ‚trɪplə'keʃən

triply 'trɪplɪ

tripod 'traɪpad

Tripoli 'trɪpəlɪ |-tan trɪ'pɑlətṇ

Tripolis 'trɪpəlɪs |-'s -ɪz

tripos 'traɪpɑs |-es -ɪz

triptych 'trɪptɪk

trireme 'traɪrim

trisect traɪ'sɛkt |-ed -ɪd |-ction -kʃən

Tristan 'trɪstən

triste *Fr* trist

Tristram 'trɪstrəm

trisyllabic ‚trɪsɪ'læbɪk, ‚traɪ- |-al -ḷ |-ally -ḷɪ,
-ɪklɪ

trisyllable trɪ'sɪləbḷ, traɪ-, 'trɪsɪl-, 'traɪ-

trite traɪt

Triton 'traɪtṇ

triturate 'trɪtʃə‚ret |-d -ɪd |-tion ‚trɪtʃə'reʃən

triumph 'traɪəmf, -mpf |-ed -t

triumphal traɪ'ʌmfḷ, -'ʌmpfḷ

triumphance traɪ'ʌmfəns, -'ʌmpf- |-cy -ɪ |-nt
-nt

triumvir traɪ'ʌmvɚ; ES -'ʌmvə(r; |-ate -ɪt

triune 'traɪjun, traɪ'jun ('trɪ‚une 'God)

trivalence traɪ'veləns, 'trɪvələns |-cy -ɪ |-lent
-lənt

trivet 'trɪvɪt

trivia 'trɪvɪə |-l 'trɪvjəl, -vɪəl

triviality ‚trɪvɪ'ælətɪ

trivialize 'trɪvɪəl‚aɪz, -vjəl- |-s -ɪz |-d -d

trivium 'trɪvɪəm |-via -vɪə

triweekly traɪ'wiklɪ ('tri‚weekly 'news)

Trix trɪks |-'s -ɪz |-y, -ie -ɪ

Troad 'troæd

Troas 'troəs, 'troæs |-'s -ɪz

Trocadero ‚trakə'dɪro (*Fr* trökade'ro)

trochaic tro'ke·ɪk

troche 'trokɪ

trochee 'trokɪ

trod trad |trodden 'tradṇ

troglodyte 'traglə‚daɪt, 'trɒg-

Troilus 'trɔɪləs, 'tro·ɪləs |-'s -ɪz—*in Chaucer
usually trisyllabic; in Shak. only twice so*

Trojan 'trodʒən

troll trol |trolled trold

trolley, -lly 'tralɪ |-ed, -ied -d

trollop 'traləp |-ed -t

Trollope 'traləp |-pian tra'lopɪən

trombone 'trambon, tram'bon ('trom‚bone
'solo)

Trondheim, -hjem 'tranhɛm, 'tranjɛm

trone tron |troned trond

troop trup |trooped trupt |-er -ɚ; ES -ə(r

trope trop

trophic 'trafɪk |-al -ḷ |-ally -ḷɪ, -ɪklɪ

trophy 'trofɪ |-ied -d

tropic 'trapɪk |-al -ḷ |-ally -ḷɪ, -ɪklɪ

tropism 'tropɪzəm |-ist -ɪst |-pistic tro'pɪstɪk

troposphere 'tropə‚sfɪr; ES -‚sfɪə(r, S+
-‚sfɛə(r

troppo 'trapo (*It* 'trɔppo)

Trossachs 'trasæks, -səks, 'trɒs-

trot trat |trotted 'tratɪd

troth trɔθ, troθ, trɒθ |-'s -θs |-ths -θs, -ðz
|-ed -t

Trotsky 'tratskɪ

trotter 'tratɚ; ES 'tratə(r

troubadour 'trubə‚dʊr, -‚dor, -‚dɔr; ES
-‚dʊə(r, -‚doə(r, E+-‚dɔə(r

Troubetskoy tru‚bɛt'skɔɪ, -'bɛtskɔɪ

trouble 'trʌbḷ |-d -d |-ling 'trʌblɪŋ, -bḷɪŋ

troublesome 'trʌbḷsəm |-ly -lɪ

troublous ˈtrʌbləs

Troubridge ˈtrubrɪdʒ, cf Trowbridge

trough trɔf, trɒf, -θ |-s -fs, -vz, -θs, -ðz— -θ
  is esp. freq. in N Engd.

trounce traʊns |trounces ˈtraʊnsɪz |-d -t

troupe trup |trouped trupt

trousered ˈtraʊzəd; ES -zəd; |-sers -z

trousseau truˈso, ˈtruso

trout traʊt |trouted ˈtraʊtɪd

trouvère truˈvɛr; ES -ˈvɛə(r

trove trov

trover ˈtrovɚ; ES ˈtrovə(r

trow tro |trowed trod

Trowbridge ˈtrobrɪdʒ |-'s -ɪz, cf Troubridge

trowel ˈtraʊəl, traʊl |-ed -d

Troy, t- trɔɪ |-an -ən |-ans -ənz

truancy ˈtruənsɪ, ˈtrɪu- |-ant -ənt

truce trus, trɪus |-s -ɪz |-d -t

truck trʌk |trucked trʌkt

truckle ˈtrʌkl̩ |-d -d |-ling ˈtrʌklɪŋ, -kl̩ɪŋ

truculence ˈtrʌkjələns, ˈtruk- |-cy -ɪ |-nt -nt

trudge trʌdʒ |trudges ˈtrʌdʒɪz |-d -d

Trudgen, t- ˈtrʌdʒən |-ed -d

true tru, trɪu |-d -d |-love -ˌlʌv

truepenny ˈtruˌpɛnɪ, ˈtrɪu-

truffle ˈtrʌfl̩, ˈtrufl̩ |-d -d

truism ˈtruɪzəm, ˈtrɪu-

trull trʌl

truly ˈtrulɪ, ˈtrɪulɪ

Truman ˈtrumən, ˈtrɪu-

Trumbull ˈtrʌmbl̩

trump trʌmp |trumped trʌmpt |-ery -ərɪ, -rɪ

trumpet ˈtrʌmpɪt |-ed -ɪd

truncate ˈtrʌŋket |-d -ɪd |-tion trʌŋˈkeʃən

truncheon ˈtrʌntʃən |-ed -d

trundle ˈtrʌndl̩ |-d -d |-ling ˈtrʌndlɪŋ, -dl̩ɪŋ

trunk trʌŋk |trunked trʌŋkt

trunnion, T- ˈtrʌnjən |-ed -d

Truro ˈtruro, ˈtrɪuro

truss trʌs |trusses ˈtrʌsɪz |trussed trʌst

trust trʌst |trusted ˈtrʌstɪd |-ee trʌsˈti

trustful ˈtrʌstfəl |-ly -ɪ

trustworthy ˈtrʌstˌwɝˈðɪ; ES -ˌwɜðɪ, -ˌwɜˈðɪ

trusty ˈtrʌstɪ

truth truθ, trɪuθ |-'s -θs |-ths -ðz, -θs

truthful ˈtruθfəl, ˈtrɪuθ- |-ly -ɪ

try traɪ |tried traɪd

trylon ˈtraɪlɑn; ES+-lɒn

try-on ˈtraɪˌɑn, -ˌɒn, -ˌɔn

Tryon ˈtraɪən

tryout ˈtraɪˌaʊt

trypanosome ˈtrɪpənəˌsom

trysail ˈtraɪˌsel, naut. ˈtraɪsl̩

try-square ˈtraɪˌskwɛr, -ˌskwær; E -ˌskwɛə(r,
  ES -ˌskwæə(r

tryst trɪst, traɪst |-ed -ɪd

tsar tsɑr; ES tsɑː(r, E+tsaː(r

tsarevitch ˈtsɑrəˌvɪtʃ; E+ˈtsɑrə-; |-'s -ɪz

tsarevna tsɑˈrɛvnə; E+tsɑ-

tsarina tsɑˈrinə; E+tsɑ-

Tschaikovsky, -wsky tʃaɪˈkɔfskɪ, -ˈkɒf-,
  -vskɪ, -ˈkaʊskɪ

tsetse ˈtsɛtsɪ

Tsingtao ˈtsɪŋˈtaʊ

T-square ˈtiˌskwɛr, -ˌskwær; E -ˌskwɛə(r, ES
  -ˌskwæə(r

Tsushima tsəˈʃimə, ˈtsuʃɪˌmɑ

Tuareg ˈtwɑrɛg

tub tʌb |tubbed tʌbd

tuba 'horn' ˈtjubə, ˈtɪubə, ˈtubə |-s -z |-bae -bi

tuba mythical tree ˈtubə

tuba nut, liquor ˈtubɑ

Tuba ˈtubə

Tubal ˈtjubl̩, ˈtɪubl̩, ˈtubl̩

Tubal-cain ˈtjubl̩ˌken, ˈtɪu-, ˈtu-

tube tjub, tɪub, tub |-bal -l̩ |-bar -ɚ; ES -ə(r

tuber ˈtjubɚ, ˈtɪu-, ˈtu-; ES -bə(r

tubercle ˈtjubɚkl̩, ˈtɪu-, ˈtu-; ES -bəkl̩

tubercular tjuˈbɝkjələ, tɪu-, tu-, tə-; ES -ˈbɝ-
  kjələ(r, -ˈbɝkjələ(r; |-lin -lɪn |-lous -ləs

tuberculosis tjuˌbɝkjəˈlosɪs, tɪu-, tu-, tə-;
  ES -ˌbɜk-, -ˌbɝk-

tuberose 'tuberous' ˈtjubəˌros, ˈtɪu-, ˈtu-

tuberose flower ˈtjubˌroz, ˈtɪub-, ˈtub- |-s -ɪz

tuberous ˈtjubərəs, ˈtɪu-, ˈtu-

tubular ˈtjubjələ, ˈtɪu-, ˈtu-; ES -lə(r

tubule ˈtjubjul, ˈtɪubjul, ˈtubjul

tuck, T- tʌk |tucked tʌkt

tuckahoe, T- ˈtʌkəˌho

tucker, T- ˈtʌkɚ; ES ˈtʌkə(r; |-ed -d |-ing
  ˈtʌkərɪŋ, ˈtʌkrɪŋ

tucket ˈtʌkɪt

Tucson tuˈsan, -ˈsɒn, -ˈsɔn—acct+ˈTucson

Tudor ˈtjudɚ, ˈtɪu-, ˈtu-; ES -də(r

Tuesday ˈtjuzdɪ, ˈtɪuz-, ˈtuz—see Monday

tufa ˈtjufə, ˈtɪufə, ˈtufə

tuff tʌf

tuft tʌft |tufted ˈtʌftɪd

tug tʌg |tugged tʌgd |-boat -ˌbot

Tuileries ˈtwilərɪz (*Fr* tɥilˈri)

tuition tjuˈɪʃən, tɪu-, tu- |-al -l̩ |-ary -ˌɛrɪ

Tulane tjuˈlen, tɪu-, tu-

Tulare tuˈlɛrɪ, -ˈlærɪ; S -ˈlærɪ

tularemia, -raem- ˌtulǝˈrimɪǝ

tulip ˈtjuləp, ˈtɪu-, ˈtu-, -ɪp

Tullamore ˌtʌləˈmor, -ˈmɔr; ES -ˈmoǝ(r, E+-ˈmɔǝ(r; (ˈTullaˌmore ˈRoad)

tulle tjul, tɪul, tul (*Fr* tyl)

Tullichewan ˌtʌlɪˈkjuǝn, -ˈkɪuǝn (*Sc* -ˈxjuǝn)

Tully ˈtʌlɪ

Tulsa ˈtʌlsǝ

tumble ˈtʌmbl̩ |-d -d |-ling ˈtʌmblɪŋ, -bl̩ɪŋ

tumble-down ˈtʌmbl̩ˈdaʊn (ˈtumble-ˌdown ˈshed)

tumbler ˈtʌmblǝ˞; ES ˈtʌmblǝ(r

tumbrel, -bril ˈtʌmbrǝl

tumefaction ˌtjumǝˈfækʃǝn, ˌtɪu-, ˌtu-

tumefy ˈtjumǝˌfaɪ, ˈtɪu-, ˈtu- |-fied -ˌfaɪd

tumescence tjuˈmɛsn̩s, tɪu-, tu- |-scent -sn̩t

tumid ˈtjumɪd, ˈtɪu-, ˈtu-

tumidity tjuˈmɪdǝtɪ, tɪu-, tu-

tumor ˈtjumǝ˞, ˈtɪu-, ˈtu-; ES -mǝ(r; |-ed -d |-ous -ǝs

tumult ˈtjumʌlt, ˈtɪu-, ˈtu- |-ed -ɪd

tumultuous tjuˈmʌltʃʊǝs, tɪu-, tu-

tumulus ˈtjumjǝlǝs, ˈtɪu-, ˈtu- |-es -ɪz |-li -ˌlaɪ

tun tʌn |tunned tʌnd

tuna ˈtunǝ

Tunbridge ˈtʌnbrɪdʒ |-'s -ɪz

tundra ˈtʌndrǝ, ˈtʊndrǝ

tune tjun, tɪun, tun |-d -d

tungsten ˈtʌŋstǝn

tunic ˈtjunɪk, ˈtɪu-, ˈtu- |-ked -t |-le -l̩

Tunis ˈtjunɪs, ˈtɪu-, ˈtu- |-'s -ɪz

Tunisia tjuˈnɪʃɪǝ, tɪu-, tu-, -ʃǝ |-n -n

Tunkhannock tʌŋkˈhænǝk

tunnel ˈtʌnl̩ |-ed -d

tunny ˈtʌnɪ

Tunstall ˈtʌnstl̩

tup tʌp |tupped tʌpt

Tupelo, t- ˈtjupǝˌlo, ˈtɪu-, ˈtu-

Turania tjuˈrenɪǝ, tɪu-, tu- |-n -n

turban ˈtɝbǝn; ES ˈtɜb-, ˈtɝb-; |-ed -d

Turberville, -vile ˈtɝbǝˌvɪl; ES ˈtɜbǝ-, ˈtɝbǝ-

turbid ˈtɝbɪd; ES ˈtɜbɪd, ˈtɝbɪd

turbidity tɝˈbɪdǝtɪ; ES tɜ-, tɝ-

turbinate *adj* ˈtɝbǝnɪt, -ˌnet; ES ˈtɜb-, ˈtɝb-

turbinate *v* ˈtɝbǝˌnet; ES ˈtɜb-, ˈtɝb-; |-d -ɪd

turbine ˈtɝbaɪn, -bɪn; ES ˈtɜ-, ˈtɝ-

turbot ˈtɝbǝt; ES ˈtɜ-, ˈtɝ-

turbulence ˈtɝbjǝlǝns; ES ˈtɜb-, ˈtɝb-; |-cy -ɪ |-lent -lǝnt

Turco ˈtɝko; ES ˈtɜko, ˈtɝko

Turcoman ˈtɝkǝmǝn; ES ˈtɜk-, ˈtɝk-; |-s -z

tureen tuˈrin, tɪuˈrin, tjuˈrin

turf *n* tɝf; ES tɜf, tɝf; |-'s -s |-s -s *or* -rves -vz

turf *v* tɝf; ES tɜf, tɝf; |-s -s |-ed -t

Turgenev turˈgɛnjɪf; ES tuǝ-; (*Rus* turˈgenjɪf)

turgent ˈtɝdʒǝnt; ES ˈtɜdʒ-, ˈtɝdʒ-

turgescence tɝˈdʒɛsn̩s; ES tɜ-, tɝ-; |-cy -ɪ |-scent -sn̩t

turgid ˈtɝdʒɪd; ES ˈtɜdʒ-, ˈtɝdʒ-

turgidity tɝˈdʒɪdǝtɪ; ES tɜ-, tɝ-

Turin ˈtjurɪn, ˈtɪu-, ˈtu-

Turk tɝk; ES tɜk, tɝk; |-ish -ɪʃ

Turkestan ˌtɝkɪˈstæn, -ˈstɑn; ES ˌtɜkɪ-, ˌtɝkɪ-

Turkey, t- ˈtɝkɪ; ES ˈtɜkɪ, ˈtɝkɪ

Turkmen ˈtɝkmɛn; ES ˈtɜk-, ˈtɝk-

Turkmenistan ˌtɝkmɛnɪˈstæn, -ˈstɑn; ES ˌtɜk-, ˌtɝk-

Turkoman ˈtɝkǝmǝn; ES ˈtɜk-, ˈtɝk-; |-s -z

Turkomen ˈtɝkǝˌmɛn; ES ˈtɜk-, ˈtɝk-

Turlock ˈtɝlɑk; ES ˈtɜ-, ˈtɝ-, -lɒk

turmoil ˈtɝmɔɪl; ES ˈtɜ-, ˈtɝ-

turn tɝn; ES tɜn, tɝn; |-ed -d |-about -ǝˌbaʊt

turnbuckle ˈtɝnˌbʌkl̩; ES ˈtɜn-, ˈtɝn-

Turnbull ˈtɝnˌbʊl; ES ˈtɜn-, ˈtɝn-

turncoat ˈtɝnˌkot; ES ˈtɜn-, ˈtɝn-; |-ed -ɪd

turndown ˈtɝnˌdaʊn; ES ˈtɜn-, ˈtɝn-

turner, T- ˈtɝnǝ˞; ES ˈtɜnǝ(r, ˈtɝnǝ(r

turnip ˈtɝnǝp, -ɪp; ES ˈtɜn-, ˈtɝn-; |-ed -t

turnkey ˈtɝnˌki; ES ˈtɜn-, ˈtɝn-

turnout ˈtɝnˌaʊt; ES ˈtɜn-, ˈtɝn-

turnover ˈtɝnˌovǝ˞; ES ˈtɜnˌovǝ(r, ˈtɝnˌovǝ(r

turnpike ˈtɝnˌpaɪk; ES ˈtɜn-, ˈtɝn-; |-d -t

turnspit ˈtɝnˌspɪt; ES ˈtɜn-, ˈtɝn-

turnstile ˈtɝnˌstaɪl; ES ˈtɜn-, ˈtɝn-

turntable ˈtɝnˌtebl̩; ES ˈtɜn-, ˈtɝn-

turpentine ˈtɝpǝnˌtaɪn, ˈtɝpm̩-; ES ˈtɜp-, ˈtɝp-; |-d -d

Turpin ˈtɝpɪn; ES ˈtɜpɪn, ˈtɝpɪn

turpitude ˈtɝpǝˌtjud, -ˌtrud, -ˌtud; ES ˈtɜp-, ˈtɝpturquoise 'tɜˑkwɔɪz, -kɔɪz; ES 'tɜ-, 'tɝ-; |-s -ɪz

turret 'tɜˑɪt, 'tʊrɪt; ES 'tɜr-, 'tʌr-, 'tɝ-, 'tʊr-; |-ed -ɪd

turtle 'tɜˑtl̩; ES 'tɜtl̩, 'tɝtl̩; |-d -d |-ling -tḷɪŋ, -tl̩ɪŋ |-dove -'dʌv, -ˌdʌv

turves tɜˑvz; ES tɜvz, tɝvz

Tuscaloosa ˌtʌskə'lusə

Tuscan 'tʌskən |-y -ɪ

Tuscarawas ˌtʌskə'rɔwəs |-'s -ɪz

Tuscarora ˌtʌskə'rorə, -'rɔrə; S -'rorə

Tusculum 'tʌskjələm

tush tʌʃ |tushes 'tʌʃɪz |tushed tʌʃt

tusk tʌsk |tusked tʌskt

Tuskegee tʌs'kigɪ

Tussaud tə'so, tʊ-

tussle 'tʌsl̩ |-d -d |-ling 'tʌslɪŋ, 'tʌsl̩ɪŋ

tussock 'tʌsək |-ed -t

tut intj ʔ (voiceless suction tongue-blade alveolar click)

tut n, v tʌt |tutted 'tʌtɪd

Tutankhamen ˌtutaŋk'amɪn, -ən

tutelage 'tutl̩ɪdʒ, 'tɪu-, 'tju-

tutelary 'tutl̩ˌɛrɪ, 'tɪu-, 'tju-

tutor 'tutɚ, 'tɪu-, 'tju-; ES -tə(r; |-ed -d

tutorial tu'torɪəl, tɪu-, tju-, -'tɔr-; S -'tor-; |-ly -ɪ

tutti-frutti 'tutɪ'frutɪ (It 'tutti'frutti)

Tuttle 'tʌtl̩

tu-whit tu'hwɪt |tu-whoo tu'hwu

Tuxedo, t- tʌk'sido, -də

Twaddell musician, linguist twa'dɛl, twɒ-, twə-, physicist 'twadl̩, 'twɒdl̩

twaddle 'twadl̩, 'twɒdl̩ |-d -d |-ling -dlɪŋ, -dl̩ɪŋ

twain, T- twen |-ed -d

twang twæŋ |twanged twæŋd

'twas 'it was' stressed 'twaz, 'twɒz, 'twʌz, ˌtwaz, ˌtwɒz, ˌtwʌz; unstr. twəz

'twasn't 'it was not' 'twazn̩t, 'twɒzn̩t, 'twʌzn̩t, ˌtwazn̩t, ˌtwɒzn̩t, ˌtwʌzn̩t

tweak twik |tweaked twikt

Tweddell 'twedl̩—the purely phonetic form of Tweed-dale; 'twidˌdel, 'twidl̩, twə'dɛl, etc., are due to other influences. Cf Tweedmouth

Tweed, t- twid

Tweeddale 'twidˌdel, 'twidl̩

Tweedle 'twidl̩

tweedle 'twidl̩ |-d -d |-ling 'twidlɪŋ, -dl̩ɪŋ

tweedledee, T- ˌtwidl̩'di |-d -d |-dum -'dʌm

Tweedmouth 'twidməθ, -ˌmaʊθ, loc. 'twɛdməθ, cf Tweddell

Tweedsmuir 'twidzˌmjʊr, -ˌmɪur; ES -ˌmjʊə(r, -ˌmɪuə(r

'tween twin

tweet-tweet 'twit'twit |-ed -ɪd

tweezers 'twizɚz; ES -zəz; |-zered -zɚd; ES -zəd

twelfth twelfθ |-ths -θs

Twelfth-night 'twelfθˌnaɪt

twelve twɛlv |-mo -mo |-month -ˌmʌnθ

twelvepenny 'twɛlvˌpɛnɪ, -pənɪ

Twemlow 'twɛmlo

twenty 'twɛntɪ |-tieth -tɪθ |-tieths -tɪθs

twentyfold 'twɛntɪ'fold ('twenty ˌfold 'loss)

'twere 'it were' stressed 'twɝ, ˌtwɝ; ES -ɝ(r, -ɝ; unstr. twɚ; ES twə(r

twice twaɪs

twice-told 'twaɪs'told ('Twice-ˌTold 'Tales)

Twickenham 'twɪkənəm, 'twɪknəm, formerly + 'twɪt- (17c Twittenham)

twiddle 'twɪdl̩ |-d -d |-ling 'twɪdlɪŋ, -dl̩ɪŋ

twig twɪg |twigged twɪgd

twilight 'twaɪˌlaɪt

twill twɪl |twilled twɪld

'twill 'it will' stressed 'twɪl, ˌtwɪl; unstr. tl̩— Unstr. twəl, twl̩ are rarely used.

twin twɪn |twins twɪnz |twinned twɪnd

twine twaɪn |twined twaɪnd

twinge twɪndʒ |twinges 'twɪndʒɪz |-d -d

twinkle 'twɪŋkl̩ |-d -d |-ling 'twɪŋklɪŋ, -kl̩ɪŋ

twinkling n 'twɪŋklɪŋ

twirl twɝl; ES twɜl, twɝl; |-ed -d

twist twɪst |twisted 'twɪstɪd

twit twɪt |twitted 'twɪtɪd

twitch twɪtʃ |twitches 'twɪtʃɪz |twitched twɪtʃt

twitter 'twɪtɚ; ES 'twɪtə(r; |-ed -d |-ing 'twɪtərɪŋ, -trɪŋ

'twixt twɪkst

two tu

two-by-four adj 'tubə'for, -'fɔr; ES -'foə(r, E+-'fɔə(r

two-by-four n 'tubəˌfor, -ˌfɔr; ES -ˌfoə(r, E+-ˌfɔə(r

two-faced 'tu'fest ('two-ˌfaced 'Janus)

two-fisted 'tu'fɪstɪd

twofold adj, adv 'tu'fold ('twoˌfold 'gain)

Key: See in full §§3–47. bee bi |pity 'pɪtɪ (§6) |rate ret |yet jɛt |sang sæŋ |angry 'æŋ·grɪ |bath bæθ; E baθ (§10) |ah ɑ |far fɑr |watch wɑtʃ, wɒtʃ (§12) |jaw dʒɔ |gorge gɔrdʒ |go go

two-handed ˈtuˈhændɪd (ˈtwo-ˌhanded ˈen-
    gine)
two-legged ˈtuˈlɛgɪd, -ˈlɛgd
twopence ˈtʌpəns |-s -ɪz
twopenny ˈtuˌpɛnɪ, -pənɪ, ˈtʌpənɪ
twosome ˈtusəm
ˈtwould ˈit would' stressed ˈtwʊd, ˌtwʊd;
    unstr. twəd
two-way ˈtuˈwe (ˈtwo-ˌway ˈbridge)
Twyford ˈtwaɪfəd; ES ˈtwaɪfəd
Tybalt ˈtɪbl̩t
Tyburn ˈtaɪbən; ES ˈtaɪbən
Tychicus ˈtɪkɪkəs |-ʼs -ɪz
Tycho ˈtaɪko
tycoon taɪˈkun
Tygart ˈtaɪgət; ES ˈtaɪgət
tying ˈtaɪɪŋ
tyke taɪk
Tyler, -lor ˈtaɪlə; ES ˈtaɪlə(r
tympan ˈtɪmpən |-ic tɪmˈpænɪk
tympanum ˈtɪmpənəm |-s -z |-na -nə |-ny -nɪ
Tynan ˈtaɪnən
Tyndale ˈtɪndl̩ |Tyndall ˈtɪndl̩
Tyne taɪn |-mouth ˈtɪnməθ, ˈtaɪn-
type taɪp |typed taɪpt |-script -ˌskrɪpt
Typee ˈtaɪˈpi |-s -z
typesetter ˈtaɪpˌsɛtə; ES -ˌsɛtə(r
typewrite ˈtaɪpˌraɪt |-wrote -ˌrot |-written
    -ˌrɪtn̩ |-r -ə; ES -ə(r
typhoid ˈtaɪfɔɪd, taɪˈfɔɪd (ˈtyˌphoid ˈfever)
typhoidal taɪˈfɔɪdl̩
typhonic taɪˈfɑnɪk; ES+-ˈfɒn-

typhoon taɪˈfun
typhous ˈtaɪfəs |typhus ˈtaɪfəs
typic ˈtɪpɪk |-al -l̩ |-ally -l̩ɪ, -ɪklɪ
typify ˈtɪpəˌfaɪ |-fied -ˌfaɪd
typist ˈtaɪpɪst
typographer taɪˈpɑgrəfə, -ˈpɒg-; ES -fə(r;
    |-phy -fɪ
typographic ˌtaɪpəˈgræfɪk |-al -l̩ |-ally -l̩ɪ,
    -ɪklɪ
typothetae taɪˈpɑθəˌti, ˌtaɪpəˈθiti; ES+-ˈpɒθ-
tyrannic tɪˈrænɪk, taɪ- |-al -l̩ |-ally -l̩ɪ |-icly
    -ɪklɪ
tyrannicide tɪˈrænəˌsaɪd, taɪ-
tyrannize ˈtɪrəˌnaɪz |-s -ɪz |-d -d
tyrannous ˈtɪrənəs |-ny -nɪ
tyrant ˈtaɪrənt |-ed -ɪd
Tyre taɪr; ES taɪə(r; |-rian ˈtɪrɪən
tyre taɪr; ES taɪə(r; |-d -d
tyro ˈtaɪro
Tyrol ˈtɪrəl, -ɑl, -ɒl, tɪˈrol
Tyrolean tɪˈrolɪən, ˌtɪrəˈliən
Tyrolese ˌtɪrəˈliz
Tyrone Irel tɪˈron, US taɪˈron, tɪ-
Tyrrell ˈtɪrəl, ˈtɛrəl, cf Terrell
Tyrrhenian tɪˈrinɪən
Tyrtaeus tɝˈtiəs; ES tɝ-, tɝ-; |-ʼs -ɪz
Tyrwhitt ˈtɪrɪt, ˈtɛrɪt, cf Tyrrell
Tyson ˈtaɪsn̩
Tytler ˈtaɪtlə; ES ˈtaɪtlə(r
tzar tsar; ES tsɑ:(r, E+tsa:(r
tzarina tsaˈrinə; E+tsa-
tzetze ˈtsɛtsɪ

U

U, u letter ju, jɪu |pl U's, Us, poss U's juz, jɪuz
ubiety juˈbaɪətɪ
ubiquitary juˈbɪkwəˌtɛrɪ |-tous -təs |-ty -tɪ
U-boat ˈjuˌbot
Udall, Udale, Udell ˈjudl̩, cf Yewdale
udder ˈʌdə; ES ˈʌdə(r; |-ed -d |-ful -ˌfʊl
udometer juˈdɑmətə; ES -ˈdɑmətə(r, -ˈdɒm-
udometric ˌjudəˈmɛtrɪk
Uffizi Gallery uˈfitsi
Uganda juˈgændə, uˈgɑndə
ugh ux & various guttural sounds
ugly ˈʌglɪ

uh-huh ˈyes' ˈʌˈhʌ, ˈno' ˈhʌʔɪʔʌ (nasal ʌ)
uhlan ˈulan, ˈulən
Uhland ˈulənd (Ger ˈuːlɑnt)
Uinta, -h juˈɪntə
uitlander, U- ˈaɪtˌlændə; ES -ˌlændə(r; (Du
    ˈœytˌlandər)
ukase ˈjukes, juˈkez
Ukraine ˈjukren, juˈkren, juˈkraɪn |-nian
    juˈkrenɪən, -ˈkraɪnɪən
ukulele ˌjukəˈlelɪ (Hawaii ˌukuˈlele)
ulcer ˈʌlsə; ES ˈʌlsə(r; |-ate -ˌet |-ous -əs
ulceration ˌʌlsəˈreʃən

|full fʊl |tooth tuθ |further ˈfɝðə; ES ˈfɝðə |custom ˈkʌstəm |while hwaɪl |how haʊ |toy tɔɪ
|using ˈjuzɪŋ |fuse fjuz, fɪuz |dish dɪʃ |vision ˈvɪʒən |Eden ˈidn̩ |cradle ˈkredl̩ |keep ʼem ˈkipm̩

Ulfilas ˈʌlfɪləs, ˈʊl- |-ˈs -ɪz
ullage ˈʌlɪdʒ |-s -ɪz |-d -d
Ullswater ˈʌlzˌwɔtɚ, -ˌwɑ-, -ˌwɒ-; ES -tə(r
Ulmus, u- ˈʌlməs
ulna ˈʌlnə |-s -z |-nae -ni
ulster, U- ˈʌlstɚ; ES ˈʌlstə(r; |-ite -ˌaɪt
ulterior ʌlˈtɪrɪɚ; ES -ˈtɪrɪ·ə(r
ultima ˈʌltəmə |-mate -mɪt
ultima Thule ˈʌltəməˈθjuli, -ˈθɪuli
ultimatum ˌʌltəˈmetəm |-s -z |-ta -tə
ultimo ˈʌltəˌmo
ultra ˈʌltrə
ultraconservative ˌʌltrəkənˈsɝvətɪv; ES -ˈsɝv-, -ˈsɝv-
ultrafashionable ˌʌltrəˈfæʃnəbl̩, -ˈfæʃənə-
ultramarine ˌʌltrəməˈrin
ultramicroscope ˌʌltrəˈmaɪkrəˌskop
ultramicroscopic ˌʌltrəˌmaɪkrəˈskɑpɪk; ES+ -ˈskɒpɪk; |-al -l̩
ultramodern ˌʌltrəˈmadɚn; ES -ˈmadən, -ˈmɒd-; |-ism -ˌɪzəm |-ist -ɪst
ultramodernistic ˌʌltrəˌmadɚnˈɪstɪk; ES -ˌmadən-, -ˌmɒdən-
ultramontane ˌʌltrəˈmɑnten; ES+-ˈmɒn-
ultramundane ˌʌltrəˈmʌnden
ultranationalism ˌʌltrəˈnæʃnəlˌɪzəm, -ʃənəl-
ultrareligious ˌʌltrərɪˈlɪdʒəs
ultraroyalist ˌʌltrəˈrɔɪəlɪst, -ˈrɔjəlɪst
ultraviolet ˌʌltrəˈvaɪəlɪt
ultra vires ˌʌltrəˈvaɪriz
ululant ˈjuljələnt |-late -ˌlet |-lated -ˌletɪd
ululation ˌjuljəˈleʃən
Ulysses juˈlɪsiz |Ulysses' juˈlɪsiz
umbel ˈʌmbl̩ |-ed -d |-lar -ɚ; ES -ə(r
umbellate ˈʌmbl̩ɪt, -ˌet |-ated -ˌetɪd
umber ˈʌmbɚ; ES ˈʌmbə(r; |-ed -d |-ing ˈʌmbərɪŋ, -brɪŋ
umbilical ʌmˈbɪlɪkl̩ |-ly -ɪ
umbilicus ʌmˈbɪlɪkəs, ˌʌmbɪˈlaɪkəs |-es -ɪz |-ci -ˌsaɪ, -ˈlaɪsaɪ
umbles ˈʌmbl̩z
umbra ˈʌmbrə |-s -z |-brae -bri
umbrage ˈʌmbrɪdʒ |-s -ɪz |-d -d
umbrageous ʌmˈbredʒəs
umbrella ʌmˈbrɛlə, əm-
Umbria ˈʌmbrɪə |-n -n
umbriferous ʌmˈbrɪfərəs
umiak, oom- ˈumɪˌæk
umlaut ˈʊmlaʊt |umlauted ˈʊmlaʊtɪd

umph m̩m̩m̩ & various other grunts and nasal puffs
umpire ˈʌmpaɪr; ES ˈʌmpaɪə(r; |-d -d
Umpqua ˈʌmpkwə
umpteen ˈʌmpˈtin |-th -θ -θ |-tieth -tɪθ
un- prefix ʌn-, ˌʌn-, ˈʌn- according to rhythm and meaning (see §19)
Una ˈjunə
unabashed ˌʌnəˈbæʃt |-bashedly -ˈbæʃɪdlɪ
unabated ˌʌnəˈbetɪd (ˈunaˌbated ˈzeal)
unable ʌnˈebl̩
unabridged ˌʌnəˈbrɪdʒd |-bridgedly -ˈbrɪdʒɪdlɪ
unaccented ʌnˈæksɛntɪd, ˌʌnækˈsɛntɪd
unacceptable ˌʌnəkˈsɛptəbl̩, -ɪk- |-bly -blɪ
unaccommodating ˌʌnəˈkɑməˌdetɪŋ; ES+ -ˈkɒm-
unaccompanied ˌʌnəˈkʌmpənɪd
unaccountable ˌʌnəˈkauntəbl̩ |-bly -blɪ
unaccounted-for ˌʌnəˈkauntɪdˌfɔr; ES -ˌfɔə(r
unaccustomed ˌʌnəˈkʌstəmd
unacquainted ˌʌnəˈkwentɪd
unaddressed ˌʌnəˈdrɛst (ˈunadˌdressed ˈnote)
unadorned ˌʌnəˈdɔrnd; ES -ˈdɔənd; |-nedly -nɪdlɪ
unadulterated ˌʌnəˈdʌltəˌretɪd
unadvisable ˌʌnədˈvaɪzəbl̩ |-bly -blɪ
unadvised ˌʌnədˈvaɪzd |-visedly -ˈvaɪzɪdlɪ
unaffected ˌʌnəˈfɛktɪd (ˈunafˌfected ˈjoy)
unafraid ˌʌnəˈfred
unaided ʌnˈedɪd (ˈunˌaided ˈeffort)
Unaka juˈnekə
Unalaska ˌunəˈlæskə, ˌʌn-
unalienable ʌnˈeljənəbl̩, -ˈelɪən- |-bly -blɪ
unallotted ˌʌnəˈlɑtɪd; ES+-ˈlɒtɪd
unallowable ˌʌnəˈlauəbl̩ |-bly -blɪ
unalloyed ˌʌnəˈlɔɪd (ˈunalˌloyed ˈpleasure)
unalterable ʌnˈɔltərəbl̩, -trə- |-bly -blɪ
unaltered ʌnˈɔltɚd; ES -ˈɔltəd
unambiguous ˌʌnæmˈbɪgjuəs
un-American ˌʌnəˈmɛrəkən (ˈun-Aˌmerican ˈway)
unaneled 'unannointed' ˌʌnəˈnild
unanimity ˌjunəˈnɪmətɪ
unanimous juˈnænəməs, ju-
unannealed 'unsoftened' ˌʌnəˈnild
unannounced ˌʌnəˈnaunst
unanswerable ʌnˈænsərəbl̩, -srə-; E+-ˈan-, -ˈɑn-; |-bly -blɪ

Key: See in full §§3–47. bee bi |pity ˈpɪtɪ (§6) |rate ret |yet jɛt |sang sæŋ |angry ˈæŋ·grɪ |bath bæθ; E baθ (§10) |ah ɑ |far fɑr |watch wɑtʃ, wɒtʃ (§12) |jaw dʒɔ |gorge gɔrdʒ |go go

unanswered ʌn'ænsəˑd; ES -'ænsəd, E+-'an-,
-'an-

unappeasable ˌʌnə'pizəbļ |-bly -blɪ

unappetizing ʌn'æpəˌtaɪzɪŋ

unappreciable ˌʌnə'priʃɪəbļ, -ʃəbļ |-bly -blɪ

unappreciated ˌʌnə'priʃɪˌetɪd |-tive -tɪv

unapproachable ˌʌnə'protʃəbļ |-bly -blɪ

unapproached ˌʌnə'protʃt

unapproved ˌʌnə'pruvd ('unapˌproved 'act)

unapt ʌn'æpt

unargued ʌn'ɑrgjʊd; ES -'ɑ:gjʊd; E+
-'ɑ:gjʊd

unarm ʌn'ɑrm; ES -'ɑ:m, E+-'a:m; |-ed -d
|-edly -ɪdlɪ

unarmored ʌn'ɑrməˑd; ES -'ɑ:məd, E+
-'a:məd

unartistic ˌʌnɑr'tɪstɪk; ES -ɑ:'tɪstɪk, E+-a:-;
|-al -ļ |-ally -ļɪ, -ɪklɪ

unashamed ˌʌnə'ʃemd |-shamedly -'ʃemɪdlɪ

unasked ʌn'æskt; E -'askt, -'æskt, -'askt

unassailable ˌʌnə'seləbļ |-bly -blɪ

unassimilated ˌʌnə'sɪməˌletɪd

unassisted ˌʌnə'sɪstɪd ('unasˌsisted 'eye)

unassuming ˌʌnə'sumɪŋ, -'sɪum-, -'sjum-

unattached ˌʌnə'tætʃt ('unatˌtached 'rope)

unattainable ˌʌnə'tenəbļ |-bly -blɪ

unattested ˌʌnə'tɛstɪd

unattractive ˌʌnə'træktɪv ('unatˌtractive 'air)

unauspicious ˌʌnə'spɪʃəs ('unauˌspicious 'day)

unauthentic ˌʌnə'θɛntɪk |-ally -ļɪ, -ɪklɪ

unauthenticated ˌʌnə'θɛntɪˌketɪd

unauthorized ʌn'ɔθəˌraɪzd |-zedly -zɪdlɪ

unavailable ˌʌnə'veləbļ |-bly -blɪ

unavailing ˌʌnə'velɪŋ ('unaˌvailing 'plea)

unavenged ˌʌnə'vɛndʒd

unavoidable ˌʌnə'vɔɪdəbļ |-bly -blɪ

unavowed ˌʌnə'vaʊd |-vowedly -'vaʊɪdlɪ

unaware ˌʌnə'wɛr, -'wær; E -'wɛə(r, ES
-'wæə(r; |-s -z

unbaked ʌn'bekt ('unˌbaked 'dough)

unbalance ʌn'bæləns |-s -ɪz |-d -t

unbaptized ˌʌnbæp'taɪzd

unbar ʌn'bɑr; ES -'bɑ:(r, E+-'ba:(r; |-red -d

unbated ʌn'betɪd ('unˌbated 'zeal)

unbearable ʌn'bɛrəbļ, -'bær-; S -'bær-; |-bly
-blɪ

unbeaten ʌn'bitņ ('unˌbeaten 'team)

unbecoming ˌʌnbɪ'kʌmɪŋ

unbeknown ˌʌnbɪ'non

unbelief ˌʌnbə'lif, -bļ'if, -bɪ'lif

unbelievable ˌʌnbə'livəbļ, -bļ'iv-, -bɪ'liv-
|-bly -blɪ

unbeliever ˌʌnbə'livəˑ, -bļ'ivəˑ, -bɪ'livəˑ; ES
-və(r; |-ving -vɪŋ

unbelt ʌn'bɛlt |-ed -ɪd

unbend ʌn'bɛnd |-bent -'bɛnt or -bended
-'bɛndɪd |-able -əbļ |-bly -blɪ

unbeseeming ˌʌnbɪ'simɪŋ

unbiased ʌn'baɪəst ('unˌbiased 'view)

unbid ʌn'bɪd |-den -ņ

unbind ʌn'baɪnd |-bound -'baʊnd

unblamable ʌn'bleməbļ |-bly -blɪ

unbleached ʌn'blitʃt ('unˌbleached 'muslin)

unblemished ʌn'blɛmɪʃt

unblessed, -st ʌn'blɛst |-sedness -sɪdnɪs

unblushing ʌn'blʌʃɪŋ

unbodied ʌn'bɑdɪd; ES+-'bɒdɪd

unbolt ʌn'bolt |-ed -ɪd

unborn ʌn'bɔrn; ES -'bɔən

unbosom ʌn'bʊzəm, -'buzəm |-ed -d

unbought ʌn'bɔt

unbounded ʌn'baʊndɪd ('unˌbounded 'joy)

unbowed 'not bowed down' ʌn'baʊd

unbowed 'not bent as a bow' ʌn'bod

unbrace ʌn'bres |-s -ɪz |-d -t

unbraid ʌn'bred |-ed -ɪd ('unˌbraided 'hair)

unbreakable ʌn'brekəbļ |-bly -blɪ

unbreathed ʌn'briðd—cf breathed

unbridle ʌn'braɪdļ |-d -d |-ling -dlɪŋ, -dļɪŋ

unbroken ʌn'brokən ('unˌbroken 'series)

unbruised ʌn'bruzd, -'brɪuzd

unbuckle ʌn'bʌkļ |-d -d |-ling -klɪŋ, -kļɪŋ

unburden ʌn'bɝdņ; ES -'bɝdņ, -'bɝˑdņ;
|-ed -d

unburied ʌn'bɛrɪd

unburned ʌn'bɝnd; ES -'bɝnd, -'bɝˑnd; |-nt
-nt

unbusinesslike ʌn'bɪznɪsˌlaɪk

unbutton ʌn'bʌtņ |-ed -d |-ing -'bʌtnɪŋ,
-tņɪŋ

uncage ʌn'kedʒ |-s -ɪz |-d -d

uncalled-for ʌn'kɔldˌfɔr; ES -ˌfɔə(r

uncanny ʌn'kænɪ |-nily -'kænļɪ, -nɪlɪ

uncanonical ˌʌnkə'nɑnɪkļ; ES+-'nɒn-; |-ly
-ɪ, -ɪklɪ

uncap ʌn'kæp |uncapped ʌn'kæpt

uncared-for ʌn'kɛrdˌfɔr, -'kærd-; E -'kɛəd-
ˌfɔə(r, ES -'kæəd-

|full fʊl |tooth tuθ |further 'fɝðəˑ; ES 'fɝðə |custom 'kʌstəm |while hwaɪl |how haʊ |toy tɔɪ
|using 'juzɪŋ |fuse fjuz, fɪuz |dish dɪʃ |vision 'vɪʒən |Eden 'idņ |cradle 'kredļ |keep 'em 'kipm̩

uncatalogued, -logged ʌnˈkæt‖ˌɔgd, -ˌɑgd, -ˌɒgd

uncaught ʌnˈkɔt

unceasing ʌnˈsisɪŋ (ˈunˌceasing ˈflow)

uncensored ʌnˈsɛnsɚd; ES -ˈsɛnsəd

uncensured ʌnˈsɛnʃɚd; ES -ˈsɛnʃəd

unceremonious ˌʌnsɛrəˈmonɪəs, -ˈmonjəs

uncertain ʌnˈsɝtn̩, -ˈsɝtɪn; ES -ˈsɝt-, -ˈsɝt-; |-ty -tɪ

unchain ʌnˈtʃen |unchained ʌnˈtʃend

unchallenged ʌnˈtʃælɪndʒd, -əndʒd

unchangeable ʌnˈtʃendʒəb‖ |-bly -blɪ

unchanged ʌnˈtʃendʒd |-ness -ˈtʃendʒɪdnɪs

unchanging ʌnˈtʃendʒɪŋ (ˈunˌchanging ˈheat)

uncharitable ʌnˈtʃærətəb‖ |-bly -blɪ

uncharted ʌnˈtʃɑrtɪd; ES -ˈtʃɑːtɪd, E+-ˈtʃɑːt-

unchaste ʌnˈtʃest

unchastened ʌnˈtʃesn̩d (ˈunˌchastened ˈheart)

unchastity ʌnˈtʃæstətɪ

unchecked ʌnˈtʃɛkt (ˈunˌchecked ˈspeed)

unchristian ʌnˈkrɪstʃən

unchurch ʌnˈtʃɝtʃ; ES -ˈtʃɝtʃ, -ˈtʃɝtʃ; |-es -ɪz |-ed -t

uncial ˈʌnʃɪəl, ˈʌnʃəl, ˈʌnsɪəl |-ly -ɪ

uncircumcised ʌnˈsɝkəmˌsaɪzd; ES -ˈsɝk-, -ˈsɝk-; |-sedness -zɪdnɪs

uncivil ʌnˈsɪv‖ |-ized -ˌaɪzd |-ly -ɪ

unclad ʌnˈklæd

unclaimed ʌnˈklemd (ˈunˌclaimed ˈhonor)

unclasp ʌnˈklæsp; E+-ˈklasp, -ˈklɑsp; |-ed -t

unclassified ʌnˈklæsəˌfaɪd

uncle ˈʌŋk‖ |uncled ˈʌŋk‖d

unclean ʌnˈklin |-ed -d

uncleanly adv ʌnˈklinlɪ, adj ʌnˈklɛnlɪ

unclench ʌnˈklɛntʃ |-es -ɪz |-ed -t

Uncle Remus ˈʌŋk‖ˈriməs |-ʼs -ɪz

Uncle Sam ˈʌŋk‖ˈsæm

Uncle Tom's Cabin ˈʌŋk‖ˌtamzˈkæbɪn, -ˌtɒmz-

uncloak ʌnˈklok |uncloaked ʌnˈklokt

unclose adj ʌnˈklos

unclose v ʌnˈkloz |-s -ɪz |-d -d

unclothe ʌnˈkloð |-s -ðz |-d -d |-dly -ɪdlɪ

uncloud ʌnˈklaʊd |-clouded -ˈklaʊdɪd

unco ˈʌŋko

uncoil ʌnˈkɔɪl |-coiled -ˈkɔɪld

uncolored ʌnˈkʌlɚd; ES -ˈkʌləd

uncomely ʌnˈkʌmlɪ (ˈunˌcomely ˈspeech)

uncomfortable ʌnˈkʌmfɚtəb‖; ES -ˈkʌmfət-, -ˈkʌmftə-; |-bly -blɪ

uncommercial ˌʌnkəˈmɝʃəl; ES -ˈmɝʃəl, -ˈmɝʃəl; |-ly -ɪ

uncommon ʌnˈkamən; ES+-ˈkɒm-

uncommunicative ˌʌnkəˈmjunəˌketɪv, -ˈmɪun-

uncomplaining ˌʌnkəmˈplenɪŋ

uncompleted ˌʌnkəmˈplitɪd (ˈuncomˌpleted ˈjob)

uncomplimentary ˌʌnkampləˈmɛntərɪ, -trɪ; ES+-kɒm-

uncomprehending ˌʌnkamprɪˈhɛndɪŋ; ES+-kɒm-

uncompromising ʌnˈkamprəˌmaɪzɪŋ; ES+-ˈkɒm-

unconcealed ˌʌnkənˈsild (ˈunconˌcealed ˈire)

unconcern ˌʌnkənˈsɝn; ES -ˈsɝn, -ˈsɝn; |-ed -d |-edly -ɪdlɪ

unconcerted ˌʌnkənˈsɝtɪd; ES -ˈsɝt-, -ˈsɝt-

unconditional ˌʌnkənˈdɪʃən‖, -ʃnəl |-ly -ɪ

unconditioned ˌʌnkənˈdɪʃənd

unconfined ˌʌnkənˈfaɪnd |-finedly -ˈfaɪnɪdlɪ

unconfirmed ˌʌnkənˈfɝmd; ES -ˈfɝmd, -ˈfɝmd; |-medly -mɪdlɪ

unconformity ˌʌnkənˈfɔrmətɪ; ES -ˈfɔəmətɪ

uncongenial ˌʌnkənˈdʒinjəl |-ly -ɪ

unconnected ˌʌnkəˈnɛktɪd

unconquerable ʌnˈkaŋkərəb‖, -ˈkɒŋ-, -ˈkɔŋ-, -krəb‖ |-bly -blɪ

unconquered ʌnˈkaŋkɚd, -ˈkɒŋ-, -ˈkɔŋ-; ES -kəd

unconscious ʌnˈkanʃəs; ES+-ˈkɒn-

unconsecrated ʌnˈkansɪˌkretɪd; ES+-ˈkɒn-

unconsidered ˌʌnkənˈsɪdɚd; ES -ˈsɪdəd; (ˈunconˌsidered ˈtrifles)

unconstant ʌnˈkanstənt; ES+-ˈkɒn-

unconstitutional ˌʌnkanstəˈtjuʃən‖, -ˈtɪu-, -ˈtu-; ES+-kɒn-; |-ly -ɪ

unconstrained ˌʌnkənˈstrend |-nedly -nɪdlɪ

uncontestable ˌʌnkənˈtɛstəb‖ |-bly -blɪ

uncontrollable ˌʌnkənˈtroləb‖ |-bly -blɪ

uncontrolled ˌʌnkənˈtrold |-ledly -lɪdlɪ

unconventional ˌʌnkənˈvɛnʃən‖, -ʃnəl |-ly -ɪ

unconverted ˌʌnkənˈvɝtɪd; ES -ˈvɝt-, -ˈvɝt-; |-tible -təb‖ |-bly -blɪ

unconvinced ˌʌnkənˈvɪnst |-cedly -sɪdlɪ

uncooked ʌnˈkʊkt (ˈunˌcooked ˈfood)

un-co-ordinated ˌʌnkoˈɔrdn̩ˌetɪd; ES -ˈɔədn̩-

uncork ʌnˈkɔrk; ES ʌnˈkɔək; |-ed -t

uncorrected ˌʌnkəˈrɛktɪd

uncorroborated ˌʌnkəˈrabəˌretɪd; ES+-ˈrɒb-

Key: See in full §§3–47. bee bi |pity ˈpɪtɪ (§6) |rate ret |yet jɛt |sang sæŋ |angry ˈæŋ·grɪ |bath bæθ; E baθ (§10) |ah·ɑ |far fɑr |watch watʃ, wɒtʃ (§12) |jaw dʒɔ |gorge gɔrdʒ |go go

uncorrupted ˌʌnkəˈrʌptɪd
uncountable ʌnˈkaʊntəbļ |-bly -blɪ
uncouple ʌnˈkʌpļ |-d -d |-ling -plɪŋ, -pļɪŋ
uncouth ʌnˈkuθ (ˈunˌcouth ˈaspect)
uncover ʌnˈkʌvɚ; ES -ˈkʌvə(r; |-ed -d |-ing -ˈkʌvərɪŋ, -vrɪŋ
uncreated ˌʌnkrɪˈetɪd (ˈuncreˌated ˈworlds)
uncredited ʌnˈkrɛdɪtɪd |-table -təbļ |-bly -blɪ
uncritical ʌnˈkrɪtɪkļ |-ly -ɪ, -ɪklɪ
uncrossed ʌnˈkrɔst, -ˈkrɒst
uncrowned ʌnˈkraʊnd (ˈunˌcrowned ˈking)
unction ˈʌŋkʃən |-tious -ʃəs |-tional -ʃənļ
unctuosity ˌʌŋktʃʊˈɑsətɪ; ES +-ˈɒs-
unctuous ˈʌŋktʃʊəs
uncultivable ʌnˈkʌltəvəbļ
uncultivatable ʌnˈkʌltəˌvetəbļ |-vated -ˌvetɪd
uncultured ʌnˈkʌltʃɚd; ES -ˈkʌltʃəd
uncurdled ʌnˈkɝdļd; ES -ˈkɜdļd, -ˈkɝdļd
uncurious ʌnˈkjʊrɪəs, -ˈkɪʊrɪəs
uncurl ʌnˈkɝl; ES -ˈkɜl, -ˈkɝl; |-ed -d
uncurtained ʌnˈkɝtņd, -tɪnd; ES -ˈkɜt-, -ˈkɝt-
uncut ʌnˈkʌt (ˈunˌcut ˈpages)
undamaged ʌnˈdæmɪdʒd
undated ʌnˈdetɪd
undaunted ʌnˈdɔntɪd, -ˈdɒntɪd, -ˈdɑntɪd
undazzled ʌnˈdæzļd (ˈunˌdazzled ˈeyes)
undebated ˌʌndɪˈbetɪd |-table -təbļ
undeceive ˌʌndɪˈsiv |-d -d
undecided ˌʌndɪˈsaɪdɪd
undecipherable ˌʌndɪˈsaɪfərəbļ, -frəbļ |-bly -blɪ
undecorated ʌnˈdɛkəˌretɪd
undefeated ˌʌndɪˈfitɪd
undefended ˌʌndɪˈfɛndɪd (ˈundeˌfended ˈisle)
undefensible ˌʌndɪˈfɛnsəbļ |-bly -blɪ
undefiled ˌʌndɪˈfaɪld |-filedly -ˈfaɪlɪdlɪ
undefined ˌʌndɪˈfaɪnd |-nedly -nɪdlɪ |-nable -nəbļ |-bly -blɪ
undelayed ˌʌndɪˈled (ˈundeˌlayed ˈmail)
undelivered ˌʌndɪˈlɪvɚd; ES -vəd; |-rable -vrəbļ, -vərəbļ
undemocratic ˌʌndɛməˈkrætɪk |-ally -ļɪ, -ɪklɪ
undemonstrative ˌʌndɪˈmɑnstrətɪv; ES+ -ˈmɒn-
undeniable ˌʌndɪˈnaɪəbļ |-bly -blɪ
undenominational ˌʌndɪˌnɑməˈneʃənļ, -ʃnəl; ES+-ˌnɒm-
undependable ˌʌndɪˈpɛndəbļ |-bly -blɪ

under- Compounds in under- vary in accent according to meaning, rhythm, and sense stress. See note at prefix over-
under ˈʌndɚ; ES ˈʌndə(r
underact ˈʌndɚˈækt |-acted -ˈæktɪd
underage ‘shortage’ ˈʌndərɪdʒ, ˈʌndrɪdʒ |-s -ɪz
underage ˈʌndɚˈedʒ (ˈunderˌage ˈpupil)
underbid n ˈʌndɚˌbɪd; ES ˈʌndəˌbɪd
underbid v ˌʌndɚˈbɪd; ES ˌʌndə-; |past & pptc -bid -ˈbɪd
underbred n ˈʌndɚˈbrɛd; ES ˈʌndəˌbrɛd
underbred adj ˈʌndɚˈbrɛd; ES ˈʌndə-
underbrush ˈʌndɚˌbrʌʃ; ES ˈʌndə-
underbuy ˈʌndɚˈbaɪ; ES ˈʌndə-; |-bought -ˈbɔt
undercarriage ˈʌndɚˌkærɪdʒ; ES ˈʌndə-; |-s -ɪz
undercharge n ˈʌndɚˌtʃɑrdʒ; ES ˈʌndə-ˌtʃɑːdʒ, E+-ˌtʃɑːdʒ; |-s -ɪz
undercharge v ˈʌndɚˈtʃɑrdʒ; ES ˈʌndəˈtʃɑːdʒ, E+-ˈtʃɑːdʒ; |-s -ɪz |-d -d
underclothed ˈʌndɚˈkloðd; ES ˈʌndə-
underclothes ˈʌndɚˌkloz, -ˌkloðz; ES ˈʌndə-
underconsumption ˈʌndɚkənˈsʌmpʃən; ES ˈʌndə-
undercover ˌʌndɚˈkʌvɚ; ES ˌʌndəˈkʌvə(r
undercurrent ˈʌndɚˌkɝənt; ES ˈʌndəˌkɜrənt, -ˌkʌrənt, -ˌkɝ-
undercut n ˈʌndɚˌkʌt; ES ˈʌndə-
undercut v ˌʌndɚˈkʌt; ES ˌʌndə-
underdo ˌʌndɚˈdu; ES ˌʌndə-; |-does -ˈdʌz |-did -ˈdɪd |-done -ˈdʌn
underdog ˈʌndɚˌdɔg, -ˈdɒg-, -ˌd-; ES ˈʌndə-
underestimate n ˈʌndɚˈɛstəmɪt, -ˌmet
underestimate v ˈʌndɚˈɛstəˌmet |-d -ɪd
underestimation ˈʌndɚˌɛstəˈmeʃən
underexpose ˈʌndɚɪkˈspoz |-s -ɪz |-d -d |-sure -ʒɚ; ES -ʒə(r
underfeed n ˈʌndɚˌfid; ES ˈʌndə-
underfeed v ˈʌndɚˈfid; ES ˈʌndə-; |-fed -ˈfɛd
underfoot ˌʌndɚˈfʊt; ES ˌʌndə-; (ˈunderˌfoot ˈvassal)
undergarment ˈʌndɚˌgɑrmənt; ES ˈʌndəˌgɑːmənt, E+-ˌgɑːmənt
undergo ˌʌndɚˈgo; ES ˌʌndə-; |-went -ˈwɛnt |-gone -ˈgɔn, -ˈgɒn
undergraduate ˌʌndɚˈgrædʒʊɪt, -ˌet; ES ˌʌndə-

|full fʊl |tooth tuθ |further ˈfɝðɚ; ES ˈfɝðə |custom ˈkʌstəm |while hwaɪl |how haʊ |toy tɔɪ |using ˈjuzɪŋ |fuse fjuz, fɪuz |dish dɪʃ |vision ˈvɪʒən |Eden ˈidņ |cradle ˈkredļ |keep 'em ˈkipm̩

underground *adj, adv* ˈʌndɚˈgraʊnd; ES
ˈʌndə-; (ˈunderˌground ˈstream)
underground *n* ˈʌndɚˌgraʊnd; ES ˈʌndə-
undergrown ˈʌndɚˈgron; ES ˈʌndə-
undergrowth ˈʌndɚˌgroθ; ES ˈʌndə-; |-ths
-θs
underhand ˈʌndɚˈhænd; ES ˈʌndə-; (ˈunder-
ˌhand ˈstroke)
underhanded ˈʌndɚˈhændɪd; ES ˈʌndə-
underhung ˌʌndɚˈhʌŋ; ES ˌʌndə-
underivable ˌʌndɪˈraɪvəbḷ
underlaid ˌʌndɚˈled; ES ˌʌndə-
underlay *n* ˈʌndɚˌle; ES ˈʌndə-
underlay *past of* underlie ˌʌndɚˈle; ES ˌʌndə-
underlay *v* ˌʌndɚˈle; ES ˌʌndə-; |-laid -ˈled
underlie ˌʌndɚˈlaɪ; ES ˌʌndə-; |-lay -ˈle
|-lain -ˈlen
underline *n* ˈʌndɚˌlaɪn; ES ˈʌndə-
underline *v* ˌʌndɚˈlaɪn; ES ˌʌndə-; |-d -d
underling ˈʌndɚlɪŋ; ES ˈʌndə-
underlip ˈʌndɚˈlɪp; ES ˈʌndə-; (ˈunderˌlip
& ˈupper ˌlip)
underman *n* ˈʌndɚˌmæn; ES ˈʌndə-; |-men
-ˌmɛn
underman *v* ˈʌndɚˈmæn; ES ˈʌndə-; |-ned -d
undermine ˌʌndɚˈmaɪn; ES ˌʌndə-; |-d -d
undermost ˈʌndɚˌmost; ES ˈʌndə-
underneath ˌʌndɚˈniθ, -ˈnɪð; ES ˌʌndə-
undernourish ˈʌndɚˈnɝɪʃ; ES ˈʌndəˈnɝɪʃ,
-ˈnʌr-, -ˈnɝ-; |-es -ɪz |-ed -t
underofficer ˈʌndɚˌɒfəsɚ, -ˌɒf-,-ˌɑf-; ES -sə(r
underpass ˈʌndɚˌpæs; ES ˈʌndə-, E+-ˌpas,
-ˌpɑs
underpay ˈʌndɚˈpe; ES ˈʌndə-; |-paid -ˈped
underpin ˌʌndɚˈpɪn; ES ˌʌndə-; |-ned -d
underpinning *n* ˈʌndɚˌpɪnɪŋ;ES ˈʌndə-
underpopulated ˈʌndɚˈpɑpjəˌletɪd; ES ˈʌndə-
ˈpɑp-, -ˈpɒp-
underprivileged ˈʌndɚˈprɪvəlɪdʒd; ES ˈʌndə-
underprize ˈʌndɚˈpraɪz; ES ˈʌndə-; |-s -ɪz
|-d -d
underproduction ˈʌndɚprəˈdʌkʃən; ES ˈʌndə-
underrate ˈʌndɚˈret; ES ˈʌndəˈret; |-d -ɪd
underripe ˈʌndɚˈraɪp; ES ˈʌndə-
underrun ˌʌndɚˈrʌn; ES ˌʌndə-; |-ran -ˈræn
|-run -ˈrʌn
underscore ˌʌndɚˈskor, -ˈskɔr; ES ˌʌndə-
ˈskoə(r, E+-ˈskɔə(r; |-d -d—*acct* + ˈunder-
ˌscore

undersea ˈʌndɚˈsi; ES ˈʌndə-; (ˈunderˌsea
ˈlife)
undersecretary ˌʌndɚˈsɛkrəˌtɛrɪ; ES ˌʌndə-
undersell ˌʌndɚˈsɛl; ES ˌʌndə-; |-sold -ˈsold
undershirt ˈʌndɚˌʃɝt; ES ˈʌndəˌʃɝt, -ˌʃɝt
undershoot *v* ˌʌndɚˈʃut; ES ˌʌndə-; |-shot
-ˈʃɑt; ES+-ˈʃɒt
undershot *adj* ˈʌndɚˌʃɑt; ES ˈʌndəˌʃɑt, -ˌʃɒt
underside ˈʌndɚˈsaɪd; ES ˈʌndə-; (ˈunder-
ˌside & ˈupper ˌside)
undersign ˌʌndɚˈsaɪn; ES ˌʌndə-; |-ed -d
undersigned *n* ˌʌndɚˈsaɪnd; ES ˌʌndə-;
(ˈunderˌsigned ˈagent)
undersize *adj* ˈʌndɚˈsaɪz; ES ˈʌndə-; |-d -d
(ˈunderˌsize(d) ˈbolt)
undersize *n* ˈʌndɚˌsaɪz; ES ˈʌndə-; |-s -ɪz
underskirt ˈʌndɚˌskɝt; ES ˈʌndəˌskɝt, -ˌskɝt
underslung ˌʌndɚˈslʌŋ; ES ˌʌndə-
understand ˌʌndɚˈstænd; ES ˌʌndə-; |-stood
-ˈstʊd
understandability ˌʌndɚˌstændəˈbɪlətɪ; ES
ˌʌndə-
understandable ˌʌndɚˈstændəbḷ; ES ˌʌndə-;
|-bly -blɪ
understate ˈʌndɚˈstet; ES ˈʌndə-; |-d -ɪd
understood ˌʌndɚˈstʊd; ES ˌʌndə-
understrapper ˈʌndɚˌstræpɚ; ES ˈʌndə-
ˌstræpə(r
understudy ˈʌndɚˌstʌdɪ; ES ˈʌndə-
undertake ˌʌndɚˈtek; ES ˌʌndə-; |-took
-ˈtʊk |-taken -ˈtekən
undertaker *'who undertakes'* ˌʌndɚˈtekɚ; ES
ˌʌndəˈtekə(r; *'funeral director'* ˈunderˌtaker
undertaking *'enterprise'* ˌʌndɚˈtekɪŋ; ES
ˌʌndə-; *'directing funerals'* ˈunderˌtaking
undertone ˈʌndɚˌton; ES ˈʌndə-; |-d -d
undertook ˌʌndɚˈtʊk; ES ˌʌndə-
undertow ˈʌndɚˌto; ES ˈʌndə-
undertrump ˌʌndɚˈtrʌmp; ES ˌʌndə-; |-ed -t
undervaluation ˈʌndɚˌvæljuˈeʃən; ES ˈʌndə-
undervalue ˈʌndɚˈvælju; ES ˈʌndə-; |-d -d
underwater *n* ˈʌndɚˌwɑtɚ, -ˌwɑtɚ, -ˌwɒtɚ; ES
-tə(r; *adj cf* ˈunderˈwater ˌwork *and* ˈunder-
ˌwater ˈmines
underwear ˈʌndɚˌwɛr, -ˌwær; E ˈʌndəˌwɛə(r,
ES ˈʌndəˌwæə(r
underweight ˈʌndɚˈwet; ES ˈʌndə-; (ˈunder-
ˌweight ˈboxer)
underwent ˌʌndɚˈwɛnt; ES ˌʌndə-

underwood, U- 'ʌndə˞ˌwʊd; ES 'ʌndə-; |-ed -ɪd

underworld 'ʌndə˞ˌwɜˑld; ES 'ʌndəˌwɜld, -ˌwɜˑld

underwrite ˌʌndə˞'raɪt; ES ˌʌndə-; |-wrote -'rot |-written -'rɪtn̩

underwriter 'ʌndə˞ˌraɪtə˞; ES 'ʌndəˌraɪtə(r

undescribable ˌʌndɪ'skraɪbəbl̩ |-bly -blɪ

undeserved ˌʌndɪ'zɜˑvd; ES -'zɜvd, -'zɜˑvd; |-vedly -vɪdlɪ

undesigning ˌʌndɪ'zaɪnɪŋ

undesirability ˌʌndɪˌzaɪrə'bɪlətɪ

undesirable ˌʌndɪ'zaɪrəbl̩ |-bly -blɪ

undesired ˌʌndɪ'zaɪrd; ES -'zaɪəd; |-ly -rɪdlɪ

undetected ˌʌndɪ'tɛktɪd

undetermined ˌʌndɪ'tɜˑmɪnd; ES -'tɜm-, -'tɜˑm-; |-nable -nəbl̩ |-bly -blɪ

undeterred ˌʌndɪ'tɜˑd; ES -'tɜd, -'tɜˑd

undeveloped ˌʌndɪ'vɛləpt

undeviating ʌn'divɪˌetɪŋ

undid ʌn'dɪd

undies 'ʌndɪz

undigested ˌʌndə'dʒɛstɪd, daɪ- |-tible -təbl̩

undignified ʌn'dɪgnəˌfaɪd

undiluted ˌʌndɪ'lutɪd, -daɪ-, -'lɪutɪd

undiminished ˌʌndə'mɪnɪʃt

undimmed ʌn'dɪmd ('unˌdimmed 'lights)

Undine 'ʌndin, 'ʌndaɪn

undiplomatic ˌʌndɪplə'mætɪk |-ally -l̩ɪ, -ɪklɪ

undiscerned ˌʌndɪ'zɜˑnd, -'sɜˑnd; ES -ɜnd, -ɜˑnd; |-nedly -nɪdlɪ

undiscernible, -able ˌʌndɪ'zɜˑnəbl̩, -'sɜˑn-; ES -ɜn-, -ɜˑn-; |-bly -blɪ

undisciplined ʌn'dɪsəˌplɪnd

undisclosed ˌʌndɪs'klozd

undiscouraged ˌʌndɪs'kɜˑɪdʒd; ES -'kɜr-, -'kʌr-, -'kɜˑ-

undiscovered ˌʌndɪ'skʌvə˞d; ES -'skʌvəd; |-verable -vərəbl̩, -vrəbl̩ ('undisˌcovered 'country)

undiscriminating ˌʌndɪ'skrɪməˌnetɪŋ

undisguised ˌʌndɪs'gaɪzd |-sedly -zɪdlɪ |-sable -zəbl̩ |-bly -blɪ

undismayed ˌʌndɪs'med ('undisˌmayed 'heart)

undisposed ˌʌndɪ'spozd

undisputed ˌʌndɪ'spjutɪd, -'sprutɪd

undissolved ˌʌndɪ'zɑlvd, -'zɒlvd; |-vable -vəbl̩ |-bly -blɪ

undistilled ˌʌndɪ'stɪld

undistinguished ˌʌndɪ'stɪŋgwɪʃt |-shable -ʃəbl̩

undistracted ˌʌndɪ'stræktɪd

undistributed ˌʌndɪ'strɪbjətɪd

undisturbed ˌʌndɪ'stɜˑbd; ES -'stɜbd, -'stɜˑbd |-bedly -bɪdlɪ

undiversified ˌʌndə'vɜˑsəˌfaɪd; ES -'vɜsə-, -'vɜˑsə-

undivided ˌʌndə'vaɪdɪd

undivulged ˌʌndə'vʌldʒd ('undiˌvulged 'purpose)

undo ʌn'du |-does -'dʌz |-did -'dɪd |-done -'dʌn

undomestic ˌʌndə'mɛstɪk |-ticated -tɪˌketɪd

undone ʌn'dʌn ('done & 'unˌdone)

undouble ʌn'dʌbl̩ |-d -d |-ling -blɪŋ, -bl̩ɪŋ

undoubted ʌn'daʊtɪd ('unˌdoubted 'fact)

undrained ʌn'drend

undramatic ˌʌndrə'mætɪk |-ally -l̩ɪ, -ɪklɪ

undrape ʌn'drep |-d -t

undreamed ʌn'drimd |-dreamt -'drɛmpt

undress n 'ʌnˌdrɛs, adj ʌn'drɛs ('unˌdress 'garb)

undress v ʌn'drɛs |-es -ɪz |-ed -t

undrilled ʌn'drɪld

undrinkable ʌn'drɪŋkəbl̩

Undset 'ʊnsɛt

undue ʌn'dju, -'dɪu, -'du ('unˌdue 'haste)

undulant 'ʌndjələnt, 'ʌndələnt

undulate adj 'ʌndjəlɪt, 'ʌndə-, -ˌlet

undulate v 'ʌndjəˌlet, 'ʌndə- |-d -ɪd

undulation ˌʌndjə'leʃən, ˌʌndə-

undulatory 'ʌndjələˌtorɪ, 'ʌndə-, -ˌtɔrɪ; S -ˌtorɪ

unduly ʌn'djulɪ, -'dɪulɪ, -'dulɪ

undutiful ʌn'djutɪfəl, -'dɪu-, -'du- |-ly -ɪ

undyed ʌn'daɪd ('unˌdyed 'wool)

undying ʌn'daɪɪŋ

unearned ʌn'ɜˑnd; ES -ɜnd, -ɜˑnd

unearth ʌn'ɜˑθ; ES -ɜθ, -ɜˑθ; |-ed -t |-ly -lɪ

uneasily ʌn'izl̩ɪ, -'izɪlɪ

uneasy ʌn'izɪ ('unˌeasy 'sleep)

uneaten ʌn'itn̩ |-table -təbl̩

uneclipsed ˌʌnɪ'klɪpst

uneconomical ˌʌnikə'nɑmɪkl̩, -ɛk-; ES+ -'nɒm-; |-ly -ɪ, -ɪklɪ

unedifying ʌn'ɛdəˌfaɪɪŋ

uneducable ʌn'ɛdʒəkəbl̩, -dʒʊ-

uneducated ʌn'ɛdʒəˌketɪd, -dʒʊ-

unembarrassed ˌʌnɪm'bærəst, -ɪst

---

unemotional ˌʌnɪˈmoʃənḷ, -ʃnəl |-ly -ɪ
unemphatic ˌʌnɪmˈfætɪk |-ally -ḷ, -ɪklɪ
unemployable ˌʌnɪmˈplɔɪəbḷ
unemployed ˌʌnɪmˈplɔɪd |-ployment -ˈplɔɪmənt
unenclosed ˌʌnɪnˈklozd
unencumbered ˌʌnɪnˈkʌmbəd; ES -ˈkʌmbəd
unending ʌnˈɛndɪŋ (ˈunˌending ˈlabor)
unendorsed ˌʌnɪnˈdɔrst; ES -ˈdɔəst
unendurable ˌʌnɪnˈdjurəbḷ, -ˈdɪur-, -ˈdur- |-bly -blɪ |-ring -ɪŋ
unenforceable ˌʌnɪnˈforsəbḷ, -ˈfɔrs-; ES -ˈfoəs-, E+-ˈfɔəs-; |-bly -blɪ
unengaged ˌʌnɪnˈgedʒd (ˈunenˌgaged ˈtime)
unenjoyable ˌʌnɪnˈdʒɔɪəbḷ
unenlightened ˌʌnɪnˈlaɪtṇd |-ning -tṇɪŋ, -tnɪŋ
unenterprising ʌnˈɛntəˌpraɪzɪŋ; ES -ˈɛntə-
unentertaining ˌʌnɛntəˈtenɪŋ; ES -ɛntə-
unenthusiastic ˌʌnɪnˌθjuzɪˈæstɪk, -ˌθɪuz-, -ˌθuz- |-ally -ḷ, -ɪklɪ
unenvied ʌnˈɛnvɪd |-viable -vɪəbḷ |-bly -blɪ
unequal ʌnˈikwəl |-ed -d |-ly -ɪ
unequipped ˌʌnɪˈkwɪpt
unequivocal ˌʌnɪˈkwɪvəkḷ |-ly -ɪ, -əklɪ
unerring ʌnˈɝɪŋ, -ˈɛr-; ES -ˈɜrɪŋ, -ˈɝɪŋ, -ˈɛrɪŋ
unescapable ˌʌnəˈskepəbḷ |-bly -blɪ
unessential ˌʌnəˈsɛnʃəl |-ly -ɪ
unestimated ʌnˈɛstəˌmetɪd
unethical ʌnˈɛθɪkḷ |-ly -ɪ, -ɪklɪ
uneven ʌnˈivən (ˈunˌeven ˈground)
uneventful ˌʌnɪˈvɛntfəl |-ly -ɪ
unexaggerated ˌʌnɪgˈzædʒəˌretɪd
unexampled ˌʌnɪgˈzæmpḷd; E+-ˈzamp-, -ˈzamp-
unexceptionable ˌʌnɪkˈsɛpʃənəbḷ, -ʃnəbḷ |-bly -blɪ
unexceptional ˌʌnɪkˈsɛpʃənḷ, -ʃnəl |-ly -ɪ
unexchanged ˌʌnɪksˈtʃendʒd |-geable -dʒəbḷ |-bly -blɪ
unexciting ˌʌnɪkˈsaɪtɪŋ (ˈunexˌciting ˈlife)
unexcused ˌʌnɪkˈskjuzd, -ˈskɪuzd |-sable -zəbḷ |-bly -blɪ
unexecuted ʌnˈɛksɪˌkjutɪd, -ˌkɪutɪd
unexhausted ˌʌnɪgˈzɔstɪd |-tible -təbḷ |-bly -blɪ
unexpected ˌʌnɪkˈspɛktɪd (ˈunexˌpected ˈguest)
unexpended ˌʌnɪkˈspɛndɪd
unexperienced ˌʌnɪkˈspɪrɪənst

unexpired ˌʌnɪkˈspaɪrd; ES -ˈspaɪəd
unexplained ˌʌnɪkˈsplend |-nedly -nɪdlɪ |-nable -nəbḷ |-bly -blɪ
unexploded ˌʌnɪkˈsplodɪd (ˈunexˌploded ˈmyth)
unexplored ˌʌnɪkˈsplord, -ˈsplɔrd; ES -ˈsploəd, E+-ˈsplɔəd
unexposed ˌʌnɪkˈspozd
unexpressed ˌʌnɪkˈsprɛst |-sable, -sible, -səbḷ |-bly -blɪ
unexpressive ˌʌnɪkˈsprɛsɪv (ˈunexˌpressive ˈshe)
unexpurgated ʌnˈɛkspəˌgetɪd, ˌʌnɪkˈspɝgetɪd; ES -ˈɛkspə-, -ɪkˈspɜ-, -ˈspɝ-
unfaded ʌnˈfedɪd |-dable -dəbḷ |-bly -blɪ
unfading ʌnˈfedɪŋ (ˈunˌfading ˈblue)
unfailing ʌnˈfelɪŋ
unfair ʌnˈfɛr, -ˈfær; E -ˈfɛə(r, ES -ˈfæə(r
unfaithful ʌnˈfeθfəl |-ly -ɪ
unfaltering ʌnˈfɔltrɪŋ, -ˈfɔltərɪŋ
unfamiliar ˌʌnfəˈmɪljə; ES -ˈmɪljə(r
unfamiliarity ˌʌnfəˌmɪlɪˈærətɪ, -ˌmɪljɪˈærətɪ, -ˌmɪlˈjærətɪ
unfashionable ʌnˈfæʃnəbḷ, -ʃənə- |-bly -blɪ
unfasten ʌnˈfæsṇ |-ed -d |-ing -ˈfæsnɪŋ, -ˈfæsṇɪŋ; E+-ˈfas-, -ˈfas-
unfathered ʌnˈfaðəd; ES -ˈfaðəd, E+-ˈfað-
unfathomed ʌnˈfæðəmd |-mable -əməbḷ |-bly -blɪ
unfavorable ʌnˈfevrəbḷ, ˈfevərə- |-bly -blɪ
unfed ʌnˈfɛd (ˈunˌfed ˈflock)
unfeeling ʌnˈfilɪŋ
unfeigned ʌnˈfend |-nedly -nɪdlɪ
unfelt ʌnˈfɛlt (ˈunˌfelt ˈsorrow)
unfenced ʌnˈfɛnst
unfermented ˌʌnfəˈmɛntɪd; ES -fəˈmɛntɪd
unfertilized ʌnˈfɝtḷˌaɪzd; ES -ˈfɜt-, -ˈfɝt-
unfetter ʌnˈfɛtə; ES -ˈfɛtə(r; |-ed -d
unfilial ʌnˈfɪlɪəl, -ˈfɪljəl |-ly -ɪ
unfilled ʌnˈfɪld (ˈunˌfilled ˈquota)
unfinished ʌnˈfɪnɪʃt
unfired ʌnˈfaɪrd; ES -ˈfaɪəd
unfit ʌnˈfɪt |-ted -ɪd
unfix ʌnˈfɪks |-es -ɪz |-ed -t
unflagging ʌnˈflægɪŋ
unflattering ʌnˈflætərɪŋ, -ˈflætrɪŋ
unflavored ʌnˈflevəd; ES -ˈflevəd
unfledged ʌnˈflɛdʒd (ˈunˌfledged ˈyouth)
unfold ʌnˈfold |-ed -ɪd

Key: *See in full §§3–47.* bee **bi** |pity ˈpɪtɪ (§6) |rate **ret** |yet jɛt |sang sæŋ |angry ˈæŋ·grɪ |bath bæθ; E baθ (§10) |ah ɑ |far fɑr |watch wɑtʃ, wɒtʃ (§12) |jaw dʒɔ |gorge gɔrdʒ |go go

unforbidden ˌʌnfɚˈbɪdn̩; ES -fəˈbɪdn̩
unforced ʌnˈfɔrst, -ˈfɔrst; ES -ˈfɔəst, E+ -ˈfɔəst; |-cedly -sɪdlɪ
unforeseeable ˌʌnforˈsiəbl̩, -fɔr-; ES -fɔə-, E+-fə-; |-bly -blɪ
unforeseen ˌʌnforˈsin, -fɔr-, -fɚ-; ES -fɔə-, -fə-, E+-fɔə-
unforgettable ˌʌnfɚˈgɛtəbl̩; ES -fə-; |-bly -blɪ
unforgiven ˌʌnfɚˈgɪvən; ES -fə-; |-givable -ˈgɪvəbl̩ |-bly -blɪ
unforgot ˌʌnfɚˈgɑt; ES -fəˈgɑt, -ˈgɒt; |-ten -n̩
unformed ʌnˈfɔrmd; ES -ˈfɔəmd
unformulated ʌnˈfɔrmjəˌletɪd; ES -ˈfɔəm-
unfortified ʌnˈfɔrtəˌfaɪd; ES -ˈfɔətəˌfaɪd
unfortunate ʌnˈfɔrtʃənɪt; ES -ˈfɔətʃənɪt
unfounded ʌnˈfaʊndɪd (ˈunˌfounded ˈrumor)
unframed ʌnˈfremd
unfree ʌnˈfri |-d -d
unfrequent ʌnˈfrikwənt |-ncy -nsɪ
unfrequented ˌʌnfrɪˈkwɛntɪd
unfriended ʌnˈfrɛndɪd
unfrock ʌnˈfrɑk; ES+-ˈfrɒk; |-ed -t
unfruitful ʌnˈfrutfəl, -ˈfrɪut- |-ly -ɪ
unfulfilled ˌʌnfʊlˈfɪld (ˈunfulˌfilled ˈhope)
unfunded ʌnˈfʌndɪd
unfurl ʌnˈfɝl; ES -ˈfɜl, -ˈfɝl; |-ed -d
unfurnished ʌnˈfɝnɪʃt; ES -ˈfɜn-, -ˈfɝn-
ungainly ʌnˈgenlɪ
ungallant ʌnˈgælənt
ungalled ʌnˈgɔld (ˈunˌgalled ˈjade)
ungarbled ʌnˈgɑrbl̩d; ES -ˈgɑːbl̩d, E+-ˈgɑːb-
ungarnished ʌnˈgɑrnɪʃt; ES -ˈgɑːn-, E+ -ˈgɑːn-
ungathered ʌnˈgæðɚd; ES -ˈgæðəd
ungenerous ʌnˈdʒɛnərəs, -ˈdʒɛnrəs
ungentle ʌnˈdʒɛntl̩ |-tly -tlɪ
ungentlemanly ʌnˈdʒɛntl̩mənlɪ
ungifted ʌnˈgɪftɪd
ungird ʌnˈgɝd; ES -ˈgɜd, -ˈgɝd; |-ed -ɪd
ungirt ʌnˈgɝt; ES -ˈgɜt, -ˈgɝt
unglazed ʌnˈglezd (ˈunˌglazed ˈchina)
ungloved ʌnˈglʌvd
unglue ʌnˈglu, -ˈglɪu |-d -d
ungodly ʌnˈgɑdlɪ, -ˈgɒdlɪ, -ˈgɔdlɪ
ungot ʌnˈgɑt; ES+-ˈgɒt; |-ten -n̩
ungoverned ʌnˈgʌvɚnd; ES -ˈgʌvənd; |-nable -nəbl̩ |-bly -blɪ
ungraceful ʌnˈgresfəl |-ly -ɪ
ungracious ʌnˈgreʃəs

ungraded ʌnˈgredɪd
ungrammatical ˌʌngrəˈmætɪkl̩ |-ly -ɪ, -ɪklɪ
ungrateful ʌnˈgretfəl |-ly -ɪ
ungrounded ʌnˈgraʊndɪd (ˈunˌgrounded ˈfear)
ungrudging ʌnˈgrʌdʒɪŋ
unguard ʌnˈgɑrd; ES -ˈgɑːd, E+-ˈgɑːd; |-ed -ɪd
unguent ˈʌŋgwənt |-ed -ɪd
unguided ʌnˈgaɪdɪd
ungulate ˈʌŋgjəlɪt, -ˌlet
unhackneyed ʌnˈhæknɪd
unhair ʌnˈhɛr, -ˈhær; E -ˈhɛə(r, ES -ˈhæə(r; |-ed -d
unhallowed ʌnˈhælod, -ˈhæləd
unhampered ʌnˈhæmpɚd; ES -ˈhæmpəd
unhand ʌnˈhænd |-ed -ɪd
unhandicapped ʌnˈhændɪˌkæpt
unhandsome ʌnˈhænsəm (ˈunˌhandsome ˈdeed)
unhandy ʌnˈhændɪ |-dily -dl̩ɪ, -dɪlɪ
unhanged ʌnˈhæŋd
unhappy ʌnˈhæpɪ |-pily -pl̩ɪ, -pɪlɪ
unhardened ʌnˈhardn̩d; ES -ˈhɑːdn̩d, E+ -ˈhɑːd-
unharmed ʌnˈharmd; ES -ˈhɑːmd, E+ -ˈhɑːmd
unharmonious ˌʌnharˈmonɪəs, -njəs; ES -ha-, E+-ha-
unharness ʌnˈharnɪs; ES -ˈhɑːnɪs, E+ -ˈhɑːnɪs; |-es -ɪz |-ed -t
unhat ʌnˈhæt |-hatted -ˈhætɪd
unhatched ʌnˈhætʃt
unhealthful ʌnˈhɛlθfəl |-ly -ɪ
unhealthily ʌnˈhɛlθəlɪ, -ɪlɪ
unhealthy ʌnˈhɛlθɪ (ˈunˌhealthy ˈfogs)
unheard ʌnˈhɝd; ES -ˈhɜd, -ˈhɝd
unheard-of ʌnˈhɝdˌav, -ˌɒv, -ˌʌv; ES -ˈhɜd-, -ˈhɝd-
unheedful ʌnˈhidfəl |-ly -ɪ
unhelm ʌnˈhɛlm |-ed -d
unheralded ʌnˈhɛrəldɪd
unheroic ˌʌnhɪˈroˌɪk, -hi- |-al -l̩ |-ally -l̩ɪ, -ɪklɪ
unhesitating ʌnˈhɛzəˌtetɪŋ
unhindered ʌnˈhɪndɚd; ES -ˈhɪndəd
unhinge ʌnˈhɪndʒ |-s -ɪz |-d -d
unhitch ʌnˈhɪtʃ |-es -ɪz |-ed -t
unholy ʌnˈholɪ |-holily -ˈholəlɪ, -lɪlɪ
unhonored ʌnˈanɚd; ES -ˈanəd, -ˈɒnəd
unhood ʌnˈhʊd |-ed -ɪd

|full fʊl |tooth tuθ |further ˈfɝðɚ; ES ˈfɜðə |custom ˈkʌstəm |while hwaɪl |how haʊ |toy tɔɪ |using ˈjuzɪŋ |fuse fjuz, fɪuz |dish dɪʃ |vision ˈvɪʒən |Eden ˈidn̩ |cradle ˈkredl̩ |keep 'em ˈkipm̩

unhook ʌnˈhʊk |-ed -t
unhoped ʌnˈhopt
unhoped-for ʌnˈhoptˌfɔr; ES -ˌfɔə(r
unhorse ʌnˈhɔrs; ES -ˈhɔəs; |-s -ɪz |-d -t
unhouse ʌnˈhaʊz |-s -ɪz |-d -d
unhung ʌnˈhʌŋ (ˈunˌhung ˈpicture)
unhurried ʌnˈhɜˑɪd; ES -ˈhɜrɪd, -ˈhʌrɪd, -ˈhɜˑɪd
unhurt ʌnˈhɜˑt; ES -ˈhɜt, -ˈhɜˑt
unhusk ʌnˈhʌsk |-ed -t
unhygienic ˌʌnhaɪdʒɪˈɛnɪk |-ally -ļɪ, -ɪklɪ
unhyphenated ʌnˈhaɪfəˌnetɪd
Uniat ˈjunɪˌæt
unicameral ˌjunɪˈkæmərəl
unicellular ˌjunɪˈsɛljələˑ; ES -lə(r
Unicoi ˈjunɪˌkɔɪ
unicorn, U- ˈjunɪˌkɔrn; ES -ˌkɔən
unidentified ˌʌnaɪˈdɛntəˌfaɪd, ˌʌnə-
unidiomatic ˌʌnɪdɪəˈmætɪk |-ally -ļɪ, -ɪklɪ
unifiable ˈjunəˌfaɪəbļ |-bly -blɪ
unification ˌjunəfəˈkeʃən
unifier ˈjunəˌfaɪəˑ; ES -ˌfaɪˑə(r
uniform ˈjunəˌfɔrm; ES -ˌfɔəm
uniformitarian ˌjunəˌfɔrməˈtɛrɪən, -ˈter-; ES -ˌfɔəmə-
uniformity ˌjunəˈfɔrmətɪ; ES -ˈfɔəm-
unify ˈjunəˌfaɪ |-fied -ˌfaɪd
unilateral ˌjunɪˈlætərəl |-ly -ɪ
unilluminated ˌʌnəˈluməˌnetɪd, -ˈlɪum-
unimaginable ˌʌnɪˈmædʒɪnəbļ, -ˈmædʒnəbļ |-bly -blɪ
unimagined ˌʌnɪˈmædʒɪnd (ˈuniˌmagined ˈjoy)
unimpaired ˌʌnɪmˈpɛrd, -ˈpærd; E -ˈpɛəd, ES -ˈpæəd
unimpassioned ˌʌnɪmˈpæʃənd
unimpeachable ˌʌnɪmˈpitʃəbļ |-bly -blɪ
unimpeded ˌʌnɪmˈpidɪd (ˈunimˌpeded ˈway)
unimportance ˌʌnɪmˈpɔrtn̩s; ES -ˈpɔətn̩s; |-nt -n̩t
unimposing ˌʌnɪmˈpozɪŋ
unimpressionable ˌʌnɪmˈprɛʃnəbļ, -ʃənəbļ
unimpressive ˌʌnɪmˈprɛsɪv
unimproved ˌʌnɪmˈpruvd (ˈunimˌproved ˈland)
uninclosed ˌʌnɪnˈklozd
unincorporated ˌʌnɪnˈkɔrpəˌretɪd; ES -ˈkɔəp-
unincumbered ˌʌnɪnˈkʌmbəˑd; ES -ˈkʌmbəd
unindorsed ˌʌnɪnˈdɔrst; ES -ˈdɔəst
uninfected ˌʌnɪnˈfɛktɪd
uninflammable ˌʌnɪnˈflæməbļ

uninflected ˌʌnɪnˈflɛktɪd (ˈuninˌflected ˈstem)
uninfluenced ʌnˈɪnfluənst, -flɪʊənst
uninformed ˌʌnɪnˈfɔrmd; ES -ˈfɔəmd
uninhabitable ˌʌnɪnˈhæbɪtəbļ |-bly -blɪ
uninhabited ˌʌnɪnˈhæbɪtɪd
uninitiated ˌʌnɪˈnɪʃɪˌetɪd
uninjured ʌnˈɪndʒəˑd; ES -ˈɪndʒəd
uninspired ˌʌnɪnˈspaɪrd; ES -ˈspaɪəd
uninstructed ˌʌnɪnˈstrʌktɪd
unintelligent ˌʌnɪnˈtɛlədʒənt |-gence -dʒəns
unintelligibility ˌʌnɪnˌtɛlədʒəˈbɪlətɪ
unintelligible ˌʌnɪnˈtɛlədʒəbļ |-bly -blɪ
unintended ˌʌnɪnˈtɛndɪd (ˈuninˌtended ˈjoke)
unintentional ˌʌnɪnˈtɛnʃənļ, -ʃnəl |-ly -ɪ
uninterested ʌnˈɪntərɪstɪd, -ˈɪntrɪstɪd, -ˈɪntəˌrɛstɪd |-ting -tɪŋ—see interesting
unintermitting ˌʌnɪntəˑˈmɪtɪŋ; ES -ɪntə-
uninterrupted ˌʌnɪntəˈrʌptɪd
uninvited ˌʌnɪnˈvaɪtɪd |-ting -tɪŋ
union ˈjunjən |-ize -ˌaɪz |-izes -ˌaɪzɪz |-ized -ˌaɪzd
unipod ˈjunəˌpɑd; ES+-ˌpɒd
unique juˈnik
unisexual ˌjunɪˈsɛkʃʊəl |-ly -ɪ
unison ˈjunəzn̩, ˈjunəsn̩
unissued ʌnˈɪʃud, -ˈɪʃjud—see issue
unit ˈjunɪt |-age -ɪdʒ |-ages -ɪdʒɪz
Unitarian, u- ˌjunəˈtɛrɪən, -ˈterɪən, -rjən
unitary ˈjunəˌtɛrɪ
unite juˈnaɪt |-d -ɪd
United States juˈnaɪtɪdˈstets, often ˈjuˌnaɪtɪdˈstets
unitive ˈjunətɪv |unity ˈjunətɪ
univalent ˌjunəˈvelənt, juˈnɪvələnt
universal ˌjunəˈvɜˑsļ; ES -ˈvɜs], -ˈvɜˑs]; |-ly -ɪ
universality ˌjunəvɜˑˈsælətɪ, -vəˈsæl-; ES -vɜ-, -vɜˑ-, -və-
universalize ˌjunəˈvɜˑsļˌaɪz; ES -ˈvɜs-, -ˈvɜˑs-; |-s -ɪz |-d -d
universe ˈjunəˌvɜˑs; ES -ˌvɜs, -ˌvɜˑs; |-s -ɪz
university ˌjunəˈvɜˑsətɪ, -ˈvɜˑstɪ; ES -ˈvɜs-, -ˈvɜˑs-; (ˈUniˌversity ˈHeights)
unjust ʌnˈdʒʌst (ˈunˌjust ˈsteward)
unjustified ʌnˈdʒʌstəˌfaɪd |-fiable -ˌfaɪəbļ |-bly -blɪ
unkempt ʌnˈkɛmpt
unkept ʌnˈkɛpt
unkind ʌnˈkaɪnd
unknit ʌnˈnɪt |-ted -ɪd

Key: *See in full §§3–47.* bee bi |pity ˈpɪtɪ (§6) |rate ret |yet jɛt |sang sæŋ |angry ˈæŋ·grɪ |bath bæθ; E baθ (§10) |ah ɑ |far fɑr |watch wɑtʃ, wɒtʃ (§12) |jaw dʒɔ |gorge gɔrdʒ |go go

unknowable ʌn'noəbļ |-bly -blɪ
unknown ʌn'non ('un͵known 'place)
unlabeled ʌn'lebļd
unlabored ʌn'lebəd; ES -'lebəd
unlace ʌn'les |-s -ɪz |-d -t
unlade ʌn'led |-laded -'ledɪd |-laden -'ledn̩
unladylike ʌn'ledɪ͵laɪk
unlaid ʌn'led ('un͵laid 'ghost)
unlamented ͵ʌnlə'mɛntɪd
unlash ʌn'læʃ |-es -ɪz |-ed -t
unlatch ʌn'lætʃ; |-es -ɪz |-ed -t
unlawful ʌn'lɔfəl |-ly -ɪ
unlearn ʌn'lɜn; ES -'lɜn, -'lɝn; |-ed -d, -t *or* -t -t
unlearned *past & pptc* ʌn'lɜnd, -'lɝnt; ES -'lɜn-, -'lɝn-; *adj* -nɪd
unlearnt ʌn'lɝnt; ES -'lɜnt, -'lɝnt
unleash ʌn'liʃ |-es -ɪz |-ed -t
unleavened ʌn'lɛvənd ('un͵leavened 'bread)
unled ʌn'lɛd
unless ən'lɛs
unlessoned ʌn'lɛsn̩d ('un͵lessoned 'girl)
unlettered ʌn'lɛtəd; ES -'lɛtəd; ('un͵lettered 'Muse)
unlicensed ʌn'laɪsənst
unlighted ʌn'laɪtɪd
unlike ʌn'laɪk |-ly -lɪ |-lihood -lɪ͵hʊd
unlimber ʌn'lɪmbə; ES -'lɪmbə(r; |-ed -d |-ing -brɪŋ, -bərɪŋ
unlimited ʌn'lɪmɪtɪd
unlined ʌn'laɪnd ('un͵lined 'fur)
unlink ʌn'lɪŋk |-ed -t
unlisted ʌn'lɪstɪd
unlit ʌn'lɪt ('un͵lit 'candle)
unload ʌn'lod |-ed -ɪd
unlock ʌn'lɑk; ES+-'lɒk; |-ed -t
unlooked-for ʌn'lʊkt͵fɔr; ES -͵fɔə(r
unloose ʌn'lus |-s -ɪz |-d -t |-n -'lusn̩
unlovable ʌn'lʌvəbļ |-bly -blɪ
unloved ʌn'lʌvd |-lovely -'lʌvlɪ
unlucky ʌn'lʌkɪ ('un͵lucky 'strike)
unmagnetic ͵ʌnmæg'nɛtɪk |-al -ļ
unmailed ʌn'meld |-lable -ləbļ
unmake ʌn'mek |-made -'med
unman ʌn'mæn |-manned -'mænd
unmanageable ʌn'mænɪdʒəbļ |-bly -blɪ
unmanly ʌn'mænlɪ
unmannered ʌn'mænəd; ES -'mænəd
unmannerly ʌn'mænəlɪ; ES -'mænəlɪ

unmanufactured ͵ʌnmænjə'fæktʃəd, -mænə-; ES -tʃəd
unmarked ʌn'mɑrkt; ES -'mɑ:kt, E+-'mɑ:kt
unmarketable ʌn'mɑrkɪtəbļ; ES -'mɑ:k-, E+-'mɑ:k-
unmarriageable ʌn'mærɪdʒəbļ
unmarried ʌn'mærɪd ('un͵married 'man)
unmask ʌn'mæsk; E+-'mask, -'mɑsk; |-ed -t
unmatched ʌn'mætʃt |-matchable -'mætʃəbļ |-bly -blɪ
unmeaning ʌn'minɪŋ
unmeant ʌn'mɛnt
unmeasurable ʌn'mɛʒrəbļ, -ʒərəbļ |-bly -blɪ
unmechanical ͵ʌnmɪ'kænɪkļ |-ly -ɪ, -ɪklɪ
unmeet ʌn'mit
unmelodious ͵ʌnmə'lodɪəs
unmelted ʌn'mɛltɪd ('un͵melted 'snow)
unmentioned ʌn'mɛnʃənd |-nable -ʃənəbļ, -ʃnəbļ |-bly -blɪ
unmerchantable ʌn'mɝtʃəntəbļ; ES -'mɝtʃ-, -'mɝtʃ-
unmerciful ʌn'mɝsɪfəl; ES -'mɜs-, -'mɝs-; |-ly -ɪ, -flɪ
unmerited ʌn'mɛrɪtɪd
unmethodical ͵ʌnmə'θɑdɪkļ; ES+-'θɒd-; |-ly -ɪ, -ɪklɪ
unmew ʌn'mju, -'mɪu |-ed -d
unmilitary ʌn'mɪlə͵tɛrɪ
unmindful ʌn'maɪndfəl, -'maɪnf- |-ly -ɪ
unmistakable ͵ʌnmə'stekəbļ |-bly -blɪ
unmistaken ͵ʌnmə'stekən
unmitigable ʌn'mɪtəgəbļ |-bly -blɪ
unmitigated ʌn'mɪtə͵getɪd
unmixed ʌn'mɪkst ('un͵mixed 'evil)
unmodified ʌn'mɑdə͵faɪd; ES+-'mɒd-
unmolested ͵ʌnmə'lɛstɪd
unmoor ʌn'mʊr; ES -'mʊə(r; |-ed -d
unmoral ʌn'mɔrəl, -'mɑrəl, -'mɒrəl |-ly -ɪ
unmorality ͵ʌnmə'rælətɪ, -mɔ-, -mɑ-, -mɒ-, -mo-
unmortgaged ʌn'mɔrgɪdʒd; ES -'mɔəgɪdʒd
unmotivated ʌn'motə͵vetɪd
unmounted ʌn'maʊntɪd ('un͵mounted 'print)
unmourned ʌn'mornd, -'mɔrnd; ES -'moənd, E+-'mɔənd
unmoved ʌn'muvd |-vable -vəbļ |-bly -blɪ |-vedly -vɪdlɪ
unmuffle ʌn'mʌfļ |-d -d |-ling -flɪŋ, -fļɪŋ
unmusical ʌn'mjuzɪkļ, -'mɪuz- |-ly -ɪ

|full fʊl |tooth tuθ |further 'fɝðɚ; ES 'fɝðə |custom 'kʌstəm |while hwaɪl |how haʊ |toy tɔɪ |using 'juzɪŋ |fuse fjuz, fɪuz |dish dɪʃ |vision 'vɪʒən |Eden 'idn̩ |cradle 'kredļ |keep 'em 'kipm̩

unmuzzle ʌn'mʌzḷ |-d -d |-ling -zlɪŋ, -zḷɪŋ
unnail ʌn'nel |-ed -d
unnamed ʌn'nemd |-mable -məbḷ
unnatural ʌn'nætʃərəl, -'nætʃrəl |-ly -ɪ
unnavigable ʌn'nævəgəbḷ |-bly -blɪ
unnecessarily ʌn'nɛsə͵sɛrəlɪ, esp. if emph.
  ͵ʌnnɛsə'sɛrəlɪ
unnecessary ʌn'nɛsə͵sɛrɪ
unneedful ʌn'nidfəl |-ly -ɪ
unnegotiable ͵ʌnnɪ'goʃɪəbḷ |-bly -blɪ
unneighborly ʌn'nebɚlɪ; ES -'nebəlɪ
unnerve ʌn'nɝv; ES -'nɝv, -'nɜv; |-d -d
unnoted ʌn'notɪd ('un͵noted 'action)
unnoticeable ʌn'notɪsəbḷ |-bly -blɪ
unnumbered ʌn'nʌmbɚd; ES -'nʌmbəd
unobjectionable ͵ʌnəb'dʒɛkʃnəbḷ, -ʃənə- |-bly
  -blɪ
unobliging ͵ʌnə'blaɪdʒɪŋ ('uno͵bliging 'boor)
unobservant ͵ʌnəb'zɝvənt; ES -'zɝv-, -'zɜv-
unobstructed ͵ʌnəb'strʌktɪd
unobtainable ͵ʌnəb'tenəbḷ |-bly -blɪ
unobtrusive ͵ʌnəb'trusɪv, -'trɪus-
unoccasioned ͵ʌnə'keʒənd
unoccupied ʌn'akjə͵paɪd; ES+-'ɒk-
unoffending ͵ʌnə'fɛndɪŋ |-fensive -'fɛnsɪv
unoffered ʌn'ɔfɚd, -'ɒf-, -'af-; ES -fəd
unofficial ͵ʌnə'fɪʃəl |-ly -ɪ
unopen ʌn'opən, -'opm̩ |-ed -d |-ing -pnɪŋ,
  -pənɪŋ
unopposed ͵ʌnə'pozd ('unop͵posed 'measure)
unorganized ʌn'ɔrgən͵aɪzd; ES -'ɔɔg-
unoriginal ͵ʌnə'rɪdʒənḷ |-ly -ɪ
unorthodox ʌn'ɔrθə͵daks; ES -'ɔɔθə͵daks,
  -͵dɒks
unostentatious ͵ʌnastən'teʃəs; ES+-ɒs-
unowned ʌn'ond ('un͵owned 'goods)
unpack ʌn'pæk |-ed -t
unpaid ʌn'ped
unpaired ʌn'perd, -'pærd; E -'pɛəd, ES
  -'pæəd
unpalatable ʌn'pælətəbḷ, -lɪtə- |-bly -blɪ
unparalleled ʌn'pærə͵lɛld
unpardonable ʌn'pardnəbḷ, -'pardn̩əbḷ; ES
  -'pɑːd-, E+-'pɑːd-; |-bly -blɪ
unparliamentary ͵ʌnparlə'mɛntərɪ, -trɪ; ES
  -pɑl-, E+-pɑl-
unpartisan, -žan ʌn'partəzn̩; ES -'pɑːt-,
  E+-'pɑːt-
unpasteurized ʌn'pæstəraɪzd, -'pæstʃə-

unpatriotic ͵ʌnpetrɪ'atɪk; ES+-'ɒtɪk; |-ally
  -ḷɪ, -ɪklɪ
unpaved ʌn'pevd ('un͵paved 'street)
unpeg ʌn'pɛg |-ged -d
unpeople ʌn'pipḷ |-d -d |-ling -plɪŋ, -pḷɪŋ
unperceivable ͵ʌnpɚ'sivəbḷ; ES -pə-; |-bly
  -blɪ
unperforated ʌn'pɝfə͵retɪd; ES -'pɝf-, -'pɜf-
unpersuaded ͵ʌnpɚ'swedɪd; ES -pə'swedɪd
unpersuasive ͵ʌnpɚ'swesɪv; ES -pə'swesɪv
unperturbed ͵ʌnpɚ'tɝbd; ES -pə'tɝbd, -pə-
  'tɜbd; |-bable -bəbḷ |-bly -blɪ
unperused ͵ʌnpə'ruzd, -'rɪuzd
unphilosophic ͵ʌnfɪlə'safɪk; ES+-'sɒf-; |-al -ḷ
  |-ally -ḷɪ, -ɪklɪ
unpicked ʌn'pɪkt ('un͵picked 'fruit)
unpierced ʌn'pɪrst; ES -'pɪəst, S+-'peəst
unpile ʌn'paɪl |-d -d
unpin ʌn'pɪn |-ned -d
unpitied ʌn'pɪtɪd ('un͵pitied 'grief)
unpitying ʌn'pɪtɪɪŋ
unplaced ʌn'plest
unplait ʌn'plet |-ed -ɪd—see unplat, unpleat
unplanned ʌn'plænd
unplanted ʌn'plæntɪd; E+-'plant-, -'plɑnt-
unplat ʌn'plæt |-ted -ɪd—see unplait, unpleat
unplayable ʌn'pleəbḷ
unpleasant ʌn'plɛznt̩
unpleasing ʌn'plizɪŋ
unpleat ʌn'plit |-ed -ɪd—see plait, unplat
unpledged ʌn'plɛdʒd
unplowed ʌn'plaud ('un͵plowed 'land)
unplumbed ʌn'plʌmd
unpoetic ͵ʌnpo'ɛtɪk |-al -ḷ |-ally -ḷɪ, -ɪklɪ
unpoised ʌn'pɔɪzd
unpolished ʌn'palɪʃt; ES+-'pɒlɪʃt
unpolitic ʌn'palə͵tɪk; ES+-'pɒl-; |-ly -lɪ
unpolitical ͵ʌnpə'lɪtɪkḷ |-ly -ɪ, -ɪklɪ
unpolled ʌn'pold
unpolluted ͵ʌnpə'lutɪd, -pə'lɪutɪd
unpopular ʌn'papjəlɚ; ES -'papjələ(r, -'pɒp-
unpopularity ͵ʌnpapjə'lærətɪ; ES+-pɒp-
unpractical ʌn'præktɪkḷ |-ly -ɪ, -ɪklɪ
unpracticed ʌn'præktɪst ('un͵practiced 'art)
unprecedented ʌn'prɛsə͵dɛntɪd |-ly -lɪ, esp. if
  emph. ͵unprece'dentedly
unpredictable ͵ʌnprɪ'dɪktəbḷ |-bly -blɪ
unprejudiced ʌn'prɛdʒədɪst
unpremeditated ͵ʌnprɪ'mɛdə͵tɛtɪd

Key: See in full §§3–47. bee bi |pity 'pɪtɪ (§6) |rate ret |yet jɛt |sang sæŋ |angry 'æŋ·grɪ
|bath bæθ; E baθ (§10) |ah ɑ |far fɑr |watch watʃ, wɒtʃ (§12) |jaw dʒɔ |gorge gɔrdʒ |go go

unprepared ˌʌnprɪˈpɛrd, -ˈpærd; E -ˈpɛəd, ES -ˈpæəd; |-ness -nɪs, -rɪdnɪs |-redly -rɪdlɪ	unratified ʌnˈrætəˌfaɪd
unprepossessing ˌʌnpripəˈzɛsɪŋ	unravel ʌnˈrævl̩ |-ed -d |-ing -ˈrævlɪŋ, -v̩lɪŋ
unpresentable ˌʌnprɪˈzɛntəbl̩ |-bly -blɪ	unread ʌnˈrɛd
unpressed ʌnˈprɛst (ˈunˌpressed ˈcheese)	unreadable ʌnˈridəbl̩ |-bly -blɪ
unpresuming ˌʌnprɪˈzumɪŋ, -ˈzɪum-, -ˈzjum-	unready ʌnˈrɛdɪ |-readily -ˈrɛdl̩ɪ, -dɪlɪ
unpretending ˌʌnprɪˈtɛndɪŋ |-tentious -ˈtɛnʃəs	unreal ʌnˈriəl, ʌnˈril, ʌnˈrɪəl |-ly -ɪ—see really
unprevailing ˌʌnprɪˈvelɪŋ (ˈunpreˌvailing ˈwoe)	unreality ˌʌnrɪˈælətɪ
unpreventable ˌʌnprɪˈvɛntəbl̩ |-bly -blɪ	unrealized ʌnˈriəlˌaɪzd, -ˈrɪəl- |-zable -zəbl̩
unpriced ʌnˈpraɪst	unreason ʌnˈrizn̩ |-ed -d |-ing -ˈriznɪŋ, -zn̩ɪŋ
unprincipled ʌnˈprɪnsəpl̩d	unreasonable ʌnˈriznəbl̩, -zn̩əbl̩ |-bly -blɪ
unprivileged ʌnˈprɪvəlɪdʒd	unrebuked ˌʌnrɪˈbjukt, -ˈbɪukt
unprocurable ˌʌnprəˈkjurəbl̩, -ˈkɪur-	unreceipted (ˈunreˌceipted ˈbill) ˌʌnrɪˈsitɪd
unproductive ˌʌnprəˈdʌktɪv	unreceived ˌʌnrɪˈsivd
unprofessional ˌʌnprəˈfɛʃənl̩, -ˈfɛʃnəl |-ly -ɪ	unreciprocated ˌʌnrɪˈsɪprəˌketɪd
unprofitable ʌnˈprɑftəbl̩, -fɪtə-; ES +-ˈprɒf-; |-bly -blɪ	unreckoned ʌnˈrɛkənd
unprogressive ˌʌnprəˈgrɛsɪv, -pro-	unrecognized ʌnˈrɛkəgˌnaɪzd |-zable -zəbl̩ |-bly -blɪ
unprohibited ˌʌnproˈhɪbɪtɪd	unreconcilable ʌnˈrɛkənˌsaɪləbl̩ |-bly -blɪ, emph. +ˌunreconˈcilable, -bly
unpromising ʌnˈprɑmɪsɪŋ; ES +-ˈprɒm-	unrecorded ˌʌnrɪˈkɔrdɪd; ES -ˈkɔədɪd
unprompted ʌnˈprɑmptɪd; ES +-ˈprɒmp-	unredeemed ˌʌnrɪˈdimd
unpronounceable ˌʌnprəˈnaʊnsəbl̩, -pɚ- |-bly -blɪ	unreel ʌnˈril |-ed -d
unpropitious ˌʌnprəˈpɪʃəs, -pro-	unreeve naut. ʌnˈriv |-rove -ˈrov or -reeved -ˈrivd
unproportioned ˌʌnprəˈporʃənd, -ˈpɔr-; ES -ˈpoə-, E+-ˈpɔə-	unrefined ˌʌnrɪˈfaɪnd (ˈunreˌfined ˈsugar)
unprotected ˌʌnprəˈtɛktɪd	unreflecting ˌʌnrɪˈflɛktɪŋ
unproved ʌnˈpruvd (ˈunˌproved ˈthesis)	unreformed ˌʌnrɪˈfɔrmd; ES -ˈfɔəmd; |-mable -məbl̩
unproven ʌnˈpruvən	unrefuted ˌʌnrɪˈfjutɪd, -ˈfrutɪd |-table -təbl̩
unprovided ˌʌnprəˈvaɪdɪd	unregarded ˌʌnrɪˈgɑrdɪd; ES -ˈgɑːdɪd, E+-ˈgɑːd-
unprovoked ˌʌnprəˈvokt |-kedly -kɪdlɪ	unregenerate ˌʌnrɪˈdʒɛnərɪt |-rated -ˌretɪd
unpublished ʌnˈpʌblɪʃt	unregistered ʌnˈrɛdʒɪstɚd; ES -ˈrɛdʒɪstəd
unpunctual ʌnˈpʌŋktʃʊəl, -tʃʊl |-ly -ɪ	unregulated ʌnˈrɛgjəˌletɪd
unpunctuality ˌʌnpʌŋktʃʊˈælətɪ	unrehearsed ˌʌnrɪˈhɝst; ES -ˈhɜst, -ˈhɜˑst
unpunctuated ʌnˈpʌŋktʃʊˌetɪd	unrelated ˌʌnrɪˈletɪd (ˈunreˌlated ˈfacts)
unpunished ʌnˈpʌnɪʃt |-shable -ʃəbl̩	unrelaxed ˌʌnrɪˈlækst
unpurchasable ʌnˈpɝtʃəsəbl̩; ES -ˈpɜtʃ-, -ˈpɜˑtʃ-	unrelenting ˌʌnrɪˈlɛntɪŋ
unpursuing ˌʌnpɚˈsuɪŋ, -ˈsɪu-, -ˈsju-; ES -pə-	unreliability ˌʌnrɪˌlaɪəˈbɪlətɪ
unquailing ʌnˈkwelɪŋ (ˈunˌquailing ˈspirit)	unreliable ˌʌnrɪˈlaɪəbl̩ |-bly -blɪ
unqualified ʌnˈkwɑləˌfaɪd, -ˈkwɒl- |-ly -lɪ	unrelieved ˌʌnrɪˈlivd |-vedly -vɪdlɪ
unquenched ʌnˈkwɛntʃt |-chable -tʃəbl̩ |-bly -blɪ	unreligious ˌʌnrɪˈlɪdʒəs
unquestionable ʌnˈkwɛstʃənəbl̩ |-bly -blɪ	unremembered ˌʌnrɪˈmɛmbɚd; ES -ˈmɛmbəd
unquestioned ʌnˈkwɛstʃənd	unremitting ˌʌnrɪˈmɪtɪŋ
unquiet ʌnˈkwaɪət (ˈunˌquiet ˈgrave)	unremovable ˌʌnrɪˈmuvəbl̩ |-bly -blɪ
unquotable ʌnˈkwotəbl̩	unremunerative ˌʌnrɪˈmjunəˌretɪv, -ˈmɪun-, -ərətɪv
unquote ʌnˈkwot |-d -ɪd	
unraised ʌnˈrezd	unrenowned ˌʌnrɪˈnaʊnd

\|full fʊl \|tooth tuθ \|further ˈfɝðɚ; ES ˈfɜðə \|custom ˈkʌstəm \|while hwaɪl \|how haʊ \|toy tɔɪ \|using ˈjuzɪŋ \|fuse fjuz, fɪuz \|dish dɪʃ \|vision ˈvɪʒən \|Eden ˈidn̩ \|cradle ˈkredl̩ \|keep 'em ˈkipm̩

unrented ʌnˈrɛntɪd (ˈunˌrented ˈfarm)
unrepair ˌʌnrɪˈpɛr, -ˈpær; E -ˈpɛə(r, ES
-ˈpæə(r; |-ed -d
unrepealed ˌʌnrɪˈpild
unrepentant ˌʌnrɪˈpɛntənt
unreported ˌʌnrɪˈportɪd, -ˈpɔrtɪd; ES -ˈpoətɪd,
E+-ˈpɔətɪd
unrepresented ˌʌnrɛprɪˈzɛntɪd |-tative -tətɪv
unrepressed ˌʌnrɪˈprɛst |-sible -səbl̩
unrequested ˌʌnrɪˈkwɛstɪd
unrequited ˌʌnrɪˈkwaɪtɪd |-table -təbl̩
unreserve ˌʌnrɪˈzɝv; ES -ˈzɝv, -ˈzɝv; |-d -d
|-dly -ɪdlɪ
unresisting ˌʌnrɪˈzɪstɪŋ
unresponsive ˌʌnrɪˈspɑnsɪv; ES+-ˈspɒn-;
|-sible -səbl̩
unrest ʌnˈrɛst |-ed -ɪd |-ful -fəl |-fully -fəlɪ
unrestrainable ˌʌnrɪˈstrenəbl̩ |-bly -blɪ
unrestrained ˌʌnrɪˈstrend |-nt -nt |-nedly
-nɪdlɪ
unrestricted ˌʌnrɪˈstrɪktɪd
unretentive ˌʌnrɪˈtɛntɪv
unretrieved ˌʌnrɪˈtrivd |-vable -vəbl̩
unrevealed ˌʌnrɪˈvild (ˈunreˌvealed ˈtruth)
unrevenged ˌʌnrɪˈvɛndʒd
unrevoked ˌʌnrɪˈvokt
unrewarded ˌʌnrɪˈwɔrdɪd; ES -ˈwɔədɪd
unrhymed ʌnˈraɪmd
unrighteous ʌnˈraɪtʃəs
unrightful ʌnˈraɪtfəl |-ly -ɪ
unrimed ʌnˈraɪmd (ˈunˌrimed ˈverse)
unrip ʌnˈrɪp |-ripped -ˈrɪpt
unripe ʌnˈraɪp |-ened -ənd, -ˈraɪpm̩d
unrivaled ʌnˈraɪvl̩d
unrobe ʌnˈrob |-robed -ˈrobd
unroll ʌnˈrol |-rolled -ˈrold
unromantic ˌʌnroˈmæntɪk |-al -l̩ |-ally -l̩ɪ,
-ɪklɪ
unroof ʌnˈruf, -ˈrʊf |-ed -t
unrove past of unreeve ʌnˈrov
unruled ʌnˈruld, -ˈrɪuld |-edly -lɪdlɪ
unsaddle ʌnˈsædl̩ |-d -d |-ling -ˈsædl̩ɪŋ, -dlɪŋ
unsafe ʌnˈsef (ˈunˌsafe ˈroad)
unsaid ʌnˈsɛd
unsalable, -saleable ʌnˈseləbl̩ |-bly -blɪ
unsalaried ʌnˈsælərɪd
unsalted ʌnˌsɔltɪd (ˈunˌsalted ˈbutter)
unsanctioned ʌnˈsæŋkʃənd
unsanitary ʌnˈsænəˌtɛrɪ

unsatisfactory ˌʌnsætɪsˈfæktrɪ, -tərɪ |-torily
-trəlɪ, -tərəlɪ
unsatisfied ʌnˈsætɪsˌfaɪd
unsaturated ʌnˈsætʃəˌretɪd
unsavory ʌnˈsevərɪ, -ˈsevrɪ
unsay ʌnˈse |-says -ˈsɛz |-said -ˈsɛd
unscared ʌnˈskɛrd, -ˈskærd; E -ˈskɛəd, ES
-ˈskæəd
unscarred ʌnˈskɑrd; ES -ˈskɑːd, E+-ˈskɑːd
unscathed ʌnˈskeðd
unscented ʌnˈsɛntɪd (ˈunˌscented ˈsoap)
unscholarly ʌnˈskɑləˌlɪ; ES -ˈskɑləlɪ, -ˈskɒl-
unschooled ʌnˈskuld
unscientific ˌʌnsaɪənˈtɪfɪk |-al -l̩ |-ally -l̩ɪ,
-ɪklɪ
unscramble ʌnˈskræmbl̩ |-d -d |-ling -blɪŋ,
-bl̩ɪŋ
unscreened ʌnˈskrind (ˈunˌscreened ˈcoal)
unscrew ʌnˈskru, -ˈskrɪu |-ed -d
unscriptural ʌnˈskrɪptʃərəl |-ly -ɪ
unscrupulous ʌnˈskrupjələs, -ˈskrɪup-
unseal ʌnˈsil |-ed -d
unseam ʌnˈsim |-ed -d
unsearchable ʌnˈsɝtʃəbl̩; ES -ˈsɜtʃ-, -ˈsɝtʃ-
unseasonable ʌnˈsiznəbl̩, -zŋ̩ə- |-bly -blɪ
unseasoned ʌnˈsiznd (ˈunˌseasoned ˈwit)
unseat ʌnˈsit |-seated -ˈsitɪd
unseaworthy ʌnˈsiˌwɝðɪ; ES -ˌwɝðɪ, -ˌwɝðɪ
unseconded ʌnˈsɛkəndɪd
unsectarian ˌʌnsɛkˈtɛrɪən, -ˈter- |-ism -ˌɪzəm
unsecured ˌʌnsɪˈkjurd, -ˈkɪurd; ES -əd
unseeing ʌnˈsiɪŋ
unseemly ʌnˈsimlɪ
unseen ʌnˈsin (ˈseen and ˈunˌseen)
unsegmented ʌnˈsɛgməntɪd
unselfish ʌnˈsɛlfɪʃ
unsentimental ˌʌnsɛntəˈmɛntl̩ |-ly -ɪ
unserviceable ʌnˈsɝvɪsəbl̩; ES -ˈsɜvɪs-,
-ˈsɝvɪs-; |-bly -blɪ
unset ʌnˈsɛt
unsettle ʌnˈsɛtl̩ |-d -d |-ling -ˈsɛtl̩ɪŋ, -tlɪŋ
unsew ʌnˈso |past -sewed -ˈsod |pptc -sewed
-ˈsod or -sewn -ˈson
unsex ʌnˈsɛks |-es -ɪz |-ed -t
unshackle ʌnˈʃækl̩ |-d -d |-ling -klɪŋ, -kl̩ɪŋ
unshaded ʌnˈʃedɪd
unshaken ʌnˈʃekən |-kable -kəbl̩ |-bly -blɪ
unshaped ʌnˈʃept |-pely -plɪ |-pen -pən
unshaven ʌnˈʃevən

Key: *See in full §§3–47.* bee **bi** |pity ˈpɪtɪ (§6) |rate ret |yet jɛt |sang sæŋ |angry ˈæŋ·grɪ
|bath bæθ; E baθ (§10) |ah ɑ |far fɑr |watch wɑtʃ, wɒtʃ (§12) |jaw dʒɔ |gorge gɔrdʒ |go go

unsheathe ʌnˈʃið |-d -d
unshed ʌnˈʃɛd
unsheltered ʌnˈʃɛltəd; ES -ˈʃɛltəd
unship ʌnˈʃɪp |-ped -t
unshod ʌnˈʃɑd; ES+-ˈʃɒd; (ˈunˌshod ˈhorse)
unshrinkable ʌnˈʃrɪŋkəbḷ
unshrinking ʌnˈʃrɪŋkɪŋ (ˈunˌshrinking ˈsta-tion)
unshrunk ʌnˈʃrʌŋk |-en -ən
unsifted ʌnˈsɪftɪd
unsight ʌnˈsaɪt |-ed -ɪd |-ly -lɪ
unsigned ʌnˈsaɪnd
unsinewed ʌnˈsɪnjud, -ˈsɪnɪud, -ˈsɪnud
unsingable ʌnˈsɪŋəbḷ
unsinkable ʌnˈsɪŋkəbḷ
unsisterly ʌnˈsɪstəlɪ; ES -ˈsɪstəlɪ
unskilled ʌnˈskɪld (ˈunˌskilled ˈlabor)
unskillful, -skilf- ʌnˈskɪlfəl |-ly -ɪ
unsling ʌnˈslɪŋ |-slung -ˈslʌŋ
unsnap ʌnˈsnæp |-ped -t
unsnarl ʌnˈsnɑrl; ES -ˈsnɑːl, E+-ˈsnɑːl; |-ed -d
unsociability ˌʌnsoʃəˈbɪlətɪ
unsociable ʌnˈsoʃəbḷ |-bly -blɪ
unsocial ʌnˈsoʃəl |-ly -ɪ
unsoiled ʌnˈsɔɪld
unsold ʌnˈsold
unsolder ʌnˈsɑdɚ; ES -ˈsɑdə(r, -ˈsɒd-
unsoldierly ʌnˈsoldʒɚlɪ; ES -ˈsoldʒəlɪ
unsolicited ˌʌnsəˈlɪsɪtɪd
unsoluble ʌnˈsɑljəbḷ; ES+-ˈsɒl-
unsolvable ʌnˈsɑlvəbḷ, -ˈsɒlv- |-bly -blɪ
unsolved ʌnˈsɑlvd, -ˈsɒlvd
unsophisticated ˌʌnsəˈfɪstɪˌketɪd
unsophistication ˌʌnsəˌfɪstɪˈkeʃən
unsorted ʌnˈsɔrtɪd; ES -ˈsɔətɪd
unsought ʌnˈsɔt (ˈunˌsought ˈhelp)
unsound ʌnˈsaʊnd |-ed -ɪd
unsowed ʌnˈsod |-sown -ˈson
unsparing ʌnˈspɛrɪŋ, -ˈspær-; S -ˈspærɪŋ
unspeakable ʌnˈspikəbḷ |-bly -blɪ
unspecified ʌnˈspɛsəˌfaɪd
unspent ʌnˈspɛnt
unspoiled ʌnˈspɔɪld |-spoilt -ˈspɔɪlt
unspoken ʌnˈspokən
unsportsmanlike ʌnˈsportsmənˌlaɪk, -ˈsports-; ES -ˈspoəts-, E+-ˈspɔəts-
unspotted ʌnˈspɑtɪd; ES+-ˈspɒtɪd
unsprung ʌnˈsprʌŋ

unstable ʌnˈstebḷ |-bly -blɪ
unstained ʌnˈstend |-nable -nəbḷ |-nedly -nɪdlɪ
unstamped ʌnˈstæmpt
unstandardized ʌnˈstændɚdˌaɪzd; ES -ˈstæn-dəd-
unstarched ʌnˈstɑrtʃt; ES -ˈstɑːtʃt, E+ -ˈstɑːtʃt
unstate ʌnˈstet |-d -ɪd
unsteady ʌnˈstɛdɪ |-dily -dḷɪ, -dɪlɪ
unsteel ʌnˈstil |-steeled -ˈstild
unstick ʌnˈstɪk |-stuck -ˈstʌk
unstinted ʌnˈstɪntɪd
unstitch ʌnˈstɪtʃ |-ed -t
unstop ʌnˈstɑp; ES+-ˈstɒp; |-ped -t
unstrained ʌnˈstrend
unstrap ʌnˈstræp |-ped -t
unstratified ʌnˈstrætəˌfaɪd
unstressed ʌnˈstrɛst (ˈunˌstressed ˈword ˈstressed & ˈunˌstressed)
unstriated ʌnˈstraɪetɪd
unstring ʌnˈstrɪŋ |-strung -ˈstrʌŋ
unstuck ʌnˈstʌk
unstudied ʌnˈstʌdɪd
unstuffed ʌnˈstʌft
unsubmissive ˌʌnsəbˈmɪsɪv
unsubstantial ˌʌnsəbˈstænʃəl |-ly -ɪ
unsubstantiality ˌʌnsəbˌstænʃɪˈælətɪ
unsubstantiated ˌʌnsəbˈstænʃɪˌetɪd
unsuccess ˌʌnsəkˈsɛs |-ful -fəl |-fully -fəlɪ
unsuggestive ˌʌnsəgˈdʒɛstɪv, -səˈdʒɛstɪv
unsuitability ˌʌnsutəˈbɪlətɪ, -sɪut-, -sjut-
unsuited ʌnˈsutɪd, -ˈsɪut-, -ˈsjut- |-table -təbḷ |-bly -blɪ
unsullied ʌnˈsʌlɪd
unsung ʌnˈsʌŋ
unsupportable ˌʌnsəˈportəbḷ, -ˈpɔrt-; ES -ˈpoət-, E+-ˈpɔət-; |-bly -blɪ
unsuppressed ˌʌnsəˈprɛst |-sible -səbḷ |-bly -blɪ
unsure ʌnˈʃur; ES -ˈʃuə(r; (ˈunˌsure ˈhopes)
unsurmounted ˌʌnsɚˈmauntɪd; ES -sə-; |-table -təbḷ |-bly -blɪ
unsurpassed ˌʌnsɚˈpæst; ES -səˈpæst, E+ -ˈpɑst, -ˈpɑst
unsusceptible ˌʌnsəˈsɛptəbḷ
unsuspected ˌʌnsəˈspɛktɪd |-ting -tɪŋ
unsuspicious ˌʌnsəˈspɪʃəs
unsustained ˌʌnsəˈstend

|full fʊl |tooth tuθ |further ˈfɝðɚ; ES ˈfɝðə |custom ˈkʌstəm |while hwaɪl |how haʊ |toy tɔɪ |using ˈjuzɪŋ |fuse fjuz, fɪuz |dish dɪʃ |vision ˈvɪʒən |Eden ˈidn̩ |cradle ˈkredḷ |keep 'em ˈkipm̩

unswathe ʌn'swe ð |-d -d
unswayed ʌn'swed
unsweetened ʌn'switn̩d
unswept ʌn'swɛpt
unswerving ʌn'swɜˑvɪŋ; ES -'swɜv-, -'swɜˑv-
unsymmetrical ˌʌnsɪ'mɛtrɪk| |-ly -ɪ, -ɪklɪ
unsympathetic ˌʌnsɪmpə'θɛtɪk |-ally -|ɪ, -ɪklɪ
unsystematic ˌʌnsɪstə'mætɪk |-al -| |-ally -|ɪ, -ɪklɪ
untactful ʌn'tæktfəl |-ly -ɪ
untainted ʌn'tentɪd ('un‚tainted 'honor)
untaken ʌn'tekən
untalented ʌn'tæləntɪd
untamed ʌn'temd |-mable, -meable -məb|
untangle ʌn'tæŋg| |-d -d |-ling -glɪŋ, -g|ɪŋ
untanned ʌn'tænd ('un‚tanned 'hides)
untarnished ʌn'tɑrnɪʃt; ES -'tɑːn-, E+-'tɑːn-
untasted ʌn'testɪd
untaught ʌn'tɔt
untaxed ʌn'tækst |-xable -ksəb|
unteachable ʌn'titʃəb| |-bly -blɪ
untenable ʌn'tɛnəb| |-bly -blɪ
untended ʌn'tɛndɪd
untented ʌn'tɛntɪd
Untermeyer 'ʌntɚˌmaɪɚ; ES 'ʌntəˌmaɪ‑ə(r
unterrified ʌn'tɛrəˌfaɪd
untested ʌn'tɛstɪd
unthanked ʌn'θæŋkt |-kful -kfəl |-kfully -kfəlɪ
unthinkable ʌn'θɪŋkəb| |-bly -blɪ |-king -kɪŋ
unthought ʌn'θɔt |-ful -fəl |-fully -fəlɪ
unthought-of ʌn'θɔtˌɑv, -ˌɒv, -ˌʌv
unthread ʌn'θrɛd |-ed -ɪd
unthrifty ʌn'θrɪftɪ ('un‚thrifty 'knave)
unthrone ʌn'θron |-d -d
untidy ʌn'taɪdɪ |-dily -d|ɪ, -dɪlɪ
untie ʌn'taɪ |-tied -'taɪd
until ən'tɪl
untilled ʌn'tɪld
untimely ʌn'taɪmlɪ
untinged ʌn'tɪndʒd
untired ʌn'taɪrd; ES -'taɪəd; |-ring -rɪŋ
untitled ʌn'taɪt|d
unto not in familiar use. Before vowel 'ʌntu;
   before cons. 'ʌntə, 'ʌntʊ; before pause 'ʌntʊ;
   in poetry often ʌn'tu
untold ʌn'told ('un‚told 'riches)
untouchability ˌʌntʌtʃə'bɪlətɪ
untouched ʌn'tʌtʃt |-chable -tʃəb| |-bly -blɪ

untoward ʌn'tord, -'tɔrd; ES -'toəd, E+
   -'tɔəd
untraceable ʌn'tresəb| |-bly -blɪ
untrained ʌn'trend
untrammeled ʌn'træm|d
untransferable ˌʌntræns'fɚb|; ES -'fɜrə-,
   -'fɜˑ-
untranslatable ˌʌntræns'letəb|, -trænz- |-bly
   -blɪ
untraveled ʌn'trævłd
untraversed ʌn'trævɚst, -'trævɜˑst; ES -'træ‑
   vəst, -'trævɜst, -'trævɜˑst
untread ʌn'trɛd |past -trod -'trɑd |pptc
   -trodden -'trɑdn̩ or -trod -'trɑd; ES+
   -'trɒd(n̩
untrimmed ʌn'trɪmd
untrod ʌn'trɑd; ES+-'trɒd; |-den -n̩
untroubled ʌn'trʌb|d
untrue ʌn'tru, -'trɪu |-ly -lɪ
untruss ʌn'trʌs |-es -ɪz |-ed -t
untrustful ʌn'trʌstfəl |-ly -ɪ
untruth ʌn'truθ, -'trɪuθ |-ths -ðz, -θs |-ful -fəl
   |-fully -fəlɪ
unturned ʌn'tɜˑnd; ES -'tɜnd, -'tɜˑnd
untutored ʌn'tutɚd, -'trutɚd, -'tjutɚd; ES
   -təd
untwine ʌn'twaɪn |-d -d
untwist ʌn'twɪst |-ed -ɪd
unused ʌn'juzd |-sable -zəb| |-bly -blɪ
unusual ʌn'juʒʊəl, -'juʒʊl, -'juʒəl |-ly -ɪ
unuttered ʌn'ʌtɚd; ES -'ʌtəd; |-rable -tərəb|
   |-bly -blɪ
unvaccinated ʌn'væksn̩ˌetɪd
unvalued ʌn'væljʊd
unvaried ʌn'vɛrɪd, -'verɪd, -'værɪd |-rying
   -rɪŋ
unvarnished ʌn'vɑrnɪʃt; ES -'vɑːn-, E+
   -'vɑːn-
unveil ʌn'vel |-ed -d
unventilated ʌn'vɛnt|ˌetɪd
unverified ʌn'vɛrəˌfaɪd |-fiable -ˌfaɪəb| |-bly
   -blɪ
unversed ʌn'vɜˑst; ES -'vɜst, -'vɜˑst
unvexed ʌn'vɛkst
unvisited ʌn'vɪzɪtɪd
unvocal ʌn'vok| |-ized -ˌaɪzd
unvoiced ʌn'vɔɪst ('un‚voiced 'thought)
unwanted ʌn'wɑntɪd, -'wɔntɪd, -'wɒntɪd; S
   -'wɔntɪd, -'wɒntɪd, -'wɑntɪd

Key: See in full §§3–47. bee bi |pity 'pɪtɪ (§6) |rate ret |yet jɛt |sang sæŋ |angry 'æŋ·grɪ
|bath bæθ; E baθ (§10) |ah ɑ |far fɑr |watch wɑtʃ, wɒtʃ (§12) |jaw dʒɔ |gorge gɔrdʒ |go go

unwarily ʌnˈwɛrəlɪ, -ˈwerəlɪ, -ˈwærəlɪ
unwarlike ʌnˈwɔrˌlaɪk; ES -ˈwɔə-
unwarned ʌnˈwɔrnd; ES -ˈwɔənd; |-nedly -nɪdlɪ
unwarranted ʌnˈwɔrəntɪd, -ˈwɑr-, -ˈwɒr- |-table -təbḷ |-bly -blɪ
unwary ʌnˈwɛrɪ, -ˈwerɪ, -ˈwærɪ—*see* wary
unwashed ʌnˈwɑʃt, -ˈwɔʃt, -ˈwɒʃt
unwatched ʌnˈwɑtʃt, -ˈwɒtʃt, -ˈwɔtʃt
unwavering ʌnˈwevrɪŋ, -ˈwevərɪŋ
unwearable ʌnˈwɛrəbḷ, -ˈwær-; S -ˈwær-
unwearied ʌnˈwɪrɪd, -ˈwir-; S+-ˈwɛrɪd; |-rying -rɪɪŋ
unweave ʌnˈwiv |*past* -wove -ˈwov *or* -weaved -ˈwivd |*pptc* -woven -ˈwovən *or* -wove -ˈwov
unwed *adj* ʌnˈwɛd |-ded -ɪd
unweight ʌnˈwet |-ed -ɪd
unwelcome ʌnˈwɛlkəm (ˈunˌwelcome ˈnews)
unwell ʌnˈwɛl
unwept ʌnˈwɛpt
unwholesome ʌnˈholsəm
unwieldy ʌnˈwildɪ
unwilling ʌnˈwɪlɪŋ
unwincing ʌnˈwɪnsɪŋ
unwind *'uncoil'* ʌnˈwaɪnd |-wound -ˈwaʊnd
unwind *'deprive of breath'* ʌnˈwɪnd |-ed -ɪd
unwinking ʌnˈwɪŋkɪŋ
unwise ʌnˈwaɪz |unwisdom ʌnˈwɪzdəm
unwished ʌnˈwɪʃt
unwitnessed ʌnˈwɪtnɪst
unwitting ʌnˈwɪtɪŋ
unwomanly ʌnˈwʊmənlɪ, -ˈwumənlɪ
unwonted ʌnˈwʌntɪd—*see* wont
unworkable ʌnˈwɝkəbḷ; ES -ˈwɜk-, -ˈwɝk-; |-bly -blɪ
unworldly ʌnˈwɝldlɪ; ES -ˈwɜld-, -ˈwɝld-
unworn ʌnˈworn, -ˈwɔrn; ES -ˈwoən, E+ -ˈwɔən
unworshipped ʌnˈwɝʃəpt; ES -ˈwɜʃ-, -ˈwɝʃ-
unworthy ʌnˈwɝðɪ; ES -ˈwɜðɪ, -ˈwɝðɪ
unwound *'uncoiled'* ʌnˈwaʊnd
unwounded *'unhurt'* ʌnˈwundɪd, -ˈwaʊndɪd
unwrap ʌnˈræp |-ped -t
unwrinkle ʌnˈrɪŋkḷ |-d -d
unwritten ʌnˈrɪtn̩ (ˈunˌwritten ˈlaw)
unwrought ʌnˈrɔt
unyielding ʌnˈjildɪŋ
unyoke ʌnˈjok |-yoked -ˈjokt

up *adv, prep, stressed* ˈʌp, ˌʌp; *unstr.* ʌp, əp
up *n, adj* ʌp, *v* ʌp |upped ʌpt
up- *prefix* ʌp-, ˌʌp-, ˈʌp- *according to rhythm and meaning; unstr.* əp-
up and down, up-and-down ˈʌpənˈdaʊn, ˈʌpm̩ˈdaʊn (ˈup-and-ˌdown ˈmotion)
up and up, up-and-up ˈʌpənˈʌp, ˈʌpəndˈʌp
Upanishad uˈpænɪˌʃæd, uˈpɑnɪˌʃɑd
upas ˈjupəs |upases ˈjupəsɪz
upborne ʌpˈborn, -ˈbɔrn; ES -ˈboən, E+ -ˈbɔən
upbraid ʌpˈbred |-ed -ɪd
upbringing *n* ˈʌpˌbrɪŋɪŋ
upbuild ʌpˈbɪld |-built -ˈbɪlt *or arch.* -ed -ˈbɪldɪd
upcast *n, adj* ˈʌpˌkæst; E+-ˌkast, -ˌkɑst—*cf* downcast
upcountry *n, adj, adv* ˈʌpˈkʌntrɪ (ˈupˈcountry ˌfolk, ˈupˌcountry ˈtown)
upend *v* ʌpˈɛnd |-ended -ˈɛndɪd
upgather ʌpˈgæðɚ; ES -ˈgæðə(r; |-ed -d |-ing -ˈgæðrɪŋ, -ˈgæðərɪŋ
upgrade *adj, adv* ˈʌpˈgred (ˈupˌgrade & ˈdownˌgrade)
upgrowth ˈʌpˌgroθ |-ths -θs
upharsin juˈfɑrsɪn; ES -ˈfɑːsɪn, E+-ˈfaːs-
upheaval ʌpˈhivḷ, ˈʌpˌhivḷ
upheave ʌpˈhiv |-heaved -ˈhivd
upheld ʌpˈhɛld
uphill *n* ˈʌpˌhɪl, ʌpˈhɪl
uphill *adj* ˈʌpˈhɪl (ˈupˌhill ˈwork)
uphill *adv* ˈʌpˈhɪl (ˈupˌhill & ˈdownˌhill)
uphold ʌpˈhold |-held -ˈhɛld |*arch. pptc*+ -holden -ˈholdən
upholster ʌpˈholstɚ; ES -stə(r; |-ed -d |-ing -strɪŋ, -stərɪŋ
upholsterer ʌpˈholstərɚ, -ˈholstrɚ; ES -rə(r
upholstery ʌpˈholstrɪ, -ˈholstərɪ
upkeep *n* ˈʌpˌkip
upkeep *v* ʌpˈkip |-kept -ˈkɛpt
upland *n, adj, adv* ˈʌplənd, ˈʌpˌlænd
uplander ˈʌpləndɚ, ˈʌpˌlændɚ; ES -də(r
uplift *n* ˈʌpˌlɪft
uplift *v* ʌpˈlɪft |-lifted -ˈlɪftɪd, *arch. past & pptc*+-lift -ˈlɪft
upmost ˈʌpˌmost
upon *stressed* əˈpɑn, əˈpɒn, əˈpɔn; *unstr. occas.* əpən; *restressed* əˈpʌn
upper ˈʌpɚ; ES ˈʌpə(r

upper-class ˈʌpɚˈklæs; ES ˈʌpəˈklæs, E+ -ˈklas, -ˈklɑs

uppercut n, v ˈʌpɚˌkʌt; ES ˈʌpə-

uppermost ˈʌpɚˌmost; ES ˈʌpə-

uppers ˈʌpɚz; ES ˈʌpəz

uppish ˈʌpɪʃ

Uppsala ˈʌpˌsɑlə (Sw ˈɔpˌsɑːlɑ)

upraise ʌpˈrez |-s -ɪz |-d -d

uprear ʌpˈrɪr; ES -ˈrɪə(r, S+-ˈrɛə(r; |-ed -d

upright n, adj, v ˈʌpˌraɪt |-ed -ɪd

upright adv ˈʌpˌraɪt, ʌpˈraɪt

uprise n ˈʌpˌraɪz |-s -ɪz

uprise v ʌpˈraɪz |-s -ɪz |-rose -ˈroz |-risen -ˈrɪzn̩

uprising n ˈʌpˌraɪzɪŋ, ʌpˈraɪzɪŋ

uproar ˈʌpˌror, -ˌrɔr; ES -ˌroə(r, E+-ˌrɔə(r; v upˈroar

uproarious ʌpˈrorɪəs, -ˈrɔrɪəs; S -ˈrorɪəs

uproot ʌpˈrut, -ˈrʊt |-ed -ɪd

uprouse ʌpˈraʊz |-s -ɪz |-d -d

Upsala ˈʌpˌsɑlə (Sw ˈɔpˌsɑːlɑ)

upset n ˈʌpˌsɛt

upset adj, v ʌpˈsɛt

upshot ˈʌpˌʃɑt; ES+-ˌʃɒt

upside ˈʌpˈsaɪd, ˈʌpˌsaɪd

upside down, upside-down ˈʌpˌsaɪdˈdaʊn

upsilon ˈjupsələn, -ˌlɑn, -ˌlɒn, Brit. jup-ˈsaɪlən

upspring n ˈʌpˌsprɪŋ

upspring v ʌpˈsprɪŋ |past -sprang -ˈspræŋ or -sprung -ˈsprʌŋ |pptc -sprung -ˈsprʌŋ

upstage adj, adv, v ˈʌpˈstedʒ |-s -ɪz |-d -d

upstairs n, ʌpˈstɛrz, -ˈstærz; E -ˈstɛəz, ES -ˈstæəz; acct+ˈupˌstairs, adj, adv ˈupˈstairs

upstanding ʌpˈstændɪŋ

upstart n, adj ˈʌpˌstɑrt; ES -ˌstɑːt, E+-ˌstɑːt

upstart v ʌpˈstɑrt; ES -ˈstɑːt, E+-ˈstɑːt; |-ed -ɪd

upstate adj, adv ˈʌpˈstet (ˈupˌstate ˈtown)

upstream adj, adv ˈʌpˈstrim; v ʌpˈstrim |-ed -d

upstroke ˈʌpˌstrok

upsweep n ˈʌpˌswip

upsweep v ʌpˈswip |-swept -ˈswɛpt

upswing n ˈʌpˌswɪŋ

upswing v ʌpˈswɪŋ |-swung -ˈswʌŋ

uptake ˈʌpˌtek

upthrust ˈʌpˌθrʌst

up-to-date ˈʌptəˈdet (ˈup-to-ˌdate ˈnews)

uptown n ʌpˈtaʊn, ˈʌpˌtaʊn

uptown adj, adv ˈʌpˈtaʊn (ˈupˌtown & ˈdown-ˌtown)

upturn n ˈʌpˌtɝn; ES -ˌtɝn, -ˌtɜn

upturn v ʌpˈtɝn; ES -ˈtɝn, -ˈtɜn; |-ed -d

upward ˈʌpwɚd; ES ˈʌpwəd; |-s -z

Ur ɝ; ES ɜ(r, ɝ

uraemia jʊˈrimɪə, -mjə |-mic -mɪk

Ural ˈjʊrəl

Ural-Altaic ˈjʊrəl·ælˈteɪk

uranalysis ˌjʊrəˈnæləsɪs |-yses -əˌsiz

Urania jʊˈrenɪə |-n -n

uranic jʊˈrænɪk

uraninite jʊˈrænəˌnaɪt

uranite ˈjʊrəˌnaɪt

uranium jʊˈrenɪəm, -njəm

Uranus ˈjʊrənəs |-ʼs -ɪz

urban, U- ˈɝbən; ES ˈɜbən, ˈɝbən

Urbana ɝˈbænə; ES ɜˈbænə, ɝˈbænə

urbane ɝˈben; ES ɜˈben, ɝˈben; |-ness -ˈben-nɪs

urbanite ˈɝbənˌaɪt; ES ˈɜb-, ˈɝb-

urbanity ɝˈbænətɪ; ES ɜˈbæn-, ɝˈbæn-

urbanize ˈɝbənˌaɪz; ES ˈɜb-, ˈɝb-; |-s -ɪz |-d -d

urchin ˈɝtʃɪn; ES ˈɜtʃɪn, ˈɝtʃɪn

Urdu ˈʊrdu, ʊrˈdu, ɝˈdu; ES ˈʊədu, ʊəˈdu, ɜˈdu, ɝˈdu

urea jʊˈriə, ˈjʊrɪə |-l -l

uredo jʊˈrido

uremia jʊˈrimɪə, -mjə |-mic -mɪk

urethra jʊˈriθrə |-s -z |-rae -ri

urethritis ˌjʊrɪˈθraɪtɪs

uretic jʊˈrɛtɪk

urge ɝdʒ; ES ɜdʒ, ɝdʒ; |-s -ɪz |-d -d |-nt -ənt |-ncy -ənsɪ

Uriah jʊˈraɪə

uric ˈjʊrɪk

Uriel ˈjʊrɪəl

Urim ˈjʊrɪm

urinal ˈjʊrənl̩

urinalysis ˌjʊrəˈnæləsɪs |-yses -əˌsiz

urinary ˈjʊrəˌnɛrɪ

urinate ˈjʊrəˌnet |-d -ɪd |-tion ˌjʊrəˈneʃən

urine ˈjʊrɪn

urn ɝn; ES ɜn, ɝn

urology jʊrˈɑlədʒɪ; ES+-ˈɒl-

Urquhart ˈɝkɚt, -kɪt; ES ˈɜk-, ˈɝk-; (Sc ˈɝxərt)

Ursa ˈɝsə; ES ˈɜsə, ˈɝsə

Key: See in full §§3–47. bee **bi** |pity ˈpɪtɪ (§6) |rate **ret** |yet jɛt |sang sæŋ |angry ˈæŋ·grɪ |bath bæθ; E baθ (§10) |ah ɑ |far fɑr |watch wɑtʃ, wɒtʃ (§12) |jaw dʒɔ |gorge gɔrdʒ |go go

Ursa Major ˈɝsəˈmedʒɚ; ES ˈɜsəˈmedʒɑ(r, ˈɝsəˈmedʒɑ(r; |gen Ursae Majoris ˈɝsi-, ˈɜsiməˈdʒɔrɪs |Minor -ˈmaɪnɚ; ES -nə(r; |gen Minoris -mɪˈnorɪs
ursine ˈɝsaɪn, -sɪn; ES ˈɜs-, ˈɝs-
Ursula ˈɝsjʊlə, ˈɝsələ; ES ˈɜs-, ˈɝs-; |-line -lɪn, -ˌlaɪn (in Shak. Ursley ˈʊrslɪ, modern ˈɝslɪ)
Ursus ˈɝsəs; ES ˈɜsəs, ˈɝsəs |-sus' -səs
Urswick ˈɝzwɪk, ˈɝzɪk; ES ˈɜz-, ˈɝz-
Uruguay ˈjʊrəˌgwe, -ˌgwaɪ (Sp ˌuruˈgwai)
Uruguayan ˌjʊrəˈgweən, -ˈgwaɪən
us stressed ˈʌs, ˌʌs; unstr. əs |-'s s (let's lɛts)
usability ˌjuzəˈbɪlətɪ
usable ˈjuzəbl̩
usage ˈjusɪdʒ, less freq. ˈjuzɪdʒ |-s -ɪz
usance ˈjuzn̩s |-s -ɪz
use n jus |uses ˈjusɪz
use v juz |uses ˈjuzɪz |used juzd |-able -əbl̩
used to adj 'accustomed to,' v 'was (were) accustomed to': before a pause ˈjustu, before vowels ˈjustʊ, before vowels or conss. ˈjustə
useful ˈjusfəl |-ly -ɪ
useless ˈjuslɪs
user ˈjuzɚ; ES ˈjuzə(r
usher, U- ˈʌʃɚ; ES ˈʌʃə(r; |-ed -d |-ing -ˌʃərɪŋ, -ˌʃrɪŋ
Usk ʌsk
usquebaugh ˈʌskwɪˌbɔ
usual ˈjuʒʊəl, ˈjuʒʊl, ˈjuʒəl |-ly -ɪ
usufruct ˈjuzjʊˌfrʌkt, ˈjus-
usurer ˈjuʒərɚ; ES ˈjuʒərə(r

usurious juˈʒʊrɪəs, -rjəs
usurp jʊˈzɝp, -ˈsɝp; ES -ʒp, -ɝp; |-ed -t
usurpation ˌjuzɚˈpeʃən, -sɚ-; ES ˌjuzɚ-, -sə-
usury ˈjuʒərɪ, ˈjuʒrɪ
Utah ˈjutɔ, ˈjutɑ |-an -ən
Ute jut, ˈjutɪ
utensil jʊˈtɛnsl̩
uterus ˈjutərəs |-es -ɪz |-ri -ˌraɪ |-rine -rɪn
Uther ˈjuθɚ; ES ˈjuθə(r
Utica ˈjutɪkə
utile ˈjutɪl
utilitarian ˌjutɪləˈtɛrɪən, jʊˌtɪlə-, -ˈter-
utility jʊˈtɪlətɪ
utilization ˌjutl̩əˈzefən, -aɪˈz-
utilize ˈjutl̩ˌaɪz |-s -ɪz |-d -d |-zable -əbl̩
utmost ˈʌtˌmost, ˈʌtməst
Utopia juˈtopɪə, -pjə |-n -n
Utrecht ˈjutrɛkt (Du ˈytrɛxt)
utricle ˈjutrɪkl̩
utter, U- ˈʌtɚ; ES ˈʌtə(r; |-ed -d
utterance ˈʌtərəns, ˈʌtrəns |-s -ɪz
utterer ˈʌtərɚ; ES ˈʌtərə(r
uttermost ˈʌtɚˌmost, -məst; ES ˈʌtə-
uvula ˈjuvjələ |-lar -lɚ; ES -lə(r
Uxbridge ˈʌksbrɪdʒ |-'s -ɪz
uxorial ʌkˈsorɪəl, ʌgˈz-, -ɔrɪəl; S -orɪəl; |-ious -ɪəs
uxoricide ʌkˈsorəˌsaɪd, ʌgˈz-, -ɔr-; S -or-
Uzbek ˈʌzbɛk |Uzbeg ˈʌzbɛg
uzzard 'izzard' ˈʌzɚd; ES ˈʌzəd
Uzziah ʌˈzaɪə
Uzziel ʌˈzaɪəl

V

V, v letter vi |pl V's, Vs, poss V's viz
vacant ˈvekənt |vacancy ˈvekənsɪ
vacate ˈveket |-cated -ketɪd
vacation veˈkeʃən, və-, vɪ- |-ed -d |-ing -ˌʃənɪŋ, -ˌʃnɪŋ
vaccinate ˈvæksn̩ˌet |-d -ɪd |-tion ˌvæksn̩ˈeʃən
vaccine ˈvæksin, -sɪn
Vachel ˈvetʃəl
vacillate ˈvæsl̩ˌet |-d -ɪd |-tion ˌvæsl̩ˈeʃən
vacillatory ˈvæsl̩əˌtorɪ, -ˌtɔrɪ; S -ˌtorɪ
vacuity væˈkjuətɪ, və-, -ˈkɪu-
vacuo ˈvækjʊˌo |-uous -juəs

vacuum ˈvækjuəm |-s -z |vacua ˈvækjuə
vade mecum ˈvedɪˈmikəm
vagabond ˈvægəˌbɑnd, -ˌbɒnd |-age -ɪdʒ
vagary vəˈgɛrɪ, ve-, -ˈgɛrɪ
vagina vəˈdʒaɪnə |-nal ˈvædʒən̩l, vəˈdʒaɪnl̩
vagrant ˈvegrənt |-grancy -grənsɪ
vagrom malapropism ˈvegrəm
vague veg
vagus ˈvegəs |-es -ɪz |-vagi ˈvedʒaɪ
vail vel |vailed veld
Vailima vaɪˈlimə
vain ven |-ness ˈvennɪs

vainglory ven'glɔrɪ, -'glɔrɪ; S -'glorɪ; |-rious
-rɪəs

vair vɛr, vær; E vɛə(r, ES væə(r

valance 'væləns |-s -ɪz |-d -t

vale *'valley'* vel

vale *'farewell'* 'veli

valediction ˌvælə'dɪkʃən

valedictorian ˌvælədɪk'tɔrɪən, -'tɔr-; S -'tor-

valedictory ˌvælə'dɪktərɪ, -trɪ

valence *chem.* 'veləns |-cy -sɪ

Valencia və'lɛnʃɪə, -ʃə |-n -n

Valenciennes vəˌlɛnsɪ'ɛnz (*Fr* valã'sjɛn)

valentine, V- 'vælənˌtaɪn

Valera, de dəvə'lɛrə, -'lɛrə, -'lɪrə

Valeria və'lɪrɪə |-ius -s |-ius's -sɪz

valet 'vælɪt |-ed -ɪd (*Fr* va'lɛ)—*A pseudo-
French* 'væle, væ'le *is sometimes heard.
Valet, with a* t, *has been English for at least
400 years.*

valetudinarian ˌvæləˌtjudn̩'ɛrɪən, -ˌtɪu-, -ˌtu-,
-'ɛrɪən

valetudinary ˌvælə'tjudn̩ˌɛrɪ, -'tɪu-, -'tu-

Valhalla væl'hælə

valiant 'væljənt |-nce -ns |-ncy -nsɪ

valid 'vælɪd

validate 'væləˌdet |-d -ɪd

validity və'lɪdətɪ

valise və'lis |-s -ɪz

Valkyrie væl'kɪrɪ

valley 'vælɪ |-ed -ɪd

Vallombrosa ˌvæləm'brosə (*It* ˌvallom'bro:sa)

valor 'vælɚ; ES 'vælə(r; |-ous -əs

valorization ˌvælərə'zeʃən, -aɪ'z-

valorize 'væləˌraɪz |-s -ɪz |-d -d

Valparaiso ˌvælpə'rezo, *in* SA +-'raɪso, -zo
(*Sp* ˌbalpara'iso)

valuable 'væljəb!, 'væljʊəb! |-bly -blɪ

valuation ˌvælju'eʃən

valuator 'væljuˌetɚ; ES -ˌetə(r

value 'vælju |valued 'væljud

valve vælv |-d -d

valvular 'vælvjələ; ES -lə(r

vamoose væ'mus |-s -ɪz |-d -t

vamp væmp |vamped væmpt

vampire 'væmpaɪr; ES 'væmpaɪə(r; |-ed -d

van væn |vanned vænd

vanadium və'nedɪəm, -djəm

Van Buren væn'bjʊrən, -'bɪurən

Vancouver væn'kuvɚ; ES -'kuvə(r

vandal, V- 'vænd! |-ism -ˌɪzəm

vandalize 'vænd!ˌaɪz |-s -ɪz |-d -d

Vanderbilt 'vændɚˌbɪlt; ES 'vændə-

Van Dieman, v- væn'dimən

Van Doren væn'dorən, -'dɔr-; S -'dor-

van Dyck, Dijk væn'daɪk

Van Dyck væn'daɪk

Vandyke, Van Dyke, van D- væn'daɪk

vane ven |vaned vend

Vanessa və'nɛsə

van Eyck væn'aɪk

vanguard 'vænˌgard; ES -ˌgɑːd, E+-ˌgaːd

vanilla və'nɪlə

vanish 'vænɪʃ |-es -ɪz |-ed -t

vanity 'vænətɪ

van Loon væn'lon

vanquish 'vænkwɪʃ, 'væŋ-

vantage 'væntɪdʒ |-s -ɪz |-d -d

vanward 'vænwɚd; ES 'vænwəd

vapid 'væpɪd |vapidity væ'pɪdətɪ, və-

vapor 'vepɚ; ES 'vepə(r; |-ous -əs, -prəs

vaporific ˌvepə'rɪfɪk

vaporization ˌvepərə'zeʃən, -aɪ'z-

vaporize 'vepəˌraɪz |-s -ɪz |-d -d |-ry -rɪ

Vargas 'vargəs; ES 'vaːg-; (*Pg* 'vargəʃ)

variability ˌvɛrɪə'bɪlətɪ, ˌver-, ˌvær-

variable 'vɛrɪəb!, 'ver-, 'vær- |-bly -blɪ

variant 'vɛrɪənt, 'ver-, 'vær- |-nce -ns

variation ˌvɛrɪ'eʃən, ˌver-, ˌvær-

varicolored 'vɛrɪˌkʌlɚd, 'ver-, 'vær-; ES
-ˌkʌləd

varicose 'værɪˌkos, 'vɛrɪ- |-d -t

varicosis ˌværɪ'kosɪs

variegate 'vɛrɪˌget, 'ver-, 'vær- |-d -ɪd

variegation ˌvɛrɪ'geʃən, ˌver-, ˌvær-

variety və'raɪətɪ |-tal -t! |-tally -t!ɪ

variola və'raɪələ

varioloid 'vɛrɪəˌlɔɪd, ˌver-, ˌvær-

variorum ˌvɛrɪ'orəm, ˌver-, ˌvær-, -'ɔrəm; S
-'orəm

various 'vɛrɪəs, 'ver-, 'vær-

varlet 'varlɪt; ES 'vaːlɪt, E+'vaːl-; |-ry -rɪ

varment, -mint 'varmənt; ES 'vaːmənt, E+
'vaːm-

Varney 'varnɪ; ES 'vaːnɪ, E+'vaːnɪ

varnish 'varnɪʃ; ES 'vaːn-, E+'vaːn-; |-es -ɪz

Varrius 'vɛrɪəs |-'s -ɪz

Varro 'vɛro

varsity 'varsətɪ, 'varstɪ; ES 'vaːs-, E+'vaːs-

Key: See in full §§3–47. bee bi |pity 'pɪtɪ (§6) |rate ret |yet jɛt |sang sæŋ |angry 'æŋ·grɪ
|bath bæθ; E baθ (§10) |ah ɑ |far fɑr |watch watʃ, wɒtʃ (§12) |jaw dʒɔ |gorge gɔrdʒ |go go

Varuna ˈværunə, ˈvʌr-

vary ˈvɛrɪ, ˈvɛːrɪ, ˈvɛrɪ, ˈværɪ |-ried -rɪd—
  Some speakers distinguish vary *from* very
  by a longer ɛ (*§55*).

vascular ˈvæskjələ˞; ES ˈvæskjələ(r

vase ves, *much less freq.* vez, (*Brit* vaz) |-s -ɪz

vaseline ˈvæsḷˌin, -ɪn

vassal ˈvæsḷ |-ed -d

vast væst; E+vast, vɑst; |-ity -ətɪ

vat væt

Vatican ˈvætɪkən

vaudeville ˈvodəˌvɪl, ˈvodv-, ˈvodəˌvɪl (*Fr*
  vodˈvil)

Vaughan, -ghn vɔn

vault vɔlt |-ed -ɪd

vaunt vɔnt, vɒnt, vant |-ed -ɪd

Vaux *Eng name* vɔks |-'s -ɪz, *Fr* vil. vo

Vauxhall ˈvɑksˈhɔl; ES+ˈvɒks-; (ˈVauxˌhall
  ˈGardens)

vavasour ˈvævəˌsur; ES -ˌsuə(r

vaward ˈvɔwɚd; ES ˈvɔwəd

've *abbr. spelling of unstressed* have v, *as in*
  I've ɑɪv, you've ˈjuv, jʊv, we've ˈwiv, wɪv,
  they've ðev

veal vil |vealed vild

vector ˈvɛktɚ; ES ˈvɛktə(r

Veda ˈvedə, ˈvidə |-dic -dɪk

vedette vəˈdɛt

vee vi

veer vɪr; ES vɪə(r; |-ed -d

Vega *star* ˈvigə, *Sp poet* ˈvegə (*Sp* ˈbega)

vegetable ˈvɛdʒtəbḷ, ˈvɛdʒətəbḷ |-tal -dʒətḷ

vegetarian ˌvɛdʒəˈtɛrɪən, -ˈter-

vegetate ˈvɛdʒəˌtet |-d -ɪd |-tive -ɪv

vegetation ˌvɛdʒəˈteʃən

vehement ˈviəmənt, ˈvihɪ- |-nce -ns

vehicle ˈviɪkḷ, ˈviəkḷ, ˈvihɪkḷ

vehicular viˈhɪkjələ˞; ES -ˈhɪkjələ(r

veil vel |veiled veld

vein ven |veined vend

velar ˈvilɚ; ES ˈvilə(r

velarize ˈviləˌrɑɪz |-s -ɪz |-d -d

Velásquez, -láz- vəˈlɑskeθ, vəˈlæskwɪz (*Sp*
  beˈlaskeθ, -ˈlaθ-) |-'s -keθs, -kwɪzɪz

veld, -dt vɛlt

vellum ˈvɛləm

velocipede vəˈlɑsəˌpid; ES+-ˈlɒs-

velocity vəˈlɑsətɪ; ES+-ˈlɒs-

velours vəˈlur; ES -ˈluə(r

velum ˈviləm

velure vəˈlur, -ˈlɪur; ES -ˈluə(r, -ˈlɪuə(r

Velutus vəˈlutəs, -ˈlɪu- |-'s -ɪz

velvet ˈvɛlvɪt |-ed -ɪd |-y -ɪ

venal ˈvinḷ |-nality viˈnælətɪ

venation viˈneʃən

vend vɛnd |-ed -ɪd |-ee vɛnˈdi

vender ˈvɛndɚ; ES ˈvɛndə(r

vendetta vɛnˈdɛtə |-s -z

vendibility ˌvɛndəˈbɪlətɪ

vendible ˈvɛndəbḷ |-bly -blɪ

vendition vɛnˈdɪʃən

vendor ˈvɛndɚ; ES -də(r; (vɛnˈdi ən vɛnˈdɔr)

vendue vɛnˈdju, -ˈdɪu, -ˈdu

veneer vəˈnɪr; ES -ˈnɪə(r; |-ed -d

venerability ˌvɛnərəˈbɪlətɪ

venerable ˈvɛnərəbḷ, -nrə- |-bly -blɪ

venerate ˈvɛnəˌret |-d -ɪd |-tion ˌvɛnəˈreʃən

venereal vəˈnɪrɪəl

venery ˈvɛnərɪ

Venetian vəˈniʃən—*The old variant* vəˈnɪʃən
  is still heard, spelt Venicyan, Venitian
  15–19cc; cf OF Venicien, *Fr* Vénitien.

Venezuela ˌvɛnəˈzwilə |-n -n (*Am Sp* ˌbene-
  ˈswela)

venge vɛndʒ |-s -ɪz |-d -d |-ful -fəl |-fully -fəlɪ

vengeance ˈvɛndʒəns |-s -ɪz

venial ˈvinɪəl, -njəl |-ly -ɪ

Venice ˈvɛnɪs |-'s -ɪz

venire facias vɪˈnɑɪriˈfeʃɪˌæs

venison ˈvɛnəzn (*Brit* ˈvɛnzn)

Venizelos ˌvɛnɪˈzelas, -lɒs, -ləs |-'s -ɪz

venom ˈvɛnəm |-ed -d |-ous -əs

venous ˈvinəs

vent vɛnt |-ed -ɪd

ventail ˈvɛntel

Ventidius vɛnˈtɪdɪəs, -ˈtɪdʒəs |-'s -ɪz

ventilate ˈvɛntḷˌet |-d -ɪd |-tor -ɚ; ES -ə(r

ventilation ˌvɛntḷˈeʃən

ventral ˈvɛntrəl |-ly -ɪ

ventricle ˈvɛntrɪkḷ

ventriloquism vɛnˈtrɪləˌkwɪzəm |-quist -kwɪst

Ventura vɛnˈturə

venture ˈvɛntʃɚ; ES -tʃə(r; |-d -d |-ring
  -tʃərɪŋ, -tʃrɪŋ |-rous -tʃərəs, -tʃrəs

venue ˈvɛnju, ˈvɛnɪu, ˈvɛnu

Venus ˈvinəs |-es -ɪz |-'s -ɪz

Vera ˈvɪrə

veracious vəˈreʃəs |-racity -ˈræsətɪ

Veracruz, V- Cruz ˈvɛrəˈkruz |-ˈs -ɪz (*Am Sp* ˈberaˈkrus)

veranda, -ah vəˈrændə |-daed, -dahed -dəd

verb vɝb; ES vɝb, vɝ̈b; |-al -l̩ |-ally -l̩ɪ

verbatim vɝˈbetɪm, vɝ̈-; ES və-, vɝ-, vɝ̈-

verbena vɝˈbinə; ES vəˈbinə

verbiage ˈvɝbɪɪdʒ, -bjɪdʒ; ES ˈvɝb-, ˈvɝ̈b-

verbose vɝˈbos, vɝ̈-; ES və-, vɝ-, vɝ̈-; |-bosity -ˈbɑsətɪ; ES+-ˈbɒs-

verboten fəˈbotn̩; ES fə-; (*Ger* fɛrˈboːtən)

verdant ˈvɝdn̩t; ES ˈvɝd-, ˈvɝ̈d-; |-ncy -n̩sɪ

Verde, Cape ˈkepˈvɝd; ES -ˈvɝd, -ˈvɝ̈d

Verdi ˈvɛrdɪ; ES ˈvɛədɪ; (*It* ˈverdi)

verdict ˈvɝdɪkt; ES ˈvɝd-, ˈvɝ̈d-

verdigris ˈvɝdɪˌgris; ES ˈvɝd-, ˈvɝ̈d-

verditer ˈvɝdɪtɚ; ES ˈvɝdɪtə(r, ˈvɝ̈dɪtə(r

Verdun vɛrˈdʌn, ˈvɛrdən; ES vɛəˈdʌn, ˈvɛədən; (*Fr* vɛrˈdœ̃)

verdure ˈvɝdʒɚ, -dʒʊr; ES ˈvɝdʒə(r, ˈvɝ̈dʒə(r, -dʒʊə(r; |-rous -rəs

Vere, de dəˈvɪr; ES dəˈvɪə(r

verge vɝdʒ; ES vɝdʒ, vɝ̈dʒ; |-s -ɪz |-d -d

verger ˈvɝdʒɚ; ES ˈvɝdʒə(r, ˈvɝ̈dʒə(r

Verges ˈvɝdʒiz, -dʒɪz; ES ˈvɝ-, ˈvɝ̈-; |-ges' -dʒiz, -dʒɪz

Vergil ˈvɝdʒəl; ES ˈvɝdʒ-, ˈvɝ̈dʒ-

Vergilian vəˈdʒɪlɪən, vɝ̈-, -ljən; ES və-, vɝ-, vɝ̈-

verify ˈvɛrəˌfaɪ |-fied -ˌfaɪd |-fiable -ˌfaɪəbl̩ |-bly -blɪ

verily ˈvɛrəlɪ

verisimilar ˌvɛrəˈsɪmələ; ES -ˈsɪmələ(r

verisimilitude ˌvɛrəsəˈmɪləˌtjud, -ˌtɪud, -ˌtud

veritable ˈvɛrətəbl̩ |-bly -blɪ |-ty ˈvɛrətɪ

verjuice ˈvɝˌdʒus, -ˌdʒɪus; ES ˈvɝ-, ˈvɝ̈-

vermeil ˈvɝml̩, -mɪl; ES ˈvɝ-, ˈvɝ̈-

vermicelli ˌvɝməˈsɛlɪ; ES ˌvɝm-, ˌvɝ̈m-; (*It* ˌvermiˈtʃɛlli)

vermiform ˈvɝməˌfɔrm; ES ˈvɝməˌfɔəm, ˈvɝ̈m-

vermifuge ˈvɝməˌfjudʒ, -ˌfɪudʒ; ES ˈvɝm-, ˈvɝ̈m-

vermilion, V- vɚˈmɪljən; ES və-

Vermillion vɚˈmɪljən; ES və-

vermin ˈvɝmɪn; ES ˈvɝmɪn, ˈvɝ̈m-; |-ous -əs

Vermont vɚˈmɑnt, vɝ̈-; ES vəˈmɑnt, və-, vɝ̈-, -ˈmɒnt

vermouth ˈvɝmuθ, vɚˈmuθ; ES ˈvɝ-, və-, ˈvɝ̈-; (*Fr* vɛrˈmut, *Ger* Wermut ˈveːrmuːt)

vernacular vɚˈnækjələ; ES vəˈnækjələ(r

vernal ˈvɝnl̩; ES ˈvɝnl̩, ˈvɝ̈-; |-ly -ɪ

Verne vɝn; ES vɝn, vɝ̈n; (*Fr* vɛrn)

Verner's law ˈvɛrnɚz ˈlɔ, ˈvɝ̈nɚz; ES ˈvɛənəz, ˈvɝnəz, ˈvɝ̈nəz

vernier ˈvɝnɪɚ; ES ˈvɝnɪ·ə(r, ˈvɝ̈nɪ·ə(r

Vernon ˈvɝnən; ES ˈvɝnən, ˈvɝ̈nən

Verona vəˈronə (*It* veˈroːna)

Veronica vəˈrɑnɪkə, -ˈrɒn-

Versailles *US* vɚˈselz; ES və-; *France* vɚ̈-ˈselz, vɛrˈsaɪ; ES və-, vɛə-; (*Fr* vɛrˈsɑːj)

versatile ˈvɝsətl̩, -tɪl; ES ˈvɝs-, ˈvɝ̈s-

versatility ˌvɝsəˈtɪlətɪ; ES ˌvɝs-, ˌvɝ̈s-

verse vɝs; ES vɝs, vɝ̈s; |-s -ɪz |-d -t

versicle ˈvɝsɪkl̩; ES ˈvɝs-, ˈvɝ̈s-

versicolor ˈvɝsɪˌkʌlɚ; ES ˈvɝsɪˌkʌlə(r, ˈvɝ̈s-

versification ˌvɝsəfəˈkeʃən; ES ˌvɝs-, ˌvɝ̈s-

versify ˈvɝsəˌfaɪ; ES ˈvɝs-, ˈvɝ̈s-; |-fied -ˌfaɪd

version ˈvɝʒən, ˈvɝʃən; ES ˈvɝ-, ˈvɝ̈-

verso ˈvɝso; ES ˈvɝso, ˈvɝ̈so

verst vɝst; ES vɝst, vɝ̈st

versus ˈvɝsəs; ES ˈvɝs-, ˈvɝ̈s-

vertebra ˈvɝtəbrə; ES ˈvɝt-, ˈvɝ̈t-; |-brae -ˌbri |-bras -brəz |-brate -ˌbret

vertex ˈvɝtɛks; ES ˈvɝt-, ˈvɝ̈t-; |-s -ɪz |-tices -təˌsiz

vertical ˈvɝtɪkl̩; ES ˈvɝt-, ˈvɝ̈t-; |-ly -ɪ, -ɪklɪ

vertiginous vɝˈtɪdʒənəs; ES vɝ-, vɝ̈-

vertigo ˈvɝtɪˌgo; ES ˈvɝt-, ˈvɝ̈t-; |-s -z, *as L* vɚˈtaɪgo |-tigines vɚˈtɪdʒəˌniz; ES və-

vertu vɝˈtu; ES vɝ-, vɝ̈-; (*It* verˈtuː)

Verulam ˈvɛrʊləm, ˈvɛrələm

vervain ˈvɝven; ES ˈvɝven, ˈvɝ̈-

verve vɝv; ES vɝv, vɝ̈v

very ˈvɛrɪ—*Some educated Americans often pronounce* very *almost like* ˈvɝɪ, *but no one regards it as standard.*

vesicle ˈvɛsɪkl̩

Vespasian vɛsˈpeʒɪən, -ʒən

vesper ˈvɛspɚ; ES ˈvɛspə(r

Vespucci vɛsˈputʃɪ (*It* vesˈputtʃi)

vessel ˈvɛsl̩ |vesseled ˈvɛsl̩d

vest vɛst |vested ˈvɛstɪd

Vesta ˈvɛstə |vestal ˈvɛstl̩

vestee vɛsˈti

vestibule ˈvɛstəˌbjul, -ˌbɪul |-d -d

vestige ˈvɛstɪdʒ |-s -ɪz

vestigial vɛsˈtɪdʒɪəl |-ly -ɪ

vestment ˈvɛstmənt |-ed -ɪd

Key: *See in full §§3–47.* bee bi |pity ˈpɪtɪ (§6) |rate ret |yet jɛt |sang sæŋ |angry ˈæŋ·grɪ |bath bæθ; E baθ (§10) |ah ɑ |far fɑr |watch wɑtʃ, wɒtʃ (§12) |jaw dʒɔ |gorge gɔrdʒ |go go

vestry 'vɛstrɪ

vesture 'vɛstʃɚ; ES -tʃə(r; |-d -d

vesuvian, V- və'suvɪən, -'sɪu-, -'sju- |-ius
-ɪəs, -vjəs |-ius's -əsɪz

vet vɛt |vetted 'vɛtɪd

vetch vɛtʃ |vetches 'vɛtʃɪz

veteran 'vɛtərən, 'vɛtrən

veterinarian ˌvɛtrə'nɛrɪən, -tərə-, -'ner-

veterinary 'vɛtrəˌnɛrɪ, 'vɛtərəˌnɛrɪ

veto 'vito |vetoed 'vitod

vex vɛks |vexes 'vɛksɪz |-ed -t |-edly -ɪdlɪ

vexation vɛks'eʃən |-tious -ʃəs

via 'vaɪə

viable 'vaɪəbl̩

viaduct 'vaɪəˌdʌkt

vial 'vaɪəl, vaɪl

viand 'vaɪənd

viaticum vaɪ'ætɪkəm |-s -z |-ca -kə

vibrant 'vaɪbrənt |-ncy -nsɪ

vibrate 'vaɪbret |-d -ɪd |-tor -ɚ; ES -ə(r

vibration vaɪ'breʃən |-tive 'vaɪbrətɪv, -bre-

vibrato vi'brato

vibratory 'vaɪbrəˌtorɪ, -ˌtɔrɪ; S -ˌtorɪ

viburnum, V- vaɪ'bɝnəm; ES -'bɜn-, -'bɝn-

vicar 'vɪkɚ; ES 'vɪkə(r

vicarial vaɪ'kɛrɪəl, vɪ-, -'ker- |-ious -ɪəs

vice n vaɪs |vices 'vaɪsɪz

vice prep 'vaɪsɪ, -sɪ

vice-admiral 'vaɪs'ædmərəl |-ty -tɪ

vice-chancellor 'vaɪs'tʃænsəlɚ, -slɚ; ES -lə(r;
|-ship -ˌʃɪp

vice-consul 'vaɪs'kɑnsl̩; ES+-'kɒn-; |-ar -ɚ,
-sjəlɚ; ES -ə(r; |-ate -ɪt |-ship -ˌʃɪp

vicegerent vaɪs'dʒɪrənt |-ncy -nsɪ |-ship -ˌʃɪp

vice-governor 'vaɪs'gʌvənɚ, -vnɚ, -'gʌvənɚ;
ES -'gʌvənə(r, -vnə(r; |-ship -ˌʃɪp—
'gʌvənɚ becomes 'gʌvənɚ by dissimilation
(§121).

vicennial vaɪ'sɛnɪəl |-ly -ɪ

vice-president 'vaɪs'prɛzədənt, -'prɛzdənt
|-ncy -nsɪ |-ship -ˌʃɪp

viceregal vaɪs'rigl̩ |-ly -ɪ

vice-regent 'vaɪs'ridʒənt |-ncy -nsɪ

viceroy 'vaɪsrɔɪ |-ship -ˌʃɪp

viceroyal vaɪs'rɔɪəl, -'rɔjəl |-ty -tɪ

vice versa 'vaɪsɪ'vɝsə; ES -'vɜsə, -'vɝsə

Vichy 'viʃɪ, 'vɪʃɪ (Fr vi'ʃi)

vicinage 'vɪsn̩ɪdʒ |-nal -sn̩əl, -sən̩l̩

vicinity və'sɪnətɪ

vicious 'vɪʃəs

vicissitude və'sɪsəˌtjud, -ˌtɪud, -ˌtud

Vicksburg 'vɪksbɝg; ES -bɜg, -bɝg

victim 'vɪktɪm |-ize -ˌaɪz |-izes -ˌaɪzɪz |-ized
-ˌaɪzd

victor 'vɪktɚ; ES 'vɪktə(r

Victoria, v- vɪk'torɪə, -'tɔr-, -rjə; S -'tor-;
|-n -n |-ious -ɪəs, -rjəs

victory 'vɪktrɪ, 'vɪktərɪ

victress 'vɪktrɪs |-es -ɪz

Victrola vɪk'trolə

victual 'vɪtl̩ |victuals 'vɪtl̩z (vittle 1575)

vicuna vɪ'kjunə, -'kɪunə (Sp bi'kuna)

Vida first name 'vaɪdə, 'vidə; It poet 'vidə
(It 'vi:da)

vide 'see' 'vaɪdɪ

videlicet, abbr. viz. vɪ'dɛləsɪt, vɪz

vie vaɪ |vied vaɪd |vying 'vaɪɪŋ

Vienna vɪ'ɛnə |-nese ˌviə'niz

view vju, vɪu |-ed -d |-point -ˌpɔɪnt

vigesimal vaɪ'dʒɛsəml̩

vigil 'vɪdʒəl

vigilant 'vɪdʒələnt |-lance -ləns

vigilante ˌvɪdʒə'læntɪ

vignette vɪn'jɛt |vignetted vɪn'jɛtɪd

vigor 'vɪgɚ; ES 'vɪgə(r; |-ous -əs

viking, V- 'vaɪkɪŋ

vile vaɪl |vilely 'vaɪllɪ

vilification ˌvɪləfə'keʃən

vilify 'vɪləˌfaɪ |-fied -ˌfaɪd

vill vɪl |villa 'vɪlə

village 'vɪlɪdʒ |-s -ɪz |-d -d

villain 'vɪlən |-ous -əs |-y -ɪ

villanage, -ain-, -en-, -ein- 'vɪlənɪdʒ

villein 'vɪlɪn

Villiers 'vɪlɚz, 'vɪljɚz; ES 'vɪləz, -ljəz

villous 'vɪləs

Vilna 'vɪlnə

vim vɪm

vinaigrette ˌvɪnə'grɛt |-d -ɪd

Vincennes US vɪn'sɛnz |-'s -ɪz |France Fr
vɛ̃'sɛn

Vincent 'vɪnsn̩t

Vincentio vɪn'sɛnʃɪˌo, -ʃjo

Vinci, Leonardo da ˌlɪə'nɑrdo də'vɪntʃɪ; ES
-'nɑːdo; (It ˌleo'nardo da'vintʃi)

vincible 'vɪnsəbl̩ |-bly -blɪ

vindicability ˌvɪndəkə'bɪlətɪ

vindicable 'vɪndəkəbl̩ |-bly -blɪ

|full fʊl |tooth tuθ |further 'fɝðɚ; ES 'fɜðə |custom 'kʌstəm |while hwaɪl |how haʊ |toy tɔɪ
|using 'juzɪŋ |fuse fjuz, fɪuz |dish dɪʃ |vision 'vɪʒən |Eden 'idn̩ |cradle 'kredl̩ |keep 'em 'kipm̩

vindicate ˈvɪndəˌket |-d -ɪd |-tor -ɚ; ES -ə(r

vindication ˌvɪndəˈkeʃən

vindicative ˈvɪndəˌketɪv, vɪnˈdɪkətɪv

vindicatory ˈvɪndəkəˌtorɪ, -ˌtɔrɪ; S -ˌtorɪ

vindictive vɪnˈdɪktɪv

vine vaɪn |vined vaɪnd

vinegar ˈvɪnɪgɚ; ES -gə(r; |-y -ɪ, -grɪ

vineyard ˈvɪnjɚd; ES ˈvɪnjəd

viniculture ˈvɪnɪˌkʌltʃɚ; ES -ˌkʌltʃə(r

vinous ˈvaɪnəs |-nosity vaɪˈnɑsətɪ; ES+-ˈnɒs-

vintage ˈvɪntɪdʒ |-s -ɪz |-d -d

vintner ˈvɪntnɚ; ES ˈvɪntnə(r

viny ˈvaɪnɪ

viol ˈvaɪəl, vaɪl

viola mus. instr. vɪˈolə, ˈvaɪələ (It viˈɔːlɑ)

viola flower ˈvaɪələ

Viola name ˈvaɪələ, vaɪˈolə, in Shak. ˈvaɪələ

violable ˈvaɪələbḷ |-bly -blɪ

violate ˈvaɪəˌlet |-d -ɪd |-tion ˌvaɪəˈleʃən

violent ˈvaɪələnt |-nce -ns |-nces -nsɪz

Violenta ˌvaɪəˈlɛntə

violet ˈvaɪəlɪt

violin ˌvaɪəˈlɪn |-ed -d

violine, -lin chem. ˈvaɪəˌlin, -lɪn

violinist ˌvaɪəˈlɪnɪst

violoncellist ˌviələnˈtʃɛlɪst, ˌvaɪələnˈsɛlɪst;
ES+-lɒn-; |-llo -lo (It ˌviolonˈtʃɛllo)

viper ˈvaɪpɚ; ES ˈvaɪpə(r; |-ous -əs, -prəs

virago vəˈrego, vaɪˈrego

virelay ˈvɪrəˌle

vireo ˈvɪrɪˌo

virgate n, adj ˈvɝgɪt, -get; ES ˈvɜ-, ˈvɝ-

virgate v ˈvɝˈget; ES ˈvɜ-, ˈvɝ-; |-d -ɪd

Virgil ˈvɝdʒəl; ES ˈvɜdʒ-, ˈvɝdʒ-

Virgilia vɚˈdʒɪlɪə, vɜ-; ES və-, vɜ-, vɝ-;
|-n -n

virgin ˈvɝdʒɪn; ES ˈvɜ-, ˈvɝ-; |-ed -d |-al -ḷ
|-ally -ḷɪ

Virginia vɚˈdʒɪnjə, esp. NEngd -ˈdʒɪnɪə; ES
və-; |-n -n

Virgin Islands ˈvɝdʒɪnˈaɪləndz; ES ˈvɜdʒ-,
ˈvɝdʒ-

virginity vɚˈdʒɪnətɪ; ES vɚ-

Virgo ˈvɝgo, gen ˈvɝdʒɪnɪs; ES ˈvɜ-, ˈvɝ-

virgule ˈvɝgjul; ES ˈvɜg- ˈvɝg-

viridescent ˌvɪrəˈdɛsṇt |-nce -ns

viridity vəˈrɪdətɪ

virile ˈvɪrəl, ˈvaɪrəl |-rility vəˈrɪlətɪ, vɪ-

virtu vɝˈtu; ES vɜ-, vɝ-; (It virˈtu:)

virtual ˈvɝtʃʊəl; ES ˈvɜ-, ˈvɝ-; |-ly -ɪ

virtue ˈvɝtʃu; ES ˈvɜ-, ˈvɝ-; |-tuous -tʃʊəs

virtuosity ˌvɝtʃʊˈɑsətɪ; ES ˌvɜtʃʊˈɑsətɪ,
-ˈɒs-, ˌvɜ-

virtuoso ˌvɝtʃʊˈoso; ES ˌvɜ-, ˌvɝ-; (It
ˌvirtuˈo:so)

virulent ˈvɪrjələnt, ˈvɪrʊlənt, ˈvɪrə- |-nce -ns

virus ˈvaɪrəs |viruses ˈvaɪrəsɪz

visa n ˈvizə |pl visas ˈvizəz=visé

visa v ˈvizə |visas ˈvizəz |visaed ˈvizəd=visé

visage ˈvɪzɪdʒ |-s -ɪz |-d -d

visard ˈvɪzɚd; ES ˈvɪzəd; |-ed -ɪd=vizard

vis-à-vis ˌvizəˈvi |pl same (Fr vizaˈvi)

Visayan viˈsajən

viscera ˈvɪsərə |rare sg viscus ˈvɪskəs

viscid ˈvɪsɪd |viscidity vɪˈsɪdətɪ

viscose ˈvɪskos |viscous ˈvɪskəs

viscosity vɪsˈkɑsətɪ; ES+-ˈkɒs-

viscount ˈvaɪkaunt |-ess -ɪs |-ess's -ɪsɪz

vise vaɪs |-s -ɪz |-d -t

visé n ˈvize |pl visés ˈvizez=visa

visé v ˈvize |visés ˈvizez |viséed ˈvized=visa

visibility ˌvɪzəˈbɪlətɪ

visible ˈvɪzəbḷ |-bly -blɪ

Visigoth ˈvɪzɪˌgɑθ, -ˌgɒθ, -ˌgɔθ

vision ˈvɪʒən |-ary -ˌɛrɪ

visit ˈvɪzɪt |-ed -ɪd |-or -ɚ; ES -ə(r

visitant ˈvɪzətənt |-itation ˌvɪzəˈteʃən

visor ˈvaɪzɚ, much less freq. ˈvɪzɚ; ES -zə(r;
|-ed -d

vista ˈvɪstə

Vistula ˈvɪstʃʊlə

visual ˈvɪʒʊəl |-ly -ɪ

visualize ˈvɪʒʊəlˌaɪz |-s -ɪz |-d -d

vital ˈvaɪtḷ |-ly -ɪ |-tality vaɪˈtælətɪ

vitals ˈvaɪtḷz

vitamin ˈvaɪtəmɪn |vitamine ˈvaɪtəˌmaɪn,
-mɪn

vitiate ˈvɪʃɪˌet |-d -ɪd |-iable ˈvɪʃɪəbḷ

viticulture ˈvɪtɪˌkʌltʃɚ; ES -ˌkʌltʃə(r

vitreous ˈvɪtrɪəs

vitrescent vɪˈtrɛsṇt |-nce -ns |-ncy -ṇsɪ

vitric ˈvɪtrɪk

vitrify ˈvɪtrəˌfaɪ |-fied -ˌfaɪd

vitriol ˈvɪtrɪəl |-ed -d

vitriolic ˌvɪtrɪˈɑlɪk; ES+-ˈɒl-

vituperate vaɪˈtupəˌret, vɪ-, -ˈtɪu-, -ˈtju- |-d
-ɪd

vituperation vaɪˌtupəˈreʃən, vɪ-, -ˌtɪu, -ˌtju-

Vitus ˈvaɪtəs |-ʼs -ɪz
viva ʼlong live!ʼ ˈvivə (It ˈviːva)
vivace viˈvatʃɪ (It viˈvaːtʃe)
vivacious vaɪˈveʃəs |-vacity -ˈvæsətɪ
vivarium vaɪˈvɛrɪəm, -ˈver- |-s -z |-ia -ɪə
viva-voce ˈvaɪvəˈvosɪ |-d -d
Vivian, -en ˈvɪvɪən, -vjən
vivid ˈvɪvɪd
vivification ˌvɪvəfəˈkeʃən
vivify ˈvɪvəˌfaɪ |-fied -ˌfaɪd
viviparous vaɪˈvɪpərəs
vivisect ˌvɪvəˈsɛkt |-ed -ɪd |-section -ˈsɛkʃən
vixen ˈvɪksn̩
viz. vɪz, vɪˈdɛləsɪt
vizard arch. var. of visor ˈvɪzɚd; ES ˈvɪzəd
vizier vɪˈzɪr, ˈvɪzjɚ, ˈvɪzɪɚ; ES vɪˈzɪə(r,
ˈvɪzjə(r, ˈvɪzɪ·ə(r
vizor ˈvaɪzɚ, ˈvɪz-; ES -zə(r; |-ed -d, cf visor
Vladivostok ˌvlædɪˈvɑstɑk; ES+-ˈvɒstɒk
vocable ˈvokəb| |-bly -blɪ
vocabulary vəˈkæbjəˌlɛrɪ, vo-
vocal ˈvok| |-ly -ɪ
vocalic voˈkælɪk
vocalize ˈvok|ˌaɪz |-s -ɪz |-d -d
vocation voˈkeʃən
vocative ˈvɑkətɪv, ˈvɑkɪ-; ES+ˈvɒk-
vociferate voˈsɪfəˌret |-d -ɪd |-rous -rəs
vodka ˈvɑdkə, ˈvɒdkə
vogue vog |vogued vogd
voice vɔɪs |-s -ɪz |-d -t
void vɔɪd |-ed -ɪd |-able -əb| |-ance -n̩s
voile vɔɪl (Fr vwal)
volant ˈvolənt
Volapük, -puk ˌvoləˈpyk, ˈvaləˌpʊk, ˈvɒl-
|-ism -ˌɪzəm |-ist -ɪst
volatile ˈvalət|, -tɪl; ES+ˈvɒl-; |-ly -lɪ
volatility ˌvaləˈtɪlətɪ; ES+ˌvɒl-
volcanic valˈkænɪk; ES+vɒl-; |-ally -|ɪ, -ɪklɪ
volcano valˈkeno; ES+vɒl-
volcanology ˌvalkənˈalədʒɪ; ES+ˌvɒlkən-
ˈɒlədʒɪ
vole vol |-d -d
volery ˈvalərɪ; ES+ˈvɒl-
Volga ˈvalgə, ˈvɒlgə
volition voˈlɪʃən |-al -| |-ally -|ɪ
volitive ˈvalətɪv; ES+ˈvɒl-
Volkslied Ger ˈfɔlksˌliːt |pl -lieder -ˌliːdər
volley ˈvalɪ; ES+ˈvɒlɪ; |-ed -d |-ball -ˌbɔl
volplane ˈvalˌplen; ES+ˈvɒl-; |-d -d

Volpone valˈponɪ, vɒl-
Volscian ˈvalʃən, ˈvɒl-, -ʃɪən |-s -z
Volstead ˈvalstɛd, -stɪd, ˈvɒl-
Volsunga Saga ˈvalsʊŋgəˌsagə, ˈvɒl-
volt volt |-age -ɪdʒ |-ages -ɪdʒɪz
voltaic valˈte·ɪk; ES+vɒl-
Voltaire valˈter, vɒl-, -ˈtær; E -ˈtɛə(r, ES
-ˈtæə(r; (Fr vɔlˈtɛːr) |-rean, -rian -ɪən
voltameter valˈtæmətɚ; ES -ˈtæmətə(r, vɒl-
voltammeter ˈvoltˈæmˌmitɚ; ES -ˌmitə(r
volte-face ˈvaltˌfas, ˈvaltə-, ˈvɒl- (Fr vɔltə-
ˈfas)
Voltemand, -ti- ˈvaltəˌmænd, ˈvɒl-
voltmeter ˈvoltˌmitɚ; ES -ˌmitə(r
volubility ˌvaljəˈbɪlətɪ; ES+ˌvɒl-
voluble ˈvaljəb|; ES+ˈvɒl-; |-bly -blɪ
volume ˈvaljəm; ES+ˈvɒl-; |-d -d
volumeter vəˈlumətɚ, -ˈlɪu-, vəlˈju-, valˈju-;
ES -tə(r, vɒl-
volumetric ˌvaljəˈmɛtrɪk; ES+ˌvɒl-; |-al -|
|-ally -|ɪ, -ɪklɪ
voluminous vəˈlumənəs, vəˈlɪu-
Volumnia vəˈlʌmnɪə, -njə |-ius -s |-ius's -sɪz
voluntary ˈvalənˌtɛrɪ; ES+ˈvɒl-; |-rily -rəlɪ,
esp. if emph. ˌvolunˈtarily
volunteer ˌvalənˈtɪr; ES -ˈtɪə(r, ˌvɒl-, S+
-ˈtɛə(r
voluptuary vəˈlʌptʃuˌɛrɪ -tuous -tʃuəs
volute vəˈlut, vəˈlɪut |-d -ɪd
vomit ˈvamɪt; ES+ˈvɒm-; |-ed -ɪd
voodoo ˈvudu |-ed -d
voracious voˈreʃəs
vortex ˈvɔrtɛks; ES ˈvɔətɛks; |-es -ɪz |-tices
-tɪˌsiz
vortical ˈvɔrtɪk|; ES ˈvɔə-; |-ly -ɪ
vortiginous vɔrˈtɪdʒənəs; ES vɔ-
Vosges voʒ |Vosgian, -gean ˈvoʒɪən |-ʼs -ɪz
votaress, -tress ˈvotərɪs, ˈvotrɪs |-es -ɪz
votary ˈvotərɪ
vote vot |voted ˈvotɪd
votive ˈvotɪv
vouch vautʃ |-es -ɪz |-ed -t
voucher ˈvautʃɚ; ES ˈvautʃə(r
vouchsafe vautʃˈsef |-s -s |-d -t
vow vau |vowed vaud
vowel ˈvauəl, vaul, ˈvauɪl |-ed -d |-like -ˌlaɪk
vox vaks, vɒks |voces ˈvosiz
voyage ˈvɔɪ·ɪdʒ, ˈvɔjɪdʒ |-s -ɪz |-d -d
voyager ˈvɔɪ·ɪdʒɚ, ˈvɔjɪdʒɚ; ES -ə(r

full fʊl |tooth tuθ |further ˈfɝðɚ; ES ˈfɝðə |custom ˈkʌstəm |while hwaɪl |how hau |toy tɔɪ
|using ˈjuzɪŋ |fuse fjuz, fɪuz |dish dɪʃ |vision ˈvɪʒən |Eden ˈidn̩ |cradle ˈkred| |keep ʼem ˈkipm̩

voyageur *Fr* vwaja'ʒœ:r
vraisemblance *Fr* vrɛsã'blã:s
Vriesland 'frizlənd, -ˌlænd
Vulcan 'vʌlkən |-canian vʌl'kenɪən
vulcanite 'vʌlkənˌaɪt
vulcanize 'vʌlkənˌaɪz |-s -ɪz |-d -d
vulcanology ˌvʌlkən'alədʒɪ; ES+-'ɒl-
vulgar 'vʌlgɚ; ES 'vʌlgə(r; |-ism -ˌɪzəm
vulgarian vʌl'gɛrɪən, -'gær-, -'ger-

vulgarity vʌl'gærətɪ
vulgarize 'vʌlgəˌraɪz |-s -ɪz |-d -d
Vulgate 'vʌlget, -gɪt
vulnerable 'vʌlnərəbl̩ |-bly -blɪ
Vulpecula vʌl'pɛkjʊlə |-lid -lɪd
vulpine 'vʌlpaɪn
vulture 'vʌltʃɚ; ES 'vʌltʃə(r
vulva 'vʌlvə
vying *ptc of* vie 'vaɪɪŋ

W

W, w *letter* 'dʌb·ljʊ, 'dʌblju, 'dʌbju |*pl* W's,
Ws, *poss* W's 'dʌb·ljuz, 'dʌbljuz, 'dʌbjuz
Wabash 'wɔbæʃ |-'s -ɪz
wabble 'wabl̩, 'wɒb- |-d -d |-ling -blɪŋ, -bl̩ɪŋ
|-bly -blɪ, -bl̩ɪ
Wace *Eng dean* wes, *Norm poet* wes, wæs,
was
Waco 'weko
wad wad, wɒd |-ded -ɪd
waddle 'wadl̩, 'wɒdl̩ |-d -d |-ling -dlɪŋ, -dl̩ɪŋ
wade wed |waded 'wedɪd
Wadsworth 'wadzwɚθ, 'wɒd-; ES -wəθ
wafer 'wefɚ; ES 'wefə(r; |-ed -d |-ing
'wefərɪŋ, 'wefrɪŋ
waffle wafl̩, 'wɒfl̩, 'wɔfl̩
waft wæft, waft, waft |-ed -ɪd
wafture 'wæftʃɚ, 'waf-, 'waf-; ES -tʃə(r
wag wæg |wagged wægd
wage wedʒ |wages 'wedʒɪz |waged wedʒd
wager 'wedʒɚ; ES 'wedʒə(r; |-ed -d |-ing
'wedʒərɪŋ, 'wedʒrɪŋ
waggery 'wægərɪ
waggle 'wægl̩ |-d -d |-ling 'wæglɪŋ, 'wægl̩ɪŋ
Wagner *Eng name* 'wægnɚ, *Ger musician*
'wægnɚ, 'vagnɚ; ES -nə(r; (*Ger* 'va:gnər)
Wagnerian wæg'nɪrɪən, vag-
wagon 'wægən, 'wægŋ |-ed -d
wagonette ˌwægən'ɛt
wagon-lit *Fr* vagõ'li
Wagram *Ger* 'va:gram
Wagstaff 'wægˌstæf; E+-ˌstaf, -ˌstaf
wagtail 'wægˌtel
Wahabi, Wahh-, -bee wa'habɪ, wə-
Wahr, *George* wɔr; ES wɔə(r
waif wef |waifed weft

Waikiki 'wɑ·iˌkiki
wail wel |wailed weld |-ful -fəl |-fully -fəlɪ
wain wen
wainscot 'wenskət, -ˌskat, -ˌskot; ES+-ˌskɒt;
|-ed -ɪd |-ing -ɪŋ
wainwright, W- 'wenˌraɪt
waist west |waisted 'westɪd
waistband 'westˌbænd, 'wes-, -bənd
waistcloth 'westˌklɔθ, -ˌklɒθ—*see* cloth
waistcoat 'westˌkot, 'wesˌkot, 'wɛskət |-ed -ɪd
waistline 'westˌlaɪn
wait wet |-ed -ɪd |-er -ɚ; ES -ə(r; |-ress -rɪs
waive wev |waived wevd |waiver 'wevɚ; ES
-ə(r
wake wek |*past* waked wekt *or* woke wok
|*pptc* waked wekt, *rarely* woken 'wokən
Wakefield 'wekˌfild
wakeful 'wekfəl |-ly -ɪ
Wake Island 'wek 'aɪlənd
wakeless 'weklɪs
waken wekən |-ed -d |-ing 'wekənɪŋ, 'weknɪŋ
wake-robin 'wekˌrabɪn; ES+-ˌrɒbɪn
Walden 'wɔldən, -dɪn
Waldenses wal'dɛnsiz, wɒl-
Waldo 'wɔldo
Waldoboro 'wɔldəˌbɝo, -ə; ES -ˌbɜr-, -ˌbʌr-,
-ˌbɝ-
Waldorf 'wɔldɔrf; ES -dɔəf
wale wel |waled weld
Wales welz |Wales's 'welzɪz
Walhalla wæl'hælə, væl'hælə
walk wɔk |walked wɔkt
walkaway 'wɔkəˌwe
walker, W- 'wɔkɚ; ES 'wɔkə(r
walkout 'wɔkˌaʊt

Key: See in full §§3–47. bee bi |pity 'pɪtɪ (§6) |rate ret |yet jɛt |sang sæŋ |angry 'æŋ·grɪ
|bath bæθ; E baθ (§10) |ah ɑ |far fɑr |watch watʃ, wɒtʃ (§12) |jaw dʒɔ |gorge gɔrdʒ |go go

walkover ˈwɔkˌovɚ; ES -ˌovə(r
walk-up ˈwɔkˌʌp
Walküre, Die *Ger* di valˈkyːrə
Walkyrie wælˈkırı, væl-
wall wɔl |walled wɔld
wallaby ˈwɑləbı, ˈwɒl-
Wallace ˈwɑlıs, ˈwɒl-, ˈwɑl- |-ˈs -ız
Wallachia wɑˈlekıə, wɒ-
wallah, -la ˈwɑlə, ˈwɒlə
Walla Walla ˈwɑləˈwɑlə, ˈwɒləˈwɒlə
Wallenstein ˈwɑlənˌstaın, ˈwɒl- (*Ger* ˈvɑlən-
ˌʃtaın)
Waller ˈwɔlɚ, ˈwɒlɚ, ˈwɑlɚ; ES -ə(r
wallet ˈwɑlıt, ˈwɒlıt, ˈwɔlıt
walleye ˈwɔlˌaı |-d -d
wallflower ˈwɔlˌflauɚ, -ˌflaur; ES -ˌflau·ə(r,
-ˌflauə(r
Wallingford ˈwɔlıŋfɚd, ˈwɒl-, ˈwɑl-; ES -fəd
Walloon wɑˈlun, wɒ-, wə-
wallop ˈwɑləp, ˈwɒləp |-ed -t
wallow ˈwɑlo, ˈwɒlo, -lə |-ed -d |-ing -ləwıŋ
wallpaper ˈwɔlˌpepɚ; ES -ˌpepə(r
walnut ˈwɔlnət, ˈwɒl-, -ˌnʌt
Walpole ˈwɔlˌpol
walrus ˈwɔlrəs, ˈwɑl-, ˈwɒl- |-es -ız
Walsh wɔlʃ, wɑlʃ, wɒlʃ |-ˈs -ız
Walsingham ˈwɔlsıŋəm, ˈwɑl-, ˈwɒl-
Walter ˈwɔltɚ; ES ˈwɔltə(r
Waltham *Engd* ˈwɔltəm, -lθəm; *Mass*
ˈwɔlθæm, -θəm—Waltham *was at first*
ˈwɑldˌham, *then* ˈwaltˌham, ˈwɑltəm,
ˈwɔltəm—*The* h *sound was lost long ago, and
the letters* -th- *wrongly taken to represent* θ.
*Now the error is established, both in America
and England.*
Walthamstow *Engd* ˈwɔlθəmˌsto, ˈwɔltəm-
Walton ˈwɔltṇ
waltz wɔlts |-es -ız |-ed -t
Walworth ˈwɔlwɚθ; ES -wəθ
Wampanoag ˌwɑmpəˈnoæg, ˌwɒm-
wampum ˈwɑmpəm, ˈwɒmpəm, ˈwɔmpəm
wampus ˈwɑmpəs, ˈwɒm-, ˈwɔm- |-es -ız
wamus, wamm- ˈwɑməs, ˈwɒm-, ˈwɑm- |-es
-ız
wan wɑn, wɒn |-ned -d
Wanamaker ˈwɑnəˌmekɚ, ˈwɒn-; ES -ˌmekə(r
wand wɑnd, wɒnd
wander ˈwɑndɚ, ˈwɒndɚ; ES -də(r; |-ed -d
|-ing -drıŋ, -dərıŋ

wanderlust ˈwɑndɚˌlʌst, ˈwɒn- (*Ger* ˈvɑndər-
ˌlust)
wane wen |waned wend
wangle ˈwæŋgḷ |-d -d |-ling ˈwæŋglıŋ, -glɪŋ
Wannamaker ˈwɑnəˌmekɚ, ˈwɒn-; ES
-ˌmekə(r
wanness ˈwɑnnıs, ˈwɒn-
want wɑnt, wɔnt, wɒnt; S wɔnt, wɒnt, wɑnt;
|-ed -ıd |want to *often* ˈwɑntə
wantage ˈwɑntıdʒ *etc. see* want
Wantage ˈwɑntıdʒ, ˈwɒn-
wanton ˈwɑntən, ˈwɒntən |-ness -tənnıs
Wapakoneta ˌwɑpəkəˈnɛtə, ˌwɒpə-
Wapello wəˈpɛlo, wɑ-, wɒ-
wapentake ˈwɑpənˌtek, ˈwɒp-, ˈwæp-
wapiti ˈwɑpətı, ˈwɒp-
war wɔr; ES wɔə(r; |-red -d
Warbeck ˈwɔrbɛk; ES ˈwɔəbɛk
warble ˈwɔrbḷ; ES ˈwɔəbḷ; |-d -d |-ling -blıŋ,
-bḷɪŋ |-bler -blɚ; ES -blə(r
Warburton ˈwɔrbɚtṇ; ES ˈwɔəbətṇ
ward, W- wɔrd; ES wɔəd; |-ed -ıd |-en -ṇ
|-er -ɚ; ES -ə(r; |-ress -rıs |-ship -ʃıp
wardrobe ˈwɔrdˌrob; ES ˈwɔədˌrob
wardroom ˈwɔrdˌrum, -ˌrum; ES ˈwɔəd-
ware, W- wɛr, wær; E wɛə(r, ES wæə(r
Wareham ˈwɛrəm, ˈwær-; S ˈwær-; *Mass*
loc.+ˈwæəhæm
warehouse *n* ˈwɛrˌhaus, ˈwær- |-ses -zız; ES
see ware
warehouse *v* ˈwɛrˌhauz, ˈwær-, -ˌhaus |-s -ız
|-d -d, -t; ES *see* ware
wareroom ˈwɛrˌrum, ˈwær-, -ˌrum; ES *see*
ware
warfare ˈwɔrˌfɛr, -ˌfær; E ˈwɔəˌfɛə(r, ES
-ˌfæə(r; |-d -d
warily ˈwɛrəlı, ˈwerəlı, ˈwærəlı—*The pron.
with* e *is esp. freq. in the* S.
warison ˈwærəsṇ
warlike ˈwɔrˌlaık; ES ˈwɔə-
warlock ˈwɔrˌlak; ES ˈwɔəˌlak, -ˌlɒk
warm wɔrm; ES wɔəm; |-ed -d
warm-blooded ˈwɔrmˈblʌdıd; ES ˈwɔəm-;
(ˈwarm-ˌblooded ˈvalor)
warmhearted ˈwɔrmˈhartıd; ES ˈwɔəm-
ˈhaːtıd, E+-ˈhaːtıd
warmth wɔrmpθ, wɔrmθ; ES wɔəm-
warn wɔrn; ES wɔən; |-ed -d
warp wɔrp; ES wɔəp; |-ed -t

|full fʊl |tooth tuθ |further ˈfɝðɚ; ES ˈfɝðə |custom ˈkʌstəm |while hwaıl |how hau |toy tɔı
|using ˈjuzıŋ |fuse fjuz, fıuz |dish dıʃ |vision ˈvıʒən |Eden ˈidṇ |cradle ˈkredḷ |keep ʼem ˈkipm̩

warpath ˈwɔrˌpæθ; ES ˈwɔə-, E+-ˌpɑθ, -ˌpɑθ; |-ths -ðz

warplane ˈwɔrˌplen; ES ˈwɔə-

warrant ˈwɔrənt, ˈwɑrənt, ˈwɒrənt |-ed -ɪd

warrantee ˌwɔrənˈti, ˌwɑr-, ˌwɒr-

warrantor ˈwɔrənˌtɔr, ˈwɑr-, ˈwɒr-; ES -tɔə(r; (ˌwarranˈtee & ˌwarranˈtor)

warranty ˈwɔrəntɪ, ˈwɑr-, ˈwɒr-

warren, W- ˈwɔrɪn, ˈwɑr-, ˈwɒr-, -ən

Warrick ˈwɔrɪk, ˈwɑrɪk, ˈwɒrɪk—see Warwick

warrior ˈwɔrɪɚ, ˈwɑr-, ˈwɒr-, -rjɚ; ES -rɪ·ə(r, -rjə(r

Warsaw ˈwɔrsɔ; ES ˈwɔəsɔ

warship ˈwɔrˌʃɪp; ES ˈwɔə-

warsle ˈwɑrsḷ; ES ˈwɑːsḷ; |-d -d |-ling -slɪŋ, -sḷɪŋ

wart wɔrt; ES wɔət; |-ed -ɪd

Warton ˈwɔrtṇ; ES ˈwɔətṇ

Warwick US ˈwɔrwɪk; ES ˈwɔəwɪk; less freq. ˈwɔrɪk, ˈwɑrɪk, ˈwɒrɪk; Engd ˈwɔrɪk, ˈwɑrɪk, ˈwɒrɪk

Warwickshire ˈwɔrɪkˌʃɪr, ˈwɑr-, ˈwɒr-, -ʃɚ; ES -ˌʃɪə(r, -ʃə(r

warworn ˈwɔrˌworn, -ˌwɔrn; ES ˈwɔəˌwoən, E+-ˌwɔən

wary ˈwɛrɪ, ˈwerɪ, ˈwærɪ—The pron. with e is esp. freq. in the S.

was stressed ˈwɑz, ˌwɑz, ˈwɒz, ˌwɒz; unstr. wəz; restressed ˈwʌz, ˌwʌz

wash wɑʃ, wɔʃ, wɒʃ |-es -ɪz |-ed -t |-able -əbḷ

washboard ˈwɑʃˌbord, ˈwɔʃ-, ˈwɒʃ-, -ˌbɔrd; ES -ˌboəd, E+-ˌbɔəd

washed-out ˈwɑʃtˌaut, ˈwɔʃt-, ˈwɒʃt-

washed-up ˈwɑʃtˈʌp, ˈwɔʃt-, ˈwɒʃt- (ˈwashed-ˌup ˈlook)

washer ˈwɑʃɚ, ˈwɔʃɚ, ˈwɒʃɚ; ES -ʃə(r; |-man, -men -mən |-woman -ˌwumən |-women -ˌwɪmɪn—see woman

Washington ˈwɑʃɪŋtən, ˈwɔʃ-, ˈwɒʃ-

Washita ˈwɑʃɪˌtɔ, ˈwɒʃ-, ˈwɔʃ-

washrag ˈwɑʃˌræg, ˈwɔʃ-, ˈwɒʃ-

washroom ˈwɑʃˌrum, ˈwɔʃ-, ˈwɒʃ-, -ˌrum

washstand ˈwɑʃˌstænd, ˈwɔʃ-, ˈwɒʃ-

washwoman ˈwɑʃˌwumən, ˈwɔʃ-, ˈwɒʃ- |-women -ˌwɪmɪn—see woman

washy ˈwɑʃɪ, ˈwɔʃɪ, ˈwɒʃɪ

wasn't ˈwɑzṇt, ˈwɒzṇt, ˈwʌzṇt, before some conss.+-zṇ (ɪt ˈwazṇ gud)

wasp wɑsp, wɔsp, wɒsp

wassail ˈwɑsḷ, ˈwɒsḷ, ˈwæsḷ, -el |-ed -d

Wasserman ˈwɑsɚmən, ˈvɑs-; ES -sə-; (Ger ˈvɑsərˌman)

wast 2 sg of was, stressed ˈwɑst, ˈwɒst, ˌwɑst, ˌwɒst; unstr. wəst

wastage ˈwestɪdʒ |-s -ɪz

waste west |-d -ɪd |-ful -fəl |-fully -fəlɪ

wastebasket ˈwestˌbæskɪt; E+-ˌbɑs-, -ˌbɑs-

wastepaper ˈwestˈpepɚ; ES -ˈpepə(r

waster ˈwestɚ; ES ˈwestə(r

wastrel ˈwestrəl

watch wɑtʃ, wɒtʃ, wɔtʃ |-es -ɪz |-ed -t

watchcase ˈwɑtʃˌkes, ˈwɒtʃ-, ˈwɔtʃ-

watchdog ˈwɑtʃˌdɔg, ˈwɒtʃ-, ˈwɔtʃ-, -ˌdɒg

watchful ˈwɑtʃfəl, ˈwɒtʃ-, ˈwɔtʃ- |-ly -ɪ

watchmaker ˈwɑtʃˌmekɚ, ˈwɒtʃ-, ˈwɔtʃ-; ES -ˌmekə(r

watchman ˈwɑtʃmən, ˈwɒtʃ-, ˈwɔtʃ- |-men -mən

watchtower ˈwɑtʃˌtauɚ, ˈwɒtʃ-, ˈwɔtʃ-; ES -ˌtau·ə(r

watchword ˈwɑtʃˌwɝd, ˈwɒtʃ-, ˈwɔtʃ-; ES -ˌwɜd, -ˌwɝd

water ˈwɔtɚ, ˈwɑtɚ, ˈwɒtɚ; ES -tə(r;—The same variants of water occur in the following compounds and derivatives.

water-borne ˈwɔtɚˌborn, -ˌbɔrn; ES ˈwɔtə-ˌboən, E+-ˌbɔən

waterbuck ˈwɔtɚˌbʌk; ES ˈwɔtə-

Waterbury ˈwɔtɚˌbɛrɪ, ˈwɔtəˌbɛrɪ, -bərɪ; ES ˈwɔtə-; Loss of ɚ in the second pron. is due to dissimilation (§121).

watercourse ˈwɔtɚˌkors, -ˌkɔrs; ES ˈwɔtə-ˌkoəs, E+-ˌkɔəs; |-s -ɪz

watercraft ˈwɔtɚˌkræft; ES ˈwɔtəˌkræft, E+-ˌkrɑft, -ˌkrɑft

watercress ˈwɔtɚˌkrɛs; ES ˈwɔtə-; |-es -ɪz

Wateree ˌwɔtɚˈri

waterfall ˈwɔtɚˌfɔl; ES ˈwɔtə-

waterfowl ˈwɔtɚˌfaul; ES ˈwɔtə-

water-inch ˈwɔtɚˈɪntʃ |-es -ɪz

wateriness ˈwɔtɚɪnɪs, ˈwɒtɪ-

waterlog ˈwɔtɚˌlɔg, -ˌlɑg, -ˌlɒg; ES ˈwɔtə-; |-ged -d |-gedness -ɪdnɪs

Waterloo ˌwɔtɚˈlu; ES ˌwɔtə-

waterman, W- ˈwɔtɚmən; ES ˈwɔtə-; |-men -mən

watermark ˈwɔtɚˌmark; ES ˈwɔtəˌmɑk, E+-ˌmɑːk; |-ed -t

Key: See in full §§3–47. bee bi |pity ˈpɪtɪ (§6) |rate ret |yet jɛt |sang sæŋ |angry ˈæŋ·grɪ |bath bæθ; E baθ (§10) |ah ɑ |far fɑr |watch wɑtʃ, wɒtʃ (§12) |jaw dʒɔ |gorge gɔrdʒ |go go

watermelon ˈwɔtɚˌmɛlən; ES ˈwɔtə-
waterproof *n, v* ˈwɔtɚˌpruf; ES ˈwɔtə-; |-ed -t
waterproof *adj* ˈwɔtɚˈpruf; ES ˈwɔtə-;
(ˈwaterˌproof ˈpaint)
waterscape ˈwɔtɚˌskep; ES ˈwɔtə-
watershed ˈwɔtɚˌʃɛd; ES ˈwɔtə-
waterside ˈwɔtɚˌsaɪd; ES ˈwɔtə-
water-soak ˈwɔtɚˌsok; ES ˈwɔtə-; |-ed -t
water-soluble ˈwɔtɚˌsaljəbḷ; ES ˈwɔtəˌsal-,
-ˌsɒl-
waterspout ˈwɔtɚˌspaʊt; ES ˈwɔtə-
watertight ˈwɔtɚˈtaɪt; ES ˈwɔtə-; (ˈwater-
ˌtight ˈjoint)
waterway ˈwɔtɚˌwe; ES ˈwɔtə-
waterwork ˈwɔtɚˌwɝk; ES ˈwɔtəˌwɜk, ˈwɔtə-
ˌwɝk; |-s -s
waterworn ˈwɔtɚˌworn, -ˌwɔrn; ES ˈwɔtə-
ˌwoən, E+-ˌwɔən
watery ˈwɔtərɪ, ˈwɔtrɪ
Watson ˈwɑtsṇ, ˈwɒtsṇ
watt, W- wɑt, wɒt |-age -ɪdʒ |-ages -ɪdʒɪz
Watteau wɑˈto, wɒˈto (*Fr* vaˈto)
watt-hour ˈwɑtˈaʊr, ˈwɒt-; ES -ˈaʊə(r
wattle ˈwɑtḷ, ˈwɒtḷ |-d -d |-ling -tḷɪŋ, -tlɪŋ
wattmeter ˈwɑtˌmitɚ, ˈwɒt-; ES -ˌmitə(r
Watts wɑts, wɒts |-'s -ɪz
Waukegan wɔˈkigən
Waukesha ˈwɔkɪˌʃɒ
wave wev |-d -d |-y -ɪ
Wavell ˈwevḷ
waver ˈwevɚ; ES -və(r; |-ed -d |-ing -vrɪŋ,
-vərɪŋ
Waverly ˈwevɚlɪ; ES ˈwevəlɪ
wax wæks |waxes ˈwæksɪz |waxed wækst
|-en -ṇ
waxwing ˈwæksˌwɪŋ
waxwork ˈwæksˌwɝk; ES -ˌwɜk, -ˌwɝk
way, W- we
waybill ˈweˌbɪl |-ed -d
wayfarer ˈweˌfɛrɚ, ˈweˌfærɚ; E -ˌfɛrə(r, ES
-ˌfærə(r
wayfaring ˈweˌfɛrɪŋ, -ˌfærɪŋ; S -ˌfærɪŋ
Wayland ˈwelənd
waylay ˌweˈle |-laid -ˈled (ˈwayˌlaid ˈtwice)
Wayne wen
wayside ˈweˌsaɪd
wayward ˈwewɚd; ES ˈwewəd
wayworn ˈweˌworn, -ˌwɔrn; ES ˈweˌwoən,
E+-ˌwɔən

we *stressed* ˈwi, ˌwi, *occas.* ˌwɪ *in* we're ˌwɪr;
unstr. wɪ, wi
weak wik
weaken ˈwikən |-ed -d |-ing ˈwikənɪŋ, -knɪŋ
weak-kneed ˈwikˈnid (ˈweak-ˌkneed ˈcoward)
weakling ˈwiklɪŋ
weal wil
weald, W- wild
wealth wɛlθ |wealthy ˈwɛlθɪ |-ily -əlɪ
wean win |weaned wind
weapon ˈwɛpən |-ed -d
wear wɛr, wær; E wɛə(r, ES wæə(r; |wore
wor, wɔr; ES woə(r, E+wɔə(r; |worn
worn, wɔrn; ES woən, E+wɔən
Wear *Eng riv.* wɪr; ES wɪə(r; |-mouth -məθ
Weare *US* wɛr, wær; E wɛə(r, ES ˈwæə(r;
Dev, Som wɪr; ES wɪə(r
wearisome ˈwɪrɪsəm
weary ˈwɪrɪ, ˈwɪrɪ; S+ˈwɛrɪ; |-ied -ɪd
weasand ˈwizṇd
weasel ˈwizḷ |-ed -d |-ing ˈwizlɪŋ, ˈwizlɪŋ
weather ˈwɛðɚ; ES ˈwɛðə(r
weather-beaten ˈwɛðɚˌbitṇ; ES ˈwɛðəˌbitṇ
weatherboard ˈwɛðɚˌbord, -ˌbɔrd; ES ˈwɛðə-
ˌboəd, E+-ˌbɔəd; |-ed -ɪd
weather-bound ˈwɛðɚˌbaʊnd; ES ˈwɛðə-
weathercock ˈwɛðɚˌkɑk; ES ˈwɛðəˌkɑk,
-ˌkɒk
Weatherford ˈwɛðɚfɚd; ES ˈwɛðəfəd
weatherglass ˈwɛðɚˌglæs; ES ˈwɛðəˌglæs,
E+-ˌglas, -ˌglas
weatherproof ˈwɛðɚˈpruf; ES ˈwɛðə-;
(ˈweatherˌproof ˈtop)
weather-wise ˈwɛðɚˌwaɪz; ES ˈwɛðə-
weatherworn ˈwɛðɚˌworn, -ˌwɔrn; ES ˈwɛðə-
ˌwoən, E+-ˌwɔən
weave wiv |wove wov |woven ˈwovən *or* wove
wov
web wɛb |webbed wɛbd
Weber *Am name* ˈwɛbɚ, ˈwibɚ, *Ger name*
ˈvebɚ; ES -bə(r; (*Ger* ˈveːbər)
weber *elec.* ˈvebɚ, ˈwibɚ; ES -bə(r
webfoot ˈwɛbˌfʊt, -ˈfʊt |-feet -ˌfit, -ˈfit
web-footed ˈwɛbˈfʊtɪd (ˈweb-ˌfooted ˈbird)
Webster, w- ˈwɛbstɚ; ES ˈwɛbstə(r
Websterian wɛbˈstɪrɪən
webworm ˈwɛbˌwɝm; ES -ˌwɜm, -ˌwɝm
wed wɛd |wedded ˈwɛdɪd |wedded ˈwɛdɪd *or*
wed wɛd

|full fʊl |tooth tuθ |further ˈfɝðɚ; ES ˈfɝðə |custom ˈkʌstəm |while hwaɪl |how haʊ |toy tɔɪ
|using ˈjuzɪŋ |fuse fjuz, fɪuz |dish dɪʃ |vision ˈvɪʒən |Eden ˈidṇ |cradle ˈkredḷ |keep 'em ˈkipm̩

we'd *abbr. spelling of* we had, we would,
  stressed ˈwɪd, ˌwɪd, *unstr.* wɪd, wid
Weddell ˈwɛdl̩, wəˈdɛl—*cf* Weddle
wedding ˈwɛdɪŋ
Weddle ˈwɛdl̩
wedge wɛdʒ |wedges ˈwɛdʒɪz |wedged wɛdʒd
wedge-shaped ˈwɛdʒˌʃept
Wedgwood, w- ˈwɛdʒˌwʊd
wedlock ˈwɛdlɑk; ES+-ˌlɒk
Wednesday ˈwɛnzdɪ—*see* Monday, Friday
wee wi
weed wid |weeded ˈwidɪd |weedy ˈwidɪ
Weedon ˈwidn̩
week wik |weekday ˈwikˌde |weekly ˈwiklɪ
week end *n* ˈwikˈɛnd
week-end *adj* ˈwikˈɛnd (ˈweek-ˈend ˌparty,
  ˈweek-ˌend ˈtrip)
week-end *v* ˈwikˈɛnd |-ed -ɪd
Weems wimz |Weems's ˈwimzɪz
ween win |weened wind
weep wip |wept wɛpt
weevil ˈwivl̩ |-ed -d
weft wɛft |-ed -ɪd
weigela, W- waɪˈdʒilə, -ˈgilə
weigelia, W- waɪˈdʒiljə, -ˈgil-, -lɪə
weigh we |weighed wed
weight wet |weighted ˈwetɪd
Wei-hai-wei ˈweˈhaɪˈwe
Weimar *Ger* ˈvaɪmɑr
weir wɪr; ES wɪə(r, S+wɛə(r; |-ed -d
weird wɪrd; ES wɪəd, S+wɛəd
Welch wɛltʃ, wɛlʃ |-'s -ɪz
welcome ˈwɛlkəm |welcomed ˈwɛlkəmd
weld wɛld |welded ˈwɛldɪd
Weldon ˈwɛldən
welfare ˈwɛlˌfɛr, -ˌfær; E -ˌfɛə(r, ES -ˌfæə(r
welkin ˈwɛlkɪn
well wɛl |welled wɛld
we'll *abbr. spelling of* we will, *stressed* ˈwil,
  ˌwil; *unstr.* wɪl, wil
Welland ˈwɛlənd
wellaway ˈwɛləˈwe
well-being ˈwɛlˈbiɪŋ
wellborn ˈwɛlˈbɔrn; ES ˈwɛlˈbɔən
well-bred ˈwɛlˈbrɛd (ˈwell-ˌbred ˈlook)
well-doer ˈwɛlˈduɚ; ES -ˈduˌə(r
Wellesley ˈwɛlzlɪ
well-favored ˈwɛlˈfevɚd; ES -ˈfevəd
well-found ˈwɛlˈfaʊnd

well-founded ˈwɛlˈfaʊndɪd (ˈwell-ˌfounded
  ˈact)
well-groomed ˈwɛlˈgrumd
wellhead ˈwɛlˌhɛd
Wellington ˈwɛlɪŋtən
well-known ˈwɛlˈnon (ˈwell-ˌknown ˈfact)
well-meaning ˈwɛlˈminɪŋ
well-nigh ˈwɛlˈnaɪ (ˈwell-ˌnigh ˈdead)
well-read ˈwɛlˈrɛd
well-spoken ˈwɛlˈspokən
wellspring ˈwɛlˌsprɪŋ
well-thought-of ˈwɛlˈθɔtˌɑv, -ˌɒv, -ˌʌv
well-to-do ˈwɛltəˈdu (ˈwell-to-ˌdo ˈfarmer)
Welsh wɛlʃ, wɛltʃ |-man, -men -mən
welt wɛlt |welted ˈwɛltɪd
Weltanschauung *Ger* ˈvɛltˌɑnˌʃaʊ-ʊŋ
welter ˈwɛltɚ; ES ˈwɛltə(r; |-ed -d |-ing
  -tərɪŋ, -trɪŋ
welterweight ˈwɛltɚˌwet; ES ˈwɛltə-
Weltpolitik *Ger* ˈvɛltpoliˌtiːk
Weltschmerz *Ger* ˈvɛltˌʃmɛrts
Wembley ˈwɛmblɪ
Wemys wimz |-'s -ɪz
wen wɛn
Wenceslaus ˈwɛnsɪsˌlɒs |-'s -ɪz
wench wɛntʃ |-es -ɪz |-ed -t
wend wɛnd |*past & pptc* wended ˈwɛndɪd *or*
  went wɛnt—went *is now associated with* go.
went *past & pptc of* wend *&* go wɛnt
wept *past of* weep wɛpt
were *past of* be: *stressed* ˈwɝ, ˌwɝ, *o.f.* ˈwɛr,
  ˌwɛr, ˈwær, ˌwær; ES ˈwɝ(r, ˌwɝ(r, ˈwɝ,
  ˌwɝ, *o.f.* ˈwɛə(r, ˌwɛə(r, ˈwæə(r, ˌwæə(r;
  unstr. wɚ; ES wə(r
we're *abbr. spelling of* we are: *stressed* ˈwir,
  ˈwɪr, ˌwir, ˌwɪr; ES -iə(r, -ɪə(r; *unstr.* wɪr;
  ES wɪə(r
weren't wɝnt; ES wɝnt, wɝnt
werewolf, werw- ˈwɪrˌwʊlf, ˈwɝ-; ES ˈwɪə-,
  ˈwɝ-, ˈwɝ-, S+ˈwɛə-
wert *stressed* ˈwɝt, ˌwɝt; ES -ɝt, -ɝt; *unstr.*
  wɚt; ES wət
Weser *Ger riv.* ˈvezɚ; ES ˈvezə(r; *rarely* ˈwiz-
  (*Ger* ˈveːzər)
Wesley ˈwɛslɪ |-an -ən (ˈwɛzlɪ *is mainly Brit*)
Wessex ˈwɛsɪks, ˈwɛsɛks |-'s -ɪz
west, W- wɛst |-er -ɚ; ES -ə(r
Westbourne ˈwɛstborn, -bɔrn, -bən; ES
  -bɔən, -bən, E+-bɔən

Key: See in full §§3–47. bee bi |pity ˈpɪtɪ (§6) |rate ret |yet jɛt |sang sæŋ |angry ˈæŋ·grɪ
|bath bæθ; E baθ (§10) |ah ɑ |far fɑr |watch wɑtʃ, wɒtʃ (§12) |jaw dʒɔ |gorge gɔrdʒ |go go

In the words below pronounced with **hw,** *many speakers replace* **hw** *with plain* **w**

Westcott, Wescott ˈwɛskət
westerly, W- ˈwɛstəlɪ; ES ˈwɛstəlɪ
western, W- ˈwɛstən; ES -tən; |-er -ɚ; ES
-ə(r; |-most -ˌmost, -məst—*occas.* ˈwɛstənɚ
by r-dissimilation (§121)
West Ham ˈwɛstˈhæm
Westinghouse ˈwɛstɪŋˌhaʊs |-'s -ˌhaʊsɪz
Westminster ˈwɛstˌmɪnstɚ, -ˈmɪn-; ES -stə(r
Westmoreland *Pa* wɛstˈmorlənd, -ˈmɔr-; ES
-ˈmoə-, E+-ˈmɔə-; *Va* ˈwɛstmələnd; ES
-mə-
Westmorland *Engd, Can* ˈwɛstmələnd; ES
-mə-
west-northwest ˈwɛstˌnɔrθˈwɛst; ES -ˌnɔəθ-
Westphalia wɛstˈfelɪə, -ljə |-n -n
west-southwest ˈwɛstˌsaʊθˈwɛst
West Virginia ˈwɛstvɚˈdʒɪnjə, *less freq.* -nɪə;
ES -və-; |-n -n
westward, W- ˈwɛstwəd; ES -wəd; |Ho -ˈho
wet wɛt |*past & pptc* wet wɛt *or* wetted ˈwɛtɪd
wether ˈwɛðɚ; ES ˈwɛðə(r
we've *abbr. spelling of* we have, *stressed* ˈwiv,
ˌwiv; *unstr.* wɪv, wiv
Weybridge ˈwebrɪdʒ |-'s -ɪz
Weygand ˈvegənd (*Fr* veˈgã)
Weyman ˈwaɪmən
Weymouth ˈweməθ
wh- —*In the vocab. only the sound* hw *is given
for the spelling* wh, *but it is to be understood
that in all such cases many speakers replace*
hw *with plain* w. *See §25.*
whack hwæk |whacked hwækt
whale hwel |whaled hweld |-back -ˌbæk |-boat
-ˌbot |-bone -ˌbon
whang hwæŋ |whanged hwæŋd
wharf hwɔrf; ES hwɔəf; |-'s -s |-ves -vz *or*
-s -s |-ed -t—*In N Engd many pronounce* w
in wharf *who use* hw *in other words; in
Delmarva the exact reverse has been reported.*
wɔəf *is also common in the* S.
wharfinger ˈhwɔrfɪndʒɚ; ES ˈhwɔəfɪndʒə(r
Wharton ˈhwɔrtn̩; ES ˈhwɔətn̩
wharve, wa- hwɔrv, wɔrv; ES -ɔəv
what *stressed* ˈhwɑt, ˌhwɑt, ˈhwɒt, ˌhwɒt,
ˈhwʌt, ˌhwʌt; *unstr.* hwət, wət
whate'er hwɑtˈɛr, hwɒt-, hwət-; ES -ˈɛə(r
whatever hwɑtˈɛvɚ, hwɒt-, hwət-; ES -ˈɛvə(r
Whatmough ˈhwɑtmo, ˈhwɒt-

whatnot ˈhwɑtˌnɑt, ˈhwɒt-; ES+-ˌnɒt
whatsoever ˌhwɑtsoˈɛvɚ, ˌhwɒt-; ES -ˈɛvə(r
wheat hwit |wheaten ˈhwitn̩
wheatear ˈhwitˌɪr; ES -ˌɪə(r, S+-ˌɛə(r
Wheatstone ˈhwitstən, -ˌston
wheedle hwidl̩ |-d -d |-ling ˈhwidlɪŋ, -dl̩ɪŋ
wheel hwil |wheeled hwild
wheelbarrow ˈhwilˌbæro, -rə—*The L.A. and
other evidence show that* ˈhwilˌbaro *is occas.
heard from cultivated speakers.*
wheel-chair ˈhwilˈtʃɛr, -ˈtʃær; E -ˈtʃɛə(r, ES
-ˈtʃæə(r
Wheeler ˈhwilɚ; ES ˈhwilə(r
wheelhouse ˈhwilˌhaʊs |-houses -ˌhaʊzɪz
wheelless ˈhwillɪs
wheelman ˈhwilmən |-men -mən
wheelwright ˈhwilˌraɪt
wheeze hwiz |wheezes ˈhwizɪz |wheezed
hwizd
whelk hwɛlk |whelked hwɛlkt
whelm hwɛlm |whelmed hwɛlmd
whelp hwɛlp |whelped hwɛlpt
when hwɛn |-as hwɛnˈæz
whence hwɛns
whencesoever ˌhwɛns·soˈɛvɚ; ES -ˈɛvə(r
whene'er hwɛnˈɛr, hwən-; ES -ˈɛə(r
whenever hwɛnˈɛvɚ, hwən-; ES -ˈɛvə(r
whensoever ˌhwɛnsoˈɛvɚ; ES -ˈɛvə(r
where hwɛr, hwær; E hwɛə(r, ES hwæə(r
whereabout *n* ˈhwɛrəˌbaʊt, ˈhwær-; S ˈhwær-;
|-s -s
whereabout *adv* ˌhwɛrəˈbaʊt, ˌhwær-; S
ˌhwær-; |-s -s
whereas hwɛrˈæz, hwær-; S hwær-
whereat hwɛrˈæt, hwær-; S hwær-
whereby hwɛrˈbaɪ, hwær-; E hwɛə-, ES
hwæə-
where'er hwɛrˈɛr, hwær-; E hwɛrˈɛə(r, ES
hwær-
wherefor hwɛrˈfɔr, hwær-; E hwɛəˈfɔə(r, ES
hwæə-
wherefore ˈhwɛrˌfor, ˈhwær-, -ˌfɔr; E ˈhwɛə-
ˌfoə(r, ˈhwæə-, -ˌfɔə(r; S ˈhwæəˌfoə(r
wherefrom hwɛrˈfrɑm, hwær-, -ˈfrɒm; E
hwɛə-, ES hwæə-
wherein hwɛrˈɪn, hwær-; S hwærˈɪn
whereinto hwɛrˈɪntu, hwær-, -tu, ˌhwɛrɪnˈtu,
hwær-; S hwærˈɪn-, ˌhwærɪnˈtu

|full fʊl |tooth tuθ |further ˈfɝðɚ; ES ˈfɝðə |custom ˈkʌstəm |while hwaɪl |how haʊ |toy tɔɪ
|using ˈjuzɪŋ |fuse fjuz, frʊz |dish dɪʃ |vision ˈvɪʒən |Eden ˈidn̩ |cradle ˈkredl̩ |keep 'em ˈkipm̩

In the words below pronounced with **hw**, *many speakers replace* **hw** *with plain* **w**

whereof hwɛrˈʌv, hwær-, -ˈɒv; S hwær-
whereon hwɛrˈɑn, hwær-, -ˈɒn, -ˈɔn; S hwær-;
-ˈɔn *is esp. freq. in the S and W.*
wheresoe'er ˌhwɛrsoˈɛr, ˌhwær-; E ˌhwɛəso-
ˈɛə(r, ES ˌhwæə-
wheresoever ˌhwɛrsoˈɛvɚ, ˌhwær-; E ˌhwɛəso-
ˈɛvə(r, ES ˌhwæə-
wherethrough hwɛrˈθru, hwær-; E hwɛə-, ES
hwæə-
whereto hwɛrˈtu, hwær-; E hwɛə-, ES
hwæə-; (ˈWhereˌto ˈtends allˌthis?)
whereunder hwɛrˈʌndɚ, hwær-; E hwɛr-
ˈʌndə(r, ES hwær-
whereunto hwɛrˈʌntu, hwær-, -tu, ˌhwɛrʌn-
ˈtu, ˌhwær-; S hwærˈʌn-, ˌhwærʌnˈtu
whereupon ˌhwɛrəˈpɑn, ˌhwær-, -ˈpɒn, -ˈpɔn;
S ˌhwær-
wherever hwɛrˈɛvɚ, hwær-; E hwɛrˈɛvə(r, ES
hwær-
wherewith hwɛrˈwɪθ, hwær-, -ˈwɪð; E hwɛə-,
ES hwæə-; hwɛrˈwɪθ *has the regular voiceless* θ *of the stressed syllable, while* hwɛrˈwɪð
imitates older unstressed wɪð. *Similarly*
herewith, therewith.
wherewithal *n* ˈhwɛrwɪðˌɔl, ˈhwær-; E ˈhwɛə-,
ES ˈhwæə-
wherewithal *adv* ˌhwɛrwɪðˈɔl, ˌhwær-; E
ˌhwɛə-, ES ˌhwæə-
wherry ˈhwɛrɪ |wherried ˈhwɛrɪd
whet hwɛt |whetted ˈhwɛtɪd |-stone -ˌston
whether ˈhwɛðɚ; ES ˈhwɛðə(r
whew hwɪu, hwju, Φju, Φɪu, xju, xɪu, *etc.*
Whewell ˈhjuəl, ˈhɪuəl
whey hwe |wheyed hwed |-face -ˌfes |-faced
-ˌfest
which hwɪtʃ |-ever hwɪtʃˈɛvɚ; ES -ˈɛvə(r
whichsoever ˌhwɪtʃsoˈɛvɚ; ES -ˈɛvə(r
whiff hwɪf |whiffed hwɪft
whiffle ˈhwɪfl̩ |-d -d |-ling ˈhwɪflɪŋ, -fl̩ɪŋ
whiffletree ˈhwɪfl̩ˌtri, -trɪ
Whig hwɪg |Whigged hwɪgd
while hwaɪl |-d -d |-s -z |-lom -əm |-st -st
whim hwɪm |-med -d |-sey, -sy -zɪ
whimper ˈhwɪmpɚ; ES -pə(r; |-ed -d |-ing
-pərɪŋ, -prɪŋ
whimsical ˈhwɪmzɪkl̩ |-ly -ɪ, -ɪklɪ
whin hwɪn
whine hwaɪn |whined hwaɪnd

whinner ˈhwɪnɚ; ES ˈhwɪnə(r
whinny ˈhwɪnɪ |whinnied ˈhwɪnɪd
whip hwɪp |whipped hwɪpt
whipcord ˈhwɪpˌkɔrd; ES -ˌkɔəd
whiplash ˈhwɪpˌlæʃ |-es -ɪz |-ed -t
whippersnapper ˈhwɪpɚˌsnæpɚ; ES ˈhwɪpə-
ˌsnæpə(r
whippet ˈhwɪpɪt |-ed -ɪd
whippletree ˈhwɪpl̩ˌtri, -trɪ
whippoorwill ˌhwɪpɚˈwɪl; ES ˌhwɪpəˈwɪl—
*acct+*ˈwhippoorˌwill
whipsaw ˈhwɪpˌsɔ |-sawed -ˌsɔd
whipsocket ˈhwɪpˌsɑkɪt; ES+-ˌsɒkɪt
whipstitch ˈhwɪpˌstɪtʃ |-ed -t
whipstock ˈhwɪpˌstɑk, -ˌstɒk
whir hwɝ; ES hwɝ(r, hwɜ; |-red -d |-ring
ˈhwɝɪŋ; ES ˈhwɜrɪŋ, ˈhwɝ-
whirl hwɝl; ES hwɜl, hwɝl; |-ed -d
whirligig ˈhwɝlɪˌgɪg; ES ˈhwɜl-, ˈhwɝl-
whirlpool ˈhwɝlˌpul; ES ˈhwɜl-, ˈhwɝl-
whirlwind ˈhwɝlˌwɪnd; ES ˈhwɜl-, ˈhwɝl-
whish hwɪʃ |whishes ˈhwɪʃɪz |whished hwɪʃt
whisht *intj* hwɪʃt
whisk hwɪsk |whisked hwɪskt
whiskers ˈhwɪskɚz; ES ˈhwɪskəz
whiskey ˈhwɪskɪ |-ed -d
whisper ˈhwɪspɚ; ES ˈhwɪspə(r; |-ed -d |-ing
-prɪŋ, -pərɪŋ
whist hwɪst |-ed -ɪd
whistle ˈhwɪsl̩ |-d -d |-ling ˈhwɪslɪŋ, -sl̩ɪŋ
whistler, W- ˈhwɪslɚ; ES -lə(r
whit hwɪt
Whitby ˈhwɪtbɪ
white, W- hwaɪt |-d -ɪd
whitebeard ˈhwaɪtˌbɪrd; ES -ˌbɪəd
whitecap ˈhwaɪtˌkæp |-capped -ˌkæpt
Whitechapel ˈhwaɪtˌtʃæpl̩
white-collar ˈhwaɪtˈkɑlɚ; ES -ˈkɑlə(r, -ˈkɒl-;
(ˈwhite-ˈcollar ˌman, ˈwhite-ˌcollar ˈjob)
white-faced ˈhwaɪtˈfest (ˈwhite-ˌfaced ˈcow)
Whitefield *Method. preacher* ˈhwɪtˌfild, ˈhwaɪt-
whitefish ˈhwaɪtˌfɪʃ |-es -ɪz
Whitefriars ˈhwaɪtˌfraɪrz; ES -ˌfraɪəz
Whitehall ˈhwaɪtˈhɔl (ˈWhiteˌhall ˈPalace),
surname ˈhwaɪtˌhɔl
white-headed ˈhwaɪtˈhɛdɪd
white-hot ˈhwaɪtˈhɑt; ES+-ˈhɒt
white-livered ˈhwaɪtˈlɪvɚd; ES -ˈlɪvəd

Key: *See in full §§3–47.* bee bi |pity ˈpɪtɪ (§6) |rate ret |yet jɛt |sang sæŋ |angry ˈæŋˌgrɪ
|bath bæθ; E baθ (§10) |ah ɑ |far fɑr |watch wɑtʃ, wɒtʃ (§12) |jaw dʒɔ |gorge gɔrdʒ |go go

In the words below pronounced with **hw,** *many speakers replace* **hw** *with plain* **w**

whiten 'hwaɪtn̩ |-ed -d |-ing 'hwaɪtn̩ɪŋ, -tnɪŋ

whitesmith 'hwaɪt‚smɪθ |-ths -θs

whitewash 'hwaɪt‚waʃ, -‚wɔʃ, -‚wɒʃ |-es -ɪz |-ed -t

whitewing 'hwaɪt‚wɪŋ

whitewood 'hwaɪt‚wʊd

whither 'hwɪðɚ; ES 'hwɪðə(r

whithersoever ‚hwɪðɚso'ɛvɚ; ES ‚hwɪðəso-'ɛvə(r

whitherward 'hwɪðɚwɚd; ES 'hwɪðəwəd

whiting, W- 'hwaɪtɪŋ

whitlow 'hwɪtlo

Whitman 'hwɪtmən

Whitmonday 'hwɪt'mʌndɪ

Whitmore 'hwɪtmor, -mɔr; ES -moə(r, E+-mɔə(r

Whitney 'hwɪtnɪ

Whitsun 'hwɪtsn̩ |-tide -‚taɪd

Whitsunday 'hwɪt'sʌndɪ, 'hwɪtsn̩‚de

Whittier 'hwɪtɪɚ; ES 'hwɪtɪ·ə(r

Whittington 'hwɪtɪŋtən

whittle 'hwɪtl̩ |-d -d |-ling 'hwɪtl̩ɪŋ, -tlɪŋ

whiz, -zz hwɪz |whizzes 'hwɪzɪz |whizzed hwɪzd

who *interrog* hu

who *rel partly stressed* ‚hu, *unstr.* hʊ

whoa hwo, wo, ho; *unstressed* hʊ:

whoe'er hu'ɛr, hu'ɛr; ES -'ɛə(r

whoever hu'ɛvɚ, hu'ɛvɚ; ES -'ɛvə(r

whole hol, hʊl; *N Engd*+hɔl (§46)

wholehearted 'hol'hɑrtɪd; ES -'hɑːtɪd, E+ -'hɑːtɪd

whole-or-none 'holɚ'nʌn; ES 'holə'nʌn

wholesale 'hol‚sel

wholesome 'holsəm

whole-souled 'hol'sold ('whole-‚souled 'friend)

wholly 'holɪ, *esp. if emph.* 'hollɪ; *N Engd*+ 'hɔlɪ

whom hum, *unstressed occas.* hʊm

whoop hup, hwup |-ed· -t

whoopee *n* 'hwupi, 'hwʊpi, 'hu-, 'hʊ-; *intj*+ 'whoo'pee

whooping-cough 'hupɪŋ‚kɔf, 'hʊpɪŋ-, -‚kɒf

whop hwap, hwɒp |-per -ɚ; ES -ə(r

whore hor, hɔr; ES hoə(r, E+hɔə(r; |-dom -dəm

whoremaster 'hor‚mæstɚ, 'hɔr-; ES 'hoə-‚mæstə(r, E+'hɔə-, -‚mas-, -‚mɑs-

whoremonger 'hor‚mʌŋgɚ, 'hɔr-; ES 'hoə-‚mʌŋgə(r, E+'hɔə-

whoreson 'horsn̩, 'hɔrsn̩; ES 'hoəsn̩, E+ 'hɔəsn̩

whorl hwɝl; ES hwɜl, hwɝl

whortleberry 'hwɝtl̩‚bɛrɪ, -bərɪ; ES 'hwɜtl̩-, 'hwɝtl̩-

whose huz, *unstressed occas.* hʊz

whoso 'huso

whosoever ‚huso'ɛvɚ; ES -'ɛvə(r

why *interrog* hwaɪ; *intj* hwaɪ, waɪ; *unstressed expletive* waɪ, hwaɪ

Wichita 'wɪtʃə‚tɔ

wick wɪk |wicked 'having wick(s)' wɪkt

wicked 'evil' 'wɪkɪd

wicker 'wɪkɚ; ES 'wɪkə(r; |-ed -d

wickerwork 'wɪkɚ‚wɝk; ES 'wɪkə‚wɜk, 'wɪkə‚wɝk

wicket 'wɪkɪt |wicketed 'wɪkɪtɪd

Wickham 'wɪkəm

wickiup, wik- 'wɪkɪ‚ʌp

Wiclif, Wy-, Wickliffe, Wy- 'wɪklɪf

wicopy 'wɪkəpɪ

Widdicombe 'wɪdɪkəm

wide waɪd |-n -n̩ |-ned -n̩d |-ning -n̩ɪŋ, -nɪŋ

wide-angle *adj* 'waɪd'æŋgl̩ ('wide-‚angle 'lens)

wide-awake 'waɪdə'wek

wide-open 'waɪd'opən, -'opm̩

widespread 'waɪd'sprɛd

widgeon, wig- 'wɪdʒən

widow 'wɪdo, -ə |-ed -d

widower 'wɪdəwɚ; ES 'wɪdəwə(r; |-ered -d

widowhood 'wɪdo‚hʊd, 'wɪdə-

width wɪdθ, wɪtθ |-ths -θs

wield wild |wielded 'wildɪd

wienerwurst 'winɚ‚wɝst, 'winɪ-; ES 'winə-‚wɜst, 'winɪ-, -‚wɝst

wife waɪf |wife's waɪfs, waɪvz (*in Shak.* wives waɪvz) |*pl* wives waɪvz—*The pronunciation* waɪvz *for* wife's *is not the plural, but the older possessive singular.*

wifely 'waɪflɪ

wig wɪg |wigged wɪgd

Wigan 'wɪgən

wiggle 'wɪgl̩ |-d -d |-ling 'wɪglɪŋ, 'wɪgl̩ɪŋ

wiggler 'wɪglɚ; ES 'wɪglə(r

wiggly 'wɪglɪ, 'wɪgl̩ɪ

wight, W- waɪt

|full fʊl |tooth tuθ |further 'fɝðɚ; ES 'fɜðə |custom 'kʌstəm |while hwaɪl |how haʊ |toy tɔɪ |using 'juzɪŋ |fuse fjuz, fɪuz |dish dɪʃ |vision 'vɪʒən |Eden 'idn̩ |cradle 'kredl̩ |keep 'em 'kipm̩

Wigton ˈwɪgtən |Wigtown ˈwɪgtən, -ˌtaʊn

Wigtownshire ˈwɪgˌtaʊnˌʃɪr, -ʃɚ; ES -ˌʃɪə(r, -ʃə(r

wigwag ˈwɪgˌwæg |wigwagged ˈwɪgˌwægd

wigwam ˈwɪgwɑm, -wɒm, -wɔm

Wilberforce ˈwɪlbɚˌfɔrs, -ˌfɔrs; ES ˈwɪlbə-ˌfɔəs, E+-ˌfɔəs

Wilbraham *Mass* ˈwɪlbrəˌhæm, *Engd* ˈwɪl-brɪəm

Wilbur ˈwɪlbɚ; ES ˈwɪlbə(r

wild, W- waɪld

wildcat ˈwaɪldˌkæt, ˈwaɪlˌkæt |-ed -ɪd

wildebeest ˈwɪldəˌbist

wilder, W- ˈwaɪldɚ; ES ˈwaɪldə(r

wilder *v* ˈwɪldɚ; ES ˈwɪldə(r; |-ed -d |-ing ˈwɪldərɪŋ, -drɪŋ

wilderness ˈwɪldɚnɪs; ES ˈwɪldənɪs; |-es -ɪz

wildfire, W- ˈwaɪldˌfaɪr; ES -ˌfaɪə(r

wilding, W- ˈwaɪldɪŋ

wildwood ˈwaɪldˌwʊd

wile waɪl |wiled waɪld

Wilfred ˈwɪlfrɪd, -frəd

Wilhelmina ˌwɪlhɛlˈminə

Wilkes wɪlks |-'s -ɪz

Wilkes-Barre ˈwɪlksˌbærɪ

Wilkinsburg ˈwɪlkɪnzˌbɝg; ES -ˌbɝg, -ˌbɝg

Wilkinson ˈwɪlkɪnsn̩

will *trans v* wɪl |willed wɪld

will *aux v stressed* ˈwɪl, ˌwɪl; *unstr.* wəl |ˈll əl, *after some conss.* l̩ (ˈnɛdl̩ go), *after vowels* l, əl (wil go, ˈðeəl go)

Willa ˈwɪlə

Willamette wɪˈlæmɪt

Willard ˈwɪlɚd; ES ˈwɪləd

Willesden ˈwɪlzdən

willful, wilf- ˈwɪlfəl |-ly -ɪ

William ˈwɪljəm |-s -z |-'s -zɪz |-son -sn̩

Williamsburg ˈwɪljəmzˌbɝg; ES -ˌbɝg, -ˌbɝg

Willimantic ˌwɪləˈmæntɪk

willing ˈwɪlɪŋ

Willis ˈwɪlɪs |-'s -ɪz

Willkie ˈwɪlkɪ

will-less ˈwɪllɪs

will-o'-the-wisp ˌwɪləðəˈwɪsp

Willoughby ˈwɪləbɪ

willow, W- ˈwɪlo, ˈwɪlə |-y ˈwɪləwɪ

willowware ˈwɪloˌwɛr, -lə-, -ˌwær; E -ˌwɛə(r, ES -ˌwæə(r

willy, W- ˈwɪlɪ |willied ˈwɪlɪd

willy-nilly ˈwɪlɪˈnɪlɪ

Willys ˈwɪlɪs |-'s -ɪz

Wilmcote ˈwɪŋkət, ˈwɪmkət

Wilmington ˈwɪlmɪŋtən

Wilno ˈvɪlnə=Vilna

Wilson ˈwɪlsn̩

wilt *aux v stressed* ˈwɪlt, ˌwɪlt; *unstr.* wəlt, əlt, l̩t (ðaʊlt si)

wilt *v* wɪlt |wilted ˈwɪltɪd

Wilton ˈwɪltn̩

Wilts *short for* Wiltshire wɪlts

Wiltshire ˈwɪltˌʃɪr, -ʃɚ; ES -ʃɪə(r, -ʃə(r

wily ˈwaɪlɪ

wimble ˈwɪmbl̩ |-d -d |-ling ˈwɪmblɪŋ, -bl̩ɪŋ

Wimbledon ˈwɪmbl̩dən

Wimborne ˈwɪmborn, -bɔrn, -bən; ES ˈwɪmboən, -bən, E+-bɔən

wimple ˈwɪmpl̩ |-d -d |-ling ˈwɪmplɪŋ, -pl̩ɪŋ

Wimpole ˈwɪmpol

win wɪn |won wʌn

Winant ˈwaɪnənt

wince wɪns |winces ˈwɪnsɪz |winced wɪnst

winch wɪntʃ |winches ˈwɪntʃɪz |winched wɪntʃt

Winchelsea ˈwɪntʃəlsɪ

Winchester ˈwɪnˌtʃɛstɚ, ˈwɪntʃɪstɚ; ES -tə(r

wind *n* wɪnd, *older and poet.* waɪnd

wind 'to exhaust' wɪnd |winded ˈwɪndɪd

wind 'blow horn' waɪnd, wɪnd |wound waʊnd *or rarely* winded ˈwaɪndɪd, ˈwɪndɪd

wind *v* 'twist' waɪnd |wound waʊnd

windable ˈwaɪndəbl̩, ˈwɪnd-, *accord. to sense—see* wind

windage 'effect of air' ˈwɪndɪdʒ

windbag ˈwɪndˌbæg, ˈwɪn- |-ged -d |-gery -ərɪ

wind-blown ˈwɪndˌblon, ˈwɪn-

wind-borne ˈwɪndˌborn, ˈwɪn-, -ˌbɔrn; ES -ˌboən, E+-ˌbɔən

windbreak ˈwɪndˌbrek, ˈwɪn-

winder ˈwaɪndɚ, ˈwɪndɚ, *acc. to sense—see* wind; ES -də(r

Windermere ˈwɪndɚˌmɪr; ES ˈwɪndəˌmɪə(r

windfall, W- ˈwɪndˌfɔl, ˈwɪn-

windflower ˈwɪndˌflaʊɚ, ˈwɪn-, -ˌflaʊr; ES -ˌflaʊ·ə(r, -ˌflaʊə(r

Windham ˈwɪndəm, *loc. in Vt+*ˈwɪndhæm, ˈwɪndæm

winding ˈwaɪndɪŋ, ˈwɪndɪŋ, *acc. to sense—see* wind

Key: *See in full §§3–47.* bee **bi** |pity ˈpɪtɪ (§6) |rate ret |yet jɛt |sang sæŋ |angry ˈæŋ·grɪ |bath bæθ; E baθ (§10) |ah ɑ |far fɑr |watch wɑtʃ, wɒtʃ (§12) |jaw dʒɔ |gorge gɔrdʒ |go go

windjammer ˈwɪndˌdʒæmɚ, ˈwɪn-; ES -ˌdʒæmə(r
windlass ˈwɪndləs |windlasses ˈwɪndləsɪz
windmill ˈwɪnˌmɪl, ˈwɪnd-
window ˈwɪndo, -də |-ed -d |-ing ˈwɪndəwɪŋ
windowpane ˈwɪndoˌpen, -də-
windpipe ˈwɪndˌpaɪp, ˈwɪn-
windrow ˈwɪnˌro, ˈwɪndˌro
wind-shaken ˈwɪndˌʃekən, ˈwɪn-
windshield ˈwɪndˌʃild, ˈwɪn-
Windsor ˈwɪnzɚ; ES ˈwɪnzə(r
windstorm ˈwɪndˌstɔrm, ˈwɪn-; ES -ˌstɔəm
wind-swept ˈwɪndˌswɛpt, ˈwɪn-
windtight ˈwɪndˈtaɪt, ˈwɪn- (ˈwɪndˌtight ˈwall)
windup ˈwaɪndˌʌp
windward, W- ˈwɪndwɚd; ES ˈwɪndwəd
windy ˈwɪndɪ, ˈwaɪndɪ, acc. to sense—see wind
wine waɪn |wined waɪnd
winebibber ˈwaɪnˌbɪbɚ; ES -ˌbɪbə(r
wineglass ˈwaɪnˌglæs; E+-ˌglas, -ˌglɑs; |-ful -ˌful
winegrower ˈwaɪnˌgroɚ; ES -ˌgro·ə(r
winery ˈwaɪnərɪ
Winesap ˈwaɪnˌsæp
wineskin ˈwaɪnˌskɪn
Winfred ˈwɪnfrɪd, -frəd
wing wɪŋ |winged wɪŋd
winged adj wɪŋd, ˈwɪŋɪd |adv -ly -ɪdlɪ
wing-footed ˈwɪŋˈfʊtɪd (ˈwing-ˌfooted ˈTime)
wingspread ˈwɪŋˌsprɛd
wing-weary ˈwɪŋˌwɪrɪ, -ˌwɪrɪ; S+-ˌwɛrɪ
wingy ˈwɪŋɪ
Winifred ˈwɪnəfrɪd, -frəd
wink wɪŋk |winked wɪŋkt
winkle, W- ˈwɪŋkl̩ |-d -d |-ling ˈwɪŋklɪŋ, -kl̩ɪŋ
Winnebago ˌwɪnəˈbego
Winnepesaukee ˌwɪnəpəˈsɔkɪ
Winnipeg ˈwɪnəˌpɛg
winnow ˈwɪno, -ə |-ed -d |-ing ˈwɪnəwɪŋ
winsome ˈwɪnsəm
Winsted ˈwɪnstɛd, -stɪd
winter, W- ˈwɪntɚ; ES ˈwɪntə(r; |-ed -d |-ing ˈwɪntərɪŋ, ˈwɪntrɪŋ
Winterbourne ˈwɪntɚˌborn, -ˌbɔrn, -ˌburn; ES ˈwɪntəˌboən, -ˌbuən, E+-ˌbɔən
wintergreen ˈwɪntɚˌgrin; ES ˈwɪntə-
winterkill ˈwɪntɚˌkɪl; ES ˈwɪntə-; |-ed -d
wintertide ˈwɪntɚˌtaɪd; ES ˈwɪntə-
Winthrop ˈwɪnθrəp

wintry ˈwɪntrɪ, ˈwɪntərɪ
wipe waɪp |wiped waɪpt
wirable ˈwaɪrəbl̩
wire waɪr; ES waɪə(r; |-ed -d
wiredancer ˈwaɪrˌdænsɚ; ES ˈwaɪəˌdænsə(r, E+-ˌdans-, -ˌdɑns-
wiredraw ˈwaɪrˌdrɔ; ES ˈwaɪə-; |-drew -ˌdru, -ˌdrɪu |-drawn -ˌdrɔn
wirehair n ˈwaɪrˌhɛr, -ˌhær; E ˈwaɪəˌhɛə(r, ES -ˌhæə(r
wire-haired ˈwaɪrˈhɛrd, -ˈhærd; E ˈwaɪəˈhɛəd, ES -ˈhæəd; (ˈwire-ˌhaired ˈpup, a ˈwire-ˈhaired one)
wireless ˈwaɪrlɪs; ES ˈwaɪəlɪs; |-es -ɪz |-ed -t
wirepulling ˈwaɪrˌpʊlɪŋ; ES ˈwaɪə-
wirespun ˈwaɪrˌspʌn; ES ˈwaɪəˌspʌn
wirework ˈwaɪrˌwɝk; ES ˈwaɪəˌwɝk, -ˌwɝk
wireworm ˈwaɪrˌwɝm; ES ˈwaɪəˌwɜm, ˈwaɪə-ˌwɝm
wiring ˈwaɪrɪŋ
wirra ˈwɪrə
wiry ˈwaɪrɪ
wis v erron. from iwis adv wɪs |-ses -ɪz |-sed -t
wis v erron. pres of wit v wɪs
Wisconsin wɪsˈkɑnsn̩; ES+-ˈkɒn-
wisdom ˈwɪzdəm
wise n, adj waɪz
wise v waɪz |-s -ɪz |-d -d
wiseacre ˈwaɪzˌekɚ, ˈwaɪzəkɚ; ES -ˌekə(r, -əkə(r
wisecrack ˈwaɪzˌkræk |-ed -t
wish wɪʃ |wishes ˈwɪʃɪz |wished wɪʃt |-edly -ɪdlɪ
wishbone ˈwɪʃˌbon
wishful ˈwɪʃfəl |-ly -ɪ
wish-wash ˈwɪʃˌwaʃ, -ˌwɔʃ, -ˌwɒʃ
wishy-washy ˈwɪʃɪˌwaʃɪ, -ˌwɔʃɪ, -ˌwɒʃɪ
wisp wɪsp |wisped wɪspt
wist n & past of v wit wɪst
wistaria, W- wɪsˈtɛrɪə, -ˈterɪə
wisteria, W- wɪsˈtɪrɪə
wistful ˈwɪstfəl |-ly -ɪ
wit arch. v: inf wɪt |pres sg, pl wot wɑt, wɒt |past & pptc wist wɪst |pres ptc witting ˈwɪtɪŋ
wit n wɪt
witan hist. n pl ˈwɪtən
witch wɪtʃ |witches ˈwɪtʃɪz |witched wɪtʃt
witchcraft ˈwɪtʃˌkræft; E+-ˌkraft, -ˌkrɑft

|full fʊl |tooth tuθ |further ˈfɝðɚ; ES ˈfɝðə |custom ˈkʌstəm |while hwaɪl |how haʊ |toy tɔɪ |using ˈjuzɪŋ |fuse fjuz, fɪuz |dish dɪʃ |vision ˈvɪʒən |Eden ˈidn̩ |cradle ˈkredl̩ |keep 'em ˈkipm̩

witchery 'wɪtʃərɪ
witching 'wɪtʃɪŋ
witenagemot, -te *hist. n* 'wɪtənəgəˌmot
with *prep* wɪð, wɪθ—*The choice between* wɪð
and wɪθ *may depend partly on phonetic con-
ditions, but there is no consistent general
practice.* wɪθ *is clearly not substandard.*
with *'binder'* wɪθ, wɪð=withe |*pl* withs -θs,
-ðz
withal *adv, prep* wɪð'ɔl, wɪθ'ɔl
Witham *Essex* 'wɪtəm (*OE* wit·ham); *riv.*
'wɪðəm (*OE* wiðma); *surnames* 'wɪð-, 'wɪθ-
withdraw wɪð'drɔ, wɪθ- |-drew -'dru, -'drɪu
|-drawn -'drɔn
withdrawal wɪð'drɔəl, wɪθ-, -'drɔl
withdrew wɪð'dru, wɪθ-, -'drɪu
withe *'binder'* waɪð, wɪθ, wɪð |withes waɪðz,
wɪθs, wɪðz
wither 'wɪðɚ; ES 'wɪðə(r; |-ed -d |-ing
'wɪðrɪŋ, 'wɪðərɪŋ
withers, W- 'wɪðɚz; ES 'wɪðəz; |-'s -ɪz
withhold wɪθ'hold, wɪð- |*past & pptc* -held
-'hɛld |*arch. pptc* -holden -'holdən
within wɪð'ɪn, wɪθ'ɪn
withindoors wɪð'ɪnˌdorz, wɪθ-, -ˌdɔrz; ES
-ˌdoəz, E+-ˌdɔəz
without wɪð'aut, wɪθ-
withoutdoors wɪð'autˌdorz, wɪθ-, -ˌdɔrz; ES
-ˌdoəz, E+-ˌdɔəz
withstand wɪθ'stænd, wɪð- |-stood -ˌstud
withy 'wɪðɪ, 'wɪθɪ
witless 'wɪtlɪs |witling 'wɪtlɪŋ
witness 'wɪtnɪs |-es -ɪz |-ed -t
Wittenberg 'wɪtn̩ˌbɝg; ES -ˌbɜg, -ˌbɝg; (*Ger*
'vɪtənˌbɛrk)
witticism 'wɪtəˌsɪzəm
witting 'wɪtɪŋ
witty 'wɪtɪ |wittily 'wɪt̩ɪ, 'wɪtɪlɪ
wive waɪv |wived waɪvd
wivern, wyv- 'waɪvɚn; ES 'waɪvən
wives, wives' waɪvz
wizard 'wɪzɚd; ES 'wɪzəd; |-ry -rɪ
wizen 'wɪzn̩ |wizened 'wɪznd |-ing -zn̩ɪŋ,
-znɪŋ
wo *intj or var. of* woe wo
woad wod
wobble 'wabl̩, 'wɒbl̩ |-d -d |-ling -blɪŋ, -bl̩ɪŋ
|-ly -blɪ, -bl̩ɪ
wobegone 'wobɪˌgɔn, -ˌgɒn

Woburn *Mass* 'wobɚn, 'wubɚn; ES -bən;
London 'wo-, *Beds* 'wu-
Wodehouse 'wudˌhaus, -dəs |-'s -ɪz
Woden, -an 'wodn̩
woe wo |-ful -fəl |-fully -fəlɪ
woebegone 'wobɪˌgɔn, -ˌgɒn
woke wok |woken 'wokən; |*N Engd*+wɜk
(§46)
Woking 'wokɪŋ
Wolcot(t) 'wulkət
wold wold
wolf wulf |wolf's wulfs, -vz |wolves wulvz
Wolfe wulf |Wolfe's wulfs
wolfhound 'wulfˌhaund
wolfish 'wulfɪʃ, 'wulvɪʃ
wolfram, W- 'wulfrəm (*Ger* 'vɔlfram)
wolframite 'wulfrəmˌaɪt
Wollaston 'wuləstn̩
Wollstonecraft 'wulstənˌkræft; E+-ˌkraft,
-ˌkrɑft
Wolseley 'wulzlɪ
Wolsey 'wulzɪ
wolverine, -ene ˌwulvə'rin
wolves wulvz
woman 'wumən, 'wumən |women 'wɪmɪn, -ən
—*The prons.* 'womən *&* 'wamən *are reported as occas., esp. in the S.*
womanhood 'wumənˌhud, 'wumən-
womankind 'wumən'kaɪnd, 'wum-, -ˌkaɪnd
womanlike 'wumənˌlaɪk, 'wum- |-manly
-mənlɪ
womb wum |wombed wumd
wombat 'wambæt, 'wɒmbæt
women 'wɪmɪn, -ən |-folk -ˌfok
won *past & pptc of* win wan
won *Korean coin* wan, wɒn
wonder 'wandɚ; ES -də(r; |-ed -d |-ing -drɪŋ,
-dərɪŋ |-ful -fəl |-fully -fəlɪ, -flɪ
wonderland, W- 'wandɚˌlænd; ES 'wandə-
wonder-stricken 'wandɚˌstrɪkən; ES 'wandə-
wonder-struck 'wandɚˌstrak; ES 'wandə-
wonderwork 'wandɚˌwɜk; ES 'wandəˌwɜk,
-ˌwɜk
wondrous 'wandrəs
wont *'custom,' 'accustomed'* want, wont, *less
freq.* wɔnt, want, wɒnt |-ed -ɪd—*To many*
wont *is not vernacular, & hence is subject to
spelling pron., & perhaps to the influence of*
won't.

Key: See in full §§3–47. bee bi |pity 'pɪtɪ (§6) |rate ret |yet jɛt |sang sæŋ |angry 'æŋ·grɪ
|bath bæθ; E baθ (§10) |ah ɑ |far fɑr |watch watʃ, wɒtʃ (§12) |jaw dʒɔ |gorge gɔrdʒ |go go

won't **wont, wʌnt,** *much less freq.* **wunt**
woo **wu** |wooed **wud**
wood **wud** |-bin -ˌbɪn |-bine -ˌbaɪn |-chuck
-ˌtʃʌk |-cock -ˌkɑk; ES+-ˌkɒk
Woodbury **ˈwudˌbɛrɪ, -bərɪ**
woodcraft **ˈwudˌkræft; E+-ˌkraft, -ˌkrɑft**
woodcut **ˈwudˌkʌt**
wooden **ˈwudn̩** |-head -ˌhɛd |-ness **ˈwudn̩nɪs**
woodenheaded **ˈwudn̩ˈhɛdɪd** (ˈwoodenˌheaded
ˈboy)
woodenware **ˈwudn̩ˌwɛr, -ˌwær; E -ˌwɛə(r, ES
-ˌwæə(r**
woodland *n* **ˈwudˌlænd, -lənd;** *adj* **ˈwudlənd**
woodlander **ˈwudləndɚ; ES -ləndə(r**
woodman, W- **ˈwudmən** |-men **-mən**
wood-note **ˈwudˌnot**
woodpecker **ˈwudˌpɛkɚ; ES -ˌpɛkə(r**
Woodrow **ˈwudro**
Woodruff **ˈwudrəf, ˈwudruf**
woodsman **ˈwudzmən** |-men **-mən**
Woodstock **ˈwudˌstɑk; ES+-ˌstɒk**
woodsy **ˈwudzɪ**
woodward *'forester'* **ˈwudˌwɔrd, -wɚd; ES
-ˌwɔəd, -wəd**
woodward *adv* **ˈwudwɚd; ES ˈwudwəd;** |-s **-z**
Woodward **ˈwudwɚd, ˈwudɚd; ES ˈwudwəd,
ˈwudəd**
wood-wind **ˈwudˌwɪnd**
woodwork **ˈwudˌwɝk; ES ˈwudˌwɜk, -ˌwɝk;**
|-er -ɚ; ES -ə(r
woody **ˈwudɪ**
wooer **ˈwuɚ; ES ˈwu·ə(r**
woof *n* **wuf;** *intj* **ˈwuf**
wool **wul** |woolen **ˈwulɪn, -ən** |woolly **ˈwulɪ**
Woolf **wulf**
woolfell **ˈwulˌfɛl**
woolgathering **ˈwulˌgæðrɪŋ, -ˌgæðərɪŋ**
woolgrower **ˈwulˌgroɚ; ES -ˌgro·ə(r**
woolpack **ˈwulˌpæk**
woolsack, W- **ˈwulˌsæk**
woolsey, W- **ˈwulzɪ**
Woolwich *Engd* **ˈwulɪdʒ, ˈwulɪtʃ** |-'s **-ɪz**
Wooster **ˈwustɚ; ES ˈwustə(r**
Wootton, Wooton, Wotton **ˈwutn̩**
Worcester **ˈwustɚ; ES ˈwustə(r;** |-shire -ˌʃɪr,
-ʃɚ; ES -ˌʃɪə(r, -ʃə(r; *loc.*+ˈustə(r, ˈustə—
The first r *in* Worcester *was lost by the 16c.*
word **wɝd; ES wɜd, wɝd;** |-ed -ɪd |-book
-ˌbuk

Wordsworth **ˈwɝdzwɚθ; ES ˈwɜdzwəθ,
ˈwɝdzwəθ**
Wordsworthian **wɝdzˈwɝθɪən, -ðɪən, -jən;
ES wɜdzˈwɜ-, wɝdzˈwɝ-**
wore **wor, wɔr; ES woə(r, E+wɔə(r**
work **wɝk; ES wɜk, wɝk;** |-ed -t *or* wrought
rɔt
workaday **ˈwɝkəˌde; ES ˈwɜk-, ˈwɝk-**
workbag **ˈwɝkˌbæg; ES ˈwɜk-, ˈwɝk-**
workbench **ˈwɝkˌbɛntʃ; ES ˈwɜk-, ˈwɝk-;**
|-es -ɪz
workday **ˈwɝkˌde; ES ˈwɜk-, ˈwɝk-**
workhouse **ˈwɝkˌhaus; ES ˈwɜk-, ˈwɝk-;**
|-ses -zɪz
workingman **ˈwɝkɪŋˌmæn; ES ˈwɜk-, ˈwɝk-;**
|-men -ˌmɛn
workman **ˈwɝkmən; ES ˈwɜk-, ˈwɝk-;** |-men
-mən |-manlike -mənˌlaɪk |-manship -mən-
ʃɪp
workout **ˈwɝkˌaut; ES ˈwɜk-, ˈwɝk-**
workpeople **ˈwɝkˌpipl̩; ES ˈwɜk-, ˈwɝk-**
workshop **ˈwɝkˌʃɑp; ES ˈwɜk-, ˈwɝk-, -ˌʃɒp**
worktable **ˈwɝkˌtebl̩; ES ˈwɜk-, ˈwɝk-**
workwoman **ˈwɝkˌwumən, -ˌwum-; ES ˈwɜk-,
ˈwɝk-;** |-women -ˌwɪmɪn, -ən
world **wɝld; ES wɜld, wɝld;** |-ling -lɪŋ
worldly-wise **ˈwɝldlɪˈwaɪz; ES ˈwɜld-, ˈwɝld-**
world-wide **ˈwɝldˈwaɪd; ES ˈwɜld-, ˈwɝld-**
worm **wɝm; ES wɜm, wɝm**
worm-eaten **ˈwɝmˌitn̩; ES ˈwɜm-, ˈwɝm-**
wormhole **ˈwɝmˌhol; ES ˈwɜm-, ˈwɝm-;**
|-d -d
Worms **wɝmz; ES wɜmz, wɝmz; (*Ger* vɔrms)**
wormseed **ˈwɝmˌsid; ES ˈwɜm-, ˈwɝm-**
wormwood **ˈwɝmˌwud; ES ˈwɜm-, ˈwɝm-**
worn **worn, wɔrn; ES woən, E+wɔən;** |-ness
-nɪs
worn-out **ˈwornˈaut, ˈwɔrn-; ES ˈwoən-,
E+ˈwɔən-; (ˈworn-ˌout ˈshoes)**
worry **ˈwɝɪ; ES ˈwɜrɪ, ˈwʌrɪ, ˈwɝɪ;** |-ied -d
worse **wɝs; ES wɜs, wɝs;** |-en -n̩ |-ened -n̩d
|-ening -n̩ɪŋ, -nɪŋ
worship **ˈwɝʃəp; ES ˈwɜʃəp, ˈwɝʃ-;** |-ped -t
worst **wɝst; ES wɜst, wɝst;** |-ed -ɪd
Worstead **ˈwustɪd**
worsted *yarn* **ˈwustɪd**
worsted *'beaten'* **ˈwɝstɪd; ES ˈwɜs-, ˈwɝs-**
wort **wɝt; ES wɜt, wɝt**
worth **wɝθ; ES wɜθ, wɝθ;** |-thy -ðɪ

|full **ful** |tooth **tuθ** |further **ˈfɝðɚ; ES ˈfɝðə** |custom **ˈkʌstəm** |while **hwaɪl** |how **hau** |toy **tɔɪ**
|using **ˈjuzɪŋ** |fuse **fjuz, fɪuz** |dish **dɪʃ** |vision **ˈvɪʒən** |Eden **ˈidn̩** |cradle **ˈkredl̩** |keep 'em **ˈkipm̩**

worth-while ˈwɝɵˈhwaɪl; ES ˈwɝɵ-, ˈwɝɵ-
wot *pres of v* wit wɑt, wɒt
Wotton ˈwɑtn̩, ˈwɑt-, ˈwɒt-, *cf* Wootton
would *stressed* ˈwʊd, ˌwʊd; *unstr.* wəd, əd, d
wouldest ˈwʊdɪst
wouldn't ˈwʊdn̩t, *before some conss.*+ˈwʊdn̩
  (ˈwʊdn̩ du)—*The pron.* ˈwʊdənt *is substandard.*
wouldst, -d'st *stressed* ˈwʊdst, ˌwʊdst; *unstr.*
  wədst, ədst, dst
wound '*hurt*' wund, *less freq.* waund |-ed -ɪd
wound *past of* wind waund
wove wov |woven ˈwovən
wow wau
wrack ræk |wracked rækt
wraith reɵ |-ths -ɵs
Wrangel *Russia* ˈræŋgl̩ |-ell *Alas* ˈræŋgl̩
wrangle ˈræŋgl̩ |-d -d |-ling ˈræŋglɪŋ, -glɪŋ
wrangler '*who wrangles*' ˈræŋglɚ, -gl̩ɚ; ES
  -ə(r
wrangler '*honors man*' ˈræŋglɚ; ES ˈræŋglə(r
wrastle ˈræsl̩ |-d -d |-ling ˈræslɪŋ, ˈræsl̩ɪŋ—
  ˈræsl̩ *is not a mispronunciation of* wrestle, *but
represents the original form* wrastle, *found in
Chauc., Shak., 1611 Bible, and still current.*
wrath ræɵ; E+raɵ, rɑɵ; |-ful -fəl |-fully -fəlɪ
  (*Brit* rɔɵ, rɒɵ)
wreak rik |wreaked rikt
wreath *n* riɵ |wreaths riðz, -ɵs |-ed -t
wreathe *v* rið |-s -z |-d -d
Wreay *Engd* re, *loc.* rɪə
wreck rɛk |-ed -t |-age -ɪdʒ |-ages -ɪdʒɪz
wren, W- rɛn
wrench rɛntʃ |wrenches ˈrɛntʃɪz |-ed -t
Wrentham ˈrɛnɵəm, ˈrɛntɵəm
wrest rɛst |wrested ˈrɛstɪd
wrestle ˈrɛsl̩ |-d -d |-ling ˈrɛslɪŋ, ˈrɛsl̩ɪŋ—*cf*
  wrastle
wretch rɛtʃ |wretches ˈrɛtʃɪz
wretched ˈrɛtʃɪd
wriggle ˈrɪgl̩ |-d -d |-ling ˈrɪglɪŋ, ˈrɪgl̩ɪŋ
wriggler ˈrɪglɚ; ES ˈrɪglə(r

wright, W- raɪt
wring rɪŋ |wrung rʌŋ
wrinkle ˈrɪŋkl̩ |-d -d |-ling ˈrɪŋklɪŋ, -kl̩ɪŋ
wrinkleless ˈrɪŋkl̩lɪs
wrinkly ˈrɪŋklɪ
Wriothesley ˈrɑtslɪ, ˈrɒtslɪ, *cf* Wrottesley
wrist rɪst |wristed ˈrɪstɪd
wristband ˈrɪstˌbænd, ˈrɪzbənd
wristlet ˈrɪstlɪt, ˈrɪslɪt
wristlock ˈrɪstˌlɑk; ES+-ˌlɒk
writ rɪt
write raɪt |wrote rot, *arch.* writ rɪt |written
  ˈrɪtn̩, *arch.* writ rɪt, wrote rot
write-up ˈraɪtˌʌp
writhe raɪð |writhed raɪðd
written *pptc of* write ˈrɪtn̩
wrong rɔŋ, rɒŋ; S+rɑŋ; |-doer -ˈduɚ; ES
  -ˈduə(r; *acct*+ˈwrongˈdoer, ˈwrongˌdoer
wrongheaded ˈrɔŋˈhɛdɪd, ˈrɒŋ-, S+ˈrɑŋ-
wrote rot
wroth rɔɵ, rɒɵ
Wrottesley ˈrɑtslɪ, ˈrɒtslɪ
wrought rɔt
wrought-iron *adj* ˈrɔtˈaɪɚn; ES -ˈaɪ·ən
wrought-up ˈrɔtˈʌp (ˈwrought-ˌup ˈtemper)
wrung rʌŋ
wry raɪ |-neck ˈraɪˌnɛk
Wulfila ˈwʊlfɪlə=Ulfilas
Wulfstan ˈwʊlfstən, -stæn, -stan
Wurlitzer ˈwɝlɪtsɚ; ES ˈwɝlɪtsə(r, ˈwɝ-
Würtemberg ˈwɝtəmˌbɝg; ES ˈwɝtəmˌbɝg,
  ˈwɝtəmˌbɝg; (*Ger* ˈvyrtəmˌbɛrk)
Wuthering ˈwʌðərɪŋ
Wyandot, -tte ˈwaɪənˌdɑt; ES+-ˌdɒt
Wyatt ˈwaɪət
Wycherley ˈwɪtʃɚlɪ; ES ˈwɪtʃəlɪ
Wycliffe, -clif, Wiclif ˈwɪklɪf |-ite -ˌaɪt
Wycombe ˈwɪkəm
wye, W- waɪ
Wykeham ˈwɪkəm
Wyoming waɪˈomɪŋ, ˈwaɪəmɪŋ
wyvern ˈwaɪvɚn; ES ˈwaɪvən

X

X, x *letter* ɛks |*pl* X's, Xs, *poss* X's ˈɛksɪz
Xanadu ˈzænəˌdu

Xanthippe, -ti- zænˈtɪpɪ
xanthous ˈzænɵəs

Key: *See in full §§3–47.*   bee bi |pity ˈpɪtɪ (§6) |rate ret |yet jɛt |sang sæŋ |angry ˈæŋ·grɪ
|bath bæɵ; E baɵ (§10) |ah ɑ |far fɑr |watch wɑtʃ, wɒtʃ (§12) |jaw dʒɔ |gorge gɔrdʒ |go go

Xavier ˈzævɪə, ˈzev-, -jə; ES -vɪ·ə(r, -vjə(r
xebec ˈzibɛk
Xenia *Ohio* ˈzinjə, ˈzinɪə
Xenocrates zəˈnɑkrəˌtiz; ES+-ˈnɒk-; |-'s -ɪz
xenomania ˌzɛnəˈmenɪə, -njə
Xenophanes zəˈnɑfəˌniz; ES+-ˈnɒf-; |-'s -ɪz
xenophobia ˌzɛnəˈfobɪə, -bjə
Xenophon ˈzɛnəfən

Xerxes ˈzɝksiz, ˈzɝkziz; ES ˈzɜk-, ˈzɝk-;
  |Xerxes' -ksiz, -kziz
xi saɪ, zaɪ (*Gk* ksi)
Xmas ˈkrɪsməs |-es -ɪz
XP ˈkaɪˈro
X-ray ˈɛksˈre |-ed -d (ˈX-ˌray ˈpicture)
xylograph ˈzaɪləˌgræf; E+-ˌgraf, -ˌgrɑf
xylophone ˈzaɪləˌfon, ˈzɪl-

Y

Y, y *letter* waɪ |*pl* Y's, Ys, *poss* Y's waɪz
-y *ending, pron.* -ɪ *or* -i, *of ns, adjs, & advs*
  (glory, glories, money, icy, fully ˈfʊlɪ, -i).
  The sound varies in America from -ɪ *toward*
  -i, *though the* -i *is seldom as high* (*close*) *as*
  in the pl of basis (bases ˈbesiz—*cf* Macy's
  ˈmesɪz, -iz) *or of* stasis (stases ˈstesiz—
  cf Stacy's). *The* -i *variant is commonest in*
  the N & E, but rare in the S. In America
  as a whole -ɪ *appears to prevail. As it is not*
  feasible in the vocabulary to give both variants
  -ɪ & -i *for the numerous words in* -y, *it must*
  be understood that, though only -ɪ *is given,*
  very many speakers use the higher vowel
  approaching -i. *The ending* -y *is often*
  omitted from the vocab.
yacht jɑt; ES+jɒt; |-ed -ɪd |-sman -smən
  |-smen -smən
Yadkin ˈjædkɪn
Yahoo, y- ˈjɑhu, ˈjehu, jəˈhu
Yahweh, -we ˈjɑwɛ |-wism -wɪzəm |-wist
  -wɪst |-wistic jɑˈwɪstɪk
yak jæk
Yakima ˈjækəmə
Yakut jɑˈkʊt
Yakutsk jɑˈkʊtsk, jə-
Yale jel
yam jæm
yammer ˈjæmɚ; ES -mə(r; |-ed -d |-ing
  ˈjæmərɪŋ, ˈjæmrɪŋ
Yancey ˈjænsɪ
Yangtze-Kiang ˈjæŋtsɪˈkjæŋ
yank jæŋk |-ed -t
Yank jæŋk |Yankee ˈjæŋkɪ |-eeism -ɪˌɪzəm
Yankee-Doodle ˈjæŋkɪˈdudl̩
yap jæp |yapped jæpt

Yap jɑp |-man -mən |-men -mən
Yaqui ˈjɑki
yard jɑrd; ES jɑːd, E+jaːd; |-ed -ɪd
yardarm ˈjɑrdˌɑrm; ES ˈjɑːdˌɑːm, E+ˈjaːd-
  ˌaːm
yardstick ˈjɑrdˌstɪk; ES ˈjɑːd-, E+ˈjaːd-
yare jɛr, jær; E jɛə(r, ES jæə(r
Yarmouth ˈjɑrməθ; ES ˈjɑːməθ, E+ˈjaːməθ
yarn jɑrn; ES jɑːn, E+jaːn; |-ed -d
yarovize ˈjɑrəˌvaɪz |-s -ɪz |-d -d
yarrow, Y- ˈjæro, ˈjærə
yataghan, -gan ˈjætəˌgæn, -gən
yaw jɔ |yawed jɔd
yawl jɔl
yawn jɔn |yawned jɔnd
yawp, yaup jɔp, jɒp, jɑp |-ed -t
Yazoo ˈjæzu
y-clad ɪˈklæd
y-clept ɪˈklɛpt
ye *pro, stressed* ˈji; *unstr.* jɪ
ye *arch. spelling for the def. art.* the ðə, ðɪ, *in*
  which y *is not the same letter as in* you, *but*
  is the old th-*letter* þ. *Ignorance has well-nigh*
  established the ridiculous pron. ji.
yea je
yean jin |yeaned jind |-ling ˈjinlɪŋ
year jɪr; ES jɪə(r, S+jɛə(r; |-book -ˌbʊk
yearling ˈjɪrlɪŋ; ES ˈjɪə-, S+ˈjɛə-;—ˈjɝlɪŋ,
  ˈjɝ-, -lɪ *are old-fashioned Am prons. The*
  corresponding ˈjɝlɪŋ, -lɪ *have recently come*
  into standard Brit use.
yearlong ˈjɪrˈlɔŋ, -ˈlɒŋ; ES ˈjɪə-, S+ˈjɛə-,
  -ˈlɒŋ
yearly ˈjɪrlɪ; ES ˈjɪəlɪ, S+ˈjɛə-
yearn jɝn; ES jɜn, jɝn; |-ed -d
yeast jist |-y ˈjistɪ, *in Shak.* ˈjɛstɪ

Yeats jets |Yeats's 'jetsız

yegg jɛg

yelk jɛlk *doublet of* yolk |yelked jɛlkt

yell jɛl |yelled jɛld

yellow 'jɛlo, -ə |-ed -d |-ing 'jɛləwıŋ

yellowhammer 'jɛloˌhæmə, 'jɛlə-; ES -ˌhæmə(r

Yellowstone 'jɛloˌston, 'jɛlə-

yellowthroat 'jɛloˌθrot, 'jɛlə-

yellowwood 'jɛloˌwʊd, 'jɛlə-

yelp jɛlp |yelped jɛlpt

Yemen 'jɛmən, 'je- |-ite -ˌaɪt

yen jɛn

yeoman 'jomən |-men -mən |-ry -rı

Yeovil 'jovıl

Yerkes 'jɝkiz; ES 'jɝkiz, 'jɝkiz; |-es' -iz

yes jɛs |yeses 'jɛsız |yesed jɛst

yester 'jɛstə; ES 'jɛstə(r

yesterday 'jɛstədı, -ˌde; ES 'jɛstə-

yesternight 'jɛstə'naɪt; ES 'jɛstə-

yestreen jɛs'trin

yesty '*yeasty*' 'jɛstı

yet jɛt

yew ju, jıu—*Many speakers distinguish* yew *from* you.

Yewdale 'juˌdel, 'judl, *cf* Udall

Yggdrasill 'ıgdrəˌsıl

Yiddish 'jıdıʃ

yield jild |yielded 'jildıd

yip jıp |yipped jıpt

Ymir 'imır, 'ımır; ES -mıə(r; |Ymer -mə; ES -mə(r

yodel 'jodl |-ed -d |-ing 'jodlıŋ, 'jodlıŋ

yoga 'jogə

yogi 'jogi |yogin 'jogın

yoick jɔɪk |-ed -t |yoicks *intj* jɔɪks

yoke jok |yoked jokt |-fellow -ˌfɛlo, -ə

yokel 'jokl

Yokohama ˌjokə'hɑmə

yolk jok, jolk |-ed -t; |*N Engd*+jɔ̃k (*§46*)

Yom Kippur 'jom'kıpə, -ʊr; ES -ə(r, -ʊə(r

yon jɑn, jɒn |-d -d |-der -də; ES -də(r

Yonge jʌŋ

Yonkers 'jɑŋkəz, 'jɒŋ-; ES -kəz |-'s -ız

yore jor, jɔr; ES joə(r, E+jɔə(r

Yorick 'jɔrık, 'jɑrık, 'jɒrık

York, -ke jɔrk; ES jɔək; |Yorkist -ıst

Yorks '*Yorkshire*' jɔrks; ES jɔəks

Yorkshire 'jɔrkʃır, -ʃə; ES 'jɔəkʃıə(r, -ʃə(r

York State 'jɔrkˌstet; ES 'jɔək-

Yorktown 'jɔrkˌtaʊn; ES 'jɔək-

Yosemite jo'sɛmətı

you *stressed* 'ju, ju; *unstr.* jʊ, jə; *combined with final* -t -'tʃu, -tʃʊ, -tʃə (don'tʃu? 'mɛtʃʊ); *or with final* -d -'dʒu, -dʒʊ, -dʒə (wʊ'dʒu? 'dɪdʒʊ?)

you'd *abbr. spelling of* you had, you would: *stressed* 'jud, ˌjud; *unstr.* jʊd, jəd

Youghiogheny *river* ˌjɑkə'gɛnı, ˌjɒk-

you'll *abbr. spelling of* you will, *stressed* 'jul, ˌjul; *unstr.* jʊl, jəl

young jʌŋ |-er 'jʌŋgə; ES -gə(r; |-est -gıst

youngish 'jʌŋıʃ

youngling 'jʌŋlıŋ

youngster 'jʌŋstə, 'jʌŋkstə; ES -stə(r

younker 'jʌŋkə; ES 'jʌŋkə(r

your *stressed* 'jʊr, ˌjʊr; ES 'jʊə(r, ˌjʊə(r, 'joə(r, ˌjoə(r, E+'jɔə(r, ˌjɔə(r; *unstr.* jʊr, jə; ES jʊə(r, joə(r, jə(r, E+jɔə(r

you're *abbr. spelling of* you are, *stressed* 'jur, ˌjur, 'jʊr, ˌjʊr; ES 'juə(r, ˌjuə(r, 'jʊə(r, ˌjʊə(r; *unstr.* jʊr, jə; ES jʊə(r, jə(r

yours jʊrz; ES jʊəz, joəz, E+jɔəz

yourself jʊr'sɛlf, jə'sɛlf; ES jʊə'sɛlf, joə'sɛlf, jə'sɛlf, E+jɔə'sɛlf; |-selves -'sɛlvz

youth juθ |-'s -θs |-s -ðz, -θs |-ful -fəl |-fully -fəlı

you've *abbr. of* you have, *stressed* 'juv, juv; *unstr.* jʊv, jəv

yow *doublet of* ewe jo—*see* ewe

yow *intj* jaʊ

yowl jaʊl |yowled jaʊld

Ypres 'iprə, 'iprəz (*Fr* ip); *often* 'waɪpəz (ES -pəz), *cf* Yreka

Ypsilanti ˌıpsə'læntı, -tə

Yreka waɪ'rikə

Yser 'aɪzə, 'izə; ES -zə(r; (*Fr* i'zɛːr)

yttrium 'ıtrıəm

Yucatan ˌjukə'tæn, -'tɑn ('Yucaˌtan 'gum)

yucca, Y- 'jʌkə

Yugoslav, J- *n* 'jugoˌslɑv, -ˌslæv

Yugoslav, J- *adj* 'jugo'slɑv, -'slæv ('Yugoˌslav 'state)

Yugoslavia, J- 'jugo'slɑvıə, -vjə |-n -n

Yugoslavic, J- ˌjugo'slɑvık, -'slæv-

Yukon 'jukɑn, -kɒn

yule, Y- jul, jıul |-tide -ˌtaɪd—*Some speakers distinguish* yule *from* you'll.

Key: See in full *§§3–47*. bee bi |pity 'pıtı (*§6*) |rate ret |yet jɛt |sang sæŋ |angry 'æŋ·grı |bath bæθ; E baθ (*§10*) |ah ɑ |far fɑr |watch watʃ, wɒtʃ (*§12*) |jaw dʒɔ |gorge gɔrdʒ |go go

Yutang ju'tæŋ—*see* Lin Yutang
Yvonne ɪ'vɑn, ɪ'vɒn, *humorous* waɪ'vɑnɪ, *cf*
  Ypres, Yreka, Gnadenhutten

Ywain, -e ɪ'wen ('Y‚waɪn *&* 'Gawain)
ywis *arch. adv* ɪ'wɪs
y-wrought ɪ'rɔt

Z

Z, z *letter* zi, *o.f.* 'ɪzɚd; ES 'ɪzəd; *Brit* zɛd |*pl*
  Z's, Zs, *poss* Z's ziz
Zabulon 'zæbjələn=Zebulun
Zacchaeus, -cheus zæ'kiəs |-'s -ɪz
Zachariah, -a ‚zækə'raɪə |-as -əs |-as's -əsɪz
Zachary 'zækərɪ
Zambezi, -si zæm'bizɪ
Zanesville 'zenzvɪl
Zangwill 'zæŋwɪl
zany 'zenɪ
Zanzibar 'zænzə‚bɑr; ES -‚bɑ:(r, E+-‚bɑ:(r
Zarathustra ‚zærə'θustrə
zareba, -reeba zə'ribə
Zdanowicz 'stænə‚vɪtʃ |-'s -ɪz
zeal, Z- zil
Zealand 'zilənd
Zeal-of-the-Land Busy 'zɪləvðə‚lænd 'bɪzɪ
zealot 'zɛlət |-ry -rɪ
zealous 'zɛləs
Zebedee 'zɛbə‚di
zebra 'zibrə
zebu 'zibju, 'zibɪu
Zebulun, -lon 'zɛbjələn
Zechariah ‚zɛkə'raɪə
zed zɛd
zee zi
Zeeland 'zilənd (*Du* 'ze:lɑnt)
Zeitgeist 'zaɪt‚gaɪst (*Ger* 'tsaɪt‚gaɪst)
zenana zɛ'nɑnə
Zend zɛnd |Zend-Avesta 'zɛndə'vɛstə
zenith 'zinɪθ |-ths -θs
Zeno *Gk phil.* 'zino, *It admiral* 'zeno (*It*
  'dze:no)
Zenobia zə'nobɪə, -bjə
Zephaniah ‚zɛfə'naɪə
zephyr 'zɛfɚ; ES 'zɛfə(r
Zephyrus 'zɛfərəs |-'s -ɪz
Zeppelin, z- 'zɛpəlɪn, 'zɛplɪn (*Ger* ‚tsɛpə'li:n)
zero 'zɪro, 'ziro
Zerubbabel zə'rʌbəb!
zest zɛst |-ed -ɪd |-ful -fəl |-fully -fəlɪ

zeta 'zetə, 'zitə
zeugma 'zjugmə, 'zɪug-, 'zug-
Zeus zus, zɪus, zjus |-'s -ɪz
zigzag 'zɪgzæg |zigzagged 'zɪgzægd
Zimbalist 'zɪmb!ɪst
zinc zɪŋk |zincked, zinced zɪŋkt
zincify 'zɪŋkə‚faɪ |-fied -‚faɪd
zincite 'zɪŋkaɪt
zing zɪŋ |zinged zɪŋd
zinnia, Z- 'zɪnɪə, 'zɪnjə
Zion 'zaɪən |-ism -‚ɪzəm |-ist -ɪst |-ite -‚aɪt
zip zɪp |zipped zɪpt
Zipangu zɪ'pæŋgu
Zipper, z- 'zɪpɚ; ES 'zɪpə(r; |-ed -d
zircon 'zɝkɑn, -kɒn; ES 'zɝk-, 'zɝ·k-
zirconium zɚ'konɪəm; ES zə-
zither 'zɪθɚ; ES 'zɪθə(r; |-ed -d |-n -n
zloty 'zlɑtɪ, 'zlɒtɪ |-ys -z
Zoar zor, zɔr, 'zoɚ, 'zɔɚ; ES zoə(r, 'zo·ə(r,
  E+zɔə(r, 'zɔ·ə(r; |-ite -‚aɪt
zodiac 'zodɪ‚æk |zodiacal zo'daɪək!
Zoe 'zo·ɪ, zo
Zola 'zolə (*Fr* zɔ'la)
Zollverein *Ger* 'tsɔlfɛr‚ʔaɪn
zombi, -bie 'zɑmbɪ, 'zɒmbɪ
zone zon |-nal -! |-nally -!ɪ
zoo zu
zoogeographical ‚zoə‚dʒiə'græfɪk! |-ly -ɪ, -ɪklɪ
zoogeography ‚zoədʒi'ɑgrəfɪ, -'ɒg-
zoological ‚zoə'lɑdʒɪk!; ES+-'lɒdʒ-; |-ly -ɪ,
  -ɪklɪ
Zoological Gardens *Lond* zu'lɑdʒɪk!, ‚zuə-
  'lɑdʒ-; ES+-'lɒdʒ-
zoology zo'ɑlədʒɪ; ES+-'ɒl-; |-ist -ɪst
zoom zum |zoomed zumd
zoomorphism ‚zoə'mɔrfɪzəm; ES -'mɔəf-
zoophyte 'zoə‚faɪt
zoosperm 'zoə‚spɝm; ES -‚spɜm, -‚spɝm
zoospore 'zoə‚spor, -‚spɔr; ES -‚spoə(r, E+
  -‚spɔə(r
Zophar 'zofɚ; ES 'zofə(r

|full fʊl |tooth tuθ |further 'fɝðɚ; ES 'fɝðə |custom 'kʌstəm |while hwaɪl |how haʊ |toy tɔɪ
|using 'juzɪŋ |fuse fjuz, fɪuz |dish dɪʃ |vision 'vɪʒən |Eden 'idn̩ |cradle 'kred! |keep 'em 'kipm̩

Zorn *Sw artist* sɔrn; ES sɔən

Zoroaster ˌzoro'æstɚ; ES -'æstə(r; |-trian -trɪən

Zouave, z- zʊ'ɑv, zwɑv

zounds zaʊndz, zaʊnz

Zuider Zee, Zuy- 'zaɪdɚ'ze, -'zi; ES 'zaɪdə-; (*Du* 'zœydər'zeː)

Zulu 'zulu |-land 'zuləˌlænd, 'zulu-

Zuñi 'zunjɪ, 'sun- (*Am Sp* 'suɲi)

Zurich 'zʊrɪk, 'zɪʊrɪk, 'zjʊrɪk (*Ger* 'tsyːrɪx)

Zutphen 'zʌtfən, 'zʊt-

Zuyder Zee—*see* Zuider Zee

zwieback 'tswiˌbɑk, 'swi- (*Ger* 'tsviːˌbɑk)

Zwingli 'zwɪŋglɪ |-an -ən |-anism -ənˌɪzəm |-anist -ənɪst (*Ger* 'tsvɪŋliː)

zymase 'zaɪmes

zyme zaɪm

zymology zaɪ'mɑlədʒɪ; ES+-'mɒl-

zymosis zaɪ'mosɪs

zymotic zaɪ'mɑtɪk; ES+-'mɒt-; |-ally -ˌlɪ, -ɪklɪ

zymurgy 'zaɪmɚdʒɪ; ES -mɝdʒɪ, -mɚdʒɪ

Key: *See in full §§3–47.* bee bi |pity 'pɪtɪ (§6) |rate ret |yet jɛt |sang sæŋ |angry 'æŋ·grɪ |bath bæθ; E baθ (§10) |ah ɑ |far fɑr |watch wɑtʃ, wɒtʃ (§12) |jaw dʒɔ |gorge gɔrdʒ |go go |full fʊl |tooth tuθ |further 'fɝðɚ; ES 'fɜðə |custom 'kʌstəm |while hwaɪl |how haʊ |toy tɔɪ |using 'juzɪŋ |fuse fjuz, fɪuz |dish dɪʃ |vision 'vɪʒən |Eden 'idn̩ |cradle 'kredl̩ |keep 'em 'kipm̩